For more resources, visit the Web site for

The American Promise

bedfordstmartins.com/roark

FREE Online Study Guide

Get instant feedback on your progress with

- Chapter self-tests
- Key terms review
- Map quizzes
- Timeline activities
- Note-taking outlines

FREE History research and writing help

Refine your research skills and find plenty of good sources with

- Suggested references for each chapter compiled by the textbook authors
- A database of useful images, maps, documents, and more at *Make History*
- A guide to online sources for history
- Help with writing history papers
- A tool for building a bibliography
- Tips on avoiding plagiarism

Learn how this book can improve your performance on tests and exams.

PREVIEW BEFORE YOU READ

Look at the chapter outline to see the topics in the chapter and the order in which they are covered.

Skim the "Reviewing the Chapter" section at the end of the chapter to see what might be important for a test.

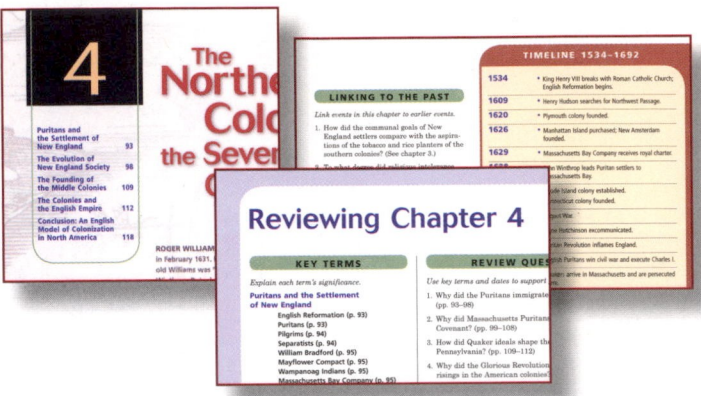

FOCUS WHILE YOU READ

Pay attention to section headings as you read.

Watch for key terms, highlighted in blue type.

Answer the review questions after each major section.

Connect photos, maps, and tables to what you are reading.

REVIEW AFTER YOU READ

Explain the significance of each key term.

Answer the Review Questions and Making Connections questions based on your readings.

Look back at earlier chapters to respond to the Linking to the Past questions.

Review the Timeline to remind yourself of the chapter's main events and chronology.

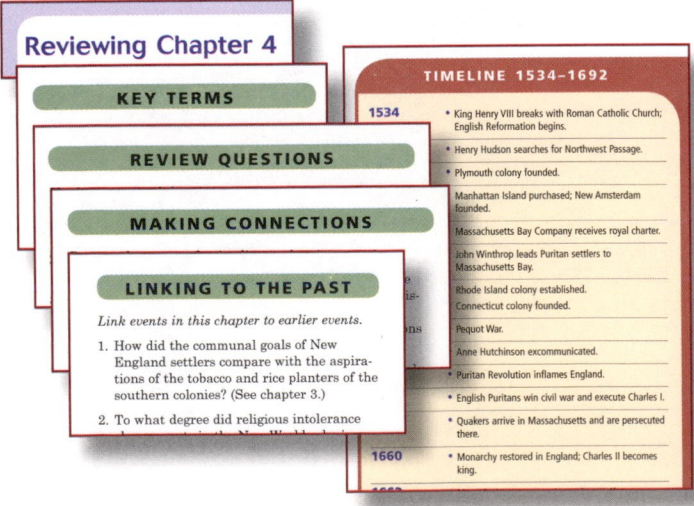

The American Promise

A History of the United States

FIFTH EDITION

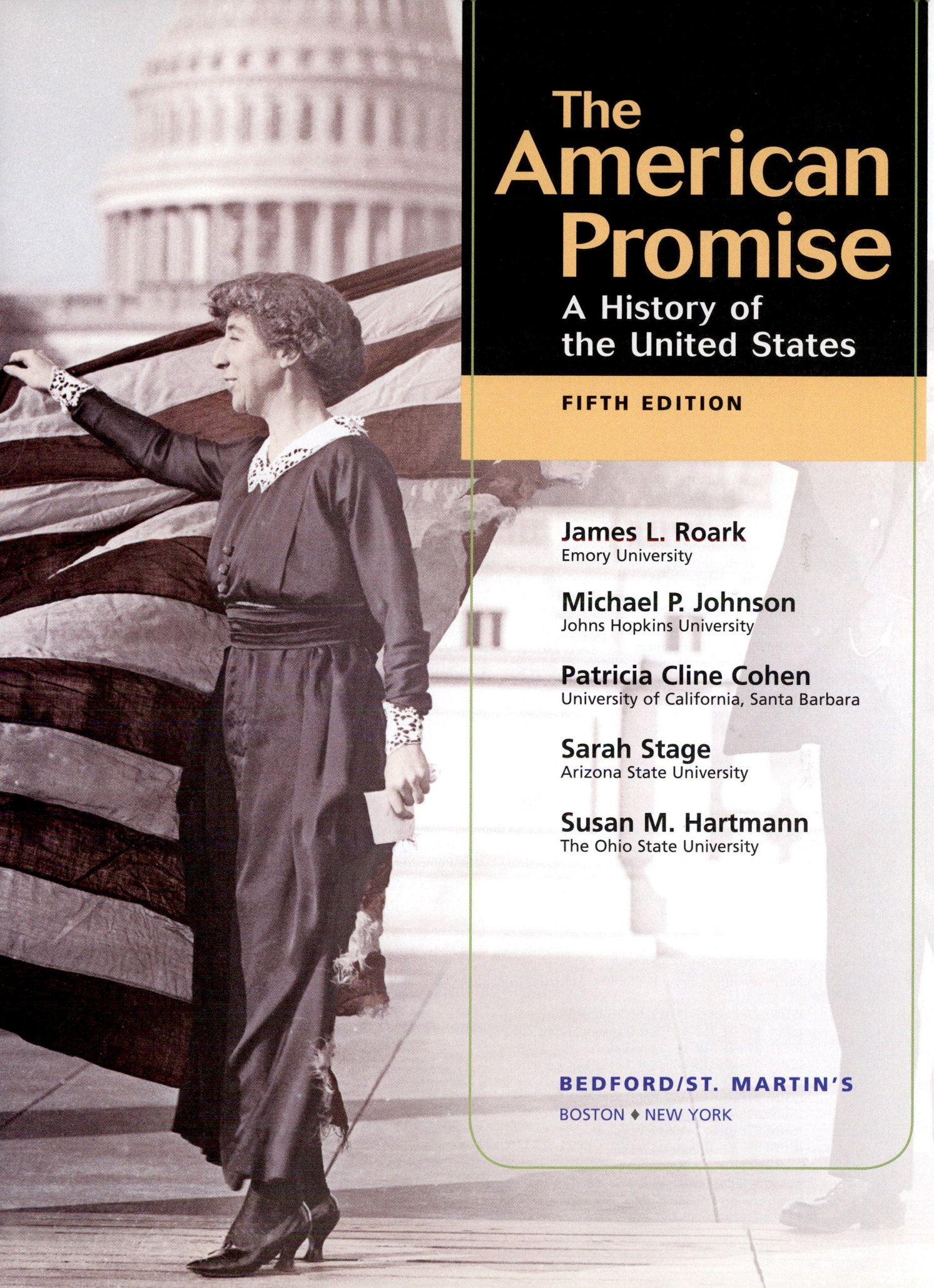

The American Promise

A History of the United States

FIFTH EDITION

James L. Roark
Emory University

Michael P. Johnson
Johns Hopkins University

Patricia Cline Cohen
University of California, Santa Barbara

Sarah Stage
Arizona State University

Susan M. Hartmann
The Ohio State University

BEDFORD/ST. MARTIN'S

BOSTON ◆ NEW YORK

FOR BEDFORD/ST. MARTIN'S

Publisher for History: Mary Dougherty
Executive Editor for History: William J. Lombardo
Director of Development for History: Jane Knetzger
Developmental Editor: Michelle McSweeney
Senior Production Editor: Bridget Leahy
Assistant Production Manager: Joe Ford
Senior Marketing Manager for U.S. History: Amy Whitaker
Editorial Assistants: Jennifer Jovin and Laura Kintz
Production Assistants: Elise Keller and Victoria Royal
Copy Editor: Linda McLatchie
Indexer: Leoni Z. McVey
Photo Researchers: Pembroke Herbert and Sandi Rygiel, Picture Research Consultants, Inc.
Permissions Manager: Kalina K. Ingham
Senior Art Director: Anna Palchik
Text Designer: Tom Carling, Carling Design, Inc.
Cover Designer: Billy Boardman
Cover Photo: Jeannette Rankin with American Flag. Congresswoman Jeannette Rankin is presented with the flag that flew
    at the House of Representatives during the passage of the suffrage amendment, January 21, 1918. © Bettman/CORBIS
Cartography: Mapping Specialists Limited
Composition: Cenveo Publisher Services
Printing and Binding: RR Donnelley and Sons

President: Joan E. Feinberg
Editorial Director: Denise B. Wydra
Director of Marketing: Karen R. Soeltz
Director of Production: Susan W. Brown
Associate Director, Editorial Production: Elise S. Kaiser
Managing Editor: Elizabeth M. Schaaf

Library of Congress Control Number: 2011939422

Manufactured in the United States of America.

7 6 5 4 3 2
f e d c b a

For information, write: Bedford/St. Martin's, 75 Arlington Street, Boston, MA 02116 (617-399-4000)

ISBN: 978–0–312–66312-4 (Combined Edition)
ISBN: 978–0–312–56953-2 (Loose-leaf Edition)
ISBN: 978–0–312–66313-1 (Vol. 1)
ISBN: 978–0–312–56948-8 (Loose-leaf Edition)
ISBN: 978–0–312–66314-8 (Vol. 2)
ISBN: 978–0–312–56946-4 (Loose-leaf Edition)
ISBN: 978–0–312–56954-9 (Vol. A)
ISBN: 978–0–312–56947-1 (Vol. B)
ISBN: 978–0–312–56944-0 (Vol. C)

Preface

As authors, we continue to be deeply gratified that *The American Promise* is one of the most widely adopted texts for the U.S. history survey, reaching students at all levels and helping instructors in all classroom environments. We know from years of firsthand experience that the survey course is the most difficult to teach and the most difficult to take, and we remain committed to making this book the most teachable and readable introductory American history text available. In creating this fifth edition, we set out to develop a resource that is both recognizable and new.

Our experience as teachers continues to inform every aspect of our text, beginning with its framework. We have found that students need *both* the structure a political narrative provides *and* the insights gained from examining social and cultural experience. To write a comprehensive, balanced account of American history, we focus on the public arena — the place where politics intersects social and cultural developments — to show how Americans confronted the major issues of their day and created far-reaching historical change. To engage students in the American story and to portray fully the diversity of the American experience, we stitch into our narrative the voices of hundreds of contemporaries, provide a vivid and compelling art program, and situate American history in the global world in which students live. To help students read, understand, and remember American history, we provide the best in pedagogical aids. While this edition rests solidly on our original goals and premises, the book has also changed, largely in response to adopters who helped us see new ways that the book could work for their students.

Users of past editions have emphasized the central role that *The American Promise* plays in their introductory courses — both as an in-class tool for them to teach from and as a resource for students to study from independently. Our goal in this fifth edition was to make our text even more successful for all students and instructors, whether they are using it in class or at home, whether in print or online. Within the book's covers, we added more contemporary voices to enliven the narrative, more visuals that promote analytical skills, and more pedagogy to facilitate independent study and class discussion. In an effort to assist instructors to help their students meet specific learning objectives, our new pedagogy highlights historical interrelationships and causality, underscores the importance of global contexts in U.S. history, and models historical thinking.

To extend the text, our array of multimedia and print supplements has never been more abundant or more impressive. A range of options — from video clips to lecture kits on CD-ROM and much more — offers instructors endless combinations to tailor *The American Promise* to fit the needs of their classroom. (See pages xii–xv.) Students of all learning styles have more ways than ever to enhance their traditional textbook experience and make history memorable. The e-book, for example, allows students to zoom in on and more closely examine the text's hundreds of historical photographs and artifacts. The book companion site links to even more primary documents, including images, texts, and audiovisual files, and its Online Study Guide provides Web-based self tests, map exercises, and visual activities. By seamlessly connecting our text to its rich storehouse of digital resources, these supplements help students better understand the people whose ideas and actions shaped their times and whose efforts still affect our lives.

Our title, *The American Promise*, reflects our agreement with playwright Arthur Miller's conviction that the essence of America has been its promise. For millions, the nation has held out the promise of a better life, unfettered worship, equality before the law, representative government, democratic politics, and other freedoms seldom found elsewhere. But none of these promises has come with guarantees. As we see it, much of American history is a continuing struggle over the definition and realization of the nation's promise. Who are we, and what do we want to be? Abraham Lincoln, in the midst of what he termed the "fiery trial" of the Civil

War, pronounced the nation "the last best hope of Earth." Kept alive by countless sacrifices, that hope has been marred by compromises, disappointments, and denials, but it still lives. We believe that our new edition of *The American Promise,* with its increased attention to human agency, will continue to show students that American history is an unfinished story and to make them aware of the legacy of hope bequeathed to them by generations of Americans stretching back more than four centuries, a legacy that is theirs to preserve and build on.

Features

We know that a history survey textbook may be unfamiliar or challenging for many students. The benefit of this full-length format is that we have room to give students *everything* they need to succeed. Our book is designed to pique students' interest and to assist them in every way in their reading, reviewing, and studying for exams. We are pleased to draw your attention to three aspects of our textbook that make *The American Promise* stand out from the crowd — our visual program, pedagogical support, and special features.

Visuals. From the beginning, readers have proclaimed this textbook a visual feast, richly illustrated in ways that extend and reinforce the narrative. The fifth edition offers more than eight hundred contemporaneous **illustrations** — one-third of them new — along with innovative techniques for increasing visual literacy. Twelve new **Visualizing History** features show students how to examine the evidence through a wide spectrum of historic objects, including archaeological artifacts, furniture, paintings, photographs, advertisements, clothing, and political cartoons. In addition, one picture in each chapter includes a special **visual activity caption** that reinforces the skill of image analysis. More than three hundred **artifacts** — from dolls and political buttons to guns and sewing machines — emphasize the importance of material culture in the study of the past and make the historical account tangible.

Our highly regarded and thoroughly redesigned **map program,** with more than 170 maps in all, rests on the old truth that "History is not intelligible without geography." Each chapter offers, on average, four **full-size maps** showing major developments in the narrative and two or three **spot maps** embedded in the narrative that emphasize an area of detail from the discussion. To help students think critically about the role of geography in American history, we include **two critical-thinking map exercises** per chapter. Revised maps in the fifth edition illustrate new scholarship on topics such as the Comanche empire in the American Southwest and highlight recent events in the Middle East. Another unique feature is our brief **Atlas of the Territorial Growth of the United States,** a series of full-color maps at the end of each volume that reveals the changing cartography of the nation.

Throughout the text, a host of tables, figures, and other graphics enhance and reinforce the content. **Thematic chronologies** summarize complex events and highlight key points in the narrative. To support our emphasis on the global context of U.S. history, **Global Comparison figures** showcase data with a focus on transnational connections. In addition, occasional **Promise of Technology** illustrations examine the ramifications — positive and negative — of technological developments in American society and culture.

Pedagogy. As part of our ongoing efforts to make *The American Promise* the most teachable and readable survey text available, we paid renewed attention to imaginative and effective pedagogy. Each chapter begins with a concise but colorful **opening vignette** that invites students into the narrative with lively accounts of individuals or groups who embody the central themes of the chapter. New vignettes in this edition include the Grimké sisters speaking out against slavery, Frederick Jackson Turner proclaiming his frontier hypothesis, migrant mother Frances Owens struggling to survive in the Great Depression, and the experience of Vietnam War veteran Frederick Downs Jr. Each vignette ends with a **narrative overview** of all of the chapter's main topics. Major sections within each chapter have **introductory paragraphs** that preview the subsections that follow and conclude with **review questions** to help students check their comprehension of main ideas. **Running heads** with dates and topical headings remind students of chronology, and **callouts** draw attention to interesting quotations from a wide range of American voices. In addition, **key terms,** set in boldface type and grouped together at the end of the chapter, highlight important people, events, and concepts. All chapters culminate in a **conclusion,** which reexamines central ideas and provides a bridge to the next chapter, and a **Selected Bibliography,** which lists important books to jump-start student research and to show students that our narrative comes from scholarship.

The two-page **Reviewing the Chapter** section at the end of each chapter provides a thorough review guide to ensure student success. A list of **Key Terms**, grouped according to chapter headings, provides a starting point for self study and suggests important relationships among major topics, while an illustrated chapter **Timeline** gives clear chronological overviews of key events. Three sets of questions prompt students to think critically and to make use of the facts they have mastered. **Review Questions,** repeated from within the narrative, focus on a specific topic or event, and **Making Connections** questions prompt students to think about broad developments within the chapter. An **all-new set of Linking to the Past** questions cross-reference developments in earlier chapters, encouraging students to make comparisons, see causality, and understand change over longer periods of time. **Online Study Guide cross-references** at the end of the review section point students to free self-assessment quizzes and other study aids.

Special Features. We have been delighted to learn that students and instructors alike use and enjoy our special features. Many instructors use them for class discussion or homework, and students report that even when the special features are not assigned, they read these features on their own because they find them interesting, informative, and exceptional entry points back into the narrative text itself. Each boxed feature concentrates on a historical thinking skill or a habit of mind. We include features that focus on analyzing written or visual primary source evidence, and other features that pose intriguing questions about the past or America's relation to the world and thereby model historical inquiry, the curiosity at the heart of our discipline. For this edition, we have added a **new Visualizing History** feature to many chapters. Images such as Native American weaponry, Puritan furniture, nineteenth-century paintings, photographs by progressive reformers, early-twentieth-century advertisements, and twenty-first-century political cartoons are all presented as sources for examination. By stressing the importance of historical context and asking critical questions, each of these new features shows students how to mine visual documents for evidence in order to reach conclusions about the past.

Fresh topics and the addition of questions in our four enduring special features further enrich this edition. Each biographical **Seeking the American Promise** essay explores a different promise of America — the promise of home ownership or the promise of higher education, for example — while recognizing that the promises fulfilled for some have meant promises denied to others. New subjects in this edition include indentured servant Anne Orthwood and her struggle in colonial America, progressive reformer Alice Hamilton, World War I servicewoman Nora Saltonstall, Chinese scientist Qian Xuesen and his encounter with anticommunism in America, and Vietnamese immigrant-turned-politician Joseph Cao. In addition to these new topics, all Seeking the American Promise features now conclude with a **new set of Questions for Consideration** that help students explore the subject further and understand its significance within the chapter and the book as a whole.

Each **Documenting the American Promise** feature juxtaposes three or four primary documents to show varying perspectives on a topic or an issue and to provide students with opportunities to build and practice their skills of historical interpretation. Feature introductions and document headnotes contextualize the sources, and **Questions for Analysis and Debate** promote critical thinking about primary sources. New topics in this edition are rich with human drama and include "Hunting Witches in Salem, Massachusetts," "Mill Girls Stand Up to Factory Owners," and "The Press and the Pullman Strike."

Historical Questions essays pose and interpret specific questions of continuing interest in order to demonstrate various methods and perspectives of historical thinking. **New question sets** accompanying each of these features focus on a particular mode of inquiry: **Thinking about Evidence, Thinking about Beliefs and Values,** and **Thinking about Cause and Effect.** New to this edition is the feature "How Did America's First Congress Address the Question of Slavery?"

Beyond America's Borders features consider the reciprocal connections between the United States and the wider world and challenge students to think about the effects of transnational connections over time. With the goal of widening students' perspectives and helping students see that this country did not develop in isolation, these features are enhanced by new end-of-feature questions, **America in a Global Context.** New essays in this edition include "European Nations and the Peace of Paris, 1783" and "Global Prosperity in the 1850s."

Updated Scholarship

We updated the fifth edition in myriad ways to reflect our ongoing effort to offer a comprehensive text that braids all Americans into the national narrative and to frame that national narrative in a more global perspective. To do so, we have paid particular attention to the most recent scholarship and, as always, appreciated and applied many suggestions from our users that keep the book fresh, accurate, and organized in a way that works best for students.

In Volume One, we focused our attention on Native Americans, especially in the West, because of the publication of exciting new scholarship. In Chapter 6, we have incorporated into the narrative more coverage of Indians and their roles in various conflicts between the British and the colonists before the Revolution. Chapter 9 expands the coverage of American conflicts with Indians in the Southwest, adding new material on Creek chief Alexander McGillivray. Chapter 10 greatly increases the coverage of Indians in the West, with a new section devoted to the Osage territory and the impressive Comanche empire known as Comanchería. In addition, several new Visualizing History features — on ancient tools used in Chaco Canyon, on Aztec weaponry and its weaknesses in the face of Spanish steel, on Mohawk clothing and accessories, and on gifts exchanged between Anglos and Indians on the Lewis and Clark trail — highlight the significance of Native American material culture over the centuries.

Volume Two also includes expanded attention to Native Americans — particularly in Chapter 17, where we improved our coverage of Indian schools, assimilation techniques used by whites, and Indian resistance strategies — but our main effort for the fifth edition in the second half of the book has been to do more of what we already do best, and that is to give even more attention to women, African Americans, and the global context of U.S. history. In the narrative, we have added coverage of women as key movers in the rise of the Lost Cause after the Civil War, and we consider the ways in which the GI Bill disproportionately benefited white men after World War II. New features and opening vignettes focus on widely recognized as well as less well-known women who both shaped and were shaped by the American experience: the depression-era struggle of Florence Owens (the face of the famous Dorothea Lange photograph *Migrant Mother*), the workplace reforms set in motion by progressive activist Alice Hamilton, and the World War I

service of overseas volunteer Nora Saltonstall. Chapter 16 includes new coverage of the Colfax massacre, arguably the single worst incidence of brutality against African Americans during the Reconstruction era. Chapter 27 provides new coverage of civil rights activism and resistance in northern states, and Chapter 28 increases coverage of black power and urban rebellions across the country. A new Visualizing History feature in Chapter 16 examines the Winslow Homer painting *A Visit from the Old Mistress*.

Because students live in an increasingly global world and need help making connections with the world outside the United States, we have continued our efforts to incorporate the global context of American history throughout the fifth edition. This is particularly evident in Volume Two, where we have expanded coverage of transnational issues in recent decades, such as the 1953 CIA coup in Iran, the U.S. bombing campaign in Vietnam, and U.S. involvement in Afghanistan.

In addition to the many changes noted above, in both volumes we have updated, revised, and improved the fifth edition in response to both new scholarship and requests from instructors. New and expanded coverage areas include, among others, taxation in the pre-Revolutionary period and the early Republic, the Newburgh Conspiracy of the 1780s, the overbuilding of railroads in the West during the Gilded Age, the 1918–1919 global influenza epidemic, finance reform in the 1930s, post–World War II considerations of universal health care, the economic downturn of the late 2000s, the Obama presidency, and the most recent developments in the Middle East.

Acknowledgments

We gratefully acknowledge all of the helpful suggestions from those who have read and taught from previous editions of *The American Promise*, and we hope that our many classroom collaborators will be pleased to see their influence in the fifth edition. In particular, we wish to thank the talented scholars and teachers who gave generously of their time and knowledge to review this book: Patricia Adams, *Chandler-Gilbert Community College*; Susan Agee, *Truckee Meadows Community College*; Jennifer Bertolet, *George Washington University*; Michael Bryan, *Greenville Technical College*; Kim Burdick, *Delaware Technical and Community College*; Monica Butler, *Seminole State College, Sanford*; Andria Crosson, *University of Texas San Antonio*; Lawrence Devaro, *Rowan University and Camden County College*;

Philip DiMare, *California State University, Sacramento*; Dorothy Drinkard-Hawkshawe, *East Tennessee State University*; Edward (Jim) Dudlo, *Brookhaven College*; John Duke, *Alvin Community College*; Aaron Edstrom, *University of Texas El Paso*; Brian Farmer, *Amarillo College*; Rafaele Fierro, *Tunxis Community College*; José Garcia, *University of Central Florida*; Cecilia Gowdy-Wygant, *Front Range Community College Westminster*; William Grose, *Wythevilla Community College*; Stephanie Lee Holyfield, *University of Delaware*; Johanna Hume, *Alvin Community College*; W. Sherman Jackson, *Miami University*; Michael Jacobs, *University of Wisconsin Baraboo/Sauk County*; Kevin Kern, *University of Akron*; Barbara Martin, *University of Southern Indiana*; Alfonso John Mooney, *University of Oklahoma*; Christopher Paine, *Lake Michigan College*; George Sochan, *Bowie State University*; Joyce Thierer, *Emporia State University*; Kathryn Wells, *Central Piedmont Community College*; Steven White, *Bluegrass Community and Technical College*; and Tom Zeiler, *University of Colorado at Boulder*.

A project as complex as this requires the talents of many individuals. First, we would like to acknowledge our families for their support, forbearance, and toleration of our textbook responsibilities. Pembroke Herbert and Sandi Rygiel of Picture Research Consultants, Inc., contributed their unparalleled knowledge, soaring imagination, and diligent research to make possible the extraordinary illustration program.

We would also like to thank the many people at Bedford/St. Martin's who have been crucial to this project. No one contributed more than freelance developmental editor Michelle McSweeney, who managed the entire revision and oversaw the development of each chapter. The results of her dedication to excellence and commitment to creating the best textbook imaginable are evident on every page. We greatly appreciate the acute intelligence, attention to detail, and limitless tolerance for the authors' eccentricities that Michelle brought to this revision. We thank freelance editors Jan Fitter and Shannon Hunt for their help with the manuscript. Thanks also go to editorial assistant Laura Kintz for her assistance preparing the manuscript and to associate editor Jennifer Jovin, who provided unflagging assistance and who coordinated the supplements. We are also grateful to Jane Knetzger, director of development for history; William J. Lombardo, executive editor for history; and Mary Dougherty, publisher for history, for their support and guidance. For their imaginative and tireless efforts to promote the book, we want to thank Jenna Bookin Barry, Amy Whitaker, John Hunger, Sean Blest, and Stephen Watson. With great skill and professionalism, Bridget Leahy, senior production editor, pulled together the many pieces related to copyediting, design, and composition, with the able assistance of Elise Keller and the guidance of managing editor Elizabeth Schaaf and assistant managing editor John Amburg. Senior production supervisor Joe Ford oversaw the manufacturing of the book. Designer Tom Carling, copyeditor Linda McLatchie, and proofreaders Janet Cocker and Mary Lou Wilshaw-Watts attended to the myriad details that help make the book shine. Leoni McVey provided an outstanding index. The book's gorgeous covers were designed by Billy Boardman. New media editor Marissa Zanetti made sure that *The American Promise* remains at the forefront of technological support for students and instructors. Editorial director Denise Wydra provided helpful advice throughout the course of the project. Finally, Charles H. Christensen, former president, took a personal interest in *The American Promise* from the start, and Joan E. Feinberg, president, guided all editions through every stage of development.

Versions and Supplements

Adopters of *The American Promise* and their students have access to abundant extra resources, including documents, presentation and testing materials, the acclaimed Bedford Series in History and Culture volumes, and much much more. See below for more information, visit the book's catalog site at **bedfordstmartins .com/roark/catalog**, or contact your local Bedford/ St. Martin's sales representative.

Get the Right Version for Your Class

To accommodate different course lengths and course budgets, *The American Promise* is available in several different formats, including three-hole punched loose-leaf Budget Books versions and e-books, which are available at a substantial discount.

- **Combined edition** (Chapters 1–31) — available in hardcover, loose-leaf, and e-book formats

- **Volume 1: To 1877** (Chapters 1–16) — available in paperback, loose-leaf, and e-book formats

- **Volume 2: From 1865** (Chapters 16–31) — available in paperback, loose-leaf, and e-book formats

- **Volume A: To 1800** (Chapters 1–10) — available in paperback format

- **Volume B: 1800–1900** (Chapters 10–20) — available in paperback format

- **Volume C: From 1900** (Chapters 21–31) — available in paperback format

The online, interactive **Bedford e-Book** can be examined or purchased at a discount at **bedfordstmartins.com/ebooks**. Your students can also purchase *The American Promise* in other popular e-book formats for computers, tablets, and e-readers.

Online Extras for Students

The book's companion site at **bedfordstmartins .com/roark** gives students a way to read, write, and study, and to find and access quizzes and activities, study aids, and history research and writing help.

FREE **Online Study Guide.** Available at the companion site, this popular resource provides students with quizzes and activities for each chapter, including multiple-choice self-tests that focus on important concepts; flashcards that test students' knowledge of key terms; timeline activities that emphasize causal relationships; and map quizzes intended to strengthen students' geography skills. Instructors can monitor students' progress through an online Quiz Gradebook or receive email updates.

FREE **Research, Writing, and Anti-plagiarism Advice.** Available at the companion site, Bedford's **History Research and Writing Help** includes the textbook authors' **Suggested References** organized by chapter; **History Research and Reference Sources,** with links to history-related databases, indexes, and journals; **More Sources and How to Format a History Paper,** with clear advice on how to integrate primary and secondary sources into research papers and how to cite and format sources correctly; **Build a Bibliography,** a simple Web-based tool known as The Bedford Bibliographer that generates bibliographies in four commonly used documentation styles; and **Tips on Avoiding Plagiarism,** an online tutorial that reviews the consequences of plagiarism and features exercises to help students practice integrating sources and recognize acceptable summaries.

Resources for Instructors

Bedford/St. Martin's has developed a wide range of teaching resources for this book and for this course. They range from lecture and presentation materials and assessment tools to course management options. Most can be downloaded or ordered at **bedfordstmartins.com/roark/catalog**.

HistoryClass for The American Promise. HistoryClass, a Bedford/St. Martin's Online Course

Space, puts the online resources available with this textbook in one convenient and completely customizable course space. There you and your students can access an interactive e-book and primary sources reader; maps, images, documents, and links; chapter review quizzes; interactive multimedia exercises; and research and writing help. In HistoryClass you can get all our premium content and tools and assign, rearrange, and mix them with your own resources. For more information, visit **yourhistoryclass.com**.

Bedford Coursepack for Blackboard, WebCT, Desire2Learn, Angel, Sakai, or Moodle. We have free content to help you integrate our rich content into your course management system. Registered instructors can download coursepacks with no hassle and no strings attached. Content includes our most popular free resources and book-specific content for *The American Promise.* Visit **bedfordstmartins.com/coursepacks** to see a demo, find your version, or download your coursepack.

Instructor's Resource Manual. The instructor's manual offers both experienced and first-time instructors tools for preparing lectures and running discussions. It includes chapter review material, teaching strategies, and a guide to chapter-specific supplements available for the text.

Guide to Changing Editions. Designed to facilitate an instructor's transition from the previous edition of *The American Promise* to the current edition, this guide presents an overview of major changes as well as of changes in each chapter.

Computerized Test Bank. The test bank includes a mix of fresh, carefully crafted multiple-choice, matching, short-answer, and essay questions for each chapter. It also contains the Historical Question, Documenting the American Promise, Seeking the American Promise, and Beyond America's Borders questions from the textbook and model answers for each. The questions appear in Microsoft Word format and in easy-to-use test bank software that allows instructors to easily add, edit, re-sequence, and print questions and answers. Instructors can also export questions into a variety of formats, including WebCT and Blackboard.

The Bedford Lecture Kit: **Maps, Images, Lecture Outlines, and i>clicker Content.** Look good and save time with *The Bedford Lecture Kit.* These presentation materials are downloadable individually from the Instructor Resources tab at **bedfordstmartins.com/roark/ catalog** and are available on *The Bedford Lecture Kit* Instructor's Resource CD-ROM. They provide ready-made and fully customizable PowerPoint multimedia presentations that include lecture outlines with embedded maps, figures, and selected images from the textbook and extra background for instructors. Also available are maps and selected images in JPEG and PowerPoint formats; content for i>clicker, a classroom response system, in Microsoft Word and PowerPoint formats; the *Instructor's Resource Manual* in Microsoft Word format; and outline maps in PDF format for quizzing or handing out. All files are suitable for copying onto transparency acetates.

Make History — **Free Documents, Maps, Images, and Web Sites.** *Make History* combines the best Web resources with hundreds of maps and images, to make it simple to find the source material you need. Browse the collection of thousands of resources by course or by topic, date, and type. Each item has been carefully chosen and helpfully annotated to make it easy to find exactly what you need. Available at **bedfordstmartins .com/makehistory**.

Reel Teaching: Film Clips for the U.S. History Survey. This DVD provides a large collection of short video clips for classroom presentation. Designed as engaging "lecture launchers" varying in length from 1 to 15 or more minutes, the 59 documentary clips were carefully chosen for use in both semesters of the U.S. survey course. The clips feature compelling images, archival footage, personal narratives, and commentary by noted historians.

America in Motion: Video Clips for U.S. History. Set history in motion with *America in Motion,* an instructor DVD containing dozens of short digital movie files of events in twentieth-century American history. From the wreckage of the battleship *Maine,* to FDR's Fireside Chats, to Oliver North testifying before Congress, *America in Motion* engages students with dynamic scenes from key events and challenges them to think critically. All files are classroom-ready, edited for brevity, and easily integrated with PowerPoint or other presentation software for electronic lectures or assignments. An accompanying guide provides each clip's historical context, ideas for use, and suggested questions.

The American Promise via **Dallas Tele-Learning Distance Learning Courses.** *The*

American Promise has been selected as the textbook for the award-winning U.S. history video-based courses *Shaping America: U.S. History to 1877* and *Transforming America: U.S. History since 1877* by Dallas TeleLearning at the LeCroy Center for Educational Telecommunications, Dallas County Community College District. Guides for students and instructors fully integrate the narrative of *The American Promise* into each course. For more information on these distance-learning opportunities, visit the Dallas TeleLearning Web site at **http://telelearning.dcccd.edu**, email **learn@dcccd.edu**, or call 972-669-6650.

Videos and Multimedia. A wide assortment of videos and multimedia CD-ROMs on various topics in U.S. History is available to qualified adopters through your Bedford/St. Martin's sales representative.

Package and Save Your Students Money

For information on free packages and discounts up to 50%, visit **bedfordstmartins.com/roark/catalog**, or contact your local Bedford/St. Martin's sales representative.

Bedford e-Book. The e-book for this title, described above, can be packaged with the print text at a discount.

***Reading the American Past,* Fifth Edition.** Edited by Michael P. Johnson, one of the authors of *The American Promise*, and designed to complement the textbook, *Reading the American Past* provides a broad selection of over 150 primary source documents, as well as editorial apparatus to help students understand the sources. Available free when packaged with the print text.

Reading the American Past e-Book. The reader is also available as an e-book. When packaged with the print or electronic version of the textbook, it is available for free.

The Bedford Series in History and Culture. More than one hundred fifty titles in this highly praised series combine first-rate scholarship, historical narrative, and important primary documents for undergraduate courses. Each book is brief, inexpensive, and focused on a specific topic or period. For a complete list of titles, visit **bedfordstmartins.com/history/series**. Package discounts are available.

Rand McNally Atlas of American History. This collection of more than eighty full-color maps illustrates key events and eras from early exploration, settlement, expansion, and immigration to U.S. involvement in wars abroad and on U.S. soil. Introductory pages for each section include a brief overview, timelines, graphs, and photos to quickly establish a historical context. Available for $3.00 when packaged with the print text.

Maps in Context: A Workbook for American History. Written by historical cartography expert Gerald A. Danzer (University of Illinois at Chicago), this skill-building workbook helps students comprehend essential connections between geographic literacy and historical understanding. Organized to correspond to the typical U.S. history survey course, *Maps in Context* presents a wealth of map-centered projects and convenient pop quizzes that give students hands-on experience working with maps. Available free when packaged with the print text.

The Bedford Glossary for U.S. History. This handy supplement for the survey course gives students historically contextualized definitions for hundreds of terms—from *abolitionism* to *zoot suit*—that they will encounter in lectures, reading, and exams. Available free when packaged with the print text.

U.S. History Matters: A Student Guide to World History Online. This resource, written by Alan Gevinson, Kelly Schrum, and the late Roy Rosenzweig (all of George Mason University), provides an illustrated and annotated guide to 250 of the most useful Web sites for student research in U.S. history as well as advice on evaluating and using Internet sources. This essential guide is based on the acclaimed "History Matters" Web site developed by the American Social History Project and the Center for History and New Media. Available free when packaged with the print text.

Trade Books. Titles published by sister companies Hill and Wang; Farrar, Straus and Giroux; Henry Holt and Company; St. Martin's Press; Picador; and Palgrave Macmillan are available at a 50% discount when packaged with Bedford/St. Martin's textbooks. For more information, visit **bedfordstmartins.com/tradeup**.

A Pocket Guide to Writing in History. This portable and affordable reference tool by Mary Lynn Rampolla provides reading, writing, and research advice useful to students in all history courses. Concise yet comprehensive advice on approaching typical history assignments, developing critical reading skills, writing effective history papers, conducting research, using and documenting sources, and avoiding plagiarism—enhanced with practical tips and examples throughout—have made this slim reference a best-seller. Package discounts are available.

A Student's Guide to History. This complete guide to success in any history course provides the practical help students need to be effective. In addition to introducing students to the nature of the discipline, author Jules Benjamin teaches a wide range of skills from preparing for exams to approaching common writing assignments, and explains the research and documentation process with plentiful examples. Package discounts are available.

Going to the Source: The Bedford Reader in American History. Developed by Victoria Bissell Brown and Timothy J. Shannon, this reader's strong pedagogical framework helps students learn how to ask fruitful questions in order to evaluate documents effectively and develop critical reading skills. The reader's wide variety of chapter topics that complement the survey course and its rich diversity of sources—from personal letters to political cartoons—provoke students' interest as it teaches them the skills they need to successfully interrogate historical sources. Package discounts are available.

America Firsthand. With its distinctive focus on ordinary people, this primary documents reader, by Anthony Marcus, John M. Giggie, and David Burner, offers a remarkable range of perspectives on America's history from those who lived it. Popular Points of View sections expose students to different perspectives on a specific event or topic, and Visual Portfolios invite analysis of the visual record. Package discounts are available.

Brief Contents

Contents

CHAPTER 1
Ancient America,
Before 1492   2

CHAPTER 2
Europeans Encounter the New World, 1492–1600   30

CHAPTER 3

The Southern Colonies in the Seventeenth Century, 1601–1700   60

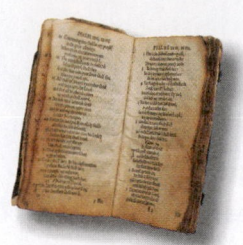

CHAPTER 4

The Northern Colonies in the Seventeenth Century, 1601–1700   90

CHAPTER 7
The War for America, 1775–1783   190

CHAPTER 8
Building a Republic, 1775–1789   226

CHAPTER 11
The Expanding Republic, 1815–1840 320

CHAPTER 12
The New West and the Free North, 1840–1860 356

CHAPTER 15
The Crucible of War,
1861–1865 460

CHAPTER 16
Reconstruction,
1863–1877 498

CHAPTER 17
The Contested West,
1865–1900   534

CHAPTER 18
Business and Politics in the Gilded Age,
1865–1900   568

CHAPTER 19
The City and Its Workers, 1870–1900   602

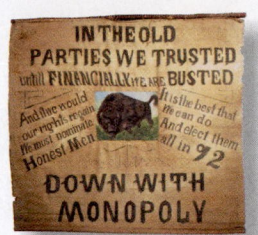

CHAPTER 20
Dissent, Depression, and War, 1890–1900   638

CHAPTER 25
The United States and the Second World War, 1939–1945   822

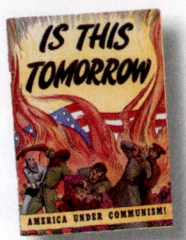

CHAPTER 26
Cold War Politics in the Truman Years, 1945–1953   862

Maps, Figures, and Tables

Maps

Special Features

VISUALIZING HISTORY

The American Promise

A History of the United States

FIFTH EDITION

The
American
Promise
A History of
the United States

FIFTH EDITION

MISSISSIPPIAN WOODEN MASK

Sometime between AD 1200 and 1350, a Native American among the Mississippian people in what is now central Illinois fashioned this mask from red cedar. A thin sheet of copper that originally covered the mask has eroded away, leaving a greenish residue streaking the face. Influenced by the culture of the vast ceremonial site at Cahokia, shown in an artist's rendering in the background, the people who used the mask in rituals probably intended it to depict the face of both worldly and supernatural power. The haunting visage evokes the long history of ancient Americans and their impressive achievements.

1

Ancient America

Before 1492

NOBODY TODAY KNOWS HIS NAME. BUT ALMOST A THOUSAND YEARS ago, more than four hundred years before Europeans arrived in the Western Hemisphere, many ancient Americans celebrated this man — let's call him Sun Falcon. They buried Sun Falcon during elaborate rituals at Cahokia, the largest residential and ceremonial site in ancient North America. (In this chapter, ancient North America refers to the giant land-mass north of present-day Mexico.) Located near the eastern shore of the Mississippi River in what is now southwestern Illinois, Cahokia stood at the spiritual and political center of the world in the eyes of the 15,000 or 20,000 ancient Americans who lived there and thousands more in the hinterlands nearby. The way Cahokians buried Sun Falcon suggests that he was a very important person who represented spiritual and political authority.

What we know about Sun Falcon and the Cahokians who buried him has been discovered by archaeologists — scientists who study artifacts, or material objects, left behind by ancient peoples. Cahokia attracted the attention of archaeologists because of the hundreds of earthen mounds that ancient Americans built in the region. The largest surviving mound, Monks Mound, is a huge terraced pyramid rising one hundred feet from a base that covers sixteen acres (an acre is about the size of a football field), making it the biggest single structure ever built by ancient North Americans.

Atop the four terraces — or platforms — on Monks Mound, political and religious leaders performed ceremonies watched by thousands of Cahokia residents and visitors who stood on a fifty-acre plaza at the base of the mound. Exactly what the leaders did in these ceremonies is unknown. Whatever they did was probably designed to demonstrate to onlookers the leaders' access to supernatural forces. Large garbage pits beside the plaza contain the bones of thousands of butchered deer, remnants of giant feasts that probably accompanied these ceremonies. At the far edge of the plaza, about a half mile from the base of Monk's Mound, Cahokians buried Sun Falcon in an oblong mound about 6 feet high and 250 feet long.

Before Cahokians lowered Sun Falcon into his grave sometime around AD 1050, they first placed the body of another man facedown in the dirt. On top of that man, Cahokians draped a large cape made of twenty thousand shell beads crafted into the likeness of a bird. They then put Sun Falcon faceup on the beaded cape with his head pointing southeast, aligned with the passage of the sun across the sky during the summer solstice at Cahokia. Experts speculate that Cahokians believed that Sun Falcon looked upward toward the life-giving light of the sun while the man

3

beneath the beaded cape communicated with the dark interior of the earth. The people who buried Sun Falcon, it appears, sought to pay homage not only to him but also to the awe-inspiring forces of darkness and light, of earth and sun, that governed their lives.

To accompany Sun Falcon, Cahokians also buried hundreds of arrows with exquisitely crafted arrowheads, thousands of shell beads, and other rare and valuable artifacts that they believed Sun Falcon would find useful in the afterlife. Near the artifacts, Cahokians buried the bodies of seven other adults, including at least one person killed at the grave site, who probably were relatives or servants of Sun Falcon. Not far away, archaeologists discovered several astonishing mass graves. One contained 53 women, all but one between the ages of fifteen and twenty-five, who had been sacrificed by poison, strangulation, or having their throats slit. Other graves contained 43 more sacrificed women, 4 men whose arms had been tied together at the elbows and whose heads and hands had been chopped off, and 39 other men and women who had been executed at the burial site. In all, more than 270 people were buried in the mound with Sun Falcon.

To date, archaeologists have found no similar burial site in ancient North America. However, they have excavated only a tiny fraction of Cahokia. Who knows what remains to be discovered there and else-where?

Nobody knows exactly who Sun Falcon was or why Cahokians buried him as they did. Archaeologists believe that Sun Falcon's burial and the human sacrifices that accompanied it were major public rituals that communicated to the many onlookers the fearsome power he wielded, the respect he commanded, and the authority his survivors intended to honor and maintain. Much remains unknown and unknowable about him and his fellow Cahokians, just as it does with other ancient Americans. The history of ancient Americans is therefore necessarily incomplete and controversial. Still, archaeologists have learned enough to understand where ancient Americans came from and many basic features of the complex cultures they created and passed along to their descendants, who dominated the history of America until 1492.

Cahokia Burial

The excavation of the ceremonial burial site at Cahokia revealed the remains of a man— presumably a revered leader—whom Cahokians buried atop a large cape or blanket in the shape of a bird, probably a raptor. Archaeologists superimposed the grid of white lines to record the precise location of each object. Covering the cape are more than 20,000 beads made of shells sewn onto an underlying fabric or animal skin (not visible). Nearby in the same mound, excavators found mass graves of scores of other Cahokians, many of them executed just before burial, evidently during ceremonies to honor their leader. Courtesy Illinois State Museum: archival photograph.

▶ Archaeology and History

Archaeologists and historians share the desire to learn about people who lived in the past, but they usually employ different methods to obtain information. Both archaeologists and historians study **artifacts** as clues to the activities and ideas of the humans who created them. They concentrate, however, on different kinds of artifacts. **Archaeologists** tend to focus on physical objects such as bones, spear points, pots, baskets, jewelry, clothing, and buildings. Historians direct their attention mostly to writings, including personal and private jottings such as letters and diary entries, and an enormous variety of public documents, such as laws, speeches, newspapers, and court cases. Although historians are interested in other artifacts and archaeologists do not neglect written sources if they exist, the characteristic concentration of historians on writings and of archaeologists on other physical objects denotes a rough cultural and chronological boundary between the human beings studied by the two groups of scholars, a boundary marked by the use of writing.

Writing is defined as a system of symbols that record spoken language. Writing originated among ancient peoples in China, Egypt, and Central America about eight thousand years ago, within the most recent 2 percent of the four hundred millennia that modern human beings (*Homo sapiens*) have existed. Writing came into use even later in most other places in the world. The ancient Americans who buried Sun Falcon at Cahokia about AD 1050 and all those who inhabited North America in 1492 possessed many forms of symbolic representation, but not writing.

The people who lived during the millennia before writing were biologically nearly identical to us. But unlike us, they did not use writing to communicate across space and time. They invented hundreds of spoken languages; they moved across the face of the globe, learning to survive in almost every natural environment; they chose and honored leaders; they traded, warred, and worshipped; and, above all, they learned from and taught one another. Much of what we would like to know about their experiences remains unknown because it took place before writing existed.

Archaeologists specialize in learning about people who did not document their history in writing. They study the millions of artifacts these people created. They also scrutinize soil, geological strata, pollen, climate, and other environmental features to reconstruct as much as possible about the world ancient peoples inhabited. Although no documents chronicle ancient Americans' births and deaths or pleasures and pains, archaeologists have learned to make artifacts, along with their natural and human environment, reveal a great deal about the people who used them.

This chapter relies on studies by archaeologists to sketch a brief overview of ancient America, the long first phase of the history of the United States. Ancient Americans and their descendants resided in North America for thousands of years before Europeans arrived. For their own reasons and in their own ways, they created societies and cultures of remarkable diversity and complexity. Because they did not use written records, their

> ### North Americans in 1492 possessed many forms of symbolic representation, but not writing.

Mexican Stone Tablet

In 2006, Mexican archaeologists announced the discovery of this stone tablet inscribed with the earliest evidence of writing in the Western Hemisphere. About three thousand years ago, somebody in what is now the Mexican state of Veracruz incised this stone with sixty-two characters, barely visible in this photograph. Experts have not yet deciphered the writing, but the repetition of certain characters has led some experts to speculate that it records poetry.
© Michael D. Coe.

history cannot be reconstructed with the detail and certainty made possible by writing. But it is better to abbreviate and oversimplify ancient Americans' history than to ignore it.

> **REVIEW** Why do historians rely on the work of archaeologists to write the history of ancient North America?

▶ The First Americans

The first human beings to arrive in the Western Hemisphere emigrated from Asia. They brought with them hunting skills, weapon- and tool-making techniques, and a full range of other forms of human knowledge developed millennia earlier in Africa, Europe, and Asia. These first Americans hunted large mammals, such as the mammoths they had learned in Europe and Asia to kill, butcher, and process for food, clothing, building materials, and many other purposes.

Most likely, these first Americans wandered into the Western Hemisphere more or less accidentally, hungry and in pursuit of their prey.

African and Asian Origins

Human beings lived elsewhere in the world for hundreds of thousands of years before they reached the Western Hemisphere. They lacked a way to travel to the Western Hemisphere because millions of years before humans existed anywhere on the globe, North and South America became detached from the gigantic common landmass scientists now call **Pangaea**. About 240 million years ago, powerful forces deep within the earth fractured Pangaea and slowly pushed continents apart to approximately their present positions (Map 1.1). This process of **continental drift** encircled the land of the Western Hemisphere with large oceans that isolated it from the other continents long before early human beings (*Homo erectus*) first appeared in Africa about two million years ago. (Hereafter in this chapter, the

MAP ACTIVITY

Map 1.1 Continental Drift
Massive geological forces separated North and South America from other continents eons before human beings evolved in Africa 1.5 million years ago.

READING THE MAP: Which continents separated from Pangaea earliest? Which ones separated from each other last? Which are still closely connected to each other?

CONNECTIONS: How does continental drift explain why human life developed elsewhere on the planet for hundreds of thousands of years before the first person entered the Western Hemisphere 15,000 years ago?

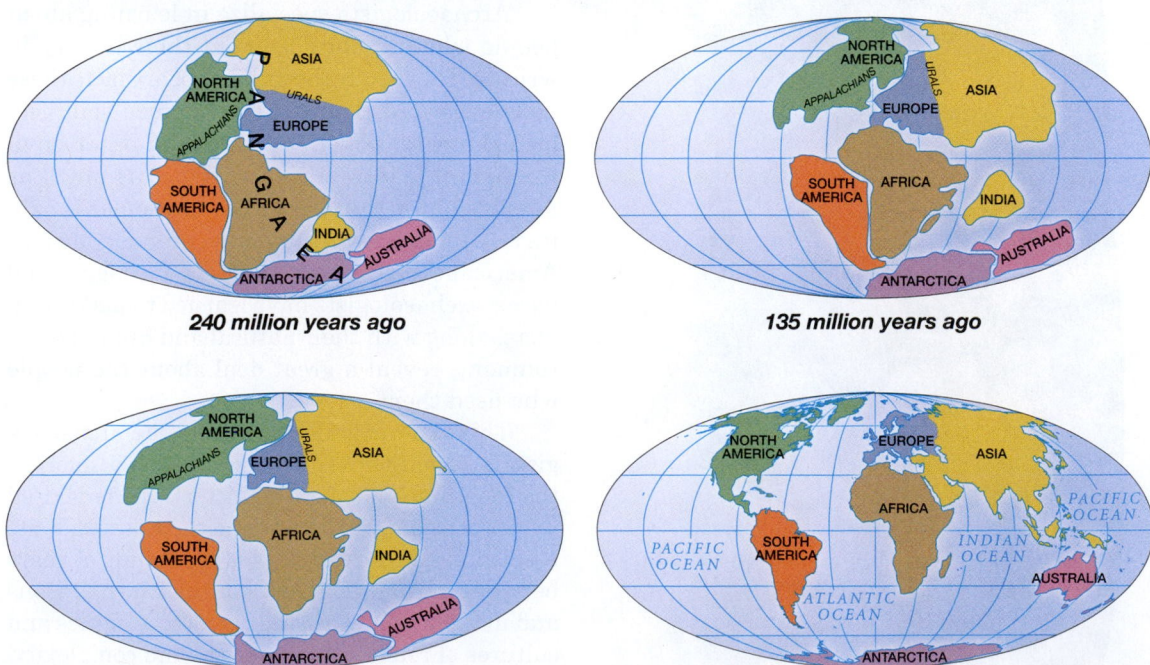

240 million years ago

135 million years ago

65 million years ago

Present day

abbreviation *BP* — archaeologists' notation for "years before the present"—is used to indicate dates earlier than two thousand years ago. Dates more recent than two thousand years ago are indicated with the common and familiar notation *AD* — for example, AD 1492.)

More than 1.5 million years after *Homo erectus* appeared, or about 400,000 BP, modern humans (*Homo sapiens*) evolved in Africa. All human beings throughout the world today are descendants of these ancient Africans. Their DNA was the template for ours. Slowly, over many millennia, **Homo sapiens** migrated out of Africa and into Europe and Asia. Unlike North and South America, Europe and Asia retained land connections to Africa, allowing ancient humans to migrate on foot. Sometimes ancient people navigated rivers and lakes in small boats, but these vessels could not survive battering by the winds and waves of the enormous oceans isolating North and South America from the Eurasian landmass. For roughly 97 percent of the time *Homo sapiens* have been on

Beringia

earth, none migrated to the Western Hemisphere.

Two major developments made it possible for ancient humans to migrate to the Western Hemisphere. First, people successfully adapted to the frigid environment near the Arctic Circle. Second, changes in the earth's climate reconnected North America to Asia.

By about 25,000 BP, *Homo sapiens* had spread from Africa throughout Europe and Asia. People, probably women, had learned to use bone needles to sew animal skins into warm clothing that permitted them to become permanent residents of extremely cold regions such as northeastern Siberia. A few of these ancient Siberians clothed in animal hides walked to North America on land that now lies submerged beneath the sixty miles of water that currently separates easternmost Siberia from westernmost Alaska. A pathway across this watery chasm opened during the last global cold spell — the Wisconsin glaciation, which endured from about 25,000 BP to 14,000 BP — when snow piled up in glaciers, causing the sea level to drop as much

FIGURE 1.1   Human Habitation of the World and the Western Hemisphere
These clock faces illustrate the long global history of modern humans (left) and of human history in the Western Hemisphere since the arrival of the first ancient Americans (right). If the total period of human life on earth is considered, American history since the arrival of Columbus in 1492 comprises less than one minute (or one-tenth of 1 percent) of modern human existence. And if the total period of human life in the New World is converted from millennia to a 12-hour clock, ancient American history makes up the first 11$\frac{1}{2}$ hours, and all history since the arrival of the Europeans in 1492 occupies only the last half hour.

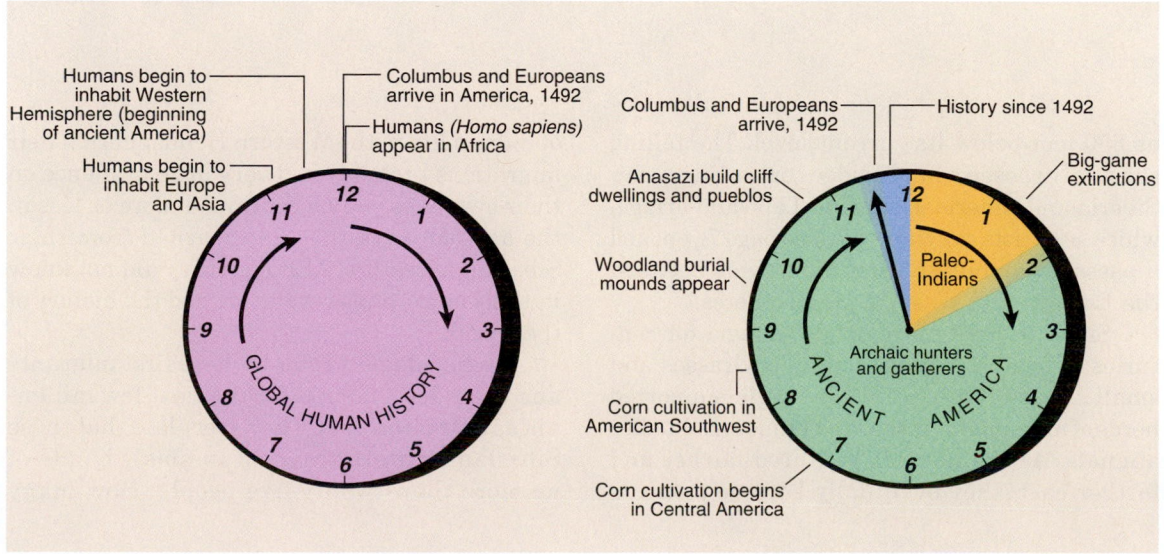

Who Were the First Americans?

To learn who the first Americans were and when they arrived requires following a trail that has grown very cold during the past 15,000 or 20,000 years.

After millennia of erosion and environmental change, much of the land they walked, hunted, and camped on is now submerged and inaccessible beneath the Bering Sea and along the Atlantic and Pacific coasts, where rising sea levels have flooded wide, previously exposed coastal plains. Most of the numerous Paleo-Indian sites archaeologists have excavated were occupied more than a hundred centuries after the first migrants arrived. These sites often yield spear points and large animal bones, but Paleo-Indian human skeletal remains are very rare. And yet evidence that Paleo-Indians inhabited the Western Hemisphere is overwhelming and indisputable. Human craftsmanship is the only credible explanation for Clovis points, and carbon dating establishes that the oldest Clovis sites are about 13,500 years old.

Scattered and controversial evidence suggests, however, that Clovis peoples were not the first arrivals. The Monte Verde excavation in Chile has persuaded many archaeologists that the first Americans resided in South America sometime between 14,750 BP and 14,000 BP. This site and a few other likely pre-Clovis sites in North America, most notably Meadowcroft in Pennsylvania, contain no Clovis-era artifacts, suggesting that their inhabitants arrived earlier and differed from the later Clovis peoples. But if the first Americans already lived in Chile and Pennsylvania 14,000 or more years ago, when did they first arrive and from where?

Some experts hypothesize that pre-Clovis peoples sailed or floated across the Pacific from Australia or Antarctica. Most scholars consider those ideas far-fetched. The Pacific is too wide and tempestuous for these ancient peoples and their small boats to have survived a long transoceanic trip.

Ancient Siberians had the means (hunting skills and adaptation to the frigid climate), motive (pursuit of game animals), and opportunity (the Beringian land bridge) to become the first humans to arrive in America, and most archaeologists believe they did just that. But when they came is difficult to determine, since the Beringian land bridge existed for thousands of years. The extreme rarity of the earliest archaeological sites in North America also makes it difficult to estimate with confidence when pre-Clovis hunters arrived. A rough guess is 15,000 BP, although it might have been earlier. The scarcity of pre-Clovis sites discovered so far strongly suggests that these ancient Americans were few in number (compared to the much more numerous Clovis-era Paleo-Indians), very widely scattered, and ultimately unsuccessful in establishing permanent residence in the hemisphere. Although they and their descendants may have survived in America for a millennium or more, pre-Clovis peoples appear to have died out. The sparse archaeological evidence discovered to date does not suggest that they evolved into Clovis peoples. Although Clovis peoples evidently were not the first humans to arrive in the Western Hemisphere, they probably represent the first Paleo-Indians to establish a permanent American presence.

To investigate where the mysterious first Americans came from, experts have supplemented archaeological evidence with careful study of modern-day Native Americans. Although many millennia separate today's Native Americans from those ancient hunters, most as 350 feet below its current level. The falling sea level exposed a land bridge connecting Asian Siberia and American Alaska. This land bridge, which scientists call **Beringia** (see page 7), opened a passageway hundreds of miles wide between the Eastern and Western Hemispheres.

Siberian hunters roamed Beringia for centuries in search of game animals. Grasses and small shrubs that covered Beringia supported herds of mammoths, bison, and numerous smaller animals. As the hunters ventured farther and farther east, they eventually became pioneers of human life in the Western Hemisphere. Their migrations probably had very little influence on their own lives, which continued more or less in the age-old ways they had learned from their Siberian ancestors. Although they did not know it, their migrations revolutionized the history of the world.

Archaeologists refer to these first migrants and their descendants for the next few millennia as **Paleo-Indians**. They speculate that these Siberian hunters traveled in small bands of no more than twenty-five people. How many

Clovis Point
This spear point excavated from a Clovis-era site along the Columbia River in what is now Washington state was crafted by Clovis people around 11,000 BP. It illustrates the shape, size, and technique of flaking — the chipping away of small fragments of stone to create the point — common to Clovis points throughout the hemisphere. Archaeologists believe that such commonalities in Clovis artifacts document a widely shared Clovis culture practiced for many human generations. Clovis hunters wedged the point into a wooden shaft, bound it with leather or twine, and then had a sharp-edged weapon for killing (and butchering) game animals.
Washington State Historical Society.

scholars agree that telltale clues to the identity of the first Americans can be gleaned from dental, linguistic, and genetic evidence collected from their descendants who still live throughout the hemisphere.

Detailed scientific analyses of the teeth of thousands of ancient and modern Native Americans have identified distinctive dental shapes — such as incisors with a scooped-out inner surface — commonly found among ancient Siberians, ancient Americans, and modern Native Americans, but rare elsewhere. This dental evidence strongly supports the Asian origins and Beringian

migration route of the first Americans.

Linguistic analysis of more than a thousand modern Native American languages demonstrates that Native Americans throughout the hemisphere speak some form of Amerind, the consequence (presumably) of its arrival with the earliest wave of ancient migrants around 13,000 BP. This migration chronology and linguistic analysis remain controversial among experts, but they suggest that Clovis peoples spoke some ancient form of Amerind.

Genetic research into the mutation rate of DNA reveals that many modern Native Americans share

genetic characteristics commonly found among Asians. Estimates of the evolutionary time required to produce the subtle differences between Asian and Native American DNA suggest a migration from Asia as early as 25,000 BP or before. But like the other high-tech evidence, this genetic evidence is sharply disputed by experts.

Fascinating as the genetic, linguistic, and dental studies are, they are unlikely to win widespread support among experts until they can be corroborated by archaeological evidence that, so far, has not been found. Until then, specialists will continue to debate when the first Americans arrived and how they were related to subsequent generations of ancient Americans.

Thinking about Evidence

1. What evidence supports the hypothesis that the first Americans came from Asia? Do you find the evidence persuasive?

2. If pre-Clovis peoples were the first Americans, what evidence suggests when they arrived and what happened to them?

3. Can you imagine archaeological evidence that, if found, would conclusively identify the first Americans and when they arrived?

such bands arrived in North America before Beringia disappeared beneath the sea will never be known.

When the first migrants came is hotly debated by experts. They probably arrived sometime after 15,000 BP. Scattered and inconclusive evidence suggests that they may have arrived several thousand years earlier. (See "Historical Question," page 8.) Certainly, humans who came from Asia — whose ancestors had left Africa hundreds of thousands of years earlier — inhabited the Western Hemisphere by 13,500 BP.

Paleo-Indian Hunters

When humans first arrived in the Western Hemisphere, massive glaciers covered most of present-day Canada. A narrow corridor not entirely obstructed by ice ran along the eastern side of Canada's Rocky Mountains, and most archaeologists believe that Paleo-Indians probably migrated through the ice-free passageway in pursuit of game. They may have also traveled along the Pacific coast in small boats, hunting marine life and hopscotching from one desirable landing spot to another. At the southern edge of the glaciers, Paleo-Indians entered a hunters' paradise. North, Central, and South America teemed with wildlife that had never before confronted wily two-legged predators armed with razor-sharp spears. The abundance of game presumably made hunting relatively easy. Ample food permitted the Paleo-Indian population to grow. Within a thousand years or so, Paleo-Indians had migrated to the tip of South America and virtually everywhere else in the Western Hemisphere, as proved by discoveries of their spear points in numerous excavations.

Early Paleo-Indians used a distinctively shaped spearhead known as a **Clovis point**, named for the place in New Mexico where it was first excavated. Archaeologists' discovery of Clovis points throughout North and Central America in sites occupied between 13,500 BP and 13,000 BP provides evidence that these nomadic hunters shared a common ancestry and way of life. Paleo-Indians hunted mammoths and bison — judging from the artifacts and bones that

> **Some Paleo-Indians refrigerated killed mammoths by filling the intestines with stones and sinking the carcasses to the bottom of an icy lake.**

have survived from this era — but they probably also hunted smaller animals. Concentration on large animals, when possible, made sense because just one mammoth kill supplied hunters with meat for weeks or, if dried, for months. Some Paleo-Indians even refrigerated killed mammoths by filling the intestines with stones and sinking the carcasses to the bottom of an icy lake to be retrieved and used later. In addition to food, mammoth kills provided hides and bones for clothing, shelter, tools, and much more.

About 11,000 BP, Paleo-Indians confronted a major crisis. The mammoths and other large mammals they hunted became extinct. The extinction was gradual, stretching over several hundred years. Scientists are not completely certain why it occurred, although environmental change probably contributed to it. About this time, the earth's climate warmed, glaciers melted, and sea levels rose. Mammoths and other large mammals probably had difficulty adapting to the warmer climate. Many archaeologists also believe, however, that Paleo-Indians probably contributed to the extinctions in the Western Hemisphere by killing large animals more rapidly than they could reproduce. Although some experts dispute this overkill hypothesis, similar environmental changes had occurred for millions of years without triggering the large-mammal extinctions that followed the arrival of Paleo-Indian hunters. Whatever the causes, Paleo-Indians faced a radical change in the natural environment within just a few thousand years of their arrival in the Western Hemisphere — namely, the extinction of large mammals. After the extinction, Paleo-Indians literally inhabited a new world.

Paleo-Indians adapted to the drastic environmental change of the big-game extinction by making at least two important changes in their way of life. First, hunters began to prey more intensively on smaller animals. Second, Paleo-Indians devoted more energy to foraging — that is, to collecting wild plant foods such as roots, seeds, nuts, berries, and fruits. When Paleo-Indians made these changes, they replaced the apparent uniformity of the big-game-oriented Clovis culture with great cultural diversity adapted to the many natural environments throughout the hemisphere, ranging from icy tundra to steamy jungles.

These post-Clovis adaptations to local environments resulted in the astounding variety of Native American cultures that existed when Europeans arrived in AD 1492. By then, more than three hundred major tribes and hundreds of lesser groups inhabited North America alone.

Ancient Petroglyphs

These petroglyphs — drawings incised onto the surface of rocks — probably depict shamans, ancient American spiritual leaders and healers who claimed the ability to communicate with supernatural powers. Shamans may well have made the petroglyphs to help them cure sicknesses, attempt to control the weather, or assure success for hunters. Petroglyphs can be found throughout North America; often they portray animals, people, or geometric designs. The petroglyphs shown here are among thousands located in the Coso Mountains on the edge of the Mojave Desert in what is now eastern California, where ancient Americans etched them onto rocks for millennia. © David Muench.

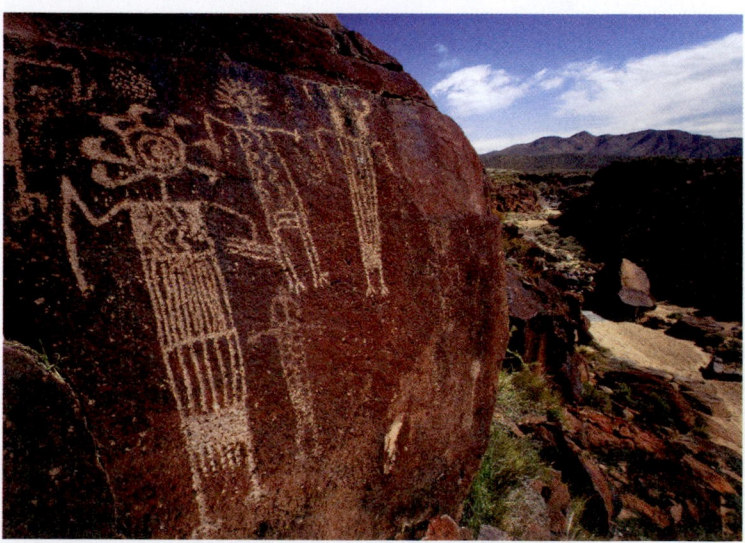

Clovis Spear Straightener
Clovis hunters used this bone spear straightener about 11,000 BP at a campsite in Arizona, where archaeologists discovered it lying among the butchered remains of two mammoth carcasses and thirteen ancient bison. Similar objects often appear in ancient sites in Eurasia, but this is the only bone artifact yet discovered in a Clovis-era site in North America. Presumably Clovis hunters stuck their spear shafts through the opening and then grasped the handle of the straightener and moved it back and forth along the length of the shaft to remove imperfections and make the spear a more effective weapon. Arizona State Museum, University of Arizona.

Hundreds more lived in Central and South America. Hundreds of other ancient American cultures had disappeared or transformed themselves as their people constantly adapted to environmental change and other challenges.

REVIEW How and why did humans migrate into North America after 15,000 BP?

▶ Archaic Hunters and Gatherers

Archaeologists use the term *Archaic* to describe the many different hunting and gathering cultures that descended from Paleo-Indians and the long period of time when those cultures dominated the history of ancient America — roughly from 10,000 BP to somewhere between 4000 BP and 3000 BP. The term describes the era in the history of ancient America that followed the Paleo-Indian big-game hunters and preceded the development of agriculture. It denotes a **hunter-gatherer** way of life that persisted in North America long after European colonization.

Like their Paleo-Indian ancestors, **Archaic Indians** hunted with spears, but they also took smaller game with traps, nets, and hooks. Unlike their Paleo-Indian predecessors, most Archaic peoples used a variety of stone tools to prepare food from wild plants. A characteristic Archaic artifact is a grinding stone used to pulverize seeds into edible form. Most Archaic Indians migrated from place to place to harvest plants and hunt animals. They usually did not establish permanent villages, although they often returned to the same river valley or fertile meadow year after year. In regions with especially rich resources — such as present-day California and the Pacific Northwest — they developed permanent settlements. Many groups became excellent basket makers in order to collect and store food they gathered from wild plants. Archaic peoples followed these practices in distinctive ways in the different environmental regions of North America (Map 1.2).

Great Plains Bison Hunters

After the extinction of large game animals, some hunters began to concentrate on bison in the huge herds that grazed the grassy, arid plains stretching hundreds of miles east of the Rocky Mountains. For almost a thousand years after the big-game extinctions, Archaic Indians hunted bison with Folsom points, named after a site near Folsom, New Mexico. In 1908, George McJunkin, an African American cowboy, discovered this site, which contained a deposit of large fossilized bones. In 1926, archaeologists excavated the site McJunkin had discovered and found evidence that proved conclusively for the first time that ancient Americans and giant bison — which were known to have been extinct for at least ten thousand years — were contemporaries. One Folsom point remained stuck between two ribs of a giant bison, where a Stone Age hunter had plunged it more than ten thousand years earlier.

Like their nomadic predecessors, Folsom hunters moved constantly to maintain contact with their prey. **Great Plains hunters** developed trapping techniques that made it easy to kill large numbers of animals. At the original Folsom site, careful study of the bones McJunkin found suggests that early one winter hunters drove bison into a narrow gulch and speared twenty-three of them. At other sites, Great Plains hunters stampeded bison herds over cliffs and then slaughtered the animals that plunged to their deaths.

Bows and arrows reached Great Plains hunters from the north about AD 500. They largely replaced spears, which had been the hunters' weapons of choice for millennia. Bows permitted

MAP ACTIVITY

Map 1.2 Native North American Cultures
Environmental conditions defined the boundaries of the broad zones of cultural similarity among ancient North Americans.

READING THE MAP: What crucial environmental features set the boundaries of each cultural region? (The topography indicated on Map 1.3, "Native North Americans about 1500," may be helpful.)

CONNECTIONS: How did environmental factors and variations affect the development of different groups of Native American cultures? Why do you think historians and archaeologists group cultures together by their regional positions?

hunters to wound animals from farther away, arrows made it possible to shoot repeatedly, and arrowheads were easier to make and therefore less costly to lose than the larger, heavier spear points. But these new weapons did not otherwise alter age-old techniques of bison hunting on the Great Plains. Although we often imagine ancient Great Plains bison hunters on horseback, in fact

they hunted on foot, like their Paleo-Indian ancestors. Horses that had existed in North America millions of years earlier had long since become extinct. Horses did not return to the Great Plains until Europeans imported them in the decades after 1492, when Native American bison hunters acquired them and soon became expert riders.

Fishhooks
Ancient Americans crafted these fishhooks sometime between AD 900 and 1600 from abalone shells collected in the waters off coastal California. Fishermen attached a line to the nub shown at the top of three of the hooks, skewered bait onto the point of the hook, then pulled up when a fish nibbled, hoping to snag the lip of the unsuspecting fish. (The numbers on the hooks were added in modern times.) The hooks illustrate Pacific Coast cultures' exploitation of their rich marine environment. ©The Field Museum #A114464_32d.

Great Basin Cultures

Archaic peoples in the Great Basin between the Rocky Mountains and the Sierra Nevada inhabited a region of great environmental diversity. Some **Great Basin Indians** lived along the shores of large marshes and lakes that formed during rainy periods, eating fish they caught with bone hooks and nets. Other cultures survived in the foothills of mountains between the blistering heat on the desert floor and the cold, treeless mountain heights. Hunters killed deer, antelope, and sometimes bison, as well as smaller game such as rabbits, rodents, and snakes. These broadly defined zones of habitation changed constantly, depending largely on the amount of rain.

Despite the variety and occasional abundance of animals, Great Basin peoples relied on plants as their most important food source. Unlike meat and fish, plant food could be collected and stored for long periods to protect against shortages caused by the fickle rainfall. Many Great Basin peoples gathered piñon nuts as a dietary staple. By diversifying their food sources and migrating to favorable locations to collect and store them, Great Basin peoples adapted to the severe environmental challenges of the region and maintained their Archaic hunter-gatherer way of life for centuries after Europeans arrived in AD 1492.

Pacific Coast Cultures

The richness of the natural environment made present-day California the most densely settled area in all of ancient North America. The land and ocean offered such ample food that **California peoples** remained hunters and gatherers for hundreds of years after AD 1492. The diversity of California's environment also encouraged corresponding variety among native peoples. The mosaic of Archaic settlements in California included about five hundred separate tribes speaking some ninety languages, each with local dialects. No other region of comparable size in ancient North America exhibited such cultural variety.

The Chumash, one of the many California cultures, emerged in the region surrounding what is now Santa Barbara about 5000 BP. Comparatively plentiful food resources — especially acorns — permitted Chumash people to establish relatively permanent villages. Conflict, evidently caused by competition for valuable acorn-gathering territory, frequently broke out among the villages, as documented by Chumash skeletons that display signs of violent deaths. Although few other

> **The richness of the natural environment made present-day California the most densely settled area in all of ancient North America.**

Ancient California Peoples

Chumash Necklace
Long before the arrival of Europeans, ancient Chumash people in southern California made this elegant necklace of abalone shell. The carefully formed, polished, and assembled pieces of shell illustrate the artistry of the Chumash and their access to the rich and diverse marine life of the Pacific coast. Since living abalone cling stubbornly to submerged rocks along the coast, Chumash divers presumably pried abalone from their rocky perches to obtain their delicious flesh; then one or more Chumash artisans recycled the inedible shell to make this necklace. Its iridescent splendor demonstrates that Chumash people wore beautiful as well as useful adornments. Natural History Museum of Los Angeles County.

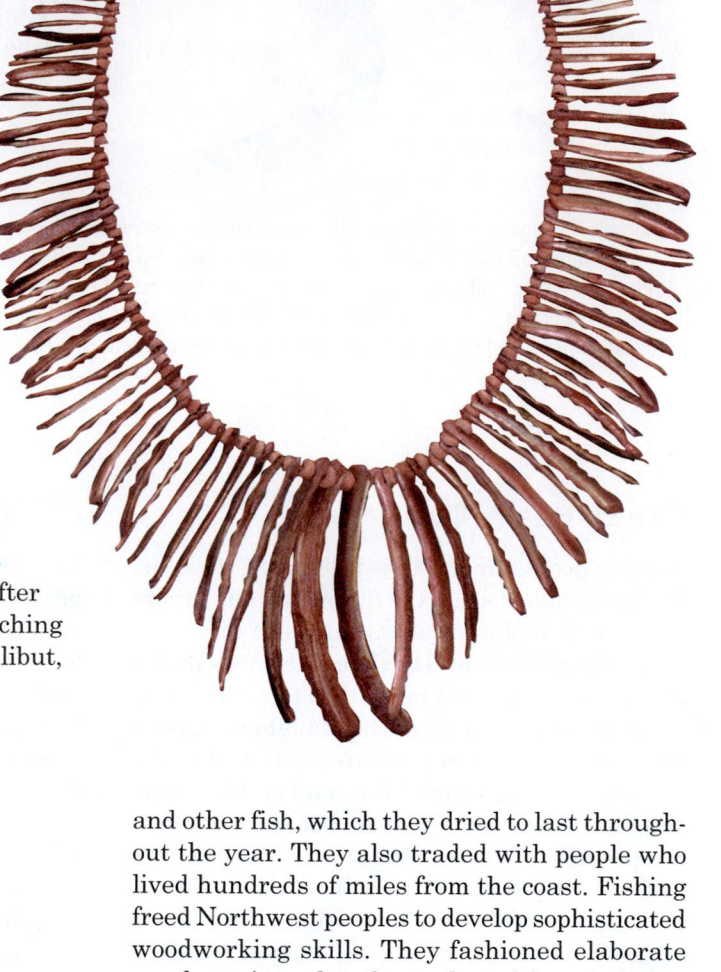

California cultures achieved the population density and village settlements of the Chumash, all shared the hunter-gatherer way of life and reliance on acorns as a major food source.

Another rich natural environment lay along the Pacific Northwest coast. Like the Chumash, **Northwest peoples** built more or less permanent villages. After about 5500 BP, they concentrated on catching whales and large quantities of salmon, halibut,

Ozette Whale Effigy
This carving of a whale fin decorated with hundreds of sea otter teeth was discovered along with thousands of other artifacts of daily life at Ozette, an ancient village on the tip of the Olympic Peninsula in present-day Washington that was inundated by a catastrophic mud slide about five hundred years ago. The fin illustrates the importance of whale hunting to the residents of Ozette, who set out in canoes, each carrying eight men armed with harpoons, to catch and kill animals weighing twenty to thirty tons each. Richard Alexander Cooke III.

and other fish, which they dried to last throughout the year. They also traded with people who lived hundreds of miles from the coast. Fishing freed Northwest peoples to develop sophisticated woodworking skills. They fashioned elaborate wood carvings that denoted wealth and status, as well as huge canoes for fishing, hunting, and conducting warfare against neighboring tribes. Much of the warfare among Archaic northwesterners grew out of attempts to defend or gain access to prime fishing sites.

Eastern Woodland Cultures

East of the Mississippi River, Archaic peoples adapted to a forest environment that included many local variants, such as the major river valleys of the Mississippi, Ohio, Tennessee, and Cumberland; the Great Lakes region; and the Atlantic coast (see Map 1.2). Throughout these diverse locales, Archaic peoples pursued similar survival strategies.

Woodland hunters stalked deer as their most important prey. Deer supplied **Woodland peoples** with food as well as hides and bones that they crafted into clothing, weapons, and many other tools. Like Archaic peoples elsewhere, Woodland Indians gathered edible plants, seeds, and nuts, especially hickory nuts, pecans, walnuts, and acorns. About 6000 BP, some Woodland groups established more or less permanent settlements of 25 to 150 people, usually near a river or lake that offered a wide variety of plant and animal resources. The existence of such settlements has permitted archaeologists to locate numerous Archaic burial sites that suggest Woodland people had a life expectancy of about eighteen years, a relatively short time to learn all the skills necessary to survive, reproduce, and adapt to change.

Around 4000 BP, Woodland cultures added two important features to their basic hunter-gatherer lifestyles: agriculture and pottery. Gourds and pumpkins that were first cultivated thousands of years earlier in Mexico spread north to Woodland peoples through trade and migration. Woodland peoples also began to cultivate local species such as sunflowers, as well as small quantities of tobacco, another import from South America. Corn, which had been grown by Mesoamerican and South American peoples since about 7000 BP, slowly traveled north with migrants and traders and eventually became a significant food crop among Eastern Woodland

peoples around 2500 BP. Most likely, women learned how to plant, grow, and harvest these crops as an outgrowth of their work gathering edible wild plants. Cultivated crops added to the quantity, variety, and predictability of Woodland food sources, but they did not alter Woodland peoples' dependence on gathering wild plants, seeds, and nuts.

Like agriculture, pottery probably originated in Mexico. Traders and migrants most likely brought pottery-making skills northward along with Mesoamerican and South American seeds. Pots were more durable than baskets for cooking and the storage of food and water, but they were also much heavier and therefore were shunned by nomadic peoples. The permanent settlements of Woodland peoples made the heavy weight of pots much less important than their advantages compared to leaky and fragile baskets. While pottery and agriculture introduced changes in Woodland cultures, ancient Woodland Americans retained the other basic features of their Archaic hunter-gatherer lifestyle, which persisted in most areas to 1492 and beyond.

REVIEW Why did Archaic Native Americans shift from big-game hunting to foraging and hunting smaller animals?

Mississippian Effigy Bowl
A Mississippian craftsman carved this effigy bowl from the mineral diorite within a century or two of AD 1200. Excavated from the Moundville site near the Black Warrior River in what is today central Alabama, the bowl was probably used in ceremonies to hold ritualistic liquids or herbs, rather than as a vessel for day-to-day drinking and eating. Depicting a crested wood duck, a figure commonly represented among the thousands of artifacts discovered at Moundville, the bowl illustrates the stunning artistry achieved by ancient Mississippians. Richard Alexander Cooke III.

► Agricultural Settlements and Chiefdoms

Among Eastern Woodland peoples and most other Archaic cultures, agriculture supplemented hunter-gatherer subsistence strategies but did not replace them. Reliance on wild animals and plants required most Archaic groups to remain small and mobile. But beginning about 4000 BP, distinctive southwestern cultures slowly began to depend on agriculture and to build permanent settlements. Later, around 2500 BP, Woodland peoples in the vast Mississippi valley began to construct burial mounds and other earthworks that suggest the existence of social and political hierarchies that archaeologists term *chiefdoms*. Although the hunter-gatherer lifestyle never entirely disappeared, the development of agricultural settlements and chiefdoms represented important innovations to the Archaic way of life.

Southwestern Cultures

Ancient Americans in present-day Arizona, New Mexico, and southern portions of Utah and Colorado developed cultures characterized by **agricultural settlements** and multiunit dwellings called pueblos. All southwestern peoples confronted the challenge of a dry climate and unpredictable fluctuations in rainfall that made the supply of wild plant food very unreliable. These ancient Americans probably adopted agriculture in response to this basic environmental uncertainty.

About 3500 BP, southwestern hunters and gatherers began to cultivate corn, their signature food crop. The demands of corn cultivation encouraged hunter-gatherers to restrict their migratory habits in order to tend the crop. A vital consideration was access to water. Southwestern Indians became irrigation experts, conserving water from streams, springs, and rainfall and distributing it to thirsty crops.

About AD 200, small farming settlements began to appear throughout southern New Mexico, marking the emergence of the **Mogollon culture**. Typically, a Mogollon settlement included a dozen pit houses, each made by digging out a rounded pit about fifteen feet in diameter and a foot or two deep and then erecting poles to support a roof of branches or dirt. Larger villages usually had one or two bigger pit houses that may have been the predecessors of the circular kivas, the ceremonial rooms that became a characteristic of nearly all southwestern settlements. About AD 900, Mogollon culture began to decline, for reasons that remain obscure. Its descendants included the Mimbres people in southwestern New Mexico, who crafted spectacular pottery adorned with human and animal designs. By about AD 1250, the Mimbres culture disappeared, for reasons unknown.

Around AD 500, while the Mogollon culture prevailed in New Mexico, other ancient people migrated from Mexico to southern Arizona and

VISUAL ACTIVITY

Ancient Agriculture

Dropping seeds into holes punched in cleared ground by a pointed stick known as a "dibble," this ancient American farmer sows a new crop while previously planted seeds — including the corn and beans immediately opposite him — bear fruit for harvest. Created by a sixteenth-century European artist, the drawing misrepresents who did the agricultural work in many ancient American cultures — namely, women rather than men. The Pierpont Morgan Library/Art Resource, NY.

READING THE IMAGE: In what ways has this ancient farmer modified and taken advantage of the natural environment?

CONNECTIONS: What were the advantages and disadvantages of agriculture compared to hunting and gathering?

Hohokam "Cigarettes"
Ancient Hohokam smokers in present-day Arizona stuffed these reeds (which probably grew near their irrigation canals) with shredded tobacco. They wrapped cotton thread around each reed to protect their fingers from heat while they inhaled the smoke of the burning tobacco. When hunting or tending their crops, Hohokam smokers probably found these "cigarettes" more convenient than their heavier and more cumbersome stone or ceramic pipes, which were better suited for sedentary occasions.
Jerry Jacka Photography.

established the distinctive **Hohokam culture**. Hohokam settlements used sophisticated grids of irrigation canals to plant and harvest crops twice a year. Hohokam settlements reflected the continuing influence of Mexican cultural practices that migrants brought with them as they traveled north. Hohokam people built sizable platform mounds and ball courts characteristic of many Mexican cultures. About AD 1400, Hohokam culture declined for reasons that remain a mystery, although the rising salinity of the soil brought about by centuries of irrigation probably caused declining crop yields and growing food shortages.

North of the Hohokam and Mogollon cultures, in a region that encompassed southern Utah and Colorado and northern Arizona and New Mexico, the **Anasazi culture** began to flourish about AD 100. The early Anasazi built pit houses on mesa tops and used irrigation much as their neighbors did to the south. Beginning around AD 1000 (again, it is not known why), some Anasazi began to move to large, multistory cliff dwellings whose spectacular ruins still exist at Mesa Verde, Colorado, and elsewhere. Other Anasazi communities—like the one whose impressive ruins can be visited at Chaco Canyon, New Mexico — erected huge stone-walled pueblos with enough rooms to house everyone in the settlement. (See "Visualizing History," page 18.) Anasazi pueblos and cliff dwellings typically included one or

Southwestern Indians became irrigation experts, conserving water from streams, springs, and rainfall and distributing it to thirsty crops.

Mexican Ball Court Model
The Mexica and other Mesoamerican peoples commonly built special courts (or playing fields) for their intensely competitive ball games. This rare model of a ball court, made in Mexico sometime between 2200 BP and AD 250, shows a game in progress, complete with players and spectators. Players wore padded belts and used their hips to hit the hard rubber ball through the goal. Spectators bet on the games, and losing players were often killed. A few ball courts have been excavated in North America, providing compelling evidence of one of the many connections between ancient Mesoamericans and North Americans. Yale University Art Gallery/Art Resource, NY.

Daily Life in Chaco Canyon

Pueblo Bonito, Chaco Canyon, New Mexico

About AD 1000, Pueblo Bonito stood at the center of Chacoan culture, which ranged over 20,000 square miles in the arid region at the intersection of present-day Utah, Colorado, Arizona, and New Mexico. The largest of more than 3,600 Chacoan archaeological sites, Pueblo Bonito originally stood four or five stories tall and housed more than 600 rooms, including 35 kivas, the circular structures visible around the perimeter of the large plazas.

Chacoans covered each kiva with a roof, creating a darkened underground space for ceremonial rituals. Why might these spaces be built belowground and separated from the other rooms of the pueblo?

The exact nature of Chacoan ceremonies remains a mystery, but less mysterious are the routines of daily life that sustained the people at Pueblo Bonito for centuries. Imagine a woman setting out from the pueblo on a spring day to plant corn,

Sandal

the most important food crop. She might first strap on sandals, like the one shown here, woven from fibers of the yucca plant. What does the

more kivas used for secret ceremonies, restricted to men, that sought to communicate with the supernatural world. The alignment of Chaco buildings with solar and lunar events (such as the summer and winter solstices) suggests that Anasazi studied the sky carefully, probably because they believed supernatural celestial powers influenced their lives.

Drought began to plague the region about AD 1130, and it lasted for more than half a century, triggering the disappearance of the Anasazi culture. By AD 1200, the large Anasazi pueblos had been abandoned. The prolonged drought probably intensified conflict among pueblos and made it impossible to depend on the techniques of irrigated agriculture that had worked for centuries. Some Anasazi migrated toward regions with more reliable rainfall and settled in Hopi, Zuñi, and Acoma pueblos that their descendants in Arizona and New Mexico have occupied ever since.

Woodland Burial Mounds and Chiefdoms

No other ancient Americans created dwellings similar to pueblos, but around 2500 BP, Woodland cultures throughout the vast watershed drained by the Mississippi River began to build burial mounds. The size of the mounds, the labor and

sandal suggest about the importance of the harvesting, processing, and weaving of yucca fibers?

To dig a hole for planting corn seeds, our imagined woman might use a digging stick like the one shown here, tipped by the horn of a mountain sheep, tightly bound with sinew to a sturdy cottonwood branch, and covered with animal hide to protect the binding. What does the digging stick suggest about the interdependence of hunting and agriculture in the daily lives of Chacoans?

Digging Stick

Once harvested and dried, corn needed to be ground in order to be cooked and eaten. By looking at the small flat stone (the *mano*) and the larger stone slab (the *metate*) shown here, can you imagine how our Chacoan woman used these tools? Some rooms at Pueblo Bonito

Mano and Metate

held numerous grinding stones like the ones shown here. What does such grouping suggest about the corn-grinding process?

To cook the cornmeal she had ground, our imagined woman would need to mix it with water. She might use a ceramic ladle like the one shown here — crafted and decorated by a pottery maker at Chaco — to dip some fresh water from a storage pot. To make a fire, she could use the Chacoan fire starter kit shown here. Can you visualize how the fire starter worked? After kindling a cooking fire, she could heat the cornmeal gruel in a ceramic pot. Once the mixture was cooked, she might use the ladle again to

Ladle

transfer servings into small bowls for eating. Why do you think the decoration at the end of the ladle's handle is blurred?

Chacoans flourished at Pueblo Bonito despite the arid climate and limited natural resources. In their daily lives, they sustained themselves by using their knowledge and skills to grow and cook corn and to craft vital items such as ceramics and footwear. Can you imagine each step in the creation of the artifacts shown here? Can you imagine the organization and scheduling of daily tasks required to make and use these basic items?

SOURCES: Pueblo Bonito, Chaco Canyon, New Mexico: Richard Alexander Cooke III; sandal, digging stick, mano and metate, fire starter kit, and ladle: Chaco Culture National Historic Park.

Fire Starter Kit

organization required to erect them, and differences in the artifacts buried with certain individuals suggest the existence of a social and political hierarchy that archaeologists term a **chiefdom**. Experts do not know the name of a single chief, nor do they know the organizational structure a chief headed. But the only way archaeologists can account for the complex and labor-intensive burial mounds and the artifacts found in them is to assume that one person — whom scholars term a *chief* — commanded the labor and obedience of very large numbers of other people, who made up the chief's chiefdom.

Between 2500 BP and 2100 BP, **Adena people** built hundreds of burial mounds radiat-

ing from central Ohio. In the mounds, the Adena usually accompanied burials with grave goods that included spear points and stone pipes as well as thin sheets of mica (a glasslike mineral) crafted into the shapes of birds, beasts, and human hands. Over the body and grave goods, Adena people piled dirt into a mound. Sometimes burial mounds were constructed all at once, but often they were built up slowly over many years.

About 2100 BP, Adena culture evolved into the more elaborate **Hopewell culture**, which lasted about five hundred years. Centered in Ohio, Hopewell culture extended throughout the enormous drainage of the Ohio and Mississippi rivers. Hopewell people built larger mounds

than did their Adena predecessors and filled them with more magnificent grave goods. Burial was probably reserved for the most important members of Hopewell groups. Most people were cremated. Burial rituals appear to have brought many people together to honor the dead person and to help build the mound. Hopewell mounds were often one hundred feet in diameter and thirty feet high. Grave goods at Hopewell sites testify to the high quality of Hopewell crafts and to a thriving trade network that ranged from present-day Wyoming to Florida. Archaeologists believe that Hopewell chiefs probably played an important role in this sprawling interregional trade.

Hopewell culture declined about AD 400 for reasons that are obscure. Archaeologists speculate that bows and arrows, along with increasing reliance on agriculture, made small settlements more self-sufficient and therefore less dependent on the central authority of the Hopewell chiefs who were responsible for the burial mounds.

Four hundred years later, another mound-building culture flourished. The **Mississippian culture** emerged in the floodplains of the major southeastern river systems about AD 800 and lasted until about AD 1500. Major Mississippian sites, such as the one at Cahokia (see pages 3–4), included huge mounds with platforms on top for ceremonies and for the residences of great chiefs. Most likely, the ceremonial mounds and ritual

practices derived from Mexican cultural expressions that were brought north by traders and migrants. At Cahokia, skilled farmers supported the large population with ample crops of corn. In addition to mounds, Cahokians erected what archaeologists call woodhenges (after the famous Stonehenge in England) — long wooden poles set upright in the ground and carefully arranged in huge circles. Although the purpose of woodhenges is unknown, experts believe that Cahokians probably built them partly for celestial observations.

Cahokia and other Mississippian cultures dwindled by AD 1500. When Europeans arrived, most of the descendants of Mississippian cultures, like those of the Hopewell culture, lived in small dispersed villages supported by hunting and gathering, supplemented by agriculture. Clearly, the conditions that caused large chiefdoms to emerge — whatever they were — had changed, and chiefs no longer commanded the sweeping powers they had once enjoyed.

REVIEW   How did food-gathering strategies influence ancient cultures across North America?

► Native Americans in the 1490s

On the eve of European colonization in the 1490s, Native Americans lived throughout North and South America, but their total population is a subject of spirited debate among scholars. Some experts claim that Native Americans inhabiting what is now the United States and Canada numbered 18 million to 20 million, while others place the population at no more than 1 million. A prudent estimate is about 4 million, or about the same as the number of people living on the small island nation of England at that time. The vastness of the territory meant that the overall population density of North America (excluding Mesoamerica) was low, just 60 people per 100 square miles, compared to more than 8,000 in England. Native Americans were spread thin across the land because of their survival strategies of hunting, gathering, and agriculture, although variations in climate and natural resources meant that some regions were more populous than others (Figure 1.2).

Cahokia Tablet
This stone tablet excavated from the largest mound at Cahokia depicts a bird-man whose sweeping wings and facial features — especially the nose and mouth — resemble those of a bird. Crafted around AD 1100, the tablet probably played some role in rituals enacted on the mound by Cahokian people. Similar bird-like human forms have been found among other Mississippian cultures. Cahokia Mounds Historic Site.

Eastern and Great Plains Peoples

About one-third of native North Americans inhabited the enormous Woodland region east of the Mississippi River; their population density approximated the average for North America as a whole (excluding Mesoamerica). Eastern Woodland peoples clustered into three broad linguistic and cultural groups: Algonquian, Iroquoian, and Muskogean.

Algonquian tribes inhabited the Atlantic seaboard, the Great Lakes region, and much of the upper Midwest (Map 1.3). The relatively mild climate along the Atlantic permitted the coastal Algonquians to grow corn and other crops as well as to hunt and fish. Around the Great Lakes and in northern New England, however, cool summers and severe winters made agriculture impractical. Instead, the Abenaki, Penobscot, Chippewa, and other tribes concentrated on hunting and fishing, using canoes both for transportation and for gathering wild rice.

Inland from the Algonquian region, **Iroquoian** tribes occupied territories centered in Pennsylvania and upstate New York, as well as the hilly upland regions of the Carolinas and Georgia. Three features distinguished Iroquoian tribes from their neighbors. First, their success in cultivating corn and other crops allowed them to build permanent settlements, usually consisting of several bark-covered longhouses up to one hundred feet long and housing five to ten families. Second, Iroquoian societies adhered to matrilineal rules of descent. Property of all sorts belonged to women. Women headed family clans and even selected the chiefs (normally men) who governed the tribes. Third, for purposes of war and diplomacy, an Iroquoian confederation — including the Seneca, Onondaga, Mohawk, Oneida, and Cayuga tribes — formed

FIGURE 1.2 Native American Population in North America about 1492 (Estimated)
On the eve of the arrival of Europeans, Native Americans lived throughout North America, as their ancestors had for millennia (see Map 1.2, page 12). Population densities varied widely, depending in large part on the availability of natural resources, but the Pacific coast, where rich marine resources supported hunter-gatherers, had the highest concentration of people. The lowest population density was in the Arctic, where the vast expanse of land offered few resources. Overall, the population density of North America was less than 1 percent of the population density of England, which helps explain why European colonists tended to view North America as a comparatively empty wilderness.

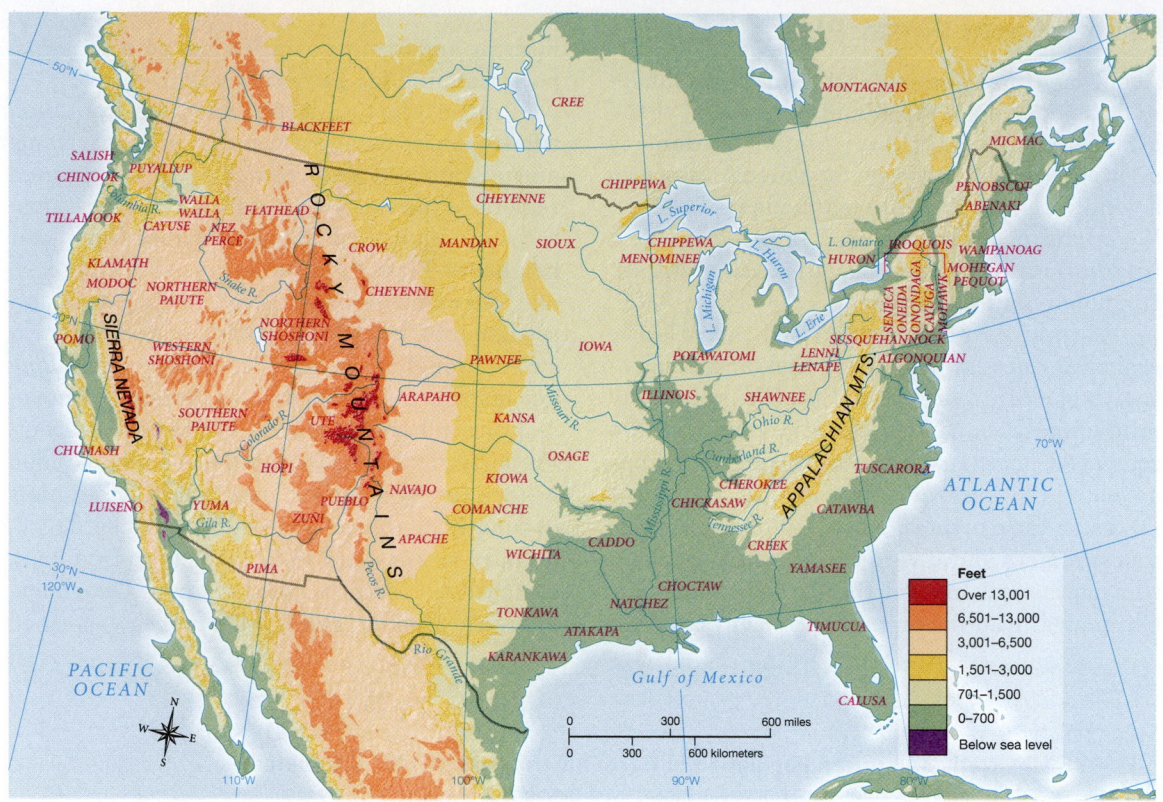

MAP 1.3
Native North Americans about 1500
Distinctive Native American peoples resided throughout the area that, centuries later, would become the United States. This map indicates the approximate location of some of the larger tribes about 1500. In the interest of legibility, many other peoples who inhabited North America at the time are omitted from the map.

the **League of Five Nations**, which remained powerful well into the eighteenth century.

Muskogean peoples spread throughout the woodlands of the Southeast, south of the Ohio River and east of the Mississippi. Including the Creek, Choctaw, Chickasaw, and Natchez tribes, Muskogeans inhabited a bountiful natural environment that provided abundant food from hunting, gathering, and agriculture. Remnants of the earlier Mississippian culture still existed in Muskogean religion. The Natchez, for example, worshipped the sun and built temple mounds modeled after those of their Mississippian ancestors, including Cahokia.

Great Plains peoples accounted for about one out of seven native North Americans. Inhabiting the huge region west of the Eastern Woodland people and east of the Rocky Mountains, many tribes had migrated to the Great Plains within the century or two before the 1490s, forced westward by Iroquoian and Algonquian tribes.

Some Great Plains tribes—especially the Mandan and Pawnee — farmed successfully, growing both corn and sunflowers. But the Teton Sioux, Blackfeet, Comanche, Cheyenne, and Crow on the northern plains and the Apache and other nomadic tribes on the southern plains depended on buffalo (American bison) for their subsistence.

Southwestern and Western Peoples

Southwestern cultures included about a quarter of all native North Americans. These descendants of the Mogollon, Hohokam, and Anasazi cultures lived in settled agricultural communities, many of them pueblos. They continued to grow corn, beans, and squash using methods they had refined for centuries.

However, their communities came under attack by a large number of warlike Athapascans who invaded the Southwest beginning around

AD 1300. The Athapascans — principally Apache and Navajo — were skillful warriors who preyed on the sedentary pueblo Indians, reaping the fruits of agriculture without the work of farming.

About a fifth of all native North Americans resided along the Pacific coast. In California, abundant acorns and nutritious marine life continued to support high population densities, but this abundance retarded the development of agriculture. Similar dependence on hunting and gathering persisted along the Northwest coast, where fishing reigned supreme. Salmon were so plentiful that at **The Dalles**, a prime fishing site on the Columbia River on the border of present-day Oregon and Washington, Northwest peoples caught millions of pounds of salmon every summer and traded their catch as far away as California and the Great Plains. Although important trading centers existed throughout North America, particularly in the Southwest, it is likely that The Dalles was the largest Native American trading center in ancient North America.

Cultural Similarities

While trading was common, all native North Americans in the 1490s still depended on hunting and gathering for a major portion of their food. Most of them also practiced agriculture. Some used agriculture to supplement hunting and gathering; for others, the balance was reversed. People throughout North America used bows, arrows, and other weapons for hunting and warfare. None of them employed writing, expressing themselves instead in many other ways: drawings sketched on stones, wood, and animal skins; patterns woven in baskets and textiles; designs painted on pottery, crafted into beadwork, or carved into effigies; and songs, dances, religious ceremonies, and burial rites.

These rich and varied cultural resources of native North Americans did not include features of life common in Europe during the 1490s. Native North Americans did not use wheels; sailing ships were unknown to them; they had no large domesticated animals such as horses, cows, or oxen; their use of metals was restricted to copper. However, the absence of these European conveniences mattered less to native North Americans than their own cultural adaptations to the natural environment local to each tribe and to the social environment among neighboring peoples. That great similarity — adaptation to natural and social environments — underlay all the cultural diversity among native North Americans.

It would be a mistake, however, to conclude that native North Americans lived in blissful harmony with nature and one another. Archaeological sites provide ample evidence of violent conflict. Skeletons, like those at Cahokia, bear the marks of wounds as well as of ritualistic human sacrifice. Religious, ethnic, economic, and familial conflicts must have occurred, but they remain in obscurity because they left few archaeological traces. In general, fear and anxiety must have been at least as common among native North Americans as feelings of peace and security.

Native North Americans not only adapted to the natural environment but also changed it in many ways. They built thousands of structures, from small dwellings to massive pueblos and enormous mounds, permanently altering the landscape. Their gathering techniques selected productive and nutritious varieties of plants, thereby shifting the balance of local plants toward useful varieties. The first stages of North American agriculture, for example, probably involved Native Americans gathering wild seeds and then sowing them in a meadow for later harvest. It is almost certain that fertile and hardy varieties of corn were developed this way, first in Mesoamerica and later in North America. To clear land for planting corn, native North Americans set fires that burned off thousands of acres of forest.

Native North Americans also used fires for hunting. Great Plains hunters often started fires to force buffalo together and make them easy to slaughter. Eastern Woodland, Southwest, and Pacific coast Indians also set fires to hunt deer and other valuable prey. Hunters crouched downwind from a brushy area while their companions set a fire upwind; as animals raced out of the burning underbrush, hunters killed them.

Throughout North America, Indians started fires along the edges of woods to burn off shrubby undergrowth and encroaching tree seedlings. These burns encouraged the growth of tender young plants that attracted deer and other game animals, bringing them within convenient range of hunters' weapons. The burns also encouraged the growth of sun-loving food plants that Indians

> **While trading was common, all native North Americans in the 1490s still depended on hunting and gathering for a major portion of their food.**

THE PROMISE OF TECHNOLOGY

Ancient American Weaving

The workbasket of a master weaver shown here illustrates the technology of ancient American textile production. Found in the Andes in a woman's grave dating from one thousand years ago, the workbasket contains tools for every stage of textile production. Weaving — like other activities such as cooking, hunting, and worship — depended above all on human knowledge passed from one person to another in cycle after cycle of teaching and learning. This cycle of teaching and learning was fragile. A weaver's knowledge could die with her if she had not taught it to somebody else. What kinds of human knowledge would have been required to make weavings with the contents of this workbasket? Museum of Fine Arts, Boston. Gift of Charles H. White, 02.680.

relished, such as blackberries, strawberries, and raspberries.

Because the fires set by native North Americans usually burned until they ran out of fuel or were extinguished by rain or wind, enormous regions of North America were burned over. In the long run, fires created and maintained light-dappled meadows for hunting and agriculture, cleared entangling underbrush from forests, and promoted a diverse and productive natural environment. Fires, like other activities of native North Americans, shaped the landscape of North America long before Europeans arrived in 1492.

> **REVIEW** What cultural similarities were shared by the diverse peoples of the Western Hemisphere in the 1490s, and why?

▶ The Mexica: A Mesoamerican Culture

The vast majority of the 80 million people who lived in the Western Hemisphere in the 1490s inhabited Mesoamerica and South America, where the population approximately equaled that of Europe. Like their much less numerous counterparts north of the Rio Grande, these people lived in a natural environment of tremendous diversity. They too developed hundreds of cultures, far too numerous to catalog here. But among all these cultures, the **Mexica** stood out. (Europeans often called these people Aztecs, a name the Mexica did not use.) Their empire stretched from coast to coast across central Mexico, encompassing between 8 million and 25 million people (experts disagree about the total population). We know more about the Mexica than about any other Native American society of the time, principally because of their massive monuments and their Spanish conquerors' well-documented interest in subduing them (as discussed in chapter 2). Their significance in the history of the New World after 1492 dictates a brief discussion of their culture and society.

The Mexica began their rise to prominence about 1325, when small bands settled on a marshy island in Lake Texcoco, the site of the future city of Tenochtitlán, the capital of the Mexican empire. Resourceful, courageous, and cold-blooded warriors, the Mexica were often hired out as mercenaries for richer, more settled tribes.

By 1430, the Mexica succeeded in asserting their dominance over their former allies and leading their own military campaigns in an ever-widening arc of empire building. Despite pockets of resistance, by the 1490s the Mexica ruled an empire that covered more land than Spain and Portugal combined and contained almost three times as many people.

The empire exemplified the central values of Mexican society. The Mexica worshipped the

Mexican Human Sacrifice
This graphic portrayal of human sacrifice was drawn by a Mexican artist in the sixteenth century. It shows the typical routine of human sacrifice practiced by the Mexica for centuries before Europeans arrived. The victim climbed the temple steps and then was stretched over a stone pillar (notice the priest's helper holding the victim's legs) to make it easier for the priest to plunge a stone knife into the victim's chest, cut out the still-beating heart, and offer it to the bloodthirsty gods. The body of the previous victim has already been pushed down from the temple heights and is about to be dragged away. Scala/Art Resource, NY; Biblioteca Nazionale, Florence, Italy.

war god **Huitzilopochtli**. Warriors held the most exalted positions in the social hierarchy, even above the priests who performed the sacred ceremonies that won Huitzilopochtli's favor. In the almost constant battles necessary to defend and extend the empire, young Mexican men exhibited the courage and daring that would allow them to rise in the carefully graduated ranks of warriors. The Mexica considered capturing prisoners the ultimate act of bravery. Warriors usually turned over the captives to Mexican priests, who sacrificed them to Huitzilopochtli by cutting out their hearts. The Mexica believed that human sacrifice fed the sun's craving for blood, which kept the sun aflame and prevented the fatal descent of everlasting darkness and chaos.

The empire contributed far more to Mexican society than victims for sacrifice. At the most basic level, the empire functioned as a military and political system that collected **tribute** from subject peoples. The Mexica forced conquered tribes to pay tribute in goods, not money. Tribute redistributed to the Mexica as much as one-third of the goods produced by conquered tribes. It included everything from candidates for human sacrifice to textiles and basic food products such as corn and beans, as well as exotic luxury items such as gold, turquoise, and rare bird feathers.

Tribute reflected the fundamental relations of power and wealth that pervaded the Mexican empire. The relatively small nobility of Mexican warriors, supported by a still smaller priesthood, possessed the military and religious power to command the obedience of thousands of non-noble Mexicans and of millions of non-Mexicans in subjugated colonies. The Mexican elite exercised their power to obtain tribute and thereby to redistribute wealth from the conquered to the conquerors, from the commoners to the nobility, from the poor to the rich. This redistribution of wealth made possible the achievements of Mexican society that eventually amazed the Spaniards: the huge cities, fabulous temples, teeming markets, and luxuriant gardens, not to mention the storehouses stuffed with gold and other treasures.

On the whole, the Mexica did not interfere much with the internal government of conquered regions. Instead, they usually permitted the traditional ruling elite to stay in power — so long as they paid tribute. The conquered provinces received very little in return from the Mexica, except immunity from punitive raids. Subjugated communities felt exploited by the constant payment of tribute to the Mexica. By depending on military conquest and the constant collection of tribute, the Mexica failed to create among their subjects a belief that Mexican domination was, at some level, legitimate and equitable. The high

By the 1490s, the Mexica ruled an empire that covered more land than Spain and Portugal combined and contained almost three times as many people.

Salado Ritual Figure
About AD 1350, this figure was carefully wrapped in a reed mat with other items and stored in a cave in a mountainous region of New Mexico by people of the Salado culture, descendants of the Mimbres, who had flourished three centuries earlier. The face of this figure is as close to a self-portrait of ancient Americans on the eve of their encounter with Europeans as we are ever likely to have. Adorned with vivid pigments, cotton string, bright feathers, and stones, the effigy testifies to the human complexity of all ancient Americans. Photography © 2000 The Art Institute of Chicago.

relied on oral rather than written communication. But much can be pieced together from artifacts they left behind at camps, kill sites, and ceremonial and residential centers such as Cahokia. Ancient Americans achieved their success through resourceful adaptation to the hemisphere's many and ever-changing natural environments. They also adapted to social and cultural changes caused by human beings — such as marriages, deaths, political struggles, and warfare — but the sparse evidence that has survived renders those adaptations almost entirely unknowable. Their creativity and artistry are unmistakably documented in their numerous artifacts. Those material objects sketch the only likenesses of ancient Americans we will ever have — blurred, shadowy images that are indisputably human but forever silent.

When European intruders began arriving in the Western Hemisphere in 1492, their attitudes about the promise of the New World were heavily influenced by the diverse peoples they encountered. Europeans coveted Native Americans' wealth, labor, and land, and Christian missionaries sought to save their souls. Likewise, Native Americans marveled at such European technological novelties as sailing ships, steel weapons, gunpowder, and horses, while often reserving judgment about Europeans' Christian religion.

level of discontent among subject peoples constituted the soft, vulnerable underbelly of the Mexican empire, a fact that Spanish intruders exploited after AD 1492 to conquer the Mexica.

REVIEW Why was tribute important in the Mexican empire?

▶ Conclusion: The World of Ancient Americans

Ancient Americans shaped the history of human beings in the New World for more than thirteen thousand years. They established continuous human habitation in the Western Hemisphere from the time the first big-game hunters crossed Beringia until 1492 and beyond. Much of their history remains irretrievably lost because they

In the four centuries following 1492, as the trickle of European strangers became a flood of newcomers from both Europe and Africa, Native Americans and settlers continued to encounter each other. Peaceful negotiations as well as violent conflicts over both land and trading rights resulted in chronic fear and mistrust. Yet even as the era of European colonization marked the beginning of the end of ancient America, the ideas, subsistence strategies, and cultural beliefs of native North Americans remained powerful among their descendants for generations and continue to persist to the present.

▶ Selected Bibliography

General Works

Robson Bonnichsen and Karen L. Turnmire, *Ice Age Peoples of North America* (1999).

Karen Olsen Bruhns and Karen R. Stothert, *Women in Ancient America* (1999).

Thomas D. Dillehay, *The Settlement of the Americas: A New Prehistory* (2000).

Brian Fagan, *Ancient North America* (2005).

Tim Flannery, *The Eternal Frontier: An Ecological History of North America and Its Peoples* (2001).

J. C. H. King, *First People, First Contacts: Native Peoples of North America* (1999).

Charles C. Mann, *1491: New Revelations of the Americas before Columbus* (2006).

Francis McManamon et al., eds., *Archaeology in America* (2008).

Steven Mithen, *After the Ice: A Global Human History, 20,000–5000 BC* (2003).

David Hurst Thomas, *Skull Wars: Kennewick Man, Archaeology, and the Battle for Native American Identity* (2000).

Nicholas Wade, *Before the Dawn: Recovering the Lost History of Our Ancestors* (2006).

Native American Cultures in Territory of Present-Day United States

Mary J. Adair, *Prehistoric Agriculture in the Central Plains* (1988).

Kenneth M. Ames and Herbert D. G. Maschner, *Peoples of the Northwest Coast: Their Archaeology and Prehistory* (1999).

Sally A. Kitt Chappell, *Cahokia: Mirror of the Cosmos* (2002).

Linda S. Cordell, *Archaeology of the Southwest* (2009).

Richard J. Dent Jr., *Chesapeake Prehistory: Old Traditions, New Directions* (1995).

E. James Dixon, *Bones, Boats, and Bison: Archeology and the First Colonization of Western North America* (1999).

Thomas E. Emerson et al., eds., *Late Woodland Societies: Tradition and Transformation across the Midcontinent* (2008).

Kendrick Frazier, *People of Chaco: A Canyon and Its Cultures* (1999).

George C. Frison, *Prehistoric Hunters of the High Plains* (2nd ed., 1991).

Sarah A. Kerr, *Beyond Chaco: Great Kiva Communities on the Mogollon Rim Frontier* (2001).

Steven A. LeBlanc, *Prehistoric Warfare in the American Southwest* (1999).

Stephen H. Lekson, *The Chaco Meridian: Centers of Political Power in the Ancient Southwest* (1999).

Jerald T. Milanich, *Archaeology of Precolumbian Florida* (1994).

Timothy R. Pauketat, *Cahokia: Ancient America's Greatest City on the Mississippi* (2009).

Jefferson Reid and Stephanie Whittlesley, *The Archaeology of Ancient Arizona* (1997).

Karl H. Schlesier, *Plains Indians, A.D. 500–1500: The Archaeological Past of Historic Groups* (1994).

Lynne Sebastian, *The Chaco Anasazi: Sociopolitical Evolution in the Prehistoric Southwest* (1992).

Lynda Shaffer, *Native Americans before 1492: The Moundbuilding Centers of the Eastern Woodlands* (1992).

Marvin T. Smith, *Coosa: The Rise and Fall of a Southeastern Mississippian Chiefdom* (2000).

Biloine Whiting Young and Melvin L. Fowler, *Cahokia: The Great Native American Metropolis* (1999).

The Mexica

David Carrasco, *City of Sacrifice: The Aztec Empire and the Role of Violence in Civilization* (1999).

Michael D. Coe and Rex Koontz, *Mexico: From the Olmecs to the Aztecs* (5th ed., 2002).

Susan Toby Evans, *Ancient Mexico and Central America: Archaeology and Culture History* (2008).

Eduardo Matos Moctezuma and Felipe Solis Olguin, *Aztecs* (2002).

▶ **FOR MORE BOOKS ABOUT TOPICS IN THIS CHAPTER,** see the Online Bibliography at **bedfordstmartins.com/roark.**

▶ **FOR ADDITIONAL PRIMARY SOURCES FROM THIS PERIOD,** see Michael Johnson, ed., *Reading the American Past*, Fifth Edition.

▶ **FOR WEB SITES, IMAGES, AND DOCUMENTS RELATED TO TOPICS AND PLACES IN THIS CHAPTER,** visit Make History at **bedfordstmartins.com/roark.**

Reviewing Chapter 1

REVIEW QUESTIONS

Use key terms and dates to support your answers.

1. Why do historians rely on the work of archaeologists to write the history of ancient America? (pp. 5–6)

2. How and why did humans migrate into North America after 15,000 BP? (pp. 6–11)

3. Why did Archaic Native Americans shift from big-game hunting to foraging and hunting smaller animals? (pp. 11–15)

4. How did food-gathering strategies influence ancient cultures across North America? (pp. 15–20)

5. What cultural similarities were shared by the diverse peoples of the Western Hemisphere in the 1490s, and why? (pp. 20–24)

6. Why was tribute important in the Mexican empire? (pp. 24–26)

MAKING CONNECTIONS

Draw on key terms, the timeline, and review questions.

1. Explain the different approaches historians and archaeologists bring to studying people in the past. How do the different kinds of evidence they draw upon shape their accounts of the human past? In your answer, cite specific examples from the history of ancient America.

2. Discuss ancient peoples' strategies for surviving in the varied climates of North America. How did their different approaches to survival contribute to the diversity of Native American cultures? What else might have contributed to the diversity?

3. For more than twelve thousand years, Native Americans both adapted to environmental change in North America and produced significant changes in the environments around them. Discuss specific examples of Native Americans' adaptation to environmental change and the changes they caused in the North American landscape.

4. Rich archaeological and manuscript sources have enabled historians to develop a detailed portrait of the Mexica on the eve of European contact. How did the Mexica establish and maintain their expansive empire?

Link events in this chapter to earlier events.

1. Did the history of ancient Americans make them unusually vulnerable to eventual conquest by European colonizers? Why or why not?

2. Do you think that ancient American history would have been significantly different if North and South America had never been disconnected from the Eurasian landmass? If so, how and why? If not, why not?

▶ **FOR PRACTICE QUIZZES AND OTHER STUDY TOOLS,** visit the Online Study Guide at bedfordstmartins.com/roark.

TIMELINE

NOTE: Major events are depicted below in chronological order, but the time scale between events varies from millennia to centuries.

(BP is an abbreviation used by archaeologists for "years before the present.")

ca. 400,000 BP	• Modern humans (*Homo sapiens*) evolve in Africa.
ca. 25,000–14,000 BP	• Wisconsin glaciation exposes Beringia, land bridge between Siberia and Alaska.
ca. 15,000 BP	• First humans arrive in North America.
ca. 13,500–13,000 BP	• Paleo-Indians in North and Central America use Clovis points to hunt big game.
ca. 11,000 BP	• Mammoths and many other big-game prey of Paleo-Indians become extinct.
ca. 10,000–3000 BP	• Archaic hunter-gatherer cultures dominate ancient America.
ca. 5000 BP	• Chumash culture emerges in southern California.
ca. 4000 BP	• Some Eastern Woodland peoples begin growing gourds and pumpkins and making pottery.
ca. 3500 BP	• Southwestern cultures begin corn cultivation.
ca. 2500 BP	• Eastern Woodland cultures start to build burial mounds, cultivate corn.
ca. 2500–2100 BP	• Adena culture develops in Ohio.
ca. 2100 BP–AD 400	• Hopewell culture emerges in Ohio and Mississippi valleys.
ca. AD 200–900	• Mogollon culture develops in New Mexico.
ca. AD 500	• Bows and arrows appear in North America south of Arctic.
ca. AD 500–1400	• Hohokam culture develops in Arizona.
ca. AD 800–1500	• Mississippian culture flourishes in Southeast.
ca. AD 1000–1200	• Anasazi peoples build cliff dwellings at Mesa Verde and pueblos at Chaco Canyon.
ca. AD 1325–1500	• Mexica conquer neighboring peoples and establish Mexican empire.
AD 1492	• Christopher Columbus arrives in New World, beginning European colonization.

29

SPANISH GOLD COIN

This Spanish gold coin celebrates the Spanish monarchs Queen Isabella and King Ferdinand, who patronized the voyages of Christopher Columbus that eventually transformed Europeans' knowledge of the world. Minted around 1500, before Spaniards captured the gold hoards of Mexico and Peru, the coin illustrates the use of gold as the premier form of currency in sixteenth-century Europe. Since gold epitomized wealth and power, Spaniards spared no effort to confiscate as much gold in the New World as possible and ship it back to the Spanish monarchy. The map in the background depicts a European view of Brazil in 1519.

Map: Bibliotheque Nationale de France; gold coin: Erich Lessing / Art Resource, NY.

2

Europeans Encounter the New World
1492–1600

TWO BABIES WERE BORN IN SOUTHERN EUROPE IN 1451, SEPARATED by about seven hundred miles and a chasm of social, economic, and political power. The baby girl, Isabella, was born in a king's castle in what is now Spain. The baby boy, Christopher, was born in the humble dwelling of a weaver near Genoa in what is now Italy. Forty-one years later, the lives and aspirations of these two people intersected in southern Spain and permanently changed the history of the world.

Isabella was named for her mother, the Portuguese second wife of King John II of Castile, whose monarchy encompassed the large central region of present-day Spain. She grew up amid the swirling countercurrents of dynastic rivalries and political conflict. Isabella's father died when she was three, and her half-brother, Henry, assumed the throne. Henry proved an ineffective ruler who made many enemies among the nobility and the clergy.

As a young girl, Isabella was educated by private tutors who were bishops in the Catholic Church, and her learning helped her become a strong, resolute woman. King Henry tried to control her and plotted to undermine her independence by arranging her marriage to one of several eligible sons of European monarchs. Isabella refused to accept Henry's choices and maneuvered to obtain Henry's consent that she would succeed him as monarch. She then selected Ferdinand, a man she had never met, to be her husband. A year younger than Isabella, Ferdinand was the king of Aragon, a region encompassing a triangular slice of northeastern Spain bordering France and the Mediterranean Sea. The couple married in 1469, and Isabella became queen when Henry died in 1474.

Queen Isabella and King Ferdinand fought to defeat other claimants to Isabella's throne, to unite the monarchies of Spain under their rule, to complete the long campaign known as the Reconquest to eliminate Muslim strongholds on the Iberian Peninsula, and to purify Christianity. In their intense decades-long campaign to defend Christianity, persecute Jews, and defeat Muslims, Isabella and Ferdinand traveled throughout their realm, staying

Spanish Tapestry
This detail from a lavish sixteenth-century tapestry depicts Columbus (kneeling) receiving a box of jewels from Queen Isabella (whose husband, King Ferdinand, stands slightly behind her) in appreciation for his voyages to the New World. These gifts and others signified the monarchs' elation about the immense promise of the lands and peoples that Columbus encountered. The exact nature of that promise did not become clear until after the deaths of both Columbus and Isabella, when Cortés invaded and eventually conquered Mexico between 1519 and 1521. © Julio Conoso/Corbis Sygma.

a month or two in one place after another, meeting local notables, hearing appeals and complaints, and impressing all with their regal splendor.

Tagging along in the royal cavalcade of advisers, servants, and assorted hangers-on that moved around Spain in 1485 was Christopher Columbus, a deeply religious man obsessed with obtaining support for his scheme to sail west across the Atlantic Ocean to reach China and Japan. An experienced sailor, Columbus had become convinced that it was possible to reach the riches of the East by sailing west. Columbus pitched his idea to the king of Portugal in 1484. The king's geography experts declared Columbus's proposal impossible: The globe was too big, the ocean between Europe and China was too wide, and no sailors or ships could possibly withstand such a long voyage.

Rejected in Portugal, Columbus made his way to the court of Isabella and Ferdinand in 1485 and joined their entourage until he finally won an audience with the monarchs in January 1486. They too rejected his plan. Doggedly, year after year Columbus kept trying to interest Isabella until finally she changed her mind. In mid-April 1492, hoping to expand the wealth and influence of her monarchy, she summoned Columbus and agreed to support his risky scheme.

Columbus hurriedly organized his expedition, and just before sunrise on August 3, 1492, three ships under his command caught the tide out of a harbor in southern Spain and sailed west. Barely two months later, in the predawn moonlight of October 12, 1492, he glimpsed an island on the western horizon. At daybreak, Columbus rowed ashore, and as the curious islanders crowded around, he claimed possession of the land for Isabella and Ferdinand.

Columbus's encounters with Isabella and those islanders in 1492 transformed the history of the world and unexpectedly made Spain the most important European power in the Western Hemisphere for more than a century. Long before 1492, other Europeans had restlessly expanded the limits of the world known to them, and their efforts helped make possible Columbus's voyage. But without Isabella's sponsorship, it is doubtful that Columbus could have made his voyage. With her support and his own unflagging determination, Columbus blazed a watery trail to a world that neither he nor anyone else in Europe knew existed. As Isabella, Ferdinand, and subsequent Spanish monarchs sought to reap the rewards of what they considered their emerging empire in the West, they created a distinctively Spanish colonial society that conquered and killed Native Americans, built new institutions, and extracted great wealth that enriched the Spanish monarchy and made Spain the envy of other Europeans.

Europe in the Age of Exploration

Historically, the East — not the West — attracted Europeans. Around the year 1000, Norsemen ventured west across the North Atlantic and founded a small fishing village at L'Anse aux Meadows on the tip of Newfoundland that lasted only a decade or so. After the world's climate cooled, choking the North Atlantic with ice, the Norse left. Viking sagas memorialized the Norse "discovery," but it had virtually no other impact in the New World or in Europe. Instead, wealthy Europeans developed a taste for luxury goods from Asia and Africa, and merchants competed to satisfy that taste. As Europeans traded with the East and with one another, they acquired new information about the world they inhabited. A few people — sailors, merchants, and aristocrats — took the risks of exploring beyond the limits of the world known to Europeans. Those risks were genuine and could be deadly. But sometimes they paid off in new information, new opportunities, and eventually the discovery of a world entirely new to Europeans.

Mediterranean Trade and European Expansion

From the twelfth through the fifteenth centuries, spices, silk, carpets, ivory, gold, and other exotic goods traveled overland from Persia, Asia Minor, India, and Africa and then were funneled into continental Europe through Mediterranean trade routes (Map 2.1). Dominated primarily by the Italian cities of Venice, Genoa, and Pisa, this lucrative trade enriched Italian merchants and bankers, who fiercely defended their near monopoly of access to Eastern goods. The vitality of the Mediterranean trade offered few incentives

MAP 2.1

European Trade Routes and Portuguese Exploration in the Fifteenth Century
The strategic geographic position of Italian cities as a conduit for overland trade from Asia was slowly undermined during the fifteenth century by Portuguese explorers who hopscotched along the coast of Africa and eventually found a sea route that opened the rich trade of the East to Portuguese merchants.

to look for alternatives. New routes to the East and the discovery of new lands were the stuff of fantasy.

Preconditions for turning fantasy into reality developed in fifteenth-century Europe. In the mid-fourteenth century, Europeans suffered a catastrophic epidemic of bubonic plague. The **Black Death**, as it was called, killed about a third of the European population. This devastating pestilence had major long-term consequences. By drastically reducing the population, it made Europe's limited supply of food more plentiful for survivors. Many survivors inherited property from plague victims, giving them new chances for advancement. The turmoil caused by the plague also prompted many peasants to move away from their homes and seek opportunities elsewhere.

Understandably, most Europeans perceived the world as a place of alarming risks where the delicate balance of health, harvests, and peace could quickly be tipped toward disaster by epidemics, famine, and violence. Most people protected themselves from the constant threat of calamity by worshipping the supernatural, by living amid kinfolk and friends, and by maintaining good relations with the rich and powerful. But the insecurity and uncertainty of fifteenth-century European life also encouraged a few people to take greater risks, such as embarking on dangerous sea voyages through uncharted waters to points unknown.

> Portugal devoted far more energy and wealth to the geographic exploration of the world between 1415 and 1460 than all other European countries combined.

In European societies, exploration promised fame and fortune to those who succeeded, whether they were kings or commoners. Monarchs such as Isabella who hoped to enlarge their realms and enrich their dynasties also had reasons to sponsor journeys of exploration. More territory meant more subjects who could pay more taxes, provide more soldiers, and participate in more commerce, magnifying the monarch's power and prestige. Voyages of exploration also could stabilize the monarch's regime by diverting unruly noblemen toward distant lands. Some explorers, such as Columbus, were commoners who hoped to be elevated to the aristocracy as a reward for their daring achievements.

Scientific and technological advances also helped set the stage for exploration. The invention of movable type by Johannes Gutenberg around 1450 in Germany made printing easier and cheaper, stimulating the diffusion of information, including news of discoveries, among literate Europeans; one such European was Isabella, who had an extensive personal library. By 1400, crucial navigational aids employed by maritime explorers such as Columbus were already available: compasses; hourglasses, which allowed for the calculation of elapsed time, useful in estimating speed; and the astrolabe and quadrant, which were devices for determining latitude. Many people throughout fifteenth-century Europe knew about these and other technological advances, but the Portuguese were the first to use them in a campaign to sail beyond the limits of the world known to Europeans.

A Century of Portuguese Exploration

With only 2 percent of the population of Christian Europe, Portugal devoted far more energy and wealth to the geographic exploration of the world between 1415 and 1460 than all other European countries combined. Facing the Atlantic on the Iberian Peninsula, the Portuguese lived on the fringes of the thriving Mediterranean trade. As a Christian kingdom, Portugal cooperated with Spain in the **Reconquest**, the centuries-long drive to expel the Muslims from the Iberian Peninsula. The religious zeal that propelled the Reconquest also justified expansion into what the Portuguese considered heathen lands. A key victory came in 1415 when Portuguese forces conquered Ceuta, the Muslim bastion at the mouth of the Strait of Gibraltar that had blocked Portugal's access to the Atlantic coast of Africa.

The most influential advocate of Portuguese exploration was **Prince Henry the Navigator**, son of the Portuguese king (and great-uncle of Queen Isabella of Spain). From 1415 until his death in 1460, Henry collected the latest information about sailing techniques and geography, supported new crusades against the Muslims, sought fresh sources of trade to fatten Portuguese pocketbooks, and pushed explorers to go farther still. Expeditions to Africa also promised to wrest wheat fields from their Moroccan owners and to obtain gold, the currency of European trade. Gold was scarce in Europe because the quickening pace of commerce increased the need for currency while purchases in the East drained gold away from Europeans.

Neither the Portuguese nor anybody else in Europe knew the immensity of Africa or the

Ivory Saltcellar
This exquisitely carved sixteenth-century ivory saltcellar combines African materials, craftsmanship, and imagery in an artifact for Portuguese tables. Designed to hold table salt in the central globe, the saltcellar portrays a victim about to be beheaded by the armed man who has already beheaded five others. To Portuguese eyes, the saltcellar dramatized African brutality and quietly suggested the superiority of Portuguese virtues and their beneficial influence in Africa. Archivio Fotografico del Museo Preistorico Etnografico L. Pigorini, Roma.

length or shape of its coastline, which, in reality, fronted the Atlantic for more than seven thousand miles — about five times the considerable distance from Genoa, Columbus's hometown, to Lisbon, the Portuguese capital. At first, Portuguese mariners cautiously hugged the west coast of Africa, seldom venturing beyond sight of land. By 1434, they had reached the northern edge of the Sahara Desert, where strong westerly currents swept them out to sea. They soon learned to ride those currents far away from the coast before catching favorable winds that turned them back toward land, a technique that allowed them to reach Cape Verde by 1444 (see Map 2.1).

To stow the supplies necessary for long periods at sea and to withstand the battering of waves in the open ocean, the Portuguese developed the caravel, a fast, sturdy ship that became explorers' vessel of choice. In caravels, Portuguese mariners sailed into and around the Gulf of Guinea and as far south as the Congo by 1480.

Fierce African resistance confined Portuguese expeditions to coastal trading posts, where they bartered successfully for gold, slaves, and ivory. Powerful African kingdoms welcomed Portuguese trading ships loaded with iron goods, weapons, textiles, and ornamental shells. Portuguese merchants learned that establishing relatively peaceful trading posts on the coast was far more profitable than attempting the violent conquest and colonization of inland regions. In the 1460s, the Portuguese used African slaves to develop sugar plantations on the Cape Verde Islands, inaugurating an association between enslaved Africans and plantation labor that would be transplanted to the New World in the centuries to come.

About 1480, Portuguese explorers, eager to bypass the Mediterranean merchants, began a conscious search for a sea route to Asia. In 1488, Bartolomeu Dias sailed around the Cape of Good Hope at the southern tip of Africa and hurried back to Lisbon with the exciting news that it appeared to be possible to sail on to India and China. In 1498, after ten years of careful preparation, Vasco da Gama commanded the first Portuguese fleet to sail to India. Portugal quickly capitalized on the commercial potential of da Gama's new sea route. By the early sixteenth century, the Portuguese controlled a far-flung commercial empire in India, Indonesia, and China (collectively referred to as the East Indies). Their new sea route to the East eliminated overland travel and allowed Portuguese merchants to charge much lower prices for the Eastern goods they imported and still make handsome profits.

Sixteenth-Century Pomander
This jewel-encrusted pomander was designed to be stuffed with aromatic spices brought to Europe through the Mediterranean trade routes dominated by Italians or through the Indian Ocean trade route around Africa dominated by the Portuguese. A wealthy European wore the pomander on a chain at the neck or waist and sniffed it to overcome noxious stenches common in daily life. Ordinary Europeans could not afford the pomander or the spices, and simply had to live with vile odors. The pomander illustrates the strong connection in the sixteenth century between fashion, luxury, and the spice trade. The Burghley House Collection, Stamford, England EWA008553.

Portugal's African explorations during the fifteenth century broke the monopoly of the old Mediterranean trade with the East, dramatically expanded the world known to Europeans, established a network of Portuguese outposts in Africa and Asia, and developed methods of sailing the high seas that Columbus employed on his revolutionary voyage west.

REVIEW Why did European exploration expand dramatically in the fifteenth century?

▶ A Surprising New World in the Western Atlantic

In retrospect, the Portuguese seemed ideally qualified to venture across the Atlantic. They had pioneered the frontiers of seafaring, exploration, and geography for almost a century. However, Portuguese and most other experts believed that sailing west across the Atlantic to Asia was literally impossible. The European discovery of America required someone bold enough to believe that the experts were wrong and that the risks were surmountable. That person was **Christopher Columbus**. His explorations inaugurated a geographic revolution that

forever altered Europeans' understanding of the world and its peoples, including themselves. Columbus's landfall in the Caribbean initiated a thriving exchange between the people, ideas, cultures, and institutions of the Old and New Worlds that continues to this day.

The Explorations of Columbus

Columbus went to sea when he was about fourteen, and he eventually made his way to Lisbon, where he married Felipa Moniz, whose father had been raised in the household of Prince Henry the Navigator. Through Felipa, Columbus gained access to explorers' maps and information about the tricky currents and winds encountered in sailing the Atlantic. Columbus himself ventured into the Atlantic frequently and at least twice sailed to the central coast of Africa.

Like other educated Europeans, Columbus believed that the earth was a sphere and that theoretically it was possible to reach the East Indies by sailing west. With flawed calculations, he estimated that Asia was only about 2,500 miles away, a shorter distance than Portuguese ships routinely sailed between Lisbon and the Congo. In fact, the shortest distance to Japan from Europe's jumping-off point was nearly 11,000 miles. Convinced by his erroneous calculations, Columbus became obsessed with a scheme to prove he was right.

In 1492, after years of unsuccessful lobbying in Portugal and Spain, plus overtures to England and France, Columbus finally won financing for his journey from the Spanish monarchs, **Queen Isabella and King Ferdinand**. They saw Columbus's venture as an inexpensive gamble: The potential loss was small, but the potential gain was huge. They gave Columbus a letter of introduction to China's Grand Khan, the ruler they hoped he would meet upon reaching the other side of the Atlantic.

After scarcely three months of frantic preparation, Columbus and his small fleet — the *Niña* and *Pinta*, both caravels, and the *Santa María*, a larger merchant vessel — headed west. Six weeks after leaving the Canary Islands, where he stopped for supplies, Columbus landed on a tiny Caribbean island about three hundred miles north of the eastern tip of Cuba.

Columbus claimed possession of the island for Isabella and Ferdinand and named it San Salvador, in honor of the Savior, Jesus Christ. He called the islanders "Indians," assuming that they inhabited the East Indies somewhere near Japan or China. The islanders called themselves **Tainos**,

which in their language meant "good" or "noble." The Tainos inhabited most of the Caribbean islands Columbus visited on his first voyage, as had their ancestors for more than two centuries. An agricultural people, the Tainos grew cassava, corn, cotton, tobacco, and other crops. Instead of dressing in the finery Columbus had expected to find in the East Indies, the Tainos "all . . . go around as naked as their mothers bore them," Columbus wrote. Although Columbus concluded that the Tainos "had no religion," in reality they worshipped gods they called *zemis*, ancestral spirits who inhabited natural objects such as trees and stones. The Tainos mined a little gold, but they had no riches. "It seemed to me that they were a people very poor in everything," Columbus wrote.

What the Tainos thought about Columbus and his sailors we can only surmise, since they left no written documents. At first, Columbus got the impression that the Tainos believed the Spaniards came from heaven. But after six weeks of encounters, Columbus decided that "the people of these lands do not understand me nor do I, nor anyone else that I have with me, [understand] them. And many times I understand one thing said by these Indians . . . for another, its contrary." The confused communication between the Spaniards and the Tainos suggests how strange each group seemed to the other. Columbus's perceptions of the Tainos were shaped by European attitudes, ideas, and expectations, just as the Tainos' perceptions of the Europeans were no doubt colored by their own culture.

Columbus and his men understood that they had made a momentous discovery, but they found it frustrating. Although the Tainos proved friendly, they did not have the riches Columbus expected to find in the East. In mid-January 1493, he started back to Spain, where Queen Isabella and King Ferdinand were overjoyed by his news. With a voyage that had lasted barely eight months, Columbus appeared to have catapulted Spain from the position of an also-ran in the race for a sea route to Asia into that of a serious challenger to Portugal, whose explorers had not yet sailed to India or China. The Spanish monarchs elevated Columbus

to the nobility and awarded him the title "Admiral of the Ocean Sea." The seven Tainos Columbus had brought to Spain were baptized as Christians, and King Ferdinand became their godfather.

Soon after Columbus returned to Spain, the Spanish monarchs rushed to obtain the pope's support for their claim to the new lands in the West. When the pope, a Spaniard, complied, the Portuguese feared that their own claims to recently discovered territories were in jeopardy. To protect their claims, the Portuguese and Spanish monarchs negotiated the **Treaty of Tordesillas** in 1494. The treaty drew an imaginary line eleven hundred miles west of the Canary Islands (Map 2.2). Land discovered west of the line (namely, the islands that Columbus discovered and any additional land that might be found) belonged to Spain; Portugal claimed land to the east (namely, its African and East Indian trading empire).

Isabella and Ferdinand moved quickly to realize the promise of their new claims. In the fall of 1493, they dispatched Columbus once again, this time with a fleet of seventeen ships and more than a thousand men who planned to locate the Asian mainland, find gold, and get rich. When Columbus returned to the island where he had left behind thirty-nine of his sailors (because of a shipwreck near the end of his first voyage), he received

Columbus's First Voyage to the New World, 1492–1493

Columbus called the islanders "Indians," assuming that they inhabited the East Indies somewhere near Japan or China.

Taino Zemi Basket
This basket is an example of the effigies Tainos made to represent zemis, or deities. The effigy illustrates the artistry of the basket maker, almost certainly a Taino woman. Crafted sometime between 1492 and about 1520, the effigy demonstrates that the Tainos readily incorporated goods obtained through contacts with Europeans into their own traditional beliefs and practices. The basket maker used African ivory and European mirrors as well as Native American fibers, dyes, and designs. © The Trustees of the British Museum.

MAP ACTIVITY

Map 2.2   European Exploration in Sixteenth-Century America
This map illustrates the approximate routes of early European explorations of the New World.

READING THE MAP: Which countries were most actively exploring the New World? Which countries were exploring later than others?

CONNECTIONS: What were the motivations behind the explorations? What were the motivations for colonization?

disturbing news. In his absence, his sailors had terrorized the Tainos by kidnapping and sexually abusing their women. In retaliation, the Tainos had killed all the sailors. This small episode prefigured much of what was to happen in encounters between Native Americans and Europeans in the years ahead.

Before Columbus died in 1506, he returned to the New World two more times (in 1498 and 1502) without relinquishing his belief that the East Indies were there, someplace. Other explorers continued to search for a passage to the East or some other source of profit. Before long, however, prospects of beating the Portuguese to Asia began to dim along with the hope of finding vast hoards of gold. Nonetheless, Columbus's discoveries forced sixteenth-century Europeans to think about the world in new ways. It was possible to sail from Europe to the western rim of the Atlantic and return to Europe. Most important, Columbus's voyages proved that lands and peoples entirely unknown to Europeans lay across the Atlantic.

The Geographic Revolution and the Columbian Exchange

Within thirty years of Columbus's initial discovery, Europeans' understanding of world geography underwent a revolution. An elite of perhaps twenty thousand people with access to Europe's royal courts and trading centers learned the exciting news about global geography. But it took a generation of additional exploration before they could comprehend the larger contours of Columbus's discoveries.

European monarchs hurried to stake their claims to the newly discovered lands. In 1497, King Henry VII of England, who had spurned Columbus a decade earlier, sent John Cabot to look for a **Northwest Passage** to the Indies across the North Atlantic (see Map 2.2). Cabot reached the tip of Newfoundland, which he believed was part of Asia, and hurried back to England, where he assembled a small fleet and sailed west in 1498. But he was never heard from again.

Three thousand miles to the south, a Spanish expedition landed on the northern coast of South America in 1499 accompanied by Amerigo Vespucci, an Italian businessman. In 1500, Pedro Álvars Cabral commanded a Portuguese fleet bound for the Indian Ocean that accidentally made landfall on the east coast of Brazil as it looped westward into the Atlantic.

By 1500, European experts knew that several large chunks of land cluttered the western Atlantic. A few cartographers speculated that these chunks were connected to one another in a landmass that was not Asia. In 1507, Martin Waldseemüller, a German cartographer, published the first map that showed the New World separate from Asia; he named the land America, in honor of Amerigo Vespucci.

Two additional discoveries confirmed Waldseemüller's speculation. In 1513, Vasco Núñez de Balboa crossed the Isthmus of Panama and reached the Pacific Ocean. Clearly, more water lay between the New World and Asia. **Ferdinand Magellan** discovered just how much water when he led an expedition to circumnavigate the globe in 1519. Sponsored by King Charles I of Spain, Magellan's voyage took him first to the New World, around the southern tip of South America, and into the Pacific late in November 1520. Crossing the Pacific took almost four months, decimating his crew with hunger and thirst. Magellan himself was killed by Philippine tribesmen. A remnant of his expedition continued on to the Indian Ocean and managed to transport a cargo of spices back to Spain in 1522.

In most ways, Magellan's voyage was a disaster. One ship and 18 men crawled back from an expedition that had begun with five ships and more than 250 men. But the geographic information it provided left no doubt that America was a continent separated from Asia by the enormous Pacific Ocean. Magellan's voyage made clear that it was possible to sail west to reach the East Indies, but that was a terrible way to go. After Magellan, most Europeans who sailed west set their sights on the New World, not on Asia.

Columbus's arrival in the Caribbean anchored the western end of what might be imagined as a sea bridge that spanned the Atlantic, connecting the Western Hemisphere to Europe. Somewhat like the Beringian land bridge traversed by the first Americans millennia earlier (see chapter 1), the new sea bridge reestablished a connection between the Eastern and Western Hemispheres. The Atlantic Ocean, which had previously isolated America from Europe, became an aquatic highway, thanks to sailing technology, intrepid seamen, and their European sponsors. This new sea bridge launched the **Columbian exchange**, a transatlantic trade of goods, people, and ideas that has continued ever since.

Maize Goddess

The arrival of Columbus in the New World started an ongoing transatlantic exchange of goods, people, and ideas. In 1493, Columbus told Isabella and Ferdinand about an amazingly productive New World plant he called *maize*, his version of the Taino word *mahiz*, which means "life-giver." This maize, or corn, goddess crafted in Peru about a thousand years before Columbus arrived in the New World suggests ancient Americans' worship of corn. Within a generation after 1493, corn had been carried across the Atlantic and was growing in Europe, the Middle East, Africa, India, and China. Bildarchiv Preussischer Kulturbesitz/Art Resource, NY.

Spaniards brought novelties to the New World that were commonplace in Europe, including Christianity, iron technology, sailing ships, firearms, wheeled vehicles, horses and other domesticated animals, and much else. Unknowingly, they also carried many Old World microorganisms that caused devastating epidemics of smallpox, measles, and other diseases that would kill the vast majority of Indians during the sixteenth century and continue to decimate survivors in later centuries. European diseases made the Columbian exchange catastrophic for Native Americans. In the long term, these diseases were decisive in transforming the dominant peoples of the New World from descendants of Asians, who had inhabited the hemisphere for millennia, to descendants of Europeans and Africans, the recent arrivals from the Old World.

Ancient American goods, people, and ideas made the return trip across the Atlantic. Europeans were introduced to New World foods such as corn and potatoes that became important staples in European diets, especially for poor people. Columbus's sailors became infected with syphilis in sexual encounters with New World women and unwittingly carried the deadly bacteria back to Europe. New World tobacco created a European fashion for smoking that ignited quickly and has yet to be extinguished. But for almost a generation after 1492, this Columbian exchange did not reward the Spaniards with the riches they yearned to find.

REVIEW   How did Columbus's discoveries help revolutionize Europeans' understanding of global geography?

▶ Spanish Exploration and Conquest

During the sixteenth century, the New World helped Spain become the most powerful monarchy in both Europe and the Americas. Initially, Spanish expeditions reconnoitered the Caribbean, scouted stretches of the Atlantic coast, and established settlements on the large islands of Hispaniola, Puerto Rico, Jamaica, and Cuba. Spaniards enslaved Caribbean tribes and put them to work growing crops and mining gold. But the profits from these early ventures barely covered the costs of maintaining the settlers. After almost thirty years of exploration, the promise of Columbus's discovery seemed illusory.

In 1519, however, that promise was spectacularly fulfilled by Hernán Cortés's march into Mexico. By about 1545, Spanish conquests extended from northern Mexico to southern Chile, and New World riches filled Spanish treasure chests. Cortés's expedition served as the model for Spaniards' and other Europeans' expectations that the New World could yield bonanza profits for its conquerors. Meanwhile, forced labor and deadly epidemics meant that native populations plummeted.

The Conquest of Mexico

Hernán Cortés, an obscure nineteen-year-old Spaniard seeking adventure and the chance to make a name for himself, arrived in the New

Smallpox Victim in Hut
This sixteenth-century Mexican drawing shows a victim of smallpox lying in a hut made of branches. Spaniards brought smallpox to Mexico where it sickened and killed millions. A highly contagious and often fatal viral infection, smallpox spread like wildfire among native Americans in the New World who, unlike most Europeans, had no previous exposure to the virus and therefore had developed no immunity to it. Smallpox and other European microbes decimated native Americans, greatly disfiguring and demoralizing many of those who survived. At the time, nearly everybody recognized the horrors of smallpox, but nobody knew how to prevent or cure it. Arxiu Mas.

World in 1504. Throughout his twenties, he fought in the conquest of Cuba and elsewhere in the Caribbean. In 1519, the governor of Cuba authorized Cortés to organize an expedition of about six hundred men and eleven ships to investigate rumors of a fabulously wealthy kingdom somewhere in the interior of the mainland.

A charismatic and confident man, Cortés could not speak any Native American language. Landing first on the Yucatán peninsula with his ragtag army, he had the good fortune to receive from a local chief of the Tobasco people the gift of a young girl named **Malinali**. She spoke several native languages, including Mayan and Nahuatl, the language of the **Mexica**, the most powerful people in what is now Mexico and Central America (see chapter 1). Malinali had acquired her linguistic skills painfully. Born into a family of Mexican nobility, she learned Nahuatl as a child. After her father died and her mother remarried, her stepfather sold her as a slave to Mayan-speaking Indians, who subsequently gave her to the Tobascans. Malinali, whom the Spaniards called Marina, soon learned Spanish and became Cortés's interpreter. She also became one of Cortés's several mistresses and bore him a son. (Several years later, after Cortés's wife arrived in New Spain, Cortés cast Marina aside, and she married one of his soldiers.) Malinali was the Spaniards' essential conduit of communication with the Indians. "Without her help," wrote one of the Spaniards who accompanied Cortés, "we would not have understood the language of New Spain and Mexico." Malinali allowed Cortés to talk and fight with Indians along the Gulf coast of Mexico as he tried to discover the location of the fabled kingdom. By the time Marina died, the people among whom she had grown up — who had taught her languages, enslaved her, and given her to Cortés — had been conquered by the Spaniards with her help.

In **Tenochtitlán**, the capital of the Mexican empire, the emperor **Montezuma** heard about some strange creatures sighted along the coast. (Montezuma and his people are often called Aztecs, but they called themselves Mexica.) He feared that the strangers were led by the god Quetzalcoatl, who was returning to Tenochtitlán to fulfill a prophecy of the Mexican religion. Marina had told Cortés about Quetzalcoatl, and when Montezuma's messengers arrived, Cortés donned the regalia they had brought, almost certain proof to the Mexica that he was indeed the god they feared. The Spaniards astounded the messengers by blasting their cannons and displaying their swords.

The messengers hurried back to Montezuma with their amazing news. The emperor sent representatives to bring the strangers large quantities of food and perhaps postpone their dreaded arrival in the capital. Before the Mexican messengers served food to the Spaniards, they sacrificed several human hostages and soaked the food in their blood. This fare disgusted the Spaniards and might have been enough to turn them back to Cuba. But along with the food, the Mexica also brought the Spaniards another gift, a "disk in the shape of a sun, as big as a cartwheel and made of very fine gold," as one of the Mexica recalled. Here was conclusive evidence that the rumors of fabulous riches heard by Cortés had some basis in fact.

In August 1519, Cortés marched inland to find Montezuma. Leading about 350 men armed with swords, lances, and muskets and supported by ten cannons, four smaller guns, and sixteen horses, Cortés had to live off the land, establishing peaceful relations with indigenous tribes when he could and killing them when he thought it necessary. On November 8, 1519, Cortés reached Tenochtitlán, where Montezuma welcomed him. After presenting Cortés with gifts, Montezuma ushered the Spaniards to the royal palace and showered them with lavish hospitality. The Spaniards were stunned by the magnificence that surrounded them. One of Cortés's soldiers recalled that "it all seemed like an enchanted vision . . . [or] a dream." Quickly, Cortés took Montezuma hostage and held him under house arrest, hoping to make him a puppet through whom the Spaniards could rule the Mexican empire. This uneasy peace existed for several months until one of Cortés's men led a brutal massacre of many Mexican nobles, causing the people of

Cortés's Invasion of Tenochtitlán, 1519–1521

0 25 50 mi.

0 25 50 km.

Gulf of Mexico

Texcoco
Otumba
Zautla
Jalapa
Veracruz
Tlaxcala
Tenochtitlán
Cholula

Cortés's original route, 1519
Cortés's retreat, 1520
Cortés's return route, 1520–1521

Cortés Arrives in Tenochtitlán

In this portrayal of Cortés and his army arriving in the Mexican capital, Malinali stands at the front of the procession, serving as the Spaniards' translator and intermediary with Montezuma (not pictured). Painted by a Mexican artist after the conquest, the work contrasts Cortés — dressed as a Spanish gentleman, respectfully doffing his hat to Montezuma — with his soldiers, who are armed and ready for battle. The painting displays the choices confronted by the Mexica: accept the pacific overtures of Cortés or face the Spanish soldiers' powerful weapons. Why were the Indians who carried the Spaniards' supplies important? Bibliothèque Nationale de France.

Tenochtitlán to revolt. Montezuma was killed (whether by his own people or Spaniards is not certain), and the Mexica mounted a ferocious assault on the Spaniards. On June 30, 1520, Cortés and about a hundred other Spaniards fought their way out of Tenochtitlán and retreated about one hundred miles to Tlaxcala, a stronghold of bitter enemies of the Mexica. The friendly Tlaxcalans — who had long resented Mexican power — allowed Cortés to regroup, obtain reinforcements, and plan a strategy to conquer Tenochtitlán.

In the spring of 1521, Cortés and tens of thousands of Indian allies laid siege to the Mexican capital. With a relentless, scorched-earth strategy, Cortés finally defeated the last Mexican defenders on August 13, 1521. The great capital of the Mexican empire "looked as if it had been ploughed up," one of Cortés's soldiers remembered.

How did a few hundred Spaniards so far away from home defeat millions of Indians fighting on their home turf? For one thing, the Spaniards had superior military technology that partially offset the Mexicans' numerical advantages. (See "Visualizing History," page 44.) They fought with weapons of iron and steel against the Mexicans' stone, wood, and copper. The muscles of Mexican warriors could not match the endurance of cannons and muskets fueled by gunpowder.

European viruses proved to be even more powerful weapons. Smallpox arrived in Mexico with Cortés, and in the ensuing epidemic thousands of Mexicans died and many others became too sick to fight. After Cortés evacuated Tenochtitlán, a plague — probably another smallpox outbreak — decimated the Mexican capital, "striking everywhere in the city and killing a vast number of our people," as one Mexican recalled. The sickness spread back along the network of trade and tribute feeding Tenochtitlán, weakening the entire Mexican empire and causing many to fear that their gods had abandoned them. "Cut us loose," one Mexican pleaded, "because the gods have died."

The Spaniards' concept of war also favored them. Mexicans tended to consider war a way to impose their tribute system on conquered people and to take captives for sacrifice. They believed that the high cost of continuing to fight would cause their adversaries to surrender and pay tribute. While Mexicans sought surrender, Spaniards sought total victory. As one Mexican described a Spanish attack, soldiers "stabbed everyone with iron lances and . . . iron swords. They stuck some in the belly, and then their entrails came spilling out. They split open the heads of some, . . . their skulls were cut up into little bits. Some they hit on the shoulders; their bodies broke open and ripped." To Spaniards, war meant destroying their enemy's ability to fight.

Politics proved decisive in Cortés's victory over the Mexicans. Cortés shrewdly exploited the tensions between the Mexica and the people they ruled in their empire (see chapter 1). Cortés reinforced his small army with thousands of Indian allies who were eager to seek revenge against the Mexica. Cortés's Indian allies fought alongside the Spaniards and provided a fairly secure base from which to maneuver against the Mexican stronghold of Tenochtitlán. Hundreds of thousands of other Indians aided Cortés by failing to come to the Mexicans' defense. In the end, the political tensions created by the Mexican empire proved to be its crippling weakness.

SPANISH EXPLORATION AND CONQUEST

Incan Gold Figure and Spanish Gold Ingot
Before conquest by the Spaniards, craftsmen in Mexico, Peru, and elsewhere in Central and South America fashioned spectacular objects from gold — like this Incan pre-conquest figure — for leaders who sought to display their wealth, status, and — probably — their supernatural power. Spaniards had no interest in the artistry or ceremonial meanings of such artifacts and routinely melted them down into ingots of gold to be shipped back to Spain, like the one shown here. This ingot was excavated in Mexico City in 1982, more than 450 years after 1521, when it was probably dropped by one of Cortés's soldiers.
Figure: Bildarchiv Preussischer Kulturbesitz/Art Resource, NY; ingot: Museo Nacional de Antropologia, conaculta-inah, 10-220012.

The Search for Other Mexicos

Lured by their insatiable appetite for gold, Spanish **conquistadors** (soldiers who fought in conquests) quickly fanned out from Tenochtitlán in search of other sources of treasure. The most spectacular prize fell to **Francisco Pizarro**, who conquered the **Incan empire** in Peru. The Incas controlled a vast, complex region that contained more than nine million people and stretched along the western coast of South America for more than two thousand miles. In 1532, Pizarro and his army of fewer than two hundred men captured the Incan emperor Atahualpa and held him hostage. As ransom, the Incas gave Pizarro the largest treasure yet produced by the conquests: gold and silver equivalent to half a century's worth of precious-metal production in Europe. With the ransom safely in their hands, the Spaniards murdered Atahualpa. The Incan treasure proved that at least one other Mexico did indeed exist, and it spurred the search for others.

Juan Ponce de León had sailed along the Florida coast in 1513. Encouraged by Cortés's success, he went back to Florida in 1521 to find riches, only to be killed in battle with Calusa Indians. A few years later, Lucas Vázquez de Ayllón explored the Atlantic coast north of Florida to present-day South Carolina. In 1526, he established a small settlement on the Georgia coast that he named San Miguel de Gualdape, the first Spanish attempt to establish a foothold in what is now the United States. This settlement was soon swept away by sickness and hostile Indians. Pánfilo de Narváez surveyed the Gulf coast from Florida to Texas in 1528, but his expedition ended disastrously with a shipwreck near present-day Galveston, Texas.

In 1539, Hernando de Soto, a seasoned conquistador who had taken part in the conquest of Peru, set out with nine ships and more than six hundred men to find another Peru in North America. Landing in Florida, de Soto literally slashed his way through much of southeastern North America for three years, searching for the rich, majestic civilizations he believed were there. After the brutal slaughter of many Native Americans and much hardship, de Soto died of a fever in 1542. His men buried him in the Mississippi River and turned back to Mexico, disappointed.

Tales of the fabulous wealth of the mythical Seven Cities of Cíbola also lured Francisco Vásquez de Coronado to search the Southwest and Great Plains of North America. In 1540, Coronado left northern Mexico with more than three hundred Spaniards, a thousand Indians, and a priest who claimed to know the way to what he called "the greatest and best of the discoveries." Cíbola turned out to be a small Zuñi pueblo of about a hundred families. When the Zuñi shot arrows at the Spaniards, Coronado attacked the pueblo and routed the defenders after a hard battle. Convinced that the rich cities must lie somewhere over the horizon, Coronado kept moving all the way to central Kansas before deciding in 1542 that the rumors he had pursued were just that.

The same year Coronado abandoned his search for Cíbola, Juan Rodríguez Cabrillo's maritime expedition sought to find wealth along the coast of California. Cabrillo died on Santa Catalina Island, offshore from present-day Los Angeles, but his men sailed on to Oregon, where a ferocious storm forced them to turn back toward Mexico.

These probes into North America by de Soto, Coronado, and Cabrillo persuaded other Spaniards that although enormous territories stretched northward, their inhabitants had little to loot

Weapons of Conquest

For centuries, Spanish soldiers and Mexican warriors wielded weapons that had proven to be effective in their respective military cultures. In Spain, royal soldiers completed the centuries-long Reconquest in 1492, driving out Muslims and affirming Christian rule in the Iberian Peninsula. In ancient Mesoamerica, the Mexica had asserted their dominance among the many regional tribes and established an empire that covered much of present-day Mexico (see chapter 1). When the Spanish conquistadors traveled to the New World during the sixteenth century, the battles of conquest revealed the deadly limitations of weaponry that the Mexica had used to build their mighty empire.

The Mexica fought with offensive weapons similar to the wooden club shown here. Razor-sharp fragments of obsidian, a glasslike min-

Mexican Warriors Battle Spanish Conquistadors

eral, studded the edges of the club, allowing Mexican warriors, like the three shown here, to deliver lacerating, even lethal, blows against an enemy at close range. The Mexica and their enemies tried to defend themselves by deflecting these weapons of wood and stone with shields made of hides, wood, and feathers, as shown here. Why do you think Mexican warriors had such elaborate and colorful shields and

Mexican Warrior's Shield

Mexican War Club

or exploit. After a generation of vigorous exploration, the Spaniards concluded that there was only one Mexico and one Peru.

Spanish Outposts in Florida and New Mexico

Disappointed by the explorers' failure to discover riches in North America, the Spanish monarchy insisted that a few settlements be established in Florida and New Mexico to give a token of reality to its territorial claims. Settlements in Florida would have the additional benefit of protecting Spanish ships from pirates and privateers who lurked along the southeastern coast, waiting for the Spanish treasure fleet sailing toward Spain.

In 1565, the Spanish king sent Pedro Menéndez de Avilés to create settlements along the Atlantic coast of North America. In early September,

Menéndez founded **St. Augustine** in Florida, the first permanent European settlement within what became the United States. By 1600, St. Augustine had a population of about five hundred, the only remaining Spanish beachhead on North America's vast Atlantic shoreline.

More than sixteen hundred miles west of St. Augustine, the Spaniards founded another outpost in 1598. Juan de Oñate led an expedition of about five hundred people to settle northern Mexico, now called New Mexico, and claim the booty rumored to exist there. Oñate had impeccable credentials for both conquest and mining. His father helped to discover the bonanza silver mines of Zacatecas in central Mexico, and his wife was Isabel Tolosa Cortés Montezuma—the granddaughter of Cortés and the great-granddaughter of Montezuma.

After a two-month journey from Mexico, Oñate and his companions reached pueblos near

Spanish Battle Sword

battle dress? Why might Mexican warriors have considered bright designs made with feathers useful for offense or defense?

In Europe, Spaniards had gone to battle for centuries with offensive weapons made of steel, like the sword shown here. This sword is inscribed with Latin mottoes that read on one side, "Turn away these troubles from us," and on the other side, "With God we achieve lofty goals but nothing by ourselves." Why might these inscriptions have been meaningful to a Spanish soldier who slashed and stabbed enemies with this sword?

On the battlefields of sixteenth-century Europe, Spanish soldiers defended themselves against the steel weapons of their enemies with steel shields and body armor, as shown here. In Mexico, the wood and stone weapons of Mexican warriors tended to bounce off the Spaniards' shields and armor, in effect disarming Mexicans' major offensive weap-

onry. Likewise, Spaniards' sword blows, which might have clanked off a European enemy's steel shield, slashed through a Mexican warrior's shield of hide and feathers, destroying this basic form of defense.

Like the Mexican club, the steel sword was effective only at close range; the sword shown here, for example, is three feet long. (The effective range of a modern military rifle is nearly a mile.) What does the relatively short effective range of the Spanish sword and the Mexican club suggest about combat during the conquest? What does each

weapon's design suggest about the fighter's ultimate goal in combat?

Horses were unknown in Mexico until Spaniards imported them. What offensive and defensive advantages did horses provide for mounted Spanish soldiers when in combat against Mexican foot soldiers? Did horses have any disadvantages for Spaniards or any advantages for the Mexica?

While the Mexica wounded and killed many Spaniards, in the end Spaniards prevailed and conquered Mexico. Although Spaniards' superior weaponry contributed to their success, can you imagine tactics that the Mexica might have used to delay, subvert, or even defeat Spanish conquest?

SOURCE: Mexican warriors and Spanish conquistadors: Biblioteca Nacional, Madrid; Spanish shield: The Royal Armory, Madrid; Spanish sword: The Metropolitan Museum of Art, Purchase, The Lauder Foundation Gift, 1984. Photograph © The Metropolitan Museum of Art Accession Number 1984.73; Mexican shield: Museum fur Volkerkunde Vienna; Mexican war club: Image # 7864 American Museum of Natural History.

Spanish Shield

present-day Albuquerque and Santa Fe. He solemnly convened the pueblos' leaders and received their oath of loyalty to the Spanish king and the Christian God. Oñate sent out scouting parties to find the legendary treasures of the region and to locate the ocean, which he believed must be nearby. Meanwhile, many of his soldiers planned to mutiny, and relations with the Indians deteriorated. When Indians in the Acoma pueblo revolted against the Spaniards, Oñate ruthlessly suppressed the uprising, killing eight hundred men, women, and children. Although Oñate's response to the **Acoma pueblo revolt** reconfirmed the Spaniards' military superiority, he did not bring peace or stability to the region. After another pueblo revolt occurred in 1599, many of Oñate's settlers returned to Mexico, leaving New Mexico as a small, dusty assertion of Spanish claims to the North American Southwest.

New Spain in the Sixteenth Century

For all practical purposes, Spain was the dominant European power in the Western Hemisphere during the sixteenth century (Map 2.3, page 47). Portugal claimed the giant territory of Brazil under the Tordesillas treaty but was far more concerned with exploiting its hard-won trade with the East Indies than with colonizing the New World. England and France were absorbed by domestic and diplomatic concerns in Europe and largely lost interest in America until late in the century. In the decades after 1519, the Spaniards created the distinctive colonial society of **New Spain**, which showed other Europeans how the New World could be made to serve the purposes of the Old.

The Spanish monarchy gave the conquistadors permission to explore and plunder what they

Connections between Spanish Christianity and Mexican Traditional Religions
Spanish missionaries struggled to eradicate all forms of Mexicans' traditional religion. The painting portrays a Catholic priest instructing two Mexican children while another priest shelters a group of children and wields a cross to protect them from the diabolical creatures seeking to tempt them to embrace evil. Even Mexicans who converted to Christianity continued to express their spirituality in traditional ways. The sixteenth-century chalice cover shown here, designed to cover the cup that contains wine for Christian communion — is made of traditional Mexican feather work and features a whirlpool design emblematic of a major Mexican goddess.
Painting: Collection Revillagigedo Historia/Archivos General de la Nacion, Palacio Nacional; chalice cover: Werner Forman/Art Resource, NY.

found. (See "Documenting the American Promise," page 48.) The crown took one-fifth, called the "royal fifth," of any loot confiscated and allowed the conquerors to divide the rest. In the end, most conquistadors received very little after the plunder was divided among leaders such as Cortés and his favorite officers. To compensate his disappointed battle-hardened soldiers, Cortés gave them towns the Spaniards had subdued.

The distribution of conquered towns institutionalized the system of **encomienda**, which empowered the conquistadors to rule the Indians and the lands in and around their towns. The concept of encomienda was familiar to Spaniards, who had used it to govern regions recaptured from Muslims during the Reconquest. Encomienda transferred to the Spanish *encomendero* (the man who "owned" the town) the tribute that the town had previously paid to the Mexican empire. In theory, encomienda involved a reciprocal relationship between the encomendero and "his" Indians. In return for the tribute and labor of the Indians, the encomendero was supposed to be responsible for their material well-being, to guarantee order and justice in the town, and to encourage the Indians to convert to Christianity.

Catholic missionaries labored earnestly to convert the Indians. They fervently believed that God expected them to save the Indians' souls by convincing them to abandon their old sinful beliefs and to embrace the one true Christian faith. (See "Seeking the American Promise," page 50.) But after baptizing tens of thousands of Indians, the

missionaries learned that many Indians continued to worship their own gods. Most priests came to believe that the Indians were lesser beings inherently incapable of fully understanding Christianity.

In practice, encomenderos were far more interested in what the Indians could do for them than in what they or the missionaries could do for the Indians. Encomenderos subjected the Indians to chronic overwork, mistreatment, and abuse. According to one Spaniard, the Indians' behavior justified the encomenderos' cruelty: "Everything [the Indians] do is slowly done and by compulsion. They are malicious, lying, [and] thievish." Economically, however, encomienda recognized a fundamental reality of New Spain: The most important treasure the Spaniards could plunder from the New World was not gold but uncompensated Indian labor.

The practice of coerced labor in New Spain grew directly out of the Spaniards' assumption that they were superior to the Indians. As one missionary put it, the Indians "are incapable of learning. . . . [They] are more stupid than asses and refuse to improve in anything." Therefore, most Spaniards assumed, Indians' labor should be organized by and for their conquerors. Spaniards seldom hesitated to use violence to punish and intimidate recalcitrant Indians.

Encomienda engendered two groups of influential critics. A few of the missionaries were horrified at the brutal mistreatment of the Indians. The cruelty of the encomenderos made it difficult for priests to persuade the Indians

MAP ACTIVITY

Map 2.3 Sixteenth-Century European Colonies in the New World

Spanish control spread throughout Central and South America during the sixteenth century, with the important exception of Portuguese Brazil. North America, though claimed by Spain under the Treaty of Tordesillas, remained peripheral to Spain's New World empire.

READING THE MAP: Track Spain's efforts at colonization by date. How did political holdings, the physical layout of the land, and natural resources influence where the Spaniards directed their energies?

CONNECTIONS: What was the purpose of the Treaty of Tordesillas? How might the location of silver and gold mines have affected Spain's desire to assert its claims over regions still held by Portugal after 1494, and Spain's interest in California, New Mexico, and Florida?

Zuñi Defend Pueblo against Coronado

This sixteenth-century drawing by a Mexican artist shows Zuñi bowmen fighting back against the arrows of Coronado's men and the entreaties of Christian missionaries. Intended to document the support some Mexican Indians gave to Spanish efforts to extend the conquest into North America, the drawing depicts the Zuñi defender at the bottom of the pueblo aiming his arrow at a Mexican missionary armed only with religious weaponry: a crucifix, a rosary, and a book (presumably the Bible). Hunterian Museum Library, University of Glasgow. Glasgow University Library, Department of Special Collections.

Justifying Conquest

The immense riches Spain reaped from its New World empire came largely at the expense of Native Americans. A few individual Spaniards raised their voices against the brutal exploitation of the Indians. Their criticisms prompted the Spanish monarchy to formulate an official justification of conquest that, in effect, blamed the Indians for resisting Spanish dominion.

DOCUMENT 1
Montecino's 1511 Sermon

In 1511, a Dominican friar named Antón Montecino delivered a blistering sermon that astonished the Spaniards gathered in the church in Santo Domingo, headquarters of the Spanish Caribbean.

Your greed for gold is blind. Your pride, your lust, your anger, your envy, your sloth, all blind. . . . You are in mortal sin. And you are heading for damnation. . . . For you are destroying an innocent people. For they are God's people, these innocents, whom you destroyed. By what right do you make them die? Mining gold for you in your mines or working for you in your fields, by what right do you unleash enslaving wars upon them? They have lived in peace in this land before you came, in peace in their own homes. They did nothing to harm you to cause you to slaughter them wholesale. . . .

Are you not under God's command to love them as you love yourselves?

Are you out of your souls, out of your minds? Yes. And that will bring you to damnation.

SOURCE: Zvi Dor-Ner, *Columbus and the Age of Discovery* (New York: William Morrow, 1991), 220–21.

DOCUMENT 2
The Requerimiento

Montecino returned to Spain to bring the Indians' plight to the king's attention. In 1512 and 1513, King Ferdinand met with philosophers, theologians, and other advisers and concluded that the holy duty to spread the Christian faith justified conquest. To buttress this claim, the king had his advisers prepare the Requerimiento.

According to the Requerimiento, Indians who failed to welcome Spanish conquest and all its blessings deserved to die. Conquistadors were commanded to read the Requerimiento to the Indians before any act of conquest. Beginning in 1514, they routinely did so, speaking in Spanish while other Spaniards brandishing unsheathed swords stood nearby.

On the part of the King . . . [and] queen of [Spain], subduers of the barbarous nations, we their servants notify and make known to you, as best we can, that the Lord our God, living and eternal, created the heaven and the earth, and one man and one woman, of whom you and we, and all the men of the world, were and are descendants. . . .

God our lord gave charge to one man called St. Peter, that he should be lord and superior to all the men in the world, that all should obey him, and that he should be the head of the whole human race, wherever men should live . . . and he gave him the world for his kingdom and jurisdiction.

And he commanded him to place his seat in Rome, as the spot most fitting to rule the world from. . . . This man was called Pope, as if to say, Admirable Great Father and Governor of men. The men who lived in that time obeyed that St. Peter and took him for lord, king, and superior of the universe. So also they have regarded the others who after him have been elected to the pontificate, and so has

of the tender mercies of the Spaniards' God. "What will [the Indians] think about the God of the Christians," Friar Bartolomé de Las Casas asked, when they see their friends "with their heads split, their hands amputated, their intestines torn open? . . . Would they want to come to Christ's sheepfold after their homes had been destroyed, their children imprisoned, their wives raped, their cities devastated, their maidens deflowered, and their provinces laid waste?" Las Casas and other outspoken missionaries softened few hearts among the encomenderos, but they did win some sympathy for the Indians from the Spanish monarchy and royal bureaucracy. The Spanish monarchy moved to abolish encomienda in an effort to replace swashbuckling it been continued even till now, and will continue till the end of the world.

One of these pontiffs, who succeeded that St. Peter as lord of the world . . . made donation of these islands and mainland to the aforesaid king and queen [of Spain] and to their successors. . . .

So their highnesses are kings and lords of these islands and mainland by virtue of this donation; and . . . almost all those to whom this has been notified, have received and served their highnesses, as lords and kings, in the way that subjects ought to do, with good will, without any resistance, immediately, without delay, when they were informed of the aforesaid facts. And also they received and obeyed the priests whom their highnesses sent to preach to them and to teach them our holy faith; and all these, of their own free will, without any reward or condition have become Christians, and are so, and their highnesses have joyfully and graciously received them, and they have also commanded them to be treated as their subjects and vassals; and you too are held and obliged to do the same. Wherefore, as best we can, we ask and require that you consider what we have said to you, and that you take the time that shall be necessary to understand and deliberate upon it, and that you acknowledge the Church as the ruler and superior of the whole world, and the high priest called Pope, and in his name the king and queen [of Spain] our lords, in his place, as superiors and lords and kings of these islands and this mainland by virtue of the said donation, and that you consent and permit that these religious fathers declare and preach to you. . . .

If you do so . . . we . . . shall receive you in all love and charity, and shall leave you your wives and your children and your lands free without servitude, that you may do with them and with yourselves freely what you like and think best, and they shall not compel you to turn to Christians unless you yourselves, when informed of the truth, should wish to be converted to our holy Catholic faith. . . . And besides this, their highnesses award you many privileges and exemptions and will grant you many benefits.

But if you do not do this or if you maliciously delay in doing it, I certify to you that with the help of God we shall forcefully enter into your country and shall make war against you in all ways and manners that we can, and shall subject you to the yoke and obedience of the Church and of their highnesses; we shall take you and your wives and your children and shall make slaves of them, and as such shall sell and dispose of them as their highnesses may command; and we shall take away your goods and shall do to you all the harm and damage that we can, as to vassals who do not obey and refuse to receive their lord and resist and contradict him; and we protest that the deaths and losses which shall accrue from this are your fault, and not that of their highnesses, or ours, or of these soldiers who come with us.

The Indians who heard the Requerimiento could not understand Spanish, of course. No native documents survive to record the Indians' thoughts upon hearing the Spaniards' official justification for conquest, even when it was translated into a language they recognized. But one conquistador reported that when the Requerimiento was translated for two chiefs in Colombia, they responded that if the pope gave the king so much territory that belonged to other people, "the Pope must have been drunk."

SOURCE: Adapted from A. Helps and M. Oppenheim, eds., *The Spanish Conquest in America and Its Relation to the History of Slavery and to the Government of the Colonies*, 4 vols. (London and New York, 1900–1904), 1:264–67.

Questions for Analysis and Debate

1. How did the Requerimiento address the criticisms of Montecino? According to the Requerimiento, why was conquest justified? What was the source of the Indians' resistance to conquest?

2. What arguments might a critic like Montecino have used to respond to the Requerimiento's justification of conquest? What arguments might the Mexican leader Montezuma have made against those of the Requerimiento?

3. Was the Requerimiento a faithful expression or a cynical violation of the Spaniards' Christian faith?

---

old conquistadors with royal bureaucrats as the rulers of New Spain.

In 1549, a reform called the ***repartimiento*** began to replace encomienda. It limited the labor an encomendero could command from his Indians to forty-five days per year from each adult male. The repartimiento, however, did not challenge the principle of forced labor, nor did it prevent encomenderos from continuing to cheat, mistreat, and overwork their Indians. Many Indians were put to work in silver mines, which required large capital investments and large groups of laborers. Silver mining was grueling and dangerous for the workers, but very profitable for the Spaniards who supervised them: During

Spreading Christianity in New Spain

Spanish officials aspired to accompany the military and political conquest of the New World with spiritual conquest. With royal support, priests flocked to New Spain to harvest the millions of souls unexpectedly disclosed by the voyages of Columbus. In 1529, a young priest named Bernardino de Sahagún sailed to New Spain, where he spent the remaining sixty-one years of his life seeking to realize the promise of spreading Christianity to people who had never heard of it.

Sahagún believed that preaching the gospel in the New World was a heaven-sent opportunity to revitalize global Christianity. In Asia, he wrote, "there are nothing but Turks and Moors"; in Africa, "there are no longer any Christians"; in Germany, "there are nothing but heretics"; and in Europe, "in most places there is no obedience to the Church." Now, Sahagún wrote, "Our Lord [ordained] the Spanish people to traverse the Ocean Sea to make discoveries in the West" and to "bring into the embrace of the Church that multitude of peoples, kingdoms, and nations." In pursuit of his goal to rescue Christianity by converting the New World Indians, Sahagún compiled the most important collection of information in existence about the lives and beliefs of sixteenth-century Mexicans.

Sahagún and other Spaniards considered Christianity the one true faith. When Cortés and his men marched into Mexico a decade before Sahagún arrived, they went out of their way to destroy effigies of Mexican gods and to replace them with crosses, the icons of Christianity. "It was necessary," Sahagún wrote, "to destroy the idolatrous things, and all the idolatrous buildings, and even the customs of the [Mexicans] . . . that were intertwined with idolatrous rites and accompanied by idolatrous ceremonies."

What Sahagún considered idolatry was rooted in individual Mexicans' belief in what he called their own "innumerable insanities and gods without number." Sahagún and other priests set out to persuade the Indians to reject belief in traditional deities and to have faith instead in the divinity of Jesus Christ and in the Catholic Church as Christ's representative on earth.

At first, the conversion campaign seemed amazingly successful. One priest claimed that more than nine million Mexicans had been baptized by 1539. But after a few years, Sahagún and other priests realized that many Indians simply "took [Jesus Christ] as yet another god . . . without . . . relinquishing their ancient gods." Adopting some of the outward rituals of Christianity while maintaining belief in what Spaniards considered pagan idols was a "twisted perversity," Sahagún wrote, one that caused the New World church "to be founded on falsehood."

Unlike many other Spaniards, Sahagún believed that in order to purge Mexicans' idolatries, church leaders needed to become familiar with Mexicans' traditional religious ideas. To diagnose what he called the Mexicans' "spiritual illnesses," Sahagún set out to record everything he could learn about the Indians' beliefs.

As a first step, Sahagún learned Nahuatl, the Mexicans' unwritten language. Next, he and other priests started schools to teach Latin and eventually Spanish to young Indian students, usually drawn from elite families. These "trilinguals," as Sahagún called them, could translate religious texts into Nahuatl, which the priests could use in their missionary efforts.

---

the entire sixteenth century, precious-metal exports from New Spain to Spain were worth twenty-five times more than the next most important export, leather hides (Figure 2.1).

For the Spaniards, life in New Spain after the conquests was relatively easy. Although the riches they won fell far short of their expectations, encomienda gave them a comfortable, leisurely life that was the envy of many Spaniards back in Europe. As one colonist wrote to his brother in Spain, "Don't hesitate [to come]. . . . This land [New Spain] is as good as ours [in Spain], for God has given us more here than there, and we shall be better off." During the century after 1492, about 225,000 Spaniards settled in the colonies. Virtually all of them were poor young men of common (non-noble) lineage who came directly from Spain. Laborers and artisans made up the largest proportion, but soldiers and sailors were also numerous. Throughout the sixteenth century, men vastly outnumbered women, although the proportion of women grew from about one in twenty before 1519 to nearly one in three by the 1580s.

The gender and number of Spanish settlers shaped two fundamental features of the society of New Spain. First, Europeans never made up more than 1 or 2 percent of the total population.

Beginning in 1558, Sahagún used his trilinguals to undertake a systematic investigation of every facet of Mexican life. Sahagún and his assistants interviewed Mexican elders, asking them not only about gods and religious ceremonies but also about farming, family life, education, poetry, songs, and even their conquest by the Spaniards. Sahagún developed great admiration for both the Mexicans and their language. "They are quick to learn," he wrote. "There is no art for which they do not have the talent to learn and use it." In fact, Sahagún declared, the Mexicans "are held to be barbarians and a people of little worth, yet in truth, in matters of culture, they are a step ahead of many nations that presume to be civilized."

For years, Sahagún edited and organized this massive treasure trove of information about Mexican life and beliefs, all in the hope that it would ultimately help priests make converts to Christianity. When church officials heard about Sahagún's great work, they obtained a royal order in 1577 to collect all copies and send them immediately to Spain for destruction. The Spanish monarchy and most church officials wanted to stamp out the Mexicans' beliefs, not preserve them. Sahagún dutifully sent his volumes to Spain, but he was still working on a final copy, which he later gave to a priest friend, who saved it, and it survives to this day. Unbeknownst to him, Sahagún's

Montezuma Receiving Tribute
This drawing from Sahagún's Florentine Codex portrays Montezuma (seated at left) receiving a rich array of featherwork, ritualistic costumes, textiles, battle shields, and other luxuries from one of his subjects. Made by a Mexican artist in the mid-sixteenth century, the drawing adapts preconquest symbols to illustrate the enormous power and respect that Montezuma commanded. By the time the drawing was made, Montezuma had been dead for about forty years, and the Spaniards, not Montezuma's descendants, collected tribute (mostly in the form of labor) from the Indians. Bridgeman Art Library Ltd.

masterwork preserved for posterity an unrivaled account of the hearts and souls of sixteenth-century Mexicans in their own words.

Questions for Consideration

1. In what ways did Sahagún's work contribute to the conquest of Mexico?

2. What ideas about the Mexicans did Sahagún hold in common with the Spanish monarchy, royal officials, and other Catholic missionaries? To what extent did his ideas conflict with those held by other Spaniards?

3. What did Sahagún believe about the global significance of his missionary work? How might his "trilinguals" and Mexican informants have interpreted his efforts?

Although Spaniards ruled New Spain, the population was almost wholly Indian. Second, the shortage of Spanish women meant that Spanish men frequently married Indian women or used them as concubines. For the most part, the relatively few women from Spain married Spanish men, contributing to a tiny elite defined by European origins.

The small number of Spaniards, the masses of Indians, and the frequency of intermarriage created a steep social hierarchy defined by perceptions of national origin and race. Natives of Spain — *peninsulares* (people born on the Iberian Peninsula) — enjoyed the highest social status

in New Spain. Below them but still within the white elite were *creoles*, the children born in the New World to Spanish men and women. Together, peninsulares and creoles made up barely 1 or 2 percent of the population. Below them on the social pyramid was a larger group of *mestizos*, the offspring of Spanish men and Indian women, who accounted for 4 or 5 percent of the population. So many of the mestizos were born out of wedlock that the term *mestizo* (after the Spanish word for "mixed") became almost synonymous with *bastard* during the sixteenth century. Some mestizos worked as artisans and labor overseers and lived well, and a few rose

Español con India,
Mestizo.

Mestizo con Española
Castizo.

Castizo con Española
Español.

Español con Mora
Mulato.

5

6

Mulato con Española
Morisco.

Morisco con Española
Chino.

7

Chino con India
Salta atras.

Salta atras con Mulata
Lobo.

VISUAL ACTIVITY

Mixed Races

The residents of New Spain maintained a lively interest in each person's racial lineage. These eighteenth-century paintings illustrate forms of racial mixture common in the sixteenth century. In the first painting, a Spanish man and an Indian woman have a mestizo son; in the fourth, a Spanish man and a woman of African descent have a mulatto son; in the fifth, a Spanish woman and a mulatto man have a *morisco* daughter. The many racial permutations led the residents of New Spain to develop an elaborate vocabulary of ancestry. The child of a morisco and a Spaniard was a *chino*; the child of a chino and an Indian was a *salta abas*; the child of a salta abas and a mulatto was a *lobo*; and so on. Can you detect hints of some of the meanings of racial categories in the clothing depicted in these paintings? Bob Schalkwijk/INAH.

READING THE IMAGE: : What do these paintings reveal about social status in New Spain?

CONNECTIONS: How do the paintings of mixed-race families illustrate the power the Spaniards exercised in their New World colonies? What were some other aspects of colonial society that demonstrated Spanish domination?

pronounced pattern in the European colonies of the New World: a society stratified sharply by social origin and race. All Europeans of whatever social origin considered themselves superior to Native Americans; in New Spain, they were a dominant minority in both power and status.

The Toll of Spanish Conquest and Colonization

By 1560, the major centers of Indian civilization had been conquered, their leaders overthrown, their religion held in contempt, and their people forced to work for the Spaniards. Profound demoralization pervaded Indian society. As a Mexican poet wrote:

> Nothing but flowers and songs of sorrow are left in Mexico . . .
>
> where once we saw warriors and wise men. . . .
>
> We are crushed to the ground; we lie in ruins. There is nothing but grief and suffering in Mexico.

Adding to the culture shock of conquest and colonization was the deadly toll of European

into the ranks of the elite, especially if their Indian ancestry was not obvious from their skin color. Most mestizos, however, were lumped with the Indians, the enormous bottom slab of the social pyramid.

The society of New Spain established the precedent for what would become a

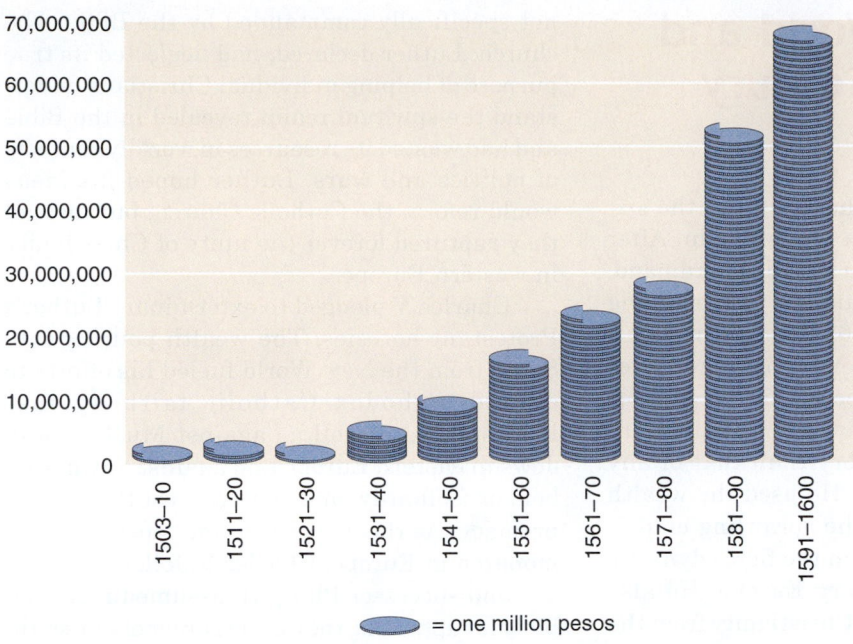

FIGURE 2.1 New World Gold and Silver Imported into Spain during the Sixteenth Century, in Pesos
Spain imported more gold than silver during the first three decades of the sixteenth century, but the total value of this treasure was quickly eclipsed during the 1530s and 1540s, when rich silver mines were developed. Silver accounted for most of the enormous growth in Spain's precious-metal imports from the New World.

diseases. As conquest spread, the Indians succumbed to virulent epidemics of measles, smallpox, and respiratory illnesses. They had no immunity to these diseases because they had not been exposed to them before the arrival of Europeans. The isolation of the Western Hemisphere before 1492 had protected ancient Americans from the contagious diseases that had raged throughout Eurasia for millennia. The new post-1492 sea bridge eliminated that isolation, and by 1570 the Indian population of New Spain had fallen about 90 percent from what it was when Columbus arrived. The destruction of the Indians was a catastrophe unequaled in human history. A Mayan Indian recalled that when sickness struck his village, "great was the stench of the dead. . . . The dogs and vultures devoured the bodies. The mortality was terrible." For most Indians, New Spain was a graveyard.

For the Spaniards, Indian deaths meant that the most valuable resource of New Spain — Indian labor — dwindled rapidly. By the last quarter of the sixteenth century, Spanish colonists felt the pinch of a labor shortage. To help supply laborers, the colonists began to import African slaves. Some Africans had come to Mexico with the conquistadors. One Mexican recalled that among Cortés's men were "some black-skinned one[s] with kink[y] hair." In the years before 1550, while Indian labor was still adequate, only 15,000 slaves were imported from Africa. Even after Indian labor began to decline, the relatively high cost of African slaves kept imports low, totaling approximately 36,000 from 1550 to the end of the century. During the sixteenth century, New Spain continued to rely primarily on a shrinking number of Indians.

REVIEW How did New Spain's distinctive colonial population shape its economy and society?

A Sign of Conquest
This skull of an Indian man in his fifties was excavated from the site of a Native American village in southwestern Georgia visited by de Soto's expedition in 1540. The skull shows that the man suffered a fatal sword wound above his right eye. Combined with slashed and severed arm and leg bones from the same site, the skull demonstrates the brutality de Soto employed against indigenous peoples on his journey through the Southeast. No native weapons could have inflicted the wounds left on this skull and the other bones. *Private Collection.*

► The New World and Sixteenth-Century Europe

The riches of New Spain helped make the sixteenth century the Golden Age of Spain. After the deaths of Queen Isabella and King Ferdinand, their sixteen-year-old grandson became King Charles I of Spain in 1516. Three years later, just as Cortés ventured into Mexico, King Charles used judicious bribes to secure his selection as Holy Roman Emperor Charles V. His empire encompassed more territory than that of any other European monarch. He used the wealth of New Spain to protect the sprawling empire and promote his interests in the fierce dynastic battles of sixteenth-century Europe. He also sought to defend orthodox Christianity from the insurgent heresy of the Protestant Reformation. The power of the Spanish monarchy spread the clear message throughout sixteenth-century Europe that a New World empire could bankroll Old World ambitions.

The Protestant Reformation and the Spanish Response

In 1517, **Martin Luther**, an obscure Catholic priest in central Germany, initiated the **Protestant Reformation** by publicizing his criticisms of the Catholic Church. Luther's ideas won the sympathy of many Catholics, but they were considered extremely dangerous by church officials and monarchs such as Charles V who believed that just as the church spoke for God, they ruled for God.

Luther preached a doctrine known as "justification by faith": Individual Christians could obtain salvation and life everlasting only by having faith that God would save them. Giving monetary offerings to the church, following the orders of priests, or participating in church rituals would not bring believers closer to heaven. Also, the only true source of information about God's will was the Bible, not the church. By reading the Bible, any Christian could learn as much about God's commandments as any priest. Indeed, Luther called for a "priesthood of all believers."

In effect, Luther charged that the Catholic Church was in many respects fraudulent. He insisted that priests were unnecessary for salvation and that they encouraged Christians to violate God's will by promoting religious practices not specifically commanded by the Bible. The church, Luther declared, had neglected its true purpose of helping individual Christians understand the spiritual realm revealed in the Bible and had wasted its resources in worldly conflicts of politics and wars. Luther hoped his ideas would reform the Catholic Church, but instead they ruptured forever the unity of Christianity in western Europe.

Charles V pledged to exterminate Luther's Protestant heresies. The wealth pouring into Spain from the New World fueled his efforts to defend orthodox Catholic faith against Protestants, as well as against Muslims and Jews in eastern Europe and against any nation bold or foolhardy enough to contest Spain's supremacy. As the wealthiest and most powerful monarch in Europe, Charles V, followed by his son and successor Philip II, assumed responsibility for upholding the existing order of sixteenth-century Europe.

American wealth, particularly Mexican silver, fueled Spanish ambitions and made the Spanish monarchy rich and powerful among the states of Europe. But Charles V's and Philip II's expenses for constant warfare far outstripped the revenues arriving from New Spain. To help meet military expenditures, both kings raised taxes in Spain more than fivefold during the sixteenth century. Since the nobility, the wealthiest Spaniards by far, were exempt from taxation, the burdensome new taxes fell mostly on poor peasants. The monarchy's ambitions impoverished the vast majority of Spain's population and brought the nation to the brink of bankruptcy. When taxes failed to produce enough revenue to fight its wars, the monarchy borrowed heavily from European bankers. By the end of the sixteenth century, interest payments on royal debts swallowed two-thirds of the crown's annual revenues. In retrospect, the riches from New Spain proved a short-term blessing but a long-term curse.

Most Spaniards, however, looked upon New Spain as a glorious national achievement that displayed Spain's superiority over Native Americans and over other Europeans. As they surveyed their many accomplishments in the New World, they saw clear signs of progress. They had added enormously to their knowledge and wealth. They had built mines, cities, Catholic churches, and even universities on the other side of the Atlantic. These military, religious, and economic achievements gave them great pride and confidence that their European rivals often considered swaggering arrogance.

Europe and the Spanish Example

The lessons of sixteenth-century Spain were not lost on Spain's European rivals. Spain proudly displayed the fruits of its New World conquests. In 1520, for example, the German artist Albrecht Dürer wrote in his diary that he "marveled over the subtle ingenuity of the men in these distant lands" who created "things which were brought to the King . . . [such as] a sun entirely of gold, a whole fathom [six feet] broad." But the most exciting news about "the men in these distant lands" was that they could serve the interests of Europeans, as Spain had shown. With a few notable exceptions, Europeans saw the New World as a place for the expansion of European influence, a place where, as one Spaniard wrote, Europeans could "give to those strange lands the form of our own."

France and England tried to follow Spain's example. Both nations warred with Spain in Europe, preyed on Spanish treasure fleets, and ventured to the New World, where they too hoped to find an undiscovered passageway to the East Indies or another Mexico or Peru.

In 1524, France sent Giovanni da Verrazano to scout the Atlantic coast of North America from North Carolina to Canada, looking for a Northwest Passage (see Map 2.2). Eleven years later, France probed farther north with Jacques Cartier's voyage up the St. Lawrence River. Encouraged, Cartier returned to the region with a group of settlers in 1541, but the colony they established — like the search for a Northwest Passage — came to nothing.

English attempts to follow Spain's lead were slower but equally ill-fated. Not until 1576, almost eighty years after John Cabot's voyages, did the

Algonquian Ceremonial Dance

When English artist John White visited the coast of present-day North Carolina in 1585 as part of Raleigh's expedition, he painted this watercolor of an Algonquian ceremonial dance. This and White's other portraits are the only surviving likenesses of sixteenth-century North American Indians that were drawn from direct observation. White's portrait captures the individuality of the Indians while depicting a ceremony that must have appeared bizarre and alien to a sixteenth-century Englishman. The significance of this ceremonial dance is still a mystery, although the portrait's obvious signs of order, organization, and collective understanding show that the dancing Indians knew its purpose. Copyright Trustees of the British Museum/Bridgeman Art Library.

English again try to find a Northwest Passage. This time Martin Frobisher sailed into the frigid waters of northern Canada (see Map 2.2). His sponsor was the Cathay Company, which hoped to open trade with China. Like many other explorers, Frobisher was mesmerized by the Spanish example and was sure he had found gold. But the tons of "ore" he hauled back to England proved worthless, the Cathay Company collapsed, and English interests shifted southward to the giant region on the northern margins of New Spain.

Roanoke Settlement, 1585–1590

English explorers' attempts to establish North American settlements were no more fruitful than their search for a northern route to China. Sir Humphrey Gilbert led expeditions in 1578 and 1583 that made feeble efforts to found colonies in Newfoundland until Gilbert vanished at sea. Sir Walter Raleigh organized an expedition in 1585 to settle Roanoke Island off the coast of present-day North Carolina. The first group of explorers left no colonists on the island, but two years later Raleigh sent a contingent of more than one hundred settlers to **Roanoke** under John White's leadership. White went back to England for supplies, and when he returned to Roanoke in 1590, the colonists had disappeared, leaving only the word *Croatoan* (whose meaning is unknown) carved in a tree. The Roanoke colonists most likely died from a combination of natural causes and unfriendly Indians. By the end of the century, England had failed to secure a New World beachhead.

> **REVIEW**   How did Spain's conquests in the New World shape Spanish influence in Europe?

▶ Conclusion: The Promise of the New World for Europeans

The sixteenth century in the New World belonged to the Spaniards who employed Columbus and to the Indians who greeted him as he stepped ashore. The Portuguese, whose voyages to Africa and Asia set the stage for Columbus's voyages, won the important consolation prize of Brazil, but Spain hit the jackpot. Isabella of Spain helped initiate the Columbian exchange between the New World and the Old, which massively benefited first Spain and later other Europeans and which continues to this day. The exchange also subjected Native Americans to the ravages of European diseases and Spanish conquest. Spanish explorers, conquistadors, and colonists forced the Indians to serve the interests of Spanish settlers and the Spanish monarchy. The exchange illustrated one of the most important lessons of the sixteenth century: After millions of years, the Atlantic no longer was an impermeable barrier separating the Eastern and Western Hemispheres. After the voyages of Columbus, European sailing ships regularly bridged the Atlantic and carried people, products, diseases, and ideas from one shore to the other.

No European monarch could forget the seductive lesson taught by Spain's example: The New World could vastly enrich the Old. Spain remained a New World power for almost four centuries, and its language, religion, culture, and institutions left a permanent imprint. By the end of the sixteenth century, however, other European monarchies had begun to contest Spain's dominion in Europe and to make forays into the northern fringes of Spain's New World preserve. To reap the benefits the Spaniards enjoyed from their New World domain, the others had to learn a difficult lesson: how to deviate from Spain's example. That discovery lay ahead.

While England's rulers eyed the huge North American hinterland of New Spain for possible exploitation, they realized that it lacked the two main attractions of Mexico and Peru: incredible material wealth and large populations of Indians to use as workers. In the absence of gold and silver booty and plentiful native labor in North America, England would need to find some way to attract colonizers to a region that — compared to New Spain — did not appear very promising. During the next century, England's leaders overcame these dilemmas by developing a distinctive colonial model, one that encouraged land-hungry settlers from England and Europe to engage in agriculture and that depended on other sources of unfree labor: indentured servants from Europe and slaves from Africa.

▶ Selected Bibliography

General Works

J. H. Elliott, *Empires of the Atlantic World: Britain and Spain in America, 1491–1830* (2006).

Jonathan Locke Hart, *Representing the New World: The English and French Uses of the Example of Spain* (2001).

Jonathan Locke Hart, *Columbus, Shakespeare, and the Interpretation of the New World* (2003).

John L. Kessell, *Spain in the Southwest: A Narrative History of Colonial New Mexico, Arizona, Texas, and California* (2002).

Kenneth F. Kiple and Stephen V. Beck, eds., *Biological Consequences of European Expansion, 1450–1800* (1997).

Diarmaid MacCulloch, *Christianity: The First Three Thousand Years* (2009).

William D. Phillips and Carla Rahn Phillips, *The Worlds of Christopher Columbus* (1992).

David J. Weber, *The Spanish Frontier in North America* (2009).

Explorers and Empires

James Horn, *A Kingdom Strange: The Brief and Tragic History of the Lost Colony of Roanoke* (2010).

Henry Arthur Francis Kamen, *Empire: How Spain Became a World Power, 1492–1763* (2004).

Karen Ordahl Kupperman, *Roanoke: The Abandoned Colony* (2nd ed., 2007).

Francesc Relaño, *The Shaping of Africa: Cosmographic Discourse and Cartographic Science in Late Medieval and Early Modern Europe* (2002).

A. J. R. Russell-Wood, *The Portuguese Empire, 1415–1808: A World on the Move* (1998).

Hugh Thomas, *Rivers of Gold: The Rise of the Spanish Empire from Columbus to Magellan* (2004).

Europeans Encounter the New World

Ricardo Alegria and Jose Arrom, *Taino: Pre-Columbian Art and Culture from the Caribbean* (1998).

Rebecca Catz, *Christopher Columbus and the Portuguese, 1476–1498* (1993).

Noble David Cook, *Born to Die: Disease and New World Conquest, 1492–1650* (1998).

Valerie J. Flint, *The Imaginative Landscape of Christopher Columbus* (1992).

Anthony Pagden, *Lords of All the World: Ideologies of Empire in Spain, Britain, and France, 1500–1800* (1995).

Irving Rouse, *The Tainos: Rise and Decline of the People Who Greeted Columbus* (1992).

Conquest and New Spain

Herman L. Bennett, *Africans in Colonial Mexico: Absolutism, Christianity, and Afro-Creole Consciousness, 1570–1640* (2003).

Louise M. Burkhart, *The Slippery Earth: Nahua-Christian Moral Dialogue in Sixteenth-Century Mexico* (1989).

David Ewing Duncan, *Hernando de Soto: A Savage Quest in the Americas* (1995).

Richard Flint and Shirley Cushing Flint, *The Coronado Expedition* (2003).

Serge Gruzinski, *The Conquest of Mexico: The Incorporation of Indian Societies into the Western World, Sixteenth–Eighteenth Centuries* (1993).

Ramón A. Gutiérrez, *When Jesus Came, the Corn Mothers Went Away: Marriage, Sexuality, and Power in New Mexico, 1500–1846* (1991).

Robert H. Jackson, *Race, Caste, and Status: Indians in Colonial Spanish America* (1999).

John L. Kessell, *Pueblos, Spaniards, and the Kingdom of New Mexico* (2010).

Andrew L. Knaut, *The Pueblo Revolt of 1680: Conquest and Resistance in Seventeenth-Century New Mexico* (1995).

Miguel León-Portilla, *Bernardino de Sahagún: First Anthropologist* (2002).

James Lockhart, *The Nahuas after Conquest: A Social and Cultural History of the Indians of Central Mexico, Sixteenth through Eighteenth Centuries* (1992).

Jerald T. Milanich, *Laboring in the Fields of the Lord: Spanish Missions and Southwestern Indians* (1999).

Stuart B. Schwartz, *All Can Be Saved: Religious Tolerance and Salvation in the Iberian Atlantic World* (2009).

Charles A. Truxillo, *By the Sword and the Cross: The Historical Evolution of the Catholic World Monarchy in Spain and the New World, 1492–1825* (2001).

Stephanie Gail Wood, *Transcending Conquest: Nahua Views of Spanish Colonial Mexico* (2003).

▶ FOR MORE BOOKS ABOUT TOPICS IN THIS CHAPTER, see the Online Bibliography at **bedfordstmartins.com/roark**.

▶ FOR ADDITIONAL PRIMARY SOURCES FROM THIS PERIOD, see in Michael Johnson, ed., *Reading the American Past*, Fifth Edition.

▶ FOR WEB SITES, IMAGES, AND DOCUMENTS RELATED TO TOPICS AND PLACES IN THIS CHAPTER, visit Make History at **bedfordstmartins.com/roark**.

Reviewing Chapter 2

REVIEW QUESTIONS

Use key terms and dates to support your answers.

1. Why did European exploration expand dramatically in the fifteenth century? (pp. 33–36)

2. How did Columbus's discoveries help revolutionize Europeans' understanding of world geography? (pp. 36–40)

3. How did New Spain's distinctive colonial population shape its economy and society? (pp. 40–53)

4. How did Spain's conquests in the New World shape Spanish influence in Europe? (pp. 54–56)

MAKING CONNECTIONS

Draw on key terms, the timeline, and review questions.

1. The Columbian exchange exposed people on both sides of the Atlantic to surprising new people and goods. It also produced dramatic demographic and political transformations in the Old World and the New. How did the Columbian exchange lead to redistributions of power and population? Discuss these changes, being sure to cite examples from both contexts.

2. Despite inferior numbers, the Spaniards were able to conquer the Mexica and maintain control of the colonial hierarchy that followed. Why did the Spanish conquest of the Mexica succeed, and how did the Spaniards govern the conquered territory to maintain their dominance?

3. Spanish conquest in North America brought new peoples into constant contact. How did the Spaniards' and Indians' perceptions of each other shape their interactions? In your answer, cite specific examples and consider how perceptions changed over time.

4. How did the astonishing wealth generated for the Spanish crown by its conquest of the New World influence European colonial exploration throughout the sixteenth century? In your answer, discuss ways it both encouraged and limited interest in exploration.

LINKING TO THE PAST

Link events in this chapter to earlier events.

1. How did the legacy of ancient Americans influence their descendants' initial encounters and subsequent economic, social, and military relations with Europeans in the sixteenth century? (See chapter 1.)

2. Before the arrival of Europeans, Native Americans in the New World had no knowledge of Christianity, just as Europeans had no knowledge of Native American religions. To what extent did contrasting religious beliefs and assumptions influence relations among Europeans and Native Americans in the New World in the sixteenth century? (See chapter 1.)

▶ **FOR PRACTICE QUIZZES AND OTHER STUDY TOOLS**, visit the Online Study Guide at **bedfordstmartins.com/roark**.

TIMELINE 1480–1599

1480	• Portuguese ships reach Congo.
1488	• Bartolomeu Dias rounds Cape of Good Hope.
1492	• Christopher Columbus lands on Caribbean island that he names San Salvador.
1493	• Columbus makes second voyage to New World.
1494	• Portugal and Spain negotiate Treaty of Tordesillas.
1497	• John Cabot searches for Northwest Passage.
1498	• Vasco da Gama sails to India.
1513	• Vasco Núñez de Balboa crosses Isthmus of Panama.
1517	• Protestant Reformation begins in Germany.
1519	• Hernán Cortés leads expedition to find wealth in Mexico. • Ferdinand Magellan sets out to sail around the world.
1520	• Mexica in Tenochtitlán revolt against Spaniards.
1521	• Cortés conquers Mexica at Tenochtitlán.
1532	• Francisco Pizarro begins conquest of Peru.
1535	• Jacques Cartier explores St. Lawrence River.
1539	• Hernando de Soto explores southeastern North America.
1540	• Francisco Vásquez de Coronado starts to explore Southwest and Great Plains.
1542	• Juan Rodríguez Cabrillo explores California coast.
1549	• Repartimiento reforms begin to replace encomienda.
1565	• St. Augustine, Florida, settled.
1576	• Martin Frobisher explores northern Canadian waters.
1587	• English settle Roanoke Island.
1598	• Juan de Oñate explores New Mexico.
1599	• Acoma pueblos revolt against Oñate.

TOBACCO CUTTER

Planters in the southern colonies of British North America shipped tobacco leaves to England, where tobacconists used machines like the one shown here to chop the leaves into small pieces for smoking. Tobacco merchants often flavored the chopped leaves with oils, herbs, and spices, much as coffeehouse baristas today add hazelnut, mocha, or vanilla flavors to lattes and cappuccinos. The illustration on the side of the cutter refers to the Native American origins of tobacco grown in the fields in the Chesapeake region, shown on the map in the background.

Tobacco cutter: Niemeyer Nederlands Tabacologisch Museum; map: Princeton University Libraries, Department of Rare Books and Special Collections.

3

The Southern Colonies in the Seventeenth Century 1601–1700

IN DECEMBER 1607, BARELY SIX MONTHS AFTER ARRIVING AT Jamestown with the first English colonists, Captain John Smith was captured by warriors of Powhatan, the supreme chief of about fourteen thousand Algonquian Indians who inhabited the coastal plain of present-day Virginia, near Chesapeake Bay. According to Smith, Powhatan "feasted him after their best barbarous manner." Then, Smith recalled, "two great stones were brought before Powhatan: then as many [Indians] as could layd hands on [Smith], dragged him to [the stones], and thereon laid his head, and being ready with their clubs, to beate out his braines." At that moment, Pocahontas, Powhatan's eleven-year-old daughter, rushed forward and "got [Smith's] head in her armes, and laid her owne upon his to save him from death." Pocahontas, Smith wrote, "hazarded the beating out of her owne braines to save mine, and . . . so prevailed with her father, that I was safely conducted [back] to James towne."

This romantic story of an Indian maiden rescuing a white soldier and saving Jamestown — and ultimately English colonization of North America — has been enshrined in the writing of American history since 1624, when Smith published his *Generall Historie of Virginia*. Historians believe that this episode happened more or less as Smith described it. But Smith did not understand why Pocahontas acted as she did.

Most likely, when Pocahontas intervened to save Smith, she was a knowing participant in an Algonquian ceremony that expressed Powhatan's supremacy and his ritualistic adoption of Smith as a subordinate chief, or *werowance*. What Smith interpreted as Pocahontas's saving him from certain death was instead a ceremonial enactment of Powhatan's willingness to incorporate Smith and the white strangers at Jamestown into Powhatan's empire. Powhatan routinely attached his sons and daughters to subordinate tribes as an expression of his protection and his dominance. By appearing to save Smith, Pocahontas was probably acting out Smith's new status as an adopted member of Powhatan's extended family.

61

Ætatis suæ 21. Aᵒ 1616.

Matoaks als Rebecka daughter to the mig. Powhatan Emperour of Attanoughkomouck converted and baptized in the Christi.. Wife to the worll Mr. Tho: Rolff.

Pocahontas in England

Shortly after Pocahontas and her husband, John Rolfe, arrived in England in 1616, she posed for this portrait dressed in English clothing, possibly including the earrings shown here, suitable for a princess. The portrait captures the dual novelty of England for Pocahontas and of Pocahontas for the English. Ornate, courtly clothing probably signified to English observers that Pocahontas was royalty and to Pocahontas that the English were accepting her as befitted the "Emperour" Powhatan's daughter. The mutability of Pocahontas's identity is displayed in the identification of her as "Matoaks" or "Rebecka." Painting: National Portrait Gallery, Smithsonian Institution/Art Resource, NY; earrings: Courtesy of Preservation Virginia.

Smith returned to England about two years after the adoption ritual. In Virginia, relations between Powhatan and the English colonists deteriorated into bloody raids by both parties. In 1613, the colonists captured Pocahontas and held her hostage at Jamestown. Within a year, she converted to Christianity and married one of the colonists, a widower named John Rolfe. After giving birth to a son named Thomas, Pocahontas, her husband, and the new baby sailed for England in the spring of 1616. There, promoters of the Virginia colony dressed her as a proper Englishwoman and arranged for her to go to a ball attended by the king and queen.

When John Smith heard that Pocahontas was in London, he went to see her. According to Smith, Pocahontas said, "You did promise Powhatan what was yours should bee his, and he the like to you; you called him father, being in his land a stranger, and by the same reason so must I doe you." It seems likely that Pocahontas believed that her incorporation into English society was a counterpart of the adoption ritual Powhatan had staged for John Smith in Virginia back in 1607.

Pocahontas died in England in 1617. Her son, Thomas, ultimately returned to Virginia, and by the time of the American Revolution his descendants numbered in the hundreds. But the world Thomas Rolfe and his descendants inhabited was shaped by a reversal of the power ritualized when his mother "saved" John Smith. By the end of the seventeenth century, Native Americans no longer dominated the newcomers who had arrived in the Chesapeake with John Smith.

During the seventeenth century, English colonists learned how to deviate from the example of New Spain (see chapter 2) by growing tobacco, a crop Native Americans had cultivated in small quantities for centuries. The new settlers grew enormous quantities of tobacco and exported most of it to England. Instead of incorporating Powhatan's people into their new society, the settlers encroached on Indian land and built new societies on the foundation of tobacco agriculture and transatlantic trade.

Producing large crop surpluses for export required hard labor and people who were willing — or could be forced — to do it. While New Spain took advantage of Native American labor, for the most part the Native Americans in British North America refused to be conscripted into the English colonists' fields. Instead, the settlers depended on the labor of family members, indentured servants, and, by the last third of the seventeenth century, African slaves.

By the end of the century, the southern colonies had become sharply different both from the world dominated by Powhatan when the Jamestown settlers first arrived and from contemporary English society. In ways unimaginable to Powhatan, Pocahontas, and John Smith, the colonists paid homage to the international market and the English monarch by working mightily to make a good living growing crops for sale to the Old World.

▶ An English Colony on Chesapeake Bay

When James I became king of England in 1603, he looked toward North America as a possible location for English colonies that could be as profitable as New Spain. In 1606, he granted the Virginia Company more than six million acres in North America in hopes of establishing the English equivalent of Spain's New World empire. Enthusiastic reports from the Roanoke voyages twenty years earlier (see chapter 2) claimed that in Virginia "the earth bringeth foorth all things in aboundance . . . without toile or labour."

Even if these reports were exaggerated, investors reasoned, perhaps some valuable exotic crop could be grown profitably. Maybe rich lodes of gold and silver awaited discovery, as they had in New Spain. Or maybe quick and easy profits could be grabbed in an occasional raid on the gold and silver stashed in the holds of Spanish ships that cruised up the Atlantic coast on their way to Spain. Such hopes failed to address the difficulties of adapting English desires and expectations to the New World already inhabited by Native Americans. The Jamestown settlement struggled to survive for nearly two decades, until the royal government replaced the private Virginia Company, which never earned a penny for its investors.

The Fragile Jamestown Settlement

Although Spain claimed all of North America under the 1494 Treaty of Tordesillas (see chapter 2),

King James believed that England could encroach on the outskirts of Spain's New World empire. In 1588, England had successfully defended itself from the Spanish Armada, a large fleet of warships sent to invade England and bring it under Spanish rule. Now, the king hoped to flex England's muscles overseas and build new colonies in areas of North America that Spain could not defend. In effect, his land grant to the **Virginia Company**, a joint-stock company, was a royal license to poach on both Spanish claims and Powhatan's chiefdom.

English merchants had pooled their capital and shared risks for many years by using joint-stock companies for trading voyages to Europe, Asia, and Africa. The London investors of the Virginia Company, however, had larger ambitions: They hoped to found an empire that would strengthen England both overseas and at home. Richard Hakluyt, a strong proponent of colonization, claimed that a colony would provide work for swarms of poor "valiant youths rusting and hurtfull by lack of employment" in England. Colonists could buy English goods and supply products that England now had to import from other nations. More trade and more jobs would benefit many people in England, but the Virginia Company investors risked their capital because they fervently hoped to reap quick profits from the new colony.

In December 1606, the ships *Susan Constant*, *Discovery*, and *Godspeed* carried 144 Englishmen toward Virginia. They arrived at the mouth of Chesapeake Bay on April 26, 1607. That night while the colonists rested onshore, one of them later recalled, a band of Indians "creeping upon all foure, from the Hills like Beares, with their Bowes in their mouthes," attacked and dangerously wounded two men. The attack by **Algonquian Indians** gave the colonists an early warning that the North American wilderness was not quite the paradise described by the Virginia Company's publications in England. A few weeks later, they went ashore on a small peninsula in the midst of the territory ruled by **Powhatan**. With the memory of their first night in America fresh in their minds, they quickly built a fort, the first building in the settlement they named **Jamestown**.

The Jamestown fort showed the colonists' awareness that they needed to protect themselves from Indians and Spaniards. Spain planned to wipe out Jamestown when the time was ripe, but that time never came. Powhatan's people defended Virginia as their own. For weeks, the settlers and Powhatan's warriors skirmished repeatedly. English muskets and cannons repelled Indian attacks on Jamestown, but the Indians' superior numbers and knowledge of the Virginia wilderness made it risky for the settlers to venture far beyond the peninsula.

The settlers soon confronted dangerous, invisible threats: disease and starvation. Salt water and freshwater mixed in the swampy marshlands surrounding Jamestown, creating an ecological zone that allowed waterborne diseases to thrive, especially since the colonists' sanitation precautions were haphazard. During the summer, many of the Englishmen lay "night and day groaning in every corner of the Fort most pittiful to heare," wrote George Percy, one of the settlers. By September, fifty colonists had died. The colonists increased their misery by bickering among themselves, leaving crops unplanted and food supplies shrinking. "For the most part [the settlers] died of meere famine," Percy wrote; "there were never Englishmen left in a forreigne Countrey in such miserie as wee were in this new discovered Virginia."

Chief Powhatan

In 1612, John Smith published a map of early Virginia that included this drawing of Powhatan, surrounded by some of his many wives, smoking a pipe, and adorned with a feathered headdress. The illustration was almost certainly made by an English artist who had never been to Virginia or seen Powhatan but who tried to imagine the scene as described by John Smith. Princeton University Libraries, Department of Rare Books and Special Collections.

Powhatan's people came to the rescue of the weakened and demoralized Englishmen. Early in September 1607, they began to bring corn to the colony for barter. Accustomed to eating food derived from wheat, English people considered corn the food "of the barbarous Indians which know no better . . . a more convenient food for swine than for man." The famished colonists soon overcame their prejudice against corn. Jamestown leader **Captain John Smith** recalled that the settlers were so hungry that "they would have sould their soules" for half a basket of Powhatan's corn. Indians' corn acquired by both trade and plunder managed to keep 38 of the original settlers alive until a fresh supply of food and 120 more colonists arrived from England in January 1608.

It is difficult to exaggerate the fragility of the early Jamestown settlement. One colonist lamented that "this place [is] a meere plantacion of sorrowes and Cropp of trobles, having been plentifull in nothing but want and wanting nothing but plenty." During the "starving time" winter of 1609–10, food became so short that one or two famished settlers resorted to eating their recently deceased neighbors. When a new group of colonists arrived in 1610, they found only 60 of the 500 previous settlers still alive. The Virginia Company sent hundreds of new settlers to Jamestown each year, each of them eager to find the paradise promised by the company. But most settlers went instead to early graves.

Cooperation and Conflict between Natives and Newcomers

Powhatan's people stayed in contact with the English settlers but maintained their distance. The Virginia Company boasted that the settlers bought from the Indians "the pearles of earth [corn] and [sold] to them the pearles of heaven [Christianity]." In fact, few Indians converted to Christianity, and the English devoted scant effort to proselytizing. Marriage between Indian women and English men also was rare, despite the acute shortage of English women in Virginia in the early years. Few settlers other than John Smith bothered to learn the Indians' language.

Powhatan's people regarded the English with suspicion, for good reason. Although the settlers often made friendly overtures to the Indians, they did not hesitate to use their guns and swords to enforce English notions of proper Indian behavior. More than once, the Indians refused to trade their corn to the settlers, evidently hoping to starve them out. Each time, the English broke the boycott by attacking the uncooperative Indians, pillaging their villages, and confiscating their corn.

The Indians retaliated against English violence, but for fifteen years they did not organize an all-out assault on the European intruders, probably for several reasons. Although Christianity held few attractions for the Indians, the power of the settlers' God impressed them. One chief told John Smith that "he did believe that our [English] God as much exceeded theirs as our guns did their bows and arrows." Powhatan probably concluded that these powerful strangers would make better allies than enemies. As allies, the English strengthened Powhatan's dominance over the tribes in the region.

They also traded with his people, usually exchanging European goods for corn. Native Virginians had some copper weapons and tools before the English arrived, but they quickly recognized the superiority of the intruders' iron and steel knives, axes, and pots, and they traded eagerly to obtain them. The trade that supplied the Indians with European conveniences provided the English settlers with a necessity: food.

> "This place [is] a meere plantacion of sorrowes and Cropp of trobles, having been plentifull in nothing but want and wanting nothing but plenty."
> — A Jamestown colonist

But why were the settlers unable to feed themselves for more than a decade? First, as the staggering death rate suggests, many settlers were too sick to be productive members of the colony. Second, very few farmers came to Virginia in the early years. Instead, most of the newcomers were gentlemen and their servants. In John Smith's words, these men "never did know what a day's work was." The proportion of gentlemen in Virginia in the early years was six times greater than in England, a reflection of the Virginia Company's urgent need for investors and settlers. John Smith declared repeatedly that in Virginia "there is no country to pillage [as in New Spain]. . . . All you can expect from [Virginia] must be by labor." For years, however, colonists clung to English notions that gentlemen should not work with their hands and that tradesmen should work only in trades for which they had been trained. These ideas made more sense in labor-rich England than in labor-poor Virginia. In the meantime, the colonists depended on the Indians' corn for food.

Becaufe many doe defire to know the manner of their Language, I haue inferted thefe few words.

KA katorawincs yowo. What call
you this.
Nemarough, a man.
Crenepo, a woman.
Marowancheffo, a boy.
Yehawkans, Houfes.
Mattcores, Skins, or garments.
Mockafins, Shooes.
Tuffan, Beds. Pokatawer, Fire.
Attawp, A bow. Attonce, Arrowes.
Monacookes, Swords.
Aumouhhowgh, A Target.
Pawcuffacks, Gunnes.
Tomahacks, Axes.
Tockahacks, Pickaxes.
Pamefacks, Kniues.
Accowprets, Sheares.
Pawpecones, Pipes. Mattaßin, Copper
Vffawaffin, Iron, Braffe, Silver, or any
white mettall. Muffes, Woods.
Attaffkuff, Leaues, weeds, or graffe.
Chepfin, Land. Shacquohocan. A ftone.
Wepenter, A cookold.
Suckahanna, Water. Noughmaff, Fifh.
Copotone, Sturgeon.
Weghfhaughes, Flefh.
Sawwehone, Bloud.
Netoppew, Friends.
Marrapough, Enemics.
Maskapow, the worft of the enemies.
Mawchick chammay, The beft of
friends
Cafacunnakack, peya quagh acquintan
vttafantafough, In how many daies
will there come hither any more
Englifh Ships.
    Their Numbers.
Necut, 1. Ningh, 2. Nuff, 3. Yowgh, 4.
Paranske, 5. Comotinch, 6. Toppawoff, 7
Nuffwafh, 8. Kekatawgh, 9. Kaskeke 10
They count no more but by tennes
as followeth.
Cafe, how many.
Ninghfapooeksku, 20.
Nuffapooeksku, 30.

Yowghapooeksku, 40.
Parankeftaffapoockfku, 50.
Comatincktaffapoockfku, 60.
Nuffwafhtaffapoockfku, 70.
Kekatanghtaffapoockfku, 90.
Necuttoughtyfinough, 100.
Necuttwevnquaough, 1000.
Rawcofowghs, Dayes.
Kefkowghes, Sunnes:
Toppquough. Nights.
Nepawwefhowghs, Moones.
Pawpaxfoughes, Yeares.
Pummahumps, Starres.
Ofies, Heavens.
Okees, Gods.
Quiyoughcofoughs, Pettie Gods, and
    their affinities.
Righcomoughes, Deaths.
Kekughes, Liues.
Mowchick woyawgh tawgh noeragh
kaquere mecher, I am very hungry?
what fhall I eate?
Tawnor nehiegh Powhatan, Where
dwels Powhatan.
Mache, nehiegh yourowgh, Orapaks.
Now he dwels a great way hence
at Orapaks.
Vittapitchewayne anpechitchs nehaw-
per Werowacomoco, You lie, he ftaid
ever at Werowacomoco.
Kator nehiegh mattagh neer vttapit-
chewayne, Truely he is there I doe
not lie.
Spaughtynere keragh werowance maw-
marinough kekatë wawgh peyaquaugh.
Run you then to the King Mawma-
rynough and bid him come hither.
Vtteke, e peya weyack wighwhip, Get
you gone, & come againe quickly.
Kekaten Pokahontas patiaquagh ningh
tanks manotyens neer mowchick raw-
renock audowgh, Bid Pokahontas
bring hither two little Baskets, and
I will giue her white Beads to make
her a Chaine.   FINIS.

John Smith's Dictionary of Powhatan's Language
In 1612, John Smith published this list of the English equivalents of words used by Powhatan's people, almost the only record of the coastal Algonquian language that exists. Smith probably compiled the list by pointing and listening carefully. Can you find any of Powhatan's words that made their way into common English usage? Princeton University Libraries, Department of Rare Books and Special Collections.

To produce enough corn for their own survival and for trade with the English required the Indians to spend more time and effort growing crops. Since Native American women did most of the agricultural work, their burden increased along with the cultural significance of their chief crop. The corn surplus grown by Indian women was bartered for desirable English goods such as iron pots, which replaced the baskets and ceramic jugs Native Americans had used for millennia. Growing enough corn to feed the English altered age-old patterns of village life. But from the Indians' viewpoint, the most important fact about the always-hungry English colonists was that they were not going away.

Powhatan died in 1618, and his brother **Opechancanough** replaced him as supreme chief. In 1622, Opechancanough organized an all-out assault on the English settlers. As an English colonist observed, "When the day appointed for the massacre arrived [March 22], a number of savages visited many of our people in their dwellings, and while partaking with them of their meal[,] the savages, at a given signal, drew their weapons and fell upon us murdering and killing everybody they could reach[,] sparing neither women nor children, as well inside as outside the dwellings." In all, the Indians killed 347 colonists, nearly a third of the English population. But the attack failed to dislodge the colonists. Instead, in the years to come the settlers unleashed a murderous campaign of Indian extermination that pushed the Indians beyond the small circumference of white settlement. Before 1622, the settlers knew that the Indians, though dangerous, were necessary to keep the colony alive. In the years after 1622, most colonists considered the Indians their perpetual enemies.

From Private Company to Royal Government

In the immediate aftermath of the 1622 uprising, the survivors became discouraged and demoralized because, as one explained, the "massacre

The persistence of the Virginia colony created difficulties for Powhatan's chiefdom. Steady contact between natives and newcomers spread European diseases among the Indians, who suffered deadly epidemics in 1608 and between 1617 and 1619. The settlers' insatiable appetite for corn introduced other tensions within Powhatan's villages.

Advertisement for Jamestown Settlers
Virginia imported thousands of indentured servants to labor in the tobacco fields, but the colony also advertised in 1631 for settlers like those pictured here. The notice features men and women equally, although men heavily outnumbered women in the Chesapeake region. How would the English experiences of the individuals portrayed in the advertisement have been useful in Virginia? Why would such individuals have wanted to leave England and go to Virginia? If indentured servants had been pictured, how might they have differed in appearance from these people?
Harvard Map Collection, Pusey Library, Harvard University.

A Lady.

A Noble-man.

A Gentleman.

A Gentle Woman.

A Citizens wife.

A Citizen.

A Countryman.

A Country Woman.

killed all our Countrie . . . [and] burst the heart of all the rest." The disaster prompted a royal investigation of affairs in Virginia. The investigators discovered that the appalling mortality among the colonists was caused more by disease and mismanagement than by Indian raids. In 1624, King James revoked the charter of the Virginia Company and made Virginia a **royal colony**, subject to the direction of the royal government rather than to the company's private investors, an arrangement that lasted until 1776.

The king now appointed the governor of Virginia and his council, but most other features of local government established under the Virginia Company remained intact. In 1619, for example, the company had inaugurated the **House of Burgesses**, an assembly of representatives (called burgesses) elected by the colony's inhabitants. (Historians do not know exactly which settlers were considered inhabitants and were thus qualified to vote.) Under the new royal government, laws passed by the burgesses had to be approved by the king's bureaucrats in England rather than by the company. Otherwise, the House of Burgesses continued as before, acquiring distinction as the oldest representative legislative assembly in the English colonies. Under the new royal government, all free adult men in Virginia could vote for the House of Burgesses, giving it a far broader and more representative constituency than the English House of Commons had.

The demise of the Virginia Company marked the end of the first phase of colonization of the Chesapeake region. From the first 105 adventurers in 1607, the population had grown to about 1,200 by 1624. Despite mortality rates higher than during the worst epidemics in London, new settlers still came. Their arrival and King James's willingness to take over the struggling colony reflected a fundamental change in Virginia. After years of fruitless experimentation, it was becoming clear that English settlers could make a fortune in Virginia by growing tobacco.

REVIEW   Why did Powhatan behave as he did toward the English colonists?

▶ A Tobacco Society

Tobacco grew wild in the New World, and Native Americans used it for thousands of years before Europeans arrived. Columbus observed Indians smoking tobacco on his first voyage to the New World. Many other sixteenth-century European explorers noticed the Indians' habit of "drinking smoke." During the sixteenth century, Spanish colonists in the New World sent tobacco to Europe, where it was an expensive luxury used sparingly by a few. During the next century,

English colonists in North America sent so much tobacco to European markets that it became an affordable indulgence used often by many people. (See "Beyond America's Borders," page 70.)

By 1700, nearly 100,000 colonists lived in the Chesapeake region, encompassing Virginia, Maryland, and northern North Carolina (Map 3.1). They exported more than 35 million pounds of tobacco, a fivefold increase in per capita production since 1620. Clearly, Chesapeake colonists mastered the demands of tobacco agriculture, and the "Stinkinge Weede" (a seventeenth-century Marylander's term for tobacco) also mastered the colonists. Settlers lived by the rhythms of tobacco agriculture, and their endless need for labor attracted droves of English indentured servants to work in tobacco fields.

Tobacco Agriculture

Initially, the Virginia Company had no plans to grow and sell tobacco. "As for tobacco," John Smith wrote, "we never then dreamt of it." **John Rolfe** — future husband of **Pocahontas** — planted West Indian tobacco seeds in 1612 and learned that they flourished in Virginia. By 1617, the colonists had grown enough tobacco to send the first commercial shipment to England, where it sold for a high price. After that, Virginia transformed itself from a colony of rather aimless adventurers who had difficulty growing enough corn to feed themselves to a society of dedicated planters who grew as much tobacco as possible.

A demanding crop, tobacco required close attention and a great deal of hand labor year-round. Primitive tools and methods made this intensive cycle of labor taxing. Like the Indians, the colonists "cleared" fields by cutting a ring of bark from each tree (a procedure known as "girdling"), thereby killing the tree. Girdling brought sunlight to clearings but left fields studded with tree stumps, making the use of plows impractical. Instead, colonists used heavy hoes to till their tobacco

Tobacco Plantation
This print illustrates the processing of tobacco on a seventeenth-century plantation. Workers cut the mature plants and put the leaves in piles to wilt (left foreground). After the leaves dried somewhat, they were suspended from poles in a drying barn (right foreground), where they were seasoned before being packed in casks for shipping. The print suggests the labor demands of tobacco by showing twenty-two individuals, all but two of them actively at work with the crop. The couple in the left foreground may be on their way to work, but it is more likely that they are overseeing the labor of their servants or employees. From "About Tobacco," Lehman Brothers.

fields. To plant, a visitor observed, they "just make holes [with a stick] into which they drop the seeds," much as the Indians did. Growing tobacco with such methods left little time for idleness, but the colonists enjoyed the fruits of their labor. "Everyone smokes while working or idling," one traveler reported, including "men, women, girls, and boys, from the age of seven years."

The English settlers worked hard because their labor promised greater rewards in the Chesapeake region than in England. One colonist proclaimed that "the dirt of this Province affords as great a profit to the general Inhabitant, as the Gold of Peru doth to . . . the Spaniard." Although he exaggerated, it was true that a hired man could expect to earn two or three times more in Virginia's tobacco fields than in England. Better still, in Virginia land was so abundant that it was extremely cheap compared with land in England.

By the mid-seventeenth century, common laborers could buy a hundred acres for less than their annual wages—an impossibility in England. New settlers who paid their own transportation to the Chesapeake received a grant of fifty acres of free land (termed a **headright**). The Virginia Company granted headrights to encourage settlement, and the royal government continued them for the same reason.

A Servant Labor System

Headrights, cheap land, and high wages gave poor English folk powerful incentives to immigrate to the New World. Yet many potential immigrants could not scrape together the money to pay for a trip across the Atlantic. Their poverty

American Tobacco and European Consumers

English colonies in the Chesapeake were "wholly built upon smoke," King Charles I observed during the second quarter of the seventeenth century. The king's shrewd observation highlighted the fundamental reason the seventeenth-century Chesapeake colonies prospered by growing ever-larger crops of tobacco: namely, because people on the eastern side of the Atlantic were willing to buy ever-greater quantities of tobacco to smoke — and to sniff, chew, drink, and even use for enemas. Europeans' desire for tobacco was the only reason it had commercial value. Without this demand, the history of both the English North American colonies and the rest of the world would have been very different.

Still, some Europeans hated tobacco, most notably England's King James I (who preceded Charles I). In *A Counterblaste to Tobacco*, a pamphlet published in 1611, James declared that smoking was "A custome lothsome to the eye, hatefull to the Nose, harmefull to the braine, dangerous to the Lungs, and in the blacke stinking fume thereof, neerest resembling the horrible : . . smoke of the pit that is bottomelesse." He reviled the "filthy smoke," the "stinking Suffumigation," the "spitting," the "lust," the "shameful imbecilitie," and the "sin" of tobacco. James's fulminations acknowledged that "the generall use of Tobacco" was "daily practiced . . . by all sorts and complexions of people." He noted, "The publike use [of tobacco], at all times, and in all places, hath now so farre prevailed that a man cannot heartily welcome his friend now, but straight they must bee in hand with Tobacco." Clearly, James championed a lost cause.

When the Spaniards first brought tobacco to Europe during the sixteenth century, physicians praised it as a wonder drug. One proclaimed that "this precious herb is so general a human need [that it is] not only for the sick but for the healthy." Such strong recommendations from learned men were reinforced by everyday experiences of commoners. Sailors returning from the New World "suck in as much smoke as they can," one Spaniard observed, "[and] in this way they say that their hunger and thirst are allayed, their strength is restored and their spirits are refreshed; [and] . . . their brains are lulled by a joyous intoxication." That joyous intoxication — "a bewitching quality," King James called it — made tobacco irresistible to most Europeans.

At the beginning of the seventeenth century, tobacco was scarce and therefore expensive. In 1603, for example, England imported only about 25,000 pounds of tobacco, all from New Spain. By 1700, England imported nearly 40 million pounds of tobacco, almost all from the Chesapeake colonies. The huge increase in the tobacco supply caused prices to plummet. A quantity of tobacco that sold for a dollar in 1600 cost less than two and a half cents by 1700.

The low prices made possible by bumper crops harvested by planters in the Chesapeake transformed tobacco consumption in England and elsewhere in Europe. Annual per capita tobacco use in England grew more than 200-fold during the seventeenth century, from less than a fifth of an ounce in the 1620s to 2.3 pounds by 1700. American tobacco became the first colonial product of mass consumption by Europeans, blazing a trail followed by New World sugar, coffee, and chocolate.

Tobacco altered European culture. It spawned new industries, new habits, and new forms of social life. Smoking was the most common form of tobacco consumption in the seven-

and the colonists' crying need for labor formed the basic context for the creation of a servant labor system.

About 80 percent of the immigrants to the Chesapeake during the seventeenth century came as **indentured servants**. Instead of a slave society, the seventeenth-century Chesapeake region was fundamentally a society of white servants and ex-servants.

Relatively few African slaves were brought to the Chesapeake in the first half century after settlement. The first known Africans arrived in Virginia in 1619 aboard the *White Lion*, an English privateer that had seized them from a Portuguese slave ship bound for South America. The "20. And odd Negroes," as John Rolfe called them, were slaves captured in Angola in west-central Africa. Virginia officials acquired them by giving the privateer captain supplies in exchange. A few more slaves trickled into the Chesapeake region during the next several decades. Until the 1670s, however, only a small number of slaves labored in Chesapeake tobacco fields. (Large numbers of slaves came in the eighteenth century, as chapter 5 explains.) Men and women of African descent occasionally became indentured servants, served out their terms of servitude, and teenth century, and smokers needed far more than tobacco to light up. They needed pipes; they needed boxes or tins to hold their tobacco and a container to hold the embers they used to light the tobacco, or a flint and steel to strike sparks; they needed pipe cleaners; they needed spittoons if they were smoking in a respectable place that disapproved of spitting on the floor. European merchants and manufacturers supplied all these needs, along with the tobacco itself, which had to be graded, chopped, flavored, packaged, stored, advertised, and sold. Men and women smoked in taverns, in smoking clubs, around dinner tables, and in bed.

The somewhat cumbersome paraphernalia of smoking caused many tobacco users to shift to snuff, which became common in the eighteenth century. Snuff use eliminated smoke, fire, and spitting, replacing them with the more refined gesture of taking a pinch of powdered, flavored tobacco from a snuffbox and sniffing it into one or both nostrils, which produced a fashionable sneeze followed by a genteel wipe with a dainty handkerchief. One snuff taker explained the health benefits of such a sneeze: "by its gently pricking and stimulating the membranes, [snuff] causes Sneezing or Contractions, whereby the Glands like so many squeezed Sponges, dismiss their Seriosities and Filth."

Whether consumed by sniffing, by smoking, or in other ways, tobacco profoundly changed European habits,

Smoking Club
In Europe, tobacco smokers congregated in clubs to enjoy the intoxicating weed. This seventeenth-century print satirizes smokers' gatherings of fashionable men, women, and children who indulged their taste for tobacco. Emblems of the tobacco trade adorn the wall; pipes, spittoons, and other smoking implements are close at hand; and the dog cleans up after those who cannot hold their smoke. Koninklijke Bibliotheek, The Hague.

economies, and societies. And its popularity turned the Chesapeake colonies into invaluable assets for England.

America in a Global Context

1. Why did European demand for tobacco grow so dramatically during the seventeenth century?

2. How did Europeans use tobacco, and why? Why did some people object to tobacco use?

3. What were the consequences of the transatlantic tobacco market both in the Chesapeake and in Europe?

became free. A few slaves purchased their way out of bondage and lived as free people, even owning land and using the local courts to resolve disputes, much as freed white servants did. These people were exceptions, however. Almost all people of African descent were slaves and remained enslaved for life.

A small number of Native Americans also became servants. But the overwhelming majority of indentured servants were white immigrants from England. To buy passage aboard a ship bound for the Chesapeake, an English immigrant had to come up with about £5, roughly a year's wages for an English servant or laborer. Earning

wages at all was difficult in England since job opportunities were shrinking. Many country landowners needed fewer farmhands because they shifted from growing crops to raising sheep in newly enclosed fields.

Unemployed people drifted into seaports such as Bristol, Liverpool, and London, where they learned about the plentiful jobs in North America. Unable to pay for their trip across the Atlantic, poor immigrants agreed to a contract called an indenture, which functioned as a form of credit. By signing an indenture, an immigrant borrowed the cost of transportation to the Chesapeake from a merchant or ship captain in

Bristol Docks
This painting of the docks in Bristol, England, portrays a scene common at ports throughout the seventeenth-century Atlantic world. Workers unload colonial commodities shipped to Bristol while merchants meet in small groups to make deals to sell the colonial goods and reload the ships with English exports, including indentured servants. Tobacco flooded into Bristol in the seventeenth century while Bristol merchants also became active in the African slave trade, trading British goods on the west African coast for slaves, who were then taken to the New World to be sold to eager sugar and tobacco planters. © Bristol City Museum and Art Gallery/UK Bridgeman Art Library.

England. To repay this loan, the indentured person agreed to work as a servant for four to seven years in North America.

Once the indentured person arrived in the colonies, the merchant or ship captain sold his right to the immigrant's labor to a local tobacco planter. To obtain the servant's labor, the planter paid about twice the cost of transportation and agreed to provide the servant with food and shelter during the term of the indenture. When the indenture expired, the planter owed the former servant "freedom dues," usually a few barrels of corn and a suit of clothes.

Ideally, indentures allowed poor immigrants to trade their most valuable assets — their freedom and their ability to work — for a trip to the New World and a period of servitude followed by freedom in a land of opportunity. Planters reaped more immediate benefits. Servants meant more hands to grow more tobacco. A planter expected a servant to grow enough tobacco in one year to cover the price the planter paid for the indenture. Servants' labor during the remaining three to six years of the indenture promised a handsome profit for the planter. No wonder one Virginian declared, "Our principall wealth . . . consisteth in servants." But roughly half of all servants became sick and died before serving out their indentures, reducing planters' gains. Planters still profited, however, since they received a headright of fifty acres of land from the colonial government for every newly purchased servant.

About three out of four servants were young men between the ages of fifteen and twenty-five when they arrived in the Chesapeake. Typically, they shared the desperation of sixteen-year-old

Francis Haires, who indentured himself for seven years because, according to his contract, "his father and mother and All friends [are] dead and he [is] a miserable wandering boy." Like Francis, most servants had no special training or skills, although the majority had some experience with agricultural work. "Hunger and fear of prisons bring to us onely such servants as have been brought up to no Art or Trade," one Virginia planter complained. A skilled craftsman could obtain a shorter indenture, but few risked coming to the colonies since their prospects were better in England.

Women were almost as rare as skilled craftsmen in the Chesapeake and more ardently desired. In the early days of the tobacco boom, the Virginia Company shipped young single women servants to the colony as prospective wives for male settlers willing to pay "120 weight [pounds] of the best leaf tobacco for each of them," in effect getting both a wife and a servant. The company reasoned that, as one official wrote in 1622, "the plantation can never flourish till families be planted, and the respect of wives and children fix the people on the soil." The company's efforts as a marriage broker proved no more successful than its other ventures. Women remained a small minority of the Chesapeake population until late in the seventeenth century.

The servant labor system perpetuated the gender imbalance. Although female servants cost about the same as males and generally served for the same length of time, only about one servant in four was a woman. Planters preferred male servants, as one explained, because they were "the mor[e] excellent and yousefull Cretuers," especially for field work. Although many servant women hoed and harvested tobacco fields, most also did household chores such as cooking, washing, cleaning, gardening, and milking.

The Rigors of Servitude

Servants — whether men or women, whites or blacks, English or African — tended to work together and socialize together. During the first half century of settlement, racial intermingling occurred, although the small number of blacks made it infrequent. Courts punished sexual relations between blacks and whites, but the court cases show that sexual desire readily crossed the color line. In general, the commonalities of servitude caused servants — regardless of their race and gender — to consider themselves apart from free people, whose ranks they longed to join eventually.

Servant life was harsh by the standards of seventeenth-century England and even by the frontier standards of the Chesapeake. Unlike servants in England, Chesapeake servants had no control over who purchased their labor — and thus them — for the period of their indenture. They were "sold here upp and downe like horses," one observer reported. Before their indentures expired, many servants were bought and sold several times. A Virginia servant protested in 1623 that his master "hath sold me for £150 sterling like a damnd slave." But tobacco planters' need for labor muffled complaints about treating servants as property.

For servants, the promise of indentured servitude that loomed large in their decision to leave England and immigrate to the Chesapeake often withered when they confronted the rigors of labor in the tobacco fields. James Revel, an eighteen-year-old thief punished by being indentured to a Virginia tobacco planter, declared he was a "slave" sent to hoe "tobacco plants all day" from dawn to dark. Severe laws aimed to keep servants in their place. Punishments for petty crimes stretched servitude far beyond the original terms of indenture. Richard Higby, for example, received six extra years of servitude for killing three hogs. After midcentury, the Virginia legislature added three or more years to the indentures of most servants by requiring them to serve until they were twenty-four years old.

Women servants were subject to special restrictions and risks. They were prohibited from marrying until their servitude had expired. A servant woman, the law assumed, could not serve two masters at the same time: one who owned her indentured labor and another who was her husband. However, the predominance of men in the Chesapeake population inevitably pressured women to engage in sexual relations. (See "Seeking the American Promise," page 74.) About a third of immigrant women were pregnant when they married. Pregnancy and childbirth sapped a woman's strength, and a new child diverted her attention, reducing her usefulness as a servant. As a rule, if a woman servant gave birth to a child, she had to serve two extra years and pay a fine. However, for some servant women, premarital pregnancy was a path out of servitude: The father of an unborn child sometimes purchased the indenture of the servant mother-to-be and then freed and married her.

> **"The plantation can never flourish till families be planted, and the respect of wives and children fix the people on the soil."**
> — An official of the Virginia Company

The Gamble of Indentured Servitude

Anne Orthwood sailed out of her native Bristol, England, in September 1662, shortly after her twenty-third birthday. Her mother, Mary, had moved there in 1640 to escape the humiliation of giving birth to Anne out of wedlock, and in Bristol she had a second daughter, also illegitimate. Mary never married. Anne and her sister grew up with the stigma of being bastards, a shameful and degraded status at a time when the vast majority of children were born to married couples.

Bristol was a thriving seaport, second only to London in its overseas trade, but poor unmarried women — especially those like Mary, with two illegitimate daughters — had little hope to share in the city's commercial prosperity. Instead, they usually worked at menial jobs such as domestic servant or washerwoman. The continual arrival and departure of ships, sailors, merchants, passengers, and cargoes of all kinds from throughout the Atlantic world made Bristol a hub of information and gossip that Anne could not have avoided. She probably heard that in Virginia jobs were plentiful and workers were few. Hundreds of people sailed from Bristol to Virginia every year, five hundred in 1662 alone, most of them poor young men who agreed to become indentured servants. Anne probably also heard about the shortage of women in Virginia, along with the tantalizing news that, as one promoter declared, if women "come of an honest stock and have a good repute, they may pick and chuse their Husbands out of the better sort of people." The promise of both work and matrimony proved irresistible to Anne, especially compared to the gloomy prospect of staying in Bristol. In August 1662, Anne signed an indenture to a ship's surgeon who agreed to pay her way to Virginia in exchange for her consent to work for four years as a servant.

Anne arrived in Virginia late in the fall of 1662, and the surgeon quickly sold her indenture — and thus her — to William Kendall, a wealthy planter and prominent official on Virginia's Eastern Shore. Kendall himself had come to Virginia as a servant in 1650, but unlike Anne, he was from a respectable family and had received a valuable education as a merchant's clerk. When he became free in 1654, he prospered, thanks in large part to his good fortune in marriage. Kendall married a wealthy widow in Virginia, and after she died, he married another wealthy widow, helping him amass more than 25,000 acres of land. When Anne joined Kendall's household, some twenty people lived there, including seven or eight servants, two slaves, a free black man, and numerous relatives, among them a nephew, John Kendall.

Like Anne, John Kendall had recently arrived in Virginia from England, was in his early twenties, and was unmarried. We can't know if Anne thought John was one of the "better sort of people" she might marry, but it appears that she and John felt a mutual attraction. William Kendall had no intention of allowing his nephew to get mixed up with a lowly servant woman, and a bastard at that. His own experience confirmed that marrying upward was the path to prosperity in Virginia. About eight months after Anne became his servant, William Kendall decided to separate her and John by selling Anne's indenture — and thus her — to a tenant farmer named Jacob Bishop, who lived several miles away.

As young people will, Anne and John found a way to get together. Anne accompanied Bishop when he went to conduct legal business at court, held at a local tavern, as was customary at the time. While there, on Saturday night and Sunday,

Harsh punishments reflected four fundamental realities of the servant labor system. First, planters' hunger for labor caused them to demand as much labor as they could get from their servants, including devising legal ways to extend the period of servitude. Second, servants hoped to survive their servitude and use their freedom to obtain land and start a family. Third, servants' hopes frequently conflicted with planters' demands. Since servants saw themselves as free people in a temporary status of servitude, they often made grudging, halfhearted workers. Finally, planters put up with this contentious arrangement because the alternatives were less desirable.

Planters could not easily hire free men and women because land was readily available and free people preferred to work for themselves on their own land. Nor could planters depend on much labor from family members. The preponderance of men in the population meant that families were few, were started late, and thus had few children. And, until the 1680s and 1690s, slaves were expensive and hard to come by. Before then, masters who wanted to expand their labor force and grow more tobacco had few alternatives to buying indentured servants.

Cultivating Land and Faith

Villages and small towns dotted the rural landscape of seventeenth-century England, but in the Chesapeake towns were few and far between. Instead, tobacco farms occupied small clearings surrounded by hundreds of acres of wilderness.

English Servants
This collective portrait of English servants painted by William Hogarth in the mid-eighteenth century features three young women who perhaps somewhat resembled indentured servant Anne Orthwood, who had immigrated to Virginia nearly a century earlier. No likeness of Orthwood exists. Unlike Orthwood, most servants who came to the Chesapeake during the seventeenth century were young boys, like the boy depicted here at top center. Tate Gallery, London/Art Resource, NY.

November 28 and 29, 1663, she met John Kendall, and they had sex. "Three tymes She thought hee had to doe with her," Anne later testified, "but twice She was Certaine."

John impregnated Anne. We don't know if Anne hoped that John would buy her indenture, free her, and marry her, but she probably did. She refused to say who was responsible for her condition; her silence suggests that she hoped John Kendall would step forward and rescue her. But he didn't. She finally identified John as the father when a midwife quizzed her during the rigors of giving birth to twin boys. One baby died shortly after birth, as did Anne. Her other son, whom she named Jasper, was indentured as an infant to a Virginia planter and, after twenty-two years of servitude, became a free man. John Kendall never acknowledged Jasper as his son, but he did follow his uncle William's advice and marry a wealthy widow.

Like so many other Virginia colonists, Anne found an early grave rather than the work, marriage, and respectability she craved. She gambled her freedom for the promise of a better life in Virginia, and she lost.

Other former servants gambled and won, grandly like William Kendall or modestly like Anne's son Jasper.

Questions for Consideration

1. How did family relationships and popular assumptions about them influence Anne Orthwood? How did they influence John Kendall?

2. How did Anne Orthwood's experiences reflect the risks and opportunities confronted by other female and male servants?

Tobacco was such a labor-intensive crop that one field worker could tend only about two acres of the plants in a year (an acre is slightly smaller than a football field), plus a few more acres for food crops. A successful farmer needed a great deal more land, however, because tobacco quickly exhausted the fertility of the soil. Since each farmer cultivated only 5 or 10 percent of his land at any one time, a "settled" area comprised swatches of cultivated land surrounded by forest. Arrangements for marketing tobacco also contributed to the dispersion of settlements. Tobacco planters sought land that fronted a navigable river in order to minimize the work of transporting the heavy barrels of tobacco onto ships. A settled region thus resembled a lacework of farms stitched around waterways.

Most Chesapeake colonists were nominally Protestants. Attendance at Sunday services and conformity to the doctrines of the Church of England were required of all English men and women. Few clergymen migrated to the Chesapeake, however, and too few of those who did were models of righteousness and piety. Certainly,

Settlement Patterns along the James River

- Farm or plantation

Hog Island
Jamestown
James River

some colonists took their religion seriously. Church courts punished fornicators, censured blasphemers, and served notice on parishioners who spent Sundays "goeing a fishing." But on the whole, religion did not awaken the zeal of Chesapeake settlers, certainly not as it did the zeal of New England settlers in these same years (as discussed in chapter 4). What quickened the pulse of most Chesapeake folk was a close horse race, a bloody cockfight, or — most of all — an exceptionally fine tobacco crop. The religion of the Chesapeake colonists was Anglican, but their faith lay in the turbulent, competitive, high-stakes gamble of survival as tobacco planters.

The situation was similar in the Catholic colony of Maryland. In 1632, England's King Charles I granted his Catholic friend **Lord Baltimore** about six and a half million acres in the northern Chesapeake region. In return, the king specified that Lord Baltimore pay him the token rent of "two Indian arrowheads" a year. Lord Baltimore intended to create a refuge for Catholics, who suffered severe discrimination in England. He fitted out two ships, the *Ark* and the *Dove*; gathered about 150 settlers; and sent them to the new colony, where they arrived on March 25, 1634. However, Maryland failed to live up to Baltimore's hopes. The colony's population grew very slowly for twenty years, and most settlers were Protestants rather than Catholics. The religious turmoil of the Puritan Revolution in England (discussed in chapter 4) spilled across the Atlantic, creating conflict between Maryland's few Catholics — most of them wealthy and prominent — and the Protestant majority, most of them neither wealthy nor prominent. During the 1660s, Maryland began to attract settlers, mostly Protestants, as readily as Virginia. Although Catholics and the Catholic faith continued to exert influence in Maryland, the colony's society, economy, politics, and culture became nearly indistinguishable from Virginia's. Both colonies shared a devotion to tobacco, the true faith of the Chesapeake.

REVIEW   Why did the vast majority of European immigrants to the Chesapeake come as indentured servants?

Jamestown Church Tower

This modern-day photograph shows the remains of the tower of the Anglican church that colonists constructed in Jamestown beginning in 1639. Nearby is the foundation of an older church, built in 1617, that also served as the site of the first meeting of the Virginia general assembly or House of Burgesses, the first representative legislative body in British North America. The churches illustrate the importance Virginia's leaders attached to maintaining the central British institution of worship and spiritual order in the fledgling colony.

Courtesy of Preservation Virginia.

▶ Hierarchy and Inequality in the Chesapeake

The system of indentured servitude sharpened inequality in Chesapeake society by the mid-seventeenth century, propelling social and political polarization that culminated in 1676 with Bacon's Rebellion. The rebellion prompted reforms that stabilized relations between elite planters and their lesser neighbors and paved the way for a social hierarchy that muted differences of landholding and wealth and amplified racial differences. (See "Historical Question," page 78.) Amid this social and political evolution, one thing did not change: Chesapeake colonists' dedication to growing tobacco.

Social and Economic Polarization

The first half of the seventeenth century in the Chesapeake was the era of the **yeoman** — a farmer who owned a small plot of land sufficient to support a family and tilled largely by servants and a few family members. A small number of elite planters had larger estates and commanded ten or more servants. But for the first several decades, few men lived long enough to accumulate fortunes sufficient to set them much apart from their neighbors. On the whole, a rough frontier equality characterized free families in the Chesapeake until about 1650.

Until midcentury, the principal division in Chesapeake society was less between rich and poor planters than between free farmers and unfree servants. Although these two groups contrasted sharply in their legal and economic status, their daily lives had many similarities. Servants looked forward to the time when their indentures would expire and they would become free and eventually own land.

Three major developments splintered the equality during the third quarter of the century. First, as planters grew more and more tobacco, the ample supply depressed tobacco prices in European markets. Cheap tobacco reduced planters' profits and made saving enough to become landowners more difficult for freed servants. Second, because the mortality rate in the Chesapeake colonies declined, more and more servants survived their indentures, and landless freemen became more numerous and grew more discontented. Third, declining mortality also encouraged the formation of a planter elite. By living longer, the most successful planters compounded their success. The wealthiest planters also began to buy slaves as well as to serve as merchants, marketing crops for their less successful neighbors, importing English goods for sale, and extending credit to hard-pressed customers.

By the 1670s, the society of the Chesapeake had become polarized. Landowners — the planter elite and the more numerous yeoman planters — clustered around one pole. Landless colonists, mainly freed servants, gathered at the other. Each group eyed the other with suspicion and mistrust. For the most part, planters saw landless freemen as a dangerous rabble rather than as fellow colonists with legitimate grievances.

Governor William Berkeley feared the political threat to the governing elite posed by "six parts in seven [of Virginia colonists who] . . . are poor, indebted, discontented, and armed."

Government Policies and Political Conflict

In general, government and politics strengthened the distinctions in Chesapeake society. The most vital distinction separated servants and masters, and the colonial government enforced it with an iron fist. Poor men such as William Tyler complained that "nether the Governor nor Counsell could or would doe any poore men right, but that they would shew favor to great men and wronge the poore." Most Chesapeake colonists, like most Europeans, assumed that "great men" should bear the responsibilities of government. Until 1670, all freemen could vote, and they routinely elected prosperous planters to the legislature. No former servant served in either the governor's council or the House of Burgesses after 1640. Yet Tyler and other poor Virginians believed that the "great men" used their government offices to promote their selfish personal interests rather than governing impartially.

As discontent mounted among the poor during the 1660s and 1670s, colonial officials tried to keep political power in safe hands. Beginning in 1661, for example, Governor William Berkeley did not call an election for the House of Burgesses for fifteen years. In 1670, the House of Burgesses outlawed voting by poor men, permitting only men who headed households and were landowners to vote.

The king also began to tighten the royal government's control of trade and to collect substantial revenue from the Chesapeake. A series of English laws funneled the colonial trade exclusively into the hands of English merchants and shippers. The **Navigation Acts** of 1650 and 1651 specified that colonial goods had to be transported in English ships with predominantly English crews. A 1660 act required colonial products to be sent only to English ports, and a 1663 law stipulated further that all goods sent to the colonies must pass through English ports and be carried on English ships manned by English sailors. Taken together, these navigation acts reflected the English government's mercantilist assumptions about the colonies: What was good for England should determine colonial policy.

Why Did English Colonists Consider Themselves Superior to Indians and Africans?

Were seeds of the racial prejudice that has been such a powerful force in American history planted in the seventeenth-century Chesapeake? To answer that question, historians have paid close attention to the language colonists used to describe Indians, Africans, and themselves.

In the mid-1500s, the English adopted the words *Indian* and *Negro* from Spanish, where they had come to mean, respectively, an aboriginal inhabitant of the New World and a black person of African ancestry. Both terms were generic, homogenizing an enormous diversity of tribal affiliations, languages, and cultures. Neither term originated with the people to whom it referred. The New England minister Roger Williams, who published a book on Indian languages in 1643, reported, "They have often asked mee, why we call them Indians," a poignant question that reveals the European origins of the term, dating back to Columbus.

After *Indians*, the word the settlers used most frequently to describe Native Americans was *savages*. The Indians were savages in the colonists' eyes because they lacked the traits of English civilization. As one Englishman put it in 1625, the natives of Virginia were "so bad a people, having little of humanitie but shape, ignorant of Civilitie, of Arts, of Religion; more brutish than the beasts they hunt, more wild and unmanly than that unmanned wild countrey, which they range rather than inhabite; captivated also to Satans tyranny in foolish pieties, mad impieties, wicked idlenesse, busie and bloudy wickednesse." Some English colonists counterbalanced this harsh indictment with admiration for certain features of Indian behavior. They praised Indians' calm dignity and poise, their tender love and care for family members, and their simple, independent way of life in apparent harmony with nature.

Color was not a feature of the Indians' savagery. During the seventeenth century, colonists never referred to Indians as "red." Instead, they saw Indians' skin color as tawny or tanned, the "Sun's livery," as one settler wrote. To the English, tanned skin denoted a member of the working class who spent his or her days toiling under the sun; pale skin was the fashion. Many settlers held the view that Indians were innately white like the English but in other ways woefully un-English.

Despite their savagery in English eyes, Indians controlled two things colonists desperately wanted: land and peace. Early in the seventeenth century, when English settlements were small and weak, peace with the Indians was a higher priority than land. In this period, English comments on Indian savagery noted the obvious differences between settlers and Indians, but the colonists' need for peace kept them attuned to ways to coexist with the Indians. By the middle of the seventeenth century, as colonial settlements grew and the desire for land increased, violent conflict with Indians erupted repeatedly. The violence convinced settlers that the only way to achieve both land and peace was to eliminate the Indians, by either killing them or pushing them far away from colonial settlements. English assumptions of their superiority to savage Indians provided justification and a gloss of respectability to the colonists' violent and relentless grab of Indian land.

The colonists identified Africans quite differently. Their most common term for Africans was *Negroes*, but the other was not *savage* or *heathen* but *black*. What struck English colonists most forcefully about Africans was not their un-English ways but their un-English skin color.

Black was not a neutral color to the colonists. According to the *Oxford English Dictionary* (which catalogs the changing meaning of words), *black* meant to the English people who settled the Chesapeake "deeply stained with dirt; soiled, dirty, foul . . . having dark or deadly purposes, malignant; pertaining to or involving death, deadly; baneful, disastrous, sinister . . .

Assumptions about **mercantilism** also underlay the import duty on tobacco inaugurated by the Navigation Act of 1660. The law assessed an import tax of two pence on every pound of colonial tobacco brought into England, about the price a Chesapeake tobacco farmer received. The tax gave the king a major financial interest in the size of the tobacco crop. During the 1660s, these tobacco import taxes yielded about a quarter of all English customs revenues, an impressive sign of the growing importance of the Chesapeake colonies in England's Atlantic empire.

European Attitudes toward Africans
This lavish portrait of two seventeenth-century aristocratic ladies illustrates common European attitudes toward Africans. Both ladies appear completely at ease with the black servant boy. One casually drapes her arm over his shoulder; the other daintily plucks fruit from the bowl he holds. While the two ladies gaze confidently at the viewer, the boy stares at the black lapdog, whose color and protruding eyes he shares, along with an ornamental collar. The portrait suggests that the ladies consider the African boy akin to the dog — an exotic pet vastly inferior to them but safely domesticated and fit to be a plaything or accessory. Réunion des Musées Nationaux/Art Resource, NY.

foul, iniquitous, atrocious, horrible, wicked." Black was the opposite of white, which connoted purity, beauty, and goodness — attributes the colonists identified with themselves. By the middle of the seventeenth century, the colonists referred to themselves not only as English but also as free, hinting that they believed that people who were not English were not free. After about 1680, colonists often referred to themselves as white, acknowledging the color of free people. By the end of the seventeenth century, blacks were triply cursed in English eyes: un-English, un-white, and un-free.

Virginians did not legally define slavery as permanent, lifelong, inherited bondage until 1660. The sparse surviving evidence demonstrates, however, that colonists practiced slavery from the start. The debasements of slavery strengthened the colonists' prejudice toward blacks, while racial prejudices buttressed slavery.

Colonists' attitudes toward Indians and Africans exaggerated and hardened English notions about social hierarchy, about superiority and inferiority. Colonists' convictions of their own superiority to Indians and Africans justified, they believed, their exploitation of Indians' land and Africans' labor.

Those justifications planted the seeds of pernicious racial prejudices that flourished in America for centuries.

Thinking about Beliefs and Attitudes

1. How did the words colonists used to describe Indians and Africans indicate their beliefs?

2. To what extent did colonists' ideas about themselves shape their attitudes toward Indians and Africans?

3. What were the consequences of English colonists' belief in their own superiority?

Bacon's Rebellion

Colonists, like residents of European monarchies, accepted class divisions and inequality as long as they believed that government officials ruled for the general good. When rulers violated that precept, ordinary people felt justified in rebelling.

In 1676, **Bacon's Rebellion** erupted as a dispute over Virginia's Indian policy. Before it was over, the rebellion convulsed Chesapeake politics and society, leaving in its wake death, destruction, and a legacy of hostility between the great planters and their poorer neighbors.

Governor William Berkeley
This portrait illustrates the distance that separated Governor Berkeley and the other Chesapeake grandees from poor planters, landless freemen, servants, and slaves. Berkeley's clothing suited the genteel homes of Jamestown, not the rustic dwellings of lesser Virginians. His haughty, satisfied demeanor suggests his lack of sympathy for poor Virginians, who, he was certain, deserved their lot. National Gallery of Art, Washington, D.C., USA/SuperStock.

Opechancanough, the Algonquian chief who had led the Indian uprising of 1622 in Virginia, mounted another surprise attack in 1644 and killed about five hundred Virginia colonists in two days. During the next two years of bitter fighting, the colonists eventually gained the upper hand, capturing and murdering the old chief. The treaty that concluded the war established policies toward the Indians that the government tried to maintain for the next thirty years. The Indians relinquished all claims to land already settled by the English. Wilderness land beyond the fringe of English settlement was supposed to be reserved exclusively for Indian use. The colonial government hoped to minimize contact between settlers and Indians and thereby maintain the peace.

If the Chesapeake population had not grown, the policy might have worked. But the number of land-hungry colonists, especially poor, recently freed servants, continued to multiply. In their quest for land, they pushed beyond the treaty limits of English settlement and encroached steadily on Indian land. During the 1660s and 1670s, violence between colonists and Indians repeatedly flared along the advancing frontier. The government, headquartered in the tidewater region near the coast, far from the danger of Indian raids, took steps to calm the disputes and reestablish the peace. Frontier settlers thirsted for revenge against what their leader, Nathaniel Bacon, termed "the protected and Darling Indians." Bacon proclaimed his "Design not only to ruine and extirpate all Indians in Generall but all Manner of Trade and Commerce with them." Indians were not the only enemies Bacon and his men singled out. Bacon also urged the colonists to "see what spounges have suckt up the Publique Treasure." He charged that **grandees**, or elite planters, operated the government for their private gain, a charge that made sense to many colonists. In fact, officeholders had profited enough to buy slaves to replace their servants; by the 1660s, they owned about 70 percent of all the colony's slaves. Bacon crystallized the grievances of the small planters and poor farmers against both the Indians and the colonial rulers in Jamestown.

Hoping to maintain the fragile peace on the frontier in 1676, Governor Berkeley pronounced Bacon a rebel, threatened to punish him for treason, and called for new elections of burgesses who, Berkeley believed, would endorse his get-tough policy. To Berkeley's surprise, the elections backfired. Almost all the old burgesses were voted out of office, and they were replaced by local leaders, including Bacon. The legislature was now in the hands of minor grandees who, like Bacon, chafed at the rule of the elite planters.

In June 1676, the new legislature passed a series of reform measures known as Bacon's Laws. Among other changes, the laws gave local settlers a voice in setting tax levies, forbade officeholders from demanding bribes or other extra fees for carrying out their duties, placed limits on holding multiple offices, and restored the vote to all freemen. Under pressure, Berkeley pardoned Bacon and authorized his campaign of Indian warfare. But elite planters soon convinced Berkeley that Bacon and his men were a greater threat than Indians.

When Bacon learned that Berkeley had once again branded him a traitor, he declared war against Berkeley and the other grandees. For three months, Bacon's forces fought the Indians, sacked the grandees' plantations, and attacked

"See what spounges have suckt up the Publique Treasure."

— NATHANIEL BACON

Jamestown. Berkeley's loyalists retaliated by plundering the homes of Bacon's supporters. The fighting continued until late October, when Bacon unexpectedly died, most likely from dysentery, and several English ships arrived to bolster Berkeley's strength. With the rebellion crushed, Berkeley hanged several of Bacon's allies and destroyed farms that belonged to Bacon's supporters.

The rebellion did nothing to dislodge the grandees from their positions of power. If anything, it strengthened them. When the king learned of the turmoil in the Chesapeake and its devastating effect on tobacco exports and customs duties, he ordered an investigation. Royal officials replaced Berkeley with a governor more attentive to the king's interests, nullified Bacon's Laws, and instituted an export tax on every hogshead (large barrel) of tobacco as a way of paying the expenses of government without having to obtain the consent of the tightfisted House of Burgesses.

In the aftermath of Bacon's Rebellion, tensions between great planters and small farmers gradually lessened. Bacon's Rebellion showed, a governor of Virginia said, that it was necessary "to steer between . . . either an Indian or a civil war." The ruling elite concluded that it was safer for the colonists to fight the Indians than to fight each other, and the government made little effort to restrict settlers' encroachment on Indian land. Tax cuts also were welcomed by all freemen. The export duty on tobacco imposed by the king allowed the colonial government to reduce taxes by 75 percent between 1660 and 1700. In the long run, however, the most important contribution to political stability was the declining importance of the servant labor system. During the 1680s and 1690s, fewer servants arrived in the Chesapeake, partly because of improving economic conditions in England. Accordingly, the number of poor, newly freed servants also declined, reducing the size of the lowest stratum of free society. In 1700, as many as one-third of the free colonists still worked as tenants on land owned by others, but the social and political distance between them and the great planters did not seem as important as it had been in 1660. The main reason was that by 1700 the Chesapeake was in the midst of transitioning to a slave labor system that minimized the differences between poor farmers and rich planters and magnified the differences between whites and blacks.

REVIEW Why did Chesapeake colonial society become increasingly polarized between 1650 and 1670?

► Toward a Slave Labor System

Although forced native labor was already a common practice under New Spain's system of *repartimiento* (see chapter 2), repeated Indian uprisings in the Spanish colonies of New Mexico and Florida kept them marginal and unprofitable. English colonists, who had been unsuccessful in conscripting Indian labor, looked to another source of workers used by the Spaniards and Portuguese: enslaved Africans. On this foundation, European colonizers built African **slavery** into the most important form of coerced labor in the New World.

During the seventeenth century, English colonies in the West Indies followed the Spanish and Portuguese examples and developed sugar plantations with slave labor. In the English North American colonies, however, a slave labor system did not emerge until the last quarter of the seventeenth century. During the 1670s, settlers from Barbados brought slavery to the new English mainland colony of Carolina, where the imprint of the West Indies remained strong for decades. In Chesapeake tobacco fields at about the same time, slave labor began to replace servant labor, marking the transition toward a society of freedom for whites and slavery for Africans.

Religion and Revolt in the Spanish Borderland

While English colonies in the Chesapeake grew and prospered with the tobacco trade, the northern outposts of the Spanish empire in New Mexico and Florida stagnated. Spanish officials seriously considered eliminating both settlements because their costs greatly exceeded their benefits. Only about fifteen hundred Spaniards lived in Florida, and roughly twice as many inhabited New Mexico, yet both colonies required regular deliveries of goods and large subsidies because their populations proved unable to sustain themselves. One royal governor complained that "no [Spaniard] comes . . . to plow and sow [crops], but only to eat and loaf."

Instead of attracting settlers and growing crops for export, New Mexico and Florida appealed to Spanish missionaries seeking to convert Indians to Christianity. In both colonies, Indians outnumbered Spaniards ten or twenty to one. Royal officials hoped that the missionaries' efforts would pacify the Indians and be a relatively cheap way to preserve Spanish footholds in North America.

Sugar Plantation
This portrait of a Brazilian sugar plantation shows the house of the Brazilian owners, attended by numerous slaves. Cartloads of sugarcane are being hauled to the mill, which is powered by a waterwheel (far right), where the cane will be squeezed between rollers to extract the sugary juice. The juice will then be distilled over a fire tended by the slaves (at the left end of the mill) until it has the desired consistency and purity. Notice that all of the working people are of African descent, and probably all of them are slaves. How does the artist differentiate slaves from their owners?
Courtesy of the John Carter Brown Library at Brown University.

The missionaries baptized thousands of Indians in Spanish North America during the seventeenth century, but they also planted the seeds of Indian uprisings against Spanish rule.

Dozens of missionaries came to Florida and New Mexico, as one announced, to free the Indians "from the miserable slavery of the demon and from the obscure darkness of their idolatry." The missionaries followed royal instructions that Indians should be taught "to live in a civilized manner, clothed and wearing shoes . . . [and] given the use of . . . bread, linen, horses, cattle, tools, and weapons, and all the rest that Spain has had." Stirrups adorned with Christian crosses on soldiers' saddles proclaimed the faith behind the Spaniards' swords, and vice versa. In effect, the missionaries sought to convert the Indians not just into Christians but also into surrogate Spaniards.

The missionaries supervised the building of scores of Catholic churches across Florida and New Mexico. Adopting practices common elsewhere in New Spain, they forced the Indians both to construct these churches and to pay tribute in the form of food, blankets, and other goods. Although the missionaries congratulated themselves on the many Indians they converted, their coercive methods subverted their goals. A missionary reported that an Indian in New Mexico asked him, "If we [missionaries] who are Christians caused so much harm and violence [to Indians], why should they become Christians?"

The Indians retaliated repeatedly against Spanish exploitation, but the Spaniards sup-pressed the violent uprisings by taking advantage of the disunity among the Indians, much as Cortés did in the conquest of Mexico (see chapter 2). In 1680, however, the native leader **Popé** organized

Spanish Stirrup
This seventeenth-century stirrup used by Spaniards on the northern frontier of New Spain illustrates the use of elaborate ornamentation and display to convey a sense of Spanish power. It is no accident that the stirrup is in the shape of a Christian cross, a vivid symbol of the Spaniards' belief in the divine source of their authority. © George H. H. Huey.

English possessions
French possessions
Spanish possessions
Carolina Grant, 1665

FALL LINE · MD. · DEL.
VIRGINIA
TUSCARORA
CHEROKEE CATAWBA
YAMASEE
CREEK
Roanoke I.
Cape Fear
Charles Towne
Ashley R.
Port Royal I.
St. Augustine
TIMUCUA
SPANISH FLORIDA
Apalachicola R.
Gulf of Mexico
ATLANTIC OCEAN
2,000 miles
60°W
30°N
20°N
10°N
80°W
70°W
Bahamas (Br.)
Cuba (Sp.)
Hispaniola (Sp.)
Jamaica (Br.)
Saint Domingue (Fr.)
Puerto Rico (Sp.)
VIRGIN IS. (Den.)
St. Kitts (Br.)
Nevis (Br.)
Antigua (Br.)
Montserrat (Br.)
Guadeloupe (Fr.)
Dominica (Br.)
Martinique (Fr.)
St. Lucia (Br.)
St. Vincent (Br.)
Barbados (Br.)
Grenada (Br.)
Tobago (Br.)
Trinidad (Sp.)
Curaçao (Neth.)
WEST INDIES
Caribbean Sea
NEW SPAIN
NEW GRANADA

0   250   500 miles
0   250   500 kilometers

N W E S

MAP ACTIVITY

Map 3.2   The West Indies and Carolina in the Seventeenth Century
Although Carolina was geographically close to the Chesapeake colonies, it was culturally closer to the West Indies in the seventeenth century because its early settlers — both blacks and whites — came from Barbados. South Carolina maintained strong ties to the West Indies for more than a century, long after the arrival of many later settlers from England, Ireland, France, and elsewhere.

READING THE MAP: Locate English colonies in America and English holdings in the Caribbean. Which European country controlled most of the mainland bordering the Caribbean? Where was the closest mainland English territory?
CONNECTIONS: Why were colonists in Carolina so interested in Barbados? What goods did they export? Describe the relationship between Carolina and Barbados in 1700.

the **Pueblo Revolt**, ordering his followers, as one recounted, to "break up and burn the images of the holy Christ, the Virgin Mary, and the other saints, the crosses, and everything pertaining to Christianity." During the revolt, Indians desecrated churches, killed two-thirds of the Spanish missionaries, and drove the Spaniards out of New Mexico to present-day El Paso, Texas. The Spaniards managed to return to New Mexico by the end of the seventeenth century, but only by curtailing the missionaries and reducing labor exploitation. Florida Indians never mounted a unified attack on Spanish rule, but they too organized sporadic uprisings and resisted conversion, causing a Spanish official to report by the end of the seventeenth century that "the law of God and the preaching of the Holy Gospel have now ceased."

The West Indies: Sugar and Slavery

The most profitable part of the English New World empire in the seventeenth century lay in the Caribbean (Map 3.2). The tiny island of **Barbados**, colonized in the 1630s, was the jewel

of the English West Indies. During the 1640s, Barbadian planters began to grow sugarcane with such success that a colonial official proclaimed Barbados "the most flourishing Island in all those American parts, and I verily believe in all the world for the production of sugar." Sugar commanded high prices in England, and planters rushed to grow as much as they could. By midcentury, annual sugar exports from the English Caribbean totaled about 150,000 pounds; by 1700, exports reached nearly 50 million pounds.

Sugar transformed Barbados and other West Indian islands. Poor farmers could not afford the expensive machinery that extracted and refined sugarcane juice, but planters with enough capital to grow sugar got rich. By 1680, the wealthiest Barbadian sugar planters were, on average, four times richer than tobacco grandees in the Chesapeake. The sugar grandees differed from their Chesapeake counterparts in another crucial

> **"Barbados is grown the most flourishing Island in all those American parts, and I verily believe in all the world for the production of sugar."**
> — A colonial official of Barbados

Figure 3.1 GLOBAL COMPARISON: Migration to the New World from Europe and Africa, 1492–1700

Before 1640, Spain and Portugal sent four out of five European migrants to the New World, virtually all of them bound for New Spain or Brazil. But from 1640 to 1700, nearly as many migrants came from England as from all other European nations combined, a measure of the growing significance of England's colonies. From 1492 to 1700, more enslaved Africans than Europeans arrived in the New World. What might explain the shifts in the destinations of enslaved Africans? Were those shifts comparable to shifts among European immigrants?

For slaves, work on a sugar plantation was a life sentence to brutal, unremitting labor. Slaves suffered high death rates. Since slave men outnumbered slave women two to one, few slaves could form families and have children. These grim realities meant that in Barbados and elsewhere in the West Indies, the slave population did not grow by natural reproduction. Instead, planters continually purchased enslaved Africans. Although sugar plantations did not gain a foothold in North America in the seventeenth century, the West Indies nonetheless exerted a powerful influence on the development of slavery in the mainland colonies.

Carolina: A West Indian Frontier

The early settlers of what became South Carolina were immigrants from Barbados. In 1663, a Barbadian planter named John Colleton and a group of seven other men obtained a charter from England's King Charles II to establish a colony south of the Chesapeake and north of the Spanish territories in Florida. The men, known as "proprietors," hoped to siphon settlers from Barbados and other colonies and encourage them to develop a profitable export crop comparable to West Indian sugar and Chesapeake tobacco. The proprietors enlisted the English philosopher John Locke to help draft the *Fundamental Constitutions of Carolina*, which provided for religious liberty and political rights for small property holders while envisioning a landed aristocracy supported by bound laborers and slaves. Following the Chesapeake example, the proprietors also offered headrights of up to 150 acres of land for each settler, a provision that eventually undermined the *Constitutions'* goal of a titled aristocracy. In 1670, the proprietors established the colony's first permanent English settlement, Charles Towne, later spelled Charleston (see Map 3.2).

As the proprietors had planned, most of the early settlers were from Barbados. In fact, Carolina was the only seventeenth-century English colony to be settled principally by colonists from other colonies rather than from England. The Barbadian immigrants brought their slaves with them. More than a fourth of the early settlers were slaves, and as the colony continued to attract settlers from Barbados, the black population multiplied. By 1700, slaves made up about half the population of Carolina. The new colony's close association with Barbados caused English officials to refer routinely to "Carolina in ye West Indies."

way: The average sugar baron in Barbados owned 115 slaves in 1680.

African slaves planted, cultivated, and harvested the sugarcane that made West Indian planters wealthy. Beginning in the 1640s, Barbadian planters purchased thousands of slaves to work their plantations, and the African population on the island mushroomed. During the 1650s, when blacks made up only 3 percent of the Chesapeake population, they had already become the majority in Barbados. By 1700, slaves constituted more than three-fourths of the island's population (Figure 3.1).

The Carolinians experimented unsuccessfully to match their semitropical climate with profitable export crops of tobacco, cotton, indigo, and olives. In the mid-1690s, colonists identified a hardy strain of rice and took advantage of the knowledge of rice cultivation among their many African slaves to build rice plantations. Settlers also sold livestock and timber to the West Indies, as well as another "natural resource": They captured and enslaved several thousand local Indians and sold them to Caribbean planters. Both economically and socially, seventeenth-century Carolina was a frontier outpost of the West Indian sugar economy.

Slave Labor Emerges in the Chesapeake

By 1700, more than eight out of ten people in the southern colonies of English North America lived in the Chesapeake. Until the 1670s, almost all Chesapeake colonists were white people from England. By 1700, however, one out of eight people in the region was a black person from Africa. A few black people had lived in the Chesapeake since the 1620s, but the black population grew fivefold between 1670 and 1700 as hundreds of tobacco planters made the transition from servant to slave labor. Only relatively prosperous planters could afford to buy slaves, concentrating slave ownership among the elite.

Planters saw several advantages to purchasing slaves rather than servants. Although slaves cost three to five times more than servants, slaves never became free. Because the mortality rate had declined by the 1680s, planters could reasonably expect a slave to live longer than a servant's period of indenture. Slaves also promised to be a perpetual labor force, since children of slave mothers inherited the status of slavery. And unlike servants, they could be controlled politically. Bacon's Rebellion had demonstrated how disruptive former servants could be when their expectations were not met. A slave labor system promised to avoid the political problems caused by the servant labor system. Slavery kept discontented laborers in permanent servitude, and their color was a badge of their bondage.

The slave labor system polarized Chesapeake society along lines of race and status: All slaves were black, and nearly all blacks were slaves; almost all free people were white, and all whites were free or only temporarily bound in indentured servitude. Unlike Barbados, however, the Chesapeake retained a vast white majority. Among whites, huge differences of wealth and

status still existed. By 1700, more than three-quarters of white families had neither servants nor slaves. Nonetheless, poor white farmers enjoyed the privileges of free status. They could own property, get married, have families, and bequeath their property and their freedom to their descendants; they could move when and where they wanted; they could associate freely with other people; they could serve on juries, vote, and hold political office; and they could work, loaf, and sleep as they chose. These privileges of freedom — none of them possessed by slaves — made lesser white folk feel they had a genuine stake in the existence of slavery, even if they did not own a single slave. By emphasizing the privileges of freedom shared by all white people, the slave labor system reduced the ten-

Tobacco Wrapper
This wrapper labeled a container of tobacco from the English colonies sold at Reighly's shop in Essex. The wrapper was much like a brand, promising consumers consistency in quality and taste. The wrapper features two black slaves enjoying a pipe of the leaves they presumably helped grow. It also illustrates tobacco growing in a field and harvested leaves ready to be packed into a barrel, ferried to the ships waiting off-shore, and transported to Reighly's and other tobacconists in England. Reighly's owners didn't worry that depicting slaves would alienate their customers. The Granger Collection, New York.

sions between poor folk and grandees that had plagued the Chesapeake region in the 1670s.

In contrast to slaves in Barbados, most slaves in the seventeenth-century Chesapeake colonies had frequent and close contact with white people. Slaves and white servants performed the same tasks on tobacco plantations, often working side by side in the fields. Slaves took advantage of every opportunity to slip away from white supervision and seek out the company of other slaves. Planters often feared that slaves would turn such seemingly innocent social pleasures to political ends, either to run away or to conspire to strike against their masters. Slaves often did run away, but they were usually captured or returned after a brief absence. Despite planters' nightmares, slave insurrections did not occur.

Although slavery resolved the political unrest caused by the servant labor system, it created new political problems. By 1700, the bedrock political issue in the southern colonies was keeping slaves in their place, at the end of a hoe. The slave labor system in the southern colonies stood roughly midway between the sugar plantations and black majority of Barbados to the south and the small farms and homogeneous villages that developed in seventeenth-century New England to the north (as discussed in chapter 4).

REVIEW   Why had slave labor largely displaced indentured servant labor by 1700 in Chesapeake tobacco production?

▶ Conclusion: The Growth of English Colonies Based on Export Crops and Slave Labor

By 1700, the colonies of Virginia, Maryland, and Carolina were firmly established. The staple crops they grew for export provided a livelihood for many, a fortune for a few, and valuable revenues for shippers, merchants, and the English monarchy. Their societies differed markedly from English society in most respects, yet the colonists considered themselves English people who happened to live in North America. They claimed the same rights and privileges as English men and women, while they denied those rights and privileges to Native Americans and African slaves.

The English colonies also differed from the example of New Spain. Settlers and servants flocked to English colonies, in contrast to Spaniards who trickled into New Spain. Few English missionaries sought to convert Indians to Protestant Christianity, unlike the numerous Catholic missionaries in the Spanish settlements in New Mexico and Florida. Large quantities of gold and silver never materialized in English North America. English colonists never adopted the system of encomienda (see chapter 2) because the Indians in these areas were too few and too hostile and their communities too small and decentralized compared with those of the Mexica. Yet some forms of coerced labor and racial distinction that developed in New Spain had North American counterparts, as English colonists employed servants and slaves and defined themselves as superior to Indians and Africans.

By 1700, the remnants of Powhatan's people still survived. As English settlement pushed north, west, and south of Chesapeake Bay, the Indians faced the new colonial world that Powhatan and Pocahontas had encountered when John Smith and the first colonists had arrived at Jamestown. By 1700, the many descendants of Pocahontas's son, Thomas, as well as other colonists and Native Americans, understood that the English had come to stay.

Economically, the southern colonies developed during the seventeenth century from the struggling Jamestown settlement that could not feed itself into a major source of profits for English merchants, shippers, and the king. The European fashion for tobacco provided livelihoods for numerous white families and riches for elite planters. But after 1700, enslaved Africans were conscripted in growing numbers to grow tobacco in the Chesapeake and rice in Carolina. The slave society that dominated the eighteenth-century southern colonies was firmly rooted in the developments of the seventeenth century.

A desire for land, a hope for profit, and a dream for security motivated southern white colonists. Realizing these aspirations involved great risks, considerable suffering, and frequent disappointment, as well as seizing Indian lands and coercing labor from servants and slaves. By 1700, despite huge disparities in individual colonists' success in achieving their goals, tens of thousands of white colonists who were immigrants or descendants of immigrants now considered the southern colonies their home, shaping the history of the region and of the nation as a whole for centuries to come.

▶ Selected Bibliography

Chesapeake Society

Kathleen Brown, *Good Wives, Nasty Wenches, and Anxious Patriarchs: Gender, Race, and Power in Colonial Virginia* (1996).

Lois Green Carr et al., *Robert Cole's World: Agriculture and Society in Early Maryland* (1991).

Alison Games, *The Web of Empire: English Cosmopolitans in the Age of Expansion, 1560–1660* (2009).

April Hatfield, *Atlantic Virginia: Intercolonial Relations in the Seventeenth Century* (2003).

Karen Ordahl Kupperman, *The Jamestown Project* (2010).

Peter C. Mancall, *The Atlantic World and Virginia, 1550–1624* (2007).

Peter C. Mancall, *Hakluyt's Promise: An Elizabethan's Obsession for an English America* (2010).

Debra Meyers, *Common Whores, Vertuous Women, and Loveing Wives: Free Will Christian Women in Colonial Maryland* (2003).

Marcy Norton, *Sacred Gifts, Profane Pleasures: A History of Tobacco and Chocolate in the Atlantic World* (2010).

Steve Sarson, *British America, 1500–1800: Creating Colonies, Imagining an Empire* (2005).

Terry L. Snyder, *Brabbling Women: Disorderly Speech and the Law in Early Virginia* (2003).

Christopher L. Tomlins, *Freedom Bound: Law, Labor, and Civic Identity in Colonizing English America, 1580–1865* (2010).

Lorena S. Walsh, *Motives of Honor, Pleasure, and Profit: Plantation Management in the Colonial Chesapeake, 1607–1763* (2010).

Indians

Alan Gallay, *The Indian Slave Trade: The Rise of the English Empire in the American South, 1670–1717* (2002).

Ramón A. Gutiérrez, *When Jesus Came, the Corn Mothers Went Away: Marriage, Sexuality, and Power in New Mexico, 1500–1846* (1991).

Pekka Hämäläinen, *The Comanche Empire* (2009).

Karen Ordahl Kupperman, *Indians and English: Facing Off in Early America* (2000).

Helen C. Rountree, *Pocahontas, Powhatan, Opechancanough: Three Indian Lives Changed by Jamestown* (2005).

Jayme A. Sokolow, *The Great Encounter: Native Peoples and European Settlers in the Americas, 1492–1800* (2003).

Margaret Holmes Williamson, *Powhatan Lords of Life and Death: Command and Consent in Seventeenth-Century Virginia* (2003).

Slavery and Indentured Servitude

Susan Dwyer Amussen, *Caribbean Exchanges: Slavery and the Transformation of English Society, 1640–1700* (2007).

Ira Berlin, *The Making of African America: The Four Great Migrations* (2010).

James F. Brooks, *Captives and Cousins: Slavery, Kinship, and Community in the Southwest Borderlands* (2002).

Tim Hashaw, *The Birth of Black America: The First African Americans and the Pursuit of Freedom at Jamestown* (2007).

Linda M. Heywood and John K. Thornton, *Central Africans, Atlantic Creoles, and the Foundation of the Americas* (2007).

Russell R. Menard, *Migrants, Servants, and Slaves: Unfree Labor in Colonial British America* (2001).

Jerald T. Milanich, *Laboring in the Fields of the Lord: Spanish Missions and Southeastern Indians* (1999).

Edmund S. Morgan, *American Slavery, American Freedom: The Ordeal of Colonial Virginia* (1975).

Jennifer L. Morgan, *Laboring Women: Reproduction and Gender in New World Slavery* (2004).

John Ruston Pagan, *Anne Orthwood's Bastard: Sex and Law in Early Virginia* (2003).

Carolina Society and the West Indies

Cara Anzilotti, *In the Affairs of the World: Women, Patriarchy, and Power in Colonial South Carolina* (2002).

S. Max Edelson, *Plantation Enterprise in Colonial South Carolina* (2006).

Kirsten Fischer, *Suspect Relations: Sex, Race, and Resistance in Colonial North Carolina* (2002).

Michael Jarvis, *In the Eye of All Trade: Bermuda, Bermudians, and the Maritime Atlantic World, 1680–1783* (2010).

Russell K. Menard, *Sweet Negotiations: Sugar, Slavery, and Plantation Agriculture in Early Barbados* (2006).

▶ **FOR MORE BOOKS ABOUT TOPICS IN THIS CHAPTER,** see the Online Bibliography at bedfordstmartins.com/roark.

▶ **FOR ADDITIONAL PRIMARY SOURCES FROM THIS PERIOD,** see Michael Johnson, ed., *Reading the American Past*, Fifth Edition.

▶ **FOR WEB SITES, IMAGES, AND DOCUMENTS RELATED TO TOPICS AND PLACES IN THIS CHAPTER,** visit Make History at bedfordstmartins.com/roark.

Reviewing Chapter 3

REVIEW QUESTIONS

Use key terms and dates to support your answers.

1. Why did Powhatan behave as he did toward the English colonists? (pp. 63–68)

2. Why did the vast majority of European immigrants to the Chesapeake come as indentured servants? (pp. 68–76)

3. Why did Chesapeake colonial society become increasingly polarized between 1650 and 1670? (pp. 76–81)

4. Why had slave labor largely displaced indentured servant labor by 1700 in Chesapeake tobacco production? (pp. 81–86)

MAKING CONNECTIONS

Draw on key terms, the timeline, and review questions.

1. Given the vulnerability of the Jamestown settlement in its first two decades, why did its sponsors and settlers not abandon it? In your answer, discuss the challenges the settlement faced and the benefits different participants in England and the New World hoped to derive from their efforts.

2. Tobacco dominated European settlement in the Chesapeake during the seventeenth century. How did tobacco agriculture shape the region's development? In your answer, be sure to address the demographic and geographic features of the colony.

3. Bacon's Rebellion highlighted significant tensions within Chesapeake society. What provoked the rebellion, and what did it accomplish? In your answer, be sure to consider causes and results in the colonies and in England.

4. In addition to making crucial contributions to the economic success of seventeenth-century English colonies, Native Americans and enslaved Africans influenced colonial politics. Describe how European colonists' relations with these populations contributed to political friction and harmony within the colony.

LINKING TO THE PAST

Link events in this chapter to earlier events.

1. How did England's colonization efforts in the Chesapeake and Carolina during the seventeenth century compare with Spain's conquest and colonization of Mexico? (See chapter 2.)

2. How did the development of the transatlantic tobacco trade exemplify the Columbian exchange? (See chapter 2.)

▶ **FOR PRACTICE QUIZZES AND OTHER STUDY TOOLS,** visit the Online Study Guide at **bedfordstmartins.com/roark.**

TIMELINE 1606–1680

1606	• Virginia Company receives royal charter.
1607	• English colonists found Jamestown settlement; Pocahontas "rescues" John Smith.
1607–1610	• Starvation plagues Jamestown.
1612	• John Rolfe begins to plant tobacco in Virginia.
1617	• First commercial tobacco shipment leaves Virginia for England.
	• Pocahontas dies in England.
1618	• Powhatan dies; Opechancanough becomes chief of the Algonquians.
1619	• First Africans arrive in Virginia.
	• House of Burgesses begins to meet in Virginia.
1622	• Opechancanough leads first Indian uprising against Virginia colonists.
1624	• Virginia becomes royal colony.
1630s	• Barbados colonized by English.
1632	• King Charles I grants Lord Baltimore land for colony of Maryland.
1634	• Colonists begin to arrive in Maryland.
1640s	• Barbados colonists begin to grow sugarcane with labor of African slaves.
1644	• Opechancanough leads second Indian uprising against Virginia colonists.
1660	• Navigation Act imposes mercantilist requirement that colonial products to be shipped only to English ports.
	• Virginia law defines slavery as inherited, lifelong servitude.
1663	• Royal charter granted for Carolina colony.
1670	• Charles Towne, South Carolina, founded.
1670–1700	• Slave labor system emerges in Carolina and Chesapeake colonies.
1676	• Bacon's Rebellion.
1680	• Pueblo Revolt.

PSALM XXII, XXIII.

25 Concerning thee shall be my prayse,
in the great assembly:
before them that him reverence
performe my vowes will I.

26 The meek shall eat & be suffic'd:
Iehovah prayse shall they
that doe him seek: your heart shall live
unto perpetuall aye.

27 All ends of th'earth remember shall
and turne unto the Lord:
and thee all heathen-families
to worship shall accord,

28 Because unto Iehovah doth
the kingdome appertaine:
and he among the nations
is ruler Soveraigne,

29 Earths-fat-ones,eat & worship shall:
all who to dust descend,
(though none can make alive his soule)
before his face shall bend,

30 With service a posterity
him shall attend upon:
to God it shall accounted bee
a generation.

31 Come shall they, & his righteousnes
by them declar'd shall bee,
unto a people yet unborne,
that done this thing hath hee.

23 A Psalme of David.

The Lord to mee a shepheard is,
want therefore shall not I.

‡ Hee

PSALME XXII, XXIIII.

2 Hee in the folds of tender-grasse,
doth cause mee downe to lie:
To waters calme me gently leads

3 Restore my soule doth hee:
he doth in paths of righteousnes:
for his names sake leade mee.

4 Yea though in valley of deaths shade
I walk, none ill I'le feare:
because thou art with mee, thy rod,
and staffe my comfort are.

5 For mee a table thou hast spread,
in presence of my foes:
thou dost annoynt my head with oyle,
my cup it over-flowes.

6 Goodnes & mercy surely shall
all my dayes follow mee:
and in the Lords house I shall dwell
so long as dayes shall bee.

Psalme 24.
A psalme of david.

The earth Iehovahs is,
and the fulnesse of it:
the habitable world, & they
that there upon doe sit.

2 Because upon the seas,
hee hath it firmly layd:
and it upon the water-floods
most sollidly hath stayd.

3 The mountaine of the Lord,
who shall thereto ascend?
and in his place of holynes

E 3

AMERICA'S FIRST BOOK
The first book printed in what is now the United States, this copy of *The Whole Book of Psalms Faithfully Translated into English Metre* was published in Cambridge, Massachusetts, in 1640. The background image shows the earliest known view of New Amsterdam (present-day New York) from around the same time. Puritans banned music, stained glass, and anything else from their worship services that might divert attention from God's word. Worshippers used this book to sing psalms, celebrating God's truth with an unadorned chorus of voices. The words of the famous twenty-third psalm, beginning near the bottom of the left-hand page, commonly echoed through Puritan churches.

Drawing: Library of Congress; book: Roger Foley/Library of Congress.

4

The Northern Colonies in the Seventeenth Century 1601–1700

ROGER WILLIAMS AND HIS WIFE, MARY, ARRIVED IN MASSACHUSETTS in February 1631. Educated at Cambridge University, the twenty-eight-year-old Williams was "a godly [Puritan] minister," noted Governor John Winthrop. But when Winthrop's Boston church asked Williams to become its minister, he refused because the church had not openly rejected the corrupt Church of England. New England's premier Puritan church was not pure enough for Roger Williams.

Williams and his wife moved to Plymouth colony for two years. While there, he spent a great deal of time among the Narragansett Indians. "My soul's desire was to do the natives good," he said. Williams believed that "Nature knows no difference between Europeans and [Native] Americans in blood, birth, [or] bodies . . . God having made of one blood all mankind." He sought to learn about the Indians' language, religion, and culture without trying to convert them to Christianity, insisting that all human beings— Christians and non-Christians alike—should live according to their consciences as revealed to them by God.

Believing that English claims were legally, morally, and spiritually invalid, Williams condemned English colonists for their "sin of unjust usurpation" of Indian land. In contrast, Massachusetts officials defended colonists' settlement on Indian land. If land "lies common, and hath never been replenished or subdued, [it] is free to any that possess or improve it," Governor Winthrop explained. Besides, he said, "if we leave [the Indians] sufficient [land] for their use, we may lawfully take the rest, there being more than enough for them and us."

In 1633, Williams became minister of the church in Salem, Massachusetts, where church members believed, like other New England Puritans, that churches and governments should enforce both godly belief and behavior according to biblical rules. They claimed that "the Word of God is . . . clear." In contrast, Williams believed that the Bible shrouded the Word of God in "mist and fog." Williams contended that devout and pious Christians could and did

differ about what the Bible said and what God expected. That observation led him to denounce the emerging New England order as impure, ungodly, and tyrannical.

Williams disagreed with the New England government's requirement that everyone attend church services. He argued that forcing non-Christians to attend church was akin to requiring "a dead child to suck the breast, or a dead man [to] feast." This "False Worshipping" only promoted "spiritual drunkenness and whoredom." He believed that to regulate religious behavior would be "spiritual rape"; that governments should tolerate all religious beliefs because only God knows the Truth; that no person and no religion can understand God with absolute certainty. "I commend that man," Williams wrote, "whether Jew, or Turk, or Papist, or whoever, that steers no otherwise than his conscience dares." In Williams's view, toleration of religious belief and liberty of conscience were the only paths to religious purity and political harmony.

New England's leaders denounced Williams's arguments and banished him for his "extreme and dangerous" opinions. In January 1636, he escaped from an attempt to ship him back to England and fled south to Narragansett Bay, wandering for "fourteen weeks in a bitter winter season," Williams later wrote, "not knowing what bed or bread did mean." In the spring, he and his followers purchased land from the Narragansetts and established the colony of Rhode Island, which enshrined "Liberty of Conscience" as a fundamental ideal and became a refuge for other dissenters. Although New England's leaders expelled Williams from their holy commonwealth, his dissenting ideas arose from orthodox Puritan doctrines, which inspired him to draw his own conclusions and stick to them.

During the seventeenth century, New England's Puritan zeal cooled, and the promise of a holy New England faded. Late in the century, the new "middle" colonies of New York, New Jersey, and Pennsylvania were founded, featuring greater religious and ethnic diversity than New England. Religion remained important throughout all the colonies, but it competed with the growing faith that a better life required less focus on salvation and more attention to worldly concerns of family, work, and trade.

Throughout the English mainland colonies, settlements encroached on Indian land, causing violent conflict to flare up repeatedly. Political conflict also arose among colonists, particularly in response to major political upheavals in England. By the end of the seventeenth century, the English monarchy exerted greater control over North America and the rest of its Atlantic empire, but the products, people, and ideas that pulsed between England and the colonies energized both.

New England

This 1677 map highlights the importance of water in the New England settlements. Why do you think roads and trails linking settlements are not shown? Rhode Island, haven for Roger Williams and other religious dissenters, is located on the left side, just below the center. The small numbers on the map indicate Indian attacks during King Philip's War.

© Massachusetts Historical Society, Boston, MA, USA/The Bridgeman Art Library.

▶ Puritans and the Settlement of New England

Puritans who emigrated to North America aspired to escape the turmoil and persecution they suffered in England, a long-term consequence of the English Reformation. They also sought to build a new, orderly, Puritan version of England. Puritans established the first small settlement in New England in 1620, followed a few years later by additional settlements by the Massachusetts Bay Company. Allowed self-government through royal charter, these Puritans were in a unique position to direct the new colonies according to their faith. Their faith shaped the colonies they established in almost every way. Although many New England colonists were not Puritans, Puritanism remained a paramount influence in New England's religion, politics, and community life during the seventeenth century.

Puritan Origins: The English Reformation

The religious roots of the Puritans who founded New England reached back to the Protestant Reformation, which arose in Germany in 1517 (see chapter 2). The Reformation spread quickly to other countries, but the English church initially remained within the Catholic fold and continued its allegiance to the pope in Rome. Henry VIII, who reigned from 1509 to 1547, saw that the Reformation offered him an opportunity to break with Rome and take control of the church in England. In 1534, Henry formally initiated the **English Reformation**. At his insistence, Parliament passed the Act of Supremacy, which outlawed the Catholic Church and proclaimed the king "the only supreme head on earth of the Church of England." Henry seized the vast properties of the Catholic Church in England as well as the privilege of appointing bishops and others in the church hierarchy.

In the short run, the English Reformation allowed Henry VIII to achieve his political goal of controlling the church. In the long run, however, the Reformation brought to England the political and religious turmoil that Henry had hoped to avoid. Henry himself sought no more than a halfway Reformation. Protestant doctrines held no attraction for him; in almost all matters of religious belief and practice, he

Queen Elizabeth
This sixteenth-century portrait of Queen Elizabeth celebrates English victory over the Spanish Armada in 1588 (shown in the panels on either side of Elizabeth's head) that resulted in England's empire reaching North America (notice her right hand covering North America on the globe). Shortly before the battle, Elizabeth rallied the English people with a famous speech, declaring that, "I have the body of a weak and feeble woman; but I have the heart and stomach of a king — and of a King of England too." In a sense, this portrait depicts a queen with the virtues of a king.
© Bettmann/Corbis.

remained an orthodox Catholic. Many English Catholics wanted to revoke the English Reformation; they hoped to return the Church of England to the pope and to restore Catholic doctrines and ceremonies. But many other English people insisted on a genuine, thoroughgoing Reformation; these people came to be called **Puritans**.

During the sixteenth century, Puritanism was less an organized movement than a set of ideas and religious principles that appealed strongly to many dissenting members of the Church of England. They sought to eliminate what they considered the offensive features of Catholicism that remained in the religious doctrines and practices of the Church of England. For example, they demanded that the church hierarchy be abolished and that ordinary Christians be given greater control over religious life. They wanted to do away with the rituals of Catholic worship and instead emphasize an individual's relationship with God developed through Bible study, prayer, and introspection. Although there were many varieties and degrees of Puritanism, all Puritans

English Monarchy and the Protestant Reformation

1509–1547	Henry VIII	Leads the English Reformation, outlawing the Catholic Church in England and establishing the English monarch as supreme head of the Church of England.
1547–1553	Edward VI	Moves religious reform in a Protestant direction.
1553–1558	Mary I	Outlaws Protestantism and strives to reestablish the Catholic Church in England.
1558–1603	Elizabeth I	Tries to position the Church of England between extremes of Catholicism and Protestantism.
1603–1625	James I	Authorizes a new, Protestant translation of the Bible but is unsympathetic to Puritan reformers.
1625–1649	Charles I	Continues move away from Puritan reformers. Beheaded during the Puritan Revolution.
1642		Puritan Revolution (English Civil War) begins.
1644–1660	Oliver Cromwell	Leads Puritan side to victory in the English Civil War. Parliament proclaims England a Puritan republic (1649) and declares Cromwell the nation's "Lord Protector" (1653).
1660–1685	Charles II	Restored to the monarchy by Parliament and attempts to enforce religious toleration of Catholics and Protestant dissenters from the Church of England.
1685–1688	James II	Ousted by Parliament for pro-Catholic policies and replaced by his Protestant son-in-law, William, and his daughter (William's wife) in the "Glorious Revolution" (1688).
1689–1694	William III and Mary II	Reassert Protestant influence in England and its empire.

shared a desire to make the English church thoroughly Protestant.

The fate of Protestantism waxed and waned under the monarchs who succeeded Henry VIII. When Henry died in 1547, the advisers of the new king, Edward VI — the nine-year-old son of Henry and his third wife, Jane Seymour — initiated religious reforms that moved in a Protestant direction. The tide of reform reversed in 1553 when Edward died and was succeeded by Mary I, the daughter of Henry and Catherine of Aragon, his first wife. Mary was a steadfast Catholic, and shortly after becoming queen, she married Philip II of Spain, Europe's most powerful guardian of Catholicism. Mary attempted to restore the pre-Reformation Catholic Church. She outlawed Protestantism in England and persecuted those who refused to conform, sentencing almost three hundred to burn at the stake.

The tide turned again in 1558 when Mary died and was succeeded by Elizabeth I, the daughter of Henry and his second wife, Anne Boleyn. During her long reign, Elizabeth reaffirmed the English Reformation and tried to position the English church between the extremes of Catholicism and Puritanism. Like her father, she was less concerned with theology than with politics. Above all, she desired a church that would strengthen the monarchy and the nation.

By the time Elizabeth died in 1603, many people in England looked on Protestantism as a defining feature of national identity.

When Elizabeth's successor, James I, became king, English Puritans petitioned for further reform of the Church of England. James authorized a new translation of the Bible, known ever since as the King James version. However, neither James I nor his son Charles I, who became king in 1625, was receptive to the ideas of Puritan reformers. James and Charles moved the Church of England away from Puritanism. They enforced conformity to the Church of England and punished dissenters, both ordinary Christians and ministers. In 1629, Charles I dissolved Parliament — where Puritans were well represented — and initiated aggressive anti-Puritan policies. Many Puritans despaired about continuing to defend their faith in England and began to make plans to emigrate. Some left for Europe, others for the West Indies. The largest number set out for America.

The Pilgrims and Plymouth Colony

One of the first Protestant groups to emigrate, later known as **Pilgrims**, espoused an unorthodox view known as separatism. These **Separatists** sought to withdraw — or separate — from the Church of England, which they considered hopelessly corrupt. In 1608, they moved to Holland; by 1620, they realized that they could not live and worship there as they had hoped. **William Bradford**, a leader of the group, recalled that "many of their children, by . . . the great licentiousness of youth in [Holland], and the manifold temptations of the place, were drawn away by evil examples." Bradford and other Separatists believed that America promised to better protect their children's piety and preserve their community. Separatists obtained permission to settle in the extensive territory granted to the Virginia Company (see chapter 3). To finance their journey, they formed a joint-stock company with English investors. The investors provided the capital; the Separatists provided their labor and lives and received a share of the profits for seven years. In August 1620, the Pilgrim families boarded the *Mayflower*, and after eleven weeks at sea all but one of the 102 immigrants arrived at the outermost tip of Cape Cod, in present-day Massachusetts.

The Pilgrims realized immediately that they had landed far north of the Virginia grants and had no legal authority to settle in the area. To provide order and security as well as a claim to legitimacy, they drew up the **Mayflower Compact** on the day they arrived. They pledged to "covenant and combine ourselves together into a civil Body Politick, for our better Ordering and Preservation." The signers (all men) agreed to enact and obey necessary and just laws.

The Pilgrims settled at Plymouth and elected William Bradford their governor. That first winter, which they spent aboard their ship, "was most sad and lamentable," Bradford wrote later. "In two or three months' time half of [our] company died . . . being the depth of winter, and wanting houses and other comforts [and] being infected with scurvy and other diseases."

In the spring, Indians rescued the floundering Plymouth settlement. First Samoset and then Squanto befriended the settlers. Samoset had learned English from previous contacts with sailors and fishermen who had visited the coast to dry fish and make repairs years before the Plymouth settlers arrived. Squanto had been kidnapped by an English trader in 1614 and taken as a slave to Spain, where he escaped to London. There he learned English and finally made his way back home. Samoset arranged for the Pilgrims to meet and establish good relations with Massasoit, the chief of the **Wampanoag Indians**, whose territory included

Plymouth. Squanto, Bradford recalled, "was a special instrument sent of God for their [the Pilgrims'] good. . . . He directed them how to set their corn, where to take fish, and to procure other commodities, and was also their pilot to bring them to unknown places." With the Indians' guidance, the Pilgrims managed to harvest enough food to guarantee their survival through the coming winter, an occasion they celebrated in the fall of 1621 with a feast of thanksgiving attended by Massasoit and other Wampanoags.

Still, the Plymouth colony remained precarious. Only seven dwellings were erected that first year, and a new group of threadbare, sickly settlers arrived in November 1621, requiring the colony to adopt stringent food rationing. The colonists quarreled with their London investors, who became frustrated when Plymouth failed to produce the expected profits.

Yet the Pilgrims persisted, living simply and coexisting in relative peace with the Indians. They paid the Wampanoags when settlers gradually encroached on Indian land. By 1630, Plymouth had become a small permanent settlement, but it failed to attract many other English Puritans.

> **"In two or three months' time half of [our] company died . . . being the depth of winter, and wanting houses and other comforts [and] being infected with scurvy and other diseases."**
> — Governor **WILLIAM BRADFORD**

The Founding of Massachusetts Bay Colony

In 1629, shortly before Charles I dissolved Parliament, a group of Puritan merchants and country gentlemen obtained a royal charter for the **Massachusetts Bay Company**. The charter provided the usual privileges granted to joint-stock companies, including land for colonization that spanned present-day Massachusetts, New Hampshire, Vermont, Maine, and upstate New York. In addition, a unique provision of the charter permitted the government of the Massachusetts Bay Company to be located in the colony rather than in England. This provision allowed Puritans to exchange their status as a harassed minority in England for self-government in Massachusetts.

To lead the emigrants, the stockholders of the Massachusetts Bay Company elected **John Winthrop**, a prosperous lawyer and landowner, to serve as governor. In March 1630, eleven ships crammed with seven hundred passengers sailed

Seal of Massachusetts Bay Colony
In 1629, the Massachusetts Bay Company designed this seal depicting an Indian man inviting English settlers to "come over and help us." Of course, such an invitation was never issued. The seal was an attempt to lend an aura of altruism to the Massachusetts Bay Company's colonization efforts. In reality, colonists in Massachusetts and elsewhere were far less interested in helping Indians than in helping themselves. For the most part, that suited the Indians, who wanted no "help" from the colonists. What does the seal suggest about English views of Indians? Courtesy of Massachusetts Archives.

for Massachusetts; six more ships and another five hundred emigrants followed a few months later. Winthrop's fleet arrived in Massachusetts Bay in early June. Unlike the Separatists, Winthrop's Puritans aspired to reform the corrupt Church of England (rather than separate from it) by setting an example of godliness in the New World. Winthrop and a small group chose to settle on the peninsula that became Boston, and other settlers clustered at promising locations nearby (Map 4.1).

In a sermon to his companions aboard the *Arbella* while they were still at sea — probably the most famous sermon in American history — Winthrop proclaimed the cosmic significance of their journey. The Puritans had "entered into a covenant" with God to "work out our salvation under the power and purity of his holy ordinances," Winthrop declared. This sanctified agreement with God meant that the Puritans had to make "extraordinary" efforts to "bring into familiar and constant practice" religious principles that most people in England merely preached. To achieve their pious goals, the Puritans had to subordinate their individual interests to the common good. "We must be knit together in this work as one man," Winthrop preached. "We must delight in each other, make others' conditions our own, rejoice together, mourn together, labor and suffer together." The stakes could not be

higher, Winthrop told his listeners: "We must consider that we shall be as a city upon a hill. The eyes of all people are upon us."

That belief shaped seventeenth-century New England as profoundly as tobacco shaped the Chesapeake. Winthrop's vision of a city on a hill fired the Puritans' fierce determination to keep their covenant and live according to God's laws, unlike the backsliders and compromisers who accommodated to the Church of England. Their resolve to adhere strictly to God's plan charged nearly every feature of life in seventeenth-century New England with a distinctive, high-voltage piety.

The new colonists, as Winthrop's son John wrote later, had "all things to do, as in the beginning of the world." Unlike the early Chesapeake settlers, the first Massachusetts Bay colonists encountered few Indians because the local population had been almost entirely exterminated by an epidemic probably caused by contact with Europeans more than a decade earlier. Still, as in the Chesapeake, the colonists fell victim to deadly ailments. More than two hundred settlers died during the first year, including one of Winthrop's sons and eleven of his servants. But Winthrop maintained a confidence that proved infectious. He wrote to his wife, "I like so well to be heer as I do not repent my comminge. . . . I would not have altered my course, though I had forseene all these Afflictions." And each year from 1630 to 1640, ship after ship followed in the wake of Winthrop's fleet. In all, more than

MAP ACTIVITY

Map 4.1   New England Colonies in the Seventeenth Century
New Englanders spread across the landscape town by town during the seventeenth century. (For the sake of legibility, only a few of the more important towns are shown on the map.)

READING THE MAP: Using the dates on the map, create a chronology of the establishment of towns in New England. What physical features correspond to the earliest habitation by English settlers?

CONNECTIONS: Why were towns so much more a feature of seventeenth-century New England than of the Chesapeake (see also chapter 3)? How did Puritan dissent influence the settlement of New England colonies?

twenty thousand new settlers came, their eyes focused on the Puritans' city on a hill.

Often, when the Church of England cracked down on a Puritan minister in England, he and many of his followers moved together to New England. Smaller groups of English Puritans moved to the Chesapeake, Barbados, and elsewhere in the New World, including New Amsterdam (present-day New York). By 1640, New England had one of the highest ratios of preachers to population in all of Christendom. Several ministers sought to carry the message of Christianity to the Indians in order to replace what missionary John Eliot termed the Indians' "unfixed, confused, and ungoverned . . . life, uncivilized and unsubdued to labor and order." They established "praying towns" to encourage Indians to leave their communities and adopt English ways. A few Indians moved to these towns and converted to Christianity, but for the most part the colonists focused less on saving Indians' souls than on saving their own.

The occupations of New England immigrants reflected the social origins of English Puritans. On the whole, the immigrants came from the middle ranks of English society. The vast majority were either farmers or tradesmen, including carpenters, tailors, and textile workers. Indentured servants, whose numbers dominated the Chesapeake settlers, accounted for only about a fifth of those headed for New England. Most New England immigrants paid their way to Massachusetts, even though the journey often took their life savings. They were encouraged by the promise of bounty in New England reported in Winthrop's letter to his son: "Here is as good land as I have seen there [in England]. . . . Here can be no want of anything to those who bring means to raise [it] out of the earth and sea."

In contrast to Chesapeake newcomers, New England immigrants usually arrived as families. In fact, more Puritans came with family members than did any other group of immigrants in all of American history. A ship that left Weymouth, England, in 1635, for example, carried 106 passengers, all but eight of them part of a family unit. Unlike immigrants to the Chesapeake, women and children made up a solid majority in New England.

As Winthrop reminded the first settlers in his *Arbella* sermon, each family was a "little commonwealth" that mirrored the hierarchy among all God's creatures. Just as humankind was subordinate to God, so young people were subordinate to their elders, children to their parents, and wives to their husbands. The immigrants' family ties reinforced their religious beliefs with universally understood notions of hierarchy and mutual dependence. Whereas immigrants to the Chesapeake were disciplined mostly by the coercions of servitude and the caprices of the tobacco market, immigrants to New England entered a social order defined by the interlocking institutions of family, church, and community.

REVIEW   Why did the Puritans immigrate to North America?

▶ The Evolution of New England Society

The New England colonists, unlike their counterparts in the Chesapeake, settled in small towns, usually located on the coast or by a river (see Map 4.1). Massachusetts Bay colonists founded 133 towns during the seventeenth century, each with one or more churches. Church

members' fervent piety, buttressed by the institutions of local government, enforced remarkable religious and social conformity in the small New England settlements. During the century, tensions within the Puritan faith and changes in New England communities splintered religious orthodoxy and weakened Puritan zeal. By 1700, however, Puritanism still maintained a distinctive influence in New England.

Church, Covenant, and Conformity

Puritans believed that the church consisted of men and women who had entered a solemn covenant with one another and with God. Winthrop and three other men signed the original covenant of the first Boston church in 1630, agreeing to "Promisse, and bind our selves, to walke in all our wayes according to the Rule of the Gospell, and in all sincere Conformity to His holy Ordinaunces." Each new member of the covenant had to persuade existing members that she or he had fully experienced conversion. By 1635, the Boston church had added more than 250 names to the four original subscribers to the covenant.

Puritans embraced a distinctive version of Protestantism derived from **Calvinism**, the doctrines of John Calvin, a sixteenth-century Swiss Protestant theologian. Calvin insisted that Christians strictly discipline their behavior to conform to God's commandments announced in the Bible. Like Calvin, Puritans believed in **predestination** — the idea that the all-powerful God, before the creation of the world, decided which few human souls would receive eternal life. Only God knows the identity of these fortunate predestined individuals — the "elect" or "saints." Nothing a person did in his or her lifetime could alter God's inscrutable choice or provide assurance that the person was predestined for salvation with the elect or damned to hell with the doomed multitude. The gloomy inevitability and exclusivity of predestination contrasted sharply with Catholic doctrines that all human beings could potentially be granted eternal life by God, acting through the Catholic Church.

Despite the looming uncertainty about God's choice of the elect, Puritans believed that if a person lived a rigorously godly life — constantly winning the daily battle against sinful temptations — his or her behavior was likely to be a hint, a visible sign, that he or she was one of God's chosen few. Puritans thought that "sainthood" would become visible in individuals'

Sabbath Breakers

These seventeenth-century prints show some of the punishments Sabbath breakers might suffer from man and God. In the upper illustration, a person who gathered sticks on the Sabbath is stoned to death as Puritans believed the Bible commanded. In the lower print, women who broke the Sabbath by preparing flax for spinning suffer God's retribution when they are burned to death. Some New Englanders thought the Sabbath started at sunset on Saturday evening; others believed it began about 3:00 p.m. on Saturday. Given the extreme punishments for Sabbath breaking, New Englanders needed to tread carefully between Saturday afternoon and Monday morning. *Divine Examples of God's Severe Judgements upon Sabbath-Breakers* (London, 1671).

behavior, especially if they were privileged to know God's Word as revealed in the Bible.

The connection between sainthood and saintly behavior, however, was far from certain. Some members of the elect, Puritans believed, had not heard God's Word as revealed in the Bible, and therefore their behavior did not necessarily signal their sainthood. One reason Puritans required all town residents to attend church services was to enlighten anyone who was ignorant of God's Truth. The slippery relationship between saintly behavior, observable by anybody, and God's predestined election, invisible and unknowable to anyone, caused Puritans to worry constantly that individuals who acted like saints were fooling themselves and others. Nevertheless, Puritans thought that **visible saints** — persons who passed their demanding tests of conversion and church membership — probably, though not certainly, were among God's elect.

Members of Puritan churches ardently hoped that God had chosen them to receive eternal life and tried to demonstrate saintly behavior. Their covenant bound them to help one another attain salvation and to discipline the entire community by saintly standards. Church members kept an eye on the behavior of everybody in town. Infractions of morality, order, or propriety were reported to Puritan elders, who summoned the wayward to a church inquiry. By overseeing every aspect of life, the visible saints enforced a remarkable degree of righteous conformity in Puritan communities. Total conformity, however, was never achieved. Ardent Puritans differed among themselves; non-Puritans shirked orthodox rules. Every community contained dissenters and recalcitrants, such as the Roxbury servant who declared that "if hell were ten times hotter, [I] would rather be there than [I] would serve [my] master."

Despite the central importance of religion, churches played no direct role in the civil government of New England communities. Puritans did not want to mimic the Church of England, which they considered a puppet of the king rather than an independent body that served the Lord. They were determined to insulate New England churches from the contaminating influence of the civil state and its merely human laws.

Seats of Power

The two chairs shown here high-light important contrasts between the dominant ideas of New England Puritans and those of Old World rulers. While neither chair is typical of furniture owned by ordinary people, both chairs illustrate designs that appealed to leaders in their respective societies.

The elaborately carved European throne chair belonged to an unknown wealthy person and dates from the late sixteenth century. The more simple New England great chair belonged to Michael Metcalf, a teacher and community leader in seventeenth-century Dedham, Massachusetts.

The magnificent carvings on the throne chair feature at least seven human images; abundant likenesses

New England Great Chair

of fruit, foliage, textiles, and architecture; and two dramatic rams' heads. What do these images convey about the wood carver who made them? What might the chair suggest about the person who sat in it? To what degree could the throne chair be viewed as an example of the handiwork of God rather than human handiwork?

The carving on Metcalf's great chair lacks the ornate artistry of that on the throne chair. How does the less skillful carving suggest the colonial origins of the great chair? Under the seat, which lifts up to reveal an enclosed compartment, Metcalf stored books, presumably including a Bible. Why would a space for book storage be important for a New Englander like Metcalf? Why do you think the throne chair lacks an obvious place for books?

Although ministers were the most highly respected figures in New England towns, they were prohibited from holding government office.

Puritans had no qualms, however, about their religious beliefs influencing New England governments. As much as possible, the Puritans tried to bring public life into conformity with their view of God's law. For example, fines were issued for Sabbath-breaking activities such as working, traveling, playing a flute, smoking a pipe, and visiting neighbors.

Puritans mandated other purifications of what they considered corrupt English practices. (See "Visualizing History," above.) They refused to celebrate Christmas or Easter because the Bible did not mention either one. They outlawed religious wedding ceremonies; couples were married by a magistrate in a civil ceremony (the first wedding in Massachusetts performed by a minister occurred in 1686). They prohibited elaborate clothing and finery such as lace trim and short sleeves — "whereby the nakedness of the

arm may be discovered." They banned cards, dice, shuffleboard, and other games of chance, as well as music and dancing. The distinguished minister Increase Mather insisted that "Mixt or Promiscuous Dancing . . . of Men and Women" could not be tolerated since "the unchaste Touches and Gesticulations used by Dancers have a palpable tendency to that which is evil." On special occasions, Puritans proclaimed days of fasting and humiliation, which, as one preacher boasted, amounted to "so many Sabbaths more."

Government by Puritans for Puritanism

It is only a slight exaggeration to say that seventeenth-century New England was governed by Puritans for Puritanism. The charter of the Massachusetts Bay Company empowered the company's stockholders, known as freemen, to meet as a body known as the General Court and make the laws needed to govern the company's affairs. The colonists transformed this arrangement for running a joint-stock company into a structure for governing

The space between the arms and seat of the great chair is solid wood, designed to block cold drafts and keep Metcalf relatively warm while he sat in the chair and read. What does the open space under the arms of the throne chair suggest about the clothing of the person who sat in it?

The carved wings that decorate the top of the back of Metcalf's chair symbolized the soul of a human being. The wings, combined with Metcalf's initials, the date 1652, and the large diamond, make the carving on the back of the great chair notably similar to the carving on New England gravestones. What might such symbolism have suggested to the carver and to Metcalf? How did the tombstone-like reference to human mortality relate to Puritanism? Does the throne chair also evoke mortality?

Imagine Metcalf sitting in his great chair and looking at the

European Throne Chair

throne chair. What might he have said about it and the ideas it represents? Likewise, imagine the owner of the throne chair sitting in it and observing the great chair. What might that person have said about the ideas represented by the great chair?

Neither the throne chair nor the great chair displays the Christian symbol of the cross or any other obvious sign of Christianity. What do you think accounts for that absence?

If the great chair hints at the importance of serious Bible study and unflinching introspection in Puritan New England, what major ideas in sixteenth-century Europe are suggested by the throne chair?

SOURCE: New England great chair: Dedham Historical Society/photo by Forrest Frasier; European throne chair: courtesy of Huntington Antiques Ltd., Gloucestershire, England.

the colony. Hoping to ensure that godly men would decide government policies, the General Court expanded the number of freemen in 1631 to include all male church members. Only freemen had the right to vote for governor, deputy governor, and other colonial officials. As new settlers were recognized as freemen, the size of the General Court grew too large to meet conveniently. So in 1634, the freemen in each town agreed to send two deputies to the General Court to act as the colony's legislative assembly. All other men were classified as "inhabitants," and they had the right to vote, hold office, and participate fully in town government.

A "town meeting," composed of a town's inhabitants and freemen, chose the selectmen and other officials who administered local affairs. New England town meetings routinely practiced a level of popular participation in political life that was unprecedented elsewhere in the world during the seventeenth century. Almost every adult man could speak out in town meetings and fortify his voice with a vote. However, all women — even church members — were prohibited from voting, and towns did not permit "contrary-minded" men to become or remain inhabitants. Although town meeting participants

wrangled from time to time, widespread political participation tended to reinforce conformity to Puritan ideals.

One of the most important functions of New England government was land distribution. Settlers who wanted to establish a new town entered a covenant and petitioned the General Court for a grant of land. The court granted town sites to suitably pious petitioners but did not allow settlement until the Indians who inhabited a grant agreed to relinquish their claim to the land, usually in exchange for manufactured goods. For instance, William Pynchon purchased the site of Springfield, Massachusetts, from the Agawam Indians for "eighteen fathams [arm's lengths] of Wampum [strings of shell-beads used in trade], eighteen coates, 18 hatchets, 18 hoes, [and] 18 knives."

Having obtained their grant, town founders apportioned land among themselves and any newcomers they permitted to join them. Normally, each family received a house lot large enough for an adjacent garden as well as one or more strips of agricultural land on the perimeter of the town. Although there was a considerable difference between the largest and smallest family plots, most clustered in the middle range — roughly

Old Ship Meeting House
Built in Hingham, Massachusetts, in 1681, this meeting house is one of the oldest surviving buildings used for church services in English North America. The unadorned walls and windows reflect the austere religious aesthetic of New England Puritanism. The family pews mark boundaries of kinship and piety visible to all. The elevated pulpit signals the superiority of God's word as preached by the minister. The open space in front of the pulpit suggests worshippers' unblocked access to biblical truth.
Old Ship Church, Hingham, MA, photo by Steve Dunwell.

fifty to one hundred acres — resulting in a more nearly equal distribution of land in New England than in the Chesapeake.

The physical layout of New England towns encouraged settlers to look inward toward their neighbors, multiplying the opportunities for godly vigilance. Most people considered the forest that lay just beyond every settler's house an alien environment that was interrupted here and there by those oases of civilization, the towns. Footpaths connecting one town to another were so rudimentary that even John Winthrop once got lost within half a mile of his house and spent a sleepless night in the forest, circling the light of his small campfire and singing psalms.

The Splintering of Puritanism

Almost from the beginning, John Winthrop and other leaders had difficulty enforcing their views of Puritan orthodoxy. In England, persecution as a dissenting minority had unified Puritan voices in opposition to the Church of England. In New England, the promise of a godly society and the Puritans' emphasis on individual Bible study led New Englanders toward different visions of godliness. Puritan leaders, however, interpreted dissent as an error caused either by a misguided believer or by the malevolent power of Satan. Whatever the cause, errors could not be tolerated. As one Puritan minister proclaimed, "The Scripture saith . . . there is no Truth but one."

Shortly after banishing **Roger Williams** (see pages 91–92), Winthrop confronted another dissenter, this time a devout Puritan woman steeped in Scripture and absorbed by religious questions: **Anne Hutchinson**. The mother of fourteen children, Hutchinson served her neighbors as a midwife. After she settled into her new home in Boston in 1634, women gathered there to hear her weekly lectures on recent sermons. As one listener observed, she was a "Woman that Preaches better Gospell then any of your blackcoates . . . [from] the Ninneversity." As the months passed, Hutchinson began to lecture twice a week, and crowds of sixty to eighty women and men assembled to listen to her.

Hutchinson expounded on the sermons of John Cotton, her favorite minister. Cotton stressed what he termed the "covenant of grace" — the idea that individuals could be saved only by God's grace in choosing them to be members of the elect. Cotton contrasted this familiar Puritan doctrine with the covenant of works, the erroneous belief that a person's behavior — one's works — could win God's favor and ultimately earn a person salvation. Belief in the covenant of works and in the possibility of salvation for all was known as **Arminianism**. Cotton's sermons strongly hinted that many Puritans, including ministers, embraced Arminianism, which claimed — falsely, Cotton declared — that human beings could influence God's will. Anne Hutchinson agreed with Cotton. Her lectures emphasized her opinion that many of the colony's leaders affirmed the Arminian covenant of works. Like Cotton, she preached that only God's covenant of grace led to salvation.

The meetings at Hutchinson's house alarmed her nearest neighbor, Governor John Winthrop, who believed that she was subverting the good order of the colony. In 1637, Winthrop had formal charges brought against Hutchinson and denounced her lectures as "not tolerable nor comely in the sight of God nor fitting for your sex." He told her, "You have stept out of your place, you have rather bine a Husband than a Wife and a preacher than a Hearer; and a Magistrate than a Subject."

In court, Winthrop interrogated Hutchinson, fishing for a heresy he could pin on her. Winthrop and other Puritan elders referred to Hutchinson and her followers as **antinomians**, people who believed that Christians could be saved by faith alone and did not need to act in accordance with God's law as set forth in the Bible and as interpreted by the colony's leaders. Hutchinson nimbly defended herself against the accusation of antinomianism. Yes, she acknowledged, she believed that men and women were saved by faith alone; but no, she did not deny the need to obey God's law. "The Lord hath let me see which was the clear ministry and which the wrong," she said. Finally, Winthrop had cornered her. How could she tell which ministry was which? "By an immediate revelation," she replied, "by the voice of [God's] own spirit to my soul." Winthrop spotted in this statement the heresy of prophecy, the view that God revealed his will directly to a believer instead of exclusively through the Bible, as every right-minded Puritan knew.

In 1638, the Boston church formally excommunicated Hutchinson. The minister decreed, "I doe cast you out and . . . deliver you up to Satan that you may learne no more to blaspheme[,] to seduce and to lye. . . . I command you . . . as a Leper to withdraw your selfe out of the Congregation." Banished, Hutchinson and her family moved first to Roger Williams's Rhode Island and then to present-day New York, where she and most of her family were killed by Indians.

The strains within Puritanism exemplified by Anne Hutchinson and Roger Williams caused communities to splinter repeatedly during the seventeenth century. **Thomas Hooker**, a prominent minister, clashed with Winthrop and other leaders over the composition of the church. Hooker argued that men and women who lived godly lives should be admitted to church membership even if they had not experienced conversion. This issue, like most others in New England, had both religious and political dimensions, for only church members could vote in Massachusetts. In 1636, Hooker led an exodus of more than eight hundred colonists from Massachusetts to the Connecticut River valley, where they founded Hartford and neighboring towns. In 1639, the towns adopted the Fundamental Orders of Connecticut, a quasi-constitution that could be altered by the vote of freemen, who did not have to be church members, though nearly all of them were.

Other Puritan churches divided and subdivided throughout the seventeenth century as acrimony developed over doctrine and church government. Sometimes churches split over the appointment of a controversial minister. Sometimes families who had a long walk to the meetinghouse simply decided to form their own church nearer their homes. These schisms arose from ambiguities and tensions within Puritan belief. As the colonies matured, other tensions developed as well.

Religious Controversies and Economic Changes

A revolutionary transformation in the fortunes of Puritans in England had profound consequences in New England. Disputes between King Charles I and Parliament, which was dominated by Puritans, escalated in 1642 to civil war in England, a conflict known as the **Puritan Revolution**. Parliamentary forces led by the staunch Puritan Oliver Cromwell were victorious, executing Charles I in 1649 and proclaiming England a Puritan republic. From 1649 to 1660, England's rulers were not monarchs who suppressed Puritanism but believers who championed it. In a half century, English Puritans had risen from a harassed group of religious dissenters to a dominant power in English government.

When the Puritan Revolution began, the stream of immigrants to New England dwindled to a trickle, creating hard times for the colonists. They could no longer consider themselves a city on a hill setting a godly example for humankind. Puritans in England, not New England, were reforming English society. Furthermore, when immigrant ships became rare, the colonists faced sky-high prices for scarce English goods and few customers for their own colonial products. As they searched to find new products and markets, they established the enduring patterns of New England's economy.

New England's rocky soil and short growing season ruled out cultivating the southern colonies' crops of tobacco and rice that found ready markets in Atlantic ports. Exports that New Englanders could not get from the soil they took instead from the forest and the sea. During the first decade of settlement, colonists traded with the Indians for animal pelts, which were in demand in Europe. By the 1640s, furbearing animals had become scarce unless traders ventured far beyond the frontiers of English settlement. Trees from the seemingly limitless forests of New England proved a longer-lasting resource. Masts for ships and staves for barrels of Spanish wine and West Indian sugar were crafted from New England timber.

The most important New England export was fish. During the turmoil of the Puritan Revolution, English ships withdrew from the rich North Atlantic fishing grounds, and New England fishermen quickly took their place. Dried, salted codfish found markets in southern Europe and the West Indies. The fish trade also stimulated colonial shipbuilding and trained generations of fishermen, sailors, and merchants, creating a commercial network that endured for more than a century. But this export econ-

omy remained peripheral to most New England colonists. Their lives revolved around their farms, their churches, and their families.

Although immigration came to a standstill in the 1640s, the population continued to boom, doubling every twenty years. In New England, almost everyone married, and women often had eight or nine children. Long, cold winters minimized the presence of warm-weather ailments such as malaria and yellow fever in the northern colonies, so the mortality rate was lower than in the South. The descendants of the immigrants of the 1630s multiplied, boosting the New England population to roughly equal that of the southern colonies (Figure 4.1).

During the second half of the seventeenth century, under the pressures of steady population growth and integration into the Atlantic economy, the red-hot piety of the founders cooled. After 1640, the population grew faster than church membership. All residents attended sermons on pain of fines and punishment, but many could not find seats in the meetinghouses. Boston's churches in 1650 could house only about a third of the city's residents. By the 1680s, women were the majority of church members throughout New England. In some towns, only 15 percent of the adult men were members. A growing fraction of New Englanders, especially men, embraced what one historian has termed "horse-shed Christianity": They attended sermons but loitered outside near the horse shed, gossiping about the weather, fishing, their crops, or the scandalous behavior of neighbors. This slackening of piety led the Puritan minister Michael Wigglesworth to ask, in verse:

> How is it that
> I find In stead of holiness Carnality;
> In stead of heavenly frames an Earthly mind,
> For burning zeal luke-warm Indifferency,
> For flaming love, key-cold Dead-heartedness. . . .
> Whence cometh it, that Pride, and Luxurie
> Debate, Deceit, Contention and Strife,
> False-dealing, Covetousness, Hypocrisie
> (With such Crimes) amongst them are so rife,
> That one of them doth over-reach another?
> And that an honest man can hardly
> Trust his Brother?

FIGURE 4.1 Population of the English North American Colonies in the Seventeenth Century The colonial population grew at a steadily accelerating rate during the seventeenth century. New England and the southern colonies each accounted for about half the total colonial population until after 1680, when growth in Pennsylvania and New York contributed to a surge in the population of the middle colonies.

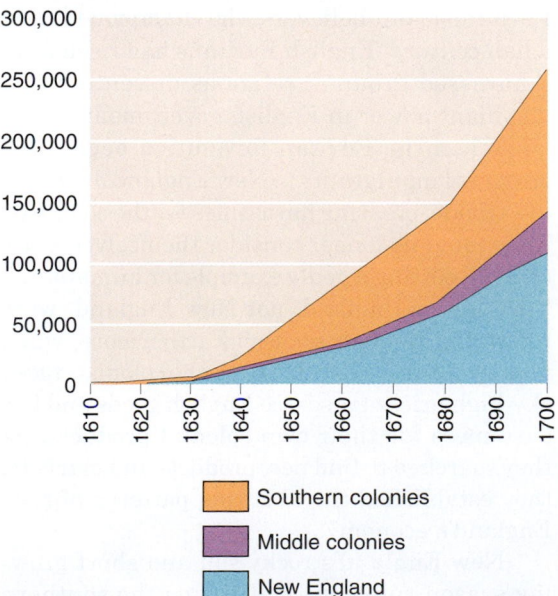

Most alarming to Puritan leaders, many of the children of the visible saints of Winthrop's generation failed to experience conversion and attain full church membership. Puritans tended

to assume that sainthood was inherited — that the children of visible saints were probably also among the elect. Acting on this premise, churches permitted saints to baptize their infant sons and daughters, symbolically cleansing them of their contamination with original sin. As these children grew up during the 1640s and 1650s, however, they seldom experienced the inward transformation that signaled conversion and qualification for church membership. The problem of declining church membership and the watering-down of Puritan orthodoxy became urgent during the 1650s when the children of saints, who had grown to adulthood in New England but had not experienced conversion, began to have children themselves. Their sons and daughters — the grandchildren of the founders of the colony — could not receive the protection that baptism afforded against the terrors of death because their parents had not experienced conversion.

Puritan churches debated what to do. To allow anyone, even the child of a saint, to become a church member without conversion was an unthinkable retreat from fundamental Puritan doctrine. In 1662, a synod of Massachusetts ministers reached a compromise known as the **Halfway Covenant**. Unconverted children of saints would be permitted to become "halfway" church members. Like regular church members, they could baptize their infants. But unlike full church members, they could not participate in communion or have the voting privileges of church membership. The Halfway Covenant generated a controversy that sputtered through Puritan churches for the remainder of the century. With the Halfway Covenant, Puritan churches came to terms with the lukewarm piety that had replaced the founders' burning zeal.

Nonetheless, New England communities continued to enforce piety with holy rigor. Beginning in 1656, small bands of **Quakers** — members of the Society of Friends, as they called themselves — began to arrive in Massachusetts. Many of their beliefs were at odds with orthodox Puritanism. Quakers believed that God spoke directly to each individual through an "inner light" and that individuals needed neither a preacher nor the Bible to discover God's Word. Maintaining that all human beings were equal in God's eyes, Quakers refused to conform to mere temporal powers such as laws and governments unless God requested otherwise. For example, Quakers refused to observe the Sabbath because, they insisted, God had not set aside any special day for worship, expecting believers to worship faithfully every day. Women often took a leading role in Quaker meetings, in contrast to Puritan congregations, where women usually outnumbered men but remained subordinate.

New England communities treated Quakers with ruthless severity. Some Quakers were branded on the face "with a red-hot iron with [an] H. for heresie." When Quakers refused to leave Massachusetts, Boston officials hanged four of them between 1659 and 1661.

New Englanders' partial success in realizing the promise of a godly society ultimately undermined the intense appeal of Puritanism. In the pious Puritan communities of New England, leaders tried to eliminate sin. In the process, they diminished the sense of utter

David, Joanna, and Abigail Mason
In this 1670 painting, which depicts the children of Bostonians Joanna and Anthony Mason, the artist lavished attention on the young subjects' elaborate clothing and adornments: fashionable slashed sleeves, fancy lace, silver-studded shoes, necklaces for the girls, and a silver-headed cane for the boy. The painting hints that the children themselves were adornments—young sprouts of the Mason lineage, which could afford such finery. Unified by trappings of wealth and sober self-importance, rather than by signs of warm affection, innocent smiles, and familial solidarity, the portrait expresses the growing respect for wealth and its worldly rewards in seventeenth-century New England.
Fine Arts Museums of San Francisco. Gift of Mr. and Mrs. John D. Rockefeller III.

Hunting Witches in Salem, Massachusetts

In the summer of 1692, many people in and around Salem, Massachusetts, accused dozens of their neighbors and kinfolk of being witches. Officials convened a special court to hear the testimony of the accusers and to examine the accused. In the end, nineteen convicted witches were hanged, and more than 150 accused witches crammed the jails before the trials were called off, in part because some people began to have doubts about whether the accused witches were truly guilty.

DOCUMENT 1
Cotton Mather, *Wonders of the Invisible World*, 1692

Cotton Mather, one of the most prominent Puritan ministers at the time, supported the trials and encouraged the witch-hunt, which he believed purged New England of the malicious handiwork of the devil. Mather summarized evidence of Satan's diabolical presence to explain and justify the need for the witch-hunt.

That the Devil, is *Come down unto us with great Wrath*, we find, we feel, we now deplore. . . . The *Devil*, Exhibiting himself ordinarily as a small *Black man*, has decoy'd a fearful Knot of Proud, Froward, Ignorant, Envious, and Malicious Creatures, to Lift themselves in his Horrid Service, by Entering their Names in a Book by him Tendered unto them. These *Witches* . . . have met in Hellish *Randezvouzes*, wherein . . . they have had their Diabolical Sacraments, imitating the *Baptism* and the *Supper* of our Lord. In these Hellish Meetings, these Monsters have associated themselves to do no less a Thing than, *To Destroy the Kingdom of our Lord Jesus Christ, in these parts of the World*. . . . These wicked Spectres, or *Devils*, . . . Seize poor people about the Country with Various and bloody *Torments*. . . . The People thus Afflicted, are miserably Scratched and Bitten, so that the Marks are most *Visible* to all the World, but the causes utterly *Invisible*; and the same *Invisible* Furies, do most *Visibly* stick *Pins* into the Bodies of the Afflicted, and *Scald* them, & hideously Distort, and Disjoint all their members. . . . Yea, they sometimes drag the poor People out of their Chambers, and Carry them over *Trees* and *Hills*, for diverse Miles together. A large part of the Persons tortured by these Diabolical *Spectres*, are horribly Tempted by them . . . to sign the *Devils Laws*, in a Spectral *Book* laid before them. . . .

SOURCE: Cotton Mather, *The Wonders of the Invisible World* (Boston, 1692), 48–50.

DOCUMENT 2
Witnesses against Accused Witch Susanna Martin, 1692

Neighbors lined up to give testimony that, in their minds, proved that the accused were witches. Like many other accused people, Susanna Martin pleaded not guilty to witchcraft. The court, persuaded by the testimony of witnesses like the following, sentenced her to death, and she was executed on July 19, 1692.

Bernard Peache testify'd, That being in Bed on a Lords-day Night, he heard a scrabbling at the Window, whereat he then saw, *Susanna Martin* come in, and jump down upon the Floor. She took hold of this Deponents Feet, and drawing his Body up into an Heap, she lay upon him, near Two Hours; in all which time he could neither speak nor stirr. At length, when he could begin to move, he laid hold on her Hand, and pulling it up to his mouth, he bit three of her Fingers, as he judged, unto the Bone. Whereupon she went from the Chamber, down the Stairs, out at the Door. . . .

    John Kembal . . . Being desirous to furnish himself with a Dog, he applied himself to buy one of this Martin. . . . But she not letting him have his Choice [Kembal went to another neighbor to get a puppy]. Within a few days after, [when] this *Kembal* . . . came below the Meeting-House, there appeared unto him, a little thing like a *Puppy*, of a Darkish Colour; and it shot Backwards and forwards between his Leggs. He had the Courage to use all possible Endeavors of Cutting it, with his Axe; but he could not Hit it; the Puppy gave a jump from him, and went, as to him, it seem'd into the Ground. Going a little further, there

appeared unto him a Black Puppy, somewhat bigger than the first; but Black as Cole. Its motions were quicker than those of his Ax; it Flew at his Belly and away; then at his Throat, also over his Shoulder. . . . His heart now began to fail him, and he thought the Dog would have Tore his Throat out. But he recovered himself, and called upon God in his Distress; and Naming the Name of JESUS CHRIST, it Vanished away at once. . . . [The next day, Susanna Martin told other people that he had been frightened by puppies, although] Kembal [said he] had mentioned the Matter to no Creature Living.

Joseph Ring . . . has been strangely carried about by *Demons,* from one *Witch-Meeting* to another, for near two years together; and for one Quarter of this Time, they have made him, and kept him Dumb, tho he is now again able to speak. . . . Afterwards . . . this poor man would be visited with unknown shapes . . . which would force him away with them, unto unknown Places, where he saw meetings, Feastings, Dancings. . . . When he was brought into these Hellish meetings, one of the First things they still did unto him, was to give him a knock on the Back, whereupon he was ever as if Bound with chains, uncapable of Stirring out of the place, till they should Release him. . . . There often came to him a man, who presented him a Book, whereto he would have him set his Hand; promising to him, that he should then have even what he would; and presenting him with all the delectable Things, persons, and places that he could imagine. But he refusing to subscribe, the business would end with dreadful Shapes, Noises and Screechings, which almost scared him out of his witts. . . . This man did now affirm, that he saw the Prisoner [Susanna Martin], at several of those Hellish Randezvouzes. Note, This Woman was one of the most Impudent, Scurrilous, wicked creatures in the world & she did now throughout her whole Trial, discover herself to be such an one. Yet when she was asked what she had to say for her self, her Cheef Plea was, *That she had Led a most virtuous and Holy Life.*

SOURCE: Cotton Mather, *The Wonders of the Invisible World* (Boston, 1692), 115–26.

DOCUMENT 3
Robert Calef, *More Wonders of the Invisible World*, 1700

A few New Englanders spoke out against the witch-hunt as the persecution of innocent people. Robert Calef, a Boston merchant, wrote a scathing criticism of the witch trials and their supporters, such as Cotton Mather. Printers in New England refused to publish Calef's book, which was eventually published in London.

And now to sum up all in a few words, we have seen a biggotted zeal, stirring up a blind, and most bloody rage, not against enemies, or irreligious, profligate persons— but . . . against as virtuous and religious as any they have left behind them in this country, which have suffered as evil doers . . . and this by the testimony of vile varlets, as not only were known before, but have been further apparent since, by their manifest lives, whoredoms, incest &c. The accusations of these, from their spectral sight, being the chief evidence against those that suffered; in which accusations they were upheld by both magistrates and ministers, so long as they apprehended themselves in no danger. And then, tho' they could defend neither the doctrine nor the practice, yet none of them have in such a publick manner as the case requires, testified against either; tho', at the same time they could not but be sensible what a stain and lasting infamy they have brought upon the whole country, to the indangering of the future welfare not only of this but of other places, induced by their example . . . occasioning the great dishonour and blasphemy of the name of God, scandalizing the Heathen, hardening of enemies; and as a natural effect thereof, to the great increase of Atheism.

SOURCE: Robert Calef, *More Wonders of the Invisible World* (London, 1700), unpaginated "Epistle to the Reader."

Questions for Analysis and Debate

1. According to Cotton Mather, why was the devil dangerous? How did the devil operate in New England? What was the significance of Mather's emphasis that invisible "Furies" could inflict visible injuries?

2. What persuaded witnesses against Susanna Martin that she was a witch? How might a critic such as Robert Calef have responded to the testimony of these witnesses? How might Cotton Mather and these witnesses have explained Martin's claim that she led "a most virtuous and Holy Life"?

3. What do these documents suggest about the status of Christianity in New England in the late seventeenth century? Why did Mather and the witch-hunters believe that the devil was such a threat, when Calef believed that the witch-hunters themselves were the greater danger?

Storage Chest
This painted storage chest made in Hadley, Massachusetts, reflects late-seventeenth-century New Englanders' delight in color and ornament, in contrast to the plain and simple styles favored by their early-seventeenth-century predecessors. The initials "SW" likely refer to the first owner of the chest, probably the daughter of a proud father who had the chest made for SW's upcoming marriage. SW would have used the chest to store textiles, another indication that by the late seventeenth century, prosperous New England families owned more than they required for daily use and needed a place to store the surplus.
Pocumtuck Valley Memorial Association Memorial Hall Museum.

human depravity that was the wellspring of Puritanism. By 1700, New Englanders did not doubt that human beings sinned, but they were more concerned with the sins of others than with their own.

Witch trials held in Salem, Massachusetts, signaled the erosion of religious confidence and assurance. From the beginning of English settlement in the New World, more than 95 percent of all legal accusations of witchcraft occurred in New England, a hint of the Puritans' preoccupation with sin and evil. The most notorious witchcraft trials took place in Salem in 1692, when witnesses accused more than one hundred people of witchcraft, a capital crime. (See "Documenting the American Promise," page 106.) Bewitched young girls shrieked in pain, their limbs twisted into strange contortions, as they pointed out the witches who tortured them. According to the trial court record, the bewitched girls declared that "the shape of [one accused witch] did oftentimes very grievously pinch them, choke them, bite them, and afflict them; urging them to write their names in a book" — the devil's book. Most of the accused witches were older women, and virtually all of them were well known to their accusers. The Salem court hanged nineteen accused witches and pressed one to death, signaling enduring belief in the supernatural origins of evil and gnawing doubt about the strength of Puritan New Englanders' faith. Why else, after all, had so many New Englanders succumbed to what their accusers and the judges believed were the temptations of Satan?

REVIEW   Why did Massachusetts Puritans adopt the Halfway Covenant?

Witches Show Their Love for Satan
Mocking pious Christians' humble obeisance to God, witches willingly debased themselves by standing in line to kneel and kiss Satan's buttocks — or so it was popularly believed. This seventeenth-century print portrays Satan with clawlike hands and feet, the tail of a rodent, the wings of a bat, and the head of a lustful ram attached to the torso of a man. Notice that women predominate among the witches eager to express their devotion to Satan and to do his bidding. UCSF Library/Center for Knowledge Management.

MAP 4.2

Middle Colonies in the Seventeenth Century
For the most part, the middle colonies in the seventeenth century were inhabited by settlers who clustered along the Hudson and Delaware rivers. The vast geographic extent of the colonies shown in this map reflects land grants authorized in England. Most of this area was inhabited by Native Americans rather than settled by colonists.

▶ The Founding of the Middle Colonies

South of New England and north of the Chesapeake, a group of middle colonies were founded in the last third of the seventeenth century. Before the 1670s, few Europeans settled in the region. For the first two-thirds of the seventeenth century, the most important European outpost in the area was the relatively small Dutch colony of New Netherland. By 1700, however, the English monarchy had seized New Netherland, renamed it New York, and encouraged the creation of a Quaker colony in Pennsylvania led by William Penn. Unlike the New England colonies, the middle colonies of New York, New Jersey, and Pennsylvania originated as land grants by the English monarch to one or more proprietors, who then possessed both the land and the extensive, almost monarchical, powers of government (Map 4.2). These middle colonies attracted settlers of more diverse European origins and religious faiths than were found in New England.

From New Netherland to New York

In 1609, the Dutch East India Company dispatched Henry Hudson to search for a Northwest Passage to the Orient. Hudson sailed along the Atlantic coast and ventured up the large river that now bears his name until it dwindled to a stream that obviously did not lead to China. A decade later, the Dutch government granted the West India Company — a group of Dutch merchants and shippers — exclusive rights to trade with the Western Hemisphere. In 1626, Peter Minuit, the resident director of the company, purchased Manhattan Island from the Manhate Indians for trade goods worth the equivalent of a dozen beaver pelts. New Amsterdam, the small settlement established at the southern tip of Manhattan Island, became the principal trading center in **New Netherland** and the colony's headquarters.

Unlike the English colonies, New Netherland did not attract many European immigrants. Like New England and the Chesapeake colonies, New Netherland never realized its sponsors' dreams of great profits. The company tried to stimulate immigration by granting patroonships — allotments of eighteen miles of land along the Hudson River — to wealthy stockholders who would bring fifty families to the colony and settle them as serflike tenants on their huge domains. Only one patroonship succeeded; the others failed to attract settlers, and the company eventually recovered much of the land.

Though few in number, New Netherlanders were remarkably diverse, especially compared with the homogeneous English settlers to the north and south. Religious dissenters and immigrants from Holland, Sweden, France, Germany, and elsewhere made their way to the colony. A minister of the Dutch Reformed Church complained to his superiors in Holland that several groups of Jews had recently arrived, adding to the religious mixture of "Papists, Mennonites and Lutherans among the Dutch [and] many Puritans . . . and many other atheists . . . who conceal themselves under the name of Christians."

The West India Company struggled to govern the motley colonists. Peter Stuyvesant, governor from 1647 to 1664, tried to enforce conformity to the Dutch Reformed Church, but the company declared that "the consciences of men should be free and unshackled," making a virtue

> **"In souls there is no sex."**
> — Quaker saying about the religious equality of men and women

New Amsterdam
The settlement on Manhattan Island — complete with a windmill — appears in the background of this 1673 Dutch portrait of New Amsterdam. In the foreground, the Dutch artist placed native inhabitants of the mainland, drawing them to resemble Africans rather than Lenni Lenape (Delaware) Indians. The artist probably had never seen Indians and depended on well-known artistic conventions about the appearance of Africans to create his Native Americans. The portrait contrasts orderly, efficient, business-like New Amsterdam with the exotic natural environment of America, to which the native woman on the left clings. © Collection of the New-York Historical Society.

of New Netherland necessity. The company never permitted the colony's settlers to form a representative government. Instead, the company appointed government officials who established policies, including taxes, that many colonists deeply resented.

In 1664, New Netherland became New York. Charles II, who became king of England in 1660 when Parliament restored the monarchy, gave his brother James, the Duke of York, an enormous grant of land that included New Netherland. Of course, the Dutch colony did not belong to the king of England, but that legal technicality did not deter the king or his brother. The duke quickly organized a small fleet of warships, which

appeared off Manhattan Island in late summer 1664, and demanded that Stuyvesant surrender. With little choice, he did.

As the new proprietor of the colony, the Duke of York exercised almost the same unlimited authority over the colony as had the West India Company. The duke never set foot in New York, but his governors struggled to impose order on the unruly colonists. Like the Dutch, the duke permitted "all persons of what Religion soever, quietly to inhabit . . . provided they give no disturbance to the publique peace, nor doe molest or disquiet others in the free exercise of their religion." This policy of religious toleration was less an affirmation of liberty of conscience than a recognition

William Penn
This portrait was drawn about a decade after the founding of Pennsylvania. At a time when extravagant clothing and a fancy wig proclaimed that the wearer was important, Penn is portrayed informally, lacking even a coat, his natural hair neat but undressed — all a reflection of his Quaker faith. Penn's full face and double chin show that his faith did not make him a stranger to the pleasures of the table. No hollow-cheeked ascetic or wild-eyed enthusiast, Penn appears sober and observant. The portrait captures the calm determination — anchored in faith — that inspired Penn's hopes for his new colony. Historical Society of Pennsylvania.

Unlike most Quakers, William Penn came from an eminent family. His father had served both Cromwell and Charles II and had been knighted. Born in 1644, the younger Penn trained for a military career, but the ideas of dissenters from the reestablished Church of England appealed to him, and he became a devout Quaker. By 1680, he had published fifty books and pamphlets and spoken at countless public meetings, although he had not won official toleration for Quakers in England.

The Quakers' concept of an open, generous God who made his love equally available to all people manifested itself in behavior that continually brought them into conflict with the English government. Quaker leaders were ordinary men and women, not specially trained preachers. Quakers allowed women to assume positions of religious leadership. "In souls there is no sex," they said. Since all people were equal in the spiritual realm, Quakers considered social hierarchy false and evil. They called everyone "friend" and shook hands instead of curtsying or removing their hats — even when meeting the king. These customs enraged many non-Quakers and provoked innumerable beatings and worse. Penn was jailed four times for such offenses, once for nine months.

Despite his many run-ins with the government, Penn remained on good terms with Charles II. Partly to rid England of the troublesome Quakers, in 1681 Charles made Penn the proprietor of a new colony of some 45,000 square miles called Pennsylvania.

of the reality of the most heterogeneous colony in seventeenth-century North America.

New Jersey and Pennsylvania

The creation of New York led indirectly to the founding of two other middle colonies, New Jersey and Pennsylvania (see Map 4.2). In 1664, the Duke of York subdivided his grant and gave the portion between the Hudson and Delaware rivers to two of his friends. The proprietors of this new colony, New Jersey, quarreled and called in a prominent English Quaker, **William Penn**, to arbitrate their dispute. Penn eventually worked out a settlement that continued New Jersey's proprietary government. In the process, Penn became intensely interested in what he termed a "holy experiment" of establishing a genuinely Quaker colony in America.

Toleration and Diversity in Pennsylvania

Quakers flocked to Pennsylvania in numbers exceeded only by the great Puritan migration to New England fifty years earlier. Between 1682 and 1685, nearly eight thousand immigrants arrived, most of them from England, Ireland, and Wales. They represented a cross section of the artisans, farmers, and laborers who predominated among English Quakers. Quaker missionaries also encouraged immigrants from the European continent, and many came, giving Pennsylvania greater ethnic diversity than any other English colony except New York. The Quaker colony prospered, and the capital city, Philadelphia, soon rivaled New York as a center of commerce. By 1700, the city's five thousand inhabitants participated in a thriving trade exporting flour and other food products to the West Indies and importing English textiles and manufactured goods.

Penn was determined to live in peace with the Indians who inhabited the region. His Indian policy expressed his Quaker ideals and contrasted sharply with the hostile policies of the other English colonies. As he explained to the chief of the Lenni Lenape (Delaware) Indians, "God has written his law in our hearts, by which we are taught and commanded to love and help and do good to one another . . . [and] I desire to enjoy [Pennsylvania lands] with your love and consent." Penn instructed his agents to obtain the Indians' consent by purchasing their land, respecting their claims, and dealing with them fairly.

Penn declared that the first principle of government was that every settler would "enjoy the free possession of his or her faith and exercise of worship towards God." Accordingly, Pennsylvania tolerated Protestant sects of all kinds as well as Roman Catholicism. All voters and officeholders had to be Christians, but the government did not compel settlers to attend religious services, as in Massachusetts, or to pay taxes to maintain a state-supported church, as in Virginia.

Despite its toleration and diversity, Pennsylvania was as much a Quaker colony as New England was a stronghold of Puritanism. Penn had no hesitation about using civil government to enforce religious morality. One of the colony's first laws provided severe punishment for "all such offenses against God, as swearing, cursing, lying, profane talking, drunkenness, drinking of healths, [and] obscene words . . . which excite the people to rudeness, cruelty, looseness, and irreligion."

As proprietor, Penn had extensive powers subject only to review by the king. He appointed a governor, who maintained the proprietor's power to veto any laws passed by the colonial council, which was elected by property owners who possessed at least one hundred acres of land or who paid taxes. The council had the power to originate laws and administer all the affairs of government. A popularly elected assembly served as a check on the council; its members had the authority to reject or approve laws framed by the council.

Penn stressed that the exact form of government mattered less than the men who served in it. In Penn's eyes, "good men" staffed Pennsylvania's government because Quakers dominated elective and appointive offices. Quakers, of course, differed among themselves. Members of the assembly struggled to win the right to debate and amend laws, especially tax laws. They finally won the battle in 1701 when a new Charter of Privileges gave the proprietor the power to appoint the council and in turn stripped the council of all its former powers and gave them to the assembly, which became the only single-house legislature in all the English colonies.

REVIEW How did Quaker ideals shape the colony of Pennsylvania?

▶ The Colonies and the English Empire

Proprietary grants to faraway lands were a cheap way for the king to reward friends. As the colonies grew, however, the grants became more valuable. After 1660, the king took initiatives to channel colonial trade through English hands and to consolidate royal authority over colonial governments. Occasioned by such economic and political considerations and triggered by King Philip's War between colonists and Native Americans, these initiatives defined the basic relationship between the colonies and England that endured until the American Revolution (Map 4.3).

Royal Regulation of Colonial Trade

English economic policies toward the colonies were designed to yield customs revenues for the monarchy and profitable business for English merchants and shippers. Also, the policies were intended to divert the colonies' trade from England's enemies, especially the Dutch and the French.

The Navigation Acts of 1650, 1651, 1660, and 1663 (see chapter 3) set forth two fundamental rules governing colonial trade. First, goods shipped to and from the colonies had to be transported in English ships using primarily English crews. Second, the Navigation Acts listed ("enumerated," in the language of the time) colonial products that could be shipped only to England or to other English colonies. While these regulations prevented Chesapeake planters from shipping their tobacco directly to the European continent, they interfered less with the commerce of New England and the middle colonies, whose principal exports — fish, lumber, and flour — were not enumerated and could legally be sent directly to their most important markets in the West Indies.

MAP ACTIVITY

Map 4.3 American Colonies at the End of the Seventeenth Century
By the end of the seventeenth century, settlers inhabited a narrow band of land that stretched more or less continuously from Boston to Norfolk, with pockets of settlement farther south. The colonies' claims to enormous tracts of land to the west were contested by Native Americans as well as by France and Spain.

READING THE MAP: What geographic feature acted as the western boundary for colonial territorial claims? Which colonies were the most settled and which the least?
CONNECTIONS: The map divides the colonies into four regions. Can you think of an alternative organization? On what criteria would it be based?

By the end of the seventeenth century, colonial commerce was defined by regulations that subjected merchants and shippers to royal supervision and gave them access to markets throughout the English empire. In addition, colonial commerce received protection from the English navy. By 1700, colonial goods (including those from the West Indies) accounted for one-fifth of all English imports and for two-thirds of all goods re-exported from England to the European continent. In turn, the colonies absorbed more than one-tenth of English exports. The commercial regulations gave economic value to England's proprietorship of the American colonies.

Beaver

North American beaver, shown here in a drawing from New France, became avidly hunted and trapped during the seventeenth century. Beaver populations in Europe, especially in Russia, had become badly depleted from overtrapping, although the demand for beaver pelts remained strong, providing an eager market for North American fur traders. Merchants and manufacturers prized beaver pelts because the fur could be shaved from the skin and felted — that is pressed together into a dense mat that was soft, warm, somewhat water repellent, and useful for making hats, like the one shown here. Drawing: Gilcrease Museum, Tulsa, Oklahoma; hat: Private collection. Image courtesy of Pilgrim Hall Museum, Plymouth, Massachusetts.

> **"[It was a] solemn sight to see so many Christians lying in their blood . . . like a company of sheep torn by wolves. All of them stripped naked by a company of hell-hounds, roaring, singing, ranting and insulting."**
>
> — MARY ROWLANDSON, describing an Indian attack

King Philip's War and the Consolidation of Royal Authority

The monarchy also took steps to exercise greater control over colonial governments. Virginia had been a royal colony since 1624; Maryland, South Carolina, and the middle colonies were proprietary colonies with close ties to the crown. The New England colonies possessed royal charters, but they had developed their own distinctively Puritan governments. Charles II, whose father, Charles I, had been executed by Puritans in England, took a particular interest in harnessing the New England colonies more firmly to the English empire. The occasion was a royal investigation following **King Philip's War**.

A series of skirmishes in the Connecticut River valley between 1636 and 1637 culminated in the Pequot War when colonists massacred hundreds of Pequot Indians. In the decades that followed, New Englanders established relatively peaceful relations with the more potent Wampanoags, but they steadily encroached on Indian land. In 1642, a native leader urged warring tribes to band together against the English. "We [must]

be one as they [the English] are," he said; "otherwise we shall be gone shortly, for our fathers had plenty of deer and skins . . . but these English having gotten our land, they with scythes cut down the grass, and with axes fell the trees, and their cows and horses eat the grass, and their hogs spoil our clam banks, and we shall all be starved."

Such grievances accumulated until 1675, when the Wampanoags attacked English settlements in western Massachusetts. Metacomet — the chief of t h e Wampanoags (and son of Massasoit), whom the colonists called King Philip — probably neither planned the attacks nor masterminded a conspiracy with the Nipmucs and the Narragansetts, as the colonists feared. But when militias from Massachusetts and other New England colonies counterattacked all three tribes, a deadly sequence of battles killed more than a thousand colonists and thousands more Indians.

The Indians destroyed thirteen English settlements and partially burned another half dozen. Mary Rowlandson, a minister's wife in Lancaster, Massachusetts, who was captured by Indians after her relatives were killed and wounded, recalled later that it was a "solemn sight to see so many Christians lying in their blood . . . like a company of sheep torn by wolves. All of them stripped naked by a company of hell-hounds, roaring, singing, ranting and insulting, as if they would have torn our very hearts out."

King Philip's War, 1675

MASSACHUSETTS
Boston
NIPMUCK
MASSACHUSET
Plymouth
Hartford
PEQUOT
NARRAGANSETT
POCASSET
WAMPANOAG
Thames
NAUSET
CONNECTICUT
MOHEGAN
SAKONNET
New Haven
RHODE ISLAND

◆ Indian settlement
◆ English settlement attacked

Wampanoag War Club

This seventeenth-century war club was used to kill King Philip, according to the Anglican missionary who obtained it from Indians early in the eighteenth century. Although the missionary's tale is probably a legend, the club is certainly a seventeenth-century Wampanoag weapon that might well have been used in King Philip's War. The heavy ball carved into the head of the club could deliver a disabling, even fatal, blow. Unlike a bow and arrow, the club needed to be wielded at very close range. For this reason, it was most useful against a wounded or utterly unaware enemy. Courtesy of the Fruitlands Museums, Harvard, Massachusetts.

By the spring of 1676, Indian warriors ranged freely within seventeen miles of Boston. The colonists finally defeated the Indians, principally with a scorched-earth policy of burning their food supplies. But King Philip's War left the New England colonists with a large war debt, a devastated frontier, and an enduring hatred of Indians. "A Swarm of Flies, they may arise, a Nation to Annoy," a colonial officer wrote in justification of destroying the Indians, "Yea Rats and Mice, or Swarms of Lice a Nation may destroy." And in 1676, an agent of the king arrived to investigate whether New England was abiding by English laws.

Not surprisingly, the king's agent found all sorts of deviations from English rules, and the monarchy decided to govern New England more directly. In 1684, an English court revoked the Massachusetts charter, the foundation of the distinctive Puritan government. Two years later, royal officials incorporated Massachusetts and the other colonies north of Maryland into the **Dominion of New England**. To govern the dominion, the English sent Sir **Edmund Andros** to Boston. Some New England merchants cooperated with Andros, but most colonists were offended by his flagrant disregard of such Puritan tradi-

tions as keeping the Sabbath. Worst of all, the Dominion of New England invalidated all land titles, confronting every landowner in New England with the horrifying prospect of losing his or her land.

Events in England, however, permitted Massachusetts colonists to overthrow Andros and retain title to their property. When Charles II died in 1685, he was succeeded by his brother James II, a zealous Catholic. James's aggressive campaign to appoint Catholics to government posts engendered such unrest that in 1688 a group of Protestant noblemen in Parliament invited the Dutch ruler William III of Orange, James's son-in-law, to claim the English throne.

When William III landed in England at the head of a large army, James fled to France, and William III and his wife, Mary II (James's daughter), became co-rulers in the relatively bloodless "Glorious Revolution," reasserting Protestant influence in England and its empire. Rumors of the revolution raced across the Atlantic and emboldened colonial uprisings against royal authority in Massachusetts, New York, and Maryland.

In Boston in 1689, rebels tossed Andros and other English officials in jail, destroyed the Dominion of New England, and reestablished the former charter government. New Yorkers followed the Massachusetts example. Under the leadership of Jacob Leisler, rebels seized the royal governor in 1689 and ruled the colony for more than a year. That same year in Maryland, the Protestant Association, led by John Coode, overthrew the colony's pro-Catholic government, fearing it would not recognize the new Protestant king.

John Sheldon's Snowshoes

John Sheldon, a resident of Deerfield, Massachusetts — first settled by colonists in 1669 — wore these snowshoes to rescue more than one hundred colonists taken hostage by the French and their Indian allies during the Deerfield Raid of 1704. The design of snowshoes, which colonists in 1666 called "a Rackett tyed to each foote," was adopted from the Native Americans, who had used them for centuries. Pocumtuck Valley Memorial Association Memorial Hall Museum.

New France and the Indians: The English Colonies' Northern Borderlands

North of New England, French explorers, traders, and missionaries carved out a distinctive North American colony that contrasted, competed, and periodically fought with the English colonies to the south.

The explorer Jacques Cartier sailed into the St. Lawrence River in 1535 and claimed the region for France. Cartier's attempts to found a permanent colony failed, but French ships followed in his wake and began to trade with Native Americans for wild animal pelts. By the time King Louis XIV made New France a royal colony in 1663, the fur trade had become the colony's economic foundation.

The French monarchy hoped to channel the fur trade through French hands into the broader European market and to compete against rival Dutch traders, whose headquarters at Albany (in what is now New York) funneled North American furs down the Hudson River to markets in the Netherlands. The crown also hoped the fur trade would allow the creation of a North American colony on the cheap.

The fur trade required little investment other than the construction and staffing of trading outposts at Quebec, Montreal, and elsewhere. In exchange for textiles and various metal trade goods, the Iroquois, Huron, Ottawa, Ojibwa, and other Native Americans did the arduous, time-consuming, and labor-intensive work of tracking, trapping, and skinning the animals and transporting the pelts — usually by canoe — to French traders. Unlike the English colonies, which attracted numerous settlers to engage in agriculture and produce food as well as valuable export crops, New France needed only a few colonists to keep the trading posts open and to maintain friendly relations with their Indian suppliers. By 1660, English colonists in North America outnumbered their French counterparts by more than twenty to one.

After England seized control of New York in 1664, English fur traders replaced the Dutch at Albany and eagerly competed to divert the northern fur trade away from New France. By then, the Iroquois — strategically located between the supply of furs to the north and west, New France to the east, and New York to the south — had become middlemen, collecting pelts from Huron, Ottawa, and other Indians and swapping them with French or English traders, depending on who offered the better deal. Able to mobilize scores of fierce warriors to threaten European traders as well as their Indian suppliers, the Iroquois managed to play the French and English off against each other and to maintain a near choke hold on the supply of furs.

Native Americans preferred English trade goods, which tended to be of higher quality and less expensive than those available at French outposts, but New France cultivated better relationships with the Indians. When English colonists had the required military strength, they seldom hesitated to kill Indians, especially those who occupied land the colonists craved. The small number of colonists in New France never had as much military power as the English colonists; hence, they sought to stay on relatively peaceful and friendly terms with the Indians. French men commonly married or cohabited with Indian women, an outgrowth of both the shortage of French women among the colonists and the acceptance of such couplings, compared with the strong taboo prevalent in the English colonies.

But these rebel governments did not last. When King William III's governor of New York arrived in 1691, he executed Leisler for treason. Coode's men ruled Maryland until the new royal governor arrived in 1692 and ended both Coode's rebellion and Lord Baltimore's proprietary government. In Massachusetts, John Winthrop's city on a hill became another royal colony in 1691. The new charter said that the governor of the colony would be appointed by the king rather than elected by the colonists' representatives. But perhaps the most unsettling change was the new qualification for voting. Possession of property replaced church membership as a prerequisite for voting in colony-wide elections. Wealth

Jesuit missionaries led the spiritual colonization of New France. Zealous enemies of what they considered Protestant heresies and stout defenders of Catholicism, the Jesuits fanned out to Indian villages throughout New France, determined to convert the Native Americans and to preserve the colony as a Catholic stronghold. Unwittingly, the missionaries also spread European diseases among the Native Americans, repeatedly causing deadly epidemics. Above all, the missionaries worked hand in hand with the fur traders and royal officials to make New France a low-cost Catholic colony on the thinly defended borders of the predominantly Protestant English colonies.

To extend the boundaries of New France far to the west and south, almost encircling the English colonies along the Atlantic coast, royal officials in 1673 sponsored a voyage by the explorer Louis Jolliet and the priest Jacques Marquette to explore the vast interior of the North American continent by canoeing down the Mississippi River to what is now Arkansas. Jolliet and Marquette made grandiose claims to the Mississippi valley, but in reality these claims amounted to little more than a colored patch on European maps. The dominant military power in New France remained the Iroquois, not the French.

England and France clashed repeatedly in North America over the fur trade and in a colonial

La pesche des Sauuages

Indians in New France
Native Americans used canoes as the most efficient form of transportation on waterways throughout North America. Heavy bundles of animal pelts, for example, were carried long distances from a remote trapping region to a fur trading post in canoes. This seventeenth-century drawing from New France illustrates Native Americans' "very amazing" skills in handling a canoe, in this case by standing up while netting and spearing fish. The figure on the right appears to be playing a flute, perhaps to attract fish. Why do you think the artist was so fascinated with the fishermen's tattoos and body paint? Gilcrease Museum, Tulsa, Oklahoma.

extension of their rivalry at home. European conflict between France and England spread to North America during King William's War (1689–1697), when the colonists and their Indian allies carried out numerous deadly raids, marking the contested boundary between New France and the English colonies as a bloody zone controlled by none of its claimants or inhabitants.

America in a Global Context

1. In what ways did New France reflect the colonial objectives of the French monarchy?

2. How did New France differ from the English colonies in seventeenth-century North America?

3. How did European rivalries influence the encounters of Indians with French and English colonists?

replaced God's grace as the defining characteristic of Massachusetts citizenship.

Much as colonists chafed under increasing royal control, they still valued English protection from hostile neighbors. Colonists worried that the Catholic colony of New France menaced frontier regions by encouraging Indian raids and by competing for the lucrative fur trade. (See "Beyond America's Borders," page 116.) Although French leaders tried to buttress the military strength of New France during the last third of the seventeenth century to block the expansion of the English colonies, most of the military efforts mustered by New France focused on defending against attacks by the powerful Iroquois. However, when the English colonies were distracted by the

Glorious Revolution, French forces from the fur-trading regions along the Great Lakes and in Canada attacked villages in New England and New York. Known as King William's War, the conflict with the French was a colonial outgrowth of William's war against France in Europe. The war dragged on until 1697 and ended inconclusively in both Europe and the colonies. But it made clear to many colonists that along with English royal government came a welcome measure of military security.

REVIEW Why did the Glorious Revolution in England lead to uprisings in the American colonies?

▶ Conclusion: An English Model of Colonization in North America

By 1700, the northern English colonies of North America had developed along lines quite different from the example set by their southern counterparts. Emigrants came with their families and created settlements unlike the scattered plantations and largely male environment of early Virginia. Puritans in New England built towns and governments around their churches and placed worship of God, not tobacco, at the center of their society. They depended chiefly on the labor of family members rather than on that of servants and slaves.

The convictions of Puritanism that motivated John Winthrop and others to reinvent England in the colonies became muted, however, as New England matured and dissenters such as Roger Williams multiplied. Catholics, Quakers, Anglicans (members of the Church of England), Jews, and others settled in the middle and southern colonies, creating considerable religious toleration, especially in Pennsylvania and New York. At the same time, northern colonists, like their southern counterparts, developed an ever-increasing need for land that inevitably led to bloody conflict with the Indians who were displaced.

During the next century, the English colonial world would undergo surprising new developments built on the achievements of the seventeenth century. Immigrants from Scotland, Ireland, and Germany streamed into North America, and unprecedented numbers of African slaves poured into the southern colonies. On average, white colonists attained a relatively comfortable standard of living, especially compared with most people in England and continental Europe. While religion remained important, the intensity of religious concern that characterized the seventeenth century waned during the eighteenth century. Colonists worried more about prosperity than about providence, and their societies grew increasingly secular, worldly, and diverse.

▶ Selected Bibliography

General Works

Virginia DeJohn Anderson, *Creatures of Empire: How Domestic Animals Transformed Early America* (2004).

Colin G. Calloway, *New Worlds for All: Indians, Europeans, and the Remaking of Early America* (1998).

Eric Jay Dolin, *Fur, Fortune, and Empire: The Epic History of the Fur Trade in America* (2010).

David D. Hall, *Worlds of Wonder, Days of Judgment: Popular Religious Belief in Early New England* (1989).

Diarmaid MacCulloch, *The Reformation* (2005).

Peter Moogk, *La Nouvelle France: The Making of French Canada—A Cultural History* (2000).

Carla Gardina Pestana, *The English Atlantic in the Age of Revolution, 1640–1661* (2004).

James Pritchard, *In Search of Empire: The French in the Americas, 1670–1730* (2007).

Native Americans

Russell Bourne, *Gods of War, Gods of Peace: How the Meeting of Native and Colonial Religions Shaped Early America* (2002).

Roger M. Carpenter, *The Renewed, the Destroyed, and the Remade: The Three Thought Worlds of the Huron and the Iroquois, 1609–1675* (2004).

Richard W. Cogley, *John Eliot's Mission to the Indians before King Philip's War* (1999).

Jill Lepore, *The Name of War: King Philip's War and the Origins of American Identity* (1998).

Daniel R. Mandell, *King Philip's War: Colonial Expansion, Native Resistance, and the End of Indian Sovereignty* (2010).

Donna Merwick, *The Shame and the Sorrow: Dutch-Amerindian Encounters in New Netherland* (2006).

Michael Leroy Oberg, *Dominion and Civility: English Imperialism and Native America, 1585–1685* (1999).

Ann Marie Plane, *Colonial Intimacies: Indian Marriages in Early New England* (2000).

New England

Louise A. Breen, *Transgressing the Bounds: Subversive Enterprises among the Puritan Elite in Massachusetts, 1630–1692* (2001).

Nick Bunker, *Making Haste from Babylon: The Mayflower Pilgrims and Their World* (2010).

James F. Cooper Jr., *Tenacious of Their Liberties: The Congregationalists in Colonial Massachusetts* (1999).

Cornelia Hughes Dayton, *Women before the Bar: Gender, Law, and Society in Connecticut, 1639–1789* (1995).

Lisa M. Gordis, *Opening Scriptures: Bible Reading and Interpretive Authority in Puritan New England* (2003).

Jane Kamensky, *Governing the Tongue: The Politics of Speech in Early New England* (1997).

Eve LaPlante, *American Jezebel: The Uncommon Life of Anne Hutchinson, the Woman Who Defied the Puritans* (2005).

Mary Beth Norton, *In the Devil's Snare: The Salem Witchcraft Crisis of 1692* (2002).

Mark A. Peterson, *The Price of Redemption: The Spiritual Economy of Puritan New England* (1998).

Nathaniel Philbrick, *Mayflower: A Story of Courage, Community, and War* (2006).

Michael P. Winship, *Making Heretics: Militant Protestantism and Free Grace in Massachusetts, 1636–1641* (2002).

Middle Colonies

Ned C. Landsman, *Crossroads of Empire: The Middle Colonies in British North America* (2010).

Peter C. Mancall, *Fatal Journey: The Final Expedition of Henry Hudson* (2009).

Cathy Matson, *Merchants and Empire: Trading in Colonial New York* (1998).

David E. Narrett, *Inheritance and Family Life in Colonial New York City* (1992).

Russell Shorto, *The Island at the Center of the World: The Epic Story of Dutch Manhattan and the Forgotten Colony That Shaped America* (2004).

Allen Tully, *Forming American Politics: Ideals, Interests, and Institutions in Colonial New York and Pennsylvania* (1994).

▶ **FOR MORE BOOKS ABOUT TOPICS IN THIS CHAPTER,** see the Online Bibliography at **bedfordstmartins.com/roark**.

▶ **FOR ADDITIONAL PRIMARY SOURCES FROM THIS PERIOD,** see Michael Johnson, ed., *Reading the American Past*, Fifth Edition.

▶ **FOR WEB SITES, IMAGES, AND DOCUMENTS RELATED TO TOPICS AND PLACES IN THIS CHAPTER,** visit Make History at **bedfordstmartins.com/roark**.

Reviewing Chapter 4

REVIEW QUESTIONS

Use key terms and dates to support your answers.

1. Why did the Puritans immigrate to North America? (pp. 93–97)

2. Why did Massachusetts Puritans adopt the Halfway Covenant? (pp. 98–108)

3. How did Quaker ideals shape the colony of Pennsylvania? (pp. 109–112)

4. Why did the Glorious Revolution in England lead to uprisings in the American colonies? (pp. 112–118)

MAKING CONNECTIONS

Draw on key terms, the timeline, and review questions.

1. How did the religious dissenters who flooded into the northern colonies address the question of religious dissent in their new homes? Comparing two colonies, discuss their different approaches and the implications of those approaches for colonial development.

2. In his sermon aboard the *Arbella*, John Winthrop spoke of the Massachusetts Bay Colony as "a city upon a hill." What did he mean? How did this expectation influence life in New England during the seventeenth century? In your answer, be sure to consider the relationship between religious and political life in the colony.

3. Religious conflict and political turmoil battered England in the seventeenth century. How did political developments in England affect life in the colonies? In your answer, consider the establishment of the colonies and the crown's attempts to exercise authority over them.

4. To what extent did the New England and middle colonies become more alike during the seventeenth century? To what extent did they remain distinctive? In your answer, consider religions, economies, systems of governance, and patterns of settlement in the colonies.

LINKING TO THE PAST

Link events in this chapter to earlier events.

1. How did the communal goals of New England settlers compare with the aspirations of the tobacco and rice planters of the southern colonies? (See chapter 3.)

2. To what degree did religious intolerance shape events in the New World colonies of Spain, France, and England? (See chapters 2 and 3.)

▶ FOR PRACTICE QUIZZES AND OTHER STUDY TOOLS, visit the Online Study Guide at bedfordstmartins.com/roark.

TIMELINE 1534–1692

1534	• King Henry VIII breaks with Roman Catholic Church; English Reformation begins.
1609	• Henry Hudson searches for Northwest Passage.
1620	• Plymouth colony founded.
1626	• Manhattan Island purchased; New Amsterdam founded.
1629	• Massachusetts Bay Company receives royal charter.
1630	• John Winthrop leads Puritan settlers to Massachusetts Bay.
1636	• Rhode Island colony established. • Connecticut colony founded.
1636–1637	• Pequot War.
1638	• Anne Hutchinson excommunicated.
1642	• Puritan Revolution inflames England.
1649	• English Puritans win civil war and execute Charles I.
1656	• Quakers arrive in Massachusetts and are persecuted there.
1660	• Monarchy restored in England; Charles II becomes king.
1662	• Many Puritan congregations adopt Halfway Covenant.
1664	• English seize Dutch colony, rename it New York. • Colony of New Jersey created.
1675–1676	• King Philip's War.
1681	• William Penn receives charter for colony of Pennsylvania.
1686	• Dominion of New England created.
1688	• England's Glorious Revolution; William III and Mary II become new rulers.
1689–1697	• King William's War.
1692	• Salem witch trials.

TEXTILE SAMPLE BOOK

This bulging collection of
cloth samples assembled by a
textile manufacturer in Norwich,
England, allowed colonial merchants to choose
combinations of colors, designs, textures, weights,
and fibers (such as wool, cotton, or linen) that they believed
their customers would purchase. The book illustrates the astonishing
variety of textiles the Norwich manufacturer could readily produce and ship
throughout the Atlantic world. The book also depicts the bewildering and
somewhat intoxicating range of choices available to British North American
consumers. The background image, of Charleston harbor in South Carolina,
portrays the bustling Atlantic commerce of the eighteenth century.

Background: Colonial Williamsburg Foundation; book: NWHCM: 1966.658 Despatch book by Ives and Basely,
1792, from the collections of Norfolk Museums and Archaeology Service.

5

Colonial America in the Eighteenth Century 1701–1770

THE BROTHERS AMBOE ROBIN JOHN AND LITTLE EPHRAIM ROBIN JOHN and their cousin Ancona Robin John lived during the 1750s and 1760s in Old Calabar on the Bight of Biafra in West Africa. The Robin Johns were part of a slave-trading dynasty headed by their kinsman Grandy King George, one of the most powerful leaders of the Efik people. Grandy King George owned hundreds of slaves whom he employed to capture and trade for still more slaves in the African interior. He sold these captives to captains of European slave ships seeking to fill their holds with human cargo for the transatlantic voyage to the sugar, tobacco, and rice fields in the New World. Old Calabar was a major contributor to the massive flow of more than 1.2 million slaves from the Bight of Biafra to the New World during the eighteenth century.

Grandy King George nearly monopolized the Old Calabar slave trade during the 1760s, allowing him to live in luxury, surrounded by fine British trade goods. British slave ship captains and Grandy King George's African rivals resented his choke hold on the supply of slaves and in 1767 conspired to trap the king and the Robin Johns, seize hundreds of their slaves, and destroy the king's monopoly. In the bloody melee, Grandy King George managed to escape, but other members of his family were less fortunate. Amboe Robin John was beheaded by the leader of the African attackers. Little Ephraim and Ancona Robin John were enslaved, packed aboard the ship Duke of York with more than 330 other slaves, and transported across the Atlantic to the West Indies.

Unlike most slaves, the Robin Johns understood, spoke, and even wrote English, an essential skill they had learned as slave traders in Old Calabar. A French physician bought the Robin Johns and, according to Ancona, "treated [them] . . . upon ye whole not badly." After seven months, the Robin Johns escaped from their owner and boarded a ship "determined to get home," Little Ephraim wrote. But the ship captain took them to Virginia instead and sold them as slaves to a merchant who traded between the

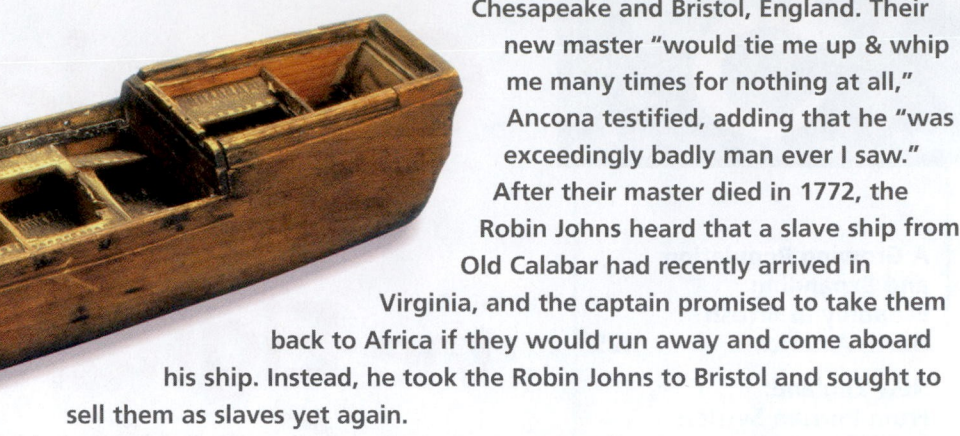

Model of a Slave Ship
Jammed into the holds of slave ships, enslaved Africans made the dreaded Middle Passage to the New World. The model of a slave ship shown here was used in parliamentary debates by anti-slavery leaders in Britain to demonstrate the inhumanity of shipping people as if they were cargo. The model does not show another typical feature of slave ships: weapons. Slaves vastly outnumbered the crews aboard the ships, and crew members justifiably feared slave uprisings. Wilberforce House, Hull City Museums and Art Galleries, UK/Bridgeman Art Library.

Chesapeake and Bristol, England. Their new master "would tie me up & whip me many times for nothing at all," Ancona testified, adding that he "was exceedingly badly man ever I saw." After their master died in 1772, the Robin Johns heard that a slave ship from Old Calabar had recently arrived in Virginia, and the captain promised to take them back to Africa if they would run away and come aboard his ship. Instead, he took the Robin Johns to Bristol and sought to sell them as slaves yet again.

While imprisoned "in this Deplorable condition" on a ship in Bristol harbor, the Robin Johns managed to smuggle letters to a Bristol slave trader they had known and dealt with in Old Calabar. With help from him and other English sympathizers, the Robin Johns appeared before Lord Mansfield, the chief justice of England, and appealed for their freedom on the grounds that they were unjustly enslaved because they "were free people . . . [who] had not done anything to forfeit our liberty." After complex negotiations, they won legal recognition of their freedom.

As free Africans in Bristol, the Robin Johns converted to Christianity under the ministry of the famous Methodists John and Charles Wesley, but they longed to return to Africa. In 1774, they left Bristol as free men on a slave ship bound for Old Calabar, where they resumed their careers as slave traders.

The Robin Johns' unrelenting quest to escape enslavement and redeem their freedom was shared but not realized by millions of Africans who were victims of slave traders such as Grandy King George and numberless merchants, ship captains, and colonists. In contrast, tens of thousands of Europeans voluntarily crossed the Atlantic to seek opportunities in North America — often by agreeing to several years of contractual servitude. Both groups illustrate the undertow of violence and deceit beneath the surface of the eighteenth-century Atlantic commerce linking Britain, Africa, the West Indies, and British North America. In the flux and uncertainty of the eighteenth-century world, many, like the Robin Johns, turned to the consolations of religious faith as a source of meaning and hope in an often cruel and unforgiving society.

The flood of free and unfree migrants crossing the Atlantic contributed to unprecedented population growth in eighteenth-century British North America. In contrast, Spanish and French colonies in North America remained thinly populated outposts of European empires interested principally in maintaining a toehold in the vast continent. While the New England, middle, and southern colonies retained regional distinctions, commercial, cultural, and political trends built unifying experiences and assumptions among British North American colonists.

▶ A Growing Population and Expanding Economy in British North America

The most important fact about eighteenth-century British America is its phenomenal population growth: In 1700, colonists numbered about 250,000; by 1770, they tallied well over 2 million. An index of the emerging significance of colonial North America is that in 1700, there were nineteen people in England for every American colonist; by 1770, there were only three. The eightfold growth of the colonial population signaled the maturation of a distinctive colonial society. That society was by no means homogeneous. Colonists of different ethnic groups, races, and religions lived in varied environments under thirteen different colonial governments, all of them part of the British empire.

In general, the growth and diversity of the eighteenth-century colonial population derived from two sources: immigration and **natural increase** (growth through reproduction). Natural increase contributed about three-fourths of the population growth, immigration about one-fourth. Immigration shifted the ethnic and racial balance among the colonists, making them by 1770 less English and less white than ever before. Fewer than 10 percent of eighteenth-century immigrants came from England; about 36 percent were Scots-Irish, mostly from northern Ireland; 33 percent arrived from Africa, almost all of them slaves; nearly 15 percent had left the many German-language principalities (the nation of Germany did not exist until 1871); and almost 10 percent came from Scotland. In 1670, more than 9 out of 10 colonists were of English ancestry, and only 1 out of 25 was of African ancestry. By 1770, only about half of the colonists were of English descent, while more than 20 percent descended from Africans. Thus, by 1770, the people of the colonies had a distinctive colonial — rather than English — profile (Map 5.1).

The booming population of the colonies hints at a second major feature of eighteenth-century colonial society: an expanding economy. In 1700, after almost a century of settlement, nearly all the colonists lived within fifty miles of the Atlantic coast. The nearly limitless wilderness stretching westward made land relatively cheap compared with its price in the Old World. The abundance of land in the colonies made labor precious, and the colonists always needed more. The insatiable demand for labor was the fundamental economic environment that sustained the mushrooming

"Dummy Board" of Phyllis, a New England Slave
This life-size portrait of a slave woman named Phyllis, a mulatto who worked as a domestic servant for her owner, Elizabeth Hunt Wendell, was painted sometime before 1753. Known as a "dummy board," it was propped against a wall or placed in a doorway or window to suggest that the residence was occupied and to discourage thieves. Phyllis's dress and demeanor suggest that she was capable, orderly, and efficient. She illustrates the integration of the mundane tasks of housekeeping with the shifting currents of transatlantic commerce. Although tens of thousands of slaves were brought from Africa to British North America during the eighteenth century, Phyllis was probably not one of them. Instead, she was most likely born in the colonies of mixed black and white parentage. Courtesy of Historic New England.

MAP 5.1

Europeans and Africans in the Eighteenth Century
This map illustrates regions where Africans and certain immigrant groups clustered. It is important to avoid misreading the map. Predominantly English and German regions, for example, also contained colonists from other places. Likewise, regions where African slaves resided in large numbers also included many whites, slave masters among them. The map suggests the diversity of eighteenth-century colonial society.

population. Economic historians estimate that free colonists (those who were not indentured servants or slaves) had a higher standard of living than the majority of people elsewhere in the Atlantic world. The unique achievement of the eighteenth-century colonial economy was this modest economic welfare of the vast bulk of the free population.

> **REVIEW**   How did the North American colonies achieve the remarkable population growth of the eighteenth century?

► New England: From Puritan Settlers to Yankee Traders

The New England population grew sixfold during the eighteenth century but lagged behind the growth in the other colonies. Most immigrants chose other destinations because of New England's relatively densely settled land and because Puritan orthodoxy made these colonies comparatively inhospitable to those of other faiths and those indifferent to religion. As the population grew, many settlers in search of farmland dispersed from towns, and Puritan communities lost much of their cohesion. Nonetheless, networks of economic exchange laced New Englanders to their neighbors, to Boston merchants, and to the broad currents of Atlantic commerce. In many ways, trade became a faith that competed strongly with the traditions of Puritanism.

Natural Increase and Land Distribution

The New England population grew mostly by natural increase, much as it had during the seventeenth century. Nearly every adult woman married. Most married women had children — often many children, thanks to the relatively low mortality rate in New England. The perils of childbirth gave wives a shorter life expectancy than husbands, but wives often lived to have six, seven, or eight babies. Anne Franklin and her husband, Josiah, a soap and candle maker in Boston, had seven children. Four months after Anne died, Josiah married his second wife, Abiah, and the couple had ten more children, including their son Benjamin, who became one of the most prominent colonial leaders of the eighteenth century. Like many other New Englanders, Benjamin Franklin felt hemmed in by family pressures and lack of opportunity and left the region when he was seventeen years old "to assert my freedom," as he put it, first in New York and then in Philadelphia.

The growing New England population pressed against a limited amount of land. Compared to colonies farther south, New England had less land for the expansion of settlement (see Map 5.1). Moreover, as the northernmost group of British colonies, New England had contested northern and western frontiers. Powerful Native Americans, especially the Iroquois and Mahican tribes, jealously guarded their territory. The French (and Catholic) colony of New France also menaced the British (and mostly Protestant) New England colonies when provoked by colonial or European disputes. (See chapter 4, "Beyond America's Borders," page 116.)

During the seventeenth century, New England towns parceled out land to individual families. In most cases, the original settlers practiced **partible inheritance** — that is, they subdivided land more or less equally among sons. By the eighteenth century, the original land allotments had to be further subdivided to accommodate grandsons and great-grandsons, and many plots of land became too small to support a family. Sons who could not hope to inherit sufficient land to farm had to move away from the town where they were born.

During the eighteenth century, colonial governments in New England abandoned the seventeenth-century policy of granting land to towns. Needing revenue, the governments of both Connecticut and Massachusetts sold land directly to individuals, including speculators. Now money, rather than membership in a community bound by a church covenant, determined whether a person could obtain land. The new land policy eroded the seventeenth-century pattern of settlement. As colonists spread north and west, they tended to settle on individual farms rather than in the towns and villages that characterized the seventeenth century. New Englanders still depended on their relatives and neighbors, but far more than in the seventeenth century, they regulated their behavior in newly settled areas by their own individual choices.

Farms, Fish, and Atlantic Trade

A New England farm was a place to get by, not to get rich. New England farmers grew food for their families, but their fields did not produce huge marketable surpluses. Instead of one big crop, a farmer grew many small ones. If farmers had extra, they sold to or traded with neighbors. Poor roads made travel difficult, time-consuming, and expensive, especially with bulky and heavy agricultural goods. The one major agricultural product the New England colonies exported — livestock — walked to market on its own legs. By 1770, New Englanders had only one-fourth as much wealth per capita as free colonists in the southern colonies.

As consumers, New England farmers participated in a diversified commercial economy that linked remote farms to markets throughout the Atlantic world. Merchants large and small stocked imported goods — British textiles, ceramics, and metal goods;

Chinese tea; West Indian sugar; and Chesapeake tobacco. Farmers' needs supported local shoemakers, tailors, wheelwrights, and carpenters. Larger towns, especially Boston, housed skilled tradesmen such as cabinetmakers, silversmiths, and printers. Shipbuilders tended to do better than other artisans because they served the most dynamic sector of the New England economy. Many New Englanders made their fortunes at sea, as they had since the seventeenth century.

Fish accounted for more than a third of New England's eighteenth-century exports; livestock and timber made up another third. The West Indies absorbed two-thirds of all New England's exports. Slaves on Caribbean sugar plantations ate dried, salted codfish caught by New England fishermen, filled barrels crafted from New England timber with molasses and refined sugar, and loaded those barrels aboard ships bound ultimately for Europeans with a sweet tooth. Almost all of the rest of New England's exports went to Britain and continental Europe (Map 5.2). This **Atlantic commerce** benefited the entire New England economy, providing jobs for laborers and tradesmen as well as for ship captains, clerks, merchants, and sailors. (See "Seeking the American Promise," page 130.)

Merchants dominated Atlantic commerce. The largest and most successful New England merchants lived in Boston at the hub of trade between local folk and the international market. Merchants not only bought and sold goods but also owned and insured the ships that carried the merchandise throughout the Atlantic world. Shrewd, diligent, and lucky merchants could make fortunes. The magnificence of a wealthy Boston merchant's home stunned John Adams, a thrifty Massachusetts lawyer who became a leader during the American Revolution and ultimately the second president of the United States. To Adams, the merchant's house seemed fit "for a noble Man, a Prince." Such luxurious Boston homes contrasted with the modest dwellings of Adams and other New Englanders, an indication of the polarization of wealth that developed in Boston and other seaports during the eighteenth century.

By 1770, the richest 5 percent of Bostonians owned about half the city's wealth; the poorest two-thirds of the population owned less than one-tenth. While the rich got richer and

> "We in New England know nothing of poverty and want, we have no idea of the thing, how much better do our poor people live than 7/8 of the people on this much famed island."
> — A Connecticut traveler, writing from England

Map labels:
- 80°N
- 60°E
- NORTH AMERICA
- NEW FRANCE
- ENGLISH COLONIES
- ENGLAND
- EUROPE
- Linens, horses
- Fish, furs, naval stores
- Manufactured goods
- New York
- Boston
- Philadelphia
- Baltimore
- Newport
- Manufactured goods
- Tobacco
- Rice, indigo, hides
- Manufactured goods
- Norfolk
- Wilmington
- Grain, fish, lumber, rum
- Manufactured goods
- SPAIN
- Charleston
- Savannah
- Rice
- Slaves
- Fish, livestock, flour, lumber
- Slaves, sugar
- Slaves, sugar
- PORTUGAL
- Wine, Fruit
- SPANISH FLORIDA
- Molasses, fruit
- ATLANTIC OCEAN
- Wine
- 100°W
- WEST INDIES
- European products
- AFRICA
- Caribbean Sea
- Manufactured goods
- 40°E
- Slaves
- Rum
- Manufactured goods
- Slaves, gold
- IVORY, GOLD, AND SLAVE COASTS
- SOUTH AMERICA
- 110°W
- 60°N
- 40°N
- 20°N
- 0°
- 20°S
- 80°W
- 60°W
- 40°W
- 20°W
- 0°
- 20°E

Legend:
- Major centers of trade
- Major ocean trade route

Scale:
- 0 500 1,000 miles
- 0 500 1,000 kilometers

MAP ACTIVITY

MAP 5.2 Atlantic Trade in the Eighteenth Century

This map illustrates the economic outlook of the colonies in the eighteenth century — east toward the Atlantic world rather than west toward the interior of North America. The long distances involved in the Atlantic trade and the uncertainties of ocean travel suggest the difficulties Britain experienced governing the colonies and regulating colonial commerce.

READING THE MAP: What were the major Atlantic markets for trade coming out of Europe? What goods did the British colonies import and export?

CONNECTIONS: In what ways did the flow of raw materials from the colonies affect British industry? How did British colonial trade policies influence the Atlantic trade?

everybody else had a smaller share of the total wealth, the incidence of genuine poverty did not change much. About 5 percent of New Englanders qualified for poor relief throughout the eighteenth century. Overall, colonists were better off than most people in England. A Connecticut traveler wrote from England in 1764, "We in New England know nothing of poverty and want, we have no idea of the thing, how much better do our poor people live than 7/8 of the people on this much famed island."

The contrast with English poverty had meaning because the overwhelming majority of New Englanders traced their ancestry to England. New England was more homogeneously English than any other colonial region. People of African ancestry (almost all of them slaves) numbered more than fifteen thousand by 1770, but they barely diversified the region's 97 percent white majority. In the Narragansett region of Rhode Island, large landowners imported numerous slaves to raise livestock. But most New Englanders had little use for slaves on their family farms. Instead, slaves were concentrated in towns, especially Boston, where most of them worked as domestic servants and laborers.

Boston Common in Needlework

Hannah Otis embroidered this exquisite needlework portrait of Boston Common in 1750, when she was eighteen years old. From the perspective of the twenty-first century, the scene gives few hints of city life. Otis populated the cityscape with more animals than people and more plants than paving stones. The large house (center right) belonged to the Hancock family. John Hancock, who later signed the Declaration of Independence, is shown on horseback in the foreground. Eighteenth-century Bostonians owned slaves, as Otis shows. What features of this portrait would suggest a city to an eighteenth-century viewer? Photograph © 2012 Museum of Fine Arts, Boston.

By 1770, the population, wealth, and commercial activity of New England differed from what they had been in 1700. Ministers still enjoyed high status, but Yankee traders had replaced Puritan saints as the symbolic New Englanders. Atlantic commerce competed with religious convictions in ordering New Englanders' daily lives.

> **REVIEW** Why did settlement patterns in New England change from the seventeenth to the eighteenth century?

▶ The Middle Colonies: Immigrants, Wheat, and Work

In 1700, almost twice as many people lived in New England as in the middle colonies of Pennsylvania, New York, New Jersey, and Delaware. But by 1770, the population of the middle colonies had multiplied tenfold — mainly from an influx of German, Irish, Scottish, and other immigrants — and nearly equaled the population of New England. Immigrants made the middle colonies a uniquely diverse society. By 1800, barely one-third of Pennsylvanians and less than half the total population of the middle colonies traced their ancestry to England. New settlers, whether free or in servitude, poured into the middle colonies because they perceived unparalleled opportunities. However, the increasing number of slaves arriving in bondage had little hope of sharing in such rewards.

German and Scots-Irish Immigrants

Germans made up the largest contingent of migrants from the European continent to the middle colonies. By 1770, about 85,000 Germans had arrived in the colonies. Their fellow colonists often referred to them as **Pennsylvania Dutch**, an English corruption of *Deutsch*, the word the immigrants used to describe themselves.

Most German immigrants came from what is now southwestern Germany, where, one observer noted, peasants were "not as well off as cattle elsewhere." Devastating French invasions of Germany during Queen Anne's War (1702–1713) made bad conditions worse and triggered the first large-scale migration. German immigrants included numerous artisans and a few merchants, but the great majority were farmers and laborers. Economically, they represented "middling folk," neither the poorest (who could not afford the trip) nor the better-off (who did not want to leave).

A Sailor's Life in the Eighteenth-Century Atlantic World

Although most eighteenth-century North American colonists made their living on farms, tens of thousands manned the vessels that ferried people, animals, commodities, consumer goods, ideas, and microorganisms from port to port throughout the Atlantic world. Built almost entirely from wood and fiber, ships were the most complex machines in the eighteenth century. Seamen needed to learn how to handle the intricacies of a vessel's working parts quickly, smoothly, and reliably. The ship, the cargo, and their own lives depended on their knowledge and dexterity. They had to endure hard physical labor for weeks or months on end in a cramped space packed with cargo and crew. Sailors followed "one of the hardest and dangerousest callings," one old salt declared.

Despite the certainty of strenuous work and spartan accommodations, young men like Ashley Bowen made their way to wharves in small ports such as Marblehead, Massachusetts — Bowen's hometown — or large commercial centers such as Boston, Philadelphia, New York, and Charleston. There they boarded vessels and launched a life of seafaring, seeking the promise of a future wafting on the surface of the deep rather than rooted below the surface of the soil.

Born in 1728, Bowen grew up in Marblehead, one of the most important fishing ports in North America. Like other boys who lived in or near ports, Bowen probably watched ships come and go; heard tales of adventure, disaster, and intrigue; and learned from neighbors and pals how to maneuver small, shallow-draft boats within sight of land. Young girls sometimes learned to handle a small boat, but they almost never worked as sailors aboard Atlantic vessels. When Bowen was only eleven years old, he sailed as a ship's boy aboard a vessel captained by the father of a friend to pick up a load of tar bound for Bristol, England. The ship then loaded a cargo of coal in Wales and carried it to Boston, where Bowen, now twelve, arrived with a yearlong seafaring education under his belt.

Most commonly, young men first went to sea when they were fifteen to eighteen years old. Like Bowen, they were single, living with their parents, and casting about for work.

They usually sailed with friends, neighbors, or kinfolk, and they sought an education in the ways of the sea. Also like Bowen, they aspired to earn some wages, to rise in the ranks eventually from seaman to mate and possibly to master (the common term for captain), to save enough to marry and support a family, and after twenty years or so to retire from the rigors of the seafaring life with a "competency" — that is, enough money to live modestly.

It typically took about four years at sea to become a fully competent seaman. Shortly after Bowen returned from his first voyage, his father apprenticed him to a sea captain for seven years. In return for a hefty payment, the captain agreed to tutor young Bowen in the art of seafaring, which ideally promised to ease his path to become a captain himself. In reality, the captain employed him as a cabin boy, taught him little except to obey, and beat him for trivial mistakes, causing Bowen to run away after four years of servitude.

Now seventeen years old, Bowen had already sailed to dozens of ports in North America, the West Indies, the British Isles, and Europe. For the next eighteen years, he shipped out as a common seaman on scores of vessels carrying nearly every kind of cargo afloat on the Atlantic. He sailed mostly aboard merchant freighters, but he also worked on whalers, fishing boats, privateers, and warships. He survived sickness, imprisonment, foul weather, accidents, and innumerable close calls. But when he retired

---

By the 1720s, Germans who had established themselves in the colonies wrote back to their friends and relatives, as one reported, "of the civil and religious liberties [and] privileges, and of all the goodness I have heard and seen." Such letters prompted still more Germans to pull up stakes and embark for America, to exchange the miserable certainties of their lives in Europe for the uncertain attractions of life in the middle colonies.

Similar motives propelled the **Scots-Irish**, who considerably outnumbered German immigrants. The "Scots-Irish" actually hailed from northern Ireland, Scotland, and northern England. Like the Germans, the Scots-Irish were Protestants, but with a difference. Most German immigrants worshipped in Lutheran or German Reformed churches; many others belonged to dissenting sects such as the Mennonites, Moravians, and Amish, whose adherents sought relief from persecution they had suffered in Europe for their refusal to bear arms and to swear oaths, practices they shared with the Quakers. In contrast, the Scots-Irish tended to be militant Presbyterians who seldom hesitated to bear arms or swear oaths. Like from seafaring at age thirty-five, he still had not managed to attain command. In twenty-four years at sea, he had worked as either a common seaman or a mate. For whatever reason, when most shipowners eyed Bowen, they did not see a man they would trust to command their vessels.

Like Bowen, about three out of ten seamen spent their entire seafaring lives as seamen or mates, earning five dollars or so a month in wages, roughly comparable to the wages of farm laborers. Another three out of ten seamen died at sea, many by drowning or as a result of injuries or, most commonly, from tropical diseases usually picked up in the West Indies. Bowen lived to the age of eighty-five, working as a rigger, crafting nautical fittings for sailing vessels. When Bowen, like thousands of other seafarers, looked at the world, his gaze did not turn west toward the farms and forests of the interior but rather turned east, toward the promise of the Atlantic deep beyond.

Questions for Consideration

1. What attracted Ashley Bowen to a seafaring life? How successful was he?

2. How did Bowen's experiences as a seaman compare to those of farmers in the colonies?

3. How might Bowen's outlook on the world compare to that of the vast majority of colonists who seldom or never went to sea?

Ashley Bowen's Journal
Ashley Bowen painted these watercolors of ships he sailed aboard in 1754, 1755, and 1756. Befitting an experienced seaman, he paid attention to the distinctive rigging and flags of each vessel, and he kept notes about the vessels' owners, masters, mates, passengers, and destinations. As the focus of Bowen's fascination, the vessels dwarf the buildings of Marblehead, Massachusetts, in the background. To Bowen, each ship had distinctive features. Can you spot the differences that caught his eye? Why might such differences be important to Bowen? Photo courtesy of The Marblehead Historical Society, Marblehead, MA.

German settlers, however, Scots-Irish immigrants were clannish, residing when they could among relatives or neighbors from the old country.

In the eighteenth century, wave after wave of Scots-Irish immigrants arrived, culminating in a flood of immigration in the years just before the American Revolution. Deteriorating economic conditions in northern Ireland, Scotland, and England pushed many toward America. Most of the immigrants were farm laborers or tenant farmers fleeing droughts, crop failures, high food prices, or rising rents. They came, they told inquisitive British officials, because of "poverty," the "tyranny of landlords," and their desire to "do better in America."

Both Scots-Irish and Germans probably heard the common saying "Pennsylvania is heaven for farmers [and] paradise for artisans," but they almost certainly did not fully understand the risks of their decision to leave their native lands. Ship captains, aware of the hunger for labor in the colonies, eagerly signed up the penniless German emigrants as **redemptioners**, a variant of indentured servants. A captain would agree to provide transportation to Philadelphia, where redemptioners would obtain the money to pay for their passage by borrowing it from a friend or relative who was already in the colonies or, as most did, by selling themselves as servants.

Many redemptioners traveled in family groups, unlike impoverished Scots-Irish emigrants, who usually traveled alone and paid for their passage by contracting as indentured servants before they sailed to the colonies.

Redemptioners and indentured servants were packed aboard ships "as closely as herring," one migrant observed. Seasickness compounded by exhaustion, poverty, poor food, bad water, inadequate sanitation, and tight quarters encouraged the spread of disease. On the sixteen immigrant ships arriving in Philadelphia in 1738, more than half the passengers died en route. When one ship finally approached land, a traveler wrote, "everyone crawls from below to the deck . . . and people cry for joy, pray, and sing praises and thanks to God." Unfortunately, their troubles were far from over. Redemptioners and indentured servants had to stay on board until somebody came to purchase their labor. Unlike indentured servants, redemptioners negotiated independently with their purchasers about their period of servitude. Typically, a healthy adult redemptioner agreed to four years of labor. Indentured servants commonly served five, six, or seven years.

"God Gives All Things to Industry": Urban and Rural Labor

An indentured servant in 1743 wrote that Pennsylvania was "the best poor Man's Country in the World." Although the servant reported that "the Condition of bought Servants is very hard" and masters often failed to live up to their promise to provide decent food and clothing, opportunity abounded in the middle colonies because there was more work to be done than workers to do it.

Most servants toiled in Philadelphia, New York City, or one of the smaller towns or villages. Artisans, small manufacturers, and shopkeepers prized the labor of male servants. Female servants made valuable additions to households, where nearly all of them cleaned, washed, cooked, or minded children. From the masters' viewpoint, servants were a bargain. A master could purchase five or six years of a servant's labor for approximately the wages a common laborer would earn in four months. Wageworkers could walk away from their jobs when they pleased, and they did so often enough to be troublesome for employers. Servants, however, could not walk away; they were legally bound to work for their masters until their terms expired.

Since a slave cost at least three times as much as a servant, only affluent colonists could afford the long-term investment in slave labor. Like many other prosperous urban residents, Benjamin Franklin purchased a few slaves after he became wealthy. But most farmers in the middle colonies used family labor, not slaves. Wheat, the most widely grown crop, did not require more labor than farmers could typically muster from relatives, neighbors, and a hired hand or two. Consequently, although people of African ancestry (almost all slaves) increased to more than thirty thousand in the middle colonies by 1770, they accounted for only about 7 percent of the total population and much less outside the cities.

Most slaves came to the middle colonies and New England after a stopover in the West Indies, as the Robin Johns did. Very few came directly from Africa. Enough slaves arrived to prompt colonial assemblies to pass laws that punished slaves much more severely than servants for the same transgressions. "For the least trespass," an indentured servant reported, slaves "undergo the severest Punishment." And slaves — unlike servants — could not charge masters with violating the terms of their contracts. A master's commands, not a written contract, set the terms of a slave's bondage. Small numbers of slaves managed to obtain their freedom, though few of them as dramatically as the Robin Johns. But free African Americans did not escape whites' firm convictions about black inferiority and white supremacy.

Whites' racism and blacks' lowly social status made African Americans scapegoats for European Americans' suspicions and anxieties. In 1741, when arson and several unexplained thefts plagued New York City, officials suspected a murderous slave conspiracy and executed thirty-one slaves. On the basis of little evidence other than the slaves' "insolence" (refusal to conform fully to whites' expectations of servile behavior), city authorities burned thirteen slaves at the stake and hanged eighteen others. Although slaves were certifiably impoverished, they were not among the poor for whom the middle colonies were reputed to be the best country in the world.

Immigrants swarmed to the middle colonies because of the availability of land. The Penn family (see chapter 4) encouraged immigration to bring in potential buyers for their enormous tracts of land in Pennsylvania. From the beginning, Pennsylvania followed a policy of negotiating with Indian tribes to purchase additional land. This policy reduced the violent frontier clashes more common elsewhere in the colonies.

Yet even the Penn family did not shrink from occasionally testing its agreement with Indians. In a dispute with tribes on the northern Delaware River in 1737, the Penns pulled out a document showing that local Indians had granted the colonists land that stretched as far as a man could walk in a day and a half. Under the terms of this infamous "Walking Purchase," the Penns sent out three runners, one of whom raced more than sixty miles in the time limit and doubled the size of the Penns' claim.

Few colonists drifted beyond the northern boundaries of Pennsylvania. Owners of the huge estates in New York's Hudson valley preferred to rent rather than sell their land, and therefore they attracted fewer immigrants. The **Iroquois Indians** dominated the lucrative fur trade of the St. Lawrence valley and eastern Great Lakes, and they vigorously defended their territory from colonial encroachment. Few settlers chose to risk having their scalps lifted by Iroquois warriors in northern New York when they could settle instead in the comparatively safe environs of Pennsylvania.

The price of farmland depended on soil quality, access to water, distance from a market town, and extent of improvements. One hundred acres of improved land that had been cleared, plowed, fenced, and ditched, and perhaps had a house and barn built on it, cost three or four times more than the same acreage of uncleared, unimproved land. Since the cheapest land always lay at the margin of settlement, would-be farmers tended to migrate to promising areas just beyond already improved farms. By midcentury, settlement had reached the eastern slopes of the Appalachian Mountains, and newcomers spilled south down the fertile valley of the Shenandoah River into western Virginia and the Carolinas. Thousands of settlers migrated from the middle colonies through this back door to the South. Abraham Lincoln's great-grandfather, John Lincoln — whose own grandfather, Mordecai, had migrated from England to Puritan Massachusetts in the 1630s — moved his family in the 1760s from Pennsylvania down the Shenandoah Valley into Virginia, where the future president's grandfather, also named Abraham, raised his family, including the future president's father, Thomas Lincoln.

Patterns of Settlement, 1700–1770

Farmers like the Lincolns made the middle colonies the breadbasket of North America. They planted a wide variety of crops to feed their families, but they grew wheat in abundance. Flour milling was the number one industry and flour the number one export, constituting nearly three-fourths of all exports from the middle colonies. Pennsylvania flour fed residents in other colonies, in southern Europe, and, above all, in the West Indies (see Map 5.2). For farmers, the

Marten Van Bergen Farm
This detail from a rare 1730s painting depicts the home of Marten and Catarina Van Bergen, prosperous Dutch colonists in New York's Hudson valley. The full-size painting, commissioned by the Van Bergens to hang over their fireplace mantel, is a panorama portraying the farm as a peaceable, small-scale kingdom governed by the couple and populated by their seven children, their slaves and indentured servants, and neighboring Native Americans. Rather than a place of fields and crops, which are absent from the painting, the farm is the locus of a happy, orderly family revolving around Marten and Catarina and the warm hearth just behind them. Copyright © New York State Historical Association, Cooperstown, NY.

VISUAL ACTIVITY

Bethlehem, Pennsylvania

This view of the small community of Bethlehem, Pennsylvania, in 1757 dramatizes the profound transformation of the natural landscape wrought in the eighteenth century by highly motivated human labor. Founded by Moravian immigrants in 1740, Bethlehem must have appeared at first like the dense woods on the upper left horizon. In less than twenty years, precisely laid-out orchards and fields replaced forests and glades. By carefully penning their livestock (lower center right) and fencing their fields (lower left), farmers safeguarded their livelihoods from the risks and disorders of untamed nature. Individual farmsteads (lower center) and impressive multistory brick town buildings (upper center) integrated the bounty of the land with the delights of community life. Few eighteenth-century communities were as orderly as Bethlehem, but many effected a comparable transformation of the environment. Print Collection, Miriam and Ira D. Wallack Division of Art, Prints and Photographs, The New York Public Library. Astor, Lenox, and Tilden Foundations.

READING THE IMAGE: What does this painting indicate about the colonists' priorities?

CONNECTIONS: Why might Pennsylvanians have been so concerned about maintaining order?

grain market in the Atlantic world proved risky but profitable. Grain prices rose steadily after 1720. By 1770, a bushel of wheat was worth twice as much (adjusted for inflation) as it had been fifty years earlier.

The standard of living in rural Pennsylvania was probably higher than in any other agricultural region of the eighteenth-century world. The comparatively widespread prosperity of all the middle colonies permitted residents to indulge in a half-century shopping spree for British imports.

The middle colonies' per capita consumption of imported goods from Britain more than doubled between 1720 and 1770, far outstripping the per capita consumption of British goods in New England and the southern colonies.

Philadelphia stood at the crossroads of trade in wheat exports and British imports. By 1776, Philadelphia had a larger population than any other city in the entire British empire except London. Merchants occupied the top stratum of Philadelphia society. In a city where only 2 percent of the residents owned enough property to qualify to vote, merchants built grand homes and dominated local government. Many of Philadelphia's wealthiest merchants were Quakers. Quaker traits of industry, thrift, honesty, and sobriety encouraged the accumulation of wealth. A colonist complained that a Quaker "prays for his neighbors on First Days [the Sabbath] and then preys on him the other six."

The lower ranks of merchants included aspiring tradesmen such as **Benjamin Franklin**. In 1728, Franklin opened a small shop, run mostly by his wife, Deborah, that sold a little of everything: cheese, codfish, coffee, goose feathers, soap, and occasionally a slave. In 1733, Benjamin Franklin began to publish *Poor Richard's Almanack*, which preached the likelihood of long-term rewards for tireless labor and quickly became Franklin's most profitable product.

The popularity of *Poor Richard's Almanack* suggests that many Pennsylvanians thought less about the pearly gates than about their pocketbooks. Poor Richard's advice that "God gives all Things to Industry" might be considered the motto for the middle colonies. The promise of a worldly payoff made work a secular faith. Poor Richard advised, "Work as if you were to live 100 years, Pray as if you were to die Tomorrow."

William Penn's Quaker utopia became a center of worldly affluence whose most famous citizen, Franklin, was neither a Quaker nor a utopian. Quakers remained influential, but Franklin spoke for most colonists with his aphorisms of work, discipline, and thrift that echoed Quaker rules for outward behavior. Franklin's maxims did not look to the Quaker's divine inner light for guidance. Instead, they celebrated the spark of ambition and the promise of gain.

REVIEW Why did immigrants flood into Pennsylvania during the eighteenth century?

▶ The Southern Colonies: Land of Slavery

Between 1700 and 1770, the population of the southern colonies of Virginia, Maryland, North Carolina, South Carolina, and Georgia grew almost ninefold. By 1770, about twice as many people lived in the South as in either the middle colonies or New England. As elsewhere, natural increase and immigration accounted for the rapid population growth. Many Scots-Irish and German immigrants funneled from the middle colonies into the southern backcountry. Other immigrants were indentured servants (mostly English and Scots-Irish) who followed their seventeenth-century predecessors. But slaves made the most striking contribution to the booming southern colonies, transforming the racial composition of the population. Slavery became the defining characteristic of the southern colonies during the eighteenth century, shaping the region's economy, society, and politics.

The Atlantic Slave Trade and the Growth of Slavery

The number of southerners of African ancestry (nearly all of them slaves) rocketed from just over 20,000 in 1700 to well over 400,000 in 1770. The black population increased nearly three times faster than the South's briskly growing white population. Consequently, the proportion of southerners of African ancestry grew from 20 percent in 1700 to 40 percent in 1770.

Southern colonists clustered into two distinct geographic and agricultural zones. The colonies in the upper South, surrounding the Chesapeake Bay, specialized in growing tobacco, as they had since the early seventeenth century. Throughout the eighteenth century, nine out of ten southern whites and eight out of ten southern blacks lived in the Chesapeake region. The upper South retained a white majority during the eighteenth century.

In the lower South, a much smaller cluster of colonists inhabited the coastal region and specialized in the production of rice and indigo (a plant used to make blue dye). Lower South colonists made up only 5 percent of the total population of the southern colonies in 1700 but inched upward to 15 percent by 1770. South Carolina was the sole British colony along the southern Atlantic coast until 1732. (North Carolina, founded in 1711, was largely an extension of the Chesapeake region.) Georgia was founded in 1732 as a refuge for poor people from England. Georgia's leaders banned slaves from 1735 to 1750, but few settlers arrived until after 1750, when the prohibition on slavery was lifted and slaves flooded in. In South Carolina, in contrast to Georgia and every other British mainland

Sources of African Slaves

- Southeast Africa 5%
- Senegambia 3%
- Sierra Leone 6%
- Gold Coast 12%
- Bight of Biafra 13%
- Bight of Benin 23%
- Congo and Angola 38%

Destinations of African Slaves

- Mexico and Central America 2%
- British North America 4%
- Europe 2%
- Guianas 6%
- Spanish South America 6%
- West Indies 42%
- Brazil 38%

Main sources of African slaves

Main destinations of African slaves in the Americas

MAP ACTIVITY

Map 5.3 The Atlantic Slave Trade

Although the Atlantic slave trade lasted from about 1450 to 1870, it peaked during the eighteenth century, when more than six million African slaves were imported to the New World. Only a small fraction of these slaves were taken to British North America. Most went to sugar plantations in Brazil and the Caribbean.

READING THE MAP: Where in Africa did most slaves originate? Approximately how far was the trip from the busiest ports of origin to the two most common New World destinations?

CONNECTIONS: Why were so many more African slaves sent to the West Indies and Brazil than to British North America?

colony, slaves outnumbered whites almost two to one; in some low-country districts, the ratio of blacks to whites exceeded ten to one.

The enormous growth in the South's slave population occurred through natural increase

TABLE 5.1	SLAVE IMPORTS, 1451–1870
Estimated Slave Imports to the Western Hemisphere	
1451–1600	275,000
1601–1700	1,341,000
1701–1810	6,100,000
1811–1870	1,900,000

and the flourishing Atlantic slave trade (Table 5.1 and Map 5.3). Slave ships brought almost 300,000 Africans to British North America between 1619 and 1780. Of these Africans, 95 percent arrived in the South and 96 percent arrived during the eighteenth century. Unlike indentured servants and redemptioners, these Africans did not choose to come to the colonies. Like the Robin Johns, most of them had been born into free families in villages located within a few hundred miles of the West African coast.

Although they shared African origins, they came from many different African cultures, including Akan, Angolan, Asante, Bambara, Gambian, Igbo, and Mandinga, among others. They spoke different languages, worshipped different deities, observed different rules of kinship, grew different crops, and recognized different rulers. The most

Olaudah Equiano
Painted more than a decade after he had bought his freedom, this portrait evokes Equiano's successful acculturation to eighteenth-century English customs. His clothing and hairstyle reflect the fashions of a respectable young Englishman. In his *Interesting Narrative*, Equiano wrote that he "looked upon [the English] . . . as men superior to us [Africans], and therefore I had the stronger desire to resemble them, to imbibe their spirit and imitate their manners." Yet Equiano did not forsake his African roots. He honored his dual identity by campaigning against slavery. His *Narrative* was one of the most important and powerful antislavery documents of the time. Library of Congress.

important experience they had in common was enslavement.

Captured in war, kidnapped, or sold into slavery by other Africans, they were brought to the coast, sold to African traders like the Robin Johns who assembled slaves for resale, and sold again to European or colonial slave traders or ship captains, who packed two hundred to three hundred or more aboard ships that carried them on the **Middle Passage** across the Atlantic and then sold them yet again to colonial slave merchants or southern planters.

Olaudah Equiano published an account of his enslavement that hints at the stories that might have been told by the millions of other Africans swept up in the slave trade. Equiano wrote that he was born in 1745 in the interior of what is now Nigeria. "I had never heard of white men or Europeans, nor of the sea," he recalled. One day when he was eleven years old, he was kidnapped by Africans, who sold him to other Africans, who in turn eventually sold him to a slave ship on the coast. Equiano feared that he was "going to be killed" and "eaten by those white men with horrible looks, red faces, and loose hair." Once the ship set sail, many of the slaves, crowded together in suffocating heat fouled by filth of all descriptions, died from sickness. "The shrieks of the women and the groans of the dying rendered the whole a scene of horror almost inconceivable," Equiano recalled. Most of the slaves on the ship were sold in Barbados,

but Equiano and other leftovers were shipped off to Virginia, where he "saw few or none of our native Africans and not one soul who could talk to me." Equiano felt isolated and "exceedingly miserable" because he "had no person to speak to that I could understand." Finally, the captain of a tobacco ship bound for England purchased Equiano, and he traveled as a slave between North America, England, and the West Indies for ten years until he succeeded in buying his freedom in 1766.

Only about 15 percent of the slaves brought into the southern colonies came aboard ships from the West Indies, as Equiano and the Robin Johns did. All the other slaves brought into the southern colonies came directly from Africa, and almost all the ships that brought them (roughly 90 percent) belonged to British merchants. Most of the slaves on board were young adults, with men usually outnumbering women two to one. Children under the age of fourteen, like Equiano, typically accounted for no more than 10 to 15 percent of a cargo.

Mortality during the Middle Passage varied considerably from ship to ship. On average, about 15 percent of the slaves died, but sometimes half or more perished. The average mortality among the white crew of slave ships was often nearly as bad. In general, the longer the voyage lasted, the more people died. Recent studies suggest that many slaves succumbed not only to virulent epidemic diseases such as smallpox and dysentery but also to acute dehydration caused by fluid loss from perspiration, vomiting, and diarrhea combined with a severe shortage of drinking water.

Normally, an individual planter purchased at any one time a relatively small number of newly arrived Africans, or **new Negroes**, as they were called. New Negroes were often profoundly depressed, demoralized, and disoriented. Planters

Negro's houses

a fire

Boys playing under that Rooff

a door

a Woman with her Child on her back

The African Slave Trade
The African slave trade existed to satisfy the New World's demand for labor and Europe's voracious appetite for New World products such as sugar, tobacco, and rice. African men, women, and children, like those pictured in this early-eighteenth-century engraving of a family residence in Sierra Leone, were kidnapped or captured in wars — typically by other Africans — and enslaved. Uprooted from their homes and kin, they were usually taken to coastal enclaves where African traders and European ship captains negotiated prices, made deals, and often branded the newly enslaved people. The collaboration between Europeans and their African trading partners is evident in the seventeenth-century Benin bronze box in the shape of a royal palace in Nigeria. The palace is guarded by two massive predatory birds and two Portuguese soldiers. Benin bronze box: Bildarchiv Preussischer Kulturbesitz/Art Resource, NY; engraving: Courtesy, Earl Gregg Swen Library, College of William and Mary, Williamsburg, Virginia.

expected their other slaves — either those born into slavery in the colonies (often called **country-born** or **creole slaves**) or Africans who had arrived earlier — to help new Negroes become accustomed to their strange new surroundings. Planters' preferences for slaves from specific regions of Africa aided slaves' acculturation (or seasoning, as it was called) to the routines of bondage in the southern colonies. Chesapeake planters preferred slaves from Senegambia, the Gold Coast, or — like Equiano and the Robin Johns — the Bight of Biafra, which combined accounted for 40 percent of all Africans imported to the Chesapeake. South Carolina planters

favored slaves from the central African Congo and Angola regions, the origin of about 40 percent of the African slaves they imported (see Map 5.3). Although slaves within each of these regions spoke many different languages, enough linguistic and cultural similarities existed that they could usually communicate with other Africans from the same region.

Seasoning acclimated new Africans to the physical as well as the cultural environment of the southern colonies. Slaves who had just endured the Middle Passage were poorly nourished, weak, and sick. In this vulnerable state, they encountered the alien diseases of North America without having developed a biological arsenal of acquired immunities. As many as 10 to 15 percent of newly arrived Africans, sometimes more, died during their first year in the southern colonies. Nonetheless, the large number of newly enslaved Africans made the influence of African culture in the South stronger in the eighteenth century than ever before — or since.

While newly enslaved Africans poured into the southern colonies, slave mothers bore children, which caused the slave population in the South to grow rapidly. Slave owners encouraged these births. Thomas Jefferson explained, "I consider the labor of a breeding [slave] woman as no object, that a [slave] child raised every 2 years is of more profit than the crop of the best laboring [slave] man." Although slave mothers loved and nurtured their children, the mortality rate among slave children was high, and the ever-present risk of being separated by sale brought grief to many slave families. Nonetheless, the growing number of slave babies set the southern colonies apart from other New World slave societies, where mortality rates were so high that deaths exceeded births. The high rate of natural increase in the southern colonies meant that by the 1740s the majority of southern slaves were country-born.

Slave Labor and African American Culture

Southern planters expected slaves to work from sunup to sundown and beyond. George Washington wrote that his slaves should "be at their work as soon as it is light, work til it is dark, and be diligent while they are at it." The conflict between the masters' desire for maximum labor and the slaves' reluctance to do more than necessary made the threat of physical punishment a constant for eighteenth-century slaves. Masters preferred black slaves to white indentured servants, not just because slaves served for life but also because colonial laws did not limit the force masters could use against slaves. As a traveler observed in 1740, "A new negro . . . [will] let a hundred men show him how to hoe, or drive a wheelbarrow; he'll still take the one by the bottom and the other by the wheel and . . . often die before [he] can be conquered." Slaves resisted their masters' demands, the traveler noted, because of their "greatness of soul" — their stubborn unwillingness to conform to their masters' definition of them as merely slaves.

Some slaves escalated their acts of resistance to direct physical confrontation with the master, the mistress, or an overseer. But a hoe raised in anger, a punch in the face, or a desperate swipe with a knife led to swift and predictable retaliation by whites. Throughout the southern colonies, the balance of physical power rested securely in the hands of whites.

Rebellion occurred, however, at Stono, South Carolina, in 1739. Before dawn on a September Sunday, a group of about twenty slaves attacked a country store, killed the two storekeepers, and confiscated the store's guns, ammunition, and powder. Enticing other slaves to join, the group plundered and burned more than half a dozen plantations and killed more than twenty white men, women, and children. A mounted force of whites quickly suppressed the rebellion. They placed the rebels' heads atop mileposts along the road, grim reminders of the consequences of rebellion. The **Stono rebellion** illustrated that eighteenth-century slaves had no chance of overturning slavery and very little chance of defending themselves in any bold strike for freedom. After the rebellion, South Carolina legislators enacted repressive laws designed to guarantee that whites would always have the upper hand. No other similar uprisings occurred during the colonial period.

Slaves maneuvered constantly to protect themselves and to gain a measure of autonomy within the boundaries of slavery. In Chesapeake tobacco fields, most slaves were subject to close supervision by whites. In the lower South, the **task system** gave slaves some control over the pace of their work and some discretion in the use of the rest of their time. A "task" was typically defined as a certain area of ground to be cultivated or a specific job to be completed. A slave who completed the assigned task might use the remainder of the day, if any, to work in a garden, fish, hunt, spin, weave, sew, or cook. When masters sought to boost productivity by increasing tasks, slaves did what they could to defend their customary work assignments.

Eighteenth-century slaves also planted the roots of African American lineages that branch out to the present. Slaves valued family ties, and, as in West African societies, kinship structured slaves' relations with one another. Slave parents often gave a child the name of a grandparent,

> **"My [slaves] should be at their work as soon as it is light, work til it is dark, and be diligent while they are at it."**
> — GEORGE WASHINGTON

Colonial Slave Drum
An African in Virginia made this drum sometime around the beginning of the eighteenth century. The drum combines deerskin and cedarwood from North America with African workmanship and designs. During rare moments of respite from their work, slaves played drums to accompany dances learned in Africa. They also drummed out messages from plantation to plantation. Whites knew that slaves used drums for communication, but they could not decipher the meanings of the rhythms and sounds. Fearful that drums signaled rebellious uprisings, whites outlawed drumming but could not eliminate it. Most likely, the messages sent included lamentations about the drummers' lives of bondage.

aunt, or uncle. In West Africa, kinship identified a person's place among living relatives and linked the person to ancestors in the past and to descendants in the future. Newly imported African slaves usually arrived alone, like Equiano, without kin. Often slaves who had traversed the Middle Passage on the same ship adopted one another as "brothers" and "sisters." Likewise, as new Negroes were seasoned and incorporated into existing slave communities, established families often adopted them as fictive kin.

When possible, slaves expressed many other features of their West African origins in their lives on New World plantations. They gave their children traditional dolls and African names such as Cudjo or Quash, Minda or Fuladi. They grew food crops they had known in Africa, such as yams and okra. They constructed huts with mud walls and thatched roofs similar to African residences. They fashioned banjos, drums, and other musical instruments, held dances, and observed funeral rites that echoed African practices. In these and many other ways, slaves drew upon their African heritages as much as the oppressive circumstances of slavery permitted.

Tobacco, Rice, and Prosperity

Slaves' labor bestowed prosperity on their masters, British merchants, and the monarchy. Slavery was so important and valuable that one

minister claimed in 1757 that "to live in Virginia without slaves is morally impossible." The southern colonies supplied 90 percent of all North American exports to Britain. Rice exports from the lower South exploded from less than half a million pounds in 1700 to eighty million pounds in 1770, nearly all of it grown by slaves. Exports of indigo also boomed. Together, rice and indigo made up three-fourths of lower South exports, nearly two-thirds of them going to Britain and most of the rest to the West Indies, where sugar-growing slaves ate slave-grown rice.

Tobacco was by far the most important export from British North America; by 1770, it represented almost one-third of all colonial exports and three-fourths of all Chesapeake exports. Under the provisions of the Navigation Acts (see chapter 4), nearly all of it went to Britain, where the monarchy collected a lucrative tax on each pound. British merchants then reexported more than 80 percent of the tobacco to the European continent, pocketing a nice markup for their troubles.

These products of slave labor made the southern colonies by far the richest in North America. The per capita wealth of free whites in the South was four times greater than that in New England and three times that in the middle colonies. At the top of the wealth pyramid stood the rice grandees of the lower South and the tobacco gentry of the Chesapeake. These elite families commonly resided on large estates in handsome mansions adorned by luxurious gardens, all maintained and supported by slaves. The extravagant lifestyle of one gentry family astonished a young tutor from New Jersey, who noted that during the winter months the family kept twenty-eight large fires roaring, requiring six oxen to haul four heavy cartloads of slave-cut firewood to the house every day. In contrast, yeoman families — who supported themselves on small plots of land with family labor — cut their own firewood and usually warmed themselves around just one fire.

The vast differences in wealth among white southerners engendered envy and occasional tension between rich and poor, but remarkably little open hostility. In private, the planter elite spoke disparagingly of humble whites, but in public the planters acknowledged their lesser neighbors as equals, at least in belonging to the superior — in their minds — white race. Looking upward, white yeomen and tenants (who owned neither land nor slaves) sensed the gentry's condescension and veiled contempt. But they also appreciated the gentry for granting favors,

Eliza Lucas Pinckney's Gown
When Eliza Lucas was sixteen years old in 1738, she took over day-to-day management of her father's rice plantations when he was called to duty in the British army. Highly educated, independent, and energetic, Lucas relished her duties and introduced numerous innovations on the plantations, including the cultivation of indigo — which became a major export crop in South Carolina — and silkworms. She married Charles Pinckney, a wealthy rice planter, in 1744 and continued her interest in agricultural innovation while raising four children. The gown shown here was made for her out of silk produced on her plantation and sent to England to be dyed and woven. Smithsonian Institution, Washington, D.C.

upholding white supremacy, and keeping slaves in their place. Although racial slavery made a few whites much richer than others, it also gave those who did not get rich a powerful reason to feel similar (in race) to those who were so different (in wealth).

The slaveholding gentry dominated the politics and economy of the southern colonies. In Virginia, only adult white men who owned at least one hundred acres of unimproved land or twenty-five acres of land with a house could vote. This property-holding requirement prevented about 40 percent of white men in Virginia from voting for representatives to the House of Burgesses. In South Carolina, the property requirement was only fifty acres of land, and therefore most adult white men qualified to vote. In both colonies, voters elected members of the gentry to serve in the colonial legislature. The gentry passed elected political offices from generation to generation, almost as if they were hereditary. Politically, the gentry built a self-perpetuating oligarchy — rule by the elite few — with the votes of their many humble neighbors.

The gentry also set the cultural standard in the southern colonies. They entertained lavishly, gambled regularly, and attended Anglican (Church of England) services more for social than for religious reasons. Above all, they cultivated the leisurely pursuit of happiness. They did not condone idleness, however. Their many pleasures and responsibilities as plantation owners kept them busy. Thomas Jefferson, a phenomenally productive member of the gentry, recalled that his earliest childhood memory was of being carried on a pillow by a family slave — a powerful image of the slave hands supporting the gentry's leisure and achievement.

REVIEW   How did slavery influence the society and economy of the southern colonies?

▶ Unifying Experiences

The societies of New England, the middle colonies, and the southern colonies became more sharply differentiated during the eighteenth century, but colonists throughout British North America also shared unifying experiences that eluded settlers in the Spanish and French colonies. The first was economic. All three British colonial regions had their economic roots in agriculture. Colonists sold their distinctive products in markets that, in turn, offered a more or less uniform array of goods to consumers throughout British North America. Another unifying experience was a decline in the importance of religion. Some settlers called for a revival of religious intensity, but most people focused less on religion and more on the affairs of the world than they had in the seventeenth century. Also, white inhabitants throughout British North America became aware that they shared a distinctive identity as *British* colonists. Thirteen different governments presided over these North American colonies, but all of them answered to the British monarchy. British policies governed not only trade but also military and diplomatic relations with the Indians, French, and Spanish arrayed along colonial borderlands. Royal officials who expected loyalty from the colonists often had difficulty obtaining obedience. The British colonists asserted their prerogatives as British subjects to defend their special colonial interests.

Commerce and Consumption

Eighteenth-century commerce whetted colonists' appetites to consume. Colonial products spurred the development of mass markets throughout the Atlantic world (Figure 5.1). Huge increases in the supply of colonial tobacco and sugar brought the price of these small luxuries within the reach of most free whites. Colonial goods brought into focus an important lesson of eighteenth-century commerce: Ordinary people, not just the wealthy elite, would buy the things that they desired in addition to what they absolutely needed. Even news, formerly restricted mostly to a few people through face-to-face conversations or private letters, became an object of public consumption through the innovation of newspapers and the rise in literacy among whites. With the appropriate stimulus, market demand seemed unlimited.

The Atlantic commerce that took colonial goods to markets in Britain brought objects of consumer desire back to the colonies. British merchants and manufacturers recognized that colonists made excellent customers, and the Navigation Acts gave British exporters privileged access to the colonial market. By midcentury, export-oriented industries in Britain were growing ten times faster than firms attuned to the home market. Most British exports went to the vast European market, where potential customers outnumbered those in the colonies by more than one hundred to one.

But as European competition stiffened, colonial markets became increasingly important. British exports to North America multiplied eightfold between 1700 and 1770, outpacing the rate of population growth after midcentury. When the colonists' eagerness to consume exceeded their ability to pay, British exporters willingly extended credit, and colonial debts soared. Imported mirrors, silver plates, spices, bed and table linens, clocks, tea services, wigs, books, and more infiltrated parlors, kitchens, and bedrooms throughout the colonies. Despite the many differences among the colonists, the consumption of British exports built a certain material uniformity across region, religion, class, and status. Buying and using British exports made the colonists look and feel more British even though they lived at the edge of a wilderness an ocean away from Britain.

The dazzling variety of imported consumer goods also presented women and men with a novel array of choices. In many respects, the choices might appear trivial: whether to buy knives and forks, teacups, a mirror, or a clock. But such small choices confronted eighteenth-century consumers with a big question: What do you want? As colonial consumers defined and expressed their desires with greater frequency during the eighteenth century, they became accustomed to thinking of themselves as individuals who had the power to make decisions that influenced the quality of their lives — attitudes of significance in the hierarchical world of eighteenth-century British North America.

Religion, Enlightenment, and Revival

Eighteenth-century colonists could choose from almost as many religions as consumer goods. Virtually all of the bewildering variety of religious denominations represented some form of Christianity, almost all of them Protestant. Slaves made up the largest group of non-Christians. A few slaves converted to Christianity in Africa or after they arrived in North America, but most continued to embrace elements of indigenous African religions. Roman Catholics concentrated in Maryland as they had since the seventeenth century, but even there they were far outnumbered by Protestants.

The varieties of Protestant faith and practice ranged across a broad spectrum. The middle colonies and the southern backcountry included militant Baptists and Presbyterians. Huguenots

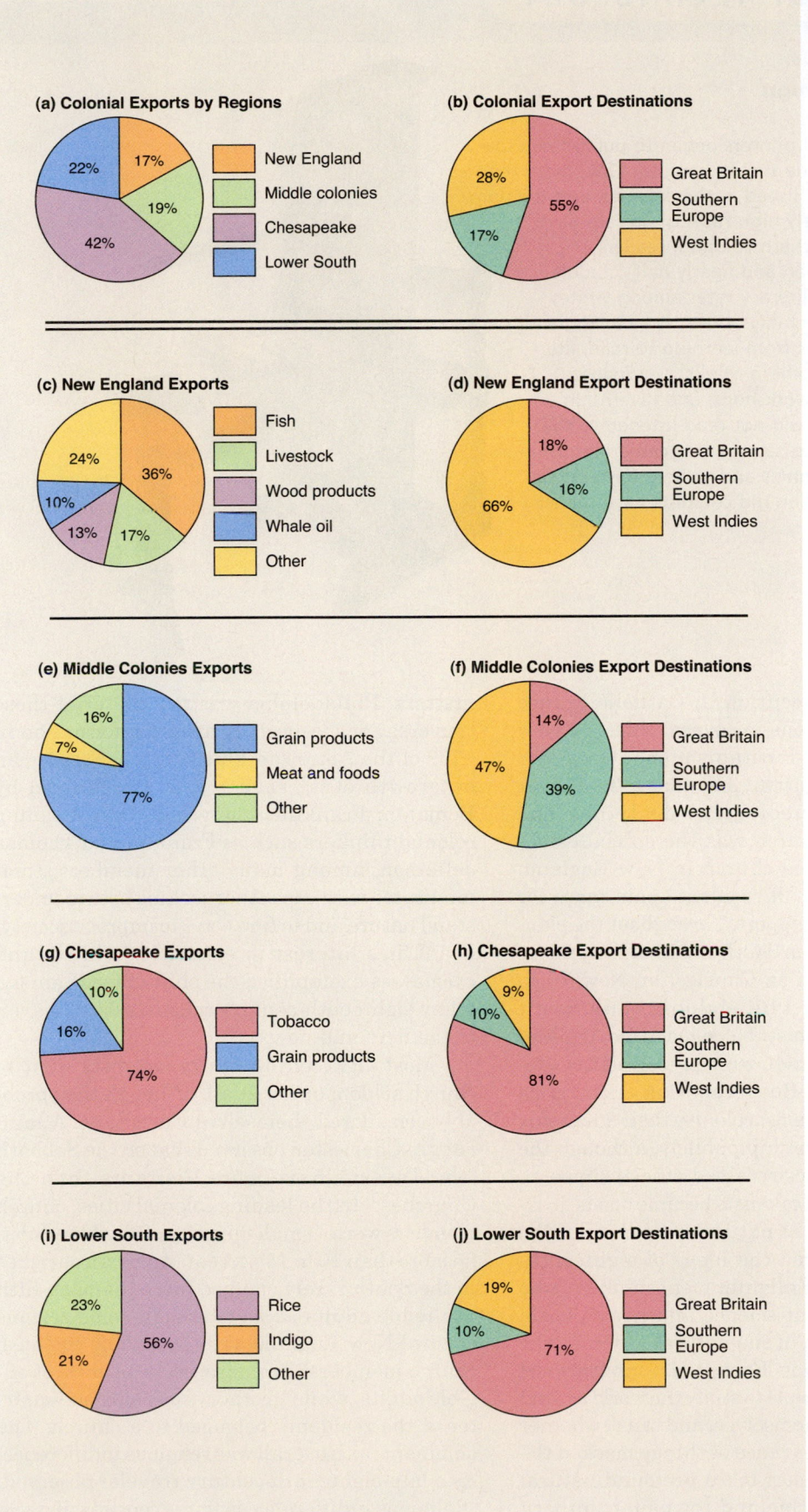

(a) Colonial Exports by Regions

- 17% New England
- 19% Middle colonies
- 42% Chesapeake
- 22% Lower South

(b) Colonial Export Destinations

- 55% Great Britain
- 17% Southern Europe
- 28% West Indies

(c) New England Exports

- 36% Fish
- 17% Livestock
- 13% Wood products
- 10% Whale oil
- 24% Other

(d) New England Export Destinations

- 18% Great Britain
- 16% Southern Europe
- 66% West Indies

(e) Middle Colonies Exports

- 77% Grain products
- 7% Meat and foods
- 16% Other

(f) Middle Colonies Export Destinations

- 14% Great Britain
- 39% Southern Europe
- 47% West Indies

(g) Chesapeake Exports

- 74% Tobacco
- 16% Grain products
- 10% Other

(h) Chesapeake Export Destinations

- 81% Great Britain
- 10% Southern Europe
- 9% West Indies

(i) Lower South Exports

- 56% Rice
- 21% Indigo
- 23% Other

(j) Lower South Export Destinations

- 71% Great Britain
- 10% Southern Europe
- 19% West Indies

FIGURE 5.1 Colonial Exports, 1768–1772

These pie charts provide an overview of the colonial export economy in the 1760s. The first two show that almost two-thirds of colonial exports came from the South and that the majority of the colonies' exports went to Great Britain. The remaining charts illustrate the distinctive patterns of exports in each colonial region. What do these patterns reveal about regional variations in Britain's North American colonies? What do they suggest about Britain's economic interest in the colonies?

THE PROMISE OF TECHNOLOGY

Newspapers and Public Opinion

In the eighteenth century, colonial printers began to publish newspapers on printing presses like the one shown here. By 1740, more than a dozen newspapers were being published in the colonies, and the number continued to increase. Relatively high rates of literacy gave them a large audience. In the northern colonies, readers included well over half of adult men and nearly half of adult women. In the southern colonies, literacy rates among whites were slightly lower but still considerably above those in England. Since whites tried to prevent slaves from learning to read, literacy rates remained low among southern blacks. Newspapers were often read aloud in homes, workshops, and taverns. In these public places, people who could not read listened to the controversial ideas and partisan accusations that caused information to spread beyond official channels and to help form public opinion. What sources of information did colonists have other than newspapers? Newport Historical Society.

who had fled persecution in Catholic France peopled congregations in several cities. In New England, old-style Puritanism splintered into strands of Congregationalism that differed over fine points of theological doctrine. The Congregational Church was the official established church in New England, and all residents paid taxes for its support. Throughout the plantation South and in urban centers such as Charleston, New York, and Philadelphia, prominent colonists belonged to the Anglican Church, which received tax support in the South. But dissenting faiths grew everywhere, and in most colonies their adherents won the right to worship publicly, although the established churches retained official support.

> ## "The Taverns have more Visitants than the Churches."
> — A Charleston minister

Many educated colonists became deists, looking for God's plan in nature more than in the Bible. **Deism** shared the ideas of eighteenth-century European Enlightenment thinkers, who tended to agree that science and reason could disclose God's laws in the natural order. In the colonies as well as in Europe, **Enlightenment** ideas encouraged people to study the world around them, to think for themselves, and to ask whether the disorderly appearance of things masked the principles of a deeper, more profound natural order. From New England towns to southern drawing rooms, individuals met to discuss such matters. Philadelphia was the center of these conversations, especially after the formation in 1769 of the American Philosophical Society, an outgrowth of an earlier group organized by Benjamin Franklin, who was a deist. Leading colonial thinkers such as Franklin and Thomas Jefferson, among many other members, communicated with each other seeking both to understand nature and to find ways to improve society. Franklin's interest in electricity, stoves, and eyeglasses exemplified the shift of focus among many eighteenth-century colonists from heaven to the here and now.

Most eighteenth-century colonists went to church seldom or not at all, although they probably considered themselves Christians. A minister in Charleston observed that on the Sabbath "the Taverns have more Visitants than the Churches." In the leading colonial cities, church members were a small minority of eligible adults, no more than 10 to 15 percent. Anglican parishes in the South rarely claimed more than one-fifth of eligible adults as members. In some regions of rural New England and the middle colonies, church membership embraced two-thirds of eligible adults, while in other areas only one-quarter of the residents belonged to a church. The dominant faith overall was religious indifference. As a late-eighteenth-century traveler observed, "Religious indifference is imperceptibly disseminated from one end of the continent to the other."

The spread of religious indifference, of deism, of denominational rivalry, and of comfortable backsliding profoundly concerned many Christians. A few despaired that, as one wrote, "religion . . . lay a-dying and ready to expire its last breath of life." To combat what one preacher called the "dead formality" of church services, some ministers set out to convert nonbelievers and to revive the piety of the faithful with a new style of preaching that appealed more to the heart than to the head. Historians have termed this wave of revivals the **Great Awakening**. In Massachusetts during the mid-1730s, the fiery Puritan minister **Jonathan Edwards** reaped a harvest of souls by reemphasizing traditional Puritan doctrines of humanity's utter depravity and God's vengeful omnipotence. The title of Edwards's most famous sermon, "Sinners in the Hands of an Angry God," conveys the flavor of his message. In Pennsylvania and New Jersey, William Tennent led revivals that dramatized spiritual rebirth with accounts of God's miraculous powers, such as raising Tennent's son from the dead.

The most famous revivalist in the eighteenth-century Atlantic world was **George Whitefield**. An Anglican, Whitefield preached well-worn messages of sin and salvation to large audiences in England using his spellbinding, unforgettable voice. Whitefield visited the North American colonies seven times, staying for more than three years during the mid-1740s and attracting tens of thousands to his sermons, including Benjamin Franklin and Olaudah Equiano. Whitefield's preaching transported many in his audience to emotion-choked states of religious ecstasy. About one revival he wrote, "The bitter cries and groans were enough to pierce the hardest heart. Some of the people were as pale as death; others were wringing their hands; others lying on the ground; others sinking into the arms of their friends; and most lifting their eyes to heaven, and crying to God for mercy."

Whitefield's successful revivals spawned many lesser imitations. Itinerant preachers, many of them poorly educated, toured the colonial backcountry after midcentury, echoing Whitefield's

George Whitefield

An anonymous artist portrayed George Whitefield preaching, emphasizing the power of his sermons to transport his audience to a revived awareness of divine spirituality. Light from above gleams off his forehead. His crossed eyes and faraway gaze suggest that he spoke in a semihypnotic trance. Notice the absence of a Bible on the pulpit. Rather than elaborating on God's Word as revealed in Scripture, Whitefield speaks from his own inner awareness. The woman below his hands appears transfixed. Her eyes and Whitefield's do not meet, yet the artist's use of light suggests that she and Whitefield see the same core of holy Truth. National Portrait Gallery, London.

medium and message as best they could. Bathsheba Kingsley, a member of Jonathan Edwards's flock, preached the revival message informally — as did an unprecedented number of other women throughout the colonies — causing her congregation to brand her a "brawling woman" who had "gone quite out of her place."

The revivals awakened and refreshed the spiritual energies of thousands of colonists struggling with the uncertainties and anxieties of eighteenth-century America. The conversions at revivals did not substantially boost the total number of church members, however. After the revivalists moved on, the routines and pressures of everyday existence reasserted their primacy in the lives of many converts. But the revivals communicated the important message that every soul mattered, that men and women could choose to be saved, that individuals had the power to make a decision for everlasting life or death. Colonial revivals expressed in religious terms many of the same democratic and egalitarian values expressed in economic terms by colonists' patterns of consumption. One colonist noted the analogy by referring to itinerant revivalists as "Pedlars in divinity." Like consumption, revivals contributed to a set of common experiences that bridged colonial divides of faith, region, class, and status.

Trade and Conflict in the North American Borderlands

British power defended the diverse inhabitants of its colonies from Indian, French, and Spanish enemies on their borders — as well as from foreign powers abroad. Each colony organized a militia, and privateers sailed from every port to prey on foreign ships. But the British navy and army bore ultimate responsibility for colonial

defense (Figure 5.2). Royal officials warily eyed the small North American settlements of New France and New Spain for signs of threats to the colonies.

Alone, neither New France nor New Spain jeopardized British North America, but with Indian allies they could become a potent force that kept colonists on their guard (Map 5.4). Native Americans' impulse to defend their territory from colonial incursions competed with their desire for trade, which tugged them toward the settlers. As a colonial official observed in 1761, "A modern Indian cannot subsist without Europeans. . . . [The European goods that were] only conveniency at first [have] now become necessity." To obtain such necessities as guns, ammunition, clothing, sewing utensils, and much more that was manufactured largely by the British, Indians trapped beavers, deer, and other furbearing animals throughout the interior.

British, French, Spanish, and Dutch officials monitored the fur trade to prevent their competitors from deflecting the flow of furs toward their own markets. Indians took advantage of this competition to improve their own prospects, playing one trader and empire off another. The Iroquois, for example, promised the French exclusive access to the furs and territory of the Great Lakes region and at the same time made the

---

FIGURE 5.2   GLOBAL COMPARISON: Large Warships in European Navies, 1660–1760

The large warships in England's navy usually outnumbered those of rival nations from 1660 to 1760. During the eighteenth century, the British fleet grew dramatically, while the fleets of rival nations declined. The British monarchy paid the enormous cost of building, manning, and maintaining the largest European navy because defending commerce and communication with its far-flung colonies was fundamental to the integrity of its empire. Although Britain's North American colonies benefited from defense by the most powerful navy in the Atlantic, colonists constantly worried about surprise attacks by other nations when British warships were someplace else. What might account for the changing numbers of warships between 1660 and 1760?

= 10 warships

| 1660 | 1710 | 1760 |

England   France   England   France   England   France

Netherlands   Denmark   Netherlands   Denmark   Netherlands   Denmark

Note: Comparable data does not exist for Spain.

same pledge of exclusive rights to the British. Indian tribes and confederacies also competed among themselves for favored trading rights with one colony or another, a competition colonists encouraged.

The shifting alliances and complex dynamics of the fur trade struck a fragile balance along the frontier. The threat of violence from all sides was ever present, and the threat became reality often enough for all parties to be prepared for the worst. In the **Yamasee War of 1715**, Yamasee and Creek Indians — with French encouragement — mounted a coordinated attack against colonial settlements in South Carolina and inflicted heavy casualties. The Cherokee Indians, traditional enemies of the Creeks, refused to join the attack. Instead, they protected their access to British trade goods by allying with the colonists and turning the tide of battle, thus triggering a murderous rampage of revenge by the colonists against the Creek and Yamasee tribes.

Relations between Indians and colonists differed from colony to colony and from year to year. But the British colonists' nagging perceptions of menace on the frontier kept them continually hoping for help from the British to keep the Indians at bay and to maintain the essential flow of trade. In 1754, the British colonists' endemic competition with the French flared into the Seven Years' War (also known as the French and Indian War), which would inflame the frontier for years (as discussed in chapter 6). Before the 1760s, neither the British colonists nor the British themselves developed a coherent policy toward the Indians. But both agreed that Indians made deadly enemies, profitable trading partners, and powerful allies. As a result, the British and their colonists kept an eye on both the French and Spanish empires and relations with the Indians.

The Spanish, in turn, were keeping an eye on the Pacific coast, where Russian hunters in search of seals and sea otters threatened to become a permanent presence on New Spain's northern frontier. To block Russian access to present-day California, officials in New Spain mounted a campaign to build forts (called **presidios**) and missions there. In 1769, an expedition headed by a military man, **Gaspar de Portolá**, and a Catholic priest, **Junípero Serra**, traveled north from Mexico to present-day San Diego, where they founded the first California mission, San Diego de Alcalá. They soon journeyed all the way to Monterey, which became the capital of Spanish California. There Portolá established a presidio in 1770 "to defend us from attacks by the Russians," he wrote. The same year, Serra founded Mission

MAP 5.4

Zones of Empire in Eastern North America
The British zone, extending west from the Atlantic coast, was much more densely settled than the zones under French, Spanish, and Indian control. The comparatively large number of British colonists made them more secure than the relatively few colonists in the vast regions claimed by France and Spain or the settlers living among the many Indian peoples in the huge area between the Mississippi River and the Appalachian Mountains. Yet the British colonists were not powerful enough to dominate the French, Spaniards, or Indians. Instead, they had to guard against attacks by powerful Indian groups allied with the French or Spaniards.

San Carlos Borroméo de Carmelo in Monterey to convert the Indians and recruit them to work to support the soldiers and other Spaniards in the presidio. By 1772, Serra had founded other missions along the path from San Diego to Monterey.

One Spanish soldier praised the work of the missionaries, writing that "with flattery and presents [the missionaries] attract the savage Indians and persuade them to adhere to life in society and to receive instruction for a knowledge of the Catholic faith, the cultivation of the land, and the arts necessary for making the instruments most needed for farming." Yet for the Indians, the Spaniards' California missions had horrendous consequences, as they had elsewhere in the Spanish borderlands. European diseases decimated Indian populations, Spanish soldiers raped Indian women, and missionaries beat Indians and subjected them to near slavery. Indian uprisings against the Spaniards occurred repeatedly (see "Documenting the American Promise," page 150), but the presidios and missions endured as feeble projections of the Spanish empire along the Pacific coast.

Colonial Politics in the British Empire

The plurality of peoples, faiths, and communities that characterized the North American colonies arose from the somewhat haphazard policies of the eighteenth-century British empire. Since the Puritan Revolution of the mid-seventeenth century, British monarchs had valued the colonies' contributions to trade and encouraged their growth and development. Unlike Spain and France — whose policies of excluding Protestants and foreigners kept the

Spanish Missions in California

Map labels:
CALIFORNIA
San Francisco (1776)
San José (1777)
San Joaquin R.
Monterey (1770)
San Antonio de Padua (1771)
San Luis Obispo (1772)
El Camino Real
Santa Barbara (1782)
Los Angeles (1781)
San Gabriel (177
San Juan Capistrano (17
San Diego (1769)
PACIFIC OCEAN
✝ Mission
✝ Presidio & mission
● Mission & town

Mission Carmel

This eighteenth-century drawing portrays a reception for a Spanish visitor at Mission Carmel in what is now Carmel, California. Lines of mission Indians dressed in robes flank the entrance to the chapel where a priest and his assistants await the visitor. During worship, priests wore lavishly decorated chasubles, like the one shown here from Mission Santa Clara. The intricate and colorful embroidery signified the magnificence of divine authority, embodied in the priests — God's representatives on earth — and their Spanish sponsors. The reception ritual dramatized the strict hierarchy that governed relations among Spanish missionaries, ruling officials, and the subordinate Indians. Reception: University of California at Berkeley, Bancroft Library; chasuble: de Saisset Museum, Santa Clara University.

Ambush of Spanish Expedition

In May 1720, the New Mexico governor sent forty-three Spanish soldiers and sixty Pueblo Indians to expel French intruders from New Spain's northern borderlands. In August, when the expedition reached present-day Nebraska, the French and their Indian allies attacked, killing thirty-three Spaniards and twelve Pueblos. Shortly afterward, an artist — whether Indian or Spanish is unknown — recorded the ambush in this hide painting. The priest in the center of the painting shown here is Father Juan Minguez, the first priest assigned to Albuquerque; he was killed in the ambush. The Indian directly in front of him is Joseph Naranjo, leader of the Spaniards' Pueblo allies, who also was killed. Courtesy of the Museum of New Mexico, Neg. No. 149804.

population of their North American colonial territories tiny — Britain kept the door to its colonies open to anyone, and tens of thousands of non-British immigrants settled in the North American colonies and raised families.

The open door did not extend to trade, however, as the seventeenth-century Navigation Acts restricted colonial trade to British ships and traders. These policies evolved because they served the interests of the monarchy and of influential groups in Britain and the colonies. The policies also gave the colonists a common framework of political expectations and experiences.

British attempts to exercise political power in their colonial governments met with success so long as British officials were on or very near the sea. Colonists acknowledged — although they did not always readily comply with — British authority to collect customs duties, inspect cargoes, and enforce trade regulations. But when royal officials tried to wield their authority in the internal affairs of the colonies on land, they invariably encountered colonial resistance. A governor appointed by the king in each of the nine royal colonies (Rhode Island and Connecticut selected their own governors) or by the proprietors in Maryland and Pennsylvania headed the government of each colony. The British envisioned colonial governors as mini-monarchs able to exert influence in the colonies much as the king did in Britain. But colonial governors were not kings, and the colonies were not Britain.

Eighty percent of colonial governors had been born in England, not in the colonies. Some governors stayed in England, close to the source of royal patronage, and delegated the grubby details of colonial affairs to subordinates. Even the best-intentioned colonial governors had difficulty developing relations of trust and respect with influential colonists because their terms of office averaged just five years and could be terminated at any time. Colonial governors controlled few patronage positions to secure political friendships in the colonies. Officials who administered the colonial customs service, for example, received their appointments through patronage networks centered in England rather than from colonial governors. Obedient and loyal to their superiors in Britain, colonial governors fought incessantly with the colonists' assemblies. They battled over governors' vetoes of colonial legislation, removal of colonial judges, creation of new courts, dismissal of the representative assemblies, and other local issues.

Spanish Priests Report on California Missions

Catholic missionaries sent regular reports to their superiors in Mexico City, New Spain's capital city. The reports described what the missionaries considered their successes in converting pagan Indians — whom they called gentiles — as well as the difficulties caused by the behavior of both Spaniards and Indians.

DOCUMENT 1
Father Luís Jayme Describes Conditions at Mission San Diego de Alcalá, 1772

Father Luís Jayme, a Franciscan missionary, reported on the deplorable behavior of some of the Spanish soldiers at Mission San Diego de Alcalá, who frequently raped Indian women, causing many Indians to resist the efforts of the missionaries.

With reference to the Indians, I wish to say that great progress [in converting Indians] would be made if there was anything to eat and the soldiers would set a good example. We cannot give them anything to eat because what Don Pedro [the governor] has given is not enough to last half a year for the Indians from the Californias who are here. Thus little progress will be made under present conditions. As for the example set by the soldiers, no doubt some of them are good exemplars and deserve to be treated accordingly, but very many of them deserve to be hanged on account of the continuous outrages which they are committing in seizing and raping the women. There is not a single mission where all the gentiles have not been scandalized, and even on the roads, so I have been told. Surely, as the gentiles themselves state, they [the soldiers] are committing a thousand evils, particularly of a sexual nature. . . .

At one of these Indian villages near this mission of San Diego, which said village is very large, and which is on the road to Monterey, the gentiles therein many times have been on the point of coming here to kill us all, and

the reason for this is that some soldiers went there and raped their women, and other soldiers who were carrying the mail to Monterey turned their animals into their fields and they ate up their crops. Three other Indian villages . . . [near] here have reported the same thing to me several times. For this reason on several occasions when . . . I have gone to see these Indian villages, as soon as they saw us they fled from their villages and fled to the woods or other remote places. . . . They do this so that the soldiers will not rape their women as they have already done so many times in the past.

No wonder the Indians here were bad when the mission was first founded. To begin with, they did not know why [the Spaniards] had come, unless they wanted to take their lands away from them. Now they all want to be Christians because they know that there is a God who created the heavens and earth and all things, that there is a Hell and Glory, that they have souls, etc., but when the mission was first founded . . . they thought they were like animals, and . . . they were very loath to pray, and they did not want to be Christians at all. . . . [Now] they all know the natural law, which, so I am informed, they have observed as well or better than many Christians elsewhere. They do not have idols; they do not go on drinking sprees; they do not marry relatives; and they have but one wife. The married men sleep with their wives only. . . . Some of the first adults whom we baptized, when we pointed out to them that it was wrong to have sexual intercourse with a woman to whom they were not married, told me that they already knew that, and that among them it was

---

Some governors developed a working relationship with the colonists' assemblies. But during the eighteenth century, the assemblies gained the upper hand.

Since British policies did not clearly define the colonists' legal powers, colonial assemblies seized the opportunity to make their own rules.

Gradually, the assemblies established a strong tradition of representative government analogous, in their eyes, to the British Parliament. Voters often returned the same representatives to the assemblies year after year, building continuity in power and leadership that far exceeded that of the governor.

considered to be very bad, and so they do not do so at all. "The soldiers," they told me, "are Christians and, although they know that God will punish them in Hell, do so, having sexual intercourse with our wives." "We," they said, "although we did not know that God would punish us for that in Hell, considered it to be very bad, and we did not do it, and even less now that we know that God will punish us if we do so." When I heard this, I burst into tears to see how these gentiles were setting an example for us Christians.

SOURCE: Maynard Geiger, trans. and ed., *The Letter of Luís Jayme, O.F.M.: San Diego, October 17, 1772* (Los Angeles, 1970), 38–42.

DOCUMENT 2
Father Junípero Serra Describes the Indian Revolt at Mission San Diego de Alcalá, 1775

Father Junípero Serra, the founder of many of the California missions, reported to his superiors in Mexico City that an Indian uprising had destroyed Mission San Diego de Alcalá. He recommended rebuilding and urged officials to provide additional soldiers to defend the missions, but not to punish the rebellious Indians.

As we are in the vale of tears, not all the news I have to relate can be pleasant. And so I make no excuses for announcing . . . the tragic news that I have just received of the total destruction of the San Diego Mission, and of the death of the senior of its two religious ministers, called Father Luís Jayme, at the hand of the rebellious gentiles and of the Christian neophytes [Indians who lived in the mission]. All this happened, November 5th, about one or two o'clock at night. The gentiles came together from forty rancherías [settlements], according to information given me, and set fire to the church, after sacking it. They then went to the storehouse, the house where the Fathers lived, the soldiers' barracks, and all the rest of the buildings. They killed a carpenter . . . and a blacksmith. . . . They wounded with their arrows the four soldiers, who alone were on guard at the . . . mission. . . .

And now, after the Father has been killed, the Mission burned, its many and valuable furnishings destroyed, together with the sacred vessels, its paintings, its baptis-

mal, marriage, and funeral records, and all the furnishings for the sacristy, the house, and the farm implements — now the forces [of soldiers] of both presidios [nearby] come together to set things right. . . . What happened was that before they set about reestablishing the Mission, they wanted to . . . lay hands on the guilty ones who were responsible for the burning of the Mission, and the death of the Fathers, and chastise them. The harassed Indians rebelled anew and became more enraged. . . . And so the soldiers there are gathered together in their presidios, and the Indians in their state of heathenism. . . .

While the missionary is alive, let the soldiers guard him, and watch over him, like the pupils of God's very eyes. That is as it should be. . . . But after the missionary has been killed, what can be gained by campaigns [against the rebellious Indians]? Some will say to frighten them and prevent them from killing others. What I say is that, in order to prevent them from killing others, keep better guard over them than they did over the one who has been killed; and, as to the murderer, let him live, in order that he should be saved — which is the very purpose of our coming here, and the reason which justifies it.

SOURCE: Antonine Tibesar, O.F.M., ed., *The Writings of Junípero Serra* (Washington, D.C., 1956), 2:401–7. Reprinted by permission of the American Academy of Franciscan History.

Questions for Analysis and Debate

1. In what ways did Jayme and Serra agree about the motivations of Indians in and around Mission San Diego de Alcalá? In what ways did they disagree? How would Serra's recommendations for rebuilding the mission have addressed the problems identified by Jayme that caused the revolt?

2. How did the goals and activities of the Spanish soldiers compare with those of the Catholic missionaries?

3. How did the religious convictions of Jayme and Serra influence their reports? What might Spanish soldiers or Indians have said about these events? What might they have said about missionaries like Jayme and Serra?

By 1720, colonial assemblies had won the power to initiate legislation, including tax laws and authorizations to spend public funds. Although all laws passed by the assemblies (except in Maryland, Rhode Island, and Connecticut) had to be approved by the governor and then by the Board of Trade in Britain, the difficulties in communication about complex subjects over long distances effectively ratified the assemblies' decisions. Years often passed before colonial laws were repealed by British authorities, and in the meantime the assemblies' laws prevailed.

The heated political struggles between royal governors and colonial assemblies that occurred throughout the eighteenth century taught colonists a common set of political lessons. They learned to employ traditionally British ideas of representative government to defend their own colonial interests. More important, they learned that power in the British colonies rarely belonged to the British government.

REVIEW What experiences tended to unify the colonists in British North America during the eighteenth century?

▶ Conclusion: The Dual Identity of British North American Colonists

During the eighteenth century, a society that was both distinctively colonial and distinctively British emerged in British North America. Tens of thousands of immigrants and slaves gave the colonies an unmistakably colonial complexion and contributed to the colonies' growing population and expanding economy. People of different ethnicities and faiths sought their fortunes in the colonies, where land was cheap, labor was dear, and — as Benjamin Franklin preached — work promised to be rewarding. Indentured servants and redemptioners risked temporary periods of bondage for the potential reward of better opportunities in the colonies than on the Atlantic's eastern shore. Slaves arrived in unprecedented numbers and endured lifelong servitude, which they neither chose nor desired but from which their masters greatly benefited.

None of the European colonies could claim complete dominance of North America. The desire to expand and defend their current claims meant that the English, French, and Spanish colonies were drawn into regular conflict with one another, as well as with the Indians upon whose land they encroached. In varying degrees, all sought control of the Native Americans and their land, their military power, their trade, and even their souls. Spanish missionaries and soldiers sought to convert Indians on the West Coast and exploit their labor; French alliances with Indian tribes posed a formidable barrier to westward expansion of the British empire.

Yet despite their attempts to tame their New World holdings, Spanish and French colonists did not develop societies that began to rival the European empires that sponsored and supported them. They did not participate in the cultural, economic, social, and religious changes experienced by their counterparts in British North America, nor did they share in the emerging political identity of the British colonists.

Identifiably colonial products from New England, the middle colonies, and the southern colonies flowed to the West Indies and across the Atlantic. Back came unquestionably British consumer goods along with fashions in ideas, faith, and politics. The bonds of the British empire required colonists to think of themselves as British subjects and, at the same time, encouraged them to consider their status as colonists. By 1750, British colonists in North America could not imagine that their distinctively dual identity — as British and as colonists — would soon become a source of intense conflict. But by 1776, colonists in British North America had to choose whether they were British or American.

Selected Bibliography

General Works

Ira Berlin, *Generations of Captivity: A History of African-American Slaves* (2003).

Holly Brewer, *By Birth or Consent: Children, Law, and the Anglo-American Revolution in Authority* (2005).

Jan de Vries, *The Industrious Revolution: Consumer Behavior and the Household Economy, 1650 to the Present* (2008).

Eric Jay Dolin, *Fur, Fortune, and Empire: The Epic History of the Fur Trade in America* (2010).

Kathleen DuVal, *The Native Ground: Indians and Colonists in the Heart of the Continent* (2006).

Julie Flavell, *When London Was Capital of America* (2010).

Patrick Griffin, *The People with No Name: Ireland's Ulster Scots, America's Scots Irish, and the Creation of a British Atlantic World, 1689–1764* (2001).

David Hancock, *Oceans of Wine: Madeira and the Emergence of American Trade and Taste* (2009).

Brendan McConville, *The King's Three Faces: The Rise and Fall of Royal America, 1688–1776* (2007).

Nancy Shoemaker, *A Strange Likeness: Becoming Red and White in Eighteenth-Century North America* (2005).

Peter Silver, *Our Savage Neighbors: How Indian War Transformed Early America* (2008).

New England

Richard Aquila, *The Iroquois Restoration: Iroquois Diplomacy on the Colonial Frontier, 1701–1754* (1997).

Elaine Forman Crane, *Ebb Tide in New England: Women, Seaports, and Social Change, 1630–1800* (1998).

Phyllis Whitman Hunter, *Purchasing Identity in the Atlantic World: Massachusetts Merchants, 1670–1780* (2001).

George M. Marsden, *Jonathan Edwards: A Life* (2003).

Lisa Norling, *Captain Ahab Had a Wife: New England Women and the Whale Fishery, 1720–1870* (2000).

Daniel Vickers, *Young Men and the Sea: Yankee Seafarers in the Age of Sail* (2005).

Middle Colonies

Katherine Carté Engel, *Religion and Profit: Moravians in Early America* (2009).

Leslie M. Harris, *In the Shadow of Slavery: African Americans in New York City, 1626–1863* (2003).

Eric Hinderaker, *Elusive Empires: Constructing Colonialism in the Ohio Valley, 1673–1800* (1997).

Jill Lepore, *New York Burning: Liberty, Slavery, and Conspiracy in Eighteenth-Century Manhattan* (2005).

James H. Merrell, *Into the American Woods: Negotiators on the Pennsylvania Frontier* (1999).

Jane T. Merritt, *At the Crossroads: Indians and Empires on a Mid-Atlantic Frontier, 1700–1763* (2003).

Donna Merwick, *The Shame and the Sorrow: Dutch-Amerindian Encounters in New Netherland* (2006).

Simon P. Newman, *Embodied History: The Lives of the Poor in Early Philadelphia* (2003).

David Waldstreicher, *Runaway America: Benjamin Franklin, Slavery, and the American Revolution* (2004).

Southern Colonies

Vincent Carretta, *Equiano the African: Biography of a Self-Made Man* (2005).

Steven W. Hackel, *Children of Coyote, Missionaries of Saint Francis: Indian-Spanish Relations in Colonial California, 1769–1850* (2005).

Robert H. Jackson, *Missions and the Frontiers of Spanish America* (2005).

Catherine Kerrison, *Claiming the Pen: Women and Intellectual Life in the Early American South* (2006).

Philip D. Morgan, *Slave Counterpoint: Black Culture in the Eighteenth-Century Chesapeake and Low Country* (1998).

Robert Olwell, *Masters, Slaves, and Subjects: The Culture of Power in the South Carolina Low Country, 1740–1790* (1998).

Jon F. Sensbach, *Rebecca's Revival: Creating Black Christianity in the Atlantic World* (2005).

Randy Sparks, *The Two Princes of Calabar: An Eighteenth-Century Atlantic Odyssey* (2004).

David J. Weber, *Bárbaros: Spaniards and Their Savages in the Age of Enlightenment* (2005).

Bradford J. Wood, *This Remote Part of the World: Regional Formation in Lower Cape Fear, North Carolina, 1725–1775* (2004).

▶ **FOR MORE BOOKS ABOUT TOPICS IN THIS CHAPTER,** see the Online Bibliography at **bedfordstmartins.com/roark**.

▶ **FOR ADDITIONAL PRIMARY SOURCES FROM THIS PERIOD,** see Michael Johnson, ed., *Reading the American Past*, Fifth Edition.

▶ **FOR WEB SITES, IMAGES, AND DOCUMENTS RELATED TO TOPICS AND PLACES IN THIS CHAPTER,** visit Make History at **bedfordstmartins.com/roark**.

Reviewing Chapter 5

KEY TERMS

Explain each term's significance.

A Growing Population and Expanding Economy in British North America
- natural increase (p. 125)

New England: From Puritan Settlers to Yankee Traders
- partible inheritance (p. 127)
- Atlantic commerce (p. 127)

The Middle Colonies: Immigrants, Wheat, and Work
- Pennsylvania Dutch (p. 129)
- Scots-Irish (p. 130)
- redemptioners (p. 131)
- Iroquois Indians (p. 133)
- Benjamin Franklin (p. 135)

The Southern Colonies: Land of Slavery
- Middle Passage (p. 137)
- Olaudah Equiano (p. 137)
- new Negroes (p. 137)
- country-born or creole slaves (p. 138)
- Stono rebellion (p. 139)
- task system (p. 139)

Unifying Experiences
- deism (p. 144)
- Enlightenment (p. 144)
- Great Awakening (p. 145)
- Jonathan Edwards (p. 145)
- George Whitefield (p. 145)
- Yamasee War of 1715 (p. 147)
- presidios (p. 147)
- Gaspar de Portolá (p. 147)
- Junípero Serra (p. 147)

REVIEW QUESTIONS

Use key terms and dates to support your answer.

1. How did the North American colonies achieve the remarkable population growth of the eighteenth century? (pp. 125–126)

2. Why did settlement patterns in New England change from the seventeenth to the eighteenth century? (pp. 126–129)

3. Why did immigrants flood into Pennsylvania during the eighteenth century? (pp. 129–135)

4. How did slavery influence the society and economy of the southern colonies? (pp. 135–141)

5. What experiences tended to unify the colonists in British North America during the eighteenth century? (pp. 141–152)

MAKING CONNECTIONS

Draw on key terms, the timeline, and review questions.

1. Colonial products such as tobacco and sugar transformed consumption patterns on both sides of the Atlantic in the eighteenth century. How did consumption influence the relationship between the American colonies and Britain? In your answer, consider how it might have strengthened and weakened connections.

2. Why did the importance of religion decline throughout the colonies from the seventeenth to the eighteenth century? How did American colonists respond to these changes?

3. How did different colonies attempt to manage relations with the Indians? How did the Indians attempt to manage relationships with the Europeans? In your answer, consider disputes over territory and trade.

4. Varied immigration patterns contributed to important differences among the British colonies. Compare and contrast patterns of immigration to the middle and southern colonies. Who came, and how did they get there? How did they shape the economic, cultural, and political character of each colony?

154

LINKING TO THE PAST

Link events in this chapter to earlier events.

1. How did the British North American colonies in 1750 differ politically and economically from those in 1650? Were there important continuities? (See chapters 3 and 4.)

2. Is there persuasive evidence that colonists' outlook on the world shifted from the seventeenth to the eighteenth century? Why or why not? (See chapters 3 and 4.)

▶ FOR PRACTICE QUIZZES AND OTHER STUDY TOOLS, visit the Online Study Guide at bedfordstmartins.com/roark.

TIMELINE 1702–1775

1711– 1713	• Queen Anne's War triggers German migration to North America.
1711	• North Carolina founded.
1715	• Yamasee War.
1730s	• Jonathan Edwards promotes Great Awakening.
1732	• Georgia founded.
1733	• Benjamin Franklin begins to publish *Poor Richard's Almanack.*
1739	• Stono rebellion.
1740s	• George Whitefield preaches religious revival in North America. • Majority of southern slaves are country-born.
1745	• Olaudah Equiano born.
1750s	• Colonists begin to move down Shenandoah Valley.
1754	• Seven Years' War begins.
1769	• American Philosophical Society founded. • First California mission, San Diego de Alcalá, established.
1770	• Mission and presidio established at Monterey, California. • British North American colonists number more than two million.
1775	• Indians destroy San Diego mission.

PATRICK HENRY'S MAP DESK

This odd little table with its pullout extensions supported large maps and larger dreams of wealth from land speculation. Patrick Henry, like many elite Virginians in the 1760s, bought thousands of acres of frontier land west of the Appalachian Mountains, hoping to resell later at a higher price to settlers. Yet his acreage was occupied by the Cherokee. To avoid frontier war, the British prohibited speculation and settlement west of the mountains. Henry soon won election to Virginia's House of Burgesses (pictured in the background in a painting made in 1851 by Pennsylvania artist Peter Frederick Rothemel), and by 1775 he spoke in favor of independence, a position that eventually would unleash settlers looking to buy western land from speculators like him.

6

The British Empire and the Colonial Crisis
1754–1775

IN 1771, THOMAS HUTCHINSON BECAME THE ROYAL GOVERNOR OF the colony of Massachusetts. Unlike most royal governors, who were British aristocrats sent over by the king for short tours of duty, Hutchinson was a fifth-generation American. A Harvard-educated member of the Massachusetts elite, from a family of successful merchants, he had served two decades in the Massachusetts general assembly. In 1758, Thomas Hutchinson was appointed lieutenant governor, and in 1760 he also became chief justice of the colony's highest court. He lived in the finest mansion in Boston. Wealth, power, and influence were his in abundance. He was proud of his connection to the British empire and loyal to his king.

Hutchinson had the misfortune to be a loyal colonial leader during the two very tumultuous decades leading up to the American Revolution. He worked hard to keep the British and colonists aligned in interests, even promoting a plan to unify the colonies with a limited government (the Albany Plan of Union) to deal with Indian policy. His plan of union ultimately failed, however, and a major war — the Seven Years' War — ensued, pitting the British and colonists against the French and their Indian allies in the backcountry of the American colonies. When the war ended and the British government began to think about taxing colonists to pay for it, Hutchinson had no doubt that the new British taxation policies were legitimate — unwise, perhaps, but legitimate.

Not everyone in Boston shared his opinion. Fervent, enthusiastic crowds protested against a succession of British taxation policies enacted after 1763 — the Sugar Act, the Stamp Act, the Townshend duties, the Tea Act, all landmark events on the road to the American Revolution. But Hutchinson maintained his steadfast loyalty to Britain. His love of order and tradition inclined him to unconditional support of the British empire, and by nature he was a measured and cautious man. "My temper does not incline to enthusiasm," he once wrote.

Privately, he lamented the stupidity of the British acts that provoked trouble, but his sense of duty required him to defend the king's policies, however misguided. Quickly, he became an inspiring villain to the emerging

Thomas Hutchinson
The only formal portrait of Thomas Hutchinson still in existence shows an assured young man in ruffles. Decades of turmoil in Boston failed to puncture his self-confidence. Doubtless he sat for other portraits, as did all the Boston leaders in the 1760s to 1780s, but no other likeness has survived. One portrait of him hung in his summer house outside Boston; a revolutionary crowd mutilated it and stabbed out the eyes. In 1775, Hutchinson fled to Britain, the country he regarded as his cultural home, only to realize how very American he was. Courtesy of the Massachusetts Historical Society.

revolutionary movement. Governor Hutchinson came to personify all that was wrong with British and colonial relations. The man not inclined to enthusiasm unleashed popular enthusiasm all around him. He never appreciated that irony.

In another irony, Thomas Hutchinson was actually one of the first Americans to recognize the difficulties of maintaining full rights and privileges for colonists so far from their supreme government, the king and Parliament in Britain. In 1769, when British troops occupied Boston in an effort to provide civil order, he wrote privately to a friend in England, "There must be an abridgement of what are called English liberties. . . . I doubt whether it is possible to project a system of government in which a colony three thousand miles distant from the parent state shall enjoy all the liberty of the parent state." What he could not imagine was the possibility of giving up the parent state and creating an independent government closer to home.

Thomas Hutchinson was a loyalist; in the 1750s, most English-speaking colonists were affectionately loyal to Britain. But the Seven Years' War, which Britain and its colonies fought together as allies, shook that affection, and imperial policies in the decade following the war shattered it completely. Over the course of 1763 to 1773, Americans insistently raised serious questions about Britain's governance of its colonies. Many came to believe what Thomas Hutchinson could never accept — that a tyrannical Britain had embarked on a course to enslave the colonists by depriving them of their traditional English liberties.

The opposite of liberty was slavery, a condition of nonfreedom and coercion. Political rhetoric about liberty, tyranny, and slavery heated up the emotions of white colonists during the many crises of the 1760s and 1770s. But this rhetoric turned out to be a two-edged sword. The call for an end to tyrannical slavery meant one thing when sounded by Boston merchants whose commercial shipping rights had been revoked, but the same call meant something quite different in 1775 when sounded by black Americans locked in the bondage of slavery.

► The Seven Years' War, 1754–1763

For the first half of the eighteenth century, Britain was at war intermittently with France or Spain. Often the colonists in America experienced reverberations from these conflicts, most acutely along the frontier of New France in northern New England.

In the 1750s, international tensions returned, this time sparked by conflicts over contested land in America's Ohio Valley. The land, variously claimed by Virginians, Pennsylvanians, and the French, was actually inhabited by more than a dozen Indian tribes. The result was the costly **Seven Years' War** (its British name), known in the colonies as the French and Indian War, in which Americans and the British shared the hardships of battle and finally the glory of victory. Before it ended in 1763, fighting had extended through Europe, into the Caribbean, and even to India. The immense costs of the war — in money, death, and desire for revenge by losers and even winners — laid the groundwork for the imperial crisis of the 1760s between the British and Americans.

French-British Rivalry in the Ohio Country

For several decades, French traders had cultivated alliances with the Indian tribes in the Ohio Country, a frontier region they regarded as part of New France (Map 6.1). Cementing their relationships with gifts, the French established a profitable exchange of manufactured goods for beaver furs. But in the 1740s, Pennsylvania traders began to infringe on the territory. Adding to the tensions, a group of enterprising Virginians, including the brothers Lawrence and Augustine Washington, formed the **Ohio Company** in 1747 and advanced into French-claimed territory. Their goal was to secure wilderness tracts to be resold later on to the exploding Anglo-American population seeking fresh land.

French soldiers began building a series of military forts to secure their trade routes and to create a western barrier to American population expansion.

In response, the royal governor of Virginia, Robert Dinwiddie, also a shareholder in the Ohio Company, dispatched a messenger in 1753 to warn the French that they were trespassing on Virginia land. For this dangerous mission, he chose the twenty-one-year-old George Washington, half-brother of the Ohio Company leaders, who did not disappoint. Washington returned with crucial intelligence confirming French military intentions.

Impressed, Dinwiddie appointed the youth to lead a small military expedition west to assert and, if need be, defend Virginia's claim. Imperial officials in London, concerned about the French fortifications, had authorized the governor "to repel force by force," only if the French attacked first. By early 1754, the French had built Fort Duquesne at the forks of the Ohio River; Washington's delicate assignment was to chase the French away without actually being the aggressor.

In the spring of 1754, Washington set out with 160 Virginians and a small contingent of Mingo Indians, who were also concerned about the French military presence in the Ohio Country. The first battle of what would become known as the French and Indian War occurred early one May morning when the Mingo chief Tanaghrisson led a detachment of Washington's soldiers to a small French encampment in the woods. Who fired first was later a matter of dispute, but fourteen Frenchmen (and no Virginians) were wounded. While Washington, lacking a translator, struggled to communicate with the injured French commander, Tanaghrisson and his men intervened to kill and then scalp the wounded soldiers, including the commander, probably with the aim of inflaming hostilities between the French and the colonists.

This sudden massacre violated Washington's instructions to avoid being the aggressor and raised the stakes considerably. Fearing retaliation, Washington ordered his men to fortify their position, resulting in the makeshift "Fort Necessity." Reinforcements amounting to several hundred more Virginians arrived, but the Mingos, sensing disaster and displeased by Washington's style of command, fled. (Tanaghrisson later said, "The Colonel was a good-natured man, but had no experience; he took upon him to

Ohio River Valley, 1753

Lake Erie

Fort Presqu'isle
Fort Le Boeuf
Fort Machault (Venango)
Allegheny R.
PA.
Fort Duquesne
Redstone Old Fort
Fort Necessity
Fort Cumberland
Scioto R.
Muskingum R.
Ohio R.
Ohio Company
VIRGINIA
Kanawha R.

† British fort
† French fort

Map 6.1　European Areas of Influence and the Seven Years' War, 1754–1763
In the mid-eighteenth century, France, Britain, and Spain claimed vast areas of North America, many of them already inhabited by various Indian peoples. The early flash points of the Seven Years' War were in regions of disputed claims where the French had allied with powerful native groups — the Iroquois and the Algonquian tribes — to put pressure on the westward-moving British and Americans.

command the Indians as his slaves, [and] would by no means take advice from the Indians.") In early July, more than six hundred French soldiers aided by one hundred Shawnee and Delaware warriors attacked Fort Necessity, killing or wounding a third of Washington's men. The message was clear: The French would not depart from the disputed territory.

The Albany Congress

Even as Virginians, Frenchmen, and Indians fought and died in the Ohio Country, British imperial leaders hoped to prevent a larger war. One obvious strategy was to strengthen frayed British alliances with once friendly Indian tribes. Since 1692, Mohawks and New York merchants in the fur trade had participated in an alliance called the Covenant Chain, but lately the Mohawks felt neglected by British officials and left open to victimization by unsavory land speculators and Albany fur traders. British authorities in London directed the governor to convene a colonial conference to repair trade relations and secure the Indians' help — or at least their neutrality — against the looming French threat.

More than just New Yorkers and Mohawks were called to the Albany meeting, held in June and July 1754. Seven colonies sent a total of twenty-four delegates, making this an unprecedented pan-colony gathering. All six constituent tribes of the Iroquois Confederacy, of which the Mohawks were the easternmost tribe, also attended. The Mohawk chief Hendrick, a gray-haired man with long-term friendships with English and Dutch colonists, gave a powerful and widely cited speech at the congress, asserting that the recent neglect would inevitably reorient Indian trade relations to the French. "Look at the French, they are men; they are fortifying every where; but we are ashamed to say it; you are like women, bare and open, without any fortifications." Hendrick urged the assembled colonists to prepare for defense against the French. (See "Visualizing History," page 162.)

Two delegates at the congress seized the occasion to push for yet more ambitious plans. Benjamin Franklin of Pennsylvania and Thomas Hutchinson of Massachusetts, both rising political stars, coauthored the **Albany Plan of Union**, a proposal for a unified but limited government to formulate Indian policy and coordinate colonial

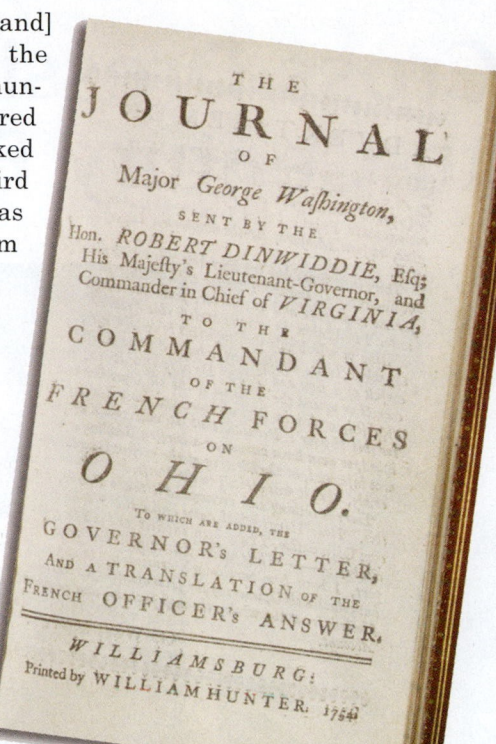

Washington's Journal, 1754
After George Washington's first mission to contact the French, he submitted to Governor Dinwiddie a report of about seven thousand words (the equivalent of a twenty-five-page paper), written in two days. He coolly narrated scenes of personal danger: traveling in deep snow, falling off a raft into an icy river, and being shot at by a lone Indian. Dinwiddie published Washington's report to inform Virginians and British leaders about the French threat in the West. With its republication in London, the pamphlet brought renown to Washington as a young man of resolute and rugged courage. Huntington Library.

military forces. Key features included a president-general, appointed by the crown, and a grand council representing the colonies, meeting annually to consider questions of war, peace, and trade with the Indians. The writers of the Albany Plan humbly reaffirmed Parliament's authority; this was no bid for enlarged autonomy of the colonies. Hutchinson and Franklin easily persuaded the conference delegates to take the plan back to their respective assemblies.

To Franklin's surprise, not a single colony approved the Albany Plan. The Massachusetts assembly feared it was "a Design of gaining power over the Colonies," especially the power of taxation. Others objected that it would be impossible to agree on unified policies toward scores of quite different Indian tribes. The British government never backed the Albany Plan either; instead, it appointed two superintendents of Indian affairs, one for the northern and another for the southern colonies, each with exclusive powers to negotiate treaties, trade, and land sales with all tribes.

The Indians at the Albany Congress were not impressed with the Albany Plan either. The Covenant Chain alliance with the Mohawk tribe was reaffirmed, but the other nations left without pledging to help the British battle the French. At this very early point in the Seven Years' War,

Cultural Cross-Dressing in Eighteenth-Century Portraits

Chief Hendrick

John Caldwell

the Iroquois figured that the French military presence around the Great Lakes would discourage the westward push of American colonists and therefore better serve their interests.

The War and Its Consequences

By 1755, George Washington's frontier skirmish had turned into a major mobilization of British and American troops against the French. At first, the British expected a quick victory on three fronts. General Edward Braddock, recently arrived from England, marched his army toward Fort Duquesne in western Pennsylvania. Farther north, British troops moved toward Fort Niagara, critically located between Lakes Erie and Ontario. And William Johnson, a New Yorker recently

appointed superintendent of northern Indian affairs, led forces north toward Lake Champlain, intending to defend the border against the French in Canada (see Map 6.1). Unfortunately for the British, the French were prepared to fight and had cemented respectful alliances with many Indian tribes throughout the region.

Braddock's march west was the first of a series of disasters for the British. Accompanied by George Washington and his Virginia soldiers, Braddock led 2,000 troops into the backcountry in July 1755. Although Indian guidance and support amounted to a mere 8 Oneida warriors, Braddock expected an easy victory with his big artillery and overwhelming numbers. One day short of reaching Fort Duquesne, in heavy woods where their cannons were useless, the British

Having one's individual likeness rendered in paint was a mark of distinction in the eighteenth century. The subjects of portraiture were typically the wealthy, who had the means to pay an artist's fee, or, less often, nonwealthy but noteworthy people with public name recognition. Rarer still were portraits that presented such sitters dressed in clothes from other cultures. Here, Chief Hendrick Peters Theyanoguin, spokesman for the Mohawk Indians at the 1754 Albany Congress, appears in fine British clothing in a 1755 engraving, while John Caldwell, a titled young Irishman and an officer in the British army, sports colorful Indian dress in a painting made in Britain in 1780.

Soon after the Albany Congress, Hendrick traveled to Philadelphia, where an elite men's club paid for a professional portrait, likely the basis for the engraving shown here. Within the year, the sixty-three-year-old Hendrick was dead, killed at Lake George in the first northern battle in the Seven Years' War. His passing sparked great public mourning. Two taverns and three sailing vessels in Philadelphia were named in his honor. In London, this engraving was published in the *Gentleman's Magazine*, and hand-colored prints were sold in British and American bookshops.

Hendrick's gold-braided coat, ruffled shirt, and three-cornered hat are all signs of a well-dressed English gentleman. Why might he have chosen this outfit for the portrait painted in Philadelphia? What statement might it have made to London purchasers about Hendrick's political allegiance? Based on this portrait, was Hendrick some kind of cultural broker? What marks his Indianness in the engraving? Is there any visual evidence indicating that this London engraving is based on the actual portrait of Hendrick posing in person, as opposed to its being a picture of a generic Indian made up from the artist's imagination? Consider, for example, the facial tattoos — a starburst over his ear, the two lines under the eye — and the long scar on his left cheek. Do they suggest a generic Indian or a particular man?

Ensign John Caldwell, born into an aristocratic family in 1756, was stationed during the Revolutionary War (see chapter 7) at Fort Detroit, a British garrison that provided aid to eastern Great Lakes tribes battling Americans. The Ojibwas of that region bestowed a high honor on Caldwell by giving him an Indian name in a ceremony, and it was likely that he then acquired the clothing and accessories shown in this portrait. Notice the headdress, breechcloth, beaded pouch, knife and sheath, tomahawk, wampum belt, red leggings and garters (showing an expanse of thigh, immodest by British standards), and fringed moccasins. What might have been the purpose of Caldwell's posing for a portrait in this garb? Was he trying to channel the power of Indian men, doubtless seen as exotic by British viewers of the painting? Did Caldwell "go native"? Or was this his way to display manly courage?

Although we cannot generalize from two images, we can place the portraits in the context of their time and draw some conclusions about what their purposes were. Hendrick's portrait was created in 1755 and was publicly disseminated to memorialize the leader of one of the few tribes loyal to Britain during the Seven Years' War. The taverns and sailing ships named for him further mark his celebrated status. Caldwell's portrait was a private possession, commissioned after the Revolutionary War when much of Britain's North American land claims had fallen to the colonies. What attitude do you think Hendrick and Caldwell intended to convey regarding the other's culture? How might each have reacted to the other's portrait?

were ambushed by 250 French soldiers joined by 640 Indian warriors, including Ottawas, Ojibwas, Potawatomis, Shawnees, and Delawares. Surviving soldiers reported that they never saw more than a half dozen Indians at a time, so hidden were they in the woods. But the soldiers could hear them. One soldier wrote weeks later that "the yell of the Indians is fresh on my ear, and the terrific sound will haunt me until the hour of my dissolution." The disciplined British troops stood their ground, making them easy targets. In the bloody Battle of the Monongahela, named for a nearby river, nearly a thousand on the British side were killed or wounded. Washington was unhurt, though two horses in succession were shot out from under him. General Braddock was killed.

Braddock's defeat stunned British leaders. For the next two years, they stumbled badly, deploying inadequate numbers of troops. Colonial assemblies, unwilling to be forced to shoulder the costs of war, held back from contributing provincial troops. What finally turned the war around was the rise to power in 1757 of **William Pitt**, Britain's prime minister, a man ready to commit massive resources to fight France and its ally Spain worldwide. Pitt treated the assemblies as allies, not subordinates, and paid them to raise and equip provincial soldiers, an intensification of manpower that led at last to the capture of Forts Duquesne, Niagara, and Ticonderoga, followed by victories over the French cities of Quebec and finally Montreal, all from 1758 to 1760.

By 1761, the war subsided in America but expanded globally, with battles in the Caribbean, Austria, Prussia, and India. The British captured the French sugar islands Martinique and Guadeloupe and then invaded Spanish Cuba with an army of some four thousand provincial soldiers from New York and New England. By the end of 1762, France and Spain capitulated, and the **Treaty of Paris** was signed in 1763.

The triumph was sweet but short-lived. In the complex peace negotiations, Britain gained control of Canada, eliminating the French threat from the north. British and American title to the eastern half of North America, precisely what Britain had claimed before the war, was confirmed. France transferred all its territory west of the Mississippi River, including New Orleans, to Spain as compensation for Spain's assistance during the war. France retained Martinique and Guadeloupe, while Cuba, where two thousand Americans had died of injury or disease in the invasion, was restored to Spain (Map 6.2).

In the aftermath of the war, Britain and the colonies, having worked as allies to defeat the French, began to eye each other warily. The British credited their mighty army for their victory and criticized the colonists for inadequate support. William Pitt was convinced that colonial smuggling — beaver pelts from French fur traders and illegal molasses in the French Caribbean — "principally, if not alone, enabled France to sustain and protract this long and expensive war." American traders, grumbled British leaders, were really traitors.

Colonists read the lessons of the war differently. American soldiers had turned out in force, they claimed, but had been relegated to grunt work by arrogant British commanders and subjected to unexpectedly harsh military discipline, ranging from frequent floggings (stealing a shirt brought a thousand lashes) to executions, the punishment for desertion. One Massachusetts army doctor avoided attending the punishments: "I saw not the men whiped, for altho' there is almost every Day more or less whiped or Piqueted [forced to stand on a sharpened stake], I've never had the curiosity to see 'm, the Shrieks and Crys" being more than he could bear.

Further, the British army did not always wage frontier warfare so brilliantly. Benjamin Franklin heard General Braddock brag that "these savages may, indeed, be a formidable enemy to your raw American militia, but upon the king's regular and disciplined troops, sir, it is impossible they should make any impression." Braddock's crushing defeat "gave us Americans," Franklin wrote, "the first suspicion that our exalted ideas of the prowess of British regulars had not been well founded."

MAP ACTIVITY

Map 6.2 Europe Redraws the Map of North America, 1763
In the peace treaty of 1763, France ceded to Britain its interior territory from Quebec to New Orleans, retaining fishing rights in the far north and several sugar islands in the Caribbean. France transferred to Spain its claim to extensive territory west of the Mississippi River.

READING THE MAP: Who actually lived on and controlled the lands ceded by France? In what sense, if any, did Britain or Spain own these large territories?
CONNECTIONS: What was the goal of the Proclamation of 1763? (See page 166.) Could it ever have worked?

Abigail Adams
Abigail Smith Adams was twenty-two when she sat for this pastel portrait in 1766. A wife for two years and a mother for one year, Adams exhibits a steady, intelligent gaze. Pearls and a lace collar anchor her femininity, while her facial expression projects a confidence and maturity not often credited to young women of the 1760s. A decade later, she was running the family's Massachusetts farm while her husband, John, attended the Continental Congress in Philadelphia. Her frequent letters gave him the benefit of her sage advice on politics and the war.
Courtesy of the Massachusetts Historical Society.

of an American Woman," defended their female patriotism: "The time is arrived to display the same sentiments which animated us at the beginning of the Revolution, when we renounced the use of teas [and] when our republican and laborious hands spun the flax."

The Loyalists

Around one-fifth of the American population remained loyal to the crown in 1776, and probably another two-fifths tried to stay neutral. With proper cultivation, this large base might have sustained the British empire in America. In general, **loyalists** of the elite classes often had strong cultural and economic ties to England; they thought that social stability depended on a government anchored by monarchy and aristocracy, and they feared democratic tyranny.

Patriots seemed to them to be unscrupulous, violent, self-interested men who simply wanted power for themselves. There were many non-elite loyalists as well, with diverse and often highly local reasons for opposing the revolutionary leaders of their region.

The most visible loyalists (called **Tories** by their enemies) were royal officials, not only governors such as Thomas Hutchinson of Massachusetts but also local judges and customs officers. Wealthy merchants gravitated toward loyalism to maintain the trade protections of navigation acts and the British navy. Conservative urban lawyers admired the stability of British law and order. Among the ordinary colonists, some chose loyalism simply to oppose traditional adversaries. Backcountry Carolina farmers leaned loyalist out of resentment of the power of the lowlands gentry, generally of patriot persuasion. Tenant farmers of the Hudson River valley in New York, who harbored decades of grievances against rich landlords now active in the Continental Congress, also tended to side with the British. And, of course, southern slaves had their own resentments against the white slave-owning class and looked to Britain in hope of freedom.

Many Indian tribes hoped to remain neutral at the war's start, seeing the conflict as a civil war between the English and Americans. Eventually, however, most were drawn in, many taking the British side. The powerful Iroquois Confederacy divided: The Mohawk, Cayuga, Seneca, and Onondaga peoples lined up with the British; the Oneida and Tuscarora tribes aided Americans. One young Mohawk leader, **Thayendanegea** (known also by his English name, **Joseph Brant**), traveled to England in 1775 to complain to King George about land-hungry American settlers. "It is very hard when we have let the King's subjects have so much of our lands for so little value," he wrote; "they should want to cheat us in this manner of the small spots we have left for our women and children to live on." Brant pledged Indian support for the king in exchange for protection from encroaching settlers. In the Ohio Country, parts of the Shawnee and Delaware tribes started out pro-American but shifted to the British side by 1779 in the face of repeated betrayals by American settlers and soldiers.

Pockets of loyalism thus existed everywhere—in the middle colonies, in the backcountry of the southern colonies, and out beyond the Appalachian Mountains in Indian country (Map 7.2). Even New England towns at the heart of the turmoil, such as Concord, Massachusetts, had a small unaccountably failed to press his advantage. Had he attacked Washington's army at Philadelphia, he could have taken the city. Instead, he parked his German troops in winter quarters along the Delaware River. Perhaps he knew that many of the Continental soldiers' enlistment periods ended on December 31, making him confident that the Americans would not attack him. He was wrong.

On December 25, in an icy rain, Washington stealthily moved his army across the Delaware River and at dawn made a quick capture of the unsuspecting German soldiers. This impressive victory lifted the sagging morale of the patriot side. For the next two weeks, Washington remained on the offensive, capturing supplies in a clever attack on British units at Princeton. Soon he was safe in Morristown, in northern New Jersey, where he settled his army for the winter. Washington finally had time to administer mass smallpox inoculations and see his men through the abbreviated course of the disease.

All in all, in the first year of declared war, the rebellious Americans had a few proud moments but also many worries. The inexperienced Continental army had barely hung on in the New York campaign. Washington had shown exceptional daring and admirable restraint, but what really saved the Americans was the repeated reluctance of the British to follow through militarily when they had the advantage.

REVIEW Why did the British initially exercise restraint in their efforts to defeat the rebellious colonies?

▶ The Home Front

Battlefields alone did not determine the outcome of the war. Struggles on the home front were equally important. In 1776, each community contained small numbers of highly committed people on both sides and far larger numbers who were uncertain about whether independence was worth a war. Both persuasion and force were used to gain the allegiance of the many neutrals. Revolutionaries who took control of local government often used it to punish loyalists and intimidate neutrals, while loyalists worked to reestablish British authority. A major factor pushing neutrals to side with the revolution was the British treatment of prisoners of war. Adding to the turbulence of the times was a very shaky wartime economy. The creative financing of the fledgling government brought hardships as well

as opportunities, forcing Americans to confront new manifestations of virtue and corruption.

Patriotism at the Local Level

Committees of correspondence, of public safety, and of inspection dominated the political landscape in patriot communities. These committees took on more than customary local governance; they enforced boycotts, picked army draftees, and policed suspected traitors. They sometimes invaded homes to search for contraband goods such as British tea or textiles.

Loyalists were dismayed by the increasing show of power by patriots. A man in Westchester, New York, described his response to intrusions by committees: "Choose your committee or suffer it to be chosen by a half dozen fools in your neighborhood — open your doors to them — let them examine your tea-cannisters and molasses-jugs, and your wives' and daughters' petty coats — bow and cringe and tremble and quake — fall down and worship our sovereign lord the mob. . . . Should any pragmatical committee-gentleman come to my house and give himself airs, I shall show him the door." Oppressive or not, the local committees were rarely challenged. Their persuasive powers convinced many middle-of-the-road citizens that neutrality was not a comfortable option.

Another group new to political life — white women — increasingly demonstrated a capacity for patriotism as wartime hardships dramatically altered their work routines. Many wives whose husbands were away on military or political service took on masculine duties. Their competence to tend farms and make business decisions encouraged some to assert competence in politics as well. Abigail Adams managed the family farm in Massachusetts while John Adams was away for several years engaged in politics, in which Abigail took a keen interest. Eliza Wilkinson managed a South Carolina plantation and talked revolutionary politics with women friends. "None were greater politicians than the several knots of ladies who met together," she remarked, alert to the unusual turn female conversations had taken. "We commenced perfect statesmen."

Women from prominent Philadelphia families took more direct action, forming the **Ladies Association** in 1780 to collect money for Continental soldiers. A published broadside, "The Sentiments

"If a good bleeding can bring those Bible-faced Yankees to their senses, the fever of independency should soon abate."
— A British general

inadequate supplies. Arnold showed heroic determination, but close to half of his men either died or turned back during the march. Arnold and Montgomery jointly attacked Quebec in December but failed to take the city. Worse yet, they encountered smallpox, which killed more men than had the battle for Quebec.

The main action of the first year of the war came not in Canada, however, but in New York, crucial to British strategy. In August 1776, some 45,000 British troops (including 8,000 German mercenaries, called **Hessians**) under the command of General Howe landed south of New York City. General Washington had anticipated this move and had relocated his army of 20,000 south from Massachusetts. The **battle of Long Island**, in late August 1776, pitted the well-trained British "redcoats" (slang referring to their red uniforms) against a very green Continental army. Howe attacked,

inflicting many casualties (1,500 dead and wounded, with another 1,000 taken prisoner). A British general crowed, "If a good bleeding can bring those Bible-faced Yankees to their senses, the fever of independency should soon abate." Howe failed to press forward, however, perhaps remembering the costly victory of Bunker Hill, and Washington evacuated his troops to Manhattan Island in the dead of a foggy night. Knowing it would be hard to hold Manhattan, he withdrew farther north to two forts on either side of the Hudson River, allowing the British command to set up headquarters in the wealthy island city. For two months, the armies engaged in limited skirmishing, but in November Howe finally captured Fort Washington and Fort Lee, taking another 3,000 prisoners.

Washington retreated quickly across New Jersey into Pennsylvania. Again Howe

Triumphal Entry of Royal Troops in New York, 1776

An artist in Germany portrayed British troops marching into New York City in September 1776, in rank and file as far as the eye can see. It looks like a peaceful take-over, with Americans watching quietly from windows and street corners. The picture shows a European-looking city, with blocks of far more substantial buildings than New York actually had. Clearly this artist was not familiar with the real New York. Just days before the British marched in, several hundred wooden buildings went up in smoke from a fire set by a disgruntled American woman. Museum of the City of New York, The J. Clarence Davies Collection.

Der Einzug der Königlichen Völcker in Neu Yorck. | L'Entré triumphale de Troupes royales a Nouvelle Yorck.

MAP ACTIVITY

Map 7.1   The War in the North, 1775–1778

After the early battles in Massachusetts in 1775, rebel forces invaded Canada but failed to capture Quebec. A large British army landed in New York in August 1776, turning New Jersey into a continual battle site in 1777 and 1778. Burgoyne arrived from England to secure Canada and attempted to pinch off New England along the Hudson River, but he was stopped at Saratoga in 1777 in the key battle of the early war.

READING THE MAP: Which general's troops traveled the farthest in each of these years: 1775, 1776, and 1777? How did the availability of water routes affect British and American strategy?

CONNECTIONS: Why did the French wait until early 1778 to join American forces against the British? What did France hope to gain from participating in the war?

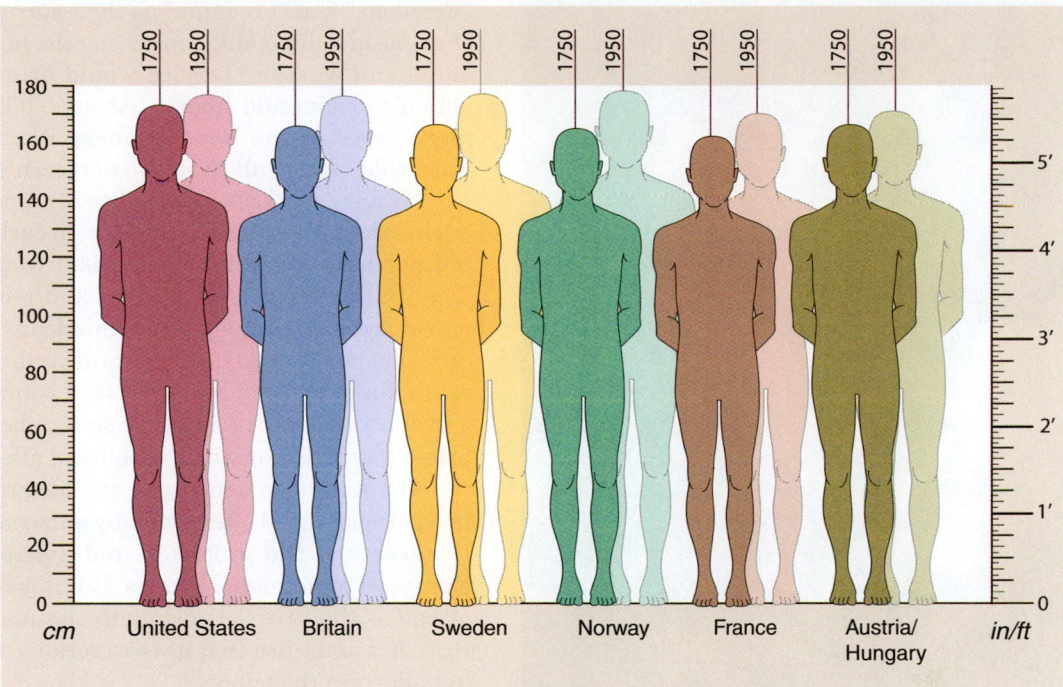

FIGURE 7.1   GLOBAL COMPARISON: How Tall Were Eighteenth-Century Men on Average?
Although individuals within a population vary in height for genetic reasons, variations between populations are generally due to differences in the basic standard of living. A key factor is inadequate nutrition, which typically stunts childhood growth and leads to shorter adults. Military enlistment records provide large data sets on male height, allowing historians to gain insight into comparative standards of living. This figure shows that American men during the Revolution were on average 8 centimeters (cm) or about 3 inches taller than British and European men, indicating an abundance of food and fewer endemic diseases than in Europe. American soldiers exhibited modest but distinct regional differences, with southerners an average of 1.3 cm taller than New Englanders. A much wider spread occurred in Britain, where officers from the gentry were a full 15 cm taller on average than soldiers recruited from the working class. What might account for these differences?

capture, pacify, and then restore to the crown, and they stretched in a long line from New Hampshire to Georgia. Clearly, a large land army was required for the job. Without the willingness to seize food from the locals, the British needed hundreds of supply ships — hence their desire to capture the ports. The British strategy also assumed that many Americans remained loyal to the king and would come to their aid.

The overall British plan was a divide-and-conquer approach, focusing first on New York, the state judged to have the greatest number of loyal subjects. New York offered a geographic advantage as well: Control of the Hudson River would allow the British to isolate the rebellious New Englanders. British armies could descend from Canada and move up from New York City along the Hudson River into western Massachusetts. Squeezed between a naval blockade on the eastern coast and army raids in the west, Massachusetts could be driven to surrender. New Jersey and

Pennsylvania would fall in line, the British thought, because of loyalist strength. Virginia was a problem, like Massachusetts, but the British were confident that the Carolinas would help them isolate and subdue Virginia.

Quebec, New York, and New Jersey

In late 1775, an American expedition was launched to capture the cities of Montreal and Quebec before British reinforcements could arrive (Map 7.1). This offensive was a clear sign that the war was not purely a reaction to the invasion of Massachusetts. A force of New York Continentals commanded by General Richard Montgomery took Montreal easily in September 1775 and then advanced on Quebec. Meanwhile, a second contingent of Continentals led by Colonel Benedict Arnold moved north through Maine to Quebec, a punishing trek through freezing rain with woefully

Flute-playing African American
This eighteenth-century portrait was displayed for many years in the State Department in Washington D.C., with artist and sitter unrecorded. One compelling hypothesis suggests it is Barzillai Lew, a talented musician from Groton, Massachusetts. As a boy, Lew served as a fifer in the Seven Years' War, and in 1775 he again was a fifer in the Revolutionary War through three enlistments, seeing action at Bunker Hill and Fort Ticonderoga. Fife and drum music supplied rhythm and mood for military marches, so this was an essential job in the army. Lew lived until 1822; many of his 13 children were also musicians.
Courtesy of Mae Theresa Bonitto; photograph courtesy of the *Boston Globe*.

"Looking at it with apparent unconcern," he wrote of the gutsy woman, "she observed that it was lucky it did not pass a little higher, for in that case it might have carried away something else."

Black Americans at first were excluded from the Continental army by slave owner George Washington's orders. But as manpower needs abruptly increased, the Continental Congress permitted free blacks and even slaves to enlist, compensating their masters up to $400 for each man released. In Rhode Island and Connecticut, black Continental soldiers served in segregated units with white officers. While some of these men were involuntary substitutes sent by their owners, others were clearly inspired by ideals of freedom in a war against tyranny. For example, twenty-three Rhode Island blacks gave "Liberty,"

"Freedom," and "Freeman" as their surnames at the time of enlistment, expressing the hope that successful wartime service would bring them actual freedom and liberty. About 5,000 black men served in the Revolutionary War on the rebel side, nearly all from the northern states.

Military service helped politicize Americans during the early stages of the war. In early 1776, independence was a risky, potentially treasonous idea. But as the war heated up and recruiters demanded commitment, some Americans discovered that apathy had its dangers as well. Anyone who refused to serve ran the risk of being called a traitor to the cause. Military service became a prime way of demonstrating political allegiance.

The American army was at times raw and inexperienced, and often woefully undermanned. It never had the precision and discipline of European professional armies. But it was never as bad as the British continually assumed. The British would learn that it was a serious mistake to underrate the enemy.

The British Strategy

The American strategy was straightforward — to repulse and defeat an invading army. The British strategy was not as clear. Britain wanted to put down a rebellion and restore monarchical power in the colonies, but the question was how to accomplish this. A decisive defeat of the Continental army was essential but not sufficient to end the rebellion, for the British would still have to contend with an armed and motivated insurgent population. Furthermore, there was no single political nerve center whose capture would spell certain victory. The Continental Congress moved from place to place, staying just out of reach of the British. During the course of the war, the British captured and occupied every major port city, but that brought no serious loss to the Americans, 95 percent of whom lived in the countryside.

King George had told Parliament at the outset that once his army subdued the rebels, "I shall be ready to receive the misled with tenderness and mercy" as soon as "the unhappy and deluded multitude . . . shall become sensible of their error." While this was calmingly deceptive talk appropriate to the start of war, it did underscore the real tension in the British position. Britain's delicate task was to restore the old governments, not to destroy an enemy country. Hence, the British generals were at first reluctant to ravage the countryside, confiscate food, or burn villages. There were thirteen distinct political entities to

Jefferson's Laptop Writing Desk

On a stagecoach ride from Virginia to Philadelphia in May 1776, thirty-three-year-old Thomas Jefferson sketched a design for a portable laptop writing desk. On arrival, he hired a Philadelphia cabinetmaker to produce it in mahogany. The adjustable book rest (notice the notches) could also open up to create a large writing surface. Pens, quills, ink, and paper were stored below. Jefferson used this desk to pen rough drafts of the Declaration of Independence. Near the end of his life, he gave the desk to his granddaughter's husband, expressing the hope that it might become esteemed for its connection to the Declaration. National Museum of American History, Smithsonian Institution, Washington, D.C.

Four men, including John Dickinson, declined to sign; several others "signed with regret . . . and with many doubts," according to John Adams. The document was then printed, widely distributed, and read aloud in celebrations everywhere.

Printed copies did not include the signers' names, for they had committed treason, a crime punishable by death. On the day of signing, they indulged in gallows humor. When Benjamin Franklin paused before signing to look over the document, John Hancock of Massachusetts teased him, "Come, come, sir. We must be unanimous. No pulling different ways. We must all hang together." Franklin replied, "Indeed we must all hang together. Otherwise we shall most assuredly hang separately."

REVIEW Why were many Americans initially reluctant to pursue independence from Britain?

▶ The First Year of War, 1775–1776

Both sides approached the war for America with uneasiness. The Americans, with inexperienced militias, were opposing the mightiest military power in the world. Also, their country was not unified; many people remained loyal to Britain. The British faced serious obstacles as well. Their disdain for the fighting abilities of the Americans required reassessment in light of the Bunker Hill battle. The logistics of supplying an army with food across three thousand miles of water were daunting. And since the British goal was to regain allegiance, not to destroy and conquer, the army was often constrained in its actions. These patterns — undertrained American troops and British troops strangely unwilling to press their advantage — played out repeatedly in the first year of war.

The American Military Forces

Americans claimed that the initial months of war were purely defensive, triggered by the British invasion. But the war also quickly became a rebellion, an overthrowing of long-established authority. As both defenders and rebels, many Americans were highly motivated to fight, and the potential manpower that could be mobilized was, in theory, very great.

Local defense in the colonies had long rested with a militia composed of all able-bodied men over age sixteen. Militias, however, were best suited for local and limited engagements, responding to conflict with Indians or slave rebellions. Such events were relatively infrequent, and the traditional militia training day in most communities had evolved into a holiday of drinking, marching, and shooting practice.

In forming the Continental army, the congress first set enlistment at one year, which proved to be too optimistic. Incentives produced longer commitments: a $20 bonus for three years of service, a hundred acres of land for enlistment for the duration of the war. For this inducement to be effective, of course, recruits had to believe that the Americans would win. Over the course of the war, some 230,000 men enlisted, about one-quarter of the white male adult population. (See Figure 7.1, page 200.)

Women also served in the Continental army, cooking, washing, and nursing the wounded. The British army established a ratio of one woman to every ten men; in the Continental army, the ratio was set at one woman to fifteen men. Close to 20,000 "camp followers," as they were called, served during the war, many of them wives of men in service. Some 12,000 children also tagged along, and babies were born in the camps. Some women helped during battles, supplying drinking water or ammunition to soldiers. One soldier recalled a woman at the battle of Monmouth whose petticoats were shot off by a cannonball that whizzed between her outstretched legs.

it; men read it aloud in taverns and coffeehouses; John Adams sent a copy to his wife, Abigail, who passed it around to neighbors in Braintree, Massachusetts. New Englanders desired independence, but other colonies, under no immediate threat of violence, remained cautious.

Abigail Adams was impatient not only for independence but also for other legal changes that would revolutionize the new country. In a series of astute letters to her husband, she outlined obstacles and gave advice. She worried that southern slave owners might shrink from a war in the name of liberty: "I have sometimes been ready to think that the passion for Liberty cannot be Equally strong in the Breasts of those who have been accustomed to deprive their fellow Creatures of theirs." And in March 1776, she expressed her hope that women's legal status would improve under the new government: "In the new Code of Laws which I suppose it will be necessary for you to make I desire you would Remember the Ladies, and be more generous and favourable to them than your ancestors." Her chief concern was husbands' legal dominion over wives: "Do not put such unlimited power into the hands of the Husbands," she advised. "Remember all Men would be tyrants if they could." Abigail Adams anticipated a more radical end to tyranny than did Thomas Paine.

The Continental Congress was, in fact, not rewriting family law; that task was left to individual states in the 1780s. John Adams dismissed his wife's concerns. But to a male politician, Adams privately rehearsed the reasons why women (and men who were free blacks, or young, or propertyless) should remain excluded from political participation. Even though he concluded that nothing should change, at least Abigail's letter had forced him to ponder the exclusion, something few men — or women — did in 1776. Urgent talk of political independence was as radical as most could imagine.

The Declaration of Independence

In addition to Paine's *Common Sense*, another factor hastening independence was the prospect of an alliance with France, Britain's archrival. France was willing to provide military supplies and naval power only if assured that the Americans would separate from Britain. News that the British were negotiating to hire German mercenary soldiers further solidified support for independence. By May 1776, all but four colonies were agitating for a declaration. The holdouts were Pennsylvania, Maryland, New York, and South Carolina, the latter two containing large loyalist populations. An exasperated Virginian wrote to his friend in the congress, "For God's sake, why do you dawdle in the Congress so strangely? Why do you not at once declare yourself a separate independent state?" In early June, the Virginia delegation introduced a resolution calling for independence. The moderates still commanded enough support to postpone a vote on the measure until July. In the meantime, the congress appointed a committee, with Thomas Jefferson and others, to draft a longer document setting out the case for independence.

On July 2, after intense politicking, all but one state voted for independence; New York abstained. The congress then turned to the document drafted by Jefferson and his committee. Jefferson began with a preamble that articulated philosophical principles about natural rights, equality, the right of revolution, and the consent of the governed as the only true basis for government. He then listed more than two dozen specific grievances against King George. The congress merely glanced at the philosophical principles, as though ideas about natural rights and the consent of the governed were accepted as "self-evident truths," just as the document claimed. The truly radical phrase declaring the natural equality of "all men" was likewise passed over without comment.

> "Do not put such unlimited power into the hands of the Husbands. Remember all Men would be tyrants if they could."
> — ABIGAIL ADAMS

For two days, the congress wrangled over the list of grievances, especially the issue of slavery. Jefferson had included an impassioned statement blaming the king for slavery, which delegates from Georgia and South Carolina struck out. They had no intention of denouncing their labor system as an evil practice. But the congress let stand another of Jefferson's fervent grievances, blaming the king for mobilizing "the merciless Indian Savages" into bloody frontier warfare, a reference to Pontiac's Rebellion (see chapter 6).

On July 4, the amendments to Jefferson's text were complete, and the congress formally adopted the **Declaration of Independence**. (See appendix I, page A-1.) The New York delegation switched from abstention to endorsement on July 15, making the vote on independence unanimous. In early August, the delegates gathered to sign the official parchment copy.

Thomas Paine and *Common Sense*
Thomas Paine, a recent immigrant to America, wrote *Common Sense* to advance the debate on independence. The pamphlet sold hundreds of thousands of copies, and Paine donated the proceeds to the Revolutionary cause. Shown here is George Washington's personal copy, with his name inscribed at the top. Paine became a soldier during the early part of the Revolution; he then worked as a clerk for the Continental Congress and the Pennsylvania assembly. He returned to Europe in 1787 and quickly became involved in the French Revolution, defending it in a major pamphlet called *The Rights of Man*. He later wrote *The Age of Reason*, a book that among other things seemed to avow atheism. In 1802, he returned to the United States, where he was welcomed by Thomas Jefferson but spurned by nearly everyone else because of his reputation for antireligious ideas. He died in obscurity in 1809, and a New York newspaper unfairly summarized his life by saying, "He had lived long, did some good and much harm." Pamphlet: Boston Athenaeum; portrait: Monticello/ Thomas Jefferson Memorial Foundation, Inc.

its author, was an English artisan and coffeehouse intellectual who had befriended Benjamin Franklin in London. He came to America in the fall of 1774 with letters of introduction from Franklin to several Philadelphia printers, one of whom hired him. He soon met delegates from the Second Continental Congress, and, with their encouragement, he wrote *Common Sense* to lay out a lively and compelling case for complete independence.

In simple yet forceful language, Paine elaborated on the absurdities of the British monarchy. Why should one man, by accident of birth, claim extensive power over others? he asked. A king might be foolish or wicked. "One of the strongest natural proofs of the folly of hereditary right in kings," Paine wrote, "is that nature disapproves it; otherwise she would not so frequently turn it into ridicule by giving mankind *an ass for a lion.*" Calling the British king an ass broke through the automatic deference most Americans still had for the monarchy. To replace monarchy, Paine advocated republican government based on the consent of the people. Rulers, according to Paine, were only representatives of the people, and the best form of government relied on frequent elections to achieve the most direct democracy possible.

Paine's pamphlet sold more than 150,000 copies in a matter of weeks. Newspapers reprinted

An Exact View of the Late Battle at Charlestown, June 17th 1775
This dramatic panorama is the earliest visual representation of the battle of Bunker Hill. On sale to the public six weeks after the battle, the engraving shows Charlestown in flames (center back) and British and American soldiers in fixed formation firing muskets at each other. The Americans, to the left, are dug in along the crest of the hill; British casualties have begun to litter the field of battle. Created by noted cartographer Bernard Romans, this illustration likely decorated many a patriot's wall. Technically, the British won the battle by taking the hill. Is that the story told by this picture? Colonial Williamsburg Foundation.

leaders to fear that the British intended to spread smallpox into the countryside as a "weapon of defense."

A week after Bunker Hill, when General Washington arrived to take charge of the new Continental army, he found enthusiastic but undisciplined troops. Sanitation was an unknown concept, with inadequate latrines fouling the campground. The amazed general attributed the disarray to the New England custom of letting militia units elect their own officers, which he felt undermined deference. Washington spotted a militia captain, a barber in civilian life, shaving an ordinary soldier, and he moved quickly to impose more hierarchy and authority. "Be easy," he advised his newly appointed officers, "but not too familiar, lest you subject yourself to a want of that respect, which is necessary to support a proper command."

While military plans moved forward, the Second Continental Congress pursued its contradictory objective: reconciliation with Britain.

Delegates from the middle colonies (Pennsylvania, Delaware, and New York), whose merchants depended on trade with Britain, urged that channels for negotiation remain open. In July 1775, congressional moderates led by John Dickinson engineered an appeal to the king called the **Olive Branch Petition**. The petition affirmed loyalty to the monarchy and strategically blamed all the troubles on the king's ministers and on Parliament. It proposed that the American colonial assemblies be recognized as individual parliaments under the umbrella of the monarchy. But **King George III** rejected the Olive Branch Petition and heatedly condemned the Americans as traitors. Reconciliation was now out of the question.

Thomas Paine, Abigail Adams, and the Case for Independence

Pressure for independence started to mount in January 1776, when a pamphlet titled *Common Sense* appeared in Philadelphia. **Thomas Paine**,

THE PROMISE OF TECHNOLOGY

Muskets and Rifles

Muskets were the weapon of choice in the Revolutionary War. Formal combat involved successive ranks (rows) of soldiers in precise formation firing row by row in unison at an enemy within a 50-yard range. The massed fire made up for the notoriously inaccurate aim of each musket. Long-barreled rifles, used to hunt game in frontier regions, offered much greater accuracy because of spiral grooves inside the barrel. Grooved (rifled) barrels imparted spin to the ball, which in turn stabilized and lengthened its flight, enabling expert marksmen to hit small targets at 150 to 200 yards. Yet rifles took twice as long to load and fire, and the longer barrels made them unwieldy for soldiers on the march. Not for another half century would there be machine-tooled, mass-produced firearms like the Colt revolver and the Remington rifle. These new repeat-fire weapons were cheaper, more accurate, and far more deadly in the hands of an individual shooter. What might happen if a close-standing rank of musketeers fired their weapons individually instead of in unison? York County Historical Society.

Pursuing Both War and Peace

Three days after the congress established the army, one of the bloodiest battles of the Revolution occurred. The British commander in Boston, Thomas Gage, had recently received troop reinforcements, including three talented generals (William Howe, John Burgoyne, and Henry Clinton), and new instructions to attack the Massachusetts rebels. But before Gage could take the offensive, the Americans fortified the hilly terrain of Charlestown, a peninsula just north of Boston, on the night of June 16, 1775.

The British generals could have closed off the peninsula to box in the Americans. But General **William Howe** insisted on a bold frontal assault, sending 2,500 soldiers across the water and up the hill in an intimidating but potentially costly attack. The American troops, 1,400 strong, turned them back twice with deadly short-range fire.

On the third assault, the British took the hill, mainly because the American ammuni-tion supply gave out, and the defenders quickly retreated. The **battle of Bunker Hill** was thus a British victory, but an expensive one. The dead numbered 226 on the British side, with more than 800 wounded; the Americans suffered 140 dead, 271 wounded, and 30 captured. As General Clinton later remarked, "It was a dear bought victory; another such would have ruined us."

Unwilling to risk more raids into the countryside, Howe retreated to Boston instead of pursuing the fleeing Americans. If the British had had any grasp of the basic instability of the American units around Boston, they might have decisively defeated the Continental army in its infancy. Instead, they lingered in Boston, abandoning it without a fight nine months later.

Howe used the time in Boston to inoculate his army against smallpox because a new epidemic of the deadly disease was spreading in port cities along the Atlantic. Inoculation worked by producing a mild but real (and therefore risky) case of smallpox, followed by lifelong immunity. Howe's instinct was right: During the American Revolution, some 130,000 people on the American continent, most of them Indians, died of smallpox. When hundreds of Bostonians began to contract the disease, Howe ordered them to leave town, causing American

Battle of Bunker Hill, 1775

Charlestown Neck
Bunker Hill
Mystic River
Breed's Hill
Charlestown
Charles River
Boston
Boston Harbor
Charles River Basin

→ American forces
→ British forces
▲▲▲ American defenses

▶ The Second Continental Congress

On May 10, 1775, nearly one month after the fighting at Lexington and Concord, the **Second Continental Congress** assembled in Philadelphia. The congress immediately set to work on two crucial but contradictory tasks: to raise and supply an army and to explore reconciliation with Britain. To do the former, they needed soldiers and a commander, they needed money, and they needed to work out a declaration of war. To do the latter, they needed diplomacy to approach the king. But the king was not receptive, and by 1776, as the war progressed and hopes of reconciliation faded, delegates at the congress began to ponder the treasonous act of declaring independence — said by some to be plain common sense.

Assuming Political and Military Authority

Like members of the First Continental Congress (see chapter 6), the delegates to the second were well-established figures in their home colonies, but they still had to learn to know and trust one another. They did not always agree. The Adams cousins John and Samuel defined the radical end of the spectrum, favoring independence. **John Dickinson** of Pennsylvania, no longer the eager revolutionary who had dashed off *Letters from a Farmer* in 1767, was now a moderate, seeking reconciliation with Britain. Benjamin Franklin, fresh off a ship from an eleven-year residence in London, was feared by some to be a British spy. Mutual suspicions flourished easily when the undertaking was so dangerous, opinions were so varied, and a misstep could spell disaster.

Most of the delegates were not yet prepared to break with Britain. Some felt that government without a king was unworkable, while others feared it might be suicidal to lose Britain's protection against its traditional enemies, France and Spain. Colonies that traded actively with Britain feared undermining their economies. Probably the vast majority of ordinary Americans were unable to envision independence. From the Stamp Act of 1765 to the Coercive Acts of 1774 (see chapter 6), the constitutional struggle with Britain had focused on the issue of parliamentary power, but almost no one had questioned the legitimacy of the monarchy.

The few men at the Continental Congress who did think that independence was desirable were, not surprisingly, from Massachusetts. Their colony had been stripped of civil government under the Coercive Acts, their capital was occupied by the British, and their blood had been shed at Lexington and Concord. Even so, those men knew that it was premature to push for a break with Britain. John Adams wrote his wife, Abigail, in June 1775: "America is a great, unwieldy body. Its progress must be slow. It is like a large fleet sailing under convoy. The fleetest sailors must wait for the dullest and slowest."

Yet swift action was needed, for the Massachusetts countryside was under threat of further attack. Even the hesitant moderates in the congress agreed that a military buildup was necessary. Around the country, militia units from New York to Georgia collected arms and trained on village greens in anticipation. On June 14, the congress voted to create the **Continental army**, choosing a Virginian, not a New Englander, as commander in chief. The appointment of **George Washington** sent the clear message that there was widespread commitment to war beyond New England.

Next the congress drew up a document titled "A Declaration on the Causes and Necessity of Taking Up Arms," which rehearsed familiar arguments about the tyranny of Parliament and the need to defend English liberties. This declaration was first drafted by a young Virginia planter, **Thomas Jefferson**, a radical on the question of independence. The moderate John Dickinson, fearing that the declaration would offend Britain, was allowed to rewrite it. However, he left intact much of Jefferson's highly charged language about choosing "to die freemen rather than to live slaves." Even a man as reluctant about independence as Dickinson acknowledged the necessity of military defense against an invading army.

To pay for the military buildup, the congress authorized a currency issue of $2 million. The Continental dollars were merely paper; they were not backed by gold or silver. The delegates somewhat naively expected that the currency would be accepted as valuable on trust as it spread in the population through the hands of soldiers, farmers, munitions suppliers, and beyond.

In just two months, the Second Continental Congress had created an army, declared war, and issued its own currency. It had taken on the major functions of a legitimate government, both except the tax on tea, kept as a symbol of Parliament's power.

The renewal of trade and the return of cooperation between Britain and the colonies gave men like Thomas Hutchinson hope that the worst of the crisis was behind them. For nearly two years, peace seemed possible, but tense incidents in 1772, followed by a renewed struggle over the tea tax in 1773, precipitated a full-scale crisis in the summer and fall of 1774.

The Calm before the Storm

Repeal of the Townshend duties brought an end to nonimportation. Trade boomed in 1770 and 1771, driven by pent-up demand. Moreover, the leaders of the popular movement seemed to be losing their power. Samuel Adams, for example, ran for a minor local office and lost to a conservative merchant. Then in 1772, several incidents again brought the conflict with Britain into sharp focus. One was the burning of the *Gaspée*, a Royal Navy ship pursuing suspected smugglers near Rhode Island. A British investigating commission failed to arrest anyone but announced that it would send suspects, if any were found, to Britain for trial on charges of high treason. This ruling seemed to fly in the face of the traditional English right to trial by a jury of one's peers.

When news of the *Gaspée* investigation spread, it was greeted with disbelief in other colonies. Patrick Henry, Thomas Jefferson, and Richard Henry Lee in the Virginia House of Burgesses proposed that a network of standing committees be established to link the colonies and pass along alarming news. By mid-1773, every colonial assembly except Pennsylvania's had a "committee of correspondence."

Another British action in 1772 further spread the communications network. Lord North proposed to pay the salaries of superior court justices out of the tea revenue, similar to Townshend's plan for paying royal governors. The Boston town meeting, fearful that judges would now be improperly influenced by their new paymasters, established a committee of correspondence and urged all Massachusetts towns to do likewise. The first message, circulated in December 1772, attacked the salary policy for judges as the latest proof of a sinister British conspiracy to undermine traditional liberties: first taxation without consent, followed by military occupation, a massacre, and now a plot to subvert the justice system. By spring 1773, more than half the towns in Massachusetts had set up **committees of correspondence**, providing local forums for debate.

These committees politicized ordinary townspeople, sparking a revolutionary language of rights and constitutional duties. They also bypassed the official flow of power and information through the colony's royal government.

The final incident shattering the relative calm of the early 1770s was the **Tea Act of 1773**. Americans had resumed buying the taxed British tea, but they were also smuggling large quantities of Dutch tea, cutting into the sales of Britain's East India Company. So Lord North proposed legislation giving favored status to the East India Company, allowing it to sell tea directly to a few selected merchants in four colonial cities, cutting out British middlemen. The appointed agents would resell the tea, collecting the three pence tax that had its origins in the Townshend duty on tea of 1767. The reduced shipping costs would lower the final price of the East India tea below that of smuggled Dutch tea, thus motivating Americans to obey the law.

Tea in Boston Harbor

In the fall of 1773, news of the Tea Act reached the colonies. Parliamentary legislation to make tea inexpensive struck many colonists as an insidious plot to trick Americans into buying the duties tea. The real goal, some argued, was the increased revenue that would pay the salaries of royal governors and judges. The Tea Act was thus a painful reminder of Parliament's claim to the power to tax and legislate for the colonies.

But how to resist the Tea Act? Nonimportation was not viable, because the tea trade was too lucrative to expect merchants to give it up willingly. Consumer boycotts seemed ineffective, because it was impossible to distinguish between duties tea (the object of the boycott) and smuggled tea (illegal but politically clean) once it was in the teapot. The appointment of official tea agents, parallel to the Stamp Act distributors, suggested one solution. In Charleston, Philadelphia, and New York, revived Sons of Liberty pressured tea agents to resign. Without agents, governors yielded, and tea cargoes either landed duty-free or were sent home.

Governor Hutchinson, however, would not bend any rules. Three ships bearing tea arrived in Boston in November 1773. The ships cleared customs, and the crews, sensing the town's extreme tension, unloaded all cargo except the tea. The captains wished to leave Boston with their tea on board, but because the ships had already cleared customs, Hutchinson would not grant them passage without paying the tea duty.

Tossing the Tea
This colored English engraving shows Boston men in Indian disguise dumping tea chests into the harbor. A large crowd on the shore cheers them on. The red rowboat stacked with chests suggests that the raiders were stealing as well as destroying the tea. This event was not dubbed the "Tea Party" until the 1830s, when a later generation celebrated the illegal destruction of the tea and made heroes out of the few surviving participants, by then well into their eighties. The bottle at right was a souvenir item of the 1830s, with tea leaves said to have been salvaged from that fateful night.
Engraving: Library of Congress; bottle: © Massachusetts Historical Society/The Bridgeman Art Library.

To add to the difficulties, another long-standing law imposed a time limit on ships in the harbor. After twenty days, the required duty had to be paid, or local authorities would confiscate the cargo.

For the full twenty days, pressure built in Boston. Daily mass meetings energized citizens from Boston and surrounding towns, alerted by the committees of correspondence. On the final day, December 16, when for a final time Hutchinson refused clearance for the ships, a large crowd gathered at Old South Church to debate a course of action. No official plan was agreed on at that meeting, but immediately following it, 100 to 150 men, disguised as Indians, boarded the ships and dumped thousands of pounds of tea into the harbor while a crowd of 2,000 watched. In admiration, John Adams wrote: "This Destruction of the Tea is so bold, so daring, so firm, intrepid and inflexible, and it must have so important Consequences."

The Coercive Acts

Lord North's response was swift and stern: He persuaded Parliament to issue the **Coercive Acts**, four laws meant to punish Massachusetts for destroying the tea. In America, those laws, along with a fifth one, the Quebec Act, were soon known as the **Intolerable Acts**.

The first act, the Boston Port Act, closed Boston harbor to all shipping as of June 1, 1774, until the destroyed tea was paid for. Britain's objective was to halt the commercial life of the city.

The second act, called the Massachusetts Government Act, greatly altered the colony's charter, underscoring Parliament's claim to supremacy over Massachusetts. The royal governor's powers were augmented, and the governor's council became an appointive, rather than elective, body. Further, the governor could now appoint all judges, sheriffs, and officers of the court. No town meeting beyond the annual spring election of town selectmen could be held without the governor's approval, and every agenda item required prior approval. Every Massachusetts town was affected.

The third Coercive Act, the Impartial Administration of Justice Act, stipulated that any royal official accused of a capital crime—for example, Captain Preston and his soldiers at the Boston Massacre—would be tried in a court in Britain. It did not matter that Preston had received a fair trial in Boston. What this act ominously suggested was that down the road, more Captain Prestons and soldiers might be firing into unruly crowds.

The fourth act amended the 1765 Quartering Act and permitted military commanders to lodge soldiers wherever necessary, even in private households. In a related move, Lord North appointed General **Thomas Gage**, commander of the Royal Army in New York, as governor of Massachusetts. Thomas Hutchinson was out, relieved at long last of his duties. Military rule, including soldiers, returned once more to Boston.

The fifth act, the Quebec Act, had nothing to do with the four Coercive Acts, but it fed American fears. It confirmed the continuation of French civil law and government form, as well as Catholicism, for Quebec—an affront to Protestant New Englanders who had recently been denied their own representative government. The act also gave Quebec control of disputed land (and the lucrative fur trade) throughout the Ohio Valley, land also claimed by Virginia, Pennsylvania, and a number of Indian tribes.

The five Intolerable Acts spread alarm in all the colonies. If Britain could squelch Massachusetts—change its charter, suspend local government, inaugurate military rule, and on top of that give Ohio to Catholic Quebec—what liberties were secure? Fearful royal governors in a half dozen colonies dismissed the sitting assemblies, adding to the sense of urgency. A few of the assemblies defiantly continued to meet in new locations. Through the committees of correspondence, colonial leaders arranged to convene in Philadelphia in September 1774 to respond to the crisis.

Beyond Boston: Rural New England

Well before the delegates assembled in Philadelphia, all of New England had arrived at the brink of open insurrection. With a British general occupying the Massachusetts governorship and some three thousand troops controlling Boston, the revolutionary momentum shifted from urban radicals to rural farmers who protested

Hutchinson the Traitor Faces Death
This hideous engraving enlivened the cover of an almanac published in Boston in December 1773, during the high drama over tea. It shows Thomas Hutchinson with the devil behind him holding up a list of his many crimes and a skeleton representing death about to spear him. The caption below the picture read: "The wicked Statesman, or the Traitor to his Country, at the Hour of DEATH." On page 2, readers of this anti-Hutchinson diatribe were invited to think about "the Horrors that Man must endure, who owes his Greatness to his Country's Ruin." The color here is probably a later addition. Granger Collection.

the Massachusetts Government Act in dozens of spontaneous, dramatic showdowns. To get around the prohibition on new meetings, some towns refused to adjourn their last authorized town meeting. More defiant towns just ignored the law. Gage's call for elections for a new provincial assembly under his control sparked elections for a competing unauthorized assembly.

In all Massachusetts counties except one, crowds of thousands of armed men converged to prevent the opening of county courts run by crown-appointed jurists. No judges were physically harmed, but they were forced to resign and made to doff their judicial wigs or run a humiliating gantlet. In Suffolk County, the courts met in troop-filled Boston, making mass intimidation of judges impossible. One by one, however, the citizen jurors called to serve in court refused. By August 1774, farmers and artisans all over Massachusetts had effectively taken full control of their local institutions.

Unfettered by the crown, ordinary citizens throughout New England began serious planning for the showdown everyone assumed would come. Town militias stockpiled gunpowder "in case of invasion." Militia officers repudiated their official chain of command to the governor and stepped up drills of their units. Town after town withheld its tax money from the royal governor and diverted it to military supplies. Governor Gage felt under heavy threat, but he could do little. He beefed up fortifications around Boston and in general rattled his sword loudly, praying for reinforcements from Britain.

At this point in the struggle, confrontations did not lead to bloodshed. But one incident, the Powder Alarm, nearly provoked violence and showed how close New England farmers were to armed insurrection. On September 1, 1774, Gage sent troops to capture a supply of gunpowder just outside Boston. In the surprise and scramble of the attack, false news spread that the troops had fired on men defending the powder, killing six. Within twenty-four hours, several thousand armed men from Massachusetts, New Hampshire, and Connecticut streamed on foot to Boston to avenge the first blood spilled. At this moment, ordinary men became insurgents, willing to kill or be killed in the face of the British clampdown. Once the error was corrected and the crisis defused, the men returned home peaceably. But Gage could no longer doubt the speed, numbers, and deadly determination of the rebellious subjects.

> **"We ask only for peace, liberty and security. We wish no diminution of royal prerogatives, we demand no new rights."**
> — The First Continental Congress

All this had occurred without orchestration by Boston radicals, Gage reported. But British leaders found it hard to believe, as one put it, that "a tumultuous Rabble, without any Appearance of general Concert, or without any Head to advise, or Leader to conduct" could pull off such effective resistance. Repeatedly in the years to come, the British would seriously underestimate their opponents.

The First Continental Congress

Every colony except Georgia sent delegates to Philadelphia in September 1774 to discuss the looming crisis in what was later called the **First Continental Congress**. The gathering included notables such as Samuel Adams and John Adams from Massachusetts and George Washington and Patrick Henry from Virginia. A few colonies purposely sent men who opposed provoking Britain, such as Pennsylvania's Joseph Galloway, to keep the congress from becoming too radical.

Delegates sought to articulate their liberties as British subjects and the powers Parliament held over them, and they debated possible responses to the Coercive Acts. Some wanted a total ban on trade with Britain to force repeal, while others, especially southerners dependent on tobacco and rice exports, opposed halting trade. Samuel Adams and Patrick Henry were eager for a ringing denunciation of all parliamentary control. The conservative Joseph Galloway proposed a plan (quickly defeated) to create a secondary parliament in America to assist the British Parliament in ruling the colonies.

The congress met for seven weeks and produced a declaration of rights couched in traditional language: "We ask only for peace, liberty and security. We wish no diminution of royal prerogatives, we demand no new rights." But from Britain's point of view, the rights assumed already to exist were radical. Chief among them was the claim that Americans were not represented in Parliament and so each colonial government had the sole right to govern and tax its own people. The one slight concession to Britain was a carefully worded agreement that the colonists would "cheerfully consent" to trade regulations for the larger good of the empire, so long as trade regulation was not a covert means of raising revenue.

To put pressure on Britain, the delegates agreed to a staggered and limited boycott of trade: imports prohibited this year, exports the following, and rice totally exempted (to keep South Carolinians happy). To enforce the boycott, they called for a Continental Association, with chapters in each town variously called committees of public safety or of inspection, to monitor all commerce and punish suspected violators of the boycott (sometimes with a bucket of tar and a bag of feathers). Its work done in under two months, the congress disbanded in late October, with agreement to reconvene the following May.

The committees of public safety, the committees of correspondence, the regrouped colonial assemblies, and the Continental Congress were all political bodies functioning defiantly without any constitutional authority. British officials did not recognize them as legitimate, but many Americans who supported the patriot cause instantly accepted them. A key reason for the stability of such unauthorized governing bodies was that they were composed of many of the same men who had held elective office before.

Britain's severe reaction to Boston's destruction of the tea finally succeeded in making many colonists from New Hampshire to Georgia realize that the problems of British rule went far beyond questions of nonconsensual taxation. The Coercive Acts infringed on liberty and denied self-government; they could not be ignored. With one colony already subordinated to military rule and a British army at the ready in Boston, the threat of a general war was on the doorstep.

REVIEW Why did Parliament pass the Coercive Acts in 1774?

▶ Domestic Insurrections, 1774–1775

Before the Second Continental Congress could meet, violence and bloodshed came to Massachusetts. Fearing the threat of domestic insurrection, General (and Governor) Thomas Gage requested more troops from Britain and prepared to subdue rebellion. On the other side, New England farmers prepared to defend their homes against an intrusive power they feared was bent on enslaving them. To the south, a different and inverted version of the same story began to unfold, as thousands of enslaved black men and women seized an unprecedented opportunity to mount a different kind of insurrection — against planter-patriots who looked over their shoulders uneasily whenever they called out for liberty from the British.

The British Retreat from Concord, April 19, 1775
Two young self-trained artists hustled to Concord and Lexington some ten days after the clash that touched off the American Revolution. After interviewing witnesses, 18-year-old Ralph Earle sketched scenes and 21-year-old Amos Doolittle, a silversmith, transferred them to copper engraving plates for mass production. This scene depicts British soldiers streaming toward Boston and under ambush by American insurgents firing from behind a stone wall. The British set fire to several houses suspected of harboring snipers. Doolittle's set of four engravings went on sale in December 1775. Miriam and Ira D. Wallach Division of Art, Prints and Photographs, The New York Public Library. Astor, Lenox and Tilden Foundations.

MAP ACTIVITY

MAP 6.3   Lexington and Concord, April 1775
When British soldiers left Boston to raid a suspected arms supply in Concord, Paul Revere and William Dawes set out to warn the patriots. Revere went by boat from Boston to Charlestown and then by horse through Medford to Lexington. Dawes casually passed British sentries guarding the narrow land route out of Boston and then rode his horse at full speed to Lexington. Once there, Revere and Dawes urged Samuel Adams and John Hancock, guests in a Lexington home, to flee to avoid capture. The two couriers then went on to Concord to warn residents of the impending attack.

READING THE MAP: How did Dawes's route differ from Revere's? What kinds of terrain and potential dangers did each man face during his ride, according to the map?
CONNECTIONS: Why send two men on the same mission? Why not send four or more?

Lexington and Concord

During the winter of 1774–75, Americans pressed on with boycotts. Optimists hoped to effect a repeal of the Coercive Acts; pessimists stockpiled arms and ammunition. In Massachusetts, militia units known as minutemen prepared to respond at a minute's notice to any threat from the British troops in Boston.

Thomas Gage soon realized how desperate the British position was. The people, Gage wrote to Lord North, were "numerous, worked up to a fury, and not a Boston rabble but the freeholders and farmers of the country." Gage requested twenty thousand reinforcements. He also strongly advised repeal of the Coercive Acts, but leaders in Britain could not admit failure. Instead, in mid-April 1775, they ordered Gage

> **"A phrenzy of revenge seems to have seized all ranks of people."**
> — THOMAS JEFFERSON, on the Battles of Lexington and Concord

to arrest the troublemakers immediately, before the Americans got better organized.

Gage quickly planned a surprise attack on a suspected ammunition storage site at Concord, a village eighteen miles west of Boston (Map 6.3). Near midnight on April 18, 1775, more than fifteen hundred British soldiers moved west across the Charles River. Boston silversmith Paul Revere and William Dawes, a tanner, learned of the attack by a prearranged signal, two lanterns hung in a church belfry, and they raced ahead to alert the minutemen. When the British arrived at **Lexington**, a village five miles east of **Concord**, they were met by some seventy armed men assembled on the village green. The British commander barked out, "Lay down your arms, you damned rebels, and disperse." The militiamen hesitated and began to comply, turning to leave the green, but then someone — nobody knows who — fired. In the next two minutes, more firing left eight Americans dead and ten wounded.

The British units continued their march to Concord, any pretense of surprise gone. Three companies of minutemen nervously occupied the town center but offered no challenge to the British, who searched in vain for the ammunition. Finally, at Old North Bridge in Concord, British troops and three hundred to four hundred local minutemen exchanged shots, killing two Americans and three British soldiers.

By now, both sides were very apprehensive. The British failed to find the expected arms, and the Americans failed to stop their raid. As the British returned to Boston, militia units from the countryside converged on the Concord road and ambushed them, bringing the bloodiest fighting of the day. In the end, 273 British soldiers were wounded or dead; the toll for the Americans stood at about 95. It was April 19, 1775, and the war had begun.

Rebelling against Slavery

News of the battles of Lexington and Concord spread rapidly. Within eight days, Virginians had heard of the fighting, and, as Thomas Jefferson reflected, "a phrenzy of revenge seems to have

Phillis Wheatley's Title Page
Phillis, born in Africa, became the slave of John Wheatley at age seven. Remarkably gifted in English, she wrote poetry and could read the Bible with ease by age sixteen. Her master took her to London in 1773, where this book of poems was published, gaining her great literary notice. The Wheatleys freed Phillis, who then married a free black man; two of their three children died in infancy, and her husband deserted her. Poetry alone could not support her, and she found work in a boardinghouse. By the end of 1784, Phillis and her remaining child had died. Library of Congress.

seized all ranks of people." The royal governor of Virginia, **Lord Dunmore**, removed a large quantity of gunpowder from the Williamsburg powder house and put it on a ship in the dead of night, out of reach of any frenzied Virginians. Next, he threatened to arm slaves, if necessary, to ward off attacks by colonists.

This was an effective threat; Dunmore understood full well how to produce panic among planters. In November 1775, he issued an official proclamation promising freedom to defecting able-bodied slaves who would fight for the British. Although Dunmore wanted to scare the planters, he had no intention of liberating all the slaves or starting a real slave rebellion. Female, young, and elderly slaves were not welcome to flee, and many were sent back to face irate masters. Astute blacks noticed that Dunmore neglected to free his own slaves. A Virginia barber named Caesar declared that "he did not know any one foolish enough to believe him [Dunmore], for if he intended to do so, he ought first to set his own free." By December 1775, around fifteen hundred slaves in Virginia had fled to Lord Dunmore, who armed them and called them his "Ethiopian Regiment." Camp diseases quickly set in: dysentery, typhoid fever, and smallpox. When Dunmore sailed for England in mid-1776, he took just three hundred black survivors with him. But the association of freedom with the British authorities had been established, and throughout the war thousands more southern slaves made bold to run away as soon as they heard the British army was approaching.

In the northern colonies as well, slaves clearly recognized the evolving political struggle with Britain as an ideal moment to bid for freedom. A twenty-one-year-old Boston domestic slave employed biting sarcasm in a 1774 newspaper essay to call attention to the hypocrisy of local slave owners: "How well the Cry for Liberty, and the reverse Disposition for exercise of oppressive Power over others agree, — I humbly think it does not require the Penetration of a Philosopher to Determine." This extraordinary young woman, **Phillis Wheatley**, had already gained international recognition through a book of poems endorsed by Governor Thomas Hutchinson and Boston merchant John Hancock and published in London in 1773. Possibly neither man fully appreciated the irony of his endorsement, however, for Wheatley's poems spoke of "Fair Freedom" as the "Goddess long desir'd" by Africans enslaved in America. At the urging of his wife, Wheatley's master freed the young poet in 1775.

Wheatley's poetic ideas about freedom found concrete expression among other discontented groups. Some slaves in Boston petitioned Thomas Gage, promising to fight for the British if he would liberate them. Gage turned them down. In Ulster County, New York, along the Hudson River, two blacks were overheard discussing gunpowder, and thus a plot unraveled that involved at least twenty slaves in four villages discovered to have ammunition stashed away.

In Maryland, soon after the news of the Lexington battle arrived, blacks exhibited impatience with their status as slaves, causing one Maryland planter to report that "the insolence of the Negroes in this county is come to such a height, that we are under a necessity of disarming them. . . . We took about eighty guns, some bayonets, swords, etc." In North Carolina, a planned uprising was uncovered, and scores of slaves were arrested. Ironically, it was the revolutionary committee of public safety that ordered the whippings to punish this quest for liberty.

By 1783, when the Revolutionary War ended, as many as twenty thousand blacks had voted against slavery with their feet by seeking refuge with the British army. Most failed to achieve the liberation they were seeking. The British generally used them for menial labor, and disease, especially smallpox, devastated encampments of runaways. But some eight thousand to ten thousand persisted through the war and later, under the protection of the British army, left America to start new lives of freedom in Canada's Nova Scotia or Africa's Sierra Leone.

REVIEW How did enslaved people in the colonies react to the stirrings of revolution?

► Conclusion: The Long Road to Revolution

In the aftermath of the Seven Years' War, Britain and its American colonies were victorious, but almost none of the warring parties came away satisfied. France lost vast amounts of North American land claims, and Indian land rights were increasingly violated or ignored. As for the victors, Britain's huge war debt and subsequent revenue-generating policies distressed Americans and set the stage for the imperial crisis of the 1760s and 1770s. The years 1763 to 1775 brought repeated attempts by the British government to subordinate the colonies into contributing partners in the larger scheme of empire.

American resistance to British policies grew slowly but steadily. In 1765, loyalist Thomas Hutchinson shared with patriot Samuel Adams the belief that it was exceedingly unwise for Britain to assert a right to taxation because Parliament did not adequately represent Americans. By temperament and office, Hutchinson was obliged to uphold British policy. Adams, in contrast, protested the policy

and made political activists out of thousands in the process.

By 1775, events propelled many Americans to the conclusion that a concerted effort was afoot to deprive them of all their liberties, the most important of which were the right to self-rule and the right to live free of an occupying army. Prepared to die for those liberties, hundreds of minutemen converged on Concord. April 19 marked the start of their rebellion.

Another rebellion under way in 1775 was doomed to be short-circuited. Black Americans who had experienced actual slavery listened to shouts of "Liberty!" from white crowds and appropriated the language of revolution swirling around them that spoke to their deepest needs and hopes. Defiance of authority was indeed contagious, but freedom for black slaves would not be fully granted in America for nearly a century.

In 1765, patriot leaders had wanted a correction, a restoration of the ancient liberty of self-taxation, but events over the next decade convinced many that a return to the old ways was impossible. Challenging Parliament's right to tax had led, step-by-step, to challenging Parliament's right to legislate over the colonies in any matter. By 1774, many in New England were willing to shoulder guns and risk death to free the colonies from Parliament's rule. Yet even after the battles of Lexington and Concord, a war with Britain seemed far from inevitable to colonists outside New England. In the months ahead, American colonial leaders pursued peaceful as well as military solutions to the question of who actually had authority over them. By the end of 1775, however, reconciliation with the crown would be unattainable.

► Selected Bibliography

General Works

Edward Countryman, *The American Revolution* (2003).
Merrill Jensen, *The Founding of a Nation: A History of the American Revolution, 1763–1776* (2004).
Robert Middlekauff, *The Glorious Cause: The American Revolution, 1763–1789* (2005).
Gordon Wood, *The Radicalism of the American Revolution* (1993).
Alfred F. Young, *Liberty Tree: Ordinary People and the American Revolution* (2006).

Native Americans and the Seven Years' War

Fred Anderson, *Crucible of War: The Seven Years' War and the Fate of Empire in British North America, 1754–1766* (2001).

Colin G. Calloway, *The Scratch of a Pen: 1763 and the Transformation of America* (2007).

Gregory Evans Dowd, *War under Heaven: Pontiac, the Indian Nations, and the British Empire* (2004).

Eric Hinderaker, *The Two Hendricks: Unraveling a Mohawk Mystery* (2010).

James H. Merrell, *Into the American Woods: Negotiators on the Pennsylvania Frontier* (2000).

Timothy J. Shannon, *Indians and Colonists at the Crossroads of Empire: The Albany Congress of 1754* (2002).

Peter Silver, *Our Savage Neighbors: How Indian War Transformed Early America* (2009).

Richard White, *The Middle Ground: Indians, Empires, and Republics in the Great Lakes Region, 1650–1815* (1991).

The Revolutionary Crisis of the 1760s and 1770s

Richard Archer, *As If an Enemy's Country: The British Occupation of Boston and the Origins of Revolution* (2010).

Bernard Bailyn, *The Ordeal of Thomas Hutchinson* (1976).

Carol Berkin, *Revolutionary Mothers: Women in the Struggle for America's Independence* (2006).

T. H. Breen, *American Insurgents, American Patriots: The Revolution of the People* (2010).

Benjamin L. Carp, *Defiance of the Patriots: The Boston Tea Party and the Making of America* (2010).

John E. Ferling, *The First of Men: A Life of George Washington* (1988).

David Hackett Fischer, *Paul Revere's Ride* (1995).

Robert A. Gross, *The Minutemen and Their World* (2001).

Joan Gundersen, *To Be Useful to the World: Women in Revolutionary America, 1740–1790* (1996).

Woody Holton, *Forced Founders: Indians, Debtors, Slaves, and the Making of the American Revolution in Virginia* (1999).

Pauline Maier, *From Resistance to Revolution: Colonial Radicals and the Development of American Opposition to Britain, 1765–1776* (1992).

Edmund S. and Helen M. Morgan, *The Stamp Act Crisis: Prologue to Revolution* (1995).

Gary B. Nash, *The Unknown American Revolution: The Unruly Birth of Democracy and the Struggle to Create America* (2006).

Mary Beth Norton, *Liberty's Daughters: The Revolutionary Experience of American Women, 1750–1800* (1996).

Ray Raphael, *The First American Revolution: Before Lexington and Concord* (2002).

Alfred F. Young, *The Shoemaker and the Tea Party: Memory and the American Revolution* (2000).

Slavery

Ira Berlin, *Many Thousands Gone: The First Two Centuries of Slavery in North America* (2000).

Douglas R. Egerton, *Death or Liberty: African Americans and Revolutionary America* (2009).

Sylvia Frey, *Water from the Rock: Black Resistance in a Revolutionary Age* (1991).

Sidney Kaplan and Emma Nogrady Kaplan, *The Black Presence in the Era of the American Revolution* (1989).

Philip Morgan, *Slave Counterpoint* (1998).

▶ **FOR MORE BOOKS ABOUT TOPICS IN THIS CHAPTER**, see the Online Bibliography at **bedfordstmartins.com/roark**.

▶ **FOR ADDITIONAL PRIMARY SOURCES FROM THIS PERIOD**, see Michael Johnson, ed., *Reading the American Past*, Fifth Edition.

▶ **FOR WEB SITES, IMAGES, AND DOCUMENTS RELATED TO TOPICS AND PLACES IN THIS CHAPTER**, visit Make History at **bedfordstmartins.com/roark**.

Reviewing Chapter 6

KEY TERMS

Explain each term's significance.

The Seven Years' War, 1754–1763
- Seven Years' War (p. 159)
- Ohio Company (p. 159)
- Albany Plan of Union (p. 161)
- William Pitt (p. 163)
- Treaty of Paris, 1763 (p. 164)
- Pontiac's Rebellion (p. 166)
- Proclamation of 1763 (p. 166)

The Sugar and Stamp Acts, 1763–1765
- George III (p. 167)
- Sugar (Revenue) Act (p. 167)
- Stamp Act (p. 168)
- virtual representation (p. 169)
- Patrick Henry (p. 169)
- Virginia Resolves (p. 169)
- Samuel Adams (p. 170)
- Sons of Liberty (p. 170)
- Thomas Hutchinson (p. 170)
- Stamp Act Congress (p. 171)
- Declaratory Act (p. 174)

The Townshend Acts and Economic Retaliation, 1767–1770
- Townshend duties (p. 174)
- nonconsumption agreements (p. 175)
- Daughters of Liberty (p. 175)
- Boston Massacre (p. 177)

The Destruction of the Tea and the Coercive Acts, 1770–1774
- committees of correspondence (p. 179)
- Tea Act of 1773 (p. 179)
- Coercive (Intolerable) Acts (p. 180)
- Thomas Gage (p. 181)
- First Continental Congress (p. 182)

Domestic Insurrections, 1774–1775
- Lexington and Concord (p. 184)
- Lord Dunmore (p. 185)
- Phillis Wheatley (p. 185)

REVIEW QUESTIONS

Use key terms and dates to support your answer.

1. How did the Seven Years' War erode relations between colonists and British authorities? (pp. 159–167)

2. Why did the Sugar Act and the Stamp Act draw fierce opposition from colonists? (pp. 167–174)

3. Why did British authorities send troops to occupy Boston in the fall of 1768? (pp. 174–178)

4. Why did Parliament pass the Coercive Acts in 1774? (pp. 178–183)

5. How did enslaved people in the colonies react to the stirrings of revolution? (pp. 183–186)

MAKING CONNECTIONS

Draw on key terms, the timeline, and review questions.

1. In the mid-eighteenth century, how did Native Americans influence relations between European nations? Between Britain and the colonies?

2. What other grievances, besides taxation, led colonists by 1775 to openly rebel against Britain?

3. How did the colonists organize to oppose British power so effectively? In your answer, discuss the role of communication in facilitating the colonial resistance, being sure to cite specific examples.

LINKING TO THE PAST

Link events in this chapter to earlier events.

1. In Bacon's Rebellion in Virginia in 1676, backcountry farmers protested the rule of a royal governor who did not seem to have the economic interests of many Virginians at heart. Compare the administration of Sir William Berkeley of Virginia with that of Thomas Hutchinson of Massachusetts in the 1760s. Are there more differences than similarities? (See chapter 3.)

2. How does the growing ethnic and religious diversity of the mid-eighteenth-century colonies help explain the evolution of anti-British feeling that would culminate in insurrection in 1775? (See chapter 5.)

▶ FOR PRACTICE QUIZZES AND OTHER STUDY TOOLS, visit the Online Study Guide at **bedfordstmartins.com/roark**.

TIMELINE 1754–1775

1754
- Seven Years' War begins in North America.
- Albany Congress proposes Plan of Union (never implemented).

1755
- Braddock defeated in western Pennsylvania.

1757
- William Pitt fully commits Britain to war effort.

1760
- Montreal falls to British.
- George III becomes British king.

1763
- Treaty of Paris ends Seven Years' War.
- Pontiac's Rebellion.
- Proclamation of 1763.
- Paxton Boys massacre friendly Indians in Pennsylvania.

1764
- Parliament enacts Sugar (Revenue) Act.

1765
- Parliament enacts Stamp Act.
- Virginia Resolves challenge Stamp Act.
- Sons of Liberty stage dozens of crowd actions.
- Stamp Act Congress meets.

1766
- Parliament repeals Stamp Act and passes Declaratory Act.

1767
- Parliament enacts Townshend duties.

1768
- British station troops in Boston.

1768–1769
- Merchants sign nonimportation agreements.

1770
- Boston Massacre.
- Parliament repeals Townshend duties.

1772
- British navy ship *Gaspée* burned.

1773
- Parliament passes Tea Act.
- Dumping of tea in Boston harbor.

1774
- Parliament passes Coercive (Intolerable) Acts.
- Powder Alarm shows colonists' readiness to engage in battle with British.
- First Continental Congress meets; Continental Association formed.

1775
- Battles of Lexington and Concord.
- Lord Dunmore promises freedom to defecting slaves.

189

CONTINENTAL ARMY UNIFORM
This uniform belonged to Colonel Peter Gansevoort, commander of Fort Stanwix in the Mohawk Valley of New York. In a cost-saving move, color-coded shoulder ribbons indicated military title; as Gansevoort rose in the ranks he changed ribbons, not coats. Young Gansevoort won fame and several promotions for successfully defending Fort Stanwix against a siege by British and Indians. Yet a related battle diminished the joy of his victory. Hundreds of neighboring militiamen hurrying to aid Gansevoort met ambush and slaughter by loyalists and Indians (pictured in the background in an artistic interpretation from the 1850s) in a battle called Oriskany.

Background: Library of Congress; uniform: National Museum of American History, Smithsonian Institution, Washington, D.C.

7

The War for America

1775–1783

ROBERT SHURTLIFF OF MASSACHUSETTS WAS A LATECOMER TO THE
American Revolution, enlisting in the Continental army months after the
last decisive battle at Yorktown had been fought. The army needed fresh
recruits as a holding action against the large British force still occupying
New York City. Both sides were waiting for the peace treaty to be finalized
in Paris — a process that would take nearly two years.

To secure those new recruits in a country exhausted by eight years of
war, some towns offered cash bounties of $50 in silver. Beardless boys who
had been children when the first shots were fired at Lexington now
stepped forward, Shurtliff among them. Reportedly eighteen, the youth
was single, poor, and at loose ends. With a muscular physique and a ready
proficiency with a musket, Shurtliff won assignment to the army's elite light
infantry unit, part of Washington's army of 10,000 men stationed along the
Hudson River, north of New York City.

That is, 10,000 men and 1 woman. "Robert Shurtliff" was actually
Deborah Sampson, age twenty-three, from Middleborough, Massachusetts.
For seventeen months, Sampson masqueraded as a man, marching through
woods, skirmishing with the enemy, and enduring the boredom of camp.
Understating her age enabled her to blend in with the beardless boys, as
did her competence as a soldier. With privacy at a minimum, she faced constant risk of discovery. Soldiers slept six to a tent, "spooning" their bodies
together for warmth. Somehow, Sampson managed to escape detection.
Although many thousands of women served the army as cooks, laundresses, and caregivers, they were never placed in combat. Not only was
Sampson defrauding the military, but she was also violating a legal prohibition on cross-dressing. Why did she run this risk?

A hard-luck childhood had left Sampson both impoverished and unusually plucky. When she was five, her father deserted the family, forcing
her mother to place the children in foster care. Deborah trained to be a
servant in a succession of families. Along the way, she learned to plow a
field and to read and write, uncommon skills for a female servant. Freed
from servitude at age eighteen, she earned a living as a weaver and then

as a teacher, low-wage jobs but also ones without supervising bosses. Marriage would have been her normal next step, but either lack of inclination or a wartime shortage of men kept her single and "masterless," rare for an eighteenth-century woman. But like most single females, she was also poor; the $50 bounty enticed her to enlist.

Sampson's true sex was finally discovered by a physician when she was hospitalized for a fever. She was discharged immediately, but her fine service record kept her superiors from prosecuting her for cross-dressing. What eventually made Sampson famous was not her war service alone — there were several other instances of women who wielded weapons in various battles — but her success in selling her story to the public. In 1797, now a middle-aged mother of three, she told her life story (a blend of fact and fiction) in a short book. During 1802–1803, she reenacted her wartime masquerade on a speaking tour of New England and New York. Once again, she was crossing gender boundaries, since women who were not actresses normally did not speak from public stages.

Except for her disguised sex, Sampson's Revolutionary War experience was similar to that of most Americans. Disruptions affected everyone's life, whether in military service or on the home front. Wartime shortages caused women and children to take up traditionally male labor. Soldiers fought for ideas, but they also fought to earn money. Hardship was widely endured. And Sampson's quest for personal independence — a freedom from the constraints of being female — was echoed in the general quest for political independence that many Americans identified as a major goal of the war.

Political independence was not everyone's primary goal at first. For more than a year after fighting began, the Continental Congress in Philadelphia resisted declaring America's independence. Some delegates cautiously hoped for reconciliation with Britain. The congress raised an army, financed it, and sought alliances with foreign countries — all while exploring diplomatic channels for peace.

Once King George III rejected all peace overtures, Americans loudly declared their independence, and the war moved into high gear. In part a classic war with professional armies and textbook battles, the Revolutionary War was also a civil war and at times a brutal guerrilla war between committed rebels and loyalists. It also had complex ethnic dimensions, pitting Indian tribes allied with the British against others allied with the Americans. And it provided an unprecedented opportunity for enslaved African Americans to win their freedom, either by joining the British, who openly encouraged slaves to desert their masters, or by joining the Continental army and state militias, fighting alongside white Americans.

Deborah Sampson
In the mid-1790s, Deborah Sampson sat for this small portrait painted by Massachusetts folk artist Joseph Stone. An engraved copy of it illustrated *The Female Review*, a short book about Sampson's unusual military career and life published in 1797. Sampson, by then a wife and mother, displays femininity in this picture. Note her long curly hair, the necklace, and the stylish gown with a low, lace-trimmed neckline filled in (for modesty's sake) with a white neckerchief. Sampson the soldier had used a cloth band to compress her breasts; Sampson the matron wore a satin band to define her bustline. Rhode Island Historical Society.

VISUAL ACTIVITY

The Bloody Massacre Perpetrated in King Street, Boston, on March 5, 1770
This mass-produced engraving by Paul Revere sold for sixpence per copy. In this patriot version of events, the soldiers are posed as a firing squad, shooting under orders at an unarmed and bewigged crowd. Actually, the shots were chaotic, and the five fatalities were all from the lower orders of youth and laborers, not the sort to wear wigs. Among them was Crispus Attucks, a dockworker of African and Indian ethnicity, but Revere shows only whites among the wounded and dead.
Anne S. K. Brown Military Collection, Providence, RI.

READING THE IMAGE: How does this picture attempt to sway its viewers' sympathies?
CONNECTIONS: Does this picture accurately represent the events of the Boston Massacre? What might account for its biases?

veneration. Crispus Attucks, a sailor and rope maker in his forties, was the son of an African man and a Natick Indian woman. A slave in his youth, he was at the time of his death a free laborer at the Boston docks. Attucks was one of the first American partisans to die in the revolutionary struggle with Britain, and certainly the first African American.

The trial of the eight soldiers came in the fall of 1770. They were defended by two young Boston attorneys, Samuel Adams's cousin John Adams and Josiah Quincy. Because Adams and Quincy had direct ties to the leadership of the Sons of Liberty, their decision to defend the British soldiers at first seems odd. But Adams was deeply committed to the idea that even unpopular defendants deserved a fair trial. Samuel Adams respected his cousin's decision to take the case, for there was a tactical benefit as well. It showed that the Boston leadership was not lawless but could be seen as defenders of British liberty and law.

The five-day trial resulted in acquittal for Preston and for all but two of the soldiers, who were convicted of manslaughter, branded on the thumbs, and released. Nothing materialized in the trial to indicate a conspiracy or concerted

plan to provoke trouble by either the British or the Sons of Liberty. To this day, the question of responsibility for the Boston Massacre remains obscure.

REVIEW   Why did British authorities send troops to occupy Boston in the fall of 1768?

▶ The Destruction of the Tea and the Coercive Acts, 1770–1774

In the same week as the Boston Massacre, yet another new British prime minister, Frederick North, acknowledged the harmful impact of the boycott on trade and recommended repeal of the Townshend duties. A skillful politician, Lord North took office in 1770 and kept it for twelve years; at last King George had stability at the helm. Seeking peace with the colonies and prosperity for British merchants, North persuaded Parliament to remove all the duties

"Perspective View of the Boston Commons, October 1, 1768"
The first regiment of British soldiers arrived in Boston on October 1, sent to maintain law and order. Christian Remick, amateur artist, captured that first moment of uneasy contact. Locals stroll on the Boston Commons— families, dogs, romancing couples—eyeing the soldiers at their tented encampment. The redcoated soldiers, no doubt glad to be on land after their journey at sea, drill with their weapons. Even in this crude rendering, the bayonets on their guns stand out. Mather Byles, a local minister and wit, remarked that the Bostonians had wished for a "redress of grievances, which grievances had returned red-dressed." Photograph courtesy of the Concord Museum, Concord, MA.

major troubles occurred that winter and through most of 1769. But as January 1, 1770, approached, marking the end of the nonimportation agreement, it was clear that some merchants—such as Thomas Hutchinson's two sons, both importers — were ready to break the boycott.

Trouble began in January, when a crowd defaced the door of the Hutchinson brothers' shop with "Hillsborough paint," a potent mixture of human excrement and urine. In February, a crowd surrounded the house of customs official Ebenezer Richardson, who panicked and fired a musket, accidentally killing a young boy passing on the street. The Sons of Liberty mounted a massive funeral procession to mark this first instance of violent death in the struggle with Britain.

For the next week, tension gripped Boston. The climax came on Monday evening, March 5, 1770, when a crowd taunted eight British soldiers guarding the customs house. Onlookers threw snowballs and rocks and dared the soldiers to fire; finally one did. After a short pause, someone yelled "Fire!" and the other soldiers shot into the crowd, hitting eleven men, killing five of them.

The **Boston Massacre**, as the event quickly became called, was over in minutes. In the immediate aftermath, Hutchinson (now acting governor after Bernard's recall to Britain) showed courage in addressing the crowd from the balcony of the statehouse. He quickly removed the regiments to an island in the harbor to prevent further bloodshed, and he jailed Captain Thomas Preston and his eight soldiers for their own protection, promising they would be held for trial.

The Sons of Liberty staged elaborate martyrs' funerals for the five victims. Significantly, the one nonwhite victim shared equally in the public's conspicuous boycotts of British-made goods. In Boston, more than three hundred women signed a petition to abstain from tea, "sickness excepted," in order to "save this abused Country from Ruin and Slavery." A nine-year-old girl visiting the royal governor's house in New Jersey took the tea she was offered, curtsied, and tossed the beverage out a nearby window.

Homespun cloth became a prominent symbol of patriotism. A young Boston girl learning to spin called herself "a daughter of liberty," noting that "I chuse to wear as much of our own manufactory as pocible." In the boycott period of 1768 to 1770, newspapers reported on spinning matches, or bees, in some sixty New England towns, in which women came together in public to make yarn. Nearly always, the bee was held at the local minister's house, and the yarn produced was charitably handed over to him for distribution to the poor. Newspaper accounts variously called the spinners "Daughters of Liberty" or "Daughters of Industry."

This surge of public spinning was related to the politics of the boycott, which infused traditional women's work with new political purpose. But the women spinners were not equivalents of the Sons of Liberty. The Sons marched in streets, burned effigies, threatened hated officials, and celebrated anniversaries of their successes with raucous drinking in taverns. The Daughters manifested their patriotism quietly, in ways marked by piety, industry, and charity. The difference was due in part to cultural ideals of gender, which prized masculine self-assertion and feminine selflessness. It also was due to class. The Sons were a cross-class alliance, with

> **A nine-year-old girl visiting the royal governor's house in New Jersey took the tea she was offered, curtsied, and tossed the beverage out a nearby window.**

leaders from the middling orders reliant on men and boys of the lower ranks to fuel their crowds. The Daughters dusting off spinning wheels and shelving their teapots were genteel ladies accustomed to buying British goods. The difference between the Sons and the Daughters also speaks to two views of how best to challenge authority: violent threats and street actions, or the self-disciplined, self-sacrificing boycott of goods?

On the whole, the anti-British boycotts were a success. Imports fell by more than 40 percent; British merchants felt the pinch and let Parliament know it. In Boston, the Hutchinson family — whose fortune rested on British trade — also endured losses, but even more alarming to the lieutenant governor, Boston seemed overrun with anti-British sentiment. The Sons of Liberty staged rollicking annual celebrations of the Stamp Act riot, and both Hutchinson and Governor Bernard concluded that British troops were necessary to restore order.

Military Occupation and "Massacre" in Boston

In the fall of 1768, Britain sent three thousand uniformed troops to occupy Boston. The soldiers drilled conspicuously on the town Common, played loud music on the Sabbath, and in general grated on the nerves of Bostonians. Although the situation was frequently   tense, no

Spinning Wheel
This wheel, used for spinning flax into linen thread, is likely the type used in the politicized 1768–1769 spinning bees in which Daughters of Liberty proclaimed their boycott of British textiles. The spinning Daughters of Liberty were praised for their virtuous industry. Responding to such praise, one young woman complained about her male counterparts: "Alas! We hear nothing of their working matches, nothing of their concern for the honor of their King or for the safety or liberties of their country." Instead, the news was of "nocturnal Carousals and Exploits; of their drinking, gaming & whoring matches; and how they disturb the quiet of honest people." Smithsonian Institution, Washington, D.C.

not represented in Parliament. Further, he argued that the new way to pay governors' salaries subverted the proper relationship between the people and their rulers. The assembly circulated a letter with Adams's arguments to other colonial assemblies for their endorsement. As with the Stamp Act Congress of 1765, colonial assemblies were starting to coordinate their protests.

In response to Adams's letter, Lord Hillsborough, the new man in charge of colonial affairs in Britain, instructed Massachusetts governor Bernard to dissolve the assembly if it refused to repudiate the letter. The assembly refused, by a vote of 92 to 17, and Bernard carried out his instruction. In the summer of 1768, Boston was in an uproar.

Nonconsumption and the Daughters of Liberty

The Boston town meeting led the way with **nonconsumption agreements** calling for a boycott of all British-made goods. Dozens of other towns passed similar resolutions in 1767 and 1768. For example, prohibited purchases in the town of New Haven, Connecticut, included carriages, furniture, hats, clothing, lace, clocks, and textiles. The idea was to encourage home manufacture and to hurt trade, causing London merchants to pressure Parliament for repeal of the duties.

Nonconsumption agreements were very hard to enforce. With the Stamp Act, there was one hated item, a stamp, and a limited number of official distributors. In contrast, an agreement to boycott all British goods required serious personal sacrifice. Some merchants were wary because it hurt their pocketbooks, and a few continued to import in readiness for the end of nonconsumption (or to sell on the side to people choosing to ignore the boycotts). In Boston, such merchants found themselves blacklisted in newspapers and broadsides.

A more direct blow to trade came from nonimportation agreements, but getting merchants to agree to these proved more difficult, because of fears that merchants in other colonies might continue to import goods and make handsome profits. Not until late 1768 could Boston merchants agree to suspend trade through a nonimportation agreement lasting one year starting January 1, 1769. Sixty signed the agreement. New York merchants soon followed suit, as did Philadelphia and Charleston merchants in 1769.

Doing without British products, whether luxury goods, tea, or textiles, no doubt was a hardship. But it also presented an opportunity,

Edenton Tea Ladies
American women in many communities renounced British apparel and tea during the early 1770s. Women in Edenton, North Carolina, publicized their pledge and drew hostile fire in the form of a British cartoon. The cartoon's message is that brazen women who meddled in politics would undermine their femininity. Neglected babies, urinating dogs, wanton sexuality, and mean-looking women would be some of the dire consequences, according to the artist. The cartoon works as humor for the British because of the gender reversals it predicts and because of the insult it directs at American men. Library of Congress.

for many of the British products specified in nonconsumption agreements were household goods traditionally under the control of the "ladies." By 1769, male leaders in the patriot cause clearly understood that women's cooperation in nonconsumption and home manufacture was beneficial to their cause. The Townshend duties thus provided an unparalleled opportunity for encouraging female patriotism. During the Stamp Act crisis, Sons of Liberty took to the streets in protest. During the difficulties of 1768 and 1769, the concept of **Daughters of Liberty** emerged to give shape to a new idea — that women might play a role in public affairs. Any woman could express affiliation with the colonial protest through

The 1763 boundary was yet a further provocation to many Americans, and most especially to land speculators (like Virginia's Patrick Henry or the men of the Ohio Company) who had already staked claims to huge tracts of land west of the Appalachians and who had no desire to lose profitable resale opportunities. The boundary also proved impossible to enforce, despite the large British military presence. Surging population growth had already sent many hundreds of settlers, many of them squatters, west of the Appalachians.

By 1774, continuous hostilities and periodic bloodshed escalated into a conflict named Lord Dunmore's War, after Virginia's royal governor. In this short but deadly war, Virginia soldiers traversed the Appalachian Mountains to attack Mingo and Shawnee peoples south of the Ohio River, thereby establishing speculators' land claims in western Virginia and Kentucky. But they left the frontier aflame with such ethnic antagonism that would-be settlers were left fearful, uncertain about their future, and increasingly wary of British claims to be a protective mother country.

REVIEW How did the Seven Years' War erode relations between colonists and British authorities?

▶ The Sugar and Stamp Acts, 1763–1765

In 1760, **George III**, twenty-two years old, became king of England. Timid and insecure, George struggled to gain his footing in his new job. He rotated through a succession of leaders, searching for a prime minister he could trust. A half dozen ministers in seven years took turns dealing with one basic, underlying British reality: A huge war debt needed to be serviced, and the colonists, as British subjects, should help pay it off. To many Americans, however, that proposition seemed in deep violation of what they perceived to be their rights and liberties as British subjects, and it created resentment that eventually erupted in large-scale street protests. The first provocative revenue acts were the work of Sir George Grenville, prime minister from 1763 to 1765.

Silver Medal to Present to Indians
After Pontiac's uprising ended, the British aimed to conciliate the Indians by distributing gifts. This silver medal of 1766 shows King George III on the front and a cozy depiction of an Indian and a Briton smoking a peace pipe on the back. The Latin words announce George's name, title, and kingly dominions.
Imagine a conversation between an Indian chief and an English translator who tried to explain what the slogan HAPPY WHILE UNITED might mean. The scene of two men with friendly body language illustrates HAPPY and UNITED. The WHILE, conveying a sense of temporariness and contingency, might have been trickier to explain. Why? The American Numismatic Society.

Grenville's Sugar Act

To find revenue, George Grenville scrutinized the customs service, which monitored the shipping trade and collected all import and export duties. Grenville found that the salaries of customs officers cost the government four times what was collected in revenue. The shortfall was due in part to bribery and smuggling, so Grenville began to insist on rigorous attention to paperwork and a strict accounting of collected duties.

The hardest duty to enforce was the one imposed by the Molasses Act of 1733 — a stiff tax of six pence per gallon on any molasses imported to British colonies from non-British sources. The purpose of the tax was to discourage trade with French Caribbean islands and to redirect the molasses trade to British sugar islands, but it did not work. French molasses remained cheap and abundant because French planters on Martinique and Guadeloupe had no use for it. A by-product of sugar production, molasses was a key ingredient in rum, a drink the French scorned. Rum-loving Americans were eager to buy French molasses, and for decades American importers lined the pockets of customs officials in order to avoid paying the tariffs.

Grenville's inspired solution was the **Revenue Act** of 1764, popularly dubbed the **Sugar Act**. It lowered the duty on French molasses to three pence, making it more attractive for shippers to obey the law, and at the same time raised penalties for smuggling. The act appeared to be in the tradition of navigation acts meant to regulate trade (see chapter 4), but Grenville's actual intent was to raise revenue. He was using an established form of law for new ends and accomplishing his goal by the novel means of lowering a duty.

The Sugar Act toughened enforcement policies. From now on, all British naval crews could act as impromptu customs officers, boarding suspicious ships and seizing cargoes found to be in violation. Smugglers caught without proper paperwork would be prosecuted, not in a local court with a friendly jury but in a vice-admiralty court located in Nova Scotia, where a single judge presided. The implication was that justice would be sure and severe.

Grenville's hopes for the Sugar Act did not materialize. The small decrease in duty did not offset the attractions of smuggling, while the increased vigilance in enforcement led to several ugly confrontations in port cities. Reaction to the Sugar Act foreshadowed questions about Britain's right to tax Americans, but in 1764 objections to the act came principally from the small numbers of Americans engaged in the shipping trades.

From the British point of view, the Sugar Act seemed to be a reasonable effort to administer the colonies. To American shippers, however, the Sugar Act was not just about regulating trade. The British supervision appeared to be a disturbing intrusion into the long-held colonial practice of self-taxation by elected colonial assemblies. Benjamin Franklin, Pennsylvania's lobbyist in London, warned that "two distinct Jurisdictions or Powers of Taxing cannot well subsist together in the same country."

The Stamp Act

By his second year in office, Grenville had made almost no dent in the national debt. So in February 1765, he escalated his revenue program with the **Stamp Act**, precipitating a major conflict between Britain and the colonies over Parliament's right to tax. The Stamp Act imposed a tax on all paper

A Philadelphia Tavern Scene
This trade card advertises the pleasures that await customers at Isaac Jones's tavern on Front Street—smoking and drinking. These men are likely drinking rum, a favorite colonial beverage frequently imbibed in taverns in sociable groups. The Sugar Act of 1763 put into question the supply of West Indies molasses, politicizing an essential ingredient in rum. Library Company of Philadelphia.

used for official documents — newspapers, pamphlets, court documents, licenses, wills, ships' cargo lists — and required an affixed stamp as proof that the tax had been paid. Unlike the Sugar Act, which regulated trade, the Stamp Act was designed plainly and simply to raise money. It affected nearly everyone who used any taxed paper but, most of all, users of official documents in the business and legal communities.

Grenville was no fool. Anticipating that the stamp tax would be unpopular—Thomas Hutchinson had forewarned him — he delegated the administration of the act to Americans, to avoid taxpayer hostility toward British enforcers. In each colony, local stamp distributors would be hired at a handsome salary of 8 percent of the revenue collected.

English tradition held that taxes were a gift of the people to their monarch, granted by the people's representatives. This view of taxes as a freely given gift preserved an essential concept of English political theory: the idea that citizens have the liberty to enjoy and use their property without fear of confiscation. The king could not demand money; only the House of Commons could grant it. Grenville agreed with the notion of taxation by consent, but he argued that the colonists were already "virtually" represented in Parliament. The House of Commons, he insisted, represented all British subjects, wherever they were.

Colonial leaders emphatically rejected this view, arguing that **virtual representation** could not withstand the stretch across the Atlantic. Colonists willingly paid local and provincial taxes, levied by their town, county, or colonial assemblies. Typically, such annual taxes were based on property valuation, with an emphasis on income-generating property, such as numbers of cultivated acres and of livestock. The taxes paid for government administrative expenses and for shared necessities like local roads, schools, and poor relief. In contrast, the stamp tax was a clear departure as a fee-per-document tax, levied by a distant Parliament on unwilling colonies.

Resistance Strategies and Crowd Politics

News of the Stamp Act arrived in the colonies in April 1765, seven months before it was to take effect. There was time, therefore, to object. Governors were unlikely to challenge the law, for most of them owed their office to the king. Instead, the colonial assemblies took the lead; eight of them held discussions on the Stamp Act.

Virginia's assembly, the House of Burgesses, was the first. At the end of its May session, after two-thirds of the members had left, **Patrick Henry**, a young political newcomer, presented a series of resolutions on the Stamp Act that were debated and passed, one by one. They became known as the **Virginia Resolves**. Henry's resolutions inched the assembly toward radical opposition to the Stamp Act. The first three stated the obvious: that Virginians were British citizens, that they enjoyed the same rights and privileges as Britons, and that self-taxation was one of those rights. The fourth resolution noted that Virginians had always taxed themselves, through their representatives in the House of Burgesses. The fifth took a radical leap by pushing the other four unexceptional statements to one logical conclusion — that the Virginia assembly alone had the right to tax Virginians.

Two more fiery resolutions were debated as Henry pressed the logic of his case to the extreme. The sixth resolution denied legitimacy to any tax law originating outside Virginia, and the seventh boldly called anyone who disagreed with these propositions an enemy of Virginia. This was too much for the other representatives. They voted down resolutions six and seven and later rescinded their vote on number five as well.

Their caution hardly mattered, however, because newspapers in other colonies printed all seven Virginia Resolves, creating the impression that a daring first challenge to the Stamp Act had occurred. Consequently, other assemblies were willing to consider even more radical questions, such as this: By what authority could Parliament legislate for the colonies without also taxing them? No one disagreed, in 1765, that Parliament had legislative power over the colonists, who were, after all, British subjects. Several assemblies advanced the argument that there was a distinction between *external* taxes, imposed to regulate trade, and *internal* taxes, such as a stamp tax or a property tax, which could only be self-imposed.

Reaction to the Stamp Act ran far deeper than political debate in assemblies. Every person whose livelihood required official paper had to decide whether to comply with the act. There were only three options: boycotting, which was within the law but impractical because of the reliance on paper; defying the law and using unstamped paper; or preventing distribution of the stamps at the source before the law took effect, thus ensuring universal noncompliance.

Newspapers Protest the Stamp Act
The Stamp Act affected newspapers more than any other business. From New Hampshire to South Carolina, papers issued in late October 1765 featured black mourning lines and funereal symbols to forecast the imminent death of the press. The *Pennsylvania Journal's* first page was designed as a tombstone complete with skull and cross-bones. A New Hampshire editor dramatically declared, "I must Die, or Submit to that which is worse than Death, Be Stamped, and lose my Freedom." All colonial newspapers resumed publication within a week or two, defiantly operating without stamped paper and with a jubilant sense of the power of the press. Library of Congress.

The first organized resistance to the Stamp Act began in Boston in August 1765 under the direction of town leaders, chief among them **Samuel Adams**, John Hancock, and Ebenezer Mackintosh. The first two, both Harvard graduates, were town officers. Adams, in his forties, had shrewd political instincts and a gift for organizing. Hancock, though not yet thirty, had recently inherited his uncle's shipping business and was one of the wealthiest men in Massachusetts. Mackintosh, the same age as Hancock, was a shoemaker and highly experienced street activist. (See "Seeking the American Promise," page 172.) Many other artisans, tradesmen, printers, tavern keepers, dockworkers, and sailors — the middling and lower orders — mobilized in resistance to the Stamp Act, taking the name "**Sons of Liberty**."

The plan hatched in Boston called for a large street demonstration highlighting a mock execution designed to convince Andrew Oliver, the designated stamp distributor, to resign. On August 14, 1765, a crowd of two thousand to three thousand demonstrators, led by Mackintosh, hung an effigy of Oliver in a tree and then paraded it around town before finally beheading and burning it. In hopes of calming tensions, the royal governor Francis Bernard took no action. The flesh-and-blood Oliver stayed in hiding; the next day he resigned his office in a well-publicized announcement. The Sons of Liberty were elated.

The demonstration provided lessons for everyone. Oliver learned that stamp distributors would be very unpopular people. Governor Bernard, with no police force to call on, learned the limitations of his power to govern. The demonstration's leaders learned that street action was effective. And hundreds of ordinary men not only learned what the Stamp Act was all about but also gained pride in their ability to have a decisive impact on politics.

Twelve days later, a second crowd action showed how well these lessons had been learned. On August 26, a crowd visited the houses of three detested customs and court officials, breaking windows and raiding wine cellars. A fourth target was the finest dwelling in Massachusetts, owned by the stiff-necked lieutenant governor and chief justice **Thomas Hutchinson**. Rumors abounded that Hutchinson had urged Grenville to adopt the Stamp Act. Although he had actually done the opposite, Hutchinson refused to set the record straight, saying curtly, "I am not obliged to give an answer to all the questions that may be put me by every lawless person." The crowd attacked his house, and by daybreak only the exterior walls were standing. Governor Bernard gave orders to call out the militia, but he was told that many militiamen were among the crowd.

The destruction of Hutchinson's house brought a temporary halt to protest activities in Boston. The town meeting issued a statement of sympathy for Hutchinson, but a large reward for the arrest and conviction of rioters failed to produce a single lead. Hutchinson assumed that Mackintosh had led the attack, under orders issued by Samuel Adams, but Adams denied involvement and professed shock at the "truly mobbish Nature" of the violence.

Essentially, the opponents of the Stamp Act in Boston had triumphed; no one replaced Oliver as distributor. When the act took effect on November 1, ships without stamped permits continued to clear the harbor. Since he could not bring the lawbreakers to court, Hutchinson, ever principled, felt obliged to resign his office as chief justice. He remained lieutenant governor, however, and within five years he became the royal governor.

Liberty and Property

Boston's crowd actions of August sparked similar eruptions by groups calling themselves Sons of Liberty in nearly fifty towns throughout the

Symbolic Death to Stamp Agents
Crowds of protesters in many American towns staged threatening demonstrations designed to make any stamp distributor think twice about selling the hated stamps. In this contemporary cartoon, a dummy wearing a hat and waistcoat is being led to destruction. One protester carries a hangman's gallows, another a large bundle of sticks to burn the dummy after it is hanged. Do you think the cartoonist was in sympathy with the demonstrators? Why or why not? Granger Collection.

colonies, and stamp distributors everywhere hastened to resign. A crowd forced one Connecticut distributor to throw his hat and powdered wig in the air while shouting a cheer for "Liberty and property!" This man fared better than another Connecticut stamp agent who was nearly buried alive by Sons of Liberty. Only when the thuds of dirt sounded on his coffin did he have a sudden change of heart, shouting out his resignation to the crowd above. Luckily, he was heard. In Charleston, South Carolina, the stamp distributor resigned after crowds burned effigies and chanted "Liberty! Liberty!" The royal governor of Virginia glumly assessed the situation in a letter to British authorities: "The flame is spread through all the continent, and one colony supports another in their disobedience to superior powers."

Some colonial leaders, disturbed by the riots, sought a more moderate challenge to parliamentary authority. In October 1765, twenty-seven delegates representing nine colonial assemblies met in New York City as the **Stamp Act Congress**. For two weeks, the men hammered out a petition about taxation addressed to the king and Parliament. Their statement closely resembled the first five Virginia Resolves, claiming that taxes were "free gifts of the people," which only the people's representatives could give. They dismissed virtual representation: "The people of these colonies are not, and from their local circumstances, cannot be represented in the House of Commons." At the same time, the delegates carefully affirmed their subordination to Parliament and monarch in deferential language. Nevertheless, the Stamp Act Congress, by the mere fact of its meeting, advanced a radical potential — the notion of intercolonial political action.

The rallying cry of "Liberty and property" made perfect sense to many white Americans of all social ranks, who feared that the Stamp Act threatened their traditional right to liberty as British subjects. The liberty in question was the right to be taxed only by representative government. "Liberty and property" came from a trinity of concepts — "life, liberty, property" — that

> **"The flame is spread through all the continent, and one colony supports another in their disobedience to superior powers."**
> — The royal governor of Virginia

Pursuing Liberty, Protesting Tyranny

In August 1765, a little-known Boston shoemaker gained sudden prominence as the leader of crowd actions opposing the Stamp Act. Ebenezer Mackintosh boldly encouraged thousands of ordinary men in Massachusetts to assert a claim to liberty against what they identified as British tyranny. Mackintosh's story offers a glimpse into the political thinking of the man in the street during the decade of pre-Revolutionary turmoil. By 1776, this quest for liberty would be a defining feature of the fledgling United States.

Born in poverty in 1737, Ebenezer Mackintosh lacked family resources to ease his way in the world. His ancestors arrived in the Puritan migration of the 1630s; a century later, his family was quite poor. Ebenezer's father, an orphan, struggled against bad fortune. He owned no land and lacked a trade; he married and buried wives at least three times. The best he could do for young Ebenezer was to apprentice him to a shoemaker. During the Seven Years' War, Ebenezer joined the army to secure a signing bonus. He saw brief action and returned to Boston in 1758 to resume shoemaking. He was twenty-one.

A major fire in Boston in 1760 marked a dramatic change in direction for Mackintosh. In the aftermath of the fire, the city looked to young, able-bodied men to reinvigorate its volunteer fire companies and picked Ebenezer to join a select firemen's association in the city's South End. Fighting fires demonstrated one's sense of civic duty and manly responsibility. Fire clubs also generated fraternal sociability, with firemen regularly meeting in taverns over pitchers of beer, cementing the team spirit so critical to successful firefighting. Mackintosh proved to be a leader of men in times of emergency; he soon became head of the South End gang, which staged a mock battle once a year against the rival North End gang. In this traditional street festival, Mackintosh gained direct experience managing rowdy crowds.

Expertise in fire and crowd control paved the way for Mackintosh's transition from community leader to community activist in 1765. Stamp Act protests erupted twice in August of that year. In the first event, Mackintosh presided over the mock hanging of a dummy representing Andrew Oliver, the stamp distributor, at a century-old elm tree known as the Liberty Tree. The shoemaker led several thousand protesters in a march on the new stamp office, which was pulled down and burned. Twelve days later, a smaller but far more destructive demonstration almost certainly led by Mackintosh demolished the mansion of Governor Thomas Hutchinson. Hutchinson ordered Mackintosh arrested, but no witnesses cared to identify him. Hours later, the sheriff — a member of Mackintosh's fire company — released him, predicting worse trouble if he was kept in jail.

The shoemaker continued to lead large demonstrations in November and December, forcing Andrew Oliver to repudiate his stamp distributor duties. Ordinary people like Mackintosh exerted a new authority and confidence, commanding their social betters to do their bidding.

In 1766, the Stamp Act was repealed, and Mackintosh went back to shoemaking. He married Elizabeth Maverick and had two children by 1769. Perhaps he took a break from activism; no record links him to protest activities when British troops came to town in 1769–1770, nor was his presence recorded at the Boston Massacre in March 1770. In 1773, he was apparently back at it, bragging later in life that he helped throw tea into Boston harbor.

A well-publicized rumor spread in 1774 that a ship en route from London carried official orders to arrest four rebellious subjects, most notably Samuel Adams and Mackintosh. Adams stayed put, but Mackintosh, still lacking resources and at a low moment in life — his young wife had recently died — decided that flight was his best option. Carrying his two young children and his meager belongings, he walked 150 miles to a village in northern New Hampshire, where he set up shop as a shoemaker. He served locally and briefly as a soldier in the Revolution and then remarried and fathered four more children.

An especially telling clue to Mackintosh's idealization of liberty appears in the unusual name he gave his son born in 1769: Paschal Paoli Mackintosh, named in honor of Pasquale Paoli of Corsica, an antimonarchical freedom fighter who battled Italian foes and who won approving coverage in American newspapers in 1767–1769. (In those years, some

had come to be regarded as the birthright of freeborn British subjects since at least the seventeenth century. A powerful tradition of British political thought invested representative government with the duty to protect individual lives, liberties, and property against potential abuse by royal authority. Up to 1765, Americans had consented to accept Parliament as a body that represented them. But now, in this matter of taxation via stamps, Parliament seemed a distant body that had failed to protect Americans' liberty and property against royal authority.

Alarmed, some Americans began to speak and write about a plot by British leaders to enslave them. A Maryland writer warned that if the colonies lost "the right of exemption from all taxes without their consent," that loss would "deprive them of every privilege distinguishing

Mackintosh the Fireman
Mackintosh's signature demonstrates his facility with a pen. The woodcut depicts advanced firefighting techniques in Boston in the 1760s. Underground water mains made from bored-out wooden logs brought pond water to Boston's center. Firemen punched a hole in the log to tap the water, moving it via hose and bucket brigade. (A fireplug resealed the hole.) Teams of vigorous men pumped the water with sufficient force to spray it on the fire. Demolition to halt the spread of fires was also essential work. Mackintosh's fire-control skills transferred easily to anti–Stamp Act actions, whether burning effigies and small buildings or pulling down Hutchinson's house. Signature: Publications of the Colonial Society of Massachusetts; fire engine: Granger Collection.

scores of babies throughout the colonies were named Paschal.) Mackintosh enjoyed his brief moment of fame, and he lived to see liberty defined and enshrined in the foundational documents of the United States. Although his life ended in 1816 in obscurity, as it had begun, Mackintosh's activism in 1765 helped ensure that the thousands of people he mobilized learned a new political language of rights and liberties — a language that still resonates loudly today.

Questions for Consideration

1. Why would a twenty-eight-year-old shoemaker of low social status get upset about Britain's passage of the Stamp Act?

2. How likely was it that Mackintosh's wife, Elizabeth Maverick Mackintosh, participated in any of the crowd actions led by her husband?

3. What was at stake for Mackintosh in the American Revolution? What did he gain? What stayed the same?

freemen from slaves." In Virginia, a group of planters headed by Richard Henry Lee issued a document called the Westmoreland Resolves, claiming that the Stamp Act was an attempt "to reduce the people of this country to a state of abject and detestable slavery." The opposite meanings of *liberty* and *slavery* were utterly clear to white Americans, but they stopped short of applying similar logic to the half million black Americans they held in bondage. Many blacks, however, could see the contradiction. When a crowd of Charleston blacks paraded with shouts of "Liberty!" just a few months after white Sons of Liberty had done the same, the town militia turned out to break up the demonstration.

Politicians and merchants in Britain reacted with distress to the American demonstrations and petitions. Merchants particularly feared trade disruptions and pressured Parliament to repeal the Stamp Act. By late 1765, yet another new minister, the Marquess of Rockingham, headed the king's cabinet and sought a way to repeal the act without losing face. The solution came in March 1766: The Stamp Act was repealed, but with the repeal came the **Declaratory Act**, which asserted Parliament's right to legislate for the colonies "in all cases whatsoever." Perhaps the stamp tax had been inexpedient, but the power to tax — one prime case of a legislative power — was stoutly upheld. As yet, the Sugar Act lowered the molasses tax, and the Stamp Act was a complete bust; very little tax revenue had been extracted from the colonies.

REVIEW   Why did the Sugar Act and the Stamp Act draw fierce opposition from colonists?

▶ The Townshend Acts and Economic Retaliation, 1767–1770

Rockingham did not last long as prime minister. By the summer of 1766, George III had persuaded William Pitt to resume that position. Pitt appointed Charles Townshend to be chancellor of the exchequer, the chief financial minister. Facing both the old war debt and the cost of the British troops in America, not successfully shifted to the Americans, Townshend turned again to taxation. But his knowledge of the changing political climate in the colonies was limited, and his plan to raise revenue touched off coordinated boycotts of British goods in 1768 and 1769. Even women were politicized as self-styled "Daughters of Liberty." Boston led the uproar, causing the British to send peacekeeping soldiers to assist the royal governor. The stage was thus set for the first fatalities in the brewing revolution.

The Townshend Duties

Townshend proposed new taxes in the old form of a navigation act. Officially called the Revenue Act of 1767, it established new duties on tea, glass, lead, paper, and painters' colors imported into the colonies, to be paid by the importer but passed on to consumers in the retail price. A

year before, the duty on French molasses had been reduced from three pence to one pence per gallon, and finally the Sugar Act was pulling in a tidy revenue of about £45,000 annually. Townshend naively assumed that external taxes on transatlantic trade would be acceptable to Americans.

The **Townshend duties** were not especially burdensome, but the principle they embodied — taxation through trade duties — looked different to the colonists in the wake of the Stamp Act crisis. Although Americans once distinguished between external and internal taxes, accepting external duties as a means to direct the flow of trade, that distinction was wiped out by an external tax meant only to raise money. John Dickinson, a Philadelphia lawyer, articulated this view in a series of articles titled *Letters from a Farmer in Pennsylvania*, widely circulated in late 1767. "We are taxed without our consent. . . . We are therefore — SLAVES," Dickinson wrote, calling for "a total denial of the power of Parliament to lay upon these colonies any 'tax' whatever."

A controversial provision of the Townshend duties directed that some of the revenue generated would pay the salaries of royal governors. Before 1767, local assemblies set the salaries of their own officials, giving them significant influence over crown-appointed officeholders. Through his new provision, Townshend aimed to strengthen the governors' position as well as to curb what he perceived to be the growing independence of the assemblies.

The New York assembly, for example, seemed particularly defiant. It refused to enforce Parliament's Quartering Act of 1765, which directed the colonies to shelter and supply British regiments still based in America. This was effectively a tax levied without consent, the assembly argued, because it required New Yorkers to pay money by order of Parliament. In response, Townshend pushed through the New York Suspending Act, which declared all the assembly's acts null and void until it met its obligations to the army. Both measures — the new compensation model for royal governors and the suspension of the governance functions of the New York assembly — struck a chill throughout the colonies. Many wondered whether legislative government was at all secure.

Massachusetts again took the lead in protesting the Townshend duties. Samuel Adams, now an elected member of the provincial assembly, argued that any form of parliamentary taxation was unjust because Americans were

Sir Jeffery Amherst in 1765
After five years in America, commander-in-chief Jeffery Amherst returned to England and basked in the glory of his military successes against the French in Canada, which had brought him knighthood. Britain's leading artist, Joshua Reynolds, painted him in a clunky, medieval suit of knight's armor—certainly not what he wore in the wilds along the St. Lawrence River, pictured behind him. Amherst's face expresses self-assured amusement, yet his arms strike a pensive and even feminine pose. An acquaintance wrote of Amherst that "his manners were grave, formal, and cold." Mead Art Museum, Amherst College, Amherst, Massachusetts.

In 1763, a renewal of commitment to Indian ways and the formation of tribal alliances led to open warfare, which the British called **Pontiac's Rebellion**, after the chief of the Ottawas. (The coordinated uprising was actually the work of many men.) In mid-May, Ottawa, Potawatomi, and Huron warriors attacked Fort Detroit. Six more attacks on forts followed within weeks, and frontier settlements were also raided by nearly a dozen tribes from western New York, the Ohio Valley, and the Great Lakes region. By the fall, Indians had captured every fort west of Detroit. More than four hundred British soldiers were dead and another two thousand colonists killed or taken captive.

Pontiac's Uprising, 1763

Not all of the attacks were instigated by Indians. The worst of a number of violent aggressions by Americans occurred in late 1763, when some fifty Pennsylvania vigilantes known as the Paxton Boys descended on a peaceful village of Conestoga Indians — friendly Indians, living not far from Philadelphia — and murdered and scalped twenty of them. The vigilantes, now numbering five hundred and out to make war on all Indians, marched on Philadelphia to try to capture and murder some Christian Indians held in protective custody there. British troops prevented that, but the Paxton Boys escaped punishment for their murderous attack on the Conestoga village.

In early 1764, the uprising faded. The Indians were short on ammunition, and the British were tired and broke. The British government recalled the imperious general Amherst, blaming him for mishandling the conflict, and his own soldiers toasted his departure. A new military leader, Thomas Gage, took command and began distributing gifts profusely among the Indians.

To minimize the violence, the British government issued the **Proclamation of 1763**, forbidding colonists to settle west of the Appalachian Mountains. More than just naming a boundary, the Proclamation offered assurances that Indian territory would be respected. It limited trade with Indians to traders licensed by colonial governors, and it forbade private sales of Indian land. But the Proclamation's language also took care not to identify western lands as belonging to the Indians. Instead, it spoke of lands that "are reserved to [Indians], as their Hunting Grounds."

Other parts of the Proclamation of 1763 referred to American and even French colonists in Canada as "our loving subjects," entitled to English rights and privileges. In contrast, the Indians were clearly rejected as British subjects and instead were described more vaguely as those "who live under our protection" and as "Tribes of Indians with whom We are connected." Of course, the British were not really well connected with any Indians, nor did they wish connections to form among the tribes. As William Johnson, the superintendent of northern Indian affairs, advised in 1764, "It will be expedient to treat with each nation separately . . . for could they arrive at a perfect union, they must prove very dangerous Neighbours."

Perhaps most important, the enormous expense of the Seven Years' War caused by Pitt's no-holds-barred military strategy cast a huge shadow over the victory. And the costs continued to mount, because British leaders decided in 1762 to maintain a force of ten thousand soldiers in North America to guard against potential hostilities with Indians or French Canadians. By 1763, Britain's national debt, double what it had been when Pitt took office, posed a formidable challenge to the next decade of leadership in Britain.

Pontiac's Rebellion and the Proclamation of 1763

One glaring omission marred the Treaty of Paris: The major powers at the treaty table failed to include the Indians. Minavavana, an Ojibwa chief of the Great Lakes region, put it succinctly to an English trader: "Englishman, although you have conquered the French, you have not yet conquered us! We are not your slaves. These lakes, these woods and mountains were left to us by our ancestors. They are our inheritance; and we will part with them to none." Furthermore, Minavavana pointedly noted, "your king has never sent us any presents, nor entered into any treaty with us, wherefore he and we are still at war."

Minavavana's complaint about the absence of British presents was significant. To Indians, gifts cemented social relationships, symbolizing honor and establishing obligation. Over many decades, the French had mastered the subtleties of gift exchange, distributing textiles and hats and receiving calumets (ceremonial pipes) in return. British military leaders, new to the practice, often discarded the calumets as trivial trinkets, thereby insulting the givers. From the British view, a generous gift might signify tribute (thus demeaning the giver), or it might be positioned as a bribe. "It is not my intention ever to attempt to gain the friendship of Indians by presents," Major General Jeffery Amherst declared. The Indian view was the opposite: Generous givers expressed dominance and protection, not subordination, in the ceremonial practices of giving.

Despite Minavavana's confident words, Indians north of the Ohio River had plenty of cause for concern. Old French trading posts all over the Northwest were beefed up by the British into military bases. Fort Duquesne, renamed Fort Pitt to honor the victorious British prime minister, was fortified with new walls sixty feet thick at their base, ten at the top, announcing that this was no fur trading post. Americans settlers were beginning to cluster around Fort

Pitt's protective sphere, further alarming the local Indians.

A religious revival among the Indians magnified feelings of antagonism toward the British. A Delaware prophet named Neolin reported a vision in which the Master of Life chastised Indians: "Whence comes it that ye permit the Whites upon your lands? Can ye not live without them?" Neolin urged a return to traditional ways, and his preaching spread quickly, gaining credence as the British bungled diplomacy and American settlers continued to penetrate western lands.

> ## "Englishman, although you have conquered the French, you have not yet conquered us! We are not your slaves."
> — Ojibwa chief MINAVAVANA

The Seven Years' War

1692–1750s	English and Iroquois create and affirm the Covenant Chain alliance in western New York.
1700–1740s	French settlers enjoy exclusive trade with Indians in Ohio Valley.
1747	Ohio Company receives land grant from British king.
1753	Mohawk chief Hendrick accuses English of breaking Covenant Chain.
	French soldiers advance from Canada into Ohio Country.
	George Washington delivers message telling French they are trespassing.
1754	French build Fort Duquesne.
	Washington returns to Ohio Country with troops and Mingo allies.
	May. Washington, guided by Mingo chief Tanaghrisson, attacks French.
	June–July. Albany Congress convenes.
	July. French and Indian soldiers defeat Washington at Fort Necessity.
1755	British authorities appoint two superintendents of Indian affairs.
	July. Braddock defeated at Monongahela.
1756	William Pitt becomes British prime minister.
1758	British capture Fort Duquesne.
1759	British capture Forts Niagara and Ticonderoga.
1760	British capture Montreal.
1762	British capture Cuba.
1763	Treaty of Paris signed.

Rivington's New-York Loyal Gazette
Not all newspaper editors supported the Revolution. James Rivington of New York City heaped abuse on Washington and others, and earned a reputation for mean-spirited polemics. In return, rioters hanged him in effigy, broke up his press, and burned down his house. When New York became British headquarters, Rivington curried favor with the British command. Yet it appears now that long-standing rumors about his duplicity are likely true: by 1781, evidence suggests he was indeed passing codes to George Washington about British military plans. Courtesy, American Antiquarian Society.

and increasingly silenced core of loyalists who refused to countenance armed revolution. On occasion, husbands and wives, fathers and sons disagreed completely on the war. (See "Documenting the American Promise," page 206.)

Loyalists were most vocal between 1774 and 1776, when the possibility of a full-scale rebellion against Britain was still uncertain. They challenged the emerging patriot side in pamphlets and newspapers. In 1776 in New York City, 547 loyalists signed and circulated a broadside titled "A Declaration of Dependence" in rebuttal to the congress's July 4 declaration, denouncing the "most unnatural, unprovoked Rebellion that ever disgraced the annals of Time."

Who Is a Traitor?

In June 1775, the Second Continental Congress declared all loyalists to be traitors. Over the next year, state laws defined as treason acts such as provisioning the British army, saying anything that undermined patriot morale, and discouraging men from enlisting in the Continental army. Punishments ranged from house arrest and suspension of voting privileges to confiscation of property and deportation. Sometimes self-appointed committees of Tory-hunters bypassed

the judicial niceties and terrorized loyalists, raiding their houses or tarring and feathering them.

Were wives of loyalists also traitors? When loyalist families fled the country, their property was typically confiscated. But if the wife stayed, courts usually allowed her to keep one-third of the property, the amount due her if widowed, and confiscated the rest, so long as she was known to be "a steady and true and faithful friend to the American states," in the case of one Connecticut woman. This legal position supported a wife's autonomy to choose political sides, if she stayed in the United States. Yet what about a wife who favored the patriot side but was obligated by her fleeing loyalist husband to join him? After the Revolution, descendants of refugee loyalists filed several lawsuits to regain property that had entered the family through the mother's inheritance. In one well-publicized Massachusetts case in 1805, the outcome confirmed the traditional view of women as political blank slates. The American son of loyalist refugee Anna Martin recovered her

"They call me a brainless Tory, but tell me . . . which is better — to be ruled by one tyrant three thousand miles away, or by three thousand tyrants not a mile away?"
— Boston loyalist MATHER BYLES

Families Divide over the Revolution

Generalizing about rebels versus loyalists is a complex historical task. Sometimes categorizing by class, race, and geographic descriptors helps explain the split. But beyond economic interests or cultural politics, sometimes the loyalist-patriot divide cut across families — and cut deeply. These documents reveal men and women pitted against loved ones over wartime allegiance.

DOCUMENT 1
A Loyalist Wife Writes to Her Patriot Husband, 1778

Mary Gould Almy, a wife and mother, lived in Newport, Rhode Island, an island town occupied by the British army in 1778. She was a Quaker and a loyalist, in contrast to her Anglican husband, Benjamin Almy, who joined the Continental army. Mary wrote to Benjamin in September 1778, sending him her account of the monthlong siege of the town by the French fleet and American troops.

September 02, 1778. Once more, my dear Mr. Almy, I am permitted to write you. . . . I am to give you an account of what passes during the siege; but first let me tell you, it will be done with spirit, for my dislike to the nation that you call your friends, is the same as when you knew me, knowing there is no confidence to be placed in them. . . .

[The 1st day]: At nine in the morning a signal was made for a fleet in sight; at ten o'clock was discovered the number to be eleven large ships . . . the French fleet. . . . With a distressed heart, I endeavor to comfort my poor children by saying, that they would not come in till morning, and then began to secure my papers and plate in the ground.

[The 9th day]: Heavens! what a scene of wretchedness before this once happy and flourishing island. . . . Neither sleep to my eyes, nor slumber to my eyelids, this night; but judge you, what preparation could I make, had I been endowed with as much presence of mind as ever woman was; six children hanging around me, the little girls crying out, "Mamma, will they kill us?" The boys endeavor to put on an air of manliness, and strive to assist, but slip up to the girls, in a whisper, "Who do you think will hurt you? Ain't your papa coming with them?" Indeed this cut me to the soul.

[The 18th day]: Still carting, still fortifying; your people encroaching nearer, throwing up new works every night. . . . And really, Mr. Almy, my curiosity was so great, as to wish to behold the entrenchment that I supposed you were behind; . . . different agitations as by turns took hold upon me. Wishing most ardently to call home my wanderer, at the same time, filled with resentment against those he calls his friends.

[The 24th day]: They kept up a smart firing till two o'clock, and then they began to bury the dead and bring in the wounded. . . . The horrors of that day will never be quite out of my remembrance. I quitted company and hid myself to mourn in silence, for the wickedness of my country. Never was a heart more differently agitated than mine. Some of my good friends in the front of the battle here; and Heaven only knows how many of the other side. . . . At last I shut myself from the family, to implore Heaven to protect you, and keep you from imprisonment and death.

SOURCE: *Mrs. Almy's Journal: Siege of Newport, R.I., August 1778* (Newport, RI: Newport Historical Publishing Company, 1881), 19–31. Reprinted with permission. Available online in select college libraries in the electronic database: *North American Women's Letters and Diaries*, Alexander Street Press.

DOCUMENT 2
Patriot Benjamin Franklin and Loyalist Son William Correspond, 1784

Benjamin Franklin, a keen advocate of the Revolution, had a son who stayed loyal to the crown. William was Benjamin's illegitimate son, resulting from a youthful indiscretion. He was raised in the Franklin family and accompanied Benjamin to England in 1757 for four years' service as Pennsylvania's colonial agent. Thanks to his father, William acquired connections at court, and in 1762, at the age of thirty-one, he was appointed royal governor of New Jersey, a post he held until 1776. When the war began, he was declared a traitor to the patriot cause and placed under house arrest. Father and son did not communicate for the next nine years, even when William was confined in a Connecticut prison for eight months. During this time, Benjamin took charge of William's oldest son, an illegitimate child born before William's legal marriage. After the war, William moved to England, and in 1784 he wrote to his father, then in Paris, asking for a meeting of reconciliation. He did not apologize for his loyalism.

Dear and honored Father,

Ever since the termination of the unhappy contest between Great Britain and America, I have been anxious to write to you. . . . There are narrow illiberal Minds in all Parties. In that which I took, and on whose Account I have so much suffered, there have not been wanting some who have insinuated that my Conduct has been founded on Collusion with you, that one of us might succeed whichever Party should prevail. . . . The Falsity of such Insinuation in our Case you well know, and I am happy that I can with Confidence appeal not only to you but to my God, that I have uniformly acted from a strong Sense of what I conceived my Duty to my King, and Regard to my Country, required. If I have been mistaken, I cannot help it. It is an Error of Judgment what the maturest Reflection I am capable of cannot rectify; and I verily believe were the same Circumstances to occur again Tomorrow, my Conduct would be exactly similar to what it was heretofore.

The father replied:
Dear Son,

I . . . am glad to find that you desire to revive the affectionate Intercourse, that formerly existed between us. It will be very agreeable to me; indeed nothing has ever hurt me so much and affected me with such keen Sensations, as to find myself deserted in my old age by my only Son; and not only deserted, but to find him taking up Arms against me, in a Cause, wherein my good Fame, Fortune and Life were all at Stake. You conceived, you say, that your Duty to your King and regard for your Country requir'd this. I ought not to blame you for differing in Sentiment with me in Public Affairs. We are Men, all subject to errors. Our opinions are not in our own Power; they are form'd and govern'd much by Circumstances, that are often as inexplicable as they are irresistible. Your Situation was such that few would have censured your remaining Neuter, *tho' there are Natural Duties which preceded political ones, and cannot be extinguish'd by them.*

This is a disagreeable Subject. I drop it. And we will endeavor, as you propose mutually to forget what has happened relating to it, as well as we can. I send your Son over to pay his Duty to you. . . . He is greatly esteem'd and belov'd in this Country, and will make his Way anywhere. . . . Wishing you Health, and more happiness than it seems you have lately experienced, I remain your affectionate father, B. Franklin

SOURCE: Courtesy of the American Philosophical Society, www.amphilsoc.org.

DOCUMENT 3
Two Oneida Brothers Confront Their Different Allegiances, 1779

Mary Jemison was captured as a girl during the Seven Years' War and adopted into the Seneca tribe of western

New York, where she remained for life. When she was eighty, her narrative was taken down and published. In this story from her narrative, she relates how some Oneida warriors siding with the British captured two Indians guiding General Sullivan's 1779 campaign of terror in central New York. One of the captors recognized his own brother.

Envy and revenge glared in the features of the conquering savage, as he advanced to his brother (the prisoner) in all the haughtiness of Indian pride, heightened by a sense of power, and addressed him in the following manner:

"Brother, you have merited death! The hatchet or the war-club shall finish your career! When I begged of you to follow me in the fortunes of war, you was deaf to my cries — you spurned my entreaties!

"Brother! You have merited death and shall have your deserts! When the rebels raised their hatchets to fight their good master, you sharpened your knife, you brightened your rifle and led on our foes to the fields of our fathers! You have merited death and shall die by our hands! When those rebels had drove us from the fields of our fathers to seek out new homes, it was you who could dare to step forth as their pilot, and conduct them even to the doors of our wigwams, to butcher our children and put us to death! No crime can be greater! But though you have merited death and shall die on this spot, my hands shall not be stained in the blood of a brother! *Who will strike?*"

Little Beard, who was standing by, as soon as the speech was ended, struck the prisoner on the head with his tomahawk, and dispatched him at once.

SOURCE: James E. Seaver, *A Narrative of the Life of Mrs. Mary Jemison, who was taken by the Indians, in the year 1755, when only about twelve years of age, and has continued to reside amongst them to the present time* (1824), chapter VII, Project Gutenberg, www.gutenberg.org/ebooks/6960 (accessed June 28, 2011).

Questions for Analysis and Debate

1. Why was Mary Almy "cut . . . to the soul" by the remarks of her sons? She was frightened for her husband's safety. Was she also angry with him? Why or why not?

2. What did Benjamin Franklin mean by the emphasized words *"Natural Duties"*? Do you think Franklin really believed that his son was entitled to his own political opinions on the Revolutionary War? What factors help explain why William remained loyal to the crown?

3. Why did the Oneida warrior believe that his brother merited death?

MAP ACTIVITY

Map 7.2   Loyalist Strength and Rebel Support

The exact number of loyalists can never be known. No one could have made an accurate count at the time, and political allegiance often shifted with the wind. This map shows the regions of loyalist strength on which the British relied — most significantly, the lower Hudson valley and the Carolina Piedmont.

READING THE MAP: Which forces were stronger, those loyal to Britain or those rebelling? (Consider the size of their respective areas, centers of population, and vital port locations.) What areas were contested? If the contested areas ultimately had sided with the British, how would the balance of power have changed?

CONNECTIONS: Who was more likely to be a loyalist and why? How many loyalists left the United States? Where did they go?

---

dowry property on the grounds that she had no independent will to be a loyalist.

Tarring and feathering, property confiscation, deportation, terrorism — to the loyalists, such denials of liberty of conscience and of freedom to own private property proved that democratic tyranny was more to be feared than the monarchical variety. A Boston loyalist named Mather Byles aptly expressed this point: "They call me a brainless Tory, but tell me . . . which is better — to be ruled by one tyrant three thousand miles away, or by three thousand tyrants not a mile away?" Byles was soon sentenced to deportation.

Throughout the war, probably 7,000 to 8,000 loyalists fled to England, and 28,000 found haven in Canada. British strategy depended on using loyalists to hold occupied territory, but for many loyalists, that was impossible without British protection. In New Jersey, for example, 3,000 Jerseyites

felt protected (or scared) enough by the occupying British army in 1776 to swear an oath of allegiance to the king. But then General Howe drew back to New York City, leaving them to the mercy of local patriot committees that pressured for new loyalty oaths to the Continental Congress. Despite the staunch backing of loyalists in 1776, the British could not build a winning strategy on their support.

Prisoners of War

The poor treatment of loyalists as traitors by the revolutionaries was more than matched by the horrendous treatment of American prisoners of war by the British. Such captives were a predictable by-product of war, and George Washington fully expected the British to provide humane treatment, as was customary among European military powers. Among these civilities were

A British Prison Ship
A carefully executed cutaway drawing of an unnamed ship by an unnamed artist shows scores of American POWs below decks being guarded by redcoats. The degree of crowding and of care—note the infirmary on the middle level to the right of the gangplank—is represented as more humane than was actually the case. The artist added these words in French on the border of the paper, "My God, Have you forgotten me?" Museum of the City of New York, Gift of Mrs. Edith Gregor Halpert.

provision of food, clothing, blankets, and laundry, all paid for by the captives' own government, and the possibility of release via prisoner exchanges. These customs recognized that captured soldiers were not common criminals subject to punishing incarceration. But British leaders refused to see the captives as foot soldiers employed by a sovereign nation. In their eyes, the captured Americans were traitors — and therefore worse than common criminals.

The British crowded their initial 4,000 prisoners on two dozen vessels anchored in the river between Manhattan and Brooklyn. The largest of these was the half-century-old HMS *Jersey*, stripped of its masts and guns. Built to house a crew of 400, the *Jersey*'s hull was packed with more than 1,100 prisoners of war. Survivors described the dark, stinking space belowdecks where more than half a dozen men died daily, wasted and parched from extreme thirst. Food and sanitation facilities were inadequate. A twenty-year-old captive seaman described his first view of the hold: "Here was a motley crew, covered with rags and filth; visages pallid with disease, emaciated with hunger and anxiety, and retaining hardly a trace of their original appearance. Here were men . . . now shriveled by a scanty and unwholesome diet, ghastly with inhaling an impure atmosphere, exposed to contagion and disease, and surrounded with the horrors of sickness and death."

The Continental Congress sent food and funds to supply rations to the prisoners, but only a fraction of the provisions reached the men; most of the supplies were diverted to British use. Washington fumed at General Howe and threatened severe treatment of British prisoners, but Howe remained uncooperative.

Treating the captives as criminals potentially triggered the Anglo-American right of habeas corpus, a central feature of English law since the thirteenth century, which guaranteed every prisoner the right to challenge his detention before a judge and to learn the charges against him. To remove that possibility, Parliament voted in early 1777 to suspend habeas corpus specifically for "persons taken in the act of high treason" in any of the colonies.

Despite the treatment of his own men, Washington insisted that captured British soldiers be treated humanely. From the initial group of Hessians taken on Christmas of 1776 to the several thousands more captured in American victories by 1778, America's prisoners of war were gathered in rural encampments that shifted location from Massachusetts to Virginia and points in between. Guarded by local townsmen, the captives typically could cultivate small gardens, move about freely during the day, and even hire themselves out to farmers suffering wartime labor shortages. Officers with money could purchase comfortable lodging with private families and mixed socially with Americans. Officers enjoyed the freedom to travel locally; many were even allowed to keep their guns as they waited for prisoner exchanges to release them.

As the war dragged on, such exchanges were negotiated out of necessity, when the British were desperate to regain valued officers. American officers benefited from these limited exchanges, but for ordinary soldiers and seamen, death — or the rare escape — was their fate. More than 15,000 men endured captivity in the prison ships during the war, and two-thirds of them died, a larger number than those who died in battle (estimated to be around 5,000). News of the horrors of the British death ships increased the revolutionaries' resolve and convinced some neutrals of the necessity of the war.

Financial Instability and Corruption

Wars cost money — for arms and ammunition, for food and uniforms, for soldiers' pay, for provisions for prisoners. The Continental Congress printed money, but its value quickly deteriorated

because the congress held no reserves of gold or silver to back the currency. In practice, it was worth only what buyers and sellers agreed it was worth. When the dollar eventually bottomed out at one-fortieth of its face value, a loaf of bread that once sold for two and a half cents then sold for a dollar. States, too, were printing paper money to pay for wartime expenses, further complicating the economy.

As the currency depreciated, the congress turned to other means to procure supplies and labor. One method was to borrow hard money (gold or silver coins) from wealthy men in exchange for certificates of debt (public securities) promising repayment with interest. The certificates of debt were similar to present-day government bonds. To pay soldiers, the congress issued land grant certificates, written promises of acreage usually located in frontier areas such as central Maine or eastern Ohio. Both the public securities

and the land grant certificates quickly became forms of negotiable currency. A soldier with no cash, for example, could sell his land grant certificate to get food for his family. These certificates soon depreciated, too.

Depreciating currency inevitably led to rising prices, as sellers compensated for the falling value of the money. The wartime economy of the late 1770s, with its unreliable currency and price inflation, was extremely demoralizing to Americans everywhere. In 1778, in an effort to impose stability, local committees of public safety began to fix prices on essential goods such as flour. Inevitably, some turned this unstable situation to their advantage. Money that fell fast in value needed to be spent quickly; being in debt was suddenly advantageous because the debt could be repaid in devalued currency. A brisk black market sprang up in prohibited luxury imports, such as tea, sugar, textiles, and wines, even though these items came from Britain. A New Hampshire delegate to the Continental Congress denounced the violation of the homespun association agreements of just a few years before: "We are a crooked and perverse generation, longing for the fineries and follies of those Egyptian task masters from whom we have so lately freed ourselves."

REVIEW   How did the patriots promote support for their cause in the colonies?

▶ The Campaigns of 1777–1779: The North and West

In early 1777, the Continental army faced bleak choices. General Washington had skillfully avoided defeat, but the minor victories in New Jersey lent only faint optimism to the American side. Meanwhile, British troops moved south from Quebec, aiming to isolate New England from the rest of the colonies by taking control of the Hudson River. Their presence drew the Continental army up into central New York, polarizing Indian tribes of the Iroquois nation and turning the Mohawk Valley into a bloody war zone. By 1779, tribes in western New York and in Indian country in the Ohio Valley were fully involved in the Revolutionary War. Most sided with the British and against the Americans. The Americans had some success in this period, such as the victory at Saratoga, but the involvement of Indians and the continuing strength of the British forced the American government to look to France for help.

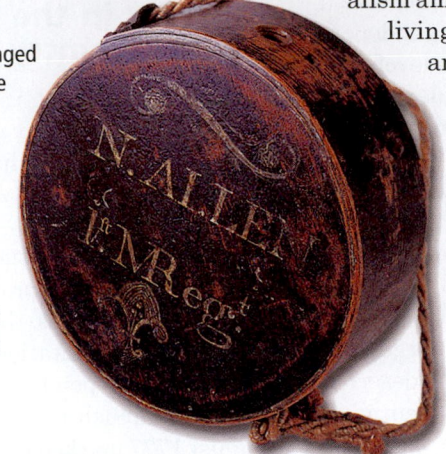

A Soldier's Canteen
This wooden canteen belonged to Noah Allen, whose name and regiment number are carved into the side. Allen was from the Sixth Continental Regiment from Massachusetts. Almost no piece of equipment surpassed the soldier's canteen in importance. The water it carried came from streams, lakes, and, when available, wells.
Fort Ticonderoga Museum.

Burgoyne's Army and the Battle of Saratoga

In 1777, British general **John Burgoyne** assumed command of an army of 7,800 soldiers in Canada and began the northern squeeze on the Hudson River valley. His goal was to capture Albany, near the intersection of the Hudson and Mohawk rivers (see Map 7.1). Accompanied by 1,000 "camp followers" (cooks, laundresses, and musicians) and some 400 Indian warriors, Burgoyne's army did not travel light. In addition to food and supplies for 9,200 people, the army carried food for the 400 horses hauling heavy artillery. Burgoyne also carted thirty trunks of personal belongings and fine wines.

In July, Burgoyne captured Fort Ticonderoga with ease. American troops stationed there spotted the approaching British and abandoned the fort without a fight. The British continued to move south, but the large army moved slowly on primitive roads through dense forests. Burgoyne lost a month hacking his way south; meanwhile, his supply lines back to Canada were severely stretched. Soldiers sent out to forage for food were beaten back by local militia units.

The logical second step in isolating New England should have been to advance troops up the Hudson from New York City to meet Burgoyne. American surveillance indicated that General Howe in Manhattan was readying his men for a major move in August 1777. But Howe surprised everyone by sailing south to attack Philadelphia.

To reinforce Burgoyne, British and Hessian troops stationed at Montreal traveled south and then east along the Mohawk River, joined there by Mohawks and Senecas of the Iroquois Confederacy. The British were counting on loyalism among the numerous Palatine Germans living in the Mohawk Valley to allow them an easy path to Albany (see Map 7.1). A hundred miles west of Albany, they encountered American Continental soldiers at Fort Stanwix, supported by Palatine German militiamen and Oneida Indians. Mohawk chief Joseph Brant led the Senecas and Mohawks in an ambush on the Germans and the Oneidas in a narrow ravine called Oriskany, killing nearly 500 out of 840 of them. On Brant's side, some 90 warriors were killed. Meanwhile, Continental defenders of Fort Stanwix forced their British and Indian attackers to retreat (see Map 7.1). The **Oriskany** and **Fort Stanwix** battles were very deadly; they were also complexly multiethnic, pitting Indians against Indians, German Americans (the Palatines) against German mercenaries, New York patriots against New York loyalists, and English Americans against British soldiers.

The British retreat at Fort Stanwix deprived General Burgoyne of the additional troops he expected. Camped at a small village called Saratoga, he was isolated, with food supplies dwindling and men deserting. His adversary at Albany, General Horatio Gates, began moving his army toward Saratoga. Burgoyne decided to attack first because every day his soldiers weakened. The British prevailed, but at the great cost of 600 dead or wounded redcoats. Three weeks later, an American attack on Burgoyne's forces at Saratoga cost the British another 600 men and most of their cannons. General Burgoyne finally surrendered to the American forces on October 17, 1777.

Americans on the side of the rebellion were jubilant. After the **battle of Saratoga**, the first decisive victory for the Continental army, a popular dance called "General Burgoyne's Surrender" swept through the country, and bookies in the major cities set odds at five to one that the war would be won in six months.

General Howe, meanwhile, had succeeded in occupying Philadelphia in September 1777. Figuring that the Saratoga loss was balanced by the capture of

Battle of Saratoga, 1777

Fort Ticonderoga
captured by British
July 6

Lake Champlain

Burgoyne

Lake George

Fort Anne

Fort Edward

Stark

1st Battle, Sept. 19
2nd Battle, Oct. 7

Saratoga
Burgoyne surrenders
Oct. 17

Gates

Hudson R.

Bennington

Albany

➡ American forces   American victory
➡ British forces   British victory

Philadelphia, the British government proposed a negotiated settlement — not including independence — to end the war. The American side refused.

Patriot optimism was not well founded. Spirits ran high, but supplies of arms and food ran precariously low. Washington moved his troops into winter quarters at Valley Forge, just west of Philadelphia. Quartered in drafty huts, the men lacked blankets, boots, stockings, and food. Some 2,000 men at Valley Forge died of disease; another 2,000 deserted over the bitter six-month encampment.

Washington blamed the citizenry for lack of support; indeed, evidence of corruption and profiteering was abundant. Army suppliers too often provided defective food, clothing, and gunpowder. One shipment of bedding arrived with blankets one-quarter their customary size. Food supplies arrived rotten. As one Continental officer said, "The people at home are destroying the Army by their conduct much faster than Howe and all his army can possibly do by fighting us."

> **"The people at home are destroying the Army by their conduct much faster than Howe and all his army can possibly do by fighting us."**
> — A Continental army officer

The War in the West: Indian Country

Burgoyne's defeat in the fall of 1777 and Washington's long stay at Valley Forge up to June 1778 might suggest that the war paused for a time, and it did on the Atlantic coast. But in the interior western areas — the Mohawk Valley, the Ohio Valley, and Kentucky — the war of Indians against the American pro-independence side heated up. For native tribes, the struggle was not about taxation, representation, or monarchical rule; it was about independence, freedom, and land.

The ambush and slaughter at Oriskany in August 1777 marked the beginning of three years of terror for the inhabitants of the Mohawk Valley. Loyalists and Indians engaged in many raids on farms throughout 1778, capturing or killing the residents. In retaliation, American militiamen destroyed Joseph Brant's home village, Onanquaga. Although they failed to capture any warriors, they killed several children in hiding. A month later, Brant's warriors attacked the town of Cherry Valley, killing 16 soldiers and 32 civilians and taking 71 people captive.

Death of Jane McCrea
In 1804, artist John Vanderlyn memorialized the martyr legend of Jane McCrea. McCrea, daughter of an American patriot family, was in love with a loyalist in Burgoyne's Army. In July 1777 she eloped to join her fiancé, guided by Indians sent by the British to escort her. But she was killed on the short journey—either shot in the crossfire of battle, as the British claimed, or murdered by Indians allied with the British, in the patriots' version. American general Horatio Gates used the story of the vulnerable, innocent maiden dressed in alluring wedding clothes as propaganda to inspire his soldiers' drive for victory at Saratoga. Wadsworth Atheneum Museum of Art, Hartford/Art Resource, NY.

The following summer, General Washington authorized a campaign to wreak "total destruction and devastation" on all the Iroquoian villages of central New York. Some 4,500 troops commanded by General John Sullivan implemented a deliberate campaign of terror in the fall of 1779. Forty Indian towns met with total obliteration; the soldiers looted and torched the dwellings and then burned cornfields and orchards. In a few towns, women and children were slaughtered, but in most, the inhabitants managed to escape, fleeing to the British at Fort Niagara. Thousands of Indian refugees, sick and starving, camped around the fort in one of the most miserable winters on record.

Much farther to the west, beyond Fort Pitt in the Ohio Valley, another complex story of alliances and betrayals between American mili-tiamen and Indians unfolded. Some 150,000 native people lived between the Appalachian Mountains and the Mississippi River, and by 1779 neutrality was no longer an option. Most sided with the British, who maintained a garrison at Fort Detroit, but a portion of the Shawnee and Delaware tribes at first sought peace with the Americans. In mid-1778, the Delaware chief White Eyes negotiated a treaty at Fort Pitt, pledging Indian support for the Americans in exchange for supplies and trade goods. But escalating violence undermined the agreement. That fall, when American soldiers killed two friendly Shawnee chiefs, Cornstalk and Red Hawk, the Continental Congress hastened to apologize, as did the governors of Pennsylvania and Virginia, but the soldiers who stood trial for the murders

MAP 7.3

The Indian War in the West, 1777–1782
The American Revolution involved many Indian tribes, most of them supporting the British. Iroquois Indians, with British aid, attacked American towns in New York's Mohawk Valley throughout 1778. In 1779, the Continental army destroyed forty Iroquois villages in central New York. Shawnee and Delaware Indians to the west of Fort Pitt tangled with American militia units in 1779, while tribes supported by the British at Fort Detroit conducted raids on Kentucky settlers, who hit back with raids of their own. Sporadic fighting continued in the West through 1782, ending with Indian attacks on Hannastown, Pennsylvania, and Fort Henry on the Ohio River.

were acquitted. Two months later, White Eyes, nominally an ally of and an informant for the Americans, died under mysterious circumstances. He was almost certainly murdered by militiamen, who repeatedly had trouble honoring distinctions between allied and enemy Indians.

West of North Carolina (today's Tennessee), the frontier war zone of the South, militias attacked Cherokee settlements in 1779, destroying thirty-six villages and burning fields and livestock. Indian raiders from north of the Ohio River, in alliance with the British, repeatedly attacked white settlements such as Boonesborough (in present-day Kentucky) (Map 7.3). In retali-

ation, a young Virginian, George Rogers Clark, led Kentucky militiamen into what is now Illinois, attacking and taking the British fort at Kaskaskia. Clark's men wore native clothing — hunting shirts and breechcloths — but their dress was not a sign of solidarity with the Indians. When they attacked British-held Fort Vincennes in 1779, Clark's troops tomahawked Indian captives and threw their still-live bodies into the river in a gory spectacle witnessed by the redcoats. "To excel them in barbarity is the only way to make war upon Indians," Clark announced. And, he might have added, it was an effective way to terrorize British soldiers as well.

VISUAL ACTIVITY

"The Balance of Power," 1780

This cartoon was published in England soon after Spain and the Netherlands declared an alliance with France to support the war in America. On the left, Britannia, a female figure representing Great Britain, cannot be moved by all the lightweights on the right-hand side of the scale. France wears a ruffled shirt, Spain has a feather in his hat, and a Dutch boy has just hopped on, saying, "I'll do anything for Money." The forlorn Indian maiden, the standard icon representing America in the eighteenth century, sits on the scale, head in hand, wailing, "My Ingratitude is Justly punished." The poem printed below the cartoon predicts, "The Americans too will with Britons Unite." This fanciful prediction was punctured nine months after it appeared, when the British surrendered to the Americans and the French at Yorktown in 1781.

Print Collection, Miriam and Ira D. Wallach Division of Art, Prints, and Photographs, The New York Public Library. Astor, Lenox, and Tilden Foundations.

READING THE IMAGE: What does this cartoon reveal about British perceptions of the American Revolution?
CONNECTIONS: How did British attitudes toward the colonies contribute to the British defeat in the war?

By 1780, very few Indians remained neutral. Violent raids by Americans drove Indians into the arms of the British at Detroit and Niagara, or into the arms of the Spaniards, who still held much of the land west of the Mississippi River. Said one officer on the Sullivan campaign, "Their nests are destroyed but the birds are still on the wing." For those who stayed near their native lands, chaos and confusion prevailed. Rare as it was, Indian support for the American side occasionally emerged out of a strategic sense that the Americans were unstoppable in their westward pressure and that it was better to work out an alliance than to lose in a war. But American treatment of even friendly Indians showed that there was no winning strategy for them.

The French Alliance

On their own, the Americans could not have defeated Britain, especially as pressure from hostile Indians increased. Essential help arrived as a result of the victory at Saratoga, which convinced the French to enter the war; a formal alliance was signed in February 1778. France recognized the United States as an independent nation and promised full military and commercial support. Most crucial was the French navy, which could challenge British supplies and troops at sea and aid the Americans in taking and holding prisoners of war.

Well before 1778, however, the French had been covertly providing cannons, muskets, gunpowder, and highly trained military advisers to the Americans. Monarchical France was understandably cautious about endorsing a democratic revolution attacking kingship. Instead, the main attraction of an alliance was the opportunity it provided to defeat archrival Britain. A victory would also open pathways to trade and perhaps result in France's acquiring the coveted British West Indies. Even an American defeat would not be a disaster for France if the war lasted many years and drained Britain of men and money.

French support materialized slowly. The navy arrived off the Virginia coast in July 1778 but then sailed south to the West Indies to defend the French sugar-producing islands. French help would prove indispensable to the American victory, but the alliance's first months brought no dramatic victories, and some Americans grumbled that the partnership would prove worthless.

REVIEW   Why did the Americans need assistance from the French to ensure victory?

▶ The Southern Strategy and the End of the War

When France joined the war, some British officials wondered whether the fight was worth continuing. A troop commander, arguing for an immediate negotiated settlement, shrewdly observed that "we are far from an anticipated peace, because the bitterness of the rebels is too widespread, and in regions where we are masters the rebellious spirit is still in them. The land is too large, and there are too many people. The more land we win, the weaker our army gets in the field." The commander of the British navy argued for abandoning the war, and even Lord North, the prime minister, agreed. But the king was determined to crush the rebellion, and he encouraged a new strategy for victory focusing on the southern colonies, thought to be more persuadably loyalist. He had little idea of the depth of anger that would produce deadly guerrilla warfare between loyalists and patriots. The king's plan was brilliant but desperate, and ultimately unsuccessful.

Georgia and South Carolina

The new strategy called for British forces to abandon New England and focus on the South, with its large slave population thought to be ready to run to the king's forces. Such desertions, the British assumed, would disrupt the economy and unnerve rebellious white slave owners. Banking on loyalism among the nonslaveholding whites of Georgia and the Carolinas, the British hoped to build a safe foothold that would allow them to recapture the southern colonies one by one, moving north to the more problematic middle colonies and saving prickly New England for last.

Georgia, the first target, fell at the end of December 1778 (Map 7.4). A small army of British soldiers occupied Savannah and Augusta, and a new royal governor and loyalist assembly were quickly installed. Taking Georgia was easy because the bulk of the Continental army was in New York and New Jersey, keeping an eye on General **Henry Clinton**, Howe's replacement as commander in chief, and the French were still in the West Indies. The British in Georgia quickly organized twenty loyal militia units, and 1,400 Georgians swore an oath of allegiance to the king. So far, the southern strategy looked as if it might work.

MAP 7.4

The War in the South, 1780–1781
After taking Charleston in May 1780, the British advanced into South Carolina and the foothills of North Carolina, leaving a bloody civil war in their wake. When the American general Horatio Gates and his men fled from the humiliating battle of Camden, Gates was replaced by General Nathanael Greene and General Daniel Morgan, who pulled off major victories at King's Mountain and Cowpens. The British general Cornwallis then moved north and invaded Virginia, but he was bottled up and finally overpowered at Yorktown in the fall of 1781.

Next came South Carolina. The Continental army put ten regiments into the port city of Charleston to defend it from attack by British troops shipped south from New York under the command of General Clinton. For five weeks in early 1780, the British laid siege to the city and took it in May 1780, in the process capturing 3,300 American soldiers, a tremendous loss for the patriots. Again, the king's new strategy seemed to be on target.

From Charleston, Clinton announced that slaves owned by rebel masters were welcome to seek refuge with his army. Several thousand responded by escaping to the coastal city. Untrained in formal warfare, they were of more immediate use to the British as knowledgeable guides to the surrounding countryside and as laborers in service to the army, building defensive earthworks and fortifications. Escaped slaves with boat piloting skills were particularly valuable to the British as they navigated the inland river systems of the southern colonies.

Clinton returned to New York, leaving the task of pacifying the rest of South Carolina to General **Charles Cornwallis** and 4,000 troops.

A bold commander, Lord Cornwallis quickly chased out the remaining Continentals and established military rule of South Carolina by midsummer. He purged rebels from government office and disarmed rebel militias. One officer under Cornwallis, Colonel Banastre Tarleton, plundered food and supplies from large plantations, using insurgent blacks to terrify wealthy whites. As in Georgia, pardons were offered to Carolinians willing to prove their loyalty by taking up arms for the British.

By August 1780, American troops arrived from the North to strike back at Cornwallis. General Gates, the hero of Saratoga, led 3,000 troops, half of them experienced Continental soldiers and others newly recruited militiamen, into battle against Cornwallis at Camden, South Carolina, on August 16 (see Map 7.4). Right from the battle's start, militia units panicked; one unit managed to return fire, but others threw down unfired muskets and fled. The remaining Continentals, seriously outnumbered, faced heavy fire and soon gave up. When regiment leaders tried to regroup the next day, only 700 soldiers showed up; the rest were dead, wounded, captured,

Battle of Cowpens
British Colonel Banastre Tarleton, widely reviled as "the Butcher" for killing surrendering Americans, attacked American troops in a South Carolina cow field sealed off by a river in January 1781. In one hour Tarleton had decisively lost. Six decades later, American painter William T. Ranney memorialized a legendary event in which Lt. Col. William Washington (second cousin to George, pictured on a white horse) taunted "Where now is the boasting Tarleton?" causing Tarleton's aide (black horse) to hoist his sword. A timely shot by a youthful African American (name unknown) saved Washington's life. By the 1840s, art patrons evidently preferred to remember slaves as loyal to patriot masters. Collection of the State of South Carolina/Picture Resource Consultants & Archives.

or still in flight. The **battle of Camden** was a devastating defeat, the worst of the entire war, and prospects seemed very grim for the Americans.

Treason and Guerrilla Warfare

Britain's southern strategy succeeded in 1780 in part because of information about American troop movements secretly conveyed by an American traitor: **Benedict Arnold**. The hero of several American battles, Arnold was a brilliant military talent but also a deeply insecure man who never felt he got his due in either honor or financial reward. Sometime in 1779, he opened secret negotiations with General Clinton in New York, trading information for money and hinting that he could deliver far more of value. When General Washington made him commander of

A Shaming Ritual Targeting the Great Traitor
In late September 1780, Philadelphians staged a ritual humiliation of Benedict Arnold, represented by an effigy with two faces and a mask, to manifest his duplicity. Behind him stands the devil, prodding him with a pitchfork and shaking a bag of coins near his ear, reminding all that Arnold sold out for money. While two fife players and a drummer keep the beat, soldiers and onlookers proceed to a bonfire, where the effigy was burned to ashes. Library of Congress.

West Point, a new fort on the Hudson River sixty miles north of New York City, Arnold's plan crystallized. West Point controlled the Hudson; its easy capture by the British might well have meant victory in the war.

Arnold's plot to sell a West Point victory to the British was foiled in the fall of 1780 when Americans captured the man carrying plans of the fort's defense from Arnold to Clinton. News of Arnold's treason created shock waves. Arnold represented all of the patriots' worst fears about themselves: greedy self-interest, like that of the war profiteers; the unprincipled abandonment of war aims, like that of turncoat southern Tories; panic, like that of the terrified soldiers at Camden. But instead of symbolizing all that was troubling about the American side of the war, Arnold's treachery was publicly denounced in a kind of displacement of the anxieties of the moment. Vilifying Arnold allowed Americans to stake out a wide distance between themselves and dastardly conduct. It inspired a renewal of patriotism at a particularly low moment.

Bitterness over Gates's defeat at Camden and Arnold's treason revitalized rebel support in western South Carolina, an area that Cornwallis thought was pacified and loyal. The backcountry of the South soon became the site of guerrilla warfare. In hit-and-run attacks, both sides burned and ravaged not only opponents' property but also the property of anyone claiming to be neutral. Loyalist militia units organized by the British were met by fierce rebel militia units whose members figured they had little to lose. In South Carolina, some 6,000 men became active partisan fighters, and they entered into at least twenty-six engagements with loyalist units. Some were classic battles, but on other occasions the fighters were more like bandits than soldiers. Guerrilla warfare soon spread to Georgia and North Carolina. Both sides committed atrocities and plundered property, clear deviations from standard military practice.

The British southern strategy depended on sufficient loyalist strength to hold reconquered

> "We had used them to good advantage, and set them free, and now, with fear and trembling, they had to face the reward of their cruel masters."
>
> — A Hessian officer, speaking of slaves expelled from the British army

Siege of Yorktown, 1781

American forces
British forces

territory as Cornwallis's army moved north. The backcountry civil war proved this assumption false. The Americans won few major battles in the South, but they ultimately succeeded by harassing the British forces and preventing them from foraging for food. In the fall of 1780, Cornwallis moved the war into North Carolina not because he thought South Carolina was secure—it was not—but because the North Carolinians were supplying the South Carolina rebels with arms and men (see Map 7.4). Then came word that 1,400 frontier riflemen had massacred loyalist troops at King's Mountain in western South Carolina, and the news sent Cornwallis hurrying back. The British were stretched too thin to hold even two of their onetime colonies.

Surrender at Yorktown

By early 1781, the war was going very badly for the British. Their defeat at King's Mountain was quickly followed by a second major defeat at the battle of Cowpens in South Carolina in January 1781. Cornwallis retreated to North Carolina and thence to Virginia, where he captured Williamsburg in June. A raiding party under Colonel Tarleton proceeded to Charlottesville, the seat of government, capturing members of the Virginia assembly but not Governor Thomas Jefferson, who escaped the soldiers by a mere ten minutes. (The slaves at Monticello, Jefferson's home, stood their ground and saved his house from plundering, but more than a dozen at two other plantations he owned sought refuge with the British.) These minor victories allowed Cornwallis to imagine he was succeeding in Virginia. His army, now swelled by some 4,000 escaped slaves, moved toward Yorktown, near Chesapeake Bay. As the general waited for backup troops by ship from British headquarters in New York City, smallpox and typhus began to set in among the black recruits.

At this juncture, the French-American alliance came into play. French regiments commanded by the Comte de Rochambeau had joined General Washington in Newport, Rhode Island, in mid-1780, and in early 1781 warships under the Comte de Grasse had sailed from France to the West Indies. Washington, Rochambeau, and de

Lafayette at Yorktown, with James
The French nobleman Lafayette came to the United States in 1777 to volunteer his services, and in 1781 he went to Virginia to fight Cornwallis. At the siege of Yorktown, Lafayette's borrowed slave James infiltrated the British command by pretending to be an escaped slave. James fed the British misinformation and brought crucial intelligence back to Lafayette. French artist Jean Baptiste Le Paon painted the two men in 1783 without ever having seen James, who appears as a mere ornament to the heroic white general. James obtained his freedom in 1786 after Lafayette wrote a letter on his behalf to the Virginia assembly. Art Gallery, Williams Center, Lafayette College.

Grasse now fixed their attention on Chesapeake Bay. The French fleet got there ahead of the British troop ships from New York; a five-day naval battle left the French navy in clear control of the Virginia coast. This proved to be the decisive factor in ending the war, because the French ships prevented any rescue of Cornwallis's army.

On land, General Cornwallis and his 7,500 troops faced a combined French and American army of 16,000. For twelve days, the Americans and French bombarded the British fortifications at Yorktown; Cornwallis ran low on food and ammunition. He also began to expel the black recruits, some of them sick and dying. A Hessian officer serving under Cornwallis later criticized this British action as disgraceful: "We had used them to good advantage, and set them free, and now, with fear and trembling, they had to face the reward of their cruel masters." Many never made it back to their masters but died in the no-man's-land between the two armies, causing an American observer to record that "an immense number of Negroes have died in the most miserable manner in York." The twelve-day siege brought Cornwallis to the realization that neither victory nor escape was possible. He surrendered on October 19, 1781.

What began as a promising southern strategy in 1778 had turned into a discouraging defeat by 1781. British attacks in the South had energized American resistance, as did the timely exposure of Benedict Arnold's treason. The arrival of the French fleet sealed the fate of Cornwallis at the **battle of Yorktown**, and major military operations came to a halt.

The Losers and the Winners

The surrender at Yorktown spelled the end for the British, but two more years of skirmishes ensued. Frontier areas in Kentucky, Ohio, and Illinois still blazed with battles pitting Americans against various Indian tribes. The British army remained in control of three coastal cities — Savannah, Charleston, and New York — and in response, an augmented Continental army stayed at the ready, north of New York City. Occasional clashes occurred, like the ones in which light infantryman Deborah Sampson saw action, while cross-dressing as a male soldier. Skirmishes continued around Savannah and Charleston as well, involving white loyalists teamed up with runaway black insurgents.

European Nations and the Peace of Paris, 1783

News of the decisive British defeat at Yorktown in late 1781 caused Britain's prime minister, Lord North, to stagger as though wounded and exclaim, "Oh, God, it is all over!" But in truth, it was far from over. A full year elapsed before the elements of a formal peace treaty could be worked out, and an additional year passed before the treaty was signed and Britain finally ended its occupation of New York City. The delay occurred in part because several European countries besides Britain had stakes in the war that had nothing to do with the chief American goal of political independence.

France had entered the war mainly to thwart and damage Britain. Certainly the French monarchy had no real sympathy for a democratic revolution in the British colonies. Indeed, for months before the victory at Yorktown, French leaders conferred covertly with the British about a plan to divide the colonies among the key European powers, with Britain to retain New York City and the rice and tobacco colonies of the South, while France and Spain would carve up the rest.

The stubbornness of Britain's George III prevented such a deal.

Even after receiving news of the defeat at Yorktown, the delusional king still imagined he could retain all thirteen rebellious colonies. After a series of antiwar votes in Parliament and the resignation of Lord North, George III briefly considered abdicating his throne. Instead, he replaced North with a new minister, Lord Shelburne, who approached the peace talks with the view that independence for America was still up for debate.

Spain's interest in the war stemmed from a secret alliance with France in 1779. The Spanish king wanted to oust the British from Gibraltar, a tiny three-square-mile territory dominated by a massive rock and situated at the southern end of the Iberian Peninsula. From this strategic location, Britain controlled the passage between the Atlantic and the Mediterranean, disrupting Spanish trade. Spain launched a siege that lasted more than three years and tied up scores of British ships and thousands of troops, military assets that were thus not available for the war in America. Another important interest for Spain was control of navigation rights on the Mississippi River. Since 1763, Spain had held the lands west

of the river, and it hoped to gain the eastern bank — and thus fully control all navigation of that major river — as a prize for its contribution to defeating Britain.

At various times, Russia, Austria, and even Poland had agents in Paris offering to mediate peace talks in order to adjust the balance of power in Europe. None of these countries viewed American independence as a priority. Only Holland offered formal diplomatic recognition of the new country, an act of faith quickly followed up by a sizable loan of money to the new government. No other country was so supportive.

The Continental Congress entrusted three Americans of great distinction to handle the treaty negotiations. Benjamin Franklin, John Adams, and John Jay considered independence as the precondition for the talks to begin, so they were taken aback when the British negotiator showed up with credentials that pointedly addressed them as "the Commissioners of the Colonies." A month later, updated credentials referenced the three as representatives "of the Thirteen United States of America," a far more satisfactory acknowledgment of their new standing. In September 1782, peace talks began in earnest. Shelburne conceded on independence and set his goal as the maintenance of favored trading status with the new country. He saw, perhaps more clearly than did his king, that although Britain's political dominance over its colonies had now ended, economic dominance might nicely replace it.

The congress also instructed its three diplomats to consult France at

---

The **Treaty of Paris**, also called the Peace of Paris, was two years in the making. (See "Beyond America's Borders," above.) Commissioners from America and Britain worked out the ten articles of peace, while a side treaty including Britain, France, Spain, and the Netherlands sealed related deals. The first article went to the heart of the matter: "His Britannic Majesty acknowledges the said United States to be free Sovereign and independent States." Other articles set the western boundary of the new country at the Mississippi River and guaranteed that creditors on both sides could collect debts owed them in sterling money, a provision especially important to British merchants. Britain agreed to withdraw its troops quickly, but more than a decade later this promise still had not been fully kept. A last-minute addition to the article about the British withdrawal prohibited the British from "carrying away any Negroes or other property of the American inhabitants." The treaty was signed on September 3, 1783.

The General P—s, or Peace.

*Say what they will,
I call this an
honourable P—.*

*I call this a free and
Independent P—.*

*Jach English we confess
your exceeding good
nature, tho' we have
wrangled you out of
America you freely
make P—, with us.*

"The P - ss of Paris"
A British broadside of 1783 offers a cheeky affront to the Peace of Paris and the diplomats who negotiated it. The Indian declares "I call this a Free and Independent P-ss" while the Frenchman on the far right gloats that "tho' we have wrangled you out of America, you freely make P-ss with us." Britain, Spain, and France all participated in the Peace, but the Indians did not. Why do you think the artist included an Indian figure? What is the point of view of this cartoon?

Library of Congress.

every step of the negotiation with Britain, a condition insisted upon by the French minister to the United States. But Jay and Adams had deep suspicions of the motives of the French foreign minister, the Count of Vergennes. They feared, with justice, that Vergennes planned on placing their nation's western boundary some distance east of the Mississippi River, to meet the demands of Spain. So the Americans sidestepped their instructions and negotiated with Britain in secret, producing an acceptable draft treaty in just a few weeks.

By January 1783, France, Britain, and Spain had produced their own treaties, involving deals with lands in India, Africa, and the Mediterranean, and in September of that year all the treaties were officially approved and signed. Franklin wrote to a friend in Massachusetts, "We are now Friends with England and with all Mankind. May we never see another War! for in my Opinion, there never was a good War, or a bad Peace."

America in a Global Context

1. Why would the monarchies of France and Spain spend vast sums to help the rebellious American colonies in their fight against Britain?

2. A 1976 book about the Treaty of Paris is titled *The Virgin Diplomats*. Does anyone in this story fit that title? Why or why not?

3. On what grounds might the United States claim all land east of the Mississippi River?

News of the treaty signing was cause for celebration among most Americans, but not among the thousands of self-liberated blacks who had joined the British under promise of freedom. Boston King, a refugee from a South Carolina plantation, now huddled with his family at New York under protection of the British. He later wrote how the treaty's article prohibiting the British from evacuating any slaves "filled us with inexpressible anguish and terror." King and others pressed the British commander in New York, Sir Guy Carleton, to honor pre-treaty British promises. Luckily, Carleton responded favorably. For all refugees able to state that they had been with the British for more than a year, he issued certificates of freedom — and hence they were no longer "property" to be returned. More than 4,000 blacks sailed out of New York for Nova Scotia, Boston King among them. As Carleton coolly explained to a protesting George Washington, "the Negroes in question . . . I found free when I arrived at New York, I had therefore no right, as I thought, to prevent their going to any part of the world they thought proper." British commanders in Savannah and Charleston followed Carleton's lead and aided the exit of perhaps 10,000 blacks from the United States.

The emancipation of slaves had never been a war goal of the British; destabilizing patriot planters and gaining manpower were their initial reasons for promises of freedom. Had the British won the war, they might well have reenslaved insurgent blacks to restore the profitable plantation economy of the South. For their part, blacks viewed British army camps as sites of refuge (not figuring on the devastations of epidemic diseases and food shortages) and had no reason to revere the British monarchy. In fact, some runaways had headed for Indian country instead.

The Treaty of Paris had nothing to say about the Indian participants in the Revolutionary War. Like the treaty ending the Seven Years' War, the 1783 treaty failed to recognize the Indians as players in the conflict. As one American told the Shawnee people, "Your Fathers the English have made Peace with us for themselves, but forgot you their Children, who Fought with them, and neglected you like Bastards." Indian lands were assigned to the victors as though they were uninhabited. Some Indian refugees fled west into present-day Missouri and Arkansas, and others, such as Joseph Brant's Mohawks, relocated to Canada. But significant numbers remained within the new United States, occupying their traditional homelands in areas west and north of the Ohio River. For them, the Treaty of Paris brought no peace at all; their longer war against the Americans would extend at least until 1795 and for some until 1813. Their ally, Britain, conceded defeat, but the Indians did not.

With the treaty finally signed, the British began their evacuation of New York, Charleston, and Savannah, a process complicated by the sheer numbers involved — soldiers, fearful loyalists, and runaway slaves by the thousands. In New York City, more than 27,000 soldiers and 30,000 loyalists sailed on hundreds of ships for England in the late fall of 1783. In a final act of mischief, on the November day when the last ships left, the losing side raised the British flag at the southern tip of Manhattan, cut away the ropes used to hoist it, and greased the flagpole.

REVIEW Why did the British southern strategy ultimately fail?

▶ Conclusion: Why the British Lost

The British began the war for America convinced that they could not lose. They had the best-trained army and navy in the world; they were familiar with the landscape from the Seven Years' War; they had the willing warrior-power of most of the native tribes of the backcountry; and they easily captured every port city of consequence in America. A majority of colonists were either neutral or loyal to the crown. Why, then, did the British lose?

Beginning in 1775 and 1776, British royal officials fled the colonies, thereby abdicating civil power, which they never really regained. The Americans created their own government structures, from the Continental Congress to local committees and militias. Staffed by many who before 1775 had been the political elites, these new government agencies had remarkably little trouble establishing their authority to rule. The basic British goal — to turn back the clock to imperial rule — receded into impossibility as the war dragged on.

Another ongoing problem facing the British was the uncertainty of supplies. Unwilling to ravage the countryside until late in the war, the army depended on a steady stream of supply ships from home. Insecurity about food helps explain their reluctance to pursue the Continental army aggressively. And although any plan to repacify the colonies required the cooperation of the loyalists and neutrals, the British repeatedly failed to support them, leaving them to the mercy of vengeful rebels.

Finally, French aid looms large in any explanation of the British defeat. Even before the formal alliance, French artillery and ammunition proved vital to the Continental army. After 1780, the French army brought a new infusion of troops to a war-weary America, and the French navy made the Yorktown victory possible.

The war for America had lasted just over six years, from Lexington to Yorktown; negotiations and the evacuation took two more. It profoundly disrupted the lives of Americans everywhere. More than a war for independence from Britain, it required people to think about politics and the legitimacy of authority. The precise disagreement with Britain about representation and political participation had profound implications for the kinds of governance the Americans would adopt, both in the moment of emergency and later when states began to write their constitutions. The rhetoric employed to justify the revolution against Britain put the words *liberty*, *tyranny*, *slavery*, *independence*, and *equality* into common usage. These words carried far deeper meanings than a mere complaint over taxation without representation, meanings not lost on unfree groups — slaves, servants, wives — excluded from politics by their dependent status. In the decades to come, the Revolution unleashed a dynamic of equality and liberty that was largely unintended and unwanted by many of the political leaders of 1776. A half century later, the language of the Declaration of Independence would emerge as a potent force offering legitimacy to antislavery and woman's rights groups.

► # Selected Bibliography

General Works

Carol Berkin, *Revolutionary Mothers: Women in the Struggle for America's Independence* (2005).

Edward Countryman, *The American Revolution* (1985).

John Fering, *Almost a Miracle: The American Victory in the War of Independence* (2009).

Piers Mackesy, *The War for America, 1775–1783* (1964).

Gary B. Nash, *The Unknown American Revolution: The Unruly Birth of Democracy and the Struggle to Create America* (2005).

Jack Rakove, *Revolutionaries: A New History of the Invention of America* (2010).

Ray Raphael, *A People's History of the American Revolution: How Common People Shaped the Fight for Independence* (2001).

Charles Royster, *A Revolutionary People at War: The Continental Army and American Character, 1775–1783* (1996).

Gordon S. Wood, *The Radicalism of the American Revolution* (1992).

The Wartime Confederation and Its Leaders

Ron Chernow, *George Washington: A Life* (2010).

Joseph J. Ellis, *His Excellency: George Washington* (2004).

John E. Ferling, *Setting the World Ablaze: Washington, Adams, Jefferson, and the American Revolution* (2000).

Eric Foner, *Tom Paine and Revolutionary America* (1976).

Edith Gelles, *Portia: The World of Abigail Adams* (1992).

Woody Holton, *Abigail Adams* (2010).

Pauline Maier, *American Scripture: Making the Declaration of Independence* (1997).

Jackson Turner Main, *The Sovereign States, 1775–1783* (1973).

Jack N. Rakove, *The Beginnings of National Politics: An Interpretive History of the Continental Congress* (1979).

Campaigns, Battles, and Soldiers

Wayne K. Bodle, *The Valley Forge Winter: Civilians and Soldiers in War* (2004).

W. Jeffrey Bolster, *Black Jacks: African American Seamen in the Age of Sail* (1998).

Edwin G. Burrows, *The Prisoners of New York* (2008).

Colin G. Calloway, *The American Revolution in Indian Country: Crisis and Diversity in Native American Communities* (1995).

E. Wayne Carp, *To Starve the Army at Pleasure: Continental Army Administration and American Political Culture, 1775–1783* (1984).

David Hackett Fischer, *Washington's Crossing* (2004).

Joseph R. Fischer, *A Well-Executed Failure: The Sullivan Campaign against the Iroquois, July–September 1779* (1997).

Sylvia Frey, *The British Soldier in America: A Social History of Military Life in the Revolutionary Period* (1965).

Robert Gross, *The Minutemen and Their World* (1976).

Sidney Kaplan and Emma Nogrady Kaplan, *The Black Presence in the Era of the American Revolution* (1989).

Richard M. Ketchum, *Saratoga: Turning Point of America's Revolutionary War* (1997).

John Komlos, ed., *Stature, Living Standards, and Economic Development: Essays in Anthropometric History* (1994).

David G. Martin, *The Philadelphia Campaign: June 1777–1778* (2003).

James Kirby Martin, *Benedict Arnold, Revolutionary Hero: An American Warrior Reconsidered* (1997).

Holly A. Mayer, *Belonging to the Army: Camp Followers and Community during the American Revolution* (1996).

David McCullough, *1776* (2005).

Alfred F. Young, *Masquerade: The Life and Times of Deborah Sampson, Continental Soldier* (2004).

► **FOR MORE BOOKS ABOUT TOPICS IN THIS CHAPTER,** see the Online Bibliography at **bedfordstmartins.com/roark.**

► **FOR ADDITIONAL PRIMARY SOURCES FROM THIS PERIOD,** see Michael Johnson, ed., *Reading the American Past*, Fifth Edition.

► **FOR WEB SITES, IMAGES, AND DOCUMENTS RELATED TO TOPICS AND PLACES IN THIS CHAPTER,** visit Make History at **bedfordstmartins.com/roark.**

Reviewing Chapter 7

KEY TERMS

Explain each term's significance.

The Second Continental Congress

Second Continental Congress (p. 193)
John Dickinson (p. 193)
Continental army (p. 193)
George Washington (p. 193)
Thomas Jefferson (p. 193)
William Howe (p. 194)
battle of Bunker Hill (p. 194)
Olive Branch Petition (p. 195)
King George III (p. 195)
Common Sense (p. 195)
Thomas Paine (p. 195)
Abigail Adams (p. 197)
Declaration of Independence (p. 197)

The First Year of War, 1775–1776

Hessians (p. 202)
battle of Long Island (p. 202)

The Home Front

Ladies Association (p. 203)
loyalists (Tories) (p. 204)
Joseph Brant (Thayendanegea) (p. 204)

The Campaigns of 1777–1779: The North and West

John Burgoyne (p. 211)
battle of Oriskany (p. 211)
battle of Fort Stanwix (p. 211)
battle of Saratoga (p. 211)

The Southern Strategy and the End of the War

Henry Clinton (p. 215)
Charles Cornwallis (p. 216)
battle of Camden (p. 217)
Benedict Arnold (p. 217)
battle of Yorktown (p. 219)
Treaty of Paris, 1783 (p. 220)

REVIEW QUESTIONS

Use key terms and dates to support your answer.

1. Why were many Americans reluctant to pursue independence from Britain? (pp. 193–198)

2. Why did the British initially exercise restraint in their efforts to defeat the rebellious colonies? (pp. 198–203)

3. How did the patriots promote support for their cause in the colonies? (pp. 203–210)

4. Why did the Americans need assistance from the French to ensure victory? (pp. 210–215)

5. Why did the British southern strategy ultimately fail? (pp. 215–222)

MAKING CONNECTIONS

Draw on key terms, the timeline, and review questions.

1. Even before the colonies had committed to independence, they faced the likelihood of serious military conflict. How did they mobilize for war? In your answer, discuss specific challenges they faced, noting the unintended consequences of their solutions.

2. Congress's adoption of the Declaration of Independence confirmed a decisive shift in the conflict between the colonies and Britain. Why did the colonies make this decisive break in 1776? In your answer, discuss some of the arguments for and against independence.

3. The question of whether the colonists would be loyal to the new government or to the old king was pivotal during the Revolutionary War. Discuss the importance of loyalty in the outcome of the conflict. In your answer, consider both military and political strategy.

4. American colonists and British soldiers were not the only participants in the Revolutionary War. How did Native Americans shape the conflict? What role did African Americans play? What benefits did these two groups hope to gain? Did they succeed?

LINKING TO THE PAST

Link events in this chapter to earlier events.

1. Most Indian tribes joined with the French and opposed the British in the Seven Years' War; yet in the American Revolution, most tribes sided with the British and opposed the Americans. What accounts for this apparent shift in alliances? (See chapter 6.)

2. Consider the leading roles of Massachusetts and Virginia in the coming of the American Revolution. With such very different origins and such very different economic, demographic, and religious histories, how could these two so readily join in partnership in the break from British rule? (See chapters 3, 4, and 5.)

▶ FOR PRACTICE QUIZZES AND OTHER STUDY TOOLS, visit the Online Study Guide at bedfordstmartins.com/roark.

TIMELINE 1775–1783

1775
- Second Continental Congress convenes; creates Continental army.
- British win battle of Bunker Hill.
- King George III rejects Olive Branch Petition.
- Americans lose battle of Quebec.

1776
- *Common Sense* published.
- British evacuate Boston.
- **July 4** Congress adopts Declaration of Independence.
- British take Manhattan.

1777
- British Parliament suspends habeas corpus for rebels.
- British take Fort Ticonderoga.
- Ambush at Oriskany; Americans hold Fort Stanwix.
- British occupy Philadelphia.
- British surrender at Saratoga.

1777–78
- Continental army endures winter at Valley Forge.

1778
- France enters war on American side.
- American militiamen destroy Mohawk chief Joseph Brant's village.
- White Eyes negotiates treaty with Americans; later mysteriously dies.
- British take Savannah, Georgia.

1779
- Militias attack Cherokee settlements in far western North Carolina.
- Americans destroy forty Iroquois villages in New York.
- Americans take Forts Kaskaskia and Vincennes.

1780
- Philadelphia Ladies Association raises money for soldiers.
- British take Charleston, South Carolina.
- French army arrives in Newport, Rhode Island.
- British win battle of Camden.
- Benedict Arnold exposed as traitor.
- Americans win battle of King's Mountain.

1781
- British forces invade Virginia.
- French fleet blockades Chesapeake Bay.
- Cornwallis surrenders at Yorktown; concedes British defeat.

1783
- Treaty of Paris ends war; United States gains all land east of Mississippi River.

A CHAIR FOR THE NEW NATION

George Washington sat in this splendid and unique mahogany chair, topped by a gold-painted sun, for three hot months in the summer of 1787. He was presiding over a convention of fifty-five delegates engaged in the difficult work of hammering out the new Constitution of the United States, pictured here in the background. On the day the delegates finished writing, Benjamin Franklin sagely observed that he had often stared at the sun on the chair, unable to tell if it was morning or evening: "But now at length I have the happiness to know that it is a rising and not a setting Sun."

Background: National Archives; chair: Independence National Historic Park.

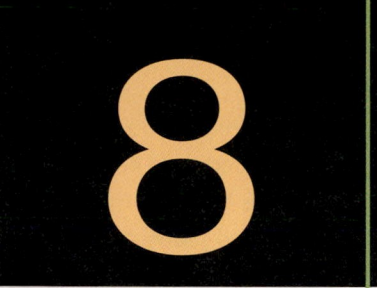

8

Building a Republic

1775–1789

JAMES MADISON GRADUATED FROM PRINCETON COLLEGE IN NEW Jersey in 1771, not knowing what to do next with his life. Certainly, the twenty-year-old had an easy fallback position. As the firstborn son of a wealthy plantation owner, he could return to the foothills of Virginia and wait to inherit substantial land and many slaves. But Madison was an intensely studious young man, uninterested in farming. Five years at boarding school had given him fluency in Greek, Latin, French, and mathematics; and three years at Princeton had acquainted him with the great thinkers, both ancient and modern. Driven by a thirst for learning, young Madison hung around Princeton for six months after graduation.

In 1772, he returned home, still adrift. He tried studying law, but his unimpressive oratorical talents discouraged him. Instead, he swapped reading lists and ideas about political theory by letter with a Princeton classmate, prolonging his student life. While Madison struggled for direction, the powerful winds before the storm of the American Revolution swirled through the colonies. In May 1774, Madison traveled north to deliver his brother to boarding school and was in Philadelphia when the startling news broke that Britain had closed the port of Boston in retaliation for the destruction of the tea. Turbulent protests over the Coercive Acts turned him into a committed revolutionary.

Back in Virginia, Madison joined his father on the newly formed committee of public safety. For a few days in early 1775, the twenty-four-year-old took up musket practice in a burst of enthusiasm for war, but it was quickly plain that his greater contribution lay in the science of politics. In the spring of 1776, he gained election to the Virginia Convention, a Revolutionary assembly replacing the defunct royal government. The convention's main task was to hammer out a state constitution with innovations such as frequent elections and limited executive power. Shy, self-effacing, and still learning the ropes, Madison mostly stayed on the sidelines, but Virginia's elder statesmen noted the young man's logical, thoughtful contributions. When his county failed to return him to the assembly in the next election, he was appointed to the governor's council, where he spent two years gaining experience in a wartime government.

**James Madison,
by Charles Willson Peale**
Philadelphia artist Charles Willson Peale painted this miniature portrait of Madison in 1783, along with a matching miniature of Madison's fiancée, Kitty Floyd, the sixteen-year-old daughter of a New York delegate to the Continental Congress. Madison's portrait was mounted in a brooch (note the pin sticking out on the right) so that his lady love might wear it on her person, but Floyd returned the miniature to Madison when she broke off the engagement. Eleven years later, Madison tried romance again when New York congressman Aaron Burr introduced him to a young Virginia widow named Dolley Payne Todd. Madison was forty-three, and Todd was twenty-six; they married four months after meeting.
Library of Congress.

In early 1780, Madison represented Virginia in the Continental Congress. Not quite twenty-nine, unmarried, and supported by his father's money, he was free of the burdens that made distant political service difficult for so many others. He stayed in the North for three years, working with men such as Alexander Hamilton of New York and Robert Morris of Pennsylvania as the congress wrestled with the chaotic economy and the ever-precarious war effort. In one crisis, Madison's negotiating skills proved crucial: He broke the deadlock over the ratification of the Articles of Confederation by arranging for the cession of Virginia's vast western lands. Those lands would soon appear on maps as the Northwest Territory, calling forth a series of western land ordinances, planned out by Madison's friend Thomas Jefferson, that exemplified the promise of and high hopes for the future of the new confederation government. But more often, service in the congress proved frustrating to Madison because the confederation government seemed to lack essential powers, chief among them the power to tax.

Madison resumed a seat in the Virginia assembly in 1784. But he did not retreat to a local point of view as so many other state politicians of the decade did. The economic hardships created by heavy state taxation programs — which in Massachusetts led to a full-fledged rebellion against state government — spurred Madison to pursue means to strengthen the government shared by the thirteen new states. In this, he was in the minority: To many Americans, it was not clear that the Articles of Confederation needed major revamping.

Madison thought the Articles did need overhauling. He worked hard to organize an all-state convention in Philadelphia in May 1787, where he took the lead in steering the delegates to a complete rewrite of the structure of the national government, investing it with considerably greater powers. True to form, Madison spent the months before the convention in feverish study of the great thinkers he had read in college, seeking the best way to constitute a government on republican principles. His lifelong passion for scholarly study, seasoned by a dozen years of energetic political experience, paid off handsomely. The United States Constitution was the result.

By the end of the 1780s, James Madison had had his finger in every kind of political pie on the local, state, confederation, and finally national level. He had transformed himself from a directionless and solitary youth into one of the leading political thinkers of the Revolutionary period. His personal history over the 1780s was deeply entwined with the path of the emerging United States.

▶ The Articles of Confederation

From 1775 to 1781, the Continental Congress met in Philadelphia and other cities without any formal constitutional basis. It took time to work out a plan of government that embodied Revolutionary principles. With monarchy gone, where would sovereignty lie? What would be the nature of representation? Who would hold the power of taxation? The resulting plan, called the **Articles of Confederation**, proved to be surprisingly difficult to implement, mainly because the thirteen states disagreed over boundaries in the land to the west of the states. Once the Articles were ratified and the active phase of the war had drawn to a close, the congress faded in importance compared with politics in the individual states.

Congress and Confederation

After the Declaration of Independence had been signed and circulated, the Continental Congress set a committee in motion to draft a document that would specify what powers the congress had and by what authority it existed. There was widespread agreement on key central governmental powers: pursuing war and peace, conducting foreign relations, regulating trade, and running a postal service. Yet the congress's attention was still mainly on the war, and so it took a year of tinkering before its members reached agreement on the Articles of Confederation in November 1777. The Articles defined the union as a loose confederation of states, characterized as "a firm league of friendship" existing mainly to foster a common defense. The structure of the government paralleled that of the existing Continental Congress. There was no national executive (that is, no president) and no national judiciary. Term limits of three years ensured rotation in congressional offices. State delegations could vary in size from two to seven, and each delegation cast a single vote. Routine decisions in the congress required a simple majority of seven states; for momentous decisions, such as declaring war, nine states needed to agree. To approve or amend the Articles required the unanimous consent both of the thirteen state delegations and of the thirteen state legislatures — giving any state an unrealistic and eventually crippling veto power. Most crucially, the Articles gave the national government no power of direct taxation.

Taxation was a necessity, since all governments require money and governments pursuing wars need even more. The congress issued bonds to finance most of the war's hefty and immediate costs (for supplies and manpower); the bonds were held in part by French and Dutch bankers but also by large numbers of middling to wealthy Americans. (Bondholders considered bonds with 6 percent interest an attractive investment, especially when they could be purchased with depreciating Continental dollars that were accepted at face value.) The congress also anticipated new peacetime expenses in addition to the large war debt and the expanding interest owed to bondholders. Trade regulation required a paid force of customs officers; a postal system required postmen, horses and wagons, and well-maintained postal roads; the western lands required surveyors; and Indian diplomacy (or war) added further large costs. Article 8 of the confederation document declared that taxes were needed to support "the common defence or general welfare" of the country, yet the congress also had to be sensitive to the rhetoric of the Revolution, which denounced heavy taxation by a distant and nonrepresentative power.

The congress hoped to solve this delicate problem with a two-step procedure. The congress would **requisition** (that is, request) money to be paid into the common treasury, and each state legislature would then levy taxes within

Revolutionary War Flag from New Hampshire
In June 1777, the Continental Congress decreed specifications for the new American flag. Thirteen red and white stripes lay adjacent to a blue corner embellished with thirteen white stars "representing a new Constellation," a powerful metaphor that anchored the fragile union of the thirteen states in the vast and timeless expanse of the heavens. Flag designers experimented with the arrangement of the stars—in a circle or a square, in rows, or, in this case of a flag made in New Hampshire, in staggered rows. Early American flags were strictly military banners; not for another half century would they become ever-present symbols of nonmilitary patriotism. American Antiques, David A. Schorsch — Eileen M. Smiles.

its borders to pay the requisition. The Articles specified that state contributions were to be assessed in proportion to the property value of the state's land; thus, large and populous states paid more than did small or sparsely populated states. Requiring that the actual tax bill be passed by the state legislatures preserved the Revolution's principle of taxation only by direct representation. However, no mechanism compelled states to pay.

The lack of centralized authority in the confederation government was exactly what many state leaders wanted in the late 1770s. A league of states with rotating personnel, no executive branch, no power of direct taxation, and a requirement of unanimity for any major change seemed to be a good way to keep government in check. Yet there were problems, and the first was the requirement that every state ratify the Articles of Confederation. This mandatory unanimity stalled the acceptance of the Articles for four additional years, until 1781.

The Problem of Western Lands

The most serious disagreement over the Articles of Confederation involved the absence of any plan for the lands to the west of the thirteen original states. This absence was deliberate; an earlier draft of the Articles gave the congress the power to set state boundaries and to administer the sales of the western lands. But states with large land claims objected. A few states — Virginia and Connecticut, for example — had old colonial charters that located their western boundaries at the Mississippi River, and they insisted that their claims be recognized. Six more states also had plausible legal claims to extensive territories (Map 8.1). Five states lacked such land claims entirely, and they preferred that the congress preserve all the western lands as a national domain that would eventually be sold off to settlers and constitute new states, administered by the congress. Financial motives loomed large, for, as one Rhode Island delegate put it, "the western world opens an amazing prospect as a national fund; it is equal to our debt."

The eight land-claiming states were ready to sign the Articles of Confederation in 1777, since it protected their interests. Three states without claims — Rhode Island, Pennsylvania, and New Jersey — eventually capitulated and

> ## "The western world opens an amazing prospect as a national fund; it is equal to our debt."
> — A Rhode Island delegate

signed, "not from a Conviction of the Equality and Justness of it," said a New Jersey delegate, "but merely from an absolute Necessity there was of complying to save the Continent." But Delaware and Maryland continued to hold out, insisting on a national domain policy. In 1779, the disputants finally compromised: Any land a state volunteered to relinquish would become the national domain. When James Madison and Thomas Jefferson ceded Virginia's huge land claim in 1781, the Articles of Confederation were at last unanimously approved. (See appendix I, page A-1.)

The western lands issue demonstrated that powerful interests divided the thirteen new states. The apparent unity of purpose inspired by fighting the war against Britain papered over sizable cracks in the new confederation.

Running the New Government

No fanfare greeted the long-awaited inauguration of the new government in 1781. The congress continued to sputter along, its problems far from solved by the signing of the Articles. Lack of a quorum often hampered day-to-day activities. The Articles required representation from seven states to conduct business and a minimum of two men from each state's delegation. But some days, fewer than fourteen men in total showed up. State legislatures were slow to select delegates, and many politicians preferred to devote their energies to state governments, especially when the congress seemed deadlocked or, worse, irrelevant. Some had difficulty learning the art of formal debate. A Pennsylvanian reflected that "I find there is a great deal of difference between sporting a sentiment in a letter, or over a glass of wine upon politics, and discharging properly the duties of a senator."

It also did not help that the congress had no permanent home. During the war, when the British army threatened Philadelphia, the congress relocated to small Pennsylvania towns such as Lancaster and York and then to Baltimore. After hostilities ceased, the congress moved from Trenton to Princeton to Annapolis to New York City. Many delegates were reluctant to travel far from home, especially if they had wives and children. Consequently, some of the most committed delegates were young bachelors, such as James Madison, and men in their fifties and sixties whose families were grown, such as Samuel Adams.

To address the difficulties of an inefficient congress, executive departments of war, finance,

MAP ACTIVITY

Map 8.1 Cession of Western Lands, 1782–1802

The thirteen new states found it hard to ratify the Articles of Confederation without settling their conflicting land claims in the West, an area larger than the original states and occupied by Indian tribes. The five states objecting to the Articles' silence over western lands policy were Maryland, Delaware, New Jersey, Rhode Island, and Pennsylvania.

READING THE MAP: Which state had the largest claims on western territory?

CONNECTIONS: In what context did the first dispute regarding western lands arise? How was it resolved? Does the map suggest a reason why Pennsylvania, a large state, joined the four much smaller states on this issue?

and foreign affairs were created in 1781 to handle purely administrative functions. When the department heads were ambitious — as was Robert Morris, a wealthy Philadelphia merchant who served as superintendent of finance — they could exercise considerable executive power. The Articles of Confederation had deliberately refrained from setting up an executive branch, but a modest one was being invented by necessity.

REVIEW   Why was the confederation government's authority so limited?

▶ The Sovereign States

In the first decade of independence, the states were sovereign and all-powerful. Only a few functions, such as declaring war and peace, had been transferred to the confederation government. As Americans discarded their British identity, they thought of themselves instead as Virginians or New Yorkers or Rhode Islanders. Familiar and close to home, state governments claimed the allegiance of citizens and became the arena in which the Revolution's innovations would first be tried. States defined who was a voter, and they also defined who would be free. Squaring slavery with Revolutionary ideals became a front-burner issue everywhere; northern states had more success ending this inconsistency than did southern states, where slavery was deeply entrenched in the economy.

The State Constitutions

In May 1776, the congress recommended that all states draw up constitutions based on "the authority of the people." By 1778, all had done so. Having been denied the unwritten rights of Englishmen, Americans wanted written contracts that guaranteed basic principles. A shared feature of all the state constitutions was the conviction that government ultimately rests on the consent of the governed. Political writers in the late 1770s embraced the concept of **republicanism** as the underpinning of the new governments. Republicanism meant more than popular elections and representative institutions. For some, republicanism invoked a way of thinking about who leaders should be: autonomous, virtuous citizens who placed civic values above private interests. For others, it suggested direct democracy, with nothing standing in the way of the will of the people. For all, it meant government that promoted the people's welfare.

Widespread agreement about the virtues of republicanism went hand in hand with the idea that republics could succeed only in relatively small units, so that the people could make sure their interests were being served. Nearly every state continued the colonial practice of a two-chamber assembly but greatly augmented the powers of the lower house. Two states, Pennsylvania and Georgia, abolished the more elite upper house altogether, and most states severely limited the term and powers of the governor. Instead, real power resided with the lower houses, constituted to be responsive to popular majorities, with annual elections and guaranteed rotation in office. If a representative displeased his constituents, he could be out of office in a matter of months. James Madison learned about such political turnover when he lost reelection to the Virginia assembly in 1777. Ever shy, he attributed the loss to his reluctance to socialize at taverns and glad-hand his constituents in the traditional Virginia style. His series of increasingly significant political posts from 1778 to 1787 all came as a result of appointment, not popular election.

Six of the state constitutions included **bills of rights** — lists of basic individual liberties that government could not abridge. Virginia passed the first bill of rights in June 1776, and many of the other states borrowed from it. Its language resembles the Declaration of Independence, which Thomas Jefferson was drafting that month in Philadelphia. The Virginia bill of rights states: "That all men are by nature equally free and independent, and have certain inherent rights, of which, when they enter into a state of society, they cannot by any compact deprive or divest their posterity; namely, the enjoyment of life and liberty, with the means of acquiring and possessing property, and pursuing and obtaining happiness and safety." Along with these inherent rights went more specific rights to freedom of speech, freedom of the press, and trial by jury.

Who Are "the People"?

When the Continental Congress called for state constitutions based on "the authority of the people," and when the Virginia bill of rights granted "all men" certain rights, who was meant by "the people"? Who exactly were the citizens of this new country, and how far would the principle of democratic government extend? Different people answered these questions differently, but in the 1770s certain limits to political participation were widely agreed upon.

One limit was defined by property. In nearly every state, candidates for the highest offices had to meet substantial property qualifications. In Maryland, candidates for governor had to be worth the large sum of £5,000, while voters had to own fifty acres of land or £30. In the most democratic state, Pennsylvania, voters and candidates simply needed to be property tax payers, large or small. Only property owners were presumed to possess the necessary independence of mind to make wise political choices. Are not propertyless men, asked John Adams, "too little acquainted with public affairs to form a right judgment, and too dependent upon other men to have a will of their own?" Property qualifications probably disfranchised from one-quarter to one-half of adult white males in all the states. Not all of them took their nonvoter status quietly. One Maryland man challenged the £30 rule: "Every poor man has a life, a personal liberty, and a right to his earnings; and is in danger of being injured by government in a variety of ways." Why restrict such a man from voting? Others noted that propertyless men were fighting and dying in the Revolutionary War; surely they had legitimate political concerns. Finally, a few radical voices challenged the notion that wealth was correlated with good citizenship; maybe the opposite was true. But ideas like this were outside the mainstream. The writers of the new constitutions, themselves men of property, viewed the right to own and preserve property as a central principle of the Revolution.

Another exclusion from voting — women — was so ingrained that few stopped to question it. Yet the logic of allowing propertied females to vote did occur to a handful of well-placed women. Abigail Adams wrote to her husband, John, in 1782, "Even in the freest countrys our property is subject to the controul and disposal of our partners, to whom the Laws have given a sovereign Authority. Deprived of a voice in Legislation, obliged to submit to those Laws which are imposed upon us, is it not sufficient to make us indifferent to the publick Welfare?" A wealthy Virginia widow named Hannah Corbin wrote to her brother, congressional delegate Richard Henry Lee, to complain of her taxation without the corresponding representation. Her letter no longer exists, but Lee wrote in his reply that women would be "out of character . . . to press into those tumultuous assemblies of men where the business of choosing representatives is conducted."

Only three states specified that voters had to be male, so powerful was the unspoken assumption that only men could vote. Still, in one state, small numbers of women began to turn out at the polls in the 1780s. New Jersey's constitution of 1776 enfranchised all free inhabitants worth more than £50, language that in theory opened the door to free blacks as well as unmarried women who met the property requirement. (Married women owned no property, for by law their husbands held title to everything.) Little fanfare accompanied this radical shift, and some historians have inferred that the inclusion of unmarried

women and blacks was an oversight. Yet other parts of the suffrage clause pertaining to residency and property were extensively debated when the clause was put in the state constitution, and no objections were raised at that time to its gender- and race-free language. Thus other historians have concluded that the law was intentionally inclusive. In 1790, a revised election law used the words *he or she* in reference to voters, making woman suffrage explicit. As one New Jersey legislator declared, "Our Constitution gives this right to maids or widows *black* or *white*." However, that legislator was complaining, not bragging, so his words do not mean that egalitarian suffrage was an accepted fact.

A Possible Voter in Essex County, New Jersey
Mrs. Elizabeth Alexander Stevens was married to John Stevens, a New Jersey delegate to the Continental Congress in 1783. Widowed in 1792, she would have then been eligible to vote in state elections according to New Jersey's unique enfranchisement of property-holding women. Essex County, where Elizabeth Stevens lived, was said to be the place where female suffrage was exercised most actively. This portrait, done around 1793–1794, represents the most likely face of that rare bird, the eighteenth-century female voter. The widow Stevens died in 1799, before suffrage was redefined to be the exclusive right of males.
New Jersey Historical Society.

In 1790, only about 1,000 free black adults of both sexes lived in New Jersey, a state with a population of 184,000. The number of unmarried adult white women was probably also small and comprised mainly widows. In view of the property requirement, the voter blocs enfranchised under this law were minuscule. Still, this highly unusual situation lasted until 1807, when a new state law specifically disfranchised both blacks and women. Henceforth, independence of mind, that essential precondition of voting, was redefined to be sex- and race-specific.

In the 1780s, voting everywhere was class-specific because of property restrictions. John Adams urged the framers of the Massachusetts constitution not even to discuss the scope of suffrage but simply to adopt the traditional colonial property qualifications. If suffrage is brought up for debate, he warned, "there will be no end of it. New claims will arise; women will demand a vote; lads from twelve to twenty-one will think their rights not enough attended to; and every man who has not a farthing, will demand an equal voice with any other."

Equality and Slavery

Restrictions on political participation did not mean that propertyless people enjoyed no civil rights and liberties. The various state bills of rights applied to all individuals who were free; unfree people were another matter.

The author of the Virginia bill of rights was George Mason, a planter who owned 118 slaves. When he wrote that "all men are by nature equally free and independent," he meant that white Americans were the equals of the British and could not be denied the liberties of British citizens. Other Virginia legislators, worried about misinterpretations, added the phrase specifying that rights belonged only to people who had entered civil society. As one wrote, with relief, "Slaves, not being constituent members of our society, could never pretend to any benefit from such a maxim." One month later, the Declaration of Independence

> **"Slaves, not being constituent members of our society, could never pretend to any benefit from such a maxim."**
> — A Virginia legislator

Legal Changes to Slavery, 1777–1804

- Abolished slavery
- Gradual emancipation
- Individual cases of emancipation

used essentially the same phrase about equality, this time without the modifying clause about entering society. Two state constitutions, for Pennsylvania and Massachusetts, also picked it up. In Massachusetts, one town suggested rewording the draft constitution to read "All men, whites and blacks, are born free and equal." The suggestion was not implemented.

Slowly, the Revolutionary ideals about natural equality and liberty began to erode the institution of slavery. Often, enslaved blacks led the challenge. In 1777, several Massachusetts slaves petitioned for their "natural & unalienable right to that freedom which the great Parent of the Universe hath bestowed equally on all mankind." They modestly asked for freedom for their children at age twenty-one and were turned down. In 1779, similar petitions in Connecticut and New Hampshire met with no success. Seven Massachusetts free men, including the mariner brothers Paul and John Cuffe, refused to pay taxes for three years on the grounds that they could not vote and so were not represented. The Cuffe brothers landed in jail in 1780 for tax evasion, but their petition to the Massachusetts legislature spurred the extension of suffrage to taxpaying free blacks in 1783.

Another way to bring the issue before lawmakers was to sue in court. In 1781, a woman called **Elizabeth Freeman** (Mum Bett) was the first to win freedom in a Massachusetts court, basing her case on the just-passed state constitution that declared "all men are born free and equal." (See "Seeking the American Promise," page 236.) Another Massachusetts slave, Quok Walker, charged his master with assault and battery, arguing that he was a freeman under that same constitutional phrase. Walker won and was set free, a decision confirmed in an appeal to the state's superior court in 1783. Several similar cases followed, and by 1789 slavery had been effectively abolished by a series of judicial decisions in Massachusetts.

Pennsylvania's legislature enacted a **gradual emancipation** law in 1780, providing that infants born to a slave mother on or after March 1, 1780, would be freed at age twenty-eight. Not until 1847 did Pennsylvania fully abolish slavery, but slaves did not wait for such slow implementation.

Black Loyalists in Canada: Passport to Freedom

This rare sketch from 1788 portrays a black woodcutter who resided in Nova Scotia along with three thousand other black loyalists who had escaped to northeastern Canada between 1783 and 1785. The inset is a passport issued by the British high command to Cato Rammsay, permitting him to leave New York in 1783. Very few of the Nova Scotia refugees were able to acquire land, and after 1786 the British authorities stopped provisioning them. Most, like the man pictured here, were forced to become servants or day laborers for whites. Low wages created dissatisfaction, and racial tensions mounted. In 1791–1792, nearly a third of the black refugees in Nova Scotia left for Sierra Leone in West Africa, where British officials promised them land and opportunities for self-rule. Sketch: William Booth, National Archives of Canada C-401621; passport: Nova Scotia Archives & Records Management.

Untold numbers in Pennsylvania simply ran away and asserted their freedom. One estimate holds that more than half of young slave men in Philadelphia joined the ranks of free blacks, and by 1790, free blacks outnumbered slaves in Pennsylvania two to one.

Rhode Island and Connecticut adopted gradual emancipation laws in 1784. In 1785, New York expanded the terms under which individual owners could free slaves, but only in 1799 did the state adopt a gradual emancipation law; New Jersey followed suit in 1804. These were the two northern states with the largest number of slaves: New York in 1800 with 20,000, New Jersey with more than 12,000. In contrast, slaves in Pennsylvania numbered just 1,700. Gradual emancipation illustrates the tension between radical and conservative implications of republican ideology. Republican government protected people's liberties and property, yet slaves were both people and property. Gradual emancipation attempted to balance the civil rights of blacks and the property rights of their owners by delaying the promise of freedom.

South of Pennsylvania, in Delaware, Maryland, and Virginia, where slavery was critical to the economy, emancipation bills were rejected. All three states, however, eased legal restrictions and allowed individual acts of emancipation for adult slaves below the age of forty-five under new manumission laws passed in 1782 (Virginia),

1787 (Delaware), and 1790 (Maryland). By 1790, close to 10,000 newly freed Virginia slaves had formed local free black communities complete with schools and churches.

In the deep South — the Carolinas and Georgia — freedom for slaves was unthinkable among whites. Yet several thousand slaves had defected to the British during the war, and between 3,000 and 4,000 shipped out of Savannah and Charleston, destined for freedom. Adding northern blacks evacuated from New York City in 1783, the probable total of emancipated blacks who left the United States was between 8,000 and 10,000. Some went to Canada, some to England, and some to Sierra Leone on the west coast of Africa. Many hundreds took refuge with the Seminole and Creek Indians, becoming permanent members of their communities in Spanish Florida and western Georgia.

Although all these instances of emancipation were gradual, small, and certainly incomplete,

A Slave Sues for Her Freedom

The stirring language about liberty, equality, and freedom that inspired American revolutionaries in the 1770s was written into many state constitutions in the 1780s. Yet unfree people, held as property, had little recourse to challenge their status.

Massachusetts law presented an unusual opportunity because it recognized slaves as persons with legal standing to bring lawsuits against whites. Less than 2 percent of the state's population consisted of slaves, who numbered well under four thousand and lived mainly in the coastal cities. Before 1780, some thirty Massachusetts slaves had sued for their freedom, but their cases had turned on particular circumstances, such as an owner's unfulfilled promise to emancipate or a dispute over a slave's parentage. In 1780, a new Massachusetts state constitution boldly declared that "all men are born free and equal," opening the door to lawsuits based on a broad right to freedom. The first to bring suit under the new constitution was Bett, a thirty-year-old slave living in the western Massachusetts town of Sheffield.

Born of African parents in the early 1740s, Bett and her sister Lizzie grew up as slaves in Claverack, New York, in the wealthy Dutch American family of Pieter Hogeboom. When Hogeboom died in 1758, Bett and Lizzie were transported twenty-four miles east into Massachusetts, where Hogeboom's daughter Hannah lived with her husband, Colonel John Ashley. A town tax list of 1771 shows that Colonel Ashley, the richest man in Sheffield and a respected leader in the patriot cause, owned five slaves. He was known as a kind and gentle man, but as one account suggests, his wife was "a shrew untamable" and "the most despotic of mistresses." One day, Hannah Ashley became enraged with Lizzie and heaved a hot kitchen shovel at her. Bett interceded to protect her sister, sustaining a burn on her arm that left a lifelong scar.

On another occasion, in 1773, Bett was, in her own words, "keepin' still and mindin' things" while she served refreshments to a dozen white men gathered at her master's house to draw up a protest petition against the British. Colonel Ashley took the lead in drafting a set of resolutions, the first of which read, "Resolved, That mankind in a state of nature are equal, free, and independent of each other, and have a right to the undisturbed enjoyment of their lives, their liberty and property." Bett well noted the import of their discussion.

In the fall of 1780, Bett overheard conversations at the Ashleys' house about the new Massachusetts state constitution. Bett pondered the words proclaiming equality and reasonably concluded that they applied to her. She sought out a young lawyer named Theodore Sedgwick, who had been present at the petition meeting in 1773. Sedgwick, Sheffield's representative in the new Massachusetts legislature, filed a writ in April 1781 requesting the recovery of unlawfully held property — in this case, the human property of Bett and a second plaintiff owned by Ashley, a man identified only as Brom, "a Negro man" and a "labourer." Ashley contested the writ, and the case, officially called *Brom and Bett v. J. Ashley, Esq.*, went to court.

When the case went to trial, a jury agreed that Bett and Brom were entitled to freedom and ordered Ashley to pay each plaintiff thirty shillings in damages as well as all the court costs. The brief court records do not reveal the legal arguments presented, but Sedgwick descendants later boasted that Theodore Sedgwick invoked the Massachusetts constitution to argue that slavery could not exist in the state.

Bett chose a new name to go with her new status: Elizabeth Freeman. She left Colonel Ashley's employ and became a paid housekeeper in the Sedgwick family, rais-

their symbolic importance was enormous. Every state from Pennsylvania north acknowledged that slavery was fundamentally inconsistent with Revolutionary ideology. On some level, white southerners also understood this, but their inability to imagine a free biracial society prevented them from taking action. George Washington owned 390 slaves and freed not one of them in the 1780s, even when his friend the French general Lafayette urged him to do so as a model for others. In his will, written in 1799, Washington provided for the eventual freedom of his slaves — but only after his wife, Martha, died. She freed them one year later, preferring loss of income to the uneasy situation of her life being the only barrier to her slaves' freedom.

Emancipation in the 1780s, limited as it was, shows that the phrase of the Declaration of Independence — "all men are created equal" — was beginning to acquire real force as a basic principle. Yet a geographic pattern was taking shape: From the 1780s on, the North was associated with freedom and the South with slavery, with profound consequences for the next two centuries of American history.

REVIEW How did states determine who would be allowed to vote?

ing the children when their mother became incapacitated by mental illness. "Her spirit spurned slavery," a Sedgwick daughter wrote, offering this quotation from Bett as evidence: "Anytime, anytime while I was a slave, if one minute's freedom had been offered to me, and I had been told I must die at the end of that minute, I would have taken it — just to stand one minute on God's earth a free woman — I would."

The Sedgwicks were especially grateful to Freeman for her commanding presence of mind during Shays's Rebellion in 1786 (see page 244). Because Sedgwick represented the legal elite of the county, he was the target of hostile crowd action. Freeman was home alone when insurgents, searching for Sedgwick and for valuables to plunder, demanded entry. Unable to prevent their entry, Freeman let the dissidents in but followed the men around with a large shovel and threatened to flatten anyone who damaged any property. When Freeman died in 1829, she was buried in the Sedgwick family plot, with a gravestone inscription supplied by the Sedgwicks that ended "Good mother, farewell."

Freeman's lawsuit of 1781 inspired others to sue, and in a case in 1783 the judge of the Massachusetts Supreme Court declared that "slavery is in my judgment as effectively abolished as it can be by the granting of rights and privileges" in the state constitution. It took several more legal challenges and additional time for that news to trickle out, but the erosion of slavery in Massachusetts gradually picked up speed as blacks demanded manumission or wages for work, or simply walked away from their masters. In 1790, the federal census listed 5,369 "other free persons" (that is, nonwhites) in the state and not a single slave.

Questions for Consideration

1. What events encouraged the slave Bett to take her master to court to sue for freedom?

Elizabeth Freeman
Solo portraits of African American women in the early Republic are incredibly rare. This 1811 watercolor of "Mum Bett" was painted by Susan Ridley Sedgwick, wife of one of the Sedgwick sons, indicating the importance of Freeman to the family. A Sedgwick son later wrote: "If there could be a practical refutation of the imagined superiority of our race to hers, the life and character of this woman would afford that refutation. . . . She had nothing of the submissive or subdued character, which succumbs to superior force. . . . She had, when occasion required it, an air of command which conferred a degree of dignity." Massachusetts Historical Society.

2. How would you characterize Mum Bett's status in the Sedgwick household? Was she merely a hired servant, or something more?

3. Compare Elizabeth Freeman's desire to pass from slavery to freedom with the claim of white revolutionaries who sought freedom in order to escape being "enslaved" by Britain.

▶ The Confederation's Problems

In 1783, the confederation government faced three interrelated concerns: paying down the large war debt, making formal peace with the Indians, and dealing with western settlement. The federal debt remained a vexing problem, since the Articles of Confederation lacked the power to enforce its tax requisitions. Making matters worse, the debt suddenly escalated in 1783 when army officers threatened to stage a coup to secure pensions. Western lands suggested a promising source of income to reduce the federal debt, but competing land claims made it difficult for states to use the proceeds of land sales to retire state debts. The Indian inhabitants of those same lands had different ideas, of course.

From 1784 to 1786, the congress struggled mightily with these three issues. Some leaders were gripped by a sense of crisis, fearing that the Articles of Confederation were too weak. Others defended the Articles as the best guarantee of liberty because real governance occurred at the state level, closer to the people. A major outbreak of civil disorder in western Massachusetts quickly crystallized the debate and propelled the critics of the Articles into decisive and far-reaching action.

The War Debt and the Newburgh Conspiracy

For nearly two years, the Continental army camped at Newburgh, a town just north of the British-occupied city of New York, awaiting news of a finalized peace treaty that would send the British army home. The soldiers at Newburgh were bored, restless, and upset about the confederation government's wobbly financial standing. Military payrolls were far in arrears, and an earlier promise of generous pensions (half pay for life), made to all officers in 1780 in a desperate effort to retain them, seemed increasingly unlikely to be honored. In December 1782, officers petitioned the congress for immediate back pay for their men so that when peace arrived, no one would go home penniless. The petition carried an unspecified threat: "The uneasiness of the soldiers, for want of pay, is great and dangerous; any further experiments on their patience may have fatal effects."

> "The uneasiness of the soldiers, for want of pay, is great and dangerous; any further experiments on their patience may have fatal effects."
> — Officers' petition to the congress

Instead of rejecting the petition outright for lack of money, several members of the congress saw an opportunity to make an especially forceful case to the states for the necessity of taxation. One of these was **Robert Morris**, a Philadelphia merchant with a gift for financial dealings, who was the government's superintendent of finance. Morris single-handedly kept the books and wheedled loans from European bankers, using his own substantial fortune as collateral. He knew better than anyone how insolvent the United States was. In 1781 and later in 1786, Morris led an effort to amend the Articles to allow the government to collect a 5 percent **impost** (an import tax), yet each time it failed by one vote. The dissenters, Rhode Island and New York, collected state import duties at their bustling ports, so it was in their interest to block a national impost. Both states acknowledged the seriousness of the confederation's taxation problem — just not at the same time. The failure of the impost vote showed how unworkable the amendment provision of the Articles was. In this context, the petition from the army officers offered a new opening to pressure the states for the power to tax.

The result was a plot called the **Newburgh Conspiracy**, the country's first and only instance of a threat-ened military coup. Morris and several other congressmen offered encouragement to officers to act as if the army would march on the congress to demand its pay. No actual coup was envisioned; both sides simply wanted a more powerful central government to arise from the threat. Yet the risks were great, for not everyone would understand that this was a ruse. What if the soldiers, incited by their grievances, could not be held in check? One congressman was confident that the risk was worth taking. He wrote privately (and guardedly) about the officers' petition: "I am glad to see things in their present train. It must terminate in giving to Government that power without which Government is just a name."

General George Washington, sympathetic to the plight of unpaid soldiers and officers, had approved the initial petition. But the plotters, knowing of his reputation for integrity, did not inform him of their collusion with congressional leaders. In March 1783, when the general learned of these developments, he delivered an emotional speech to a meeting of five hundred officers, reminding them in stirring language of honor, heroism, and sacrifice. He urged them to put their faith in the congress, and he denounced the plotters as "subversive of all order and discipline." In essence, Washington asserted the key principle that civilian government takes precedence over the military. His audience was left speechless and tearful, and the plot was immediately defused.

In the midst of the crisis, congressman Robert Morris put forward his own threat, to resign. He complained that a government that could incur debts with no assured way to pay them, including the debts owed the soldiers, was unworkable: "I will never be the Minister of Injustice." Morris was not universally admired, for just a few years earlier he had left the congress amid accusations that he had unfairly profited from public service. But his threat to quit now, at this crucial juncture, sent shock waves around the country. Morris continued to work to find money to pay the soldiers, as did Washington. In the end, a trickle of money from a few states was too little and too late, coming after the army began to disband. For its part, the congress voted to endorse a plan to *commute*, or transform, the lifetime pension promised the officers into a lump-sum payment of full pay for five years. But no lump sum of money was available. Instead, the officers were issued "commutation certificates," promising future payment with interest, which quickly depreciated like other forms of public debt in the 1780s.

Lucky Man in Massachusetts?
This New Englander posed for a formal portrait around 1790, proudly holding a lottery ticket. Has this man just won the lottery, or is he merely hopeful? State taxes and confederation requisitions often proved hard to collect in the 1780s. Lotteries became a common way to raise supplementary state financing for schools and public works in the earliest years of the Republic. Portrait: Milwaukee Art Museum, Purchase, Layton Art Collection; ticket: Massachusetts Historical Society.

Massachusetts LOTTERY. (Nº 702 —)
THIS TICKET entitles the Possessor to such Prize as may be drawn against its Number, agreeable to an Act of the General Assembly of this State, passed *February* 19th, 1781.
B   Sam Barrett

In 1783, the soldiers' pay issue added some $5 million to the rising public debt, forcing the congress to press for larger requisitions from the states. The confederation, however, had one new source of enormous untapped wealth: the extensive western territories, attractive to the fast-growing white population but currently inhabited by Indians.

The Treaty of Fort Stanwix

Although the Indians were excluded from the 1783 Treaty of Paris, the confederation government now recognized the need to formalize treaties that would end ongoing hostilities between Indians and settlers and secure land cessions. The congress was particularly concerned with the land inhabited by the **Iroquois Confederacy**, a league of six tribes, but now claimed by the states of New York and Massachusetts based on their colonial charters (see Map 8.1). The Massachusetts charter was older by four decades, but New York felt entitled because the disputed land bordered its territory. The tension between the two states was such that it struck a southern delegate as "the seeds of dissension which I think will not end without a civil war."

At issue was the revenue stream that land sales would generate. The congress summoned the Iroquois to a meeting in October 1784 at Fort Stanwix, on the upper reaches of the Mohawk River. The Articles of Confederation gave the congress (as opposed to individual states) the right to manage diplomacy, war, and "all affairs with the Indians, not members of any of the States." Although Massachusetts accepted the confederation's authority, New York's governor seized on the ambiguous language in the Articles, claiming

that the Iroquois were in fact "members" of his state and that New York had sole rights to negotiate. He called his own meeting with the Iroquois at Fort Stanwix in September. Suspecting that New York might be superseded by the congress, the most important chiefs declined to come and instead sent deputies without authority to negotiate. The Mohawk leader Joseph Brant shrewdly identified the problem of divided authority that afflicted the confederation government: "Here lies some Difficulty in our Minds, that there should be two separate bodies to manage these Affairs." No deal was struck with New York.

Three weeks later, U.S. commissioners opened proceedings at Fort Stanwix with the Seneca chief Cornplanter and Captain Aaron Hill, a Mohawk leader, accompanied by six hundred Indians from the six tribes. The U.S. commissioners arrived with a security detail of one hundred New Jersey militiamen.

The Americans demanded a return of prisoners of war; recognition of the confederation's authority to negotiate, rather than that of individual states; and an all-important cession of a strip of land from Fort Niagara due south, which established U.S.-held territory adjacent to the border with Canada. This crucial change enclosed the Iroquois land within the United States and made it impossible for the Indians to claim to be *between* the United States and Canada. When the tribal leaders balked, one of the commissioners sternly replied, "You are mistaken in supposing that, having been excluded from the treaty between the United States and the King of England, you are become a free and independent nation and may make what terms you please. It is not so. You are a subdued people."

Cornplanter

Cornplanter, whose Indian name was Kaintwakon ("what one plants"), headed the Seneca delegation at Fort Stanwix in 1784. Raised fully Indian, he was the son of a Dutch fur trader and a highborn Seneca woman of the Wolf Clan. Evidently, the Dutch trader did not stick around for long, as Cornplanter never learned either Dutch or English. But during the Revolution, when his father faced capture by Indians, Cornplanter recognized him by his name and released him. The Seneca chief sat for this formal portrait in full finery in the 1790s; he died in 1836, at about age ninety. © Collection of the New-York Historical Society.

In the end, the treaty was signed, gifts were given, and six high-level Indian hostages were kept at the fort awaiting the release of the American prisoners taken during the Revolutionary War, mostly women and children. In addition, a significant side deal sealed the release of much of the Seneca tribe's claim to the Ohio Valley to the United States. This move was a major surprise and aggravation to the Delaware, Mingo, and Shawnee Indians who lived there. In the months to come, tribes not at the meeting tried to disavow the **Treaty of Fort Stanwix** as a document signed under coercion by virtual hostages. But the confederation government

Treaty of Fort Stanwix, 1784

ignored those complaints and made plans to survey and develop the Ohio Territory.

New York's governor astutely figured that the congress's power to implement the treaty terms was limited. The confederation's financial coffers were nearly empty, and its leadership was stretched. So New York quietly began surveying and then selling the very land it had failed to secure by individual treaty with the Iroquois. As that fact became generally known, it pointed up the weakness of the confederation government. One Connecticut leader wondered, "What is to defend us from the ambition and rapacity of New York, when she has spread over that vast territory, which she claims and holds? Do we not already see in her the seeds of an over-bearing ambition?"

Land Ordinances and the Northwest Territory

The congress ignored western New York and turned instead to the Ohio Valley to make good on the promise of western expansion. Delegate Thomas Jefferson, charged with drafting a policy, proposed dividing the territory north of the Ohio River and east of the Mississippi — called the **Northwest Territory** — into nine new states with evenly spaced east-west boundaries and townships ten miles square. He at first advocated giving the land to settlers, rather than selling it, arguing that future property taxes on the improved land would be payment enough. Jefferson's aim was to encourage rapid and democratic settlement, to build a nation of freeholders (as opposed to renters), and to discourage land speculation. Jefferson also insisted on representative governments in the new states; they would not become colonies of the older states. Finally, Jefferson's draft prohibited slavery in the nine new states.

The congress adopted parts of Jefferson's plan in the Ordinance of 1784: the rectangular grid, the nine states, and the guarantee of self-government and eventual statehood. What the congress found too radical was the proposal to give away the land; the national domain was the confederation's only source of independent wealth. The slavery prohibition also failed, by a vote of seven to six states.

A year later, the congress revised the legislation with procedures for mapping and selling the land. The Ordinance of 1785 called for three to five states, divided into townships six miles square, further divided into thirty-six sections of 640 acres, each section enough for four family farms (Map 8.2). Property was thus reduced to easily mappable squares. Land would be sold by public auction at a minimum price of one dollar an acre, with highly desirable land bid up for more. Two further restrictions applied: The minimum purchase was 640 acres, and payment had to be in hard money or in certificates of debt from Revolutionary days. This effectively meant that the land's first owners would be prosperous speculators. The grid of invariant squares further enhanced speculation, allowing buyers and sellers to operate without ever setting foot on the acreage. The commodification of land had been taken to a new level.

Speculators usually held the land for resale rather than inhabiting it. Thus they avoided direct contact with the most serious obstacle to settlement: the dozens of Indian tribes that claimed the land as their own. The treaty signed at Fort Stanwix in 1784 was followed in 1785 by the Treaty of Fort McIntosh, which similarly coerced partial cessions of land from the Delaware, Wyandot, Chippewa, and Ottawa tribes. Finally, in 1786, a united Indian meeting near Detroit issued an ultimatum: No cession would be valid without the unanimous consent of the tribes. The Indians advised the United States to "prevent your surveyors and other people from coming upon our side of the Ohio river." For two more decades, violent Indian wars in Ohio and Indiana would continue to impede white settlement (see chapter 9).

In 1787, a third land act, called the **Northwest Ordinance**, set forth a three-stage process by which settled territories would advance to statehood. First, the congress would appoint officials for a sparsely populated territory who would adopt a legal code and appoint local magistrates to administer justice. When the free male population of voting age and landowning status (fifty acres) reached 5,000, the territory could elect its own legislature and send a nonvoting delegate to the congress. When the population of voting citizens reached 60,000, the territory could write a state constitution and apply for full admission to the Union. At all three territorial stages, the inhabitants were subject to taxation to support the Union, in the same manner as were the original states.

The Northwest Ordinance of 1787 was perhaps the most important legislation passed by the confederation government. It ensured that the new United States, so recently released from colonial dependency, would not itself become a colonial power—at least not with respect to white citizens. The mechanism it established allowed for the successful and orderly expansion of the United States across the continent in the next century.

MAP 8.2   The Northwest Territory and Ordinance of 1785

Surveyors ventured into the eastern edge of the Northwest Territory in the 1780s and produced this first plat map (at right), showing the 6-mile square townships neatly laid out. Each township was subdivided into one-mile squares each containing sixteen 40-acre farms. Jefferson got his straight lines and right angles after all; compare this map to his on page 242.

Plat Map © TNGenNet Inc. 2002.

VISUAL ACTIVITY

Jefferson's Map of the Northwest Territory
Thomas Jefferson sketched out borders for nine new states in his initial plan for the Northwest Territory in 1784 and additional anticipated states below the Ohio River. Straight lines and right angles held a strong appeal for him. But such regularity ignored inconvenient geographic features such as rivers and even more inconvenient political facts such as Indian territorial claims, most unlikely to be ceded by treaty in orderly blocks. Jefferson also submitted a list of distinctive names for the states. Number 9, for example, was Polypotamia, "land of many rivers" in Greek. Other proposed names were Sylvania, Michigania, Assenisipia, and Metropotamia. William L. Clements Library.

READING THE IMAGE: What does this map indicate about Jefferson's vision of the Northwest Territory?
CONNECTIONS: What were the problems with Jefferson's design for the division of the territory? Why did the congress alter it in the land ordinances of 1784, 1785, and 1787?

Nonwhites were not forgotten or neglected in the 1787 ordinance. The brief document acknowledged the Indian presence in the Northwest Territory and promised that "the utmost good faith shall always be observed towards the Indians; their lands and property shall never be taken from them without their consent; and, in their property, rights, and liberty, they shall never be invaded or disturbed, unless in just and lawful wars authorized by Congress." The 1787 ordinance further pledged that "laws founded in justice and humanity, shall from time to time be made for preventing wrongs being done to them, and for preserving peace and friendship

with them." Such promises were full of noble intentions, but they were not generally honored in the decades to come.

Jefferson's original and remarkable suggestion to prohibit slavery in the Northwest Territory resurfaced in the 1787 ordinance, passing this time without any debate. Probably the addition of a fugitive slave provision in the act set southern congressmen at ease: Escaped slaves caught north of the Ohio River would be returned south. Also, abundant territory south of the Ohio remained available for the spread of slavery. The ordinance thus acknowledged and supported slavery even as it barred it from one region. Still,

View of a Farm Near Detroit, 1789
In French, Detroit means "the narrows," in this case the narrow river connecting Lake Huron and Lake Erie. Detroit was founded in 1701 by the French as a fur-trading and defensive fort; the British took it over in 1763. In 1783, it became part of the Northwest Territory, but the British failed to vacate until the Jay Treaty of 1795 forced them out. This watercolor scene was painted in 1789 on a piece of silk by Anne Powell, a loyalist refugee from Boston whose family fled to Canada and then Detroit. Royal Ontario Museum.

the prohibition of slavery in the Northwest Territory perpetuated the dynamic of gradual emancipation in the North. North-South sectionalism based on slavery was slowly taking shape.

The Requisition of 1785 and Shays's Rebellion, 1786–1787

Without an impost amendment and with public land sales projected but not yet realized, the confederation turned again to the states in the 1780s to contribute revenue to the central government. The amount requested was $3 million, four times larger than the previous year's requisition. Of this sum, 30 percent was needed for the operating costs of the government. Another 30 percent was earmarked to pay debts owed to foreign lenders, who insisted on payment in gold or silver. The remaining 40 percent was to go to Americans who owned government bonds, the IOUs of the Revolutionary years. A significant slice of that 40 percent represented the interest (but not the principal) owed to army officers for their recently issued "commutation certificates." This was a tax that, if collected, was going to hurt.

At this time, states were struggling under state tax levies. Several states without major ports (and the import duties that ports generated) were already asking a great deal of their farmer citizens in order to retire state debts from the Revolution. New Jersey and Connecticut fit this profile, and both state legislatures voted to ignore the requisition. In other states, like New Hampshire, town meetings voted to refuse to pay, on the grounds that the towns didn't have the money. In late 1786, a group of two hundred armed insurgents surrounded the New Hampshire capitol to protest the taxes but were driven off by a hastily called and armed militia. The shocked assemblymen pulled back from an earlier order to haul delinquent taxpayers into courts. Some states (Rhode Island, North Carolina, and Georgia) responded to their constituents' protests by issuing abundant amounts of paper money and allowing taxes to be paid in greatly depreciated currency.

Nowhere were the tensions so extreme as in Massachusetts. For four years in a row, a fiscally conservative legislature, dominated by the coastal commercial centers, had passed tough tax laws to pay state creditors who required

payment in hard money, not cheap paper. Then in March 1786, the legislature in Boston loaded the federal requisition onto the bill. In June, farmers in southeastern Massachusetts marched on a courthouse in an effort to close it down, and petitions of complaint about oppressive taxation poured in from the western two-thirds of the state. In July 1786, when the legislature adjourned, having yet again ignored their complaints, dissidents held a series of conventions and called for revisions to the state constitution to promote democracy, eliminate the elite upper house, and move the capital farther west in the state.

Still unheard in Boston, the dissidents in six counties targeted the county courts, the local symbol of state authority. In the fall of 1786, several thousand armed men in each protest event forced bewildered judges to close their courts until the state constitution was revised. Sympathetic local militias did not intervene. The insurgents were not predominantly poor or debt-ridden farmers; they included veteran soldiers and officers in the Continental army as well as town leaders. One was a farmer and onetime army captain, Daniel Shays.

The governor of Massachusetts, James Bowdoin, once a protester against British taxes, now characterized the western dissidents as illegal rebels. He vilified Shays as the chief leader (he was not), and a Boston newspaper claimed that Shays planned to burn Boston to the ground and overthrow the government, a report that created panic. Another former radical, Samuel Adams, took the extreme position that "the man who dares rebel against the laws of a republic ought to suffer death." Those aging revolutionaries had little considered that representatives in a state legislature could seem to be as oppressive as monarchs. The dissidents challenged the assumption that popularly elected governments would always be fair and just.

Members of the Continental Congress had much to worry about. In nearly every state, the requisition of 1785 spawned some combination of crowd protests, threats to state authorities, demands for inflationary paper money, and emotional diatribes about greedy money speculators. The Massachusetts insurgency was the worst episode, and it seemed to be spinning out of control. In October 1786, the congress began to anticipate the need for armed intervention. But

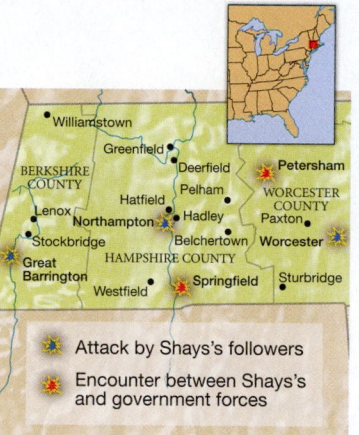

Shays's Rebellion, 1786–1787

🌟 Attack by Shays's followers

🌟 Encounter between Shays's and government forces

when it called for enlistments to triple the size of the federal army, fewer than 100 men responded. So Governor Bowdoin raised a private army, gaining the services of some 3,000 men with pay provided by wealthy and fearful Boston merchants.

In January 1787, the insurgents learned of the private army marching west from Boston, and 1,500 of them moved swiftly to capture a federal armory in Springfield to obtain weapons. But a militia band loyal to the state government beat them to the weapons facility and met their attack with gunfire; 4 rebels were killed and another 20 wounded. The final and bloodless encounter came at Petersham, where Bowdoin's army surprised the rebels on a freezing February morning and took 150 prisoners; the others fled into the woods, but most were soon rounded up and jailed. Daniel Shays escaped capture by fleeing to the self-declared independent republic of Vermont.

In the end, 2 men were executed for rebellion; 16 more sentenced to hang were reprieved at the last moment on the gallows. Some 4,000 men gained leniency by confessing their misconduct and swearing an oath of allegiance to the state. A special Disqualification Act prohibited the penitent rebels from voting, holding public office, serving on juries, working as schoolmasters, or operating taverns for up to three years.

Shays's Rebellion caused leaders throughout the country to worry about the confederation's ability to handle civil disorder. Inflammatory Massachusetts newspapers wrote about bloody mob rule; perhaps, some feared, similar "combustibles" in other states were awaiting the spark that would set off a dreadful political conflagration. New York lawyer John Jay wrote to George Washington, "Our affairs seem to lead to some crisis, some revolution — something I cannot foresee or conjecture. I am uneasy and apprehensive; more so than during the war." Benjamin Franklin, in his eighties, shrewdly observed that in 1776 Americans had feared "an excess of power in the rulers" but now the problem was perhaps "a defect of obedience" in the subjects. Among such leaders, the sense of crisis in the confederation had greatly deepened.

REVIEW   Why did farmers in western Massachusetts revolt against the state legislature?

Two Rebel Leaders and a Silver Bowl for an Anti-Shays General
A Boston almanac of 1787 yields the only rough depiction of Daniel Shays
in existence. Shays is standing with another rebel leader, Job Shattuck, from
the town of Groton. This particular almanac series was quite pro-Constitution
in 1788, so very likely this picture was intended to mock the rebels by showing
them in fancy uniforms and armed with swords, trappings beyond their presumed
lowly means. The silver bowl was a present to an official general, William Shepard of
Springfield, from his militiamen, who honored his victory over the insurgents. Presenta-
tional silver conveyed a double message: It announced gratitude and praise in engraved
words, and it transmitted considerable monetary value in the silver itself. General Shepard could display his trophy on a
shelf, use it as a punch bowl, will it to descendants to keep his moment of fame alive, or melt it down in hard times.
Bowl: Yale University Art Gallery, Mabel Brady Garvan Collection; illustration: National Portrait Gallery, Smithsonian Institution/Art Resource, NY.

▶ The United States Constitution

Shays's Rebellion provoked an odd mixture of fear and hope that the government under the Articles of Confederation was losing its grip on power. A small circle of Virginians decided to try one last time to augment the powers granted to the government by the Articles. Their call for a meeting to discuss trade regulation led, more quickly than they could have imagined in 1786, to a total reworking of the national government.

From Annapolis to Philadelphia

Led by **James Madison**, the Virginians convinced the confederation congress to allow a September 1786 meeting of delegates at Annapolis, Maryland, to try again to revise the trade regulation powers of the Articles. Only five states participated, and the delegates rescheduled the meeting for Philadelphia in May 1787. The congress reluctantly endorsed the Philadelphia meeting and limited its scope to "the sole and express purpose of revising the Articles of Confederation." But at least one representative at the Annapolis meeting had more ambitious plans. **Alexander Hamilton**

of New York hoped the Philadelphia meeting would do whatever was necessary to strengthen the federal government. Young Hamilton was suited for such bold steps. Born in impoverished circumstances in the West Indies, he had made his way into the elite circles of New York society (via talent, hard work, and a well-connected marriage) and now fully identified with the elite and their fear of democratic disorder.

The fifty-five men who assembled at Philadelphia in May 1787 for the **constitutional convention** were generally those who had already concluded that there were weaknesses in the Articles of Confederation. Few attended who were opposed to revising the Articles. Patrick Henry, author of the Virginia Resolves in 1765 and more recently state governor, refused to go to the con-

vention, saying he "smelled a rat." Rhode Island declined to send delegates. Two men sent by New York's legislature to check the influence of fellow-delegate Alexander Hamilton left in dismay in the middle of the convention, leaving Hamilton as the sole representative of the state.

This gathering of white men included no artisans, day laborers, or ordinary farmers. Two-thirds of the delegates were lawyers. Half had been officers in the Continental army. The majority had served in the confederation congress and knew its strengths and weaknesses. Seven men had been governors of their states and knew firsthand the frustrations of thwarted executive power. A few elder statesmen attended, such as Benjamin Franklin and George Washington, but on the whole the delegates were young, like Madison and Hamilton.

The Pennsylvania Statehouse
The constitutional convention assembled at the Pennsylvania statehouse to sweat out the summer of 1787. Despite the heat, the delegates nailed the windows shut to eliminate the chance of being heard by eavesdroppers, so intent were they on secrecy. The statehouse, built in the 1740s to house the colony's assembly, accommodated the Continental Congress at various times in the 1770s and 1780s. The building is now called Independence Hall in honor of the signing of the Declaration of Independence there in 1776.
Historical Society of Pennsylvania.

The Virginia and New Jersey Plans

The convention worked in secrecy, which enabled the men to freely explore alternatives without fear that their honest opinions would come back to haunt them. The Virginia delegation first laid out a fifteen-point plan for a complete restructuring of the government. This **Virginia Plan** was a total repudiation of the principle of a confederation of states. Largely the work of Madison, the plan set out a three-branch government composed of a two-chamber legislature, a powerful executive, and a judiciary. It practically eliminated the voices of the smaller states by pegging representation in both houses of the congress to population. The theory was that government operated directly on people, not on states. Among the breathtaking powers assigned to the congress were the rights to veto state legislation and to coerce states militarily to obey national laws. To prevent the congress from having absolute power, the executive and judiciary could jointly veto its actions.

In mid-June, delegates from New Jersey, Connecticut, Delaware, and New Hampshire — all small states — unveiled an alternative proposal. The **New Jersey Plan**, as it was called, maintained the existing single-house congress of the Articles of Confederation in which each state had one vote. Acknowledging the need for an executive, it created a plural presidency to be shared by three men elected by the congress from among its membership. Where it sharply departed from the existing government was in the sweeping powers it gave to the new congress: the right to tax, regulate trade, and use force on unruly state governments. In favoring national power over states' rights, it aligned itself with the Virginia Plan. But the New Jersey Plan retained the confederation principle that the national government was to be an assembly of states, not of people.

For two weeks, delegates debated the two plans, focusing on the key issue of representation. The small-state delegates conceded that one house in a two-house legislature could be apportioned by population, but they would never agree that both houses could be. Madison was equally vehement about bypassing representation by state, which he viewed as the fundamental flaw in the Articles.

The debate seemed deadlocked, and for a while the convention was "on the verge of dissolution, scarce held together by the strength of a hair," according to one delegate. Only in mid-July did the so-called **Great Compromise** break the stalemate and produce the basic structural features of the emerging **United States Constitution**. Proponents of the competing plans agreed on a bicameral legislature. Representation in the lower house, the House of Representatives, would be apportioned by population, and representation in the upper house, the Senate, would come from all the states equally. Instead of one vote per state in the upper house, as in the New Jersey Plan, the compromise provided two senators who voted independently.

Representation by population turned out to be an ambiguous concept once it was subjected to rigorous discussion. Who counted? Were slaves, for example, people or property? As people, they would add weight to the southern delegations in the House of Representatives, but as property they would add to the tax burdens of those states. What emerged was the compromise known as the **three-fifths clause**: All free persons plus "three-fifths of all other Persons" constituted the numerical base for the apportionment of representatives.

Using "all other Persons" as a substitute for "slaves" indicates the discomfort delegates felt in acknowledging in the Constitution the existence of slavery. The words *slave* and *slavery* appear nowhere in the document, but slavery figured in two places besides the three-fifths clause. Government power over trade regulation naturally included the slave trade, which the Constitution euphemistically described as "the Migration or Importation of such Persons as any of the States now shall think proper to admit." Another provision contrived to guarantee the return of fugitive slaves using awkward, lawyer-like prose: "No person, held to Service or Labour in one State, under the Laws thereof, escaping into another, shall, in Consequence of any Law or Regulation therein, be discharged from such Service or Labour but shall be delivered up on Claim of the party to whom such Service or Labour may be due." Although slavery was nowhere named, it was nonetheless recognized, protected, and thereby perpetuated by the U.S. Constitution.

Democracy versus Republicanism

The delegates in Philadelphia made a distinction between *democracy* and *republicanism* new to the American political vocabulary. Pure democracy was now taken to be a dangerous thing. As a Massachusetts delegate put it, "The evils we experience flow from the excess of democracy." The delegates still favored republican institutions, but they created a government that gave direct voice to the people only in

> **"The evils we experience flow from the excess of democracy."**
> — A Massachusetts delegate

the House and that granted a check on that voice to the Senate, a body of men elected not by direct popular vote but by the state legislatures. Senators served for six years, with no limit on reelection; they were protected from the whims of democratic majorities, and their long terms fostered experience and maturity in office.

Similarly, the presidency evolved into a powerful office out of the reach of direct democracy. The delegates devised an electoral college whose only function was to elect the president and vice president. Each state's legislature would choose the electors, whose number was the sum of representatives and senators for the state, an interesting blending of the two principles of representation. The president thus would owe his office not to the Congress, the states, or the people, but to a temporary assemblage of distinguished citizens who could vote their own judgment on the candidates. His term of office was four years, but he could be reelected without limitation.

The framers had developed a far more complex form of federal government than that provided by the Articles of Confederation. To curb the excesses of democracy, they devised a government with limits and checks on all three of its branches. They set forth a powerful president who could veto legislation passed in Congress, but they gave Congress the power to override presidential vetoes. They set up a national judiciary to settle disputes between states and citizens of different states. They separated the branches of government not only by functions and by reciprocal checks but also by deliberately basing the election of each branch on different universes of voters — voting citizens (the House), state legislators (the Senate), and the electoral college (the presidency).

The convention carefully listed the powers of the president and of Congress. The president could initiate policy, propose legislation, and veto acts of Congress; he could command the military and direct foreign policy; and he could appoint the entire judiciary, subject to Senate approval. Congress held the purse strings: the power to levy taxes, to regulate trade, and to coin money and control the currency. States were expressly forbidden to issue paper money. Two more powers of Congress — to "provide for the common defence and general Welfare" of the country and "to make all laws which shall be necessary and proper" for carrying out its powers — provided elastic language that came closest to Madison's wish to grant sweeping powers to the new government.

While no one was entirely satisfied with every line of the Constitution, only three dissenters refused to sign the document. The Constitution specified a mechanism for ratification that avoided the dilemma faced earlier by the confederation government: Nine states, not all thirteen, had to ratify it, and special ratifying conventions elected only for that purpose, not state legislatures, would make the crucial decision.

REVIEW   Why did the government proposed by the constitutional convention employ multiple checks on each branch?

▶ Ratification of the Constitution

Had a popular vote been taken on the Constitution in the fall of 1787, it probably would have been rejected. In populous Virginia, Massachusetts, and New York, substantial majorities opposed a powerful new national government. North Carolina and Rhode Island refused to call ratifying conventions. Seven states were easy victories for the Constitution, but securing the approval of the nine required for ratification proved difficult. Pro-Constitution forces, called Federalists, had to strategize very shrewdly to defeat anti-Constitution forces, called Antifederalists.

The Federalists

Proponents of the Constitution moved into action swiftly. To silence the criticism that they had gone beyond their charge, they submitted the document to the congress. The congress withheld explicit approval but resolved to send the Constitution to the states for their consideration. The pro-Constitution forces shrewdly secured another advantage by calling themselves **Federalists**. By all logic, this label was more suitable for the backers of the confederation concept, because the Latin root of the word *federal* means "league." Their opponents thus became known as Antifederalists, a label that made them sound defensive and negative, lacking a program of their own.

To gain momentum, the Federalists targeted the states most likely to ratify quickly. Delaware provided unanimous ratification by early December, before the Antifederalists had even begun to campaign. Pennsylvania, New Jersey, and Georgia followed within a month (Map 8.3). Delaware and New Jersey were small states

NEW HAMPSHIRE
9th
June 21, 1788

MAINE
(part of MASS.)

MASSACHUSETTS
6th
Feb. 16, 1788

NEW YORK
11th
July 26, 1788

RHODE ISLAND
13th
May 29, 1790

CONNECTICUT
5th
Jan. 9, 1788

PENNSYLVANIA
2nd
Dec. 12, 1787

NEW JERSEY
3rd
Dec. 18, 1787

DELAWARE
1st
Dec. 8, 1787

VIRGINIA
10th
June 26, 1788

MARYLAND
7th
Apr. 26, 1788

SPANISH LOUISIANA

Kentucky District

Tennessee District

NORTH CAROLINA
12th
Nov. 21, 1789

SOUTH CAROLINA
8th
May 23, 1788

GEORGIA
4th
Jan. 2, 1788

Disputed with Spain

SPANISH FLORIDA

Majority for ratification

Majority against ratification

Divided

No returns (unsettled areas)

1st Order in which the 13 states ratified

MAP ACTIVITY

Map 8.3 Ratification of the Constitution, 1788–1790
Populated areas cast votes for delegates to state ratification conventions. This map shows Antifederalist strength generally concentrated in backcountry, noncoastal, and non-urban areas, but with significant exceptions (for example, Rhode Island).

READING THE MAP: Where was Federalist strength concentrated? How did the distribution of Federalist and Antifederalist sentiment affect the order of state ratifications of the Constitution?
CONNECTIONS: What objections did Antifederalists have to the new United States Constitution? How did their locations affect their view of the Federalist argument?

surrounded by more powerful neighbors; a government that would regulate trade and set taxes according to population was an attractive proposition. Georgia sought the protection that a stronger national government would afford against hostile Indians and Spanish Florida to the south. "If a weak State with the Indians on its back and the Spaniards on its flank does not see the necessity of a General Government there must I think be wickedness or insanity in the way," said Federalist George Washington.

Another three easy victories came in Connecticut, Maryland, and South Carolina. As in Pennsylvania, merchants, lawyers, and urban artisans in general favored the new Constitution,

as did large landowners and slaveholders. This tendency for the established political elite to be Federalist enhanced the prospects of victory, for Federalists already had power and influence disproportionate to their number. Antifederalists in these states tended to be rural, western, and noncommercial, men whose access to news was limited and whose participation in state government was tenuous.

Massachusetts was the first state to give the Federalists serious difficulty. The vote to select the ratification delegates decidedly favored the Antifederalists, whose strength lay in the western areas of the state, home to Shays's Rebellion. One rural delegate from Worcester County voiced widely

Mercy Otis Warren
The sister of James Otis and the wife of James Warren, both prominent leaders in the pre-revolutionary movement in Massachusetts, Mercy Otis Warren was well positioned to learn about revolutionary politics from the ground up. An ardent advocate for independence, she counted Abigail and John Adams among her close friends but broke with them in the late 1780s when she took up the Antifederalist cause. In 1788 Warren published a pamphlet explaining her well-argued objections to the Constitution. She declined to put her name on the publication, choosing instead to give "Columbian Patriot" as a pseudonym. Why might she have done that?
Photograph © 2012 Museum of Fine Arts, Boston, Bequest of Winslow Warren, 31.212.

shared suspicions: "These lawyers and men of learning and money men that talk so finely, and gloss over matters so smoothly, to make us poor illiterate people swallow down the pill, expect to get into Congress themselves; they expect to be the managers of the Constitution and get all the power and all the money into their own hands, and then they will swallow up all us little folks." Nevertheless, the Antifederalists' lead was slowly eroded by a vigorous newspaper campaign. In the end, the Federalists won in Massachusetts by a very slim margin and only with promises that amendments to the Constitution would be taken up in the first Congress.

By May 1788, eight states had ratified; only one more was needed. North Carolina and Rhode Island were hopeless for the Federalist cause, and New Hampshire seemed nearly as bleak. More worrisome was the failure to win over the largest and most economically critical states, Virginia and New York.

The Antifederalists

The **Antifederalists** were a composite group, united mainly in their desire to block the Constitution. Although much of their strength came from back-country areas long suspicious of eastern elites, many Antifederalist leaders came from the same well-connected social background as Federalist leaders; economic class alone did not differentiate them. The Antifederalists also drew strength in states such as New York that were already on sure economic footing and could afford to remain independent. Probably the biggest appeal of the Antifederalists' position lay in the long-nurtured fear that distant power might infringe on people's liberties. The language of the earlier Revolutionary movement was not easily forgotten.

But by the time eight states had ratified the Constitution, the Antifederalists faced a far harder task than they had once imagined. First, they were no longer defending the status quo now that the momentum lay with the Federalists. Second, it was difficult to defend the confederation government with its admitted flaws. Even so, they remained genuinely fearful that the new government would be too distant from the people and could thus become corrupt or tyrannical. "The difficulty, if not impracticability, of exercising the equal and equitable powers of government by a single legislature over an extent of territory that reaches from the Mississippi to the western lakes, and from them to the Atlantic ocean, is an insuperable objection to the adoption of the new system," wrote one articulate Antifederalist in a compelling and much-read political pamphlet. The author, "A Columbia Patriot," was an alias for Mercy Otis Warren, a Massachusetts woman whose father, brother, and husband had all been active leaders in the Revolutionary movement in Boston.

The new government was indeed distant. In the proposed House of Representatives, the only directly democratic element of the Constitution, one member represented some 30,000 people. How could that member really know or communicate with his whole constituency, Antifederalists worried. One Antifederalist essayist contrasted the proposed model with the personal character of state-level representation: "The members of our state legislature are annually elected — they are subject to instructions — they are chosen within small circles — they are sent but a small distance from their respective homes. Their conduct is constantly known to their constituents. They frequently see, and are seen, by the men whose servants they are."

Antifederalists also feared that representatives would always be elites and thus "ignorant of the sentiments of the middling and much more of the lower class of citizens, strangers to their ability, unacquainted with their wants, difficulties, and distress," a Maryland man worried. None of this would be a problem under a confederation system, according to the Antifederalists, because real power would continue to reside in the state governments.

The Federalists generally agreed that the elite would be favored for national elections. Indeed, Federalists wanted power to reside with intelligent, virtuous leaders like themselves. They did not envision a government constituted of every class of people. "Fools and knaves have voice enough in government already," quipped one Federalist, without being guaranteed representation in proportion to their total population. Alexander Hamilton claimed that mechanics and laborers

preferred to have their social betters represent them. Antifederalists disagreed: "In reality, there will be no part of the people represented, but the rich.... It will literally be a government in the hands of the few to oppress and plunder the many." (See "Historical Question," page 252.)

Antifederalists fretted over many specific features of the Constitution. It prohibited state-issued paper money. It regulated the time and place of congressional elections, leading to fears that only one inconvenient polling place might be authorized, disfranchising rural voters. The most widespread objection was the Constitution's glaring omission of any guarantees of individual liberties in a bill of rights like those contained in many state constitutions.

Despite Federalist campaigns in the large states, it was a small state — New Hampshire — that

"Fools and knaves have voice enough in government already."
— A Federalist

Silk Banner of the New York Society of Pewterers
As soon as nine states ratified the Constitution, the Federalists held spectacular victory celebrations meant to demonstrate national unity behind the new government. New York City's parade, coming three days before the state's own ratification vote in July 1788, involved five thousand participants marching under seventy-six occupational banners representing farmers, brewers, tobacconists, lawyers, and others. This banner was carried by the Society of Pewterers, metalsmiths who made household utensils. Despite the broad spectrum of male workers represented in the parade, many of whom could not vote, no working women participated. Why? © Collection of the New-York Historical Society.

Was the New United States a Christian Country?

Rebecca Samuel, a Jewish resident of Virginia, conveyed her excitement about the new U.S. Constitution when she wrote her German parents in 1791 that finally "Jew and Gentile are as one" in the realm of politics and citizenship. Other voices were distinctly less approving. An Antifederalist pamphlet warned that the pope could become president; another feared that "a Turk, a Jew, a Roman Catholic, and what is worse than all, a Universalist, may be President."

The document that produced such wildly different reactions was indeed remarkable for the conspicuous absence of religion. The Constitution did not invoke Christianity as a state religion. It made no reference to an almighty being, and it specifically promised, in Article 6, section 3, that "no religious test shall ever be required as a qualification to any office or public trust under the United States."

More than a few Christian leaders were stunned at the Constitution's near silence on religion, a clear turnabout from state constitutions of the 1770s and 1780s. A New Yorker warned that "should the Citizens of America be as irreligious as her Constitution, we will have reason to tremble, lest the Governor of the universe . . . crush us to atoms." A delegate to North Carolina's ratifying convention predicted that the Constitution was "an invitation for Jews and pagans of every kind to come among us." A concerned Presbyterian minister asked Alexander Hamilton why religion was

not in the Constitution. Hamilton reportedly quipped, "Indeed, Doctor, we forgot it."

Measured against the practices of state governments, Hamilton's observation is hardly credible. The men who wrote the state constitutions actively debated principles of inclusion and exclusion for voting rights and officeholding. Along with factors like property ownership, race, gender, and age, many also argued for religious qualifications.

Most leaders of the 1780s took for granted that Christianity was the one true faith and the essential foundation of morality. All but two state constitutions assumed the primacy of Protestantism, and one-third of them collected public taxes to support Christian churches. Every state but one required officeholders to take a Christian oath. For example, every member of Pennsylvania's legislature swore to "acknowledge the Scripture of the Old and New Testament to be given by divine inspiration."

Other common political practices affirmed Christian practice. Governors proclaimed fast days and public thanksgivings in the name of the Holy Trinity. Chaplains led legislatures in Christian prayer. Jurors and witnesses swore Christian oaths. New England states passed Sabbath laws prohibiting all work or travel on Sunday. Blasphemy laws punished people who cursed the Christian God or Jesus.

Although close to half the state constitutions did include freedom of

religious conscience as an explicit right, this right promised nothing about political equality. How then did the U.S. Constitution come to be such a break from the immediate past? Had the Constitution's writers really just forgotten about religion?

Not James Madison of Virginia. Madison arrived at the constitutional convention fresh from a hard-fought battle in Virginia to establish religious liberty free from all state interference. Opponents sponsored a bill to support Christian ministers with tax money; Madison instead secured passage in 1786 of the Virginia Statute for Religious Freedom, a document written several years earlier by Thomas Jefferson. The statute guaranteed freedom of conscience and prohibited any distinctions in "civil capacities" based on religion. In Jefferson's distinctive formulation, the statute asserted "that our civil rights have no dependence on our religious opinions any more than our opinions in physics or geometry." There could be no religious tests for officeholding thereafter in that state and no state funding of ministers.

The Virginia Statute expressed Madison's ideal, but on practical grounds he thought it best for the U.S. Constitution to say as little as possible about religion, since state laws reflected a variety of positions. When Antifederalists demanded a bill of rights, Madison drew up a list for the first Congress to consider. Two on his list dealt with religion, but only one was approved by Congress to become part of the First Amendment: "Congress shall make no law respecting an establishment of religion, or prohibiting the free exercise thereof." In a stroke, Madison placed religious worship and the privileging of any one church beyond Congress's power. Significantly, his second proposal

provided the decisive ninth vote for ratification on June 21, 1788. Federalists there succeeded in getting the convention postponed from February to June and conducted an intense and successful lobbying effort on specific delegates in the interim.

The Big Holdouts: Virginia and New York

With nine states voting in favor, the Constitution was ensured passage, but four states still opposed ratification. A glance at a map demonstrated

Touro Synagogue

A Jewish community inhabited the coastal shipping city of Newport, Rhode Island, as early as the 1650s. In 1759, the thriving group built a synagogue, the oldest Jewish house of worship still standing in the United States. It is sited diagonally on its property so that worshippers face east, the direction of Jerusalem. President Washington visited Newport in 1790 and wrote to "the Hebrew Congregation" a few days later: "It is now no more that toleration is spoken of, as if it was by the indulgence of one class of people, that another enjoyed the exercise of their inherent natural rights." Touro Synagogue/photo John T. Hopf.

failed to gain traction in congressional debate: "No State shall violate the equal rights of conscience." Evidently, the states wanted to be able to keep their Christian-only rules — rules that would violate dissenters' consciences and thus keep them out of office.

Gradually, states deleted restrictive laws, but as late as 1840 Jews still could not hold public office in four states; even into the twentieth century, Sunday laws in some states forced business closings on the Christian Sabbath, creating economic hardship for both owners and workers whose religion prohibited work on Saturday. The guarantee of freedom of conscience in religion was implanted in various founding documents in the 1770s and 1780s, but it has taken many years to fulfill Jefferson's and Madison's larger vision of what true religious liberty means: the freedom for religious belief to be independent of civil status.

Thinking about Beliefs and Attitudes

1. Why do you think so many state constitutions allowed only Protestants to hold political office?

2. What point was Jefferson making when he compared opinions about religion to opinions about physics or geometry as relevant factors for officeholding?

3. Why did Madison's language guaranteeing that Congress would not establish a federal religion appeal to Antifederalists? Why did other representatives in Congress reject Madison's additional proposal that states be prohibited from violating "the equal rights of conscience"?

the necessity of pressing the Federalist case in the two largest, Virginia and New York (see Map 8.3). Although Virginia was home to Madison and Washington, an influential Antifederalist group led by Patrick Henry and George Mason made the outcome uncertain. The Federalists finally but barely won ratification in Virginia by proposing twenty specific amendments that the new government would promise to consider.

New York voters tilted toward the Antifederalists out of a sense that a state so large

and powerful need not relinquish so much authority to the new federal government. But New York was also home to some of the most persuasive Federalists. Starting in October 1787, Alexander Hamilton collaborated with James Madison and New York lawyer John Jay on a series of eighty-five essays on the political philosophy of the new Constitution. Published in New York newspapers and later republished as *The Federalist Papers*, the essays brilliantly set out the failures of the Articles of Confederation and offered an analysis of the complex nature of the Federalist position. In one of the most compelling essays, number 10, Madison challenged the Antifederalists' heartfelt conviction that republican government had to be small-scale. Madison argued that a large and diverse population was itself a guarantee of liberty. In a national government, no single faction could ever be large enough to subvert the freedom of other groups. "Extend the sphere, and you take in a greater variety of parties and interests; you make it less probable that a majority of the whole will have a common motive to invade the rights of other citizens," Madison asserted. He called it "a republican remedy for the diseases most incident to republican government."

At New York's ratifying convention, Antifederalists predominated, but impassioned debate and lobbying — plus the dramatic news of Virginia's ratification — finally tipped the balance to the Federalists. Still, the Antifederalists' approval of the document was delivered with a list of twenty-four individual rights they hoped would be protected and thirty-three structural changes they hoped to see in the Constitution. New York's ratification ensured the legitimacy of the new government, yet it took another year and a half for Antifederalists in North Carolina to come around. Fiercely independent Rhode Island held out until May 1790, and even then it ratified by only a two-vote margin.

In less than twelve months, the U.S. Constitution was both written and ratified. (See appendix I, page A-1.) An amazingly short time by twenty-first-century standards, it is even more remarkable for the late eighteenth century, with its horse-powered transportation and hand-printed communications. The Federalists had faced a formidable task, but by building momentum and ensuring consideration of a bill of rights, they did indeed carry the day.

REVIEW Why did Antifederalists oppose the Constitution?

Conclusion: The "Republican Remedy"

Thus ended one of the most intellectually tumultuous and creative periods in American history. American leaders experimented with ideas and drew up plans to embody their evolving and conflicting notions of how a society and a government ought to be formulated. There was widespread agreement that government should derive its power and authority from the people, but a narrow vision of "the people" prevailed. With limited exceptions — New Jersey, for example — free blacks and women were excluded from government. Indians, even when dubiously called "members" of a state, were never considered political participants, and neither were slaves. Even taking free white males as "the people," men disagreed fiercely over the degree of democracy — the amount of direct control of government by the people — that would be workable in American society.

The period began in 1775 with a confederation government that could barely be ratified because of its requirement of unanimity for approval. Amendments also required unanimity, which proved impossible to achieve on questions dealing with western lands, an impost, and the proper way to respond to unfair taxation in a republican state. The new Constitution offered a different approach to these problems by loosening the grip of impossible unanimity and by embracing the ideas of a heterogeneous public life and a carefully balanced government that together would prevent any one part of the public from tyrannizing another. The genius of James Madison was to anticipate that diversity of opinion was not only an unavoidable reality but also a hidden strength of the new society beginning to take shape. This is what he meant in *Federalist* essay number 10 when he spoke of the "republican remedy" for the troubles most likely to befall a government in which the people are the source of authority.

Despite Madison's optimism, political differences remained keen and worrisome to many. The Federalists still hoped for a society in which leaders of exceptional wisdom would discern the best path for public policy. They looked backward to a society of hierarchy, rank, and benevolent rule by an aristocracy of talent, but they created a government with forward-looking checks and balances as a guard against corruption, which they figured would most likely emanate from the people. The Antifederalists also looked backward, but to an old order of small-scale direct

democracy and local control, in which virtuous people kept a close eye on potentially corruptible rulers. The Antifederalists feared a national government led by distant, self-interested leaders who needed to be held in check. In the 1790s, these two conceptions of republicanism and of leadership would be tested in real life. And to a degree, these competing visions of leadership, diversity, democracy, and corruption still animate American public life today.

▶ Selected Bibliography

General Works

Lance Banning, *The Sacred Fire of Liberty: James Madison and the Founding of the Federal Republic* (1995).

Gary B. Nash, *The Unknown American Revolution: The Unruly Birth of Democracy and the Struggle to Create America* (2006).

Peter S. Onuf and Cathy D. Matson, *A Union of Interests: Political and Economic Thought in Revolutionary America* (1990).

Jack Rakove, *Revolutionaries: A New History of the Invention of America* (2010).

Robert E. Shalhope, *The Roots of Democracy: American Thought and Culture, 1760–1800* (2004).

Alan Taylor, *The Divided Ground: Indians, Settlers, and the Northern Borderland of the American Revolution* (2006).

Gordon Wood, *The Creation of the American Republic, 1776–1787* (1969).

Alfred F. Young, ed., *Beyond the American Revolution: Explorations in the History of American Radicalism* (1993).

The Confederation Government and the States

Daniel M. Friedenberg, *Life, Liberty, and the Pursuit of Land: The Plunder of Early America* (1992).

Marc W. Kruman, *Between Authority and Liberty: State Constitution Making in Revolutionary America* (1997).

Peter S. Onuf, *Statehood and Union: A History of the Northwest Ordinance* (1987).

Charles Rappleye, *Robert Morris, Financier of the American Revolution* (2010).

Jack N. Rakove, *The Beginnings of National Politics: An Interpretive History of the Continental Congress* (1979).

Citizenship

Ira Berlin, *Many Thousands Gone: The First Two Centuries of Slavery in North America* (1998).

Linda K. Kerber, *Women of the Republic: Intellect and Ideology in Revolutionary America* (1980).

Joanne Pope Melish, *Disowning Slavery: Gradual Emancipation and "Race" in New England, 1780–1860* (1998).

Gary B. Nash and Jean R. Sonderlund, *Freedom by Degrees: Emancipation in Pennsylvania and Its Aftermath* (1991).

Leonard L. Richards, *Shays's Rebellion: The American Revolution's Final Battle* (2002).

Marylynn Salmon, *Women and the Law of Property in Early America* (1986).

Rosemarie Zagarri, *A Woman's Dilemma: Mercy Otis Warren and the American Revolution* (1995).

The Constitution and Ratification

John K. Alexander, *The Selling of the Constitutional Convention: A History of News Coverage* (1990).

Richard Beeman, *Plain, Honest Men: The Making of the American Constitution* (2010).

Carol Berkin, *A Brilliant Solution: Inventing the American Constitution* (2003).

Richard Brookhiser, *Gentleman Revolutionary: Gouverneur Morris, the Rake Who Wrote the Constitution* (2003).

Saul Cornell, *The Other Founders: Anti-Federalism and the Dissenting Tradition in America, 1788–1828* (1999).

Michael Allen Gillespie and Michael Lienesch, eds., *Ratifying the Constitution* (1989).

Woody Holton, *Unruly Americans and the Origins of the Constitution* (2007).

John P. Kaminski and Richard Leffler, *Federalists and Antifederalists: The Debate over the Constitution* (1998).

Cecelia M. Kenyon, *Men of Little Faith: Selected Writings by Cecelia Kenyon* (2003).

Leonard W. Levy, *The Establishment Clause: Religion and the First Amendment* (1994).

Jackson Turner Main, *The Antifederalists: Critics of the Constitution, 1781–1788* (2006).

William Lee Miller, *The First Liberty: Religion and the American Republic* (1986).

Richard B. Morris, *Witnesses at the Creation: Hamilton, Madison, Jay, and the Constitution* (1985).

Jack N. Rakove, *Original Meanings: Politics and Ideas in the Making of the Constitution* (1996).

▶ FOR MORE BOOKS ABOUT TOPICS IN THIS CHAPTER, see the Online Bibliography at bedfordstmartins.com/roark.

▶ FOR ADDITIONAL PRIMARY SOURCES FROM THIS PERIOD, see Michael Johnson, ed., *Reading the American Past*, Fifth Edition.

▶ FOR WEB SITES, IMAGES, AND DOCUMENTS RELATED TO TOPICS AND PLACES IN THIS CHAPTER, visit Make History at bedfordstmartins.com/roark.

Reviewing Chapter 8

REVIEW QUESTIONS

Use key terms and dates to support your answer.

1. Why was the confederation government's authority so limited? (pp. 229–231)

2. How did states determine who would be allowed to vote? (pp. 232–236)

3. Why did farmers in western Massachusetts revolt against the state legislature? (pp. 237–244)

4. Why did the government proposed by the constitutional convention employ multiple checks on each branch? (pp. 245–248)

5. Why did Antifederalists oppose the Constitution? (pp. 248–254)

MAKING CONNECTIONS

Draw on key terms, the timeline, and review questions.

1. Leaders in the new nation held that voting should be restricted to citizens who possessed independence of mind. What did they mean by "independence of mind," and why did they provide for this restriction? How did this principle limit voters in the early Republic?

2. Why did many Revolutionary leaders shaping the government of the new nation begin to find the principle of democracy troubling? How did they attempt to balance democracy with other concerns in the new government?

3. Twenty-first-century Americans see a profound tension between the Revolutionary ideals of liberty and equality and the persistence of American slavery. Did Americans in the late eighteenth century see a tension? How do the official documents cited in this chapter reflect their feelings on the topic of slavery? In your answer, be sure to discuss factors that might have shaped varied responses, such as region, race, and class.

4. The Northwest Territory was the confederation's greatest asset. Discuss the proposals to manage settlement of the new territory. How did they shape the nation's expansion? Which proposals succeeded, and which ones failed?

LINKING TO THE PAST

Link events in this chapter to earlier events.

1. Compare and contrast the complaints against taxation connected with the Stamp Act in 1765 and those resulting from the congressional requisition of 1785. What were the principal arguments in each case? In either case, was it simply a matter of people refusing to pay to support government functions? Why do you think anti–Stamp Act activists like Samuel Adams took a negative view of the 1786 tax protests? (See chapter 6.)

2. Thomas Paine's pamphlet *Common Sense*, which sharply criticized the monarchy, was widely circulated and hailed by rebellious colonists in 1776. In light of the colonists' negative view toward monarchical power leading up to the Revolutionary War, how do you explain the powerful presidency that the victorious Americans set up in 1787? (See chapter 7.)

▶ FOR PRACTICE QUIZZES AND OTHER STUDY TOOLS, visit the Online Study Guide at bedfordstmartins.com/roark.

TIMELINE 1775–1804

1775
- Second Continental Congress begins to meet.

1776
- Declaration of Independence adopted.
- Virginia adopts state bill of rights.

1777
- Articles of Confederation sent to states.

1778
- State constitutions completed.

1780
- Pennsylvania institutes gradual emancipation.

1781
- Articles of Confederation ratified.
- Creation of executive departments.
- Slaves Mum Bett and Quok Walker successfully sue for freedom in Massachusetts.

1782
- Virginia relaxes state manumission law.

1783
- Newburgh Conspiracy exposed.
- Treaty of Paris signed, ending the Revolutionary War.
- Massachusetts extends suffrage to taxpaying free blacks.

1784
- Gradual emancipation laws passed in Rhode Island and Connecticut.
- Treaty of Fort Stanwix.

1785
- Treaty of Fort McIntosh.
- Congress issues requisition for $3 million to the states.

1786
- Shays's Rebellion begins.

1787
- Shays's Rebellion crushed.
- Northwest Ordinance.
- Delaware provides manumission law.
- Constitutional convention meets in Philadelphia.
- *The Federalist Papers* begin to appear in New York newspapers.

1788
- U.S. Constitution ratified.

1789
- Slavery ended in Massachusetts by judicial decision.

1790
- Maryland provides manumission law.

1799
- Gradual emancipation law passed in New York.

1804
- Gradual emancipation law passed in New Jersey.

INAUGURAL BALUSTRADE
This gold-painted iron railing graced the balcony of Federal Hall in New York City, where George Washington took the president's oath of office in 1789 (pictured here in a contemporary engraving). Thirteen arrows, distinct yet united, form the centerpiece of the ornate balustrade. Frenchman Pierre l'Enfant designed it for the inauguration, symbolically turning the much older building into the home of the new Federal Congress. L'Enfant came to revolutionary America with Lafayette, wintered at Valley Forge with Washington, and fought in the southern campaign. His major assignment of the 1790s was the design and planning of an entire city, Washington, D.C.

Balustrade: © Collection of the New-York Historical Society Gift of the Chamber of Commerce of the State of New York; engraving: Library of Congress.

9

The New Nation Takes Form
1789–1800

ALEXANDER HAMILTON, THE NATION'S FIRST SECRETARY OF THE treasury, exercised vast influence over the economic and domestic policy of the new government. Heralded as a brilliant unifier of the pro-Constitution Federalists of 1788, Hamilton in his new role soon proved to be the most polarizing figure of the 1790s.

Determination marked his disadvantaged childhood. Hamilton grew up on a small West Indies island. His parents never married. His father, the impoverished fourth son of a Scottish lord, disappeared when Alexander was nine, and his mother, a woman with a checkered past, died two years later. Jeered as a "whore child," Hamilton developed a fierce ambition to make good. He clerked for a merchant who was so impressed with the lad that he sent him to the mainland colonies for an education. Hamilton started at King's College (now Columbia University) in 1773, but the war intruded. Political articles he wrote for a New York newspaper brought him to the attention of General George Washington, who made the nineteen-year-old his close aide and an officer. After the war, Hamilton practiced law in New York and participated in the constitutional convention in Philadelphia. His astute *Federalist* essays — he produced more than fifty in just a few months — helped secure the ratification of the Constitution.

Hamilton's private life was similarly upwardly mobile. Handsome and now well connected, he married Betsey Schuyler, daughter of a very wealthy New Yorker. Hamilton's magnetic charm attracted both men and women at dinner parties and social gatherings. Late-night socializing, however, never interfered with Hamilton's prodigious capacity for work.

As secretary of the treasury, Hamilton quickly moved into high gear. "If a Government appears to be confident of its own powers, it is the surest way to inspire the same confidence in others," he once remarked. He immediately secured big loans from two banks and started to track tax revenues from trade, the government's main source of income. Most trade was with Britain, so Hamilton sought ways to protect Anglo-American relations. Next he tackled the country's unpaid Revolutionary War debt, writing in three months a forty-thousand-word report for Congress explaining how to fund the debt and pump millions of dollars into the U.S. economy. His bold plan for a national banking system aimed to enhance and control the money supply. Finally, he wrote a richly detailed analysis of ways to promote manufacturing via government subsidies and tariff policies.

Hamilton was both visionary and practical. No one could deny that he was a gifted man with remarkable political intuitions. Yet this magnetic man made enemies in the 1790s, as the "founding fathers" of the Revolution and Constitution became competitors and even bitter rivals. To some extent, jealousy over Hamilton's talents and his access to President Washington explains the chill, but serious differences in political philosophy drove the divisions deeper.

Personalities clashed. Hamilton's charm no longer worked with James Madison, now a representative in Congress and an opponent of all of Hamilton's plans. His charm had never worked with John Adams, the new vice president, who privately called him "the bastard brat of a Scotch pedlar" motivated by "disappointed Ambition and unbridled malice and revenge." Years later, when asked why he had deserted Hamilton, Madison coolly replied, "Colonel Hamilton deserted me." Hamilton assumed that government was safest when in the hands of "the rich, the wise, and the good" — words he used to describe America's commercial elite. For Hamilton, economic and political power naturally belonged together, creating an energetic force for economic growth. By contrast, agrarian values ran deep with Jefferson and Madison, and they were suspicious of get-rich-quick speculators, financiers, and manufacturing development. Differing views of European powers also loomed large in the rivalries. Hamilton admired everything British, while Jefferson was enchanted by France, where he had lived in the 1780s. These loyalties governed foreign relations in the late 1790s, when the United States tangled with both overseas rivals.

The personal and political antagonisms of this first generation of American leaders left their mark on the young country. Leaders generally agreed on Indian policy in the new republic — peace when possible, war when necessary — but on little else. No one was prepared for the intense and passionate polarization over economic and foreign policy. The disagreements were articulated around particular events and policies: taxation and the public debt, a new farmers' rebellion in a western region, policies favoring commercial development, a treaty with Britain, a rebellion in Haiti, and the Quasi-War with France, which led to severe strictures on sedition and free speech. But at their heart, these disagreements sprang from opposing ideologies on the value of democracy, the nature of leadership, and the limits of federal power.

By 1800, the oppositional politics ripening between Hamiltonian and Jeffersonian politicians would begin to crystallize into political parties, the Federalists and the Republicans. To the citizens of that day, this was an unhappy development.

Alexander Hamilton, by John Trumbull
Hamilton was confident, handsome, audacious, brilliant, and very hardworking. Ever slender, in marked contrast to the more corpulent leaders of his day, he posed for this portrait in 1792, at the age of thirty-seven and at the height of his power. CSFB Collection of Americana, NYC.

▶ The Search for Stability

After the struggles of the 1780s, the most urgent task in establishing the new government was to secure stability. Leaders sought ways to heal old divisions, and the first presidential election offered the means to do that in the person of George Washington, who enjoyed widespread veneration. People trusted him to exercise the untested and perhaps elastic powers of the presidency.

Congress had important work as well in initiating the new government. Congress quickly agreed on the Bill of Rights, which answered the concerns of many Antifederalists. In the cultural realm, the private virtue of women was mobilized to bolster the public virtue of male citizens and to enhance political stability. Republicanism was forcing a rethinking of women's relation to the state.

Liverpool Souvenir Pitcher, 1789
A British pottery manufacturer produced this commemorative pitcher for the American market to capture sales at the time of George Washington's inauguration in 1789. The design shows Liberty as a woman dressed in a golden gown, her liberty cap on a pole. She is holding a laurel wreath (signifying classical honors) over Washington's head. Fifteen labeled links encircle the scene, representing the states, although in 1789 Rhode Island and North Carolina had not yet ratified the Constitution, and Vermont and Kentucky were merely anticipated states. The Liverpool manufacturer was looking ahead; commemorative pitchers, jugs, and mugs were commonplace articles of consumer culture produced in Britain for the American market. Smithsonian Institution, Washington, D.C.

Washington Inaugurates the Government

The unanimous election of George Washington in February 1789 was quick work, the tallying of the 69 votes by the electoral college a mere formality. (By contrast, John Adams became vice president with just 34 electoral votes, with the remaining 35 votes split among a variety of candidates; Adams's pride was wounded.) Washington perfectly embodied the republican ideal of disinterested, public-spirited leadership. Indeed, he cultivated that image through astute ceremonies such as the dramatic surrender of his sword to the Continental Congress at the end of the war, symbolizing the subservience of military power to the law, a point he had made previously during the Newburgh Conspiracy (see chapter 8).

Once in office, Washington calculated his moves, knowing that every step set a precedent and that any misstep could be dangerous for the fragile government. Congress debated a title for Washington, ranging from "His Highness, the President of the United States of America and Protector of Their Liberties" to "His Majesty, the President"; Washington favored "His High Mightiness." But in the end, republican simplicity prevailed. The final title was simply "President of the United States of America," and the established form of address became "Mr. President," a subdued yet dignified title in a society where only property-owning adult white males could presume to be called "Mister."

Washington's genius in establishing the presidency lay in his capacity for implanting his own reputation for integrity into the office itself. He was not a brilliant thinker or a shrewd political strategist. He was not even a particularly congenial man. In the political language of the day, he was "virtuous," meaning that he took pains to elevate the public good over private interest and projected honesty and honor over ambition. He remained aloof, resolute, and dignified, to the point of appearing wooden at times. He encouraged pomp and ceremony to create respect for the office, traveling with six horses to pull his coach, hosting formal balls, and surrounding himself with uniformed servants. He even held weekly "levees," as European monarchs did, hour-long audiences granted to distinguished visitors (including women), at which Washington appeared attired in black velvet, with a feathered hat and a polished sword. The president and his guests bowed, avoiding the egalitarian familiarity of a handshake. But he always managed, perhaps just barely, to avoid the extreme of royal splendor.

How Did America's First Congress Address the Question of Slavery?

In its opening months, the First Congress had an ambitious agenda. It established executive departments, the judiciary, and a federal postal system. It crafted the Bill of Rights, debated Alexander Hamilton's *Report on Public Credit*, and ratified its first Indian treaty. Tackling slavery was nowhere on its agenda. Congressmen assumed that key North-South compromises embedded in the Constitution had resolved the issue. But they were wrong: An angry debate over slavery burst forth in early 1790.

In mid-February, citizens of Pennsylvania and New York petitioned Congress to "exercise justice and mercy" and to end the "trafficking in the persons of fellow-men" — that is, the slave trade. The petitioners were Quakers, members of a religion with a long-standing moral objection to slavery. The pragmatic James Madison urged the representatives to refer the petitions to a congressional committee, thus keeping them out of public view. Representatives from South Carolina and Georgia instead urged immediate dismissal, citing the Constitution's ban on interference with the slave trade before 1808. Reaching no agreement, the Congress postponed discussion for a day.

But the next day brought another petition, not coincidentally. Drawn up by a largely Quaker group called the Pennsylvania Abolition Society, it asked Congress "to discourage every species of traffic in the persons of our fellow-men" and to "countenance the restoration of liberty" to slaves. The petition quoted the Constitution to prove the government's duty to "promote the general welfare, and secure the blessings of liberty" for all. That Benjamin Franklin's signature topped the list of petitioners gave it significant political clout.

This second petition was not just about the Atlantic slave trade, which was indeed protected for twenty years by the Constitution. It called for Congress to legislate on the domestic buying and selling of slaves, about which the Constitution was silent. Further, restoring liberty to slaves required an emancipation law, again something not barred by the Constitution. No method was specified "for removing this inconsistency from the character of the American people," but the petitioners expressed confidence in a merciful Congress.

The petitions touched off an explosive debate in the House. Several northern representatives tried to use them to reopen up the contentious issue; representatives from the deep South were adamantly opposed. A rare moment of humor surfaced when a South Carolina member asserted that during ratification, "We took each other, with our mutual bad habits and respective evils, for better, for worse; the Northern States adopted us with our slaves, and we adopted them with their Quakers." No other levity was to be heard. Southerners cited biblical justifications for slavery, argued that slavery civilized slaves, predicted economic collapse if slavery ended, and called the petitioners fanatics. Madison finally got his way: The petitions were referred to a committee, amid mounting concern that newspaper coverage of the debate would create rebelliousness among slaves.

A month later, that committee's report defined a middle road in clarifying the powers of Congress over slavery. As expected, the report affirmed that Congress could not end the slave trade before 1808, but it also concluded that Congress could neither force emancipation nor deny it. And while the report held that Congress had no authority to regulate slave treatment, it urged southern legislatures to pass humanitarian laws regulating the provision of food and housing and the protection of slave women and families. Southern representatives strongly objected to this third pronouncement, touching off yet another bitter public debate in Congress.

Washington chose talented and experienced men to preside over the newly created Departments of War, Treasury, and State. For the Department of War, Washington selected General **Henry Knox**, former secretary of war in the confederation government. For the Treasury — an especially tough job in view of revenue conflicts during the confederation (see chapter 8) — the president appointed **Alexander Hamilton**, known for his general brilliance and financial astuteness. To lead the Department of State, the foreign policy arm of the executive branch, Washington chose **Thomas Jefferson**, a master of diplomatic relations and the current minister to France. For attorney general, Washington picked Edmund Randolph, a Virginian who had attended the

In the end, a shorter report was hammered out in debate as the formal reply to the petitioners, in which the key provision read: "The Congress have no authority to interfere in the emancipation of slaves, or in the treatment of them within any of the States; it remaining with the several States alone to provide any regulation therein, which humanity and true policy may require." The final vote on this amended report was a squeaker, with 29 ayes to 25 nays.

The Quaker groups conceded and ceased filing petitions, but a discouraged Benjamin Franklin made one last attempt to shape public opinion by writing a satirical essay for a Philadelphia newspaper. In it, the elder statesman ridiculed the proslavery speeches by transposing their exact arguments into a bogus document by a purported North African Muslim leader explaining why his country's fifty thousand Christian slaves were better off enslaved than free. It was vintage Franklin — funny, smart, and cutting. It was also Franklin's final public pronouncement; he died suddenly three weeks later, at the age of eighty-four. The congressional report launched by his 1790 petition stood for more than four decades as the silencing mechanism against any attempt at the federal level to disrupt slavery.

Thinking about Cause and Effect

1. Why did Congress answer the Quaker petitioners? Did it have to?

2. What was the result of the Quakers' efforts to abolish slavery? Do you think they were astute political strategists?

3. What was the South Carolina representative implying when he ironically referred to southern slaves and northern Quakers as "mutual bad habits and respective evils"? Do you think he was he talking about slavery as an institution, or slaves as people, in this statement?

constitutional convention but who had turned Antifederalist during ratification. For chief justice of the Supreme Court, Washington designated **John Jay**, a New York lawyer who, along with Madison and Hamilton, had vigorously defended the Constitution in *The Federalist Papers*.

Soon Washington began to hold regular meetings with these men, thereby establishing the precedent of a presidential cabinet. (Vice President John Adams was not included; his only official duty, to preside over the Senate, he found "a punishment." To his wife he complained, "My country has in its wisdom contrived for me the most insignificant office.") No one anticipated that two decades of party turbulence would emerge from the brilliant but explosive mix of Washington's first cabinet.

The Bill of Rights

An important piece of business for the First Congress, meeting in 1789, was the passage of the **Bill of Rights**. Seven states had ratified the Constitution on the condition that guarantees of individual liberties and limitations to federal power be swiftly incorporated. The Federalists of 1787 had thought an enumeration of rights unnecessary, but in 1789 Congressman James Madison understood that healing the divisions of the 1780s was of prime importance. He said, "It will be a desirable thing to extinguish from the bosom of every member of the community, any apprehensions that there are those among his countrymen who wish to deprive them of the liberty for which they valiantly fought and honorably bled."

Madison pulled much of his wording of rights directly from various state constitutions with bills of rights. He enumerated guarantees of freedom of speech, press, and religion; the right to petition and assemble; and the right to be free from unwarranted searches and seizures. One amendment asserted the right to keep and bear arms in support of a "well-regulated militia," to which Madison added, "but no person religiously scrupulous of bearing arms, shall be compelled to render military service in person." That provision for what a later century would call "conscientious objector" status failed to gain acceptance in Congress.

In September 1789, Congress approved a set of twelve amendments and sent them to the states for approval. The process of state ratification took another two years, but there was no serious doubt about the outcome. By 1791, ten amendments were eventually ratified. The First through Eighth Amendments dealt with individual liberties, and the Ninth and Tenth concerned the boundary between federal and state authority. (See the amendments to the U.S. Constitution in appendix I, page A-12.)

Still, not everyone was entirely satisfied. State ratifying conventions had submitted some eighty proposed amendments. Congress never considered proposals to change structural features of the new government, and Madison had no intention of reopening debates about the length of the president's term or the power to levy excise taxes. He also had no thought to use the Bill of Rights to address the status of enslaved people. But others capitalized on the First Amendment's right to petition to force the First Congress into a bitter debate over slavery (see "Historical Question," page 262).

Significantly, no one complained about one striking omission in the Bill of Rights: the right to vote. Only much later was voting seen as a fundamental liberty requiring protection by constitutional amendment — indeed, by four amendments. The Constitution deliberately left the definition of eligible voters to the states because of the existing wide variation in local voting practices. Most of these practices were based on property qualifications, but some touched on religion and, in one unusual case (New Jersey), on sex and race (see chapter 8).

The Republican Wife and Mother

The exclusion of women from political activity did not mean they had no civic role or responsibility. A flood of periodical articles in the 1790s by both male and female writers reevaluated courtship, marriage, and motherhood in light of republican ideals. Tyrannical power in the ruler, whether king or husband, was declared a thing of the past. Affection, not duty, bound wives to their husbands and citizens to their government. In republican marriages, the writers claimed, women had the capacity to reform the morals and manners of men. One male author promised women that "the solidity and stability of the liberties of your country rest with you; since Liberty is never sure, 'till Virtue reigns triumphant. . . . While you thus keep our country virtuous, you maintain its independence."

Until the 1790s, public virtue was strictly a masculine quality. But another sort of virtue enlarged in importance: sexual chastity, a private asset prized as a feminine quality. Essayists of the 1790s explicitly advised young women to use sexual virtue to increase public virtue in men. "Love and courtship . . . invest a lady with more authority than in any other situation that falls to the lot of human beings," one male essayist proclaimed. If women spurned selfish suitors, they could promote good morals more than any social institution could, essayists promised.

Republican ideals also cast motherhood in a new light. Throughout the 1790s, advocates for female education, still a controversial proposition, argued that education would produce better mothers, who in turn would produce better citizens, a concept historians call **republican motherhood**. Benjamin Rush, a Pennsylvania physician and educator, called for female education because "our ladies should be qualified . . . in instructing their sons in the principles of liberty and government." A woman speaker at a Fourth of July picnic in Connecticut in 1799 articulated family duty in service to the state to her all-female audience: "As mothers, wives, sisters, and daughters, we may all be important, [and] teach our little boys, the inestimable value of Freedom, how to blend and harmonize the natural and social rights of man, and as early impressions are indelible, thus assist our dear country, to be as glorious in maintaining, as it was great in gaining her immortal independence." A Massachusetts essayist named **Judith Sargent Murray** favored education that would remake women into self-confident, rational beings. Her first essay of 1790 was boldly titled "On the Equality of the Sexes," but a subsequent essay on education reassured readers that educated women would retain their "characteristic trait" of sweetness. Even Murray had to justify female education in the context of family duty.

This shift in understanding about women's relation to the state was subtle but profoundly important. Politics was still a masculine preserve, but now women's domestic obligations were infused with political meaning, and a few women became so bold as to claim an expanded scope for women's intellectual development as well. But nothing about this shift altered traditional gender relations. The analogy between marriage and civil society worked precisely because of the self-subordination inherent in the term *virtue*. Men should put the public good first, before selfish desires, just as women must put their husbands and families first, before themselves. Women might gain literacy and knowledge, but only in the service of improved domestic duty. In Federalist America, wives and citizens alike should feel affection for and trust in their rulers; neither should ever rebel.

> **REVIEW**   How did political leaders in the 1790s attempt to overcome the divisions of the 1780s?

Republican Womanhood: Judith Sargent Murray
The young woman in this 1772 portrait became known in the 1790s as America's foremost spokeswoman for woman's equality. Judith Sargent Murray wrote essays for the *Massachusetts Magazine* under the pen name "Constantia." Her 1790 essay, "On the Equality of the Sexes," asserted that women had "natural powers" of mind fully the equal of men's. In 1798, she published her collected "Constantia" essays in a book titled *The Gleaner;* George Washington and John Adams each bought a copy. John Singleton Copley, Terra Foundation for American, Chicago/Art Resource, NY.

▶ Hamilton's Economic Policies

The new government had the luck to be launched in flush economic times. Compared to the severe financial instability of the 1780s, the 1790s brimmed with opportunity, as seen in increased agricultural trade and improvements in transportation and banking. In 1790, the federal government moved from New York City to Philadelphia, a more central location with a substantial mercantile class. There, Alexander Hamilton, secretary of the treasury, embarked on his innovative plan to solidify the government's economic base. But controversy arose at every turn. Hamilton's plan to combine the large national debt with unpaid state debts produced a crisis in the First Congress. And his plan to raise revenues via taxation on whiskey brought on the country's first domestic rebellion.

Agriculture, Transportation, and Banking

Dramatic increases in international grain prices motivated American farmers to boost agricultural production for the export trade. Europe's rising population needed grain, and the French Revolutionary and Napoleonic Wars, which engulfed Europe after 1793 for a dozen years, severely compromised production there. From the Connecticut River valley to the Chesapeake, farmers planted more wheat, generating new jobs for millers, coopers, dockworkers, and ship and wagon builders.

Cotton production also underwent a boom, spurred by market demand and a mechanical invention. Limited amounts of smooth-seed cotton had long been grown in the coastal areas of the South, but this variety of cotton did not thrive in the drier inland regions. Greenseed cotton grew well inland, but its rough seeds stuck to the cotton fibers and were labor-intensive to remove. In 1793, Yale graduate Eli Whitney devised a machine called a gin that easily separated out the seeds; cotton production soared, giving a boost to transatlantic trade with Britain, whose factories eagerly processed the raw cotton into cloth.

A surge of road building further stimulated the economy. Before 1790, one bumpy road connected Maine to Georgia, but with the establishment of the U.S. Post Office in 1792, road mileage increased sixfold to facilitate the transport of mail. Private companies also built toll roads, such as the Lancaster Turnpike west of Philadelphia, the Boston-to-Albany turnpike, and a third road from Virginia to Tennessee. By 1800, a dense network of dirt, gravel, and plank roadways connected towns in southern New England and the Middle Atlantic states, spurring commercial stage companies to regularize and speed up passenger traffic. A trip from New York to Boston took four days; from New York to Philadelphia, less than two (Map 9.1). In 1790, Boston had only three stagecoach companies; by 1800, there were twenty-four.

> ### "A national debt if not excessive will be to us a national blessing; it will be a powerful cement of our union."
> — **ALEXANDER HAMILTON**

A third development signaling economic resurgence was the growth of commercial banking. During the 1790s, the number of banks nationwide multiplied tenfold, from three to twenty-nine in 1800. Banks drew in money chiefly through the sale of stock. They then made loans in the form of banknotes, paper currency backed by the gold and silver that stockholders paid in. Because banks issued two or three times as much money in banknotes as

they held in hard money, they were creating new money for the economy.

The U.S. population expanded along with economic development, propelled by large average family size and better than adequate food and land resources. As measured by the first two federal censuses in 1790 and 1800, the population grew from 3.9 million to 5.3 million, an increase of 35 percent.

The Public Debt and Taxes

The upturn in the economy, plus the new taxation powers of the government, suggested that the government might soon repay its wartime debt, amounting to more than $52 million owed to foreign and domestic creditors. But Hamilton had a different plan. He issued a *Report on Public Credit* in January 1790, recommending that the debt be funded — but not repaid immediately — at full value. This meant that old certificates of debt would be rolled over into new bonds, which would earn interest until they were retired several years later. There would still be a public debt, but it would be secure, giving its holders a direct financial stake in the new government. The bonds would circulate, injecting millions of dollars of new money into the economy. "A national debt if not excessive will be to us a national blessing; it will be a powerful cement of our union," Hamilton wrote to a financier. The debt was the "price of liberty," he further argued, and had to be honored, not repudiated. But it would not paid off either: Hamilton's goal was to make the new country creditworthy, not debt-free.

Funding the debt in full was controversial because speculators had already bought up debt certificates cheaply, and Hamilton's report touched off further speculation. (Hamilton himself held no certificates, but his father-in-law held some with a face value of $60,000.) Philadelphia and New York speculators sent agents into backcountry regions looking for certificates of debt whose unwary owners were ignorant about the proposed face-value funding.

Hamilton compounded controversy with his proposal to add to the federal debt another $25 million that some state governments still owed to individuals. During the war, states had obtained supplies by issuing

Major Roads in the 1790s

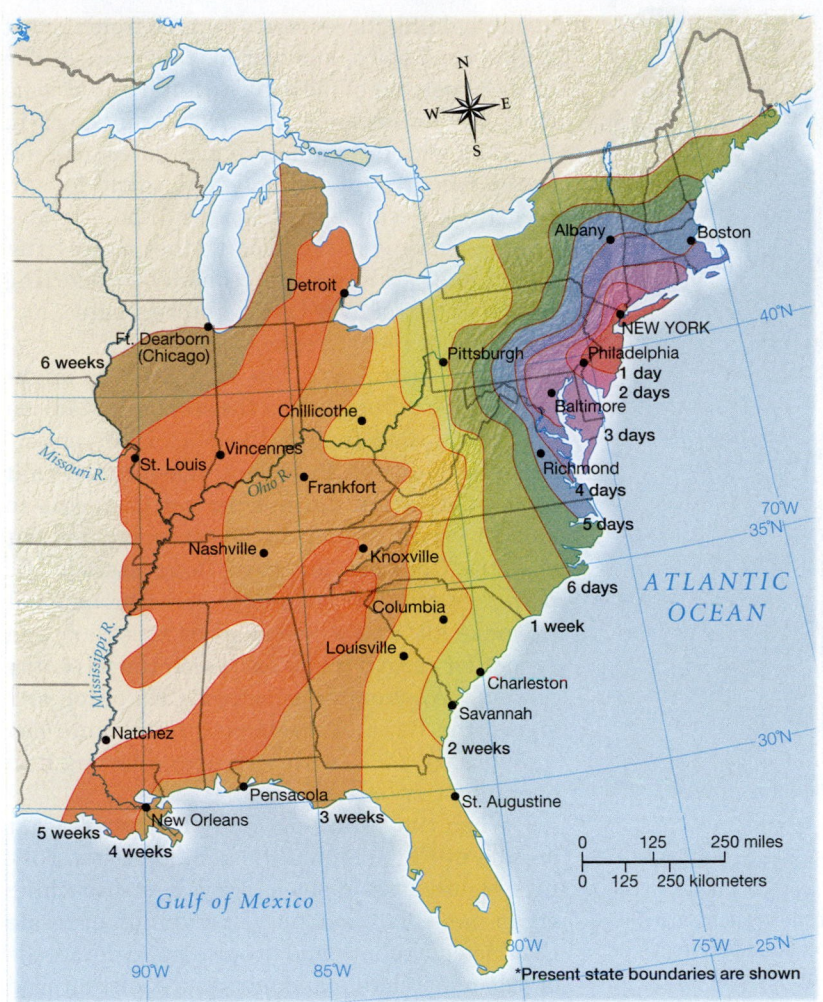

MAP ACTIVITY

Map 9.1 Travel Times from New York City in 1800

Notice that travel out of New York extends over a much greater distance in the first week than in subsequent weeks. River corridors in the West and East speeded up travel — but only if one were going downriver. Also notice that travel by sea (north and south along the coast) was much faster than land travel.

READING THE MAP: Compare this map to the map "Major Roads in the 1790s" (page 266) and to Map 9.2 (page 273). What physical and cultural factors account for the slower travel times west of Pittsburgh?

CONNECTIONS: Why did Americans in the 1790s become so interested in traveling long distances? How did travel times affect the U.S. economy?

IOUs to farmers, merchants, and moneylenders. Some states, such as Virginia and New York, had paid off these debts entirely. Others, such as Massachusetts, had partially paid them off through heavy taxation of the people. About half the states had made little headway. Hamilton called for the federal government to assume these state debts and combine them with the federal debt, in effect consolidating federal power over the states.

Congressman James Madison strenuously objected to putting windfall profits in the pockets of speculators. He instead proposed a complex scheme to pay both the original holders of the federal debt and the speculators, each at fair fractions of the face value. Hamilton countered that tracking the history of traded certificates would be impossible, and further, each prior sale at a devalued price was the correct market price at that moment and could not be undone by the government. Madison also strongly objected to assumption of all the states' debts. A large debt

was dangerous, Madison warned, especially because it would lead to high taxation. Secretary of State Jefferson also was fearful of Hamilton's proposals: "No man is more ardently intent to see the public debt soon and sacredly paid off than I am. This exactly marks the difference between Colonel Hamilton's views and mine, that I would wish the debt paid tomorrow; he wishes it never to be paid, but always to be a thing where with to corrupt and manage the legislature."

A solution to this impasse arrived when Jefferson invited Hamilton and Madison to dinner. Over good food and wine, Hamilton secured the reluctant Madison's promise to restrain his opposition. In return, Hamilton pledged to back efforts to locate the nation's new capital city in the South, along the Potomac River, an outcome that was sure to please Virginians. In early July 1790, Congress voted for the Potomac site, and in late July Congress passed the debt package, assumption and all.

RATE OF TOLL

	Cts
Each foot passenger	3
Horse rider	8
Two wheeled Pleasure carriage	20
Four wheeled do. do.	30
Curricle	30
Cart or waggon by one beast	10
Drawn by two beasts	15
Loaded do.	25
By three do. empty	20
Loaded do.	30
By four do. empty	25
Loaded do.	37½
Each additional beast	5
Sleigh drawn by one beast	10
By two do.	15
Sled by one do.	6¼
By two do.	12½
By four do.	25
Each additional beast	5
Horse jack or mule	4
Neat cattle	3
Sheep & swine each	1

Bridge Toll Sign, 1796
This sign lists an amazing variety of tolls charged for crossing a bridge over the Connecticut River between Cornish, New Hampshire, and Windsor, Vermont, in 1796. Owners of bridges and toll roads collected fees from users of their privately built rights-of-way. Can you deduce any principle of pricing in this list? Is the list exhaustive? What if a boy with a dog attempted to cross the bridge? Do you imagine there were traffic jams at the tollgate? New Hampshire Historical Society.

The First Bank of the United States and the *Report on Manufactures*

The second and third major elements of Hamilton's economic plan were his proposal to create a national **Bank of the United States** and his program to encourage domestic manufacturing. Arguing that banks were the "nurseries of national wealth," Hamilton modeled his bank plan on European central banks, such as the Bank of England, a private corporation that used the government's money to invigorate the British economy. According to Hamilton's plan, the central bank was to be capitalized at $10 million, a sum larger than all the hard money in the entire nation. The federal government would hold 20 percent of the bank's stock, making the bank in effect the government's fiscal agent, holding its revenues derived from import duties, land sales, and various other taxes. The other 80 percent of the bank's capital would come from private investors, who could buy stock in the bank with either hard money (silver or gold) or the recently funded and thus sound federal securities. Because of its size and the privilege of being the only national bank, the central bank would help stabilize the economy by exerting prudent control over credit, interest rates, and the value of the currency.

Concerned that a few rich bankers might have undue influence over the economy, Madison tried but failed to stop the plan in Congress. Jefferson advised President Washington that the Constitution did not permit Congress to charter banks. Hamilton, however, pointed out that the Constitution gave Congress specific powers to regulate commerce and a broad right "to make all laws which shall be necessary and proper for carrying into execution the foregoing powers." Washington sided with Hamilton and signed the Bank of the United States into law in February 1791, with a charter allowing it to operate for twenty years.

When the bank's privately held stock went on sale in Philadelphia, Boston, and New York City in July, it sold out in a few hours, touching off an immediate mania of speculation in resale that lasted a month and drew in many hundreds of urban merchants and artisans. A discouraged Madison reported that in New York "the Coffee House is an eternal buzz with the gamblers," some of them self-interested congressmen intent on "public plunder." Stock prices shot upward and then plunged in mid-August, causing Jefferson to fret about the risk to morality inherent in gambling in stocks: "The spirit of gaming, once it has seized a subject, is incurable. The tailor who has made thousands in one day, tho' he has lost them the next, can never again be content with the slow and moderate earnings of his needle."

The third component of Hamilton's plan was issued in December 1791 in the **Report on Manufactures**, a proposal to encourage the production of American-made goods. Domestic manufacturing was in its infancy, and Hamilton aimed to mobilize the new powers of the federal government to grant subsidies to manufacturers and to impose moderate tariffs on those same products from overseas. Hamilton's plan targeted manufacturing of iron goods, arms and ammunition, coal, textiles, wood products, and glass. Among the blessings of manufacturing, he counted the new employment opportunities that would open to children and unmarried young women, who he assumed were under-utilized in agricultural societies. The *Report on Manufactures*, however, was never approved by Congress, and indeed never even voted on. Many confirmed agriculturalists in Congress feared that manufacturing was a curse rather than a blessing. Madison and Jefferson in particular were alarmed by stretching the "general welfare" clause of the Constitution to include public subsidies to private businesses.

The Whiskey Rebellion

Hamilton's plan to restore public credit required new taxation to pay the interest on the large national debt. In deference to the merchant class, Hamilton did not propose a general increase in import duties, nor did he propose land taxes, which would have fallen hardest on the nation's wealthiest landowners. Instead, he convinced Congress in 1791 to pass a 25 percent excise tax on whiskey, to be paid by farmers when they brought their grain to the distillery, then passed on to individual whiskey consumers in the form of higher prices. Members of Congress from eastern states favored the tax — especially New Englanders, where the favorite drink was rum. A New Hampshire representative observed that the country would be "drinking down the national debt," an idea he evidently found acceptable. More seriously, Virginia representative James Madison hoped that the tax might promote "sobriety and thereby prevent disease and untimely deaths."

Not surprisingly, the new excise tax proved unpopular with grain farmers in the western regions and whiskey drinkers everywhere. In 1791, farmers in Kentucky and the western parts of Pennsylvania, Virginia, Maryland, and the Carolinas forcefully conveyed to Congress their resentment of Hamilton's tax. One farmer complained that he had already paid half his grain to the local distillery for distilling his rye, and now the distiller was taking the new whiskey tax out of the farmer's remaining half. This "reduces the balance to less than one-third of the original quantity. If this is not an oppressive tax, I am at a loss to describe what is so," the farmer wrote. Congress responded with modest modifications to the tax in 1792, but even so, discontent was rampant.

Simple evasion of the law was the most common response. In some places, crowds threatened to tar and feather federal tax collectors, and distilleries underreported their production. Four counties in Pennsylvania established committees of correspondence and held assemblies

The Return for SOUTH CAROLINA having been made since the foregoing Schedule was originally printed, the whole Enumeration is here given complete, except for the N. Western Territory, of which no Return has yet been published.

DISTICTS	Free white Males of 16 years and upwards, including heads of families.	Free white Males under sixteen years.	Free white Females, including heads of families.	All other free persons.	Slaves.	Total.
Vermont	22435	22328	40505	255	16	85539
N. Hampshire	36086	34851	70160	630	158	141885
Maine	24384	24748	46870	538	NONE	96540
Massachusetts	95453	87289	190582	5463	NONE	378787
Rhode Island	16019	15799	32652	3407	948	68825
Connecticut	60523	54403	117448	2808	2764	237946
New York	83700	78122	152320	4654	21324	340120
New Jersey	45251	41416	83287	2762	11423	184139
Pennsylvania	110788	106948	206363	6537	3737	434373
Delaware	11783	12143	22384	3899	8887	59094
Maryland	55915	51339	101395	8043	103036	319728
Virginia	110936	116135	215046	12866	292627	747610
Kentucky	15154	17057	28922	114	12430	73677
N. Carolina	69988	77506	140710	4975	100572	393751
S. Carolina	35576	37722	66880	1801	107094	249073
Georgia	13103	14044	25739	398	29264	82548
	807094	791850	1541263	59150	694280	3893635

Total number of Inhabitants of the United States exclusive of S. Western and N. Territory.	Free white Males of 21 years and upwards.	Free Males under 21 years of age.	Free white Females.	All other persons.	Slaves.	Total
S. W. territory	6271	10277	15365	361	3417	35691
N. Ditto						

VISUAL ACTIVITY

1790 Census Page

This page displays the final tally of the first federal census in 1790, mandated by the U.S. Constitution as the means to determine both representation in Congress and proportional taxation of the states. Notice the choice of five classifications for the count: free white males age sixteen or older, free white males under age sixteen, free white females, all other free persons, and slaves. To implement the Constitution's three-fifths clause (counting slaves as three-fifths of a person), slaves had to be counted separately from all free persons. Separating white males into two broad age groups at sixteen provided a measure of military strength, important to know in times of Indian (or other) wars. U.S. Census Bureau.

READING THE IMAGE: Which northern states still had slaves? Which state had the largest population? Which had the largest white population?

CONNECTIONS: Why did the census separate males from females? Who might "all other free persons" include? Since women, children, and "all other free persons" counted for purposes of apportionment, could it be said that those groups were represented in the new government?

to carry their message to Congress. Hamilton admitted to Congress that the revenue was far less than anticipated. But rather than abandon the law, he tightened up the prosecution of tax evaders.

This will make the 'Squire ... be our fill of grog.

come friend bum I'll take thee to thy mother

for thou art our old friend the long noted pensioner

Just where he hung the people meet.
To see him swinglong musse sweet.

AN EXCISEMAN.

An Exciseman, 1792
This rough cartoon threatens the hated figure of the whiskey tax collector, shown making off with two barrels of the drink. An evil spirit hooks him by the nose to deliver him to the gallows where is he roasted over a flaming barrel of whiskey. The ghoulish poem under the gallows begins: "Just where he hung the people meet/To see him swing was music sweet." Text below the cartoon (not shown here) explains that "Distillers and Farmers pay all due deference and respect to Congress" and will "contribute amply" to government, but they hate harassment by a tax collector. Courtesy of the Historical Society of Pennsylvania Collection Atwater Kent Museum of Philadelphia.

In western Pennsylvania, Hamilton had one ally, a stubborn tax collector named John Neville who refused to quit even after a group of spirited farmers burned him in effigy. In May 1794, Neville filed charges against seventy-five farmers and distillers for tax evasion. His action touched off the **Whiskey Rebellion**. In July, he and a federal marshal were ambushed in Allegheny County by a group of forty men. Neville's house was then burned to the ground by a crowd estimated at five hundred, and one man in the crowd was killed. At the end of July, seven thousand Pennsylvania farmers planned a march — or perhaps an attack, some thought — on Pittsburgh to protest the hated tax.

In response, President Washington nationalized the Pennsylvania militia and set out, with Hamilton at his side, at the head of thirteen thousand soldiers. A worried Philadelphia newspaper criticized the show of force: "Shall Pennsylvania be converted into a human slaughter house because the dignity of the United States will not admit of conciliatory measures? Shall torrents of blood be spilled to support an odious excise system?" But in the end, no blood was spilled. By the time the army arrived in late September, the demonstrators had dispersed. No battles were fought, and no shots were exchanged. Twenty men were rounded up as rebels and charged with high treason, but only two were convicted, and both were soon pardoned by Washington.

Had the federal government overreacted? Thomas Jefferson thought so; he saw the event as a replay of Shays's Rebellion of 1786, when a protest against government taxation had been met with unreasonable government force (see chapter 8). The rebel farmers agreed; they felt entitled to protest oppressive taxation. Hamilton and Washington, however, thought that laws passed by a republican government must be obeyed. To them, the Whiskey Rebellion presented an opportunity for the new federal government to flex its muscles and stand up to civil disorder.

REVIEW   Why were Hamilton's economic policies controversial?

▶ Conflict on America's Borders and Beyond

While the whiskey rebels challenged federal leadership from within the country, disorder threatened the United States from external sources as well. From 1789 onward, serious trouble brewed in four directions. To the southwest, the loosely confederated Creek Indians pushed back against the western thrust of the white southern population, which gave George Washington the opportunity to test the use of diplomacy and avoid costly war. To the northwest, a powerful confederation of Indian tribes in the Ohio Country went to formidable lengths to scare away white settlers, resulting in six years of brutal warfare. At the same time, conflicts between the major European powers forced Americans to take sides and nearly thrust the country into another war, this time across the Atlantic. And to the south, a Caribbean slave rebellion raised fears that racial war could arise in the United States. Despite these conflicts and the grave threats they posed to the young country, Washington won reelection to the presidency unanimously in the fall of 1792.

Creeks in the Southwest

An urgent task of the new government was to take charge of Indian affairs, ending the ambiguous divided authority between state and confederation government that had characterized the 1780s. Washington and his secretary of war, Henry Knox, hoped to secure peace with the Indians, partly out of a sense of fair play but also over worries about the expense of warfare. Some twenty thousand Indians affiliated with the Creeks occupied lands extending from Georgia into what is now Mississippi, and border skirmishes with land-hungry Georgians were becoming a frequent occurrence. Knox and Washington singled out one Creek chief, **Alexander McGillivray**, and sent a delegation to Georgia for preliminary treaty negotiations.

McGillivray, the son of a Scottish trader and a French-Creek mother, had an unusual history that prepared him to be a major cultural broker. His maternal line conferred a legitimate claim to Creek leadership; his paternal line afforded him access to the literacy and numeracy taught in American schools. Fluent in English and near fluent in Spanish, McGillivray spoke several Creek languages and had even studied Greek and Latin. In the 1770s, he worked for the British distributing gifts to various southern tribes; in the 1780s, he gained renown for brokering negotiations with the Spanish in Florida. The chief agreed to meet with Knox's delegates with some reluctance, since the Creeks' military strength at that point was quite sufficient to keep Georgia settlers at bay.

The American negotiators offered substantial terms to McGillivray, most notably a guarantee of the Creeks' extensive tribal lands and a promise to protect their borders from white settlers. In return, they asked him to cede a disputed tract of land where settlers already lived. But McGillivray sent the negotiators away, enjoying, as he wrote to a Spanish trader, the spectacle of the self-styled "masters of the new world" having "to bend and supplicate for peace at the feet of a people whom shortly before they despised."

A year later, Secretary Knox renewed efforts for a treaty. Georgia settlers and land speculators continued to push onto Creek land. Because of the war brewing north of the Ohio River with the much more belligerent tribes of the Northwest, the federal government had no military resources to spare. To coax McGillivray to the treaty table, Knox invited him to New York City to meet with the president himself. McGillivray arrived in a triumphal procession, joined by twenty-seven lesser chiefs and their entourages. The Creek leader was accorded the honors of a head of state.

The negotiations stretched out for a month in the capital city. In the end, the 1790 **Treaty of New York** incorporated Knox's original plan: Creek tribal lands were guaranteed, with a promise of boundary protection by federal troops against land-seeking settlers. The Creeks were assured of annual payments in money and trade goods, including "domestic animals and implements of husbandry" — words that hinted at a future time when the Creeks would become more agricultural and thus less in need of expansive hunting grounds. The Creeks promised to accept the United States alone as its trading partner, shutting out Spain. At the signing ceremony, Washington read the treaty aloud, with a translator repeating each article to the assembled

Alexander McGillivray, 1790

When the Creek delegation came to New York City to negotiate a treaty, artist Jonathan Trumball was on hand. He showed the guests a portrait he had just completed of George Washington; the Indians professed amazement. "I had been desirous of obtaining portraits of some of the principal men, who possessed a dignity of manner, form, countenance and expression, worthy of Roman Senators," Trumball recalled, but all declined to sit for him. So the artist made five drawings "by stealth." McGillivray is shown wearing an American military coat, a present from Washington, with epaulettes of the rank of brigadier general. Charles Allen Munn Collection, Fordham University Library, Bronx, New York.

chiefs. But both sides had made promises they could not keep. McGillivray thought that the Creeks' interests were best served by maintaining creative tension between the American and Spanish authorities, and by 1792, he had signed an agreement with the Spanish governor of New Orleans, in which each side offered mutual pledges to protect against encroachments by Georgia settlers. By the time Alexander McGillivray died in 1793, his purported leadership of the Creeks was in serious question, and the Treaty of New York joined the list of treaties never fully implemented. Its promise of federal border protection of Creek boundaries was unrealistic from the start, and its pledge of full respect for Creek sovereignty also was only a promise on paper.

At the very start of the new government, in dealing with the Creeks, Washington and Knox tried to find a different way to approach Indian affairs, one rooted more in British than in American experience. But in the end, the demographic imperative of explosive white population growth and westward-moving, land-seeking settlers, together with the economic imperative of land speculation, meant that confrontation with the native population was nearly inevitable. As Washington wrote in 1796, "I believe scarcely any thing short of a Chinese Wall, or line of Troops will restrain Land Jobbers, and the encroachment of Settlers, upon Indian Territory."

Ohio Indians in the Northwest

In the 1783 Treaty of Paris, Britain had yielded all land east of the Mississippi River to the United States without regard to the resident Indian population. The 1784 Treaty of Fort Stanwix (see chapter 8) had attempted to solve that omission by establishing terms between the new confederation government and native peoples, but the various key tribes of the Ohio Valley — the Shawnee, Delaware, and Miami — had not been involved in those negotiations. To confuse matters further, British troops still occupied half a dozen forts in the northwest, protecting an ongoing fur trade between British traders and Indians and thereby sustaining Indians' claims to that land.

The doubling of the American population from two million in 1770 to nearly four million in 1790 greatly intensified the pressure for western land. Several thousand settlers a year moved down the Ohio River in the mid-1780s. Most

"I have always been of the opinion that we never should have a permanent peace with those Indians until they were made to experience our superiority."
—General ANTHONY WAYNE

headed for Kentucky on the south bank of the river, but some eyed the forests to the north, in Indian country. By the late 1780s, government land sales in eastern Ohio had commenced, although actual settlement lagged.

Meanwhile, the U.S. Army entered the western half of Ohio, where white settlers did not dare to go. Fort Washington, built on the Ohio River in 1789 at the site of present-day Cincinnati, became the command post for three major invasions of Indian country (Map 9.2). General Josiah Harmar, under orders to subdue the Indians of western Ohio, marched with 1,400 men into Ohio's northwest region in the fall of 1790, burning Indian villages. His inexperienced troops were ambushed by Miami and Shawnee Indians led by their chiefs, **Little Turtle** and **Blue Jacket**. Harmar lost one-eighth of his soldiers.

Harmar's defeat spurred efforts to clear Ohio for permanent American settlement. General **Arthur St. Clair**, the military governor of the Northwest Territory, had pursued peaceful tactics in the 1780s, signing treaties with Indians for land in eastern Ohio — dubious treaties, as it happened, since the Indian negotiators were not authorized to yield land. In the wake of Harmar's bungled operation, St. Clair geared up for military action, and in the fall of 1791 he led two thousand men (accompanied by two hundred women camp followers) north from Fort Washington to claim Ohio territory from the Miami and Shawnee tribes. Along the route, St. Clair's men quickly built two forts, named for Hamilton and Jefferson. However, when the Indians attacked at daybreak on November 4 at the headwaters of the Wabash River, St. Clair's army was not protected by fortifications.

Before noon, 55 percent of the Americans were dead or wounded; only three of the women escaped alive. "The savages seemed not to fear anything we could do," wrote an officer afterward. "The ground was literally covered with the dead." The Indians captured valuable weaponry, scalped and dismembered the dying, and pursued fleeing survivors for miles. With more than nine hundred lives lost, this was the most stunning American loss in the history of the U.S.-Indian wars. Grisly tales of St. Clair's defeat became instantly infamous, increasing the level of terror that Americans brought to their confrontations with the Indians.

Washington doubled the U.S. military presence in Ohio and appointed a new commander, General Anthony Wayne of Pennsylvania, nicknamed "Mad Anthony" for his headstrong, hard-drinking style of leadership. About the Ohio natives, Wayne wrote, "I have always been of the opinion that we never should have a permanent peace

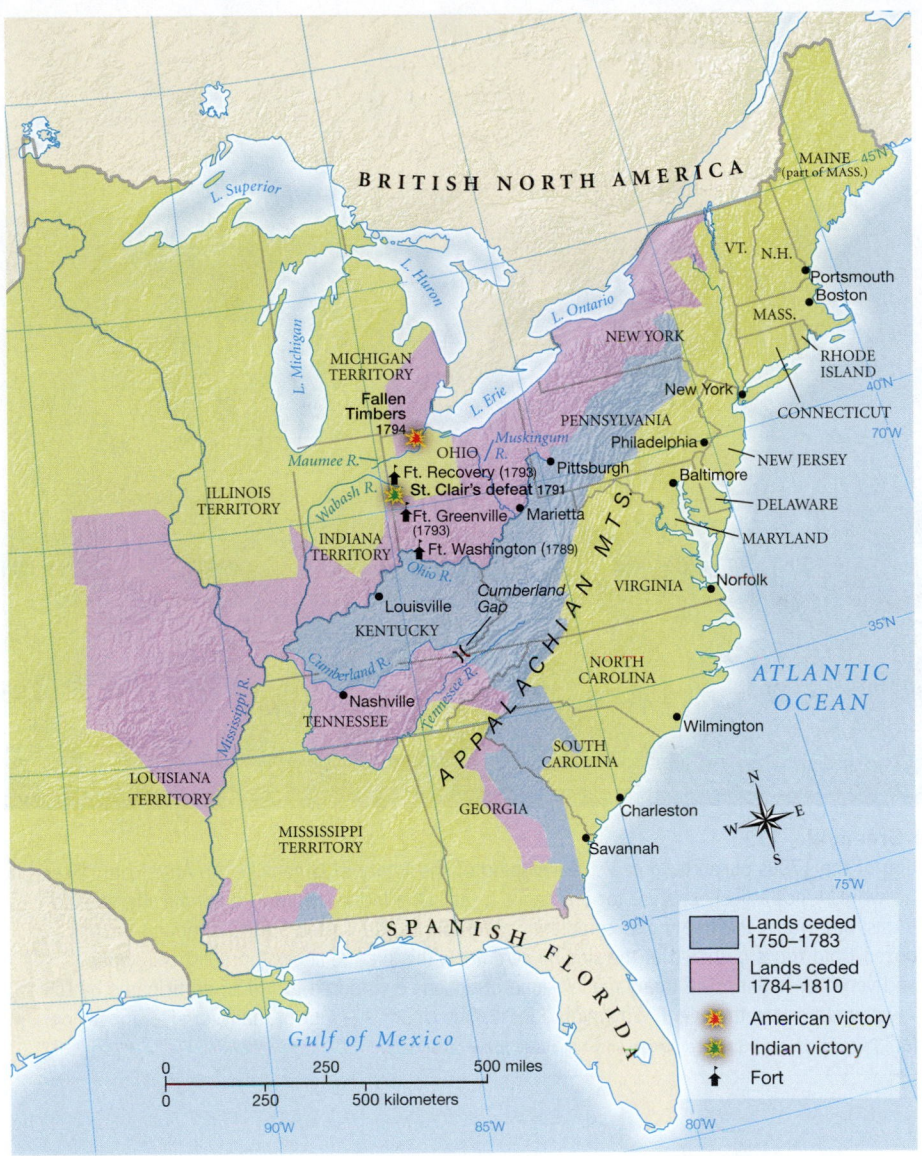

MAP ACTIVITY

Map 9.2   Western Expansion and Indian Land Cessions to 1810
By the first decade of the nineteenth century, intense Indian wars had resulted in significant cessions of land to the U.S. government by treaty.

READING THE MAP: Locate the Appalachians. The Proclamation Line of 1763 that ran along these mountains forbade colonists to settle west of the line. How well was that purpose met?

CONNECTIONS: How much did the population of the United States grow between 1750 and 1790? How did this growth affect western settlement?

with those Indians until they were made to experience our superiority." Throughout 1794, Wayne's army engaged in skirmishes with Shawnee, Delaware, and Miami Indians. Chief Little Turtle of the Miami tribe advised negotiation; in his view, Wayne's large army looked overpowering. But Blue Jacket of the Shawnees counseled continued warfare, and his view prevailed.

The decisive action came in August 1794 at the **battle of Fallen Timbers**, near the Maumee River where a recent tornado had felled many trees. The confederated Indians — mainly Ottawas, Potawatomis, Shawnees, and Delawares numbering around eight hundred — ambushed the Americans but were underarmed, and Wayne's troops made effective use of their guns and bayonets. The Indians withdrew and sought refuge at nearby Fort Miami, still held by the British, but their former allies locked the gate and refused

protection. The surviving Indians fled to the woods, their ranks decimated.

Fallen Timbers was a major defeat for the Indians. The Americans had destroyed cornfields and villages on the march north, and with winter approaching, the Indians' confidence was sapped. They reentered negotiations in a much less powerful bargaining position. In 1795, about a thousand Indians representing nearly a dozen tribes met with Wayne and other American emissaries to work out the **Treaty of Greenville**. The Americans offered treaty goods (calico shirts, axes, knives, blankets, kettles, mirrors, ribbons, thimbles, and abundant wine and liquor casks) worth $25,000 and promised additional shipments every year. The government's idea was to create a dependency on American goods to keep the Indians friendly. In exchange, the Indians ceded most of Ohio to the Americans;

Treaty of Greenville, 1795
This painting of the 1790s purports to depict the signing of the Treaty of Greenville. An American officer kneels and writes—not a likely posture for drafting a treaty. One Indian gestures emphatically, as if to dictate terms, but in fact the treaty was completely favorable to the United States. Although Indians from a dozen Ohio tribes gathered at the signing ceremony, this picture shows unrealistically open spaces and very few Indians. The treaty medal—one of dozens distributed to Indian participants by U.S. officials—commemorates the event. Why might "E Pluribus Unum"—"Out of many, one"—appear on the medal? Painting: Chicago Historical Society; medal: Indiana Historical Society.

only the northwest part of the territory was reserved solely for the Indians.

The treaty brought temporary peace to the region, but it did not restore a peaceful life to the Indians. The annual allowance from the United States too often came in the form of liquor. "More of us have died since the Treaty of Greenville than we lost by the years of war before, and it is all owing to the introduction of liquor among us," said Chief Little Turtle in 1800. "This liquor that they introduce into our country is more to be feared than the gun and tomahawk."

France and Britain

While Indian battles engaged the American military in the west, another war overseas to the east was also closely watched. Since 1789, revolution had been raging in France. At first, the general American reaction was positive, for it was flattering to think that the American Revolution had inspired imitation in France. As monarchy and privilege were overthrown in France, towns throughout America celebrated the victory of the French people with civic feasts and public festivities. Dozens of pro-French political clubs, called democratic or republican societies, sprang up around the country.

Many American women exhibited solidarity with revolutionary France by donning tricolor cockades, decorative knots of red, white, and blue ribbons. Pro-French headgear for committed women included an elaborate turban, leading one horrified Federalist newspaper editor to chastise the "fiery frenchified dames" thronging Philadelphia's streets. In Charleston, South Carolina, a pro-French pageant in 1793 united two women as partners, one representing France and the other America. The women repudiated their husbands "on account of ill treatment" and "conceived the design of living together in the strictest union and friendship," while a gun salute

Revolutionary Solidarity

In the early 1790s, those Americans enthused by the French Revolution might accessorize with a tricolor cockade — a distinctive bow made from red, white, and blue ribbons. American newspapers avidly reported details of Parisian revolutionary fashions for women, as shown in this French picture. Another short-lived, pro-French fad appeared in marriage announcements in Boston, Hartford, and Philadelphia newspapers in the early months of 1793, in which grooms adopted *Citizen* as their title of address, with the corresponding term *Citess* for brides. (*Citess* was invented on the spot and spelled eighteenth-century style with a character shaped like the letter *f*.) In France, *Citoyen* and *Citoyenne* enjoyed widespread use as egalitarian titles of address. Outfit: Bibliothèque Nationale de France; Announcement: Courtesy, American Antiquarian Society.

MARRIED,
By Citizen *Thacher*, Citizen FREDERICK W. GEYER, jun. to Citess REBECCA, daughter to Citizen NATHAN FRAZER.
— On Thursday Evening last, by Citizen *Lathrop*, Citizen JONATHAN WILD, to Citess MARY, daughter to Citizen SAMUEL RIDGWAY.

sealed the pledge. Most likely, this ceremony was not the country's first civil union but instead a richly metaphorical piece of street theater in which the spurned husbands represented the French and British monarchies. In addition to these purely symbolic actions, the growing exchange of political and intellectual ideas across the Atlantic helped plant the seeds of a woman's rights movement in America (see "Beyond America's Borders," page 276).

Anti–French Revolution sentiments also ran deep. Vice President John Adams, who lived in France in the 1780s, trembled to think of radicals in France or America. "Too many Frenchmen, after the example of too many Americans, pant for the equality of persons and property," Adams said. "The impracticability of this, God Almighty has decreed, and the advocates for liberty, who attempt it, will surely suffer for it."

Support for the French Revolution remained a matter of personal conviction until 1793, when Britain and France went to war and French versus British loyalty became a critical foreign policy debate. France had helped America substantially during the American Revolution, and the confederation government had signed an alliance in 1778 promising aid if France were ever under attack. Americans optimistic about the eventual outcome of the French Revolution wanted to deliver on that promise. But those shaken by the report of the guillotining of thousands of French people — including the king and queen — as well as those with strong commercial ties to Britain sought ways to stay neutral.

In May 1793, President Washington issued the Neutrality Proclamation, which contained friendly assurances to both sides, in an effort to stay out of European wars. Yet American ships continued to trade between the French West Indies and France. In late 1793 and early 1794, the British expressed their displeasure by capturing more than three hundred of these vessels near the West Indies. Clearly, something had to be done to assert American power.

President Washington sent John Jay, the chief justice of the Supreme Court and a man of strong pro-British sentiments, to England in 1794 to negotiate commercial relations in the British West Indies and secure compensation for the seizure of American ships. In addition, Jay was supposed to resolve several long-standing problems. Southern planters wanted reimbursement for the slaves lured away by the British army during the war, and western settlers wanted Britain to vacate the frontier

France, Britain, and Woman's Rights in the 1790s

During the 1770s and 1780s, no one in America wondered publicly about rights for women. Boycotts by the Daughters of Liberty before the Revolution did not challenge gender hierarchy, nor did New Jersey's handful of women voters (see chapter 8). It took radical ideas from France and Britain to spark new ideas challenging women's subordinate status in American society.

In France between 1789 and 1793, the revolution against monarchy enlarged ideas about citizenship and led some women to call themselves *citoyennes*, female citizens. Women's political clubs, such as the Society of Republican Revolutionary Women in Paris, sent petitions and gave speeches to the National Assembly, demanding education, voting rights, and a curbing of patriarchal powers of men over women. In 1791, Frenchwoman Olympe de Gouges rewrote the male revolutionaries' document *The Declaration of the Rights of Man* into *The Rights of Woman*, a manifesto asserting that "all women are born free and remain equal to men in rights." Another prominent woman, Anne Josèphe Théroigne de Méricourt, maintained

a political *salon* (intellectual gathering), marched around Paris in masculine riding attire, and addressed crowds engaged in violent street actions. Her vision went beyond political rights to the social customs that dictated women's subordination: "It is time for women to break out of the shameful incompetence in which men's ignorance, pride, and injustice have so long held us captive."

Although the male National Assembly never approved voting rights for French women in that era, it did reform French civil and family law in the early 1790s. Marriage was removed from the control of the church, divorce was legalized, and the age of majority for women was lowered. A far-reaching change in inheritance law required division of a patriarch's estate among all his children, regardless of age, sex, and even legitimacy. By contrast, most American states adopted traditional English family law virtually unchanged.

French feminism traveled across the Channel to Britain and directly inspired a talented woman named Mary Wollstonecraft. Born into a respectable but downwardly mobile

family, the self-educated Wollstonecraft took work as a governess before establishing herself as a writer in London. There she met the radical Thomas Paine and the philosopher William Godwin, along with other leading artists and intellectuals. In 1792, she published *A Vindication of the Rights of Woman*, offering a contrast to Paine's 1791 book *The Rights of Man*. Where Paine talked about property and politics as fundamental rights and never considered women, Wollstonecraft argued that women, as humans, also had inherent rights. She spoke forcefully about the intellectual equality of the sexes that would become evident once women could get an equal education. She championed female economic independence and, most radically, suggested that traditional marriage at its worst was legalized prostitution.

Wollstonecraft's book created an immediate sensation in America. Excerpts appeared in periodicals, bookstores stocked the London edition, and by 1795 there were three American reprints. Some women readers were cautious. A sixty-year-old Philadelphian, Elizabeth Drinker, reflected in her diary, "In very many of her sentiments, she, as some of our friends say, speaks my mind; in some others, I do not altogether coincide with her. I am not for quite so much independence." Others embraced Wollstonecraft's ideas. In 1794, a youthful Priscilla Mason delivered a biting commencement address at a Philadelphia girls' academy, inspired by Wollstonecraft to condemn "the high and mighty

forts still occupied because of their proximity to the Indian fur trade.

Jay returned from his diplomatic mission with a treaty that no one could love. First, the **Jay Treaty** failed to address the captured cargoes or the lost property in slaves. Second, it granted the British a lenient eighteen months to withdraw from the frontier forts, as well as continued rights in the fur trade. (This provision disheartened the Indians just then negotiating the Treaty of Greenville in Ohio. It was a significant factor in their decision to make peace.) Finally, the treaty

called for repayment with interest of the debts that some American planters still owed to British firms dating from the Revolutionary War. In exchange for such generous terms, Jay secured limited trading rights in the West Indies and agreement that some issues — boundary disputes with Canada and the damage and loss claims of shipowners — would be decided later by arbitration commissions.

When newspapers published the terms of the treaty, powerful opposition emerged from Maine to Georgia. In Massachusetts, graffiti

FRONTISPIECE.

Publish'd at Philad.ᵃ Dec.ʳ 1.ˢᵗ 1792.

Woman's Rights in the _Lady's Magazine_, 1792
A new Philadelphia publication aimed at women readers commissioned this engraving to accompany excerpts from Mary Wollstonecraft's _A Vindication of the Rights of Woman_. Lady Liberty, on the left in Greek dress, shares a paper titled "Rights of Woman" with a young woman in eighteenth-century garb. Notice the objects arranged below Liberty: a book, a musical instrument, an artist's palette, a globe, and a page of geometrical shapes. The kneeling figure seems to gesture toward them. What do they suggest about the nature of the "rights of woman" that this picture endorses? Library Company of Philadelphia.

that same July Fourth rejected Wollstonecraft with the claim that woman's rights really meant a woman's duty "to submit to the control of that government she has voluntarily chosen" — namely, the government of a husband.

The interest in the rights of woman faded fast, however. The unhappy fate of de Gouges, guillotined in France in 1794 for her criticism of French leaders, was soon followed by the news of Wollstonecraft's death in childbirth in 1797. Soon thereafter, William Godwin, father of her infant daughter, revealed details of her unconventional personal life, including news of love affairs, two children conceived out of wedlock, and two suicide attempts. "Her licentious practice renders her memory odious to every friend of virtue," declared a prominent American minister in 1801, shutting down nearly all possibility for continued public admiration of Wollstonecraft and her ideas about women.

America in a Global Context

1. Contrast the radical ideas of Mary Wollstonecraft with the more moderate concept of "republican motherhood," which summarizes American women's contributions to civil society and family life.

2. Why might Wollstonecraft's unconventional personal life cast doubt on the value of her ideas about the rights of woman?

lords" (men) who denied women education and professional opportunities. "Happily, a more liberal way of thinking begins to prevail. . . . Let us by suitable education, qualify ourselves for those high departments," Mason said.

Male readers' responses were varied as well. Aaron Burr, a senator from New York, called Wollstonecraft's book "a work of genius." A Fourth of July speaker in New Jersey in 1793 proclaimed that "the Rights of Woman are no longer strange sounds to an American ear" and called for revisions in state law codes. Critics of Wollstonecraft's ideas were not in short supply. A New York orator on

appeared on walls: "Damn John Jay! Damn everyone who won't damn John Jay! Damn everyone who won't stay up all night damning John Jay!" Bonfires in many places burned effigies of Jay and copies of the treaty. Nevertheless, the treaty passed the Senate in 1795 by a vote of 20 to 10. Some representatives in the House, led by Madison, tried to undermine the Senate's approval by insisting on a separate vote on the funding provisions of the treaty, on the grounds that the House controlled all spending bills. Finally, in 1796, the House approved funds to implement

the various commissions mandated by the treaty, but by only a three-vote margin. The bitter vote in both houses of Congress divided along the same lines as the Hamilton-Jefferson split on economic policy.

The Haitian Revolution

In addition to the Indian troubles and the European wars across the Atlantic, yet another bloody conflict to the south polarized and even terrorized many Americans in the 1790s. The French colony

of Saint Domingue, in the western third of the large Caribbean island of Hispaniola, became engulfed in revolution starting in 1791. Bloody war raged for more than a decade, resulting in 1804 in the birth of the Republic of Haiti, the first and only independent black state to arise out of a successful slave revolution.

The **Haitian Revolution** was a complex event involving many participants, including the diverse local population and, eventually, three European countries. Some 30,000 whites dominated the island in 1790, running sugar and coffee plantations with the enslaved labor of close to half a million blacks, two-thirds of them of African birth. The white French colonists were not the only plantation owners, however. About 28,000 free mixed-race people (*gens de couleur*) owned one-third of the island's plantations and nearly a quarter of the slave labor force. Despite their economic status, these mixed-race planters were barred from political power, but they aspired to it.

The French Revolution of 1789 was the immediate catalyst for rebellion in this already tense society. First, white colonists challenged the white royalist government in an effort to link Saint Domingue with the new revolutionary government in France. Next, the mixed-race planters rebelled in 1791, demanding equal civil rights with the whites. No sooner was this revolt viciously suppressed than another part of the island's population rose up; thousands of slaves armed with machetes and torches wreaked devastation and slaughter. In 1793, the civil war escalated to include French, Spanish, and British troops fighting the inhabitants and also one another. Led by former slave Toussaint L'Ouverture, slaves and free blacks in alliance with Spain occupied the northern

Haitian Revolution, 1791–1804

- Beginning of slave revolt, 1791
- Border of Saint Domingue/ Santo Domingo, 1790
- Border of Haiti/ Santo Domingo, 1820

CUBA (Sp.)

HISPANIOLA   *ATLANTIC OCEAN*

Le Cap   Fort Dauphin

SAINT DOMINGUE (France)   SANTO DOMINGO (Spain)

Port-au-Prince

Caribbean Sea

regions of the island, leaving a thousand plantations in ruins and tens of thousands of people dead. Thousands of white and mixed-race planters, along with some of their slaves, fled to Spanish Louisiana and southern cities in the United States. Charleston alone accepted so many refugees that the city's population was one-sixth French in the early nineteenth century.

White Americans followed the revolution in fascinated horror through newspapers and refugees' accounts. A few sympathized with the impulse for liberty, but others feared that violent black insurrection might spread to the United States. White refugees were welcomed in Charleston, Norfolk, and Richmond, but French-speaking blacks, whether free or slave, were eventually barred from entry to all southern states except Virginia. Many black American slaves also fastened on news of the

Toussaint L'Ouverture
This French engraving made around 1800 depicts the Haitian leader in full military dress and feathered hat commandingly issuing a document to French officers. Library of Congress.

revolution, hearing about it from dockworkers, black sailors, and refugees and through oral networks in taverns and shops. The amazing news of the success of a first-ever massive revolution by slaves traveled quickly in this oral culture. Whites complained of behaviors that might prefigure plots and conspiracies, such as increased insolence and higher runaway rates among slaves.

The Haitian Revolution provoked naked fear of a race war in white southerners. Jefferson, agonizing over the contagion of liberty in 1797, wrote another Virginia slaveholder that "if something is not done, and soon done, we shall be the murderers of our own children . . . ; the revolutionary storm, now sweeping the globe, will be upon us, and happy if we make timely provision to give it an easy passage over our land. From the present state of things in Europe and America, the day which brings our combustion must be near at hand; and only a single spark is wanting to make that day to-morrow."

Jefferson's cataclysmic fears were not shared by New Englanders. Timothy Pickering of Massachusetts, in Washington's cabinet since 1795, chastised the inconsistent Jefferson for supporting French revolutionaries while condemning black Haitians fighting for freedom just because they had "a skin not colored like our own." Not that Pickering supported either type of violent revolutionary — he did not. But he and his political allies, soon to be called the Federalists, were far more willing to contemplate trade and diplomatic relations with the emerging black republic of Haiti.

REVIEW   Why did the United States feel vulnerable to international threats in the 1790s?

▶ Federalists and Republicans

By the mid-1790s, polarization over the French Revolution, Haiti, the Jay Treaty, and Hamilton's economic plans had led to two distinct and consistent rival political groups: **Federalists** and **Republicans**. Politicians and newspapers adopted these labels, words that summarized conflicting political positions. Federalist leaders supported Britain in foreign policy and commercial interests at home, while Republicans rooted for liberty in France and worried about monarchical Federalists at home. The labels did not yet describe full-fledged political parties; such division was still thought to be a sign of failure of the experiment in government. Even so, Washington's decision not to seek a third term led to serious partisan electioneering in the presidential and congressional elections of 1796. Federalist John Adams won the presidency, but party strife accelerated over failed diplomacy in France, bringing the United States to the brink of war. Pro-war and antiwar antagonism created a major crisis over political free speech, militarism, and fears of sedition and treason.

The Election of 1796

Washington struggled to appear to be above party politics, and in his farewell address he stressed the need to maintain a "unity of government" reflecting a unified body politic. He also urged the country to "steer clear of permanent alliances with any portion of the foreign world." The leading contenders for his position, John Adams of Massachusetts and Thomas Jefferson of Virginia, in theory agreed with him, but around them raged a party contest split along pro-British versus pro-French lines.

Adams and Jefferson were not adept politicians in the modern sense, skilled in the arts of persuasion and intrigue. Bruised by his conflicts with Hamilton, Jefferson had resigned as secretary of state in 1793 and retreated to Monticello, his home in Virginia. Adams's job as vice president kept him closer to the political action, but his personality often put people off. He was temperamental, thin-skinned, and quick to take offense.

The leading Federalists informally caucused and chose Adams as their candidate, with Thomas Pinckney of South Carolina to run with him. The Republicans settled on Aaron Burr of New York to pair with Jefferson. The Constitution did not anticipate parties and tickets. Instead, each electoral college voter could cast two votes for any two candidates, but on only one ballot. The top vote-getter became president, and the next-highest assumed the vice presidency. (This procedural flaw was corrected by the Twelfth Amendment, adopted in 1804.) With only one ballot, careful maneuvering was required to make sure that the chief rivals for the presidency did not land in the top two spots.

Into that maneuverable moment stepped Alexander Hamilton. No longer in the cabinet, Hamilton had returned to his law practice in 1795, but he kept a firm hand on political developments. Hamilton did not trust Adams; he preferred Pinckney, and he tried to influence southern electors to switch from Jefferson to the

slave-owning Pinckney by publishing a series of anonymous biting satires directed against Jefferson. But his plan failed: Adams was elected president with 71 electoral votes; Jefferson came in second with 68 and thus became vice president. Pinckney got 59 votes, while Burr trailed with 30.

Adams's inaugural speech pledged neutrality in foreign affairs and respect for the French people, based on his several years of residence there, which made Republicans hopeful. To please Federalists, Adams retained three cabinet members from Washington's administration — the secretaries of state, treasury, and war. But the three were Hamilton loyalists, passing off Hamilton's judgments and advice as their own to the unwitting Adams. Vice President Jefferson extended a conciliatory hand to Adams when the two old friends met in Philadelphia, still the capital. They even took temporary lodging in the same boardinghouse, as if expecting to work closely together. But the Hamiltonian cabinet ruined the honeymoon. Jefferson's advice was spurned, and he withdrew from active counsel of the president.

The XYZ Affair

From the start, Adams's presidency was in crisis. France retaliated for the British-friendly Jay Treaty by abandoning its 1778 alliance with the United States. In 1796, it refused to recognize the U.S. minister sent by President Washington to France. Next, French privateers — armed private vessels — started detaining American ships carrying British goods; by March 1797, more than three hundred American vessels had been seized. To avenge these insults, Federalists started murmuring openly about war with France. Adams preferred negotiations and dispatched a three-

man commission to France in the fall of 1797. But at the same time, the president recommended new expenditures for military defense. Negotiations, it appeared, would be backed by the muscle of military preparedness. Congress approved money for building three new naval frigates, for arming merchant vessels, and for reinforcing and improving defenses in coastal cities.

When the three American commissioners arrived in Paris, French officials would not receive them. Finally, the French minister of foreign affairs, Talleyrand, sent three French agents — unnamed and soon known to the American public as X, Y, and Z — to the American commissioners with the information that $250,000 might grease the wheels of diplomacy and that a $12 million loan to the French government would be the price of a peace treaty. Incensed, the commissioners brought news of the bribery attempt to the president.

Americans reacted to the **XYZ affair** with shock and anger. Even staunch pro-French Republicans began to reevaluate their allegiance. The Federalist-dominated Congress appropriated money for an army of ten thousand soldiers and repealed all prior treaties with France. In 1798, twenty naval warships launched the United States into its first undeclared war, called the **Quasi-War** by historians to underscore its uncertain legal status. The main scene of action was the Caribbean, where more than one hundred French ships were captured.

There was no home-front unity in this time of undeclared war; antagonism only intensified between Federalists and Republicans. Because there seemed to be very little chance of a land invasion by France, leading Republicans feared, with some justification, that the Federalists' real aim might be to raise the army to threaten domestic dissenters. Some claimed that Hamilton had

John and Abigail Adams
The artist Gilbert Stuart began painting these companion portraits in 1800; Adams was 65 and his wife was 56. A friend once listed Adams's shortcomings as a politician: "He can't dance, drink, game, flatter, promise, dress, swear with gentlemen, and small talk and flirt with the ladies." But, luckily, Adams had a secret weapon to keep him resilient: Abigail, his wife, a woman of astute intellect and wisdom. National Gallery of Art, Washington, D.C.

masterminded the army buildup and was lobbying to be second in command, behind the aging ex-president Washington, presumed to be the man to lead the army. President Adams was increasingly mistrustful of members of his cabinet, but they backed the military buildup, and Adams was too weak politically to prevail. He was, moreover, beginning to suspect that his cabinet was more loyal to Hamilton than to the president.

Antagonism spiraled out of control between Federalists and Republicans. Republican newspapers heaped abuse on Adams. One denounced him as "a person without patriotism, without philosophy, and a mock monarch." Pro-French mobs roamed the streets of Philadelphia, the capital, and Adams, fearing for his personal safety, stocked weapons in his presidential quarters. Federalists, too, went on the offensive. In Newburyport, Massachusetts, they lit a huge bonfire and burned issues of the state's Republican newspapers. Officers in a New York militia unit drank a menacing toast on July 4, 1798: "One and but one party in the United States." A Federalist editor ominously declared that "he who is not for us is against us."

The Alien and Sedition Acts

With tempers so dangerously high and fears that political dissent was perhaps akin to treason, Federalist leaders moved to muffle the opposition.

In mid-1798, Congress hammered out the Sedition Act, which not only made conspiracy and revolt illegal but also penalized speaking or writing anything that defamed the president or Congress. Criticizing government leaders became a criminal offense. One Federalist in Congress justified his vote for the law this way: "Let gentlemen look at certain papers printed in this city and elsewhere, and ask themselves whether an unwarrantable and dangerous combination does not exist to overturn and ruin the government by publishing the most shameless falsehoods against the representatives of the people." In all, twenty-five men, almost all Republican newspaper editors, were charged with sedition; twelve were convicted. (See "Documenting the American Promise," page 282.)

Congress also passed two Alien Acts. The first extended the waiting period for an alien to achieve citizenship from five to fourteen years and required all aliens to register with the federal government. The second empowered the president in time of war to deport or imprison without trial any foreigner suspected of being a danger to the United States. The clear intent of these laws was to harass French immigrants already in the United States and to discourage others from coming.

Republicans strongly opposed the **Alien and Sedition Acts** on the grounds that they were in conflict with the Bill of Rights, but they did not have the votes to revoke the acts in Congress,

Cartoon of the Lyon-Griswold Fight in Congress
The political tensions of 1798 were not merely intellectual; two men brawled on the floor of Congress. Roger Griswold, a Connecticut Federalist, called Matthew Lyon, a Vermont Republican, a coward. Lyon responded with some well-aimed spit, the first departure from the gentleman's code of honor. Griswold responded by raising his cane to Lyon, whereupon Lyon grabbed nearby fire tongs to beat back his assailant. Madison wrote to Jefferson that the two should have dueled, the honorable way to avenge insults. But Lyon, a recent Scots-Irish immigrant, preferred rough-and-tumble fighting as the best response to insult.
Library of Congress.

The Crisis of 1798: Sedition

As President John Adams inched toward an undeclared war with France, criticism of his foreign policy reached an all-time high. Newspaper editors and politicians favorable to France blasted him with such intemperate language that his supporters feared that the United States could be pushed to the brink of civil war. Federalists in Congress tried to muffle the opposition by criminalizing seditious words, believing it to be the only way to preserve the country. Republicans just redoubled their opposition.

DOCUMENT 1
Abigail Adams Complains of Sedition, 1798

Throughout the spring of 1798, a beleaguered Abigail Adams complained repeatedly in confidential letters to her sister Mary Cranch about the need for a sedition law to put a stop to the political criticisms of her husband, the president, by Benjamin Bache, the pro-French editor of the Philadelphia Aurora.

(April 26): . . . Yet dairingly do the vile incendaries keep up in Baches paper the most wicked and base, voilent & calumniating abuse—It was formerly considerd as leveld against the Government, but now it . . . insults the Majesty of the Sovereign People. But nothing will have an Effect until Congress passes a Sedition Bill. . . . (April 28): . . . We are now wonderfully popular except with Bache & Co who in his paper calls the President old, querilous, Bald, blind, cripled, Toothless Adams. (May 10): . . . This Bache is cursing & abusing daily. If that fellow . . . is not surpressd, we shall come to a civil war. (May 26): . . . I wish the Laws of our Country were competant to punish the stirer up of sedition, the writer and Printer of base and unfounded calumny. This would contribute as much to the Peace and harmony of our Country as any measure. . . . (June 19): . . . In any other Country Bache & all his papers would have been seazd and ought to be here, but congress are dilly dallying about passing a Bill enabling the President to seize suspisious persons, and their papers. (June 23): . . . I wish our Legislature would set the example & make a sedition act, to hold in order the base Newspaper calumniators. In this State, you could not get a verdict, if a prosecution was to be commenced.

SOURCE: *New Letters of Abigail Adams, 1788–1801*, edited by Stewart Mitchell, pp. 165, 167, 172, 179, 193, 196. Copyright © 1974 by The American Antiquarian Society. Reprinted by permission of Houghton Mifflin Company. All rights reserved.

DOCUMENT 2
The Sedition Act of 1798

On July 14, 1798, Congress approved a bill making sedition with malicious intent a crime.

SECTION 1. . . . if any persons shall unlawfully combine or conspire together, with intent to oppose any measure or measures of the government of the United States . . . , or to impede the operation of any law of the United States, or to intimidate or prevent any person holding . . . office in or under the government of the United States, from undertaking, performing or executing his trust or duty, and if any person or persons, with intent as aforesaid, shall counsel, advise or attempt to procure any insurrection, riot, unlawful assembly, or combination . . . , he or they shall be deemed guilty of a high misdemeanor, and on conviction . . . shall be punished by a fine not exceeding five thousand dollars, and by imprisonment during a term not less than six months nor exceeding five years. . . .

SEC. 2. . . . If any person shall write, print, utter or publish, or shall cause or procure to be written, printed, uttered or published . . . , any false, scandalous and malicious writing or writings against the government of the United States, or either house of the Congress of the United States, or the President of the United States, with intent to defame the said government . . . or to bring them . . . into contempt or disrepute; or to excite against them . . . the hatred of the good people of the United States . . . , or to aid, encourage or abet any hostile designs of any foreign nation against the United States . . . , then such person, being thereof convicted . . . shall be punished by a fine not exceeding two thousand dollars, and by imprisonment not exceeding two years.

SOURCE: Excerpted text from congressional bill, July 14, 1798.

DOCUMENT 3
Matthew Lyon Criticizes John Adams, 1798

Matthew Lyon, a member of Congress from Vermont, published this criticism of President Adams in a letter to the editor of Spooner's Vermont Journal *(July 31, 1798). It became the first of three counts against him in a sedition trial. Lyon drew a four-month sentence and a fine of $1,000. From jail, he ran for reelection to Congress — and won.*

As to the Executive, when I shall see the efforts of that power bent on the promotion of the comfort, the happiness, and the accommodation of the people, that Executive shall have my zealous and uniform support. But when I see every consideration of the public welfare swallowed up in a continual grasp for power, in an unbounded thirst for ridiculous pomp, foolish adulation, or selfish avarice; when I shall behold men of real merit daily turned out of office for no other cause but independence of sentiment; when I shall see men of firmness, merit, years, abilities, and experience, discarded on their application for office, for fear they possess that independence; and men of meanness preferred for the ease with which they take up and advocate opinions, the consequence of which they know but little of; when I shall see the sacred name of religion employed as a State engine to make mankind hate and persecute one another, I shall not be their humble advocate.

SOURCE: Matthew Lyon, Letter in *Spooner's Vermont Journal*, July 31, 1798. Quoted in *Matthew Lyon: New Man of the Democratic Revolution, 1749–1822* by Aleine Austin, pp. 108–9. Copyright © 1981 Aleine Austin. Reprinted with permission of Pennsylvania State University Press.

DOCUMENT 4
The Virginia Resolution, December 24, 1798

James Madison drafted the Virginia Resolution and had a trusted ally present it to the Virginia legislature, which was dominated by Republicans. (Jefferson did the same for Kentucky.) The Virginia document denounces the Alien and Sedition Acts and declares that states have the right to "interpose" to stop unconstitutional actions by the federal government.

RESOLVED . . . That this assembly most solemnly declares a warm attachment to the Union of the States, to maintain which it pledges all its powers; and that for this end, it is

their duty to watch over and oppose every infraction of those principles which constitute the only basis of that Union, because a faithful observance of them, can alone secure its existence and the public happiness.

That this Assembly doth explicitly and peremptorily declare, that it views the powers of the federal government, as resulting from the compact, to which the states are parties; as limited by the plain sense and intention of the instrument constituting the compact; as no further valid that they are authorized by the grants enumerated in that compact; and that in case of a deliberate, palpable, and dangerous exercise of other powers, not granted by the said compact, the states who are parties thereto, have the right, and are in duty bound, to interpose for arresting the progress of the evil, and for maintaining within their respective limits, the authorities, rights and liberties appertaining to them. . . .

That the General Assembly doth particularly protest against the palpable and alarming infractions of the Constitution, in the two late cases of the "Alien and Sedition Acts" . . . ; the first of which exercises a power no where delegated to the federal government . . . ; and the other of which acts, exercises in like manner, a power not delegated by the constitution, but on the contrary, expressly and positively forbidden by one of the amendments thereto; a power, which more than any other, ought to produce universal alarm, because it is levelled against that right of freely examining public characters and measures, and of free communication among the people thereon, which has ever been justly deemed, the only effectual guardian of every other right.

SOURCE: Avalon Project, Yale Law School, 1996. www.yale.edu. © 1996–2007 The Avalon Project at Yale Law School. Reprinted with permission.

Questions for Analysis and Debate

1. Why did the Federalists believe that the Sedition Act was necessary? What exactly was the threat, according to Abigail Adams? What threat is implied by the wording of the act?

2. Does Matthew Lyon's criticism of President Adams rise to the level of threat that the Federalists feared? How do you explain Lyon's guilty verdict? His reelection to Congress?

3. What might Madison have meant by "interpose" as the desired action by states? What could states actually do?

4. Which side had the stronger argument in 1798–1799? Do you think there should be limits on what can be said publicly about high government officials? Why or why not?

nor could the federal judiciary, dominated by Federalist judges, be counted on to challenge them. Jefferson and Madison turned to the state legislatures, the only other competing political arena, to press their opposition. Each man anonymously drafted a set of resolutions condemning the acts and had the legislatures of Virginia and Kentucky present them to the federal government in late fall 1798. The **Virginia and Kentucky Resolutions** put forth the decidedly novel argument that state legislatures have the right to judge the constitutionality of federal laws and even to nullify them. These were amazing assertions of state power, in view of Madison's role in 1787 in creating a federal government that superseded the states, and in view of Jefferson's position as the vice president. By their action, both men ran the risk of being charged with sedition. The resolutions made little dent in the Alien and Sedition Acts, but the idea of a state's right to nullify federal law did not disappear. It would resurface several times in decades to come, most notably in a major tariff dispute in 1832 and in the sectional arguments that led to the Civil War.

> **"We are all republicans, we are all federalists."**
> —President THOMAS JEFFERSON

Amid all the war hysteria and sedition fears in 1798, President Adams regained his balance. He was uncharacteristically restrained in pursuing opponents under the Sedition Act, and he finally refused to declare war on France, as extreme Federalists wished. No doubt he was beginning to realize how much he had been the dupe of Hamilton. He also shrewdly realized that France was not eager for war and that a peaceful settlement might be close at hand. In January 1799, a peace initiative from France arrived in the form of a letter assuring Adams that diplomatic channels were open again and that new peace commissioners would be welcomed in France.

Adams accepted this overture and appointed new negotiators. By late 1799, the Quasi-War with France had subsided, and in 1800 the negotiations resulted in a treaty declaring "a true and sincere friendship" between the United States and France. But Federalists were not pleased; Adams lost the support of a significant part of his own party and sealed his fate as the first one-term president of the United States.

The election of 1800 was openly organized along party lines. The self-designated national leaders of each group met to handpick their candidates for president and vice president. Adams's chief opponent was Thomas Jefferson. When the election was finally over, President Jefferson mounted the inaugural platform to announce,

"We are all republicans, we are all federalists," an appealing rhetoric of harmony appropriate to an inaugural address. But his formulation perpetuated a denial of the validity of party politics, a denial that ran deep in the founding generation of political leaders.

REVIEW Why did Congress pass the Alien and Sedition Acts in 1798?

▶ Conclusion: Parties Nonetheless

American political leaders began operating the new government in 1789 with great hopes of unifying the country and overcoming selfish factionalism. The enormous trust in President Washington was the central foundation for those hopes, and Washington did not disappoint, becoming a model Mr. President with a blend of integrity and authority. Stability was further aided by easy passage of the Bill of Rights (to appease Antifederalists) and by attention to cultivating a virtuous citizenry of upright men supported and rewarded by republican womanhood. Diplomatic attempts were made to secure a peace treaty with the Creeks in the southwest and to offer them protection. (Overtures to the Indians in the northwest were less successful.) Yet the hopes of the honeymoon period soon turned to worries and then fears as major political disagreements flared up.

At the core of the conflict was a group of talented men — Hamilton, Madison, Jefferson, and Adams — so recently allies but now opponents. They diverged over Hamilton's economic program, over relations with the British and the Jay Treaty, over the French and Haitian revolutions, and over preparedness for war abroad and free speech at home. Hamilton was perhaps the driving force in these conflicts, but the antagonism was not about mere personality. Parties were taking shape not around individuals, but around principles, such as ideas about what constituted enlightened leadership, how powerful the federal government should be, who was the best ally in Europe, and when oppositional political speech turned into treason. The Federalists were pro-British, pro-commerce, and ever alarmed about the potential excesses of democracy. The Republicans celebrated, up to a point, the radical republicanism of France and opposed the Sedition Act as an alarming example of an overbearing government cutting off freedom of speech.

When Jefferson in his inaugural address of 1800 offered his conciliatory assurance that Americans were at the same time "all republicans" and "all federalists," he probably mystified some listeners. Possibly, he meant to suggest that both groups shared two basic ideas—the value of republican government, in which power derived from the people, and the value of the unique federal system of shared governance structured by the Constitution. But by 1800, *Federalist* and *Republican* defined competing philosophies of government. To at least some of his listeners, Jefferson's assertion of harmony across budding party lines could only have seemed bizarre. For the next two decades, these two groups would battle each other, each fearing that the success of the other might bring about the demise of the country. And meanwhile, leaders continued to worry that partisan spirit itself was a bad thing.

▶ Selected Bibliography

Politics

Bernard Bailyn, *To Begin the World Anew: The Genius and Ambiguities of the American Founders* (2003).

Ron Chernow, *Alexander Hamilton* (2004).

Ron Chernow, *Washington: A Life* (2010).

Jerry A. Clouse, *The Whiskey Rebellion: Southwestern Pennsylvania's Frontier People Test the American Constitution* (1995).

Stanley Elkins and Eric McKitrick, *The Age of Federalism: The Early American Republic, 1788–1800* (1993).

Joseph J. Ellis, *American Creation: Triumphs and Tragedies in the Founding of the Republic* (2008).

Joseph J. Ellis, *Founding Brothers: The Revolutionary Generation* (2000).

John E. Ferling, *Adams vs. Jefferson: The Tumultuous Election of 1800* (2005).

John E. Ferling, *The Ascent of George Washington: The Hidden Political Genius of an American Icon* (2010).

David P. Geggus, ed., *The Impact of the Haitian Revolution in the Atlantic World* (2002).

David Patrick Geggus and Norman Fiering, eds., *The World of the Haitian Revolution* (2008).

Peter P. Hill, *French Perceptions of the Early American Republic, 1783–1793* (1988).

Ralph Ketcham, *Presidents above Party: The First American Presidency, 1789–1829* (1984).

David McCullough, *John Adams* (2001).

Jeffrey L. Pasley, *The Tyranny of Printers: Newspaper Politics in the Early American Republic* (2001).

Thomas P. Slaughter, *The Whiskey Rebellion: Frontier Epilogue to the American Revolution* (1986).

Larry E. Tise, *The American Counterrevolution: A Retreat from Liberty, 1783–1800* (1999).

Richard J. Twomey, *Jacobins and Jeffersonians: Anglo-American Radicalism in the United States, 1790–1820* (1989).

Henry Wiencek, *An Imperfect God: George Washington, His Slaves, and the Creation of America* (2003).

Society and Culture

Susan Branson, *These Fiery Frenchified Dames: Women and Political Culture in Early National Philadelphia* (2001).

Richard D. Brown, *Knowledge Is Power: The Diffusion of Information in Early America, 1700–1865* (1989).

Nancy Cott, *The Bonds of Womanhood: Women's Sphere in New England, 1780–1835* (1997).

Joanne B. Freeman, *Affairs of Honor: National Politics in the New Republic* (2001).

Richard R. John, *Spreading the News: The American Postal System from Franklin to Morse* (1996).

Linda Kerber, *Women of the Republic: Intellect and Ideology in Revolutionary America* (1997).

Clare A. Lyons, *Sex among the Rabble: An Intimate History of Gender and Power in the Age of Revolution, Philadelphia, 1730–1830* (2006).

Bruce H. Mann, *Republic of Debtors: Bankruptcy in the Age of American Independence* (2002).

Simon P. Newman, *Parades and the Politics of the Street: Festive Culture in the Early American Republic* (2000).

Sheila L. Skemp, *Judith Sargent Murray: A Brief Biography with Documents* (1998).

Rosemarie Zagarri, *Revolutionary Backlash: Women and Politics in the Early American Republic* (2007).

Indians and the Frontier

Andrew R. L. Cayton, *Frontier Republic: Ideology and Politics in the Ohio Country, 1780–1825* (1989).

Gregory E. Dowd, *A Spirited Resistance: The North American Indian Struggle for Unity, 1745–1815* (1992).

R. Douglas Hurt, *The Ohio Frontier: Crucible of the Old Northwest, 1720–1830* (1998).

Claudio Saunt, *A New Order of Things: Property, Power, and the Transformation of the Creek Indians, 1733–1816* (1999).

Wiley Sword, *President Washington's Indian War: The Struggle for the Old Northwest, 1790–1795* (1993).

▶ FOR MORE BOOKS ABOUT TOPICS IN THIS CHAPTER, see the Online Bibliography at bedfordstmartins.com/roark.

▶ FOR ADDITIONAL PRIMARY SOURCES FROM THIS PERIOD, see Michael Johnson, ed., *Reading the American Past*, Fifth Edition.

▶ FOR WEB SITES, IMAGES, AND DOCUMENTS RELATED TO TOPICS AND PLACES IN THIS CHAPTER, visit Make History at bedfordstmartins.com/roark.

Reviewing Chapter 9

KEY TERMS

Explain each term's significance.

The Search for Stability
Henry Knox (p. 262)
Alexander Hamilton (p. 262)
Thomas Jefferson (p. 262)
John Jay (p. 263)
Bill of Rights (p. 264)
republican motherhood (p. 264)
Judith Sargent Murray (p. 265)

Hamilton's Economic Policies
Report on Public Credit (p. 266)
national debt (p. 266)
Bank of the United States (p. 268)
Report on Manufactures (p. 268)
Whiskey Rebellion (p. 270)

Conflict on America's Borders and Beyond
Alexander McGillivray (p. 271)
Treaty of New York (p. 271)
Little Turtle (p. 272)
Blue Jacket (p. 272)
Arthur St. Clair (p. 272)
battle of Fallen Timbers (p. 273)
Treaty of Greenville (p. 273)
Jay Treaty (p. 276)
Haitian Revolution (p. 278)

Federalists and Republicans
Federalists (p. 279)
Republicans (p. 279)
XYZ affair (p. 280)
Quasi-War (p. 280)
Alien and Sedition Acts (p. 281)
Virginia and Kentucky Resolutions (p. 284)

REVIEW QUESTIONS

Use key terms and dates to support your answer.

1. How did political leaders in the 1790s attempt to overcome the divisions of the 1780s? (pp. 261–265)

2. Why were Hamilton's economic policies controversial? (pp. 265–270)

3. Why did the United States feel vulnerable to international threats in the 1790s? (pp. 270–279)

4. Why did Congress pass the Alien and Sedition Acts in 1798? (pp. 279–284)

MAKING CONNECTIONS

Draw on key terms, the timeline, and review questions.

1. Why did the Federalist alliance of the late 1780s fracture in the 1790s? Why was this development troubling to the nation? In your answer, cite specific ideological and political developments that hindered cooperation.

2. What provoked the Whiskey Rebellion? How did the government respond? In your answer, discuss the foundations and precedents of the conflict, as well as the significance of the government's response.

3. Americans held that virtue was pivotal to the success of their new nation. What did they mean by *virtue*? How did they hope to ensure that their citizens and their leaders possessed virtue?

4. The domestic politics of the new nation were profoundly influenced by conflicts beyond the nation's borders. Discuss how conflicts abroad contributed to domestic political developments in the 1790s.

LINKING TO THE PAST

Link events in this chapter to earlier events.

1. Americans fought against the French in the Seven Years' War but welcomed them as allies during the Revolutionary War. Did either or both of those earlier experiences with France have any bearing on the sharp division in the 1790s between pro-French and anti-French political leaders in the United States? (See chapters 6 and 7.)

2. Shays's Rebellion appeared to some in 1786 to underscore the need for a stronger national government. Compare the Whiskey Rebellion to Shays's Rebellion. How were they similar, and how were they different? Did the Constitution of 1787 make a difference in the authorities' response to rebellion? (See chapter 8.)

▶ **For practice quizzes and other study tools**, see the Online Study Guide at **bedfordstmartins.com/roark**.

TIMELINE 1789–1800

1789
- George Washington inaugurated first president.
- French Revolution begins.
- First Congress meets.
- Fort Washington erected in western Ohio.

1790
- Congress approves Hamilton's debt plan.
- Judith Sargent Murray publishes "On the Equality of the Sexes."
- National capital moved from New York City to Philadelphia.
- Shawnee and Miami Indians in Ohio defeat General Josiah Harmar.

1791
- States ratify Bill of Rights.
- Congress and president charter Bank of the United States.
- Ohio Indians defeat General Arthur St. Clair.
- Congress passes whiskey tax.
- Haitian Revolution begins.
- Hamilton issues *Report on Manufactures*.

1793
- Anglo-French Wars commence in Europe.
- Washington issues Neutrality Proclamation.
- Eli Whitney invents cotton gin.

1794
- Whiskey Rebellion.
- Battle of Fallen Timbers.

1795
- Treaty of Greenville.
- Jay Treaty.

1796
- Federalist John Adams elected second president.

1797
- XYZ affair.

1798
- Quasi-War with France erupts.
- Alien and Sedition Acts.
- Virginia and Kentucky Resolutions.

1800
- Republican Thomas Jefferson elected third president.

PATRIOTIC PITCHER, 1800

This earthenware pitcher celebrates American military readiness. A militia officer strikes a springy pose near a cannon that juts out aggressively. Martial words frame the picture and provide a toast: "Success to America Whose Militia Is Better Than Standing Armies." The picture's swagger implies a military preparedness that was in fact woefully off the mark in 1800. Thousands of American-themed pitchers — with eagles and flags, Miss Liberty and George Washington — were marketed by British manufacturers. Pitchers saw daily use wherever people gathered to eat or drink, as in this country tavern scene painted by Philadelphia artist John Lewis Krimmel.

Pitcher: Kahn Fine Antiques/photo courtesy of Antiques and Fine Arts; background: Toledo Museum of Art.

10

Republicans in Power
1800–1824

THE NAME TECUMSEH TRANSLATES AS "SHOOTING STAR," A FITTING name for the Shawnee chief who reached meteoric heights of fame among Indians during Thomas Jefferson's presidency. From Canada to Georgia and west to the Mississippi, Tecumseh was accounted a charismatic leader, for which white Americans praised (and feared) him. Graceful, eloquent, compelling, astute: Tecumseh was all these and more, a gifted natural commander, equal parts politician and warrior.

The Ohio Country, where Tecumseh was born in 1768, was home to some dozen Indian tribes, including the Shawnee, recently displaced from the South. During the Revolutionary War, the region became a battleground with the "Big Knives," as the Shawnee people called the Americans. Tecumseh's childhood was marked by repeated violence and the loss of his father and two brothers in battle. The Revolution's end in 1783 brought no peace to Indian country. American settlers pushed west, and the youthful Tecumseh honed his warrior skills by ambushing pioneers flatboating down the Ohio River. He fought at the battle of Fallen Timbers, a major Indian defeat, but avoided the 1795 negotiations of the Treaty of Greenville, in which half a dozen dispirited tribes ceded much of Ohio to the Big Knives. In frustration, he watched as seven treaties between 1802 and 1805 whittled away more Indian land.

Some Indians, resigned and tired, looked for ways to accommodate, taking up farming, trade, and even intermarriage with the Big Knives. Others spent their treaty payments on alcohol. Tecumseh's younger brother Tenskwatawa led an embittered life of idleness and drink. But Tecumseh rejected accommodation and instead campaigned for a return to ancient ways. Donning traditional animal-skin garb, he traveled around the Great Lakes region after 1805 persuading tribes to join his pan-Indian confederacy. The territorial governor of Indiana, William Henry Harrison, reported, "For four years he has been in constant motion. You see him today on the Wabash, and in a short time hear of him on the shores of Lake Erie or Michigan, or on the banks of the Mississippi, and wherever he goes he makes an impression favorable to his purpose."

Even Tecumseh's dissolute brother was born anew. After a near-death experience in 1805, Tenskwatawa revived and recounted a startling vision of meeting the Master of Life. Renaming himself the Prophet, he urged

289

Indians everywhere to regard whites as children of the Evil Spirit, destined to be destroyed.

Tecumseh and the Prophet established a new village called Prophetstown, located in present-day Indiana, offering a potent blend of spiritual regeneration and political unity that attracted thousands of followers. Governor Harrison admired and feared Tecumseh, calling him "one of those uncommon geniuses which spring up occasionally to produce revolutions."

President Thomas Jefferson worried about an organized Indian confederacy and its potential for a renewed alliance with the British in Canada. Those worries became a reality during Jefferson's second term in office (1805–1809). Although his first term (1801–1805) brought notable successes, such as the Louisiana Purchase and the Lewis and Clark expedition, his second term was consumed by the threat of war with either Britain or France, in a replay of the late-1790s tensions. When war came in 1812, the enemy was Britain, bolstered by a reenergized Indian-British alliance. Among the causes of the war were insults over international shipping rights and the capture of U.S. vessels. But the war also derived compelling strength from Tecumseh's confederacy. Significant battles pitted U.S. soldiers against Indians in the Great Lakes, Tennessee, and Florida.

In the end, the War of 1812 settled little between the United States and Britain, but it was tragically conclusive for the Indians. Eight hundred warriors led by Tecumseh helped defend Canada against U.S. attacks, but the British did not reciprocate when the Indians were under threat. Tecumseh died on Canadian soil at the battle of the Thames in the fall of 1813. No Indian leader with his star power would emerge again east of the Mississippi.

The briefly unified Indian confederacy under Tecumseh had no counterpart in the young Republic's confederation of states, where widespread unity behind a single leader proved impossible to achieve. Republicans did battle with Federalists during the Jefferson and Madison administrations, but then Federalists doomed their party by opposing the War of 1812. After 1815, they ceased to be a major force in political life. The next two presidents, James Monroe and John Quincy Adams, congratulated themselves on the Federalists' demise and Republican unity, but in fact divisions within their own party were extensive. Wives of politicians increasingly inserted themselves into this dissonant mix, managing their husbands' politicking and enabling them to appear above the fray and maintain the fiction of a nonpartisan state. That it was a fiction became sharply apparent in the most serious political crisis of this period, the Missouri Compromise of 1820.

Tecumseh

Several portraits of Tecumseh exist, but they all present a different visage, and none of them enjoys verified authenticity. This one perhaps comes closest to how Tecumseh actually looked. It is an 1848 engraving adapted from an earlier drawing that no longer exists, sketched by a French trader in Indiana named Pierre Le Dru in a live sitting with the Indian leader in 1808. The engraver has given Tecumseh a British army officer's uniform, showing that he fought on the British side in the War of 1812. Notice the head covering and the medallion around Tecumseh's neck, marking his Indian identity.
Library of Congress.

▶ Jefferson's Presidency

The nerve-wracking election of 1800, decided in the House of Representatives, stoked fears that party divisions would ruin the country. A panicky Federalist newspaper in Connecticut predicted that a victory by **Thomas Jefferson** would produce a bloody civil war and usher in an immoral reign of "murder, robbery, rape, adultery and incest." Similar fears were expressed in the South, where a frightful slave uprising seemed a possible outcome of Jefferson's victory. But nothing nearly so dramatic occurred. Jefferson later called his election the "revolution of 1800," referring to his repudiation of Federalist practices and his cutbacks in military spending and taxes. While he cherished a republican simplicity in governance, he inevitably encountered events that required decisive and sometimes expensive government action. One early example came when pirates repeatedly threatened American ships off the north coast of Africa.

Turbulent Times: Election and Rebellion

The result of the election of 1800 (Map 10.1) remained uncertain from polling times in the late fall to repeated roll call votes in the House of Representatives in February 1801. Federalist John Adams, never secure in his leadership of the Federalist Party, was no longer in the presidential race once it reached the House. Instead, the contest was between Jefferson and his running mate, Senator **Aaron Burr** of New York. Republican voters in the electoral college slipped up, giving Jefferson and Burr an equal number of votes, an outcome possible because of the single balloting to choose both president and vice president. (To fix this problem, the Twelfth Amendment to the Constitution, adopted in 1804, provided for distinct ballots for the two offices.) The vain and ambitious Burr declined to concede, so the sitting Federalist-dominated House of Representatives got to choose the president.

Each state delegation had one vote, and nine were needed to win. Some Federalists preferred Burr, believing that his character flaws made him susceptible to Federalist pressure. But the influential Alexander Hamilton, though no friend of Jefferson, recognized that the high-strung Burr would be more dangerous in the presidency. Jefferson was a "contemptible hypocrite" in Hamilton's opinion, but at least he was not corrupt. Jefferson received the votes of eight states on the first ballot. Thirty-six ballots and six days later, he got the critical ninth vote, as well as a tenth. This election demonstrated a remarkable feature of the new government: No matter how hard fought the campaign, the leadership of the nation could shift from one group to its rivals in a peaceful transfer of power effected by ballots, not bullets.

As the country struggled over its white leadership crisis, a twenty-four-year-old blacksmith named Gabriel, the slave of Thomas Prossor, plotted rebellion in Virginia. Inspired by the Haitian Revolution (see chapter 9), and perhaps directly informed of it by French slaves new to the Richmond area, Gabriel was said to be organizing a thousand slaves to march on the state capital of Richmond and take the governor, James Monroe, hostage. On the appointed day, however, a few nervous slaves went to the authorities with news of **Gabriel's rebellion**, and within days scores of implicated conspirators were jailed and brought to trial.

> **"I have nothing more to offer than what General Washington would have had to offer, had he been taken by the British and put to trial by them."**
> — A jailed slave accused of contemplating rebellion

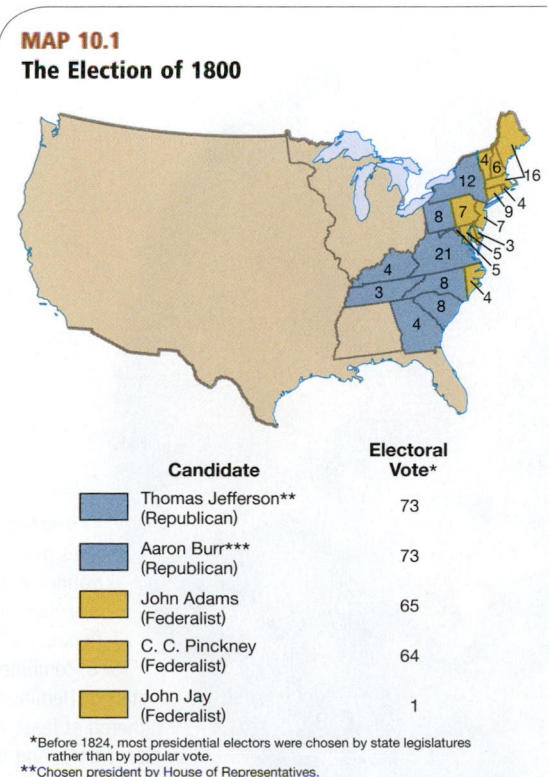

MAP 10.1
The Election of 1800

Candidate	Electoral Vote*
Thomas Jefferson** (Republican)	73
Aaron Burr*** (Republican)	73
John Adams (Federalist)	65
C. C. Pinckney (Federalist)	64
John Jay (Federalist)	1

*Before 1824, most presidential electors were chosen by state legislatures rather than by popular vote.
**Chosen president by House of Representatives.
***Chosen vice president by House of Representatives.

Pistols from the Burr-Hamilton Duel

In 1804, Vice President Aaron Burr shot and killed Alexander Hamilton with a .54-caliber pistol. Hamilton had long scorned Burr, and when a newspaper published Hamilton's disdain, Burr felt obliged to avenge his honor. Dueling, fully accepted in the South as an extralegal remedy for insult, had recently been outlawed in northern states. Burr was charged with a misdemeanor in New York, where the challenge was issued, and with homicide in New Jersey, where the duel was fought. After four months as a fugitive in the South, Burr resumed his official duties in Washington. He was never arrested. Courtesy of Chase Manhattan Archives.

One of the jailed rebels compared himself to the most venerated icon of the early Republic: "I have nothing more to offer than what General Washington would have had to offer, had he been taken by the British and put to trial by them." Such talk invoking the specter of a black George Washington worried white Virginians, and in the fall of 1800 twenty-seven black men were hanged for allegedly contemplating rebellion. Finally, Jefferson advised Governor Monroe to halt the hangings. "The world at large will forever condemn us if we indulge a principle of revenge," Jefferson wrote.

The Jeffersonian Vision of Republican Simplicity

Once elected, Thomas Jefferson turned his attention to establishing his administration in clear contrast to the Federalists. For his inauguration, held in the village called Washington City, he dressed in everyday clothing to strike a tone of republican simplicity, and he walked to the Capitol for the modest swearing-in ceremony. As president, he scaled back Federalist building plans for Washington and cut the government budget.

Martha Washington and Abigail Adams had received the wives of government officials at weekly teas, thereby cementing social relations in the governing class. But Jefferson, a longtime widower, disdained female gatherings and avoided the women of Washington City. He abandoned George Washington's practice of holding weekly formal receptions, limiting these drop-in gatherings to just two a year. His preferred social event was the small dinner party with carefully chosen politicos, either all Republicans or all Federalists (and all male). At these intimate dinners, the president exercised influence and strengthened informal relationships that would help him govern.

Thomas Jefferson, by John Trumbull

This miniature portrait of Jefferson was made in the late 1780s, when the young widower lived with his two daughters and their attendant, the slave Sally Hemings. In 1802, a scandal erupted when a journalist charged that Jefferson had fathered several children by Hemings. DNA evidence from 1998, combined with historical evidence about Jefferson's whereabouts at the start of Hemings's six pregnancies, makes a powerful case that Jefferson fathered at least some of her children. Jefferson never commented about Hemings in his writings, and the written record on her side is entirely mute. Two of her four surviving children were allowed to slip away to freedom in the 1820s; the other two were freed in Jefferson's will. Monticello/Thomas Jefferson Memorial Foundation, Inc.

Jefferson's Duplicating Machine

Jefferson wrote tens of thousands of letters during his lifetime. For some years, he made copies of his work by pressing very thin tissue paper against manuscript pages whose patented slow-drying ink was still wet. In 1804, Jefferson acquired his first polygraph, or duplicating machine, which could produce four identical copies of a handwritten page. Patented by an Englishman and a Philadelphian in 1803, the polygraph linked up to five pens. The motion of the first pen, held in Jefferson's hand, was perfectly mimicked by the other pens, poised over tautly held paper. National Museum of American History, Smithsonian Institution, Behring Center.

Jefferson was no Antifederalist. He had supported the Constitution in 1788, despite his concern about the unrestricted reelection allowed to the president. But events of the 1790s had caused him to worry about the stretching of powers in the executive branch. Jefferson had watched with distrust as Hamiltonian policies refinanced the public debt, established a national bank, and secured commercial ties with Britain (see chapter 9). These policies seemed to Jefferson to promote the interests of money-hungry speculators and profiteers at the expense of the rest of the country. Financial schemes that seemed merely to allow rich men to become richer were corrupt and worthless, he believed, and their promotion by the federal government was not authorized by the Constitution. In Jefferson's vision, the source of true liberty in America was the independent farmer, someone who owned and worked his land both for himself and for the market.

Jefferson set out to dismantle Federalist innovations. He reduced the size of the army by a third, preferring "a well-disciplined militia" for defense, and he cut back the navy to just half a dozen ships. With the consent of Congress, he abolished all federal taxes based on population or whiskey. Government revenue would now derive solely from customs duties and the sale of western land. This strategy benefited the South, where three-fifths of the slaves counted for representation but not for taxation now. By the end of his first term, Jefferson had deeply reduced Hamilton's cherished national debt.

A properly limited federal government, according to Jefferson, was responsible merely for running a postal system, maintaining the federal courts, staffing lighthouses, collecting customs duties, and conducting a census once every ten years. The president had one private secretary, a young man named Meriwether Lewis, to help with his correspondence, and Jefferson paid him out of his own pocket. The Department of State employed only 8 people:

Secretary James Madison, 6 clerks, and a messenger. The Treasury Department was by far the largest unit, with 73 revenue commissioners, auditors, and clerks, plus 2 watchmen. The entire payroll of the executive branch amounted to a mere 130 people in 1801.

However, one large set of government workers lay beyond Jefferson's command. His predecessor, John Adams, had made 217 last-minute appointments of Federalists to various judicial and military posts. Jefferson refused to honor those "midnight judges" who had not yet been fully processed. One disappointed job seeker, William Marbury, sued the new secretary of state, James Madison, for failure to make good on the appointment. This action gave rise to a landmark Supreme Court case, **_Marbury v. Madison_**, decided in 1803. The Court ruled that although Marbury's commission was valid and the new president should have delivered it, the Court could not compel him to do so. What made the case significant was little noted at the time: The Court found that the grounds of Marbury's suit, resting in the Judiciary Act of 1789, were in conflict with the Constitution. For the first time, the Court acted to disallow a law on the grounds that it was unconstitutional.

Dangers Overseas: The Barbary Wars

Jefferson's desire to keep government and the military small met a severe test in the western Mediterranean Sea, where U.S. trading interests ran afoul of local Muslim states, leading to the first formal declaration of war against the United States by a foreign power. For well over a cen-

The Burning of the Frigate *Philadelphia* in Tripoli Harbor, 1804
After losing the warship *Philadelphia* to Tripolitan forces in 1803, American naval leaders decided to destroy it to prevent its use by the so-called pirates of North Africa. Commander Stephen Decatur engineered the daring nighttime raid. With his men concealed below decks of a modest trading vessel, Decatur entered the harbor and had his Arabic-speaking pilot secure permission to tie up next to the *Philadelphia*. The American raiding party quickly boarded, sending the Tripolitan guards into the water to swim to shore. In twenty minutes the warship was ablaze; Decatur departed with only one injured man and no fatalities. The Mariners Museum, Newport News, Virginia.

tury, four Muslim states on the northern coast of Africa — Morocco, Algiers, Tunis, and Tripoli, called the Barbary States by Americans — controlled all Mediterranean shipping traffic by demanding large annual payments (called "tribute") for safe passage. Countries electing not to pay found their ships at risk for seizure, with cargoes plundered and crews captured and sold into slavery. By the mid-1790s, the United States was paying $50,000 a year. About a hundred American merchant ships annually traversed the Mediterranean, trading lumber, tobacco, sugar, and rum for regional delicacies such as raisins, figs, capers, and medicinal opium.

In May 1801, when the pasha (military head) of Tripoli failed to secure a large increase in his tribute, he declared war on the United States. Jefferson had long considered such payments extortion, and he sent four warships to the Mediterranean to protect U.S. shipping. From 1801 to 1803, U.S. frigates engaged in skirmishes with Barbary privateers.

Then, in late 1803, the USS *Philadelphia* ran aground near Tripoli's harbor. Its three-hundred-man crew was captured along with the ship. In retaliation, a U.S. naval ship commanded by Lieutenant Stephen Decatur sailed into the harbor after dark, guided by an Arabic-speaking pilot to fool harbor sentries. Decatur's crew set the *Philadelphia* on fire, rendering the ship useless to its hijackers and making Decatur an instant hero in America. A later foray into the harbor to try to blow up the entire Tripoli fleet with a bomb-laden boat failed when the explosives detonated prematurely, killing eleven Americans.

In 1804, William Eaton, an American officer stationed in Tunis, felt the humiliation of his country's ineffectiveness. He requested a thousand Marines to invade Tripoli, but Secretary of State James Madison rejected the plan and another scheme to ally with the pasha's exiled brother to effect regime change. On his own, Eaton contacted the brother, assembled a force of four hundred men (mostly Greek and Egyptian mercenaries plus his Marines), and marched them over five hundred miles of desert for a surprise attack on Derne, Tripoli's second-largest city. Amazingly, he succeeded. The pasha of Tripoli yielded, released — for a fee — the prisoners taken from the *Philadelphia*, and negotiated a treaty with the United States that terminated tribute. One significant clause of the treaty stipulated that the United States "has in itself no character of enmity against the Laws, Religion or Tranquility of Musselmen [Muslims]" and that "no pretext arising from Religious Opinions, shall ever produce an interruption of the Harmony existing between the two Nations." Peace with the other Barbary States came in a second treaty in 1812.

The **Barbary Wars** of 1801–1805 cost Jefferson's government more money than the tribute demanded. But the honor of the young country was thought to be at stake. At political gatherings, the slogan "Millions for defense, but not a cent for tribute" became a popular toast.

REVIEW How did Jefferson attempt to undo the Federalist innovations of earlier administrations?

▶ Opportunities and Challenges in the West

While Jefferson remained cautious about exercising federal power, he quickly learned that circumstances sometimes required him to enlarge the authority of the presidency. Shifting politics in Europe in 1803 opened an unexpected door to the spectacular purchase from France of the Louisiana Territory. To explore the largely unmarked boundaries of this huge acquisition, Jefferson sent four separate expeditions into the prairie and mountains. The powerful Osage of the Arkansas River valley responded to overtures for an alliance and were soon lavishly welcomed by Jefferson in Washington City, but the even more powerful Comanche of the southern Great Plains stood their ground against all invaders. Meanwhile, the expedition by Lewis and Clark, the longest and northernmost trek of the four launched by Jefferson, mapped U.S. terrain all the way to the Pacific Ocean, giving a boost to expansionist aspirations.

The Louisiana Purchase

When the map of North America was redrawn in 1763, at the end of the Seven Years' War, a large expanse of the territory west of the Mississippi River shifted from France to Spain (see Map 6.2, page 164). Spain never controlled or settled the area centered on the Great Plains, which was already peopled by many Indian tribes, most notably the powerful and expansionist Comanche nation. New Orleans was Spain's principal stronghold in the region, a onetime French city strategically sited on the Mississippi River near its outlet to the Gulf of Mexico. Spain profited modestly from trade taxes it imposed on the small but growing flow of agricultural products shipped down the river from American farms in the western parts of Kentucky and Tennessee (to be sold at New Orleans or Caribbean destinations).

The biggest concern of the Spanish governor of New Orleans was that the sparse population of lower Louisiana was insufficient to ward off an anticipated westward movement of Americans. Spanish officials took steps to encourage European immigration, but only small numbers of Germans and French came. Up the river at St. Louis, the Spanish governor happily welcomed Native American refugees from the Northwest Territory who had been pushed out by what was termed

a "plague of locusts" — American settlers — in the 1790s. Hoping that a Spanish-Indian alliance might be able to stop the expected demographic wave, he promised that the Spanish would "receive you in their homes as if you all belonged to our nation." Still, defending many hundreds of miles of the river against Americans on the move was a daunting prospect. "You can't put doors on open country," said an adviser to the Spanish king.

Thus, in 1800 Spain struck a secret deal to return this trans-Mississippi territory to France, in the hopes that a French Louisiana would provide a buffer zone between Spain's more valuable holdings in Mexico and the land-hungry Americans. The French emperor Napoleon accepted the transfer and agreed to Spain's condition that France could not sell Louisiana to anyone without Spain's permission.

From the U.S. perspective, Spain had proved a weak western neighbor, but France was another story. Jefferson was so alarmed by the rumored transfer that he instructed Robert R. Livingston, America's minister in France, to approach the French and offer to buy New Orleans. At first, the French denied they owned the city. But when Livingston hinted that the United States might seize it if buying was not an option, the French negotiator asked him to name his price for the entire Louisiana Territory from the Gulf of Mexico north to Canada. Livingston stalled, and the Frenchman made suggestions: $125 million? $60 million? Livingston shrewdly stalled some more and within days accepted the bargain price of $15 million (Map 10.2).

> **"You can't put doors on open country."**
> — An advisor to the Spanish king

On the verge of war with Britain, France needed both money and friendly neutrality from the United States, and it got both from the quick sale of the Louisiana Territory. In addition, the recent and costly loss of Haiti as a colony made a French presence in New Orleans less feasible as well. But in selling Louisiana to the United States, France had broken its agreement with Spain, which protested that the sale was illegal.

Moreover, there was no consensus on the western border of this land transfer. Spain claimed that the border was about one hundred miles west of the Mississippi River, while in Jefferson's eyes it was some eight hundred miles farther west, defined by the crest of the Rocky Mountains. When Livingston pressured the French negotiator to clarify his country's understanding of the

MAP ACTIVITY

Map 10.2   Jefferson's Expeditions in the West, 1804–1806

The Louisiana Purchase of 1803 brought the U.S. a large territory without clear boundaries. Jefferson sent off four scientific expeditions to take stock of the land's possibilities and to assess the degree of potential antagonism from Indian and Spanish inhabitants.

READING THE MAP: How did the size of the newly acquired territory compare to the land area of the existing American states and territories? What natural features of the land might have suggested boundaries for the Louisiana Purchase? Did those natural features coincide with actual patterns of human habitation already in place?

CONNECTIONS: What political events in Europe created the opportunity for the Jefferson administration to purchase Louisiana? How did the acquisition of Louisiana affect Spain's hold on North America?

boundary, the negotiator replied, "I can give you no direction. You have made a noble bargain for yourself, and I suppose you will make the most of it."

Jefferson and most members of Congress were delighted with the **Louisiana Purchase**. In late 1803, the American army took formal control of the Louisiana Territory, and the United States nearly doubled in size — at least on paper. The Spanish inhabitants of New Orleans had relinquished the city to a few French officials just a month before the Americans arrived to claim it, and now many of the Spaniards left for Texas or West Florida (along the Gulf coast), lands still in Spanish hands. One departing Spanish officer expressed his loathing for the "ambitious, restless, lawless, conniving, changeable, and turbulent" Americans, writing, "I am so disgusted with hearing them that I can hardly wait to leave them behind me."

The Lewis and Clark Expedition

Jefferson quickly launched four government-financed expeditions up the river valleys of the new territory to establish relationships with Indian tribes and to determine Spanish influence and presence. The first set out in 1804 to explore the upper reaches of the Missouri River. Jefferson appointed twenty-eight-year-old Meriwether Lewis, his secretary, to head the expedition and instructed him to investigate Indian cultures, to collect plant and animal specimens, and to chart the geography of the West, with particular attention to locating the headwaters of the rivers "running southwardly" to Spain's settlements. (See "Visualizing History," page 298.) The expedition was also charged with scouting locations for military posts, negotiating fur trade agreements, and identifying river routes to the West (see Map 10.2).

For his co-leader, Lewis chose Kentuckian William Clark, a veteran of the 1790s Indian wars. Together, they handpicked a crew of forty-five, including expert rivermen, gunsmiths, hunters, interpreters, a cook, and Clark's slave named York. The explorers left St. Louis in the spring of 1804, working their way northwest up the Missouri River. They camped for the winter at a Mandan village in what is now central North Dakota. The Mandan Indians were familiar with British and French traders from Canada, but the black man York created a sensation. Reportedly, the Indians rubbed moistened fingers over the man's skin to see if the color was painted on.

The following spring, the explorers headed west, accompanied by a sixteen-year-old Shoshoni woman named **Sacajawea**. Kidnapped by Mandans at about age ten, she had been sold to a French trapper as a slave/wife. Hers was not a unique story among Indian women, and such women knew several languages, making them valuable translators and mediators. Further, Sacajawea and her new baby allowed the American expedition to appear peaceful to suspicious tribes. As Lewis wrote in his journal, "No woman ever accompanies a war party of Indians in this quarter."

The **Lewis and Clark expedition** reached the Pacific Ocean at the mouth of the Columbia River in November 1805. When the two leaders returned home the following year, they were greeted as national heroes. They had established favorable relations with dozens of Indian tribes; they had collected invaluable information on the peoples, soils, plants, animals, and geography of the West; and they had inspired a nation of restless explorers and solitary imitators.

Osage and Comanche Indians

The three additional U.S. expeditions set forth between 1804 and 1806 from the Mississippi River to probe the contested southwestern border of the Louisiana Purchase. The first exploring

Comanche Feats of Horsemanship, 1834
Pennsylvania artist George Catlin toured the Great Plains and captured Comanche equestrian warfare in training. "Every young man," Catlin wrote, learned "to drop his body upon the side of his horse at the instant he is passing, effectually screened from his enemies' weapons. . . . [H]e will hang whilst his horse is at fullest speed, carrying with him his bow and his shield, and also his long lance . . . which he will wield upon his enemy as he passes; rising and throwing his arrows over the horse's back, or with equal ease and equal success under the horse's neck."
Smithsonian American Art Museum, Washington, DC/Art Resource, NY.

Cultural Exchange on the Lewis and Clark Trail

Lewis and Clark carried many gifts for the Indians they anticipated meeting as they traveled up the Missouri River toward the Rocky Mountains. Intended to signal goodwill and respect, some of the gifts held other subtle meanings as well.

Upon encountering new tribes, the explorers presented high-ranking Indian leaders with silver medals bearing the likeness of President Jefferson, in two, three-, or four-inch sizes. Imagine the Indian recipients' reactions. What specific message might the image of the president convey? On what basis do you think the explorers chose to distribute the various sizes?

Thomas Jefferson's Peace Medal, 1801

The explorers traveled with ornamental trinkets ("ear bobs," silk handkerchiefs, ivory combs, ribbons) as well as practical goods (brass buttons, needles and thread, blankets, calico shirts) that demonstrated American manufacturing and handcraft. They carried a few small mirrors and magnifying glasses but on one occasion found that making fire with the latter engendered suspicion, not goodwill. Blue glass beads — portable and inexpensive — were a sought-after gift, leading Clark to observe that beads "may be justly compared to gold and Silver among civilized nations."

Blue Trade Beads

party left from Natchez, Mississippi, and ascended the Red River to the Ouachita River, ending at a hot springs in present-day Arkansas. Two years later, the second group of explorers followed the Red River west into eastern Texas, and the third embarked from St. Louis and traveled west, deep into the Rockies. This third group, led by Zebulon Pike, had gone too far, in the view of the Spaniards: Pike and his men were arrested, taken to northern Mexico, and soon released.

Of the scores of Indian tribes in this lower Great Plains region, two enjoyed reputations for territorial dominance. The **Osage** ruled the land between the Missouri and the lower Arkansas rivers, while the trading and raiding grounds of the **Comanche** stretched from the upper Arkansas River to the Rockies and south into Texas, a vast area called Comanchería. Both were formidable tribes that proved equal to the Spaniards. The Osage accomplished this through careful diplomacy and periodic shows of strength. The Comanche cemented their dominance by expert horsemanship; a brisk trade in guns, captives, and goods; and a constant readiness to employ strong-arm tactics and violence.

Jefferson turned his attention to cultivating the Osage, whose attractive lands (in present-day southern Missouri) beckoned as farmland in America's future. He directed Meriwether Lewis, on his way west, to invite the Osage to Washington City. When the delegation of eleven Osage leaders arrived in 1804, Jefferson greeted them as heads of state, with elaborate ceremonies and generous gifts. He positioned the Osage as equals of the Americans: "The great spirit has given you strength & has given us strength, not that we might hurt one another, but to do each other all the good in our power." Jefferson's goal was to make the Osage a strong trading partner, but he also had firm notions about what items to offer for trade: hoes and ploughs for the men; spinning wheels and looms for the women. These highly gendered tools signified a departure from the native gender system in which women tended crops while men hunted game. As Jefferson saw it, such equipment would bring the Indians the blessings of an agricultural civilization. Diminished reliance on the hunt would reduce the amount of land that tribes needed to sustain their communities. Jefferson expressed his hope that "commerce is the great engine by which we are to coerce them, & not war."

For their part, the Osage wanted Jefferson primarily to provide protection against Indian refugees displaced by American settlers east of the Mississippi. Jefferson's Osage alliance soon

Jefferson pointedly urged Lewis to take small hand-cranked corn mills, to acculturate the native women to American household technology. Indian women, with full charge of corn agriculture and its preparation as food, used mortars and pestles to pulverize dried kernels. Each time Lewis and Clark presented tribal chiefs with a corn mill and demonstrated its use, the recipients professed to be "highly pleased." Yet a year later, a fur trader visiting the Mandan nation wrote, "I saw the remains of an excellent large corn mill, which the foolish fellows had demolished to barb their arrows." Did the explorers perhaps fail in their mission by giving the mill to male leaders instead of to

Corn Mill Grinder

women? Or could this repurposing of the food grinder be read as a rejection by the women themselves of Americans' gendered practices?

The explorers received gifts as well. The most impressive was the necklace shown here, made of thirty-five four-inch grizzly bear claws. The explorers encountered a number of Indian men wearing bear claw "collars" (Lewis's term for it). For many tribes, bears were sacred animals, and their claws embodied spiritual power. Grizzlies are large (up to nine hundred pounds) and aggressive, so acquiring so many claws without firearms clearly took extraordinary courage. Can you imagine the impact of wearing such an ornament when meeting visitors from a distant and unknown society? Was it a forceful show of courage and power? Why might Indians bestow this rare necklace on the explorers? Did it honor their manly

Grizzly Bear Claw Necklace

courage? Or promote a spiritual brotherhood? Or might it have been intended to discourage further shootings of the sacred bears?

SOURCE: Jefferson's medal: Research Division of the Oklahoma Historical Society; trade beads: Ralph Thompson Collection of the North Dakota Lewis & Clark Bicentennial Foundation, Washburn, ND; corn mill: The Colonial Williamsburg Foundation; bear claw necklace: Peabody Museum, Harvard University, Photo 99-12-10/99700.

proved to be quite expensive, with costs arising from ransoming prisoners, providing defense, brokering treaties, and giving gifts all around. In 1806, a second ceremonial visit to Washington and other eastern cities by a dozen Osage leaders cost the federal government $10,000.

These promising peace initiatives were short-lived. By 1808, intertribal warfare was on the rise, and the governor of the Louisiana Territory declared that the U.S. government no longer had an obligation to protect the Osage. Jefferson's presidency was waning, and soon the practice of whittling away Indian lands through coercive treaties, so familiar to men like Tecumseh, reasserted itself. A treaty in 1808, followed by others in 1818, 1825, and 1839, shrank the Osage lands, and by the 1860s they were forced onto a small region in present-day Oklahoma.

By contrast, the Comanche managed to resist attempts to dominate them. For nearly a century, several branches of the tribe extended control over other tribes and over the Spaniards, holding the latter in check in small settlements clustered around Santa Fe in New Mexico and a few locations in Texas. Maps drawn in Europe marking Spanish ownership of vast North American lands simply did not correspond

to the reality on the ground. One sign of Comanche success was their demographic surge during the mid- to late eighteenth century, owing both to their ability to take captives and blend them into their tribe and to their superior command of food resources, especially buffalo.

In 1807, a Comanche delegation arrived at Natchitoches in Louisiana, where a newly appointed U.S. Indian agent entertained them lavishly to demonstrate American power and wealth. In a highly imaginative speech, the agent proclaimed an improbable solidarity with the Comanche: "It is now so long since our Ancestors came from beyond the great Water that we have no remembrance of it. We ourselves are Natives of the Same land that you are, in other words white Indians, we therefore Should feel & live together like brothers & Good Neighbours."

The Comanche welcomed the United States as a new trading partner and invited traders to travel into Comanchería to their market fairs. Into the late 1820s, this trade flourished on an extensive scale, with Americans selling weapons, cloth, and household metal goods in exchange for horses, mules, bison, and furs. And despite maps of the United States that showed the Red River just inside the southwestern border of the Louisiana

Purchase, the land from the Red north to the Arkansas River, west of Arkansas, remained under Indian control and thus off-limits to settlement by white Americans until the late nineteenth century (see Map 10.2).

> **REVIEW** Why was Spain concerned that France sold the Louisiana Territory to the United States?

▶ Jefferson, the Madisons, and the War of 1812

Jefferson easily retained the presidency in the election of 1804, with his 162 electoral votes trouncing the 14 won by Federalist Charles Cotesworth Pinckney of South Carolina. Jefferson faced seriously escalating tensions with both France and Britain, leading him to try a novel tactic, an embargo, to stave off war. His Republican secretary of state, James Madison, followed Jefferson as president in 1808, again defeating Pinckney but by a much narrower margin.

Madison continued with a modified embargo, but he broke from Jefferson's all-male style of social networking by involving his gregarious wife, Dolley Madison, in serious politics. Under James Madison's leadership, the country declared war in 1812 on Britain and on Tecumseh's Indian confederacy. The two-year war cost the young nation its White House and its Capitol, but victory was proclaimed at the end nonetheless.

Impressment and Embargo

In 1803, France and Britain went to war, and both repeatedly warned the United States not to ship arms to the other. Britain acted on these threats in 1806, stopping U.S. ships to inspect cargoes for military aid to France and seizing suspected deserters from the British navy, along with many Americans. Ultimately, 2,500 U.S. sailors were "impressed" (taken by force) by the British, who needed them for their war with France.

In retaliation against the **impressment** of American sailors, Jefferson convinced Congress to pass a nonimportation law banning a variety of British-made goods, such as leather products, window glass, and beer.

One incident made the usually cautious Jefferson nearly belligerent. In June 1807, the American ship *Chesapeake*, harboring some British deserters, was ordered to stop by the British frigate *Leopard*. The *Chesapeake* refused, and the *Leopard* opened fire, killing three Americans and capturing four alleged deserters—right at the mouth of the Chesapeake Bay, well within U.S. territorial waters. In response, Congress passed the **Embargo Act of 1807**, banning all importation of British goods into the country. Though a drastic measure, the embargo was meant to forestall war and make Britain suffer. All foreign ports were declared off-limits to American merchants to discourage illegal trading through secondary ports. Jefferson was convinced that Britain needed America's agricultural products far more than America needed British goods.

The Embargo Act of 1807 was a disaster. From 1790 to 1807, U.S. exports had increased fivefold, but the embargo brought commerce to a standstill. In New England, the heart of the shipping industry, unemployment rose. Grain plummeted in value, river traffic halted, tobacco rotted in the South, and cotton went unpicked. Protest petitions flooded Washington. The federal government suffered, too, for import duties were a significant source of revenue. Jefferson paid political costs as well and decided not to run for a third term. The Federalist Party, in danger of fading away after its weak showing in the election of 1804, began to revive.

James Madison was chosen to be the Republican candidate by party caucuses — informal political groups that orchestrated the selection of candidates for state and local elections. The Federalist caucuses again chose Pinckney, and in the election he secured 47 electoral votes, compared to 14 in 1804; Madison's total was 122. Support for the Federalists remained centered in New England, whose shipping industry suffered heavy losses in the embargo. The Republicans still held the balance of power nationwide.

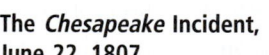

The *Chesapeake* Incident, June 22, 1807

***Dolley Madison*, by Gilbert Stuart**
The "presidentress" of the Madison administration sat for this official portrait in 1804. She wears an empire-style dress, at the height of French fashion in 1804 and a style worn by many women at the coronation of the emperor Napoleon in Paris. The hallmarks of such a dress were a light fabric (muslin or chiffon), short sleeves, a high waistline from which the fabric fell straight to the ground, and usually a low, open neckline, as shown here. © White House Historical Association.

Dolley Madison and Social Politics

As wife of the highest-ranking cabinet officer, **Dolley Madison** developed elaborate social networks during her first eight years in Washington. Hers constituted the top level of female politicking in the highly political city, since Jefferson had no First Lady. Although women could not vote and supposedly left politics to men, the female relatives of Washington politicians took on several overtly political functions that greased the wheels of the affairs of state. They networked through dinners, balls, receptions, and the intricate custom of "calling," in which men and women paid brief visits and left calling cards at each other's homes. Webs of friendship and influence in turn facilitated female political lobbying. It was not uncommon for women in this social set to write letters of recommendation for men seeking government work. Hostessing was no trivial or leisured business; it significantly influenced the federal government's patronage system.

When James Madison became president, Dolley Madison, called by some the "presidentress," struck a balance between queenliness and republican openness. She dressed the part in resplendent clothes, choosing a plumed velvet turban for her headdress at her husband's inauguration. She opened three elegant rooms in the executive mansion for a weekly open-house party called "Mrs. Madison's crush" or "squeeze." In contrast to George and Martha Washington's stiff, brief receptions, the Madisons' parties went on for hours, with scores or even hundreds of guests milling about, talking, and eating. Members of Congress, cabinet officers, distinguished guests, envoys from foreign countries, and their womenfolk attended with regularity. The affable and generous Mrs. Madison made her guests comfortable with small talk, but a female partygoer reported that "Mr. Madison had no leisure for the ladies; every moment of his time is engrossed by the crowd of male visitors who court his notice, and after passing the first complimentary salutations, his attention is unavoidably withdrawn to more important objects." His wife's weekly squeeze established informal channels of information and provided crucial political access, a key element of smooth governance.

In 1810–1811, the Madisons' house acquired its present name, the White House, probably in reference to its white-painted sandstone exterior. The many guests at the weekly parties experienced simultaneously the splendor of the executive mansion and the atmosphere of republicanism that made it accessible to so many. Dolley Madison, ever an enormous political asset to her rather shy husband, understood well the symbolic function of the White House to enhance the power and legitimacy of the presidency.

> **"Mr. Madison had no leisure for the ladies; every moment of his time is engrossed by the crowd of male visitors who court his notice."**
> — A female guest at Mrs. Madison's "squeeze"

Tecumseh and Tippecanoe

While the Madisons cemented alliances at home, difficulties with Britain and France overseas and with Indians in the old Northwest continued to increase. The Shawnee chief **Tecumseh** (see pages 289–90) actively solidified his confederacy, while the more northern tribes renewed their ties with supportive British agents and fur traders in Canada, a potential source of food and weapons. If the United States went to war with Britain, there would clearly be serious repercussions on the frontier.

MAP 10.3

Indian Lands Ceded by Treaties in the Northwest Territory, 1795–1809

The Treaty of Greenville (1795) transferred two-thirds of Ohio to the Americans. For more than a decade thereafter, officials such as William Henry Harrison managed to acquire for the United States vast tracts along the Ohio and Mississippi rivers by negotiating with Indians whose authority to speak for their tribes was often unclear or dubious. "Land Cessions in the Old Northwest, 1795–1809." From *Tecumseh: A Life* by John Sugden. Copyright 1997 by John Sugden. Reprinted with the permission of Henry Holt and Company LLC.

Shifting demographics raised the stakes for both sides. The 1810 census counted some 230,000 Americans in Ohio only seven years after it achieved statehood. Another 40,000 Americans inhabited the territories of Indiana, Illinois, and Michigan. The Indian population of the entire region (the old Northwest Territory) was much smaller, probably about 70,000, a number unknown to the Americans but certainly gauged by Tecumseh during his extensive travels.

Up to 1805, Indiana's territorial governor, William Henry Harrison, had negotiated a series of treaties in a divide-and-conquer strategy aimed at extracting Indian lands for paltry payments (Map 10.3). But with the rise to power of Tecumseh and his brother **Tenskwatawa**, the Prophet, Harrison's strategy faltered. A fundamental part of Tecumseh's message was the assertion that all Indian lands were held in common by all the tribes. "No tribe has the right to sell [these lands], even to each other, much less to strangers . . . ," Tecumseh said. "Sell a country! Why not sell the air, the great sea, as well as the earth? Didn't the Great Spirit make them all for the use of his children?" In 1809, while Tecumseh was away on a recruiting trip, Harrison assembled the leaders of the Potawatomi, Miami, and Delaware tribes to negotiate the Treaty of Fort Wayne. After promising (falsely) that this was the last cession of land the United States would seek, Harrison secured three million acres at about two cents per acre.

When he returned, Tecumseh was furious with both Harrison and the tribal leaders. Leaving his brother in charge at Prophetstown on the Tippecanoe River, the Shawnee chief left to seek alliances with tribes in the South. In November 1811, Harrison decided to attack Prophetstown with a thousand men. The two-hour battle resulted in the deaths of sixty-two Americans and forty

Indians before the Prophet's forces fled the town, which Harrison's men set on fire. The **battle of Tippecanoe** was heralded as a glorious victory for the Americans, but Tecumseh was now more ready than ever to make war on the United States.

The War of 1812

The Indian conflicts in the old Northwest soon merged into the wider conflict with Britain, now known as the War of 1812. In 1809, Congress replaced Jefferson's stringent embargo with the Non-Intercourse Act, which prohibited trade only with Britain and France and their colonies, thus restoring trade with other European countries to alleviate somewhat the anguish of shippers, farmers, and planters. By 1811, the country was seriously divided and on the verge of war.

The new Congress seated in March 1811 contained several dozen young Republicans eager to avenge the insults from abroad. Thirty-four-year-old **Henry Clay** from Kentucky and twenty-nine-year-old John C. Calhoun from South Carolina became the center of a group informally known as the **War Hawks**. Mostly lawyers by profession, they came from the West and South and welcomed a war with Britain both to justify attacks on the Indians and to bring an end to impressment. Many were also expansionists, looking to occupy Florida and threaten Canada. Clay was elected Speaker of the House, an extraordinary honor for a newcomer. Calhoun won a seat on the Foreign Relations Committee. The War Hawks approved major defense expenditures, and the army soon quadrupled in size.

In June 1812, Congress declared war on Great Britain in a vote divided along sectional lines: New England and some Middle Atlantic states opposed the war, fearing its effect on commerce, while the South and West were strongly for it. Ironically, Britain had just announced

Battle of Tippecanoe, 1811

that it would stop the search and seizure of American ships, but the war momentum would not be slowed. The Foreign Relations Committee issued an elaborate justification titled *Report on the Causes and Reasons for War*, written mainly by Calhoun and containing extravagant language about Britain's "lust for power," "unbounded tyranny," and "mad ambition." These were fighting words in a war that was in large measure about insult and honor.

The War Hawks proposed an invasion of Canada, confidently predicting victory in four weeks. Instead, the war lasted two and a half years, and Canada never fell. The northern invasion turned out to be a series of blunders that revealed America's grave unpreparedness for war against the unexpectedly powerful British and Indian forces. Detroit quickly fell, as did Fort Dearborn, site

MAP 10.4

The War of 1812

During the War of 1812, battles were fought along the Canadian border and in the Chesapeake region. The most important American victory came in New Orleans two weeks after a peace agreement had been signed in England.

The Burning of Washington City
On August 24, 1814, the British army entered the nation's capital and set government buildings ablaze. This British line engraving celebrates that victory, showing disciplined troops armed with torches. To the left behind the soldiers, the White House burns, as does the round dome of the Capitol in the distance. Some soldiers plundered for trophies of war that night. Shown here is James Madison's personal medicine chest, taken back to England by a British soldier. One of the soldier's descendants returned the souvenir to President Franklin D. Roosevelt in 1939. Engraving: Anne S. K. Brown Military Collection, Brown University Library; medicine chest: FDR Library.

of the future Chicago (Map 10.4). By the fall of 1812, the outlook was grim.

Worse, the New England states dragged their feet in raising troops, and some New England merchants carried on illegal trade with Britain. While President Madison fumed about Federalist disloyalty, Bostonians drank East India tea in Liverpool cups. The fall presidential election pitted Madison against DeWitt Clinton of New York, nominally a Republican but able to attract the Federalist vote. Clinton picked up all of New England's electoral votes, with the exception of Vermont's, and also took New York, New Jersey, and part of Maryland. Madison won in the electoral college, 128 to 89, but his margin of victory was considerably smaller than in 1808.

In late 1812 and early 1813, the tide began to turn in the Americans' favor. First came some reassuring victories at sea. Then the Americans attacked York (now Toronto) and burned it in April 1813. A few months later, Commodore Oliver Hazard Perry defeated the British fleet at the western end of Lake Erie. Emboldened, General Harrison drove an army into Canada from Detroit and in October 1813 defeated the British and Indians at the battle of the Thames, where Tecumseh was killed.

Creek Indians in the South who had allied with Tecumseh's confederacy were also plunged into all-out war. Some 10,000 living in the Mississippi Territory put up a spirited fight against U.S. forces for ten months in 1813–1814. Even without Tecumseh's recruitment trip of 1811 or the War of 1812, the Creeks had grievances aplenty, sparked by American settlers moving into their territory. Using guns obtained from Spanish Florida, the Creeks mounted a strong defense. But the **Creek War** ended suddenly in March 1814 when a general named Andrew Jackson led 2,500 Tennessee militiamen in a bloody attack called the Battle of Horseshoe Bend. More than 550 Indians were killed, and several hundred more died trying to escape across a river. Later that year, General Jackson extracted from the defeated tribe a treaty relinquishing thousands of square miles of their land to the United States.

Washington City Burns: The British Offensive

In August 1814, British ships sailed into the Chesapeake Bay, landing 5,000 troops and throwing the capital into a panic. Families evacuated, banks hid their money, and government clerks carted away boxes of important papers. Dolley Madison, with dinner for guests cooking over the fire, fled with her husband's papers, leaving several struggling servants to rescue a portrait of George Washington. As the cook related, "When the British did arrive, they ate up the very dinner, and drank the wines, &c.,

that I had prepared for the President's party." Then they torched the White House. They also burned the Capitol, a newspaper office, and a well-stocked arsenal. Instead of trying to hold the city, the British headed north and attacked Baltimore, but a fierce defense by the Maryland militia thwarted that effort.

In another powerful offensive that same month, British troops marched from Canada into New York State, but a series of mistakes cost them a naval skirmish at Plattsburgh on Lake Champlain, and they retreated to Canada. Five months later, another large British army landed in lower Louisiana and, in early January 1815, encountered General Andrew Jackson and his militia just outside New Orleans. Jackson's forces dramatically carried the day. The British suffered between 2,000 and 3,000 casualties, the Americans fewer than 80. Jackson became an instant hero. The **battle of New Orleans** was the most glorious victory the Americans had experienced, allowing some Americans to boast that the United States had won a second war of independence from Britain. No one in the United States knew that negotiators in Europe had signed a peace agreement two weeks earlier.

The Treaty of Ghent, signed in December 1814, settled few of the surface issues that had led to war. Neither country could claim victory, and no land changed hands. Instead, the treaty reflected a mutual agreement to give up certain goals. The Americans dropped their plea for an end to impressments, which in any case subsided as soon as Britain and France ended their war in 1815. They also gave up any claim to Canada. The British agreed to stop all aid to the Indians. Nothing was said about shipping rights. The most concrete result was a plan for a commission to determine the exact boundary between the United States and Canada.

Antiwar Federalists in New England could not gloat over the war's ambiguous conclusion because of an ill-timed and seemingly unpatriotic move on their part. The region's leaders had convened a secret meeting in Hartford, Connecticut, in December 1814 to discuss dramatic measures to curb the South's power. They proposed abolishing the Constitution's three-fifths clause as a basis of representation; requiring a two-thirds vote instead of a simple majority for imposing embargoes, admitting states, or declaring war; limiting the president to one term; and prohibiting the election of successive presidents from the same state. The cumulative aim of these proposals was to reduce the South's political power and break Virginia's lock on the

presidency. New England wanted to make sure that no sectional party could again lead the country into war against the clear interests of another. The Federalists at Hartford even discussed secession from the Union but rejected that path. Coming just as peace was achieved, however, the **Hartford Convention** looked very unpatriotic. The Federalist Party never recovered its grip, and within a few years it was reduced to a shadow of its former self, even in New England.

No one really won the War of 1812; however, Americans celebrated as though they had, with parades and fireworks. The war gave rise to a new spirit of nationalism. The paranoia over British tyranny evident in the 1812 declaration of war was laid to rest, replaced by pride in a more equal relationship with the old mother country. Indeed, in 1817 the two countries signed the Rush-Bagot disarmament treaty (named after its two negotiators), which limited each country to a total of four naval vessels, each with just a single cannon, to patrol the vast watery border between them. The Rush-Bagot treaty was perhaps the most successful disarmament treaty for a century to come.

The biggest winners in the War of 1812 were the young men, once called War Hawks, who took up the banner of the Republican Party and carried it in new, expansive directions. These young politicians favored trade, western expansion, internal improvements, and the energetic development of new economic markets. The biggest losers of the war were the Indians. Tecumseh was dead, his brother the Prophet was discredited, the prospects of an Indian confederacy were dashed, the Creeks' large homeland was seized, and the British protectors were gone.

REVIEW   Why did Congress declare war on Great Britain in 1812?

▶ Women's Status in the Early Republic

Dolley Madison's pioneering role as "presidentress" showed that at the pinnacles of power, elite women could assume an active presence in civic affairs. But, as with the 1790s cultural compromise that endorsed female education to make women into better wives and mothers (see chapter 9), Mrs. Madison and her female circle practiced politics to further their husbands' careers. There was little talk of the "rights of woman."

From 1800 to 1825, key institutions central to the shaping of women's lives — the legal system, marriage, and religion — proved fairly resistant to change. State legislatures and the courts maintained the legal dependency of married white women in a country whose defining characteristic for men was independence. Marriage laws for whites continued to support unequal power between men and women, while religious organizations reconsidered the role of women in church governance in the face of rising church membership rates for women. The most dramatic opportunity for women came with the flowering of female academies whose rigorous curricula fostered high-level literacy and rational thought. Even when advertised as institutions to prepare girls to be intelligent mothers, many academies built up their students' self-confidence and implanted expectations that their mental training would find a use beyond the kitchen and nursery.

Women and the Law

The Anglo-American view of women, embedded in English common law, was that wives had no independent legal or political personhood. The legal doctrine of *feme covert* (covered woman) held that a wife's civic life was completely subsumed by her husband's. A wife was obligated to obey her husband; her property was his, her domestic and sexual services were his, and even their children were legally his. Women had no right to keep their wages, to make contracts, or to sue or be sued.

State legislatures generally passed up the opportunity to rewrite the laws of domestic relations even though they redrafted other British laws in light of republican principles. Lawyers never paused to defend, much less to challenge, the assumption that unequal power relations lay at the heart of marriage.

The one aspect of family law that changed in the early Republic was divorce. Before the Revolution, only New England jurisdictions recognized a limited right to divorce; by 1820, every state except South Carolina did so. However, divorce was uncommon and in many states could be obtained only by petition to the state's legislature, a daunting obstacle for many ordinary people. A mutual wish to terminate a marriage was never sufficient grounds for a legal divorce. A New York judge affirmed that "it would be aiming a deadly blow at public morals to decree a dissolution of the marriage contract merely because the parties requested it.

Divorces should never be allowed, except for the protection of the innocent party, and for the punishment of the guilty." States upheld the institution of marriage both to protect persons they thought of as naturally dependent (women and children) and to regulate the use and inheritance of property. (Unofficial self-divorce, desertion, and bigamy were remedies that ordinary people sometimes chose to get around the law, but all were socially unacceptable.) Legal enforcement of marriage as an unequal relationship played a major role in maintaining gender inequality in the nineteenth century.

Single adult women could own and convey property, make contracts, initiate lawsuits, and pay taxes. They could not vote (except in New Jersey before 1807), serve on juries, or practice law, so their civil status was limited. Single women's economic status was often limited as well, by custom as much as by law. Job prospects were few and low-paying. Unless they had inherited adequate property or could live with married siblings, single adult women in the early Republic very often were poor.

None of the legal institutions that structured white gender relations applied to black slaves. As property themselves, under the jurisdiction of slave owners, they could not freely consent to any contractual obligations, including marriage. The protective features of state-sponsored unions were thus denied to black men and women in slavery. But this also meant that slave unions did not establish unequal power relations between partners backed by the force of law, as did marriages among the free.

Women and Church Governance

In most Protestant denominations around 1800, white women made up the majority of congregants. Yet church leadership of most denominations rested in men's hands. There were some exceptions, however. In Baptist congregations in New England, women served along with men on church governance committees, deciding on the admission of new members, voting on hiring ministers, and even debating doctrinal points. Quakers, too, had a history of recognizing women's spiritual talents. Some were accorded the status of minister, capable of leading and speaking in Quaker meetings.

Between 1790 and 1820, a small and highly unusual set of women actively engaged in open preaching. Most were from Freewill Baptist

Women and the Church: Jemima Wilkinson
In this early woodcut, Jemima Wilkinson, "the Publick Universal Friend," wears a clerical collar and body-obscuring robe, in keeping with the claim that the former Jemima was now a person without gender. With hair pulled back tight on the head and curled at the neck in a masculine style of the 1790s, was Wilkinson masculinized, or did the "Universal Friend" truly transcend gender? Rhode Island Historical Society.

in men's clothes, wore her hair in a masculine style, shunned gender-specific pronouns, and preached openly in Rhode Island and Philadelphia. In the early nineteenth century, Wilkinson established a town called New Jerusalem in western New York with some 250 followers. Her fame was sustained by periodic newspaper articles that fed public curiosity about her lifelong transvestism and her unfeminine forcefulness.

The decades from 1790 to the 1820s marked a period of unusual confusion, ferment, and creativity in American religion. New denominations blossomed, new styles of religiosity gripped adherents, and an extensive periodical press devoted to religion popularized all manner of theological and institutional innovations. In such a climate, the age-old tradition of gender subordination came into question here and there among the most radically democratic of the churches. But the presumption of male authority over women was deeply entrenched in American culture. Even denominations that had allowed women to participate in church governance began to pull back, and most churches reinstated patterns of hierarchy along gender lines.

Female Education

First in the North and then in the South, states and localities began investing in public schools to foster an educated citizenry deemed essential to the healthy functioning of a republic. Young girls attended district schools, sometimes along with boys or, in rural areas, more often in separate summer sessions. Basic literacy and numeracy formed the curriculum taught to white children aged roughly six to eleven. By 1830, girls had made rapid gains, in many places approaching male literacy rates. (Far fewer schools addressed the needs of free black children, whether male or female.)

More advanced female education came from a growing number of private academies. Judith Sargent Murray, the Massachusetts author who had called for equality of the sexes around 1790 (see chapter 9), predicted in 1800 that "a new era in female history" would emerge because "**female academies** are everywhere establishing." Some dozen female academies were established in the 1790s, and by 1830 that number had grown to nearly two hundred. Candidates for admission were primarily daughters of elite families as well as those of middling families with elite or intellectual aspirations, such as ministers' daughters.

groups centered in New England and upstate New York. Others came from small Methodist sects, and yet others rejected any formal religious affiliation. Probably fewer than a hundred such women existed, but several dozen traveled beyond their local communities, creating converts and controversy. They spoke from the heart, without prepared speeches, often exhibiting trances and claiming to exhort (counsel or warn) rather than to preach.

The best-known exhorting woman was **Jemima Wilkinson**, who called herself "the Publick Universal Friend." After a near-death experience from a high fever, Wilkinson proclaimed her body no longer female or male but the incarnation of the "Spirit of Light." She dressed

One Woman's Quest to Provide Higher Education for Women

Talented young men seeking the mental enrichment and career boost of higher education saw their opportunities expand rapidly in the early Republic. By 1830, six dozen private and state-chartered institutions offered them training in science, history, religion, literature, and philosophy. Yet not a single one admitted females.

With the spread of district schools and female academies, however, the number of girls trained for advanced study was on the rise. The winning rationale for female education — that mothers molded the character of rising generations — worked well to justify basic schooling. But a highly intellectual woman, negatively termed a "bluestocking," was thought to put her very femininity at risk. Some critics sounded a more practical note: "When girls become scholars, who is to make the puddings and pies?"

The academic aspirations of Emma Hart — born in Connecticut in 1787 as the sixteenth in a farm family of seventeen children — were encouraged by her father, who read Shakespeare at night to his large brood. After graduating from the local district school and then an academy for girls, Emma taught for a term at the district school before moving to Vermont to head the Middlebury Female Academy, founded in 1800. There, she taught sixty adolescents in an underheated building.

Emma ran the academy for two years until her marriage in 1809 to an established Middlebury physician and banker named John Willard. Marriage for white women usually brought an end to employment outside the home. Yet despite caring for a baby and attending to her domestic duties, Emma found time to read books from her husband's well-stocked library. She read widely, from political philosophy to medical treatises, physiology texts, and even Euclid's geometry.

Four years into their marriage, John Willard suffered severe financial losses. This turn of events led Emma Willard to open an advanced girls' school in her home. She patterned her courses on those at nearby Middlebury College for men, and her rigorous curriculum soon drew students from all over the Northeast. One satisfied father with political connections persuaded the Willards to relocate to his home state of New York with the promise to help them secure state funding for a school.

Emma drew up a formal proposal in 1819, arguing that advanced female education would both enhance motherhood and supply excellent teachers needed for a projected state-supported school system. Though her proposal was endorsed by Governor DeWitt Clinton, John Adams, and Thomas Jefferson, the New York assembly failed to fund Willard's school. Local citizens in Troy supplied Willard with a building, however, and in 1821 the Troy Female Seminary opened with students coming from many states. Willard deliberately chose the modest term "seminary" instead of "college," which was "the province of the men." Yet her rigorous curriculum did include "masculine" subjects such as Latin, Greek, mathematics, and science in addition to modern languages and

The three-year curriculum included both ornamental arts and solid academics. The former strengthened female gentility: drawing, needlework, music, and French conversation. The academic subjects included English grammar, literature, history, the natural sciences, geography, and elocution (the art of effective public speaking). Academy catalogs show that, by the 1820s, the courses and reading lists at the top female academies equaled those at male colleges such as Harvard, Yale, Dartmouth, and Princeton. The girls at these academies studied Latin, rhetoric, logic, theology, moral philosophy, algebra, geometry, and even chemistry and physics.

Two of the best-known female academies were the Troy Female Seminary in New York, founded by Emma Willard in 1821, and the Hartford Seminary in Connecticut, founded by Catharine Beecher in 1822. (See "Seeking the American Promise," page 308.) Unlike theological seminaries that trained men for the clergy, Troy and Hartford prepared their female students to teach, on the grounds that women made better teachers than did men. Author Harriet Beecher Stowe, educated at her sister's school and then a teacher there, agreed: "If men have more knowledge they have less talent at communicating it. Nor have they the patience, the long-suffering, and gentleness necessary to superintend the formation of character."

literature. Willard taught geometry and trigonometry herself and hired other teachers for classes in astronomy, botany, geology, chemistry, and zoology. She soon forged a cooperative alliance with the neighboring Rensselaer Polytechnic Institute. In direct emulation of Harvard and Princeton, her seminary also offered a required course in moral philosophy, which Willard herself taught to all senior students using the same texts employed at the male colleges.

Willard invited the public to weeklong examinations, where students solved algebra problems and geometry proofs on chalkboards and gave twenty-minute discourses on history and philosophy. Educated men were particularly encouraged to question the students, to put to rest any "lurking suspicion, that the learning which a female possesses must be superficial." One minister was astonished, and pleased, to see "Euclid discussed by female lips." By emphasizing geometry, Willard vindicated her claim that women could equal men in logic. But she took pains to make sure her students preserved "feminine delicacy" and avoided "the least indelicacy of language or behavior, such as too much exposure of the person."

More than the rigorous curriculum inspired these young women. Willard was an exemplary role model, beloved by many of her students for her dedication and confidence. A student named Elizabeth Cady, who attended the seminary in the 1830s and later became an important figure in the woman's rights movement, recalled that Willard had a "profound self respect (a rare quality in a woman) which gave her a dignity truly regal." Willard graciously gave much of the credit to her unusually supportive husband: "He entered into the full spirit of my views, with a disinterested zeal for the sex whom, as he had come to believe, his own had unjustly neglected."

The Troy Female Seminary flourished; it still exists today as the Emma Willard School. From 1821 to 1871, more than 12,000 girls attended; it was larger than most men's colleges. Ministers' daughters received a discount on tuition, and many girls were allowed to defer payment until they were wage-earning teachers. Nearly 5,000 graduates in the first fifty years became teachers, and some 150 directed their own schools scattered across the nation. When the marquis de Lafayette, aging hero of the American Revolution, visited Willard's school in 1824, he pronounced it a "Female University." Surely, Willard took pleasure in his recognition of her success.

Portrait of Emma Willard
Emma Hart Willard's calm composure shines through in this portrait. Emma Willard School.

Questions for Consideration

1. How did Emma Willard's own life demonstrate the importance of female education for a family's financial security?

2. Compare the occupation of Emma Willard with that of Dolley Madison. In what ways were these women similar? How did they differ?

The most immediate value of advanced female education lay in the self-cultivation and confidence it provided. Following the model of male colleges, female graduation exercises showcased speeches and recitations performed in front of a mixed-sex audience of family, friends, and local notables. Here, the young women's elocution studies paid off; they had learned the art of persuasion along with correct pronunciation and the skill of fluent speaking. Academies also took care to promote a pleasing female modesty. Female pedantry or intellectual immodesty triggered the stereotype of the "bluestocking," a British term of hostility for a too-learned woman doomed to fail in the marriage market.

By the mid-1820s, the total annual enrollment at the female academies and seminaries equaled enrollment at the near six dozen male colleges in the United States. Both groups accounted for only about 1 percent of their age cohorts in the country at large, indicating that advanced education was clearly limited to a privileged few. Among the men, this group disproportionately filled the future rosters of ministers, lawyers, judges, and political leaders. Most female graduates in time married and raised families, but first many of them became teachers at academies and district schools. A large number also became authors, contributing essays and poetry to newspapers,

An Academy Student's Embroidery
Girls in the burgeoning female academies studied grammar, history, geography, arithmetic, French, and sometimes Greek, Latin, and geometry, although study of ancient languages and abstruse math was sometimes criticized as an intrusion into male domains. Female students also learned ornamental sewing. This work of silk embroidery comes from South Carolina and probably dates from around 1800–1810, judging from the high-waisted dress style. It shows an accomplished student, with map and globe on the table. What do you think would be more challenging for a 14-year-old girl: to learn basic arithmetic or to embroider so expertly? Rivers Collection, Charleston.

editing periodicals, and publishing novels. The new attention to the training of female minds laid the foundation for major changes in the gender system as girl students of the 1810s matured into adult women of the 1830s.

> REVIEW   How did the civil status of American women and men differ in the early Republic?

▶ Monroe and Adams

With the elections of 1816 and 1820, Virginians continued their hold on the presidency. In 1816, **James Monroe** beat Federalist Rufus King of New York, garnering 183 electoral votes to King's 34. In 1820, the Republican Monroe was reelected with all but one electoral vote. The collapse of the Federalist Party ushered in an apparent period of one-party rule, but politics remained highly contentious. At the state level, increasing voter engagement sparked a drive for universal white male suffrage.

Many factors promoted increased partisanship. Monroe and his aloof wife, Elizabeth, sharply curtailed social gatherings at the White House, driving the hard work of social networking into competing channels. Ill feelings were stirred by a sectional crisis over the admission of Missouri to the Union, and foreign policy questions involving European claims to Latin America animated sharp disagreements as well. The election of 1824 brought forth an abundance of candidates, all claiming to be Republicans. The winner was John Quincy Adams in an election decided by the House of Representatives and, many believed, a backroom bargain. Put to the test of practical circumstances, the one-party political system failed and then fractured.

From Property to Democracy

Up to 1820, presidential elections occurred in the electoral college, at a remove from ordinary voters. The excitement generated by state elections, however, created an insistent pressure for greater democratization of presidential elections.

In the 1780s, twelve of the original thirteen states enacted property qualifications based on the time-honored theory that only male freeholders — landowners, as distinct from tenants or servants — had sufficient independence of mind to be entrusted with the vote. Of course, not everyone accepted that restricted idea of the people's role in government (see chapter 8). In the 1790s, Vermont became the first state to enfranchise all adult males, and four other states soon broadened suffrage considerably by allowing all male taxpayers to vote, a status that could be triggered simply by owning a cow, since local property taxes were an ever-present and generally nonburdensome reality. Between 1800 and 1830, greater democratization became a lively issue both in established states and in new states emerging in the West.

In the established states, lively newspaper exchanges and petition campaigns pushed state after state to hold constitutional conventions, where questions of suffrage, balloting procedures, apportionment, and representation were hotly debated. Both political philosophy and practical politics were entwined in these debates: Who are "the people" in a government founded on popular sovereignty, and whose party or interest group gains the most from expanded suffrage?

In new states, small populations together with yet smaller numbers of large property owners meant that few men could vote under typical restrictive property qualifications. Congress initially set a fifty-acre freehold as the threshold

Painting on a patriotic motif by John A. Woodside of Philadelphia in the early 1800s.

for voting, but in Illinois fewer than three hundred men met that test at the time of statehood. When Indiana, Illinois, and Mississippi became states, their constitutions granted suffrage to all taxpayers. Five additional new western states abandoned property and taxpayer qualifications altogether.

The most heated battles over suffrage occurred in eastern states, where expanding numbers of commercial men, renters, and mortgage holders of all classes contended with entrenched landed elites who, not surprisingly, favored the status quo. Still, by 1820, half a dozen states passed suffrage reform. Some stopped short of complete male suffrage, instead tying the vote to tax status or militia service. In the remainder of the states, the defenders of landed property qualifications managed to delay expanded suffrage for two more decades. But it was increasingly hard to persuade the disfranchised that landowners alone had a stake in government. Proponents of the status quo began to argue instead that the "industry and good habits" necessary to achieve a propertied status in life were what gave landowners the right character to vote. Opponents fired back blistering attacks. One delegate to New York's constitutional convention said, "More integrity and more patriotism are generally found in the labouring class of the community than in the higher orders."

Owning land was no more predictive of wisdom and good character than it was of a person's height or strength, said another observer.

Both sides of the debate generally agreed that character mattered, and many ideas for ensuring an electorate of proper wisdom came up for discussion. The exclusion of paupers and felons convicted of "infamous crimes" found favor in legislation in many states. Literacy tests and raising the voting age to a figure in the thirties were debated but ultimately discarded. The exclusion of women required no discussion in the constitutional conventions, so firm was the legal power of *feme covert*. But in one exceptional moment, at the Virginia convention in 1829, a delegate wondered aloud why unmarried women over the age of twenty-one could not vote; he was quickly silenced with the argument that all women lacked the "free agency and intelligence" necessary for wise voting.

Free black men's enfranchisement was another story, generating much discussion at all the conventions. Under existing freehold qualifications, a small number of propertied black men could vote; universal or taxpayer suffrage would inevitably enfranchise many more. Many delegates at the various state conventions spoke against that extension, claiming that blacks as a race lacked prudence, independence, and knowledge. With the exception of New York, which

The House of Representatives, by Samuel F. B. Morse, 1822
In this large chamber, arising in 1815–1819 from the ashes of the old Capitol, Congress debated the various Missouri statehood bills. Built in a grand classical style, the room had towering marble columns and a cast-steel dome. A window in the dome provided natural light; the oil chandelier, lowered and lighted by hand, permitted evening sessions. Unfortunately, echoes bouncing off the smooth dome ruined the room's acoustics. Various fixes were tried — hanging draperies, rearranging the desks. In 1850 Congress finally authorized a bigger chamber. The room shown here is now called Statuary Hall, where Capitol visitors can experience for themselves the poor acoustics. Samuel F. B. Morse, *The House of Representatives*, completed 1822; probably reworked 1823; oil on canvas, 86-7/8 x 130-5/8 inches. The Corcoran Gallery of Art, Washington, D.C., Museum Purchase, Gallery Fund 11.14.

into the state. Tallmadge's model was New York's gradual emancipation law of 1799 (see chapter 8). It did not strip slave owners of their current property, and it allowed them full use of the labor of newborn slaves well into their prime productive years. Still, southern congressmen objected because in the long run the amendments would make Missouri a free state, presumably no longer allied with southern economic and political interests. Just as southern economic power rested on slave labor, southern political power drew extra strength from the slave population because of the three-fifths rule. In 1820, the South owed seventeen of its seats in the House of Representatives to its slave population.

Tallmadge's amendments passed in the House by a close and sharply sectional vote of North against South. The ferocious debate led a Georgia representative to observe that the question had started "a fire which all the waters of the ocean could not extinguish. It can be extinguished only in blood." The Senate, with an even number of slave and free states, voted down the amendments, and Missouri statehood was postponed until the next congressional term.

In 1820, a compromise emerged. Maine, once part of Massachusetts, applied for statehood as a free state, balancing against Missouri as a slave state. The Senate further agreed that the southern boundary of Missouri — latitude 36°30' — extended west, would become the permanent line dividing slave from free states, guaranteeing the North a large area where slavery was banned (Map 10.5). The House also approved the **Missouri Compromise**, thanks to expert deal brokering by Kentucky's Henry Clay, who earned the nickname "the Great Pacificator" for his superb negotiating skills. The whole package passed because seventeen northern congressmen decided that minimizing sectional conflict was the best course and voted with the South.

President Monroe and former president Jefferson at first worried that the Missouri crisis would reinvigorate the Federalist Party as the party of the North. But even ex-Federalists agreed that the split between free and slave states was too dangerous a fault line to be permitted to become a shaper of national politics. When new parties did develop in the 1830s, they

retained the existing property qualification for black voters as it removed it for whites, the general pattern was one of expanded suffrage for whites and a total eclipse of suffrage for blacks.

The Missouri Compromise

The politics of race produced the most divisive issue during Monroe's term. In February 1819, Missouri—so recently the territory of the powerful Osage Indians—applied for statehood. Since 1815, four other states had joined the Union (Indiana, Mississippi, Illinois, and Alabama) following the blueprint laid out by the Northwest Ordinance of 1787. But Missouri posed a problem. Although much of its area was on the same latitude as the free state of Illinois, its territorial population included ten thousand slaves brought there by southern planters.

Missouri's unusual combination of geography and demography led a New York congressman, James Tallmadge Jr., to propose two amendments to the statehood bill. The first stipulated that slaves born in Missouri after statehood would be free at age twenty-five, and the second declared that no new slaves could be imported

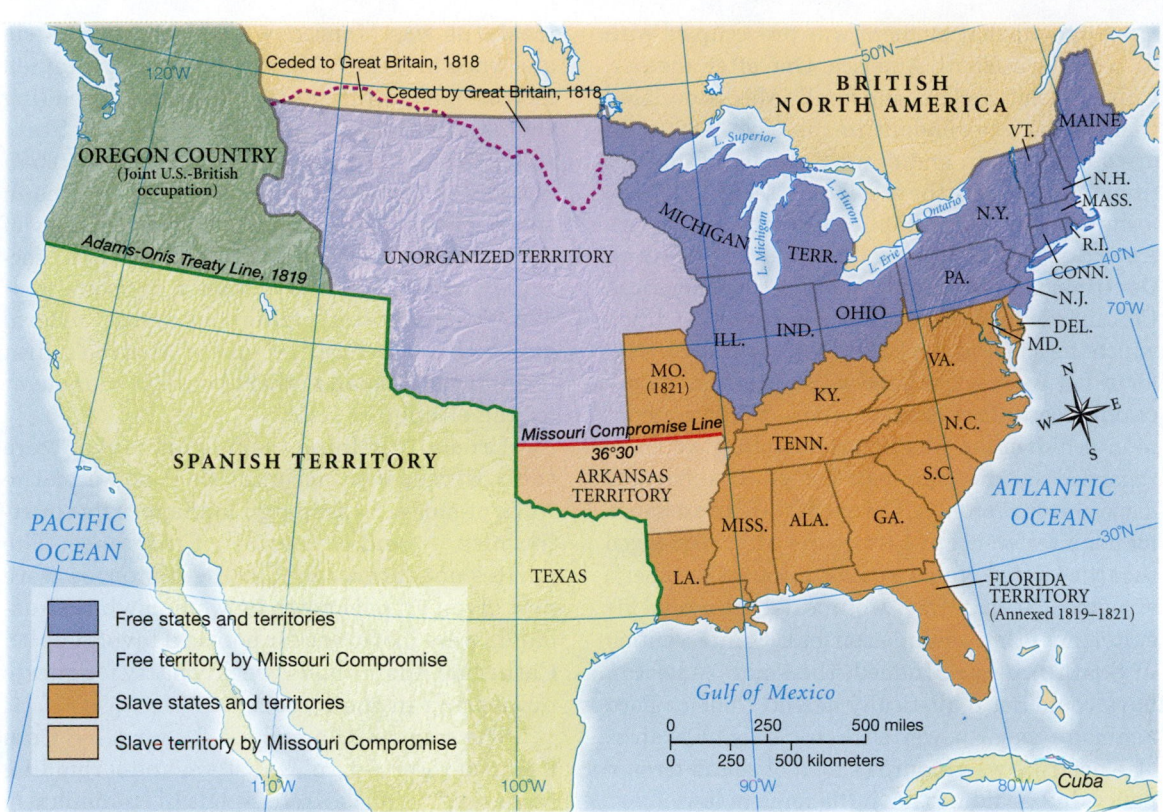

Free states and territories

Free territory by Missouri Compromise

Slave states and territories

Slave territory by Missouri Compromise

MAP ACTIVITY

Map 10.5 The Missouri Compromise, 1820

After a difficult battle in Congress, Missouri entered the Union in 1821 as part of a package of compromises. Maine was admitted as a free state to balance slavery in Missouri, and a line drawn at latitude 36°30' put most of the rest of the Louisiana Territory off-limits to slavery in the future.

READING THE MAP: How many free and how many slave states were there prior to the Missouri Compromise? What did the admission of Missouri as a slave state threaten to do?

CONNECTIONS: Who precipitated the crisis over Missouri, what did he propose, and where did the idea come from? Who proposed the Missouri Compromise, and who benefited from it?

took pains to bridge geography, each party developing a presence in both North and South. Monroe and Jefferson also worried about the future of slavery. Both understood slavery to be deeply problematic, but, as Jefferson said, "we have the wolf by the ears, and we can neither hold him, nor safely let him go. Justice is in one scale, and self-preservation in the other."

The Monroe Doctrine

As Congress struggled with the slavery issue, new foreign policy challenges also arose. In 1816, U.S. troops led by General Andrew Jackson invaded Spanish Florida in search of Seminole Indians harboring escaped slaves. Once there, Jackson declared himself the commander of northern Florida, demonstrating his power in 1818 by executing two British men who he claimed were dangerous enemies. In asserting rule over the territory, and surely in executing the two British subjects on Spanish land, Jackson had gone too far. Privately, President Monroe was distressed and pondered court-martialing Jackson, prevented only by Jackson's immense popularity as the hero of the battle of New Orleans. Instead, John Quincy Adams, the secretary of state, negotiated with Spain the Adams-Onís Treaty, which delivered all of Florida to the United States in 1819 and finally settled the disputed borders of the Louisiana Purchase. In exchange, the Americans agreed to abandon any claim to Texas or Cuba. Southerners viewed this as a large concession, having eyed both places as potential acquisitions for future slave states.

Spain at that moment was preoccupied with its colonies in South America. One after another, Chile, Colombia, Peru, and finally Mexico declared themselves independent in the early 1820s. To discourage Spain and other European countries from reconquering these colonies, Monroe in 1823 formulated a declaration of principles on South America, known in later years as the **Monroe Doctrine**. The president warned that "the American Continents, by the free and independent condition which they have assumed and maintain, are henceforth not to be considered as subjects for future colonization by any European power." Any attempt to interfere in the Western Hemisphere would be regarded as "the manifestation of an unfriendly disposition towards the United States." In exchange for noninterference by Europeans, Monroe pledged that the United States would stay out of European struggles. At that time, Monroe did not intend his statement to lay a foundation for U.S. intervention in South America. Indeed, the small American navy could not realistically defend Chile or Peru against a major power such as Spain or France. The doctrine was Monroe's idea of sound foreign policy, but it did not have the force of law.

The Election of 1824

Monroe's nonpartisan administration was the last of its kind, a throwback to eighteenth-century ideals, as was Monroe, with his powdered wig and knee breeches. Monroe's cabinet contained men of sharply different philosophies, all calling themselves Republicans. Secretary of State **John Quincy Adams** represented the urban Northeast; South Carolinian John C. Calhoun spoke for the planter aristocracy as secretary of war; and William H. Crawford of Georgia, secretary of the treasury, was a proponent of Jeffersonian states' rights and limited federal power. Even before the end of Monroe's first term, these men and others began to maneuver for the election of 1824.

Crucially helping them to maneuver were their wives, who accomplished some of the work of modern campaign managers by courting men — and women — of influence. The parties not thrown by Elizabeth Monroe were now given all over town by women whose husbands were jockeying for political favor. Louisa Catherine Adams had a weekly party for guests numbering in the hundreds.

The somber Adams lacked charm — "I am a man of reserved, cold, austere, and forbidding manners," he once wrote — but his abundantly charming (and hardworking) wife made up for that. She attended to the etiquette of social calls, sometimes making two dozen in a morning, and counted sixty-eight members of Congress as her regular guests. This was smart politics, in case

Election Sewing or Trinket Boxes from 1824

Women could express their support for a presidential candidate by purchasing a sewing box emblazoned with his face. On the left is a box with John Quincy Adams's picture inside the cover; the top of the box (not visible here) has a velvet pincushion printed with the slogan "Be Firm for Adams." The competing box on the right features Andrew Jackson's likeness under glass on top of the cover. The lithographic portrait was hand-colored with watercolors. Notice that Jackson is shown in his military uniform, with the title of general and a rather younger-looking face than he actually had in 1824. Collection of Janice L. and David J. Frent.

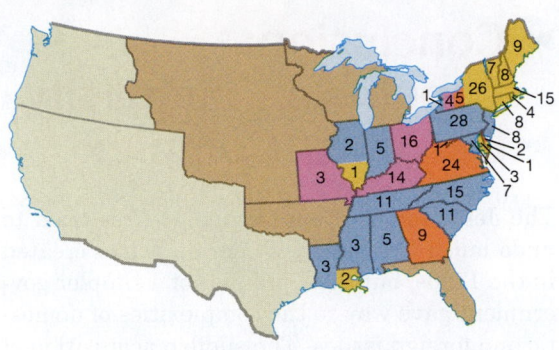

Candidate*	Electoral Vote	Popular Vote	Percent of Popular Vote
John Q. Adams	84	108,740	30.5
Andrew Jackson	99	153,544	43.1
Henry Clay	37	47,136	13.2
W. H. Crawford	41	46,618	13.1

*No distinct political parties

Note: Because no candidate garnered a majority in the electoral college, the election was decided in the House of Representatives. Although Clay was eliminated from the running, as Speaker of the House he influenced the final decision in favor of Adams.

MAP 10.6
The Election of 1824

the House of Representatives wound up deciding the 1824 election — which it did.

John Quincy Adams (as well as Louisa Catherine) was ambitious for the presidency, but so were others. Candidate Henry Clay, Speaker of the House and negotiator of the Treaty of Ghent with Britain in 1814, promoted a new "American System," a package of protective tariffs to encourage manufacturing and federal expenditures for internal improvements such as roads and canals. Treasurer William Crawford was a favorite of Republicans from Virginia and New York, even after he suffered an incapacitating stroke in mid-1824. Calhoun was another serious contender, having served in Congress and in several cabinets. A southern planter, he attracted northern support for his backing of internal improvements and protective tariffs.

The final candidate was an outsider and a latecomer: General **Andrew Jackson** of Tennessee. Jackson had far less national political experience than the others, but he enjoyed great celebrity from his military career. In 1824, on the anniversary of the battle of New Orleans, the Adamses threw a spectacular ball in his honor, hoping that some of Jackson's charisma would rub off on Adams, who was not yet think-

ing of Jackson as a rival for office. Not long after, Jackson's supporters put his name forward for the presidency, and voters in the West and South reacted with enthusiasm. Adams was dismayed, while Calhoun dropped out of the race and shifted his attention to winning the vice presidency.

Along with democratizing the vote, eighteen states (out of the full twenty-four) had put the power to choose members of the electoral college directly in the hands of voters, making the 1824 election the first one to have a popular vote tally for the presidency. Jackson proved by far to be the most popular candidate, winning 153,544 votes. Adams was second with 108,740, Clay won 47,136 votes, and the debilitated Crawford garnered 46,618. This was not a large turnout, probably amounting to just over a quarter of adult white males. Nevertheless, the election of 1824 marked a new departure in choosing presidents. Partisanship energized the electorate; apathy and a low voter turnout would not recur until the twentieth century.

In the electoral college, Jackson received 99 votes, Adams 84, Crawford 41, and Clay 37 (Map 10.6). Jackson lacked a majority, so the House of Representatives stepped in for the second time in U.S. history. Each congressional delegation had one vote; according to the Constitution's Twelfth Amendment, passed in 1804, only the top three candidates joined the runoff. Thus Henry Clay was out of the race and in a position to bestow his support on another candidate.

Jackson's supporters later characterized the election of 1824 as the "corrupt bargain." Clay backed Adams, and Adams won by one vote in the House in February 1825. Clay's support made sense on several levels. Despite strong mutual dislike, he and Adams agreed on issues such as federal support to build roads and canals. Moreover, Clay was uneasy with Jackson's volatile temperament and unstated political views and with Crawford's diminished capacity. What made Clay's decision look "corrupt" was that immediately after the election, Adams offered to appoint Clay secretary of state — and Clay accepted.

In fact, there probably was no concrete bargain; Adams's subsequent cabinet appointments demonstrated his lack of political astuteness. But Andrew Jackson felt that the election had been stolen from him, and he wrote bitterly that "the Judas of the West [Clay] has closed the contract and will receive the thirty pieces of silver."

The Adams Administration

John Quincy Adams, like his father, was a one-term president. His career had been built on diplomacy, not electoral politics, and despite his wife's deftness in the art of political influence, his own political horse sense was not well developed. With his cabinet choices, he welcomed his opposition into his inner circle. He asked Crawford to stay on in the Treasury. He retained an openly pro-Jackson postmaster general even though that position controlled thousands of nationwide patronage appointments. He even asked Jackson to become secretary of war. With Calhoun as vice president (elected without opposition by the electoral college) and Clay at the State Department, the whole argumentative crew would have been thrust into the executive branch. Crawford and Jackson had the good sense to decline the appointments.

Adams had lofty ideas for federal action during his presidency, and the plan he put before Congress was so sweeping that it took Henry Clay aback. Adams called for federally built roads, canals, and harbors. He proposed a national university in Washington as well as government-sponsored scientific research. He wanted to build observatories to advance astronomical knowledge and to promote precision in timekeeping, and he backed a decimal-based system of weights and measures. In all these endeavors, Adams believed he was continuing the legacy of Jefferson and Madison, using the powers of government to advance knowledge. But his opponents feared he was too Hamiltonian, using federal power inappropriately to advance commercial interests.

Whether he was more truly Federalist or Republican was a moot point. Lacking the give-and-take political skills required to gain congressional support, Adams was unable to implement much of his program. He scorned the idea of courting voters to gain support and using the patronage system to enhance his power. He often made appointments (to posts such as customs collectors) to placate enemies rather than to reward friends. A story of a toast offered to the president may well have been mythical, but as humorous folklore it made the rounds during his term and came to summarize Adams's precarious hold on leadership. A dignitary raised a glass and said, "May he strike confusion to his foes," to which another voice scornfully chimed in, "as he has already done to his friends."

REVIEW   How did the collapse of the Federalist Party influence the administrations of James Monroe and John Quincy Adams?

▶ Conclusion: Republican Simplicity Becomes Complex

The Jeffersonian Republicans at first tried to undo much of what the Federalists had created in the 1790s, but their promise of a simpler government gave way to the complexities of domestic and foreign issues. The sudden acquisition of the Louisiana Purchase promised land and opportunity to settlers but first required intricate federal-level dealings with powerful western Indians. British impressments of American sailors challenged Jefferson and Madison to stand up to the onetime mother country, culminating in the War of 1812. Fighting both the British and their Indian allies, the Americans engaged in two years of inconclusive battles, mostly on American soil. Their eventual triumph at the battle of New Orleans allowed them the illusion that they had fought a second war of independence.

The War of 1812 was the Indians' second lost war for independence. Tecumseh's vision of an unprecedentedly large confederacy of Indian tribes that would halt westward expansion by white Americans was cut short by the war and by his death. When Canada was under attack, the British valued its defense more than they valued their promises to help the Indians.

The war elevated to national prominence General Andrew Jackson, whose popularity with voters in the 1824 election surprised traditional politicians (and their politically astute wives) and threw the one-party rule of Republicans into a tailspin. New western states with more lenient voter qualifications and eastern states with reformed suffrage laws further eroded the old political elite. Appeals to the mass of white male voters would be the hallmark of all nineteenth-century elections after 1824. In such a system, John Quincy Adams and men like him were at a great disadvantage.

Ordinary American women, whether white or free black, had no place in government. Male legislatures maintained women's *feme covert* status, keeping wives dependent on husbands. A few women claimed greater personal autonomy through religion, while many others benefited from expanded female schooling in schools and academies. These increasingly substantial gains in education would blossom into a major transformation of gender starting in the 1830s and 1840s.

Amid the turmoil of the early Republic, two events in particular sparked developments that would prove momentous in later decades. The bitter debate over slavery that surrounded the Missouri Compromise accentuated the serious divisions between northern and southern states — divisions that would only widen in the decades to come. And Jefferson's long embargo and Madison's wartime trade stoppage gave a big boost to American manufacturing by removing competition with British factories. When peace returned in 1815, the years of independent development burst forth into a period of sustained economic growth that continued nearly unabated into the mid-nineteenth century.

▶ Selected Bibliography

Politics

Andrew Burstein and Nancy Isenberg, *Madison and Jefferson* (2010).

Saul Cornell, *The Other Founders: Anti-Federalism and the Dissenting Tradition in America, 1788–1828* (1999).

Joseph J. Ellis, *American Sphinx: The Character of Thomas Jefferson* (1997).

Joanne B. Freeman, *Affairs of Honor: National Politics in the New Republic* (2001).

Nancy Isenberg, *Fallen Founder: The Life of Aaron Burr* (2008).

Alexander Keyssar, *The Right to Vote: The Contested History of Democracy in the United States* (2000).

Jon Kukla, *A Wilderness So Immense: The Louisiana Purchase and the Destiny of America* (2003).

Jeffrey L. Pasley, Andrew W. Robertson, and David Waldstreicher, *Beyond the Founders: New Approaches to the Political History of the Early American Republic* (2003).

Stephen Watts, *The Republic Reborn: War and the Making of Liberal America, 1790–1820* (1987).

Sean Wilentz, *The Rise of American Democracy: Jefferson to Lincoln* (2005).

Richard Zacks, *The Pirate Coast: Thomas Jefferson, the First Marines, and the Secret Mission of 1805* (2006).

Indians, the War of 1812, and the West

Stephen E. Ambrose, *Undaunted Courage: Meriwether Lewis, Thomas Jefferson, and the Opening of the American West* (1996).

Carl Benn, *The Iroquois in the War of 1812* (1998).

James F. Brooks, *Captives and Cousins: Slavery, Kinship, and Community in the Southwest Borderlands* (2002).

Kathleen DuVal, *The Native Ground: Indians and Colonists in the Heart of the Continent* (2007).

R. David Edmunds, *Tecumseh and the Quest for Indian Leadership* (1984).

Albert Furtwangler, *Acts of Discovery: Visions of America in the Lewis and Clark Journals* (1993).

Pekka Hämäläinen, *The Comanche Empire* (2009).

John Sugden, *Tecumseh: A Life* (1997).

Alan Taylor, *The Civil War of 1812: American Citizens, British Subjects, Irish Rebels, and Indian Allies* (2010).

Richard White, *The Middle Ground: Indians, Empires, and Republics in the Great Lakes Region, 1650–1815* (1991).

Slavery

Douglas Egerton, *Gabriel's Rebellion* (1993).

Annette Gordon-Reed, *The Hemingses of Monticello: An American Family* (2009).

James Oliver Horton and Lois E. Horton, *In Hope of Liberty: Culture, Community, and Protest among Northern Free Blacks, 1700–1860* (1997).

Gary B. Nash, *Forging Freedom: The Formation of Philadelphia's Black Community, 1720–1840* (1988).

Shane White, *Somewhat More Independent: The End of Slavery in New York City, 1710–1810* (1991).

Women, Marriage, and Religion

Catherine Allgor, *Parlor Politics: In Which the Ladies of Washington Help Build a City and a Government* (2000).

Norma Basch, *Framing American Divorce: From the Revolutionary Generation to the Victorians* (1999).

Norma Basch, *In the Eyes of the Law: Women, Marriage, and Property in Nineteenth-Century New York* (1982).

Catherine A. Brekus, *Strangers and Pilgrims: Female Preaching in America, 1740–1845* (1998).

Nancy Cott, *Public Vows: A History of Marriage and the Nation* (2001).

Susan Juster, *Disorderly Women: Sexual Politics and Evangelicalism in Revolutionary New England* (1994).

Mary Kelley, *Learning to Stand and Speak: Women, Education, and Public Life in America's Republic* (2006).

Susan E. Klepp, *Revolutionary Conceptions: Women, Fertility, and Family Limitation in America, 1760–1820* (2009).

Mary Beth Sievens, *Stray Wives: Marital Conflict in Early National New England* (2005).

▶ FOR MORE BOOKS ABOUT TOPICS IN THIS CHAPTER, see the Online Bibliography at **bedfordstmartins.com/roark**.

▶ FOR ADDITIONAL PRIMARY SOURCES FROM THIS PERIOD, see Michael Johnson, ed., *Reading the American Past*, Fifth Edition.

▶ FOR WEB SITES, IMAGES, AND DOCUMENTS RELATED TO TOPICS AND PLACES IN THIS CHAPTER, visit Make History at **bedfordstmartins.com/roark**.

Reviewing Chapter 10

Explain each term's significance.

Jefferson's Presidency
- Thomas Jefferson (p. 291)
- Aaron Burr (p. 291)
- Gabriel's rebellion (p. 291)
- *Marbury v. Madison* (p. 293)
- Barbary Wars (p. 294)

Opportunities and Challenges in the West
- Louisiana Purchase (p. 296)
- Sacajawea (p. 297)
- Lewis and Clark expedition (p. 297)
- Osage (p. 298)
- Comanche (p. 298)

Jefferson, the Madisons, and the War of 1812
- Impressment (p. 300)
- Embargo Act of 1807 (p. 300)
- Dolley Madison (p. 301)
- Tecumseh (p. 301)
- Tenskwatawa (p. 302)
- battle of Tippecanoe (p. 303)
- Henry Clay (p. 303)
- War Hawks (p. 303)
- Creek War (p. 304)
- battle of New Orleans (p. 305)
- Hartford Convention (p. 305)

Women's Status in the Early Republic
- *feme covert* (p. 306)
- Jemima Wilkinson (p. 307)
- female academies (p. 307)

Monroe and Adams
- James Monroe (p. 310)
- Missouri Compromise (p. 312)
- Monroe Doctrine (p. 314)
- John Quincy Adams (p. 314)
- Andrew Jackson (p. 315)

REVIEW QUESTIONS

Use key terms and dates to support your answer.

1. How did Jefferson attempt to undo the Federalist innovations of earlier administrations? (pp. 291–294)

2. Why was Spain concerned that France sold the Louisiana Territory to the United States? (pp. 295–300)

3. Why did Congress declare war on Great Britain in 1812? (pp. 300–305)

4. How did the civil status of American women and men differ in the early Republic? (pp. 305–310)

5. How did the collapse of the Federalist Party influence the administrations of James Monroe and John Quincy Adams? (pp. 310–316)

MAKING CONNECTIONS

Draw on key terms, the timeline, and review questions.

1. When Jefferson assumed the presidency following the election of 1800, he expected to transform the national government. Describe his republican vision and his successes and failures in implementing it. Did subsequent Republican presidents advance the same objectives?

2. How did the United States expand and strengthen its control of territory in North America in the early nineteenth century? In your answer, discuss the roles of diplomacy, military action, and political leadership in contributing to this development.

3. Regional tensions emerged as a serious danger to the American political system in the early nineteenth century. Discuss specific conflicts that had regional dimensions. How did Americans resolve, or fail to resolve, these tensions?

4. Although the United States denied its female citizens equality in public life, some women were able to exert considerable influence. How did they do so? In your answer, discuss the legal, political, and educational status of women in the early Republic.

LINKING TO THE PAST

Link events in this chapter to earlier events.

1. Compare the British-Indian alliance in the Revolutionary War with the British-Indian alliance in the War of 1812. Were there any reasons for men like Tecumseh to think that the alliance might work out better the second time? (See chapter 7.)

2. How do you think the Federalist supporters of the Constitution in 1787–1788 felt about the steady decline in states' property qualifications for male voters that occurred between 1800 and 1824? Did the democratization of voting necessarily undermine the Constitution's restrictions on direct democracy in the federal government? (See chapter 8.)

▶ FOR PRACTICE QUIZZES AND OTHER STUDY TOOLS, visit the Online Study Guide at **bedfordstmartins.com/roark**.

TIMELINE 1800–1825

1800
- Republicans Thomas Jefferson and Aaron Burr tie in electoral college.
- Fears of slave rebellion led by Gabriel in Virginia result in twenty-seven executions.

1801
- House of Representatives elects Thomas Jefferson president after thirty-six ballots.
- Pasha of Tripoli declares war on United States.

1803
- *Marbury v. Madison*.
- Britain and France each warn United States not to ship war-related goods to the other.
- United States purchases Louisiana Territory.

1804
- U.S. Marines and foreign mercenaries under William Eaton take Derne, Tripoli.
- President Jefferson meets with Osage leaders in Washington City.

1804–1806
- Lewis and Clark expedition travels from St. Louis to Pacific Ocean.

1807
- British attack and search *Chesapeake*.
- Embargo Act.
- United States establishes trade with Comanche Indians.

1808
- Republican James Madison elected president; Dolley Madison soon dubbed "presidentress."

1809
- Treaty of Fort Wayne.
- Non-Intercourse Act.

1811
- Battle of Tippecanoe.

1812
- United States declares war on Great Britain.

1813
- Tecumseh dies at battle of the Thames.

1814
- British attack Washington City.
- Treaty of Ghent.
- New England Federalists meet at Hartford Convention.

1815
- Battle of New Orleans.

1816
- Republican James Monroe elected president.

1819
- Adams-Onís Treaty.

1820
- Missouri Compromise.

1823
- Monroe Doctrine asserted.

1825
- John Quincy Adams elected president by House of Representatives.

HOUSEHOLD CLOCK

Massachusetts clockmaker Simon Willard patented this short pendulum clock in 1802, touching off a revolutionary period in the history of timekeeping. Before 1800, sundials and church bells answered most timekeeping needs. With the speed-up of commerce and transportation, as illustrated in this 1834 drawing of New York City's busy South Street docks, many people needed affordable timepieces to facilitate punctuality. Willard's small handcraft workshop made only 4,000 of his wall clocks; he was soon outpaced by Connecticut entrepreneurs who devised a cheap compact clock made entirely of machine-cut wood. By the mid 1820s, clocks could be found in most households of the middle ranks and above.

Clock: Willard House and Clock Museum; background:

11

The Expanding Republic
1815–1840

IN 1837, LARGE AUDIENCES THROUGHOUT MASSACHUSETTS WITNESSED the astonishing spectacle of two sisters from a wealthy southern family delivering long, impassioned speeches about the evils of slavery. Sarah and Angelina Grimké showed no fear or hesitation. They were women on a mission, channeling a higher power to authorize their outspokenness. As Angelina, thirty-two, wrote to a friend after one event: "Whilst in the act of speaking I am favored to forget little 'I' entirely & to feel altogether hid behind the great cause I am pleading. Were it not for this feeling, I know not how I could face such audiences without embarrassment." In their seventy-nine speaking engagements, some forty thousand women — and men — came to hear them.

Not much in their family background predicted the sisters' radical break with tradition. And radical it was: The abolitionist movement was in its infancy in the 1830s, centered around Boston editor William Lloyd Garrison, who demanded an immediate end to slavery. Nearly as radical as Garrison, the Grimké sisters had crossed a gender line by speaking their own unscripted words of moral politics in front of mixed-sex audiences.

The Grimké sisters grew up in Charleston, South Carolina, in a prominent family whose wealth derived from slavery. With a dozen siblings, an invalid mother, and a busy father — he was chief justice of the State Supreme Court — the two sisters evaded familial surveillance enough to develop independent minds and explore alternative churches that opposed slavery. By the late 1820s, both sisters had moved to Philadelphia and joined the Quakers' Society of Friends.

Until 1835, they refrained from activism and remained aloof from Philadelphia's growing antislavery community. That year, the British abolitionist George Thompson lectured in town, inspiring Angelina to write to Garrison, describing herself as a white southern exile from slavery. When Garrison published her letter in his weekly paper, the *Liberator*, her rare voice of personal testimony caused a great stir. Angelina next wrote *An Appeal to the Christian Women of the South*, urging southern women to take political action against slavery; Charleston postmasters burned copies sent by mail. A year later, she issued *An Appeal to the Women of the Nominally Free States*, setting forth the ideas that would be articulated on her Massachusetts lecture tour.

Grimké Sisters
Sarah M. and Angelina E. Grimké sat for these portraits probably sometime around 1840, when Sarah was 48 and Angelina was 35. Quaker women typically wore plain headdresses, but these day caps—sheer fabric with ruffles—are not very austere. Such caps were common indoor wear, to keep hair in place and protected, while outdoors, a large-brimmed sun-screening bonnet would go over the cap. The thousands of abolitionist women who did not take to lecture platforms instead contributed major financial support to the movement by making handcraft items, such as this silk drawstring purse, and selling them at giant fairs. Portraits: Library of Congress; purse: The Daughters of the American Revolution Museum, Washington, D.C., Gift of Mrs. Erwin L. Broecker.

The extended tour of Massachusetts caused a sensation and led to a doubling of membership in northern antislavery societies. Newspapers and state church leaders fiercely debated the Grimkés' position. And the issue of women's right to speak in public was open for full examination. The Grimké sisters defended their stand: "Whatever is morally right for a man to do is morally right for a woman to do," Angelina wrote. "I recognize no rights but human rights." Sarah produced a set of essays titled *Letters on the Equality of the Sexes* (1838), the first American treatise asserting women's equality with men.

The Grimké sisters' innovative radicalism was part of a vibrant, contested public life that came alive in the United States of the 1830s. This decade — often summed up as the Age of Jackson, in honor of the two-term president who left his distinctive mark on the period — was a time of rapid economic, political, and social change. Andrew Jackson's bold self-confidence mirrored the new confidence of American society in the years after 1815. An entrepreneurial spirit gripped the country, producing a market revolution of unprecedented scale. Old social hierarchies eroded; ordinary men dreamed of moving high up the ladder of success. Stunning advances in transportation and economic productivity fueled such dreams and propelled thousands to travel west or to cities. Urban growth and technological change fostered the diffusion of a distinctive and lively public culture, spread mainly through the increased circulation of newspapers and also by thousands of public lecturers, like the Grimké sisters, allowing popular opinions to coalesce and intensify.

Expanded communication transformed politics dramatically. Sharp disagreements over the best way to promote individual liberty, economic opportunity, and national prosperity in the new market economy defined key differences between presidential candidates in the election of 1828. By the early 1830s, these political differences were embedded in new political parties, which attracted increasing numbers of white male voters into their ranks. Religion became democratized as well. A nationwide evangelical revival brought its adherents the certainty that salvation was now available to all and that the moral perfection of society was within reach.

But perfection proved elusive. Steamboats blew up, banks and businesses periodically collapsed, alcoholism rates soared, Indians were killed or relocated farther west, and slavery continued to expand. The brash confidence that turned some people into rugged, self-promoting individuals inspired others to think about the human costs of rapid economic expansion and thus about reforming society in dramatic ways. The common denominator was a faith that people and societies could shape their own destinies.

► The Market Revolution

The return of peace in 1815 unleashed powerful forces that revolutionized the organization of the economy. Spectacular changes in transportation facilitated the movement of commodities, information, and people, while textile mills and other factories created many new jobs, especially for young unmarried women. Innovations in banking, legal practices, and tariff policies promoted swift economic growth.

This was not yet an industrial revolution, as was beginning in Britain, but rather a market revolution fueled by traditional sources — water, wood, beasts of burden, and human muscle. What was new was the accelerated pace of economic activity and the scale of the distribution of goods. Men and women were drawn out of old patterns of rural self-sufficiency into the wider realm of national market relations. At the same time, the nation's money supply enlarged considerably, leading to speculative investments in commerce, manufacturing, transportation, and land. The new nature and scale of production and consumption changed Americans' economic behavior, attitudes, and expectations. But in 1819 and again in 1837 and 1839, serious crashes of the economy punctured their optimistic expectations.

Improvements in Transportation

Before 1815, transportation in the United States was slow and expensive; it cost as much to ship a crate over thirty miles of domestic roads as it did to send it across the Atlantic Ocean. A stagecoach trip from Boston to New York took four days. But between 1815 and 1840, networks of roads, canals, steamboats, and finally railroads dramatically raised the speed and lowered the cost of travel (Map 11.1).

MAP ACTIVITY

Map 11.1 Routes of Transportation in 1840

By the 1830s, transportation advances had cut travel times significantly. By way of the Erie Canal, goods and people could move from New York City to Buffalo in four days, a trip that had taken two weeks by road in 1800. Similarly, the trip from New York to New Orleans, which had taken four weeks in 1800, could now be accomplished in less than half that time on steamboats plying the western rivers.

READING THE MAP: In what parts of the country were canals built most extensively? Were most of them within a single state's borders, or did they encourage interstate travel and shipping?

CONNECTIONS: What impact did the Erie Canal have on the development of New York City? How did improvements in transportation affect urbanization in other parts of the country?

Improved transportation moved goods into wider markets. It moved passengers, too, broadening their horizons and allowing young people as well as adults to take up new employment in cities or factory towns. Transportation also facilitated the flow of political information via the U.S. mail with its bargain postal rates for newspapers, periodicals, and books. Enhanced public transport was expensive and produced uneven economic benefits, so presidents from Jefferson to Monroe were reluctant to fund it with federal dollars. Only the National Road, begun in 1806, was government sponsored. By 1818, it linked Baltimore with Wheeling, in western Virginia. In all other cases, private investors pooled resources and chartered transport companies, receiving significant subsidies and monopoly rights from state governments. Turnpike and roadway mileage increased dramatically after 1815, reducing shipping costs. Stagecoach companies proliferated, and travel time on main routes was cut in half.

Water travel was similarly transformed. In 1807, Robert Fulton's steam-propelled boat, the *Clermont*, churned up the Hudson River from New York City to Albany, touching off a steamboat craze. By 1820, a dozen boats left New York City daily, and scores more operated on midwestern rivers and the Great Lakes. By the early 1830s, more than seven hundred steamboats were in operation on the Ohio and Mississippi rivers. A voyager on one of the first steamboats to go down the Mississippi reported that the Chickasaw Indians called the vessel a "fire canoe" and considered it "an omen of evil."

Indeed, steamboats were not benign advances. The urgency to cut travel time for competitive gain over rival steamboat companies — or to win impromptu races — led to overstoked furnaces, sudden boiler explosions, and terrible mass fatalities. An investigation of an accident near Cincinnati in 1838, in which 150 passengers were killed, charged: "Such disasters have their foundation in the present mammoth evil of our country, an inordinate love of gain. We are not satisfied with getting rich, but we must get rich in a day. We are not satisfied with traveling at a speed of ten miles an hour, but we must fly." By that year, nearly three thousand Americans had been killed in steamboat accidents, leading to initial federal attempts — at first unsuccessful — to regulate safety on ships used for interstate commerce. The environment also paid a huge price: Steamboats had to load fuel — "wood up" — every twenty miles or so, resulting in mass deforestation. By the 1830s, the banks of many main rivers were denuded of trees, and

THE PROMISE OF TECHNOLOGY

Early Steamboats

The American traveling public fell in love with steamboats for their speed and power. People and products could now go upriver, against the current, under the enthralling and modern power of steam. On every boat, a furnace heated water under pressure in a boiler to produce that steam, powering an engine that drove large paddlewheels. However, with innovation came risk. Between 1811 and 1851, accidents destroyed nearly a thousand boats, a third of all steam vessels built in that period, and killed a total of several thousand travelers. Fires and boiler explosions made for horrifying spectacles, as this lithograph by the famed printmakers Currier and Ives attests. In 1840, the *Lexington* caught fire in Long Island Sound. Despite having the latest safety features, only 4 people survived; many of the 139 victims froze to death in the icy winter waters. How did Americans' fondness for steamboats reflect the attitudes of this era? The Mariners Museum, Newport News, VA.

Awful Conflagration of the Steam Boat **LEXINGTON** In Long Island Sound on Monday Eve! Jan! 13th 1840, by which melancholy occurrence, over 100 PERSONS PERISHED.

The Erie Canal at Lockport
The Erie Canal, completed in 1825, struck many as the eighth wonder of the world, both for its length of 350 miles and for its impressive elevation, requiring the construction of eighty-three locks. The biggest engineering challenge came at Lockport, twenty miles from Buffalo, where the canal had to traverse a steep slate escarpment. Work crews — mostly immigrant Irishmen — used gunpowder and grueling physical labor to blast the deep artificial gorge shown here. Next, a series of double locks was constructed to move boats in stages up and down the 60-foot elevation. Department of Rare Books and Special Collections, Rush Rhees Library, University of Rochester.

forests miles back from the rivers fell to the ax. Wood combustion transferred the carbon stored in trees into the atmosphere, creating America's first significant air pollution.

Canals were another major innovation of the transportation revolution. These shallow highways of water allowed passage for boats pulled by mules. Travel was slow — less than five miles per hour — but the low-friction water enabled one mule to pull a fifty-ton barge. Pennsylvania in 1815 and New York in 1817 commenced major state-sponsored canal enterprises. Pennsylvania's Schuylkill Canal stretched 108 miles west from Philadelphia when it was completed in 1826. Much more impressive was the **Erie Canal**, finished in 1825, covering 350 miles between Albany and Buffalo and linking the port of New York City with the entire Great Lakes region. Wheat and flour moved east, household goods and tools moved west, and passengers went in both directions. By the 1830s, the cost of shipping by canal fell to less than one-tenth of the cost of overland transport, and New York City quickly blossomed into the premier commercial city in the United States.

In the 1830s, private railroad companies began to give canals competition. The nation's first railroad, the Baltimore and Ohio, laid thirteen miles of track in 1829. During the 1830s, three thousand more miles of track materialized nationwide, the result of a speculative fever in railroad construction masterminded by bankers, locomotive manufacturers, and state legislators who provided subsidies, charters, and land rights-of-way. Rail lines in the 1830s were generally short, on the order of twenty to one hundred miles. They did not yet provide an efficient distribution system for goods, but passengers flocked to experience the marvelous speeds of fifteen to twenty miles per hour. Railroads and other advances in transportation made possible enormous change by unifying the country culturally and economically.

Factories, Workingwomen, and Wage Labor

Transportation advances promoted the expansion of manufacturing after 1815, creating an ever-expanding market for goods. The two leading industries, textiles and shoes, altered methods of production and labor relations. Textile production was greatly spurred by the development of water-driven machinery built near fast-coursing rivers. Shoe manufacturing, still using the power and skill of human hands, involved only a reorganization of production. Both industries pulled young women into wage-earning labor for the first time.

The earliest factory was built by English immigrant Samuel Slater in Pawtucket, Rhode Island, in the 1790s. It featured a mechanical spinning machine that produced thread and yarn. By 1815, nearly 170 spinning mills had been built along New England rivers. In British manufacturing cities, entire families worked in low-wage, health-threatening factories. By contrast, American factories targeted young women as employees; they were cheap to hire because of their limited employment options. Mill girls would "retire" to marriage, replaced by fresh recruits earning beginners' wages.

In 1821, a group of Boston entrepreneurs founded the town of Lowell on the Merrimack River, centralizing all aspects of cloth production: combing, shrinking, spinning, weaving, and dyeing. By 1836, the eight mills in Lowell employed more than five thousand young women, who lived in carefully managed company-owned boardinghouses. Corporation rules at the **Lowell mills** required church attendance and prohibited drinking and unsupervised courtship; dorms were locked at 10 P.M. A typical mill worker earned $2 to $3 for a seventy-hour week, more than a seamstress or domestic servant could earn but less than a young man's wages. The job consisted of tending noisy power looms in rooms kept hot and humid, ideal for thread but not for people.

Despite the discomforts, young women embraced factory work as a means to earn spending money and build savings before marriage;

Cotton Textile Industry, ca. 1840

Largest circle represents 8,000 employees

several banks in town held the nest eggs of thousands of workers. Also welcome was the unprecedented, though still limited, personal freedom of living in an all-female social space, away from parents and domestic tasks. In the evening, the women could engage in self-improvement activities, such as writing for the company's periodical, the *Lowell Offering*, or attending lectures on literary, scientific, or even political topics. In 1837, 1,500 mill girls squeezed into Lowell's city hall to hear the Grimké sisters speak about the evils of slavery.

In the mid-1830s, worldwide growth and competition in the cotton market impelled mill owners to speed up work and decrease wages. The workers protested, emboldened by their communal living arrangement and by their relative independence as temporary employees. In 1834 and again in 1836, hundreds of women at Lowell went out on strike (see "Documenting the American Promise," page 328). All over New England, female mill workers led strikes and formed unions. In 1834, mill workers in Dover, New Hampshire, denounced their

Mill Worker Tending a Power Loom, 1850

The young woman pictured here is tending a power loom in a textile mill. The inset shows spindles of pink and blue thread next to a shuttle, which wove the woof — the crosswise threading —into the warp already mounted on the loom. The mill worker's main task was to replace the spindle when it ran out of thread; she also had to be alert for sudden breaks in the warp, which required a fast shutdown of the loom and a quick repair of the thread. In the 1830s, women weavers generally tended two of these machines at a time. Mill worker: American Textile History Museum; Shuttle with spindles: Picture Research Consultants & Archives.

owners for trying to turn them into "slaves": "However freely the epithet of 'factory slaves' may be bestowed upon us, we will never deserve it by a base and cringing submission to proud wealth or haughty insolence." Their assertiveness surprised many, but ultimately the ease of replacing them undermined their bargaining power, and owners in the 1840s began to shift to immigrant families as their primary labor source.

The shoe manufacturing industry centered in eastern New England reorganized production and hired women, including wives, as shoebinders. Male shoemakers still cut the leather and made the soles in shops, but female shoebinders working from home now stitched the upper parts of the shoes. Working from home meant that wives could contribute to family income — unusual for most wives in that period — and still perform their domestic chores.

In the economically turbulent 1830s, shoebinder wages fell. Unlike mill workers, female shoebinders worked in isolation, a serious hindrance to organized protest. In Lynn, Massachusetts, a major shoemaking center, women used female church networks to organize resistance, communicating via religious newspapers. The Lynn shoebinders who demanded higher wages in 1834 built on a collective sense of themselves as women, even though they did not work together daily. "Equal rights should be extended to all — to the weaker sex as well as the stronger," they wrote in a document establishing the Female Society of Lynn.

In the end, the Lynn shoebinders' protests failed to achieve wage increases. At-home workers all over New England continued to accept low wages, and even in Lynn many women shied away from organized protest, preferring to situate their work in the context of family duty (helping their husbands to finish the shoes) instead of market relations.

Bankers and Lawyers

Entrepreneurs like the Lowell factory owners relied on innovations in the banking system to finance their ventures. Between 1814 and 1816, the number of state-chartered banks in the United States more than doubled from fewer than 90 to 208. By 1830, there were 330, and by 1840 hundreds more. Banks stimulated the economy by making loans to merchants and manufacturers and by enlarging the money supply. Borrowers were issued loans in the form of banknotes — certificates unique to each bank — that were used as money for all transactions. Neither fed-

Fancy Wedding Shoes Made in Lynn, Massachusetts Emily Lucinda Alden wore these shoes when she married Addison Davis in 1840. The soles are flat, with no heels, and the upper parts of the shoes are made of hand-stitched white satin. An extraordinary clue about women and marriage is revealed in the bride's name-to-be affixed to the shoe box. Etiquette books of the 1840s uniformly decreed her married name would be Mrs. Addison Davis. Emily might not have entirely grasped the eclipse of her own public and legal personage that would be imposed by marriage. Even Elizabeth Cady Stanton, a prominent woman's rights leader who also married in 1840, had to do battle not to be called Mrs. Henry Stanton. Lynn Historical Society.

eral nor state governments issued paper money, so banknotes became the country's currency.

In theory, a note could always be traded in at a bank for its hard-money equivalent in gold or silver, a transaction known as a "**specie payment**." A note from a solid local bank might be worth exactly what it was written for, but the face value of a note from a distant or questionable bank would be discounted. Buying and selling banknotes in this era required knowledge and caution. Not surprisingly, counterfeiting flourished.

Bankers exercised great power over the economy, deciding who would get loans and what the discount rates would be. The most powerful bankers sat on the board of directors for the **second Bank of the United States**, headquartered in Philadelphia and featuring eighteen branches throughout the country. The twenty-year charter of the first Bank of the United States had expired in 1811, and the second Bank of the United States opened for business in 1816 under another twenty-year charter. The rechartering of this bank would become a major issue in the 1832 presidential campaign.

Accompanying the market revolution was a revolution in commercial law, fashioned by politicians to enhance the prospects of private investment. In 1811, states started to rewrite their laws of incorporation (allowing the chartering

Mill Girls Stand Up to Factory Owners, 1834

Lowell's first large "turn out" by mill girls came in February 1834, after the factory owners announced a 15 percent wage cut. Workers began to circulate petitions and hold female-only meetings to plan a response, and on February 14 hundreds walked off the job. Newspaper accounts seized on the groundbreaking spectacle of young women, thought to be docile and polite, taking to the streets in protest. Four days later, the strike fizzled when the inexperienced workers realized that the owners could ignore and easily replace them. But lessons were learned, and a later Lowell "turn out," in 1836, was sustained for several months.

DOCUMENT 1
The Lowell Journal Reports the Strike, February 18, 1834

A town newspaper favorable to the factory owners characterized the work stoppage as a delusional farce led by a small number of "wicked girls."

THE FACTORY GIRLS.—It has become known, from rumor, that a considerable number of the girls employed in the mills of this town turned out on Friday last, to prevent a reduction in wages. . . . It was proposed, some time since, to make a very small reduction in the wages of all of the hands on the first of March, and notices to that effect were posted in the mills. . . .

Upon this, several wicked and malicious girls . . . undertook to get up a *turn out*, with a view to threaten the agents with an entire stoppage of the works, in order to exact the higher rates of wages. . . . On Friday and Saturday from 800 to 1000 girls revolted under the most laughable delusions, that mischief could invent. The first day, processions were formed of about 700 girls, who listened to sundry stimulative exhortations, . . . and marched through the streets, ankle-deep in mud, with waving handkerchiefs and scarfs, and signals of beckonings to all who kept the peace, and conducted wisely. Saturday became a day of repentance to many; and they would gladly have returned to their business, but for a pledge, cunningly devised, that each who did so, should forfeit five dollars to the rebels. The Sabbath afforded opportunity for a little more cool reflection, and on Monday morning, a large concourse attended by a parcel of idle men and boys, heard another speech, . . . which was followed by a well-timed prayer and a judicious exhortation from a clergyman of the Methodist persuasion. The result of the whole matter is, that a few of the ring-leaders are refused entrance into the mills, and most of the disaffected, having learned the truth, and becoming sensible of the wicked misrepresentations of which they had nearly been the victims, are returning to their work, ready to take a diminished price, and continue to labor at wages which will give them from one and a half, to two and a half dollars per week, more than their board. — This, to be sure, is not so much as they have had in past times, nor so much as we hope they will soon have again, but it is more than they can get in any other occupation in New England.

The most amusing part of the farce, for it deserves no other name, was the eagerness with which an attempt was made to break the banks. A large sum, in the total, was withdrawn from the Savings' Bank, which, in addition to wages due, was presented at the Lowell and Rail Road Banks for specie — a flock of girls about as numerous and dense as the wild pigeons of the West, thronged the counters and pocketed the hard cash. The Banks, notwithstanding the severe pressure outside their counters have felt none within, and the public generally, and the factory girls in particular, are still invited to call.

SOURCE: *The Lowell Journal*, February 18, 1834, as reprinted in the *New-York Spectator*, March 6, 1834. Gale Database, "Nineteenth-century U.S. Newspapers."

DOCUMENT 2
Anonymous Mill Girls, "Union Is Power"

A position paper, quickly drafted, framed the strikers' goals in terms of "rights" and appealed to the patriotic spirit of the American Revolution and their heritage as "daughters of freemen" to justify their actions.

Our present object is to have union and exertion, and we remain in possession of our own unquestionable rights. We circulate this paper, wishing to obtain the names of all who imbibe the spirit of our patriotic ancestors, who preferred privation to bondage, and parted with all that renders life desirable — and even life itself — to procure independence for their children. The oppressing hand of avarice would enslave us; and to gain their object, they very gravely tell us of the pressure of the times; this we are already sensible of, and deplore it. If any are in want of assistance, the Ladies will be compassionate, and assist them; but we prefer to have the disposing of our charities in our own hands; and as we are free, we would remain in possession of what kind Providence has bestowed upon us, and remain daughters of freemen still.

All who patronize this effort, we wish to have discontinue their labors until terms of reconciliation are made.

Resolved, That we will not go back into the mills to work unless our wages are continued to us as they have been.

Resolved, That none of us will go back unless they receive us all as one.

Resolved, That if any have not money enough to carry them home, that they shall be supplied.

SOURCE: Printed in *The Man*, February 22, 1834. Published in New York City by G. H. Evans. American Periodicals Series Online.

DOCUMENT 3
Support from Workingmen, March, 1834

Periodicals aimed at working-class men championed the striking women of Lowell.

Some of the Eastern papers severely censure the Lowell girls for their recent "Turn out," and for not submitting to the reduction announced by their employers. Those females had as good a right to fix a price on their labor, and to refuse to reduce it, as their employers have to fix a price on their manufactures, and if they were to resign that right, they would be altogether at the mercy of their employers. . . .

The price of female labor is already too low, and the amount of labor that females have to perform too great. Many of those young women . . . must, out of their small earning, which rarely exceeds two dollars and fifty cents a week, provide board and clothing, and lay by something to support themselves when they are sick or unemployed.

SOURCE: *The National Trades' Union* (published weekly by the General Trades' Union of the City of New York), as reprinted in the *Workingman's Advocate* (New York), March 8, 1834. American Periodical Series Online.

DOCUMENT 4
A Strike Leader Speaks Out, mid-March, 1834

A month later, one of the leaders explained that the strike was caused not only by reduced wages but also by anger at the insolence and tyranny of wealthy factory owners. Her remarks were published in a New York daily, The Man, *a paper established in 1834 to advocate for workingmen's issues.*

The Lowell Girls have been censured in no measured terms by the Federal press of the east, for the "turn out.". . . One of the girls has turned round on her accusers, and while she does not outstep the modesty of her sex, her spirit would do credit to any parentage in these or other days. Hear the yankee girl:

"We do not estimate our *Liberty* by dollars and cents; consequently it was not the reduction of *wages* alone which caused the excitement, but that *haughty, overbearing disposition* — that *purse proud insolence*, which was becoming more and more apparent — that spirit of tyranny so manifest at present among the *avaricious* and wealthy manufacturers of this and the old country.

"I have only to add, that if the proprietors and agents are not satisfied with alluring us from our homes — from the peaceful abodes of our childhood, under the false promises of a great reward, and then casting us upon the world, . . . merely because we would not be slaves — . . . let them bring down upon us the whole influence of the *rich* and *noble*, the *proud* and the *mighty*, all piled upon the *United States Bank* — steep us in poverty to the very dregs, but we beseech them not to asperse our characters, or *stigmatize* us as *disorderly* persons. Grant us this favor, and give us the privilege of breathing the air of freedom in its *purity*, and we will be content."

SOURCE: *The Man*, March 20, 1834. Published in New York City by G. H. Evans. American Periodicals Series Online.

Questions for Analysis and Debate

1. Does the *Lowell Journal* adequately explain how a few "ringleaders" could motivate over eight hundred female workers to engage in street protests and a run on the local banks?

2. In the strikers' statement of purpose, what is the significance of the references to Revolutionary-era ideals of independence and liberty and the phrase "daughters of freemen"? What did their final resolution promise? Do these young women feel subordinate and deferential to the factory owners? Were they in fact subordinates?

3. What do the several references to banks and money tell us about the class dimensions of this situation? How did the *Lowell Journal* excuse the wage reduction? What did the strike leader mean by "purse proud insolence"?

of businesses by states), and the number of corporations expanded rapidly, from about twenty in 1800 to eighteen hundred by 1817. Incorporation protected individual investors from being held liable for corporate debts. State lawmakers also wrote laws of eminent domain, empowering states to buy land for roads and canals even from unwilling sellers. In such ways, entrepreneurial lawyers of the 1820s and 1830s created the legal foundation for an economy that favored ambitious individuals interested in maximizing their own wealth.

Not everyone applauded these developments. The skillful lawyer-turned-politician **Andrew Jackson** spoke for a large and mistrustful segment of the population when he warned about the potential abuses of power "which the moneyed interest derives from a paper currency which they are able to control, from the multitude of corporations with exclusive privileges which they have succeeded in obtaining in the different states, and which are employed altogether for their benefit." Jacksonians believed that ending government-granted privileges was the way to maximize individual liberty and economic opportunity.

Booms and Busts

One aspect of the economy that the lawyer-politicians could not control was the threat of financial collapse. The boom years from 1815 to 1818 exhibited a volatility that resulted in the first sharp, large-scale economic downturn in U.S. history. Americans called this downturn a "panic," and the pattern was repeated in the 1830s. Rapidly rising consumer demand stimulated price increases, and speculative investment opportunities offering the possibility of high payoffs abounded — in bank stocks, western land sales, urban real estate, and commodities markets. High inflation made some people wealthy but created hardships for workers on fixed incomes.

> "[Credit is like] a man pissing in his breeches on a cold day to keep his arse warm — very comfortable at first but I dare say . . . you know how it feels afterwards."
> — A farmer in debt in 1819

When the bubble burst in 1819, the overnight rich suddenly became the overnight poor. Some blamed the **panic of 1819** on the second Bank of the United States for failing to control state banks that had suspended specie payments in their eagerness to expand the economic bubble. By mid-1818, when the Bank of the United States called in its loans and insisted that the state banks do likewise, the contracting of the money supply sent tremors throughout the economy. The crunch was made worse by a financial crisis in Europe in the spring of 1819. Overseas, prices for American cotton, tobacco, and wheat plummeted by more than 50 percent. Thus, when the banks began to call in their outstanding loans, American debtors involved in the commodities trade could not come up with the money. Business and personal bankruptcies skyrocketed. The intricate web of credit and debt relationships meant that almost everyone with even a toehold in the new commercial economy was affected by the panic. Thousands of Americans lost their savings and property, and unemployment estimates suggest that half a million people lost their jobs.

Recovery took several years. Unemployment declined, but bitterness lingered, ready to be stirred up by politicians in the decades to come. The dangers of a system dependent on extensive credit were now clear. In one folksy formulation that circulated around 1820, a farmer compared credit to "a man pissing in his breeches on a cold day to keep his arse warm — very comfortable at first but I dare say . . . you know how it feels afterwards."

By the mid-1820s, the economy was back on track, driven by increases in productivity, consumer demand for goods, and international trade, as well as a restless and calculating people moving goods, human labor, and investment capital in expanding circles of commerce. Despite the panic of 1819, credit financing continued to fuel the system. With the growth of manufacturing and transportation networks, buyers and sellers operated in a much larger arena, using credit transactions on paper instead of moving actual (and scarce) hard money around. A merchant in Ohio who bought goods in New York City on credit hoped to repay the loan with interest when he sold the merchandise — often on credit — for a profit. Slave owners might obtain loans to purchase additional land or slaves, using currently owned slaves as collateral. A network of credit and debt relations grew dense by the 1830s in a system that encouraged speculation and risk taking. A pervasive optimism about continued growth supported the elaborate system, but a single business failure could produce many innocent victims. Well after the panic of 1819, an undercurrent of anxiety about rapid economic change continued to shape the political views of many Americans.

REVIEW Why did the United States experience a market revolution after 1815?

The Spread of Democracy

Just as the market revolution held out the promise, if not the reality, of economic opportunity for all who worked, the political transformation of the 1830s held out the promise of political opportunity for hundreds of thousands of new voters. During Andrew Jackson's presidency (1829–1837), the second American party system took shape. Not until 1836, however, would the parties have distinct names and consistent programs transcending the particular personalities running for office. Over those years, more men could and did vote, responding to new methods of arousing voter interest. In 1828, Jackson's charismatic personality defined his party, and his victory over incumbent president John Quincy Adams turned on questions of character. Once in office, Jackson championed ordinary citizens against the power elite — democracy versus aristocracy, in Jackson's terminology. A lasting contribution of the Jackson years was the notion that politicians needed to have the common touch in their dealings with voters.

Popular Politics and Partisan Identity

The election of 1828 was the first presidential contest in which the popular vote determined the outcome. In twenty-two out of twenty-four states, voters — not state legislatures — designated the number of electors committed to a particular candidate. More than a million voters participated, three times the number in 1824 and nearly half the free male population, reflecting the high stakes that voters perceived in the Adams-Jackson rematch. Throughout the 1830s, voter turnout continued to rise and reached 70 percent in some localities, partly because of the disappearance of property qualifications in all but three states and partly because of heightened political interest.

The 1828 election inaugurated new campaign styles. State-level candidates routinely gave speeches at rallies, picnics, and banquets. Adams and Jackson still declined such appearances as undignified, but **Henry Clay** of Kentucky, campaigning for Adams, earned the nickname "the Barbecue Orator." Campaign rhetoric became more informal and even blunt. The Jackson camp established many Hickory Clubs, trading on Jackson's popular nickname, "Old Hickory," from a common Tennessee tree suggesting resilience

TABLE 11.1	THE GROWTH OF NEWSPAPERS, 1820–1840			
	1820	1830	1835	1840
U.S. population (in millions)	9.6	12.8	15.0	17.1
Number of newspapers published	500	800	1,200	1,400
Daily newspapers	42	65	—	138

and toughness. (Jackson was the first presidential candidate to have an affectionate and widely used nickname.)

Partisan newspapers in ever-larger numbers defined issues and publicized political personalities as never before. Improved printing technology and rising literacy rates fueled a great expansion of newspapers of all kinds (Table 11.1). Party leaders dispensed subsidies and other favors to secure the support of papers, even in remote towns and villages. In New York State, where party development was most advanced, a pro-Jackson group called the Bucktails controlled fifty weekly publications. Stories from the leading Jacksonian paper in Washington, D.C., were reprinted two days later in a Boston or Cincinnati paper, for example, as fast as the mail stage could carry them. Presidential campaigns were now coordinated in a national arena.

Politicians at first identified themselves as Jackson or Adams men, honoring the fiction of Republican Party unity. By 1832, however, the terminology had evolved to National Republicans, who favored federal action to promote commercial development, and Democratic Republicans, who promised to be responsive to the will of the majority. Between 1834 and 1836, National Republicans came to be called **Whigs**, while Jackson's party became simply the **Democrats**.

The Election of 1828 and the Character Issue

The campaign of 1828 was the first national election in which scandal and character questions reigned supreme. They became central issues because voters used them to comprehend the kind of public official each man would make. Character issues conveyed in shorthand larger questions about morality, honor, and discipline. Jackson and Adams presented two radically different styles of manhood.

John Quincy Adams was vilified by his opponents as an elitist, a bookish academic, and even a monarchist. Critics pointed to his White House billiard table and ivory chess set as symbols of his aristocratic degeneracy. They also attacked

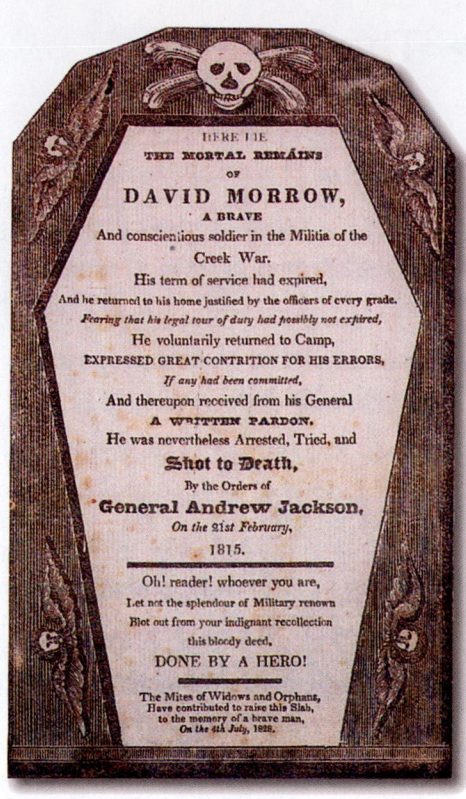

Campaign Posters from 1828

The poster on the left praises Andrew Jackson as a war hero and "man of the people" and reminds readers that Jackson, who won the popular vote in 1824, did not stoop to "bargain for the presidency," as John Quincy Adams presumably had in his dealings with Henry Clay (see chapter 10). The poster with the ominous tombstone and coffin graphics accuses Jackson of an unjustified killing of a Kentucky militiaman (one of six executed) during the Creek War in 1815. The text implores readers to think of the "hero" as a man capable of "this bloody deed."

Pro-Jackson broadside: © Collection of the New-York Historical Society; anti-Jackson broadside: Smithsonian Institution, Washington, D.C.

his "corrupt bargain" of 1824 — the alleged election deal between Adams and Henry Clay (see chapter 10). Adams's supporters returned fire with fire. They played on Jackson's fatherless childhood to portray him as the bastard son of a prostitute. Worse, the cloudy circumstances around his marriage to Rachel Donelson Robards in 1791 gave rise to the story that Jackson was a seducer and an adulterer, having married a woman whose divorce from her first husband was not entirely legal. Pro-Adams newspapers howled that Jackson was sinful and impulsive, while portraying Adams as pious, learned, and virtuous.

Editors in favor of Adams played up Jackson's violent temper, as evidenced by his participation in many duels, brawls, and canings. Jackson's supporters used the same stories to project Old Hickory as a tough frontier hero who knew how to command obedience. As for learning, Jackson's rough frontier education gave him a "natural sense," wrote a Boston editor, that "can never be acquired by reading books — it can only be acquired,

in perfection, by reading men." Jackson won a sweeping victory, with 56 percent of the popular vote and 178 electoral votes to Adams's 83 (Map 11.2). Old Hickory took most of the South and West and carried Pennsylvania and New York as well; Adams carried the remainder of the East. Jackson's vice president was **John C. Calhoun**, who had just served as vice president under Adams but had broken with Adams's policies.

After 1828, national politicians no longer deplored the existence of political parties. They were coming to see that parties mobilized and delivered voters, sharpened candidates' differences, and created party loyalty that surpassed loyalty to individual candidates and elections. Adams and Jackson clearly symbolized the competing ideas of the emerging parties: a moralistic, top-down party (the Whigs) ready to make major decisions to promote economic growth competing against a contentious, energetic party (the Democrats) ready to embrace liberty-loving individualism.

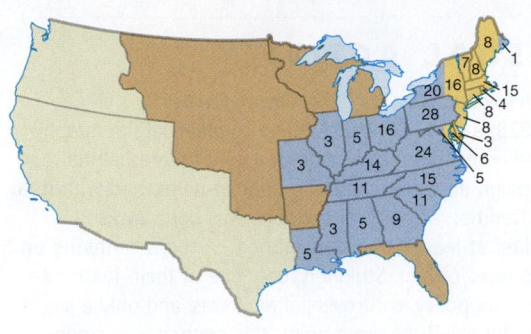

Candidate	Electoral Vote	Popular Vote	Percent of Popular Vote
Andrew Jackson (Democratic Republican)	178	647,286	56
John Q. Adams (National Republican)	83	508,064	44

MAP 11.2
The Election of 1828

Jackson's Democratic Agenda

Before the inauguration in March 1829, Rachel Jackson died. Certain that the ugly campaign had hastened his wife's death, the president went into deep mourning, his depression worsened by constant pain from a bullet still lodged in his chest from an 1806 duel and by mercury poisoning from the medicines he took. Aged sixty-two, Jackson carried only 140 pounds on his six-foot-one frame. His adversaries doubted that he would make it to a second term. His supporters, however, went wild at the inauguration. Thousands cheered his ten-minute inaugural address, the shortest in history. An open reception at the White House turned into a near riot as well-wishers jammed the premises, used windows as doors, stood on furniture for a better view of the great man, and broke thousands of dollars' worth of china and glasses.

During his presidency, Jackson continued to offer unprecedented hospitality to the public. Twenty spittoons newly installed in the East Room of the White House accommodated the tobacco chewers among the throngs that arrived daily to see the president. The courteous Jackson, committed to his image as president of the "common man," held audiences with unannounced visitors throughout his two terms.

Past presidents had tried to lessen party conflict by including men of different factions in their cabinets, but Jackson would have only loyalists, a political tactic followed by most later presidents. For secretary of state, the key job, he tapped New Yorker Martin Van Buren, one

of the shrewdest politicians of the day. Throughout the federal government, from postal clerks to ambassadors, Jackson replaced competent civil servants with party loyalists. "To the victor belong the spoils," said a Democratic senator from New York, expressing approval of patronage-driven appointments. Jackson's appointment practices became known as the **spoils system**; it was a concept the president strenuously defended.

Jackson's agenda quickly emerged. Fearing that intervention in the economy inevitably favored some groups at the expense of others, Jackson favored a Jeffersonian limited federal government. He therefore opposed federal support of transportation and grants of monopolies and charters that benefited wealthy investors. Like Jefferson, he anticipated the rapid settlement of the country's interior, where land sales would spread economic democracy to settlers. Thus, establishing a federal policy to remove the Indians from this area had high priority. Unlike Jefferson, Jackson exercised his presidential veto power over Congress. In 1830, he vetoed a highway project in Maysville, Kentucky — Henry Clay's home state — that Congress had backed. The Maysville Road veto articulated Jackson's principled stand that citizens' tax dollars could be spent only on projects of a "general, not local" character. In all, Jackson used the veto twelve times; all previous presidents combined had exercised that right a total of nine times.

> **"To the victor belong the spoils."**
> — A Democratic senator from New York, praising patronage appointments

REVIEW   Why did Andrew Jackson defeat John Quincy Adams so dramatically in the 1828 election?

▶ Jackson Defines the Democratic Party

In his two terms as president, Andrew Jackson worked to implement his vision of a politics of opportunity for all white men. To open land for white settlement, he favored the relocation of all eastern Indian tribes. He dramatically confronted John C. Calhoun and South Carolina when that state tried to nullify the tariff of 1828. Disapproving of all government-granted privilege, Jackson challenged what he called the "monster" Bank of the United States and took it down to defeat. In all this, he greatly enhanced the power of the presidency.

Indian Policy and the Trail of Tears

Probably nothing defined Jackson's presidency more than his efforts to solve what he saw as the Indian problem. Thousands of Indians lived in the South and the old Northwest, and many remained in New England and New York. In his first message to Congress in 1829, Jackson, who rose to fame fighting the Creek and Seminole tribes in the 1810s, declared that removing the Indians to territory west of the Mississippi was the only way to save them. White civilization destroyed Indian resources and thus doomed the Indians, he claimed: "That this fate surely awaits them if they remain within the limits of the states does not admit of a doubt. Humanity and national honor demand that every effort should be made to avert so great a calamity." Jackson never publicly wavered from this seemingly noble theme, returning to it in his next seven annual messages.

Prior administrations had experimented with different Indian policies. Starting in 1819, Congress funded missionary associations eager to "civilize" native peoples by converting them to Christianity and encouraging English literacy and agricultural practices. Missionaries also promoted white gender customs, but Indian women were reluctant to embrace practices that accorded them less power than their tribal systems did. The federal government had also pursued aggressive treaty making with many tribes, dealing with the Indians as foreign nations (see chapters 9 and 10).

Privately, Jackson thought it was "absurd" to treat the Indians as foreigners; he saw them as subjects of the United States. Jackson also did not approve of assimilation; that way lay extinction, he said. Removal was the answer. Congress backed Jackson's goal and passed the **Indian Removal Act of 1830**, appropriating $500,000 to relocate eastern tribes west of the Mississippi. About 100 million acres of eastern land would be vacated for eventual white settlement under this act authorizing ethnic expulsion (Map 11.3).

Jackson's frequent claim that removal would save the Indians from extinction was in part formulated in response to the widespread controversy generated by the Indian Removal Act. Newspapers, public lecturers, and local clubs debated the expulsion law, and public opinion, especially in the North, was heated. "One would think that the guilt of African slavery was enough for the nation to bear, without the additional

MAP ACTIVITY

Map 11.3 Indian Removal and the Trail of Tears
The federal government under President Andrew Jackson pursued a vigorous policy of Indian removal in the 1830s. Tribes were forcibly moved west to land known as Indian Territory (present-day Oklahoma). In 1838, as many as a quarter of the Cherokee Indians died on the route known as the Trail of Tears.

READING THE MAP: From which states were most of the Native Americans removed? Through which states did the Trail of Tears go?

CONNECTIONS: Before Jackson's presidency, how did the federal government view Native Americans, and what policy initiatives were undertaken by the government and private groups? How did Jackson change the government's policy toward Native Americans?

crime of injustice to the aborigines," one writer declared in 1829. In an unprecedented move, thousands of northern white women signed petitions opposing the removal policy. The right to petition for redress of grievances, part of the Constitution's First Amendment, had long been used by individual women acting on a personal cause — say, a military widow requesting her husband's pension. But mass petitioning by women was something new; it directly challenged the

prevailing assumption that women could not be political actors. Between 1830 and 1832, women's petitions rolled into Washington, arguing specifically that the Cherokee Indians of Georgia were a sovereign people on the road to Christianity and entitled to stay on their land. Jackson ignored the petitions.

For the northern tribes, their numbers diminished by years of war, gradual removal was already well under way. But not all the Indians went quietly. In 1832 in western Illinois, Black Hawk, a leader of the Sauk and Fox Indians who had fought in alliance with Tecumseh in the War of 1812 (see chapter 10), resisted removal. Volunteer militias attacked and chased the Indians into southern Wisconsin, where, after several skirmishes and a deadly battle (later called the Black Hawk War), Black Hawk was captured and some four hundred of his people were massacred.

The large southern tribes — the Creek, Chickasaw, Choctaw, Seminole, and Cherokee — proved even more resistant to removal. The tribal leadership of the Cherokee in Georgia chose a unique path of resistance by taking their case to the U.S. Supreme Court. Georgia Cherokees had already taken several assimilationist steps. Spurred by dedicated missionaries, these leaders had incorporated written laws, including, in 1827, a constitution modeled on the U.S. Constitution. Two hundred of the wealthiest Cherokee men had intermarried with whites, adopting white styles of housing, dress, and cotton agriculture, including the ownership of slaves. They developed a written alphabet and published a newspaper and Christian prayer books in their language. These features helped make their cause attractive to the northern white women who petitioned the government on their behalf. Yet most of the seventeen thousand Cherokees maintained cultural continuity with past traditions.

In 1831, when Georgia announced its plans to seize all Cherokee property, the tribal leaders asked the U.S. Supreme Court to restrain Georgia. The Court held that the Cherokee people lacked standing to sue, not being citizens of either the United States or any foreign state. In the Court's view, tribes residing within U.S. boundaries were "domestic dependent nations," in effect wards of the state. A year later, they brought suit again, this time using an ally, a white missionary, as their stand-in plaintiff. In *Worcester v. Georgia* (1832), the Supreme Court upheld the territorial sovereignty of the Cherokee people, recognizing their existence as "a distinct community, occupying its own territory, in which the laws of Georgia can have no force." An angry President Jackson ignored the Court and pressed the Cherokee tribe to move west: "If they now refuse to accept the liberal terms offered, they can only be liable for whatever evils and difficulties may arise. I feel conscious of having done my duty to my red children."

The Cherokee tribe remained in Georgia for two more years without significant violence. Then, in 1835, a small, unauthorized faction of the acculturated leaders signed a treaty selling all the tribal lands to the state, which rapidly resold the land to whites. Chief John Ross, backed by several thousand Cherokees, petitioned the U.S. Congress to ignore the bogus treaty. "By the stipulations of this instrument," he wrote, "we are stripped of every attribute of freedom and eligibility for legal self-defense. Our property may be plundered before our eyes; violence may be committed on our persons; even our lives may be taken away. . . . We are denationalized; we are disfranchised."

As the Cherokees stubbornly held out, other tribes capitulated to Jackson's mandate and endured forcible relocation. Fifteen thousand Creek, twelve thousand Choctaw, five thousand Chickasaw, and several thousand Seminole Indians moved to Indian Territory (which became the state of Oklahoma in 1907). In his farewell address to the nation in 1837, Jackson assured white listeners of his faith in the humanitarian benefits of Indian removal: "This unhappy race . . . are now placed in a situation where we may well hope that they will share in the blessings of civilization and be saved from the degradation and destruction to which they were rapidly hastening while they remained in the states."

When the Cherokees refused to move by the voluntary evacuation deadline of May 1838, Jackson's successor, Martin Van Buren, sent federal troops to remove them. Under armed guard, the Cherokees embarked on a 1,200-mile journey west that came to be called the **Trail of Tears**. A newspaperman in Kentucky described the forced march: "Even aged females, apparently, nearly ready to drop into the grave, were traveling with heavy burdens attached to the back. . . . They buried fourteen to fifteen at every

Cherokee Deer Hide Coat
Durable, supple, and nearly airtight, tanned deer hides made excellent clothing material. This knee-length coat, decorated with red paint, red buttons, and fringe, has extra layers of hide on the shoulders for additional protection against rain and snow. It dates from the first quarter of the nineteenth century and was still in the possession of Cherokees in Oklahoma in the 1930s. It seems entirely plausible to surmise that it traveled to Oklahoma with its owner on the Trail of Tears in 1838. Courtesy, Museum of the American Indian, Smithsonian Institution, Washington, D.C.

stopping place." Nearly a quarter of the Cherokees died en route from the hardship. Perhaps Jackson had genuinely believed that exile to the West was necessary to save Indian cultures from destruction. But for the forcibly removed tribes, the costs of relocation were high.

The Tariff of Abominations and Nullification

Jackson's Indian policy happened to harmonize with the principle of states' rights; the president supported Georgia's right to ignore the Supreme Court's decision in *Worcester v. Georgia*. But in another pressing question of states' rights, Jackson contested South Carolina's attempt to ignore federal tariff policy.

Federal tariffs as high as 33 percent on imports such as textiles and iron goods had been passed in 1816 and again in 1824 in an effort to shelter new American manufacturers from foreign competition. Some southern congressmen opposed the steep tariffs, fearing they would reduce overseas shipping and thereby hurt cotton exports. In 1828, Congress passed a revised tariff that came to be known as the **Tariff of Abominations**. A bundle of conflicting duties, some as high as 50 percent, the legislation contained provisions that pleased and angered every economic and sectional interest.

South Carolina in particular suffered from the Tariff of Abominations. Worldwide prices for cotton had declined in the late 1820s, and the falloff in shipping caused by the high tariffs further hurt the South. In 1828, a group of South Carolina politicians headed by John C. Calhoun advanced a doctrine called **nullification**. The Union, they argued, was a confederation of states that had yielded some but not all power to the federal government. When Congress overstepped its powers, states had the right to nullify Congress's acts. As precedents, they pointed to the Virginia and Kentucky Resolutions of 1798, intended to invalidate the Alien and Sedition Acts (see chapter 9). Congress had erred in using tariff policy to benefit specific industries, they claimed; tariffs should be used only to raise revenue.

On assuming the presidency in 1829, Jackson ignored the South Carolina statement of nullification and shut out Calhoun, his new vice president, from influence or power. Tariff revisions in early 1832 brought little relief to the South. Sensing futility, Calhoun resigned the vice presidency and became a senator to better serve his state. Finally, strained to their limit,

South Carolina leaders took the radical step of declaring federal tariffs null and void in their state as of February 1, 1833. The constitutional crisis was out in the open.

Opting for a dramatic confrontation, Jackson sent armed ships to Charleston harbor and threatened to invade the state. He pushed through Congress the Force Bill, defining South Carolina's stance as treason and authorizing military action to collect federal tariffs. At the same time, Congress moved quickly to pass a revised tariff that was more acceptable to the South. The conciliating Senator Henry Clay rallied support for a moderate bill that gradually reduced tariffs down to the 1816 level. On March 1, 1833, Congress passed both the new tariff and the Force Bill. In response, South Carolina withdrew its nullification of the old tariff — and then nullified the Force Bill. It was a symbolic gesture, since Jackson's show of muscle was no longer necessary. Both sides were satisfied: Federal power had prevailed over an assertion of states' rights, and South Carolina got the lower tariff it wanted.

Yet the question of federal power versus states' rights was far from settled. The implied threat behind nullification was secession, a position articulated in 1832 by some South Carolinians whose concerns went beyond tariff policy. In the 1830s, the political moratorium on discussions of slavery agreed on at the time of the Missouri Compromise (see chapter 10) was coming unglued, and new northern voices opposed to slavery gained increasing attention. If and when a northern-dominated federal government decided to end slavery, the South Carolinians thought, the South should nullify such laws or else remove itself from the Union.

The Bank War and Economic Boom

Along with the tariff and nullification, President Jackson fought another political battle, over the Bank of the United States. After riding out the panic of 1819, the bank finally prospered. With twenty-nine branches, it handled the federal government's deposits, extended credit and loans, and issued banknotes — by 1830, the most stable currency in the country. Jackson, however, did not find the bank's functions sufficiently valuable to offset his criticism of the concept of a national bank: that it concentrated undue economic power in the hands of a few.

National Republican (Whig) senators Daniel Webster and Henry Clay decided to force the issue.

They convinced the bank to apply for charter renewal in 1832, well before the fall election, even though the existing charter ran until 1836. They fully expected that Congress's renewal would force Jackson to follow through on his rhetoric with a veto, that the unpopular veto would cause Jackson to lose the election, and that the bank would survive on an override vote by a new Congress swept into power on the anti-Jackson tide.

At first, the plan seemed to work. The bank applied for rechartering, Congress voted to renew, and Jackson, angry over being manipulated, issued his veto. But it was a brilliantly written veto, full of fierce language about the privileges of the moneyed elite who oppressed the democratic masses in order to enrich themselves. "Many of our rich men have not been content with equal protection and equal benefits, but have besought us to make them richer by act of Congress," Jackson wrote.

Clay and his supporters found Jackson's economic ideas and his language of class antagonism so absurd that they distributed thousands of copies of the bank veto as campaign material for their own party. A confident Henry Clay headed his party's ticket for the presidency. But the plan backfired. Jackson's translation of the bank controversy into a language of class antagonism and egalitarian ideals resonated with many Americans. Old Hickory won the election easily, gaining 55 percent of the popular vote and 219 electoral votes to Clay's 49. Jackson's party still controlled Congress, so

no override was possible. The second Bank of the United States would cease to exist after 1836. Distraught over the election, Clay condemned the "reign of Jackson," which he termed a "reign of corruption." "The dark cloud," he wrote, "has become more dense, more menacing, more alarming."

Confirming Clay's fears, Jackson took steps to destroy the bank sooner than 1836. Calling it a "monster," he ordered the sizable federal deposits to be removed from its vaults and redeposited into Democratic-inclined state banks. In retaliation, the Bank of the United States raised interest rates and called in loans. This action caused a brief decline in the economy in 1833 and actually enhanced Jackson's claim that the bank was too powerful for the good of the country.

Unleashed and unregulated, the economy went into high gear in 1834. Just at this moment, an excess of silver from Mexican mines made its way into American banks, giving bankers license to print ever more banknotes. From 1834 to 1837, inflation soared; prices of basic goods rose more than 50 percent. States quickly chartered hundreds of new private banks, each issuing its own banknotes. Entrepreneurs borrowed and invested money, and the webs of credit and debt relationships that were the hallmark of the American economy grew denser yet.

The market in western land sales also heated up. In 1834, about 4.5 million acres of the public domain had been sold, the highest annual volume since 1818. By 1836, the total reached an astonishing 20 million acres (Figure 11.1). Some of this was southern land in Mississippi and Louisiana, which slave owners rushed to bring under cultivation, but much more was in the North, where land offices were deluged with buyers. The Jackson administration worried that the purchasers were overwhelmingly eastern capitalist land speculators instead of independent farmers intending to settle on the land.

In one respect, the economy attained an admirable goal: The national debt disappeared, and from 1835 to 1837, for the only time in American history, the government had a monetary surplus. But much of that surplus consisted of questionable bank currencies — "bloated, diseased" currencies, in Jackson's vivid terminology. While the boom was on, however, few stopped to worry about the consequences if and when the bubble burst.

FIGURE 11.1 Western Land Sales, 1810–1860
Land sales peaked in the 1810s, 1830s, and 1850s as Americans rushed to speculate in western land sold by the federal government. The surges in 1818 and 1836 demonstrate the volatile, speculative economy that suddenly collapsed in the panics of 1819 and 1837.

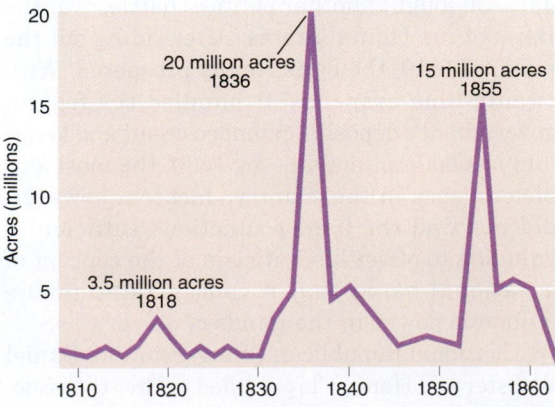

REVIEW Why did Jackson promote Indian removal?

▶ Cultural Shifts, Religion, and Reform

The growing economy, booming by the mid-1830s, transformed social and cultural life. For many families, especially in the commercialized Northeast, standards of living rose, consumption patterns changed, and the nature and location of work were altered. All this had a direct impact on the duties of men and women and on the training of youths for the economy of the future.

Along with economic change came an unprecedented revival of evangelical religion known as the Second Great Awakening. Just as universal male suffrage allowed all white men to vote, democratized religion offered salvation to all who embraced it. Among the most serious adherents of evangelical Protestantism were men and women of the new merchant classes, whose self-discipline in pursuing market ambitions meshed well with the message of self-discipline in pursuit of spiritual perfection. Not content with individual perfection, many of these people sought to perfect society as well, by defining excessive alcohol consumption, nonmarital sex, and slavery as three major evils of modern life in need of correction.

The Family and Separate Spheres

The centerpiece of new ideas about gender relations was the notion that husbands found their status and authority in the new world of work, leaving wives to tend the hearth and home. Sermons, advice books, periodicals, and novels reinforced the idea that men and women inhabited **separate spheres** and had separate duties. "To woman it belongs . . . to elevate the intellectual character of her household [and] to kindle the fires of mental activity in childhood," wrote Mrs. A. J. Graves in a popular book titled *Advice to American Women*. For men, by contrast, "the absorbing passion for gain, and the pressing demands of business, engross their whole attention." In particular, the home, now said to be the exclusive domain of women, was sentimentalized as the source of intimacy, love, and safety, a refuge from the cruel and competitive world of market relations.

Images of the Family at Home
Hundreds of itinerant amateur artists journeyed the back roads and small villages of antebellum America, earning a modest living painting individuals and families. This picture from the 1830s exhibits a common convention—the arrangement of family members by age and by sex, as if to emphasize the ideal of separate spheres. In contrast, the handpainted snuff box depicts a cozy and more realistic scene where a husband rocks the cradle while his wife lies in bed, perhaps recuperating from childbirth. Note the scampering pets, the kettle on the stove, and the chamber pot under the bed, all emblems of unvarnished everyday life. Portrait: Museum of Fine Arts, Boston, Gift of Maxim Karolik for the M. and M. Karolik Collection of American Watercolors and Drawings, 1800–1875; snuff box: Historic Deerfield, photo by Penny Leveritt.

	Nineteenth Century		Twentieth Century		
	1800	*1850*	*1900*	*1960*	*2000*
United States	21	23	23	20	25
England	20	24	24	22	28
Netherlands	—	28	26	25	28
Russia	—	19	—	25	22

Note: Dates are approximate. Dashes indicate a lack of reliable information.

FIGURE 11.2   GLOBAL COMPARISON: Changing Trends in Age at First Marriage for Women
Average age at first marriage is a remarkably complex indicator of social, economic, and cultural factors. In general, women marry younger if existing conditions provide young couples with early financial support: abundant affordable farmland, coresidence with parents, or steady employment for men. Factors that postpone marriage include a lack of farmland, deterioration in male employment prospects, a changed economy requiring more years of pre-job education and training, or enhanced employment for women that makes the job market more attractive than the marriage market. In Europe and the United States, women's age at marriage rose steeply in the nineteenth century. The northeastern United States led the way in the 1820s and 1830s. Can you suggest reasons why? Population experts note that rising age at first marriage is often accompanied by rising rates of nonmarriage, sometimes as high as 20 percent. How might these two trends be connected?

Some new aspects of society gave substance to this formulation of separate spheres. Men's work was undergoing profound change after 1815 and increasingly brought cash to the household, especially in the manufacturing and urban Northeast. Farmers and tradesmen sold products in a market, and bankers, bookkeepers, shoemakers, and canal diggers earned regular salaries or wages. Furthermore, many men now worked away from the home, at an office or a store.

A woman's domestic role was more complicated than the cultural prescriptions indicated (Figure 11.2). Although the vast majority of married white women did not hold paying jobs, their homes required time-consuming labor. But the advice books treated housework as a loving familial duty, thus rendering it invisible in an economy that evaluated work by how much cash it generated. In reality, wives contributed directly to family income in many ways. Some took in boarders; others earned pay for shoebinding or needlework done at home. Wives in the poorest classes, including most free black wives, did not have the luxury of husbands earning adequate wages; for them, wage-paying work as servants or laundresses helped augment family income.

> **"Females can be educated cheaper, quicker, and better, and will teach cheaper after they are qualified."**
> — A Massachusetts report on education

Idealized notions about the feminine home and the masculine workplace gained acceptance in the 1830s (and well beyond) because of the cultural ascendancy of the commercialized Northeast, with its domination of book and periodical publication. Men seeking manhood through work and pay could embrace competition and acquisitiveness, while women established femininity through dutiful service to home and family. This particular formulation of gender difference helped smooth the path for the first generation of Americans experiencing the market revolution, and both men and women of the middle classes benefited. Men were set free to pursue wealth, and women gained moral authority within the home. Beyond white families of the middle and upper classes, however, these new gender ideals had limited applicability. And new voices like those of the Grimké sisters challenged whether "virtue" and "duty" had separate masculine and feminine manifestations. Despite their apparent authority in printed material of the period, these gender ideals were never all-pervasive.

The Education and Training of Youths

The market economy required expanded opportunities for training youths of both sexes. By the 1830s, in both the North and the South,

Women Graduates of Oberlin College, Class of 1855
Oberlin College, founded in Ohio by evangelical and abolitionist activists in the 1830s, admitted men and women, both white and black. In the early years, the black students were all male, and the women students, who attended classes in the separate Ladies' Department, were all white. By 1855, as this daguerreotype shows, black women had integrated the Ladies' Department. Each student is dressed in the latest fashion: a dark taffeta dress with a detachable white lace collar. Hairstyles were similarly uniform in the 1850s: hair parted down the middle, dressed with oil, and lustrously coiled over the ears. Oberlin College Archives, Oberlin, OH.

state-supported public school systems were the norm, designed to produce pupils of both sexes able, by age twelve to fourteen, to read, write, and participate in marketplace calculations. Literacy rates for white females climbed dramatically, rivaling the rates for white males for the first time. The fact that taxpayers paid for children's education created an incentive to seek an inexpensive teaching force. By the 1830s, school districts replaced male teachers with young females, for, as a Massachusetts report on education put it, "females can be educated cheaper, quicker, and better, and will teach cheaper after they are qualified." Many were trained in private female academies, now numbering in the hundreds (see chapter 10).

Advanced education continued to expand in the 1830s, with an additional two dozen colleges for men and several more female seminaries offering education on a par with the male colleges. Mount Holyoke Seminary in western Massachusetts, founded by educator Mary Lyon in 1837, developed a rigorous scientific curriculum, and Oberlin College in Ohio, founded by Presbyterians in 1835, became the first coeducational college when it opened its doors to women in 1837. Oberlin's goal was to train young men for the ministry and to prepare young women to be ministers' wives.

Still, only a very small percentage of young people attended institutions of higher learning. The vast majority of male youths left public school at age fourteen to apprentice in specific trades or to embark on business careers by seeking entry-level clerkships, abundant in the growing urban centers. Young women headed for mill towns or cities in unprecedented numbers, seeking work in the expanding service sector as seamstresses and domestic servants. Changes in patterns of youth employment meant that large numbers of youngsters escaped the watchful eyes of their parents. Moralists fretted about the dangers of unsupervised youths, and following the lead of the Lowell mill owners, some established apprentices' libraries and uplifting lecture series to keep young people honorably occupied. Advice books published by the hundreds instructed youths in the virtues of hard work and delayed gratification.

The Second Great Awakening

A newly invigorated version of Protestantism gained momentum in the 1820s and 1830s as the economy reshaped gender and age relations. The earliest manifestations of this fervent piety, which historians call the **Second Great Awakening**, appeared in 1801 in Kentucky, when a crowd of ten thousand people camped out on a hillside at Cane Ridge for a revival meeting that lasted several weeks. By the 1810s and 1820s, "camp meetings" had spread to the Atlantic seaboard states. The outdoor settings permitted huge attendance, intensifying the emotional impact of the revival.

The gatherings attracted women and men hungry for a more immediate access to spiritual peace, one not requiring years of soul-searching. One eyewitness reported that "some of the people were singing, others praying, some crying for mercy. . . . At one time I saw at least five hundred swept down in a moment as if a battery of a thousand guns had been opened upon them, and then immediately followed shrieks and shouts that rent the very heavens."

From 1800 to 1820, church membership doubled in the United States, much of it among the evangelical groups. Methodists, Baptists, and Presbyterians formed the core of the new movement; Episcopalians, Congregationalists, Unitarians, Dutch Reformed, Lutherans, and Catholics maintained strong skepticism about the emotional enthusiasm. Women more than men were attracted to the evangelical movement, and wives and mothers typically recruited husbands and sons to join them.

The leading exemplar of the Second Great Awakening was a lawyer turned minister named **Charles Grandison Finney**. Finney lived in western New York, where the completion of the Erie Canal in 1825 fundamentally altered the social and economic landscape overnight. Towns swelled with new inhabitants who brought

remarkable prosperity along with other, less admirable side effects, such as prostitution, drinking, and gaming. Finney saw New York canal towns as especially ripe for evangelical awakening. In Rochester, he sustained a six-month revival through the winter of 1830–31, generating thousands of converts.

Finney's message was directed primarily at the business classes. He argued that a reign of Christian perfection loomed, one that required public-spirited outreach to the less-than-perfect to foster their salvation. Evangelicals promoted Sunday schools to bring piety to children; they battled to honor the Sabbath by ending mail delivery, stopping public transport, and closing shops on Sundays. Many women formed missionary societies that distributed millions of Bibles and religious tracts. Through such avenues, evangelical religion offered women expanded spheres of influence. Finney adopted the tactics of Jacksonian-era politicians — publicity, argumentation, rallies, and speeches — to sell his cause. His object, he said, was to get Americans to "vote in the Lord Jesus Christ as the governor of the Universe."

Sunday School

In the 1820s, American Protestantism embraced the idea of Sunday Schools for indigent children, and by 1832, the American Sunday School Union formed to generate curriculum materials for what had quickly become a popular nationwide movement. Leadership came from coalitions of lay people mainly from the newly awakened variety of Protestant churches, while teachers both male and female usually volunteered their labor. The target student population consisted of poor children both white and free black, many of whom worked six days a week and had only the Sabbath free for schooling. The schools imparted basic literacy along with an education in Christianity. The Granger Collection, NYC.

SUNDAY SCHOOL.

The Temperance Movement and the Campaign for Moral Reform

The evangelical disposition — a combination of faith, energy, self-discipline, and righteousness — animated vigorous campaigns to eliminate alcohol abuse and eradicate sexual sin. Millions of Americans took the temperance pledge to abstain from strong drink, and thousands became involved in efforts to end prostitution.

Alcohol consumption had risen steadily in the decades up to 1830, when the average person over age thirteen annually consumed an astonishing nine gallons of hard liquor plus thirty gallons of hard cider, beer, and wine. All classes imbibed. A lively saloon culture fostered masculine camaraderie along with extensive alcohol consumption among laborers, while in elite homes the after-dinner whiskey or sherry was commonplace. Colleges before 1820 routinely served students a pint of ale with meals, and the military included rum in the daily ration.

Organized opposition to drinking first surfaced in the 1810s among health and religious reformers. In 1826, Lyman Beecher, a Connecticut minister of an "awakened" church, founded the **American Temperance Society**, which warned that drinking led to poverty, idleness, crime, and family violence. Adopting the methods of evangelical ministers, temperance lecturers traveled the country expounding the damage of drink. By 1833, some six thousand local affiliates of the American Temperance Society boasted more than a million members. Middle-class drinking began a steep decline. One powerful tool of persuasion was the temperance pledge, which many business owners began to require of employees.

In 1836, leaders of the temperance movement regrouped into a new society, the American Temperance Union, which demanded total abstinence from its adherents. The intensified war against alcohol moved beyond individual moral suasion into the realm of politics as reformers sought to deny taverns liquor licenses. By 1845, temperance advocates had put an impressive dent in alcohol consumption, which diminished to one-quarter of the per capita consumption of 1830. In 1851, Maine became the first state to ban entirely the manufacture and sale of all alcoholic beverages.

More controversial than temperance was a social movement called "moral reform," which first aimed at public morals in general but quickly narrowed to a campaign to eradicate sexual sin. In 1833, a group of Finneyite women started the New York Female Moral Reform Society. Its members insisted that uncontrolled male sexual expression posed a serious threat to society in general and to women in particular. The society's nationally distributed newspaper, the *Advocate of Moral Reform*, was the first major paper in the country that was written, edited, and typeset by women. In it, they condemned men who visited brothels or seduced innocent women. Within five years, more than four thousand auxiliary groups of women had sprung up, mostly in New England, New York, Pennsylvania, and Ohio.

In its analysis of the causes of licentiousness and its conviction that women had a duty to speak out about unspeakable things, the Moral Reform Society pushed the limits of what even the men in the evangelical movement could tolerate. Yet these women did not regard themselves

"Signing the Pledge"
This lithograph from the 1840s captures and celebrates a hard-won moment in the life of a hard-luck (but fictive) family. A temperance worker convinces the man of the household to give his solemn word to abstain from all alcohol, while his wife exhibits prayerful gratitude. What message does this picture send about the consequences of alcohol abuse? And about the possibilities of redemption? The temperance pledge was a major tool used by anti-alcohol advocates to curb drinking: Could it have really worked? Consider the power of religious oaths in a society infused with religious belief. The Granger Collection, NYC.

as radicals. They were simply pursuing the logic of a gender system that defined home protection and morality as women's special sphere and a religious conviction that called for the eradication of sin.

Organizing against Slavery

More radical still was the movement in the 1830s to abolish the sin of slavery. The abolitionist movement had its roots in Great Britain in the late 1700s. (See "Beyond America's Borders," page 344.) Previously, the American Colonization Society, founded in 1817 by Maryland and Virginia planters, aimed to promote gradual individual emancipation of slaves followed by colonization in Africa. By the early 1820s, several thousand ex-slaves had been transported to Liberia on the West African coast. But not surprisingly, newly freed men and women often were not eager to emigrate; their African roots were three or more generations in the past. Colonization was too gradual (and expensive) to have much impact on American slavery.

Transatlantic Abolition

Abolitionism blossomed in the United States in the 1830s, but its roots stretched back to the 1780s in Britain and America. Developments in both countries led to a transatlantic antislavery movement with shared ideas, strategies, activists, songs, and, eventually, victories.

An important source of antislavery sentiment derived from the Quaker religion, with its deep convictions regarding human equality. But moral sentiment alone does not make a political movement. English Quakers, customarily an apolitical group, awoke to sudden antislavery zeal in 1783, triggered in part by the loss of the imperial war for America and the debate it spurred about citizenship and slavery. The end of the war also brought a delegation of Philadelphia Quakers to meet with the London group, and an immediate result was the first petition requesting that Parliament abolish the slave trade.

The English Quakers, now joined by a scattering of evangelical Anglicans and Methodists, formed the Society for Effecting the Abolition of the Slave Trade in 1787 and in just five years became a force to be reckoned with. They amassed thousands of signatures on petitions to Parliament. They organized a boycott of slave-produced sugar from the British West Indies that involved 300,000 Britons. (Women, the traditional cooks of English families, were essential to the effort.) In 1789, the society scored a publicity coup by publishing two chilling illustrations of slave ships stacked with human cargo. These images, reprinted by the thousands, created a sensation. The society mobilized the resulting groundswell of antislavery sentiment to pressure Parliament once again. A sympathetic member of that body, the Methodist William Wilberforce, brought the anti–slave trade issue to a debate and vote in 1791; it lost.

Meanwhile, Pennsylvania Quakers in 1784 launched their own Society for Promoting the Abolition of Slavery, which worked to end slavery in that state and petitioned the confederation congress — unsuccessfully — to end American participation in the international slave trade. When the First Congress met in 1790, this antislavery society delivered two petitions in quick succession, one to ban the slave trade and a second to ban slavery itself (see chapter 9, "Historical Question," page 262). In rejecting both petitions, Congress pointed to the U.S. Constitution's clause that prohibited federal regulation of the trade before 1808.

The antislavery movement also took root in France, with the founding of the Société des Amis des Noirs (Society of the Friends of Blacks) in 1788. Inspired by Quaker groups in London and Philadelphia, the Société sent petitions to the French National Assembly. All three antislavery groups, in close communication, agreed that ending the slave trade was the critical first step in abolishing slavery. That goal was achieved once the revolution of *liberté and égalité* came to France; a 1794 decree of the National Assembly freed all French colonial slaves and termed them citizens.

Success came more slowly in Britain and America. In 1807, Parliament finally made it illegal for British ships to transport Africans into slavery. A year later, the United States also banned the international slave trade. The rapid natural increase of the African American population made passage of this law relatively easy. Older slave states along the coast supported the ban because it actually increased the value of their native-born slaves who were sold and transported west in the domestic slave trade.

Around 1830, northern challenges to slavery surfaced with increasing frequency and resolve, beginning in free black communities. In 1829, a Boston printer named David Walker published *An Appeal . . . to the Coloured Citizens of the World*, which condemned racism, invoked the egalitarian language of the Declaration of Independence, and hinted at racial violence if whites did not change their prejudiced ways. In 1830, at the inaugural National Negro Convention meeting in Philadelphia, forty blacks from nine states discussed the racism of American society and proposed emigration to Canada. In 1832 and 1833, a twenty-eight-year-old black woman named **Maria Stewart** delivered public lectures on slavery and racial prejudice to black audiences in Boston.

Although Stewart's arguments against slavery were welcomed, her voice — that of a woman — created problems even among her sympathetic audiences. Few American-born women had yet engaged in public speaking beyond theatrical performances or religious prophesying. Stewart was breaking a social taboo, an offense made more challenging by her statements suggesting that black women should rise above housework:

DESCRIPTION OF A SLAVE SHIP.

Description of a Slave Ship
This powerful and often-reprinted image combines a precise technical rendering of a British ship (normally evoking pride in Britons) with the horrors of a crowded mass of dark human flesh. Peabody Essex Museum, Salem, MA.

provided financial compensation for owners (£20 million), a key proviso made possible by the relatively small number of slave owners in the British slaveholding colonies.

The success of the British movement generated even greater transatlantic communication. In 1840, British and American abolitionists came together in full force at the World Anti-Slavery Convention in London. Most of the 409 delegates were from Britain and the West Indies, although 53 Americans and half a dozen French delegates also attended. Ten days of meetings produced speeches and reports on the worldwide practice of slavery, along with debates over various economic and religious strategies to end it. A key plan was to publicize throughout America the British movement's success in achieving emancipation. The delegates closed their meeting fully energized by their international congress, called to propose international solutions to an international problem.

British antislavery forces took a new tack in the 1820s, when women became active and pushed beyond the ban on trade. Quaker widow Elizabeth Heyrick authored *Immediate Not Gradual Abolition* in 1824, prompting the formation of scores of all-women societies. American women abolitionists soon followed suit. Abolitionists again bombarded Parliament with a massive petition campaign, and 30 percent of the 1.3 million signatures submitted in 1833 were women's. That year, Parliament finally passed the Abolition of Slavery Act, which freed all slave children under age six and gradually phased out slavery for everyone older during a four-year apprenticeship. The act also

America in a Global Context

1. What were some of the tactics that British abolitionists used to advance their cause?

2. What factors help explain why the emancipation of slaves came earliest in France, and then four decades later in Britain and seven decades later in the United States?

"How long shall the fair daughters of Africa be compelled to bury their minds and talents beneath a load of iron pots and kettles?" She retired from the platform in 1833 but took up writing and published her lectures in a national publication called the *Liberator*, giving them much wider circulation.

The *Liberator*, founded in 1831 in Boston, took antislavery agitation to new heights. Its founder and editor, an uncompromising twenty-six-year-old white printer named **William Lloyd Garrison**, advocated immediate abolition: "On this subject, I do not wish to think, or speak, or write, with moderation. No! No! Tell a man whose house is on fire to give a moderate alarm; tell him to moderately rescue his wife from the hands of the ravisher; tell the mother to gradually extricate her babe from the fire into which it has fallen; — but urge me not to use moderation in a cause like the present." In 1832, Garrison's supporters started the New England Anti-Slavery Society.

Similar groups were organized in Philadelphia and New York in 1833. Soon a dozen antislavery newspapers and scores of antislavery lecturers were spreading the word and inspiring

Controversy over Abolitionism
Mob violence erupted in northern cities with regularity when abolitionist speakers came to town. This 1837 poster from Poughkeepsie, New York, exemplifies the inflammatory language that kindled riots. The abolitionist speaker is framed as seditious, evil, and fanatical, while the citizens are called to the noble task of defending the Constitution and the Union. Antislavery societies raised money to support these lecture tours, one way being the weekly pledge. Families committed to the cause kept a contribution box like this one, inscribed with biblical passages and the symbolic yet disturbing image of the slave in chains. Poster: Library of Congress; box: Boston Public Library/Rare Books Department—Courtesy of the Trustees.

the formation of new local societies, which numbered thirteen hundred by 1837. Confined entirely to the North, their membership totaled a quarter of a million men and women.

Many white northerners, even those who opposed slavery as a blot on the country's ideals, were not prepared to embrace the abolitionist call for emancipation. From 1834 to 1838, there were more than a hundred eruptions of serious mob violence against abolitionists and free blacks. On one occasion, antislavery headquarters in Philadelphia and a black church and orphanage were burned to the ground. In another incident, Illinois abolitionist editor Elijah Lovejoy was killed by a rioting crowd attempting to destroy his printing press.

Women played a prominent role in abolition, just as they did in moral reform and evangelical religion. They formed women's auxiliaries and held fairs to sell handmade crafts to support male lecturers in the field. They circulated antislavery petitions, presented to the U.S. Congress with tens of thousands of their signatures. Up to 1835, women's petitions were framed as respectful memorials to Congress about the evils of slavery, but by mid-decade these petitions used urgent language to call for political action, instructing Congress to outlaw slavery in the District of Columbia (the only area under Congress's sole power). By such fervent tactics, antislavery women asserted their claim to be heard on political issues independently of their husbands and fathers.

Garrison particularly welcomed women's activity, despite the potential for danger. The 1837 Massachusetts speaking tour of the **Grimké sisters** (see pages 321–322) brought out respectful audiences of thousands but also drew intimidation from some quarters. The state leaders of the Congregational Church banned the sisters from speaking in their churches. They claimed that while a modest woman deserved deference and protection, an immodest woman presumptuously instructing men in public forfeited her privileges and invited male attack. "When she assumes the place and tone of man as a public reformer, our care and protection of her seem unnecessary; we put ourselves in self-defence against her . . . her character becomes unnatural." Serious violence occurred in 1838, when a mob attacked a female antislavery convention in Philadelphia. Rocks shattered windows as Angelina Grimké gave her speech, and after the women vacated the building, it was burned to the ground.

In the late 1830s, the cause of abolition divided the nation as no other issue did. Even among abolitionists, significant divisions emerged. The Grimké sisters, radicalized by the public reaction to their speaking tour, began to write and speak about woman's rights. Angelina Grimké compared the silencing of women to the silencing of slaves: "The denial of our duty to act, is a bold denial of our right to act; and if *we* have no right to act, then may we well be termed 'the white slaves of the North' — for, like our brethren in bonds, we must seal our lips in silence and despair." The Grimkés were opposed by moderate abolitionists who were unwilling to mix the new and controversial issue of woman's rights with their first cause, the rights of blacks. A few radical men, such as Garrison, embraced woman's rights fully, working to get women some leadership positions in the national antislavery group.

The many men and women active in reform movements in the 1830s found their initial inspiration in evangelical Protestantism's dual message: Salvation was open to all, and society needed to be perfected. Their activist mentality squared well with the interventionist tendencies of the party forming in opposition to Andrew Jackson's Democrats. Generally, reformers gravitated toward the Whig Party, the males as voters and the females as rallying supporters in the 1830s campaigns.

REVIEW How did evangelical Protestantism contribute to the social reform movements of the 1830s?

▶ Van Buren's One-Term Presidency

By the mid-1830s, a vibrant and tumultuous political culture occupied center stage in American life. A colorful military hero had left his stamp on the nation, but Andrew Jackson was too ill to stand for a third term. His vice president and handpicked successor, the northerner Martin Van Buren, inherited a strong Democratic organization, but he faced doubts from slave-owning Jacksonians and outright opposition from increasingly combative Whigs. Abolitionist tactics had pushed slavery into the political debate, but Van Buren managed to defuse that conflict somewhat and even use it to his advantage. What could not be forestalled, however, was the collapse of the economic boom so celebrated by both Democrats and Whigs. The shattering panic of 1837, followed by another panic in 1839, brought the country its worst economic depression yet.

The Politics of Slavery

Sophisticated party organization was the specialty of **Martin Van Buren**. Nicknamed "the Little Magician" for his consummate political skills, the New Yorker had built his career by pioneering many of the loyalty-enhancing techniques the Democrats used in the 1830s. First a senator and then governor, Van Buren became Jackson's secretary of state and then his running mate in 1832, replacing John C. Calhoun. His eight years

in the volatile Jackson administration required the full measure of his political deftness as he sought repeatedly to save Jackson from both his enemies and his own obstinacy.

Jackson clearly favored Van Buren for the nomination in 1836, but starting in 1832, the major political parties had developed nominating conventions to choose their candidates. In 1835, Van Buren got the convention nod unanimously, to the dismay of his archrival, Calhoun, who then worked to discredit Van Buren among southern proslavery Democrats. Van Buren spent months assuring them that he was a "northern man with southern principles." This was not hard, since his Dutch family hailed from the Hudson River counties where New York slavery had once flourished, and his own family had owned at least one slave as late as the 1810s, although he chose not to broadcast that fact. (Slavery was only gradually phased out in New York starting in 1799.) Calhoun's partisans whipped up controversy over Van Buren's support of suffrage for New York's propertied free blacks at the 1821 state convention on suffrage. Van Buren's partisans countered by emphasizing that the Little Magician had argued that the mass of "poor, degraded blacks" were incapable of voting; he had merely favored retaining the existing stiff property qualifications for the handful of elite blacks who had always voted in New York, while simultaneously removing all such qualifications for white men.

Calhoun was able to stir up trouble for Van Buren because southerners were becoming increasingly alarmed by the rise of northern antislavery sentiment. When, in late 1835, abolitionists prepared to circulate in the South a million pamphlets condemning slavery, a mailbag of their literature was hijacked at the post office in Charleston, South Carolina, and ceremoniously burned along with effigies of leading abolitionists. President Jackson condemned the theft but issued approval for individual postmasters to exercise their own judgment about whether to allow incendiary materials to reach their destination. Abolitionists saw this as censorship of the mail.

The petitioning tactics of abolitionists escalated sectional tensions. As petitions demanding that Congress "purify" the District of Columbia by outlawing slavery grew into the hundreds, proslavery congressmen sought to short-circuit the appeals by passing a "gag rule" in 1836. The gag rule prohibited entering the documents into the public record on the

> **"The South already turns pale at the number [of antislavery petitions] sent."**
> — ANGELINA GRIMKÉ

Going Ahead or Gone to Smash: An Entrepreneur Struggles in the 1830s

The spectacular economic boom of the 1830s gave life to the dream of get-rich-quick entrepreneurship. America's newfound abundance and progress promised a level of comfort and even opulence previously unimagined. A new slang term, *go-aheadism*, captured the enthusiasm of the day. But this cocky confidence also had a downside, identified by a New York diarist who lamented that *go-aheadism* had made Americans "the most careless, reckless, headlong people on the face of the earth." Soon enough, a rich vocabulary also defined business failure: *gone to smash, fizzled, wiped out, busted, up a tree,* and *GTT* — for "gone to Texas," a location outside the United States (until 1845) and therefore out of reach of U.S. law.

Benjamin Rathbun epitomized both *go-aheadism* and *gone to smash* failure in the turbulent 1830s. A shy man who was never seen to smile, he shrewdly identified Buffalo, New York, as the perfect location for his new business venture, an opulent hotel. Buffalo, a boomtown, linked the Erie Canal with the Great Lakes,

where scores of steamboats departed daily for the interior of the country. The town's population nearly doubled from 1830 to 1835, and then doubled again, to eighteen thousand inhabitants, by 1840. Fueling this boom were brokerage houses that lined Buffalo's streets, lending money at high interest rates to borrowers speculating in real estate and business.

The success of the Eagle Hotel enabled Rathbun to become Buffalo's biggest self-made man. In eight years, he built a vast empire of real estate, building construction, banks, stores, and transportation. More than two thousand employees — more than a third of all adult males in Buffalo — were on his payroll. This empire required business acumen, astute management, and a steady influx of borrowed banknotes issued by New York City creditors. Rathbun's trusted younger brother, Lyman, headed financial operations, while Rathbun kept his eye on the big picture: designing the grand architecture of Buffalo (ninety-nine buildings) and buying up all the land on the American side of Niagara Falls

for profitable resale. Some people even said that Rathbun owned the falls themselves.

Collapse came suddenly in 1836. Rathbun learned that his creditors in New York City had lost faith in him and were selling his IOUs to brokers at a steep discount, a process known as "note shaving." To cover the much higher interest rates charged by the new note holders, the Rathbuns negotiated more loans, supposedly backed by a dozen cosigners from the Buffalo business community guaranteeing payment if the brothers failed. When Rathbun applied for a $500,000 loan in an attempt to consolidate his debt, the dozen endorsements were revealed to be forgeries. Benjamin Rathbun was convicted of fraud and sentenced to five years' hard labor in state prison; brother Lyman disappeared with trunks full of money — "GTT," many people said.

Rathbun's spectacular failure plunged Buffalo into a severe depression eight months in advance of the panic of 1837. Although deliberate fraud brought him down, his *wipeout* highlighted the inherent difficulties in an economy of note shaving and discounting, where loans of millions of dollars were granted on the basis of a few signatures. Historians calculate that something like one-fifth of all businessmen in the 1830s *fizzled* or went *up a tree*.

Massive failures in the five years after 1837 led to two striking innovations in business law and loan practices. First, the federal government passed the U.S. Bankruptcy Act of 1841, a controversial and short-term law that enabled failed debtors to wipe debts away legally, paying creditors a fraction of what was owed. Debtors gained release from crushing

grounds that what the abolitionists prayed for was unconstitutional and, further, an assault on the rights of white southerners, as one South Carolina representative put it. Abolitionists like the Grimké sisters considered the gag rule to be an abridgment of free speech. They also argued that, tabled or not, the petitions were effective. "The South already turns pale at the number

sent," Angelina Grimké said in a speech exhorting more petitions to be circulated.

Van Buren shrewdly seized on both mail censorship and the gag rule to express his prosouthern sympathies. Abolitionists were "fanatics," he repeatedly claimed, possibly under the influence of "foreign agents" (British abolitionists). He dismissed the issue of abolition in the District of

The Eagle Hotel, Buffalo, 1825
Benjamin Rathbun (shown here scowling) bought this three-story building in 1825, doubled it in size with a building behind it, and turned it into the finest hotel west of New York City. Located on Main Street in Buffalo, the Eagle became the meeting place for all civic and professional groups in early Buffalo. The marquis de Lafayette, French hero of the American Revolution, stayed at the Eagle in 1825 on his U.S. tour. *The Picture Book of Earlier Buffalo*, Frank H. Severance, vol. 16, 1912, page 161.

debt but had to endure the humiliation of having notices of their bankruptcies printed in the newspapers.

Second, the credit rating industry was born in 1841 when a failed businessman opened the Mercantile Agency in New York City. For a $50 subscription fee, lenders could tap into large books containing confidential information gathered by hundreds of agents around the country who assessed the creditworthiness of local businessmen. Church (and saloon) attendance, family stability, and punctuality were often factors in grading businessmen's reputations for prudence and reliability.

Had it been in existence in 1836, the Mercantile Agency might have unmasked Rathbun's fraud through semiannual checks on his reputation. The Bankruptcy Act no doubt helped the many debt-saddled Buffalo men who had been caught out by Rathbun's failure. His liquidated estate paid out first to the thousands of workers on his payroll, second to the lawyers, and third to preferred creditors, leaving hundreds of thousands of dollars of debt unpaid.

When Rathbun left prison in 1843, he rejoined his wife, now running a boardinghouse in Buffalo to make ends meet. Soon the Rathbuns

moved to New York City, where the onetime proprietor of Buffalo's Eagle Hotel returned to his first occupation. With financial help from cousins, he leased a building for the first in a series of increasingly seedy hotels that he ran until his death.

Questions for Consideration

1. What factors led to the Rathbuns' downfall?

2. How did the new credit rating agency, established in reaction to the panic of 1837, intend to prevent economic crises?

Columbia as "inexpedient" and promised that if he was elected president, he would not allow any interference in southern "domestic institutions."

Elections and Panics

Although the elections of 1824, 1828, and 1832 clearly bore the stamp of Jackson's personality,

by 1836 the party apparatus was sufficiently developed to give Van Buren, a backroom politician, a shot at the presidency. Local and state committees existed throughout the country. Democratic candidates ran in every state election, succeeding even in the old Federalist stronghold of New England. More than four hundred newspapers self-identified as Democratic partisans.

349

The Whigs had also built state-level organizations and newspaper loyalty. They had no top contender with nationwide support, so three regional candidates opposed Van Buren. Senator Daniel Webster of Massachusetts could deliver New England, home to reformers, merchants, and manufacturers; Senator Hugh Lawson White of Tennessee attracted proslavery voters still suspicious of the northern Magician; and the aging General William Henry Harrison, now residing in Ohio and remembered for his Indian war heroics in 1811, pulled in the western anti-Indian vote. Not one of the three candidates had the ability to win the presidency, but together they came close to denying Van Buren a majority vote. Van Burenites called the three-Whig strategy a deliberate plot to derail the election and move it to the House of Representatives.

In the end, Van Buren won with 170 electoral votes, while the other three received a total of 113. The popular vote told a somewhat different story. Van Buren's narrow majorities, where he won, were far below those Jackson had commanded. Although Van Buren had pulled together a national Democratic Party with wins in both the North and the South, he had done it at the cost of committing northern Democrats to the proslavery agenda. And running three candidates had maximized the Whigs' success by drawing Whigs into office at the state level.

When Van Buren took office in March 1837, the financial markets were already quaking; by April, the country was plunged into crisis. The causes of the **panic of 1837** were multiple and far-ranging. Bad harvests in Europe and a large trade imbalance between Britain and the United States caused the Bank of England to start calling in loans to American merchants. Failures in various crop markets and a 30 percent downturn in international cotton prices fed the growing

The Panic of 1837

A sad family with an unemployed father faces sudden privation in this cartoon showing the consequences of the panic of 1837. The wife and children complain of hunger, the house is stripped nearly bare, and rent collectors loom in the doorway. Faint pictures on the wall show Andrew Jackson and Martin Van Buren presiding over the economic devastation of the family. The only support system for the unemployed in 1837 was the local almshouse, where families were split up and living conditions were harsh. Library of Congress.

disaster. Cotton merchants in the South could no longer meet their obligations to New York creditors, whose firms began to fail — ninety-eight of them in March and April 1837 alone. Frightened citizens thronged the banks to try to get their money out, and businesses rushed to liquefy their remaining assets to pay off debts. Prices of stocks, bonds, and real estate fell 30 to 40 percent. The familiar events of the panic of 1819 unfolded again, with terrifying rapidity, and the credit market tumbled like a house of cards. Newspapers describing the economic free fall generally used the language of emotional states — excitement, anxiety, terror, panic. Such words focused on human reactions to the crisis rather than on the structural features of the economy that had interacted to amplify the downturn. The vocabulary for understanding the wider economy was still quite limited, making it hard to track the bigger picture of the workings of capitalism. (See "Seeking the American Promise," page 348.)

Instead, many observers looked to politics, religion, and character flaws to explain the crisis. Some Whig leaders were certain that Jackson's antibank and hard-money policies were responsible for the ruin. New Yorker Philip Hone, a wealthy Whig, called the Jackson administration "the most disastrous in the annals of the country" for its "wicked interference" in banking and monetary matters. Others framed the devastation as retribution for an immoral frenzy of speculation that had gripped the nation. A religious periodical in Boston hoped that Americans would now moderate their greed: "We were getting to think that there was no end to the wealth, and could be no check to the progress of our country; that economy was not needed, that prudence was weakness." In this view, the panic was a wakeup call, a blessing in disguise. Others identified the competitive, profit-maximizing capitalist system as the cause and looked to Britain and France for new socialist ideas calling for the common ownership of the means of production. American socialists, though few in number, were vocal and imaginative, and in the early 1840s several thousand developed utopian alternative communities (as discussed in chapter 12).

The panic of 1837 subsided by 1838, but in 1839 another run on the banks and ripples of business failures deflated the economy, creating a second panic. President Van Buren called a special session of Congress to consider creating an independent treasury system to perform some of the functions of the defunct Bank of the United States. Such a system, funded by government deposits, would deal only in hard money and would exert a powerful moderating influence on inflation and the credit market. But Van Buren encountered strong resistance in Congress, even among Democrats. The treasury system finally won approval in 1840, but by then Van Buren's chances of winning a second term in office were virtually nil.

In 1840, the Whigs settled on **William Henry Harrison** to oppose Van Buren. The campaign drew on voter involvement as no other presidential campaign ever had. The Whigs borrowed tricks from the Democrats: Harrison was touted as a common man born in a log cabin (in reality, he was born on a Virginia plantation), and raucous campaign parades featured toy log cabins held aloft. His Indian-fighting days, now thirty years behind him, were played up to give him a Jacksonian aura. Whigs staged festive rallies around the country, drumming up mass appeal with candlelight parades and song shows, and women participated in rallies as never before. Some 78 percent of eligible voters cast ballots — the highest percentage ever in American history.

Harrison took 53 percent of the popular vote and won a resounding 234 electoral college votes to Van Buren's 60. A Democratic editor lamented, "We have taught them how to conquer us!"

REVIEW How did slavery figure as a campaign issue in the election of 1836?

▶ Conclusion: The Age of Jackson or the Era of Reform?

Harrison's election closed a decade that had brought the common man and democracy to the forefront of American politics. Economic transformations loom large in explaining the fast-paced changes of the 1830s. Transportation advances put goods and people in circulation, augmenting urban growth and helping to create a national culture, and water-powered manufacturing began to change the face of wage labor. Trade and banking mushroomed, and western land once occupied by Indians was auctioned off in a landslide of sales. Two periods of economic downturn — including the panic of 1819 and the panics of 1837 and

1839 — offered sobering lessons about speculative fever.

For many people, Andrew Jackson symbolized this age of opportunity. His fame as an aggressive general, Indian fighter, champion of the common man, and defender of slavery attracted growing numbers of voters to the emergent Democratic Party, which championed personal liberty, free competition, and egalitarian opportunity for all white men.

Jackson's constituency was challenged by a small but vocal segment of the population troubled by serious moral problems that Jacksonians preferred to ignore. Reformers drew sustenance from the message of the Second Great Awakening: that all men and women were free to choose salvation and that personal and societal sins could be overcome. Reformers targeted personal vices (illicit sex and intemperance) and social problems (prostitution, poverty, and slavery) and joined forces with evangelicals and wealthy lawyers and merchants (North and South) who appreciated a national bank and protective tariffs. The Whig Party was the party of activist moralism and state-sponsored entrepreneurship. Whig voters were, of course, male, but thousands of reform-minded women broke new ground by signing political petitions on the issues of Indian removal and slavery. A few exceptional women, like Sarah and Angelina Grimké, captured the national limelight by offering powerful testimony against slavery and in the process pioneering new pathways for women to contribute a moral voice to politics.

National politics in the 1830s were more divisive than at any time since the 1790s. The new party system of Democrats and Whigs reached far deeper into the electorate than had the Federalists and Republicans. Stagecoaches and steamboats carried newspapers from the cities to the backwoods, politicizing voters and creating party loyalty. Politics acquired immediacy and excitement, causing nearly four out of five white men to cast ballots in 1840.

High rates of voter participation would continue into the 1840s and 1850s. Unprecedented urban growth, westward expansion, and early industrialism marked those decades, sustaining the Democrat-Whig split in the electorate. But critiques of slavery, concerns for free labor, and an emerging protest against women's second-class citizenship complicated the political scene of the 1840s, leading to third-party political movements. One of these third parties, called

the Republican Party, would achieve dominance in 1860 with the election of an Illinois lawyer, Abraham Lincoln, to the presidency.

▶ Selected Bibliography

The Market Revolution

Edward J. Balleisen, *Navigating Failure: Bankruptcy and Commercial Society in Antebellum America* (2001).

Mary H. Blewett, *Men, Women, and Work: Class, Gender, and Protest in the New England Shoe Industry, 1780–1910* (1988).

Jeanne Boydston, *Home and Work: Housework, Wages, and the Ideology of Labor in the Early Republic* (1990).

Thomas Dublin, *Transforming Women's Work: New England Lives in the Industrial Revolution* (1994).

John Lauritz Larson, *The Market Revolution in America: Liberty, Ambition, and the Eclipse of the Common Good* (2009).

Stephen Mihm, *A Nation of Counterfeiters: Capitalists, Con Men, and the Making of the United States* (2009).

Seth Rockman, *Scraping By: Wage Labor, Slavery, and Survival in Early Baltimore* (2008).

Charles G. Sellers, *The Market Revolution: Jacksonian America, 1815–1846* (1991).

Carol Sheriff, *The Artificial River: The Erie Canal and the Paradox of Progress, 1817–1862* (1996).

Politics

Andrew Burstein, *The Passions of Andrew Jackson* (2003).

John Ehle, *Trail of Tears: The Rise and Fall of the Cherokee Nation* (1997).

Daniel Walker Howe, *What Hath God Wrought: The Transformation of America, 1815–1845* (2009).

Jon Meacham, *American Lion: Andrew Jackson in the White House* (2009).

Sean Michael O'Brien, *In Bitterness and in Tears: Andrew Jackson's Destruction of the Creeks and Seminoles* (2003).

Theda Perdue, *Cherokee Women: Gender and Culture Change, 1700–1835* (1998).

Merrill D. Peterson, *The Great Triumvirate: Webster, Clay, and Calhoun* (1987).

Sean Wilentz, *The Rise of American Democracy, Jefferson to Lincoln* (2005).

Culture, Religion, and Reform

Bruce Dorsey, *Reforming Men and Women: Gender in the Antebellum City* (2002).

Lori D. Ginzberg, *Women and the Work of Benevolence: Morality, Politics, and Class in the Nineteenth-Century United States* (1990).

Nathan O. Hatch, *The Democratization of American Christianity* (1991).

Julie Roy Jeffrey, *The Great Silent Army of Abolitionism: Ordinary Women in the Antislavery Movement* (1998).

Richard R. John, *Spreading the News: The American Postal System from Franklin to Morse* (1995).

Catherine E. Kelly, *In the New England Fashion: Reshaping Women's Lives in the Nineteenth Century* (1999).

Bruce Laurie, *Beyond Garrison: Antislavery and Social Reform* (2005).

Gerda Lerner, *The Grimké Sisters from South Carolina: Pioneers for Women's Rights and Abolition* (2009).

Richard S. Newman, *The Transformation of American Abolitionism: Fighting Slavery in the Early Republic* (2002).

Mark Perry, *Lift Up Thy Voice: The Grimké Family's Journey from Slaveholders to Civil Rights Leaders* (2002).

Alisse Portnoy, *Their Right to Speak: Women's Activism in the Indian and Slave Debates* (2005).

Patrick Rael, *Black Identity and Black Protest in the Antebellum North* (2002).

Stacey M. Robertson, *Hearts Beating for Liberty: Women Abolitionists in the Old Northwest* (2010).

Scott A. Sandage, *Born Losers: A History of Failure in America* (2005).

Kathryn Kish Sklar and James Brewer Stewart, *Women's Rights and Transatlantic Slavery in the Era of Emancipation* (2007).

Richard B. Stott, *Jolly Fellows: Male Milieus in Mid-Nineteenth Century America* (2009).

Daniel S. Wright, *"The First of Causes to Our Sex": The Female Moral Reform Movement in the Antebellum Northeast, 1834–1848* (2006).

Ronald J. Zboray, *Literary Dollars and Social Sense: A People's History of the Mass Market Book* (2005).

▶ **FOR MORE BOOKS ABOUT TOPICS IN THIS CHAPTER,** see the Online Bibliography at **bedfordstmartins.com/roark.**

▶ **FOR ADDITIONAL PRIMARY SOURCES FROM THIS PERIOD,** see Michael Johnson, ed., *Reading the American Past*, Fifth Edition.

▶ **FOR WEB SITES, IMAGES, AND DOCUMENTS RELATED TO TOPICS AND PLACES IN THIS CHAPTER,** visit Make History at **bedfordstmartins.com/roark.**

Reviewing Chapter 11

KEY TERMS

Explain each term's significance.

The Market Revolution
Erie Canal (p. 325)
Lowell mills (p. 326)
specie payment (p. 327)
second Bank of the United
   States (p. 327)
Andrew Jackson (p. 330)
panic of 1819 (p. 330)

The Spread of Democracy
Henry Clay (p. 331)
Whigs (p. 331)
Democrats (p. 331)
John C. Calhoun (p. 332)
spoils system (p. 333)

Jackson Defines the Democratic Party
Indian Removal Act of 1830 (p. 334)
Trail of Tears (p. 336)
Tariff of Abominations (p. 337)
nullification (p. 337)

Cultural Shifts, Religion, and Reform
separate spheres (p. 339)
Second Great Awakening (p. 341)
Charles Grandison Finney (p. 342)
American Temperance Society
  (p. 343)
Maria Stewart (p. 344)
William Lloyd Garrison (p. 345)
Grimké sisters (p. 346)

Van Buren's One-Term Presidency
Martin Van Buren (p. 347)
panic of 1837 (p. 350)
William Henry Harrison (p. 351)

REVIEW QUESTIONS

Use key terms and dates to support your answer.

1. Why did the United States experience a market revolution after 1815? (pp. 323–330)

2. Why did Andrew Jackson defeat John Quincy Adams so dramatically in the 1828 election? (pp. 331–333)

3. Why did Jackson promote Indian removal? (pp. 333–339)

4. How did evangelical Protestantism contribute to the social reform movements of the 1830s? (pp. 339–347)

5. How did slavery figure as a campaign issue in the election of 1836? (pp. 347–351)

MAKING CONNECTIONS

Draw on key terms, the timeline, and review questions.

1. Describe the market revolution that began in the 1810s. How did it affect Americans' work and domestic lives? In your answer, be sure to consider how gender contributed to these developments.

2. Andrew Jackson's presidency coincided with important changes in American politics. Discuss how Jackson benefited from, and contributed to, the vibrant political culture of the 1830s. Cite specific national developments in your answer.

3. Describe Andrew Jackson's response to the "Indian problem" during his presidency. How did his policies revise or continue earlier federal policies toward Native Americans? How did Native Americans respond to Jackson's actions?

4. While a volatile economy buffeted the United States in the 1830s, some Americans looked to reform the nation. Discuss the objectives and strategies of two reform movements. What was the relationship of these reform movements to larger political and economic trends of the 1830s?

Link events in this chapter to earlier events.

1. How were the economic circumstances and social anxieties that gave rise to the Second Great Awakening similar to, and different from, those that encouraged the First Great Awakening? (See chapter 5.)

2. Compare the development of political parties in the 1790s (Federalists and Republicans) with the second development of parties in the 1830s (Whigs and Democrats). Were the parties of the 1830s in any way the descendants of the two of the 1790s? Or were they completely different? (See chapter 9.)

▶ **For practice quizzes and other study tools,** see the Online Study Guide at **bedfordstmartins.com/roark.**

TIMELINE 1807–1840

1807	• Robert Fulton's *Clermont* sets off steamboat craze.
1816	• Second Bank of the United States chartered.
1817	• American Colonization Society founded.
1818	• National Road links Baltimore to western Virginia.
1819	• Economic panic.
1821	• Mill town of Lowell, Massachusetts, founded.
1825	• Erie Canal completed in New York.
1826	• American Temperance Society founded. • Schuylkill Canal completed in Pennsylvania.
1828	• Congress passes Tariff of Abominations. • Democrat Andrew Jackson elected president.
1829	• David Walker's *Appeal . . . to the Coloured Citizens of the World* published. • Baltimore and Ohio Railroad begun.
1830	• Indian Removal Act. • Women's petitions for Indian rights begin.
1830–1831	• Charles Grandison Finney preaches in Rochester, New York.
1831	• William Lloyd Garrison starts *Liberator*.
1832	• Massacre of Sauk and Fox Indians led by Chief Black Hawk. • *Worcester v. Georgia*. • Jackson vetoes charter renewal of Bank of the United States. • New England Anti-Slavery Society founded.
1833	• Nullification of federal tariffs declared in South Carolina. • New York and Philadelphia antislavery societies founded. • New York Female Moral Reform Society founded.
1834	• Female mill workers strike in Lowell, Massachusetts, and again in 1836.
1836	• Democrat Martin Van Buren elected president. • American Temperance Union founded.
1837	• Economic panic.
1838	• Trail of Tears: Cherokees forced to relocate west.
1839	• Economic panic.
1840	• Whig William Henry Harrison elected president.

GOLD NUGGET

Gold! Nuggets like this one scooped from a California river drove easterners crazy with excitement. The quarter of a million men who joined the gold rush in the five years after gold's discovery in 1848 sought to escape routine jobs and mundane lives by "making their pile" in California. The great rush for western riches fulfilled the hopes of only a few, but the rest participated in one of the great adventures of the nineteenth century and rarely regretted their experiences. The background image reminds us that gold mining meant hard work.

Nugget: Collection of the Oakland Museum of California; background: Library of Congress.

12

The New West and the Free North
1840–1860

EARLY IN NOVEMBER 1842, ABRAHAM LINCOLN AND HIS NEW WIFE, Mary, moved into their first home in Springfield, Illinois, a rented room measuring eight by fourteen feet on the second floor of the Globe Tavern. The small, noisy room above the tavern and next door to a blacksmith shop was the nicest place that Abraham Lincoln had ever lived. It was the worst place that Mary Todd Lincoln had ever inhabited. She grew up in Lexington, Kentucky, attended by slaves in the elegant home of her father, a prosperous merchant, banker, and politician. In March 1861, nineteen years after their marriage, the Lincolns moved into what would prove to be their last home, the presidential mansion in Washington, D.C.

Abraham Lincoln climbed from the Globe Tavern to the White House by relentless work, unslaked ambition, and immense talent — traits he had honed since boyhood. Lincoln and many others celebrated his rise from humble origins as an example of the opportunities that beckoned in the free-labor economy of the North and West. They attributed his spectacular ascent to his individual qualities and tended to ignore the help he received from Mary and many others.

Born in a Kentucky log cabin in 1809, Lincoln grew up on small, struggling farms as his family migrated west. His father, Thomas Lincoln, who had been born in Virginia, never learned to read and, as his son recalled, "never did more in the way of writing than to bunglingly sign his own name." Lincoln's mother, Nancy, could neither read nor write. In December 1816, Thomas Lincoln moved his young family from Kentucky to the Indiana wilderness. On the Indiana farmstead, Abraham learned the arts of agriculture practiced by families throughout the nation. Although only eight years old, he "had an axe put into his hands at once" and used it "almost constantly" for the next fifteen years, as he recalled later. When he could be spared from work, the boy attended school, less than a year in all. "There was absolutely nothing to excite ambition for education," Lincoln recollected. In contrast, Mary Todd received ten years of schooling in Lexington's best private academies for young women.

357

In 1830, Thomas Lincoln decided to move farther west. The Lincolns hitched up the family oxen and headed to central Illinois. The next spring, Thomas moved yet again, but this time Abraham stayed behind and set out on his own, a "friendless, uneducated, penniless boy," as he described himself.

By dogged striving, Abraham Lincoln gained an education and the respect of his Illinois neighbors, although a steady income eluded him for years. Mary Todd had many suitors, including Stephen A. Douglas, Lincoln's eventual political rival. After she married Lincoln, she said, "Intellectually my husband towers above Douglas . . . [and he] has no equal in the United States." The newlyweds received help from Mary's father, including eighty acres of land and a yearly allowance of about $1,100 for six years that helped them move out of their room above the Globe Tavern and into their own home. Abraham eventually built a thriving law practice in Springfield, Illinois, and served in the state legislature and then in Congress. Mary helped him in many ways, rearing their sons, tending their household, and integrating him into her wealthy and influential extended family in Illinois and Kentucky. Mary also shared Abraham's keen interest in politics and ambition for power. With Mary's support, Abraham's striving ultimately propelled them into the White House, where he became the first president born west of the Appalachian Mountains.

Like Lincoln, millions of Americans believed they could make something of themselves, whatever their origins, so long as they were willing to work. Individuals who refused to work — who were lazy, undisciplined, or foolish — had only themselves to blame if they failed. Work was a prerequisite for success, not a guarantee. This emphasis on work highlighted the individual efforts of men and tended to slight the many crucial contributions of women, family members, neighbors, and friends to the successes of men like Lincoln. In addition, the rewards of work were skewed toward white men and away from women and free African Americans. Nonetheless, the promise of such rewards spurred efforts that shaped the contours of America, pushing the boundaries of the nation ever westward to the Pacific Ocean. The nation's economic, political, and geographic expansion raised anew the question of whether slavery should also move west, the question that Lincoln and other Americans confronted again and again following the Mexican-American War, yet another outgrowth of the nation's ceaseless westward movement.

Lincoln's Log Cabin and Springfield Home
Abraham Lincoln grew up in Indiana between 1816, when he was eight years old, and 1830, when he became twenty-one. In Indiana, Lincoln, his father, his stepmother, and assorted kinfolk lived in the log cabin shown here. After moving to Illinois and becoming a successful lawyer and politician in Springfield, Lincoln and his wife Mary moved in 1844 to the home shown here. The contrast between the rustic log cabin and the spacious home highlights the opportunities the free labor system offered to all Americans, according to Lincoln. Log cabin: Meserve-Kunhandt collection; Springfield home: © Bettmann/Corbis.

Economic and Industrial Evolution

During the 1840s and 1850s, Americans experienced a profound economic transformation whose roots reached back to the beginning of the nineteenth century. Since 1800, the total output of the U.S. economy had multiplied twelvefold. Four fundamental changes in American society fueled this remarkable economic growth. First, millions of Americans moved from farms to towns and cities, Abraham Lincoln among them. Second, factory workers (primarily in towns and cities) increased to about 20 percent of the labor force by 1860. Third, a shift from water power to steam as a source of energy raised productivity, especially in factories and transportation. Railroads in particular harnessed steam power, speeding transport and cutting costs. Fourth, agricultural productivity nearly doubled during Lincoln's lifetime, spurring the nation's economic growth more than any other factor.

Historians often refer to this cascade of changes as an industrial revolution. However, these changes did not cause an abrupt discontinuity in America's economy or society, which remained overwhelmingly agricultural. Old methods of production continued alongside the new. The changes in the American economy during the 1840s and 1850s might better be termed "industrial evolution."

Agriculture and Land Policy

While cities, factories, and steam engines multiplied throughout the North and West, the foundation of the United States' economic growth lay in agriculture. A French traveler in the United States noted that Americans had "a general feeling of hatred against trees." Although the traveler exaggerated, his observation contained an important truth. Trees limited agricultural productivity because farmers had to spend a great deal of time and energy clearing land for planting. As farmers pushed westward in a quest for cheap land, they encountered the Midwest's comparatively treeless prairie, where they could spend less time with an ax and more time with a plow and hoe. Rich prairie soils yielded bumper crops, enticing farmers such as the Lincolns to migrate to the Midwest by the tens of thousands between 1830 and 1860. The populations of Indiana, Illinois, Michigan, Wisconsin, and Iowa exploded tenfold between 1830 and 1860, four times faster than the growth of the nation

as a whole. Lincoln's home state of Illinois added more people during the 1850s than any other state in the Union.

Labor-saving improvements in farm implements also boosted agricultural productivity. Inventors tinkered to craft stronger, more efficient plows to furrow the earth with as little effort as possible. In 1837, **John Deere** made a strong, smooth steel plow that sliced through prairie soil so cleanly that farmers called it the "singing plow." Deere's company became the leading plow manufacturer in the Midwest, turning out more than ten thousand plows a year by the late 1850s. Humans and animals (rather than steam) provided the energy for plowing, but better plows permitted farmers to break more ground and plant more crops.

Improvements in wheat harvesting also increased farmers' productivity. In 1850, most farmers harvested wheat by hand, cutting two or three acres a day with backbreaking labor. In the 1840s, Cyrus McCormick and others experimented with designs for **mechanical reapers**, and by the 1850s a McCormick reaper that cost between $100 and $150 allowed a farmer to harvest twelve acres a day. Farmers had purchased about eighty thousand reapers by 1860, but most continued to cut their grain by hand. Still, improved reapers and plows, usually powered by horses or oxen, allowed farmers to cultivate more land, doubling the corn and wheat harvests between 1840 and 1860.

Federal land policy made possible the agricultural productivity that fueled the nation's economy. Up to 1860, the United States continued to be land-rich and labor-poor. Territorial acquisitions made the nation a great deal richer in land, adding more than a billion acres with the Louisiana Purchase (see chapter 10) and the annexation of Florida, Oregon, and vast territories following the Mexican-American War. The federal government made most of this land available for purchase to attract settlers and to generate revenue. Wily speculators found ways to claim large tracts of the most desirable plots and sell them to settlers at a generous markup. But millions of ordinary farmers bought federal land for just $1.25 an acre, or $50 for a forty-acre farm that could support a family. Millions of other farmers squatted on unclaimed federal land, carved

> "There is . . . in America a general feeling of hatred against trees."
> — A French visitor to the United States

Harvesting Grain with Cradles
This late-nineteenth-century painting shows a grain harvest during the mid-nineteenth century at Bishop Hill, Illinois, a Swedish community where the artist, Olof Krans, and his parents settled in 1850. The men swing cradles, slowly cutting a swath through the grain; the women gather the cut grain into sheaves to be hauled away later for threshing. Although most Bishop Hill farmers had only a few family members and a hired hand or two, they could call upon the labor of the many men and women from the community at harvest time. Notice that all the work is done by hand; there is no machine in sight. Bishop Hill State Historic Site, Illinois Historic Preservation Agency.

out farms, and, if they still lacked funds to buy the land after a few years, usually moved farther west to squat on federal land elsewhere. By making land available to millions of Americans on relatively easy terms, the federal government achieved the goal of attracting settlers to the new territories in the West, which in due course joined the Union as new states. Above all, federal land policy facilitated the increase in agricultural productivity that underlay the nation's impressive economic growth.

Manufacturing and Mechanization

Changes in manufacturing arose from the nation's land-rich, labor-poor economy. European countries had land-poor, labor-rich economies; there, meager opportunities in agriculture kept factory laborers plentiful and wages low. In the United States, western expansion and government land policies buoyed agriculture, keeping millions of people on

the farm — 80 percent of the nation's 31 million people lived in rural areas in 1860 — and thereby limiting the supply of workers for manufacturing and elevating wages. Because of this relative shortage of workers, American manufacturers searched constantly for ways to save labor.

Mechanization allowed manufacturers to produce more with less labor. In general, factory workers produced twice as much (per unit of labor) as agricultural workers. The practice of manufacturing and then assembling interchangeable parts spread from gun making to other industries and became known as the **American system**. Standardized parts produced by machine allowed manufacturers to employ unskilled workers, who were much cheaper and more readily available than highly trained craftsmen. A visitor to a Springfield, Massachusetts, gun factory in 1842 noted, for example, that standardized parts made the trained gunsmith's "skill of the eye and the hand, [previously] acquired by practice alone . . . no longer indispensable." Even in heavily mechanized industries, few factories had more than twenty or thirty employees.

Manufacturing and agriculture meshed into a dynamic national economy. New England led the nation in manufacturing, shipping goods such as guns, clocks, plows, and axes west and south, while southern and western states sent commodities such as wheat, pork, whiskey, tobacco, and cotton north and east. In the 1840s, mines in Pennsylvania, Ohio, and elsewhere began to produce millions of tons of coal for industrial fuel, accelerating the shift to steam power. Between 1840 and 1860, coal production multiplied eightfold, cutting prices in half and permitting coal-fired steam engines to power ever more factories, railroads, and ships. Even so, by 1860 coal accounted for less than a fifth of the nation's energy consumption while, in manufacturing, people and work animals provided thirty times more energy than steam did.

American manufacturers specialized in producing for the gigantic domestic market rather than for export. British goods dominated the international market and, on the whole, were cheaper and better than American-made products. U.S. manufacturers supported tariffs to minimize British competition, but their best protection from British competitors was to strive harder to please their American customers, most of them farmers. The burgeoning national economy was further fueled by the growth of the railroads, which served to link farmers and factories in new ways.

Railroads: Breaking the Bonds of Nature

A Swedish visitor in 1849 noticed that American schoolboys drew sketches of locomotives, always in motion, belching smoke. Railroads captured Americans' imagination because they seemed to break the bonds of nature. (See "Visualizing History," page 364.) When canals and rivers froze in winter or became impassable during summer droughts, trains steamed ahead. When becalmed sailing ships went nowhere, locomotives kept on chugging, averaging more than twenty miles an hour during the 1850s. Above all, railroads gave cities not blessed with canals or navigable rivers a way to compete for rural trade.

In 1850, trains steamed along 9,000 miles of track, almost two-thirds of it in New England and the Middle Atlantic states. By 1860, several railroads spanned the Mississippi River, connecting frontier farmers to the nation's 30,000 miles of track, approximately as much as in all of the rest of the world combined (Map 12.1). In 1857, for example, France had 3,700 miles of track; England and Wales had 6,400 miles. The massive expansion of American railroads helped catapult

THE PROMISE OF TECHNOLOGY

The Telegraph

Samuel F. B. Morse is credited with inventing the telegraph because of his patent in June 1840, but, as one contemporary observed, Morse's talent consisted of "combining and applying the discoveries of others in the invention of a particular instrument and process for telegraphic purposes." Morse sent the first message in 1844 on this telegraph using a code he devised that represented each letter and number with dots and dashes. With a series of taps on a telegraph key, operators sent short and long pulses of electricity. By 1846, most eastern cities were connected by telegraph. By 1850, of the states east of the Mississippi River, only Florida remained without it. More than fifty thousand miles of wires webbed the nation by 1861, when the telegraph reached California. The telegraph obliterated distance, and cheap, efficient, and fast communication changed American businesses, newspapers, government, and everyday life. The telegraph made it possible to synchronize

clocks, which in turn allowed railroads to run safely according to precise schedules. Newspapers could gather information from around the country and have it in the headlines within hours. On a personal level, families across the continent could communicate more quickly than letter writing allowed. The telegraph met the needs of the vigorous, sprawling nation. Division of Political History, Smithsonian Institution, Washington, D.C.

MAP ACTIVITY

Map 12.1   Railroads in 1860

Railroads were a crucial component of the revolutions in transportation and communications that transformed nineteenth-century America. The railroad system reflected the differences in the economies of the North and South.

READING THE MAP: In which sections of the country was most of the railroad track laid by the middle of the nineteenth century? What cities served as the busiest railroad hubs?

CONNECTIONS: How did the expansion of railroad networks affect the American economy? Why was the U.S. government willing to grant more than twenty million acres of public land to the private corporations that ran the railroads?

the nation into position as the world's second-greatest industrial power, after Great Britain.

In addition to speeding transportation, railroads propelled the growth of other industries, such as iron and communications. Iron production grew five times faster than the population during the decades up to 1860, in part to meet

railroads' demand. Railroads also stimulated the fledgling telegraph industry. In 1844, **Samuel F. B. Morse** persuasively demonstrated the potential of his telegraph by transmitting a series of dots and dashes that instantly conveyed an electronic message along forty miles of wire strung between Washington, D.C., and Baltimore. By

1861, more than fifty thousand miles of wire stretched across the continent to the Pacific Ocean, often alongside railroad tracks, making trains safer and more efficient and accelerating communications of all sorts.

In contrast to the government ownership of railroads common in other industrial nations, private corporations built and owned almost all American railroads. But the railroads received massive government aid, especially federal land grants. Up to 1850, the federal government had granted a total of seven million acres of federal land to various turnpike, highway, and canal projects. In 1850, Congress approved a precedent-setting grant to railroads of six square miles of federal land for each mile of track laid. By 1860, Congress had granted railroads more than twenty million acres of federal land, thereby underwriting construction costs and promoting the expansion of the rail network, the settlement of federal land, and the integration of the domestic market.

The railroad boom of the 1850s signaled the growing industrial might of the American economy. An Illinois farmer praised railroads' "cheap and easy conveyance of commodities to foreign markets." Like other industries, railroads succeeded because they served both farms and cities. But transportation was not revolutionized overnight. Most Americans in 1860 were still far more familiar with horses than with locomotives. And even by 1875, trains carried only about one-third of the mail; most of the rest still went by stagecoach or horseback.

The economy of the 1840s and 1850s linked an expanding, westward-moving population in farms and cities with muscles, animals, machines, steam, and railroads. Abraham Lincoln cut trees, planted corn, and split rails as a young man before he moved to Springfield, Illinois, and became a successful attorney who defended, among others, railroad corporations. His mobility — westward, from farm to city, from manual to mental labor, and upward — illustrated the direction of economic change and the opportunities that beckoned enterprising individuals.

> **REVIEW** Why did the United States become a leading industrial power in the nineteenth century?

▶ Free Labor: Promise and Reality

The nation's impressive economic performance did not reward all Americans equally. Native-born white men tended to do better than immigrants. With few exceptions, women were excluded from opportunities open to men. Tens of thousands of women worked as seamstresses, laundresses,

Hiring a Domestic Servant
This 1849 painting portrays a middle-class woman (seated) at an employment office looking over women to hire as domestic servants. The employment agent (center) advertised his services in the newspaper (crumpled on the floor) and attracted a supply of poor women seeking jobs. The agent appears to be explaining the qualifications of the two standing women. The middle-class woman would want a servant who knew how to do domestic chores and was obedient, honest, and virtuous. While the agent talks, the two women for hire appear uncomfortable and look away from their potential boss. © Collection of the New-York Historical Society.

The Path of Progress

Westward the Star of Empire Takes Its Way — near Council Bluffs, Iowa

domestic servants, factory hands, and teachers but had little opportunity to aspire to higher-paying jobs. In the North and West, slavery was slowly eliminated in the half century after the American Revolution, but most free African Americans were relegated to dead-end jobs as laborers and servants. Discrimination against immigrants, women, and free blacks did not trouble most white men. With certain notable exceptions, they considered it proper and just.

The Free-Labor Ideal

During the 1840s and 1850s, leaders throughout the North and West emphasized a set of ideas that seemed to explain why the changes under way in their society benefited some people more than others. They referred again and again to the advantages of what they termed *free labor*. (The word *free* referred to laborers who were not slaves. It did not mean laborers who worked for

nothing.) By the 1850s, free-labor ideas described a social and economic ideal that accounted for both the successes and the shortcomings of the economy and society taking shape in the North and West.

Spokesmen for the **free-labor ideal** celebrated hard work, self-reliance, and independence. They proclaimed that the door to success was open not just to those who inherited wealth or status but also to self-made men such as Abraham Lincoln. Free labor, Lincoln argued, was "the just and generous, and prosperous system, which opens the way for all — gives hope to all, and energy, and progress, and improvement of condition to all." Free labor permitted farmers and artisans to enjoy the products of their own labor, and it also benefited wageworkers. "The prudent, penniless beginner in the world," Lincoln asserted, "labors for wages awhile, saves a surplus with which to buy tools or land, for himself; then labors on his own account another while, and at

This painting depicts a mid-nineteenth-century landscape of agricultural and industrial progress. Created by Andrew Melrose to celebrate the recently built railroad connecting Chicago and Council Bluffs, Iowa, almost four hundred miles to the west, the painting contrasts the irregularity of nature with the new principles of order imposed on the natural landscape by human beings.

What principles of order are suggested by the locomotive and the railroad tracks? How do they contrast with the natural order represented by the forest on the right side of the painting, by the rock-studded vegetation on either side of the rail bed, and by the deer scampering across the tracks?

The locomotive barreling down the tracks is barely visible behind its blazing headlight, which illuminates the way forward and startles the deer accustomed to shadowed hiding places in the forest. What does the contrast between the immense power of the locomotive and the skittish, vulnerable deer suggest about industrial progress?

Detail of Farmhouse

Likewise, how do the speed, direction, and glaring headlight of the locomotive contrast with the obstacles to progress in the painting? Are the deer headed toward progress? Why or why not?

The left side of the painting shows a frontier farm cultivated by a family standing in the shadow of the log cabin. How do the principles of agricultural order represented by the farm compare with those of the industrial order represented by the railroad and the natural order represented by the forest? What attributes of familial order are visible in the depiction of the farm? Do these attributes differ from the attributes of order among the deer?

Detail of Deer Crossing Tracks

To what extent does the farm suggest agricultural progress? Why have so many trees been chopped down? Why are the stumps littering the fields? What do these farming practices suggest about the farm family's attitudes toward nature?

Notice that the family is not watching the natural beauty of the setting sun bathing the landscape in a golden twilight but instead is looking toward the artificial light of the locomotive. Why might they have gathered outside their cabin to watch the train? What does their interest in the locomotive suggest about their attitudes toward the railroad?

The smoke rises vertically from the chimney of the log cabin, yet it trails backward from the smokestack of the locomotive. What does this contrast suggest about the differences between agricultural and industrial progress?

Overall, what does this painting suggest about the benefits and costs of progress for the farm family, the forest, the deer, the railroad, and American society in general?

SOURCE: Museum of the American West, Autry National Center.

length hires another new beginner to help him." Wage labor, he claimed, was the first rung on the ladder toward self-employment and eventually hiring others.

The free-labor ideal affirmed an egalitarian vision of human potential. Lincoln and other spokesmen stressed the importance of **universal education** to permit "heads and hands [to] cooperate as friends" (Figure 12.1). Throughout the North and West, communities supported public schools to make the rudiments of learning available to young children. By 1860, many cities and towns had public schools that boasted that up to 80 percent of children ages seven to thirteen attended school at least for a few weeks each year. In rural areas, where the labor of children was more difficult to spare, schools typically enrolled no more than half the school-age children. Lessons included more than arithmetic, penmanship, and a smattering of other subjects. Textbooks and teachers — most of whom were young women — drummed into students the lessons of the free-labor system: self-reliance, discipline, and, above all else, hard work. "Remember that all the ignorance, degradation, and misery in the world is the result of indolence and vice," one textbook intoned. Both in and outside school, free-labor ideology emphasized labor as much as freedom.

Economic Inequality

The free-labor ideal made sense to many Americans, especially in the North and West, because it seemed to describe their own experiences. Lincoln frequently referred to his humble beginnings as a hired laborer and implicitly invited his listeners to consider how far he had come. In 1860, his assets of $17,000 easily placed him in the wealthiest 5 percent of the population. The opportunities presented by the expanding economy made a few men much, much richer. In 1860, the nation

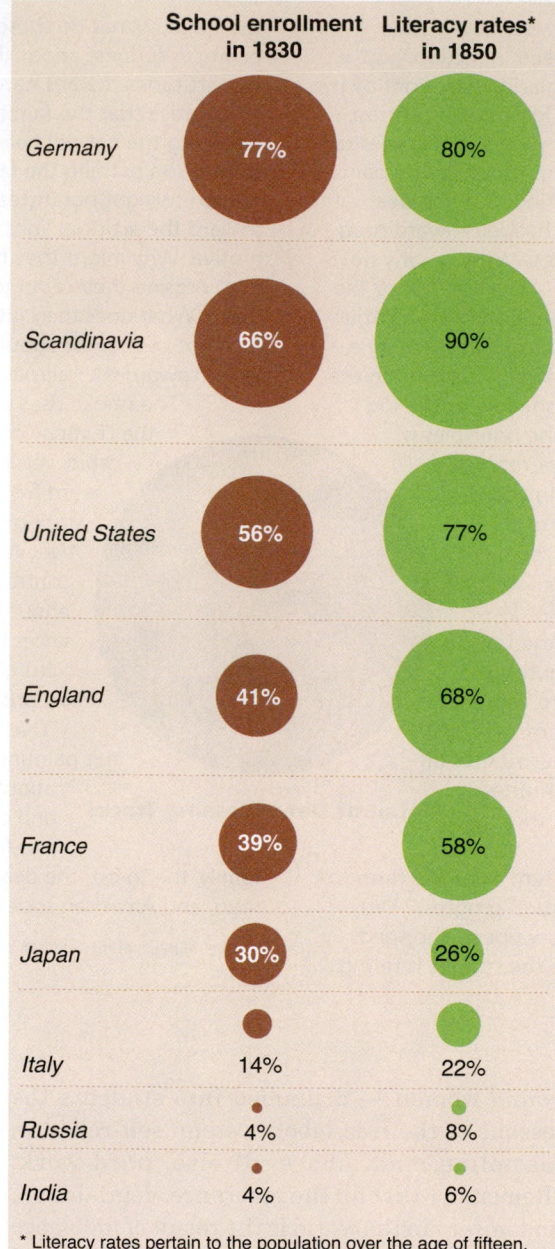

	School enrollment in 1830	Literacy rates* in 1850
Germany	77%	80%
Scandinavia	66%	90%
United States	56%	77%
England	41%	68%
France	39%	58%
Japan	30%	26%
Italy	14%	22%
Russia	4%	8%
India	4%	6%

* Literacy rates pertain to the population over the age of fifteen.

FIGURE 12.1 GLOBAL COMPARISON: Nineteenth-Century School Enrollment and Literacy Rates
In the first half of the nineteenth century, school enrollment and literacy rates in northern and western Europe and the United States were high compared to those in the rest of the world. U.S. figures would be even higher but for the South, where less than 10 percent of black slaves were literate and whites were less likely to attend school than in the North. The ability to read and write facilitates communication, business transactions, acquisition of skills, and perhaps even greater openness to change, all building blocks of rapid economic growth. But mass literacy has not always been a prerequisite for economic development. When England underwent industrialization between 1780 and 1830, less than half of the nation's children attended school. By 1850, England was the world's greatest industrial power, but where did it rank in literacy?

had about forty millionaires. Most Americans, however, measured success in more modest terms. The average wealth of adult white men in the North in 1860 barely topped $2,000. Nearly half of American men had no wealth at all; about 60 percent owned no land. Because property possessed by married women was normally considered to belong to their husbands, women typically had less wealth than men. Free African Americans had still less; 90 percent of them were propertyless. (See "Beyond America's Borders," page 368.)

Free-labor spokesmen considered these economic inequalities a natural outgrowth of freedom — the inevitable result of some individuals being both luckier and more able and willing to work. These inequalities also demonstrate the gap between the promise and the performance of the free-labor ideal. Economic growth permitted many men to move from being landless squatters to landowning farmers and from being hired laborers to independent, self-employed producers. But many more Americans remained behind, landless and working for wages. Even those who realized their aspirations often had a precarious hold on their independence. Bad debts, market volatility, crop failure, sickness, or death could quickly eliminate a family's gains.

Seeking out new opportunities in pursuit of free-labor ideals created restless social and geographic mobility. While fortunate people such as Abraham Lincoln rose far beyond their social origins, others shared the misfortune of a merchant who, an observer noted, "has been on the sinking list all his life." In search of better prospects, roughly two-thirds of the rural population moved every decade, and population turnover in cities was even greater. This constant coming and going weakened community ties to neighbors and friends and threw individuals even more on their own resources in times of trouble.

Immigrants and the Free-Labor Ladder

The risks and uncertainties of free labor did not deter millions of immigrants from entering the United States during the 1840s and 1850s. Almost 4.5 million immigrants arrived between 1840 and 1860, six times more than had come during the previous two decades (Figure 12.2). By 1860, foreign-born residents made up about one-eighth of the U.S. population, a fraction that held steady well into the twentieth century.

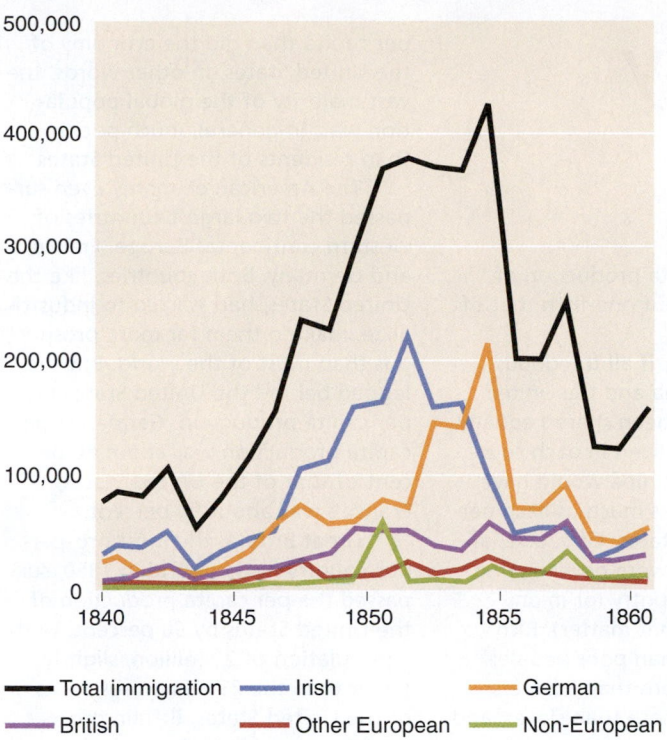

500,000
400,000
300,000
200,000
100,000
0
1840   1845   1850   1855   1860

—— Total immigration   —— Irish   —— German
—— British   —— Other European   —— Non-European

FIGURE 12.2 **Antebellum Immigration, 1840–1860**
After increasing gradually for several decades, immigration shot up in the mid-1840s. Between 1848 and 1860, nearly 3.5 million immigrants entered the United States.

entered during these years were skilled tradesmen and their families. Roughly a quarter were farmers, some of whom settled in Texas. German butchers, bakers, beer makers, carpenters, shopkeepers, and machinists settled mostly in the Midwest, often congregating in cities. On the whole, German Americans were often Protestants and occupied the middle stratum of independent producers celebrated by free-labor spokesmen; relatively few worked as wage laborers or domestic servants.

Irish immigrants, in contrast, entered at the bottom of the free-labor ladder and struggled to climb up. Nearly 1.7 million Irish immigrants arrived between 1840 and 1860, nearly all of them desperately poor and often weakened by hunger and disease. Potato blight struck Ireland in 1845 and returned repeatedly in subsequent years, spreading a catastrophic famine throughout the island. Many of the lucky ones crowded into the holds of ships and set out for America, where

Nearly three-fourths of the immigrants who arrived in the United States between 1840 and 1860 came from either Germany or Ireland. The majority of the 1.4 million Germans who

A German Immigrant in New York
This 1855 painting depicts a German immigrant in New York City asking directions from an African American man who is cutting firewood. Like many other German immigrants, the man shown here appears relatively well off. Compare his clothing with that of the sawyer and the white laborer on the right. Unlike most Irish immigrants, who arrived without family members, the German immigrant is accompanied by his daughter and son. The German appears to be speaking respectfully to the black sawyer, suggesting that he did not fully share assumptions of white supremacy common among native-born white working men. North Carolina Museum of Art, Raleigh, purchased with funds from the State of North Carolina (52.9.2).

Global Prosperity in the 1850s

By the 1850s, the U.S. economy had achieved a remarkable economic transformation. In 1801, when president-elect Thomas Jefferson rode horseback the 180 miles from his home in Monticello, Virginia, to Washington, D.C., he and his horse had to swim across several rivers that lacked bridges or ferries. In 1861, when president-elect Abraham Lincoln traveled more than 1,000 miles to Washington from his home in Springfield, Illinois, he did not need to get wet swimming across rivers. He rode the entire way on railroads. The changes that made Lincoln's journey possible created an American economy that produced more goods and services per capita than that of any other country in the world, except one — Great Britain.

In the 1850s, some countries in the world produced more total goods and services than the United States. But since they had much larger populations than the United States, they produced much less per capita. For example, China produced huge quantities of goods and services, roughly four times more than the United States did. But since the Chinese population was about twenty times greater than that of the United States, the per capita production of China was only about one-fifth that of the United States.

In other words, if all the goods and services in China and the United States in 1850 had been shared equally by the people who lived in each country, each person in China would have had only one-fifth as much as each person in the United States. Of course, all goods and services were never shared equally in either country (or in any other country for that matter). Rich people had more than poor people; landowners had more than laborers; slave owners had more than slaves; and so on. Still, per capita production can serve as an imperfect but revealing indicator of the general prosperity of a country's economy.

Like China, African countries were about one-fifth as prosperous as the United States. India, Japan, Mexico, and Brazil had somewhat more prosperous economies, with per capita production about one-third that of the United States. European countries such as Russia, Spain, and Italy were about half as prosperous as the United States. Overall, more than 90 percent of the people in the world in 1850 lived in countries whose economies produced half or less (much less, for most people)

per capita than did the economy of the United States. In other words, the vast majority of the global population was, in general, much poorer than residents of the United States.

The American economy even surpassed the two largest countries of western continental Europe, France and Germany. Both countries, like the United States, had started to industrialize, making them far more prosperous than most of the world. But they lagged behind the United States in per capita production. Germany's per capita production was about 80 percent of that of the United States; France's was about 90 percent.

Great Britain, the most prosperous country in the world in 1850, surpassed the per capita production of the United States by 30 percent. With a population of 21 million, slightly fewer than the 23 million residents of the United States, Britain produced a whopping 45 percent of the world's manufactured goods.

Many factors contributed to Britain's economic leadership, but three were especially important. First, most people in Britain had moved to towns and cities by 1850. Rural folks made up only 22 percent of Britain's population, compared to 85 percent of the U.S. population. Many urban dwellers worked in industries that, in general, were more productive than agriculture, boosting British output. Second, wages were relatively high in Britain, giving manufacturers a big incentive to replace costly labor with machinery. Although machinery

they congregated in northeastern cities. As one immigrant group declared, "All we want is to get out of Ireland; we must be better anywhere than here." Death trailed after them. So many died crossing the Atlantic that ships from Ireland were often termed "coffin ships."

Roughly three out of four Irish immigrants worked as laborers or domestic servants. Irish men dug canals, loaded ships, laid railroad track, and did odd jobs while Irish women worked in the homes of others — cooking, washing and ironing, minding children, and cleaning house. Almost all Irish immigrants were Catholic, a fact that set them apart from the overwhelmingly Protestant native-born residents. Many natives regarded the Irish as hard-drinking, unruly, half-civilized folk. Such views lay behind the discrimination reflected in job announcements that commonly stated, "No Irish need apply." Despite such prejudices, native residents hired Irish immigrants because they accepted low pay and worked hard.

required capital outlays to set up and maintain, it was far more efficient and tireless than wageworkers.

Manufacturers in both Britain and the United States had similar incentives to industrialize, but British producers did so first and with far greater effectiveness than did those in the United States, in large measure because Britain had a cheap and nearly inexhaustible source of energy — coal, the third crucial factor in Britain's economic leadership. Britain had a unique endowment of coal resources that could be mined relatively inexpensively, making coal prices much lower than in the rest of the world. Low coal prices gave manufacturers a cheap energy source, making it less costly for them to adopt innovative industrial techniques that boosted production — such as steam power. In 1850, coal consumption in Britain was ten times greater than in France and seven times greater than in Germany and the United States. Britain's unique combination of cheap energy, high wages, and a large urban population helped make it the most productive and prosperous country in the world in 1850.

America in a Global Context

1. In 1850, how did U.S. prosperity compare to that in the rest of the world?

2. Why did Britain have the world's leading economy in 1850?

3. To what extent is per capita production a misleading measure of prosperity? Can you think of better measures?

4. What questions does the pattern of global prosperity and poverty in 1850 raise about immigration to the United States?

In America's labor-poor economy, Irish laborers could earn more in one day than in several weeks in Ireland, where opportunities were often scarce. In America, one immigrant explained in 1853, there was "plenty of work and plenty of wages plenty to eat and no land lords thats enough what more does a man want." But some immigrants wanted more, especially respect and decent working conditions. One immigrant complained that he was "a slave for the Americans as the generality of the Irish . . . are."

Such testimony illustrates that the free-labor system, whether for immigrants or native-born laborers, often did not live up to the optimistic vision outlined by Abraham Lincoln and others. Many wage laborers could not realistically aspire to become independent, self-sufficient property holders, despite the claims of free-labor proponents.

REVIEW How did the free-labor ideal account for economic inequality?

▶ The Westward Movement

The nation's swelling population, booming economy, and boundless confidence propelled a new era of rapid westward migration beginning in the 1840s. Until then, the overwhelming majority of Americans lived east of the Mississippi River. Native Americans inhabited the plains, deserts, and rugged coasts to the west. The British claimed the Oregon Country, and the Mexican flag flew over the vast expanse of the Southwest. But by 1850, the nation's limits pushed far beyond the boundaries of the 1803 Louisiana Purchase. The United States stretched to the Pacific and had more than doubled in size. By 1860, the great migration had carried four million Americans west of the Mississippi River.

Frontier settlers took the land and then, with the exception of the Mormons, lobbied their government to acquire the territory they had settled. The human cost of aggressive expansionism was high. The young Mexican nation lost a war and half of its territory. Two centuries of Indian wars east of the Mississippi ended during the 1830s, but the fierce struggle between native inhabitants and invaders continued for another half century in the West. Americans believed it was their destiny to conquer the continent.

Manifest Destiny

Most Americans believed that the superiority of their institutions and white culture bestowed on them a God-given right to spread their civilization across the continent. They imagined the West as a howling wilderness, empty and undeveloped. If they recognized Indians and Mexicans at all, they dismissed them as primitive drags on progress who would have to be redeemed, shoved aside, or exterminated. The West provided young men especially an arena in which to "show their manhood." The sense of uniqueness and mission was as old as the Puritans, but by the 1840s the conviction of superiority had been bolstered by the United States' amazing success. Most Americans believed that the West needed the civilizing power of the hammer and the plow, the ballot box and the pulpit, which had transformed the East.

In 1845, a New York political journal edited by John L. O'Sullivan coined the term *manifest destiny* as the latest justification for white settlers to take the land they coveted. O'Sullivan called on Americans to resist any foreign power — British, French, or Mexican — that attempted to thwart "the fulfillment of our manifest destiny to overspread the continent allotted by Providence for the free development of our yearly multiplying millions . . . [and] for the development of the great experiment of liberty and federative self-government entrusted to us." Almost overnight, the magic phrase *manifest destiny* swept the nation and provided an ideological shield for conquering the West.

As important as national pride and racial arrogance were to manifest destiny, economic gain made up its core. Land hunger drew hundreds of thousands of average Americans westward. Some politicians, moreover, had become convinced that national prosperity depended on capturing the rich trade of the Far East. To trade with Asia, the United States needed the Pacific coast ports that stretched from San Diego to Puget Sound. "The sun of civilization must shine across the sea: socially and commercially," Missouri senator Thomas Hart Benton declared. The United States and Asia must "talk together, and trade together. Commerce is a great civilizer." In the 1840s, American economic expansion came wrapped in the rhetoric of uplift and civilization.

Oregon and the Overland Trail

The Oregon Country — a vast region bounded on the west by the Pacific Ocean, on the east by the Rocky Mountains, on the south by the forty-second parallel, and on the north by Russian Alaska — caused the pulse of American expansionists to race. But the British also coveted the area. They argued that their claim lay with Sir Francis Drake's discovery of the Oregon coast in 1579. Americans countered with historic claims of their own. Unable to agree, the United States and Great Britain decided in 1818 on "joint occupation" that would leave Oregon "free and open" to settlement by both countries. A handful of American fur traders and "mountain men" roamed the region in the 1820s.

By the late 1830s, settlers began to trickle along the **Oregon Trail**, following a trail blazed by the mountain men (Map 12.2). The first wagon trains headed west in 1841, and by 1843 about 1,000 emigrants a year set out from Independence, Missouri. By 1869, when the first transcontinental railroad was completed, approximately 350,000 migrants had traveled west to the Pacific in wagon trains.

Emigrants encountered the Plains Indians, a quarter of a million Native Americans scattered over the area between the Mississippi River and

MAP 12.2
Major Trails West
In the 1830s, wagon trains began snaking their way to the Southwest and the Pacific coast. Deep ruts, some of which can still be seen today, soon marked the most popular routes.

the Rocky Mountains. Some were farmers who lived peaceful, sedentary lives, but a majority —the Sioux, Cheyenne, Shoshoni, and Arapaho of the central plains and the Kiowa, Wichita, and Comanche of the southern plains — were horse-mounted, nomadic, nonagricultural peoples whose warriors symbolized the "savage Indian" in the minds of whites.

Horses, which had been brought to North America by Spaniards in the sixteenth century, permitted the Plains tribes to become highly mobile hunters of buffalo. They came to depend on buffalo for nearly everything — food, clothing, shelter, and fuel. Competition for buffalo led to war between the tribes. Young men were introduced to warfare early, learning to ride ponies at breakneck speed while firing off arrows and, later, rifles with astounding accuracy. "A Comanche on his feet is out of his element," observed western artist George Catlin, "but the moment he lays his hands upon his horse, his *face* even becomes handsome, and he gracefully flies away like a different being."

The Plains Indians struck fear in the hearts of whites on the wagon trains. But Native Americans had far more to fear from whites. Indians killed fewer than four hundred emigrants on the trail between 1840 and 1860, while whites brought alcohol and deadly epidemics of smallpox, measles, cholera, and scarlet fever. Moreover, white hunters slaughtered buffalo for the international hide market and sometimes just for sport. The buffalo still numbered some twelve million in 1860, but the herds were shrinking rapidly, intensifying conflict among the Plains tribes.

Emigrants insisted that the federal government provide them with more protection. The government constructed a chain of forts along the Oregon Trail (see Map 12.2). More important, it adopted a new Indian policy: "concentration." In 1851, the government called the Plains tribes to a conference at Fort Laramie, Wyoming. Some ten thousand Indians showed up, hopeful that

> **"A woman that can not endure almost as much as a horse has no business here."**
> — An Oregon settler

Kee-O-Kuk, the Watchful Fox, Chief of the Tribe, by George Catlin, 1835
In the 1830s, Pennsylvania-born artist George Catlin traveled the West painting Native Americans. Catlin was the first artist to portray Indians in their own environments and one of the few to present them as human beings, not savages. Convinced that western Indian cultures would soon disappear, Catlin sought to document Indian life through hundreds of paintings and prints. Keokuk, chief of the Sauk and Fox, struggled with the warrior Black Hawk (see chapter 11) about how to deal with whites. Black Hawk fought American expansion; Keokuk believed that war was fruitless and signed over land in Illinois, Missouri, and Wisconsin.
Smithsonian American Art Institution, Washington, D.C. Gift of Mrs. Joseph Harrison Jr.

something could be done to protect them from the ravages of the wagon trains. Instead, government negotiators at the **Fort Laramie conference** persuaded the chiefs to sign agreements that cleared a wide corridor for wagon trains by restricting Native Americans to specific areas that whites promised they would never violate. This policy of concentration became the seedbed for the subsequent policy of reservations. But whites would not keep out of Indian territory, and Indians would not easily give up their traditional ways of life. Struggle for control of the West meant warfare for decades to come.

Still, Indians threatened emigrants less than life on the trail did. The men, women, and children who headed west each spring could count on at least six months of grueling travel. With nearly two thousand miles to go and traveling no more than fifteen miles a day, the pioneers endured parching heat, drought, treacherous rivers, disease, physical and emotional exhaustion, and, if the snows closed the mountain passes before they got through, freezing and starvation. Women sometimes faced the dangers of trailside childbirth. It was said that a person could walk from Missouri to the Pacific stepping only on the graves of those who had died head-

ing west. Such tribulations led one miserable woman, trying to keep her children dry in a rainstorm and to calm them as they listened to Indian shouts, to wonder "what had possessed my husband, anyway, that he should have thought of bringing us away out through this God forsaken country."

Men usually found Oregon "one of the greatest countries in the world." From "the Cascade mountains to the Pacific, the whole country can be cultivated," exclaimed one eager settler. When women reached Oregon, they found that neighbors were scarce and things were in a "primitive state." One young wife arrived with only her husband, one stew kettle, and three knives. Necessity blurred the traditional division between men's and women's work. "I am maid of all traids," one busy woman remarked in 1853. Work seemed unending. "I am a very old woman," declared twenty-nine-year-old Sarah Everett. "My face is thin sunken and wrinkled, my hands bony withered and hard." Another settler observed, "A woman that can not endure almost as much as a horse has no business here." Yet despite the ordeal of the trail and the difficulties of starting from scratch, emigrants kept coming.

Plains Indians and Trails West in the 1840s and 1850s

BRITISH NORTH AMERICA

CREE
BLACKFEET
ASSINIBOINE
GROS VENTRE
FLATHEAD
HIDATSA
MANDAN
CROW   ARIKARA   DAKOTA SIOUX
SHOSHONI
TETON SIOUX   YANKTON SIOUX
CHEYENNE   PONCA   OMAHA
Ft. Laramie
ARAPAHO   PAWNEE   OTO
ROCKY MTS   KANSA
UTE
KIOWA
PLAINS   KIOWA APACHE
APACHE
NAVAJO
PUEBLO   WICHITA
COMANCHE
MEXICO   TONKAWA

Mississippi R.

↑ Fort
—— Trails west
▨ United States, 1848

VISUAL ACTIVITY

Pioneer Family on the Trail West
In 1860, W. G. Chamberlain photographed these unidentified travelers momentarily at rest by the upper Arkansas River in Colorado. We do not know their fates, but we can only hope that they fared better than the Sager family. Henry and Naomi Sager and their six children set out from St. Joseph, Missouri, in 1844. "Father," one of Henry and Naomi's daughters remembered, "was one of those restless men who are not content to remain in one place long at a time. [He] had been talking of going to Texas. But mother, hearing much said about the healthfulness of Oregon, preferred to go there." Still far from Oregon, Henry Sager died of fever. Twenty-six days later, Naomi died, leaving seven children, the last delivered on the trail. The Sager children, under the care of other families in the wagon train, pressed on. After traveling two thousand miles in seven months, the migrants arrived in Oregon, where Marcus and Narcissa Whitman, whose own daughter had drowned, adopted all seven of the Sager children. Denver Public Library, Western History Division # F3226.

READING THE IMAGE: Based on this photograph, what were some of the difficulties faced by pioneers traveling west?

CONNECTIONS: How did wagon trains change the western United States?

The Mormon Exodus

Not every wagon train heading west was bound for the Pacific Slope. One remarkable group of religious emigrants halted near the Great Salt Lake in what was then Mexican territory. The **Mormons** deliberately chose the remote site as a refuge. After years of persecution in the East, they fled west to find religious freedom and communal security.

In 1820, an upstate New York farm boy named **Joseph Smith Jr.** had begun to experience revelations that were followed, he said, by a visit from an angel who led him to golden tablets buried near his home. With the aid of magic stones, he translated the mysterious language on the tablets to produce *The Book of Mormon*, which he published in 1830. It told the story of an ancient Hebrew civilization in the New World and predicted the appearance of an American prophet who would reestablish Jesus Christ's undefiled kingdom in America. Converts, attracted to the promise of a pure faith in the midst of antebellum America's social turmoil and rampant materialism, flocked to the new Church of Jesus Christ of Latter-Day Saints (the Mormons).

Neighbors branded Mormons heretics and drove Smith and his followers from New York to Ohio, then to Missouri, and finally in 1839 to Nauvoo, Illinois, where they built a prosperous community. But a rift in the church developed after Smith sanctioned "plural marriage" (polygamy). Non-Mormons caught wind of the controversy and eventually arrested Smith and his brother. On June 27, 1844, a mob stormed the jail and shot both men dead.

The embattled church turned to an extraordinary new leader, **Brigham Young**, who oversaw a great exodus. In 1846, traveling in 3,700 wagons, 12,000 Mormons made their way to eastern Iowa, then the following year to their new home beside the Great Salt Lake. Young described the region as a barren waste, "the paradise of the lizard, the cricket and the rattlesnake." Within ten years, however, the Mormons developed an irrigation system that made the desert bloom. Under Young's stern leadership, the Mormons built a thriving community using cooperative labor, not the individualistic and competitive enterprise common among most emigrants.

In 1850, the Mormon kingdom was annexed to the United States as Utah Territory. The nation's attention focused on Utah in 1852 when Brigham Young announced that many Mormons practiced polygamy. Although only one Mormon man in five had more than one wife (Young had twenty-three), Young's statement caused a popular outcry that forced the U.S. government to establish its authority in Utah. In 1857, 2,500 U.S. troops invaded Salt Lake City in what was known as the Mormon War. The bloodless occupation illustrated that most Americans viewed the Mormons as a threat to American morality, law, and institutions. The invasion did not dislodge the Mormon Church from its central place in Utah, however, and for years to come, most Americans perceived the Mormon settlement as strange and suitably isolated.

The Mexican Borderlands

In the Mexican Southwest, westward-moving Anglo-American pioneers confronted northern-moving Spanish-speaking frontiersmen. On this frontier as elsewhere, national cultures, interests, and aspirations collided. Since 1821, when Mexico won its independence from Spain, the Mexican flag had flown over the vast expanse that stretched from the Gulf of Mexico to the Pacific and from the Oregon Country to Guatemala (Map 12.3). But Mexico's northern provinces were sparsely populated, and the young nation was plagued by civil wars, economic crises, quarrels with the Roman Catholic Church, and devastating raids by the Comanche, Apache, and Kiowa. Mexico found it increasingly difficult to defend its borderlands, especially when faced with a northern neighbor convinced of its superiority and bent on territorial acquisition.

The American assault began quietly. In the 1820s, Anglo-American trappers, traders, and settlers drifted into Mexico's far northern provinces. Santa Fe, a remote outpost in the province of New Mexico, became a magnet for American

Mormon Family
The rest of America found the Mormon practice of polygamy deeply offensive. Five years after American troops occupied Utah in 1857, President Abraham Lincoln signed anti-polygamy legislation, and in 1890 the Mormons officially abandoned plural marriages. But in this photograph from Salt Lake City in the 1850s, a husband, his three wives, and their five children sit proudly for a family portrait. No matter national opinion, they clearly are at ease with their unusual family constellation. ©The Church of Jesus Christ of Latter Day Saints, Intellectual Property Division.

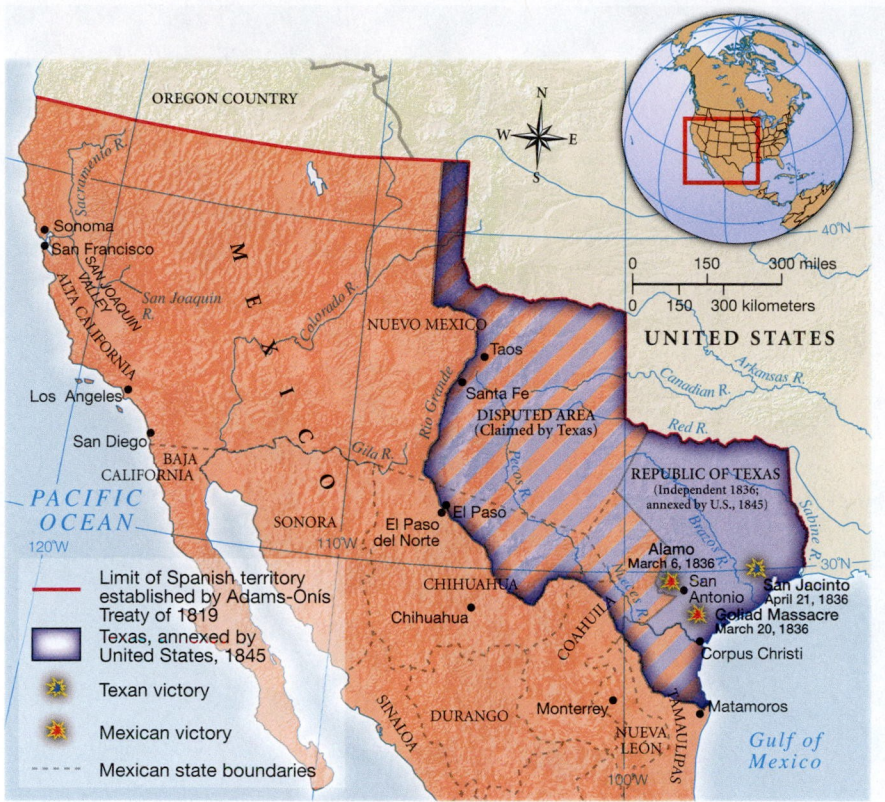

MAP 12.3

Texas and Mexico in the 1830s
As Americans spilled into lightly populated and loosely governed northern Mexico, Texas and then other Mexican provinces became contested territory.

enterprise. Each spring, American traders gathered at Independence, Missouri, for the long trek southwest along the Santa Fe Trail (see Map 12.2). They crammed their wagons with inexpensive American manufactured goods and returned home with Mexican silver, furs, and mules.

The Mexican province of Texas attracted a flood of Americans who had settlement, not long-distance trade, on their minds (see Map 12.3). Wanting to populate and develop its northern territory, the Mexican government granted the American **Stephen F. Austin** a huge tract of land along the Brazos River. In the 1820s, Austin became the first Anglo-American *empresario* (colonization agent) in Texas, offering land at only ten cents an acre. Thousands of Americans poured across the border. Most were Southerners who brought cotton and slaves with them.

By the 1830s, the settlers had established a thriving plantation economy in Texas. Americans numbered 35,000, while the *Tejano* (Spanish-speaking) population was less than 8,000. Few Anglo-American settlers were Roman Catholic, spoke Spanish, or cared about assimilating into Mexican culture. Afraid of losing Texas to the new arrivals, the Mexican government in 1830 banned further immigration to Texas from the United States and outlawed the introduction of

additional slaves. The Anglo-Americans made it clear that they wanted to be rid of the "despotism of the sword and the priesthood" and to govern themselves. In Mexico City, however, General **Antonio López de Santa Anna** seized political power and set about restoring order to the northern frontier.

When the Texan settlers rebelled, Santa Anna ordered the Mexican army northward. In February 1836, the army arrived at the outskirts of San Antonio. Commanded by Colonel William B. Travis from Alabama, the rebels included the Tennessee frontiersman Davy Crockett and the Louisiana adventurer James Bowie, as well as a handful of Tejanos. They took refuge in a former Franciscan mission known as the Alamo. Santa Anna sent wave after wave of his 2,000-man army crashing against the walls until the attackers finally broke through and killed all 187 rebels. A few weeks later, outside the small town of Goliad, Mexican forces captured a

Texas War for Independence, 1836

Fandango, by Theodore Gentilz, 1844
Although Spanish and Mexican authorities failed to entice many Hispanic settlers to distant provinces such as Texas, a small and resourceful Tejano community managed to develop a ranching economy in the harsh frontier conditions. The largest Hispanic population was concentrated in the vicinity of San Antonio, where settlers reproduced as best they could the cultural traditions they carried with them. Here, a group of animated, well-dressed men and women perform a Spanish dance called the fandango while musicians play in triple time. Daughters of the Republic of Texas Library, Alamo Collection.

garrison of Texans. Mexican firing squads executed almost 400 of the men as "pirates and outlaws." In April 1836, at San Jacinto, General Sam Houston's army adopted the massacre of Goliad as a battle cry and crushed Santa Anna's troops in a surprise attack. The Texans had succeeded in establishing the **Lone Star Republic**, and the following year the United States recognized the independence of Texas from Mexico.

Earlier, in 1824, in an effort to increase Mexican migration to the province of California, the Mexican government granted *ranchos* — huge estates devoted to cattle raising — to new settlers. *Rancheros* ruled over near-feudal empires worked by Indians whose condition sometimes approached that of slaves. Not satisfied, the rancheros coveted the vast lands controlled by the Franciscan missions. In 1834, they persuaded the Mexican govern-

ment to confiscate the missions and make their lands available to new settlement, a development that accelerated the decline of the California Indians. Devastated by disease, the Indians, who had numbered approximately 300,000 when the Spanish arrived in 1769, had declined to half that number by 1846.

Despite the efforts of the Mexican government, California in 1840 had a population of only 7,000 Mexican settlers. Non-Mexican settlers numbered only 380, but among them were Americans who championed manifest destiny. They sought to woo American emigrants to California. In the 1840s, wagon after wagon left the Oregon Trail to head southwest on the California Trail (see Map 12.2). As the trickle of Americans became a river, Mexican officials grew alarmed. As a New York newspaper put it in 1845, "Let the tide of emigration flow toward California and the American population will soon be sufficiently numerous to play the Texas game." Only a few Americans in California wanted a war for independence, but many dreamed of living again under the U.S. flag.

The U.S. government made no secret of its desire to acquire California. In 1835, President Andrew Jackson tried unsuccessfully to purchase it. In 1846, American settlers in the Sacramento Valley took matters into their own hands. Prodded by John C. Frémont, a former army captain and explorer who had arrived with a party of sixty buckskin-clad frontiersmen spoiling for a fight, the Californians raised an independence movement known as the Bear Flag Revolt. By then, James K. Polk, a champion of aggressive expansion, sat in the White House.

REVIEW Why did westward migration expand dramatically in the mid-nineteenth century?

▶ Expansion and the Mexican-American War

Although emigrants acted as the advance guard of American empire, there was nothing automatic about the U.S. annexation of territory in the West. Acquiring territory required political action. In the 1840s, the politics of expansion became entangled with sectionalism and the slavery question. Texas, Oregon, and the Mexican borderlands also thrust the United States into dangerous diplomatic crises with Great Britain and Mexico.

Aggravation between Mexico and the United States escalated to open antagonism in 1845 when the United States annexed Texas. Absorbing territory still claimed by Mexico ruptured diplomatic relations between the two countries and set the stage for war. But it was President James K. Polk's insistence on having Mexico's other northern provinces that made war certain. The war was not as easy as Polk anticipated, but it ended in American victory and the acquisition of a new American West. One of the nation's new territories, California, proved immediately profitable; the discovery of gold prompted a massive wave of emigration to the western coast, a rush that nearly destroyed Native American and Californio society.

The Politics of Expansion

Texans had sought admission to the Union almost since winning their independence from Mexico in 1836. Almost constant border warfare between Mexico and the Republic of Texas in the decade following the revolution underscored the precarious nature of independence. It also made clear that annexing Texas to the United States risked precipitating war, for Mexico had never relinquished its claim to its lost province. But any suggestion of adding another slave state to the Union outraged most Northerners, who applauded westward expansion but imagined the expansion of liberty, not slavery.

President **John Tyler**, who became president in April 1841 when William Henry Harrison died one month after taking office, understood that Texas was a dangerous issue. Adding to the danger, Great Britain began sniffing around Texas, apparently contemplating adding the young republic to its growing empire. Tyler, an ardent expansionist, decided to risk annexing the Lone Star Republic. However, when he laid an annexation treaty before the Senate in 1844, howls of protest erupted across the North. Future Massachusetts senator Charles Sumner deplored the "insidious" plan to annex Texas and carve from it "great slaveholding states." The Senate soundly rejected the treaty, and it appeared that Tyler had succeeded only in inflaming sectional conflict.

Polk and Dallas Banner, 1844
In 1844, Democratic presidential nominee James K. Polk and vice presidential nominee George M. Dallas campaigned under this cotton banner. The extra star spilling over into the red and white stripes symbolizes Polk's vigorous support for annexing the huge slave republic of Texas, which had declared its independence from Mexico eight years earlier. Henry Clay, Polk's Whig opponent, ran under a banner that was similar but conspicuously lacked the additional star. Collection of Janice L. and David J. Frent.

The issue of Texas had not died down by the 1844 election. In an effort to appeal to northern voters, the Whig nominee for president, **Henry Clay**, came out against annexation of Texas. "Annexation and war with Mexico are identical," he declared. The Democrats chose Tennessean **James K. Polk**, a passionate expansionist who vigorously backed annexation. To make annexation palatable to Northerners, the Democrats shrewdly yoked Texas to Oregon, thus tapping the desire for expansion in the free states of the North as well as in the slave states of the South. The Democratic platform called for the "reannexation of Texas" and the "reoccupation of Oregon." The suggestion that the United States was merely reasserting existing rights was poor history but good politics.

When Clay finally recognized the popularity of expansion, he waffled, hinting that he might accept the annexation of Texas after all. His retreat succeeded only in alienating antislavery opinion in the North. James G. Birney, the candidate of the fledgling Liberty Party, picked up the votes of thousands of disillusioned Clay supporters. In the November election, Polk received 170 electoral votes and Clay 105. New York's 35 electoral votes proved critical to Clay's defeat. A shift of just one-third of Birney's 15,000 votes to Clay would have given Clay the state and the presidency.

In his inaugural address on March 4, 1845, Polk underscored his faith in America's manifest destiny. "This heaven-favored land," he proclaimed, enjoyed the "most admirable and wisest system of well-regulated self-government . . . ever devised by human minds." He asked, "Who shall assign limits to the achievements of free minds and free hands under the protection of this glorious Union?"

The nation did not have to wait for Polk's inauguration to see results from his victory. One month after the election, President Tyler announced that the triumph of the Democratic Party provided a mandate for the annexation of Texas "promptly and immediately." In February 1845, after a fierce debate between antislavery and proslavery forces, Congress approved a joint resolution offering the Republic of Texas admission to the United States. Texas entered as the fifteenth slave state.

Tyler delivered Texas, but Polk had promised Oregon, too. Westerners particularly demanded that the new president make good on the Democrats' pledge "Fifty-four Forty or Fight" —that is, all of Oregon, right up to Alaska (54°40′ was the southern latitude of Russian Alaska).

But Polk was close to war with Mexico and could not afford a war with Britain over U.S. claims in Canada. He renewed an old offer to divide Oregon along the forty-ninth parallel. When Britain accepted the compromise, some Americans cried betrayal, but most celebrated the agreement that gave the nation an enormous territory peacefully. When the Senate finally approved the treaty in June 1846, the United States and Mexico were already at war.

The Mexican-American War, 1846–1848

From the day he entered the White House, Polk craved Mexico's remaining northern provinces: California and New Mexico, land that today makes up California, Nevada, Utah, most of New Mexico and Arizona, and parts of Wyoming and Colorado. Since the 1830s, Comanches, Kiowas, Apaches, and others had attacked Mexican ranches and towns, killing thousands, and the Polk administration invoked Mexico's inability to control its northern provinces to denigrate its claims to them. Polk hoped to buy the territory, but when the Mexicans refused to sell, he concluded that military force would be needed to realize the United States' manifest destiny.

Polk had already ordered General **Zachary Taylor** to march his 4,000-man army 150 miles south from its position on the Nueces River, the southern boundary of Texas according to the Mexicans, to the banks of the Rio Grande, the boundary claimed by Texans (Map 12.4). Viewing the American advance as aggression, the Mexican general in Matamoros ordered Taylor back to the Nueces. Taylor refused, and on April 25, 1846, Mexican cavalry attacked a party of American soldiers, killing or wounding sixteen and capturing the rest. Even before news of the battle arrived in Washington, Polk had obtained his cabinet's approval of a war message.

On May 11, the president told Congress, "Mexico has passed the boundary of the United States, has invaded our territory, and shed American blood upon American soil." Thus "war exists, and, notwithstanding all our efforts to avoid it, exists by the act of Mexico herself." Congress passed a declaration of war and began raising an army. Despite years of saber rattling toward Mexico and Britain, the U.S. Army was pitifully small, only 8,600 soldiers. Faced with the nation's first foreign war, against a Mexican army that numbered more than 30,000, Polk called for volunteers. Eventually, more than 112,000 white Americans (40 percent of whom

MAP 12.4

The Mexican-American War, 1846–1848
American and Mexican soldiers skirmished across much of northern Mexico, but the major battles took place between the Rio Grande and Mexico City.

were immigrants; blacks were banned) joined the army to fight in Mexico.

Despite the flood of volunteers, the war divided the nation. Northern Whigs in particular condemned the war. The Massachusetts legislature claimed that the war was being fought for the "triple object of extending slavery, of strengthening the slave power, and of obtaining control of the free states." On January 12, 1848, a gangly freshman Whig representative from Illinois rose in the House of Representatives to deliver his first important speech in Congress. Before Abraham Lincoln sat down, he had questioned Polk's intelligence, honesty, and sanity. The president ignored the upstart representative, but antislavery, anti-

war Whigs kept up the attack throughout the conflict. In their effort to undercut national support, they labeled it "Mr. Polk's War."

Since most Americans backed the war, it was not really Polk's war, but the president acted as if it were and directed the war personally. He planned a short war in which U.S. armies would occupy Mexico's northern provinces and defeat the Mexican army in a decisive battle or two, after which Mexico would sue for peace and the United States would keep the territory its armies occupied.

At first, Polk's strategy seemed to work. In May 1846, Zachary Taylor's troops drove south from the Rio Grande and routed the Mexican army, first at Palo Alto, then at Resaca de la

***Batalla del Sacramento*, by Julio Michaud y Thomas**
Most images of the Mexican-American War were created by artists from the United States, but Mexicans also recorded the war. In this hand-colored lithograph, Mexican artist Julio Michaud y Thomas depicts the February 1847 battle in which 1,100 American troops engaged 3,000 Mexicans on the banks of the Sacramento River near Chihuahua. Michaud accurately portrays the first moments of the bold Mexican cavalry charge, but American artillery forced the Mexican lancers to retreat, with "great confusion in their ranks." When the fighting ended, the Mexicans had suffered some 700 casualties, while American casualties amounted to about a half dozen. Yale Collection of Western Americana, Beinecke Rare Book and Manuscript Library.

Palma (see Map 12.4). "Old Rough and Ready," as Taylor was affectionately known among his adoring troops, became an instant war hero. Polk rewarded Taylor for his victories by making him commander of the Mexican campaign.

A second prong of the campaign centered on Colonel Stephen Watts Kearny, who led a 1,700-man army from Missouri into New Mexico. Without firing a shot, U.S. forces took Santa Fe in August 1846. Kearny then marched into San Diego three months later, encountering a major Mexican rebellion against American rule. In January 1847, after several clashes and severe losses, the U.S. forces occupied Los Angeles. California and New Mexico were in American hands.

By then, Taylor had driven deep into the interior of Mexico. In September 1846, after house-to-house fighting, he took the city of Monterrey. Taylor then pushed his 5,000 troops

> **"I can assure you that fighting is the least dangerous & arduous part of a soldier's life."**
> — An American soldier in the Mexican-American War

southwest, where the Mexican hero of the Alamo, General Antonio López de Santa Anna, was concentrating an army of 21,000. On February 23, 1847, Santa Anna's troops attacked Taylor at Buena Vista. Superior American artillery and accurate musket fire won the day, but the Americans suffered heavy casualties, including Henry Clay Jr., the son of the man who had opposed Texas annexation for fear it would precipitate war. The Mexicans suffered even greater losses (some 3,400 dead, wounded, and missing, compared with 650 Americans). During the night, Santa Anna withdrew his battered army, much to the "profound disgust of the troops," one Mexican officer remembered. "They are filled with grief that they were going to lose the benefit of all the sacrifices that they had made; that the conquered field would be abandoned, and that the victory would be given to the enemy."

The series of uninterrupted victories in northern Mexico fed the American troops' sense of invincibility. "No American force has ever thought of being defeated by any amount of Mexican troops," one soldier declared. The Americans worried about other hazards, however. "I can assure you that fighting is the least dangerous & arduous part of a soldier's life," one young man declared. Letters home told of torturous marches across arid wastes alive with tarantulas, scorpions, and rattlesnakes. Others recounted dysentery, malaria, smallpox, cholera, and yellow fever. Of the 13,000 American soldiers who died (some 50,000 Mexicans perished), fewer than 2,000 fell to Mexican bullets and shells. Disease killed most of the others. Medicine was so primitive that, as one Tennessee man observed, "nearly all who take sick die."

Victory in Mexico

Although the Americans won battle after battle, President Polk's strategy misfired. Despite heavy losses on the battlefield, Mexico refused to trade land for peace. One American soldier captured the Mexican mood: "They cannot submit to be deprived of California after the loss of Texas, and nothing but the conquest of their Capital will force them to such a humiliation." Polk had arrived at the same conclusion. While Taylor occupied the north, General **Winfield Scott** would land an army on the Gulf coast of Mexico and march 250 miles inland to Mexico City. Polk's plan entailed enormous risk because Scott would have to cut himself off from supplies and lead his men deep into enemy country against a much larger army.

An amphibious landing on March 9, 1847, near Veracruz put some 10,000 American troops ashore. After a siege of two weeks and furious shelling, Veracruz surrendered. In April 1847, Scott's forces moved westward, following the path blazed more than three centuries earlier by Hernán Cortés to "the halls of Montezuma" (see chapter 2).

After the defeat at Buena Vista, Santa Anna had returned to Mexico City, where he rallied his ragged troops and marched them east to set a trap for Scott in the mountain pass at Cerro Gordo. Knifing through Mexican lines, the Americans almost captured Santa Anna, who fled the field on foot. So complete was the victory that Scott gloated to Taylor, "Mexico no longer has an army." But Santa Anna, ever resilient, again rallied the Mexican army. Some 30,000 troops took up defensive positions on the outskirts of Mexico City and began melting down church bells to cast new cannons.

In August 1847, Scott began his assault on the Mexican capital. The fighting proved the

Mexican Family
This family had its portrait taken in 1847, in the middle of the war. Where were the adult males? Mexican civilians were vulnerable to atrocities committed by the invading army, a large part of which were volunteers who received little training and resisted discipline. The "lawless Volunteers stop at no outrage," Brigadier General William Worth declared. "Innocent blood has been basely, cowardly, and barbarously shed in cold blood." Generals Zachary Taylor and Winfield Scott gradually tamed the volunteers with stern military justice. Unknown photographer. Daguerrotype, ca. 1847, 2-7/8 x 3/16 inches, Amon Carter Museum, Fort Worth, Texas, P1981.65.18.

most brutal of the war. Santa Anna backed his army into the city, fighting each step of the way. At the battle of Churubusco, the Mexicans took 4,000 casualties in a single day and the Americans more than 1,000. At the castle of Chapultepec, American troops scaled the walls and fought the Mexican defenders hand to hand. After Chapultepec, Mexico City officials persuaded Santa Anna to evacuate the city to save it from destruction, and on September 14, 1847, Scott rode in triumphantly.

On February 2, 1848, American and Mexican officials signed the **Treaty of Guadalupe Hidalgo** in Mexico City. Mexico agreed to give up all claims to Texas north of the Rio Grande and to cede the provinces of New Mexico and California — more than 500,000 square miles — to the United States (see Map 12.4). The United States agreed to pay Mexico $15 million and to assume $3.25 million in claims that American citizens had against Mexico. In March 1848, the Senate ratified the treaty. Polk had his Rio Grande border, his Pacific ports, and all the land that lay between.

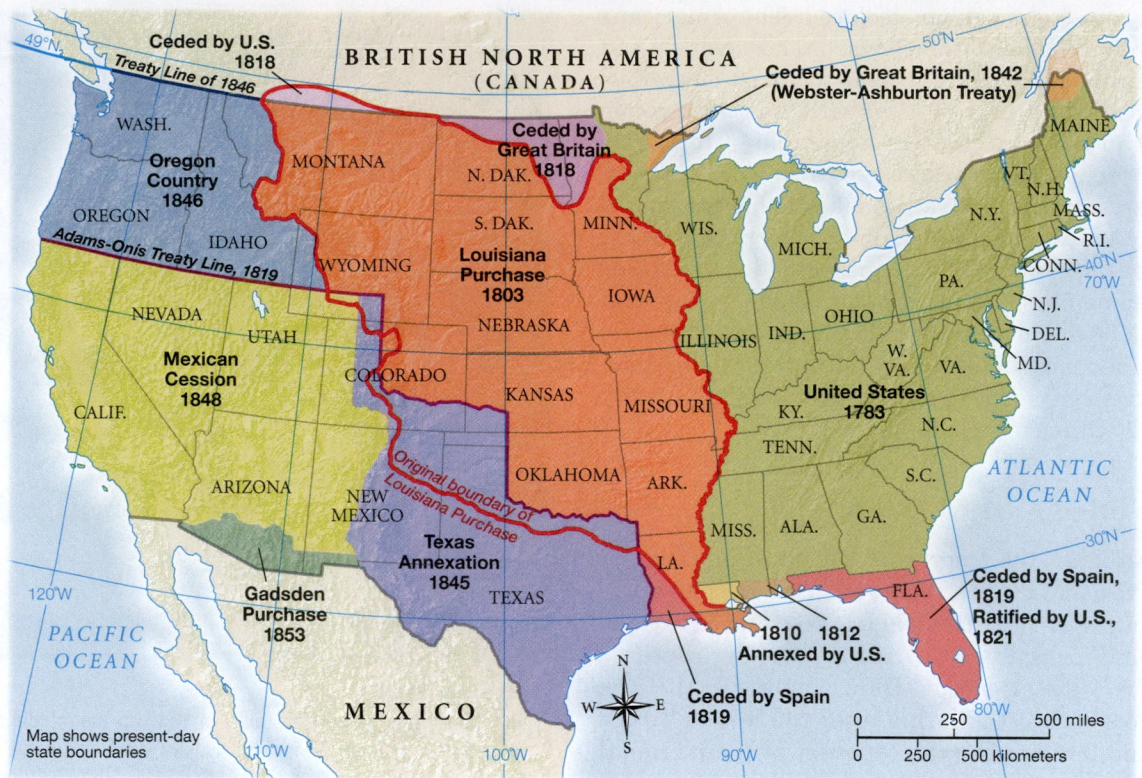

MAP ACTIVITY

MAP 12.5 Territorial Expansion by 1860
Less than a century after its founding, the United States spread from the Atlantic seaboard to the Pacific coast. War, purchase, and diplomacy had gained a continent.

READING THE MAP: List the countries from which the United States acquired land. Which nation lost the most land because of U.S. expansion?

CONNECTIONS: Who coined the phrase *manifest destiny*? When? What does it mean? What areas targeted for expansion were the subjects of debate during the presidential campaign of 1844?

The American triumph had enormous consequences. Less than three-quarters of a century after its founding, the United States had achieved its self-proclaimed manifest destiny to stretch from the Atlantic to the Pacific (Map 12.5). It would enter the industrial age with vast new natural resources and a two-ocean economy, while Mexico faced a sharply diminished economic future.

Golden California

Another consequence of the Mexican defeat was that California gold poured into American, not Mexican, pockets. In January 1848, just weeks before the formal transfer of territory, James Marshall discovered gold in the American River in the foothills of the Sierra Nevada. Marshall's

discovery set off the **California gold rush**, one of the wildest mining stampedes in the world's history. Between 1849 and 1852, more than 250,000 "forty-niners," as the would-be miners were known, descended on the Golden State. In less than two years, Marshall's discovery transformed California from foreign territory to statehood.

Gold fever quickly spread around the world. A stream of men of various races and nationalities, all bent on getting rich, remade the quiet California world of Mexican ranches into a raucous, roaring mining and town economy. Only a few struck it rich, and life in the goldfields was nasty, brutish, and often short. Men faced miserable living conditions, sometimes sheltering in holes and brush lean-tos. They also faced cholera and scurvy, exorbitant prices for food (eggs cost a dollar apiece), deadly encounters with claim jumpers, and endless backbreaking labor. An individual with gold in his pocket could find only temporary relief in the saloons, card games, dogfights, gambling dens, and brothels that flourished in the mining camps.

By 1853, San Francisco had grown into a raw, booming city of 50,000 that depended as much on gold as did the mining camps inland. Like the towns that dotted the San Joaquin and Sacramento valleys, it suffered from overcrowding, fire, crime, and violence. But enterprising individuals had learned that there was money to be made tending to the needs of the miners. Hotels, saloons, restaurants, laundries, and stores of all kinds exchanged services and goods for miners' gold.

In 1851, the Committee of Vigilance determined to bring order to the city. Members pledged that "no thief, burglar, incendiary or assassin shall escape punishment, either by the quibbles of the law, the insecurity of prisons, the carelessness or corruption of the police, or a laxity of those who pretended to administer justice." Lynchings proved that the committee meant business. In time, merchants, tradesmen, and professionals made the city their home and brought their families from back east. Gunfights declined, but many years would pass before anyone pacified San Francisco.

Establishing civic order was made more difficult by California's diversity and Anglo bigotry. The Chinese attracted special scrutiny. By 1851, 25,000 Chinese lived in California, and their religion, language, dress, queues (long pigtails), eating habits, and recreational use of opium convinced many Anglos that they were not fit citizens of the Golden State. In 1850, the California legislature passed the Foreign Miners' Tax Law, which levied high taxes on non-Americans to drive them from the goldfields, except as hired laborers working on claims owned by Americans. The Chinese were segregated residentially and occupationally and made ineligible for citizenship. Along with blacks and Indians, Chinese were denied public education and the right to testify in court.

As early as 1852, opponents demanded a halt to Chinese immigration. Chinese leaders in San Francisco fought back. Admitting deep cultural differences, they insisted that "in the important matters we are good men. We honor our parents; we take care of our children; we are industrious and peaceable; we trade much; we are trusted for small and large sums; we pay our debts; and are honest,

Miner with Pick, Pan, and Shovel
This young man exhibits the spirit of individual effort that was the foundation of free-labor ideals. Posing with a pick and shovel to loosen gold-bearing deposits and a pan to wash away debris, the man appears determined to succeed as a miner by his own muscles and sweat. Hard work with these tools, the picture suggests, promised rewards and maybe riches. Collection of Matthew Isenburg.

and of course must tell the truth." Their protestations offered little protection, however, and racial violence grew.

Anglo-American prospectors asserted their dominance over other groups, especially Native Americans and the Californios, Spanish and Mexican settlers who had lived in California for decades. Despite the U.S. government's pledge to protect Mexican and Spanish land titles after the cession of 1848, Americans took the land of the rancheros and through discriminatory legislation pushed Hispanic professionals, merchants, and artisans into the ranks of unskilled labor. Mariano Vallejo, a leading Californio, said of the forty-niners, "The good ones were few and the wicked many."

For Indians, the gold rush was catastrophic. Numbering about 150,000 in 1848, the Indian population of California fell to 25,000 by 1854. Starvation, disease, and a declining birthrate took a heavy toll. Indians also fell victim to wholesale murder. The nineteenth-century historian Hubert Howe Bancroft described

Chinese Man
This daguerreotype of an unidentified Chinese man was made by Isaac Wallace Baker, a photographer who traveled through California's mining camps in his wagon studio. One of the earliest known portraits of an Asian in California, the portrait shows a proud man boldly displaying his queue (long braid). This was almost certainly an act of defiance, for Anglos ridiculed Chinese cultural traditions, and vigilantes chased down men who wore queues. Collection of the Oakland Museum of California, Gift of Anonymous Donor.

white behavior toward Indians during the gold rush as "one of the last human hunts of civilization, and the basest and most brutal of them all." To survive, Indians moved to the most remote areas of the state and tried to stay out of the way.

The forty-niners created dazzling wealth: In 1852, 81 million ounces of gold, nearly half of the world's production, came from California. However, most forty-niners eventually took up farming, opened small businesses, or worked for wages for the corporations that took over the mining industry. Others looked beyond the land, for California's ports were connected to a vast trade network throughout the Pacific. Americans traded furs, hides, and lumber and engaged in whaling and the China trade in tea, silk, and porcelain. Still, as California's first congressional representative observed, the state was separated "by thousands of miles

of plains, deserts, and almost impossible mountains" from the rest of the Union. Some dreamers imagined a railroad that would someday connect the Golden State with the thriving agriculture and industry of the East. Others imagined a country transformed not by transportation but by progressive individual and institutional reform.

> **REVIEW** Why was the annexation of Texas such a controversial policy?

▶ Reforming Self and Society

While manifest destiny, the Mexican-American War, and the California gold rush transformed the nation's boundaries, many Americans sought personal and social reform. The emphasis on self-discipline and individual effort at the core of the free-labor ideal led Americans to believe that insufficient self-control caused the major social problems of the era. Evangelical Protestants struggled to control individuals' propensity to sin. Temperance advocates exhorted drinkers to control their urge for alcohol. In the midst of the worldly disruptions of geographic expansion and economic change, about one-third of Americans belonged to a church in 1850. Although many — like Abraham Lincoln — remained outside churches, the influence of evangelical religion reached far beyond church members.

The evangelical temperament — a conviction of righteousness coupled with energy, self-discipline, and faith that the world could be improved — animated most reformers. However, a few activists pointed out that certain fundamental injustices lay beyond the reach of individual self-control. Transcendentalists and utopians believed that perfection could be attained only by rejecting the competitive, individualistic values of mainstream society. Woman's rights activists and abolitionists sought to reverse the subordination of women and to eliminate the enslavement of blacks by changing laws and social institutions as well as attitudes and customs. They confronted the daunting challenge of repudiating widespread assumptions about male supremacy and white supremacy and somehow challenging the entrenched institutions that reinforced those assumptions: the family and slavery.

The Mansion of Happiness
Unlike the modern day board game Monopoly, which encourages players to greedily amass real estate and wealth, The Mansion of Happiness, designed by a minister in 1843, rewarded players for traits of pious, middle-class respectability. Players spun a small top to determine how many spaces to advance. Players who landed on spaces labeled Piety, Chastity, or Temperance, got to advance six more spaces. Landing on Idleness sent a player back to Industry. A player who settled on Passion had to return to the water to cool off. The winner made it to the central Mansion of Happiness: Heaven. Rare Book & Special Collections Division, Library of Congress.

The Pursuit of Perfection: Transcendentalists and Utopians

A group of New England writers who came to be known as transcendentalists believed that individuals should conform neither to the dictates of the materialistic world nor to the dogma of formal religion. Instead, people should look within themselves for truth and guidance. The leading transcendentalist, Ralph Waldo Emerson — an essayist, poet, and lecturer — proclaimed that the power of the solitary individual was nearly limitless. Henry David Thoreau, Margaret Fuller, and other transcendentalists agreed with Emerson that "if the single man plant himself indomitably on his instincts, and there abide, the huge world will come round to him." In many ways, the inward gaze and confident egoism of **transcendentalism** represented less an alternative to mainstream values than an exaggerated form of the rampant individualism of the age.

Unlike transcendentalists who sought to turn inward, a few reformers tried to change the world by organizing utopian communities as alternatives to prevailing social arrangements. Although these communities never attracted more than a few thousand people, the activities of their members demonstrated both dissatisfaction with the larger society and their efforts to realize their visions of perfection.

Some communities set out to become models of perfection whose success would point the way toward a better life for everyone. During the 1840s, more than two dozen communities organized themselves around the ideas of Charles

Fourier, a French critic of contemporary society. Members of **Fourierist phalanxes**, as these communities were called, believed that individualism and competition were evils that denied the basic truth that "men . . . are brothers and not competitors." Phalanxes aspired to replace competition with harmonious cooperation based on communal ownership of property. But Fourierist communities failed to realize their lofty goals, and few survived more than two or three years.

The **Oneida community** went beyond the Fourierist notion of communalism. John Humphrey Noyes, the charismatic leader of Oneida, believed that American society's commitment to private property made people greedy and selfish. Noyes claimed that the root of private property lay in marriage, in men's conviction that their wives were their exclusive property. Drawing from a substantial inheritance, Noyes organized the Oneida community in New York in 1848 to abolish marital property rights through the practice of what he called "complex marriage." Sexual intercourse was not restricted to married couples but was permitted between any consenting man and woman in the community. Noyes also required all members to relinquish their economic property to the community, which developed a lucrative business manufacturing animal traps. Oneida's sexual and economic communalism attracted several hundred members, but most of their neighbors considered Oneidans adulterers, blasphemers, and worse. Yet the practices that set Oneida apart from its mainstream neighbors strengthened the community, and it survived long after the Civil War.

Woman's Rights Activists

Women participated in the many reform activities that grew out of evangelical churches. Women church members outnumbered men two to one and worked to put their religious ideas into practice by joining peace, temperance, antislavery, and other societies. Involvement in reform organizations gave a few women activists practical experience in such political arts as speaking in public, running a meeting, drafting resolutions, and circulating petitions. Along with such experience came confidence. The abolitionist Lydia Maria Child pointed out in 1841 that "those who urged women to become missionaries and form tract societies . . . have changed the household utensil to a living energetic being and they have no spell to turn it into a broom again."

In 1848, about three hundred reformers led by **Elizabeth Cady Stanton** and Lucretia Mott gathered at Seneca Falls, New York, for the first national woman's rights convention in the United States. As Stanton recalled, "The general discontent I felt with women's portion as wife, mother, housekeeper, physician, and spiritual guide, [and] the wearied anxious look of the majority of women impressed me with a strong feeling that some active measure should be taken to right the wrongs of society in general, and of women in particular." The **Seneca Falls Declaration of Sentiments** set an ambitious agenda to demand civil liberties for women and to right the wrongs of society. The declaration proclaimed that "the history of mankind is a history of repeated injuries and usurpations on the part of man toward woman, having in direct object the establishment of an absolute tyranny over her." In the style of the Declaration of Independence (see appendix I, page A-1), the Seneca Falls declaration demanded that women "have immediate admis-

Bloomers and Woman's Emancipation
This 1851 British cartoon lampoons bloomers, the trouserlike garment worn beneath shortened skirts by two cigar-smoking American women. Bloomers were invented in the United States as an alternative to the uncomfortable, confining, and awkward dresses worn by fashionable women, suggested here by the clothing of the "respectable" women on the right. In the 1850s, Elizabeth Cady Stanton and other woman's rights activists wore bloomers and urged all American women to do likewise. Ridiculed as unfeminine by critics, American reformers eventually abandoned bloomers and focused on more important woman's rights issues. The "bloomerism" controversy illustrates the immense power of conventional notions of femininity confronted by woman's rights advocates. Miriam and Ira D. Wallach Division of Art, Prints, and Photographs, The New York Public Library. Astor, Lenox, and Tilden Foundations.

BLOOMERISM—AN AMERICAN CUSTOM.

sion to all the rights and privileges which belong to them as citizens of the United States," particularly the "inalienable right to the elective franchise."

Nearly two dozen other woman's rights conventions assembled before 1860, repeatedly calling for suffrage and an end to discrimination against women. But women had difficulty receiving a respectful hearing, much less achieving legislative action. Even so, the Seneca Falls declaration served as a pathbreaking manifesto of dissent against male supremacy and of support for woman suffrage, and it inspired many women to challenge the barriers that limited their opportunities.

Stanton and other activists sought fair pay and expanded employment opportunities for women by appealing to free-labor ideology. Woman's rights advocate Paula Wright Davis urged Americans to stop discriminating against able and enterprising women: "Let [women] . . . open a Store, . . . plant and tend an Orchard, . . . learn any of the lighter mechanical Trades, . . . study for a Profession, . . . be called to the lecture-room, [and] . . . the Temperance rostrum . . . [and] let her be appointed [to serve in the Post Office]." Some women pioneered in these and many other occupations during the 1840s and 1850s. Woman's rights activists also succeeded in protecting married women's rights to their own wages and property in New York in 1860. But discrimination against women persisted, as most men believed that free-labor ideology required no compromise of male supremacy.

Abolitionists and the American Ideal

During the 1840s and 1850s, abolitionists continued to struggle to draw the nation's attention to the plight of slaves and the need for emancipation. Former slaves **Frederick Douglass**, Henry Bibb, and Sojourner Truth lectured to reform audiences throughout the North about the cruelties of slavery. Abolitionists published newspapers, held conventions, and petitioned Congress, but they never attracted a mass following among white Americans. Many white Northerners became convinced that slavery was wrong, but they still believed that blacks were inferior. Many other white Northerners shared the common view of white Southerners that slavery was necessary and even desirable. The westward extension of the nation during the 1840s offered abolitionists an opportunity to link their unpopular ideal to a goal that many white Northerners found much more attractive — limiting the geographic expansion of slavery, an issue that moved to the center of national politics during the 1850s (as discussed in chapter 14).

Black leaders rose to prominence in the abolitionist movement during the 1840s and 1850s. African Americans had actively opposed slavery for decades, but a new generation of leaders came to the forefront in these years. Frederick Douglass, Henry Highland Garnet, William Wells Brown, Martin R. Delany, and others became impatient with white abolitionists' appeals to the conscience of the white majority. In 1843, Garnet urged slaves to choose "Liberty or Death"

Abolitionist Meeting
This rare daguerreotype was made by Ezra Greenleaf Weld in August 1850 at an abolitionist meeting in Cazenovia, New York. Frederick Douglass, who had escaped from slavery in Maryland twelve years earlier, is seated on the platform next to the woman at the table. One of the nation's most brilliant and eloquent abolitionists, Douglass also supported equal rights for women. The man behind Douglass is Gerrit Smith, a wealthy and militant abolitionist whose funds supported many reform activities. Notice the two black women on either side of Smith and the white woman next to Douglass. Most white Americans considered such voluntary racial proximity scandalous and promiscuous. Collection of the J. Paul Getty Museum, Malibu, CA.

and rise in insurrection against their masters, an idea that alienated almost all white people and carried little influence among slaves. To express their own uncompromising ideas, black abolitionists founded their own newspapers and held their own antislavery conventions, although they still cooperated with sympathetic whites.

The commitment of black abolitionists to battling slavery grew out of their own experiences with white supremacy. The 250,000 free African Americans in the North and West constituted less than 2 percent of the total population in 1860. They confronted the humiliations of racial discrimination in nearly every arena of daily life. Only Maine, Massachusetts, New Hampshire, and Vermont permitted black men to vote; New York imposed a special property-holding requirement on black — but not white — voters, effectively excluding most black men from the franchise. The pervasive racial discrimination both handicapped and energized black abolitionists. Some cooperated with the efforts of the **American Colonization Society** to send freed slaves and other black Americans to Liberia in West Africa. Others sought to move to Canada, Haiti, or elsewhere. They were convinced that, as an African American from Michigan wrote, "it is impracticable, not to say impossible, for the whites and blacks to live together, and upon terms of social and civil equality, under the same government." Most black American leaders refused to embrace emigration and worked against racial prejudice in their own communities, organizing campaigns against segregation, particularly in transportation and education. Their most notable success came in 1855 when Massachusetts integrated its public schools. Elsewhere, white supremacy continued unabated.

Outside the public spotlight, free African Americans in the North and West contributed to the antislavery cause by quietly aiding fugitive slaves. **Harriet Tubman** escaped from slavery in Maryland in 1849 and repeatedly risked her freedom and her life to return to the South to escort slaves to freedom. When the opportunity arose, free blacks in the North provided fugitive slaves with food, a safe place to rest, and a helping hand. An outgrowth of the antislavery sentiment and opposition to white supremacy that unified nearly all African Americans in the North, this "**underground railroad**" ran mainly through black neighborhoods, black churches, and black homes.

REVIEW Why were women especially prominent in many nineteenth-century reform efforts?

► Conclusion: Free Labor, Free Men

During the 1840s and 1850s, a cluster of interrelated developments — population growth, steam power, railroads, and the growing mechanization of agriculture and manufacturing — meant greater economic productivity, a burst of output from farms and factories, and prosperity for many. Diplomacy with Great Britain and war with Mexico handed the United States 1.2 million square miles and more than 1,000 miles of Pacific coastline. One prize of manifest destiny, California, almost immediately rewarded its new owners with tons of gold. To most Americans, new territory and vast riches were appropriate accompaniments to the nation's stunning economic progress and superior institutions.

To Northerners, industrial evolution confirmed the choice they had made to eliminate slavery and promote free labor as the key to independence, equality, and prosperity. Like Abraham Lincoln, millions of Americans could point to their personal experiences as evidence of the practical truth of the free-labor ideal. But millions of others had different stories to tell. They knew that in the free-labor system, poverty and wealth continued to rub shoulders. By 1860, more than half of the nation's free-labor workforce toiled for someone else. Free-labor enthusiasts denied that the problems were inherent in the country's social and economic systems. Instead, they argued, most social ills — including poverty and dependency — sprang from individual deficiencies. Consequently, many reformers focused on personal self-control and discipline, on avoiding sin and alcohol. Other reformers focused on woman's rights and the abolition of slavery. They challenged widespread conceptions of male supremacy and black inferiority, but neither group managed to overcome the prevailing free-labor ideology based on individualism, racial prejudice, and notions of male superiority.

By midcentury, half of the nation had prohibited slavery, and half permitted it. The North and the South were animated by different economic interests, cultural values, and political aims. Each celebrated its regional identity and increasingly disparaged that of the other. Not even the victory over Mexico could bridge the deepening divide between North and South.

▶ Selected Bibliography

The Economy and Free Labor

Jeanne Boydston, *Home and Work: Housework, Wages, and the Ideology of Labor in the Early Republic* (1990).

J. Matthew Gallman, *Receiving Erin's Children: Philadelphia, Liverpool, and the Irish Famine Migration, 1854–1855* (2000).

Jonathan A. Glickstein, *Concepts of Free Labor in the Antebellum United States* (1991).

Donald R. Hoke, *Ingenious Yankees: The Rise of the American System of Manufactures in the Private Sector* (1990).

Jonathan Hughes and Louis P. Cain, *American Economic History* (2011).

Robert A. Margo, *Wages and Labor Markets in the United States, 1820–1860* (2000).

David R. Meyer, *The Roots of American Industrialization* (2003).

Scott A. Sandage, *Born Losers: A History of Failure in America* (2005).

Kenneth J. Winkle, *The Young Eagle: The Rise of Abraham Lincoln* (2001).

Westward Expansion and the Mexican-American War

H. W. Brand, *Lone Star Nation* (2004).

Christopher Corbett, *The Poker Bride: The First Chinese in the Wild West* (2009).

David Dary, *The Oregon Trail: An American Saga* (2004).

Brian DeLay, *War of a Thousand Deserts: Indian Raids and the U.S.-Mexican War* (2008).

Jared Farmer, *On Zion's Mount: Mormons, Indians, and the American Landscape* (2008).

Paul W. Foos, *A Short, Offhand, Killing Affair: Soldiers and Social Conflict during the Mexican-American War* (2002).

Amy S. Greenberg, *Manifest Manhood and the Antebellum American Empire* (2005).

Timothy J. Henderson, *A Glorious Defeat: Mexico and Its War with the United States* (2007).

Benjamin Heber Johnson, *Revolution in Texas: How a Forgotten Rebellion and Its Bloody Suppression Turned Mexicans into Americans* (2003).

Susan Lee Johnson, *Roaring Camp: The Social World of the California Gold Rush* (2000).

Robert W. Merry, *A Country of Vast Designs: James K. Polk, the Mexican War, and the Conquest of the American Continent* (2009).

Gregory H. Nobles, *American Frontiers: Cultural Encounters and Continental Conquest* (1997).

Malcolm Rohrbough, *Days of Gold: The California Gold Rush and the American Nation* (1997).

James A. Sandos, *Converting California: Indians and Franciscans in the Missions* (2004).

Joel H. Sibley, *Storm over Texas: The Annexation Controversy and the Road to Civil War* (2005).

Richard White, *"It's Your Misfortune and None of My Own": A New History of the American West* (1993).

Richard Bruce Winders, *Mr. Polk's Army: The American Military Experience in the Mexican War* (1997).

Antebellum Culture and Reform

Bruce Dorsey, *Reforming Men and Women: Gender in the Antebellum City* (2002).

Lori D. Ginzberg, *Elizabeth Cady Stanton: An American Life* (2009).

Bruce Laurie, *Beyond Garrison: Antislavery and Social Reform* (2005).

Sally McMillen, *Seneca Falls and the Origins of the Women's Rights Movement* (2008).

Patrick Rael, *Black Identity and Black Protest in the Antebellum North* (2002).

Susan M. Ryan, *The Grammar of Good Intentions: Race and the Antebellum Culture of Benevolence* (2003).

Beth A. Salerno, *Sister Societies: Women's Antislavery Organizations in Antebellum America* (2005).

Susan Zaeske, *Signatures of Citizenship: Petitioning, Antislavery, and Women's Political Identity* (2003).

▶ FOR MORE BOOKS ABOUT TOPICS IN THIS CHAPTER, see the Online Bibliography at bedfordstmartins.com/roark.

▶ FOR ADDITIONAL PRIMARY SOURCES FROM THIS PERIOD, see Michael Johnson, ed., *Reading the American Past*, Fifth Edition.

▶ FOR WEB SITES, IMAGES, AND DOCUMENTS RELATED TO TOPICS AND PLACES IN THIS CHAPTER, visit Make History at bedfordstmartins.com/roark.

Reviewing Chapter 12

KEY TERMS

Explain each term's significance.

Economic and Industrial Evolution
John Deere (p. 359)
mechanical reapers (p. 359)
American system (p. 360)
Samuel F. B. Morse (p. 362)

Free Labor: Promise and Reality
free-labor ideal (p. 364)
universal education (p. 365)

The Westward Movement
manifest destiny (p. 370)
Oregon Trail (p. 370)
Fort Laramie conference (p. 372)
Mormons (p. 373)
Joseph Smith Jr. (p. 373)
Brigham Young (p. 374)
Stephen F. Austin (p. 375)
Antonio López de Santa Anna (p. 375)
Lone Star Republic (p. 376)

Expansion and the Mexican-American War
John Tyler (p. 377)
Henry Clay (p. 378)
James K. Polk (p. 378)
Zachary Taylor (p. 378)
Winfield Scott (p. 381)
Treaty of Guadalupe Hidalgo (p. 381)
California gold rush (p. 382)

Reforming Self and Society
transcendentalism (p. 385)
Fourierist phalanxes (p. 386)
Oneida community (p. 386)
Elizabeth Cady Stanton (p. 386)
Seneca Falls Declaration of Sentiments (p. 386)
Frederick Douglass (p. 387)
American Colonization Society (p. 388)
Harriet Tubman (p. 388)
underground railroad (p. 388)

REVIEW QUESTIONS

Use key terms and dates to support your answer.

1. Why did the United States become a leading industrial power in the nineteenth century? (pp. 359–363)

2. How did the free-labor ideal account for economic inequality? (pp. 363–369)

3. Why did westward migration expand dramatically in the mid-nineteenth century? (pp. 370–377)

4. Why was the annexation of Texas such a controversial policy? (pp. 377–384)

5. Why were women especially prominent in many nineteenth-century reform efforts? (pp. 384–388)

MAKING CONNECTIONS

Draw on key terms, the timeline, and review questions.

1. Varied political, economic, and technological factors promoted westward migration in the mid-nineteenth century. Considering these factors, discuss migration to two different regions (for instance, Texas, Oregon, Utah, or California). What drew migrants to the regions? How did the U.S. government contribute to their efforts?

2. How did the ideology of manifest destiny contribute to the mid-nineteenth-century drive for expansion? Discuss its implications for individual migrants and the nation. In your answer, consider how manifest destiny built on, or revised, earlier understandings of the nation's history and racial politics.

3. The Mexican-American War reshaped U.S. borders and more. Discuss the consequences of the war for national political and economic developments in subsequent decades. What resources did the new territory give the United States? How did debate over annexation revive older political disputes?

4. Some nineteenth-century reform movements drew on the free-labor ideal, while others challenged it. Discuss the free-labor ideal in relation to two reform movements (such as abolitionism and utopian communalism). How did the reform movements draw on the ideal to pursue specific reforms? How did these minority movements try to influence national developments?

LINKING TO THE PAST

Link events in this chapter to earlier events.

1. In what ways were the North's economy, society, and political structure during the 1840s and 1850s shaped by the American Revolution and the Constitution? (See chapters 7 and 8.)

2. The nation's mighty push westward in the 1840s and 1850s extended a history of expansion that was as old as the nation itself. How was expansion to the West between 1840 and 1860 similar to and different from expansion between 1800 and 1820? (See chapter 10.)

▶ FOR PRACTICE QUIZZES AND OTHER STUDY TOOLS, visit the Online Study Guide at **bedfordstmartins.com/roark**.

TIMELINE 1830–1861

1830	• Joseph Smith Jr. publishes *The Book of Mormon*.
1836	• Battle of the Alamo.
	• Texas declares independence from Mexico.
1837	• John Deere patents steel plow.
1840s	• Practical mechanical reapers created.
	• Fourierist phalanxes founded.
1841	• First wagon trains head west on Oregon Trail.
	• Vice President John Tyler becomes president when William Henry Harrison dies.
1844	• Democrat James K. Polk elected president.
	• Samuel F. B. Morse demonstrates telegraph.
1845	• Term *manifest destiny* coined.
	• United States annexes Texas, which enters Union as slave state.
	• Potato blight in Ireland spurs immigration to United States.
1846	• Bear Flag Revolt in California.
	• Congress declares war on Mexico.
	• United States and Great Britain agree to divide Oregon Country.
1847	• Mormons settle in Utah.
1848	• Treaty of Guadalupe Hidalgo.
	• Oneida community organized in New York.
	• First U.S. woman's rights convention takes place at Seneca Falls, New York.
1849	• California gold rush begins.
1850	• Mormon community annexed to United States as Utah Territory.
	• Congress grants railroads six square miles of land for every mile of track laid.
1851	• Conference at Fort Laramie, Wyoming, marks the beginning of government policy of Indian concentration.
1855	• Massachusetts integrates public schools.
1857	• U.S. troops invade Salt Lake City in Mormon War.
1861	• California connected to rest of nation by telegraph.

CLAY JUG

Enslaved African American potters created tens of thousands of ceramic pots to hold water and store food. Renowned South Carolina slave potter, Dave, created this three-foot-tall pot in 1857. Although teaching slaves to read and write was illegal, Dave usually signed his work; he also inscribed some of his pots with verse. "I wonder where is all my relations / Friendship to all and every nation" probably refers to the slave sales that sent some of his family to Louisiana. While Dave worked in his potter's shed, most slaves toiled in cotton fields.

Jug: Collection of McKissick Museum, University of South Carolina; background image: Schomburg Center for Research in Black Culture / General Research and Reference Division / The New York Public Library.

13

The Slave South
1820–1860

NAT TURNER WAS BORN A SLAVE IN SOUTHAMPTON COUNTY, VIRGINIA, in October 1800. People in his neighborhood claimed that he had always been different. His parents noticed special marks on his body, which they said were signs that he was "intended for some great purpose." His master said that he learned to read without being taught. As an adolescent, he adopted an austere lifestyle of Christian devotion and fasting. In his twenties, he received visits from the "Spirit," the same spirit, he believed, that had spoken to the ancient prophets. In time, Nat Turner began to interpret these things to mean that God had appointed him an instrument of divine vengeance for the sin of slaveholding.

In the early morning of August 22, 1831, he set out with six trusted friends — Hark, Henry, Sam, Nelson, Will, and Jack — to punish slave owners. Turner struck the first blow, an ax to the head of his master, Joseph Travis. The rebels killed all of the white men, women, and children they encountered. By noon, they had visited eleven farms and slaughtered fifty-seven whites. Along the way, they had added fifty or sixty men to their army. Word spread quickly, and soon the militia and hundreds of local whites gathered. By the next day, whites had captured or killed all of the rebels except Turner, who hid out for about ten weeks before being captured in nearby woods. Within a week, he was tried, convicted, and executed. By then, forty-five slaves had stood trial, twenty had been convicted and hanged, and another ten had been banished from Virginia. Frenzied whites had killed another hundred or more blacks — insurgents and innocent bystanders — in their counterattack against the rebellion.

Virginia's bewildered governor, John Floyd, struggled to understand why Turner's band of "assassins and murderers" assaulted the "unsuspecting and defenseless" citizens of "one of the fairest counties" of the state. White Virginians prided themselves on having the "mildest" slavery in the South, but sixty black rebels on a rampage challenged the comforting theory of the contented slave. Nonetheless, whites found explanations that allowed them to feel safer. They placed the blame on outside agitators. In 1829, David Walker, a freeborn black man living in Boston, had published his *Appeal . . . to the Coloured Citizens of the World*, an invitation to slaves to rise up in bloody rebellion, and copies had fallen into the hands of Virginia slaves. Moreover, on January 1, 1831, in Boston, the Massachusetts

Horrid Massacre in Virginia
No contemporary images of Nat Turner
are known to exist. This woodcut simply
imagines the rebellion as a nightmare in
which black brutes took the lives of
innocent whites. Although there was
never another rebellion as large as
Turner's, images of black violence
continued to haunt white imaginations.
Library of Congress.

abolitionist William Lloyd Garrison had published the first issue of the
Liberator, his fiery newspaper (see chapter 11). White Virginians also
dismissed the rebellion's leader, Nat Turner, as insane. "He is a complete
fanatic, or plays his part admirably," wrote Thomas R. Gray, the lawyer
who was assigned to defend Turner.

In the months following the insurrection, the Virginia legislature reaffirmed the state's determination to preserve black bondage by passing
laws that strengthened the institution of slavery and further restricted
free blacks. A professor at the College of William and Mary, Thomas R.
Dew, published a vigorous defense of slavery that became the bible of
Southerners' proslavery arguments. More than ever, the nation was
divided along the Mason-Dixon line, the surveyors' mark that in colonial
times had established the boundary between Maryland and Pennsylvania
but half a century later divided the free North and the slave South.

Black slavery increasingly molded the South into a distinctive region.
In the decades after 1820, Southerners, like Northerners, raced westward,
but unlike Northerners who spread small farms, manufacturing, and free
labor, Southerners spread slavery, cotton, and plantations. Geographic
expansion meant that slavery became more vigorous and more profitable
than ever, embraced more people, and increased the South's political
power. Antebellum Southerners included diverse people who at times
found themselves at odds with one another — not only slaves and free
people but also women and men; Indians, Africans, and Europeans; and
aristocrats and common folk. Nevertheless, beneath this diversity, a distinctively southern society and culture were forming. The South became
a slave society, and most white Southerners were proud of it.

▶ The Growing Distinctiveness of the South

From the earliest settlements, inhabitants of the southern colonies had shared a great deal with northern colonists. Most whites in both sections were British and Protestant, spoke a common language, and shared an exuberant pride in their victorious revolution against British rule. The creation of the new nation under the Constitution in 1789 forged political ties that bound all Americans. The beginnings of a national economy fostered economic interdependence and communication across regional boundaries. White Americans everywhere celebrated the achievements of the prosperous young nation, and they looked forward to its seemingly boundless future.

Despite these national similarities, Southerners and Northerners grew increasingly different. The French political observer Alexis de Tocqueville believed he knew why. "I could easily prove," he asserted in 1831, "that almost all the differences which may be noticed between the character of the Americans in the Southern and Northern states have originated in slavery." Slavery made the South different, and it was the differences between the North and South, not the similarities, that increasingly shaped antebellum American history.

Cotton Kingdom, Slave Empire

In the first half of the nineteenth century, millions of Americans migrated west. In the South, the stampede began after the Creek War of 1813–1814, which divested the Creek Indians of 24 million acres and initiated the government campaign to remove Indian people living east of the Mississippi River to the West (see chapters 10 and 11). Hard-driving slaveholders seeking virgin acreage for new plantations, striving farmers looking for patches of cheap land for small farms, herders and drovers pushing their hogs and cattle toward fresh pastures — anyone who was restless and ambitious felt the pull of Indian land.

But more than anything it was cotton that propelled Southerners westward. South of the **Mason-Dixon line**, climate and geography were ideally suited for the cultivation of cotton. Cotton's requirements are minimal: two hundred frost-free days from planting to picking, and plentiful rain, conditions found in much of the South. By the 1830s, cotton fields stretched from the Atlantic seaboard to central Texas. Heavy migration led to statehood for Arkansas in 1836 and for Texas and Florida in 1845. Production soared from 300,000 bales in 1830 to nearly 5 million in 1860, when the South produced three-fourths of the world's supply. The South — especially that tier of states from South Carolina west to Texas called the Lower South — had become the **cotton kingdom** (Map 13.1).

The cotton kingdom was also a slave empire. The South's cotton boom rested on the backs of slaves, most of whom toiled in gangs under the direct supervision of whites. As cotton agriculture expanded westward, whites shipped more than a million enslaved men and women from the Atlantic coast across the continent in what has been called the "Second Middle Passage," a massive deportation that dwarfed the transatlantic slave trade to North America. Victims of this brutal domestic slave trade marched hundreds of miles southwest to new plantations in the Lower South. The earliest arrivals faced the hardest work, literally cutting plantations from forests. One observer noted that young male slaves in Alabama who were no more than nineteen or twenty looked twice their age. Cotton, slaves, and plantations moved west together.

The slave population grew enormously. Southern slaves numbered fewer than 700,000 in 1790, about 2 million in 1830, and almost 4 million by 1860. By 1860, the South contained more slaves than all the other slave societies in the New World combined. The extraordinary growth was not the result of the importation of slaves, which the federal government outlawed in 1808. Instead, the slave population grew through natural reproduction; by midcentury, most U.S. slaves were native-born Southerners. In comparison, Cuba and Brazil, slave societies that kept their slave trades open until the mid-nineteenth century, had more African-born slaves and thus stronger ties to Africa.

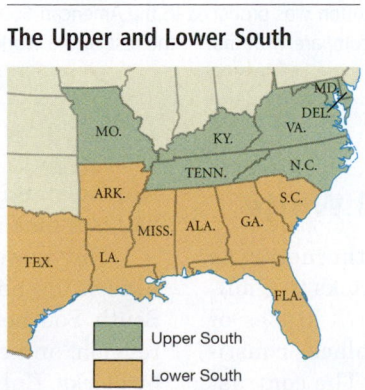

The Upper and Lower South

MO.   KY.   VA.   MD.   DEL.

TENN.   N.C.

ARK.   S.C.

MISS.   ALA.   GA.

TEX.   LA.

FLA.

◻ Upper South
◻ Lower South

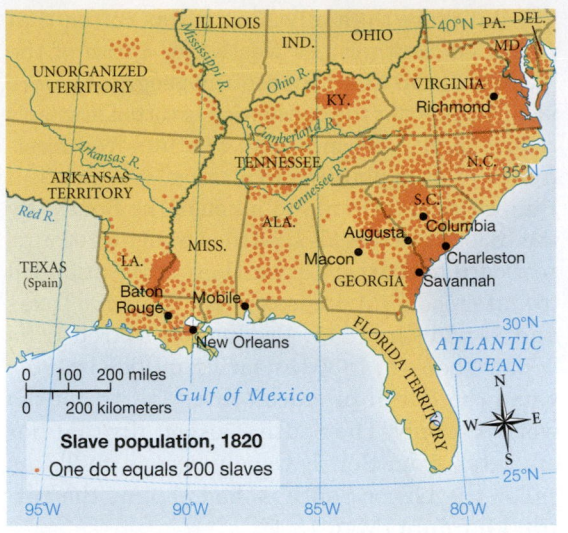

Slave population, 1820
• One dot equals 200 slaves

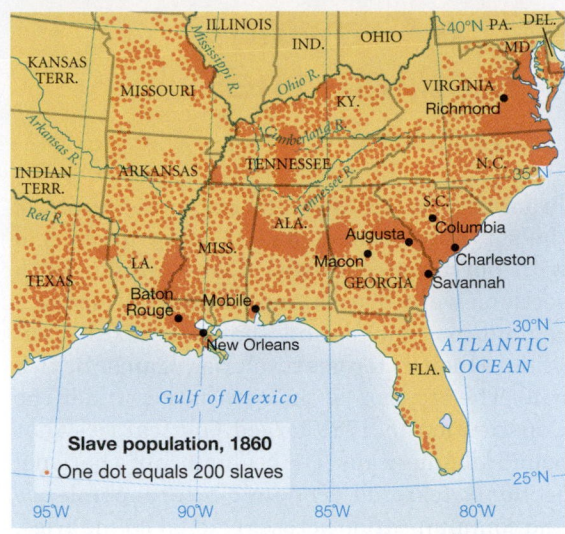

Slave population, 1860
• One dot equals 200 slaves

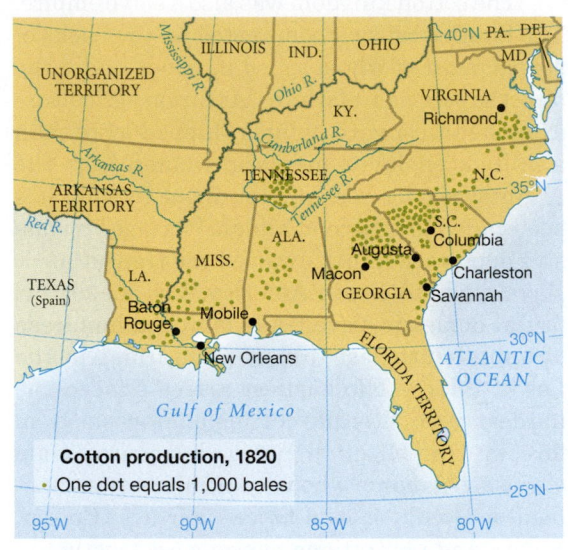

Cotton production, 1820
• One dot equals 1,000 bales

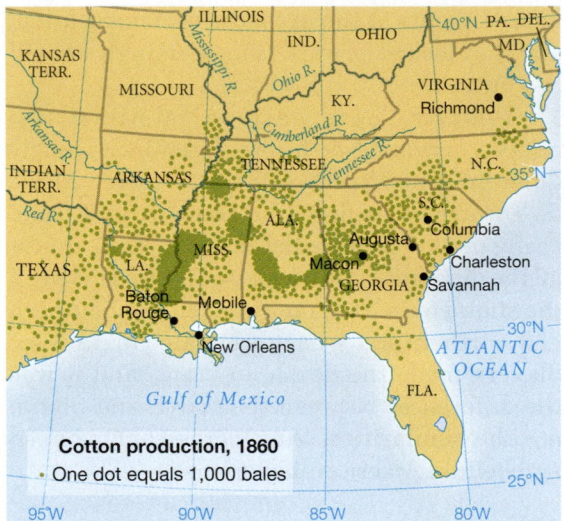

Cotton production, 1860
• One dot equals 1,000 bales

MAP ACTIVITY

Map 13.1   Cotton Kingdom, Slave Empire: 1820 and 1860
As the production of cotton soared, the slave population increased dramatically. Slaves continued to toil in tobacco and rice fields, but in Alabama, Mississippi, and Texas, they increasingly worked on cotton plantations.

READING THE MAP: Where was slavery most prevalent in 1820? In 1860? How did the spread of slavery compare with the spread of cotton?

CONNECTIONS: How much of the world's cotton was produced in the American South in 1860? How did the number of slaves in the American South compare with that in the rest of the world? What does this suggest about the South's cotton kingdom?

The South in Black and White

By 1860, one in every three Southerners was black (approximately 4 million blacks to 8 million whites). In the Lower South states of Mississippi and South Carolina, blacks constituted the majority (Figure 13.1). The contrast with the North was striking: In 1860, only one Northerner in seventy-six was black (about 250,000 blacks to 19 million whites).

The presence of large numbers of African Americans had profound consequences for the South. Southern culture — language, food, music, religion, and even accents — was in part shaped by blacks. But the most direct consequence of the South's biracialism was southern whites' commit-

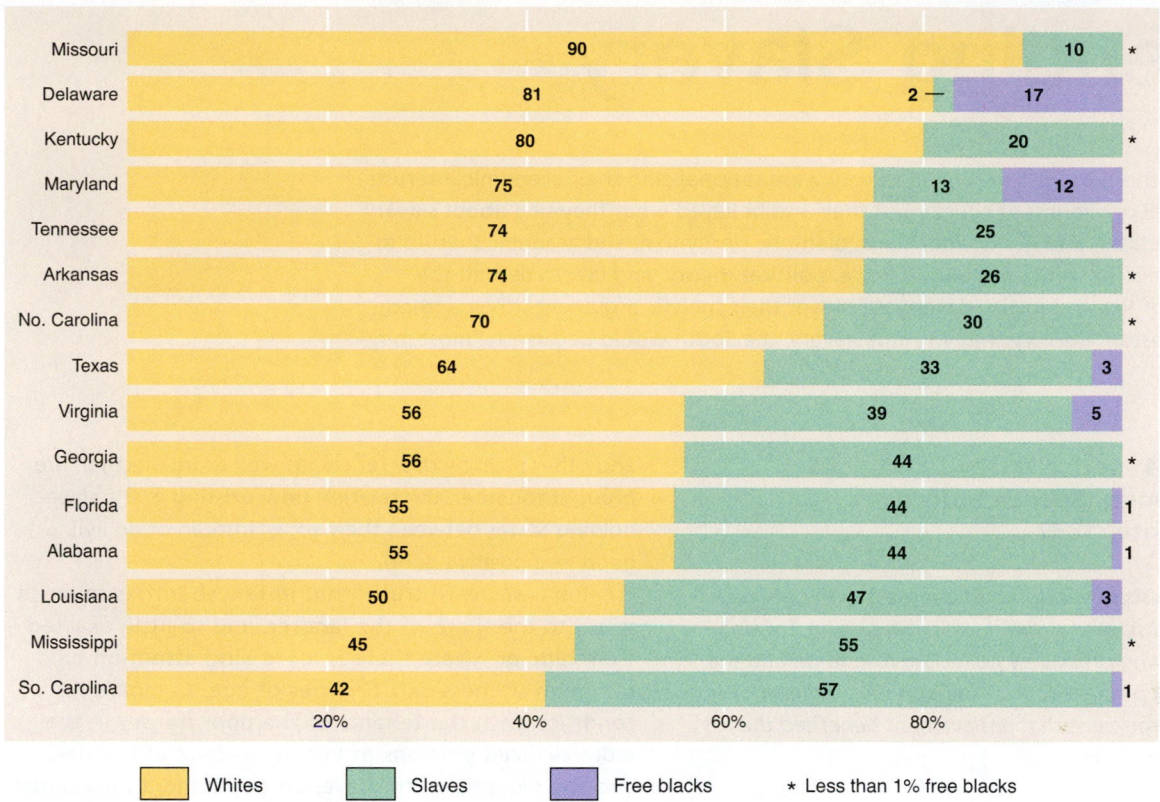

State	Whites	Slaves	Free blacks
Missouri	90	10	*
Delaware	81	2	17
Kentucky	80	20	*
Maryland	75	13	12
Tennessee	74	25	1
Arkansas	74	26	*
No. Carolina	70	30	*
Texas	64	33	3
Virginia	56	39	5
Georgia	56	44	*
Florida	55	44	1
Alabama	55	44	1
Louisiana	50	47	3
Mississippi	45	55	*
So. Carolina	42	57	1

20% 40% 60% 80%

☐ Whites   ☐ Slaves   ☐ Free blacks   * Less than 1% free blacks

FIGURE 13.1 Black and White Populations in the South, 1860
Blacks represented a much larger fraction of the population in the South than in the North, but considerable variation existed from state to state. Only one Missourian in ten, for example, was black, while Mississippi and South Carolina had black majorities. States in the Upper South were "whiter" than states in the Lower South, despite the Upper South's greater number of free blacks.

ment to white supremacy. Northern whites believed in racial superiority, too, but their dedication to white supremacy lacked the intensity and urgency increasingly felt by white Southerners who lived among millions of blacks who had every reason to hate them and to strike back, as Nat Turner had.

After 1820, attacks on slavery—from blacks and a handful of white Southerners opposed to slavery and from Northern abolitionists—jolted southern slaveholders into a distressing awareness that they lived in a dangerous world. As the only slave society embedded in an egalitarian, democratic republic, the South made extraordinary efforts to strengthen slavery. In the 1820s and 1830s, state legislatures constructed **slave codes** (laws) that required the total submission of slaves. As the Louisiana code stated, a slave "owes his master . . . a respect without bounds, and an absolute obedience." The laws also underlined the authority of all whites, not just masters. Any white could "correct" slaves who did not stay "in their place."

Intellectuals joined legislators in the campaign to strengthen slavery. The South's academics, writers, and clergy employed every imaginable defense. They argued that in the South slaves were legal property, and wasn't the protection of property the bedrock of American liberty? History also endorsed slavery, they claimed. Weren't the great civilizations — such as those of the Hebrews, Greeks, and Romans — slave societies? They claimed that the Bible, properly interpreted, also sanctioned slavery. Old Testament patriarchs owned slaves, they observed, and in the New Testament, Paul returned the runaway slave Onesimus to his master. Proslavery spokesmen played on the fears of Northerners and Southerners alike by charging that giving blacks equal rights would lead to the sexual mixing of the races, or **miscegenation**.

Another of slavery's champions, George Fitzhugh of Virginia, attacked the North's free-labor economy and society. He claimed that behind the North's grand slogans lay a heartless

Defending Slavery

White Southerners who defended slavery were rationalizing their economic interests and racial privileges, of course, but they also believed what they said about slavery being just, necessary, and godly. Politicians, planters, clergymen, and academics wrote essays on economics, religion, morality, science, political theory, and law to defend the southern way of life and justify slavery. Whatever their specific arguments, they agreed with the *Charleston Mercury* that without slavery, the South would become a "most magnificent jungle."

DOCUMENT 1
John C. Calhoun, Speech before the U.S. Senate, 1837

When abolitionists began to flood Congress with petitions that denounced slavery as sinful and odious, John C. Calhoun, the South's leading proslavery politician, rose to defend the institution as "a positive good." Calhoun devoted part of his speech to the argument that enslavement benefited the slaves themselves.

Be it good or bad, it [slavery] has grown up with our society and institutions, and is so interwoven with them, that to destroy it would be to destroy us as a people. But let me not be understood as admitting, even by implication, that the existing relations between the two races in the slave-holding States is an evil: far otherwise; I hold it to be a good, as it has thus far proved to be to both, and will continue to prove so if not disturbed by the fell spirit of abolition. I appeal to facts. Never before has the black race of Central Africa, from the dawn of history to the present day, attained a condition so civilized and so improved, not only physically, but morally and intellectually. It came to us in a low, degraded, and savage condition, and in the course of a few generations, it has grown up under the fostering care of our institutions, reviled they have been, to its present comparatively civilized condition. This, with the rapid increase of numbers, is conclusive proof of the general happiness of the race, in spite of all the exaggerated tales to the contrary. . . .

I hold that in the present state of civilization, where two races of different origin, and distinguished by color, and other physical differences, as well as intellectual, are brought together, the relation now existing in the slave-holding States between the two, is, instead of an evil, a good — a positive good. . . .

I may say with truth, that in few countries so much is left to the share of the laborer, and so little exacted from him, or where there is more kind attention paid to him in sickness or infirmities of age. Compare his condition with the tenants of the poor houses in the more civilized portions of Europe — look at the sick, and the old and infirm slave, on one hand, in the midst of his family and friends, under the kind superintending care of his master and mistress, and compare it with the forlorn and wretched condition of the pauper in the poor house.

SOURCE: John C. Calhoun, "Speech on the Reception of Abolition Petitions, Delivered in the Senate, February 6th, 1837," in *Speeches of John C. Calhoun, Delivered in the House of Representatives and in the Senate of the United States.* Edited by Richard K. Cralle (Appleton, 1853), 625–33.

DOCUMENT 2
William Harper, *Memoir on Slavery*, 1837

Unlike Calhoun, who defended slavery by pointing to what he considered slavery's concrete benefits for blacks, William Harper — judge, politician, and academic — defended slavery by denouncing abolitionists, particularly the "atrocious philosophy" of "natural equality and inalienable rights" that they used to support their attacks on slavery.

philosophy: "Every man for himself, and the devil take the hindmost." Gouging capitalists exploited wageworkers unmercifully, Fitzhugh declared, and he contrasted the North's vicious free-labor system with the humane relations that he said prevailed between masters and slaves because slaves were valuable capital that masters sought to protect.

But at the heart of the defense of slavery lay the claim of black inferiority. Black enslavement was both necessary and proper, slavery's defenders argued, because Africans were lesser

All men are born free and equal. Is it not palpably nearer the truth to say that no man was ever born free, and that no two men were ever born equal? . . . Wealth and poverty, fame or obscurity, strength or weakness, knowledge or ignorance, ease or labor, power or subjection, mark the endless diversity in the condition of men. . . .

It is the order of nature and of God, that the being of superior faculties and knowledge, and therefore of superior power, should control and dispose of those who are inferior. It is as much in the order of nature, that men should enslave each other, as that other animals should prey upon each other. I admit that he does this under the highest moral responsibility, and is most guilty if he wantonly inflicts misery or privation on beings more capable of enjoyment or suffering than brutes, without necessity or any view to the great good which is to result. . . .

Moralists have denounced the injustice and cruelty which have been practiced towards our aboriginal Indians, by which they have been driven from their native seats and exterminated.

. . . No doubt, much fraud and injustice has been practiced in the circumstances and manner of their removal. Yet who has contended that civilized man had no moral right to possess himself of the country? That he was bound to leave this wide and fertile continent, which is capable of sustaining uncounted myriads of a civilized race, to a few roving and ignorant barbarians? Yet if any thing is certain, it is certain that there were no means by which he could possess the country, without exterminating or enslaving them. Slave and civilized man cannot live together, and the savage can only be tamed by being enslaved or by having slaves.

SOURCE: William Harper, *Memoir of Slavery* (J. S. Burges, 1838).

DOCUMENT 3
Thornton Stringfellow, "The Bible Argument: or, Slavery in the Light of Divine Revelation," 1856

Reverend Thornton Stringfellow, a Baptist minister from Virginia, offered a defense of human bondage based on his reading of the Bible. In these passages, he makes a case that Jesus himself approved of the relationship between master and slave.

Jesus Christ recognized this institution [slavery] as one that was lawful among men, and regulated its relative duties. . . . I affirm then, first, (and no man denies,) that Jesus Christ has not abolished slavery by a prohibitory command: and second, I affirm, he has introduced no new moral principle which can work its destruction, under the gospel dispensation; and that the principle relied on for this purpose, is a fundamental principle of the Mosaic law, under which slavery was instituted by Jehovah himself. . . .

To the church at Colosse, a city of Phrygia, in the lesser Asia, Paul in his letter to them, recognizes the three relations of wives and husbands, parents and children, servants and masters, as relations existing among the members . . . and to the servants and masters he thus writes: "Servants obey in all things your masters, according to the flesh: not with eye service, as men pleasers, but in singleness of heart, fearing God: and whatsoever you do, do it heartily, as to the Lord and not unto men; knowing that of the Lord ye shall receive the reward of the inheritance, for ye serve the Lord Christ. . . . Masters give unto your servants that which is just and equal, knowing that you also have a master in heaven."

SOURCE: *Slavery Defended: The Views of the Old South* by Eric L. McKitrick, editor. Published by Prentice-Hall, 1963. Reprinted with permission. *Cotton Is King and Pro-Slavery Arguments* by Thornton Stringfellow (Pritchard, Abbott & Loomis, 1860), 459–546.

Questions for Analysis and Debate

1. According to John C. Calhoun, what were slavery's chief benefits for blacks? How did his proslavery convictions shape his argument?

2. Why do you suppose William Harper interjected Americans' treatment of Indians into his defense of slavery?

3. According to Thornton Stringfellow, the Bible instructs both masters and slaves about their duties. What are their respective obligations?

beings. Rather than exploitative, slavery was a mass civilizing effort that lifted lowly blacks from barbarism and savagery, taught them disciplined work, and converted them to soul-saving Christianity. According to Virginian **Thomas R. Dew**, most slaves were grateful. He declared that "the slaves of a good master are his warmest, most constant, and most devoted friends."

Whites gradually moved away from defending slavery as a "necessary evil"—the halfhearted argument popular at the time of the American Revolution—and toward an aggressive defense

THE FRUITS OF AMALGAMATION.

The Fruits of Amalgamation
In this lithograph from 1839, Edward W. Clay of Philadelphia attacked abolitionists by imagining the miscegenation (also known as "amalgamation") that would come from their misguided campaign. He drew a beautiful white woman, her two black children, and her dark-skinned, ridiculously overdressed husband, resting his feet in his wife's lap. The couple is attended by a white servant. Another interracial couple has come calling. Abolitionists denied the charge of amalgamation and pointed to the lasciviousness of southern slaveholders as the true source of racial mixing in antebellum America. Courtesy, American Antiquarian Society.

of slavery as a "positive good." **John C. Calhoun**, an influential southern politician, declared that in the states where slavery had been abolished, "the condition of the African, instead of being improved, has become worse," while in the slave states, the Africans "have improved greatly in every respect." (See "Documenting the American Promise," page 398.)

Black slavery encouraged southern whites to unify around race rather than to divide by class. The grubbiest, most tobacco-stained white man could proudly proclaim his superiority to all blacks and his equality with the most refined southern patrician. Because of racial slavery, Georgia attorney Thomas R. R. Cobb observed, every white Southerner "feels that he belongs to an elevated class. It matters not that he is no slaveholder; he is not of the inferior race; he is

a freeborn citizen." Consequently, the "poorest meets the richest as an equal; sits at his table with him; salutes him as a neighbor; meets him in every public assembly, and stands on the same social platform." In the South, Cobb boasted, "there is no war of classes."

In reality, slavery did not create perfect harmony among whites or ease every strain along class lines. But by providing every white Southerner membership in the ruling race, slavery helped whites bridge differences in wealth, education, and culture.

The Plantation Economy

As important as slavery was in unifying white Southerners, only about a quarter of the white population lived in slaveholding families. Most slaveholders owned fewer than five slaves. Only about 12 percent of slave owners owned twenty or more, the number of slaves that historians consider necessary to distinguish a **planter** from a farmer. Despite their small numbers, planters dominated the southern economy. In 1860, 52 percent of the South's slaves lived and worked on **plantations**. Plantation slaves produced more than 75 percent of the South's export crops, the backbone of the region's economy. Slavery was dying elsewhere in the New World (only Brazil and Cuba still defended slavery at midcentury), but slave plantations increasingly dominated southern agriculture.

The South's major cash crops — tobacco, sugar, rice, and cotton — grew on plantations (Map 13.2). Tobacco, the original plantation crop in North America, had shifted westward in the nineteenth century from the Chesapeake to Tennessee and Kentucky. Large-scale sugar production began in 1795, when Étienne de Boré built a modern sugar mill in what is today New Orleans, and sugar plantations were confined almost entirely to Louisiana. Commercial rice production began in the seventeenth century, and like sugar, rice was confined to a small geographic area, a narrow strip of coast stretching from the Carolinas into Georgia.

Tobacco, sugar, and rice were labor-intensive crops that relied on large numbers of slaves to do the backbreaking work. Most phases of tobacco cultivation — planting, transporting, thinning, picking off caterpillars, cutting, drying, packing — required laborers to stoop or bend down. Work on sugarcane plantations was particularly physically demanding. During the harvest, slaves worked eighteen hours a day, and so hard was the slaves' task that one visitor concluded that "nothing but 'involuntary servitude' could go through the toil and suffering required to produce sugar." Working in water and mud in the heat of a Carolina summer regularly threatened slaves engaged in rice production with malaria, yellow fever, and other diseases.

But by the nineteenth century, cotton was king of the South's plantation crops. Cotton became commercially significant in the 1790s after the invention of a new cotton gin by Eli Whitney dramatically increased the production of raw cotton (see chapter 9). Cotton was relatively easy to grow and took little capital to get started — just enough to

purchase land, seed, and simple tools. Thus, small farmers as well as planters grew cotton. But planters, whose fields were worked by gangs of slaves, produced three-quarters of the South's cotton, and cotton made planters rich.

Plantation slavery also enriched the nation. By 1840, cotton accounted for more than 60 percent of American exports. Most of the cotton was shipped to Great Britain, the world's largest manufacturer of cotton textiles. Much of the profit from the sale of cotton overseas returned to planters, but some went to northern middlemen who bought, sold, insured, warehoused, and shipped cotton to the mills in Great Britain and

> ### "Nothing but 'involuntary servitude' could go through the toil and suffering required to produce sugar."
> — A visitor to a sugarcane plantation

MAP ACTIVITY

Map 13.2   The Agricultural Economy of the South, 1860
Cotton dominated the South's agricultural economy, but the region grew a variety of crops and was largely self-sufficient in foodstuffs.

READING THE MAP: In what type of geographic areas were rice and sugar grown? After cotton, what crop commanded the greatest agricultural area in the South? In which region of the South was this crop predominantly found?
CONNECTIONS: What role did the South play in the U.S. economy in 1860? How did the economy of the South differ from that of the North?

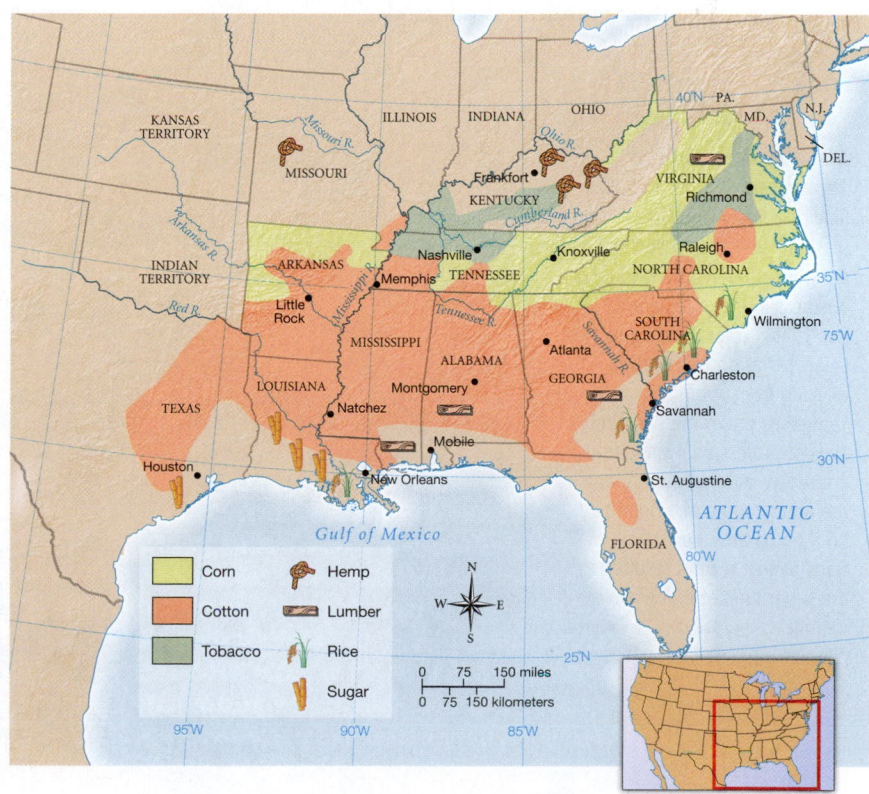

THE PROMISE OF TECHNOLOGY

The Cotton Gin

Machines for separating cotton fibers from seeds that clung to the fiber — cotton gins (the word *gin* is short for *engine*) — had been around for centuries, but none cleaned cotton quickly and efficiently. In 1793, Eli Whitney, a young New Englander living on a Georgia plantation, built a simple little device that was crude but effective. It was not much more than wire teeth set in a wooden cylinder that, when rotated, reached through narrow slats to pull cotton fibers away from the sticky seeds while a brush swept the fibers from the revolving teeth. News of the invention spread like wildfire. The cotton gin enabled southern farmers to supply huge quantities of clean cotton for the world market. Planters in particular profited hugely as cotton pushed out indigo, then tobacco, as the South's major cash crop. The commercial production of cotton eventually bound millions of African Americans to slavery. Why did the cotton gin have such different consequences for planters and for slaves? Smithsonian Institution, National Museum of American History, Behring Center.

elsewhere. As one New York merchant observed, "Cotton has enriched all through whose hands it has passed." As middlemen invested their profits in the booming northern economy, industrial development received a burst of much-needed capital. Furthermore, southern plantations benefited northern industry by providing an important market for textiles, agricultural tools, and other manufactured goods.

The economies of the North and South steadily diverged. While the North developed a mixed economy — agriculture, commerce, and manufacturing — the South remained overwhelmingly agricultural. Year after year, planters funneled the profits they earned from land and slaves back into more land and more slaves. With its capital flowing into agriculture, the South did not develop many factories. By 1860, only 10

Slave Traders: Sold to Tennessee

Slave trading — or "Negro speculation," as it was called by contemporaries — was a booming business in the antebellum South. This color drawing by Lewis Miller portrays slaves walking from Virginia to Tennessee under the watchful eyes of professional slave traders. A few children accompany the adults, some of whom may be their parents. Forced migrations almost always resulted in the separation of black family members. Abby Aldrich Rockefeller Folk Art Center, Williamsburg, VA.

Arise! Arise! and weep no more dry up your tears, we shall part no more. Come rose we go to Tennessee, that happy shore. To old virginia never — never — return.

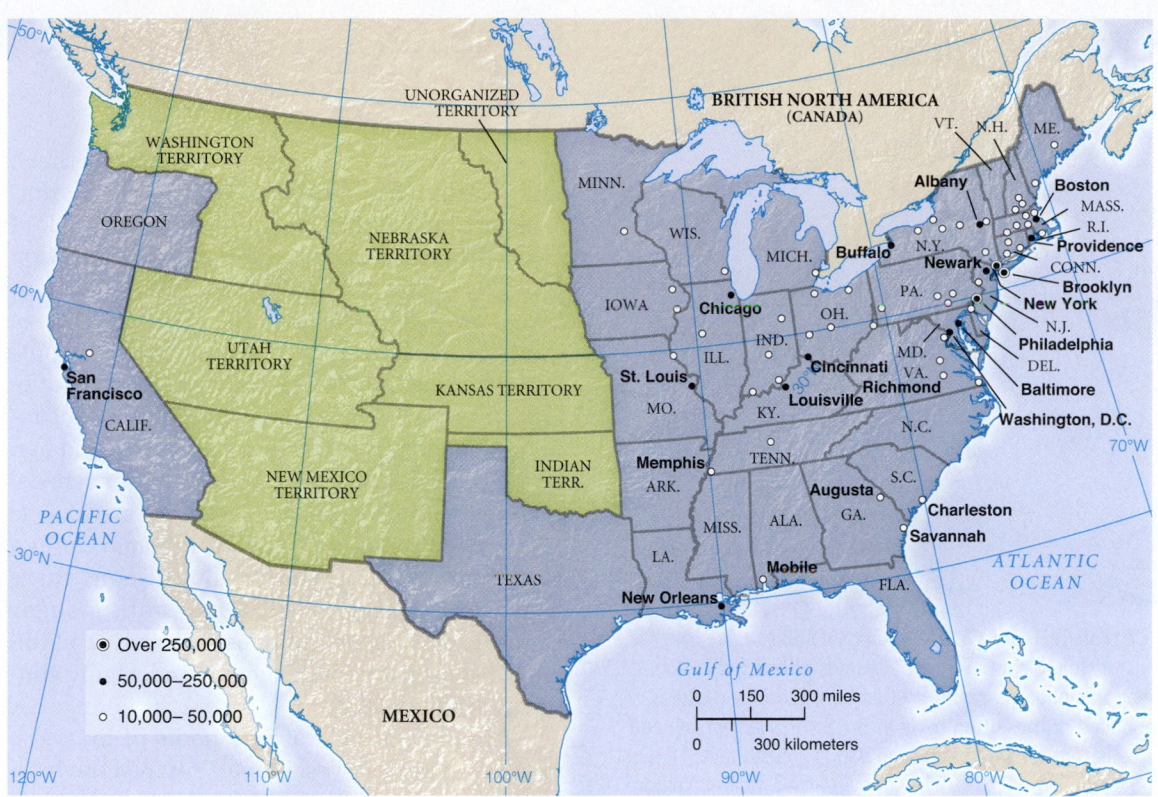

MAP 13.3

Major Cities in 1860

By 1860, northern cities were more numerous and larger than southern cities. In the slave states, cities were usually seaports or river ports that served the needs of agriculture, especially cotton.

percent of the nation's industrial workers lived in the South. Some cotton mills sprang up, but the region that produced 100 percent of the nation's cotton manufactured less than 7 percent of its cotton textiles.

Without significant economic diversification, the South developed fewer cities than the North and West (Map 13.3). In 1860, it was the least urban region in the country. Whereas nearly 37 percent of New England's population lived in cities, less than 12 percent of Southerners were urban dwellers. Southern cities were mostly port cities and were busy principally with exporting the agricultural products of plantations in the interior. Urban merchants provided agriculture with indispensable services, such as hauling, insuring, and selling cotton, rice, and sugar, but they were the tail on the plantation dog.

Immigrants as a Percentage of State Populations, 1860

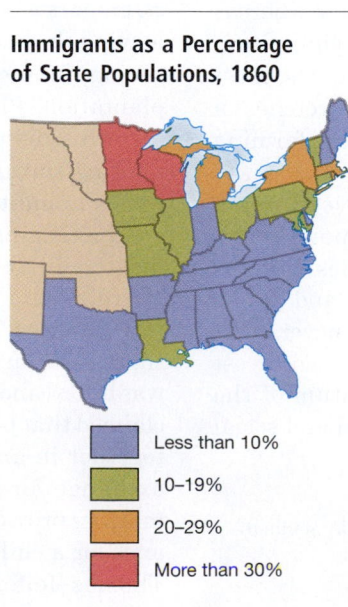

- Less than 10%
- 10–19%
- 20–29%
- More than 30%

Because the South had so few cities and industrial jobs, it attracted small numbers of European immigrants. Seeking economic opportunity, not competition with slaves (whose labor would keep wages low), immigrants steered northward. In 1860, 13 percent of all Americans were born abroad. But in nine of the fifteen slave states, only 2 percent or less of the population was foreign-born.

Not every Southerner celebrated the region's commitment to cotton and slaves. Critics bemoaned what one called the "deplorable scarcity" of factories. Diversification, reformers promised, would make the South economically independent and more prosperous. State governments encouraged economic development by helping to create banking systems that supplied credit for a wide range of projects and by constructing railroads, but they

Steamboats and Cotton in New Orleans, circa 1858
Smokestacks of dozens of steamboats overlook hundreds of bales of cotton at the foot of Canal Street. This photograph by Jay Dearborn Edwards captures something of the magnitude of the cotton trade in the South's largest city and major port. A decade earlier, visitor Solon Robinson had expressed awe: "It must be seen to be believed; and even then, it will require an active mind to comprehend acres of cotton bales standing upon the levee. . . ." Amid the sea of cotton, few Southerners doubted that cotton was king. Historic New Orleans Collection.

failed to create some of the essential services modern economies required. By the mid-nineteenth century, for example, no southern legislature had created a statewide public school system. Planters failed to see any benefit in educating the children of small farmers, especially with their tax money. Despite the flurry of railroad building, the South's mileage in 1860 was less than half that of the North. Moreover, whereas railroads crisscrossed the North carrying manufactured goods and agricultural products, most railroads in the South were short stretches of track that ran from port cities back into farming areas in order to transport cotton.

Northerners claimed that slavery was a backward labor system, and compared with Northerners, Southerners invested less of their capital in industry, transportation, and public education. But planters' pockets were never fuller than in the 1850s. Planters' decisions to reinvest in agriculture ensured the momentum of the plantation economy and the political and social relationships rooted in it.

REVIEW Why did the nineteenth-century southern economy remain primarily agricultural?

▶ Masters and Mistresses in the Big House

Nowhere was the contrast between northern and southern life more vivid than on the plantations of the South. Located on a patchwork of cleared fields and dense forests, a plantation typically included a "big house," where the plantation owner and his family lived, and a slave quarter. Scattered about were numerous outbuildings, each with a special function. Near the big house were the kitchen, storehouse, smokehouse (for curing and preserving meat), and hen coop. More distant were the barns, toolsheds, artisans' workshops, and overseer's house. Large plantations sometimes had an infirmary and a chapel for slaves. Depending on the crop, there was also a tobacco shed, a rice mill, a sugar refinery, or a cotton gin house. Lavish or plain, plantations everywhere had an underlying similarity (Figure 13.2).

The plantation was the home of masters, mistresses, and slaves. Slavery shaped the lives of all the plantation's inhabitants, from work to leisure activities, but it affected each differently. A hierarchy of rigid roles and duties governed relationships. Presiding was the master, who ruled his wife, children, and slaves, none of whom had many legal rights and all of whom were designated by the state as dependents under his dominion and protection.

Paternalism and Male Honor

Whereas smaller planters supervised the labor of their slaves themselves, larger planters hired **overseers** who went to the fields with the slaves, leaving the planters free to concentrate on marketing, finance, and the general affairs of the plantation. Planters also found time to escape to town to discuss cotton prices, to the courthouse and legislature to debate politics, and to the woods to hunt and fish.

Increasingly, planters characterized their mastery in terms of what they called "Christian guardianship" and what historians have called **paternalism**. The concept of paternalism denied that the form of slavery practiced in the South was brutal and exploitative. Instead, paternalism claimed that plantations joined master and slave together in an enterprise that benefited all. In exchange for the slaves' labor and obedience, masters provided basic care and necessary guidance for a childlike, dependent people. In 1814, Thomas Jefferson captured the essence of the

SAVANNAH RIVER

BRICK WALL

LEGEND

1	MANSION	6	LOT
2	KITCHEN	7	SUNKEN GARDEN
3	SMOKEHOUSE	8	OVERSEER'S HOUSE
4	STABLES	9	HOSPITAL
5	COACH HOUSE	10	SLAVE HUTS

FIGURE 13.2   A Southern Plantation
Slavery determined how masters laid out their plantations, where they situated their "big houses" and slave quarters, and what kinds of buildings they constructed. This model of the Hermitage, the mansion built in 1830 for Henry McAlpin, a Georgia rice planter, shows the overseer's house poised in a grove of oak trees halfway between the owner's mansion and the slave huts. The placement of the mansion at the end of an extended road leading up from the river underscored McAlpin's affluence and authority. Adapted from *Back of the Big House: The Architecture of Plantation Slavery* by John Michael Vlach. Copyright © 1993 by the University of North Carolina Press. Reprinted with permission of the University of North Carolina Press. Original illustration property of the Historic American Buildings Survey, a division of the National Park Service.

slave owner declared in 1849, "It behooves those who own them to make them last as long as possible." Another planter instructed his overseer to pay attention to "whatever tends to promote their health and render them prolific."

One consequence of this paternalism and economic self-interest was a small improvement in slaves' welfare. Diet improved, although nineteenth-century slaves still ate mainly fatty pork and cornmeal. Housing improved, although the cabins still had cracks large enough, slaves said, for cats to slip through. Clothing improved, although slaves seldom received much more than two crude outfits a year and perhaps a pair of cheap shoes. In the fields, workdays remained sunup to sundown, but planters often provided a rest period in the heat of the day. And most owners ceased the colonial practice of punishing slaves by branding and mutilation.

> **"I manage them as my children."**
> — A South Carolina rice planter, speaking of his slaves

Paternalism should not be mistaken for "Ol' Massa's" kindness and goodwill. It encouraged better treatment because it made economic sense to provide at least minimal care for valuable slaves. Nor did paternalism require that planters put aside their whips. They could whip and still claim that they were only fulfilling their responsibilities as guardians of their naturally lazy and at times insubordinate black dependents. State laws gave masters nearly "uncontrolled authority over the body" of the slave, according to one North Carolina judge. Paternalism offered slaves some informal protection against the most brutal

advancing ideal: "We should endeavor, with those whom fortune has thrown on our hands, to feed & clothe them well, protect them from ill usage, require such reasonable labor only as is performed voluntarily by freemen, and be led by no repugnancies to abdicate them, and our duties to them." A South Carolina rice planter insisted, "I manage them as my children."

Paternalism was part propaganda and part self-delusion. But it was also economically shrewd. Masters increasingly recognized slaves as valuable assets, particularly after the nation closed its external slave trade in 1808 and the cotton boom simultaneously stimulated the demand for slaves. Planters realized that the expansion of the slave labor force could come only from natural reproduction. As one

How Often Were Slaves Whipped?

There is little doubt that the whipping of slaves was widespread and acceptable in the South. We know from white sources that whipping was the prescribed method of physical punishment on most antebellum plantations. Masters' instructions to overseers authorized whippings and often established the number of strokes an overseer could administer. Some planters allowed fifteen lashes, some fifty, and some one hundred. But slave owners' instructions, as revealing as they are, tell us more about the severity of beating than about their frequency.

Remembrances of former slaves confirm that whipping was widespread and frequent. In the 1930s, a government program gathered testimony from more than 2,300 elderly African Americans about their experiences as slaves. Their accounts offer grisly evidence of the cruelty of slavery. "You say how did our Master treat his slaves?" asked one woman. "Scandalous, they treated them just like dogs." She was herself whipped "till the blood dripped to the ground." Bert Strong never personally felt the sting of the lash, but he recalled hearing slaves on other farms "hollering when they get

beat." He said, "They beat them till it a pity." Beatings occurred often, but how often?

The diary of Bennet H. Barrow, the master of Highland plantation in West Feliciana Parish, Louisiana, provides a rare picture of a master's punishment of his slaves. For a twenty-three-month period in 1840–1841, Barrow meticulously recorded every one of the 160 whippings he administered or ordered, which amounted to one whipping every four and a half days. Barrow's records establish that 60 of the 77 slaves who worked in his fields were whipped in this period, with 80 percent of the males and 70 percent of the females being whipped at least once. Most of the 17 field slaves who escaped being beaten were children and pregnant women.

In most instances, Barrow recorded not only the fact of a whipping but also his reasons for administering it. All sorts of "rascallity" made Barrow reach for his whip. The provocations included family quarrels in the slave quarter, impudence, running away, and failure to keep curfew. But nearly 80 percent of the reasons were related to poor work. Barrow gave beatings for picking "very trashy cotton," for "not picking

as well as he can," and for failing to pick the prescribed weight of cotton. One slave claimed to have lost his eyesight and for months refused to work, until Barrow "gave him 25 cuts yesterday morning & ordered him to work Blind or not." Some planters used whips that raised welts, caused blisters, and bruised. Others resorted to rawhide and cowhide whips that broke the skin, caused scarring, and sometimes permanently maimed. Occasionally, slaves were beaten to death.

Whipping was not Barrow's only means of inflicting pain. His diary mentions confining slaves to a plantation jail, putting them in chains, shooting them, breaking a "sword cane" over one slave's head, having slaves mauled by dogs, placing them in stocks, "staking down" slaves for hours, holding their heads under water, and a variety of punishments intended to ridicule and to shame, including making men wear women's clothing and do "women's work," such as the laundry. Still, Barrow's preferred instrument of punishment was the whip.

On the Barrow plantation, as on many others, whipping was public. Victims were often tied to a stake in the quarter, and the other slaves were made to watch. In a real sense, the entire slave population on the plantation experienced a whipping every four and a half days, and all were familiar with its terror and agony.

Was whipping effective? Did it produce a hardworking, efficient, and conscientious labor force? Not

punishments, but whipping remained the planters' essential form of coercion. (See "Historical Question," above.)

Paternalism never won universal acceptance among planters, but by the nineteenth century it had become a kind of communal standard. With its notion that slavery imposed on masters a burden and a duty, paternalism provided slaveholders with a means of rationalizing their rule. But it also provided some slaves with leverage in controlling the conditions of their lives. Slaves learned to manipulate the slaveholder's need to see himself as a good master. To avoid a reputa-

tion as a cruel tyrant, planters sometimes negotiated with slaves, rather than just resorting to the whip. Masters sometimes granted slaves small garden plots in which they could work for themselves after working all day in the fields, or they gave slaves a few days off and a dance when they had gathered the last of the cotton.

Virginia statesman Edmund Randolph argued that slavery created in white southern men a "quick and acute sense of personal liberty" and a "disdain for every abridgement of personal independence." Indeed, prickly individualism and aggressive independence became crucial features according to Barrow's own record. No evidence indicates that whipping changed the slaves' behavior. What Barrow considered bad work continued. Unabated whipping is itself evidence of the failure of punishment to achieve the master's will. Slaves knew the rules, yet they continued to act "badly." And they continued to suffer.

Did Barrow whip as often as other planters whipped? We simply do not know. Still, the Barrow evidence allows us to speculate profitably on the frequency of whipping by large planters. We do know that Barrow did not consider himself a cruel man. He bitterly denounced his neighbor as "the most cruel Master i ever knew of" for castrating three of his slaves. Like most whites, he believed that the lash was essential to get the work done, and he used it no more than he believed absolutely necessary. Still, Barrow's whip fell on someone's back every few days.

Thinking about Beliefs and Attitudes

1. How could slaveholders, who increasingly saw themselves as "Christian guardians" to their slaves, have justified whipping them?

2. Why do you suppose masters relied on whipping as the preferred form of punishment?

3. Why do you suppose Barrow gave the overwhelming majority of whippings because of poor work?

Gordon
This photograph of Gordon, a runaway slave from Baton Rouge, Louisiana, was taken on April 2, 1863. Frederick W. Mercer, an assistant surgeon with the Forty-seventh Massachusetts Regiment, examined four hundred other runaways and found many "to be as badly lacerated." Publication of Gordon's photograph in the popular *Harper's Weekly* made him a symbol of slavery's terrible brutality. Courtesy of the Massachusetts Historical Society.

of the southern concept of honor. Social standing, political advancement, and even self-esteem rested on an honorable reputation. Defending honor became a male passion. Andrew Jackson's mother reportedly told her son, "Never tell a lie, nor take what is not your own, nor sue anybody for slander or assault and battery. *Always settle them cases yourself*." Among planters, such advice sometimes led to dueling, a ritual that had arrived from Europe in the eighteenth century. It died out in the North, but in the South, even after legislatures banned it, gentlemen continued to defend their honor with pistols at ten paces.

Southerners also expected an honorable gentleman to be a proper patriarch. Nowhere in America was masculine power more accentuated. Planters brooked no opposition from any of their dependents, black or white. The master's absolute dominion sometimes led to miscegenation. Laws prohibited interracial sex, but how many trips masters and their sons made to slave cabins is impossible to tell. As long as slavery gave white men extraordinary power, however, slave women were forced to submit to the sexual appetites of the men who owned them.

Southern Man with Children and Their Mammy
Obviously prosperous and looking like a man accustomed to giving orders and being obeyed, this patriarch poses around 1848 with his young daughters and their nurse. Why does the black woman appear in the daguerreotype? The absent mother may be dead, and her death might account for the inclusion of the African American woman in the family circle. In any case, her presence signals her importance in the household. Fathers left the raising of daughters to mothers and nurses. Collection of the J. Paul Getty Museum, Malibu, CA.

In time, as the children of one elite family married the children of another, ties of blood and kinship, as well as ideology and economic interest, linked planters to one another. Conscious of what they shared as slaveholders, planters worked together to defend their common interests. The values of the big house — slavery, honor, male domination — washed over the boundaries of plantations and flooded all of southern life.

The Southern Lady and Feminine Virtues

Like their northern counterparts, southern ladies were expected to possess the feminine virtues of piety, purity, chastity, and obedience within the context of marriage, motherhood, and domesticity. Countless toasts praised the southern lady as the perfect complement to her husband, the commanding patriarch. She was physically weak, "formed only for the less laborious occupations," and thus dependent on male protection. To gain this protection, she exhibited modesty and delicacy, possessed beauty and grace, and cultivated refinement and charm.

For women, this image of the southern lady was no blessing. **Chivalry** — the South's romantic ideal of male-female relationships — glorified the lady while it subordinated her. Chivalry's underlying assumptions about the weakness of women and the protective authority of men resembled the paternalistic defense of slavery.

Indeed, the most articulate spokesmen for slavery also vigorously defended the subordination of women. George Fitzhugh insisted that "a woman, like children, has but one right and that is the right to protection. The right to protection involves the obligation to obey. A husband, a lord and master, nature designed for every woman. . . . If she be obedient she stands little danger of maltreatment." Just as the slaveholder's mastery was written into law, so too were the paramount rights of husbands. Married women lost almost all their property rights to their husbands. Women throughout the nation found divorce difficult, but southern women found it almost impossible.

Daughters of planters confronted chivalry's demands at an early age. Their education aimed at fitting them to become southern ladies. At their private boarding schools, they read literature, learned languages, and studied the appropriate drawing-room arts. Elite women began courting at a young age and married early. Kate Carney exaggerated only slightly when she despaired in her diary: "Today, I am seventeen, getting quite old, and am not married." Yet marriage meant turning their fates over to their husbands and making enormous efforts to live up to their region's lofty ideal. One mother told her daughter: "A single life has fewer troubles; but then it is not the one for which our maker designed us."

Proslavery advocates claimed that slavery freed white women from drudgery. Surrounded "by her domestics," declared Thomas R. Dew, "she ceases to be a mere beast of burden" and "becomes the cheering and animating center of the family circle." In reality, however, having servants required the plantation mistress to work long hours. She managed the big house, directly supervising as many as a dozen slaves. But unlike her husband, the mistress had no overseer. All house servants answered directly to her. She assigned them tasks each morning, directed their work throughout the day, and punished them when she found fault. Southern ladies did not often lead lives of leisure.

Bird Store, 626 Royal Street, New Orleans
Most elite white women lived on plantations, but when they visited cities, they shopped. Here a wealthy mother and daughter shop for a pet in a New Orleans bird store. The attentive proprietor and attractive shop provide everything they need — birds, cages, food, even an inviting couch in case they want to rest before moving on. Elite white women were, in a way, like birds kept in golden cages. Could it be that they were attracted to the thought of owning birds of their own, something they could care for, train, and control? Historic New Orleans Collection.

Whereas masters used their status as slaveholders as a springboard into public affairs, mistresses' lives were circumscribed by the plantation. Masters left the plantation when they pleased, but mistresses needed chaperones to travel. When they could, they went to church, but women spent most days at home, where they often became lonely. In 1853, Mary Kendall wrote how much she enjoyed her sister's letter: "For about three weeks I did not have the pleasure of seeing one white female face, there being no white family except our own upon the plantation." Grand parties and balls occasionally broke the daily routine, but the burden of planning and supervising the preparation of the food and drink fell on the mistress.

As members of slaveholding families, mistresses lived privileged lives. But they also had significant grounds for discontent. No feature of plantation life generated more anguish among mistresses than miscegenation. Mary Boykin Chesnut of Camden, South Carolina, confided in her diary, "Ours is a monstrous system, a wrong and iniquity. Like the patriarchs of old, our men live all in one house with their wives and their concubines; and the mulattos one sees in every family partly resemble the white children. Any lady is ready to tell you who is the father of all the mulatto children in everybody's household but her own. Those, she seems to think drop from the clouds."

Most planters' wives, including Chesnut, accepted slavery. After all, the mistress's world

VISUAL ACTIVITY

The Price of Blood

This 1868 painting by T. S. Noble depicts a transaction between a slave trader and a rich planter. The trader nervously pretends to study the contract, while the planter waits impatiently for the completion of the sale. The planter's mulatto son, who is being sold, looks away. The children of white men and slave women were property and could be sold by the father/master. Morris Museum of Art, Augusta, GA.

READING THE IMAGE: Who is absent from the painting, and what does this suggest about the tragedy of miscegenation?

CONNECTIONS: The white, male planter represented the pinnacle of southern society. How did white women, black men, and black women fit into this strict hierarchy?

rested on slave labor, just as the master's did. By acknowledging the realities of male power, mistresses enjoyed the rewards of their class and race. But these rewards came at a price. Still, the heaviest burdens of slavery fell not on those who lived in the big house, but on those who toiled to support them.

REVIEW Why did the ideology of paternalism gain currency among planters in the nineteenth century?

▶ Slaves in the Quarter

On most plantations, only a few hundred yards separated the big house and the slave quarter. But the distance was great enough to provide slaves with some privacy. Out of eyesight and earshot of the big house, slaves drew together and built lives of their own. They created families, worshipped God, and developed an African American community and culture. Individually and collectively, slaves found subtle and not so subtle ways to resist their bondage.

Despite the rise of plantations, a substantial minority of slaves lived and worked elsewhere. Most labored on small farms, where they wielded a hoe alongside another slave or two and perhaps their master. But by 1860, almost half a million slaves (one in eight) did not work in agriculture at all. Some lived in towns and cities, where they worked in the homes and shops of their masters as domestics, day laborers, bakers, barbers, tailors, and more. Other slaves, far from urban centers, toiled as fishermen, lumbermen, railroad workers, and deckhands on riverboats. Slaves could also be found in most of the South's factories. Nevertheless, a majority of slaves (52 percent) counted plantations as their workplaces and homes.

Work

Ex-slave Albert Todd recalled, "Work was a religion that we were taught." Whites enslaved blacks for their labor, and all slaves who were capable of productive labor worked. Former slave Carrie Hudson recalled that children who were "knee high to a duck" were sent to the fields to carry water to thirsty workers or to protect ripening crops from hungry birds. Others helped in the slave nursery, caring for children even younger than themselves, or in the big house, where they swept floors or shooed flies in the dining room. When slave boys and girls reached the age of eleven or twelve, masters sent most of them to the fields, where they learned farmwork by laboring alongside their parents. After a lifetime of labor, old women left the fields to care for the small children and spin yarn, and old men moved on to mind livestock and clean stables.

The overwhelming majority of plantation slaves worked as field hands, and most grew cotton. Cotton had a long growing season, and work never stopped, from the clearing of the fields in January and February to the planting and cultivating in the spring and summer until the picking in the fall. Planters sometimes assigned men and women to separate gangs, the women working at lighter tasks and the men doing the heavy work of clearing and breaking the land. But women also did heavy work. "I had to work hard," Nancy Boudry remembered, and "plow and go and split wood just like a man." The backbreaking labor and the monotonous routines caused one ex-slave to observe that the "history of one day is the history of every day."

A few slaves (about one in ten) became house servants. Nearly all of those (nine out of ten) were women. They cooked, cleaned, babysat, washed clothes, and did the dozens of other tasks the master and mistress required. House servants enjoyed somewhat less physically demanding work than field hands, but they were constantly on call, with no time that was entirely their own. Since no servant could please constantly, most bore the brunt of white frustration and rage. Ex-slave Jacob Branch of Texas remembered, "My poor mama! Every washday old Missy give her a beating."

Even rarer than house servants were skilled artisans. In the cotton South, no more than one slave in twenty (almost all men) worked in a skilled trade. Most were blacksmiths and carpenters, but slaves also worked as masons, mechanics, millers, and shoemakers. Slave craftsmen took pride in their skills and often exhibited the independence of spirit that caused slaveholder James H. Hammond of South Carolina to declare in disgust that when a slave became a skilled artisan, "he is more than half freed." Skilled slave fathers took pride in teaching their crafts to their sons. "My pappy was one of the black smiths and worked in the shop," John Mathews remembered. "I had to help my pappy in the shop when I was a child and I learnt how to beat out the iron and make wagon tires, and make plows."

> **"My poor mama! Every washday old Missy give her a beating."**
> — Ex-slave JACOB BRANCH of Texas

Rarest of all slave occupations was that of **slave driver**. Probably no more than one male slave in a hundred worked in this capacity. These men were well named, for their primary task was driving other slaves to work harder in the fields. In some drivers' hands, the whip never rested. Ex-slave Jane Johnson of South Carolina called her driver the "meanest man, white or black, I ever see." But other drivers showed all the restraint they could. "Ole Gabe didn't like that whippin' business," West Turner of Virginia remembered. "When Marsa was there, he would lay it on 'cause he had to. But when old Marsa wasn't lookin', he never would beat them slaves."

Normally, slaves worked from what they called "can to can't," from "can see" in the morning to "can't see" at night. Even with a break at noon for a meal and rest, it made for a long day. For slaves, Lewis Young recalled, "work, work, work, 'twas all they do."

Family and Religion

From dawn to dusk, slaves worked for the master, but at night, when the labor was done, and all day Sunday and usually Saturday afternoon, slaves were left largely to themselves. Bone tired perhaps, they nonetheless used the time to develop

Isaac Jefferson
In this 1845 daguerreotype, seventy-year-old Isaac Jefferson proudly poses in the apron he wore while practicing his crafts as a tinsmith and nail maker. Slaves of Thomas Jefferson, Isaac, his wife, and their two children were deeded to Jefferson's daughter Mary when she married in 1797. Isaac worked at Jefferson's home, Monticello, until 1820, when he moved to Petersburg, Virginia. When work was slow on the home plantation, slave owners often would hire out their skilled artisans to neighbors who needed a carpenter, blacksmith, mason, or tinsmith. Special Collections Department, University of Virginia Library.

and enjoy what mattered most: family, religion, and community.

One of the most important consequences of slaves' limited autonomy was the preservation of the family. Though severely battered, the black family survived slavery. No laws recognized slave marriage, and therefore no master or slave was legally obligated to honor the bond. Nevertheless, plantation records show that slave marriages were often long-lasting. Young men and women in the quarter fell in love, married, and set up housekeeping in cabins of their own. The primary cause of the ending of slave marriages was death, just as it was in white families. But the second most frequent cause was the sale of the husband or wife, something no white family ever had to fear. Precise figures are unavailable, but during the massive deportation associated with the Second Middle Passage, sales destroyed hundreds of thousands of slave marriages.

In 1858, a South Carolina slave named Abream Scriven wrote a letter to his wife, who lived on a neighboring plantation. "My dear wife," he began, "I take the pleasure of writing you . . . with much regret to inform you I am Sold to man by the name of Peterson, a Treader and Stays in New Orleans." Scriven promised to send some things when he got to his new home in Louisiana, but he admitted that he was not sure how he would "get them to you and my children." He asked his wife to "give my love to my father and mother and tell them good Bye for me. And if we do not meet in this world I hope to meet in heaven. . . . My dear wife for you and my children my pen cannot express the griffe I feel to

be parted from you all." He closed with words no master would have permitted in a slave's marriage vows: "I remain your truly husband until Death." The letter makes clear Scriven's love for his family; it also demonstrates slavery's massive assault on family life in the quarter.

Masters sometimes permitted slave families to work on their own. In the evenings and on Sundays, they tilled gardens, raised pigs and fowl, and chopped wood, selling the products in the market for a little pocket change. This "overwork," as it was called, allowed slaves to supplement their insufficient diets and even enjoy small luxuries. "Den each fam'ly have some chickens and sell dem and de eggs and maybe go huntin' and sell de hides and git some money," a former Alabama slave remembered. "Den us buy what am Sunday clothes with dat money, sech as hats and pants and shoes and dresses." Slave children remembered the extraordinary efforts their parents made to sustain their families. They held their parents in high esteem, grateful for the small bits of refuge from the rigors of slavery they provided.

Religion also provided slaves with a refuge and a reason for living. Evangelical Baptists and Methodists had great success in converting slaves from their African beliefs. By the mid-nineteenth century, perhaps as many as one-quarter of all slaves claimed church membership, and many of the rest would not have objected to being called Christians.

Planters promoted Christianity in the quarter because they believed that the slaves' salvation was part of the obligation of paternalism; they also hoped that religion would make slaves more obedient. South Carolina slaveholder

Slave Cabin, circa 1860
While slave dwellings varied from plantation to plantation, this crude cabin outside Savannah, Georgia, was typical. Constructed of logs, it was about fifteen feet square, with a dirt floor, shingled roof, and no glass. As one slave observed, "The wind and rain would come in and the smoke will not go out." While it has a substantial brick chimney, the cabin is also leaning and looks in danger of falling over. This photograph by an unknown photographer may have been taken on a Sunday, when the family is home and busy with domestic chores. Collection of the New-York Historical Society.

Charles Colcock Jones, the leading missionary to the slaves, published his *Catechism for Colored Persons* in 1834. It instructed slaves "to count their Masters 'worthy of all honour,' as those whom God has placed over them in this world." But slaves laughed up their sleeves at such messages. "That old white preacher just was telling us slaves to be good to our masters," one ex-slave said with a chuckle. "We ain't cared a bit about that stuff he was telling us 'cause we wanted to sing, pray, and serve God in our own way."

Meeting in their cabins or secretly in the woods, slaves created an African American Christianity that served their needs, not the masters'. Laws prohibited teaching slaves to read, but a few could read enough to struggle with the Bible. They interpreted the Christian message themselves. Rather than obedience, their faith emphasized justice. Slaves believed that God kept score and that the accounts of this world would be settled in the next. "The idea of a revolution in the conditions of the whites and blacks is the corner-stone" of the slaves' religion, recalled one ex-slave. But the slaves' faith also spoke to their experiences in this world. In the Old Testament, they discovered Moses, who delivered his people from slavery,

and in the New Testament, they found Jesus, who offered salvation to all. Jesus' message of equality provided a potent antidote to the planters' claim that blacks were an inferior people whom God condemned to slavery.

Christianity did not entirely drive out traditional African beliefs. Even slaves who were Christians sometimes continued to believe that conjurers, witches, and spirits possessed the power to injure and protect. Moreover, slaves' Christian music, preaching, and rituals reflected the influence of Africa, as did many of their secular activities, such as wood carving, quilt making, dancing, and storytelling. But by the mid-nineteenth century, black Christianity had assumed a central place in slaves' quest for freedom. In the words of one spiritual, "O my Lord delivered Daniel / O why not deliver me too?"

Gourd Fiddle
Found in St. Marys County, Maryland, this slave-made gourd fiddle is an example of the musical instruments that African Americans crafted and played throughout the South. A hybrid of African and European elements, this fiddle offers material evidence of the cultural transformation of African slaves. Although Africans lost much in their forced journey to the Americas, they braided the traditions of Africa and the South to create something new — an African American culture. Music, a crucial component of that sustaining culture, provided slaves with a creative outlet and relief from the rigors of slavery. Smithsonian Institution/ photo by Aldo Tutino.

Resistance and Rebellion

Slaves did not suffer slavery passively. They were, as whites said, "troublesome property." Slaves understood that accommodation to what they could not change was the price of survival, but in a hundred ways they protested their bondage. Theoretically, the master was all-powerful and the slave powerless. But sustained by their families, religion, and community, slaves engaged in day-to-day resistance against their enslavers.

The spectrum of slave resistance ranged from mild to extreme. Telling a pointed story by the fireside in a slave cabin was probably the mildest form of protest. But when the weak got the better of the strong, as they did in tales of Br'er Rabbit and Br'er Fox (*Br'er* is a contraction of *Brother*), listeners could enjoy the thrill of a vicarious victory over their masters. Protest in the fields was riskier and included putting rocks in their cotton bags before having them weighed, feigning illness, and pretending to be so thick-headed that they could not understand the simplest instruction. Slaves broke so many hoes that owners outfitted the tools with oversized handles. Slaves so mistreated the work animals that masters switched from horses to mules, which could absorb more abuse. Although slaves worked hard in the master's fields, they also sabotaged his interests.

Running away was a common form of protest, but except along the borders with northern states and with Mexico, escape to freedom was almost impossible. Most runaways could hope only to escape for a few days. Seeking temporary respite from hard labor or avoiding punishment, they usually stayed close to their plantations, keeping to the deep woods or swamps and slipping back into the quarter at night to get food. "Lying out," as it was known, usually ended when the runaway, worn-out and ragged, gave up or was finally chased down by slave-hunting dogs.

Although resistance was common, outright rebellion — a violent assault on slavery by large numbers of slaves — was very rare. The scarcity of revolts in the South is not evidence of the slaves' contentedness, however. Rather, conditions gave rebels almost no chance of success. By 1860, whites in the South outnumbered blacks two to one and were heavily armed. Moreover, communication between plantations was difficult, and the South provided little protective wilderness into which rebels could retreat and defend themselves. Rebellion, as **Nat Turner**'s experience showed (see pages 393–394), was virtual suicide.

Despite steady resistance and occasional rebellion, slaves did not have the power to end their bondage. Slavery thwarted their hopes and

"$50.00 Reward!!"
Slave owners often used notices — reward posters like this one and newspaper advertisements — to recover runaway slaves. Typically, notices provided precise information about the runaway's physical appearance and clothing, since slaves often fled with only the clothes on their backs. Louis Manigault, a prominent rice planter, apparently could not accept that a trusted house servant like Dolly would flee on her own, and thus he suggests that "some white man" had enticed her away. What distinguishes this runaway notice from almost all others is Dolly's photograph. Manigault had apparently rewarded this favorite servant with a photograph, which he then used to track her down. Manigault Papers, Southern Historical Collection, North Carolina Collection, The Library of the University of North Carolina, Chapel Hill, collection #P484.

Freedom Paper

This legal document attests to the free status of the Reverend John F. Cook of Washington, D.C., his daughter Mary, and his son George. Cook was a free black man who kept his "freedom paper" in this watertight tin, which he probably carried with him at all times. Free blacks had to be prepared to prove their free status anytime a white man challenged them, for southern law presumed that a black person was a slave unless he or she could prove otherwise. Without such proof, free blacks risked enslavement. Moorland-Spingarn Research Center, Howard University, Washington, D.C.

aspirations. It broke some and crippled others. But slavery's destructive power had to contend with the resiliency of the human spirit. Slaves fought back physically, culturally, and spiritually. Not only did they survive bondage, but they also created in the quarter a vibrant African American culture that buoyed them up during long hours in the fields and brought them joy and hope in the few hours they had to themselves.

REVIEW What types of resistance did slaves participate in, and why did slave resistance rarely take the form of rebellion?

▶ The Plain Folk

Most whites in the South did not own slaves, not even one. In 1860, more than six million of the South's eight million whites lived in slaveless households. Some slaveless whites lived in cities and worked as artisans, mechanics, and traders. Others lived in the country and worked as storekeepers, parsons, and schoolteachers. But most "plain folk" were small farmers. Perhaps three out of four were **yeomen**, small farmers who owned their own land. As in the North, farm ownership provided a family with an economic foundation, social respectability, and political standing. Unlike their northern counterparts, however, southern yeomen lived in a region whose economy and society were increasingly dominated by unfree labor.

In an important sense, the South had more than one white yeomanry. The huge southern landscape provided space enough for two yeoman societies, separated roughly along geographic lines. Yeomen throughout the South had much in common, but the life of a small farm family in the cotton belt — the flatlands that spread from South Carolina to east Texas — differed from the life of a family in the upcountry — the area of hills and mountains. And some rural slaveless whites were not yeomen; they owned no land at all and were sometimes desperately poor.

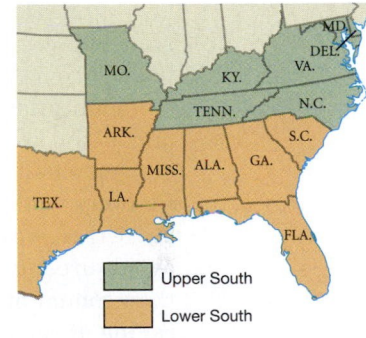

Upper South
Lower South

The Cotton Belt

Plantation Belt Yeomen

Plantation belt yeomen lived within the orbit of the planter class. Small farms outnumbered plantations in the **plantation belt**, but they were dwarfed in importance. Small farmers grew mainly food crops, particularly corn, but they also devoted a portion of their land to cotton. With only family labor to draw on, they produced just a few 400-pound bales each year, whereas large planters measured their crop in hundreds of bales. The small farmers' cotton tied them to planters. Unable to afford cotton gins or baling presses of their own, they relied on slave owners to gin and bale their cotton. With no link to merchants in the port cities, plantation belt yeomen also turned to better-connected planters to ship and sell their cotton.

A network of relationships laced small farmers and planters together. Planters hired out surplus slaves to ambitious yeomen who wanted to expand cotton production. They sometimes chose overseers from among the sons of local farm families. Plantation mistresses occasionally nursed ailing neighbors. Family ties could span class lines, making planter and yeoman kin as well as neighbors. Yeomen helped police slaves by riding in slave patrols, which nightly scoured country roads to make certain that no slaves were moving about without permission. On Sundays, plantation dwellers and plain folk came together in church to worship and afterward lingered to gossip and to transact small business.

Plantation belt yeomen may have envied, and at times even resented, wealthy slaveholders, but small farmers learned to accommodate. Planters made accommodation easier by going out of their way to behave as good neighbors and avoid direct exploitation of slaveless whites in their community. As a consequence, rather than raging at the oppression of the planter regime, the typical plantation belt yeoman sought entry into it. He dreamed of adding acreage to his farm, buying a few slaves of his own, and retiring from exhausting field work.

Upcountry Yeomen

By contrast, the hills and mountains of the South resisted the spread of slavery and plantations. In the western parts of Virginia, North Carolina, and South Carolina; in northern Georgia and Alabama; and in eastern Tennessee and Kentucky, the higher elevation, colder climate, rugged terrain, and poor transportation made it difficult for commercial agriculture to make headway. As a result, yeomen dominated these isolated areas, and planters and slaves were scarce.

At the core of this **upcountry** society was the independent farm family working its own

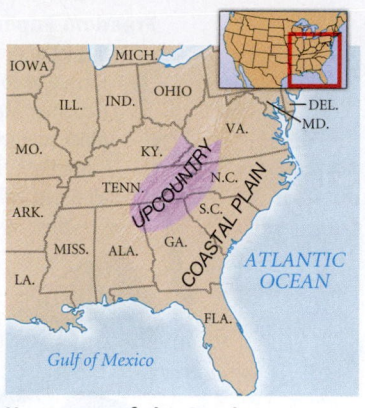

Upcountry of the South

patch of land; raising hogs, cattle, and sheep; and seeking self-sufficiency and independence. Toward that end, all members of the family worked, their tasks depending on their sex and age. Husbands labored in the fields, and with their sons they cleared, plowed, planted, and cultivated primarily food crops — corn, wheat, beans, sweet potatoes, and perhaps some fruit. Women and their daughters labored in and about the cabin most of the year. One upcountry farmer remembered that his mother "worked in the house cooking, spinning, weaving [and doing] patchwork." Women also tended the vegetable garden, kept a cow and some chickens, preserved food, cleaned their homes, fed their families, and cared for their children. Male and female tasks were equally crucial to the farm's success, but as in other white southern households, the domestic sphere was subordinated to the will of the male patriarch.

The typical upcountry yeoman also grew a little cotton or tobacco, but food production was more important than cash crops. Not much currency changed hands in the upcountry. Barter was common. A yeoman might trade his small cotton or tobacco crop to a country store owner for a little salt, bullets, needles, and nails, or swap extra sweet potatoes for a plow from a blacksmith or for leather from a tanner. Networks of exchange and mutual assistance tied individual homesteads to the larger community. Farm families joined together in logrolling, house and barn raising, and cornhusking.

Even the hills had some plantations and slaves, but the few upcountry folks who owned slaves usually had only two or three. As a result, slaveholders had much less social and economic power, and yeomen had more. But the upcountry did not oppose slavery. As long as upcountry plain folk were free to lead their own lives, they defended slavery and white supremacy just as staunchly as other white Southerners.

Poor Whites

The majority of slaveless white Southerners were hardworking, landholding small farmers, but Northerners held a different image of this group. They believed that slavery had condemned most whites to poverty and backwardness. One antislavery advocate charged that the South harbored

North Carolina Emigrants: Poor White Folks, 1845
James Henry Beard spent several years as a traveling portrait painter, counting among his sitters distinguished men like Henry Clay. But here his subject is a poor white family on the move. The wife clings to a child while perched on the back of a runty horse along with the family's entire belongings, which include a skillet and a pot. Two older children stand barefoot nearby, charged no doubt with looking after the family's cow and dog. The patriarch leans against a road sign, cradling his rifle. We don't know anything about the family's journey, but the painting suggests extreme poverty and desperation. Cincinnati Art Museum, Bridgeman Art Library.

three classes: "the slaves on whom devolves all the regular industry, the slaveholders who reap all the fruits, and an idle and lawless rabble who live dispersed over vast plains little removed from absolute barbarism." Critics called this third class a variety of derogatory names: hillbillies, crackers, rednecks, and poor white trash. According to critics, poor whites were not just whites who were poor. They were also supposedly ignorant, diseased, and degenerate. Even slaves were known to chant, "I'd rather be a nigger an' plow ol' Beck / Than a white hillbilly with a long red neck."

Contrary to northern opinion, only about one in four nonslaveholding rural white men was landless and very poor. Some worked as tenants, renting land and struggling to make a go of it. Others survived by herding pigs and cattle. And still others worked for meager wages, ditching, mining, logging, and laying track for railroads. A Georgian remembered that his "father worked by the day when ever he could get work."

Some poor white men earned reputations for mayhem and violence. One visitor claimed that a "bowie-knife was a universal, and a pistol a not at all unusual companion." Edward Isham, an illiterate roustabout, spent about as much time fighting as he did working. When he wasn't engaged in ear-biting, eye-gouging free-for-alls, he was fighting with sticks, shovels, rocks, axes, tomahawks, knives, and guns. Working at what he could find, he took up with and abandoned

many women, gambled, drank, stole, had run-ins with the law, and in 1860 murdered a respected slaveholder, for which he was hanged.

Unlike Isham, most poor white men did not engage in ferocious behavior but instead lived responsible lives. Although they sat at the bottom of the white pecking order, they were ambitious people eager to climb into the yeomanry. The Lipscomb family illustrates the possibility of upward mobility. In 1845, Smith and Sally Lipscomb and their children abandoned their worn-out land in South Carolina for Benton County, Alabama. "Benton is a mountainous country but ther is a heep of good levil land to tend in it," Smith wrote back to his brother. Alabama, Smith said, "will be better for the rising generation if not for ourselves but I think it will be the best for us all that live any length of time." Indeed, primitive living conditions made life precarious. All of the Lipscombs fell ill, but all recovered, and the entire family went to work.

Because they had no money to buy land, they squatted on seven unoccupied acres. With the help of neighbors, they built a 22-by-24-foot cabin, a detached kitchen, and two stables. From daylight to dark, Smith and his sons worked the land, and the first year they produced several bales of cotton and enough food for the table. The women worked just as hard in the cabin, and Sally contributed to the family's income by selling homemade shirts and socks. In time, the Lipscombs bought land and joined the Baptist church, completing their transformation to respectable yeomen.

Many poor whites succeeded in climbing the economic ladder, but in the 1850s upward mobility slowed. The cotton boom of that decade caused planters to expand their operations, driving the price of land beyond the reach of poor families. Whether they gained their own land or not, however, poor whites shared common cultural traits with yeoman farmers.

The Culture of the Plain Folk

Situated on scattered farms and in tiny villages, rural plain folk lived isolated lives. Bad roads and a lack of newspapers meant that life revolved around family, a handful of neighbors, the local church, and perhaps a country store.

Work occupied most hours, but plain folk still found time for pleasure. "Dancing they are all fond of," a visitor to North Carolina discovered, "especially when they can get a fiddle, or bagpipe." They also loved their tobacco. Men smoked and chewed (and spat), while women dipped snuff. But the most popular pastimes of men and boys were fishing and hunting. A traveler in Mississippi recalled that his host sent "two

> ## "Education is not extended to the masses here as at the North."
> — A northern woman visiting the south in the 1850s

of his sons, little fellows that looked almost too small to shoulder a gun," for food. "One went off towards the river and the other struck into the forest, and in a few hours we were feasting on delicious venison, trout and turtle."

Plain folk did not usually associate "book learning" with the basic needs of life. A northern woman visiting the South in the 1850s observed, "Education is not extended to the masses here as at the North." Private academies charged fees that yeomen could not afford, and public schools were scarce. Although most people managed to pick up the "three R's," approximately one southern white man in five was illiterate in 1860, and the rate for white women was even higher. "People here prefer talking to reading," a Virginian remarked. Telling stories, reciting ballads, and singing hymns were important activities in yeoman culture.

Plain folk spent more hours in revival tents than in classrooms. Not all rural whites were religious, but many were, and the most characteristic feature of their evangelical Christian faith was the revival. Preachers spoke day and night to save souls. Revivalism crossed denominational lines, but Baptists and Methodists adopted it most readily and by midcentury had become the South's largest religious groups. By emphasizing free choice and individual worth, the plain folk's religion was hopeful and affirming. Hymns and spirituals provided guides to

Camp Meeting, mid-19th Century
Camp meetings, or revivals, were a key feature of southern evangelical Christianity. Many preachers were itinerants who spoke wherever they could draw a crowd. Here an earnest clergyman preaches his message in an open field, with a tent in the background where coffee is being sold. The colorful individuals who surround the preacher include both the reverent and the not-so-reverent. Some of the audience is clearly skeptical, while others, like the two men sitting on the log, appear merely bemused. And still others have their backs to the preacher and pay no attention at all. Evangelical Christians, however, took their camp meetings, and their religion, seriously. Private Collection/Picture Research Consultants & Archives.

right and wrong — praising humility and steadfastness, condemning drunkenness and profanity. Above all, hymns spoke of the eventual release from worldly sorrows and the assurance of eternal salvation.

REVIEW   Why did the lives of plantation belt yeomen and upcountry yeomen diverge?

▶ Black and Free: On the Middle Ground

All white Southerners — slaveholders and slaveless alike — considered themselves superior to all blacks, both slave and free. Not every black Southerner was a slave. In 1860, some 260,000 (approximately 6 percent) of the region's 4.1 million African Americans were free (see Figure 13.1, page 397). What is surprising is not that their numbers were small but that they existed at all. "**Free black**" seemed increasingly a contradiction to most white Southerners. According to the emerging racial thinking, blacks were supposed to be slaves; only whites were supposed to be free. Blacks who were free stood out, and whites made them more and more targets of oppression. Free blacks stood precariously between slavery and full freedom, on what a free black artisan in Charleston characterized in 1848 as "a middle ground." But they made the most of their freedom, and a few found success despite the restrictions placed on them by white Southerners.

Precarious Freedom

The population of free blacks swelled after the Revolutionary War, when the natural rights philosophy of the Declaration of Independence and the egalitarian message of evangelical Protestantism joined to challenge slavery. A brief flurry of emancipation — the act of freeing from slavery — visited the Upper South, where the ideological assault on slavery coincided with a deep depression in the tobacco economy. By 1810, free blacks in the South numbered more than 100,000, a fact that worried white Southerners, who, because of the cotton boom, wanted more slaves, not more free blacks.

In the 1820s and 1830s, state legislatures acted to stem the growth of the free black population and to shrink the liberty of those blacks who had gained their freedom. New laws denied masters the right to free their slaves. Other laws humiliated and restricted free blacks by subjecting them to special taxes, prohibiting them from interstate travel, denying them the right to have schools and to participate in politics, and requiring them to carry "freedom papers" to prove they were not slaves. Increasingly, whites subjected free blacks to the same laws as slaves. Free blacks could not testify under oath in a court of law or serve on juries. Like slaves, they were liable to whipping and the treadmill, a wooden wheel with steps on which victims were made to walk until they dropped. Free blacks were forbidden to strike whites, even to defend themselves. "Free negroes belong to a degraded caste of society," a South Carolina judge said in 1848. "They are in no respect on a perfect equality with the white man. . . . They ought, by law, to be compelled to demean themselves as inferiors."

> "Free negroes belong to a degraded caste of society. They are in no respect on a perfect equality with the white man. . . . They ought, by law, to be compelled to demean themselves as inferiors."
>
> — A South Carolina judge in 1848

Laws confined most free African Americans to a constricted life of poverty and dependence. Typically, free blacks were rural, uneducated, unskilled agricultural laborers and domestic servants who had to scramble to survive. Opportunities of any kind — for work, education, or community — were slim. Planters believed that free blacks set a bad example for slaves, subverting the racial subordination that was the essence of slavery.

Whites feared that free blacks might cherish their race more than their status as free people and that as a consequence they would lead slaves in rebellion. In 1822, whites in Charleston accused **Denmark Vesey**, a free black carpenter, of conspiring with plantation slaves to slaughter Charleston's white inhabitants. The authorities rounded up scores of suspects, who, prodded by torture and the threat of death, implicated others in the plot "to riot in blood, outrage, and rapine." Although the city fathers never found any weapons and Vesey and most of the accused steadfastly denied the charges of conspiracy, officials hanged thirty-five black men, including Vesey, and banished another thirty-seven blacks from the state.

Achievement despite Restrictions

Despite increasingly harsh laws and stepped-up persecution, free African Americans made the most of the advantages their status offered.

Unlike slaves, free blacks could legally marry. They could protect their families from arbitrary disruption and pass on their heritage of freedom to their children. Freedom also meant that they could choose occupations and own property. For most, however, these economic rights proved only theoretical, for a majority of the South's free blacks remained propertyless.

Still, some free blacks escaped the poverty and degradation whites thrust on them. Particularly in the cities of Charleston, Savannah, Mobile, and New Orleans, a small elite of free blacks emerged. Urban whites enforced restrictive laws only sporadically, allowing free blacks room to maneuver. The free black elite consisted overwhelmingly of light-skinned African Americans who worked at skilled trades, as tailors, carpenters, mechanics, and the like. The free black elite operated schools for their children and traveled in and out of their states, despite laws forbidding both activities. They worshipped with whites (in separate seating) in the finest churches and lived scattered about in white neighborhoods, not in ghettos. And like elite whites, some owned slaves. Blacks could own slaves because they had the right to own property, which in the South included human property. Of the 3,200 black slaveholders (barely 1 percent of the free black population), most owned only a few family members whom they could not legally free. Others owned slaves in large numbers and exploited them for labor.

One such free black slave owner was William Ellison of South Carolina. Born a slave in 1790, Ellison bought his freedom in 1816 and moved to a thriving plantation district about one hundred miles north of Charleston. He set up business as a cotton gin maker, a trade he had learned as a slave, and by 1835 he was prosperous enough to purchase the home of a former governor of the state. By the time of his death in 1861, he had become a cotton planter, with sixty-three slaves and an 800-acre plantation.

Most free blacks neither became slaveholders nor sought to raise a slave rebellion, as whites accused Denmark Vesey of doing. Rather, most free blacks simply tried to preserve their freedom, which was under increasing attack. Unlike blacks in the North whose freedom was secure, free blacks in the South clung to a precarious freedom by seeking to impress whites with their reliability, economic contributions, and good behavior.

REVIEW   Why did many state legislatures pass laws restricting free blacks' rights in the 1820s and 1830s?

▶ The Politics of Slavery

By the mid-nineteenth century, all southern white men — planters and plain folk alike — and no southern black man, even those who were free, could vote. But even after the South's politics became democratic for the white male population, political power remained unevenly distributed. The non-slaveholding white majority wielded less political power than their numbers indicated. The slave-holding white minority wielded more. Self-conscious, cohesive, and with a well-developed sense of class interest, slaveholders busied themselves with party politics, campaigns, and officeholding and made demands of state governments. As a result, they received significant benefits. Nonslaveholding whites were concerned mainly with preserving their liberties and keeping their taxes low. Collectively, they asked government for little of an economic nature, and they received little.

Slaveholders sometimes worried about non-slaveholders' loyalty to slavery, but the majority of whites accepted the planters' argument that the existing social order served *all* Southerners' interests. Slavery rewarded every white man — no matter how poor — with membership in the South's white ruling race. It also provided the means by which nonslaveholders might someday advance into the ranks of the planters. White men in the South argued furiously about many things, but they agreed that they should take land from Indians, promote agriculture, uphold white supremacy and masculine privilege, and defend slavery from its enemies.

The Democratization of the Political Arena

The political reforms that swept the nation in the first half of the nineteenth century reached deeply into the South. Southern politics became democratic politics — for white men. Southerners eliminated the wealth and property requirements that had once restricted political participation. By the 1850s, every state had extended the right to vote to all adult white males. Most southern states also removed the property requirements for holding state offices. To be sure, undemocratic features lingered. Plantation districts still wielded disproportionate power in several state legislatures. Nevertheless, southern politics took place within an increasingly democratic political structure.

White male suffrage ushered in an era of vigorous electoral competition in the South. Eager voters rushed to the polls to exercise their new rights. High turnouts — often approaching 80 percent — became a hallmark of southern elections. Candidates crisscrossed their electoral districts, speaking to voters who demanded stirring oratory and also good entertainment — barbecues and bands, rum and races. In the South, it seemed, "everybody talked politics everywhere," even the "illiterate and shoeless."

As politics became aggressively democratic, it also grew fiercely partisan. From the 1830s to the 1850s, **Whigs** and **Democrats** battled for the electorate's favor. Both parties presented themselves as the plain white folk's best friend. All candidates declared their allegiance to republican equality and pledged themselves to defend the people's liberty. And each party sought to portray the other as a collection of rich, snobbish, selfish men who had antidemocratic designs up their silk sleeves.

The Whig and Democratic parties sought to serve the people differently, however. Southern Whigs tended, as Whigs did elsewhere in the nation, to favor government intervention in the economy, and Democrats tended to oppose it. Whigs backed state support of banks, railroads, and corporations, arguing that government aid would stimulate the economy, enlarge opportunity, and thus increase the general welfare. Democrats claimed that by granting favors to special economic interests, government intervention threatened individual liberty and restricted the common man's economic opportunity. Beginning with the panic of 1837 (see chapter 11), the parties clashed repeatedly on concrete economic and financial issues.

Planter Power

Whether Whig or Democrat, southern officeholders were likely to be slave owners. The power that slaveholders exerted over slaves did not translate directly into political authority over whites, however. In the nineteenth century, political power could be won only at the ballot box, and almost everywhere nonslaveholders were in the majority. Yet year after year, proud and noisily egalitarian common men elected wealthy slaveholders.

By 1860, the percentage of slave owners in state legislatures ranged from 41 percent in Missouri to nearly 86 percent in North Carolina (Table 13.1). Legislators not only tended to own slaves; they also often owned large numbers. The percentage of planters (individuals with twenty or more slaves) in southern legislatures in 1860 ranged from 5.3 percent in Missouri to 55.4 percent in South Carolina. Even in North Carolina, where only 3 percent of the state's white families belonged to the planter class, more than 36 percent of state legislators

were planters. The democratization of politics in the nineteenth century meant that more ordinary citizens participated in elections, but yeomen did not throw the planters out of office.

Upper-class dominance of southern politics reflected the elite's success in persuading the yeoman majority that what was good for slaveholders was also good for plain folk. In reality, the South had, on the whole, done well by common white men. Most had farms of their own. They participated as equals in a democratic political system. They enjoyed an elevated social status, above all blacks and in theory equal to all other whites. They commanded patriarchal authority over their households. And as long as slavery existed, they could dream of joining the planter class. Slaveless white men found much to celebrate in the slave South.

Most slaveholders took pains to win the plain folk's trust and to nurture their respect. One South Carolinian told his wealthy neighbor that he had a bright political future because he never thought himself "too good to sit down & talk to a poor man." Mary Boykin Chesnut complained about the fawning attention her husband, U.S. senator from South Carolina, showed to poor men, including one who had "mud sticking up through his toes." Smart candidates found ways to convince wary plain folk of their democratic

TABLE 13.1	PERCENT OF SLAVEHOLDERS AND PLANTERS IN SOUTHERN LEGISLATURES, 1860	
Legislature	Slaveholders	Planters*
North Carolina	85.8%	36.6%
South Carolina	81.7	55.4
Alabama	76.3	40.8
Mississippi	73.4	49.5
Georgia	71.6	29.0
Virginia	67.3	24.2
Tennessee	66.0	14.0
Louisiana	63.8	23.5
Kentucky	60.6	8.4
Florida	55.4	20.0
Texas	54.1	18.1
Maryland	53.4	19.3
Arkansas	42.0	13.0
Missouri	41.2	5.3

*Planters: Owned 20 or more slaves.

SOURCE: Adapted from Ralph A. Wooster, *The People in Power: Courthouse and Statehouse in the Lower South, 1850–1860*, page 40. Copyright © 1975 by Ralph A. Wooster. Courtesy of the University of Tennessee Press.

convictions and egalitarian sentiments, whether they were genuine or not.

In 1846 when Walter L. Steele ran for a seat in the North Carolina legislature, he commented sarcastically to a friend that he was "busily engaged in proving to the people, the soundness of my political faith, and the purity of my personal character & playing fool to a considerable extent, as you know, all candidates are obliged to do." He detested pandering to the crowd, but he had learned to speak with "candied tongue."

Georgia politics illustrate how well planters protected their interests in state legislatures. In 1850, about half of the state's revenues came from taxes on slaves, the characteristic form of planter wealth. However, the tax rate on slaves was trifling, only about one-fifth the rate on land. Moreover, planters benefited from public spending far more than other groups did. Financing railroads — which carried cotton to market — was the largest state expenditure. The legislature also established low tax rates on land, the characteristic form of yeoman wealth, which meant that the typical yeoman's annual tax bill was small. Still, relative to their wealth, large slaveholders paid less than did other whites. Relative to their numbers, they got more in return. Slaveholding legislators protected planters' interests while giving the impression of protecting the small farmers' interests as well.

The South's elite defended slavery in other ways. In the 1830s, whites decided that slavery was too important to debate. "So interwoven is [slavery] with our interest, our manners, our climate and our very being," one man declared ominously in 1833, "that no change can ever possibly be effected without a civil commotion from which the heart of a patriot must turn with horror." To end free speech on the slavery question, powerful whites dismissed slavery's critics from college faculties, drove them from pulpits, and hounded them from political life. Sometimes antislavery Southerners fell victim to vigilantes and mob violence. One could defend slavery; one could even delicately suggest mild reforms. But no Southerner could any longer safely call slavery evil or advocate its destruction.

In the South, therefore, the rise of the common man occurred alongside the continuing, even growing, power of the planter class. Rather than pitting slaveholders against nonslaveholders, elections remained an effective means of binding the region's

> **"So interwoven is [slavery] with our interest, our manners, our climate and our very being that no change can ever possibly be effected without a civil commotion."**
> — A southern man in 1833

whites together. Elections affirmed the sovereignty of white men, whether planter or plain folk, and the subordination of African Americans. Those twin themes played well among white women as well. Though unable to vote, white women supported equality for whites and slavery for blacks. In the antebellum South, the politics of slavery helped knit together all of white society.

REVIEW How did planters benefit from their control of state legislatures?

▶ Conclusion: A Slave Society

By the early nineteenth century, northern states had either abolished slavery or put it on the road to extinction, while southern states were building the largest slave society in the New World. Regional differences increased over time, not merely because the South became more and more dominated by slavery, but also because developments in the North rapidly propelled it in a very different direction.

One-third of the South's population was enslaved by 1860. Bondage saddled blacks with enormous physical and spiritual burdens: hard labor, harsh treatment, broken families, and, most important, the denial of freedom itself. Although degraded and exploited, they were not defeated. Out of African memories and New World realities, blacks created a life-affirming African American culture that sustained and strengthened them. Their families, religion, and community provided defenses to white racism and power. Defined as property, they refused to be reduced to things. Perceived as inferior beings, they rejected the notion that they were natural slaves.

Slavery was crucial to the South's distinctiveness and to the loyalty and regional identification of its whites. The South was not merely a society with slaves; it had become a slave society. Slavery shaped the region's economy, culture, social structure, and politics. Whites south of the Mason-Dixon line believed that racial slavery was necessary and just. By making all blacks a pariah class, all whites gained a measure of equality and harmony.

Many features of white southern life helped to confine class tensions: the wide availability of land, rapid economic mobility, the democratic nature of political life, the patriarchal power among all white men, and, most of all, slavery. All stress along class lines was not erased, however, and anxious slaveholders continued to worry that yeomen would defect from the proslavery consensus. But during the 1850s, white Southerners' near universal acceptance of slavery would increasingly unite them in political opposition to their northern neighbors.

► Selected Bibliography

Slaveholders and the Economy

David L. Carlton and Peter A. Coclanis, *The South, the Nation, and the World: Perspectives on Southern Economic Development* (2003).

Steven Deyle, *Carry Me Back: The Domestic Slave Trade in American Life* (2005).

Richard Follett, *The Sugar Masters: Planters and Slaves in Louisiana's Cane World, 1820–1860* (2005).

Jonathan Martin, *Divided Mastery: Slave Hiring in the American South* (2004).

James David Miller, *South by Southwest: Planter Emigration and Identity in the Slave South* (2002).

Gavin Wright, *The Political Economy of the Cotton South: Households, Markets, and Wealth in the Nineteenth Century* (1978).

Slaves, Slavery, and Race Relations

Ira Berlin, *Generations of Captivity: A History of African-American Slaves* (2003).

Thomas C. Buchanan, *Black Life on the Mississippi: Slaves, Free Blacks, and the Western Steamboat World* (2004).

Erskine Clarke, *Dwelling Place: A Plantation Epic* (2005).

Eugene D. Genovese, *Roll, Jordan, Roll: The World the Slave Made* (1974).

Gwendolyn Midlo Hall, *Slavery and African Ethnicities in the Americas: Restoring the Links* (2005).

Anthony E. Kaye, *Joining Places: Slave Neighborhoods in the Old South* (2007).

Dylan C. Penningroth, *The Claims of Kinfolk: African American Property and Community in the Nineteenth-Century South* (2003).

Brenda E. Stevenson, *Life in Black and White: Family and Community in the Slave South* (1996).

Leonard Todd, *Carolina Clay: The Life and Legend of the Slave Potter Dave* (2008).

Society and Culture

Ira Berlin, *Slaves without Masters: The Free Negro in the Antebellum South* (1974).

Charles C. Bolton and Scott P. Culclasure, eds., *The Confessions of Edward Isham: A Poor White Life of the Old South* (1998).

Christine Jacobson Carter, *Southern Single Blessedness: Unmarried Women in the Urban South, 1800–1865* (2006).

Craig T. Friend and Lorri Glover, eds., *Southern Manhood: Perspectives on Masculinity in the Old South* (2004).

Steven Hahn, *The Roots of Southern Populism: Yeoman Farmers and the Transformation of the Georgia Upcountry, 1850–1890* (1983).

Christine Leigh Heyrman, *Southern Cross: The Beginnings of the Bible Belt* (1997).

Anya Jabour, *Scarlett's Sisters: Young Women in the Old South* (2007).

Michael P. Johnson and James L. Roark, *Black Masters: A Free Family of Color in the Old South* (1984).

Stephanie McCurry, *Masters of Small Worlds: Yeoman Households, Gender Relations, and the Political Culture of the Antebellum South* (1995).

Adam Rothman, *Slave Country: American Expansion and the Deep South* (2005).

Bertram Wyatt-Brown, *Southern Honor: Ethics and Behavior in the Old South* (1982).

Jeffrey Robert Young, *Domesticating Slavery: The Master Class in Georgia and South Carolina, 1670–1837* (1999).

Politics and Political Culture

Anthony Gene Carey, *Parties, Slavery, and the Union in Antebellum Georgia* (1997).

William J. Cooper Jr., *Liberty and Slavery: Southern Politics to 1860* (1983).

Lacy K. Ford Jr., *Deliver Us from Evil: The Slavery Question in the Old South* (2009).

Michael Perman, *Pursuit of Unity: A Political History of the American South* (2009).

Elizabeth R. Varon, *We Mean to Be Counted: White Women and Politics in Antebellum Virginia* (1998).

Peter Wallenstein, *From Slave South to New South: Public Policy in Nineteenth-Century Georgia* (1987).

► **FOR MORE BOOKS ABOUT TOPICS IN THIS CHAPTER,** see the Online Bibliography at **bedfordstmartins.com/roark**.

► **FOR ADDITIONAL PRIMARY SOURCES FROM THIS PERIOD,** see Michael Johnson, ed., *Reading the American Past*, Fifth Edition.

► **FOR WEB SITES, IMAGES, AND DOCUMENTS RELATED TO TOPICS AND PLACES IN THIS CHAPTER,** visit Make History at **bedfordstmartins.com/roark**.

Reviewing Chapter 13

REVIEW QUESTIONS

Use key terms and dates to support your answer.

1. Why did the nineteenth-century southern economy remain primarily agricultural? (pp. 495–404)

2. Why did the ideology of paternalism gain currency among planters in the nineteenth century? (pp. 404–410)

3. What types of resistance did slaves participate in, and why did slave resistance rarely take the form of rebellion? (pp. 410–415)

4. Why did the lives of plantation belt yeomen and upcountry yeomen diverge? (pp. 415–419)

5. Why did many state legislatures pass laws restricting free blacks' rights in the 1820s and 1830s? (pp. 419–420)

6. How did planters benefit from their control of state legislatures? (pp. 420–422)

MAKING CONNECTIONS

Draw on key terms, the timeline, and review questions.

1. By the mid-nineteenth century, the South had become a "cotton kingdom." How did cotton's profitability shape the region's antebellum development? In your answer, discuss the region's distinctive demographic and economic features.

2. How did southern white legislators and intellectuals attempt to strengthen the institution of slavery in the 1820s? What prompted them to undertake this work? In your answer, be sure to explore regional and national influences.

3. Although bondage restricted slaves' autonomy and left slaves vulnerable to extreme abuse, they resisted slavery. Discuss the variety of ways in which slaves attempted to lessen the harshness of slavery. What were the short- and long-term effects of their efforts?

4. Despite vigorous political competition in the South, by 1860 legislative power was largely concentrated in the hands of a regional minority — slaveholders. Why were slaveholders politically dominant? In your answer, be sure to consider how the region's biracialism contributed to its politics.

LINKING TO THE PAST

Link events in this chapter to earlier events.

1. Compare and contrast Northerners' defense of free labor and white Southerners' defense of slave labor. (See chapter 12.)

2. How did President Andrew Jackson's Indian removal policies pave the way for the South's cotton empire? (See chapter 11.)

▶ FOR PRACTICE QUIZZES AND OTHER STUDY TOOLS, visit the Online Study Guide at bedfordstmartins.com/roark.

TIMELINE 1808–1860

1808	• External slave trade outlawed.
1810s–1850s	• Suffrage extended throughout South to all adult white males.
1813–1814	• Creek War opens Indian land to white settlement.
1820s–1830s	• Southern legislatures enact slave codes to strengthen slavery.
	• Southern legislatures enact laws to restrict growth of free black population.
	• Southern intellectuals fashion systematic defense of slavery.
1822	• Denmark Vesey executed for fomenting slave rebellion.
1829	• *Appeal . . . to the Coloured Citizens of the World* published.
1830	• Southern slaves number approximately two million.
1831	• Nat Turner's slave rebellion.
	• First issue of the *Liberator* published.
1834	• *Catechism for Colored Persons* published.
1836	• Arkansas admitted to Union as slave state.
1840	• Cotton accounts for more than 60 percent of nation's exports.
1845	• Texas and Florida admitted to Union as slave states.
1860	• Southern slaves number nearly four million, one-third of South's population.

JOHN BROWN'S PIKES

Scorning what he called "milk-and-water" abolitionists who only talked about slavery, John Brown favored "action!" In 1859, when he brought his abolitionist war to Harpers Ferry, Virginia, he carried with him 950 pikes — handsome but deadly spears made by a Connecticut blacksmith, which he expected to put into the hands of rebelling slaves. Bloody pikes, he thought, would end slavery in America. After Brown's failure at Harpers Ferry, townspeople sold many of the weapons as souvenirs. Earlier in the 1850s, violence — such as this gun fight between antislavery and proslavery forces — had erupted in what became known as "Bleeding Kansas."

Pikes: Chicago Historical Society; background image: © Bettmann/Corbis.

14

The House Divided
1846–1861

OTHER THAN TWENTY CHILDREN, JOHN BROWN DID NOT HAVE MUCH to show for his life in 1859. Grizzled, gnarled, and fifty-nine years old, he had for decades lived like a nomad, hauling his large family back and forth across six states as he tried desperately to better himself. He turned his hand to farming, raising sheep, running a tannery, and selling wool, but failure dogged him. The world had given John Brown some hard licks — and yet it had not budged a conviction he had held since childhood: that slavery was wrong and ought to be destroyed. In the wake of the fighting that erupted over the future of slavery in Kansas in the 1850s, his beliefs turned violent. On May 24, 1856, he led an eight-man antislavery posse in the midnight slaughter of five allegedly proslavery men at Pottawatomie, Kansas. He told Mahala Doyle, whose husband and two oldest sons he killed, that if a man stood between him and what he thought right, he would take that man's life as calmly as he would eat breakfast.

After the killings, Brown slipped out of Kansas and reemerged in the East. More than ever, he was a man on fire for abolition. He spent thirty months begging money to support his vague plan for military operations against slavery. He captivated genteel easterners who were awed by his iron-willed determination and courage, but most could not accept violence. "These men are all talk," Brown declared. "What is needed is action — action!" But enough donated to the hypnotic-eyed Brown that he was able to gather a small band of antislavery warriors.

On the night of October 16, 1859, Brown took his war against slavery into the South. With only twenty-one men, including five African Americans, he invaded Harpers Ferry, Virginia. His band seized the town's armory and rifle works, but the invaders were immediately surrounded, first by local militia and then by Colonel Robert E. Lee, who commanded the U.S. troops in the area. When Brown refused to surrender, federal soldiers charged with bayonets. Although a few of Brown's raiders escaped, federal forces killed ten of his men (including two of his sons) and captured seven, among them Brown.

"When I strike, the bees will begin to swarm," Brown told Frederick Douglass a few months before the raid. As slaves rushed to Harpers Ferry, Brown said, he would arm them with the pikes he carried with him and with weapons stolen from the armory. They would then fight a war of liberation. Brown, however, neglected to inform the slaves when he had arrived in Harpers Ferry, and the few who knew of his arrival wanted nothing to do with his enterprise. "It was not a slave insurrection," Abraham Lincoln observed. "It was an attempt by white men to get up a revolt among slaves, in which the slaves refused to participate. In fact, it was so absurd that the slaves, with all their ignorance, saw plainly enough it could not succeed."

Although Brown's raid ended in utter defeat, white Southerners viewed it as proof of their growing suspicion that Northerners actively sought to incite slaves in bloody rebellion. For more than a decade, Northerners and Southerners had accused one another of hostile intentions, and by 1859 emotions were raw. Sectional tension was as old as the Constitution, but hostility had escalated with the outbreak of war with Mexico in May 1846 (see chapter 12). Only three months after the war began, national expansion and the slavery issue intersected when Representative David Wilmot introduced a bill to prohibit slavery in any territory that might be acquired as a result of the war. After that, the problem of slavery in the territories became the principal wedge that divided the nation.

"Mexico is to us the forbidden fruit," South Carolina senator John C. Calhoun declared at the war's outset. "The penalty of eating it [is] to subject our institutions to political death." For a decade and a half, the slavery issue intertwined with the fate of former Mexican land, poisoning the national political debate. Slavery proved powerful enough to transform party politics into sectional politics. Rather than Whigs and Democrats confronting one another across party lines, Northerners and Southerners eyed one another hostilely across the Mason-Dixon line. Sectional politics encouraged the South's separatist impulses. Southern separatism, a fitful tendency before the Mexican-American War, gained strength with each confrontation. As the nation lurched from crisis to crisis, southern disaffection and alienation mounted, and support for compromise and conciliation eroded. The era began with a crisis of union and ended with the Union in even graver peril. As Abraham Lincoln predicted in 1858, "A house divided against itself cannot stand."

John Brown
In this 1859 photograph, John Brown appears respectable, even statesmanlike, but contemporaries debated his mental state and moral character, and the debate still rages. Critics argue that he was a bloody terrorist, a religious fanatic who believed that he was touched by God for a great purpose, one for which he was willing to die. Admirers see a resolute and selfless hero, a rare white man who believed that black people were the equals of whites, and a shrewd political observer who recognized that only violence would end slavery in America. Library of Congress.

▶ The Bitter Fruits of War

Between 1846 and 1848, the nation grew by 1.2 million square miles, an incredible two-thirds. The gold rush of 1849 transformed the sleepy frontier of California into a booming, thriving economy (see chapter 12). The 1850s witnessed new "rushes," for gold in Colorado and silver in Nevada's Comstock Lode. People from around the world flocked to the West, where they produced a vibrant agriculture as well as tons of gold and silver. But it quickly became clear that Northerners and Southerners had very different visions of the West, particularly the place of slavery in its future.

History provided contradictory precedents for handling slavery in the territories. In 1787, the Northwest Ordinance banned slavery north of the Ohio River. In 1803, slavery was allowed to remain in the newly acquired Louisiana Territory. The Missouri Compromise of 1820 prohibited slavery in part of that territory but allowed it in the rest. In 1846, when the war with Mexico made likely the acquisition of new territory for the United States, politicians offered various plans. But when the war ended in 1848, Congress had made no headway in solving the issue of slavery in the land acquired from Mexico, called the Mexican cession. In 1850, Congress patched together a settlement, one that Americans hoped would be permanent.

The Wilmot Proviso and the Expansion of Slavery

In the years leading up to the Civil War, Americans focused not on slavery where it existed but on the possibility that slavery might expand into areas where it did not exist. Most Americans agreed that the Constitution left the issue of slavery to the individual states to decide. Northern states had done away with slavery, while southern states

"Guarding the Corn Fields," 1850
Neither proslavery southerners nor antislavery northerners were much concerned about the Native Americans who inhabited the western lands they coveted. But Seth Eastman, a young military officer posted to Indian Territory in Minnesota in the 1830s, had married the daughter of a chief, learned the Sioux language, and recorded sympathetically the lives he encountered. Women were responsible for agriculture, and when the corn began to ripen, they built scaffolds from which they could repel the flocks of blackbirds that preyed on the corn. Corn supplemented the game, fish, berries, and wild rice that formed the bulk of the Sioux diet.
W. Duncan and Nivin MacMillan Foundation. Photo courtesy Minneapolis Institute of Arts.

had retained it. But what about slavery in the nation's territories? The Constitution states that "Congress shall have power to . . . make all needful rules and regulations respecting the territory . . . belonging to the United States." The debate about slavery, then, turned toward Congress.

The spark for the national debate appeared in August 1846 when a Democratic representative from Pennsylvania, David Wilmot, proposed that Congress bar slavery from all lands acquired in the war with Mexico. The Mexicans had abolished slavery in their country, and Wilmot declared, "God forbid that we should be the means of planting this institution upon it."

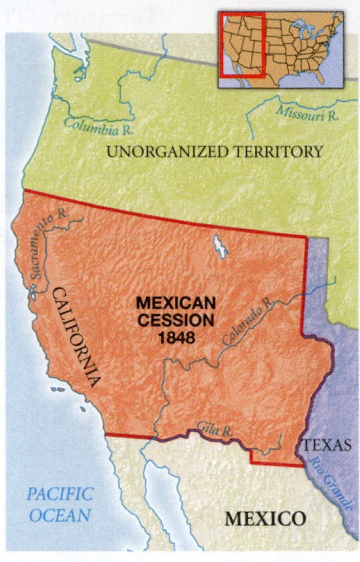

Mexican Cession, 1848

Regardless of party affiliation, Northerners lined up behind the **Wilmot Proviso**. Many supported free soil, by which they meant territory in which slavery would be prohibited, because they wanted to preserve the West for **free labor**, for hardworking, self-reliant free men, not for slaveholders and slaves. But support also came from those who were simply anti-South. New slave territories would eventually mean new slave states, and Northerners opposed magnifying the political power of Southerners. Wilmot himself said his proposal would blunt "*the power of slaveholders*" in the national government.

Additional support for free soil came from Northerners who were hostile to blacks and wanted to reserve new land for whites. Wilmot himself blatantly encouraged racist support when he declared, "I would preserve for free white labor a fair country, a rich inheritance, where the sons of toil, of my own race and own color, can live without the disgrace which association with negro slavery brings upon free labor." It is no wonder that some called the Wilmot Proviso the "White Man's Proviso."

The thought that slavery might be excluded in the territories outraged white Southerners. Like Northerners, they regarded the West as a ladder for economic and social opportunity. They also believed that the exclusion of slavery was a slap in the face to veterans of the Mexican-American War, at least half of whom were Southerners. "When the war-worn soldier returns home," one Alabaman asked, "is he to be told that he cannot carry his property to the country won by his blood?"

Southern leaders also sought to maintain political parity with the North to protect the South's interests, especially slavery. The need seemed especially urgent in the 1840s, when the North's population and wealth were booming. James Henry Hammond of South Carolina predicted that ten new states would be carved from the acquired Mexican land. If free soil won, the North would "ride over us roughshod" in Congress, he claimed. "Our only safety is in *equality* of power."

The two sides squared off in the nation's capital. Because Northerners had a majority in the House, they easily passed the Wilmot Proviso. In the Senate, however, where slave states outnumbered free states fifteen to fourteen, Southerners defeated it in 1847. Senator **John C. Calhoun** of South Carolina boldly denied that Congress had the constitutional authority to exclude slavery from the nation's territories. He argued that because the territories were the "joint and common property" of all the states, Congress could not bar citizens of one state from migrating with their property (including slaves) to the territories. Whereas Wilmot demanded that Congress slam shut the door to slavery, Calhoun called on Congress to hold the door wide open.

In 1847, Senator **Lewis Cass** of Michigan offered a compromise through the doctrine of **popular sovereignty**, by which the people who settled the territories would decide for themselves slavery's fate. This solution, Cass argued, sat squarely in the American tradition of democracy and local self-government. It had the added attraction of removing the incendiary issue of the expansion of slavery from the nation's capital and lodging it in distant territorial legislatures, where it would excite fewer passions.

Popular sovereignty's most attractive feature was its ambiguity about the precise moment when settlers could determine slavery's fate. Northern advocates believed that the decision on slavery could be made as soon as the first territorial legislature assembled. With free-soil majorities likely because of the North's greater population, they would shut the door to slavery almost before the first slave arrived. Southern supporters believed that popular sovereignty guaranteed that slavery would be unrestricted throughout the entire territorial period. Only at

THE PROMISE OF TECHNOLOGY

Daguerreotypes

In the late 1830s, Frenchman Louis Daguerre improved on existing technology when he discovered how to keep photographic images from fading, a technique that arrived in New York City by 1839. The daguerreotype photographic process was cumbersome and complex and required several minutes of exposure, making candid shots impossible. Despite their shortcomings, daguerreotypes were an instant success, and by the 1850s Americans were buying millions of images each year.

No early American photographer was more important than Mathew Brady. In 1844, he opened his first gallery in New York City. Seeing himself as a historian of the nation, he shot portraits of distinguished citizens — presidents, congressmen, senators, and statesmen — as well as of everyday people who walked into his gallery. In 1850, Brady shot this image of a hollow-cheeked and dark-eyed John C. Calhoun, who had only months to live. Brady hoped that the new technology of photography would serve as a moral agent furthering political reconciliation and peace. By 1860, however, daguerreotypes had all but disappeared from American life, replaced by more efficient photographic processes, and the Union remained imperiled. Can you imagine why Mathew Brady believed that photographs could encourage "political reconciliation and peace"? National Portrait Gallery, Smithsonian Institution/Art Resource, NY.

the very end, when settlers in a territory drew up a constitution and applied for statehood, could they decide the issue of slavery. By then, slavery would have sunk deep roots. As long as the matter of timing remained vague, popular sovereignty gave hope to both sides.

When Congress ended its session in 1848, no plan had won a majority in both houses. Northerners who demanded no new slave territory anywhere, ever, and Southerners who demanded entry for their slave property into all territories, or else, staked out their extreme positions. Unresolved in Congress, the territorial question naturally became an issue in the presidential election of 1848.

The Election of 1848

When President Polk, worn-out and ailing, chose not to seek reelection, the Democratic convention nominated Lewis Cass of Michigan, the man most closely associated with popular sovereignty. The Whigs nominated a Mexican-American War hero, General **Zachary Taylor**. The Whigs declined to adopt a party platform, betting that the combination

of a military hero and total silence on the slavery issue would unite their divided party. Taylor, who owned more than one hundred slaves on plantations in Mississippi and Louisiana, was hailed by Georgia politician Robert Toombs as a "Southern man, a slaveholder, a cotton planter."

Antislavery Whigs balked and looked for an alternative. Senator **Charles Sumner** called for a major political realignment, "one grand Northern party of Freedom." In the summer of 1848, antislavery Whigs and antislavery Democrats founded the **Free-Soil Party**, nominating a Democrat, Martin Van Buren, for president and a Whig, Charles Francis Adams, for vice president. The platform boldly proclaimed, "Free soil, free speech, free labor, and free men."

The November election dashed the hopes of the Free-Soilers. Although they succeeded in making slavery the campaign's central issue, they did not carry a single state. The major parties went through contortions to present their candidates favorably in both North and South, and their evasions succeeded. Taylor won the

General Taylor Cigar Case
This papier-mâché cigar case portrays General Zachary Taylor, Whig presidential candidate in 1848, in a colorful scene from the Mexican-American War. Shown here as a dashing, elegant officer, Taylor was in fact a short, thickset, and roughly dressed Indian fighter who had spent his career commanding small frontier garrisons. The inscription reminds voters that Taylor was a victor in the first four battles fought in the war and directs attention away from the fact that in politics he was a rank amateur. Collection of Janice L. and David J. Frent.

all-important electoral vote 163 to 127, carrying eight of the fifteen slave states and seven of the fifteen free states (Map 14.1). (Wisconsin had entered the Union earlier in 1848 as the fifteenth free state.) Northern voters were not yet ready for Sumner's "one grand Northern party of Freedom," but the struggle over slavery in the territories had shaken the major parties badly.

Debate and Compromise

Southern slaveholder Zachary Taylor entered the White House in March 1849 and almost immediately shocked the nation by championing a free-soil solution to the Mexican cession. Believing that he could avoid further sectional strife if California and New Mexico skipped the

territorial stage, the new president encouraged the settlers to apply for admission to the Union as states. Predominantly antislavery, the settlers began writing free-state constitutions. "For the first time," Mississippian Jefferson Davis lamented, "we are about permanently to destroy the balance of power between the sections."

Congress convened in December 1849, beginning one of the most contentious and most significant sessions in its history. President Taylor urged Congress to admit California as a free state immediately and to admit New Mexico, which lagged behind a few months, as soon as it applied. Southerners exploded. A North Carolinian declared that Southerners who would "consent to be thus degraded and enslaved, ought to be whipped through their fields by their own negroes."

Into this rancorous scene stepped Senator Henry Clay of Kentucky, the architect of Union-saving compromises in the Missouri and nullification crises (see chapters 10 and 11). Clay offered a series of resolutions meant to answer and balance "all questions in controversy between the free and slave states, growing out of the subject of slavery." Admit California as a free state, he proposed, but organize the rest of the Southwest without restrictions on slavery. Require Texas to abandon its claim to parts of New Mexico, but compensate it by assuming its preannexation debt. Abolish the domestic slave trade in Washington, D.C., but confirm slavery itself in the nation's capital. Reassert Congress's lack of authority to interfere with the interstate slave trade, and enact a more effective fugitive slave law.

Both antislavery advocates and "fire-eaters" (as radical Southerners who urged secession from the Union were called) savaged Clay's plan. Senator Salmon P. Chase of Ohio ridiculed it as "sentiment for the North, substance for the South." Senator

MAP 14.1
The Election of 1848

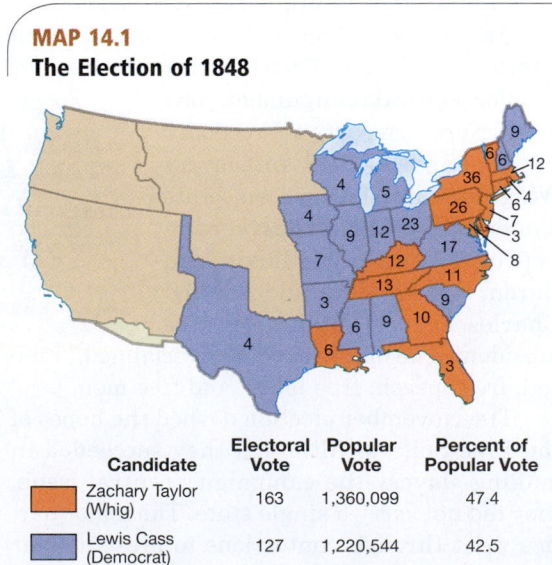

Candidate	Electoral Vote	Popular Vote	Percent of Popular Vote
Zachary Taylor (Whig)	163	1,360,099	47.4
Lewis Cass (Democrat)	127	1,220,544	42.5
Martin Van Buren (Free-Soil)	0	291,263	10.1

Henry S. Foote of Mississippi denounced it as more offensive to the South than the speeches of abolitionists William Lloyd Garrison, Wendell Phillips, and Frederick Douglass combined. The most ominous response came from John C. Calhoun, who charged that unending northern agitation on the slavery question had "snapped" many of the "cords which bind these states together in one common union." He argued that the fragile political unity of North and South depended on continued equal representation in the Senate, which Clay's plan for a free California destroyed. "As things now stand," he said in February 1850, the South "cannot with safety remain in the Union."

After Clay and Calhoun had spoken, it was time for the third member of the "great triumvirate," Senator Daniel Webster of Massachusetts,

Henry Clay Offering His California Compromise to the Senate on 5 February 1850
Pennsylvania-born artist Peter F. Rothermel, who specialized in dramatic historical paintings, captures the high intensity of the seventy-three-year-old Kentuckian's last significant political act. The citizens who packed the galleries of the U.S. Senate had come to hear "the lion of the day," and they were not disappointed. A renowned orator, Clay eloquently explained that his package of compromises required mutual concessions from both North and South but no sacrifice of "great principle" from either. Friends called his performance the "crowning grace to his public life." The Granger Collection, NY.

to address the Senate. Like Clay, Webster defended compromise. He told Northerners that the South had legitimate complaints, but he told Southerners that secession from the Union would mean civil war. He appealed for an end to reckless proposals and, to the dismay of many Northerners, mentioned by name the Wilmot Proviso. A legal ban on slavery in the territories was unnecessary, he said, because the harsh climate effectively prohibited the expansion of cotton and slaves into the new American Southwest. "I would not take pains uselessly to reaffirm an ordinance of nature, nor to reenact the will of God," Webster declared.

Free-soil forces recoiled from what they saw as Webster's desertion. Boston clergyman and abolitionist Theodore Parker could only conclude that "Southern men" must have offered Webster the presidency. Senator William H. Seward of New York responded that Webster's and Clay's compromise with slavery was "radically wrong and essentially vicious." He flatly rejected Calhoun's argument that Congress lacked the constitutional authority to exclude slavery from the territories. In any case, Seward said, in the most sensational moment in his address, there was a "higher law than the Constitution" — the law of God — to ensure freedom in all the public domain. Claiming that God was a Free-Soiler did nothing to cool the superheated political atmosphere.

> "As things now stand, [the South] cannot with safety remain in the Union."
> — HENRY CLAY

In May 1850, the Senate considered a bill that joined Clay's resolutions into a single comprehensive package, known as the Omnibus Bill because it was a vehicle on which "every sort of passenger" could ride. Clay bet that a majority of Congress wanted compromise and that the members would vote for the package, even though it might contain provisions they disliked. But the omnibus strategy backfired. Free-Soilers and proslavery Southerners voted down the comprehensive plan.

Fortunately for those who favored a settlement, Senator **Stephen A. Douglas**, a rising Democratic star from Illinois, broke the bill into its parts and skillfully ushered each through Congress. The agreement Douglas won in September 1850 was very much the one Clay had proposed in January. California entered the Union as a free state. New Mexico and Utah became territories where slavery would be decided by popular sovereignty. Texas accepted its boundary with New Mexico and received $10 million from the federal government. Congress ended the slave trade in the District of Columbia but

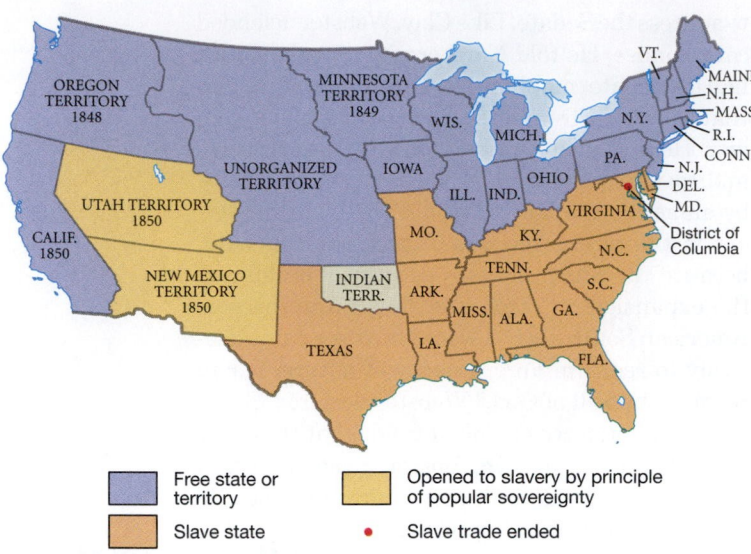

MAP 14.2

The Compromise of 1850

The patched-together sectional agreement was both clumsy and unstable. Few Americans — in either North or South — supported all five parts of the Compromise.

Legend for map:
- Free state or territory
- Slave state
- Opened to slavery by principle of popular sovereignty
- Slave trade ended

enacted a more stringent fugitive slave law. In September, Millard Fillmore, who had become president when Zachary Taylor died in July, signed into law each bill, collectively known as the **Compromise of 1850** (Map 14.2).

Actually, the Compromise of 1850 was not a true compromise at all. Douglas's parliamentary skill, not a spirit of conciliation, was responsible for the legislative success. Still, the nation breathed a sigh of relief, for the Compromise preserved the Union and peace for the moment. Some recognized, however, that the Compromise scarcely touched the deeper conflict over slavery. Free-Soiler Salmon Chase observed, "The question of slavery in the territories has been avoided. It has not been settled."

> **REVIEW** Why did responses to the Wilmot Proviso split along sectional rather than party lines?

▶ The Sectional Balance Undone

The Compromise of 1850 began to come apart almost immediately. The thread that unraveled it was not slavery in the Southwest, the crux of the disagreement, but runaway slaves in New England, a part of the settlement that had pre-

viously received little attention. Instead of restoring calm, the Compromise brought the horrors of slavery into the North.

Millions of Northerners who had never seen a runaway slave confronted slavery in the early 1850s. Harriet Beecher Stowe's *Uncle Tom's Cabin*, a novel that vividly depicts the brutality of the South's "peculiar institution," aroused passions so deep that many found goodwill toward white Southerners nearly impossible. But no groundswell of antislavery sentiment compelled Congress to reopen the slavery controversy. Politicians did it themselves. Four years after Congress stitched the sectional compromise together, it ripped the threads out. With the Kansas-Nebraska Act, it again posed the question of slavery in the territories, the deadliest of all sectional issues.

The Fugitive Slave Act

The issue of runaway slaves was as old as the Constitution, which contained a provision for the return of any "person held to service or labor in one state" who escaped to another. In 1793, a federal law gave muscle to the provision by authorizing slave owners to enter other states to recapture their slave property. Proclaiming the 1793 law a license to kidnap free blacks, northern states in the 1830s began passing "personal liberty laws" that provided fugitives with some protection.

Some northern communities also formed vigilance committees to help runaways. Each year, a few hundred slaves escaped into free states and found friendly northern "conductors" who put them aboard the **underground railroad**, which was not a railroad at all but a series of secret "stations" (hideouts) on the way to Canada. Harriet Tubman, an escaped slave from Maryland, returned to the South more than a dozen times and guided more than three hundred slaves to freedom in this way.

Furious about northern interference, Southerners in 1850 insisted on the stricter fugitive slave law that was passed as part of the Compromise. According to the **Fugitive Slave Act**, to seize an alleged slave, a slaveholder simply had to appear before a commissioner and swear that the runaway was his. The commissioner earned $10 for every individual returned to slavery but only $5 for those set free. Most galling to Northerners, the law stipulated that all citizens were expected to assist officials in apprehending runaways.

Abolitionist Theodore Parker denounced the law as "a hateful statute of kidnappers." In Boston in February 1851, an angry crowd overpowered federal marshals and snatched a runaway named Shadrach from a courtroom, put him on the underground railroad, and whisked him off to Canada. Three years later, when another Boston crowd rushed the courthouse in a failed attempt to rescue Anthony Burns, who had recently fled slavery in Richmond, a guard was shot dead. Martha Russell, a writer for the antislavery journal *National Era*, was among the angry crowd that watched Burns being escorted to the ship that would return him to Virginia. "Did you ever feel every drop of blood in you boiling and seething, throbbing and burning, until it seemed you should suffocate?" she asked. "I have felt all this today. I have seen that poor slave, Anthony Burns, carried back to slavery!"

To white Southerners, it seemed that fanatics of the "higher law" creed had whipped Northerners into a frenzy of massive resistance. Actually, the overwhelming majority of fugitives claimed by slaveholders were reenslaved peacefully. But brutal enforcement of the unpopular law had a radicalizing effect in the North, particularly in New England. To Southerners it seemed that Northerners had betrayed the Compromise. "The continued existence of the United States as one nation," warned the *Southern Literary Messenger*, "depends upon the full and faithful execution of the Fugitive Slave Bill."

> **"The continued existence of the United States as one nation depends upon the full and faithful execution of the Fugitive Slave Bill."**
> — *Southern Literary Messenger*

Ellen Craft in Disguise

In 1848, William and Ellen Craft, a slave couple from Macon, Georgia, executed a daring escape. Light-skinned, Ellen disguised herself as a sickly southern gentleman who was traveling to Philadelphia for medical treatment. She carried her right arm in a sling to explain why she couldn't sign travel documents. William acted as her personal servant as they anxiously made their way by train to Savannah, then on to Philadelphia by boat and train. The Crafts told their daring story throughout the North until the Fugitive Slave Law of 1850 drove them to Britain, where adoring crowds greeted them as celebrities. The Library of the University of North Carolina, Chapel Hill.

ELLEN CRAFT,
The fugitive Slave.

Uncle Tom's Cabin

The spectacle of shackled African Americans being herded south seared the conscience of every Northerner who witnessed such a scene. But even more Northerners were turned against slavery by a novel. **Harriet Beecher Stowe**, a white Northerner who had never set foot on a plantation, made the South's slaves into flesh-and-blood human beings almost more real than life.

A member of a famous clan of preachers, teachers, and reformers, Stowe despised the slave catchers and wrote to expose the sin of slavery. Published as a book in 1852, *Uncle Tom's Cabin, or Life among the Lowly* became a blockbuster hit, selling 300,000 copies in its first year and more than 2 million copies within ten years. Stowe's characters leaped from the page. Here was the gentle slave Uncle Tom, a Christian saint who forgave those who beat him to death; the courageous slave Eliza, who fled with her child across the frozen Ohio River; and the fiendish overseer Simon Legree, whose Louisiana plantation was a nightmare of torture and death.

135,000 SETS, 270,000 VOLUMES SOLD.

UNCLE TOM'S CABIN

FOR SALE HERE.

AN EDITION FOR THE MILLION, COMPLETE IN 1 Vol., PRICE 37 1-2 CENTS.
" " IN GERMAN, IN 1 Vol., PRICE 50 CENTS.
" " IN 2 Vols,. CLOTH, 6 PLATES, PRICE $1.50.
SUPERB ILLUSTRATED EDITION, IN 1 Vol., WITH 153 ENGRAVINGS,
PRICES FROM $2.50 TO $5.00.

The Greatest Book of the Age.

***Uncle Tom's Cabin* Poster**
After Congress passed the Fugitive Slave Act in 1850, Harriet Beecher Stowe's outraged sister-in-law told her, "Now Hattie, if I could use a pen as you can, I would write something that will make this whole nation feel what an accursed thing slavery is." This poster advertising the novel Stowe wrote calls it "The Greatest Book of the Age." The novel's vivid characters gripped readers' imaginations and fueled the growing antislavery crusade. The Granger Collection, NY.

Mother of seven children, Stowe aimed her most powerful blows at slavery's destructive impact on the family. Her character Eliza succeeds in keeping her son from being sold away, but other mothers are not so fortunate. When told that her infant has been sold, Lucy drowns herself. Driven half mad by the sale of a son and daughter, Cassy decides "never again [to] let a child live to grow up!" She gives her third child an opiate and watches as "he slept to death."

Northerners shed tears and sang praises to *Uncle Tom's Cabin*. The poet Henry Wadsworth Longfellow judged it "one of the greatest triumphs recorded in literary history." What Northerners accepted as truth, Southerners denounced as slander. The Virginian George F. Holmes proclaimed Stowe a member of the "Woman's Rights" and "Higher Law" schools and dismissed the novel as a work of "intense fanaticism." Although

it is impossible to measure precisely the impact of a novel on public opinion, *Uncle Tom's Cabin* clearly helped to crystallize northern sentiment against slavery and to confirm white Southerners' suspicion that they no longer received any sympathy in the free states.

Other writers — ex-slaves who knew life in slave cabins firsthand — also produced stinging indictments of slavery. Solomon Northup's compelling *Twelve Years a Slave* (1853) sold 27,000 copies in two years, and the powerful *Narrative of the Life of Frederick Douglass, as Told by Himself* (1845) eventually sold more than 30,000 copies. But no work touched the North's conscience as did the novel by a free white woman. A decade after its publication, when Stowe visited Abraham Lincoln at the White House, he reportedly said, "So you are the little woman who wrote the book that made this great war."

The Kansas-Nebraska Act

As the 1852 election approached, the Democrats and Whigs sought to close the sectional rifts that had opened within their parties. For their presidential nominee, the Democrats turned to Franklin Pierce of New Hampshire. Pierce's well-known sympathy with southern views on public issues caused his northern critics to include him among the "**doughfaces**," northern men malleable enough to champion southern causes. The Whigs were less successful in bridging differences. Adopting the formula that had worked in 1848, they chose another Mexican-American War hero, General Winfield Scott of Virginia. But the Whigs' northern and southern factions were hopelessly divided, and the party suffered a humiliating defeat. The Democrat Pierce carried twenty-seven states to Scott's four and won the electoral college vote 254 to 42 (see Map 14.4, page 442). In the afterglow of the Compromise of 1850, the Free-Soil Party lost almost half of the voters who had turned to it in the tumultuous political atmosphere of 1848.

Eager to leave the sectional controversy behind, the new president turned swiftly to foreign expansion. Manifest destiny remained robust. (See "Beyond America's Borders," page 440–441.) Pierce's major objective was Cuba, which was owned by Spain and in which slavery flourished, but antislavery Northerners blocked Cuba's acquisition to keep more slave territory from entering the Union.

Pierce's fortunes improved in Mexico. In 1853, diplomat James Gadsden negotiated a $10 million purchase of some 30,000 square miles of land in present-day Arizona and New Mexico. The **Gadsden Purchase** stemmed from the dream of a transcontinental railroad to California and Pierce's desire for a southern route through Mexican territory. The booming population of the Pacific coast made it obvious that the vast, loose-jointed Republic needed a railroad to bind it together. Talk of a railroad ignited rivalries in cities from New Orleans to Chicago as they maneuvered to become the eastern terminus. The desire for a transcontinental railroad evolved into a sectional contest, which by the 1850s inevitably involved slavery.

Illinois's Democratic senator Stephen A. Douglas badly wanted the transcontinental railroad for Chicago, and his chairmanship of the Senate Committee on Territories provided him with an opportunity. Any railroad that ran west from Chicago would pass through a region that Congress in 1830 had designated a "permanent" Indian reserve (see chapter 11). Douglas proposed giving this vast area between the Missouri River and the Rocky Mountains an Indian name, Nebraska, and then throwing the Indians out. Once the region achieved territorial status, whites could survey and sell the land, establish a civil government, and build a railroad.

Nebraska lay within the Louisiana Purchase and, according to the Missouri Compromise of 1820, was closed to slavery (see chapter 10). Since Douglas could not count on New England to back western economic development, he needed southern votes to pass his Nebraska legislation. But Southerners had no incentive to create another free territory or to help a northern city win the transcontinental railroad. Southerners, however, agreed to help if Congress organized Nebraska according to popular sovereignty. That meant giving slavery a chance in Nebraska Territory and reopening the dangerous issue of slavery expansion, which Douglas himself had helped to resolve only four years earlier.

In January 1854, Douglas introduced his bill to organize Nebraska Territory, leaving to the settlers themselves the decision about slavery. At southern insistence, and even though he knew it would "raise a hell of a storm," Douglas added an explicit repeal of the Missouri Compromise. Indeed, the Nebraska bill raised a storm of controversy. Free-Soilers branded Douglas's plan "a gross violation of a sacred pledge" and an "atrocious plot" to transform free land into a "dreary region of despotism, inhabited by masters and slaves."

Undaunted, Douglas skillfully shepherded the explosive bill through Congress in May 1854. Nine-tenths of the southern members (Whigs and Democrats) and half of the northern Democrats cast votes in favor of the bill. Like Douglas, most northern supporters believed that popular sovereignty would make Nebraska free territory. Ominously, however, half of the northern Democrats broke with their party and opposed the bill. In its final form, the **Kansas-Nebraska Act** divided the huge territory in two: Nebraska and Kansas (Map 14.3). With this act, the government pushed the Plains Indians farther west, making way for farmers and railroads.

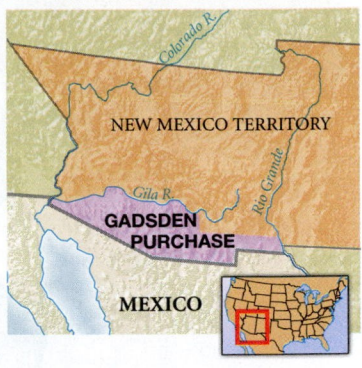

Gadsden Purchase, 1853

REVIEW Why did the Fugitive Slave Act provoke such strong opposition in the North?

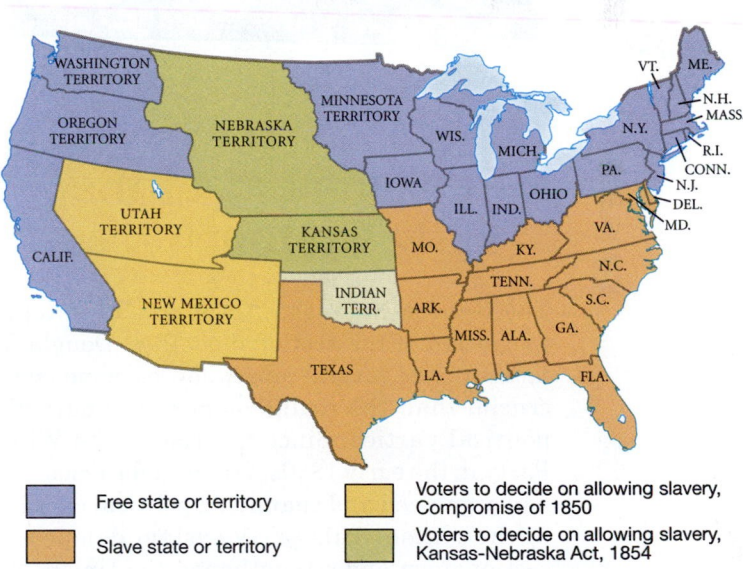

▉ Free state or territory	▉ Voters to decide on allowing slavery, Compromise of 1850
▉ Slave state or territory	▉ Voters to decide on allowing slavery, Kansas-Nebraska Act, 1854

MAP ACTIVITY

MAP 14.3 The Kansas-Nebraska Act, 1854
Americans hardly thought twice about dispossessing the Indians of land guaranteed them by treaty, but many worried about the outcome of repealing the Missouri Compromise and opening up the region to slavery.

READING THE MAP: How many slave states and how many free states does the map show? Estimate the percentage of new territory likely to be settled by slaveholders.

CONNECTIONS: Who would be more likely to support changes in government legislation to discontinue the Missouri Compromise — slaveholders or free-soil advocates? Why?

had what one critic disdainfully called "geographic" parties. Parties now sharpened ideological and policy differences between the sections and no longer muffled moral issues such as slavery. The new party system also thwarted political compromise and instead promoted political polarization that further jeopardized the Union.

The Old Parties: Whigs and Democrats

As early as the Mexican-American War, members of the Whig Party had clashed over the future of slavery in annexed Mexican lands. By 1852, the Whig Party could please its proslavery southern wing or its antislavery northern wing but not both. The Whigs' miserable showing in the election of 1852 made a despairing New York Whig ask, "Was there ever such a deluge since Noah's time?" It was clear that the Whigs were no longer a strong national party. By 1856, after more than two decades of contesting the Democrats, they were hardly a party at all (Map 14.4).

The collapse of the Whig Party left the Democrats as the country's only national party. Although the Democrats were not immune to the disruptive pressures of the territorial question, they discovered in popular sovereignty a doctrine that many Democrats could support. Even so, popular sovereignty very nearly undid the party. When Stephen Douglas applied the doctrine to the part of the Louisiana Purchase where slavery had been barred, he divided northern Democrats and destroyed the dominance of the Democratic Party in the free states. After 1854, even though the Democrats were a southern-dominated party, they remained a national political organization. Gains in the South more than balanced Democratic losses in the North. During the 1850s, Democrats elected two presidents and won majorities in Congress in almost every election.

The breakup of the Whigs and the disaffection of significant numbers of northern

▶ Realignment of the Party System

The Kansas-Nebraska Act marked a fateful escalation of the sectional conflict. Douglas's measure had several consequences, none more crucial than the realignment of the nation's political parties. Since the rise of the Whig Party in the early 1830s, Whigs and Democrats had organized and channeled political conflict in the nation. This party system dampened sectionalism and strengthened the Union. To achieve national political power, the Whigs and Democrats had to retain their strength in both North and South. Strong northern and southern wings required that each party compromise and find positions acceptable to both wings.

The Kansas-Nebraska controversy shattered this stabilizing political system. In place of two national parties with bisectional strength, the mid-1850s witnessed the development of one party heavily dominated by one section and another party entirely limited to the other section. Rather than "national" parties, the country

Democrats set many Americans politically adrift. As they searched for new political harbors, Americans found that the death of the old party system created a multitude of fresh political alternatives.

The New Parties: Know-Nothings and Republicans

Dozens of new political organizations vied for voters' attention. Out of the confusion, two emerged as true contenders. One grew out of the slavery controversy, a coalition of indignant antislavery Northerners. The other arose from an entirely different split in American society, between Roman Catholic immigrants and native Protestants.

The tidal wave of immigrants that broke over America from 1845 to 1855 produced a nasty backlash among Protestant Americans, who believed that the American Republic was about to drown in a sea of Roman Catholics from Ireland and Germany (see Figure 12.2, page 367). Most immigrants became Democrats because they perceived that party as more tolerant of newcomers than were the Whigs. But in the 1850s, they met sharp political opposition when nativists (individuals who were anti-immigrant) began to organize, first into secret fraternal societies and then in 1854 into a political party. Recruits swore never to vote for either foreign-born or Roman Catholic candidates and not to reveal any information about the organization. When questioned, they said, "I know nothing." Officially, they were the American Party, but most Americans called them **Know-Nothings**.

The Know-Nothings exploded onto the political stage in 1854 and 1855 with a series of dazzling successes. They captured state legislatures in the Northeast, West, and South and claimed dozens of seats in Congress. Their greatest triumph came in Massachusetts, a favorite destination for Irish immigrants. Know-Nothings elected the Massachusetts governor, all of the state senators, all but two of the state representatives, and all of the congressmen. Members of the Democratic and Whig parties described the phenomenal success of the Know-Nothings as a "tornado," a "hurricane," and "a freak of political insanity." By 1855, an observer might reasonably have concluded that the Know-Nothings had emerged as the successor to the Whigs.

The Know-Nothings were not the only new party making noise, however. One of the new

The Realignment of Political Parties

Whig Party

1848   Whig Party divides into two factions over slavery; Whigs adopt no platform and nominate war hero Zachary Taylor, who is elected president.

1852   Whigs nominate war hero General Winfield Scott for president; deep divisions in party result in humiliating loss.

1856   Shattered by sectionalism, Whig Party fields no presidential candidate.

Democratic Party

1848   President Polk declines to run again; Democratic Party nominates Lewis Cass, the man most closely associated with popular sovereignty, but avoids firm platform position on expansion of slavery.

1852   To bridge rift in party, Democrats nominate northern war veteran with southern views, Franklin Pierce, for president; he wins with 50.9 percent of popular vote.

1856   Democrat James Buchanan elected president on ambiguous platform; his prosouthern actions in office alienate northern branch of party.

1860   Democrats split into northern Democrats and southern Democrats; each group fields its own presidential candidate.

Free-Soil Party

1848   Breakaway antislavery Democrats and antislavery Whigs found Free-Soil Party; presidential candidate Martin Van Buren takes 10.1 percent of popular vote, mainly from Whigs.

1852   Support for Free-Soil Party ebbs in wake of Compromise of 1850; Free-Soil presidential candidate John P. Hale wins only 5 percent of popular vote.

American (Know-Nothing) Party

1851   Anti-immigrant American (Know-Nothing) Party formed.

1854–   American Party succeeds in state elections
1855   and attracts votes from northern and southern Whigs in congressional elections.

1856   Know-Nothing presidential candidate Millard Fillmore wins only Maryland; party subsequently disbands.

Republican Party

1854   Republican Party formed to oppose expansion of slavery in territories; attracts northern Whigs, northern Democrats, and Free-Soilers.

1856   Republican presidential candidate John C. Frémont wins all but five northern states, establishing Republicans as main challenger to Democrats.

1860   Republican Abraham Lincoln wins all northern states except New Jersey and is elected president in four-way race against divided Democrats and southern Constitutional Union Party.

Filibusters: The Underside of Manifest Destiny

Each year, the citizens of Caborca, a small town in the northern state of Sonora, Mexico, celebrate the defeat there in 1857 of an American army. The invaders did not wear the uniform of the U.S. Army, but instead marched as the private "Arizona Colonization Company." Their commander, Henry A. Crabb, a Mississippian who had followed the gold rush to California, saw fresh opportunity in the civil disorder that reigned south of the border. When the governor of Sonora faced an insurrection, he invited Crabb to help him repress his enemies in exchange for mineral rights and land.

Crabb marched his band of sixty-eight heavily armed ex-miners south from Los Angeles, but by the time the Americans arrived, the governor had put down the insurgency, and the Mexicans turned on the American invaders. Every American except one died either in battle or at the hands of Mexican firing squads. Crabb's head was preserved in alcohol and placed on display as a symbol of victory.

Henry Crabb was one of thousands of American adventurers, known as "filibusters" (from the Spanish *filibustero*, meaning "free-booter" or "pirate"), who in the mid-nineteenth century joined private armies that invaded foreign countries throughout the Western Hemisphere. Although these expeditions violated the U.S. Neutrality Act of 1818, private American armies attacked Canada, Mexico, Ecuador, Honduras, Cuba, and Nicaragua and planned invasions of places as far away as the Hawaiian kingdom. The federal government usually cracked down on filibusters, fearing that private invasions would jeopardize legitimate diplomatic efforts to promote trade and acquire territory.

Filibusters joined invading armies for reasons that ranged from personal gain to validating manhood. Many saw themselves as carrying on the work of manifest destiny, extending America's reach beyond Texas, California, and Oregon, the prizes of the 1830s and 1840s. In addition, during the 1840s and 1850s, when Northerners insisted on containing slavery's spread to the North and West, Southerners joined filibustering expeditions to expand slavery south beyond the U.S. border. A leading proslavery ideologue, George Fitzhugh, defended filibustering through historical comparison: "They who condemn the modern filibuster . . . must also condemn the discoverers and settlers of America, of the East Indies of Holland, and of the Indian and Pacific Oceans."

One of the most vigorous filibusters to appeal to southern interests was Narciso López, a Venezuelan-born Cuban who dedicated himself to the liberation of Cuba from Spanish rule. López claimed that Spain was planning to free Cuba's slaves, and he told Southerners that "self-preservation" demanded that they seize the island. In 1850, after gaining the support of Governor John Quitman of Mississippi, López and an army of 500 landed on the northwest coast of Cuba, but Spanish troops quickly drove them off. Two months later, he tried again. This time, the Spaniards crushed the invasion, killing 200 filibusters, shipping 160 prisoners to Spain, executing 50 invaders by firing squad, and publicly garroting López. John Quitman gathered another army of several thousand, but federal authorities seized one of his ships and ended the threat to Cuba.

The most successful of all filibusters was William Walker of Tennessee, a restless dreamer who longed for an empire of his own south of the border. In May 1855, Walker and an army of fifty-six men sailed from San Francisco to the west coast of Nicaragua. Two thousand reinforcements and a civil war in Nicaragua gave Walker his victory. He had himself proclaimed president, legalized slavery, and called on Southerners to come raise cotton, sugar, and coffee in "a magnificent country." Hundreds of Southerners took up land grants, but Walker's

antislavery organizations provoked by the Kansas-Nebraska Act called itself the **Republican Party**. The Republicans attempted to unite all those who opposed the extension of slavery into any territory of the United States, including Whigs, Free-Soilers, anti-Nebraska Democrats, and even Know-Nothings.

The Republican creed tapped into the basic beliefs and values of Northerners. Slavery, the Republicans believed, degraded the dignity of white labor by associating work with blacks and servility. As evidence, they pointed to the South, where, one Republican claimed, three-quarters of whites "retire to the outskirts of civilization, where they live a semi-savage life, sinking deeper and more hopelessly into barbarism with every succeeding generation." Republicans warned that the insatiable slaveholders of the South, whom antislavery Northerners called the "Slave Power," were conspiring through their control regime survived only until 1857, when a coalition of Central American countries sent Walker packing. Walker doggedly launched four other attacks on Nicaragua, but in 1860 Honduran forces captured and shot him.

Filibustering had lost steam by the time of the U.S. Civil War, but the Confederacy paid a diplomatic price for its association with filibustering. The Guatemalan minister Antonio José de Irisarri declared that there was "no foreign Nation which can have less cause for sympathy with the enemies of the American Union, than the Republics of Central America, because from the Southern States were set on foot those filibustering expeditions." No Central American nation recognized Confederate independence.

The peoples of Central America and the Caribbean, like the inhabitants of Sonora, still harbor bitter memories of filibusters' private wars of imperialism and honor those who fought off American advances. When U.S. Marines occupied Nicaragua in the 1920s, insurgents found inspiration in their country's defeat of William Walker's army of freebooters eighty years earlier. In 1951, on the centennial of López's invasion, Cubans erected a monument at the very spot where his ill-fated army came ashore. Costa Ricans celebrate Juan Santamaria as their national martyr for his courage in battling William Walker. Memories of the invasions by nineteenth-century filibusters set the stage for anti-American sentiment in Latin America that lingers to this day.

America in a Global Context

1. How did supporters of filibustering justify the practice?

2. What was the relationship between filibustering and sectional politics in the United States in the 1840s and 1850s?

3. Why would an expansionist-minded U.S. government frown on filibustering?

of the Democratic Party to expand slavery, subvert liberty, and undermine the Constitution.

Only if slavery was restricted to the South, Republicans believed, could the system of free labor flourish elsewhere. In the North, one Republican declared in 1854, "every man holds his fortune in his own right arm; and his position in society, in life, is to be tested by his own individual character" (see chapter 12). Without slavery, western territories would provide vast economic opportunity for free men. Powerful images of liberty and opportunity attracted a wide range of Northerners to the Republican cause.

Women as well as men rushed to the new Republican Party. Indeed, three women helped found the party in Ripon, Wisconsin, in 1854. Although they could not vote before the Civil War and suffered from a raft of other legal handicaps, women nevertheless participated in partisan politics by writing campaign literature,

1848

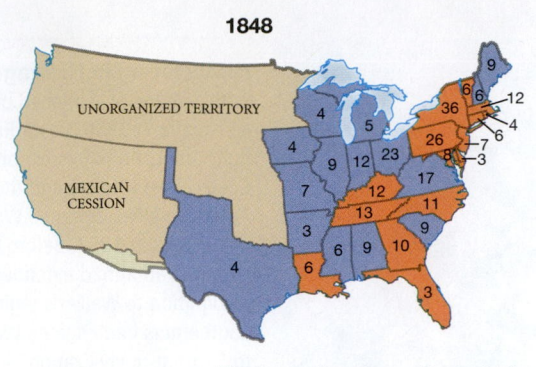

Candidate	Electoral Vote	Popular Vote	Percent of Popular Vote
Zachary Taylor (Whig)	163	1,360,099	47.4
Lewis Cass (Democrat)	127	1,220,544	42.5
Martin Van Buren (Free-Soil)	0	291,263	10.1

1852

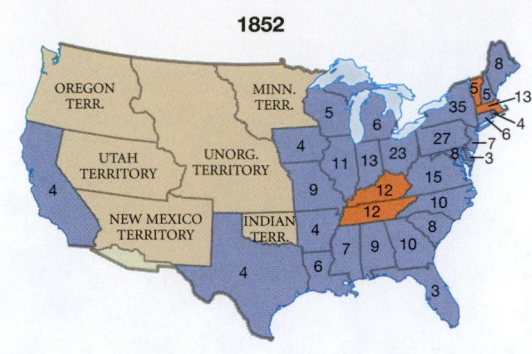

Candidate	Electoral Vote	Popular Vote	Percent of Popular Vote
Franklin Pierce (Democrat)	254	1,601,274	50.9
Winfield Scott (Whig)	42	1,386,580	44.1
John P. Hale (Free-Soil)	5	155,825	5.0

1856

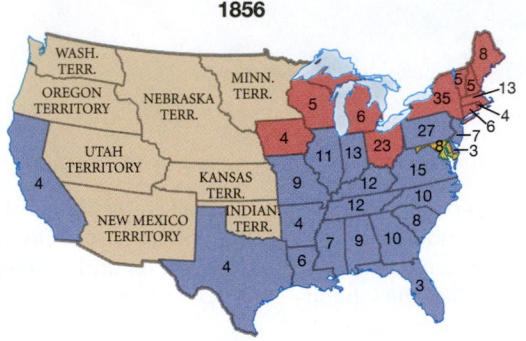

Candidate	Electoral Vote	Popular Vote	Percent of Popular Vote
James Buchanan (Democrat)	174	1,838,169	45.3
John C. Frémont (Republican)	114	1,341,264	33.1
Millard Fillmore (American)	8	874,534	21.6

1860

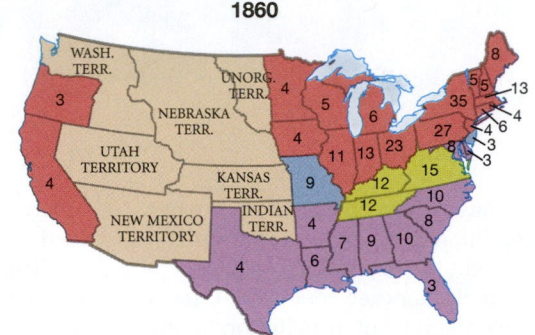

Candidate	Electoral Vote	Popular Vote	Percent of Popular Vote
Abraham Lincoln (Republican)	180	1,866,452	39.9
John C. Breckinridge (Southern Democrat)	72	847,953	18.1
Stephen A. Douglas (Northern Democrat)	12	1,375,157	29.4
John Bell (Constitutional Union)	39	590,631	12.6

MAP ACTIVITY

MAP 14.4   Political Realignment, 1848–1860

In 1848, slavery and sectionalism began taking their toll on the country's party system. The Whig Party was an early casualty. By 1860, national parties — those that contended for votes in both North and South — had been replaced by regional parties.

READING THE MAP: Which states did the Democrats pick up in 1852 compared to 1848? Which of these states did the Democrats lose in 1856? Compare the general geographic location of the states won by the Republicans in 1856 versus those won in 1860.

CONNECTIONS: In the 1860 election, which party benefited the most from the western and midwestern states added to the Union since 1848? Why do you think these states chose to back this party?

marching in parades, giving speeches, and lobbying voters. Women's antislavery fervor attracted them to the Republican Party, and participation in party politics in turn nurtured the woman's rights movement. Susan B. Anthony, who attended Republican meetings throughout the 1850s, found that her political activity made her disfranchisement all the more galling. She and other women

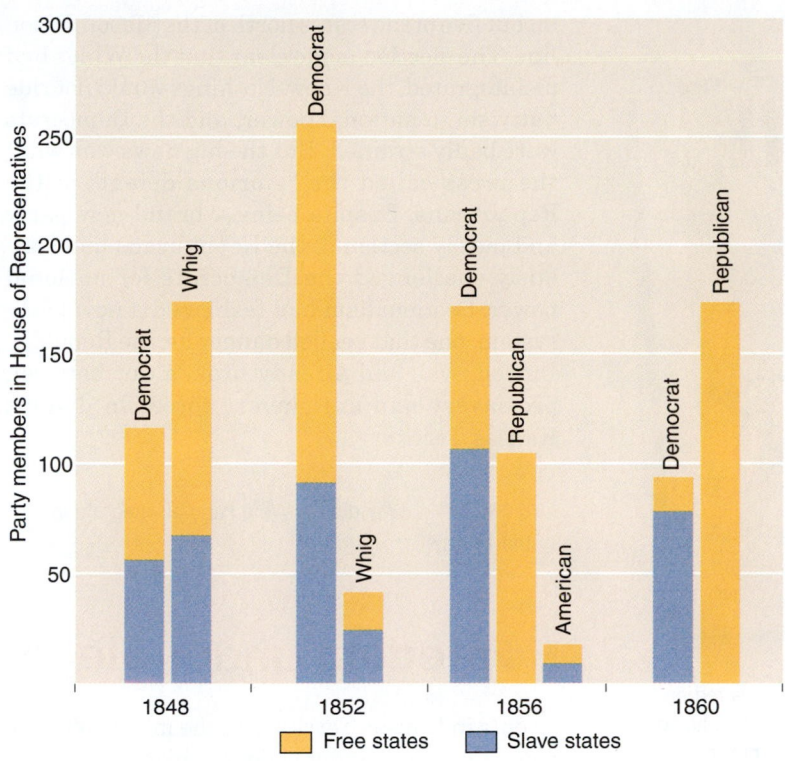

FIGURE 14.1   **Changing Political Landscape, 1848–1860**
The polarization of American politics between free states and slave states occurred in little more than a decade.

in the North worked on behalf of antislavery and to secure both woman suffrage and the right of married women to control their own property. (See "Seeking the American Promise," page 446.)

The Election of 1856

The election of 1856 revealed that the Republicans had become the Democrats' main challenger, and slavery in the territories, not nativism, was the election's principal issue. When the Know-Nothings insisted on a platform that endorsed the Kansas-Nebraska Act, most of the Northerners walked out, and the party came apart. The few Know-Nothings who remained nominated ex-president Millard Fillmore.

The Republicans adopted a platform that focused almost exclusively on "making every territory free." When they labeled slavery a "relic of barbarism," they signaled that they had written off the South. For president, they nominated the dashing soldier and California adventurer **John C. Frémont**, "Pathfinder of the West." Frémont lacked political credentials,

Know-Nothing Banner
Convinced that the incendiary issue of slavery had blinded Americans to the greater dangers of uncontrolled immigration and foreign influence, the Know-Nothings nominated Millard Fillmore for president in 1856. There is more than a little irony in this banner's appeal to "Native Americans" to stem the invasion from abroad. The Know-Nothings were referring to native-born Americans, but bona fide Native Americans — American Indians — also faced an invasion, and to them it made little difference whether the aggressors were fresh off the boat or born in the United States. Milwaukee County Historical Society.

John and Jessie Frémont Poster
The election of 1856 marked the first time a candidate's wife appeared on campaign items. In this poster, Jessie Benton Frémont rides a spirited horse alongside her husband, John C. Frémont, the Republican Party's presidential nominee. Jessie helped plan her husband's campaign, coauthored his election biography, and drew northern women into political activity as never before. "What a shame that women can't vote!" declared abolitionist Lydia Maria Child. "We'd carry 'our Jessie' into the White House on our shoulders, wouldn't we." Critics of Jessie's violation of women's traditional sphere ridiculed both Frémonts. A San Francisco man pronounced Jessie "the better man of the two." Museum of American Political Life.

but his wife, **Jessie Frémont**, the daughter of Senator Thomas Hart Benton of Missouri, knew the political map as well as her husband knew the western trails. Though careful to maintain a proper public image, the vivacious young mother and antislavery zealot helped attract voters and draw women into politics.

The Democrats, successful in 1852 in bridging sectional differences by nominating a northern man with southern principles, chose another "doughface," James Buchanan of Pennsylvania. They took refuge in the ambiguity of popular sovereignty and portrayed the Republicans as extremists ("Black Republican Abolitionists") whose support for the Wilmot Proviso risked pushing the South out of the Union.

The Democratic strategy carried the day for Buchanan, but Frémont did astonishingly well. Buchanan won 174 electoral votes against Frémont's 114 and Fillmore's 8 (see Map 14.4, page 442). Campaigning under the banner "Free soil, Free men, Frémont," the Republican carried all but five of the states north of the Mason-Dixon line. The election made clear that the Whigs had disintegrated, the Know-Nothings would not ride nativism to national power, and the Democrats were badly strained. But the big news was what the press called the "glorious defeat" of the Republicans. Despite being a brand-new party and purely sectional, the Republicans had seriously challenged the Democrats for national power. Sectionalism had fashioned a new party system, one that spelled danger for the Republic. Indeed, war had already broken out between proslavery and antislavery forces in distant Kansas Territory.

REVIEW   Why did the Whig Party disintegrate in the 1850s?

▶ Freedom under Siege

Events in Kansas Territory in the mid-1850s provided the young Republican organization with an enormous boost and help explain its strong showing in the election of 1856. Republicans organized around the premise that the slaveholding South provided a profound threat to "free soil, free labor, and free men," and now Kansas reeled with violence that Republicans argued was southern in origin. Kansas, Republicans claimed, opened a window to southern values and intentions. Republicans also pointed to the brutal beating by a Southerner of a respected northern senator on the floor of Congress. Even the Supreme Court, in the Republicans' view, reflected the South's drive toward tyranny and minority rule. Then, in 1858, the issues dividing North and South received an extraordinary airing in a senatorial contest in Illinois, when the nation's foremost Democrat debated a resourceful Republican.

"Bleeding Kansas"

Three days after the House of Representatives approved the Kansas-Nebraska Act in 1854, Senator William H. Seward of New York boldly challenged the South. "Come on then, Gentlemen of the Slave States," he cried, "since there is no escaping your challenge, I accept it in behalf of the cause of freedom. We will engage in competition for the virgin soil of Kansas, and God give the victory to the side which is stronger in numbers as it is in right." Because of Stephen Douglas, popular sovereignty would determine whether Kansas became slave or free. No one really expected New Mexico and Utah, with their harsh landscapes, to become slave states when Congress instituted popular sovereignty there in 1850, but many believed that Kansas could go either way. Free-state and slave-state settlers each sought a majority at the ballot box, claimed God's blessing, and kept their rifles ready.

In both North and South, emigrant aid societies sprang up to promote settlement from free states or slave states. The most famous, the New England Emigrant Aid Company, sponsored some 1,240 settlers in 1854 and 1855. Tiny rural communities from Virginia to Texas raised money to support proslavery settlers.

Missourians, already bordered on the east by the free state of Illinois and on the north by the free state of Iowa, especially thought it important to secure Kansas for slavery. Thousands of rough frontiersmen, egged on by Missouri senator David Rice Atchison, invaded Kansas. "There are eleven hundred coming over from Platte County to vote," Atchison reported, "and if that ain't enough we can send five thousand — enough to kill every God-damned abolitionist in the Territory." Not surprisingly, proslavery candidates swept the territorial elections in November 1854. When Kansas's first territorial legislature met, it enacted a raft of proslavery laws. Antislavery men, for example, were barred from holding office or serving on juries. Ever-pliant President Pierce endorsed the work of the fraudulently elected legislature. Free-soil Kansans did not. They elected their own legislature, which promptly banned both slaves and free blacks from the territory.

Organized into two rival governments and armed to the teeth, Kansans verged on civil war.

Fighting broke out on the morning of May 21, 1856, when several hundred proslavery men raided the town of Lawrence, the center of free-state settlement. Only one man died, but the "Sack of Lawrence," as free-soil forces called it, inflamed northern opinion. Elsewhere in Kansas, news of events in Lawrence provoked **John Brown**, a free-soil settler, to announce that "it was better that a score of bad men should die than that one man who came here to make Kansas a Free State should be driven out" and to lead the posse that massacred five allegedly proslavery settlers along Pottawatomie Creek (see pages 427–428). After that, guerrilla war engulfed the territory.

Just as **"Bleeding Kansas"** gave the fledgling Republican Party fresh ammunition for its battle against the Slave Power, so too did an event that occurred in the national capital. In May 1856, Senator Charles Sumner of Massachusetts delivered a speech titled "The Crime against Kansas," which included a scalding personal attack on South Carolina senator Andrew P. Butler. Sumner described Butler as a "Don Quixote" who had taken as his mistress "the harlot, slavery."

Preston Brooks, a young South Carolina member of the House and a kinsman of Butler's,

"Bleeding Kansas," 1850s

Armed Settlers Near Lawrence, Kansas
Armed with rifles, knives, swords, and pistols, these tough antislavery men gathered for a photograph near the free-soil town of Lawrence in 1856. Equally well-armed proslavery men attacked and briefly occupied Lawrence that same year. Kansas State Historical Society.

"A Purse of Her Own": Petitioning for the Right to Own Property

In the early Republic, as today, having money and deciding how to spend it was a fundamental aspect of independent adulthood. Yet antebellum married women were denied this privilege, because of the laws of *coverture*, which placed wives under the full legal control of their husbands (see chapter 10). By law, husbands made all the financial decisions in a household. Even money that a wife earned or brought into a marriage from gifts or inheritance was not hers to control as long as she remained married. Ernestine Potowsky Rose of New York City thought that was wrong, and she became the first woman in the United States to take action to change the law.

Born in Poland in 1810, Ernestine Potowsky was the daughter of a rabbi, which meant that her destiny was fixed: an arranged marriage, many children, and a life strictly governed by religious law. Ernestine rejected this fate and left home for London. There, at age nineteen, she married William Rose, a like-minded socialist intellectual. The couple later emigrated to the United States and settled in New York City, where William, a jeweler, started a business.

Ernestine soon learned of a bill presented in 1837 in the New York assembly proposing that married women, "equally with males and unmarried females, possess the rights of *life*, *liberty*, and PROPERTY, and are equally entitled to be protected in all three." But opponents feared that it would undermine a central pillar of marriage: the assumption that husband and wife shared identical interests. How could a wife not trust her husband to control the money? Predictably, the bill failed to pass.

The devastating panics of 1837 and 1839 (see chapter 11), and the resulting bankruptcies, soon changed some traditionalists' minds about wives and property. Men in several state legislatures crafted laws that shielded a wife's inherited property from creditors collecting debts from her husband. Mississippi led the way in 1839, and by 1848 eighteen states had modified property laws in the name of family protection.

In New York, as support for such a law grew, Ernestine Rose mobilized a new constituency of women activists around the far more egalitarian argument that married women should be able to own and control property. She circulated petitions and spoke from public platforms, often joined by Elizabeth Cady Stanton, a young wife from western New York.

In April 1848, three months before the Seneca Falls woman's rights convention (see chapter 12), the New York assembly finally awarded married women sole authority over property they brought to a marriage.

Rose welcomed the new law but recognized its key shortcoming: It made no provision for wages earned by a married woman. Nor did it alter inheritance laws that limited a widow's share of her husband's estate. Speaking at every national woman's rights convention from 1850 to 1860, Rose argued for women's economic independence. In 1853, she itemized the limited belongings allowed to a widow if her husband died without a will: "As to the personal property, after all debts and liabilities are discharged, the widow receives one-half of it; and, in addition, the law allows her, her own wearing apparel, her own ornaments, proper to her station, one bed, with appurtenances for the same, a stove, the Bible, family pictures, and all the school-books; also all spinning wheels and weaving looms, one table, six chairs, ten cups and saucers, one tea-pot, one sugar dish, and six spoons." While her audience laughed appreciatively, Rose questioned whether the spoons would be teaspoons, "since a widow might live on tea only." Spinning wheels, long gone in 1853, needed no elaboration from her to make the law sound pathetically out-of-date.

Of particular concern to Rose was the plight of poor wives. She and Susan B. Anthony traveled the state of New York and encountered women trapped in marriages with husbands who failed to support their dependents. Anthony, herself a life-

---

felt compelled to defend the honor of both his aged relative and his state. On May 22, Brooks entered the Senate, where he found Sumner working at his desk. He beat Sumner over the head with his cane until Sumner lay bleeding and unconscious on the floor. Brooks resigned his seat in the House, only to be promptly reelected. In the North, the southern hero became an archvillain. Like "Bleeding Kansas," "Bleeding Sumner" provided the Republican Party with a potent symbol of the South's "twisted and violent civilization."

The *Dred Scott* Decision

Political debate over slavery in the territories became so heated in part because the Constitution lacked precision on the issue. In 1857, in the long single woman, recalled that "as I passed from town to town I was made to feel the great evil of women's utter dependence on man. . . . Woman must have a purse of her own."

Rose's efforts paid off. In 1860, New York amended its law to include a wife's wages as her own, but only if she earned the money outside the household. Money earned selling eggs or caring for boarders still went directly into the husband's pocket. Perhaps the most significant beneficiaries of this law were women whose husbands were incompetent to support them or who had deserted them. These husbands now had no right to their wives' hard-gained earnings.

The revised New York law made other important changes to coverture. A wife could now sue (or be sued), make legal contracts of her own, and serve as joint guardian of her children, "with equal powers, rights and duties in regard to them." These changes, adopted in many states after 1860, began the long (and still ongoing) process of elevating married women to near equality with men.

Questions for Consideration

1. What do the laws of coverture reveal about how married women were viewed in antebellum America?

2. Why did a woman need "a purse of her own"?

3. Why did men eventually agree to grant married women property rights?

Ernestine Rose
Ernestine Rose, in her mid-forties when this photograph was taken, managed to hold a smile for the several minutes required to capture her image on a photographic plate. Schlesinger Library, Radcliffe Institute for Advanced Study, Harvard University.

case of *Dred Scott v. Sandford*, the Supreme Court announced its understanding of the meaning of the Constitution regarding slavery in the territories. The Court's decision demonstrated that it enjoyed no special immunity from the sectional and partisan passions that were convulsing the land.

In 1833, an army doctor bought the slave Dred Scott in St. Louis, Missouri, and took him as his personal servant to Fort Armstrong, Illinois, and then to Fort Snelling in Wisconsin Territory. Back in St. Louis in 1846, Scott, with the help of white friends, sued to prove that he and his family were legally entitled to their freedom. Scott based his claim on his travels and residences. He argued that living in Illinois, a free state, and Wisconsin, a free territory, had made his family free and that they remained free even after returning to Missouri, a slave state.

In 1857, the U.S. Supreme Court ruled in the case. Chief Justice **Roger B. Taney**, who hated Republicans and detested racial equality, wrote the Court's decision. First, the Court ruled in the *Dred Scott decision* that Scott could not legally claim violation of his constitutional rights because he was not a citizen of the United States. When the Constitution was written, Taney said, blacks "were regarded as beings of an inferior order . . . so far inferior, that they had no rights which the white man was bound to respect." Second, the laws of Dred Scott's home state, Missouri, determined his status, and thus his travels in free areas did not make him free. Third, Congress's power to make "all needful rules and regulations" for the territories did not include the right to prohibit slavery. The Court explicitly declared the Missouri Compromise unconstitutional, even though it had already been voided by the Kansas-Nebraska Act.

The Taney Court's extreme proslavery decision outraged Republicans. By denying the federal government the right to exclude slavery in the territories, it cut the legs out from under the Republican Party. Moreover, as the *New York Tribune* lamented, the decision cleared the way for "all our Territories . . . to be ripened into Slave States." Particularly frightening to African Americans in the North was the Court's declaration that free blacks were not citizens and had no rights.

The Republican rebuttal to the *Dred Scott* ruling relied heavily on the dissenting opinion of Justice Benjamin R. Curtis. Scott *was* a citizen of the United States, Curtis argued. At the time of the writing of the Constitution, free black men could vote in five states and participated in the ratification process. Scott *was* free. Because slavery was prohibited in Wisconsin, the "involuntary servitude of a slave, coming into the Territory with his master, should cease to exist." The Missouri Compromise *was* constitutional. The Founders had meant exactly what they said:

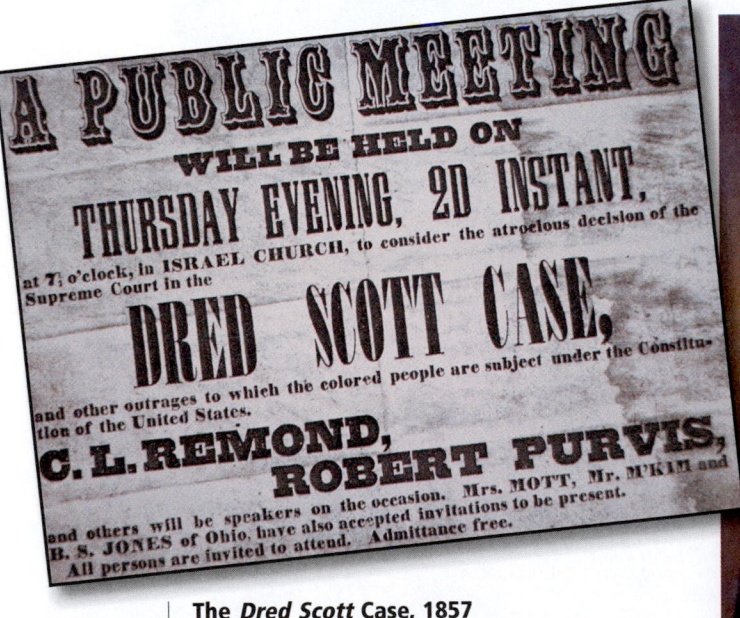

The *Dred Scott* Case, 1857
The *Dred Scott* case aroused enormous curiosity about the man suing for freedom. This portrait of Dred Scott was painted in 1857, the year of the Supreme Court's decision. African Americans in the North were particularly alarmed by the Court's ruling. The poster announces that two black leaders, Charles L. Remond and Robert Purvis, will speak at a public meeting about the "atrocious decision." Although the Court rejected his suit, he gained his freedom in May 1857 when a white man purchased and freed Scott and his family. Scott died of tuberculosis in September 1858. Poster: © Private Collection/Peter Newark American Pictures/The Bridgeman Art Library; Nationality/copyright status: American/out of copyright; Portrait: Collection of the New-York Historical Society.

Congress had the power to make "*all* needful rules and regulations" for the territories, including barring slavery.

In a seven-to-two decision, the Court rejected Curtis's arguments, thereby validating an extreme statement of the South's territorial rights. John C. Calhoun's claim that Congress had no authority to exclude slavery became the law of the land. White Southerners cheered, but the *Dred Scott* decision actually strengthened the young Republican Party. Indeed, that "outrageous" decision, one Republican argued, was "the best thing that could have happened," for it provided dramatic evidence of the Republicans' claim that a hostile "Slave Power" conspired against northern liberties.

Prairie Republican: Abraham Lincoln

By reigniting the sectional flames, the *Dred Scott* case provided Republican politicians with fresh challenges and fresh opportunities. **Abraham Lincoln** had long since put behind him his hardscrabble log-cabin beginnings in Kentucky and Indiana. He lived in a fine two-story house in Springfield, Illinois, and earned good money as a lawyer. The law provided Lincoln's living, but politics was his life. "His ambition was a little engine that knew no rest," observed his law partner William Herndon. Lincoln had served as a Whig in the Illinois state legislature and in the House of Representatives, but he had not held public office since 1849.

The disintegration of the Whig Party meant that Lincoln had no political home, but the Know-Nothings held no appeal. "How can anyone who abhors the oppression of negroes be in favor of degrading classes of white people?" he asked in 1855. "As a nation, we began by declaring that 'all men are created equal.' We now practically read it 'all men are created equal, except negroes.' When the Know-Nothings get control, it will read 'All men are created equal, except Negroes and foreigners and Catholics.'"

Convinced that slavery was a "monstrous injustice," a "great moral wrong," and an "unqualified evil to the negro, the white man, and the State," Lincoln gravitated toward the Republican Party. He condemned Douglas's Kansas-Nebraska Act of 1854 for giving slavery a new life and in 1856 joined the Republican Party. He accepted that the Constitution permitted slavery in those states where it existed, but he believed that Congress could contain its spread. Penned in, Lincoln believed, plantation slavery would wither,

and in time Southerners would end slavery themselves.

Lincoln held what were, for his times, moderate racial views. Although he denounced slavery and defended black humanity, he also viewed black equality as impractical and unachievable. "Negroes have natural rights . . . as other men have," he said, "although they cannot enjoy them here." Insurmountable white prejudice made it impossible to extend full citizenship to blacks in America, he believed. Freeing blacks and allowing them to remain in this country would lead to a race war. In Lincoln's mind, social stability and black progress required that slavery end and that blacks leave the country.

Lincoln envisioned the western territories as "places for poor people to go to, and better their conditions." The "*free* labor system," he said, "opens the way for all — gives hope to all, and energy, and progress, and improvement of condition to all." But slavery's expansion threatened free men's basic right to succeed. The Kansas-Nebraska Act and the *Dred Scott* decision persuaded him that slaveholders were engaged in a dangerous conspiracy to nationalize slavery. The next step, Lincoln warned, would be "another Supreme Court decision, declaring that the Constitution of the United States does not permit a State to exclude slavery from its limits." Unless the citizens of Illinois woke up, he warned, the Supreme Court would make "Illinois a slave State."

In Lincoln's view, the nation could not "endure, permanently half slave and half free." Either opponents of slavery would arrest its spread and place it on the "course of ultimate extinction," or its advocates would see that it became legal in "*all* the States, *old* as well as *new* — *North* as well as *South*." Lincoln's convictions that slavery was wrong and that Congress must stop its spread formed the core of the Republican ideology. Lincoln so impressed his fellow Republicans in Illinois that in 1858 they chose him to challenge the nation's premier Democrat, who was seeking reelection to the U.S. Senate.

The Lincoln-Douglas Debates

When Stephen Douglas learned that the Republican Abraham Lincoln would be his opponent for the Senate, he observed: "He is the strong man of the party — full of wit, facts, dates — and the best stump speaker, with his droll ways and dry jokes, in the West. He is as honest as he is shrewd, and if I beat him my victory will be hardly won."

The Herald in the Country, by William Sidney Mount, 1853
William Sidney Mount was the first American painter to achieve fame for his vivid depictions of everyday life. His motto was "Never paint for the few but for the many." Here, two men from the country keep up with the news by reading a copy of the *New York Herald*. Men like these increasingly accepted Abraham Lincoln's portrait of the Republican Party as the guardian of the common people's liberty and economic opportunity. When Lincoln claimed that southern slaveholders threatened free labor and democracy, northern men listened. The Long Island Museum of American Art, History and Carriages. Gift of Mr. and Mrs. Ward Melville, 1955.

Not only did Douglas have to contend with a formidable foe, but he also carried the weight of a burden not of his own making. The previous year, the nation's economy had experienced a sharp downturn. Prices had plummeted, thousands of businesses had failed, and many were unemployed. As a Democrat, Douglas had to go before the voters as a member of the party whose policies stood accused of causing the panic of 1857.

Douglas's response to another crisis in 1857, however, helped shore up his standing in Illinois. Proslavery forces in Kansas met in the town of Lecompton, drafted a proslavery constitution, and applied for statehood. Everyone knew that free-soilers outnumbered proslavery settlers, but President Buchanan instructed Congress to admit Kansas as the sixteenth slave state. Republicans denounced the "Lecompton swindle." Senator Douglas broke with the Democratic administration and denounced the **Lecompton constitution**; Congress killed the Lecompton bill. (When Kansans reconsidered the Lecompton constitution in an honest election, they rejected it six to one. Kansas entered the Union in 1861 as a free state.) By denouncing the fraudulent proslavery constitution, Douglas declared his independence from the South and, he hoped, made himself acceptable at home.

A relative unknown and a decided underdog in the Illinois election, Lincoln challenged Douglas to debate him face-to-face. The two met in seven communities for what would become a legendary series of debates. To the thousands who stood straining to see and hear, they must have seemed an odd pair. Douglas was five feet four inches tall, broad, and stocky; Lincoln was six feet four inches tall, angular, and lean. Douglas was in perpetual motion, darting across the platform, shouting, and jabbing the air; Lincoln stood still and spoke deliberately. Douglas wore the latest fashions and dazzled audiences with his flashy vests; Lincoln wore good suits but managed to look rumpled anyway.

The two men debated the crucial issues of the age — slavery and freedom. They showed the citizens of Illinois (and much of the nation because of widespread press coverage) the difference between an anti-Lecompton Democrat and a true Republican. Lincoln badgered Douglas with the question of whether he favored the spread of slavery. He tried to force Douglas into the damaging admission that the Supreme Court had repudiated Douglas's own territorial solution, popular sovereignty. At Freeport, Illinois, Douglas admitted that settlers could not now pass legislation barring slavery, but he argued that they could ban slavery just as effectively by not passing protective laws, such as those found in slave states. Southerners condemned Douglas's "Freeport Doctrine" and charged him with trying to steal the victory they had gained with the *Dred Scott* decision. Lincoln chastised his opponent for his "don't care" attitude about slavery, for "blowing out the moral lights around us."

Douglas worked the racial issue. He called Lincoln an abolitionist and an egalitarian enamored of "our colored brethren." Put on the defensive, Lincoln reaffirmed his faith in white rule: "I will say, then, that I am not, nor ever have been, in favor of bringing about in any way the social and political equality of the white and black race." But unlike Douglas, who told racist jokes, Lincoln was no negrophobe. He tried to steer the debate back to what he considered the true issue: the morality and future of slavery. "Slavery is wrong," Lincoln repeated, because "a man has the right to the fruits of his own labor."

As Douglas predicted, the election was hard-fought and closely contested. Until the adoption of the Seventeenth Amendment in 1911, citizens voted for state legislators, who in turn selected U.S. senators. Since Democrats won a slight majority in the Illinois legislature, the members returned Douglas to the Senate. But the **Lincoln-Douglas debates** thrust Lincoln, the prairie Republican, into the national spotlight.

REVIEW   Why did the *Dred Scott* decision strengthen northern suspicions of a "Slave Power" conspiracy?

▶ The Union Collapses

Lincoln's thesis that the "slavocracy" conspired to make slavery a national institution now seems exaggerated. But from the northern perspective, the Kansas-Nebraska Act, the Brooks-Sumner affair, the *Dred Scott* decision, and the Lecompton constitution amounted to irrefutable evidence of the South's aggressiveness. White Southerners, of course, saw things differently. They were the ones who were under siege, they declared. Signs were everywhere that the North planned to use its numerical advantage to attack slavery, and not just in the territories. Republicans had made it clear that they were unwilling to accept the *Dred Scott* ruling as the last word on the issue of slavery expansion. And John Brown's attempt to incite a slave insurrection in Virginia in 1859 proved that Northerners were unwilling to be bound by Christian decency and reverence for life.

Threats of secession increasingly laced the sectional debate. Talk of leaving the Union had been heard for years, but until the final crisis, Southerners had used secession as a ploy to gain concessions within the Union, not to destroy it. Then the 1850s delivered powerful blows to Southerners' confidence that they could remain in the Union and protect slavery. When the Republican Party won the White House in 1860, many Southerners concluded that they would have to leave.

The Aftermath of John Brown's Raid

For his attack on Harpers Ferry, John Brown stood trial for treason, murder, and incitement of slave insurrection. "To hang a fanatic is to make a martyr of him and fledge another brood of the same sort," cautioned one newspaper, but on December 2, 1859, Virginia executed Brown. In life, he was a ne'er-do-well, but, as the poet Stephen Vincent Benét observed, "he knew how to die." Brown told his wife that he was "determined to make the utmost possible out of a defeat." He told the court: "If it is deemed necessary that I should forfeit my life for the furtherance of the ends of justice, and mingle my blood further with the blood of . . . millions in this slave country whose rights are disregarded by wicked, cruel, and unjust enactments, I say, let it be done."

After Brown's execution, Americans across the land contemplated the meaning of his life and death. Northern denunciation of Brown as a dangerous fanatic gave way to grudging respect. Some even celebrated his "splendid martyrdom." Ralph Waldo Emerson likened Brown to Christ when he declared that Brown made "the gallows as glorious as the cross." Some abolitionists explicitly endorsed Brown's resort to violence. William Lloyd Garrison, who usually professed pacifism, announced, "I am prepared to say 'success to every slave insurrection at the South and in every country.'"

Most Northerners did not advocate bloody rebellion, however. Like Lincoln, they concluded that Brown's noble antislavery ideals could not "excuse violence, bloodshed, and treason." Still, when northern churches marked John Brown's hanging with tolling bells, hymns, and prayer vigils, white Southerners contemplated what they had in common with people who "regard John Brown as a martyr and a Christian hero, rather than a murderer and robber." Georgia senator Robert Toombs announced solemnly that Southerners must "never permit this Federal government to pass into the traitorous hands of the black Republican party." At that moment, the presidential election was only months away.

Republican Victory in 1860

Events between Brown's hanging and the presidential election only heightened sectional hostility. Across the South, whites feverishly searched for other John Browns and whipped and sometimes lynched those they suspected. A southern business convention meeting in Nashville shocked

VISUAL ACTIVITY

***John Brown Going to His Hanging,* by Horace Pippin, 1942**
The grandparents of Horace Pippin, a Pennsylvania artist, were slaves. His grandmother witnessed the hanging of John Brown, and this painting recalls the scene she so often described to him. Pippin used a muted palette to establish the bleak setting and to tell the grim story, but he managed to convey a striking intensity nevertheless. Historically accurate, the painting depicts Brown tied and sitting erect on his coffin, passing resolutely before the silent, staring white men. The black woman in the lower right corner presumably is Pippin's grandmother. Romare Bearden, a leading twentieth-century African American artist, recalled the central place of John Brown in black memory: "Lincoln and John Brown were as much a part of the actuality of the Afro-American experience, as were the domino games and the hoe cakes for Sunday morning breakfast. I vividly recall the yearly commemorations for John Brown and see my grandfather reading Brown's last speech to the court, which was a regular part of the ceremony at Pittsburgh's Shiloh Baptist Church." Pennsylvania Academy of Fine Arts, Philadelphia. John Lambert Fund.

READING THE IMAGE: What was the artist trying to convey about the tone of John Brown's execution? According to the painting, what were the feelings of those gathered to witness the event?
CONNECTIONS: How did Brown's trial and execution contribute to the growing split between North and South?

the nation (including many Southerners) by calling for the reopening of the African slave trade, closed since 1808 and considered an abomination almost everywhere in the Western world. Chief Justice Taney provoked new indignation when he ruled northern personal liberty laws unconstitutional and reaffirmed the Fugitive Slave Act. Then, the normally routine business of electing a Speaker of the House threatened to turn bloody as Democrats and Republicans battled over control of the office. After two months of acrimonious debate, one congressman observed that the "only persons who do not have a revolver and a knife are those who have two revolvers." A last-minute compromise may have averted a shootout.

When the Democrats converged on Charleston for their convention in April 1860, fire-eating Southerners denounced Stephen Douglas and demanded a platform that featured a federal slave code for the territories, a goal of extreme proslavery Southerners for years. Not only was Congress powerless to block slavery's spread, they argued, but it was obligated to offer slavery all "needful protection." But northern Democrats knew that northern voters would not stomach a federal slave code. When the delegates approved a platform with popular sovereignty, representatives from the entire Lower South and Arkansas stomped out of the convention. The remaining Democrats adjourned to meet a few weeks later in Baltimore, where they nominated Douglas for president.

Bolting southern Democrats immediately reconvened in Richmond, where they approved a platform with a federal slave code and nominated their own candidate for president: John C. Breckinridge of Kentucky, who was serving as vice president under Buchanan. Southern moderates, however, refused to support Breckinridge. They formed the **Constitutional Union Party** to provide voters with a Unionist choice. Instead of adopting a platform and confronting the slavery question, the Constitutional Union Party merely approved a vague resolution pledging "to recognize no political principle other than *the Constitution . . . the Union . . . and the Enforcement of the Laws.*" For president, they nominated former senator John Bell of Tennessee.

The Republicans smelled victory, but they estimated that they needed to carry nearly all the free states to win. To make their party more appealing, they expanded their platform beyond antislavery. They hoped that free homesteads, a protective tariff, a transcontinental railroad, and a guarantee of immigrant political rights would provide an economic and social agenda broad enough to unify the North. While reasserting their commitment to stop the spread of slavery, they also denounced John Brown's raid as "among the gravest of crimes" and confirmed the security of slavery in the South.

Republicans cast about for a moderate candidate to go with their evenhanded platform. The foremost Republican, William H. Seward, had made enemies with his radical "higher law" doctrine, which claimed that there was a higher moral law than the Constitution, and with his "irrepressible conflict" speech, in which he declared that North and South were fated to collide. Lincoln, however, since bursting onto the national scene in 1858 had demonstrated his clear purpose, good

judgment, and solid Republican credentials. That, and his residence in Illinois, a crucial state, made him attractive to the party. On the third ballot, the delegates chose Lincoln. Defeated by Douglas in a state contest less than two years earlier, Lincoln now stood ready to take him on for the presidency.

The election of 1860 was like none other in American politics. It took place in the midst of the nation's severest crisis. Four major candidates crowded the presidential field. Rather than a four-cornered contest, however, the election broke into two contests, each with two candidates. In the North, Lincoln faced Douglas;

Abraham Lincoln
Lincoln actively sought the Republican presidential nomination in 1860. While in New York City to give a political address, he had his photograph taken by Mathew Brady. "While I was there I was taken to one of the places where they get up such things," Lincoln explained, sounding more innocent than he was, "and I suppose they got my shadow, and can multiply copies indefinitely." Multiply they did. Later, Lincoln credited his victory to his New York speech and to this dignified photograph by Brady. The Lincoln Museum, Fort Wayne, Indiana, #0-17.

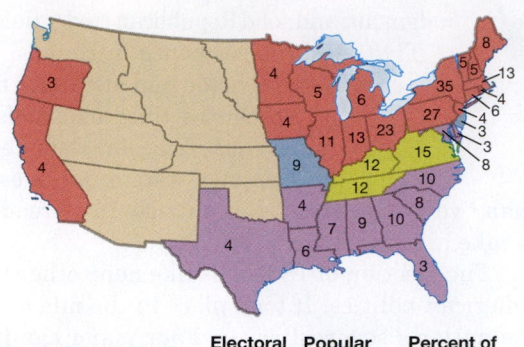

Candidate	Electoral Vote	Popular Vote	Percent of Popular Vote
Abraham Lincoln (Republican)	180	1,866,452	39.9
John C. Breckinridge (Southern Democrat)	72	847,953	18.1
Stephen A. Douglas (Northern Democrat)	12	1,375,157	29.4
John Bell (Constitutional Union)	39	590,631	12.6

MAP 14.5
The Election of 1860

Secession Winter

Across the country, telegraphs tapped out the news of Lincoln's victory. Antislavery advocate Charles Francis Adams of Massachusetts could hardly believe the results: "There is now scarcely a shadow of a doubt that the great revolution has actually taken place, and that the country has once and for all thrown off the domination of the Slaveholders." What Adams celebrated as liberation, anxious white Southerners feared was the onset of Republican tyranny. Throughout the South, they began debating what to do. Although Breckinridge had carried the South, a vote for "southern rights" was not necessarily a vote for secession. Besides, slightly more than half of the Southerners who had voted had cast ballots for Douglas and Bell, two stout defenders of the Union.

Southern Unionists tried to calm the fears that Lincoln's election triggered. Let the dust settle, they pleaded. Former congressman Alexander Stephens of Georgia asked what Lincoln had done to justify something as extreme as secession. Had he not promised to respect slavery where it existed? In Stephens's judgment, the fire-eater cure would be worse than the Republican disease. Secession might lead to war, which would loosen the hinges of southern society and possibly even open the door to slave insurrection. "Revolutions are much easier started than controlled," he warned. "I consider slavery much more secure in the Union than out of it."

Secessionists emphasized the dangers of delay. "Mr. Lincoln and his party assert that this doctrine of equality applies to the negro," former Georgia governor Howell Cobb declared, "and necessarily there can exist no such thing as property in our equals." Lincoln's election without a single electoral vote from the South meant that Southerners were no longer able to defend themselves within the Union, Cobb argued. Why wait, he asked, for Lincoln to appoint abolitionist judges, marshals, customs collectors, and postmasters to federal posts throughout the South? As for war, there would be none. The Union was a voluntary compact, and Lincoln would not coerce patriotism. If Northerners did resist with force, secessionists argued, one southern woodsman could whip five of Lincoln's greasy mechanics.

For all their differences, southern whites agreed that they had to defend slavery. John Smith Preston of South Carolina spoke for the overwhelming majority when he declared, "The

in the South, Breckinridge confronted Bell. So outrageous did Southerners consider the Republican Party that they did not even permit Lincoln's name to appear on the ballot in ten of the fifteen slave states.

An unprecedented number of voters cast their ballots on November 6, 1860. Approximately 82 percent of eligible northern men and 70 percent of eligible southern men went to the polls. Lincoln swept all of the eighteen free states except New Jersey, which split its electoral votes between him and Douglas. Although Lincoln received only 39 percent of the popular vote, he won easily in the electoral college with 180 votes, 28 more than he needed for victory (Map 14.5). Lincoln did not win because his opposition was splintered. Even if the votes of his three opponents had been combined, Lincoln still would have won. He won because his votes were concentrated in the free states, which contained a majority of electoral votes. Ominously, however, Breckinridge, running on a southern-rights platform, won the entire Lower South, plus Delaware, Maryland, and North Carolina.

> "Mr. Lincoln and his party assert that this doctrine of equality applies to the negro, and necessarily there can exist no such thing as property in our equals."
> — Former Georgia governor HOWELL COBB

"The Union Is Dissolved!"
On December 20, 1860, the *Charleston Mercury* put out this special edition of the paper to celebrate South Carolina's secession from the Union. Six weeks earlier, upon hearing the news that Lincoln had won the presidency, the *Mercury* had predicted as much, announcing, "The revolution of 1860 has been initiated." Chicago Historical Society.

South cannot exist without slavery." They disagreed about whether the mere presence of a Republican in the White House made it necessary to exercise what they considered a legitimate right to secede.

The debate about what to do was briefest in South Carolina; it seceded from the Union on December 20, 1860. By February 1861, the six other Lower South states marched in South Carolina's footsteps. In some states, the vote was close. In general, slaveholders spearheaded secession, while nonslaveholders in the Piedmont and mountain counties, where slaves were relatively few, displayed the greatest attachment to the Union. In February, representatives from South Carolina, Georgia, Florida, Alabama, Mississippi, Louisiana, and Texas met in Montgomery, Alabama, where they celebrated the birth of the **Confederate States of America**. Mississippi senator Jefferson Davis became president, and Alexander Stephens of Georgia, who had spoken so eloquently about the dangers of revolution, became vice president. In March 1861, Stephens declared that the Confederacy's "cornerstone" was "the great truth that the negro is not equal to the white man; that slavery, subordination to the superior race, is his natural and moral condition."

Lincoln's election had split the Union. Now secession split the South. Seven slave states seceded during the winter, but the eight slave states of the Upper South rejected secession, at least for the moment. The Upper South had a smaller stake in slavery. Barely half as many white families in the Upper South held slaves (21 percent) as in the Lower South (37 percent). Slaves represented twice as large a percentage of the population in the Lower South (48 percent) as in the Upper South (23 percent). Consequently, whites in the Upper South had fewer fears that Republican ascendancy meant economic

Secession of the Lower South, December 1860–February 1861

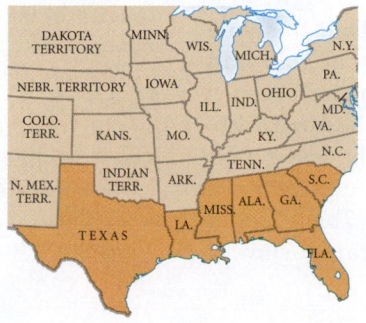

catastrophe, social chaos, and racial war. Lincoln would need to do more than just be elected to provoke them into secession.

The nation had to wait until March 4, 1861, when Lincoln took office, to see what he would do. (Presidents-elect waited four months to take office until 1933, when the Twentieth Amendment to the Constitution shifted the inauguration to January 20.) After his election, Lincoln chose to stay in Springfield and to say nothing. "Lame-duck" president James Buchanan sat in Washington and did nothing. Buchanan demonstrated,

William H. Seward said mockingly, that "it is the President's duty to enforce the laws, unless somebody opposes him." In Congress, efforts at cobbling together a peace-saving compromise came to nothing.

Lincoln began his inaugural address with reassurances to the South. He had "no lawful right" to interfere with slavery where it existed, he declared again, adding for emphasis that he had "no inclination to do so." Conciliatory about slavery, Lincoln proved inflexible about the Union. The Union, he declared, was "perpetual." Secession was "anarchy" and "legally void." The Constitution required him to execute the law "in all the States." The decision for civil war or peace rested in the South's hands, Lincoln said: "You can have no conflict, without being yourselves the aggressors. *You* have no oath registered in Heaven to destroy the government, while I shall have the most solemn one to 'preserve, protect, and defend' it." What Confederates in Charleston held in their hands at that very moment were the cords for firing the cannons aimed at the federal garrison at Fort Sumter.

REVIEW   Why did some southern states secede immediately after Lincoln's election?

▶ Conclusion: Slavery, Free Labor, and the Failure of Political Compromise

As their economies, societies, and cultures diverged in the nineteenth century, Northerners and Southerners expressed different concepts of the American promise and the place of slavery within it. Their differences crystallized into political form in 1846 when David Wilmot proposed banning slavery in any territory won in the Mexican-American War. "As if by magic," a Boston newspaper observed, "it brought to a head the great question that is about to divide the American people." Discovery of gold and other precious metals in the West added urgency to the controversy over slavery in the territories. Congress attempted to address the issue with the Compromise of 1850, but the Fugitive Slave Act and the publication of *Uncle Tom's Cabin* hardened northern sentiments against slavery

and confirmed southern suspicions of northern ill will. The bloody violence that erupted in Kansas in 1856 and the incendiary *Dred Scott* decision in 1857 further eroded hope for a solution to this momentous question.

During the extended crisis of the Union that stretched from 1846 to 1861, the slavery question intertwined with national politics. The traditional Whig and Democratic parties struggled to hold together as new parties, most notably the Republican Party, emerged. Politicians fixed their attention on the expansion of slavery, but from the beginning the nation recognized that the controversy had less to do with slavery in the territories than with the future of slavery in America.

For more than seventy years, statesmen had found compromises that accepted slavery and preserved the Union. But as each section grew increasingly committed to its labor system and the promise it offered, Americans discovered that accommodation had limits. In 1859, John Brown's militant antislavery pushed white Southerners to the edge. In 1860, Lincoln's election convinced whites in the Lower South that slavery and the society they had built on it were at risk in the Union, and they seceded. In his inaugural address, Lincoln pleaded, "We are not enemies but friends. We must not be enemies." By then, however, seven southern states had ceased to sing what he called "the chorus of the Union." It remained to be seen whether disunion would mean war.

▶ Selected Bibliography

General Works

Don E. Fehrenbacher, *The Slaveholding Republic: An Account of the United States Government's Relations to Slavery* (2001).

Michael Holt, *Fate of Their Country: Politicians, Slavery Extension, and the Coming of the Civil War* (2004).

Bruce C. Levine, *Half Slave and Half Free: The Roots of the Civil War* (1992).

James M. McPherson, *Ordeal by Fire: The Civil War and Reconstruction* (1982).

Mark E. Neely, *Boundaries of American Political Culture in the Civil War Era* (2005).

Eric H. Walther, *The Shattering of the Union: America in the 1850s* (2004).

Sean Wilentz, *The Rise of American Democracy: Jefferson to Lincoln* (2005).

Northern Sectionalism

Tom Chaffin, *Pathfinder: John Charles Frémont and the Course of American Empire* (2002).

Rodney O. Davis and Douglas L. Wilson, eds., *The Lincoln-Douglas Debates* (2008).

Eric Foner, *Free Labor, Free Soil, Free Men: The Ideology of the Republican Party before the Civil War* (1970).

William E. Gienapp, *The Origins of the Republican Party, 1852–1856* (1987).

Susan-Mary Grant, *North over South: Northern Nationalism and American Identity in the Antebellum Era* (2000).

David Grimsted, *American Mobbing, 1828–1865: Toward Civil War* (1998).

Joan D. Hedrick, *Harriet Beecher Stowe: A Life* (1994).

Pamela Herr, *Jessie Benton Frémont: A Biography* (1987).

Nancy Isenberg, *Sex and Citizenship in Antebellum America* (1998).

David S. Reynolds, *John Brown, Abolitionist: The Man Who Killed Slavery, Sparked the Civil War, and Seeded Civil Rights* (2005).

James Brewer Stewart, *Wendell Phillips, Liberty's Hero* (1986).

Wendy Hamand Venet, *Neither Ballots nor Bullets: Women Abolitionists and the Civil War* (1991).

Douglas L. Wilson, *Honor's Voice: The Transformation of Abraham Lincoln* (1998).

Kenneth J. Winkle, *The Young Eagle: The Rise of Abraham Lincoln* (2001).

Southern Sectionalism

William J. Cooper Jr., *The South and the Politics of Slavery, 1828–1856* (1978).

John Patrick Daly, *When Slavery Was Called Freedom: Evangelicalism, Proslavery, and the Causes of the Civil War* (2002).

Lacy K. Ford Jr., *Origins of Southern Radicalism: The South Carolina Upcountry, 1800–1860* (1988).

William W. Freehling, *The Road to Disunion, vol. 1, Secessionists at Bay, 1776–1854* (1990).

William A. Link, *Roots of Secession: Slavery and Politics in Antebellum Virginia* (2002).

Robert E. May, *Manifest Destiny's Underworld: Filibustering in Antebellum America* (2002).

Christopher J. Olsen, *Political Culture and Secession in Mississippi: Masculinity, Honor, and the Antiparty Tradition, 1830–1860* (2002).

Manisha Sinha, *The Counterrevolution of Slavery: Politics and Ideology in Antebellum South Carolina* (2000).

Mitchell Snay, *Gospel of Disunion: Religion and Separatism in the Antebellum South* (1993).

Secession

Daniel Crofts, *Reluctant Confederates: Upper South Unionists in the Secession Crisis* (1989).

Charles B. Dew, *Apostles of Disunion: Southern Secession Commissioners and the Causes of the Civil War* (2001).

Michael P. Johnson, *Toward a Patriarchal Republic: The Secession of Georgia* (1977).

David M. Potter, *Lincoln and His Party in the Secession Crisis* (1942).

Lorman A. Ratner and Dwight L. Teeter Jr., *Fanatics and Fire-Eaters: Newspapers and the Coming of the Civil War* (2003).

▶ **FOR MORE BOOKS ABOUT TOPICS IN THIS CHAPTER,** see the Online Bibliography at **bedfordstmartins.com/roark**.

▶ **FOR ADDITIONAL PRIMARY SOURCES FROM THIS PERIOD,** see Michael Johnson, ed., *Reading the American Past*, Fifth Edition.

▶ **FOR WEB SITES, IMAGES, AND DOCUMENTS RELATED TO TOPICS AND PLACES IN THIS CHAPTER,** visit Make History at **bedfordstmartins.com/roark**.

Reviewing Chapter 14

KEY TERMS

Explain each term's significance.

The Bitter Fruits of War
Wilmot Proviso (p. 430)
free labor (p. 430)
John C. Calhoun (p. 430)
Lewis Cass (p. 430)
popular sovereignty (p. 430)
Zachary Taylor (p. 431)
Charles Sumner (p. 431)
Free-Soil Party (p. 431)
Stephen A. Douglas (p. 433)
Compromise of 1850 (p. 434)

The Sectional Balance Undone
Uncle Tom's Cabin (p. 434)
underground railroad (p. 434)
Fugitive Slave Act (p. 434)
Harriet Beecher Stowe (p. 435)
doughfaces (p. 436)
Gadsden Purchase (p. 437)
Kansas-Nebraska Act (p. 437)

Realignment of the Party System
Know-Nothings (p. 439)
Republican Party (p. 440)
John C. Frémont (p. 443)
Jessie Frémont (p. 444)

Freedom under Siege
John Brown (p. 445)
"Bleeding Kansas" (p. 445)
Roger B. Taney (p. 448)
Dred Scott decision (p. 448)
Abraham Lincoln (p. 449)
Lecompton constitution (p. 450)
Lincoln-Douglas debates (p. 451)

The Union Collapses
Constitutional Union Party (p. 453)
southern Unionists (p. 454)
secessionists (p. 454)
Confederate States of America (p. 455)

REVIEW QUESTIONS

Use key terms and dates to support your answer.

1. Why did responses to the Wilmot Proviso split along sectional rather than party lines? (pp. 429–434)

2. Why did the Fugitive Slave Act provoke such strong opposition in the North? (pp. 434–437)

3. Why did the Whig Party disintegrate in the 1850s? (pp. 438–444)

4. Why did the *Dred Scott* decision strengthen northern suspicions of a "Slave Power" conspiracy? (pp. 444–451)

5. Why did some southern states secede immediately after Lincoln's election? (pp. 451–456)

MAKING CONNECTIONS

Draw on key terms, the timeline, and review questions.

1. The process of compromise that had successfully contained tensions between slave and free states since the nation's founding collapsed with secession. Why did compromise fail at this moment? In your answer, address specific political conflicts and attempts to solve them between 1846 and 1861.

2. In the 1850s, many Americans supported popular sovereignty as the best solution to the explosive question of slavery in the western territories. Why was this solution so popular, and why did it ultimately prove inadequate? In your answer, be sure to address popular sovereignty's varied critics as well as its champions.

3. In the 1840s and 1850s, the United States witnessed the realignment of its long-standing two-party system. Why did the old system fall apart, what emerged to take its place, and how did this process contribute to the coming of the Civil War?

4. Abraham Lincoln believed that he had staked out a moderate position on the question of slavery, avoiding the extremes of immediate abolitionism and calls for the unlimited protection of slavery. Why, then, did some southern states determine that his election necessitated the radical act of secession?

LINKING TO THE PAST

Link events in this chapter to earlier events.

1. How did social and economic developments in the South during the first half of the nineteenth century influence the decisions that southern politicians made in the 1840s and 1850s? (See chapter 13.)

2. How did the policies of the Republican Party reflect the free-labor ideals of the North? (See chapter 12.)

▶ FOR PRACTICE QUIZZES AND OTHER STUDY TOOLS, visit the Online Study Guide at bedfordstmartins.com/roark.

TIMELINE 1820–1861

1820	• Missouri Compromise.
1846	• Wilmot Proviso introduced in Congress.
1847	• Wilmot Proviso defeated in Senate.
	• Compromise of "popular sovereignty" offered.
1848	• Free-Soil Party founded.
	• Whig Zachary Taylor elected president.
1849	• California gold rush.
1850	• Taylor dies; Vice President Millard Fillmore becomes president.
	• Compromise of 1850 becomes law.
1852	• *Uncle Tom's Cabin* published.
	• Democrat Franklin Pierce elected president.
1853	• Gadsden Purchase.
1854	• American (Know-Nothing) Party emerges.
	• Kansas-Nebraska Act.
	• Republican Party founded.
1856	• "Bleeding Kansas."
	• "Sack of Lawrence."
	• Preston Brooks canes Charles Sumner.
	• Pottawatomie massacre.
	• Democrat James Buchanan elected president.
1857	• *Dred Scott* decision.
	• Congress rejects Lecompton constitution.
	• Panic of 1857.
1858	• Abraham Lincoln and Stephen A. Douglas debate slavery; Douglas wins Senate seat.
1859	• John Brown raids Harpers Ferry, Virginia.
1860	• Republican Abraham Lincoln elected president.
	• South Carolina secedes from Union.
1861	• Six other Lower South states secede.
	• Confederate States of America formed.
	• Lincoln takes office.

UNION PARADE DRUM

This drum from Belfast, Maine, was made of wood cut into thin layers, then steamed and shaped into a round shell. The drum heads were made from calfskin that was stretched tight by ropes. The fierce eagle, flag, and motto announced the cause. Drums got soldiers up in the morning; signaled them to report for breakfast, roll call, and guard duty; and announced lights out. The most important use of drums was on the battlefield where they communicated orders from commanding officers to their troops. The life of a drummer seemed glorious, and boys as young as ten eagerly served in northern units.

Drum: photo courtesy Allan Katz Americana, Woodbridge, CT; background image: Library of Congress.

15

The Crucible of War
1861–1865

ON THE RAINY NIGHT OF SEPTEMBER 21, 1862, IN WILMINGTON, North Carolina, twenty-four-year-old William Gould and seven other runaway slaves crowded into a small boat on the Cape Fear River and quietly pushed away from the dock. They rowed hard throughout the night, reaching the Atlantic Ocean by dawn. They plunged into the swells and made for the Union navy patrolling offshore. At 10:30 that morning, the USS *Cambridge* took the men aboard.

Astonishingly, on the same day that Gould reached the federal ship, President Abraham Lincoln revealed his intention to issue a proclamation of emancipation freeing the slaves in the Confederate states. Because the proclamation would not take effect until January 1863, Gould was not legally free in the eyes of the U.S. government. But the U.S. Navy, suffering from a shortage of sailors, cared little about the formal status of runaway slaves. Within days, all eight runaways became sailors in the U.S. Navy.

William Gould could read and write, and he began making almost daily entries in his diary. In some ways, Gould's naval experience looked like that of a white sailor. He found duty on a ship in the blockading squadron both boring and exhilarating. Long days of tedious work were sometimes interrupted by a "period of daring exploit." When Gould's ship closed on a Confederate vessel, he declared that "we told them good morning in the shape of a shot." In a five-day period in 1862, the *Cambridge* helped capture four blockade runners and ran another aground.

But Gould's Civil War experience was shaped by his race. Like most black men in the Union military, he saw service as an opportunity to fight slavery. From the beginning, Gould linked union and freedom, which he called "the holiest of all causes." Gould witnessed a number of ugly racial incidents on federal ships, however. "There was A malee [melee] on Deck between the white and colard [colored] men," he observed. Later, when a black regiment came aboard, "they were treated verry rough by the crew," he said. The white sailors "refused to let them eat off the mess pans and called them all kinds of names[;] . . . in all they was treated shamefully."

Still, Gould was proud of his service in the navy and monitored the progress of racial equality during the war. On shore leave in 1863, he cheered the "20th Regmt of U.S. (collard) Volunteers . . . pronounce[d] by all to be A splendid Regement." In March 1865, he celebrated the "passage of an amendment of the Con[sti]tution prohibiting slavery througho[ut] the United States." And a month later, he thrilled to the "Glad Tidings that the Stars and Stripe[s] had been planted over the Capital of the D—nd

Confederacy by the invincible Grant." He added, we must not forget the "Mayrters to the cau[se] of Right and Equality."

Slaves like the eight runaways from Wilmington took the first steps toward making the war for union also a war for freedom. Early in the fighting, black abolitionist Frederick Douglass challenged the friends of freedom to *"be up and doing; — now is your time."* But for the first eighteen months of the war, federal soldiers fought solely to uphold the Constitution and preserve the nation. With the Emancipation Proclamation, however, the northern war effort took on a dual purpose: to save the Union and to free the slaves.

Even if the Civil War had not touched slavery, the conflict still would have transformed America. As the world's first modern war, it mobilized the entire populations of North and South, harnessed the productive capacities of both economies, and produced battles that fielded 200,000 soldiers and created casualties in the tens of thousands. The carnage lasted four years and cost the nation an estimated 620,000 lives, nearly as many as in all of its other wars combined. The war helped mold the modern American nation-state, and the federal government emerged with new power and responsibility over national life. The war encouraged industrialization. It tore families apart and pushed women into new work and roles. But because the war for union also became a war against slavery, the northern victory had truly revolutionary meaning.

Recalling the Civil War years, Frederick Douglass said, "It is something to couple one's name with great occasions." It *was* something — for William Gould and millions of other Americans. Poet Walt Whitman believed that the war was the "very centre, circumference, umbilicus" of his life. Whether they fought for the Confederacy or the Union, whether they labored behind the lines to supply Yankee or rebel soldiers, whether they prayed for the safe return of Northerners or Southerners, all Americans endured the crucible of war. But the war affected no group more than the 4 million African Americans who saw its beginning as slaves and emerged as free people.

The Crew of the USS *Hunchback*
African Americans served as sailors in the federal military long before they were permitted to become soldiers. Blacks initially served only as coal heavers, cooks, and stewards, but within a year some black sailors joined their ships' gun crews. The *Hunchback* was one of the Union's innovative ironclad ships. Although ironclads made wooden navies obsolete, they were far from invincible. During the assault on Charleston in 1863, five of the nine federal ironclads were partially or wholly disabled. National Archives.

▶ "And the War Came"

Abraham Lincoln faced the worst crisis in the history of the nation: disunion. He revealed his strategy on March 4, 1861, in his inaugural address, which was firm yet conciliatory. First, he sought to stop the contagion of secession by avoiding any act that would push the skittish Upper South (North Carolina, Virginia, Maryland, Delaware, Kentucky, Tennessee, Missouri, and Arkansas) out of the Union. Second, he sought to reassure the seceding Lower South (South Carolina, Georgia, Florida, Alabama, Mississippi, Louisiana, and Texas) that the Republicans would not abolish slavery. Lincoln believed that Unionists there would assert themselves and overturn the secession decision. Always, Lincoln denied the right of secession and upheld the Union.

His counterpart, **Jefferson Davis**, fully intended to establish the Confederate States of America as an independent republic. To achieve permanence, Davis had to sustain the secession fever that had carried the Lower South out of the Union. Even if the Lower South held firm, however, the Confederacy would remain weak without additional states. Davis watched for opportunities to add new stars to the Confederate flag.

Neither man sought war; both wanted to achieve their objectives peacefully. As Lincoln later observed, "Both parties deprecated war, but one of them would *make* war rather than let the nation survive, and the other would *accept* war rather than let it perish. And the war came."

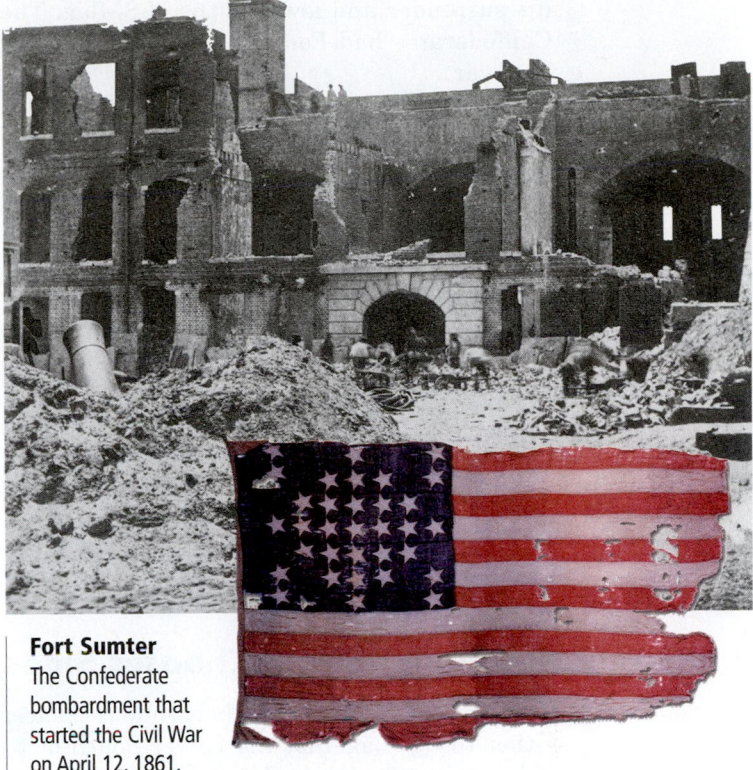

Fort Sumter
The Confederate bombardment that started the Civil War on April 12, 1861, lobbed more than 4,000 rounds at Fort Sumter, located on an artificial island inside the entrance to Charleston harbor. Cannonballs pulverized the outer walls, while hot shot ignited the wooden buildings inside. Shrapnel from thirty-three hours of cannon fire shredded this flag, which flew over the fort throughout the bombardment. When Union major Robert Anderson surrendered on April 13, he and his men marched out of the fort under this tattered banner. When Anderson returned to Fort Sumter in April 1865, he triumphantly raised this very flag. Photograph: Minnesota Historical Society; flag: Confederate Museum, United Daughters of the Confederacy.

Attack on Fort Sumter

Major Robert Anderson and some eighty U.S. soldiers occupied **Fort Sumter**, which was perched on a tiny island at the entrance to Charleston harbor in South Carolina. The fort with its American flag became a hated symbol of the nation that Southerners had abandoned, and they wanted federal troops out. Sumter was also a symbol to Northerners, a beacon affirming federal sovereignty in the seceded states.

Lincoln decided to hold Fort Sumter, but to do so, he had to provision it, for Anderson was running dangerously short of food. In the first week of April 1861, Lincoln authorized a peaceful expedition to bring supplies, but not military reinforcements, to the fort. The president understood that he risked war, but his plan honored his inaugural promises to defend federal property and to avoid using military force unless first attacked. Masterfully, Lincoln

had shifted the fateful decision of war or peace to Jefferson Davis.

On April 9, Davis and his cabinet met to consider the situation in Charleston harbor. The territorial integrity of the Confederacy demanded the end of the federal presence, Davis argued. But his secretary of state, Robert Toombs of Georgia, pleaded against military action. "Mr. President," he declared, "at this time it is suicide, murder, and will lose us every friend at the North. You will wantonly strike a hornet's nest which extends from mountain to ocean, and legions now quiet will swarm out and sting us to death." But Davis sent word to Confederate troops in Charleston to take the fort before the relief expedition arrived. Thirty-three hours of bombardment on April 12 and 13 reduced the fort to rubble. Miraculously, not a single Union soldier died. On April 14, with the fort ablaze, Major Anderson offered his surrender and lowered the U.S. flag. The Confederates had Fort Sumter, but they also had war.

On April 15, when Lincoln called for 75,000 militiamen to serve for ninety days to put down the rebellion, several times that number rushed to defend the flag. Democrats responded as fervently as Republicans. Stephen A. Douglas, the recently defeated Democratic candidate for president, pledged his support. "There are only two sides to the question," he said. "Every man must be for the United States or against it. There can be no neutrals in this war, *only patriots — or traitors*." But the people of the Upper South found themselves torn.

> **"Every man must be for the United States or against it. There can be no neutrals in this war, *only patriots — or traitors*."**
>
> — Senator
> **STEPHEN A. DOUGLAS**

The Upper South Chooses Sides

The Upper South faced a horrendous choice: either to fight against the Lower South or to fight against the Union. Many who only months earlier had rejected secession now embraced the Confederacy. To vote against southern independence was one thing, to fight fellow Southerners quite another. Thousands felt betrayed, believing that Lincoln had promised to achieve a peaceful reunion by waiting patiently for Unionists to retake power in the seceding states. It was a "politician's war," one man declared, but he conceded that "this is no time now to discuss the causes, but it is the duty of all who regard Southern institutions of value to side with the South, make common cause with the Confederate States and sink or swim with them."

One by one, the states of the Upper South jumped off the fence. Virginia, Arkansas, Tennessee, and North Carolina joined the Confederacy (Map 15.1). But in the border states of Delaware, Maryland, Kentucky, and Missouri, Unionism triumphed. Only in Delaware, where slaves accounted for less than 2 percent of the population, was the victory easy. In Maryland, Unionism needed a helping hand. Rather than allow the state to secede and make Washington, D.C., a federal island in a Confederate sea, Lincoln suspended the writ of habeas corpus, essentially setting aside constitutional guarantees that protect citizens from arbitrary arrest and detention, and he ordered U.S. troops into Baltimore. Maryland's legislature rejected secession.

The struggle turned violent in the West. In Missouri, Unionists won a narrow victory, but southern-sympathizing guerrilla bands roamed the state for the duration of the war, terrorizing civilians and soldiers alike. In Kentucky, Unionists also narrowly defeated secession, but the prosouthern minority claimed otherwise. The Confederacy, not especially careful about counting votes, eagerly made Missouri and Kentucky the twelfth and thirteenth stars on the Confederate flag.

Throughout the border states, but especially in Kentucky, the Civil War divided families. Seven of Senator Henry Clay's grandsons fought: four for the Confederacy and three for the Union. Lincoln understood that the border states — particularly Kentucky — contained indispensable resources, population, and wealth and also controlled major rivers and railroads. "I think to lose Kentucky is nearly the same as to lose the whole game," Lincoln said. "Kentucky gone, we can not hold Missouri, nor, as I think, Maryland. These all against us, . . . we would as well consent to separation at once."

In the end, only eleven of the fifteen slave states joined the Confederate States of America. Moreover, the four seceding Upper South states contained significant numbers of people who felt little affection for the Confederacy. Dissatisfaction was so rife in the western counties of Virginia

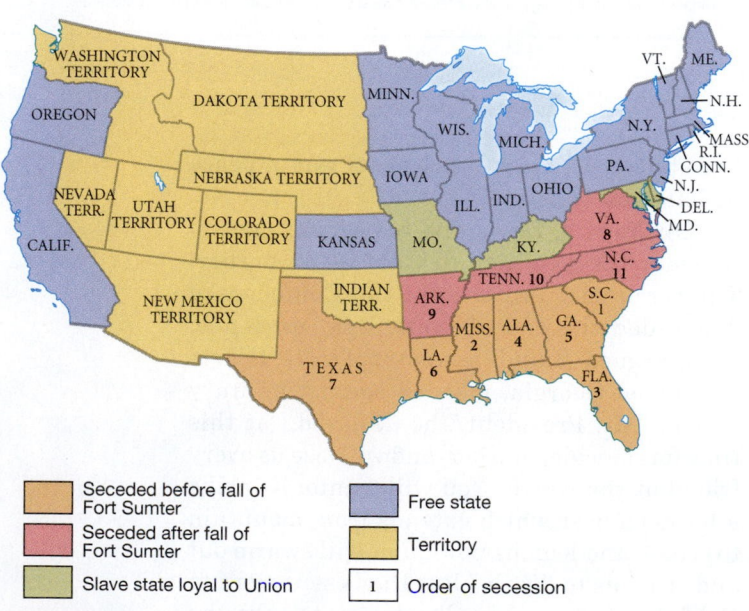

Legend:
- Seceded before fall of Fort Sumter
- Seceded after fall of Fort Sumter
- Slave state loyal to Union
- Free state
- Territory
- 1 Order of secession

MAP 15.1
Secession, 1860–1861
After Lincoln's election, the fifteen slave states debated what to do. Seven states quickly left the Union, four left after the firing on Fort Sumter, and four remained loyal to the Union.

that in 1863 citizens there voted to create the separate state of West Virginia, loyal to the Union. Still, the acquisition of four new states greatly strengthened the Confederacy's drive for national independence.

REVIEW Why did both the Union and the Confederacy consider control of the border states crucial?

▶ The Combatants

Only slaveholders had a direct economic stake in preserving slavery (estimated at some $3 billion in 1860), but most whites in the Confederacy defended the institution, the way of life built on it, and the Confederate nation. The degraded and subjugated status of blacks elevated the status of the poorest whites. "It matters not whether slaves be actually owned by many or by few," one Southerner declared. "It is enough that one simply belongs to the superior and ruling race, to secure consideration and respect." Moreover, Yankee "aggression" was no longer a mere threat; it was real and at the South's door. Southern whites equated the secession of 1861 with the declaration of independence from tyrannical British rule in 1776. As one Georgia woman said, Southerners wanted "nothing from the North but — to *be let alone.*"

For Northerners, rebel "treason" threatened to destroy the best government on earth. The South's failure to accept the democratic election of a president and its firing on the nation's flag challenged the rule of law, the authority of the Constitution, and the ability of the people to govern themselves. As an Indiana soldier told his wife, a "good government is the best thing on earth. Property is nothing without it, because it is not protected; a family is nothing without it, because they cannot be educated." Only a Union victory, Lincoln declared, would secure America's promise "to elevate the condition of man."

Northerners and Southerners rallied behind their separate flags, fully convinced that they were in the right and that God was on their side. But no one could argue that the Confederacy's resources and forces equaled the Union's. Yankees took heart from their superior power, but the rebels believed they had advantages that nullified every northern strength. Both sides mobilized swiftly in 1861, and each devised what it believed would be a winning military and diplomatic strategy.

How They Expected to Win

The balance sheet of northern and southern resources reveals enormous advantages for the Union (Figure 15.1). The twenty-three states remaining in the Union had a population of 22.3 million; the eleven Confederate states had a population of only 9.1 million, of whom 3.67 million (40 percent) were slaves. The North's economic advantages were even more overwhelming. Yet Southerners expected to win — for some good reasons — and they came very close to doing so.

Southerners knew they bucked the military odds, but hadn't the liberty-loving colonists in 1776 also done so? "Britain could not conquer three million," a Louisianan proclaimed, and "the world cannot conquer the South." How could anyone doubt the outcome of

> "Britain could not conquer three million, the world cannot conquer the South."
> — A Louisianan

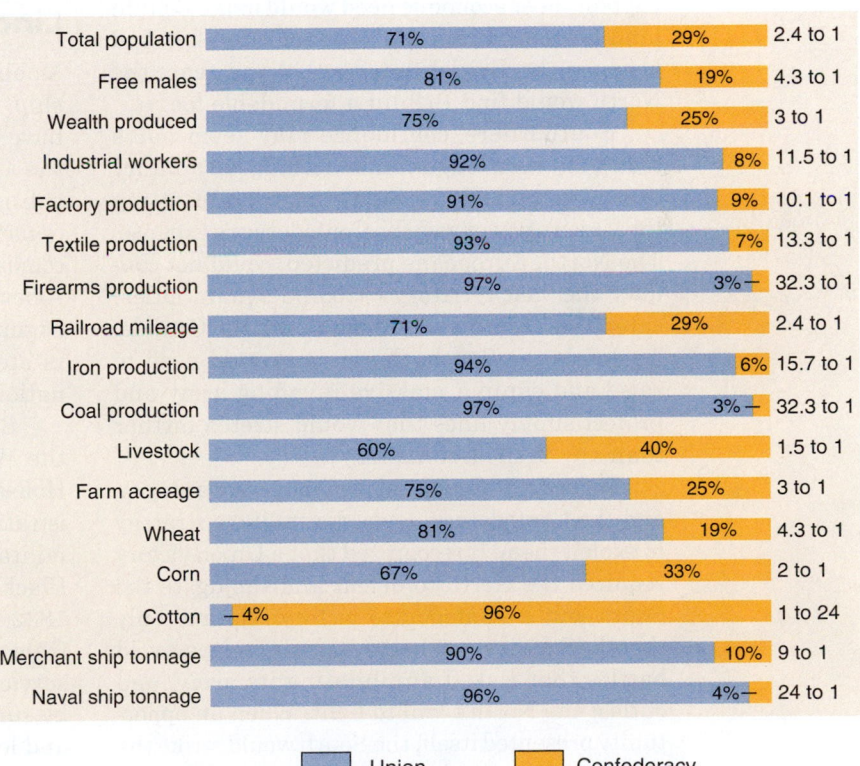

FIGURE 15.1 **Resources of the Union and the Confederacy**
The Union's enormous statistical advantages failed to convince Confederates that their cause was doomed.

a contest between lean, hard, country-born rebel warriors defending family, property, and liberty, and soft, flabby, citified Yankee mechanics waging an unconstitutional war?

The South's confidence also rested on its belief that northern prosperity depended on the South's cotton. Without cotton, New England textile mills would stand idle. Without planters purchasing northern manufactured goods, northern factories would drown in their own unsold surpluses. And without the foreign exchange earned by the overseas sales of cotton, the financial structure of the entire Yankee nation would collapse. A Virginian spoke for most Confederates when he declared that in the South's ability to "withhold the benefits of our trade, we hold a power over the North more powerful than a powerful army in the field."

King Cotton diplomacy would also make Europe a powerful ally of the Confederacy, Southerners reasoned. After all, they said, Britain's economy (and, to a lesser degree, France's) also depended on cotton. Of the 900 million pounds of cotton Britain imported annually, more than 700 million pounds came from the American South. If the supply was interrupted, sheer economic need would make Britain (and perhaps France) a Confederate ally. And because the British navy ruled the seas, the North would find Britain a formidable foe.

Southerners' confidence may seem naive today, but even tough-minded European military observers picked the South to win. Offsetting the Union's power was the Confederacy's expanse. The North, Europeans predicted, could not conquer the vast territory (750,000 square miles) extending from the Potomac to the Rio Grande. To defeat the South, the Union would need to raise and equip a massive invading army and protect supply lines that would stretch farther than any in modern history.

Indeed, the South enjoyed major advantages, and the Confederacy devised a military strategy to exploit them. It recognized that a Union victory required the North to defeat and subjugate the South, but a Confederate victory required only that the South stay at home, blunt invasions, avoid battles that risked annihilating its army, and outlast the North's will to fight. When an opportunity presented itself, the South would strike the invaders. Like the American colonists, the South could win independence by not losing the war.

If the North did nothing, the South would by default establish itself as a sovereign nation. The Lincoln administration, therefore, adopted an offensive strategy that applied pressure at many points. Lincoln declared a naval blockade of the Confederacy to deny it the ability to sell cotton abroad, giving the South far fewer dollars to pay for war goods. Even before the North could mount an effective blockade, however, Jefferson Davis decided voluntarily to cease exporting cotton. He wanted to create a cotton "famine" that would enfeeble the northern economy and precipitate European intervention. But the cotton famine Davis created devastated the South, not the North, and kept Europe on the diplomatic sidelines. Lincoln also ordered the Union army into Virginia, at the same time planning a march through the Mississippi valley that would cut the Confederacy in two. Dubbed the **Anaconda Plan**, this ambitious strategy took advantage of the Union's superior resources.

Neither side could foresee the magnitude and duration of the war. Americans thought of war in terms of the Mexican-American War of the 1840s, a conflict that had cost relatively few lives and had inflicted only light damage on the countryside. On the eve of the fighting, they could not know that four ghastly years of bloodletting lay ahead.

Lincoln and Davis Mobilize

Mobilization required effective political leadership, and at first glance the South appeared to have the advantage. Jefferson Davis brought to the Confederate presidency a distinguished political career, including experience in the U.S. Senate. He was also a West Point graduate, a combat veteran and authentic hero of the Mexican-American War, and a former secretary of war. Dignified and ramrod straight, with "a jaw sawed in steel," Davis appeared to be everything a nation could want in a wartime leader.

By contrast, Abraham Lincoln brought to the White House one lackluster term in the House of Representatives and almost no administrative experience. His sole brush with anything military was as a captain in the militia in the Black Hawk War, a brief struggle in Illinois in 1832 in which whites expelled the last Indians from the state. Lincoln later joked about his service in the Black Hawk War as the time when he survived bloody encounters with mosquitoes and led raids on wild onion patches. The lanky, disheveled Illinois lawyer-politician looked anything but military or presidential in his bearing.

In fact, the hardworking Davis proved to be less than he appeared. He had no gift for military strategy yet intervened often in military affairs. He was an even less able political leader. Quarrelsome and proud, he had an acid tongue that made enemies the Confederacy could ill afford. The Confederacy's intimidating problems might have defeated an even more talented leader, however. For example, state sovereignty, which was enshrined in the Confederate constitution, made Davis's task of organizing a new nation and fighting a war difficult in the extreme.

With Lincoln the North got far more than met the eye. He proved himself a master politician and a superb leader. When forming his cabinet, Lincoln appointed the ablest men, no matter that they were often his chief rivals and critics. He appointed Salmon P. Chase secretary of the treasury, knowing that Chase had presidential ambitions. As secretary of state, he chose his chief opponent for the Republican nomination in 1860, William H. Seward. Despite his civilian background, Lincoln displayed an innate understanding of military strategy. No one was more crucial in mapping the Union war plan. Moreover, Lincoln's eloquent letters and speeches helped galvanize the northern people in defense of the nation he called "the last best hope of earth."

Lincoln and Davis began gathering their armies. Confederates had to build almost everything from scratch, and Northerners had to channel their superior numbers and industrial resources to the purposes of war. On the eve of the war, the federal army numbered only 16,000 men, most of them scattered over the West subjugating Indians. One-third of the officers followed the example of the Virginian Robert E. Lee, resigning their commissions and heading south. The U.S. Navy was in better shape. Forty-two ships were in service, and a large merchant

Northern Volunteers, 1861
Lincoln called the Civil War a "People's Contest," a "struggle for maintaining in the world that form and substance of government, whose leading object is to elevate the condition of men — to lift artificial weights from all shoulders — clear the paths of laudable pursuit for all — to afford all an unfettered start, and a fair chance, in the race of life." Northerners shared Lincoln's vision, and in countless small towns from Iowa to Maine, when word arrived that soldiers were needed, scores of young men like these in Illinois rushed to volunteer. Private Collection/Picture Research Consultants & Archives.

marine would in time provide more ships and sailors for the Union cause. Possessing a much weaker navy, the South pinned its hopes on its armies.

The Confederacy made prodigious efforts to build new factories to produce tents, blankets, shoes, and its gray uniforms, but many rebel soldiers slept in the open air without blankets and were sometimes without shoes. Even when factories managed to produce what the soldiers needed, southern railroads — captured, destroyed, or left in disrepair — often could not deliver the goods. Food production proved less of a problem, but food sometimes rotted before it reached the soldiers. The one bright spot was the Confederacy's Ordnance Bureau, headed by Josiah Gorgas, a near miracle worker when it came to manufacturing gunpowder, cannons, and rifles.

In April 1864, Gorgas proudly observed: "Where three years ago we were not making a gun, a pistol nor a sabre, no shot nor shell . . . we now make all these in quantities to meet the demands of our large armies."

Recruiting and supplying huge armies required enormous

The Minié Ball
The Union army was one of the best-equipped armies in history, but none of its weaponry proved more vital than a French innovation by Captain Claude Minié. In 1848, Minié created an inch-long bullet that was rammed down a rifle barrel and would spin at great speed as it left the muzzle. The spin gave the bullet greater distance and accuracy than bullets fired from smoothbore weapons. When the war began, most soldiers carried smoothbore muskets, but by 1863 infantry on both sides fought with rifles. Bullets caused more than 90 percent of battle wounds, and minié balls proved extremely destructive to human bodies on impact. Picture Research Consultants & Archives.

new revenues. At first, the Union and the Confederacy sold war bonds, which essentially were loans from patriotic citizens. In addition, both sides turned to taxes. The North raised one-fifth of its wartime revenue from taxes; the South raised only one-twentieth. Eventually, both began printing paper money. Inflation soared, but the Confederacy suffered more because it financed a greater part of its wartime costs through the printing press. Prices in the Union rose by about 80 percent during the war, while inflation in the Confederacy topped 9,000 percent.

Within months of the bombardment of Fort Sumter, both sides found men to fight and ways to supply them. But the underlying strength of the northern economy gave the Union the decided advantage. With their military and industrial muscles beginning to ripple, Northerners became itchy for action that would smash the rebellion. Horace Greeley's *New York Tribune* began to chant: "Forward to Richmond! Forward to Richmond!"

> **REVIEW** Why did the South believe it could win the war despite numerical disadvantages?

▶ Battling It Out, 1861–1862

During the first year and a half of the war, armies fought major campaigns in both East and West. Because the rival capitals — Richmond and Washington, D.C. — were only ninety miles apart and each was threatened more than once with capture, the eastern campaign was especially dramatic. But the battles in the West proved more decisive. As Yankee and rebel armies pounded each other on land, the navies fought on the seas and on the rivers of the South. In Europe, Confederate and U.S. diplomats competed for advantage in the corridors of power. All the while, casualty lists on both sides reached appalling lengths.

> **"If General McClellan does not want to use the army I would like to *borrow* it."**
> — ABRAHAM LINCOLN

Stalemate in the Eastern Theater

In the summer of 1861, Lincoln ordered the 35,000 Union troops assembling outside Washington to attack the 20,000 Confederates defending Manassas, a railroad junction in Virginia about thirty miles southwest of Washington. On July 21, the army forded Bull Run, a branch of the Potomac River, and engaged the southern forces (Map 15.2). But fast-moving southern reinforcements blunted the Union attack and then counterattacked. What began as an orderly Union retreat turned into a panicky stampede. Demoralized federal troops ran over shocked civilians as the soldiers raced back to Washington.

By Civil War standards, the casualties (wounded and dead) at the **battle of Bull Run** (or **Manassas**, as Southerners called the battle) were light, about 2,000 Confederates and 1,600 Federals. The significance of the battle lay in the lessons Northerners and Southerners drew from it. For Southerners, it confirmed the superiority of rebel fighting men and the inevitability of Confederate nationhood. Manassas was "*one of the decisive battles of the world*," a Georgian proclaimed. It "*has* secured our independence." While victory fed southern pride, defeat sobered Northerners. It was a major setback, admitted the *New York Tribune*, but "let us go to work, then, with a will." Bull Run taught Lincoln that victory would be neither quick nor easy. Within four days of the disaster, the president authorized the enlistment of 1 million men for three years.

Lincoln also found a new general, the young **George B. McClellan**, whom he appointed commander of the newly named Army of the Potomac. Having graduated from West Point second in his class, the thirty-four-year-old McClellan believed that he was a great soldier and that Lincoln was a dunce, the "original Gorilla." A superb administrator and organizer, McClellan energetically whipped his dispirited soldiers into shape, but he was reluctant to send them into battle. For all his energy, McClellan lacked decisiveness. Lincoln wanted a general who would advance, take risks, and fight, but McClellan went into winter quarters. "If General McClellan does not want to use the army I would like to *borrow* it," Lincoln declared in frustration.

Finally, in May 1862, McClellan launched his long-awaited offensive. He transported his highly polished army, now 130,000 strong, to the mouth of the James River and began slowly moving up the Yorktown peninsula toward Richmond. When he was within six miles of the Confederate capital, General Joseph Johnston hit him like a hammer. In the assault, Johnston was wounded and was replaced by **Robert E. Lee**, who would become the South's most celebrated general. Lee named his command the Army of Northern Virginia.

MAP ACTIVITY

Map 15.2   The Civil War, 1861–1862
While most eyes were focused on the eastern theater, especially the ninety-mile stretch of land between Washington, D.C., and the Confederate capital of Richmond, Virginia, Union troops were winning strategic victories in the West.

READING THE MAP: In which states did the Confederacy and the Union each win the most battles during this period? Which side used or followed water routes most for troop movements and attacks?

CONNECTIONS: Which major cities in the South and West fell to Union troops in 1862? Which strategic area did those Confederate losses place in Union hands? How did this outcome affect the later movement of troops and supplies?

The contrast between Lee and McClellan could hardly have been greater. McClellan brimmed with conceit and braggadocio; Lee was courteous and reserved. On the battlefield, McClellan grew timid and irresolute, and Lee became audaciously, even recklessly, aggressive. And Lee had at his side in the peninsula campaign military men of real talent: Thomas J. Jackson, nicknamed "Stonewall" for holding the line at Manassas, and James E. B. ("Jeb") Stuart, a dashing twenty-nine-year-old cavalry commander who rode circles around Yankee troops. Jackson ranks among the most brilliant commanders of the war, but in May 1863 he died at the battle of Chancellorsville.

Lee's assault initiated the Seven Days Battle (June 25–July 1) and began McClellan's march back down the peninsula. By the time McClellan reached safety, 30,000 men from both sides had died or been wounded. Although Southerners suffered twice the casualties of Northerners, Lee had saved Richmond. Lincoln wired McClellan

Peninsula Campaign, 1862

to abandon the peninsula campaign and replaced him with General John Pope.

In August, north of Richmond, at the second battle of Bull Run, Lee's smaller army battered Pope's forces and sent them scurrying back to Washington. Lincoln ordered Pope to Minnesota to pacify the Indians and restored McClellan to command. Lincoln had not changed his mind about McClellan's capacity as a warrior, but he reluctantly acknowledged that "if he can't fight himself, he excels in making others ready to fight." Lee could fight, and he pushed his army across the Potomac and invaded Maryland. A victory on northern soil would dislodge Maryland from the Union, Lee reasoned, and might even cause Lincoln to sue for peace.

On September 17, 1862, McClellan's forces engaged Lee's army at Antietam Creek (see Map 15.2). Earlier, a Union soldier had found a copy of Lee's orders to his army dropped by a careless Confederate officer, so McClellan had a clear picture of Lee's position. While McClellan's characteristic caution cost him the opportunity to destroy the opposing army, he still did severe damage. With "solid shot . . . cracking skulls like eggshells," according to one observer, the armies went after each other. At Miller's Cornfield, the firing was so intense that "every stalk of corn in the . . . field was cut as closely as could have been done with a knife." By nightfall, 6,000 men lay dead or dying on the battlefield, and 17,000 more had been wounded. **The battle of Antietam** would be the bloodiest day of the war. Instead of being the war-winning fight Lee had anticipated when he came north, Antietam sent the battered Army of Northern Virginia limping back home. McClellan claimed to have saved the North, but Lincoln again removed him from command of the Army of the Potomac and appointed General Ambrose Burnside.

Though bloodied, Lee found an opportunity in December to punish the enemy at Fredericksburg, Virginia, where Burnside's 122,000 Union troops faced 78,500 Confederates dug in behind a stone wall on the heights above the Rappahannock River. Half a mile of open ground separated the armies. "A chicken could not live on that field when we open on it," a Confederate artillery officer predicted. Yet Burnside ordered a frontal assault. When the shooting ceased, the Federals counted nearly 13,000 casualties, the Confederates fewer than 5,000. The battle of Fredericksburg was one of the Union's worst defeats. As 1862 ended, the North seemed no nearer to ending the rebellion than it had been when the war began. Rather than checkmate, military struggle in the East had reached stalemate.

The Battle of Savage's Station, by Robert Knox Sneden, 1862
In 1862, thirty-year-old Robert Sneden joined the Fortieth New York Volunteers and soon found himself in Virginia, part of George McClellan's peninsula campaign. A gifted artist and an eloquent writer, Sneden captured an early Confederate assault in what became known as the Seven Days Battle. The "storm of lead was continuous and deadly on the approaching lines of the Rebels," Sneden observed. "They bravely rushed up, however, to within twenty feet of our artillery." Sneden produced hundreds of vivid drawings and thousands of pages of remembrances, providing one of the most complete accounts of a Union soldier's Civil War experience.
© 1996, Lora Robbins Collection of Virginia Art, Virginia Historical Society.

The Dead of Antietam

In October 1862, photographer Mathew Brady opened an exhibition at his New York gallery that shocked the nation. The exhibition consisted of ninety-five photographs that presented the battle of Antietam as the soldiers saw it. The image here is of Confederate soldiers killed near the Dunkard Church, photographed two days later by Alexander Gardner. A New York Times reporter observed, "Mr. Brady has done something to bring to us the terrible reality and earnestness of the war. If he has not brought bodies and laid them in our door-yards and along [our] streets, he had done something very like it." Library of Congress.

Union Victories in the Western Theater

While most eyes focused on events in the East, the decisive early encounters of the war were taking place between the Appalachian Mountains and the Ozarks (see Map 15.2). Confederates wanted Missouri and Kentucky, states they claimed but did not control. Federals wanted to split Arkansas, Louisiana, and Texas from the Confederacy by taking control of the Mississippi River and to occupy Tennessee, one of the Confederacy's main producers of food, mules, and iron — all vital resources.

Before Union forces could march on Tennessee, they needed to secure Missouri to the west. Union troops swept across Missouri to the border of Arkansas, where in March 1862 they encountered a 16,000-man Confederate army, which included three regiments of Indians from the so-called Five Civilized Tribes — the Choctaw, Chickasaw, Creek, Seminole, and Cherokee. Although Indians fought on both sides during the war, Native Americans who sided with the South hoped that the Confederacy would grant them more independence than had the United States. The Union victory at the battle of Pea Ridge left Missouri free of Confederate troops, but Missouri was not free of Confederate fighters. Guerrilla bands led by the notorious William Clarke Quantrill and "Bloody Bill" Anderson burned, tortured, scalped, and murdered Union civilians and soldiers until the final year of the war.

Even farther west, Confederate armies sought to fulfill Jefferson Davis's vision of a slaveholding empire stretching all the way to the Pacific. Both sides recognized the immense value of the gold and silver mines of California, Nevada, and Colorado. And both sides bolstered their armies in the Southwest with Mexican Americans, some 2,500 fighting for the Confederacy and 1,000 joining Union forces. A quick strike by Texas troops took Santa Fe, New Mexico, in the winter of 1861–62. Then in March 1862, a band of Colorado miners ambushed and crushed southern forces at Glorieta Pass, outside Santa Fe. Confederate military failures in the far West meant that there would be no Confederate empire beyond Texas.

The principal western battles took place in Tennessee, where General **Ulysses S. Grant** emerged as the key northern commander. Grant had graduated from West Point and served bravely in Mexico. When the Civil War began, he was a thirty-nine-year-old dry-goods clerk in Galena, Illinois. Gentle at home, he became pugnacious on the battlefield. "The art of war is simple," he said. "Find out where your enemy is, get at him as soon as you can and strike him as hard as you can, and keep moving on." Grant's philosophy of war as attrition would take a huge toll in human life, but it played to the North's superiority in manpower. In his private's uniform and slouch hat, Grant did not look much like a general. But Lincoln, who did not look much like a president, learned his worth. Later, to critics who wanted the president to sack Grant because of his drinking, Lincoln would say, "*I can't spare this man. He fights.*"

In February 1862, operating in tandem with U.S. Navy

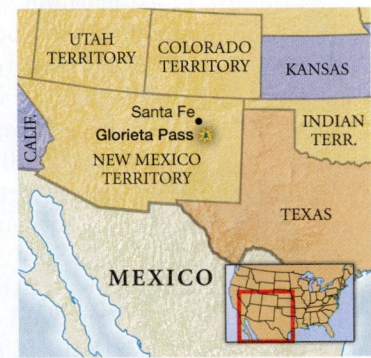

Battle of Glorieta Pass, 1862

Native American Recruits
Both the Union and the Confederacy enrolled Indian soldiers. Here, a Union recruiter swears in two recruits. The Confederates promised to assume the financial obligations of the old treaties with the United States, guarantee slavery, respect tribal independence, and permit the tribes to send delegates to Richmond. Cherokee chief John Ross, who signed with the Confederacy, likened his difficult choice to that of a man in a flood who sees a log floating by: "By refusing [the log] he is a doomed man. By seizing hold of it he has a chance for his life." Approximately 20,000 Indians fought in the Civil War, sometimes against each other. Wisconsin Historical Society.

of Memphis; and the South's largest city, New Orleans. By the end of 1862, the far West and most — but not all — of the Mississippi valley lay in Union hands. At the same time, the outcome of the struggle in another theater of war was also becoming clearer.

The Atlantic Theater

When the war began, the U.S. Navy's blockade fleet consisted of about three dozen ships to patrol more than 3,500 miles of southern coastline, and rebel merchant ships were able to slip in and out of southern ports nearly at will. Taking on cargoes in the Caribbean, sleek Confederate blockade runners brought in vital supplies — guns and medicine. But with the U.S. Navy commissioning a new blockader almost weekly, the naval fleet eventually numbered 150 ships on duty, and the Union navy dramatically improved its score.

Unable to build a conventional navy equal to the expanding U.S. fleet, the Confederates experimented with a radical new maritime design: the ironclad warship. At Norfolk, Virginia, the wooden hull of the frigate *Merrimack* was layered with two-inch-thick armor plate. Rechristened *Virginia*, the ship steamed out in March 1862 and sank two wooden federal ships, killing at least 240 Union sailors (see Map 15.2). When the *Virginia* returned to finish off the federal blockaders the next morning, it was challenged by the *Monitor*, a federal ironclad of even more

gunboats, Grant captured Fort Henry on the Tennessee River and Fort Donelson on the Cumberland (see Map 15.2). Defeat forced the Confederates to withdraw from all of Kentucky and most of Tennessee, but Grant followed.

On April 6, General Albert Sidney Johnston's army surprised Grant at Shiloh Church in Tennessee. Union troops were badly mauled the first day, but Grant remained cool and brought up reinforcements throughout the night. The next morning, the Union army counterattacked, driving the Confederates before it. The **battle of Shiloh** was terribly costly to both sides; there were 20,000 casualties, among them General Johnston. Grant later said that after Shiloh he "gave up all idea of saving the Union except by complete conquest."

Although no one knew it at the time, Shiloh ruined the Confederacy's bid to control the theater of operations in the West. The Yankees quickly captured the strategic town of Corinth, Mississippi; the river city

THE PROMISE OF TECHNOLOGY

The World's First Successful Submarine

As the federal blockade of southern ports gradually began to strangle Confederate shipping, Southerners were forced to innovate in naval technology: the iron-clad, floating mines (called torpedoes), and, most spectacular of all, the submarine. Three years of trial and error, experimentation, and wartime innovation produced the CSS *H. L. Hunley.* A sleek, forty-foot, nine-man vessel, the *Hunley* was an engineering marvel that exhibited both sophisticated technology and primitive features. General P. G. T. Beauregard felt compelled to explain to men who were considering volunteering for its crew the "desperately hazardous nature of the service required." On the night of February 17, 1864, the *Hunley* sank the Union blockader USS *Housatonic* and then itself sank with its entire crew. No other submarine would sink an enemy ship until World War I, more than half a century later. The *Hunley* is shown here at Charleston in 1863 in a painting by Conrad Wise Chapman.

How does the *Hunley* confirm the adage "Necessity is the mother of invention"? Museum of the Confederacy.

radical design, topped with a revolving turret holding two eleven-inch guns. On March 9, the two ships hurled shells at each other for two hours, but when neither could penetrate the other's armor, the battle ended in a draw.

The Confederacy never found a way to break the **Union blockade** despite exploring many naval innovations, including a new underwater vessel — the submarine. Each month, the Union fleet tightened its noose. By 1863, the South had abandoned its embargo policy and desperately wanted to ship cotton to pay for imports of arms, shoes, and uniforms needed to fight the war. The growing effectiveness of the federal blockade, a southern naval officer observed, "shut the Confederacy out from the world, deprived it of supplies, weakened its military and naval strength." By 1865, the blockaders were intercepting about half of the southern ships attempting to break through. The Confederacy was sealed off, with devastating results.

International Diplomacy

What the Confederates could not achieve on the seas, they sought to achieve through international diplomacy. Confederates and Unionists both realized that the world was watching the struggle in North America. Nationalists everywhere understood that the American Civil War engaged issues central to their own nation-building efforts. The

Confederates rested their claims to separate nationhood on the principles of self-determination and rightful rebellion against despotic power, and they desperately wanted Europe to intervene. The Lincoln

Major Battles of the Civil War, 1861–1862

April 12–13, 1861	Attack on Fort Sumter
July 21, 1861	First battle of Bull Run (Manassas)
February 6, 1862	Battle of Fort Henry
February 16, 1862	Battle of Fort Donelson
March 6–8, 1862	Battle of Pea Ridge
March 9, 1862	Battle of the *Merrimack* (the *Virginia*) and the *Monitor*
March 26, 1862	Battle of Glorieta Pass
April 6–7, 1862	Battle of Shiloh
May–July 1862	McClellan's peninsula campaign
June 6, 1862	Fall of Memphis
June 25–July 1, 1862	Seven Days Battle
August 29–30, 1862	Second battle of Bull Run (Manassas)
September 17, 1862	Battle of Antietam
December 13, 1862	Battle of Fredericksburg

FIGURE 15.2   GLOBAL COMPARISON: European Cotton Imports, 1860–1870
In 1860, the South enjoyed a near monopoly in supplying cotton to Europe's textile mills, but the Civil War almost entirely halted its exports. Figures for Europe's importation of cotton for 1861 to 1865 reveal one of the reasons the Confederacy's King Cotton diplomacy failed: Europeans found other sources of cotton. Which countries were most important in filling the void? When the war ended in 1865, cotton production resumed in the South, and exports to Europe again soared. Did the South regain its near monopoly? How would you characterize the United States' competitive position five years after the war?

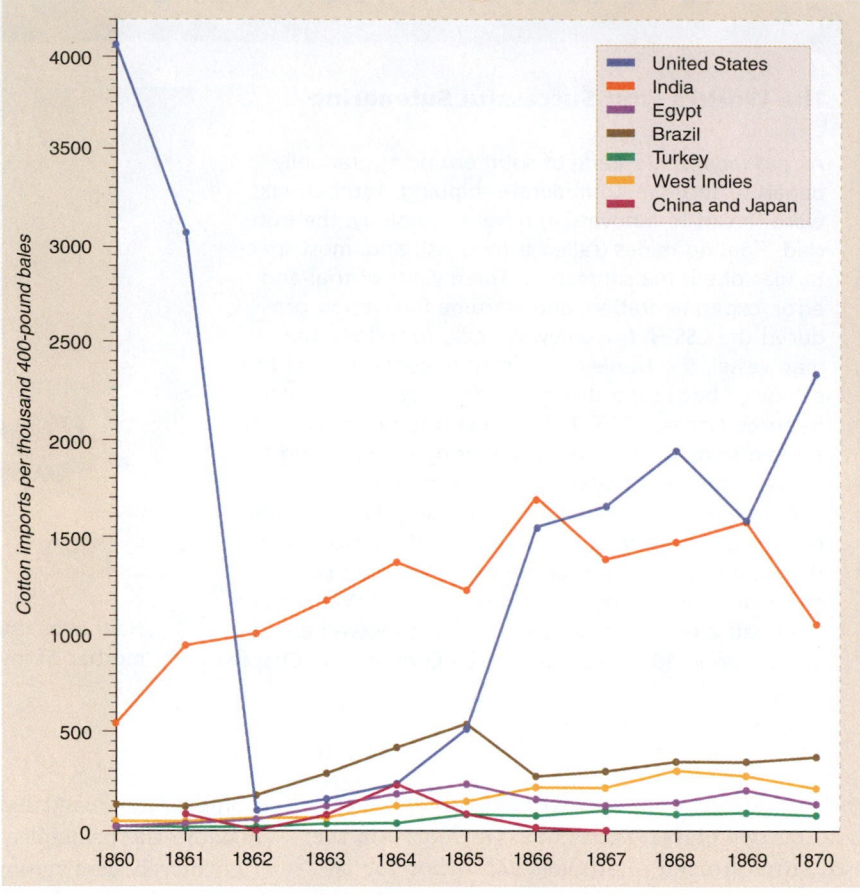

administration explained why the Union had to be preserved and why Europe had to remain neutral. "The question," Lincoln noted, is "whether a constitutional republic, or a democracy — a government of the people, by the same people — can or cannot, maintain its territorial integrity, against its own domestic foes."

More practically, the Confederates based their hope for European support on King Cotton. In theory, cotton-starved European nations would have no choice but to break the Union blockade and recognize the Confederacy. Southern hopes were not unreasonable, for at the height of the "cotton famine" in 1862, when 2 million British workers were unemployed, Britain tilted toward recognition. Along with several other European nations, Britain granted the Confederacy "belligerent" status, which enabled it to buy goods and build ships in European ports. The British-built Confederate cruiser *Alabama* sank or captured sixty-four Union merchant ships before the USS *Kearsarge* sank it off the coast of France in 1864. But no country challenged the Union blockade or recognized the Confederate States of America as

a nation, a bold act that probably would have drawn that country into war.

King Cotton diplomacy failed for several reasons. A bumper cotton crop in 1860 meant that the warehouses of British textile manufacturers bulged with surplus cotton throughout 1861. In 1862, when a cotton shortage did occur, European manufacturers found new sources in India, Egypt, and elsewhere (Figure 15.2). In addition, the development of a brisk trade between the Union and Britain — British war materiel for American grain and flour — helped offset the decline in textiles and encouraged Britain to remain neutral.

Europe's temptation to intervene disappeared for good in 1862. Union military successes in the West made Britain and France think twice about linking their fates to the struggling Confederacy. Moreover, in September 1862, Lincoln announced a new policy that made an alliance with the Confederacy an alliance with slavery — a commitment the French and British, who had outlawed slavery in their empires and looked forward to its eradication worldwide, were not willing to make. After 1862, the South's cause was linked irrevocably with slavery and reaction, and the Union's cause was linked with freedom and democracy. The Union, not the Confederacy, had won the diplomatic stakes.

REVIEW   Why did the Confederacy's bid for international support fail?

▶ Union *and* Freedom

For a year and a half, Lincoln insisted that the North fought strictly to save the Union and not to abolish slavery. Despite Lincoln's repeated pronouncements, however, the war for union became a war for African American freedom. Each month the conflict dragged on, it became clearer that the Confederate war machine depended heavily on slavery. Rebel armies used slaves to build fortifications, haul materiel, tend horses, and perform camp chores. On the home front, slaves labored in ironworks and shipyards, and they grew the food that fed both soldiers and civilians. Slavery undergirded the Confederacy as certainly as it had the Old South. As Frederick Douglass put it, slavery was "the stomach of this rebellion." Union military commanders and politicians alike gradually realized that to defeat the Confederacy, the North would have to destroy slavery. "I am a slow walker," Lincoln said, "but I never walk back."

From Slaves to Contraband

Lincoln detested human bondage, but as president he felt compelled to act prudently in the interests of the Union. He doubted his right under the Constitution to tamper with the "domestic institutions" of any state, even states in rebellion. An astute politician, Lincoln worked within the tight limits of public opinion. The issue of black freedom was particularly explosive in the loyal border states, where slaveholders threatened to jump into the arms of the Confederacy at even the hint of emancipation.

Black freedom also raised alarms in the free states. The Democratic Party gave notice that adding emancipation to the goal of union would make the war strictly a Republican affair. Moreover, many white Northerners were not about to risk their lives to satisfy what they considered abolitionist "fanaticism." "We Won't Fight to Free the Nigger," one popular banner read. They feared that emancipation would pro-pel "two or three million semi-savages" northward, where they would crowd into white neighborhoods, compete for white jobs, and mix with white "sons and daughters." Thus, emancipation threatened to dislodge the loyal slave states from the Union, alienate the Democratic Party, deplete the armies, and perhaps even spark race warfare.

Yet proponents of emancipation pressed Lincoln as relentlessly as did the anti-emancipation forces. Abolitionists argued that by seceding, Southerners had forfeited their right to the protection of the Constitution and that Lincoln could — as the price of their treason — legally confiscate their property in slaves. When Lincoln refused, abolitionists scalded him. Frederick Douglass labeled him "the miserable tool of traitors and rebels."

The Republican-dominated Congress declined to leave slavery policy entirely in President Lincoln's hands. In August 1861, Congress approved the Confiscation Act, which allowed the seizure of any slave employed directly by the Confederate military. It also fulfilled the free-soil dream of prohibiting slavery in the territories and abolished slavery in Washington, D.C. Democrats and border-state representatives voted against even these mild measures, but Congress's attitude was clearly stiffening against slavery.

Slaves, not politicians, became the most insistent force for emancipation. By escaping their masters by the tens of thousands and running away to Union lines, they forced slavery on the North's wartime agenda. Runaways made Northerners answer a crucial question: Were the runaways now free, or were they still slaves who, according to the fugitive slave law, had to be returned to their masters? At first, Yankee military officers sent the fugitives back. But Union armies needed laborers. At Fort Monroe, Virginia, General Benjamin F. Butler refused to turn them over to their owners, calling them **contraband of war**, meaning "confiscated property," and put them to work. Congress made Butler's practice national policy in March 1862 when it forbade returning fugitive slaves to their masters. Slaves were still not legally free, but there was a tilt toward emancipation.

Lincoln's policy of noninterference with slavery gradually crumbled. To calm Northerners' racial fears, Lincoln offered colonization, the deportation of African Americans from the United

> ### "The miserable tool of traitors and rebels."
> — FREDERICK DOUGLASS, speaking of Lincoln, when he refused to confiscate the slaves of Southerners

Human Contraband
These refugees from slavery crossed the Rappahannock River in Virginia in August 1862 to seek sanctuary with a federal army. Most slaves fled with little more than the clothes on their backs, but not all escaped slavery empty-handed. The oxen, horse, wagon, and goods seen here could have been procured by a number of means — purchased during slavery, "borrowed" from the former master, or gathered during flight. Refugees who possessed draft animals and a wagon had much more economic opportunity than those who had only their labor to sell. Library of Congress.

From Contraband to Free People

On August 22, 1862, Lincoln replied to an angry abolitionist who demanded that he attack slavery. "My paramount objective in this struggle *is* to save the Union," Lincoln said deliberately, "and is *not* either to save or destroy slavery. If I could save the Union without freeing *any* slave I would do it, and if I could save it by freeing *all* the slaves I would do it; and if I could save it by freeing some and leaving others alone I would also do that." Instead of simply restating his old position that union was the North's sole objective, Lincoln announced that slavery was no longer untouchable and that he would emancipate every slave if doing so would preserve the Union.

By the summer of 1862, events were tumbling rapidly toward emancipation. On July 17, Congress adopted the second Confiscation Act. The first had confiscated slaves employed by the Confederate military; the second declared all slaves of rebel masters "forever free of their servitude." In theory, this breathtaking measure freed most Confederate slaves, for slaveholders formed the backbone of the rebellion. Congress had traveled far since the war began.

Lincoln had, too. In July 1862, the president told two members of his cabinet that he had "about come to the conclusion that we must free the slaves or be ourselves subdued." A few days later, before the entire cabinet, he read a draft of a preliminary emancipation proclamation that promised to free *all* the slaves in the seceding states on January 1, 1863. Lincoln described emancipation as an "act of justice," but it was the lengthening casualty lists that finally brought him around. Emancipation, he declared, was "a military necessity, absolutely essential to the preservation of the Union." Only freeing the slaves would "strike at the heart of the rebellion." On September 22, Lincoln issued his preliminary **Emancipation Proclamation** promising freedom to slaves in areas still in rebellion on January 1, 1863.

The limitations of the proclamation — it exempted the loyal border states and the Union-occupied areas of the Confederacy — caused some to ridicule the act. The *Times* (London) observed cynically, "Where he has no power Mr. Lincoln will set the negroes free, where he retains

States to Haiti, Panama, or elsewhere. In the summer of 1862, he told a delegation of black visitors that deep-seated racial prejudice among whites made it impossible for blacks to achieve equality in the United States. One African American responded, "This is our country as much as it is yours, and we will not leave." Congress voted a small amount of money to underwrite colonization, but after one miserable experiment on a small island in the Caribbean, practical limitations and stiff black opposition sank further efforts.

While Lincoln was developing his own antislavery initiatives, he snuffed out actions that he believed would jeopardize northern unity. He was particularly alert to Union commanders who tried to dictate slavery policy from the field. In August 1861, when John C. Frémont, former Republican presidential nominee and now commander of federal troops in Missouri, freed the slaves belonging to Missouri rebels, Lincoln forced the general to revoke his edict. The following May, when General David Hunter freed the slaves in Georgia, South Carolina, and Florida, Lincoln countermanded his order. Events moved so rapidly, however, that Lincoln found it impossible to control federal policy on slavery.

power he will consider them as slaves." But Lincoln had no power to free slaves in loyal states, and invading Union armies would liberate slaves in the Confederacy as they advanced.

By presenting emancipation as a "military necessity," Lincoln hoped he had disarmed his conservative critics. Emancipation would deprive the Confederacy of valuable slave laborers, shorten the war, and thus save lives. Democrats, however, fumed that the "shrieking and howling abolitionist faction" had captured the White House and made it "a nigger war." Democrats made political hay out of Lincoln's action in the November 1862 elections, gaining thirty-four congressional seats. House Democrats quickly proposed a resolution branding emancipation "a high crime against the Constitution." The Republicans, who maintained narrow majorities in both houses of Congress, barely beat it back.

As promised, on New Year's Day 1863, Lincoln issued the final Emancipation Proclamation. Later in 1863 at Gettysburg, Pennsylvania, Lincoln famously confirmed the war's new purpose: "that this nation, under God, shall have a new birth of freedom — and that government of the people, by the people, for the people, shall not perish from the earth." In addition to freeing the slaves in the rebel states, the Emancipation Proclamation also committed the federal government to the fullest use of African Americans to defeat the Confederate enemy.

The War of Black Liberation

Even before Lincoln proclaimed emancipation a Union war aim, African Americans in the North had volunteered to fight. Military service, one black volunteer declared, would mean "the elevation of a downtrodden and despised race." But the War Department, doubtful of blacks' abilities and fearful of white reaction to serving side by side with them, refused to make black men soldiers. Instead, the army employed black men as manual laborers; black women sometimes found employment as laundresses and cooks. The navy, however, accepted blacks from the outset, including runaway slaves such as **William Gould** (see pages 461–62).

As Union casualty lists lengthened, Northerners gradually and reluctantly turned to African Americans to fill the army's blue uniforms. With

Black Men Working along the Wharf, 1860–1865
The black men seen here with picks and shovels working at the federal supply depot at City Point, Virginia, were likely fugitive slaves. Hundreds of thousands of able-bodied runaways cleared forests, built roads, erected bridges, constructed fortifications, and transported supplies for the U.S. army. They were overworked, paid irregularly, given inadequate food and clothing, and even physically assaulted, but they kept pouring into Union lines. Their labor became indispensable to the war effort, and as one Northerner remembered, "The truth was we never could get enough of them." Library of Congress.

The Right to Fight: Black Soldiers in the Civil War

"**A** war undertaken and brazenly carried on for the perpetual enslavement of colored men, calls logically and loudly for colored men to help suppress it," black leader Frederick Douglass declared at the beginning of the war. But it was only in 1863 that the lengthening casualty lists finally convinced the Lincoln administration to begin aggressively recruiting black soldiers.

In February 1863, James Henry Gooding, a twenty-six-year-old seaman from New Bedford, enlisted in the 54th Massachusetts Colored Regiment. Like most black soldiers, Gooding viewed military service as an opportunity to strike blows against slavery and white prejudice. The destruction of slavery, he believed, "depends on the free black men of the North" because "those who are in bonds must have some one to open the door; when the slave sees the white soldier approach, he dares not trust him and why? Because he has heard that *some* have treated him worse than their owners in rebellion. But if the slave sees a black soldier, he knows he has got a friend." Fighting for the Union also offered a chance to attack white racism. In military service lay "the germs of the elevation of a downtrodden and despised race," Gooding believed, the chance for African Americans "to make themselves a people."

Fighting, Gooding said, offered blacks a chance to destroy the "foul aspersion that they were not men." According to the white commander of the 59th U.S. Colored Infantry, when an ex-slave put on a uniform of army blue, the change was dramatic: "Yesterday a filthy, repulsive 'nigger,' to-day a neatly-attired man; yesterday a slave, to-day a freeman; yesterday a civilian, to-day a soldier." Others noticed the same transformation: "Put a United States uniform on his back and the *chattel* is a man." Black veterans agreed. "This was the biggest thing that ever happened in my life," one ex-soldier remembered. "I felt like a man with a uniform and a gun in my hand." Another said, "I felt freedom in my bones."

Black courage under fire ended skepticism about the capabilities of African American troops. As one white officer observed after a battle, "They seemed like men who were fighting to vindicate their manhood and they did it well." The truth is, another remarked, "they have fought their way into the respect of all the army." After the 54th served courageously in South Carolina, Gooding reported: "It is not for us to blow our horn; but when a regiment of white men gave us three cheers as we were passing them, it shows that we did our duty as men should."

Yet discrimination within the Union army continued. When the government refused to pay blacks the same as whites, the 54th refused to accept unequal pay. Gooding wrote to President Lincoln himself to explain his regiment's decision: "Now the main question is, Are we Soldiers, or are we Labourers? . . . Now your Excellency, we have done a Soldier's Duty. Why Can't we have a Soldier's pay?" The 54th's principled stance helped reverse the government's position, and in June 1864 Congress equalized the pay of black and white soldiers.

As Union troops advanced deeper into the Confederacy, former slaves greeted black soldiers as heroes. In March 1865, the white officer of a black regiment in North Carolina reported that black soldiers "stepped like lords & conquerors. The frantic demonstrations of the negro population will never die out of my memory. Their cheers & heartfelt 'God bress ye's' & cries of 'De chains is broke; De chains is broke' mingled

the Militia Act of July 1862, Congress authorized enrolling blacks in "any military or naval service for which they may be found competent." After the Emancipation Proclamation, whites — like it or not — were fighting and dying for black freedom, and few insisted that blacks remain out of harm's way behind the lines. Indeed, whites insisted that blacks share the danger, especially after March 1863, when Congress resorted to the draft to fill the Union army.

The military was far from color-blind. The Union army established segregated black regiments, paid black soldiers $10 per month rather than the $13 it paid whites, refused blacks the opportunity to become commissioned officers, punished blacks as if they were slaves, and assigned blacks to labor battalions rather than to combat units. Still, when the war ended, 179,000 African American men had served in the Union army, approximately 10 percent of all soldiers. An astounding 71 percent of black men ages eighteen to forty-five in the free states wore Union blue, a participation rate that was substantially higher than that of white men. More than 130,000 black soldiers came from the slave states, perhaps 100,000 of them ex-slaves.

In time, whites allowed blacks to put down their shovels and to shoulder rifles. At the sublimely with the lusty shout of our brave soldiery." Hardened and disciplined by their military service, black soldiers drew tremendous strength from their participation in the Union effort. Despite their second-class status, they found army life a great counterweight to the degradation and dependency of slavery.

Eager to shoulder the rights, privileges, and responsibilities of freedom, black veterans often took the lead in the hard struggle for equality after the war. Blacks in the Union army that occupied the South after 1865 assumed a special obligation to protect former slaves. "The fact is," one black chaplain said, "when colored soldiers are about they [whites] are afraid to kick colored women and abuse colored people on the Streets, as they usually do." Black veterans believed that their military service entitled African Americans not only to freedom but also to civil and political rights. Sergeant Henry Maxwell announced: "We want two more boxes besides the cartridge box — the ballot and the jury box." Black men had demonstrated what they could do if permitted to become soldiers; they now demanded the chance to perform as citizens.

James Henry Gooding did not have a chance to participate in the postwar struggle for equal rights. Wounded and captured at the battle of Olustee in Florida, he was sent to the infamous Confederate prison Andersonville, where he died on July 19, 1864.

Company E, 4th U.S. Colored Infantry, Fort Lincoln, Virginia
The Lincoln administration was slow to accept black soldiers into the Union army, in part because of doubts about their fighting ability. But eventually, the battlefield valor of black troops eroded white skepticism. Colonel Thomas W. Higginson, the white commander of the Union's 1st South Carolina Infantry, made up of former slaves, celebrated the courage his men displayed in their first skirmish: "No officer in this regiment now doubts that the key to the successful prosecution of this war lies in the unlimited employment of black troops. . . . Instead of leaving their homes and families to fight they are fighting for their homes and families." Library of Congress.

Questions for Consideration

1. Why did the Union resist enrolling black troops?

2. Why was the right to fight so important to black men?

3. How did military service affect black men?

---

battles of Port Hudson and Milliken's Bend on the Mississippi River and at Fort Wagner in Charleston harbor, black courage under fire finally dispelled notions that African Americans could not fight. More than 38,000 black soldiers died in the Civil War, a mortality rate that was higher than that of white troops. Blacks played a crucial role in the triumph of the Union and the destruction of slavery in the South. (See "Seeking the American Promise," page 478.)

REVIEW Why did the Union change policy in 1863 to allow black men to serve in the army?

▶ The South at War

Most white Southerners shifted their allegiance from the Union to the Confederacy easily, convinced that their new nation embodied the principles of the American Revolution. But by seceding, Southerners brought on themselves a firestorm of unimaginable fury. Monstrous losses on the battlefield nearly bled the Confederacy to death. Southerners on the home front also suffered, even at the hands of their own government. Efforts by the Davis administration in Richmond to centralize power in

VISUAL ACTIVITY

Confederate Soldiers and Their Slaves
Soldiers of the Seventh Tennessee Cavalry pose with their slaves. Many slaveholders took "body servants" with them to war. These slaves cooked, washed, and cleaned for the white soldiers. In 1861, James H. Langhorne reported to his sister: "Peter . . . is charmed with being with me & 'being a soldier.' I gave him my old uniform overcoat & he says he is going to have his picture taken . . . to send to the servants." Do you think Peter was "puttin' on ol' massa" or just glad to be free of plantation labor? Daguerreotype courtesy of Tom Farish. Photographed by Michael Latil.

READING THE IMAGE: What can we glean from this image about a Confederate soldier's life in the military? **CONNECTIONS:** This daguerreotype likely was not taken for any purpose other than to capture the camaraderie of four southern cavalrymen, yet the inclusion of the two slaves speaks volumes. What are the possible ramifications of slaveholders bringing "body servants" to war?

order to fight the war tested the loyalty of some men and women. Wartime economic changes hurt everyone, some more than others. By 1863, planters and yeomen who had stood together began to drift apart. Most disturbing of all, slaves became open participants in the destruction of slavery and the Confederacy.

Revolution from Above

As a Confederate general observed, Southerners were engaged in a total war "in which the whole population and the whole production . . . are to be put on a war footing, where every institution is to be made auxiliary to war." Jefferson Davis faced the task of building an army and navy from almost nothing, supplying them from factories that were scarce and anemic, and paying for it all from a treasury that did not exist. Finding eager soldiers proved easiest. Hundreds of officers defected from the U.S. Army, and hundreds of thousands of eager young rebels volunteered to follow them. Very quickly, the Confederacy developed formidable striking power.

The Confederacy's economy and finances proved tougher problems. Because of the Union blockade, the government had no choice but to build an industrial sector itself. Government-owned clothing and shoe factories, mines, arsenals, and powder works sprang up. The government also harnessed private companies, such as the huge Tredegar Iron Works in Richmond, to the war effort. Paying for the war became the most difficult task. A flood of paper money caused debilitating inflation. By 1863, people in Charleston paid ten times more for food than they had paid at the start of the war. By Christmas 1864, a Confederate soldier's monthly pay no longer bought a pair of socks. The Confederacy manufactured much more than most people imagined possible, but it never produced all that the South needed.

Richmond's war-making effort brought unprecedented government intrusion into the private lives of Confederate citizens. In April 1862, the Confederate Congress passed the first **conscription** (draft) law in American history. All able-bodied white males between the ages of eighteen and thirty-five (later seventeen and fifty) were liable to serve in the rebel army. The government adopted a policy of **impressment**, which allowed officials to confiscate food, horses, wagons, and whatever else they wanted from private citizens and to pay for them at below-market rates. After March 1863, the Confederacy legally impressed slaves, employing them as military laborers.

Richmond's centralizing efforts ran head-on into the South's traditional values of **states' rights** and unfettered individualism. Southerners lashed out at what Georgia governor Joseph E. Brown denounced as the "dangerous usurpation by Congress of the reserved right of the States." Richmond and the states struggled for control of money, supplies, and soldiers, with damaging

The Texas Brigade in Camp, 1861
Rebel soldiers who did not have slave servants to attend them spent much of their time doing chores. Standing in front of their winter quarters near Dumfries, Virginia, the Texans here are busy washing dishes, washing clothes, chopping firewood, and cooking. The soldier with the skillet displays the corn bread he has just cooked. Confederate troops ate salted meat and corn bread more than anything else, and soldiers grew very tired of the old standbys. "If any person offers me cornbread after this war comes to a close," a Louisianan declared just before Lee's surrender, "I shall probably tell him to — go to hell!" Photograph: Austin History Center, Austin Public Library; Skillet: Photograph Courtesy of the Concord Museum, Concord, MA; Sifter: Museum of the Confederacy/Southern Progress.

consequences for the war effort. Despite the strain, popular commitment to the new nation endured.

Hardship Below

Hardships on the home front fell most heavily on the poor. Flour, which cost three or four cents a pound in 1861, cost thirty-five cents in 1863. The draft stripped yeoman farms of men, leaving the women and children to grow what they ate. Government agents took 10 percent of harvests as a "tax-in-kind" on agriculture. Like inflation, shortages afflicted the entire population, but the rich lost luxuries while the poor lost necessities. In the spring of 1863, **bread riots** broke out in a dozen cities and villages across the South. In Richmond, a mob of nearly a thousand hungry women broke into shops and took what they needed.

"Men cannot be expected to fight for the Government that permits their wives & children to starve," one Southerner observed. Although a few wealthy individuals shared their bounty and the Confederate and state governments made efforts at social welfare, every attempt fell short. In late 1864, one desperate farmwife told her husband, "I have always been proud of you, and since your connection with the Confederate army, I have been prouder of you than ever before. I would not have you do anything wrong for the world, but before God, Edward, unless you come home, we must die." When the war ended, one-third of the soldiers had already gone home. A Mississippi deserter explained, "We are poor men and are willing to defend our country but our families [come] first."

Yeomen perceived a profound inequality of sacrifice. They called it "a rich man's war and a poor man's fight." The draft law permitted a man who had money to hire a substitute to take his place. Moreover, the **"twenty-Negro law"** exempted

> **"Men cannot be expected to fight for the Government that permits their wives & children to starve."**
> — A Southerner

Maria Isabella ("Belle") Boyd, Spy
Only seventeen when the war broke out, Belle Boyd became, in the words of a northern journalist, "insanely devoted to the rebel cause." Her first act for the Confederacy came on July 3, 1861, when she shot a drunken federal soldier who barged into her Virginia home and insulted her mother. Her relations with occupying northern troops improved, and soon this compelling young woman was eavesdropping on officers' conversations and slipping messages to Confederate armies. Boyd's information handed Stonewall Jackson an easy victory at Front Royal, Virginia, in May 1862. Imprisoned several times for spying, Boyd took up a theatrical career when the war ended. Courtesy Warren Rifles Confederate Museum, Front Royal, VA.

one white man on every plantation with twenty or more slaves. The government intended this law to provide protection for white women and to see that slaves tended the crops, but yeomen perceived it as rich men evading military service. A Mississippian complained that stay-at-home planters sent their slaves into the fields to grow cotton while in plain view "poor soldiers' wives are plowing with *their own* hands to make a subsistence for themselves and children — while their husbands are suffering, bleeding and dying for their country." In fact, most slaveholders went off to war, but the extreme suffering of common folk and the relative immunity of planters increased class friction.

The Richmond government hoped that the crucible of war would mold a region into a nation. Officials actively promoted Confederate nationalism to "excite in our citizens an ardent and enduring attachment to our Government and its institutions." Patriotic songwriters, poets, authors, and artists extolled southern culture. Clergymen assured their congregations that God had blessed slavery and the new nation. Jefferson Davis claimed that the Confederacy was part of a divine plan and asked citizens to observe national days of fasting and prayer. Although these efforts failed to win over thousands of die-hard Unionists and the animosity between yeomen and planters increased, the Confederacy succeeded in inspiring loyalty and pride among the majority of whites. Still, the war threatened to rip the southern social fabric along its racial seam.

The Disintegration of Slavery

The legal destruction of slavery was the product of presidential proclamation, congressional legislation, and eventually constitutional amendment, but the practical destruction of slavery was the product of war, what Lincoln called war's "friction and abrasion." Slaves took advantage of the upheaval to reach for freedom. Some half a million of the South's 4 million slaves ran away to Union military lines. More than 100,000 runaways took up arms as federal soldiers and sailors and attacked slavery directly. Other men and women stayed in the slave quarter, where they staked their claim to more freedom.

War disrupted slavery in a dozen ways. Almost immediately, it called the master away, leaving the mistress to assume responsibility for the plantation. But mistresses could not maintain traditional standards of slave discipline in wartime, and the balance of power shifted. Slaves got to the fields late, worked indifferently, and quit early. Some slaveholders responded violently; most saw no alternative but to strike bargains — offering gifts or part of the crop — to keep slaves at home and at work. An Alabama woman complained that she "begged . . . what little is done." Slaveholders had believed that they "knew" their slaves, but they learned that they did not. When the war began, a North Carolina woman praised her slaves as "diligent and respectful." When it ended, she said, "As to the idea of a *faithful servant, it is all a fiction.*"

As military action sliced through the southern countryside, some slaveholders fled, leaving their slaves behind. Many more took their slaves with them, but flight meant additional chaos and offered slaves new opportunities to resist bondage. Whites' greatest fear — retaliatory violence — rarely occurred, however. Slaves who stayed home steadily undermined white mastery and expanded control over their own lives.

REVIEW   How did wartime hardship in the South contribute to class friction?

▶ The North at War

Although little fighting took place on northern soil, Northerners could not avoid being touched by the war. Almost every family had a son, husband, father, or brother in uniform. A New Hampshire man reported in 1863 that "there is mourning all over the land, for there is scarcely a place but what some one has lost a friend or an acquaintance either in battle or the Hospital." Moreover, total war blurred the distinction between home front and battlefield. Men marched off to fight, but preserving the country was also women's work. For civilians as well as soldiers, for women as well as men, war was transforming.

The need to build and fuel the Union war machine boosted the economy. The Union sent nearly 2 million men into the military and still increased production in almost every area. But because the rewards and burdens of patriotism were distributed unevenly, the North experienced sharp, even violent, divisions. Workers confronted employers, whites confronted blacks, and Democrats confronted Republicans. Still, Northerners on the home front remained fervently attached to the Union.

The Government and the Economy

When the war began, the United States had no national banking system, no national currency, and no federal income tax. But the secession of eleven slave states cut the Democrats' strength in Congress in half and destroyed their capacity to resist Republican economic programs. The Legal Tender Act of February 1862 created a national currency, paper money that Northerners called "greenbacks." With the passage of the National Banking Act in February 1863, Congress

Union Army Horse Artillery, 1860–1865
As the North successfully harnessed its enormous industrial capacity to meet the needs of war, cannon, shells, and carriages poured out of its factories. A fraction of that abundance is seen here in Virginia as a powerful battery of Union field artillery moves forward to assist infantry units. Each cannon required more than a dozen men and many horses to service it. Assignment to an artillery battery was dangerous for man and beast. Life expectancy for an artillery horse was less than eight months, and it is estimated that 1.5 million horses died in the war. © Bettmann/Corbis.

established a system of national banks that by the 1870s had largely replaced the antebellum system of decentralized state banks. Congress also enacted a series of sweeping tax laws. By revolutionizing the country's banking, monetary, and tax structures, the Republicans generated enormous economic power.

The Republicans' wartime legislation also aimed at integrating the West more thoroughly into the Union. In May 1862, Congress approved the Homestead Act, which offered 160 acres of public land to settlers who would live and labor on it. The Homestead Act bolstered western loyalty and in time resulted in more than a million new farms. The Pacific Railroad Act in July 1862 provided massive federal assistance for building a transcontinental railroad that ran from Omaha to San Francisco when completed in 1869. Congress further bound East and West by subsidizing the Pony Express mail service and a transcontinental telegraph.

Two additional initiatives had long-term economic consequences. Congress created the Department of Agriculture and passed the Land-Grant College Act (also known as the Morrill Act after its sponsor, Representative Justin Morrill of Vermont), which set aside public land to support universities that emphasized "agriculture and mechanical arts." The Lincoln administration immeasurably strengthened the North's effort to win the war, but its ideas also permanently changed the nation.

Women and Work at Home and at War

More than a million farm men were called to the military, so farm women added men's chores to their own. "I met more women driving teams on the road and saw more at work in the fields than men," a visitor to Iowa reported in the fall of 1862. Rising production testified to their success in plowing, planting, and harvesting. Rapid mechanization assisted farm women in their new roles. Cyrus McCormick sold 165,000 of his reapers during the war years. The combination of high prices for farm products and increased production ensured that war and prosperity joined hands in the rural North.

A few industries, such as textiles (which depended on southern cotton), declined during the war, but many more grew. Huge profits prompted one Pennsylvania ironmaster to remark, "I am in no hurry for peace." With orders pouring in and a million nonfarmworkers at war, unemployment declined and wages often rose. The boom proved friendlier to owners than to workers, however. Inflation and taxes cut so deeply into workers' paychecks that their standard of living actually fell.

In cities, women stepped into jobs vacated by men, particularly in manufacturing, and also into essentially new occupations such as government secretaries and clerks. The number of women working for wages rose 40 percent during the war. As more and more women entered the workforce, employers cut wages.

Women Doing Laundry for Federal Soldiers, ca. 1861
Northern women eagerly joined the Union war effort. Thousands aided in the work of the U.S. Christian Commission, the U.S. Sanitary Commission, and other philanthropic organizations to provide soldiers with Bibles, fresh food, and new socks. But some women were forced by their desperate financial circumstances to wash soldiers' dirty clothes to make a living. Army camps were difficult places for "respectable" women to work. One Union soldier discouraged his wife even from visiting, noting, "It is not a fit place for any woman, for there is all kinds of talk, songs and everything not good for them 2 hear." © Bettmann/Corbis.

In 1864, New York seamstresses working fourteen-hour days earned only $1.54 a week. Urban workers resorted increasingly to strikes to wrench decent salaries from their employers, but their protests rarely succeeded. Nevertheless, tough times failed to undermine the patriotism of most workers.

Most middle-class white women stayed home and contributed to the war effort in traditional ways. They sewed, wrapped bandages, and sold homemade goods at local fairs to raise money to aid the soldiers. Other women expressed their patriotism in an untraditional way — as wartime nurses. Thousands of women on both sides defied prejudices about female delicacy and volunteered to nurse the wounded. Many northern female volunteers worked through the **U.S. Sanitary Commission**, a huge civilian organization that coordinated the efforts of seven thousand local women's groups to buy and distribute clothing, food, and medicine; recruit doctors and nurses; and bury the dead.

Some volunteers went on to become paid military nurses. **Dorothea Dix**, well known for her efforts to reform insane asylums, was named superintendent of female nurses in April 1861. Dix appointed some 3,000 nurses by 1863, when the power to select nurses was taken from her and given to army surgeons. Most nurses worked in hospitals behind the battle lines, but some, like **Clara Barton**, who later founded the American Red Cross, worked in battlefield units. Women who served in the war went on to lead the postwar movement to establish training schools for female nurses.

Politics and Dissent

At first, the bustle of economic and military mobilization seemed to silence politics, but bipartisan unity did not last. Within a year, Democrats were labeling the Republican administration a "reign of terror" and denouncing Republican policies — expanding federal power, subsidizing private business, emancipating the slaves — as unconstitutional, arguing that the "Constitution is as binding in war as in peace." In turn, Republicans were calling Democrats the party of "Dixie, Davis, and the Devil."

When the Republican-dominated Congress enacted the draft law in March 1863, Democrats had another grievance. The law required that all men between the ages of twenty and forty-five enroll and make themselves available for a lottery that would decide who went to war. What poor men found particularly galling were provisions that allowed a draftee to hire a substitute or simply to pay a $300 fee and get out of his military obligation. As in the South, common folk could be heard chanting, "A rich man's war and a poor man's fight."

Linking the draft and emancipation, Democrats argued that Republicans employed an unconstitutional means (the draft) to achieve an unconstitutional end (emancipation). In the summer of 1863, antidraft, antiblack mobs went on rampages in northern cities. In July in New York City, Democratic Irish workingmen — crowded into filthy tenements, gouged by inflation, enraged by the draft, and dead set against fighting to free blacks — erupted in four days of rioting. The **New York City draft riots** killed at least 105 people, most of them black, and left the Colored Orphan Asylum a smoking ruin.

Lincoln called Democratic opposition to the war "the fire in the rear" and believed that it was even more threatening to national survival than were Confederate armies. The antiwar wing of the Democratic Party, the Peace Democrats — whom some called "Copperheads," after the poisonous snake — found their chief spokesman in Ohio congressman **Clement Vallandigham**. He argued that the Confederacy could never be conquered and that Lincoln's attempt had "made this country one of the worst despotisms on earth." Vallandigham demanded: "Stop fighting. Make an armistice. . . . Withdraw your army from the seceding States."

> **"A rich man's war and a poor man's fight."**
> — A chant of common folk

In September 1862, in an effort to stifle opposition to the war, Lincoln placed under military arrest any person who discouraged enlistments, resisted the draft, or engaged in "disloyal" practices. Before the war ended, his administration imprisoned nearly 14,000 individuals, most in the border states. The administration's heavy-handed tactics suppressed free speech, but the campaign fell short of a reign of terror, for the majority of the prisoners were not northern Democratic opponents but Confederates, blockade runners, and citizens of foreign countries, and most of those arrested gained quick release. Still, Lincoln's net did capture Vallandigham, who was arrested, convicted of treason, and eventually banished. In May 1863, Union soldiers escorted the Ohioan to Confederate lines in Tennessee.

REVIEW   Why was the U.S. Congress able to pass such a bold legislative agenda during the war?

▶ Grinding Out Victory, 1863–1865

In the early months of 1863, the Union's prospects looked bleak, and the Confederate cause stood at high tide. Then, in July 1863, the tide began to turn. The military man most responsible for this shift was Ulysses S. Grant. Elevated to supreme command, Grant knit together a powerful war machine that integrated a sophisticated command structure, modern technology, and complex logistics and supply systems. But the arithmetic of this plain man remained unchanged: Killing more of the enemy than he kills of you equaled "the complete overthrow of the rebellion."

The North ground out the victory battle by bloody battle. The balance tipped in the Union's favor in 1863, but Southerners were not deterred. The fighting escalated in the last two years of the war. As national elections approached in the fall of 1864, Lincoln expected a war-weary North to reject him. Instead, northern voters declared their willingness to continue the war in the defense of the ideals of union and freedom.

Vicksburg and Gettysburg

Vicksburg, Mississippi, situated on the eastern bank of the Mississippi River, stood between Union forces and complete control of the river. In May 1863, Union forces under Grant laid siege to the city in an effort to starve out the enemy. Civilian residents moved into caves to escape the incessant Union bombardment, and as the **siege of Vicksburg** dragged on, they ate mules and rats to survive. After six weeks, on July 4, 1863, nearly 30,000 rebels marched out of Vicksburg, stacked their arms, and surrendered unconditionally. A Yankee

Vicksburg Campaign, 1863

Battle of Gettysburg, July 1–3, 1863

captain wrote home to his wife: "The backbone of the Rebellion is this day broken. The Confederacy is divided. . . . Vicksburg is ours. The Mississippi River is opened, and Gen. Grant is to be our next President."

On the same Fourth of July, word arrived that Union forces had crushed General Lee at Gettysburg, Pennsylvania (Map 15.3). Emboldened by his victory at Chancellorsville in May, Lee and his 75,000-man army had invaded Pennsylvania. On June 28, Union forces under General George G. Meade intercepted the Confederates at the small town of Gettysburg, where Union soldiers occupied the high ground. Three days of furious fighting involving 165,000 troops could not dislodge the Federals from the hills. Lee ached for a decisive victory, and on July 3 he ordered a major assault against the Union center on Cemetery Ridge. The dug-in Yankees enjoyed three-quarters of a mile of clear vision, and they raked the line of Confederate soldiers under General George E. Pickett with cannon and rifle fire. The **battle of Gettysburg** cost Lee more than one-third of his army — 28,000 casualties. "It's all my fault," he lamented. On the night of July 4, 1863, he marched his battered army back to Virginia.

The twin disasters at Vicksburg and Gettysburg proved to be the turning point of the war. The Confederacy could not replace the nearly 60,000 soldiers who were captured, wounded, or killed. Lee never launched another major offensive north of the Mason-Dixon line. It is hindsight, however, that permits us to see the pair of battles as decisive. At the time, the Confederacy still controlled the heartland of the South, and Lee still had a vicious sting. War-weariness threatened to erode the North's will to win before Union armies could destroy the Confederacy's ability to go on.

MAP ACTIVITY

Map 15.3   The Civil War, 1863–1865

Ulysses S. Grant's victory at Vicksburg divided the Confederacy at the Mississippi River. William Tecumseh Sherman's march from Chattanooga to Savannah divided it again. In northern Virginia, Robert E. Lee fought fiercely, but Grant's larger, better-supplied armies prevailed.

READING THE MAP: Describe the difference between Union and Confederate naval capacity. Were the battles shown on the map fought primarily in Union-controlled or in Confederate-controlled territory? (Look at the land areas on the map.)

CONNECTIONS: Did former slaves serve in the Civil War? If so, on which side(s), and what did they do?

Grant Takes Command

In September 1863, Union general William Rosecrans placed his army in a dangerous situation in Chattanooga, Tennessee, where he had retreated after defeat at the battle of Chickamauga (see Map 15.3). Rebels surrounded the disorganized bluecoats and threatened to starve them into submission. Grant, now commander of Union forces between the Mississippi River and the Appalachians, arrived in Chattanooga in October. Within weeks, he opened an effective supply line, broke the siege, and routed the Confederate army. The victory at Chattanooga on November 25 opened the door to Georgia. It also confirmed Lincoln's estimation of Grant. In March 1864, the president asked Grant to come east to become the general in chief of all Union armies.

Why Did So Many Soldiers Die?

The American Civil War was the bloodiest conflict in American history (Figure 15.3). Some 260,000 rebel soldiers and 360,000 Union soldiers died. Why were the Civil War totals so horrendous?

This question is almost as old as the war itself, and in answering it historians have traditionally pointed to a variety of explanations: the scale and duration of the fighting; military strategy; battlefield technology; and the backward state of medicine. The sheer size of the armies — some battles involved more than 200,000 soldiers — ensured that battlefields would turn red with blood. Moreover, what most Americans expected to be a short war extended for four full years. In addition, armies fought with antiquated Napoleonic strategy. In the generals' eyes, the ideal soldier advanced with his comrades in a compact, close-order formation. But by the 1860s, military technology had made such frontal assaults deadly. Weapons with rifled barrels were replacing smoothbore muskets and cannons, and the new weapons' greater range and accuracy made sitting ducks of charging infantry units. As a result, battles took thousands of lives in a single day. On July 2, 1862, the morning after the battle at Malvern Hill in Virginia, a Union officer surveyed the scene: "Over 5,000 dead and wounded men were on the ground . . . enough were alive and moving to give to the field a singular crawling effect."

When the war began, Union and Confederate medical departments could not cope with skirmishes, much less large-scale battles. They had no ambulance corps to remove the wounded from the scene. They had no field hospitals. Wounded soldiers often lay on battlefields for hours, sometimes days. Only the shock of massive casualties compelled reform. Gradually, both North and South organized effective ambulance corps, built hospitals, and hired trained surgeons and nurses.

Soldiers did not always count speedy transportation to a hospital as a blessing, however. As one Union soldier said, "I had rather risk a battle than the Hospitals." Field doctors gained a reputation as butchers, but a wounded man's real enemy was medical ignorance. Physicians had almost no knowledge of the cause and transmission of disease or the benefits of antiseptics. Unaware of basic germ theory, surgeons spread infection almost every time they operated. They wore the same bloody smocks for days and washed their hands and their scalpels and saws in buckets of dirty water. Although surgeons used anesthesia (both ether and chloroform), soldiers often did not survive amputations, not because of the operations

but because of the gangrene that inevitably followed. A Union doctor discovered in 1864 that bromine arrested gangrene, but the best that most amputees could hope for was maggots, which ate dead flesh on the stump and thus inhibited the spread of infection. The growing ranks of nurses, including Dorothea Dix and Clara Barton, improved wounded men's odds and alleviated their suffering. Still, during the Civil War, nearly one of every five wounded rebel soldiers died, and one of every six Yankees. A century later, in Vietnam, only one wounded American soldier in four hundred died.

Soldiers who avoided battlefield wounds and hospital infections still faced sickness. Deadly diseases such as dysentery and typhoid swept through crowded army camps, where latrines were often dangerously close to drinking-water supplies, and mosquitoes, flies, and body lice were more than nuisances. Pneumonia and malaria also cut down thousands. Quinine from South America proved an effective treatment for malaria, but by the end of the war the going price was $500 an ounce. Civilian relief agencies promoted hygiene in army camps and made some head-

---

FIGURE 15.3 Civil War Deaths
The loss of life in the Civil War — 620,000 — was almost equal to the losses in all other American wars through the Vietnam War combined.

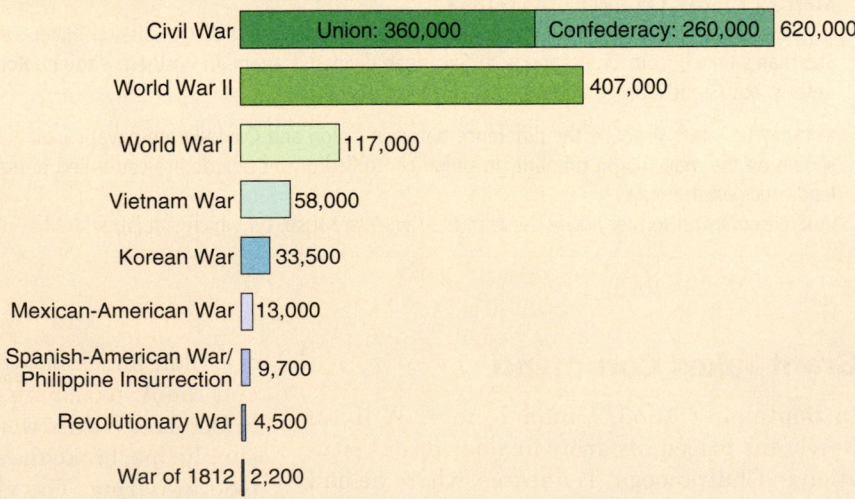

War	Deaths
Civil War	Union: 360,000 / Confederacy: 260,000 — 620,000
World War II	407,000
World War I	117,000
Vietnam War	58,000
Korean War	33,500
Mexican-American War	13,000
Spanish-American War/Philippine Insurrection	9,700
Revolutionary War	4,500
War of 1812	2,200

Wounded Men at Savage's Station

Misery did not end when the cannons ceased firing. Northern and southern surgeons performed approximately 60,000 amputations with simple instruments such as those included in this surgical kit. The wounded men shown here were but a fraction of those injured or killed during General George McClellan's peninsula campaign in 1862. Photo: Library of Congress; Surgical kit: Chicago Historical Society.

way. Nevertheless, disease killed nearly twice as many soldiers as did combat. Many who died of disease were prisoners of war. Approximately 30,000 Northerners died in Confederate prisons, and approximately 26,000 Southerners died in Union prisons.

Recently, historians have probed another explanation for the death toll, turning to soldiers' cultural attitudes and values to explain why they were willing to die in such great numbers. Some have explored how the nineteenth-century code of masculinity propelled valor on the battlefields, and how patriotism, for either the Union or the Confederacy, moved soldiers to risk everything. But scholars have focused most especially on how soldiers' religious beliefs about death made it easier for them to negotiate dying. The triumph of evangelical Protestantism in the early nineteenth century meant that Civil War soldiers faced death with calm resignation. They believed in a heaven that promised bodily resurrection and family reunion; the assurance of everlasting life, therefore, made it easier to face death. Culture, then, as well as the scope and length of the war, strategy, technology, and primitive medicine, helps explain the war's tremendous carnage.

Thinking about Cause and Effect

1. In what ways were Civil War strategists fighting the world's first "modern" war? In what ways were they still fighting a traditional-style war? How does this contrast account for the number of dead and wounded soldiers?

2. How did the high casualty rates lead to new opportunities for both women and blacks?

Major Battles of the Civil War, 1863–1865

May 1–4, 1863	Battle of Chancellorsville
July 1–3, 1863	Battle of Gettysburg
July 4, 1863	Fall of Vicksburg
September 16–20, 1863	Battle of Chickamauga
November 23–25, 1863	Battle of Chattanooga
May 5–7, 1864	Battle of the Wilderness
May 7–19, 1864	Battle of Spotsylvania Court House
June 3, 1864	Battle of Cold Harbor
June 27, 1864	Battle of Kennesaw Mountain
September 2, 1864	Fall of Atlanta
November–December 1864	Sheridan sacks Shenandoah Valley Sherman's "March to the Sea"
December 15–16, 1864	Battle of Nashville
December 22, 1864	Fall of Savannah
April 2–3, 1865	Fall of Petersburg and Richmond
April 9, 1865	Lee surrenders at Appomattox Court House

In Washington, General Grant implemented his grand strategy for a war of attrition. He ordered a series of simultaneous assaults from Virginia all the way to Louisiana. Two actions proved particularly significant. In one, General **William Tecumseh Sherman**, whom Grant appointed his successor to command the western armies, plunged southeast toward Atlanta. In the other, Grant, who took control of the Army of the Potomac, went head-to-head with Lee in Virginia for almost four straight weeks.

Grant and Lee met in the first week of May 1864 in a dense tangle of scrub oaks and small pines. Often unable to see more than ten paces, the armies pounded away at each other until approximately 18,000 Yankees and 11,000 rebels had fallen. The savagery of the **battle of the Wilderness** did not compare with that at Spotsylvania Court House a few days later. Frenzied men fought hand to hand for eighteen hours in the rain. One veteran remembered men "piled upon each other in some places four layers deep, exhibiting every ghastly phase of mutilation." (See "Historical Question," page 488.) Spotsylvania cost Grant another 18,000 casualties and Lee 10,000, but the Yankee bulldog would not let go. Grant kept moving and tangled with Lee again at Cold Harbor, where he suffered 13,000 additional casualties to Lee's 5,000.

Twice as many Union soldiers as rebel soldiers died in four weeks of fighting in Virginia in May and June, but because Lee had only half as many troops as Grant, his losses were equivalent to Grant's. Grant knew that the South could not replace the losses. Moreover, the campaign carried Grant to the outskirts of Petersburg, just south of Richmond, where he abandoned the costly tactic of the frontal assault and began a siege that immobilized both armies and dragged on for nine months.

Grant Planning the Attack at Cold Harbor

On June 2, 1864, General Ulysses S. Grant moved his headquarters to Bethesda Church, Maryland, carried the pews outdoors, and planned the attack he would make at Cold Harbor. Here, Grant leans over a pew to study a map. The next day, he ordered frontal assaults against entrenched Confederate forces, resulting in enormous Union losses. "I am disgusted with the generalship displayed," young Brigadier General Emory Upton observed. "Our men have, in many cases, been foolishly and wantonly slaughtered." Years later, Grant said that he regretted the assault at Cold Harbor, but in 1864 he kept pushing toward Richmond. Library of Congress.

***The Dead Line*, by Robert Sneden, Andersonville Prison, 1864**
The train carrying prisoner of war Robert Sneden arrived at Andersonville in February 1864 as the Confederates were completing the stockade surrounding their newest prison. Soon the sixteen and a half acres in southwestern Georgia were crammed with humanity and had to be expanded. Andersonville's 33,000 Union prisoners made it the fifth-largest city in the Confederacy. Sneden sketched this scene of a man being shot by a guard while trying to take part of a fence (the "dead line" that prisoners could not cross) for firewood. More than 13,000 prisoners perished at Andersonville. Smallpox, dysentery, scurvy, malnutrition, and infections proved far greater threats to them than bullets. © 1996, Lora Robbins Collection of Virginia Art, Virginia Historical Society.

Simultaneously, Sherman invaded Georgia. Grant instructed Sherman to "get into the interior of the enemy's country as far as you can, inflicting all the damage you can against their War resources." In May, Sherman moved 100,000 men south against 65,000 rebels. Skillful maneuvering, constant skirmishing, and one pitched battle, at Kennesaw Mountain, brought Sherman to Atlanta, which fell on September 2.

Intending to "make Georgia howl," Sherman marched out of Atlanta on November 15 with 62,000 battle-hardened veterans, heading for Savannah, 285 miles away on the Atlantic coast. One veteran remembered, "[We] destroyed all we could not eat, stole their niggers, burned their cotton & gins, spilled their sorghum, burned & twisted their R. Roads and raised Hell generally." **Sherman's March to the Sea** aimed at destroying the will of the southern people. A few weeks earlier, General **Philip H. Sheridan** had carried out his own scorched-earth campaign in the Shenandoah Valley, complying with Grant's order to turn the valley into "a barren waste . . . so that crows flying over it for the balance of this season will have to carry their provender [food] with them." When Sherman's troops entered an undefended Savannah in mid-December, the general telegraphed Lincoln that he had "a Christmas gift" for him. A month earlier, Union voters had bestowed on the president an even greater gift.

The Election of 1864

In the summer of 1864, with Sherman temporarily checked outside Atlanta and Grant bogged down in the siege of Petersburg, the Democratic Party smelled victory in the fall elections. Rankled by a seemingly never-ending war, inflation, the draft, the attack on civil liberties, and the commitment to blacks, Northerners appeared ready for a change. Lincoln himself concluded, "It seems exceedingly probable that this administration will not be re-elected."

The Democrats were badly divided, however. Peace Democrats insisted on an armistice, while "war" Democrats supported the conflict but opposed Republican means of fighting it. The party tried to paper over the chasm by nominating a war candidate, General George McClellan, but adopting a peace platform that demanded that "immediate efforts be made for a cessation of hostilities." Republicans denounced the peace plank as a cut-and-run plan that "virtually

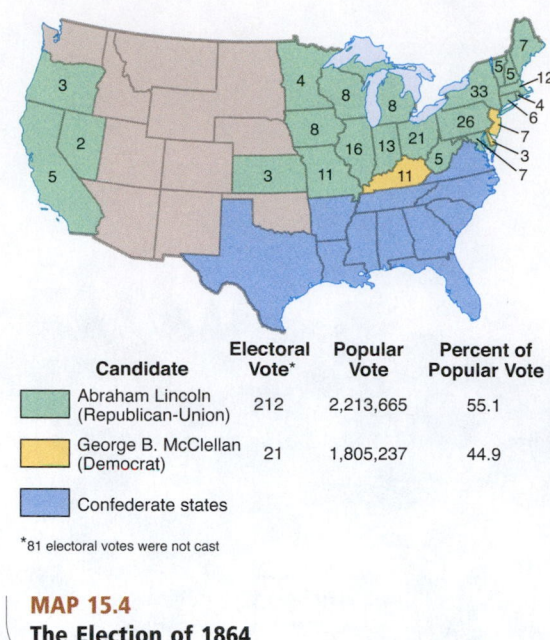

Candidate	Electoral Vote*	Popular Vote	Percent of Popular Vote
Abraham Lincoln (Republican-Union)	212	2,213,665	55.1
George B. McClellan (Democrat)	21	1,805,237	44.9
Confederate states			

*81 electoral votes were not cast

MAP 15.4
The Election of 1864

Robert E. Lee and Friends, by Mathew Brady, 1865
One week after his surrender at Appomattox Court House, Robert E. Lee sat for this portrait by Mathew Brady, the country's foremost photographer. Lee is joined by his eldest son, Major General George Washington Custis Lee (left), and a longtime aide, Lieutenant Colonel Walter H. Taylor (right). Lee's sober, weary expression reflects four hard years of war and his final defeat. Already a matchless hero among white Southerners, Lee was well on his way toward saintly immortality. In 1868, one woman described Lee as "bathed in the white light which falls directly upon him from the smile of an approving and sustaining God." Library of Congress.

proposed to surrender the country to the rebels in arms against us."

The capture of Atlanta in September turned the political tide in favor of the Republicans. Lincoln received 55 percent of the popular vote, but his electoral margin was a whopping 212 to McClellan's 21(Map 15.4). Lincoln's party won a resounding victory, one that gave him a mandate to continue the war until slavery and the Confederacy were dead.

The Confederacy Collapses

As 1865 dawned, military disaster littered the Confederate landscape. With the destruction of John B. Hood's army at Nashville in December 1864, the interior of the Confederacy lay in Yankee hands (see Map 15.3). Sherman's troops, resting momentarily in Savannah, eyed South Carolina hungrily. Farther north, Grant had Lee's army pinned down in Petersburg, a few miles from Richmond.

In the final days, some Confederates turned their backs on the rebellion. News from the battlefield made it difficult not to conclude that the Yankees had beaten them. Soldiers' wives begged their husbands to return home to keep their families from starving, and the stream of deserters grew dramatically. In most cases, when white Southerners lost the will to continue, it was not because they lost faith in independence but because they had been battered into submission. Despite the deep divisions within the Confederacy, white Southerners had demonstrated a remarkable endurance for their cause. Half of the 900,000 Confederate soldiers had been killed or wounded, and ragged, hungry women and children had sacrificed throughout one of the bloodiest wars then known to history.

The end came with a rush. On February 1, 1865, Sherman's troops stormed out of Savannah into South Carolina, the "cradle of the Confederacy." In Virginia, Lee abandoned Petersburg on April 2, and Richmond fell on April 3. Grant pursued Lee until he surrendered on April 9, 1865, at Appomattox Court House, Virginia. Grant offered generous peace terms. He allowed Lee's men to return home and to keep their horses to help "put in a crop to carry themselves and their families through the next winter." With Lee gone, the remaining Confederate armies lost hope and gave up within two weeks. After four years, the war was over.

No one was more relieved than Lincoln, but his celebration was restrained. He told his cabinet that his postwar burdens would weigh almost as heavily as those of wartime. Seeking a distraction, Lincoln attended Ford's Theatre on the evening of Good Friday, April 14, 1865. John Wilkes Booth, an actor with southern sympathies, slipped into the president's box and shot Lincoln in the head. He died at 7:22 the following morning. Vice President Andrew Johnson became president. The man who had led the nation through the war would not lead it during the postwar search for a just peace.

REVIEW Why were the siege of Vicksburg and the battle of Gettysburg crucial to the outcome of the war?

▶ Conclusion: The Second American Revolution

A transformed nation emerged from the crucible of war. Antebellum America was decentralized politically and loosely integrated economically. To bend the resources of the country to a Union victory, Congress enacted legislation that reshaped the nation's political and economic character. It created a national currency and banking system and turned to free land, a transcontinental railroad, and miles of telegraph lines to bind the West to the rest of the nation. Congress also established the sovereignty of the federal government and permanently increased its power. To most citizens before the war, Washington meant the post office and little more. During the war, the federal government drafted, taxed, and judged Americans in unprecedented ways. The massive changes brought about by the war — the creation of a national government, a national economy, and a national spirit — led one historian to call the American Civil War the "Second American Revolution."

The Civil War also had a profound effect on individual lives. When the war began in 1861, millions of men dropped their hoes, hammers, and pencils; put on blue or gray uniforms; and fought and suffered for what they passionately believed was right. The war disrupted families, leaving women at home with additional responsibilities and giving others wartime work in factories, offices, and hospitals. It offered blacks new and more effective ways to resist slavery and agitate for equality.

The war devastated the South. Three-fourths of southern white men of military age served in the Confederate army, and half of them were wounded or killed or died of disease. The war destroyed two-fifths of the South's livestock, wrecked half of the farm machinery, and blackened dozens of cities and towns. The immediate impact of the war on the North was more paradoxical. The struggle cost the North a heavy price: 360,000 lives. But rather than devastating the land, the war set the countryside and cities humming with business activity. The radical shift in power from South to North signaled a new direction in American development: the long decline of agriculture and the rise of industrial capitalism.

Most revolutionary of all, the war ended slavery. Ironically, the South's war to preserve slavery destroyed it. Nearly 200,000 black men, including ex-slave William Gould, dedicated their wartime service to its eradication. Because slavery was both a labor and a racial system, the institution was entangled in almost every aspect of southern life. Slavery's uprooting inevitably meant fundamental change. But the full meaning of abolition remained unclear in 1865. Determining the new economic, political, and social status of nearly 4 million ex-slaves would be the principal task of reconstruction.

▶ Selected Bibliography

General Works

Orville Vernon Burton, *The Age of Lincoln* (2007).
James M. McPherson, *The Battle Cry of Freedom: The Civil War Era* (1988).
Adam I. P. Smith, *The American Civil War* (2007).

Military History

Michael J. Bennett, *Union Jacks: Yankee Sailors in the Civil War* (2004).
Joseph T. Glatthaar, *General Lee's Army: From Victory to Collapse* (2008).
Mark Grimsley, *The Hard Hand of War: Union Military Policy toward Southern Civilians, 1861–1865* (1995).
Chandra Manning, *What This Cruel War Was Over: Soldiers, Slavery, and the Civil War* (2007).
James M. McPherson, *Tried by War: Abraham Lincoln as Commander in Chief* (2008).
Brooks D. Simpson, *Ulysses S. Grant: Triumph over Adversity, 1822–1865* (2000).
Russell F. Weigley, *A Great Civil War: A Military and Political History, 1861–1865* (2000).

The North and South at War

Stephen V. Ash, *When the Yankees Came: Conflict and Chaos in the Occupied South, 1861–1865* (1995).
Iver Bernstein, *The New York City Draft Riots: Their Significance for American Society and Politics in the Age of the Civil War* (1990).
William A. Blair, *Virginia's Private War: Feeding Body and Soul in the Confederacy, 1861–1865* (1998).
William J. Cooper, *Jefferson Davis, American* (2000).
Drew Gilpin Faust, *This Republic of Suffering: Death and the American Civil War* (2008).
William W. Freehling, *The South vs. the South: How Anti-Confederate Southerners Shaped the Course of the Civil War* (2001).
Gary W. Gallagher, *The Confederate War* (1997).
Judith Ann Giesberg, *Civil War Sisterhood: The U.S. Sanitary Commission and Women's Politics in Transition* (2000).
Mark E. Neely Jr., *The Fate of Liberty: Abraham Lincoln and Civil Liberties* (1991).
George C. Rable, *Civil Wars: Women and the Crisis of Southern Nationalism* (1989).
Heather Cox Richardson, *The Greatest Nation of the Earth: Republican Economic Policies during the Civil War* (1997).
James L. Roark, *Masters without Slaves: Southern Planters in the Civil War and Reconstruction* (1977).
Anne Sarah Rubin, *A Shattered Nation: The Rise and Fall of the Confederacy, 1861–1868* (2005).
Mark S. Schantz, *Awaiting the Heavenly Country: The Civil War and America's Culture of Death* (2008).
Nina Silber, *Daughters of the Union: Northern Women Fight the Civil War* (2006).
Margaret M. Storey, *Loyalty and Loss: Alabama's Unionists in the Civil War and Reconstruction* (2004).
Amy Murrell Taylor, *The Divided Family in Civil War America* (2005).
Jennifer L. Weber, *Copperheads: The Rise and Fall of Lincoln's Opponents in the North* (2008).

The Struggle for Freedom

Ira Berlin et al., eds., *Freedom: A Documentary History of Emancipation, 1861–1867*, 5 vols. (1982–2008).
Eric Foner, *The Fiery Trial: Abraham Lincoln and American Slavery* (2010).

Joseph T. Glatthaar, *Forged in Battle: The Civil War Alliance of Black Soldiers and White Officers* (1990).

William B. Gould IV, ed., *Diary of a Contraband: The Civil War Passage of a Black Sailor* (2002).

Michael P. Johnson, ed., *Abraham Lincoln, Slavery, and the Civil War: Selected Writings and Speeches* (2011).

Bruce Levine, *Confederate Emancipation: Southern Plans to Free and Arm Slaves during the Civil War* (2006).

James Oakes, *The Radical and the Republican: Frederick Douglass, Abraham Lincoln, and the Triumph of Antislavery Politics* (2007).

▶ **FOR MORE BOOKS ABOUT TOPICS IN THIS CHAPTER,** see the Online Bibliography at **bedfordstmartins.com/roark.**

▶ **FOR ADDITIONAL PRIMARY SOURCES FROM THIS PERIOD,** see Michael Johnson, ed., *Reading the American Past,* Fifth Edition.

▶ **FOR WEB SITES, IMAGES, AND DOCUMENTS RELATED TO TOPICS AND PLACES IN THIS CHAPTER,** visit Make History at **bedfordstmartins.com/roark.**

Reviewing Chapter 15

REVIEW QUESTIONS

Use key terms and dates to support your answer.

1. Why did both the Union and the Confederacy consider control of the border states crucial? (pp. 463–465)

2. Why did the South believe it could win the war despite numerical disadvantages? (pp. 465–468)

3. Why did the Confederacy's bid for international support fail? (pp. 468–475)

4. Why did the Union change policy in 1863 to allow black men to serve in the army? (pp. 475–479)

5. How did wartime hardship in the South contribute to class friction? (pp. 483–485)

6. Why was the U.S. Congress able to pass such a bold legislative agenda during the war? (pp. 485–486)

7. Why were the siege of Vicksburg and the battle of Gettysburg crucial to the outcome of the war? (pp. 486–493)

MAKING CONNECTIONS

Draw on key terms, the timeline, and review questions.

1. Despite loathing slavery, Lincoln embraced emancipation as a war objective late and with great caution. Why? In your answer, trace the progression of Lincoln's position, considering how legal, political, military, and moral concerns influenced his policies.

2. The Emancipation Proclamation did not accomplish the destruction of slavery on its own. How did a war over union bring about the end of slavery? In your answer, consider the direct actions of slaves and Union policymakers as well as indirect factors within the Confederacy.

3. In addition to restoring the Union and destroying slavery, what other significant changes did the war produce on the home front and in the nation's capital? In your answer, discuss economic, governmental, and social developments, being attentive to regional variations.

4. Brilliant military strategy alone did not determine the outcome of the war; victory also depended on generating revenue, materiel mobilization, diplomacy, and politics. In light of these considerations, explain why the Confederacy believed it would succeed and why it ultimately failed.

LINKING TO THE PAST

Link events in this chapter to earlier events.

1. Why were white slaveholders surprised by the wartime behavior of slaves? (See chapter 13.)

2. In what ways did the Lincoln administration's wartime policies fulfill the prewar aspirations of Northerners? (See chapters 12 and 14.)

▶ **FOR PRACTICE QUIZZES AND OTHER STUDY TOOLS**, visit the Online Study Guide at **bedfordstmartins.com/roark.**

TIMELINE 1861–1865

1861
- **April** Attack on Fort Sumter.
- **April–May** Four Upper South states join Confederacy.
- **July** Union forces routed in first battle of Bull Run (Manassas).
- **August** First Confiscation Act.

1862
- **February** Grant captures Fort Henry and Fort Donelson.
- **March** Confederates defeated at battle of Glorieta Pass.
- **March** Union victory at battle of Pea Ridge.
- **April** Battle of Shiloh in Tennessee ends Confederate bid to control Mississippi valley.
- **April** Confederate Congress authorizes draft.
- **May** Homestead Act.
- **May–July** Union forces defeated during Virginia peninsula campaign.
- **July** Second Confiscation Act.
- **July** Militia Act.
- **September** Battle of Antietam stops Lee's advance into Maryland.

1863
- **January** Emancipation Proclamation becomes law.
- **February** National Banking Act.
- **March** Congress authorizes draft.
- **July** Fall of Vicksburg to Union forces.
- **July** Lee defeated at battle of Gettysburg.
- **July** New York City draft riots.

1864
- **March** Grant appointed Union general in chief.
- **May–June** Wilderness campaign.
- **September** Fall of Atlanta to Sherman.
- **November** Lincoln reelected.
- **December** Fall of Savannah to Sherman.

1865
- **April 2–3** Fall of Petersburg and Richmond.
- **April 9** Lee surrenders to Grant.
- **April 15** Lincoln dies from bullet wound; Vice President Andrew Johnson becomes president.

CARPETBAG

A carpetbag was a nineteenth-century suitcase made from carpet, often brightly colored. Applied first to wildcat bankers on the western frontier, the term "carpetbagger" was a derogatory name for rootless and penniless adventurers who could carry everything they owned in a single bag. Critics of Republican administrations in the South hurled the name "carpetbaggers" at white Northerners who moved South during Reconstruction and became active in politics. The background image of bombed-out Richmond provides a reminder that one of the central tasks of the Reconstruction governments was the rebuilding of the South's battered cities and devastated agricultural economy.

Carpetbag: Nancy Gewirz/Antique Textile Resource; background: Library of Congress.

16

Reconstruction
1863–1877

IN 1856, JOHN RAPIER, A FREE BLACK BARBER IN FLORENCE, ALABAMA, urged his four freeborn sons to flee the increasingly repressive and dangerous South. Searching for a color-blind society, the brothers scattered around the world. James T. Rapier chose Canada, where he went to live with his uncle in a largely black community and studied Greek and Latin in a log schoolhouse. After his conversion at a Methodist revival, James wrote to his father: "I have not thrown a card in 3 years[,] touched a woman in 2 years[,] smoked nor drunk any Liquor in going on 2 years." He vowed, "I will endeavor to do my part in solving the problems [of African Americans] in my native land."

The Union victory in the Civil War gave James Rapier the opportunity to redeem his pledge. In 1865, after more than eight years of exile, the twenty-seven-year-old Rapier returned to Alabama, where he presided over the first political gathering of former slaves in the state. Alabama freedmen produced a petition that called on the federal government to thoroughly reconstruct the South, to guarantee suffrage, free schools, and equal rights for all men, regardless of color.

Rapier soon discovered that Alabama's whites found it agonizingly difficult to accept defeat and black freedom. They responded to the revolutionary changes under the banner "White Man — Right or Wrong — Still the White Man!" In 1868, when Rapier and other Alabama blacks vigorously supported the Republican presidential candidate, former Union general Ulysses S. Grant, the recently organized Ku Klux Klan went on a bloody rampage of whipping, burning, and shooting. A mob of 150 outraged whites scoured Rapier's neighborhood seeking four black politicians they claimed were trying to "Africanize Alabama." They caught and hanged three, but the "nigger carpetbagger from Canada" escaped. Rapier considered fleeing the state, but he decided to stay and fight.

By the early 1870s, Rapier had emerged as Alabama's most prominent black leader. Demanding that the federal government end the violence against ex-slaves, guarantee their civil rights, and give them land, he won election in 1872 to the House of Representatives, where he joined six other black congressmen. Defeated for reelection in 1874 in a campaign marked by white violence and ballot-box stuffing, Rapier turned to cotton farming, generously giving thousands of dollars of his profits to black schools and churches.

But persistent black poverty and unrelenting racial violence convinced Rapier that blacks could never achieve equality and prosperity in the South. He purchased land in Kansas and urged Alabama's blacks to escape with

James T. Rapier
Black suffrage sent fourteen African American congressmen to Washington, D.C., during Reconstruction, among them James T. Rapier of Alabama. Temporarily at least, he and his black colleagues helped shape post-emancipation society. In 1874, when Rapier spoke on behalf of a civil rights bill, he described the humiliation of being denied service at inns all along his route from Montgomery to Washington. Elsewhere in the world, he said, class and religion were invoked to defend discrimination. In Europe, "they have princes, dukes, lords"; in India, "brahmans or priests, who rank above the sudras or laborers." But in America, "our distinction is color." Alabama Department of Archives and History.

him. In 1883, however, before he could leave Alabama, Rapier died of tuberculosis at the age of forty-five.

In 1865, Union general Carl Schurz had foreseen many of the troubles Rapier would encounter in the postwar South. Schurz concluded that the Civil War was "a revolution but half accomplished." Northern victory had freed the slaves, he observed, but it had not changed former slaveholders' minds about blacks' unfitness for freedom. Left to themselves, whites would "introduce some new system of forced labor, not perhaps exactly slavery in its old form but something similar to it." To defend their freedom, Schurz concluded, blacks would need federal protection, land of their own, and voting rights. Until whites "cut loose from the past, it will be a dangerous experiment to put Southern society upon its own legs."

As Schurz discovered, the end of the war did not mean peace. The United States was one of only two societies in the New World in which slavery ended in a bloody war. (The other was Haiti.) Not surprisingly, racial turmoil continued in the South after the armies quit fighting in 1865. The nation entered one of its most chaotic and conflicted eras — Reconstruction, a violent period that would define the defeated South's status within the Union and the meaning of freedom for ex-slaves.

The place of the South within the nation and the extent of black freedom were determined not only in Washington, D.C., where the federal government played an active role, but also in the state legislatures and county seats of the South, where blacks eagerly participated in the process. Moreover, on farms and plantations from Virginia to Texas, ex-slaves struggled to become free workers while ex-slaveholders clung to the Old South. A small band of white women joined in the struggle for racial equality, and soon their crusade broadened to include gender equality. Their attempts to secure voting rights for women were thwarted, however.

Reconstruction witnessed a gigantic struggle to determine the consequences of Confederate defeat and emancipation. In the end, white Southerners prevailed. Their New South was a different South from the one to which most whites wished to return but also vastly unlike the one of which James Rapier dreamed.

▶ Wartime Reconstruction

Reconstruction did not wait for the end of war. As the odds of a northern victory increased, thinking about reunification quickened. Immediately, a question arose: Who had authority to devise a plan for reconstructing the Union? President Abraham Lincoln firmly believed that reconstruction was a matter of executive responsibility. Congress just as firmly asserted its jurisdiction. Fueling the argument were significant differences about the terms of reconstruction. Lincoln's primary aim was the restoration of national unity, which he sought through a program of speedy, forgiving political reconciliation. Congress feared that the president's program meant restoring the old southern ruling class to power. It wanted assurances of white loyalty and guarantees of black rights.

In their eagerness to formulate a plan for political reunification, neither Lincoln nor Congress gave much attention to the South's land and labor problems. But as the war rapidly eroded slavery and traditional plantation agriculture, Yankee military commanders in the Union-occupied areas of the Confederacy had no choice but to oversee the emergence of a new labor system.

"To Bind Up the Nation's Wounds"

On March 4, 1865, in his second inaugural address, President Lincoln surveyed the history of the war and then looked ahead to peace. "With malice toward none; with charity for all; with firmness in the right, as God gives us to see the right," Lincoln said, "let us strive on to finish the work we are in; to bind up the nation's wounds . . . to do all which may achieve and cherish a just, and a lasting peace." Lincoln had contemplated reunion for nearly two years. While deep compassion for the enemy guided his thinking about peace, his plan for reconstruction aimed primarily at shortening the war and ending slavery.

Lincoln's Proclamation of Amnesty and Reconstruction in December 1863 set out his terms. He offered a full pardon, restoring property (except slaves) and political rights, to rebels willing to renounce secession and to accept emancipation. His offer excluded only high-ranking Confederate military and political officers and a few other groups. When 10 percent of a state's voting population had taken an oath of allegiance, the state could organize a new government and be readmitted into the Union. Lincoln's plan did not require ex-rebels to extend social or political rights to ex-slaves, nor did it anticipate a program of long-term federal assistance to freedmen. Clearly, the president looked forward to the rapid, forgiving restoration of the broken Union.

Lincoln's easy terms enraged abolitionists such as Wendell Phillips of Boston, who charged that the president "makes the negro's freedom a mere sham." He "is willing that the negro should be free but seeks nothing else for him." He compared Lincoln to the most passive of the Civil War generals: "What McClellan was on the battlefield — 'Do as little hurt as possible!' — Lincoln is in civil affairs — 'Make as little change as possible!'" Phillips and other northern radicals called instead for a thorough overhaul of southern society. Their ideas proved to be too drastic for most Republicans during the war years, but Congress agreed that Lincoln's plan was inadequate.

In July 1864, Congress put forward a plan of its own. Congressman Henry Winter Davis of Maryland and Senator Benjamin Wade of Ohio jointly sponsored a bill that demanded that at least half of the voters in a conquered rebel state take the oath of allegiance before reconstruction could begin. The **Wade-Davis bill** also banned all ex-Confederates from participating in the drafting of new state constitutions. Finally, the bill guaranteed the equality of freedmen before the law. Congress's reconstruction would be neither as quick nor as forgiving as Lincoln's. When Lincoln refused to sign the bill and let it die, Wade and Davis charged the president with usurpation of power. They warned Lincoln to confine himself to "his executive duties — to obey and execute, not make the laws — to suppress by arms armed rebellion, and leave political organization to Congress."

Undeterred, Lincoln continued to nurture the formation of loyal state governments under his own plan. Four states — Louisiana, Arkansas, Tennessee, and Virginia — fulfilled the president's requirements, but Congress refused to seat representatives from the "Lincoln states." In his last public address in April 1865, Lincoln defended his plan but for the first time expressed publicly his endorsement of suffrage for southern blacks, at least "the very intelligent, and . . . those who serve our cause as soldiers." The announcement demonstrated that Lincoln's thinking about reconstruction was still evolving. Four days later, he was dead.

Wartime Reconstruction

This cartoon from the presidential campaign of 1864 shows the "Rail Splitter" Abraham Lincoln leveraging the broken nation back together while his running mate, Andrew Johnson, who once was a tailor by trade, stitches the Confederate states securely back into the Union. Optimism that the task of reconstructing the nation after the war would be both quick and easy shines through the cartoon. The Granger Collection, NY.

Land and Labor

Of all the problems raised by the North's victory in the war, none proved more critical than the South's transition from slavery to free labor. As federal armies invaded and occupied the Confederacy, hundreds of thousands of slaves became free workers. In addition, Union armies controlled vast territories in the South where legal title to land had become unclear. The Confiscation Acts passed during the war punished "traitors" by taking away their property. The question of what to do with federally occupied land and how to organize labor on it engaged former slaves, former slaveholders, Union military commanders, and federal government officials long before the war ended.

> **"What's the use of being free if you don't own land enough to be buried in?"**
> — A former slave

In the Mississippi valley, occupying federal troops announced a new labor code. It required slaveholders to sign contracts with ex-slaves and to pay wages. It obligated employers to provide food, housing, and medical care. It outlawed whipping, but it reserved to the army the right to discipline blacks who refused to work. The code required black laborers to enter into contracts, work diligently, and remain subordinate and obedient. Military leaders clearly had no intention of promoting a social or economic revolution. Instead, they sought to restore plantation agriculture with wage labor. The effort resulted in a hybrid system that one contemporary called "compulsory free labor," something that satisfied no one.

Planters complained because the new system fell short of slavery. Blacks could not be "transformed by proclamation," a Louisiana sugar planter declared. Yet under the new system, blacks "are expected to perform their new obligations without coercion, & without the fear of punishment which is essential to stimulate the idle and correct the vicious." Without the right to whip, he argued, the new labor system did not have a chance. Either Union soldiers must "*compel* the negroes to work," planters insisted, or the planters themselves must "be authorized and sustained in using force."

African Americans found the new regime too reminiscent of slavery to be called free labor. Its chief deficiency, they believed, was the failure to provide them with land of their own. Freedmen believed they had a moral right to land because they and their ancestors had worked it without compensation for more than two centuries. "What's the use of being free if you don't own land enough to be buried in?" one man asked. Several wartime developments led freedmen to believe that the federal government planned to undergird black freedom with landownership.

In January 1865, General William Tecumseh Sherman set aside part of the coast south of Charleston for black settlement. He devised the plan to relieve himself of the burden of thousands of impoverished blacks who trailed desperately behind his army. By June 1865, some 40,000 freedmen sat on 400,000 acres of "Sherman land." In addition, in March 1865, Congress passed a bill establishing the Bureau of Refugees, Freedmen, and Abandoned Lands. The **Freedmen's Bureau**, as it was called, distributed food and clothing to destitute Southerners and eased the transition of blacks from slaves to free persons. Congress also authorized the agency to divide abandoned and confiscated land into 40-acre plots, to rent them to freedmen, and eventually to sell them "with such title as the United States can convey." By June 1865, the bureau had situated nearly 10,000 black families on a half million acres abandoned by fleeing planters. Other ex-slaves eagerly anticipated farms of their own.

Despite the flurry of activity, wartime reconstruction failed to produce agreement about whether the president or Congress had the authority to devise policy or what proper policy should be.

The African American Quest for Autonomy

Ex-slaves never had any doubt about what they wanted from freedom. They had only to contemplate what they had been denied as slaves. (See "Documenting the American Promise," page 504.) Slaves had to remain on their plantations; freedom allowed blacks to see what was on the other side of the hill. Slaves had to be at work in the fields by dawn; freedom permitted blacks to sleep through a sunrise. Freedmen also tested the etiquette of racial subordination. "Lizzie's maid passed me today when I was coming from church *without speaking to me*," huffed one plantation mistress.

To whites, emancipation looked like pure anarchy. Blacks, they said, had reverted to their natural condition: lazy, irresponsible, and wild. Without the discipline of slavery, whites predicted, blacks would go the way of "the Indian and the buffalo." Actually, former slaves were experimenting with freedom, but they could not long afford to roam the countryside, neglect work, and casually provoke whites. Soon, most were back at work in whites' kitchens and fields.

But other items on ex-slaves' agenda of freedom endured. They continued to dream of land and economic independence. "The way we can best take care of ourselves is to have land," one former slave declared in 1865, "and turn it and till it by our own labor." Freedmen also wanted to learn to read and write. Many black soldiers had become literate in the Union army, and they understood the value of the pen and book. "I wishes the Childern all in School," one black veteran asserted. "It is beter for them then to be their Surveing a mistes [mistress]."

The restoration of broken families was another persistent black aspiration. Thousands of freedmen took to the roads in 1865 to look for kin who had been sold away or to free those who were being held illegally as slaves. A black soldier from Missouri wrote his daughters that he was coming for them. "I will have you if it cost me my life," he declared. "Your Miss Kitty said that I tried to steal you," he told them. "But I'll let her know that god never intended for a man to steal his own flesh and blood." And he swore that "if she meets me with ten thousand soldiers, she [will] meet her enemy."

Independent worship was another continuing aspiration. African Americans greeted freedom with a mass exodus from white churches, where they had been required to worship when slaves. Some joined the newly established southern branches of all-black northern churches, such as the African Methodist Episcopal Church. Others formed black versions of the major southern denominations, Baptists and Methodists. Freedmen interpreted the events of the Civil War and reconstruction as Christian people. One

The Meaning of Freedom

The Emancipation Proclamation states that "all persons held as slaves" within the states still in rebellion on January 1, 1863, "are, and henceforward shall be, free." Although the proclamation in and of itself did not free any slaves, it transformed the character of the war. Despite often intolerable conditions, black people focused on the possibilities of freedom.

DOCUMENT 1
Letter from John Q. A. Dennis to Edwin M. Stanton, July 26, 1864

John Q. A. Dennis, formerly a slave in Maryland, wrote to ask Secretary of War Edwin M. Stanton for help in reuniting his family.

BOSTON. Dear Sir I am Glad that I have the Honour to Write you a few line I have been in troble for about four yars my Dear wife was taken from me Nov 19th 1859 and left me with three Children and I being a Slave At the time Could Not do Anny thing for the poor little Children for my master it was took me Carry me some forty mile from them So I Could Not do for them and the man that they live with half feed them and half Cloth them & beat them like dogs & when I was admitted to go to see them it use to brake my heart & Now I say again I am Glad to have the honour to write to you to see if you Can Do Anny thing for me or for my poor little Children I was keap in Slavy untell last Novr 1863. then the Good lord sent the Cornel borne [federal colonel William Birney?] Down their in Marland in worsester Co So as I have been recently freed I have but letle to live on but I am Strieving Dear Sir but what I went too know of you Sir is it possible for me to go & take my Children from those men that keep them in Savery if it is possible will you pleas give me a permit from your hand then I think they would let them go. . . .

Hon sir will you please excuse my Miserable writeing & answer me as soon as you can I want get the little Children out of Slavery, I being Criple would like to know of you also if I Cant be permited to rase a Shool Down there & on what turm I Could be admited to Do so No more At present Dear Hon Sir

SOURCE: *Freedom: A Documentary History of Emancipation, 1861–1867*, ser. 1, vol. 1, *The Destruction of Slavery*, 386, edited by Ira Berlin, Joseph P. Reidy, and Leslie S. Rowland. Copyright © 1985. Reprinted with the permission of Cambridge University Press.

DOCUMENT 2
Report from Reverend A. B. Randall, February 28, 1865

A. B. Randall, the white chaplain of a black regiment stationed in Little Rock, Arkansas, affirmed the importance of legal marriage to freed slaves and emphasized their conviction that emancipation was only the first step toward full freedom.

Weddings, just now, are very popular, and abundant among the Colored People. They have just learned, of the Special Order No. 15. of Gen Thomas [Adjutant General Lorenzo Thomas] by which, they may not only be lawfully married, but have their Marriage Certificates, Recorded; in a book furnished by the Government. This is most desirable. . . . Those who were captured . . . at Ivy's Ford, on the 17th of January, by Col Brooks, had their Marriage Certificates, taken from them; and destroyed; and then were roundly cursed, for having such papers in their posession. I have married, during the month, at this Post; Twenty five couples; mostly, those, who have families; & have been living together for years. I try to dissuade single men, who are soldiers, from marrying, till their time of enlistment is out: as that course seems to me, to be most judicious. The Colord People here, generally consider, this war not only; their exodus, from bondage; but the road, to Responsibility; Competency; and an honorable Citizenship — God grant that their hopes and expectations may be fully realized.

SOURCE: *Freedom: A Documentary History of Emancipation, 1861–1867*, ser. 2, vol. 1, *The Black Military Experience*, 712, edited by Ira Berlin, Joseph P. Reidy, and Leslie S. Rowland. Copyright © 1982. Reprinted with the permission of Cambridge University Press.

DOCUMENT 3
Petition "to the Union Convention of Tennessee Assembled in the Capitol at Nashville," January 9, 1865

In January 1865, black Tennesseans petitioned a convention of white Unionists debating the reorganization of state government.

We the undersigned petitioners, American citizens of African descent, natives and residents of Tennessee, and devoted friends of the great National cause, do most respectfully ask a patient hearing of your honorable body in regard to matters deeply affecting the future condition of our unfortunate and long suffering race.

First of all, however, we would say that words are too weak to tell how profoundly grateful we are to the Federal Government for the good work of freedom which it is gradually carrying forward; and for the Emancipation Proclamation which has set free all the slaves in some of the rebellious States, as well as many of the slaves in Tennessee. . . .

We claim freedom, as our natural right, and ask that in harmony and co-operation with the nation at large, you should cut up by the roots the system of slavery, which is not only a wrong to us, but the source of all the evil which at present afflicts the State. For slavery, corrupt itself, corrupted nearly all, also, around it, so that it has influenced nearly all the slave States to rebel against the Federal Government, in order to set up a government of pirates under which slavery might be perpetrated.

In the contest between the nation and slavery, our unfortunate people have sided, by instinct, with the former. We have little fortune to devote to the national cause, for a hard fate has hitherto forced us to live in poverty, but we do devote to its success, our hopes, our toils, our whole heart, our sacred honor, and our lives. We will work, pray, live, and, if need be, die for the Union, as cheerfully as ever a white patriot died for his country. The color of our skin does not lessen in the least degree, our love either for God or for the land of our birth. . . .

We know the burdens of citizenship, and are ready to bear them. We know the duties of the good citizen, and are ready to perform them cheerfully, and would ask to be put in a position in which we can discharge them more effectually. . . .

This is a democracy — a government of the people. It should aim to make every man, without regard to the color of his skin, the amount of his wealth, or the character of his religious faith, feel personally interested in its welfare. Every man who lives under the Government should feel that it is his property, his treasure, the bulwark and defence of himself and his family. . . .

This is not a Democratic Government if a numerous, law-abiding, industrious, and useful class of citizens, born and bred on the soil, are to be treated as aliens and enemies, as an inferior degraded class, who must have no voice in the Government which they support, protect and defend, with all their heart, soul, mind, and body, both in peace and war. . . .

The possibility that the negro suffrage proposition may shock popular prejudice at first sight, is not a conclusive argument against its wisdom and policy. No proposition ever met with more furious or general opposition than the one to enlist colored soldiers in the United States army. The opponents of the measure exclaimed on all hands that the negro was a coward; that he would not fight; that one white man, with a whip in his hand could put to flight a regiment of them. . . . Yet the colored man has fought so well, on almost every occasion, that the rebel government is prevented, only by its fears and distrust of being able to force him to fight for slavery as well as he fights against it, from putting half a million of negroes into its ranks.

The Government has asked the colored man to fight for its preservation and gladly has he done it. It can afford to trust him with a vote as safely as it trusted him with a bayonet.

SOURCE: *Freedom: A Documentary History of Emancipation, 1861–1867*, ser. 2, vol. 1, *The Black Military Experience*, 811–16, edited by Ira Berlin, Joseph P. Reidy, and Leslie S. Rowland. Copyright © 1982. Reprinted with the permission of Cambridge University Press.

Questions for Analysis and Debate

1. How does John Q. A. Dennis interpret his responsibility as a father?

2. Why do you think ex-slaves wanted their marriages legalized?

3. Why, according to petitioners to the Union Convention of Tennessee, did blacks deserve voting rights?

AML. DOVE wishes to know of the whereabouts of his mother, Areno, his sisters Maria, Neziah, and Peggy, and his brother Edmond, who were owned by Geo. Dove, of Rockingham county, Shenandoah Valley, Va. Sold in Richmond, after which Saml. and Edmond were taken to Nashville, Tenn., by Joe Mick; Areno was left at the Eagle Tavern, Richmond
Respectfully yours,
SAML. DOVE.
Utica, New York, Aug. 5, 1865–3m
U. S. CHRISTIAN COMMISSION,
NASHVILLE, TENN., July 19, 1865.

Harry Stephens and Family, 1866, and Samuel Dove Ad, 1865
Dressed in their Sunday best, this Virginia family sits proudly for a photograph. Many black families were not as fortunate as the Stephens family. Separated by slavery or war, former slaves desperately sought news of missing family members through newspaper advertisements like the one posted by Samuel Dove in August 1865. We do not know whether he succeeded in locating his mother, brother, and sisters. Ad: Chicago Historical Society; Family: The Metropolitan Museum of Art, Gilman Collection, Purchase, The Horace W. Goldsmith Foundation Gift, 2005 (2005.100.277)/Art Resource, NY.

black woman thanked Lincoln for the Emancipation Proclamation, declaring, "When you are dead and in Heaven, in a thousand years that action of yours will make the Angels sing your praises I know it."

REVIEW Why did Congress object to Lincoln's wartime plan for reconstruction?

▶ Presidential Reconstruction

Abraham Lincoln died on April 15, 1865, just hours after John Wilkes Booth shot him at a Washington, D.C., theater. Chief Justice Salmon P. Chase immediately administered the oath of office to Vice President **Andrew Johnson** of Tennessee. Congress had adjourned in March and would not reconvene until December. Throughout the summer and fall, the "accidental president" made critical decisions about the future of the South without congressional advice. With dizzying speed, he drew up and executed a plan of reconstruction.

Congress returned to the capital in December to find that, as far as the president and former Confederates were concerned, reconstruction was completed. Most Republicans, however, thought Johnson's puny demands of ex-rebels made a mockery of the sacrifice of Union soldiers. Instead of honoring the dead by insisting on "a new birth of freedom," as Lincoln had promised in his 1863 speech at Gettysburg, Johnson had acted as midwife to the rebirth of the Old South and the stillbirth of black liberty. They proceeded to dismantle Johnson's program and substitute a program of their own.

***A Pastoral Visit*, 1881**
Freedom from bondage permitted blacks to flee white ministers and churches, to "come out from under the yoke," as one ex-slave put it. In *A Pastoral Visit*, Virginia-born artist Richard Norris Brooke portrays a dignified elderly black minister seated at a table with a family of his parishioners. In this sympathetic and respectful depiction, the poor family shares what it has. It is safe to say that no white minister had ever sat down for a meal in this humble northern Virginia cabin. In the Collection of the Corcoran Gallery of Art, Washington, D.C.

Johnson's Program of Reconciliation

Born in 1808 in Raleigh, North Carolina, Andrew Johnson was the son of illiterate parents. Self-educated and ambitious, Johnson moved to Tennessee, where he worked as a tailor, accumulated a fortune in land, acquired five slaves, and built a career in politics championing the South's common white people and assailing its "illegitimate, swaggering, bastard, scrub aristocracy." The only senator from a Confederate state to remain loyal to the Union, Johnson held the planter class responsible for secession. Less than two weeks before he became president, he announced what he would do to planters if he ever had the chance: "I would arrest them — I would try them — I would convict them and I would hang them."

Despite such statements, Johnson was no friend of the Republicans. A Democrat all his life, Johnson occupied the White House only because the Republican Party in 1864 had needed a vice presidential candidate who would appeal to loyal, Union-supporting Democrats. Johnson vigorously defended states' rights (but not secession) and opposed Republican efforts to expand the power of the federal government. A steadfast supporter of slavery, Johnson had owned slaves until 1862, when Tennessee rebels, angry at his Unionism, confiscated them. When he grudgingly accepted emancipation, it was more because he hated planters than sympathized with slaves. "Damn the negroes," he said. "I am fighting those traitorous aristocrats, their masters." At a time when the nation confronted the future of black Americans, the new president harbored unshakable racist convictions. Africans, Johnson said, were "inferior to the white man in point of intellect — better calculated in physical structure to undergo drudgery and hardship."

> "Damn the negroes. I am fighting those traitorous aristocrats, their masters."
> — President ANDREW JOHNSON

Like Lincoln, Johnson stressed the rapid restoration of civil government in the South. Like Lincoln, he promised to pardon most, but not all, ex-rebels. Johnson recognized the state governments created by Lincoln but set out his own requirements for restoring the other rebel states to the Union. All that the citizens of a state had to do was to renounce the right of secession, deny that the debts of the Confederacy were legal and binding, and ratify the Thirteenth Amendment abolishing slavery, which became part of the Constitution in December 1865.

Johnson's eagerness to restore relations with southern states and his lack of sympathy for blacks also led him to return to pardoned ex-Confederates all confiscated and abandoned land, even if it was in the hands of freedmen. Reformers were shocked. They had expected the president's hatred of planters to mean the permanent confiscation of the South's plantations and the distribution of the land to loyal freedmen. Instead, his instructions canceled the promising beginnings made by General Sherman and the Freedmen's Bureau to settle blacks on land of their own. As one freedman observed, "Things was hurt by Mr. Lincoln getting killed."

White Southern Resistance and Black Codes

In the summer of 1865, delegates across the South gathered to draw up the new state constitutions required by Johnson's plan of reconstruction. Rather than take their medicine, delegates choked on even the president's mild requirements. Refusing to renounce secession, the South Carolina and Georgia conventions merely "repudiated" their secession ordinances, preserving in principle their right to secede. South Carolina and Mississippi refused to disown their Confederate war debts. Mississippi rejected the Thirteenth Amendment outright, and Alabama rejected it in part. Despite these defiant acts, Johnson did nothing. White Southerners began to think that by standing up for themselves they — not victorious Northerners — would shape reconstruction.

In the fall of 1865, newly elected southern legislators across the South adopted a series of laws known as **black codes**, which made a travesty of black freedom. The codes sought to keep ex-slaves subordinate to whites by subjecting them to every sort of discrimination. Several states made it illegal for blacks to own a gun. Mississippi made insulting gestures and language

by blacks a criminal offense. The codes barred blacks from jury duty. Not a single southern state granted any black the right to vote.

At the core of the black codes, however, lay the matter of labor. Faced with the death of slavery, legislators sought to hustle freedmen back to the plantations. Whites were almost universally opposed to black landownership. Whitelaw Reid, a northern visitor to the South, found that the "man who should sell small tracts to them would be in actual personal danger." South Carolina attempted to limit blacks to either farmwork or domestic service by requiring them to pay annual taxes of $10 to $100 to work in any other occupation. Mississippi declared that blacks who did not possess written evidence of employment could be declared vagrants and be subject to involuntary plantation labor. Under so-called apprenticeship laws, courts bound thousands of black children — orphans and others whose parents they deemed unable to support them — to work for planter "guardians."

Johnson refused to intervene. A staunch defender of states' rights, he believed that the citizens of every state should be free to write their own constitutions and laws. Moreover, Johnson was as eager as other white Southerners to restore white supremacy and black subordination. As he remarked in 1865, "White men alone must manage the South."

But Johnson also followed the path that he believed offered him the greatest political return. A conservative Tennessee Democrat at the head of a northern Republican Party, he began to look southward for political allies. Despite tough talk about punishing traitors, he personally pardoned fourteen thousand wealthy or high-ranking ex-Confederates. By pardoning powerful whites, by accepting governments even when they failed to satisfy his minimal demands, and by acquiescing in the black codes, he won useful southern friends.

In the fall elections of 1865, white Southerners dramatically expressed their mood. To represent them in Congress, they chose former Confederates. Of the eighty senators and representatives they sent to Washington, fifteen had served in the Confederate army, ten of them as generals. Another sixteen had served in civil and judicial posts in the Confederacy. Nine others had served in the Confederate Congress. One — Alexander Stephens — had been vice president of the Confederacy. As one Georgian remarked, "It looked as though Richmond had moved to Washington."

The Black Codes
Titled "Selling a Freeman to Pay His Fine at Monticello, Florida," this 1867 drawing from a northern magazine equates black codes with the reinstitution of slavery. The laws stopped short of reenslavement but sharply restricted blacks' freedom. In Florida, as in other southern states, certain acts, such as breaking a labor contract, were made criminal offenses, the penalty for which could be involuntary plantation labor for a year. The Granger Collection, NYC.

Expansion of Federal Authority and Black Rights

Southerners had blundered monumentally. They had assumed that what Andrew Johnson was willing to accept, Republicans would accept as well. But southern intransigence compelled even moderates to conclude that ex-rebels were a "generation of vipers," still untrustworthy and dangerous. So angry were Republicans with the rebels that the federal government refused to supply artificial limbs to disabled Southerners, as they did for Union veterans.

The black codes became a symbol of southern intentions to "restore all of slavery but its name." Northerners were hardly saints when it came

to racial justice, but black freedom had become a hallowed war aim. "We tell the white men of Mississippi," the *Chicago Tribune* roared, "that the men of the North will convert the State of Mississippi into a frog pond before they will allow such laws to disgrace one foot of the soil in which the bones of our soldiers sleep and over which the flag of freedom waves."

The moderate majority of the Republican Party wanted only assurance that slavery and treason were dead. They did not champion black equality, the confiscation of plantations, or black voting, as did the radical minority within the party. But southern obstinacy had succeeded in forging unity (at least temporarily) among Republican factions. In December 1865, exercising

Congress's right to determine the qualifications of its members, Republicans refused to seat the southern representatives elected in the fall elections. Rather than accept Johnson's claim that the "work of restoration" was done, Congress challenged his executive power.

Republican senator Lyman Trumbull declared that the president's policy meant that an ex-slave would "be tyrannized over, abused, and virtually reenslaved without some legislation by the nation for his protection." Early in 1866, the moderates produced two bills that strengthened the federal shield. The first, the Freedmen's Bureau bill, prolonged the life of the agency established by the previous Congress. It had distributed food, supervised labor contracts, and sponsored schools for freedmen. Arguing that the Constitution never contemplated a "system for the support of indigent persons," President Andrew Johnson vetoed the bill. Congress failed by a narrow margin to override the president's veto.

The moderates designed their second measure, what would become the **Civil Rights Act of 1866**, to nullify the black codes by affirming African Americans' rights to "full and equal benefit of all laws and proceedings for the security of person and property as is enjoyed by white

citizens." The act boldly required the end of racial discrimination in state laws and represented an extraordinary expansion of black rights and federal authority. The president argued that the civil rights bill amounted to "unconstitutional invasion of states' rights" and vetoed it. In essence, he denied that the federal government possessed the authority to protect the civil rights of blacks.

In April 1866, an incensed Republican Party again pushed the civil rights bill through Congress and overrode the presidential veto. In July, it passed another Freedmen's Bureau bill and overrode Johnson's veto. For the first time in American history, Congress had overridden presidential vetoes of major legislation. As a worried South Carolinian observed, Johnson had succeeded in uniting the Republicans and probably touched off "a fight this fall such as has never been seen."

REVIEW   How did the North respond to the passage of black codes in the southern states?

▶ Congressional Reconstruction

By the summer of 1866, President Andrew Johnson and Congress had dropped their gloves and stood toe-to-toe in a bare-knuckle contest unprecedented in American history. Johnson made it clear that he would not budge on either constitutional issues or policy. Moderate Republicans responded by amending the Constitution. But the obstinacy of Johnson and white Southerners pushed Republican moderates ever closer to the radicals and to acceptance of additional federal intervention in the South. Congress also voted to impeach the president for the first time since the nation was formed. In time, Congress debated whether to make voting rights color-blind, while women sought to make voting sex-blind as well.

The Fourteenth Amendment and Escalating Violence

In June 1866, Congress passed the **Fourteenth Amendment** to the Constitution, and two years later it gained the necessary ratification of three-fourths of the states. The most important provisions of this complex amendment made all native-born or naturalized persons American citizens and prohibited states from abridging the "privileges and immunities" of citizens, depriving them of "life, liberty, or property without due

Reconstruction Cartoon

Most white southerners had difficulty adjusting to defeat, but no one defied and damned the Yankees like white women. This 1865 cartoon pokes fun at two Richmond ladies as they pass by a Union officer on their way to receive free government rations. One says sourly to the other, "Don't you think that Yankee must feel like shrinking into his boots before such high-toned Southern ladies as we?" Just a step behind the white women is a smiling black woman, who obviously views the Yankee through different eyes. Miriam and Ira D. Wallach Division of Art, Prints and Photographs, The New York Public Library. Astor, Lenox and Tilden Foundations.

process of law," and denying them "equal protection of the laws." By making blacks national citizens, the amendment provided a national guarantee of equality before the law. In essence, it protected blacks against violation by southern state governments.

The Fourteenth Amendment also dealt with voting rights. It gave Congress the right to reduce the congressional representation of states that withheld suffrage from some of its adult male population. In other words, white Southerners could either allow black men to vote or see their representation in Washington slashed. Whatever happened, Republicans stood to benefit from the Fourteenth Amendment. If southern whites granted voting rights to freedmen, Republicans would gain valuable black votes. If whites refused, the representation of southern Democrats would plunge.

The Fourteenth Amendment's suffrage provisions ignored the small band of politicized women who had emerged from the war demanding "the ballot for the two disenfranchised classes, negroes and women." Founding the **American Equal Rights Association** in 1866, **Susan B. Anthony** and **Elizabeth Cady Stanton** lobbied for "a government by the people, and the whole people; for the people and the whole people." They felt betrayed when their old antislavery allies refused to work for their goals. "It was the Negro's hour," Frederick Douglass explained. Senator Charles Sumner suggested that woman suffrage could be "the great question of the future."

The Fourteenth Amendment provided for punishment of any state that excluded voters on the basis of race but not on the basis of sex. The amendment also introduced the word *male* into the Constitution when it referred to a citizen's right to vote. Stanton predicted that "if that word 'male' be inserted, it will take us a century at least to get it out."

Tennessee approved the Fourteenth Amendment in July, and Congress promptly welcomed the state's representatives and senators back. Had President Johnson counseled other southern states to ratify this relatively mild amendment and warned them that they faced the fury of an outraged Republican Party if they refused, they might have listened. Instead, Johnson advised Southerners to reject the Fourteenth Amendment and to rely on him to trounce the Republicans in the fall congressional elections.

Johnson had decided to make the Fourteenth Amendment the overriding issue of the 1866 elections and to gather its white opponents into

Elizabeth Cady Stanton and Susan B. Anthony, 1870
Outspoken suffragists Elizabeth Cady Stanton (left) and Susan B. Anthony (right) were veteran reformers who advocated, among other things, better working conditions for labor, married women's property rights, liberalization of divorce laws, and women's admission into colleges and trade schools. Their passion for other causes led some conservatives to oppose women's political rights because they equated the suffragist cause with radicalism in general. Women could not easily overcome such views, and the long struggle for the vote eventually drew millions of women into public life. ©Bettmann/Corbis.

a new conservative party, the National Union Party. The president's strategy suffered a setback when whites in several southern cities went on rampages against blacks. When a mob in New Orleans assaulted delegates to a black suffrage convention, thirty-four blacks died. In Memphis, white mobs killed at least forty-six people. The slaughter shocked Northerners and renewed skepticism about Johnson's claim that southern whites could be trusted. "Who doubts that the Freedmen's Bureau ought to be abolished forthwith," a New Yorker observed sarcastically, "and the blacks remitted to the paternal care of their old masters, who 'understand the nigger, you know, a great deal better than the Yankees can.'"

The 1866 elections resulted in an overwhelming Republican victory. Johnson had bet that Northerners would not support federal protection of black rights and that a racist backlash would blast the Republican Party. But the war was still fresh in northern minds, and as one Republican explained, southern whites "with all their intelligence were traitors, the blacks with all their ignorance were loyal."

> "If that word 'male' be inserted [in the Fourteenth Amendment], it will take us a century at least to get it out."
> — ELIZABETH CADY STANTON

Memphis Riots, May 1866
On May 1, 1866, two carriages, one driven by a white man and the other by a black man, collided on a busy street in Memphis, Tennessee. This minor incident led to three days of bloody racial violence in which dozens of blacks and two whites died. South Memphis, pictured in this lithograph from *Harper's Weekly*, was a shantytown where the families of black soldiers stationed at nearby Fort Pickering lived. The army commander refused to send troops to protect soldiers' families and property, and white mobs ran wild. The Granger Collection, NYC.

Radical Reconstruction and Military Rule

When Johnson continued to urge Southerners to reject the Fourteenth Amendment, every southern state except Tennessee voted it down. "The last one of the sinful ten," thundered Representative James A. Garfield of Ohio, "has flung back into our teeth the magnanimous offer of a generous nation." After the South rejected the moderates' program, the radicals seized the initiative.

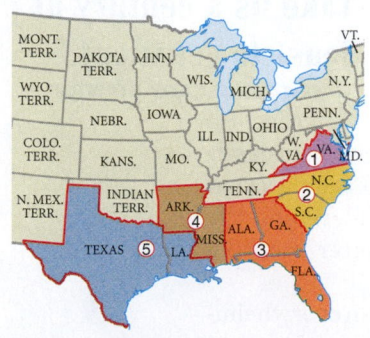

Reconstruction Military Districts, 1867

Each act of defiance by southern whites had boosted the standing of the radicals within the Republican Party. Except for freedmen themselves, no one did more to make freedom the "mighty moral question of the age." Radicals such as Massachusetts senator Charles Sumner and Pennsylvania representative Thaddeus Stevens did not speak with a single voice, but they united in demanding civil

and political equality. Southern states were "like clay in the hands of the potter," Stevens declared in January 1867, and he called on Congress to begin reconstruction all over again.

In March 1867, Congress overturned the Johnson state governments and initiated military rule of the South. The **Military Reconstruction Act** (and three subsequent acts) divided the ten unreconstructed Confederate states into five military districts. Congress placed a Union general in charge of each district and instructed him to "suppress insurrection, disorder, and violence" and to begin political reform. After the military had completed voter registration, which would include black men, voters in each state would elect delegates to conventions that would draw up new state constitutions. Each constitution would guarantee black suffrage. When the voters of each state had approved the constitution and the state legislature had ratified the Fourteenth Amendment, the state could submit its work to Congress. If Congress approved, the state's senators and representatives could be seated, and political reunification would be accomplished.

Radicals proclaimed the provision for black suffrage "a prodigious triumph," for it extended far beyond the limited suffrage provisions of the Fourteenth Amendment. Republicans now believed that only the voting power of ex-slaves could bring about a permanent revolution in the South. When combined with the disfranchisement of thousands of ex-rebels, it promised to cripple any neo-Confederate resurgence and guarantee Republican state governments in the South.

Despite its bold suffrage provision, the Military Reconstruction Act of 1867 disappointed those who also advocated the confiscation of southern plantations and their redistribution to ex-slaves. Thaddeus Stevens agreed with the freedman who said, "Give us our own land and we take care of ourselves, but without land, the old masters can hire us or starve us, as they please." But most Republicans believed they had provided blacks with what they needed: equal legal rights and the ballot. If blacks were to get land, they would have to gain it themselves.

Declaring that he would rather sever his right arm than sign such a formula for "anarchy and chaos," Andrew Johnson vetoed the Military Reconstruction Act. Congress overrode his veto the very same day, dramatizing the shift in power from the executive to the legislative branch of government. With the passage of the Reconstruction Acts of 1867, congressional reconstruction was virtually completed. Congress left whites owning most of the South's land but, in a departure that justified the term "radical reconstruction," had given black men the ballot. In 1867, the nation began an unprecedented experiment in interracial democracy — at least in the South, for Congress's plan did not touch the North. But before the spotlight swung away from Washington to the South, the president and Congress had one more scene to play.

Impeaching a President

Despite his defeats, Andrew Johnson had no intention of yielding control of reconstruction. In a dozen ways, he sabotaged Congress's will and encouraged southern whites to resist. He issued a flood of pardons, waged war against the

Andrew Johnson Cartoon
Appearing in 1868 during President Andrew Johnson's impeachment trial, this cartoon includes captions that read: "This little boy would persist in handling books above his capacity" and "And this was the disastrous result." The cartoonist's portrait of Johnson being crushed by the Constitution refers to the president's flouting of the Tenure of Office Act, which caused Republicans to vote for his impeachment. The cartoon's celebration of Johnson's destruction proved premature, however. The Granger Collection, NYC.

THIS LITTLE BOY WOULD PERSIST IN HANDLING BOOKS ABOVE HIS CAPACITY.

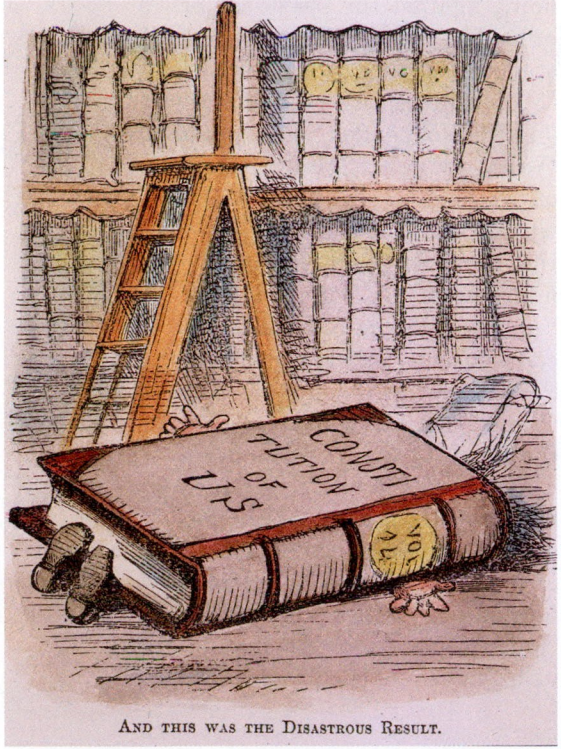

AND THIS WAS THE DISASTROUS RESULT.

Freedmen's Bureau, and replaced Union generals eager to enforce Congress's Reconstruction Acts with conservative officers eager to defeat them. Johnson claimed that he was merely defending the "violated Constitution." At bottom, however, the president subverted congressional reconstruction to protect southern whites from what he considered the horrors of "Negro domination."

When Congress realized that overriding Johnson's vetoes did not ensure that it got its way, it looked for other ways to exert its will. According to the Constitution, the House of Representatives can impeach and the Senate can try any federal official for "treason, bribery, or other high crimes and misdemeanors." Radicals argued that Johnson's abuse of constitutional powers and his failure to fulfill constitutional obligations to enforce the law were impeachable offenses. But moderates interpreted the constitutional provision to mean violation of criminal statutes. As long as Johnson refrained from breaking the law, impeachment (the process of formal charges of wrongdoing against the president or other federal official) remained stalled.

Then, in August 1867, Johnson suspended Secretary of War Edwin M. Stanton from office. The Tenure of Office Act, which had been passed earlier in the year, demanded the approval of the Senate for the removal of any government official who had been appointed with Senate approval. As required by the act, the president requested the Senate to consent to Stanton's dismissal. When the Senate balked, Johnson removed Stanton anyway. "Is the President crazy, or only drunk?" asked a dumbfounded Republican moderate. "I'm afraid his doings will make us all favor impeachment."

News of Johnson's open defiance of the law convinced every Republican in the House to vote for a resolution impeaching the president. Supreme Court chief justice Salmon Chase presided over the Senate trial, which lasted from March until May 1868. Chase refused to allow Johnson's opponents to raise broad issues of misuse of power and forced them to argue their case exclusively on the narrow legal grounds of Johnson's removal of Stanton. Johnson's lawyers argued that the president had not committed a criminal offense, that the Tenure of Office Act was unconstitutional, and that in any case it did not apply to Stanton, who had been appointed by Lincoln. When the critical vote came, thirty-

Major Reconstruction Legislation, 1865–1875

1865

Thirteenth Amendment (ratified 1865)	Abolishes slavery.

1865 and 1866

Freedmen's Bureau Acts	Establish the Freedmen's Bureau to distribute food and clothing to destitute Southerners and help freedmen with labor contracts and schooling.
Civil Rights Act of 1866	Affirms the rights of blacks to enjoy "full and equal benefit of all laws and proceedings for the security of person and property as is enjoyed by white citizens" and effectively requires the end of legal discrimination in state laws.
Fourteenth Amendment (ratified 1868)	Makes native-born blacks citizens and guarantees all citizens "equal protection of the laws." Threatens to reduce representatives of a state that denies suffrage to any of its male inhabitants.

1867

Military Reconstruction Acts	Impose military rule in the South, establish rules for readmission of ex-Confederate states to the Union, and require those states to guarantee the vote to black men.

1869

Fifteenth Amendment (ratified 1870)	Prohibits racial discrimination in voting rights in all states in the nation.

1875

Civil Rights Act of 1875	Outlaws racial discrimination in transportation, public accommodations, and juries.

five senators voted guilty and nineteen not guilty. The impeachment forces fell one vote short of the two-thirds needed to convict.

After his trial, Johnson called a truce, and for the remaining ten months of his term, congressional reconstruction proceeded unhindered by presidential interference. Without interference from Johnson, Congress revisited the suffrage issue.

The Fifteenth Amendment and Women's Demands

In February 1869, Republicans passed the **Fifteenth Amendment** to the Constitution, which prohibited states from depriving any citizen of the right to vote because of "race, color, or previous condition of servitude." The Reconstruction Acts of 1867 already required black suffrage in the South; the Fifteenth Amendment extended black voting nationwide. Partisan advantage played an important role in the amendment's passage. Gains by northern Democrats in the 1868 elections worried Republicans, and black voters now represented the balance of power in several northern states. By giving the ballot to northern blacks, Republicans could lessen their own political vulnerability. As one Republican congressman observed, "Party expediency and exact justice coincide for once."

Some Republicans, however, found the final wording of the Fifteenth Amendment "lame and halting." Rather than absolutely guaranteeing the right to vote, the amendment merely prohibited exclusion on grounds of race. The distinction would prove to be significant. In time, white Southerners would devise tests of literacy and property and other apparently nonracial measures that would effectively disfranchise blacks yet not violate the Fifteenth Amendment. But an amendment that fully guaranteed the right to vote courted defeat outside the South. Rising antiforeign sentiment — against the Chinese in California and European immigrants in the Northeast — caused states to resist giving up total control of suffrage requirements. In March 1870, after three-fourths of the states had ratified it, the Fifteenth Amendment became part of the Constitution. Republicans generally breathed a sigh of relief, confident that black suffrage was "the last great point that remained to be settled of the issues of the war."

Woman suffrage advocates, however, were sorely disappointed with the Fifteenth Amendment's failure to extend voting rights to women. The amendment denied states the right to forbid suffrage only on the basis of race. Elizabeth Cady Stanton and Susan B. Anthony condemned the Republicans' "negro first" strategy and pointed out that women remained "the only class of citizens wholly unrepresented in the government." Stanton wondered aloud why ignorant black men should legislate for educated and cultured white women. Increasingly, activist women concluded that woman "must not put her trust in man." The Fifteenth Amendment severed the early feminist movement from its abolitionist roots. Over the next several decades, feminists established an independent suffrage crusade that drew millions of women into political life.

Republicans took enough satisfaction in the Fifteenth Amendment to promptly scratch the "Negro question" from the agenda of national politics. Even that steadfast crusader for equality Wendell Phillips concluded that the black man now held "sufficient shield in his own hands. . . . Whatever he suffers will be largely now, and in future, his own fault." Northerners had no idea of the violent struggles that lay ahead.

REVIEW   Why did Johnson urge the southern states to reject the Fourteenth Amendment?

▶ The Struggle in the South

Northerners believed they had discharged their responsibilities with the Reconstruction Acts and the amendments to the Constitution, but Southerners knew that the battle had just begun. Black suffrage established the foundation for the rise of the Republican Party in the South. Gathering together outsiders and outcasts, southern Republicans won elections, wrote new state constitutions, and formed new state governments.

Challenging the established class for political control was dangerous business. Equally dangerous were the confrontations that took place on southern farms and plantations, where blacks sought to give economic meaning to their newly won legal and political equality. Ex-masters had their own ideas about the labor system that should replace slavery. Freedom remained contested territory, and Southerners fought pitched battles with one another to determine the contours of their new world.

What Did the Ku Klux Klan Really Want?

In 1866, six Confederate veterans in Pulaski, Tennessee, founded the Ku Klux Klan for fun and fellowship. But by 1868, when congressional reconstruction went into effect, the Klan had spread across the South, and members had shifted to more serious matters.

According to former Confederate general and Georgia Democratic politician John B. Gordon, the Klan owed its popularity to the "instinct of self-preservation . . . the sense of insecurity and danger, particularly in those neighborhoods where the Negro population largely predominated." Everywhere whites looked, he said, they saw "great crime." Republican politicians marched ignorant freedmen to the polls, where they blighted honest government. Ex-slaves drove overseers from plantations and claimed the land for themselves. Black rapists made white women cower behind barred doors. It was necessary, Gordon declared, "in order to protect our families from outrage and preserve our own lives, to have something that we could regard as a brotherhood — a combination of the best men of the country, to act purely in self-defense."

Behind the Klan's high-minded and self-justifying rhetoric, however, lay another agenda. It was revealed in their actions, not their words. Klansmen embarked on a campaign to reverse history. Garbed in robes and hoods, they engaged in guerrilla warfare against free labor, civil equality, and political democracy. They aimed to terrorize their enemies — ex-slaves and white Republicans — into submission. Changes in four particular areas of southern life proved flash points for Klan violence: racial etiquette, education, labor, and politics.

The Klan punished those blacks and whites who broke the Old South's racial code. The Klan considered "impudence" a punishable offense. Asked to define "impudence" before a congressional investigating committee, one white man responded: "Well, it is considered impudence for a negro not to be polite to a white man — not to pull off his hat and bow and scrape to a white man, as was done formerly." Klansmen whipped blacks for speaking disrespectfully, refusing to yield the sidewalk, and dressing well. Black women who "dress up and fix up like ladies" risked a midnight visit from the Klan. The Klan sought to restore racial subordination in every aspect of private and public life.

Klansmen also took aim at black education. White men found the sight of blacks in classrooms hard to stomach. Schools were easy targets, and scores of them went up in flames. Teachers, male and female, were flogged, or worse. Klansmen drove northern-born teacher Alonzo B. Corliss from North Carolina for "teaching niggers and making them like white men." In Cross Plains, Alabama, the Klan hanged an Irish-born teacher along with four black men. Planters wanted ex-slaves back in the fields, not at desks. In 1869, an Alabama newspaper announced that the burning of a black school should be "a warning for them to stick hereafter to 'de shovel and de hoe,' and let their dirty-backed primers go."

Planters turned to the Klan as part of their effort to preserve plantation agriculture. An Alabama white admitted that in his area the Klan was "intended principally for the negroes who failed to work." Hooded bands "punished Negroes whose landlords had complained of them." Sharecroppers who disputed their share at "settling up time" risked a visit from the night riders. It was dangerous for freedmen to consider changing employers. "If we got out looking for some other place to go," an ex-slave from Texas remembered, "them KKK they would tend to Mister negro good and plenty."

Above all, the Klan terrorized Republicans. Klansmen became the military arm of the Democratic Party. They drove blacks from the polls on election day and assaulted Republican officeholders. Klansmen gave Andrew Flowers, a black politician in Chattanooga, a brutal beating and told him that they "did not intend any nigger to hold office in the United States." Jack Dupree, president of the Republican Club in Monroe County, Mississippi, a man known to "speak his mind," had his throat cut and was disemboweled while his wife was forced to watch.

Political violence reached astounding levels. Arkansas experienced nearly three hundred political killings in the three months before the fall elections

Freedmen, Yankees, and Yeomen

African Americans made up the majority of southern Republicans. After gaining voting rights in 1867, nearly all eligible black men registered to vote as Republicans, grateful to the party that had freed them and granted them the franchise.

"It is the hardest thing in the world to keep a negro away from the polls," observed an Alabama white man. Black women, like white women, remained disfranchised, but they mobilized along with black men. In the 1868 presidential election, they bravely wore buttons supporting the Republican candidate, Ulysses S. Grant. Southern blacks did not all have identical political priorities, but they

Ku Klux Klan Rider in Tennessee about 1868 and Klan Banner

The white robes that we associate with the Ku Klux Klan are a twentieth-century phenomenon. During Reconstruction, Klansmen wore robes of various designs and colors. Hooded horses added another element to the Klan's terror. The Klansman holds a flag that looks very much like the satanic dragon on the colorful Klan banner shown here, which contains a Latin motto from Saint Augustine's definition of Catholic truth: "that which [has been believed] always, everywhere, by all." Among Klansmen, this motto was likely to refer to the truth of white supremacy.

Rider: Tennessee State Museum Collection; banner: Chicago Historical Society.

in 1868. Louisiana was even bloodier, suffering more than one thousand killings in the same year. In Georgia, the Klan murdered three scalawag members of the legislature and drove ten others from their homes. As one Georgia Republican commented after a Klan attack: "We don't call them [D]emocrats, we call them southern murderers."

It proved hard to arrest Klansmen and harder still to convict them. "If a white man kills a colored man in any of the counties of this State," observed a Florida sheriff, "you cannot convict him." Federal intervention — in the Ku Klux Klan Acts of 1870 and 1871— signaled an end to much of the Klan's power but not to counterrevolutionary violence in the South. Other groups continued the terror in the cause of white supremacy.

Thinking about Beliefs and Attitudes

1. What changes during Reconstruction particularly provoked the Klan? Why do you think these issues were so important to Klansmen?

2. Why did Klansmen believe that their actions were justified? Why do you think they hid their identities?

3. What southern traditions did the Klan seek to perpetuate?

---

united in their desire for education and equal treatment before the law.

Northern whites who made the South their home after the war were a second element of the South's Republican Party. Conservative white Southerners called them **carpetbaggers**, men so poor that they could stuff all their earthly belongings in a single carpet-sided suitcase and swoop southward like buzzards to "fatten on our misfortunes." But most Northerners who moved south were young men who looked upon the South as they did the West — as a promising place to make a living. Northerners in the southern Republican Party consistently supported programs that encouraged vigorous economic development along the lines of the northern free-labor model.

A Southern Legislature in the Carpet-Bagger Days
This late-nineteenth-century wood engraving reveals the southern Democratic view of Republican state governments during Reconstruction. It drips with prejudice and misinformation. Contrary to fact, the legislators are depicted as overwhelmingly black. Rather than serious men, they are lazy, drunk, and disorderly. While some lie about on cushions, others have literally drunk themselves under the table, which is spread with food rather than legislative documents. The white man in the foreground who calmly observes the circus is probably meant to be a manipulative carpetbagger, while the white man in the rear with the hat, pipe, and rifle slung over his shoulder is probably a treasonous scalawag. The Granger Collection, NYC.

also played a part in the political struggle by joining in parades and rallies, attending stump speeches, and even campaigning.

Reconstruction politics was not for cowards. Most whites in the South condemned southern Republicans as illegitimate and felt justified in doing whatever they could to stamp them out. Violence against blacks — the "white terror" — took brutal institutional form in 1866 with the formation in Tennessee of the **Ku Klux Klan**, a social club of Confederate veterans that quickly developed into a paramilitary organization supporting Democrats. The Klan went on a rampage of whipping, hanging, shooting, burning, and throat-cutting to defeat Republicans and restore white supremacy. (See "Historical Question," page 516.) Rapid demobilization of the Union army after the war left only twenty thousand troops to patrol the entire South. Without effective military protection, southern Republicans had to take care of themselves.

Republican Rule

In the fall of 1867, southern states held elections for delegates to state constitutional conventions, as required by the Reconstruction Acts. About 40 percent of the white electorate stayed home because they had been disfranchised or because they had decided to boycott politics. Republicans won three-fourths of the seats. About 15 percent of the Republican delegates to the conventions were Northerners who had moved south, 25 percent were African Americans, and 60 percent were white Southerners. As a British visitor observed, the delegate elections reflected "the mighty revolution that had taken place in America." But Democrats described the state conventions as zoos of "baboons, monkeys, mules . . . and other jackasses." In fact, the conventions brought together serious, purposeful men who hammered out the legal framework for a new order.

The reconstruction constitutions introduced two broad categories of changes in the South: those that reduced aristocratic privilege and increased democratic equality and those that expanded the state's responsibility for the general welfare. In the first category, the constitutions adopted universal male suffrage, abolished property qualifications for holding office, and made

Southern whites made up the third element of the South's Republican Party. Approximately one out of four white Southerners voted Republican. The other three condemned the one who did as a traitor to his region and his race and called him a **scalawag**, a term for runty horses and low-down, good-for-nothing rascals. Yeoman farmers accounted for the majority of southern white Republicans. Some were Unionists who emerged from the war with bitter memories of Confederate persecution. Others were small farmers who wanted to end state governments' favoritism toward plantation owners. Yeomen supported initiatives for public schools and for expanding economic opportunity in the South.

The South's Republican Party, then, was made up of freedmen, Yankees, and yeomen — an improbable coalition. The mix of races, regions, and classes inevitably meant friction as each group maneuvered to define the party. But Reconstruction represents an extraordinary moment in American politics: Blacks and whites joined together in the Republican Party to pursue political change. Formally, of course, only men participated in politics — casting ballots and holding offices — but white and black women more offices elective and fewer appointed. In the second category, they enacted prison reform; made the state responsible for caring for orphans, the insane, and the deaf and mute; and exempted debtors' homes from seizure.

To Democrats, however, the new state constitutions looked like wild revolution. They were blind to the fact that no constitution confiscated and redistributed land, as virtually every former slave wished, or disfranchised ex-rebels wholesale, as most southern Unionists advocated. And Democrats were convinced that the new constitutions initiated "Negro domination" in politics. In fact, although four out of five Republican voters were black men, more than four out of five Republican officeholders were white. Southerners sent fourteen black congressmen and two black senators to Washington, but only 6 percent of Southerners in Congress during Reconstruction were black (Figure 16.1). The sixteen black men in Congress included exceptional men, such as Representative **James T. Rapier** of Alabama (see pages 499–500) and Mississippi senator Blanche K. Bruce, who was born a slave in Virginia and became a local school superintendent in Mississippi, a position that paved his way to the Senate. No state legislature experienced "Negro rule," despite black majorities in the populations of some states.

FIGURE 16.1 Southern Congressional Delegations, 1865–1877
The statistics contradict the myth of black domination of congressional representation during Reconstruction.

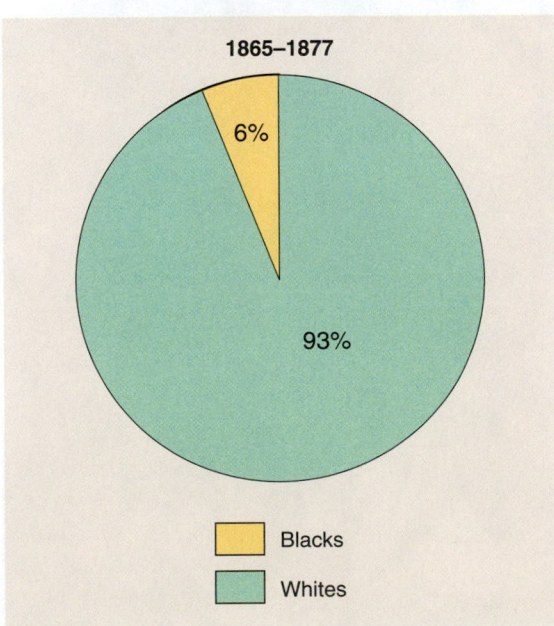

Southern voters ratified the new constitutions and swept Republicans into power. When the former Confederate states ratified the Fourteenth Amendment, Congress readmitted them. Southern Republicans then turned to a staggering array of problems. Wartime destruction — burned cities, shattered bridges, broken levees, devastated railroads — littered the landscape. The South's share of the nation's wealth had fallen from 30 percent to only 12 percent. Manufacturing, always a small contributor to the southern economy, limped along at a fraction of prewar levels, and once-powerful agricultural production remained anemic. Without the efforts of the Freedmen's Bureau, black and white Southerners would have starved. Making matters worse, racial harassment and reactionary violence dogged Southerners who sought reform. In this desperate context, Republicans struggled to breathe life into the region.

Activity focused on three areas — education, civil rights, and economic development. Every state inaugurated a system of public education. Before the Civil War, whites had deliberately kept slaves illiterate, and planter-dominated governments rarely spent tax money to educate the children of yeomen. By 1875, half of Mississippi's and South Carolina's eligible children (the majority of whom were black) were attending school. Although schools were underfunded, literacy rates rose sharply. Public schools were racially segregated, but education remained for many blacks a tangible, deeply satisfying benefit of freedom and Republican rule.

State legislatures also attacked racial discrimination and defended civil rights. Republicans especially resisted efforts to segregate blacks from whites in public transportation. Mississippi levied fines of up to $1,000 and three years in jail for owners of railroads and steamboats that pushed blacks into "smoking cars" or to lower decks. Well-off blacks took particular aim at hotels and theaters that denied "full and equal rights." But passing color-blind laws was one thing; enforcing them was another. A Mississippian complained: "Education amounts to nothing, good behavior counts for nothing, even money cannot buy for a colored man or woman decent treatment and the comforts that white people claim and can obtain." Despite the laws, segregation — later called Jim Crow — developed at white insistence and became a feature of southern life long before the end of the Reconstruction era.

Republican governments also launched ambitious programs of economic development. They envisioned a South of diversified agriculture, roaring factories, and booming towns. State legislatures chartered scores of banks and industrial companies, appropriated funds to fix ruined levees and drain swamps, and went on a railroad-building binge. These efforts fell far short of solving the South's economic troubles, however. In addition, Republican spending to stimulate economic growth meant rising taxes and enormous debt that siphoned funds from schools and other programs.

The southern Republicans' record, then, was mixed. To their credit, the biracial party adopted an ambitious agenda to change the South, even though money was scarce, the Democrats continued their harassment, and factionalism threatened the Republican Party from within. However, corruption infected Republican governments in the South. Public morality reached new lows everywhere in the nation after the Civil War, and the chaos of the postwar South proved fertile soil for bribery, fraud, and influence peddling. Despite shortcomings, however, the Republican Party made headway in its efforts to purge the South of aristocratic privilege and racist oppression. Republican governments had less success in overthrowing the long-established white oppression of black farm laborers in the rural South.

Students at a Freedmen's School in Virginia, ca. 1870s, and a One-Cent Primer

"The people are hungry and thirsty after knowledge," a former slave observed immediately after the Civil War. African American leader Booker T. Washington remembered "a whole race trying to go to school." The students at this Virginia school stand in front of their log-cabin classroom reading books, but more common were eight-page primers that cost a penny. These simple readers offered ex-slaves the elements of literacy. For people long forbidden to learn to read and write, literacy symbolized freedom. Literacy also allowed those who were deeply religious to experience the joy of reading the Bible for themselves and those who were merely practical to understand labor contracts and participate knowledgeably in politics. Primer: Gladstone Collection; students: Valentine Museum, Cook Collection.

Black Woman in Cotton Fields, Thomasville, Georgia
Few images of everyday black women during the Reconstruction era survive. Taken in 1895, this photograph nevertheless goes to the heart of the labor struggle following the Civil War, when white landlords wanted emancipated slaves to continue working in the fields. Freedom allowed some women to escape field labor, but not this Georgian, who probably worked to survive. The photograph reveals a strong person with a clear sense of who she is. Though worn to protect her head and body from the fierce heat, her intricately wrapped headdress dramatically expresses her individuality. Her bare feet also reveal something about her life. Courtesy, Georgia Department of Archives and History, Atlanta, GA.

White Landlords, Black Sharecroppers

Ex-slaves who wished to escape slave labor and ex-masters who wanted to reinstitute old ways clashed repeatedly. Except for having to pay subsistence wages, planters had not been required to offer many con-cessions to emancipation. They continued to believe that African Americans would not work without coercion. Whites moved quickly to restore the antebellum (pre–Civil War) world of work gangs, white overseers, field labor for black women and children, clustered cabins, minimal personal freedom, and even whipping whenever they could get away with it.

Ex-slaves resisted every effort to turn back the clock. They argued that if any class could be described as "lazy," it was the planters, who, as one former slave noted, "lived in idleness all their lives on stolen labor." Ex-slaves believed that land of their own would anchor their economic independence and end planters' interference in their personal lives. They could then, for example, make their own decisions about whether women and children would labor in the fields. Indeed, within months after the war, perhaps one-third of black women abandoned field labor to work on chores in their own cabins just as poor white women did. Hundreds of thousands of black children enrolled in school. But without their own land, ex-slaves had little choice but to work on plantations, and they feared that their return to the planters' fields would undermine their independence.

Freedmen resisted efforts by ex-masters to restore slavelike conditions on plantations. Instead of working for wages, David Golightly Harris of South Carolina observed, "the negroes all seem disposed to rent land," which increased their independence from whites. By rejecting wage labor, by striking, and by abandoning the most reactionary employers, blacks sought to force concessions. Out of this tug-of-war between white landlords and black laborers emerged a new system of southern agriculture.

Sharecropping was a compromise that offered something to both ex-masters and ex-slaves but satisfied neither. Under the new system, planters divided their cotton plantations into small farms that freedmen rented, paying with a share of each year's crop, usually half. Sharecropping gave blacks more freedom than the system of wages and labor gangs and released them from day-to-day supervision by whites. Black families abandoned the old slave quarters and scattered over plantations, building separate cabins for themselves on the patches of land they rented (Map 16.1). Black families now decided who would work, for how long, and how hard. Black women negotiated with ex-mistresses about work the white women wanted done

A Post-Slavery Encounter

A Visit from the Old Mistress, 1876

Winslow Homer, one of the nation's foremost painters, was widely recognized for his ability to convey drama and emotion on canvas. Homer typically sketched and painted ordinary people in their everyday lives. During the Civil War, Homer worked as an illustrator for *Harper's Weekly,* depicting scenes of the war for curious Northerners. In 1875, he traveled from his home in New York City to Virginia, where he observed firsthand the transformation of relationships between former slaves and their former owners.

A Visit from the Old Mistress captures the moment when a white woman arrives in the humble cabin of former slaves and encounters three black women, one of whom holds a toddler. Homer typically said little about his paintings, and there is much we don't know about the story being told in this work. Why has the old mistress come? We can imagine that she has come to talk about work she wants done in the big house. If so, she would have come asking, not commanding, for the end of slavery meant that ex-slaves had control over their own labor and negotiated what they would be paid and the conditions under which they would work.

Notice the way Homer has arranged the subjects of his painting, with the former slaves on one side of the room and the former mistress on the other. What does the generous space between them suggest? How do the two sides compare? Look particularly at the women's clothing and their stance. What does the white woman's posture suggest? How are the three black women positioned, and what does this say about their attitude toward the old mistress? What do you detect in the facial expressions of the people in this image?

The end of slavery required wrenching readjustments in the lives of Southerners, black and white. Do you think Homer's simple domestic scene reveals an opinion about what the artist witnessed, or does *A Visit from the Old Mistress* try merely to capture truthfully a complex moment? How might this painting have looked different if it had been created before emancipation?

SOURCE: Smithsonian American Art Museum, Washington, D.C./Art Resource, NY.

MAP ACTIVITY

Map 16.1   A Southern Plantation in 1860 and 1881

These maps of the Barrow plantation in Georgia illustrate some of the ways in which ex-slaves expressed their freedom. Freedmen and freedwomen deserted the clustered living quarters behind the master's house, scattered over the plantation, built family cabins, and farmed rented land. The former Barrow slaves also worked together to build a school and a church.

READING THE MAP: Compare the number and size of the slave quarters in 1860 with the homes of the former slaves in 1881. How do they differ? Which buildings were prominently located along the road in 1860, and which could be found along the road in 1881?

CONNECTIONS: How might the former master feel about the new configuration of buildings on the plantation in 1881? In what ways did the new system of sharecropping replicate the old system of plantation agriculture? In what ways was it different?

in the big house. (See "Visualizing History," page 522.) Still, most black families remained dependent on white landlords, who had the power to evict them at the end of each growing season. For planters, sharecropping offered a way to resume agricultural production, but it did not allow them to restore the old slave plantation.

Sharecropping introduced a new figure — the country merchant — into the agricultural equation. Landlords supplied sharecroppers with land, mules, seeds, and tools, but blacks also needed credit to obtain essential food and clothing before they harvested their crops. Thousands of small crossroads stores sprang up to offer

credit. Under an arrangement called a **crop lien**, a merchant would advance goods to a sharecropper in exchange for a *lien*, or legal claim, on the farmer's future crop. Some merchants charged exorbitant rates of interest, as much as 60 percent, on the goods they sold. At the end of the growing season, after the landlord had taken half of the farmer's crop for rent, the merchant took most of the rest. Sometimes, the farmer's debt to the merchant exceeded the income he received from his remaining half of the crop, and the farmer would have no choice but to borrow more from the merchant and begin the cycle all over again.

An experiment at first, sharecropping spread quickly and soon dominated the cotton South. Lien merchants forced tenants to plant cotton, which was easy to sell, instead of food crops. The result was excessive production of cotton and falling cotton prices, developments that cost thousands of small white farmers their land and pushed them into the great army of sharecroppers. The new sharecropping system of agriculture took shape just as the political power of Republicans in the South began to buckle under Democratic pressure.

REVIEW   What brought the elements of the South's Republican coalition together?

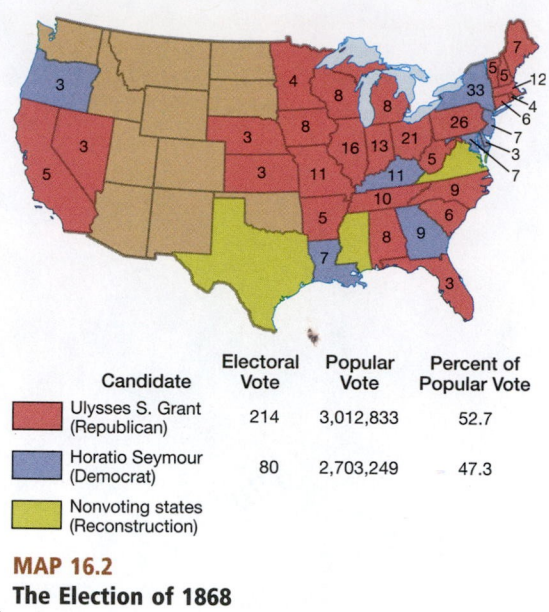

Candidate	Electoral Vote	Popular Vote	Percent of Popular Vote
Ulysses S. Grant (Republican)	214	3,012,833	52.7
Horatio Seymour (Democrat)	80	2,703,249	47.3
Nonvoting states (Reconstruction)			

MAP 16.2
The Election of 1868

▶ Reconstruction Collapses

By 1870, after a decade of war and reconstruction, Northerners wanted to put "the southern problem" behind them. Increasingly, practical, business-minded men came to the forefront of the Republican Party, replacing the band of reformers and idealists who had been prominent in the 1860s. While northern commitment to defend black freedom eroded, southern commitment to white supremacy intensified. Without northern protection, southern Republicans were no match for the Democrats' economic coercion, political fraud, and bloody violence. One by one, Republican state governments fell in the South. The election of 1876 both confirmed and completed the collapse of reconstruction.

> **"His imperturbability is amazing. I am in doubt whether to call it greatness or stupidity."**
> — Congressman JAMES A. GARFIELD, speaking of President Grant

Grant's Troubled Presidency

In 1868, the Republican Party's presidential nomination went to **Ulysses S. Grant**, the North's favorite general. Hero of the Civil War and a supporter of congressional reconstruction, Grant was the obvious choice. His Democratic opponent, Horatio Seymour of New York, ran on a platform that blasted congressional reconstruction as "a flagrant usurpation of power . . . unconstitutional, revolutionary, and void." The Republicans answered by **"waving the bloody shirt"** — that is, they reminded voters that the Democrats were "the party of rebellion." During the campaign, the Ku Klux Klan erupted in a reign of terror across the South, murdering hundreds of Republicans. Fear of violence cost Grant votes, but he gained a narrow 309,000-vote margin in the popular vote and a substantial victory (214 votes to 80) in the electoral college (Map 16.2).

Grant was not as good a president as he was a general. The talents he had demonstrated on the battlefield — decisiveness, clarity, and resolution — were less obvious in the White House. He hoped to forge a policy that secured both justice for blacks and sectional reconciliation, but he took office at a time when a majority of white Northerners had grown weary of the "Southern Question" and were increasingly willing to let southern whites manage their own affairs. Moreover, Grant surrounded himself with fumbling kinfolk and old friends from his army days. He made a string of dubious appointments that led to a series of damaging scandals. Charges of corruption tainted his vice president, Schuyler Colfax, and brought down two of his cabinet officers. Though never personally implicated in any scandal, Grant was aggravatingly naive and blind to the rot that filled his administration. Republican congressman James A. Garfield declared: "His imperturbability is amazing. I am in doubt whether to call it greatness or stupidity."

In 1872, anti-Grant Republicans bolted and launched the Liberal Party. To clean up the graft and corruption,

"I BEG TO REPEAT THAT THESE FRAUDS ON THE GOVERNMENT SHALL BE PROBED TO THE VERY BOTTOM."

Grant and Scandal

This anti-Grant cartoon by Thomas Nast, the nation's most celebrated political cartoonist, shows the president falling headfirst into the barrel of fraud and corruption that tainted his administration. During Grant's eight years in the White House, many members of his administration failed him. Sometimes duped, sometimes merely loyal, Grant stubbornly defended wrongdoers, even to the point of perjuring himself to keep an aide out of jail. Library of Congress.

READING THE IMAGE: How does Thomas Nast portray President Grant's role in corruption? According to this cartoon, what caused the problems?
CONNECTIONS: How responsible was President Grant for the corruption that plagued his administration?

Liberals proposed ending the spoils system, by which victorious parties rewarded loyal workers with public office, and replacing it with a non-partisan civil service commission that would oversee competitive examinations for appointment to office (as discussed in chapter 18). Liberals also demanded that the federal government remove its troops from the South and restore "home rule" (southern white control). Democrats liked the Liberals' southern policy and endorsed the Liberal presidential candidate, Horace Greeley, the long-time editor of the *New York Tribune*. The nation, however, still felt enormous affection for the man who had saved the Union and reelected Grant with 56 percent of the popular vote.

Grant's ambitions for his administration extended beyond reconstruction, but not even foreign affairs could escape the problems of the South. Grant coveted Santo Domingo (present-day Dominican Republic) in the Caribbean and argued that the acquisition of this tropical land would permit the United States to expand its trade and would also provide a new home for the South's blacks, who were so desperately harassed by the Klan. Aggressive foreign policy had not originated with the Grant administration. Lincoln's and Johnson's secretary of state, William H. Seward, had thwarted French efforts to set up a puppet empire under Maximilian in Mexico, and his purchase of Alaska ("Seward's Ice Box") from Russia in 1867 for only $7 million fired Grant's imperialist ambition. But in the end, Grant could not convince Congress to approve

the treaty annexing Santo Domingo. The South preoccupied Congress and undermined Grant's initiatives.

Northern Resolve Withers

Although Grant genuinely wanted to see blacks' civil and political rights protected, he understood that most Northerners had grown weary of reconstruction and were increasingly willing to let southern whites manage their own affairs. Citizens wanted to shift their attention to other issues, especially after the nation slipped into a devastating economic depression in 1873. More than eighteen thousand businesses collapsed, leaving more than a million workers on the streets. Northern businessmen wanted to invest in the South but believed that recurrent federal intrusion was itself a major cause of instability in the region. Republican leaders began to question the wisdom of their party's alliance with the South's lower classes — its small farmers and sharecroppers. One member of Grant's administration proposed allying with the "thinking and influential native southerners . . . the intelligent, well-to-do, and controlling class."

Congress, too, wanted to leave reconstruction behind, but southern Republicans made that

Grant's Proposed Annexation of Santo Domingo

difficult. When the South's Republicans begged for federal protection from Klan violence, Congress enacted three laws in 1870 and 1871 that were intended to break the back of white terrorism. The severest of the three, the **Ku Klux Klan Act** (1871), made interference with voting rights a felony. Federal marshals arrested thousands of Klansmen and came close to destroying the Klan, but they did not end all terrorism against blacks. Congress also passed the **Civil Rights Act of 1875**, which boldly outlawed racial discrimination in transportation, public accommodations, and juries. But federal authorities never enforced the law aggressively, and segregated facilities remained the rule throughout the South.

By the early 1870s, the Republican Party had lost its leading champions of African American rights to death or defeat at the polls. Other Republicans concluded that the quest for black equality was mistaken or hopelessly naive. In May 1872, Congress restored the right of office-holding to all but three hundred ex-rebels. Many Republicans had come to believe that traditional white leaders offered the best hope for honesty, order, and prosperity in the South.

Underlying the North's abandonment of reconstruction was unyielding racial prejudice. Northerners had learned to accept black freedom during the war, but deep-seated prejudice prevented many from accepting black equality. Even the actions they took on behalf of blacks often served partisan political advantage. Northerners generally supported Indiana senator Thomas A. Hendricks's harsh declaration that "this is a white man's Government, made by the white man for the white man."

The U.S. Supreme Court also did its part to undermine reconstruction. The Court issued a series of decisions that significantly weakened the federal government's ability to protect black Southerners. In the *Slaughterhouse* cases (1873), the Court distinguished between national and state citizenship and ruled that the Fourteenth Amendment protected only those rights that stemmed from the federal government, such as voting in federal elections and interstate travel. Since the Court decided that most rights derived from the states, it sharply curtailed the federal government's authority to defend black citizens. Even more devastating, the *United States v. Cruikshank* ruling (1876) said that the reconstruction amendments gave Congress the power to legislate against discrimination only by states, not by individuals. The "suppression of ordinary crime," such as assault, remained a state responsibility. The Supreme Court did not declare reconstruction unconstitutional but eroded its legal foundation.

The mood of the North found political expression in the election of 1874, when for the first time in eighteen years the Democrats gained control of the House of Representatives. As one Republican observed, the people had grown tired of the "negro question, with all its complications, and the reconstruction of Southern States, with all its interminable embroilments." Reconstruction had come apart. The people were tired of it. Grant grew increasingly unwilling to enforce it. Congress gradually abandoned it. And the Supreme Court denied the constitutionality of significant parts of it. Rather than defend reconstruction from its southern enemies, Northerners steadily backed away from the challenge. By the early 1870s, southern Republicans faced the forces of reaction largely on their own.

White Supremacy Triumphs

Reconstruction was a massive humiliation to most white Southerners. Republican rule meant intolerable insults: Black militiamen patrolled town streets, black laborers negotiated contracts with former masters, black maids stood up to former mistresses, black voters cast ballots, and black legislators such as James T. Rapier enacted laws. Whites resisted the consequences of their defeat in the Civil War by making it clear that military failure did not discredit their "civilization." They expressed their devotion to all that was good in the South — racial hierarchy, honor, vigorous masculinity — by making an idol of Robert E. Lee, the embodiment of the southern gentleman. They celebrated the "great Confederate cause," or **Lost Cause**, by extolling the deeds of their soldiers, "the noblest band of men who ever fought or ever took pen to record." Southern women took the lead in erecting monuments to the Confederate dead and, with pageantry, oratory, and flowers, in keeping alive the memory of the Lost Cause throughout the old Confederacy.

But the most important way white Southerners responded to the humiliation of reconstruction was their assault on Republican governments in the South, which attracted more hatred than did any other political regimes in American history. The northern retreat from reconstruction permitted southern Democrats to harness white rage to politics. Taking the name **Redeemers**, Democrats in the South promised to replace "bayonet rule" (a few federal troops continued to be stationed in the South) with "home rule." They branded Republican governments a carnival of extravagance, waste, and fraud and promised that honest, thrifty Democrats would supplant the irresponsible tax-and-spend Republicans. Above all, Redeemers swore to save southern civilization from a descent into "African barbarism." As one man put it, "We must render this either a white man's government, or convert the land into a Negro man's cemetery."

Southern Democrats adopted a multipronged strategy to overthrow Republican governments. First, they sought to polarize the parties around color. They went about gathering all the South's white voters into the Democratic Party, leaving the Republicans to depend on blacks, who made up a minority of the population in almost every southern state. To dislodge whites from the Republican Party, Democrats fanned the flames of racial prejudice. A South Carolina Democrat crowed that his party appealed to the "proud Caucasian race, whose sovereignty on earth God has proclaimed." Local newspapers published the names of whites who kept company with blacks, and neighbors ostracized offenders. One victim proclaimed, "No white man can live in the South in the future and act with any other than the Democratic party unless he is willing and prepared to live a life of social isolation."

Democrats also exploited the severe economic plight of small white farmers by blaming it on Republican financial policy. Government spending soared during reconstruction, and small farmers saw their tax burden skyrocket. "This is tax time," a South Carolinian reported. "We are nearly all on our head about them. They are so high &

"White Man's Country"
White supremacy emerged as a central tenet of the Democratic Party before the Civil War, and Democrats kept up a vicious racist attack on Republicans throughout Reconstruction. This silk ribbon from the 1868 presidential campaign between Republican Ulysses S. Grant and his Democratic opponent, New York governor Horatio Seymour, openly declares the Democrats' racial goal. During the campaign, Democratic vice presidential nominee Francis P. Blair Jr. promised that a Seymour victory would restore "white people" to power by declaring the reconstruction governments in the South "null and void." Collection of Janice L. and David J. Frent.

so little money to pay with" that farmers were "selling every egg and chicken they can get." In 1871, Mississippi reported that one-seventh of the state's land — 3.3 million acres — had been forfeited for nonpayment of taxes. The small farmers' economic distress had a racial dimension. Because few freedmen succeeded in acquiring land, they rarely paid taxes. In Georgia in 1874, blacks made up 45 percent of the population but paid only 2 percent of the taxes. From the perspective of a small white farmer, Republican rule meant that he was paying more taxes and paying them to aid blacks.

"Of Course He Wants to Vote the Democratic Ticket"
This Republican cartoon from the October 21, 1876, issue of *Harper's Weekly* comments sarcastically on the possibility of honest elections in the South. The caption reads: "You're free as air, ain't you? Say you are or I'll blow yer black head off." The cartoon demonstrates not only some Northerners' concern that violence would deliver the election to the Democrats but also the perception that white Southerners were crude, drunken, ignorant brutes. The Granger Collection, NY.

If racial pride, social isolation, and financial hardship proved insufficient to drive yeomen from the Republican Party, Democrats turned to terrorism. "Night riders" targeted white Republicans as well as blacks for murder and assassination. Whether white or black, a "dead Radical is very harmless," South Carolina Democratic leader Martin Gary told his followers.

But the primary victims of white violence were black Republicans, especially local leaders. Emanuel Fortune, whom the Klan drove from Jackson County, Florida, declared: "The object of it is to kill out the leading men of the republican party." But violence targeted all black voters, not just leaders. And it escalated to an unprecedented ferocity on Easter Sunday in 1873 in tiny Colfax, Louisiana. The black majority in the area had made Colfax a Republican stronghold until 1872, when Democrats turned to intimidation and fraud to win the local election. Republicans refused to accept the result and eventually occupied the courthouse in the middle of the town. After three weeks, 165 white men attacked. They overran the Republicans' defenses and set the courthouse on fire. When the blacks tried to surrender, the

whites murdered them. At least 81 black men were slaughtered that day. Although the federal government indicted the attackers, the Supreme Court ruled that it did not have the right to prosecute. And since local whites would not prosecute neighbors who killed blacks, the defendants in the **Colfax massacre** went free.

Even before adopting the all-out white supremacist tactics of the 1870s, Democrats had taken control of the governments of Virginia, Tennessee, and North Carolina. The new campaign brought fresh gains. The Redeemers retook Georgia in 1871, Texas in 1873, and Arkansas and Alabama in 1874. Mississippi became a scene of open, unrelenting, and often savage intimidation of black voters and their few remaining white allies. As the state election approached in 1876, Governor Adelbert Ames appealed to Washington for federal troops to control the violence, only to hear from the attorney general that the "whole public are tired of these annual autumnal outbreaks in the South." Abandoned, Mississippi Republicans succumbed to the Democratic onslaught in the fall elections. By 1876, only three Republican state governments survived in the South (Map 16.3).

MAP ACTIVITY

Map 16.3 The Reconstruction of the South
Myth has it that Republican rule of the former Confederacy was not only harsh but long. In most states, however, conservative southern whites stormed back into power in months or just a few years. By the election of 1876, Republican governments could be found in only three states, and they soon fell.

READING THE MAP: List in chronological order the readmission of the former Confederate states to the Union. Which states reestablished conservative governments most quickly?

CONNECTIONS: What did the former Confederate states need to do in order to be readmitted to the Union? How did reestablished conservative governments react to reconstruction?

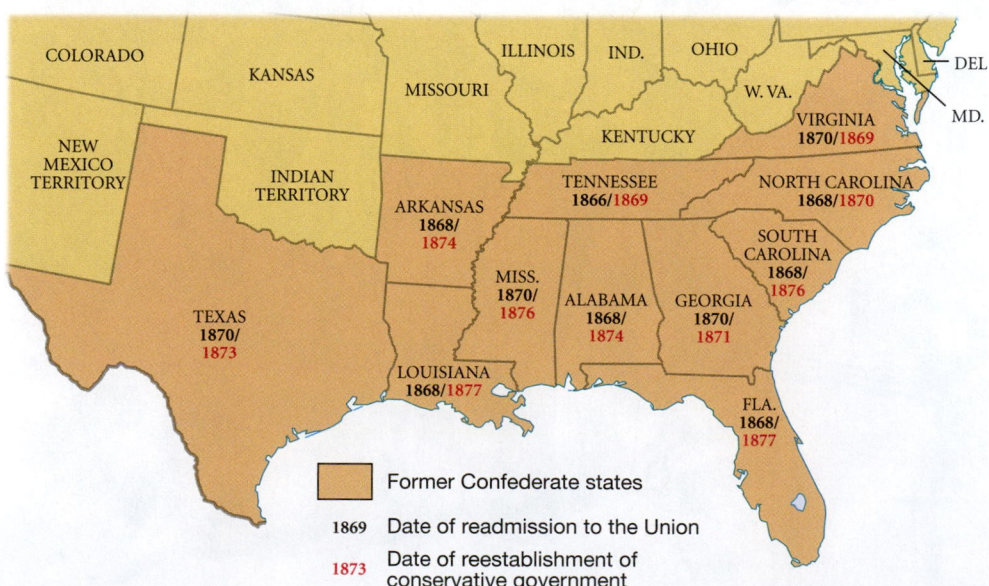

An Election and a Compromise

The centennial year of 1876 witnessed one of the most tumultuous elections in American history. Its chaos and confusion provided a fitting conclusion to the experiment known as reconstruction. The election took place in November, but not until March 2 of the following year did the nation know who would be inaugurated president on March 4. The Democrats nominated New York's governor, **Samuel J. Tilden**, who immediately targeted the corruption of the Grant administration and the "despotism" of Republican reconstruction. The Republicans put forward **Rutherford B. Hayes**, governor of Ohio. Privately, Hayes considered "bayonet rule" a mistake but concluded that waving the bloody shirt—reminding voters that the Democrats were the "party of rebellion"—remained the Republicans' best political strategy.

On election day, Tilden tallied 4,288,590 votes to Hayes's 4,036,000. But in the all-important electoral college, Tilden fell one vote short of the majority required for victory. The electoral votes of three states—South Carolina, Louisiana, and Florida, the only remaining Republican governments in the South—remained in doubt because both Republicans and Democrats in those states claimed victory. To win, Tilden needed only one of the nineteen contested votes. Hayes had to have all of them.

Congress had to decide who had actually won the elections in the three southern states and thus who would be president. The Constitution provided no guidance for this situation. Moreover, Democrats controlled the House, and Republicans controlled the Senate. Congress created a special electoral commission to arbitrate the disputed returns. All of the commissioners voted their party affiliation, giving every state to the Republican Hayes and putting him over the top in electoral votes (Map 16.4).

Some outraged Democrats vowed to resist Hayes's victory. Rumors flew of an impending coup and renewed civil war. But the impasse was broken when negotiations behind the scenes resulted in an informal understanding known as the **Compromise of 1877**. In exchange for a Democratic promise not to block Hayes's inauguration and to deal fairly with the freedmen, Hayes vowed to refrain from using the army to uphold the remaining Republican regimes in the South and to provide the South with substantial federal subsidies for railroads. Two days later, the nation celebrated Hayes's peaceful inauguration.

Stubborn Tilden supporters bemoaned the "stolen election" and damned "His Fraudulency," Rutherford B. Hayes. Old-guard radicals such as William Lloyd Garrison denounced Hayes's bargain as a "policy of compromise, of credulity, of weakness, of subserviency, of surrender." But the nation as a whole celebrated, for the country had weathered a grave crisis. The last three Republican state governments in the South fell quickly once Hayes abandoned them and withdrew the U.S. Army. Reconstruction came to an end.

REVIEW How did the Supreme Court undermine the Fourteenth and Fifteenth Amendments?

MAP 16.4
The Election of 1876

Candidate	Electoral Vote	Popular Vote	Percent of Popular Vote
Rutherford B. Hayes (Republican)	185*	4,036,298	47.9**
Samuel J. Tilden (Democrat)	184	4,288,590	51.0

*19 electoral votes were disputed.
**Percentages do not total 100 because some popular votes went to other parties.

▶ Conclusion: "A Revolution But Half Accomplished"

In 1865, when General Carl Schurz visited the South, he discovered "a revolution but half accomplished." White Southerners resisted the passage from slavery to free labor, from white racial despotism to equal justice, and from white political monopoly to biracial democracy. The old elite wanted to get "things back as near to slavery as possible," Schurz reported, while African Americans such as James T. Rapier and some whites were eager to exploit the revolutionary implications of defeat and emancipation.

The northern-dominated Republican Congress pushed the revolution along. Although it refused to provide for blacks' economic welfare, Congress employed constitutional amendments to require ex-Confederates to accept legal equality and share political power with black men. Congress was not willing to extend such power to women, however. Conservative southern whites fought ferociously to recover their power and privilege. When Democrats regained control of politics, whites used both state power and private violence to wipe out many of the gains of Reconstruction, leading one observer to conclude that the North had won the war but the South had won the peace.

The Redeemer counterrevolution, however, did not mean a return to slavery. Northern victory in the Civil War ensured that ex-slaves no longer faced the auction block and could send their children to school, worship in their own churches, and work independently on their own rented farms. Sharecropping, with all its hardships, provided more autonomy and economic welfare than bondage had. It was limited freedom, to be sure, but it was not slavery.

The Civil War and emancipation set in motion the most profound upheaval in the nation's history, and nothing reactionary whites did entirely erased its revolutionary impact. War destroyed the largest slave society in the New World. The world of masters and slaves succumbed to that of landlords and sharecroppers, a world in which white racial dominance continued, though with greater freedom for blacks. War also gave birth to a modern nation-state, and Washington increased its role in national affairs. When the South returned to the Union, it did so as a junior partner. The victorious North set the nation's compass toward the expansion of industrial capitalism and the final conquest of the West.

Despite massive changes, however, the Civil War remained only a "half accomplished" revolution. By not fulfilling the promises the nation seemed to hold out to black Americans at war's end, Reconstruction represents a tragedy of enormous proportions. The failure to protect blacks and guarantee their rights had enduring consequences. Almost a century after Reconstruction, the nation would embark on what one observer called a "second reconstruction." The solid achievements of the Thirteenth, Fourteenth, and Fifteenth Amendments to the Constitution would provide a legal foundation for the renewed commitment. It is worth remembering, though, that it was only the failure of the first reconstruction that made the modern civil rights movement necessary.

▶ Selected Bibliography

General Works

Michael W. Fitzgerald, *Splendid Failure: Postwar Reconstruction in the American South* (2007).
Eric Foner, *Reconstruction: America's Unfinished Revolution* (1988).
James M. McPherson, *Ordeal by Fire: The Civil War and Reconstruction* (3rd ed., 2000).

The Meaning of Freedom

Ira Berlin et al., eds., *Freedom: A Documentary History of Emancipation, 1861–1867,* 5 vols. to date (1982–).
John Hope Franklin and Loren Schweninger, *In Search of the Promised Land: A Slave Family in the Old South* (2006).
Thavolia Glymph, *Out of the House of Bondage: The Transformation of the Plantation Household* (2008).
Leon F. Litwack, *Been in the Storm So Long: The Aftermath of Slavery* (1979).
Susan Eva O'Donovan, *Becoming Free in the Cotton South* (2007).
Howard N. Rabinowitz, *Race Relations in the Urban South, 1865–1890* (1978).
Roger L. Ransom and Richard Sutch, *One Kind of Freedom: The Economic Consequences of Emancipation* (1977).
Loren Schweninger, *James T. Rapier and Reconstruction* (1978).
Clarence E. Walker, *A Rock in a Weary Land: The African Methodist Episcopal Church during the Civil War and Reconstruction* (1982).

The Politics of Reconstruction

Richard F. Bensel, *Yankee Leviathan: The Origins of Central State Authority in America, 1859–1877* (1990).
Philip Dray, *Capitol Men: The Epic Story of Reconstruction through the Lives of the First Black Congressmen* (2008).
Ellen Carol DuBois, *Feminism and Suffrage: The Emergence of an Independent Women's Movement in America, 1848–1869* (1978).
Richard L. Hume and Jerry B. Gough, *Blacks, Carpetbaggers, and Scalawags: The Constitutional Conventions of Radical Reconstruction* (2008).
Heather Cox Richardson, *The Death of Reconstruction: Race, Labor, and Politics in the Post–Civil War North, 1865–1901* (2001).
Leslie A. Schwalm, *Emancipation's Diaspora: Race and Reconstruction in the Upper Midwest* (2009).
Brooks D. Simpson, *The Reconstruction Presidents* (1998).
Mark Wahlgren Summers, *A Dangerous Stir: Fear, Paranoia, and the Making of Reconstruction* (2009).

C. Vann Woodward, *Reunion and Reaction: The Compromise of 1877 and the End of Reconstruction* (1951).

The Struggle in the South

James Alex Baggett, *The Scalawags: Southern Dissenters in the Civil War and Reconstruction* (2003).

Nancy D. Bercaw, *Gendered Freedoms: Race, Rights, and the Politics of Household in the Delta, 1861–1875* (2003).

Stephen Budiansky, *The Bloody Shirt: Terror after the Civil War* (2008).

Jane Turner Censer, *The Reconstruction of White Southern Womanhood, 1865–1895* (2003).

Paul A. Cimbala, *Under the Guardianship of the Nation: The Freedmen's Bureau and the Reconstruction of Georgia, 1865–1870* (1997).

Jane E. Dailey, *Before Jim Crow: The Politics of Race in Post-Emancipation Virginia* (2000).

Laura F. Edwards, *Gendered Strife and Confusion: The Political Culture of Reconstruction* (1997).

Sarah E. Gardner, *Blood and Irony: Southern White Women's Narratives of the Civil War, 1861–1937* (2004).

Stephen Kantrowitz, *Ben Tillman and the Reconstruction of White Supremacy* (2000).

Charles Lane, *The Day Freedom Died: The Colfax Massacre, the Supreme Court, and the Betrayal of Reconstruction* (2008).

George C. Rable, *But There Was No Peace: The Role of Violence in the Politics of Reconstruction* (1984).

James L. Roark, *Masters without Slaves: Southern Planters in the Civil War and Reconstruction* (1977).

Hyman Rubin III, *South Carolina Scalawags* (2006).

Peter Wallenstein, *From Slave South to New South: Public Policy in Nineteenth-Century Georgia* (1987).

▶ **FOR MORE BOOKS ABOUT TOPICS IN THIS CHAPTER,** see the Online Bibliography at **bedfordstmartins.com/roark.**

▶ **FOR ADDITIONAL PRIMARY SOURCES FROM THIS PERIOD,** see Michael Johnson, ed., *Reading the American Past*, Fifth Edition.

▶ **FOR WEB SITES, IMAGES, AND DOCUMENTS RELATED TO TOPICS AND PLACES IN THIS CHAPTER,** visit Make History at **bedfordstmartins.com/roark.**

Reviewing Chapter 16

REVIEW QUESTIONS

Use key terms and dates to support your answer.

1. Why did Congress object to Lincoln's wartime plan for reconstruction? (pp. 501–506)

2. How did the North respond to the passage of black codes in the southern states? (pp. 506–510)

3. Why did Johnson urge the southern states to reject the Fourteenth Amendment? (pp. 510–515)

4. What brought the elements of the South's Republican coalition together? (pp. 515–524)

5. How did the Supreme Court undermine the Fourteenth and Fifteenth Amendments? (pp. 524–529)

MAKING CONNECTIONS

Draw on key terms, the timeline, and review questions.

1. Reconstruction succeeded in advancing black civil rights but failed to secure them over the long term. Why and how did the federal government retreat from defending African Americans' civil rights in the 1870s? In your answer, cite specific actions by Congress and the Supreme Court.

2. Why was distributing plantation land to former slaves such a controversial policy? In your answer, discuss why landownership was important to freedmen and why Congress rejected redistribution as a general policy.

3. At the end of the Civil War, it remained to be seen exactly how emancipation would transform the South. How did emancipation change political and labor organization in the region? In your answer, discuss how ex-slaves exercised their new freedoms and how white Southerners attempted to limit them.

4. The Republican Party shaped Reconstruction through its control of Congress and state legislatures in the South. How did the identification of the Republican Party with Reconstruction policy affect the party's political fortunes in the 1870s? In your answer, be sure to address developments on the federal and state levels.

LINKING TO THE PAST

Link events in this chapter to earlier events.

1. In what ways did the attitudes and actions of President Johnson increase northern resolve to reconstruct the South and the South's resolve to resist reconstruction?

2. White women, abolitionists, and blacks all had hopes for a brighter future that were in some ways dashed during the turmoil of reconstruction. What specific goals of these groups slipped away? What political allies abandoned their causes, and why?

▶ FOR PRACTICE QUIZZES AND OTHER STUDY TOOLS, see the Online Study Guide at bedfordstmartins.com/roark.

TIMELINE 1863–1877

1863
- Proclamation of Amnesty and Reconstruction.

1864
- Lincoln refuses to sign Wade-Davis bill.

1865
- Freedmen's Bureau established.
- President Abraham Lincoln shot; dies on April 15; succeeded by Andrew Johnson.
- Black codes enacted.
- Thirteenth Amendment becomes part of Constitution.

1866
- Congress approves Fourteenth Amendment.
- Civil Rights Act.
- American Equal Rights Association founded.
- Ku Klux Klan founded.

1867
- Military Reconstruction Act.
- Tenure of Office Act.

1868
- Impeachment trial of President Johnson.
- Republican Ulysses S. Grant elected president.

1869
- Congress approves Fifteenth Amendment.

1871
- Ku Klux Klan Act.

1872
- Liberal Party formed.
- President Grant reelected.

1873
- Economic depression sets in for remainder of decade.
- *Slaughterhouse* cases.
- Colfax massacre.

1874
- Democrats win majority in House of Representatives.

1875
- Civil Rights Act.

1876
- *United States v. Cruikshank.*

1877
- Republican Rutherford B. Hayes assumes presidency; Reconstruction era ends.

LAKOTA VEST

This Lakota vest demonstrates how Native Americans adopted Euro-American articles of clothing and decorative motifs while employing materials that perpetuated native traditions. The vest belonged to Thomas American Horse, who had his initials worked into the beads at the neck. The American flag, as the vest demonstrates, figured frequently as a design in Indian art. The coming of the American flag, and with it the railroads and the slaughter of the buffalo pictured on the cover of *Leslie's Weekly* in 1871, points to the great changes that Indians faced in the struggle to control the vast land and resources of the American West.

Vest: Private Collection, photograph American Hurrah Archive, NYC; background: Library of Congress.

17

The Contested West
1865–1900

TO CELEBRATE THE FOUR HUNDREDTH ANNIVERSARY OF COLUMBUS'S voyage to the New World, Chicago hosted the World's Columbian Exposition in 1893. Architects and landscapers created a magical White City on the shores of Lake Michigan, complete with a Midway Plaisance where the first Ferris wheel awed and delighted the four million fairgoers.

Among the organizations vying to hold meetings in the White City was the American Historical Association, whose members — dedicated to the advancement of historical studies — gathered on a warm July evening to hear Frederick Jackson Turner deliver his landmark essay "The Significance of the Frontier in American History." Turner began by noting that the 1890 census could no longer discern a clear frontier line. His tone was elegiac: "The existence of an area of free land, its continuous recession, and the advance of settlement westward," he observed, "explained American development."

Of course, *west* has always been a comparative term in American history. Until the gold rush focused attention on California, the West for settlers lay beyond the Appalachians and east of the Mississippi in lands drained by the Ohio River, a part of the country now known as the Old Northwest. But by the second half of the nineteenth century, with the end of the Mexican-American War, the West now stretched from Canada to Mexico, from the Mississippi River to the Pacific Ocean.

Turner, who had originally studied the old frontier east of the Mississippi, viewed the West as a process as much as a place. The availability of land provided a "safety valve," releasing social tensions and providing opportunities for social mobility that worked to Americanize Americans. The West demanded strength and nerve, fostered invention and adaptation, and produced self-confident, individualistic Americans. Turner's theory underscored the exceptionalism of America's history, highlighting its difference from the rest of the world. His "frontier thesis" would earn him a professorship at Harvard and a permanent place in American history.

Yet the historians who applauded Turner in Chicago had short memories. That afternoon, they had crossed the midway to attend Buffalo Bill Cody's Wild West extravaganza, which featured exhibitions of riding, shooting, and roping and presented dramatic reenactments of great moments in western lore. Part circus, part theater, the show included 100 cowboys, 97 Indians,

535

180 horses, and 18 American bison. The troupe performed the "Attack on the Settler's Cabin" and their own version of "Custer's Last Stand," ending with Buffalo Bill galloping to the rescue through a cloud of dust only to mouth the words "Too late." The historians cheering in the stands that July afternoon no doubt dismissed Buffalo Bill's history as amateur, but he made a point that Turner's thesis ignored: The West was neither free nor open. The story of the country was a story of fierce and violent contest for land and resources.

In the decades following the Civil War, the United States pursued empire in the American West in Indian wars that lasted until 1890. Pushed off their land and onto reservations, Native Americans resisted as they faced waves of miners and settlers and the transformation of the environment by railroads, mines, barbed wire, and mechanized agriculture. The pastoral agrarianism Turner celebrated in his frontier thesis belied the urban, industrial West already emerging on the Comstock Lode in Nevada and in the commercial farms of California.

Buffalo Bill's mythic West, with its heroic cowboys and noble savages, obscured the complex reality of the West as a fiercely contested terrain. Competing groups of Anglos, Hispanics, former slaves, Chinese, and a host of others arrived seeking the promise of land and riches, while the Indians who inhabited the vast territory struggled to preserve their sovereignty and their cultural identity. And, with its emphasis on the rugged individualism of white men pioneering the frontier, Turner's vision of the West overlooked racial diversity and failed to acknowledge the role of women in community building.

Yet in the waning decade of the nineteenth century, as history blurred with nostalgia, Turner's evocation of the frontier as a crucible for American identity hit a nerve in a population facing rapid changes. A major depression started in May 1893, even before the Columbian Exposition opened its doors. Americans already worried about the economy, immigration, and urban industrialism found in Turner's message a new cause for concern. Would America continue to be America now that the frontier was closed? As they struggled with the question, it became clear that the West did not exist out of place and time. Nor was it particularly exceptional. The problems confronting the United States at the turn of the twentieth century — the exploitation of land and labor, the consolidation of capital, and vicious ethnic and racial rivalries — all played themselves out under western skies.

Buffalo Bill Poster
Buffalo Bill Cody used colorful posters to publicize his Wild West show during the 1880s and 1890s. One of his most popular features was the reenactment of Custer's Last Stand, which he performed for Queen Victoria in London and at the World's Columbian Exposition in Chicago. Sitting Bull, who fought at the Battle of the Little Big Horn, toured with the company in 1885 and traveled to England with the show. Cody's romantic depictions of western history helped create the myth of the Old West. Buffalo Bill Historical Center, Cody, Wyoming.

▶ Conquest and Empire in the West

While the European powers expanded their authority and wealth through imperialism and colonialism, establishing far-flung empires in Asia, Africa, and South America, the United States focused its attention on the West. As posited by **Frederick Jackson Turner**, American exceptionalism stressed how the history of the United States differed from that of European nations, citing America's western frontier as a case in point. Yet recent historians have argued that the process by which the United States expanded its borders in the nineteenth century can best be understood in the global context of imperialism and colonialism — language applied to European powers in this period that makes explicit how expansion in the American West involved the conquest, displacement, and rule over native peoples. (See "Beyond America's Borders," page 542.)

The federal government, through chicanery and conquest, pushed the Indians off their lands (Map 17.1) and onto designated Indian territories or reservations. The Indian wars that followed the Civil War depleted the Native American population and handed the lion's share of Indian land over to white settlers. The decimation of the bison herds inevitably pushed the Plains Indians onto reservations, where they lived as wards of the state. Through the lens of colonialism, we can see how the United States, with its commitment to an imperialist, expansionist ideology, colonized the West.

Indian Removal and the Reservation System

Beginning in the early days of the Republic, the government advocated a policy of **Indian removal**. With plenty of land open in the West, the army removed eastern tribes — often against their will — to territory west of the Mississippi. In the 1830s, President Andrew Jackson pushed the Five Civilized Tribes — the Cherokee, Choctaw, Chickasaw, Creek, and Seminole peoples — off their land in the southern United States. Jackson's Indian removal forced thousands of men, women, and children to leave their homes in Georgia and Tennessee and walk hundreds of miles west. So many died of hunger, exhaustion, and disease along the way that the Cherokees called their path "the trail on which we cried." At the end of this trail of tears stood land set aside as Indian Territory (present-day Oklahoma). Here, the government promised, the Indians could remain "as long as grass shall grow." But hunger for western land soon negated that promise.

Manifest destiny — the belief that the United States had a "God-given" right to aggressively spread the values of white civilization and expand the nation from ocean to ocean — dictated U.S. policy. In the name of manifest destiny, Americans forced the removal of the Five Civilized Tribes to Oklahoma; colonized Texas and won its independence from Mexico in 1836; conquered California, Arizona, New Mexico, and parts of Utah and Colorado in the Mexican-American War of 1846–1848; and invaded Oregon in the mid-1840s.

By midcentury, western land no longer seemed inexhaustible, and instead of removing Indians to the west, the government sought to take control of Indian lands and promised in return to pay annuities and put the Indians on lands reserved for their use — **reservations**. In 1851, some ten thousand Plains Indians came together at Fort Laramie in Wyoming to negotiate a treaty that ceded a wide swath of their land to allow passage of wagon trains headed west. In return, the government promised that the rest of the Indian land would remain inviolate.

The Indians who "touched the pen" to the 1851 **Treaty of Fort Laramie** hoped to preserve their culture in the face of the white onslaught, which had already decimated their population and despoiled their environment. White invaders cut down trees, miners polluted streams, and hunters killed off bison and small game. Whites brought alcohol, guns, and something even more deadly — disease. Smallpox was the biggest killer of Native Americans in the West. Epidemics spread from Mexico up to Canada. Between 1780 and 1870, the population of the Plains tribes declined by half. Cholera, diphtheria, measles, scarlet fever, and other contagious diseases also took their toll. "If I could see this thing, if I knew where it came from, I would go there and fight it," a Cheyenne warrior anguished. Disease shifted the balance of power on the plains from Woodland agrarian tribes like the Mandan and Hidatsa (who died at the rate of 79 percent) to the Lakota (Western) Sioux, who fled the contagion of villages to take up life as equestrian (horse-riding) nomads on the western plains. As the Sioux pushed west, they displaced weaker tribes.

In the Southwest, the Navajo people, like the Cherokee, endured a forced march called the "Long Walk" from their homeland to the desolate Bosque Redondo Reservation in New Mexico in 1864. "This ground we were brought on, it is not productive," complained the Navajo leader Barboncito. "We plant but it does not yield. All the stock we brought here have nearly all died."

MAP ACTIVITY

Map 17.1   The Loss of Indian Lands, 1850–1890

By 1890, western Indians were isolated on small, scattered reservations. Native Americans had struggled to retain their land in major battles, from the Santee Uprising in Minnesota in 1862 to the massacre at Wounded Knee, South Dakota, in 1890.

READING THE MAP: Where was the largest reservation located in 1890? Which states on this map show no reservations in 1890? Compare this map to Map 17.3, Federal Land Grants to Railroads and the Development of the West.

CONNECTIONS: Why did the federal government force Native Americans onto reservations? What developments prompted these changes?

Poverty and starvation stalked the reservations. Confined by armed force, the Indians eked out an existence on stingy government rations. These once proud peoples found themselves dependent on government handouts and the assistance of Indian agents who, in the words of Paiute Sarah Winnemucca, did "nothing but fill their pockets." Winnemucca launched a lecture campaign in the United States and Europe denouncing the government's reservation policy.

Styled as stepping-stones on the road to "civilization," Indian reservations closely resembled

Waiting for Rations on the Reservation
Indians who agreed to give up land and go onto reservations received food and clothing rations from the local Indian agency. Here a group of Lakota Sioux gather to receive their goods at the Standing Rock Reservation in 1881. On the right is a ration card from the Rosebud reservation. Indian agencies were notorious for their paltry provisions. Often Indians outwitted the government by taking rations during the winter, when they were hungry, only to leave the reservation to resume their nomadic hunting life during the summer season. The decimation of the great bison herds drove them permanently onto the reservations in the 1880s. Photograph: National Anthropological Archives, Smithsonian Institution, Washington, D.C.; ration ticket: National Museum of the American Indian, Smithsonian Institution (239391), Washington, D.C. Photos by Photo Services.

colonial societies where native populations, ruled by outside bureaucrats, saw their culture assaulted, their religious practices outlawed, their children sent away to school, and their way of life attacked in the name of progress and civilization. Self-styled "friends of the Indians," many of them easterners with little experience in the West, maintained that reservations would provide a classroom of civilization where Indians could be taught to speak English, to worship a Christian god, to give up hunting for farming, and to reject tribal ways.

To Americans raised on theories of racial superiority, the Indians constituted, in the words of one Colorado militia major, "an obstacle to civilization . . . [and] should be exterminated." This attitude pervaded the military, and the cavalry annihilated entire villages with ruthless efficiency. In November 1864 at the Sand Creek massacre in Colorado Territory, Colonel John M. Chivington and his Colorado militia descended on a village of Cheyenne, mostly women and children. Their leader, Black Kettle, raised a white flag and an American flag to signal surrender, but the charging cavalry ignored his signal and butchered 270 Indians. Chivington watched as his men scalped and mutilated their victims and later justified the killing of Indian children with the terse remark, "Nits make lice." The city of Denver treated Chivington and his men as heroes, but a congressional inquiry castigated the soldiers for their "fiendish malignity" and condemned the "savage cruelty" of the massacre.

The Decimation of the Great Bison Herds

In the centuries following the arrival of the first European settlers, the great herds of buffalo (American bison), once numbering as many as thirty million, fell into serious decline. A host of environmental and human factors contributed to the destruction of the bison. The dynamic ecology of the Great Plains, with its droughts, fires, and blizzards, combined with the ecological imperialism of humans (Indian buffalo-robe traders as well as whites and their cattle), put increasing pressure on the bison. By the 1850s,

SLAUGHTERED FOR THE HIDE.—[See Page 1002.]

VISUAL ACTIVITY

"Slaughtered for the Hide"

In 1874, *Harper's Weekly* featured this cover with its illustration of a buffalo hide hunter skinning a carcass on the southwestern plains. By 1872, the Santa Fe railroad reached Kansas, making Dodge City the center for the shipment of buffalo hides to the East, where they were made into leather belting used to run the nation's machinery. In a matter of months, hunters decimated the great southern bison herds. City father Colonel Richard Dodge wrote of the carnage, "The air was foul with sickening stench, and the vast plain which only a short twelve months before teemed with animal life, was a dead, solitary putrid desert." Dodge estimated that hunters slaughtered more than three million bison between 1872 and 1874. The grim reality of the trade makes the magazine's subtitle, "A Journal of Civilization," highly ironic. Library of Congress.

READING THE IMAGE: What virtues and stereotypes of the West does this magazine cover extol?

CONNECTIONS: How might the notion of "civilization" have differed according to the Native American perspective?

---

a combination of drought and commerce had driven the great herds onto the far western plains.

After the Civil War, the accelerating pace of industrial expansion brought about the near extinction of the bison. Industrial demand for heavy leather belting used in machinery and the development of larger, more accurate rifles combined to hasten the slaughter of the bison. At the same time, the nation's growing transcontinental rail system cut the range in two and divided the herds. For the Sioux and other nomadic tribes of the plains, the buffalo constituted a way of life — a source of food, fuel, and shelter and a central part of their religion and rituals. To the railroads, the bison were a nuisance, at best a cheap source of meat for their workers and a target for sport. "It will not be long before all the buffaloes are extinct near and between the railroads," Ohio senator John Sherman predicted in 1868.

In the end, the army took credit for the conquest of the Plains Indians, but victory came about largely as a result of the decimation of the great bison herds. General Philip Sheridan acknowledged as much when he applauded white hide hunters for "destroying the Indians' commissary." With their food supply gone, Indians had to choose between starvation and the reservation. "A cold wind blew across the prairie when the last buffalo fell," the great Sioux leader **Sitting Bull** lamented, "a death wind for my people."

On the southern plains in 1867, more than five thousand warring Comanches, Kiowas, and Southern Arapahos gathered at Medicine Lodge Creek in Kansas to negotiate a treaty. Satak, or Sitting Bear, a prominent Kiowa chief and medicine man, explained why the Indians sought peace: "In the far-distant past . . . the world seemed large enough for both the red man and the white man." But, he observed, "its broad plains seem now to contract, and the white man grows jealous of his red brother." To preserve their land from white encroachment, the Indians signed the Treaty of Medicine Lodge, agreeing to move to a reservation. Yet they continued to leave the reservation's confines to hunt during the summer months. After 1870, hide hunters poured into the region, and within a decade they had nearly exterminated the southern bison herds. Luther Standing Bear recounted the sight and stench: "I saw the bodies of hundreds of dead buffalo lying about, just wasting, and the odor was terrible. . . . They were letting our food lie on the plains to rot." With the buffalo gone, the Indians faced starvation and reluctantly moved to the reservations.

Indian Wars and the Collapse of Comanchería

The Indian wars in the West marked the last resistance of a Native American population devastated by disease and demoralized by the removal policy pursued by the federal government. More accurately called "settlers' wars" (since they began with "peaceful settlers," often miners, overrunning Native American land), the wars flared up again only a few years after the signing of the Fort Laramie treaty. The Dakota Sioux in Minnesota went to war in 1862. For years, under the leadership of Chief Little Crow, the Dakota, also known as the Santee, had pursued a policy of accommodation, ceding land in return for the promise of annuities. But with his people on the verge of starvation (the local Indian agent told the hungry Dakota, "Go and eat grass"), Little Crow reluctantly led his angry warriors in a desperate campaign against the intruders, killing more than 1,000 settlers. American troops quelled what was called the Great Sioux Uprising (also called the Santee Uprising) and marched 1,700 Sioux to Fort Snelling, where 400 Indians were put on trial for murder and 38 died in the largest mass execution in American history.

After the Civil War, President Ulysses S. Grant faced the prospect of protracted Indian war on the Great Plains. Reluctant to spend more money and sacrifice more lives in battle, Grant adopted a "peace policy" designed to segregate and control the Indians while opening up land to white settlers. This policy won the support of both friends of the Indians, who feared for their survival, and Indian haters, who coveted their land and wished to confine them to the least desirable areas in the West. General William Tecumseh Sherman summed up the new Indian policy succinctly: "Remove all to a safe place and then reduce them to a helpless condition." The army herded the Indians onto reservations (see Map 17.1), where the U.S. Bureau of Indian Affairs supposedly ministered to their needs. But peace in the West remained elusive.

The great Indian empire of **Comanchería**, which in the eighteenth century stretched from the Canadian plains to Mexico, by 1865 numbered fewer than five thousand Comanches, who ranged from west Texas north to Oklahoma. Through decades of dealings with the Spanish and French, the Comanches had built a complex empire based on trade in horses, hides, guns, and captives. Expert equestrians, the Comanches inaugurated the horse-centered way of life that eventually came to characterize the Plains Indians.

In 1871, Grant's peace policy in the West gave way to all-out warfare as the U.S. Army dispatched three thousand soldiers to wipe out the remains of the Comanche empire. Comanchería had been greatly reduced, but Comanche raiding parties took a toll in lives and livestock and virtually obliterated white settlements in west Texas. To defeat the Indians, the army adopted the tactics General William Sherman had used in his march through Confederate Georgia during the Civil War. At the decisive battle of Palo Duro Canyon in 1874, only three Comanche warriors died in battle, but U.S. soldiers took the Indians' camp, burning more than two hundred tepees, hundreds of robes and blankets, and thousands of pounds of winter supplies and shooting more than a thousand horses. Coupled with the decimation of the bison, the army's scorched-earth policy led to the final collapse of the Comanche people — more an economic than a military defeat. Crippled by poverty, malnutrition, and the loss of their trading-raiding economy, the surviving Indians of Comanchería, now numbering fewer than 1,500, reluctantly retreated to the reservation at Fort Sill.

The Fight for the Black Hills

On the northern plains, the fever for gold fueled the conflict between Indians and Euro-Americans. In 1866, the Cheyenne united with the Sioux in Wyoming to protect their hunting grounds in the Powder River valley, which were threatened by the construction of the Bozeman Trail connecting Fort Laramie with the goldfields in Montana. Captain William Fetterman, who had boasted that with eighty men he could ride through the Sioux nation, was killed along with all of his troops in an Indian attack. The Sioux's impressive victories led to the second **Treaty of Fort Laramie** in 1868, in which the United States agreed to abandon the Bozeman Trail and guaranteed the Indians control of the **Black Hills**, land sacred to the Lakota Sioux.

The second Treaty of Fort Laramie was full of contradictions — in one breath promising to preserve Indian land and in the next forcing the tribes to relinquish all territory outside their reservations. A controversial provision of the treaty guaranteed the Indians access to their traditional hunting grounds "so long as the buffalo may range thereon in such numbers as to justify the chase." With the bison facing extermination, the provision was ominous. Yet the government's fork-tongued promises induced some of the tribes to accept the treaty. The great Sioux chief Red Cloud led many of his people onto the reservation. Red Cloud soon

Imperialism, Colonialism, and the Treatment of the Sioux and the Zulu

Viewed through the lens of colonialism, the British war with the Zulu in South Africa offers a compelling contrast to the United States' war against the Lakota Sioux. The Zulu, like the Sioux, came to power as a result of devastating intertribal warfare. In the area that is today the KwaZulu-Natal province of the Republic of South Africa, the Zulu king Shaka united his empire by 1826 with an army of more than twenty thousand. And like the Sioux, the Zulu earned a formidable reputation as brave warriors who fought to protect their land from white encroachment.

In 1806, the British seized the Cape of Good Hope to secure shipping interests, leading to conflicts with Dutch-speaking settlers there known as the Boers, who had inhabited the southern tip of Africa since the seventeenth century. Clashes between Britons and Boers eventually resulted in the Great Trek, the migration of nearly twelve thousand Boers northeastward beginning in 1835. There they claimed land and established the South African Republic (the Transvaal) in 1853 and the Orange Free State in 1854, both independent of British rule. But the Great Trek brought the Boers into Zululand, where they met with bloody resistance.

The Zulu lived in a highly complex society, with all the young men organized into *amabutho*, regiments of warriors arranged by age and bound to local chiefs under the supreme command of the Zulu king, who demanded obedience and bravery. During his harsh reign, Shaka inspected his regiments after each battle, picking out cowards and putting them to death on the spot. Young men could not start their own households without the local chief's permission, thus ensuring an ample stock of warriors and making the Zulu army, in the words of one English observer, "a celibate, man-slaying machine." The Boer settlers repeatedly faced the wrath of the Zulu, who slaughtered the first trekkers to arrive in Zululand and raided Boer settlements to steal cattle.

The British entered the fray in 1879, sparking the Anglo-Zulu War, which a recent historian has condemned as being "as unnecessary as it was unjust." Sir Theophilus Shepstone, British secretary for native affairs, hinted at Britain's motive when he wrote in 1878, "Had [its] 30,000 warriors been in time changed to labourers working for wages, Zululand would have been a prosperous peaceful country instead of what it is now, a source of perpetual danger to itself and its neighbors."

With aims of both placating the Boers and securing a source of labor for British economic expansion — made paramount by the discovery of diamonds in the region — British troops under Lord Chelmsford invaded Zululand. Leading soldiers armed with the latest rifles and artillery, Chelmsford — with a confidence reminiscent of that of George Armstrong Custer — expected to subdue the Zulu easily. But in January 1879, at the battle of Isandhlwana, the Zulu army of

Zululand and Cape Colony, 1878

British / Boer Republics

KALAHARI DESERT · TRANSVAAL · ORANGE FREE STATE · ZULULAND · Isandlwana · CAPE COLONY · Cape Town · ATLANTIC OCEAN · INDIAN OCEAN

---

regretted his decision. "Think of it!" he told a visitor to the Pine Ridge Reservation. "I, who used to own . . . country so extensive that I could not ride through it in a week . . . must tell Washington when I am hungry. I must beg for that which I own." Several Sioux chiefs, among them **Crazy Horse** of the Oglala band and Sitting Bull of the Hunkpapa, refused to sign the treaty. Crazy Horse said that he wanted no part of the "piecemeal penning" of his people.

In 1874, the discovery of gold in the Black Hills of the Dakotas led the government to break its promise to Red Cloud. Miners began pouring into the region, and the Northern Pacific Railroad made plans to lay track. Lieutenant Colonel **George Armstrong Custer**, whose troopers found gold in the area, trumpeted news of the strike. At first, the government offered to purchase the Black Hills. But to the Lakota Sioux, the Black Hills were sacred — "the heart of everything that is." They refused to sell. The army responded by issuing an ultimatum ordering all Lakota Sioux and Northern Cheyenne bands onto the Pine Ridge Reservation and threatening to hunt down those who refused.

more than 25,000 surprised a British encampment. In less than two hours, more than 4,000 Zulu and British were killed. Only a handful of British soldiers managed to escape, and Chelmsford lost 1,300 officers and men.

When news of Isandhlwana reached London, commentators compared the massacre to Custer's defeat at the Little Big Horn three years earlier and noted that native forces armed with spears had defeated a modern army. The military disaster shocked and outraged the nation, damaging the British military's reputation of invincibility.

Vowing that the Zulu would "pay dearly for their triumph of a day," the British immediately launched unconditional war against the Zulu. In the ensuing battles, neither side took prisoners. The Zulu beat the British twice more, but after seven months the British finally routed the Zulu army and abandoned Zululand to its fate — partition, starvation, and civil war.

Historians would later compare the British victory to the U.S. Army's defeat of the Sioux in the American West, but the Zulu and Sioux met different economic fates. As Shepstone hinted in 1878, the British goal had been to subdue the Zulu and turn them into cheap labor. Compared to the naked economic exploitation of the Zulu, the U.S. policy toward the Sioux, with its forced assimilation on reservations and its misguided attempts to turn the nomadic tribes into sedentary, God-fearing farmers, may seem less exploitative if no less ruthless in its cultural imperialism.

Zulu Warriors
Chief Ngoza (center) poses with Zulu men in full war dress. Their distinctive cowhide shields date to the reign of King Shaka. Each warrior also carried two or three throwing spears and an *ikwa*, or flat-bladed stabbing spear used in close combat. Zulu warriors marched at the double and could cover up to fifty miles a day. Campbell Collections of the University of KwaZulu-Natal.

Both the Little Big Horn and Isandhlwana became legends that spawned a romantic image of the "noble savage": fierce in battle, honored in defeat. Describing this myth, historian James Gump, who has chronicled the subjugation of the Sioux and the Zulu, observed, "Each western culture simultaneously dehumanized and glamorized the Sioux and Zulu," and noted that the noble savage mythology was "a product of the racist ideologies of the late nineteenth century as well as the guilt and compassion associated with the bloody costs of empire building."

Imperial powers, both Britain and the United States defeated indigenous rivals and came to dominate their lands (and, in the case of the Zulu, their labor) in the global expansion that marked the nineteenth century.

America in a Global Context

1. How was the British war with the Zulu similar to and different from the American war with the Sioux?

2. Compare the fate of the defeated Zulu with that of the Sioux.

In the summer of 1876, the army launched a three-pronged attack led by Custer, General **George Crook**, and Colonel John Gibbon. Crazy Horse stopped Crook at the Battle of the Rosebud. Custer, leading the second prong of the army's offensive, divided his troops and ordered an attack. On June 25, he spotted signs of the Indians' camp. Crying "Hurrah Boys, we've got them," he led 265 men of the Seventh Cavalry into the largest Indian camp ever assembled on the Great Plains, more than 8,000 Indians. Nomadic bands of Sioux, Cheyenne, and Arapaho had come together for a summer buffalo hunt and camped along the banks of the Greasy Grass River (whites called it the Little Big Horn). Indian warriors led by Sitting Bull and Crazy Horse set upon Custer and his men and quickly annihilated them. "It took us about as long as a hungry man to eat his dinner," the Cheyenne chief Two Moons recalled. Gibbon arrived two days later to discover the carnage.

"Custer's Last Stand," as the **Battle of the Little Big Horn** was styled in myth, turned out to be the last stand for the Sioux. The Indians'

Crazy Horse at the Little Big Horn
This pictograph by Amos Bad Heart Bull, an Oglala Sioux from the Pine Ridge Reservation, pictures Crazy Horse at the center of the battle of the Little Big Horn. Although the artist was only seven years old in 1876, he based his pictures on the recollections of his uncle and other Oglala elders. Crazy Horse ritually prepared for battle by painting hail stones on his body, wearing a small stone tied behind one ear, and placing a single eagle feather in his hair. According to one of the Arapaho warriors who fought beside him against Custer, Crazy Horse "was the bravest man he ever saw." The Granger Collection, New York.

nomadic way of life meant they could not remain a combined force for long. The bands that had massed at the Little Big Horn scattered, and the army hunted them down. "Wherever we went," wrote the Oglala holy man Black Elk, "the soldiers came to kill us." In 1877, Crazy Horse was captured and killed. Four years later, in 1881, Sitting Bull surrendered. The government took the Black Hills and confined the Lakota to the Great Sioux Reservation. The Sioux never accepted the loss of the Black Hills. In 1923, they filed suit, demanding the return of the land illegally taken from them. After a protracted court battle lasting nearly sixty years, the U.S. Supreme Court ruled in 1980 that the government had illegally abrogated the Treaty of Fort Laramie and upheld an award of $122.5 million in compensation to the tribes. The Sioux refused the settlement and continue to press for the return of the Black Hills.

REVIEW How did the slaughter of the bison contribute to the Plains Indians' removal to reservations?

▶ Forced Assimilation and Resistance Strategies

More than two hundred years of contact with whites utterly transformed Native American societies. The indigenous peoples Christopher Columbus had mistakenly dubbed "Indians" included more than five hundred distinct tribal entities with different languages, myths, religions, and physical appearance. According to the census of 1900, the Indian population in the continental United States stood at 250,000 (admittedly an undercount), down from estimates as high as 15 million at the time of first contact with Europeans. Not only had the population been decimated by war, disease, and the obliteration of the bison, but Indian lands had shrunk so much that by 1890 Euro-Americans controlled 97.5 percent of the territory formerly occupied by Native Americans.

Imperialistic attitudes of whites toward Indians continued to evolve in the late nineteenth

century. To "civilize" the Indians, the U.S. government sought to force assimilation on their children. Reservations, once designed as stepping-stones to civilization, became increasingly unpopular among whites who coveted Indian land. A new policy of allotment gained favor. It promised to put Indians on parcels of land, forcing them into farming, and then to redistribute the rest of the land to settlers. In the face of this ongoing assault on their way of life, Indians actively resisted, contested, and adapted to colonial rule.

Indian Schools and the War against Indian Culture

Indian schools constituted the cultural battleground of the Indian wars in the West, their avowed purpose being "to destroy the Indian in him and save the man." In 1877, Congress appropriated funds for Indian education, reasoning that "it was less expensive to educate Indians than to kill them." Virginia's Hampton Institute, created in 1868 to school newly freed slaves, accepted its first Indian students in 1878. Although many Indian schools operated on the reservations, authorities much preferred boarding facilities that isolated students from the "contamination" of tribal values.

Many Native American parents resisted sending their children away. When all else failed, the military kidnapped the children and sent them off to school. An agent at the Mescalero Apache Agency in Arizona Territory reported in 1886 that "it became necessary to visit the camps unexpectedly with a detachment of police, and seize such children as were proper and take them away to school, willing or unwilling." The parents put up a struggle. "Some hurried their children off to the mountains or hid them away in camp, and the police had to chase and capture them like so many wild rabbits," the agent observed. "This unusual proceeding created quite an outcry. The men were sullen and muttering, the women loud in their lamentations and the children almost out of their wits with fright." Once at school, the children were stripped and scrubbed, their clothing and belongings were confiscated, and their hair was hacked off and doused with kerosene to kill lice. Issued stiff new uniforms, shoes, and what one boy recalled as the "torture" of woolen long underwear, the children often lost not only their possessions but also their names: Hehakaavita (Yellow Elk) became Thomas Goodwood; Polingaysi Qoyawayma became Elizabeth White.

Hampton Pageant, 1892
The Indian students in this picture are dressed for Columbia's Roll Call, a pageant at Hampton Institute honoring the nation's heroes on Indian Citizen Day, 1892. Among others portrayed are Christopher Columbus, Pocahontas, George Washington, and, in the center, a student dressed as Columbia, symbol of the Republic, draped in the American flag. There was no mention of Crazy Horse, Sitting Bull, or Geronimo, all Indians who resisted white encroachment and appropriation of their land in the West. Courtesy of Hampton University Archives.

The curriculum featured agricultural and manual arts for boys and domestic skills for girls, training designed to make Indians "willing workers" who would no longer be a burden to the government. The **Carlisle Indian School** in Pennsylvania, founded in 1879, became the model for later institutions. To encourage assimilation, Carlisle pioneered the "outing system" — sending students to live with white families during summer vacations. The policy reflected the school's slogan: "To civilize the Indian, get him into civilization. To keep him civilized, let him stay."

Merrill Gates, a member of the Board of Indian Commissioners, summed up the goal of Indian education: "To get the Indian out of the blanket and into trousers, — and trousers with a pocket in them, *and with a pocket that aches to be filled with dollars!*" Gates's faith in the "civilizing" power of the dollar reflected the unabashed materialism of the Gilded Age. But the cultural annihilation that Gates cheerfully predicted did not prove so easy.

The Dawes Act and Indian Land Allotment

In the 1880s, the practice of rounding up Indians and herding them onto reservations lost momentum in favor of allotment — a new policy designed to encourage assimilation through farming and the ownership of private property. Americans vowing to avenge Custer urged the government to get tough with the Indians. Reservations, they argued, took up too much good land that white settlers could put to better use. At the same time, people sympathetic to the Indians were appalled at the desperate poverty on the reservations and feared for the Indians' survival. Helen Hunt Jackson, in her classic work *A Century of Dishonor* (1881), convinced many readers that the Indians had been treated unfairly. "Our Indian policy," the *New York Times* concluded, "is usually spoliation behind the mask of benevolence."

> **"Our Indian policy is usually spoliation behind the mask of benevolence"**
> — The *New York Times*

The Indian Rights Association, a group of mainly white easterners formed in 1882, campaigned for the dismantling of the reservations, now viewed as obstacles to progress. To "cease to treat the Indian as a red man and treat him as a man" meant putting an end to tribal communalism and fostering individualism. "Selfishness," declared Senator Henry Dawes of Massachusetts, "is at the bottom of civilization." Dawes called for "allotment in severalty" — the institution of private property.

In 1887, Congress passed the **Dawes Allotment Act**, dividing up reservations and allotting parcels of land to individual Indians as private property. Each unmarried Indian man and woman as well as married men and children (married women were excluded) became eligible to receive 160 acres of land from reservation property. Indians who took allotments earned U.S. citizenship. To protect Indians from land speculators, the government held most of the allotted land in trust, and the Indians could not sell it for twenty-five years. Since Indian land far surpassed the acreage needed for allotments, the government reserved the right to sell the "surplus" to white settlers.

The Dawes Act effectively reduced Indian land from 138 million acres to a scant 48 million. The legislation, in the words of one critic, worked "to despoil the Indians of their lands and to make them vagabonds on the face of the earth." The Dawes Act completed the dispossession of the western Indian peoples and dealt a crippling blow to traditional tribal culture. Amended in 1891 and again in 1906, it remained in effect until 1934, when the United States restored the right of Native Americans to own land communally (as discussed in chapter 24).

Indian Resistance and Survival

Faced with the extinction of their entire way of life, different groups of Indians responded in different ways in the waning decades of the nineteenth century. In the 1870s, Comanche and Kiowa raiding parties frustrated the U.S. Army by using the reservation at Fort Sill as an asylum, knowing that troops could not pursue them onto reservation land. They brazenly used the reservations as a seasonal supply base during the winter months, taking the meager annuities doled out by the Indian agents, only to resume their nomadic ways when spring came. Soon other tribes followed their lead.

Some tribes, including the Crow, Arikara, Pawnee, and Shoshoni, chose to fight alongside the army against their old enemies, the Sioux. The Crow chief Plenty Coups explained why he allied with the United States: "Not because we loved the white man . . . or because we hated the Sioux . . . but because we plainly saw that this course was the only one which might save our beautiful country for us." The Crow and Shoshoni got to stay in their homelands and avoided the fate of other tribes shipped to reservations far away.

Indians who refused to stay on reservations risked being hunted down — a clear indication that reservations were intended to keep Indians in, not to keep whites out, as the friends of the Indians had intended. The Nez Percé war of 1877 is perhaps the most harrowing example of the army's policy. In 1863, the government dictated a treaty drastically reducing Nez Percé land. Most of the chiefs refused to sign the treaty and did not move to the reservation. In 1877, the army issued an ultimatum — come in to the reservation or be hunted down. Some eight hundred Nez Percé people, many of them women and children, fled across the mountains of Idaho, Wyoming, and Montana, heading for the safety of Canada. At the end of their 1,300-mile trek, 50 miles from freedom, they stopped to rest in the snow. The army's Indian scouts spotted their tepees, and the soldiers attacked. Yellow Wolf recalled their plight: "Children crying with cold. No fire. There could be no light. Everywhere the crying, the death wail." After a five-day siege, the Nez Percé leader, **Chief Joseph**, surrendered.

Chief Joseph
Chief Joseph came to symbolize the heroic resistance of the Nez Percé. General Nelson Miles promised the Nez Percé that they could return to their homeland if they surrendered. But he betrayed them, as he would betray the Apache people seven years later. The Nez Percé were shipped off to Indian Territory (Oklahoma). In 1879, Chief Joseph traveled to Washington, D.C., to speak for his people. "Let me be a free man," he pleaded, "free to choose my own teachers, free to follow the religion of my fathers, free to think and talk and act for myself — and I will obey every law." National Anthropological Archives, Smithsonian Institution, Washington, D.C. (#2906).

His speech, reported by a white soldier, would become famous. "I am tired of fighting," he said as he surrendered his rifle. "Our chiefs are killed. It is cold and we have no blankets. The little children are freezing to death. . . . I am tired.

My heart is sick and sad. From where the sun now stands, I will fight no more forever."

In the Southwest, the Apaches resorted to armed resistance. They roamed the Sonoran Desert of southern Arizona and northern Mexico, perfecting a hit-and-run guerrilla warfare that terrorized white settlers and bedeviled the army in the 1870s and 1880s. General George Crook combined a policy of dogged pursuit with judicious diplomacy. Crook relied on Indian scouts to track the raiding parties, recruiting nearly two hundred, including Apaches, Navajos, and Paiutes. By 1882, Crook had succeeded in persuading most of the Apaches to settle on the San Carlos Reservation in Arizona Territory. A desolate piece of desert inhabited by scorpions and rattlesnakes, San Carlos, in the words of one Apache, was "the worst place in all the great territory stolen from the Apaches."

Geronimo, a respected shaman (medicine man) of the Chiricahua Apache, refused to stay at San Carlos and repeatedly led raiding parties in the early 1880s. His warriors attacked ranches to obtain ammunition and horses. Among Geronimo's band was **Lozen**, a woman who rode with the warriors, armed with a rifle and a cartridge belt. The sister of a great chief who described her as being as "strong as a man, braver than most, and cunning in strategy," Lozen never married and remained a warrior in Geronimo's band even after her brother's death. In the spring of 1885, Geronimo and his followers, including Lozen, went on a ten-month offensive, moving from the Apache sanctuary in the Sierra Madre to raid and burn ranches and towns on both sides of the Mexican border. General Crook caught up with Geronimo in the fall and persuaded him to return to San Carlos, only to have him slip away on the way back to the reservation. Chagrined, Crook resigned his post. General **Nelson Miles**, Crook's replacement, adopted a policy of hunt and destroy.

Geronimo's band of thirty-three Apaches, including women and children, managed to elude Miles's troops for more than five months. In the end, this small band fought two thousand soldiers to a stalemate. After months of pursuit, Lieutenant Leonard Wood, a member of Miles's spit-and-polish cavalry, discarded his horse and most of his clothes until he was reduced to wearing nothing "but a pair of canton flannel drawers, and an old blue blouse, a pair of moccasins and a hat without a crown."

Eventually, Miles's scouts cornered Geronimo in 1886 at Skeleton Canyon. Caught between Mexican regulars and the U.S. Army, Geronimo agreed to march north with the soldiers and

negotiate a settlement. "We have not slept for six months," he admitted, "and we are worn out." Although fewer than three dozen Apaches had been considered "hostile," when General Miles induced them to surrender, the government rounded up nearly five hundred Apaches, including the scouts who had helped track Geronimo, and sent them as prisoners to Florida. By 1889, more than a quarter of them had died, some as a result of illnesses contracted in the damp lowland climate and some by suicide. Their plight roused public opinion, and in 1892 they were moved to Fort Sill in Oklahoma and later to New Mexico.

Geronimo lived to become something of a celebrity. He appeared at the St. Louis Exposition in 1904, and he rode in President Theodore Roosevelt's inaugural parade in 1905. In a newspaper interview, he confessed, "I want to go to my old home before I die. . . . Want to go back to the mountains again. I asked the Great White Father to allow me to go back, but he said no." None of the Apaches were permitted to return to Arizona; when Geronimo died in 1909, he was buried in Oklahoma.

On the plains, many tribes turned to a nonviolent form of resistance — a compelling new religion called the **Ghost Dance**. The Paiute shaman Wovoka, drawing on a cult that had developed in the 1870s, combined elements of Christianity and traditional Indian religion to found the Ghost Dance religion in 1889. Wovoka claimed that he had received a vision in which the Great Spirit spoke through him to all Indians, prophesying that if they would unite in the Ghost Dance ritual, whites would be destroyed in an apocalypse. The shaman promised that Indian warriors slain in battle would return to life and that buffalo once again would roam the land unimpeded. This religion, born of despair and with a message of hope, spread like wildfire over the plains. The Ghost Dance was performed in Idaho, Montana, Utah, Wyoming, Colorado, Nebraska, Kansas, the Dakotas, and Indian Territory by tribes as diverse as the Sioux, Arapaho, Cheyenne, Pawnee, and Shoshoni. Dancers often went into hypnotic trances, dancing until they dropped from exhaustion.

The Ghost Dance was nonviolent, but it frightened whites, especially when the Sioux taught that wearing a white ghost shirt made Indians immune to soldiers' bullets. Soon whites began to fear an uprising. "Indians are dancing in the snow and are wild and crazy," wrote the Bureau of Indian Affairs agent at the Pine Ridge Reservation in South Dakota. Frantic, he pleaded for reinforcements. "We are at the mercy of these dancers. We need protection, and we need it now." President Benjamin Harrison dispatched several thousand federal troops to Sioux country to handle any outbreak.

Ghost Dancers
Arapaho women at the Darlington Agency in Indian Territory (Oklahoma) participate in the Ghost Dance. Different tribes performed variations of the dance, but generally dancers formed a circle and danced until they reached the trance-like state shown here. The ceremonial drum (right) features a drawing of a thunderbird. Whites feared the dancers and demanded that the army dispatch troops to subdue them. The result was the killing of Sitting Bull and the massacre at Wounded Knee.
Ghost Dance: National Anthropological Archives, Smithsonian Institution, Washington, D.C. (#81-9626); Drum: Collection of Charles Stoneroad, Courtesy of the Oakland Museum of California.

In December 1890, when Sitting Bull joined the Ghost Dance, he was killed by Indian police as they tried to arrest him at his cabin on the Standing Rock Reservation. His people, fleeing the scene, joined with a larger group of Miniconjou Sioux, who were apprehended by the Seventh Cavalry, Custer's old regiment, near Wounded Knee Creek, South Dakota. As the Indians laid down their arms, a soldier attempted to take a rifle from a deaf Miniconjou man, and the gun went off. The soldiers opened fire. In the ensuing melee, Indian men, women, and children were mowed down in minutes by the army's brutally efficient Hotchkiss rapid-fire guns. Caught in the crossfire, one Indian recounted, "I saw my friends sinking about me, and heard the whine of many bullets." In a matter of minutes, eighty-three Indian men lay dead. The cavalry then hunted down women and children attempting to flee into the bluffs and canyons. The next day, more than two hundred Sioux lay dead or dying in the snow.

Settler Jules Sandoz surveyed the scene the day after the massacre at **Wounded Knee**. "Here in ten minutes an entire community was as the buffalo that bleached on the plains," he wrote. "There was something loose in the world that hated joy and happiness as it hated brightness and color, reducing everything to drab agony and gray." It had taken Euro-Americans 250 years to wrest control of the eastern half of the United States from the Indians. It took them less than 40 years to take the western half. The subjugation of the American Indians marked the first chapter in a national mission of empire that would presage overseas imperialistic adventures in Asia, Latin America, the Caribbean, and the Pacific islands.

> **REVIEW**   In what ways did different Indian groups defy and resist colonial rule?

▶ Gold Fever and the Mining West

Mining stood at the center of the United States' quest for empire in the West. The California gold rush of 1849 touched off the frenzy. The four decades following witnessed equally frenetic rushes for gold and other metals, most notably on the **Comstock Lode** in Nevada and later in New Mexico, Colorado, the Dakotas, Montana, Idaho, Arizona, and Utah. Each rush built on the last, producing new mining technologies and innovations in financing as hordes of miners,

eager to strike it rich, moved from one boomtown to the next. Mining in the West, however, was a story not only of boom and bust but also of community building and the development of territories into states (Map 17.2).

At first glance, the mining West may seem much different from the East, but by the 1870s the term *urban industrialism* described Virginia City, Nevada, as accurately as it did Pittsburgh or Cleveland. A close look at mining on the Comstock Lode indicates some of the patterns and paradoxes of western mining. The diversity of peoples drawn to the West by the promise of mining riches and land made the region the most cosmopolitan in the nation, as well as the most contested. And a look at territorial government uncovers striking parallels with the corruption and cupidity in politics east of the Mississippi.

Mining on the Comstock Lode

By 1859, refugees from California's played-out goldfields flocked to the Washoe basin in Nevada. There prospectors found the gold they sought mired in blackish sand they called "that blasted blue stuff." Eventually, an enterprising miner had the stuff assayed, and it turned out that the Washoe miners had stumbled on the richest vein of silver ore on the continent — the legendary Comstock Lode, named for prospector Henry Comstock.

To exploit even potentially valuable silver claims required capital and expensive technology well beyond the means of the prospector. An active San Francisco stock market sprang up to finance operations on the Comstock. Shrewd businessmen soon recognized that the easiest way to get rich was not to mine at all but to sell their claims or to form mining companies and sell shares of stock. The most unscrupulous mined the wallets of gullible investors by selling shares in bogus mines. Speculation, misrepresentation, and outright thievery ran rampant. In twenty years, more than $300 million poured from the earth in Nevada alone. A little stayed in Virginia City, but a great deal more went to speculators in California, some of whom got rich without ever leaving San Francisco.

The promise of gold and silver drew thousands to the mines of the West, the honest as well as the unprincipled. As author Mark Twain observed in Virginia City's *Territorial Enterprise*, "All the peoples of the earth had representative adventures in the Silverland." Irish, Chinese, Germans, English, Scots, Welsh, Canadians, Mexicans, Italians, Scandinavians, French, Swiss,

MAP 17.2

Western Mining, 1848–1890

Rich deposits of gold, silver, copper, lead, and iron larded the mountains of the West, from the Sierra Nevada of California to the Rockies of Colorado and the Black Hills of South Dakota. Beginning with the gold strike on Sutter's Creek in California in 1848 and continuing through the rush for gold in Cripple Creek, Colorado, in 1890, miners from all over the world flocked to the West. Few struck it rich, but many stayed on as paid workers in the increasingly mechanized corporate mines.

became Nevada, as many as 30 percent of the people came from outside the United States, compared to 25 percent in New York and 21 percent in Massachusetts.

Irish immigrants formed the largest ethnic group in the mining district. In Virginia City, fully one-third of the population claimed at least one parent from Ireland. Irish and Irish American women constituted the largest group of women on the Comstock. As servants, boarding-house owners, and washerwomen, they made up a significant part of the workforce. By contrast, the Chinese community, numbering 642 in 1870, remained overwhelmingly male. Virulent anti-Chinese sentiment barred the men from work in the mines, but despite the violent anti-Asian rhetoric, the mining community came to depend on Chinese labor. Many boardinghouses and affluent homes employed a Chinese cook or servant along with an Irish parlor maid.

As was so often the case in the West, where Euro-American ambitions clashed with Native American ways, the discovery of precious metals on the Comstock spelled disaster for the Indians. No sooner had the miners struck pay dirt than they demanded that army troops "hunt Indians" and establish forts to protect transportation to and from the diggings. This sudden and dramatic intrusion left Nevada's native tribes — the Northern Paiute and Bannock Shoshoni — exiles in their own land. At first they resisted, but over time they made peace with the invaders and developed resourceful strategies to adapt and preserve their culture and identity despite the havoc wreaked by western mining and settlement.

In 1873, Comstock miners uncovered a new vein of ore, a veritable cavern of gold and silver. This "Big Bonanza" speeded the transition from small-scale industry to corporate oligopoly, creating a radically new social and economic environment. The Comstock became a laboratory for new mining technology. Huge stamping mills pulverized rock with pistonlike hammers driven by steam engines. Enormous Cornish pumps sucked water from the mine shafts, and huge ventilators circulated air in the underground chambers. No backwoods mining camp, Virginia City was an industrial center with more than 1,200 stamping mills working on average a ton of ore every day. Almost 400 men worked in milling, nearly 300 labored in manufacturing

Chileans, and other South and Central Americans came to share in the bonanza. With them came a sprinkling of Russians, Poles, Greeks, Japanese, Spaniards, Hungarians, Portuguese, Turks, Pacific Islanders, and Moroccans, as well as other North Americans, African Americans, and American Indians. This polyglot population, typical of mining boomtowns, made Virginia City in the 1870s more cosmopolitan than New York or Boston. In the part of Utah Territory that eventually

industries, and roughly 3,000 toiled in the mines. The Gould and Curry mine covered sixty acres. Most of the miners who came to the Comstock ended up as laborers for the big companies.

New technology eliminated some of the dangers of mining but often created new ones. In the hard-rock mines of the West, accidents in the 1870s disabled one out of every thirty miners and killed one in eighty. Ross Moudy, who worked as a miner in Cripple Creek, Colorado, recalled how a stockholder visiting the mine nearly fell to his death. The terrified visitor told the miner next to him that "instead of being paid $3 a day, they ought to have all the gold they could take out." Moudy's biggest worry was carbon dioxide, which often filled the tunnels because of poor ventilation. "Many times," he confessed, "I have been carried out unconscious." Those who avoided accidents still breathed air so dangerous that respiratory diseases eventually disabled them.

After a year on the job, Moudy joined a labor union "because I saw it would help me to keep in work and for protection in case of accident or sickness." The union provided good sick benefits and hired nurses, "so if one is alone and sick he is sure to be taken care of." On the Comstock Lode, because of the difficulty of obtaining skilled labor, the richness of the ore, and the need for a stable workforce, labor unions formed early and held considerable bargaining power. Comstock miners commanded $4 a day, the highest wage in the mining West.

The mining towns of the "Wild West" are often portrayed as lawless outposts, filled with saloons and rough gambling dens and populated almost exclusively by men, except for the occasional dance-hall floozy. The truth is more complex, as Virginia City's development attests. An established urban community built to serve an industrial giant, Virginia City in its first decade boasted

"Mining on the Comstock"

This illustration, made at Gold Hill, Nevada, in 1876, shows a sectional view of a mine, highlighting the square-set timber method, an innovation in mining that assembled prefabricated timbers into cubes stacked on cubes that could support virtually any underground chasm. Note also the tunnels, incline, cooling-off room, blower, and air shaft, along with a collection of miner's tools. Mines like the one pictured here honeycombed the hills of Gold City and neighboring Virginia City on the Comstock Lode in Nevada. University of California at Berkeley, Bancroft Library.

churches, schools, theaters, an opera house, and hundreds of families. By 1870, women composed 30 percent of the population, and 75 percent of the women listed their occupation in the census as housekeeper. Mary McNair Mathews, a widow from Buffalo, New York, who lived on the Comstock in the 1870s, worked as a teacher, nurse, seamstress, laundress, and lodging-house operator. She later published a book on her adventures.

By 1875, Virginia City boasted a population of 25,000 people, making it one of the largest cities between St. Louis and San Francisco. A must-see stop on the way west, the "Queen of the Comstock" hosted American presidents as well as legions of lesser dignitaries. No rough outpost of the Wild West, Virginia City represented, in the words of a recent chronicler, "the distilled essence of America's newly established course — urban, industrial, acquisitive, and materialistic, on the move, 'a living polyglot' of cultures that collided and converged."

The Diverse Peoples of the West

The West of the late nineteenth century was indeed a polyglot place, as much so as the big cities of the East. The sheer number of peoples who mingled in the West produced a complex blend of racism and prejudice. One historian has noted, not entirely facetiously, that there were at least eight oppressed "races" in the West — Indians, Latinos, Chinese, Japanese, blacks, Mormons, strikers, and radicals.

African Americans who ventured out to the territories faced hostile settlers determined to keep the West "for whites only." In response, they formed all-black communities such as Nicodemas, Kansas. That settlement, founded by thirty black Kentuckians in 1877, grew to a community of seven hundred by 1880. Isolated and often separated by great distances, small black settlements grew up throughout the West, in Nevada, Utah, and the Pacific Northwest, as well as in Kansas. Black soldiers who served in the West during the Indian wars often stayed on as settlers. Called **buffalo soldiers** because Native Americans thought their hair resembled that of the bison, these black troops numbered up to 25,000. In the face of discrimination, poor treatment, and harsh conditions, the buffalo soldiers served with distinction and boasted the lowest desertion rate in the army.

Hispanic peoples had lived in Texas and the Southwest since Juan de Oñate led pioneer settlers up the Rio Grande in 1598. Hispanics had occupied the Pacific coast since San Diego was founded in 1769. Overnight, they were reduced to a "minority"

after the United States annexed Texas in 1845 and took land stretching to California after the Mexican-American War ended in 1848. At first, the Hispanic owners of large *ranchos* in California, New Mexico, and Texas greeted conquest as an economic opportunity — new markets for their livestock and buyers for their lands. But racial prejudice soon ended their optimism. Californios (Mexican residents of California), who had been granted American citizenship by the Treaty of Guadalupe Hidalgo (1848), faced discrimination by Anglos who sought to keep them out of California's mines and commerce. Whites illegally squatted on *rancho* land while protracted litigation over Spanish and Mexican land grants forced the Californios into court. Although the U.S. Supreme Court eventually validated most of their claims, it took so long — seventeen years on average — that many Californios sold their property to pay taxes and legal bills. The city of Oakland, California, sits on what was once a 19,000-acre ranch owned by the Peralta family, who lost the land to Anglos.

Swindles, chicanery, and intimidation dispossessed scores of Californios. Many ended up segregated in urban barrios (neighborhoods) in their own homeland. Their percentage of California's population declined from 82 percent in 1850 to 19 percent in 1880 as Anglos migrated to the state. In New Mexico and Texas, Mexicans remained a majority of the population but became increasingly impoverished as Anglos dominated business and took the best jobs. Skirmishes between Hispanics and whites in northern New Mexico over the fencing of the open range lasted for decades. Groups of Hispanics with names such as *Las Manos Negras* (the Black Hands) cut fences and burned barns. In Texas, violence along the Rio Grande pitted Tejanos (Mexican residents of Texas) against the Texas Rangers, who saw their role as "keeping Mexicans in their place."

Even more than the Mexicans, the Chinese suffered brutal treatment at the hands of employers and other laborers. Drawn by the promise of gold, more than 20,000 Chinese had joined the rush to California by 1852. Miners determined to keep "California for Americans" succeeded in passing prohibitive foreign license laws to keep the Chinese out of the mines. But Chinese immigration continued. In the 1860s, when white workers moved on to find riches in the bonanza mines of Nevada, Chinese laborers took jobs abandoned by the whites. Railroad magnate Charles Crocker hired Chinese gangs to work on the Central Pacific, reasoning that "the race that built the Great Wall" could lay tracks across the treacherous Sierra Nevada. Some 12,000

Buffalo Soldiers to the Rescue in Colorado
In this painting, artist Frederic Remington portrays the bravery of African American "buffalo soldiers." In 1879 the Ute went on the warpath in Colorado when an Indian agent threatened to destroy their ponies to force them into farming. The Ute killed the whites, and the soldiers pursuing them soon found themselves pinned down and under siege. Captain Francis Dodge and his troop of thirty-five buffalo soldiers rode twenty-three hours to the rescue. Remington's picture is imagined — painted well after the fact. Although Remington spent a stint tracking Geronimo in Arizona for *Harper's Magazine*, he returned to the East and there gained renown for his depictions of the mythic Old West. The Granger Collection, New York.

Chinese, representing 90 percent of Crocker's workforce, completed America's first transcontinental railroad in 1869.

By 1870, more than 63,000 Chinese immigrants lived in America, 77 percent of them in California. A 1790 federal statute that limited naturalization to "white persons" was modified after the Civil War to extend naturalization to blacks ("persons of African descent"). But the Chinese and other Asians continued to be denied access to citizenship. As perpetual aliens, they constituted a reserve army of transnational laborers that many saw as a threat to American labor. For the most part, the Chinese did not displace white workers but instead found work as railroad laborers, cooks, servants, and farmhands while white workers sought out more lucrative fields. In the 1870s, when California and the rest of the nation weathered a major economic depression, the Chinese became easy scapegoats. California workingmen rioted and fought to keep Chinese workers out of the state, claiming they were "coolie labor" — involuntary contract laborers recruited by business interests determined to keep wages at rock bottom.

In 1876, the Workingmen's Party formed to fight for Chinese exclusion. Racial and cultural animosities stood at the heart of anti-Chinese agitation. Denis Kearney, the fiery San Francisco leader of the movement, made clear this racist bent when he urged legislation to "expel every one of the moon-eyed lepers." Nor was California alone in its anti-immigrant nativism. As the country confronted growing ethnic and racial diversity with the rising tide of global immigration in the decades following the Civil War, many questioned the principle of racial equality at the same time they argued against the assimilation of "nonwhite" groups. In this climate, Congress passed the **Chinese Exclusion Act** in 1882, effectively barring Chinese immigration and setting a precedent for further immigration restrictions.

> **"Expel every one of the moon-eyed lepers."**
> — San Francisco leader
> **DENIS KEARNEY, speaking of Chinese immigrants**

Chinese Workers
Chinese section hands, wearing their distinctive conical hats, are shown here in 1898 shoveling dirt for the North Pacific Coast Railroad in Corte Madera, California. Charles Crocker was the first railroad executive to hire Chinese laborers to work on the Central Pacific railroad in the 1860s, reasoning that the race that built the Great Wall could build tracks through the Sierra Nevada. California Historical Society, FN-25345.

The Chinese Exclusion Act led to a sharp drop in the Chinese population — from 105,465 in 1880 to 89,863 in 1900 — because Chinese immigrants, overwhelmingly male, did not have families to sustain their population. Eventually, Japanese immigrants, including women as well as men, replaced the Chinese, particularly in agriculture. As "nonwhite" immigrants, they could not become naturalized citizens, but their children born in the United States claimed the rights of citizenship. Japanese parents, seeking to own land, purchased it in their children's names. Although anti-Asian prejudice remained strong in California and elsewhere in the West, Asian immigrants formed an important part of the economic fabric of the western United States.

The Mormons, who had fled west to Utah Territory in 1844 to avoid religious persecution, established Salt Lake City, a thriving metropolis of more than 150,000 residents by 1882. To counter criticism of the Mormon practice of polygamy (church leader Brigham Young had twenty-seven wives), the Utah territorial legislature gave women the right to vote in 1870, the first universal woman suffrage act in the nation. (Wyoming had granted suffrage to white women in 1869.) Although woman's rights advocates argued that the newly enfranchised women would "do away with the horrible institution of polygamy," it remained in force. Not until 1890 did the church hierarchy yield to pressure and renounce polygamy. The fierce controversy over polygamy postponed statehood for Utah until 1896.

Territorial Government

The federal government practiced a policy of benign neglect when it came to territorial government in the West. The president appointed a governor, a secretary, and two to four judges, along with an attorney and a marshal. In Nevada Territory, that meant that a handful of officials governed an area the size of New England. Originally a part of the larger Utah Territory, Nevada, propelled by mining interests, moved on the fast track to statehood, entering the Union in 1864, long before its population or its development merited statehood.

More typical were the territories extant in 1870 — New Mexico, Utah, Washington, Colorado, Dakota, Arizona, Idaho, Montana, and Wyoming. These areas remained territories for inordinately long periods ranging from twenty-three to sixty-two years. While awaiting statehood, they were subject to territorial governors who were underpaid, often unqualified, and largely ignored in Washington. Most territorial governors won their posts because of party loyalty and had little knowledge of the areas they served, little notions of their duties, and limited ability to perform them.

In theory, territorial governors received adequate salaries, as high as $3,500 in an era when the average workingman earned less than $500 a year. In practice, the funds rarely arrived in a timely fashion, and more than one governor found that he had to pay government expenses out of his own pocket. As one cynic observed, "Only the rich or those having 'no visible means of support,' can afford to accept office." John C. Frémont, the governor of Arizona Territory, complained he was so poor that he could not inspect the Grand Canyon because he didn't have money to keep a horse.

Territorial governors with fewer scruples accepted money from special interests — mine owners and big ranchers. Nearly all territorial appointees tried to make ends meet by maintaining business connections with the East or by taking advantage of investment opportunities in the West. Distance and the lack of funds made it difficult to summon officers from Washington to investigate charges of corruption. Officials who ventured west to look into such charges often felt intimidated by gun-packing westerners. One judge sent to New Mexico Territory in 1871 reported that he "stayed three days, made up his mind that it would be dangerous to do any investigating, . . . and returned to his home without any action." Underfunded and overlooked, victims of political cronyism, and prey to special interests, territorial governments were rife with conflicts of interest and corruption, mirroring the self-serving political and economic values of the country as a whole in the rush for riches that followed the Civil War.

REVIEW How did industrial technology change mining in Nevada?

▶ Land Fever

In the three decades following 1870, more land was settled than in all the previous history of the country. Americans by the hundreds of thousands packed up and moved west, goaded if not by the hope of striking gold, then by the promise of owning land. The agrarian West shared with the mining West a persistent restlessness, an equally pervasive addiction to speculation, and a penchant for exploiting natural resources and labor.

Two factors stimulated the land rush in the trans-Mississippi West. The **Homestead Act of 1862** promised 160 acres free to any citizen or

Admission of States in the Trans-Mississippi West

Year	State	Year	State
1821	Missouri	1889	North Dakota
1836	Arkansas	1889	South Dakota
1845	Texas	1889	Montana
1846	Iowa	1889	Washington
1850	California	1890	Idaho
1858	Minnesota	1890	Wyoming
1859	Oregon	1896	Utah
1861	Kansas	1907	Oklahoma
1864	Nevada	1912	New Mexico
1867	Nebraska	1912	Arizona
1876	Colorado		

prospective citizen, male or female, who settled on the land for five years. Even more important, **transcontinental railroads** opened up new areas and actively recruited settlers. After the completion of the first transcontinental railroad in 1869, homesteaders abandoned the covered wagon, and by the 1880s they could choose from four competing rail lines and make the trip west in a matter of days.

Although the country was rich in land and resources, not all who wanted to own land achieved their goal. During the transition from the family farm to large commercial farming, small farms gave way to vast spreads worked by migrant labor or paid farmworkers. Just as industry corporatized and consolidated in the East, the period from 1870 to 1900 witnessed corporate consolidation in mining, ranching, and agriculture.

Moving West: Homesteaders and Speculators

A Missouri homesteader remembered packing as her family pulled up stakes and headed west to Oklahoma in 1890. "We were going to God's Country," she wrote. "You had to work hard on that rocky country in Missouri. I was glad to be leaving it. . . . We were going to a new land and get rich."

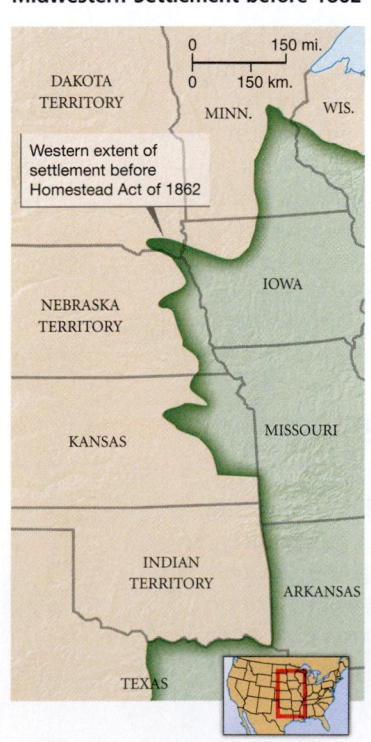

Norwegian Immigrant and Sod House
Norwegian immigrant Beret Olesdater sits in front of her sod house in Lac qui Parle, Minnesota, in 1896. On the plains, where trees were scarce and lumber was often prohibitively expensive, settlers built with the materials at hand. The dugout was the most primitive dwelling, carved into a hillside. Huts cut from blocks of sod, like the one pictured here, marked a step up. Life for women on the plains proved especially lonely and hard. © Minnesota Historical Society/ Corbis.

People who ventured west searching for "God's Country" faced hardship, loneliness, and deprivation. To carve a farm from the raw prairie of Iowa, the plains of Nebraska, or the forests of the Pacific Northwest took more than fortitude and backbreaking toil. It took luck. Blizzards, tornadoes, grasshoppers, hailstorms, drought, prairie fires, accidental death, and disease were only a few of the catastrophes that could befall even the best farmer. Homesteaders on free land still needed as much as $1,000 for a house, a team of farm animals, a well, fencing, and seed. Poor farmers called "sodbusters" did without even these basics, living in dugouts carved into hillsides and using muscle instead of machinery.

"Father made a dugout and covered it with willows and grass," one Kansas girl recounted. When it rained, the dugout flooded, and "we carried the water out in buckets, then waded around in the mud until it dried." Rain wasn't the only problem. "Sometimes the bull snakes would get in the roof and now and then one would lose his hold and fall down on the bed. . . . Mother would grab the hoe . . . and after the fight was over Mr. Bull Snake was dragged outside." The sod house, a step up from the dugout, had walls cut from blocks of sod and a roof of sod, lumber, or tin. (See "Documenting the American Promise," page 558.)

For women on the frontier, obtaining simple daily necessities such as water and fuel meant backbreaking labor. Out on the plains, where water was scarce, women often had to trudge to the nearest creek or spring. "A yoke was made to place across [Mother's] shoulders, so as to carry at each end a bucket of water," one daughter recollected, "and then water was brought a half mile from spring to house." Gathering fuel was another heavy chore. Without ready sources of coal or firewood, settlers on the plains turned to what substitutes they could scavenge — twigs, tufts of grass, corncobs, sunflower stalks. But by far the most prevalent fuel was "chips" — chunks of dried cattle and buffalo dung, found in abundance on the plains.

Despite the hardships, some homesteaders succeeded in building comfortable lives. The sod hut made way for a more substantial house; the log cabin yielded to a white clapboard home with a porch and a rocking chair. For others, the promise of the West failed to materialize. Already by the 1870s, much of the best land had been taken. Too often, homesteaders found that only the least desirable tracts were left — poor land, far from markets, transportation, and society. "There is plenty of land for sale in California," one migrant complained in 1870, but "the majority of the available lands are held by speculators, at prices far beyond the reach of a poor man." The railroads, flush from land grants provided by the state and federal governments, owned huge swaths of land in the West and actively recruited settlers. Altogether, the land grants totaled approximately 180 million acres — an area almost one-tenth the size of the United States (Map 17.3). Of the 2.5 million farms established between 1860 and 1900,

Midwestern Settlement before 1862

homesteading accounted for only one in five; the vast majority of farmland sold for a profit.

As land grew scarce on the prairie in the 1870s, farmers began to push farther west, moving into western Kansas, Nebraska, and eastern Colorado — the region called the **Great American Desert** by settlers who had passed over it on their way to California and Oregon. Many agricultural experts warned that the semiarid land (where less than twenty inches of rain fell annually) would not support a farm on the 160 acres allotted to homesteaders. But their words of caution were drowned out by the extravagant claims of western promoters, many employed by the railroads to sell off their land grants. "Rain follows the plow" became the slogan of western boosters, who insisted that cultivation would alter the climate of the region and bring more rainfall. Instead, drought followed the plow. Droughts were a cyclical fact of life on the Great Plains. Plowed up, the dry topsoil blew away in the wind. A period of relatively good rainfall in the early 1880s encouraged farming; then a protracted drought in the late 1880s and early 1890s sent starving farmers reeling back from the plains. Thousands left, some in wagons carrying the slogan "In God we trusted, in Kansas we busted."

Fever for fertile land set off a series of spectacular land runs in Oklahoma. When two million acres of land in former Indian Territory opened for settlement in 1889, thousands of homesteaders massed on the border. At the opening pistol shot, "with a shout and a yell the swift riders shot out, then followed the light buggies or wagons," a reporter wrote. "Above all, a great cloud of dust hover[ed] like smoke over a battlefield." By nightfall, Oklahoma boasted two tent cities with more than ten thousand residents. In the last frenzied land rush on Oklahoma's Cherokee strip in 1893, several settlers were killed in the stampede, and nervous men guarded their claims with rifles. As public land grew scarce, the hunger for land grew fiercer for both farmers and ranchers.

Ranchers and Cowboys

Cattle ranchers followed the railroads onto the plains, establishing a cattle kingdom from Texas to Wyoming between 1865 and 1885. Cowboys drove huge herds, as many as three thousand head of cattle that grazed on public lands as they followed cattle tracks like the Chisholm Trail from Texas to railheads in Kansas. More than 1.5 million Texas longhorns went to market before the range began to close in the 1880s.

Barbed wire revolutionized the cattle business and sounded the death knell for the open range. In 1874, Joseph F. Glidden, an Illinois sheriff, invented and patented barbed wire. Gambler and promoter John "Bet a Million" Gates made his fortune by corralling a herd of Texas longhorns in downtown San Antonio, proving the merit of the flimsy-looking wire he went on to market profitably. As the largest ranches in Texas began to fence, nasty fights broke out between big ranchers and "fence cutters," who resented the end of the free

Railroad Locomotive
In the years following the Civil War, the locomotive replaced the covered wagon, enabling settlers to travel from Chicago or St. Louis to the West Coast in two days. By the 1890s, more than 72,000 miles of track stretched west of the Mississippi River. The first transcontinental railroad, completed in 1869, soon led to the creation of competing systems, so that by the 1880s travelers going west could choose from four railroad lines. In this photograph, men and women perched on a locomotive celebrate the completion of a section of track. Library of Congress.

Cattle Trails, 1860–1890

Young Women Homesteaders and the Promise of the West

"**Y**oung men! Poor men! Widows! Resolve to have a home of your own!" urged New York editor Horace Greeley. "If you are able to buy and pay for one in the East, very well; if not, make one in the broad and fertile West!" In his exhortation to go west, Greeley did not speak to men alone. Many women, and not just widows, heeded the call. The Homestead Act of 1862 allowed unmarried women and female heads of households to claim free land. Many did. The number of women establishing homesteads in the West ranged from 5 percent of homesteaders in the early settlements to more than 20 percent after 1900.

Among the women homesteaders were Clara and Mary Troska and their two cousins Helen and Christine Sonnek, who headed to North Dakota. "Mary, Helen, Christine and I packed our suitcases," Clara wrote. "I took my mandolin, Christine took hers and her rifle. . . . We were on our way to Minot." Young women like Clara between the ages of twenty-one and twenty-five constituted the largest percentage of women (53 percent) taking up claims in the Dakotas.

Like Christine Sonnek, who took her mandolin along with her rifle, homesteading women prepared to enjoy their new environment despite its challenges. Their letters, diaries, and reminiscences reveal not only the hardships they faced but also the sense of promise that lured them west. Adventurous, resourceful, and exuberant, many of these young homesteading women seemed to relish their experiences.

DOCUMENT 1
The Varied Activities of a Woman Homesteader

Dakota homesteader Bess Cobb's letter to a friend reveals the optimism and high spirits that energized the young women who filed homesteading claims.

Suppose you girls are saying "poor Bess" and feeling dreadfully sorry for me out here in the wild and wooly uncivilized regions of America. But really time just seems to fly. I haven't done half I had planned and I am afraid winter will be here before we are ready for it. I've sewed some, done a little fancy-work and lots of darning and mending but most of my time has been spent out of doors digging in the garden and riding. . . . You can see a team miles away — up one valley we can see ten miles, up to the Cannon Ball river — so when any one starts to our shack, if we see them in time we can comb our hair, change our gowns and get a good meal in running order before they arrive. You see Dakota has some redeeming qualities. Wish you could come out, but I suppose you think I am too far away. I have the neatest little shack I've ever seen and "my crops" are tip top. I know you would enjoy our camp life for a short time.

SOURCE: "Excerpts from a letter written by Bess Cobb, Guide to Manuscripts 1364, State Historical Society, North Dakota Heritage Center, Bismarck," from pages 140–41 in *Land in Her Own Name: Women as Homesteaders in North Dakota* by H. Elaine Lindgren. Copyright © 1996. Reprinted with permission of University of Oklahoma Press.

DOCUMENT 2
A Hard Winter

Lucy Goldthorpe, a young schoolteacher, came from Iowa to Dakota in 1905. Here she describes to a reporter her survival during the winter and contrasts her childhood fantasies with homestead reality.

There were many long, cold days and nights in my little homestead shack that winter! The walls were only single board thickness, covered with tar paper on the outside. I'd spent money sparingly, because I didn't have much, but I had worked hard all during summer and fall in an effort to winterize the structure. Following the pattern used by many of the settlers, I covered the interior walls with a blue building paper. Everything was covered, including the ceiling, and the floor. To help seal out the cold I'd added layers of gunny sacks over the paper on the floor and then the homemade wool rugs I'd shipped from home.

Regardless of what I did the cold crept in through the thin walls. With no storm entry at the door and only single windows my little two-lid laundry stove with oven attached to the pipe had a real struggle to keep the place livable. . . .

A neighbor family returning to their claim "from the outside" brought me fresh vegetables. They were such a prized addition to my meals that I put the bag in bed with me at night to keep them from freezing. Night after night I stored food and my little alarm clock in the stove pipe oven; that was the only way I could keep the clock running and be sure of a non-frozen breakfast.

Each day brought new, unexpected challenges and at times I wondered if I would be able to stay with it until the land was mine. Could any land be worth the lonely hours and hardships? The howling wind and driving snow, the mournful wail of coyotes searching the tormented land for food did nothing to make the winter any more pleasant. . . .

As a child I had enjoyed hearing my father tell of the hardships of the early days. They seemed so exciting to me as I listened in the warmth and security of our well built, fully winterized Iowa home. Like most youngsters I'd wished for the thrill of those other days. Little did I think that an opportunity for just that would come through homesteading alone, far out in the windswept, unsettled land. Believe me, it wasn't nearly as glamorous as the imagination would have it!

SOURCE: Roberta M. Starry, "Petticoat Pioneer." Excerpt from page 48 in *The West* 7, no. 5, October 1967. Copyright © 1967. Reprinted with permission.

DOCUMENT 3
Socializing and Entertainment

Homesteading wasn't all hard times. Young, single homesteaders found time for fun. Here Effie Vivian Smith describes a "shack party" during the winter of 1906 on her Dakota claim.

I never enjoyed myself better in my life than I have this winter. We go some place or some one is here from 1 to 4 times a week. A week ago last Fri. a load of 7 drove out to my claim. Cliff, Clara, David, and I had gone out the Wed. before and such a time as we had. My shack is 10 feet 3 inches by 16 feet and I have only 2 chairs and a long bench for seats, a table large enough for 6, a single bed, and only 3 knives so 2 of them ate with paring knives & 1 with the butcher knife. We had two of them sit on the bed and moved the table up to them. . . . We played all the games we could think of both quiet and noisy and once all but Clara went out & snowballed. They brought a

bu[shel] of apples, & a lot of nuts, candy, & gum & we ate all night. . . .

We have just started a literary society in our neighborhood. Had our first debate last Fri. The question was Resolved that city life is better than country life. All the judges decided in the negative. . . . Tomorrow our crowd is going to a literary [society] 6 or 7 miles from here, and the next night to a dance at the home of one of our bachelor boys. We always all go in our sleigh. I am learning to dance this winter but don't attend any except the ones we get up ourselves and they are just as nice & just as respectable as the parties we used to have at Ruthven [Iowa]. I just love to dance. . . .

SOURCE: H. Elaine Lindgren, "Letter to her cousin, written on January 9, 1906." From pages 177–78 in *Land in Her Own Name: Women as Homesteaders in North Dakota*. Copyright © 1996 University of Oklahoma Press. Reprinted with permission.

DOCUMENT 4
Homesteading Pays Off

Homesteading proved rewarding for many women, not only economically but also because of the sense of accomplishment they experienced. Here Theona Carkin tells how the sale of her Dakota homestead helped finance her university degree.

Life in general was dotted with hardships but there were many good times also. I have always felt that my efforts on my homestead were very worthwhile and very rewarding, and I have always been proud of myself for doing it all.

By teaching off and on . . . and upon selling the homestead, I was able to pay all my own college expenses.

SOURCE: "99-Year-Old U Graduate Recalls Early Childhood." From page 5 in *Alumni Review*, June 1985. Published by the University of North Dakota, Grand Forks.

Questions for Analysis and Debate

1. What sorts of hardships did the young women homesteaders encounter in the Dakotas?

2. How did their youth affect how they reacted to hardship?

3. What did the young women find particularly appealing about their experiences as homesteaders?

4. What did they wish to convey about their experiences?

5. How did homesteading benefit women who chose not to remain on the land?

MAP ACTIVITY

Map 17.3   Federal Land Grants to Railroads and the Development of the West, 1850–1900
Generous federal land grants meant that railroads could sell the desirable land next to the track at a profit
or hold it for speculation. Railroads received more than 180 million acres, an area as large as Texas. Built
well ahead of demand, the western railroads courted settlers, often onto land not fit for farming.

READING THE MAP: Which mining cities and towns were located directly on a railroad line? Which towns
were located at the junction of more than one line or railroad branch?
CONNECTIONS: In what ways did the growth of the railroads affect the population of the West? What
western goods and products did the railroads help bring east and to ports for shipping around the world?

range. One old-timer observed, "Those persons,
Mexicans and Americans, without land but who
had cattle were put out of business by fencing."
Fencing forced small-time ranchers
who owned land but could not
afford to buy barbed wire or
sink wells to sell out for the
best price they could get. The
displaced ranchers, many of them Mexicans,
ended up as wageworkers on the huge spreads
owned by Anglos or by European syndicates.

On the range, the cowboy gave way to the
cattle king and, like the miner, became a wage
laborer. Many cowboys were African Americans
(as many as five thousand in Texas alone). Writers
of western literature chose to ignore the presence
of black cowboys like Deadwood Dick (Nat Love),
who was portrayed as a white man in the dime
novels of the era.

By 1886, cattle overcrowded the range. Severe
blizzards during the winter of 1886–87 decimated
the herds. "A whole generation of cowmen," wrote

THE PROMISE OF TECHNOLOGY

Barbed Wire

The original working model of Joseph Glidden's barbing machine, patented in 1874, consisted of an old-fashioned coffee mill with its casing cut away and its grinder altered to cut and coil small lengths of wire. The barbs were strung by hand between strands of plain wire. Despite its flimsiness, barbed wire could contain cattle, as master promoter John "Bet a Million" Gates demonstrated by corralling a herd of Texas longhorns in downtown San Antonio in 1879. How did barbed wire transform cattle ranching in the West? Ellwood House Museum, De Kalb, IL.

one chronicler, "went dead broke." Fencing worsened the situation. During blizzards, cattle stayed alive by keeping on the move. But when they ran up against barbed wire fences, they froze to death. In the aftermath of the "Great Die Up," new labor-intensive forms of cattle ranching replaced the open-range model.

Tenants, Sharecroppers, and Migrants

In the post–Civil War period, as agriculture became a big business tied by the railroads to national and global markets, an increasing number of laborers worked land that they would never own. In the southern United States, farmers labored under particularly heavy burdens. The Civil War wiped out much of the region's capital, which had been invested in slaves, and crippled the plantation economy. Newly freed slaves rarely obtained land of their own and often ended up as farm laborers. "The colored folks stayed with the old boss man and farmed and worked on the plantations," a black Alabama sharecropper observed bitterly. "They were still slaves, but they were free slaves." Some freedpeople did manage to pull together enough resources to go west. In 1879, more than fifteen thousand black **Exodusters** moved from Mississippi and Louisiana to take up land in Kansas.

California's Mexican cowboys, or *vaqueros*, commanded decent wages throughout the Southwest. Skilled horsemen, the vaqueros boasted that five of them could do the work of thirty Anglo cowboys. The vocabulary of ranching, with words such as *rodeo*, *lasso*, and *lariat*, testified to the centrality of the vaqueros' place in the cattle industry. But by 1880, as the coming of the railroads ended the long cattle drives and as large feedlots began to replace the open range, the value of their skills declined. Many vaqueros ended up as migrant laborers, often on land their families had once owned. Similarly, in Texas, Tejanos found themselves displaced. After the heyday of cattle ranching ended in the late 1880s, cotton production rose in the southeastern regions of the state. Ranchers turned their pastures into sharecroppers' plots and hired displaced cowboys, most of them Mexicans, as seasonal laborers for as little as seventy-five cents a day, thereby creating a growing army of agricultural wageworkers.

Land monopoly and large-scale farming fostered tenancy and migratory labor on the West Coast. By the 1870s, less than 1 percent of California's population owned half the state's available agricultural land. The rigid economics of large-scale commercial agriculture and the seasonal nature of the crops spawned a ragged army of migratory agricultural laborers. Derisively labeled "blanket men" or "bindle stiffs," these transients worked the fields in the growing season and wintered in the flophouses of San Francisco. Most farm laborers were Chinese immigrants. After passage of the Chinese Exclusion Act of 1882, Mexicans, Filipinos, and Japanese immigrants filled the demand for migratory workers.

A Vaquero
Rafael "Chappo" Remudas is pictured here in Burns, Oregon, around 1890. He came as a vaquero to the high desert in 1872 and became boss of the P Ranch, handing down his skills to a new generation of white "buckaroos," who replaced the vaqueros. Chappo proudly sits his horse, surrounded by the tools of his trade: his lasso wound tightly around his saddle horn, his kerchief tied at his neck, *tapederos* (covered stirrups to protect his feet), heavy leggings, a flat-crowned sombrero, and his silver-mounted bridle.
Photo courtesy of the Harney County Historical Society, Burns, OR.

Commercial Farming and Industrial Cowboys

In the late nineteenth century, the population of the United States remained overwhelmingly rural. The 1870 census showed that nearly 80 percent of the nation's people lived on farms and in villages of fewer than 8,000 inhabitants. By 1900, the figure had dropped to 66 percent (Figure 17.1). At the same time, the number of farms rose. Rapid growth in the West increased the number of the nation's farms from 2 million in 1860 to more than 5.7 million in 1900.

Despite the hardships individual farmers experienced, new technology and farming techniques revolutionized American farm life. Mechanized farm machinery halved the time and labor cost of production and made it possible to cultivate vast tracts of land. Meanwhile, urbanization provided farmers with expanding markets for their produce, and railroads carried crops to markets thousands of miles away. Even before the start of the twentieth century, American agriculture had entered the era of what would come to be called agribusiness — farming as a big business — with the advent of huge commercial farms.

As farming moved onto the prairies and plains, mechanization took command. Steel plows, reapers, mowers, harrows, seed drills, combines, and threshers replaced human muscle. Horse-drawn implements gave way to steam-powered machinery. By 1880, a single combine could do the work of twenty men, vastly increasing the acreage a farmer could cultivate. Mechanization spurred the growth of bonanza wheat farms, some more than 100,000 acres, in California and

FIGURE 17.1 Changes in Rural and Urban Populations, 1870–1900
Between 1870 and 1900, both the number of urban dwellers and the number of farms increased, even as the number of rural inhabitants fell. Mechanization made it possible to farm with fewer hands, fueling the exodus from farm to city throughout the second half of the nineteenth century.

Mechanical Corn Planter
Mechanical planters came into use in the 1860s. The Farmers Friend Manufacturing Company of Dayton, Ohio, advertised its lever and treadle corn planter in the early 1880s. Although this planter, which featured attachments for grain drilling and fertilizing, appears to have been designed to be drawn by farm animals, steam-powered farm implements would soon replace animal power. Notice how the female figure on the left, symbolizing the bucolic farm life, is offset by the company's impressive factory in Dayton on the right.
Ohio Historical Society.

the Red River Valley of North Dakota and Minnesota. This agricultural revolution meant that Americans raised more than four times the corn, five times the hay, and seven times the wheat and oats they had before the Civil War.

Like cotton farmers in the South, western grain and livestock farmers increasingly depended on foreign markets for their livelihood. A fall in global market prices meant that a farmer's entire harvest went to pay off debts. In the depression that followed the panic of 1893, many heavily mortgaged farmers lost their land to creditors. As a Texas cotton farmer complained, "By the time the World Gets their Liveing out of the Farmer as we have to Feed the World, we the Farmer has nothing Left but a Bear Hard Liveing." Commercial farming, along with mining, represented another way in which the West developed its own brand of industrialism. The far West's industrial economy sprang initially from California gold and the vast territory that came under American control following the Mexican-American War. In the ensuing rush on land and resources, environmental factors interacted with economic and social forces to produce enterprises as vast in scale and scope as anything found in the East.

Two Alsatian immigrants, Henry Miller and Charles Lux, pioneered the West's mix of agriculture and industrialism. Beginning as meat wholesalers, Miller and Lux quickly expanded their business to encompass cattle, land, and land reclamation projects such as dams and irrigation systems. With a labor force of migrant workers, a highly coordinated corporate system, and large sums of investment capital, the firm of **Miller & Lux** became one of America's industrial behemoths. Eventually, these "industrial cowboys" grazed a herd of 100,000 cattle on 1.25 million acres of company land in California, Oregon, and Nevada and employed more than 1,200 migrant laborers on their corporate ranches. Miller & Lux dealt with the labor problem by offering free meals to migratory workers, thus keeping wages low while winning goodwill among an army of unemployed who competed for the work. When the company's Chinese cooks rebelled at washing the dishes resulting from the free meals, the migrant laborers were forced to eat

Loggers in Washington, 1890
Loggers pose on and beside one huge felled tree. The loggers worked in all-male crews with a "faller" cutting down the tree, "buckers" cutting it into manageable pieces, and "whistle punks" relaying information. By 1890, loggers using only axes and handsaws had harvested over one billion board feet of timber in the state of Washington alone. The massive deforestation continued and picked up speed as steam power replaced brawn and horse-power. Loggers lived a hard, dirty life in remote migratory camps, working long hours and sometimes wearing the same clothes for months on end. ©Bettmann/Corbis.

after the ranch hands and use their dirty plates. By the 1890s, more than eight hundred migrants a year followed what came to be known as the "Dirty Plate Route" on Miller & Lux ranches throughout California.

Since the days of Thomas Jefferson, agrarian life had been linked with the highest ideals of a democratic society. Now agrarianism itself had been transformed. The farmer was no longer a self-sufficient yeoman but often a businessman or a wage laborer tied to a global market. And even as farm production soared, industrialization outstripped it. More and more farmers left the fields for urban factories or found work in the "factories in the fields" of the new industrialized agribusiness. Now that the future seemed to lie not with the small farmer but with industrial enterprises, was democracy itself at risk? This question would ignite a farmers' revolt in the 1880s and dominate political debate in the 1890s.

REVIEW Why did many homesteaders find it difficult to acquire good land in the West?

▶ Conclusion: The West in the Gilded Age

In 1871, author Mark Twain published *Roughing It*, a chronicle of his days spent in mining towns in California and Nevada. There he found corrupt politics, vulgar display, and mania for speculation, the same cupidity he later skewered in *The Gilded Age* (1873), his biting satire of greed and corruption in the nation's capital. Far from being an antidote to the meretricious values of the East — an innocent idyll out of place and time — the American West, with its get-rich-quick ethos and its addiction to gambling and speculation, helped set the tone for the Gilded Age.

Twain's view countered that of Frederick Jackson Turner and perhaps better suited a West that witnessed the overbuilding of railroads, the consolidation of business in mining and ranching; the rise of commercial farming; corruption and a penchant for government handouts; racial animosity, whether in the form of Indian wars or Chinese exclusion; the exploitation of labor and natural resources, which led to the decimation of the great bison herds, the pollution of rivers with mining wastes, and the overgrazing of the plains; and the beginnings of an imperial policy that would provide a template for U.S. adventures abroad. Turner, intent on promoting what was unique about the frontier, failed to note that the same issues that came to dominate debate east of the Mississippi — the growing power of big business, the exploitation of land and labor, corruption in politics, and ethnic and racial tensions exacerbated by colonial expansion and unparalleled immigration — took center stage in the West at the end of the nineteenth century.

▶ Selected Bibliography

General

Najia Aarin-Heriot, *Chinese Immigrants, African Americans, and Racial Anxiety in the United States, 1848–1882* (2003).

Robert V. Hine and John Mack Faragher, *The American West: A New Interpretive History* (2000).

Patricia Nelson Limerick, *Something in the Soil: Legacies and Reckonings in the New West* (2000).

Valerie Matsumoto and Blake Allmendinger, eds., *Over the Edge: Remapping the American West* (1999).

Louis S. Warren, *Buffalo Bill's America: William Cody and the Wild West Show* (2005).

Richard White, *"It's Your Misfortune and None of My Own": A New History of the American West* (1991).

Richard White, *Railroaded: The Transcontinentals and the Making of Modern America* (2011).

David M. Wrobel, *Promised Lands: Promotion, Memory, and the Creation of the American West* (2002).

Indians

David Wallace Adams, *Education for Extinction: American Indians and the Boarding School Experience, 1875–1928* (1995).

Gary Clayton Anderson, *The Conquest of Texas: Ethnic Cleansing in the Promised Land, 1820–1875* (2005).

Stuart Banner, *How the Indians Lost Their Land: Law and Power on the Frontier* (2005).

Ned Blackhawk, *Violence over the Land: Indian Empires in the Early American West* (2006).

Colin Calloway, *First Peoples: A Documentary Survey of American Indian History* (3rd ed., 2008).

James O. Gump, *The Dust Rose like Smoke: The Subjugation of the Zulu and the Sioux* (1994).

Pekka Hamalainen, *The Comanche Empire* (2008).

Andrew C. Isenberg, *The Destruction of the Bison: An Environmental History, 1730–1920* (2000).

Edward Lazarus, *Black Hills, White Justice: The Sioux Nation versus the United States, 1775 to the Present* (1991).

Jeffrey Ostler, *The Plains Sioux and U.S. Colonialism from Lewis and Clark to Wounded Knee* (2004).

Nathaniel Philbrick, *The Last Stand: Custer, Sitting Bull, and the Battle of the Little Bighorn* (2010).

Francis Paul Prucha, *The Great Father: The United States Government and the American Indian* (1986).

Charles M. Robinson III, *A Good Year to Die: The Story of the Great Sioux War* (1995).

Alan Trachtenberg, *Shades of Hiawatha: Staging Indians, Making Americans, 1880–1930* (2004).

Mining, Ranching, and Farming

Suchen Chan, *This Bittersweet Soil: The Chinese in American Agriculture, 1860–1919* (1986).

Suchen Chan, Douglas Henry Daniels, Mario T. Garcia, and Terry P. Wilson, *Peoples of Color in the American West* (1994).

Roger Daniels, *Asian American: Chinese and Japanese in the United States since 1850* (1997).

Deborah Fitzgerald, *Every Farm a Factory: The Industrial Ideal in American Agriculture* (2003).

Manuel G. Gonzales, *Mexicanos: A History of Mexicans in the United States* (1999).

J. S. Holliday, *Rush for Riches: Gold Fever and the Making of California* (1999).

David Igler, *Industrial Cowboys: Miller & Lux and the Transformation of the Far West, 1850–1920* (2001).

Andrew C. Isenberg, *Mining California: An Ecological History* (2005).

Ronald M. James, *The Roar and the Silence: The History of Virginia City and the Comstock Lode* (1998).

William Loren Katz, *Black West: A Documentary and Pictorial History of the African American Role in the Westward Expansion of the United States* (2005).

Karen R. Merrill, *Public Lands and Political Meaning: Ranchers, the Government, and the Property between Them* (2002).

Rodman Wilson Paul, *Mining Frontiers of the Far West, 1848–1880* (rev. ed., 2001).

William G. Robbins, *Colony and Empire: The Capitalist Transformation of the American West* (1994).

Steven Stoll, *Larding the Lean Earth: Soil and Society in Nineteenth-Century America* (2002).

FOR MORE BOOKS ABOUT TOPICS IN THIS CHAPTER, see the Online Bibliography at bedfordstmartins.com/roark.

FOR ADDITIONAL PRIMARY SOURCES FROM THIS PERIOD, see Michael Johnson, ed., *Reading the American Past*, Fifth Edition.

FOR WEB SITES, IMAGES, AND DOCUMENTS RELATED TO TOPICS AND PLACES IN THIS CHAPTER, visit Make History at bedfordstmartins.com/roark.

Reviewing Chapter 17

REVIEW QUESTIONS

Use key terms and dates to support your answer.

1. How did the slaughter of the bison contribute to the Plains Indians' removal to reservations? (pp. 537–544)

2. In what ways did different Indian groups defy and resist colonial rule? (pp. 544–559)

3. How did industrial technology change mining in Nevada? (pp. 549–555)

4. Why did many homesteaders find it difficult to acquire good land in the West? (pp. 555–564)

MAKING CONNECTIONS

Draw on key terms, the timeline, and review questions.

1. Westward migration brought settlers into conflict with Native Americans. What was the U.S. government's policy toward Indians in the West, and how did it evolve over time? How did the Indians resist and survive white encroachment? In your answer, discuss the cultural and military features of the conflict.

2. The economic and industrial developments characteristic of the East after the Civil War also made their mark on the West. How did innovations in business and technology transform mining and agriculture in the West? In your answer, be sure to consider effects on production and the consequences for the lives of miners and agricultural laborers.

3. Settlers from all over the world came to the American West seeking their fortunes but found that opportunity was not equally available to all. In competition for work and land, why did Anglo-American settlers usually have the upper hand? How did legal developments contribute to this circumstance?

4. Railroads had a profound impact on the development of the western United States. What role did railroads play in western settlement, industrialization, and agriculture? How did railroads affect Indian populations in the West?

LINKING TO THE PAST

Link events in this chapter to earlier events.

1. In what ways were the goals of migrants to the West similar to those of the northerners who moved to the South after the Civil War? How did they differ? (See chapter 16.)

2. How did the racism of the West compare with the racist attitudes against African Americans in the Reconstruction South? (See chapter 16.)

▶ FOR PRACTICE QUIZZES AND OTHER STUDY TOOLS, visit the Online Study Guide at bedfordstmartins.com/roark.

TIMELINE 1851–1900

1851	• First Treaty of Fort Laramie.
1862	• Homestead Act. • Great Sioux Uprising (Santee Uprising).
1864	• Sand Creek massacre.
1867	• Treaty of Medicine Lodge.
1868	• Second Treaty of Fort Laramie.
1869	• First transcontinental railroad completed.
1870	• Hunters begin to decimate bison herds.
1873	• "Big Bonanza" discovered on Comstock Lode.
1874	• Discovery of gold in Black Hills.
1876	• Battle of the Little Big Horn.
1877	• Chief Joseph surrenders. • Crazy Horse arrested and killed.
1878	• Indian students enroll at Hampton Institute in Virginia.
1879	• Carlisle Indian School opens in Pennsylvania. • More than fifteen thousand Exodusters move to Kansas.
1881	• Sitting Bull surrenders.
1882	• Chinese Exclusion Act. • Indian Rights Association formed.
1886	• Geronimo surrenders.
1886–1888	• Severe blizzards decimate cattle herds.
1887	• Dawes Allotment Act.
1889	• Rise of Ghost Dance. • Two million acres in Oklahoma opened for settlement.
1890	• Sitting Bull killed. • Massacre at Wounded Knee, South Dakota.
1893	• Last land rush takes place in Oklahoma Territory. • Frederick Jackson Turner presents "frontier thesis."
1900	• Census finds 66 percent of population lives in rural areas, compared to 80 percent in 1870.

CAMPAIGN PINS

These gilt campaign pins depicting James G. Blaine thumbing his nose at rival Grover Cleveland proved ironic—the Democrat Cleveland won the presidency in 1884 by campaigning for honest government. Public concern about the lucrative partnership of government and business made Thomas Kepler's 1889 cartoon, "The Bosses of the Senate," a defining symbol of the Gilded Age. The trusts are caricatured as bloated moneybags who dominate the Senate chambers. The motto "This is a Senate of the Monopolists, by the Monopolists, and for the Monopolists" hangs prominently on the wall.

Pins: Collection of Janice L. and David J. Frent; background: Library of Congress.

18

Business and Politics in the Gilded Age
1865–1900

ONE NIGHT OVER DINNER, AUTHORS MARK TWAIN AND CHARLES Dudley Warner teased their wives about the sentimental novels they read. When the two women challenged them to write something better, they set to work. Warner supplied the melodrama, while Twain "hurled in the facts." The result was a runaway best seller, a savage satire of the "get-rich-quick" era that would forever carry the book's title, *The Gilded Age* (1873).

Twain left no one unscathed in the novel — political hacks, Washington lobbyists, Wall Street financiers, small-town boosters, and the "great putty-hearted public" that tolerated the plunder. Underneath the glitter of the Gilded Age lurked vulgarity, crass materialism, and political corruption. Twain had witnessed the crooked partnership of business and politics in the administration of Ulysses S. Grant. Here he describes how a lobbyist finagled to get a bill through Congress:

> Why the matter is simple enough. A Congressional appropriation costs money. . . . A majority of the House Committee, say $10,000 apiece — $40,000; a majority of the Senate Committee, the same each — say $40,000; a little extra to one or two chairmen of one or two such committees, say $10,000 each — $20,000; and there's $100,000 of the money gone, to begin with. Then, seven male lobbyists, at $3,000 each — $21,000; one female lobbyist, $3,000; a high moral Congressman or Senator here and there — the high moral ones cost more, because they give tone to a measure — say ten of these at $3,000 each, is $30,000; then a lot of small fry country members who won't vote for anything whatever without pay — say twenty at $500 apiece, is $10,000 altogether; lot of jimcracks for Congressmen's wives and children — those go a long way — you can't spend too much money in that line — well, those things cost in a lump, say $10,000 — along there somewhere; — and then comes your printed documents. . . . [W]ell, never mind the details, the total in clean numbers foots up $118,254.42 thus far!

In Twain's satire, Congress is for sale to the highest bidder. The corrupt interplay of business and politics raised serious questions about the health of American democracy.

The Gilded Age seemed to tarnish all who touched it. No one would learn that better than Twain, who, even as he attacked it as an "era of incredible rottenness," fell prey to its enticements. Born Samuel Langhorne Clemens, he grew up in a rough Mississippi River town, where he became a

Mark Twain and *The Gilded Age*
Popular author Mark Twain (Samuel Langhorne Clemens) wrote acerbically about the excesses of the Gilded Age in his novel of that name written with Charles Dudley Warner and published in 1873. No one knew the meretricious lure of the era better than Twain, who succumbed to a get-rich-quick scheme that led him to the brink of bankruptcy. Photo: Beinecke Rare Book and Manuscript Library, Yale University; book: Newberry Library.

riverboat pilot. Taking the pen name Mark Twain, he gained fame chronicling western mining booms. In 1866, he came east to launch a career as an author, public speaker, and itinerant humorist. Twain played to packed houses, but his work was judged too vulgar for the genteel tastes of the time because he wrote about common people using common language. His masterpiece, *The Adventures of Huckleberry Finn*, was banned in Boston when it appeared in 1884.

Huck Finn's creator eventually stormed the citadels of polite society, hobnobbing with the wealthy and living in increasingly lavish style. Succumbing to the money fever of his age, Twain plunged into a scheme in the hope of making millions. By the 1890s, he faced bankruptcy and began a dogged climb out of debt.

Twain's tale was common in an age when the promise of wealth led as many to ruin as to riches. In the Gilded Age, fortunes were made and lost with dizzying frequency. Those who pursued riches, whether in the mines of the West or in the stock market, found many rocks in their path. Wall Street panics in 1873 and 1893 periodically interrupted the boom times and plunged the country into economic depression. But with railroad overbuilding and industry expanding on every level, the mood of the country remained buoyant.

The rise of industrialism in the United States and the interplay of business and politics strike the key themes in the Gilded Age. From 1870 to 1890, the transition from a rural, agricultural economy to urban industrialism, global in its reach, transformed American society. The growth of old industries and the creation of new ones, along with the rise of big business, signaled the coming of age of industrial capitalism. Economic issues increasingly shaped party politics, although old divisions engendered by sectionalism and slavery by no means disappeared. Meanwhile, new concerns over lynchings, temperance, and suffrage propelled women into more active roles in society.

Perhaps nowhere were the hopes and fears that industrialism inspired more evident than in the public's attitude toward the business moguls of the day. Men like Andrew Carnegie, John D. Rockefeller, and J. P. Morgan sparked the popular imagination as the heroes and villains in the high drama of industrialization. And as concern grew over the power of big business and the growing chasm between rich and poor, many Americans looked to the government for solutions.

► Old Industries Transformed, New Industries Born

In the years following the Civil War, the American economy underwent a transformation. Where once wealth had been measured in tangible assets — property, livestock, buildings — the economy now ran on money and the new devices of business — paper currency, securities, and anonymous corporate entities. Wall Street, the heart of the country's financial system, increasingly affected Main Street. The scale and scope of American industry expanded dramatically. Old industries like iron transformed into modern industries typified by the behemoth U.S. Steel. Discovery and invention stimulated new industries, from oil refining to electric light and power. The expansion of the nation's rail system in the decades after the Civil War played the key role in the transformation of the American economy.

Jay Gould, Andrew Carnegie, John D. Rockefeller, and other business leaders pioneered new strategies to seize markets and consolidate power in the rising railroad, steel, and oil industries. Always with an eye to the main chance, these business tycoons set the tone in the get-rich-quick era of freewheeling capitalism that came to be called the **Gilded Age**.

Railroads: America's First Big Business

The military conquest of America's inland empire and the dispossession of Native Americans (see chapter 17) relied on an elaborate new railroad system, which allowed businesses to expand on a nationwide scale. The first transcontinental railroad, completed in 1869, linked new markets in the West to the nation's eastern and midwestern farms and cities. Between 1870 and 1880, overbuilding doubled the amount of track in the country and it nearly doubled again in the following decade. By 1900, the nation boasted more than 193,000 miles of railroad track — more than in all of Europe and Russia combined (Map 18.1). The railroads had become America's first big business. Privately owned but publicly financed by enormous land grants from the federal government and the states, the railroads epitomized the insidious nexus of business and politics in the Gilded Age.

To understand how the railroads came to dominate American life, there is no better place to start than with the career of **Jay Gould**, who pioneered the expansion of America's railway system and became the era's most notorious speculator. Jason "Jay" Gould bought his first railroad before he turned twenty-five. It was only sixty-two miles long, in bad repair, and on the brink of failure, but within two years he sold it at a profit of $130,000.

Gould, by his own admission, knew little about railroads and cared less about their operation. The secretive Gould operated in the stock market like a shark, looking for vulnerable railroads, buying enough stock to take control, and threatening to undercut his competitors until they bought him out at a high profit. The railroads that fell into his hands fared badly and often went bankrupt. Gould's genius lay not in providing transportation, but in cleverly buying and selling railroad stock on Wall Street, the nerve center of the new economy.

> ## "The most hated man in America."
> — Railroad tycoon JAY GOULD, speaking of himself

JUSTICE IN THE WEB.

Jay Gould as a Spider
In this 1885 political cartoon titled "Justice in the Web," artist Fredrick Burr Opper portrays Jay Gould as a hideous spider whose web, formed by Western Union telegraph lines, has entrapped "justice" through its monopoly of the telegraph industry. The telegraph, by transmitting coded messages across electric wire, formed the nervous system of the new industrial order. Gould, who controlled Western Union as well as the Erie and the Union Pacific Railroads, made his fortune by stock speculation. Images like this one fueled the public's distaste for Gould and made him, in his own words, "the most hated man in America." Granger Collection.

MAP ACTIVITY

MAP 18.1   Railroad Expansion, 1870–1890
Railroad mileage nearly quadrupled between 1870 and 1890, with the greatest growth occurring in the trans-Mississippi West. The western railroads — the Great Northern, Northern Pacific, Southern Pacific, and Atlantic and Pacific — were completed in the 1880s. Fueled by speculation and built ahead of demand, the western railroads made fortunes for individual speculators. But they rarely paid for themselves and often left disaster in their wake. At the same time, they fed a culture of insider dealing and political corruption.

READING THE MAP: Where were most of the railroad lines located in 1870? By 1890, how many railroads reached the west coast? What was the end point of the only western route?

CONNECTIONS: Why were so many rails laid between 1870 and 1890? How did the railroads affect the nation's economy?

The New York Stock Exchange, dating back to 1792, expanded as the volume of stock increased sixfold between 1869 and 1901. Where on one sleepy day in 1830 only thirty-one stocks traded, by 1886 more than a million shares a day changed hands. As the scale and complexity of the financial system increased, the line between investment and speculation blurred, causing many Americans to question if the concern with paper profits fueled the boom and bust cycles that led to panic and depression, putting hardworking Americans out of jobs. Yet however crass their motives, millionaire speculators like Jay Gould built America's rail system. In the 1880s, Gould moved to put together a second transcontinental railroad. His competitors had little choice but to adopt his strategy of expansion and consolidation, which in turn encouraged overbuilding and stimulated a national market.

The dramatic growth of the railroads created the country's first big business. Before the Civil War, even the largest textile mill in New England employed no more than 800 workers. By contrast, the Pennsylvania Railroad by the 1870s boasted a payroll of more than 55,000 workers. Capitalized at more than $400 million, the Pennsylvania Railroad constituted the largest private enterprise in the world.

The big business of railroads bestowed enormous riches on a handful of tycoons. Both Gould and his competitor "Commodore" Cornelius Vanderbilt amassed fortunes estimated at $100 million. Such staggering wealth eclipsed that of upper-class Americans from previous generations and left a legacy of lavish spending for an elite crop of ultrarich heirs. (See "Visualizing History," page 574.)

The Republican Party, firmly entrenched in Washington, worked closely with business interests, subsidizing the transcontinental railroad system with land grants of a staggering 100 million acres of public land and $64 million in tax incentives and direct aid. States and local communities joined the railroad boom, knowing that only those towns and villages along the tracks would grow and flourish. The combined federal and state land giveaway amounted to more than 180 million acres, an area larger than Texas.

A revolution in communication accompanied and supported the growth of the railroads. The telegraph, developed by Samuel F. B. Morse, marched across the continent alongside the railroad. By transmitting coded messages along electrical wire, the telegraph formed the "nervous system" of the new industrial order. Telegraph service quickly replaced Pony Express mail carriers in the West and transformed business by providing instantaneous communication. Again Jay Gould took the lead. In 1879, through stock manipulation, he seized control of Western Union, the company that monopolized the telegraph industry. By the end of the century, the telegraph carried 63 million messages a year and made it possible to move money around the world. Financiers in London and New York could follow the markets on ticker tape and transfer funds by wire.

The railroads soon fell on hard times. Already by the 1870s, lack of planning led to overbuilding. Across the nation, railroads competed fiercely for business. A manufacturer in an area served by competing railroads could get substantially reduced shipping rates in return for promises of steady business. Because railroad owners lost money through this kind of competition, they tried to set up agreements, or "pools," to end cutthroat competition by dividing up territory and setting rates. But these informal gentlemen's agreements invariably failed because men like Jay Gould, intent on undercutting all competitors, refused to play by the rules.

Novelist Charles Dudley Warner described how the rail speculators operated:

> [They fasten upon] some railway that is prosperous, pays dividends, pays a liberal interest on its bonds, and has a surplus. They contrive to buy, no matter at what the cost, a controlling interest in it. . . . Then they absorb its surplus; let it run down so that it pays no dividends and by-and-by cannot even pay its interest; then they squeeze the bondholders, who may be glad to accept anything that is offered out of the wreck, and perhaps then they throw the property into the hands of a receiver, or consolidate it with some other road at a value enormously greater than it cost them in stealing it. Having in one way or another sucked it dry, they look around for another road.

The public's alarm at the control wielded by the new railroad magnates and the tactics they employed provided a barometer of attitudes toward big business itself. When Gould died in 1892, the press described him as "the world's richest man." Rival Cornelius Vanderbilt judged Gould "the smartest man in America." But to the public, he was, as he himself admitted shortly before his death, "the most hated man in America."

Andrew Carnegie, Steel, and Vertical Integration

If Jay Gould was the man Americans loved to hate, **Andrew Carnegie** became one of America's heroes. Unlike Gould, for whom speculation was the game and wealth the goal, Carnegie turned his back on speculation and worked to build something enduring — Carnegie Steel, the biggest steel business in the world during the Gilded Age.

The growth of the steel industry proceeded directly from railroad building. The first railroads ran on iron rails, which cracked and broke with alarming frequency. Steel, both stronger and more flexible than iron, remained too expensive for use in rails until Englishman Henry Bessemer developed a way to make steel more cheaply from pig iron. Andrew Carnegie, among the first to champion the new "King Steel," came to dominate the emerging industry.

The Vanderbilts and the Gilded Age

Nothing represented the Gilded Age better than the Gold Room of Marble House, the "cottage" Alva Vanderbilt opened in Newport, Rhode Island, in 1892. William K. Vanderbilt, Alva's husband, was the grandson of Cornelius Vanderbilt, the founder of the New York Central Railway and the richest man of his era. His sons doubled his wealth, and his grandsons spent it lavishly. Alva, who enjoyed building houses, judged Marble House her triumph and liked to describe it as "Versailles improved." Modeled after Marie Antoinette's château, the Petit Trianon, on the grounds of Versailles, the mansion suited Alva's ambition to bring French culture to America. Designed by Richard Morris Hunt, the architect of the plutocracy, Marble House replicated the glory of the seventeenth-century French royal palaces Alva had admired when she visited France in her youth. Why might Alva have chosen to model her Newport home after a French queen's château?

The Gold Room, Alva's miniature version of Versailles's Hall of Mirrors, is a riot of neoclassical exuberance, with panels of Greek gods and goddesses adorning the walls. Above the striated black-and-white marble mantelpiece, bronze figures bear a vast candelabra, while cupids cavort and cherubs blow

Marble House: The Vanderbilt Mansion in Newport, Rhode Island

The Gold Room in Marble House

Carnegie, a Scottish immigrant, landed in New York in 1848 at the age of twelve. He rose from a job cleaning bobbins in a textile factory to become one of the richest men in America. Before he died, he gave away more than $300 million, most notably to public libraries. His generosity, combined with his own rise from poverty, burnished his public image.

When Carnegie was a teenager, his skill as a telegraph operator caught the attention of Tom Scott, superintendent of the Pennsylvania Railroad. Scott hired Carnegie, soon promoted him, and lent him the money for his first foray into Wall Street investment. As a result of this crony capitalism, Carnegie became a millionaire before his thirtieth birthday. At point, Carnegie turned

574

trumpets on the walls and ceilings. Why do you think the Vanderbilts chose classical figures for their decoration? The enormous chandeliers and wood panels painted in red, green, and gold are multiplied in their dazzling magnificence by vast mirrors hung over the four doors, above the mantelpiece, and on the south wall. Critics charged that Marble House, with its Gold Room, was "a symbol of the heartless, glittering emptiness of the Gilded Age." What did they mean by this criticism?

The Vanderbilts' wealth and their lavish spending made it hard for old-money New Yorkers, living in their staid brownstones, to compete. Alva and William's Fifth Avenue mansion in New York City had a ballroom that could accommodate 1,600 guests. At their legendary costume ball in 1883, the Vanderbilts released live doves to astound their guests.

Alva Vanderbilt, pictured right at her famous costume ball dressed as a Venetian princess, flouted convention by divorcing William in 1895. Her indomitable will, her quest for recognition, and her fearless defiance of convention led her to the women's rights cause. She would become a principal supporter of the National Woman's Party and serve as its president.

In 1909, Alva organized two highly successful suffrage meetings at Marble House and prevailed upon her old friends to give to the cause. Many bought tickets to the meetings just to have the opportunity to tour the mansion. Crowds of more than five hundred thronged the grounds. In 1932, shortly before she died, Alva sold Marble House with the

Alva Vanderbilt Releasing the Doves

assurance that it would be kept as she had designed it. In the 1960s, the Preservation Society of Newport County took over the house, and today it is a National Historic Landmark open to the public. Alva Vanderbilt no doubt felt a deep pride in her creation, once describing it as "like a fourth child," and she had no trouble opening it to raise funds for the suffragist cause.

How might she feel about paying visitors wandering the rooms of Marble House today?

SOURCE: Marble House: © Dave G. Houser/Corbis; Gold Room: © Kelly-Mooney Photography/Corbis; Alva Vanderbilt: photo courtesy of The Preservation Society of Newport County.

away from speculation and struck out on his own to reshape the iron and steel industry. "My preference was always manufacturing," he wrote. "I wished to make something tangible." By applying the lessons of cost accounting and efficiency that he had learned from twelve years with the Pennsylvania Railroad, Carnegie turned steel into the nation's first manufacturing big business.

In 1872, Andrew Carnegie acquired one hundred acres in Braddock, Pennsylvania, on the outskirts of Pittsburgh, convenient to two railroad lines and fronted by the Monongahela River, a natural highway to Pittsburgh and the Ohio River and to the coal and iron mines farther north. There Carnegie built the largest, most up-to-date Bessemer steel plant in the world. At

Andrew Carnegie in 1894
"The man who dies rich . . . dies disgraced," asserted Andrew Carnegie. A classic rags-to-riches hero, Carnegie gave away more than $300 million before he died in 1919. Public libraries were among his favorite philanthropies; he contributed to the building of more than 2,500. But Carnegie was not so benign to his workers, whom he drove mercilessly, demanding a twelve-hour day, six days a week.
©Bettmann/Corbis.

that time, steelmakers produced about 70 tons a week. Within two decades, Carnegie's blast furnaces poured out an incredible 10,000 tons a week. He soon cut the cost of making rails by more than half, from $58 to $25 a ton. His formula for success was simple: "Cut the prices, scoop the market, run the mills full; watch the costs and profits will take care of themselves."

To guarantee the lowest costs and the maximum output, Carnegie pioneered a system of business organization called **vertical integration**. All aspects of the business were under Carnegie's control — from the mining of iron ore, to its transport on the Great Lakes, to the production of steel. Vertical integration, in the words of one observer, meant that "from the moment these crude stuffs were dug out of the earth until they flowed in a stream of liquid steel in the ladles, there was never a price, profit, or royalty paid to any outsider."

Always Carnegie kept his eyes on the account books, looking for ways to cut costs. The great productivity Carnegie encouraged came at a high price. He deliberately pitted his managers against one another, firing the losers and rewarding the winners with a share in the company. Workers achieved the output Carnegie demanded by enduring low wages, dangerous working conditions, and twelve-hour days six days a week. One worker, commenting on the contradiction between Carnegie's generous philanthropy in endowing public libraries and his tightfisted labor policy, observed, "After working twelve hours, how can a man go to a library?"

By 1900, Andrew Carnegie had become the best-known manufacturer in the nation, and

FIGURE 18.1   Iron and Steel Production, 1870–1900
Iron and steel production in the United States grew from nearly none in 1870 to 10 million tons a year by 1900. The secrets to the great increase in steel production were the use of the Bessemer process and vertical integration, pioneered by Andrew Carnegie. By 1900, Carnegie's mills alone produced more steel than all of Great Britain. With corporate consolidation after 1900, the rate of growth in steel proved even more spectacular.

the age of iron had yielded to an age of steel. Steel from Carnegie's mills supported the elevated trains in New York and Chicago, formed the skeleton of the Washington Monument, supported the first steel bridge to span the Mississippi, and girded America's first skyscrapers. Carnegie steel armored the naval fleet that helped make the United States a world military power. As a captain of industry, Carnegie's only rival was the titan of the oil industry, John D. Rockefeller.

John D. Rockefeller, Standard Oil, and the Trust

Edwin Drake's discovery of oil in Pennsylvania in 1859 sent thousands rushing to the oil fields in search of "black gold." In the days before the automobile and gasoline, crude oil was refined into lubricating oil for machinery and kerosene for lamps, the major source of lighting in nineteenth-century houses before the invention of gas lamps and electric lighting. The amount of capital needed to buy or build an oil refinery in the 1860s and 1870s remained relatively low — less than $25,000, or roughly what it cost to lay one mile of railroad track. With start-up costs so low, the new petroleum industry experienced riotous competition among many small refineries. Ultimately, **John D. Rockefeller** and his Standard Oil Company succeeded in controlling nine-tenths of the oil-refining business.

Rockefeller grew up the son of a shrewd Yankee who peddled quack cures for cancer. Under his father's rough tutelage, he learned how to drive a hard bargain. "I trade with the boys and skin 'em and just beat 'em every time I can," "Big Bill" Rockefeller boasted. "I want to make 'em sharp." John D. learned his lessons well. In 1865, at the age of twenty-five, he controlled the largest oil refinery in Cleveland. Like a growing number of business owners, Rockefeller abandoned partnership or single proprietorship to embrace the corporation as the business structure best suited to maximize profit and minimize personal liability. In 1870, he incorporated his oil business, founding the Standard Oil Company, a behemoth so huge that it served as the precursor not only of today's ExxonMobil but also of Amoco, Chevron, Sunoco, and ConocoPhillips.

As the largest refiner in Cleveland, Rockefeller demanded secret rebates from the railroads in exchange for his steady business. Rebates enabled Rockefeller to drive out his competitors through predatory pricing.

The railroads, facing the pressures of cutthroat competition, needed Rockefeller's business so badly that they gave him a share of the rates that his competitors paid. A Pennsylvania Railroad official later confessed that Rockefeller extracted such huge rebates that the railroad, which could not risk losing his business, sometimes ended up paying him to transport Standard's oil. Secret deals, predatory pricing, and rebates enabled Rockefeller to undercut his competitors and pressure competing refiners to sell out or face ruin.

To gain legal standing for Standard Oil's secret deals, Rockefeller in 1882 pioneered a new form of corporate structure — the **trust**. The trust differed markedly from Carnegie's vertical approach in steel. Instead of attempting to control all aspects of the oil business, from the well to the consumer, Rockefeller used horizontal integration to control the refining process. Several trustees held stock in various refinery companies "in trust" for Standard's stockholders. This elaborate stock swap allowed the trustees to coordinate policy among the refineries, giving Rockefeller a virtual monopoly on the oil-refining business. The Standard Oil trust, valued at more than $70 million, paved the way for trusts in sugar, whiskey, matches, and many other products.

When the federal government responded to public pressure to outlaw the trust as a violation of free trade, Standard Oil changed tactics and reorganized as a holding company. Instead of stockholders in competing companies acting through trustees to set prices and determine territories, the holding company simply brought competing companies under one central administration. No longer technically separate businesses, they could act in concert without violating antitrust laws that forbade companies from forming "combinations in restraint of trade." As Standard Oil's empire grew, Rockefeller ended the independence of the refinery operators and closed inefficient plants. Next he moved to control sources of crude oil and took charge of the transportation and marketing of petroleum products. By the 1890s, Standard Oil ruled more than 90 percent of the oil business, employed 100,000 people, and was the biggest, richest, most feared, and most admired business organization in the world.

John D. Rockefeller enjoyed enormous success in business, but he was not well liked by the public. Before he died in 1937 at the age of ninety-eight, Rockefeller had become the country's first billionaire. But despite his modest habits, his pious Baptist

VISUAL ACTIVITY

"What a Funny Little Government"

The power wielded by John D. Rockefeller and the Standard Oil Company is captured in this political cartoon by Horace Taylor, which appeared in the January 22, 1900, issue of the *Verdict*. Rockefeller is pictured holding the White House and the Treasury Department in the palm of his hand, while in the background the U.S. Capitol has been converted into an oil refinery. Rockefeller and the company he ran held so much power that many feared democracy itself was threatened in the Gilded Age. Collection of the New-York Historical Society.

READING THE IMAGE: According to Horace Taylor, what kind of relationship did John D. Rockefeller have with the federal government? What benefits did he accrue from it?

CONNECTIONS: How much influence did industrialists such as Rockefeller exert over the national government in the late nineteenth century?

faith, and his many charitable gifts, he never shared in the public affection that Carnegie enjoyed. Editor and journalist Ida M. Tarbell's "History of the Standard Oil Company," which ran for three years (1902–1905) in serial form in *McClure's Magazine*, largely shaped the public's harsh view of Rockefeller.

Ida M. Tarbell had grown up in the Pennsylvania oil region, and her father had owned one of the small refineries gobbled up by Standard Oil. Her devastatingly thorough history chronicled the methods Rockefeller had used to take over the oil industry. Publicly, Rockefeller refused to respond to her allegations, although in private he dubbed her "Miss Tarbarrel." "If I step on that worm I will call attention to it," he explained. "If I ignore it, it will disappear." Yet by the time

Tarbell finished publishing her story, Rockefeller slept with a loaded revolver by his bed in fear of would-be assassins. Standard Oil and the man who created it had become the symbol of heartless monopoly.

New Inventions: The Telephone and Electricity

The second half of the nineteenth century was an age of invention. Men like Thomas Alva Edison and Alexander Graham Bell became folk heroes. But no matter how dramatic the inventors or the inventions, the new electric and telephone industries pioneered by Edison and Bell soon eclipsed their inventors and fell under the control of bankers and industrialists.

Ida M. Tarbell, Scourge of Standard Oil
Inquisitive and determined to have a career as a writer, Ida M. Tarbell became one of America's first investigative reporters. Pictured here shortly before she became an editor at *McClure's Magazine*, Tarbell would earn her reputation from a scathing inquiry into "The History of the Standard Oil Company," which first ran as a series of nineteen articles (see inset) and came out in book form in 1904. Tarbell grew up in Pennsylvania's oil region, where her family suffered from the underhanded practices that John D. Rockefeller used to seize control of the refining business. She was particularly focused on the illegal rebates he wrung from railroads. Tarbell: Library of Congress; magazine: Special Collections, The Ida Tarbell Collection, Pelletier Library, Allegheny College.

Alexander Graham Bell came to America from Scotland at the age of twenty-four with a passion to find a way to teach the deaf to speak (his wife and mother were deaf). Instead, he developed a way to transmit voice over wire — the telephone. Bell's invention astounded the world when he demonstrated it at the Philadelphia Centennial Exposition in 1876. Dumbfounded by the display, the emperor of Brazil cried out, "My God, it talks!"

In 1880, Bell's company, American Bell, pioneered "long lines" (long-distance telephone service), creating American Telephone and Telegraph (AT&T) as a subsidiary. In 1900, AT&T became the parent company of the system as a whole, controlling Western Electric, which manufactured and installed the equipment, and coordinating the Bell regional divisions. This complicated organizational structure meant that Americans could communicate not only locally but also across the country. And unlike a telegraph message, which had to be written out and taken to a telegraph station, sent over the wire, and then delivered by hand to the recipient, the telephone connected both parties immediately and privately. Bell's invention proved a boon to business, contributing to speed and efficiency. The number of telephones soared, reaching 310,000 in 1895 and more than 1.5 million in 1900.

Notable American Inventions 1865–1899

Year	Invention
1865	Railroad sleeping car
1867	Typewriter
1868	Railroad refrigerator car
1870	Stock ticker
1874	Barbed wire
1876	Telephone
1877	Phonograph
1879	Incandescent lightbulb
1882	Electric fan
1885	Adding machine
1886	Coca-Cola
1888	Kodak camera
1890	Electric chair
1891	Zipper
1895	Safety razor
1896	Electric stove
1899	Tape recorder

Thomas Edison and Moving Pictures
Edison's "greatest marvel," the Vitascope, was actually not his own invention. Edison was slow to develop a projection system, but the market for a machine that would project films for large audiences led him to acquire the Vitascope, pictured here in a postcard, from Thomas Armat and C. Francis Jenkins. The first theatrical exhibition took place in New York City in 1896. The Vitascope became a popular attraction in variety and vaudeville theaters, where rapt audiences like the one pictured here dressed up and enjoyed moving pictures accompanied by a live orchestra. Library of Congress.

Even more than Alexander Graham Bell, inventor **Thomas Alva Edison** embodied the old-fashioned virtues of Yankee ingenuity and rugged individualism that Americans most admired. A self-educated dynamo, he worked twenty hours a day in his laboratory in Menlo Park, New Jersey, vowing to turn out "a minor invention every ten days and a big thing every six months or so." He almost made good on his promise. At the height of his career, he averaged a patent every eleven days and invented such "big things" as the phonograph, the motion picture camera, and the filament for the incandescent lightbulb.

Edison, in competition with George W. Westinghouse, pioneered the use of electricity as an energy source. By the late nineteenth century, electricity had become a part of American urban life. It powered trolley cars and lighted factories, homes, and office buildings. Indeed, electricity became so prevalent in urban life that it symbolized the city, whose bright lights contrasted with rural America, left largely in the dark because private enterprise judged it not profitable enough to run electric lines to outlying farms and ranches.

While Americans thrilled to the new electric cities and the changes wrought by inventors, the day of the inventor quietly yielded to the heyday of the corporation. In 1892, the electric industry consolidated. Reflecting a nationwide trend in business, Edison General Electric dropped the name of its inventor, becoming simply General Electric (GE). For years, an embittered Edison

THE PROMISE OF TECHNOLOGY

Electrifying America

This 1889 cartoon was part of a campaign Thomas Edison waged against George Westinghouse in what came to be known as the "war of the currents." With the system of how best to provide electric current to the nation at stake, Edison launched a massive public relations campaign to discredit the high-voltage alternating current (AC) favored by Westinghouse. In the cartoon, innocent pedestrians are electrocuted by the wires as a policeman runs for help. The skull in the wires attached to the electric lightbulb warns that this new technology can be deadly. Although the direct current (DC) Edison championed was less dangerous to handle, it could reach only a one-mile radius from a power station. Despite his campaign to discredit Westinghouse, Edison lost the war of the currents. Cities that wanted electric lighting found Westinghouse's alternating current, despite the dangers of high voltage, less expensive and better suited to their needs. Was Edison taking a risk in trying to discredit alternating current? Granger Collection.

AN UNRESTRAINED DEMON.

refused to set foot inside a GE building. General Electric could afford to overlook the slight. A prime example of the trend toward business consolidation taking place in the 1890s, GE soon dominated the market.

REVIEW What devices did John D. Rockefeller use to gain control of 90 percent of the oil-refining business by 1890?

▶ From Competition to Consolidation

Even as Rockefeller and Carnegie built their empires, the era of the "robber barons," as they were dubbed by their detractors, was drawing to a close. Increasingly, businesses replaced partnerships and sole proprietorships with the anonymous corporate structure that would come to dominate the twentieth century. At the same time, mergers led to the creation of huge new corporations.

Banks and financiers played a key role in this consolidation, so much so that the decades at the turn of the twentieth century can be characterized as a period of **finance capitalism** — investment sponsored by banks and bankers. When the depression that followed the panic of 1893 bankrupted many businesses, bankers stepped in to bring order and to reorganize major industries. During these years, a new social philosophy based on the theories of naturalist Charles Darwin helped to justify consolidation and to inhibit state or federal regulation of business. A conservative Supreme Court further frustrated attempts to control business by consistently declaring unconstitutional legislation designed to regulate railroads or to outlaw trusts and monopolies.

J. P. Morgan and Finance Capitalism

John Pierpont Morgan, the preeminent finance capitalist of the late nineteenth century, loathed competition and sought whenever possible to eliminate it by substituting consolidation and

J. P. Morgan, Photograph by Edward Steichen
Few photographs of J. P. Morgan exist. Morgan, who suffered from a skin condition that left him with a misshapen strawberry of a nose, rarely allowed his picture to be taken. But it was his eyes that people remembered — eyes so piercing that Edward Steichen, who took this photograph, observed that "meeting his gaze was a little like confronting the headlights of an express train." George Eastman House. Reprinted with permission of Joanna T. Steichen.

and moved to eliminate competition by creating what he called "a community of interest" among the managers he handpicked. By the time he finished "Morganizing" the railroads, a handful of directors controlled two-thirds of the nation's track.

Banker control of the railroads helped to coordinate the industry. But reorganization came at a high price. To keep investors happy and to guarantee huge profits from the sale of stock, Morgan heavily "watered" the stock of the railroads, issuing more shares than the assets of the company warranted. J. P. Morgan & Co. made millions of dollars from commissions and from blocks of stock acquired through reorganization. The flagrant overcapitalization created by the watered stock hurt the railroads in the long run, saddling them with enormous debt. Equally harmful was the management style of the Morgan directors. Bankers, not railroad men, they aimed at short-term profit and discouraged the continued technological and organizational innovation needed to run the railroads effectively.

In 1898, Morgan moved into the steel industry, directly challenging Andrew Carnegie. Morgan supervised the mergers of several smaller steel companies, which soon expanded from the manufacture of finished goods to compete head-to-head with Carnegie in steel production. The pugnacious Carnegie cabled his partners in the summer of 1900: "Action essential: crisis has arrived . . . have no fear as to the result; victory certain." The press trumpeted news of the impending fight between the feisty Scot and the haughty Wall Street banker, but what the papers called the "battle of the giants" in the end proved little more than the wily maneuvering of two businessmen so adept that even today it is difficult to say who won. For all his belligerence, the sixty-six-year-old Carnegie yearned to retire to Skibo Castle, his home in Scotland. He may well have welcomed Morgan's bid for power. Morgan, who disdained haggling, agreed to pay Carnegie's asking price, $480 million (the equivalent of about $10 billion in today's currency). According to legend, when Carnegie later teased Morgan, saying that he should have asked $100 million more, Morgan replied, "You would have got it if you had."

Morgan's acquisition of Carnegie Steel signaled the passing of the old entrepreneurial order personified by Andrew Carnegie and the arrival of a new, anonymous corporate world. The banker quickly moved to pull together Carnegie's chief competitors to form a huge new

central control. Morgan's passion for order made him the architect of business mergers. The son of a prominent banker, **J. P. Morgan** inherited along with his wealth the stern business code of the old-fashioned merchant bankers, men who valued character and reputation. Aloof and silent, Morgan looked down on the climbers and the speculators with a haughtiness that led his rivals to call him "Jupiter," after the ruler of the Roman gods. At the turn of the twentieth century, he dominated American banking, exerting an influence so powerful that his critics charged he controlled a vast "money trust" even more insidious than Rockefeller's Standard Oil.

Morgan acted as a power broker in the reorganization of the railroads and the creation of industrial giants such as General Electric and U.S. Steel. When the railroads fell on hard times in the 1890s, he used his access to capital to rescue embattled, wrecked, and ruined companies. Morgan quickly took over the struggling railroads

Homestead Steelworks
The Homestead steelworks, outside Pittsburgh, is pictured shortly after J. P. Morgan bought out Andrew Carnegie and created U.S. Steel, the precursor of today's USX. Try to count the smokestacks in the picture. Air pollution on this scale posed a threat to the health of citizens and made for a dismal landscape. Workers complained that trees would not grow in Homestead. Hagley Museum & Library.

corporation, United States Steel, known today as USX. Created in 1901 and capitalized at $1.4 billion, U.S. Steel was the largest corporation in the world. Yet for all its size, it did not hold a monopoly in the steel industry. Significant small competitors, such as Bethlehem Steel, remained independent, creating a competitive system called an oligopoly, in which several companies control production. The smaller manufacturers simply followed the lead of U.S. Steel in setting prices and dividing the market so that each company held a comfortable share. Although oligopoly did not entirely eliminate competition, it did effectively blunt it.

When J. P. Morgan died in 1913, his estate totaled $68 million, not counting an estimated $50 million in art treasures. Andrew Carnegie, who gave away more than $300 million before his death six years later, is said to have quipped, "And to think he was not a rich man!" But Carnegie's gibe missed the mark. The quest for power, not wealth, had motivated J. P. Morgan, and his power could best be measured not in the millions he owned but in the billions he controlled. Even more than Carnegie or Rockefeller, Morgan left his stamp on the twentieth century and formed the model for corporate consolidation

that economists and social scientists soon justified with a new social theory known as social Darwinism.

Social Darwinism, Laissez-Faire, and the Supreme Court

John D. Rockefeller Jr., the son of the founder of Standard Oil, once remarked to his Baptist Bible class that the Standard Oil Company, like the American Beauty rose, resulted from "pruning the early buds that grew up around it." The elimination of smaller, inefficient units, he said, was "merely the working out of a law of nature and a law of God." The comparison of the business world to the natural world gave rise to a theory of society paralleling the relatively new notion of evolution formulated by the British naturalist Charles Darwin. In his monumental work *On the Origin of Species* (1859), Darwin theorized that in the struggle for survival, adaptation to the environment triggered among species a natural selection process that led to

> "The drunkard in the gutter is just where he ought to be, according to the fitness and tendency of things. . . . Millionaires are the product of natural selection."
> — Social Darwinist
> **WILLIAM GRAHAM SUMNER**

Social Darwinism: Did Wealthy Industrialists Practice What They Preached?

Darwinism, with its emphasis on tooth-and-claw competition, seemed ideally suited to the get-rich-quick mentality of the Gilded Age. By placing the theory of evolution in an economic context, social Darwinism argued against government intervention in business while at the same time insisting that reforms to ameliorate the evils of urban industrialism would only slow evolutionary progress. Most of the wealthy industrialists of the day probably never read Charles Darwin or the exponents of social Darwinism. Nevertheless, the catchphrases of social Darwinism larded the rhetoric of business in the Gilded Age.

Andrew Carnegie, alone among the American business moguls, not only championed social Darwinism but also avidly read the works of its primary exponent, the British social philosopher Herbert Spencer. Significantly, Spencer, not Darwin, coined the catchphrase "survival of the fittest." Carnegie spoke of his indebtedness to Spencer in terms usually reserved for religious conversion: "Before Spencer, all for me had been darkness, after him, all had become light — and right." In his autobiography, Carnegie wrote, "I had found the truth of evolution. 'All is well since all grows better' became my motto, my true source of comfort."

Not content to worship Spencer from afar, Carnegie assiduously worked to make his acquaintance and then would not rest until he had convinced the reluctant Spencer to come to America. In Pittsburgh, Carnegie promised, Spencer could best view his evolutionary theories at work in the world of industry. Clearly, Carnegie viewed his steelworks as the apex of America's new industrial order, a testimony to the playing out of evolutionary theory in the economic world.

In 1882, Spencer undertook an American tour. Carnegie personally invited him to Pittsburgh, squiring him through the Braddock steel mills. But Spencer failed to appreciate Carnegie's achievement. The heat, noise, and pollution of Pittsburgh reduced Spencer to near collapse, and he could only choke out, "Six months' residence here would justify suicide." Carnegie must have been devastated.

How well Carnegie actually understood the principles of social Darwinism is debatable. In his 1900 essay "Popular Illusions about Trusts," Carnegie spoke of the "law of evolution that moves from the heterogeneous to the homogeneous," citing Spencer as his source. Spencer, however, had written of the movement "from an indefinite incoherent homogeneity to a definite coherent heterogeneity." Instead of acknowledging that the history of human evolution moved from the simple to the more complex, Carnegie seemed to insist that evolution moved from the complex to the simple. This confusion of the most basic evolutionary theory calls into question Carnegie's grasp of Spencer's ideas or indeed of Darwin's. Other business leaders too busy making money to read no doubt understood even less about the working of evolutionary theory and social Darwinism, which they so often claimed as their own.

evolution. Herbert Spencer in Britain and William Graham Sumner in the United States developed the theory of **social Darwinism**. The social Darwinists concluded that societal progress came about as a result of relentless competition in which the strong survived and the weak died out.

In social terms, the idea of the "survival of the fittest," coined by Herbert Spencer, had profound significance, as Sumner, a professor of political economy at Yale University, made clear in his book *What Social Classes Owe to Each Other* (1883). "The drunkard in the gutter is just where he ought to be, according to the fitness and tendency of things," Sumner insisted. Conversely, "millionaires are the product of

natural selection," and although "they get high wages and live in luxury," Sumner claimed, "the bargain is a good one for society."

Social Darwinists equated wealth and power with "fitness" and believed that the unfit should be allowed to die off to advance the progress of humanity. Any efforts by the rich to aid the poor would only tamper with the rigid laws of nature and slow down evolution. Social Darwinism acted to curb social reform while at the same time glorifying great wealth. In an age when Rockefeller and Carnegie amassed hundreds of millions of dollars (billions in today's currency) and the average worker earned $500 a year, social Darwinism justified economic inequality (See "Historical Question," above.)

The distance between preachment and practice is boldly evident in the example of William Graham Sumner, America's foremost social Darwinist. Ironically, Sumner, who often sounded like an apologist for the rich, aroused the wrath of the very group he championed. The problem was that strict social Darwinists like Sumner insisted absolutely that the government ought not to meddle in the economy. The purity of Sumner's commitment to laissez-faire led him to adamantly oppose the protective tariffs the pro-business Republicans enacted to inflate the prices of manufactured goods produced abroad so that U.S. businesses could compete against foreign rivals. Sumner outspokenly attacked the tariff and firmly advocated free trade from his chair in political economy at Yale University. In 1890, the same year Congress passed the McKinley tariff, Sumner's fulminations against this highest tariff in the nation's history so outraged Yale's wealthy alumni that they mounted a campaign (unsuccessful) to have him fired.

Inconsistency never seemed to trouble Andrew Carnegie, who did not acknowledge a contradiction between his worship of Spencer and his strong support for the tariff. The comparison of Carnegie's position and Sumner's underscores the reality that although in theory laissez-faire constrained the government from playing an active role in business affairs, in practice industrialists fought for government favors — whether tariffs, land grants, or subsidies — that worked to their benefit. Only when legislatures proposed taxes or regulation did business leaders cry foul and invoke the "natural laws" of social Darwinism and its corollary, laissez-faire.

Herbert Spencer
The British writer and philosopher Herbert Spencer became a hero to industrialist Andrew Carnegie, who orchestrated Spencer's trip to America in 1882. The sage of social Darwinism proved a great disappointment to Carnegie. A cautious hypochondriac, Spencer guarded himself zealously against any painful contact with that teeming competitive world that he extolled. Once on American soil, Spencer spurned Carnegie's offer of hospitality during his visit to Pittsburgh and insisted on staying in a hotel. And when Carnegie eagerly demonstrated the wonders of the world's most modern steel mill to his guest, the tour reduced Spencer to a state of near collapse. Hulton Archives/ Getty Images.

Thinking about Beliefs and Attitudes

1. In what ways did American business moguls think that the notion of evolution applied to them?

2. Why were most industrialists inconsistent in invoking the principles of social Darwinism?

Andrew Carnegie softened some of the harshness of social Darwinism in his essay "The Gospel of Wealth," published in 1889. The millionaire, Carnegie wrote, acted as a "mere trustee and agent for his poorer brethren, bringing to their service his superior wisdom, experience, and ability to administer, doing for them better than they could or would do for themselves." Carnegie preached philanthropy and urged the rich to "live unostentatious lives" and "administer surplus wealth for the good of the people." His **gospel of wealth** earned much praise but won few converts. Most millionaires followed the lead of J. P. Morgan, who contributed to charity but hoarded private treasures in his marble library.

Social Darwinism nicely suited an age in which the gross inequalities accompanying industrialization seemed to cry out for action. Assuaging the nation's conscience, social Darwinism justified neglect of the poor in the name of "race progress." With so many of the poor coming from different races and ethnicities, social Darwinism fueled racism. A new "scientific racism" purported to prove "Anglo-Saxons" superior to all other groups. Social Darwinism buttressed the status quo and reassured comfortable, white Americans that all was as it should be. Even the gospel of wealth, which mitigated the harshest dictates of social Darwinism, insisted that Americans lived in the best of all possible worlds and that the rich were the natural rulers.

With its emphasis on the free play of competition and the survival of the fittest, social Darwinism encouraged the economic theory of **laissez-faire** (French for "let it alone"). Business argued that government should not meddle in economic affairs, except to protect private property. A conservative Supreme Court agreed. During the 1880s and 1890s, the Court increasingly reinterpreted the Constitution to protect business from taxation, regulation, labor organization, and antitrust legislation.

In a series of landmark decisions, the Court used the Fourteenth Amendment, originally intended to protect freed slaves from state laws violating their rights, to protect corporations. Defining corporations as "persons," the Court reiterated the amendment's language, that no state can "deprive any person of life, liberty, or property, without due process of law." In 1886 in *Santa Clara County v. Southern Pacific Railroad*, the Court reasoned that legislation designed to regulate the railroad deprived the corporation of "due process." Using the same reasoning, the Court struck down state laws regulating railroad rates, declared income tax unconstitutional, and judged labor unions a "conspiracy in restraint of trade." The Court's elevation of the rights of property over other rights stemmed from the conservatism of its justices. According to Justice Stephen J. Field, the Constitution "allows no impediments to the acquisition of property." Field, born into a wealthy New England family, spoke with the bias of the privileged class to whom property rights were sacrosanct. Imbued with this ideology, the Court refused to impede corporate consolidation and did nothing to curb the excesses of big business or promote the humane treatment of workers. Only in the arena of politics did Americans tackle the issues raised by corporate capitalism.

REVIEW Why did the ideas of social Darwinism appeal to many Americans in the late nineteenth century?

▶ Politics and Culture

For many Americans, politics provided a source of identity, a means of livelihood, and a ready form of entertainment. No wonder voter turnout averaged a hefty 77 percent (compared to 57 percent in the 2008 presidential election). A variety of factors contributed to the complicated interplay of politics and culture. Patronage provided an economic incentive for voter participation, but ethnicity, religion, sectional loyalty, race, and gender all influenced the political life of the period.

Political Participation and Party Loyalty

Patronage proved a strong motivation for party loyalty among many voters. Political parties in power doled out federal, state, and local government jobs to their loyal supporters. With hundreds of thousands of jobs to be filled, the choice of party affiliation could mean the difference between a paycheck and an empty pocket. Money greased the wheels of this system of patronage, dubbed the **spoils system** from the adage "to the victor go the spoils." With their livelihoods tied to their party identity, government employees in particular had an incentive to vote in great numbers.

Political affiliation provided a powerful sense of group identity for many voters proud of their loyalty to the Democrats or the Republicans.

Hayes Campaign Lantern, 1876
Republicans carried this lantern in the presidential campaign of 1876. Designed for nighttime rallies, the lantern featured paper transparencies that allowed light to shine through the stars and illuminate the portrait of the candidate, Rutherford B. Hayes. Marching men with lighted lanterns held aloft must have been a dramatic sight in small towns across the country, where politics constituted a major form of entertainment in the nineteenth century.
Collection of Janice L. and David J. Frent.

Democrats, who traced the party's roots back to Thomas Jefferson, called theirs "the party of the fathers." The Republican Party, founded in the 1850s, still claimed strong loyalties in the North as a result of its alignment with the Union during the Civil War. Republicans proved particularly adept at evoking Civil War loyalty, using a tactic called "waving the bloody shirt" — reminding voters which side they had fought for in the Civil War. Noting the power of old sectional loyalties, one of the party faithful observed, "Iowa will go Democratic when Hell goes Methodist."

Religion and ethnicity also played a significant role in politics. In the North, Protestants from the old-line denominations, particularly Presbyterians and Methodists, flocked to the Republican Party, which championed a series of moral reforms, including local laws requiring businesses to close in observance of the Sabbath. In the burgeoning cities, the Democratic Party courted immigrants and working-class Catholic and Jewish voters, charging, rightly, that Republican moral crusades often masked attacks on immigrant culture.

Sectionalism and the New South

After the end of Reconstruction, most white voters in the former Confederate states remained loyal Democrats, voting for Democratic candidates in every presidential election for the next seventy years. Labeling the Republican Party the agent of "Negro rule," Democrats urged white southerners to "vote the way you shot." Yet the so-called solid South proved far from solid on the state and local levels. The economic plight of the South led to shifting political alliances and to third-party movements that challenged Democratic attempts to define politics along race lines and maintain the Democratic Party as the white man's party.

The South's economy, devastated by the war, foundered at the same time the North experienced an unprecedented industrial boom. Soon an influential group of southerners called for a **New South** modeled on the industrial North. Henry Grady, the ebullient young editor of the *Atlanta Constitution*, used his paper's influence (it boasted the largest circulation of any weekly in the country) to extol the virtues of a new industrial South. Part bully, part booster, Grady exhorted the South to use its natural advantages — cheap labor and abundant natural resources — to go head-to-head in competition with northern industry.

Grady's message fell on receptive ears. Many southerners, men and women, black and white, joined the national migration from farm to city, leaving the old plantations to molder and decay. With the end of military rule in 1877, southern Democrats took back state governments, calling themselves "Redeemers." Yet rather than restore the economy of the old planter class, they embraced northern promoters who promised prosperity and profits.

The railroads came first, opening up the region for industrial development. Southern railroad mileage grew fourfold from 1865 to 1890. The number of cotton spindles also soared as textile mill owners abandoned New England in search of the cheap labor and proximity to raw materials promised in the South. By 1900, the South had become the nation's leading producer of cloth, and more than 100,000 southerners, many of them women and children, worked in the region's textile mills.

The New South prided itself most on its iron and steel industry, which grew up in the area surrounding Birmingham, Alabama. During this period, the smokestack replaced the white-pillared plantation as the symbol of the New South. Andrew Carnegie toured the region in 1889 and observed, "The South is Pennsylvania's most formidable industrial enemy." But southern industry remained controlled by northern investors, who had no intention of letting the South beat the North at its own game. Elaborate mechanisms rigged the price of southern steel, inflating it, as one northern insider confessed, "for the purpose of protecting the Pittsburgh mills and in turn the Pittsburgh steel users." Similarly, in the lumber and mining industries, investors in the North and abroad, not southerners, reaped the lion's share of the profits.

In only one industry did the South truly dominate — tobacco. Capitalizing on the invention of a machine for rolling cigarettes, the American Tobacco Company, founded by the Duke family of North Carolina, eventually dominated the industry. As cigarettes replaced chewing tobacco in popularity at the turn of the twentieth century, a booming market developed for Duke's "ready mades." Soon the company sold 400,000 cigarettes a day.

In practical terms, the industrialized New South proved an illusion. Much of the South remained agricultural, caught in the grip of the insidious crop lien system (see chapter 16). White

"Iowa will go Democratic when Hell goes Methodist."
— A Northern Republican

southern farmers, desperate to get out of debt, sometimes joined with African Americans to pursue their goals politically. Between 1865 and 1900, voters in every state south of the Mason-Dixon line experimented with political alliances that crossed the color line and threatened the status quo.

Gender, Race, and Politics

Gender — society's notion of what constitutes acceptable masculine or feminine behavior — influenced politics throughout the nineteenth century. From the early days of the Republic, citizenship had been defined in male terms. Citizenship and its prerogatives (voting and officeholding) served as a badge of manliness and rested on its corollary, patriarchy — the power and authority men exerted over their wives and families. With the advent of universal (white) male suffrage in the early nineteenth century, gender eclipsed class as the defining feature of citizenship; men's dominance over women provided the common thread that knit all white men together politically. The concept of **separate spheres** dictated political participation for men only. Once the public sphere of political participation became equated with manhood, women found themselves increasingly restricted to the private sphere of home and hearth.

Women were not alone in their limited access to the public sphere. Though Reconstruction legislation had guaranteed their freedom, blacks continued to face discrimination, especially in the New South. Segregation, commonly practiced under the rubric of **Jim Crow** laws (as discussed in chapter 21), prevented ex-slaves from riding in the same train cars as whites, from eating in the same restaurants, or from using the same toilet facilities.

Amid the turmoil of the post-Reconstruction South, some groups struck cross-racial alliances in search of political might. In Virginia, the "Readjusters," a coalition of blacks and whites determined to "readjust" (lower) the state debt and spend more money on public education, captured state offices from 1879 to 1883. Groups like the Readjusters rested on the belief that universal political rights (voting, officeholding, patronage) could be extended to black males in the public sphere while maintaining racial segregation in the private sphere. Democrats, for their part, fought back by trying to convince voters that black voting would inevitably lead

to miscegenation (racial mixing). Black male political power and sexual power, they warned, went hand in hand. Ultimately, their arguments prevailed, and many whites returned to the Democratic fold to protect "white womanhood" and with it white supremacy.

The notion that black men threatened white southern womanhood reached its most vicious form in the practice of lynching — the killing and mutilation of black men by white mobs. By 1892, the practice had become so prevalent that a courageous black editor, **Ida B. Wells**, launched an antilynching movement. That year, a white mob lynched a friend of Wells's whose grocery store competed too successfully with a white-owned store. Wells shrewdly concluded that lynching served "as an excuse to get rid of Negroes who were acquiring wealth and property and thus keep the race terrorized." She began to collect data on lynching and discovered that in the decade between 1882 and 1892 lynching rose in the South by an overwhelming 200 percent, with more than 241 black people killed. The vast increase in lynching testified to the retreat of the federal government following Reconstruction and to white southerners' determination to maintain supremacy through terrorism and intimidation.

In the face of this carnage, Wells struck back. As the first salvo in her attack, she put to rest the "old threadbare lie that Negro men assault white women." As she pointed out, violations of black women by white men, which were much more frequent than black attacks on white women, went unnoticed and unpunished. Wells articulated lynching as a problem of race and gender. She insisted that the myth of black attacks on white southern women masked the reality that mob violence had more to do with economics and the shifting social structure of the South than with rape. She demonstrated in a sophisticated way how the southern patriarchal system, having lost its control over blacks with the end of slavery, used its control over white women to circumscribe the liberty of black men.

Wells's strong stance immediately resulted in reprisal. While she was traveling in the North, vandals ransacked her office in Tennessee and destroyed her printing equipment. Yet the warning that she would be killed on sight if she ever returned to Memphis only stiffened her resolve. As she wrote in her autobiography, *Crusade for Justice* (1928), "Having lost my paper, had a price put on my life and been made an exile . . . , I felt that I owed it to myself and to my race to

SOUTHERN HORRORS.

LYNCH LAW

IN ALL

ITS PHASES

Miss IDA B. WELLS,

Price,   -   -   Fifteen Cents.

THE NEW YORK AGE PRINT.
1892.

Ida B. Wells

Ida B. Wells began her antilynching campaign in 1892 after a friend's murder led her to examine the problem of lynching in the South. She spread her message in lectures and pamphlets like this one, distributed for fifteen cents. Wells brought the horror of lynching to a national and international audience and mobilized other African American women to undertake social action under the auspices of the National Association of Colored Women. She later became a founding member of the National Association for the Advancement of Colored People (NAACP). Manuscript, Archives and Rare Books Division, Schomburg Center for Research in Black Culture, The New York Public Library, Astor, Lenox, and Tilden Foundations.

issue to national and international prominence. At her funeral in 1931, black leader W. E. B. Du Bois eulogized Wells as the woman who "began the awakening of the conscience of the nation." Wells's determined campaign against lynching provided just one example of women's political activism during the Gilded Age. The suffrage and temperance movements, along with the growing popularity of women's clubs, dramatized how women refused to be relegated to a separate sphere that kept them out of politics.

Women's Activism

No one better recognized the potency of the gendered notion of political rights than Elizabeth Cady Stanton, who lamented the introduction of the word *male* into the Fourteenth Amendment (see chapter 16). The explicit linking of manhood with citizenship and voting rights in the Constitution marked a major setback for reformers who supported the vote for women. In 1869, Stanton along with Susan B. Anthony formed the National Woman Suffrage Association, the first independent woman's rights organization in the United States (discussed in chapter 20). Women found ways to act politically long before they voted and cleverly used their moral authority as wives and mothers to move from the domestic sphere into the realm of politics.

The extraordinary activity of women's clubs in the period following the Civil War provides just one example. Women's clubs proliferated from the 1860s to the 1890s, often in response to the exclusionary policies of men's organizations. In 1868, newspaper reporter Jane Cunningham Croly (pen name Jennie June) founded the Sorosis Club in New York City after the New York Press Club denied entry to women journalists wishing to attend a banquet honoring the British author Charles Dickens. In 1890, Croly brought state and local clubs together under the umbrella of the **General Federation of Women's Clubs** (GFWC). Not wanting to alienate southern women, the GFWC barred black women's clubs from joining, despite their vehement objections. Women's clubs soon abandoned literary pursuits to devote themselves to "civic usefulness," endorsing an end to child labor, supporting the eight-hour workday, and helping pass pure food and drug legislation.

The temperance movement (the movement to end drunkenness) attracted by far the largest number of organized women in the late nineteenth century. By the late 1860s and the

tell the whole truth now that I was where I could do so freely." As a reporter, first for the *New York Age* and later for the *Chicago Inter-Ocean*, she used every opportunity to hammer home her message. Beginning in 1894 and continuing for decades, antilynching bills were introduced in Congress, only to be defeated by southern opposition.

Lynching did not end during Ida B. Wells's lifetime, but Wells's forceful voice brought the

"Woman's Holy War"
This political cartoon from 1874 styles the temperance campaign as "Woman's Holy War" and shows a woman knight in armor (demurely seated sidesaddle on her charger), wielding a battle-ax and trampling on barrels of liquor. The image of temperance women as ax-wielding Amazons proved a popular satiric image. The temperance movement experienced a resurgence in the 1870s after Bible-toting women marched to shut down saloons from New York to Michigan. Their activism led to the creation of the Woman's Christian Temperance Union in 1874.
Picture Research Consultants & Archives.

1870s, the liquor business was flourishing, with about one saloon for every fifty males over the age of fifteen. During the winter of 1873–74, temperance women adopted a radical new tactic. Armed with Bibles and singing hymns, they marched on taverns and saloons and refused to leave until the proprietors signed a pledge to quit selling liquor. Known as the Woman's Crusade, the movement spread like a prairie fire through small towns in Ohio, Indiana, Michigan, and Illinois and soon moved east into New York, New England, and Pennsylvania. Before it was over, more than 100,000 women had marched in more than 450 cities and towns.

The women's tactics may have been new, but the temperance movement dated back to the 1820s. Originally, the movement was led by Protestant men who organized clubs to pledge voluntary abstinence from liquor. By the 1850s, temperance advocates won significant victories when states, starting with Maine, passed laws to prohibit the sale of liquor (known as "Maine laws"). The Woman's Crusade dramatically brought the issue of temperance back into the national spotlight and led to the formation of a new organization, the **Woman's Christian Temperance Union** (WCTU) in 1874. Composed entirely of women, the WCTU advocated total abstinence from alcohol.

Temperance provided women with a respectable outlet for their increasing resentment of women's inferior status and their growing recognition of women's capabilities. In its first five years, the WCTU relied on education and moral suasion, but when Frances Willard became president in 1879, she politicized the organization (as discussed in chapter 20). When the women of the WCTU joined with the Prohibition Party (formed in 1869 by a group of evangelical clergymen), one wag observed, "Politics is a man's game, an' women, childhern, and prohyibitionists do well to keep out iv it." By sharing power with women, the Prohibitionist men violated the old political rules and risked attacks on their honor and manhood.

Even though they could not yet vote, women found ways to affect the political process. Like men, they displayed strong party loyalties and rallied around traditional Republican and Democratic candidates. Third parties courted women, recognizing that their volunteer labor and support could be key assets in party building. Nevertheless, despite growing political awareness among women, politics, particularly presidential politics, remained an exclusively male prerogative.

REVIEW   How did race and gender influence politics?

▶ Presidential Politics

The presidents of the Gilded Age, from Rutherford B. Hayes (1877–1881) to William McKinley (1897–1901), are largely forgotten men, primarily because so little was expected of them. In wartime, Lincoln had expanded the power of the presidency, but following the war, even as the nation addressed western expansion, economic transformation, and nascent urban industrialism, the power of the presidency waned. The dominant creed of laissez-faire, coupled with the dictates of social Darwinism, warned the president and the government to leave business alone. Still, presidents in the Gilded Age grappled with corruption and party strife and struggled toward the creation of new political ethics designed to replace patronage with a civil service system that promised to award jobs on the basis of merit, not party loyalty.

Corruption and Party Strife

The political corruption and party factionalism that characterized the administration of Ulysses S. Grant (1869–1877) (see chapter 16) continued to trouble the nation in the 1880s. The spoils system — awarding jobs for political purposes — remained the driving force in party politics at all levels of government in the Gilded Age. Pro-business Republicans generally held a firm grip on the White House, while Democrats had better luck in Congress. Both parties relied on patronage to cement party loyalty. Corruption was rampant, with senators and representatives, and sometimes members of the executive branch, on the payrolls of business interests. The notion of "conflict of interest" did not exist; nor did a standard of accepted ethical behavior. Reformers eager to end corruption and the replace the spoils system with a merit-based civil service system faced an uphill battle.

A small but determined group of reformers championed a new ethics that would preclude politicians from getting rich from public office. The selection of U.S. senators particularly concerned them. Under the Constitution, senators were selected by state legislatures, not directly elected by the voters. Powerful business interests often contrived to control state legislatures and through them U.S. senators. As journalist Henry Demarest Lloyd quipped, Standard Oil "had done everything to the Pennsylvania legislature except to refine it." Nothing prevented a senator from collecting a paycheck from any of the great corporations. So many did so that political cartoonists often portrayed senators as huge money bags labeled with the names of the corporations they served. In this climate, a constitutional amendment calling for the direct election of senators faced stiff opposition from entrenched interests.

Republican president **Rutherford B. Hayes**, whose disputed election in 1876 signaled the end of Reconstruction in the South, tried to steer a middle course between spoilsmen and reformers. Although the Democratic press ridiculed him as "Rutherfraud" because he had not been popularly elected (see chapter 16), Hayes proved a hardworking, well-informed executive who wanted peace, prosperity, and an end to party strife. Yet the Republican Party remained divided into factions led by strong party bosses who boasted that they could make or break any president.

Foremost among the Republican bosses in the Senate stood Roscoe Conkling of New York, a master spoilsman who ridiculed civil service as "snivel service." He and his followers, called the "Stalwarts," represented the Grant faction of the party. Conkling's archrival, Senator James G. Blaine of Maine, led the "Half Breeds." Not as openly corrupt as the Grant wing of the party, the Half Breeds and their champion were nevertheless tainted with charges of corruption. A third group, called the "Mugwumps," consisted primarily of reform-minded Republicans from Massachusetts and New York who deplored the spoils system and advocated **civil service reform**. The name "Mugwump" came from the Algonquian word for "chief," but critics used the term derisively, punning that the Mugwumps straddled the fence on issues of party loyalty, "with their mug on one side and wump on the other."

President Hayes's middle course pleased no one, and he soon managed to alienate all factions of his party. No one was surprised when he announced that he would not seek reelection in 1880. To avoid choosing among its factions, the Republican Party in 1880 nominated a dark-horse candidate, Representative **James A. Garfield** of Ohio. To foster party unity, they picked Stalwart Chester A. Arthur as the vice presidential candidate. The Democrats made an attempt to overcome sectionalism and establish a national party by selecting as their presidential standard-bearer an old Union general, Winfield Scott Hancock. But as one observer noted, "It is a peculiarly constituted party that sends rebel brigadiers to Congress because of their rebellion, and then nominates a Union General as its candidate for president because of his loyalty." Hancock garnered only lukewarm support, receiving just 155 electoral votes to Garfield's 214, although the popular vote was less lopsided.

> **"[Standard Oil] had done everything to the Pennsylvania legislature except to refine it."**
> — Journalist
> **HENRY DEMAREST LLOYD**

Garfield's Assassination and Civil Service Reform

"My God," Garfield swore after only a few months in office, "what is there in this place that a man should ever want to get into it?" Garfield, like Hayes, faced the difficult task of remaining independent while pacifying the party bosses and placating the reformers. As the federal bureaucracy grew to nearly 150,000 jobs, thousands of office seekers swarmed to the nation's capital, each clamoring for a position. In the days before Secret Service protection, the White House door stood open to all comers. Garfield took a fatalistic view. "Assassination," he told a friend, "can no more be guarded against than death by lightning, and it is best not to worry about either."

On July 2, 1881, less than four months after taking office, Garfield was shot. His assailant,

Civil Service Exams

In this 1890s photograph, prospective police officers in Chicago take the written civil service exam. Civil service meant that politicians and party bosses could no longer use jobs in the government to reward the party faithful. Many people worried that merit examinations would favor the educated elite at the expense of immigrant groups such as the Irish, who had made a place for themselves in the political system by the late nineteenth century. Chicago Historical Society.

Charles Guiteau, though clearly insane, turned out to be a disappointed office seeker who claimed to be motivated by political partisanship. He told the police officer who arrested him, "I did it; I will go to jail for it; Arthur is president, and I am a Stalwart." Throughout the hot summer, the country kept a deathwatch as Garfield lingered. When he died in September, Chester A. Arthur became president. The press almost universally condemned Republican factionalism for creating the political climate that produced Guiteau and led to the second political assassination in a generation.

Stalwart Roscoe Conkling saw his hopes for the White House dashed. Attacks on the spoils system increased, and the public joined the chorus calling for reform. Both parties claimed credit for passage of the Pendleton Civil Service Act of 1883, which established a permanent Civil Service Commission consisting of three members appointed by the president. Some fourteen thousand jobs came under a merit system that required examinations for office and made it impossible to remove jobholders for political reasons. The new law also prohibited federal jobholders from contributing to political campaigns, thus drying up the major source of the party bosses' revenue. Soon, business interests stepped in to replace officeholders as the nation's chief political contributors. Ironically, civil service reform thus gave business an even greater influence in political life.

Reform and Scandal: The Campaign of 1884

With Conkling's downfall, James G. Blaine assumed leadership of the Republican Party and at long last captured the presidential nomination in 1884. A magnetic Irish American, Blaine inspired such devotion that his supporters called themselves Blainiacs. But Mugwumps like editor Carl Schurz insisted that Blaine "wallowed in spoils like a rhinoceros in an African pool." They bolted the party and embraced the Democrats' presidential nominee, the stolid **Grover Cleveland**, reform governor of New York. The burly, beer-drinking Cleveland distinguished himself from an entire generation of politicians by the simple motto "A public office is a public trust." First as mayor of Buffalo and later as governor of New York, he built a reputation for honesty, economy, and administrative efficiency. The Democrats, who had not won the presidency since 1856, had high hopes for his candidacy,

"Another Voice for Cleveland"
This political cartoon ran in the magazine *Judge* in the fall of 1884 during the presidential campaign. Grover Cleveland, the Democratic candidate, is pictured cringing from the cries of a babe in arms — an allusion to his admission that he had fathered an illegitimate child. Despite the lurid publicity, Cleveland won the election. Library of Congress.

especially after the Mugwumps threw their support to Cleveland. As the Mugwumps insisted, "The paramount issue this year is moral rather than political."

The Mugwumps soon regretted their words. The 1884 contest degenerated so far into scandal and nasty mudslinging that one disgusted journalist styled it "the vilest campaign ever waged." In July, Cleveland's hometown paper, the *Buffalo Telegraph*, dropped the bombshell that the candidate had fathered an illegitimate child in an affair with a local widow. Cleveland, a bachelor, stoically accepted responsibility for the child. Crushed by the scandal, the Mugwumps lost much of their enthusiasm. At public rallies, Blaine's partisans taunted Cleveland, chanting, "Ma, Ma, where's my Pa?" Silent but fuming, Cleveland waged his campaign in the traditional fashion by staying home.

Blaine set a new campaign style by launching a whirlwind national tour. On a last-minute stop in New York City, the exhausted candidate committed a misstep that may have cost him the election. He overlooked a remark by a supporter, a local clergyman who cast a slur on Catholic voters by styling the Democrats as the party of "Rum, Romanism, and Rebellion." Linking drinking (rum) and Catholicism (Romanism) offended Irish Catholic voters, whom Blaine had counted on to desert the Democratic Party and support him because of his Irish background.

With less than a week to go until the election, Blaine had no chance to recover from the negative publicity. He lost New York State by fewer than 1,200 votes and with it the election. In the final tally, Cleveland defeated Blaine by a scant 23,005 votes nationwide but won with

Candidate	Electoral Vote	Popular Vote	Percent of Popular Vote
Grover Cleveland (Democrat)	219	4,874,986	48.5*
James G. Blaine (Republican)	182	4,851,981	48.3

*Percentages do not total 100 because some popular votes went to other parties.

MAP 18.2
The Election of 1884

219 electoral votes to Blaine's 182 (Map 18.2), ending twenty-four years of Republican control of the presidency. Cleveland's followers had the last word. To the chorus of "Ma, Ma, where's my Pa?" they retorted, "Going to the White House, ha, ha, ha."

REVIEW   How did the question of civil service reform contribute to divisions within the Republican Party?

► Economic Issues and Party Realignment

Four years later, in the election of 1888, fickle voters turned Cleveland out, electing Republican Benjamin Harrison, the grandson of President William Henry Harrison. Then, in the only instance in American history when a president once defeated at the polls returned to office, the voters brought Cleveland back in the election of 1892. What factors account for such a surprising turnaround? The 1880s witnessed a remarkable political realignment as a set of economic concerns replaced appeals to Civil War sectional loyalties. The tariff, federal regulation of the railroads and trusts, and the campaign for free silver restructured American politics. A Wall Street panic in 1893 set off a major depression that further fed political unrest.

The Tariff and the Politics of Protection

The tariff became a potent political issue in the 1880s. The concept of a protective tariff to raise the price of imported goods and stimulate American industry dated back to Alexander Hamilton in the founding days of the Republic. The Republicans turned the tariff to political ends in 1861 by enacting a measure that both raised revenues for the Civil War and rewarded their industrial supporters, who wanted protection from foreign competition. After the war, the pro-business Republicans continued to revise and enlarge the tariff. Manufactured goods such as steel and textiles, and some agricultural products, including sugar and wool, benefited from protection. Most farm products, notably wheat and cotton, did not. By the 1880s, the tariff produced more than $2.1 billion in revenue. Not only did the high tariff pay off the nation's Civil War debt and fund pensions for Union soldiers, but it also created a huge surplus that sat idly in the Treasury's vaults while the government argued about how (or even whether) to spend it.

To many Americans, particularly southern and midwestern farmers who sold their crops in a world market but had to buy goods priced artificially high because of the protective tariff, the answer was simple: Reduce the tariff. Advocates of free trade and moderates agitated for tariff reform. But those who benefited from the tariff—industrialists insisting that America's "infant industries" needed protection and some westerners producing protected raw materials such as wool, hides, and lumber—firmly opposed lowering the tariff. Many argued that workers, too, benefited from high tariffs that protected American wages by giving American products an edge over imported goods.

The Republican Party seized on the tariff question to forge a new national coalition. "Fold up the bloody shirt and lay it away," Blaine advised a colleague in 1880. "It's of no use to us. You want to shift the main issue to protection." By encouraging an alliance among industrialists, labor, and western producers of raw materials — groups seen to benefit from the tariff — Blaine hoped to solidify the North, Midwest, and West against the solidly Democratic South. Although the tactic failed for Blaine in the presidential election of 1884, it worked for the Republicans four years later.

Cleveland, who had straddled the tariff issue in the election of 1884, startled the nation in 1887 by calling for tariff reform. Cleveland attacked the tariff as a tax levied on American consumers by powerful industries. And he pointed out that high tariffs impeded the expansion of American markets abroad at a time when American industries needed to expand if they were to keep growing. The Republicans countered by arguing that "tariff tinkering" would only unsettle prosperous industries, drive down wages, and shrink the farmers' home market. Republican Benjamin Harrison, who supported the high tariff, ousted Cleveland from the White House in 1888, carrying all the western and northern states except Connecticut and New Jersey.

Back in power, the Republicans brazenly passed the highest tariff in the nation's history in 1890. The new tariff, sponsored by Republican representative William McKinley of Ohio and signed into law by Harrison, stirred up a hornet's nest of protest across the United States. The American people had elected Harrison to preserve protection but not to enact a higher tariff. Democrats condemned the **McKinley tariff** and labeled the Republican Congress that passed it the "Billion Dollar Congress" for its carnival of spending, which depleted the nation's surplus by enacting a series of pork barrel programs shamelessly designed to bring federal money to congressmen's own constituents. In the congressional election of 1890, angry voters swept the hapless Republicans, including tariff sponsor McKinley, out of office. Two years later, Harrison himself was defeated. Grover Cleveland, whose call for tariff revision had cost him the election in 1888, triumphantly returned to the White House vowing to lower the tariff. Such were the changes in the political winds whipped up by the tariff issue.

Controversy over the tariff masked deeper divisions in American society. Conflict between workers and farmers on the one side and bankers and corporate giants on the other erupted throughout the 1880s and came to a head in the 1890s. Both sides in the tariff debate spoke to concern over class conflict when they insisted that their respective plans, whether McKinley's high tariff or Cleveland's tariff reform, would bring prosperity and harmony. For their part, many working people shared the sentiment voiced by one labor leader that the tariff was "only a scheme devised by the old parties to throw dust in the eyes of laboring men."

Railroads, Trusts, and the Federal Government

American voters may have divided on the tariff, but increasingly they agreed on the need for federal regulation of the railroads and federal legislation to curb the power of the "trusts" (a term loosely applied to all large business combinations). As early as the 1870s, angry farmers in the Midwest who suffered from the unfair shipping practices of the railroads organized to fight for railroad regulation. The Patrons of Husbandry, or the Grange, founded in 1867 as a social and educational organization for farmers, soon became an independent political movement. By electing Grangers to state office, farmers made it possible for several midwestern states to pass laws in the 1870s and 1880s regulating the railroads. At first, the Supreme Court ruled in favor of state regulation (*Munn v. Illinois*, 1877). But in 1886, the Court reversed itself, ruling that because railroads crossed state boundaries, they fell outside state jurisdiction (*Wabash v. Illinois*). With more than three-fourths of railroads crossing state lines, the Supreme Court's decision effectively quashed the states' attempts at railroad regulation.

Anger at the *Wabash* decision finally led to the first federal law regulating the railroads, the Interstate Commerce Act, passed in 1887 during Cleveland's first administration. The act established the nation's first federal regulatory agency, the **Interstate Commerce Commission (ICC)**, to oversee the railroad industry. In its early years, the ICC was never strong enough to pose a serious threat to the railroads. For example, it could not end rebates to big shippers. In its early decades, the ICC proved more important as a precedent than effective as a watchdog.

Concern over the growing power of the trusts led Congress to pass the **Sherman Antitrust Act** in 1890. The act outlawed pools and trusts, ruling that businesses could no longer enter into agreements to restrict competition. It did nothing to restrict huge holding companies such as Standard Oil, however, and proved to be a weak sword against the trusts. In the following decade, the government successfully struck down only six trusts but used the law four times against labor by outlawing unions as a "conspiracy in restraint of trade." In 1895, the conservative Supreme Court dealt the antitrust law a crippling

> **"[The tariff is] only a scheme devised by the old parties to throw dust in the eyes of laboring men."**
> — A labor leader

blow in *United States v. E. C. Knight Company*. In its decision, the Court ruled that "manufacture" did not constitute "trade." This semantic quibble drastically narrowed the law, in this case allowing the American Sugar Refining Company, which had bought out a number of other sugar companies (including E. C. Knight) and controlled 98 percent of the production of sugar, to continue its virtual monopoly.

Both the ICC and the Sherman Antitrust Act testified to the nation's concern about corporate abuses of power and to a growing willingness to use federal measures to intervene on behalf of the public interest. As corporate capitalism became more and more powerful, public pressure toward government intervention grew. Yet not until the twentieth century would more active presidents sharpen and use these weapons effectively against the large corporations.

The Fight for Free Silver

While the tariff and regulation of the trusts gained many backers, the silver issue stirred passions like no other issue of the day. On one side stood those who believed that gold constituted the only honest money. Although other forms of currency circulated, notably paper money such as banknotes and greenbacks, the government's support of the gold standard meant that anyone could redeem paper money for gold. Many who supported the gold standard were eastern creditors who did not wish to be paid in devalued dollars. On the opposite side stood a coalition of western silver barons and poor farmers from the West and South who called for **free silver**. The mining interests, who had seen the silver bonanza in the West drive down the price of the precious metal, wanted the government to buy silver and mint silver dollars. Farmers from the West and South who had suffered from deflation during the 1870s and 1880s hoped that increasing the money supply with silver dollars, thus causing inflation, would give them some debt relief by enabling them to pay off their creditors with cheaper dollars.

During the depression following the panic of 1873, critics of hard money organized the Greenback Labor Party, an alliance of farmers and urban wage laborers. The Greenbackers favored issuing paper currency not tied to the gold supply, citing the precedent of the greenbacks issued during the Civil War. The government had the right to define what constituted legal tender, the Greenbackers reasoned: "Paper is equally money, when . . . issued according to law." They proposed that the nation's currency be based on its wealth — land, labor, and capital — and not simply on its reserves of gold. The Greenback Labor Party captured more than a million votes and elected fourteen members to Congress in 1878. Although conservatives considered the Greenbackers dangerous cranks, their views eventually prevailed in the 1930s, when the country abandoned the gold standard.

After the Greenback Labor Party collapsed, proponents of free silver came to dominate the monetary debate in the 1890s. Advocates of free silver pointed out that until 1873 the country had enjoyed a system of bimetallism — the minting of both silver and gold into coins. In that year, at the behest of those who favored gold, the Republican Congress had voted to stop buying and minting silver, an act silver supporters denounced as the "crime of '73." By sharply contracting the money supply at a time when the nation's economy was burgeoning, the Republicans had enriched bankers and investors at the expense of cotton and wheat farmers and industrial wageworkers. In 1878 and again in 1890, with the Sherman Silver Purchase Act, Congress took steps to ease the tight money policy and appease advocates of silver by passing legislation requiring the government to buy silver and issue silver certificates. Though good for the mining interests, the laws did little to promote the inflation desired by farmers. Soon monetary reformers began to call for "the free and unlimited coinage of silver," a plan whereby nearly all the silver mined in the West would be minted into coins circulated at the rate of sixteen ounces of silver — equal in value to one ounce of gold.

By the 1890s, the silver issue crossed party lines. The Democrats hoped to use it to achieve a union between western and southern voters. Unfortunately for them, Democratic president Grover Cleveland remained a staunch conservative in money matters and supported the gold standard as vehemently as any Republican. After a panic on Wall Street in the spring of 1893, Cleveland called a special session of Congress and bullied the legislature into repealing the Silver Purchase Act because he believed it threatened economic confidence. Repeal proved disastrous for Cleveland, not only economically but also politically. It did nothing to bring prosperity and dangerously divided the country. Angry farmers, furious at the president's harsh monetary policy, warned Cleveland not to travel west of the Mississippi River if he valued his life.

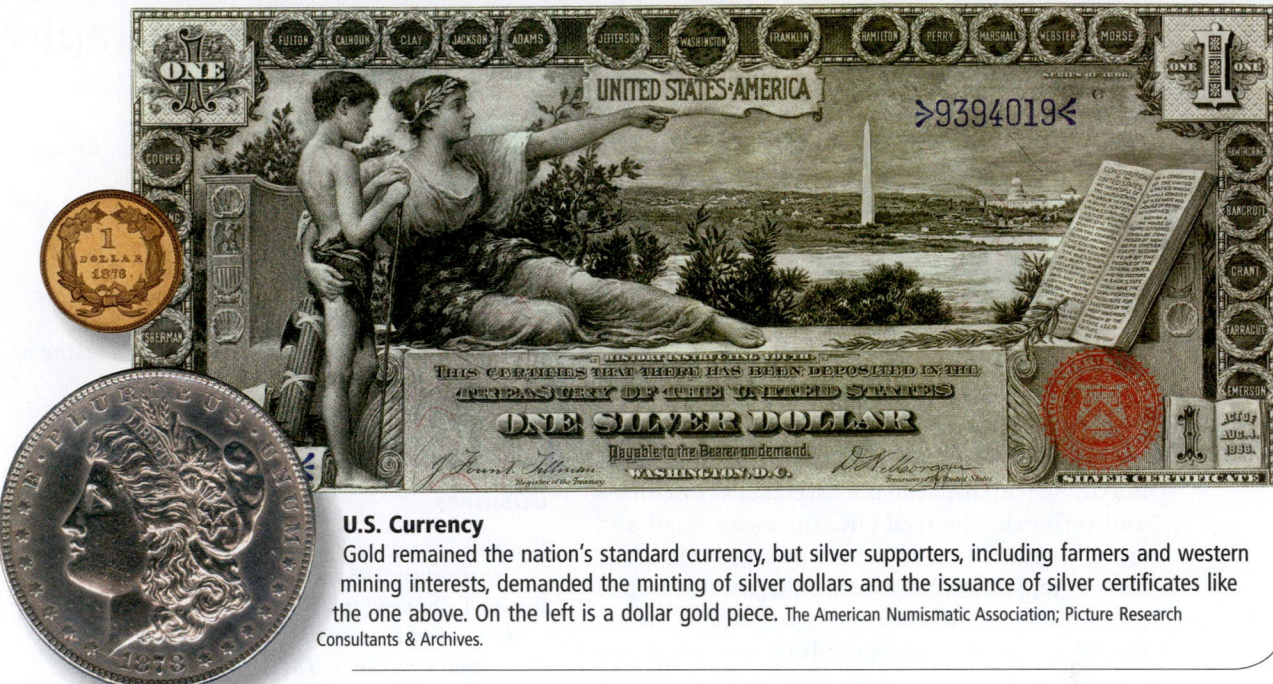

U.S. Currency
Gold remained the nation's standard currency, but silver supporters, including farmers and western mining interests, demanded the minting of silver dollars and the issuance of silver certificates like the one above. On the left is a dollar gold piece. The American Numismatic Association; Picture Research Consultants & Archives.

Panic and Depression

President Cleveland had scarcely begun his second term in office in 1893 when the country faced the worst depression it had yet seen. In the face of economic disaster, Cleveland clung to the economic orthodoxy of the gold standard. In the winter of 1894–95, the president walked the floor of the White House, sleepless over the prospect that the United States might go bankrupt. Individuals and investors, rushing to trade in their banknotes for gold, strained the country's monetary system. The Treasury's gold reserves dipped so low that unless they could be buttressed, the unthinkable might happen: The U.S. Treasury might not be able to meet its obligations.

At this juncture, J. P. Morgan stepped in and suggested a plan. A group of bankers would purchase $65 million in U.S. government bonds, paying in gold. Cleveland knew that such a scheme would unleash a thunder of protest, yet to save the gold standard, the president had no choice but to accept Morgan's help. A storm of controversy erupted over the deal. The press claimed that Cleveland had lined his own pockets and rumored that Morgan had made $8.9 million. Neither allegation was true. Cleveland had not profited a penny, and Morgan made far less than the millions his critics claimed.

But if President Cleveland's action managed to salvage the gold standard, it did not save the country from hardship. The winter of 1894–95 was one of the worst times in American history. People faced unemployment, cold, and hunger. A firm believer in limited government, Cleveland insisted that nothing could be done to help: "I do not believe that the power and duty of the General Government ought to be extended to the relief of individual suffering which is in no manner properly related to the public service or benefit." Nor did it occur to Cleveland that his great faith in the gold standard prolonged the depression, favored creditors over debtors, and caused immense hardship for millions of Americans.

REVIEW Why were Americans split on the question of the tariff and currency?

▶ Conclusion: Business Dominates an Era

The gold deal between J. P. Morgan and Grover Cleveland underscored a dangerous reality: The federal government was so weak that its solvency depended on a private banker. This lopsided power relationship signaled the dominance of business in the era Mark Twain satirically but accurately characterized as the Gilded Age. Perhaps no other era in American history spawned

greed, corruption, and vulgarity on so grand a scale — an era when speculators like Jay Gould not only built but wrecked railroads to turn paper profits; an era when the get-rich-quick ethic of the western prospector infused the whole continent; and an era when business boasted openly of buying politicians, who in turn lined their pockets at the public's expense.

Nevertheless, the Gilded Age was not without its share of solid achievements, many inextricably linked to its empire in the West (see chapter 17). Where dusty roads and cattle trails once sprawled across the continent, steel rails now bound the country together, creating a national market that enabled America to make the leap into the industrial age. Factories and refineries poured out American steel and oil at unprecedented rates. Businessmen like Carnegie, Rockefeller, and Morgan developed new strategies to consolidate American industry. New inventions, including the telephone and electric light and power, changed Americans' everyday lives. By the end of the nineteenth century, the country had achieved industrial maturity. It boasted the largest, most innovative, most productive economy in the world. No other era in the nation's history witnessed such a transformation.

Yet the changes that came with these developments worried many Americans and gave rise to the era's political turmoil. Race and gender profoundly influenced American politics, leading to new political alliances. Fearless activist Ida B. Wells fought racism in its most brutal form — lynching. Women's organizations championed causes, notably suffrage and temperance, and challenged prevailing views of woman's proper sphere. Reformers fought corruption by instituting civil service. And new issues — the tariff, the regulation of the trusts, and currency reform — restructured the nation's politics.

The Gilded Age witnessed a nation transformed. Fueled by expanding industry, cities grew exponentially, not only with new inhabitants from around the globe but also with new bridges, subways, and skyscrapers. The frenzied growth of urban America brought wealth and opportunity, but also the exploitation of labor, racism toward newcomers, and social upheaval that lent a new urgency to calls for social reform.

▶ Selected Bibliography

General Works

Charles W. Calhoun, ed., *The Gilded Age: Essays on the Origins of Modern America* (1996).

Sean Dennis Cashman, *America in the Gilded Age: From the Death of Lincoln to the Rise of Theodore Roosevelt* (1993).

Rebecca Edwards, *New Spirits: Americans in the Gilded Age, 1865–1905* (2006).

Jackson Lears, *Rebirth of a Nation: The Making of Modern America, 1877–1920* (2009).

Richard While, *Railroaded: The Transcontinentals and the Making of Modern America* (2011).

Business

Kathleen Brady, *Ida Tarbell: Portrait of a Muckraker* (1984).

Edward Chancellor, *Devil Take the Hindmost: A History of Financial Speculation* (1999).

Ron Chernow, *Titan: The Life of John D. Rockefeller, Sr.* (1998).

Steve Fraser, *Every Man a Speculator: A Cultural History of Wall Street in America* (2005).

Morton J. Horowitz, *The Transformation of American Law, 1870–1960* (1992).

Walter Licht, *Industrializing America* (1995).

David Nasaw, *Andrew Carnegie* (2006).

T. J. Stiles, *The First Tycoon: The Epic Life of Cornelius Vanderbilt* (2009).

Jean Strouse, *Morgan: American Financier* (1999).

Viviana A. Zelizer, *The Social Meaning of Money* (1994).

Politics

Paula Baker, *The Moral Framework of Public Life* (1991).

Richard F. Bensel, *The Political Economy of American Industrialization, 1877–1900* (2000).

Ruth Bordin, *Women and Temperance: The Quest for Power and Liberty, 1873–1900* (1990).

Alyn Brodsky, *Grover Cleveland: A Study in Character* (2000).

Robert W. Cherny, *American Politics in the Gilded Age, 1868–1900* (1997).

Jane Dailey, Glenda Elizabeth Gilmore, and Bryant Simon, eds., *Jumpin' Jim Crow: Southern Politics from the Civil War to Civil Rights* (2000).

Rebecca Edwards, *Angels in the Machinery: Gender in American Party Politics from the Civil War to the Progressive Era* (1997).

Dana Frank, *Buy American: The Untold Story of Economic Nationalism* (1999).

Paula Giddings, *Ida, a Sword among Lions: Ida B. Wells and the Campaign against Lynching* (2008).

Steven Hahn, *A Nation under Our Feet: Black Political Struggles in the Rural South from Slavery to the Great Migration* (2003).

Darlene Clark Hine and Kathleen Thompson, *A Shining Thread of Hope: The History of Black Women in America* (1998).

Ari Hoogenboom, *Rutherford B. Hayes: Warrior and President* (1995).

H. Paul Jeffers, *An Honest President: The Life and Presidencies of Grover Cleveland* (2000).

Ross Evans Paulson, *Liberty, Equality, and Justice: Civil Rights, Women's Rights, and the Regulation of Business, 1865–1932* (1997).

Dorothy Salem, *To Better Our World: Black Women in Organized Reform, 1890–1920* (1990).

Ian Tyrell, *Woman's World, Woman's Empire: The Woman's Christian Temperance Union in International Perspective, 1880–1930* (1991).

LeeAnn Whites, *Gender Matters: Civil War, Reconstruction, and the Making of the New South* (2005).

Culture

Judy Arlene Hilkey, *Character Is Capital: Success Manuals and Manhood in Gilded Age America* (1997).

Jane H. Hunter, *How Young Ladies Became Girls: The Victorian Origins of American Girlhood* (2002).

Paulette D. Kilmer, *The Fear of Sinking: The American Success Formula in the Gilded Age* (1996).

Alan Trachtenberg, *The Incorporation of America: Culture and Society in the Gilded Age* (anniversary edition, 2009).

For more books about topics in this chapter, see the Online Bibliography at **bedfordstmartins.com/roark**.

For additional primary sources from this period, see Michael Johnson, ed., *Reading the American Past*, Fifth Edition.

For Web sites, images, and documents related to topics and places in this chapter, visit Make History at **bedfordstmartins.com/roark**.

Reviewing Chapter 18

KEY TERMS

Explain each term's significance.

Old Industries Transformed, New Industries Born
- Gilded Age (p. 571)
- Jay Gould (p. 571)
- Andrew Carnegie (p. 573)
- vertical integration (p. 576)
- John D. Rockefeller (p. 577)
- trust (p. 577)
- Ida M. Tarbell (p. 578)
- Thomas Alva Edison (p. 580)

From Competition to Consolidation
- finance capitalism (p. 581)
- J. P. Morgan (p. 582)
- social Darwinism (p. 584)
- gospel of wealth (p. 585)
- laissez-faire (p. 586)

Politics and Culture
- spoils system (p. 586)
- New South (p. 587)
- separate spheres (p. 588)
- Jim Crow (p. 588)
- Ida B. Wells (p. 588)
- General Federation of Women's Clubs (GFWC) (p. 589)
- Woman's Christian Temperance Union (WCTU) (p. 590)

Presidential Politics
- Rutherford B. Hayes (p. 591)
- civil service reform (p. 591)
- James A. Garfield (p. 591)
- Grover Cleveland (p. 592)

Economic Issues and Party Realignment
- McKinley tariff (p. 595)
- Interstate Commerce Commission (ICC) (p. 595)
- Sherman Antitrust Act (p. 595)
- free silver (p. 596)

REVIEW QUESTIONS

Use key terms and dates to support your answer.

1. What devices did John D. Rockefeller use to gain control of 90 percent of the oil-refining business by 1890? (pp. 571–581)

2. Why did the ideas of social Darwinism appeal to many Americans in the late nineteenth century? (pp. 581–586)

3. How did race and gender influence politics? (pp. 586–590)

4. How did the question of civil service reform contribute to divisions within the Republican Party? (pp. 590–594)

5. Why were Americans split on the question of the tariff and currency? (pp. 594–597)

MAKING CONNECTIONS

Draw on key terms, the timeline, and review questions.

1. How did the railroads contribute to the growth of American industry? In your answer, discuss the drawbacks and benefits of these developments.

2. Late-nineteenth-century industrialization depended on developments in technology and business strategy. What were some of the key innovations in both arenas? How did they facilitate the maturation of American industry?

3. By the 1870s, several new concerns had displaced slavery as the defining question of American politics. What were these new issues, and how did they shape new regional, economic, and racial alliances and rivalries? In your answer, consider the part that political parties played in this process.

4. Energetic political activity characterized Gilded Age America, both within and beyond formal party politics. How did the activism of women denied the vote contribute to the era's electoral politics? In your answer, be sure to cite specific examples of political action.

5. The U.S. Congress and the Supreme Court facilitated the concentration of power in the hands of private business concerns during the Gilded Age. Citing specific policies and court decisions, discuss how government helped augment the power of big business in the late nineteenth century.

LINKING TO THE PAST

Link events in this chapter to earlier events.

1. In what ways did the military conquest of the trans-Mississippi West, with its dislocation of Native Americans, play a significant role in the industrial boom of the Gilded Age? (See chapter 17.)

2. In what ways did the rampant get-rich-quick mentality of western miners and land speculators help set the tone for the Gilded Age? Is the West the herald of the Gilded Age, or must we look to New York and Washington? (See chapter 17.)

▶ FOR PRACTICE QUIZZES AND OTHER STUDY TOOLS, visit the Online Study Guide at **bedfordstmartins.com/roark**.

TIMELINE 1869–1901

1869	• First transcontinental railroad completed.
	• National Woman Suffrage Association founded.
1870	• John D. Rockefeller incorporates Standard Oil Company.
1872	• Andrew Carnegie builds the largest, most up-to-date Bessemer steel plant in the world.
1873	• Wall Street panic leads to major economic depression.
1874	• Woman's Christian Temperance Union (WCTU) founded.
1876	• Alexander Graham Bell demonstrates telephone.
1877	• Republican Rutherford B. Hayes sworn in as president.
	• "Redeemers" come to power in South.
	• *Munn v. Illinois.*
1880	• Republican James A. Garfield elected president.
1881	• Garfield assassinated; Vice President Chester A. Arthur becomes president.
1882	• John D. Rockefeller develops the trust.
1883	• Pendleton Civil Service Act.
1884	• Democrat Grover Cleveland elected president.
1886	• *Wabash v. Illinois.*
1887	• Interstate Commerce Act.
1888	• Republican Benjamin Harrison elected president.
1890	• McKinley tariff.
	• General Federation of Women's Clubs (GFWC) founded.
	• Sherman Antitrust Act.
1892	• Ida B. Wells launches antilynching campaign.
1893	• Wall Street panic touches off national depression.
1895	• J. P. Morgan bails out U.S. Treasury.
1901	• U.S. Steel incorporated and capitalized at $1.4 billion.

BROOKLYN BRIDGE FAN

Advertisers used images of the Brooklyn Bridge to sell everything from patent medicine to soap. The front side of this colorful commemorative fan celebrates the opening of the bridge on May 24, 1883; the reverse side promotes a furniture company. The background photograph shows the wooden platforms that connected the gothic towers as the huge cables went into place high over the East River. It took fourteen years and cost the lives of twenty-seven men to complete the bridge.

Fan: Museum of the City of New York; background: ©Bettmann/Corbis.

19

The City and its Workers
1870–1900

"A TOWN THAT CRAWLED NOW STANDS ERECT, AND WE WHOSE BACKS were bent above the hearths know how it got its spine," boasted a steel-worker surveying New York City. Where once wooden buildings stood rooted in the mire of unpaved streets, cities of stone and steel sprang up in the last decades of the nineteenth century. The labor of millions of workers, many of them immigrants, laid the foundations for urban America.

No symbol better represented the new urban landscape than the Brooklyn Bridge, opened in May 1883. The great bridge soared over the East River in a single mile-long span. Begun in 1869, the bridge was the dream of builder John Roebling, who died in a freak accident almost as soon as construction began.

Building the Brooklyn Bridge took fourteen years and cost the lives of twenty-seven men. Nearly three hundred workers labored around the clock in three shifts, six days a week, most for $2 a day. To sink the foundation deep into the riverbed, common laborers tunneled down through mud and debris, working in reinforced wooden boxes called caissons, which were open at the bottom and pressurized to keep the water from flooding in. Before long, the workers experienced a mysterious malady they called "bends" because it left them doubled over in pain after they came to the surface. Scientists later discovered that nitrogen bubbles trapped in the bloodstream caused the condition and that it could be prevented if the men came up slowly to allow for decompression.

The first death occurred when the caissons reached a depth of seventy-one feet. On April 22, 1872, a heavyset German immigrant named John Meyers complained that he did not feel well and headed home to his boardinghouse. Before he could reach his bed, he collapsed and died. Eight days later, another man dropped dead, and the entire workforce in the cais-sons went out on strike. Conditions had become so hazardous and terrify-ing that the workers demanded a higher wage for fewer hours of work.

One worker, Frank Harris, remembered the men's fear of working in the caissons. As a scrawny sixteen-year-old from Ireland, Harris started to work a few days after landing in America. He described his experience:

The six of us were working naked to the waist in the small iron chamber with the temperature of about 80 degrees Fahrenheit: In five minutes the

603

sweat was pouring from us, and all the while we were standing in icy water that was only kept from rising by the terrific pressure. No wonder the headaches were blinding.

By the fifth day, Harris experienced terrible shooting pains in his ears, and fearing he might go deaf, he quit. Like Harris, many immigrant workers walked off the job, often as many as a hundred a week. But a ready supply of immigrants meant that the work never slowed or stopped; new workers eagerly entered the caissons, where they could earn in a day more than they made in a week in Ireland or Italy.

Washington Roebling, who took over as chief engineer after his father's death, routinely worked twelve to fourteen hours six days a week. Soon he, too, fell victim to the bends and ended up an invalid, directing the completion of the bridge through a telescope from his window in Brooklyn Heights. His wife, Emily Warren Roebling, acted as site superintendent and general engineer of the project. At the dedication of the bridge, Roebling turned to his wife and said, "I want the world to know that you, too, are one of the Builders of the Bridge."

At the end of the nineteenth century, the Brooklyn Bridge stood as a symbol of many things: the industrial might of the United States; the labor of the nation's immigrants; the ingenuity and genius of its engineers and inventors; the rise of iron and steel; and, most of all, the ascendancy of urban America. Poised on the brink of the twentieth century, the nation was shifting inexorably from a rural, agricultural society to an urban, industrial nation. In the burgeoning cities, tensions would erupt into conflict as workers squared off to fight for their rights to organize into labor unions and to demand safer working conditions, shorter hours, and better pay. And the explosive growth of the cities would foster political corruption as unscrupulous bosses and entrepreneurs cashed in on the building boom. Immigrants, political bosses, middle-class managers, poor laborers, and the very rich populated the nation's cities, crowding the streets, laboring in the stores and factories, and taking their leisure at the new ballparks, amusement parks, dance halls, and municipal parks that dotted the urban landscape. As the new century dawned, the city and its workers moved to center stage in American life.

Workers in the Caissons

In 1870 *Frank Leslie's Illustrated Weekly* ran an article on the construction of the Brooklyn Bridge. Illustrations show the workers inside the caissons below the East River. Crews entered through a cylindrical airlock that took them down more than seventy feet. There in the wooden caissons they worked with pick and shovel to break up the big boulders and haul the rock away. "What with the flaming lights, the deep shadows, the confusing noise of hammer, drills, and chains, the half-naked forms flitting about," wrote one reporter, the scene resembled hell. The hot, dangerous work fell primarily to Irish immigrant workers. Library of Congress.

▶ The Rise of the City

"We cannot all live in cities, yet nearly all seem determined to do so," New York editor Horace Greeley complained. The last three decades of the nineteenth century witnessed an urban explosion. Cities and towns grew more than twice as rapidly as the total population. Among the fastest-growing cities, Chicago expanded at a meteoric rate, doubling its population each decade. The number of cities with more than 100,000 inhabitants jumped from eighteen in 1870 to thirty-eight in 1900. Most of the nation's largest cities were east of the Mississippi, although St. Louis and San Francisco both ranked among the top ten urban areas. By 1900, the United States boasted three cities with more than a million inhabitants—New York, Chicago, and Philadelphia.

Patterns of **global migration** contributed to the rise of the city. In the port cities of the East Coast, more than fourteen million people arrived, many from southern and eastern Europe, and huddled together in dense urban ghettos. The word *slum* entered the American vocabulary along with a growing concern over the rising tide of newcomers. In the city, the widening gap between rich and poor became more visible, exacerbated by changes in the city landscape brought about by advances in transportation and technology.

The Urban Explosion: A Global Migration

The United States grew up in the country and moved to the city, or so it seemed by the end of the nineteenth century. Between 1870 and 1900, eleven million people moved into cities. Burgeoning industrial centers such as Pittsburgh, Chicago, New York, and Cleveland acted as giant magnets, attracting workers from the countryside. But rural Americans were by no means the only ones migrating to cities. Worldwide in scope, the movement from rural areas to urban industrial centers attracted millions of immigrants to American shores in the waning decades of the nineteenth century.

By the 1870s, the world could be conceptualized as three interconnected geographic regions (Map 19.1). At the center stood an industrial core bounded by Chicago and St. Louis in the west; Toronto, Glasgow, and Berlin in the north; Warsaw in the east; and Milan, Barcelona, Richmond, and Louisville in the south.

Surrounding this industrial core lay a vast agricultural domain encompassing Canada, much of Scandinavia, Russia and Poland, Hungary, Greece, Italy and Sicily, southern Spain, the South and the western plains of America, central and northern Mexico, the hinterlands of northern China, and the southern islands of Japan. Capitalist development in the late nineteenth century shattered traditional patterns of economic activity in this rural periphery. As old patterns broke down, these rural areas exported, along with other raw materials, new recruits for the industrial labor force.

> "We cannot all live in cities, yet nearly all seem determined to do so."
> — New York editor
> HORACE GREELEY

Beyond this second circle lay an even larger third world including the Caribbean, Central and South America, the Middle East, Africa, India, and most of Asia. Ties between this part of the world and the industrial core strengthened in the late nineteenth century, but most of the people living there stayed put. They worked on plantations and railroads, and in mines and ports, as part of a huge export network managed by foreign powers that staked out spheres of influence and colonies in this vast region.

In the 1870s, railroad expansion and low steamship fares gave the world's peoples a new-found mobility, enabling industrialists to draw on a global population for cheap labor. When Andrew Carnegie opened his first steel mill in 1872, his superintendent hired workers he called "buckwheats" — young American boys just off the farm. By the 1890s, however, Carnegie's workforce was liberally sprinkled with other rural boys, Hungarians and Slavs who had migrated to the United States, willing to work for low wages.

Altogether, more than 25 million immigrants came to the United States between 1850 and 1920. They came from all directions: east from Asia, south from Canada, north from Latin America, and west from Europe (Map 19.2). Part of a worldwide migration, immigrants traveled to South America and Australia as well as to the United States. Yet more than 70 percent of all European immigrants chose North America as their destination.

The largest number of immigrants to the United States came from the British Isles and from German-speaking lands (Figure 19.1). The vast majority of immigrants were white; Asians accounted for fewer than one million immigrants, and other people of color numbered even fewer. Yet ingrained racial prejudices

MAP ACTIVITY

Map 19.1   Economic Regions of the World, 1890s

The global nature of the world economy at the turn of the twentieth century is indicated by three interconnected geographic regions. At the center stands the industrial core — western Europe and the northeastern United States. The second region — the agricultural periphery — supplied immigrant laborers to the industries in the core. Beyond these two regions lay a vast area tied economically to the industrial core by colonialism.

READING THE MAP: What types of economic regions were contained in the United States in this period? Which continents held most of the industrial core? Which held most of the agricultural rural domain? Which held the greatest portion of the third world?

CONNECTIONS: Which of these three regions provided the bulk of immigrant workers to the United States? What major changes prompted the global migration at the end of the nineteenth century?

increasingly influenced the country's perception of immigration patterns. One of the classic formulations of the history of European immigration divided immigrants into two distinct waves that have been called the "old" and the "new" immigration. According to this theory, before 1880 the majority of immigrants came from northern and western Europe, with Germans, Irish, English, and Scandinavians making up approximately 85 percent of the newcomers. After 1880, the pattern shifted, with more and more ships carrying passengers from southern and eastern Europe. Italians, Hungarians, eastern European Jews, Turks, Armenians, Poles, Russians, and other Slavic peoples accounted for more than 80 percent of all immigrants by 1896 (Figure 19.2). Implicit in the distinction was an invidious comparison between "old" pioneer settlers and "new" unskilled laborers. Yet this sweeping general-

ization spoke more to perception than to reality. In fact, many of the earlier immigrants from Ireland, Germany, and Scandinavia came not as settlers or farmers, but as wageworkers, and they were met with much the same disdain as the Italians and Slavs who followed them.

The "new" immigration resulted from a number of factors. Improved economic conditions in western Europe coupled with increased immigration to Australia and Canada slowed the flow of immigrants coming into the United States from northern and western Europe. At the same time, economic depression in southern Italy, the persecution of Jews in eastern Europe, and a general desire to avoid conscription into the Russian army led many people from southern and eastern Europe to move to the United States. The need of America's industries for cheap, unskilled labor during prosperous years also stimulated immigration.

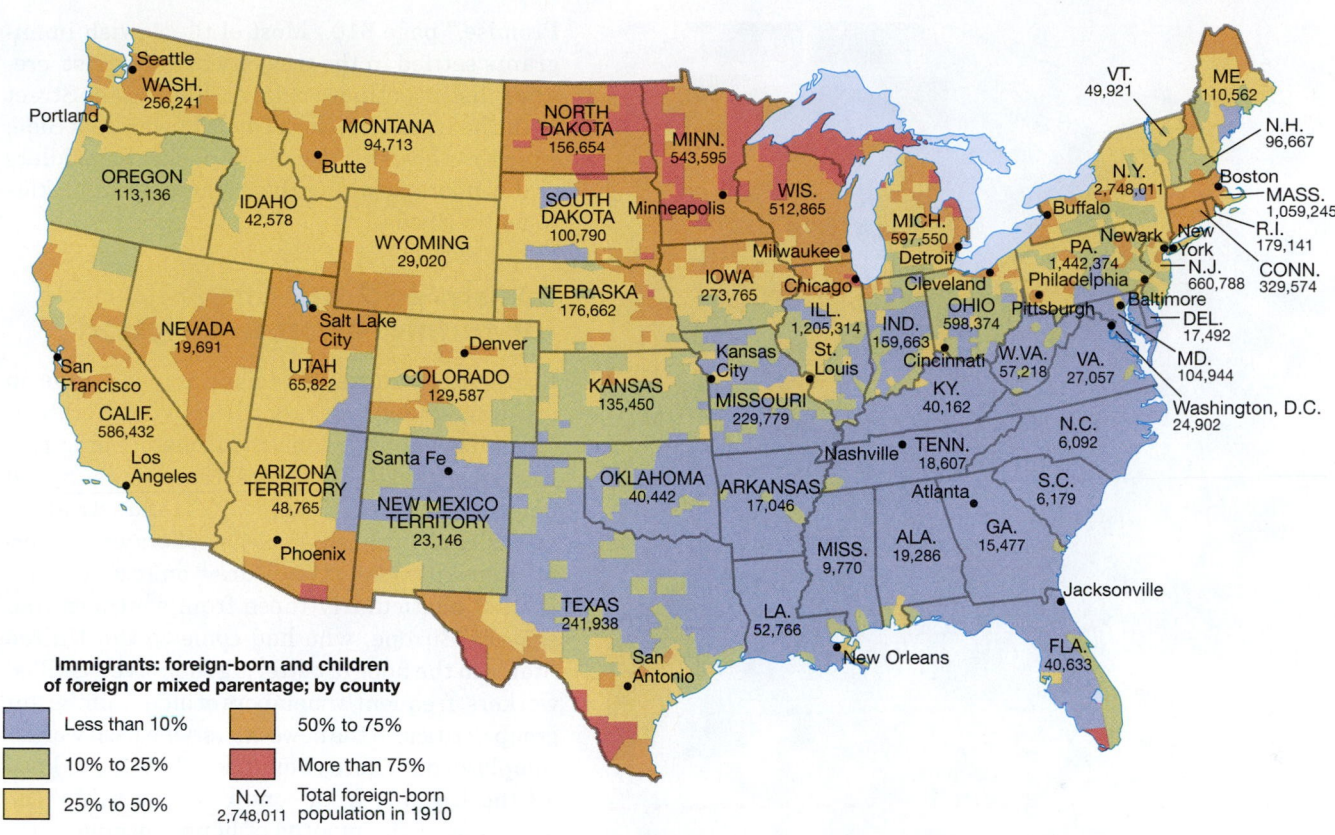

Immigrants: foreign-born and children of foreign or mixed parentage; by county

- Less than 10%
- 10% to 25%
- 25% to 50%
- 50% to 75%
- More than 75%

N.Y. 2,748,011 Total foreign-born population in 1910

MAP ACTIVITY

Map 19.2 The Impact of Immigration, to 1910

Immigration flowed in all directions — south from Canada, north from Mexico and Latin America, east from Asia, and west from Europe.

READING THE MAP: Which states had high percentages of immigrants? Which cities attracted the most immigrants? Which cities attracted the fewest?

CONNECTIONS: Why did most immigrants gravitate toward the cities? Why do you think the South drew such a low percentage of immigrants?

Steamship companies courted immigrants — a highly profitable, self-loading cargo. By the 1880s, the price of a ticket from Liverpool had dropped to less than $25. Would-be immigrants eager for information about the United States relied on letters from friends and relatives, advertisements, and word of mouth — sources that were not always dependable or truthful. Even photographs proved deceptive: Workers dressed in their Sunday best looked more prosperous than they actually were to relatives in the old country, where only the very wealthy wore white collars or silk dresses. No wonder people left for the United States believing, as one Italian immigrant observed, "that if they were ever fortunate enough to reach America, they would fall into a pile of manure and get up brushing the diamonds out of their hair."

Most of the newcomers stayed in the nation's cities. By 1900, almost two-thirds of the country's immigrant population resided in cities, many of the immigrants too poor to move on. (The average laborer immigrating to the United States carried only about $21.50.) Although the foreign-born population rarely outnumbered the native-born population, taken together immigrants and their American-born children did constitute a majority in some areas, particularly in the nation's largest cities: Philadelphia, 55 percent; Boston, 66 percent; Chicago, 75 percent; and New York City, an amazing 80 percent in 1900.

Not all the newcomers came to stay. Perhaps eight million European immigrants — most of them young men — worked for a year or a season and then returned to their homelands. Immigration officers called these immigrants,

Russian Immigrant Family
A Russian immigrant family is shown leaving Ellis Island in 1900. Notice the white slips of paper pinned to their coats indicating that they have been processed. The family is well dressed, but the paucity of their possessions testifies to the struggles they face. She carries her belongings in a white cloth sack, and he has a suitcase in one hand and bedding draped over his arm. An immigration official in uniform stands on the left. Keystone-Mast Collection, UCR/California Museum of Photography, University of California, Riverside.

Promise," page 610.) Most of the Jewish immigrants settled in the port cities of the East, creating distinct ethnic enclaves, like Hester Street in the heart of New York City's Lower East Side, which rang with the calls of pushcart peddlers and vendors hawking their wares, from pickles to feather beds.

Racism and the Cry for Immigration Restriction

Ethnic diversity and racism played a role in dividing skilled workers (those with a craft or specialized ability) from the globe-hopping proletariat of unskilled workers (those who supplied muscle or tended machines). As industrialists mechanized to replace skilled workers with lower-paid unskilled labor, they drew on recent immigrants, particularly those from southern and eastern Europe, who had come to the United States in the hope of bettering their lives. Skilled workers, frequently members of older immigrant groups, criticized the newcomers. One Irish worker complained, "There should be a law . . . to keep all the Italians from comin' in and takin' the bread out of the mouths of honest people."

The Irish worker's resentment brings into focus the impact of racism on America's immigrant laborers. Throughout the nineteenth century and into the twentieth, members of the educated elite as well as the uneducated viewed ethnic and even religious differences as racial characteristics, referring to the Polish or the Jewish "race." Americans judged "new" immigrants of southern and eastern European "races" as inferior. Each wave of newcomers was deemed somehow inferior to the established residents. The Irish who criticized the Italians so harshly had themselves been stigmatized as a lesser "race" a generation earlier.

Immigrants not only brought their own religious and racial prejudices to the United States but also absorbed the popular prejudices of American culture. Social Darwinism, with its strongly racist overtones, decreed that whites stood at the top of the evolutionary ladder. But who was "white"? Skin color supposedly served as a marker for the "new" immigrants — "swarthy" Italians; dark-haired, olive-skinned Jews. But even blond, blue-eyed Poles were not considered white. The social construction of "race" is nowhere more apparent than in the testimony of an Irish dockworker who boasted that he hired only "white men," a category that he insisted excluded "Poles and Italians." For the new immigrants, Americanization and assimilation would prove inextricably part of becoming "white."

many of them Italians, "birds of passage" because they followed a regular pattern of migration to and from the United States. By 1900, almost 75 percent of the new immigrants were young, single men.

Women generally had less access to funds for travel and faced tighter family control. Because the traditional sexual division of labor relied on women's unpaid domestic labor and care of the very young and the very old, women most often came to the United States as wives, mothers, or daughters, not as single wage laborers. Only among the Irish did women immigrants outnumber men by a small margin from 1871 to 1891.

Jews from eastern Europe most often came with their families and came to stay. Beginning in the 1880s, a wave of violent **pogroms**, or persecutions, in Russia and Poland prompted the departure of more than a million Jews in the next two decades. (See "Seeking the American

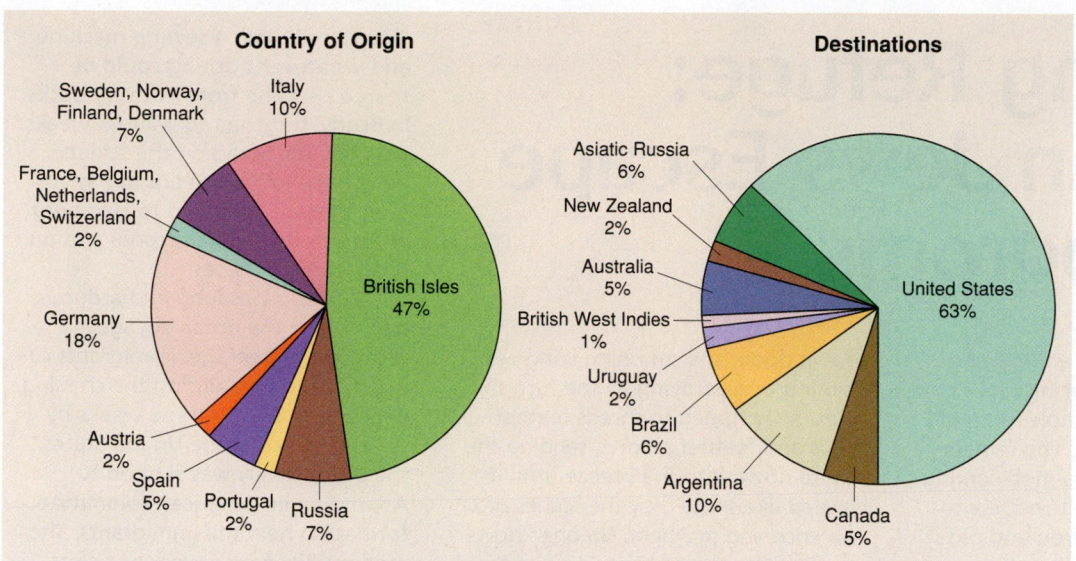

FIGURE 19.1   GLOBAL COMPARISON: European Emigration, 1870–1890
A look at European emigration between 1870 and 1890 shows that emigrants from Germany, Austria, and the British Isles (including England, Ireland, Scotland, and Wales) formed the largest group of out-migrants during those decades. After 1890, the origin of European emigrants tilted south and east, with Italians and eastern Europeans growing in number (see Figure 19.2). The United States, by far the most popular destination for global emigrants in this period, took in nearly two-thirds of the Europeans who left their homelands. What factors might account for the United States being the most popular destination for European emigrants?

For African Americans, the cities of the North promised not just economic opportunity but an escape from institutionalized segregation and persecution. Throughout the South, Jim Crow laws — restrictions that segregated blacks — became common in the decades following Reconstruction. Intimidation and lynching terrorized blacks. "To die from the bite of frost is far more glorious than

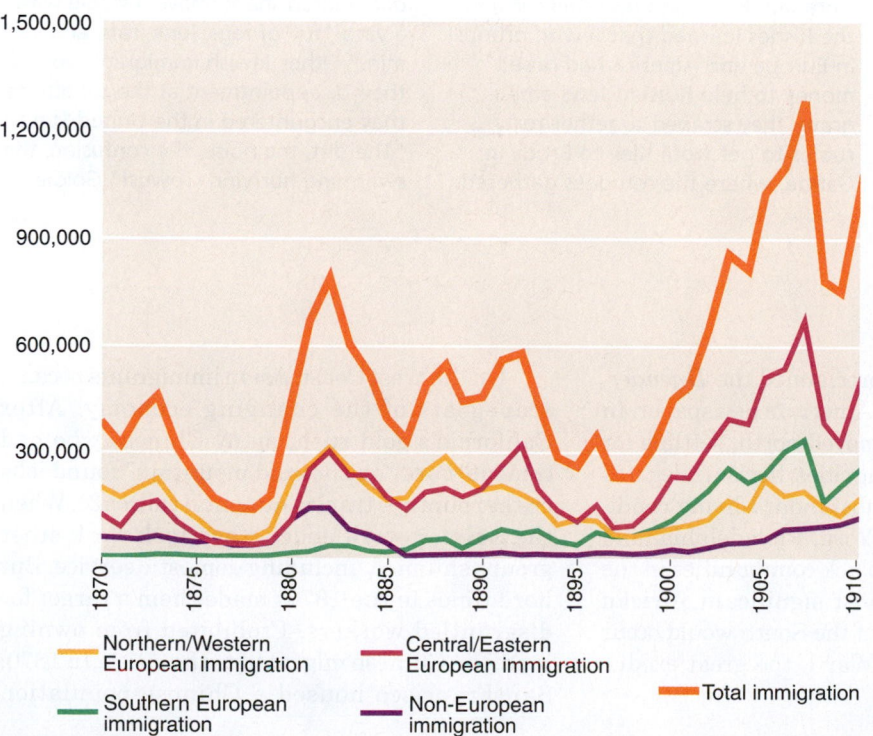

FIGURE 19.2   European Immigration, 1870–1910
Before 1880, more than 85 percent of U.S. immigrants came from northern and western Europe—Germany, Ireland, England, and the Scandinavian countries. After 1880, 80 percent of the "new" immigrants came from Italy, Turkey, Hungary, Armenia, Poland, Russia, and other Slavic countries.

Northern/Western European immigration

Central/Eastern European immigration

Southern European immigration

Non-European immigration

Total immigration

Seeking Refuge: Russian Jews Escape the Pogroms

Fifteen-year-old Abraham Bisno recalled running for his life. "I hid myself in a clay hole in an old brickyard on a hillside," he remembered. "I witnessed the mob coming down the hill to assault the Jewish settlement. I saw children and old people beaten — buildings burned — I heard women screaming."

Violent pogroms — deadly riots against Jews — erupted in Russia in 1881 in the wake of the assassination of Czar Alexander II, sparked by rumors that he had been murdered by Jews. Kiev, where Abraham Bisno lived with his parents, became the scene of a pogrom in late April. "For days on end," Bisno wrote, "entire neighborhoods were looted and largely destroyed by crowds estimated at over four thousand." Fanatical priests fed anti-Semitism (hatred of Jews) by denouncing the Jews as heartless "Christ-killers" who used the blood of Christian children in their rituals. The government failed to move quickly to put down the violence, even after only one of the ten who plotted the czar's assassination turned out to be Jewish.

Bands of Russians swarmed through the Jewish quarters, breaking down doors and smashing windows, looting or destroying all the furnishings. They ripped to shreds feather beds and feather pillows, sending the white down into the breeze until it settled like snow over the scenes of violence and mayhem. No one knows precisely how many Jews died at the hands of the mob, but estimates range as high as five hundred. "The building we lived in and the place we worked in were assaulted at the same time," Bisno recalled. "Mother ran for her life while we struggled for ours; we were all separated by the mob — the shop was destroyed, the goods carried away."

These and subsequent pogroms and persecutions prompted a great wave of Jewish migration. Between 1880 and 1914, more than 2.7 million Jews sought refuge from religious persecution, the vast majority of them heading to the United States. Among the first to emigrate were Abraham Bisno and his family. When the Bisnos learned that Jewish groups in Europe and America had raised money to help Russian Jews emigrate, they scraped together forty rubles to get from Kiev to Brody in Galicia, where the refugees gathered.

"Our family sold a sewing machine and whatever clothing could be spared — some from our very backs." In Brody, they had to wait six weeks, begging for bread on the streets, before they received aid to pay for their passage overland to Hamburg and from there to Liverpool and on to the United States.

The trip was long and arduous, particularly the ocean voyage. Crowded in steerage, immigrants suffered seasickness during the crossing, which took two to three weeks by steamer. Once in the United States, the Bisno family was sent on to Atlanta by an American committee formed to help the immigrants. The men quickly found work as tailors. Bisno struck out on his own, moving to Chattanooga, where he apprenticed to an English-speaking tailor and quickly picked up the language by reading signs and advertisements. But the Bisnos were unhappy in the South. Abraham's mother complained that she could not find a butcher who sold kosher meat, and his father fretted that there was no Orthodox synagogue in the neighborhood. So after nine months, the family moved to a larger Jewish community in Chicago.

The slums of the nation's big cities, where many of the Jewish immigrants ended up, were far from a "promised land." The Bisnos lived in a dilapidated shack above a stable with a yard "full of rags, junk, rats, and vermin." Other Jewish immigrants voiced their disappointment at the conditions they encountered in the United States. "The dirt, the noise, the confusion, the swarming hurrying crowds!" Goldie

at the hands of a mob," proclaimed the *Defender*, Chicago's largest African American newspaper. In the 1890s, many blacks moved north, settling for the most part in the growing cities. Racism relegated them to poor jobs and substandard living conditions, but by 1900 New York, Philadelphia, and Chicago had the largest black communities in the nation. Although the most significant African American migration out of the South would occur during and after World War I, the great exodus was already under way.

On the West Coast, Asian immigrants became scapegoats of the changing economy. After California's gold rush, many Chinese who had come to work "on the gold mountain" found jobs on the country's transcontinental railroads. When the railroad work ended, they took work other groups shunned, including domestic service. But hard times in the 1870s made them a target for disgruntled workers. Prohibited from owning land, the Chinese migrated to the cities. In 1870, San Francisco housed a Chinese population

Stone exclaimed. "My heart sank. This was all so different from what I had expected or dreamed."

Bad as conditions were, the immigrant Jews appreciated the safe haven the United States afforded. And although the sweatshops where Bisno and other Jewish immigrants labored were dark and bleak, for most Jews the slums proved a temporary prison. The United States provided not only a refuge but also a chance to start over and prosper. Bisno watched as many of his friends and relatives, after saving or borrowing a little money, opened small businesses of their own. "All had to begin in a very small way," he recalled. "With a hundred or two hundred dollars they were able to start grocery stores, markets, cigar stores." Bisno quickly moved up in his trade, becoming a contractor in a sweatshop by the time he reached the age of sixteen. But then his life took a different course. Moved by the Haymarket martyrs, he converted to socialism in 1886, joined the Knights of Labor, and went on to become a labor organizer. The first president of the Chicago Cloak Makers' Union, he worked until his death in 1929 to improve the lot of garment workers.

Jewish Refugees from the Pogroms
In this colorful depiction, Liberty, dressed in the Stars and Stripes, opens the gates of the country to a Jewish immigrant couple and their children fleeing the pogroms in Russia. Abraham Bisno and his family were among the first group of immigrants to flee Kiev after the pogroms of 1881 and to seek refuge in the United States. Yivo Institute for Jewish Research.

Questions for Consideration

1. Compare the Jewish immigrants from Russia with other immigrant groups discussed in this chapter. What attracted each group to America? What were their expectations? How did each group fare?

2. What aspects of Bisno's life in America led him to join the labor movement? How may his childhood in Russia have influenced him in this direction?

---

estimated at 12,022, and it continued to grow until passage of the Chinese Exclusion Act in 1882 (see chapter 17). For the first time in the nation's history, U.S. law excluded an immigrant group on the basis of race.

Huang Zunxian came to San Francisco in 1882 as Chinese consul general. Disillusioned with the anti-Chinese violence he saw all around him, he wrote a series of angry poems that took Americans to task for their hypocrisy. One of them read:

They have sealed the gates tightly
Door after door with guards beating alarms.
Anyone with a yellow-colored face
Is beaten even if guiltless.
The American eagle strides the heavens soaring
With half of the globe clutched in his claw.
Although the Chinese arrived later,
Couldn't you leave them a little space?

Despite the Chinese Exclusion Act, some Chinese managed to come to America using a loophole that allowed relatives to join their

Rags to Riches
The formulaic novels of popular author Horatio Alger feature fatherless young men who, through the right combination of "pluck and luck," move ahead in the world. Alger's message of rags to riches fueled the dreams of countless young people in the late nineteenth century. Yet despite the myth, few Americans rose from rags to riches. Even Alger's heroes, such as his popular character Ragged Dick, pictured here, more often traded their rags for respectability, not for great wealth.
Picture Research Consultants & Archives.

Give me your tired, your poor,
Your huddled masses yearning to breathe free,
The wretched refuse of your teeming shore,
Send these, the homeless, tempest-tost to me,
I lift my lamp beside the golden door!

The tide of immigrants to New York City soon swamped the immigration office at Castle Garden in lower Manhattan. After the federal government took over immigration in 1890, it built a facility on **Ellis Island** in New York harbor, opened in 1892. After a fire gutted the wooden building, an imposing new brick edifice replaced it in 1900. Its overcrowded halls became the gateway to the United States for millions.

To many Americans, the "new" immigrants seemed uneducated, backward, and uncouth — impossible to assimilate. "These people are not Americans," editorialized the popular journal *Public Opinion*, "they are the very scum and offal of Europe." Terence V. Powderly, head of the broadly inclusive Knights of Labor, complained that the newcomers "herded together like animals and lived like beasts." Blue-blooded Yankees led by Senator Henry Cabot Lodge of Massachusetts formed an unlikely alliance with leaders of organized labor — who feared that immigrants would drive down wages — to press for immigration restrictions. Lodge and his supporters championed a literacy test as a requirement for immigration, knowing that the vast majority of Italian and Slavic peasants could neither read nor write. In 1896, Congress approved a literacy test for immigrants, but President Grover Cleveland promptly vetoed it. "It is said," the president reminded Congress, "that the quality of recent immigration is undesirable. The time is quite within recent memory when the same thing was said of immigrants, who, with their descendants, are now numbered among our best citizens." Cleveland's veto forestalled immigration restriction but did not stop anti-immigrant forces from seeking to close the gates. They would continue to press for restrictions until they achieved their goal in the 1920s (as discussed in chapter 23).

families. By contrast, the nation's small Japanese community of about 3,000 expanded rapidly after 1890, until pressures to keep out all Asians led in 1910 to the creation of an immigration station at Angel Island in San Francisco Bay. Asian immigrants were detained there, sometimes for months, and many were deported as "undesirable." Their sad stories can be read in the graffiti on the barracks walls.

On the East Coast, the volume of immigration from Europe in the last two decades of the century proved unprecedented. In 1888 alone, more than half a million Europeans landed in America, 75 percent of them in New York City. The Statue of Liberty, a gift from the people of France erected in 1886, stood sentinel in the harbor. The verse inscribed at Liberty's base was penned by a young Jewish woman named Emma Lazarus:

The Social Geography of the City

During the Gilded Age, cities experienced demographic and technological changes that greatly altered the social geography of the city. Cleveland, Ohio, provides a good example. In the 1870s, Cleveland was a small city in both population and area. Oil magnate John D. Rockefeller could, and often did, walk from his large brick house on Euclid Avenue to his office downtown. On his

Knife and Scissors Sharpener Pushcart
Joseph Antonucci, an Italian immigrant, used this knife and scissors sharpener cart on Chicago's West Side in 1900. After a day's work, Antonucci usually parked the cart in a fire station or a customer's stable and then took the train home. Sometimes he pushed his cart for miles to ply his trade beyond the city limits in towns such as Hammond, Indiana. For poor immigrants who could not afford rent, pushcarts provided a cheap and portable means of livelihood. The cries of street peddlers, vendors, and scissors sharpeners like Antonucci added to the cacophony of the urban streets. Chicago Historical Society.

way, he passed the small homes of his clerks and other middle-class families. Behind these homes ran miles of alleys crowded with the dwellings of Cleveland's working class. Farther out, on the shores of Lake Erie, close to the factories and foundries, clustered the shanties of the city's poorest laborers.

Within two decades, the Cleveland that Rockefeller knew no longer existed. The coming of mass transit transformed the walking city. In its place emerged a central business district surrounded by concentric rings of residences organized by ethnicity and income. First the horse car in the 1870s and then the electric streetcar in the 1880s made it possible for those who could afford the five-cent fare to work downtown and flee after work to the "cool green rim" of the city, with its single-family homes, lawns, gardens, and trees. Social segregation — the separation of rich and poor, and of ethnic and old-stock Americans — was one of the major social changes engendered by the rise of the industrial metropolis, evident not only in Cleveland but in cities across the nation.

Race and ethnicity affected the way cities evolved. Newcomers to the nation's cities faced hostility and not surprisingly sought out their kin and country folk as they struggled to survive. Distinct ethnic neighborhoods often formed around a synagogue or church. African Americans typically experienced the greatest residential segregation, but every large city had its ethnic enclaves — Little Italy, Chinatown, Bohemia Flats, Germantown — where English was rarely spoken.

Poverty, crowding, dirt, and disease constituted the daily reality of New York City's immigrant poor — a plight documented by photojournalist **Jacob Riis** in his best-selling book *How the Other Half Lives* (1890). By taking his camera into the hovels of the poor, Riis opened the nation's eyes to conditions in the city's slums (see chapter 21, "Visualizing History," page 688). Riis invited his readers into a Bottle Street tenement:

> One, two, three beds are there, if the old boxes and heaps of foul straw can be called by that name; a broken stove with a crazy pipe from which the smoke leaks at every joint; a table of rough boards propped up on boxes, piles of rubbish in the corner. The closeness and smell are appalling.

While Riis's audience shivered at his revelations about the "other half," many middle-class Americans worried equally about the excesses of the wealthy. They feared the class antagonism fueled by the growing chasm between rich and poor so visible in the nation's cities, and shared Riis's view that "the real danger to society comes not only from the tenements, but from the ill-spent wealth which reared them."

The excesses of the Gilded Age's newly minted millionaires were nowhere more visible than in the lifestyle of the Vanderbilts. "Commodore"

The Electric Streetcar
This colorful electric streetcar ran in Washington, D.C., from 1888 to 1913, replacing horse-drawn vehicles. By 1900 over 200 miles of track ran through the nation's capital. The electric cars revolutionized the social geography of the city. The token shown gave riders the opportunity to travel from the city center to the suburbs for just a few cents. Streetcar: National Museum of American History, Smithsonian Institution, Behring Center; token: Picture Research Consultants & Archives.

Cornelius Vanderbilt, an uncouth ferryman who built the New York Central Railroad, died in 1877, leaving his son $90 million. William Vanderbilt doubled that sum, and his two sons proceeded to spend lavishly on Fifth Avenue mansions and "cottages" in Newport, Rhode Island, that sought to rival the palaces of Europe (see chapter 18, "Visualizing History," page 574). In 1883, Alva (Mrs. William) Vanderbilt launched herself into New York society by throwing a costume party so opulent that not even old New York society, which turned up its nose at the nouveau riche, could resist an invitation. Dressed as a Venetian princess, the hostess greeted her twelve hundred guests. But her sister-in-law Alice Vanderbilt stole the show by appearing as that miraculous new invention, the electric light, resplendent in a white satin evening dress studded with diamonds. The *New York World* speculated that Alva Vanderbilt's party cost more than a quarter of a million dollars (more than $4 million today).

Such ostentatious displays of wealth became especially alarming when they were coupled with disdain for the well-being of ordinary people. When a reporter in 1882 asked William Vanderbilt whether he considered the public good when running his railroads, he shot back, "The public be damned." The fear that America had become a plutocracy — a society ruled by the rich — gained credence from the fact that the wealthiest 1 percent of the population owned more than half the real and personal property

in the country. As the new century dawned, reformers would form a progressive movement to address the problems of urban industrialism and the substandard living and working conditions it produced.

> **REVIEW**   Why did American cities experience explosive growth in the late nineteenth century?

► At Work in Industrial America

The number of industrial wageworkers in the United States exploded in the second half of the nineteenth century, more than tripling from 5.3 million in 1860 to 17.4 million in 1900. More than half of the country's men, women, and children made up the laboring class that performed manual work for wages. These workers toiled in a variety of settings. Many skilled workers and artisans still earned a living in small workshops. But with the rise of corporate capitalism, large factories, mills, and mines increasingly dotted the landscape. Sweatshops and outwork — the contracting of piecework, including finishing garments by hand, to be performed in the home — provided work experiences different from those of factory operatives and industrial workers. Pick-and-shovel labor, whether on the railroads or in the building trades, constituted yet another kind of work. Managers, as well as women "typewriters" and salesclerks, formed a new white-collar segment of America's workforce.

America's Diverse Workers

Common laborers formed the backbone of the American labor force. They built the railroads and subways, tunneled under New York's East River to anchor the Brooklyn Bridge, and helped lay the foundation of industrial America. These "human machines" stood at the bottom of the country's economic ladder and generally came from the most recent immigrant groups. Initially, the Irish wielded the picks and shovels that built American cities, but by the turn of the century, as the Irish bettered their lot, Slavs and Italians took up their tools.

At the opposite end of labor's hierarchy stood skilled craftsmen like iron puddler James J. Davis, a Welsh immigrant who worked in the Pennsylvania mills. Using brains along with brawn, puddlers took up the melted pig iron in the heat of the furnace and, with long, heavy "spoons" (poles), formed the cooling metal into 200-pound balls, relying on eye and intuition to make each ball uniform. Davis likened his work to baking bread: "I am like some frantic baker in the inferno. . . . My spoon weighs twenty-five pounds, my porridge is pasty iron, and the heat of my kitchen is so great that if my body was not hardened to it the ordeal would drop me in my tracks."

Possessing such a skill meant earning good wages. Davis made up to $7 a day, when there was work. But most industry and manufacturing work in the nineteenth century remained seasonal; few workers could count on year-round pay. In addition, two major depressions only twenty years apart, beginning in 1873 and 1893, spelled unemployment and hardship. In an era before unemployment insurance, workers' compensation, or old-age pensions, even the best worker could not guarantee security for his family. "The fear of ending in the poor-house is one of the terrors that dog a man through life," Davis confessed.

Skilled workers like Davis wielded power on the shop floor. Employers attempted to limit workers' control by replacing people with machines, breaking down skilled work into ever-smaller tasks that could be performed by unskilled factory operatives. New England's textile mills provide a classic example of the effects of mechanized factory labor in the nineteenth century. Mary, a weaver at the mills in Fall River, Massachusetts, went to work in the 1880s at the age of twelve. By then, mechanization of the

Sweatshop Worker
Sweatshop workers endured crowded and often dangerous conditions. Most were young women, like the one shown here sewing pants in New York City. Young working women earned little money but prided themselves on their independence. Notice the young woman's stylish hairdo, white shirtwaist, and necklace (an indication that she did not turn over all the money in her pay envelope to her father, as was often the case). George Eastman House.

looms had reduced the job of the weaver to watching for breaks in the thread. "At first the noise is fierce, and you have to breathe the cotton all the time, but you get used to it," Mary told a reporter from *Independent* magazine. "When the bobbin flies out and a girl gets hurt, you can't hear her shout — not if she just screams, you can't. She's got to wait, 'till you see her. . . . Lots of us is deaf."

During the 1880s, the number of foreign-born mill workers almost doubled. At Fall River, Mary and her Scots-Irish family resented the new immigrants. "The Polaks learn weavin' quick," she remarked, using a common derogatory term to identify a rival group. "They just as soon live on nothin' and work like that. But it won't do 'em much good for all they'll make out of it." Employers encouraged racial and ethnic antagonism because it inhibited labor organization.

The majority of factory operatives in the textile mills were young, unmarried women like Mary. They worked from six in the morning to six at night six days a week, and they took home about $1 a day. The seasonal nature of the work also drove wages down. "Like as not your mill will 'shut down' three months," and "some weeks you only get two or three days' work," Mary recounted. After twenty years of working in the mill, Mary's family had not been able to scrape together enough money to buy a house: "We saved some, but something always comes."

Mechanization transformed the garment industry as well. With the introduction of the foot-pedaled sewing machine in the 1850s and the use of mechanical cloth-cutting knives in the 1870s, independent tailors were replaced with workers hired by contractors to sew pieces of cloth into suits and dresses. Working in **sweatshops**, small rooms hired for the season or even in the contractor's own tenement, women and children formed an important segment of garment workers. Discriminated against in the marketplace, where they earned less than men, women generally worked for wages for only eight to ten years, until they married.

Sadie Frowne, a sixteen-year-old Polish Jew, went to work in a Brooklyn sweatshop in the 1890s. Frowne sewed for eleven hours a day in a 20-by-14-foot room containing fourteen machines. "The machines go like mad all day, because the faster you work the more money you get," she recalled. Paid by the piece, she earned about $4.50 a week and, by rigid economy, tried to save $2. Young and single, Frowne typified the woman wage earner in the late nineteenth century. In 1890, the average workingwoman was twenty-two and had been working since the age of fifteen, laboring twelve hours a day six days a week and earning less than $6 a week. Only marriage delivered women from dead-end jobs. No wonder single working women scrimped to buy ribbons and finery to make themselves attractive to young men.

The Family Economy: Women and Children

In 1900, the typical male worker in manufacturing earned $435 a year, about $12,000 in today's dollars. Many working-class families, whether native-born or immigrant, lived in or near poverty, their economic survival dependent on the contributions of all family members, regardless of sex or age. "Father," asked one young immigrant girl, "does everybody in America live like this? Go to work early, come home late, eat and go to Sleep? And the next day again work, eat, and sleep?" Most workers did. The **family economy** meant that everyone needed to contribute to maintain even the most meager household. Children dutifully turned over their wages to their fathers and kept only a tiny portion for themselves. One statistician estimated that in 1900 as many as 64 percent of working-class families relied on income other than the husband's wages to make ends meet. The paid and unpaid work of women and children proved essential for family survival, let alone economic advancement.

In the cities, boys as young as six years old plied their trades as bootblacks and newsboys. Often working under an adult contractor, these children earned as little as fifty cents a day. Many of them were homeless — orphaned or

Bootblacks

The faces and hands of the two bootblacks shown here with a third boy on a New York City street in 1896 testify to their grimy trade. Boys as young as six years old found work on city streets as bootblacks and newsboys. Often they worked for contractors who took a cut of their meager earnings. When families could no longer afford to feed their children, boys often headed out on their own at a young age. For these child workers, even free education was a luxury they could not afford. Alice Austin photo, Staten Island Historical Society.

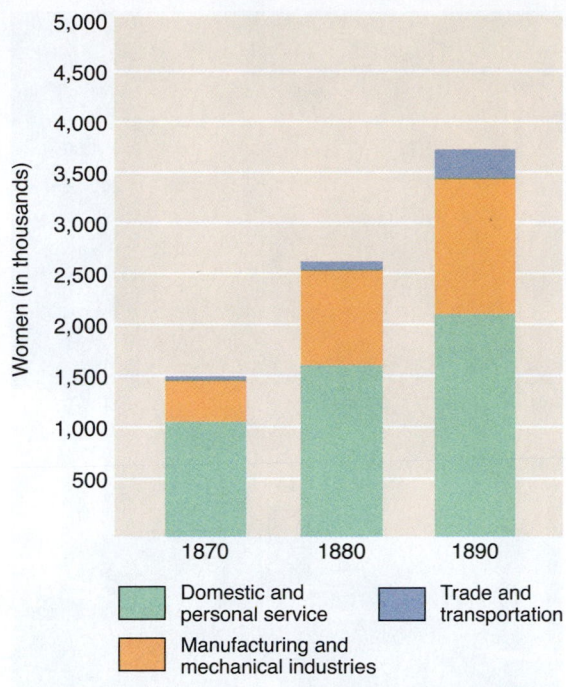

FIGURE 19.3 Women and Work, 1870–1890
In 1870, close to 1.5 million women worked in nonagricultural occupations. By 1890, that number had more than doubled to 3.7 million. More and more women sought work in manufacturing and mechanical industries, although domestic service still constituted the largest employment arena for women.

working class, rarely worked for wages outside the home. In 1890, only 3 percent were employed. Nevertheless, working-class married women found ways to contribute to the family economy. In many Italian families, for example, piecework such as making artificial flowers allowed married women to contribute to the family economy without leaving their homes. Black women, married and unmarried, worked for wages in much greater numbers. The 1890 census showed that 25 percent of married African American women were employed, often as domestics in the houses of white families.

> "Father, does everybody in America live like this? Go to work early, come home late, eat and go to Sleep? And the next day again work, eat, and sleep?"
> — A young immigrant girl

White-Collar Workers: Managers, "Typewriters," and Salesclerks

In the late nineteenth century, business expansion and consolidation led to a managerial revolution, creating a new class of white-collar workers who worked in offices and stores. As skilled workers saw their crafts replaced by mechanization, some moved into management positions. "The middle class is becoming a salaried class," a writer for the *Independent* magazine observed, "and is rapidly losing the economic and moral independence of former days." As large business organizations consolidated, corporate development separated management from ownership, and the job of directing the firm became the province of salaried executives and managers, the majority of whom were white men drawn from the 8 percent of Americans who held high school diplomas.

Until late in the century, when engineering schools began to supply recruits, many skilled workers moved from the shop floor to positions of considerable responsibility. William "Billy" Jones, the son of a Welsh immigrant, was one such worker. Beginning as an apprentice at the age of ten, Jones rose through the ranks to become plant superintendent at Andrew Carnegie's Pittsburgh steelworks in 1872. By all accounts, Jones was the best steel man in the industry, and Carnegie rewarded him with a "hell of a big salary," $25,000 — the same salary as the president of the United States. Most middle managers averaged far less, $1,100 a year being counted as a good salary. Senior executives, generally recruited from the college-educated elite, took home $4,000

cast off by their families. "We wuz six, and we ain't got no father," a child of twelve told reporter Jacob Riis. "Some of us had to go."

Child labor increased decade by decade after 1870. The percentage of children under fifteen engaged in paid labor did not drop until after World War I. The 1900 census estimated that 1,750,178 children ages ten to fifteen were employed, an increase of more than a million over thirty years. Children in this age range constituted more than 18 percent of the industrial labor force. Many younger children not counted by the census worked beside their older siblings in mills, in factories, and on the streets.

In the late nineteenth century, the number of women workers also rose sharply, with their most common occupations changing slowly from domestic service to factory work and then to office work. In 1870, the census listed 1.5 million women working for wages in nonagricultural occupations. By 1890, the number had more than doubled, with 3.7 million women working for pay (Figure 19.3). Women's working patterns varied considerably according to race and ethnicity. White married women, even among the or more, and a company's general manager could earn as much as $15,000 a year, approximately 30 times what the average worker earned. (Today's top CEOs on average earn 550 times more than the average worker receives.) At the top of the economic pyramid, the great industrialists amassed fortunes that rank John D. Rockefeller, Andrew Carnegie, and Cornelius Vanderbilt among the top ten richest men in American history, easily outpacing today's billionaires.

The new white-collar workforce also included women **"typewriters"** and salesclerks. In the decades after the Civil War, as businesses became larger and more far-flung, the need for more elaborate and exact records, as well as the greater volume of correspondence, led to the hiring of more office workers. Mechanization transformed business as it had industry and manufacturing. The adding machine, the cash register, and the typewriter came into general use in the 1880s. Employers seeking literate workers soon turned to nimble-fingered women. Educated men had many other career choices, but for middle-class white women, secretarial work constituted one of the very few areas where they could put their literacy to use for wages.

Sylvie Thygeson was typical of the young women who went to work as secretaries. Thygeson grew up in an Illinois prairie town and went to work as a country schoolteacher after graduating high school in 1884. Realizing that teaching school did not pay a living wage, she mastered typing and stenography and found work as a secretary to help support her family. According to her account, she made "a fabulous sum of money" (possibly $25 a month). Nevertheless, she gave up her job after a few years when she met and married her husband.

Called "typewriters," women workers like Thygeson were seen as indistinguishable from the machines they operated. Far from viewing their jobs as dehumanizing, women typewriters took pride in their work and relished the economic independence it afforded them. But the entry of women into the workplace challenged traditional gender roles. Society distinguished between "ladies" (who stayed at home) and "working girls" (by definition lower-class women and a term often used for prostitutes). When white middle-class women entered offices as court reporters, typewriters, and stenographers, issues of class and gender clashed. Could a "lady" work? And if she did, did her economic independence threaten men and marriage? Some of this ambivalence can be seen in a poem published in 1896 in the

Clerical Worker
A stenographer takes dictation in an 1890s office. Notice that the apron, a symbol of feminine domesticity, has accompanied women into the workplace. In the 1880s, with the invention of the typewriter, many women put their literacy skills to use in the nation's offices. Brown Brothers.

Boston *Courier*. The poet waxes eloquent on his attraction to the "typewriter":

> The click of the keys, as her fingers fly,
>   And the ring of the silvery bell,
> I hardly hear, though I sit quite near,
>   Enchained by her magic spell.

After several verses, however, he ruefully abandons his ardor in the face of her modesty and professional manner. And, more telling, he acknowledges that the independent working woman may not need him at all.

> So, to her of my love I shall never speak,
>   Twould be vain I can clearly see.
> Why, she gets sixteen dollars a week.
>   And what does she want of me?

As Sylvie Thygeson's story shows, most women chose marriage and the home over the office, despite concerns to the contrary. But by the 1890s, secretarial work was the overwhelming choice of native-born, single white women, who constituted more than 90 percent of the female clerical force. Not only considered more genteel than factory work or domestic labor, office work also meant more money for shorter hours. In 1883, Boston's clerical workers on average made more than $6 a week, compared with less than $5 for women working in manufacturing.

As a new consumer culture came to dominate American urban life in the late nineteenth century, department stores offered another employment opportunity for women in the cities. Boasting ornate facades, large plate-glass display windows, and marble and brass fixtures, stores such as Macy's in New York, Wanamaker's in Philadelphia, and Marshall Field in Chicago stood as monuments to the material promise of the era. Within these palaces of consumption, cash girls, stock clerks, and wrappers earned as little as $3 a week, while at the top of the scale, buyers like Belle Cushman of the fancy goods department at Macy's earned $25 a week, an unusually high salary for a woman in the 1870s. Salesclerks counted themselves a cut above factory workers. Their work was neither dirty nor dangerous, and even when they earned less than factory workers, they felt a sense of superiority.

REVIEW How did business expansion and consolidation change workers' occupations in the late nineteenth century?

▶ Workers Organize

By the late nineteenth century, industrial workers were losing ground in the workplace. In the fierce competition to reduce prices and cut costs, industrialists, led by Andrew Carnegie, invested heavily in new machinery that replaced skilled workers with unskilled labor. The erosion of skills and the redefinition of labor as mere "machine tending" left the worker with a growing sense of individual helplessness that served as a spur to collective action. In 1877, in the midst of a depression that left many workers destitute, labor flexed its muscle in the Great Railroad Strike and showed the power of collective action. This and other strikes underscored the tensions produced by rapid industrialization.

In the 1870s and 1880s, labor organizations grew, and the Knights of Labor and the American Federation of Labor attracted workers. Convinced of the inequity of the wage-labor system, labor organizers spoke eloquently of abolishing class privileges and monopoly. Their rhetoric as well as the violence often associated with strikes frightened many middle-class Americans and caused them to equate the labor movement with the specter of class war and anarchism.

The Great Railroad Strike of 1877

Economic depression following the panic of 1873 threw as many as three million people out of work. Those who were lucky enough to keep their jobs watched as pay cuts eroded their wages until they could no longer feed their families. In the summer of 1877, the Baltimore and Ohio (B&O) Railroad announced a 10 percent wage cut at the same time it declared a 10 percent dividend to its stockholders. Angry brakemen in West Virginia, whose wages had already fallen from $70 to $30 a month, walked out on strike. One B&O worker described the hardship that drove him to take such desperate action: "We eat our hard bread and tainted meat two days old on the sooty cars up the road, and when we come home, find our wives complaining that they cannot even buy hominy and molasses for food."

The West Virginia brakemen's strike touched off the **Great Railroad Strike** of 1877, a nationwide uprising that spread rapidly to Pittsburgh and Chicago, St. Louis and San Francisco (Map 19.3). Within a few days, nearly 100,000 railroad workers walked off the job. The spark of rebellion soon led an estimated 500,000 laborers to join the train workers. In Reading, Pennsylvania, militiamen refused to fire on the strikers, saying, "We may be militiamen, but we are workmen first." Rail traffic ground to a halt; the nation lay paralyzed.

Violence erupted as the strike spread. In Pittsburgh, strikers clashed with militia brought in from Philadelphia, who arrogantly boasted

MAP 19.3

The Great Railroad Strike of 1877

Starting in West Virginia and Pennsylvania, the strike spread as far north as Albany, New York, and as far west as San Francisco, bringing rail traffic to a standstill. Called the Great Uprising, the strike heralded the beginning of a new era of working-class protest and trade union organization.

they would clean up "the workingmen's town." Charging with bayonets leveled, the troops opened fire on the crowds, killing twenty people.

> **"The railroad strikers, as a rule, are good men, sober, intelligent, and industrious."**
>
> — President
> RUTHERFORD B. HAYES

Angry workers retaliated by reducing an area two miles long beside the tracks to smoldering rubble. Before the day ended, twenty more workers had been shot, and the railroad had sustained millions of dollars' worth of property damage. Nothing like the Pittsburgh riots had ever happened in American history. Armed workers had chased the Philadelphia militia out of town. Now business pressured the federal government to step in.

Within eight days, the governors of nine states, acting at the prompting of the railroad owners and managers, defined the strike as an "insurrection" and called for federal troops. President Rutherford B. Hayes, after hesitating briefly, called out the army. By the time the troops arrived, the violence had run its course. Federal troops did not shoot a single striker in 1877. But they struck a blow against labor by acting as strikebreakers — opening rail traffic, protecting nonstriking train crews (known by the derogatory term "scabs"), and maintaining peace along the line. In three weeks, the strike was over.

Although many middle-class Americans initially sympathized with the conditions that led to the strike, they condemned the strikers for the violence and property damage that occurred. The *New York Times* editorialized about the "dangerous classes," and the *Independent* magazine offered the following advice on how to deal with "rioters": "If the club of a policeman, knocking out the brains of the rioter, will answer then well and good; but if it does not promptly meet the exigency, then bullets and bayonets . . . constitutes [*sic*] the one remedy and one duty of the hour."

"The strikes have been put down by force," President Hayes noted in his diary on August 5. "But now for the real remedy. Can't something be done by education of the strikers, by judicious control of the capitalists, by wise general policy

Destruction from the Great Railroad Strike of 1877
Pictures of the devastation caused in Pittsburgh during the strike shocked many Americans. When militiamen fired on striking workers, killing more than twenty strikers, the mob retaliated by destroying a two-mile area along the track, reducing it to a smoldering rubble. Property damage totaled $2 million. Curious pedestrians came out to view the destruction. Carnegie Library of Pittsburgh.

to end or diminish the evil? The railroad strikers, as a rule, are good men, sober, intelligent, and industrious." While Hayes acknowledged the workers' grievances, most businessmen and industrialists did not and fought the idea of labor unions, arguing that workers and employers entered into contracts as individuals and denying the right of unions to bargain collectively for their workers. For their part, workers quickly recognized that they held little power individually and flocked to join unions. As labor leader Samuel Gompers noted, the nation's first national strike dramatized the frustration and unity of the workers and served as an alarm bell to labor "that sounded a ringing message of hope to us all."

The Knights of Labor and the American Federation of Labor

The **Knights of Labor**, the first mass organization of America's working class, proved the chief beneficiary of labor's newfound consciousness. The Noble and Holy Order of the Knights of Labor had been founded in 1869 by Uriah Stephens, a Philadelphia garment cutter. A secret society of workers, the Knights envisioned a "universal brotherhood" of all workers, from common laborers to master craftsmen. The organization's secrecy and ritual served to bind Knights together at the same time that it discouraged company spies and protected members from reprisals.

Although the Knights played no active role in the 1877 railroad strike, membership swelled as a result of the growing interest in labor organizing that followed the strike. In 1878, the Knights abandoned secrecy and launched an ambitious campaign to organize workers, attempting to bridge the boundaries of ethnicity, gender, ideology, race, and occupation in a badly fragmented society. **Leonora Barry** served as general investigator for women's work from 1886 to 1890, helping the Knights recruit teachers, waitresses, housewives, and domestics along with factory and sweatshop workers. Women composed perhaps 20 percent of the membership. The Knights also made good on its vow to include African Americans, organizing more than 95,000 black workers. That the Knights of Labor often fell short of its goals to unify the working class proved less surprising than the scope of its efforts.

Under the direction of Grand Master Workman **Terence V. Powderly**, the Knights became the dominant force in labor during the 1880s. The organization advocated a kind of workers' democracy that embraced reforms including public ownership of the railroads, an income tax, equal pay for women workers, and the abolition of child labor. A loose mix of ideology, unionism, culture, fraternalism, and mysticism, the Knights called for one big union to create a cooperative commonwealth that would supplant the wage system and remove class distinctions. Only the "parasitic" members of society — gamblers, stockbrokers, lawyers, bankers, and liquor dealers — were denied membership.

In theory, the Knights of Labor opposed strikes. Powderly championed arbitration and preferred to use boycotts. But in practice, much of the organization's appeal came from the Knights' sweeping victory against railroad tycoon Jay Gould in the Great Southwest Strike of 1885. Despite the reservations of its leadership, the Knights became a militant labor organization that won passionate support from working people with the slogan "An injury to one is the concern of all."

The Knights of Labor was not without rivals. Many skilled workers belonged to craft unions organized by trade. Among the largest and richest of these unions stood the Amalgamated Association of Iron and Steel Workers, founded in 1876 and counting twenty thousand skilled workers as members. Trade unionists spurned the broad reform goals of the Knights and focused on workplace issues. **Samuel Gompers**, a cigar maker born in London of Dutch Jewish ancestry, promoted what he called "pure and simple" unionism. Gompers founded the Organized Trades and Labor Unions in 1881 and reorganized it in 1886 into the **American Federation of Labor** (AFL), which coordinated the activities of craft unions throughout the United States. His plan was simple: organize skilled workers such as machinists and locomotive engineers — those with the most bargaining power — and use strikes to gain immediate objectives such as higher pay and better working conditions. Gompers at first drew few converts. The AFL had only 138,000 members in 1886, compared with 730,000 for the Knights of Labor. But events soon brought down the Knights, and Gompers's brand of unionism came to prevail.

Haymarket and the Specter of Labor Radicalism

While the AFL and the Knights of Labor competed for members, more radical labor groups, including socialists and anarchists, believed that reform was futile and called instead for social revolution. Both the socialists and the anarchists, sensitive to criticism that they preferred revolution in theory to improvements here and now, rallied around the popular issue of the eight-hour day.

Since the 1840s, labor had sought to end the twelve-hour workday, which was standard in industry and manufacturing. By the mid-1880s, it seemed clear to many workers that labor shared too little in the new prosperity of the decade, and pressure mounted for the eight-hour day. Labor championed the popular issue and launched major rallies in cities across the nation. Supporters of the movement set May 1, 1886, as the date for a nationwide general strike in support of the eight-hour workday.

All factions of the nascent labor movement came together in Chicago on May Day for what was billed as the largest demonstration to date. A group of labor radicals led by anarchist Albert Parsons, a *Mayflower* descendant, and August Spies, a German socialist, spearheaded the eight-hour movement in Chicago. Chicago's Knights of Labor rallied to the cause even though Terence Powderly and the union's national leadership, worried about the increasing activism of the rank and file, refused to endorse the movement for shorter hours. Samuel Gompers was on hand, too, to lead the city's trade unionists, although he privately urged the AFL assemblies not to participate in the general strike.

Gompers's skilled workers were labor's elite. Many still worked in small shops where negotiations between workers and employers took place in an environment tempered by personal relationships. Well dressed in their frock coats and starched

THE CHICAGO RIOT

A RECORD OF THE
Terrible Scenes of May 4, 1886.

Chicago and New York:
BELFORD, CLARKE & CO.,
1886.

VISUAL ACTIVITY

"The Chicago Riot"

Inflammatory pamphlets like this one, published in the wake of the Haymarket bombing, presented a one-sided view of the incident and stirred public passion. In this charged atmosphere, the anarchist speakers at the rally were tried and convicted for the bombing even though witnesses testified that none of them had thrown the bomb. The identity of the bomb thrower remains uncertain. Chicago Historical Society.

READING THE IMAGE: What does the cover suggest about the views of the author of the pamphlet?

CONNECTIONS: In what ways does this pamphlet reflect the public climate following the Haymarket bombing?

shirts, the AFL's skilled workers stood in sharp contrast to the dispossessed workers out on strike across town at Chicago's huge McCormick reaper works. There strikers watched helplessly as the company brought in strikebreakers to take their jobs and marched the "scabs" to work under the protection of the Chicago police and security guards supplied by the Pinkerton Detective Agency. Cyrus McCormick Jr., son of the inventor of the mechanical reaper, viewed labor organization as a threat to his power as well as to his profits; he was determined to smash the union.

During the May Day rally, 45,000 workers paraded peacefully down Michigan Avenue in support of the eight-hour day, many singing the song that had become the movement's anthem:

We want to feel the sunshine;
We want to smell the flowers,
We're sure that God has willed it,
And we mean to have eight hours.
Eight hours for work, eight hours for rest,
eight hours for what we will!

Trouble came two days later, when strikers attacked strikebreakers outside the McCormick works and police opened fire, killing or wounding six men. Angry radicals rushed out a circular urging workers to "arm yourselves and appear in full force" at a rally in Haymarket Square.

On the evening of May 4, the turnout at Haymarket was disappointing. No more than two or three thousand gathered in the drizzle to hear Spies, Parsons, and the other speakers. Mayor Carter Harrison, known as a friend of labor, mingled conspicuously in the crowd, pronounced the meeting peaceable, and went home to bed. Sometime later, police captain John "Blackjack" Bonfield, who had made his reputation cracking skulls, marched his men into the crowd, by now fewer than three hundred people, and demanded that it disperse. Suddenly, someone threw a bomb into the police ranks. After a moment of stunned silence, the police drew their revolvers. "Fire and kill all you can," shouted a police lieutenant. When the melee ended, seven policemen and an unknown number of other people lay dead. An additional sixty policemen and thirty or forty civilians suffered injuries.

News of the "Haymarket riot" provoked a nationwide convulsion of fear, followed by blind rage directed at anarchists, labor unions, strikers, immigrants, and the working class in general. Eight men, including Parsons and Spies, went on trial in Chicago, although witnesses testified that none of them had thrown the bomb. "Convict these men," thundered the state's attorney, Julius S. Grinnell, "make examples of them, hang them, and you save our institutions." Although the state could not link any of the defendants to the **Haymarket bombing**, the jury nevertheless found them all guilty. Four were executed, one committed suicide, and three received prison sentences. On the gallows, Spies spoke for the Haymarket martyrs: "The time will come when our silence will be more powerful than the voices you throttle today."

The bomb blast at Haymarket had lasting repercussions. To commemorate the death of the Haymarket martyrs, labor made May 1 an annual international celebration of the worker. But the Haymarket bomb, in the eyes of one observer, proved "a godsend to all enemies of the labor movement." It effectively scotched the eight-hour-day movement and dealt a blow to the Knights of Labor, already wracked by internal divisions. With the labor movement everywhere under attack, many skilled workers turned to the American Federation of Labor. Gompers's narrow economic strategy made sense at the time and enabled one segment of the workforce — the skilled — to organize effectively and achieve tangible gains. But the nation's unskilled workers remained untouched by the AFL's brand of trade unionism. The vast majority of America's workers would have to wait another forty years before a mainstream labor union, the Congress of Industrial Organizations (CIO), moved to organize the unskilled (as discussed in chapter 24).

REVIEW   Why did the fortunes of the Knights of Labor rise in the late 1870s and decline in the 1890s?

Maids and Domestics

These Swedish immigrant women were working as maids in the Merchant's Hotel in Black River Falls, Wisconsin, when they posed for this picture in 1890. Each carries a tool of her trade—broom and dustpan, iron, potato peeler, dishcloth, pie plate, serving tray. The women, young and well dressed, have similar collars, but no clear uniform. Domestic work could be hard and lonely. Only the largest private house would have so many women employed. Wisconsin Historical Society (WHi (V22d) 1386).

▶ At Home and at Play

The growth of urban industrialism not only dramatically altered the workplace but also transformed home and family life and gave rise to new forms of commercialized leisure. Industrialization redefined the very concepts of work and home. Increasingly, men went out to work for wages, while most white married women stayed home, either working in the home without pay — cleaning, cooking, and rearing children — or supervising paid domestic servants who did the housework.

Domesticity and "Domestics"

The separation of the workplace and the home that marked the shift to industrial society redefined the home as a "haven in the heartless world," presided over by a wife and mother who made the household her separate sphere. The growing separation of workplace and home led to a new ideology, one that sentimentalized the home and women's role in it. The cultural ideology that dictated woman's place in the home began to develop in the early 1800s and has been called the **cult of domesticity**, a phrase used to prescribe an ideal of middle-class, white womanhood that dominated the period from 1820 to the end of the nineteenth century.

The cult of domesticity and the elaboration of the middle-class home led to a major change in patterns of hiring household help. The live-in servants, or **domestics**, became a fixture in the North, replacing the hired girl of the previous century. In American cities by 1870, 15 to 30 percent of all households included live-in domestic servants, more than 90 percent of them women. Earlier in the mid-nineteenth century, native-born women increasingly took up other work and left domestic service to immigrants. In the East, the maid was so often Irish that "Bridget" became a generic term for female domestics. (The South continued to rely on black female labor, first slave and later free.)

Servants by all accounts resented the long hours and lack of privacy. "She is liable to be rung up at all hours," one study of domestics reported. "Her very meals are not secure from interruption, and even her sleep is not sacred." No wonder tension between domestic servants and their female employers proved endemic. Domestic service became the occupation of last resort, a "hard and lonely life" in the words of one female servant.

For women of the white middle class, domestics were a boon, freeing them from household drudgery and giving them more time to spend with their children or to pursue club work or reform. Thus, while domestic service supported the cult of domesticity, it created for those women who could afford it opportunities that expanded their horizons outside the home in areas such as women's clubs and the temperance and suffrage movements.

Such benefits of middle-class respectability contrasted sharply with the austerity of the working-class home. Reformer Margaret Byington recounted her visit with the family of a Slavic worker in Homestead, the Carnegie mill town outside Pittsburgh. The family lived in a two-room dwelling, and Byington found the young mother doing the family laundry in a big washtub set on a chair in the middle of the downstairs room, struggling to keep her two babies from tumbling into the scalding water. Further describing the congested home, Byington noted the room's single large bed and "the inevitable cook stove upon which in the place of honor was simmering the evening's soup. Upstairs in a second room, a boarder and the man of the house were asleep. Soon they would get up and turn their beds over to two more boarders, who were out at work." In the eyes of Byington and many middle-class reformers, the Slavs' crowded tenement, with its lack of privacy, scarcely qualified as a "home."

Cheap Amusements

Growing class divisions manifested themselves in patterns of leisure as well as in work and home life. The poor and working class took their leisure, when they had any, not in the crowded tenements that housed their families, but increasingly in the cities' new dance halls, music houses, ballparks, and amusement arcades, which by the 1890s formed a familiar part of the urban landscape.

The growing anonymity of urban industrial society posed a challenge to traditional rituals of courtship. Young workingwomen no longer

Beach Scene at Coney Island
Coney Island became a symbol of commercialized leisure and mechanical excitement at the turn of the twentieth century. This fanciful rendering captures the frenetic goings-on. Men and women, along with costumed clowns, frolic in the waves. Notice the woolen bathing outfits, with their leggings, modest skirts and blouses, and bathing hats. Men box and play ball, a woman flies on a parachute, while a uniformed policeman wades into the fray, brandishing his billy club. On the shore are the rides — with the Ferris wheel dominating the skyline — and the famous hotel in the shape of an elephant. Sunday crowds on the island reportedly reached 100,000. Beach scene: Library of Congress; Sand pail: Private Collection.

met prospective husbands only through their families. Fleeing crowded tenements, the young sought each other's company in dance halls and other commercial retreats. Scorning proper introductions, working-class youths "picked up" partners at dance halls, where drinking was part of the evening's entertainment. Young workingwomen, who rarely could afford more than trolley fare when they went out, counted on being "treated" by men, a transaction that often implied sexual payback. Young women's need to negotiate sexual encounters if they wished to participate in commercial amusements blurred the line between respectability and promiscuity and made the dance halls a favorite target of reformers who feared they lured teenaged girls into prostitution.

For men, baseball became a national pastime in the 1870s — then, as now, one force in urban life capable of uniting a city across class lines. Cincinnati mounted the first entirely paid team, the Red Stockings, in 1869. Soon professional teams proliferated in cities across the nation, and Mark Twain hailed baseball as "the very symbol, the outward and visible expression, of the drive and push and rush and struggle of the raging, tearing, booming nineteenth century."

The increasing commercialization of entertainment in the late-nineteenth-century city was best seen at **Coney Island**. A two-mile stretch of sand nine miles from Manhattan by trolley or steamship, Coney Island in the 1870s and 1880s attracted visitors to its beaches, dance pavilions, and penny arcades, where they consumed treats ranging from oysters to saltwater taffy. In the 1890s, Coney Island was transformed into the site of some of the largest and most elaborate amusement parks in the country. Promoter George Tilyou built Steeplechase Park in 1897, advertising "10 hours of fun for 10 cents." With its mechanical thrills and fun-house laughs, the amusement park encouraged behavior that one schoolteacher aptly described as "everyone with the brakes off." By 1900, as many as a million New Yorkers flocked to Coney Island on any given weekend, making the amusement park the unofficial capital of a new mass culture.

> ### "Everyone with the brakes off."
> — A schoolteacher's description of behavior at Coney Island's Steeplechase Amusement park

REVIEW How did urban industrialism shape the world of leisure?

▶ City Growth and City Government

Private enterprise, not planners, built the cities of the United States. Boosters, builders, businessmen, and politicians all had a hand in creating the modern metropolis. With a few notable exceptions, such as Washington, D.C., and Savannah, Georgia, there was no such thing as a comprehensive city plan. Cities simply mushroomed, formed by the dictates of profit and the exigencies of local politics. With the rise of the city came the need for public facilities, transportation, and services that would tax the imaginations of America's architects and engineers and set the scene for the rough-and-tumble of big-city government, politics, and politicians.

Building Cities of Stone and Steel

Skyscrapers and mighty bridges dominated the imagination and the urban landscape. Less imposing but no less significant were the paved streets, the parks and public libraries, and the subways and sewers. In the late nineteenth century, Americans rushed to embrace new technology of all kinds, making their cities the most modern in the world.

Structural steel made enormous advances in building possible. A decade after the completion of the **Brooklyn Bridge** (see pages 603–604), engineers used the new technology to construct the Williamsburg Bridge just to the north. More prosaic and utilitarian than its neighbor, the new bridge was never as acclaimed, but it was longer by four feet and completed in half the time. It became the model for future building as the age of steel supplanted the age of stone and iron.

Chicago, not New York, gave birth to the modern skyscraper. Rising from the ashes of the Great Fire of 1871, which destroyed three square miles and left eighteen thousand people homeless, Chicago offered a generation of skilled architects and engineers the chance to experiment. Commercial architecture became an art form at the hands of a skilled group of architects who together constituted the "Chicago school." Men of genius such as Louis Sullivan gave Chicago some of the world's finest commercial buildings. Employing the dictum "Form follows

VIEW OF CONSTRUCTION OF "THE FAIR" BUILDING, CHICAGO.
Illustrating Paper by W. L. B. JENNEY, Architect, published in this number.

Chicago Skyscraper Going Up
With the advent of structural steel, skyscrapers like this one in progress in Chicago in 1891 became prominent features of the American urban landscape. This architect's rendering of the Fair Building, a department store designed by William Le Baron Jenney, shows a modern skyscraper whose foundations supported the structural steel skeleton so that the walls could simply "hang" on the outside of the building, because they no longer had to support the structure. Newberry Library (*Inland Architect*, Nov. 1891).

function," they built startlingly modern structures. A fitting symbol of modern America, the skyscraper expressed the domination of corporate power.

Alongside the skyscrapers rose new residential apartments for the rich and the middle class. The "French flat" — apartments with the latest plumbing and electricity — gained popularity in the 1880s as affluent city dwellers overcame their distaste for multifamily housing (which carried the stigma of the tenement) and gave in to "flat fever." "Housekeeping isn't fun," cried one New York woman. "Give us flats!" In 1883 alone, more than one thousand new apartments went up in Chicago.

Across the United States, municipal governments undertook public works on a scale never before seen. They paved streets, built sewers and water mains, replaced gas lamps with electric lights, ran trolley tracks on the old horsecar lines, and dug underground to build subways, tearing down the unsightly elevated tracks that had clogged city streets. In San Francisco, Andrew Smith Hallidie mastered the city's hills, building a system of cable cars in 1873. Boston completed the nation's first subway system in 1897, and New York and Philadelphia soon followed.

Cities became more beautiful with the creation of urban public parks to complement the new buildings that quickly filled city lots. Much of the credit for America's greatest parks goes to one man — landscape architect **Frederick Law Olmsted**. The indefatigable Olmsted designed parks in Atlanta, Boston, Brooklyn, Hartford, Detroit, Chicago, and Louisville, as well as the grounds for the U.S. Capitol. But he is best remembered for the creation of New York City's Central Park. Completed in 1873, it became the first landscaped public park in the United States. Olmsted and his partner, Calvert Vaux, directed the planting of more than five million trees, shrubs, and vines to transform the eight hundred acres between 59th and 110th streets into an oasis for urban dwellers. "We want a place," he wrote, where people "may stroll for an hour, seeing, hearing, and feeling nothing of the bustle and jar of the streets."

American cities did not overlook the mind in their efforts at improvement. They created a comprehensive free public school system that educated everyone from the children of the middle class to the sons and daughters of immigrant workers. Yet the exploding urban population strained the system and led to crowded

The Boston Public Library

When the first public library in the country moved to its new site in Boston's Copley Square in 1895, the best artists and architects of the day lent their talents to build "a palace for the people." Architect Charles F. McKim designed the library around a cloistered courtyard in the style of a Renaissance palazzo. Sculptor Augustus Saint-Gaudens modeled the Sienna marble lions that guard the grand stairway. French muralist Puvis de Chavannes contributed the allegorical mural representing literature and learning. A frolicking nude Bacchante by Frederick MacMonnies graced the courtyard fountain for a few days until scandalized Bostonians demanded its removal. Today it has been restored to its place. Library photograph: ©Richard Cheek for the Boston Public Library; statue: image copyright ©The Metropolitan Museum of Art/Art Resource, NY.

and inadequate facilities. In 1899, more than 544,000 pupils attended school in New York's five boroughs. Municipalities across the United States provided free secondary school education for all who wished to attend, even though only 8 percent of Americans completed high school.

To educate those who couldn't go to school, American cities created the most extensive free public library system in the world. In 1895, the Boston Public Library opened its bronze doors under the inscription "Free to All." Designed in the style of a Renaissance palazzo, with more than 700,000 books on the shelves ready to be checked out, the library earned the description "a palace of the people."

Despite the Boston Public Library's legend "Free to All," the poor did not share equally in the advantages of city life. The parks, the libraries, and even the subways and sewers benefited some city dwellers more than others. Few library cards were held by Boston's laborers, who worked six days a week and found the library closed on Sunday. And in the 1890s, there was nothing central about New York's Central Park. It was a four-mile walk from the tenements of Hester Street to the park's entrance at 59th Street and Fifth Avenue. Then, as now, the comfortable majority, not the indigent minority, reaped a disproportionate share of the benefits in the nation's big cities.

Any story of the American city, it seems, must be a tale of two cities — or, given the cities' great diversity, a tale of many cities within each metropolis. At the turn of the twentieth century, a central paradox emerged: The enduring monuments of America's cities — the bridges, skyscrapers, parks, and libraries — stood as the undeniable achievements of the same system of municipal government that reformers dismissed as boss-ridden, criminal, and corrupt.

City Government and the "Bosses"

The physical growth of the cities required the expansion of public services and the creation of entirely new facilities: streets, subways, elevated trains, bridges, docks, sewers, and public utilities. There was work to be done and money to be made. The professional politician — the colorful big-city boss — became a phenomenon of urban growth and **bossism** a national phenomenon. Though corrupt and often criminal, the boss saw to the building of the city and provided needed social services for the new residents. Yet not even the big-city boss could be said to rule the unruly city. The governing of America's cities resembled more a tug-of-war than boss rule.

The most notorious of all the city bosses was **William Marcy "Boss" Tweed** of New York. At midcentury, Boss Tweed's Democratic Party "machine" held sway. A machine was really no more than a political party organized at the grassroots level. Its purpose was to win elections and reward its followers, often with jobs on the city's payroll. New York's citywide Democratic machine, **Tammany Hall**, commanded an army of party functionaries. At the bottom were district captains. In return for votes, they provided services for their constituents, everything from a scuttle of coal in the winter to housing for an evicted family. At the top were powerful ward bosses who distributed lucrative franchises for subways and streetcars. They formed a shadow government more powerful than the city's elected officials.

As chairman of the Tammany general committee, Tweed kept the Democratic Party together and ran the city through the use of bribery and graft. "As long as I count the votes," he shamelessly boasted, "what are you going to do about

Tammany Bank
This cast-iron bank, a campaign novelty, bears the name of the New York City Democratic machine. It conveys its political reform message graphically: When you put a penny in the politician's hand, he puts it in his pocket. Tammany Hall dominated city politics for more than a century, dispensing contracts and franchises worth millions of dollars. Some of those dollars invariably found their way into the pockets of Tammany politicians.
Collection of Janice L. and David J. Frent.

it?" The excesses of the Tweed ring soon led to a clamor for reform and cries of "Throw the rascals out." Cartoonist Thomas Nast pilloried Tweed in the pages of *Harper's Weekly*. His cartoons, easily understood even by those who could not read, did the boss more harm than hundreds of outraged editorials. Tweed's rule ended in 1871. Eventually, he was tried and convicted and later died in jail.

New York was not the only city to experience bossism and corruption. The British visitor James Bryce concluded in 1888, "There is no denying that the government of cities is the one conspicuous failure of the United States." More than 80 percent of the nation's thirty largest cities experienced some form of boss rule in the decades around the turn of the twentieth century. However, infighting among powerful ward bosses often meant that no single boss enjoyed exclusive power in the big cities.

"As long as I count the votes, what are you going to do about it?"
— New York's BOSS TWEED

Urban reformers and proponents of good government (derisively called "goo goos" by their rivals) challenged machine rule and sometimes succeeded in electing reform mayors. But the reformers rarely managed to stay in office for long. Their detractors called them "mornin' glories," observing that they "looked lovely in the mornin' and withered up in a short time." The bosses enjoyed continued success largely because the urban political machine helped the cities' immigrants and poor, who remained the bosses' staunchest allies. "What tells in holding your district," a Tammany ward boss observed, "is to go right down among the poor and help them in the different ways they need help. It's philanthropy, but it's politics, too — mighty good politics." Saloons were the epicenter of ward politics. They played a crucial role in workers' lives and often served informally as political headquarters, as well as employment agencies and union halls.

A few reform mayors managed to achieve success and longevity by following the bosses' model. **Hazen S. Pingree** of Detroit exemplified the successful reform mayor. A businessman who went into politics in the 1890s, Pingree, like most good-government candidates, promised to root out dishonesty and inefficiency. But when the depression of 1893 struck, Pingree emerged as a champion of the working class and the poor. He hired the unemployed to build schools, parks, and public baths. By providing jobs and needed services, he built a powerful political organization based on working-class support. Detroit's

Chicago's White City

This painting by H. D. Nichols captures the monumental architecture of the White City built for the World's Columbian Exposition in 1893. In the foreground, the central Court of Honor features a Frederick MacMonnies fountain, with Christopher Columbus at the prow of his ship. In the distance is Daniel Chester French's sixty-foot gilded statue *Republic*. Monumental, harmonious, and pristine, the White City was designed by Daniel Burnham and Frederick Law Olmsted to awe and overwhelm fairgoers. And so it did, drawing millions of visitors from America and abroad, who eagerly snapped up souvenirs, such as the playing cards pictured here, to commemorate their visit. Painting: Chicago Historical Society; Cards: Compliments of Columbus Antique Mall & Museum.

voters kept him in the mayor's office for four terms and then helped elect him governor twice.

The big-city boss, through the skillful orchestration of rewards, exerted powerful leverage and lined up support for his party from a broad range of constituents, from the urban poor to wealthy industrialists. In 1902, when journalist **Lincoln Steffens** began "The Shame of the Cities," a series of articles exposing city corruption, he found that business leaders who fastidiously refused to mingle socially with the bosses nevertheless struck deals with them. "He is a self-righteous fraud, this big businessman," Steffens concluded. "I found him buying boodlers [bribers] in St. Louis, defending grafters in Minneapolis, originating corruption in Pittsburgh, sharing with bosses in Philadelphia, deploring reform in Chicago, and beating good government with corruption funds in New York."

The complexity of big-city government, apparent in the many levels of corruption that Steffens uncovered, pointed to one conclusion: For all the color and flamboyance of the big-city boss, he was simply one of many actors in the drama of municipal government. Old-stock aristocrats, new professionals, saloon-keepers, pushcart peddlers, and politicians all fought for their interests in the hurly-burly of city government. They didn't much like each other, and they sometimes fought savagely. But they learned to live with one another. Compromise and accommodation — not boss rule — best characterized big-city government by the turn of the twentieth century, although the cities' reputation for corruption left an indelible mark on the consciousness of the American public.

White City or City of Sin?

Americans have always been of two minds about the city. They like to boast of its skyscrapers and bridges, its culture and sophistication, and they pride themselves on its bigness and bustle. At the same time, they fear it as the city of sin, the home of immigrant slums, the center of vice and crime. Nowhere did the divided view of the American city take form more graphically than in Chicago in 1893. In that year, Chicago hosted the **World's Columbian Exposition**, the grandest world's fair in the nation's history. (See "Beyond America's Borders," page 632.) The fairground on Lake Michigan offered a lesson in what Americans on the eve of the twentieth century imagined a city might be. Only five miles down the shore from downtown Chicago, the White City, as the fairground became known,

seemed light-years away from Chicago, with its stockyards, slums, and bustling terminals. Frederick Law Olmsted and architect Daniel Burnham supervised the transformation of a swampy wasteland into a pristine paradise of lagoons, fountains, wooded islands, gardens, and imposing buildings.

"Sell the cookstove if necessaray and come," novelist Hamlin Garland wrote to his parents on the farm. And come they did, in spite of the panic and depression that broke out only weeks after the fair opened in May 1893. In six months, fairgoers purchased more than 27 million tickets, turning a profit of nearly a half million dollars for promoters. Visitors from home and abroad strolled the elaborate grounds and visited the exhibits — everything from a model of the Brooklyn Bridge carved in soap to the latest goods and inventions. Half carnival, half culture, the great fair offered something for everyone. On the Midway Plaisance, crowds thrilled to the massive wheel built by Mr. Ferris and watched agog as Little Egypt danced the hootchy-kootchy.

In October, the fair closed its doors in the midst of the worst depression the country had yet seen. During the winter of 1894, Chicago's unemployed and homeless took over the grounds, vandalized the buildings, and frightened the city's comfortable citizens out of their wits. When reporters asked Daniel Burnham what should be done with the moldering remains of the White City, he responded, "It should be torched." And it was. In July 1894, in a clash between federal troops and striking railway workers, incendiaries set fires that leveled the fairgrounds.

In the end, the White City remained what it had always been, a dreamscape. Buildings that looked like marble were actually constructed of staff, a plaster substance that began to crumble even before fire destroyed the fairgrounds. Perhaps it was not so strange, after all, that the legacy of the White City could be found on Coney Island, where two new amusement parks, Luna and Dreamland, sought to combine, albeit in a more tawdry form, the beauty of the White City and the thrill of the Midway Plaisance. More enduring than the White City itself was what it represented: the emergent industrial might of the United States, at home and abroad, with its inventions, manufactured goods, and growing consumer culture.

REVIEW   How did municipal governments respond to the challenges of urban expansion?

The World's Columbian Exposition and Nineteenth-Century World's Fairs

The 1893 World's Columbian Exposition in Chicago and the other great world's fairs of the nineteenth century represented a unique phenomenon of industrial capitalism and a testament to the expanding global market economy. The Chicago fair, named to celebrate the four hundredth anniversary of Columbus's arrival in the New World, offered a cornucopia of international exhibits testifying to growing international influences ranging from cultural to technological exchange.

Great cities vied to host world's fairs, as much to promote commercial growth as to demonstrate their cultural refinement. Each successive fair sought to outdo its predecessor. Chicago's fair followed on the great success of the 1889 Universal Exposition in Paris. The Paris Exposition featured as its crowning glory the 900-foot steel tower constructed by Alexandre-Gustav Eiffel. How could Chicago, a prairie upstart, top that?

The answer was the creation of the White City, with its monumental architecture, landscaped grounds, and first Ferris wheel. The White City celebrated the classicism of the French Beaux Arts school, which borrowed heavily from the massive geometric styling and elaborate detailing of Greek and Renaissance architecture. Beneath its Renaissance facade, the White City acted as an enormous emporium dedicated to the unabashed materialism of the Gilded Age. Fairgoers could view virtually every kind of manufactured product in the world inside the imposing Manufactures and Liberal Arts Building, including Swiss glassware and clocks, Japanese lacquerware and bamboo, British woolen products, and French perfumes and linens. The German pavilion displayed fine wooden furniture as well as tapestries, porcelain, and jewelry belonging to the ruling family.

As suited an industrial age, manufactured products and heavy machinery drew the largest crowds. Displays introduced visitors to the latest mechanical and technological innovations, many the result of international influences. For five cents, fairgoers could put two hard rubber tubes into their ears and listen for the first time to a Gramophone playing the popular tune "The Cat Came Back." The Gramophone, which signaled the beginning of the recorded music industry, was itself the work of a German immigrant, Emile Berliner (Thomas Edison later claimed credit for a similar invention, calling it the phonograph).

Such international influences were evident throughout the Columbian Exposition. At the Tiffany pavilion, one of the most popular venues at the fair, visitors oohed and aahed over the display of lamps, ornamental metalwork, and fine jewelry that Louis Comfort Tiffany credited to the influence of Japanese art forms. Juxtaposed with Tiffany's finery stood a display of firearms in the Colt gallery. An American company since 1836, Colt had opened a factory in England in 1851, and its revolvers enjoyed an international reputation — the best-known firearms not only in America but also in Canada, Mexico, and many European countries. Colt's new automatic weapon, the machine gun, would soon play a major role on the world stage in both the Boxer uprising in China and the Spanish-American War.

All manner of foodstuffs — teas from India, Irish whiskey, and pastries and other confectionery from Germany and France — tempted fairgoers. American food products such as Shredded Wheat, Aunt Jemima syrup, and Juicy Fruit gum debuted at the fair, where they competed for ribbons. Winners such as Pabst "Blue Ribbon" Beer used the award in advertisements. And the fair introduced two new foods — carbonated soda and the hamburger — destined to become America's best-known contributions to international cuisine.

The Columbian Exposition also served as a testimony to American technological achievement and progress. By displaying technology in action, the White City tamed it and made it accessible to American and world consumers. The fair helped promote new technologies, particularly electric light and power. With 90,000 electric lights, 5,100 arc lamps, electric fountains, an electric elevated railroad, and electric launches plying the lagoons, the White City provided a glowing advertisement for electricity. In the Electricity Building, fairgoers visited the Bell Telephone Company exhibit,

ALL NATIONS ARE WELCOME TO THE WORLD'S COLUMBIAN EXPOSITION CHICAGO 1893.

"All Nations Are Welcome"
Uncle Sam, flanked by the city of Chicago, welcomes representatives carrying the flags of many nations to the World's Columbian Exposition in 1893. In the background are the fairgrounds on the shores of Lake Michigan. More than one hundred nations participated in the fair by sending exhibits and mounting pavilions to showcase their cultures and products. Chicago Historical Society.

marveled at General Electric's huge dynamo (electric generator), and gazed into the future at the all-electric home and model demonstration kitchen.

Consumer culture received its first major expression and celebration at the Columbian Exposition. Not only did this world's fair anticipate the mass marketing, packaging, and advertising of the twentieth century, but the vast array of products on display also cultivated the urge to consume. Thousands of concessionaires with products for sale sent a message that tied enjoy-ment inextricably to spending money and purchasing goods, both domestic and foreign. The Columbian Exposition set a pattern for the twentieth-century world's fairs that followed, making a powerful statement about the possibilities of urban life in an industrial age and encouraging the rise of a new middle-class consumer culture. As G. Brown Goode, head of the Smithsonian Institution observed, the Columbian Exposition was in many ways "an illustrated encyclopedia of civilization."

America in a Global Context

1. Would you describe the Columbian Exposition as a commercial venture, a cultural display, or an entertainment? Why?

2. What role did the fair play in popularizing new technologies?

3. What was meant by the observation that the fair was "an illustrated encyclopedia of civilization"?

4. How did the international flavor of the White City compare with the reality of global migration into America's fast-growing cities?

▶ # Conclusion: Who Built the Cities?

As much as the great industrialists and financiers, as much as eminent engineers like John and Washington Roebling, common workers, most of them immigrants, built the nation's cities. The unprecedented growth of urban, industrial America resulted from the labor of millions of men, women, and children who toiled in workshops and factories, in sweatshops and mines, on railroads and construction sites across America.

America's cities in the late nineteenth century teemed with life. Immigrants and blue bloods, poor laborers and millionaires, middle-class managers and corporate moguls, secretaries, salesgirls, sweatshop laborers, and society matrons lived in the cities and contributed to their growth. Town houses and tenements jostled for space with skyscrapers and great department stores, while parks, ball fields, amusement arcades, and public libraries provided the city masses with recreation and entertainment.

Municipal governments, straining to build the new cities, experienced the rough-and-tumble of machine politics as bosses and their constituents looked to profit from city growth. Reformers deplored the graft and corruption that accompanied the rise of the cities. But they were rarely able to oust the party bosses for long because they failed to understand the services the political machines provided for their largely immigrant and poor constituents; nor did reformers account for the ties between city politicians and wealthy businessmen who sought to benefit from franchises and contracts.

For America's workers, urban industrialism along with the rise of big business and corporate consolidation drastically changed the workplace. Industrialists replaced skilled workers with new machines that could be operated by cheaper unskilled labor. And during hard times, employers did not hesitate to cut workers' already meager wages. As the Great Railroad Strike of 1877 demonstrated, when labor united, it could bring the nation to attention. Organization held out the best hope for the workers; first the Knights of Labor and later the American Federation of Labor won converts among the nation's working class.

The rise of urban industrialism challenged the American promise, which for decades had been dominated by Jeffersonian agrarian ideals. Could such a promise exist in the changing world of cities, tenements, immigrants, and huge corporations? In the great depression that came in the 1890s, mounting anger and frustration would lead farmers and workers to join forces and create a grassroots movement to fight for change under the banner of a new People's Party.

▶ # Selected Bibliography

Immigration

John Bodnar, *The Transplanted: A History of Immigration in Urban America* (1985).

Vincent J. Cannato, *American Passage: The History of Ellis Island* (2010).

Roger Daniels, *Guarding the Golden Door: American Immigration Policy and Immigrants since 1882* (2004).

Martha Gardner, *The Qualities of a Citizen: Women, Immigration, and Citizenship, 1870–1965* (2005).

Dirk Hoerder, *Cultures in Contact: World Migrations in the Second Millennium* (2002).

Matthew Frye Jacobson, *Whiteness of a Different Color: European Immigrants and the Alchemy of Race* (1998).

David M. Reimers, *Unwelcome Strangers* (1998).

David R. Roediger, *Working toward Whiteness: How America's Immigrants Became White* (2005).

Ronald Takaki, *Strangers from a Different Shore: A History of Asian Americans* (1998).

Workers and Unions

Susan Porter Benson, *Counter Cultures: Saleswomen, Managers, and Customers in American Department Stores, 1890–1940* (1986).

Ileen A. DeVault, *United Apart: Gender and the Rise of Craft Unionism* (2004).

Hasia Diner, *Lower East Side Memories: A Jewish Place in America* (2000).

Leon Fink, *Workingman's Democracy: The Knights of Labor and American Politics* (1983).

James Green, *Death in the Haymarket: A Story of Chicago, the First Labor Movement, and the Bombing That Divided Gilded Age America* (2006).

Hamilton Hold, ed., *The Life Stories of Undistinguished Americans as Told by Themselves* (2000).

Jacqueline Jones, *American Work: Four Centuries of Black and White Labor* (1998).

Jackson Lears, *Rebirth of a Nation: The Making of Modern America, 1877–1920* (2009).

Susan Levine, *Labor's True Women: Carpet Weavers, Industrialization, and Labor Reform in the Gilded Age* (1984).

David Montgomery, *The Fall of the House of Labor: The Workplace, the State, and American Labor Activism, 1865–1925* (1987).

Roy Rosenzweig, *Eight Hours for What We Will: Workers and Leisure in an Industrial City, 1870–1920* (1983).

Timothy Spears, *Chicago Dreaming: Midwesterners and the City, 1871–1919* (2005).

Carole Srole, *Transcribing Class and Gender: Masculinity and Femininity in Nineteenth Century Courts and Offices* (2009).

Sharon Hartman Strom, *Beyond the Typewriter: Gender, Class, and the Origins of Modern American Office Work, 1900–1930* (1992).

Robert E. Weir, *Knights Unhorsed: Internal Conflict in a Gilded Age Social Movement* (2000).

The City and Its Amusements

LeRoy Ashby, *With Amusement for All: A History of American Popular Culture since 1830* (2006).

Sven Beckert, *The Monied Metropolis: New York City and the Consolidation of the American Bourgeoisie, 1850–1896* (2001).

Gary S. Cross and John K. Walton, *The Playful Crowd: Pleasure Places in the Twentieth Century* (2005).

Sarah Deutsch, *Women and the City: Gender, Space, and Power in Boston, 1870–1940* (2000).

Nan Enstad, *Ladies of Labor, Girls of Adventure: Working Women, Popular Culture, and Labor Politics at the Turn of the Twentieth Century* (1999).

Margaret Garb, *City of American Dreams: A History of Home Ownership and Housing Reform in Chicago, 1871–1919* (2005).

Richard Haw, *The Brooklyn Bridge: A Cultural History* (2005).

Elizabeth Hawes, *New York, New York: How the Apartment House Transformed Life in the City, 1869–1930* (1993).

Kathy Peiss, *Cheap Amusements: Working Women and Leisure in Turn-of-the-Century New York* (1986).

Roy Rosenzweig and Elizabeth Blackmar, *The Park and the People: A History of Central Park* (1992).

Witold Rybczynski, *A Clearing in the Distance: Frederick Law Olmsted and America in the Nineteenth Century* (1999).

Jules Tygiel, *Past Time: Baseball as History* (2000).

▶ FOR MORE BOOKS ABOUT TOPICS IN THIS CHAPTER, see the Online Bibliography at **bedfordstmartins.com/roark**.

▶ FOR ADDITIONAL PRIMARY SOURCES FROM THIS PERIOD, see Michael Johnson, ed., *Reading the American Past*, Fifth Edition.

▶ FOR WEB SITES, IMAGES, AND DOCUMENTS RELATED TO TOPICS AND PLACES IN THIS CHAPTER, visit Make History at **bedfordstmartins.com/roark**.

Reviewing Chapter 19

REVIEW QUESTIONS

Use key terms and dates to support your answer.

1. Why did American cities experience explosive growth in the late nineteenth century? (pp. 605–614)

2. How did business expansion and consolidation change workers' occupations in the late nineteenth century? (pp. 614–619)

3. Why did the fortunes of the Knights of Labor rise in the late 1870s and decline in the 1890s? (pp. 619–624)

4. How did urban industrialism shape the world of leisure? (pp. 624–626)

5. How did municipal governments respond to the challenges of urban expansion? (pp. 626–633)

MAKING CONNECTIONS

Draw on key terms, the timeline, and review questions.

1. Americans expressed both wonder and concern at the nation's mushrooming cities. Why did cities provoke such divergent responses? In your answer, discuss the dramatic demographic, environmental, and political developments associated with urbanization.

2. Why did patterns of immigration to the United States in the late nineteenth century change? How did Americans respond to the immigrants who arrived late in the century? In your answer, consider how industrial capitalism, nationally and globally, contributed to these developments.

3. How did urban industrialization affect Americans' lives outside of work? Describe the impact of late-nineteenth-century economic developments on home life and leisure. In your answer, consider how class, race, gender, and ethnicity contributed to diverse urban experiences.

4. When workers began to embrace organization in the late 1870s, what did they hope to accomplish? Were they successful? Why or why not? In your answer, discuss both general conditions and specific events that shaped these developments.

LINKING TO THE PAST

Link events in this chapter to earlier events.

1. Compare the lives of migrant workers and industrial cowboys in the West to workers in the nation's cities. What are the major similarities? (See chapter 17.)

2. You have already looked at the development of America's industries in the nineteenth century from the vantage point of moguls such as Andrew Carnegie and John D. Rockefeller. How does your view of industrialism change when the focus is shifted to the nation's workers? (See chapter 18.)

▶ FOR PRACTICE QUIZZES AND OTHER STUDY TOOLS, visit the Online Study Guide at bedfordstmartins.com/roark.

TIMELINE 1869–1897

1869
- Knights of Labor founded.
- Cincinnati mounts first paid baseball team, the Red Stockings.

1871
- Boss Tweed's rule in New York ends.
- Chicago's Great Fire.

1873
- Panic on Wall Street touches off depression.
- San Francisco's cable car system opens.

1877
- Great Railroad Strike.

1880s
- Immigration from southern and eastern Europe rises.

1882
- Chinese Exclusion Act.

1883
- Brooklyn Bridge opens.

1886
- American Federation of Labor (AFL) founded.
- Haymarket bombing.

1890s
- African American migration from the South begins.

1890
- Jacob Riis publishes *How the Other Half Lives*.

1892
- Ellis Island opens in New York harbor to process immigrants.

1893
- World's Columbian Exposition.
- Panic on Wall Street touches off major economic depression.

1895
- Boston Public Library opens.

1896
- President Grover Cleveland vetoes immigrant literacy test.

1897
- Steeplechase Park opens on Coney Island.
- Nation's first subway system opens in Boston.

IN THE OLD
PARTIES WE TRUSTED
untill FINANCIALLY WE ARE BUSTED

And if we would
our rights regain
We must nominate
Honest Men

It is the best that
We can do
And elect them
all in 92

DOWN WITH
MONOPOLY

PEOPLE'S PARTY BANNER

This buffalo banner from the 1892 Populist convention declares "In the Old Parties We Trusted until Financially we are Busted" and promises to elect "Honest Men." In the background some of those men stand, along with women and children, on the steps of the capitol in Topeka in 1893, after being elected to the Kansas House of Representatives. Perhaps taking the buffalo as a mascot was a poor choice for the new party, for just as the great herds on the western plains had been decimated in the 1880s, the People's (or Populist) Party would go down to defeat in 1896.
Banner: Nebraska State Historical Society; background: Kansas State Historical Society.

20

Dissent, Depression, and War 1890–1900

FRANCES WILLARD TRAVELED TO ST. LOUIS IN FEBRUARY 1892 WITH high hopes. Political change was in the air, and Willard was there to help fashion a new reform party, one that she hoped would embrace her two passions — temperance and woman suffrage. As head of the Woman's Christian Temperance Union, an organization with members in every state and territory in the nation, Willard wielded considerable clout. At her invitation, twenty-eight of the country's leading reformers had already met in Chicago to draft a set of principles to bring to St. Louis. Always expedient, Willard had settled for a statement condemning the saloon rather than an endorsement for a stronger measure to prohibit the sale of alcohol. But at the convention, she hoped to press the case for woman suffrage and prohibition. Willard knew it would not be easy, but in the heady atmosphere of 1892 she determined to try. No American woman before her had played such a central role in a political movement. At the height of her political power, Willard took her place among the leaders on the podium in St. Louis.

Exposition Music Hall presented a colorful spectacle. "The banners of the different states rose above the delegates throughout the hall, fluttering like the flags over an army encamped," wrote one reporter. The fiery orator Ignatius Donnelly attacked the money kings of Wall Street. Mary Elizabeth Lease, a veteran campaigner from Kansas known for exhorting farmers to "raise less corn and more hell," added her powerful voice to the cause. Terence V. Powderly, head of the Knights of Labor, called on workers to join hands with farmers against the "nonproducing classes." Frances Willard urged the crowd to outlaw the liquor traffic and give the vote to women. Between speeches, the crowd sang labor songs like "Hurrah for the Toiler" and "All Hail the Power of Laboring Men."

Over the next few days, delegates hammered out a series of demands, breathtaking in their scope. They tackled the tough questions of the day — the regulation of business, the need for banking and currency reform, the right of labor to organize and bargain collectively, and the role of the federal government in regulating business, curbing monopoly, and guaranteeing democracy. But the new party determined to stick to economic issues and

Frances Willard

Frances Willard, the forward-thinking leader of the Woman's Christian Temperance Union, learned to ride a bicycle at age fifty-three. The bicycle became hugely popular in the 1890s, even though traditionalists fulminated that it was unladylike for women to straddle a bike and immodest for them to wear the divided skirts that allowed them to pedal. Shown here in 1895, Willard declared bicycling a "harmless pleasure" that encouraged "clear heads and steady hands." Willard brought her progressive ideas to the People's Party 1892 convention, where she shared a place on the platform with the new party's leaders. Photo: Courtesy of the Frances E. Willard Memorial Library and Archives (WCTU).

resisted endorsing either temperance or woman suffrage. As a member of the platform committee, Willard fought for both and complained of the "crooked methods . . . employed to scuttle these planks." Outmaneuvered in committee, she brought the issues to the floor of the convention, only to go down to defeat by a vote of 352 to 238.

Despite Willard's disappointment, the convention ended its work amid a chorus of cheers. According to one eyewitness, "Hats, paper, handkerchiefs, etc., were thrown into the air; . . . cheer after cheer thundered and reverberated through the vast hall reaching the outside of the building where thousands who had been waiting the outcome joined in the applause till for blocks in every direction the exultation made the din indescribable."

What was all the shouting about? The cheering crowd was celebrating the birth of a new political party, officially named the People's Party. Fed up with the Democrats and Republicans, a broad coalition of groups came together in St. Louis to fight for change. They resolved to reconvene in Omaha in July to nominate candidates for the upcoming presidential election. Defeated but not willing to abandon the new party, Willard resolved to work for the nomination of a presidential candidate committed to temperance and suffrage.

The St. Louis gathering marked an early milestone in one of the most turbulent decades in U.S. history. Unrest, agitation, agrarian revolt, labor strikes, a severe financial panic and depression, and a war of expansion shook the 1890s. As the decade opened, Americans dissatisfied with the two major political parties were already flocking to organizations including the Farmers' Alliance, the American Federation of Labor, and the Woman's Christian Temperance Union, and they worked together to create the political alliance that gave birth to the People's (or Populist) Party. In a decade of unrest and uncertainty, the People's Party countered laissez-faire economics by insisting that the federal government play a more active role to ensure greater economic equity in industrial America. This challenge to the status quo culminated in 1896 in one of the most hotly contested presidential elections in the nation's history. At the close of the tumultuous decade, the Spanish-American War helped to bring the country together, with Americans rallying to support the troops. But disagreement over American imperialism and overseas expansion raised questions about the nation's role on the world stage as the United States stood poised to enter the twentieth century.

► The Farmers' Revolt

Hard times in the 1880s and 1890s created a groundswell of agrarian revolt. A bitter farmer wrote from Minnesota, "I settled on this Land in good Faith Built House and Barn. Broken up Part of the Land. Spent years of hard Labor in grubbing fencing and Improving." About to lose his farm to foreclosure, he lamented, "Are they going to drive us out like trespassers . . . and give us away to the Corporations?"

Crop prices for the nation's six million farmers fell decade after decade, even as their share of the world market grew (Figure 20.1). In parts of Kansas, wheat sold for so little that angry farmers burned their crops for fuel rather than take them to market. At the same time, consumer prices soared (Figure 20.2). Farmers couldn't make ends meet. In Kansas alone, almost half the farms had fallen into the hands of the banks by 1894 through foreclosure.

The Farmers' Alliance

At the heart of the farmers' problems stood a banking system dominated by eastern commercial banks committed to the gold standard, a railroad rate system that was capricious and unfair, and rampant speculation that drove up the price of land. In the West, farmers rankled under a system that allowed railroads to charge them exorbitant freight rates while granting rebates to large shippers (see chapter 18). In the South, lack of currency and credit drove farmers to the stopgap credit system of the crop lien, turning the entire region into "a vast pawn shop." Determined to do something, farmers banded together to fight for change.

Farm protest was not new. In the 1870s, farmers had supported the Grange and the Greenback Labor Party. As the farmers' situation grew more desperate, they organized, forming regional alliances. The first **Farmers' Alliance** came together in Lampasas County, Texas, to fight "landsharks and horse thieves." During the 1880s, the movement spread rapidly. In frontier farmhouses in Texas, in log cabins in the backwoods of Arkansas, and in the rural parishes of Louisiana, separate groups of farmers formed similar alliances for self-help.

As the movement grew, farmers' groups consolidated into two regional alliances: the Northwestern Farmers' Alliance, active in Kansas, Nebraska, and other midwestern Granger states; and the more radical Southern Farmers' Alliance. In the 1880s, traveling lecturers preached the Alliance message. Worn-out men and careworn women did not need to be convinced that something was wrong. By 1887, the Southern Farmers' Alliance had grown to more than 200,000 members, and by 1890 it counted more than 3 million members.

> "We are going to get out of debt and be free and independent people once more."
> — A Georgia farmer, on the effects of the Alliance movement

Kansas Farm Family Forced Off Their Farm
Hard times in the 1880s sent farmers reeling back from the plains. In 1894, almost half the farmers in Kansas lost their land because they could not make mortgage payments. The Owens family of Greeley County, pictured here, were among the defeated, forced to pack up their belongings and head east. The simple writing on their wagon tells the chronology of their retreat. Kansas State Historical Society.

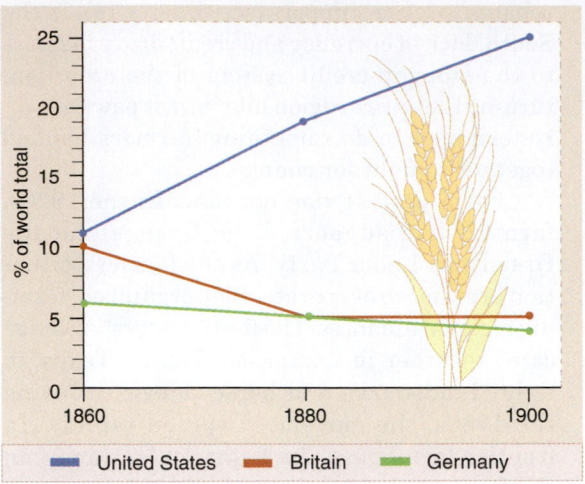

FIGURE 20.1 GLOBAL COMPARISON: Share of the World Wheat Market, 1860–1900
Although many countries produced wheat for home use, Britain, Germany, and the United States were among the largest wheat exporters. Exporting wheat worldwide became viable in the United States only after the completion of the transcontinental railroad in 1869. The resulting growth of the railroads, coupled with the development of improved mechanical reapers throughout the second half of the century, led to the mechanization of U.S. agriculture, allowing wheat farmers to harvest ever-larger crops. From 1860 to 1900, the United States' percentage of world wheat production more than doubled, while Germany's declined and Britain's was cut in half as a result of its growing emphasis on industrialization. What was the impact of entering a world market for U.S. wheat farmers?

Radical in its inclusiveness, the Southern Alliance reached out to African Americans, women, and industrial workers. Through cooperation with the **Colored Farmers' Alliance**, an African American group founded in Texas in the 1880s, blacks and whites attempted to make common cause. As Georgia's Tom Watson, a Southern Alliance stalwart, pointed out, "The colored tenant is in the same boat as the white tenant, . . . and . . . the accident of color can make no difference in the interests of farmers, croppers, and laborers."

The political culture of the Alliance encouraged the inclusion of women and children and used the family as its defining symbol. Women rallied to the Alliance banner along with their menfolk, drawn to meetings that combined picnic, parade, revival, country fair, and political convention. "I am going to work for prohibition, the Alliance, and for Jesus as long as I live," swore one woman.

In wagon trains, men and women in the thousands thronged to Alliance meetings to listen to speeches and to debate and discuss the issues of the day. The Alliance leaders aimed to do more than exhort their followers; they aimed to educate them. The Farmers' Alliance produced and distributed "a perfect avalanche of literature" — speeches, newspapers, books, and tracts — full of damning details about the political collusion between business and politics, along with detailed analyses of the securities and commodities markets, the tariff and international trade, and credit and currency. Alliance lecturers reached out to the illiterate, often speaking for hours under the broiling sun to educate their rapt audiences on the fine points of economics and politics.

At the heart of the Alliance movement stood a series of farmers' cooperatives. By "bulking" their cotton —

FIGURE 20.2 Consumer Prices and Farm Income, 1865–1910
Around 1870, consumer prices and farm income were about equal. During the 1880s and 1890s, however, farmers suffered great hardships as prices for their crops steadily declined and the cost of consumer goods continued to rise.

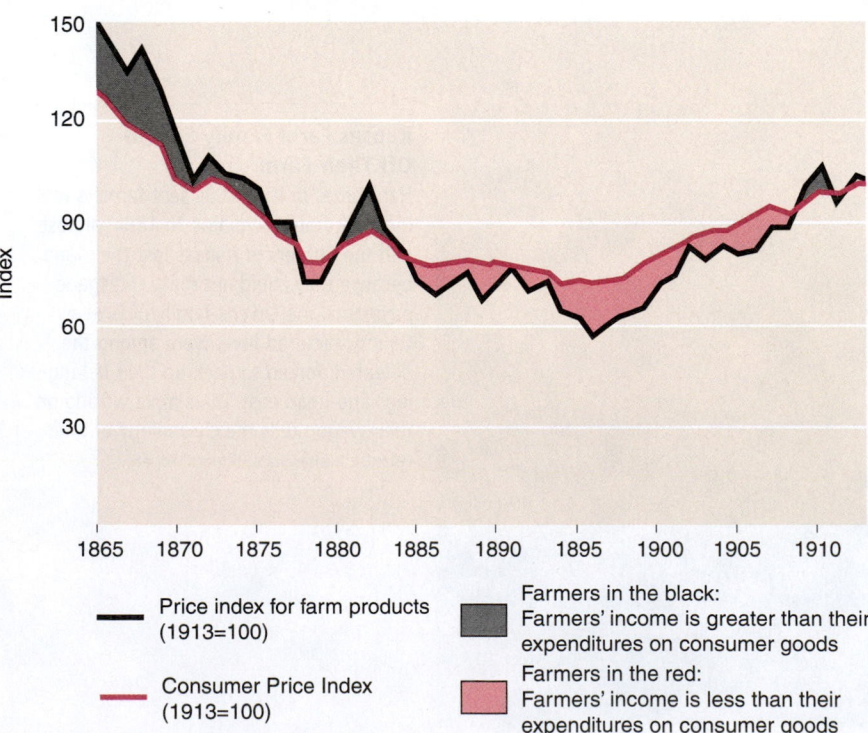

Price index for farm products (1913=100)

Consumer Price Index (1913=100)

Farmers in the black: Farmers' income is greater than their expenditures on consumer goods

Farmers in the red: Farmers' income is less than their expenditures on consumer goods globe. As part of the spoils of war, the United States acquired Cuba, Puerto Rico, Guam, and the Philippines. Yielding to pressure from American sugar growers, President McKinley expanded the empire further, annexing Hawai'i in July 1898.

Contemptuous of the Cubans, whom General William Shafter declared "no more fit for self-government than gun-powder is for hell," the U.S. government directed the writing of a new Cuban constitution in 1900 and refused to give up military control of the island until the Cubans accepted the so-called Platt Amendment — a series of provisions that granted the United States the right to intervene to protect Cuba's "independence," as well as the power to oversee Cuban debt so that European creditors would not find an excuse for intervention. For good measure, the United States gave itself a ninety-nine-year lease on a naval base at Guantánamo. In return, McKinley promised to implement an extensive sanitation program to clean up the island, making it more attractive to American investors.

MAP ACTIVITY

Map 20.4   U.S. Overseas Expansion through 1900

The United States extended its interests abroad with a series of territorial acquisitions. Although Cuba was granted independence, the Platt Amendment kept the new nation firmly under U.S. control. In the wake of the Spanish-American War, the United States woke up to find that it held an empire extending halfway around the globe.

READING THE MAP: Does the map indicate that more territory was acquired by purchase or by war, occupation, or unilateral decision? How many purchases of land outside the continental United States did the government make?
CONNECTIONS: What foreign policy developments occurred in the 1890s? How did American political leaders react to them? Where was U.S. expansion headed and why?

in low esteem, blamed "the warlike atmosphere in Congress and the press, and the natural tendency to look for reasons for the loss that did not reflect on the Navy." Judging the sinking an accident, Rickover warned, "We must make sure that those in 'high places' do not without more careful consideration of the consequences, exert our prestige and might."

Two decades later, the pendulum swung back. A 1995 study of the *Maine* published by the Smithsonian Institution concluded that zealot followers of General Weyler sank the battleship: "They had the opportunity, the means, and the motivation, and they blew up the *Maine* with a small low-strength mine they made themselves." According to this theory, the terrorists' homemade bomb burst the *Maine*'s hull, triggering a massive explosion. And in 1998 *National Geographic* employed computer models to show that an external explosion (bomb) was capable of sinking the *Maine*.

Thinking about Evidence

1. How have explanations for the sinking of the *Maine* changed over time? Has the evidence changed, or have interpretations of the evidence shifted?

2. What does the word *terrorism* suggest about how our understanding of the event may have changed in the twenty-first century?

"Maine Explosion Caused by Bomb or Torpedo"
The yellow press wasted no time claiming foul play in the explosion of the *Maine*. The front page of the New York *World* on February 17, 1898, two days after the blast, trumpeted the news and graphically portrayed the destruction of the ship. The text hinted at a plot to blow up the *Maine* and insisted that the explosion was not accidental, although there was no evidence to back up the assertion. The extent of the destruction and the deaths of 267 sailors fueled war fever. ©Collection of the New-York Historical Society.

the likes of New York socialite William Tiffany busting broncos in competition with Dakota cowboy Jim "Dead Shot" Simpson. When the Rough Riders shipped out to Cuba, journalists fought for a berth with the colorful regiment. The Rough Riders' charge up Kettle Hill and Roosevelt's role in the decisive battle of San Juan Hill made front-page news. Overnight, Roosevelt became the most famous man in America. By the time he sailed home from Cuba, a coalition of independent Republicans was already plotting his political future.

The Debate over American Imperialism

After a few brief campaigns in Cuba and Puerto Rico brought the Spanish-American War to an end, the American people woke up in possession of an empire that stretched halfway around the

Did Terrorists Sink the *Maine*?

At 9:40 p.m. on the evening of February 15, 1898, the U.S. battleship *Maine* blew up in Havana harbor. "The shock threw us backward," reported one eyewitness. "From the deck forward of amidships shot a streak of fire as high as the tall buildings on Broadway. Then the glare of light widened out like a funnel at the top, and down through this bright circle fell showers of wreckage and mangled sailors." In all, 267 sailors drowned or burned to death in one of the worst naval catastrophes to occur during peacetime.

Captain Charles Dwight Sigsbee, the last man to leave the burning ship, filed a terse report saying that the *Maine* had blown up and "urging [that] public opinion should be suspended until further report." But the yellow press, led by William Randolph Hearst's *New York Journal*, ran banner headlines proclaiming, "The War Ship *Maine* Was Split in Two by an Enemy's Secret Infernal Machine!"

Public opinion quickly divided between those who suspected foul play and those who believed the explosion had been an accident. Foremost among the accident theorists was the Spanish government, along with U.S. business interests who hoped to avoid war. The "jingoes," as proponents of war were

called, rushed to blame Spain. Even before the details were known, Assistant Secretary of the Navy Theodore Roosevelt wrote, "The *Maine* was sunk by an act of dirty treachery on the part of the Spaniards I believe; though we shall never find out definitely, and officially it will go down as an accident."

In less than a week, the navy formed a court of inquiry, and divers inspected the wreckage. The panel reported on March 25, 1898, that a mine had exploded under the bottom of the ship, igniting gunpowder in the forward magazine. The panel could not determine whether the mine had been planted by the Spanish government or by recalcitrant followers of Valeriano Weyler. The infamous Weyler had been ousted after the American press dubbed him "the Butcher" for his harsh treatment of the Cubans.

As time passed, however, more people came to view the explosion of the *Maine* as an accident. European experts concluded that the *Maine* had exploded accidentally, from a fire in the coal bunker adjacent to the reserve gunpowder. Perhaps poor design, not treachery, had sunk the *Maine*.

In 1910, New York congressman William Sultzer put it succinctly:

"The day after the ship was sunk, you could hardly find an American who did not believe that she had been foully done to death by a treacherous enemy. Today you can hardly find an American who believes Spain had anything to do with it." The *Maine* still lay in the mud of Havana harbor, a sunken tomb containing the remains of many sailors. The Cuban government asked for the removal of the wreck, and veterans demanded a decent burial for the sailors. So in March 1910, Congress voted to raise the *Maine* and reinvestigate.

The "Final Report on Removing the Wreck of Battleship *Maine* from the Harbor of Habana, Cuba" appeared in April 1913. This report confirmed that the original naval inquiry was in error, but it ruled out the accident theory by concluding that the nature of the initial explosion indicated a homemade bomb — once again casting suspicion on Weyler's fanatic followers. Following the investigation and removal of human remains, the wreckage of the *Maine* was towed out to sea and, with full funeral honors, sunk in six hundred fathoms of water.

Controversy over the *Maine* proved harder to sink. In the Vietnam era, when faith in the "military establishment" plummeted, Admiral Hyman Rickover launched yet another investigation. Viewing the 1913 "Final Report" as a cover-up, he complained that the ship had been sunk so deep "that there will be no chance of the true facts being revealed." Rickover, a maverick who held the naval brass

few Americans had ever heard of the Philippines. Even McKinley confessed that he could not immediately locate the archipelago on the map. He nevertheless recognized the strategic importance of the Philippines and dispatched U.S. troops to secure the islands.

The war in Cuba ended almost as quickly as it began. The first troops landed on June 22, and after a handful of battles the Spanish forces surrendered on July 17. The war lasted just long

enough to elevate Theodore Roosevelt to the status of bona fide war hero. Roosevelt resigned his navy post and formed the Rough Riders, a regiment composed of a sprinkling of Ivy League polo players and a number of western cowboys. Roosevelt admired horsemanship and had gained the cowboys' respect during his stint as a cattle rancher in the Dakotas. While the troops languished in Tampa awaiting their orders, Roosevelt and his men staged rodeos for the press, with

Spain opened up the prospect of expansion into Asia as well, since Spain controlled not only Cuba and Puerto Rico but also Guam and the Philippine Islands. Appointed assistant secretary of the navy in April 1897, Roosevelt took the helm in the absence of his boss and audaciously ordered the U.S. fleet to Manila in the Philippines. In the event of conflict with Spain, Roosevelt would have the navy in a position to capture the islands and gain an entry point to China.

President McKinley slowly moved toward intervention. In a show of American force, he dispatched the battleship *Maine* to Cuba. On the night of February 15, 1898, a mysterious explosion destroyed the *Maine*, killing 267 crew members. The source of the explosion remained unclear, but inflammatory stories in the press enraged Americans, who immediately blamed the Spanish government. (See "Historical Question," page 666.) Rallying to the cry "Remember the *Maine*," Congress declared war on Spain in April. In a surge of patriotism, more than a million men rushed to enlist. War brought with it a unity of purpose and national harmony that ended a decade of political dissent and strife. "In April, everywhere over this good fair land, flags were flying," wrote Kansas editor William Allen White. "At the stations, crowds gathered to hurrah for the soldiers, and to throw hats into the air, and to unfurl flags."

Soon they had something to cheer about. Five days after McKinley signed the war resolution, a U.S. Navy squadron commanded by Admiral George Dewey destroyed the Spanish fleet in Manila Bay (Map 20.3). Dewey's stunning victory caught the United States by surprise. Although naval strategists including Theodore Roosevelt had been orchestrating the move for some time,

MAP ACTIVITY

Map 20.3   The Spanish-American War, 1898

The Spanish-American War was fought in two theaters, the Philippine Islands and Cuba. Five days after President William McKinley called for a declaration of war, Admiral George Dewey captured Manila without the loss of a single American sailor. The war lasted only eight months. Troops landed in Cuba in mid-June and by mid-July had taken Santiago and Havana and destroyed the Spanish fleet.

READING THE MAP: Which countries held imperial control over countries and territories immediately surrounding the Philippine Islands and Cuba?

CONNECTIONS: What role did American newspapers play in the start of the war? How did the results of the war serve American aims in both Asia and the Western Hemisphere?

launched a fight for independence against the Spanish colonial regime in 1895. In an attempt to isolate the guerrillas, the Spanish general Valeriano Weyler herded Cubans into crowded and unsanitary concentration camps, where thousands died of hunger, disease, and exposure. Starvation soon spread to the cities. Tens of thousands of Cubans died, and countless others were left without food, clothing, or shelter. By 1898, fully a quarter of the island's population had perished in the Cuban revolution.

> **"You furnish the pictures and I'll furnish the war."**
> — Newspaper owner, WILLIAM RANDOLPH HEARST

As the Cuban rebellion dragged on, pressure for American intervention mounted. American newspapers fueled public outrage at Spain. A fierce circulation war raged in New York City between William Randolph Hearst's *Journal* and Joseph Pulitzer's *World*. Their competition provoked what came to be called **yellow journalism**, named for the colored ink used in a popular comic strip. Practitioners of yellow journalism pandered to the public's appetite for sensationalism. The Cuban war provided a wealth of dramatic copy. Newspapers fed the American people a daily diet of "Butcher" Weyler and Spanish atrocities. Hearst sent artist Frederic Remington to document the horror, and when Remington wired home, "There is no trouble here. There will be no war," Hearst shot back, "You furnish the pictures and I'll furnish the war."

American interests in Cuba were, in the words of the U.S. minister to Spain, more than "merely theoretical or sentimental." American business had more than $50 million invested in Cuban sugar, and American trade with Cuba, a brisk $100 million a year before the rebellion, had dropped to near zero. Nevertheless, the business community balked, wary of a war with Spain. When industrialist Mark Hanna, the Republican kingmaker and senator from Ohio, urged restraint, a hotheaded **Theodore Roosevelt** exploded, "We will have this war for the freedom of Cuba, Senator Hanna, in spite of the timidity of commercial interests."

To expansionists like Roosevelt, more than Cuban independence was at stake. War with

WAR IS HELL"—SHERMAN.
PEACE IN CUBA UNDER SPANISH RULE IS WORSE THAN HELL

Yellow Journalism
Most cartoonists followed the lead of Hearst and Pulitzer in promoting war with Spain. Cartoonist Grant Hamilton drew this cartoon for *Judge* magazine in March 1898. It shows a brutish Spain (the "Devil's Deputy") with bloody hands trampling on a sailor from the *Maine*. Cuba is prostrate, and a pile of skulls represents civilians "starved to death by Spain." Such vicious representations of Spain became common in the American press in the weeks leading up to the Spanish-American War. What does the cartoon say about American attitudes toward race? Collection of the New-York Historical Society.

saber rattling, the British backed down and accepted U.S. mediation in the area despite their territorial claims in Guiana.

In Central America, American business triumphed in a bloodless takeover that saw French and British interests routed by behemoths such as the United Fruit Company of Boston. United Fruit virtually dominated the Central American nations of Costa Rica and Guatemala, while an importer from New Orleans turned Honduras into a "banana republic" (a country run by U.S. business interests). Thus, by 1895, the United States, through business as well as diplomacy, had successfully achieved hegemony in Latin America and the Caribbean, forcing even the British to concur with the secretary of state that "the infinite resources [of the United States] combined with its isolated position render it master of the situation and practically invulnerable as against any or all other powers."

At the same time that American foreign policy warned European powers to stay out of the Western Hemisphere, the United States competed for trade in the Eastern Hemisphere. As American interests in China grew, the United States became more aggressive in defending its presence in Asia and the Pacific. The United States risked war with Germany in 1889 to guarantee the U.S. Navy access to Pago Pago in the Samoan Islands, a port for refueling on the way to Asia. Germany, seeking dominance over the islands, challenged the United States by sending warships to the region. But before fighting broke out, a great typhoon destroyed the German and American ships. Acceding to the will of nature, the potential combatants later divided the islands amicably in the 1899 Treaty of Berlin.

The biggest prize in Asia remained the China market. In the 1890s, China, weakened by years of internal warfare, was beginning to be partitioned into spheres of influence by Britain, Japan, Germany, France, and Russia. Concerned about the integrity of China and no less about American trade, Secretary of State John Hay in 1899–1900 wrote a series of notes calling for an "open door" policy that would ensure trade access to all and maintain

Chinese sovereignty. The notes — sent to Britain, Germany, and Russia and later to France, Japan, and Italy — were greeted by the major powers with polite evasion. Nevertheless, Hay skillfully managed to maneuver the major powers into doing his bidding, and in 1900 he boldly announced the Open Door as international policy. The United States, by insisting on the **Open Door policy**, managed to secure access to Chinese markets, expanding its economic power while avoiding the problems of maintaining a far-flung colonial empire on the Asian mainland. But as the Spanish-American War soon demonstrated, Americans found it hard to resist the temptations of overseas empire.

"A Splendid Little War"

The **Spanish-American War** began as a humanitarian effort to free Cuba from Spain's colonial grasp and ended with the United States itself acquiring territory overseas and fighting a dirty guerrilla war with Filipino nationalists who, like the Cubans, sought independence. Behind the contradiction stood the twin pillars of American foreign policy: The Monroe Doctrine made Spain's presence in Cuba unacceptable, and U.S. determination to keep open the door to Asia made the Philippines attractive as a stepping-stone to China. Precedent for the nation's imperial adventures also came from the recent Indian wars in the American West, which provided a template for the subjugation of native peoples in the name of civilization.

Looking back on the Spanish-American War of 1898, Secretary of State John Hay judged it "a splendid little war; begun with the highest motives, carried on with magnificent intelligence and spirit, favored by that fortune which loves the brave." At the close of a decade marred by bitter depression, social unrest, and political upheaval, the war offered Americans a chance to wave the flag and march in unison. War fever proved as infectious as the tune of a John Philip Sousa march. Few argued the merits of the conflict until it was over and the time came to divide the spoils.

The war began with moral outrage over the treatment of Cuban revolutionaries, who had

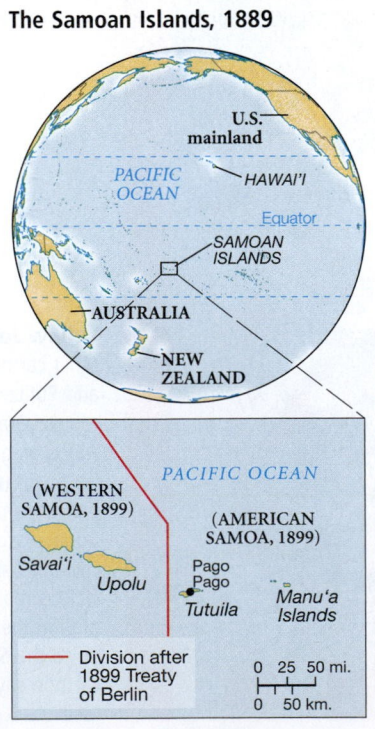

The Samoan Islands, 1889

U.S. mainland
PACIFIC OCEAN
HAWAI'I
Equator
SAMOAN ISLANDS
AUSTRALIA
NEW ZEALAND

PACIFIC OCEAN
(WESTERN SAMOA, 1899)
(AMERICAN SAMOA, 1899)
Savai'i
Upolu
Pago Pago
Tutuila
Manu'a Islands

— Division after 1899 Treaty of Berlin

0   25   50 mi.
0   50 km.

VISUAL ACTIVITY

The Open Door

The trade advantage gained by the United States through the Open Door policy, enunciated by Secretary of State John Hay in 1900, is portrayed graphically in this political cartoon. Uncle Sam stands prominently in the "open door," while representatives of the other great powers seek admittance to the "Flowery Kingdom" of China. Uncle Sam holds the golden key of "American diplomacy," while the Chinese man on the other side of the door beams with pleasure. In fact, the Open Door policy promised equal access for all powers to the China trade, not U.S. preeminence as the cartoon implies. Culver Pictures.

READING THE IMAGE: How does the cartoon portray the United States' role in international diplomacy?

CONNECTIONS: In what ways does this image misrepresent the reality of American and European involvement in China and of the Open Door policy?

The Monroe Doctrine and the Open Door Policy

The emergence of the United States as a world power pitted the nation against other colonial powers, particularly Germany and Japan, which posed a threat to the twin pillars of America's expansionist foreign policy — one dating back to President James Monroe in the 1820s, the other formalized in 1900 under President William McKinley. The first, the **Monroe Doctrine**, came to be interpreted as establishing the Western Hemisphere as an American "sphere of influence" and warned European powers to stay away or

risk war. The second, the Open Door, dealt with maintaining market access to China.

American diplomacy actively worked to buttress the Monroe Doctrine, with its assertion of American hegemony (domination) in the Western Hemisphere. In the 1880s, Republican secretary of state James G. Blaine promoted hemispheric peace and trade through Pan-American cooperation but at the same time used American troops to intervene in Latin American border disputes. In 1895, President Cleveland risked war with Great Britain to enforce the Monroe Doctrine when a conflict developed between Venezuela and British Guiana. After American of his confederates seized control of a government building and proclaimed themselves a "provisional government." Minister Stevens promptly recognized the revolutionaries as the legitimate government of Hawai'i.

To avoid bloodshed, Queen Lili'uokalani agreed to step aside. But in a masterstroke, she composed a letter addressed not to her enemies in the provisional government, but to the U.S. government. Protesting her overthrow, she yielded her authority "until such time as the Government of the United States, shall, upon the facts being presented to it, undo the action of its representatives and reinstate me in the authority which I claim as the constitutional sovereign of the Hawai'ian Islands." The action now shifted to Washington, where Grover Cleveland, a Democrat skeptical of America's adventures abroad, quickly squelched plans for annexation and supported the Hawai'ian queen. The provisional government, however, enjoyed the support of Republicans in Congress and refused to step down, biding its time, waiting for the Republicans to take back the White House.

In 1898, as the taste for empire swept the United States in the wake of the Spanish-American War, President William McKinley quietly signed a treaty annexing Hawai'i. His action pleased not only Hawai'i's sugar growers but also American expansionists, who judged Hawai'i

Queen Lili'uokalani (1838–1917)
An accomplished woman who straddled two cultures, Lydia Kamakaeha Dominis, or Queen Lili'uokalani, spoke English as easily as her native Hawai'ian and was fluent in French and German as well. She traveled widely in Europe and the United States. Despite President Cleveland's belief that the monarchy should be restored, Lili'uokalani never regained her throne. In 1898, she published *Hawai'i's Story by Hawai'i's Queen*, outlining her version of the events that had led to her downfall. In 1993, on the one hundredth anniversary of the revolution that deposed her, Congress passed and President Bill Clinton signed a resolution offering an apology to native Hawai'ians for the overthrow of their queen. Courtesy of the Lili'uokalani Trust.

strategically important in expanding U.S. trade with China.

"Hawai'i is ours," Grover Cleveland wrote sadly. "As I look back upon the first steps in this miserable business, and as I contemplate the means used to complete the outrage, I am ashamed of the whole affair."

America in a Global Context

1. How did economic issues on the mainland affect the status of Hawai'i?

2. What role did party politics play in the annexation of Hawai'i?

---

force sent to rescue the foreigners and put down the uprising in the Chinese capital of Beijing (Peking). The European powers imposed the humiliating Boxer Protocol in 1901, giving themselves the right to maintain military forces in Beijing and requiring the Chinese government to pay an exorbitant indemnity of $333 million for the loss of life and property resulting from the **Boxer uprising**.

In the aftermath of the uprising, missionaries voiced no concern at the paradox of bringing Christianity to China

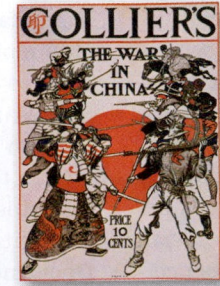

at gunpoint. "It is worth any cost in money, worth any cost in bloodshed," argued one bishop, "if we can make millions of Chinese true and intelligent Christians." Merchants and missionaries alike shared such moralistic reasoning. Indeed, they worked hand in hand; trade and Christianity marched into Asia together. "Missionaries," admitted the American clergyman Charles Denby, "are the pioneers of trade and commerce. . . . The missionary, inspired by holy zeal, goes everywhere and by degrees foreign commerce and trade follow."

Regime Change in Hawai'i

Queen Lili'uokalani came to the throne in Hawai'i in 1891 determined to take back power for her monarchy and her people. As a member of Hawai'i's native royalty, or *ali'i*, she had received a first-rate education in missionary school. As a young woman, she converted to Christianity, adopted the English name Lydia, and married the white (*haole*) governor of Maui. Yet she maintained a reverence for traditional Hawai'ian ways and resented the treatment of her people by the white minority. Her brother, King Kalakaua, had proven a weak leader, coerced by the white elite into signing the "Bayonet Constitution," which put the government squarely in the hands of the whites. Determined to rule, not simply to reign, Lili'uokalani moved ahead with plans to wrest power from the minority she referred to as Hawai'i's "guests."

American missionaries first came to Hawai'i in 1820. Some intermarried with their Christian converts, creating a group of *hapa haole* (half whites), as well as a growing number of children born in Hawai'i to white parents. The temptations of wealth led many missionaries, like Amos Starr Cooke, to acquire land and take up sugar planting. In 1851, he founded Castle & Cooke, which became one of the world's largest sugar producers. By the end of the century, missionaries and planters had blended into one ruling class and gained control of extensive tracts of land. Thanks to the "Bayonet Constitution," they controlled the islands, even though native Hawai'ians and the Japanese and Chinese "coolie" laborers imported to work on the sugar plantations outnumbered them ten to one.

Sugar became a booming business in Hawai'i as a result of favorable reciprocity treaties with the United States. But hard times came to the islands with the passage of the McKinley tariff in 1890. The tariff wiped out the advantage Hawai'ian sugar had enjoyed in the American market, with devastating results. Within two years, the value of Hawai'ian sugar exports plummeted from $13 million to $8 million.

One way to avoid the tariff was by incorporating Hawai'i into the United States through annexation. Foremost among those who championed this scheme was Lorrin Thurston, the thirty-five-year-old grandson of American missionaries. Thurston, born in Hawai'i and educated in the United States, was zealous in his belief that Hawai'i should be ruled by "the intelligent part of the community" — white Americans and their children. In 1892, he founded the secret Annexation Club and traveled to Washington, D.C., where he won the support of Republican secretary of state James G. Blaine, an enthusiastic supporter of American expansion. Thurston returned to Hawai'i armed with the knowledge that annexation had influential friends in Washington.

Queen Lili'uokalani picked Saturday, January 14, 1893, as the day to promulgate her new constitution. Her aim was to return Hawai'i to Hawai'ians by allowing only those with native ancestry the right to vote. Learning of her intentions, Thurston quickly hatched a plot to overthrow the monarchy. Thurston's daring plan could work only with the cooperation of the United States. So late that night, he called on John L. Stevens, the American minister to Hawai'i. Laying out his plan, he urged Stevens, a staunch annexationist, to support the overthrow of the queen and to pledge U.S. support for Thurston's actions. Without hesitating, Stevens promised to land Marines from the USS *Boston* "to protect American lives and property."

Two days later, 162 American Marines and sailors marched into Honolulu armed with carbines, howitzers (small cannons), and Gatling guns. The next day, Thurston and 17

---

force." Much of that moral tone was set by American missionaries intent on spreading the gospel of Christianity to the "heathen." No area on the globe constituted a greater challenge than China.

An 1858 agreement, the Tianjin (Tientsin) treaty admitted foreign missionaries to China. Although Christians converted only 100,000 in a population of 400 million, the Chinese nevertheless resented the interference of missionaries in village life. Opposition to foreign missionaries took the form of antiforeign secret societies, most notably the Boxers, whose Chinese name translated to "Righteous Harmonious Fist." No simple boxing club, the Boxers in 1899 began to hunt down and kill Chinese Christians and missionaries in northwestern Shandong (Shan-tung) Province. With the tacit support of China's Dowager Empress, the Boxers became bolder. Under the slogan "Uphold the Ch'ing Dynasty, Exterminate the Foreigners," they marched on the cities. Their rampage eventually led to the massacre of some 30,000 Chinese converts and 250 foreign nuns, priests, and missionaries along with their families. In August 1900, 2,500 U.S. troops joined an international

FIGURE 20.3 **Expansion in U.S. Trade, 1870–1910**
Between 1870 and 1910, American exports more than tripled. Imports generally rose, but they were held in check by the high protective tariffs championed by Republican presidents from Ulysses S. Grant to William Howard Taft. A decline in imports is particularly noticeable after the passage of the prohibitive McKinley tariff in 1890.

they will or not, Americans must now begin to look outward. The growing production of the country requires it." As the depression deepened, one diplomat warned that Americans "must turn [their] eyes abroad, or they will soon look inward upon discontent."

Exports constituted a small but significant percentage of the profits of American business in the 1890s (Figure 20.3). And where American interests led, businessmen expected the government's power and influence to follow to protect their investments. Companies like Standard Oil actively sought to use the U.S. government as their agent, often putting foreign service employees on the payroll. "Our ambassadors and ministers and consuls," wrote John D. Rockefeller appreciatively, "have aided to push our way into new markets and to the utmost corners of the world." Whether "our" referred to the United States or to Standard Oil remained ambiguous; in practice, the distinction was of little importance in late-nineteenth-century foreign policy.

America's foreign policy often appeared little more than a sidelight to business development. In Hawai'i (first called the Sandwich Islands), American sugar interests fomented a rebellion in 1893, toppling the increasingly independent Queen Lili'uokalani. (See "Beyond America's Borders," page 660.) They pushed Congress to annex the islands, which would allow planters to avoid the high McKinley tariff on sugar. When President Cleveland learned that Hawai'ians opposed annexation, he withdrew the proposal from Congress. But expansionists still coveted the islands and continued to look for an excuse to push through annexation.

However compelling the economic arguments about overseas markets proved, business interests alone did not account for the new expansionism that seized the nation during the 1890s. As Mahan confessed, "Even when material interests are the original exciting cause, it is the sentiment to which they give rise, the moral tone which emotion takes that constitutes the greater

Mei Foo Lamp
The Standard Oil Company sold more than a million Mei Foo ("beautiful companion") lamps in China during the 1890s to promote the sale of kerosene in the China market. The first oil tankers were square-rigged kerosene clipper ships that plied the Pacific beginning in 1892 as the petroleum industry rushed to capture the China trade. Standard Oil ads admonished, "If a person wishes to have luck, longevity, health and peace, he or she must live in a world of light." Courtesy of ExxonMobil Corporation.

Wednesday morning." Intimidation alone did not explain the failure of urban labor to rally to Bryan. Republicans repeatedly warned workers that if the Democrats won, the inflated silver dollar would be worth only fifty cents. However much farmers and laborers might insist that they were united as producers against the non-producing bosses, it was equally true that inflation did not offer the boon to urban laborers that it did to western farmers.

On election day, four out of five voters went to the polls in an unprecedented turnout. In the critical midwestern states, as many as 95 percent of the eligible voters cast their ballots. In the end, the election hinged on between 100 and 1,000 votes in several key states, including Wisconsin, Iowa, and Minnesota. Although McKinley won twenty-three states to Bryan's twenty-two, the electoral vote showed a lopsided 271 to 176 in McKinley's favor (Map 20.2).

The biggest losers in 1896 turned out to be the Populists. On the national level, they polled fewer than 300,000 votes, a million less than in 1894. In the clamor to support Bryan, Populists in the South, determined to beat McKinley at any cost, swallowed their differences and drifted back to the Democratic Party. The People's Party was crushed, and with it the agrarian revolt.

But if Populism proved unsuccessful at the polls, it nevertheless set the domestic political agenda for the United States in the next decades, highlighting issues such as railroad regulation, banking and currency reform, electoral reforms, and an enlarged role for the federal government in the economy. Meanwhile, as the decade ended, the bugle call to arms turned America's attention to foreign affairs and effectively drowned out the trumpet of reform. The struggle for social justice gave way to a war for empire as the United States asserted its power on the world stage.

REVIEW Why was the People's Party unable to translate national support into victory in the 1896 election?

▶ The United States and the World

Throughout much of the second half of the nineteenth century, U.S. interest in foreign policy took a backseat to territorial expansion in the American West. The United States stood aloof while Great Britain, France, Germany, Spain, Belgium, and an increasingly powerful Japan competed for empires in Asia, Africa, Latin America, and the Pacific. Between 1870 and 1900, European nations colonized more than 20 percent of the world's landmass and 10 percent of the world's population.

At the turn of the twentieth century, the United States pursued a foreign policy consisting of two currents—isolationism and expansionism. Although the determination to remain detached from European politics had been a hallmark of U.S. foreign policy since the nation's founding, Americans simultaneously believed in manifest destiny—the "obvious" right to expand the nation from ocean to ocean. With its own inland empire secured, the United States looked outward. Determined to protect its sphere of influence in the Western Hemisphere and to expand its trading in Asia, the nation moved away from isolationism and toward a more active role on the world stage. The push for commercial expansion joined with a sense of Christian mission and led both to the strengthening of the Monroe Doctrine in the Western Hemisphere and to a more assertive policy in Asia. All of these trends were in evidence during the Spanish-American War and the debates that followed.

Markets and Missionaries

The depression of the 1890s provided a powerful impetus to American commercial expansion. As markets weakened at home, American businesses looked abroad for profits. As early as 1890, Captain Alfred Thayer Mahan, leader of a growing group of American expansionists, prophesied, "Whether

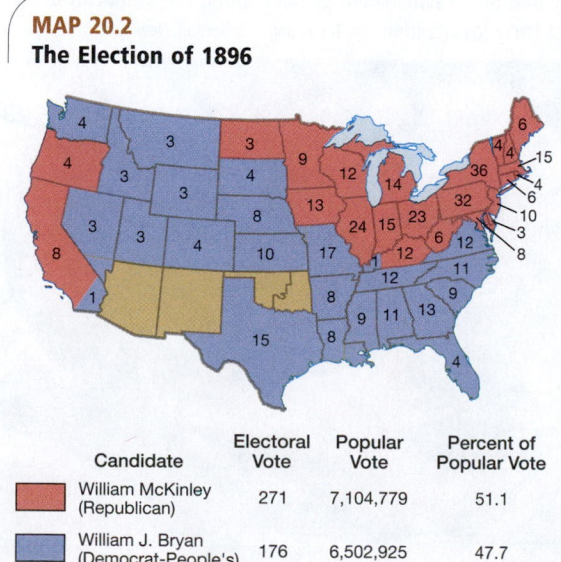

MAP 20.2
The Election of 1896

Candidate	Electoral Vote	Popular Vote	Percent of Popular Vote
■ William McKinley (Republican)	271	7,104,779	51.1
■ William J. Bryan (Democrat-People's)	176	6,502,925	47.7

Gold Elephant Campaign Button and Silver Ribbon from St. Louis, 1896
Mechanical elephant badges that opened to show portraits of William McKinley and his running mate, Garret Hobart, were popular campaign novelties in the election of 1896. The elephant, the mascot of the Republican Party, is gilded to indicate the party's support of the gold standard. By contrast, the delegate ribbon from the St. Louis National Silver Convention in 1896 features a silver eagle and fringe testifying to the power of free silver as a campaign issue. The Democrats nominated William Jennings Bryan on a free-silver platform, and the Populists put him on their ticket as well. Elephant: Collection of Janice L. and David J. Frent; ribbon: Nebraska State Historical Society.

paved the way for the selection of Bryan by a lopsided vote. The Populists did not know it, but their cheers for Bryan signaled not a chorus of victory but the death knell for the People's Party.

Few contests in the nation's history have been as fiercely fought and as full of emotion as the presidential election of 1896. On one side stood Republican William McKinley, backed by the wealthy industrialist and party boss Mark Hanna. Hanna played on the business community's fears of Populism to raise a Republican war chest more than double the amount of any previous campaign. On the other side, William Jennings Bryan, with few assets beyond his silver tongue, struggled to make up in energy and eloquence what his party lacked in campaign funds, crisscrossing the country in a whirlwind tour, traveling more than eighteen thousand miles and delivering more than six hundred speeches in three months. According to his own reckoning, he visited twenty-seven states and spoke to more than five million Americans.

As election day approached, the silver states of the Rocky Mountains lined up solidly for Bryan. The Northeast stood solidly for McKinley. Much of the South, with the exception of the border states, abandoned the Populists and returned to the Democratic "party of the fathers," leaving Tom Watson to lament that

"[Populists] play Jonah while [Democrats] play the whale." The Midwest hung in the balance. Bryan intensified his campaign in Illinois, Michigan, Ohio, and Indiana. But midwestern farmers proved less receptive than western voters to the blandishments of free silver.

In the cities, Democrats charged the Republicans with mass intimidation. "Men, vote as you please," the head of New York's Steinway Piano Company reportedly announced to his workers on the eve of the election, "but if Bryan is elected tomorrow the whistle will not blow

"Swallowed!"
This political cartoon from 1900 shows William Jennings Bryan as a python swallowing the Democratic Party's donkey mascot. Bryan, who ran unsuccessfully in 1896, won the Democratic nomination again in 1900 and in 1908. Ironically, it was not the Democratic party so much as the Populist party that Bryan swallowed. By nominating the Democrat Bryan on their ticket in 1896, the Populist Party lost its identity. The Granger Collection, New York.

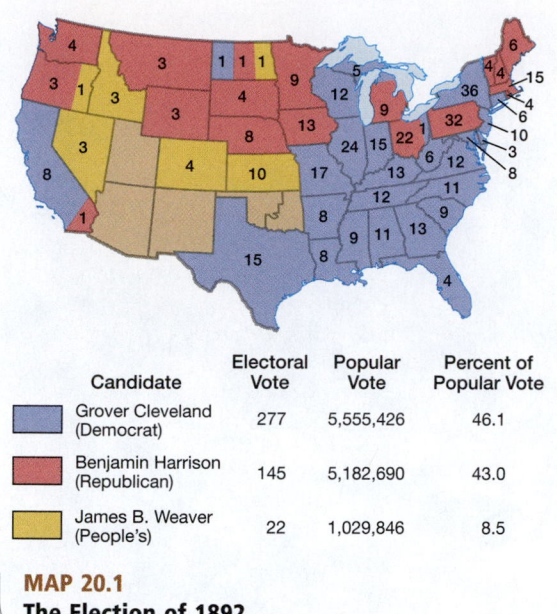

Candidate	Electoral Vote	Popular Vote	Percent of Popular Vote
Grover Cleveland (Democrat)	277	5,555,426	46.1
Benjamin Harrison (Republican)	145	5,182,690	43.0
James B. Weaver (People's)	22	1,029,846	8.5

MAP 20.1
The Election of 1892

lynch a black Populist preacher, Watson rallied two thousand gun-toting Populists to the man's defense. Although many Populists remained racist in their attitudes toward African Americans, the spectacle of white Georgians riding through the night to protect a black man from lynching was symbolic of the enormous changes the Populist Party promised in the South.

As the presidential election of 1896 approached, the depression intensified cries for reform not only from the Populists but also throughout the electorate. Depression worsened the tight money problem caused by the deflationary pressures of the gold standard. Once again, proponents of free silver stirred rebellion in the ranks of both the Democratic and the Republican parties. When the Republicans nominated Ohio governor **William McKinley** on a platform pledging the preservation of the gold standard, western advocates of free silver representing miners and farmers walked out of the convention. Open rebellion also split the Democratic Party as vast segments in the West and South repudiated President Grover Cleveland because of his support for gold. In South Carolina, Benjamin Tillman won his race for Congress by promising, "Send me to Washington and I'll stick my pitchfork into [Cleveland's] old ribs!"

The spirit of revolt animated the Democratic National Convention in Chicago in the summer of 1896. **William Jennings Bryan** of Nebraska, the thirty-six-year-old "boy orator from the Platte," whipped the convention into a frenzy with his passionate call for free silver. In his speech in favor of the silver plank in the party's platform, Bryan masterfully cataloged the grievances of farmers and laborers, closing his dramatic speech with a ringing exhortation: "Do not crucify mankind upon a cross of gold." Pandemonium broke loose as delegates stampeded to nominate Bryan, the youngest candidate ever to run for the presidency.

The juggernaut of free silver rolled out of Chicago and on to St. Louis, where the People's Party met a week after the Democrats adjourned. Smelling victory, many western Populists urged the party to ally with the Democrats and endorse Bryan. A major obstacle in the path of fusion, however, was Bryan's running mate, Arthur M. Sewall. A Maine railway director and bank president, Sewall, who had been placed on the ticket to appease conservative Democrats, embodied everything the Populists detested.

Populism's regional constituencies remained as divided over tactics as they were uniform in their call for change. Western Populists, including a strong coalition of farmers and miners in states such as Idaho and Colorado, championed free silver. In these largely Republican states, Populists had joined forces with Democrats in previous elections and saw no problem with becoming "Popocrats" once Bryan led the Democratic ticket on a free silver platform. Similarly in the Midwest, a Republican stronghold, Populists who had used fusion with the Democrats as a tactic to win elections had little trouble backing Bryan. But in the South, where Democrats had resorted to fraud and violence to steal elections from the Populists in 1892 and 1894, support for a Democratic ticket proved especially hard to swallow. Die-hard southern Populists wanted no part of fusion.

All of these tactical differences emerged as the Populists met in St. Louis in 1896 to nominate a candidate for president. To show that they remained true to their principles, delegates first voted to support all the planks of the 1892 platform, added to it a call for public works projects for the unemployed, and only narrowly defeated a plank for woman suffrage. To deal with the problem of fusion, the convention selected the vice presidential candidate first. The nomination of Tom Watson undercut opposition to Bryan's candidacy. And although Bryan quickly sent a telegram to protest that he would not drop Sewall as his running mate, mysteriously his message never reached the convention floor. Fusion triumphed. Watson's vice presidential nomination

Coxey's Army
A contingent of Coxey's army stops to rest on its way to Washington, D.C. A "petition in boots," Coxey's followers were well dressed, as evidenced by the men in this photo wearing white shirts, vests, neckties, and bowler hats. Music was an important component of the march, including the anthem "Marching with Coxey," sung to the tune of "Marching through Georgia." Band members are pictured on the right with their instruments. Despite their peaceful pose, the marchers stirred the fears of many conservative Americans, who predicted an uprising of the unemployed. Instead, Coxey and a contingent of his marchers were arrested and jailed for "walking on the grass" when they reached the nation's capital. Ohio Historical Society.

By August, the leaderless, tattered armies dissolved. Although the "On to Washington" movement proved ineffective in forcing federal relief legislation, Coxey's army dramatized the plight of the unemployed and acted, in the words of one participant, as a "living, moving object lesson." Like the Populists, Coxey's army called into question the underlying values of the new industrial order and demonstrated how ordinary citizens turned to means outside the regular party system to influence politics in the 1890s.

The People's Party and the Election of 1896

Even before the depression of 1893 gave added impetus to their cause, the Populists had railed against the status quo. "We meet in the midst of a nation brought to the verge of moral, political, and material ruin," Ignatius Donnelly had declared in his keynote address at the creation of the People's Party in St. Louis in 1892. "The fruits of the toil of millions are boldly stolen to build up colossal fortunes for a few. . . . From the same prolific womb of governmental injustice we breed the two great classes — tramps and millionaires."

The fiery rhetoric frightened many who saw in the People's Party a call not to reform but to revolution. Throughout the country, the press denounced the Populists as "cranks, lunatics, and idiots." When one self-righteous editor dismissed them as "calamity howlers," Populist governor Lorenzo Lewelling of Kansas shot back, "If that is so I want to continue to howl until those conditions are improved."

The People's Party captured more than a million votes in the presidential election of 1892, a respectable showing for a new party (Map 20.1). But increasingly, sectional and racial animosities threatened its unity. In the South, the Populists' willingness to form common cause with black farmers made them anathema. Realizing that race prejudice obscured the common economic interests of black and white farmers, **Tom Watson** of Georgia openly courted African Americans, appearing on platforms with black speakers and promising "to wipe out the color line." When angry Georgia whites threatened to compared Pullman's model town to a "gilded cage" for workers.

The depression brought hard times to Pullman. Workers saw their wages slashed five times between May and December 1893, with cuts totaling at least 28 percent. At the same time, Pullman refused to lower the rents in his model town, insisting that "the renting of the dwellings and the employment of workmen at Pullman are in no way tied together." When workers went to the bank to cash their paychecks, they found that the rent had been taken out. One worker discovered only forty-seven cents in his pay envelope for two weeks' work. When the bank teller asked him whether he wanted to apply it to his back rent, he retorted, "If Mr. Pullman needs that forty-seven cents worse than I do, let him have it." At the same time, Pullman continued to pay his stockholders an 8 percent dividend, and the company accumulated a $25 million surplus.

At the heart of the labor problems at Pullman lay not only economic inequity but also the company's attempt to control the work process, substituting piecework for day wages and undermining skilled craftsworkers. The Pullman workers rebelled. During the spring of 1894, Pullman's desperate workers, seeking help, flocked to the ranks of the **American Railway Union** (ARU), led by the charismatic **Eugene V. Debs**. The ARU, unlike the skilled craft unions of the AFL, pledged to organize all railway workers — from engineers to engine wipers. "It has been my life's desire," wrote Debs, "to unify railroad employees and to eliminate the aristocracy of labor, which unfortunately exists, and organize them so all will be on an equality." The ARU's belief in industrial democracy, however, was not matched by a commitment to racial equality; by a narrow margin, union members voted to exclude African American workers.

George Pullman responded to union organization at his plant by firing three of the union's leaders the day after they led a delegation to protest wage cuts. Angry men and women walked off the job in disgust. What began as a spontaneous protest in May 1894 quickly blossomed into a strike that involved more than 90 percent of Pullman's 3,300 workers. "We do not know what the outcome will be, and in fact we do not much care," one worker confessed. "We do know that we are working for less wages than will maintain ourselves and families in the necessaries of life, and on that proposition we refuse to work any longer." Pullman countered by shutting down the plant.

A Pullman Craftsworker
Pullman Palace cars were known for their luxurious details. Here, a painter working in the 1890s applies elaborate decoration to the exterior of a Pullman car. In the foreground is an intricately carved door, an example of fine hand-detailing. The Pullman workers' strike in 1894 stemmed in part from the company's efforts to undermine the status of craftsworkers by reducing them to low-paid piecework. Control of the workplace, as much as issues related to wages and hours, fueled the labor wars of the 1890s. Chicago Historical Society.

In June, the Pullman strikers appealed to the ARU to come to their aid. Debs hesitated to commit his fledgling union to a major strike in the midst of a depression. He pleaded with the workers to find

The Press and the Pullman Strike: Framing Class Conflict

Press coverage of the 1894 Pullman strike and the subsequent American Railway Union boycott was extensive and usually partisan. How newspapers covered the Pullman strike provides a window into the way the press framed class conflict in the United States in the 1890s. The *Chicago Times*, for example, clearly supported the ARU, as was evident in its coverage of events. By contrast, the *Chicago Tribune* and most other Chicago newspapers sided with George M. Pullman and the General Managers Association. Nellie Bly, the era's most colorful investigative reporter, wrote a personal account of her experience with ARU members for the *New York World*.

DOCUMENT 1
***Chicago Tribune*, May 12, 1894**

PULLMAN MEN OUT
Discharges the Cause

Two thousand employees in the Pullman car works struck yesterday, leaving 800 others at their posts. This was not enough to keep the works going, so a notice was posted on the big gates at 6 o'clock . . . saying: "These shops closed until further notice."

Mr. Pullman said last night he could not tell when work would be resumed. The American Railway Union, which has been proselytizing for a week among the workmen, announces that it will support the strikers . . . [intimating] that the trainmen on the railways on which are organized branches of the union might refuse to handle any of the Pullman rolling stock.

DOCUMENT 2
***Chicago Times*, May 12, 1894**

PULLMAN MEN OUT
Firing Three Men Starts It

Almost the entire force of men employed in the Pullman shops went on strike yesterday. Out of the 4,800 men and women employed in the various departments there were probably not over 800 at work at 6 o'clock last evening. The immediate cause of the strike was the discharge or laying off of three men in the iron machine shop. The real but remote cause is the question of wages over which the men have long been dissatisfied and on account of which they had practically resolved to strike a month ago. . . .

The position of the company is that no increase in wages is possible. . . . President George M. Pullman told the committee that the company was doing business at a loss even at the reduced wages paid the men and offered to show his books in support of his assertion.

DOCUMENT 3
***Chicago Times*, May 15, 1894**

SKIMS OFF THE FAT
Pullman Company Declares a Dividend Today

Full Pockets Swallow $600,000 While Honest Labor Is Starving

Today the Pullman Company will declare a quarterly dividend of 2 per cent on its capital stock of $30,000,000 and President George M. Pullman is authority for the statement that his company owes no man a cent. This despite the assertion of Mr. Pullman that the works have been run at a loss for eight months. Six hundred thousand dollars to shareholders, while starvation threatens the workmen.

DOCUMENT 4
***Chicago Tribune*, July 1, 1894**

MOBS BENT ON RUIN
Men Who Attempt to Work Are Terrorized and Beaten

Continued and menacing lawlessness marked the progress yesterday of Dictator Debs and those who obey his orders in their efforts at coercing the railroads of the country into obeying the mandates of the American Railway Union. The Rock Island was the chief sufferer from the mob spirit which broke loose the moment its men struck. . . . At 10 o'clock the officials threw up their hands and discontinued service for the night. At Blue Island, anarchy reigned. The Mayor and police force of that town could do nothing to repress the riotous strikers and they did their own sweet will. . . .

On the Illinois Central it was the same old story of destruction of the company's property without interference from the police. . . . Dictator Debs was as blatant as ever yesterday. He asserted . . . that the fight against Pullman was now a thing of the past. He is waging his warfare against the General Managers, who had committed the sin of combining against him.

DOCUMENT 5
Chicago Tribune, July 7, 1894

YARDS FIRE SWEPT
Rioters Prevent Firemen from Saving the Property

From Brighton Park to Sixty-First Street the yards of the Pan-Handle road were last night put to the torch by the rioters. Between 600 and 700 freight cars have been destroyed, many of them loaded. Miles and miles of costly track are in a snarled tangle of heat-twisted rails. Not less than $750,000 — possibly a whole $1,000,000 of property — has been sacrificed to the caprice of a mob of drunken Anarchists and rebels. That is the record of the night's work by the Debs strikers in the Stock-Yards District.

DOCUMENT 6
Chicago Times, July 7, 1894

MEN NOT AWED BY SOLDIERS
Railway Union Is Confident of Winning against Armed Capital

Despite the presence of United States troops and the mobilization of five regiments of state militia, despite threats of martial law and total extermination of the strikers by bullet and bayonet, the great strike inaugurated by the American Railway Union holds three-fourths of the roads running out of Chicago in its strong fetters, and last night traffic was more fully paralyzed than at any time since the inception of the tie-up. . . . With the exception of an occasional car or two moved by the aid of the military, not a wheel is turning. . . .

If the soldiers are sent to this district, bloodshed and perhaps death will follow today, for this is the most lawless element in the city, as is shown by their riotous work yesterday. . . . But the perpetrators are not American Railway Union men. The people engaged in this outrageous work of destruction are not strikers, most of them are not even grown men. The persons who set the fires yesterday on the authority of the firemen and police are young hoodlums. . . . The setting fire to the cars yesterday was done openly where anyone could see it and when the slightest effort would have resulted in the apprehension

of the guilty ones, but no such effort was made. The firemen were overwhelmed with the work of attending to a dozen different fires and could not, and the police on the scene apparently didn't care to or would not make arrests.

DOCUMENT 7
New York World, July 14, 1894

CHEERS FOR NELLIE BLY
Nellie Bly Covers the Strike

I found in my mail this morning an earnest request from the Pullman A. R. U. for me to be present at a meeting which was to be held in the Turner Hall, Kensington. . . .

Several of the workmen made speeches this afternoon trying to cheer the spirits of their hungry and disheartened brothers. I was introduced and asked to say a few words to the men. . . .

So I took my nerves in hand and my place before the table near where the speakers sat. I don't intend to repeat what I said, but I told them several truths. They were especially amused when I told them that I had come to Chicago very bitterly set against the strikers; that so far as I understood the question, I thought the inhabitants of the model town of Pullman hadn't a reason on earth to complain. With this belief I visited the town, intending in my articles to denounce the riotous and bloodthirsty strikers. Before I had been half a day in Pullman I was the most bitter striker in the town.

That is true. I've [flip]flopped, as they call it, and I am brave enough to confess it. If ever men and women had cause to strike, those men and women are in Pullman. I also said to these men, sitting so quietly and peaceably before me, hungry for a word of sympathy or a word of hope, that if any of them wished to make any statements to me I would be glad to have them do so. After the meeting I was besieged. If I attempted to tell half the tales of wrong I've listened to I could fill an entire copy of *The World*.

Questions for Analysis and Debate

1. How do the *Tribune* and *Times* articles differ in their portrayal of events and actors in the strike?

2. Which version of the strike do you think most middle-class readers, who tended to be sympathetic to the strikers but fearful of violence, would find most compelling?

3. Which version of the strike do you think was favored by business owners, who provided advertising revenue to the newspapers?

4. Do you think readers found Nellie Bly's article persuasive? Why or why not?

another solution. But when George Pullman adamantly refused arbitration, the ARU membership voted to boycott all Pullman cars. Beginning on June 29, switchmen across the United States refused to handle any train that carried Pullman cars.

The conflict escalated quickly. The General Managers Association (GMA), an organization of managers from twenty-four different railroads, acted in concert to quash the **Pullman boycott**. Determined to kill the ARU, they recruited strikebreakers and fired all the protesting switchmen. Their tactics set off a chain reaction. Entire train crews walked off the job in a show of solidarity with the Pullman workers. In a matter of days, the boycott/strike spread to more than fifteen railroads and affected twenty-seven states and territories. By July 2, rail lines from New York to California lay paralyzed. Even the GMA was forced to concede that the railroads had been "fought to a standstill."

The boycott remained surprisingly peaceful. In contrast to the Great Railroad Strike of 1877, no major riots broke out, and no serious property damage occurred. Debs, in a whirlwind of activity, fired off telegrams to all parts of the country advising his followers to avoid violence and respect law and order. But the nation's newspapers, fed press releases by the GMA, distorted the issues and misrepresented the strike. Across the country, papers ran headlines like "Wild Riot in Chicago" and "Mob Is in Control." (See "Documenting the American Promise," page 648.)

In Washington, Attorney General Richard B. Olney, a lawyer with strong ties to the railroads, determined to put down the strike. In his way stood the governor of Illinois, John Peter Altgeld, who, observing that the boycott remained peaceful, refused to call out troops. To get around Altgeld, Olney convinced President Grover Cleveland that federal troops had to intervene to protect the mails. To further cripple the boycott, two conservative Chicago judges issued an injunction so sweeping that it prohibited Debs from speaking in public. By issuing the injunction, the court made the boycott a crime punishable by a jail sentence for contempt of court, a civil process that did not require a jury trial. Even the conservative *Chicago Tribune* judged the injunction "a menace to liberty … a weapon ever ready for the capitalist." Furious, Debs risked jail by refusing to honor it.

Olney's strategy worked. President Grover Cleveland called out the army. On July 5, nearly 8,000 troops marched into Chicago. The GMA was jubilant. "It has now become a fight between the United States Government and the American Railway Union," a spokesman observed, "and we shall leave them to fight it out." Violence

Nellie Bly in Her Traveling Clothes, 1890
The journalist Elizabeth Jane Cochran took the pen name Nellie Bly (from a popular song by composer Stephen Foster) when she began her career writing for the *Pittsburg Dispatch* in 1880. Best known for her vow to travel around the world in fewer than 80 days, she is shown here in her travel costume. Her dispatches to the *New York World* documenting her trip made her an international celebrity. But some of her best writing involved gritty stories about society's poor and outcast. In 1894 she interviewed striking workers at the Pullman Palace Car company. In direct defiance of her editor, Joseph Pulitzer, Bly declared her allegiance with the strikers. Library of Congress.

immediately erupted. In one day, troops killed 25 workers and wounded more than 60. In the face of bullets and bayonets, the strikers held firm. "Troops cannot move trains," Debs reminded his followers, a fact that was borne out as the railroads remained paralyzed despite the military intervention. But if the army could not put down the boycott, the injunction could and did. Debs was arrested and imprisoned for contempt of court. With its leader in jail, its headquarters raided and ransacked, and its members demoralized, the ARU was defeated along with

National Guard Occupying Pullman, Illinois
After President Grover Cleveland called out the troops to put down the Pullman strike in 1894, the National Guard occupied the town of Pullman to protect George M. Pullman's property. Here, guardsmen ring the Arcade building, the town shopping center, while curious men and women look on. The intervention of troops at Homestead and Pullman enabled the owners to bring in strikebreakers and defeat the unions. In Cripple Creek, Colorado, where a Populist governor used the militia to keep the peace and not fight the strikers, the miners won the day in 1894. Chicago Historical Society.

the boycott. Pullman reopened his factory, hiring new workers to replace many of the strikers and leaving 1,600 workers without jobs.

In the aftermath of the strike, a special commission investigated the events at Pullman, taking testimony from 107 witnesses, from the lowliest workers to George M. Pullman himself. Stubborn and self-righteous, Pullman spoke for the business orthodoxy of his era, steadfastly affirming the right of business to safeguard its interests through confederacies such as the GMA and at the same time denying labor's right to organize. "If we were to receive these men as representatives of the union," he stated, "they could probably force us to pay any wages which they saw fit."

From his jail cell, Eugene Debs reviewed the events of the Pullman strike. With the courts and the government ready to side with industrialists in the interest of defending private property, Debs realized that labor had little recourse. Strikes seemed futile, and unions remained helpless; workers would have to take control of the state itself. Debs went into jail a trade unionist and came out six months later a socialist. At first, he turned to the Populist Party, but after its demise he formed the Socialist Party in 1900 and ran for president on its ticket five times. Debs's dissatisfaction with the status quo was shared by another group even more alienated from the political process — women.

> **REVIEW** What tactics led to the defeat of the strikers in the 1890s? Where were they able to succeed and why?

▶ Women's Activism

"Do everything," **Frances Willard** urged her followers in 1881 (see pages 639–40). The new president of the Woman's Christian Temperance Union (WCTU) meant what she said. The WCTU followed a trajectory that was common for women in the late nineteenth century. As women organized to deal with issues that touched their homes and families, they moved into politics, lending new urgency to the cause of woman suffrage. Urban industrialism dislocated women's lives no less than men's. Like men, women sought political change and organized to promote issues central to their lives, campaigning for temperance and woman suffrage.

Frances Willard and the Woman's Christian Temperance Union

A visionary leader, Frances Willard spoke for a group left almost entirely out of the U.S. electoral process. In 1890, only one state, Wyoming, allowed women to vote in national elections. But lack of the franchise did not mean that women were apolitical. The WCTU demonstrated the breadth of women's political activity in the late nineteenth century.

Women supported the temperance movement because they felt particularly vulnerable to the effects of drunkenness. Dependent on men's wages, women and children suffered when money went for drink. The drunken, abusive husband epitomized the evils of a nation in which women remained second-class citizens. The WCTU, composed entirely of women, viewed all women's interests as essentially the same and therefore did not hesitate to use the singular *woman* to emphasize gender solidarity. Although mostly white and middle-class, WCTU members resolved to speak for their entire sex.

Woman's Christian Temperance Union Postcards
The Woman's Christian Temperance Union distributed postcards like these to attack the liquor trade. These cards are typical in their portrayal of saloon backers as traitors to the nation. In the top card, notice the man trampling on the American flag as he casts his ballot—a sly allusion to the need for woman suffrage. The second card shows a saloon keeper recruiting an "army of drunkards." Collection of Joyce M. Tice.

> **"All this work has tended more toward the liberation of women than it has toward the extinction of the saloon."**
> — FRANCES WILLARD, on the activities of the WCTU

When Frances Willard became president in 1879, she radically changed the direction of the organization. Social action replaced prayer as women's answer to the threat of drunkenness. Viewing alcoholism as a disease rather than a sin and poverty as a cause rather than a result of drink, the WCTU became involved in labor issues, joining with the Knights of Labor to press for better working conditions for women workers. Describing workers in a textile mill, a WCTU member wrote in the organization's *Union Signal* magazine, "It is dreadful to see these girls, stripped almost to the skin . . . and running like racehorses from the beginning to the end of the day." She concluded, "The hard slavish work is drawing the girls into the saloon."

Willard capitalized on the cult of domesticity as a shrewd political tactic to move women into public life and gain power to ameliorate social problems. Using "home protection" as her watchword, she argued as early as 1884 that women needed the vote to protect home and family. By the 1890s, the WCTU's grassroots network of local unions had spread to all but the most isolated rural areas of the country. Strong and rich, with more than 200,000 dues-paying members, the WCTU was a formidable group.

Willard worked to create a broad reform coalition in the 1890s, embracing the Knights of Labor, the People's Party, and the Prohibition Party. Until her death in 1898, she led, if not a woman's rights movement, then the first organized mass movement of women united around a women's issue. By 1900, thanks largely to the WCTU, women could claim a generation of experience in political action — speaking, lobbying, organizing, drafting legislation, and running private charitable institutions. As Willard observed, "All this work has tended more toward the liberation of women than it has toward the extinction of the saloon."

Elizabeth Cady Stanton, Susan B. Anthony, and the Movement for Woman Suffrage

Unlike the WCTU, the organized movement for woman suffrage remained small and relatively weak in the late nineteenth century. The U.S. woman's rights movement was begun by **Elizabeth Cady Stanton** at the first woman's rights convention in the United States, at Seneca Falls, New York, in 1848. Women's rights advocates split in 1867 over whether the Fourteenth and Fifteenth Amendments, which granted voting

rights to African American males, should have extended the vote to women as well. Stanton and her ally, **Susan B. Anthony**, launched the National Woman Suffrage Association in 1869, demanding the vote for women (see chapter 18). A more conservative group, the American Woman Suffrage Association (AWSA), formed the same year. Composed of men as well as women, the AWSA believed that women should vote in local but not national elections.

By 1890, the split had healed, and the newly united **National American Woman Suffrage Association** (NAWSA) launched campaigns on the state level to gain the vote for women. Twenty years had made a great change. Woman suffrage, though not yet generally supported, was no longer considered a crackpot idea. Thanks to the WCTU's support of the "home protection" ballot, suffrage had become accepted as a means to an end even when it was not embraced as a woman's natural right. The NAWSA honored Elizabeth Cady Stanton by electing her its first president, but Susan B. Anthony, who took the helm in 1892, emerged as the leading figure in the new united organization.

Stanton and Anthony, both in their seventies, were coming to the end of their public careers. Since the days of the Seneca Falls

Campaigning for Woman Suffrage
In 1896, women voted in only four states — Wyoming, Colorado, Idaho, and Utah. The West led the way in the campaign for woman suffrage, with Wyoming Territory granting women the vote as early as 1869. Sparse population meant that only sixteen votes were needed in the state's territorial legislature to obtain passage of woman suffrage. The poster calls on Nebraska to join the suffrage column, while the flag illustrates the number of states in which women could vote. Poster: Nebraska State Historical Society; Flag: Smithsonian Institution, Washington, D.C.

woman's rights convention, they had worked for reforms for their sex, including property rights, custody rights, and the right to education and gainful employment. But the prize of woman suffrage still eluded them. Suffragists won victories in Colorado in 1893 and Idaho in 1896. One more state joined the suffrage column in 1896 when Utah entered the Union. But women suffered a bitter defeat in a California referendum on woman suffrage that same year. Never losing faith, Susan B. Anthony remarked in her last public appearance, in 1906, "Failure is impossible." It would take until 1920 for all women to gain the vote with the ratification of the Nineteenth Amendment, but the unification of the two woman suffrage groups in 1890 signaled a new era in women's fight for the vote, just as Frances Willard's place on the platform in 1892 in St. Louis symbolized women's growing role in politics and reform.

> **REVIEW** How did women's temperance activism contribute to the cause of woman suffrage?

▶ Depression Politics

The depression that began in the spring of 1893 and lasted for more than four years put nearly half of the labor force out of work, a higher percentage than during the Great Depression of the 1930s (as discussed in chapters 23 and 24). The human cost of the depression was staggering. "I Take my pen in hand to let you know that we are Starving to death," a Kansas farm woman wrote to the governor in 1894. "Last cent gone," wrote a young widow in her diary. "Children went to work without their breakfasts." The burden of feeding and sheltering the unemployed and their families fell to private charity, city government, and some of the stronger trade unions. Following the harsh dictates of social Darwinism and laissez-faire, the majority of America's elected officials believed that it was inappropriate for the government to intervene. But the scope of the depression made it impossible for local agencies to supply sufficient relief, and increasingly Americans called on the federal government to take action. Armies of the unemployed marched on Washington to demand relief, and the Populist Party experienced a surge of support as the election of 1896 approached.

> **"I Take my pen in hand to let you know that we are Starving to death."**
>
> —A Kansas farm woman in 1894

Coxey's Army

Masses of unemployed Americans marched to Washington, D.C., in the spring of 1894 to call attention to their plight and to urge Congress to enact a public works program to end unemployment. Jacob S. Coxey of Massilon, Ohio, led the most publicized contingent. Convinced that men could be put to work building badly needed roads for the nation, Coxey proposed a scheme to finance public works through non-interest-bearing bonds. "What I am after," he maintained, "is to try to put this country in a condition so that no man who wants work shall be obliged to remain idle." His plan won support from the AFL and the Populists.

Starting out from Ohio with one hundred men, **Coxey's army**, as it was dubbed, swelled as it marched east through the spring snows of the Alleghenies. In Pennsylvania, Coxey recruited several hundred from the ranks of those left unemployed by the Homestead lockout. Called by Coxey the Commonweal of Christ, the army advanced to the tune of "Marching through Georgia":

> We are not tramps nor vagabonds,
>   that's shirking honest toil,
> But miners, clerks, skilled artisans,
>   and tillers of the soil
> Now forced to beg our brother worms
>   to give us leave to toil,
> While we are marching with Coxey.
> Hurrah! hurrah! for the unemployed's appeal
> Hurrah! hurrah! for the marching commonweal!

On May 1, Coxey's army arrived in Washington. When Coxey defiantly marched his men onto the Capitol grounds, police set upon the demonstrators with nightsticks, cracking skulls and arresting Coxey and his lieutenants. Coxey went to jail for twenty days and was fined $5 for "walking on the grass."

Those who had trembled for the safety of the Republic heaved a sigh of relief after Coxey's arrest, hoping that it would halt the march on Washington. But other armies of the unemployed, totaling possibly as many as five thousand people, were still on their way. Too poor to pay for railway tickets, they rode the rails as "freeloaders." The more daring contingents commandeered entire trains, stirring fears of revolution. Journalists who covered the march did little to quiet the nation's fears. They delighted in military terminology, describing themselves as "war correspondents." To boost newspaper sales, they gave to the episode a tone of urgency and heightened the sense of a nation imperiled.

unionism, already associated in the public mind as a result of the Haymarket bombing in 1886 (see chapter 19). Hugh O'Donnell later wrote, "The bullet from Berkman's pistol, failing in its foul intent, went straight through the heart of the Homestead strike."

In the end, the workers capitulated. The Homestead mill reopened in November, and the men returned to work, except for the union leaders, now blacklisted in every steel mill in the country. With the owners firmly in charge, the company slashed wages, reinstated the twelve-hour day, and eliminated five hundred jobs.

In the drama of events at Homestead, the significance of what occurred often remained obscured: The workers at Homestead had been taught a lesson. They would never again, in the words of the National Guard commander, "believe the works are their's [sic] quite as much as Carnegie's." Another forty-five years would pass before steelworkers, unskilled as well as skilled, successfully unionized. In the meantime, Carnegie's production tripled, even in the midst of a depression. "Ashamed to tell you profits these days," Carnegie wrote a friend in 1899. And no wonder: Carnegie's profits had grown from $4 million in 1892 to $40 million in 1900.

The Cripple Creek Miners' Strike of 1894

Less than a year after the Homestead lockout, a panic on Wall Street in the spring of 1893 touched off a bitter economic depression. In the West, silver mines fell on hard times, leading to the **Cripple Creek miners' strike of 1894**. When mine owners moved to lengthen the workday from eight to ten hours, the newly formed Western Federation of Miners (WFM) vowed to hold the line in Cripple Creek, Colorado. In February 1894, the WFM threatened to strike all mines working more than eight-hour shifts. The mine owners divided: Some quickly settled with the WFM; others continued to demand ten hours, provoking a strike.

The striking miners received help from many quarters. Working miners paid $15 a month to a strike fund, and miners in neighboring districts sent substantial contributions. The miners enjoyed the support and assistance of local businesses and grocers, who provided credit to the strikers. With these advantages, the Cripple Creek strikers could afford to hold out for their demands.

Even more significant, Governor Davis H. Waite, a Populist elected in 1892, had strong ties to the miners and refused to use the power of the state against the strikers. Governor Waite asked the strikers to lay down their arms and demanded that the mine owners disperse their hired deputies. The miners agreed to arbitration and selected Waite as their sole arbitrator. By May, the recalcitrant mine owners capitulated, and the union won an eight-hour day.

Governor Waite's intervention demonstrated the pivotal power of the state in the nation's labor wars. Having a Populist in power made a difference. A decade later, in 1904, with Waite out of office, mine owners relied on state troops to take back control of the mines, defeating the WFM and blacklisting all of its members. In retrospect, the Cripple Creek miners' strike of 1894 proved the exception to the rule of state intervention on the side of private property. More typical was the outcome of another strike in 1894 in Pullman, Illinois.

Eugene V. Debs and the Pullman Strike

The economic depression that began in 1893 swelled the ranks of the unemployed to three million, almost half of the working population. "A fearful crisis is upon us," wrote a labor publication. Nowhere were workers more demoralized than in the model town of Pullman, on the outskirts of Chicago.

In the wake of the Great Railroad Strike of 1877, **George M. Pullman**, the builder of Pullman railroad cars, had moved his plant and workers away from the "snares of the great city." In 1880, he purchased 4,300 acres nine miles south of Chicago and built a model town. The town of Pullman boasted parks, fountains, playgrounds, an auditorium, a library, a hotel, shops, and markets, along with 1,800 units of housing. Noticeably absent was a saloon.

The housing in Pullman was clearly superior to that in neighboring areas, but workers paid a high price to live in the model town. George M. Pullman expected a 6 percent return on his investment. As a result, Pullman's rents ran 10 to 20 percent higher than housing costs in nearby communities. And a family in Pullman could never own its own home. George Pullman refused to "sell an acre under any circumstances." As long as he controlled the town absolutely, he held the powerful whip of eviction over his employees and could quickly get rid of "troublemakers." Although observers at first praised the beauty and orderliness of the town, critics by the 1890s

Pinkertons hoisted a white flag and arranged with O'Donnell to surrender. With three workers dead and scores wounded, the crowd, numbering perhaps ten thousand, was in no mood for conciliation. As the hated "Pinks" came up the hill, they were forced to run a gantlet of screaming, cursing men, women, and children. When a young guard dropped to his knees, weeping for mercy, a woman used her umbrella to poke out his eye. One Pinkerton had been killed in the siege on the barges. In the grim rout that followed their surrender, not one avoided injury.

The "battle of Fort Frick" ended in a dubious victory for the workers. They took control of the plant and elected a council to run the community. At first, public opinion favored their cause. Newspapers urged Frick to negotiate or submit to arbitration. A congressman castigated Carnegie for "skulking in his castle in Scotland." Populists, meeting in St. Louis, condemned the use of "hireling armies."

The action of the Homestead workers struck at the heart of the capitalist system, pitting the workers' right to their jobs against the rights of private property. The workers' insistence that "we are not destroying the property of the company — merely protecting our rights" did not prove as compelling to the courts and the state as the property rights of the mill owners. Four days after the confrontation, Pennsylvania's governor, who sympathized with the workers, nonetheless yielded to pressure from Frick and ordered eight thousand National Guard troops into Homestead to protect Carnegie's property. The strikers, thinking they had nothing to fear from the militia, welcomed the troops with a brass band. But they soon understood the reality. The troops' ninety-five-day occupation not only protected Carnegie's property but also enabled Frick to reopen the mills and bring in strikebreakers. "We have been deceived," one worker complained bitterly. "We have stood idly by and let the town be occupied by soldiers who come here, not as our protectors, but as the protectors of non-union men. . . . If we undertake to resist the seizure of our jobs, we will be shot down like dogs."

Then, in a misguided effort to ignite a general uprising, **Alexander Berkman**, a Russian immigrant and anarchist, attempted to assassinate Frick. Berkman bungled his attempt. Shot twice and stabbed with a dagger, Frick survived and showed considerable courage, allowing a doctor to remove the bullets but refusing to leave his desk until the day's work

FRANK LESLIE'S
ILLUSTRATED
HOMESTEAD TROUBLES.
WEEKLY

NEW YORK, JULY 14, 1892.

THE LABOR TROUBLES AT HOMESTEAD, PENNSYLVANIA—ATTACK OF THE STRIKERS AND THEIR SYMPATHIZERS ON THE SURRENDERED PINKERTON MEN.

Homestead Workers Attack the Pinkertons
The nation's attention was riveted on labor strife at the Homestead steel mill in the summer of 1892. *Frank Leslie's Illustrated Weekly* ran a cover story on the violence that Pinkerton agents faced from a crowd of men, women, and children armed with clubs, guns, and ax handles.

The workers, who had been locked out by Henry Clay Frick, were enraged that Frick had hired the Pinkertons to bring in strikebreakers. Overwhelmed by the strikers, the Pinkertons surrendered. Although the mob was armed (note the boy with a gun in the foreground), not one of the Pinkertons was shot as they ran the gantlet. All, however, were beaten. The New York Society Library.

was completed. "I do not think that I shall die," Frick remarked coolly, "but whether I do or not, the Company will pursue the same policy and it will win." After the assassination attempt, public opinion turned against the workers.

Berkman was quickly tried and sentenced to prison. Although the Amalgamated and the AFL denounced his action, the incident linked anarchism and means of a referendum. Because the Populists shared common cause with labor against corporate interests, they also supported the eight-hour workday and an end to contract labor.

The sweeping array of Populist reforms enacted in the Populist platform changed the agenda of politics for decades to come. More than just a response to hard times, Populism presented an alternative vision of American economic democracy.

REVIEW Why did American farmers organize alliances in the late nineteenth century?

▶ The Labor Wars

While farmers united to fight for change, industrial laborers fought their own battles in a series of bloody strikes so fiercely waged on both sides that historians have called them the "labor wars." Industrial workers felt increasingly threatened as businesses combined into huge corporations, and in the 1890s labor took a stand. At issue was the right of workers to organize and to speak through unions to bargain collectively and fight for better working conditions, higher wages, shorter hours, and greater worker control in the face of increased mechanization.

Three major conflicts of the period — the lockout of steelworkers in Homestead, Pennsylvania, in 1892; the miners' strike in Cripple Creek, Colorado, in 1894; and the Pullman strike in Illinois that same year — raised fundamental questions about the rights of labor and the sanctity of private property.

The Homestead Lockout

In 1892, steelworkers in Pennsylvania squared off against Andrew Carnegie in a decisive struggle over the right to organize in the Homestead steel mills. Carnegie was unusual among industrialists as a self-styled friend of labor. In 1886, he had written, "The right of the workingmen to combine and to form trade unions is no less sacred than the right of the manufacturer to enter into associations and conferences with his fellows."

"If we undertake to resist the seizure of our jobs, we will be shot down like dogs."
— A Homestead striker

Yet as much as he cherished his liberal beliefs, Carnegie cherished his profits more. In 1892, Carnegie resolved to crush the Amalgamated Iron and Steel Workers, one of the largest and richest craft unions in the American Federation of Labor (AFL). When the Amalgamated attempted to renew its contract at Carnegie's Homestead mill, its leaders were told that since "the vast majority of our employees are Non union, the Firm has decided that the minority must give place to the majority." While it was true that only 800 skilled workers belonged to the elite Amalgamated, the union had long enjoyed the support of the plant's 3,000 non-union workers. Slavs, who did much of the unskilled work, made common cause with the Welsh, Scottish, and Irish skilled workers who belonged to the union. Never before had the Amalgamated been denied a contract.

Carnegie preferred not to be directly involved in the union busting that lay on the horizon, so that spring he sailed to Scotland and left **Henry Clay Frick**, the toughest antilabor man in the industry, in charge of the Homestead plant. By summer, a strike looked inevitable. Frick prepared by erecting a fifteen-foot fence around the plant and topping it with barbed wire. Workers aptly dubbed it "Fort Frick." To defend his fort and protect strikebreakers, Frick hired 316 mercenaries from the Pinkerton National Detective Agency at the rate of $5 per day, more than double the wage of the average Homestead worker.

The Pinkerton Agency, founded before the Civil War, came into its own in the 1880s as a private security force for hire. Pinkerton agents were a motley crew, recruited from all levels of society, from urban thugs to college boys. The "Pinks" earned the hatred of workers by protecting strikebreakers and acting as company spies.

On June 28, the **Homestead lockout** began when Frick locked the workers out of the mills and prepared to bring in strikebreakers, whom the workers derogatorily referred to as "scabs." Hugh O'Donnell, the young Irishman who led the union, vowed to prevent scabs from entering the plant. On July 6 at 4 a.m., a lookout spotted two barges moving up the Monongahela River in the fog. Frick was attempting to smuggle Pinkertons into Homestead.

Workers sounded the alarm, and within minutes a crowd of more than a thousand, hastily armed with rifles, hoes, and fence posts, rushed to the riverbank to meet the enemy. When the Pinkertons attempted to come ashore, gunfire broke out, and more than a dozen Pinkertons and some thirty strikers fell, killed or wounded. The Pinkertons retreated to the barges. For twelve hours, the workers, joined by their family members, threw everything they had at the barges, from fireworks to dynamite. Finally, the that is, selling it together — farmers could negotiate a better price. And by setting up trade stores and exchanges, they sought to escape the grasp of the merchant/creditor. Through the cooperatives, the Farmers' Alliance promised to change the way farmers lived. "We are going to get out of debt and be free and independent people once more," exulted one Georgia farmer.

Cooperatives sprang up throughout the South and West. But the Alliance faced insurmountable difficulties in running successful cooperatives. Opposition by merchants, bankers, wholesalers, and manufacturers made it impossible for the cooperatives to get credit. As the cooperative movement died, the Farmers' Alliance moved toward direct political action. Confounded by the failure of the Democrats and Republicans to break with commercial interests and support the farmers, Alliance leaders moved, often reluctantly, toward the formation of a third party.

The Populist Movement

In the earliest days of the Alliance movement, a leader of the Southern Farmers' Alliance insisted, "The Alliance is a strictly white man's nonpolitical, secret business association." But by 1892, it was none of those things. Advocates of a third party carried the day at the convention of laborers, farmers, and common folk in 1892 in St. Louis, where the Farmers' Alliance gave birth to the **People's Party** and launched the Populist movement. "There is something at the back of all this turmoil more than the failure of crops or the scarcity of ready cash," a journalist observed in 1892.

The same spirit of religious revival that animated the Farmers' Alliance infused the People's Party. The Populists built on the work of the Alliance to mount a critique of industrial society and a call for action. Convinced that the money and banking systems worked to the advantage of the wealthy few, they demanded economic democracy. To help farmers get the credit they needed at reasonable rates, southern farmers hit on the ingenious idea of a **subtreasury** — a plan that would allow farmers to store their nonperishable crops until prices rose and to receive commodity credit from the federal government to obtain needed supplies. The subtreasury promised to get rid of the crop lien system once and for all. Although the idea would be enacted piecemeal in progressive and New Deal legislation in the twentieth century, conservatives in the 1890s dismissed it as far-fetched "corn tassel communism."

Mary Elizabeth Lease
This painting of Lease, taken in 1895 at the height of her political activities in Kansas, shows a well-dressed, mild-eyed woman — belying her reputation as a hell-raiser who supposedly exhorted Kansas farmers to "raise less corn and more hell." Lease's admirers styled her "The People's Joan of Arc." But in the eyes of her detractors, who attacked not only her speeches but also the propriety of a woman who dared to pursue a career as a public speaker, she was "a lantern-jawed, google-eyed nightmare" and "a petticoated smut-mill." Kansas State Historical Society.

To the western farmer, the Populists promised land reform, championing a plan that would claim excessive land granted to railroads or sold to foreign investors. The Populists' boldest proposal called for government ownership of the railroads and the telegraph system to put an end to discriminatory rates. Citing examples of how the powerful railroads had corrupted the political system, the Populists did not shrink from advocating what their opponents branded state socialism.

The Populists also demanded currency reform. Farmers in all sections rallied to the cry for cheaper currency, calling for free silver and greenbacks — attempts to increase the nation's tight money supply and thus make credit easier to obtain. And to empower the common people, the Populist platform called for the direct election of senators (then chosen by state legislatures) and for other electoral reforms, including the secret ballot and the right to initiate legislation, to recall elected officials, and to submit issues to the people by

Columbia's Easter Bonnet
The United States, symbolized by the female figure of Columbia, tries on "World Power" in this cartoon from *Puck* that appeared in 1901 after the Spanish-American War left the United States in control of Spain's former colonies in Guam, the Philippines, and Puerto Rico. The bonnet, in the shape of an American battleship, indicates the key role the U.S. Navy played in the conflict. "Expansion," spelled out in the smoke from the ship's smokestack, points to a new overseas direction for American foreign policy at the turn of the twentieth century. Library of Congress.

In the formal Treaty of Paris (1898), Spain ceded the Philippines to the United States along with the former Spanish colonies of Puerto Rico and Guam (Map 20.4). Empire did not come cheap. When Spain initially balked at these terms, the United States agreed to pay an indemnity of $20 million for the islands. Nor was the cost measured in money alone. Filipino revolutionaries under **Emilio Aguinaldo**, who had greeted U.S. troops as liberators, bitterly fought the new masters. It would take seven years and 4,000 American dead — almost ten times the number killed in Cuba — not to mention an estimated 20,000 Filipino casualties, to defeat Aguinaldo and secure American control of the Philippines, America's coveted stepping-stone to China.

At home, a vocal minority, mostly Democrats and former Populists, resisted the country's foray into overseas empire, judging it unwise, immoral, and unconstitutional. William Jennings Bryan, who enlisted in the army but never saw action, concluded that American expansionism only distracted the nation from problems at home. Pointing to the central paradox of the war, Representative Bourke Cockran of New York admonished, "We who have been the destroyers of oppression are asked now to become its agents." Mark Twain, lending his bitter eloquence to the cause of anti-imperialism, lamented that the United States had become "yet another Civilized Power, with its banner of the Prince of Peace in one hand and its loot-basket and its butcher-knife in the other."

The anti-imperialists were soon drowned out by cries for empire. As Senator Knute Nelson of Minnesota assured his colleagues, "We come as ministering angels, not as despots." Fresh from the conquest of Native Americans in the West, the nation largely embraced the heady mixture of racism and missionary zeal that fueled American adventurism abroad. The *Washington Post* trumpeted, "The taste of empire is in the mouth of the people," thrilled at the prospect of "an imperial policy, the Republic renascent, taking her place with the armed nations."

REVIEW Why did the United States largely abandon its isolationist foreign policy in the 1890s?

▶ Conclusion: Rallying around the Flag

A decade of domestic strife ended amid the blare of martial music and the waving of flags. The Spanish-American War drowned out the calls for social reform that had fueled the Populist politics of the 1890s. During that decade, angry farmers facing hard times looked to the Farmers' Alliance to fight for their vision of economic democracy, workers staged bloody battles across the country to assert their rights, and women attacked drunkenness and the conditions that fostered it and mounted a suffrage movement to secure their basic political rights. In St. Louis in 1892, Frances Willard joined with other disaffected Americans to form a new People's Party to fight for change.

The bitter depression that began in 1893 led to increased labor strife. The Pullman boycott brutally dramatized the power of property and the conservatism of the laissez-faire state. Even the miners' victory in Cripple Creek,

Colorado, in 1894 proved short-lived. But workers' willingness to confront capitalism on the streets of Chicago, Homestead, Cripple Creek, and a host of other sites across America eloquently testified to labor's growing determination, unity, and strength.

As the depression deepened, the sight of Coxey's army of unemployed marching on Washington to demand federal intervention in the economy signaled a growing shift in the public mind against the stand-pat politics of laissez-faire personified by President William McKinley. The call for the government to take action to better the lives of workers, farmers, and the dispossessed manifested itself in the fiercely fought presidential campaign of William Jennings Bryan in 1896. With the outbreak of the Spanish-American War in 1898, the decade ended on a harmonious note with patriotic Americans rallying around the flag. Few questioned America's foray into overseas empire. The United States took its place on the world stage, buttressing its hemispheric domination with the Monroe Doctrine and employing the Open Door policy, which promised access to the riches of China. But even though Americans basked in patriotism and contemplated empire, old grievances had not been laid to rest. The People's Party had been beaten, but the Populist spirit lived on in the demands for greater government involvement in the economy, expanded opportunities for direct democracy, and a more equitable balance of profits and power between the people and the big corporations. This reform agenda would be taken up by a new generation of progressive reformers in the first decades of the twentieth century.

▶ Selected Bibliography

The Farmers Alliance, the Labor Wars, and Women's Activism

Peter H. Argersinger, *The Limits of Agrarian Radicalism: Western Populism and American Politics* (1995).

Jean H. Baker, *Sisters: The Lives of America's Suffragists* (2005).

Ruth Bordin, *Frances Willard: A Biography* (1986).

Ellen Carol DuBois, *Woman Suffrage and Women's Rights* (1998).

Michel Lewis Goldberg, *An Army of Women: Gender and Politics in Gilded Age Kansas* (1997).

Steven Hahn, *A Nation under Our Feet: Black Political Struggles in the Rural South from Slavery to the Great Migration* (2003).

Elizabeth Jameson, *All That Glitters: Class, Conflict, and Community in Cripple Creek* (1998).

Michael Kazin, *The Populist Persuasion: An American History* (rev. ed., 1998).

Paul Krause, *The Battle for Homestead, 1880–1892* (1992).

Jackson Lears, *The Rebirth of a Nation: The Making of Modern America, 1877–1920* (2009).

Connie L. Lester, *Up from the Mudsills of Hell: The Farmers' Alliance, Populism, and Progressive Agriculture in Tennessee, 1870–1915* (2006).

Michael McGerr, *A Fierce Discontent: The Rise and Fall of the Progressive Movement in America* (2005).

David Nasaw, *Andrew Carnegie* (2006).

Charles Postel, *The Populist Vision (2007)*.

Nick Salvatore, *Eugene V. Debs: Citizen and Socialist* (1982).

Depression and the Election of 1896

Steve Fraser, *Every Man a Speculator: A Cultural History of Wall Street in America* (2005).

Stephen Kantrowitz, *Ben Tillman and the Reconstruction of White Supremacy* (2000).

Michael Kazin, *A Godly Hero: The Life of William Jennings Bryan* (2006).

Kenneth L. Kusmer, *Down and Out, on the Road: The Homeless in American History* (2002).

Gretchen Ritter, *Goldbugs and Greenbacks: The Antimonopoly Tradition in the Politics of Finance in America* (1997).

Troy Rondinone, *The Great Industrial War: Framing Class Conflict in the Media, 1865–1950* (2010).

Carol A. Schwantes, *Coxey's Army: An American Odyssey* (1985).

Douglas Steeples and David O. Whitten, *Democracy in Desperation: The Depression of 1893* (1998).

U.S. Foreign Policy and the Spanish-American War

Fred Anderson and Andrew Cayton, *The Domination of War: Empire and Liberty in North America, 1500–2000* (2005).

Kristin Hoganson, *Fighting for American Manhood: How Gender Politics Provoked the Spanish-American and Philippine-American Wars* (1998).

Matthew Frye Jacobson, *Barbarian Virtues: The United States Encounters Foreign Peoples at Home and Abroad, 1876–1917* (2000).

Amy Kaplan, *The Anarchy of Empire in the Making of U.S. Culture* (2002).

Stephen Kinzer, *Overthrow: America's Century of Regime Change from Hawaii to Iraq* (2006).

Walter LaFeber, *The American Search for Opportunity, 1865–1913* (1994).

Brian Linn, *The Philippine War, 1899–1902* (2000).

Paul T. McCartney, *Power and Progress: American National Identity, the War of 1898, and the Rise of American Imperialism* (2006).

Ivan Musicant, *Empire by Default: The Spanish American War and the Dawn of the American Century* (1998).

Diana Preston, *Besieged in Peking: The Story of the 1900 Boxer Uprising* (1999).

Margaret Strobel, *Gender, Sex, and Empire* (1993).

Evan Thomas, *The War Lovers: Roosevelt, Lodge, Hearst, and the Rush to Empire, 1898* (2010).

▶ **FOR MORE BOOKS ABOUT TOPICS IN THIS CHAPTER,** see the Online Bibliography at **bedfordstmartins.com/roark**.

▶ **FOR ADDITIONAL PRIMARY SOURCES FROM THIS PERIOD,** see Michael Johnson, ed., *Reading the American Past*, Fifth Edition.

▶ **FOR WEB SITES, IMAGES, AND DOCUMENTS RELATED TO TOPICS AND PLACES IN THIS CHAPTER,** visit Make History at **bedfordstmartins.com/roark**.

Reviewing Chapter 20

REVIEW QUESTIONS

Use key terms and dates to support your answer.

1. Why did American farmers organize alliances in the late nineteenth century? (pp. 641–644)

2. What tactics led to the defeat of the strikers in the 1890s? Where were they able to succeed and why? (pp. 644–651)

3. How did women's temperance activism contribute to the cause of woman suffrage? (pp. 651–654)

4. Why was the People's Party unable to translate national support into victory in the 1896 election? (pp. 654–658)

5. Why did the United States largely abandon its isolationist foreign policy in the 1890s? (pp. 658–669)

MAKING CONNECTIONS

Draw on key terms, the timeline, and review questions.

1. In the late nineteenth century, Americans clashed over the disparity of power brought about by industrial capitalism. Why did many farmers and urban workers look to the government to help advance their vision of economic justice? In your answer, discuss specific reforms working-class Americans pursued and the strategies they employed.

2. In the 1890s, workers mounted labor protests and strikes. What circumstances gave rise to these actions? How did they differ from earlier strikes, such as the Great Railroad Strike of 1877? In your answer, discuss specific actions, being sure to consider how local and national circumstances contributed to their ultimate resolution.

3. How did women's activism in the late nineteenth century help advance the cause of woman suffrage? In your answer, discuss specific gains made in the late nineteenth century, as well as shifts in reformers' strategies.

4. Given the farmers' unrest in the 1890s, why did the Populist Party fail to defeat Republican William McKinley in the election of 1896? What coalitions failed to come together?

Link events in this chapter to earlier events.

1. How did the conquest of Native Americans in the West foreshadow U.S. expansion abroad? In what ways did the assumptions of racial superiority evident in U.S. Indian policy affect the treatment of Cubans and Filipinos? (See chapter 17.)

2. Why in the midst of burgeoning growth did the United States experience a major depression in the 1890s? Draw on your knowledge of the development of U.S. industries such as the railroads. (See chapter 18.)

▶ FOR PRACTICE QUIZZES AND OTHER STUDY TOOLS, visit the Online Study Guide at **bedfordstmartins.com/roark**.

TIMELINE 1884–1901

1884
- Frances Willard, head of Woman's Christian Temperance Union, calls for woman suffrage.

1890
- National American Woman Suffrage Association (NAWSA) formed.
- Wyoming only state allowing women to vote in national elections.
- Southern Farmers' Alliance numbers three million members.

1892
- People's (Populist) Party founded.
- Homestead lockout.

1893
- Stock market crash touches off severe economic depression.
- President Grover Cleveland nixes attempt to annex Hawai'i.

1894
- Miners' strike in Cripple Creek, Colorado.
- Coxey's army marches to Washington, D.C.
- Federal troops and court injunction crush Pullman boycott.

1895
- President Grover Cleveland enforces Monroe Doctrine in border dispute between British Guiana and Venezuela.

1896
- Democrats and Populists support William Jennings Bryan for president.
- Republican William McKinley elected president.

1898
- U.S. battleship *Maine* explodes in Havana harbor.
- Congress declares war on Spain.
- Admiral George Dewey destroys Spanish fleet in Manila Bay, the Philippines.
- U.S. troops defeat Spanish forces in Cuba.
- Treaty of Paris ends war with Spain and cedes Philippines, Puerto Rico, and Guam to the United States.
- United States annexes Hawai'i.

1899–1900
- Secretary of State John Hay enunciates Open Door policy in China.
- Boxer uprising in China.

1901
- Boxer Protocol imposed on Chinese government.

WE WANT OUR TEDDY BACK

THE PROGRESSIVE PARTY

BORN 1912

PROGRESSIVE PARTY SOUVENIR BANDANA

This colorful bandana from the 1912 presidential race celebrates the Progressive Party and its candidate, Theodore Roosevelt. The progressive reform movement began at the grassroots, growing out of the crises of the 1890s to emerge full-blown in 1900. The appalling conditions in New York's tenements, documented by Jacob Riis in photographs like this one of a Baxter Street courtyard, goaded reformers to action. Roosevelt would become the Progressives' champion, challenging laissez-faire liberalism and arguing for government action to ensure greater social justice. In 1912 Roosevelt's followers broke with Republicans to form the new Progressive Party, demanding "We Want Our Teddy Back."

Bandana: Collection of Janice L. and David J. Frent; background: The Jacob A. Riis Collection, #108, Museum of the City of New York.

21

Progressivism from the Grass Roots to the White House
1890–1916

IN THE SUMMER OF 1889, JANE ADDAMS LEASED TWO FLOORS OF A dilapidated mansion on Chicago's West Side. Her Italian and Russian Jewish neighbors must have scratched their heads, wondering why this well-dressed woman, who surely could afford a better house in a better neighborhood, chose to live on South Halsted Street. Yet the house, built by Charles Hull, precisely suited Addams's needs.

Personal action marked the first step in Addams's search for solutions to the social problems created by urban industrialism. Her object was two-fold: She wanted to help her immigrant neighbors, and she wanted to offer an opportunity for educated women like herself to find meaningful work. Addams's emphasis on the reciprocal relationship between the social classes made Hull House different from other philanthropic enterprises. She wished to do things with, not just for, Chicago's poor.

In the next decade, Hull House expanded from two rented floors in the old brick mansion wedged between a saloon and an undertaker to some thirteen buildings housing a remarkable variety of activities. Addams converted the basement bathroom into public baths, opened a restaurant for workingwomen too tired to cook after their long shifts, and sponsored a nursery and kindergarten. Hull House offered classes, lectures, art exhibits, musical instruction, and college extension courses. It boasted a gymnasium, a theater, a manual training workshop, a labor museum, and the first public playground in Chicago.

From the first, Hull House attracted an extraordinary set of reformers. Some stayed for decades, as did Julia Lathrop before she went to Washington, D.C., in 1912 to head the Children's Bureau. Others, like Gerard Swope, who later became president of the General Electric Company, came for only a short time. Hull House residents pioneered the scientific investigation of urban ills. Armed with statistics, they launched campaigns to improve housing, end child labor, fund playgrounds, mediate between labor and management, and lobby for laws to protect workers.

Addams quickly learned that it was impossible to deal with urban problems without becoming involved in political action. Her determination to clean up the garbage on Halsted Street led her into politics. Piles of decaying garbage overflowed the street's wooden trash bins, breeding flies and disease. Investigation revealed that the local ward boss got a kickback from a contractor who didn't bother to provide adequate service. To end the graft, Addams got herself appointed garbage inspector. Out on the streets at six in the morning, she rode atop the garbage wagon to make sure it made its rounds. Eventually, her struggle to aid the urban poor led her not only to city hall but on to the state capitol and to Washington, D.C., as well.

Under Jane Addams's leadership, Hull House became a "spearhead for reform," part of a broader movement that contemporaries called progressivism. The transition from personal action to political activism that Addams personified became one of the hallmarks of this reform period, which lasted from the 1890s to World War I.

By the 1890s, many Americans recognized that the laissez-faire approach of government toward business no longer worked. The classical liberalism of the nation's Founders, which opposed the tyranny of centralized government, had not foreseen the enormous private wealth and power of the Gilded Age's business giants. As the gap between rich and poor widened in the 1890s, progressive

Jane Addams

Jane Addams was twenty-nine years old when she founded Hull House on South Halsted Street in Chicago. She and her college roommate, Ellen Gates Starr, established America's premier social settlement. Her desire to live among the poor and her insistence that settlement house work benefited educated women such as herself as well as her immigrant neighbors separated her from the charity workers who had come before her and marked the distance from philanthropy to progressive reform. Her autobiographical *Twenty Years at Hull-House*, published in 1910, is shown in the inset. Photo: Jane Addams Memorial Collection (JAMC neg. 14), Special Collections, University of Illinois at Chicago, photographer: Max Platz; Book: Newberry Library.

reformers began demanding government intervention to guarantee a more equitable society. The willingness to use the government to promote change and to counterbalance the power of private interests redefined liberalism in the twentieth century.

Faith in activism in both the political and the private realms united an otherwise diverse group of progressive reformers. A sense of Christian mission inspired some. Others, fearing social upheaval, sought to remove some of the worst evils of urban industrialism — tenements, child labor, and harsh working conditions. A belief in technical expertise and scientific management infused progressivism and made the cult of efficiency part and parcel of the movement.

Progressives shared a growing concern about the power of wealthy individuals and corporations and a strong dislike of the trusts, but they were not immune to the prejudices of the era. Although they pressed for direct democracy, many progressives sought to restrict the rights of African Americans, Asians, and even the women who formed the backbone of the movement.

All of these elements — uplift and efficiency, social justice and social control, direct democracy and discrimination — came together in the Progressive Era both at the grass-roots level in the cities and states and in the presidencies of Theodore Roosevelt and Woodrow Wilson.

Grassroots Progressivism

Much of progressive reform began at the grassroots level and percolated upward into local, state, and eventually national politics as reformers attacked the social problems fostered by urban industrialism. Although **progressivism** flourished in many different settings across the country, urban problems inspired the progressives' greatest efforts. In their zeal to "civilize the city," reformers founded settlement houses, professed a new Christian social gospel, and campaigned against vice and crime in the name of "social purity." Allying with the working class, they sought to better the lot of sweatshop garment workers and to end child labor. Their reform efforts often began on the local level but ended up being debated in state legislatures and in the U.S. Congress.

Civilizing the City

Progressives attacked the problems of the city on many fronts. The settlement house movement attempted to bridge the distance between the classes. The social gospel called for churches to play a new role in social reformation. And the social purity movement campaigned to clean up vice, particularly prostitution.

The **settlement house** movement, which began in England, came to the United States in 1886 with the opening of the University Settlement House in New York City. The needs of poor urban neighborhoods provided the impetus for these social settlements. In 1893, Lillian Wald, a nurse attending medical school in New York, went to care for a woman living in a dilapidated tenement. The experience led Wald to leave medical school and recruit several other nurses to move to New York City's Lower East Side "to live in the neighborhood as nurses, identify ourselves with it socially, and . . . contribute to it our citizenship." Wald's Henry Street settlement expanded in 1895, pioneering public health nursing. Although Wald herself was Jewish, she insisted that the settlement remain independent of religious ties, making it different from the avowedly religious settlements in England.

Women, particularly college-educated women like **Jane Addams** and Lillian Wald, formed the backbone of the settlement house movement and

Children Playing at Hull House

A young settlement house worker leads neighborhood children in a circle game in this photograph taken at Hull House at the turn of the twentieth century. Jane Addams recognized early on that Chicago's working mothers needed safe, reliable child care. Hull House filled the need by providing day nurseries. Older children, like the boys and girls pictured here in their short pants and pinafores, could find at Hull House a snack and a place to play after school. Adena Rich Miller Scrapbook (JAMC neg. 435b), Special Collection, University Library, University of Illinois at Chicago.

Making the Workplace Safer: Alice Hamilton Explores the Dangerous Trades

Nothing in Alice Hamilton's middle-class, midwestern upbringing hinted at the leading role she would play in the progressive movement as a pioneer in the field of occupational health and safety. Yet at an early age, she resolved to become a doctor, because, as she wrote, "as a doctor I could go anywhere I pleased — to the far-off lands or to city slums — and be quite sure that I could be of use anywhere."

This desire to be of use prompted Hamilton to earn a medical degree at the University of Michigan and to study bacteriology in Germany and at Johns Hopkins University. In September 1897, she fulfilled a longtime dream by moving into Hull House, where she, like most of the residents, worked a day job (at Northwestern University's Medical School) and participated in settlement activities in the evenings and on weekends. Hamilton soon focused on the area of public health, particularly the link between occupation and illness.

Through her work, Hamilton came to believe that the poor health of many immigrants resulted from unsafe conditions and noxious chemicals, especially lead dust, in the industrial workplace. Employers insisted that lead poisoning resulted from workers' failure to wash their hands before they ate, or they blamed workers' ill health on alcoholism, but Hamilton disagreed. As she noted, the United States was far behind Europe in the field of industrial toxicology and in the regulation of dangers in the workplace. "The employers [here] could, if they wished, shut their eyes to the dangers their workmen faced," Hamilton observed, "for nobody held them responsible, while the workers [largely immigrants] accepted the risks with fatalistic submissiveness as part of the price one must pay for being poor."

In 1910, at the age of thirty-two, Hamilton was appointed to the newly created Occupational Disease Commission of Illinois, the first inves-

tigative body of its kind in the United States. For the next decade, she relied primarily on "shoe leather epidemiology" to explore the dangerous trades. With her assistants, she visited factories, read hospital records, and interviewed workers in their homes to discover instances of lead poisoning. "No young doctor," she wrote, "can hope for work as exciting and rewarding." Lead poisoning builds up slowly in the body, leading to colic and convulsions. Lead harms the nervous system, causing paralysis and wristdrop, a condition in which the hands and fingers cannot be extended. In cases of chronic lead poisoning, victims suffer from weight loss, constipation, high blood pressure, anemia, abdominal pain, fatigue, and premature senility. One of Hamilton's case studies tells the grim story.

A Hungarian, thirty-six years old, worked for seven years grinding lead paint. During this time he had three attacks of colic, with vomiting and headache. I saw him in the hospital, a skeleton of a man, looking almost twice his age, his limbs soft and flabby, his muscles wasted. He was extremely emaciated, his color was a dirty grayish yellow, his eyes dull and expressionless. He lay in an apathetic condition, rousing when spoken to and answering rationally but slowly, with often an appreciable delay, then sinking back into apathy.

In 1911, Hamilton prepared a report making clear the connection

---

stood in the vanguard of the progressive movement. Settlement houses gave college-educated women eager to use their knowledge a place to put their talents to work in the service of society and to champion progressive reform. (See "Seeking the American Promise," above.) Largely because of women's efforts, settlements like Hull House grew in number from six in 1891 to more than four hundred in 1911. In the process, settlement

house women created a new profession — social work — and stimulated the new reform movement of progressivism.

For their part, churches confronted urban social problems by enunciating a new **social gospel**, one that saw its mission as not simply to reform individuals but to reform society. The social gospel offered a powerful corrective to social Darwinism and the gospel of wealth, between occupation and illness, leading to needed reforms in Illinois. In 1913, the U.S. commissioner of labor asked her to undertake a national study. "I had, as a Federal agent," she wrote, "no right to enter any establishment — that depended on the courtesy of the employer. I must discover for myself where the plants were, and the method of investigation to be followed. . . . Nobody would keep tabs on me, I should not even receive a salary." Using her intelligence and charm, she was rarely denied entry, and her experience at Hull House led her directly to the workers in their homes when she wanted the facts. Her powers of persuasion prompted several employers to institute reforms in their plants to cut down on lead dust.

By 1915, Hamilton had become the foremost American authority on lead poisoning and one of a handful of prominent specialists in industrial disease. When the Harvard Medical School began a program in industrial hygiene in 1916, Hamilton became the first woman invited to join the faculty. Until her retirement in 1935, she alternated a semester of teaching at Harvard with her field work "exploring the dangerous trades." In her long retirement (she lived to be 101), she continued to blend her commitment to social justice and civil rights, political activism, and concern for the poorest workers. Hamilton died on September 22, 1970, three months before Congress passed the Occupational Safety and Health Act, institutionalizing the reforms she had fought for her whole life.

Alice Hamilton

This picture of Alice Hamilton was taken the year she graduated from the University of Michigan medical school in 1893. A resident of Hull House, she pioneered the field of occupational health and safety. Schlesinger Library, Radcliffe Institute for Advanced Study, Harvard University.

Questions for Consideration

1. What was the importance of Hull House in Alice Hamilton's career?

2. Hamilton observed that regulation of industry was much more advanced in Europe than in the United States, where, as she put it, the "subject was tainted with Socialism or with feminine sentimentality for the poor." In her own work, how did she overcome this attitude?

which fostered the belief that riches somehow signaled divine favor (see chapter 18). Washington Gladden, a prominent social gospel minister, challenged that view when he urged Congregationalists to turn down a gift from John D. Rockefeller, arguing that it was "tainted money." In place of the gospel of wealth, progressive clergy exhorted their congregations to put Christ's teachings to work in their daily lives.

Charles M. Sheldon's popular book *In His Steps* (1898) called on men and women to Christianize capitalism by asking the question "What would Jesus do?"

Ministers also played an active role in the **social purity movement**, the campaign to attack vice. The Reverend Charles H. Parkhurst shocked his Madison Square congregation in the 1890s by donning a disguise and touring

New York City's brothels to uncover the links between political corruption and urban vice. Armed with eyewitness accounts and affidavits, he demanded reform. To end the "social evil," as reformers delicately referred to prostitution, the social purity movement brought together ministers who wished to stamp out sin, doctors concerned about the spread of venereal disease, and women reformers determined to fight the double standard that made premarital and extramarital sex acceptable for men but demanded chastity of women. Advanced progressive reformers linked prostitution to poverty and championed higher wages for women. "Is it any wonder," asked the Chicago vice commission, "that a tempted girl who receives only six dollars per week working with her hands sells her body for twenty-five dollars per week when she learns there is a demand for it and men are willing to pay the price?"

Attacks on alcohol went hand in hand with the push for social purity. In the early twentieth century, the Anti-Saloon League, formed in 1895 under the leadership of Protestant clergy, added to the efforts of the Woman's Christian Temperance Union in campaigning to end the sale of liquor. Reformers pointed to links between drinking, prostitution, wife and child abuse, unemployment, and industrial accidents. The powerful liquor lobby fought back, spending liberally in election campaigns, fueling the charge that liquor corrupted the political process.

An element of nativism (dislike of foreigners) ran through the movement for prohibition, as it did in a number of progressive reforms. The Irish, the Italians, and the Germans were among the groups stigmatized by temperance reformers for their drinking. Even though most workers toiled six days a week and had only Sunday for recreation and relaxation, some progressives campaigned on the local level to enforce the Sunday closing of taverns, stores, and other commercial establishments. To further deny the working class access to alcohol, these progressives pushed for state legislation to outlaw the sale of liquor. By 1912, seven states were "dry."

Progressives' efforts to civilize the city demonstrated their willingness to take action; their belief that environment, not heredity alone, determined human behavior; and their optimism that conditions could be corrected through government action without radically altering America's economy or institutions. All of these attitudes characterized the progressive movement.

Progressives and the Working Class

Day-to-day contact with their neighbors made settlement house workers particularly sympathetic to labor unions. When Mary Kenney O'Sullivan complained that her bookbinders' union met in a dirty, noisy saloon, Jane Addams invited the union to meet at Hull House. And during the Pullman strike in 1894 (see chapter 20, "Documenting the American Promise," page 648), Hull House residents organized strike relief. "Hull-House has been so unionized," grumbled one Chicago businessman, "that it has lost its usefulness and become a detriment and harm to the community." But to the working class, the support of middle-class reformers marked a significant gain.

Attempts to forge a cross-class alliance became institutionalized in 1903 with the creation of the **Women's Trade Union League** (WTUL). The WTUL brought together women workers and middle-class "allies." Its goal was to organize workingwomen into unions under the auspices of the American Federation of Labor (AFL). However, as one workingwoman confided, "The men think that the girls should not get as good work as the men and should not make half as much money as a man." Samuel Gompers, president of the AFL, endorsed the principle of equal pay for equal work, shrewdly observing that it would help male workers more than women, since many employers hired women precisely because they could be paid less.

Although the alliance between workingwomen, primarily immigrants and daughters of immigrants, and their middle-class allies was not without tension, the WTUL helped workingwomen achieve significant gains. Its most notable success came in 1909 in the "uprising of the twenty thousand," when hundreds of women employees of the Triangle Shirtwaist Company in New York City went on strike to protest low wages, dangerous working conditions, and management's refusal to recognize their union, the International Ladies' Garment Workers Union. In support, an estimated twenty thousand garment workers, most of them teenage girls and many of them Jewish and Italian immigrants, stayed out on strike through the winter, picketing in the bitter cold. By the time the strike ended in February 1910, the workers had won important demands in many shops. The solidarity shown by the women workers proved to be the strike's greatest achievement. As Clara Lemlich, one of the strike's leaders, exclaimed, "They used to say that you couldn't even organize women. They wouldn't come to union meetings. They were 'temporary' workers. Well we showed them!"

The WTUL made enormous contributions to the strike. It provided volunteers for the picket lines, posted more than $29,000 in bail, protested police brutality, organized a parade of ten thousand strikers, took part in the arbitration conference, appealed for funds, and generated publicity for the strike. Under the leadership of the WTUL, women from every class of society, from J. P. Morgan's daughter Anne to socialists on New York's Lower East Side, joined the strikers in a dramatic display of cross-class alliance.

But for all its success, the uprising of the twenty thousand failed fundamentally to change conditions for women workers, as the tragic Triangle fire dramatized in 1911. A little over a year after the shirtwaist makers' strike ended, fire alarms sounded at the Triangle Shirtwaist factory. The ramshackle building, full of lint and combustible cloth, burned to rubble in half an hour. A WTUL member described the scene below on the street: "Two young girls whom I knew to be working in the vicinity came rushing toward me, tears were running from their eyes and they were white and shaking as they caught me by the arm. 'Oh,' shrieked one of them, 'they are jumping. Jumping from ten stories up! They are going through the air like bundles of clothes.'"

The terrified Triangle workers had little choice but to jump. Flames blocked one exit, and the other door had been locked to prevent workers from pilfering. The flimsy, rusted fire escape collapsed under the weight of fleeing workers, killing dozens. Trapped, 54 workers on the top floors jumped to their deaths. Of 500 workers, 146 died and scores of others were injured. The owners of the Triangle firm went to trial for negligence, but they avoided conviction when authorities determined that the fire had been started by a careless smoker. The Triangle Shirtwaist Company reopened in another firetrap within a matter of weeks.

Outrage and a sense of futility overwhelmed Rose Schneiderman, a leading WTUL organizer, who made a bitter speech at the memorial service for the dead Triangle workers. "I would be a traitor to those poor burned bodies if I came here to talk good fellowship," she told her audience. "We have tried you good people of the public and we have found you wanting. . . . I know from my experience it is up to the working people to save themselves . . . by a strong working class movement." The Triangle fire severely tested the bonds

> "They used to say that you couldn't even organize women. . . . Well we showed them!"
> — Strike leader CLARA LEMLICH

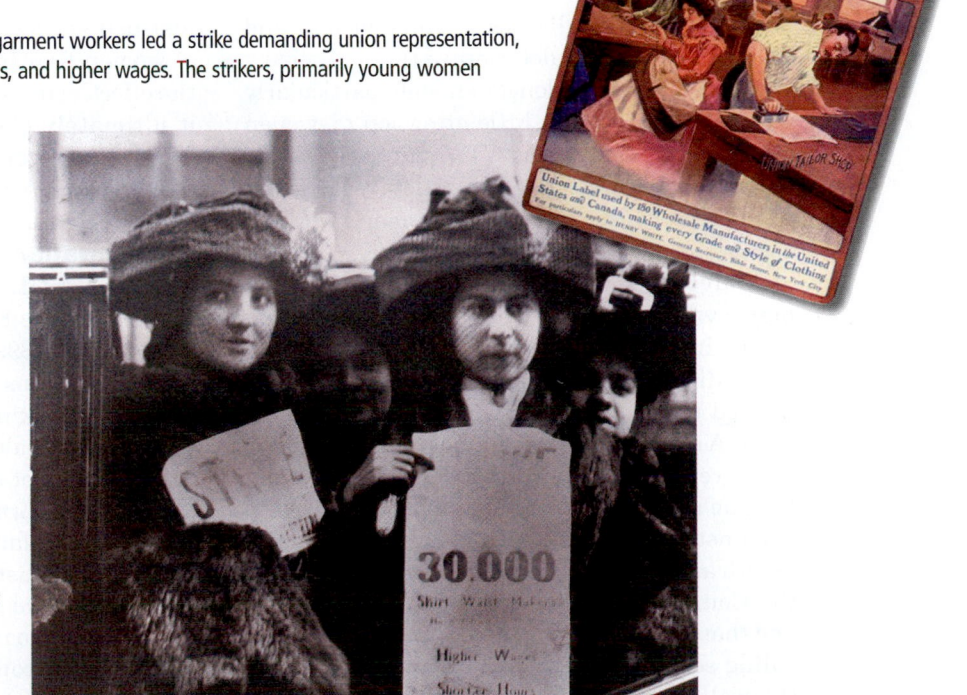

Women Strikers
Throughout the bitter winter of 1909, garment workers led a strike demanding union representation, shorter hours, better working conditions, and higher wages. The strikers, primarily young women from the Jewish and Italian immigrant communities, joined the International Ladies' Garment Workers Union and proved that women could be unionized and mount an effective strike. The Women's Trade Union League, a cross-class alliance of working women and middle-class "allies," contributed money and offered moral support to the strikers. The women pictured here claim 30,000 are on strike, but historically the strike has been called the "uprising of the 20,000." With their tailored dress and fancy hats, the workers could easily be mistaken for their middle-class WTUL "allies." The illustration on the right urges consumers to fight sweatshops by buying only garments that carry the union label.
Strikers: Brown Brothers; ad: Picture Research Consultants & Archives.

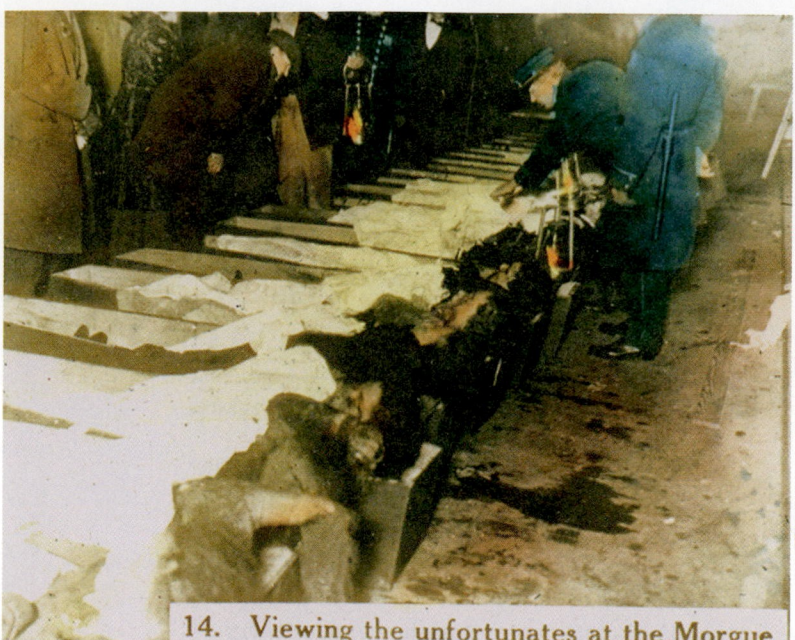

14. Viewing the unfortunates at the Morgue

Triangle Fire Morgue
After the Triangle fire on March 26, 1911, New York City set up a makeshift morgue at the end of Manhattan's Charities Pier. There, the remains of more than a hundred young women and two dozen young men were laid out in coffins for their friends and relatives to identify. Those trapped in the building were burned beyond recognition. A ring, a charred shoe, a melted hair comb often provided the only clues to the identity of a sister, a daughter, or a sweetheart. Artist John Sloan created the striking image, with its dark triangle representing the capitalist triumvirate of Rent, Profit, and Interest. A bloated businessman weeps over his lost profits while a young woman worker lies burning on the pavement and a leering skeleton poses on the left. Photo: Hadwin Collection, Kheel Center, Cornell University, Ithaca, NY; illustration: Granger Collection.

of the cross-class alliance. Schneiderman and other WTUL leaders determined that organizing and striking were no longer enough, particularly when the AFL paid so little attention to women workers. Increasingly, the WTUL turned its efforts to lobbying for protective legislation — laws that would limit hours and regulate women's working conditions.

Advocates of protective legislation won a major victory in 1908 when the U.S. Supreme Court, in *Muller v. Oregon*, reversed its previous rulings and upheld an Oregon law that limited to ten the hours women could work in a day. A mass of sociological evidence put together by Florence Kelley of the National Consumers' League and Josephine Goldmark of the WTUL demonstrated the ill effects of long hours on the health and safety of women. The data convinced the Court that long hours endangered women and therefore the entire human race. The Court's ruling set a precedent, but one that separated the well-being of women workers from that of men by arguing that women's reproductive role

justified special treatment. Later generations of women fighting for equality would question the effectiveness of this strategy and argue that it ultimately closed good jobs to women. The WTUL, however, greeted protective legislation as a first step in the attempt to ensure the safety of all workers.

The **National Consumers' League** (NCL), like the WTUL, fostered cross-class alliance. When Florence Kelley took over the leadership of the NCL in 1899, she urged middle-class women to boycott stores and exert pressure for decent wages and working conditions for women employees, primarily saleswomen. The league published a "white list" of stores that met its standards. Like the WTUL, the NCL increasingly promoted protective legislation to better working conditions for women. Frustrated by the reluctance of the private sector to respond to the need for reform, progressives turned to government at all levels. Aware that European governments had assumed a social role, providing regulation of industries and benefits to workers, American progressives wanted their own state and federal governments to help level the playing field between workers and industrialists. Critics would later charge that the progressives assumed too easily that government regulation could best solve social problems.

Reform also fueled the fight for woman suffrage. For women like Jane Addams and Florence Kelley, involvement in social reform led inevitably to support for woman suffrage. These new suffragists emphasized the reforms that could be accomplished if women had the vote. Addams insisted that in an urban, industrial society, a good housekeeper could not be sure the food she fed her family or the water and milk they drank were pure unless she became involved in politics and wielded the ballot — and not just the broom — to protect her family. The concept of **municipal housekeeping** encouraged women to put their talents to work in the service of society.

REVIEW What types of people were drawn to the progressive movement, and what motivated them?

▶ Progressivism: Theory and Practice

Progressive reformers developed a theoretical basis for their activist approach by countering social Darwinism with a dynamic new reform Darwinism. The progressives emphasized action and experimentation. Dismissing the view that humans should leave progress to the dictates of natural selection, progressive reform Darwinists argued that human intelligence could shape change and improve society. In their zeal for action, progressives often showed an unchecked admiration for speed and efficiency that promoted scientific management and a new cult of efficiency. These varied strands of progressive theory found practical application in state and local politics, where reformers challenged traditional laissez-faire government.

Reform Darwinism and Social Engineering

The active, interventionist approach of the progressives directly challenged social Darwinism, with its insistence that the world operated on the principle of survival of the fittest and that human beings stood powerless in the face of the law of natural selection. Without abandoning the evolutionary framework of Darwinism, a new group of sociologists argued that evolution could be advanced more rapidly if men and women used their intellects to alter the environment. Sociologist Lester Frank Ward put it clearly in his book *Dynamic Sociology* (1883). "I insist that the time must soon come," he wrote, "when control of blind natural forces in society must give way to human foresight." Dubbed **reform Darwinism**, the new sociological theory condemned the laissez-faire approach, insisting that the liberal state should play a more active role in solving social problems.

Efficiency and *expertise* became watchwords in the progressive vocabulary. In *Drift and Mastery* (1914), journalist and critic Walter Lippmann called for skilled "technocrats" to use scientific techniques to control social change, substituting social engineering for aimless drift. Progressive reformers' emphasis on expertise inevitably fostered a kind of elitism. Unlike the Populists, who advocated a greater voice for the masses, progressives, for all their interest in social justice, insisted that experts be put in charge.

At its extreme, the application of expertise and social engineering took the form of **scientific management**, whose mechanized routine alienated the working class. Frederick Winslow Taylor pioneered "systematized shop management." After dropping out of Harvard, Taylor went to work as a machinist at Midvale Steel in Philadelphia in the 1880s. Obsessed with making humans and machines produce more and faster, he earned a master's of engineering degree in 1885 and went back to Midvale to restructure the workplace. With a stopwatch in his hand, he meticulously timed workers and attempted to break down their work into its simplest components, one repetitious action after another, on the theory that productivity would increase if tasks could be simplified. An advocate of piecework, quotas, and pay incentives for productivity, Taylor insisted that unions were unnecessary. As a consulting engineer, he spread his gospel of efficiency and won many converts among corporate managers. Workers hated the monotony of systematized shop management and argued that it led to the speedup — pushing workers to produce more in less time and for less pay. But many progressives applauded the increased productivity and efficiency of Taylor's system.

> "I insist that the time must soon come when control of blind natural forces in society must give way to human foresight."
> — Sociologist **LESTER FRANK WARD**

Progressive Government: City and State

The politicians who became premier progressives were generally the followers, not the leaders, in a movement already well advanced at the grassroots level. Yet they left their stamp on the movement. Tom Johnson made Cleveland a model of progressive reform, Robert M. La Follette turned Wisconsin into a laboratory for progressivism, and Hiram Johnson ended the domination of the Southern Pacific Railroad in California politics.

Progressivism burst forth at every level of government in 1900, but nowhere more forcefully than in Cleveland with the election of Democrat **Thomas Loftin Johnson** as mayor. A self-made millionaire by age forty, Johnson moved to Cleveland in 1899, where he began his career in politics. During his mayoral campaign, he pledged to reduce the streetcar fare from five cents to three cents. His election touched off a seven-year war between Johnson and the streetcar moguls, who argued that they couldn't meet costs with the lower fare. To get his three-cent fare, Johnson had the city buy the streetcar system, a tactic of municipal ownership progressives called "gas and water socialism." Under Johnson's administration, Cleveland became, in the words of journalist Lincoln Steffens, the "best governed city in America." Reelected four times, Johnson fought for fair taxation and championed greater democracy through the use of the initiative, referendum, and recall — devices that allowed voters to have a direct say in legislative and judicial matters.

In Wisconsin, Republican **Robert M. La Follette** converted to the progressive cause early in the 1900s. An astute politician, La Follette capitalized on the grassroots movement for reform to launch his long political career as governor (1901–1905) and U.S. senator (1906–1925). A graduate of the University of Wisconsin, La Follette brought scientists and professors into his administration and used the university, just down the street from the statehouse in Madison, as a resource in drafting legislation.

As governor, La Follette lowered railroad rates, raised railroad taxes, improved education, preached conservation, established factory regulation and workers' compensation, instituted the first direct primary in the country, and inaugurated the first state income tax. Under his leadership, Wisconsin earned the title "laboratory of democracy." A fiery orator, "Fighting Bob" La Follette united his supporters around issues that transcended party loyalties. This emphasis on reform characterized progressivism, which attracted followers from both major parties. Democrats like Tom Johnson and Republicans like Robert La Follette could lay equal claim to the label "progressive." Democrats and Republicans alike crossed party lines to work for reform.

West of the Rockies, progressivism arrived somewhat later and found a champion in Republican **Hiram Johnson** of California, who served as governor from 1911 to 1917 and later as a U.S. senator. Since the 1870s, California

Tom Johnson
Tom Johnson, the reform mayor of Cleveland from 1901 to 1909, is shown here campaigning in Cleveland's Wade Park in 1908. For more than seven years, Mayor Johnson fought for a three-cent streetcar fare, winning the support of the working class and angering the businessmen who ran the city's streetcars. To get this low fare, Johnson finally instituted municipal ownership of the transit system. The Western Reserve Historical Society, Cleveland, OH.

politics had been dominated by the Southern Pacific Railroad, a corporation so rapacious that novelist Frank Norris styled it *The Octopus* (1901). Johnson ran for governor in 1910 on the promise to "kick the Southern Pacific out of politics." With the support of the reform wing of the Republican Party and the promise "to return the government to the people," he handily won. As governor, he introduced the direct primary; supported the initiative, referendum, and recall; strengthened the state's railroad commission; supported conservation; and signed an employer's liability law.

> **REVIEW**   How did progressives justify their demand for more activist government?

Theodore Roosevelt
Aptly described by a contemporary observer as "a steam engine in trousers," Theodore Roosevelt, at forty-two, was the youngest president ever to occupy the White House. He brought to the office energy, intellect, and activism in equal measure. Roosevelt boasted that he used the presidency as a "bully pulpit" — a forum from which he advocated reforms ranging from trust-busting to conservation.
Library of Congress.

▶ Progressivism Finds a President: Theodore Roosevelt

On September 6, 1901, President William McKinley was shot by Leon Czolgosz, an anarchist, while attending the Pan-American Exposition in Buffalo, New York. Eight days later, McKinley died. When news of his assassination reached his friend and political mentor Mark Hanna, Hanna is said to have growled, "Now that damned cowboy is president." He was speaking of Vice President Theodore Roosevelt, the colorful hero of the battle of San Juan Hill, who had indeed punched cattle in the Dakotas in the 1880s.

In the first hours of his presidency, Roosevelt reassured the shocked nation that he intended "to continue absolutely unbroken" the policies of McKinley. But Roosevelt was as different from McKinley as the twentieth century was from the nineteenth. An activist and a moralist, imbued with the progressive spirit, Roosevelt would turn the White House into a "bully pulpit," advocating conservation and antitrust reforms and championing the nation's emergence as a world power. In the process, Roosevelt would work to shift the nation's center of power from Wall Street to Washington.

After serving nearly two full terms as president, Roosevelt left office at the height of his powers. Any man would have found it difficult to follow in his footsteps, but his handpicked successor, William Howard Taft, proved hopelessly ill suited to the task. Taft's presidency was marked by a progressive stalemate, a bitter break with Roosevelt, and a schism in the Republican Party.

The Square Deal

At age forty-two, Theodore Roosevelt became the youngest man ever to move into the White House. A patrician by birth and an activist by temperament, Roosevelt brought to the job enormous talent and energy. By the time he graduated from Harvard, he was already an accomplished naturalist, an enthusiastic historian, and a naval strategist. He could have chosen from any of those promising careers; instead, he chose politics, not a bad choice for a man who relished competition and craved power.

Roosevelt was shrewd enough to realize that the path to power did not lie in the good government leagues formed by his well-bred friends. "If it is the muckers that govern," he wrote, "then I want to see if I cannot hold my own with them." So he apprenticed himself early on to the local Republican ward boss Thomas C. Platt, who held court in a grimy, smoke-filled club above a Manhattan saloon. Roosevelt's rise in politics was swift and sure. He went from the New York assembly at the age of twenty-three to the presidency in less than twenty years, with time out as a cowboy in the Dakotas, police commissioner of New York City, assistant secretary of the navy, colonel of the Rough Riders, and governor of New York. Elected governor in 1898 as a moderate reformer, Roosevelt soon clashed with Platt, who finagled to get him "kicked upstairs" as a candidate for the vice presidency in 1900. As vice president, the party bosses reasoned, Roosevelt could do little harm. But one bullet proved the error of their logic.

As president, Roosevelt would harness his explosive energy to strengthen the power of the federal government, putting business on notice that it could no longer count on a laissez-faire government to give it free rein. In Roosevelt's eyes, self-interested capitalists like John D. Rockefeller, whose Standard Oil trust monopolized the refinery business, constituted "the most dangerous members of the criminal class — the criminals of great wealth." The "absolutely vital question" facing the country, Roosevelt wrote to a friend in 1901, was "whether or not the government has the power to control the trusts." The Sherman Antitrust Act of 1890 had been badly weakened by a conservative Supreme Court and by attorneys general more willing to use it against labor unions than against monopolies. To determine whether the law had any teeth left, Roosevelt, in one of his first acts as president, ordered his attorney general to begin a secret antitrust investigation of the Northern Securities Company.

> **"Wall Street is paralyzed at the thought that a President of the United States would sink so low as to try to enforce the law."**
> — A newspaper editor

He picked a good target. Northern Securities had resulted from one of the most controversial mergers of the era. Two railroad magnates had fought a ruinous rate war that precipitated a panic on Wall Street, bankrupting thousands of small investors. To bring peace to the warring factions, financier J. P. Morgan stepped in and created the Northern Securities Company in 1901, linking three competing railroads under one management. This new behemoth monopolized railroad traffic in the Northwest. Small investors still smarting from their losses, farmers worried about freight rates, and the public in general saw in Northern Securities the symbol of corporate highhandedness.

In February 1902, just five months after Roosevelt took office, Wall Street rocked with the news that the government had filed an antitrust suit against Northern Securities. As one newspaper editor sarcastically observed, "Wall Street is paralyzed at the thought that a President of the United States would sink so low as to try to enforce the law." An indignant J. P. Morgan

demanded to know why he had not been consulted. "If we have done anything wrong," he told the attorney general, "send your man to my man and they can fix it up." Roosevelt, amused, later noted that Morgan "could not help regarding me as a big rival operator." Roosevelt's thunderbolt put Wall Street on notice that the new president expected to be treated as an equal and was willing to use government as a weapon to curb business excesses. Perhaps sensing the new mood, the Supreme Court, in a significant turnaround, upheld the Sherman Act and called for the dissolution of Northern Securities in 1904.

"Hurrah for Teddy the Trustbuster," cheered the papers. Roosevelt went on to use the Sherman Act against forty-three trusts, including such giants as American Tobacco, Du Pont, and Standard Oil. Always the moralist, he insisted on a "rule of reason." He would punish "bad" trusts (those that broke the law) and leave "good" ones alone. In practice, he preferred regulation to antitrust suits. In 1903, he pressured Congress to pass the Elkins Act, outlawing railroad rebates. And he created the new cabinet-level Department of Commerce and Labor with the subsidiary Bureau of Corporations to act as a corporate watchdog.

Observing Roosevelt in action, journalist Joseph Pulitzer remarked, "He has subjugated Wall Street." Pulitzer exaggerated, but Roosevelt had masterfully asserted the moral and political authority of the executive, underscoring, in his words, the "duty of the President to act upon the theory that he is the steward of the people." In his handling of the anthracite coal strike in 1902, Roosevelt again demonstrated his willingness to assert the authority of the presidency, this time to mediate between labor and management.

In May, 147,000 coal miners in Pennsylvania went on strike. The United Mine Workers (UMW) demanded a reduction in the workday from twelve to ten hours, an equitable system of weighing each miner's output, and a 10 percent wage increase, along with recognition of the union. When asked about the appalling conditions in the mines that led to the strike, George Baer, the mine operators' spokesman, scoffed, "The miners don't suffer, why they can't even speak English." Buttressed by social Darwinism, Baer observed that "God in his infinite wisdom" had placed "the rights and interests of the laboring man" in the hands of the capitalists, not "the labor agitators."

The strike dragged on through the summer and into the fall. Hoarding and profiteering drove the price of coal from $2.50 to $6.00 a

Breaker Boys
Child labor in America's mines and mills was common at the turn of the twentieth century, despite state laws that tried to restrict it. Here, "breaker boys," some as young as seven years old, pick over coal in a Pennsylvania mine. Their unsmiling faces bear witness to the difficulty and danger of their work. A committee investigating child labor found more than ten thousand children illegally employed in the Pennsylvania coalfields. Brown Brothers.

ton. As winter approached, coal shortages touched off near riots in the nation's big cities. At this juncture, Roosevelt stepped in to mediate, inviting representatives from both sides to meet in Washington in October. His unprecedented intervention served notice that government counted itself an independent force in business and labor disputes. At the same time, it gave unionism a boost by granting the UMW a place at the table.

At the meeting, Baer and the mine owners refused to talk with the union representative — a move that angered the attorney general and insulted the president. The meeting ended in an impasse. Beside himself with rage over the "woodenheaded obstinacy and stupidity" of management, Roosevelt threatened to seize the mines and run them with federal troops. It was a powerful bluff, one that called into question not only the supremacy of private property but also the rule of law. But the specter of federal troops being used to operate the mines quickly brought management around. In the end, the miners won a reduction in hours and a wage increase, but the owners succeeded in preventing formal recognition of the UMW.

Taken together, Roosevelt's actions in the Northern Securities case and the anthracite coal strike marked a dramatic departure from the presidential passivity of the Gilded Age. Roosevelt's actions demonstrated conclusively that government intended to act as a countervailing force to the power of the big corporations. Pleased with his role in the anthracite strike, Roosevelt announced that all he had tried to do was give labor and capital a square deal.

The phrase **Square Deal** became Roosevelt's campaign slogan in the 1904 election. But to win the presidency in his own right, Roosevelt needed to wrest control of the Republican Party from kingmaker and party boss Mark Hanna. Roosevelt adroitly used patronage to win supporters and weaken Hanna's power. Hanna died of typhoid fever in 1904, leaving Roosevelt the undisputed leader of the party.

In the presidential election of 1904, Roosevelt easily defeated the Democrats, who abandoned their former candidate, William Jennings Bryan, to support Judge Alton B. Parker, a "safe" choice they hoped would lure business votes away from Roosevelt. In the months before the election, the president prudently toned down his criticism of

The Birth of Photojournalism

Photography changed the way Americans viewed their world and strongly influenced American memory. By the 1840s, Americans had embraced photography, importing the technology of Frenchman Louis Daguerre to make portraits called daguerreotypes. During the Civil War, Mathew Brady carried his darkroom on wheels into the battlefields and took pictures that brought the bloody war into focus. By the 1890s, Americans could purchase a Kodak camera that George Eastman marketed with the slogan "You push the button, we do the rest." As the poet Oliver Wendell Holmes observed, the camera became not just "the mirror of reality" but "the mirror with a memory." How do you think photography affected American memory?

Yet for Jacob Riis, the progressive reformer who wished to document the grim horrors of tenement life, photography was useless because it required daylight or careful studio lighting. Riis, who covered the police beat for the *New York Tribune*, never thought of buying a camera. He could only crudely sketch the dim hovels, the criminal nightlife, and the windowless tenement rooms of New

Five Cents a Spot

York. Then came the breakthrough: "One morning scanning my newspaper at my breakfast table, I put it down with an outcry. . . . There it was, the thing I had been looking for all these years. . . . A way had been

big business. Wealthy Republicans like J. P. Morgan may have grumbled privately, branding Roosevelt a class traitor, but they remained loyal to the party. Roosevelt swept into office with the largest popular majority — 57.9 percent — any candidate had polled up to that time.

Roosevelt the Reformer

"Tomorrow I shall come into my office in my own right," Roosevelt is said to have remarked on the eve of his election. "Then watch out for me!" Roosevelt's stunning victory gave him a mandate for reform. He would need all the popularity and political savvy he could muster, however, to guide his reform measures through

Congress. The Senate remained controlled by a staunchly conservative Republican "old guard," with many senators on the payrolls of the corporations Roosevelt sought to curb. Roosevelt's pet project remained railroad regulation. The Elkins Act prohibiting rebates had not worked. No one could stop big shippers like Standard Oil from wringing concessions from the railroads. Roosevelt determined that the only solution lay in giving the Interstate Commerce Commission (ICC) real power to set rates and prevent discriminatory practices. But the right to determine the price of goods or services was an age-old prerogative of private enterprise, and one that business had no intention of yielding to government.

Five Cents a Spot

flash. By looking at a line drawing side by side with the corresponding photograph, we can compare the impact of the two mediums. Look at Riis's line drawing of a "Five Cents a Spot" lodgers' tenement that appeared in *How the Other Half Lives*, and compare it with the photograph on which it was based. Riis had followed a policeman who was raiding the tenement to evict the lodgers. In his book, he describes the room as "not thirteen feet either way," in which "slept twelve men and women, two or three in bunks in a sort of alcove, the rest on the floor." Note how the flash catches the sleepy faces and tired bodies, the crowding, dirt, and disorder. What details visible in the photograph are lost in the drawing? Which portrayal has a greater impact on the viewer?

Riis's pioneering photojournalism shocked the nation and led not only to tenement reform but also to the development of city playgrounds, neighborhood parks, and child labor laws. Would you agree that his photographs are "a mirror of reality," or did Riis interpret and frame the "reality" he photographed?

SOURCE: *Five Cents a Spot*, drawing and photo: Library of Congress.

discovered to take pictures by flashlight." Armed with new magnesium cartridge flash pistols, Riis set out to shine light in the dark corners of New York. "Our party carried terror wherever it went," Riis recalled. "The spectacle of strange men invading a house in the midnight hours armed with [flash] pistols which they shot off recklessly was hardly reassuring." But the results were a huge step forward for photojournalism.

Riis's book *How the Other Half Lives* (1890) made photographic history. Along with Riis's text and engravings of his drawings, it contained reproductions of seventeen photographs taken with his camera and

To ensure passage of the **Hepburn Act**, which would increase the power of the ICC, Roosevelt worked skillfully behind the scenes. In its final form, the Hepburn Act, passed in May 1906, gave the ICC the power to set rates subject to court review. Committed progressives like La Follette judged the law a defeat for reform. Die-hard conservatives branded it a "piece of populism." Both sides exaggerated. The law left the courts too much power and failed to provide adequate means for the ICC to determine rates, but its passage proved a landmark in federal control of private industry. For the first time, a government commission had the power to investigate private business records and to set rates.

Always an apt reader of the public temper, Roosevelt witnessed a growing appetite for reform. Revelations of corporate and political wrongdoing and social injustice filled the papers and boosted the sales of popular magazines. Roosevelt, who wielded publicity like a weapon in his pursuit of reform, counted many of the new investigative journalists, including Jacob Riis, among his friends. (See "Visualizing History," above.) But he warned them against going too far, citing the allegorical character in *Pilgrim's Progress* who was so busy raking muck that he took no notice of higher things. Roosevelt's criticism gave the American vocabulary a new word, *muckraker*, which journalists soon appropriated as a title of honor.

Muckraking, as Roosevelt well knew, provided enormous help in securing progressive legislation. In the spring of 1906, publicity generated by the muckrakers about poisons in patent medicines goaded the Senate, with Roosevelt's backing, into passing a pure food and drug bill. Opponents in the House of Representatives hoped to keep the legislation locked up in committee. There it would have died, were it not for the publication of Upton Sinclair's novel *The Jungle* (1906), with its sensational account of filthy conditions in meatpacking plants.

The Jungle

Upton Sinclair, a lifelong socialist, wrote *The Jungle* to expose the evils of capitalism. But readers were more horrified by his descriptions of the unsanitary conditions in the meatpacking industry, where the novel's hapless hero sees rats, filth, and diseased animals processed into meat products. After reading the book, President Theodore Roosevelt could no longer stomach sausage for breakfast. The president immediately ordered a study of conditions in the meatpacking industry. The public outcry surrounding *The Jungle* contributed to the enactment of pure food and drug legislation and a federal meat inspection law. Sinclair ruefully remarked, "I aimed at the public's heart, but I hit them in the stomach." Picture Research Consultants, Inc.

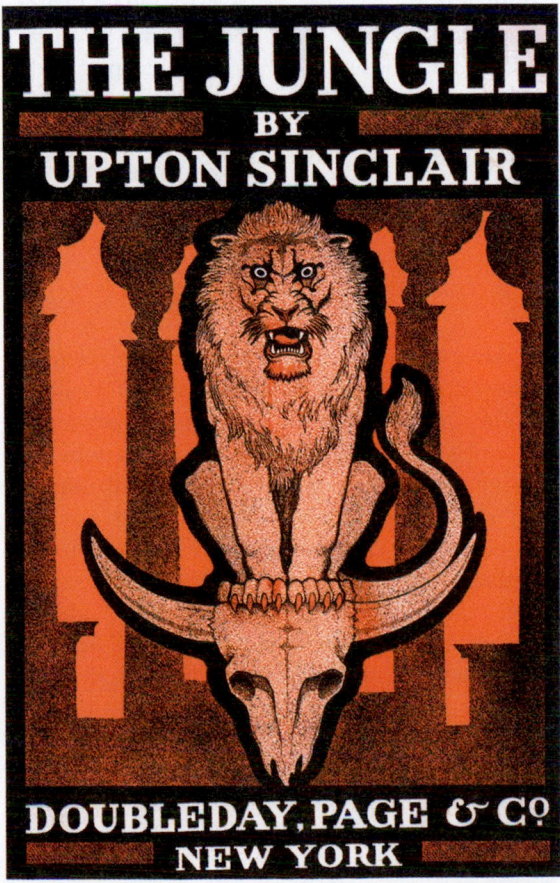

A massive public outcry led to the passage of the **Pure Food and Drug Act** and the Meat Inspection Act in 1906.

In the waning years of his administration, Roosevelt allied with the more progressive elements of the Republican Party. In speech after speech, he attacked "malefactors of great wealth." Styling himself a "radical," he claimed credit for leading the "ultra conservative" party of McKinley to a position of "progressive conservatism and conservative radicalism."

When an economic panic developed in the fall of 1907, business interests quickly blamed the president. The panic of 1907 proved severe but short. Once again, J. P. Morgan stepped in to avert disaster, this time switching funds from one bank to another to prop up weak institutions. For his services, he claimed the Tennessee Coal and Iron Company, an independent steel business that had long been coveted by the U.S. Steel Corporation. Morgan dispatched his lieutenants to Washington, where they told Roosevelt that the sale of the company would aid the economy "but little benefit" U.S. Steel. Willing to take the word of a gentleman, Roosevelt tacitly agreed not to institute antitrust proceedings against U.S. Steel over the acquisition. Roosevelt later learned that Morgan had been less than candid. U.S. Steel acquired Tennessee Coal and Iron for a price well below market value, doing away with a competitor and undercutting the economy of the Southeast. Roosevelt's promise not to institute antitrust proceedings against U.S. Steel would give rise to the charge that he acted as a tool of the Morgan interests.

The charge of collusion between business and government underscored the extent to which corporate leaders like Morgan found federal regulation preferable to unbridled competition or harsher state measures. During the Progressive Era, enlightened business leaders cooperated with government in the hope of avoiding antitrust prosecution. Convinced that regulation and not trust-busting offered the best way to deal with big business, Roosevelt never acknowledged that his regulatory policies fostered an alliance between business and government that today is called corporate liberalism.

Roosevelt and Conservation

In the area of conservation, Roosevelt proved indisputably ahead of his time. When he took office, some 43 million acres of forestland remained as government reserves. He more than quadrupled that number to 194 million acres. To conserve natural resources, he fought western

cattle barons, lumber kings, mining interests, and powerful leaders in Congress, including Speaker of the House Joseph Cannon, who vowed to spend "not one cent for scenery."

As the first president to have lived and worked in the West, Roosevelt came to the White House convinced of the need for better management of the nation's rivers and forests and the preservation of wildlife and wilderness. During his presidency, he placed the nation's conservation policy in the hands of scientifically trained experts like his chief forester, Gifford Pinchot. Pinchot preached conservation — the efficient use of natural resources. Willing to permit grazing, lumbering, and the development of hydroelectric power, conservationists fought private interests only when they felt business acted irresponsibly or threatened to monopolize water and electric power. Preservationists like John Muir, founder of the Sierra Club, believed that the wilderness needed to be protected. Roosevelt, who hiked Yosemite with Muir, understood the need for both preservation and conservation. (See "Historical Question," page 692.)

Roosevelt's multifaceted personality encompassed many contradictions. A fervent Darwinian naturalist and an (overly) enthusiastic game hunter, a conservationist who built big dams and a preservationist who saved the redwoods, Roosevelt aimed to have it both ways. And he did.

One of Roosevelt's first acts as president was to establish a pelican refuge in Florida. An avid bird-watcher since his youth, he added 50 more bird reservations from Florida to Alaska

MAP ACTIVITY

Map 21.1 National Parks and Forests

The national park system in the West began with Yellowstone in 1872. Grand Canyon, Yosemite, Kings Canyon, and Sequoia followed in the 1890s. During his presidency, Theodore Roosevelt added six parks — Crater Lake, Wind Cave, Petrified Forest, Lassen Volcanic, Mesa Verde, and Zion.

READING THE MAP: Collectively, do national parks or national forests encompass more land? According to the map, how many national parks were created before 1910? How many were created after 1910?

CONNECTIONS: How do conservation and preservation differ? Why did Roosevelt believe that saving land in the West was important? What principles guided the national land use policy of the Roosevelt administration?

Progressives and Conservation: Should Hetch Hetchy Be Dammed or Saved?

In 1890, President Benjamin Harrison signed into law an act setting aside two million acres in California's Yosemite Valley and designating Yosemite a national park. For naturalist John Muir, the founder of the Sierra Club, the act marked a victory in his crusade to guarantee that "incomparable Yosemite" would be preserved for posterity. But Muir's fight was not yet over.

The growing city of San Francisco needed water and power, and Mayor James Phelan soon sought to obtain water rights in Hetch Hetchy, a spectacular mountain valley within Yosemite's borders. There, the Tuolumne River could easily be dammed and the valley flooded to create a reservoir large enough to ensure the city's water supply for one hundred years.

When Muir heard of the plan, he sprang into action to save Hetch Hetchy. "That any one would try to destroy such a place seems incredible," he wrote, describing the valley as "one of Nature's rarest and most precious mountain temples." All of Yosemite National Park, he argued, should remain sacrosanct. In 1903, the secretary of the interior concurred, denying San Francisco

supervisors commercial use of Hetch Hetchy on the grounds that it lay within the national park.

But the San Francisco earthquake and resulting fire in 1906 created a groundswell of sympathy for the devastated city. In this climate, San Francisco renewed its efforts to obtain Hetch Hetchy and in 1907 succeeded in gaining authorization to proceed with plans to dam the river and flood the valley.

Given President Theodore Roosevelt's commitment to conservation, how could his administration have agreed to the destruction of the Hetch Hetchy valley? Historians traditionally have styled the struggle as one that pitted conservationists against preservationists. Roosevelt's chief forester, Gifford Pinchot, represented the forces of conservation, or managed use. To him, the battle was not over preservation but over public versus private control of water and power. Roosevelt somewhat reluctantly agreed, although he softened the blow by designating a redwood sanctuary north of San Francisco a national monument in 1907 and naming it Muir Woods.

California progressives, who swept into office with the election of

Hiram Johnson as governor in 1910, argued that if Congress did not grant the city of San Francisco the right to control Hetch Hetchy, the powerful Pacific Gas and Electric Company (PG&E) would monopolize the city's light and power industry. These progressives dismissed Muir and his followers as "nature fakers" and judged them little more than dupes in the machinations of PG&E.

For their part, Muir and the preservationists, although they fought for the integrity of the national parks, did not champion the preservation of wilderness for its own sake. The urban professional men and women who joined the Sierra Club saw nature as a retreat and restorative for city dwellers. The club hosted an annual camping trip to popularize Yosemite and spoke in glowing terms of plans to build new roads and hotels that would make the "healing power of Nature" accessible to "thousands of tired, nerve-shaken, over-civilized people." As historian Robert Righter has pointed out, the battle over Hetch Hetchy represented not so much conservation versus preservation, or managed use versus wilderness, as it did the victory of water and power over tourism and recreation.

Nevertheless, the engineers and irrigation men who dammed Hetch Hetchy demonstrated a breathtaking arrogance. Speaking for them, Franklin Lane, interior secretary under Woodrow Wilson, proclaimed, "The mountains are our enemy. We must pierce them and make them serve. The sinful rivers we must curb." Lane and the conservationists won the day. In 1913, Congress passed the Raker Act authorizing the building of the O'Shaughnessy Dam, completed a decade later. To build the dam, the

during his presidency. The passage of the Antiquities Act in 1906 gave the president unchecked power to protect archaeological, scientific, and environmentally significant federal lands instead of "dilly dallying" with a "tortoise-paced Congress." Roosevelt wielded his power

with relish, creating 18 national monuments, 6 national parks, and 150 national forests. He prided himself on saving the Grand Canyon from miners and developers. At the same time, he supported the Newlands Reclamation Act (1902), much criticized by today's ecologists, as

Hetch Hetchy valley was first denuded of its trees and then flooded under two hundred feet of water. Muir did not live to see the destruction of Hetch Hetchy. He died in 1914, cursing the "dark damn-dam-damnation." But his fight to save Hetch Hetchy galvanized the preservation movement and led to the passage of the National Park Service Act in 1916 creating a federal agency to protect the nation's parks.

The last chapter in the battle over Hetch Hetchy may yet be written. In 1987, President Ronald Reagan's secretary of the interior, Donald Hodel, shocked San Francisco by suggesting the removal of the O'Shaughnessy Dam and the restoration of the Hetch Hetchy valley. Although it is unlikely that the dam will be demolished (it supplies San Francisco not only with water but also with revenue from electric power), advocates for the restoration of the Hetch Hetchy valley continue to rally to the cause. As Ken Browner of the Sierra Club wrote, "Waiting in Yosemite National Park, under water, is a potential masterpiece of restoration" and a chance "to correct the biggest environmental mistake ever committed against the National Park System."

Thinking about Beliefs and Attitudes

1. What does the damming of Hetch Hetchy tell us about the Roosevelt administration's conservation policies in the West?

2. Given Roosevelt's conservation policies overall, are critics right in accusing him of failing to preserve the wilderness?

Roosevelt and Muir in Yosemite

This 1903 photograph shows President Theodore Roosevelt on a camping trip in Yosemite National Park with John Muir. Roosevelt and Muir later clashed over the flooding of the Hetch Hetchy valley in Yosemite. Roosevelt and his chief forester, Gifford Pinchot, favored giving San Francisco the right to dam the valley to supply water and power. Muir bitterly noted that Pinchot had never bothered to visit the valley he condemned to a watery grave. Theodore Roosevelt Collection, Harvard College Library.

a measure to irrigate the West by building large dams and reservoirs in the "conquest" of the desert ecosystem and the promotion of population growth.

In 1907, Congress attempted to put the brakes on Roosevelt's conservation program by passing a law limiting his power to create forest reserves in six western states. In the days leading up to the law's enactment, Roosevelt feverishly created twenty-one new reserves and enlarged eleven more, saving 16 million acres from development. Once again, Roosevelt had outwitted his adversaries.

"Opponents of the forest service turned hand-springs in their wrath," he wrote, "but the threats . . . were really only a tribute to the efficiency of our action." Worried that private utilities were gobbling up waterpower sites and creating a monopoly of hydroelectric power, he connived with Pinchot to withdraw 2,565 power sites from private use by designating them "ranger stations." Firm in his commitment to wild America, Roosevelt proved willing to stretch the law when it served his ends. His legacy is more than 234 million acres of American wilderness saved for posterity (Map 21.1).

The Big Stick

Roosevelt's activism extended to his foreign policy, where he worked to buttress the nation's newly won place among world leaders. A fierce proponent of America's interests abroad, he believed that Congress was inept in foreign affairs, and he relied on executive power to pursue a vigorous foreign policy, sometimes stretching the powers of the presidency beyond legal limits. In his relations with the European powers, he relied on military strength and diplomacy, a combination he aptly described with the aphorism "Speak softly but carry a big stick." In the Caribbean, Roosevelt jealously guarded the U.S. sphere of influence defined in the Monroe Doctrine. His proprietary attitude toward the Western Hemisphere became evident in the case of the Panama Canal. Roosevelt had long been a supporter of a canal linking the Caribbean and the Pacific. By enabling ships to move quickly from the Atlantic to the Pacific, a canal would trim 8,000 miles from a coast-to-coast voyage and effectively double the U.S. Navy's power.

VISUAL ACTIVITY

"The World's Constable"
In this political cartoon from 1905, President Theodore Roosevelt, dressed as a constable, wields the club of "The New Diplomacy" in one hand with "Arbitration" tucked under his arm. The Roosevelt Corollary to the Monroe Doctrine made the United States the Western Hemisphere's policeman, a role Roosevelt relished. The Granger Collection, NYC.

READING THE IMAGE: How does this political cartoon visually represent Roosevelt's foreign policy? Does it appear to be supportive or critical of his policies? How does it treat the other peoples of the world?
CONNECTIONS: What aspects of Roosevelt's foreign policy ideas and actions are depicted in the cartoon?

THE WORLD'S CONSTABLE.

Having decided on a route across the Panamanian isthmus (a narrow strip of land connecting North and South America), then part of Colombia, Roosevelt in 1902 offered the Colombian government a one-time sum of $10 million and an annual rent of $250,000. When the government in Bogotá refused to accept the offer, Roosevelt became incensed at what he called the "homicidal corruptionists" in Colombia for trying to "blackmail" the United States. At the prompting of a group of New York investors, the Panamanians staged an uprising in 1903, and with unseemly haste the U.S. government recognized the new government within twenty-four hours. The Panamanians promptly accepted the $10 million, and the building got under way. The canal would take eleven years and $375 million to complete; it opened in 1914 (Map 21.2).

In the wake of the Panama affair, a confrontation with Germany over Venezuela, and yet another default on a European debt, this time in the Dominican Republic, Roosevelt announced in 1904 what became known as the **Roosevelt Corollary** to the Monroe Doctrine. Couched in the moralistic rhetoric typical of Roosevelt, the corollary declared that the United States would not intervene in Latin America as long as nations there conducted their affairs with "decency." But the United States would step in if any Latin American nation proved guilty of "brutal wrongdoing." The Roosevelt Corollary in effect made the United States the policeman of the Western Hemisphere and served notice to the European powers to keep out.

In Asia, Roosevelt inherited the Open Door policy initiated by Secretary of State John Hay in 1899, designed to ensure U.S. commercial entry into China. As Britain, France, Russia, Japan, and Germany raced to secure Chinese trade and territory, Roosevelt was tempted to use force to enter the fray and gain economic or possibly territorial concessions. As a result of victory in the Spanish-American War, the United States already enjoyed a foothold in the Philippines. Realizing that Americans would not support an aggressive Asian policy, Roosevelt sensibly held back.

In his relations with Europe, Roosevelt sought to establish the United States, fresh from its victory over Spain, as a rising force in world affairs. When tensions flared between France and Germany in Morocco in 1905, Roosevelt mediated at a conference in Algeciras, Spain, where he worked to maintain a balance of power that helped neutralize German ambitions. His skillful mediation gained him a reputation as an astute player on the world stage and demonstrated the nation's new presence in world affairs.

The Roosevelt Corollary in Action

MAP ACTIVITY

Map 21.2   The Panama Canal, 1914
The Panama Canal, completed in 1914, bisects the isthmus in a series of massive locks and dams. As Theodore Roosevelt had planned, the canal greatly strengthened the U.S. Navy by allowing ships to move from the Atlantic to the Pacific in a matter of days.

READING THE MAP: How long was the trip from New York to San Francisco before the Panama Canal was built? After it was built?

CONNECTIONS: How did Roosevelt's desire for a canal lead to independence for Panama? How did the canal benefit the U.S. Navy?

Roosevelt earned the Nobel Peace Prize in 1906 for his role in negotiating an end to the Russo-Japanese War, which had broken out when the Japanese invaded Chinese Manchuria, threatening Russia's sphere of influence in the area. Once again, Roosevelt sought to maintain a balance of power, in this case working to curb Japanese expansionism. Roosevelt admired the Japanese, judging them "the most dashing fighters in the world," but he did not want Japan to become too strong in Asia.

When good relations with Japan were jeopardized by discriminatory legislation in California calling for segregated public schools for Asians, Roosevelt smoothed over the incident and negotiated the "Gentlemen's Agreement" in 1907, which allowed the Japanese to save face by voluntarily restricting immigration to the United States. To demonstrate America's naval power and to counter Japan's growing bellicosity, Roosevelt dispatched the Great White Fleet, sixteen of the navy's most up-to-date battleships, on a "goodwill mission" around the world. U.S. relations with Japan improved, and in the 1908 Root-Takahira agreement the two nations pledged to maintain the Open Door and support the status quo in the Pacific. Roosevelt's show of American force constituted a classic example of his dictum "Speak softly but carry a big stick."

The Troubled Presidency of William Howard Taft

Roosevelt had promised on the eve of his election in 1904 that he would not seek another term. So he retired from the presidency in 1909 at age fifty and removed himself from the political scene by going on safari in Africa. He turned the White House over to **William Howard Taft**, a lawyer who had served as governor-general of the Philippines. In the presidential election of 1908, Taft soundly defeated the perennial Democratic candidate, William Jennings Bryan, in the electoral college. But Taft's popular majority amounted to only half of Roosevelt's record win in 1904.

A genial man with a talent for law, Taft had no experience in elective office, no feel for politics, and no nerve for controversy. His ambitious wife coveted the office and urged him to seek it. He would have been better off listening to his mother, who warned, "Roosevelt is a good fighter and enjoys it, but the malice of politics would make you miserable." Her words proved prophetic.

Once in office, Taft proved a perfect tool in the hands of Republicans who yearned for a return to the days of a less active executive. A lawyer by training and instinct, Taft believed that it was up to the courts, not the president, to arbitrate social issues. Roosevelt had carried presidential power to a new level, often flouting the separation of powers and showing thinly veiled contempt for Congress and the courts. A legalist, Taft found it difficult to condone Roosevelt's actions. Wary of the progressive insurgents in Congress, Taft relied increasingly on conservatives in the Republican Party. As a progressive senator lamented, "Taft is a ponderous and amiable man completely surrounded by men who know exactly what they want."

Taft's troubles began on the eve of his inaugural, when he called a special session of Congress to deal with the tariff, which had grown inordinately high under Republican rule. Roosevelt had been too politically astute to tackle the troublesome tariff issue, even though he knew that rates needed to be lowered. Taft blundered into the fray. The House of Representatives passed a modest downward revision, but the conservative Senate struck down the tax and added more than eight hundred crippling amendments to the tariff. The Payne-Aldrich bill that emerged actually raised the tariff, benefiting big business and the trusts at the expense of consumers. As if paralyzed, Taft neither fought for changes nor vetoed the measure. On a tour of the Midwest in 1909, he was greeted with jeers when he claimed, "I think the Payne bill is the best bill that the Republican Party ever passed." In the eyes of a growing number of Americans, Taft's praise of the tariff made him either a fool or a liar.

Taft's legalism soon got him into hot water in the area of conservation. He undid Roosevelt's work to preserve hydroelectric power sites when he learned that they had been improperly designated as ranger stations. And when Gifford Pinchot publicly denounced Taft's secretary of the interior as a tool of western land-grabbers, Taft fired Pinchot, touching off a storm of controversy that damaged Taft and alienated Roosevelt.

When Roosevelt returned to the United States in June 1910, he received a hero's welcome and attracted a stream of visitors and reporters seeking his advice and opinions. Hurt, Taft kept his distance. By late summer, Roosevelt had taken sides with the progressive insurgents in his party. "Taft is utterly hopeless as a leader," Roosevelt confided to his son as he set out on a speaking tour of the West. Reading the mood of the country, Roosevelt began to sound more and more like a candidate.

With the Republican Party divided, the Democrats swept the congressional elections of

William Howard Taft

William Howard Taft had little aptitude for politics. When Theodore Roosevelt tapped him as his successor in 1908, Taft had never held an elected office. A legalist by training and temperament, Taft moved congenially in the conservative circles of the Republican Party. His actions dismayed progressives and eventually led Roosevelt to challenge him for the presidency in 1912. The break with Roosevelt saddened and embittered Taft. One symptom of his unhappiness was his weight. Already a hefty 320 pounds when he was elected, Taft ballooned to more than 355 pounds by the time he left office. Library of Congress.

amendments — the Sixteenth Amendment, which provided for a modest graduated income tax, and the Seventeenth Amendment, which called for the direct election of senators (formerly chosen by state legislatures) — went to the states, where they would win ratification in 1913. While Congress rode the high tide of progressive reform, Taft sat on the sidelines.

In foreign policy, Taft continued Roosevelt's policy of extending U.S. influence abroad, but here, too, Taft had a difficult time following in Roosevelt's footsteps. His policy of **dollar diplomacy** championed commercial goals rather than the strategic aims Roosevelt had pursued. Taft naively assumed he could substitute "dollars for bullets." In the Caribbean, he provoked anti-American feeling by attempting to force commercial treaties on Nicaragua and Honduras and by dispatching U.S. Marines to Nicaragua and the Dominican Republic in 1912 pursuant to the Roosevelt Corollary. In Asia, he openly avowed his intent to promote "active intervention to secure for . . . our capitalists opportunity for profitable investment." Lacking Roosevelt's understanding of power politics, Taft never recognized that an aggressive commercial policy could not exist without the willingness to use military might to back it up.

Taft faced the limits of dollar diplomacy when revolution broke out in Mexico in 1911. Under pressure to protect American investments, which amounted to more than $4 billion, he mobilized troops along the border. In the end, however, with no popular support for a war with Mexico, he had to fall back on diplomatic pressure to salvage American interests.

Taft hoped to encourage world peace through the use of a world court and arbitration. He unsuccessfully sponsored a series of arbitration treaties that Roosevelt, who prized national honor more than international law, vehemently opposed as weak and cowardly. By 1910, Roosevelt had become a vocal critic of Taft's foreign policy, which he dismissed as "maudlin folly." The final breach between Taft and Roosevelt came in 1911, when Taft's attorney general filed an antitrust suit against U.S. Steel. In its brief against the corporation, the government cited Roosevelt's agreement with the Morgan interests in the 1907 acquisition

1910. Branding the Payne-Aldrich tariff "the mother of trusts," they captured a majority in the House of Representatives and won several key governorships. The revitalized Democratic Party could look to new leaders, among them the progressive governor of New Jersey, Woodrow Wilson.

The new Democratic majority in the House, working with progressive Republicans in the Senate, achieved a number of key reforms, including legislation to regulate mine and railroad safety, to create the Children's Bureau in the Department of Labor, and to establish an eight-hour day for federal workers. Two significant constitutional

Taft's "Dollar Diplomacy"

of Tennessee Coal and Iron. The incident greatly embarrassed Roosevelt. Thoroughly enraged, he lambasted Taft's "archaic" antitrust policy and hinted that he might be persuaded to run for president again.

> **REVIEW**   In what ways did Roosevelt's domestic policies respond to progressive demands?

▶ Woodrow Wilson and Progressivism at High Tide

Progressives' disillusionment with Taft resulted in a split in the Republican Party and the creation of a new Progressive Party led by Theodore Roosevelt. In the election of 1912, four candidates, including Socialist Eugene V. Debs, styled themselves "progressives." Democrat **Woodrow Wilson**, with a minority of the popular vote, won the election. Born in Virginia and raised in Georgia, he became the first southerner to be elected president since 1844 and only the second Democrat to occupy the White House since Reconstruction. A believer in states' rights, Wilson nevertheless promised legislation to break the hold of the trusts.

> **"We shall not falter, we stand at Armageddon and do battle for the Lord."**
> — THEODORE ROOSEVELT, speaking at the Bull Moose Party convention

This lean, ascetic scholar was, as one biographer conceded, a man whose "political convictions were never as fixed as his ambition." Although he owed his governorship to the Democratic machine, he quickly turned his back on the bosses and, with his eye on the presidency, put New Jersey in the vanguard of progressivism. He brought to the White House a gift for oratory, a stern will, and a set of fixed beliefs. Wilson proved rarely able to compromise. His tendency to turn differences of opinion into personal hatreds would impair his leadership and damage his presidency. Fortunately for Wilson, he came to power with a Democratic Congress eager to do his bidding.

Progressive Insurgency and the Election of 1912

Convinced that Taft was "hopelessly inept," Roosevelt announced his candidacy for the Republican nomination with the colorful phrase "My hat is in the ring." But for all his popularity, Roosevelt no longer controlled the party machinery. Taft, with uncharacteristic strength, refused to step aside. As he bitterly told a journalist, "Even a rat in a corner will fight." Roosevelt took advantage of newly passed primary election laws and ran in thirteen states, winning 278 delegates to Taft's 48. But at the Chicago convention, Taft's bosses refused to seat the Roosevelt delegates. Fistfights broke out on the convention floor as Taft won nomination on the first ballot. Crying robbery, Roosevelt's supporters bolted the party.

Seven weeks later, in the same Chicago auditorium, the hastily organized Progressive Party met to nominate Roosevelt. Amid a thunder of applause, Jane Addams seconded Roosevelt's nomination. Full of reforming zeal, the delegates chose Roosevelt and Hiram Johnson to head the new party and approved the most ambitious platform since that of the Populists. Planks called for woman suffrage, presidential primaries, conservation of natural resources, an end to child labor, workers' compensation, a minimum wage that would include women workers, social security, and a federal income tax.

Roosevelt arrived in Chicago to accept the nomination and announced that he felt "as fit as a bull moose," giving the new party a nickname and a mascot. But for all the excitement and the cheering, the new Progressive Party was doomed, and the candidate knew it. The people may have supported the party, but the politicians, even progressives such as La Follette, stayed within the Republican fold. "I am under no illusion about it," Roosevelt confessed to a friend. "It is a forlorn hope." But he had gone too far to turn back. He led the Bull Moose Party into the fray, exhorting his followers in ringing biblical tones, "We shall not falter, we stand at Armageddon and do battle for the Lord."

The Democrats, delighted at the split in the Republican ranks, smelled victory. Their convention turned into a bitter fight for the nomination. After forty-six ballots, Woodrow Wilson became the party's nominee. Wilson's career in politics was nothing short of meteoric. He was elected governor of New Jersey in 1910, and after only eighteen months in office the former professor of political science and president of Princeton University found himself running for president of the United States.

Voters in 1912 could choose among four candidates who claimed to be progressives. Taft, Roosevelt, and Wilson each embraced the label, and even the Socialist candidate, Eugene V. Debs, styled himself a progressive. That the term *progressive* could stretch to cover these diverse candidates underscored major disagreements in

1912 Election Cartoon
In this 1912 political cartoon, an elephant — the mascot of the Republican Party (the Grand Old Party, or GOP) — and a donkey — representing the Democratic Party — react in alarm as a bull moose charges into the fray. The bull moose, with its spectacles and gleaming teeth, caricatures Theodore Roosevelt, the new Progressive Party's presidential candidate. Granger Collection.

progressive thinking about the relationship between business and government. Taft, in spite of his trust-busting, was generally viewed as the candidate of the old guard. The real contest for the presidency was between Roosevelt and Wilson and the two political philosophies summed up in their respective campaign slogans: "**The New Nationalism**" and "**The New Freedom**."

The New Nationalism expressed Roosevelt's belief in federal planning and regulation. He accepted the inevitability of big business but demanded that government act as "a steward of the people" to regulate the giant corporations. Wilson, schooled in the Democratic principles of limited government and states' rights, set a markedly different course with his New Freedom. Wilson promised to use antitrust legislation to get rid of big corporations and to give small businesses and farmers better opportunities in the marketplace.

The energy and enthusiasm of the Bull Moosers made the race seem closer than it was. In the end, the Republican vote split, while the Democrats remained united. No candidate claimed a majority in the race. Wilson captured a bare 42 percent of the popular vote. Roosevelt and his Bull Moose Party won 27 percent, an unprecedented tally for a new party. Taft came in third with 23 percent. The Socialist Party, led by Debs, captured 6 percent. In the electoral college, however, Wilson won a decisive 435 votes, with 88 going to Roosevelt and only 8 to Taft (Map 21.3). The Republican Party moved in a conservative direction, while the Progressive Party essentially collapsed after Roosevelt's defeat. It had always been, in the

words of one astute observer, "a house divided against itself and already mortgaged."

Wilson's Reforms: Tariff, Banking, and the Trusts

Although he endorsed states' rights and opposed big government in his campaign, Wilson was prepared to work on the base built by Roosevelt to strengthen presidential power, exerting leadership to achieve banking reform and working through his party in Congress to accomplish the

MAP 21.3
The Election of 1912

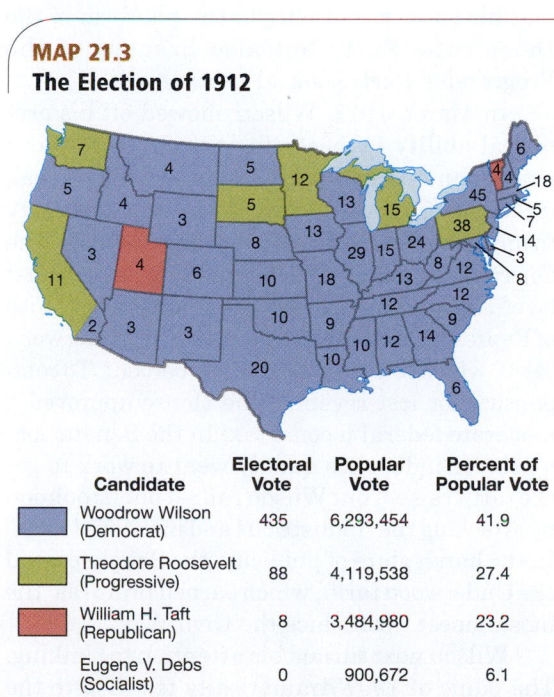

Candidate	Electoral Vote	Popular Vote	Percent of Popular Vote
Woodrow Wilson (Democrat)	435	6,293,454	41.9
Theodore Roosevelt (Progressive)	88	4,119,538	27.4
William H. Taft (Republican)	8	3,484,980	23.2
Eugene V. Debs (Socialist)	0	900,672	6.1

Wilson Ribbon

With the Republicans divided in 1912, the Democrats turned to Woodrow Wilson to lead the party, nominating him on the forty-sixth ballot. In those days, prospective candidates generally did not attend the nominating convention. The ribbon in the photograph belonged to a member of the Democratic National Committee, who traveled to Wilson's summer home in Sea Girt, New Jersey, on August 7, 1912, to inform Wilson officially of his nomination. Democrats hoping for a wild celebration at Wilson's inauguration had their hopes dashed when Wilson, a Presbyterian teetotaler, called instead for a day of prayer. Collection of Janice L. and David J. Frent.

failure of the banking system. That year, Roosevelt, like President Grover Cleveland before him, had to turn to J. P. Morgan to avoid economic catastrophe. But by the time Wilson came to office, Morgan's legendary power had come under close scrutiny. In 1913, a Senate committee investigated the "money trust," calling J. P. Morgan himself to testify. The committee uncovered an alarming concentration of banking power. J. P. Morgan and Company and its affiliates held 341 directorships in 112 corporations, controlling assets of more than $22 billion ($500 billion in today's dollars). The sensational findings created a mandate for banking reform.

The **Federal Reserve Act** of 1913 marked the most significant piece of domestic legislation of Wilson's presidency. It established a national banking system composed of twelve regional banks, privately controlled but regulated and supervised by the Federal Reserve Board, appointed by the president. It gave the United States its first efficient banking and currency system and, at the same time, provided for a greater degree of government control over banking. The new system made currency more elastic and credit adequate for the needs of business and agriculture. It did not, however, attempt to take control of the boom and bust cycles in the U.S. economy, which would produce the Great Depression of the 1930s (as discussed in chapters 23 and 24).

Wilson, flush with success, tackled the trust issue next. When Congress reconvened in January 1914, he supported the introduction and passage of the Clayton Antitrust Act to outlaw "unfair competition" — practices such as price discrimination and interlocking directorates (directors from one corporation sitting on the board of another). By spelling out unfair practices, Wilson hoped to guide business activity back to healthy competition without resorting to regulation. In the midst of the successful fight for the Clayton Act, Wilson changed course and threw his support behind the creation of the **Federal Trade Commission** (FTC), precisely the kind of federal regulatory agency that Roosevelt had advocated in his New Nationalism platform. The FTC, created in 1914, had not only wide investigatory powers but also the authority to prosecute corporations for "unfair trade practices" and to enforce its judgments by issuing "cease and desist" orders. Despite his campaign promises, Wilson's antitrust program worked to regulate rather than to break up big business.

By the fall of 1914, Wilson had exhausted the stock of ideas that made up the New Freedom. He alarmed progressives by declaring that the progressive movement had fulfilled its mission

Democratic agenda. Before he was finished, Wilson presided over progressivism at high tide and lent his support not only to the platform of the Democratic Party but also to many of the Progressive Party's social reforms.

In March 1913, Wilson showed off his oratorical ability by becoming the first president since John Adams to go to Capitol Hill and speak directly to Congress. With the Democratic Party firmly in control, he called for tariff reform. "The object of the tariff," Wilson told Congress, "must be effective competition." The Democratic House of Representatives hastily passed the Underwood tariff, which lowered rates by 15 percent. To compensate for lost revenue, the House approved a moderate federal income tax. In the Senate, lobbyists for industries quietly went to work to get the tariff raised, but Wilson rallied public opinion by attacking the "industrious and insidious lobby." In the harsh glare of publicity, the Senate passed the Underwood tariff, which earned praise as "the most honest tariff since the Civil War."

Wilson next turned his attention to banking. The panic of 1907 dramatically testified to the and that the country needed "a time of healing." Disgruntled progressives also disapproved of Wilson's conservative appointments. Having fought provisions in the Federal Reserve Act that would give bankers control, Wilson promptly named a banker as the first chief of the Federal Reserve Board. Appointments to the new FTC also went to conservative businessmen. The progressive penchant for expertise helps explain Wilson's choices. Believing that experts in the field could best understand the complex issues at stake, Wilson appointed bankers to oversee the banks and businessmen to regulate business.

Wilson, Reluctant Progressive

As Wilson repeatedly obstructed or obstinately refused to endorse further progressive reforms, progressives watched in dismay. He failed to support labor's demand for an end to court injunctions against labor unions. He twice threatened to veto legislation providing farm credits for nonperishable crops. He refused to support child labor legislation or woman suffrage. Wilson used the rhetoric of the New Freedom to justify his actions, claiming that his administration would condone "special privileges to none." But, in fact, his stance often reflected the interests of his small-business constituency.

In the face of Wilson's obstinacy, reform might have ended in 1913 had not politics intruded. In the congressional elections of 1914, the Republican Party, no longer split by Roosevelt's Bull Moose faction, won substantial gains. Democratic strategists, with their eyes on the 1916 presidential race, recognized that Wilson needed to pick up support in the Midwest and the West by capturing votes from former Bull Moose progressives. Wilson responded belatedly by lending his support to reform in the months leading up to the election of 1916. In a sharp about-face, he cultivated union labor, farmers, and social reformers. To please labor, he appointed progressive Louis Brandeis to the Supreme Court. To woo farmers, he threw his support behind legislation to obtain rural credits. And he won praise from labor by supporting workers' compensation and the Keating-Owen child labor law (1916), which outlawed the regular employment of children younger than sixteen. When a railroad strike threatened in the months before the election, Wilson practically ordered Congress to establish an eight-hour day on the railroads. He had moved a long way from his position in 1912 to embrace many of the social reforms championed by Theodore Roosevelt. As Wilson boasted, the Democrats had "opened their hearts to the demands of social justice" and had "come very near to car-

Progressive Poster Condemning Child Labor
This poster attacks child labor, borrowing the convention of the business flowchart to portray graphically how industries employing children were "making human junk." Progressives' concern for the plight of poor children won them the label "child savers." Although activists worked hard to pass the Keating-Owen Act prohibiting child labor in 1916, the Supreme Court declared the law unconstitutional two years later on the grounds that Congress had no right to regulate manufacturing within states. In its appeal to end child labor, what does this poster emphasize more — concern for children or concern for society? Library of Congress.

rying out the platform of the Progressive Party." Wilson's shift toward reform, along with his claim that he had kept the United States out of the war in Europe (as discussed in chapter 22), helped him win reelection in 1916.

REVIEW How and why did Wilson's reform program evolve during his first term?

▶ The Limits of Progressive Reform

While progressivism called for a more active role for the liberal state, at heart it was a movement that sought reforms designed to preserve American institutions and stem the tide of more radical change. Its basic conservatism can be seen by comparing it with the more radical movements of socialism, radical labor, and birth control — and by looking at the groups progressive reform left behind, including women and African Americans.

Radical Alternatives

The year 1900 marked the birth of the Social Democratic Party in America, later called simply the **Socialist Party**. Like the progressives, the socialists were middle-class and native-born. They had broken with the older, more militant Socialist Labor Party precisely because of its dogmatic approach and immigrant constituency. The new group of socialists proved eager to appeal to a broad mass of disaffected Americans.

The Socialist Party chose as its presidential standard-bearer Eugene V. Debs, whose experience in the Pullman strike of 1894 (see chapter 20) convinced him that "there is no hope for the toiling masses of my countrymen, except by the pathways mapped out by Socialism." Debs would run for president five times, in every election (except 1916) from 1900 to 1920. The socialism Debs advocated preached cooperation over competition and urged men and women to liberate themselves from "the barbarism of private ownership and wage slavery." In the 1912 election, Debs indicted both old parties as "Tweedledee and Tweedledum," each dedicated to the preservation of capitalism and the continuation of the wage system. Only through socialism, he argued, could democracy exist. Styling the Socialist Party the "revolutionary party of the working class," he urged voters to rally to his standard. Debs's best showing came in 1912, when his 6 percent of the popular vote totaled more than 900,000 votes.

Farther to the left than the socialists stood the **Industrial Workers of the World** (IWW), nicknamed the Wobblies. In 1905, Debs, along with Western Federation of Miners leader William Dudley "Big Bill" Haywood, created the IWW, "one big union" dedicated to organizing the most destitute segment of the workforce, the unskilled workers disdained by Samuel Gompers's AFL: western miners, migrant farmworkers, lumbermen, and immigrant textile workers. Haywood, a craggy-faced miner with one eye (he had lost the other in a childhood accident), was a charismatic leader and a proletarian intellectual. Seeing workers on the lowest rung of the social ladder as the victims of violent repression, the IWW advocated direct action, sabotage, and the general strike — tactics designed to trigger a workers' uprising. The IWW never had more than 10,000 members at any one time, although possibly as many as 100,000 workers belonged to the union at one time or another in the early twentieth century. Nevertheless, the IWW's influence on the country extended far beyond its numbers (as discussed in chapter 22).

In contrast to political radicals like Debs and Haywood, **Margaret Sanger** promoted birth control as a movement for social change. Sanger, a nurse who had worked among the poor on New York's Lower East Side, coined the term *birth control* in 1915 and launched a movement with broad social implications. Sanger and her followers saw birth control not only as a sexual and medical reform but also as a means to alter social and political power relationships and to alleviate human misery.

The desire for family limitation was widespread, and in this sense birth control was nothing new. The birthrate in the United States had been falling consistently throughout the nineteenth century. The average number of children per family dropped from 7.0 in 1800 to 3.6 by 1900. But the open advocacy of *contraception*, the use of artificial means to prevent pregnancy, struck many people as both new and shocking. And it was illegal. Anthony Comstock, New York City's commissioner of vice, promoted laws in the 1870s making it a felony not only to sell contraceptive devices like condoms and cervical caps but also to publish information on how to prevent pregnancy.

When Margaret Sanger used her militant feminist newspaper, the *Woman Rebel*, to promote birth control, the Post Office confiscated Sanger's publication and brought charges of obscenity against her. Facing arrest, she fled to Europe, only to return in 1916 as something of a national celebrity. In her absence, birth control had become linked with free speech and had been taken up as a liberal cause. Under public pressure, the government dropped the charges against Sanger, who undertook a nationwide tour to publicize the birth control cause.

Sanger then turned to direct action, opening the nation's first birth control clinic in the Brownsville section of Brooklyn in October 1916. Located in the heart of a Jewish and Italian immigrant

WE WANT DEBS

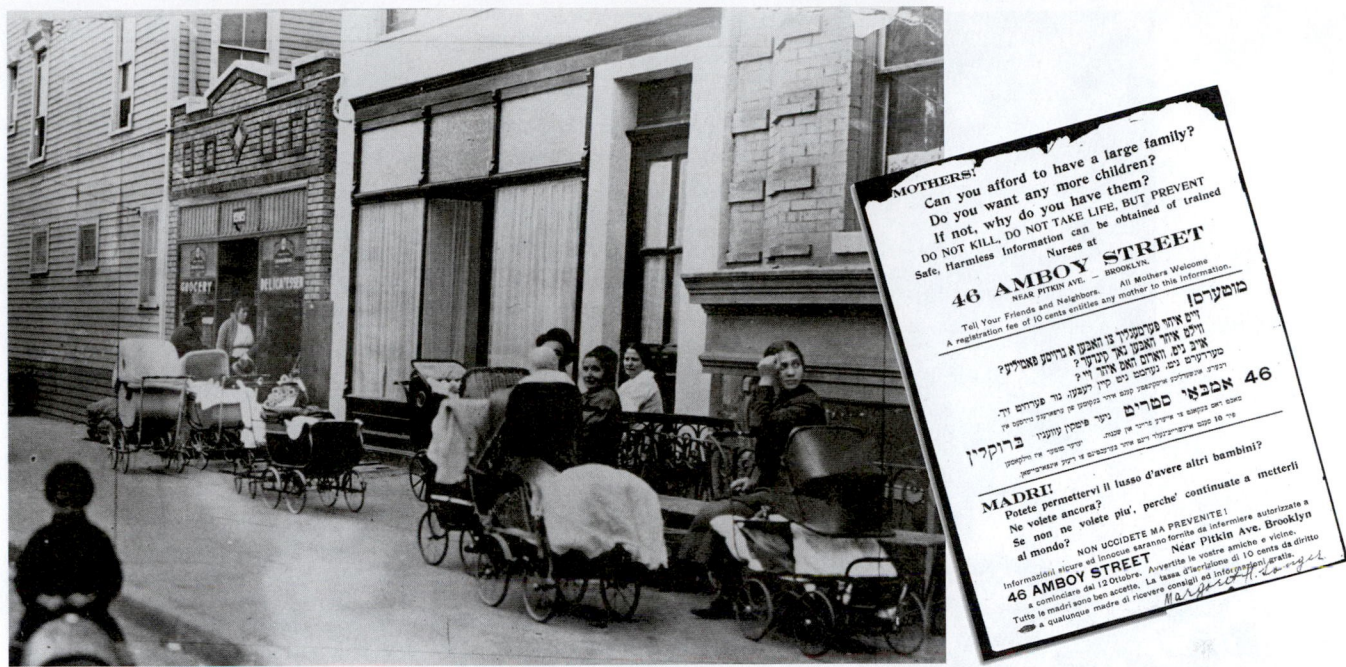

Margaret Sanger's Brownsville Birth Control Clinic
Margaret Sanger opened the first birth control clinic in the United States in the Brownsville section of Brooklyn in 1916. During the nine days it operated before police shut it down, more than four hundred women visited the clinic. Here, they are shown waiting patiently in line with their baby carriages. Sanger published her fliers in English, Yiddish, and Italian. Her clinic, located in the heart of an immigrant neighborhood, proved that immigrant women — including Italian Catholics and Russian Jews — wanted information about birth control as much as their middle- and upper-class Protestant counterparts did. Sophia Smith Collection, Smith College.

neighborhood, the clinic attracted 464 clients. On the tenth day, police shut down the clinic and threw Sanger in jail. By then, she had become a national figure, and the cause she championed had gained legitimacy, if not legality. After World War I, the birth control movement would become much less radical as Sanger turned to medical doctors for support and mouthed popular racist genetic theories. But in its infancy, the movement Sanger led was part of a radical vision for reforming the world that made common cause with the socialists and the IWW in challenging the limits of progressive reform.

Progressivism for White Men Only

The day before President Woodrow Wilson's inauguration in March 1913, the largest mass march to that date in the nation's history took place as more than five thousand demonstrators took to the streets in Washington to demand the vote for women. A rowdy crowd on hand to celebrate the Democrats' triumph attacked the marchers. Men spat at the suffragists and threw lighted cigarettes and matches at their clothing. "If my wife were where you are," a burly cop told one suffragist, "I'd break her head." But for all the marching, Wilson pointedly ignored woman suffrage in his inaugural address the next day.

The march served as a reminder that the political gains of progressivism were not spread equally throughout the population. As the twentieth century dawned, women still could not vote in most states, although they had won major victories in the West. Increasingly, however, woman suffrage had become an international movement. In Great Britain, Emmeline Pankhurst and her daughters Cristabel and Sylvia promoted a new, militant suffragism. They seized the spotlight in a series of marches, mass meetings, and acts of civil disobedience that sometimes escalated into riots, violence, and arson.

Alice Paul, a Quaker social worker who had visited England and participated in suffrage activism there, returned to the United States in 1910 in time to plan the mass march on the eve of Wilson's inauguration and to lobby for a federal amendment to give women the vote. Paul's

> "If my wife were where you are, I'd break her head."
> —A Washington cop to a suffragist marcher

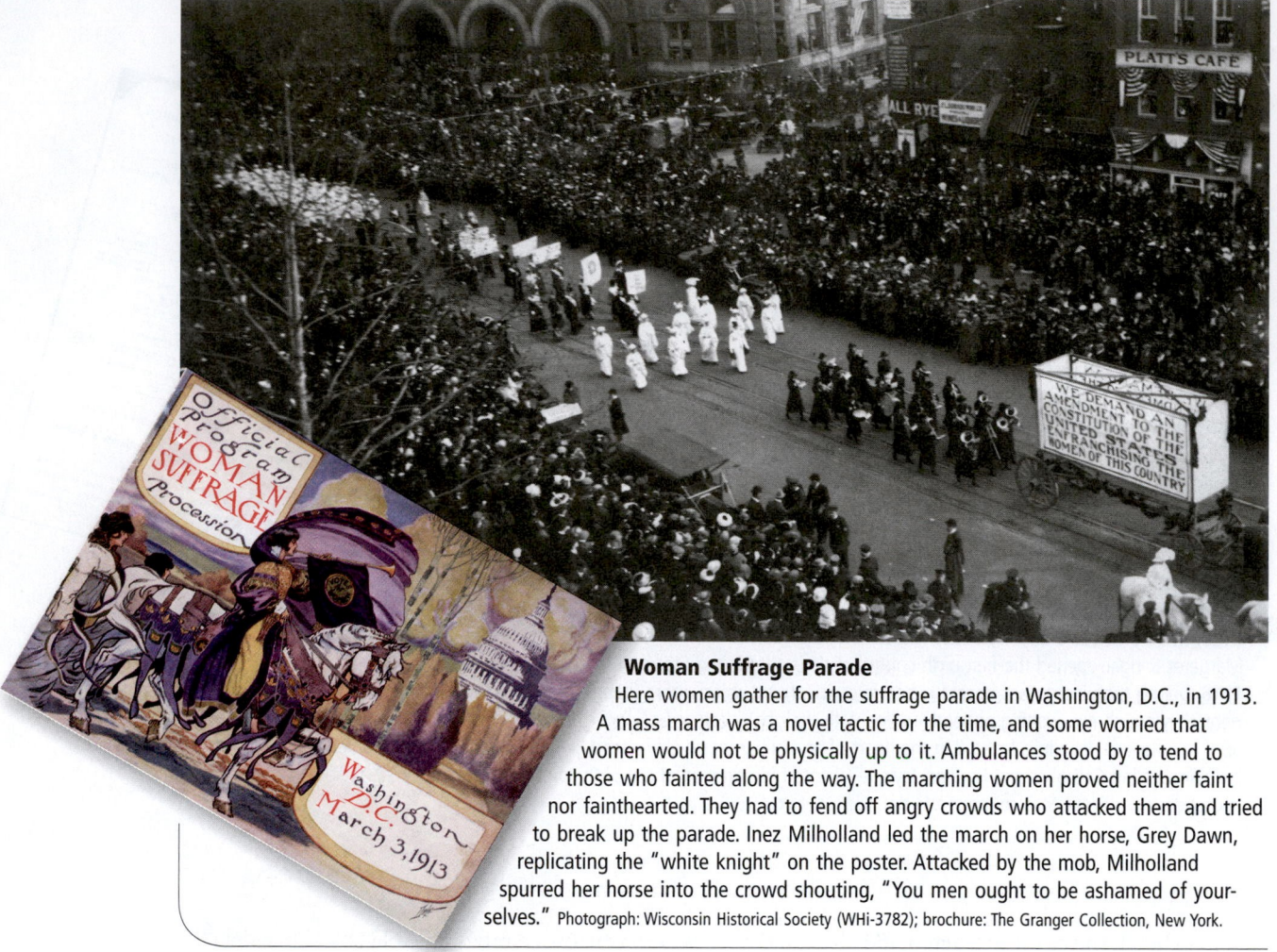

Woman Suffrage Parade

Here women gather for the suffrage parade in Washington, D.C., in 1913. A mass march was a novel tactic for the time, and some worried that women would not be physically up to it. Ambulances stood by to tend to those who fainted along the way. The marching women proved neither faint nor fainthearted. They had to fend off angry crowds who attacked them and tried to break up the parade. Inez Milholland led the march on her horse, Grey Dawn, replicating the "white knight" on the poster. Attacked by the mob, Milholland spurred her horse into the crowd shouting, "You men ought to be ashamed of yourselves." Photograph: Wisconsin Historical Society (WHi-3782); brochure: The Granger Collection, New York.

dramatic tactics alienated many in the National American Woman Suffrage Association. In 1916, Paul founded the militant National Woman's Party, which became the radical voice of the suffrage movement, advocating direct action such as mass marches and civil disobedience.

Women weren't the only group left out in progressive reform. Progressivism, as it was practiced in the West and South, was tainted with racism and sought to limit the rights of African and Asian Americans. Anti-Asian bigotry in the West led to a renewal of the Chinese Exclusion Act in 1902. At first, California governor Hiram Johnson stood against the strong anti-Asian prejudice of his state. But in 1913, he caved in to popular pressure and signed the Alien Land Law, which barred Japanese immigrants from purchasing land in California. The law was largely symbolic — ineffectual in practice because Japanese children born in the United States were U.S. citizens and property could be purchased in their names.

South of the Mason-Dixon line, the progressives' racism targeted African Americans.

Progressives preached the disfranchisement of black voters as a "reform." During the bitter electoral fights that had pitted Populists against Democrats in the 1890s, the party of white supremacy held its power by votes purchased or coerced from African Americans. Southern progressives proposed to "reform" the electoral system by eliminating black voters. Beginning in 1890 with Mississippi, southern states curtailed the African American vote through devices such as poll taxes (fees required for voting) and literacy tests. The racist intent of southern voting legislation became especially clear after 1900 when states resorted to the grandfather clause, a legal provision that allowed men who failed a literacy test to vote if their grandfathers had cast a ballot. Grandfathering thus permitted illiterate southern white men to vote while excluding illiterate blacks.

The Progressive Era also witnessed the rise of Jim Crow laws to segregate public facilities. The new railroads precipitated segregation in the South where it had rarely existed before, at least on paper. Soon, separate railcars, separate waiting rooms, separate bathrooms, and separate dining facilities for blacks sprang up across the South. In courtrooms in Mississippi, blacks were required to swear on a separate Bible.

In the face of this growing repression, **Booker T. Washington**, the preeminent black leader of the day, urged caution and restraint. A former slave, Washington had opened the Tuskegee Institute in Alabama in 1881 to teach vocational skills to African Americans. He emphasized education and economic progress for his race and urged African Americans to put aside issues of political and social equality. In an 1895 speech in Atlanta that came to be known as the **Atlanta Compromise**, he stated, "In all things that are purely social we can be as separate as the fingers, yet one as the hand in all things essential to mutual progress." Washington's accommodationist policy appealed to whites and elevated "the wizard of Tuskegee" to the role of national spokesman for African Americans.

The year after Washington proclaimed the Atlanta Compromise, the Supreme Court upheld the legality of racial segregation, affirming in *Plessy v. Ferguson* (1896) the constitutionality of the doctrine of "separate but equal." Blacks could be segregated in separate schools, restrooms, and other facilities as long as the facilities were "equal" to those provided for whites. Of course, facilities for blacks rarely proved equal. In the North, where racism of a different sort led to a clamor for legislation to restrict immigration, support for African American equality found few advocates. And with anti-Asian bigotry strong in the West, the doctrine of "white supremacy" found increasing support in all sections of the country.

When Theodore Roosevelt invited Booker T. Washington to dine at the White House in 1901, a storm of racist criticism erupted. One southern editor fumed that the White House "had been painted black." But Roosevelt summoned Washington to talk politics and patronage, not African American rights. Roosevelt's unquestioned racial prejudice became clear in the Brownsville incident in 1906, when he dishonorably discharged an entire battalion of 167 black soldiers because he suspected (although there was no proof) that they were shielding the murderer of a white saloon-keeper killed in a shoot-out in the Texas town.

Woodrow Wilson brought to the White House southern attitudes toward race and racial segregation. He instituted segregation in the federal workforce, especially the Post Office, and approved segregated drinking fountains and restrooms in the nation's capital. When critics attacked the policy, Wilson insisted that segregation was "in the interest of the Negro."

In 1906, a major race riot in Atlanta called into question Booker T. Washington's strategy of uplift and accommodation. For three days in September, the streets of Atlanta ran red with blood as angry white mobs chased and cornered any blacks they happened upon, pulling passengers from streetcars and invading black

DINNER GIVEN AT THE WHITE HOUSE BY PRESIDENT ROOSEVELT TO BOOKER T. WASHINGTON, OCTOBER 17th, 1901

Booker T. Washington and Theodore Roosevelt Dine at the White House
When Theodore Roosevelt invited Booker T. Washington to the White House in 1901, he stirred up a hornet's nest of controversy that continued into the election of 1904. This Republican campaign piece gives the meeting a positive slant, showing Roosevelt and a light-skinned Washington sitting under a portrait of Abraham Lincoln, a symbol of the party's historic commitment to African Americans. Democrats portrayed the meeting in a very different light; their campaign buttons pictured Washington with darker skin and implied that Roosevelt favored "race mingling" and had "painted the White House black." Collection of Janice L. and David J. Frent.

neighborhoods to kill and loot. An estimated 250 African Americans died in the riots — members of Atlanta's black middle class along with the poor and derelict. Professor William Crogman of Clark College noted the central irony of the riot: "Here we have worked and prayed and tried to make good men and women of our colored population," he observed, "and at our very doorstep the whites kill these good men." In Dark Town, a working-class neighborhood, blacks fought back to defend their homes, shooting into the white mob and driving off the attackers. In the aftermath of the riot, the city's leaders, black and white, managed to quash any nascent black unity by falling back on the old strategy of allying "the best white people and the best colored people." Yet the riot caused many African Americans to question Washington's strategy of gradualism and accommodation.

Foremost among Washington's critics stood **W. E. B. Du Bois**, a Harvard graduate who urged African Americans to fight for civil rights and racial justice. In *The Souls of Black Folk* (1903),

Du Bois attacked the "Tuskegee Machine," comparing Washington to a political boss who used his influence to silence his critics and reward his followers. Du Bois founded the Niagara movement in 1905, calling for universal male suffrage, civil rights, and leadership composed of a black intellectual elite. The Atlanta riot only bolstered his resolve. In 1909, the Niagara movement helped found the **National Association for the Advancement of Colored People** (NAACP), a coalition of blacks and whites that sought legal and political rights for African Americans through the courts. In the decades that followed, the NAACP came to represent the future for African Americans, while Booker T. Washington, who died in 1915, represented the past.

REVIEW How did race, class, and gender shape the limits of progressive reform?

► Conclusion: The Transformation of the Liberal State

Progressivism was never a radical movement. Its goal remained to reform the existing system — by government intervention if necessary — but without uprooting any of the traditional American political, economic, or social institutions. As Theodore Roosevelt, the bellwether of the movement, insisted, "The only true conservative is the man who resolutely sets his face toward the future." Roosevelt was such a man, and progressivism was such a movement. But although progressivism was never radical, neither was it the laissez-faire liberalism of the previous century. Progressives' willingness to use the power of government to regulate business and achieve a measure of social justice redefined liberalism in the twentieth century, tying it to the expanded power of the state.

Progressivism contained many paradoxes. A diverse coalition of individuals and interests, the progressive movement began at the grass roots but left as its legacy a stronger presidency and unprecedented federal involvement in the economy and social welfare. A movement that believed in social justice, progressivism often promoted social control. And while progressives called for greater democracy, they fostered elitism with their worship of experts and efficiency and often failed to champion equality for women and minorities.

Whatever its inconsistencies and limitations, progressivism took action to deal with the problems posed by urban industrialism. Progressivism

W. E. B. Du Bois

W. E. B. Du Bois grew up in Great Barrington, Massachusetts, and in 1895 he became the first African American to earn a doctorate from Harvard. Throughout his life, he urged African Americans not only to focus on their own education and economic prospects but also to work politically for racial equality. In *The Souls of Black Folk* (1903), he wrote that he wished "to make it possible for a man to be both a Negro and an American, without being cursed and spit upon by his fellows, without having the doors of Opportunity closed roughly in his face." Special Collections Department, W. E. B. Du Bois Library, University of Massachusetts Amherst.

saw grassroots activists address social problems on the local and state levels and search for national solutions. By increasing the power of the presidency and expanding the power of the state, progressives worked to bring about greater social justice and to achieve a better balance between government and business. Jane Addams and Theodore Roosevelt could lay equal claim to the movement that redefined liberalism and launched the liberal state of the twentieth century. War on a global scale would provide progressivism with yet another challenge even before it had completed its ambitious agenda.

▶ Selected Bibliography

General

Maureen A. Flanagan, *America Reformed: Progressives and Progressivisms, 1890s–1920s* (2007).

Jackson Lears, *Rebirth of a Nation: The Making of Modern America, 1877–1920* (2009).

Michael McGerr, *A Fierce Discontent: The Rise and Fall of the Progressive Movement in America* (2005).

Eric Ruchway, *Blessed among Nations: How the World Made America* (2006).

Grassroots Progressivism

Victoria Bissell Brown, *The Education of Jane Addams* (2004).

Robert Kanigel, *The One Best Way: Frederick Winslow Taylor* (1997).

Louise W. Knight, *Citizen: Jane Addams and the Struggle for Democracy* (2005).

Seth Koven and Sonya Michel, eds., *Mothers of a New World: Maternalist Politics and the Origins of the Welfare State* (1993).

Robyn Muncy, *Creating a Female Dominion in American Reform* (1991).

Kathryn Kish Sklar, *Florence Kelley and the Nation's Work: The Rise of Women's Political Culture, 1830–1900* (1995).

Landon R. Y. Storre, *Civilizing Capitalism: The National Consumers' League, Women's Activism, and Labor Standards in the New Deal Era* (2000).

Nancy C. Unger, *Fighting Bob La Follette: The Righteous Reformer* (2000).

David Von Drehle, *Triangle: The Fire That Changed America* (2003).

Progressive Politics and Diplomacy

Douglas Brinkley, *The Wilderness Warrior: Theodore Roosevelt and the Crusade for America* (2009).

John Milton Cooper, *Woodrow Wilson: A Biography* (2009).

Alan Dawley, *Changing the World: American Progressives in War and Revolution* (2003).

Lewis L. Gould, *Four Hats in the Ring: The 1912 Election and the Birth of Modern American Politics* (2008); *William Howard Taft: Presidency* (2009).

Kristin Hoganson, *Consumers' Imperium: The Global Production of American Domesticity, 1865–1920* (2007).

Matthew Frye Jacobson, *Barbarian Virtues: The United States Encounters Foreign Peoples at Home and Abroad, 1876–1917* (2000).

Robert Johnston, *The Radical Middle Class: Populist Democracy and the Question of Capitalism in Progressive Era Portland, Oregon* (2003).

Walter LaFeber, *The American Search for Opportunity, 1865–1913* (1994).

Kevin Matson, *Creating a Democratic Public: The Struggle for Urban Participatory Democracy during the Progressive Era* (1998).

Robert W. Righter, *The Battle over Hetch Hetchy: America's Most Controversial Dam and the Birth of Modern Environmentalism* (2005).

Daniel T. Rodgers, *Atlantic Crossings: Social Politics in a Progressive Age* (1998).

Radicals, Race Relations, and Woman Suffrage

Mary Jo Buhle, *Women and American Socialism, 1870–1920* (1981).

Ellen Chesler, *Woman of Valor: Margaret Sanger and the Birth Control Movement in America* (1993).

Melvyn Dubofsky, *"Big Bill" Haywood* (1987).

Gary Gerstle, *American Crucible: Race and Nation in the Twentieth Century* (2002).

Glenda Elizabeth Gilmore, *Gender and Jim Crow: Women and the Politics of White Supremacy in North Carolina, 1896–1920* (1996).

David Fort Godshalk, *Veiled Visions: The 1906 Atlanta Race Riot and the Reshaping of American Race Relations* (2005).

Evelyn Higginbotham, *Righteous Discontent: The Women's Movement in the Black Baptist Church, 1880–1920* (1993).

David Levering Lewis, *W. E. B. Du Bois: Biography of a Race, 1868–1919* (1993).

Rebecca J. Mead, *How the Vote Was Won: Woman Suffrage in the Western United States, 1868–1914* (2004).

Nick Salvatore, *Eugene V. Debs: Citizen and Socialist* (1982).

▶ **For more books about topics in this chapter,** see the Online Bibliography at **bedfordstmartins.com/roark**.

▶ **For additional primary sources from this period,** see Michael Johnson, ed., *Reading the American Past*, Fifth Edition.

▶ **For Web sites, images, and documents related to topics and places in this chapter,** visit Make History at **bedfordstmartins.com/roark**.

Reviewing Chapter 21

REVIEW QUESTIONS

Use key terms and dates to support your answer.

1. What types of people were drawn to the progressive movement, and what motivated them? (pp. 677–683)

2. How did progressives justify their demand for more activist government? (pp. 683–685)

3. In what ways did Roosevelt's domestic policies respond to progressive demands? (pp. 685–698)

4. How and why did Wilson's reform program evolve during his first term? (pp. 698–701)

5. How did race, class, and gender shape the limits of progressive reform? (pp. 702–706)

MAKING CONNECTIONS

Draw on key terms, the timeline, and review questions.

1. Diverse approaches to reform came under the umbrella of progressivism. Discuss the work of three progressive reformers working at the grassroots or local government level. What do your examples reveal about progressivism? What characteristics connected their reform efforts? What separated them?

2. Theodore Roosevelt's foreign policy was summed up in the dictum "Speak softly but carry a big stick." Using two examples, describe how this policy worked. By contrast, why did Taft's policy of dollar diplomacy fail?

3. Opponents on the campaign stump, Theodore Roosevelt and Woodrow Wilson shared a commitment to domestic reform. Compare their legislative programs, including the evolution of their policies over time and their ability to respond to shifting political circumstances. What do their policies reveal about their understandings of the roles of the executive and the federal government?

4. What contemporary movements lay beyond the limits of progressive reform? Why did progressive reform coincide with the restriction of minority rights? In your answer, discuss how radical movements provide insights into the character of progressivism itself.

LINKING TO THE PAST

Link events in this chapter to earlier events.

1. In what ways did Populism and progressivism differ? In what ways were they similar? (See chapter 20.)

2. During the Gilded Age, industrial capitalism concentrated power in the hands of corporations. How did Theodore Roosevelt respond to this problem? How did his approach differ from that of the Gilded Age presidents? Was his strategy effective? (See chapter 18.)

► FOR PRACTICE QUIZZES AND OTHER STUDY TOOLS, visit the Online Study Guide at bedfordstmartins.com/roark.

TIMELINE 1889–1916

1889
- Jane Addams opens Hull House.

1895
- Booker T. Washington enunciates Atlanta Compromise.

1896
- *Plessy v. Ferguson.*

1900
- Socialist Party founded.

1901
- William McKinley assassinated; Theodore Roosevelt becomes president.

1902
- Antitrust lawsuit filed against Northern Securities Company.
- Roosevelt mediates anthracite coal strike.

1903
- Women's Trade Union League (WTUL) founded.
- United States begins construction of Panama Canal.
- Elkins Act.

1904
- Roosevelt Corollary to Monroe Doctrine.

1905
- Industrial Workers of the World (IWW) founded.
- W. E. B. Du Bois founds Niagara movement.

1906
- Pure Food and Drug Act and Meat Inspection Act.
- Atlanta race riot.
- Hepburn Act.

1907
- Panic on Wall Street.
- Roosevelt signs "Gentlemen's Agreement" with Japan restricting immigration.

1908
- *Muller v. Oregon.*
- Republican William Howard Taft elected president.

1909
- Garment workers' strike in New York City.
- National Association for the Advancement of Colored People (NAACP) formed.

1910
- Hiram Johnson elected governor of California.

1911
- Triangle fire in New York City.
- Taft launches antitrust suit against U.S. Steel.

1912
- Roosevelt runs for president on Progressive Party ticket.
- Democrat Woodrow Wilson elected president.

1913
- Suffragists march in Washington, D.C.
- Federal Reserve Act.

1914
- Federal Trade Commission (FTC) created.
- Clayton Antitrust Act.

1916
- Alice Paul launches National Woman's Party.
- Margaret Sanger opens first U.S. birth control clinic.
- Keating-Owen child labor law.

GAS MASK

Before World War I, the use of poison gas was considered uncivilized, but on April 22, 1915, the Germans used poison gas for the first time in battle. The Allies condemned the German innovation as diabolic but quickly developed poison gas of their own. Despite the crude appearance of this gas mask, filter respirators (using charcoal or antidote chemicals) proved highly effective. Fewer than 1500 American soldiers died from gas, but many of those who were gassed and survived were disabled and likely to die young. The soldiers trudging along this muddy road in France in 1918 kept their masks handy.

Mask: Collection of Colonel Stuart S. Corning Jr./Picture Research Consultants & Archives; background: Library of Congress.

22

World War I: The Progressive Crusade at Home and Abroad
1914–1920

GEORGE "BROWNIE" BROWNE WAS ONE OF 2 MILLION SOLDIERS WHO crossed the Atlantic during World War I to serve in the American Expeditionary Force (AEF) in France. The twenty-three-year-old civil engineer from Waterbury, Connecticut, volunteered in July 1917, three months after the United States entered the war, serving with the 117th Engineers Regiment, 42nd Division. Two-thirds of the "doughboys" (American soldiers in Europe) saw action during the war, and few white troops saw more than Brownie did.

When Brownie and the 42nd arrived at the front in northeastern France, veteran French troops provided advanced instruction in the techniques of trench warfare. They taught Brownie's regiment of engineers how to build and maintain trenches, barbed-wire entanglements, and artillery and machine-gun positions. Although his sector of the front was deemed "quiet," Brownie came under German artillery, machine-gun, and rifle fire each day. Still, in February 1918, he wrote Martha Johnson, his girlfriend back home, "the longer I'm here the more spirit I have to 'stick it out' for the good of humanity and the U.S. which is the same thing."

Training ended abruptly in the spring of 1918 when the Germans launched a massive offensive, and the 42nd entered the trenches in the Champagne region. The German bombardment made the night "as light as daytime, and the ground . . . was a mass of flames and whistling steel from the bursting shells." Wave after wave of German soldiers rushed forward. One doughboy from the 42nd remembered, "The destruction was terrible and the advancing waves were torn and split apart. The great gaps [in the line of soldiers] were filled, only to be again torn and shattered by the direct artillery fire." Another said, "Dead bodies were all around me. Americans, French, Hun [Germans] in all phases and positions of death." A third declared that soon "the odor was something fierce. We had to put on our gas masks to keep from getting sick." In Champagne, the engineers became infantry. After helping to stop the German advance during eight days of combat, the 42nd suffered nearly 6,500 dead, wounded, and missing, 20 percent of the division.

Brownie came through the campaign unscathed, but he had not had a bath in four weeks, was covered with "cooties" (body lice), and was bone tired. After only ten days' rest, however, his unit joined in the first major American offensive, an attack against German defenses at Saint-Mihiel. To maintain secrecy, the 42nd marched sixty miles in six rainy nights. Widespread misery and confusion prompted one doughboy to remark, "Now I know why they call us the A.E.F. It means 'Ass End First.'" At 1:00 a.m. on September 12, 3,000 American artillery launched more than a million rounds against German positions. This time the engineers preceded the advancing infantry, cutting through or blasting any barbed wire that remained. The battle cost the 42nd another 1,200 casualties, but Brownie was not among them.

At the end of September, the 42nd shifted to the Meuse-Argonne region, where it participated in the most brutal American fighting of the war. And it was there that Brownie's war ended. While the engineers were clearing paths through the barbed wire for the infantry, the Germans fired thousands of poison gas shells. The gas, "so thick you could cut it with a knife," felled Brownie. When the war ended on November 11, 1918, he was recovering from his respiratory wounds at a camp behind the lines. Discharged from the army in February 1919, Brownie returned home, where he and Martha married. Like the rest of the country, they were eager to get on with their lives.

President Woodrow Wilson had never expected to lead the United States into the Great War, as the Europeans called it. When war erupted in 1914, he declared America's absolute neutrality. But trade and principle entangled the United States in Europe's troubles and gradually drew the nation into the conflict. Wilson claimed that America's participation would serve grand purposes and uplift both the United States and the entire world.

At home, the war helped progressives finally achieve their goals of national prohibition and woman suffrage, but it also promoted a vicious attack on Americans' civil liberties. While George Browne and the other doughboys were helping to win the war in Europe, hyperpatriotism meant intolerance, repression, and vigilante violence at home. In 1919, Wilson sailed for Europe to secure a just peace. Unable to dictate terms to the victors, Wilson accepted disappointing compromises. Upon his return to the United States, he met a crushing defeat that marked the end of Wilsonian internationalism. Crackdowns on dissenters, immigrants, racial and ethnic minorities, and unions signaled the end of the Progressive Era at home.

George "Brownie" Browne

Mobilizing an army was easy compared with preparing men for battle. Training at Fort Slocum, New York, Brownie complained about the Army's red tape, bad food, shortage of equipment, inexperienced officers, lack of sleep, and physical exhaustion. Writing to his girlfriend just before evening taps in August 1917, Brownie said, "Believe me I *am* tired." Despite the hardships, however, Brownie enjoyed the camaraderie of the camp and was, as this photograph reveals, a happy soldier. When his unit arrived at Saint-Nazaire in October 1917, Brownie was proud to be one of the first doughboys to set foot in France. Courtesy of Janet W. Hansen.

► Woodrow Wilson and the World

Shortly after winning election to the presidency in 1912, **Woodrow Wilson** confided to a friend: "It would be an irony of fate if my administration had to deal with foreign affairs." Indeed, Wilson had focused his life and career on domestic concerns, seldom venturing far from home and traveling abroad only on brief vacations. As president of Princeton University and then governor of New Jersey, he had remained rooted in local affairs. In his campaign for the presidency, Wilson spoke passionately about domestic reform but hardly mentioned foreign affairs.

Wilson, however, could not avoid the world and the rising tide of militarism, nationalism, and violence that beat against American shores. Economic interests compelled the nation outward. Moreover, Wilson was drawn abroad by his own progressive political principles. He believed that the United States had a moral duty to champion national self-determination, peaceful free trade, and political democracy. "We have no selfish ends to serve," he proclaimed. "We desire no conquest, no dominion. . . . We are but one of the champions of the rights of mankind." Yet as president, Wilson revealed that he was as ready as any American president to apply military solutions to problems of foreign policy.

Taming the Americas

When he took office, Wilson sought to distinguish his foreign policy from that of his Republican predecessors. To Wilson, Theodore Roosevelt's "big stick" and William Howard Taft's "dollar diplomacy" appeared crude flexing of military and economic muscle. To signal a new direction, Wilson appointed **William Jennings Bryan** as secretary of state. A pacifist on religious grounds, Bryan immediately

MAP 22.1

U.S. Involvement in Latin America and the Caribbean, 1895–1941

Victory against Spain in 1898 made Puerto Rico an American possession and Cuba a protectorate. The United States later gained control of the Panama Canal Zone. The nation was quick to protect expanding economic interests with military force by propping up friendly, though not necessarily democratic, governments.

- U.S. possessions in 1900
- U.S. protectorates or areas of temporary occupation

Border dispute, Jan. 1916–Feb. 1917

U.S. intervention, Apr.–Nov. 1914

Protectorate, 1898–1934 Occupied, 1898–1902; 1906–1909; 1912; 1917–1922

Protectorate, 1905–1941 Occupied, 1916–1924

Ceded to U.S. by Spain, 1898

Protectorate, 1915–1936 Occupied, 1915–1934

Purchased from Denmark for $25 million, 1917

U.S. intervention, 1912

CANAL ZONE Leased, 1903 Completed, 1914

U.S. intervention, 1909–1910 Occupied, 1912–1925; 1926–1933

Independent from Colombia, 1903 Protectorate, 1903–1939

U.S. intervention in border dispute, 1895–1896 U.S. intervention in monetary dispute, 1902

Francisco "Pancho" Villa
The dashing Mexican revolutionary Pancho Villa gallops along a column of his soldiers in 1914. After Villa's raid into New Mexico in 1916 to punish Americans for aiding his revolutionary rivals, General John J. Pershing dove across the border, pursued Villa for three hundred miles into Mexico, and then returned home almost a year later empty-handed. Brown Brothers.

turned his attention to making agreements with thirty nations for the peaceful settlement of disputes.

But Wilson and Bryan, like Roosevelt and Taft, also believed that the Monroe Doctrine gave the United States special rights and responsibilities in the Western Hemisphere. Issued in 1823 to warn Europeans not to attempt to colonize the Americas again, the doctrine had become a cloak for U.S. domination. Thus, when it appeared that unrest might undermine American interests in Nicaragua, Haiti, and the Dominican Republic, Wilson authorized U.S. military intervention, paving the way for U.S. banks and corporations to assert financial control. All the while, Wilson believed that U.S. actions were promoting order and democracy. "I am going to teach the South American Republics to elect good men!" he declared (Map 22.1).

Wilson's most serious involvement in Latin America

U.S. Intervention in Mexico, 1916–1917

ARIZ.   N. MEX.
Culberson's Ranch
Columbus March 9
El Paso
TEXAS
Ascensión
Colonia Dublán
Carrizal June 21
Casas Grandes
Rio Grande
Galeana
Namiquipa
MEXICO
Bachiniva
Guerrero March 29
Chihuahua
Tomochic April 21
San Francisco de Borja
✶ Raids and clashes
→ U.S. main force
→ U.S. cavalry
Parral April 12

came in Mexico, where revolution broke out in 1910. When General Victoriano Huerta seized power by violent means three years later, most European nations promptly recognized Mexico's new government, but Wilson refused, declaring that he would not support a "government of butchers." In April 1914, Wilson sent 800 Marines to seize the port of Veracruz to prevent the unloading of a large shipment of arms for Huerta, who was by then involved in a civil war of his own. Huerta fled to Spain, and the United States welcomed a more compliant government.

Wilson could not tame Mexico that easily, however. A rebellion erupted among desperately poor farmers who believed that the new government of Venustiano Carranza, aided by U.S. business interests, had betrayed the revolution's promise to help the common people. In January 1916, the rebel army, commanded by **Francisco "Pancho" Villa**, seized a train carrying gold to

Texas from an American-owned mine in Mexico and killed the 17 American engineers aboard. In March, a band of some 400 to 500 of Villa's men crossed the border for a predawn raid on Columbus, New Mexico. They stayed for less than two hours, but they burned much of the town and killed 18 Americans. Wilson promptly dispatched 12,000 troops, led by Major General John J. Pershing. The wily Villa avoided capture, and in January 1917 Wilson recalled Pershing so that the general might prepare the army for the possibility of fighting in the Great War.

The European Crisis

Before 1914, Europe had enjoyed decades of peace, but just beneath the surface lay the potentially destructive forces of nationalism and imperialism. The consolidation of the German and Italian states into unified nations and the similar ambition of Russia to create a Pan-Slavic union initiated new rivalries throughout Europe. As the conviction spread that colonial possessions were a mark of national greatness, competition expanded onto the world stage. Most ominously, Germany under Kaiser **Wilhelm II** meant to challenge Great Britain's world supremacy by creating industrial muscle at home, an empire abroad, and a mighty navy. The German challenge threatened the balance of power and thus the peace.

European nations sought to avoid an explosion by developing a complex web of military and diplomatic alliances. By 1914, Germany, Austria-Hungary, and Italy (the **Triple Alliance**) stood opposed to Great Britain, France, and Russia (the **Triple Entente**, also known as "the Allies"). But in their effort to prevent war through a balance of power, Europeans had actually magnified the possibility of large-scale conflict by creating trip wires along the boundaries of two heavily armed power blocs (Map 22.2). Treaties, some of them secret, obligated members of the alliances to come to the aid of another member if attacked.

The fatal sequence began on June 28, 1914, in the Bosnian city of Sarajevo, when a Bosnian Serb terrorist assassinated **Archduke Franz Ferdinand**, heir to the Austro-Hungarian throne. On July 18, Austria-Hungary declared war on Serbia, holding it accountable for the killing. The elaborate alliance system meant that the war could not remain local. Russia announced that it would back the Serbs. Compelled by treaty to support Austria-Hungary, Germany on August 3 attacked Russia and France. In response, Great Britain, upholding its pact with France, declared

war on Germany on August 4. Within weeks, Europe was engulfed in war. The conflict became a world war when Japan, seeing an opportunity to rid itself of European competition in China, joined the cause against Germany. The evenly matched alliances would fight a disastrous war lasting more than four years, at a cost of 8.5 million soldiers' lives — an entire generation of young men. A war that started with a solitary murder proved impossible to stop. Indeed, Britain's foreign secretary, Edward Grey, announced sadly: "The lamps are going out all over Europe. We shall not see them lit again in our lifetime."

The Ordeal of American Neutrality

Woodrow Wilson promptly announced that the war was purely a European matter. Because it engaged no vital American interest and involved no significant principle, he said, the United States would remain neutral and continue normal relations with the warring nations. America had traditionally insisted that "free ships made free goods" — that neutral nations were entitled to trade safely with all nations at war. But more was involved than lofty principle. In the year before Europe went to war, the U.S. economy had slipped into a recession that wartime disruption of European trade could drastically worsen.

Although Wilson proclaimed neutrality, his sympathies, like those of many Americans, lay with Great Britain and France. Americans gratefully remembered crucial French assistance in the American Revolution and shared with the British a language, a culture, and a commitment to liberty. Germany, by contrast, was a monarchy with strong militaristic traditions. The British portrayed the German ruler, Kaiser Wilhelm II, as personally responsible for the war's atrocities, and before long American newspapers were labeling him "the Mad Dog of Europe" and "the Beast of Berlin." Still, Wilson insisted on neutrality, in part because he feared the conflict's effects on the United States as a nation of immigrants, millions of whom had only recently come from countries now at war. As he told the German ambassador, "We definitely have to be neutral, since otherwise our mixed populations would wage war on each other."

Britain's powerful fleet controlled the seas and quickly set up an economic blockade of Germany. The United States

MAP 22.2

European Alliances after the Outbreak of World War I

With Germany and Austria-Hungary wedged between their Entente rivals and all parties fully armed, Europe was poised for war when Archduke Franz Ferdinand of Austria-Hungary was assassinated in Sarajevo in June 1914.

vigorously protested, but Britain refused to give up its naval advantage. The blockade actually had little economic impact on the United States. Between 1914 and the spring of 1917, while trade with Germany evaporated, war-related exports to Britain — food, clothing, steel, and munitions — escalated by some 400 percent, enough to pull the American economy out of its prewar slump. Although the British blockade violated American neutrality, the Wilson administration gradually acquiesced, thus beginning the fateful process of alienation from Germany.

Germany retaliated with a submarine blockade of British ports. This terrifying new form of combat by *Unterseebooten*, or **U-boats**, threatened traditional rules of war. Unlike surface warships that could harmlessly stop freighters and prevent them from entering a war zone, submarines relied on sinking their quarry. And once they sank a ship, the tiny U-boats could not possibly pick up survivors. Britain portrayed the submarine as an outlaw weapon that violated notions of "civilized" warfare. Nevertheless, in February 1915, Germany announced that it intended to sink on sight enemy ships en route to the British Isles. On May 7, 1915, a German U-boat torpedoed the British passenger liner **Lusitania**, killing 1,198 passengers, 128 of them U.S. citizens.

American newspapers featured drawings of drowning women and children, and some demanded war. Calmer voices pointed out that Germany had warned prospective passengers and that the *Lusitania* carried millions of rounds of ammunition and so was a legitimate target. Secretary of State Bryan resisted the hysteria and declared that a ship carrying war materiel

Sinking of the *Lusitania*, 1915

"should not rely on passengers to protect her from attack — it would be like putting women and children in front of an army." He counseled Wilson to warn American citizens that they traveled on ships of belligerent countries at their own risk.

Wilson sought a middle course that would retain his commitment to peace and neutrality without condoning German attacks on passenger ships. On May 10, 1915, he rejected American intervention, declaring that "there is such a thing as a man being too proud to fight." But Wilson also rejected Bryan's position. Any further destruction of ships, Wilson announced, would be regarded as "deliberately unfriendly" and might lead the United States

to break off diplomatic relations with Germany. Wilson essentially demanded that Germany abandon unrestricted submarine warfare. Bryan resigned, predicting that the president had placed the United States on a collision course with Germany. Wilson's replacement for Bryan, **Robert Lansing**, was far from neutral. He believed that Germany's antidemocratic character and goal of "world dominance" meant that it "must not be permitted to win this war or even to break even."

> **"There is such a thing as a man being too proud to fight."**
> —WOODROW WILSON

After Germany apologized for the civilian deaths on the *Lusitania*, tensions subsided. But in 1916, to ensure continued U.S. neutrality, Germany went further, promising no more submarine attacks without warning and without provisions for the safety of civilians. Wilson's supporters celebrated the success of his middle-of-the-road strategy that steered a course between belligerence and pacificism.

Wilson's diplomacy proved helpful in his bid for reelection in 1916. In the contest against Republican Charles Evans Hughes, the Democratic Party ran Wilson under the slogan "He kept us out of war." Wilson felt uneasy with the claim, recognizing that any "little German lieutenant can push us into the war at any time by some calculated outrage." But the Democrats' case for Wilson's neutrality appealed to enough of those in favor of peace to eke out a majority. Wilson won, but only by the razor-thin margins of 600,000 popular and 23 electoral votes.

The United States Enters the War

Step-by-step, the United States backed away from "absolute neutrality" and more forthrightly sided with the Allies (the Triple Entente). The consequence of protesting the German blockade of Great Britain but accepting the British blockade of Germany was that by 1916 the United States was supplying the Allies with 40 percent of their war materiel. When France and Britain ran short of money to pay for U.S. goods and asked for loans, Wilson argued that "loans by American bankers to any foreign government which is at war are inconsistent with the true spirit of neutrality." But rather than jeopardize America's wartime prosperity, Wilson relaxed his objections, and billions of dollars in loans kept American goods flowing to Britain and France.

In January 1917, Germany decided that it could no longer afford to allow neutral shipping

"Enlist"

This poster depicting a young mother and her baby sinking beneath the cold waters of the Atlantic Ocean brought home the terrible cost of Germany's sinking of the British passenger liner *Lusitania* in 1915. When a German propagandist in the United States sought to defend the sinking, the American response was so ferocious that the German ambassador was forced to send him back to Germany. Burned into American memory, the sinking of the *Lusitania* remained a compelling reason to enlist in the armed forces after the United States entered the war in 1917. Library of Congress.

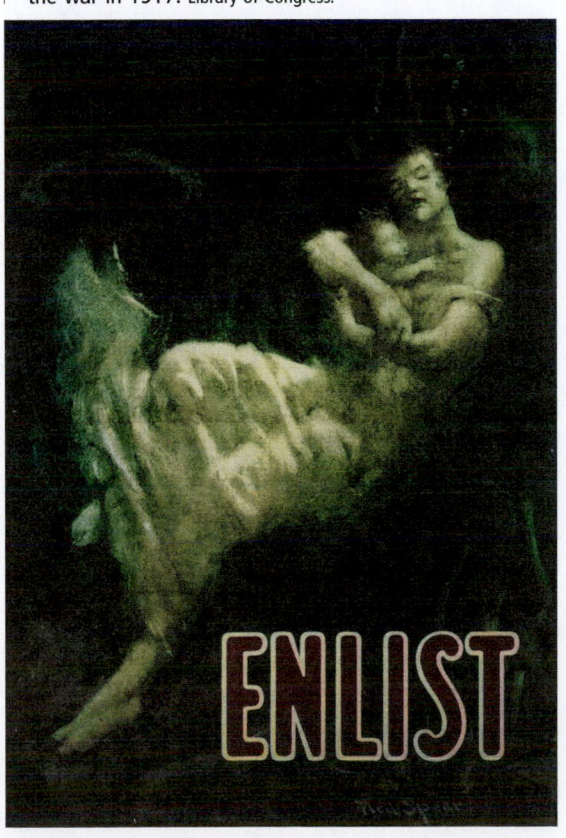

to reach Great Britain while Britain's blockade gradually starved Germany. It announced that its navy would resume unrestricted submarine warfare and sink without warning any ship, enemy or neutral, found in the waters off Great Britain. Germany understood that the decision would probably bring the United States into the war but gambled that the submarines would strangle the British economy and allow German armies to win a military victory in France before American troops arrived in Europe.

Resisting demands for war, Wilson continued to hope for a negotiated peace and only broke off diplomatic relations with Germany. Then on February 25, 1917, British authorities informed Wilson of a secret telegram sent by the German foreign secretary, Arthur Zimmermann, to the German minister in Mexico. It promised that in the event of war between Germany and the United States, Germany would see that Mexico regained its "lost provinces" of Texas, New Mexico, and Arizona if Mexico would declare war against the United States. Wilson angrily responded to the **Zimmermann telegram** by asking Congress to approve a policy of "armed neutrality" that would allow merchant ships to fight back against any attackers. Germany's overture to Mexico convinced Wilson that the war was, indeed, a defense of democracy against German aggression.

In March, German submarines sank five American vessels off Britain, killing 66 Americans. On April 2, the president asked Congress to issue a declaration of war. He accused Germany of "warfare against all mankind." Still, he called for a "war without hate" and insisted that the destruction of Germany was not the goal of the United States. Rather, America fought to "vindicate the principles of peace and justice." He promised a world made "safe for democracy." On April 6, 1917, by majorities of 373 to 50 in the House and 82 to 6 in the Senate, Congress voted to declare war. Among those voting no was Representative Jeannette Rankin of Montana, the first woman elected to Congress.

Wilson feared what war would do at home. He said despairingly, "Once lead this people into war, and they'll forget there ever was such a thing as tolerance. To fight you must be brutal and ruthless, and the spirit of ruthless brutality will infect Congress, the courts, the policeman on the beat, the man in the street."

REVIEW   Why did President Wilson fail to maintain U.S. neutrality during World War I?

▶ "Over There"

American soldiers sailed for France with songwriter George M. Cohan's rousing "Over There" ringing in their ears:

> Over there, over there
> Send the word, send the word over there,
> That the Yanks are coming, the Yanks are coming
> The drums rum-tumming ev'rywhere.

America's military venture in Europe was by far the largest the nation had ever undertaken on foreign soil. Filled with a sense of democratic mission and trained to be morally upright as well as fiercely effective, some doughboys, such as George Browne, found the adventure exhilarating and maintained their idealism to the end. The majority, however, saw little that was gallant in rats, lice, and poison gas and — despite the progressives' hopes — little to elevate the human soul in a landscape of utter destruction and death. Most were dedicated simply to defeating the "Huns" and returning home.

The Call to Arms

When America entered the war, Britain and France were nearly exhausted after almost three years of conflict. Millions of soldiers had perished; food and morale were dangerously low. Another Allied power, Russia, was in turmoil. In March 1917, a revolution had forced Czar Nicholas II to abdicate, and eight months later, in a separate peace with Germany, the **Bolshevik** revolutionary government withdrew Russia from the war. Peace with Russia allowed Germany to withdraw hundreds of thousands of its soldiers from the eastern front and to deploy them against the Allies on the western front in France.

On May 18, 1917, to meet the demand for fighting men, Wilson signed a sweeping **Selective Service Act**, authorizing a draft of all young men into the armed forces. Conscription helped transform a tiny volunteer armed force of 80,000 men into a vast army and navy. Although almost 350,000 inductees either failed to report or claimed conscientious objector status, draft boards eventually inducted 2.8 million men into the armed services, in addition to the 2 million, including George Browne, who volunteered.

Among the 4.8 million men under arms, 370,000 were black Americans. Although African Americans remained understandably skeptical about President Wilson's war for democracy, most followed W. E. B. Du Bois's advice to "close ranks" and to temporarily "forget our special

"Men Wanted for the United States Army"
The exuberant soldiers swarming over this truck were so thrilled with their task of recruiting new men that they managed to display the flag backward. Their urgency reflects the fact that when America declared war on Germany in April 1917, its army numbered only 127,000, roughly the size of Chile's army. Unwilling to trust voluntary enlistments, Wilson called for a draft, and within months nearly 10 million American men had registered for the draft. When the war ended, 2 million men had volunteered for military service, and 2.8 million had been drafted. The navy was as desperate for men as the army. This heroic poster helped attract thousands of volunteers. Photo: Brown Brothers; Poster: Image by © Swim Ink 2, LLC/Corbis.

grievances" until the nation had won the war. During training, black recruits suffered the same prejudices that they encountered in civilian life. Rigidly segregated, they faced crude abuse and miserable conditions, and they were usually assigned to labor battalions, where they shouldered shovels more often than rifles.

Training camps sought to transform raw white recruits into fighting men. Progressives in the government were also determined that the camps turn out soldiers with the highest moral and civic values. Secretary of War Newton D. Baker created the Commission on Training Camp Activities, staffed by YMCA workers and veterans of the settlement house and playground movements.

Military training included games, singing, and college extension courses. The army asked soldiers to stop thinking about sex, explaining that a "man who is thinking below the belt is not efficient." The Military Draft Act of 1917 prohibited prostitution and alcohol near training camps.

Wilson's choice to command the **American Expeditionary Force (AEF)** on the battlefields of France, Major General **John "Black Jack" Pershing**, was as morally upright as he was militarily uncompromising. "The standards for the American Army will be those of West Point," the ramrod-straight Pershing announced early in the war. "The upright bearing, attention to detail, uncomplaining obedience to instruction required of the cadet will be required of every officer and soldier of our armies in France." Described by one observer as "lean, clean, keen," he gave progressives perfect confidence.

The War in France

At the front, the AEF discovered a desperate situation. The war had degenerated into a stalemate of armies defensively dug into hundreds of miles of trenches that stretched across France. Huddling in the mud among the corpses and rats, soldiers were separated from the enemy by only a few hundred yards of "no-man's-land." When ordered "over the top," troops raced desperately toward the enemy's trenches, only to be entangled in barbed wire, enveloped in poison gas, and mowed down by machine guns. In three days of fighting at the battle of the Somme in 1916, French and British forces lost 600,000 dead and wounded and the Germans 500,000. The deadliest battle of the war allowed the Allies to advance their trenches only a few meaningless miles across devastated land.

> **"Why, then, fight the Germans, only for the benefit of the Wall Street robbers?"**
> — A German leaflet given to African American troops

Still, U.S. troops saw almost no combat in 1917. The major exception was the 92nd Division of black troops. When Pershing received an urgent call for troops from the French, he sent the 92nd to the front because he did not want to lose command over the white troops he valued more. In the 191 days they spent in battle — longer than any other American outfit — the 369th Regiment of the 92nd Division won more medals than any other American combat unit. Black soldiers recognized the irony of having to serve with the French to gain respect. Pershing told the French that their failure to draw the color line risked "spoiling the Negroes." German propagandists raised some painful questions. In a leaflet that aviators dropped among black troops, the Germans reminded them of their second-class citizenship and asked, "Why, then, fight the Germans, only for the benefit of the Wall Street robbers and to protect the millions they have loaned to the British, French, and Italians?"

White troops continued to train and used their free time to explore places that most of them otherwise could never have hoped to see. True to the crusader image, American officials allowed only morally uplifting tourism. Paris's temptations were off limits, and French premier

Doughboys in France
Stretched out in the mud in the middle of what used to be a forest, men in the 23rd Infantry of the 2nd Division fire a 37 mm gun at German positions. The black tree trunks offer dramatic testimony to the devastating power of the massive artillery bombardments. We can only imagine the cost to soldiers who were dug in here when the artillery opened up. One doughboy described a German bombardment like this: "The intensity of it simply enters your heart and brain, and tears every nerve to pieces." National Archives.

Georges Clemenceau's offer to supply U.S. troops with licensed prostitutes was declined with the half-serious remark that if Wilson found out, he would stop the war.

Sightseeing and training ended abruptly in March 1918. When the Brest-Litovsk treaty signed that month by Germany and the Bolsheviks officially took Russia out of the war, the Germans launched a massive offensive aimed at French ports on the Atlantic. After 6,000 cannons unleashed the heaviest barrage in history, a million German soldiers smashed a hole in the Allied lines at a cost of 250,000 casualties on each side. Pershing, who believed the right moment for U.S. action had finally come, visited Ferdinand Foch, head of the French army, to ask for the "great honor" of becoming "engaged

in the greatest battle in history." Foch agreed to Pershing's terms of a separate American command and in May assigned the Americans to the central sector.

In May and June, at Cantigny and then at Château-Thierry, the eager but green Americans checked the German advance with a series of dashing assaults (Map 22.3). Then they headed toward the forest stronghold of Belleau Wood, moving against streams of retreating Allied soldiers who cried defeat: "La guerre est finie!" (The war is over!) A French officer commanded the Americans to retreat with them, but the American commander replied sharply, "Retreat, hell. We just got here." After charging through a wheat field against withering machine-gun fire, the Marines plunged into hand-to-hand

MAP ACTIVITY

Map 22.3 The American Expeditionary Force, 1918
In the last year of the war, the AEF joined the French army on the western front to respond to the final German offensive and pursue the retreating enemy until surrender.

READING THE MAP: Across which rivers did the Germans advance in 1918? Where did the armistice line of November 11, 1918, lie in relation to the stabilized front of 1915–1917? Through which countries did the armistice line run?

CONNECTIONS: What events paved the way for the AEF to join the combat effort in 1918? What characteristic(s) differentiated American troops from other Allied forces and helped them achieve victory?

VISUAL ACTIVITY

Life in the Trenches
One U.S. soldier in a rat-infested trench tensely looks out for danger, while three others sit or lie in exhausted sleep. They offer a glimpse of the reality of the Great War, minus the noise, stench, and danger. This trench is dry for the moment, but with the rains came mud so deep that wounded men drowned in it. By the time American doughboys arrived in Europe, hostile troops had faced each other for more than three years, burrowed into a double line of trenches that were protected by barbed wire, machine-gun nests, and mortars and backed by heavy artillery. Trenches with millions of combatants stretched from French ports on the English Channel all the way to Switzerland. Nothing could make living in such holes anything better than miserable, but a decent shave with a Gillette safety razor and a friendly game of checkers offered doughboys temporary relief. Inevitably, however, the whistles would blow, sending the young men "over the top" and rushing toward enemy lines. Photo: Imperial War Museum; shaving kit and checkers set: Collection of Colonel Stuart S. Corning Jr./Picture Research Consultants, Inc.

READING THE IMAGE: What do these images suggest about the reality of life for American soldiers during World War I?
CONNECTIONS: How does the photograph of the trench contrast with the larger tactical approach to war employed by the American Expeditionary Force in France?

combat. Victory came hard, but a German report praised the enemy's spirit, noting that "the Americans' nerves are not yet worn out." Indeed, it was German morale that was on the verge of cracking.

In the summer of 1918, the Allies launched a massive counteroffensive that would end the war. A quarter of a million U.S. troops joined in the rout of German forces along the Marne River. In September, more than a million Americans took part in the assault that threw the Germans back from positions along the Meuse River. In four brutal days during the Meuse-Argonne offensive, the AEF sustained 45,000 casualties. Pershing had predicted that German defenses would crack in thirty-six hours; six weeks later, the Germans gave way. In November, a revolt against the German government sent Kaiser Wilhelm II fleeing to Holland. On November 11, 1918, a delegation from the newly established

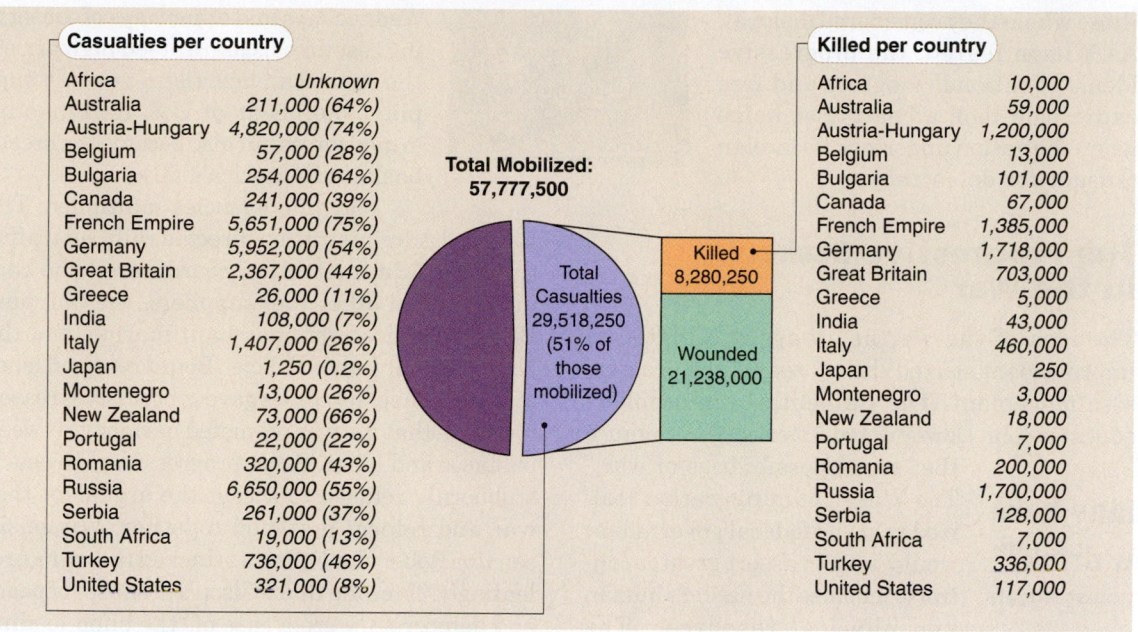

Casualties per country	
Africa	Unknown
Australia	211,000 (64%)
Austria-Hungary	4,820,000 (74%)
Belgium	57,000 (28%)
Bulgaria	254,000 (64%)
Canada	241,000 (39%)
French Empire	5,651,000 (75%)
Germany	5,952,000 (54%)
Great Britain	2,367,000 (44%)
Greece	26,000 (11%)
India	108,000 (7%)
Italy	1,407,000 (26%)
Japan	1,250 (0.2%)
Montenegro	13,000 (26%)
New Zealand	73,000 (66%)
Portugal	22,000 (22%)
Romania	320,000 (43%)
Russia	6,650,000 (55%)
Serbia	261,000 (37%)
South Africa	19,000 (13%)
Turkey	736,000 (46%)
United States	321,000 (8%)

Total Mobilized: 57,777,500

Total Casualties 29,518,250 (51% of those mobilized)

Killed 8,280,250

Wounded 21,238,000

Killed per country	
Africa	10,000
Australia	59,000
Austria-Hungary	1,200,000
Belgium	13,000
Bulgaria	101,000
Canada	67,000
French Empire	1,385,000
Germany	1,718,000
Great Britain	703,000
Greece	5,000
India	43,000
Italy	460,000
Japan	250
Montenegro	3,000
New Zealand	18,000
Portugal	7,000
Romania	200,000
Russia	1,700,000
Serbia	128,000
South Africa	7,000
Turkey	336,000
United States	117,000

FIGURE 22.1   GLOBAL COMPARISON: Casualties of the First World War
There is no agreement about the number of casualties in World War I. Record keeping in many countries was only rudimentary. Moreover, the destructive nature of the war meant that countless soldiers were wholly obliterated or instantly buried. The chart above provides estimates of casualties (the combined number of wounded and killed soldiers) per country. The percentage listed with each casualty figure represents the portion of soldiers mobilized who were killed. However approximate, these figures make clear that the conflict that raged from 1914 to 1918 was a truly catastrophic world war. Although soldiers came from almost every part of the globe, the human devastation was not evenly distributed. Which country suffered the most casualties? Which country suffered the greatest percentage of casualties? What do you think was the principal reason that the United States suffered a smaller percentage of casualties than most other nations?

German republic met with the French high command to sign an armistice that brought the fighting to an end.

The adventure of the AEF was brief, bloody, and victorious. When Germany had resumed unrestricted U-boat warfare in 1917, it had been gambling that it could defeat Britain and France before the Americans could raise and train an army and ship it to France. The German military had miscalculated badly. Of the 2 million American troops in Europe, 1.4 million saw some action. By the end, 112,000 AEF soldiers perished from wounds and disease, while another 230,000 Americans, including George Browne, suffered casualties but survived. Only the Civil War, which lasted much longer, had been more costly in American lives. European nations, however, suffered much greater losses: 2.2 million Germans, 1.9 million Russians, 1.4 million French, and 900,000 Britons (Figure 22.1). Where they had fought, the landscape was as blasted and barren as the moon.

REVIEW   How did the American Expeditionary Force contribute to the defeat of Germany?

▶ The Crusade for Democracy at Home

Many progressives hoped that the war would improve the quality of American life as well as free Europe from tyranny and militarism. Mobilization helped propel the crusades for woman suffrage and prohibition to success. Progressives enthusiastically channeled industrial and agricultural production into the war effort. Labor shortages caused by workers entering the military provided new opportunities for women in the booming wartime economy. With labor at a premium, unionized workers gained higher pay and shorter hours. To instill loyalty in Americans whose ancestry was rooted in the belligerent nations, Wilson launched a campaign to foster patriotism. The campaign included the creation of a government agency to promote official propaganda, indoctrination in the schools, and parades, rallies, and films. But fanning patriotism led to suppressing dissent. When the government launched a harsh assault on civil liberties, mobs gained license to attack those whom they considered disloyal. As Wilson feared, the progressive ideals of rational progress and free expression took a beating at home when the nation undertook its foreign crusade for democracy.

The Progressive Stake in the War

> **"Shall the many have food or the few drink?"**
> —Prohibitionist slogan

The idea of the war as an agent of national improvement stirred the old zeal of the progressive movement. The influential philosopher-educator John Dewey urged Americans to embrace the "social possibilities of war." The Wilson administration realized that the federal government would have to assert greater control to mobilize the nation's human and physical resources. The nation's capital soon bristled with agencies charged with managing the war effort. Bernard Baruch headed the War Industries Board, created to stimulate and direct industrial production. A wealthy Wall Street stockbroker and a reform Democrat, Baruch brought industrial management and labor together into a team that produced everything from boots to bullets and made U.S. troops the best-equipped soldiers in the world.

Herbert Hoover, a self-made millionaire engineer, headed the Food Administration. He led remarkably successful "Hooverizing" campaigns for "meatless" Mondays and "wheatless"

Wednesdays and other ways of conserving resources. Guaranteed high prices, the American heartland not only supplied the needs of U.S. citizens and armed forces but also became the breadbasket of America's allies.

Wartime agencies multiplied: The Railroad Administration directed railroad traffic, the Fuel Administration coordinated the coal industry and other fuel suppliers, the Shipping Board organized the merchant marine, and the National War Labor Policies Board resolved labor disputes. Their successes gave progressives reason to believe that the war promoted harmony between business and labor. Some progressives, however, stubbornly refused to accept the argument that war and reform marched together. Wisconsin senator Robert La Follette attacked the war unrelentingly, claiming that Wilson's promises of peace and democracy were a case of "the blind leading the blind" at home and abroad.

Industrial leaders found that wartime agencies enforced efficiency, which helped corporate profits triple. Some working people also had cause to celebrate. Mobilization meant high prices for farmers and plentiful jobs at high wages in the new war industries (Figure 22.2). Because increased industrial production required peaceful labor relations, the National War Labor Policies Board enacted the eight-hour day, a living minimum wage, and collective bargaining rights in some industries. Wages rose sharply during the war (as did prices), and the American Federation

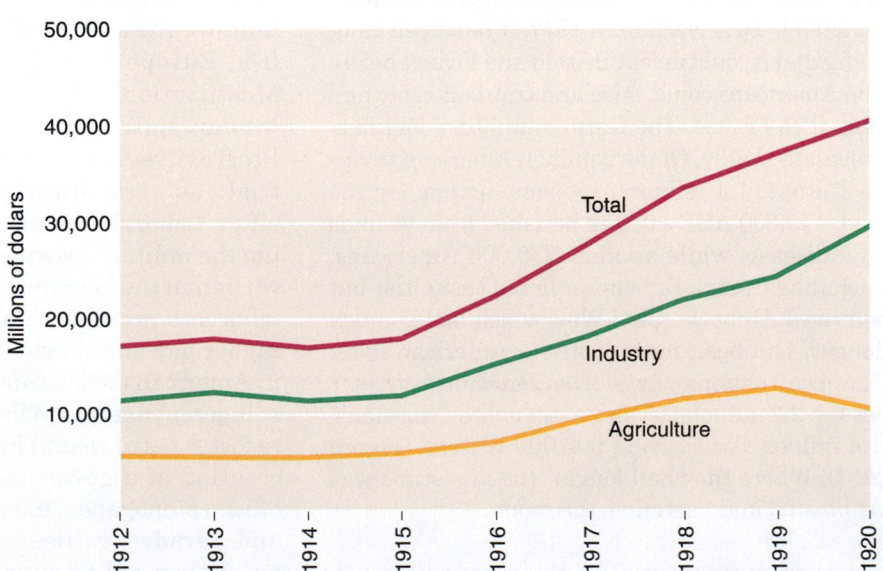

FIGURE 22.2
Industrial Wages, 1912–1920
With help from unions and progressive reformers, wageworkers gradually improved their economic condition. The entry of millions of young men into the armed forces during World War I caused labor shortages and led to a rapid surge in industrial wages.

Agriculture: cash receipts.
Industry: includes mining, electric power, manufacturing, construction, and communications.

of Labor (AFL) saw its membership soar from 2.7 million to more than 5 million.

The war also provided a huge boost to the stalled moral crusade to ban alcohol. By 1917, prohibitionists had convinced nineteen states to go dry. Liquor's opponents now argued that banning alcohol would make the cause of democracy powerful and pure. At the same time, shutting down the distilleries would save millions of bushels of grain that could feed the United States and its allies. "Shall the many have food or the few drink?" the drys asked. Prohibitionists added a patriotic twist by arguing that closing breweries with German names such as Schlitz, Pabst, and Anheuser-Busch would deal a blow to the German cause. In December 1917, Congress passed the **Eighteenth Amendment**, which banned the manufacture, transportation, and sale of alcohol. After swift ratification by the states, the amendment went into effect on January 1, 1920.

Women, War, and the Battle for Suffrage

Women had made real strides during the Progressive Era, and war presented new opportunities. More than 25,000 women served in France. About half were nurses. The others drove ambulances; ran canteens for the Salvation Army, Red Cross, and YMCA; worked with French civilians in devastated areas; and acted as telephone operators and war correspondents. (See "Seeking the American Promise," page 726.) Like men who joined the war effort, they believed that they were taking part in a great national venture. "I am more than willing to live as a soldier and know of the hardships I would have to undergo," one canteen worker declared when applying to go overseas, "but I want to help my country. . . . I want . . . to do the *real* work." And like men, women struggled against disillusionment in France. One woman explained: "Over in America, we thought we knew something about the war . . . but when you get here the difference is [like the one between] studying the laws of electricity and being struck by lightning."

At home, long-standing barriers against hiring women fell when millions of workingmen became soldiers and few new immigrant workers crossed the Atlantic. Tens of thousands of women found work in defense plants as welders, metalworkers, and heavy machine operators — jobs traditionally reserved for men — and with the railroads. A black woman, a domestic before the war, celebrated her job as a laborer in a railroad

yard: "We are making more money at this than any work we can get, and we do not have to work as hard as at housework which requires us to be on duty from six o'clock in the morning until nine or ten at night, with might[y] little time off and at very poor wages." Other women found white-collar work. Between 1910 and 1920, the number of women clerks doubled. Before the war ended, more than a million women had found work in war industries.

The most dramatic advance for women came in the political arena. Since the Seneca Falls convention of 1848, where women voiced their first formal demand for the ballot, the struggle for woman suffrage had inched forward. Adopting a state-by-state approach, suffragists had achieved some success, but before 1910 only four sparsely populated western states had adopted woman suffrage (Map 22.4). Elsewhere, voting rights for women met strong hostility and defeat. After 1910, suffrage leaders added a federal campaign to amend the Constitution, targeting Congress and the president, to the traditional state-by-state strategy for suffrage.

MAP ACTIVITY

Map 22.4 Women's Voting Rights before the Nineteenth Amendment
The long campaign for women's voting rights reversed the pioneer epic that moved from east to west. From its first successes in the new democratic West, suffrage rolled eastward toward the entrenched, male-dominated public life of the Northeast and South.

READING THE MAP: What was the first state to grant woman suffrage? How many states extended full voting rights to women before 1914? How many extended these rights during World War I (1914–1918)?

CONNECTIONS: Suffragists redirected their focus during the war. What strategies did they use then?

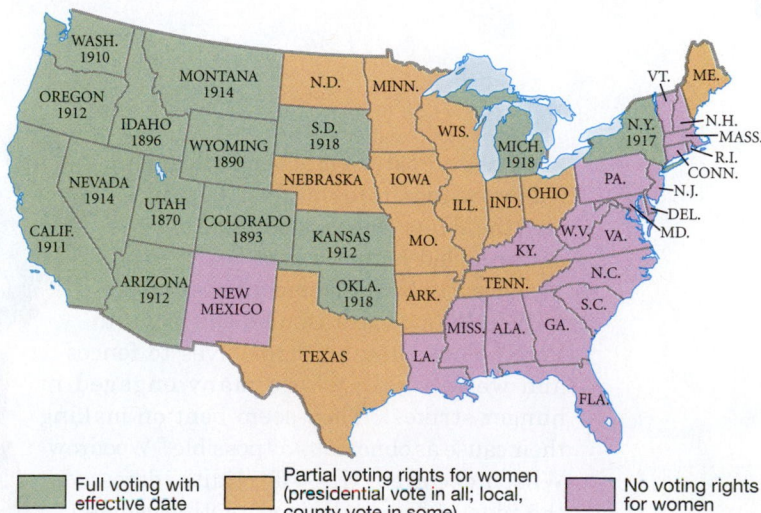

Full voting with effective date

Partial voting rights for women (presidential vote in all; local, county vote in some)

No voting rights for women

Seeking to Serve: An American Woman in Wartime France

When World War I broke out in Europe in 1914, nineteen-year-old Nora Saltonstall was vacationing in Maine with other wellborn young people. A daughter of privilege, she belonged to one of Massachusetts's most distinguished families. But she was no silly, idle debutante. The Saltonstalls instilled in their children a strong sense of the obligation to serve. Within months, she was rolling bandages for the Red Cross in Boston and raising money for the relief of Belgian refugees. By the time the United States entered the war in April 1917, her two Harvard-educated brothers had already volunteered for military service. In October 1917, she volunteered for Red Cross work in France.

After an eleven-day voyage across the submarine-infested Atlantic, Saltonstall arrived in Bordeaux without any idea what she would be doing. She was assigned to long hours of dull work in Paris finding housing for refugees, and like many other American women in France, she contracted "frontline fever," an obsession with getting as far forward in the war zone as she could. She longed for what she called a "man's size job,"

something that would test her mettle and contribute to victory.

By January 1918, Saltonstall had found "real work," which would be "a direct help, even if it is the tiniest drop in the bucket." She joined a group of female Red Cross volunteers attached to a mobile surgical hospital that followed closely behind the French armies. Lacking training as a nurse, she became the unit's driver, responsible for chauffeuring personnel, transporting the wounded, and hauling supplies as the unit moved from place to place. Soon she was driving on muddy, shell-pocked roads in the dark without lights. She also became a mechanic, with the responsibility for maintaining and repairing the vehicles. "I usually cover myself with grease and oil every morning, tinker about a bit and do more harm than good," she wrote home shortly after arriving. But before long, she announced proudly, "I fixed the steering shaft on the Ford all by myself." Her life, she told her mother, consisted of "choked carburetors, broken springs, long hours on the road, food snatched when you can get it, and sleep." Her work brought changes. "I have developed a most

enormous muscle in my right arm, and I am really rather ashamed of it because it literally stands out." She joked, "I'll have to try to direct it into a tennis stroke after the war."

But Saltonstall's sense of humor was tested by the death and destruction she confronted every day. The "stream of wounded men and refugees still makes me ache," she said. "I never hated the war so much before. I have seen enough wounds to hate them, and I don't see how people who have been in it for 3½ years can bear up at all, just one long unending hashing up of people." She lived, she said, in an "insane asylum."

At the same time, she never felt more alive. She believed that she was "learning more . . . than I could learn in years of regular living at home." Saltonstall loved being in the thick of things and "at last feeling as if I were doing something necessary here." She felt proud: "Because we are here, work is being done better and lives saved which might otherwise have been lost. . . . I love my job." She never expressed regrets about coming to France: "If I had not come over I would have felt not to have belonged to this generation and would have felt all my life as if there were something lacking to me on a level with all the up and coming crowd of my own age." Of this she was certain: "After the war there is going to be a difference between those who were in France and those not."

In November 1918, after nearly a year at the front, she scribbled in

---

The radical wing of the suffragists, led by the indomitable Alice Paul, picketed the White House, where the marchers unfurled banners that proclaimed "America Is Not a Democracy. Twenty Million Women Are Denied the Right to Vote." They chained themselves to fences and went to jail, where many engaged in hunger strikes. "They seem bent on making their cause as obnoxious as possible," Woodrow Wilson declared. His wife, Edith, detested the idea of "masculinized" voting women.

But membership in the mainstream organization, the National American Woman Suffrage Association (NAWSA), led by Carrie Chapman Catt, soared to some two million. The NAWSA even accepted African American women into its ranks, though not on an equal basis. Seeing the handwriting on the wall, the Republican and Progressive parties endorsed woman suffrage in 1916.

In 1918, Wilson gave his support to suffrage, calling the amendment "vital to the winning of the war." He conceded that it her diary: "Great excitement, guns stopped firing at midnight. Peace in the air." She celebrated the armistice with the others, but she also realized that her great adventure was almost over. She contemplated her return to the ordinariness of her civilian life: "I wonder when I get to Boston whether I will ever have the courage to motor 80 miles to a party, arrive at midnight, dance until 5 A.M. and then after a wonderful lunch and supper, motor back the next evening." Demobilization left her with a "very flat feeling." In December, the French government decorated Nora and her unit with the Croix de Guerre for their courageous service, and in March 1919 she sailed for home. Nora Saltonstall never got to confront her concerns about reentering American life, however. Just months after returning, on a camping trip in the West, she contracted typhoid fever and died.

Questions for Consideration

1. How did Nora Saltonstall's gender shape her wartime service? How was her experience different from or similar to that of George "Brownie" Browne?

2. Considering domestic developments during and just after the war (discussed later in this chapter), do you think that Saltonstall's worries about life in America after the war were justified? Why or why not?

Nora Saltonstall
Born into Boston's elite, Nora Saltonstall, seen here at the wheel of the yawl *Comanche* off the coast of Maine, grew into a self-assured, adventurous young woman. Although no rebel (she wasn't a suffragist, for example), she was certain that she had something to offer to America's war effort. Unlike most Americans who arrived in Paris during the war, she was no stranger to Europe. While her brothers studied at Harvard, she had spent a year studying art and history while touring the continent. Photo no. 33.3192, Saltonstall-Brooks-Lewis Papers, Massachusetts Historical Society, Boston.

would be wrong not to reward the wartime "partnership of suffering and sacrifice" with a "partnership of privilege and right." By linking their cause to the wartime emphasis on national unity, the advocates of woman suffrage finally triumphed. In 1919, Congress passed the **Nineteenth Amendment**, granting women the vote, and by August 1920 the required two-thirds of the states had ratified it. (See "Documenting the American Promise," page 728.) But rather than being the end of the long road to women's full equality, as some suffragists contended, woman suffrage proved to be only the beginning.

Rally around the Flag — or Else

When Congress committed the nation to war, most peace advocates rallied around the flag. The Carnegie Endowment for International Peace adopted new stationery with the heading "Peace through Victory" and issued a resolution saying that "the most effectual means of promoting peace is to prosecute the war against the Imperial German Government."

The Final Push for Woman Suffrage

By the early twentieth century, the women's movement had mobilized millions, who increasingly concentrated on the passage of an amendment to the U.S. Constitution to ensure women's voting rights. Nothing came easily to the suffragists, but in 1920 their passion and courage were rewarded by the ratification of the Nineteenth Amendment.

DOCUMENT 1
Passing the Baton

Elizabeth Cady Stanton and Susan B. Anthony were best friends and close colleagues in the woman suffrage movement. In this October 1902 letter to Stanton, Anthony acknowledges that neither of them would live to see victory, but she nevertheless remains confident that the campaign will succeed. Stanton died days after receiving this letter, and Anthony died four years later.

My dear Mrs. Stanton . . .

It is fifty-one years since first we met and we have been busy through every one of them, stirring up the world to recognize the rights of women. The older we grow, the more keenly we feel the humiliation of disfranchisement and the more vividly we realize its disadvantages in every department of life and most of all in the labor market.

We little dreamed when we began this contest, optimistic with the hope and buoyancy of youth, that half a century later we would be compelled to leave the finish of the battle to another generation of women. But our hearts are filled with joy to know that they enter upon this task equipped with a college education, with business experience, with the fully admitted right to speak in public — all of which were denied to women fifty years ago. They have practically but one point to gain — the suffrage; we had all. These strong, courageous, capable young women will take our place and complete our work. There is an army of them, where we were but a handful. Ancient prejudice has become so softened, public sentiment so liberalized and women have so thoroughly demonstrated their ability as to leave not a shadow of doubt that they will carry our cause to victory. . . .

Ever lovingly yours, Susan B. Anthony

SOURCE: From *The Elizabeth Cady Stanton–Susan B. Anthony Reader: Correspondence, Writings, Speeches*, 298–99, edited by Ellen Carol DuBois. By permission of Northeastern University Press, 1992.

DOCUMENT 2
Politicking for Suffrage

While radical suffragists chained themselves to the White House fence and went on hunger strikes, other women followed more traditional political channels — methodically gathering petitions, lobbying legislators, building alliances, and rounding up votes. Mary Garrett Hay, vice president of the National American Woman Suffrage Association (NAWSA), reports her efforts with New York state legislators.

New York City, N.Y.
March 13th, 1919

Mrs. Maud Wood Park
1626 Rhode Island Avenue
Washington, D.C.

Dear Mrs. Park,
. . . I kept in very close touch on the telephone and telegraph wire with New York Congressmen and they reported to me, really twice a day what was going on, as far as Speaker, Floor Leader and Suffrage Committee was concerned. I can do more in the House than in the Senate, and I have asked Mr. Hays on the long distance telephone to try and see that things are perfectly straight for our Cause there.

Things will be all right, I believe, but I have made up my mind not to trust either Democrats or Republicans, until the Suffrage Amendment is passed; however, I do not say this to the men[,] only to you, and I shall keep my eyes and ears open and busy, and on the job all I can.

SOURCE: *Women and Social Movements in the United States, 1600–2000*, "How Did Suffragists Lobby to Obtain Congressional Approval of a Woman Suffrage Amendment to the U.S. Constitution, 1917–1920?" Document #10. Courtesy of the Schlesinger Library, Radcliffe Institute, Harvard University (Cambridge, MA).

DOCUMENT 3
The President Intervenes

Although some people urged suffragists to muffle their demands during the war so that the nation could concentrate on victory, Carrie Chapman Catt, president of the NAWSA since 1915, pressed on, recognizing that the war offered a special opportunity. Catt prodded President Woodrow Wilson quietly but persistently, and on September 30, 1918, Wilson finally intervened directly, urging the Senate to pass the Nineteenth Amendment. His argument on behalf of democracy mirrored precisely that of radical suffragists who were protesting in front of the White House.

[The Senate's] adoption is, in my judgment, clearly necessary to the successful prosecution of the war and the successful realization of the objects for which the war is being fought.

. . . If we be indeed democrats and wish to lead the world to democracy, we can ask other peoples to accept in proof of our sincerity and our ability to lead them whither they wish to be led, nothing less persuasive and convincing than our actions.

. . . They are looking to the great, powerful, famous democracy of the West to lead them to a new day for which they have so long waited; and they think, in their logical simplicity, that democracy means that women shall play their part in affairs alongside men and upon an equal footing with them. . . . We have made partners of the women in this war. Shall we admit them only to a partnership of suffering and sacrifice and toil and not to a partnership of privilege and right?

This war could not have been fought, either by the other nations engaged or by America, if it had not been for the services of the women — services rendered in every sphere. . . .

. . . I tell you plainly that this measure which I urge upon you is vital to the winning of the war and to the energies alike of preparation and of battle.

. . . And not to winning the war only. It is vital to the right solution of the great problems which we must settle, and settle immediately, when the war is over. We shall need in our vision of affairs, as we have never needed them before, the sympathy and insight and clear moral instinct of the women of the world. . . . We shall need their moral sense to preserve what is right and fine and worthy in our system of life as well as to discover just what it is that ought to be purified and reformed. Without their counsellings we shall be only half wise.

SOURCE: "Appeal of President Wilson to the Senate of the United States to Submit the Federal Amendment for Woman Suffrage Delivered in Person Sept. 20, 1918," in *History of Woman Suffrage*, Vol. 5: 1900–1920, 760–63.

DOCUMENT 4
Reflections on Victory

Carrie Chapman Catt celebrates the passage of the Nineteenth Amendment in this letter to her staff at the NAWSA on Thanksgiving Day 1920. She reflects on the long road to victory and considers the satisfactions of the journey.

I have kept Thanksgiving sacred to reflections upon the long trail behind us, and the triumph which was its inevitable conclusion. John Adams said long after the Revolution that only about one third of the people were for it, a third being against it, and the remaining third utterly indifferent. Perhaps this proportion applies to all movements. At least a third of the women were for our cause at the end. . . . As I look back over the years . . . I realize that the greatest thing in the long campaign for us was not its crowning victory, but the discipline it gave us all. . . . It was a great crusade, the world has seen none more wonderful. . . . My admiration, love and reverence go out to that band which fought and won a revolution . . . with congratulations that we were permitted to establish a new and good thing in the world.

SOURCE: Carrie Chapman Catt to NAWSA Office Staff, Thanksgiving Day 1920, in Elizabeth Frost and Kathryn Cullen-DuPont, *Women's Suffrage in America: An Eyewitness History* (1992), 335–36.

Questions for Analysis and Debate

1. Why was Susan B. Anthony confident that woman suffrage would soon become a reality?

2. Why were some legislators in New York and elsewhere willing to work closely with suffragists such as Mary Garrett Hay?

3. What, according to Woodrow Wilson, would America's rejection of the Nineteenth Amendment have jeopardized?

4. What do you suppose Carrie Chapman Catt meant when she said that the greatest gain for women in the suffrage campaign was "discipline"?

D. W. Griffith's *Hearts of the World*
Hollywood joined in the government's efforts to stir up rage against the "brutal Huns," as Germans were often called. In a film made for the British and French governments by America's leading filmmaker, D. W. Griffith, a hulking German is about to whip a defenseless farm woman (played by Lillian Gish, one of the nation's favorite actors). When the film premiered in Washington, D.C., in 1918, First Lady Edith Wilson wrote to Griffith, pleading with him to cut or soften the violent whipping scene. Edith Wilson was one of the few people in the nation's capital who sought to moderate the hate campaign. Library of Congress.

Only a handful of reformers resisted the tide of patriotism. A group of professional women, led by settlement house leader Jane Addams and economics professor Emily Greene Balch, denounced what Addams described as "the pathetic belief in the regenerative results of war." The Women's Peace Party, which emerged in 1915, and its foreign affiliates in the Women's International League for Peace and Freedom led the struggle to persuade governments to negotiate peace and spare dissenters from harsh punishment. After America entered the conflict, advocates for peace were routinely labeled

cowards and traitors, their efforts crushed by the steamroller of conformity.

To suppress criticism of the war, Wilson stirred up patriotic fervor. In 1917, the president created the **Committee on Public Information** under the direction of George Creel, a journalist, who became the nation's cheerleader for war. He sent "Four-Minute Men," a squad of 75,000 volunteers, around the country to give brief pep talks that celebrated successes on the battlefields and in the factories. Posters, pamphlets, and cartoons depicted brave American soldiers and sailors defending freedom and democracy against the evil "Huns."

America rallied around Creel's campaign. The film industry cranked out melodramas about battle-line and home-front heroes and taught audiences to hiss at the German kaiser. A musical, *The Kaiser: The Beast of Berlin*, opened on Broadway in 1918. Faculties of colleges and universities generated war propaganda in the guise of scholarship. When Professor James McKeen Cattell of Columbia University urged that America seek peace with Germany short of victory, university president Nicholas Murray Butler fired him on the grounds that "what had been folly is now treason."

A firestorm of anti-German passion erupted. Across the nation, "100% American" campaigns enlisted ordinary people to sniff out disloyalty. German, the most widely taught foreign language in 1914, practically disappeared from the nation's schools. Targeting German-born Americans, the *Saturday Evening Post* declared that it was time to rid the country of "the scum of the melting pot." Rabid anti-German action reached its extreme with the lynching of Robert Prager, a baker in Collinsville, Illinois. In the eyes of the mob, it was enough that Prager was German-born and had socialist leanings, even though he had not opposed American participation in the war. Persuaded by the defense lawyer who praised what he called a "patriotic murder," the jury at the trial of the killers took only twenty-five minutes to acquit.

As hysteria increased, the campaign reached absurd levels. In Montana, a school board barred a history text that had good things to say about medieval Germany. Menus across the nation changed German toast to French toast and sauerkraut to liberty cabbage. In Milwaukee, vigilantes mounted a machine gun outside the Pabst Theater to prevent the staging of Schiller's *Wilhelm Tell*, a powerful protest against tyranny. One vigilant citizen claimed to see a periscope in the Great Lakes, and the fiancée of one of the war's leading critics, caught dancing on the dunes of Cape Cod, was held on suspicion of signaling to German submarines.

The Wilson administration's zeal in suppressing dissent contrasted sharply with its war aims of defending democracy. In the name of self-defense, the Espionage Act (June 1917), the Trading with the Enemy Act (October 1917), and the Sedition Act (May 1918) gave the government sweeping powers to punish any opinion or activity it considered "disloyal, profane, scurrilous, or abusive." When Postmaster General Albert Burleson blocked mailing privileges for dissenting publications, dozens of journals were forced to close down. Of the 1,500 individuals eventually charged with sedition, all but a dozen had merely spoken words the government found objectionable. One of them was Eugene V. Debs, the leader of the Socialist Party, who was convicted under the Espionage Act for speeches condemning the war as a capitalist plot and sent to the Atlanta penitentiary.

The president hoped that national commitment to the war would silence partisan politics, but his Republican rivals used the war as a weapon against the Democrats. The trick was to oppose Wilson's conduct of the war but not the war itself. Republicans outshouted Wilson on the nation's need to mobilize for war but then complained that Wilson's War Industries Board was a tyrannical agency that crushed free enterprise. Such attacks appealed to widely diverse business, labor, and patriotic groups. As the war progressed, Republicans gathered power against the Democrats, who had narrowly reelected Wilson in 1916.

In 1918, Republicans gained a narrow majority in both the House and the Senate. The end of Democratic control of Congress not only halted further domestic reform but also meant that the United States would advance toward military victory in Europe with political power divided between a Democratic president and a Republican Congress likely to challenge Wilson's plans for international cooperation.

REVIEW   How did progressive ideals fare during wartime?

▶ A Compromised Peace

Wilson decided to reaffirm his noble war ideals by announcing his peace aims before the end of hostilities. He hoped the victorious Allies would adopt his plan for international democracy, but he was sorely disappointed. The leaders of Britain, France, and Italy (which had joined the Allies in 1915 in hopes of postwar gains) understood that Wilson's principles jeopardized their own postwar plans for the acquisition of enemy territory, new colonial empires, and reparations. Wilson also faced strong opposition at home from those who feared that his enthusiasm for international cooperation would undermine American sovereignty.

Wilson's Fourteen Points

On January 8, 1918, President Wilson revealed to Congress his **Fourteen Points**, his blueprint for a new democratic world order. The first five points affirmed basic liberal ideals: an end to secret treaties; freedom of the seas; removal of economic barriers to free trade; reduction of weapons of war; and recognition of the rights of colonized peoples. The next eight points supported the right to self-determination of European peoples who had been dominated by Germany or its allies. Wilson's fourteenth point called for a "general association of nations" — a **League of Nations** — to provide "mutual guarantees of political independence and territorial integrity to great and small states alike." A League of Nations reflected Wilson's lifelong dream of a "parliament of man." Only such an organization of "peace-loving nations," he believed, could justify the war and secure a lasting peace.

Citizens of the United States and of every Allied country greeted the Fourteen Points enthusiastically. Wilson felt confident that he could prevail against undemocratic and selfish forces at the peace table. During the final year of the war, he pressured the Allies to accept the Fourteen Points as the basis of the postwar settlement.

The Paris Peace Conference

From January 18 to June 28, 1919, the eyes of the world focused on Paris. There, powerful men wrestled with difficult problems. Although no other American president had ever gone to Europe while in office, Wilson, inspired by his mission, decided to head the U.S. delegation. He said he owed it to the American soldiers. "It is now my duty," he announced, "to play my full part in making good what they gave their life's blood to obtain." A dubious British diplomat retorted that Wilson was drawn to Paris "as a debutante is

> **"God himself was content with ten commandments."**
> — French premier GEORGES CLEMENCEAU, disparaging Wilson's Fourteen Points

entranced by the prospect of her first ball." The decision to leave the country at a time when his political opponents challenged his leadership was risky enough, but his stubborn refusal to include prominent Republicans in the delegation proved foolhardy and eventually cost him his dream of a new world order with the United States at its center.

After four terrible years of war, the common people of Europe almost worshipped Wilson, believing that he would create a safer, more decent world. When the peace conference convened at Louis XIV's magnificent palace at Versailles, however, Wilson encountered a different reception. Representing the Allies were the decidedly unidealistic David Lloyd George, prime minister of Britain; Georges Clemenceau,

premier of France; and Vittorio Orlando, former prime minister of Italy. To the Allied leaders, Wilson appeared a naive and impractical moralist. His desire to gather former enemies within a new international democratic order showed how little he understood hard European realities. Clemenceau claimed that Wilson "believed you could do everything by formulas" and "empty theory." Disparaging the Fourteen Points, he added, "God himself was content with ten commandments."

The Allies wanted to fasten blame for the war on Germany, totally disarm it, and make it pay so dearly that it would never threaten its neighbors again. The French demanded retribution in the form of territory containing Germany's richest mineral resources. The British made it

Leaders of the Paris Peace Conference
The three leaders in charge of putting the world back together after the Great War — from left to right, British prime minister David Lloyd George, French premier Georges Clemenceau, and U.S. president Woodrow Wilson — amiably and confidently stride toward the peace conference at the Versailles palace. Clemenceau is caught offering animated instruction to Wilson, whom he considered naively idealistic. Indeed, in an unguarded moment, Clemenceau expressed his contempt for the entire United States as a country that was unique in having passed directly from barbarism to decadence without an intervening period of civilization. Gamma Liaison/Getty Images.

clear that they were not about to give up the powerful weapon of naval blockade for the vague principle of freedom of the seas.

The Allies forced Wilson to make drastic compromises. In return for France's moderating its territorial claims, he agreed to support Article 231 of the peace treaty, assigning war guilt to Germany. Though saved from permanently losing Rhineland territory to the French, Germany was outraged at being singled out as the instigator of the war and being saddled with more than $33 billion in damages. Many Germans felt that their nation had been betrayed. After agreeing to an armistice in the belief that peace terms would be based in Wilson's generous Fourteen Points, they faced hardship and humiliation instead.

Wilson had better success in establishing the principle of self-determination. But from the beginning, Secretary of State Robert Lansing knew that the president's concept of self-determination was "simply loaded with dynamite." Lansing won-

dered, "What unit has he in mind? Does he mean a race, a territorial area, or a community?" Even Wilson was vague about what self-determination actually meant. "When I gave utterance to those words," he admitted, "I said them without the knowledge that nationalities existed, which are coming to us day after day." Lansing suspected that the notion "will raise hopes which can never be realized. It will, I fear, cost thousands of lives. In the end it is bound to be discredited, to be called the dream of an idealist who failed to realize the danger until it was too late."

Yet partly on the basis of self-determination, the conference redrew the map of Europe and parts of the rest of the world. Portions of Austria-Hungary were ceded to Italy, Poland, and Romania, and the remainder was reassembled into Austria, Hungary, Czechoslovakia, and Yugoslavia — independent republics whose boundaries were drawn with attention to concentrations of major ethnic groups. More arbitrarily, the Ottoman empire was carved

MAP 22.5

Europe after World War I
The post–World War I settlement redrew boundaries to create new nations based on ethnic groupings. Within defeated Germany and Russia, this outcome left bitter peoples who resolved to recover the territory taken from them.

up into small mandates (including Palestine) run by local leaders but under the control of France and Great Britain. The conference reserved the mandate system for those regions it deemed insufficiently "civilized" to have full independence. Thus, the reconstructed nations — each beset with ethnic and nationalist rivalries — faced the challenge of making a new democratic government work (Map 22.5). Many of today's bitterest disputes — in the Balkans and Iraq, between Greece and Turkey, between Arabs and Jews — have roots in the decisions made in Paris in 1919.

Wilson hoped that self-determination would also dictate the fate of Germany's colonies in Asia and Africa. But the Allies, who had taken over the colonies during the war, allowed the League of Nations only a mandate to administer them. Technically, the mandate system rejected imperialism, but in reality it allowed the Allies to maintain control. Thus, while denying Germany its colonies, the Allies retained and added to their own far-flung territories.

The cause of democratic equality suffered another setback when the peace conference rejected Japan's call for a statement of racial equality in the treaty. Wilson's belief in the superiority of whites, as well as his apprehension about how white Americans would respond to such a declaration, led him to oppose the clause. To soothe hurt feelings, Wilson agreed to grant Japan a mandate over the Shantung Peninsula in northern China, which had formerly been controlled by Germany. The gesture mollified Japan's moderate leaders, but the military faction preparing to take over the country used bitterness toward racist Western colonialism to build support for expanding Japanese power throughout Asia.

Closest to Wilson's heart was finding a new way to manage international relations. In Wilson's view, war had discredited the old strategy of balance of power. Instead, he proposed a League of Nations that would provide collective security. The league would establish rules of international conduct and resolve conflicts between nations through rational and peaceful means. When the Allies agreed to the league, Wilson was overjoyed. He believed that the league would rectify the errors his colleagues had forced on him in Paris. The league would solidify and extend the noble work he had begun.

To some Europeans and Americans, the **Versailles treaty** came as a bitter disappointment. Wilson's admirers were shocked that the president dealt in compromise like any other politician. But without Wilson's presence, the treaty that was signed on June 28, 1919, surely would have been more vindictive. Wilson returned home in July 1919 consoled that, despite his frustrations, he had gained what he most wanted — a League of Nations. In Wilson's judgment, "We have completed in the least time possible the greatest work that four men have ever done."

The Fight for the Treaty

The tumultuous reception Wilson received when he arrived home persuaded him, probably correctly, that the American people supported the treaty. When the president submitted the treaty to the Senate in July 1919, he warned that failure to ratify it would "break the heart of the world." By then, however, criticism of the treaty was mounting, especially from Americans convinced that their countries of ethnic origin had not been given fair treatment. Irish Americans, Italian Americans, and German Americans launched especially sharp attacks. Others worried that the president's concessions at Versailles had jeopardized the treaty's capacity to provide a generous plan for rebuilding Europe and to guarantee world peace.

Some of the most potent critics were found in the Senate. Bolstered by a slight Republican majority in Congress, a group of Republican "irreconcilables," which included such powerful isolationist senators as Hiram Johnson of California and William Borah of Idaho, condemned the treaty for entangling the United States in world affairs. A larger group of Republicans did not object to American participation in world politics but feared that membership in the League of Nations would jeopardize the nation's ability to act independently. No Republican, in any case, was eager to hand Wilson and the Democrats a foreign policy victory with the 1920 presidential election little more than a year away.

At the center of Republican opposition was Wilson's archenemy, Senator **Henry Cabot Lodge** of Massachusetts. Lodge's hostility was in part personal. "I never thought I could hate a man as much as I hate Wilson," he once admitted. But Lodge also raised cogent objections to the treaty and the league. Lodge was no isolationist, but he thought that much of the Fourteen Points was a "general bleat about virtue being better than vice." Lodge expected the United States' economic and military power to propel the nation into a major role in world affairs. But he insisted that membership in the League of Nations, which would require collective action to maintain peace, threatened the nation's independence in foreign relations.

"Refusing to Give the Lady a Seat"
Woodrow Wilson promised that the League of Nations would usher in an age of international peace. When stiff opposition to American membership in the league developed in the United States, friends of the league mounted a counterattack. This cartoon skewers the three leading Republican opponents of the league — Senators William Borah of Idaho, Henry Cabot Lodge of Massachusetts, and Hiram Johnson of California — who stubbornly refuse to budge an inch for the angel of peace. Clever cartoons could not save the league, however. Only shrewd diplomacy could do that, and Wilson was not able to deliver. Picture Research Consultants & Archives.

Lodge used his position as chairman of the Senate Foreign Relations Committee to air every sort of complaint. Out of the committee hearings came several amendments, or "reservations," that sought to limit the consequences of American membership in the league. For example, several reservations required approval of both the House and the Senate before the United States could participate in league-sponsored economic sanctions or military action.

It gradually became clear that ratification of the treaty depended on acceptance of the Lodge reservations. Democratic senators, who overwhelmingly supported the treaty, urged Wilson to accept Lodge's terms, arguing that they left the essentials of the treaty intact. Wilson, however, insisted that the reservations cut "the very heart out of the treaty." He expressed personal hatred as well. "*Lodge* reservations?" he thundered. "Never! I'll never consent to adopt any policy with which that impossible name is so prominently identified."

Wilson decided to take his case directly to the people. On September 3, 1919, still exhausted from the peace conference and against the objections of his doctors, he set out by train on the most ambitious speaking tour ever undertaken by a president. On September 25 in Pueblo, Colorado, Wilson collapsed and had to return to Washington. There, he suffered a massive stroke that partially paralyzed him. From his bedroom, Wilson sent messages instructing Democrats in the Senate to hold firm against any and all reservations. Wilson commanded enough loyalty to ensure a vote against the Lodge reservations. But when the treaty without reservations came before the Senate in March 1920, the combined opposition of the Republican irreconcilables and reservationists left Wilson six votes short of the two-thirds majority needed for passage. Wilson told his doctor, "The Devil is a busy man."

The nations of Europe organized the League of Nations at Geneva, Switzerland. Although Woodrow Wilson received the Nobel Peace Prize in 1920 for his central role in creating the league, the United States never became a member. In refusing to accept relatively minor compromises with Senate moderates, Wilson lost his treaty and American membership in the league. Whether American membership could have prevented the world war that would begin in Europe in 1939 is highly unlikely, but the United States' failure to join certainly weakened the league from the start. Woodrow Wilson and Henry Cabot Lodge both died in 1924, never seeing international order or security, never knowing the whirlwind of resentment and violence that would eventually follow the Great War's failure to make the world safe for democracy.

REVIEW   Why did the Senate fail to ratify the Versailles treaty?

▶ Democracy at Risk

The defeat of Wilson's plan for international democracy proved the crowning blow to progressives who had hoped that the war could boost reform at home. When the war ended, Americans wanted to demobilize swiftly. In the process, servicemen, defense workers, and farmers lost their war-related jobs. The volatile combination — of unemployed veterans returning home, a stalled economy, and leftover wartime patriotism looking for a new cause — threatened to explode. Wartime anti-German passion was quickly followed by

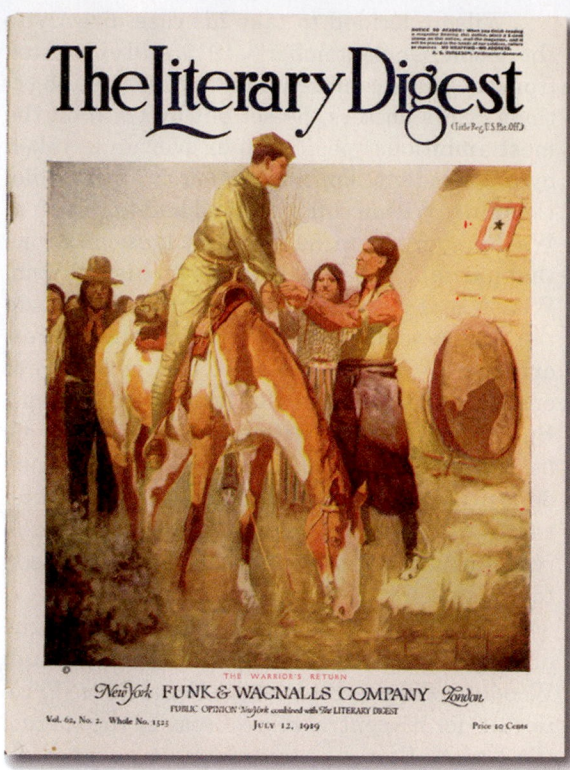

"The Warrior's Return"
About 16,000 Native Americans served in the U.S. armed forces during World War I. This magazine cover offers a romanticized reconstruction of one homecoming. The young soldier, still in uniform and presumably fresh from France, rides his pony to the tepee of his parents, who proudly welcome their brave warrior. The tepee is decorated with a star, a national symbol that families with sons in the military displayed on their homes. The painting sought to demonstrate that even Americans on the margins of national life were sufficiently assimilated and loyal to join the national sacrifice to defeat the enemy. Picture Research Consultants & Archives.

antiradicalism, a fevered campaign that ensnared unionists, socialists, dissenters, and African Americans and Mexicans who had committed no offense but to seek to escape rural poverty. The 1920 election marked the end of Wilson's two terms in the White House and his crusades.

Economic Hardship and Labor Upheaval

Americans greeted peace with a demand that the United States return to a peacetime economy. The government abruptly abandoned its wartime economic controls and canceled war contracts worth millions of dollars. In a matter of months, 3 million soldiers mustered out of the military and flooded the job market just as war production ceased. Unemployment soared. At the same time, consumers went on a postwar spending spree that drove inflation skyward. In 1919, prices rose 75 percent over prewar levels, and in 1920 prices rose another 28 percent.

Most of the gains workers had made during the war evaporated. Freed from government controls, business turned against the eight-hour day and attacked labor unions. With inflation eating up their paychecks, workers fought back. The year 1919 witnessed nearly 3,600 strikes involving 4 million workers. The

most spectacular strike occurred in February 1919 in Seattle, where shipyard workers had been put out of work by demobilization. When a coalition of the radical Industrial Workers of the World (IWW, called Wobblies) and the moderate American Federation of Labor called a general strike, the largest work stoppage in American history shut down the city. Newspapers claimed that the walkout was "a Bolshevik effort to start a revolution." The suppression of the **Seattle general strike** by city officials cost the AFL many of its wartime gains and contributed to the destruction of the IWW soon afterward.

A strike by Boston policemen in the fall of 1919 underscored postwar hostility toward labor militancy. Although the police had received no raise since before the war and were paid less than pick-and-shovel laborers, they won little sympathy. Once the officers stopped walking their beats, looters sacked the city. Massachusetts governor Calvin Coolidge called in the National Guard to restore order and broke the **Boston police strike**. The public, yearning for peace and security in the wake of war, welcomed Coolidge's anti-union assurance that "there is no right to strike against the public safety by anybody, anywhere, any time." Labor strife climaxed in the grim **steel strike of 1919**. Faced with the industry's plan to revert to seven-day

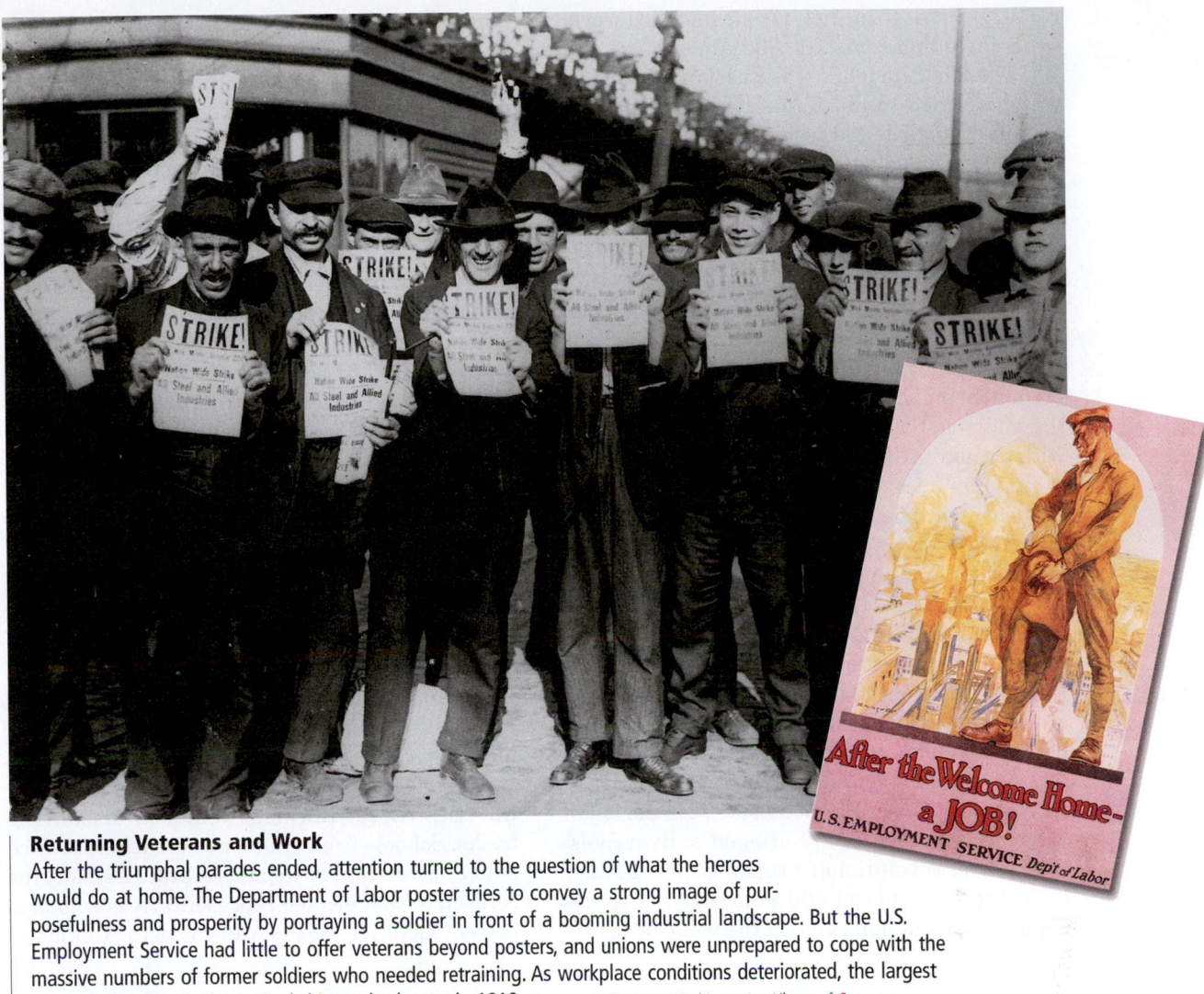

Returning Veterans and Work
After the triumphal parades ended, attention turned to the question of what the heroes would do at home. The Department of Labor poster tries to convey a strong image of purposefulness and prosperity by portraying a soldier in front of a booming industrial landscape. But the U.S. Employment Service had little to offer veterans beyond posters, and unions were unprepared to cope with the massive numbers of former soldiers who needed retraining. As workplace conditions deteriorated, the largest number of strikes in the nation's history broke out in 1919. Veterans: © Bettmann/Corbis; poster: Library of Congress.

weeks, twelve-hour days, and weekly wages of about $20, Samuel Gompers, head of the AFL, called for a strike. In September, 350,000 workers in fifteen states walked out. The steel industry hired 30,000 strikebreakers (many of them African Americans) and convinced the public that the strikers were radicals bent on subverting democracy and capitalism. In January 1920, after 18 striking workers were killed, the strike collapsed. That devastating defeat initiated a sharp decline in the fortunes of the labor movement, a trend that would continue for almost twenty years.

The Red Scare

Suppression of labor strikes was one response to the widespread fear of internal subversion that swept the nation in 1919. The **Red scare** ("Red" referred to the color of the Bolshevik flag) far outstripped even the assault on civil liberties during the war. It had homegrown causes: the postwar recession, labor unrest, terrorist acts, and the difficulties of reintegrating millions of returning veterans. But unsettling events abroad also added to Americans' anxieties.

Two epidemics swept the globe in 1918. One was Spanish influenza, which brought on a lethal accumulation of fluid in the lungs. A nurse near the front lines in France observed that victims "run a high temperature, so high that we can't believe it's true. . . . It is accompanied by vomiting and dysentery. When they die, as about half of them do, they turn a ghastly dark gray and are taken out at once and cremated." Before the flu virus had run its course, 40 million people had died worldwide, including some 700,000 Americans.

The other epidemic was Russian bolshevism, which seemed to most Americans at the time equally contagious and deadly. Bolshevism became even more menacing in March 1919, when the new Soviet leaders created the Comintern, a worldwide association of Communists intent on fomenting revolution in capitalist countries. (See "Beyond America's Borders," page 740.) A Communist revolution in the United States was extremely unlikely, but edgy Americans, faced with a flurry of terrorist acts, believed otherwise. Dozens of prominent individuals had received bombs through the mail. On September 16, 1920, a wagon filled with dynamite and iron exploded on Wall Street, killing 38 and maiming 143 others. Authorities never caught the terrorists, and the successful attack on America's financial capital fed the nation's fear, anger, and uncertainty.

Even before the Wall Street bombing, the government had initiated a hunt for domestic revolutionaries. Led by Attorney General **A. Mitchell Palmer**, the campaign targeted men and women who harbored ideas that Palmer believed could lead to violence, even though the individuals may not have done anything illegal. In January 1920, Palmer ordered a series of raids that netted 6,000 alleged subversives. Finding no revolutionary conspiracies, Palmer nevertheless ordered 500 noncitizen suspects deported. His action came in the wake of a campaign against the most notorious radical alien, Russian-born **Emma Goldman**. Before the war, Goldman's passionate support of labor strikes, women's rights, and birth control had made her a symbol of radicalism. Finally, after a stay in prison for denouncing military conscription, she was ordered deported by J. Edgar Hoover, the eager director of the Justice Department's Radical Division. In December 1919, as Goldman and 250 others boarded a ship for exile in Russia, she turned defiantly to thumb her nose at a jeering crowd.

The effort to rid the country of alien radicals was matched by efforts to crush troublesome citizens. Law enforcement officials and vigilante groups joined hands against so-called Reds. In November 1919 in the rugged lumber town of Centralia, Washington, a menacing crowd gathered in front of the IWW hall. Nervous Wobblies inside opened fire, killing three people. Three IWW members were arrested and later convicted of murder, but another, ex-soldier Wesley Everett, was carried off by the mob, which castrated him, hung him from a bridge, and then riddled his body with bullets. His death was officially ruled a suicide.

Public institutions joined the attack on civil liberties. Local libraries removed dissenting books. Schools fired unorthodox teachers. Police shut down radical newspapers. State legislatures refused to seat elected representatives who professed socialist ideas. And in 1919, Congress

Emergency Hospital
Despite its name, the Spanish flu was first observed in the spring of 1918 in Kansas. Army camps, with their close troop quarters, proved perfect incubators. This emergency hospital at Camp Funston, Kansas, is filled with soldiers who were among the flu's early victims. Crowded troopships quickly spread the virus to Europe. Civilians were not immune. In October 1918 in Philadelphia, more than 4500 people died in a single week. Contracting the Spanish flu was not a death sentence, but it disproportionately killed young adults. National Museum of Health & Medicine, Armed Forces Institute of Pathology.

Rooting out Reds
On January 2, 1920, Attorney General A. Mitchell Palmer ordered hundreds of federal agents to thirty-three American cities to smash the alleged Bolshevik conspiracy. Led by J. Edgar Hoover, the agents arrested more than six thousand individuals on charges of plotting to overthrow the government. The agents who carried out Palmer's Red-hunting were not particularly careful about protecting the property of those they targeted. This photograph of the Industrial Workers of the World (IWW) headquarters in New York City shows the results of one raid. Labadie Collection, University of Michigan.

removed its lone socialist representative, Victor Berger, on the pretext that he was a threat to national safety.

That same year, the Supreme Court provided a formula for restricting free speech. In upholding the conviction of socialist Charles Schenck for publishing a pamphlet urging resistance to the draft during wartime (*Schenck v. United States*), the Court established a "clear and present danger" test. Such utterances as Schenck's during a time of national peril, Justice Oliver Wendell Holmes wrote, were equivalent to shouting "Fire!" in a crowded theater. But Schenck's pamphlet had little power to provoke a public firmly opposed to its message.

In 1920, the assault on civil liberties provoked the creation of the **American Civil Liberties Union (ACLU)**, which was dedicated to defending the individual rights that the Constitution guaranteed. One of the ACLU's founders, Roger Baldwin, declared, "So long as we have enough people in this country willing to fight for their rights, we'll be called a democracy." The ACLU championed the targets of Attorney General Palmer's campaign — politically radical immigrants, trade unionists, socialists and Communists, and antiwar activists who still languished in jail.

But in the end, the Red scare collapsed because of its excesses. In particular, the antiradical campaign lost credibility after Palmer warned in the spring of 1920 that radicals were planning to celebrate the Bolshevik Revolution with a nationwide wave of violence on May 1, international workers' day. Officials called out state militias, mobilized bomb squads, and even placed machine-gun nests at major city intersections. When May 1 came and went without a single disturbance, the public mood turned from fear to scorn.

The Great Migrations of African Americans and Mexicans

Before the Red scare lost steam, the government raised alarms about the loyalty of African Americans. A Justice Department investigation concluded that Reds were fomenting racial unrest among blacks. Although the report was wrong about Bolshevik influence, it was correct in noticing a new stirring among African Americans, an assertiveness born of participation in the war effort and the massive migration out of the South.

In 1900, nine of every ten blacks still lived in the South, where poverty, disfranchisement, segregation, and violence dominated their lives. A majority of black men continued to toil in agriculture as dirt-poor tenants or sharecroppers or worked for wages of 60 cents a day. Black women worked in the homes of whites as domestics for $2 a week. Whites remained committed to keeping blacks down. "If we own a good farm or horse, or cow, or bird-dog, or yoke of oxen," a

Bolshevism

In March 1917, revolutionaries overthrew the Russian czar, whose conservative autocracy was the target of peasants and urban workers seeking a more democratic government. But Marxist radicals, who called themselves Bolsheviks, were not satisfied with the regime change. In November, the Bolsheviks seized control of Russia and made their leader, Vladimir Ilyich Lenin, ruler. Lenin scoffed at the idea that the Allies were fighting for democracy and insisted that greedy capitalists were waging war for international dominance. In March 1918, he shocked Woodrow Wilson and the Allies by signing a separate peace with Germany and withdrawing Russia from the war. Still locked in the desperate struggle with Germany, the Allies cried betrayal.

The Bolshevik regime dedicated itself to ending capitalism in Russia (known as the Soviet Union after 1922) and to instituting what it called a "dictatorship of the proletariat." In theory, workers — agricultural and industrial — would control the economy and exercise political power. But very quickly a gap opened between the workers and party leaders, who instituted a top-down apparatus that institutionalized the bloody repression of their opponents.

Prodded by British leader Winston Churchill, who declared that "the Bolshevik infant should be strangled in its cradle," Britain and France urged the United States to join them in sending troops to Russia in support of Russian democrats opposing the new revolutionary regime. Several prominent Americans spoke out against American intervention. Senator William Borah of Idaho declared: "The Russian people have the same right to establish a Socialist state as we have to establish a republic." But Wilson concluded that the Bolsheviks were a dictatorial party that had come to power through a violent coup that denied Russians political choice, and in September 1918 he ordered 14,000 U.S. troops to join British and French forces in Russia. U.S., British, and French troops fought to overthrow Lenin and annul the Bolshevik Revolution, but the Bolsheviks (by now calling themselves Communists) prevailed. U.S. troops withdrew from Russia in June 1919, after the loss of more than 200 American lives.

The Bolshevik regime also committed itself to overthrowing capitalist and imperialist regimes around the world. Clearly, Lenin's imagined future was at odds with Wilson's proposed liberal new world order. Wilson withheld U.S. diplomatic recognition of the Soviet Union (a policy that persisted until 1934) and joined the Allies in an economic boycott to bring down the Bolshevik government. Unbowed, Lenin promised that his party would "incite rebellion among all the peoples now oppressed," and revolutionary agitation became central to Soviet foreign policy. Just after the armistice, Communist revolutions erupted in Bavaria and Hungary. Though short-lived, the Communist regimes there sent shock waves throughout the West. In 1919, moreover, a Russian official bragged that monies being sent to Europe to foment Bolshevik rebellion were "nothing compared to the funds transmitted to New York for the purpose of spreading bolshevism in the United States." American attention shifted from revolutionaries in Europe to revolutionaries at home. The Red scare was on.

Attorney General A. Mitchell Palmer perceived a "blaze of Revolution sweeping over every American institution of law and order . . . licking the altars of churches . . . crawling into the sacred corners of American homes." In 1919, the U.S. government launched an all-out attack on the Communist ("Red") menace. In the same year, disgruntled socialists founded the American Communist Party, but it attracted only a handful of members, who spent most of their time arguing the fine points of doctrine, not manufacturing bombs. However, the few radicals who did resort to bombs prompted near panic

black sharecropper in Mississippi observed in 1913, "we are harassed until we are bound to sell, give away, or run away, before we can have any peace in our lives."

The First World War provided African Americans with the opportunity to escape the South's cotton fields and kitchens. War channeled almost 5 million American workers into military service and caused the number of European immigrants to fall from more than a million in 1914 to 31,000 in 1918. Deprived of their traditional sources of laborers just as production

demands were increasing, northern industrialists turned to black labor. Young black men, who made up the bulk of the early migrants, found work in steel mills, shipyards, munitions plants, railroad yards, automobile factories, and mines. From 1915 to 1920, a half million blacks (approximately 10 percent of the South's black population) boarded trains bound for Philadelphia, Detroit, Cleveland, Chicago, St. Louis, and other industrial cities.

Thousands of migrants wrote home to tell family and friends about their experiences in the in some quarters. Even mild dissenters faced bullying and threats. Workers seeking better wages and conditions, women and African Americans demanding equal rights, and anyone else pushing for change found the government hurling the epithet "Red" at them. Before the hysteria subsided, the nation witnessed beatings, jailings, and deportations.

The Bolshevik Revolution had endless consequences. In the Soviet Union, it initiated a brutal reign of terror that lasted for more than seven decades. In international politics, it set up a polarity that lasted nearly as long. In a very real sense, the Cold War, which set the United States and the Soviet Union at each other's throats after World War II, began in 1917. America's abortive military intervention against the Bolshevik regime and the Bolsheviks' call for worldwide revolution convulsed relations from the very beginning. In the United States, the rabid antiradicalism of the Red scare threatened traditional American values. Commitment to the protection of dissent succumbed to irrational anticommunism. Even mild reform became tarred with the brush of bolshevism. Although the Red scare quickly withered, the habit of crushing dissent in the name of security would live on. Years later, in the 1950s, when Americans' anxiety mounted and their confidence waned once again, witch-hunts against radicalism reemerged to undermine American democracy.

Vladimir Ilyich Lenin
After the Bolshevik success in Russia in 1917, Lenin became the face of the Communist revolution. His call for workers everywhere to rise against the ruling classes and end capitalism and imperialism sent chills down spines throughout much of Western Europe and the United States. Rather than viewing Lenin as a bloodthirsty monster, however, this dramatic portrait presents him as the courageous hero of the people's revolution. Lenin admitted that in the United States revolution would "probably not come soon," but that gave Americans little comfort. AP/Wide World Photos.

America in a Global Context

1. Why did U.S.-Bolshevik relations get off to such a rocky start? Were harsh relations the result of certain policy decisions or inherent in the clashing value systems?

2. In the United States, is there an inevitable tension between national security and free expression? Why or why not?

North. One man announced proudly that he had recently been promoted to "first assistant to the head carpenter." He added, "I should have been here twenty years ago. I just begin to feel like a man. . . . My children are going to the same school with the whites and I don't have to [h]umble to no one. I have registered — will vote the next election and there ain't any 'yes sir' — it's all yes and no and Sam and Bill."

But the North was not the promised land. Black men stood on the lowest rungs of the labor ladder. Jobs of any kind proved scarce for black women, and most worked as domestic servants as they did in the South. The existing black middle class sometimes shunned the less educated, less sophisticated rural southerners crowding into northern cities. Many whites, fearful of losing jobs and status, lashed out against the new migrants. Savage race riots ripped through two dozen northern cities. The worst occurred in July 1917 when a mob of whites invaded a section of East St. Louis, Illinois, crowded with blacks who had been recruited to help break a strike. The mob murdered at least

If You are a Stranger in the City

If you want a job   If you want a place to live
If you are having trouble with your employer
If you want information or advice of any kind
CALL UPON

The CHICAGO LEAGUE ON URBAN
CONDITIONS AMONG NEGROES
3719 South State Street

Telephone Douglas 9098   T. ARNOLD HILL, Executive Secretary

No charges — no fees. We want to help YOU

SELF-HELP

1. Do not loaf. Get a job at once.
2. Do not live in crowded rooms. Others can be obtained.
3. Do not carry on loud conversations in street cars and public places.
4. Do not keep your children out of school.
5. Do not send for your family until you get a job.
6. Do not think you can hold your job unless you are industrious, sober, efficient and prompt.

Cleanliness and fresh air are necessary for good health. In case of sickness send immediately for a good physician. Become an active member in some church as soon as you reach the city.

Issued by

African Americans Migrate North
Wearing their Sunday best and carrying the rest of what they owned in two suitcases, this southern family waits to board a northern-bound train in 1912. In Chicago, the League on Urban Conditions among Negroes, which eventually became the Urban League, sought to ease the transition of southern blacks to life in the North by distributing cards such as the one shown here (front and back). Other cards advised hard work, sobriety, cleanliness, finding a church, getting children into school, and speaking softly in public places. Photo: Photographs and Prints Division, Schomburg Center for Research in Black Culture, New York Public Library, Astor, Lenox, and Tilden Foundations; card: Arthur and Graham Aldis papers (Aldis neg-1A & 1B), Special Collections, The University Library, University of Illinois at Chicago.

39 people and left most of the black district in flames. In 1918, the nation witnessed 96 lynchings of blacks, some of them decorated war veterans still in uniform.

Still, most black migrants stayed in the North and encouraged friends and family to follow. By 1940, more than one million blacks had left the South, profoundly changing their own lives and the course of the nation's history. Black enclaves such as Harlem in New York and the South Side of Chicago, "cities within cities," emerged in the North. These assertive communities provided a foundation for black protest and political organization in the years ahead.

At nearly the same moment that black Americans streamed into northern cities, another migration was under way in the American Southwest. Between 1910 and 1920, the Mexican-born population in the United States soared from 222,000 to 478,000. Mexican immigration resulted from developments on both sides of the border. In Mexico, dictator Porfirio Díaz initiated land policies that decimated poor farmers. When the Mexicans revolted against Díaz in 1910, initiating a ten-year civil war, the trickle of migration became a flood. North of the border, the Chinese Exclusion Act of 1882 and later the disruption of World War I cut off the supply of cheap foreign labor and caused western employers in the expanding rail, mining, construction, and agricultural industries to look south to Mexico for workers.

As a result of Americans' racial stereotyping of Mexicans — a U.S. government economist

Mexican Women Arriving in El Paso, 1911
These Mexican women, carrying bundles and wearing traditional shawls, try to get their bearings upon arriving in El Paso, Texas — the Ellis Island for Mexican immigrants. Perhaps they are looking for a family member who preceded them, or perhaps they are alone and calculating their next step. In any case, they were part of the first modern wave of Mexican immigration to the United States. Women like them found work in the cotton and sugar beet fields, canneries, and restaurants of the Southwest, as well as at home taking in sewing, laundry, and boarders. Whatever their work, their journey across the border was life changing. Courtesy of the Rio Grande Historical Collections, New Mexico State University, Las Cruces, NM.

described them as "docile, patient, usually orderly in camp, fairly intelligent under competent supervision, obedient and cheap" — Mexicans were considered excellent prospects for manual labor but not for citizenship. Employers tried to dampen racial fears by stressing that the immigrants were only temporary residents, not a lasting threat. In 1917, when anti-immigration advocates convinced Congress to do something about foreigners coming into the United States, the restrictive legislation bowed to southwestern industry and exempted Mexicans. By 1920, ethnic Mexicans made up about three-fourths of California's farm laborers. They were also crucial to the Texas economy, accounting for three-fourths of laborers in the cotton fields and in construction there.

Like immigrants from Europe and black migrants from the South, Mexicans in the American Southwest dreamed of a better life. And like the others, they found both opportunity and disappointment. Wages were better than in Mexico, but life in the fields, mines, and factories was hard, and living conditions — in boxcars, labor camps, or urban barrios — often were dismal. Signs warning "No Mexicans Allowed" increased rather than declined. Mexican women nurtured families, but many also worked picking cotton or as domestics. Among Mexican Americans, some of whom had lived in the Southwest for a century or more, *los recién llegados* (the recent arrivals) encountered mixed reactions. One Mexican American expressed this ambivalence: "We are all Mexicans anyway because the gueros [Anglos] treat us all alike." But he also called for immigration quotas because the recent arrivals drove down wages and incited white prejudice that affected all ethnic Mexicans.

Despite friction, large-scale immigration into the Southwest meant a resurgence of the Mexican cultural presence, which became the basis for greater solidarity and political action for the ethnic Mexican population. In 1929 in Texas, Mexican Americans formed the League of United Latin American Citizens.

Postwar Politics and the Election of 1920

A thousand miles away in Washington, D.C., President Woodrow Wilson, bedridden and paralyzed, stubbornly ignored the mountain of domestic troubles — labor strikes, the Red Scare, race riots, immigration backlash — and insisted that the 1920 election would be a "solemn referendum" on the League of Nations. Dutifully, the Democratic nominees for president, James M. Cox of Ohio, and for vice president, Franklin Delano Roosevelt of New York, campaigned on Wilson's international ideals. The Republican Party chose the handsome, gregarious Warren Gamaliel Harding, senator from Ohio. Harding's rise in Ohio politics was a tribute to his amiability, not his mastery of the issues.

Harding found the winning formula when he declared that "America's present need is not heroics, but healing; not nostrums [questionable remedies] but normalcy." But what was "normalcy"? Harding explained: "By 'normalcy' I don't mean the old order but a regular steady order of things. I mean normal procedure, the

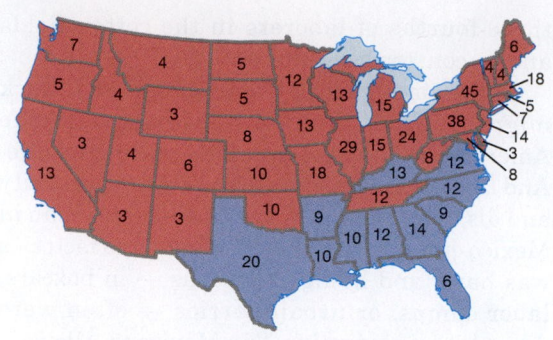

Candidate	Electoral Vote	Popular Vote	Percent of Popular Vote
Warren G. Harding (Republican)	404	16,143,407	60.5
James M. Cox (Democrat)	127	9,130,328	34.2
Eugene V. Debs (Socialist)	0	919,799	3.4

MAP 22.6
The Election of 1920

natural way, without excess." Eager to put wartime crusades and postwar strife behind them, voters responded by giving Harding the largest presidential victory ever: 60.5 percent of the popular vote and 404 out of 531 electoral votes (Map 22.6). Once in office, Harding and his wife, Florence, threw open the White House gates, which had been closed since the declaration of war in 1917. Their welcome brought throngs of visitors and lifted the national pall, signaling a new, more easygoing era.

REVIEW   How did the Red scare contribute to the erosion of civil liberties after the war?

▶ Conclusion: Troubled Crusade

America's experience in World War I was exceptional. For much of the world, the Great War produced great destruction, endless blackened fields, thousands of ruined factories, and millions of casualties. But in the United States, war and prosperity marched hand in hand. America emerged from the war with the strongest economy in the world and a position of international preeminence.

Still, the nation paid a heavy price both at home and abroad. American soldiers like George Browne encountered unprecedented horrors — submarines, poison gas, machine guns — and

more than 100,000 died. On Memorial Day 1919, at the Argonne Cemetery, where 14,200 Americans lie, General John J. Pershing said, "It is . . . for us to uphold the conception of duty, honor and country for which they fought and for which they died. It is for the living to carry forward their purpose and make fruitful their sacrifice." Rather than redeeming their sacrifice as Pershing intoned and Wilson promised, however, the peace that followed the armistice tarnished it. The flawed treaty forced a humiliating peace on Germany and contributed to the rise of Adolf Hitler and a second world war even more catastrophic than the first.

At home, rather than permanently improving working conditions, advancing public health, and spreading educational opportunity, as progressives had hoped, the war threatened to undermine the achievements of the previous two decades. Moreover, rather than promoting democracy in the United States, the war bred fear, intolerance, and repression that led to a crackdown on dissent and a demand for conformity. Reformers could count only woman suffrage as a permanent victory and prohibition as, ultimately, a temporary one.

Woodrow Wilson had promised more than anyone could deliver. Progressive hopes of extending democracy and liberal reform nationally and internationally were dashed. In 1920, a bruised and disillusioned society stumbled into a new decade. The era coming to an end had called on Americans to crusade and sacrifice. The new era promised peace, prosperity, and a good time.

▶ Selected Bibliography

General Works

John Milton Cooper, *Woodrow Wilson: A Biography* (2009).

Thomas Fleming, *The Illusion of Victory: America in World War I* (2003).

Robert H. Zieger, *America's Great War: World War I and the American Experience* (2000).

"Over There"

Gerald Astor, *The Right to Fight: A History of African Americans in the Military* (1998).

Peter Boyle, *American-Soviet Relations: From the Russian Revolution to the Fall of Communism* (1993).

Edward M. Coffman, *The War to End All Wars: The American Military Experience in World War I* (1968).

Byron Farwell, *Over There: The United States in the Great War, 1917–1918* (1999).

Lloyd C. Gardner, *Safe for Democracy: The Anglo-American Response to Revolution, 1913–1923* (1987).

Judith S. Graham, ed., *"Out Here at the Front": The World War I Letters of Nora Saltonstall* (2004).

Jennifer D. Keene, *Doughboys, the Great War, and the Remaking of America* (2001).

Thomas Knock, *To End All Wars: Woodrow Wilson and the Quest for a New World Order* (1992).

Edward G. Lengel, *To Conquer Hell: The Meuse-Argonne, 1918* (2008).

Margaret Olwen Macmillan, *Paris 1919: Six Months That Changed the World* (2002).

Gary Mead, *The Doughboys: America and the First World War* (2000).

Emily S. Rosenberg, *Financial Missionaries to the World: The Politics and Culture of Dollar Diplomacy, 1890–1930* (1999).

Gene Smith, *Until the Last Trumpet Sounds: The Life of General of the Armies John J. Pershing* (1998).

David L. Snead, ed., *An American Soldier in World War I: George Browne* (2006).

David F. Trask, *The AEF and Coalition Warmaking, 1917–1918* (1993).

Susan Zeiger, *In Uncle Sam's Service: Women with the AEF, 1917–1919* (1999).

The Home Front

Jean Baker, *Sisters: The Lives of America's Suffragists* (2005).

Nancy Cott, *The Grounding of American Feminism* (1987).

Leslie Midkiff DeBauche, *Reel Patriotism: The Movies and World War I* (1997).

Marc A. Eisner, *From Warfare State to Welfare State: World War I, Compensatory State Building, and the Limits of the Modern Order* (2000).

Ernest Freeberg, *Democracy's Prisoner: Eugene V. Debs, the Great War, and the Right to Dissent* (2008).

Elizabeth Frost and Kathryn Cullen-DuPont, eds., *Women's Suffrage in America: An Eyewitness History* (1992).

Maurine Weiner Greenwald, *Women, War, and Work: The Impact of World War I on Women Workers in the United States* (1980).

James N. Gregory, *Southern Diaspora: How the Great Migrations of Black and White Southerners Transformed America* (2005).

James R. Grossman, *Land of Hope: Chicago, Black Southerners, and the Great Migration* (1989).

David Kennedy, *Over Here: The First World War and American Society* (1980).

David Levering Lewis, *W. E. B. Du Bois: Biography of a Race, 1868–1919* (1993).

Robert K. Murray, *Red Scare: A Study in National Hysteria, 1919–1920* (1955).

Tammy M. Proctor, *Civilians in a World at War, 1914–1918* (2010).

George J. Sanchez, *Becoming Mexican American: Ethnicity, Culture, and Identity in Chicano Los Angeles, 1900–1945* (1993).

William H. Thomas Jr., *Unsafe for Democracy: World War I and the U.S. Justice Department's Covert Campaign to Suppress Dissent* (2008).

Joe William Trotter Jr., ed., *The Great Migration in Historical Perspective* (1991).

▶ **For more books about topics in this chapter,** see the Online Bibliography at **bedfordstmartins.com/roark**.

▶ **For additional primary sources from this period,** see Michael Johnson, ed., *Reading the American Past*, Fifth Edition.

▶ **For web sites, images, and documents related to topics and places in this chapter,** visit Make History at **bedfordstmartins.com/roark**.

Reviewing Chapter 22

KEY TERMS

Explain each term's significance.

Woodrow Wilson and the World
Woodrow Wilson (p. 713)
William Jennings Bryan (p. 713)
Francisco "Pancho" Villa (p. 714)
Wilhelm II (p. 715)
Triple Alliance (p. 715)
Triple Entente (p. 715)
Archduke Franz Ferdinand (p. 715)
U-boats (p. 716)
Lusitania (p. 716)
Robert Lansing (p. 717)
Zimmermann telegram (p. 718)

"Over There"
Bolshevik (p. 718)
Selective Service Act (p. 718)
American Expeditionary Force (AEF)
  (p. 719)
John "Black Jack" Pershing (p. 719)

The Crusade for Democracy at Home
Eighteenth Amendment (prohibition)
  (p. 725)
Nineteenth Amendment (woman
  suffrage) (p. 727)
Committee on Public Information
  (p. 730)

A Compromised Peace
Fourteen Points (p. 731)
League of Nations (p. 731)
Versailles treaty (p. 734)
Henry Cabot Lodge (p. 734)

Democracy at Risk
Seattle general strike (p. 736)
Boston police strike (p. 736)
steel strike of 1919 (p. 736)
Red scare (p. 737)
A. Mitchell Palmer (p. 738)
Emma Goldman (p. 738)
Schenck v. United States (p. 739)
American Civil Liberties Union
  (ACLU) (p. 739)

REVIEW QUESTIONS

Use key terms and dates to support your answer.

1. Why did President Wilson fail to maintain U.S. neutrality during World War I? (pp. 713–718)

2. How did the American Expeditionary Force contribute to the defeat of Germany? (pp. 718–723)

3. How did progressive ideals fare during wartime? (pp. 723–731)

4. Why did the Senate fail to ratify the Versailles treaty? (pp. 731–735)

5. How did the Red scare contribute to the erosion of civil liberties after the war? (pp. 735–743)

MAKING CONNECTIONS

Draw on key terms, the timeline, and review questions.

1. Why did the United States at first resist intervening in World War I? Why did it later retreat from this policy and send troops? In your answer, discuss whether these decisions revised or reinforced earlier U.S. foreign policy.

2. Some reformers were optimistic that World War I would advance progressive ideals at home. Discuss specific wartime domestic developments that displayed progressivism's influence. How did the war contribute to these developments? Did they endure in peacetime? Why or why not?

3. A conservative reaction in American politics followed peace, most vividly in the labor upheaval and Red scare that swept the nation. What factors drove these developments? How did they shape the postwar political spectrum?

4. During World War I, the nation witnessed important demographic changes. What drove African American and Mexican migration north? How did the war facilitate these changes? In your answer, explain the significance of these developments to the migrants and the nation.

LINKING TO THE PAST

Link events in this chapter to earlier events.

1. How did America's experience in World War I compare with its experience during the Spanish-American War, its previous war abroad? Discuss the decision to go to war in each case, the military aspects, and the outcome. (See chapter 20.)

2. How did the experience of America's workers during World War I compare with their experience in the previous three decades? Consider the composition of the workforce, wages, conditions, and labor's efforts to organize. (See chapters 20 and 21.)

▶ FOR PRACTICE QUIZZES AND OTHER STUDY TOOLS, visit the Online Study Guide at **bedfordstmartins.com/roark**.

TIMELINE 1914–1920

1914
- **April** U.S. Marines occupy Veracruz, Mexico.
- **June 28** Assassination of Archduke Franz Ferdinand.
- **July 18** Austria-Hungary declares war on Serbia.
- **August 3** Germany attacks Russia and France.
- **August 4** Great Britain declares war on Germany.

1915
- *Lusitania* sunk.
- Women's Peace Party formed.
- Italy joins Allies.

1916
- Pancho Villa attacks Americans in Mexico and New Mexico.
- Wilson reelected.

1917
- Zimmermann telegram intercepted.
- **April 6** United States declares war on Germany.
- Committee on Public Information created.
- Selective Service Act.
- Espionage Act and Trading with the Enemy Act.
- East St. Louis, Illinois, race riot.

1918
- **January 8** President Wilson gives Fourteen Points speech.
- **March** Russia arranges separate peace with Germany.
- **May** Sedition Act.
- **May–June** U.S. Marines see first major combat at Cantigny and Château-Thierry.
- **November 11** Armistice signed ending World War I.

1919
- **January** Paris peace conference begins.
- **June** Treaty of Versailles signed.
- **September** Wilson undertakes speaking tour.
- Wave of labor strikes.

1920
- American Civil Liberties Union founded.
- **January** Prohibition begins.
- **January** Palmer raids.
- **March** Senate votes against ratification of Treaty of Versailles.
- **August** Nineteenth Amendment ratified.
- **November** Republican Warren G. Harding elected president.

MODEL T FORD

Nothing symbolized the 1920s more than the automobile. When Henry Ford introduced the Model T in 1908, Americans thought of automobiles as toys of the rich, far too costly for average people. But by the 1920s, millions of Americans owned Fords, and their lives were never the same. One of novelist Booth Tarkington's characters expressed some reservations about automobiles: "With all their speed forward, they may be a step backward in civilization." But most Americans loved their automobiles and sped away into the future. Behind this Model T, workers install the wheels on a Ford chassis on a moving assembly line.

Car: National Museum of American History, Smithsonian Institution, Behring Center; background: From the Collections of The Henry Ford.

23

From New Era to Great Depression
1920–1932

AMERICANS IN THE 1920S CHEERED HENRY FORD AS AN AUTHENTIC American hero. When the decade began, he had already produced six million automobiles; by 1927, the figure reached fifteen million. In 1920, one car rolled off the Ford assembly line every minute; in 1925, one appeared every ten seconds. In 1920, a Ford car cost $845; in 1928, the price was less than $300, within range of most of the country's skilled workingmen. Henry Ford put America on wheels, and in the eyes of most Americans he was an honest man who made an honest car: basic, inexpensive, and reliable. He became the greatest example of free enterprise's promise and achievement. But like the age in which he lived, Henry Ford was many-sided, more complex and more contradictory than this simple image suggests.

Born in 1863 on a farm in Dearborn, Michigan, Ford hated the drudgery of farmwork and loved tinkering with machines. At sixteen, he fled rural life for Detroit, where he became a journeyman machinist and experimented with internal combustion engines. In 1893, he put together one of the first successful gasoline-driven carriages in the United States. His ambition, he said, was to "make something in quantity." The product he chose reflected American restlessness, the desire to be on the move. "Everybody wants to be someplace he ain't," Ford declared. "As soon as he gets there he wants to go right back." In 1903, with $28,000 from a few backers, Ford gathered twelve workers in a 250-by-50-foot shed and created the Ford Motor Company.

Ford's early cars were custom-made one at a time. By 1914, his cars were being built along a continuously moving assembly line: Workers bolted on parts brought to them by cranes and conveyor belts. Ford made only one kind of car, the Model T, which became synonymous with mass production. A boxlike black vehicle, it was cheap, easy to drive, and simple to repair. The Model T dominated the market. Throughout the rapid expansion of the automotive industry, the Ford Motor Company remained the

Henry Ford, 1921
A dapper Henry Ford inspects a new Model T in Buffalo, New York, in 1921, while curious onlookers inspect him. Henry Ford was a man of genius whose compelling vision of modern mass production led the way in the 1920s, but he was also cranky, pinched, and mean-spirited. He hated Jews and Catholics, bankers and doctors, and liquor and tobacco, and his millions allowed him to act on his prejudices. Still, his name became synonymous with American success. From the Collections of The Henry Ford.

industry leader, peaking in 1925, when it outsold all its rivals combined (Map 23.1).

Nobody entertained grander or more contradictory visions of the new America he had helped to create than Henry Ford himself. When he began his rise, progressive critics condemned the industrial giants of the nineteenth century as "robber barons" who lived in luxury while reducing their workers to wage slaves. Ford, however, identified with the common folk and saw himself as the benefactor of Americans yearning to be free and mobile.

Ford's automobile plants made him a billionaire, but their highly regimented assembly lines reduced Ford workers to near robots. On the cutting edge of modern technology, Ford nevertheless remained nostalgic about rural values. He sought to revive the past in Greenfield Village, a museum outside Detroit, where he relocated buildings from a bygone era, including his parents' farmhouse. His museum contrasted sharply with the roaring Ford plant farther along the Detroit River at River Rouge. The African American and immigrant workers who worked at the plant found no place in Greenfield Village. Yet all would be well, Ford insisted, if Americans remained true to their agrarian past and somehow managed to be modern and scientific at the same time.

Tension between traditional values and modern conditions lay at the heart of the conflicted 1920s. For the first time, more Americans lived in urban than in rural areas, yet Americans remained nostalgic about farms and small towns. Although the nation generally prospered, the new wealth widened the gap between rich and poor. While millions admired urban America's sophisticated new style and consumer products, others condemned postwar society for its vulgar materialism. A great outpouring of artistic talent led, ironically, to incessant critiques of America's artistic barrenness. The Ku Klux Klan and other champions of an idealized older America resorted to violence as well as words when they chastised the era's "new woman," "New Negro," and surging immigrant populations.

The public, disillusioned with the outcome of World War I, turned away from the Christian moralism and idealism of the Progressive Era. In the 1920s, Ford and businessmen like him replaced political reformers such as Theodore Roosevelt and Woodrow Wilson as the models of progress. The U.S. Chamber of Commerce crowed, "The American businessman is the most influential person in the nation." Social justice gave way to individual advancement. At the center of it all, President Calvin Coolidge spoke in praise of those in power when he declared, "The business of America is business." The fortunes of the era rose, then crashed, according to the values and practices of the business community.

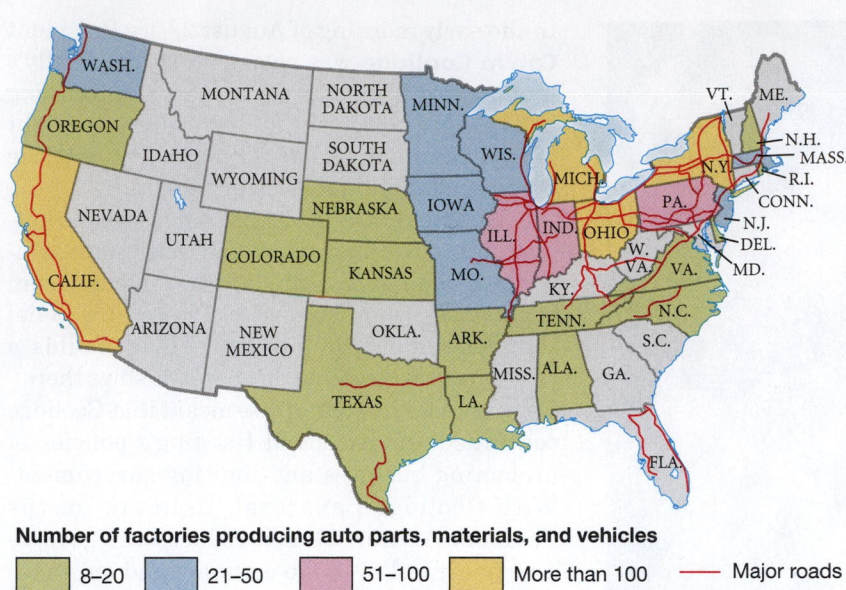

Number of factories producing auto parts, materials, and vehicles

8–20   21–50   51–100   More than 100   — Major roads

▶ The New Era

The 1920s were a time of contradiction and ambivalence. Once Woodrow Wilson left the White House, the energy flowed away from government activism and civic reform and toward private economic endeavor. The rise of a free-wheeling economy and a heightened sense of individualism caused Secretary of Commerce Herbert Hoover to declare that America had entered a "New Era," one of many labels used to describe the complex 1920s. Some terms focus on the decade's high-spirited energy and cultural changes: Roaring Twenties, Jazz Age, Flaming Youth, Age of the Flapper. Others echo the rising importance of money—Dollar Decade, Golden Twenties, Prosperity Decade—or reflect the sinister side of gangster profiteering—Lawless Decade. Still others emphasize the lonely confusion of the Lost Generation and the stress and anxiety of the Aspirin Age.

America in the twenties was many things, but there was no getting around the truth of Calvin Coolidge's insight: The business of America *was* business. Politicians and diplomats proclaimed business the heart of American civilization. Average men and women bought into the idea that business and its wonderful products were what made America great, as they snatched up the flood of new consumer items American factories sent forth.

A Business Government

Republicans controlled the White House from 1921 to 1933. The first of the three Republican presidents was **Warren Gamaliel Harding**, the Ohio senator who in his 1920 campaign called for a "return to normalcy," by which he meant the end of public crusades and a return to private pursuits. Harding promised a government run by the best minds, and he appointed a few men of real stature to his cabinet. Herbert Hoover, the energetic and ambitious former head of the wartime Food Administration, became secretary of commerce. However, wealth also counted: Andrew Mellon, one of the richest men in America, became secretary of the treasury. And friendship counted, too. Harding handed out jobs to members of his old "Ohio gang," whose only qualification was their friendship. This curious combination of merit and cronyism made for a disjointed administration in which a few men debated national needs, while other men looked for ways to advance their own interests.

When Harding was elected in 1920 in a landslide over Democratic opponent James Cox (see chapter 22, Map 22.6), the unemployment rate hit 20 percent, the highest ever up to that point. Farmers fared the worst; their bankruptcy rate increased tenfold. Harding pushed measures to regain national prosperity — high tariffs to protect American businesses (the Fordney-McCumber tariff in 1922 raised duties

Warren G. Harding and Babe Ruth
President Warren G. Harding shakes hands with New York Yankee home run king George Herman "Babe" Ruth Jr. during an April 4, 1923, visit to Yankee Stadium. The 1920s were the Golden Age of Sports, and Ruth was the best-paid and most highly acclaimed athlete of the decade. In 1920, a man died of excitement when Ruth slugged a ball into the bleachers. Even when he struck out, "the Babe" usually attracted more attention than any politician—even the president of the United States. © Bettmann/Corbis.

to unprecedented levels), price supports for agriculture, and the dismantling of wartime government control over industry in favor of unregulated private business. "Never before, here or anywhere else," the U.S. Chamber of Commerce said proudly, "has a government been so completely fused with business."

Harding's policies to boost American enterprise made him very popular, but ultimately his small-town congeniality and trusting ways did him in. Some of his friends in the Ohio gang were up to their necks in lawbreaking. Three of Harding's appointees would go to jail. Interior Secretary Albert Fall was convicted of accepting bribes of more than $400,000 for leasing oil reserves on public land in Teapot Dome, Wyoming, and "**Teapot Dome**" became a synonym for political corruption.

Baffled about how to deal with "my Goddamned friends," Harding in the summer of 1923 took a trip to Alaska to escape his troubles. But the president found no rest, and his health declined.

> **"Never before, here or anywhere else, has a government been so completely fused with business."**
>
> — U.S. Chamber of Commerce

In the early morning of August 2, Vice President **Calvin Coolidge** was awakened at his family's farmhouse in Vermont with the news that Harding had died of a heart attack. By the flickering light of an oil lamp, Coolidge's father, a justice of the peace, swore his son in as president.

This rustic drama calmed a nation confronting the death of a president and continuing scandal in Washington. Coolidge was a modest man of integrity who had once expressed his belief that "the man who builds a factory builds a temple, the man who works there worships there." Reverence for free enterprise meant that Coolidge continued and extended Harding's policies of promoting business and limiting government. With Coolidge's approval, Secretary of the Treasury Andrew Mellon reduced the government's control over the economy and cut taxes for corporations and wealthy individuals. New rules for the Federal Trade Commission severely limited its power to regulate business. Secretary of Commerce Herbert Hoover limited government authority by encouraging trade associations that would keep business honest and efficient through voluntary cooperation.

Coolidge found a staunch ally in the Supreme Court. For many years, the Court had opposed federal regulation of hours, wages, and working conditions on the grounds that such legislation was the proper concern of the states. With Coolidge, the Court also found ways to curtail a state's ability to regulate business. It ruled against closed shops — businesses where only union members could be employed — while confirming the right of owners to form exclusive trade associations. In 1923, the Court declared unconstitutional the District of Columbia's minimum-wage law for women, asserting that the law interfered with the freedom of employer and employee to make labor contracts. The Court and the president attacked government intrusion in the free market, even when the prohibition of government regulation threatened the welfare of workers.

The election of 1924 confirmed the defeat of the progressive principle that the state should take a leading role in ensuring the general welfare. To oppose Coolidge, the Democrats nominated John W. Davis, a corporate lawyer whose conservative views differed little from Republican principles. Only the Progressive Party and its presidential nominee, Senator Robert La Follette of Wisconsin, offered a genuine alternative. When La Follette championed labor unions, regulation of business, and protection of civil liberties, Republicans coined the

slogan "Coolidge or Chaos." Turning their backs on what they considered labor radicalism and reckless reform, voters chose Coolidge in a landslide. Coolidge was right when he declared, "This is a business country, and it wants a business government." What was true of the government's relationship to business at home was also true abroad.

Promoting Prosperity and Peace Abroad

After orchestrating the Senate's successful effort to block U.S. membership in the League of Nations, Henry Cabot Lodge boasted, "We have torn Wilsonism up by the roots." But repudiation of Wilsonian internationalism and rejection of collective security through the League of Nations did not mean that the United States retreated into isolationism. The United States emerged from World War I with its economy intact and enjoyed a decade of stunning growth. Economic involvement in the world and the continuing chaos in Europe made withdrawal impossible. New York replaced London as the center of world finance, and the United States became the world's chief creditor.

One of the Republicans' most ambitious foreign policy initiatives was the Washington Disarmament Conference, which convened to establish a global balance of naval power. Secretary of State Charles Evans Hughes shaped the **Five-Power Naval Treaty of 1922** committing Britain, France, Japan, Italy, and the United States to a proportional reduction of naval forces. The treaty led to the scrapping of more than two million tons of warships, by far the world's greatest success in disarmament. Americans celebrated President Harding for safeguarding the peace while remaining outside the League of Nations. By fostering international peace, he also helped make the world a safer place for American trade.

A second major effort on behalf of world peace came in 1928, when Secretary of State Frank Kellogg joined French foreign minister Aristide Briand to produce the **Kellogg-Briand pact**. Nearly fifty nations signed the solemn pledge to renounce war and settle international disputes peacefully. Most Americans considered the nation's signature an affirmation of its commitment to peace rather than to Wilson's foolish notion of a progressive, uplifting war.

But Republican administrations preferred private-sector diplomacy to state action. With the blessing of the White House, a team of American

Charles Evans Hughes and Disarmament
As Secretary of State, Charles Evans Hughes, the distinguished man in the white beard in the middle of this 1921 photograph, brought the world's major powers to Washington for naval disarmament talks. The gathering resulted in the United States's greatest diplomatic achievement of the 1920s. A former presidential candidate and Supreme Court justice, Hughes lent respectability and high-mindedness to his office, although few Americans cared about foreign affairs. The handwritten page is from the treaty that President Coolidge signed in 1923. Photo: Library of Congress; treaty: ©Bettmann/Corbis.

financiers led by Chicago banker Charles Dawes swung into action when Germany suspended its war reparation payments in 1923. Impoverished, Germany was staggering under the massive bill of $33 billion presented by the victorious Allies in the Versailles treaty. When Germany failed to meet its annual payment, France occupied Germany's industrial Ruhr Valley, creating the worst international crisis since the war. In 1924, American corporate leaders produced the **Dawes Plan**, which halved Germany's annual reparation payments, initiated fresh American loans to Germany, and caused the French to retreat from the Ruhr. Although the United States failed to join the league, it continued to exercise significant economic and diplomatic influence abroad. These Republican successes overseas helped fuel prosperity at home.

Automobiles, Mass Production, and Assembly-Line Progress

The automobile industry emerged as the largest single manufacturing industry in the nation. Aided by the federal government's decision to spend more on roads than on anything else, cars, trucks, and buses surged past railroads as the primary haulers of passengers and freight. **Henry Ford** shrewdly located his company in Detroit, knowing that key materials for his automobiles were manufactured in nearby states (see Map 23.1). Keystone of the American economy, the automobile industry not only employed hundreds of thousands of workers directly but also brought whole industries into being — filling stations, garages, fast-food restaurants, and "guest cottages" (motels). The need for tires, glass, steel, highways, oil, and refined gasoline for automobiles provided millions of related jobs. By 1929, one American in four found employment directly or indirectly in the automobile industry. "Give us our daily bread" was no longer addressed to the Almighty, one commentator quipped, but to Detroit.

Automobiles altered the face of America. Cars changed where people lived, what work they did, how they spent their leisure, even how they thought. Hundreds of small towns decayed because the automobile enabled rural people to bypass them in favor of more distant cities and towns. Urban streetcars began to disappear as workers moved to the suburbs and commuted to work along crowded highways. In Los Angeles, which boasted of the nation's most extensive system of electronic trolleys, almost a thousand miles of track suffered a slow death at the hands of the automobile. Nothing shaped modern America more than the automobile, and efficient mass production made the automobile revolution possible.

Mass production by the assembly-line technique had become standard in almost every factory, from automobiles to meatpacking to cigarettes. To improve efficiency, corporations reduced assembly-line work to the simplest, most repetitive tasks. They also established specialized divisions — purchasing, production, marketing, and employee relations — each with its own team of professionally trained managers. Changes on the assembly line and in management, along with technological advances, significantly boosted overall efficiency. Between 1922 and 1929, productivity in manufacturing increased 32 percent. Average wages, however, increased only 8 percent. As assembly lines became standard, workers lost many of the skills in which they had once taken pride, but corporations reaped great profits from these changes.

Industries also developed programs for workers that came to be called **welfare capitalism**. Some businesses improved safety and sanitation inside factories and instituted paid vacations and pension plans. Welfare capitalism encouraged loyalty to the company and discouraged traditional labor unions. Not wanting to relive the chaotic strikes of 1919, industrialists sought to eliminate reasons for workers to join unions. One labor organizer in the steel industry bemoaned the success of welfare capitalism. "So many workmen here had been lulled to sleep by the company union, the welfare plans, the social organizations fostered by the employer," he declared, "that they had come to look upon the employer as their protector, and had believed vigorous trade union organization unnecessary for their welfare."

Consumer Culture

Mass production fueled corporate profits and national economic prosperity. During the 1920s, per capita income increased by a third, the cost of living stayed the same, and unemployment remained low. But the rewards of the economic boom were not evenly distributed. Americans who labored with their hands inched ahead, while white-collar workers enjoyed significantly more spending money and more leisure time to spend it. Mass production of a broad range of new products — automobiles, radios, refrigerators, electric irons, washing machines — produced a consumer goods revolution.

In this new era of abundance, more people than ever conceived of the American dream in terms of the things they could acquire. In *Middletown* (1929), a study of the inhabitants of Muncie, Indiana, sociologists Robert and Helen Lynd revealed how the business boom and business values of the 1920s affected average Americans. Muncie was,

Detroit and the Automobile Industry in the 1920s

Centers of iron and steel production

Automobiles and ancillary industries

Oil and gas

THE PROMISE OF TECHNOLOGY

Household Appliances

By the end of the 1920s, most urban homes in America had electricity, and middle-class urban families began acquiring household appliances that transformed women's daily lives. Before electricity, most chores were day-long ordeals. Washing machines saved housewives long hours spent hauling and heating water and hand-washing clothes. Ironing had been one of the most dreaded chores, especially in the summer when the kitchen stove had to be kept hot for heavy irons that needed frequent reheating. Electric irons eased the burden enormously. Vacuum cleaners saved the labor of hauling rugs out of the house to be beaten. Although household appliances relieved women of backbreaking labor, housework did not take less time. With the appearance of appliances, standards of cleanliness rose, and so did the frequency of many household chores. Nevertheless, an advertisement from a leading women's magazine insisted that "the wise woman delegates to electricity all that electricity can do." Ads like this promoted new technologies and reminded prospective buyers that this beautiful Eden washing machine could be theirs through an "easy-payment plan." How did housekeeping change with the introduction of electrical appliances? Picture Research Consultants & Archives.

above all, "a culture in which everything hinges on money." Moreover, faced with technological and organizational change beyond their comprehension, many citizens had lost confidence in their ability to play an effective role in civic affairs. More and more they became passive consumers, deferring to the supposed expertise of leaders in politics and economics.

The pied piper of these disturbing changes was the rapidly expanding business of advertising, which stimulated the desire for new products and hammered away at the traditional values of thrift and saving. Newspapers, magazines, radios, and billboards told Americans what they had to have in order to be popular, secure, and successful. Advertising linked material goods to the fulfillment of every spiritual and emotional need. Americans increasingly defined and measured their social status, and indeed their personal worth, on the yardstick of material possessions. Happiness itself rode on owning a car and choos-

ing the right cigarettes and toothpaste. (See "Visualizing History," page 758.)

By the 1920s, the United States had achieved the physical capacity to satisfy Americans' material wants (Figure 23.1). The economic problem shifted from production to consumption: Who would buy the goods flying off American assembly lines? One solution was to expand America's markets in foreign countries, and government and business joined in that effort. Another solution to the problem of consumption was to expand the market at home.

Henry Ford realized early on that "mass production requires mass consumption." He understood that automobile workers not only produced cars but would also buy them if they made enough money. "One's own employees ought to be one's own best customers," Ford said. In 1914, he raised wages in his factories to $5 a day, more than twice the going rate. High wages made for workers who were more loyal and more

VISUAL ACTIVITY

Colorado Filling Station and Gas Pump

Gulf Oil Company gave away the first free road map in 1914. By 1929, when Conoco (Continental Oil Company) produced this lavish map with Colorado's spectacular mountains looming in the background, nearly every oil company was supplying road maps as part of its campaign to attract the booming tourist trade. This appealing drive-through station is a far cry from the first retail outlets for gas — blacksmith shops and hardware stores, the same places individuals bought kerosene to burn in their lamps. Because motorists did not trust what they could not see, companies in the 1910s introduced glass-cylinder, gravity-flow gas pumps. Courtesy, Colorado Historical Society.

READING THE IMAGE: What does this road map and accompanying image of a gravity-flow gasoline pump tell us about American consumer culture on the eve of the Great Depression?

CONNECTIONS: Does the road map accurately reflect the economic direction of the U.S. economy in 1929?

---

exploitable, and high wages returned as profits when workers bought Fords.

Not all industrialists were as farseeing as Ford. Because the wages of many workers barely edged upward, many people's incomes were too puny to satisfy the growing desire for consumer goods. Business supplied the solution: Americans could realize their dreams through credit. Installment buying — a little money down, a payment each month — allowed people to purchase expensive items they could not otherwise afford or to purchase items before saving the

necessary money. As one newspaper announced, "The first responsibility of an American to his country is no longer that of a citizen, but of a consumer." During the 1920s, America's motto became spend, not save. Old values — "Use it up, wear it out, make it do or do without" — seemed about as pertinent as a horse and buggy. American culture had shifted.

REVIEW   How did the spread of the automobile transform the United States?

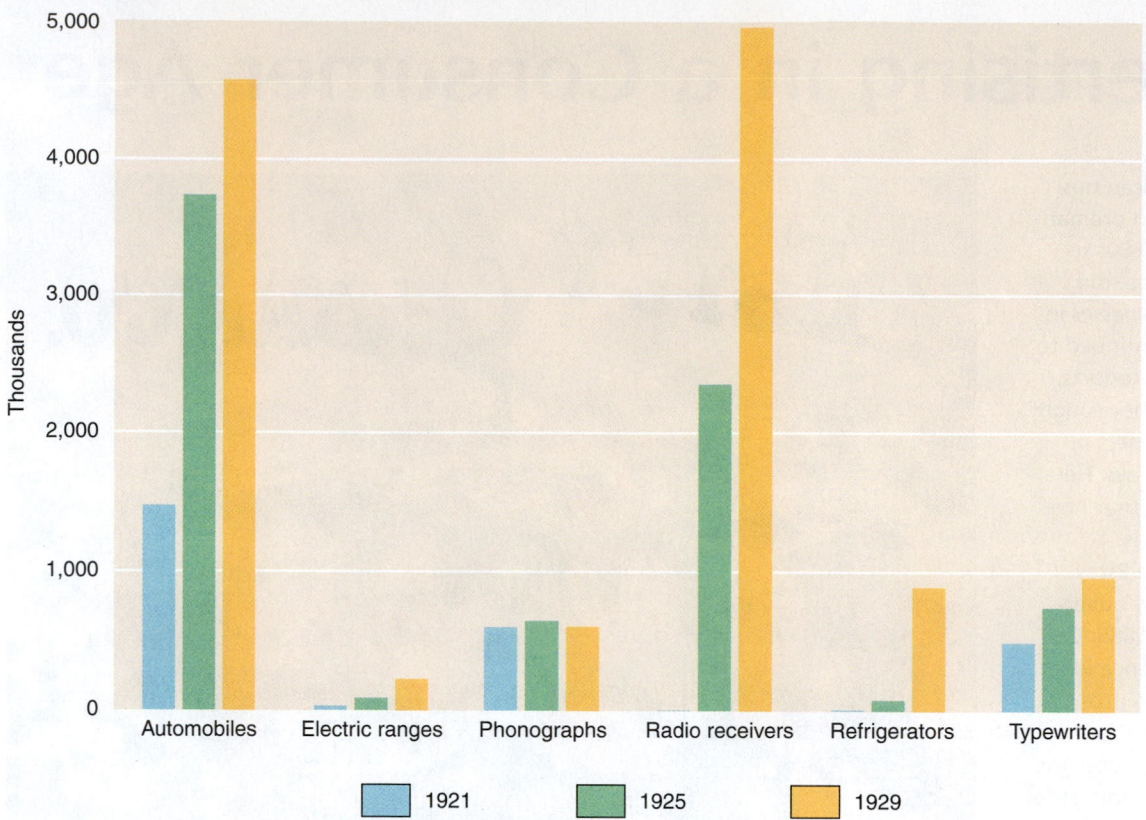

FIGURE 23.1   Production of Consumer Goods, 1921–1929
Transportation, communications, and entertainment changed the lives of consumers in the 1920s. Laborsaving devices for the home were popular, but the vastly greater sales of automobiles and radios showed that consumerism was powerful in moving people's attention beyond their homes.

▶ The Roaring Twenties

By the beginning of the decade, psychoanalyst **Sigmund Freud** had become a household name. Most Americans knew little of the complexity of his pioneering work in the psychology of the unconscious, but people realized that Freud offered a way of looking at the world that was radically different. In the twenties, much to Freud's disgust, the American media turned his ideas about the sexual origins of behavior on its head. If it is wrong to deny that we are sexual beings, some reasoned, then the key to health and fulfillment must lie in following impulse freely. Those who doubted this reasoning were simply "repressed." The new ethic of personal freedom excited many Americans to seek pleasure without guilt in a whirl of activity that earned the decade the name "Roaring Twenties." Prohibition made lawbreakers of millions of

otherwise decent folk. Flappers and "new women" challenged traditional gender boundaries. Other Americans enjoyed the Roaring Twenties through the words and images of vastly expanded mass communication. Motion pictures, radio, and magazines marketed celebrities. In the freedom of America's big cities, particularly New York, a burst of creativity produced the "New Negro," who confounded and disturbed white Americans. The "Lost Generation" of writers, profoundly disillusioned with mainstream America's cultural direction, fled the country.

Prohibition

Republicans generally sought to curb the powers of government, but the twenties witnessed a great exception to this rule when the federal government implemented one of the last reforms of the Progressive Era: the Eighteenth Amendment, which banned the manufacture and sale of alcohol

Advertising in a Consumer Age

Just as American business changed dramatically from the 1880s to the 1920s, so, too, did advertising. Businesses in the New Era continued to promote their products, of course, but they sought to attract customers in very different ways. Here are two images that illustrate the changes.

Look at the Estey Organ Company advertisement from 1885. Can you tell at a glance what product is being promoted? First and foremost, the ad features the company's huge industrial complex — two red brick kilns with smoke belching from their chimneys, surrounded by lumberyards and milling, woodworking, metalworking, and varnishing shops. If the prospective customer somehow failed to get the message, the advertisement announces that Estey's plant is "The Most Extensive

Estey Organ Company

in the World." Indeed, Estey was the world's largest organ manufacturer, selling 1,800 organs a year around the globe. Why do you think the size of the factory was featured so prominently in the ad? How might

customers in 1885 have responded to such an ad?

The men who presided over Estey's impressive manufacturing operation — founder Jason Estey; his son, Julius; and his son-in-law, Levi

and took effect in January 1920 (see chapter 22). Drying up the rivers of liquor that Americans consumed, supporters of **prohibition** claimed, would eliminate crime, boost production, and lift the nation's morality. Instead, prohibition initiated a fourteen-year orgy of lawbreaking unparalleled in the nation's history.

Charged with enforcing prohibition, the Treasury Department faced a staggering task. Although it smashed more than 172,000 illegal stills in 1925 alone, there were never enough Treasury agents. Moreover, loopholes in the law almost guaranteed failure. Sacramental wine was permitted, allowing fake clergy to party with bogus congregations. Farmers were allowed to ferment their

own "fruit juices." Doctors and dentists could prescribe liquor for medicinal purposes. America's wettest city was probably Detroit, known widely as "the city on a still." Detroit was home to more than 20,000 illegal drinking establishments, making the alcohol business the city's second-largest industry, behind automobile manufacturing.

In 1929, a Treasury agent in Indiana reported intense local resistance to enforcement of prohibition. "Conditions in most important cities very bad," he declared. "Lax and corrupt public officials great handicap . . . prevalence of drinking among minor boys and the . . . middle or better classes of adults." The "speakeasy," an illegal nightclub, became a common feature of the urban

UPHOLD 18TH AMENDMENT

REPEAL 18TH AMENDMENT

Fuller — appear in the lower right corner. What is the purpose of including the company founder and managers in the advertisement? In the other corner, the ad imagines an Estey organ in the parlor of a well-to-do family that gathers to hear one of its accomplished daughters play. How might this image influence potential customers?

Based on this advertisement, what did the Estey Organ Company believe was its most important selling factor? What other factors were important?

By the 1920s, companies employed advertising specialists who created ads that would appeal to the consumer's anxieties and personal needs and would even stimulate needs that didn't yet exist. As a result, advertisements changed dramatically.

In this 1929 advertisement for Lucky Strike cigarettes, the factory and its owners are nowhere to be found. Instead, it offers a woman in a bathing suit. What does she have to do with cigarettes? Millions of Americans smoked billions of cigarettes in the 1920s. In countless tobacco advertisements, smoking promised instant maturity, sophistication, and worldliness. What is this ad's promise to smokers? To whom is it appealing?

Look at the various elements of the ad — the headline, the pictures, the quoted slogans, the text, and the footnote. What health claims are made? Does the ad's small print undermine the main message?

Before the 1920s, advertising often focused on production. Even small businesses presented themselves as powerful and efficient producers of consumer goods such as organs, furniture, and stoves. In the consumer society of the 1920s, companies sought to teach Americans to judge themselves and others by what they bought, rather than by what they produced. How might an ad for Lucky Strike have looked if it had been done in 1885? What might an Estey Organ Company ad have looked like in the 1920s?

SOURCE: Organ ad: Collection of Norman Pease; Lucky Strike ad: Picture Research Consultants & Archives.

Lucky Strike

---

landscape. Speakeasies' dance floors led to the sexual integration of the formerly all-male drinking culture, changing American social life forever. One liquor dealer, trading on common knowledge that whiskey still flowed in the White House, distributed cards advertising himself as the "President's Bootlegger."

Eventually, serious criminals took over the liquor trade. Alphonse "Big Al" Capone became the era's most notorious gang lord by establishing in Chicago a bootlegging empire that the government estimated brought in $95 million a year, when a chicken dinner cost 5 cents. During the first four years of prohibition, Chicago witnessed more than two hundred gang-related killings as rival mobs struggled for control of the lucrative liquor trade. The most notorious event came on St. Valentine's Day 1929, when Capone's Italian-dominated mob machine-gunned seven members of a rival Irish gang. Federal authorities finally sent Capone to prison for income tax evasion. Capone never denied being a bootlegger. "I violate the Prohibition law — sure," he told a reporter. "Who doesn't? The only difference is, I take more chances than the man who drinks a cocktail before dinner."

While prohibition did cut down on drinking and alcohol-related illnesses, Americans overwhelmingly favored the repeal of the Eighteenth Amendment.

> "I violate the Prohibition law — sure. Who doesn't? The only difference is, I take more chances than the man who drinks a cocktail before dinner."
> —AL CAPONE

Confiscated Liquor
Revenue agents, some holding rifles, proudly display the bootleg liquor they have confiscated during a raid in Washington, D.C., in 1922. The carefully staged scene and the photographer on the roof indicate that the agents were eager to publicize their success. Successes like this were common during prohibition, but the criminalization of liquor could not permanently defeat "Satan in a bottle." The Granger Collection, NYC.

When the Nineteenth Amendment, ratified in 1920, granted women the vote, feminists felt liberated and expected women to reshape the political landscape. A Kansas woman declared, "I went to bed last night a *slave*[;] I awoke this morning a *free woman*." Women began pressuring Congress to pass laws that especially concerned women, including measures to protect women in factories and grant federal aid to schools. Black women lobbied particularly for federal courts to assume jurisdiction over the crime of lynching. But women's only significant national legislative success came in 1921 when Congress enacted the Sheppard-Towner Act, which extended federal assistance to states seeking to reduce high infant mortality rates. Rather than the beginning of women's political success, the act marked the high tide of women's influence in the 1920s.

A number of factors helped thwart women's political influence. Male domination of both political parties, the rarity of female candidates, and lack of experience in voting, especially among recent immigrants, kept many women away from the polls. In some places, male-run election machines actually disfranchised women, despite the Nineteenth Amendment. In the South, poll taxes, literacy tests, and outright terrorism continued to decimate the vote of African Americans, men and women alike.

Most important, rather than forming a solid voting bloc, feminists divided. Some argued for women's right to special protection; others demanded equal protection. The radical National Woman's Party fought for an **Equal Rights Amendment** that stated flatly: "Men and women shall have equal rights throughout the United States." The more moderate League of Women Voters feared that the amendment's wording threatened state laws that provided women special protection, such as preventing them from working on certain machines. Put before Congress in 1923, the Equal Rights Amendment went down to defeat, and radical women were forced to work for the causes of birth control, legal equality for minorities, and the end of child labor through other means.

Economically, more women worked for pay — approximately one in four by 1930 — but they clustered in "women's jobs." The proportion of women working in manufacturing fell, while the number of women working as secretaries, stenographers, and typists skyrocketed. Women almost monopolized the occupations of librarian,

In 1931, a panel of distinguished experts reported that prohibition, which supporters had defended as "a great social and economic experiment," had failed. The social and political costs of prohibition outweighed the benefits. Prohibition fueled criminal activity, corrupted the police, demoralized the judiciary, and caused ordinary citizens to disrespect the law. In 1933, the nation ended prohibition with the Twenty-first Amendment, making the Eighteenth Amendment the only constitutional amendment to be repealed.

The New Woman

Of all the changes in American life in the 1920s, none sparked more heated debate than the alternatives offered to the traditional roles of women. Increasing numbers of women worked and went to college, defying older gender hierarchies and norms. Even mainstream magazines such as the *Saturday Evening Post* began publishing stories about young, college-educated women who drank gin cocktails, smoked cigarettes, and wore skimpy dresses and dangly necklaces. Before the Great War, the **new woman** dwelt in New York City's bohemian Greenwich Village, but afterward the mass media brought her into middle-class America's living rooms.

nurse, elementary school teacher, and telephone operator. Women also represented 40 percent of salesclerks by 1930. More female white-collar workers meant that fewer women were interested in protective legislation for women; new women wanted salaries and opportunities equal to men's.

Increased earnings gave working women more buying power in the new consumer culture. A stereotype soon emerged of the **flapper**, so called because of the short-lived fad of wearing unbuckled galoshes. The flapper had short "bobbed" hair and wore lipstick and rouge. She spent freely on the latest styles — dresses with short skirts and drop waists, no sleeves, and no petticoats — and she danced all night to wild jazz.

The new woman both reflected and propelled the modern birth control movement. Margaret Sanger, the crusading pioneer for contraception during the Progressive Era (see chapter 21), restated her principal conviction in 1920: "No woman can call herself free until she can choose consciously whether she will or will not be a mother." By shifting strategy in the twenties, Sanger courted the conservative American Medical Association; linked birth control with the eugenics movement, which advocated limiting reproduction among "undesirable" groups; and thus made contraception a respectable subject for discussion.

Flapper style and values spread from coast to coast through films, novels, magazines, and advertisements. New women challenged American convictions about separate spheres for women and men, the double standard of sexual conduct, and Victorian ideas of proper female appearance and behavior. (See "Historical Question," page 762.) Although only a minority of American women became flappers, all women, even those who remained at home, felt the great changes of the era.

The New Negro

The 1920s witnessed the emergence not only of the "new woman" but also of the "New Negro." Both new identities riled conservatives and reactionaries. African Americans who challenged the caste system that confined dark-skinned Americans to the lowest levels of society confronted whites who insisted that race relations would not change. Cheers for black soldiers quickly faded after their return from World War I, and African Americans soon faced grim days of economic hardship and race riots (see chapter 22).

The prominent African American intellectual W. E. B. Du Bois and the National Association for the Advancement of Colored People (NAACP) aggressively pursued the passage of a federal antilynching law to counter mob violence against blacks in the South. Many poor blacks, however, disillusioned with mainstream politics, turned for new leadership to a Jamaican-born visionary named **Marcus Garvey**. Garvey urged African Americans to rediscover the heritage of Africa, take pride in their own achievements, and maintain racial purity by avoiding miscegenation. In 1917, Garvey launched the Universal Negro Improvement Association (UNIA) to help African Americans gain economic and political independence entirely outside white society. In 1919, the UNIA created its own shipping company, the Black Star Line, to support the "Back to Africa" movement among black Americans. But the business was an economic failure, and in 1927 the federal government pinned charges of illegal practices on Garvey and deported him to Jamaica. Nevertheless, the issues Garvey raised

"The Girls' Rebellion"
The August 1924 cover of *Redbook*, a popular women's magazine, portrays the kind of postadolescent girl who was making respectable families frantic. Flappers scandalized their middle-class parents by flouting the old moral code. This young woman sports the "badges of flapperhood," including what one critic called an "intoxication of rouge." The cover promises a story inside about girls gone wild. Fictionalized, emotion-packed stories such as this brought the new woman into every woman's home. Picture Research Consultants & Archives.

25 Cents
THE
REDBOOK
MAGAZINE
August 1924
"The Girls' Rebellion"
A startling and revealing story of "the younger generation" that everyone should read

Was There a Sexual Revolution in the 1920s?

"Cigarette in hand, shimmying to the music of the masses, the New Woman and the New Morality have made their theatric debut upon the modern scene," lamented one commentator in 1926. A moral chasm, the *Atlantic* magazine declared, had opened between the generations. The old and young in America "were as far apart in point of view, codes, and standards as if they belonged to different races." Charlotte Perkins Gilman represented many older feminists who were disappointed with the outcome of recent advances for women: "It is sickening to see so many of the newly freed abusing that freedom in a mere imitation of masculine weakness and vice." Older Americans wholeheartedly agreed that the younger generation was in full-fledged revolt against traditional standards of morality and that America was in danger of going to hell in a handbasket.

Critics had, it seemed, plenty of evidence. Between newspapers, movies, and magazines, even the small towns of America were "literally saturated with sex," one observer complained. Flappers and college coeds claimed the privileges of men, smoking cigarettes, drinking from hip flasks, and staying out all night. When eight hundred college women met to discuss life on campus and what "nice girls" should do, they concluded, "Learn temperance in petting, not abstinence." Anxious observers counseled intervention. The

Ohio legislature debated whether to prohibit any "female over fourteen years of age" from wearing a "skirt which does not reach to that part of the foot known as the instep." The *Ladies' Home Journal* urged "legal prohibition" of jazz dancing.

But were the concerned observers correct? Was there really a sexual revolution in the 1920s? The principal movers of the new morality were youths, and without a doubt young, middle-class men and women felt freer than ever to express openly their feelings about sex. But we must separate the new candor from actual sexual behavior. Although solid evidence is difficult to come by, correspondence, diaries, and other personal documents; physicians' records; divorce proceedings; advice literature; and a few early sex surveys provide important clues.

A good place to begin the investigation is where youth congregated: college campuses. Campus life included a self-conscious ethos of experimentation and innovation, but as students demolished old rules, they also created new ones. One major innovation was "dating" — that is, going out unsupervised rather than receiving callers at home or meeting at church socials. Dating was encouraged by the automobile, that "house of prostitution on wheels," as one juvenile judge in Indiana labeled it. Dating led to a second innovation: "petting," or any sexual activity short

of intercourse. One examination of coed behavior at the end of the 1920s found that 92 percent of women admitted engaging in petting.

Like dating, petting represented a significant change in female behavior. But it was not a total rejection of traditional morality because it took place within the search for the ideal marriage partner. There was also a modest increase in premarital sexual intercourse, made possible by the widespread acceptance of contraceptives. But sexual intercourse usually took place between partners who assumed they would marry. The new woman of the 1920s, though freer sexually, continued to focus on romance, marriage, and family.

Did the new sexual behavior mark a drastic change from the past? Evidence of sexual habits before World War I is even more difficult to come by than for the 1920s, but it appears that changes in attitudes and behaviors had been under way for decades. Nineteenth-century Victorian notions of sexless women who felt little or no passion had been eroding since at least the 1890s. A small survey of the sexual practices of middle-class women in the 1890s conducted by Dr. Clelia Duel Mosher, a physician at Stanford University, found that women were enthusiastic about sex and often found satisfaction. The primary ideologues of the sexual revolution, Havelock Ellis, who celebrated female passion, and Sigmund Freud, who stressed the centrality of sex in human endeavor, reached large American audiences before World War I.

Changes in sexual morality, therefore, were evolutionary rather than revolutionary. Still, liberal attitudes and behaviors had their greatest impact in the 1920s. American culture was being remade, and young people, especially women,

about racial pride, black identity, and the search for equality persisted, and his legacy remains at the center of black nationalist thought.

Still, most African Americans maintained hope in the American promise. In New York City, hope and talent came together. Poor blacks

from the South, as well as sophisticated immigrants from the West Indies, poured into Harlem in uptown Manhattan. New York City's black population jumped 115 percent (from 152,000 to 327,000) in the 1920s, while its white population increased only 20 percent. Similar

Heroes and Heroines
Two kinds of women look up adoringly at two kinds of 1920s heroes. A wholesome image is seen on the left in a 1927 cover of *People's Popular Monthly* magazine. The healthy outdoor girl, smartly turned out in her raccoon coat and pennant, flatters a naive college football hero. On the right, the pale, sensitive Vilma Banky kneels imploringly before the hypnotic gaze of the movies' greatest heartthrob, Rudolph Valentino. Magazine: Picture Research Consultants & Archives; Poster: Billy Rose Theatre Collection, The New York Public Library at Lincoln Center.

were at the cutting edge. Now equal at the polling booth, women were also growing more economically independent. Changes in women's political and economic lives were reflected in their sexual attitudes and behaviors. In place of the idea that women were naturally pure, the new morality proclaimed the equality of desire. Only the boldest women rejected a "double standard" (the notion that the sexual behavior of women should be more circumscribed than that of men), but many jettisoned notions of female submission, obedience, and endless childbearing. Charges that the giddy flapper and her partner were bringing down American civilization were overblown, but young women certainly were changing the culture.

Thinking about Evidence

1. Is there any evidence for the contention that changes in sexual behavior in the 1920s were more evolutionary than revolutionary?

2. How did changes in women's political and economic lives affect their sexual behaviors?

demographic changes occurred on a smaller scale throughout the North. Overcrowding and unsanitary housing accompanied this black population explosion, but so too did a new self-consciousness and self-confidence that fed into artistic accomplishment.

In Harlem, an extraordinary mix of black artists, sculptors, novelists, musicians, and poets deliberately set out to create a distinctive African American culture that drew on their identities as Americans and Africans. As scholar Alain Locke put it in 1925, they introduced to the world

Duke Ellington at the Cotton Club
Duke Ellington, at the piano, presides over the floor show at the Cotton Club in Harlem, where black performers played for white audiences. The chorus girls—who were all supposed to be "tall, tan, and terrific"—dance in the "jungle style" that whites expected. During the years from 1927 to 1931 that his orchestra was the house band at the Cotton Club, Ellington recorded more than one hundred of his compositions, establishing him as America's greatest jazz composer and bandleader. The Frank Driggs Collection.

the "**New Negro**," who rose from the ashes of slavery and segregation to proclaim African Americans' creative genius.

The emergence of the New Negro came to be known as the **Harlem Renaissance**. Building on the independence and pride displayed by black soldiers during the war, black artists sought to defeat the fresh onslaught of racial discrimination and violence with poems, paintings, and plays. "We younger Negro artists . . . intend to express 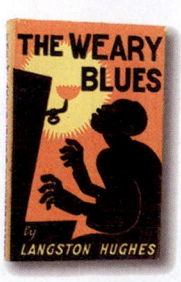 our individual dark-skinned selves without fear or shame," poet Langston Hughes said of the Harlem Renaissance. "If white people are pleased, we are glad. If they are not, it doesn't matter. We know we are beautiful. And ugly, too."

The Harlem Renaissance produced dazzling talent. Black writer James Weldon Johnson, who in 1903 had written the Negro national anthem, "Lift Every Voice," wrote *God's Trombones* (1927), in which he expressed the wisdom and beauty of black folktales from the South. The poetry of Langston Hughes, Claude McKay, and Countee Cullen celebrated the vitality of life in Harlem. Zora Neale Hurston's novel *Their Eyes Were Watching God* (1937) explored the complex passions of black people in a southern community. Black painters, led by Aaron Douglas, linked African art, which had recently inspired European modernist artists, to the concept of the New Negro.

Despite such vibrancy, Harlem for most whites remained a separate black ghetto known only for its lively nightlife. Fashionable whites crowded into Harlem's segregated nightclubs, the most famous of which was the Cotton Club, where they believed they could hear "real" jazz, a relatively new musical form, in its "natural" surroundings. The vigor of the Harlem Renaissance left a powerful legacy for black Americans, but the creative burst did little in the short run to dissolve the prejudice of white society. (See "Seeking the American Promise," page 766.)

Entertainment for the Masses

By the late 1920s, jazz had captured the nation, and jazz giants such as Louis Armstrong, Jelly Roll Morton, Duke Ellington, and Bessie Smith performed for huge audiences. Jazz was only one of the entertainment choices of Americans in the 1920s. Popular culture, like consumer goods, was mass-produced and mass-consumed. The proliferation of movies, radios, music, and sports meant that Americans found plenty to do, and in doing the same things, they helped create a national culture.

Nothing offered escapist delights like the movies. Hollywood, California, discovered the successful formula of combining opulence, sex, and adventure. By 1929, the movies were drawing more than 80 million people in a single week, as

many as lived in the entire country. Admission was cheap, and blacks as well as whites attended, although they entered theaters through different entrances and sat separately. Rudolph Valentino, described as "catnip to women," and Clara Bow, the "It Girl" (everyone knew what *it* was), became household names. Most loved of all was the comic Charlie Chaplin, whose famous character, the wistful Little Tramp, showed an endearing inability to cope with the rules and complexities of modern life.

Americans also found heroes in sports. Baseball, professionalized since 1869 and segregated into white and black leagues, solidified its place as the national pastime in the 1920s. It remained essentially a game played by and for the working class. In George Herman "Babe" Ruth, baseball had the most cherished free spirit of the time. "The Sultan of Swat" mixed his record-setting home runs with rowdy escapades, demonstrating to fans that sports offered a way to break out of the ordinariness of everyday life. By "his sheer exuberance," one sportswriter declared, Ruth "has lightened the cares of the world."

The public also fell in love with a young boxer from the grim mining districts of Colorado. As a teenager, Jack Dempsey had made his living hanging around saloons betting he could beat anyone in the house. When he took the heavyweight crown just after World War I, he was revered as the people's champ, an American equalizer who was a stand-in for the average American who felt increasingly confined by bureaucracy and machine-made culture. In Philadelphia in 1926, a crowd of 125,000 fans saw challenger Gene Tunney pummel and defeat the people's champ.

Football, essentially a college sport, held greater sway with the upper classes. The most famous coach, Knute Rockne of Notre Dame, celebrated football for its life lessons of hard work and teamwork. Let the professors make learning as interesting and significant as football, Rockne advised, and the problem of getting young people to learn would disappear. But in keeping with the times, football moved toward a more commercial spectacle. Harold "Red" Grange, "the Galloping Ghost," led the way by going from stardom at the University of Illinois to the Chicago Bears in the new professional football league.

The decade's hero worship reached its zenith in the celebration of **Charles Lindbergh**, a young pilot who set out on May 20, 1927, from Long Island in his single-engine plane, *The Spirit of St. Louis*, to become the first person to fly nonstop across the Atlantic. Newspapers tagged Lindbergh "the Lone Eagle" — the perfect hero for an age

that celebrated individual accomplishment. "Charles Lindbergh," one journalist proclaimed, "is the stuff out of which have been made the pioneers that opened up the wilderness. His are the qualities which we, as a people, must nourish." Lindbergh realized, however, that technical and organizational complexity was fast reducing chances for solitary achievement. Consequently, he titled his book about the flight *We* (1927) to include the machine that had made it all possible.

Another machine — the radio — became important to mass culture. The nation's first licensed radio station, KDKA in Pittsburgh, began broadcasting in 1920, and soon American airwaves buzzed with news, sermons, soap operas, sports, comedy, and music. For the first time, Americans on the West Coast laughed at the latest jokes from New York, and citizens everywhere listened to the voices of political candidates without leaving home. Because they could now reach prospective customers in their own homes, advertisers bankrolled radio's rapid growth. Between 1922 and 1929, the number of radio stations in the United States increased from 30 to 606. In just seven years, homes with radios jumped from 60,000 to a staggering 10.25 million.

Radio added to the spread of popular music, especially jazz. Jazz — with its energy and freedom — provided the sound track for a new, distinct social class of youths. As the traditional bonds of community, religion, and family loosened, the young felt less pressure to imitate their elders and more freedom to develop their own culture. An increasing number of college students helped the "rah-rah" style of college life become a fad promoted in movies, songs, and advertisements. The collegiate set was the vanguard of the decade's "flaming youth."

The Lost Generation

Some writers and artists felt alienated from America's mass-culture society, which they found shallow, anti-intellectual, and materialistic. Adoration of silly movie stars disgusted them. Moreover, they believed that business culture blighted American life. To their minds, Henry Ford made a poor hero. Young, white, and mostly college educated, these expatriates, as they came to be called, felt embittered by the war and renounced the progressives who had promoted it as a crusade. For them, Europe — not Hollywood or Harlem — seemed the place to seek their renaissance.

The American-born writer Gertrude Stein, long established in Paris, remarked famously as the young exiles gathered around her, "They are

The Quest for Home Ownership in Segregated Detroit

Owning a place of one's own has always been important in America. In the nineteenth century, with the rise of industry and cities, the goal of a family farm gave way to the goal of a single-family house. Home ownership has been widely realized today, with roughly two-thirds of Americans (with the assistance of mortgage companies) owning their own homes.

In the 1920s, decent housing was in short supply in Detroit, America's great boomtown, as thousands poured in to work in Henry Ford's automobile factories. Arriving before World War I, blue-collar German, Irish, and Polish immigrants found homes in working-class neighborhoods scattered around the city center. The great migration out of the South sent Detroit's black population soaring, and the newcomers frightened white property owners who believed that blacks would drive down property values, cause neighborhood decay, and fill their streets with criminals.

The property owners resolved to keep their neighborhoods all-white by channeling blacks into Black Bottom, the downtown ghetto. Although the U.S. Supreme Court had struck down a law mandating segregated housing in 1917, inventive white homeowners created other means to draw racial boundaries. Real estate agents refused to show blacks houses in white neighborhoods. Banks turned down blacks for mortgages. Whites signed restrictive covenants, promising not to sell their homes to blacks. If a black family managed to slip through their defenses, whites resorted to violence.

Dr. Ossian Sweet, a black physician, arrived in Detroit in 1921. He set up his medical practice in Black Bottom and prospered. He soon had the down payment for a home, but he refused to settle his wife and baby daughter in the congested, rat-infested ghetto. In 1925, Sweet bought a substantial bungalow at 2905 Garland Avenue, several blocks inside a working-class white neighborhood. His brother said later, "He wasn't looking for trouble. He just wanted to bring up his little girl in good surroundings." Sweet understood the danger; whites had recently run other black professionals out of their Detroit neighborhoods. "Well, we have decided we are not going to run," Sweet told a friend. "We're not going to look for any trouble, but we're going to be prepared to protect ourselves if trouble arises." When Gladys and Ossian Sweet moved into their home on September 8, 1925, nine friends and family members accompanied them. The moving van that brought their furniture also carried a shotgun, two rifles, six pistols, and four hundred rounds of ammunition.

Hundreds of white men quickly filled the streets, greatly outnumbering the few police who hoped to keep the peace. Shouting that they would send the "niggers" back where they belonged, the mob began throwing rocks, breaking windows, and advancing. Suddenly, gunfire erupted from the second story of the Sweet house, and two white men were shot; one was killed. The police kept the mob away long enough for a paddy wagon to haul the eleven blacks to the police station, where they were all indicted for murder.

Asked why he wanted to move to a white neighborhood, where there was likely to be trouble, Sweet said, "Because I bought the house, and it was my house, and I felt I had a right to live in it." The NAACP, which saw the case as an opportunity to strike a legal blow in favor of self-defense against racial violence, hired Clarence Darrow to defend the accused. Darrow was the most celebrated defense lawyer in the country and fresh from the Scopes trial in Tennessee (see page 770). Darrow told the jury that the facts were simple: "When they defended their home, they were arrested and charged with murder." He reminded the all-white jury that "every man's home is his castle, which even the king may not enter. Every man has a right to kill to defend himself or his family, or others, either in defense of the home, or in defense of themselves." A split jury caused the judge to declare a mistrial. A second trial

the lost generation." Most of the expatriates, however, believed to the contrary that they had finally found themselves. The **Lost Generation** helped launch the most creative period in American art and literature in the twentieth century. The novelist whose spare, clean style best exemplified the expatriate efforts to make art mirror basic reality was Ernest Hemingway. Hemingway's experience in the Great War convinced him that the world in which he was raised, with its Christian moralism and belief in progress, was bankrupt. Admirers found the terse language and hard lessons of his novel *The Sun Also Rises* (1926) to be perfect expressions of a world stripped of illusions.

Many writers who remained in America were exiles in spirit. Before the war, intellectuals had eagerly joined progressive reform movements.

Dr. Ossian Sweet and His House
Dr. Ossian Sweet's substantial two-story brick home is listed on the National Register of Historic Places. In September 1925, Sweet tried to move his family into the then all-white Detroit suburb where the house is located. Residents reacted violently, determined to uphold "the present high standards of the neighborhood." The Detroit News.

ended in not guilty verdicts for all the defendants.

Over the next several decades, housing discrimination became entrenched throughout the nation. Blacks succeeded in breaking out of the inner cities and moving into the suburbs, where today more than one-third of African Americans live, but breaching city boundaries did not mean leaving residential segregation behind. Of all the nation's segregated cities, none was more segregated than Detroit. As late as 1963, Martin Luther King Jr. declared: "I have a dream this afternoon that one day right here in Detroit Negroes will be able to buy a house or rent a house anywhere their money will carry them." As for Sweet, he moved back into his home on Garland Avenue in 1928, but without his wife and daughter, both of whom had died. He stayed in the bungalow for more than twenty-five years, and when he left, the neighborhood around him was still largely white.

Questions for Consideration

1. Why did whites in Dr. Sweet's neighborhood oppose his living there?

2. Why didn't the Supreme Court's 1917 decision and Dr. Sweet's acquittal end residential segregation in Detroit and other American cities?

Afterward, they were more likely critics of American cultural vulgarity. Novelist Sinclair Lewis in *Main Street* (1920) and *Babbitt* (1922) satirized his native Midwest as a cultural wasteland. Humorists such as James Thurber created outlandish characters to poke fun at American stupidity and inhibitions. And southern writers, led by William Faulkner, explored the South's grim class and race heritage. Worries about alienation surfaced as well. Although F. Scott Fitzgerald gained fame as the chronicler of flaming youth, he spoke sadly in *This Side of Paradise* (1920) of a disillusioned generation "grown up to find all Gods dead, all wars fought, all faiths in man shaken."

REVIEW   How did the new freedoms of the 1920s challenge older conceptions of gender and race?

▶ Resistance to Change

Large areas of the country did not share in the wealth of the 1920s. By the end of the decade, 40 percent of the nation's farmers were landless, and 90 percent of rural homes lacked indoor plumbing, gas, or electricity. Rural America's wariness and distrust of urban America turned to despair in the 1920s when the census reported that the majority of the population had shifted to the city (Map 23.2). Urban domination over the nation's political and cultural life and sharply rising economic disparity drove rural Americans in often ugly, reactionary directions.

Cities seemed to stand for everything rural areas stood against. Rural America imagined itself as solidly Anglo-Saxon (despite the presence of millions of African Americans in the South and Mexican Americans, Native Americans, and Asian Americans in the West), and the cities seemed to be filled with undesirable immigrants. Rural America was the home of old-time Protestant religion, and the cities teemed with Catholics, Jews, liberal Protestants, and atheists. Rural America championed old-fashioned moral standards — abstinence and self-denial — while the cities spawned every imaginable vice. In the 1920s, frustrated rural people sought to recapture their country by helping to push through prohibition, dam the flow of immigrants, revive the Ku Klux Klan, defend the Bible as literal truth, and defeat an urban Roman Catholic for president.

MAP ACTIVITY

Map 23.2   The Shift from Rural to Urban Population, 1920–1930

The movement of whites and Hispanics toward urban and agricultural opportunity made Florida, the West, and the Southwest the regions of fastest population growth. By contrast, large numbers of blacks left the rural South to find a better life in the North. Because almost all migrating blacks went from the countryside to cities in distant parts of the nation, while white and Hispanic migrants tended to move shorter distances toward familiar places, the population shift brought more drastic overall change to blacks than to whites and Hispanics.

READING THE MAP: Which states had the strongest growth? To which cities did southern blacks predominantly migrate?

CONNECTIONS: What conditions in the countryside made the migration to urban areas appealing to many rural Americans? In what social and cultural ways did rural America view itself as different from urban America?

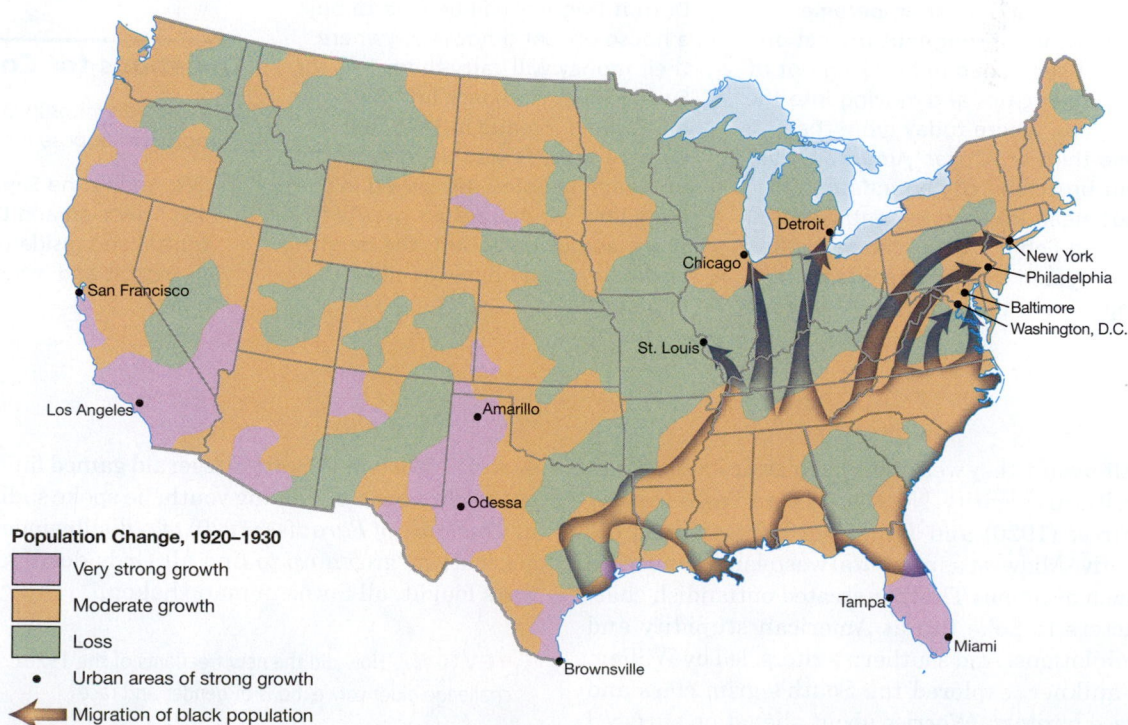

Population Change, 1920–1930

- Very strong growth
- Moderate growth
- Loss
- • Urban areas of strong growth
- ← Migration of black population

Rejecting the Undesirables

Before the war, when about a million immigrants arrived each year, some Americans warned that unassimilable foreigners were smothering the nation. War against Germany and its allies expanded nativist and antiradical sentiment. After the war, large-scale immigration resumed (another 800,000 immigrants arrived in 1921) at a moment when industrialists no longer needed new factory laborers. Returning veterans, as well as African American and Mexican migration, had relieved labor shortages. Moreover, union leaders feared that millions of poor immigrants would undercut their efforts to organize American workers. Rural America's God-fearing Protestants were particularly alarmed that most of the immigrants were Catholic or Jewish. In 1921, Congress responded by severely restricting immigration.

In 1924, Congress very nearly slammed the door shut. The **Johnson-Reed Act** limited the number of immigrants to no more than 161,000 a year and gave each European nation a quota based on 2 percent of the number of people from that country in America in 1890. The act revealed the fear and bigotry that fueled anti-immigration legislation. While it cut immigration by more than 80 percent, it squeezed some nationalities far more than others. Backers of Johnson-Reed openly declared that America had become the "garbage can and the dumping ground of the world," and they manipulated quotas to ensure entry only to "good" immigrants. By basing quotas on the 1890 census, in which western Europeans predominated, the law effectively reversed the trend toward immigration from southern and eastern Europe, which by 1914 had amounted to 75 percent of the yearly total. For example, the Johnson-Reed Act allowed Great Britain 62,458 entries, but Russia could send only 1,992.

The 1924 law reaffirmed the 1880s legislation barring Chinese immigrants and added Japanese and other Asians to the list of the excluded. But it left open immigration from the Western Hemisphere. Farmers in the Southwest demanded continued access to cheap agricultural labor, and during the 1920s some 500,000 Mexicans crossed the border. In addition, Congress in 1924 passed the Indian Citizenship Act, which extended suffrage and citizenship to all American Indians. Indian veterans of World World I had already been made citizens, but now Congress deemed every Indian worthy of participating in American democracy.

Rural Americans, who had most likely never laid eyes on a Polish packinghouse worker, a Slovak coal miner, an Armenian sewing machine operator, or a Chinese laundry worker, strongly supported the Johnson-Reed Act, as did industrialists and labor leaders. The immigration restriction laws of the 1920s provided the framework for immigration policy until the 1960s. These laws marked the end of an era — the denial of the Statue of Liberty's open-arms welcome to Europe's "huddled masses yearning to breathe free."

Antiforeign hysteria climaxed in the trial of two anarchist immigrants from Italy, **Nicola Sacco and Bartolomeo Vanzetti.** Arrested in 1920 for robbery and murder in South Braintree, Massachusetts, the men were sentenced to death by a judge who openly referred to them as "anarchist bastards." In response to doubts about the

Sacco and Vanzetti

After the guilty verdicts were announced, American artist Ben Shahn produced a series of paintings to preserve the memory of Nicola Sacco and Bartolomeo Vanzetti, who many immigrants, liberals, and civil libertarians believed were falsely accused and unfairly convicted. Even today, the 1927 executions symbolize for some the shortcomings of American justice. Digital Image © Museum of Modern Art/Licensed by Scala/Art Resource, NY.

fairness of the verdict, a blue-ribbon review committee found the trial judge guilty of a "grave breach of official decorum" but refused to recommend a motion for retrial. Massachusetts's execution of Sacco and Vanzetti on August 23, 1927, provoked international outrage. Fifty thousand American mourners followed the caskets in the rain, convinced that the men had died because they were immigrants and radicals, not because they were murderers.

The Rebirth of the Ku Klux Klan

The nation's sour antiforeign mood struck a responsive chord in members of the **Ku Klux Klan**. The Klan first appeared in the South during Reconstruction to thwart black freedom and expired with the reestablishment of white supremacy (see chapter 16). In 1915, the Klan was reborn at Stone Mountain, Georgia, but when the new Klan extended its targets beyond black Americans, it quickly spread beyond the South. Under a banner proclaiming "100 percent Americanism," the Klan promised to defend family, morality, and traditional American values against the threats posed by blacks, immigrants, radicals, feminists, Catholics, and Jews.

Building on the frustrations of rural America, the Klan attracted three million to four million members — women as well as men. By the mid-1920s, the Klan had spread throughout the nation, almost controlling Indiana and influencing politics in Illinois, California, Oregon, Texas, Louisiana, Oklahoma, and Kansas. In 1926, Klan imperial wizard Hiram Wesley Evans described the assault of modernity: "One by one all our traditional moral standards went by the boards or were so disregarded that they ceased to be binding," he explained. "The sacredness of our Sabbath, of our homes, of chastity, and finally even of our right to teach our own children in schools [represented] fundamental facts and truth torn away from us." The Klan's uniforms and rituals offered a certain counterfeit dignity to old-stock, Protestant, white Americans who felt passed over, and the hoods allowed members to beat and intimidate their victims with little fear of consequences.

WKKK Badge
Some half a million women were members of the Women of the Ku Klux Klan (WKKK). Young girls could join the female youth auxiliary, the Tri-K for Girls. Klanswomen fit perfectly within the KKK because the organization proclaimed itself the defender of the traditional virtues of pure womanhood and decent homes. This badge from Harrisburg, Pennsylvania, advertises the local WKKK's support for a home for "orphan and dependent children." Klanswomen also joined in boycotts of businesses owned by Jews and others whom they did not consider "100% American." Collection of Janice L. and David J. Frent.

Eventually, social changes, along with lawless excess, crippled the Klan. Immigration restrictions eased the worry about invading foreigners, and sensational wrongdoing by Klan leaders cost it the support of traditional moralists. Grand Dragon David Stephenson of Indiana, for example, went to jail for the kidnapping and rape of a woman who subsequently committed suicide. Yet the social grievances, economic problems, and religious anxieties of the countryside and small towns remained, ready to be ignited.

The Scopes Trial

In 1925 in a Tennessee courtroom, old-time religion and the new spirit of science went head-to-head. The confrontation occurred after several southern states passed legislation against the teaching of Charles Darwin's theory of evolution in the public schools. Fundamentalist Protestants insisted that the Bible's creation story be taught as the literal truth. Scientists and civil liberties organizations clamored for a challenge to the law, and John Scopes, a young biology teacher in Dayton, Tennessee, offered to test his state's ban on teaching evolution. When Scopes came to trial, Clarence Darrow, a brilliant defense lawyer from Chicago, volunteered to defend him. Darrow, an avowed agnostic, took on the prosecution's fundamentalist William Jennings Bryan. Bryan, a three-time Democratic nominee for president and a symbol of rural America, was eager to defeat the proposition that humans had evolved from apes.

The **Scopes trial** quickly degenerated into a media circus. The first trial to be covered live on

radio, it attracted a nationwide audience. Most of the reporters from big-city newspapers were hostile to Bryan, none more so than the cynical H. L. Mencken, who painted Bryan as a sort of Darwinian missing link ("a sweating anthropoid" and a "gaping primate"). When, under relentless questioning by Darrow, Bryan declared on the witness stand that he did indeed believe that the world had been created in six days and that Jonah had lived in the belly of a whale, his humiliation in the eyes of most urban observers was complete. Nevertheless, the Tennessee court upheld the law and punished Scopes with a $100 fine. Although fundamentalism won the battle, it lost the war. Mencken had the last word in a merciless obituary for Bryan, who died just a week after the trial ended. Portraying the "monkey trial" as a battle between the country and the city, Mencken flayed Bryan as a "charlatan, a mountebank, a zany without shame or dignity," motivated solely by "hatred of the city men who had laughed at him for so long."

As Mencken's acid prose indicated, Bryan's humiliation was not purely a victory of reason and science. It also revealed the disdain urban people felt for country people and the values they clung to. The Ku Klux Klan revival and the Scopes trial dramatized and inflamed divisions between city and country, intellectuals and the uneducated, the privileged and the poor, the scoffers and the faithful.

Al Smith and the Election of 1928

The presidential election of 1928 brought many of the developments of the 1920s — prohibition, immigration, religion, and the clash of rural and urban values — into sharp focus. Republicans emphasized the economic success of their party's pro-business government and turned to Herbert Hoover, the energetic secretary of commerce and leading public symbol of 1920s prosperity. But because both parties generally agreed that the American economy was basically sound, the campaign turned on social issues that divided Americans.

The Democrats nominated four-time governor of New York **Alfred E. Smith**. Smith adopted "The Sidewalks of New York" as a campaign theme song and seemed to represent all that rural Americans feared and resented. A child of immigrants, Smith got his start in politics with the help of Tammany Hall, New York City's Irish-dominated political machine and to many

the epitome of big-city corruption. He denounced immigration quotas, signed New York State's anti-Klan bill, and opposed prohibition, believing that it was a nativist attack on immigrant customs. When Smith supposedly asked reporters in 1922, "Wouldn't you like to have your foot on the rail and blow the foam off some suds?" prohibition forces dubbed him "Alcohol Al."

Smith's greatest vulnerability in the heartland, however, was his religion. He was the first Catholic to run for president. A Methodist bishop in Virginia denounced Roman Catholicism as "the Mother of ignorance, superstition, intolerance and sin" and begged Protestants not to vote for a candidate who represented "the kind of dirty people that you find today on the sidewalks of New York." The magazine *Baptist and Commoner* argued that Smith's election would mean "granting the Pope the right to dictate to this government what it should do."

Hoover, who neatly combined the images of morality, efficiency, service, and prosperity, won the election by a landslide (Map 23.3). He received nearly 58 percent of the vote and gained 444 electoral votes to Smith's 87. The Republicans' most notable success came in the previously solid Democratic South, where Smith's religion, views

> **"The Mother of ignorance, superstition, intolerance, and sin."**
> — A Methodist bishop, speaking of Roman Catholicism

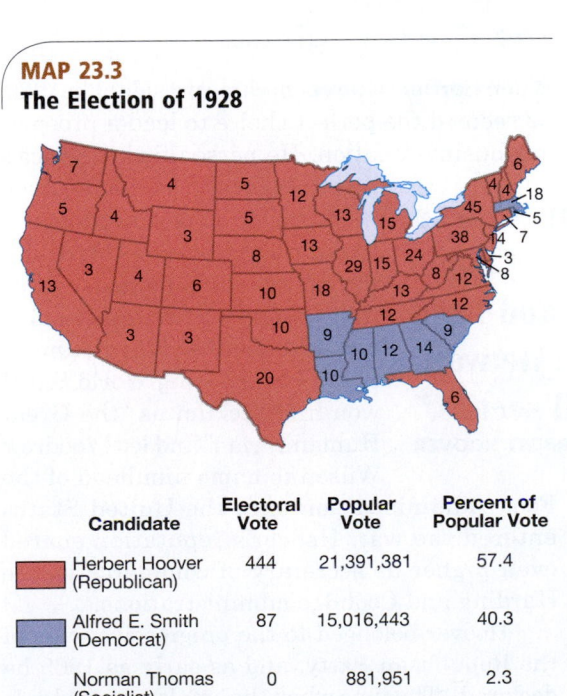

MAP 23.3
The Election of 1928

Candidate	Electoral Vote	Popular Vote	Percent of Popular Vote
Herbert Hoover (Republican)	444	21,391,381	57.4
Alfred E. Smith (Democrat)	87	15,016,443	40.3
Norman Thomas (Socialist)	0	881,951	2.3

on prohibition, and big-city persona allowed them to take four states. The only bright spot for Democrats was the nation's cities, which voted Democratic, indicating the rising strength of ethnic minorities, including Smith's fellow Catholics.

> **REVIEW** Why did the relationship between urban and rural America deteriorate in the 1920s?

▶ The Great Crash

At his inauguration in 1929, Herbert Hoover told the American people, "Given a chance to go forward with the policies of the last eight years, we shall soon with the help of God be in sight of the day when poverty will be banished from this nation." Those words came back to haunt Hoover, for within eight months the Roaring Twenties came to a crashing halt. The prosperity Hoover touted collapsed with the stock market, and the nation ended nearly three decades of barely interrupted economic growth. Like much of the world, the United States fell into the most serious economic depression of all time. Hoover and his reputation were among the first casualties, along with the reverence for business that had been the hallmark of the New Era.

Herbert Hoover: The Great Engineer

When **Herbert Hoover** became president in 1929, he seemed the perfect choice to lead a prosperous business nation. He personified America's rags-to-riches ideal, having risen from poor Iowa orphan to one of the world's most celebrated mining engineers by the time he was thirty. His success in managing efforts to feed civilian victims of the fighting during World War I won him acclaim as "the Great Humanitarian" and led Woodrow Wilson to name him head of the Food Administration once the United States entered the war. Hoover's reputation soared even higher as secretary of commerce in the Harding and Coolidge administrations.

> **"We want to see a nation built of home owners and farm owners. . . . We want them all secure."**
> — President HERBERT HOOVER

Hoover belonged to the progressive wing of the Republican Party, and as early as 1909 he declared, "The time when the employer could ride roughshod over his labor[ers] is disappearing with the doctrine of 'laissez-faire' on which it is founded." He urged a limited business-government partnership that would manage the sweeping changes Americans experienced. When Hoover entered the White House, he brought a reform agenda: "We want to see a nation built of home owners and farm owners. We want to see their savings protected. We want to see them in steady jobs. We want to see more and more of them insured against death and accident, unemployment and old age. We want them all secure."

But Hoover also had ideological and political liabilities. Principles that appeared strengths in the prosperous 1920s — individual self-reliance, industrial self-management, and a limited federal government — became straitjackets when economic catastrophe struck. Moreover, Hoover had never held an elected public office, had a poor political touch, and was too thin-skinned to be an effective politician. Even so, most Americans considered him "a sort of superman" able to solve any problem. Prophetically, he confided to a friend his fear that "if some unprecedented calamity should come upon the nation . . . I would be sacrificed to the unreasoning disappointment of a people who expected too much." The distorted national economy set the stage for the calamity Hoover so feared.

The Distorted Economy

In the spring of 1929, the United States enjoyed a fragile prosperity. Although America had become the world's leading economy, it had done little to help rebuild Europe's shattered economy after World War I. Instead, the Republican administrations demanded that Allied nations repay their war loans, creating a tangled web of debts and reparations that sapped Europe's economic vitality. Moreover, to boost American business, the United States enacted tariffs that prevented other nations from selling their goods to Americans. Fewer sales meant that foreign nations had less money to buy American goods, which were pouring out in record abundance. American banks propped up the nation's export trade by extending credit to foreign customers, and fresh debt piled onto existing debt in an absurd pyramid.

American prosperity was real enough, but the domestic economy was also in trouble. Wealth was badly distributed. Farmers continued to suffer from low prices and chronic indebtedness; the average income of families working the land

Hoover Campaign Poster
This poster effectively illustrates Herbert Hoover's 1928 campaign message: Republican administrations in the 1920s had produced middle-class prosperity, complete with a house in the suburbs and the latest automobile. To remind voters that Hoover as secretary of commerce had promoted industry that made the suburban dream possible, the poster portrays smoking chimneys at a discreet distance. The poster gives no hint that this positive message would give way to outright religious bigotry in the campaign against Democrat (and Catholic) Al Smith. Collection of Janice L. and David J. Frent.

amounted to only $240 per year. The wages of industrial workers, though rising during the decade, failed to keep up with productivity and corporate profits. Overall, nearly two-thirds of all American families lived on less than the $2,000 per year that economists estimated would "supply only basic necessities." Statistics captured the grim reality. The wealthiest 1 percent of the population received 15 percent of the nation's income — the same amount received by the poorest 42 percent. The Coolidge administration worsened the deepening inequality by cutting taxes on the wealthy.

By 1929, the inequality of wealth produced a serious problem in consumption. The rich spent lavishly, but they could absorb only a tiny fraction of the nation's output. Ordinary folk, on whom the system ultimately depended, were unable to take up the slack. For a time, the new device of installment buying — buying on credit — kept consumer demand up. By the end of the decade, four out of five cars and two out of three radios were bought on credit.

Signs of economic trouble began to appear at mid-decade. New construction slowed down. Automobile sales faltered. Companies began cutting back production and laying off workers. Between 1921 and 1928, as investment and loan opportunities faded, five thousand banks failed, wiping out the life savings of hundreds of thousands of people. Still, the boom seemed to roar on, muffling the sounds of economic distress just beneath the surface.

The Crash of 1929

Even as the international and domestic economies faltered, Americans remained remarkably upbeat. Hoping for even bigger slices of the economic pie, Americans speculated wildly in the stock market on Wall Street. Between 1924 and 1929, the values of stocks listed on the New York Stock Exchange increased by more than 400 percent. In September 1929, General Electric traded at $396 a share, three times the price of a year earlier. Buying stocks on margin — that is, putting up only part of the money at the time of purchase — accelerated. Many people got rich this way, but those who bought on credit could finance their loans only if their stocks increased in value. Speculators could not imagine that the market might fall and that they would be forced

Stock Market Crash
Edward Laning, a mural painter who lost his personal fortune in the stock market crash, gained a measure of revenge in this melodramatic version of the panic on the Stock Exchange floor. Stock Exchange president Richard Whitney stands illuminated and unperturbed in the center as prices and brokers collapse around him. A few years later, however, Whitney went to prison for stealing from other people's accounts to cover his own losses. Laning went on to fame for his murals at Ellis Island and the New York Public Library. Collection of John P. Axelrod/Picture Research Consultants & Archives.

to meet their margin loans with cash they did not have. A Yale economist assured doubters that stock prices had reached "a permanently high plateau."

Finally, in the autumn of 1929, the market hesitated. Investors nervously began to sell their overvalued stocks. The dip quickly became a panic on October 24, the day that came to be known as Black Thursday. Brokers jammed the stock exchange desperately trying to unload shares. The giants of finance gathered in the offices of J. P. Morgan Jr., son of the nineteenth-century Wall Street lion, to plot ways of restor-

ing confidence. They injected $100 million of their assets to bolster the market and issued brave declarations of faith. But more panic selling came on **Black Tuesday**, October 29, the day the market suffered a greater fall than ever before. In the next six months, the stock market lost six-sevenths of its total value.

It was once thought that the crash alone caused the Great Depression. It did not. In 1929, the national and international economies were already riddled with severe problems. But the dramatic losses in the stock market crash and the fear of risking what was left acted as a great brake on economic activity. The collapse on Wall Street shattered the New Era's confidence that America would enjoy perpetually expanding prosperity.

Hoover and the Limits of Individualism

At first, Americans expressed relief that Herbert Hoover resided in the White House when the bubble broke. Unlike some conservatives who believed that the government should do nothing during economic downturns, Hoover believed that "we should use the powers of government to cushion the situation." Not surprisingly for a man who had been such an active secretary of commerce, Hoover acted quickly to arrest the decline.

In November 1929, to keep the stock market collapse from ravaging the entire economy, Hoover called a White House conference of business and labor leaders and urged them to join in a voluntary plan for recovery: Businesses would maintain production and keep their workers on the job; labor would accept existing wages, hours, and conditions. Within a few months, however, the bargain fell apart. As demand for their products declined, industrialists cut production, sliced wages, and laid off workers. Poorly paid or unemployed workers could not buy much, and their decreased spending led to further cuts in production and further loss of jobs. Thus began the terrible spiral of economic decline.

To deal with the problems of rural America, Hoover got Congress to pass the Agricultural Marketing Act in 1929. The act created the **Farm Board**, which used its budget of $500 million to buy up agricultural surpluses and thus, it was hoped, raise prices. But prices declined. To help end the decline, Hoover joined conservatives in urging protective tariffs on agricultural goods, and the **Hawley-Smoot tariff** of 1930 established the highest rates in history. The same year, Congress also authorized $420 million for public

works projects to give the unemployed jobs and create more purchasing power. In three years, the Hoover administration nearly doubled federal public works expenditures.

But with each year of Hoover's term, the economy weakened. Tariffs did not end the suffering of farmers because foreign nations retaliated with increased tariffs of their own that crippled American farmers' ability to sell abroad. In 1932, Hoover hoped to help hard-pressed industry with the **Reconstruction Finance Corporation (RFC)**, a federal agency empowered to lend government funds to endangered banks and corporations. The theory was **trickle-down economics**: Pump money into the economy at the top, and in the long run the people at the bottom would benefit. Or as one wag put it, "Feed the sparrows by feeding the horses." In the end, very little of what critics of the RFC called a "millionaires' dole" trickled down to the poor.

And the poor multiplied. Hundreds of thousands of workers lost their jobs each month. By 1932, an astounding one-quarter of the American workforce — some thirteen million people — were unemployed. There was no direct federal assistance, and state services and private charities were swamped. The depression that began in 1929 devastated much of the world, but no other industrialized nation provided such feeble support to the jobless. Cries grew louder for the federal government to give hurting people relief.

Hoover was no do-nothing president, but there were limits to his activism. He intended a limited role for the federal government in fighting the economic disaster. He compared direct federal aid to the needy to the "dole" in Britain, which he thought destroyed the moral fiber of the chronically unemployed. "Prosperity cannot be restored by raids upon the public Treasury," he declared. Besides, he said, the poor could rely on the charitable spirit of their neighbors to protect them "from hunger and cold." In 1931, he allowed the Red Cross to distribute government-owned agricultural surpluses to the hungry. In 1932, he relaxed his principles further to offer small federal loans, not gifts, to the states to help them in their relief efforts. But Hoover's circumscribed notions of legitimate government action proved vastly inadequate to address the problems of restarting the economy and ending human suffering.

REVIEW Why did the American economy collapse in 1929?

► Life in the Depression

In 1930, suffering on a massive scale set in. Despair settled over the land. Men and women hollow-eyed with hunger grew increasingly bewildered and angry in the face of cruel contradictions. They saw agricultural surpluses pile up in the countryside and knew that their children were going to bed hungry. They saw factories standing idle and knew that they and millions of others were willing to work. The gap between the American people and leaders who failed to resolve these contradictions widened as the depression deepened. By 1932, America's economic problems had created a dangerous social and political crisis.

The Human Toll

Statistics only hint at the human tragedy of the Great Depression. When Herbert Hoover took office in 1929, the American economy stood at its peak. When he left in 1933, it had reached its twentieth-century low (Figure 23.2). In 1929, national income was $88 billion. By 1933, it had declined to $40 billion. In 1929, unemployment was 3.1 percent, or 1.5 million workers. By 1933, unemployment stood at 25 percent, almost 13 million workers. In Cleveland, Ohio, 50 percent of the workforce was jobless, and in Toledo, 80 percent. The nation's steel industry operated at only 12 percent of capacity. By 1932, more than 9,000 banks had shut their doors, wiping out some 9 million savings accounts.

Jobless, homeless victims wandered in search of work, and the tramp, or hobo, became one of the most visible figures of the decade. Riding the rails or hitchhiking, a million vagabonds moved southward and westward looking for seasonal agricultural work. Other unemployed men and women, sick or less hopeful, huddled in doorways, overcome, one man remembered, by "helpless despair and submission." Scavengers haunted alleys behind restaurants in search of food. One writer told of an elderly woman who always took off her glasses to avoid seeing the maggots crawling over the garbage she ate. The Children's Bureau announced that one in five schoolchildren did not get enough to eat. "I don't want to steal," a Pennsylvania man wrote to the governor in 1931,

> "I don't want to steal, but I won't let my wife and boy cry for something to eat. . . . How long is this going to keep up? I cannot stand it any longer."
> —A Pennsylvania man in 1931

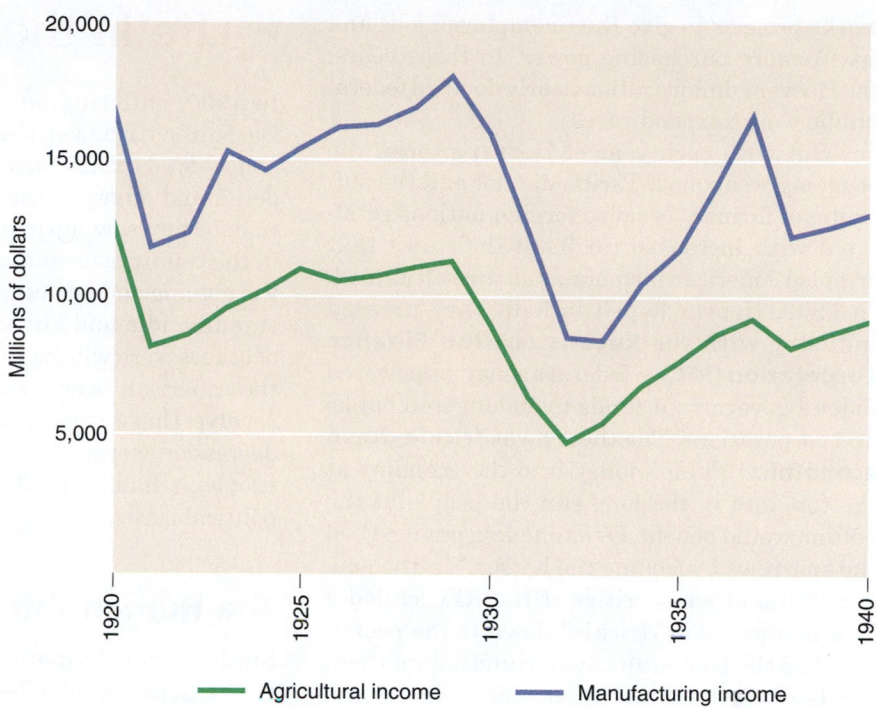

FIGURE 23.2 Manufacturing and Agricultural Income, 1920–1940
After economic collapse, recovery in the 1930s began under New Deal auspices. The sharp declines in 1937–1938, when federal spending was reduced, indicated that New Deal stimuli were still needed to restore manufacturing and agricultural income.

"but I won't let my wife and boy cry for something to eat. . . . How long is this going to keep up? I cannot stand it any longer."

Rural poverty was most acute. Tenant farmers and sharecroppers, mainly in the South, came to symbolize how poverty crushed the human spirit. Eight and a half million people, three million of them black, crowded into cabins without plumbing, electricity, or running water. They subsisted — just barely — on salt pork, cornmeal, molasses, beans, peas, and whatever they could hunt or fish. All the diseases of dietary and vitamin deficiencies wracked them. When economist John Maynard Keynes was asked whether anything like this degradation had existed before, he replied, "Yes, it was called the Dark Ages and it lasted four hundred years."

There was no federal assistance to meet this human catastrophe. Instead, Hoover relied on a patchwork of strapped charities and destitute

An Unemployed Youth
Joblessness was frightening and humiliating. Brought up to believe that if you worked hard, you got ahead, the unemployed had difficulty seeing failure to find work as anything other than personal failure. Many slipped into despair and depression. We can only imagine this young man's story. Utterly alone, sitting on a bench that might be his bed, his hat on the ground and his head in his hands, he looks emotionally battered and perhaps defeated. Whether he found work, joined the throngs of beggars and panhandlers on the streets, or cast his lot with the army of hoboes who rode the rails looking for something better is unknown. Library of Congress.

state and local agencies. For a family of four without any income, the best the city of Philadelphia could do was provide $5.50 per week. That was not enough to live on but was still comparatively generous. New York City provided only $2.39 per week. Detroit, devastated by the auto industry's failure, allotted 60 cents a week before the city ran out of money altogether, joining a hundred other cities in 1932 that appropriated no money at all for the indigent.

The deepening crisis roused old fears and caused some Americans to look for scapegoats. Among the most thoroughly scapegoated were Mexican Americans. During the 1920s, cheap agricultural labor from Mexico flowed legally across the U.S. border, welcomed by the large farmers. In the 1930s, however, the public denounced the newcomers as dangerous aliens who took jobs from Americans. Government officials, most prominently those in Los Angeles County, targeted Mexican residents for deportation regardless of citizenship status. As many as half a million Mexicans and Mexican Americans were deported or fled to Mexico.

The depression deeply affected the American family. Young people postponed marriage; between 1929 and 1932, marriages declined by 31 percent. When they did marry, they produced few children. For the first time in American history, the birthrate was on the verge of dropping below the death rate. Moreover, white women, who generally worked in low-paying service areas, did not lose their jobs as often as men who worked in steel, automobile, and other heavy industries. Idle husbands suffered a loss of self-esteem. "Before the depression," one unemployed man reported, "I wore the pants in this family, and rightly so." Jobless, he lost "self-respect" and also "the respect of my children, and I am afraid that I am losing my wife." Another unemployed father said, "A man is not a man without work." Employers discriminated against married women workers, but necessity continued to drive women into the marketplace. As a result, by 1940 some 25 percent more women were employed for wages than in 1930.

Denial and Escape

President Hoover had no idea of how to reach out to the suffering nation. To express his optimism about economic recovery, he maintained formal dress and manners in the White House and continued to keep a retinue of valets and waiters to attend him. All he did was to repeat that economic recovery was on its way. Contradicting the president's optimism were makeshift shantytowns, called "**Hoovervilles**," that sprang up on the edges of America's cities. Newspapers used as cover by those sleeping on the streets were "Hoover blankets." An empty pocket turned inside out was a "Hoover flag," and jackrabbits caught for food were "Hoover hogs." Bitter jokes circulated about the increasingly unpopular president. One told of Hoover asking for a nickel to telephone a friend. Flipping him a dime, an aide said, "Here, call them both."

Deportation to Mexico
A crowd gathered at the train depot in Miami, Arizona, to say good-bye to friends and family who were being pushed to leave depression-wracked America. Scenes like this one were repeated throughout the Southwest. In 1931, Los Angeles County chartered trains to carry Mexicans and Mexican Americans out of the country, arguing that the $15,000 expense "would be recovered within six weeks in saving on charity." But contrary to popular belief, immigrants did not put undue pressure on social services. Moreover, some of the deportees were American citizens who had never been south of the border. Arizona State University Library.

While Hoover practiced denial, other Americans sought refuge from reality at the movies. Throughout the depression, between 60 million and 75 million people (nearly two-thirds of the nation) scraped together enough change to fill the movie palaces every week. Box office hits such as *Forty-second Street* and *Gold Diggers of 1933* capitalized on the hope that prosperity lay just around the corner. But a few filmmakers grappled with realities rather than escape them. *The Public Enemy* (1931) taught hard lessons about gangsters' ill-gotten gains. Indeed, under the new production code of 1930, designed to protect public morals, all movies had to find some way to show that crime did not pay.

Despite Hollywood's efforts to keep Americans on the right side of the law, crime increased. Out in the countryside, the plight of people who had lost their farms to bank foreclosures led to the romantic idea that bank robbers were only getting back what banks had stolen from the poor. Woody Guthrie, the populist folksinger from Oklahoma, captured the public's tolerance for outlaws in his tribute to a murderous bank robber with a choirboy face, "The Ballad of Pretty Boy Floyd":

> Yes, as through this world I ramble,
> I see lots of funny men,
> Some will rob you with a six-gun,
> Some will rob you with a pen.
> But as through your life you'll travel,
> Wherever you may roam,
> You won't never see an outlaw drive
> A family from their home.

Working-Class Militancy

It was the nation's working class that bore the brunt of the economic collapse. In Chicago, workingwomen received less than twenty-five cents an hour. Sawmill workers in the West got a nickel. By 1931, William Green, head of the American Federation of Labor (AFL), had turned militant. "I warn the people who are exploiting the workers," he shouted, "that they can drive them only so far before they will turn on them and destroy them. They are taking no account of the history of nations in which governments have been overturned. Revolutions grow out of the depths of hunger."

The American people were slow to anger, but on March 7, 1932, several thousand unemployed autoworkers massed at the gates of Henry Ford's River Rouge factory in Dearborn, Michigan, to demand work. Pelted with rocks, Ford's private security forces responded with gunfire, killing four demonstrators. Forty thousand outraged citizens turned out for the unemployed men's funerals.

Farmers mounted uprisings of their own. When Congress refused to guarantee farm prices that would at least equal the cost of production, several thousand farmers created the National Farmers' Holiday Association in 1932, so named because its members planned to take a "holiday" from shipping crops to market. When some farmers persisted, militants barricaded roads and dumped thousands of gallons of milk in ditches. Farm militants also resorted to what they called "penny sales." When banks foreclosed and put farms up for auction, neighbors warned others not to bid, bought the foreclosed property for a few pennies, and returned it to the bankrupt owners. Under this kind of pressure, some states suspended debts or reduced mortgages. In California in 1933, when landowners cut their laborers' already substandard wages, more than 50,000 farmworkers, most of them Mexicans, went on strike. Militancy won farmers little in the way of long-term solutions, but one individual observed that "the biggest and finest crop of revolutions you ever saw is sprouting all over the country right now."

Even those who had proved their patriotism by serving in World War I rose up in protest against the government. In June and July 1932, tens of thousands of unemployed veterans traveled to Washington, D.C., to petition Congress for the immediate payment of the pension (known as a "bonus") that Congress had promised them in 1924. The throng included, according to a Washington reporter, "truck drivers and blacksmiths, steel workers and coal miners, stenographers and common laborers," in all "a fair cross section" of the nation. President Hoover feared that the veterans would spark a riot and ordered the U.S. Army to evict the **Bonus Marchers** from their camp on the outskirts of the city. Tanks decimated the squatters' encampments while five hundred soldiers wielding bayonets and tear gas sent the ragtag protesters fleeing. The mayhem, which was captured on newsreels, appalled the nation and further undermined public support for the beleaguered Hoover. "So all the misery and suffering had finally come to this," reported one journalist, "soldiers

"Scottsboro Boys"
Nine black youths, ranging in age from thirteen to twenty-one, stand in front of rifle-bearing National Guard troops called up by Alabama governor B. M. Miller, who feared a mob lynching after two white women accused the nine of rape in March 1931. In less than two weeks, an all-white jury heard flimsy evidence, convicted the nine of rape, and sentenced them to death. Although none was executed, all nine spent years in jail. Eventually, the state dropped the charges against the youngest four and granted paroles to the others. The last "Scottsboro Boy" left jail in 1950.
© Bettmann/Corbis.

marching with their guns against American citizens."

Such scenes during the Great Depression — the massive failure of capitalism — brought socialism back to life in the United States and catapulted the Communist Party to its greatest size and influence in American history. Some 100,000 Americans — workers, intellectuals, college students — joined the Communist Party in the belief that only an overthrow of the capitalist system could save the victims of the depression. In 1931, the party, through its National Miners Union, moved into Harlan County, Kentucky, to support a strike by brutalized coal miners. The mine owners unleashed thugs against the strikers and eventually beat the miners down. But the Communist Party gained a reputation as the most dedicated and fearless champion of the union cause.

The left also led the fight against racism. While both major parties refused to challenge segregation in the South, the Socialist Party, led by Norman Thomas, attacked the system

Harlan County Coal Strike, 1931

of sharecropping that left many African Americans in near servitude. The Communist Party also took action. When nine young black men in Scottsboro, Alabama (the **Scottsboro Boys**), were arrested on trumped-up rape charges in 1931, a team of lawyers sent by the party saved the defendants from the electric chair.

Radicals on the left often sparked action, but protests by moderate workers and farmers occurred on a far greater scale. Breadlines, soup kitchens, foreclosures, unemployment, government violence, and cold despair drove patriotic men and women to question American capitalism. "I am as conservative as any man could be," a Wisconsin farmer explained, "but any economic system that has in its power to set me and my wife in the streets, at my age — what can I see but red?"

REVIEW How did the depression reshape American politics?

▶ Conclusion: Dazzle and Despair

In the aftermath of World War I, America turned its back on progressive crusades and embraced conservative Republican politics, the growing influence of corporate leaders, and business values. Changes in the nation's economy — Henry Ford's automobile revolution, advertising, mass production — propelled fundamental change throughout society. Living standards rose, economic opportunity increased, and Americans threw themselves into private pleasures — gobbling up the latest household goods and fashions, attending baseball and football games and boxing matches, gathering around the radio, and going to the movies. As big cities came to dominate American life, the culture of youth and flappers became the leading edge of what one observer called a "revolution in manners and morals." At home in Harlem and abroad in Paris, American literature, art, and music flourished.

For many Americans, however, none of the glamour and vitality had much meaning. Instead of seeking thrills at speakeasies, plunging into speculation on Wall Street, or escaping abroad, the vast majority struggled to earn a decent living. Blue-collar America did not participate fully in white-collar prosperity. Rural America was almost entirely left out of the Roaring Twenties. Country folk, deeply suspicious and profoundly discontented, championed prohibition, revived the Klan, attacked immigration, and defended old-time Protestant religion.

Just as the dazzle of the Roaring Twenties hid deep divisions in society, extravagant prosperity masked structural flaws in the economy. The crash of 1929 and the depression that followed starkly revealed the economy's crises of international trade and consumption. Hard times swept high living off the front pages of the nation's newspapers. Different images emerged: hoboes hopping freight trains, strikers confronting police, malnourished sharecroppers staring blankly into the distance, empty apartment buildings alongside cardboard shantytowns, and mountains of food rotting in the sun while guards with shotguns chased away the hungry.

The depression hurt everyone, but the poor were hurt most. As farmers and workers sank into aching hardship, businessmen rallied around Herbert Hoover to proclaim that private enterprise would get the country moving again. But things fell apart, and Hoover faced increasingly radical opposition. Membership in the Socialist and Communist parties surged, and more and more Americans contemplated desperate measures. By 1932, the depression had nearly brought the nation to its knees. America faced its greatest crisis since the Civil War, and citizens demanded new leaders who would save them from the "Hoover Depression."

▶ Selected Bibliography

General Works

David M. Kennedy, *Freedom from Fear: The American People in Depression and War, 1929–1945* (1999).

William E. Leuchtenburg, *The Perils of Prosperity, 1914–1932* (1958).

Michael Parrish, *Anxious Decades: America in Prosperity and Depression, 1920–1941* (1992).

Politics and Economy

Kristi Anderson, *After Suffrage: Women in Partisan and Electoral Politics before the New Deal* (1996).

Douglas Brinkley, *Wheels for the World: Henry Ford, His Company, and a Century of Progress, 1903–2003* (2003).

Kendrick A. Clements, *Hoover, Conservation, and Consumerism: Engineering the Good Life* (2000).

Warren I. Cohen, *Empire without Tears: America's Foreign Relations, 1921–1933* (1987).

Steve Fraser, *Every Man a Speculator: A History of Wall Street* (2005).

Colin Gordon, *New Deals: Business, Labor, and Politics in America, 1920–1935* (1994).

David Greenberg, *Calvin Coolidge* (2006).

Owen Gutfreund, *Twentieth-Century Sprawl: Highways and the Reshaping of the American Landscape* (2004).

Jill Jonnes, *Empires of Light: Edison, Tesla, and Westinghouse, and the Race to Electrify the World* (2003).

William E. Leuchtenburg, *Herbert Hoover: 31st President, 1929–1933* (2009).

Martha L. Olney, *Buy Now, Pay Later: Advertising, Credit, and Consumer Durables in the 1920s* (1991).

Lorrai Schuyler, *Weight of Their Votes: Southern Women and Political Leverage in the 1920s* (2006).

Steven Watts, *People's Tycoon: Henry Ford and the American Century* (2005).

Society and Culture

Douglas Carl Abrams, *Selling the Old-Time Religion: American Fundamentalists and Mass Culture, 1920–1940* (2001).

Francisco E. Balderrama and Raymond Rodriguez, *Decade of Betrayal: Mexican Repatriation in the 1930s* (1995).

Kevin Boyle, *Arc of Justice: A Saga of Race, Civil Rights, and Murder in the Jazz Age* (2004).

Liz Conor, *Spectacular Modern Woman: Feminine Visibility in the 1920s* (2004).

Ruth Schwartz Cowan, *More Work for Mother: The Ironies of Household Technology from the Open Hearth to the Microwave* (1983).

Roger Daniels, *Guarding the Golden Door: American Immigration Policy and Immigrants since 1882* (2004).

Paula S. Fass, *The Damned and the Beautiful: American Youth in the 1920s* (1977).

David J. Goldberg, *Discontented America: The United States in the 1920s* (1999).

David M. Kennedy, *Birth Control in America: The Career of Margaret Sanger* (1970).

David E. Kyvig, *Daily Life in the United States, 1920–1940* (2002).

Edward J. Larson, *Summer of the Gods: The Scopes Trial and America's Continuing Debate over Science and Religion* (1997).

David Levering Lewis, *W. E. B. Du Bois: The Fight for Equality and the American Century, 1919–1963* (2000).

Nancy MacLean, *Behind the Mask of Chivalry: The Making of the Second Ku Klux Klan* (1994).

David E. Nye, *Electrifying America: Social Meanings of a New Technology, 1880–1940* (1990).

Daniel Okrent, *Last Call: The Rise and Fall of Prohibition* (2010).

David M. Reimers, *Unwelcome Strangers: American Identity and the Turn against Immigration* (1998).

Susan Smulyan, *Selling Radio: The Commercialization of American Broadcasting, 1920–1934* (1994).

Judith Stein, *The World of Marcus Garvey* (1986).

Andrew Wiese, *Places of Their Own: African American Suburbanization in the Twentieth Century* (2004).

▶ **FOR MORE BOOKS ABOUT TOPICS IN THIS CHAPTER,** see the Online Bibliography at **bedfordstmartins.com/roark.**

▶ **FOR ADDITIONAL PRIMARY SOURCES FROM THIS PERIOD,** see Michael Johnson, ed., *Reading the American Past*, Fifth Edition.

▶ **FOR WEB SITES, IMAGES, AND DOCUMENTS RELATED TO TOPICS AND PLACES IN THIS CHAPTER,** visit Make History at **bedfordstmartins.com/roark.**

Reviewing Chapter 23

REVIEW QUESTIONS

Use key terms and dates to support your answer.

1. How did the spread of the automobile transform the United States? (pp. 751–756)

2. How did the new freedoms of the 1920s challenge older conceptions of gender and race? (pp. 757–767)

3. Why did the relationship between urban and rural America deteriorate in the 1920s? (pp. 768–772)

4. Why did the American economy collapse in 1929? (pp. 772–775)

5. How did the depression reshape American politics? (pp. 775–779)

MAKING CONNECTIONS

Draw on key terms, the timeline, and review questions.

1. In the 1920s, Americans' wariness of the concentration of power in the hands of industrial capitalists gave way to unrestrained confidence in American business. What drove this shift in popular opinion? How did it influence Republicans' approach to governance and the development of the American economy in the 1920s?

2. Americans' encounters with the wealth and increased personal freedom characteristic of the 1920s varied greatly. Discuss the impact such variation had on Americans' responses to new circumstances. Why did some embrace the era's changes, while others resisted them? Ground your answer in a discussion of specific political, legal, or cultural conflicts.

3. How did shifting government policy contribute to both the boom of the 1920s and the bust of 1929? In your answer, consider the part domestic and international policy played in these developments, including taxation, tariffs, and international banking.

4. The Great Depression plunged the nation into a profound crisis with staggering personal and national costs. How did Americans attempt to lessen the impact of these circumstances? In your answer, discuss and compare the responses of individual Americans and the federal government.

LINKING TO THE PAST

Link events in this chapter to earlier events.

1. How did America's experience in World War I — both at home and abroad — help shape the 1920s? (See chapter 22.)

2. How did attitudes toward government in the Progressive Era differ from those in the 1920s? (See chapter 21.)

▶ **FOR PRACTICE QUIZZES AND OTHER STUDY TOOLS,** visit the Online Study Guide at **bedfordstmartins.com/roark.**

TIMELINE 1920–1932

1920
- Eighteenth Amendment goes into effect.
- Nineteenth Amendment ratified.
- Republican Warren G. Harding elected president.

1921
- Sheppard-Towner Act.
- Congress restricts immigration.

1922
- Fordney-McCumber tariff.
- Five-Power Naval Treaty.

1923
- Equal Rights Amendment defeated in Congress.
- Harding dies; Vice President Calvin Coolidge becomes president.

1924
- Dawes Plan.
- Coolidge elected president.
- Johnson-Reed Act.
- Indian Citizenship Act.

1925
- Scopes trial.

1927
- Charles Lindbergh flies nonstop across the Atlantic.
- Nicola Sacco and Bartolomeo Vanzetti executed.

1928
- Kellogg-Briand pact.
- Republican Herbert Hoover elected president.

1929
- St. Valentine's Day murders.
- Agricultural Marketing Act.
- Publication of *Middletown*.
- Stock market collapses.

1930
- Congress authorizes $420 million for public works projects.
- Hawley-Smoot tariff.

1931
- Scottsboro Boys arrested.
- Harlan County, Kentucky, coal strike.

1932
- River Rouge factory demonstration.
- Reconstruction Finance Corporation established.
- National Farmers' Holiday Association formed.

NEW DEAL CAMPAIGN POSTER
This 1936 presidential campaign poster boasts that President Franklin D. Roosevelt is a "Real Depression Buster," without even mentioning his name. The acronyms on the poster (such as CCC and NRA) refer to an alphabet soup of New Deal programs that exemplified Roosevelt's commitment to an activist government that could bring both help and hope to the nation. The poster highlight's Roosevelt's confident smile, perhaps the New Deal's most potent symbol. The background image depicts men lined up for free food, a common sight during the Great Depression, as joblessness and poverty rates skyrocketed.
Poster: Collection of Janice L. and David J. Frent; background: © Bettmann/Corbis.

24

The New Deal Experiment
1932–1939

IN EARLY MARCH 1936, FLORENCE OWENS PILED HER SEVEN CHILDREN, ages one to fourteen, into an old Hudson. Owens and her family had been picking beets in the Imperial Valley of southern California, near the Mexican border, but the harvest was over now. Owens headed north toward Watsonville, where she hoped to find work picking lettuce. About halfway there, near the small town of Nipomo, her car broke down. She coasted into a labor camp of more than two thousand migrant workers who were hungry, out of work, and stuck, lacking the money to look for work elsewhere. They had been attracted by growers' advertisements of work in the pea fields, only to find the crop ruined by a heavy frost. Owens set up a lean-to shelter and prepared food for her family while two of her sons worked on the car. They ate half-frozen peas from the field and small birds the children killed. Owens recalled later, "I started to cook dinner for my kids, and all the little kids around the camp came in. 'Can I have a bite? Can I have a bite?' And they was hungry, them people was."

Florence Owens was born in 1903 in Oklahoma, or what was then Indian Territory. Both of Florence's parents were Cherokee. When she was a baby, her father abandoned her mother, who soon remarried a Choctaw man, and the young family moved to a small farm near Tahlequah, Oklahoma, where Florence grew up. When she was seventeen, Florence married Cleo Owens, a farmer who, after a few years, moved his growing family to California, where he worked in sawmills. Cleo died of tuberculosis in 1931, leaving Florence a widow with six young children.

Florence began to work as a farm laborer in California's Central Valley to support herself and her children. She picked cotton, earning about $2 a day. "I'd leave home before daylight and come in after dark," she explained. "We just existed! Anyway, we survived, let's put it that way." To survive, she worked nights as a waitress, making "50-cents a day and the leftovers." Sometimes, she remembered, "I'd carry home two water buckets full" of leftovers to feed her children.

Like tens of thousands of other migrant laborers, Owens followed the crops, planting, cultivating, and harvesting as jobs opened up in the fields along the West Coast from California to Oregon and Washington. Joining Owens and other migrants — many of whom were Mexicans and Filipinos — were Okie refugees from the Dust Bowl, the large swath of Great Plains states that suffered drought, failed crops, and foreclosed mortgages during the 1930s. As one Okie told a government official in California about the Dust Bowl, "Back there we like to starve to death"; working as a migrant laborer, tough as it was, he said, "beats starvin to death."

Soon after Florence Owens fed her children at the pea pickers' camp, a car pulled up, and a woman with a camera got out and began to take photographs of Owens. The woman was Dorothea Lange, a photographer employed by a New Deal agency to document conditions among farmworkers in California. Lange snapped six photos of Owens, moving closer each time until, with the last shot, she filled the frame with Owens and three of her children. After about ten minutes, Lange climbed back in her car and headed to Berkeley. Owens and her family, their car now repaired, drove off to the lettuce fields of Watsonville.

Within days, Lange's last photograph of Owens was published in San Francisco, and news of the near-famine conditions in the pea pickers' camp reached Washington, D.C. Federal officials rushed twenty thousand pounds of food to the camp, but Owens and her children were long gone when it arrived. The photograph of Owens, however, subsequently known as *Migrant Mother*, became an icon of the desperation among Americans that President Franklin Roosevelt's New Deal sought to alleviate. *Migrant Mother* became Dorothea Lange's most famous photograph, but Florence Owens continued to work in the fields, "ragged, hungry, and broke," as a San Francisco newspaper noted. One of Owens's daughters recalled, "That photo never gave mother or us kids any relief."

Unlike Owens, her children, and other migrant workers, many Americans received government help from Roosevelt's New Deal initiatives to provide relief for the needy, to speed economic recovery, and to reform basic economic and governmental institutions. Roosevelt's New Deal elicited bitter opposition from critics on the right and the left and failed to satisfy fully its own goals of relief, recovery, and reform. But within the Democratic Party, the New Deal energized a powerful political coalition that helped millions of Americans withstand the privations of the Great Depression. In the process, the federal government became a major presence in the daily lives of most American citizens.

Florence Owens and Children

This classic photograph of migrant farm laborer Florence Owens and her children, known as *Migrant Mother*, was taken in 1936 in the labor camp of a pea field in California by New Deal photographer Dorothea Lange. The photo depicts the privations common among working people during the depression, but it also evokes a mother's leadership, dignity, and affection, qualities that helped shelter her family from poverty and joblessness. The photo suggests the depression's cruel assault on most Americans' first safety net — their families — a reality that the New Deal sought to remedy with its proposals for relief, recovery, and reform. Library of Congress.

▶ Franklin D. Roosevelt: A Patrician in Government

Unlike the millions of impoverished Americans, Franklin Roosevelt came from a wealthy and privileged background that contributed to his optimism, self-confidence, and vitality. He constantly drew on these personal qualities in his political career to bridge the economic, social, and cultural chasm that separated him from the struggles of ordinary people like Florence Owens. During the twelve years he served as president (1933–1945), many elites came to hate him as a traitor to his class, while millions more Americans, especially the hardworking poor and dispossessed, revered him because he cared about them and their problems.

The Making of a Politician

Born in 1882, **Franklin Delano Roosevelt** grew up on his father's leafy estate at Hyde Park on the Hudson River, north of New York City. Roosevelt was steeped at home and school in high-minded doctrines of public service and Christian duty to help the poor and weak. He prepared for a career in politics, hoping to follow in the political footsteps of his fifth cousin, Theodore Roosevelt. In 1905, Franklin married his distant cousin, Eleanor Roosevelt. Theodore Roosevelt — the current president of the United States — gave the bride away, an indication of Franklin's gilt-edged connections.

Unlike his cousin Teddy, Franklin Roosevelt sought his political fortune in the Democratic Party. He served in Woodrow Wilson's administration as assistant secretary of the navy, fueling a lifelong interest in maritime matters. In 1920, he catapulted to the second spot on the national Democratic ticket as the vice presidential candidate of presidential nominee James M. Cox. Although Cox lost the election (see chapter 22), Roosevelt's energetic campaigning convinced Democratic leaders that he had a bright future in national politics.

In the summer of 1921, at the age of thirty-nine, Roosevelt caught polio, which paralyzed both his legs. For the rest of his life, he wore heavy steel braces, and he could walk a few steps only by leaning on another person. Tireless physical therapy helped him regain his vitality and intense desire for

Roosevelt's Common Touch
Understanding the political importance of appearing both neighborly and physically robust, Franklin Roosevelt set up a friendly chat outside the polls during his bid for reelection as New York's governor in 1930. In this photograph with working-class voter Ruben Appel, Roosevelt's upright position was a feat of stagecraft. His legs rendered useless by polio, Roosevelt could remain standing only by propping himself up on his cane. Rare photos like this and a taboo against showing Roosevelt in his wheelchair kept the public from thinking of Roosevelt as a "cripple" and unfit for office; many did not even realize he was disabled. Franklin D. Roosevelt Library.

high political office. But he recaptured his political momentum mostly from a sitting position, although he carefully avoided being photographed in the wheelchair he used routinely.

Fascism: Adolf Hitler and National Socialism

The Great Depression paralyzed economies around the globe and seemed to demonstrate that capitalism had failed. Individual working people and even businesses could do little to restore prosperity. Only governments had the power to kick-start the economy. Many people believed that democracies such as the United States were too weak and divided to take the necessary steps.

President Franklin Roosevelt optimistically declared that the "democratic faith" of Americans in 1933 was "too sturdy" to turn to "alien ideologies like communism and fascism." But authoritarian, anti-democratic Communist and fascist parties battled to seize control of national governments across Europe. In Germany, Adolf Hitler and his fascist National Socialist Party, also known as the Nazis, came to power in 1933 and improved the economy while crushing democracy.

Hitler rose to power as the leader of a political coalition (composed of Nazis, other conservative parties, and the army) that sought to bring order to Germany in the years following World War I. Hitler stoked discontent by proclaiming his fantasy that an international conspiracy of Communists and financiers — mostly Jews — caused Germany's defeat and was responsible for its postwar woes. During the 1920s, economic distress and political turmoil increased support for Hitler's National Socialist Party among disgruntled veterans, farmers, residents of small towns, shopkeepers, artisans, and other members of the middle and lower-middle classes. The Nazis became the most popular political party by 1932, but they still commanded only one-third of the vote when Hitler became head of the German government in January 1933.

Within a few months, Hitler seized dictatorial power. The Nazis outlawed all political opposition, murdering hundreds and imprisoning more than 100,000 Communists, socialists, union members, and others in the summer of 1933, creating a one-party government. To stifle any lingering dissent, the Nazis seized control of every institution in German society, from local governments to choirs and hiking clubs. They created an elaborate system of spies who punished anyone suspected of questioning Nazi rule. Hitler boasted that "every person should know for all time that if he raises his hand to strike at the [Nazi] State, certain death will be his lot." The Nazi Gestapo (secret police) routinely carried out Hitler's threat, making lawless, life-threatening terror a reality throughout German society.

Hitler's obsessive anti-Semitism made Jews a special target of the Nazi police state. The Nazis organized boycotts of Jewish businesses, destroyed and confiscated Jews' property, purged Jews from civilian and military employment, and passed laws prohibiting marriages between Jews and non-Jews. In reality, Jews accounted for only about 1 percent of the German population, and most of them were fully acculturated members of German society. Hitler claimed, however, that Jews and other "enemies of the people" — such as Gypsies, homosexuals, the chronically ill, and the mentally or physically disabled — polluted the purity of the German race. Hitler and the Nazis relished the persecution of Jews, profited from robbing Jews of their property, and constantly warned about the grave threat Jews posed to Germany — a claim that was completely false.

Hitler's fascist dictatorship had one overriding goal: to rearm Germany and expand German territory until it encompassed all of Europe and much of the Soviet Union. Hitler grandiosely planned a campaign of conquest that would result in the Nazis' thousand-year dominion over the world. He announced in 1933 that "the re-armament of the German people . . . must always and everywhere stand in the foreground." In consultation

---

After his polio attack, Roosevelt frequented a polio therapy facility at Warm Springs, Georgia. There, he combined the health benefits of the soothing waters with political overtures to southern Democrats, which helped make him a rare political creature: a New Yorker from the Democratic Party's urban and immigrant wing with whom whites from the Democratic Party's entrenched southern wing felt comfortable.

By 1928, Roosevelt had recovered sufficiently to campaign to become governor of New York, and he squeaked out a victory. As governor of the nation's most populous state, Roosevelt showcased his leadership and his suitability for a presidential campaign of his own. His activist policies as governor became a dress rehearsal for his presidency.

As the Great Depression spread hard times throughout the nation, Governor Roosevelt believed that government should intervene to protect citizens from economic hardships rather than wait for the law of supply and demand to improve the economy. According to the with military leaders, the Nazis mobilized German industries to build tanks, ships, aircraft, and weapons as rapidly as possible, all in violation of the terms of the Versailles treaty.

Unlike the Communists in the Soviet Union, fascists in Nazi Germany worked with privately owned industrial firms, which welcomed military production that brought them increased investment, productivity, and profits. The rearmament campaign reduced unemployment from more than 11 million in 1933 to less than 1 million by 1937. Likewise, although the peace treaty limited the size of the German military to 100,000 men, the Nazis had nearly 2.5 million men in uniform by 1939. They financed this massive militarization by forcing civilians to consume less and work more and by extortion and robbery of private wealth.

The Nazis barraged Germany with propaganda designed to promote a cult of Hitler worship. The führer (leader) was portrayed as having almost superhuman powers. The famous Nazi film director Leni Riefenstahl echoed this Hitler cult when she wrote to the führer, "You exceed anything human imagination has the power to conceive, achieving deeds without parallel in the history of mankind." Hitler welcomed such flattery, which masked the underlying terror, lawlessness, and corruption of his fascist dictatorship. The Nazis reduced unemployment and brought a measure of

Germans Salute a Nazi Parade
This photograph depicts the enthusiasm of German men, women, and children who raise their hands in the Nazi salute as fascist officials parade through the streets of Nuremberg in 1938. Although Hitler's police state never won the allegiance of all Germans, most welcomed the economic prosperity and political order imposed by Hitler, and they willingly cooperated with the Nazis' reign of terror, persecution, and rearmament. United States Holocaust Memorial Museum.

prosperity to many Germans during the 1930s by outlawing democracy, suppressing dissent, imprisoning and murdering tens of thousands of people, and preparing for a war that would leave Germany a smoldering ruin twelve years after Hitler seized power.

America in a Global Context

1. How did Hitler's Nazism compare with Roosevelt's New Deal?

2. To what degree was Roosevelt correct about the "democratic faith" of Americans compared, for example, with that of Germans?

laissez-faire views of many conservatives — especially Republicans, but also numerous Democrats — the depression simply represented market forces separating strong survivors from weak losers. Unlike Roosevelt, conservatives believed that government help for the needy sapped individual initiative and impeded the self-correcting forces of the market by rewarding people for losing the economic struggle to survive. Roosevelt lacked a full-fledged counterargument to these conservative claims, but he sympathized with the plight of poor people.

"To these unfortunate citizens," he proclaimed, "aid must be extended by governments, not as a matter of charity but as a matter of social duty. . . . [No one should go] unfed, unclothed, or unsheltered."

The highlight of Roosevelt's efforts to relieve the economic woes of New Yorkers was the Temporary Emergency Relief Administration, created in 1931. It provided an unprecedented $20 million in aid for the poor, earning him the gratitude of needy New Yorkers and the attention of national politicians.

To his supporters, Roosevelt seemed to be a leader determined to attack the economic crisis without deviating from democracy — unlike the fascist parties gaining strength in Europe — or from capitalism — unlike the Communists in power in the Soviet Union. (See "Beyond America's Borders," page 788.) Roosevelt's ideas about precisely how to revive the economy were vague. A prominent journalist described Roosevelt in 1931 as "a kind of amiable boy scout . . . a pleasant man who, without any important qualifications for the office, would very much like to be president." Such sneering comments did not sway his many supporters who appreciated his energy and activism. His conviction that government should do something to help Americans climb out of the economic abyss propelled him into the front ranks of the national Democratic Party.

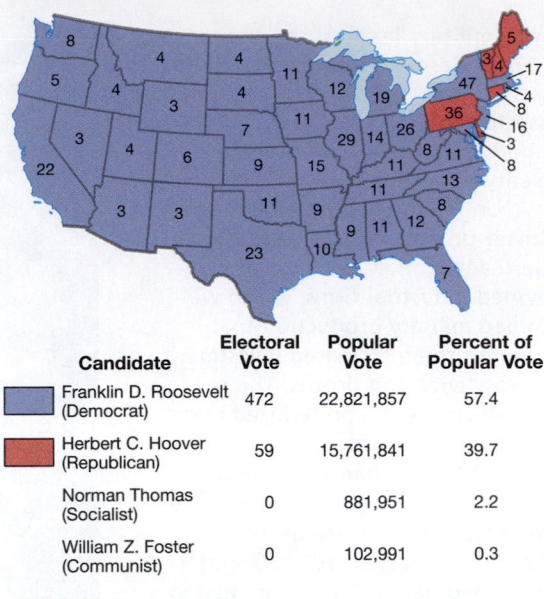

Candidate	Electoral Vote	Popular Vote	Percent of Popular Vote
Franklin D. Roosevelt (Democrat)	472	22,821,857	57.4
Herbert C. Hoover (Republican)	59	15,761,841	39.7
Norman Thomas (Socialist)	0	881,951	2.2
William Z. Foster (Communist)	0	102,991	0.3

MAP 24.1
The Election of 1932

The Election of 1932

Democrats knew that Herbert Hoover's unpopularity gave them a historic opportunity to recapture the White House in 1932. Since Abraham Lincoln's election, Republicans had occupied the White House three-fourths of the time, a trend Democrats hoped to reverse. Democrats, however, had to overcome warring factions that divided the party by region, religion, culture, and commitment to the status quo. Southern Democrats chaired powerful committees in Congress thanks to their continual reelection in a one-party South devoted to white supremacy. This southern, native-born, white, rural, Protestant, conservative wing of the Democratic Party found little common ground with the northern, immigrant, urban, disproportionately Catholic, liberal wing. Rural and native-born drys (supporters of prohibition) clashed with urban and foreign-born wets (opponents of prohibition). Eastern-establishment Democratic dignitaries shared few goals with angry farmers and factory workers. Still, this unruly coalition managed to agree on Franklin Roosevelt as its presidential candidate.

In his acceptance speech, Roosevelt vowed to help "the forgotten man at the bottom of the pyramid" with "bold, persistent experimentation." Highlighting his differences with Hoover and the Republicans, he pledged "a new deal for the American people." Few details about what Roosevelt meant by "a new deal" emerged in the presidential campaign. He declared that "the people

of America want more than anything else . . . two things: work . . . with all the moral and spiritual values that go with work . . . and a reasonable measure of security . . . for themselves and for their wives and children." Although Roosevelt never explained exactly how the federal government could provide either work or security, voters decided that whatever his new deal might be, it was better than reelecting Hoover.

Roosevelt won the 1932 presidential election in a historic landslide. He received 57 percent of the nation's votes, the first time a Democrat had won a majority of the popular vote since 1852 (Map 24.1). He amassed 472 electoral votes to Hoover's 59, carrying state after state that had voted Republican for years (Map 24.2). Roosevelt's coattails swept Democrats into control of Congress by large margins. The popular mandate for change was loud and clear.

Roosevelt's victory represented the emergence of what came to be known as the **New Deal coalition**. Attracting support from farmers, factory workers, immigrants, city folk, African Americans, women, and progressive intellectuals, Roosevelt launched a realignment of the nation's political loyalties. The New Deal coalition dominated American politics throughout Roosevelt's presidency and remained powerful long after his death in 1945.

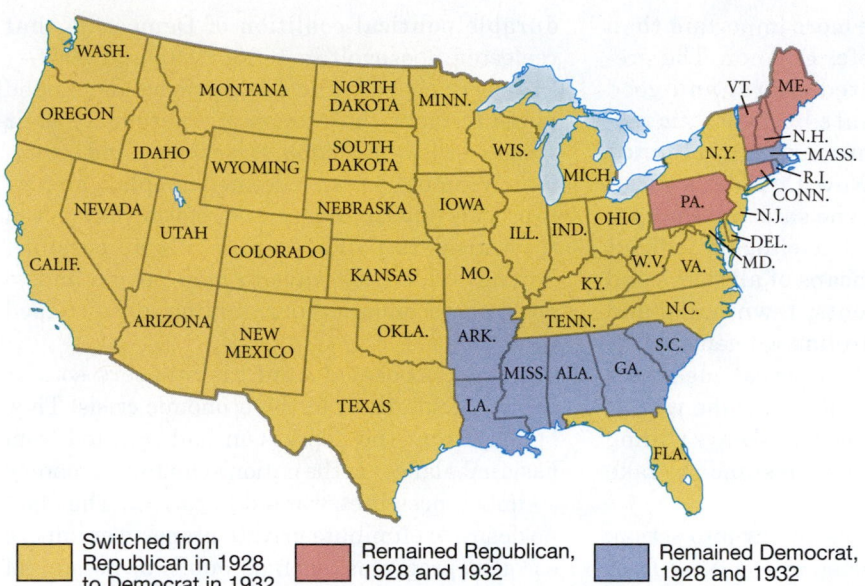

MAP ACTIVITY

Map 24.2   Electoral Shift, 1928–1932
The Democratic victory in 1932 signaled the rise of a New Deal coalition within which women and minorities, many of them new voters, made the Democrats the majority party for the first time in the twentieth century.

READING THE MAP: How many states voted Democratic in 1928? How many states voted Republican in 1932? How many states shifted from Republican to Democratic between 1928 and 1932?

CONNECTIONS: What factions within the Democratic Party opposed Franklin Roosevelt's candidacy in 1932, and why did they do so? To what do you attribute his landslide victory?

Map legend:
- Switched from Republican in 1928 to Democrat in 1932
- Remained Republican, 1928 and 1932
- Remained Democrat, 1928 and 1932

United less by ideology or support for specific policies, voters in the New Deal coalition instead expressed faith in Roosevelt's promise of a government that would, somehow, change things for the better. Nobody, including Roosevelt, knew exactly what the New Deal would change or whether the changes would revive the nation's ailing economy and improve Americans' lives. But Roosevelt and many others knew that the future of American capitalism and democracy was at stake.

REVIEW   Why did Franklin D. Roosevelt win the 1932 presidential election by such a large margin?

▶ Launching the New Deal

At noon on March 4, 1933, Americans gathered around their radios to hear the inaugural address of the newly elected president. Roosevelt began by asserting his "firm belief that the only thing we have to fear is fear itself — nameless, unreasoning, unjustified terror which paralyzes needed efforts to convert retreat into advance." He promised "direct, vigorous action," and the first months of his administration, termed "the Hundred Days," fulfilled that promise in a whirlwind of government initiatives that launched the New Deal.

Roosevelt and his advisers had three interrelated objectives: to provide relief to the destitute, especially the one out of four Americans who were unemployed; to foster the economic recovery of farms and businesses, thereby creating jobs and reducing the need for relief; and to reform the government and economy in ways that would reduce the risk of devastating consequences in future economic slumps. The New Deal never fully achieved these goals of relief, recovery, and reform. But by aiming for them, Roosevelt's experimental programs enormously expanded government's role in the nation's economy and society.

The New Dealers

To design and implement the New Deal, Roosevelt needed ideas and people. He convened a "Brains Trust" of economists and other leaders to offer suggestions and advice about the problems facing the nation. Among the most important reformers to join the Roosevelt administration were two veterans of Roosevelt's New York governorship: **Harry Hopkins** and **Frances Perkins**. Hopkins, a social worker, administered New Deal relief efforts and served as one of the president's loyal confidants. Perkins, who had extensive experience trying to improve working conditions in shops and factories, served as secretary of labor, making her the first woman cabinet member in American history.

> "One of my great pleasures was meeting Mrs. Roosevelt. . . . [S]he was so free of prejudice . . . and she was always willing to take a stand, and there were stands to take about blacks and women."
> —A North Carolina women's rights activist

No New Dealers were more important than the president and his wife, Eleanor. The gregarious president radiated charm and good cheer, giving the New Deal's bureaucratic regulations a benevolent human face. **Eleanor Roosevelt** became the New Deal's unofficial ambassador. She served, she said, as "the eyes and ears of the New Deal," traveling throughout the nation meeting Americans of all colors and creeds in church basements, town halls, and front parlors. A North Carolina women's rights activist recalled, "One of my great pleasures was meeting Mrs. Roosevelt. . . . [S]he was so free of prejudice . . . and she was always willing to take a stand, and there were stands to take about blacks and women."

As Roosevelt's programs swung into action, the millions of beneficiaries of the New Deal became grassroots New Dealers who expressed their appreciation by voting Democratic on election day. In this way, the New Deal created a durable political coalition of Democrats that reelected Roosevelt in 1936, 1940, and 1944.

As Roosevelt and his advisers developed plans to meet the economic emergency, their watchwords were *action*, *experiment*, and *improvise*. Without a sharply defined template for how to provide relief, recovery, and reform, they moved from ideas to policies as quickly as possible, hoping to identify ways to help people and to boost the economy. Four guiding ideas shaped their policies.

First, Roosevelt and his advisers sought capitalist solutions to the economic crisis. They believed that the depression had resulted from basic imbalances in the nation's capitalist economy — imbalances they wanted to correct. They had no desire to eliminate private property or impose socialist programs, such as public ownership of productive resources. Instead, they hoped to save the capitalist economy by remedying its flaws.

Second, Roosevelt's Brains Trust persuaded him that the greatest flaw of America's capitalist economy was **underconsumption**, the root cause of the current economic paralysis. Underconsumption, New Dealers argued, resulted from the gigantic productive success of capitalism. Factories and farms produced more than they could sell to consumers, causing factories to lay off workers and farmers to lose money on bumper crops. Workers without wages and farmers without profits shrank consumption and choked the economy. Somehow, the balance between consumption and production needed to be restored.

Third, New Dealers believed that the immense size and economic power of American corporations needed to be counterbalanced by government and by organization among workers and small producers. Unlike progressive trust-busters, New Dealers did not seek to splinter big businesses. Huge businesses had developed for good economic reasons and were here to stay. Roosevelt and his advisers hoped to counterbalance big economic institutions with government programs focused on protecting individuals and the public interest.

Fourth, New Dealers felt that government must somehow moderate the imbalance of wealth created by American capitalism. Wealth concentrated in a few hands reduced consumption by most

Eleanor Roosevelt Serving Unemployed Women

Eleanor Roosevelt used her First Lady status to highlight New Dealers' sympathy for the poor, the unemployed, and neglected working people. Shown here in December 1932, Roosevelt serves soup to jobless women and their children. The carefully posed scene contrasts Roosevelt's broad smile with the somewhat awed concern on the faces of the two women facing her and with the casual, workaday indifference of the kitchen workers in the background. The photo depicts both the value of personal, face-to-face relief efforts and the impossibility of such limited, private gestures to help the millions of Americans in need. © Bettmann/Corbis.

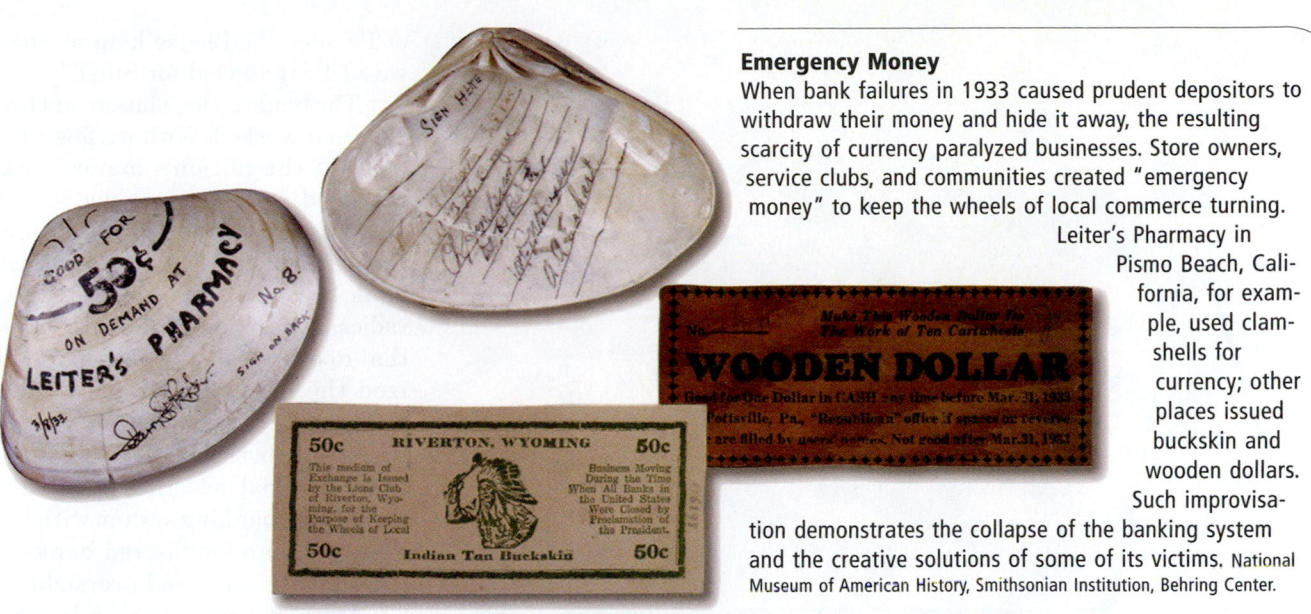

Emergency Money
When bank failures in 1933 caused prudent depositors to withdraw their money and hide it away, the resulting scarcity of currency paralyzed businesses. Store owners, service clubs, and communities created "emergency money" to keep the wheels of local commerce turning. Leiter's Pharmacy in Pismo Beach, California, for example, used clamshells for currency; other places issued buckskin and wooden dollars. Such improvisation demonstrates the collapse of the banking system and the creative solutions of some of its victims. National Museum of American History, Smithsonian Institution, Behring Center.

Americans and thereby contributed to the current economic gridlock. In the long run, government needed to find a way to permit ordinary working people to share more fully in the fruits of the economy. In the short term, New Dealers sought to lend a helping hand to poor people who suffered from the maldistribution of wealth.

Banking and Finance Reform

Roosevelt wasted no time making good on his inaugural pledge for "action now." As he took the oath of office on March 4, the nation's banking system was on the brink of collapse. Roosevelt immediately declared a four-day "bank holiday" to devise a plan to shore up banks and restore depositors' confidence. Working round the clock, New Dealers drafted the Emergency Banking Act, which gave the secretary of the treasury the power to decide which banks could be safely reopened and to release funds from the Reconstruction Finance Corporation to bolster banks' assets. To secure the confidence of depositors, Congress passed the Glass-Steagall Banking Act, setting up the **Federal Deposit Insurance Corporation (FDIC)**, which guaranteed bank

Fireside Chat
President Roosevelt explained New Deal programs to ordinary Americans in his frequent radio broadcasts. People throughout the nation, like the man shown here, listened to Roosevelt's fireside chats in the quiet of their homes. The chats reassured many Americans that Washington cared about their suffering and was trying to relieve it. One New Yorker wrote the president that he felt Roosevelt had "walked into my home, sat down, and in plain and forceful language explained to me how he was tackling the job I and my fellow citizens gave him." Franklin D. Roosevelt Library.

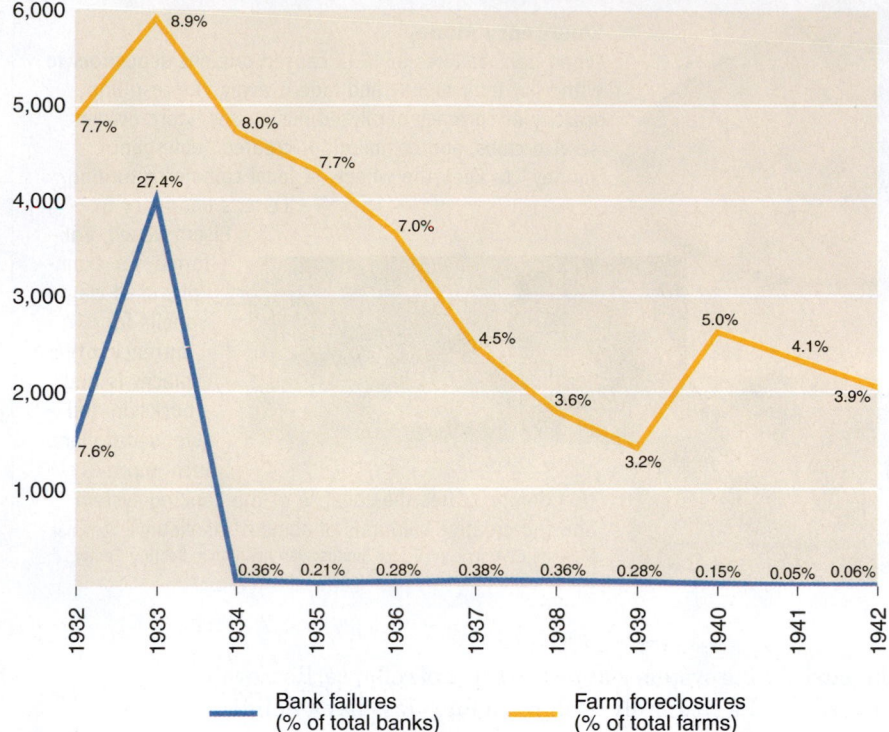

FIGURE 24.1   Bank Failures and Farm Foreclosures, 1932–1942
New Deal legislation to stabilize the economy had its most immediate and striking effect in preventing banks, along with their depositors, from going under and farmers from losing their land.

customers that the federal government would reimburse them for deposits if their banks failed. In addition, the act required the separation of commercial banks (which accept deposits and make loans to individuals and small businesses) and investment banks (which make speculative investments with their funds), in an effort to insulate the finances of Main Street America from the risky speculations of Wall Street wheeler-dealers.

On Sunday night, March 12, while the banks were still closed, Roosevelt broadcast the first of a series of **fireside chats**. Speaking in a friendly, informal manner, he explained the new banking legislation that, he said, made it "safer to keep your money in a reopened bank than under the mattress." With such plain talk, Roosevelt translated complex matters into common sense. This and subsequent fireside chats forged a direct connection — via radio waves — between Roosevelt and millions of Americans, a connection felt by a man from Paris, Texas, who wrote to Roosevelt, "You are the one & only President that ever helped a Working Class

of People. . . . Please help us some way I Pray to God for relief."

The banking legislation and fireside chat worked. Within a few days, most of the nation's major banks reopened, and they remained solvent as reassured depositors switched funds from their mattresses to their bank accounts (Figure 24.1). Some radical critics of the New Deal believed that Roosevelt should have nationalized the banks and made them a cornerstone of economic planning by the federal government. Instead, these first New Deal measures propped up the private banking system with federal funds and subjected banks to federal regulation and oversight.

In his inaugural address, Roosevelt criticized financiers for their greed and incompetence. To prevent the fraud, corruption, and insider trading that had tainted Wall Street and contributed to the crash of 1929, Roosevelt pressed Congress to regulate the stock market. Legislation in 1934 created the **Securities and Exchange Commission (SEC)** to oversee financial markets by licensing investment dealers, monitoring all stock transactions, and requiring corporate officers to make full disclosures about their companies. To head the SEC, Roosevelt named an abrasive and ambitious Wall Street financier, Joseph P. Kennedy, who had a somewhat shady reputation for stock manipulation. When critics complained about his selection, Roosevelt replied, "Set a thief to catch a thief." Under Kennedy's leadership, the SEC helped a cleaned-up and regulated Wall Street to recover slowly, although the stock market stayed well below its frothy heights during the 1920s.

Relief and Conservation Programs

Patching the nation's financial structure provided little relief for the hungry and unemployed. A poor man from Nebraska asked Eleanor Roosevelt "if the folk who was borned here in America . . . are this Forgotten Man, the President had in mind, [and] if we are this Forgotten Man then we are still Forgotten." Since its founding, the federal government had never assumed responsibility for needy people, except in moments of natural disaster or emergencies such as the Civil War. Instead, churches, private charities, county and municipal governments, and occasionally states assumed the burden of poor relief, usually with meager payments. The depression necessitated unprecedented federal relief efforts, according to Harry Hopkins and other New Dealers. As one New Yorker who still had a job wrote the government, "We work, ten hours a day for six days. In the grime and dirt of a nation [for] . . . low pay [making us] . . . slaves — slaves of the depression!"

Hopkins galvanized support for the **Federal Emergency Relief Administration (FERA)**, established in May 1933, which supported four million to five million households with $20 or $30 a month. FERA also created jobs for the unemployed on thousands of public works projects, organized by Hopkins into the Civil Works Administration (CWA), which put paychecks worth more than $800 million into the hands of previously jobless workers. Earning wages between 40 and 60 cents an hour, laborers renovated schools, dug sewers, and rebuilt roads and bridges. FERA extended the scope of relief to include health and education, funding literacy classes and providing vaccinations for millions.

The most popular work relief program was the **Civilian Conservation Corps (CCC)**, established in March 1933. It offered unemployed young men a chance to earn wages while working to conserve natural resources, a long-standing interest of Roosevelt. Women were excluded from working in the CCC until Eleanor Roosevelt demanded that a token number of young women be hired. One of the young men who enlisted in the CCC, Blackie Gold, had been out of work and had to "beg for coal, [and] buy bread that's two, three days old" to support his large family. After he joined the CCC, Gold earned $30 a month and was required to send all but $5 of it home to his family. By the end of the program in 1942, the three million CCC workers had checked soil erosion, tamed rivers, and planted more than two billion trees. CCC workers left a legacy of vast new recreation areas, along with roads that made those areas accessible to millions of Americans. Just as important, the CCC, CWA, and other work relief efforts replaced the

Civil Conservation Corps (CCC)
During the New Deal, the Civilian Conservation Corps provided work and wages for about two-and-a-half million young men to improve parks, build roads, plant trees, and engage in other conservation projects, as symbolized by the evergreen tree emblazoned on the CCC insignia patch. The CCC workers shown here carrying cross-cut saws for clearing trees from roads and trails in Yosemite National Park marched in quasi-military order. The U.S. Army administered the CCC, but offered no military training. Instead, CCC workers earned wages of about $30 a month, all but $5 of which went to their parents. Photograph: National Archives Pacific Region; patch: ©Bettmann/Corbis.

stigma of welfare with the dignity of jobs. As one woman said about her husband's work relief job, "We aren't on relief anymore. My husband is working for the Government."

The New Deal also sought to harness natural resources for hydroelectric power. Continuing a project begun under Hoover, the New Deal completed the colossal Hoover Dam across the Colorado River in Nevada, providing not only electricity but also flood control and irrigation water for Arizona and southern California. Building the dam also provided badly needed jobs and wages for thousands of unemployed workers.

The New Deal's most ambitious and controversial natural resources development project was the **Tennessee Valley Authority (TVA)**, created in May 1933 to build dams along the Tennessee River to supply impoverished rural communities with cheap electricity (Map 24.3). The TVA planned model towns for power station workers and new homes for the farmers who would benefit from electricity and flood control. The most ambitious example of New Deal enthusiasm for planning,

MAP ACTIVITY

Map 24.3 The Tennessee Valley Authority

The New Deal created the Tennessee Valley Authority to modernize a vast impoverished region with hydroelectric power dams and, at the same time, to reclaim eroded land and preserve old folkways.

READING THE MAP: How many states were affected by the TVA? How many miles of rivers (approximately) were affected?

CONNECTIONS: What kinds of benefits — economic as well as social and cultural — did TVA programs bring to the region? How might the lives of a poor farming family in Alabama or Tennessee have changed after the mid-1930s owing to these programs?

the TVA set out to demonstrate that a partnership between the federal government and local residents could overcome the barriers of state governments and private enterprises to make efficient use of abundant natural resources and break the ancient cycle of poverty. The TVA never fully realized these utopian ends, but it improved the lives of millions in the region with electric power, flood protection, soil reclamation, and jobs.

New sources of hydroelectric power helped the New Deal bring the wonders of electricity to country folk, fulfilling an old progressive dream. When Roosevelt became president, 90 percent of rural Americans lacked electricity. Private electric companies refused to build transmission lines into the sparsely settled countryside when they had a profitable market in more accessible and densely populated urban areas. Beginning in 1935, the **Rural Electrification Administration (REA)** made low-cost loans available to local cooperatives for power plants and transmission lines to serve rural communities. Within ten years, the REA delivered electricity to nine out of ten farms, giving rural Americans access for the first time to modern conveniences that urban people had enjoyed for decades.

Agricultural Initiatives

Farmers had been mired in a depression since the end of World War I. New Dealers diagnosed the farmers' plight as a classic case of overproduction and underconsumption. Following age-old practices, farmers tried to compensate for low crop prices by growing more crops, hoping to boost their earnings by selling larger quantities. Instead, producing more crops pushed prices lower still. Farm income sank from a disastrously low $6 billion in 1929 to a catastrophically low $2 billion in 1932. Income among farm families plunged to $167 a year, barely one-tenth of the national average.

New Dealers sought to cut agricultural production, thereby raising crop prices and farmers' income. With more money in their pockets, farm families — who made up one-third of all Americans — would then buy more goods and lift consumption in the entire economy. To reduce production, the **Agricultural Adjustment Act (AAA)** authorized the "domestic allotment plan," which paid farmers *not* to grow crops. Individual farmers who agreed not to plant crops on a portion of their fields (their "allotment") would receive a government payment compensating them for the crops they did not plant. Since crops were already in the ground by the time the act was passed in May 1933, drastic measures were necessary to reduce production immediately. While millions of Americans like Florence Owens and her children went to bed hungry, farmers slaughtered countless cattle, hogs, sheep, and other livestock and destroyed untold acres of crops to qualify for their allotment payments.

With the formation of the Commodity Credit Corporation, the federal government allowed farmers to hold their harvested crops off the market and wait for a higher price. In the meantime, the government stored the crop and gave farmers a "commodity loan" based on a favorable price. In effect, commodity loans addressed the problem of underconsumption by making the federal government a major consumer of agricultural goods and reducing farmers' vulnerability to low prices. New Dealers also sponsored the Farm Credit Act (FCA) to provide long-term credit on mortgaged farm property, allowing debt-ridden farmers to avoid foreclosures that were driving thousands off their land (see Figure 24.1).

Crop allotments, commodity loans, and mortgage credit made farmers major beneficiaries of the New Deal. Crop prices rose impressively, farm income jumped 50 percent by 1936, and FCA loans financed 40 percent of farm mortgage debt by the end of the decade. These gains were distributed fairly equally among farmers in the corn, hog, and wheat region of the Midwest. In the South's cotton belt, however, landlords controlled the distribution of New Deal agricultural benefits and shamelessly rewarded themselves while denying benefits to many sharecroppers and tenant farmers — blacks and whites — by taking the land they worked out of production and assigning it to the allotment program. When that happened, tenants and sharecroppers got booted off the land they worked, and their privation worsened. As the president of the Oklahoma Tenant Farmers' Union explained, large farmers who got "Triple-A" payments often used the money to buy tractors and then "forced their tenants and [share]croppers off the land," causing these "Americans to be starved and dispossessed of their homes in our land of plenty."

Industrial Recovery

Unlike farmers, industrialists cut production with the onset of the depression. Between 1929 and 1933, industrial production fell more than 40 percent in an effort to balance low demand with

Rural Electrification and Running Water
New Deal programs brought housing and electricity to rural families like those in this east-central Tennessee village. The Tennessee Valley Authority provided the houses shown here as well as the electric power they received. The New Deal's Rural Electrification Administration built the necessary infrastructure to bring running water to villages like these, where the pump operated by the children in the foreground was the only source of water. The REA used posters like this one to increase awareness of the benefits of running water. What difference do you think electricity and running water made in the daily lives of the people in this village? Pump: FDR Library; poster: Digital Image ©The Museum of Modern Art/Licensed by SCALA/Art Resource, NY.

low supply and thereby maintain prices. But falling industrial production meant that millions of working people lost their jobs. Unlike farmers, most working people lived in towns and cities and needed jobs to eat. Mass unemployment also reduced consumer demand for industrial products, contributing to a downward spiral in both production and jobs, with no end in sight. Industries responded by reducing wages for employees who still had jobs, further reducing demand — a trend made worse by competition among industrial producers. New Dealers struggled to find a way to break this cycle of unemployment and underconsumption — a way consistent with corporate profits and capitalism.

The New Deal's National Industrial Recovery Act opted for a government-sponsored form of industrial self-government through the **National Recovery Administration (NRA)**, established in June 1933. The NRA encouraged industrialists in every part of the economy to agree on rules,

Textile Workers Strike for Better Wages and Working Conditions

" The 'Stretch-out System' is the cause of the whole trouble," a textile worker declared in 1930, echoing the sentiments of thousands of other mill workers. The "stretch-out" was the term coined by mill workers for the cost-cutting efficiencies implemented by mill owners that led to layoffs and poor working conditions for textile workers during the 1920s and 1930s. Textile manufacturers drastically increased the workload of their employees to cut labor costs and raise productivity. A mill worker who tended thirty looms in 1920 was responsible for ninety or more looms by 1929 — if she or he still had a job. Layoffs of mill hands in the midst of the Great Depression contributed to further deterioration in wages and working conditions. So many people were desperate for work, no matter what the wage, that manufacturers were able to cut wages in half. The result, as one textile worker wrote Roosevelt, was that "the ones who are Still at Work are Being Treated as Bad or Worse tha[n] the Slaves were in Slavery times."

Like so many other textile workers who faced the tough choice of working with the stretch-out or not working, Icy Norman was relieved to find work in 1929 at Burlington Mills in Piedmont Heights, North Carolina, where the supervisor happened to be a friend of her deceased father's. He hired Norman to wind thread onto bobbins for weaving. At first, she earned only 15 cents a day, but as she became more skilled, her wages rose to $10 a week, a little over 15 cents an hour. "After I got used to being in there," Norman recalled, "I really loved my work. . . . I got pleasure out of it and it made me happy to do my job." Still, as one mill worker wrote to Roosevelt, "every textile worker in the South would walk out of the mill today if they were not afraid of starvation."

In September 1934, hundreds of thousands of textile workers throughout the nation overcame their fears and walked out of the mills in the largest strike in American history. Strikers shut down mills from Maine to Alabama. More than half of all textile workers nationwide and about two-thirds of mill hands in the southern heartland of the textile industry walked out, including Icy Norman. Loosely organized by the Textile Workers' Union, the strikers demanded better working conditions and wages through enforcement of the textile code established by the New Deal's National Recovery Administration (NRA).

Like other NRA codes, the textile code was written and administered by the leading textile manufacturers. It provided for a maximum forty-hour workweek, a minimum weekly wage of $12 for southern mill hands, and the right of workers to organize unions. Textile workers celebrated the passage of the NRA in June 1933. "It seemed too good to be true," one textile worker observed. Mill hands told a New Dealer, "We trust in the Supreme Being and Franklin Roosevelt. . . . [We] know that the President will see that [we] have work and proper wages; and that the stretchout will be abandoned."

But their faith was misplaced, and the code was widely ignored. When workers complained that mill owners continued the stretch-out, cutting wages and firing any mill hands they suspected of union sympathies, their grievances were heard by the textile manufacturers who headed the NRA code authority. In the year before the strike, the textile code authority received nearly 4,000 complaints, investigated 96, and resolved just 1 in favor of a worker. Boiling with frustration over the failure of the textile code, more than 400,000 mill hands went on strike. Seeking to realize what they viewed as the unfulfilled promises of the New Deal's NRA, they aimed to organize a union to bargain with mill owners to improve wages and working conditions.

The strike lasted three weeks and led to numerous violent confrontations with police and National Guardsmen. It ended because of the

known as codes, to define fair working conditions, to set prices, and to minimize competition. The idea behind codes was to stabilize existing industries and maintain their workforces while avoiding what both industrialists and New Dealers termed "destructive competition," which forced employers to cut wages and jobs. Industry after industry wrote elaborate codes addressing detailed features of production, pricing, and competition. In exchange for the relaxation of federal antitrust regulations that prohibited such business agreements, the participating businesses promised to recognize the right of working people to organize and engage in collective bargaining. To encourage consumers to patronize businesses participating in NRA codes, the New Deal mounted a

Striking Mill Workers Jeer Strikebreakers
Textile workers on strike against the Cannon Textile Mills in North Carolina in September 1934 shouted taunts and curses at "scabs," the derogatory term for employees who refused to honor the strikers' picket line. Notice the contrast between the clothing of the strikers and that of the strikebreakers. What might explain this contrast? Although thousands of women like Icy Norman joined the strike, there are no women among the strikers shown here. What might account for the absence of women mill hands in this picket line? © Bettmann/Corbis.

combination of the mill owners' intransigence, the Textile Workers' Union's lack of resources, the mill workers' increasingly desperate financial situation, and Roosevelt's focus on the need for industrial peace to achieve economic recovery.

The mill hands achieved virtually nothing as a result of the strike. Mill owners continued to flout the textile codes, the stretch-out continued without interruption, and working conditions did not improve. Angry mill owners fired and blacklisted strike leaders, succeeding in their efforts to crush workers' organizations.

Icy Norman went back to work after the strike ended, and since she was not a union activist, she managed to keep her job until she retired in 1976, after forty-seven years at Burlington Mills. For her efforts, the company rewarded her with a free visit to a local hairdresser, a tour of the Burlington executive suite, and a farewell handshake.

Questions for Consideration

1. How did the stretch-out contribute to unemployment for textile workers?

2. Why was textile workers' faith in Roosevelt and NRA codes misplaced?

3. Why do you think unions failed to organize textile workers when they succeeded in organizing autoworkers, for example?

public relations campaign that displayed the NRA's Blue Eagle in shop windows and on billboards throughout the nation.

New Dealers hoped that NRA codes would yield businesses with a social conscience, ensuring fair treatment of workers and consumers and promotion of the general economic welfare. Instead, NRA codes tended to strengthen conventional business practices. Large corporations wrote codes that served primarily their own interests rather than the needs of workers or the welfare of the national economy. (See "Seeking the American Promise," page 798.) The failure of codes to cover domestic workers or agricultural laborers like Florence Owens led one woman to complain to Roosevelt that the NRA "never mentioned the

Major Legislation of the New Deal's First Hundred Days

	Name of Act	Basic Provisions
March 9, 1933	Emergency Banking Act	Provides for reopening stable banks and authorizing the Reconstruction Finance Corporation to supply funds.
March 31, 1933	Civilian Conservation Corps Act	Provides jobs for unemployed young men.
May 12, 1933	Agricultural Adjustment Act	Provides funds to pay farmers for not growing crops.
May 12, 1933	Federal Emergency Relief Act	Provides relief funds for the destitute.
May 18, 1933	Tennessee Valley Authority Act	Creates the TVA to bring electric power and conservation to the area.
June 16, 1933	National Industrial Recovery Act	Specifies cooperation among business, government, and labor in setting fair prices and working conditions.
June 16, 1933	Glass-Steagall Banking Act	Creates the Federal Deposit Insurance Corporation (FDIC) to insure bank deposits.

robbery of the Housewives" by the privations caused by the depression.

Many business leaders criticized NRA codes as heavy-handed government regulation of private enterprise. Some even claimed that the NRA was a homegrown version of Benito Mussolini's fascism, then taking shape in Italy. In reality, however, compliance with NRA codes was voluntary, and government enforcement efforts were weak to nonexistent. The NRA did little to reduce unemployment, raise consumption, or relieve the depression. In effect, it represented a peace offering to business leaders by Roosevelt and his advisers, conveying the message that the New Deal did not intend to wage war against profits or private enterprise. The peace offering failed, however. Most corporate leaders became active and often bitter opponents of Roosevelt and the New Deal.

REVIEW   How did the New Dealers try to steer the nation toward recovery from the Great Depression?

▶ Challenges to the New Deal

The first New Deal initiatives engendered fierce criticism and political opposition. From the right, Republicans and business people charged that New Deal programs were too radical, undermining private property, economic stability, and democracy. Critics on the left faulted the New Deal for its failure to allay the human suffering caused by the depression and for its timidity in attacking corporate power and greed.

Resistance to Business Reform

New Deal programs rescued capitalism, but business leaders lambasted Roosevelt, even though their economic prospects improved more than those of most other Americans during the depression. Republicans and business leaders denounced New Deal efforts to regulate or reform what they considered their private enterprises. Although concentrated corporate power avoided reform, business leaders still conducted stridently anti–New Deal campaigns that expressed their resentment and fear of regulations, taxes, and unions. One opponent called the president "Stalin Delano Roosevelt" and insisted that the New Deal was really a "Raw Deal."

By 1935, two major business organizations, the National Association of Manufacturers and the Chamber of Commerce, had become openly anti–New Deal. Their critiques were amplified by the American Liberty League, founded in 1934, which blamed the New Deal for betraying basic constitutional guarantees of freedom and individualism. To them, the AAA was a "trend toward fascist control of agriculture," relief programs marked "the end of democracy," and the NRA was a plunge into the "quicksand of visionary experimentation." Although the Liberty League's membership never exceeded 125,000, its well-financed publicity campaign widened the rift between Roosevelt and business people.

Economists who favored rational planning in the public interest and labor leaders who sought to influence wages and working conditions by organizing unions attacked the New Deal from the left. In their view, the NRA stifled enterprise by permitting monopolistic practices. They pointed out that industrial trade associations twisted NRA codes to suit their aims, thwarted competition, and engaged in price gouging. Labor leaders especially resented the NRA's willingness to allow businesses to form company-controlled unions while blocking workers from organizing genuine grassroots unions to bargain for themselves.

The Supreme Court stepped into this cross fire of criticisms in May 1935 and declared that the NRA unconstitutionally conferred powers reserved to Congress on an administrative agency staffed by government appointees. The NRA codes soon lost the little authority they had. The failure of the NRA demonstrated the depth of many Americans' resistance to economic planning and the stubborn refusal of business leaders to yield to government regulations or reforms.

Casualties in the Countryside

The AAA weathered critical battering by champions of the old order better than the NRA. Allotment checks for keeping land fallow and crop prices high created loyalty among farmers with enough acreage to participate. As a white farmer in North Carolina declared, "I stand for the New Deal and Roosevelt . . . , the AAA . . . and crop control." Agricultural processors and distributors, however, criticized the AAA. They objected that the program reduced the volume of crop production — the only source of their profits — while they paid a tax on processed crops that funded the very program that disadvantaged them. In 1936, the Supreme Court agreed with their contention that they were victims of an illegal attempt to tax one group (processors and distributors) to enrich another (farmers).

Evicted Sharecroppers
An unintended consequence of the New Deal's Agricultural Adjustment Administration's plan to maintain farm prices by reducing acreage in production was the eviction of tenant farmers when the land they worked was left idle. These African American sharecroppers were part of a squatters camp that stretched for 150 miles along the western floodplain of the Mississippi River in southeastern Missouri in January 1939. They protested AAA policies that caused cotton farmers to evict them from their homes. Homeless and jobless, camping out with all their earthly belongings, these families were among the many rural laborers whose lives were made worse by New Deal agricultural policies. © Bettmann/Corbis.

Down but not out, the AAA rebounded from the Supreme Court ruling by eliminating the offending tax and funding allotment payments from general government revenues.

Protests stirred, however, among those who did not qualify for allotments. The Southern Farm Tenants Union argued passionately that the AAA enriched large farmers while it impoverished small farmers who rented rather than owned their land. One black sharecropper explained why only $75 a year from New Deal agricultural subsidies trickled down to her: "De landlord is landlord, de politicians is landlord, de judge is landlord, de shurf [sheriff] is landlord, ever'body is landlord, en we [sharecroppers] ain' got nothin'!" Such testimony showed that the AAA, like the NRA, tended to help most those who least needed help. Roosevelt's political dependence on southern Democrats caused him to avoid confronting such economic and racial inequities in the South's entrenched order.

Displaced tenants often joined the army of migrant workers like Florence Owens who straggled across rural America during the 1930s, some to flee Great Plains dust storms. Many migrants came from Mexico to work Texas cotton, Michigan beans, Idaho sugar beets, and California crops of all kinds. But since the number of people willing to take agricultural jobs usually exceeded the number of jobs available, wages fell and native-born white migrants fought to reserve even these low-wage jobs for themselves. Hundreds of thousands of "Okies" streamed out of the **Dust Bowl** of Oklahoma, Kansas, Texas, and Colorado, where chronic drought and harmful agricultural practices blasted crops and hopes. Parched, poor, and windblown, Okies — like the Joad family immortalized in John Steinbeck's novel *The Grapes of Wrath* (1939) — migrated to the lush fields and orchards of California, congregating in labor camps and hoping to find work and a future. But migrant laborers seldom found steady or secure work. As one Okie said, "When they need us they call us migrants, and when we've picked their crop, we're bums and we got to get out."

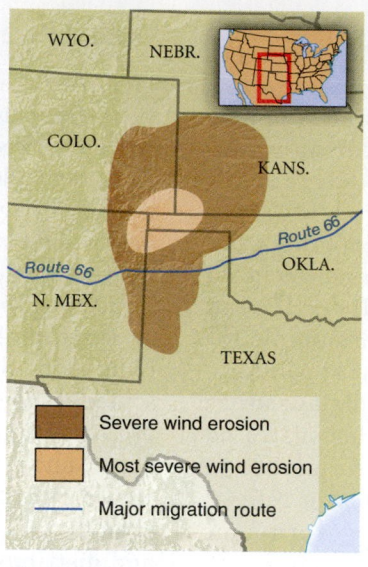

Severe wind erosion

Most severe wind erosion

Major migration route

The Dust Bowl

Politics on the Fringes

Politically, the New Deal's staunchest opponents were in the Republican Party — organized, well heeled, mainstream, and determined to challenge Roosevelt at every turn. But the New Deal also faced challenges from the political fringes, fueled by the hardship of the depression and the hope for a cure-all.

Socialists and Communists accused the New Deal of being the handmaiden of business elites and of rescuing capitalism from its self-inflicted crisis. Socialist author **Upton Sinclair** ran for governor of California in 1934 on a plan he called "End Poverty in California." Sinclair demanded that the state take ownership of idle factories and unused land and give them to cooperatives of working people, a first step toward what he envisioned as a "Cooperative Commonwealth" that would put the needs of people above profits. Sinclair lost the election, ending the most serious socialist electoral challenge to the New Deal.

Some intellectuals and artists sought to advance the cause of more radical change by joining left-wing organizations, including the American Communist Party. At its high point in the 1930s, the party had about thirty thousand members, the large majority of them immigrants, especially Scandinavians in the upper Midwest and eastern European Jews in major eastern and midwestern cities. Individual Communists worked to organize labor unions, protect the civil rights of black people, and help the destitute, but the party preached the overthrow of "bourgeois democracy" and the destruction of capitalism in favor of Soviet-style communism. Party spokesmen termed the NRA a "fascist slave program" and likened Roosevelt and the New Deal to Hitler and the Nazis. Such talk attracted few followers among the nation's millions of poor and unemployed. They wanted jobs and economic security within American capitalism and democracy, not violent revolution to establish a dictatorship of the Communist Party.

Okie Family
This tenant farmer worked land near Eagleton, Oklahoma, but became sick with pneumonia and lost his farm. The county he had lived in for fifteen years refused to give him Works Progress Administration benefits because he briefly left the county after recovering from his illness. Accompanied by his five children, he carted all his possessions in a toy wagon along a highway while looking for work. Such poor, jobless migrants were common along America's roads during the 1930s. Library of Congress.

More powerful radical challenges to the New Deal sprouted from homegrown roots. Many Americans felt overlooked by New Deal programs that concentrated on finance, agriculture, and industry but did little to produce jobs or aid the poor. The merciless reality of the depression also continued to erode the security of people who still had jobs but worried constantly that they, too, might be pushed into the legions of the unemployed and penniless.

A Catholic priest in Detroit named **Charles Coughlin** spoke to and for many worried Americans in his weekly radio broadcasts, which reached a nationwide audience of 40 million. Father Coughlin expressed outrage at the suffering and inequities that he blamed on Com-munists, bankers, and "predatory capitalists" who, he claimed, appealing to widespread anti-Semitic sentiments, were mostly Jews. In 1932, Coughlin applauded Roosevelt's election and declared, "The New Deal is Christ's deal." But Coughlin became frustrated by Roosevelt's refusal to grant him influence, turned against the New Deal, and in 1935 founded the National Union for Social Justice, or Union Party, to challenge Roosevelt in the 1936 presidential election.

Dr. **Francis Townsend**, of Long Beach, California, also criticized the timidity of the New Deal. Angry that many of his retired patients lived in misery, Townsend proposed in 1934 the creation of the Old Age Revolving Pension, which would pay every American over age sixty a pension of $200 a month. To receive the pension, senior citizens had to agree to spend the entire amount within thirty days, thereby stimulating the economy.

Townsend organized pension clubs with more than two million paying members and petitioned the federal government to enact his scheme. When the major political parties rebuffed his impractical plan, Townsend merged his forces with Coughlin's Union Party in time for the 1936 election.

A more formidable challenge to the New Deal came from the powerful southern wing of the Democratic Party. **Huey Long**, son of a backcountry

> ## "Every man a king, but no one wears a crown."
> —Campaign slogan of Louisiana governor **HUEY LONG**

Louisiana farmer, was elected governor of the state in 1928 with his slogan "Every man a king, but no one wears a crown." Unlike nearly all other southern white politicians who harped on white supremacy, Long championed the poor over the rich, country people over city folk, and the humble over elites. As governor, "the Kingfish" — as he liked to call himself — delivered on his promises to provide jobs and build roads, schools, and hospitals, but he also behaved ruthlessly to achieve his goals. Journalists routinely referred to him as the "dictator of Louisiana." Swaggering and bullying to get his way, Long delighted his supporters, who elected him to the U.S. Senate in 1932. Senator Long introduced a sweeping "soak the rich" tax bill that would outlaw personal incomes of more than $1 million and inheritances of more than $5 million. When the Senate rejected his proposal, Long decided to run for president, mobilizing more than five million Americans behind his "Share Our Wealth" plan. Like Townsend's scheme, Long's program promised far more than it could deliver. The Share Our Wealth campaign died when Long was assassinated in 1935, but his constituency and the wide appeal of a more equitable distribution of wealth persisted.

The challenges to the New Deal from both Republicans and more radical groups stirred Democrats to solidify their winning coalition. In the midterm congressional elections of 1934 — normally a time when a president loses support — voters gave New Dealers a landslide victory. Democrats increased their majority in the House of Representatives and gained a two-thirds majority in the Senate.

REVIEW   Why did groups at both ends of the political spectrum criticize the New Deal?

Huey Long
Huey Long's ability to adapt his captivating stump-speech style to the radio made him the one rival politician who gave Roosevelt serious concern in the mid-1930s. Long is shown here in 1932 campaigning in Arkansas in support of Hattie Carraway's bid for election to the U.S. Senate. Stigmatized as both a woman and a populist reformer, Carraway seemed a sure loser until Long crossed the border from Louisiana on her behalf. In two weeks of speaking and pressing the flesh, Long brushed aside criticism that he was an interloper and boosted Carraway to victory as part of his crusade to share the wealth. Corbis.

► Toward a Welfare State

The popular mandate for the New Deal revealed by the congressional elections persuaded Roosevelt to press ahead with bold new efforts to achieve relief, recovery, and reform. Despite the initiatives of the Hundred Days, the depression still strangled the economy. Rumbles of discontent from Father Coughlin, Huey Long, and their supporters showed that New Deal programs had fallen far short of their goals. In 1935, Roosevelt capitalized on his congressional majorities to enact major new programs that signaled the emergence of an American welfare state.

Taken together, these New Deal efforts stretched a safety net under the lives of ordinary Americans. Although many citizens remained unprotected, New Deal programs helped millions with jobs, relief, and government support. Knitting together the safety net was the idea that when individual Americans suffered because of forces beyond their control, the federal government bore responsibility to support and protect them. The safety net of welfare programs tied the political loyalty of working people to the New Deal and the Democratic Party. As a North Carolina mill worker said, "Mr. Roosevelt is the only man we ever had in the White House who would understand that my boss is a sonofabitch."

Relief for the Unemployed

First and foremost, Americans still needed jobs. Since the private economy left eight million people jobless by 1935, Roosevelt and his advisers launched a massive work relief program. Roosevelt believed that direct government handouts crippled recipients with "spiritual and moral disintegration . . . destructive to the human spirit." Jobs, by contrast, bolstered individuals' "self-respect, . . . self-confidence, . . . courage, and determination." With a congressional appropriation of nearly $5 billion — more than all government revenues in 1934 — the New Deal created the **Works Progress Administration (WPA)** to

VISUAL ACTIVITY

City Activities Mural

During the 1930s, artists — many of them employed by New Deal agencies — painted thousands of murals depicting the variety and vigor of American life. These murals often appeared in public buildings. The mural shown here, by Missouri-born artist Thomas Hart Benton, illustrates urban life, emphasizing the intoxicating and seductive pleasures of the flesh and the spirit to be found in American cities. © AXA Financial, Inc. Thomas Hart Benton, City Activities with Subway, from America Today, 1930. Distemper and egg tempera on gessoed linen with oil glaze 92 x 134$^{1}/_{2}$". Collection of AXA Financial, Inc., through its subsidiary, The Equitable Life Assurance Society of the U.S.

READING THE IMAGE: What features of urban experience does Benton emphasize in this mural? What ideas and attitudes, if any, link the people shown here?

CONNECTIONS: To what extent does the mural highlight activities distinct to U.S. cities, compared with urban life in Europe, Africa, or Asia?

give unemployed Americans government-funded jobs on public works projects. The WPA put millions of jobless citizens to work on roads, bridges, parks, public buildings, and more. In addition, Congress passed — over Roosevelt's veto — the bonus long sought by the Bonus Marchers (see chapter 23), giving veterans an average of $580 and further stimulating the economy.

By 1936, WPA funds provided jobs for 7 percent of the nation's labor force. In effect, the WPA made the federal government the employer of last resort, creating useful jobs when the capitalist economy failed to do so. In hiring, WPA officials tended to discriminate in favor of white men and against women and racial minorities. But by the time the WPA ended in 1943 — because mobilization for World War II created full employment — it had made major contributions to both relief and recovery. Overall, WPA jobs put thirteen million men and women to work and gave them paychecks worth $10 billion.

About three out of four WPA jobs involved construction and renovation of the nation's physical infrastructure. WPA workers built 572,000 miles of roads, 78,000 bridges, 67,000 miles of city streets, 40,000 public buildings, 8,000 parks, 350 airports, and much else. In addition, the WPA gave jobs to thousands of artists, musicians, actors, journalists, poets, and novelists. The WPA also organized sewing rooms for jobless women, giving them work and wages and allowing them to produce more than 100 million pieces of clothing that were donated to the needy. The WPA reached the most isolated corners of the nation, funding librarians and nurses on horseback to deliver books and health care to remote cabins in Appalachia. Throughout the nation, WPA projects displayed tangible evidence of the New Deal's commitment to public welfare.

Empowering Labor

During the Great Depression, factory workers who managed to keep their jobs worried constantly about being laid off while their wages and working hours were cut. When workers tried to organize labor unions to protect themselves, municipal and state governments usually sided with employers. Since the Gilded Age, state and federal governments had been far more effective at busting unions than at busting trusts. The New Deal dramatically reversed the federal government's stance toward unions. With legislation and political support, the New Deal encouraged an unprecedented wave of union organizing among the nation's working people. When the head of the United Mine Workers, John L. Lewis, told coal miners that "the President wants you to join a union," he exaggerated only a little. New Dealers believed that unions would counterbalance the organized might of big corporations by defending working people, maintaining wages, and replacing the bloody violence that often accompanied strikes with economic peace and commercial stability.

Grand Coulee Dam
The New Deal's Works Progress Administration helped pay for these and other workers to construct the giant Grand Coulee Dam on the Columbia River in eastern Washington state. Like other WPA projects, the Grand Coulee Dam gave employment to thousands of Americans and harnessed natural resources for what officials considered the public good. Once completed in 1942, the dam provided electricity for major war industries in Oregon and Washington, including uranium processing for the wartime Manhattan Project that resulted in the atomic bomb. Library of Congress.

Violent battles on the nation's streets and docks showed the determination of militant labor leaders to organize unions that would protect jobs as well as wages. In 1934, striking workers in Toledo, Minneapolis, San Francisco, and elsewhere were beaten and shot by police and the National Guard. In Congress, labor leaders lobbied for the National Labor Relations Act, a bill sponsored by Senator Robert Wagner of New York that authorized the federal government to intervene in labor disputes and supervise the organization of labor unions. Justly considered a "Magna Carta for labor," the **Wagner Act**, as it came to be called, guaranteed industrial workers the right to organize unions, putting the might of federal law behind the appeals of labor leaders. The Wagner Act created the National Labor Relations Board to sponsor and oversee elections for union representation. If the majority of workers at a company voted for a union, the union became the sole bargaining agent for the entire workplace, and the employer was required to negotiate with the elected union leaders. Roosevelt signed the Wagner Act in July 1935, for the first time providing federal support for labor organization — the most important New Deal reform of the industrial order.

The achievements that flowed from the Wagner Act and renewed labor militancy were impressive. When Roosevelt became president

Women's Emergency Brigade Supports Sit-Down Strikers

During the depression, General Motors cut employment and wages in half, leading to a wave of strikes. In February 1937, the wives of strikers occupying a plant in Flint, Michigan, organized the Women's Emergency Brigade, shown here. Not shown are the thousands of armed police and National Guardsmen surrounding the plant. Strikers and their supporters smashed the windows of the plant to vent tear gas deployed by security agents. The marching women carried clubs to deflect the blows of the General Motors cops. The American flag asserted the patriotism of the strikers and their supporters, whom General Motors and other strike opponents labeled "outside agitators, radicals, and Communists." © Bettmann/Corbis.

in 1933, union membership — composed almost entirely of skilled workers in trade unions affiliated with the American Federation of Labor (AFL) — stood at three million, down by half since the end of World War I. With the support of the Wagner Act, union membership expanded almost fivefold, to fourteen million, by the time of Roosevelt's death in 1945. By then, 30 percent of the workforce was unionized, the highest union representation in American history.

Most of the new union members were factory workers and unskilled laborers, many of them immigrants, women, and African Americans. For decades, established AFL unions had no desire to organize factory and unskilled workers, who struggled along without unions. In 1935, under the aggressive leadership of the mine workers' John L. Lewis and the head of the Amalgamated Clothing Workers, Sidney Hillman, a coalition of unskilled workers formed the **Committee for Industrial Organization** (CIO; later the Congress of Industrial Organizations). The CIO, helped by the Wagner Act, mobilized organizing drives in major industries. The exceptional courage and organizing skill of labor militants earned the CIO the leadership role in the campaign to organize the bitterly anti-union automobile and steel industries.

The bloody struggle by the CIO-affiliated United Auto Workers (UAW) to organize workers at General Motors climaxed in January 1937. Striking workers occupied the main assembly plant in Flint, Michigan, in a **sit-down strike** that slashed the plant's production of 15,000 cars a week to a mere 150. Stymied, General Motors eventually surrendered and agreed to make the UAW the sole bargaining agent for all the company's workers and to refrain from interfering with union activity. Having subdued the auto industry's leading producer, the UAW expanded its campaign until, after much violence, the entire industry was unionized when the Ford Motor Company capitulated in 1941.

The CIO hoped to ride organizing success in auto plants to victory in the steel mills. But after unionizing the industry giant U.S. Steel, the CIO ran up against ruthless opposition from smaller steel firms. Following a police attack that killed ten strikers at Republic Steel outside Chicago in May 1937, the battered steelworkers halted their organizing campaign. In steel and other major industries, such as the stridently anti-union southern textile mills, organizing efforts stalled until after 1941, when military mobilization created labor shortages that gave workers greater bargaining power.

Social Security and Tax Reform

The single most important feature of the New Deal's emerging welfare state was **Social Security**. An ambitious, far-reaching, and permanent reform, Social Security was designed to provide a modest income to relieve the poverty of elderly people. Only about 15 percent of older Americans had private pension plans, and during the depression corporations and banks often failed to pay the meager pensions they had promised. Corporations routinely fired or demoted employees to avoid or reduce pension payments. Prompted by the popular but impractical panaceas of Dr. Townsend, Father Coughlin, and Huey Long, Roosevelt became the first president to advocate protection for the elderly. He told Congress that "it is our plain duty to provide for that security upon which welfare depends . . . and undertake the great task of furthering the security of the citizen and his family through social insurance."

The political struggle for Social Security highlighted class differences among Americans. Support for the measure came from a coalition of advocacy groups for the elderly and the poor, traditional progressives, leftists, social workers, and labor unions. Arrayed against them were economic conservatives, including the American Liberty League, the National Association of Manufacturers, the Chamber of Commerce, and the American Medical Association. Enact the Social Security system, these conservatives and their representatives in the Republican Party warned, and the government will ruin private property, destroy initiative, and reduce proud individuals to spineless loafers.

The large New Deal majority in Congress passed the Social Security Act in August 1935. The act provided that contributions from workers and their employers would fund pensions for the elderly, giving contributing workers a personal stake in the system and making it politically invulnerable. When eligible workers reached retirement age, they were not subject to a means test to prove that they were needy. Instead, they had earned benefits based on their contributions

> "It is our plain duty to provide for that security upon which welfare depends . . . and undertake the great task of furthering the security of the citizen and his family through social insurance."
> —President FRANKLIN ROOSEVELT to Congress

Social Security Card
The Social Security Act required each working American who participated in the system to register with the government and obtain a unique number — the "SSN" familiar to every citizen today — inscribed on an identity card, making benefits portable from one job and one state to another. For the first time in the nation's history, millions of ordinary citizens were numbered, registered, and identified by a federal government bureau-cracy. Picture Research Con-sultants & Archives.

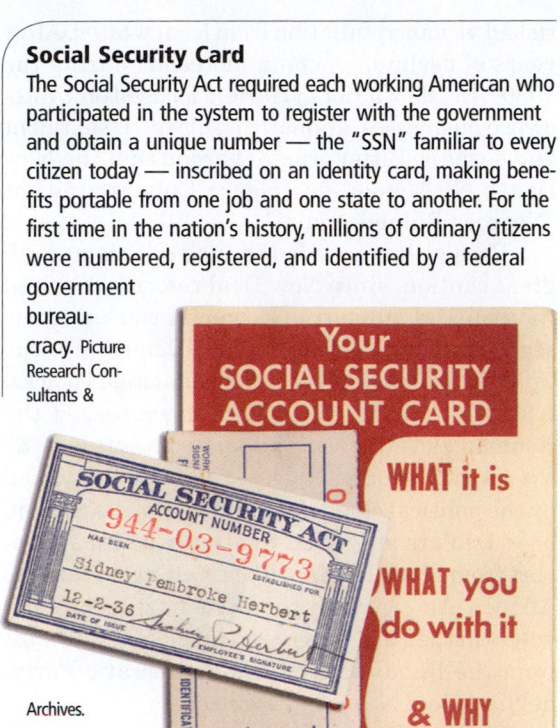

and years of work. Social Security also created unemployment insurance that provided modest benefits for workers who lost their jobs.

Not all workers benefited from the Social Security Act. It excluded domestic and agricultural workers like Florence Owens, thereby making ineligible about half of all African Americans and more than half of all employed women — about five million people in all. In addition, the law excluded workers employed by religious and nonprofit organizations, such as schools and hospitals, rendering ineligible even more working women and minorities.

In a bow to traditional beliefs about local governments' responsibility for public assistance, Social Security issued multimillion-dollar grants to the states to help support dependent children, public health services, and the blind. After the Supreme Court in 1937 upheld Social Security, the program was expanded to include benefits for dependent survivors of deceased recipients. Although the first Social Security check (for

$41.30) was not issued until 1940, the system gave millions of working people the assurance that when they became too old to work, they would receive a modest income from the federal government. This safety net protected many ordinary working people from fears of a penniless and insecure old age.

Fervent opposition to Social Security struck New Dealers as evidence that the rich had learned little from the depression. Roosevelt had long felt contempt for the moneyed elite who ignored the suffering of the poor. He looked for a way to redistribute wealth that would weaken conservative opposition, advance the cause of social equity, and defuse political challenges from Huey Long and Father Coughlin. In June 1935, as the Social Security Act was being debated, Roosevelt delivered a message to Congress outlining comprehensive tax reform. Charging that large fortunes put "great and undesirable concentration of control in [the hands of] relatively few individuals," Roosevelt urged a graduated tax on corporations, an inheritance tax, and an increase in maximum personal income taxes. Congress endorsed Roosevelt's basic principle by taxing those with higher incomes at a somewhat higher rate.

Neglected Americans and the New Deal

The patchwork of New Deal reforms erected a two-tier welfare state. In the top tier, organized workers in major industries were the greatest beneficiaries of New Deal initiatives. In the bottom tier, millions of neglected Americans — women, children, and old folks, along with the unorganized, unskilled, uneducated, and unemployed — often fell through the New Deal safety net. Many working people remained more or less untouched by New Deal benefits. The average unemployment rate for the 1930s stayed high — 17 percent. Workers in industries that resisted unions received little help from the Wagner Act or the WPA. Tens of thousands of women in southern textile mills, for example, commonly received wages of less than ten cents an hour and were fired if they protested. Domestic workers — almost all of them women — and agricultural workers — many of them African, Hispanic, or Asian Americans — were neither unionized nor eligible for Social Security.

The New Deal neglected few citizens more than African Americans. About half of black Americans in cities were jobless, more than double the unemployment rate among whites.

In the rural South, where the vast majority of African Americans lived, conditions were worse, given the New Deal agricultural policies such as the AAA that favored landowners, who often pushed blacks off the land they farmed. Only 11 of more than 10,000 WPA supervisors in the South were black, even though African Americans accounted for a third of the region's population. Disfranchisement by intimidation and legal subterfuge prevented southern blacks from protesting their plight at the ballot box. Protesters

Mary McLeod Bethune
At the urging of Eleanor Roosevelt, Mary McLeod Bethune, a southern educational and civil rights leader, became director of the National Youth Administration's Division of Negro Affairs. The first black woman to head a federal agency, Bethune used her position to promote social change. Here, Bethune takes her mission to the streets to protest the discriminatory hiring practices of the Peoples Drug Store chain in the nation's capital. Moorland-Spingarn Research Center, Howard University.

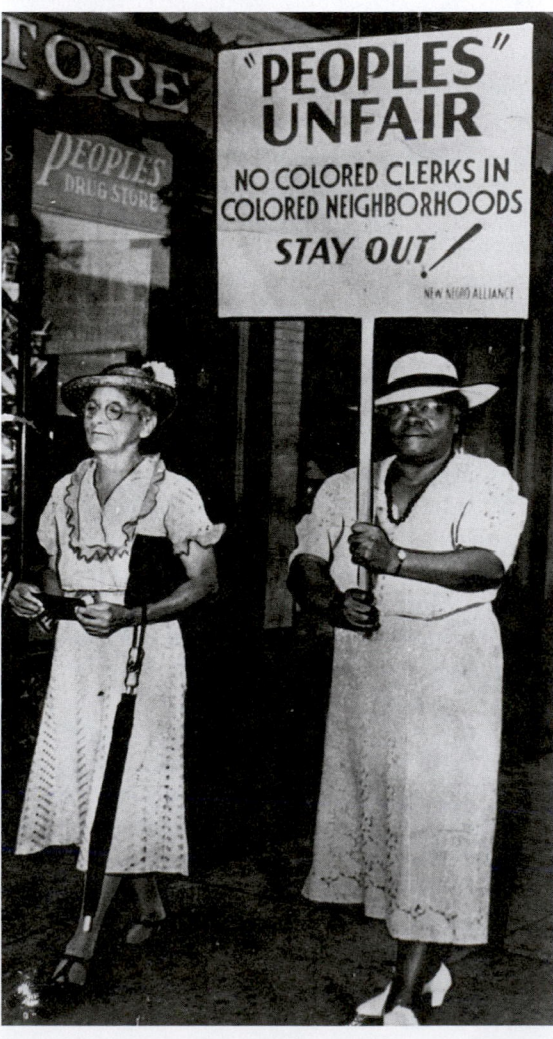

risked vicious retaliation from local whites. After years of decline, lynching increased during the 1930s. In 1935, a riot in Harlem focused on white-owned businesses, dramatizing blacks' resentment and despair. Bitter critics charged that the New Deal's NRA stood for "Negro Run Around" or "Negroes Ruined Again."

Roosevelt responded to such criticisms with great caution, since New Deal reforms required the political support of powerful conservative, segregationist, southern white Democrats who would be alienated by programs that aided blacks. A white Georgia relief worker expressed the common view that "any Nigger who gets over $8 a week is a spoiled Nigger, that's all." Stymied by the political clout of entrenched white racism, New Dealers still tried to attract political support from black leaders. Roosevelt's overtures to African Americans prompted northern black voters in the 1934 congressional elections to shift from the Republican to the Democratic Party, helping elect New Deal Democrats.

Eleanor Roosevelt sponsored the appointment of **Mary McLeod Bethune** — the energetic cofounder of the National Council of Negro Women — as head of the Division of Negro Affairs in the National Youth Administration. The highest-ranking black official in Roosevelt's administration, Bethune used her position to guide a small number of black professionals and civil rights activists to posts within New Deal agencies. Nicknamed the "Black Cabinet," these men and women composed the first sizable representation of African Americans in white-collar posts in the federal government, and they ultimately helped about one in four African Americans get access to New Deal relief programs.

Despite these gains, by 1940 African Americans still suffered severe handicaps. Most of the thirteen million black workers toiled at low-paying menial jobs, unprotected by the New Deal safety net. Making a mockery of the "separate but equal" doctrine, segregated black schools had less money and worse facilities than white schools, and only 1 percent of black students earned college degrees. In southern states, there were no black police officers or judges and hardly any black lawyers. Vigilante violence against blacks went unpunished. For these problems of black Americans, the New Deal offered few remedies.

Hispanic Americans fared no better. About a million Mexican Americans lived in the United States in the 1930s, most of them first- or second-generation immigrants who worked crops throughout the West. During the depression,

Mexican Migrant Farmworkers
These Mexican immigrants are harvesting sugar beets in 1937 in northwestern Minnesota. Between 1910 and 1940, when refugees from the Mexican revolution poured across the American border, the Hispanic-American Alliance and other such organizations sought to protect Mexican Americans' rights against nativist fears and hostility. Alliance banners such as this one flew in opposition to the deportation of Mexican aliens, the disproportionately high use of the death penalty against convicted Mexicans, and a 1926 attempt to bar Mexican Americans from city jobs in Los Angeles. The alliance steadfastly emphasized Mexican Americans' desire to receive permanent legal status in the United States. Photo: Library of Congress; Banner: Collection of the Oakland Museum of California, Gift of the Arizona Historical Society.

field workers saw their low wages plunge lower still to about a dime an hour. Ten thousand Mexican American pecan shellers in San Antonio, Texas, earned only a nickel an hour. To preserve scarce jobs for U.S. citizens, the federal government choked off immigration from Mexico, while state and local officials prohibited the employment of aliens on work relief projects and deported tens of thousands of Mexican Americans, many with their American-born children. Local white administrators of many New Deal programs throughout the West discriminated against Hispanics and other people of color. A New Deal study concluded that "the Mexican is . . . segregated from the rest of the community as effectively as the Negro . . . [by] poverty and low wages."

Asian Americans had similar experiences. Asian immigrants were still excluded from U.S. citizenship and in many states were not permit-

ted to own land. By 1930, more than half of Japanese Americans had been born in the United States, but they were still liable to discrimination. One young Asian American expressed the frustration felt by many others: "I am a fruit-stand worker. I would much rather it were doctor or lawyer . . . but my aspirations [were] frustrated long ago by circumstances. . . . I am only what I am, a professional carrot washer."

Native Americans also suffered neglect from New Deal agencies. As a group, they remained the poorest of the poor. Since the Dawes Act of 1887 (see chapter 17), the federal government had encouraged Native Americans to assimilate — to

John Collier Meets with Navajo Representatives
Commissioner of Indian Affairs John Collier receives a Navajo delegation protesting restrictions in the Indian Reorganization Act (IRA) of 1934. The Navajos dyed and wove the wool of their sheep into beautiful designs like those shown here. The importance of their weavings caused them to protest the IRA's limits on the number of sheep they could raise. Collier had designed the act to revive Native American society by granting tribes an independent land base and many self-governing powers. However, his attempt to make the reservations economically viable through conservation measures, including restrictions on grass-devouring sheep, roused resistance by Indians who chose traditional ways of using resources. Photo: Wide World Photos, Inc.; rug: Morning Star Gallery/Photo by Addison Doty.

abandon their Indian identities and adopt the cultural norms of the majority society. Under the leadership of the New Deal's commissioner of Indian affairs, John Collier, the New Deal's **Indian Reorganization Act (IRA)** of 1934 largely reversed that policy. Collier claimed that "the most interesting and important fact about Indians" was that they "do not expect much, often they expect nothing at all; yet they are able to be happy." Given such views, the IRA provided little economic aid to Native Americans, but it did restore their right to own land communally and to have greater control over their own affairs, including a vote on whether they should live under the IRA, as more than two-thirds opted to do. The IRA brought little immediate benefit to Native Americans and remained a divisive issue for decades, but it provided an important foundation for Indians' economic, cultural, and political resurgence a generation later.

Voicing common experiences among Americans neglected by the New Deal, singer and songwriter Woody Guthrie traveled the nation for eight years during the 1930s and heard other rambling men tell him "the story of their life": "how the home went to pieces, how . . . the crops got to where they wouldn't bring nothing, work in factories would kill a dog . . . and — always, always [you] have to fight and argue and cuss and swear . . . to try to get a nickel more out of the rich bosses."

REVIEW   What features of a welfare state did the New Deal create and why?

▶ The New Deal from Victory to Deadlock

To accelerate the sputtering economic recovery, Roosevelt shifted the emphasis of the New Deal in the mid-1930s. Instead of seeking cooperation from conservative business leaders, he decided to rely on the growing New Deal coalition to enact reforms over the strident opposition of the Supreme Court, Republicans, and corporate interests.

Added to New Deal strength in farm states and big cities were some new allies on the left. Throughout Roosevelt's first term, socialists and Communists denounced the slow pace of change and accused the New Deal of failing to serve the interests of the workers who produced the nation's wealth. But in 1935, the Soviet Union, worried about the threat of fascism in Europe, instructed Communists throughout the world to join hands with non-Communist progressives in a "Popular Front" to advance the fortunes of the working class. With varying degrees of enthusiasm, many radicals switched from opposing the New Deal to supporting its relief programs and encouragement of labor unions.

Roosevelt's conservative opponents reacted to the massing of New Deal force by intensifying their opposition to the welfare state. To Roosevelt, the situation seemed part of a historic drama that dated to the nation's origins, pitting a Hamiltonian faction of wealth and privilege against the heirs of Jefferson, who like Roosevelt, favored a more equitable distribution of wealth and opportunity.

The Election of 1936

Roosevelt believed that the presidential election of 1936 would test his leadership and progressive ideals. The depression still had a stranglehold on the economy. Nearly eight million Americans remained jobless, and millions more were stuck in poverty. Conservative leaders believed that the New Deal's failure to lift the nation out of the depression indicated that Americans were ready for a change. Left-wing critics insisted that the New Deal had missed the opportunity to displace capitalism with a socialist economy and that voters would embrace candidates who recommended more radical remedies.

Republicans turned to the Kansas heartland to select Governor Alfred (Alf) Landon as their presidential nominee. A moderate who had supported some New Deal measures, Landon stressed mainstream Republican proposals to achieve a balanced federal budget and to ease the perils of illness and old age with old-fashioned neighborliness instead of faceless government bureaucracies such as Social Security.

Roosevelt believed that the growing coalition of New Deal supporters would help him liberate the nation from a long era of privilege and wealth for a few and "economic slavery" for the rest. Roosevelt assailed his "old enemies . . . business and financial monopoly, speculation, reckless banking, [and] class antagonism," and proclaimed, "Never before in all our history have these forces been so united against one candidate. . . . They are unanimous in their hate for me — and I welcome their hatred."

Roosevelt triumphed spectacularly. He won 60.8 percent of the popular vote, making it the widest margin of victory in a presidential election to date. Third parties — including the Socialist and Communist parties — fell pitifully short of the support they expected and never again mounted a significant challenge to the New Deal. Congressional results were equally lopsided, with Democrats outnumbering Republicans more than three to one in both houses. In his inaugural address, Roosevelt pledged to use his mandate to help all citizens achieve a decent standard of living. He announced, "I see one third of a nation ill-housed, ill-clad, [and] ill-nourished," and he promised to devote his second term to alleviating their hardship.

New Deal "Needle-Book"

In the 1936 presidential campaign, Democrats distributed this sewing-needle book to celebrate New Deal achievements during Roosevelt's first term. The illustrations on the cover emphasize the return of harmony in agriculture, of booming factories providing plenty of jobs, and above all of "happiness restored" at a prosperous home. Notice that the working people in factories are faceless but the white-collar worker and the family are individualized sympathetically. The needle-book signifies Democrats' attempt to mobilize women to vote in gratitude for the happiness supplied by Roosevelt and the New Deal. Like most campaign materials, the needle-book's claims of New Deal success were greatly exaggerated. Collection of Janice L. and David J. Frent.

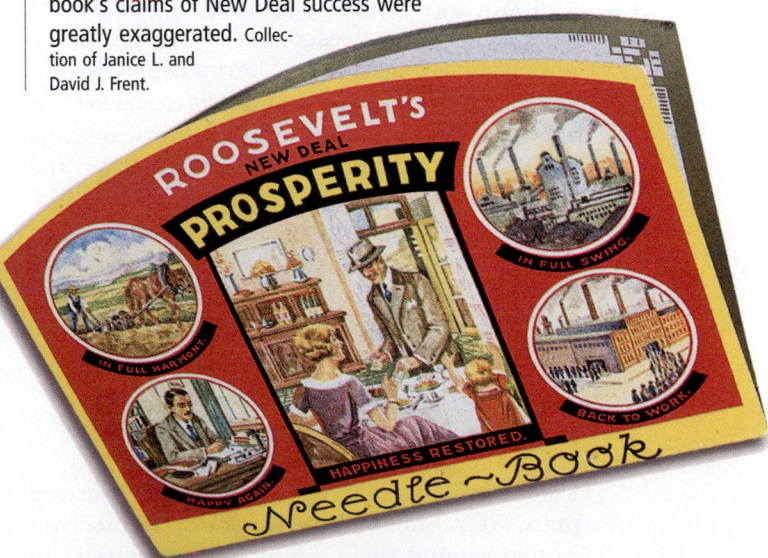

Court Packing

In the afterglow of his reelection triumph, Roosevelt pondered how to remove the remaining obstacles to New Deal reforms. He decided to target the Supreme Court. Laden with conservative justices appointed by Republican presidents, the Court had invalidated eleven New Deal measures as unconstitutional interferences with free enterprise. Now, Social Security, the Wagner Act, the Securities and Exchange Commission, and other New Deal innovations were about to be considered by the justices.

To ensure that the Supreme Court's "horse and buggy" notions did not dismantle the New Deal, Roosevelt proposed a **court-packing plan** that added one new justice for each existing judge who had served for ten years and was over the age of seventy. In effect, the proposed law would give Roosevelt the power to pack the Court with up to six New Dealers who could outvote the elderly, conservative, Republican justices.

But the president had not reckoned with Americans' deeply rooted deference to the independent authority of the Supreme Court. More than two-thirds of Americans believed that the Court should be free from political interference. Even New Deal supporters were disturbed by the court-packing scheme. The suggestion that individuals over age seventy had diminished mental capacity offended many elderly members of Congress, and the Senate defeated the bill in 1937.

Although Roosevelt's court-packing plan failed, Supreme Court justices got the message. After the furor abated, Chief Justice Charles Evans Hughes and fellow moderate Owen Roberts changed their views enough to keep the Court from invalidating the Wagner Act and Social Security. Then the most conservative of the elderly justices — the "four horsemen of reaction," one New Dealer called them — retired. Roosevelt eventually named eight justices to the Court — more than any other president — ultimately giving New Deal laws safe passage through the Court.

> **"[The New Deal is the] repudiation of Democracy [and] the Republican Party alone [is] the guardian of . . . the charter of freedom."**
>
> —Former President
> **HERBERT HOOVER**

Reaction and Recession

Emboldened by their defeat of the court-packing plan, Republicans and southern Democrats rallied around their common conservatism to obstruct additional reforms. Former president Herbert Hoover proclaimed that the New Deal was the "repudiation of Democracy" and that "the Republican Party alone [was] the guardian of . . . the charter of freedom." Democrats' arguments over whether the New Deal needed to be expanded — and if so, how — undermined the consensus among reformers and sparked antagonism between Congress and the White House. The ominous rise of belligerent regimes in Germany, Italy, Japan, and elsewhere slowed reform as some Americans began to worry more about defending the nation than changing it.

Roosevelt himself favored slowing the pace of the New Deal. He believed that existing New Deal measures had steadily boosted the economy and largely eliminated the depression crisis. In fact, the gross national product in 1937 briefly equaled the 1929 level before dropping lower for the rest of the decade. Unemployment declined to 14 percent in 1937 but quickly spiked upward and stayed higher until 1940. Roosevelt's unwarranted optimism about the economic recovery persuaded him that additional deficit spending by the federal government was no longer necessary.

Roosevelt's optimism failed to consider the stubborn realities of unemployment and poverty, and the reduction in deficit spending reversed the improving economy. Even at the high-water mark of recovery in the summer of 1937, seven million people lacked jobs. In the next few months, national income and production slipped so steeply that almost two-thirds of the economic gains since 1933 were lost by June 1938. Farm prices dropped 20 percent, and unemployment rose by more than two million.

This economic reversal hurt the New Deal politically. Conservatives argued that this recession proved that New Deal measures produced only an illusion of progress. The way to weather the recession was to tax and spend less and wait for the natural laws of supply and demand to restore prosperity. Many New Dealers insisted instead that the continuing depression demanded that Roosevelt revive federal spending and redouble efforts to stimulate the economy. In 1938, Congress heeded such pleas and enacted a massive new program of federal spending.

The recession scare of 1937–1938 taught the president the lesson that economic growth had to be carefully nurtured. The English economist John Maynard Keynes, in a theory that became known as **Keynesian economics**, argued in his influential work *The General Theory of Employment, Interest, and Money* (1936) that

Distributing Surplus Food to the Needy
When bountiful harvests produced surplus crops that would depress prices if they were sent to market, the New Deal arranged to distribute some of them to needy Americans. Here, farmworkers in east-central Arizona near the New Mexico border line up to receive a ration of potatoes authorized by the New Deal agent checking the box of index cards. Surplus commodity distribution represented New Dealers' attempt to provide relief for the hungry with crops that otherwise would rot or need to be destroyed in order to limit supply and thereby maintain agricultural prices. Library of Congress.

only government intervention could pump enough money into the economy to restore prosperity. Roosevelt never had the inclination or time to master Keynesian theory. But in a commonsense way, he understood that escape from the depression required a plan for large-scale spending to alleviate distress and stimulate economic growth (Figure 24.2).

The Last of the New Deal Reforms

From the moment he was sworn in, Roosevelt sought to expand the powers of the presidency. He believed that the president needed more authority to meet emergencies such as the depression and to administer the sprawling federal bureaucracy. In September 1938, Congress passed the Administrative Reorganization Act, which gave Roosevelt (and future presidents) new influ-

ence over the bureaucracy. Combined with a Democratic majority in Congress, a now-friendly Supreme Court, and the revival of deficit spending, the newly empowered White House seemed to be in a good position to move ahead with a revitalized New Deal.

Resistance to further reform was also on the rise, however. Conservatives argued that the New Deal had pressed government centralization too far. Even the New Deal's friends became weary of one emergency program after another while economic woes continued to shadow New Deal achievements. By the midpoint of Roosevelt's second term, restive members of Congress balked at new initiatives. Clearly, the New Deal was losing momentum, but enough support remained for one last burst of reform.

Agriculture still had strong claims on New Deal attention in the face of drought, declining crop prices, and impoverished sharecroppers and

FIGURE 24.2 GLOBAL COMPARISON: National Populations and Economies, ca. 1938

Throughout the Great Depression, the United States remained more productive than any other nation in the world. Despite the lingering effects of the depression, by 1938 the United States produced more than twice as much as Germany and the Soviet Union, nearly three times as much as Britain, more than four times as much as France and Japan, and more than five times as much as Italy. From the viewpoint of Germany, if the European nations listed here could be brought under German control, its economy would be greater than that of the United States and would become the mightiest in the world. Economically, how important were colonies to the major powers? In general, what do these data suggest about the relationship between population and gross domestic product?

	Population (millions)	Gross Domestic Product (millions of dollars)
United States		
Britain		
British Colonies		
France		
French Colonies		
Italy		
Italian Colonies		
Netherlands		
Dutch Colonies		
USSR		
Japan		
Japanese Colonies		
Germany		
Austria		
Czechoslovakia		
Poland		
Hungary		
Yugoslavia		
Romania		

= 10 million people
= 10 million dollars

tenants. In 1937, the Agriculture Department created the Farm Security Administration (FSA) to provide housing and loans to help tenant farmers become independent. A black tenant farmer in North Carolina who received an FSA loan told a New Deal interviewer, "I wake up in the night sometimes and think I must be half-dead and gone to heaven." But relatively few tenants received loans, because the FSA was starved for funds and ran up against major farm organizations intent on serving their own interests. For those who owned farms, the New Deal offered renewed prosperity with a second Agricultural Adjustment Act (AAA) in 1938. To moderate price swings by regulating supply, the plan combined production quotas on five staple crops — cotton, tobacco, wheat, corn, and rice — with storage loans through its Commodity Credit Corporation. The most prosperous farmers benefited most, but the act's Federal Surplus Commodities Corporation added an element of charity by issuing food stamps so that the poor could obtain surplus food. The AAA of 1938 brought stability to American agriculture and ample food to most — but not all — tables.

Advocates for the urban poor also made modest gains after decades of neglect. New York senator Robert Wagner convinced Congress to pass the **National Housing Act** in 1937. By 1941, some 160,000 residences had been made available to poor people at affordable rents. The program did not come close to meeting the need for affordable housing, but for the first time the federal government took an active role in providing decent urban housing.

The last major piece of New Deal labor legislation, the **Fair Labor Standards Act** of June 1938, reiterated the New Deal pledge to provide workers with a decent standard of living. After lengthy haggling and compromise that revealed the waning strength of the New Deal, Congress finally agreed to intervene in the long-sacrosanct realm of worker contracts. The new law set wage and hours standards and at long last curbed the use of child labor. The minimum-wage level was modest — twenty-five cents an hour for a maximum of forty-four hours a week. To critics of the minimum wage law who said it was "government interference," one New Dealer responded, "It was. It interfered with the fellow running that pecan shelling plant . . . [and] told him he couldn't pay that little widow seven cents an hour." To attract enough conservative votes, the act exempted merchant seamen, fishermen, domestic help, and farm laborers — relegating most women and African Americans to lower wages. Enforcement of the minimum-wage standards was weak and haphazard. Nevertheless, the Fair Labor Standards Act slowly advanced Roosevelt's inaugural promise to improve the living standards of the poorest Americans.

The final New Deal reform effort failed to make much headway against the hidebound system of racial injustice. Although Roosevelt denounced lynching as murder, he would not jeopardize his vital base of southern political support by demanding antilynching legislation, and Congress voted down attempts to make lynching a federal crime. Laws to eliminate the poll tax — used to deny blacks the opportunity to vote — encountered the same overwhelming resistance. The New Deal refused to confront racial injustice with the same vigor it brought to bear on economic hardship.

By the end of 1938, the New Deal had lost steam and encountered stiff opposition. In the congressional elections of 1938, Republicans made gains that gave them more congressional influence than they had enjoyed since 1932. New Dealers could claim unprecedented achievements since 1933, but nobody needed reminding that those achievements had not ended the depression. In his annual message to Congress in January 1939, Roosevelt signaled a halt to New Deal reforms by speaking about preserving the progress already achieved rather than extending it. Roosevelt pointed to the ominous threats posed by fascist aggressors in Germany and Japan, and he proposed defense expenditures that surpassed New Deal appropriations for relief and economic recovery.

REVIEW Why did political support for New Deal reforms decline?

▶ Conclusion: Achievements and Limitations of the New Deal

The New Deal reflected Roosevelt's confidence, optimism, and energetic pragmatism. A growing majority of Americans agreed with Roosevelt that the federal government should help those in need, thereby strengthening the political coalition that propelled the New Deal. Through programs that sought relief, recovery, and reform, the New Deal vastly expanded the size and influence of the federal government and changed the way many Americans viewed Washington. New Dealers achieved significant victories, such as Social Security, labor's right to organize, and guarantees that farm prices would be maintained through controls on production and marketing. New Deal measures marked the emergence of a welfare state, but the New Deal's limited, two-tier character left many needy Americans like Florence Owens and her children with little aid.

Full-scale relief, recovery, and reform eluded New Deal programs. Even though millions of Americans benefited from New Deal initiatives, both relief and recovery were limited and temporary. In 1940, the depression still plagued the economy. Perhaps the most impressive achievement of the New Deal was what did not happen. Although authoritarian governments and anticapitalist policies were common outside the United States during the 1930s, they were shunned by the New Deal. The greatest economic crisis the nation had ever faced did not cause Americans to abandon democracy, as happened in Germany, where Adolf Hitler seized dictatorial power. Nor did the nation turn to radical alternatives such as socialism or communism.

Republicans and other conservatives claimed that the New Deal amounted to a form of socialism that threatened democracy and capitalism. But rather than attack capitalism, Franklin Roosevelt sought to save it. And he succeeded. That success also marked the limits of the New Deal's achievements. Franklin Roosevelt believed that a shift of authority toward the federal government would allow capitalist enterprises to be balanced by the nation's democratic tradition. The New Deal stopped far short of challenging capitalism either by undermining private property or by imposing strict national planning.

New Dealers repeatedly described their programs as a kind of warfare against the depression of the 1930s. In the next decade, the Roosevelt administration had to turn from the economic crisis at home to participate in a worldwide conflagration to defeat the enemies of democracy abroad.

Nonetheless, many New Deal reforms continued for decades to structure the basic institutions of banking, the stock market, union organizations, agricultural markets, Social Security, minimum-wage standards, and more. Opponents of these measures and of the basic New Deal notion of an activist government remained powerful, especially in the Republican Party. They claimed that government was the problem, not the solution — a slogan that Republicans championed during and after the 1980s and that led, with the cooperation of some Democrats, to the dismantling of a number of New Deal programs, including the regulation of banking. The deregulation of financial institutions was in large part responsible for the economic collapse that began in 2008.

▶ Selected Bibliography

General Works

Gary Dean Best, *The Retreat from Liberalism: Collectivists versus Progressives in the New Deal Years* (2002).

William H. Chafe, ed., *The Achievement of American Liberalism: The New Deal and Its Legacies* (2003).

Morris Dickstein, *Dancing in the Dark: A Cultural History of the Great Depression* (2010).

Ronald Edsforth, *The New Deal: America's Response to the Great Depression* (2000).

David M. Kennedy, *Freedom from Fear: The American People in Depression and War, 1929–1945* (1999).

Alan Lawson, *A Commonwealth of Hope: The New Deal Response to Crisis* (2006).

William Edward Leuchtenburg, *Franklin D. Roosevelt and the New Deal, 1932–1940* (2009).

Eric Rauchway, *The Great Depression and the New Deal: A Very Short Introduction* (2008).

Amity Shlaes, *The Forgotten Man: A New History of the Great Depression* (2008).

New Deal Politics

Roger Biles, *The South and the New Deal* (2006).

Blanche Wiesen Cook, *Eleanor Roosevelt*, 2 vols. (1992, 1999).

Kirstin Downey, *The Woman behind the New Deal: The Life and Legacy of Frances Perkins* (2010).

Alonzo L. Hamby, *For the Survival of Democracy: Franklin Roosevelt and the World Crisis of the 1930s* (2004).

Joseph E. Lowndes, *From the New Deal to the New Right: Race and the Southern Origins of Modern Conservatism* (2009).

Marian C. McKenna, *Franklin Roosevelt and the Great Constitutional War: The Court-Packing Crisis of 1937* (2002).

Kim Phillips-Fein, *Invisible Hands: The Businessmen's Crusade against the New Deal* (2010).

Theodore Rosenof, *Economics in the Long Run: New Deal Theorists and Their Legacies, 1933–1993* (1997).

Robert Shogan, *Backlash: The Killing of the New Deal* (2006).

Mary Triece, *On the Picket Line: Strategies of Working-Class Women during the Depression* (2007).

Clyde P. Weed, *The Nemesis of Reform: The Republican Party during the New Deal* (1994).

New Deal Policies

Lizbeth Cohen, *Making a New Deal: Industrial Workers in Chicago, 1919–1939* (1990).

Kathleen G. Donohue, *Freedom from Want: American Liberalism and the Idea of the Consumer* (2004).

Jan Goggans, *California on the Breadlines: Dorothea Lange, Paul Taylor, and the Making of a New Deal Narrative* (2010).

Linda Gordon, *Dorothea Lange: A Life beyond Limits* (2009).

Michael R. Grey, *New Deal Medicine: The Rural Health Programs of the Farm Security Administration* (1999).

Janet Irons, *Testing the New Deal: The General Textile Strike of 1934 in the American South* (2000).

Jennifer Klein, *For All These Rights: Business, Labor, and the Shaping of America's Public-Private Welfare State* (2003).

Lawrence Levine et al., *The Fireside Conversations: America Responds to FDR during the Great Depression* (2010).

Julie Novkov, *Constituting Workers, Protecting Women: Gender, Law, and Labor in the Progressive Era and New Deal Years* (2001).

Sarah Phillips, *This Land, This Nation: Conservation, Rural America, and the New Deal* (2007).

Patrick D. Reagan, *Designing a New America: The Origins of New Deal Planning, 1890–1936* (1999).

John A. Salmond, *The General Textile Strike of 1934: From Maine to Alabama* (2002).

Jason Scott Smith, *Building New Deal Liberalism: The Political Economy of Public Works, 1933–1956* (2005).

Landon R. Y. Stors, *Civilizing Capitalism: The National Consumers' League, Women's Activism, and Labor Standards in the New Deal Era* (2000).

David A. Taylor, *Soul of a People: The WPA Writers' Project Uncovers Depression America* (2010).

▶ FOR MORE BOOKS ABOUT TOPICS IN THIS CHAPTER, see the Online Bibliography at **bedfordstmartins.com/roark.**

▶ FOR ADDITIONAL PRIMARY SOURCES FROM THIS PERIOD, see Michael Johnson, ed., *Reading the American Past*, Fifth Edition.

▶ FOR WEB SITES, IMAGES, AND DOCUMENTS RELATED TO TOPICS AND PLACES IN THIS CHAPTER, visit Make History at **bedfordstmartins.com/roark.**

Reviewing Chapter 24

KEY TERMS

Explain each term's significance.

Franklin D. Roosevelt: A Patrician in Government

Launching the New Deal

Challenges to the New Deal

Toward a Welfare State

The New Deal from Victory to Deadlock

REVIEW QUESTIONS

Use key terms and dates to support your answer.

1. Why did Franklin D. Roosevelt win the 1932 presidential election by such a large margin? (pp. 787–791)

2. How did the New Dealers try to steer the nation toward recovery from the Great Depression? (pp. 791–800)

3. Why did groups at both ends of the political spectrum criticize the New Deal? (pp. 800–804)

4. What features of a welfare state did the New Deal create and why? (pp. 804–812)

5. Why did political support for New Deal reforms decline? (pp. 812–817)

MAKING CONNECTIONS

Draw on key terms, the timeline, and review questions.

1. Franklin Roosevelt's landslide victory in 1932 changed the political landscape. How did Roosevelt build an effective interregional political coalition for the Democratic Party? How did the challenges of balancing interests within the coalition shape the policies of the New Deal? In your answer, discuss the character of the coalition and specific reforms.

2. New Dealers experimented with varied solutions to the economic disorder of the 1930s. Compare reform efforts targeting rural and industrial America. Were they effective? Why or why not? What do they reveal about how the Roosevelt administration understood the underlying causes of the Great Depression?

3. Although the New Deal enjoyed astonishing popularity, some Americans were consistently critical of Roosevelt's reforms. Why? In your answer, discuss three opponents of the New Deal, being attentive to changes over time in their opinions. Were they able to influence the New Deal? If so, how?

4. Although the New Deal extended help to many Americans, all did not benefit equally from the era's reforms. Who remained outside the reach of New Deal assistance? Why? In your answer, consider how politics shaped the limits of reform, both in constituents' ability to demand assistance and in the federal government's response to their demands.

LINKING TO THE PAST

Link events in this chapter to earlier events.

1. To what degree did the New Deal reflect a continuation of the progressive movement of the late nineteenth and early twentieth centuries? In what ways was the New Deal a departure from progressive ideals? In general, how new was the New Deal? (See chapters 21 and 22.)

2. How did the New Deal coalition compare to the long-standing political coalition that had elected Republicans to the presidency since 1920? What accounted for the differences and similarities? (See chapter 23.)

▶ FOR PRACTICE QUIZZES AND OTHER STUDY TOOLS, visit the Online Study Guide at bedfordstmartins.com/roark.

TIMELINE 1933–1938

1933
- Democrat Franklin D. Roosevelt becomes president.
- **March–June** Legislation of the Hundred Days establishes the New Deal.
- Roosevelt closes the nation's banks for a four-day "bank holiday."
- Federal Emergency Relief Administration (FERA) established.

1934
- Securities and Exchange Commission (SEC) created.
- Upton Sinclair loses bid for governorship of California.
- American Liberty League founded.
- Dr. Francis Townsend devises Old Age Revolving Pension scheme.
- Indian Reorganization Act.

1935
- Legislation creates Works Progress Administration (WPA).
- Wagner Act.
- Committee for Industrial Organization (CIO) founded.
- Social Security Act.
- Father Charles Coughlin begins National Union for Social Justice.

1936
- John Maynard Keynes publishes *The General Theory of Employment, Interest, and Money.*
- Franklin Roosevelt elected to a second term by a landslide.

1937
- United Auto Workers stages successful sit-down strike at General Motors plant in Flint, Michigan.
- Roosevelt's court-packing legislation defeated in the Senate.
- Economic recession slows recovery from depression.

1938
- Second Agricultural Adjustment Act and Fair Labor Standards Act.
- Congress rejects administration's antilynching bill.
- Administrative Reorganization Act.

GI MAIL

After the United States entered World War II, millions of American men and tens of thousands of American women served in the military, more than in all previous wars combined. Although soldiers engaged in deadly combat — like those in the Pacific theater depicted in the background — they also stayed in touch with family and friends back home. Soldiers who drew the pictures on envelopes shown here emphasized the positive: Uncle Sam crushing leaders of Germany and Japan; airplanes launching attacks from a carrier at sea; and a sailor digging money from his pocket to buy war bonds.

Background: National Archives; envelopes: Archives Center, National Museum of American History, Behring Center, Smithsonian Institution; Sumner Grant, Artifact, Veterans History Project Collection, American Folklore Center, Library of Congress.

25

The United States and the Second World War
1939–1945

ON A SUN-DRENCHED FLORIDA AFTERNOON IN JANUARY 1927, twelve-year-old Paul Tibbets cinched on a leather helmet and clambered into the front seat of the open cockpit of a biplane for his first airplane ride. While the pilot sitting behind him brought the plane in low over the Hialeah racetrack in Miami, Tibbets pitched Baby Ruth candy bars tethered to small paper parachutes to racing fans in the grandstands below. After two more candy-bar drops over the racetrack, the pilot raced to the beach, and Tibbets tossed out the remaining candy bars and watched the bathers scramble for chocolate from heaven. After this stunt, sales of Baby Ruths soared, and Tibbets was hooked on flying.

In 1937, Tibbets joined the Army Air Corps and became a military pilot. Shortly after the Japanese attack on Pearl Harbor in December 1941, Tibbets led a squadron of airplanes flying antisubmarine patrol against German U-boats lurking along the East Coast. When the heavily armored B-17 Flying Fortress bombers began to come off American assembly lines early in 1942, he took a squadron of the new planes from the United States to England. On August 17, 1942, he led the first American daytime bombing raid on German-occupied Europe, releasing 1,100 pounds of bombs from his B-17, nicknamed *Butcher Shop*, on railroad yards in northern France, the first of some 700,000 tons of explosives dropped by American bombers during the air war in Europe.

After numerous raids over Europe, Tibbets was reassigned to the North African campaign, where his duties included ferrying the American commander, General Dwight D. Eisenhower, into the battle zone. After eight months of combat missions, Tibbets returned to the United States and was ordered to test the new B-29 Super Fortress being built in Wichita, Kansas. The B-29 was much bigger than the B-17 and could fly higher and faster, making it ideal for the campaign against Japan. Tibbets's mastery of the B-29 caused him to be singled out in September 1944 to command a top-secret unit training for a special mission.

The mission was to be ready to drop on Japan a bomb so powerful that it might end the war. No such bomb yet existed, but American scientists

823

Colonel Paul Tibbets
Before taking off to drop the world's first atomic bomb on Hiroshima, Tibbets posed on the tarmac next to his customized B-29 Super Fortress bomber, named *Enola Gay* in honor of his mother. A crew of eleven handpicked airmen accompanied Tibbets on the top-secret mission. After the war, President Harry S. Truman invited Tibbets to the White House and told him, "Don't you ever lose any sleep over the fact that you planned and carried out that mission. It was my decision. You had no choice." © Bettmann/Corbis.

and engineers were working around the clock to build one. Tibbets kept this secret from his men but took them and his B-29s to Utah to develop a way to drop such a powerful weapon without getting blown up by it. In May 1945, Tibbets and his men went to Tinian Island in the Pacific, where they trained for their secret mission by flying raids over Japanese cities and dropping ordinary bombs. The atomic bomb arrived on Tinian on July 26, just ten days after a successful test explosion in the New Mexico desert. Nicknamed "Little Boy," the bomb packed the equivalent of 40 million pounds of TNT, or 200,000 of the 200-pound bombs Tibbets and other American airmen had dropped on Europe.

At 2:30 a.m. on August 6, 1945, Tibbets, his crew, and their atomic payload took off in the B-29 bomber *Enola Gay*, named for Tibbets's mother, and headed for Japan. Less than seven hours later, over the city of Hiroshima, Tibbets and his men released Little Boy from the *Enola Gay's* bomb bay. The plane bucked upward after dropping the 4.5-ton explosive, while Tibbets struggled to maintain control as the shock wave from the explosion blasted past and a purple cloud mushroomed nearly ten miles into the air. Three days later, airmen from Tibbets's command dropped a second atomic bomb on Nagasaki, and within five days Japan surrendered.

Paul Tibbets's experiences traced an arc followed by millions of Americans during World War II, from the innocence of bombarding Miami with candy bars to the deadly nuclear firestorms that rained down on Japan. Like Tibbets, Americans joined their allies to fight the Axis powers in Europe and Asia. Like his *Enola Gay* crewmen — who hailed from New York, Texas, California, New Jersey, New Mexico, Maryland, North Carolina, Pennsylvania, Michigan, and Nevada — Americans from all regions united to defeat the fascist aggressors. American industries mobilized to produce advanced bombers — like the ones Tibbets piloted — along with enough other military equipment to supply the American armed forces and their allies. At enormous cost in human life and suffering, the war resulted in employment and prosperity to most Americans at home, ending the depression, providing new opportunities for women, and ushering the nation into the postwar world as a triumphant economic and — on the wings of Tibbets's *Enola Gay* — atomic superpower.

▶ Peacetime Dilemmas

The First World War left a dangerous and ultimately deadly legacy. The victors — especially Britain, France, and the United States — sought to avoid future wars at almost any cost. The defeated nation, Germany, aspired to reassert its power and avenge its losses by means of renewed warfare. Italy and Japan felt humiliated by the Versailles peace settlement and saw war as a legitimate way to increase their global power. Japan invaded the northern Chinese province of Manchuria in 1931 with ambitions to expand throughout Asia. Italy, led by the fascist **Benito Mussolini** since 1922, hungered for an empire in Africa. In Germany, National Socialist **Adolf Hitler** rose to power in 1933 in a quest to dominate Europe and the world. (See chapter 24, "Beyond America's Borders," page 788.) These aggressive, militaristic, antidemocratic regimes seemed a smaller threat to most people in the United States during the 1930s than did the economic crisis at home. Shielded from external threats by the Atlantic and Pacific oceans, Americans hoped to avoid entanglement in foreign woes and to concentrate on climbing out of the nation's economic abyss.

Roosevelt and Reluctant Isolation

Like most Americans during the 1930s, Franklin Roosevelt believed that the nation's highest priority was to attack the domestic causes and consequences of the depression. But unlike most Americans, Roosevelt had long advocated an active role for the United States in international affairs. After World War I, Roosevelt embraced Woodrow Wilson's vision that the United States should take the lead in making the world "safe for democracy," and he continued to advocate American membership in the League of Nations during the isolationist 1920s.

The depression forced Roosevelt to retreat from his previous internationalism. He came to believe that energetic involvement in foreign affairs diverted resources and political support from domestic recovery. Once in office, Roosevelt sought to combine domestic economic recovery with a low-profile foreign policy that encouraged free trade and disarmament.

Roosevelt's pursuit of international amity was constrained by economic circumstances and American popular opinion. After an opinion poll demonstrated popular support for recognizing the Soviet Union — an international pariah since the Bolshevik Revolution in 1917 — Roosevelt established formal diplomatic relations in 1933. But when the League of Nations condemned Japanese and German aggression, Roosevelt did not support the league's attempts to keep the peace because he feared jeopardizing isolationists' support for New Deal measures in Congress. America watched from the sidelines when Japan withdrew from the league and ignored the limitations on its navy imposed after World War I. The United States also looked the other way when Hitler rearmed Germany and recalled its representative to the league in 1933, declaring that the international organization sought to thwart Germany's national ambitions. Roosevelt worried that German and Japanese violations of league sanctions and the Versailles settlement threatened world peace. But he re-assured Americans that the nation would not "use its armed forces for the settlement of any [international] dispute anywhere."

> "[The nation will not] use its armed forces for the settlement of any [international] dispute anywhere."
> — President FRANKLIN ROOSEVELT in 1933

The Good Neighbor Policy

In his 1933 inaugural address, Franklin Roosevelt announced that the United States would pursue "the policy of the good neighbor" in international relations. A few weeks later, he emphasized that this policy applied specifically to Latin America, where U.S. military forces had often intervened in local affairs (see Map 22.1, page 713). In December 1933, Secretary of State Cordell Hull formalized the good neighbor pledge that no nation had the right to intervene in the internal or external affairs of another.

The **good neighbor policy** did not indicate a U.S. retreat from empire in Latin America. Instead, it declared that the United States would not depend on military force to exercise its influence in the region. When Mexico nationalized American oil holdings and revolution boiled over in Nicaragua, Guatemala, and Cuba during the 1930s, Roosevelt refrained from sending troops to defend the interests of American corporations. In 1934, Roosevelt even withdrew American Marines from Haiti, which they had occupied since 1916. While nonintervention honored the principle of national self-determination, it also permitted the rise of dictators, such as Anastasio Somoza in Nicaragua and Fulgencio Batista in Cuba, who exploited and terrorized their nations

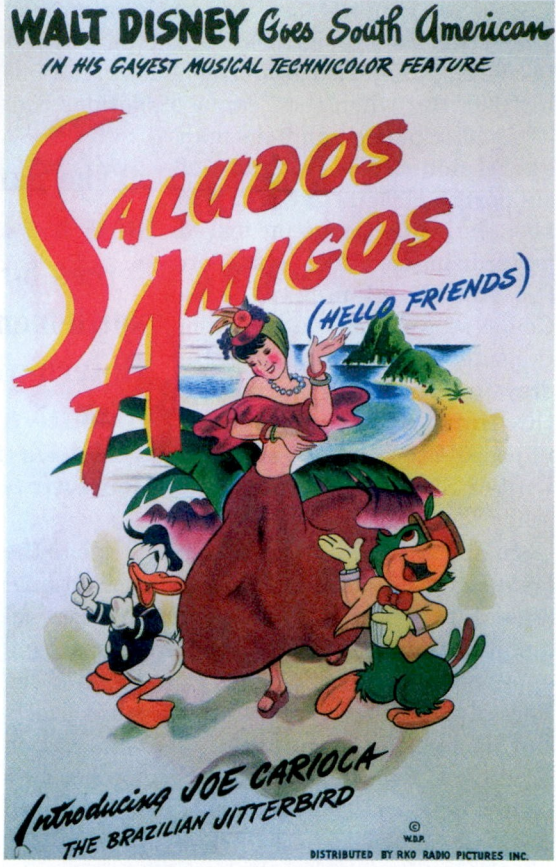

WALT DISNEY *Goes South American*
IN HIS GAYEST MUSICAL TECHNICOLOR FEATURE

SALUDOS AMIGOS *(HELLO FRIENDS)*

Introducing **JOE CARIOCA**
THE BRAZILIAN JITTERBIRD

DISTRIBUTED BY RKO RADIO PICTURES INC.

Promoting the Good Neighbor Policy
To encourage continuing friendly relations with Latin America during World War II, the Roosevelt administration urged Walt Disney to make the 1942 film *Saludos Amigos* — starring Donald Duck, Goofy, and "the Brazilian Jitterbird," Joe Carioca — largely for distribution south of the border. The good neighbor policy helped prevent Latin American nations from developing meaningful military alliances with the Axis powers during World War II. © Disney Enterprises, Inc.

The Price of Noninvolvement

In Europe, fascist governments in Italy and Germany threatened military aggression. Italian dictator Benito Mussolini proclaimed, "War is to the man what maternity is to the woman. . . . Peace [is] . . . depressing and a negation of all the fundamental virtues of man." Hitler rebuilt Germany's military strength, openly defying the terms of the Versailles peace treaty. Britain and France only made verbal protests. Emboldened, Hitler plotted to avenge defeat in World War I by recapturing territories with German inhabitants, all the while accusing Jews of polluting the purity of the Aryan master race. The virulent anti-Semitism of Hitler and his Nazi Party unified non-Jewish Germans and attracted sympathizers among many other Europeans, even in France and Britain, thereby weakening support for those who opposed Hitler or defended Jews.

In Japan, a stridently militaristic government planned to follow the invasion of Manchuria in 1931 with conquests extending throughout Southeast Asia. The Manchurian invasion bogged down in a long and vicious war when Chinese Nationalists rallied around their leader, **Jiang Jieshi (Chiang Kai-shek)**, to fight against the Japanese. Preparations for new Japanese conquests continued, however. In 1936, Japan openly violated naval limitation treaties it had agreed to and began to build a battle-ready fleet to achieve naval superiority in the Pacific.

In the United States, the hostilities in Asia and Europe reinforced isolationist sentiments. Popular disillusionment with the failure of Woodrow Wilson's idealistic goals caused many Americans to question the nation's participation in World War I. In 1933, Gerald Nye, a Republican from North Dakota, chaired a Senate committee that investigated why the United States had gone to war in 1917. The Nye committee concluded that greedy "merchants of death" — American weapons makers, bankers, and financiers — dragged the nation into the war to line their own pockets. The Nye committee persuaded many Americans that war profiteers might once again push the nation into a world war. International tensions and the Nye committee report prompted Congress to pass a series of **neutrality acts** between 1935 and 1937 designed to avoid entanglement in foreign wars. The neutrality acts prohibited making loans and selling arms to nations at war.

with private support from U.S. businesses and the hands-off policy of Roosevelt's administration.

Military nonintervention also did not prevent the United States from exerting its economic influence in Latin America. In 1934, Congress passed the Reciprocal Trade Agreements Act, which gave the president the power to reduce tariffs on goods imported into the United States from nations that agreed to lower their own tariffs on U.S. exports. By 1940, twenty-two nations had agreed to reciprocal tariff reductions, helping to double U.S. exports to Latin America and contributing to the New Deal's goal of boosting the domestic economy through free trade. Although the economic power of the United States continued to overshadow that of its neighbors, the nonintervention policy planted seeds of friendship and hemispheric solidarity.

By 1937, the growing conflicts overseas caused some Americans to call for a total embargo on all trade with warring countries. Roosevelt and Congress worried that such an embargo would hurt the nation's economy by reducing production and boosting unemployment. The Neutrality Act of 1937 attempted to reconcile the nation's desire for both peace and foreign trade with a "cash-and-carry" policy that required warring nations to pay cash for nonmilitary goods and to transport them in their own ships. This policy supported foreign trade and thereby benefited the nation's economy, but it also helped foreign aggressors by supplying them with goods and thereby undermining peace.

The desire for peace in France, Britain, and the United States led Germany, Italy, and Japan to launch offensives on the assumption that the Western democracies lacked the will to oppose them. In March 1936, Nazi troops marched into the industry-rich Rhineland on Germany's western border, in blatant violation of the Treaty of Versailles. One month later, Italian armies completed their conquest of Ethiopia, projecting fascist power into Africa. In December 1937, Japanese invaders captured Nanjing (Nanking) and celebrated their triumph in the "Rape of Nanking," a deadly rampage of murder, rape, and plunder that killed 200,000 Chinese civilians.

In Spain, a bitter civil war broke out in July 1936 when the Nationalists, fascist rebels led by General Francisco Franco, attacked the democratically elected Republican government. Both Germany and Italy reinforced Franco with soldiers, weapons, and aircraft, while the Soviet Union provided much less aid to the Republican Loyalists. The **Spanish civil war** seemed to many observers a dress rehearsal for a coming worldwide conflict, but it did not cause European democracies or the U.S. government to help the Loyalists, despite sympathy for their cause. More than 3,000 individual Americans enlisted in the Russian-sponsored Abraham Lincoln Brigade to fight on the Republican side. But, abandoned by the Western nations, the Republican Loyalists and their allies were defeated in 1939, and Franco built a fascist bulwark in southwestern Europe.

Hostilities in Europe, Africa, and Asia alarmed Roosevelt and some Americans. The president sought to persuade most Americans to moderate their isolationism and find a way to support the victims of fascist aggression. Speaking in Chicago in October 1937, Roosevelt declared that the "epidemic of world lawlessness is spreading" and warned that "mere isolation or neutrality" offered no remedy. Instead, he proposed that the United States "quarantine" aggressor nations and stop the spread of war's contagion.

Roosevelt's speech ignited a storm of protest from isolationists. Critics accused the president of seeking to replace "Americanism" with "internationalism." Disappointed by the strength of isolationism and the absence of congressional support for his quarantine policy, Roosevelt remarked, "It's a terrible thing to look over your shoulder when you are trying to lead and find no one there." The popularity of isolationist sentiment convinced Roosevelt that he needed to maneuver carefully if the United States were to help prevent fascist aggressors from conquering Europe and Asia, leaving the United States an isolated and imperiled island of democracy.

REVIEW Why did isolationism during the 1930s concern Roosevelt?

The Onset of War

Between 1939 and 1941, fascist victories overseas eventually eroded American isolationism. Continuing German and Japanese aggression caused more and more Americans to believe that it was time for the nation to take a stand. At first, taking a stand was limited to providing material support to the enemies of Germany and Japan, principally Britain, China, and the Soviet Union. But Japan's surprise attack on Pearl Harbor eliminated that restraint, and the nation began to mobilize for an all-out assault on foreign foes.

Nazi Aggression and War in Europe

Under the spell of isolationism, Americans passively watched Hitler's relentless campaign to dominate Europe. In 1938, Hitler bullied Austria into accepting incorporation — *Anschluss* — into

Spanish Civil War, 1936–1939

Nationalist, July 1936
Nationalist gains, Oct. 1937
Nationalist gains, July 1938
Nationalist gains, Feb. 1939
Republican, Feb. 1939

the Third Reich, the Nazis' name for Germany. Next, Hitler turned his attention to the German-speaking Sudetenland, granted to Czechoslovakia by the World War I peace settlement. Hoping to avoid war, British prime minister Neville Chamberlain went to Munich, Germany, in September 1938 and offered Hitler terms of **appeasement** that would give the Sudetenland to Germany if Hitler agreed to leave the rest of Czechoslovakia alone. Hitler accepted Chamberlain's offer and promised that he would make no more territorial claims in Europe. But he never intended to honor his promise. In March 1939, the German army boldly marched into Czechoslovakia and conquered it without firing a shot (Map 25.1).

MAP 25.1

Axis Aggression through 1941

For different reasons, Hitler and Mussolini launched a series of surprise military strikes before 1942. Mussolini sought to re-create the Roman empire in the Mediterranean. Hitler struck to reclaim German territories occupied by France after World War I and to annex Austria. When the German dictator began his campaign to rule "inferior" peoples beyond Germany's border by attacking Poland, World War II broke out.

THE ONSET OF WAR

Nazi Invasion of Poland
Adolf Hitler relished the early success of the German army's *blitzkrieg* against Poland in 1939. This photo shows Hitler reviewing a victory parade of his soldiers in Warsaw. Nazi insignia hanging from every lamp post declare the German conquest of Poland. After the conquest, Germans systematically murdered hundreds of thousands of Polish civilians and confined even more to slave labor camps. Notably, the photo shows no Poles celebrating Hitler's victory. PHoto by Hugo Jaeger/Timepix/Time Life Pictures/Getty Images.

In April 1939, Hitler demanded that Poland return the German territory it had been awarded after World War I. Recognizing that appeasement had failed, Britain and France assured Poland that they would go to war with Germany if Hitler launched an attack across the Polish border. In turn, Hitler negotiated with his bitter enemy, Soviet premier **Joseph Stalin**, offering him concessions in order to prevent the Soviet Union from joining Britain and France in opposing a German attack on Poland. Despite the enduring hatred between fascist Germany and the Communist Soviet Union, the two powers signed the Nazi-Soviet treaty of nonaggression in August 1939, exposing Poland to an onslaught by both the German Wehrmacht (army) and the Soviet Red Army.

At dawn on September 1, 1939, Hitler unleashed his *blitzkrieg* (literally, "lightning war") on Poland. "Act brutally!" Hitler exhorted his generals. "Send [every] man, woman, and child of Polish descent and language to their deaths, pitilessly and remorselessly." The attack triggered Soviet attacks on eastern Poland and declarations of war from France and Britain two days later, igniting a conflagration that raced around the globe. In September 1939, Germany seemed invincible, causing many people to fear that all of Europe would soon share Poland's fate.

After the Nazis overran Poland, Hitler paused for a few months before launching a westward blitzkrieg. In April 1940, German forces smashed through Denmark and Norway. In May, Germany invaded the Netherlands, Belgium, Luxembourg, and France. The French believed that their Maginot Line, a concrete fortification built after World War I, would halt the German attack (see Map 25.1). But the Maginot Line proved little more than a detour for Hitler's mechanized divisions, which wheeled around it and raced south toward Paris.

The speed of the German attack trapped more than 300,000 British and French soldiers, who retreated to the port of Dunkirk, where an improvised armada of British vessels hurriedly ferried them to safety across the English Channel. By mid-June 1940, France had surrendered the largest army in the world, signed an armistice that gave Germany control of the entire French coastline and nearly two-thirds of the countryside, and installed a collaborationist government at Vichy in southern France. With an empire that stretched across Europe from Poland to France, Hitler seemed poised to attack Britain.

The new British prime minister, **Winston Churchill**, vowed that Britain, unlike France, would never surrender to Hitler. "We shall fight on the seas and oceans [and] . . . in the air," he proclaimed, "whatever the cost may be, we shall fight on the beaches, . . . and in the fields and in the streets." Churchill's defiance stiffened British resolve for a defense against Hitler's attack, which began in mid-June 1940 when wave after wave of German bombers targeted

British military installations and cities, killing tens of thousands of civilians. The undermanned and outgunned Royal Air Force fought as doggedly as Churchill had predicted and finally won the **Battle of Britain** by November, clearing German bombers from British skies and handing Hitler his first defeat. Churchill praised the valiant British pilots, declaring that "never . . . was so much owed by so many to so few." Advance knowledge of German plans aided British pilots. The British made use of the new technology of radar and also learned to decipher Germany's top-secret military codes. Battered and exhausted by German attacks, Britain needed American help to continue to fight, as Churchill repeatedly wrote Roosevelt in private.

From Neutrality to the Arsenal of Democracy

When Hitler attacked Poland, Roosevelt issued an official proclamation of American neutrality. Most Americans condemned German aggression and favored Britain and France, but isolationism remained powerful. Roosevelt feared that if Congress did not repeal the arms embargo mandated by the Neutrality Act of 1937, France and Britain would soon succumb to the Nazi onslaught. After heated debate, Congress voted in November 1939 to revise the neutrality legislation and allow belligerent nations to buy arms, as well as nonmilitary supplies, on a cash-and-carry basis.

In practice, the revised neutrality law permitted Britain and France to purchase American war materiel and carry it across the Atlantic in their own ships, thereby shielding American vessels from attack by German submarines lurking in the Atlantic. Roosevelt wrote a friend, "What worries me is that public opinion . . . is patting itself on the back every morning and thanking God for the Atlantic Ocean (and the Pacific Ocean)" and underestimating "the serious implications" of the European war "for our own future." Roosevelt searched for a way to aid Britain short of entering a formal alliance or declaring war against Germany. Churchill pleaded for American destroyers, aircraft, and munitions, but he had no money to buy them under the prevailing cash-and-carry neutrality law. By late summer in 1940, as the Battle of Britain raged, Roosevelt concocted a scheme to deliver fifty old destroyers to Britain in exchange for American access to British bases in the Western Hemisphere. Claiming the constitutional power to strengthen America's defenses by swapping destroyers for bases, Roosevelt took the first steps toward building a firm Anglo-American alliance against Hitler.

While German Luftwaffe (air force) pilots bombed Britain, Roosevelt decided to run for an unprecedented third term as president in

Battle of Britain Survivors
During the Battle of Britain, German bombers targeted civilians in British cities. Luftwaffe pilots destroyed the Liverpool home (in the background) of Sarah Manson, the sixty-eight-year-old woman shown here with her daughter and grandchildren. Thousands of other British families suffered similar fates before the Royal Air Force managed to sweep the Luftwaffe from the skies over Britain. Subsequently, the British Bomber Command conducted saturation bombing raids against German cities, causing hundreds of thousands of civilian casualties. During World War II, more civilians were killed in military engagements than in any previous war.
© Bettmann/Corbis.

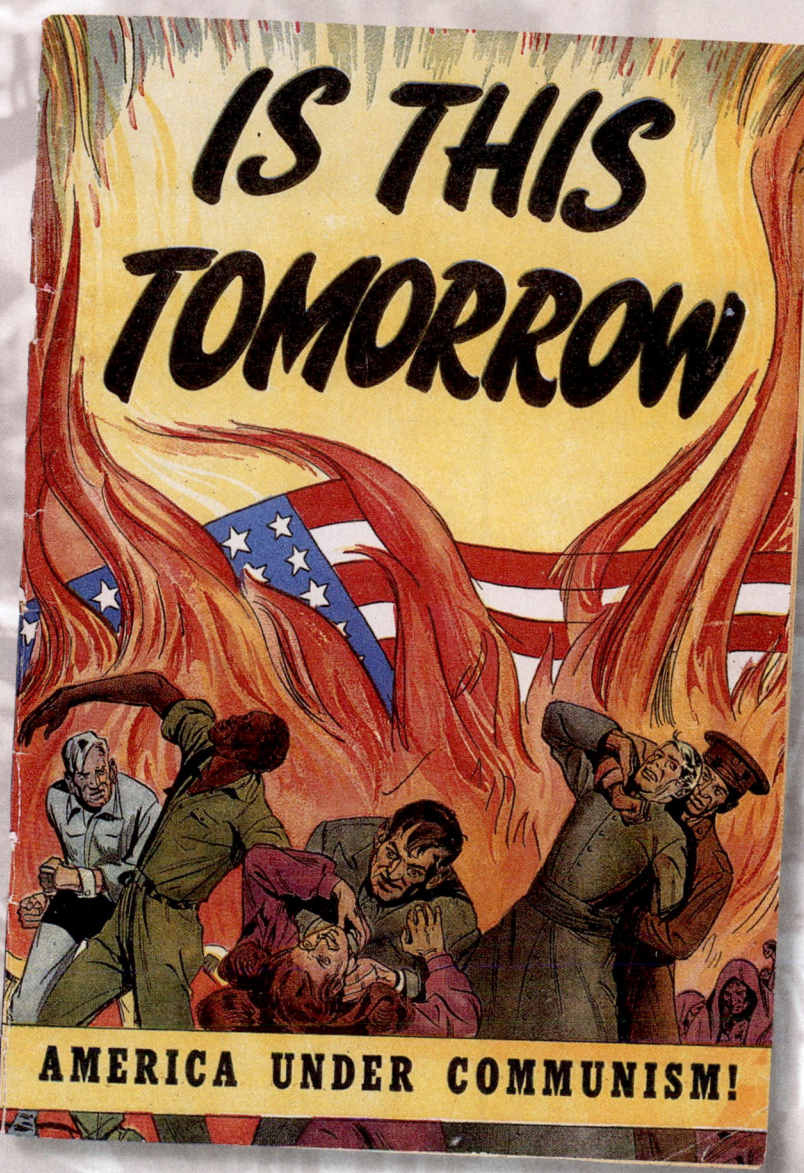

IS THIS TOMORROW

AMERICA UNDER COMMUNISM!

COLD WAR COMIC BOOK

In August 1945, Americans all over the world celebrated the end of World War II, as did these servicemen and -women stationed in London, shown in the background photo. Very quickly, however, a new threat emerged. Fear of communism dominated much of postwar American life and politics, even invading popular culture. Four million copies of this comic book, published by a religious organization in 1947, painted a terrifying picture of what would happen to Americans if the Soviets took over the country. Such takeover stories appeared in movies, cartoons, and magazines as well as in other comic books.

Comic book: Collection of Charles H. Christensen; background: National Archives.

LINKING TO THE PAST

Link events in this chapter to earlier events.

1. How did America's involvement in World War II differ from its participation in World War I? Consider diplomacy, allies and enemies, wartime military and economic policies, and social and cultural changes. (See chapter 22.)

2. Why did World War II succeed in creating the full economic recovery that remained elusive during the New Deal? Consider specifically the scope and limits of New Deal economic reforms and how they changed, if at all, during World War II. (See chapter 24.)

▶ **For practice quizzes and other study tools,** visit the Online Study Guide at **bedfordstmartins.com/roark**.

TIMELINE 1935–1945

1935–1937	• Congress passes neutrality acts.
1936	• Nazi Germany occupies Rhineland.
	• Italian armies conquer Ethiopia.
	• Spanish civil war begins.
1937	• Japanese troops capture Nanjing.
	• Roosevelt introduces his quarantine policy.
1938	• Hitler annexes Austria.
1939	• German troops occupy Czechoslovakia.
	• Nazi-Soviet nonaggression pact.
	• **September 1.** Germany's attack on Poland begins World War II.
1940	• Germany invades Denmark, Norway, France, Belgium, Luxembourg, and the Netherlands.
	• British and French evacuate from Dunkirk.
	• Vichy government installed in France.
	• Battle of Britain.
	• Tripartite Pact signed by Japan, Germany, and Italy.
1941	• Lend-Lease Act.
	• **June.** Germany invades Soviet Union.
	• **August.** Atlantic Charter issued.
	• **December 7.** Japanese attack Pearl Harbor.
1942	• Roosevelt authorizes internment of Japanese Americans.
	• Japan captures Philippines.
	• Congress of Racial Equality founded.
	• Battles of Coral Sea and Midway.
	• Roosevelt authorizes Manhattan Project.
	• **November.** U.S. forces invade North Africa.
1943	• Allied leaders demand unconditional surrender of Axis powers.
	• Race riots in 47 cities.
	• U.S. and British forces invade Sicily.
1944	• **June 6.** D Day.
1945	• **February.** Yalta Conference.
	• **April 12.** Roosevelt dies; Vice President Harry Truman becomes president.
	• **May 7.** Germany surrenders.
	• **July.** United States joins United Nations.
	• **August 6, 9.** United States drops atomic bombs on Hiroshima and Nagasaki.
	• **August 14.** Japan surrenders, ending World War II.

861

Reviewing Chapter 25

REVIEW QUESTIONS

Use key terms and dates to support your answer.

1. Why did isolationism during the 1930s concern Roosevelt? (pp. 825–827)

2. How did Roosevelt attempt to balance American isolationism with the increasingly ominous international scene of the late 1930s? (pp. 827–833)

3. How did the Roosevelt administration mobilize the human and industrial resources necessary to fight a two-front war? (pp. 833–838)

4. How did the United States seek to counter the Japanese in the Pacific and the Germans in Europe? (pp. 838–843)

5. How did the war influence American society? (pp. 843–848)

6. Why did Truman elect to use the atomic bomb against Japan? (pp. 849–857)

MAKING CONNECTIONS

Draw on key terms, the timeline, and review questions.

1. Did isolationism bolster or undermine national security and national economic interests? Discuss Roosevelt's evolving answer to this question as revealed in his administration's policies toward Europe. In your answer, consider how other constraints (such as politics, history, and ethics) affected administration policies.

2. World War II brought new prosperity to many Americans. Who benefited most from the wartime economy? What financial limitations did various members of society face, and why?

3. Japan's attack on Pearl Harbor plunged the United States into war with the Axis powers. How did the United States recover from this attack to play a decisive role in the Allies' victory? Discuss three American military or diplomatic actions and their contribution to the defeat of the Axis powers.

4. As the United States battled racist regimes abroad, the realities of discrimination at home came sharply into focus. How did minorities' contributions to the war effort as soldiers and laborers draw attention to these problems? What were the political implications of these developments? In your answer, consider both grassroots political action and federal policy.

war, as the Soviets seized political control of eastern Europe, a Communist revolution swept China, and national liberation movements emerged in the colonial empires of Britain and France. The forces unleashed by World War II would shape the United States and the rest of the world for decades to come. Before the ashes of World War II had cooled, America's wartime alliance with the Soviet Union fractured, igniting a Cold War between the superpowers. To resist global communism, the United States became, in effect, the policeman of the free world, repudiating the pre–World War II legacy of isolationism.

▶ Selected Bibliography

General Works

Max Arthur, ed., *Forgotten Voices of the Second World War: A New History of World War Two in the Words of the Men and Women Who Were There* (2004).

Michael Beschloss, *The Conquerors: Roosevelt, Truman, and the Destruction of Hitler's Germany, 1941–1945* (2002).

Richard Evans, *The Third Reich at War* (2010).

Thomas Fleming, *The New Dealers' War: Franklin D. Roosevelt and the War within World War II* (2001).

Martin Folly, *The U.S. and World War II: The Awakening Giant* (2002).

Peter Fritzsche, *Life and Death in the Third Reich* (2009).

David M. Kennedy, *Freedom from Fear: The American People in Depression and War, 1929–1945* (1999).

Mark Mazower, *Hitler's Empire: How the Nazis Ruled Europe* (2008).

Timothy Snyder, *Bloodlands: Europe between Hitler and Stalin* (2010).

Paul W. Tibbets Jr., *The Tibbets Story* (1978).

John Toland, *The Rising Sun: The Decline and Fall of the Japanese Empire, 1936–1945* (2001).

Adam Tooze, *The Wages of Destruction: The Making and Breaking of the Nazi Economy* (2006).

Foreign Policy

Tokomo Akami, *Internationalizing the Pacific: The U.S., Japan, and the Institute of Pacific Relations in War and Peace, 1919–1945* (2002).

Elizabeth Borgwardt, *A New Deal for the World: America's Vision for Human Rights* (2005).

Tsuyoshi Hasegawa, *Racing the Enemy: Stalin, Truman, and the Surrender of Japan* (2005).

J. Robert Moskin, *Mr. Truman's War: The Final Victories of World War II and the Birth of the Postwar World* (2002).

David Reynolds, *From Munich to Pearl Harbor: Roosevelt's America and the Origins of the Second World War* (2001).

Gaddis Smith, *American Diplomacy during the Second World War, 1941–1945* (1985).

Mobilization and the Home Front

Gerald Astor, *The Right to Fight: A History of African Americans in the Military* (1998).

Jeffrey F. Burton et al., *Confinement and Ethnicity: An Overview of World War II Japanese American Relocation Sites* (2002).

Stephanie A. Carpenter, *On the Farm Front: The Women's Land Army in World War II* (2003).

Mark Jonathan Harris, Franklin D. Mitchell, and Steve J. Schechter, *The Home Front: America during World War II* (1985).

Susan Hartmann, *The Home Front and Beyond: American Women in the 1940s* (1982).

John W. Jeffries, *Wartime America: The World War II Home Front* (1996).

Christopher Moore, *Fighting for America: Black Soldiers — The Unsung Heroes of World War II* (2005).

Wendy Ng, *Japanese American Internment during World War II* (2002).

Military Events

Rick Atkinson, *The Day of Battle: The War in Sicily and Italy, 1943–1944* (2008).

Antony Beevor, *D-Day: The Battle for Normandy* (2009).

John Dower, *War without Mercy: Race and Power in the Pacific War* (1986).

Max Hastings, *Overlord: D-Day and the Battle for Normandy* (2006).

Gerald F. Linderman, *The World within War: America's Combat Experience in World War II* (1997).

Peter Novick, *The Holocaust in American Life* (1999).

Richard Overy, *Why the Allies Won* (1996).

Peter Schrijvers, *The GI War against Japan: American Soldiers in Asia and the Pacific during World War II* (2002).

Thomas W. Zeiler, *Unconditional Defeat: Japan, America, and the End of World War II* (2004).

▶ FOR MORE BOOKS ABOUT TOPICS IN THIS CHAPTER, see the Online Bibliography at **bedfordstmartins.com/roark**.

▶ FOR ADDITIONAL PRIMARY SOURCES FROM THIS PERIOD, see Michael Johnson, ed., *Reading the American Past*, Fifth Edition.

▶ FOR WEB SITES, IMAGES, AND DOCUMENTS RELATED TO TOPICS AND PLACES IN THIS CHAPTER, visit Make History at **bedfordstmartins.com/roark**.

Hiroshima
This photo shows part of Hiroshima shortly after the atomic bomb dropped from the *Enola Gay*, leveling the densely populated city. The watch shown here was recovered from the incinerated rubble; it stopped at 8:16, when the bomb exploded. The destructive force unleashed by the atomic bomb included not only the heat and blast of the explosion itself but also the deadly radiation that maimed and killed Japanese civilians for years afterward. National Archives.

fall apart. American mobilization for World War II disproved Hitler's arrogant prophecy, as Paul Tibbets's historic flight dramatized. At a cost of 405,399 American lives, the nation united with its allies to crush the Axis aggressors into unconditional surrender. Almost all Americans believed they had won a "good war" against totalitarian evil. The Allies saved Asia and Europe from enslavement and finally halted the Nazis' genocidal campaign against Jews and many others whom the Nazis considered inferior. To secure human rights and protect the world against future wars, the Roosevelt administration took the lead in creating the United Nations.

Wartime production lifted the nation out of the Great Depression. The gross national product soared to four times what it had been when Roosevelt became president in 1933. Jobs in defense industries eliminated chronic unemployment, provided wages for millions of women workers and African American migrants from southern farms, and boosted Americans' prosperity. Ahead stretched the challenge of maintaining that prosperity while reintegrating millions of uniformed men and women.

By the end of the war, the United States had emerged as a global superpower. Wartime mobilization made the American economy the strongest in the world, buttressed by the military clout of the nation's nuclear monopoly. Although the war left much of the world a rubble-strewn wasteland, the American mainland had enjoyed immunity from attack. The Japanese occupation of China had left 50 million people without homes and millions more dead, maimed, and orphaned. The German offensive against the Soviet Union had killed more than 20 million Russian soldiers and civilians. Germany and Japan lay in ruins, their economies and societies as shattered as their military forces. But in the gruesome balance sheet of war, the Axis powers had inflicted far more grief, misery, and destruction on the global victims of their aggression than they had suffered in return.

As the dominant Western nation in the postwar world, the United States asserted its leadership in the reconstruction of Europe while occupying Japan and overseeing its economic and political recovery. America soon confronted new challenges in the tense aftermath of the surrender unconditionally or face utter ruin. When the Japanese failed to respond by the deadline, Truman ordered that an atomic bomb be dropped on a Japanese city not already heavily damaged by American raids. The bomb that Colonel Paul Tibbets and his crew released over **Hiroshima** on August 6 leveled the city and incinerated about 100,000 people. Three days later, after the Japanese government still refused to surrender, the second atomic bomb killed nearly as many civilians at **Nagasaki**. Robert Oppenheimer celebrated the bombings with other Los Alamos scientists responsible for creating the weapons by declaring that "his only regret was that we hadn't developed the bomb in time to have used it against the Germans."

With American assurance that the emperor could retain his throne after the Allies took over, Japan surrendered on August 14. On a troop ship departing from Europe for what would have been the final assault on Japan, an American soldier spoke for millions of others when he heard the wonderful news that the killing was over: "We are going to grow to adulthood after all."

While all Americans welcomed peace, Robert Oppenheimer and others worried about the consequences of unleashing atomic power. Shortly after the war, Oppenheimer warned: "We have made a thing, a most terrible weapon that has altered abruptly and profoundly the nature of the world . . . a thing that by all the standards of the world we grew up in is an evil thing." Almost every American, including Oppenheimer, believed that the "evil thing" had brought peace in 1945, but nobody knew what it would bring in the future, although everybody knew it would inevitably shape the world to come, as in fact it did.

REVIEW Why did Truman elect to use the atomic bomb against Japan?

▶ Conclusion: Allied Victory and America's Emergence as a Superpower

Shortly after Pearl Harbor, Hitler pronounced America "a decayed country . . . half Judaized, and the other half Negrified"; a country "where everything is built on the dollar" and bound to

Major Campaigns and Battles of World War II, 1939–1945

September 1, 1939	Germany attacks Poland.
September 3, 1939	Britain and France declare war on Germany.
April 1940	Germany attacks Denmark and Norway.
May 1940	Germany invades Netherlands, Belgium, Luxembourg, and France.
June 1940	Italy joins Germany in war against Allies.
June–November 1940	Battle of Britain.
June 22, 1941	Germany invades Soviet Union.
December 7, 1941	Japan attacks Pearl Harbor.
December 8, 1941	U.S. Congress declares war on Japan.
December 11, 1941	Germany and Italy declare war on United States.
January 2–May 6, 1942	Battles of Bataan and Corregidor.
May 7–8, 1942	Battle of the Coral Sea.
June 3–6, 1942	Battle of Midway.
August 1942–February 1943	Battle of Guadalcanal.
August 21, 1942–January 31, 1943	Battle of Stalingrad.
October 23–November 5, 1942	British halt Germans at Battle of El-Alamein.
November 1942–May 1943	Allies mount North African campaign.
July 10, 1943	Allies begin Italian invasion through Sicily.
June 4, 1944	Allies liberate Rome from German occupation.
June 6, 1944	D Day — Allied forces invade Normandy.
August 25, 1944	Allies liberate Paris.
September 12, 1944	Allies enter Germany.
October 23–26, 1944	Battle of Leyte Gulf.
December 16, 1944–January 31, 1945	Battle of the Bulge.
February 19–March 16, 1945	Battle of Iwo Jima.
April 1–June 21, 1945	Battle of Okinawa.
May 2, 1945	Soviet forces capture Berlin.
August 6, 1945	United States drops atomic bomb on Hiroshima.
August 9, 1945	United States drops atomic bomb on Nagasaki.

Marine Attack on Saipan
Marines fought Japanese soldiers on Saipan in close-quarter combat in 1944, as in many subsequent island campaigns in the Pacific theater. Here, Marines have overtaken a Japanese position and are fighting in the midst of enemy soldiers they have just killed. Japanese soldiers were commanded to fight to their deaths rather than surrender, even after their ultimate defeat was certain — a command they mostly obeyed. Such determined, suicidal resistance drastically increased American casualties and delayed American progress in the Pacific island-hopping campaign. National Archives.

Atomic Warfare

In mid-July 1945, as Allied forces prepared for the final assault on Japan, American scientists tested a secret weapon at an isolated desert site near Los Alamos, New Mexico. In 1942, Roosevelt had authorized the top-secret **Manhattan Project** to find a way to convert nuclear energy into a superbomb before the Germans added such a weapon to their arsenal. More than 100,000 Americans, led by scientists, engineers, and military officers at Los Alamos, worked frantically to win the race for an atomic bomb. Germany surrendered two and a half months before the test on July 16, 1945, when scientists first witnessed an atomic explosion that sent a mushroom cloud of debris eight miles into the atmosphere. After watching the successful test of the bomb, J. Robert Oppenheimer, the head scientist at Los Alamos, remarked soberly, "Lots of boys not grown up yet will owe their life to it."

President Truman heard about the successful bomb test when he was in Potsdam, Germany, negotiating with Stalin about postwar issues. Truman realized that the atomic bomb could hasten the end of the war with Japan, perhaps before the Russians could attack the Japanese, as Stalin had pledged at Yalta. Within a few months after the defeat of Germany, Truman also recognized that the bomb gave the United States a devastating atomic monopoly that could be used to counter Soviet ambitions and advance American interests in the postwar world.

Truman saw no reason not to use the atomic bomb against Japan if doing so would save American lives. Despite numerous defeats, Japan still had more than 6 million reserves at home for a last-ditch defense against the anticipated Allied assault, which U.S. military advisers estimated would kill at least 250,000 Americans. But first he issued an ultimatum: Japan must

МЫ ЗЛОМУ ВРАГУ ВСЕ ОТРЕЖЕМ ПУТИ,
ИЗ ПЕТЛИ, ИЗ ЭТОЙ ЕМУ НЕ УЙТИ!

СОГЛАШЕНИЕ

ДОГОВОР

МЕЖДУ СССР
АНГЛИЕЙ и США

VISUAL ACTIVITY

The Allied War Effort
The Russian poster shown here illustrates the combined efforts of the Allies, declaring, "We won't let the evil enemy escape the noose. He will not evade it." Museum of World War II, Natick, MA, www.museumofworldwarii.com.

READING THE IMAGE: What does the depiction of Hitler on the Russian poster suggest about his leadership and character?
CONNECTIONS: What does the poster suggest about the importance of the alliance among the major Allied powers?

new tanks, aircraft, and artillery to rearm the Soviet military. Through sheer hard work, the productivity of Soviet war industries more than doubled during the war. Meanwhile, food production plummeted, allowing the average Russian only one-fourth the amount of food available to the average German. Soviet casualties dwarfed the losses of the other Allies. For every American killed during the war, forty-five Soviets died. No contribution to Allied victory was more important than the monumental success of the Soviet Union on the eastern front.

Thinking about Cause and Effect

1. Specifically, how did the Allies help one another defeat the Axis powers?

2. Why was the eastern front so important to the Allied victory?

Joseph Steinbacher and other GIs who had suffered "horrendous" casualties in the Philippines were now told by their commanding officer, "Men, in a few short months we are going to invade [Japan]. . . . We will be going in on the first wave and are expecting ninety percent casualties the first day. . . . For the few of us left alive the war will be over." Steinbacher later recalled his mental attitude at that moment: "I know that I am now a walking dead man and will not have a snowball's chance in hell of making it through the last great battle to conquer the home islands of Japan."

Why Did the Allies Win World War II?

An indispensable factor in Allied victory in World War II was the alliance among the major powers: the United States, Great Britain, and the Soviet Union. Fighting alone, none of the Allies could have prevailed against Nazi Germany. Together, they were able to defeat what had been the strongest military power in the world.

The major Axis nations — Germany and Japan — did almost nothing to help each other. In the Pacific, Japan fought alone against the United States and its other allies, especially Australia and China. Britain and the Soviet Union contributed relatively little to Allied efforts in the Pacific.

In Europe, Germany enjoyed the support of Hungary, Romania, Bulgaria, and Italy, but none of these nations had the resources and industrial might to field a fully modern army. The Germans conscripted tens of thousands of men from the territories they occupied as their armies swept east, but such coerced recruits made poorly motivated soldiers.

In contrast, the Allies had a single galvanizing purpose: to defeat Hitler. The United States devoted only about 15 percent of its war effort to defeat Japan; the remaining 85 percent was directed against Germany. Little else united the Allies. Political and ideological differences between the capitalist democracies and a Communist dictatorship produced suspicion and mistrust. Nonetheless, the Allies collaborated to force the unconditional surrender of Germany. Three militarily significant consequences of the wartime alliance stand out as decisive ingredients of Allied victory: American material support for Britain and the Soviet Union; American and British bombing campaigns and the D Day invasion of Europe; and the Red Army's success in stopping the eastward advance of the German army at Stalingrad, then relentlessly driving it back to Berlin.

The flood of military supplies that poured out of American factories during the war made Allied victory possible. In total, the United States produced two-thirds of all Allied military equipment. In addition to shipping hundreds of millions of tons of supplies to Britain and stockpiling equipment for the D Day invasion, the United States sent more than half a million military vehicles to the Soviet Union, accounting for the bulk of the Red Army's motorized transportation. By 1944, American refineries supplied 90 percent of the Allies' high-octane gasoline, prompting Stalin to raise a toast at the Teheran conference "to the American auto industry and the American oil industry," which met the needs of "this . . . war of engines and octanes." American food shipments provided the equivalent of one meal a day for each Russian soldier. The American canned meat Spam was distributed so widely that Soviet troops called it "The Second Front," a sarcastic reference to the Americans' delay in opening a second front in western Europe.

The British and American bombing campaign against German targets in western Europe served as a crucial second-front surrogate until D Day, and it eventually allowed Allied pilots to rule the skies. The bombing campaign reduced the production of tanks, airplanes, and trucks by more than a third and diverted two-thirds of Germany's aircraft and three-quarters of its antiaircraft weapons from supporting the infantry on the eastern front to protecting German cities from Allied air attacks. In addition, improvements in Allied fighter planes allowed British and American pilots to decimate the Luftwaffe. Although the German civilian population and Allied air crews suffered huge casualties as a result of the air campaign, it decisively aided the Soviets' battle against the Germans on the eastern front.

But neither the bombing campaign nor the mountains of American supplies would have won the war if the Soviet Union had not stopped the seemingly unstoppable advance of the German Wehrmacht in the east. Within six months of Hitler's surprise attack on the Soviet Union in June 1941, Stalin's army had lost 4 million soldiers and nearly all its tanks and airplanes, and German armies threatened Moscow. U.S. military officials expected Stalin to capitulate within two or three months. Instead, the Red Army regrouped and managed to halt the Germans' eastward advance by early 1943.

Reversal of the German assault required colossal sacrifices by the people of the Soviet Union. As the German army swept east during 1941, Russians frantically dismantled more than 1,500 industrial plants about to be captured by the Nazis, shipped them east of the Ural Mountains, and reassembled them there. They also built new plants and soon began producing thousands of

way for Allied victory in the Philippines. While the Philippine campaign was under way, American forces captured two crucial islands — Iwo Jima and Okinawa — from which they planned to launch an attack on the Japanese homeland. To defend Okinawa, Japanese leaders ordered thousands of suicide pilots, known as *kamikaze*, to crash their bomb-laden planes into Allied ships. But instead of destroying the American fleet, they demolished the last vestige of the Japanese air force. By June 1945, the Japanese were nearly defenseless on the sea and in the air. Still, their leaders prepared to fight to the death for their homeland.

MAP ACTIVITY

Map 25.5 The Pacific Theater of World War II, 1941–1945

To drive the Japanese from their far-flung empire, the Allies launched two combined naval and military offensives — one to recapture the Philippines and then attack Japanese forces in China, the other to hop from island to island in the Central Pacific toward the Japanese mainland.

READING THE MAP: What was the extent of Japanese control up until August 1942? Which nations in the Pacific theater sided with the Allies? Which nations remained neutral?

CONNECTIONS: Describe the economic and military motivations behind Japanese domination of the region. How and when did they achieve this dominance? Judging from this map, what strategic and geographic concerns might have prompted Truman and his advisers to consider using the atomic bomb against Japan?

inch-by-inch combat to root Japanese fighters out of bunkers and caves.

While the island-hopping campaign kept pressure on Japanese forces, the Allies invaded the Philippines in the fall of 1944. In the four-day **Battle of Leyte Gulf**, one of the greatest naval battles in world history, the American fleet crushed the Japanese armada, clearing the sweeping in from the west reached the banks of the Elbe River, the agreed-upon rendezvous with the Red Army, and paused while the Soviets smashed into Berlin. In three weeks of vicious house-to-house fighting, the Red Army captured Berlin on May 2. Hitler committed suicide on April 30, and the provisional German government surrendered unconditionally on May 7. The war in Europe was finally over, with the sacrifice of 135,576 American soldiers, nearly 250,000 British troops, and 9 million Russian combatants. (See "Historical Question," page 854.)

Roosevelt did not live to witness the end of the war. On April 12, while resting in Warm Springs, Georgia, he suffered a fatal stroke. Americans grieved for the man who had led them through years of depression and world war, and they worried about his untested successor, Vice President Harry Truman.

The Defeat of Japan

After the punishing defeats in the Coral Sea and at Midway, Japan had to fend off Allied naval and air attacks. In 1943, British and American forces, along with Indian and Chinese allies, launched an offensive against Japanese outposts in southern Asia, pushing through Burma and into China, where Jiang's armies continued to resist conquest. In the Pacific, Americans and their allies attacked Japanese strongholds by sea, air, and land, moving island by island toward the Japanese homeland (Map 25.5).

The island-hopping campaign began in August 1942, when American Marines landed on Guadalcanal in the southern Pacific. For the next six months, a savage battle raged for control of the strategic area. Finally, during the night of February 8, 1943, Japanese forces withdrew. The terrible losses on both sides indicated to the Marines how costly it would be to defeat Japan. After the battle, Joseph Steinbacher, a twenty-one-year-old from Alabama, sailed from San Francisco to New Guinea, where, he recalled, "all the cannon fodder waited to be assigned" to replace the killed and wounded.

In mid-1943, Allied forces launched offensives in New Guinea and the Solomon Islands that gradually secured the South Pacific. In the Central Pacific, amphibious forces conquered the Gilbert and Marshall islands, which served as forward bases for air assaults on the Japanese home islands. As the Allies attacked island after island, Japanese soldiers were ordered to refuse to surrender no matter how hopeless their plight. The fierce Japanese resistance spurred remorseless Allied bombing attacks on Japanese-occupied islands, followed by amphibious landings by Marines and grinding,

Yalta Conference
In February 1945, U.S. president Franklin Roosevelt (middle) and British prime minister Winston Churchill (left) met with Russian leader Joseph Stalin (right) at the Black Sea resort of Yalta to plan the postwar reconstruction of Europe. Roosevelt, near the end of his life, and Churchill, soon to suffer a reelection defeat, look weary next to the resolute "Man of Steel." Controversy would later arise over whether a stronger stand by the American and British leaders could have prevented the Soviet Union from imposing Communist rule on eastern Europe. U.S. Army.

1945), as the Allies termed it, German forces drove fifty-five miles into Allied lines before being stopped at Bastogne. More than 70,000 Allied soldiers were killed, including more Americans than in any other battle of the war. The Nazis lost more than 100,000 men and hundreds of tanks, fatally depleting Hitler's reserves.

In February 1945, while Allied armies relentlessly pushed German forces backward, Churchill, Stalin, and Roosevelt met secretly at the **Yalta Conference** (named for the Russian resort town where it was held) to discuss their plans for the postwar world. Seriously ill and noticeably frail, Roosevelt managed to secure Stalin's promise to permit votes of self-determination in the eastern European countries occupied by the Red Army. The Allies pledged to support Jiang Jieshi (Chiang Kai-shek) as the leader of China. The Soviet Union obtained a role in the postwar governments of Korea and Manchuria in exchange for entering the war against Japan after the defeat of Germany.

The "Big Three" also agreed on the creation of a new international peacekeeping organization, the **United Nations (UN)**. All nations would have a place in the UN General Assembly, but the Security Council would wield decisive power, and its permanent representatives from the Allied powers — China, France, Great Britain, the Soviet Union, and the United States — would possess a veto over UN actions. The Senate ratified the United Nations Charter in July 1945 by a vote of 89 to 2, reflecting the triumph of internationalism during the nation's mobilization for war.

While Allied armies sped toward Berlin, Allied warplanes dropped more bombs after D Day than in all the previous European bombing raids combined. By April 11, Allied armies

D-Day Invasion
"Taxi to Hell—and Back" is what Robert Sargent called his photograph of the D-Day invasion of Normandy on June 6, 1944. Amid a dense fleet of landing craft, men lucky enough to have made it through rough seas and enemy fire struggle onto the beach to open a second front in Europe. Most of the soldiers in this first wave were cut down by enemy fire from the cliffs beyond the beach. Library of Congress.

Legend

- Axis powers, including annexed territory
- Extent of Axis control, early Nov. 1942
- Allied powers
- Neutral nations
- → Allied forces
- ✳ Major battle (Allied victory)

ATLANTIC OCEAN
ICELAND
North Sea
GREAT BRITAIN
IRELAND
London
NORWAY
SWEDEN
DENMARK
Baltic Sea
FINLAND
Murmansk
Archangel
Leningrad Besieged Sept. 1942–Jan. 1943
Moscow
SOVIET UNION
Danzig
Warsaw
Berlin Captured May 2, 1945
GERMANY
NETH.
BELG.
Normandy D Day June 6, 1944
LUX.
Battle of the Bulge Dec. 16, 1944–Jan. 31, 1945
FRANCE
Paris Liberated Aug. 25, 1944
Apr. 1945
Sept. 1944
July 1944
Mar. 1944
Aug. 1944
Aug. 1943
Stalingrad Aug. 21, 1942–Jan. 31, 1943
UKRAINE
POLAND
SLOVAKIA
AUSTRIA
SWITZ.
HUNGARY
ROMANIA
CROATIA
SERBIA
BULGARIA
MONTENEGRO
VICHY FRANCE
Aug. 1944
ITALY
Corsica
Sardinia
Rome Liberated June 4, 1944
Adriatic Sea
ALBANIA (It.)
GREECE
Black Sea
TURKEY
PORTUGAL
SPAIN
Casablanca
SP. MOROCCO
MOROCCO
Nov. 1942
FRENCH NORTH AFRICA (Vichy France) Joined Allies Nov. 1942
Jul 1943
Tunis Occupied May 12, 1943
Sicily
Kasserine Pass Feb. 14–26, 1943
TUNISIA
ALGERIA
LIBYA (It.)
Mediterranean Sea
Nov. 1942
Rhodes (It.)
Crete (Gr.)
Cyprus (Br.)
LEBANON (Fr.)
SYRIA
IRAQ
PALESTINE (Br.)
Suez Canal
TRANSJORDAN
SAUDI ARABIA
El-Alamein Oct. 23–Nov. 5, 1942
Alexandria
EGYPT

N W E S

0   200   400 miles
0   200   400 kilometers

MAP ACTIVITY

Map 25.4 The European Theater of World War II, 1942–1945

The Russian reversal of the German offensive at Stalingrad and Leningrad, combined with Allied landings in North Africa and Normandy, trapped Germany in a closing vise of Allied armies on all sides.

READING THE MAP: By November 1942, which nations or parts of nations in the European theater were under Axis control? Which had been absorbed by the Axis powers before the war? Which nations remained neutral? Which ones were affiliated with the Allies?

CONNECTIONS: What were the three fronts in the European theater? When did the Allies initiate actions on each front, and why did Churchill, Stalin, and Roosevelt disagree on the timing of the opening of these fronts?

▶ Toward Unconditional Surrender

By February 1943, Soviet defenders had finally defeated the massive German offensive against **Stalingrad**, turning the tide of the war in Europe. After gargantuan sacrifices in fighting that had lasted for eighteen months and killed more than 95 percent of the Russian soldiers and noncommissioned officers engaged at Stalingrad, the Red Army forced Hitler's Wehrmacht to turn back toward the west. Stalin continued to urge Britain and the United States to open a second front in France, but that offensive was postponed for more than a year after the victory at Stalingrad. In the Pacific, the Allies had halted the expansion of the Japanese empire but now had the deadly task of dislodging Japanese defenders from the far-flung outposts they still occupied. Allied military planners devised a strategy to annihilate Axis resistance by taking advantage of America's industrial superiority.

From Bombing Raids to Berlin

While the Allied campaigns in North Africa and Italy were under way, British and American pilots flew bombing missions from England to German-occupied territories and to Germany itself as an airborne substitute for the delayed second front on the ground. During night raids, British bombers targeted general areas, hoping to hit civilians, create terror, and undermine morale. Beginning with Paul Tibbets's flight in August 1942, American pilots flew heavily armored B-17s from English airfields in daytime raids on industrial targets vital for the German war machine.

German air defenses took a fearsome toll on Allied pilots and aircraft. In 1943, two-thirds of American airmen did not survive to complete their twenty-five-mission tours of duty. In all, 85,000 American airmen were killed in the skies over Europe. Many others were shot down and held as prisoners of war. In February 1944, the arrival of America's durable and deadly P-51 Mustang fighter gave Allied bombers superior protection. The Mustangs slowly began to sweep the Luftwaffe from the skies, allowing bombers to penetrate deep into Germany and pound civilian and military targets around the clock.

In November 1943, Churchill, Roosevelt, and Stalin met in Teheran to discuss wartime strategy and the second front. Roosevelt conceded to Stalin that the Soviet Union would exercise de facto control of the eastern European countries that the Red Army occupied as it rolled back the still-potent German Wehrmacht. Stalin agreed to enter the war against Japan once Germany finally surrendered, in effect promising to open a second front in the Pacific theater. Roosevelt and Churchill promised that they would at last launch a massive second-front assault in northern France, code-named Overlord, scheduled for May 1944.

General Eisenhower was assigned overall command of Allied forces and stockpiled mountains of military supplies in England. German defenders, directed by General Erwin Rommel, fortified the cliffs and mined the beaches of northwestern France. But the huge deployment of Hitler's armies in the east, which were trying to halt the Red Army's westward offensive, left too few German troops to stop the millions of Allied soldiers waiting to attack. More decisive, years of Allied air raids had decimated the German Luftwaffe, which could send aloft only 300 fighter planes against 12,000 Allied aircraft.

> **"[We] were exhausted and we were exultant. We had survived D Day!"**
> —Naval officer TRACY SUGARMAN

After frustrating delays caused by stormy weather, Eisenhower launched the largest amphibious assault in world history on **D Day**, June 6, 1944 (Map 25.4). Rough seas and deadly fire from German machine guns slowed the assault, but Allied soldiers finally succeeded in securing the beachhead. As naval officer Tracy Sugarman recalled, "What I thought were piles of cordwood [on the beach] I later learned were the bodies of 2,500 men killed by withering fire from the Nazi gun emplacements." An officer told his men, "The only people on this beach are the dead and those that are going to die — now let's get the hell out of here." And they did, finally surmounting the cliffs that loomed over the beach and destroying the German defenses. Sugarman reported that he and the other GIs who made the landing "were exhausted and we were exultant. We had survived D Day!"

Within a week, a flood of soldiers, tanks, and other military equipment swamped the Normandy beaches and propelled Allied forces toward Germany. On August 25, the Allies liberated Paris from four years of Nazi occupation. As the giant pincers of the Allied and Soviet armies closed on Germany in December 1944, Hitler ordered a counterattack to capture the Allies' essential supply port at Antwerp, Belgium. In the Battle of the Bulge (December 16, 1944, to January 31,

The Holocaust, 1933–1945

Principal German concentration and extermination camp

Reaction to the Holocaust

Since the 1930s, the Nazis had persecuted Jews in Germany and every German-occupied territory, causing many Jews to seek asylum beyond Hitler's reach. (See "Beyond America's Borders," page 846.) Roosevelt sympathized with the refugees' pleas for help, but he did not want to jeopardize his foreign policy or offend American voters. After Hitler's Anschluss in 1938, thousands of Austrian Jews sought to immigrate to the United States, but 82 percent of Americans opposed admitting them, and they were turned away. Roosevelt tried to persuade countries in Latin America and Africa to accept Jewish refugees, but only the Dominican Republic agreed to do so, eventually providing refuge for about 800 people.

In 1942, numerous reports reached the United States that Hitler was sending Jews, Gypsies, religious and political dissenters, homosexuals, and others to concentration camps, where old people, children, and others deemed too weak to work were systematically slaughtered and cremated, while the able-bodied were put to work at slave labor until they died of starvation and abuse. Despite such reports, U.S. officials refused to grant asylum to Jewish refugees. Most Americans, including top officials, believed that reports of the killing camps were exaggerated. Only 152,000 of Europe's millions of Jews managed to gain refuge in the United States prior to America's entry into the war. Afterward, the number of refugees admitted dropped steadily, to just 2,400 by 1944.

Desperate to stem the killing, the World Jewish Congress appealed to the Allies to bomb the death camps and the railroad tracks leading to them in order to hamper the killing and block further shipments of victims. Intent on achieving military victory as soon as possible, the Allies repeatedly turned down such bombing requests, arguing that the air forces could not spare resources from their military missions.

The nightmare of the **Holocaust** was all too real. When Russian troops arrived at Auschwitz in Poland in January 1945, they found emaciated prisoners, skeletal corpses, gas chambers, pits filled with human ashes, and loot the Nazis had stripped from the dead, including hair, gold fillings, and false teeth. At last, the truth about the Holocaust began to be known beyond the Germans who had perpetrated and tolerated these atrocities and the men, women, and children who had succumbed to the genocide. By then, it was too late for the 11 million civilian victims — mostly Jews — of the Nazis' crimes against humanity.

REVIEW   How did the war influence American society?

Mass Execution of Jewish Women and Children
On October 14, 1942, Jewish women and children from the village of Mizocz in present-day Ukraine were herded into a ravine, forced to undress and lie facedown, and then shot at point-blank range by German police. This rare photograph, taken by one of the authorities at the scene, shows German officers killing the women who survived the initial gunfire. Throughout the war, Germans routinely murdered defenseless people they considered subhuman. To centralize such executions, the Nazis built death camps, where they systematically slaughtered millions of Jews and other "undesirables." Taken together, such atrocities amounted to genocide, which became known as the Holocaust. United States Holocaust Memorial Museum.

In early October 1939, as Hitler's blitzkrieg swept through Poland, Roosevelt received Einstein's letter and immediately grasped the central point, exclaiming, "What you are after is to see that the Nazis don't blow us up." Roosevelt quickly convened a small group of distinguished American scientists, who convinced the president to mount an all-out effort to learn whether an atomic bomb could be built and, if so, to build it. Only weeks before the Japanese attack on Pearl Harbor, Roosevelt decided to launch the Manhattan Project, the top-secret atomic bomb program.

Leading scientists from the United States and Britain responded to the government's appeal: "No matter what you do with the rest of your life, nothing will be as important to the future of the World as your work on this Project right now." Many of the most creative, productive, and irreplaceable scientists involved in the Manhattan Project were physicists who had fled Nazi Germany. Their efforts had brought the possibility of an atomic bomb to Roosevelt's attention. Having personally experienced Nazi anti-Semitism, they understood what was at stake — a world in which either Hitler had the atomic bomb or his enemies did.

In the end, Hitler's scientists failed to develop an atomic bomb, and Germany surrendered before the American bomb was ready to go. But

Einstein Becomes a U.S. Citizen
Nazi anti-Semitism caused Albert Einstein to renounce his German citizenship, immigrate to the United States, and — in the 1940 naturalization ceremony recorded in this photo — officially become an American citizen. He is joined here by his secretary, Helen Dukas (right), and his stepdaughter, Margot Einstein (left). Courtesy, American Institute of Physics Emilio Segré Visual Archives/Brown Brothers.

the Manhattan Project succeeded, as Paul Tibbets proved over Hiroshima, Japan, on August 6, 1945. After the war, Leo Szilard, a leader among the refugee physicists, remarked, "If Congress knew the true history of the atomic energy project . . . it would create a special medal to be given to meddling foreigners for distinguished services."

America in a Global Context

1. How did German anti-Semitism contribute to the United States' willingness to build and employ the atomic bomb?

2. In what ways were the United States' development and use of the atomic bomb "important to the future of the World"?

of GIs to better themselves and their families after the war.

After twelve turbulent years in the White House, Roosevelt was exhausted and gravely ill with heart disease, but he was determined to remain president until the war ended. His poor health made the selection of a vice presidential candidate unusually important. Convinced that many Americans had soured on liberal reform, Roosevelt chose Senator **Harry S. Truman** of Missouri as his running mate. A reliable party man from a southern border state, Truman satisfied urban Democratic leaders while not worrying white southerners who were nervous about challenges to racial segregation.

The Republicans, confident of a strong conservative upsurge in the nation, nominated as their presidential candidate the governor of New York, Thomas E. Dewey, who had made his reputation as a tough crime fighter. In the 1944 presidential campaign, Roosevelt's failing health alarmed many observers, but his frailty was outweighed by Americans' unwillingness to change presidents in the midst of the war and by Dewey's failure to persuade most voters that the New Deal was a creeping socialist menace. Voters gave Roosevelt a 53.5 percent majority, his narrowest presidential victory, ensuring his continued leadership as Dr. Win-the-War.

Nazi Anti-Semitism and the Atomic Bomb

During the 1930s, Jewish physicists fled Adolf Hitler's fanatical anti-Semitic persecutions and came to the United States, where they played a leading role in the research and development of the atomic bomb. In this way, Nazi anti-Semitism contributed to making the United States the first atomic power.

One of Germany's greatest scientists, Albert Einstein, won the Nobel Prize for physics in 1921. Among other things, Einstein's work demonstrated that the nuclei of atoms of physical matter stored almost inconceivable quantities of energy. A fellow scientist praised Einstein's discoveries as "the greatest achievements in the history of human thought." But Einstein was a Jew, and his ideas were ridiculed by German anti-Semites. A German physicist who had won the Nobel Prize in 1905 attacked Einstein for his "Jewish nonsense," which was "hostile to the German spirit." Einstein wrote to a friend, "Anti-Semitism is strong here [in Berlin] and political reaction is violent." Einstein's associates warned him that the anti-Semites had targeted him for assassination.

In his manifesto, *Mein Kampf*, Hitler proclaimed that Jews were "a foreign people," "inferior beings," the "personification of the devil," "a race of dialectical liars," "parasites," and "eternal bloodsuckers," who had the "clear aim of ruining the . . . white race." Hitler's rantings attracted a huge audience in Germany, and his personal Nazi army, which numbered 400,000 by 1933, terrorized and murdered anyone who got in the way.

In January 1933, just weeks before Franklin Roosevelt's inauguration as president of the United States, Hitler became chancellor of Germany on a tidal wave of popular support for his Nazi Party. Within months, he abolished freedom of speech and assembly, outlawed all political opposition, and exercised absolute dictatorial power. On April 7, Hitler announced the Law for the Restoration of the Professional Civil Service, which stipulated that "civil servants of non-Aryan descent must retire." A non-Aryan was defined as any person "descended from non-Aryan, especially Jewish, parents or grandparents." The law meant that scientists of Jewish descent who worked for state institutions, including universities, no longer had jobs. About 1,600 intellectuals in Germany immediately lost their livelihood and their future in Hitler's Reich. Among them were about a quarter of the physicists in Germany, including Einstein and ten other Nobel Prize winners. The Nazis' anti-Semitism laws forced many leading scientists to leave Germany. Between 1933 and 1941, Einstein and about 100 other Jewish physicists joined hundreds of Jewish intellectuals in an exodus from Nazi Germany to the safety of the United States.

The refugee physicists scrambled to find positions at American universities and research institutes that would allow them to continue their studies. The accelerating pace of research in physics during the 1930s raised the possibility that a way might exist to release the phenomenal energy bottled up in atomic nuclei, perhaps even to create a superbomb. Einstein and other scientists considered that possibility remote. But many worried that if scientists loyal to Germany discovered a way to harness nuclear energy, Hitler would have the power to spread Nazi terror throughout the world. The refugee physicists asked Einstein to write a letter to President Roosevelt explaining the military and political threats posed by the latest research in nuclear physics.

Wartime Politics and the 1944 Election

Americans rallied around the war effort in unprecedented unity. Despite the consensus on war aims, the strains and stresses of the nation's massive wartime mobilization made it difficult for Roosevelt to maintain his political coalition. Whites often resented blacks who migrated to northern cities, took jobs, and made themselves at home. Many Americans complained about government price controls and the rationing of scarce goods while the war dragged on. Republicans seized the opportunity to roll back New Deal reforms. A conservative coalition of Republicans and southern Democrats succeeded in abolishing several New Deal agencies in 1942 and 1943, including the Works Progress Administration and the Civilian Conservation Corps.

In June 1944, Congress recognized the sacrifices made by millions of veterans, unanimously passing the landmark **GI Bill of Rights**, which gave GIs government funds for education, housing, and health care and provided loans to help them start businesses and buy homes. The GI Bill put the financial resources of the federal government behind the abstract goals of freedom and democracy for which veterans were fighting, and it empowered millions

Home Front Patriotism
To support the war effort, Americans on the home front were encouraged to be frugal—save tin cans and newspapers; grow vegetables in Victory Gardens; and preserve surplus food by canning it, using the aluminum pressure cooker to sterilize food, then storing it in jars for later use. In order to funnel supplies to the military, the federal government rationed food, gasoline, and many other items consumers might otherwise have purchased. The poster's slogan (obscured by the pressure cooker) announces, "I'm as patriotic as can be — And ration points [that restricted food purchases] won't worry me." Poster: Courtesy of Northwestern University Library; canning implements: Atlanta History Museum. Photograph by Rod Smith.

Progress came slowly, however. In 1940, nine out of ten black Americans lived below the federal poverty line, and those who worked earned an average of just 39 percent of whites' wages. In search of better jobs and living conditions, 5.5 million black Americans migrated from the South to centers of industrial production in the North and West, making a majority of African Americans city dwellers for the first time in U.S. history. Many discovered that unskilled jobs were available but that unions and employers often barred blacks from skilled trades. At least eighteen major unions explicitly prohibited black members. Severe labor shortages and government fair employment standards opened assembly-line jobs in defense plants to African Americans, causing black unemployment to drop by 80 percent during the war. But more jobs did not mean equal pay for blacks. The average income of black families rose during the war, but by the end of the conflict it still stood at only half of what white families earned.

Blacks' migration to defense jobs intensified racial antagonisms, which boiled over in the hot summer of 1943, when 242 race riots erupted in 47 cities. In the "zoot suit riots" in Los Angeles, hundreds of white servicemen, claiming they were punishing draft dodgers, chased and beat young Mexican American men who dressed in distinctive broad-shouldered, peg-legged zoot suits. The worst mayhem occurred in Detroit, where a long-simmering conflict between whites and blacks over racially segregated housing ignited into a race war. Whites with clubs smashed through black neighborhoods, and blacks retaliated by destroying and looting white-owned businesses. In two days of violence, twenty-five blacks and nine whites were killed, and scores more were injured.

Racial violence created the impetus for the Double V campaign, officially supported by the National Association for the Advancement of Colored People (NAACP), which asserted black Americans' demands for the rights and privileges enjoyed by all other Americans — demands reinforced by the Allies' wartime ideology of freedom and democracy. While the NAACP focused on court challenges to segregation, a new organization founded in 1942, the Congress of Racial Equality, organized picketing and sit-ins against racially segregated restaurants and theaters. The Double V campaign greatly expanded membership in the NAACP but achieved only limited success against racial discrimination during the war.

Sleeping Car Porters, promised that 100,000 African American marchers would descend on Washington if the president did not eliminate discrimination in defense industries. Roosevelt decided to risk offending his white allies in the South and in unions and issued Executive Order 8802 in mid-1941. It authorized the **Committee on Fair Employment Practices** to investigate and prevent racial discrimination in employment. Civil rights champions hailed the act, and Randolph triumphantly called off the march.

into a series of battles to liberate Italy from German occupation.

German troops dug into strong fortifications and fought to defend every inch of Italy's rugged terrain. Only after a long, deadly, and frustrating campaign up the Italian peninsula did the Allies finally liberate Rome in June 1944. Allied forces continued to push into northern Italy against stubborn German defenses for the remainder of the war, making the Italian campaign the war's deadliest for American infantrymen. One soldier wrote that his buddies "died like butchered swine."

Stalin denounced the Allies' Italian campaign because it left "the Soviet Army, which is fighting not only for its country, but also for its Allies, to do the job alone, almost single-handed." The Italian campaign exacted a high cost from the Americans and British, bringing the Nazis no closer to surrender and consuming men and materiel that might have been reserved for a second front in France.

REVIEW   How did the United States seek to counter the Japanese in the Pacific and the Germans in Europe?

▶ The Wartime Home Front

The war effort mobilized Americans as never before. Factories churned out ever more bombs, bullets, tanks, ships, and airplanes, which workers rushed to assemble, leaving their farms and small towns and congregating in cities. Women took jobs with wrenches and welding torches, boosting the nation's workforce and fraying traditional notions that a woman's place was in the home rather than on the assembly line. Despite rationing and shortages, unprecedented government expenditures for war production brought prosperity to many Americans after years of depression-era poverty. Although Americans in uniform risked their lives on battlefields in Europe and Asia, Americans on the U.S. mainland enjoyed complete immunity from foreign attack — in sharp contrast to their Soviet and British allies. The wartime ideology of human rights provided justification for the many sacrifices Americans were required to make in support of the military effort. It also established a standard of basic human equality that became a potent weapon in the campaign for equal rights at home and in condemning the

atrocities of the Holocaust perpetrated by the Nazis.

Women and Families, Guns and Butter

Millions of American women gladly took their places on assembly lines in defense industries. At the start of the war, about a quarter of adult women worked outside the home, most as teachers, nurses, social workers, and domestic servants. Few women worked in factories, except for textile mills and sewing industries, because employers and male workers often discriminated against them. But wartime mobilization of the economy and the siphoning of millions of men into the armed forces left factories begging for women workers.

> "If you've sewed on buttons, or made buttonholes, on a [sewing] machine, you can learn to do spot welding on airplane parts."
> —Proclaimed on a billboard

Government advertisements urged women to take industrial jobs by assuring them that their household chores had prepared them for work on the "Victory Line." One billboard proclaimed, "If you've sewed on buttons, or made buttonholes, on a [sewing] machine, you can learn to do spot welding on airplane parts." Millions of women responded. Advertisers often referred to a woman who worked in a war industry as "**Rosie the Riveter**," a wartime term that became popular. By the end of the war, women working outside the home numbered 18 million, 50 percent more than in 1939. Contributing to the war effort also paid off in wages. A Kentucky woman remembered her job at a munitions plant, where she earned "the fabulous sum of $32 a week. To us it was an absolute miracle." Although men were paid an average of $54 for comparable wartime work, women accepted the pay differential and welcomed their chance to earn wages and help win the war at the same time.

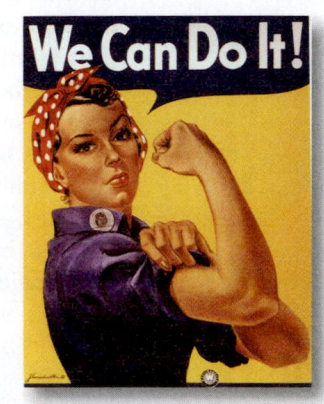

The majority of married women remained at home, occupied with domestic chores and child care. But they, too, supported the war effort, planting Victory Gardens to provide homegrown vegetables, saving tin cans and newspapers for recycling into war materiel, and hoarding pennies and nickels to buy war bonds. Many families scrimped to cope with the 30 percent inflation during the war, but families supported by men and women

Riveting Rosies
American women flocked to war industries, and manufacturers welcomed them in jobs previously restricted to men. Here Dora Miles and Dorothy Johnson rivet an airplane frame in a plant in Long Beach, California. The tool in Miles's hands drove a rivet into the metal and another tool (not shown) held by Johnson smashed the end of the rivet snug against the airframe, securing it. War industries employed an unprecedented number of African American women and men who often worked alongside whites, as shown here. Workers wore identification badges, like the one here from a shipyard in Baltimore, Maryland. Photo: Library of Congress; badge: World War II, National Homefront National Historical Park.

in manufacturing industries enjoyed wages that grew twice as fast as inflation.

The war influenced how all families spent their earnings. Buying a new washing machine or car was out of the question, since factories that formerly built them now made military goods. Many other consumer goods — such as tires, gasoline, shoes, and meat — were rationed at home to meet military needs overseas. But most Americans had more money in their pockets than ever before, and they readily found things to buy, including movie tickets, cosmetics, and music recordings.

The wartime prosperity and abundance enjoyed by most Americans contrasted with the experiences of their hard-pressed allies. Personal consumption fell by 22 percent in Britain, and food output plummeted to just one-third of prewar levels in the Soviet Union, creating widespread hunger and even starvation. Few went hungry in the United States. New Deal restraints on agricultural production were lifted, and farm output grew by 25 percent each year during the war, providing a cornucopia of food to be exported to the Allies.

The Double V Campaign

Fighting against Nazi Germany and its ideology of Aryan racial supremacy, Americans were confronted with the extensive racial prejudice in their own country. The *Pittsburgh Courier*, a leading black newspaper, asserted that the wartime emergency called for a **Double V campaign** seeking "victory over our enemies at home and victory over our enemies on the battlefields abroad." It was time, the *Courier* proclaimed, "to persuade, embarrass, compel and shame our government and our nation . . . into a more enlightened attitude."

In 1941, black organizations demanded that the federal government require companies receiving defense contracts to integrate their workforces. **A. Philip Randolph**, head of the Brotherhood of the Communists and made an eventual Allied attack on western France more likely to succeed. Churchill and Roosevelt promised Stalin that they would open a second front, but they decided to strike first in North Africa, a region of long-standing British influence that could help secure Allied control of the Mediterranean.

In October and November 1942, British forces at El-Alamein in Egypt halted German general Erwin Rommel's drive to capture the Suez Canal, Britain's lifeline to the oil of the Middle East and to British colonies in India and South Asia (see Map 25.4, page 850). In November, an American army under General **Dwight D. Eisenhower** landed far to the west, in French Morocco. Propelled by American tank units commanded by General **George Patton**, the Allied armies defeated the Germans in North Africa in May 1943. The North African campaign killed and captured 350,000 Axis soldiers, pushed the Germans out of Africa, made the Mediterranean safe for Allied shipping, and opened the door for an Allied invasion of Italy.

In January 1943, while the North African campaign was still under way, Roosevelt and Churchill met in Casablanca and announced that they would accept nothing less than the "unconditional surrender" of the Axis powers, ruling out peace negotiations. They concluded that while continuing to amass forces for the cross-Channel invasion of France, they should capitalize on their success in North Africa and strike against Italy, consigning the Soviet Union to bear the brunt of the Nazi war machine for another year.

On July 10, 1943, combined American and British amphibious forces landed 160,000 troops in Sicily. The badly equipped Italian defenders quickly withdrew to the mainland. Soon afterward, Mussolini was deposed in Italy, ending the reign of Italian fascism. Quickly, the Allies invaded the mainland, and the Italian government surrendered unconditionally. The Germans responded by rushing reinforcements to Italy and seizing control of Rome, turning the Allies' Italian campaign

Relief Column, Tunisia, North Africa

This eyewitness painting depicts a column of American soldiers moving toward the front lines to relieve exhausted and wounded comrades in Tunisia in 1943. The artist, Peter Sanfilippo, a twenty-three-year-old private from Brooklyn, New York, wrote that the "arrival of a relief column of fresh soldiers . . . reassures a battered man's faith in his fellow comrades. The unnerved and wounded are resurrected in spirit to thrive, and thus persevere into a new day." Painting watercolors allowed Sanfilippo to "maintain a mental toughness that would defy the savagery of war's violence." Peter Sanfilippo/Veterans History Project, Library of Congress, Institute on World War II and the Human Experience, Florida State University, Tallahassee, FL.

Flamethrower in Combat in the Solomon Islands
American soldiers used flamethrowers in both the Pacific and European theaters. They were especially effective against enemy soldiers dug into bunkers that were difficult to penetrate by rifle or machine-gun fire. The Marine shown here, fighting in the Solomon Islands in 1943, carried on his back canisters of jellied gasoline and compressed air that were combined and projected through the gunlike machine. The dangerous, deadly weapon ignited the mixture and spouted an intensely hot flame. Carrying a flamethrower made one a high-priority target for enemy sharpshooters, and a stray piece of hot shrapnel could cause the weapon to explode on impact. National Museum of American History, Smithsonian Institution, Behring Center, National Archives.

ficient destroyer escorts for merchant vessels allowed the Allies to prey upon the lurking U-boats. After suffering a 75 percent casualty rate among U-boat crews, Hitler withdrew German submarines from the North Atlantic in late May 1943, allowing thousands of American supply ships to cross the Atlantic unimpeded. Winning the battle of the Atlantic allowed the United States to continue to supply its British and Soviet allies for the duration of the war and to reduce the imminent threat of a German invasion of Britain.

The most important strategic questions confronting the United States and its allies were when and where to open a second front against the Nazis. Stalin demanded that America and Britain mount an immediate and massive assault across the English Channel into western France to force Hitler to divert his armies from the eastern front and relieve the pressure on the Soviet Union. Churchill and Roosevelt instead delayed opening a second front, allowing the Germans and the Soviets to slug it out. This drawn-out conflict weakened both the Nazis and

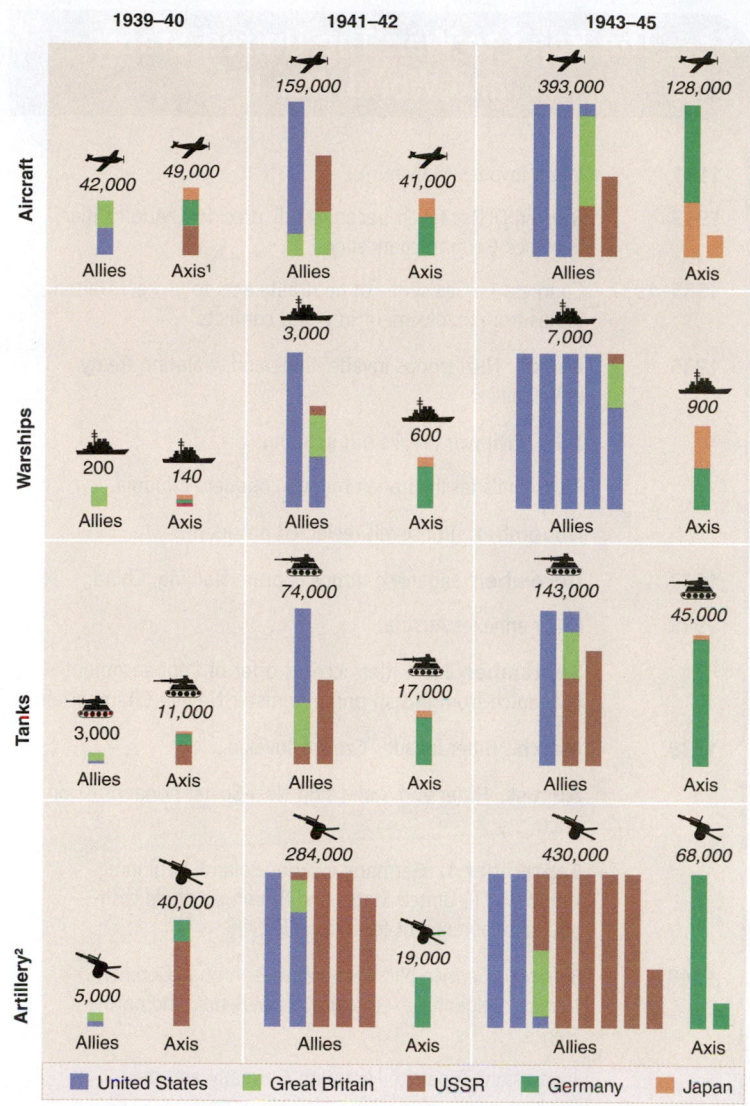

¹ The USSR was allied with Germany 1939–40.
² No reliable data exist for Japan.

FIGURE 25.1   GLOBAL COMPARISON: Weapons Production by the Axis and Allied Powers during World War II

This chart demonstrates the massive contribution of the United States to Allied weapons production during World War II. In the air and on the sea, U.S. weapons predominated, after 1940 accounting for more aircraft and many more warships than those of Britain and the Soviet Union combined. Together, the three Allied powers produced about three times as many aircraft and five to eight times as many warships as the two Axis powers. On the ground, the Soviet Union led the other Allies in the production of tanks and artillery, an outgrowth of the colossal battles on the eastern front. What do these data suggest about the significance of America's entry into the war in December 1941? What do they suggest about the kind of warfare emphasized by each of the belligerents? What does the chronology of weapons production suggest about the course of the war?

Japanese Pilot's Flag
Japanese pilots often carried small flags covered with admonitions to fight hard and well. This flag belonged to a pilot named Imano, whose relatives sent him aloft with an inscription that read, "Let your divine plane soar in the sky. We who are left behind pray only for your certain success in sinking an enemy ship." Notably, the inscription emphasized harming Japan's enemies rather than returning home safely. © U.S. Naval Academy Museum/photo by Richard D. Bond Jr.

ships and planes delivered a devastating blow to the Japanese navy.

The **Battle of Midway** reversed the balance of naval power in the Pacific and put the Japanese at a disadvantage for the rest of the war. Japan managed to build only six more large aircraft carriers during the war, while the United States launched dozens, proving the wisdom of Yamamoto's prediction. But the Japanese still occupied and defended the many places they had conquered.

The Campaign in Europe

After Pearl Harbor, Hitler's eastern-front armies marched ever deeper into the Soviet Union while his western-front forces prepared to invade Britain. As in World War I, the Germans attempted to starve the British into submission by destroying their seaborne lifeline. In 1941 and 1942, they sank Allied ships faster than new ones could be built. Overall, the U-boat campaign sank 4,700 merchant vessels and nearly 200 warships and killed 40,000 Allied seamen.

Until mid-1943, the outcome of the war in the Atlantic remained in doubt. Then, newly invented radar detectors and production of sufon the United States. To fight back effectively against Germany and Japan, the United States had to coordinate military and political strategy with its allies and muster all its human and economic assets. But in 1941, nobody knew whether that would be enough.

Turning the Tide in the Pacific

In the Pacific theater, Japan's leading military strategist, Admiral Isoroku Yamamoto, believed that if his forces did not quickly conquer and secure the territories they targeted, Japan would eventually lose the war as a result of America's far greater resources. Swiftly, the Japanese assaulted American airfields in the Philippines and captured U.S. outposts on Guam and Wake Island. After capturing Singapore and Burma, Japan sought to complete its domination of the southern Pacific with an attack on the American stronghold in the Philippines.

The Japanese unleashed a withering assault against the Philippines in January 1942 (see Map 25.5, page 853). American defenders surrendered to the Japanese in May. The Japanese victors sent captured American and Filipino soldiers on the infamous Bataan Death March to a concentration camp, causing thousands to die. By the summer of 1942, the Japanese war machine had conquered the Dutch East Indies and was poised to strike Australia and New Zealand.

In the spring of 1942, U.S. forces launched a major two-pronged counteroffensive that military officials hoped would reverse the Japanese advance. Forces led by General **Douglas MacArthur**, commander of the U.S. armed forces in the Pacific theater, moved north from Australia and eventually attacked the Japanese in the Philippines. Far more decisively, Admiral **Chester W. Nimitz** sailed his battle fleet west from Hawai'i to retake Japanese-held islands in the southern and mid-Pacific. On May 7–8, 1942, in the Coral Sea just north of Australia, the American fleet and carrier-based warplanes defeated a Japanese armada that was sailing around the coast of New Guinea.

Nimitz then learned from an intelligence intercept that the Japanese were massing an invasion force aimed at Midway Island, an outpost guarding the Hawai'ian Islands. Nimitz maneuvered his carriers and cruisers into the Central Pacific to surprise the Japanese. In a furious battle that raged on June 3–6, American

The Road to War: The United States and World War II

1931	Japan invades Manchuria.
1933	Franklin D. Roosevelt becomes U.S. president. Adolf Hitler becomes German chancellor.
1935–1937	Congress passes series of neutrality acts to protect United States from involvement in world conflicts.
1936	**March.** Nazi troops invade Rhineland, violating Treaty of Versailles.
	July. Civil war breaks out in Spain.
	Mussolini's fascist Italian regime conquers Ethiopia.
	November. Roosevelt reelected president.
1937	**December.** Japanese troops capture Nanjing, China.
1938	Hitler annexes Austria.
	September 29. Hitler accepts offer of "appeasement" in Munich from British prime minister Neville Chamberlain.
1939	**March.** Hitler invades Czechoslovakia.
	August. Hitler and Stalin sign Nazi-Soviet nonaggression pact.
	September 1. Germany invades Poland, beginning World War II. United States and Britain conclude cash-and-carry agreement for arms sales.
1940	**Spring.** German blitzkrieg smashes through Denmark, Norway, Belgium, Luxembourg, Netherlands, and northern France.
	Japan signs Tripartite Pact with Germany and Italy.
	May–June. German armies flank Maginot Line. British and French evacuated from Dunkirk. France surrenders to Germany.
	Summer/Fall. Germany conducts bombing campaign against England.
	November. Roosevelt wins third term as president. Royal Air Force wins Battle of Britain.
1941	**March.** Congress approves Lend-Lease Act, making arms available to Britain.
	June 22. Hitler invades Soviet Union.
	August. Roosevelt and Churchill issue Atlantic Charter.
	October. Militarists led by Hideki Tojo take over Japan.
	December 7. Japanese bomb Pearl Harbor. United States declares war on Japan.
	December 11. Germany and Italy declare war on United States.

Airplane Production Milestone
The Douglas Aircraft Corporation, like many other manufacturers, employed both women and men to make military equipment. Douglas built thousands of military aircraft in its facilities in California and Oklahoma. Here, hundreds of male and female workers celebrate the completion of the 3,000th C-47 Skytrain, a workhorse transport plane that carried soldiers and equipment throughout the world during the war. In all, more than 10,000 were built, and they continued in military and civilian use for decades after World War II. © Bettmann/Corbis.

To organize and oversee this tidal wave of military production, Roosevelt called upon business leaders to come to Washington and, for the token payment of a dollar a year, head new government agencies such as the **War Production Board**, which, among other things, set production priorities and pushed for maximum output. Contracts flowed to large corporations, often on a basis that guaranteed their profits. During the first half of 1942, the government issued contracts worth more than the entire gross national product in 1941.

Booming wartime employment swelled union membership. To speed production, the government asked unions to pledge not to strike. Despite the relentless pace of work, union members kept their no-strike pledge, with the important exception of members of the United Mine Workers, who walked out of the coal mines in 1943, demanding a pay hike and earning the enmity of many Americans.

Overall, conversion to war production achieved Roosevelt's ambitious goal of "crushing superiority" in military goods. At a total cost of $304 billion during the war, the nation produced an avalanche of military equipment, more than double the combined production of Germany, Japan, and Italy (Figure 25.1). This outpouring of military goods supplied not only U.S. forces but also America's allies, giving tangible meaning to Roosevelt's pledge to make America the "arsenal of democracy."

REVIEW   How did the Roosevelt administration mobilize the human and industrial resources necessary to fight a two-front war?

recalled. Another gay GI remarked, "Who in the hell is going to worry about [homosexuality]" in the midst of the life-or-death realities of war?

Conversion to a War Economy

In 1940, the American economy remained mired in the depression. Nearly one worker in seven was still without a job, factories operated far below their productive capacity, and the total federal budget was under $10 billion. Shortly after the attack on Pearl Harbor, Roosevelt announced the goal of converting the economy to produce "overwhelming . . . , crushing superiority of equipment in any theater of the world war." Factories were converted from making passenger cars to assembling tanks and airplanes, and production soared to record levels. By the end of the war, jobs exceeded workers, plants operated at full capacity, and the federal budget topped $100 billion.

▶ Fighting Back

The United States confronted a daunting military challenge in December 1941. The attack on Pearl Harbor destroyed much of its Pacific Fleet, crippling the nation's ability to defend against Japan's offensive throughout the southern Pacific. In the Atlantic, Hitler's U-boats sank American ships, while German armies occupied most of western Europe and relentlessly advanced eastward into the Soviet Union. Roosevelt and his military advisers believed that defeating Germany took top priority. To achieve that victory required preventing Hitler from defeating America's allies, Britain and the Soviet Union. If they fell, Hitler would command all the resources of Europe in a probable assault that I was segregated, that I was taken away, even though it goes back forty years. . . .

I was separated from my husband; he went to the Santa Fe, New Mexico, camp. All our letters were censored; all our letters were cut in parts and all that. So we were not too sure what messages was getting through and not getting through, but I do know that I informed him many times of his mother's condition. He should have been allowed to come back to see her, because I thought she wouldn't live too long, but they never did allow him to come back, even for her funeral. They did not allow that. I learned that a lot of the messages didn't get to him; they were crossed out. I now have those letters with me.

In 1944 I was left with his parents and our kids. But I had no time to think of what was going to happen because my child was always sick and I had been quite sick. . . .

My son knew what was going on, and he too had many times asked me why . . . you know, why? why? Of course, I had no explanation why this was happening to us.

SOURCE: Excerpt from *And Justice for All*, by John Tateishi. Copyright © 1999 by John Tateishi. Reprinted by permission of the University of Washington Press.

DOCUMENT 3
The Kikuchi Diary

Charles Kikuchi, a student at the University of California at Berkeley, sought in his prison camp diary to make sense of the internment and to judge where it would lead.

December 7, 1941
Berkeley, California
Pearl Harbor. We are at war! Jesus Christ, the Japs bombed Hawai'i and the entire fleet has been sunk. I just can't believe it. I don't know what in the hell is going to happen to us, but we will all be called into the Army right away.

. . . The next five years will determine the future of the Nisei [Japanese American citizens]. They are now at the crossroads. Will they be able to take it or will they go under? If we are ever going to prove our Americanism, this is the time. The Anti-Jap feeling is bound to rise to hysterical heights, and it is most likely that the Nisei will be included as Japs. I wanted to go to San Francisco tonight, but Pierre says I am crazy. He says it's best we stick on campus. In any event, we can't remain on the fence, and a positive approach must be taken if we are to have a place in fulfilling the Promise of America. I think the U.S. is in danger of going Fascist too, or maybe Socialist. . . .

I don't know what to think or do. Everybody is in a daze.

April 30, 1942, Berkeley
Today is the day that we are going to get kicked out of Berkeley. It certainly is degrading. . . .

I'm supposed to see my family at Tanforan as Jack told me to give the same family number. I wonder how it is going to be living with them as I haven't done this for years and years? I should have gone over to San Francisco and evacuated with them, but I had a last final to take. I understand that we are going to live in the horse stalls. I hope that the Army has the courtesy to remove the manure first. . . .

July 14, 1942
Marie, Ann, Mitch, Jimmy, Jack, and myself got into a long discussion about how much democracy meant to us as individuals. Mitch says that he would even go in the army and die for it, in spite of the fact that he knew he would be kept down. Marie said that although democracy was not perfect, it was the only system that offered any hope for a future, if we could fulfill its destinies. Jack was a little more skeptical. He even suggested that we [could] be in such grave danger that we would then realize that we were losing something. Where this point was he could not say. I said that this was what happened in France and they lost all. Jimmy suggested that the colored races of the world had reason to feel despair and mistrust the white man because of the past experiences. . . .

In reviewing the four months here, the chief value I got out of this forced evacuation was the strengthening of the family bonds. I never knew my family before this and this was the first chance that I have had to really get acquainted.

SOURCE: Excerpts (pp. 43, 51, 183, 252) from *The Kikuchi Diary: Chronicle from an American Concentration Camp*, edited by John Modell. Copyright © 1973 by the Board of Trustees of the University of Illinois. Used with the permission of the University of Illinois Press and the author.

Questions for Analysis and Debate

1. What explains General DeWitt's insistence on evacuating the Japanese after he received the report of military investigators that no acts of sabotage had occurred?

2. How do the Kikuchi diary and the oral histories of life in the camps describe the meaning of internment for the detainees?

3. Despite the internment of their families and friends in concentration camps, the Japanese American army unit in Italy earned a larger number of citations for combat heroism than any comparable army group. What hints in the documents here might help explain this combat record?

4. How did the internment camp experience influence the detainees' attitudes about their identity as Americans of Japanese descent?

Japanese Internment

Determined that the bombing of Pearl Harbor would not be followed by more sneak attacks, military and political leaders on the West Coast targeted persons of Japanese descent — aliens and citizens alike — as potential saboteurs.

DOCUMENT 1
Final Recommendations of the Commanding General, Western Defense Command and Fourth Army, Submitted to the Secretary of War

Early in 1942, General John DeWitt, commander of the Western Defense Command, persuaded President Franklin Roosevelt to issue an executive order authorizing the removal of Japanese living in the United States.

Subsequently, 110,000 Japanese Americans were confined to relocation camps for the duration of the war. DeWitt's recommendation expressed concern for military security by appealing to racist conceptions long used to curb Asian immigration. Japanese Americans and their supporters fought the internment order in the courts as a violation of fundamental constitutional rights, an argument rejected during the war by the U.S. Supreme Court. Long after the war ended, the U.S. government officially apologized for Japanese American internment and issued modest monetary payments to survivors.

February 14, 1942
Memorandum for the Secretary of War

Subject: Evacuation of Japanese and Other Subversive Persons from the Pacific Coast.
1. In presenting a recommendation for the evacuation of Japanese and other subversive persons from the Pacific Coast, the following facts have been considered:
a. Mission of the Western Defense Command and Fourth Army.
1) Defense of the Pacific Coast of the Western Defense Command, as extended, against attacks by sea, land, or air;
2) Local protection of establishment and communications vital to the National Defense for which adequate defense cannot be provided by local civilian authorities.
b. Brief Estimate of the Situation.
1) . . . The following are possible and probable enemy activities: . . .
(a) Naval attack on shipping on coastal waters;

(b) Naval attack on coastal cities and vital installations;
(c) Air raids on vital installations, particularly within two hundred miles of the coast;
(d) Sabotage of vital installations throughout the Western Defense Command. . . .
Hostile Naval and air raids will be assisted by enemy agents signaling from the coastline and the vicinity thereof; and by supplying and otherwise assisting enemy vessels and by sabotage. . . .

In the war in which we are now engaged racial affinities are not severed by migration. The Japanese race is an enemy race and while many second and third generation Japanese born on United States soil, possessed of United States citizenship, have become "Americanized," the racial strains are undiluted. To conclude otherwise is to expect that children born of white parents on Japanese soil sever all racial affinity and become loyal Japanese subjects, ready to fight and, if necessary, to die for Japan in a war against the nation of their parents. . . .

It, therefore, follows that along the vital Pacific Coast over 112,000 potential enemies, of Japanese extraction, are at large today. There are indications that these are organized and ready for concerted action at a favorable opportunity. The very fact that no sabotage has taken place to date is a disturbing and confirming indication that such action will be taken.

SOURCE: *Final Recommendations*, report by General John Lesesne DeWitt to the United States Secretary of War, February 14, 1942.

DOCUMENT 2
An Oral History of Life in the Japanese American Detention Camps

Imprisoned in bleak surroundings far from home, Japanese American internees sometimes succumbed to despair and bitterness. Looking back after forty years, Kazue Yamane recalled her confinement as a disturbing and baffling experience.

In April 1942, my husband and I and our two children left for camp, and my mother-in-law and father-in-law came about a month later. I wasn't afraid, but I kept asking in my mind, how could they? This is impossible. Even today I still think it was a nightmarish thing. I cannot reconcile myself to the fact that I had to go, that I was interned,

MAP 25.3
Western Relocation Authority Centers

Responding to prejudice and fear of sabotage, President Roosevelt authorized the roundup and relocation of all Americans of Japanese descent in 1942. Taken from their homes in the cities and fertile farmland of the far West, more than 120,000 Japanese Americans were confined in desolate camps scattered as far east as the Mississippi River.

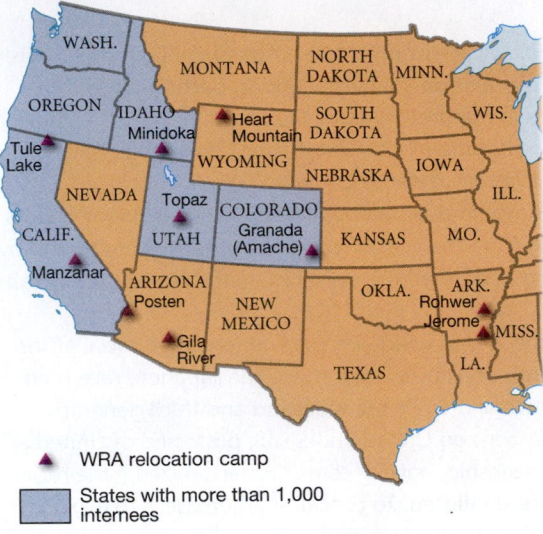

▲ WRA relocation camp

States with more than 1,000 internees

GI did on his way to the European front, "Why fight for America when you have not been treated as an American?" Only black Americans were trained in segregated camps, confined in segregated barracks, and assigned to segregated units. Most black Americans were consigned to manual labor, and relatively few served in combat until late in 1944, when the need for military manpower in Europe intensified. Then, as General George Patton told black soldiers in a tank unit in Normandy, "I don't care what color you are, so long as you go up there and kill those Kraut sonsabitches."

Homosexuals also served in the armed forces, although in much smaller numbers than black Americans. Allowed to serve as long as their sexual preferences remained covert, gay Americans, like other minorities, sought to demonstrate their worth under fire. "I was superpatriotic," a gay combat veteran

African American Pilot

This poster urging Americans to buy war bonds featured Robert Deiz, one of nearly 1,000 African American pilots who trained for military service at Tuskegee University in Alabama. The Tuskegee airmen served with distinction in the European theater. Although the American military — like much else in American society — was racially segregated, the poster illustrates the patriotic appeal for all Americans to contribute to the war effort. The poster also hints that war against Nazi racism somewhat discredited white supremacy at home. National Archives.

Supreme Court, in its 1944 *Korematsu* decision, upheld Executive Order 9066's blatant violation of constitutional rights as justified by "military necessity."

Building a Citizen Army

In 1940, Roosevelt encouraged Congress to pass the **Selective Service Act** to register men of military age who would be subject to a draft if the need arose. More than 6,000 local draft boards registered more than 30 million men and, when war came, rapidly inducted them into military service. In all, more than 16 million men and women served in uniform during the war, two-thirds of them draftees, mostly young men. Women were barred from combat duty, but they worked at nearly every noncombatant task, eroding traditional barriers to women's military service.

The Selective Service Act prohibited discrimination "on account of race or color," and almost a million African American men and women donned uniforms, as did half a million Mexican Americans, 25,000 Native Americans, and 13,000 Chinese Americans. The racial insults and discrimination suffered by all people of color made some soldiers ask, as a Mexican American isolationist-era military to fighting strength for a two-front war. The war emergency also required economic mobilization unparalleled in the nation's history. As Dr. Win-the-War, Roosevelt set aside the New Deal goal of reform and plunged headlong into transforming the American economy into the world's greatest military machine, thereby achieving full employment and economic recovery, goals that had eluded the New Deal.

Home-Front Security

Shortly after declaring war against the United States, Hitler dispatched German submarines to hunt American ships along the Atlantic coast from Maine to Florida, where Paul Tibbets and other American pilots tried to destroy them. The U-boats had devastating success for about eight months, sinking hundreds of U.S. ships and threatening to disrupt the Lend-Lease lifeline to Britain and the Soviet Union. But by mid-1942, the U.S. Navy had chased German submarines away from the East Coast and into the mid-Atlantic, reducing the direct threat to the nation.

> **"A Jap's a Jap. . . . It makes no difference whether he is an American citizen or not."**
> —A U.S. official in the West

Within the continental United States, Americans remained sheltered from the chaos and destruction the war was bringing to hundreds of millions in Europe and Asia. Nevertheless, the government worried constantly about espionage and internal subversion. The campaign for patriotic vigilance focused on German and Japanese foes, but Americans of Japanese descent became targets of official and popular persecution because of Pearl Harbor and long-standing racial prejudice against people of Asian descent.

About 320,000 people of Japanese descent lived in U.S. territory in 1941, two-thirds of them in Hawai'i, where they largely escaped such wartime persecution because they were essential and valued members of society. On the mainland, however, Japanese Americans were a tiny minority — even along the West Coast, where most of them worked on farms and in small businesses — subject to frenzied wartime suspicions and persecution. Although an official military survey concluded that Japanese Americans posed no danger, popular hostility fueled a campaign to round up all mainland Japanese Americans — two-thirds of them U.S. citizens. "A Jap's a Jap. . . . It makes no difference whether he is an American citizen or not," one official declared.

On February 19, 1942, Roosevelt issued Executive Order 9066, which authorized sending all Americans of Japanese descent to ten makeshift **internment camps** — euphemistically termed "relocation centers" — located in remote areas of the West (Map 25.3). Allowed little time to secure or sell their property, Japanese Americans lost homes and businesses worth about $400 million and lived out the war penned in by barbed wire and armed guards. (See "Documenting the American Promise," page 836.) Although several thousand Japanese Americans served with distinction in the U.S. armed forces and no case of subversion by a Japanese American was ever uncovered, the

Japanese Internment Camp at Manzanar, California
Japanese American families line up to enter the mess hall at the Manzanar, California, internment camp in May 1943. The camp was located on the barren, windswept eastern slope of the Sierra Nevada. The artist, Kango Takamura, immigrated to the United States in 1921. Like other internees, he was utterly loyal to the United States, and he tried to make the best of a bad situation. He recalled that the people at Manzanar "had plenty of food . . . not gourmet stuff, but good enough for health." After the war, Takamura returned to his work in Los Angeles movie studios. Gift of Kango Takamura, Department of Special Collections, Charles E. Young Research Library, UCLA.

Southeast Asia and ignored American demands to stop its campaign of aggression.

In 1940, Japan signaled a new phase of its imperial designs by entering a defensive alliance with Germany and Italy — the Tripartite Pact. To thwart Japanese plans to invade the Dutch East Indies, in July 1941 Roosevelt announced a trade embargo that denied Japan access to oil, scrap iron, and other goods essential for its war machines. Roosevelt hoped the embargo would strengthen factions within Japan that opposed the militarists and sought to restore relations with the United States.

Instead, the American embargo played into the hands of Japanese militarists headed by General Hideki Tojo, who seized control of the government in October 1941 and persuaded other leaders, including Emperor Hirohito, that swift destruction of American naval bases in the Pacific would leave Japan free to follow its

destiny. On December 7, 1941, 183 attack aircraft lifted off six Japanese carriers and attacked the U.S. Pacific Fleet at **Pearl Harbor** on the Hawai'ian island of Oahu. The devastating surprise attack sank or disabled eighteen ships, including all of the fleet's battleships; killed more than 2,400 Americans; and wounded more than 1,000, almost crippling U.S. war-making capacity in the Pacific. Luckily for the United States, Japanese pilots failed to destroy the vital machine shops and oil storage facilities at Pearl Harbor, and none of the nation's aircraft carriers happened to be in port at the time of the attack.

Bombing of Pearl Harbor, December 7, 1941

The Japanese scored a stunning tactical victory at Pearl Harbor, but in the long run the attack proved a colossal blunder. The victory made many Japanese commanders overconfident about their military prowess. Worse for the Japanese, Americans instantly united in their desire to fight and avenge the attack, which Roosevelt termed "dastardly and unprovoked." The president vowed that "this form of treachery shall never endanger us again." On December 8, Congress endorsed the president's call for a declaration of war. Neither Hitler nor Mussolini knew about the Japanese attack in advance, but they both declared war against America on December 11, bringing the United States into all-out war with the Axis powers in both Europe and Asia.

REVIEW How did Roosevelt attempt to balance American isolationism with the increasingly ominous international scene of the late 1930s?

Pearl Harbor Attack

This Japanese postcard celebrates the successful surprise attack on Pearl Harbor on December 7, 1941, highlighting the airborne supremacy of the Japanese, the weak defenses of the United States, and the smoking destruction caused by Japanese carrier-based aircraft. Photo: Museum of World War II, Natick, MA, www.museumofworldwarii.com.

▶ Mobilizing for War

The time had come, Roosevelt announced, for the prescriptions of "Dr. New Deal" to be replaced by the stronger medicines of "Dr. Win-the-War." Military and civilian leaders rushed to secure the nation against possible attacks, causing Americans of Japanese descent to be stigmatized and sent to internment camps. Roosevelt and his advisers lost no time enlisting millions of Americans in the armed forces to bring the

Japan Attacks America

Although the likelihood of war with Germany preoccupied Roosevelt, Hitler exercised a measure of restraint in directly provoking America. Japanese ambitions in Asia clashed more openly with American interests and commitments, especially in China and the Philippines. And unlike Hitler, the Japanese high command planned to attack the United States if necessary to pursue Japan's aspirations to rule an Asian empire it termed the Greater East Asia Co-Prosperity Sphere. Appealing to widespread Asian bitterness toward such white colonial powers as the British in India and Burma, the French in Indochina (now Vietnam), and the Dutch in the East Indies (now Indonesia), the Japanese campaigned to preserve "Asia for the Asians." Japan's invasion of China — which had lasted for ten years by 1941 — proved that its true goal was Asia for the Japanese (Map 25.2). Japan coveted the raw materials available from China and

MAP 25.2

Japanese Aggression through 1941

Beginning with the invasion of Manchuria in 1931, Japan sought to extend its imperialist control over most of East Asia. Japanese aggression was driven by the need for raw materials for the country's expanding industries and by the military government's devotion to martial honor.

Enigma Machine
German commanders used the Enigma machine throughout World War II to send top-secret military messages. British agents broke the Enigma code in late August 1941 and began deciphering German messages, dubbing the decoded intelligence "Ultra." Since the Germans made several Enigma code changes during the war, temporary Ultra blackouts occurred until the new codes could be decrypted. Still, Allied military planners used Ultra to sink submarines, anticipate German movement, and send disinformation to the German command. After World War II, Allied intelligence agencies gave thousands of Enigma machines to other nations, permitting the United States and Britain to eavesdrop on unwitting recipients of these "gifts." Museum of World War II, Natick, MA, museum of worldwarii.com.

1940. He hoped to woo voters away from their complacent isolationism to back the nation's international interests as well as New Deal reforms. But the presidential election, which Roosevelt won handily, provided no clear mandate for American involvement in the European war. The Republican candidate, Wendell Willkie, a former Democrat who generally favored New Deal measures and Roosevelt's foreign policy, attacked Roosevelt as a warmonger. Willkie's accusations caused the president to promise voters, "Your boys are not going to be sent into any foreign wars," a pledge counterbalanced by his repeated warnings about the threats to America posed by Nazi aggression.

Once reelected, Roosevelt maneuvered to support Britain in every way short of war. In a fireside chat shortly after Christmas 1940, he proclaimed that it was incumbent on the United States to become "the great arsenal of democracy" and send "every ounce and every ton of munitions and supplies that we can possibly spare to help the defenders who are in the front lines."

In January 1941, Roosevelt proposed the **Lend-Lease Act**, which allowed the British to obtain arms from the United States without paying cash but with the promise to reimburse the United States when the war ended. The purpose of Lend-Lease, Roosevelt proclaimed, was to defend democracy and human rights throughout the world, specifically the Four Freedoms: "freedom of speech and expression . . . freedom of every person to worship God in his own way . . .

freedom from want . . . [and] freedom from fear." The Lend-Lease Act passed in March 1941 and started a flow of support to Britain that totaled more than $50 billion during the war, far more than all federal expenditures combined since Roosevelt had become president in 1933.

Stymied in his plans for an invasion of England, Hitler turned his massive army eastward and on June 22, 1941, sprang a surprise attack on the Soviet Union, his ally in the 1939 Nazi-Soviet nonaggression pact. Neither Roosevelt nor Churchill had any love for Joseph Stalin or communism, but they both welcomed the Soviet Union to the anti-Nazi cause. Both Western leaders understood that Hitler's attack on Russia would provide relief for the hard-pressed British. Roosevelt quickly persuaded Congress to extend Lend-Lease to the Soviet Union, beginning the shipment of millions of tons of trucks, jeeps, and other equipment that, in all, supplied about 10 percent of Russian war materiel.

As Hitler's Wehrmacht raced across the Russian plains and Nazi U-boats tried to choke off supplies to Britain and the Soviet Union, Roosevelt met with Churchill aboard a ship near Newfoundland to cement the Anglo-American alliance. In August 1941, the two leaders issued the **Atlantic Charter**, pledging the two nations to freedom of the seas and free trade as well as the right of national self-determination.

> **"We must be the great arsenal of democracy."**
> — President FRANKLIN ROOSEVELT in late 1940

26

Cold War Politics in the Truman Years
1945–1953

HEADS TURNED WHEN CONGRESSWOMAN HELEN GAHAGAN DOUGLAS walked through the U.S. Capitol. When she served there from 1945 to 1951, she had no more than 10 female colleagues in the 435-member House of Representatives. Not only did she stand out as a woman in a thoroughly male institution, but she also drew attention as a strikingly attractive former Broadway star and opera singer. She served in Congress when the fate of the New Deal was up for grabs and the nation charted a dramatic new course in foreign policy.

Born in 1900, Helen Gahagan grew up in Brooklyn, New York. Drawn to the theater as a child, she defied her father and left Barnard College for the stage after her sophomore year. She quickly won fame on Broadway, starring in show after show until she fell in love with one of her leading men, Melvyn Douglas. They married in 1931, and she followed him to Hollywood, where he hoped to advance his movie career. During the 1930s, she bore two children and continued to appear onstage, but her career was on the wane.

Helen Gahagan Douglas admired Franklin D. Roosevelt's leadership during the depression, and both she and her husband were drawn into Hollywood's liberal political circles. The Douglases were shaken by the anti-Semitism and militarism that they witnessed on a visit to Germany in 1937, and they subsequently joined the Anti-Nazi League in California. But it was the plight of poor migrant farmworkers moving to California from Oklahoma and other states that pushed Helen Douglas into politics. Visiting migrant camps, she saw "faces stamped with poverty and despair," a "human calamity" that prompted her to head the John Steinbeck Committee to Aid Migratory Workers.

Douglas's work on behalf of migrant farmworkers connected her to the White House. She testified before Congress and became a friend of Eleanor Roosevelt and a campaigner for the president in 1940. In California, she rose fast in party politics, becoming vice chair of the state Democratic Party and head of the Women's Division. In 1944, she won election to Congress, representing not the posh Hollywood district where she lived, but the multiracial population of the Fourteenth Congressional District in downtown Los Angeles, which cemented her dedication to progressive politics.

863

Like many liberals devoted to Roosevelt, Douglas was devastated by his death and unsure of his successor, Harry S. Truman. "Who was Harry Truman anyway?" she asked. A compromise choice for the vice presidency, this "accidental president" lacked the charisma and political skills with which Roosevelt had transformed foreign and domestic policy, won four presidential elections, and forged a Democratic Party coalition that dominated national politics. Truman faced a resurgent Republican Party, which had gained strength in Congress, as well as revolts from within his own party. Besides confronting domestic problems that the New Deal had not solved — how to avoid another depression without the war to fuel the economy — Truman faced new international challenges that threatened to undermine the nation's security.

By 1947, a new term described the intense rivalry that had emerged between the United States and the Soviet Union: Cold War. Truman and his advisers became convinced that the Soviet Union posed a major threat to the United States, and they gradually shaped a policy to contain Soviet power wherever it threatened to spread. As a member of the House Foreign Affairs Committee, Douglas urged cooperation with the Soviet Union, and she initially opposed aid to Greece and Turkey, the first step in the new containment policy. Yet thereafter, Douglas was Truman's loyal ally, supporting the Marshall Plan, the creation of the North Atlantic Treaty Organization, and the war in Korea. The containment policy achieved its goals in Europe, but communism spread in Asia, and at home a wave of anti-Communist hysteria — a second Red scare — harmed many Americans and stifled dissent and debate.

Douglas's earlier links with leftist groups and her advocacy of civil rights, women's rights, and social welfare programs made her and other liberals easy targets for conservative politicians seeking to capitalize on anti-Communist fervor. When she ran for the U.S. Senate in 1950, she faced Republican Richard M. Nixon, who had gained national attention as a member of the House Un-American Activities Committee, which sought to expose Communists in government. Nixon's campaign labeled Douglas as "pink right down to her underwear" and telephoned thousands of homes with the anonymous message, "I think you should know Helen Douglas is a Communist." Nixon won a decisive victory but throughout his life carried the appellation Douglas gave him, "Tricky Dick." Douglas's political career ended in defeat, just as much of Truman's domestic agenda fell victim to the Red scare.

Helen Gahagan Douglas at the Democratic National Convention
Long accustomed as an actress to appearing before an audience, the congresswoman from California was a popular campaigner for the Democrats and a featured speaker at Democratic National Conventions. Her appeal, shown in this photo from the 1948 convention, sparked interest in her for higher office. *The Washington Post* called it the "first genuine boom in history for a woman for vice-president," but she made it clear that she was not in the running. © Bettmann/Corbis.

► From the Grand Alliance to Containment

With Japan's surrender in August 1945, Americans besieged the government for the return of their loved ones. Baby booties arrived at the White House with a note, "Please send my daddy home." Americans wanted to dismantle the large military establishment and expected the Allies, led by the United States and working within the United Nations, to cooperate in the management of international peace. Postwar realities quickly dashed these hopes. New threats arose as the wartime alliance forged by the United States, Great Britain, and the Soviet Union crumbled, and the United States began to focus on strategies for containing the spread of Soviet power around the globe.

The Cold War Begins

"The guys who came out of World War II were idealistic," reported Harold Russell, a young paratrooper who had lost both hands in a training accident. "We felt the day had come when the wars were all over." Public opinion polls echoed the veterans' confidence in the promise of peace. But these hopes were quickly dashed. Once the Allies had overcome a common enemy, the prewar mistrust and antagonism between the Soviet Union and the West resurfaced over their very different visions of the postwar world.

The Western Allies' delay in opening a second front in Western Europe aroused Soviet suspicions during the war. The Soviet Union made supreme wartime sacrifices, losing more than twenty million citizens and vast portions of its agricultural and industrial capacity. Soviet leader **Joseph Stalin** wanted to make Germany pay for Soviet economic reconstruction and to expand Soviet influence in the world. Above all, he wanted friendly governments on the Soviet Union's borders in Eastern Europe, especially in Poland, through which German troops had marched to attack Russia twice in the past twenty-five years. A ruthless dictator, Stalin also wanted to maintain his own power.

In contrast to the Soviet devastation, enemy fire had never touched the mainland of the United States, and its 405,000 dead amounted to just 2 percent of the Soviet loss. With a vastly expanded economy and a monopoly on atomic weapons, the United States was the most powerful nation on the planet. That sheer power, along with U.S. economic interests, policymakers' views about how the recent war might have been avoided, and a belief in the superiority of American institutions and intentions, all affected how American leaders approached the Soviet Union.

Fearing a return of the depression, U.S. officials believed that a healthy economy depended on opportunities abroad. American companies needed access to raw materials, markets for their goods, and security for their investments overseas. These needs could be met best in countries with similar economic and political systems, not in those where government controls interfered with the free flow of products and dollars. As President **Harry S. Truman** put it in 1947, "The American system can survive in America only if it becomes a world system." Yet leaders and citizens alike regarded their foreign policy not as a self-interested campaign to guarantee economic interests, but as the means to preserve national security and bring freedom, democracy, and capitalism to the rest of the world. Laura Briggs, a woman from Jerome, Idaho, spoke for many Americans who believed "it was our destiny to prove that we were the children of God and that our way was right for the world."

Recent history also shaped postwar foreign policy. Americans believed that World War II might have been avoided had Britain and France resisted rather than appeased Hitler's initial aggression. Navy Secretary James V. Forrestal argued against trying to "buy [the Soviets'] understanding and sympathy. We tried that once with Hitler." This "appeasement" analogy would be invoked repeatedly when the United States faced challenges to the international status quo.

The man with ultimate responsibility for U.S. policy was a keen student of history but came to the White House with little international experience. Harry S. Truman anticipated Soviet-American cooperation, as long as the Soviet Union conformed to U.S. plans for the postwar world and restrained its expansionist impulses. Proud of his ability to make quick decisions, Truman determined to be firm with the Soviets, knowing well that America's nuclear monopoly gave him the upper hand.

Soviet and American interests clashed first in Eastern Europe. Stalin insisted that the Allies' wartime agreements gave him a free hand in the countries defeated or liberated by the Red Army, just as the United States was unilaterally

> "The American system can survive in America only if it becomes a world system."
> — President HARRY S. TRUMAN

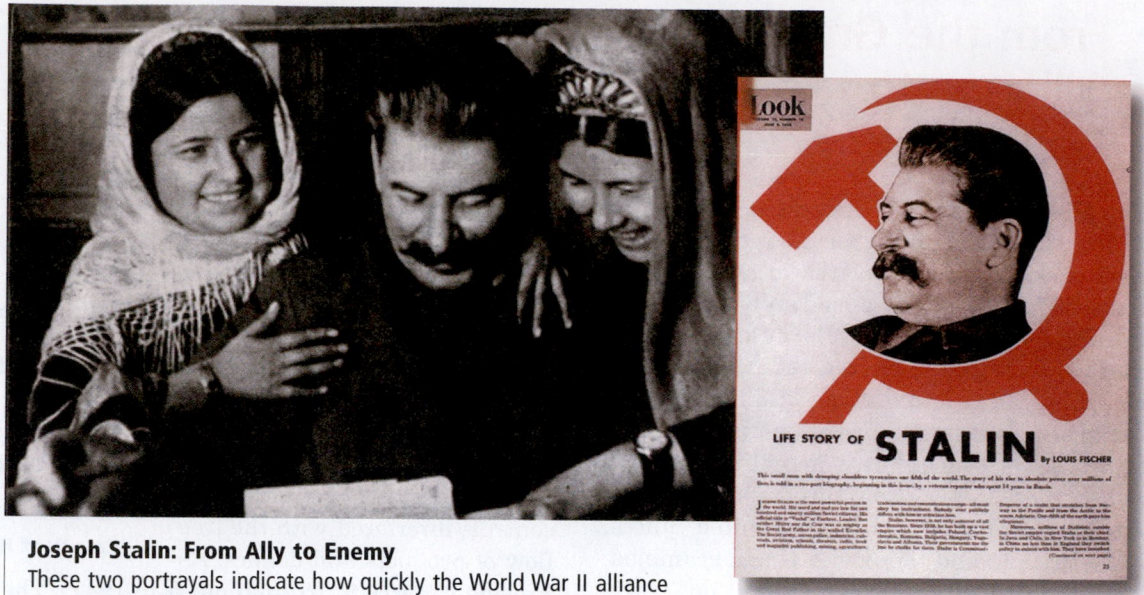

Joseph Stalin: From Ally to Enemy
These two portrayals indicate how quickly the World War II alliance disintegrated into the Cold War. The photograph on the left, from a 1944 issue of the popular magazine *Look*, shows Stalin with two adoring schoolchildren. Only four years later, in 1948, *Look* published Stalin's life story, framing his photo with communism's emblem, the hammer and sickle. The 1944 piece called Stalin a "man of indomitable will and extraordinary mental capacity [and a] lover of literature." The 1948 article depicted him as a "small man with drooping shoulders [who] tyrannizes one-fifth of the world." What do these two items suggest about the role of the press in American society? The Michael Barson Collection/Past Perfect.

reconstructing governments in Italy and Japan. The Soviet dictator used harsh methods to install Communist governments in neighboring Poland and Bulgaria. Elsewhere, the Soviets initially tolerated non-Communist governments in Hungary and Czechoslovakia. In the spring of 1946, Stalin responded to pressure from the West and removed troops from Iran on the Soviet Union's southwest border, allowing U.S. access to the rich oil fields there.

Stalin considered U.S. officials hypocritical in demanding democratic elections in Eastern Europe while supporting dictatorships friendly to U.S. interests in Latin America. The United States clung to its sphere of influence while opposing Soviet efforts to create its own. But the Western Allies were unwilling to match tough words with military force against the largest army in the world. They issued sharp protests but failed to prevent the Soviet Union from establishing satellite countries throughout Eastern Europe.

In 1946, the wartime Allies contended over Germany's future. Both sides wanted to demilitarize Germany, but U.S. policymakers sought rapid industrial revival there to foster European economic recovery and thus America's own long-term prosperity. By contrast, the Soviet Union wanted Germany weak both militarily and economically, and Stalin demanded heavy reparations from Germany to help rebuild the devastated Soviet economy. Unable to settle their differences, the Allies divided Germany. The Soviet Union installed a puppet Communist government in the eastern section, and Britain, France, and the United States began to unify their occupation zones, a process that eventually established the Federal Republic of Germany — West Germany — in 1949 (Map 26.1).

The war of words escalated early in 1946. Boasting of the superiority of the Soviet system, Stalin told a Moscow audience in February that capitalism inevitably produced war. One month later, Truman accompanied Winston Churchill to Westminster College in Fulton, Missouri, where the former prime minister denounced Soviet interference in Eastern and central Europe. "From Stettin in the Baltic to Trieste in the Adriatic, an **iron curtain** has descended across the Continent," Churchill said. (See "Documenting the American Promise," page 868.) Stalin saw Churchill's proposal for joint British-

Legend:
- European members of NATO, 1955
- Communist bloc countries
- Neutral countries
- Iron curtain

BERLIN inset:
- EAST GERMANY
- East Berlin
- West Berlin
- Berlin Wall, 1961
- U.S. zone
- British zone
- French zone
- Soviet zone

MAP ACTIVITY

Map 26.1   The Division of Europe after World War II

The "iron curtain," a term coined by Winston Churchill to refer to the Soviet grip on Eastern and central Europe, divided the continent for nearly fifty years. Communist governments controlled the countries along the Soviet Union's western border. The only exception was Finland, which remained neutral.

READING THE MAP: Is the division of Europe between NATO, Communist, and neutral countries about equal? Why would the location of Berlin pose a problem for the Western allies?

CONNECTIONS: When was NATO founded, and what was its purpose? How did the postwar division of Europe compare with the wartime alliances?

American action to combat Soviet aggression as "a call to war against the USSR."

In February 1946, **George F. Kennan**, a career diplomat and expert on Russia, wrote a comprehensive rationale for hard-line foreign policy. Downplaying the influence of Communist ideology in Soviet policy, he instead stressed the Soviets' insecurity and Stalin's need to maintain authority at home. These factors, he believed, prompted Stalin to exaggerate threats from abroad and motivated the Soviet government to try to "fill every nook and cranny available to it in the basin of world power." Kennan believed that the Soviet Union would retreat from its expansionist efforts if the United States would respond with "unalterable counterforce." He predicted that this approach, which came to be called **containment**, would eventually end in "either the breakup or the gradual mellowing of Soviet power." Kennan later expressed dismay when his ideas were used to justify what he considered indiscriminate American interventions wherever

The Emerging Cold War

Although antagonism between the Soviet Union and the West stretched back to the Russian Revolution of 1917, the United States, the Soviet Union, Britain, and other powers had cooperated to win World War II. Early in 1946, however, Soviet and Western leaders publicly expressed distrust and attributed hostile motivations to each other. Within the United States, disagreement arose about how to deal with the Soviet Union.

DOCUMENT 1
Joseph Stalin Addresses a Rally in Moscow, February 9, 1946

In early 1946, Premier Joseph Stalin called on the Soviet people to support his program for economic development. Although Stalin did not address Cold War issues, leaders in the West viewed his comments about communism and capitalism and his boasts about the strength of the Red Army as a threat to peace.

The [Second World War] arose as the inevitable result of the development of the world economic and political forces on the basis of monopoly capitalism. . . .

. . . The uneven development of the capitalist countries leads in time to sharp disturbances in their relations, and the group of countries which consider themselves inadequately provided with raw materials and export markets try usually to change this situation and to change the position in their favor by means of armed force. As a result of these factors, the capitalist world is split into two hostile camps and war follows. . . . The Soviet social system has proved to be more capable of life and more stable than a non-Soviet social system. . . .

. . . The Red Army heroically withstood all the adversities of the war, routed completely the armies of our enemies and emerged victoriously from the war. This is recognized by everybody — friend and foe.

[Stalin talks about his new Five-Year Plan.] Apart from the fact that in the very near future the rationing system will be abolished, special attention will be focused on expanding the production of goods for mass consumption, on raising the standard of life of the working people by consistent and systematic reduction of the costs of all goods, and on wide-scale construction of all kinds of scientific research institutes to enable science to develop its forces. I have no doubt that if we render the necessary assistance to our scientists they will be able not only to overtake but also in the very near future to surpass the achievements of science outside the boundaries of our country.

SOURCE: Excerpts from Joseph Stalin, *Vital Speeches of the Day*, February 9, 1946.

DOCUMENT 2
Winston Churchill Delivers His "Iron Curtain" Speech at Westminster College in Fulton, Missouri, March 5, 1946

With Truman sitting on the podium, Winston Churchill, former prime minister of Great Britain, assessed Soviet actions in harsh terms. In response, Stalin equated Churchill with Hitler, as a "firebrand of war."

The United States stands at this time at the pinnacle of world power. It is a solemn moment for the American democracy. With primacy in power is also joined an awe-inspiring accountability to the future. [Churchill then speaks of the need to support the United Nations.]

It would nevertheless be wrong and imprudent to intrust the secret knowledge or experience of the atomic bomb, which the United States, Great Britain and Canada now share, to the world organization [the United Nations], while it is still in its infancy. It would be criminal madness to cast it adrift in this still agitated and ununited world. . . .

. . . I have a strong admiration and regard for the valiant Russian people and for my war-time comrade, Marshal Stalin. . . . We understand the Russians need to be secure on her western frontiers from all renewal of German aggression. . . . It is my duty, however, to place before you certain facts. . . .

From Stettin in the Baltic to Trieste in the Adriatic, an iron curtain has descended across the Continent. Behind that line lie all the capitals of the ancient states of central and eastern Europe. Warsaw, Berlin, Prague, Vienna,

Budapest, Belgrade, Bucharest and Sofia, all these famous cities and the populations around them lie in the Soviet sphere and all are subject in one form or another, not only to Soviet influence but to a very high and increasing measure of control from Moscow. . . . The Communist parties, which were very small in all these eastern states of Europe, have been raised to preeminence and power far beyond their numbers and are seeking everywhere to obtain totalitarian control. Police governments are prevailing in nearly every case. . . .

. . . In a great number of countries, far from the Russian frontiers and throughout the world, Communist fifth columns are established and work in complete unity and absolute obedience to the directions they receive from the Communist center.

I do not believe that Soviet Russia desires war. What they desire is the fruits of war and the indefinite expansion of their power and doctrines. . . . Our difficulties and dangers will not be removed by . . . mere waiting to see what happens; nor will they be relieved by a policy of appeasement. . . . I am convinced that there is nothing [the Russians] admire so much as strength, and there is nothing for which they have less respect than for military weakness.

SOURCE: Excerpts from Winston Churchill, *Vital Speeches of the Day*, March 5, 1946.

DOCUMENT 3
Henry A. Wallace Addresses an Election Rally at Madison Square Garden, New York, September 12, 1946

Throughout 1946, Henry A. Wallace, Truman's secretary of commerce and predecessor as vice president, urged the president to take a more conciliatory approach toward the Soviet Union, a position reflected in a speech Wallace gave to a rally of leftist and liberal groups in New York City. Truman believed that Wallace's words undermined his foreign policy and demanded Wallace's resignation.

We cannot rest in the assurance that we invented the atom bomb — and therefore that this agent of destruction will work best for us. He who trusts in the atom bomb will sooner or later perish by the atom bomb — or something worse. . . .

To achieve lasting peace, we must study in detail just how the Russian character was formed — by invasions of Tartars, Mongols, Germans, Poles, Swedes, and French; by the czarist rule based on ignorance, fear and force; by the

intervention of the British, French and Americans in Russian affairs from 1919 to 1921; by the geography of the huge Russian land mass situated strategically between Europe and Asia; and by the vitality derived from the rich Russian soil and the strenuous Russian climate. Add to all this the tremendous emotional power which Marxism and Leninism gives to the Russian leaders — and then we can realize that we are reckoning with a force which cannot be handled successfully by a "Get tough with Russia" policy. "Getting tough" never bought anything real and lasting — whether for schoolyard bullies or businessmen or world powers. The tougher we get, the tougher the Russians will get. . . .

. . . We want cooperation. And I believe that we can get cooperation once Russia understands that our primary objective is neither saving the British Empire nor purchasing oil in the Near East with the lives of American soldiers. . . .

On our part we should recognize that we have no more business in the political affairs of Eastern Europe than Russia has in the political affairs of Latin America, Western Europe and the United States. . . . We have to recognize that the Balkans are closer to Russia than to us — and that Russia cannot permit either England or the United States to dominate the politics of that area. . . .

. . . Under friendly peaceful competition the Russian world and the American world will gradually become more alike. The Russians will be forced to grant more and more of the personal freedoms; and we shall become more and more absorbed with the problems of social-economic justice.

SOURCE: Excerpts from Henry A. Wallace, *Vital Speeches of the Day*, September 12, 1946. Reprinted with permission.

Questions for Analysis and Debate

1. What lessons did these three leaders draw from World War II? What did they see as the most critical steps to preventing another war?

2. What differences did these men see between the political and economic systems of the Soviet Union and those of the United States and Western Europe? How do their predictions about these systems differ?

3. What motives did these three men ascribe to Soviet actions? How do Churchill's and Wallace's proposals for the Western response to the Soviet Union differ?

4. Which leader do you think was most optimistic about the prospects for good relationships between Russia and the West? Which was most correct? Why?

communism seemed likely to arise. Nonetheless, his analysis marked a critical turning point in the development of the **Cold War**, providing a compelling rationale for wielding U.S. power throughout the world.

Not all public figures accepted the toughening line. In September 1946, Secretary of Commerce Henry A. Wallace urged greater understanding of the Soviets' concerns about their nation's security, insisting that "we have no more business in the political affairs of Eastern Europe than Russia has in the political affairs of Latin America." (See "Documenting the American Promise," page 868.) State Department officials were furious at this challenge to the hardening of U.S. policy, and Truman fired Wallace.

The Truman Doctrine and the Marshall Plan

In 1947, the United States began to implement the doctrine of containment that would guide foreign policy for the next four decades. It was not an easy transition; Americans approved taking a hard line against the Soviet Union, but they wanted to keep their soldiers and tax dollars at home. In addition to selling containment to the public, Truman had to gain the support of a Republican-controlled Congress, which included a forceful bloc opposed to a strong U.S. presence in Europe.

Crises in two Mediterranean countries triggered the implementation of containment. In February 1947, Britain informed the United States that its crippled economy could no longer sustain military assistance either to Greece, where the autocratic government faced a leftist uprising, or to Turkey, which was trying to resist Soviet pressures. Truman promptly sought congressional authority to send the two countries military and economic missions, along with $400 million in aid. Meeting with congressional leaders, Undersecretary of State Dean Acheson predicted that if Greece and Turkey fell, communism would soon consume three-fourths of the world. After a stunned silence, Michigan senator Arthur Vandenberg, the Republican foreign policy leader and a recent convert from isolationism, warned that to get approval, Truman would have to "scare hell out of the country."

Truman did just that. Outlining what would later be called the "domino theory," he warned that if Greece fell to the rebels, "confusion and disorder might well spread throughout the entire Middle East" and then create instability in Europe.

Failure to act, he said, "may endanger the peace of the world — and shall surely endanger the welfare of the nation." According to what came to be called the **Truman Doctrine**, the United States would not only resist Soviet military power but also "support free peoples who are resisting attempted subjugation by armed minorities or by outside pressures." The president failed to convince Helen Gahagan Douglas and some of her colleagues in Congress, who wanted the United States to work through the United Nations before acting unilaterally and who opposed propping up the authoritarian Greek government. But the administration won the day, setting a precedent for forty years of Cold War interventions that would aid any kind of government if the only alternative appeared to be communism. Said one World War II veteran in response to the Truman Doctrine, "I told my wife to dust off my uniform."

A much larger assistance program for Europe followed aid to Greece and Turkey. In May 1947, Acheson described a war-ravaged Western Europe, with "factories destroyed, fields impoverished, transportation systems wrecked, populations scattered and on the borderline of starvation." American citizens were sending generous amounts of private aid, but most Europeans were surviving on diets of 1,500 calories a day. Acheson insisted that Europe needed large-scale assistance to keep desperate citizens from turning to socialism or communism.

When British Foreign Secretary Ernest Bevin heard Secretary of State George C. Marshall propose the European Recovery Program, Bevin compared it to "a lifeline to a sinking man." Congress approved the measure, which came to be called the **Marshall Plan**, in March 1948, and over the next five years the United States spent $13 billion ($117 billion in 2010 dollars) to restore the economies of sixteen Western European nations. Marshall invited all European nations and the Soviet Union to cooperate in a request for aid, but as administration officials expected, the Soviets objected to the American terms of free trade and financial disclosure and ordered their Eastern European satellites likewise to reject the offer.

Humanitarian impulses as well as the goal of keeping Western Europe free of communism drove the adoption of this enormous aid program, one of the outstanding achievements of U.S. postwar foreign policy. But the Marshall Plan also helped boost the U.S. economy because the participating European nations spent most of

Marshall Plan Bread for Greek Children
Greece was one of sixteen European nations that participated in the European Recovery Program. In this photograph taken in 1949, Greek children receive loaves of bread made from the first shipment of Marshall Plan flour from the United States. © Bettmann/Corbis.

the dollars to buy American products and Europe's economic recovery created new markets and opportunities for American investment. In addition, by insisting that the recipient nations work together, the Marshall Plan marked the first step toward the European Union.

While Congress had been debating the Marshall Plan, in February 1948 the Soviets staged a brutal coup and installed a Communist regime in Czechoslovakia, the last democracy left in Eastern Europe. Next, Stalin threatened Western access to Berlin. That former capital of Germany lay within Soviet-controlled East Germany, but all four Allies jointly occupied Berlin, dividing it into separate administrative units. As the Western Allies moved to organize West Germany as a separate nation, the Soviets retaliated by blocking roads and rail lines between West Germany and the Western-held sections of Berlin, cutting off food, fuel, and other essentials to two million inhabitants.

Berlin Divided, 1948

"We stay in Berlin, period," Truman vowed. To avoid a confrontation with Soviet troops, for nearly a year U.S. and British pilots airlifted 2.3 million tons of goods to sustain the West Berliners. Stalin hesitated to shoot down these cargo planes, and in 1949 he lifted the blockade. The city was then divided into East Berlin, under Soviet control, and West Berlin, which became part of West Germany.

For many Americans, the **Berlin airlift** confirmed the wisdom of containment: When challenged, the Russians backed down, as George Kennan had predicted.

Building a National Security State

During the Truman years, advocates of the new containment policy fashioned a six-pronged defense strategy: (1) development of atomic weapons, (2) strengthening of traditional military power, (3) military alliances with other nations,

The Berlin Airlift

After the Soviet Union blockaded land routes into West Berlin in June 1948, the Western allies used airplanes to deliver food, fuel, and other necessities to Germans living there. At the peak of the airlift, U.S. or British planes landed every three minutes twenty-four hours a day. These children may have been watching for Air Force pilot Gail S. Halvorsen, who, after meeting hungry schoolchildren, began to drop candy and gum as his plane approached the landing strip. The vulnerability of Germans like these helped to ease hostile feelings that Americans and other Europeans felt toward their former enemies. Photo: Charles Fenno Jacobs/Hulton Archive/Getty Images; candy bar: Haraz N. Ghanbari.

(4) military and economic aid to friendly nations, (5) an espionage network and secret means to subvert Communist expansion, and (6) a propaganda offensive to win popular admiration for the United States around the world.

In September 1949, the United States lost its nuclear monopoly when the Soviet Union detonated its own atomic bomb. To keep the United States ahead, in January 1950 Truman approved the development of a **hydrogen bomb**, equivalent to five hundred atomic bombs. He rejected the counterarguments of several scientists who had worked on the atomic bomb and of George Kennan, who warned of an endless arms race. The "super bomb" was ready by 1954, but the U.S. advantage was brief. In November 1955, the Soviets exploded their own hydrogen bomb.

From the 1950s through the 1980s, deterrence formed the basis of American nuclear strategy. To deter the Soviet Union from attacking, the United States strove to maintain a nuclear force more powerful than the Soviets'. Because the Russians pursued a similar policy, the superpowers became locked in an ever-escalating nuclear weapons race. Albert Einstein, whose mathematical discoveries had laid the founda-

tions for nuclear weapons, commented grimly on the enormous destructive force the superpowers now possessed. The war that came after World War III, he warned, would "be fought with sticks and stones."

Implementing the second component of its containment strategy, the United States beefed up its conventional military power to deter Soviet threats that might not warrant nuclear retaliation. The National Security Act of 1947 streamlined defense planning by uniting the military branches under a single secretary of defense and creating the National Security Council (NSC) to advise the president. During the Berlin crisis in 1948, Congress hiked military appropriations and enacted a peacetime draft. In addition, Congress granted permanent status to the women's military branches, though it limited their numbers and rank and banned them from combat. General Dwight D. Eisenhower had recognized the contributions women could make in such traditionally female jobs as office work and nursing, and he assured Congress that "after an enlistment or two women will ordinarily — and thank God — they will get married." With 1.5 million men and women in uniform in 1950, the military strength of the United States had

Cold War Spying
"Intelligence," the gathering of information about the capabilities and intentions of the enemy, is as old as human warfare, but it took on new importance with the onset of the Cold War. Created in 1947, the Central Intelligence Agency (CIA) became an important Cold War tool. While much of the intelligence work took place in Washington, where analysts combed through Communist newspapers, official reports, and speeches, secret agents operating behind the iron curtain gathered information with bugs and devices such as these cameras hidden in cigarette packs. Spying soon gained a prominent place in popular culture, most notably in more than a dozen movies featuring James Bond, British agent 007. Jack Naylor Collection/Picture Research Consultants & Archives.

quadrupled since the 1930s, and defense expenditures claimed one-third of the federal budget.

Collective security, the third prong of containment strategy, marked a sharp reversal of the nation's traditional foreign policy. In 1949, the United States joined Canada and Western European nations in its first peacetime military alliance, the **North Atlantic Treaty Organization (NATO)**, designed to counter a Soviet threat to Western Europe (see Map 26.1). For the first time in its history, the United States pledged to go to war if one of its allies was attacked.

The fourth element of defense strategy involved foreign assistance programs to strengthen friendly countries, such as aid to Greece and Turkey and the Marshall Plan. In addition, in 1949 Congress approved $1 billion of military aid to its NATO allies, and the government began economic assistance to nations in other parts of the world.

The fifth ingredient of containment improved the government's espionage capacities and ability to thwart communism through covert activities. The National Security Act of 1947 created the **Central Intelligence Agency (CIA)** not only to gather information but also to perform any activities "related to intelligence affecting the national security" that the NSC might authorize. Such functions included propaganda, sabotage, economic warfare, and support for "anti-communist elements in threatened countries of the free world." In 1948, secret CIA operations helped defeat

Italy's Communist Party. Subsequently, CIA agents would intervene even more actively, helping to topple legitimate foreign governments and violating the rights of U.S. citizens.

Finally, the U.S. government sought, through cultural exchanges and propaganda, to win "hearts and minds" throughout the world. The government expanded the Voice of America, created during World War II to broadcast U.S. propaganda abroad. In addition, the State Department sent books, exhibits, jazz musicians, and other performers to foreign countries as "cultural ambassadors."

By 1950, the United States had abandoned age-old tenets of foreign policy. Isolationism and neutrality had given way to a peacetime military alliance and efforts to control events far beyond U.S. borders. Short of war, the United States could not stop the descent of the iron curtain, but it aggressively and successfully promoted economic recovery and a military shield for the rest of Europe.

Superpower Rivalry around the Globe

Efforts to implement containment moved beyond Europe. In Africa, Asia, and the Middle East, World War II accelerated a tide of national liberation movements against war-weakened imperial powers. By 1960, forty countries, with more than a quarter of the world's people, had won

Louis Armstrong in Düsseldorf
As one of its Cold War weapons, the United States sent representatives of American culture abroad. Jazz was especially popular around the world, and the State Department sponsored tours by black jazz artists in part to counter the image of the United States as a racist nation. Louis Armstrong, the great trumpet player, singer, and jazz innovator, is shown here captivating a German crowd in 1952. Later, when Armstrong became disillusioned with President Eisenhower's failure to act vigorously on civil rights, he canceled a tour of the Soviet Union, explaining, "The people over there ask me what's wrong with my country, what am I supposed to say?" AP Photo.

mination gave way to American leaders' concern about the nature of the new governments supplanting the old empires. Policymakers wanted to preserve opportunities for American trade, and U.S. corporations coveted the vast oil reserves in the Middle East. The United States viewed its own Revolution as the best model for independence movements and expected newly emerging nations to create institutions in the American democratic and capitalist image.

Yet leaders of many liberation movements, impressed with Russia's rapid economic growth, adopted socialist or Communist ideas. Although few of these movements had formal ties with the Soviet Union, American leaders saw them as a threatening extension of Soviet power. Seeking to hold communism at bay by fostering economic development and political stability, the Truman administration initiated the Point IV Program in 1949, providing technical aid to developing nations.

Civil war raged in China, where the Communists, led by **Mao Zedong** (Mao Tse-tung), fought the official Nationalist government under Jiang Jieshi (Chiang Kai-shek) as it sought to recover from the Japanese occupation. While the Communists gained support among the peasants for their land reforms and valiant stand against the Japanese, Jiang's corrupt and incompetent government alienated much of the population. Failing to promote negotiations between Jiang and Mao, the United States provided almost $3 billion in aid to the Nationalists during the civil war. Yet, recognizing the ineptness of Jiang's government, Truman and his advisers refused to divert further resources from Europe to China.

In October 1949, Mao established the People's Republic of China (PRC), and the Nationalists fled to the island of Taiwan. Fearing a U.S.-supported invasion to recapture China for the Nationalists, Mao signed a mutual defense treaty with the Soviet Union in which each nation pledged to defend the other in case of attack. The United States refused to recognize the PRC, blocked its admission to the United Nations, and supported the Nationalist government in Taiwan. Only a massive U.S. military commitment could have stopped the Chinese Communists, yet some Republicans charged that Truman and "pro-Communists

their independence. These nations, along with Latin America, came to be referred to collectively as the third world, a term denoting countries outside the Western (first world) and Soviet (second world) orbits that had not yet developed industrial economies.

Like Woodrow Wilson during World War I, Roosevelt and Truman promoted the ideal of self-determination. The United States granted independence to the Philippines in 1946, applauded the British withdrawal from India, and encouraged France to give up its control of Indochina. At the same time, both the United States and the Soviet Union cultivated governments in emerging nations that were friendly to their own interests. As the Cold War intensified, however, the ideal of self-deter-

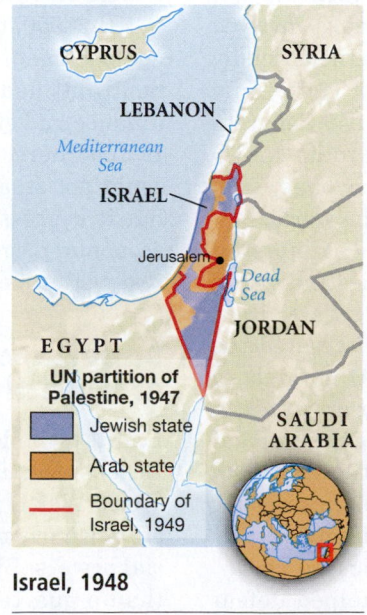

CYPRUS
SYRIA
LEBANON
Mediterranean Sea
ISRAEL
Jerusalem
Dead Sea
JORDAN
EGYPT

UN partition of Palestine, 1947
◼ Jewish state
◼ Arab state
— Boundary of Israel, 1949

SAUDI ARABIA

Israel, 1948

Mao Zedong on the Way to Victory
During World War II, Mao Zedong, leader of China's Communist Party, mobilized peasants around his revolution by implementing land reform where the Communists had control and by fighting valiantly against the Japanese. By the end of 1944, when this photo of Mao addressing his followers was taken, the Communists had a military force of more than half a million and control of more than eighty million Chinese. © Bettmann/Corbis.

in the State Department" had "lost" China. China became a political albatross for the Democrats, who resolved never again to be vulnerable to charges of being soft on communism.

With China in turmoil, the administration reconsidered its plans for postwar Japan. U.S. policy shifted to helping Japan rapidly reindustrialize and secure access to natural resources and markets in Asia. In a short time, the Japanese economy was flourishing, and the official military occupation ended when the two nations signed a peace treaty and a mutual security pact in September 1951. Like West Germany, Japan now sat squarely within the American orbit, ready to serve as an economic hub in a vital area.

The one place where Cold War considerations did not control American policy was Palestine. In 1943, then-senator Harry Truman spoke passionately about Nazi Germany's annihilation of the Jews, asserting, "This is not a Jewish problem, it is an American problem — and we must . . . face it squarely and honorably." As president, he made good on his words. Jews had been migrating to Palestine, their biblical homeland, since the nineteenth century, resulting in tension and hostilities with the Palestinian Arabs. After World War II, as hundreds of thousands of European Jews sought refuge and the creation of a national homeland in Palestine, fighting escalated into brutal terrorism on both sides.

Truman's foreign policy experts sought American-Arab friendship as a barrier against Soviet influence in the Middle East and as a means to secure access to Arabian oil. Uncharacteristically defying his advisers, the president responded instead to pleas from Jewish organizations, his moral commitment to Holocaust survivors, and his interest in the American Jewish vote for the 1948 election. When Jews in Palestine declared the state of Israel in May 1948, Truman quickly recognized the new country and made its defense the cornerstone of U.S. policy in the Middle East.

REVIEW Why did relations between the United States and the Soviet Union deteriorate after World War II?

▶ Truman and the Fair Deal at Home

Referring to the Civil War general who coined the phrase "War is hell," Truman said in December 1945, "Sherman was wrong. I'm telling you I find peace is hell." Challenged by crises abroad, Truman also faced shortages, strikes, inflation, and other problems as the economy shifted to peacetime production. At the same time, he tried to expand New Deal reform with his own **Fair Deal** agenda of initiatives in civil rights, housing, education, and health care — efforts hindered by the wave of anti-Communist hysteria sweeping the country. In sharp contrast to his success with Congress in foreign policy, Truman achieved but a modest slice of his domestic agenda.

Reconverting to a Peacetime Economy

Despite scarcities and deprivations during World War II, most Americans had enjoyed a higher standard of living than ever before. Economic

TRYING TO CATCH UP WITH YOUR DEMANDS...THOUSANDS OF NEW PROCTOR IRONS AND TOASTERS

Here they come!

PROCTOR
AUTOMATIC ELECTRIC APPLIANCES

Women's Role in Peacetime
Like many manufacturers forced to convert to war production during World War II, Proctor Electric Company, which had switched from making appliances to producing bomb fuses, cartridges, and airplane wing flaps, hoped to profit after the war from pent-up consumer demand. Even before the company had fully reconverted its plants, ads tempted consumers with products soon to come and asked them to be patient until Proctor could meet their needs, as this 1946 ad indicates. Why do you think a woman was featured in this ad? What message about women's employment during and after the war is conveyed here? Picture Research Consultants & Archives.

experts as well as ordinary citizens worried about sustaining that standard and providing jobs for millions of returning soldiers. Truman wasted no time unveiling his plan, asking Congress to enact a twenty-one-point program of social and economic reforms. He wanted to maintain the government's power to regulate the economy while it adjusted to peacetime production, and he sought government programs to provide basic essentials such as housing and health care to those in need, programs that had been on the drawing board during the New Deal. "Not even President Roosevelt ever asked for as much at one sitting," exploded Republican leader Joseph W. Martin Jr.

Congress approved one of Truman's key proposals — full-employment legislation — but even that was watered down. The Employment Act of 1946 invested the federal government with the responsibility "to promote maximum employ-

ment, production, and purchasing power," thereby formalizing what had been implicit in Roosevelt's antidepression measures — government's responsibility for maintaining a healthy economy. The law created the Council of Economic Advisors to assist the president, but it authorized no new powers to translate the government's obligation into effective action.

Inflation, not unemployment, turned out to be the most severe problem in the early postwar years. Consumers had $30 billion in wartime savings to spend, but shortages of meat, automobiles, housing, and other items persisted. Until industry could convert fully to civilian production and make more goods available, consumer demand would continue to drive up prices. With a basket of groceries on her arm to dramatize rising costs, Helen Gahagan Douglas urged Congress to support Truman's efforts to maintain price and rent controls. Those efforts fell, however, to pressures from business groups and others determined to trim government powers.

Labor relations were another thorn in Truman's side. Organized labor survived the war stronger than ever, its 14.5 million members making up 35 percent of the civilian workforce. Yet union members feared the erosion of wartime gains and launched an intense struggle to preserve them. Turning to the weapon they had set aside during the war, 5 million workers went out on strike in 1946, affecting nearly every major industry. Workers saw corporate executives profiting at their expense. Shortly before voting to strike, a former Marine and his coworkers calculated that a lavish party given by a company executive had cost more than they would earn in a whole year at the steel mill. "That sort of stuff made us realize, hell we had to bite the bullet. . . . The bosses sure didn't give a damn for us." Although most Americans approved of unions in principle, they became fed up with strikes, blamed unions for shortages and rising prices, and called for government restrictions on organized labor. When the wave of strikes subsided, workers had won wage increases of about 20 percent, but the loss of overtime pay along with rising prices left their purchasing power only slightly higher than in 1942.

Women workers fared even worse. Polls indicated that as many as 68 to 85 percent wanted to keep their wartime jobs, but most who remained in the workforce had to settle for relatively low-paying jobs in light industry or the service sector (Figure 26.1). Displaced from her shipyard work, Marie Schreiber took a cashier's job, lamenting, "You were back to women's wages, you know . . . practically in half." (See "Historical Question," page 878.) With the backing of women's organizations and union women, Congresswoman Douglas sponsored bills to require equal pay for equal work, to provide child care for employed mothers, and to create a government commission to study the status of women. But at a time when women were viewed primarily as wives and mothers and a strong current of opinion resisted further expansion of federal powers, these initiatives got nowhere.

By 1947, the economy had stabilized, avoiding the postwar depression that so many had feared. Wartime profits enabled businesses to expand. Consumers could now spend their wartime savings on houses, cars, and appliances that had lain beyond their reach during the depression and war. Defense spending and foreign aid that enabled war-stricken countries to purchase American products also stimulated the economy. A soaring birthrate further sustained consumer demand.

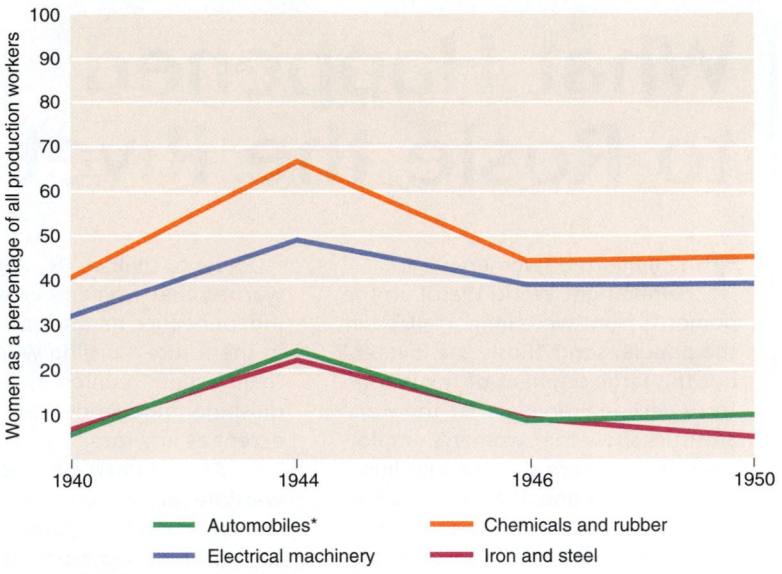

Legend:
- Automobiles*
- Chemicals and rubber
- Electrical machinery
- Iron and steel

*During World War II, this industry did not produce cars, but rather military transportation such as jeeps, tanks, aircraft, etc.

FIGURE 26.1 Women Workers in Selected Industries, 1940–1950
Women demolished the idea that some jobs were "men's work" during World War II, but they failed to maintain their gains in the manufacturing sector after the war.

Although prosperity was far from universal, the United States entered into a remarkable economic boom that lasted through the 1960s (as discussed in chapter 27).

Another economic boost came from the only large welfare measure passed after the New Deal. The **Servicemen's Readjustment Act (GI Bill)**, enacted in 1944, offered 16 million veterans job training and education; unemployment compensation while they looked for jobs; and low-interest loans to purchase homes, farms, and small businesses. By 1948, some

Veterans Go to College
So many World War II veterans wanted to use their GI benefits for higher education that colleges were overwhelmed. Many institutions had to turn away students, and they frequently limited the enrollments of women so that they could accommodate veterans. At the University of Iowa, where this photo was taken, veterans like these men comprised 60 percent of the student body. Veterans' organizations helped former GIs gain access to benefits with pamphlets like the one shown here. Photo: Margaret Bourke-White/Time Life Pictures /Getty Images; brochure: Minnesota Historical Society.

What Happened to Rosie the Riveter?

The millions of women who helped fight World War II on the domestic front were immortalized in the popular song "Rosie the Riveter," but this large segment of the work-force declined rapidly after the war. Statistics show that women's employment fell by more than two million between 1945 and 1947. Gross statistics, however, do not reveal which women left the labor force and why, and they obscure the experiences of women who continued to work but in different jobs.

Undoubtedly, public officials and business and labor leaders expected women who had taken up men's work during the war to return to domestic life. With the shadow of depression-era unemployment still hovering, women were bombarded with the message that they should quit their jobs "for the sake of their homes as well as the labor situation." The company newspaper at Kaiser shipyards in the Pacific Northwest proclaimed in May 1945, "The Kitchen — Women's Big Post-War Goal." A General Electric ad predicted that women would welcome a return to "their old house-keeping routine" because GE intended to transform housework with new appliances. Some experts connected married women's employment to their husbands' ability to

readjust to civilian life. A psychiatrist warned that women's economic independence might "raise problems in the future," urging women to realize that "reunion means relinquishing [independence] — to some extent at any rate."

Many women gave up their wartime jobs eagerly. Skyrocketing marriage and birth rates reveal the attraction of domesticity to people compelled to postpone marriage and childbearing by depression and war. The accumulation of wartime savings along with veterans' benefits enabled most families to rely on a single wage earner. Moreover, the double burdens placed on married women and mothers who took wartime jobs provided another reason for women's voluntary withdrawal from the workforce.

Yet surveys reported that 75 percent of women in wartime jobs wanted — and usually needed — to keep working. As two women employed at a Ford plant put it, "Women didn't stop eating when the war stopped." Those who struggled to remain in the workforce experienced the most wrenching changes. The vast majority managed to find jobs; in fact, women's work-force participation began growing again in 1947 and equaled the war-time peak by 1950. But women lost

the traditionally male, higher-paying jobs in heavy industries such as steel and automobile production and were pushed back into the lower-paying light manufacturing and service industries that had customarily welcomed them.

Statistics tell part of the story of this displacement. Women virtually disappeared from shipbuilding, and their share of jobs in the auto industry fell from 25 percent in 1944 to 10 percent in 1950. In light manufacturing, such as the electrical goods industry, where women had claimed one-third of the prewar jobs, women maintained their numbers but were bumped down to lower-paying work. During the war, women had narrowed the wage gap between men and women, but in 1950 employed women earned only 53 percent of what men did.

How women felt about their displacement can be pieced together to some extent from what they said to reporters and oral history interviewers and what they wrote to government agencies and labor unions. "Women do not expect or want to hold jobs at the expense of returning soldiers," resolved the Women's Trade Union League. Tina Hill, a black worker laid off from North American Aircraft in Los Angeles, remembered, "I was just glad that the war was over . . . [and] my husband had a job." Nonetheless, after doing domestic work, she leaped at the chance when North American called her back: "Was I a happy soul!"

1.3 million veterans had bought houses with government loans. Helping 2.2 million ex-soldiers attend college, the subsidies sparked a boom in higher education. A drugstore clerk before his military service, Don Condren was able to get an engineering degree and buy his first house. "I think the GI Bill gave the whole country an upward boost economically," he said.

Condren overlooked the disparate ways in which the GI Bill operated. As wives and daughters of veterans, women did benefit indirectly from the GI subsidies. Yet because women had

filled just a small proportion of military slots during the war, most women did not qualify for the employment and educational preferences available to some 15 million men. As a result, while women's enrollments increased after the war, their share of college degrees plunged below the prewar level.

Like key New Deal programs such as unemployment insurance and aid to mothers with dependent children, GI programs were administered at the state and local levels, which especially in the South routinely discriminated

When management violated women's seniority rights by hiring nonveterans, some women protested bitterly. According to one automobile worker, "We have women laid off with seniority . . . and every day they hire in new men off the street. They hire men, they say, to do the heavy work. . . . During the war they didn't care what kind of work we did." When Ford laid off women with as much as twenty-seven years' seniority, 150 women picketed with signs that read, "The Hand That Rocks the Cradle Can Build Tractors, Too."

Protests from a minority of women workers could not save the jobs that the "Rosies" had held during the war. Despite women's often exemplary performance, most employers — and most Americans — still saw women and men as different species fit for different roles and deserving of different rewards. Labor unions paid lip service to representing all their members, but few gave high priority to protecting women's seniority rights. In the absence of any federal laws against sex discrimination or a feminist movement that could have given visibility and credibility to their claims for equal treatment, most Rosie the Riveters resigned themselves to "women's work."

Sisters under the apron—Yesterday's war worker becomes today's housewife.

What's Become of Rosie the Riveter?

Women's Postwar Future
This photograph headed a *New York Times Magazine* article in June 1946. The article discussed the needs of women workers, stressing their right to work and to receive equal pay, but it also assumed that women would all but vanish from heavy manufacturing. Ellen Kaiper Collection, Oakland.

Thinking about Evidence

1. What can statistics tell us about women's work after World War II? What can we learn about women's postwar employment experiences by examining individual women's statements, letters, and interviews?

2. What are the limitations of the types of sources mentioned in this feature? How does combining different types of sources help to overcome those limitations? What other kinds of sources might be useful?

3. Based on the evidence in this feature, for what reasons did women leave the labor force? For what reasons did they remain in it?

against African Americans. Southern universities remained segregated, and the small historically black colleges could not accommodate all who wanted to attend. Black veterans who sought jobs for which the military had trained them were shuttled into menial labor. One decorated veteran said that the GI Bill "draws no color line," yet "my color bars me from most decent jobs, and if, instead of accepting menial work, I collect my $20 a week readjustment allowance, I am classified as a 'lazy nigger.'" Thousands of black veterans did benefit from

the GI Bill, but it did not help all ex-soldiers equally.

Blacks and Mexican Americans Push for Their Civil Rights

"I spent four years in the army to free a bunch of Frenchmen and Dutchmen," an African American corporal declared, "and I'm hanged if I'm going to let the Alabama version of the Germans kick me around when I get home." Black veterans as well as civilians resolved that the return to peace would not be a return to the racial injustices of prewar America. Their political clout had grown with the migration of two million African Americans to northern and western cities, where they could vote and participate in ongoing struggles to end discrimination in housing and education. Pursuing civil rights through the courts and Congress, the National Association for the Advancement of Colored People (NAACP) counted half a million members.

In the postwar years, individual African Americans broke through the color barrier, achieving several "firsts." Jackie Robinson integrated major league baseball, playing for the Brooklyn Dodgers and braving abuse from fans and players to win the Rookie of the Year Award in 1947. In 1950, Ralph J. Bunche received the Nobel Peace Prize for his United Nations work, and Gwendolyn Brooks won the Pulitzer Prize for poetry. Charlie "Bird" Parker, Ella Fitzgerald, and a host of other black musicians were hugely popular across racial lines.

Still, for most African Americans little had changed, especially in the South, where most blacks still lived and where violence greeted their attempts to assert their rights. Armed white men turned back Medgar Evers (who would become a key civil rights leader in the 1960s) and four other veterans trying to vote in Mississippi. A mob lynched Isaac Nixon for voting in Georgia, and an all-white jury acquitted the men accused of his murder. In the South, political leaders and local vigilantes routinely intimidated potential black voters with threats of violence and warnings that they could lose their livelihoods.

The Cold War heightened American leaders' sensitivity to racial issues, as the superpowers vied for the allegiance of newly independent nations with nonwhite populations. Soviet propaganda repeatedly highlighted racial injustice in the United States. Republican senator Henry Cabot Lodge called race relations "our Achilles' heel before the world," while Secretary of State Dean Acheson noted that systematic segregation and discrimination endangered "our moral leadership of the free and democratic nations of the world."

"My very stomach turned over when I learned that Negro soldiers just back from overseas were being dumped out of army trucks in Mississippi and beaten," wrote Truman. Despite his need for southern white votes, Truman spoke more boldly

Segregation
The segregation visible on this bus was a feature of life in the South from the late nineteenth century until the 1960s. State and local laws mandated separation from the cradle to the grave. African Americans could not use white hospitals, cemeteries, schools, libraries, swimming pools, restrooms, or drinking fountains. They were relegated to balconies in movie theaters and kept apart from whites in all public meetings. Segregated buses would become the target of the first large-scale civil rights protest, in Montgomery, Alabama, in 1955–1956.
Stan Wayman/Time Life Pictures/Getty Images.

on civil rights than any previous president had, thus appealing more to northern black and liberal voters. In 1946, he created the President's Committee on Civil Rights, and in February 1948 he asked Congress to enact the committee's recommendations. The first president to address the NAACP, Truman asserted that all Americans should have equal rights to housing, education, employment, and the ballot.

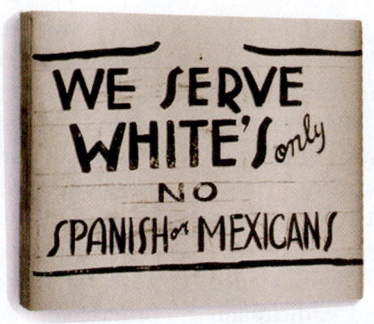

As with much of his domestic program, the president failed to act aggressively on his bold words. Congress rejected Truman's proposals for national civil rights legislation, although some northern and western states did pass laws against discrimination in employment and public accommodations. Running for reelection in 1948, Truman issued an executive order to desegregate the armed services, but it lay unimplemented until the Korean War, when the cost of segregation to military efficiency became apparent. Army officers gradually integrated their ranks, and by 1953, 95 percent of all African Americans served in mixed units. Despite the gap between Truman's words and what his administration actually accomplished, desegregation of the military and the administration's support of civil rights cases in the Supreme Court contributed to far-reaching changes, while his Committee on Civil Rights set an agenda for years to come.

Although discussion of race and civil rights usually focused on African Americans, Mexican Americans endured similar injustices. In 1929, they had formed the League of United Latin-American Citizens (LULAC) to combat discrimination and segregation in the Southwest. Like black soldiers after World War II, Mexican American veterans believed, as one of them insisted, that "we had earned our credentials as American citizens. We had paid our dues." Problems with getting their veterans' benefits spurred the formation of a new organization in 1948 in Corpus Christi, Texas — the **American GI Forum**. Dr. **Héctor Peréz García**, president of the local LULAC chapter and a combat surgeon who had received the Bronze Star, led the GI Forum, which became a key national organization for battling discrimination against Latinos and electing sympathetic officials.

"Education is our freedom," read the GI Forum's motto, yet Mexican American children were routinely segregated in public schools. In 1945, with the help of LULAC, parents filed a class action suit in southern California, challenging several school districts that barred their children from white schools. In the resulting decision, *Mendez v. Westminster* (1947), a federal court for the first time struck down school segregation. NAACP lawyer Thurgood Marshall filed a supporting brief in the case, which foreshadowed the landmark *Brown* decision in 1954 (as discussed in chapter 27). Efforts to gain equal education, along with challenges to discrimination in employment and campaigns for political representation, demonstrated a growing mobilization of Mexican Americans in the Southwest.

Dr. Héctor P. García

Héctor García, shown here with patients, came from Mexico to the United States as a small boy and, like all of his five siblings, became a doctor. While leading the G.I. Forum and advocating for Mexican-American rights, García treated all who needed his medical care regardless of whether they could pay for it. An associate referred to García, who also became active in politics, as "a man who in the space of one week delivers 20 babies, 20 speeches, and 20 thousand votes." He was appointed as an alternate U.S. Ambassador to the United Nations and served on the U.S. Commission on Civil Rights. Héctor P. García Papers, Special Collections & Archives, Texas A&M. University, Corpus Christi, Bell Library.

The Fair Deal Flounders

Republicans capitalized on public frustrations with strikes and shortages in the 1946 congressional election, accusing the administration of "confusion, corruption, and communism." Helen Gahagan Douglas hung on to her seat, but the Republicans captured control of Congress for the first time in fourteen years. Many had campaigned against New Deal "bureaucracy" and "radicalism" in 1946, and in the Eightieth Congress they suc-

ceeded in weakening some reform programs and enacting tax cuts favoring higher-income groups.

Organized labor took the most severe blow when Congress passed the **Taft-Hartley Act** over Truman's veto in 1947. Called a "slave labor" law by unions, the measure reduced the power of organized labor and made it more difficult to organize workers. For example, states could now pass "right-to-work" laws, which banned the practice of requiring all workers to join a union once a majority had voted for it. Many states,

VISUAL ACTIVITY

Harry Truman rallies a crowd from his campaign train in Bridgeport, Pennsylvania, in October 1948. This was the last presidential election in which pollsters predicted the wrong winner. They stopped taking polls in mid-October, after which many voters apparently changed their minds. One commentator praised the American citizenry, who "couldn't be ticketed by the polls, knew its own mind, and had picked the rather unlikely but courageous figure of Truman to carry on its banner." Truman's support for civil rights cost him four southern states but helped him win votes from liberals and blacks. Photo: Truman Library; campaign button: Collection of Janice L. and David J. Frent.

READING THE IMAGE: This photo was taken one month before the election. Why might his opponent's campaign have dismissed the importance of these large crowds in support of Truman?

CONNECTIONS: President Truman was under attack by the Republicans and could not enact the Fair Deal. Almost everyone thought he would lose the election. Why do you think the American people responded so well to his campaign? In what ways have presidential campaigns changed since Harry Truman's time?

especially in the South and West, rushed to enact such laws, encouraging industries to relocate there. Taft-Hartley maintained the New Deal principle of government protection for collective bargaining, but it put the government more squarely between labor and management.

In the 1948 elections, Truman faced not only a resurgent Republican Party headed by New York governor Thomas E. Dewey but also two revolts within his own party. On the left, Henry A. Wallace, whose foreign policy views had cost him his cabinet seat, led the new Progressive Party. On the right, South Carolina governor J. Strom Thurmond headed the States' Rights Party — the Dixiecrats — formed by southern Democrats who had walked out of the 1948 Democratic Party convention when it passed a liberal civil rights plank.

Almost alone in believing he could win, Truman crisscrossed the country by train, answering supporters' cries of "Give 'em hell, Harry." So bleak were Truman's prospects that on election night the *Chicago Daily Tribune* printed its next day's issue with the headline "Dewey Defeats Truman." But even though the Dixiecrats won four southern states, Truman took 303 electoral votes to Dewey's 189, and his party regained control of Congress (Map 26.2). His unexpected victory attested to the broad support for his foreign policy and the enduring popularity of New Deal reform.

While the major New Deal programs survived Republican attacks, Truman failed to enact his Fair Deal agenda. Congress made modest improvements in Social Security and raised the minimum wage, but it passed only one significant reform measure. Enacted with significant Republican support, the **Housing Act of 1949** authorized 810,000 units of government-constructed housing over the next six years and represented a landmark commitment by the government to address the housing needs of the poor. Yet it fell far short of actual need — just 61,000 units had been built when Truman left office — and slum clearance frequently displaced the poor without providing decent alternatives.

With southern Democrats posing a primary obstacle, Congress rejected Truman's proposals for civil rights, a powerful medical lobby blocked plans for a universal health care program based on the Social Security model, and conflicts over race and religion thwarted federal aid to education. Truman's efforts to revise immigration policy were mixed. The McCarran-Walter Act of 1952 ended the outright ban on immigration and citizenship for Japanese and other Asians, but it also authorized the government to bar suspected Communists and homosexuals and maintained the discriminatory quota system established in the 1920s. The president denounced that provision as "unworthy of our traditions and our ideals," but Congress overrode his veto.

Truman's concentration on foreign policy rather than domestic proposals contributed to the failure of his Fair Deal. Moreover, by late 1950, the Korean War embroiled the president in controversy and depleted his power as a legislative leader (see pages 887–892). Truman's failure to make good on his domestic proposals and expand the framework of the welfare state begun by Roosevelt set the United States apart from most European nations. By the 1950s, most other industrial democracies had in place comprehensive health, housing, and employment security programs to underwrite the material well-being of their populations.

The Domestic Chill: McCarthyism

Truman's domestic program also suffered from a wave of anticommunism that weakened liberal and leftist forces. "Red-baiting" (attempts to discredit individuals or ideas by associating them with communism) and official retaliation against leftist critics of the government had flourished during the Red scare at the end of World War I (see chapter 22). A second Red

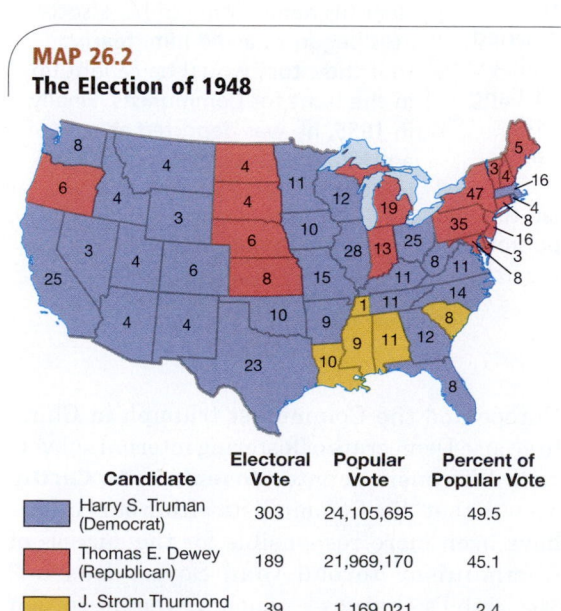

MAP 26.2
The Election of 1948

Candidate	Electoral Vote	Popular Vote	Percent of Popular Vote
Harry S. Truman (Democrat)	303	24,105,695	49.5
Thomas E. Dewey (Republican)	189	21,969,170	45.1
J. Strom Thurmond (States' Rights)	39	1,169,021	2.4
Henry A. Wallace (Progressive)	0	1,156,103	2.4

An Immigrant Scientist Encounters the Anti-Communist Crusade

Qian Xuesen (Tsien Hsue-shen) was born to a privileged family in Hangzhou, China, in 1911. Qian's father, an education official, encouraged academic excellence in his son from the start, giving him a name that means "study to be wise." After spending most of his youth in Beijing (Peking), Qian attended Jiaotong University in Shanghai, graduating at the top of his class from China's best engineering school. Deciding that aviation was the wave of the future and aware of how far behind his country lagged in this area, Qian looked abroad to further his education. In 1935, with his country torn by Japanese aggression and internal opposition to the Nationalist government, he accepted an American-sponsored scholarship and quickly earned a master's degree in aeronautical engineering from the Massachusetts Institute of Technology (MIT). One year later, he began doctoral work at the California Institute of Technology (Caltech) in Pasadena.

At Caltech, Qian joined a group of scientists working on questions about flight and contributed to the development of theoretical aerodynamics and jet propulsion, which eventually provided a foundation for America's space program. School officials were so impressed with Qian's work that they helped him get a visa extension, and in 1942 the government gave him security clearance so that he could work on the military's secret projects. Qian served on the air force's Scientific Advisory Board, and after World War II he went on a U.S. mission to interview Nazi scientists in Germany. He spent a year on the faculty at MIT and then traveled home to China amid the turmoil of a civil war between the Communists, led by Mao Zedong (Mao Tse-tung), and the Nationalist government of Jiang Jieshi (Chiang Kai-shek). While in China, Qian spent time with his father, gave motivational speeches to large audiences of students, and married a woman he had known in childhood, an opera singer named Jiang Ying (Tsiang Ying), who was the daughter of one of Jiang Jieshi's generals.

In 1949, when he returned to Caltech to direct the Jet Propulsion Center, teach, continue his research, and entertain a close circle of colleagues with classical music and elaborate dinners, Qian seemed to have everything necessary to lead a rich life and pursue his lifelong passion for science. He applied for U.S. citizenship. One year later, after the Communists had taken control of China, the U.S. government revoked Qian's security clearance. The FBI interrogated him about his associations with a group he had socialized with in the 1930s, which the FBI said was a cell of the Communist Party. Qian denied any participation in Communist activities, but the proud, angry, and humiliated scientist concluded that, given the "cloud of suspicion . . . the only gentlemanly thing left to do is to depart." The promise of a brilliant career shattered, he resisted the entreaties of Caltech officials who begged him to remain; instead, he readied a shipment of his belongings to send on to China. The government seized the shipment and accused Qian of taking secret documents. Although the claim was later refuted, the Immigration and Naturalization Service arrested him. He was released after two weeks, but for the next five years the government refused to let him go, and he and his family were kept under constant surveillance. Although Caltech administrators worked furiously to clear his name, some of his associates began to avoid him, fearing that they, too, would be caught up in the hunt for Communists. Finally, in 1955, he was deported as part of a prisoner of war exchange following the Korean War.

Qian disembarked in China with his wife and two children to a hero's reception and a career that

scare followed World War II, born of partisan political maneuvering, the collapse of the Soviet-American alliance, setbacks in U.S. foreign policy, and disclosures of Soviet espionage in the United States, Canada, and Great Britain.

Republicans who had attacked the New Deal as a plot of radicals now jumped on such Cold War events as the Soviet takeover of Eastern Europe and the Communist triumph in China to accuse Democrats of fostering internal subversion. Wisconsin senator **Joseph R. McCarthy** avowed that "the Communists within our borders have been more responsible for the success of Communism abroad than Soviet Russia." McCarthy's charges — such as the allegation that retired general George C. Marshall belonged to a Communist conspiracy — were reckless and would eventually earn him the title of "father of Chinese rocketry." Denied the full use of his talents by the United States, he organized and led China's rocketry program, developing its ballistic missiles and satellites. He became a trusted Communist Party official and loyal supporter of the government, as did anyone who hoped to have a successful career in China. Though the extremely private Qian said little about his experiences in the United States, he refused to return in 1979 to accept Caltech's Distinguished Alumni Award. Qian had lost faith in the U.S. government, but former colleagues who visited him reported that he maintained affection for the American people, and both his son and his daughter studied at American universities. Qian died in China in 2009 at the age of ninety-eight.

Questions linger about Qian's associations and intentions in the United States. A 1999 congressional report maintained that he had been a spy, but his supporters claimed that the report lacked evidence. Every one of his Caltech colleagues vouched for his integrity, and some went to great lengths to defend him against government charges. Dan A. Kimball, who was secretary of the navy in the early 1950s, later said that Qian's deportation "was the stupidest thing this country ever did. He was no more a Communist than I was — and we forced him to go." The Red scare dashed Qian's belief that America promised an opportunity for any talented individual to live a free and prosperous life. It also delivered a brilliant scientist to the nation's enemy.

Qian Xuesen
Qian Xuesen, the Chinese-American rocket scientist, teaches a class at the California Institute of Technology in 1955, shortly before he was deported back to China. Students who worked with him in the 1940s were "awe-struck" by his brilliance. He generously mentored those whose mental powers matched his, but was impatient, unbending, and harsh toward those he deemed intellectually incapable. "Students were scared stiff of him," remembered one. By the 1950s, however, students found Qian to be kinder and more supportive, perhaps because of his own ordeal with the FBI. © Bettmann/Corbis.

Questions for Consideration

1. What particular aspects of American life and institutions attracted Qian to the United States in the first place, and what made him want to stay in the country?

2. How did the timing of events in Qian's case correlate with domestic and international developments related to the Cold War and McCarthyism?

often ludicrous, but the press covered him avidly, and McCarthyism became a term synonymous with the anti-Communist crusade.

Revelations of Soviet espionage gave some credibility to fears of internal communism. For example, a number of ex-Communists, including Whittaker Chambers and Elizabeth Bentley, testified that they and others had provided secret documents to the Soviets. Chambers asserted that Alger Hiss, a former New Dealer who had served in the wartime State Department, had belonged to a secret Communist cell. Although Hiss denied the charges and prominent Democrats defended him, in 1950 a jury convicted him of lying to congressional investigators about his connections with Chambers, and he spent four years in prison. Most alarming of all, in 1950 a British physicist working on the atomic bomb project confessed that he was a spy and implicated several Americans, including Ethel and Julius Rosenberg. The Rosenbergs pleaded not guilty but were convicted of conspiracy to commit espionage and electrocuted in 1953, the only Americans to be executed for treason during the Red scare.

Records opened in the 1990s showed that the Soviet Union did receive secret documents from Americans that probably hastened its development of nuclear weapons by a year or two. Yet the vast majority of individuals hunted down in the Red scare had done nothing more than at one time joining the Communist Party, associating with Communists, or supporting radical causes. And most of those activities had taken place long before the Cold War had made the Soviet Union an enemy. Investigators often cared little for such distinctions, however.

The hunt for subversives was conducted by both Congress and the executive branch. Stung by charges of communism in the 1946 midterm elections, Truman issued Executive Order 9835 in March 1947, establishing loyalty review boards to investigate every federal employee. "A nightmare from which there [was] no awakening" was how State Department employee Esther Brunauer described it when she and her husband, a chemist in the navy, both lost their jobs because he had joined a Communist youth organization in the 1920s and associated with suspected radicals. Government investigators routinely violated the Bill of Rights by allowing anonymous informers to make charges and by placing the burden of proof on the accused. More than two thousand civil service employees lost their jobs, and another ten thousand resigned as **Truman's loyalty program** continued into the mid-1950s. Hundreds of homosexuals resigned or were fired over charges of "sexual perversion," which anti-Communist crusaders said could subject them to blackmail. Years later, Truman admitted that the loyalty program had been a mistake.

Congressional committees, such as the **House Un-American Activities Committee (HUAC)**, also investigated individuals' past and present political associations. When those under scrutiny refused to name names, investigators charged that silence was tantamount to confession, and these "unfriendly witnesses" lost their jobs and suffered public ostracism. In 1947, HUAC inves-

> "[If you called for] a square deal for the underdog, will they call you a Commie? . . . Are they going to scare us into silence?"
> — Singer FRANK SINATRA

Senator Joseph R. McCarthy
The Wisconsin senator made his reputation on anticommunism, seizing that issue when he needed to have a platform for his 1950 reelection campaign. McCarthy had loved politics since his high school days in Appleton, Wisconsin, and he easily distorted the truth to promote his political ambitions. The 1946 campaign poster in this photograph highlights his service in World War II, which he presented as involving dangerous combat missions as a tail gunner. In fact, he spent his time as an intelligence officer debriefing combat pilots. His only missions were flights over islands no longer controlled by the Japanese.
© Bettmann/Corbis.

tigated radical activity in Hollywood. Singer Frank Sinatra protested, wondering if someone called for "a square deal for the underdog, will they call you a Commie? . . . Are they going to scare us into silence?" Some actors and directors cooperated, but ten refused, citing their First Amendment rights. The "Hollywood Ten" served jail sentences for contempt of Congress — a punishment that Helen Gahagan Douglas fought — and then found themselves blacklisted in the movie industry.

The Truman administration went after the Communist Party directly, prosecuting its leaders under the Smith Act of 1940, which made it a crime to "advocate the overthrow and destruction of the Government of the United States by force and violence." Although civil libertarians argued that the guilty verdicts violated First Amendment rights of freedom of speech, press, and association, the Supreme Court ruled in

The Red Scare in Popular Culture
In 1949, producer Howard Hughes provided fodder for the Red scare with his movie *I Married a Communist*. Featuring an all-star cast, the movie tells the story of a dockworker who rose to become a shipping executive and then was used by the Communists, who threatened to expose his left-wing associations in the 1930s. The Michael Barson Collection/Past Perfect.

1951 (*Dennis v. United States*) that the Communist threat overrode constitutional guarantees.

The domestic Cold War spread beyond the nation's capital. State and local governments investigated citizens, demanded loyalty oaths, fired employees suspected of disloyalty, banned books from public libraries, and more. College professors and public school teachers lost their jobs in New York, California, and elsewhere. (See "Seeking the American Promise," page 884.) Because the Communist Party had helped organize unions and championed racial justice, labor and civil rights activists fell prey to McCarthyism as well. African American activist Jack O'Dell remembered that segregationists pinned the tag of Communist on "anybody who supported the right of blacks to have civil rights."

McCarthyism caused untold harm to thousands of innocent individuals. Anti-Communist crusaders humiliated and discredited law-abiding citizens, hounded them from their jobs, and in some cases even sent them to prison. Throughout the nearly ten years of the second Red scare, fundamental constitutional rights of freedom of speech and association were violated, the expression of dissenting ideas was stifled, and unpopular causes were removed from public contemplation.

REVIEW Why did Truman have limited success in implementing his domestic agenda?

▶ The Cold War Becomes Hot: Korea

The Cold War erupted into a shooting war in June 1950 when troops from Communist North Korea invaded South Korea. For the first time, Americans went into battle to implement containment. Confirming the global reach of the Truman Doctrine, U.S. involvement in Korea also marked the militarization of American foreign policy. The United States, in concert with the United Nations, ultimately held the line in Korea, but at a great cost in lives, dollars, and domestic unity.

Korea and the Military Implementation of Containment

The war grew out of the artificial division of Korea after World War II. Having expelled the Japanese, who had controlled Korea since 1904, the United States and the Soviet Union created two occupation zones separated by the thirty-eighth parallel (Map 26.3). With Moscow and Washington unable to agree on a unification plan, the United Nations sponsored elections in South Korea in July 1948. The American-favored candidate, Syngman Rhee, was elected president, and the United States withdrew most of its troops. In the fall of 1948, the Soviets established the People's Republic of North Korea under Kim Il-sung and also withdrew. Although doubting that Rhee's repressive government could sustain popular support, U.S. officials appreciated his staunch anticommunism and provided small amounts of economic and military aid to South Korea.

Insurgencies of workers and peasants against factory owners, landlords, and the Rhee government claimed 100,000 lives between 1946 and

MAP ACTIVITY

Map 26.3   The Korean War, 1950–1953
Although each side had plunged deep into enemy territory, the war ended in 1953 with the dividing line between North and South Korea nearly where it had been before the fighting began.

READING THE MAP: How far south did the North Korean forces progress at the height of their invasion? How far north did the UN forces get? What countries border Korea? **CONNECTIONS:** What dangers did the forays of MacArthur's forces to within forty miles of the Korean-Chinese border pose? Why did Truman forbid MacArthur to approach that border? What political considerations on the home front influenced Truman's policy and military strategy regarding Korea?

mid-1950, and skirmishes between North and South Korean troops at the thirty-eighth parallel began in 1948. Then, in June 1950, 90,000 North Koreans swept into South Korea. Truman's advisers assumed that the Soviet Union or China had instigated the attack, but later revelations pinned the initiative on Kim Il-sung, who won only reluctant acquiescence from China and

Russia. Truman wasted little time deciding to intervene, viewing Korea as "the Greece of the Far East." With the Soviet Union boycotting the UN Security Council to protest the council's refusal to seat a representative from the People's Republic of China, the United States obtained UN sponsorship of a collective effort to repel the attack. Authorized to appoint a commander for the UN force, Truman named General **Douglas MacArthur**, World War II hero and head of the postwar occupation of Japan.

Sixteen nations, including many NATO allies, sent troops to Korea, but the United States furnished most of the personnel and weapons, deploying almost 1.8 million troops and dictating military strategy. By dispatching troops without asking Congress for a declaration of war, Truman violated the spirit if not the letter of the Constitution and contributed to the expansion of executive power that would characterize the Cold War. Congress did appropriate funds to fight the **Korean War**, but the absence of a congressional declaration of war enabled the president's political opponents to call it "Truman's war" when the military situation worsened.

The first American soldiers rushed to Korea unprepared and ill equipped. One regimental commander grumbled that troops had "spent a lot of time listening to lectures on the differences between communism and Americanism and not enough time crawling on their bellies on maneuvers [or learning] how to clear a machine gun when it jams." U.S. forces suffered severe defeats in the first three months of the war. The North Koreans took the capital of Seoul and drove deep into South Korea, forcing UN troops to retreat to Pusan. Then, in September 1950, General MacArthur launched a bold counteroffensive at Inchon, 180 miles behind North Korean lines. The attack succeeded, and by October UN and South Korean forces had retaken Seoul and pushed the North Koreans back to the thirty-eighth parallel. These victories posed the momentous decision of whether to invade North Korea and seek to unify the country.

From Containment to Rollback to Containment

"Troops could not be expected . . . to march up to a surveyor's line and stop," remarked Secretary of State Dean Acheson, reflecting popular and official support for transforming the military objective from containment to elimination of the enemy and unification of Korea. Thus, for the only time during the Cold War, the United States

POWs in Korea
These demoralized U.S. soldiers reflect the grim situation for U.S. forces during the early months of the Korean War. Their North Korean captors forced them to march through Seoul in July 1950 carrying a banner proclaiming the righteousness of the Communist cause and attacking U.S. intervention. AP Images.

tried to roll back communism by force. With UN approval, on September 27, 1950, Truman authorized MacArthur to cross the thirty-eighth parallel. Concerned about possible intervention by China or the Soviet Union, the president directed him to keep UN troops away from the Korean-Chinese border. Disregarding the order, MacArthur sent UN forces to within forty miles of China, whereupon 300,000 Chinese soldiers crossed the Yalu River into Korea. With Chinese help, the North Koreans recaptured Seoul.

After three months of grueling battle, UN forces fought their way back to the thirty-eighth parallel. At that point, Truman decided to seek a negotiated settlement. MacArthur was furious when the goal of the war reverted to containment, which to him represented defeat. In comments to the press and letters to sympathetic members of Congress, the general challenged both the president's authority to conduct foreign policy and the principle of civilian control of the military. Fed up with MacArthur's insubordination, Truman relieved him of command in April 1951. Many Americans, however, sided with MacArthur. "Quite an explosion. . . . Letters of abuse by the dozens," Truman recorded in his diary. The adulation for MacArthur reflected Americans' frustration with containment. Why should Americans die simply to preserve the status quo? Why not destroy the enemy once and for all? In siding with MacArthur, Americans assumed that the United States was all-powerful and that stalemate in Korea resulted from the government's ineptitude or willingness to shelter subversives.

When Congress investigated MacArthur's dismissal, all of the top military leaders supported

> **"Troops could not be expected . . . to march up to a surveyor's line and stop."**
> — **Secretary of State DEAN ACHESON**

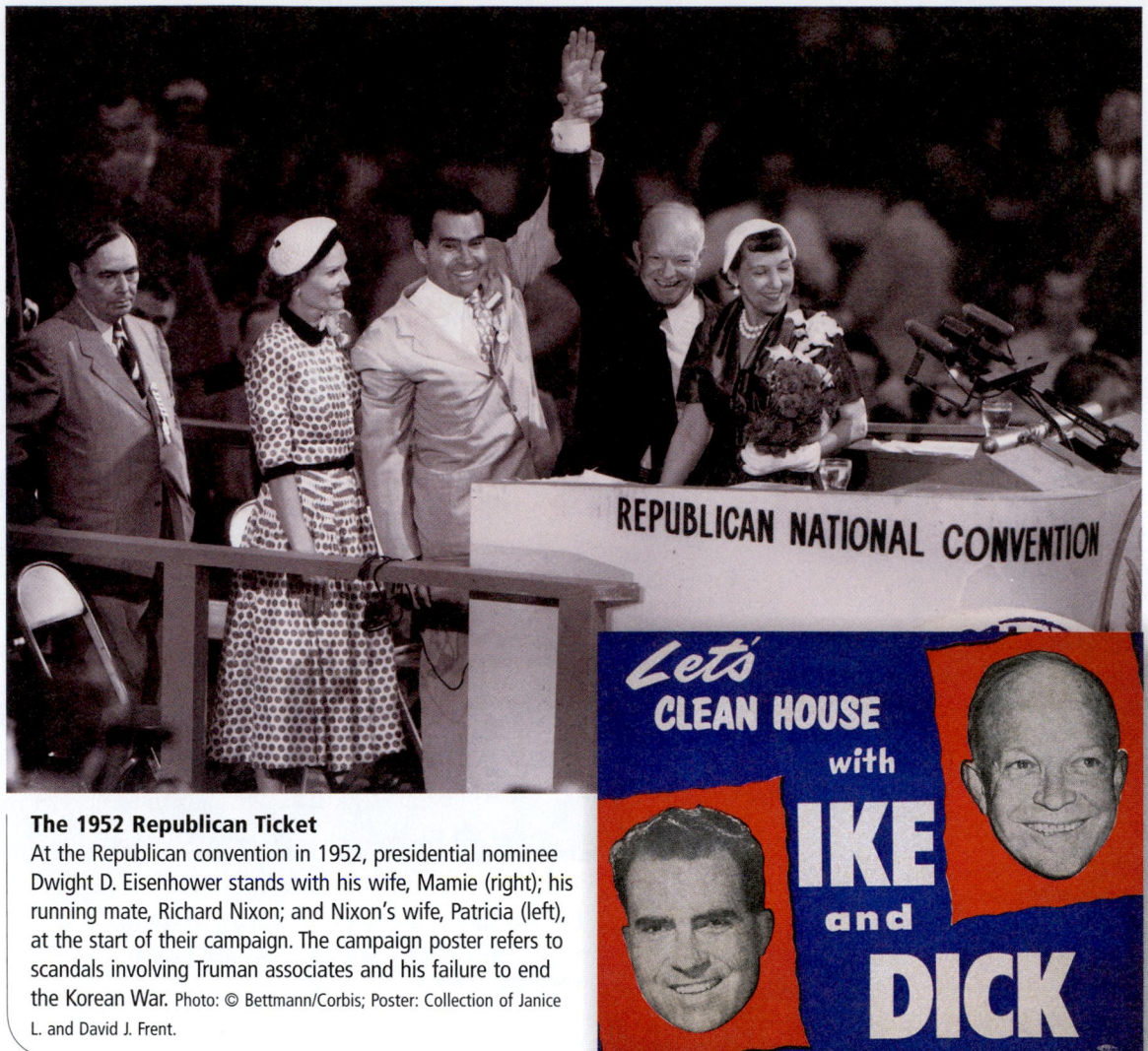

The 1952 Republican Ticket
At the Republican convention in 1952, presidential nominee Dwight D. Eisenhower stands with his wife, Mamie (right); his running mate, Richard Nixon; and Nixon's wife, Patricia (left), at the start of their campaign. The campaign poster refers to scandals involving Truman associates and his failure to end the Korean War. Photo: © Bettmann/Corbis; Poster: Collection of Janice L. and David J. Frent.

the president. According to the chairman of the Joint Chiefs of Staff, MacArthur wanted to wage "the wrong war, at the wrong place, at the wrong time, with the wrong enemy." Yet Truman never recovered from the political fallout. Nor was he able to end the war. Negotiations began in July 1951, but peace talks dragged on for two more years while twelve thousand more U.S. soldiers died.

Korea, Communism, and the 1952 Election

Popular discontent with President Truman's war boosted Republican candidates in the 1952 election. The Republicans' presidential nominee, General **Dwight D. Eisenhower**, had emerged from World War II with immense popularity. Reared in modest circumstances in Abilene, Kansas, Eisenhower attended West Point and

rose steadily through the army ranks. As supreme commander in Europe, he won widespread acclaim for leading the Allied armies to victory over Germany. After the war, he served as army chief of staff, and in 1950 Truman appointed Eisenhower the first supreme commander of NATO forces.

Both Republicans and Democrats had courted Eisenhower for the presidency in 1948. Although Eisenhower believed that professional soldiers should stay out of politics, he found compelling reasons to run in 1952. He largely agreed with Democratic foreign policy, but he deplored the Democrats' propensity to solve domestic problems with costly new federal programs. He equally disliked the foreign policy views of the leading Republican presidential contender, Senator Robert A. Taft, an opponent of NATO, who sought to cut defense spending and limit the nation's involvement abroad. Eisenhower decided to run both to stop Taft and the conservative wing of the

Republican Party and to turn the Democrats out of the White House.

Eisenhower defeated Taft for the nomination, but the old guard prevailed on the party platform. It excoriated containment as "negative, futile, and immoral" and charged the Truman administration with shielding "traitors to the Nation in high places." By choosing thirty-nine-year-old Senator **Richard M. Nixon** for his running mate, Eisenhower helped to appease the right wing of the party and ensured that anticommunism would be a major theme of the campaign.

Richard Milhous Nixon grew up in southern California, worked his way through college and law school, served in the navy, and briefly practiced law. In 1946, he helped the Republicans recapture Congress by defeating a liberal incumbent for a seat in the House of Representatives. Nixon quickly made a name for himself as a member of HUAC (see page 886) and a key anti-Communist, moving to the Senate with his victory over Helen Gahagan Douglas in 1950.

With his public approval ratings plummeting, Truman decided not to run for reelection. The Democrats nominated Adlai E. Stevenson, the popular governor of Illinois, who was acceptable to both liberals and southerners. Stevenson could not escape the domestic fallout from the Korean War, however; nor could he match the widespread appeal of Eisenhower. The Republican campaign stumbled just once, over the last item of its "Korea, Communism, and Corruption" policy. When the press reported that Nixon had accepted money from a private political fund supported by wealthy Californians, Democrats jumped to the attack, even though such gifts were common and legal. While Eisenhower deliberated about whether to dump Nixon from the ticket, Nixon saved himself by making an emotional nationwide appeal on the new medium of television. He disclosed his finances and documented his modest standard of living. Conceding that the family pet, Checkers, might be considered an illegal gift, Nixon refused to break his daughters' hearts by returning the cocker spaniel. The overwhelmingly positive response to the "Checkers speech" kept Nixon on the ticket.

Shortly before the election, Eisenhower announced dramatically, "I shall go to Korea," and voters registered their confidence in his ability to end the war. Cutting sharply into traditional Democratic territory, Eisenhower won several southern states and garnered 55 percent of the popular vote overall. His coattails carried a narrow Republican majority to Congress.

An Armistice and the War's Costs

Eisenhower made good on his pledge to end the Korean War. In July 1953, the two sides reached an armistice that left Korea divided, again roughly at the thirty-eighth parallel, with North and South separated by a two-and-a-half-mile-wide demilitarized zone (see Map 26.3). The war took the lives of 36,000 Americans and wounded more than 100,000. Nick Tosques, one of thousands of U.S. soldiers taken as prisoners of war, spent more than two years in a POW camp. "They interrogated us every day," he recalled. "Pretty soon I was telling them anything, just to keep from getting hit." South Korea lost more than 1 million people to war-related causes, and more than 1.8 million North Koreans and Chinese were killed or wounded.

The Truman administration judged the war a success for containment, since the United States had backed up its promise to help nations that were resisting communism. Both Truman and Eisenhower managed to contain what amounted to a world war — involving twenty nations altogether — within a single country and to avoid the use of nuclear weapons.

The Korean War had an enormous effect on defense policy and spending. In April 1950, two months before the war began, the National Security Council completed a top-secret report, known as **NSC 68**, on the United States' military strength. It warned that the survival of the nation required a massive military buildup and a tripling of the defense budget. Truman took no immediate action on these recommendations, but the Korean War brought about nearly all of the military expansion called for in NSC 68, vastly increasing U.S. capacity to act as a global power. Military spending shot up from $14 billion in 1950 to $50 billion in 1953 and remained above $40 billion thereafter. By 1952, defense spending claimed nearly 70 percent of the federal budget, and the size of the armed forces had tripled.

To General Matthew Ridgway, MacArthur's successor as commander of the UN forces, Korea taught the lesson that U.S. forces should never again fight a land war in Asia. Eisenhower concurred. Nevertheless, the Korean War induced the Truman administration to expand its role in Asia by increasing aid to the French, who were fighting to hang on to their colonial empire in Indochina. As U.S. Marines retreated from a battle against Chinese soldiers in 1950, they sang, prophetically, "We're Harry's police force on call, / So put back your pack on, / The next step is Saigon, / Cheer up, me lads, bless 'em all."

> **REVIEW**   How did the Korean War shape American foreign policy in the 1950s?

▶ Conclusion: The Cold War's Costs and Consequences

Arguing that the United Nations rather than unilateral American intervention should be the means of resolving foreign crises, Helen Gahagan Douglas opposed the implementation of containment with aid to Greece and Turkey in 1947, and she initially resisted designating the Soviet Union as an enemy. By 1948, however, Douglas had gotten behind Truman's decision to fight communism throughout the world, which marked the most momentous foreign policy initiative in the nation's history.

More than any development in the postwar world, the Cold War defined American politics and society for decades to come. It transformed the federal government, shifting its priorities from domestic to external affairs, greatly expanding its budget, and substantially increasing the power of the president. Military spending helped transform the nation itself, as defense contracts encouraged economic and population booms in the West and Southwest. The nuclear arms race put the people of the world at risk, consumed resources that might have been used to improve living standards, and skewed the economy toward dependence on military projects.

In sharp contrast to foreign policy, the domestic policies of the postwar years reflected continuity with the past. Most of the New Deal reforms remained in place despite Republicans' promises to turn back the clock. Helen Gahagan Douglas had come to Congress hoping to expand the New Deal, to help find "a way by which all people can live out their lives in dignity and decency." She avidly supported Truman's proposals for new programs in education, health, and civil rights, but a majority of her colleagues did not. Consequently, the poor and minorities suffered even while a majority of Americans enjoyed a higher standard of living in an economy boosted by Cold War spending and the reconstruction of Western Europe and Japan.

Another high cost of the early Cold War years was the anti-Communist hysteria that swept the nation, denying Douglas a Senate seat and more generally stifling debate and narrowing the range of ideas acceptable for political discussion. Partisan politics and Truman's warnings about the Communist menace fueled McCarthyism, but the obsession with subversion also fed on popular frustrations over the failure of containment to produce clear-cut victories. Convulsing the nation in bitter disunity, McCarthyism reflected a loss of confidence in American power. The Korean War, which ended in stalemate rather than the defeat of communism, exacerbated feelings of frustration. It would be a major challenge of the Eisenhower administration to restore national unity and confidence.

▶ Selected Bibliography

General Works

Rodolfo Acuña, *Occupied America: A History of Chicanos* (5th ed., 2004).

Carol Anderson, *Eyes off the Prize: The United Nations and the African American Struggle for Human Rights, 1944–1955* (2003).

Peter L. Hahn, *Caught in the Middle East: U.S. Policy toward the Arab-Israeli Conflict, 1945–1961* (2004).

Alonzo L. Hamby, *Man of the People: A Life of Harry S. Truman* (1995).

Ira Katznelson, *When Affirmative Action Was White: An Untold History of Racial Inequality in Twentieth-Century America* (2005).

James T. Patterson, *Grand Expectations: The United States, 1945–1974* (1996).

Brenda Gayle Plummer, *Rising Wind: Black Americans and U.S. Foreign Affairs, 1935–1960* (1996).

Ingrid Winther Scobie, *Center Stage: Helen Gahagan Douglas: A Life* (1992).

Domestic Politics and Policies

Glenn C. Altschuler and Stuart M. Blumin, *The GI Bill: A New Deal for Veterans* (2009).

Jonathan Bell, *The Liberal State on Trial: The Cold War and American Politics in the Truman Years* (2004).

Kevin Boyle, *The UAW and the Heyday of American Liberalism, 1945–1968* (1995).

Griffin Fariello, *Red Scare: Memories of the American Inquisition* (1995).

Kari Frederickson, *The Dixiecrat Revolt and the End of the Solid South, 1932–1968* (2001).

Ignacio M. García, *Hector P. García: In Relentless Pursuit of Justice* (2002).

David K. Johnson, *The Lavender Scare: The Cold War Persecution of Gays and Lesbians in the Federal Government* (2004).

Suzanne Mettler, *Soldiers to Citizens: The G.I. Bill and the Making of the Greatest Generation* (2005).

Richard Gid Powers, *Not without Honor: The History of American Anticommunism* (1995).

Henry A. J. Ramos, *The American GI Forum: In Pursuit of the Dream, 1948–1983* (1998).

Ellen W. Schrecker, *Many Are the Crimes: McCarthyism in America* (1998).

The Cold War

Greg Behrman, *The Most Noble Adventure: The Marshall Plan and the Time When America Helped Save Europe* (2007).

Robert L. Beisner, *Dean Acheson: A Life in the Cold War* (2006).

Campbell Craig and Fredric Logevall, *America's Cold War: The Politics of Insecurity* (2009).

Carolyn Eisenberg, *Drawing the Line: The American Decision to Divide Germany, 1944–1949* (1996).

John L. Gaddis, *The Cold War: A New History* (2005).

Lawrence S. Kaplan, *1948: The Birth of the Transatlantic Alliance* (2007).

Melvyn Leffler, *For the Soul of Mankind: The United States, the Soviet Union, and the Cold War* (2007).

Arnold A. Offner, *Another Such Victory: President Truman and the Cold War, 1945–1953* (2002).

Richard Rhodes, *Dark Sun: The Making of the Hydrogen Bomb* (1995).

Katherine A. S. Sibley, *Red Spies in America: Stolen Secrets and the Dawn of the Cold War* (2004).

Julian E. Zelizer, *Arsenal of Democracy: The Politics of National Security—From World War II to the War on Terrorism* (2010).

Asia and the Korean War

Gordon H. Chang, *Friends and Enemies: The United States, China, and the Soviet Union, 1948–1972* (1990).

Bruce Cumings, *The Korean War* (2010).

Allen R. Millett, *The War for Korea, 1945–1950: A House Burning* (2005).

Michael Schaller, *Altered States: The United States and Japan since the Occupation* (1997).

William Stueck, *Rethinking the Korean War: A New Diplomatic and Strategic History* (2002).

Stanley Weintraub, *MacArthur's War: Korea and the Undoing of an American Hero* (2000).

▶ **FOR MORE BOOKS ABOUT TOPICS IN THIS CHAPTER,** see the Online Bibliography at **bedfordstmartins.com/roark.**

▶ **FOR ADDITIONAL PRIMARY SOURCES FROM THIS PERIOD,** see Michael Johnson, ed., *Reading the American Past,* Fifth Edition.

▶ **FOR WEB SITES, IMAGES, AND DOCUMENTS RELATED TO TOPICS AND PLACES IN THIS CHAPTER,** visit Make History at **bedfordstmartins.com/roark.**

Reviewing Chapter 26

KEY TERMS

Explain each term's significance.

From the Grand Alliance to Containment

Joseph Stalin (p. 865)

Harry S. Truman (p. 865)

iron curtain (p. 866)

George F. Kennan (p. 867)

containment (p. 867)

Cold War (p. 870)

Truman Doctrine (p. 870)

Marshall Plan (p. 870)

Berlin airlift (p. 871)

hydrogen bomb (p. 872)

North Atlantic Treaty Organization (NATO) (p. 873)

Central Intelligence Agency (CIA) (p. 873)

Mao Zedong (p. 874)

Truman and the Fair Deal at Home

Fair Deal (p. 875)

Servicemen's Readjustment Act (GI Bill) (p. 877)

American GI Forum (p. 881)

Héctor Peréz García (p. 881)

Mendez v. Westminster (p. 881)

Taft-Hartley Act (p. 882)

Housing Act of 1949 (p. 883)

Joseph R. McCarthy (p. 884)

Truman's loyalty program (p. 886)

House Un-American Activities Committee (HUAC) (p. 886)

The Cold War Becomes Hot: Korea

Douglas MacArthur (p. 888)

Korean War (p. 888)

Dwight D. Eisenhower (p. 890)

Richard M. Nixon (p. 891)

NSC 68 (p. 891)

REVIEW QUESTIONS

Use key terms and dates to support your answer.

1. Why did relations between the United States and the Soviet Union deteriorate after World War II? (pp. 865–875)

2. Why did Truman have limited success in implementing his domestic agenda? (pp. 875–887)

3. How did the Korean War shape American foreign policy in the 1950s? (pp. 887–892)

MAKING CONNECTIONS

Draw on key terms, the timeline, and review questions.

1. What was the containment policy, and how successful was it up to 1953? In your answer, discuss both the supporters and the critics of the policy.

2. How did returning American servicemen change postwar domestic life in the areas of education and civil rights? In your answer, discuss how wartime experiences influenced their demands.

3. Why did anti-Communist hysteria sweep the country in the early 1950s? How did it shape domestic politics? In your answer, be sure to consider the influence of developments abroad and at home.

LINKING TO THE PAST

Link events in this chapter to earlier events.

1. What events and decisions during World War II contributed to the rise of the Cold War in the late 1940s? (See chapter 25.)

2. What did the anti-Communist hysteria of the late 1940s and the 1950s have in common with the Red scare that followed World War I, and how did these two phenomena differ? (See chapter 22.)

▶ FOR PRACTICE QUIZZES AND OTHER STUDY TOOLS, visit the Online Study Guide at bedfordstmartins.com/roark.

TIMELINE 1945–1953

1945
- Roosevelt dies; Vice President Harry S. Truman becomes president.

1946
- Postwar labor unrest.
- President's Committee on Civil Rights created.
- George F. Kennan drafts a containment policy.
- United States grants independence to Philippines.
- Employment Act.
- Republicans gain control of Congress.

1947
- National Security Act: National Security Council (NSC) and Central Intelligence Agency (CIA) created.
- Truman asks for aid to Greece and Turkey and announces Truman Doctrine.
- Truman establishes loyalty program.
- *Mendez v. Westminster* invalidates segregation of Mexican Americans in California schools.

1948
- Congress approves Marshall Plan.
- Women become permanent part of armed services.
- Truman orders desegregation of armed services.
- American GI Forum founded.
- United States recognizes state of Israel.
- Truman elected president.

1948–1949
- Berlin crisis and airlift.

1949
- Communists take over mainland China; Nationalists retreat to Taiwan.
- North Atlantic Treaty Organization (NATO) formed.
- Soviet Union explodes atomic bomb.

1950
- Senator Joseph McCarthy begins to accuse U.S. government of harboring Communists.
- Truman approves development of hydrogen bomb.
- United States sends troops to South Korea.

1951
- Truman relieves General Douglas MacArthur of command in Korea.
- United States ends occupation of Japan and signs peace treaty and mutual security pact.

1952
- Republican Dwight D. Eisenhower elected president.

1953
- Armistice halts Korean War.

1956 CADILLAC CONVERTIBLE

The automobile reflected both corporate and family prosperity in the 1950s. By 1960, three of every four households had a car, and the automotive industry generated one of every six jobs. This Cadillac was the top-of-the-line product manufactured by General Motors, the biggest and richest corporation in the world. Even the cheaper models purchased by average Americans featured the gas-guzzling size and space-age design of this Cadillac. The background photo shows a piece of the massive interstate highway system begun in 1956 and suburban housing developments in Los Angeles, both of which fueled Americans' mobility and devotion to consumption.

Car: Ron Kimball/Kimball Stock; background: Picture Research Consultants & Archives.

The Politics and Culture of Abundance
1952–1960

TRAILED BY REPORTERS, U.S. VICE PRESIDENT RICHARD M. NIXON LED Soviet premier Nikita Khrushchev through the American National Exhibition in Moscow in July 1959. The display of American consumer goods followed an exhibition of Soviet products in New York, part of a cultural exchange between the two superpowers that reflected a slight thaw in the Cold War after Khrushchev replaced Stalin. In Moscow, both Khrushchev and Nixon seized on the propaganda potential of the moment. As they made their way through the display, their verbal sparring turned into a slugfest of words and gestures that reporters dubbed the kitchen debate.

Showing off a new color television set, Nixon said the Soviet Union "may be ahead of us . . . in the thrust of your rockets for . . . outer space," but he insisted to Khrushchev that the United States outstripped the Soviets in consumer goods. Nixon linked capitalism with democracy, asserting that the array of products represented "what freedom means to us . . . our right to choose." Moreover, "any steelworker could buy this house," Nixon boasted, as they walked through a model of a six-room ranch-style home. Khrushchev retorted that in the Soviet Union "you are entitled to housing," whereas in the United States the homeless slept on pavements.

While the two men inspected household appliances, Nixon declared, "These are designed to make things easier for our women." Khrushchev responded that his country did not have "the capitalist attitude toward women" and appreciated women's contributions to the economy, not their domesticity. The Soviet leader found many of the items on display interesting, but he said, "they are not needed in life. . . . They are merely gadgets." In reply, Nixon insisted, "Isn't it far better to be talking about washing machines than machines of war?" Khrushchev agreed, yet Cold War tensions surfaced when he later blustered, "We too are giants. You want to threaten — we will answer threats with threats."

The Eisenhower administration (1953–1961) in fact had begun with threats to the Soviet Union. During the 1952 campaign, Republicans had vowed to roll back communism and liberate "enslaved" peoples under Soviet rule. In practice, however, President Dwight D. Eisenhower settled for a containment policy much like that of his predecessor, Harry S. Truman, though Eisenhower relied more on nuclear weapons and on secret actions

The Kitchen Debate
Soviet premier Nikita Khrushchev (left) and Vice President Richard M. Nixon (center) debate the relative merits of their nations' economies at the American National Exhibition held in Moscow in 1959. "You are a lawyer for capitalism and I am a lawyer for communism," Khrushchev told Nixon as each tried to outdo the other. Howard Sochurek/TimePix/Getty.

by the Central Intelligence Agency (CIA) against left-leaning governments. Yet as Nixon's visit to Moscow demonstrated, Eisenhower seized on political changes in the Soviet Union to reduce tensions in Soviet-American relations.

Continuity with the Truman administration also characterized domestic policy. Although Eisenhower favored corporations with tax cuts and opposed strong federal efforts in health care, education, and race relations, he did not propose to roll back New Deal programs. He even extended the reach of the federal government with a massive highway program, and he remained immensely popular through his two terms in office.

Although poverty clung stubbornly to some 20 percent of the population, the Moscow display testified to the unheard-of material gains savored by most Americans in the postwar era. Cold War weapons production spurred the economy, whose vitality stimulated suburban development, contributed to the burgeoning population and enterprise in the West and Southwest (the Sun Belt), and enabled millions of Americans to buy a host of new products.

As new homes, television sets, and household appliances transformed living patterns, Americans took part in a consumer culture that celebrated marriage, family, and traditional gender roles, even as more and more married women took jobs outside the home. Also challenging dominant norms were an emerging youth culture and dissenting writers known as the Beats.

The Cold War and the economic boom helped African Americans mount the most dramatic challenge of the 1950s, a struggle against the system of segregation and disfranchisement that had replaced slavery. Large numbers of African Americans took direct action against the institutions of injustice, developing the organizations, leadership, and strategies to mount a civil rights movement of unprecedented size and influence.

► Eisenhower and the Politics of the "Middle Way"

Moderation was the guiding principle of Eisenhower's domestic agenda and leadership style. In 1953, he pledged a "middle way between untrammeled freedom of the individual and the demands for the welfare of the whole Nation," promising that his administration would "avoid government by bureaucracy as carefully as it avoids neglect of the helpless." On the one hand, Eisenhower generally resisted expanding the federal government's power, he acted reluctantly when the Supreme Court ordered schools to desegregate, and his administration terminated the federal trusteeship of dozens of Indian tribes.

On the other hand, as a moderate Republican, Eisenhower supported the continuation, and in some cases the expansion, of New Deal programs. He signed key legislation establishing a national highway system and enlarged the federal bureaucracy with a new Department of Health, Education, and Welfare. Nicknamed "Ike," the confident war hero remained popular, but he was not able to lift the Republican Party to national dominance.

allowing federal executives to dismiss thousands of employees on grounds of loyalty, security, or "suitability." Reflecting his inclination to avoid controversial issues, Eisenhower refused to denounce Senator Joseph McCarthy publicly. In 1954, McCarthy began to destroy himself when he went after the army. As he hurled reckless charges of communism against military personnel during weeks of televised hearings, public opinion turned against him. When the army's lawyer demanded of McCarthy, "Have you left no sense of decency?" those in the hearing room applauded. A Senate vote to condemn McCarthy in December 1954 marked the end of his influence, but not the end of searching out radicals.

Eisenhower sometimes echoed the conservative Republicans' conviction that government was best left to the states and economic decisions to private business. "If all Americans want is security, they can go to prison," he commented about social welfare in 1949. Yet the welfare state grew somewhat during his administration, and Eisenhower signed laws bringing ten million

> **"Should any political party attempt to abolish social security and eliminate labor laws and farm programs, you would not hear of that party again."**
> —President
> **DWIGHT D. EISENHOWER**

Modern Republicanism

In contrast to the old guard conservatives in his party who criticized containment and wanted to repeal much of the New Deal, **Dwight D. Eisenhower** preached "modern Republicanism." This meant resisting additional federal intervention in economic and social life, but it did not mean turning the clock back to the 1920s. "Should any political party attempt to abolish social security and eliminate labor laws and farm programs," he wrote to his brother in 1954, "you would not hear of that party again in our political history." Democratic control of Congress after the elections of 1954 further contributed to Eisenhower's moderate approach, which overall maintained the course charted by Roosevelt and Truman.

The new president attempted to distance himself from the anti-Communist fervor that had plagued the Truman administration, even as he intensified Truman's loyalty program,

Polio Vaccine Distribution in the South
In 1954, American children lined up to be inoculated with the new vaccine to prevent polio. But as this scene from Blytheville, Arkansas, shows, children waiting to receive the vaccine stood in strictly segregated lines. Charles Bell, *Memphis Commercial Appeal.*

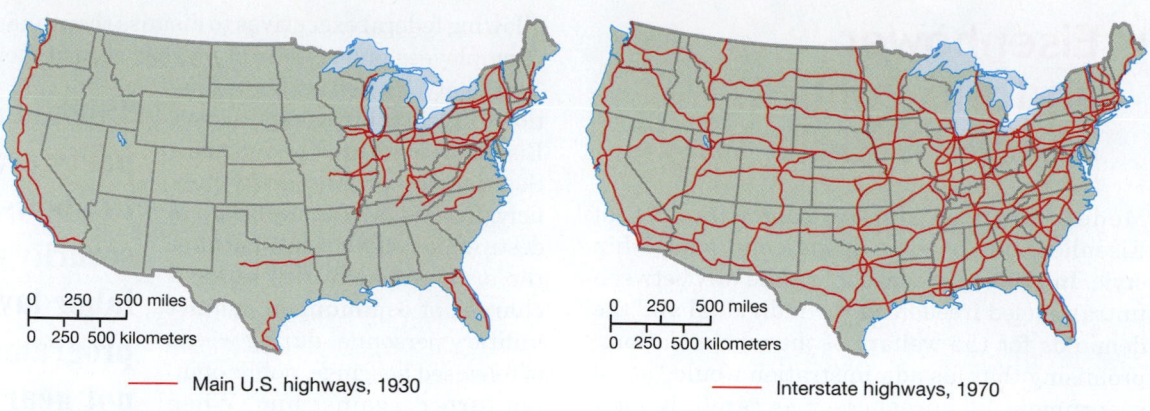

— Main U.S. highways, 1930

— Interstate highways, 1970

MAP ACTIVITY

Map 27.1   The Interstate Highway System, 1930 and 1970
Built with federal funds authorized in the Interstate Highway and Defense System Act of 1956, superhighways soon crisscrossed the nation. Trucking, construction, gasoline, and travel were among the industries that prospered, but railroads suffered from the subsidized competition.

READING THE MAP: What regions of the United States had main highways in 1930? What regions did not? How had the situation changed by 1970?

CONNECTIONS: What impact did the growth of the interstate highway system have on migration patterns in the United States? What benefits did the new interstate highways bring to Americans and at what costs?

more workers into Social Security, increasing the minimum wage, and continuing the federal government's modest role in financing public housing. He created a new Department of Health, Education, and Welfare, appointing as its head former Women's Army Corps commander Oveta Culp Hobby, the second woman to hold a cabinet post. And when the spread of polio neared epidemic proportions and terrified parents, Eisenhower obtained funds from Congress to distribute a vaccine, even though conservatives wanted to leave that responsibility to the states.

Eisenhower's greatest domestic initiative was the **Interstate Highway and Defense System Act of 1956** (Map 27.1), which involved the federal government in activities previously left to the states and localities. Promoted as essential to national defense and an impetus to economic growth, the act authorized the construction of a national highway system, with the federal government paying most of the costs through increased fuel and vehicle taxes. The new highways accelerated the mobility of Americans and the movement of goods and spurred suburban expansion, shopping malls, and growth in the fast-food and motel industries. The trucking, construction, and automobile industries had lobbied hard for the law and benefited substantially from it. Eventually, the monumental highway project exacted unforeseen costs in the form of air pollution, energy consumption, declining railroads and mass transportation, and decay of central cities.

In other areas, Eisenhower restrained federal activity in favor of state governments and private enterprise. His large tax cuts directed most benefits to business and the wealthy, he resisted federal aid to primary and secondary education, and he avoided strong White House leadership on behalf of civil rights. Eisenhower opposed national health insurance, preferring the growing practice of private insurance through employment. Moreover, whereas Democrats sought to keep nuclear power in government hands, Eisenhower signed legislation authorizing the private manufacture and sale of nuclear energy. The first commercial nuclear power plant in the United States opened in 1958 in Shippingport, Pennsylvania, northwest of Pittsburgh.

Termination and Relocation of Native Americans

Eisenhower's efforts to limit the federal government were consistent with a new direction in Indian policy, which reversed the emphasis on strengthening tribal governments and preserving Indian culture that had been established in the 1930s (see chapter 24). After World War II, when some 25,000 Indians had left their homes for military service and another 40,000 for work in defense industries, policymakers began to favor assimilating Native Americans and ending their special relationships with the government.

To some officials, who reflected the Cold War emphasis on conformity to dominant American values, the communal practices of Indians resembled socialism and stifled individual initiative. Eisenhower's commissioner of Indian affairs, Glenn Emmons, did not believe that tribal lands could produce income sufficient to lift Indians from poverty, but he also revealed the ethnocentrism of policymakers when he insisted that Indians wanted to "work and live like Americans." Moreover, government treaties with Indian nations protected Indian rights to water, land, minerals, and other resources that were increasingly attractive to state governments and private entrepreneurs.

By 1960, the government had implemented a three-part program of compensation, termination, and relocation. In 1946, Congress established the Indian Claims Commission to discharge outstanding claims by Native Americans for land taken by the government. When it closed in 1978, the commission had settled 285 cases, with compensation exceeding $800 million. Yet the awards were based on land values at the time the land was taken and did not include interest.

The second policy, termination, also originated in the Truman administration, during which Commissioner Dillon S. Myer asserted that his Bureau of Indian Affairs should do "nothing for Indians which Indians can do for themselves." Beginning in 1953, Eisenhower signed bills transferring jurisdiction over tribal land to state and local governments and ending the trusteeship relationship between Indians and the federal government. The loss of federal hospitals, schools, and other special arrangements devastated Indian tribes. As had happened after passage of the Dawes Act in 1887 (see chapter 17), some corporate interests and individuals took advantage of the opportunity to purchase Indian land cheaply. For many Indians, termination was "like the strike of doom." The government abandoned termination in the 1960s after some 13,000 Indians and more than one million acres of their land had been affected. Several tribes, including the Menominee and the Klamath, fought successfully to reverse termination and to secure restoration of their tribal status.

The **Indian Relocation Program**, the third piece of Native American policy, began in 1948 and involved more than 100,000 Native Americans by 1973. The government encouraged Indians to move to cities, where relocation centers were supposed to help with housing, job training, and

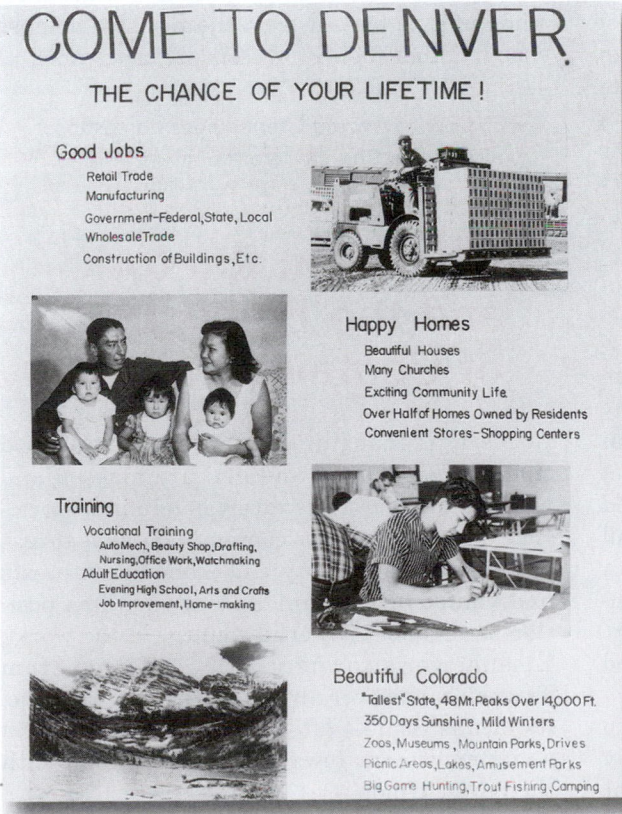

VISUAL ACTIVITY

Indian Relocation

As part of its new emphasis on assimilation in the late 1940s and the 1950s, the Bureau of Indian Affairs distributed this leaflet to entice Native Americans to move from their reservations to cities. Either with government assistance or on their own, thousands of Indians relocated in the years after World War II. In 1950, just 13.4 percent of Indians lived in urban areas. By 1970, 44 percent did so, and by 1990 the figure had reached 63 percent. National Archives.

READING THE IMAGE: Which of the features shown in this leaflet do you think would have been the most appealing to Native Americans living on reservations? Which might have evoked little interest?

CONNECTIONS: In what ways did the government's plan to assimilate Native Americans succeed? In what ways did it fail?

medical care. Even though government officials made it difficult to return home by sending Indians far away from their reservations, about one-third returned to the reservation.

Most who stayed in cities faced racism, lack of adequately paying jobs for which they had skills, poor housing, and the loss of their traditional culture. "I wish we had never left home," said one woman whose husband was out of work and drinking heavily. "It's dirty and noisy, and people all around, crowded. . . . It seems like I never see the sky or trees." Moreover, Native Americans who relocated to cities found them to be on the decline, as urban wealth began to shift to the suburbs throughout the 1950s and 1960s. Like African Americans who migrated to cities in great numbers in the 1950s, Indians found declining opportunities for economic progress (see page 912).

Reflecting long-standing disagreements among Indians themselves, some who overcame these obstacles applauded the program. But most urban Indians remained in or near poverty, and even many who had welcomed relocation began to worry that "we would lose our identity as Indian people, lose our culture and our [way] of living." Within two decades, a national pan-Indian movement emerged to resist assimilation and to demand much more for Indians (as discussed in chapter 28). The new militancy and connections across tribal lines that arose were a by-product of the urbanization of Native Americans.

The 1956 Election and the Second Term

Not all citizens were living the American dream, but with the nation at peace and the economy booming, Eisenhower easily defeated Adlai Stevenson in 1956, doubling his victory margin of 1952. Yet Democrats kept control of Congress, and in the midterm elections two years later, they all but wiped out the Republican Party, gaining a 64–34 majority in the Senate and a 282–135 advantage in the House. Although Ike captured voters' hearts, a majority of Americans remained wedded to the programs and policies of the Democrats.

Eisenhower faced more serious leadership challenges in his second term. When the economy plunged into a recession in late 1957, he fought

Major Indian Relocations, 1950–1970

with Congress over the budget and vetoed bills to expand housing, urban development, and public works projects. The president and Congress did reach agreement in two key areas: enacting the first, though largely symbolic, civil rights legislation in a century and extending the federal government's role in education, largely in the interest of national security (as discussed on pages 906–908 and 915).

In the end, the first Republican administration after the New Deal left the size and functions of the federal government intact, though it tipped policy somewhat more in favor of corporate interests. Unparalleled prosperity graced the Eisenhower years, and inflation was kept low. The economy weathered two recessions without testing the president's aversion to substantial federal intervention. Eisenhower celebrated what he called the "wide diffusion of wealth and incomes" across the United States. Yet neglected amid the remarkable abundance were some forty million Americans who lived below the poverty level. Rural deprivation was particularly pronounced, as was poverty among African Americans and other minorities, who failed to benefit from the massive defense spending that fueled the economy as a whole.

REVIEW How did Eisenhower's domestic policies reflect his moderate political vision?

► Liberation Rhetoric and the Practice of Containment

At his 1953 inauguration, Eisenhower warned that "forces of good and evil are massed and armed and opposed as rarely before in history." Like Truman, he saw communism as a threat to the nation's security and economic interests and wanted to maintain the United States' position as the most powerful country in the world. Eisenhower's foreign policy differed from Truman's, however, in three areas: its rhetoric, its means, and — after Stalin's death in 1953 — its movement toward accommodation with the Soviet Union.

Republican rhetoric, voiced most prominently by Secretary of State John Foster Dulles, deplored containment as "negative, futile, and immoral" because it accepted the existing Soviet sphere of control. Yet despite promises to roll back Soviet power, the Eisenhower administration continued the containment policy. The United States intervened at the margins of Communist power — in Asia, the Middle East, and Latin America — but not at its core in Europe. Eisenhower assigned nuclear weapons and CIA secret operations larger roles in defense strategy, and he took steps to ease tensions between the two superpowers.

The "New Look" in Foreign Policy

To meet his goals of balancing the budget and cutting taxes, Eisenhower was determined to control military expenditures. Moreover, he feared that massive defense spending would threaten the nation's economic strength. As he declared in 1953, "Every gun that is made, every warship launched, every rocket fired signifies, in the final sense, a theft from those who hunger and are not fed, those who are cold and not clothed."

Reflecting Americans' confidence in technology and their opposition to a large peacetime army, Eisenhower's defense strategy concentrated U.S. military strength in nuclear weapons and the planes and missiles to deliver them. Instead of maintaining large ground forces of its own, the United States would give friendly nations American weapons and back them up with an ominous nuclear arsenal, providing, according to the secretary of defense, "more bang for the buck." This was Eisenhower's "New Look" in foreign policy. Secretary of State Dulles believed that America's willingness to "go to the brink" of war with its intimidating nuclear weapons — a strategy called brinksmanship — would block any Soviet efforts to expand.

Throughout the 1950s, the United States far outpaced the Soviet Union in nuclear warheads and delivery missiles, yet its superiority did not ensure security. Nuclear weapons could not stop a Soviet nuclear attack. In response to one, however, they could inflict enormous destruction. This certainty of "massive retaliation" was meant to deter the Soviets from launching an attack. Because the Soviet Union could respond similarly to an American first strike, this nuclear standoff became known as **mutually assured destruction, or MAD**. Leaders of both nations pursued an ever-escalating arms race.

Missiles in the Nuclear Arms Race
After World War II, both the United States and the Soviet Union dug for information about rocketry from German installations and German scientists and engineers, who were leaders in the development of missiles. By the 1950s, both nations were arming missiles with nuclear weapons. In 1957, the United States began building intercontinental ballistic missiles (ICBMs) that could hit the Soviet Union from a launching site in the American Midwest. Shown here are missiles being manufactured by Boeing, a leading corporation in the aerospace industry, housed in Seattle, Washington. Photo by B. Anthony Stewart/ National Geographic/Getty Images.

Nuclear weapons could not roll back the iron curtain. When a revolt against the Soviet-controlled government began in Hungary in 1956, Dulles's liberation rhetoric proved to be empty. As Soviet tanks arrived to crush the revolt, a radio plea from freedom fighters cried, "SOS! They just brought us a rumor that the American troops will be here within one or two hours." But help did not come. Eisenhower was unwilling to risk U.S. soldiers and possible nuclear war, and Soviet troops soon suppressed the insurrection, killing or wounding thousands of Hungarians.

Applying Containment to Vietnam

A major challenge to the containment policy came in Southeast Asia. During World War II, Ho Chi Minh, a Vietnamese nationalist who also embraced communism, had founded a coalition called the Vietminh to fight both the occupying Japanese forces and the French colonial rulers. In 1945, the Vietminh declared Vietnam's independence from France, and when France fought to maintain its colony, the area plunged into war. After the Communists won control of China, the Truman administration quietly began to provide aid to the French and recognized their puppet government in the southern part of Vietnam (see chapter 29, Map 29.2). American principles of national self-determination took a backseat to the battle against communism.

Eisenhower viewed communism in Vietnam much as Truman had regarded it in Greece and Turkey, a view that became known as the **domino theory**. "You have a row of dominoes," Eisenhower explained, and "you knock over the first one, and what will happen to the last one is the certainty that it will go over very quickly." A Communist victory in Southeast Asia, he warned, could trigger the fall of Japan, Taiwan, and the Philippines. By 1954, the United States was contributing 75 percent of the cost of France's war, but Eisenhower resisted a larger role. When the French asked for troops and airplanes from the United States to avert almost certain defeat at Dien Bien Phu, Eisenhower, conscious of U.S. losses in the Korean War (see chapter 26), said no.

Dien Bien Phu fell in May 1954 and with it the French colony of Vietnam. Two months later in Geneva, France signed a truce. The **Geneva accords** temporarily partitioned Vietnam at the seventeenth parallel, separating the Vietminh in the north from the puppet government established by the French in the south. Within two years, the Vietnamese people were to vote in elections for a unified government. Some officials warned against U.S. involvement in Vietnam. Defense Secretary Charles Wilson saw "nothing but grief in store for us if we remained in that area." Eisenhower and Dulles nonetheless moved to prop up the dominoes with a new alliance. In September 1954, the United States joined with Britain, France, Australia, New Zealand, Thailand, Pakistan, and the Philippines in the Southeast Asia Treaty Organization, committed to the defense of Cambodia, Laos, and South Vietnam. Shortly thereafter, Eisenhower began to send weapons and military advisers to South Vietnam and put the CIA to work infiltrating and destabilizing North Vietnam. Fearing a Communist victory in the elections mandated by the Geneva accords, the United States supported South Vietnamese prime minister Ngo Dinh Diem's refusal to hold the vote.

Geneva Accords, 1954

Between 1955 and 1961, the United States provided $800 million to the South Vietnamese army (the Army of the Republic of Vietnam, or ARVN). Yet the ARVN proved grossly unprepared for the guerrilla warfare that began in the late 1950s. With military assistance from Ho Chi Minh's government in Hanoi, Vietminh rebels in the south stepped up their guerrilla attacks on the Diem government. The insurgents gained support from the largely Buddhist peasants, who were outraged by the repressive regime of the Catholic, Westernized Diem. Unwilling to abandon containment, Eisenhower left his successor with the deteriorating situation and a firm commitment to defend South Vietnam against communism.

Interventions in Latin America and the Middle East

While supporting friendly governments in Asia, the Eisenhower administration worked secretly to topple unfriendly ones in Latin America and the Middle East. Officials saw internal civil wars in terms of the Cold War conflict between the superpowers and tended to view nationalist uprisings as Communist threats to democracy. They acted against governments that not only seemed too leftist but also threatened U.S. economic interests. The Eisenhower administration took this course of action out of sight of Congress and the public, making the CIA an important arm of foreign policy.

The government of Guatemala, under the popularly elected reformist president Jacobo Arbenz, was not Soviet controlled, but it accepted support from the local Communist Party (see chapter 29, Map 29.1). In 1953, Arbenz moved to help landless, poverty-stricken peasants by nationalizing uncultivated land owned by the United Fruit Company, a U.S. corporation whose annual profits were twice the size of the Guatemalan government's budget. United Fruit refused Arbenz's offer to compensate the company at the value of the land it had declared for tax purposes. Then, in response to the nationalization program, the CIA organized and supported an opposition army that overthrew the elected government and installed a military dictatorship in 1954. United Fruit kept its land, and Guatemala descended into a series of destructive civil wars that lasted through the 1990s.

In 1959, the desire for political and economic autonomy erupted into the **Cuban revolution**, led by **Fidel Castro**. At the time, a CIA agent promised "to take care of Castro just like we took care of Arbenz." American companies had long controlled major Cuban resources, and decisions made in Washington directly influenced the lives of the Cuban people. The 1959 uprising drove out the U.S.-supported dictator Fulgencio Batista and led the CIA to warn Eisenhower that "Communists and other extreme radicals appear to have penetrated the Castro movement." When the United States denied Castro's requests for loans, he turned to the Soviet Union. And when U.S. companies refused Castro's offer to purchase them at their assessed value, he began to nationalize their property. Many anti-Castro Cubans fled to the United States and reported his atrocities, including the execution of hundreds of Batista's supporters. (See "Seeking the American Promise," page 906.) Before leaving office, Eisenhower broke off diplomatic relations with Cuba and authorized the CIA to train Cuban exiles for an invasion.

In the Middle East, the CIA intervened to oust an elected government, support an unpopular dictatorship, and maintain Western access to Iranian oil (see chapter 30, Map 30.3). In 1951, the Iranian parliament, led by **Mohammed Mossadegh**, the nationalist prime minister, nationalized the country's oil fields and refineries. Most of the oil operations had been held by a British company for decades, and Iran received less than 20 percent of the profits from its own resources. The British strongly objected to the takeover and eventually sought help from the United States.

Advisers convinced Eisenhower that Mossadegh, whom *Time* magazine had called "the Iranian George Washington," left Iran vulnerable to communism, and the president wanted to keep oil-rich areas "under the control of people who are friendly." With his authorization, CIA agents instigated a coup by bribing army officers and financing demonstrations against the government. In August 1953, Iranian army officers captured the prime minister and reestablished the authority of the shah of Iran, Mohammad Reza Pahlavi, known for favoring Western interests and the Iranian wealthy classes. Iran renegotiated its oil concessions, giving U.S. companies a 40 percent share. Resentment over this use of force would poison U.S.-Iranian relations into the twenty-first century.

Elsewhere in the Middle East, the Eisenhower administration continued Truman's support of

The CIA Helps Restore the Shah of Iran
In 1952, *Time* magazine called Iranian premier Mohammed Mossadegh "the Iranian George Washington," for his passionate commitment to nationalism and democracy. But Secretary of State John Foster Dulles believed that restoring the power of Shah Reza Pahlevi would produce a more stable U.S. ally and persuaded President Eisenhower to approve a CIA-supported coup. Here an Iranian army officer rallies supporters of the shah outside the home of Mossadegh, who was eventually forced out. The shah had dozens of Mossadegh's supporters executed, and the elderly Mossadegh spent three years in prison and the rest of his life under house arrest. AP Images.

Israel but also sought to foster friendships with Arab nations to secure access to oil and build a bulwark against communism. Yet U.S. officials demanded that smaller nations take the American side in the Cold War, even when those nations preferred to remain nonaligned, with the opportunity for assistance from both Western and Communist nations. In 1955, as part of the U.S. effort to win Arab allies, Secretary of State Dulles began talks with Egypt about American support to build the Aswan Dam on the Nile River. The following year, Egypt's leader, **Gamal Abdel Nasser**, sought arms from Communist Czechoslovakia, formed a military alliance with other Arab nations, and recognized the People's Republic of China. Unwilling to tolerate such independence, Dulles called off the deal for the dam.

On July 26, 1956, Nasser responded by seizing the Suez Canal, then owned by Britain

The Suez Crisis, 1956

Operation Pedro Pan: Young Political Refugees Take Flight

Six-year-old María was awakened before dawn one summer day in Cuba in 1962. Her parents drove her to the Havana airport, with one suitcase and her favorite doll. A paper pinned to her gingham dress gave her name and the phone number of family friends in Miami who were to meet her. She traveled with a six-year-old boy whose father in Miami had obtained the visa waivers the children would need to enter the United States. María, excited but anxious, had never been away from her parents before; she would not see them for four months.

On a different flight that summer, ten-year-old Carlos flew to Miami with his older brother, leaving behind a father they would never see again. Because of their age difference, the boys were separated on arrival and sent to different refugee camps in rural Florida. A family acquaintance — a Cuban lawyer working as a janitor in Miami — helped them gain temporary placement with foster families just ten blocks apart. A few months later, they were transferred to a juvenile delinquent facility that provided only one meal a day. Finally, a Cuban uncle arrived and took them with him to a small midwestern town where no one spoke Spanish. After three years of traumatic separation, their mother fled Cuba and joined them.

María and Carlos were just two of more than fourteen thousand unaccompanied children, ages six to eighteen, who left Cuba as part of a special U.S. government–facilitated program called Operation Pedro Pan, which functioned from December 1960 to October 1962. With little money, no knowledge of English, and often no friends or relatives to receive them, the children faced daunting loneliness and possibly neglect. What drove the parents of these children to take such an extraordinary step?

The U.S. government had already made unusual accommodation for the large exodus of adults fleeing Cuba after Fidel Castro came to power in 1959. Assuming that the refugees would return to Cuba as soon as Castro's government fell, the United States relaxed immigration restrictions for Cubans, allowed refugees to work, and authorized millions of dollars in relief and resettlement funds for people "subjected to the captivity of Communist despotism." The U.S. government felt an obligation to shelter Cubans who had worked in the government or military of deposed dictator Fulgencio Batista, a close U.S. ally. Many other Cubans who fled to the United States after the revolution had worked for U.S.-owned businesses. Still others were wealthy merchants and professionals — doctors, lawyers, university professors. By the fall of 1962, 248,000 Cubans had chosen to flee communism, furnishing the United States with a powerful symbolic statement of Cold War politics.

An even more potent symbol was Operation Pedro Pan, with its implication that Castro's Cuba had to be truly terrible for parents to part with their children, even though they expected to see their children soon. Cuban parents who opposed Castro feared not for their children's lives, but for their minds. Public schools in Cuba reportedly taught an escalating rhetoric of revolution, while private schools were shut down. Compulsory military service

and France but scheduled to revert to Egypt within seven years. In response to the seizure, Israel, whose forces had been skirmishing with Egyptian troops along their common border since 1948, attacked Egypt, with military help from Britain and France. Eisenhower opposed the intervention, recognizing that the Egyptians had claimed their own territory and that Nasser "embodie[d] the emotional demands of the people . . . for independence." He put economic pressure on Britain and France while calling on the United Nations to arrange a truce. The French and British soon pulled back, forcing Israel to retreat.

Despite staying out of the **Suez crisis**, Eisenhower made it clear that the United States would actively combat communism in the Middle East. In March 1957, Congress passed a joint resolution approving aid to any Middle Eastern nation "requesting assistance against armed aggression from any country controlled by international communism." The president invoked this **Eisenhower Doctrine** to send aid to Jordan in 1957 and troops to Lebanon in 1958 to counter anti-Western pressures on those governments.

The Nuclear Arms Race

While Eisenhower moved against perceived Communist inroads abroad, he also sought to reduce superpower tensions. After Stalin's death for boys and summer programs relocating teenagers to jobs teaching literacy in the rural countryside threatened parental rights to determine their children's activities. Relatively prosperous Cuban families did not benefit from Castro's reforms, which focused on improving health and education for the impoverished masses. Their fears of socialized child rearing were reinforced by a program of disinformation allegedly broadcast from a CIA radio station, which warned parents that "the Revolutionary Government will take [your children] away from you when they turn five and will keep them until they are eighteen." Rumors of Communist indoctrination ran rampant.

Fear of communism gripped the United States in the 1950s, and the Pedro Pan exodus both demonstrated and heightened that fear. The belief that Communists brainwashed children and turned them against their parents led some Cuban parents to try to save their children by sending them to a country that celebrated freedom. And, as with the adult refugees who had fled Cuba for the United States, parents of the Pedro Pan children believed that the trip would be temporary, until the fall of Castro's regime. But some of the children themselves, now grown, have questioned whether coming to America was worth the trauma they endured

and have speculated that Cold War politics might have shaped the operation more than humanitarian concerns. María de los Angeles Torres and Carlos Eire, two among the thousands, grew up to become university professors in the United States. Like the majority of Pedro Pan children, they are now glad they came here, but they also wonder about the choices their families made.

Leaving Havana
A family camera captures María de los Angeles Torres (far left) at the airport in Havana, before her flight to Miami in July 1961. AP Images.

Questions for Consideration

1. What were the parents of the boys and girls in Operation Pedro Pan trying to save their children from?

2. What did the United States stand to gain from harboring Cuban exiles, especially children?

in 1953, a more moderate leadership under **Nikita Khrushchev** emerged. Like Eisenhower, who remarked privately that the arms race would lead "at worst to atomic warfare, at best to robbing every people and nation on earth of the fruits of their own toil," Khrushchev wanted to reduce defense spending and the threat of nuclear devastation. Eisenhower and Khrushchev met in Geneva in 1955 at the first summit conference since the end of World War II. Although the meeting produced no new agreements, it symbolized what Eisenhower called "a new spirit of conciliation and cooperation."

In August 1957, the Soviets test-fired their first intercontinental ballistic missile (ICBM) and two months later beat the United States

into space by launching *Sputnik*, the first artificial satellite to circle the earth. The United States launched a successful satellite of its own in January 1958, but *Sputnik* raised fears that the United States lagged behind the Soviets not only in missile development and space exploration but also in science and education. In response, Eisenhower established the National Aeronautics and Space Administration (NASA), approving a huge budget increase for space research and development. Also in 1958, Congress passed the National Defense Education Act, providing support for instruction at all levels in math, foreign languages, and science and technology. Eisenhower assured the public that the United States possessed nuclear superiority.

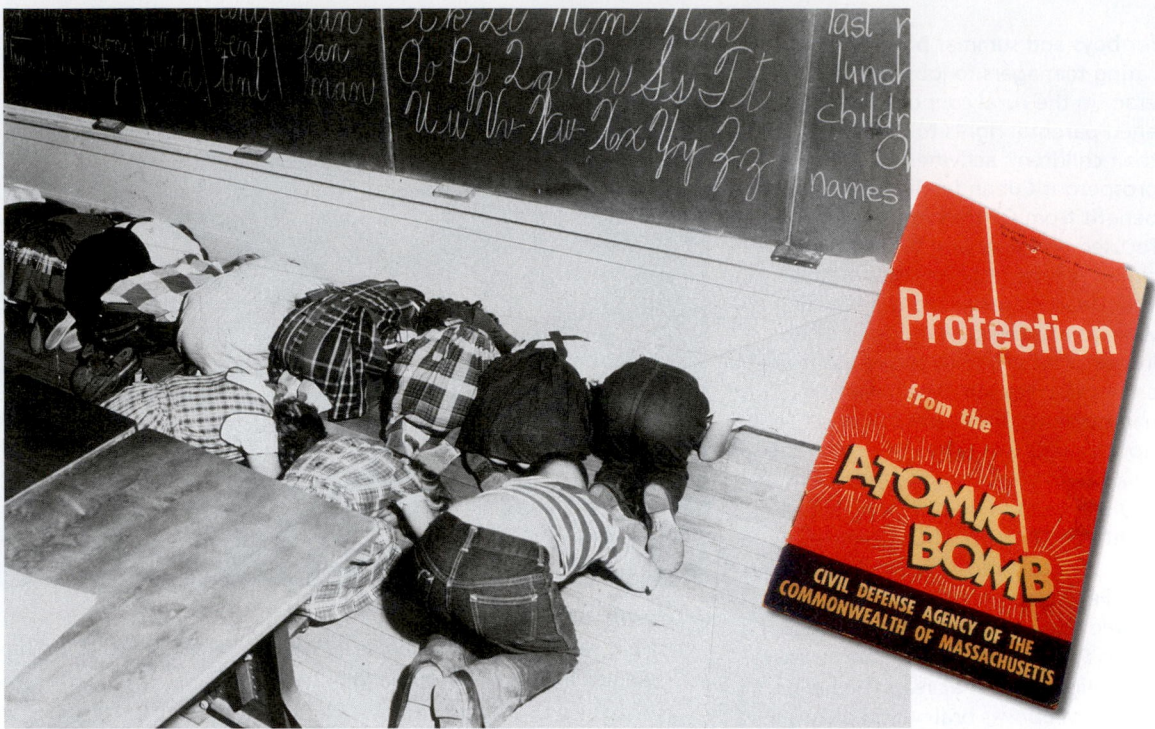

The Age of Nuclear Anxiety
As schools routinely held drills to prepare for possible Soviet attacks, children directly experienced the anxiety and insecurity of the 1950s nuclear arms race. This pamphlet about how to protect oneself from an atomic attack was published by the federal government and distributed to the general public. How effective do you think the strategy pictured here would be in a nuclear attack? Why would the government publish a pamphlet indicating that civilians could protect themselves? Photo: Archive Photos/Getty Images; Pamphlet: Lynn Historical Society

In fact, during his presidency, the stockpile of nuclear weapons more than quadrupled; the United States had installed ICBMs at home and in Britain and was prepared to deploy more in Italy and Turkey. The first Polaris submarine carrying nuclear missiles was launched in November 1960. Yet these weapons could not guarantee security because both superpowers possessed sufficient nuclear capacity to devastate each other. Most Americans did not follow Civil Defense Administration recommendations to construct home bomb shelters, but they did realize how precarious nuclear weapons had made their lives.

In the midst of the arms race, the superpowers continued to talk. In 1959, Khrushchev visited the United States, and Nixon went to the Soviet Union, where he engaged in the famous kitchen debate. By 1960, the two sides were close to a ban on nuclear testing. But just before a planned summit in Paris, a Soviet missile shot down an American U-2 spy plane over Soviet territory. The State Department first denied that U.S. planes had been violating Soviet airspace, but the Soviets produced the pilot and the photos taken on his flight. Eisenhower and Khrushchev met briefly in Paris, but the U-2 incident dashed all prospects for a nuclear arms agreement.

As Eisenhower left office, he warned about the growing influence of the **military-industrial complex** in American government and life. Eisenhower had struggled against persistent pressures from defense contractors who, in tandem with the military, sought more dollars for newer, more powerful weapons systems. In his farewell address, he warned that the "conjunction of an immense military establishment and a large arms industry . . . exercised a total influence . . . in every city, every state house, every office of the federal government." The Cold War had created a warfare state.

REVIEW Where and how did Eisenhower practice containment?

▶ New Work and Living Patterns in an Economy of Abundance

Stimulated in part by Cold War spending, economic productivity increased enormously in the 1950s. A multitude of new items came on the market, and consumption became the order of the day. Millions of Americans enjoyed new homes in the suburbs, and higher education enrollments skyrocketed. Although every section of the nation enjoyed the new abundance, the West and Southwest — the **Sun Belt** — especially boomed in production, commerce, and population.

Work itself was changing. Fewer people labored on farms, service sector employment overtook manufacturing jobs, and women's employment grew. These economic shifts disadvantaged some Americans, and they did little to help the forty million who lived in poverty. Most Americans, however, enjoyed a higher standard of living, prompting economist John Kenneth Galbraith to call the United States "the affluent society."

Technology Transforms Agriculture and Industry

Between 1940 and 1960, agricultural output mushroomed even while the number of farmworkers declined by almost one-third. Farmers achieved nearly miraculous productivity through greater crop specialization, intensive use of fertilizers, and, above all, mechanization. A single mechanical cotton picker, for example, replaced fifty people and cut the cost of harvesting a bale of cotton from $40 to $5.

The decline of family farms and the growth of large commercial farming, or agribusiness, were both causes and consequences of mechanization. Benefiting handsomely from federal price supports begun in the New Deal, larger farmers could afford technological improvements, whereas smaller producers lacked capital to invest in the machinery necessary to compete. Consequently, average farm size more than doubled between 1940 and 1964, and the number of farms fell by more than 40 percent.

Many small farmers who hung on constituted a core of rural poverty often overlooked in the

Technology Transforms Agriculture
The years from 1945 to 1970 saw a second agricultural revolution in the United States. In 1954, tractors outnumbered mules and horses on farms for the first time. In 1940, one farmer could feed 10.7 people. By 1960, one farmer could supply 25.8 people, and in 1970 that ratio was 1 to 75.8. Threshing machines sweeping across a midwestern wheat field in 1960 exemplify the onslaught of agribusiness. The advertisement shows how one person could plant several rows of corn by barely lifting a finger. Threshing machine: © Bettmann/Corbis; Advertisement: International Harvester Company.

Poverty in an Era of Abundance
The Whiteheads, a coal-mining family in Kentucky, represented the hidden side of the affluent 1950s. Mrs. John Whitehead lived with her husband, their six children, and their six grandchildren in this three-room house. It had neither running water nor electricity, and the only access to the house was over a mountain trail. National Archives.

celebration of affluence. Southern landowners replaced sharecroppers and tenants with machines, forcing them off the land. Hundreds of thousands of African Americans joined an exodus to cities, where racial discrimination and a lack of jobs for which they could qualify mired many in urban poverty. A Mississippi mother whose family had worked on a plantation since slavery reported that most of her relatives headed for Chicago when they realized that "it was going to be machines now that harvest the crops." Worrying that "it might be worse up there" for her children, she agonized, "I'm afraid to leave and I'm afraid to stay."

Industrial production was also transformed by new technologies. Between 1945 and 1960, for example, the number of labor-hours needed to manufacture a car fell by 50 percent. Technology transformed industries such as electronics, chemicals, and air transportation and promoted the growth of television, plastics, computers, and other newer industries. American businesses enjoyed access to cheap oil, ample markets abroad, and little foreign competition. Moreover, even with Eisenhower's conservative fiscal policies, government spending reached $80 billion annually and created new jobs.

Labor unions enjoyed their greatest success during the 1950s, and real earnings for production workers shot up 40 percent. The merger in 1955 of the American Federation of Labor (AFL) and the Congress of Industrial Organizations (CIO) improved labor's bargaining position. As one worker put it, "We saw continual improvement in wages, fringe benefits like holidays, vacation, medical plans . . . all sorts of things that provided more security for people." In most industrial nations, government programs underwrote their citizens' security, but the United States developed a mixed system in which company-funded programs won by unions through collective bargaining played a much larger role in providing for retirement, health care, and the like. This system, often called a private welfare state, resulted in wide disparities among workers, severely disadvantaging those not represented by unions and those with irregular employment.

While the absolute number of organized workers continued to grow, union membership peaked at 27.1 percent of the labor force in 1957. Technological advances eliminated jobs in heavy industry, reducing the number of workers in the steel, copper, and aluminum industries by 17 percent. "You are going to have trouble collecting union dues from all of these machines," commented a Ford manager to union leader Walter Reuther. Moreover, the economy as a whole was shifting from production to service as more workers distributed goods, performed services, provided education, and carried out government work. Unions made some headway in these fields, especially among government employees, but most service industries resisted unionization.

The growing clerical and service occupations swelled the demand for female workers. By the end of the 1950s, 35 percent of all women over age sixteen worked outside the home, and women held nearly one-third of all jobs. The vast majority of them worked in offices, light manufacturing, domestic service, teaching, and nursing; because these occupations were occupied primarily by women, wages were relatively low. In 1960, the average female full-time worker earned just 60 percent of the average male worker's wages. At the bottom of the employment ladder, black women took home only 42 percent of what white men earned.

Burgeoning Suburbs and Declining Cities

Although suburbs had existed since the nineteenth century, nothing symbolized the affluent society more than their tremendous expansion in the 1950s. Eleven million new homes went up in the suburbs, and by 1960 one in four Americans lived there. As Nixon boasted to Khrushchev during the **kitchen debate** (see pages 897–98), the suburbs were accessible to families with modest incomes. Builder William

J. Levitt adapted the factory assembly-line process to home building, planning nearly identical units so that individual construction workers could move from house to house and perform the same single operation in each one. In 1949, families could purchase mass-produced houses in his 17,000-home development, called Levittown, on Long Island, New York, for just under $8,000 each. Developments similar to Levittown, as well as more luxurious ones, quickly went up throughout the country. The government underwrote home ownership by guaranteeing low-interest mortgages through the Federal Housing Administration and the Veterans Administration and by making interest on mortgages tax deductible. Thousands of miles of government-funded interstate highway running through urban areas indirectly subsidized suburban development.

The growing suburbs helped polarize society, especially along racial lines. Each Levittown homeowner signed a contract pledging not to rent or sell to a non-Caucasian. The Supreme Court declared such covenants unenforceable in 1948, but suburban America remained dramatically segregated. Social critic Lewis Mumford blasted the suburbs as "a multitude of uniform, unidentifiable houses in a treeless communal wasteland, inhabited by people of the same class, the same income, the same age group." By the 1960s, suburbs also came under attack for bulldozing the natural environment, creating

> ### "A multitude of uniform, unidentifiable houses in a treeless communal wasteland."
> —Social critic LEWIS MUMFORD, describing the suburbs

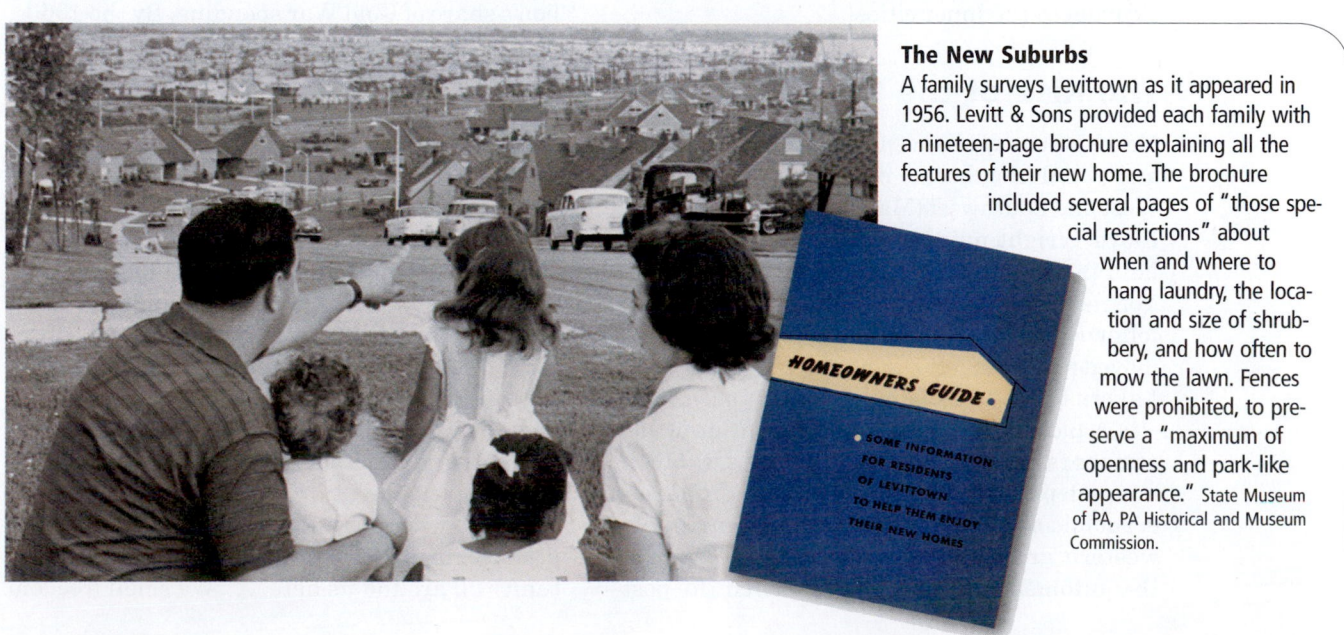

The New Suburbs
A family surveys Levittown as it appeared in 1956. Levitt & Sons provided each family with a nineteen-page brochure explaining all the features of their new home. The brochure included several pages of "those special restrictions" about when and where to hang laundry, the location and size of shrubbery, and how often to mow the lawn. Fences were prohibited, to preserve a "maximum of openness and park-like appearance." State Museum of PA, PA Historical and Museum Commission.

HOMEOWNERS GUIDE
SOME INFORMATION FOR RESIDENTS OF LEVITTOWN TO HELP THEM ENJOY THEIR NEW HOMES

An African American Suburb
The pioneer of mass-produced suburban housing, William J. Levitt, reflected the racism that kept blacks out of suburbia when he said, "We can solve a housing problem, or we can try and solve a racial problem, but we cannot combine the two." These African Americans developed their own suburb, a planned community for middle-class blacks in Richmond, California, which welcomed the first families in 1950. Richmond Public Library.

groundwater contamination, and disrupting wildlife patterns.

Although some African Americans joined the suburban migration, most moved to cities in search of economic opportunity, increasing their numbers in most cities by 50 percent during the 1950s. These migrants, however, came to cities that were already in decline, losing not only population but also commerce and industry to the suburbs or to southern and western states. Shoppers gradually chose new suburban malls over downtown department stores. Many of the new jobs lay beyond the reach of the recent black arrivals to the inner cities.

The Rise of the Sun Belt

No regions experienced the postwar economic and population booms more intensely than the West and Southwest (Map 27.2). Architect Frank Lloyd Wright quipped, "Everything loose will land in Los Angeles." California overtook New York as the most populous state. Sports franchises followed fans: In 1958, the Brooklyn Dodgers moved to Los Angeles, joined by the Minneapolis Lakers three years later.

A pleasant natural environment drew new residents to the West and Southwest, but no magnet proved stronger than the promise of economic opportunity. As railroads had fueled western growth in the nineteenth century, so the automobile and airplane spurred the post–

World War II surge. The technology of air-conditioning facilitated industrial development and by 1960 cooled nearly eight million homes in the so-called Sun Belt, which stretched from Florida to California.

So important was the defense industry to the South and West that the area was later referred to as the "Gun Belt." The aerospace industry boomed in Seattle–Tacoma, Los Angeles, and Dallas–Fort Worth, and military bases helped underwrite prosperity in cities such as San Diego and San Antonio. Although defense dollars benefited other regions, the Sun Belt captured the lion's share of Cold War spending. By the 1960s, nearly one of every three California workers held a defense-related job.

The surging populations and industries soon threatened the environment. Providing sufficient water and power to cities and to agribusiness meant building dams and reservoirs on free-flowing rivers. Native Americans lost fishing sites on the Columbia River, and dams on the Upper Missouri displaced nine hundred Indian families. Sprawling urban and suburban settlement without efficient public transportation contributed to blankets of smog over Los Angeles and other cities.

The high-technology basis of postwar economic development drew well-educated, highly skilled workers to the West, but the economic promise also attracted the poor. "We see opportunity all around us here. . . . We smell freedom

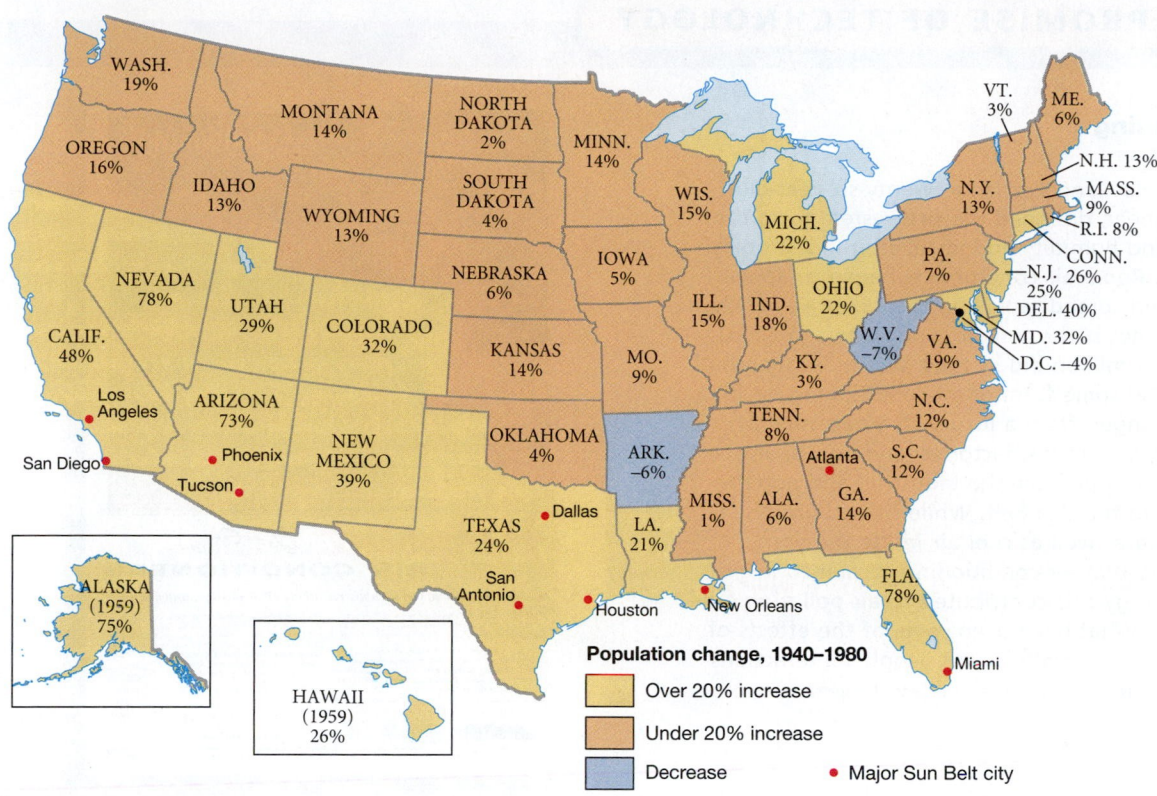

Population change, 1940–1980

- Over 20% increase
- Under 20% increase
- Decrease   • Major Sun Belt city

MAP ACTIVITY

Map 27.2   The Rise of the Sun Belt, 1940–1980
The growth of defense industries, a non-unionized labor force, and the spread of air-conditioning all helped spur economic development and population growth in the West and South, which made the Sun Belt the fastest-growing region of the country between 1940 and 1980.

READING THE MAP: Which states experienced population growth of more than 20 percent? Which states experienced the largest population growth?
CONNECTIONS: What stimulated the population boom in the Southwest? What role did the Cold War play in this expansion? What developments made the Southwest diverse in the composition of its population?

here, and maybe soon we can taste it," commented a black mother in California. Between 1945 and 1960, more than one-third of the African Americans who left the South moved west.

The Mexican American population also grew, especially in California and Texas. To supply California's vast agribusiness industry, the government continued the *bracero* program begun during World War II, under which Mexican laborers were permitted to enter the United States to work for a limited period. Until the program ended in 1964, more than 100,000 Mexicans entered the United States each year to labor in the fields — and many of them stayed, legally or illegally. But permanent Mexican immigration was not as welcome as Mexicans' low-wage labor. In 1954, the government launched a series of raids called "Operation Wetback," resulting in

the deportation of more than three million Mexicans. Even Mexicans with legal status felt unwelcome and vulnerable to incidents of mistaken identity.

At the same time, Mexican American citizens gained a victory in their ongoing struggle for civil rights in *Hernandez v. Texas*. When a Texas jury convicted Pete Hernandez of murder, lawyers from the American GI Forum and the League of United Latin-American Citizens (see chapter 26) appealed on the grounds that persons of Mexican origin had been routinely excluded from jury service. In 1954, the Supreme Court decided its first Mexican American civil rights case of the post–World War II era, ruling unanimously that Mexican Americans constituted a distinct group and that their systematic exclusion from juries violated the Fourteenth Amendment guarantee

THE PROMISE OF TECHNOLOGY

Air-Conditioning

In 1902, Willis Haviland Carrier, a twenty-six-year-old American engineer, designed the first system to control temperature and humidity and installed it in a Brooklyn printing plant. Room air conditioners began to appear in the 1930s and spread rapidly in the 1950s. Fewer than one million homes had room air conditioners in 1950, but nearly eight million did in 1960, and more than half of all homes had some form of air-conditioning by 1975, as its status changed from a luxury to a necessity. By cooling homes, businesses, factories, and hotels, air-conditioning made possible the industrial and population explosion in the Sun Belt. While this ad promised consumers clean as well as cool air inside the house, it failed to note that air-conditioning consumed large amounts of energy and contributed to air pollution outside the house. What have been some of the effects of air-conditioning on social life and people's interactions with their neighbors? Hotpoint/General Electric Company.

of equal protection. Legal scholar Ian Haney-López called the *Hernandez* ruling "huge for the Mexican American community. They now had the highest court in the land saying it's unconstitutional to treat Mexicans as if they're an inferior race."

Free of the discrimination faced by minorities, white Americans enjoyed the fullest prosperity in the West. In April 1950, when California developers opened Lakewood, a large housing development in Los Angeles County, thirty thousand people lined up to buy houses at prices ranging from $71,000 to $89,000 in 2010 dollars. Many of the new homeowners were veterans, blue-collar, and lower-level white-collar workers whose defense-based jobs at aerospace corporations enabled them to fulfill the American dream of the 1950s. A huge shopping mall, Lakewood Center, offered myriad products of the consumer

Rounding Up Undocumented Migrants

Not all Mexican Americans who wanted to work in the United States were accommodated by the *bracero* program. In 1953, Los Angeles police arrested these men, who did not have legal documents and were hiding in a freight train. Some Americans used the crude term "wetback" to refer to illegal Mexican immigrants because many of them swam across the Rio Grande, which forms part of the border between the United States and Mexico. © Bettmann/Corbis.

culture, and the workers' children lived within commuting distance of community colleges and six state universities.

The Democratization of Higher Education

California's university system exemplified a spectacular transformation of higher education. Between 1940 and 1960, college enrollments in the United States more than doubled. More than 40 percent of young Americans attended college by the mid-1960s, up from 15 percent in the 1940s. Prosperity enabled more families to keep their children in school longer, and the federal government subsidized the education of more than two million veterans. The Cold War also sent millions of federal dollars to universities for defense-related research. And state governments vastly expanded the number of public colleges and universities, while municipalities began to build two-year community colleges.

All Americans did not benefit equally from the democratization of higher education. Although their college enrollments surged from 37,000 in 1941 to 90,000 in 1961, African Americans constituted only about 5 percent of all college students. Black men and women attended college in nearly equal numbers, but for a time the educational gap between white men and women grew, even while the number of women attending college increased. In 1940, women had earned 40 percent of undergraduate degrees, but as veterans flocked to college campuses, women's proportion fell to 25 percent in 1950 and rebounded to only 33 percent by 1960. The large veteran enrollments moved colleges to relax rules that had forbidden students to marry. Unlike men, however, women tended to drop out of college after marriage and to take jobs so their husbands could stay in school. Reflecting gender norms of the 1950s, most college women agreed that "it is natural for a woman to be satisfied with her husband's success and not crave personal achievement."

> **REVIEW** How did technology contribute to changes in the economy, suburbanization, and the growth of the Sun Belt?

▶ The Culture of Abundance

Prosperity in the 1950s intensified the transformation of the nation into a consumer society, changing the way Americans lived and converting the traditional work ethic into an ethic of consumption. People married at earlier ages, the birthrate soared, and dominant values celebrated family life and traditional gender roles. Religious observance expanded even as Americans sought satisfaction in material possessions. Television entered the homes of most Americans, both reflecting and helping to promote a consumer culture. Undercurrents of rebellion, especially among young people, and women's increasing employment defied some of the dominant norms but did not greatly disrupt the complacency of the 1950s.

Consumption Rules the Day

Journalist Robert Samuelson remembered that in the 1950s "you were a daily witness to the marvels of affluence . . . a seemingly endless array of new gadgets and machines." Scorned by Khrushchev during the kitchen debate as unnecessary contrivances, consumer items flooded American society. Although the purchase and display of consumer goods was not new (see chapter 23), by the 1950s consumption had become a reigning value, vital for economic prosperity and essential to individuals' identity and status. In place of the traditional emphasis on work and savings, the consumer culture encouraged satisfaction and happiness through the purchase and use of new products.

The consumer culture rested on a firm material base. Between 1950 and 1960, both the gross national product (the value of all goods and services produced) and median family income grew by 25 percent in constant dollars (Figure 27.1). Economists claimed that 60 percent of Americans enjoyed middle-class incomes in 1960. Referring to the popular ranch-style houses in the new suburbs, *House Beautiful* magazine boasted, "Our houses are all on one level, like our class structure." Though ignoring the one in five Americans who still lived in poverty, the statement did reflect the increasing ability of people to consume products that made class differences less visible. By 1960, four out of every five families owned a television set, nearly all had a refrigerator, and most owned at least one car. The number of shopping centers quadrupled between 1957 and 1963.

Several forces spurred this unparalleled abundance. A population surge — from 152 million in 1950 to 180 million in 1960 — expanded the demand for products and boosted industries ranging from housing to baby goods. Consumer borrowing also fueled the economic boom, as people increasingly made purchases on installment plans and began to use credit cards. In what *Life* magazine referred to as a "revolution in consumer purchasing,"

> "You were a daily witness to the marvels of affluence . . . a seemingly endless array of new gadgets and machines."
>
> —Journalist ROBERT SAMUELSON, speaking of life in the 1950s

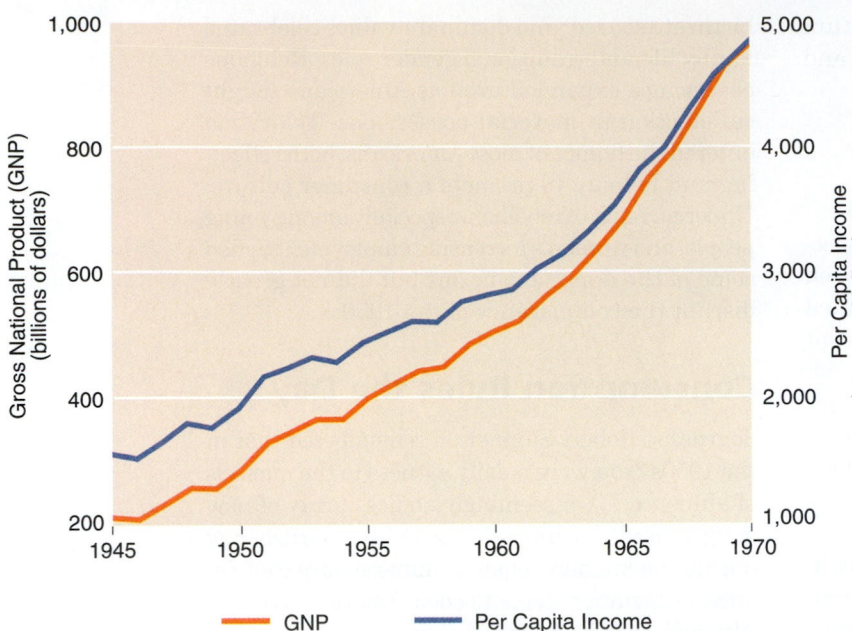

FIGURE 27.1   The Postwar Economic Boom: GNP and Per Capita Income, 1945–1970
American dominance of the worldwide market, innovative technologies that led to new industries such as computers and plastics, population growth, and increases in worker productivity all contributed to the enormous economic growth of the United States after World War II.

Americans now enjoyed their possessions while they paid for them instead of saving their money for future purchases.

Although the sheer need to support themselves and their families explained most women's employment, a desire to secure some of the new abundance sent growing numbers of women to work. In fact, married women's employment rose more than that of any other group in the 1950s. As one woman remarked, "My Joe can't put five kids through college . . . and the washer had to be replaced, and Ann was ashamed to bring friends home because the living room furniture was such a mess, so I went to work." The standards for family happiness imposed by the consumer culture increasingly required a second income.

The Revival of Domesticity and Religion

Despite married women's growing employment, a dominant ideology celebrated traditional family life and conventional gender roles. Both popular culture and public figures defined the ideal family as a male breadwinner, a full-time homemaker, and three or four children. The emphasis on home and family life reflected in part the desire for security amid anxieties about the Cold War and the nuclear menace. Writer and feminist **Betty Friedan** gave a name to the idealization of women's domestic roles in her 1963 book *The Feminine Mystique*. Friedan criticized scholars, advertisers, and public officials for promulgating a set of ideas

based on the assumption that biological differences dictated different roles for men and women. According to this feminine mystique, women should find fulfillment in devotion to their homes, families, and serving others. Not many women directly challenged these ideas, but Edith Stern, a college-educated writer, maintained that "many arguments about the joys of housewifery have been advanced, largely by those who have never had to work at it."

Although the glorification of domesticity clashed with women's increasing employment, many Americans' lives did embody the family ideal. Postwar prosperity enabled people to marry earlier and to have more children. The American birthrate soared between 1945 and 1960, peaking in 1957 with 4.3 million births and producing the **baby boom** generation (Figure 27.2 and appendix II, page A-33). Experts encouraged mothers to devote even more attention to child rearing, while they also urged fathers to cultivate family "togetherness" by spending more time with their children.

The 1950s also witnessed a surge of interest in religion. From 1940 to 1960, membership in churches and synagogues rose from 50 to 63 percent of all Americans. Polls reported that 95 percent of the population believed in God. Evangelism took on new life, most notably in the nationwide crusades of Baptist minister **Billy Graham**. Congress linked religion more closely to the state by adding "under God" to the pledge of allegiance and by requiring that "In God We Trust" be printed on all currency.

Religion helped to calm anxieties in the nuclear age, while ministers such as Graham made the Cold War a holy war, labeling communism "a great sinister anti-Christian movement masterminded by

	Live Births per 1,000
Brazil	
Canada	
China	
Cuba	
Egypt	
West Germany	
Great Britain	
Iran	
Israel	
Mexico	
Sweden	
United States	
USSR	

FIGURE 27.2   GLOBAL COMPARISON: The Baby Boom in International Perspective
The United States was not alone in welcoming bumper crops of babies in the 1950s. High fertility continued in nonindustrialized countries, while in Europe, as in the United States, birthrates rebounded from low levels during the Great Depression and World War II. Which countries had birthrates comparable to those of the United States? What might explain why countries such as Brazil, China, Iran, and Mexico had birthrates so much higher than those in the United States? What might explain why birthrates in Europe were lower than those in the United States?

Satan." Some critics questioned the depth of the religious revival, attributing the growth in church membership to a desire for conformity and a need for social outlets. One commentator, for example, noted that 53 percent of Americans could not name any book of the Christian Bible's New Testament.

Television Transforms Culture and Politics

Just as family life and religion offered a respite from Cold War anxieties, so too did the new medium of television. By 1960, close to 90 percent of American homes boasted a television set, and the average viewer spent more than five hours each day in front of the screen. Audiences were especially attracted to situation comedies, which projected the family ideal and the feminine mystique into millions of homes. On TV, married women did not have paying jobs, and they deferred to their husbands, though they often got the upper hand through subtle manipulation. In the most popular television show of the early 1950s, *I Love Lucy*, the husband-and-wife team of Lucille Ball and Desi Arnaz played the couple Lucy and Ricky Ricardo. Ricky would not let Lucy get a

Evangelist Billy Graham Preaches in New York City

Billy Graham, a young Baptist minister from North Carolina, electrified mass audiences, exhorting them to find salvation in Jesus Christ and to uphold Christian moral standards. Americans flocked to his crusades, even as he implicitly condemned their avid participation in consumerism as "materialistic, worldly, secular, greedy, and covetous." Here he addresses a crowd of 500,000 in Madison Square Garden during a crusade in New York City over the summer of 1957. One hundred thousand people heard Graham preach in Yankee Stadium, and millions watched the revivals on television. Martin Luther King Jr. joined Graham at one of the New York rallies. Photo: Gjon Mili/Time Life Pictures/Getty Images; brochure: Archives of the Billy Graham Center, Wheaton, Illinois.

The Made-for-TV Family
The Adventures of Ozzie and Harriet ran on television from 1952 to 1966. Like other family sitcoms, it idealized white family life, in which no one got divorced, no one took drugs or seriously misbehaved, fathers held white-collar jobs, and mothers did not work outside the home. Following the 1950s norm, Ozzie sought to fulfill his role as head of the household, but the impeccably dressed Harriet more often appeared as the wise and sensible one who rescued Ozzie and the teenage boys, David and Ricky, from their misadventures. In what ways do today's sitcoms differ from those of the 1950s? Picture Research Consultants & Archives.

job, and many plots depicted her zany attempts to get around him.

Television also began to affect politics. Eisenhower's 1952 presidential campaign used TV ads for the first time, although he was not happy that "an old soldier should come to this." By 1960, television played a key role in election campaigns. Reflecting on his narrow victory in 1960, president-elect John F. Kennedy remarked, "We wouldn't have had a prayer without that gadget."

Television transformed politics in other ways. Money played a much larger role in elections because candidates needed to pay for expensive TV spots. The ability to appeal directly to voters in their living rooms put a premium on personal attractiveness and encouraged candidates to build their own campaign organizations, relying less on political parties. The declining strength of parties and the growing power of money in elections were not new trends, but TV helped accelerate them.

Unlike government-financed television in Europe, American TV was paid for by private enterprise. What NBC called a "selling machine in every living room" became the major vehicle for hawking the products of the affluent society and creating a consumer culture. In the mid-1950s, advertisers spent $10 billion to push their goods on TV, and they did not hesitate to interfere with shows that might jeopardize the sale of their products. The cigarette company that sponsored the *Camel News Caravan* banned any news film clips showing "No Smoking" signs. Television programs also tantalized viewers with things to buy. On *Queen for a Day*, for example, the women with the most pitiful personal stories won fur coats, vacuum cleaners, and other merchandise.

In 1961, Newton Minow, chairman of the Federal Communications Commission, called television a "vast wasteland." While acknowledging some of TV's great achievements, particularly documentaries and drama, Minow depicted it as "a procession of game shows, . . . formula comedies about totally unbelievable families, blood and thunder, mayhem, violence, sadism, murder . . . and cartoons." But viewers kept tuning in. In little more than a decade, television came to dominate Americans' leisure time, influence their consumption patterns, and shape their perceptions of the nation's leadership.

Countercurrents

Pockets of dissent underlay the complacency of the 1950s. Some intellectuals took exception to the materialism and conformity of the era. In *The Lonely Crowd* (1950), sociologist David Riesman lamented a shift from the "inner-directed" to the "other-directed" individual, as Americans replaced independent thinking with an eagerness to adapt to external standards of behavior and belief. Sharing that distaste for the importance of "belonging," William H. Whyte Jr., in his popular book *The Organization Man* (1956), blamed the modern corporation for making employees tailor themselves to the group. Vance Packard's 1959 best seller, *The Status Seekers*, decried "the vigorous merchandising of goods as status-symbols" and argued that "class lines . . . appear to be hardening."

Implicit in much of the critique of consumer culture was concern about the loss of traditional masculinity. Consumption itself was associated with women and their presumed greater susceptibility to manipulation. Men, required to conform to get ahead, moved farther away from the nineteenth-century masculine ideals of individualism and aggressiveness. Moreover, the increase in married women's employment compromised the male ideal of breadwinner.

Into this gender confusion came *Playboy*, which began publication in 1953 and quickly gained a circulation of one million. The new magazine idealized masculine independence in the form of bachelorhood and assaulted the reigning middle-class norms of domesticity and respectability. By associating the sophisticated bachelor with good wine, music, furnishings, and the like, the magazine made consumption more masculine while promoting sexual freedom, at least for men.

In fact, new research on Americans' sexual behavior disclosed that it often departed from the postwar family ideal. Two books published by **Alfred Kinsey** and other researchers at Indiana University — *Sexual Behavior in the Human Male* (1948) and *Sexual Behavior in the Human Female* (1953)

— uncovered a surprising range of sexual conduct. In a large survey, Kinsey found that 85 percent of the men and 50 percent of the women had had sex before marriage, half of the husbands and a quarter of the wives had engaged in adultery, and one-third of the men and one-seventh of the women reported homosexual experiences. Although Kinsey's sampling procedures later cast doubt on his ability to generalize across the population, the books became best sellers. They also drew a firestorm of outrage, especially because Kinsey insisted on the natural variability of human sexuality and refused to make moral judgments.

Less direct challenges to mainstream standards appeared in the everyday behavior of young Americans. "Roll over Beethoven and tell Tchaikovsky the news!" belted out Chuck Berry in his 1956 hit record celebrating **rock and roll**, a new form of music that combined country sounds and black rhythm and blues. White teenagers lionized Elvis Presley, who shocked their parents with his tight pants, hip-rolling gestures, and sensuous rock-and-roll music. "Before there was Elvis . . . I started going crazy for 'race music,'" recalled a white man of his

Elvis Presley
Elvis Presley began recording in 1954, and within two years — by the age of 21 — he was a national star, appearing frequently on television and scoring his first number one single hit, "Heartbreak Hotel." He drew adoring teenage crowds wherever he performed, including this appearance in his hometown of Tupelo, Mississippi, in 1956. His fans' parents were not so enthralled, complaining about his "grunt and groin antics" and "unnecessary bump and grind routine." Those trademark moves were captured on this button, which, when moved slightly, created an illusion of Elvis's gyrations. Photograph: Elvis Presley Enterprises, Inc.; button: Elvis Presley Enterprises, Inc.

Jackson Pollock
The leading artist of the post–World War II revolution in painting, Jackson Pollock often worked with the canvas on the floor, dripping paint onto it with sticks, turkey basters, and hard brushes, prompting *Time* magazine to dub him, "Jack the Dripper." He struggled with alcohol and died in 1956, at the age of forty-four, crashing his car while drunk and speeding near his Long Island home. He is shown here in 1949 with his painting, *Number 9*. Photo by Arnold Newman/Getty Images.

teenage years. "That got me into trouble with my parents and the schools." His recollection underscored African Americans' contributions to rock and roll, as well as the rebellion expressed by white youths' attraction to black music.

The most blatant revolt against conventionality came from the self-proclaimed **Beat generation**, a small group of primarily male literary figures based in New York City and San Francisco. Rejecting nearly everything in mainstream culture — patriotism, consumerism, technology, conventional family life, discipline — the Beats celebrated spontaneity and absolute personal freedom, including drug consumption and free-wheeling sex. In his landmark poem *Howl* (1956), Allen Ginsberg denounced the social forces that "frightened me out of my natural ecstasy!" Jack Kerouac, who gave the Beat generation its name, published the best-selling novel *On the Road* (1957), whose energetic, stream-of-consciousness, bebop-style prose narrated the impetuous cross-country travels of two young men. "The only people for me," he wrote, "are the mad ones . . . the ones who never yawn or say a commonplace thing, but burn, burn, burn like fabulous yellow roman candles exploding like spiders across the stars." The Beats' lifestyles shocked "square" Americans, but they would provide a model for a much larger movement of youthful dissidents in the 1960s.

Bold new styles in the visual arts also showed the 1950s to be more than a decade of bland conventionality. In New York City, an artistic revolution known as "action painting" or "abstract expressionism" flowered, rejecting the idea that painting should represent recognizable forms. Jackson Pollock and other abstract expressionists, emphasizing spontaneity, poured, dripped, and threw paint on canvases or substituted sticks and other implements for brushes. The new form of painting so captivated and redirected the Western art world that New York replaced Paris as its center.

REVIEW Why did American consumption expand so dramatically in the 1950s, and what aspects of society and culture did it influence?

▶ The Emergence of a Civil Rights Movement

Building on the civil rights initiatives begun during World War II, African Americans posed the most dramatic challenge to the status quo of the 1950s as they sought to overcome the political, economic, and social barriers that had replaced the literal bonds of slavery. Every southern state mandated rigid segregation in public settings ranging from hospitals and schools to drinking fountains and restrooms. Voting laws and practices in the South disfranchised the vast majority of African Americans; employment discrimination kept them at the bottom of the economic ladder throughout the country; and schools, restaurants, and other public spaces were often as segregated, though not usually by law, in the North as they were in the South.

Although black protest was as old as American racism, in the 1950s grassroots movements arose that attracted national attention and the support of white liberals. Pressed by civil rights groups, the Supreme Court delivered significant institutional reforms, but the most important changes of all occurred among blacks themselves. Ordinary African Americans in substantial numbers sought their own liberation, building a movement that would transform race relations in the United States.

African Americans Challenge the Supreme Court and the President

Several factors spurred black protest in the 1950s. Between 1940 and 1960, more than three million African Americans moved from the South into areas where they had a political voice. Black leaders made sure that foreign policy officials realized how racist practices at home tarnished the U.S. image abroad and handicapped the United States in its competition with the Soviet Union. The very system of segregation meant that African Americans controlled certain organizational resources, such as churches, colleges, and newspapers, where leadership skills could be honed, networks developed, and information spread.

The legal strategy of the major civil rights organization, the National Association for the Advancement of Colored People (NAACP), reached its crowning achievement with the Supreme Court decision in **Brown v. Board of Education** in 1954.

Brown consolidated five separate suits that reflected the growing determination of black Americans to fight for their rights. Oliver Brown, a World War II veteran in Topeka, Kansas, filed suit because his daughter had to pass by a white school just seven blocks from their home to attend a black school more than a mile away. In Virginia, sixteen-year-old Barbara Johns initiated a student strike over wretched conditions in her black high school, leading to another of the suits joined in *Brown*.

The NAACP's lead lawyer, future Supreme Court justice Thurgood Marshall, urged the Court to overturn the "separate but equal" precedent established in *Plessy v. Ferguson* in 1896 (see chapter 21). A unanimous Court, headed by Chief Justice Earl Warren, declared, "Separate educational facilities are inherently unequal" and thus violated the Fourteenth Amendment.

Ultimate responsibility for enforcement of the decision lay with President Eisenhower, but he refused to endorse *Brown*. He also kept silent in 1955 when whites murdered Emmett Till, a fourteen-

School Integration in Little Rock, Arkansas
The nine African American teenagers who integrated Central High School in Little Rock, Arkansas, endured nearly three weeks of threats and hateful taunts before they even got through the doors. Here Elizabeth Eckford tries to ignore angry students and adults as she approaches the entrance to the school, only to be blocked by Arkansas National Guardsmen. Even after President Eisenhower intervened to enable the "Little Rock Nine" to attend school, they were called names, tripped, spat upon, and otherwise harassed by some white students. Francis Miller/TimePix/Getty.

The *Brown* Decision

Brown v. Board of Education of Topeka was the principal Supreme Court decision in the transformation of African Americans' legal and political status during the 1950s and 1960s. Responding to lawsuits argued by NAACP lawyers, *Brown* was the culmination of a series of Supreme Court rulings between 1938 and 1950 that chipped away at an earlier Court's decision in *Plessy v. Ferguson* (1896) permitting "separate but equal" public facilities.

DOCUMENT 1
Brown v. Board of Education of Topeka, May 1954

In 1954, Chief Justice Earl Warren delivered the unanimous opinion of the Supreme Court in Brown v. Board of Education of Topeka, *declaring racial segregation in public education unconstitutional and explaining why.*

In these days, it is doubtful that any child may reasonably be expected to succeed in life if he is denied the opportunity of an education. Such an opportunity, if the state has undertaken to provide it, is a right that must be made available to all on equal terms. . . .

We come then to the question presented: Does segregation of children in public schools solely on the basis of race, even though the physical facilities and other "tangible" factors may be equal, deprive the children of the minority group of equal educational opportunities?

We believe that it does. . . . In *McLaurin* [a 1950 case], the Court, in requiring that a Negro admitted to a white graduate school be treated like all other students, again resorted to intangible considerations: ". . . his ability to study, to engage in discussions and exchange views with other students, and, in general, to learn his profession." Such considerations apply with added force to children in grade and high schools. To separate them from others of similar age and qualifications solely because of their race generates a feeling of inferiority as to their status in the community that may affect their hearts and minds in a way unlikely ever to be undone.

We conclude that in the field of public education the doctrine of "separate but equal" has no place. Separate educational facilities are inherently unequal

SOURCE: *Brown*, 347 U.S. 483 (1954).

DOCUMENT 2
Southern Manifesto on Integration, March 1956

The Brown *decision outraged many southern whites. In 1956, more than one hundred members of Congress signed a manifesto pledging resistance to the ruling.*

We regard the decision of the Supreme Court in the school cases as a clear abuse of judicial power. It climaxes a trend in the Federal judiciary undertaking to legislate . . . and to encroach upon the reserved rights of the states and the people.

The original Constitution does not mention education. Neither does the Fourteenth Amendment nor any amendment. . . . The Supreme Court of the United States, with no legal basis for such action, undertook to exercise their naked judicial power and substituted their personal political and social ideas for the established law of the land.

This unwarranted exercise of power by the court, contrary to the Constitution, is creating chaos and confusion in the states principally affected. It is destroying the amicable relations between the white and negro races that have been created through ninety years of patient effort by the good people of both races. It has planted hatred and suspicion where there has been heretofore friendship and understanding. . . .

We pledge ourselves to use all lawful means to bring about a reversal of this decision which is contrary to the Constitution and to prevent the use of force in its implementation.

SOURCE: "Southern Manifesto on Integration" (1956).

In the face of white hostility, black children carried the burden of implementing the Brown *decision. The following accounts by black students reflect varied experiences, but even those who entered white schools fairly easily faced obstacles to their full participation in school activities. Nonetheless, they cherished the new opportunities, favoring integration for reasons different from those given by the Supreme Court.*

DOCUMENT 3
A High School Boy in Oak Ridge, Tennessee, 1957

I like it a whole lot better than the colored school. You have a chance to learn more and you have more sports.

I play forward or guard on the basketball team, only I don't get to participate in all games. Some teams don't mind my playing. Some teams object not because of the fellows on the team, but because of the people in their community. Mostly it's the fans or the board of education that decides against me. . . . The same situation occurs in baseball. I'm catcher, but the first game I didn't get to participate in. A farm club of the major league wrote the coach that they were interested in seeing me play so maybe I'll get to play the next time.

SOURCE: Dorothy Sterling, *Tender Warriors* (New York: Hill and Wang, 1958), 83. Copyright © 1958 by Hill and Wang. Reprinted with permission.

DOCUMENT 4
A High School Girl in Louisville, Kentucky, 1957

I'm accepted now as an individual rather than as a person belonging to the Negro race. People say to me, "I'm glad I met you because if I met someone else I might not have liked them." I don't think it's fair, this individual acceptance. I feel like I was some ambassador from some foreign country.

I couldn't go out for any extracurricular activities. Cheerleading, band, drum majorettes, the people who are members of these organizations, they go to camps in the summer which are segregated. Well, what can you do? It just leaves me out. It's not the school, it's the community.

SOURCE: Dorothy Sterling, *Tender Warriors* (New York: Hill and Wang, 1958), 83. Copyright © 1958 by Hill and Wang. Reprinted with permission.

DOCUMENT 5
A High School Girl in the Deep South, May 1966

The first day a news reporter rode the bus with us. All around us were state troopers. In front of them were federal marshals. When we got to town there were lines of people and cars all along the road. A man without a badge or anything got on the bus and started beating up the newspaper reporter. . . . He was crying and bleeding. When we got to the school the students were all around looking through the windows. The mayor said we couldn't come there because the school was already filled to capacity [and] if six of us came in it would be a fire hazard. He told us to turn around and go back. We turned around and the students started yelling and clapping. When we went back [after obtaining a court order] there were no students there at all. There were only two

teachers left so they had to bring a couple of teachers from other places. [The white students did not return, so the six black students finished the year by themselves.] The shocking thing was during the graduation ceremonies. All six of the students got together to make a speech. After we finished, I looked around and saw three teachers crying. The principal had tears in his eyes and he got up to make a little speech about us. He said at first he didn't think he would enjoy being around us. You could see in his face that he was really touched. We said something like we really enjoyed school together and that we were glad they stuck it out and all that kind of stuff.

SOURCE: *In Their Own Words: A Student Appraisal of What Happened after School Desegregation* (Washington, D.C.: Department of Health, Education, and Welfare, Office of Education, 1966), 17–18.

DOCUMENT 6
A High School Girl in the Deep South, May 1966

I chose to go because I felt that I could get a better education here. I knew that the [black] school that I was then attending wasn't giving me exactly what I should have had. As far as the Science Department was concerned, it just didn't have the chemicals we needed and I just decided to change. When I went over the students there weren't very friendly and when I graduated they still weren't. They didn't want us there and they made that plain, but we went there anyway and we stuck it out. The lessons there were harder, lots harder, but I studied and I managed to pass all my subjects.

SOURCE: *In Their Own Words: A Student Appraisal of What Happened after School Desegregation* (Washington, D.C.: Department of Health, Education, and Welfare, Office of Education, 1966), 44.

Questions for Analysis and Debate

1. What reasons did the Supreme Court give in favor of desegregation? What reasons did black students give for wanting to attend integrated schools? How do these reasons differ?

2. What arguments did the southern legislators make against the Supreme Court decision?

3. What obstacles remained for African American students to confront once they had been admitted to integrated schools?

4. What conditions do you feel would be worth enduring to obtain a better education?

year-old black boy who had allegedly whistled at a white woman in Mississippi. Reflecting his own prejudice, his preference for limited federal intervention in the states, and a leadership style that favored consensus and gradual progress, Eisenhower kept his distance from civil rights issues. Such inaction fortified southern resistance to school desegregation and contributed to the gravest constitutional crisis since the Civil War.

The crisis came in Little Rock, Arkansas, in September 1957, when Governor Orval Faubus sent Arkansas National Guard troops to block the enrollment of nine black students in Little Rock's Central High School. Later, he allowed them to enter but withdrew the National Guard, leaving the students to face an angry white mob. "During those years when we desperately needed approval from our peers," Melba Patillo Beals remembered, "we were victims of the most harsh rejection imaginable." As television cameras transmitted the ugly scene, Eisenhower was forced to send regular army troops to Little Rock, the first federal military intervention in the South since Reconstruction. Paratroopers escorted the "**Little Rock Nine**" into the school, but forty-four teachers who had supported them lost their jobs. Despite Eisenhower's explanation that he had acted to preserve the law, not to promote integration, southern leaders were outraged. Other southern cities avoided integration by closing public schools and using tax dollars to support private ones. Seven years after *Brown*, only 6.4 percent of southern black students attended integrated schools. (See "Documenting the American Promise," page 922.)

School segregation outside the South was not usually sanctioned by law, but northern school districts separated black and white students through manipulation of neighborhood boundaries and through other devices. Even before *Brown*, black parents in dozens of northern cities challenged the assignment of their children to inferior "colored" schools. While their boycotts reaped some successes, the structure of residential segregation, often supported by official action, made school segregation a severe disadvantage for African Americans in the North as well as in the South.

Although Eisenhower rejected an aggressive approach to racial issues, he did order the integration of public facilities in Washington, D.C., and on military bases, and he supported the first federal civil rights legislation since Reconstruction. Yet southern members of Congress made sure that the Civil Rights Acts of 1957 and 1960 were little more than symbolic. Baseball star Jackie Robinson spoke for many African Americans when he wired Eisenhower in 1957, "We disagree that half a loaf is better than none. Have waited this long for a bill with meaning—can wait a little longer." Eisenhower appointed the first black professional to the White House staff, E. Frederick Morrow, but Morrow confided in his diary, "I feel ridiculous . . . trying to defend the administration's record on civil rights."

Montgomery and Mass Protest

What set the civil rights movement of the 1950s and 1960s apart from earlier acts of black protest was its widespread presence in the South, the large number of people involved, their willingness to confront white institutions directly, and the use of nonviolent protest and civil disobedience to bring about change. The Congress of Racial Equality and other groups had experimented with these tactics in the 1940s, organizing, for example, to integrate movie theaters in Cincinnati, restaurants in Chicago, swimming pools in New Jersey, and a public playground in Washington, D.C. In the South, African Americans boycotted the segregated bus system in Baton Rouge, Louisiana, in 1953, but the first sustained protest to claim national attention began in Montgomery, Alabama, on December 1, 1955.

That day, police arrested **Rosa Parks** for violating a local segregation ordinance. Riding a crowded bus home from her job as a seamstress in a department store, she refused to give up her seat so that a white man could sit down. "People always say that I didn't give up my seat because I was tired, but that isn't true," Parks recalled. "I was not tired physically. . . . I was not old. . . . I was forty-two. No, the only tired I was, was tired of giving in." The bus driver called the police, who promptly arrested her.

Parks had long been active in the local NAACP, headed by E. D. Nixon. They had already talked about challenging bus segregation. So had the Women's Political Council (WPC), composed of black professional women and led by Jo Ann Robinson, an English professor at Alabama State, who had once been humiliated by a bus driver when she accidentally sat in the white section. Such local individuals and organizations, long committed to improving conditions for African Americans, laid critical foundations for the black freedom struggle throughout the South.

When word came that Parks would fight her arrest, WPC leaders mobilized teachers and students to distribute fliers calling for blacks to stay off the buses. E. D. Nixon called a mass meeting at the Holt Street Baptist Church, where those assembled founded the Montgomery Improvement Association (MIA) to organize a bus boycott. The MIA arranged volunteer car pools and marshaled more than 90 percent of the black community to sustain the yearlong **Montgomery bus boycott**.

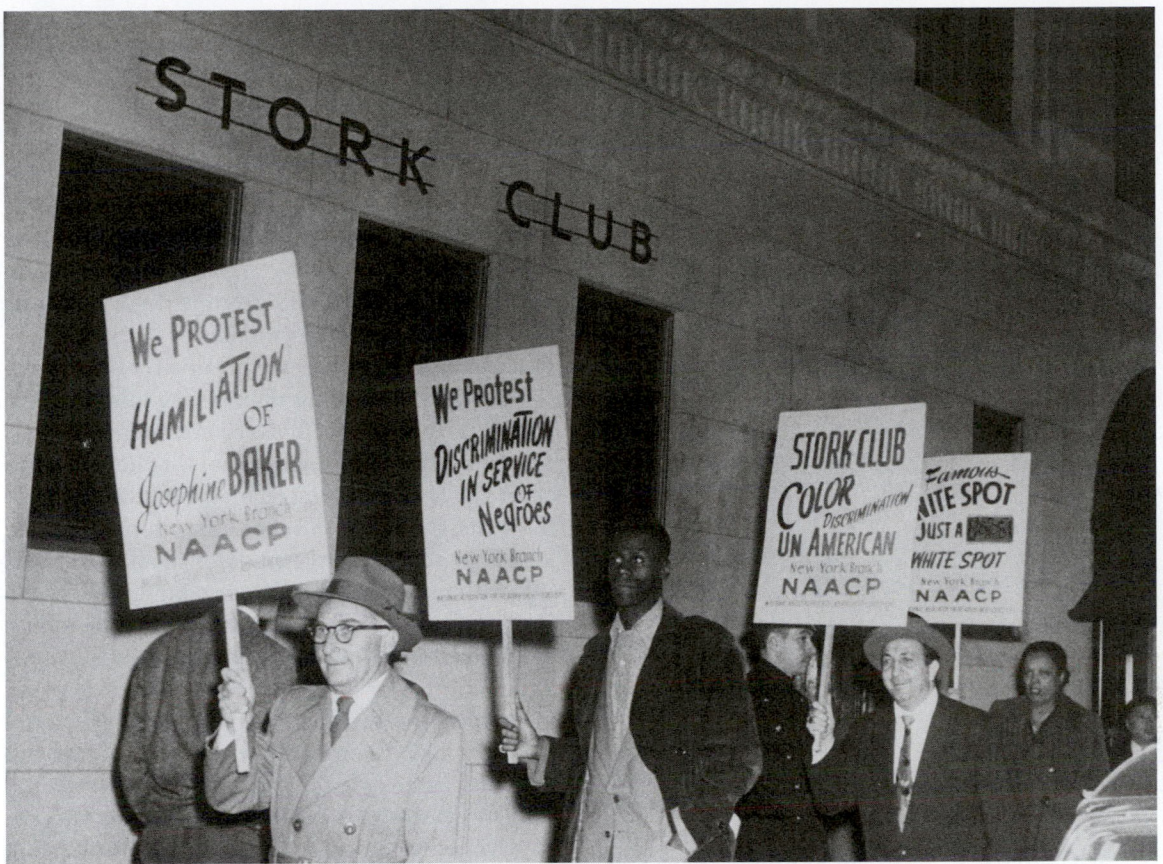

Civil Rights Activism in the North
While civil rights activism in the South gained national attention in the 1950s and 1960s, black protest had a long history in the North. Especially after the birth of the NAACP in 1909, African Americans and their allies mobilized against job discrimination and against segregation in the schools, housing, and public accommodations. In this photo, demonstrators march outside the Stork Club in New York City in 1951, protesting its refusal to serve the world famous dancer, singer, and actress Josephine Baker. Photo by FPG/Hulton Archive/Getty Images.

Elected to head the MIA was twenty-six-year-old **Martin Luther King Jr.**, a young Baptist pastor with a doctorate in theology from Boston University. As a seminary student in 1950, he had been denied service in a New Jersey restaurant and refused to leave until the owner chased him and his friends out with a gun. A captivating speaker, King addressed mass meetings at churches throughout the bus boycott, inspiring blacks' courage and commitment by linking racial justice to Christianity. He promised, "If you will protest courageously and yet with dignity and Christian love . . . historians will have to pause and say, 'There lived a great people — a black people — who injected a new meaning and dignity into the veins of civilization.'"

Montgomery blacks summoned their courage and determination in abundance. An older woman insisted, "I'm not walking for myself, I'm walking for my children and my grandchildren." Boycotters walked miles or carpooled to get to work, contributed their meager financial resources, and stood up with dignity to intimidation and police

harassment. Jo Ann Robinson, a cautious driver, got seventeen tickets in the space of two months. Authorities arrested several leaders, and whites firebombed King's house. Yet the movement persisted until November 1956, when the Supreme Court declared unconstitutional Alabama's laws requiring bus segregation. African Americans had demonstrated that they could sustain a lengthy protest and would not be intimidated.

King's face on the cover of *Time* magazine in February 1957 marked his rapid rise to national and international fame. In January, black clergy from across the South had chosen King to head the **Southern Christian Leadership Conference (SCLC)**, newly established to coordinate local protests against segregation and disfranchisement. The prominence of King and other ministers obscured the substantial

> **"People always say that I didn't give up my seat because I was tired, but that isn't true. I was not tired physically. . . . I was tired of giving in."**
> —Civil rights activist
> **ROSA PARKS**

Martin Luther King, Jr.
The twenty-six-year-old Martin Luther King, Jr. had been in Montgomery, Alabama, for less than two years when he was selected in 1955 to lead the city-wide bus boycott, which had been started by more-seasoned community leaders. Here he is shown greeting members of his Dexter Avenue Baptist Church congregation near the Montgomery State Capitol. King's philosophy of nonviolent resistance to injustice derived in part from his study of the principles of the Indian nationalist leader Mahatma Gandhi, and in 1964, he became the youngest person to be awarded the Nobel Peace Prize. Dan Weiner, Courtesy Sandra Weiner.

► Conclusion: Peace and Prosperity Mask Unmet Challenges

At the American National Exhibition in Moscow in 1959, the consumer goods that Nixon proudly displayed to Khrushchev and the Cold War competition that crackled through their dialogue reflected two dominant themes of the 1950s: the prosperity of the U.S. economy and the superpowers' success in keeping their antagonism within the bounds of peace. The tremendous economic growth of the 1950s, which raised the standard of living for most Americans, resulted in part from the Cold War: One of every ten American jobs depended directly on defense spending.

Affluence changed the very landscape of the United States. Suburban housing developments sprang up, interstate highways began to cut up cities and connect the country, farms declined in number but grew in size, and population and industry moved south and west. Daily habits and even the values of ordinary people shifted as the economy became more service oriented and the appearance of a host of new products intensified the growth of a consumer culture that had begun decades earlier.

The prosperity, however, masked a number of developments and problems that Americans would face head-on in later years: rising resistance to racial injustice, a 20 percent poverty rate, married women's movement into the labor force, and the emergence of a self-conscious youth generation. Although the federal government's defense spending and housing, highway, and education subsidies helped to sustain the economic boom, in general Eisenhower tried to curb domestic programs and let private enterprise have its way. His administration maintained the welfare state inherited from the New Deal but resisted the expansion of federal programs.

In global affairs, Eisenhower exercised restraint on large issues, recognizing the limits of U.S. power. In the name of deterrence, he promoted the development of more destructive atomic weapons, but he withstood pressures for even larger defense budgets. Nonetheless, Eisenhower shared Truman's fundamental assumption that the United States must fight communism everywhere, and when movements in Iran, Guatemala, Cuba, and Vietnam seemed too radical, too friendly to communism, or too inimical to American economic interests, he tried to undermine them, often with secret operations and severe consequences for native populations.

numbers and critical importance of black women in the movement. In fact, the SCLC owed much of its success to Ella Baker, a seasoned activist who came from New York to manage its office in Atlanta. King's prominence and the media's focus on the South also hid the national scope of racial injustice and the struggles for racial equality in the North that both encouraged and benefited from the black freedom struggle in the South.

REVIEW   What were the goals and strategies of civil rights activists in the 1950s?

Although Eisenhower presided over eight years of peace and prosperity, his foreign policy inspired anti-Americanism, established dangerous precedents for the expansion of executive power, and forged commitments and interventions that future generations would deem unwise. As Eisenhower's successors took on the struggle against communism and grappled with the domestic challenges of race, poverty, and urban decay that he had avoided, the tranquility and consensus of the 1950s would give way to the turbulence and conflict of the 1960s.

▶ Selected Bibliography

Eisenhower's Administration

Steven Z. Freiberger, *Dawn over Suez: The Rise of American Power in the Middle East, 1953–1957* (1992).

David Halberstam, *The Fifties* (1993).

George C. Herring, *America's Longest War: The United States and Vietnam, 1950–1975* (2nd rev. ed., 1986).

Stephen Kinzer, *All the Shah's Men: An American Coup and the Roots of Middle East Terror* (2003).

David A. Nichols, *A Matter of Justice: Eisenhower and the Beginning of the Civil Rights Revolution* (2007).

Chester J. Pach Jr. and Elmo Richardson, *The Presidency of Dwight D. Eisenhower* (rev. ed., 1991).

Stephen G. Rabe, *Eisenhower and Latin America: The Foreign Policy of Anticommunism* (1988).

Economic and Social Developments

Lizabeth Cohen, *A Consumers' Republic: The Politics of Mass Consumption in Postwar America* (2003).

Gail Cooper, *Air-Conditioning America: Engineers and the Controlled Environment, 1900–1960* (1998).

Kenneth T. Jackson, *Crabgrass Frontier: The Suburbanization of the United States* (1985).

Tom Lewis, *Divided Highways: Building the Interstate Highways, Transforming American Life* (1999).

David Oshinsky, *Polio: An American Story* (2005).

Adam Rome, *The Bulldozer in the Countryside: Suburban Sprawl and the Rise of American Environmentalism* (2001).

Bruce J. Schulman, *From Cotton Belt to Sunbelt: Federal Policy, Economic Development, and the Transformation of the South, 1938–1980* (1994).

Gender, the Family, and Culture

Glenn C. Altschuler, *All Shook Up: How Rock 'n' Roll Changed America* (2004).

Erik Barnouw, *Tube of Plenty: The Evolution of American Television* (rev. ed., 1982).

Stephanie Coontz, *The Way We Never Were: American Families and the Nostalgia Trip* (1992).

Robert Ellwood, *The Fifties Spiritual Marketplace: American Religion in a Decade of Conflict* (1997).

Elizabeth Fraterrigo, *"Playboy" and the Making of the Good Life in Modern America* (2009).

James Gilbert, *Men in the Middle: Searching for Masculinity in the 1950s* (2005).

James Howard Jones, *Alfred C. Kinsey: A Public/Private Life* (1998).

Elaine Tyler May, *Homeward Bound: American Families in the Cold War Era* (1988).

Joanne Meyerowitz, ed., *Not June Cleaver: Women and Gender in Postwar America, 1945–1960* (1994).

Alan Petigny, *The Permissive Society: America, 1941–1965* (2009).

Lynn Spigel, *Make Room for TV: Television and the Family Ideal in Postwar America* (1992).

Steven Watson, *The Birth of the Beat Generation: Visionaries, Rebels, and Hipsters, 1944–1960* (1995).

Minorities and Civil Rights

Melba Patillo Beals, *Warriors Don't Cry: A Searing Memoir of the Battle to Integrate Little Rock's Central High* (1994).

Taylor Branch, *Parting the Waters: America in the King Years, 1954–1963* (1988).

Mary L. Dudziak, *Cold War Civil Rights: Race and the Image of American Democracy* (2000).

Donald L. Fixico, *Termination and Relocation: Federal Indian Policy, 1945–1960* (1986).

David J. Garrow, ed., *The Montgomery Boycott and the Women Who Started It: The Memoir of Jo Ann Gibson Robinson* (1987).

James T. Patterson, Brown v. Board of Education: *A Civil Rights Milestone and Its Troubled Legacy* (2001).

Barbara Ransby, *Ella Baker and the Black Freedom Movement* (2003).

Thomas J. Sugrue, *Sweet Land of Liberty: The Forgotten Struggle for Civil Rights in the North* (2008).

Juan Williams, *Thurgood Marshall: American Revolutionary* (1998).

▶ **FOR MORE BOOKS ABOUT TOPICS IN THIS CHAPTER,** see the Online Bibliography at **bedfordstmartins.com/roark.**

▶ **FOR ADDITIONAL PRIMARY SOURCES FROM THIS PERIOD,** see Michael Johnson, ed., *Reading the American Past*, Fifth Edition.

▶ **FOR WEB SITES, IMAGES, AND DOCUMENTS RELATED TO TOPICS AND PLACES IN THIS CHAPTER,** visit Make History at **bedfordstmartins.com/roark.**

Reviewing Chapter 27

REVIEW QUESTIONS

Use key terms and dates to support your answer.

1. How did Eisenhower's domestic policies reflect his moderate political vision? (pp. 899–902)

2. Where and how did Eisenhower practice containment? (pp. 902–908)

3. How did technology contribute to changes in the economy, suburbanization, and the growth of the Sun Belt? (pp. 909–915)

4. Why did American consumption expand so dramatically in the 1950s, and what aspects of society and culture did it influence? (pp. 915–920)

5. What were the goals and strategies of civil rights activists in the 1950s? (pp. 920–926)

MAKING CONNECTIONS

Draw on key terms, the timeline, and review questions.

1. Eisenhower was the first Republican president since the New Deal had transformed the role of the federal government. How did his "modern Republicanism" address Roosevelt's legacy? How did the shape and character of government change or not change during Eisenhower's administration?

2. The 1950s brought significant changes to the everyday lives of many Americans. Discuss the economic and demographic changes that contributed to the growth of suburbs and the Sun Belt. In your answer, consider both Americans who participated in these trends and those who did not.

3. What actual developments in American society in the 1950s were at odds with prevailing norms and values?

4. During the 1950s, actions by the federal government and the courts had a significant impact on African Americans, Native Americans, and Mexican Americans. Discuss how new policies and court actions came about and how laws affected these groups for better and for worse.

LINKING TO THE PAST

1. How did the policies of termination and relocation differ from the New Deal's policy toward Indians? (See chapter 24.)

2. What developments stemming from World War II influenced U.S. foreign policy in such areas as Vietnam and Latin America? (See chapter 25.)

▶ For practice quizzes and other study tools, visit the Online Study Guide at bedfordstmartins.com/roark.

TIMELINE 1952–1960

1952
- Republican Dwight D. Eisenhower elected president.

1953
- Termination of special status of Native Americans and relocation of thousands off reservations.
- CIA engineers coup against government of Iran.

1954
- CIA stages coup against government of Guatemala.
- France signs Geneva accords, withdrawing from Vietnam.
- United States begins aid to South Vietnam.
- Government launches Operation Wetback.
- *Hernandez v. Texas.*
- *Brown v. Board of Education.*
- Senate condemns Senator Joseph McCarthy.

1955
- Eisenhower and Khrushchev meet in Geneva.

1955–1956
- Montgomery, Alabama, bus boycott.

1956
- Interstate Highway and Defense System Act.
- Eisenhower reelected by landslide to second term.
- *Howl* published.

1957
- Southern Christian Leadership Conference (SCLC) founded.
- Soviets launch *Sputnik.*
- Labor union membership peaks at 27.1 percent of labor force.
- Civil Rights Act of 1957.
- *On the Road* published.

1958
- National Aeronautics and Space Administration (NASA) established.
- National Defense Education Act.

1959
- Kitchen debate between Nixon and Khrushchev.

1960
- Soviets shoot down U.S. U-2 spy plane.
- One-quarter of Americans live in suburbs.
- Thirty-five percent of women work outside the home.

PROTEST BANNER

Banners flew in streets across the nation during the 1960s as millions of Americans made visible their positions on issues ranging from racial justice to the Vietnam War to women's equality. This pennant represents the earliest protest movement, the black freedom struggle, which invigorated a host of other movements and contributed to reforms that transformed the role of the federal government in securing individual rights. The background image captures the 1963 March on Washington for Jobs and Justice at which Martin Luther King, Jr. gave his famous "I Have a Dream" speech.

Banner: Collection of Mark Hooper; background: © Bettmann/Corbis.

Reform, Rebellion, and Reaction
1960–1974

ON AUGUST 31, 1962, FANNIE LOU HAMER BOARDED A BUS CARRYING eighteen African Americans from Ruleville, Mississippi, to the county seat in Indianola, where they intended to register to vote. Blacks accounted for more than 60 percent of Sunflower County's population but only 1.2 percent of registered voters. Before civil rights activists arrived in Ruleville to start a voter registration drive, Hamer recalled, "I didn't know that a Negro could register and vote." Her forty-five years of poverty, exploitation, and political disfranchisement typified the lives of most blacks in the rural South. The daughter of sharecroppers, Hamer began work in the cotton fields at age six, attending school in a one-room shack from December to March and only until she was twelve. After marrying Perry Hamer, she moved onto a plantation, where she worked in the fields, did domestic work for the owner, and recorded the cotton that sharecroppers harvested.

At the Indianola County courthouse, Hamer and her companions had to pass through a hostile, white, gun-carrying crowd. Using a common practice to deny blacks the vote, the registrar tested Hamer on an obscure section of the state constitution. She failed the test but resolved to try again. When the plantation owner ordered Hamer to withdraw her registration application or get off his land, she left the plantation. Ten days later, bullets flew into the home of friends who had taken her in. Refusing to be intimidated, she registered to vote on her third attempt, attended a civil rights leadership training conference, and began to mobilize others to vote. In 1963, she and other activists were arrested in Winona, Mississippi, and brutally beaten. Hamer went from jail to the hospital, where her sister could not recognize her battered face.

Fannie Lou Hamer's courage and determination made her a prominent figure in the black freedom struggle. Such activists shook the nation's conscience, provided a protest model for other groups, and pushed the government to enact not only civil rights legislation but also a host of other liberal policies. Although the federal government often tried to curb civil rights

protest, the two Democratic presidents of the 1960s favored using government to ameliorate social and economic problems. After John F. Kennedy was assassinated in November 1963, Lyndon B. Johnson launched the Great Society — a multitude of efforts to promote racial justice, education, medical care, urban development, environmental and economic health, and more. Those who struggled for racial justice lost property and sometimes their lives, but by the end of the decade American law had caught up with the American ideal of equality.

Yet strong civil rights legislation and pathbreaking Supreme Court decisions could not alone mitigate the deplorable economic conditions of African Americans nationwide, on which Hamer and others increasingly focused after 1965. Nor were liberal politicians reliable supporters, as Hamer found out in 1964 when President Johnson and his allies rebuffed black Mississippi Democrats' efforts to be represented at the Democratic National Convention. "We followed all the laws," she said, only to find that "the white man is not going to give up his power to us. . . . We have to take [it] for ourselves." By 1966, a minority of African American activists were demanding black power; the movement soon splintered, and white support sharply declined. The war in Vietnam stifled liberal reform, while a growing conservative movement, protesting that the Great Society went too far, condemned the challenge to American traditions and institutions mounted by blacks, students, and others.

Though disillusioned and often frustrated, Fannie Lou Hamer remained an activist until her death in 1977, participating in new social movements stimulated by the black freedom struggle. In 1969, she supported students at Mississippi Valley State College who demanded black studies courses and a voice in campus decisions. In 1972, she attended the first conference of the National Women's Political Caucus, established to achieve greater representation for women in government. The caucus was part of a diverse feminist movement that transformed women's legal status as well as everyday relationships between women and men.

Feminists and other groups, including ethnic minorities, environmentalists, and gays and lesbians, carried the tide of reform into the 1970s. They pushed Richard M. Nixon's Republican administration to sustain the liberalism of the 1960s, with its emphasis on a strong government role in regulating the economy, guaranteeing the welfare and rights of all individuals, and improving the quality of life. Despite its conservative rhetoric, the Nixon administration implemented school desegregation and affirmative action and adopted pathbreaking measures in environmental regulation, equality for women, and justice for Native Americans. The years between 1960 and 1974 witnessed the greatest efforts to reconcile America's promise with reality since the New Deal.

Mississippi Freedom Democratic Party Rally
Fannie Lou Hamer (left foreground) and other activists sing at a rally outside the Democratic National Convention hall in 1964, supporting the Mississippi Freedom Democratic Party (MFDP) in its challenge to the all-white delegation sent by the regular state Democratic Party. Next to Hamer is Eleanor Holmes Norton, a civil rights lawyer, and Ella Baker (far right), who helped organize the Southern Christian Leadership Conference and later managed MFDP headquarters in Washington, D.C. In the rear is SNCC leader, Stokely Carmichael (in the straw hat).
© George Ballis/Take Stock/The Image Works.

▶ Liberalism at High Tide

At the Democratic National Convention in 1960, John F. Kennedy announced "a New Frontier" that would confront "unsolved problems of peace and war, unconquered pockets of ignorance and prejudice, unanswered questions of poverty and surplus." Four years later, Lyndon B. Johnson invoked the ideal of a "Great Society, [which] rests on abundance and liberty for all [and] demands an end to poverty and racial injustice." Acting under the liberal faith that government should use its power to solve social and economic problems, end injustice, and promote the welfare of all citizens, the Democratic administrations of the 1960s won legislation on civil rights, poverty, education, medical care, housing, consumer safeguards, and environmental protection. These measures, along with path-breaking Supreme Court decisions, advanced the unfulfilled agendas of the New Deal and Fair Deal, responded to demands for rights from African Americans and other groups, and addressed problems arising from rapid economic growth.

The Unrealized Promise of Kennedy's New Frontier

John F. Kennedy grew up in privilege, the child of an Irish Catholic businessman who served as ambassador to Great Britain and nourished political ambitions for his sons. Helped by a distinguished World War II navy record, Kennedy won election to the House of Representatives in 1946 and the Senate in 1952. With a powerful political machine, his family's fortune, and a dynamic personal appeal, Kennedy won the Democratic presidential nomination in 1960. He stunned many Democrats by choosing as his running mate Lyndon B. Johnson of Texas, a rival for the presidential nomination whom liberals disparaged as a typical southern conservative.

Kennedy defeated his Republican opponent, Vice President Richard M. Nixon, in an excruciatingly close election (Map 28.1). African American voters contributed to his victory, helping to offset the 52 percent of the white vote cast for Nixon and contributing to Kennedy's 118,550-vote margin overall. Lyndon Johnson helped carry most of the South, and a rise in unemployment in 1960 also favored the Democrats. Finally, Kennedy benefited from the nation's

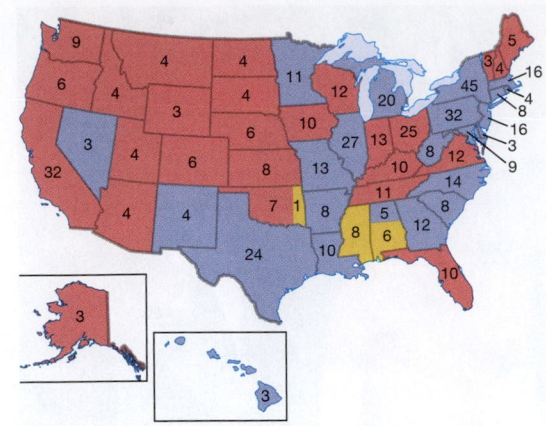

Candidate	Electoral Vote	Popular Vote	Percent of Popular Vote
▉ John F. Kennedy (Democrat)	303	34,227,096	49.9
▉ Richard M. Nixon (Republican)	219	34,108,546	49.6
▉ Harry F. Byrd (Independent)	15	501,643	0.7

MAP 28.1   The Election of 1960

first televised presidential debates, at which he appeared cool and confident beside a nervous and pale Nixon.

The Kennedy administration projected energy, idealism, and glamour, although Kennedy was in most ways a cautious, pragmatic politician. The first president to hold televised press conferences, Kennedy charmed the audience with his grace and wit. Journalists kept from the public Kennedy's serious health problems and extramarital affairs, instead projecting warm images of a vigorous president with his chic and cultured wife, Jacqueline.

At his inauguration, the forty-three-year-old Kennedy called on Americans to serve the common good. "Ask not what your country can do for you," he implored, "ask what you can do for your country." Although Kennedy's idealism inspired many, he failed to redeem campaign promises to expand the welfare state with federal education and health care programs. Moreover, he resisted leadership on behalf of racial justice until civil rights activists gave him no choice and he issued a dramatic call for a comprehensive civil rights bill, marking a turning point in his domestic agenda.

Moved by the desperate conditions he observed while campaigning in Appalachia, Kennedy pushed poverty onto the national agenda. In 1962, he read Michael Harrington's

The Kennedy Appeal
The youth and glamour of the Kennedy administration are apparent in this photo of the president and his wife hosting a White House dinner for French Minister of Culture André Malraux in May 1962. Jacqueline Kennedy had a keen interest in history and the arts, and she designed White House social events to elevate Washington's cultural life by featuring artists, writers, scholars, and musicians. Well aware of the First Lady's appeal to the public, the president once asked their driver to "turn on the lights so they can see Jackie." John F. Kennedy Library.

The Other America, which described the poverty that left more than one in five Americans "maimed in body and spirit, existing at levels beneath those necessary for human decency." By 1962, Kennedy had won support for a $2 billion urban renewal program that offered incentives to businesses to locate in economically depressed areas and a training program for the unemployed. In the summer of 1963, he asked aides to plan a full-scale attack on poverty. Kennedy had promised to make economic growth a key objective. "A rising tide lifts all boats" expressed his belief that economic growth could eradicate poverty. To that end, he asked Congress to pass an enor-

mous tax cut in 1963, arguing that reducing taxes would infuse money into the economy and thus increase demand, boost production, and reduce unemployment. Passed in February 1964, the law contributed to an economic boom, as unemployment dropped to 4.1 percent and the gross national product shot up by 7 to 9 percent annually between 1964 and 1966. Some liberal critics of the tax cut, however, pointed out that it favored the well-off and that economic growth alone would not eliminate poverty. They argued instead for increased spending on social programs.

Kennedy's antipoverty, civil rights, and economic initiatives had not reached fruition when an assassin's bullets struck him down on November 22, 1963. Within minutes of the shooting — which occurred as Kennedy's motorcade passed through Dallas, Texas — radio and television broadcast the unfolding horror to the nation. Millions watched as *Air Force One* returned to Washington bearing the president's coffin, his widow in a bloodstained suit, and the new president, Lyndon Baines Johnson.

Stunned Americans struggled to understand what had happened. Soon after the assassination, police arrested Lee Harvey Oswald and concluded that he had fired the shots from a nearby building. Two days later, while officers were transferring Oswald from one jail to another, a local nightclub operator, Jack Ruby, killed him. Suspicions arose that Ruby murdered Oswald to cover up a conspiracy by ultraconservatives who hated Kennedy, or by Communists who supported Castro's Cuba (as discussed in chapter 29). To get at the truth, President Johnson appointed a commission headed by Chief Justice Earl Warren, which concluded that both Oswald and Ruby had acted alone. Although some contested the lone-killer explanation, most scholars agreed that no conspiracy had existed.

Debate continued over how to assess Kennedy's domestic record. It had been unremarkable in his first two years, but his proposals on taxes, civil rights, and poverty in 1963 suggested an important shift. Whether Kennedy could have persuaded Congress to enact them remained in question. In the words of journalist James Reston, "What was killed was not only the president but the promise. . . . He never reached his meridian: We saw him only as a rising sun."

Johnson Fulfills the Kennedy Promise

Lyndon B. Johnson assumed the presidency with a wealth of political experience. A self-made man from Texas's Hill Country, he had won

election in 1937 to the House of Representatives and in 1948 to the Senate, where, after 1955, he served skillfully as Senate majority leader. Although his Texas base required caution on civil rights and issues affecting oil and other big businesses, Johnson's presidential aspirations led him to take more liberal stands. His own modest upbringing in an impoverished area, his admiration for Franklin Roosevelt, and his fierce ambition to outdo the New Deal president all spurred his commitment to reform in order to build what he called a **Great Society**. Equally compelling were external pressures generated by the black freedom struggle and the host of movements it helped inspire.

Johnson's coarse wit and vanity repulsed those who preferred the sophisticated Kennedy style. Lacking his predecessor's charm and eloquence, Johnson excelled behind the scenes, where he could entice, maneuver, or threaten legislators to support his objectives. His persuasive power, known as the "Johnson treatment," became legendary. In his ability to achieve consensus around his goals, Johnson had few peers in American history.

Johnson entreated Congress to act so that "John Fitzgerald Kennedy did not live or die in vain." He signed Kennedy's tax cut bill in February 1964. More remarkable was passage of the **Civil Rights Act of 1964**, which Kennedy had proposed in response to black protest. The strongest such measure since Reconstruction, the law required every ounce of Johnson's political skill to pry sufficient votes from Republicans to balance the "nays" of southern Democrats. Senate Republican leader Everett Dirksen's aide reported that Johnson "never left him alone for thirty minutes."

Antipoverty legislation followed fast on the heels of the Civil Rights Act. Just two months after Johnson announced "an unconditional war on poverty" in his January 1964 State of the Union message, the administration rushed a draft bill to Congress, which responded with equal haste in August. The Economic Opportunity Act of 1964 authorized ten new programs, allocating $800 million—about 1 percent of the federal budget — for the first year. Many provisions targeted children and youths, including Head Start for preschoolers, work-study grants for college students, and the Job Corps for unemployed young people. The Volunteers in Service to America (VISTA) program paid modest wages to volunteers working with the disadvantaged, and a legal services program provided lawyers for the poor.

The most novel and controversial part of the law, the Community Action Program (CAP), required "maximum feasible participation" of the poor themselves in antipoverty projects. Poor people began to organize community action programs to take control of their neighborhoods and to make welfare agencies, school boards, police departments, and housing authorities more accountable to the people they served. When mayors complained that activists were challenging local governments and "fostering class struggle," Johnson backed off from pushing genuine representation for the poor. Nonetheless, CAP gave people usually excluded from government an opportunity to act on their own behalf and develop leadership skills. To a Mississippi sharecropper, the local CAP literacy program "meant more to me than I can express," providing him basic skills and self-respect.

Policymaking for a Great Society

As the 1964 election approached, Johnson projected stability and security in the midst of a booming economy. Few voters wanted to risk the dramatic change promised by his Republican opponent, Arizona senator Barry M. Goldwater, who attacked the welfare state and suggested using nuclear weapons if necessary to crush communism in Vietnam.

The "Johnson Treatment"

Abe Fortas, a distinguished lawyer who had argued a major criminal rights case, *Gideon v. Wainwright* (1963), before the Supreme Court, was a close friend of and adviser to President Johnson. This photograph of the president and Fortas taken in July 1965 illustrates how Johnson used his body as well as his voice to bend people to his will. Yoichi R. Okamoto/LBJ Library Collection.

Although Goldwater captured five southern states, Johnson achieved a record-breaking landslide of 61 percent of the popular vote, and Democrats won resounding majorities in the House (295–140) and Senate (68–32). Still, Goldwater's campaign aroused considerable grassroots support, and a movement on the right grew alongside the more visible left-wing and liberal movements (as discussed in chapter 30).

"I want to see a whole bunch of coonskins on the wall," Johnson told his aides, using a hunting analogy to stress his ambitious legislative goals for what he called the "Great Society." The large Democratic majorities in Congress, his own political skills, and pressure from the black freedom struggle enabled Johnson to succeed mightily. He persuaded Congress to act on discrimination, poverty, education, medical care, housing, consumer and environmental protection, and more. Reporters called the legislation of the Eighty-ninth Congress (1965–1966) "a political miracle."

The Economic Opportunity Act of 1964 was the opening shot in the **War on Poverty**. Congress doubled the program's funding in 1965, enacted new economic development measures for depressed regions, and authorized more than $1 billion to improve the nation's slums. Direct aid included a new food stamp program, giving poor people greater choice in obtaining food, and rent supplements that provided alternatives to public housing projects for some poor families. Moreover, a movement of welfare mothers, the National Welfare Rights Organization, assisted by antipoverty lawyers, pushed administrators of Aid to Families with Dependent Children (AFDC) to ease restrictions on welfare recipients. The number of families receiving assistance jumped from less than one million in 1960 to three million by 1972, benefiting 90 percent of those eligible.

Central to Johnson's War on Poverty were efforts to equip the poor with the skills necessary to find jobs. A former schoolteacher, Johnson saw federal support for public education as a natural extension of the New Deal; it had been on the Democratic Party agenda for two decades. His Elementary and Secondary Education Act of 1965 marked a turning point by involving the federal government in K–12

education. The measure sent federal dollars to local school districts based on the number of poor children they enrolled, and it provided equipment and supplies to private and parochial schools serving the poor. That same year, Congress passed the Higher Education Act, vastly expanding federal assistance to colleges and universities for buildings, programs, scholarships, and loans.

The federal government's responsibility for health care marked an even more significant watershed. Faced with a powerful medical lobby that opposed national health insurance as "socialized medicine," Johnson pared down Truman's proposal for government-sponsored universal care. Instead, he focused on the elderly, who constituted a large portion of the nation's poor. Congress responded with the **Medicare** program, providing the elderly with universal compulsory medical insurance financed largely through Social Security taxes. A separate program, **Medicaid**, authorized federal grants to supplement state-paid medical care for poor people. By the twenty-first century, these two programs covered 87 million Americans, nearly 30 percent of the population.

Whereas programs such as Medicare fulfilled New Deal and Fair Deal promises, the Great Society's civil rights legislation represented a break with tradition and an expansion of liberalism. Racial minorities were neglected or discriminated against in many New Deal programs, and Truman's civil rights proposals bore few results. By contrast, the Civil Rights Act of 1964 made discrimination in employment, education, and public accommodations illegal. The **Voting Rights Act of 1965** banned literacy tests like the one that had stymied Fannie Lou Hamer and authorized federal intervention to ensure access to the voting booth.

Another form of bias fell with the **Immigration and Nationality Act of 1965**, which abolished the

A Tribute to Johnson for Medicare
George Niedermeyer, who lived in Hollywood, Florida, and received a Social Security pension, painted pieces of wood and glued them together to create this thank-you to President Johnson for establishing Medicare. Niedermeyer entrusted his congressional representative, Claude Pepper, known for his support of the interests of the elderly, to deliver the four-foot-tall tribute to Johnson in 1967.
LBJ Library, photo by Henry Groskinsky.

fifty-year-old quota system based on national origins that discriminated against immigrants from areas outside northern and western Europe (see chapter 23). The law maintained caps on the total number of immigrants and for the first time limited those from the Western Hemisphere; preference was now given to immediate relatives of U.S. citizens and to those with desirable skills. Massachusetts senator Edward Kennedy predicted that "our cities will not be flooded with a million citizens annually," but the measure's unanticipated consequences did nearly that, triggering a surge of immigration near the end of the century (as discussed in chapter 31).

Great Society benefits reached well beyond victims of discrimination and the poor. Medicare, for example, covered the elderly, regardless of income. A groundswell of consumer activism fueled by Ralph Nader's exposé of the auto industry, *Unsafe at Any Speed* (1965), won legislation making cars safer and raising standards for the food, drug, and cosmetics industries.

Johnson himself insisted that the Great Society meet "not just the needs of the body but the desire for beauty and hunger for community." In 1965, he sent Congress the first presidential message on the environment, obtaining measures to control water and air pollution and to preserve the natural beauty of the American landscape. First Lady "Lady Bird" Johnson made beautification of the environment her primary public project. In addition, the National Arts and Humanities Act of 1965 funded artists, musicians, writers, and scholars and brought their work to public audiences.

The flood of reform legislation dwindled after 1966, when Democratic majorities in Congress diminished and a backlash against government programs arose. Some Americans expressed their opposition with buttons reading "I fight poverty — I work." The Vietnam War dealt the largest blow to Johnson's ambitions, diverting his attention, spawning an antiwar movement that crippled his leadership, and devouring tax dollars that might have been used for reform (as discussed in chapter 29).

Against these odds, in 1968 Johnson pried out of Congress one more civil rights law, which banned discrimination in housing and jury service (see page 944). He also signed the National Housing Act of 1968, which authorized an enormous increase in low-income housing — 1.7 million units over three years — and, by leaving construction and ownership in private hands, a new way of providing it.

Assessing the Great Society

Measured by statistics, the reduction in poverty in the 1960s was considerable. The number of poor Americans fell from more than 20 percent of the population in 1959 to around 13 percent in 1968. Those who in Johnson's words "live on the outskirts of hope" gained more control of their circumstances and a sense of their right to a fairer share of America's bounty. To Rosemary Bray, what turned her family of longtime welfare recipients into taxpaying workers "was the promise of the civil rights movement and the war on poverty." A Mexican American who learned to be a sheet metal worker through a jobs program reported, "[My children] will finish high school and maybe go to college. . . . I see my family and I know the chains are broken."

> **"[My children] will finish high school and maybe go to college. . . . I see my family and I know the chains are broken."**
> —A Mexican American who trained in a jobs program

Certain groups fared better than others. Many of the aged and many male-headed families rose out of poverty, while impoverishment among female-headed families actually increased. Whites escaped poverty at a faster rate than racial and ethnic minorities. Great Society programs contributed to a burgeoning black middle class, and the proportion of African Americans who were poor fell by 10 percentage points between 1966 and 1974. Still, one out of three remained poverty-stricken (Figure 28.1).

Conservative critics charged that Great Society programs discouraged initiative and sustained a "cycle of poverty" across generations by giving the poor "handouts." Liberal critics claimed that focusing on training and education wrongly placed the cause of poverty on the poor themselves rather than on an economic system that could not provide enough adequately paying jobs. Most government training programs prepared graduates for low-skilled labor and could not guarantee employment. In contrast to the New Deal, the Great Society avoided structural reform of the economy and spurned public works projects as a means of providing jobs for the disadvantaged.

Who reaped the greatest advantages from Great Society programs? Programs such as Medicare and those addressing consumer safety and environmental reform benefited Americans across the board. Funds for economically depressed areas built highways, benefiting the construction industry. Real estate developers, investors, and moderate-income families benefited most from

*Statistics on blacks for years 1960–1965 not available.
**Statistics on the elderly for years 1960–1966 not available.

FIGURE 28.1 Poverty in the United States, 1960–1974
The short-term effects of economic growth and the Great Society's attack on poverty are seen here. Which groups experienced the sharpest decline in poverty, and what might account for the differences?

The Judicial Revolution

A key element of liberalism's ascendancy emerged in the Supreme Court under Chief Justice Earl Warren (1953–1969). In contrast to the federal courts of the Progressive Era and New Deal, which blocked reform, the **Warren Court** often moved out in front of Congress and public opinion. Expanding the Constitution's promise of equality and individual rights, the Court's decisions supported an activist government to prevent injustice and provided new protections to disadvantaged groups and accused criminals.

Following the pathbreaking *Brown v. Board of Education* school desegregation decision of 1954 (see chapter 27), the Court struck down southern states' educational plans to avoid integration and defended civil rights activists' rights to freedom of assembly and speech. In addition, a unanimous Court in *Loving v. Virginia* (1967) struck down state laws banning interracial marriage. The justices' declaration that marriage was one of the "basic civil rights of man" would later be repeated by gay men and lesbians seeking the right to marry.

Chief Justice Warren considered *Baker v. Carr* (1963) his most important decision. The case grew out of a complaint that Tennessee electoral districts were drawn so inequitably that sparsely populated rural districts had far more representatives than densely populated urban areas. Using the Fourteenth Amendment guarantee of "equal protection of the laws," *Baker* established the principle of "one person, one vote" for both state legislatures and the House of Representatives. As states redrew electoral districts, legislatures became more responsive to metropolitan interests.

The Warren Court also reformed the criminal justice system, overturning a series of convictions on the grounds that the accused had been deprived of "life, liberty, or property, without due process of law," guaranteed in the Fourteenth Amendment. In decisions that dramatically altered law enforcement practices and the treatment of individuals accused of crimes, the Court declared that states, as well as the federal government, were subject to the Bill of Rights. *Gideon v. Wainwright* (1963) ruled that when an accused criminal could not afford to hire a lawyer, the

the National Housing Act of 1968. Urban renewal often relied on slum clearance programs, which displaced the poor and caused blacks to refer to it as "Negro removal." Physicians' fees and hospital costs soared after the enactment of Medicare and Medicaid, resulting in advantages for both health care providers and the elderly and poor.

Some critics argued that ending poverty required a redistribution of income — raising taxes and using those funds to create jobs, overhaul welfare systems, and rebuild slums. Great Society programs did invest more heavily in the public sector, but they were funded from economic growth rather than from new taxes on the rich or middle class. There was no significant redistribution of income, despite large increases in subsidies for food stamps, housing, medical care, and AFDC. Economic prosperity allowed spending for the poor to rise and improved the lives of millions, but that spending never approached the amounts necessary to claim victory in the War on Poverty. Between 1965 and 1968, the Office of Economic Opportunity spent an average of $40 to $65 each year for each poor person in the country.

Reforms of the Great Society, 1964–1968

1964

Twenty-fourth Amendment	Abolishes poll tax as prerequisite for voting.
Tax Reduction Act	Provides $10 billion in tax cuts in 1964 and 1965.
Civil Rights Act	Bans discrimination in public accommodations, public education, and employment and extends protections to American Indians on reservations.
Economic Opportunity Act	Creates programs for the disadvantaged, including Head Start, VISTA, the Job Corps, and CAP.

1965

Elementary and Secondary Education Act	Provides $1.3 billion in aid to elementary and secondary schools.
Medical Care Act	Provides health insurance (Medicare) for all citizens age sixty-five and over and extends federal health benefits to welfare recipients (Medicaid).
Voting Rights Act	Bans literacy tests and other voting restrictions and authorizes the federal government to act directly to enable African Americans to both register and vote.
Executive Order 11246	Bans discrimination on the basis of race, religion, and national origin by employers awarded government contracts and requires them to "take affirmative action to ensure equal opportunity."
Department of Housing and Urban Development	Created to provide programs to improve housing and neighborhoods in urban areas.
National Arts and Humanities Act	Creates National Endowment for the Arts (NEA) and Humanities (NEH) to support the work of artists, musicians, writers, and scholars.
Water Quality Act	Requires states to set and enforce water quality standards.
Immigration and Nationality Act	Abolishes fifty-year-old discriminatory quotas based on national origins and sets equal limits for all countries.
Air Quality Act	Imposes air pollution standards for motor vehicles.
Higher Education Act	Expands federal assistance to colleges and universities.

1966

National Traffic and Motor Vehicle Safety Act	Establishes federal safety standards.
Department of Transportation	Created to administer transportation programs and policies.
Model Cities Act	Authorizes more than $1 billion to ameliorate the nation's slums.

1967

Executive Order 11375	Extends an earlier executive order banning discrimination and requiring affirmative action by federal contractors to cover women.

1968

Civil Rights Act of 1968	Bans discrimination in housing and jury service.
National Housing Act	Subsidizes the private construction of 1.7 million units of low-income housing.

state had to provide one. In 1966, *Miranda v. Arizona* required police officers to inform suspects of their rights upon arrest. The Court also overturned convictions based on evidence obtained by unlawful arrest, by electronic surveillance, or without a search warrant. Critics accused the justices of "handcuffing the police" and letting criminals go free; liberals argued that these rulings promoted equal treatment in the criminal justice system.

The Court's decisions on religion provoked even greater outrage. *Abington School District v. Schempp* (1963) ruled that requiring Bible reading and prayer in the schools violated the First Amendment principle of separation of church and state. Later judgments banned official prayer in public schools even if students were not required to participate. These decisions left students free to pray on their own, but an infuriated Alabama legislator complained, "They put Negroes in the schools and now they've driven God out." The Court's supporters, however, declared that the religion cases protected the rights of non-Christians and atheists.

Critics of the Court, part of a larger backlash mounting against Great Society liberalism, worked to pass laws or constitutional amendments that would upset despised decisions, and billboards demanded, "Impeach Earl Warren." Nonetheless, the Court's major decisions withstood the test of time.

> **REVIEW** How did the Kennedy and Johnson administrations exemplify a liberal vision of the federal government?

▶ The Second Reconstruction

As much as Supreme Court decisions, the black freedom struggle distinguished the liberalism of the 1960s from that of the New Deal. Before the Great Society reforms — and, in fact, contributing to them — African Americans had mobilized a movement that struck down legal separation and discrimination in the South. Whereas the first Reconstruction reflected the power of northern Republicans in the aftermath of the Civil War, the second Reconstruction depended heavily on the courage and determination of black people themselves. Sheyann Webb, one of the thousands of marchers in the 1965 Selma, Alabama, campaign for voting rights, recalled, "We were just people, ordinary people, and we did it."

"We were just people, ordinary people, and we did it."
—Selma voting-rights activist SHEYANN WEBB

Civil rights activism that focused on the South and on voting and other legal rights won widespread acceptance. But when African Americans stepped up protest against racial injustice in the rest of the country and challenged the economic deprivation that equal rights left untouched, a strong backlash developed, and Martin Luther King's vision faced challenges from other black activists.

The Flowering of the Black Freedom Struggle

The Montgomery bus boycott of 1955–1956 gave racial issues national visibility and produced a leader in **Martin Luther King Jr.** In the 1960s, protest expanded dramatically, mobilizing blacks into direct confrontation with the people and institutions that segregated and discriminated against them: retail establishments, public parks and libraries, buses and depots, voting registrars, and police forces.

Massive direct action in the South began in February 1960, when four African American college students in Greensboro, North Carolina, requested service at the whites-only Woolworth's lunch counter. Within days, hundreds of young people joined them, and others launched sit-ins in thirty-one southern cities.

From Southern Christian Leadership Conference headquarters, Ella Baker telephoned her young contacts at black colleges: "What are you going to do? It's time to move." Baker organized a meeting of student activists in April 1960 and supported their decision to form a new organization, the **Student Nonviolent Coordinating Committee (SNCC)**, pronounced "snick." Embracing civil disobedience and the nonviolence principles of Martin Luther King Jr., activists would confront their oppressors and stand up for their rights, but they would not respond if attacked. In the words of SNCC leader James Lawson, "Nonviolence nurtures the atmosphere in which reconciliation and justice become actual possibilities." SNCC, however, rejected the top-down leadership of King and the established civil rights organizations, adopting a decentralized structure that fostered decision making and the development of leadership at the grassroots level.

The activists' optimism and commitment to nonviolence soon underwent severe tests. Although some cities quietly met student demands, more typically activists encountered violence. Hostile whites poured food over demonstrators, burned them with cigarettes, called them "niggers," and pelted them with rocks. Local police attacked protesters with dogs, clubs, fire hoses, and tear gas; they arrested more than 3,600 demonstrators in the year following the Greensboro sit-in.

Another wave of protest occurred in May 1961, when the Congress of Racial Equality

VISUAL ACTIVITY

Lunch Counter Sit-in

John Salter Jr., a professor at Tougaloo College, and students Joan Trumpauer and Anne Moody take part in a 1963 sit-in at the Woolworth's lunch counter in Jackson, Mississippi. Shortly before this photograph was taken, whites had thrown two students to the floor, and police had arrested one student. Salter was spattered with mustard and ketchup. In 1968, Moody published *Coming of Age in Mississippi*, a popular book about her experiences in the black freedom struggle. State Historical Society of Wisconsin.

READING THE IMAGE: What does the photograph tell you about black civil rights activity of the early 1960s?

CONNECTIONS: How would you describe the changes in race relations between African Americans and whites in the United States in the first half of the 1960s?

(CORE) organized Freedom Rides to integrate interstate transportation in the South. When a group of six whites and seven blacks reached Alabama, whites bombed their bus and beat them with baseball bats so fiercely that an observer "couldn't see their faces through the blood." CORE rebuffed President Kennedy's pleas to call off the rides. But after a huge mob attacked the riders in Montgomery, Alabama, Attorney General Robert Kennedy dispatched federal marshals to restore order. Although violence against the riders abated, Freedom Riders arriving in Jackson, Mississippi, were promptly arrested, and several hundred spent weeks in jail. All told, more than four hundred blacks and whites participated

Civil Rights Freedom Rides, May 1961

in the Freedom Rides, which typified the black freedom struggle: administration efforts to stop the protests, officials' reluctance to intervene to protect demonstrators, and the steely courage of civil rights activists in the face of violence.

Encouraged by Kennedy administration officials who preferred voter registration to civil disobedience, SNCC and other groups began the Voter Education Project in the summer of 1961. They, too, met violence. Whites bombed black churches, threw tenant farmers out of their homes, and beat and jailed activists such as **Fannie Lou Hamer** (see pages 931–932). In June 1963, a white man gunned down Mississippi NAACP leader Medgar Evers in front of his house in Jackson. Similar violence met King's 1963

941

campaign in Birmingham, Alabama, to integrate public facilities and open jobs to blacks. The police attacked demonstrators with dogs, cattle prods, and fire hoses — brutalities that television broadcast around the world.

The largest demonstration drew 250,000 blacks and whites to the nation's capital in August 1963 in the **March on Washington for Jobs and Freedom**, inspired by the strategy of A. Philip Randolph in 1941 (see chapter 25). Its chief architect was Bayard Rustin, a radical Christian and pacifist, who had helped Martin Luther King develop the principles and practice of nonviolence. Speaking from the Lincoln Memorial, King put his indelible stamp on the day, drawing on all the passion and skills that made him the greatest orator of his day. "I have a dream," he repeated again and again, imagining the day "when all of God's children . . . will be able to join hands and sing . . . 'Free at last, free at last; thank God Almighty, we are free at last.'"

The euphoria of the March on Washington faded as activists returned to face continued violence in the South. In 1964, the **Mississippi Freedom Summer Project** mobilized more than a thousand northern black and white college students to conduct voter registration drives. Resistance was fierce, intensified by the sight of white activist women working alongside black men. By the end of the summer, only twelve hundred new voters had been allowed to register. Southern whites had killed several activists, beaten eighty, arrested more than a thousand, and burned thirty-five black churches. Hidden resistance came from the federal government itself, as the FBI spied on King and other leaders and expanded its activities to "expose, disrupt, misdirect, discredit, or otherwise neutralize" black protest.

Still, the movement persisted. In March 1965, Alabama state troopers used such violent force to turn back a voting rights march from Selma to the state capitol in Montgomery that the incident earned the name "Bloody Sunday" and compelled President Johnson to call up the Alabama National Guard to protect the marchers. Battered and hospitalized on Bloody Sunday, John Lewis, chairman of SNCC (and later a congressman from Georgia), managed to make the final stretch of the **Selma march** to the capitol. Calling the Voting Rights Act, which passed that October, "every bit as momentous as the Emancipation Proclamation," he said, "we all felt we'd had a part in it."

The Response in Washington

Civil rights leaders would have to wear sneakers, Lyndon Johnson said, if they were going to keep up with him. But both Kennedy and Johnson, reluctant to alienate southern voters and their congressional representatives, tended to move only when events gave them little choice. Kennedy sent federal marshals to protect the Freedom Riders, dispatched troops to enable air force veteran James H. Meredith to enroll in the all-white University of Mississippi in 1962, and called up the Alabama National Guard during the Birmingham demonstrations. But, aware of the political costs of deploying federal force, he told activists pleading for more protection that law enforcement was a local matter.

The Children's Crusade
A month into the civil rights campaign in Birmingham, Alabama, in May 1963, children and teenagers poured out of the Sixteenth Street Baptist Church to demonstrate in the downtown business section. As shown here, police stopped the children and led them into jail. After the jails filled with more than one thousand young people, police turned on the next stream of demonstrators with high-pressure water hoses and dogs, bringing national attention and sympathy to the protesters, who ultimately forced Birmingham leaders to accede to many of their demands. AP Photo/Bill Hudson.

The Selma March for Voting Rights
In 1963, the Student Nonviolent Coordinating Committee began a campaign for voting rights in Selma, Alabama, where white officials had registered only 335 of the 15,000 eligible African Americans. In March 1965, demonstrators began a fifty-four-mile march from Selma to Montgomery, the state capital, to insist that blacks be registered. In this photograph, young African Americans march with nuns, priests, and other supporters. During the march, Juanita Williams wore out her shoes (shown here), which are now displayed at the National Museum of History in Washington, D.C. What do you think motivated the marchers to carry the American flag? Photo: Steve Shapiro/TimePix/Getty; Shoes: Smithsonian Institution, Washington, D.C.

In June 1963, Kennedy finally made good on his promise to seek strong antidiscrimination legislation. Pointing to the injustice suffered by blacks, Kennedy asked white Americans, "Who among us would then be content with the counsels of patience and delay?" Johnson took up Kennedy's commitment with passion, as scenes of violence against peaceful demonstrators appalled television viewers across the nation. The resulting public support, the "Johnson treatment," and the president's appeal to memories of the martyred Kennedy all produced the most important civil rights law since Reconstruction.

The Civil Rights Act of 1964 guaranteed access for all Americans to public accommodations, public education, employment, and voting. It sounded the death knell for the South's system of segregation, outlawed job discrimination that was rampant throughout the nation, and extended constitutional protections to Indians on reservations. Title VII of the measure, banning discrimination in employment, not only attacked racial discrimination but also outlawed discrimination against women. Because Title VII applied to every aspect of employment, including wages, hiring, and promotion, it represented a giant step toward equal employment opportunity for white women as well as for racial minorities.

Responding to black voter registration drives in the South, Johnson demanded legislation to remove "every remaining obstacle to the right and the opportunity to vote." In August 1965, he signed the Voting Rights Act, empowering the federal government to intervene directly to enable African Americans to register and vote, thereby launching a major transformation in southern politics. Black voting rates shot up dramatically (Map 28.2). In turn, the number of African Americans holding political office in the South increased from a handful in 1964 to more than a thousand by 1972. Such gains translated into tangible benefits as black officials upgraded public facilities, police protection, and other basic services for their constituents. When Unita Blackwell became the first black female mayor in Mississippi, a resident of her town recalled, "She brought in the water tower. . . . Sewage, too. There wasn't nothing but those little outdoor houses."

Johnson also declared the need to realize "not just equality as a right and theory, but equality as fact and result." To this end, he issued an executive order in 1965 to require employers holding government contracts (affecting about one-third of the labor force) to take affirmative action to ensure equal opportunity. Extended to cover women

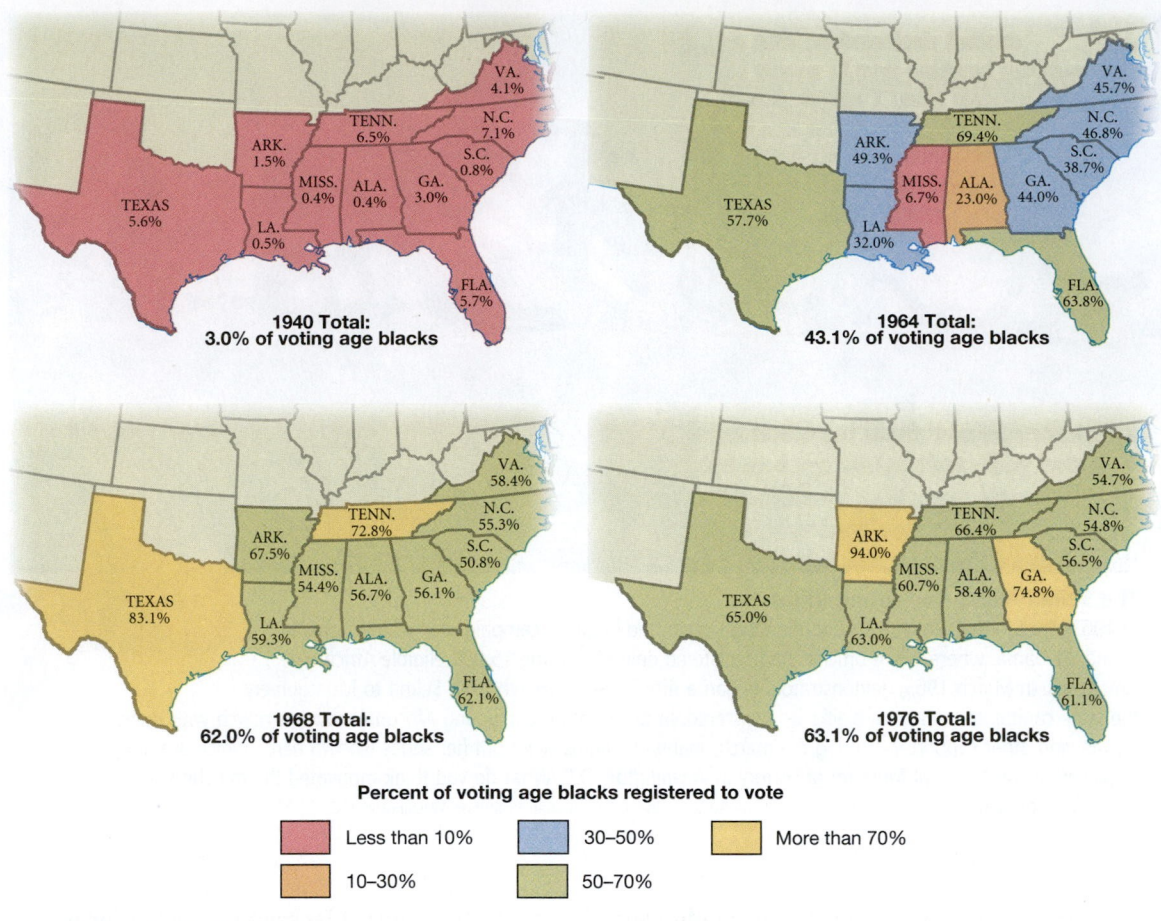

Percent of voting age blacks registered to vote

Less than 10%   30–50%   More than 70%

10–30%   50–70%

MAP ACTIVITY

Map 28.2   The Rise of the African American Vote, 1940–1976
Voting rates of southern blacks increased gradually in the 1940s and 1950s but shot up dramatically in the deep South after the Voting Rights Act of 1965 provided for federal agents to enforce African Americans' right to vote.

READING THE MAP: When did the biggest change in African American voter registration occur in the South? In 1968, which states had the highest and which had the lowest voter registration rates?
CONNECTIONS: What role did African American voters play in the 1960 election? What were the targets of three major voting drives in the 1960s?

in 1967, the affirmative action program was called "reverse discrimination" by people who incorrectly thought that it required quotas and the hiring of unqualified candidates. In fact, it required employers to counter the effects of centuries of oppression by acting forcefully to align their labor force with the available pool of qualified candidates. Most corporations came to see affirmative action as a good employment practice.

In 1968, Johnson maneuvered one final bill through Congress. While those in other regions often applauded the gains made by the black freedom struggle in the South, they were just as likely to resist claims for racial justice in their own locations. In 1963, for example, California

voters rejected a law passed by the legislature banning discrimination in housing; a majority of voters were more concerned with their right to do as they pleased with their property than with the rights of minorities to be free of discrimination. And when Martin Luther King Jr. launched a campaign against de facto segregation in Chicago in 1966, thousands of whites jeered and threw stones at demonstrators. Johnson's efforts to get a federal open-housing law succeeded only in the wake of King's assassination in 1968. The **Civil Rights Act of 1968** banned racial discrimination in housing and jury selection and authorized federal intervention when states failed to protect civil rights workers from violence.

Black Power and Urban Rebellions

By 1966, black protest was visible throughout the nation, demanding not just legal equality but also economic justice and no longer holding non-violence as a basic principle. These developments were not entirely new. African Americans had waged campaigns for decent jobs, housing, and education outside the South since the 1930s. Moreover, some African Americans had always armed themselves in self-defense, and even in the early 1960s many activists doubted that their passive suffering would change the hearts of racists. Still, the black freedom struggle began to appear more threatening to the white majority.

The new emphases resulted from a combination of heightened activism and unrealized promise.

Legal equality could not quickly improve the material conditions of blacks, and black rage at oppressive conditions erupted in waves of urban uprisings from 1965 to 1968 (Map 28.3). In a situation where virtually all-white police forces patrolled black neighborhoods, incidents between police and local blacks typically sparked rioting and resulted in looting, destruction of property, injuries, and deaths. The worst looting and property damage occurred in the Watts district of Los Angeles in August 1965, Newark and Detroit in July 1967, and the nation's capital in April 1968, but violence visited hundreds of cities. The Detroit riots ended in 43 deaths (30 at the hands of law enforcement officers, with most of the victims black), 7,000 arrests, and 1,300 destroyed buildings.

Rioting and looting seemed to many young blacks the only means available to protest the

MAP ACTIVITY

Map 28.3   Urban Uprisings, 1965–1968

When a white police officer in the Watts district of Los Angeles struck a twenty-one-year-old African American, whom he had just pulled over for driving drunk, one onlooker shouted, "We've got no rights at all — it's just like Selma." The altercation escalated into a five-day uprising, during which young blacks set fires, looted, and attacked police and firefighters. When National Guardsmen and police finally quelled the riot, 34 people were dead, 900 blacks had been injured and 4,000 arrested, hundreds of families had lost their homes, and scores of businesses had been wiped out. Similar violence, though usually not on such a large scale, erupted in dozens of cities across the nation during the next three summers, as this map indicates.

READING THE MAP: In what regions and cities of the United States were the 1960s uprisings concentrated? What years saw the greatest unrest?

CONNECTIONS: What were some of the causes of racial unrest in America's cities during this period? Whom did whites generally hold responsible for the violence and why?

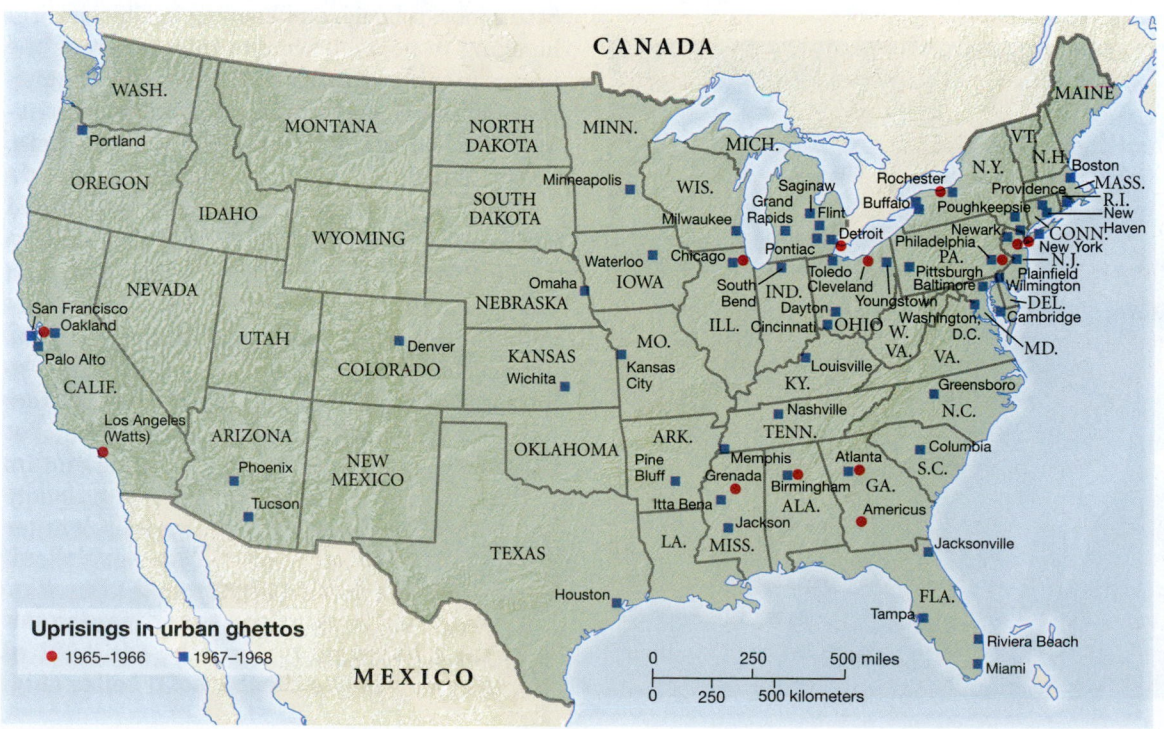

Uprisings in urban ghettos
● 1965–1966   ■ 1967–1968

poverty, lack of opportunity, and official insensitivity they experienced daily. "Since the riot, we're not niggers anymore. We're black men," reported a New Jersey activist. In Los Angeles, an observer said to a reporter, "I don't understand all this talk about 'looting.' They rob us every day. They rob us on the rent, on the food, on the job. They rob our kids on education." Most whites, however, saw the riots as criminal activity, plain and simple, blaming them on radicals who were challenging the principles of King.

Malcolm X was one of those who resisted an emphasis on integration and passive resistance. In 1952, he joined the Nation of Islam, whose adherents called themselves Black Muslims and drew on the long tradition of black nationalism. Calling for black pride and autonomy, separation from the "corrupt [white] society," and self-defense against white violence, Malcolm X attracted a large following, especially in urban ghettos.

At a June 1966 rally in Greenwood, Mississippi, SNCC chairman **Stokely Carmichael** gave the ideas espoused by Malcolm X a new name when he shouted, "We want black power." Those words quickly became the rallying cry in SNCC and CORE, and the **black power movement** riveted national attention in the late 1960s. Carmichael called integration "a subterfuge for the maintenance of white supremacy" and rejected assimilation because it implied white superiority. African Americans were encouraged to develop independent businesses and control their own schools, communities, and political organizations. The phrase "Black is beautiful" emphasized pride in African American culture and connections to dark-skinned people around the world, who were claiming their independence from colonial domination. According to black power advocates, nonviolence brought only more beatings and killings. After police killed an unarmed black teenager in San Francisco in 1966, Huey Newton and Bobby Seale organized the Black Panther Party for Self-Defense to combat police brutality.

The press paid inordinate attention to black radicals, and the civil rights movement encountered a severe white backlash. Although the urban riots of the mid-1960s erupted spontaneously, triggered by specific incidents of alleged police mistreatment, horrified whites blamed black power militants. By 1966, 85 percent of the white population — up from 34 percent two years earlier — thought that African Americans were pressing for too much too quickly.

Agreeing with black power advocates about the need for "a radical reconstruction of society," Martin Luther King Jr. expanded the scope of the struggle. In 1965, he mounted a drive for better jobs, schools, and housing in Chicago. Yet he clung to nonviolence and integration as the means to this end. In April 1968, the thirty-nine-year-old leader went to Memphis to support striking municipal sanitation workers. There, on April 4, he was murdered by an escaped white convict.

Although black power organizations captured the headlines, they failed to gain the massive support from African Americans that King and other leaders had attracted. Nor could they alleviate the poverty and racism entrenched in the urban North and West. Black radicals were harassed by the FBI and jailed; some encounters left both black militants and police dead. Yet black power's emphasis on racial pride and its critique of American institutions resonated loudly and helped shape the protest activities of other groups.

Malcolm X in Egypt
Malcolm X stands in front of the pyramids in Egypt during a trip to Africa and the Middle East in 1964. Partly as a result of meeting Muslims of all colors, as well as other whites who were committed to ending racism, he no longer equated whites with the devil. "The white man is not inherently evil," he concluded, "but America's racist society influences him to act evilly."
John Launois/Black Star/Stockphoto.com.

REVIEW How and why did the civil rights movement change in the mid-1960s?

Afro Rake

In a movement that paralleled the white counterculture in the 1960s and 1970s, young African Americans began to reject middle-class blacks' tendency to fashion their appearance after that of whites. They adopted African modes of dress and let their hair grow into a natural Afro style. In her poem "Homage to My Hair," Lucille Clifton celebrated the expression of authentic black identity: "when I feel her jump up and dance / i hear the music! my God / i'm talking about my nappy hair!" African Americans used combs like this Afro rake, or pick, which makes further political statements with its clenched fist and peace symbol. Private Collection.

▶ A Multitude of Movements

The civil rights movement's undeniable moral claims helped make protest more respectable, while its successes encouraged other groups with grievances. Native Americans, Latinos, college students, women, gay men and lesbians, and others drew on the black freedom struggle for inspiration and models of activism. Many of these groups engaged in direct-action protests, expressed their own cultural nationalism, and challenged dominant institutions and values. Like participants in the black freedom struggle, they met strong resistance, and their accomplishments fell far below their aims. Still, their grievances gained attention in the political arena, and they expanded justice and opportunity for many of their constituents.

Native American Protest

The cry "red power" reflected the influence of black radicalism on young Native Americans, whose activism took on fresh militancy and goals in the 1960s. The termination and relocation programs of the 1940s and 1950s, contrary to their intent, stirred a sense of Indian identity across tribal lines and a determination to preserve traditional culture. Native Americans demonstrated and occupied land and public buildings, claiming rights to natural resources and territory they had owned collectively before European settlement.

In 1969, Native American militants captured world attention when several dozen seized Alcatraz Island, an abandoned federal prison in San Francisco Bay, claiming their right of "first discovery" of this land. They held the island for nineteen months, using the occupation to publicize injustices against Indians, promote pan-Indian cooperation, and celebrate traditional cultures. One of the organizers, Dr. LaNada Boyer, the first Native American to attend the University of California, Berkeley, said of Alcatraz, "We were able to reestablish our identity as Indian people, as a culture, as political entities."

In Minneapolis in 1968, two Chippewa Indians, Dennis Banks and George Mitchell, founded the **American Indian Movement (AIM)** to attack problems in cities, where about 300,000 Indians lived. AIM sought to protect Indians from police harassment, secure antipoverty funds, and establish "survival schools" to teach Indian history and values. The movement's appeal quickly

> **"We were able to reestablish our identity as Indian people, as a culture, as political entities."**
> —Dr. LANADA BOYER, on the Alcatraz occupation

Native Americans Occupy Alcatraz Island
Alcatraz Island, in San Francisco Bay, housed the first U.S. military post on the West Coast and from 1936 to 1963 a federal penitentiary. In November 1969, claiming original possession of the island, Indian students and others from the Bay Area began what would become a nineteen-month-long occupation. Some one hundred Native Americans occupied the island, calling themselves "Indians of All Tribes" to reflect their diversity. They demanded the deed to the island and the creation there of an Indian university, museum, and cultural center. Although failing to achieve their goals, they brought attention to the Native American cause and spurred further activism. Photo by Ralph Crane/Time Life Pictures/Getty Images.

AIM leaders helped organize the "Trail of Broken Treaties" caravan to the nation's capital in 1972, when activists occupied the Bureau of Indian Affairs to express their outrage at the bureau's policies and bureaucratic interference in Indians' lives. In 1973, a much longer siege occurred on the Lakota Sioux reservation in South Dakota. Conflicts there between AIM militants and older tribal leaders led AIM to take over for seventy-two days the village of Wounded Knee, where U.S. troops had massacred more than one hundred Sioux Indians in 1890 (see chapter 17).

Although these dramatic occupations failed to achieve their specific goals, Indians won the end of relocation and termination policies, greater tribal sovereignty and control over community services, protection of Indian religious practices, and a measure of respect and pride. A number of laws and court decisions restored rights to ancestral lands and compensated tribes for land seized in violation of treaties.

Latino Struggles for Justice

The fastest-growing minority group in the 1960s was Latino, or Hispanic American, an extraordinarily varied population encompassing people of Mexican, Puerto Rican, Caribbean, and other Latin American origins. (The term *Latino* stresses their common bonds as a minority group in the United States. The older, less political term *Hispanic* also includes people with origins in Spain.) People of Puerto Rican and Caribbean descent flocked to East Coast cities, but more than half of the nation's Latino population — including some six million Mexican Americans — lived in the Southwest. In addition, thousands illegally crossed the border between Mexico and the United States yearly in search of economic opportunity. Political organization of Mexican Americans dated back to the League of United Latin-American Citizens (LULAC), founded in 1929, which fought segregation and discrimination through litigation (see chapter 26). In the 1960s, however, young Mexican Americans increasingly rejected traditional politics in favor of direct action. One symbol of this generational challenge was young activists' adoption of the term *Chicano* (from *mejicano*, the Spanish word for "Mexican").

Chicano protest drew national attention to California, where **Cesar Chavez** and **Dolores Huerta** organized a movement to improve the wretched conditions of migrant agricultural workers. As a child moving from farm to farm with his family, living in soggy tents and exploited by

spread and filled many Indians with a new sense of purpose. AIM members did not have "that hangdog reservation look I was used to," Lakota activist and author Mary Crow Dog wrote, and their visit to her South Dakota reservation "loosened a sort of earthquake inside me."

labor contractors, Chavez changed schools frequently and encountered indifference and discrimination. One teacher, he recalled, "hung a sign on me that said, 'I am a clown, I speak Spanish.'" After serving in World War II, Chavez began to organize voter registration drives among Mexican Americans.

In contrast to Chavez, Dolores Huerta grew up in an integrated urban neighborhood where she avoided the farmworkers' grinding poverty but witnessed subtle forms of discrimination. Once, a high school teacher challenged her authorship of an essay because it was so well written. Believing that a labor union was the key to prog-

Cesar Chavez and Dolores Huerta
Under posters showing Senator Robert Kennedy and Mahatma Gandhi, Chavez and Huerta confer in 1968 during the United Farm Workers' five-year struggle with grape growers for better wages and working conditions and union recognition. Chavez, like Martin Luther King, had studied the ideas of Gandhi, who used civil disobedience and nonviolence to gain independence for India. People across the country supported the UFW's grape boycott, including Robert Kennedy. Huerta left her teaching job to organize workers, saying, "I thought I could do more by organizing farm workers than by trying to teach their hungry children." Arthur Schatz/TimePix/Getty Images.

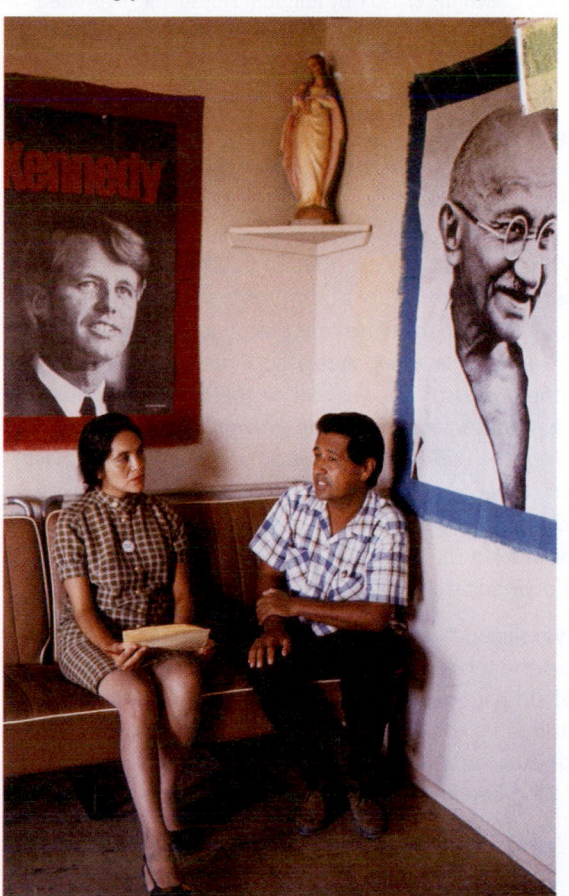

ress, she and Chavez founded the United Farm Workers (UFW) in 1962. Although Chavez headed the union until his death in 1993, Huerta was indispensable to its vitality.

To gain leverage for striking workers, the UFW mounted a nationwide boycott of California grapes, which drew support from millions of Americans and helped win a wage increase for the workers in 1970. Although the UFW struggled and lost membership during the 1970s, it helped politicize Mexican Americans and improve farmworkers' lives.

Other Chicanos mobilized to force the Equal Employment Opportunity Commission (EEOC), the enforcement agency of Title VII of the Civil Rights Act of 1964, to act against job discrimination against Mexican Americans. LULAC, the American GI Forum (see chapter 26), and other groups picketed government offices. President Johnson responded in 1967 by appointing Vicente T. Ximenes as the first Mexican American EEOC commissioner and by creating a special committee on Mexican American affairs.

Claiming "brown power," Chicanos organized to end discrimination in education, gain political power, and combat police brutality. In Denver, Rodolfo "Corky" Gonzales set up "freedom schools" where Chicano children studied the Spanish language and Mexican American history. The nationalist strains of Chicano protest were evident in La Raza Unida (the United Race), a political party founded in 1970 in Texas and based on cultural pride and brotherhood. Along with blacks and Native Americans, Chicanos continued to be disproportionately represented among the poor, but they gradually won more political offices, more effective enforcement of antidiscrimination legislation, and greater respect for their culture.

Student Rebellion, the New Left, and the Counterculture

Although materially and legally more secure than their African American, Indian, and Latino counterparts, white youths also expressed dissent, supporting the black freedom struggle and launching student protests, the antiwar movement, and the new feminist movement. Challenging establishment institutions and traditional values, young activists helped change higher education, the family, the national government, and other key institutions. They were part of a larger international phenomenon, as student movements arose in Mexico, Germany, Turkey, Czechoslovakia, Japan, and other nations around the globe. (See chapter 29, "Beyond America's Borders," page 984.)

Student Protest

The waves of student protest that rolled across college campuses in the 1960s were all the more surprising because observers had found the "silent generation" of the 1950s so complacent and conformist. Although the majority of college students did not participate in the rebellions, a sizable number of students at all kinds of colleges and universities challenged traditional authority, criticized established institutions, and demanded a voice in the decisions that affected their lives.

DOCUMENT 1
Edward Schwartz on Student Power, October 1967

Student activist Edward Schwartz wrote this statement to represent the views of the National Student Association, the largest college student organization in the 1960s. Ironically, this association, which contributed to the student upheaval of the sixties, had been founded a decade earlier, with secret funding from the CIA, as a liberal group to counter communism.

The educational premise behind demands for student power reflects the notion that people learn through living, through the process of integrating their thoughts with their actions, through testing their values against those of a community, through a capacity to act. College presidents who invoke legal authority to prove educational theory assume that growth is the ability to accept what the past has created. Student power is a medium through which people integrate their own experience with a slice of the past which seems appropriate, with their efforts to intensify the relationships between the community within the university.

Let this principle apply — he who must obey the rule should make it.

Students should make the rules governing dormitory hours, boy-girl visitation, student unions, student fees, clubs, newspapers, and the like. Faculty and administrators should advise — attempt to persuade, even. Yet the student should bear the burden of choice.

Students and faculty should co-decide curricular policy.

Students, faculty, and administration should co-decide admissions policy, overall college policy affecting the community, even areas like university investment. . . . Student power should not be argued on legal grounds. It is not a legal principle. It is an educational principle.

Student power is threatening to those who wield power now, but this is understandable. A student should threaten his administrators outside of class, just as bright students threaten professors inside of class.

Student power ultimately challenges everyone in the university — the students who must decide; the faculty and administrators who must rethink their own view of community relations in order to persuade.

People who say that student power means anarchy imply really that students are rabble who have no ability to form community and to adhere to decisions made by community. Student power is not the negation of rules — it is the creation of a new process for the enactment of rules. Student power is not the elimination of authority, it is the development of a democratic standard of authority.

SOURCE: Excerpt from "He Who Must Obey the Rule Should Make It," from *The University Crisis Reader*, vol. 1, *The Liberal University under Attack* by Immanuel Wallerstein and Paul Starr, eds., pp. 482–84. Copyright © 1971 by Random House, Inc. Reprinted with permission.

DOCUMENT 2
SDS Explanation of the Columbia Strike, September 1968

One of the longest and most violent student protests occurred in New York City at Columbia University in April and May 1968, when white and black students occupied five buildings for a week. A subsequent student strike closed the university for the rest of the academic year. One of the key issues arose from the university's expansion through buying up land in neighboring Harlem and evicting black tenants. The members of the Columbia chapter of Students for a Democratic Society (SDS), one of various factions among the protesters, rationalized their actions in the following statement.

When we seized five buildings at Columbia University, we engaged the force of wealth, privilege, property — and the force of state violence that always accompanies them — with little more than our own ideals, our fears, and a vague sense of outrage at the injustices of our society. Martin Luther King had just been shot, his name demeaned by

Columbia officials who refused to grant a decent wage to Puerto Rican workers, and who had recently grabbed part of Harlem for a student gym. . . .

For years Columbia Trustees had evicted tenants from their homes, taken land through city deals, and fired workers for trying to form a union. For years they had trained officers for Vietnam who, as ROTC literature indicates, killed Vietnamese peasants in their own country. In secret work for the IDA [Institute for Defense Analysis] and the CIA, in chemical-biological war research for the Department of War, the Trustees implicated their own University in genocide. They had consistently . . . lied to their own constituents and published CIA books under the guise of independent scholarship. . . . We lived in an institution that channeled us, marked us, ranked us, failed us, used us, and treated masses of humanity with class contempt. . . .

Columbia, standing at the top of a hill, looked down on Harlem. . . . People who survived in Harlem had been evicted by the Trustees from Morningside or still paid rent to Columbia. . . . We walked to our classrooms across land that had been privatized; we studied in buildings that had once been homes in a city that is underhoused; and we listened to the apologies for Cold War and capital in our classes.

Columbia professors often claim that the University is a neutral institution. . . . Many professors pursue all sides of a question as an end in itself. They find a certain refuge in the difficulty of defining good and evil. The result is a clogging of their moral sense, their capacity for collective justice. . . . What liberals call neutrality is really one of the ways by which the faculty protects its special status in society.

A University could not, even if it wanted, choose to be really value-free. It can choose good values; it can choose bad values; or it can remain ignorant of the values on which it acts. . . . A social institution should at least articulate its own perspective, so that its own values may be consciously applied or modified. It is a typical fallacy of American teaching, that to remain silent on crucial issues is to be objective with your own constituents. Actually a "neutral" institution is far more manipulative than a University committed to avowed goals and tasks.

SOURCE: Excerpt from "The Columbia Statement," Columbia SDS, from *The University Crisis Reader*, vol. 1, *The Liberal University under Attack* by Immanuel Wallerstein and Paul Starr, eds., pp. 23–47. Copyright © 1971 by Random House, Inc. Reprinted with permission.

DOCUMENT 3
Counterthrust on Student Power, Spring 1967

While the majority of students simply avoided involvement in campus rebellions, some students actively criticized the protesters. The largest conservative student organization was Young Americans for Freedom, which more than doubled in size during the 1960s. The following selection, from a leaflet titled "Student Power Is a Farce," reflected the views of Counterthrust, a conservative group at Wayne State University in Michigan.

Our University is being treated to the insanity of Left-Wing students demanding the run of the University. . . . Wayne students are told by the Left that "student power" merely means more democracy on campus. This is an outright lie! Student power is a Left-Wing catchword symbolizing campus militancy and radicalism. In actuality, the Left-Wing, spearheaded by the SDS [Students for a Democratic Society], want to radically alter the university community. . . .

The Leftists charge a sinister plot by private enterprise to train students for jobs at taxpayers' expense. Evidently it never occurred to the SDS that private enterprise is also the biggest single taxpayer for schools. But, of course, that would require a little thought on the part of the SDS which they have already demonstrated they are incapable of. . . .

The byword of student power-union advocates is Radicalism. . . . Fraternities and student Governments will have no place in student power-unions since both are considered allies of the status quo and thus useless. . . . As responsible Wayne students, we cannot allow our University to be used by Leftists for their narrow purposes. We were invited to this campus by the Michigan Taxpayer to receive an education. Let us honor that invitation.

SOURCE: "Student Power Is a Farce," Counterthrust, from *The University Crisis Reader*, vol. 1, *The Liberal University under Attack* by Immanuel Wallerstein and Paul Starr, eds., pp. 487–88. Copyright © 1971 by Random House, Inc. Reprinted with permission.

Questions for Analysis and Debate

1. How do the statements by Edward Schwartz and the Columbia SDS chapter differ in terms of the issues they address?

2. What did Counterthrust see as the biggest problem with student protesters?

3. Do you agree or disagree with the Columbia SDS chapter's assertion that it is impossible for a university to be neutral or value-free? Explain your position.

4. To what extent do your own campus policies and practices suggest that student protest during the 1960s and 1970s made a difference?

5. What changes that the protesters demanded have not been implemented at your college or university? Should they be?

Anti-Establishment Clothing

Youthful hippies embraced distinctive and colorful clothing to help define their identities as rebels in the new counterculture taking shape in the late 1960s. The well-worn artifacts shown here typify the self-expression of young people who scorned the older generation's button-down shirts, business suits, teased bouffant hair, sheath dresses, and all that they stood for.

Hippie first emerged as a new word in 1965, derived from *hip* and *hipster*, slang words from the realm of jazz and beatniks. But the teenagers and young adults morphing into hippies came disproportionately from the middle-class suburbs that at the time symbolized the success of the American dream. Hippies rejected the classic aspirations of steady work, home ownership, and consumer goods. In the summer of 1967, some 100,000 of them converged on the Haight-Ashbury district of San Francisco, lured by the call of the "Summer of Love." Those who stayed beyond the summer lived in voluntary poverty, relying on panhandling, crash pads, soup kitchens, and free clinics to support their freedom from middle-class values. Hippie enclaves sprouted in low-rent districts of coastal cities and in rural communes.

Clothing provided an obvious way for hippies to express their disdain for the "Establishment." What other attitudes can you decode in this

Bell-bottom Jeans

pair of bell-bottom jeans? Is it is a men's or a women's garment? Consider the degree of sewing expertise required to repurpose straight-leg pants into the bell-bottom flare. Who among the hippies was trained to do that work? Think about the typical stress points in pants. Are the patches here functional or decorative?

The fringed jacket illustrates two common themes: the Native American/cowboy-style fringe, and the red-white-blue motif. How might mainstream patriots have regarded this jacket? Was it intentionally inflammatory, or might the wearer be expressing an alternative form of patriotism? Most states had decades-old laws forbidding the desecration of the U.S. flag. Would this jacket have put its wearer at risk for arrest? In Massachusetts, a young man sporting a 4-by-6-inch flag on the left rear of his jeans was jailed for treating the flag "contemptuously," but in 1974 the U.S. Supreme Court overturned his conviction on grounds that the law's contempt provision was unconstitutionally vague.

What was rebellious about the denim shorts and halter top? Can you think of any time or place when such immodest dress would have

---

The central organization of white student protest was **Students for a Democratic Society (SDS)**, formed in 1960. In 1962, the organizers wrote in their statement of purpose, "We are people of this generation, bred in at least modest comfort, housed now in universities, looking uncomfortably at the world we inherit." The idealistic students criticized the complacency of their elders, the remoteness of decision makers from those affected by their actions, and the powerlessness and alienation generated by a bureaucratic society. SDS aimed to mobilize a "New Left" around the goals of civil rights, peace, and universal economic

security. Other forms of student activism soon followed.

The first large-scale white student protest arose at the University of California, Berkeley, in 1964, when university officials banned students from setting up tables to recruit support for various causes. Led by whites returning from civil rights work in the South, the students claimed the right to freedom of expression and political action. Members of the "free speech" movement occupied the administration building, and more than seven hundred students were arrested before the California Board of Regents overturned the new restrictions.

Fringed Jacket

Halter and Shorts

been acceptable? Can you guess how high school dress codes responded to these innovations? How the fashion industry responded? (Hint: Hot pants and miniskirts soon hit the fashion runways.)

Authentic hippie clothing remains rare; most of it probably fell apart and was junked by the mid-1970s, with occasional garments showing up in thrift stores or vintage clothing shops. By the 1980s, patterned bell-bottoms and daring short shorts looked as old-fashioned as a flapper dress from the 1920s. Nevertheless, the impact of counterculture clothing on mainstream dress was profound, leading within a few years to a much greater informality in everyday attire, even among the Establishment.

SOURCE: Jacket: Collection of Mark Hooper / Nancy Gewirz / Antique Textile Research; jeans: Nancy Gewirz / Antique Textile Research; halter and shorts: Picture Research Consultants & Archives.

Hundreds of student rallies and building occupations followed on campuses across the country, especially after 1965, when opposition to the Vietnam War mounted and students protested against universities' ties with the military (as discussed in chapter 29). Students also changed the collegiate environment. Women at the University of Chicago, for example, charged in 1969 that all universities "discriminate against women, impede their full intellectual development, deny them places on the faculty, exploit talented women and mistreat women students." At Howard University, African American students called for a "Black Awareness Research Institute," demanding that academic departments "place more emphasis on how these disciplines may be used to effect the liberation of black people." Across the country, students won curricular reforms such as black studies and women's studies programs, more financial aid for minority and poor students, independence from paternalistic rules, and a larger voice in campus decision making. (See "Documenting the American Promise," page 950.)

Student protest bewildered and angered older Americans, even more so when it blended into a cultural revolution against nearly every conventional standard of behavior. Drawing on the ideas of the Beats of the 1950s (see chapter 27), the "hippies," as they were called, rejected mainstream values such as materialism, order, and sexual control. Seeking personal rather than political change, they advocated "Do your own thing" and drew attention with their long hair, wildly colorful clothing, and use of marijuana, LSD, and other illegal drugs. Across the country, thousands of radicals established communes in cities or on farms, where they renounced private property and shared everything, often including sexual partners. (See "Visualizing History," page 952.)

Rock and folk music defined both the counterculture and the political left. English groups such as the Beatles and the Rolling Stones and homegrown performers such as Bob Dylan, Janis Joplin, and the Grateful Dead took American youth by storm. Music during the 1960s often carried insurgent political and social messages that reflected radical youth culture. "Eve of Destruction," a top hit of 1965, reminded young men at a time when the voting age was twenty-one, "You're old enough to kill but not for votin'." The Woodstock Music Festival epitomized the centrality of music to the youth rebellion. Woodstock featured the greatest rock and folk musicians of the era and drew 400,000 young people to a farm in Bethel, New York, in 1969.

Hippies faded away in the 1970s, but many elements of the counterculture — rock music, jeans, and long hair, as well as new social attitudes — filtered into the mainstream. More tolerant approaches to sexual behaviors spawned what came to be called the "sexual revolution," with help from the birth control pill, which became available in the 1960s. Self-fulfillment became a dominant concern of many Americans, and questioning of authority became more widespread.

Rock Music

Rock music provided the sound track for the youth rebellion of the 1960s. Heavily influenced by the blues as she grew up in east Texas, Janis Joplin developed a style that captivated audiences with her raw emotions and passionate delivery, paving the way for women to break into the male-dominated rock culture. Here she appears (second from left) in 1968 with the psychedelic rock band, Big Brother and the Holding Company, at Fillmore East, a famous New York City rock venue known for its fabulous light shows. Still wildly popular, Joplin died from a drug overdose in 1970. © Elliot Landy / The Image Works.

Gay Men and Lesbians Organize

More permissive sexual norms did not stretch easily to include tolerance of homosexuality. Gay men and lesbians escaped discrimination and ridicule only by concealing their very identities. Those who couldn't or wouldn't found themselves fired from jobs, arrested for their sexual activities, deprived of their children, or accused of being "perverted." While most kept their sexuality hidden, in the 1950s some gays and lesbians began to organize.

Gay Rights Protests

In the 1960s, inspired by the black freedom struggle, homosexual rights groups began to demonstrate at the White House and at government offices. This photograph, published on the cover of the *Ladder*, a magazine launched by the lesbian rights group Daughters of Bilitis in October 1956, shows a protest in front of the Civil Service Commission. Although the demonstrators agreed to look "conservative and conventional," one *Washington Post* reporter remembered, "I thought they must be totally reckless or weird." Courtesy of Department of Special Collections, Stanford University Libraries.

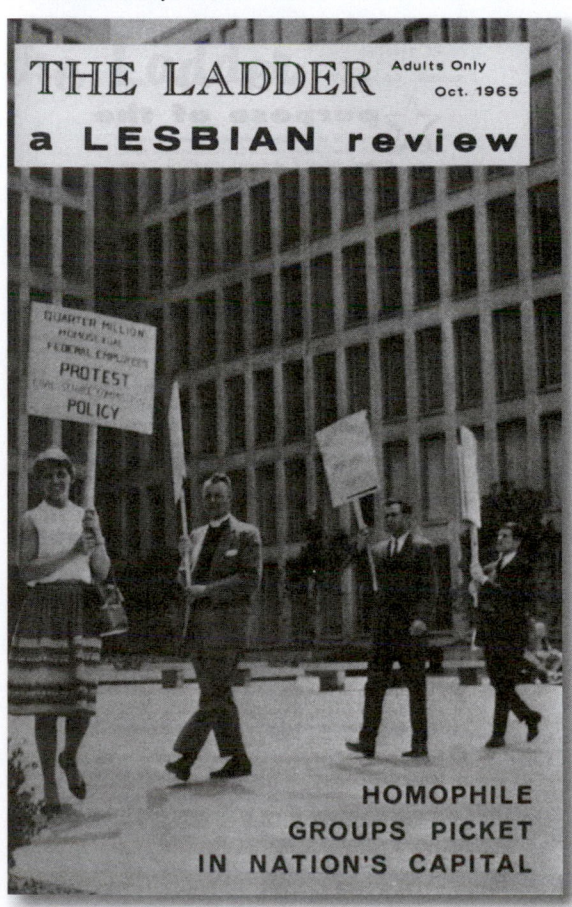

THE LADDER Adults Only Oct. 1965
a LESBIAN review

QUARTER MILLION
HOMOSEXUAL
FEDERAL EMPLOYEES
PROTEST
CIVIL SERVICE COMMISSION
POLICY

HOMOPHILE GROUPS PICKET IN NATION'S CAPITAL

Some of the first gay activism challenged the government's aggressive efforts to keep homosexuals out of the civil service. In October 1965, a picket line formed outside the White House with signs calling discrimination against homosexuals "as immoral as discrimination against Negroes and Jews." Not until ten years later, however, did the Civil Service Commission formally end its antigay policy.

The spark that ignited a larger movement was struck in 1969 when police raided a gay bar, the Stonewall Inn, in New York City's Greenwich Village, and gay men and lesbians fought back. "Suddenly, they were not submissive anymore," a police officer remarked. Energized by the defiance shown at the **Stonewall riots**, gay men and lesbians organized a host of new groups, such as the Gay Liberation Front. A more reformist organization, the National Gay and Lesbian Task Force, was founded in 1973 to ensure that gay issues received sustained national attention.

The gay rights movement struggled much longer and harder to win recognition than did other social movements. In 1972, Ann Arbor, Michigan, passed the first antidiscrimination ordinance, and two years later Elaine Noble's election to the Massachusetts legislature marked the first time an openly gay candidate won state office. In 1973, gay activists persuaded the American Psychiatric Association to withdraw its designation of homosexuality as a mental disease. It would take decades for these initial gains to improve conditions for most homosexuals, but by the mid-1970s gay men and lesbians had established a movement through which they could claim equal rights and express pride in their identities.

REVIEW How did the black freedom struggle influence other reform movements of the 1960s and 1970s?

▶ The New Wave of Feminism

On August 26, 1970, fifty years after women won the right to vote, tens of thousands of women across the country — from radical women in jeans to conservatively dressed suburbanites, peace activists, and politicians — took to the streets. They carried signs reading "Sisterhood Is Powerful" and "Don't Cook Dinner — Starve a Rat Today." Some of the banners opposed the

THE PROMISE OF TECHNOLOGY

The Pill

Longtime birth control advocate Margaret Sanger (see chapter 21) believed that the Pill was "the key to liberty" for women. In the early 1950s, she enlisted Katharine Dexter McCormick to bankroll research on oral contraception, which was conducted principally by biologists Gregory Pincus and Min-Chueh Chang and physician John Rock. They found that the hormones estrogen and progestin prevented ovulation, and in 1960 the Food and Drug Administration approved the first birth control pill, which soon became the leading form of contraception for American women. Condoms and diaphragms had been available for decades, but they required action at the time of sexual relations and were subject to failure. Surgical procedures for both men and women were also options for the prevention of pregnancy, but they were largely irreversible. After early Pill users raised concerns about its safety, manufacturers reduced the amounts of estrogen and progestin to decrease side effects and the risk for stroke, cancer, and other illnesses. This 1965 ad shows doctors how the

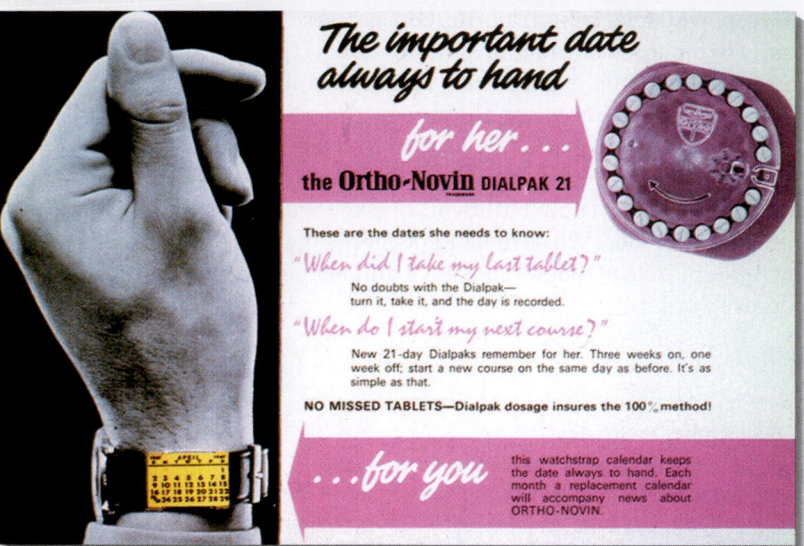

Ortho-Novin Dialpak will help women remember to take the daily tablet. What assumptions does this ad make about women and about physicians? From a woman's perspective, what are the advantages and disadvantages of the Pill compared to other contraceptive methods? National Museum of American History, Smithsonian Institution, Behring Center.

war in Vietnam, others demanded racial justice, but women's own liberation stood at the forefront.

Becoming visible by the late 1960s, the women's movement reached its high tide in the 1970s and persisted into the twenty-first century. By that time, despite a powerful countermovement, women had experienced tremendous transformations in their legal status, public opportunities, and personal and sexual relationships, and popular expectations about appropriate gender roles had shifted dramatically.

A Multifaceted Movement Emerges

Beginning in the 1940s, large demographic changes laid the preconditions for a resurgence of feminism. As more and more women took jobs, the importance of their paid work to the economy and their families belied the idea of women as dependent, domestic beings and awakened many women workers, especially labor union women, to the inferior conditions of their employment. The democratization of higher education brought more women to college campuses, where their aspirations exceeded the confines of domesticity and of routine, subordinate jobs.

Policy initiatives in the early 1960s reflected both these larger transformations and the efforts of women's rights activists. In 1961, Assistant Secretary of Labor Esther Peterson persuaded President Kennedy to create the President's Commission on the Status of Women (PCSW). In 1963, the commission reported widespread discrimination against women and recommended remedies, although it did not challenge women's domestic roles. Counterparts of the PCSW sprang up in every state, filled with women eager for action. One of the commission's concerns was addressed even before it issued its report, when Congress passed the Equal Pay Act of 1963, making it illegal to pay women less than men for the same work.

Like other movements, the rise of feminism owed much to the black freedom struggle. Women gained protection from employment discrimination through Title VII of the Civil Rights Act of 1964 and the extension of affirmative action to women by piggybacking onto civil rights measures. They soon grew impatient when the government failed to take these new policies seriously.

Women's Strike for Equality
On the fiftieth anniversary of the Nineteenth Amendment granting woman suffrage, Betty Friedan and others organized a nationwide Women's Strike for Equality. While the numbers who participated were relatively small, in New York City more than ten thousand women marched down Fifth Avenue, in defiance of police who tried to keep them on the sidewalks. The three central demands of the protest were equal opportunity in employment and education, child care, and abortion rights. During what were still the early days of second-wave feminism, ABC News showed a U.S. senator calling the demonstrators "a small band of bra-less bubble heads." Getty John Olson/Time & Life Pictures/Getty Images.

Outraged by the government's slowness in enforcing Title VII, Betty Friedan, civil rights activist Pauli Murray, several union women, and others founded the **National Organization for Women (NOW)** in 1966.

Simultaneously, a more radical feminism grew among civil rights and New Left activists. In 1965, two white women, Mary King and Casey Hayden, wrote that their work in SNCC had awakened them to sex discrimination. Although most black women did not consider themselves to be marginalized in the movement, King and Hayden presented their ideas to white male radicals in the New Left, who responded with indifference or ridicule. By contrast, their message invigorated other white women who shared their frustration with subordinate roles. Many women walked out of New Left organizations and created an independent women's liberation movement composed of small groups across the nation.

Women's liberation began to gain public attention, especially when dozens of women picketed the Miss America beauty pageant in 1968, protesting against being forced "to compete for male approval [and] enslaved by ludicrous 'beauty' standards." Women began to speak publicly about personal experiences that had always been shrouded in secrecy, such as rape and abortion. Throughout the country, women joined consciousness-raising groups, where they discovered that what they had considered "personal" problems reflected an entrenched system of discrimination against and devaluation of women.

Radical feminists, who called their movement "women's liberation," differed from feminists in NOW and other more mainstream groups in several ways. NOW focused on equal treatment for women in the public sphere; women's liberation emphasized ending women's subordination in family and other personal relationships. Groups such as NOW wanted to integrate

Transnational Feminisms

Organizations of women across national borders originated in the nineteenth century, but global connections among women increased dramatically in 1945 with the creation of the United Nations. Its charter affirmed "the equal rights of men and women," and in 1947 it established the Commission on the Status of Women, creating a forum for women from around the globe to meet and be heard. The UN helped launch a global feminist movement of unparalleled size and diversity when it declared 1975 International Women's Year and sponsored a conference in Mexico City. Six thousand women came to Mexico City on their own; official delegates from 125 nations approved the World Plan of Action for Women and prompted the UN to declare 1976 to 1985 the UN Decade for Women.

In response to the call for action in individual countries, the U.S. government funded the National Women's Conference in Houston, Texas, in 1977. More than two thousand state delegates attended, representing a cross section of American womanhood. They adopted the National Plan of Action, not only supporting ratification of the ERA and reproductive freedom but also addressing the needs of specific groups of women, including the elderly, lesbians, racial minorities, women with disabilities, rural women, and homemakers. For the first time, the U.S. women's movement had a comprehensive national agenda setting goals for decades to come.

The three themes of the UN Decade for Women — equality, development, and peace — reflected an effort to address the enormously diverse needs of women throughout the world. Feminists from Western nations who focused on equal rights met criticism from women who represented impoverished third world countries and insisted that "to talk feminism to a woman who has no water, no food, and no home is to talk nonsense." Ever larger UN-sponsored meetings followed Mexico City — Copenhagen in 1980, Nairobi in 1985, and Beijing in 1995, where twenty thousand women gathered. These global exchanges taught American feminists that to participate in a truly international movement, they would have to revise their Western-centered perspective on women's needs and understand that women's issues must include economic development and anticolonialism.

American feminists also learned that theirs was not always the most advanced nation when it came to women's welfare and status. Employed women in most industrialized countries had access to paid maternity leave and public child care. By 2010, women had headed governments in more than thirty countries, including India, Israel, Britain, and Germany. Many nations, such as Argentina, Egypt, and members of the European Union, had some form of affirmative action to increase the numbers of women in government. And whereas American women held just 17 percent of the seats in Congress, women constituted more than 35 percent of national legislatures in such countries as Sweden, South Africa, Costa Rica, and Belgium.

Despite enormous differences among women around the world, internationally minded feminists continued to seek common ground. As women into existing institutions; radical groups insisted that women's liberation required a total transformation of economic, political, and social institutions. Differences between these two strands of feminism blurred in the 1970s, as NOW and other mainstream groups embraced many of the issues raised by radicals.

> ## "My mother took care of rich white kids. I didn't think they were oppressed."
> —A black woman, speaking about feminism

Although NOW elected a black president, Aileen Hernandez, in 1970, the new feminism's leadership and constituency were predominantly white and middle-class. Women of color criticized white feminists for their inadequate attention to the disproportionate poverty experienced by minority women and to the additional layers of discrimination based on race or ethnicity. One black woman said, "My mother took care of rich white kids. I didn't think they were oppressed." To black women, who were much more frequently compelled to work in the lowest-paying jobs for their families' survival, employment did not necessarily look like liberation.

In addition to struggling with vast differences among women, feminism also contended with the refusal of the mass media to take women's grievances seriously. When the House of Representatives passed an equal rights amendment to the U.S. Constitution in 1970, the *New*

International Women's Year Tribune

Along with the official UN conference in Mexico City in 1975, nongovernmental organizations associated with the UN sponsored a tribune, where six thousand women gathered. Participants expressed the conflicting priorities of Western women and women from developing countries, and they argued over whether issues such as apartheid in South Africa and self-government for Palestinians were women's issues. Despite their disagreements, most women left Mexico City enlightened and energized. © Bettye Lane

Gertrude Mongella, secretary general of the Beijing conference, insisted in 1995, "A revolution has begun and there is no going back. . . . This revolution is too just, too important, and too long overdue."

America in a Global Context

1. What were the three themes of the UN Decade for Women? How were these three themes related to women's status and well-being?

2. In what ways were women in the United States ahead of women in other countries? In what ways were they behind? What might account for the differences?

York Times criticized it in an editorial titled "The Henpecked House." After Gloria Steinem founded *Ms: The New Magazine for Women* in 1972, feminists had their own mass-circulation periodical controlled by women and featuring articles on a broad range of feminist issues.

Ms. reported on a movement that was exceedingly multifaceted. Most African American women worked through their own groups, such as the older National Council of Negro Women and the National Black Feminist Organization, founded in 1973. Similarly, in the early 1970s,

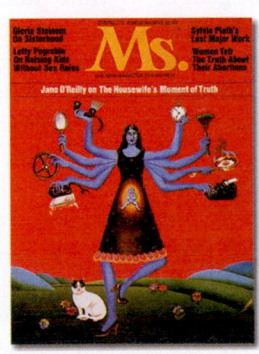

Native American women and Mexican American women founded national organizations, and Asian American women formed local movements.

Labor union women, who had long struggled for workplace gender justice, organized the National Coalition of Labor Union Women in 1974. Lesbians established collectives throughout the country, as well as their own caucuses in organizations such as NOW. Welfare mothers formed the National Welfare Rights Organization, and religious women mobilized in the National Council of Churches of Christ to "place the question of women's liberation in the main stream of the church's concern." Other new groups focused on single issues such as health, abortion rights, education, and violence against women. In addition, U.S. feminists interacted with women abroad, joining a movement that crossed national boundaries. (See "Beyond America's Borders," page 958.)

Common threads underlay the great diversity of organizations, issues, and activities. Above all, feminism represented the belief that women were barred from, unequally treated in, or poorly served by the male-dominated public arena, encompassing politics, medicine, law, education, culture, and religion. Many feminists also sought equality in the private sphere, challenging traditional norms that identified women primarily as wives and mothers or sex objects, subservient to men.

Feminist Gains Spark a Countermovement

Although more an effect than a cause of women's rising employment, feminism lifted female aspirations and helped lower barriers to posts monopolized by men. Between 1970 and 2000, women's share of law degrees shot up from 5 percent to nearly 50 percent, and their proportion of medical degrees from less than 10 percent to more than 35 percent. Women gained political offices very slowly; yet by 2010, they constituted about 17 percent of Congress and more than 20 percent of all state executives and legislators.

Feminists encountered frustrations along with achievements. Despite some inroads into male-dominated occupations, women still tended to concentrate in low-paying, traditionally female jobs, and their earnings lagged below men's well into the twenty-first century. Employed women continued to bear primary responsibility for their homes and families, thereby working a "double day."

Although public opinion polls registered support for most feminist goals, by the mid-1970s feminism faced a powerful countermovement, organized around opposition to a central goal of the women's movement: an **Equal Rights Amendment (ERA)** that would outlaw differential treatment of men and women under all state and federal laws. After Congress passed the ERA in 1972, Phyllis Schlafly, a conservative activist in the Republican Party, mobilized thousands of women at the grassroots level who feared that the ERA would devalue their own God-given roles as wives and mothers. These women, marching on state capitols, persuaded some male legislators to block ratification. When the time limit ran out in 1982, only thirty-five states had ratified the amendment, three short of the necessary three-fourths majority. (See chapter 30, "Historical Question," page 1026.)

Powerful opposition likewise arose to feminists' quest for the right to abortion. "Without the full capacity to limit her own reproduction," abortion rights activist Lucinda Cisler insisted, "a woman's other 'freedoms' are tantalizing mockeries that cannot be exercised." In 1973, the Supreme Court issued the landmark *Roe v. Wade* decision, ruling that the Constitution protects the right to abortion, which states cannot prohibit in the early stages of pregnancy. This decision galvanized many Americans who believed that human life begins with conception and equated abortion with murder. Like ERA opponents, with whom they often overlapped, activists in the right-to-life movement mobilized thousands of women who believed that abortion disparaged motherhood and that feminism threatened their traditional roles. Beginning in 1977, abortion foes successfully pressured Congress to restrict the right to abortion by prohibiting coverage under Medicaid and other government-financed health programs, and the Supreme Court allowed states to impose additional obstacles.

Despite resistance, feminists won other lasting gains. **Title IX** of the Education Amendments Act of 1972 banned sex discrimination in all aspects of education, such as admissions, athletics, and hiring. Congress also outlawed sex discrimination in credit in 1974, opened U.S. military academies to women in 1976, and prohibited discrimination against pregnant workers in 1978. Moreover, the Supreme Court struck down laws that treated men and women differently in Social Security, welfare and military benefits, and workers' compensation.

At the state and local levels, women saw reforms in areas that radical feminists had first introduced. They won laws forcing police departments and the legal system to treat rape victims more justly and humanely. Activists also pushed domestic violence onto the public agenda, obtaining government financing for shelters for battered women as well as laws ensuring both greater protection for victims of domestic violence and more effective prosecution of abusers.

REVIEW What were the key goals of feminist reformers, and why did a countermovement arise to resist them?

▶ Liberal Reform in the Nixon Administration

Opposition to civil rights measures, Great Society reforms, and protest groups — along with frustrations surrounding the war in Vietnam (as discussed in chapter 29) — delivered the White House to Republican **Richard M. Nixon** in 1968. Nixon attacked the Great Society for "pouring billions of dollars into programs that have failed," and he promised to represent the "forgotten Americans, the non-shouters, the non-demonstrators." Yet despite Nixon's desire to capitalize on the backlash against civil rights and the Great Society, his administration either promoted or accepted substantially greater federal assistance to the poor, new protections for minorities and women, major environmental regulations, and financial policies deviating sharply from traditional Republican economics.

Extending the Welfare State and Regulating the Economy

A number of factors shaped the liberal policies of the Nixon administration. Not only did the Democrats continue to control Congress, but Nixon also saw political advantages in accepting some liberal programs. Nor could he entirely ignore grassroots movements, and several of his advisers were sympathetic to particular concerns, such as environmentalism and Native American rights. Serious economic problems also compelled new approaches, and although Nixon's real passion lay in foreign policy, he knew that his domestic record would in part determine whether he enjoyed history's approving gaze.

Under Nixon, government assistance programs grew. Congress resisted his attempts to eliminate the Office of Economic Opportunity. Key programs such as Medicaid, Head Start, and Legal Services remained intact. Social Security benefits increased and were now required to rise with the cost of living; subsidies for low-income housing tripled; a new billion-dollar program provided Pell grants for low-income students to attend college; and the food stamp program expanded to benefit 12.5 million recipients. Noting the disparity between what Nixon said and what he did, his speechwriter, the archconservative Pat Buchanan, grumbled, "Vigorously did we inveigh against the Great Society, enthusiastically did we fund it."

> **"Vigorously did we inveigh against the Great Society, enthusiastically did we fund it."**
>
> —Archconservative PAT BUCHANAN, speaking of the Nixon administration

Nixon also acted contrary to his antigovernment rhetoric when economic crises and energy shortages induced him to increase the federal government's power in the marketplace. By 1970, both inflation and unemployment had surpassed 6 percent, an unprecedented combination dubbed "stagflation." Domestic troubles were compounded by the decline of American dominance in the international economy. With the productive capacity of Japan and Western Europe fully recovered from World War II, foreign cars, electronic equipment, and other products now competed favorably

Nixon's 1968 Campaign

Seeking the presidency in 1968, Richard Nixon tried to appeal to a broad spectrum of voters. Prominent Republicans of all stripes appear in this campaign poster, including the liberal Nelson Rockefeller and the conservative Barry Goldwater. While Nixon's slogan "Champion of Forgotten America" spoke to white Americans alienated by Great Society programs for minorities and the poor, the poster's inclusion of black Republican senator Edward Brooke and basketball player Wilt Chamberlain of the Los Angeles Lakers gave a nod to African Americans. Nixon also appealed to youths by supporting the vote for eighteen-year-olds and promising to end the draft. Collection of Janice L. and David J. Frent.

with American goods. In 1971, for the first time in decades, the United States imported more than it exported. Because the amount of dollars in foreign hands exceeded U.S. gold reserves, the nation could no longer back up its currency with gold.

In 1971, Nixon abandoned the convertibility of dollars into gold and devalued the dollar to increase exports. To protect domestic manufacturers, he imposed a 10 percent surcharge on most imports, and he froze wages and prices, thus enabling the government to stimulate the economy without fueling inflation. In the short run, these policies worked, and Nixon was resoundingly reelected in 1972. Yet by 1974, unemployment had crept back up and inflation soared, leaving to Nixon's successor the most severe economic crisis since the 1930s.

Skyrocketing energy prices intensified stagflation. Throughout the post–World War II economic boom, the nation's abundant oil deposits and access to cheap Middle Eastern oil had encouraged the building of large cars and skyscrapers with no concern for fuel efficiency. By the 1970s, the United States was consuming one-third of the world's fuel resources.

In the fall of 1973, the United States faced its first energy crisis. Arab nations, furious at the administration's support of Israel during the Yom Kippur War (as discussed in chapter 29), cut off oil shipments to the United States. Long lines formed at gas stations, where prices had nearly doubled, and many homes were cold. In response, Nixon authorized temporary emergency measures allocating petroleum and establishing a national 55-mile-per-hour speed limit to save gasoline. The energy crisis eased, but the nation had yet to come to grips with its seemingly unquenchable demand for fuel and dependence on foreign oil.

Responding to Environmental Concerns

The oil crisis dovetailed with a rising environmental movement, which was pushing the government to conserve energy and protect nature and human beings from the hazards of rapid economic growth. Like the conservation movement born in the Progressive Era (see chapter 21), the new environmentalists sought to preserve natural areas for recreational and aesthetic purposes and to conserve natural resources for future use. Especially in the West, the post–World War II explosion of economic growth and mushrooming population, with the resulting demands for electricity and water, made such efforts seem even more critical. Environmental groups began mobilizing in the 1950s to stop the construction of dams that would disrupt national parks and wilderness areas.

The new environmentalists, however, went beyond conservationism to attack the ravaging effects of industrial development and technological advances on human life and health. To the leaders of a new organization, Friends of the Earth, unlimited economic growth was "no longer healthy, but a cancer."

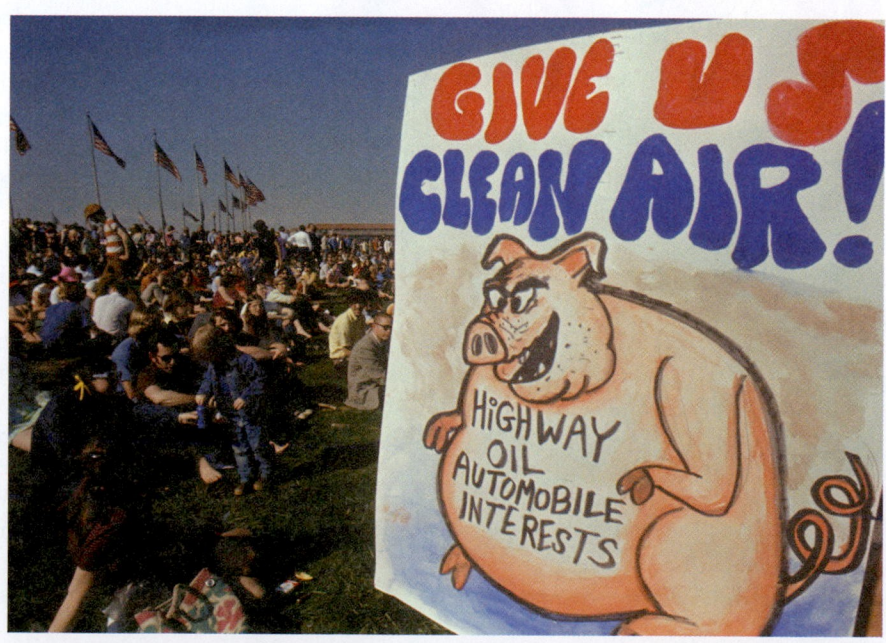

Earth Day in the Nation's Capital
Building on the success of teach-ins about the Vietnam War, Democratic senator Gaylord Nelson of Wisconsin came up with the idea of Earth Day "to shake up the political establishment and force this issue [environmentalism] onto the national agenda." As a result, on April 22, 1970, some twenty million people participated in grassroots demonstrations all over the country. This banner displayed on the Mall in Washington, D.C., focused on clean air. Other activists dramatized oil spills, toxic dumps, pesticides, polluted rivers and lakes, the loss of wilderness, and the extinction of wildlife. Dennis Brack/Black Star/Stockphoto.com.

Biologist Rachel Carson drew national attention in 1962 with her best seller *Silent Spring*, which described the harmful effects of toxic chemicals such as the pesticide DDT. The Sierra Club and other older conservation organizations expanded their agendas, and a host of new groups arose. Millions of Americans expressed environmental concerns on the first observation of Earth Day in April 1970.

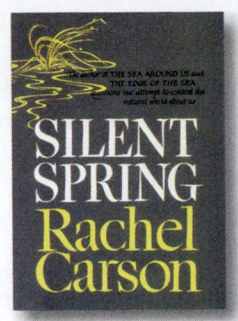

Responding to these concerns, Nixon built on the efforts begun in the Johnson administration. He called "clean air, clean water, open spaces . . . the birthright of every American" and urged Congress to "end the plunder of America's natural heritage." In 1970, he created the **Environmental Protection Agency (EPA)** to conduct research, enforce environmental laws, and reduce human health and environmental risks from pollutants. He also signed the Occupational Safety and Health Act, protecting workers against job-related accidents and disease, and the Clean Air Act of 1970, setting national standards for air quality and restricting factory and automobile emissions of carbon dioxide and other pollutants. Environmentalists claimed that Nixon failed to do enough, pointing particularly to his veto — for budgetary reasons — of the Clean Water Act of 1972, which Congress overrode. Yet his environmental initiatives surpassed those of previous administrations.

Expanding Social Justice

Nixon's 1968 campaign had exploited hostility to black protest and new civil rights policies to appeal to southern Democrats and white workers, but his administration had to answer to the courts and to Congress. In 1968, fourteen years after the *Brown* decision, school desegregation had barely touched the South. Like Eisenhower, Nixon was reluctant to use federal power to compel integration, but the Supreme Court overruled the administration's efforts to delay court-ordered desegregation and compelled it to enforce the law. By the time Nixon left office, fewer than one in ten southern black children attended totally segregated schools.

Nixon also began to implement affirmative action among federal contractors and unions and awarded more government contracts and loans to minority businesses. Congress took the initiative in other areas. In 1970, it extended the Voting Rights Act of 1965, and in 1972 it strengthened the Civil Rights Act of 1964 by enlarging the powers of the Equal Employment Opportunity Commission. In 1971, Congress also responded to the massive youth movement with the Twenty-sixth Amendment to the Constitution, which reduced the voting age to eighteen.

Women as well as minority groups benefited from the implementation of affirmative action and the strengthened EEOC, but several measures of the Nixon administration also specifically attacked sex discrimination. The president privately expressed patronizing attitudes about women. "Thank God we don't have any in the Cabinet," he told aides. Yet again, he confronted a growing movement that included Republican feminists. Nixon vetoed a comprehensive child care bill and publicly opposed abortion, but he signed the pathbreaking Title IX, guaranteeing equality in all aspects of education, and allowed his Labor Department to push affirmative action.

President Nixon gave more public support for justice to Native Americans than to any other protest group. While not bowing to radical demands, the administration dealt cautiously with extreme protests, such as the occupation of the Bureau of Indian Affairs in Washington, D.C. Nixon signed measures recognizing claims of Alaskan and New Mexican Indians and set in motion legislation restoring tribal lands and granting Indians more control over their schools and other service institutions.

REVIEW Why and how did Republican president Richard Nixon expand the liberal reforms of previous administrations?

▶ Conclusion: Achievements and Limitations of Liberalism

Senate majority leader Mike Mansfield was not alone in concluding that Lyndon Johnson "has done more than FDR ever did, or ever thought of doing." Building on initiatives from John F. Kennedy's New Frontier, the Great Society expanded the New Deal's focus on economic security, refashioning liberalism to embrace individual rights and to extend material well-being to groups left out of or discriminated against in New Deal programs. Yet opposition to Johnson's leadership grew so strong that by 1968 his liberal vision lay in ruins. "How," he asked, "was it possible that all these people could be so ungrateful to me after I have given them so much?"

Fannie Lou Hamer could have responded by pointing out how slowly the government acted when efforts to win African Americans' rights met with violence. In addition, Hamer's failed attempts to use Johnson's antipoverty programs to help poor blacks in Mississippi resulted in part from internal problems, but those failures also reflected some of the more general shortcomings of the War on Poverty. Hastily planned and inadequately funded, antipoverty programs focused more on remediating individual shortcomings than on reforms that would ensure adequately paying jobs for all. Because Johnson launched an all-out war in Vietnam and refused to ask for sacrifices from prosperous Americans, the Great Society never commanded the resources necessary for victory over poverty.

Furthermore, black aspirations exceeded white Americans' commitment to genuine equality. When the civil rights movement attacked racial barriers long entrenched throughout the nation and sought equality in fact as well as in law, it faced a powerful backlash. By the end of the 1960s, the revolution in the legal status of African Americans was complete, but the black freedom struggle had lost momentum, and African Americans remained, with Native Americans and Chicanos, at the bottom of the economic ladder.

Johnson's critics overlooked the Great Society's more successful and lasting elements. Medicare and Medicaid continue to provide access to health care for the elderly and the poor. Federal aid for education and housing became permanent elements of national policy. Moreover, Richard Nixon's otherwise conservative administration implemented school desegregation in the South and affirmative action, initiated substantial environmental reforms, and secured new rights for Native Americans and women. Women especially benefited from the decline of discrimination, and significant numbers of African Americans and other minority groups began to enter the middle class.

Yet the perceived shortcomings of government programs contributed to social turmoil and fueled the resurgence of conservative politics. Young radicals launched direct confrontations with the government and universities, calling for both domestic reform and an end to the war in Vietnam. The combination of racial conflict and youth activism escalated into widespread political discord and social disorder. The Vietnam War polarized American society as much as did racial issues or the behavior of young people, and it devoured resources that might have been used for social reform even as it undermined faith in presidential leadership.

▶ Selected Bibliography

The Black Freedom Struggle

Raymond Arsenault, *Freedom Riders: 1961 and the Struggle for Racial Justice* (2006).

Taylor Branch, *America in the King Years*, 3 vols. (1988, 1998, 2006).

Michael Eric Dyson, *Making Malcolm: The Myth and Meaning of Malcolm X* (1995).

Wesley C. Hogan, *Many Minds, One Heart: SNCC's Dream for a New America* (2009).

Chana Kai Lee, *For Freedom's Sake: The Life of Fannie Lou Hamer* (1999).

Jeffrey O. G. Ogbar, *Black Power: Radical Politics and African American Identity* (2005).

Charles Payne, *I've Got the Light of Freedom: The Organizing Tradition and the Mississippi Freedom Struggle* (1995).

Barbara Ransby, *Ella Baker and the Black Freedom Movement: A Radical Democratic Vision* (2003).

Stephen Tuck, *We Ain't What We Ought to Be: The Black Freedom Struggle from Emancipation to Obama* (2010).

Timothy Tyson, *Radio Free Dixie: Robert F. Williams and the Roots of Black Power* (1999).

Bruce Watson, *Freedom Summer: The Savage Season That Made Mississippi Burn and Made America a Democracy* (2010).

Politics, Policies, and Court Decisions

Robert Dallek, *An Unfinished Life: John F. Kennedy, 1917–1963* (2003).

Maurice Isserman and Michael Kazin, *America Divided: The Civil War of the 1960s* (2000).

Michael B. Katz, *The Undeserving Poor: From the War on Poverty to the War on Welfare* (1989).

Nancy MacLean, *Freedom Is Not Enough: The Opening of the American Workplace* (2006).

Gerald Posner, *Case Closed: Lee Harvey Oswald and the Assassination of JFK* (1993).

Lucas A. Powe Jr., *The Warren Court and American Politics* (2000).

John D. Skrentny, *The Minority Rights Revolution* (2002).

Irwin Unger, *The Best of Intentions: The Triumph and Failure of the Great Society* (1996).

Tom Wicker, *One of Us: Richard Nixon and the American Dream* (1991).

Randall B. Woods, *LBJ: Architect of American Ambition* (2006).

Protest Movements

Terry H. Anderson, *The Movement and the Sixties* (1995).

David Barber, *A Hard Rain Fell: SDS and Why It Failed* (2010).

Daniel M. Cobb, *Native Activism in Cold War America: The Struggle for Sovereignty* (2008).

John D'Emilio, William B. Turner, and Urvashi Vaid, *Creating Change: Sexuality, Public Policy, and Civil Rights* (2000).

Troy R. Johnson, *The American Indian Occupation of Alcatraz Island: Red Power and Self-Determination* (2008).

F. Arturo Rosales, *Chicano! The History of the Mexican American Civil Rights Movement* (1997).

Randy Shaw, *Beyond the Fields: Cesar Chavez, the UFW, and the Struggle for Justice in the Twenty-first Century* (2008).

William Wei, *The Asian American Movement* (1993).

Cultural Change, Sexual Revolution, and Feminism

David Allyn, *Make Love, Not War: The Sexual Revolution, an Unfettered History* (2000).

Glenn C. Altschuler, *All Shook Up: How Rock 'n' Roll Changed America* (2004).

Sara Evans, *Tidal Wave: How Women Changed America at Century's End* (2003).

David Garrow, *Liberty and Sexuality: The Right to Privacy and the Making of Roe v. Wade* (1994).

Carol Giardina, *Freedom for Women: Forging the Women's Liberation Movement, 1953–1970* (2010).

Elaine Tyler May, *America and the Pill: A History of Promise, Peril, and Liberation* (2010).

Benita Roth, *Separate Roads to Feminism: Black, Chicana, and White Feminist Movements in America's Second Wave* (2004).

▶ **FOR MORE BOOKS ABOUT TOPICS IN THIS CHAPTER,** see the Online Bibliography at **bedfordstmartins.com/roark.**

▶ **FOR ADDITIONAL PRIMARY SOURCES FROM THIS PERIOD,** see Michael Johnson, ed., *Reading the American Past*, Fifth Edition.

▶ **FOR WEB SITES, IMAGES, AND DOCUMENTS RELATED TO TOPICS AND PLACES IN THIS CHAPTER,** visit Make History at **bedfordstmartins.com/roark.**

Reviewing Chapter 28

KEY TERMS

Explain each term's significance.

Liberalism at High Tide

John F. Kennedy (p. 933)
Lyndon B. Johnson (p. 934)
Great Society (p. 935)
Civil Rights Act of 1964 (p. 935)
War on Poverty (p. 936)
Medicare (p. 936)
Medicaid (p. 936)
Voting Rights Act of 1965 (p. 936)
Immigration and Nationality Act
 of 1965 (p. 936)
Warren Court (p. 938)

The Second Reconstruction

Martin Luther King Jr. (p. 940)
Student Nonviolent Coordinating
 Committee (SNCC) (p. 940)
Fannie Lou Hamer (p. 941)
March on Washington for Jobs
 and Freedom (p. 942)
Mississippi Freedom Summer Project
 (p. 942)
Selma march (p. 942)
Civil Rights Act of 1968 (p. 944)
Malcolm X (p. 946)
Stokely Carmichael (p. 946)
black power movement (p. 946)

A Multitude of Movements

American Indian Movement (AIM) (p. 947)
Cesar Chavez (p. 948)
Dolores Huerta (p. 948)
Students for a Democratic Society (SDS)
 (p. 952)
Stonewall riots (p. 955)

The New Wave of Feminism

National Organization for Women (NOW)
 (p. 957)
Equal Rights Amendment (ERA) (p. 960)
Roe v. Wade (p. 960)
Title IX (p. 960)

Liberal Reform in the Nixon
Administration

Richard M. Nixon (p. 961)
Environmental Protection Agency (EPA)
 (p. 963)

REVIEW QUESTIONS

Use key terms and dates to support your answer.

1. How did the Kennedy and Johnson administrations exemplify a liberal vision of the federal government? (pp. 933–940)

2. How and why did the civil rights movement change in the mid-1960s? (pp. 940–946)

3. How did the black freedom struggle influence other reform movements of the 1960s and 1970s? (pp. 947–955)

4. What were the key goals of feminist reformers, and why did a countermovement arise to resist them? (pp. 955–960)

5. Why and how did Republican president Richard Nixon expand the liberal reforms of previous administrations? (pp. 961–963)

MAKING CONNECTIONS

Draw on key terms, the timeline, and review questions.

1. In what ways did Lyndon Johnson's Great Society build on the initiatives of John F. Kennedy? Why were Johnson's reforms so much more far-reaching?

2. During the 1960s, African Americans made substantial gains in asserting their freedoms and rights. What specific gains did the civil rights movement achieve? Were there limits to its success? What part did government play in this process?

3. Women participated in various ways in the feminism that emerged in the 1960s. How can we explain the rise of this movement? What assumptions and goals were held in common in this diverse movement?

4. Most of the reform movements of the 1960s sought equality as one of their key priorities, but significant differences existed among Americans in general about what equality meant. Should equality be limited to equal treatment under the law, or should it extend to economic welfare, education, sexual relations, and other aspects of life? Examining two reform movements, discuss how different ideas of equality contributed to the accomplishments and disappointments of each movement.

LINKING TO THE PAST

Link events in this chapter to earlier events.

1. Both Franklin Roosevelt's New Deal and Lyndon Johnson's Great Society attacked poverty. How was Johnson's approach different from Roosevelt's? Which was more successful, and what contributed to the relative successes and failures of each approach? (See chapter 24.)

2. What changes that had been taking place in the United States since 1940 laid a foundation for the rise of a feminist movement in the 1960s? (See chapters 25 and 26.)

▶ FOR PRACTICE QUIZZES AND OTHER STUDY TOOLS, visit the Online Study Guide at bedfordstmartins.com/roark.

TIMELINE 1960–1973

1960
- Democrat John F. Kennedy elected president.
- Student Nonviolent Coordinating Committee (SNCC) established.
- Students for a Democratic Society (SDS) founded.

1961
- Congress of Racial Equality (CORE) sponsors Freedom Rides.

1962
- United Farm Workers (UFW) founded.

1963
- President's Commission on the Status of Women issues report.
- Equal Pay Act.
- *Baker v. Carr.*
- *Abington School District v. Schempp.*
- March on Washington for Jobs and Freedom.
- President Kennedy assassinated; Lyndon B. Johnson becomes president.

1964
- Civil Rights Act.
- Mississippi Freedom Summer Project.
- Economic Opportunity Act.
- Major tax cuts enacted.

1965
- Voting Rights Act.

1965–1966
- Congress passes most of Johnson's Great Society domestic programs.

1965–1968
- Riots in major cities.

1966
- Black Panther Party for Self-Defense founded.
- *Miranda v. Arizona.*
- National Organization for Women (NOW) founded.

1967
- *Loving v. Virginia.*

1968
- Martin Luther King Jr. assassinated.
- American Indian Movement (AIM) founded.
- Republican Richard M. Nixon elected president.

1969
- Stonewall riots.

1970
- First Earth Day celebrated.
- Environmental Protection Agency (EPA) established.
- Clean Air Act.

1971
- Constitutional amendment lowers voting age to eighteen.

1972
- Title IX of Education Amendments Act.
- Congress passes Equal Rights Amendment; sends it to states for ratification.
- American Indians' "Trail of Broken Treaties" caravan to Washington, D.C.

1973
- *Roe v. Wade.*

FATIGUE HAT
This fatigue hat belonged to a soldier who served two tours of duty in Vietnam. The button reflects some veterans' response to the many Americans who just wanted to forget the war that had torn the country apart and that it had failed to win. Because their war was so different from other American wars, Vietnam veterans often returned home to hostility or indifference. Gradually attitudes about those who fought shifted, symbolized by the erection of the Vietnam Veterans Memorial, shown in the background. After the memorial was dedicated in 1982, millions of Americans visited it each year.

29

Vietnam and the End of the Cold War Consensus
1961–1975

LIEUTENANT FREDERICK DOWNS GREW UP ON A FARM IN INDIANA, played football in high school, and finished three years of college before enlisting in the army at the age of twenty-two. Leaving a ten-month-old daughter behind, he graduated from officer candidate school at Fort Benning, Georgia, and arrived in Vietnam in September 1967, prepared to lead an infantry platoon. He and his fellow soldiers went to Vietnam, "cocky and sure of our destiny, gung ho, invincible."

That confidence was tempered by the conditions he found in Vietnam. Unlike most of America's previous wars, there was no fixed battle front; helicopters ferried fighting units all over South Vietnam, as U.S. and South Vietnamese troops attempted to defeat the South Vietnamese rebels and their North Vietnamese allies. In a civil conflict characterized by guerrilla warfare, Downs led his men out on search-and-destroy missions in areas where they struggled to distinguish civilians from combatants and burned down villages just because they might be used by the enemy. He had faith that his country could win the war, but he found its ally, the South Vietnamese army, to be lazy and ineffective. "Maybe the people in Nam are worth saving, but their army isn't worth shit," he wrote in his memoir. Downs won several medals for bravery, but his one-year stint in Vietnam was cut short when a land mine blew off his left arm and wedged shrapnel into his legs and back.

Downs's service in Vietnam came at the height of a U.S. engagement that began with the Cold War commitments made in the 1940s and 1950s by Presidents Harry S. Truman and Dwight D. Eisenhower. John F. Kennedy wholeheartedly took on those commitments, promising more flexible and vigorous efforts to thwart communism. The most memorable words of his 1961 inaugural address declared that the United States would "pay any price, bear any burden, meet any hardship, support any friend, oppose any foe to assure the survival and the success of liberty."

Lieutenant Frederick Downs, Jr., in 1967
Frederick Downs—shown here before he lost his arm in Vietnam—returned from the war with a shoulder full of medals and spent the rest of his life helping other soldiers. After earning a masters degree in business administration, he worked for the Veterans Administration and eventually became director of its prosthetics and sensory aids program. In the 1980s, Downs visited Vietnam several times. As he got to know the former enemy as individuals, he lost the hatred he had once harbored, feeling "only sorrow at the ways of man." Collection of Frederick Downs.

Vietnam became the foremost test of John F. Kennedy's anticommunism. He sent increasing amounts of American arms and personnel to sustain the South Vietnamese government, but it was Lyndon B. Johnson who dramatically escalated that commitment in 1965 and turned a civil war among the Vietnamese into America's war. At peak strength in 1968, 543,000 U.S. military personnel served in Vietnam; all told, some 2.6 million saw duty there. Yet this massive intervention not only failed to defeat North Vietnam but also created intense discord at home, "poisoning the soul of America," as Downs put it. It cost President Johnson another term in office and contributed to the downfall of his Republican successor, Richard M. Nixon. Some Americans supported the government's goal in Vietnam and decried only its failure to pursue it effectively. Others believed that preserving a non-Communist South Vietnam was neither in the best interests of the United States nor within its capacity or moral right to achieve. Back home in college after months of surgery, Downs encountered a man who asked about the hook descending from his sleeve. When he said that he had lost his arm in Vietnam, the man shot back, "Serves you right."

This internal conflict was just one of the war's great costs. Like Downs, more than 150,000 soldiers suffered severe wounds, and more than 58,000 lost their lives. Martin Luther King Jr. mourned "the promises of the Great Society . . . shot down on the battlefield of Vietnam." In addition to derailing domestic reform, the war depleted the federal budget, disrupted the economy, kindled internal conflict, and led to the violation of protesters' rights, leaving a lasting mark on the nation.

Even while fighting communism in Vietnam and, on a much smaller scale, in other third world countries, American leaders moved to ease Cold War tensions with the major Communist powers. After a dramatic standoff with the Soviet Union during the Cuban missile crisis, the United States began to cooperate with its Cold War enemy to limit the spread of nuclear weapons. In addition, Nixon's historic visit to China in 1972 marked the abandonment of the policy of isolating China and paved the way for normal diplomatic relations by the end of the 1970s.

▶ New Frontiers in Foreign Policy

John F. Kennedy moved quickly to pursue containment more aggressively and with more flexible means. In contrast to the Eisenhower administration's emphasis on nuclear weapons, Kennedy expanded not only the nation's nuclear capacity but also its ability to fight conventional battles and to engage in guerrilla warfare. To ensure U.S. superiority over the Soviet Union in every domain, Kennedy accelerated the nation's space exploration program and increased attention to the third world. When the Soviets tried to establish a nuclear outpost in the Western Hemisphere in Cuba in 1962, he took the United States to the brink of war. Less dramatically but no less resolutely, Kennedy sent increasing amounts of American arms and personnel to save the South Vietnamese government from Communist insurgents.

Meeting the "Hour of Maximum Danger"

Underlying Kennedy's foreign policy was an assumption that the United States had "gone soft — physically, mentally, spiritually soft," as he put it in 1960. Calling the Eisenhower era "years of drift and impotency," he associated that administration with femininity when he mocked Nixon's celebration of American consumer goods in the kitchen debate with **Nikita Khrushchev**. "I would rather take my television black and white and have the largest rockets in the world,"

MAP ACTIVITY

Map 29.1   U.S. Involvement in Latin America and the Caribbean, 1954–1994
During the Cold War, the United States frequently intervened in Central American and Caribbean countries to suppress Communist or leftist movements.

READING THE MAP: How many and which Latin American countries did the United States invade directly? What was the extent of indirect U.S. involvement in other upheavals in the region?
CONNECTIONS: What role, if any, did geographic proximity play in U.S. policy toward the region? What was the significance of the Cuban missile crisis for U.S. foreign policy?

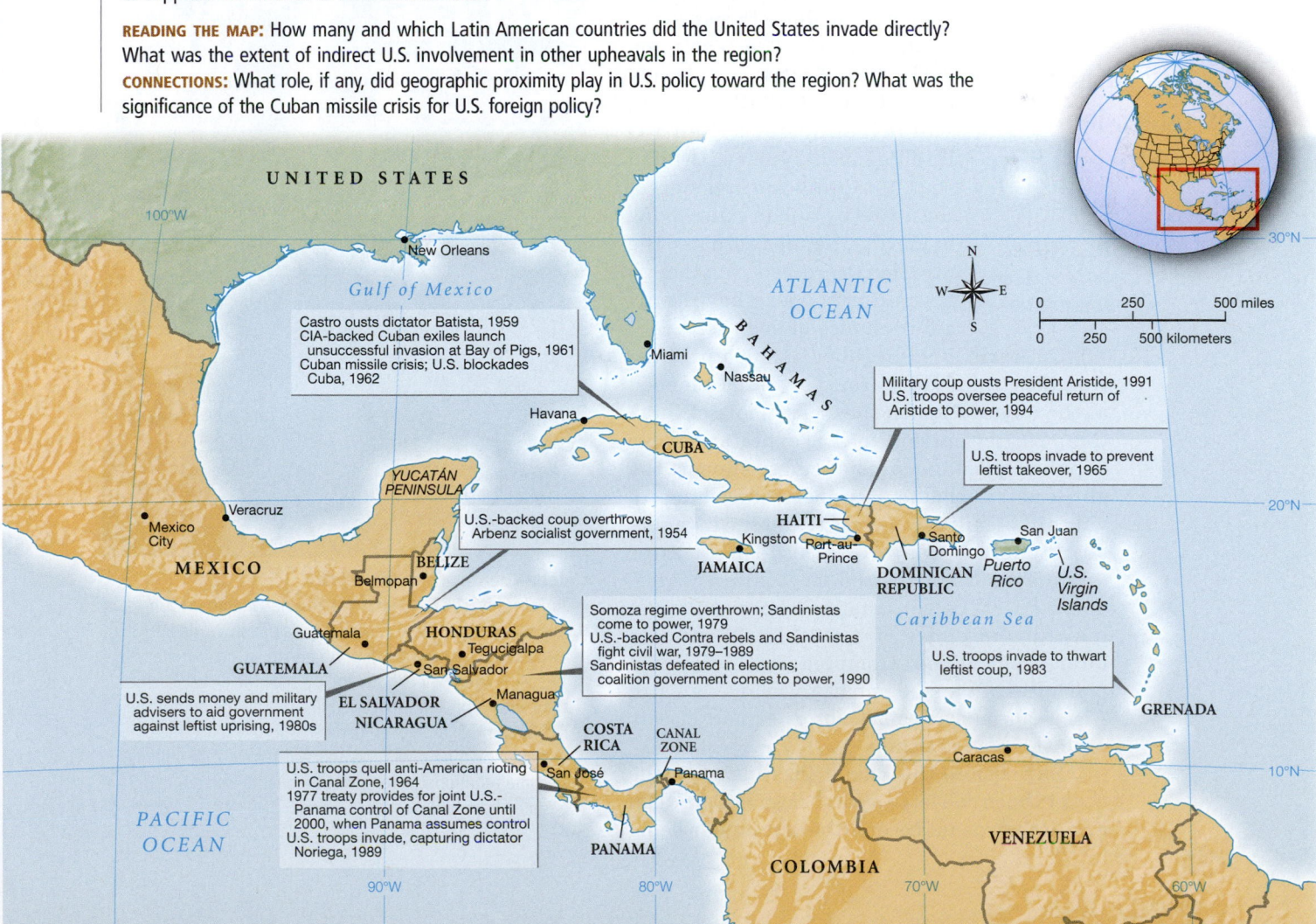

Kennedy declared. Criticizing the Eisenhower administration for relying too heavily on nuclear weapons, Kennedy built up conventional ground forces to provide a flexible response to Communist expansion. He also charged that limits on defense spending had caused the United States to fall behind even in nuclear capability. In January 1961, Kennedy warned that the nation faced a grave peril: "Each day the crises multiply. . . . Each day we draw nearer the hour of maximum danger."

Kennedy exaggerated the threat to national security; the United States remained ahead of the Soviets in nuclear capacity. Yet several developments in 1961 heightened the sense of crisis and provided a rationalization for his military buildup. Shortly before Kennedy's inauguration, Khrushchev publicly encouraged "wars of national liberation," thereby aligning the Soviet Union with independence movements in the third world that were often anti-Western. His statement reflected in part the Soviet competition with China for the allegiance of emerging nations, but U.S. officials saw in his words a threat to the status quo of containment.

Cuba, just ninety miles off the Florida coast, posed the most immediate threat to the United States. The revolution led by **Fidel Castro** had already moved Cuba into the Soviet orbit, and Eisenhower's Central Intelligence Agency (CIA) had been planning an invasion of the island by Cuban exiles living in Florida. Kennedy ordered the invasion to proceed even though his military advisers gave it only a fair chance of success.

> **"I would rather take my television black and white and have the largest rockets in the world."**
>
> — President
> **JOHN F. KENNEDY**

On April 17, 1961, about 1,400 anti-Castro exiles trained and armed by the CIA landed at the **Bay of Pigs** on the south shore of Cuba (Map 29.1). Contrary to U.S. expectations, no popular uprising materialized to support the anti-Castro brigade. Kennedy refused to provide direct military support, and the invaders quickly fell to Castro's forces. The disaster humiliated Kennedy and the United States, posing a stark contrast to the president's inaugural promise of a new, more effective foreign policy. The attempted invasion evoked memories of Yankee imperialism among Latin Americans and aligned Cuba even more closely with the Soviet Union.

Days before the Bay of Pigs invasion, the Soviet Union delivered a psychological blow when a Soviet astronaut became the first human being to orbit the earth. In May 1961, Kennedy called for a huge new commitment to the space program, with the goal of sending a man to the moon by 1970. Congress authorized the **Apollo program** and boosted appropriations for space exploration. John H. Glenn orbited the earth in 1962, and the United States beat the Soviets to the moon, landing two astronauts there in 1969.

Early in his presidency, Kennedy determined to show American toughness to Khrushchev. But when the two met in June 1961 in Vienna, Austria, Khrushchev was belligerent and shook the president's confidence. The stunned Kennedy reported privately, "He just beat [the] hell out of me. . . . If he thinks I'm inexperienced and have no guts . . . we won't get anywhere with him." Khrushchev demanded an agreement recognizing the existence of two Germanys and made veiled threats about America's occupation rights in and access to West Berlin.

Khrushchev was concerned about the massive exodus of East Germans into West Berlin,

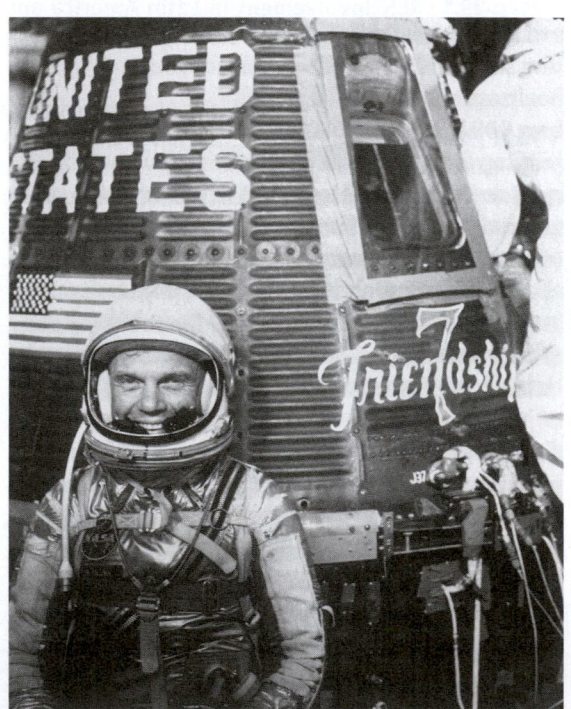

John Glenn Orbits the Earth
In February 1962, 40-year-old Marine Lieutenant John Glenn, who had flown combat missions in World War II and Korea, became the first American to circle the earth in space. The Soviets had already sent their own cosmonaut into orbit ten months earlier, but by the end of the 1960s the U.S. took over leadership in the space race. Glenn, shown here with his spacecraft before the flight, became a national hero and subsequently served as U.S. Senator from Ohio. © Bettmann/Corbis.

a major embarrassment for the Communists. To stop this flow, in August 1961 East Germany shocked the world by erecting a wall between East and West Berlin. With the **Berlin Wall** stemming the tide of migration and Kennedy insisting that West Berlin was "the great testing place of Western courage and will," Khrushchev backed off from his threats. But not until 1972 did the superpowers recognize East and West Germany as separate nations and guarantee Western access to West Berlin.

Kennedy used the Berlin crisis to add $3.2 billion to the defense budget. He increased draft calls and mobilized the reserves and National Guard, adding 300,000 troops to the military. This buildup of conventional forces provided for a "flexible response," offering "a wider choice than humiliation or all-out nuclear action." Still, Kennedy also pushed for the development of new nuclear weapons and delivery systems, more than doubling the nation's nuclear force within three years.

Peace Corps Volunteers Build a School in Gabon
Young men and women who joined the Peace Corps helped increase food production, build public works, and curb diseases in developing countries, but the majority worked on educational projects. In this photo taken in 1964, volunteers work side-by-side with a local resident to build a school in the west central African nation of Gabon, which had won its independence from France in 1960. James P. Blair/National Geographic/Getty Images.

New Approaches to the Third World

Complementing Kennedy's hard-line policy toward the Soviet Union were fresh approaches to the nationalist movements that had multiplied since the end of World War II. In 1960 alone, seventeen African nations gained their independence. Much more than his predecessors, Kennedy publicly supported third world aspirations, believing that the United States could win the hearts and minds of people in developing nations by helping to fulfill hopes for autonomy and democracy.

To that end, Kennedy created the Alliance for Progress in 1961, pledging $20 billion in Latin American aid over the next decade. Like the Marshall Plan (see chapter 26), the Alliance for Progress was designed to thwart communism and hold nations within the American sphere by fostering economic development. Yet by 1969, the United States had provided only half of the promised $20 billion, much of which went to military projects or corrupt ruling elites.

Kennedy launched his most dramatic third world initiative in 1961 with an idea borrowed from Senator Hubert H. Humphrey: the **Peace Corps**. The program recruited young people to work in developing countries, attracting many who had been moved by Kennedy's appeal for idealism and sacrifice in his inaugural address. One volunteer's service eased his guilt at having been "born between clean sheets when others were issued into the dust with a birthright of hunger." After studying a country's language and culture, Peace Corps volunteers went to work directly with its people, opening schools, providing basic health care, and assisting with agriculture and small economic enterprises. By the mid-1970s, more than 60,000 volunteers had served in Latin America, Africa, and Asia. Peace Corps projects were generally welcomed, but they did not address the receiving countries' larger economic and political structures.

Kennedy also used direct military means to bring political stability to the third world. He rapidly expanded the elite special forces corps established under Eisenhower to aid groups fighting against Communist-leaning movements. These counterinsurgency forces, including the army's Green Berets and the navy's SEALs, were trained to wage guerrilla warfare and equipped with the latest technology. They would get their first test in Vietnam.

The Arms Race and the Nuclear Brink

The final piece of Kennedy's defense strategy was to strengthen American nuclear dominance. He upped the number of nuclear weapons based in Europe from 2,500 to 7,200 and multiplied fivefold the supply of intercontinental ballistic missiles (ICBMs). Concerned that this buildup would enable the United States to launch a first strike and wipe out Soviet missile sites before they could respond, the Soviet Union stepped up its own ICBM program. Thus began the most intense arms race in history.

The superpowers came perilously close to using their weapons during the **Cuban missile crisis** in 1962. Khrushchev decided to install nuclear missiles in Cuba to protect Castro's regime from further U.S. attempts at intervention and to balance the U.S. missiles aimed at the Soviet Union from Britain, Italy, and Turkey. The thirteen-day crisis began on October 16, when the CIA showed Kennedy aerial photographs of missile launching sites under construction. Considering this an intolerable threat to the United States, the president decided to react. On October 22, he announced to a television audience that the military was on full alert and that the navy would turn back any Soviet vessel suspected of carrying offensive missiles to Cuba. Kennedy warned that any attack launched from Cuba would trigger a full nuclear assault against the Soviet Union.

Projecting the appearance of toughness was paramount to President Kennedy. Conceding that the missiles did not "alter the strategic balance in fact," one of his aides insisted that "that balance would have been

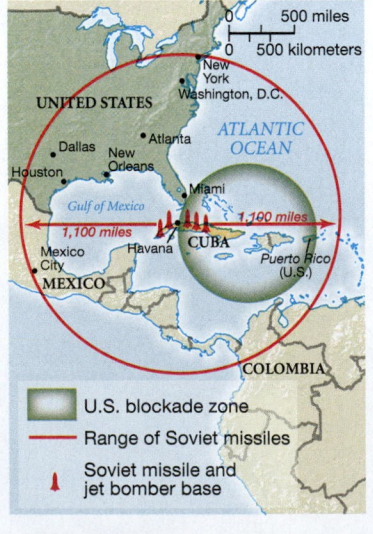

Cuban Missile Crisis, 1962

substantially altered in appearance; and in matters of national will and world leadership such appearances contribute to reality." Kennedy also worried that "Communism and Castroism are going to be spread [in Latin America] as governments frightened by this new evidence of power [fall]."

But if Kennedy risked nuclear war for appearances, both he and Khrushchev also exercised caution. Kennedy refused advice from the military to bomb the missile sites. On October 24, Russian ships carrying nuclear warheads toward Cuba suddenly turned back. When one ship crossed the blockade line, Kennedy ordered the navy to follow the ship rather than attempt to stop it.

While Americans experienced the Cold War's most dangerous days, Kennedy and Khrushchev negotiated an agreement. The Soviets removed the missiles and pledged not to introduce new offensive weapons into Cuba. The United States promised not to invade the island. Secretly, Kennedy also agreed to remove U.S. missiles from Turkey. The Cuban crisis contributed to Khrushchev's fall from power two years later, while Kennedy emerged triumphant. "I cut his balls off," Kennedy rejoiced in private. The image of an inexperienced president fumbling the Bay of Pigs invasion gave way to that of a strong leader bearing the United States through its "hour of maximum danger."

Having proved his toughness, Kennedy worked with Khrushchev to prevent future confrontations by installing a special "hot line" to speed top-level communication. In a major speech at American University in June 1963, Kennedy called for a reexamination of Cold War assumptions, asking Americans "not to see conflict as inevitable." Acknowledging the superpowers' differences, Kennedy stressed

Preparing for the Worst during the Cuban Missile Crisis
Waiting out the tense days after President Kennedy issued the ultimatum to the Soviet Union to halt shipments of missile materials to Cuba, many Americans prepared for the worst possible outcome. Owners of Chalet Suzanne, a hotel in Lake Wales, Florida—less than 500 miles from Cuba—canned several thousand cases of well water, labeled "NASK" for Nuclear Attack Survival Kit. The background is a U.S. Navy reconnaissance photo taken on October 23, 1962, showing details of the missile site in Cuba. Can of water: Courtesy Chalet Suzanne Foods, Inc., Lake Wales, Florida. Photo by David Woods; reconnaissance photo: © Bettmann/Corbis.

U.S. Involvement in Vietnam

1954 French colonial presence ends with Vietnamese victory at Dien Bien Phu.

Geneva accords establish temporary division of North and South Vietnam at seventeenth parallel and provide for free elections.

United States joins with European, East Asian, and other nations to form Southeast Asia Treaty Organization.

Eisenhower administration begins to send weapons and military advisers to South Vietnam to bolster Diem government.

1955– 1961 United States sends $800 million in aid to South Vietnamese army (ARVN) to support its struggle with South Vietnamese rebels and their North Vietnamese allies.

1961– 1963 Under Kennedy administration, military aid to South Vietnam doubles, and number of military advisers reaches 9,000.

1963 South Vietnamese military overthrows Diem's government.

1964 President Johnson uses Gulf of Tonkin incident to escalate war.

1965 Johnson administration initiates Operation Rolling Thunder, intensifying bombing of North Vietnam.

1965– 1967 Number of U.S. troops in Vietnam increases, reaching 543,000 in 1968, but U.S. and ARVN forces make only limited progress against the guerrilla forces, resulting in a stalemate.

1968 Tet Offensive causes widespread destruction and heavy casualties.

Johnson announces reduction in bombing of North Vietnam, plans for peace talks, and his decision not to run for another presidential term.

1969 Nixon administration initiates secret bombing of Cambodia, increases bombing of North Vietnam while reducing U.S. troops in the South, and pursues peace talks.

1970 Nixon orders joint U.S.-ARVN invasion of Cambodia.

1970– 1971 U.S. troops in Vietnam decrease from 334,600 to 140,000.

1972 With peace talks stalled in December, Nixon administration orders the war's most devastating bombing of North Vietnam.

1973 On January 27, United States, North Vietnam, and South Vietnam sign formal accord in Paris marking end of U.S. involvement.

1975 North Vietnam launches new offensive in South Vietnam, defeating ARVN. Vietcong troops occupy Saigon, renaming it Ho Chi Minh City.

what they had in common: "We all breathe the same air. We all cherish our children's future and we are all mortal." In August 1963, the United States, the Soviet Union, and Great Britain signed a limited nuclear test ban treaty, reducing the threat of radioactive fallout from nuclear testing and raising hopes for further superpower accord.

A Growing War in Vietnam

In his American University speech, Kennedy criticized the idea of "a Pax Americana enforced on the world by American weapons of war," but in 1961 he began to increase the flow of those weapons into South Vietnam. Kennedy's strong anticommunism and attachment to a vigorous foreign policy prepared him to expand the commitment in Vietnam that he had inherited from Eisenhower. Convinced that China and the Soviet Union were behind the efforts of North Vietnamese leader **Ho Chi Minh** to unify Vietnam under communism, Kennedy's key military adviser, General Maxwell Taylor, argued that holding firm in Vietnam would show the Soviets and Chinese that wars of national liberation were "costly, dangerous, and doomed to failure."

By the time Kennedy took office, more than $1 billion in aid and seven hundred U.S. military advisers had failed to stabilize South Vietnam. Two major obstacles stood in the way. First, the South Vietnamese insurgents — whom Americans called Vietcong, short for *Vietnam Cong-san* ("Vietnamese Communists") — were an indigenous force whose initiative came from within, not from the Soviet Union or China. Because the Saigon government refused to hold elections, the rebels saw no choice but to take up arms. Increasingly, Ho Chi Minh's Communist government in North Vietnam supplied them with weapons and soldiers.

Second, the South Vietnamese government refused to satisfy the demands of the insurgents, but the **Army of the Republic of Vietnam (ARVN)** could not defeat them militarily. Ngo Dinh Diem, South Vietnam's premier from 1954 to 1963, chose self-serving military leaders for their personal loyalty rather than for their effectiveness. Many South Vietnamese, the majority of whom were Buddhists, saw the Catholic Diem as a corrupt and brutal tool of the West. Even Secretary of State Dean Rusk called him "an oriental despot."

The growing intervention by North Vietnam made matters worse. In 1960, the Hanoi government established the **National Liberation Front (NLF)**, composed of South Vietnamese rebels but directed by the northern army. In addition, Hanoi constructed a network of infiltration routes, called the Ho Chi Minh Trail, in neighboring Laos and Cambodia, through which it sent people and supplies to help liberate the South (Map 29.2). Violence escalated between 1960 and 1963, bringing the Saigon government close to collapse.

Kennedy responded to the deteriorating situation with measured steps. Some advisers called for using any force necessary to save South Vietnam from communism. Others questioned whether such a victory was either necessary or possible. Taking the middle ground, Kennedy gradually escalated the U.S. commitment. By the spring of 1963, military aid had doubled, and the 9,000 Americans serving in Vietnam as military advisers occasionally participated in actual combat. The South Vietnamese government promised reform but never made good on its promises.

Reflecting racist attitudes of American superiority over nonwhite populations, officials assumed that U.S. technology and sheer power could win in Vietnam. Yet advanced weapons were ill suited to the guerrilla warfare practiced by the enemy, whose surprise attacks were designed to weaken support for the South Vietnamese government. In addition, U.S. weapons and strategy harmed the very people they were intended to save. Thousands of peasants were uprooted and resettled in "strategic hamlets," supposedly secure from the Communists. Those left in the countryside fell victim to bombs — containing the highly flammable substance napalm — dropped by the South Vietnamese air force to quell the Vietcong. In January 1962, U.S. planes began to spray herbicides such as **Agent Orange** to destroy the Vietcong's jungle hideouts and food supply.

With tacit permission from Washington, South Vietnamese military leaders executed a coup against Diem and his brother, who headed the secret police, in November 1963. Kennedy expressed shock when the two were murdered but indicated no change in policy. In a speech to be given on the day he was assassinated, Kennedy referred specifically to Southeast Asia and warned, "We dare not weary of the task." At his death, 16,700 Americans were stationed in Vietnam, and 100 had died there.

REVIEW Why did Kennedy believe that engagement in Vietnam was crucial to his foreign policy?

MAP ACTIVITY

Map 29.2 The Vietnam War, 1964–1975
The United States sent 2.6 million soldiers to Vietnam and spent more than $150 billion on the longest war in American history, but it was unable to prevent the unification of Vietnam under a Communist government.

READING THE MAP: What accords divided Vietnam into two nations? When were these accords signed, and where was the line of division drawn? Through what countries did the Ho Chi Minh Trail go?
CONNECTIONS: What was the Gulf of Tonkin incident, and how did the United States respond? What was the Tet Offensive, and how did it affect the war?

► Lyndon Johnson's War against Communism

The Cold War assumptions that had shaped Kennedy's foreign policy underlay his successor's approach to Southeast Asia and Latin America. Retaining Kennedy's key advisers — Secretary of State Rusk, Secretary of Defense Robert McNamara, and National Security Adviser McGeorge Bundy — **Lyndon B. Johnson** continued the massive buildup of nuclear weapons and conventional and counterinsurgency forces. In 1965, Johnson made the fateful decisions to order U.S. troops into combat in Vietnam and to initiate sustained bombing of the North. That same year, Johnson sent U.S. Marines to the Dominican Republic to crush a leftist rebellion.

> **"I don't think it's worth fighting for and I don't think we can get out."**
> — President LYNDON B. JOHNSON, speaking of Vietnam

An All-Out Commitment in Vietnam

The president who wanted to make his mark on domestic policy was compelled to deal with the commitments his predecessors had made in Vietnam. Some advisers, politicians, and international leaders raised questions about the wisdom of a greater commitment there, viewing the situation as a civil war rather than Communist aggression. Most U.S. allies did not consider Vietnam crucial to containing communism and were not prepared to share the military burden in more than token ways. Senate majority leader Mike Mansfield wondered whether Vietnam could be won with a "limited expenditure of American lives and resources somewhere commensurate with our national interests." Johnson expressed his own doubt privately: "I don't think it's worth fighting for and I don't think we can get out."

Believing that the nation's reputation as a staunch defender against communism was on the line, the president expanded the United States' military involvement. Moreover, like Kennedy, he remembered how Truman had suffered politically when the Communists took over China. Johnson wanted to prevent Republicans from charging that Democrats were weak on national security, and he believed that conceding defeat in Vietnam would undermine his ability to achieve his Great Society.

Johnson understood the ineffectiveness of his South Vietnamese allies and agonized over sending young men into combat. Yet he continued to dispatch more military advisers, weapons, and economic aid and, in August 1964, seized an opportunity to increase the pressure on North Vietnam. While spying in the Gulf of Tonkin, off the coast of North Vietnam, two U.S. destroyers reported that North Vietnamese gunboats had fired on them (see Map 29.2). Johnson quickly ordered air strikes on North Vietnamese torpedo bases and oil storage facilities. Concealing the uncertainty about whether the second attack

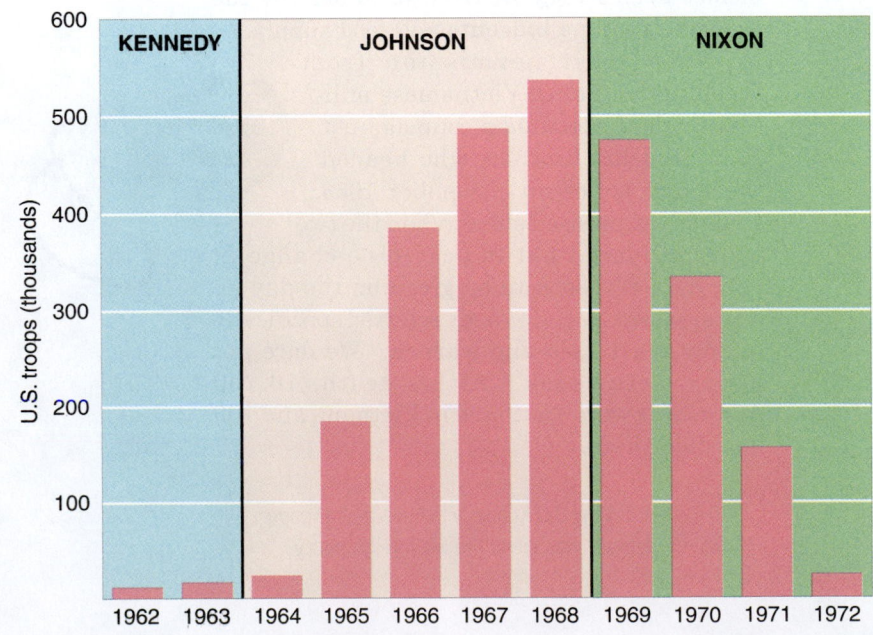

FIGURE 29.1 U.S. Troops in Vietnam, 1962–1972
The steepest increases in the American military presence in Vietnam came with Johnson's escalation of the war in 1965 and 1966. Although Nixon reduced troop levels significantly in 1971 and 1972, the United States continued massive bombing attacks.

had even occurred and the provocative U.S. operations along the North Vietnamese coast, he won from Congress the **Gulf of Tonkin Resolution**, authorizing him to take "all necessary measures to repel any armed attacks against the forces of the United States and to prevent further aggression."

The president's tough stance only two months before the 1964 election helped counter the charges made by his opponent, Arizona senator Barry Goldwater, that he was "soft on communism." Yet Johnson also presented himself as the peace candidate, assuring Americans that "we are not going to send American boys nine or ten thousand miles away from home to do what Asian boys ought to be doing for themselves."

Johnson might have used the political capital from his overwhelming reelection victory to disengage from Vietnam. Instead he widened the war, rejecting peace overtures from North Vietnam, because it insisted on American withdrawal and a coalition government in South Vietnam as steps toward ultimate unification of the country. In February 1965, Johnson authorized **Operation Rolling Thunder**, a strategy of gradually intensified bombing of North Vietnam. Less than a month later, Johnson ordered the first U.S. combat troops to South Vietnam, and in July he shifted U.S. troops from defensive to offensive operations, dispatching 50,000 more soldiers (Figure 29.1). Although the administration downplayed the import of these decisions, they marked a critical turning point. Now it was genuinely America's war.

Preventing Another Castro in Latin America

Closer to home, Johnson faced persistent problems in Latin America. Thirteen times during the 1960s, military coups toppled Latin American governments, and local insurgencies grew apace. The administration's response varied from case to case but centered on the determination to prevent any more Castro-type revolutions.

In 1964, riots erupted in the Panama Canal Zone, which the United States had seized and made a U.S. territory early in the century (see chapter 21). Instigated by Panamanians who viewed the United States as a colonial power, the riots left four U.S. soldiers and more than twenty Panamanians dead. Johnson sent troops to quell the disturbance, but he also initiated negotiations that eventually returned the canal to Panamanian authority in 2000.

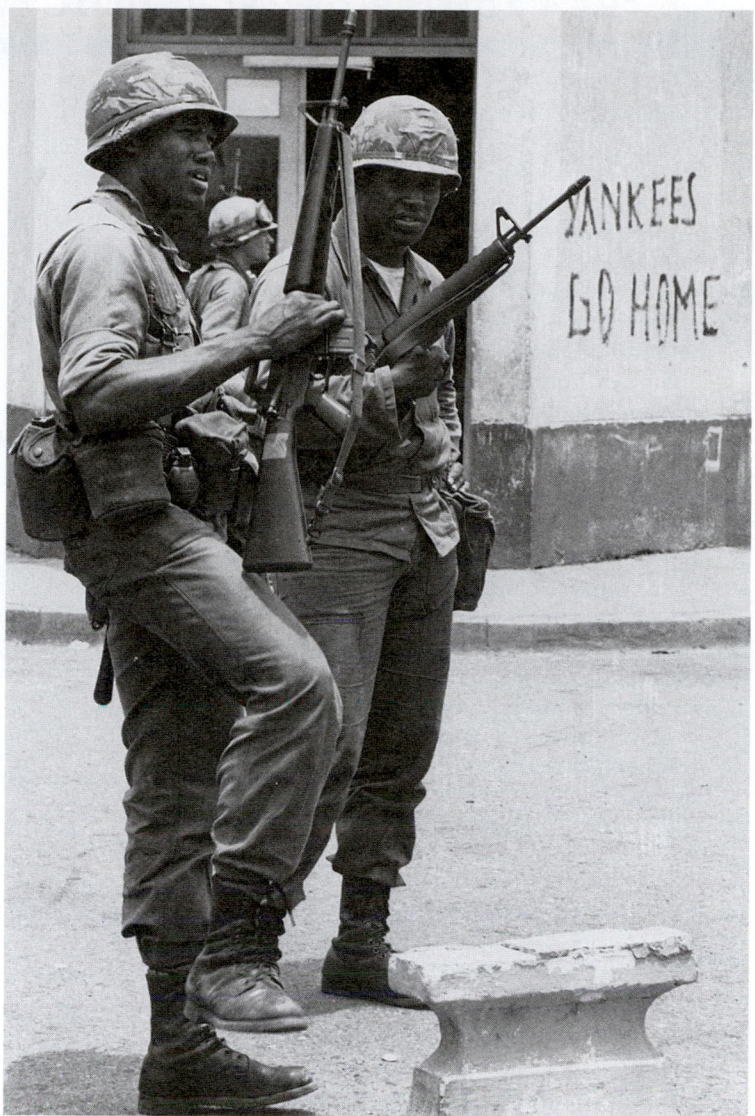

U.S. Troops in the Dominican Republic
These U.S. paratroopers were among the 20,000 troops sent to the Dominican Republic in April and May 1965. The American invasion helped restore peace but kept the popularly elected government of Juan Bosch from regaining office. Dominicans expressed their outrage in anti-American slogans that greeted troops throughout the capital, Santo Domingo. Bosch himself said, "This was a democratic revolution smashed by the leading democracy in the world." © Bettmann/Corbis.

Elsewhere, Johnson's Latin American policy generated new cries of "Yankee imperialism." In 1961, voters in the Dominican Republic ousted a longtime dictator and elected a constitutional government headed by reformist Juan Bosch, who was overthrown by a military coup two years later. In 1965, when Bosch supporters launched an uprising against the military government, Johnson sent more than 20,000 soldiers to quell what he perceived to be a leftist revolt and to take control of the island. A truce was arranged,

THE PROMISE OF TECHNOLOGY

The Military Helicopter

The U.S. military employed helicopters for medical evacuations in Korea, but not until smaller, lighter gas-turbine engines replaced piston engines did helicopters play a central role in war. Particular conditions in Vietnam — the guerrilla tactics of the enemy, the conduct of fighting all over South Vietnam rather than across a fixed battlefront, and the mountains and dense jungles with limited landing areas — put a premium on the helicopter's mobility and maneuverability. Choppers carried infantry units all over South Vietnam, transported artillery and ammunition, performed reconnaissance, picked up downed pilots, and evacuated the dead and wounded. Mounted with machine guns and grenade launchers, helicopters also served as attack vehicles. Here men of the First Squadron, Ninth Cavalry, First Cavalry Division leap from a Bell UH-1 Iro-

quois ("Huey") helicopter near Chu Lai, South Vietnam, in 1967 as they begin a reconnaissance mission. © Bettmann/ Corbis.

and in 1966 Dominicans voted in a constitutional government under a moderate rightist.

This first outright show of Yankee force in Latin America in four decades damaged the administration at home and abroad. Although Johnson had justified intervention as necessary to prevent "another Cuba," no Communists were found among the rebels, and U.S. intervention kept the reform-oriented Boschists from returning to power. Moreover, the president had not consulted the Dominicans or the Organization of American States (OAS), to which the United States had promised it would respect national sovereignty in Latin America.

The Americanized War

The military success in the Dominican Republic no doubt encouraged the president to press on in Vietnam. From 1965 to early 1968, the United States gradually escalated the war. While increasing numbers of U.S. troops fought the National Liberation Front in South Vietnam, Operation Rolling Thunder sought to break the will and capacity of the North Vietnamese to support the insurgents. Johnson carefully calibrated the attacks, boasting, "They can't even bomb an outhouse without my approval."

Some military officials chafed at the restrictions placed on the air war, but Johnson remembered what had happened in Korea and that "China is there on the [North Vietnamese] border with 700 million men." The administration banned strikes near that border and on sites where Chinese or Soviet advisers might be present, determined to avoid provoking intervention by either China or the Soviet Union, both of which now possessed nuclear weapons. To contain both domestic and international criticism of the war, Johnson also prohibited bombing targets where high civilian casualties might result.

Despite restrictions, U.S. pilots dropped 643,000 tons of bombs on North Vietnam and more than twice that amount in the South, a total surpassing all the explosives the United States dropped in World War II. Yet the bombing was no match for the determination and ingenuity of the North Vietnamese. Their sheer effort compensated for the destruction of transportation lines, industry sites, and power plants. For example, when bombs struck a rail line, civilians rushed in with bicycles to unload a train's cargo, carry it beyond the break, and load it onto a second train. In South Vietnam, the massive U.S. bombing campaign destroyed villages and fields, alienating the very population that the Americans had come to save.

On the ground, General William Westmoreland's strategy of attrition was designed to seek out and kill the Vietcong and North Vietnamese regular army. With no fixed battle front, officials calculated progress not in territory seized but in "body counts" and "kill ratios" — the number of enemies killed relative to the cost in American and ARVN lives. According to Lieutenant Frederick Downs, "To win a battle, we had to kill them. For them to win, all they had to do was survive." He realized that "we would fight and bleed to take ground," and the enemy would withdraw "after they had exacted their toll"; but then U.S. forces would leave, and the Vietcong could come back whenever they liked. The Americans, Downs said, "never owned anything except the ground they stood on."

Those Who Served

Teenagers fought the Vietnam War, in contrast to World War II, in which the average soldier was twenty-six years old. All the men in Lieutenant Downs's platoon were between the ages of eighteen and twenty-one, and the average age for all soldiers was nineteen. Until a constitutional amendment dropped the voting age from twenty-one to eighteen in 1971, most could not even vote for the officials who sent them to war. Men of all classes had fought in World War II, but in Vietnam the poor and working class constituted about 80 percent of the troops. More privileged youths avoided the draft by using college deferments or family connections to get into the National Guard. Sent from Plainville, Kansas, to Vietnam in 1965, Mike Clodfelter could not recall "a single middle-class son of the town's businessmen, lawyers, doctors, or ranchers from my high school graduating class who experienced the Armageddon of our generation."

Much more than World War II, Vietnam was a men's war. Because the United States did not undergo full mobilization for Vietnam, officials did not seek women's sacrifices for the war effort. Still, between 7,500 and 10,000 women served in Vietnam, the vast majority of them nurses. Some women were exposed to enemy fire, and eight lost their lives. Many more struggled with their helplessness in the face of the dead and maimed bodies they tended. "When you finally saved a life," said Peggy DuVall, "you wondered what kind of life you had saved."

Early in the war, African Americans constituted 31 percent of combat troops, often choosing

Counting the Days in Vietnam
Unlike previous wars, most soldiers served tours of duty in Vietnam lasting just one year. The soldier who carried this calendar expressed an obsession with time "in country" that many of his comrades shared. Soldiers considered themselves "short" when they had fewer than 100 days left. Bobby McMaster was thinking of either his wife or of the woman he would marry when, and if, he returned home. What might his inscription of the Bible verse suggest about his feelings about the woman he left behind? © Bettmann/Corbis.

the military over the meager opportunities in the civilian economy. Special forces ranger Arthur E. Woodley Jr. recalled, "I was just what my country needed. A black patriot.... The only way I could possibly make it out of the ghetto was to be the best soldier I possibly could." Death rates among black soldiers were disproportionately high until 1966, when the military adjusted personnel assignments to achieve a better racial balance.

The young troops faced extremely difficult conditions. Frederick Downs's platoon fought in

Chemical Weapons
In 1964, the U.S. military began to use the tear gas CS (o-chlorobenzylidenemalononitrile) in grenades in Vietnam, discharging more than two million pounds of CS a year by 1969. Here, a Marine has just thrown a CS grenade into a tunnel to flush out the enemy and make the tunnel unusable for several months. Military planes also dispersed CS to rid large areas of enemy forces. CS is incapacitating but usually not lethal; nonetheless, its use evoked criticism both at home and abroad, including condemnation by the UN. Marine: James H. Pickerell/Stock Connection; Gas: Ordinance Museum/Aberdeen Proving Grounds.

thick jungles filled with leeches, in rain and oppressive heat, always vulnerable to sniper bullets and land mines. He remembered that "the terror of an explosion never failed to send a shiver through our guts." Soldiers in previous wars had served "for the duration," but in Vietnam a soldier served a one-year tour of duty. A commander called it "the worst personnel policy in history," because men had less incentive to fight near the end of their tours, wanting merely to stay alive and whole.

The U.S. military inflicted great losses on the enemy, yet the war remained a stalemate. Dispatched to an area thick with Vietcong sympathizers, Downs wondered how to win the people's hearts and minds: "How could we compete with countrymen who could speak to them, live with them, were related to them?" He remained convinced that his country was doing the right thing yet recognized that "all Vietnamese had a common desire — to see us go home."

The South Vietnamese government was an enormous obstacle to victory, even though in 1965 it settled into a period of stability when it was headed by two military leaders. Graft and corruption continued to flourish in the government. In the intensified fighting and with the inability to distinguish friend from foe, ARVN and American troops killed and wounded thousands of South Vietnamese civilians and destroyed their villages. By 1968, nearly 30 percent of the population had become refugees. The failure to stabilize South Vietnam even as the U.S. military presence expanded enormously created grave challenges for the administration at home.

REVIEW Why did massive amounts of airpower and ground troops fail to bring U.S. victory in Vietnam?

▶ A Nation Polarized

Soon President Johnson was fighting a war on two fronts. Domestic opposition to the war swelled after 1965 as daily television broadcasts made it the first "living-room war." In March 1968, torn between his domestic critics and the military's clamor for more troops, Johnson announced a halt to the bombing, a new effort at negotiations, and his decision not to pursue reelection. Throughout 1968, demonstrations, violence, and assassinations convulsed the increasingly polarized nation. Vietnam took center stage in the election, and voters narrowly favored the Republican candidate, former vice president Richard Nixon, who promised to achieve "peace with honor."

The Widening War at Home

Johnson's authorization of Operation Rolling Thunder expanded the previously quiet doubts and criticism into a mass movement against the war. In April 1965, Students for a Democratic Society (SDS) recruited 20,000 people for the first major demonstration against the war in Washington, D.C. SDS chapters sprang up on more than three hundred college campuses. Thousands of students protested against Reserve Officers Training Corps (ROTC) programs, CIA recruiters, military research projects, and manufacturers of war materiel. Martin Luther King Jr. deployed his moral authority, rebuking the U.S. government in 1967 as "the greatest purveyor of violence in the world today."

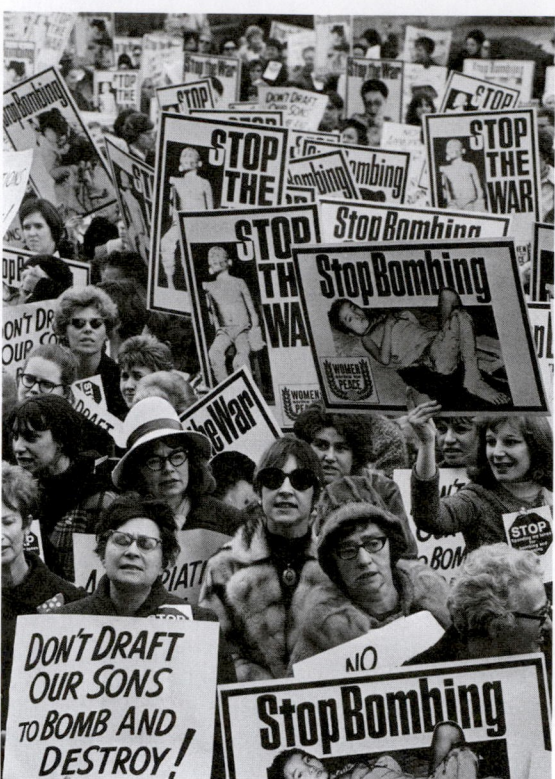

Mothers against the War
Founded in 1961 to work for nuclear disarmament, Women Strike for Peace (WSP) began to "alert the public to the dangers and horrors of the war in Vietnam" in 1963. Identifying themselves as "concerned housewives" and mothers, members mobilized around the slogan "Not Our Sons, Not Your Sons, Not Their Sons." In February 1967, WSP held the first antiwar protest at the Pentagon. More than 2,000 women, some shown here, banged their shoes on Pentagon doors, which were locked as they approached. What characteristics of the war did these women focus on? How were their objections to the war similar to and different from those of other protesters? © Bettmann/Corbis.

Environmentalists attacked the use of chemical weapons, such as the deadly Agent Orange.

Antiwar sentiment entered society's mainstream. The *New York Times* began questioning the war in 1965, and by 1968 media critics included the *Wall Street Journal, Life* magazine, and popular TV anchorman Walter Cronkite. Clergy, business people, scientists, and physicians formed their own groups to pressure Johnson to stop the bombing and start negotiations. Prominent Democratic senators, including J. William Fulbright, George McGovern, and Mike Mansfield, urged Johnson to substitute negotiation for force.

Opposition to the war took diverse forms: letters to officials, teach-ins on college campuses, mass marches, student strikes, withholding of federal taxes, draft card and flag burnings, and attempts to stop trains carrying troops. Although the peace movement never claimed a majority of the population, it focused media attention on the war and severely limited the administration's options. The twenty-year-old consensus around Cold War foreign policy had broken down.

Many would not fight in the war. The World Boxing Association stripped Muhammad Ali of his world heavyweight title when he refused to serve in what he called a "white man's war." More than 170,000 men who opposed the war on moral or religious grounds gained conscientious objector status and performed nonmilitary duties at home or in Vietnam. About 60,000 fled the country to escape the draft, and more than 200,000 were accused of failing to register or of committing other draft offenses.

Opponents of the war held diverse views. Those who saw the conflict in moral terms wanted total withdrawal, insisting that their country had no right to interfere in a civil war and stressing the suffering of the Vietnamese people. A larger segment of antiwar sentiment reflected practical considerations — the belief that the war could not be won at a bearable cost. Those activists wanted Johnson to stop bombing North Vietnam and seek negotiations.

Working-class people were no more antiwar than other groups, but they recognized the class dimensions of the war and the antiwar movement. A firefighter whose son had died in Vietnam said bitterly, "It's people like us who give up our sons for the country. The businesspeople, they run the country and make money from it. The college types . . . go to Washington and tell the government what to do. . . . But their sons don't end up in the swamps over there, in Vietnam." The antiwar movement outraged millions of Americans who supported the war. Some members of the generation who had fought against Hitler could not understand younger men's refusal to support their government. They expressed their anger at war protesters with bumper stickers that read "America: Love It or Leave It."

By 1967, the administration realized that "discontent with the war is now wide and deep." President Johnson used various means to silence critics. He equated opposition to the war with communism and assistance to the enemy. To avoid focusing attention on the war's costs, he eschewed measures to control inflation and delayed asking for a tax increase to pay for the

1968: A Year of Protest

To many people living through it, 1968 looked like the start of a worldwide political revolution. A surge of protests against the U.S. war in Vietnam and demands for greater democracy and economic justice jumped over borders and challenged authorities in many countries around the world. Although local grievances ignited many of the protests in 1968, a common feature of them all was the central role played by university students. The protests of 1968 unfolded rapidly, giving rise to excitement and apprehension. From February to December, demonstrations erupted in North and South America, Europe, and Asia. Many demonstrators expressed transnational solidarity by carrying the flag of Vietnam's National Liberation Front or placards bearing the image of Ernesto "Che" Guevara, a Latin American radical killed by the Bolivian military in 1967. And yet there was in fact little international coordination of events or any shared plan for remaking the world.

One of the first large-scale protests occurred in February at West Berlin's Free University, where some 10,000 participants from ten countries at the "Vietnam Congress" called for "an international manifestation of solidarity" with the people of Vietnam. Protests continued throughout the spring, prompting the West German government to pass emergency laws to stifle disorder. In February and March, demonstrations flared up in Madrid, Warsaw, Rome, São Paulo, and London, met by police with clubs. As with the protesters, police also took their cues from worldwide events, reacting more forcefully to demonstrations in light of commotions in other countries. Charges of police brutality, disseminated in television and newspaper reports, fed the cycle of protest further.

In April and May, violence erupted in the United States. Martin Luther King Jr.'s assassination on April 4 ignited riots in many U.S. cities. Less than a month later, students at Columbia University in New York City seized buildings and shut down the campus, leading to a bloody showdown between police and protesters.

In May, rebellion paralyzed France. It began with students' complaints about services at a university north of Paris and spread to the Sorbonne in the capital city. Police teargassed a small rally, only to face tens of thousands of students streaming into Paris over the next few days. Violence escalated as protesters barricaded streets. Independent radio stations broadcast live interviews with demonstrators, and soon a million people were in the streets. Workers joined the rebellion, shutting down factories across France. Students proclaimed that "exceptional domestic and international conditions" had brought powerless students and workers together around the world. By late May, France was in deep crisis.

Prague, the capital of Communist Czechoslovakia, also stirred in May. A liberal president, Alexander Dubček, pushed for reforms against heavy-handed Soviet control, giving rise to hopes for greater freedom. Students demonstrated, and thousands signed manifestos. But this "Prague Spring" was cut short in August when Soviet tanks rumbled into the country and Dubček was arrested. Throughout Europe, students marched on Soviet embassies to protest the crackdown. At the same moment in the United States, Chicago police battled young protesters near the Democratic National Convention.

In July, Mexican police attacked marchers carrying posters of Fidel Castro and Che Guevara. When thousands rallied against the violence, police fired into the crowd, killing several students. Violent clashes continued into August and September, as activists protested the Olympic Games, scheduled to open in Mexico City in October. Insisting that the money spent on the Olympics should have been used to alleviate the country's widespread poverty, protesters chanted, "We don't want Olympic Games; we want revolution." The upcoming Olympics created pressure for the authorities to clear the city of dissidents. When some 10,000 students assembled for a rally on October 2, jeeps with machine guns arrived. At

war. Not until June 1968 did Congress pass a 10 percent income tax surcharge. Great Society programs suffered, and the surcharge failed to check inflation.

The administration deceived the public by making optimistic statements and concealing officials' ever-graver doubts about the possibility of success in Vietnam. Johnson ordered the CIA to spy on peace advocates, and without the president's specific authorization, the FBI infiltrated the peace movement, disrupted its work, and spread false information about activists. Even the resort to illegal measures failed to subdue the opposition.

The Tet Offensive and Johnson's Move toward Peace

The year 1968 was marked by violent confrontations around the world. Protests against governments erupted from Mexico City to Paris to Tokyo, usually led by students in collaboration with

Students Protest in Mexico City
After riot police reacted violently to skirmishes between students from rival schools in Mexico City in July 1968, students began to demonstrate against the repressive measures of the government and political interference in their universities. These students, marching on August 13, 1968, were part of a movement that two weeks later swelled to a demonstration of a half million and was then dispersed by soldiers and tanks. One of their signs promises to defend their demands until "total victory." Marcel·lí Perelló.

least 100 to 200 protesters were killed, and another several hundred were wounded. The Olympic Games went on as scheduled ten days later.

In the wake of the massacre, protesters staged demonstrations and attacks on Mexican embassies in Latin America and Europe. By December, more episodes of violence against protesters occurred in Spain, Pakistan, and Northern Ireland. In the United States, violence diminished generally, but not in urban ghettos.

By year's end, a kind of stunned exhaustion set in. The Soviets had shut down the Prague Spring, the student-led protests in France and Germany had reached a stalemate, and Republican Richard Nixon had won the U.S. presidential election with promises to maintain law and order at home and to end the war in Vietnam. The year of global protest ended with despair and fear on all sides. Student protest did not disappear, but the excitement of worldwide revolutionary solidarity was blunted by

the very real threat of fatal consequences faced by protesters.

America in a Global Context

1. What did the global protests of 1968 have in common?

2. How did protest in the United States differ from that in other countries, both in the composition of the protesters and in the reaction from authorities?

---

workers. (See "Beyond America's Borders," page 984.) American society also became increasingly polarized. On one side, the so-called hawks charged that the United States was fighting with one hand tied behind its back and called for intensification of the war. The doves wanted de-escalation or withdrawal. As U.S. troop strength neared half a million and military deaths approached 20,000 by the end of 1967, most people were torn between weariness with the war and a desire to fulfill the U.S. commitment.

As one woman said, "I want to get out but I don't want to give up."

Grave doubts penetrated the administration itself in 1967. Secretary of Defense **Robert McNamara**, a principal architect of U.S. involvement, now believed that the North Vietnamese "won't quit no matter how much bombing we do." He feared for the image of the United States, "the world's greatest superpower, killing or seriously injuring 1,000 noncombatants a week, while trying to pound a tiny, backward nation into submission

The Battle for Hue
During the Tet Offensive in early 1968, North Vietnamese troops captured the city of Hue, the ancient capital of Vietnam, rich with the country's history and culture. It took nearly a month of brutal house-to-house fighting for U.S. and ARVN troops to retake the city, eighty percent of which had by then been destroyed. The great cost in lives, housing, and cultural treasure contributed to the mounting disaffection of Americans for the war, even though the Tet Offensive was ultimately a military victory for the U.S. and South Vietnam. Here U.S. Marines are pinned down near the center of Hue. © Bettmann/Corbis.

on an issue whose merits are hotly disputed." McNamara did not publicly oppose the war, but in early 1968 he left the administration.

A critical turning point came with the **Tet Offensive**. On January 30, 1968, the North Vietnamese and Vietcong launched attacks on key cities, every major American base in South Vietnam, and the U.S. Embassy in Saigon. This was the biggest surprise of the war, and not simply because both sides had customarily observed a truce during Tet, the Vietnamese New Year holiday. The offensive displayed the Communists' vitality and refusal to be intimidated by the presence of half a million American soldiers. Militarily, the enemy suffered a defeat, losing ten times as many soldiers as ARVN and U.S. forces. Psychologically, however, Tet was devastating to the United States.

> **"What the hell is going on? I thought we were winning the war."**
> — TV anchorman **WALTER CRONKITE**

The Tet Offensive underscored the credibility gap between official statements and the war's actual progress. TV anchorman Walter Cronkite wondered, "What the hell is going on? I thought we were winning the war." The attacks created a million more South Vietnamese refugees as well as widespread destruction. Explaining how he had defended a village, a U.S. Army official said, "We had to destroy the town to save it." The statement epitomized for more and more Americans the brutality and senselessness of the war. Public approval of Johnson's handling of it dropped to 26 percent.

In the aftermath of Tet, Johnson conferred with advisers in the Defense Department and an unofficial group of foreign policy experts who had been key architects of Cold War policies for two decades. Dean Acheson, Truman's secretary of state, summarized their conclusion: "We can no longer do the job we set out to do in the time we have left and we must begin to take steps to disengage."

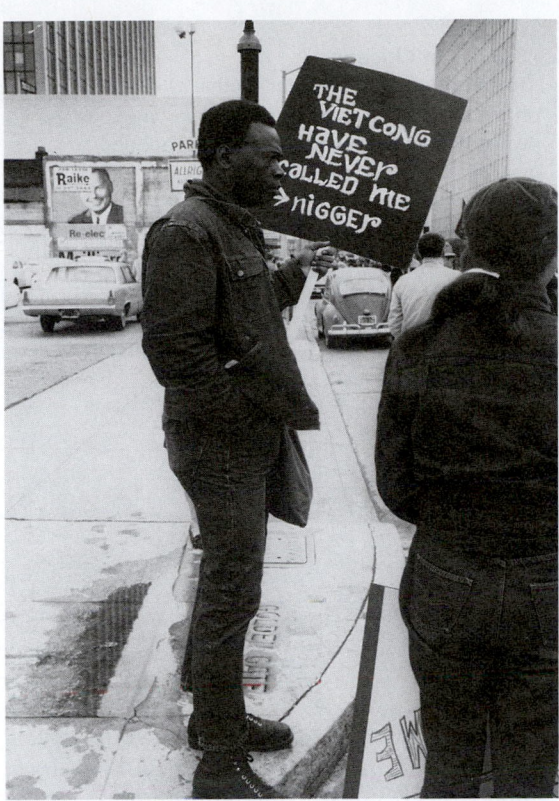

African American Antiwar Protest
The first expression of African American opposition to the war in Vietnam occurred in Mississippi in July 1965 when a group of civil rights workers called for draft resistance. Blacks should not fight for freedom in Vietnam "until all the Negro People are free in Mississippi," the activists said, and they should not risk their lives "and kill other Colored People in Santo Domingo and Viet Nam." This protester on the West Coast expresses similar sentiments in April 1967. Joe Flowers/Black Star/Stockphoto.com.

On March 31, 1968, Lyndon Johnson announced in a televised speech that the United States would sharply curtail its bombing of North Vietnam and that he was prepared to begin peace talks. He added the stunning declaration that he would not run for reelection. The gradual escalation of the war was over, and military strategy shifted from "Americanization" to "Vietnamization" of the war. But this was not a shift in policy. The goal remained a non-Communist South Vietnam; the United States would simply rely more heavily on the South Vietnamese to achieve it.

Negotiations began in Paris in May 1968. The United States would not agree to recognition of the Hanoi government's National Liberation Front, to a coalition government, or to American withdrawal. The North Vietnamese would agree to nothing less. Although the talks continued, so did the fighting.

Meanwhile, violence escalated at home. Protests occurred on two hundred college campuses in the spring of 1968, and as many as one million students participated in nationwide strikes. In the bloodiest action, students occupied buildings at Columbia University in New York City, making demands connected to the university's war-related research and to its treatment of African Americans. (See chapter 28, "Documenting the American Promise," page 950.) When negotiations failed, university officials called in the city police, who cleared the buildings, injuring scores of demonstrators and arresting hundreds. An ensuing student strike prematurely ended the academic year.

The Tumultuous Election of 1968

Disorder and violence also entered the election process. In June, two months after the murder of Martin Luther King Jr. and the riots that followed, another assassination shook the nation. Antiwar candidate Senator Robert F. Kennedy, campaigning in California for the Democratic Party's presidential nomination, was shot by a Palestinian Arab refugee who was outraged by Kennedy's support for Israel.

In August, protesters battled the police in Chicago, where the Democratic Party had convened to nominate its presidential ticket. Several thousand demonstrators came to the city, some to support the peace candidate Senator Eugene McCarthy, others to cause disruption. The Youth International Party (Yippies), a splinter group of SDS, urged protesters to demonstrate their hatred of the establishment by provoking the police and creating chaos. On August 25, when demonstrators jeered at orders to disperse, police attacked them with tear gas and clubs. Street battles continued for three days, culminating in a police riot on the night of August 28. Taunted by the crowd, the police used Mace and nightsticks, clubbing not only those who had come to provoke violence but also reporters, peaceful demonstrators, and convention delegates.

Although the bloodshed in Chicago horrified those who saw it on television, it had little effect on the convention's outcome. An assassin had ended Robert Kennedy's promising campaign in June, and Vice President **Hubert H. Humphrey**

Protest in Chicago
The worst violence surrounding the 1968 Democratic National Convention in Chicago came on August 28 when protesters assembled in Grant Park and marched to the convention site. Near the Hilton Hotel, where most of the delegates stayed, some 3,000 protesters came up against a line of police. The police attacked not only the demonstrators but also reporters, hotel guests, and bystanders with nightsticks and Mace, driving a crowd through the plate-glass window of the hotel and injuring hundreds. AP Photo/Michael Boyer.

trounced the remaining antiwar candidate, McCarthy, by nearly three to one for the Democratic nomination.

In contrast to the turmoil around the Democratic convention, the Republican convention met peacefully and nominated former vice president Richard Nixon on the first ballot. For his running mate, Nixon chose Maryland governor Spiro T. Agnew, hoping to gather southern support. A strong third candidate entered the electoral scene when the American Independent Party nominated former Alabama governor and staunch segregationist **George C. Wallace**. Wallace appealed to Americans' dissatisfaction with the reforms and rebellions of the 1960s and their outrage at the assaults on traditional values. Nixon guardedly played on resentments that fueled the Wallace campaign, calling for "law and order" and attacking liberal Supreme Court decisions, busing for school desegregation, and protesters.

Nixon and Humphrey differed little on the central issue of Vietnam. Nixon promised "an honorable end" to the war but did not indicate how he would do it. Humphrey had strong reservations about U.S. policy in Vietnam, yet as vice president he was tied to Johnson's policies. With nearly 13 percent of the total popular vote, the American Independent Party produced the strongest third-party finish since 1924. Nixon edged out Humphrey by just half a million popular votes but garnered 301 electoral college votes to Humphrey's 191 and Wallace's 46 (Map 29.3). The Democrats maintained control of Congress.

The 1968 election revealed deep cracks in the coalition that had kept the Democrats in power for most of the previous thirty years. Johnson's liberal policies on race shattered a century of Democratic Party dominance in the South, which delivered all its electoral votes to Wallace and

MAP 29.3
The Election of 1968

Candidate	Electoral Vote	Popular Vote	Percent of Popular Vote
Richard M. Nixon (Republican)	301	31,770,237	43.4
Hubert H. Humphrey (Democrat)	191	31,270,533	42.7
George C. Wallace (American Independent)	46	9,906,141	13.5

3 ⬛ Washington, D.C.

Note: North Carolina split its vote, with one elector voting for Wallace.

Nixon. Elsewhere, large numbers of blue-collar workers broke with labor's traditional support for the Democratic Party to vote for Wallace or Nixon, as did other groups that associated the Democrats with racial turmoil, poverty programs, changing sexual mores, and failure to turn the tide in Vietnam. These resentments would soon be mobilized into a resurging right in American politics (as discussed in chapter 30).

REVIEW   How did the Vietnam War shape the election of 1968?

▶ Nixon, Détente, and the Search for Peace in Vietnam

Richard M. Nixon took office with ambitious foreign policy goals, hoping to make his mark on history by applying his broad understanding of international relations to a changing world. Diverging from Republican orthodoxy, he made dramatic overtures to the Soviet Union and China. Yet anticommunism remained central to U.S. policy. In Latin America, Africa, and the Middle East, Nixon backed repressive regimes when the alternatives suggested victories for the left. Relying even more than his predecessor on public deception, secrecy, and silencing opponents, Nixon aggressively pursued the war in Vietnam. He expanded the conflict into Cambodia and Laos and ferociously bombed North Vietnam. Yet in the end, he was forced to settle for peace without victory.

Moving toward Détente with the Soviet Union and China

In Nixon's view, the "rigid and bipolar world of the 1940s and 1950s" was giving way to "the fluidity of a new era of multilateral diplomacy." America's European allies were seeking to ease East-West tensions. Moreover, Nixon and his national security adviser **Henry A. Kissinger** recognized the increasing conflict between the Soviet Union and China and believed they could exploit the situation. This Soviet-Chinese hostility, according to Nixon, "served our purpose best if we maintained closer relations with each side than they did with each other." In addition, these two nations might be used to help the United States extricate itself from Vietnam.

Following two years of secret negotiations, in February 1972 Nixon became the nation's first president to set foot on Chinese soil — an astonishing act by a man whose career had rested on fervent anticommunism. In fact, his anti-Communist credentials enabled him to conduct this shift in U.S.-Chinese relations with no significant domestic repercussions. Although his visit was largely symbolic, cultural and scientific exchanges followed, and American manufacturers began to find markets in China — small steps in the process of globalization that would take giant strides in the 1990s (as discussed in chapter 31). China had been

> **"[Soviet-Chinese hostility] served our purpose best if we maintained closer relations with each side than they did with each other."**
> — President **RICHARD M. NIXON**

Nixon in China
"This was the week that changed the world," proclaimed President Nixon in February 1972, emphasizing the stunning turnaround in relations with America's former enemy, the People's Republic of China. Nixon's trip was meticulously planned to dramatize the event on television and, aside from criticism from some conservatives, won overwhelming support from Americans. The Great Wall of China forms the setting for this photograph of Nixon and his wife, Pat. Nixon Presidential Materials Project, National Archives and Record Administration.

admitted to the United Nations in 1971, and in 1979 the United States and China would establish formal diplomatic relations.

As Nixon and Kissinger had hoped, the warming of U.S.-Chinese relations furthered their strategy of **détente**, their term for easing conflict with the Soviet Union. Détente did not mean abandoning containment but instead meant focusing on issues of common concern, such as arms control and trade. Containment would be achieved not only by military threat but also by ensuring that the Soviets and Chinese had stakes in a stable international order. Nixon's goal was "a stronger healthy United States, Europe, Soviet Union, China, Japan, each balancing the other."

Arms control, trade, and stability in Europe were three areas where the United States and the Soviet Union had common interests. In May 1972, Nixon visited Moscow, signing several agreements on trade and cooperation in science and space. Most significantly, Soviet and U.S. leaders concluded arms limitation treaties that had grown out of the **Strategic Arms Limitation Talks (SALT)** begun in 1969, agreeing to limit antiballistic missiles (ABMs) to two each. Giving up pursuit of a defense against nuclear weapons was a crucial move, because it prevented either nation from building so secure an ABM defense against a nuclear attack that it would risk a first strike.

Although the policy of détente made little progress after 1974, U.S., Soviet, and European leaders signed a historic agreement in 1975 in Helsinki, Finland, that formally recognized the post–World War II boundaries in Europe. The **Helsinki accords** were controversial because they acknowledged Soviet domination over Eastern Europe — a condition that had triggered the Cold War thirty years earlier. Yet they also contained a clause committing the signing countries to recognize "the universal significance of human rights and fundamental freedoms." Dissidents in the Soviet Union and its Eastern European satellites used this official promise of rights to challenge the Soviet dictatorship and help force its overthrow fifteen years later.

Shoring Up U.S. Interests around the World

Nixon promised in 1973 that "the time has passed when America will make every other nation's conflict our own . . . or presume to tell the people of other nations how to manage their own affairs." Yet in Vietnam and elsewhere, Nixon and Kissinger continued to view left-wing movements as threats to U.S. interests and actively resisted social revolutions that might lead to communism.

Consequently, the Nixon administration helped to overthrow **Salvador Allende**, a self-proclaimed Marxist who was elected president of Chile in 1970. Since 1964, the CIA and U.S. corporations concerned about nationalization of their Chilean properties had assisted Allende's opponents. After Allende became president, Nixon ordered the CIA director to destabilize his government by making the Chilean economy "scream." In 1973, the CIA helped the Chilean military engineer a coup, killing Allende and establishing a brutal dictatorship under General Augusto Pinochet. Representative government did not return until 1990.

In other parts of the world, too, the Nixon administration stood by repressive regimes. In southern Africa, it eased pressures on white minority governments that tyrannized blacks. In the Middle East, the United States sent massive arms shipments to support the shah of Iran's harsh regime because Iran had enormous petroleum reserves and seemed a stable anti-Communist ally. Unnoticed by most Americans, the administration cemented a relationship that turned many Iranians against the United States and would ignite a new crisis when the shah was overthrown in 1979 (as discussed in chapter 30).

Like his predecessors, Nixon pursued a delicate balance between defending Israel's security and seeking the goodwill of Arab nations strategically and economically important to the United States. Conflict between Israel and the Arab nations had escalated into the **Six-Day War** in 1967, when Israel attacked Egypt after that nation had massed troops on the Israeli border and cut off sea passage to

Chile

GUYANA
SURINAME
FRENCH GUIANA
VENEZUELA
COLOMBIA
ECUADOR
PERU
BRAZIL
BOLIVIA
PACIFIC OCEAN
PARAGUAY
Santiago
URUGUAY
CHILE
ARGENTINA
ATLANTIC OCEAN

0   250 500 mi.

0   500 km.

Israel's southern port. Although Syria and Jordan joined the war on Egypt's side, Israel won a stunning victory, seizing territory that amounted to twice its original size. Israeli forces took control of the Sinai Peninsula and the Gaza Strip from Egypt, the Golan Heights from Syria, and the West Bank, where hundreds of thousands of Palestinians lived, from Jordan.

That decisive victory did not quell Middle Eastern turmoil. In October 1973, on the Jewish holiday Yom Kippur, Egypt and Syria surprised Israel with a full-scale attack. When the Nixon administration sided with Israel in the **Yom Kippur War**, Arab nations retaliated with an oil embargo that created severe shortages in the United States. After Israel repulsed the attack, Kissinger attempted to mediate between Israel and the Arab nations, but with very limited success. The Arab countries refused to recognize Israel's right to exist, Israel began to settle its citizens in the West Bank and other territories occupied during the Six-Day War, and no solution could be found for the Palestinian refugees who had been displaced by the creation of Israel in the late 1940s (see chapter 26). The simmering conflict contributed to anti-American sentiment among Arabs who viewed the United States as Israel's supporter.

Vietnam Becomes Nixon's War

"I'm not going to end up like LBJ, holed up in the White House afraid to show my face on the street," the new president asserted. "I'm going to stop that war. Fast." Nixon gradually withdrew U.S. ground troops, but he was no more willing than Eisenhower, Kennedy, or Johnson to be the president who allowed South Vietnam to fall to the Communists. That goal was tied to the larger objective of maintaining American credibility. Regardless of the wisdom of the initial intervention, Kissinger asserted, "the commitment of 500,000 Americans has settled the importance of Vietnam. For what is involved now is confidence in American promises."

From 1969 to 1972, Nixon and Kissinger pursued a four-pronged approach. First, they tried

Israeli Territorial Gains in the Six-Day War, 1967

to strengthen the South Vietnamese military and government. Second, to disarm the antiwar movement at home, Nixon gradually replaced U.S. forces with South Vietnamese soldiers and American technology and bombs. Third, the United States negotiated with both North Vietnam and the Soviet Union. Fourth, the military applied intensive bombing to persuade Hanoi to accept American terms at the bargaining table.

As part of the Vietnamization of the war, ARVN forces grew to more than a million, and the South Vietnamese air force became the fourth largest in the world. The United States also promoted land reform, village elections, and the building of schools, hospitals, and transportation facilities. Meanwhile, U.S. forces withdrew, decreasing from 543,000 in 1968 to 140,000 by the end of 1971, a move that critics called merely "changing the color of the corpses." Even with the reduction of U.S. forces, however, more than 20,000 Americans perished in Vietnam between 1969 and 1973.

In the spring of 1969, Nixon began a ferocious air war in Cambodia, carefully hiding it from Congress and the public for more than a year. Seeking to knock out North Vietnamese sanctuaries in Cambodia, Americans dropped more than 100,000 tons of bombs but succeeded only in sending the North Vietnamese to other hiding places. Echoing Johnson, Kissinger believed that a "fourth-rate power like North Vietnam" had to have a "breaking point," but the massive bombing failed to find it.

To support a new, pro-Western Cambodian government installed through a military coup in 1970 and "to show the enemy that we were still serious about our commitment in Vietnam," Nixon ordered a joint U.S.-ARVN invasion of Cambodia in April 1970. That

U.S. Invasion of Cambodia, 1970

VISUAL ACTIVITY

Pro-War Demonstrators
Advocates as well as opponents of the war in Vietnam took to the streets, as these New Yorkers did in support of the U.S. invasion of Cambodia in May 1970. Construction workers — called "hard hats" — and other union members marched with American flags and posters championing President Nixon's policies and blasting New York mayor John Lindsay for his antiwar position. Following the demonstration, sympathetic union leaders presented Nixon with an honorary hard hat. Paul Fusco/Magnum Photos, Inc.

READING THE IMAGE: What do the hard hats in the photograph symbolize in terms of identity and politics?

CONNECTIONS: What, if anything, was the relationship between President Nixon being presented with a hard hat after a pro-war demonstration and the unraveling of the Democratic Party coalition?

order made Vietnam "Nixon's war" and provoked outrage at home. Nixon made a belligerent speech defending his move and emphasizing the importance of U.S. credibility: "If when the chips are down, the world's most powerful nation acts like a pitiful helpless giant, the forces of totalitarianism and anarchy will threaten free nations" everywhere.

Upon reading a draft of the speech, a cabinet member predicted, "This will make the students puke." They did more than that. In response, more than 100,000 people protested in Washington, D.C., and students boycotted classes on hundreds of campuses. At **Kent State University** in Ohio, National Guard troops were dispatched after protesting students burned an old ROTC building. Then, at a rally there on May 4, when some students threw rocks at the

troops, they fired at the students, killing four and wounding ten others. "They're starting to treat their own children like they treat us," commented a black woman in Harlem. In a confrontation at **Jackson State College** in Mississippi on May 14, police shot into a dormitory, killing two black students. And in August, police in Los Angeles used tear gas and clubs against Chicano antiwar protesters.

Congressional reaction to the invasion of Cambodia revealed increasing concern about abuses of presidential power. In the name of national security, presidents since Franklin Roosevelt had conducted foreign policy without the consent or sometimes even the knowledge of Congress — for example, Eisenhower in Iran and Johnson in the Dominican Republic. But in their determination to win the war in Vietnam, Johnson and Nixon had taken extreme measures to deceive the public and silence their critics. The bombing and invasion of Cambodia infuriated enough legislators that the Senate voted to terminate the Gulf of Tonkin Resolution, which had given the president virtually a blank check in Vietnam, and to cut off funds for the Cambodian operation. The House refused to go along, but by the end of June 1970 Nixon had pulled all U.S. troops out of Cambodia.

The Cambodian invasion failed to break the will of North Vietnam, but it set in motion a terrible tragedy for the Cambodian people. The North Vietnamese moved farther into Cambodia and strengthened the Khmer Rouge, Communist insurgents attempting to overthrow the U.S.-supported government of Lon Nol. A brutal civil war raged until 1975, when the Khmer Rouge triumphed and imposed a savage rule, slaughtering millions of Cambodians and giving the name "killing fields" to the land of a historically peaceful people.

In 1971, Vietnam veterans became a visible part of the peace movement, the first men in U.S. history to protest a war in which they had fought. They held a public investigation of "war crimes" in Vietnam, rallied in front of the Capitol, and cast away their war medals. In May 1971, veterans numbered among the 40,000 protesters who engaged in civil disobedience in an effort to shut down Washington. Officials made more than 12,000 arrests, which courts later ruled violations of protesters' rights.

After the spring of 1971, there were fewer massive antiwar demonstrations, but protest continued. Public attention focused on the court-martial of Lieutenant William Calley, which began in November 1970. During the trial,

Americans learned that in March 1968 Calley's company had systematically killed every inhabitant of the hamlet of **My Lai**, even though the soldiers had encountered no enemy forces and the four hundred villagers were nearly all old men, women, and children. The military covered up the atrocity for more than a year before a journalist exposed it. Eventually, twelve officers and enlisted men were charged with murder or assault, but only Calley was convicted.

Administration policy suffered another blow in June 1971 when the *New York Times* published the **Pentagon Papers**, secret government documents consisting mostly of an internal study of the war begun in 1967. Nixon sent government lawyers to court to stop further publication, in part out of fear that other information would be leaked. The Supreme Court, however, ruled that the attempt to stop publication was a "flagrant, indefensible" violation of the First Amendment. Subsequent circulation of the *Pentagon Papers*, which revealed considerable pessimism among officials even as they made rosy promises, heightened disillusionment with the war by casting doubts on the government's credibility. More than 60 percent of Americans polled in 1971 considered it a mistake to have sent American troops to Vietnam; 58 percent believed the war to be immoral.

Military morale sank in the last years of the war. Having been exposed to the antiwar movement at home, many of the remaining soldiers had less faith in the war than their predecessors had had. Racial tensions among soldiers mounted, many soldiers sought escape in illegal drugs, and enlisted men committed hundreds of "fraggings," attacks on officers. In a 1971 report, "The Collapse of the Armed Forces," a retired Marine Corps colonel described the lack of discipline: "Our army that now remains in Vietnam [is] near mutinous."

The Peace Accords

Nixon and Kissinger continued to believe that intensive firepower could bring the North Vietnamese to their knees. In March 1972, responding to a strong North Vietnamese offensive, the United States resumed sustained bombing of the North, mined Haiphong and other harbors for the first time, and announced a naval blockade. With peace talks stalled, in December Nixon ordered the most devastating bombing of North Vietnam yet, producing worldwide condemnation. The intense bombing, which Kissinger

Students Killed at Kent State
On May 4, 1970, John Filo, a photojournalism student at Kent State University in Ohio, took his camera to a student demonstration against President Nixon's decision to invade Cambodia. He observed some protesters throwing rocks at National Guardsmen, who in turn sprayed tear gas. Suddenly, some guardsmen opened fire, killing four students and wounding ten. Filo took this photograph of Mary Ann Vecchio sobbing over the dead body of Jeffrey Miller. He sent his photographs to the Associated Press, which published this photo around the world. Filo won a Pulitzer Prize for this picture. John Filo.

called "jugular diplomacy," was costly to both sides, but it brought renewed negotiations. On January 27, 1973, representatives of the United States, North Vietnam, South Vietnam, and the Vietcong (now called the People's Revolutionary Government) signed a formal peace accord in Paris. The agreement required removal of all U.S. troops and military advisers from South Vietnam but allowed North Vietnamese forces to remain. Both sides agreed to return prisoners of war. Nixon called the agreement "peace with honor," but in fact it allowed only a face-saving withdrawal for the United States.

Fighting resumed immediately among the Vietnamese. Nixon's efforts to support the South

From the Fall of Saigon to the House of Representatives

Three days before the end of April 1975, eight-year-old Anh Quang Cao was rushed to the crowded airfield near Saigon, South Vietnam, along with his brother and sister. His mother entrusted the children to their aunt, who accompanied them on a flight out of Vietnam. Anh's father had been an officer in the South Vietnamese army, which put the entire family at extreme risk as the People's Army of Vietnam approached from the north for its final assault on Saigon. Anh's mother could send only three of her children; five more remained with their parents.

South Vietnam's capital was in an uproar, with tens of thousands of inhabitants seeking escape. Anyone who had worked for or cooperated with the Americans feared bloody reprisals at the hands of the North Vietnamese. Two days after Anh's plane departed, rockets and artillery fire heavily damaged the airport. Thereafter helicopters took over, shuttling thousands out of Saigon; thousands more made for the docks to get passage on any seaworthy vessel. Both the helicopters and the boats were trying to reach the many ships of the U.S. Seventh Fleet, anchored just beyond Vietnamese territorial waters.

The ships and planes headed for a U.S. military base on Guam, 2,600 miles away, where large camps had been rapidly constructed. Anh found himself among some 64,000 other refugees in a huge tent city pitched on freshly bulldozed land. Among them, the boy located an uncle. Three times a day, the refugees lined up for eggs and bacon, hamburgers, mashed potatoes, fruit cocktail, and other classics of the American diet. The new food was part of a U.S. program dubbed "Operation New Life," rolled out in May to deal with the refugees, who by summer's end numbered 130,000.

After three weeks on Guam, Anh and his uncle joined an airlift of five hundred flights taking refugees to four military bases in the United States. The two were sent to Fort Chaffee, an army reserve base in northwest Arkansas. There they received a limited program of English-language instruction and awaited resettlement.

The U.S. plan for the initial wave of refugees was to disperse them in small numbers to communities in all fifty states. Charitable groups were encouraged to sponsor refugees with minimal government assistance — just $500 per person. Anh and his uncle were sponsored by a Lutheran church in Goshen, Indiana, where the boy entered first grade and his uncle worked in a fast-food restaurant. Anh learned to love snow, and he took an Americanized name: Joseph Cao. After four years in Goshen, Cao and his uncle moved to Texas.

By 1978, a second and larger exodus began leaving Vietnam by boat. Some 20,000 "boat people" per month paid extortionate fees and endured great hardship in crossing the South China Sea. Bad weather and inadequate food and water were less dreaded than horrific attacks by pirates, who robbed, raped, and murdered the expatriates on approximately one-third of the boats. As many as 100,000 people perished, but some half a million came to the United States, aided by the Refugee Act of 1980, which accepted the international definition of a refugee as a person unable to return to his or her country because of a "well-founded fear of persecution." Among late arrivals in this migration stream were Cao's family, his father severely traumatized by nearly seven years of imprisonment and torture in a Communist "reeducation" camp.

An able student, Cao completed high school and earned degrees in physics at Baylor University, in philosophy at Fordham University, and in law at Loyola University. Along the way, he

---

Vietnamese government, and indeed his ability to govern at all, were increasingly eroded by what came to be known as the Watergate scandal (as discussed in chapter 30). Nixon had been forced to give up his office by 1975, when North Vietnam launched a new offensive. On April 30, it occupied Saigon and renamed it Ho Chi Minh City to honor the Communist leader. The Americans hastily evacuated, along with 150,000 of their South Vietnamese allies. (See "Seeking the American Promise," above.)

Confusion, humiliation, and tragedy marked the rushed departure. The United States lacked sufficient transportation capabilities and time to evacuate all the South Vietnamese who had supported the South Vietnamese government and were desperate to leave. Former lieutenant Philip Caputo, who had returned to South Vietnam as a journalist, reported that his departing helicopter "took some ground fire from South Vietnamese soldiers who probably felt that the Americans had betrayed them."

continued to practice Catholicism, the religion of his childhood in Saigon, and he spent six years in a Jesuit seminary, doing missionary work among the poor. He became an immigration lawyer, serving the Vietnamese community in New Orleans. After Hurricane Katrina destroyed his house, he developed political ambitions and ran as an independent for the Louisiana state legislature.

Cao failed in that bid, but Republican Party leaders in Louisiana tapped him to run for Congress in 2008 in a heavily Democratic district. Cao agreed to run as a Republican, citing the debt he felt to John McCain, that year's Republican presidential candidate, who had spent five and a half years in a Hanoi POW camp. In a close election, Cao defeated the incumbent (who was embroiled in corruption charges) and thus became the first Vietnamese American to be elected to the House of Representatives.

In office, Cao proved to be an unconventional Republican, one who called out Wall Street bankers in hearings and cast the lone Republican vote for the first version of the health care reform bill in late 2009. His 2010 campaign for reelection was an uphill battle, and he lost decisively to a Democrat. Cao has returned to his law practice and his young family in New Orleans. In a *New York Times* interview before the election, he credited his philosophical studies for teaching him that "life is absurd but one cannot succumb to the absurdity of it," a fitting adage for his remarkable life story.

Congressman Cao
Vietnamese-American Ahn "Joseph" Cao speaks to constituents at a town hall meeting in Westwego, Louisiana in August 2009. AP Photo/Bill Haber.

Questions for Consideration

1. What were some of the fortunate circumstances in Cao's turbulent life?

2. How was Cao similar to and different from other immigrants in the United States?

During the four years it took Nixon to end the war, he had expanded the conflict into Cambodia and Laos and launched massive bombing campaigns. Although increasing numbers of legislators criticized the war, Congress never denied the president the funds to fight it. Only after the peace accords did the legislative branch try to reassert its constitutional authority in the making of war. The War Powers Act of 1973 required the president to secure congressional approval for any substantial, long-term deployment of troops abroad. The new law, however, did little to dispel the distrust of and disillusionment with the government that resulted from Americans' realization that their leaders had not told the truth about Vietnam.

The Legacy of Defeat

The disorder that had accompanied antiwar protests and bitter divisions among Americans were other legacies of the war. Vietnam diverted

Evacuating South Vietnam
As Communist troops rolled south toward Saigon in the spring of 1975, desperate South Vietnamese attempted to flee along with the departing Americans. These South Vietnamese, carrying little or nothing, attempt to scale the wall of the U.S. Embassy to reach evacuation helicopters. Thousands of Vietnamese who wanted to be evacuated were left behind. Even though space for evacuees was desperately limited, South Vietnamese president Nguyen Van Thieu fled to Taiwan on a U.S. plane, taking with him fifteen tons of baggage. AP Images

of 1975, the rest of Southeast Asia did not. When China and Vietnam reverted to their historically hostile relationship, the myth of a monolithic Communist power overrunning Asia evaporated.

The long pursuit of victory in Vietnam complicated the United States' relations with other nations, as even its staunchest ally, Britain, doubted the wisdom of the war. The spectacle of terrifying American power used against a small Asian country alienated many in the third world and compromised efforts to win the hearts and minds of people in developing nations.

The cruelest legacy of Vietnam fell on those who had served. "The general public just wanted to ignore us," remembered Frederick Downs, while opponents of the war "wanted to argue with us until we felt guilty about what we had done over there." The failure of the United States to win the war, its unpopularity at home, and its character as a guerrilla war denied veterans the traditional soldiers' homecoming. Veterans themselves expressed different reactions to the defeat. Many believed in the war's purposes and felt betrayed by the government for not letting them win it. Other veterans blamed the government for sacrificing the nation's youth in an immoral, unnecessary, or useless war, expressing their sense of the war's futility by referring to their dead comrades as having been "wasted." Some veterans belonging to minority groups had more reason to doubt the nobility of their purpose. A Native American soldier assigned to resettle Vietnamese civilians found it to be "just like when they moved us to the rez [reservation]. We shouldn't have done that."

Because the Vietnam War was a civil war involving guerrilla tactics, combat was especially brutal (Table 29.1). The terrors of conventional warfare were multiplied, and so were the motivations to commit atrocities. The 1968 massacre at My Lai was only the most widely publicized war crime. To demonstrate the immorality of the war, peace advocates stressed the atrocities, contributing to a distorted image of the Vietnam veteran as dehumanized and violent. "Antiwar types considered us to be psychopathic killers," Downs maintained.

Most veterans came home to public neglect. Government benefits were less generous to Vietnam veterans than they had been to those of the previous two wars. While two-thirds of Vietnam veterans said that they would serve again, and while most veterans readjusted well to civilian life, some suffered long after the

money from domestic programs and sounded the death knell for Johnson's Great Society. It created federal budget deficits and triggered inflation that contributed to ongoing economic crises throughout the 1970s (as discussed in chapter 30).

Four presidents had declared that the survival of South Vietnam was essential for U.S. containment policy, but their dire predictions that a Communist victory in South Vietnam would set the dominoes cascading did not materialize. Although Vietnam, Laos, and Cambodia all fell within the Communist camp in the spring

TABLE 29.1	VIETNAM WAR CASUALTIES
United States	
Battle deaths	47,434
Other deaths	10,786
Wounded	153,303
South Vietnam	
Killed in action	110,357
Military wounded	499,026
Civilians killed	415,000
Civilians wounded	913,000
Communist Regulars and Guerrillas	
Killed in action	66,000

Source: U.S. Department of Defense

war ended. The Veterans Administration estimated that nearly one-sixth of the veterans suffered from post-traumatic stress disorder, with its symptoms of recurring nightmares, feelings of guilt and shame, violence, drug and alcohol abuse, and suicidal tendencies. Thirty years after performing army intelligence work in Saigon, Doris Allen "still hit the floor sometimes when [she heard] loud bangs." Many of those who had served in Vietnam began to produce children with deformities and fell ill themselves with cancer, severe skin disorders, and other ailments. Veterans claimed a link between those illnesses and Agent Orange, which had exposed many to the deadly poison dioxin in Vietnam. Not until 1991 did Congress provide assistance to veterans with diseases linked to the poison.

By then, the climate had changed. The war began to enter the realm of popular culture, with novels, TV shows, and hit movies depicting a broad range of military experience — from soldiers reduced to brutality, to men and women serving with courage and integrity. The incorporation of the Vietnam War into the collective experience was symbolized most dramatically in the Vietnam Veterans Memorial unveiled in Washington, D.C., in November 1982. Designed by Yale architecture student Maya Lin, the black, V-shaped wall inscribed with the names of 58,200 men and women lost in the war became one of the most popular sites in the nation's capital. In an article describing the memorial's dedication, a Vietnam combat veteran spoke to and for his former comrades: "Welcome home. The war is over."

REVIEW What strategies did Nixon implement to bring American involvement in Vietnam to a close?

The Three Servicemen Statue
This statue was added as an integral part of the Vietnam Veterans Memorial in 1984, after some veterans and politicians protested that the stark, black wall was not an appropriate tribute to the fallen soldiers. Frederick Hart, the sculptor who had placed third in the original competition, created this more traditional memorial. He said, "The contrast between the innocence of their youth and the weapons of war underscores the poignancy of their sacrifice."
© Bettmann/Corbis.

▶ Conclusion: An Unwinnable War

Lieutenant Frederick Downs fought in America's longest war. The United States spent more than $150 billion (more than $800 billion in 2011 dollars) and sent 2.6 million young men and women to Vietnam. Of those, 58,200 never returned, and 150,000, like Downs, suffered serious injury. The war shattered consensus at home, increased presidential power at the expense of congressional authority and public accountability, weakened the economy, and contributed to the downfall of two presidents.

Even as Nixon and Kissinger took steps to ease Cold War tensions with the major Communist powers — the Soviet Union and China — they also acted vigorously throughout the third world to install or prop up anti-Communist governments. They embraced their predecessors' commitment to South Vietnam as a necessary Cold War engagement: To do otherwise would threaten American credibility and make the United States appear weak. Defeat in Vietnam did not make the United States the "pitiful helpless giant" predicted by Nixon, but it did mark a relative decline of U.S. power and the impossibility of containment on a global scale.

One of the constraints on U.S. power was the tenacity of revolutionary movements determined to achieve national independence. Overestimating the effectiveness of American technological superiority, U.S. officials badly underestimated the sacrifices that the enemy was willing to make and failed to realize how easily the United States could be perceived as a colonial intruder. Simply put, Americans were not well prepared for a guerrilla war. "It's a hell of a thing," Downs discovered, "to try to fight a war with all these goddamn civilians around."

A second constraint on Eisenhower, Kennedy, Johnson, and Nixon was their resolve to avoid a major confrontation with the Soviet Union or China. For Johnson, who conducted the largest escalation of the war, caution was critical so as not to provoke direct intervention by the Communist superpowers. After China exploded its first atomic bomb in 1964, the potential heightened for the Vietnam conflict to escalate into worldwide disaster.

Third, in Vietnam the United States sought to prop up an extremely weak ally engaged in a civil war. The South Vietnamese government failed to win the support of its people, and the intense devastation the war brought to civilians only made things worse. Short of taking over the South Vietnamese government and military, the United States could do little to strengthen South Vietnam's ability to resist communism.

Finally, domestic opposition to the war, which by 1968 had spread to mainstream America, constrained the options of Johnson and Nixon. As the war dragged on, with increasing American casualties and growing evidence of the damage being inflicted on innocent Vietnamese, more and more civilians wearied of the conflict. Even some who had fought in the war joined the peace movement, sending their military ribbons and bitter letters of protest to the White House. In 1973, Nixon and Kissinger bowed to the resolution of the enemy and the limitations of U.S. power. As the war wound down, passions surrounding it contributed to a rising conservative movement that would substantially alter the post–World War II political order.

▶ Selected Bibliography

Foreign Policy under Kennedy, Johnson, and Nixon

H. W. Brands, *The Wages of Globalism: Lyndon Johnson and the Limits of American Power* (1995).

Robert Dallek, *Nixon and Kissinger: Partners in Power* (2007).

Michael Dobbs, *One Minute to Midnight: Kennedy, Khrushchev, and Castro on the Brink of Nuclear War* (2008).

Lawrence Freedman, *Kennedy's Wars: Berlin, Cuba, Laos, and Vietnam* (2000).

Michael Grow, *U.S. Presidents and Latin American Interventions: Pursuing Regime Change in the Cold War* (2008).

Elizabeth Cobbs Hoffman, *All You Need Is Love: The Peace Corps and the Spirit of the 1960s* (1998).

Howard Jones, *The Bay of Pigs* (2008).

Margaret Macmillan, *Nixon and Mao: The Week That Changed the World* (2007).

Walter A. McDougall, *The Heavens and the Earth: A Political History of the Space Age* (1985).

Keith L. Nelson, *The Making of Détente: Soviet-American Relations in the Shadow of Vietnam* (1995).

Stephen G. Rabe, *The Most Dangerous Area in the World: John F. Kennedy Confronts Communist Revolution in Latin America* (1999).

Jeremi Suri, *Power and Protest: Global Revolution and the Rise of Détente* (2003).

The War in Vietnam

Arnold R. Isaacs, *Vietnam Shadows: The War, Its Ghosts, and Its Legacy* (1997).

David Kaiser, *American Tragedy: Kennedy, Johnson, and the Origins of the Vietnam War* (2000).

Jeffrey P. Kimball, *Nixon's Vietnam War* (1998).

A. J. Langguth, *Our Vietnam / Nuoc Viet Ta: A History of the War, 1954–1975* (2000).

Fredrik Logevall, *Choosing War: The Lost Chance for Peace and the Escalation of the War in Vietnam* (1999).

David F. Schmitz, *The Tet Offensive: Politics, War, and Public Opinion* (2005).

Marilyn B. Young, *The Vietnam Wars, 1945–1990* (1991).

Those Who Served

Christian G. Appy, *Working-Class War: American Combat Soldiers in Vietnam* (1993).

Philip Caputo, *A Rumor of War* (1977).

David Donovan, *Once a Warrior King: Memories of an Officer in Vietnam* (1985).

Frederick Downs, *The Killing Zone: My Life in the Vietnam War (1978); Aftermath: A Soldier's Return from Vietnam (1984); No Longer Enemies, Not Yet Friends: An American Soldier Returns to Vietnam* (1991).

Kathryn Marshall, *In the Combat Zone: Vivid Personal Recollections of the Vietnam War from the Women Who Served There* (1987).

Harry Maurer, *Strange Ground: Americans in Vietnam, 1945–1975, an Oral History* (1998).

Al Santoli, *Everything We Had: An Oral History of the Vietnam War* (1981).

James E. Westheider, *Fighting on Two Fronts: African Americans and the Vietnam War* (1997).

Politics and the Antiwar Movement

Dan T. Carter, *The Politics of Race: George Wallace, the Origins of the New Conservatism, and the Transformation of American Politics* (1995).

Charles DeBenedetti, with Charles Chatfield, *An American Ordeal: The Antiwar Movement in the Vietnam Era* (1990).

Michael S. Foley, *Confronting the War Machine: Draft Resistance during the Vietnam War* (2003).

Andrew E. Hunt, *The Turning: A History of Vietnam Veterans against the War* (1999).

Rhodri Jeffreys-Jones, *Peace Now! American Society and the Ending of the Vietnam War* (1999).

David Rudenstine, *The Day the Presses Stopped: A History of the Pentagon Papers Case* (1996).

Amy Swerdlow, *Women Strike for Peace: Traditional Motherhood and Radical Politics in the 1960s* (1993).

▶ **FOR MORE BOOKS ABOUT TOPICS IN THIS CHAPTER,** see the Online Bibliography at **bedfordstmartins.com/roark.**

▶ **FOR ADDITIONAL PRIMARY SOURCES FROM THIS PERIOD,** see Michael Johnson, ed., *Reading the American Past*, Fifth Edition.

▶ **FOR WEB SITES, IMAGES, AND DOCUMENTS RELATED TO TOPICS AND PLACES IN THIS CHAPTER,** visit Make History at **bedfordstmartins.com/roark.**

Reviewing Chapter 29

KEY TERMS

Explain each term's significance.

New Frontiers in Foreign Policy

John F. Kennedy (p. 971)
Nikita Khrushchev (p. 971)
Fidel Castro (p. 972)
Bay of Pigs (p. 972)
Apollo program (p. 972)
Berlin Wall (p. 973)
Peace Corps (p. 974)
Cuban missile crisis (p. 974)
Ho Chi Minh (p. 976)
Army of the Republic of Vietnam
   (ARVN) (p. 976)
National Liberation Front (NLF) (p. 976)
Agent Orange (p. 977)

Lyndon Johnson's War against Communism

Lyndon B. Johnson (p. 978)
Gulf of Tonkin Resolution (p. 979)
Operation Rolling Thunder (p. 979)

A Nation Polarized

Robert McNamara (p. 985)
Tet Offensive (p. 986)
Hubert H. Humphrey (p. 987)
George C. Wallace (p. 988)

Nixon, Détente, and the Search for Peace in Vietnam

Richard M. Nixon (p. 989)
Henry A. Kissinger (p. 989)
détente (p. 990)
Strategic Arms Limitation Talks (SALT)
   (p. 990)
Helsinki accords (p. 990)
Salvador Allende (p. 990)
Six-Day War (p. 990)
Yom Kippur War (p. 991)
Kent State University (p. 992)
Jackson State College (p. 992)
My Lai (p. 993)
Pentagon Papers (p. 993)

REVIEW QUESTIONS

Use key terms and dates to support your answer.

1. Why did Kennedy believe that engagement in Vietnam was crucial to his foreign policy? (pp. 971–977)

2. Why did massive amounts of airpower and ground troops fail to bring U.S. victory in Vietnam? (pp. 978–982)

3. How did the Vietnam War shape the election of 1968? (pp. 982–989)

4. What strategies did Nixon implement to bring American involvement in Vietnam to a close? (pp. 989–997)

MAKING CONNECTIONS

Draw on key terms, the timeline, and review questions.

1. Cuba featured prominently in the most dramatic foreign policy actions of the Kennedy administration. Citing specific events, discuss why Cuba was an area of great concern to the administration. How did Cuba figure into Kennedy's Cold War policies? Were his actions regarding Cuba effective?

2. Explain the Gulf of Tonkin incident and its significance to American foreign policy. How did President Lyndon Johnson respond to the incident? What considerations, domestic and international, contributed to his course of action?

3. The United States' engagement in Vietnam divided the nation. Discuss the range of American responses to the war. How did they change over time? How did the war shape domestic politics in the 1960s and early 1970s?

4. What was détente, and how did it affect the United States' Cold War foreign policy? What were its achievements and limitations? In your answer, discuss how Nixon's approach to communism built on and departed from the approaches of the previous two administrations.

LINKING TO THE PAST

Link events in this chapter to earlier events.

1. What commitments were made in the Truman and Eisenhower administrations that resulted in the United States' full-scale involvement in Vietnam? (See chapters 26 and 27.)

2. Compare public sentiment during America's involvement in World War II to that during its involvement in Vietnam. What policies, events, attitudes, and technological advancements contributed to the differences? (See chapter 25.)

▶ FOR PRACTICE QUIZZES AND OTHER STUDY TOOLS, visit the Online Study Guide at bedfordstmartins.com/roark.

TIMELINE 1961–1975

1961
- Bay of Pigs invasion.
- Berlin Wall erected.
- Kennedy administration increases military aid to South Vietnam.
- Alliance for Progress established.
- Peace Corps created.

1962
- Cuban missile crisis.

1963
- Limited nuclear test ban treaty signed.
- President Kennedy assassinated; Lyndon B. Johnson becomes president.

1964
- Anti-American rioting brings U.S. troops to Panama Canal Zone.
- Gulf of Tonkin Resolution.

1965
- First major demonstration against Vietnam War.
- Operation Rolling Thunder begins.
- Johnson orders first combat troops to Vietnam.
- U.S. troops invade Dominican Republic.

1967
- Arab-Israeli Six-Day War.

1968
- Demonstrations against Vietnam War increase.
- Tet Offensive.
- Johnson decides not to seek second term.
- Police and protesters clash near Democratic convention in Chicago.
- Republican Richard Nixon elected president.

1969
- American astronauts land on moon.

1970
- Nixon orders invasion of Cambodia.
- Students killed during protests at Kent State and Jackson State.

1971
- *New York Times* publishes *Pentagon Papers*.

1972
- Nixon becomes first U.S. president to visit China.
- Nixon visits Moscow to sign arms limitation treaties with Soviets.

1973
- Paris Peace Accords.
- War Powers Act.
- CIA-backed military coup in Chile.
- Arab oil embargo following Yom Kippur War.

1975
- North Vietnam takes over South Vietnam, ending the war.
- Helsinki accords.

MAKING AMERICA "REAGAN COUNTRY"

This delegate badge from the 1980 Republican National Convention displayed themes that would characterize Ronald Reagan's presidential campaigns and politics in the 1980s. Images of the flag, the Statue of Liberty, and the space program invoked patriotic sentiments, and Reagan's image as a cowboy spoke to the rugged individualism of the West, where he had made his home. The West housed key elements in the surge of conservatism that ensured Reagan's victory in 1980, shaped his administration's antigovernment, anti-Communist agenda, and helped reverse the liberal direction that national politics had taken in the 1960s. In the background conventional delegates cheer for their nominee. Badge: National Museum of American History, Smithsonian Institution, Behring Center; background: Ronald Reagan Presidential Library.

30

America Moves to the Right
1969–1989

PHYLLIS SCHLAFLY CALLED IT "ONE OF THE MOST EXCITING DAYS OF my life" when she heard conservative Republican Barry Goldwater address the National Federation of Republican Women in 1963. Like Goldwater, Schlafly opposed the moderate stance of the Eisenhower administration and current Republican leadership. Both Schlafly and Goldwater wanted the United States to do more than just contain communism — they wanted to eliminate that threat entirely. They also wanted to cut back the federal government, especially its role in providing social welfare and enforcing civil rights. Goldwater's loss to Lyndon Johnson in 1964 did not diminish Schlafly's conservative commitment. She assailed the policy innovations and turmoil of the 1960s, adding new issues to the conservative agenda and cultivating a grassroots movement that would redefine the Republican Party and American politics into the twenty-first century.

Phyllis Stewart was born in St. Louis in 1924, attended Catholic schools, and worked her way through Washington University testing ammunition at a World War II defense plant. She earned a master's degree in government from Radcliffe College in 1945 and went to work at the American Enterprise Institute, where she imbibed the think tank's conservatism. Returning to the Midwest, she married Fred Schlafly, an Alton, Illinois, attorney whose anticommunism and antigovernment passions equaled hers. The mother of six children, Schlafly claimed, "I don't think there's anything as much fun as taking care of a baby," and she asserted that she would "rather scrub bathroom floors" than write political articles.

Yet while insisting that caring for home and family was women's most important career, Schlafly spent much of her time on the road — writing, speaking, leading Republican women's organizations, and testifying before legislative committees. She ran twice for Congress but lost in her heavily Democratic district in Illinois. Her book, *A Choice Not an Echo*, pushed Barry Goldwater for president and sold more than three million copies. In 1967, she began publishing *The Phyllis Schlafly Report*, a monthly newsletter about current political issues. Throughout the 1950s and 1960s, Schlafly called for stronger efforts to combat communism at home and abroad, a more powerful military, and a less active government in domestic affairs — all traditional conservative goals.

In the 1970s, Schlafly began to address new issues, including feminism and the Equal Rights Amendment, abortion, gay rights, busing for racial integration, and religion in the schools. Her positions resonated with many Americans who were fed up with the expansion of government, the Supreme Court decisions, the protest movements, the challenges to authority, and the loosening of moral standards that seemed to define the 1960s. And the votes of those Americans began to reshape politics — in Richard Nixon's victories in 1968 and 1972; in the presidency of Jimmy Carter, whose policies stood to the right of his Democratic predecessors; and in the conservative Ronald Reagan's capture of the Republican Party, the presidency, and the political agenda in 1980.

Although Richard Nixon did not embrace the entire conservative agenda, he sought to make the Republicans the dominant party by appealing to disaffected blue-collar and southern white Democrats. The Watergate revelations forced Nixon to resign the presidency in 1974, and his Republican successor, Gerald Ford, occupied the Oval Office for little more than two years, but the shift of the political spectrum to the right continued even when Democrat Jimmy Carter captured the White House in 1976.

Antigovernment sentiment grew out of the deceptions of the Johnson administration, Nixon's abuse of presidential powers, and the inability of Presidents Ford and Carter to resolve domestic and foreign crises. As Americans saw their incomes shrink from an unprecedented combination of unemployment and inflation — called stagflation — their confidence in government and willingness to pay taxes eroded.

In 1980, Phyllis Schlafly's earlier call for "a choice not an echo" was realized when Ronald Reagan won the presidency. Cutting taxes and government regulations, attacking social programs, expanding the nation's military capacity, and pressuring the Soviet Union and communism in the third world, Reagan addressed the hopes of traditional conservatives. Like Schlafly, he also championed the concerns of Christian conservatives, who opposed abortion and sexual permissiveness and supported a larger role for religion in public life.

Reagan's goals encountered resistance from feminists, civil rights groups, environmentalists, and others who fought to keep what they had won in the 1960s and 1970s. Although Reagan failed to enact the entire conservative agenda, enormously increased the national debt, and engaged in illegal activities to thwart communism in Latin America, his popularity helped send his vice president, George H. W. Bush, to the White House at the end of his second term. And Reagan's determined optimism and spirited leadership contributed to a revival in national pride and confidence.

The *Phyllis Schlafly Report*

Phyllis Schlafly began her newsletter in 1967 with articles attacking federal social programs and calling for stronger measures and weapons to fight communism. When Congress passed the Equal Rights Amendment in 1972, the *Report* added antifeminism and other concerns of the New Right to its agenda, including opposition to abortion rights, to sex education in the schools, and to protections for gays and lesbians. Schlafly had more than 35,000 newsletter subscribers in the mid-1970s; she also had many adversaries. Feminist leader Betty Friedan told Schlafly, "I consider you a traitor to your sex. I consider you an Aunt Tom." Courtesy of Phyllis Schlafly.

The Phyllis Schlafly Report

VOL. 5, NO. 10, SECTION 2   Box 618, ALTON, ILLINOIS 62002   MAY, 1972

The Fraud Called The Equal Rights Amendment

If there ever was an example of how a tiny minority can cram its views down the throats of the majority, it is the Equal Rights Amendment, called ERA. A noisy claque of women's lib agitators rammed ERA through Congress, intimidating the men into voting for it so they would not be labeled "anti-woman."

The ERA passed Congress with big majorities on March 22, 1972 and was sent to the states for ratification. When it is ratified by 38 states, it will become the law of the land. Within two hours of Senate passage, Hawaii ratified it. New Hampshire and Nebraska, both anxious to be second, rushed their approval the next day. Then in steady succession came Iowa, Idaho, Delaware, Kansas, Texas, Maryland, Tennessee, Alaska, Rhode Island, and New Jersey. As this goes to press, 13 states have ratified it and others are on the verge of doing so.

Three states have rejected it: Oklahoma, Vermont and Connecticut.

What is ERA? The Amendment reads: "Equality of rights under the law shall not be denied or abridged by the United States or by any state on account of sex."

Does that sound good? Don't kid yourself. This innocuous-sounding amendment will take away far more important rights than it will ever give. This was made abundantly clear by the debate in Congress. Senator Sam Ervin (D., N.C.) called it "the most drastic measure in Senate history." He proved this by putting into the *Congressional Record* an article from the *Yale Law Journal* of April 1971.

The importance of this *Yale Law Journal* article is that both the proponents and the opponents of ERA agree that it is an accurate analysis of the consequences of ERA. Congresswoman Martha Griffiths, a leading proponent of ERA, sent a copy of this article to every member of Congress, stating that "It will help us understand the purposes and effect [...] Rights Amendment.... The arti[...] ERA will work in [...]

the most important of all women's rights.

"In all states husbands are primarily liable for the support of their wives and children.... The child support sections of the criminal nonsupport laws ... could not be sustained where only the male is liable for support." (YLJ, pp. 944-945).

"The Equal Rights Amendment would bar a state from imposing greater liability for support on a husband than on a wife merely because of his sex." (YLJ, p. 945)

"Like the duty of support during marriage and the obligation to pay alimony in the case of separation or divorce, nonsupport would have to be eliminated as a ground for divorce against husbands only...." (YLJ, p. 951)

"The Equal Rights Amendment would not require that alimony be abolished but only that it be available equally to husbands and wives." (YLJ, p. 952)

2. ERA will wipe out the laws which protect only women against sex crimes such as rape.

"Courts faced with criminal laws which do not apply equally to men and women would be likely to invalidate the laws rather than extending or rewriting them to apply to women and men alike." (YLJ, p. 966)

"Seduction laws, statutory rape laws, laws prohibiting obscene language in the presence of women, prostitution and 'manifest danger' laws ... The Equal Rights Amendment would not permit such laws, which base their sex discriminatory classification on social stereotypes." (YLJ, p. 954)

"The statutory rape laws, which punish men for having sexual intercourse with any woman under an age specified by law ... suffer from [...]fect under the Equal Rights Amendment [...]

"To h[...] [...]ngling out

► Nixon, Conservatism, and Constitutional Crisis

As we saw in chapter 28, Nixon acquiesced in continuing most Great Society programs and even approved pathbreaking environmental and minority and women's rights measures. Yet his public rhetoric and some of his actions signaled the country's rightward move. Whereas Kennedy had appealed to Americans to contribute to the common good, Nixon invited Americans to "let each of us ask — not just what will government do for me, but what can I do for myself?" His words invoked individualism and reliance on private enterprise rather than on government. These preferences would grow stronger in the nation during the 1970s and beyond, as a new strand of conservatism joined the older movement that focused on anticommunism, a strong national defense, and a limited federal role in domestic affairs. New conservatives, whom **Phyllis Schlafly** helped mobilize, wanted to restore what they considered traditional moral values by increasing the presence of Christianity in public life.

Nixon won a resounding victory in the 1972 election. Two years later, however, his abuse of power and efforts to cover up crimes committed by subordinates, revealed in the so-called Watergate scandal, forced the first presidential resignation in history. His handpicked successor, Gerald Ford, faced the aftermath of Watergate and severe economic problems, which returned the White House to the Democrats in 1976. Nonetheless, the rising conservative tide challenged the Democratic administration that followed.

Emergence of a Grassroots Movement

Hidden beneath Lyndon Johnson's landslide victory over Arizona senator Barry Goldwater in 1964 lay a rising conservative movement. Defining his purpose as "enlarging freedom at home and safeguarding it from the forces of tyranny abroad," Goldwater echoed the ideas of conservative intellectuals who argued that government intrusions into economic life hindered prosperity, stifled personal responsibility, and interfered with individuals' rights to determine their own values. Conservatives assailed big government in domestic affairs but demanded a strong military to eradicate "Godless communism."

Behind Goldwater's nomination was a growing grassroots movement. Vigorous especially in the South and West, it included middle-class suburban women and men, members of the rabidly anti-Communist John Birch Society, and college students in the new Young Americans for Freedom (YAF). They did not give up when Goldwater lost the election. In California, newly energized conservatives helped Ronald Reagan defeat the incumbent liberal governor, Edmund Brown, in 1966. Linking Brown with the Watts riot and student disruptions at the University of California at Berkeley (see chapter 28), Reagan exploited popular fears about rising taxes, student rebellion, and black demands for justice.

Grassroots conservatism was not limited to the West and South, but a number of Sun Belt characteristics made it especially strong in places such as Orange County, California; Dallas, Texas; and Scottsdale, Arizona. Such predominantly white areas contained relatively homogeneous, skilled, and economically comfortable populations, as well as military bases and defense production facilities. The West harbored a long-standing tradition of Protestant morality, individualism, and opposition to interference by a remote federal government. That tradition continued with the growing conservative movement, even though it was hardly consistent with the Sun Belt's economic dependence on defense spending and on huge federal projects providing water and power for the burgeoning population and its economy.

The South, which also benefited from military bases and the space program, shared the West's antipathy toward the federal government. Hostility to racial change, however, was much more central to the South's conservatism. After signing the Civil Rights Act of 1964, President Lyndon Johnson remarked privately, "I think we just delivered the South to the Republican Party." Indeed, Barry Goldwater carried five southern states in 1964.

Grassroots movements proliferated around what conservatives believed marked the "moral decline" of their nation. For example, in 1962 Mel and Norma Gabler succeeded in getting the Texas board of education to drop books that they found not in conformity with "the Christian-Judeo morals, values, and standards as given to us by God through . . . the Bible." Sex education roused the ire of Eleanor

> **"Nothing [in the sex education curriculum] depicted my values. . . . It wasn't so much the information. It was the shift in values."**
>
> —ELEANOR HOWE, a parent from Anaheim, California

A Mother Campaigns for a Say in Her Children's Education

Although historians usually trace the rise of conservatism through national politics, the most intense political battles of the 1970s and 1980s were often fought at the local level. None were more impassioned than those mounted by parents over what their children should be taught in the public schools. The introduction of sex education and new textbooks in the Kanawha County, West Virginia, school district prompted Alice Moore to challenge instruction she deemed harmful to her children and to organize a movement to gain parents' control over their children's education.

The diverse school district of Kanawha County encompassed the state capital of Charleston as well as surrounding towns and rural areas containing chemical plants, coal mines, and small hamlets. Alice Moore, a native of Mississippi, and her husband, a fundamentalist minister, lived in a small town on the outskirts of Charleston, where their four children attended local schools. When she heard that sex education was coming to Kanawha County, she rallied like-minded citizens and won a seat on the five-person school board in 1970. She failed to terminate the sex education program, which she found a "humanistic, atheistic attack on God," but managed to dilute the curriculum.

The district's adoption of a new English language arts curriculum in 1974 provoked even greater controversy. The program, similar to those sweeping school districts across the country, sought to teach children about the larger world, incorporated writings by African Americans and other minority groups, and encouraged students to think critically and independently.

Objecting to both the philosophy and the content of the new curriculum, Alice Moore began to mobilize opposition, calling on fundamentalist ministers and holding meetings in churches. In June 1974, at a meeting before an impassioned crowd of more than a thousand, she persuaded the school board to eliminate 8 of the curriculum's 325 books but failed to prevent adoption of the curriculum by a vote of three to two. Opponents then redoubled their efforts, and the textbook war was on, echoing concerns that were energizing the Christian Right across the country.

Protesters condemned what they considered disrespect for authority, American patriotism, and the free enterprise system in the new materials. One of Moore's allies, a conservative chemical company owner, vilified the curriculum as "liberal, socialist, even communist-inspired." Textbook

opponents also challenged the authority of distant "experts" to decide what was best for their children.

Furthermore, Moore and her supporters objected to the curriculum's multicultural materials, designed to illustrate the diversity of American society. Antitextbook forces disliked the nonstandard English that appeared in some of the literature, as well as what they considered the "trashy" aspects of urban ghetto life. "Why the hell do we have to indoctrinate our children out here in semi-rural communities with the problems of the inner city?" a protester asked.

The new sexual permissiveness emerging in the 1960s also aroused antitextbook forces. The sexual realism in some of the materials inflamed fundamentalist protesters above all because it defied their belief in the system of right and wrong laid out in the Bible, which they interpreted literally. To Moore, morality was not a relative issue: "God's law is absolute."

Such deeply held beliefs inspired opponents to keep their children home when school opened in September, achieving an absentee rate of around 20 percent. Defying their union leadership, thousands of miners went out on a sympathy strike while protesters set up picket lines and staged demonstrations. Three schools were bombed, district headquarters were dynamited, and guns were fired on both sides. Antitextbook supporters streamed into Charleston, including representatives from the Heritage Foundation, the John Birch Society, and the Ku Klux Klan. The violence gradually subsided, but protests went on through April 1975.

The school board ended up keeping most of the new curriculum, but

Howe in Anaheim, California, who felt that "nothing [in the sex education curriculum] depicted my values. . . . It wasn't so much the information. It was the shift in values." (See "Seeking the American Promise," above.) The Supreme Court's liberal decisions on issues such as school prayer, obscenity, and abortion also galvanized conservatives to restore "traditional values" to the nation.

In the 1970s, grassroots protests against taxes grew alongside concerns about morality. As Americans struggled with inflation and unemployment, many found themselves paying higher taxes, especially higher property taxes as the value of their homes increased. In 1978, Californians revolted in a popular referendum, reducing property taxes by more than one-half

parents were allowed to designate those books they did not want their children to read, and many teachers avoided hassles by not using any of the new books. The board also set new guidelines for choosing textbooks, which included banning materials that contained profanity, that looked favorably on different forms of government, or that "intrude[d] into the privacy of students' homes by asking personal questions about the inner feelings or behavior of themselves or their parents."

Conflicts over public school curricula, involving such topics as evolution, continued to strike communities throughout the nation into the twenty-first century, although none equaled the war in Kanawha County. Some conservative parents retreated from the public schools entirely. By 2007, parents were homeschooling 1.5 million children, and the number of private Christian schools soared, accommodating parents who, in Moore's words, "can't put their children in public schools and allow them to have their beliefs torn away." Those who believed that students should be exposed to a diversity of ideas in order to form their own beliefs were in the majority, but Christian conservatives such as Moore continued to fight for control over what their children were taught.

Questions for Consideration

1. What specific features of the new English arts curriculum did Alice Moore and her supporters object to?

2. What values of the New Right were reflected in the antitextbook campaign?

RE-ELECT
ALICE MOORE
FOR
BOARD of EDUCATION

Dear Friends,

The schools belong to the people who pay for them, not Washington Bureaucrats, not School Administrators, not National Education Organizations.

Nationally, education is costing us more than **61 billion dollars** a year, more than is spent on education by all the rest of the world combined. This is a **1000 percent increase** in 20 years while enrollment has barely doubled. Yet, almost **one third** of our high school graduates cannot pass college placement exams and this number increases annually.

Are your children getting the education you want for them? I am convinced most parents expect the schools, for which we pay and for which we provide the children, to:

- Offer the best academic education possible with emphasis on basic skills.

- Respect family privacy and our right as parents to rear our children according to **our own moral, ethical and religious beliefs** without interference.

- Provide a disciplined and morally up-lifting educational climate for the safety and peace of mind for both students and teachers. **Stop coddling the class trouble-makers at the expense of serious minded students.**

- Operate the schools as efficiently as private enterprise.

As a board member, I have tried to represent the **public interest**, not an Educational Bureaucracy. This is the kind of education I want for my five children. If this is what you want, please give me your vote and contact your friends on my behalf.

Sincerely yours,

(Mrs.) Alice Moore

The **final** board vote is at the May 11 primary. Democrats, Republicans and Independents can vote for me, for this non-partisan position.

Alice Moore Campaigns for the School Board
Alice Moore's campaign for reelection to the Kanawha County Board of Education in 1976 emphasized moral issues and fiercely attacked "Washington Bureaucrats" and government expenditures. Moore had run her first campaign for the board with the slogan "We need a mother on the board of education." She bore her fifth child while serving on the board, but one of the policies she championed prohibited pregnant girls from attending high school because she considered them "disruptive." Moore left Charleston in 1980 when her husband moved to a new church in Ohio. WV Division of Culture & History.

and limiting the state legislature's ability to raise taxes. Howard Jarvis, leader of the antitax movement, insisted, "You will have to take control of the government again, or else it is going to control you." What a newspaper called a "primal scream by the People against Big Government" spread to similar antitax crusades in other states.

Nixon Courts the Right

In his 1968 presidential campaign, Richard Nixon exploited hostility to black protest and new civil rights policies, wooing white southerners and a considerable number of northern voters away from the Democratic Party. As president, he used this "southern strategy" to make further

The Tax Revolt
Neighbors gather on the lawn of Los Angeles homeowner Mark Slade to rally for Proposition 13, an initiative campaign launched by conservative activist Howard Jarvis in 1978. Many homeowners rallied to Jarvis's antitax movement because rising land values and new assessments had increased their property taxes sharply, as their signs indicate. After Californians passed Proposition 13 by a large majority, tax revolts spread across the nation. Some thirty-seven states cut property taxes, and twenty-eight reduced income taxes. The tax issue helped the Republican Party end nearly half a century of Democratic dominance. Tony Korody/Getty Images.

"We've had all we can take of judicial interference with local schools," Phyllis Schlafly railed in 1972.

Children had been riding buses to school for decades, but busing for racial integration provoked fury. Violence erupted in Boston in 1974 when a district judge found that school officials had maintained what amounted to a dual system based on race and ordered busing "if necessary to achieve a unitary school system." When black students began to attend the formerly all-white South Boston High School, white students boycotted classes, and angry whites threw rocks at black students getting off buses. The whites most affected by busing came from working-class families who remained in cities abandoned by the more affluent and whose children often rode buses to predominantly black, overcrowded schools with deficient facilities. Clarence McDonough decried the liberal officials who bused his "kid half way around Boston so that a bunch of politicians can end up their careers with a clear conscience." African Americans themselves were conflicted about sending their children on long rides to schools where white teachers might not welcome or respect them.

White parents eventually became more accepting of integration, especially after the creation of magnet schools and other new mechanisms for desegregation offered more choice. Nonetheless, integration propelled white flight to the suburbs. By 1987, the number of white students in Boston public schools was just one-third of what it had been in 1974. Nixon failed to persuade Congress to end court-ordered busing, but after he had appointed four new justices, the Supreme Court imposed strict limits on the use of that tool to achieve racial balance.

Nixon's judicial appointments also reflected the southern strategy. He criticized the Supreme Court under Chief Justice Earl Warren for being "unprecedentedly politically active . . . using their interpretation of the law to remake American society according to their own social, political, and ideological precepts." When Warren resigned in 1969, Nixon replaced him with **Warren E. Burger**, a federal appeals court judge who was a strict constructionist — someone inclined to interpret the Constitution narrowly and to limit government intervention on behalf of individual rights. The Burger Court proved

inroads into traditional Democratic strongholds in the 1972 election.

The Nixon administration reluctantly enforced court orders to achieve high degrees of integration in southern schools, but it resisted efforts to deal with segregation outside the South. In northern and western cities, where segregation resulted from discrimination in housing and in the drawing of school district boundaries, half of all African American children attended nearly all-black schools. After courts began to order the transfer of students between schools in white and black neighborhoods to achieve desegregation, busing became "political dynamite," according to a Gallup poll.

Integration of Public Schools, 1968

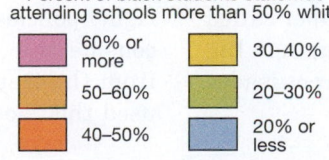

Percent of black students statewide attending schools more than 50% white

- 60% or more
- 50–60%
- 40–50%
- 30–40%
- 20–30%
- 20% or less

School Busing
Controversy over busing as a means to integrate public schools erupted in Boston when the 1974–1975 school year started. Opposition was especially high in white ethnic neighborhoods such as South Boston. Residents there resented liberal judges from the suburbs assigning them the burden of integration. Clashes between blacks and whites in South Boston, such as this one in February 1975 outside Boston's Hyde Park High School, prompted authorities to dispatch police to protect black students.
AP Photo.

more sympathetic than the Warren Court to the president's agenda, restricting somewhat the protections of individual rights established by the previous Court, but continuing to uphold many of the liberal programs of the 1960s. For example, the Court limited the range of affirmative action in *Regents of the University of California v. Bakke* (1978), but it allowed universities to consider race as one factor in admission decisions if they avoided strict quotas.

Nixon's southern strategy and other repercussions of the civil rights revolution of the 1960s ended the Democratic hold on the "solid South." In 1964, South Carolina senator Strom Thurmond, leader of the Dixiecrat challenge to Truman in 1948 (see chapter 26), changed his party affiliation to Republican. North Carolina senator Jesse Helms followed suit in 1971, and politicians throughout the South began to realize that the future for Democratic candidates had darkened there. By 2005, Republicans held the majority of southern seats in Congress and governorships in seven southern states.

In addition to exploiting racial fears, Nixon aligned himself with those anxious about women's changing roles and new demands. In 1971, he vetoed a bill providing federal funds for day care centers with a message that combined the old and new conservatism. Parents should purchase child care services "in the private, open market," he insisted, not rely on government. He appealed to social conservatives by warning about the measure's "family-weakening implications." In response to the movement to liberalize abortion laws, Nixon sided with "defenders of the right to life of the unborn." He did not comment publicly on *Roe v. Wade* (1973), which legalized abortion, but his earlier stance against abortion anticipated the Republican Party's eventual embrace of this as a key issue.

The Election of 1972

Nixon's ability to attract Democrats and appeal to concerns about Vietnam, race, law and order, and traditional morality heightened his prospects for reelection in 1972. Although the war in Vietnam continued, antiwar protests diminished with the decrease in American ground forces and casualties. Nixon's economic initiatives had temporarily checked inflation and unemployment (see chapter 28), and his attacks on busing and antiwar protesters had won increasing support from the right.

A large field of contenders vied for the Democratic nomination, including New York congresswoman **Shirley Chisholm**, the first African American to make a serious bid for the

presidency. South Dakota senator George S. McGovern came to the Democratic convention as the clear leader, and the new makeup of the convention delegates made his position even stronger. After the bitter 1968 convention in Chicago (see chapter 29), the Democrats reformed their rules, requiring delegations to represent the proportions of minorities, women, and young people in their states. These newcomers displaced many regular Democrats — officeholders, labor leaders, and representatives of older ethnic groups. One labor leader grumbled that "the Democratic party was taken over by the kooks," referring to the considerable numbers of young people and women who were to the left of party regulars. Though easily nominated, McGovern struggled against Nixon from the outset. Republicans portrayed him as a left-wing extremist, and his support for busing, a generous welfare program, and immediate withdrawal from Vietnam alienated conservative Democrats.

Nixon achieved a landslide victory, winning 60.7 percent of the popular vote and every state except Massachusetts. Although the Democrats maintained control of Congress, Nixon won majorities among traditional Democrats — southerners, Catholics, urbanites, and blue-collar workers. The president, however, had little time to savor his triumph, as revelations began to emerge about crimes committed to ensure the victory.

Watergate

During the early-morning hours of June 17, 1972, five men working for Nixon's reelection campaign crept into Democratic Party headquarters in the Watergate complex in Washington, D.C. Intending to repair a bugging device installed in an earlier break-in, they were discovered and arrested. Nixon and his aides then tried to cover up the intruders' connection to administration officials, setting in motion the most serious constitutional crisis since the Civil War. Reporters dubbed the scandal **Watergate**.

Over the next two years, Americans learned that Nixon and his associates had engaged in other abuses, such as accepting illegal contributions and unlawfully attempting to silence critics of the administration. Nixon was not the first president to lie to the public or to misuse power. Every president since Franklin D. Roosevelt had enlarged the powers of his office in the name of national security. This expansion of executive powers, often called the "imperial presidency," weakened the traditional checks and balances on the executive branch and opened the door to abuses. No president, however, had dared go as far as Nixon, who saw opposition to his policies as a personal attack and was willing to violate the Constitution to stop it.

Upon the arrest of the Watergate burglars, Nixon publicly denied any connection to them, while plotting secretly to have the CIA keep the FBI from investigating the crime. In April 1973, after investigations by a grand jury and the Senate suggested that White House aides had been involved in the cover-up effort, Nixon accepted official responsibility for Watergate but denied any knowledge of the break-in or cover-up. He also announced the resignations of three White House aides and the attorney general. In May, he authorized the appointment of an independent special prosecutor, Archibald Cox, to conduct an investigation.

The Gap in the Watergate Tapes
Franklin Roosevelt installed the first recording apparatus in the White House in 1940, but Nixon was the first president to use a voice-activated system, taping about 2,800 hours of conversations. When Nixon turned over the tapes during the Watergate investigation, an eighteen-and-a-half-minute gap appeared in a conversation between Nixon and his chief of staff, H. R. Haldeman, just three days after the Watergate break-in. Nixon's secretary, Rose Mary Woods, said that her foot must have slipped on the controls while she was transcribing the tape, using the transcription machine pictured here. Others suspected that Nixon had tampered with the evidence. Nixon Presidential Materials Project, National Archives and Records Administration.

Meanwhile, sensational revelations exploded in testimony before the Senate investigating committee, headed by Democrat Samuel J. Ervin of North Carolina. White House counsel John Dean described projects to harass "enemies" through tax audits and other illegal means and implicated the president in efforts to cover up the Watergate break-in. Another White House aide struck the most damaging blow when he disclosed that all conversations in the Oval Office were taped. Both Cox and the Ervin committee immediately asked for the tapes related to Watergate. When Nixon refused, citing executive privilege and separation of powers, Cox and Ervin won a unanimous decision from the Supreme Court ordering him to release the tapes.

Additional disclosures exposed Nixon's misuse of federal funds and tax evasion. In August 1973, Vice President Spiro Agnew resigned after an investigation revealed that he had taken bribes while governor of Maryland. Although Nixon's choice of House minority leader Gerald Ford of Michigan to succeed Agnew won widespread approval, Agnew's resignation further tarnished the administration, and Nixon's popular support plummeted to 27 percent.

In February 1974, the House of Representatives voted to begin an impeachment investigation. Upon reading passages from the White House tapes, House Republican leader Hugh Scott of Pennsylvania abandoned his support of the president, calling the transcripts a "deplorable, shabby, disgusting, and immoral performance by all." The transcripts revealed Nixon's orders to aides in March 1973: "I don't give a shit what happens. I want you all to stonewall it, let them plead the Fifth Amendment, cover up or anything else, if it'll save it — save the plan."

In July 1974, the House Judiciary Committee voted to impeach the president on three counts: obstruction of justice, abuse of power, and contempt of Congress. Seven or eight Republicans on the committee sided with the majority, and it seemed certain that the House would follow suit. Georgia state legislator and civil rights activist Julian Bond commented, "The prisons of Georgia are full of people who stole $5 or $10, and this man tried to steal the Constitution."

To avoid impeachment, Nixon announced his resignation to a national television audience on August 8, 1974. Acknowledging some incorrect judgments, he insisted that he had always tried to do what was best for the nation. The next morning, Nixon ended a rambling, emotional farewell to his staff with some advice: "Always give your best, never get discouraged, never get petty; always remember, others may hate you, but those who hate you don't win unless you hate them, and then you destroy yourself." Had he practiced that advice, he might have saved his presidency.

The Ford Presidency and the 1976 Election

Gerald R. Ford, who had represented Michigan in the House of Representatives since 1948, had built a reputation as a middle-of-the-road party

Nixon Resigns
The first president in U.S. history to resign his office, Nixon refused to admit guilt, even though tapes of his conversations indicated that he had obstructed justice, abused his power, and lied. In the decades after his resignation, he gradually rehabilitated his reputation and became an elder statesman and foreign policy adviser. All the living presidents attended his funeral in 1994. Here, he and his wife, Pat, are escorted by his successor, Gerald Ford, and his wife, Betty, as they leave the White House. © Bettmann/Corbis.

loyalist known for his integrity, humility, and dedication to public office. "I'm a Ford, not a Lincoln," he acknowledged. Most of official Washington and the American public looked favorably on his succession as president.

Upon taking office, Ford announced, "Our long national nightmare is over." But he shocked many Americans one month later by granting Nixon a pardon "for all offenses against the United States which he . . . has committed or may have committed or taken part in" during his presidency. Prompted by Ford's concern for Nixon's physical and mental health and by his hope to get the country beyond Watergate, this sweeping pardon saved Nixon from nearly certain indictment and trial, and it provoked a tremendous outcry from Congress and the public. Democrats made impressive gains in the November congressional elections, while Ford's action gave Nixon a new political life. Having gained a pardon without having to admit that he had violated the law, Nixon rebuilt his image over the next two decades into that of an elder statesman. Thirty of his associates ultimately pleaded guilty to or were convicted of crimes related to Watergate.

Congress's efforts to guard against the types of abuses revealed in the Watergate investigations had only limited effects. The **Federal Election Campaign Act of 1974** established public financing of presidential campaigns and imposed some restrictions on contributions to help prevent the selling of political favors. Yet politicians found other ways of raising money—for example, through political action committees (PACs), to which individuals could contribute more than they could to candidates. Moreover, in the 1976 case *Buckley v. Valeo*, the Supreme Court struck down limitations on campaign spending as violations of freedom of speech. Ever-larger campaign donations flowed to candidates from interest groups, corporations, labor unions, and wealthy individuals.

Special congressional investigating committees discovered a host of illegal FBI and CIA activities stretching back to the 1950s, including harassment of political dissenters and plots to assassinate Fidel Castro and other foreign leaders. In response to these revelations, President Ford established new controls on covert operations, and Congress created permanent committees to oversee the intelligence agencies. Yet these measures did little to diminish the public's cynicism about their government.

Disillusionment grew as the Ford administration struggled with serious economic problems: a low growth rate, high unemployment, a foreign trade deficit, and soaring energy prices. Ford carried these burdens into the election campaign of 1976, while contending with a major challenge from the Republican right. Blasting Nixon's and Ford's foreign policy of détente for causing the "loss of U.S. military supremacy," California governor Reagan came close to capturing the nomination.

The Democrats nominated **James Earl "Jimmy" Carter Jr.**, former governor of Georgia. A graduate of the U.S. Naval Academy, Carter spent seven years as a nuclear engineer in the navy before returning to Plains, Georgia, to run the family peanut farming business. Carter prided himself on his knowledge of policy issues, but people responded most to his promise of honesty and decency in government. He stressed his faith as a "born-again Christian" and his distance from the government in Washington. Although he selected liberal senator **Walter F. Mondale** of Minnesota as his running mate, Carter's nomination nonetheless marked a rightward turn in the party.

Carter had considerable appeal as a candidate who carried his own bags, lived modestly, and taught a Bible class at his Baptist church. He also benefited from Ford's failure to solve the country's economic problems, which helped him win the traditional Democratic coalition of blacks, organized labor, and ethnic groups and even

MAP 30.1
The Election of 1976

Candidate	Electoral Vote	Popular Vote	Percent of Popular Vote
Jimmy Carter (Democrat)	297	40,830,763	50.1
Gerald R. Ford (Republican)	240	39,147,793	48.0
Ronald Reagan (Independent Republican)	1	n/a	n/a

recapture some of the white southerners who had voted for Nixon in 1972. Still, Carter received just 50 percent of the popular vote to Ford's 48 percent (Map 30.1), although Democrats retained substantial margins in Congress.

REVIEW How did Nixon's policies reflect the increasing influence of conservatives on the Republican Party?

▶ The "Outsider" Presidency of Jimmy Carter

Carter promised a government that was "competent" as well as "decent, open, fair, and compassionate." He also warned Americans "that even our great Nation has its recognized limits, and that we can neither answer all questions nor solve all problems." Carter's humility and personal integrity helped revive trust in the presidency, but he faltered in the face of domestic and foreign crises.

Energy shortages and stagflation worsened, exposing Carter's deficiencies in working with Congress and rallying the public to his objectives. His administration achieved notable advances in environmental and energy policies, and he oversaw foreign policy successes concerning the Panama Canal, China, and the Middle East. Yet near the end of his term, Soviet-American relations deteriorated, new crises emerged in the Middle East, and the economy plummeted, all costing him a second term.

Retreat from Liberalism

Jimmy Carter vowed "to help the poor and aged, to improve education, and to provide jobs," but at the same time "not to waste money." When these goals conflicted, reform took second place to budget balancing. Carter's approach pleased increasing numbers of Americans unhappy about their tax dollars being used to benefit the disadvantaged while stagflation eroded their own standard of living. But his fiscal stringency frustrated liberal Democrats pushing for major welfare reform and a national health insurance program. Carter himself said, "In many cases I feel more at home with the conservative Democratic and Republican members of Congress than I do with the others."

Carter did fulfill liberals' desire to make government more inclusive. He appointed Andrew Young, former congressman and assistant to Martin Luther King Jr., as the first African American ambassador to the United Nations; and he named four women, including the first two black women, as cabinet heads. Moreover, Carter began to transform the federal judiciary. He appointed forty women to federal judgeships, five times as many as had

> **"In many cases I feel more at home with the conservative Democratic and Republican members of Congress than I do with the others."**
> —President
> **JIMMY CARTER**

Jimmy Carter Honors Martin Luther King Jr.
On January 14, 1979, the day before the anniversary of King's birthday, President Carter and his wife, Rosalyn, worshipped at Ebenezer Baptist Church in Atlanta, Georgia, where both King and his father had been pastors. Carter had been pushing to establish King's birthday as a national holiday, but Congress did not enact such a law until 1983. Here the Carters sing with Martin Luther King Sr.; Andrew Young, a minister who had worked with King, served in the U.S. House of Representatives, and was currently Carter's Ambassador to the United Nations; and Coretta Scott King. Jimmy Carter Presidential Library.

all his predecessors combined. He also increased the numbers of African American and Latino and Latina judges and named the first Latino ambassador to Mexico.

In contrast to his appointments, a number of factors hindered Carter's ability to transform his goals into policy. His outsider status helped him win the election but left him without strong ties to party leaders in Congress. Democrats complained of inadequate consultation and Carter's tendency to flood them with comprehensive proposals without devising a strategy to get them enacted. In addition, Carter refused to offer simple solutions to the American people, who were impatient for quick action against the forces that were squeezing their pocketbooks.

Even if he had possessed Lyndon Johnson's political skills, Carter might not have done much better. The economic problems he inherited — unemployment, inflation, and sluggish economic growth — confounded economic doctrine. Usually, rising prices accompanied a humming economy with a strong demand for labor. Now, however, stagflation burdened the economy with both steep inflation and high unemployment.

Carter first targeted unemployment. Although liberals complained that his programs did not do enough, Carter signed bills pumping $14 billion into the economy through public works and public service jobs programs and cutting taxes by $34 billion. Unemployment receded, but then inflation surged. Working people, wrote one journalist, "winced and ached" as their paychecks bought less and less, "hollowing their hopes and dreams, their plans for a house or their children's

college education." To curb inflation, Carter curtailed federal spending, and the Federal Reserve Board tightened the money supply. Not only did these measures fail to halt inflation, which surpassed 13 percent in 1980, but they also contributed to rising unemployment, reversing the gains made in Carter's first two years.

Carter's commitment to holding down the federal budget frustrated Democrats pushing for comprehensive welfare reform, national health insurance, and a substantial jobs program that would make government the employer of last resort. His refusal to propose a comprehensive national health insurance plan, long a key Democratic Party objective, led to a bitter split with Massachusetts senator Ted Kennedy, who fought Carter for the 1980 presidential nomination. Carter did sign legislation to ensure solvency in the Social Security system, but the measure increased both employer and employee contributions, thereby increasing the tax burden on lower- and middle-income Americans.

By contrast, corporations and wealthy individuals gained from new legislation, such as a sharp cut in the capital gains tax. When the Chrysler Corporation approached bankruptcy in 1979, Congress provided $1.5 billion in loan guarantees to bail out the tenth-largest corporation in the country. Congress also acted on Carter's proposals to deregulate airlines in 1978 and the banking, trucking, and railroad industries in 1980. Carter's successor, Ronald Reagan, would move much further, implementing conservatives' attachment to a free market and unfettered private enterprise.

VISUAL ACTIVITY

The Fuel Shortage

This billboard was sponsored by the Outdoor Advertising Association of America in 1980, while Iran held Americans hostage in Teheran (see page 1018) and gasoline shortages and rising gas prices vexed motorists all over the country. The shortages and high prices were sparked by the Iranian revolution, which brought to power Ayatollah Ruholla Khomeini, pictured on the billboard. The ad appeals to drivers to observe the fuel-saving 55-mile-per-hour national speed limit imposed in 1974 during the first oil crisis. John W. Hartman Center/Duke University Special Collections Library.

READING THE IMAGE: What assumptions does the billboard make about Americans' reactions to the Iran hostage crisis? What reasons does the ad give for drivers to respect the speed limit? What reasons are not mentioned?

CONNECTIONS: What impact did the hostage and oil crises have on American politics?

Energy and Environmental Reform

Complicating the government's efforts to deal with stagflation was the nation's enormous consumption of energy and its dependence on foreign nations to fill one-third of its energy demands. Consequently, Carter proposed a comprehensive program to conserve energy, and he elevated its importance by establishing the Department of Energy. Beset with competing demands among energy producers and consumers, Congress picked Carter's program apart. The **National Energy Act of 1978** penalized manufacturers of gas-guzzling automobiles and provided other incentives for conservation and development of alternative fuels, such as wind and solar power, but the act fell far short of a long-term, comprehensive program, and Carter's successor dismantled much of the regulation that did succeed.

In 1979, a new upheaval in the Middle East, the Iranian revolution, created the most severe energy crisis yet. In midsummer, shortages caused 60 percent of gasoline stations to close down; frustrated drivers waited in long lines and paid unprecedentedly high prices for gas. "We are struggling with a profound transition from a time of abundance to a time of growing scarcity in energy," Carter told the nation, asking for additional measures to address the shortages. Congress reduced controls on the oil and gas industry to stimulate American production and imposed a windfall profits tax on producers to redistribute some of the profits they would reap from deregulation.

Congress rejected a key Carter proposal to conserve oil by taxing it at the wellhead and thus ultimately increasing its cost to consumers. European nations were just as dependent on foreign oil as was the United States, but they more successfully controlled consumption. They levied high taxes on gasoline, which impelled people to rely more on public transportation and manufacturers to produce more energy-efficient cars. In the automobile-dependent United States, however, with inadequate public transit, people accustomed to driving long distances, and an aversion to taxes, politicians dismissed that approach. By the end of the century, the United States, with 6 percent of the world's population, would consume more than 25 percent of global oil production (Figure 30.1 and Map 30.2).

One alternative fuel, nuclear energy, aroused opposition from a vigorous environmental movement. Activists warned of radiation leakage, potential accidents, and the hazards of radioactive wastes from nuclear power plants, which provided about 10 percent of the nation's electricity in the 1970s. In 1976, hundreds of members of the Clamshell Alliance went to jail for attempting

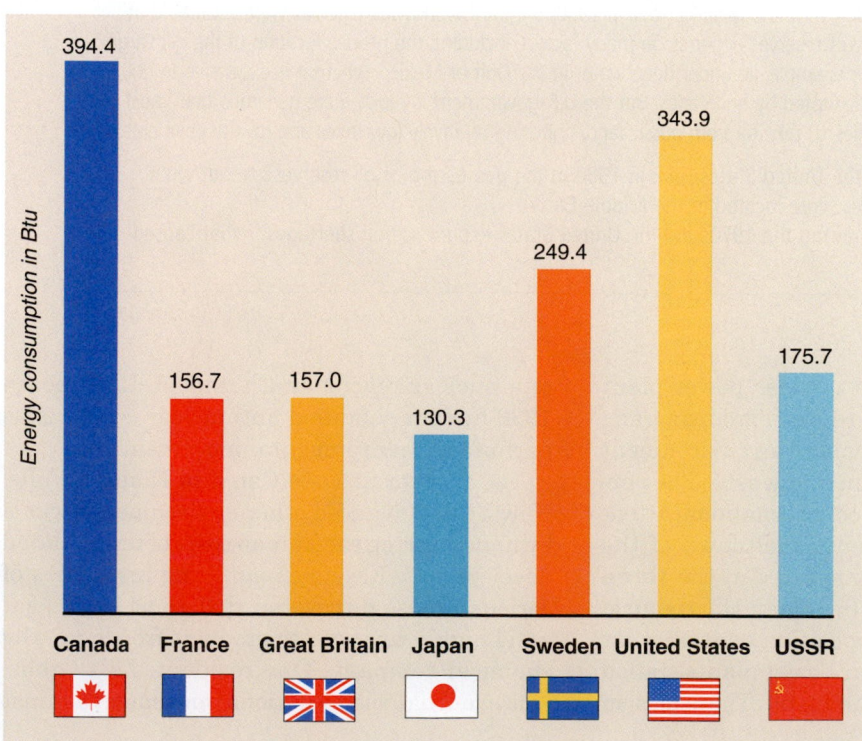

FIGURE 30.1 GLOBAL COMPARISON: Energy Consumption per Capita, 1980 Relative to most other industrialized nations, the United States consumed energy voraciously, with a per capita rate of consumption in 1980 that was more than twice as high as that of Britain, France, and Japan and nearly twice as high as that of the Soviet Union. A number of factors influence a nation's energy consumption (shown here in British thermal units, or Btu), including standard of living, climate, size of landmass and dispersal of population, availability and price of energy, and government policies such as support for public transportation. What country had a per capita rate of consumption even higher than that of the United States?

Countries with major oil reserves, 1980

Oil Reserves	Billions of Barrels
1. Saudi Arabia	166.5
2. Kuwait	68.5
3. Soviet Union	67.0
4. Iran	58.0
5. Mexico	31.3
6. Iraq	31.0
7. United States	29.8
8. U.A.E.	29.4
9. Libya	23.5
10. China	20.0

MAP ACTIVITY

Map 30.2   Worldwide Oil Reserves, 1980

Data produced by geologists and engineers enable experts to estimate the size of "proved oil reserves," quantities that are recoverable with existing technology and prices. In 1980, the total worldwide reserves were estimated at 645 billion barrels. The recovery of reserves depends on many factors, including the precise location of the oil. Large portions of the U.S. reserves, for example, lie under deep water in the Gulf of Mexico, where it is expensive to drill and where operations can be disrupted by hurricanes. But the U.S. government is much more generous than most nations in allowing oil companies to take oil from public land, imposing relatively low taxes and royalty payments.

READING THE MAP: Where did the United States rank in 1980 in the possession of oil reserves? About what portion of the total oil reserves were located in the Middle East?

CONNECTIONS: At what points during the 1970s did the United States experience oil shortages? What caused these shortages?

to block construction of a nuclear power plant in Seabrook, New Hampshire; other groups sprang up across the country to demand an environment safe from nuclear radiation and waste. The perils of nuclear energy claimed international attention in March 1979, when a meltdown of the reactor core was narrowly averted at the **Three Mile Island** nuclear facility near Harrisburg, Pennsylvania. Popular opposition and the great expense of building nuclear power plants stalled further development of the industry. The explosion of a nuclear reactor in Chernobyl, Ukraine, in 1986 further solidified antinuclear concerns as part of the environmental movement.

A disaster at Love Canal in Niagara Falls, New York, advanced other environmental goals by underscoring the human costs of unregulated development. Residents suffering high rates of serious illness discovered that their homes sat amid highly toxic waste products from a nearby chemical company. One resident, Lois Gibbs, who eventually led a national movement against

toxic wastes, explained how women were galvanized to become environmentalists: "I never thought of myself as an activist. I was a housewife, a mother, but all of a sudden it was my family, my children, and my neighbors." Finally responding to the residents' claims in 1978, the state of New York agreed to help families relocate, and the Carter administration sponsored legislation in 1980 that created the so-called Superfund, $1.6 billion for cleanup of hazardous wastes left by the chemical industry around the country.

Carter's environmental legislation did not stop there. He signed bills to improve clean air and water programs; to expand the Arctic National Wildlife Refuge (ANWR) preserve in Alaska; and to control strip-mining, which left destructive scars on the land. During the 1979 gasoline crisis, Carter attempted to balance the development of domestic fuel sources with environmental concerns, winning legislation to conserve energy and to provide incentives for the development of solar energy and environmentally friendly alternative fuels.

Promoting Human Rights Abroad

"We're ashamed of what our government is as we deal with other nations around the world," Jimmy Carter charged. Asserting that his predecessors' foreign policy violated the nation's principles of freedom and dignity, he promised to reverse the cynical support of dictators, secret diplomacy, interference in the internal affairs of other countries, and excessive reliance on military solutions.

Human rights formed the cornerstone of his approach. The Carter administration applied economic pressure on governments that denied their citizens basic rights, refusing aid or trading privileges to nations such as Chile and El Salvador, as well as to the white minority governments of Rhodesia and South Africa, which brutally violated the rights of their black majorities. Yet in other instances, Carter sacrificed human rights ideals to strategic and security considerations. He invoked no sanctions against repressive governments in Iran, South Korea, and the Philippines, for example, and he established formal diplomatic relations with the People's Republic of China in 1979, even though its government blatantly withheld democratic rights.

Carter's human rights principles faced another test when a popular movement overthrew an oppressive dictatorship in Nicaragua. U.S. officials were uneasy about the leftist Sandinistas who led the rebellion and had ties to Cuba. Once they assumed power in 1979, however, Carter recognized the new government and sent economic aid, signaling that the way a government treated its citizens was as important as how anti-Communist and friendly to American interests it was.

Applying moral principles to relations with Panama, Carter sped up negotiations over control of the Panama Canal and in 1977 signed a treaty providing for Panama's takeover of the canal in 2000. Supporters viewed the treaty as recompense for the barefaced use of U.S. power to obtain the canal in 1903. Opponents insisted on retaining the vital waterway. "We bought it, we paid for it, it's ours," claimed Ronald Reagan during the presidential primaries of 1976. It took a massive effort by the administration to get Senate ratification of the **Panama Canal treaty**, which passed by just one vote.

Seeking to promote peace in the Middle East, Carter seized on the courage of Egyptian president Anwar Sadat, the first Arab leader to risk his political career by talking directly with Israeli officials. In 1979, Carter invited Sadat and Israeli prime minister Menachem Begin to the presidential retreat at Camp David, Maryland, where he applied his tenacious diplomacy for thirteen days. These talks led to the **Camp David accords**, whereby Egypt became the first Arab state to recognize Israel, and Israel agreed to gradual withdrawal from the Sinai Peninsula, which it had seized in the 1967 Six-Day War (Map 30.3). Although the issues of Palestinian self-determination in other Israeli-occupied territories (the West Bank and Gaza) and the plight of Palestinian refugees remained unresolved, Carter had nurtured the first meaningful steps toward peace in the Middle East.

The Cold War Intensifies

Consistent with his human rights approach, Carter preferred to pursue national security through nonmilitary means and initially sought accommodation with the nation's Cold War enemies. In June 1979, Carter and Soviet premier Leonid Brezhnev signed a second strategic arms reduction treaty, setting limits on strategic missiles. Earlier that year, Carter had also followed up on another Nixon initiative, formally recognizing the People's Republic of China.

Yet that same year, Carter decided to pursue a military buildup when the Soviet Union invaded neighboring Afghanistan (see Map 30.3). Afghanistan's recently installed Communist government was threatened by Muslim opposition, which even before the invasion had received secret support from the CIA. Announcing that

MAP ACTIVITY

Map 30.3 The Middle East, 1948–1989

Determination to preserve access to the rich oil reserves of the Middle East and commitment to the security of Israel were the fundamental — and often conflicting — principles of U.S. foreign policy in that region.

READING THE MAP: Where did the United States become involved diplomatically or militarily in the Middle East between 1948 and 1989?

CONNECTIONS: What role did U.S. foreign policy regarding the Middle East and events in Israel play in provoking the 1973 Arab oil embargo against the United States? What precipitated the taking of U.S. hostages in Iran in 1979? Was U.S. intervention in the country a factor? If so, why?

the Soviet action "could pose the greatest threat to peace since the Second World War," Carter imposed economic sanctions on the Soviet Union, barred U.S. participation in the 1980 Summer Olympic Games in Moscow, and obtained legislation requiring all nineteen-year-old men to register for the draft.

Claiming that Soviet actions jeopardized oil supplies from the Middle East, the president announced the "Carter Doctrine," threatening the use of any means necessary to prevent an outside force from gaining control of the Persian Gulf. His human rights policy fell by the wayside as the United States stepped up aid to the military dictatorship in Afghanistan's neighbor, Pakistan, and the CIA funneled secret aid through Pakistan to the Afghan rebels. Finally, Carter called for hefty increases in defense spending.

Events in Iran also encouraged this hard-line approach. All the U.S. arms and aid had not enabled the shah to crush Iranian dissidents who still

resented the CIA's role in the overthrow of the Mossadegh government in 1953 (see chapter 27). Dissidents condemned the shah's savage attempts to silence opposition and detested his adoption of Western culture and values. These grievances erupted into a revolution in 1979 that forced the shah out of Iran and brought to power Shiite Islamic fundamentalists led by Ayatollah Ruholla Khomeini, whom the shah had exiled in 1964.

Carter's decision to allow the shah into the United States for medical treatment enraged Iranians, who believed that the United States would restore the shah to power as it had done in 1953. Anti-American demonstrations escalated in the capital city of Teheran. On November 4, 1979, a crowd broke into the U.S. Embassy and seized sixty-six U.S. diplomats, CIA officers, citizens, and military attachés. Refusing the captors' demands that the shah be returned to Iran for trial, Carter froze Iranian assets in U.S. banks and placed an embargo on Iranian oil. In

American Hostages in Iran

For more than a year — from November 4, 1979, to January 20, 1981 — Americans regularly saw TV images of the hostages taken by Iranian militants when they occupied the U.S. Embassy in Teheran. Early in the crisis, Ayatollah Khomeini ordered the release of thirteen of the sixty-six hostages, all of them women or African Americans, because he believed they were not spies and had already endured "the oppression of American society." Here the thirteen are presented to the press shortly before their release. © Sygma/Corbis.

April 1980, he sent a small military operation into Iran, but the rescue mission failed.

The disastrous rescue attempt and scenes of blindfolded U.S. citizens paraded before TV cameras fed Americans' feelings of impotence, simmering since the defeat in Vietnam. These frustrations in turn increased support for a more militaristic foreign policy. Opposition to Soviet-American détente, combined with the Soviet invasion of Afghanistan, nullified the thaw in superpower relations that had begun in the 1960s. The **Iran hostage crisis** dominated the news during the 1980 presidential campaign and contributed to Carter's defeat. Iran freed the hostages the day he left office, but relations with the United States remained tense.

REVIEW How and where did Carter implement his commitment to human rights, and where and why did human rights give way to other priorities?

▶ Ronald Reagan and the Conservative Ascendancy

The election of Ronald Reagan in 1980 marked the most important turning point in politics since Franklin D. Roosevelt won the presidency in 1932. Eisenhower and Nixon were middle-of-the-road Republicans, but Reagan's victory established conservatism's dominance in the Republican Party. Since the 1930s, the Democrats had defined the major issues. In the 1980s, the Republicans assumed that initiative, while Democrats searched for voter support by moving toward the right. The United States was not alone in this political shift. Conservatives rose to power in Britain with Prime Minister Margaret Thatcher, and they led governments in Germany, Canada, and Sweden, while socialist and social democratic governments elsewhere trimmed their welfare states.

Ronald Reagan Addresses Religious Conservatives
Reagan's victory in the 1980 election helped to reshape the Republican party by attracting millions of evangelical Christians who had favored Jimmy Carter in 1976. In his March 1983 address to the National Association of Evangelicals, he took a hard line on anticommunism, calling the Soviet Union an "evil empire." He also echoed the sentiments of religious conservatives with strong words about abortion and prayer in the schools and rejoiced that "America is in the midst of a spiritual awakening and a moral renewal." Ronald Reagan Presidential Library.

On the domestic front, the Reagan administration embraced the conservative Christian values of the New Right, but it left its most important mark on the economy: victory over inflation, deregulation of industry, enormous tax cuts, and a staggering federal budget deficit. Economic expansion, which took off after 1983, helped the middle class and brought great wealth to some, but the percentage of poor Americans increased, and income inequality grew. Although the Reagan era did not see a policy revolution comparable to that of the New Deal, it dealt a sharp blow to the liberalism that had informed American politics since the 1930s.

Appealing to the New Right and Beyond

Sixty-nine-year-old **Ronald Reagan** was the oldest candidate ever nominated for the presidency. Born in Tampico, Illinois, Reagan attended a small religious college and worked as a sportscaster before becoming a movie actor. He initially shared the politics of his staunchly Democratic father but moved to the right in the 1940s and 1950s and campaigned for Goldwater in 1964.

Reagan's political career took off when he was elected governor of California in 1966. He ran as a conservative, but in office he displayed considerable flexibility, approving a major tax increase, a strong water pollution bill, and a liberal abortion law. Displaying similar agility in the 1980 presidential campaign, he softened earlier attacks on programs such as Social Security and chose the moderate George H. W. Bush as his running mate.

Nonetheless, some Republicans balked at his nomination and at the party platform, which reflected the concerns of the party's right wing. For example, after Phyllis Schlafly persuaded the party to reverse its forty-year support for the Equal Rights Amendment, moderate and liberal Republican women protested outside the convention hall. (See "Historical Question," page 1026.) Some Republicans found a more acceptable presidential candidate in Illinois representative

John B. Anderson, who deserted his party to run as an independent.

Reagan's campaign capitalized on the economic recession and the international challenges symbolized by the Americans held hostage in Iran. Repeatedly, Reagan asked voters, "Are you better off now than you were four years ago?" He promised to "take government off the backs of the people" and to restore Americans' morale and other nations' respect. Fifty-one percent of voters responded favorably to Reagan's upbeat message, while Carter won 41 percent, and 7 percent went to Anderson. Republicans won control of the Senate for the first time since the 1950s.

While the economy and the Iran hostage crisis sealed Reagan's victory, he also benefited from the burgeoning grassroots conservative movements. An extraordinarily adept politician, Reagan appealed to a wide spectrum of groups and sentiments: free market advocates, militant anti-Communists, fundamentalist Christians, white southerners, and white working-class Democrats — the so-called Reagan Democrats disenchanted with the Great Society and suffering from the stagflation of the 1970s.

Reagan's support from religious conservatives, predominantly Protestants, constituted a relatively new phenomenon in politics known as the **New Right** or **New Christian Right**. During the 1970s, evangelical and fundamentalist Christianity claimed thousands of new adherents. Evangelical ministers such as Pat Robertson preached to huge television audiences, attacking feminism, abortion, and homosexuality and calling for the restoration of old-fashioned "family values." They wanted prayer back in the schools and sex education out of them. A considerable number of Catholics, such as Phyllis Schlafly, shared the fundamentalists' goal of a return to "Christian values."

Conservatives created political organizations such as the Moral Majority, founded by the Reverend Jerry Falwell in 1979, to fight "left-wing, social welfare bills, . . . pornography, homosexuality, [and] the advocacy of immorality in school textbooks." Dr. James Dobson, a clinical psychologist with a popular Christian talk show, founded the Family Research Council in 1983 to lobby Congress for measures to curb abortion, divorce, homosexuality, and single motherhood. The instruments of more traditional conservatives, who stressed limited government at home and militant anticommunism abroad, likewise flourished. Decades-old institutions like the *National Review* and the American Enterprise Institute were joined by new institutions such as the Heritage Foundation, a think tank that formulated and promoted conservative ideas. The monthly *Phyllis Schlafly Report* merged the sentiments of the old and new right.

Reagan embraced the full spectrum of conservatism, but he actually delivered more to the traditional right. He spoke for the New Right on such issues as abortion and school prayer, but he did not push hard for so-called moral or social policies. Instead, his major achievements fulfilled goals of the older right — strengthening the nation's anti-Communist posture and reducing taxes and government restraints on free enterprise. "In the present crisis," Reagan declared, "government is not the solution to our problem, government is the problem."

Reagan's admirers stretched far beyond conservatives. The extraordinarily popular president was liked even by Americans who opposed his policies and even when he made glaring mistakes. Reagan's optimism, confidence, and easygoing humor formed a large part of his appeal. Ignoring the darker moments of the American past, he presented a version of history that Americans could feel good about. Listeners understood his declaration that it was "morning in America" as a promise that the best was yet to come. Reagan also gained public sympathy after being shot by a would-be assassin in March 1981. Just before surgery to remove the bullet, Reagan joked to physicians, "I hope you're Republicans." His tremendous popularity helped him withstand serious charges of executive branch misconduct in his second term.

Unleashing Free Enterprise

Reagan's first domestic objective was a massive tax cut. Although tax cuts in the face of a large budget deficit contradicted traditional Republican economic doctrine, Reagan relied on a new theory called **supply-side economics**, which held that cutting taxes would actually increase revenue by enabling businesses to expand and encouraging individuals to work harder because they could keep more of their earnings. Business expansion would increase the production of goods and services — the supply — which in turn would boost demand. Reagan promised that the economy would grow so much that the government would recoup the lost taxes, but instead it incurred a galloping deficit.

In the summer of 1981, Congress passed the **Economic Recovery Tax Act**, the largest tax reduction in U.S. history. Rates were cut from 14 percent to 11 percent for the lowest-income individuals and from 70 percent to 50 percent for the wealthiest. The law gave corporations tax breaks and reduced levies on capital gains, gifts, and inheritances. A second measure, the Tax Reform Act of 1986, went even further, lowering the maximum rate on individual income to 28 percent and on business income to 35 percent. Although the 1986 law narrowed loopholes used primarily by the wealthy, affluent Americans saved far more on their tax bills than did average taxpayers, and the distribution of wealth tipped further in favor of the rich. Moreover, the total federal tax burden barely declined, from 19.4 percent of national income in 1981 to 19.3 percent in 1989.

> **"Hack, chop, crunch!"**
> —*Time* magazine, on Reagan's efforts to free private enterprise from government restraints

"Hack, chop, crunch!" were *Time* magazine's words for Reagan's efforts to free private enterprise from government restraints. Carter had confined deregulation to particular industries, such as air transportation and banking, while increasing health, safety, and environmental regulations. The Reagan administration, by contrast, pursued across-the-board deregulation. It declined to enforce the Sherman Antitrust Act (see chapter 18), which limited monopolies, against an unprecedented number of business mergers and takeovers. Reagan also loosened regulations protecting employee health and safety, and he weakened labor unions. When members of the Professional Air Traffic Controllers Organization — one of the few unions to support him in 1980 — struck in 1981, Reagan pointed to the illegality of the strike, gave workers two days to go back to work, and then fired thousands who didn't. Although federal workers had struck before without being penalized, Reagan demonstrated decisiveness and toughness, destroying the union and intimidating organized labor.

Ronald Reagan loved the outdoors and his remote ranch in southern California, where altogether he spent nearly one-eighth of his two-term presidency. Yet he blamed environmental laws for the nation's sluggish economic growth and targeted them for deregulation. His first secretary of the interior, James Watt, declared, "We will mine more, drill more, cut more timber," and released federal lands to private exploitation. Meanwhile, the head of the Environmental Protection Agency relaxed enforcement of air and water pollution standards. Of environmentalists, Reagan wisecracked, "I don't think they'll be happy until the White House looks like a bird's nest," but their numbers grew in opposition

to his policies. Popular support for environmental protection forced several officials to resign and blocked full realization of Reagan's deregulatory goals.

Deregulation of the banking industry, begun under Carter with bipartisan support, created a crisis in the savings and loan industry. Some of the newly deregulated savings and loan institutions (S&Ls) extended enormous loans to real estate developers and invested in other high-yield but risky ventures. S&L owners reaped lavish profits, and their depositors enjoyed high interest rates. But when real estate values began to plunge, hundreds of S&Ls went bankrupt. After Congress voted to bail out the S&L industry in 1989, American taxpayers bore the burden of the largest financial scandal in U.S. history, estimated at more than $100 billion.

Deregulation did little to reduce the size of government or the federal deficit. The administration cut funds for food stamps, job training, student aid, and other social welfare programs, and hundreds of thousands of people lost benefits. Yet increases in defense spending far exceeded the budget cuts, and the deficit climbed from $74 billion in 1981 to a high of $220 billion in 1986. Under Reagan, the nation's debt tripled to $2.3 trillion, and interest on the debt consumed one-seventh of all federal expenditures. Despite Reagan's antigovernment rhetoric, the number of federal employees increased from 2.9 million to 3.1 million during his presidency.

It took the severest recession since the 1930s to squeeze inflation out of the U.S. economy. Unemployment approached 11 percent late in 1982, and record numbers of banks and businesses closed. The threat of unemployment further undermined organized labor, forcing unions to make concessions that management insisted were necessary for industry's survival. In 1983, the economy recovered and entered a period of unprecedented growth.

That economic upswing and Reagan's own popularity posed a formidable challenge to the Democrats in the 1984 election. They nominated Carter's vice president, Walter F. Mondale, to head the ticket, but even his precedent-breaking move in choosing a woman as his running mate — New York representative Geraldine A. Ferraro — did not save the Democrats from a humiliating defeat. Reagan charged his opponents with concentrating on America's failures, while he emphasized success and possibility. Democrats, he claimed, "see an America where every day is April 15th [the deadline for income tax returns] . . . we see an America where every day is the Fourth of July."

Voters responded to the president's sunny vision and the economic comeback, giving him a landslide victory with 59 percent of the popular vote and every state but Minnesota. Stung by Republican charges that the Democratic Party was captive to "special interests" such as labor, women, and minorities, some Democratic leaders, including the young Arkansas governor, Bill Clinton, urged the party to shift more toward the right.

Winners and Losers in a Flourishing Economy

After the economy took off in 1983, some Americans won great fortunes. Popular culture celebrated making money and displaying wealth. Books by business wizards topped best seller lists, the press described lavish million-dollar parties, and a new television show, *Lifestyles of the Rich and Famous*, drew large audiences. College students listed making money as their primary ambition.

Participating conspicuously in the new affluence were members of the baby boom generation, known popularly as "yuppies," short for "young urban professionals." These mostly white, well-educated young men and women lived in urban condominiums and consumed lavishly — fancy cars, health clubs, expensive vacations, and electronic gadgets. Though definitely a minority, they established consumption standards that many tried to emulate. And, in fact, millions of Americans enjoyed larger houses that they filled with such new products as VCRs, microwave ovens, and personal computers.

Many of the newly wealthy got rich from moving assets around rather than from producing goods. Notable exceptions included Steven Jobs, who invented the Apple computer in his garage; Bill Gates, who transformed the software industry; and Liz Claiborne, who created a billion-dollar fashion enterprise. But many others made money by manipulating debt and restructuring corporations through mergers and takeovers. "To say these guys are entrepreneurs is like saying Jesse James was an entrepreneur," said Texas businessman Ross Perot, who defined entrepreneurship as making things rather than making money. Most financial wizards operated within the law, but greed sometimes led to criminal convictions.

Older industries faced increasing international pressures. Americans bought more Volkswagens and Hondas and fewer Fords and Chevrolets, as German and Japanese corporations overtook U.S. manufacturing in steel, automobiles, and electronics. International competition forced the collapse of some older companies. Others moved factories and jobs abroad to be closer to foreign markets or to benefit from the low wages in countries such as Mexico and Korea. Service industries expanded and created new jobs at home, but this work paid substantially lower wages than did manufacturing jobs. When David Ramos was laid off in 1982 from his $12.75-an-hour job in a steel plant, his wages fell to $5 an hour as a security guard, forcing his family to rely on food stamps. The number of full-time workers earning wages below the poverty level ($12,195 for a family of four in 1990) rose from 12 percent to 18 percent of all workers in the 1980s.

The weakening of organized labor combined with the decline in manufacturing to erode the

The S&L Crisis
These workers are removing the company's name from the Denver-based Silverado Banking, Savings and Loan Association, which collapsed in 1988, along with many other so-called "thrifts" that had speculated in risky loans for commercial real estate development. Neil Bush, son of President George H.W. Bush and one of Silverado's directors, was found by federal investigators to have had engaged in conflicts of interest, but he was not indicted on criminal charges. The Silverado failure cost the government more than a billion dollars. In 1989 Congress enacted strict regulations over the savings and loan industry. ©Bettmann/Corbis.

Homelessness
The increased presence of homeless people in cities across the nation challenged the view of the 1980s as a decade of prosperity. Hundreds of homeless people could be found on the sidewalks of the nation's capital every night. In November 1987, during the first snowfall of the season, a homeless man sleeps in Washington, D.C.'s Lafayette Square, across from the White House. What might the location of this homeless man suggest to viewers of the photograph? © Bettmann/Corbis.

position of blue-collar workers. Chicago steelworker Ike Mazo, who contemplated the $6-an-hour jobs available to him, fumed, "It's an attack on the living standards of workers." Increasingly, a second income was needed to stave off economic decline. By 1990, nearly 60 percent of married women with young children worked outside the home. Yet even with two incomes, families struggled. Speaking of her children, Mazo's wife confessed, "I worry about their future every day. Will we be able to put them through college?" The average $10,000 gap between men's and women's annual earnings made things even harder for the nearly 20 percent of families headed by women.

In keeping with conservative philosophy, Reagan adhered to trickle-down economics, insisting that a booming economy would benefit everyone. Average personal income did rise during his tenure, but the trend toward greater economic inequality that had begun in the 1970s intensified in the 1980s, encouraged in part by his tax policies. Between 1979 and 1987, personal income shot up sharply for the wealthiest 20 percent of Americans, while it fell by 9.8 percent for the

poorest. During Reagan's presidency, the percentage of Americans living in poverty increased from 11.7 to 13.5, the highest poverty rate in the industrialized world. Social Security and Medicare helped to stave off destitution among the elderly. Less fortunate were other groups that the economic boom had bypassed: racial minorities, female-headed families, and children. One child in five lived in poverty.

Even as the economy boomed, affluent urbanites walked past men and women sleeping in subway stations and on park benches. Experts debated the number of homeless Americans — estimates ranged from 350,000 upward — but no one doubted that homelessness had increased. Those without shelter included the victims of long-term unemployment, the erosion of welfare benefits, and slum clearance, as well as Vietnam veterans and individuals suffering from mental illness, drug addiction, and alcoholism.

REVIEW Why did economic inequality increase during the Reagan administration?

Continuing Struggles over Rights

The rise of conservatism put liberal social movements on the defensive, as the Reagan administration moved away from the national commitment to equal opportunity undertaken in the 1960s and the president's federal court appointments reflected that shift. Feminists and minority groups fought to keep protections they had recently won, and they achieved some limited gains. The gay and lesbian rights movement actually grew in numbers, edging attitudes toward greater tolerance and winning important protections in some states and cities.

Battles in the Courts and Congress

Ronald Reagan agreed with conservatives that the nation had moved too far in guaranteeing rights to minority groups. Crying "reverse discrimination," conservatives maintained that affirmative action unfairly hurt whites. Brian Weber, a Kaiser Aluminum production worker, filed a lawsuit when some African Americans with less seniority were admitted to a training program to which he had applied. Ignoring the discrimination that had prevented blacks from accruing seniority, he insisted that he should not "be made to pay for what someone did 150 years ago." Weber and other critics of affirmative action called for "color-blind" policies, ignoring statistics showing that minorities and white women still lagged far behind white men in opportunities and income.

Intense mobilization by civil rights groups, educational leaders, labor, and even corporate America prevented the administration from abandoning affirmative action, and the Supreme Court upheld important antidiscrimination policies, including the one that Weber challenged. Moreover, against Reagan's wishes, Congress voted to extend the Voting Rights Act with veto-proof majorities. The administration did, however, put the brakes on civil rights enforcement by appointing conservatives to the Justice Department, the Civil Rights Commission, and other agencies and by slashing their budgets.

Congress stepped in to defend antidiscrimination programs after the Justice Department persuaded the Supreme Court to severely weaken Title IX of the Education Amendments Act of 1972, a key law promoting equal opportunity in education. *Grove City v. Bell* (1984) allowed the Justice Department to abandon dozens of civil rights cases against schools and colleges, which in turn galvanized a coalition of civil rights organizations and groups representing women, the aged, and the disabled, along with their allies. In 1988, Congress passed the Civil Rights Restoration Act over Reagan's veto, reversing the administration's victory in *Grove City* and banning government funding of any organization that practiced discrimination on the basis of race, color, national origin, sex, disability, or age.

The *Grove City* decision reflected a rightward movement in the federal judiciary, upon which liberals had counted as a powerful ally. With the opportunity to appoint half of the 761 federal court judges and three new Supreme Court justices, President Reagan encouraged this trend by carefully selecting conservative candidates. He endured only one setback, when in 1987 the Senate denied confirmation of arch-conservative Robert Bork. Thus, Reagan's appointments turned the tide back toward strict construction — the literal interpretation of the Constitution that narrowly adheres to the words of its authors, thereby limiting judicial power to protect individual rights. The full impact of these appointments became clear after Reagan left office, as the Court allowed states to impose restrictions that weakened access to abortion for poor and uneducated women, reduced protections against employment discrimination, and whittled down legal safeguards against the death penalty.

Feminism on the Defensive

A signal achievement of the New Right was taking control of the Republican Party's position on women's rights. For the first time in its history, the Republican Party took an explicitly anti-feminist tone, opposing both the **Equal Rights Amendment (ERA)** and a woman's right to abortion, key goals of women's rights activists. When the time limit for ratification of the ERA ran out in 1982, Phyllis Schlafly celebrated victory on the issue that had first galvanized her antifeminist campaign, while amendment supporters looked for the silver lining. Sonia Johnson, who was excommunicated by the Mormon Church for her feminism in 1979, exag-

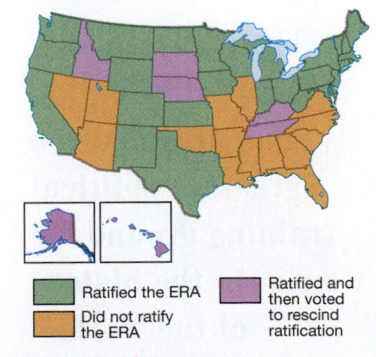

| Ratified the ERA | Ratified and then voted to rescind ratification |
| Did not ratify the ERA | |

The Fight for the Equal Rights Amendment

Why Did the ERA Fail?

The proposed Equal Rights Amendment to the U.S. Constitution guaranteed simply that "Equality of rights under the law shall not be denied or abridged by the United States or by any State on account of sex." Two more short sections gave Congress enforcement powers and provided that the ERA would take effect two years after ratification. By the 1970s, it had become the symbol of the women's movement, and the controversy it sparked revealed profound differences in beliefs and values among the American public.

The National Woman's Party, a militant suffrage organization that had helped win the vote for women in 1920, first proposed an equal rights amendment to the Constitution in 1923. The proposal won little support, however, before the resurgence of feminism in the late 1960s, when the National Organization for Women and other major women's groups made the ERA a key objective.

Both houses of Congress passed the ERA in March 1972 by overwhelming margins, 354 to 23 in the House and 84 to 8 in the Senate. Within three hours, Hawaii rushed to become the first state to ratify, and twenty-three states quickly followed. Public opinion heavily favored ratification, peaking at 74 percent in favor in 1974 and never falling below 52 percent, while opposition never topped 31 percent. Yet even after Congress extended the ratification period until 1982, the ERA fell three short of the three-fourths of the states required by the Constitution (see the map on page 1025). Why did a measure with so much congressional and popular support fail?

The ERA encountered well-organized and passionate opposition linked to the growing conservative forces in the 1970s. Conservatives' opposition to the ERA reflected in part their distaste for big government, but even more it signaled the New Right's determination to preserve traditional gender roles and "family values." What feminists saw as a simple measure to ensure equal rights for all citizens, ERA opponents saw as a threat to women's God-given and natural right to be protected and supported by men. They raised fears by suggesting extravagant ways in which courts might interpret the amendment. Senator Samuel J. Ervin Jr. claimed that the ERA would eliminate laws against rape, require coed housing for prisoners, and deprive women of alimony and child support. Others claimed it would legalize homosexual marriage and send women into combat.

Anti-ERA arguments drew on conservative Christian beliefs. Evangelical minister and politician Jerry Falwell declared the ERA "a definite violation of holy Scripture [and its] mandate that 'the husband is the head of the wife.'" Anti-ERA rhetoric also appealed to some women's understandings of their own self-interest. Many ERA opponents were full-time housewives who had no stake in equal treatment in the marketplace and who feared that the amendment would eliminate the duty of men to support their families.

Phyllis Schlafly and other conservative leaders skillfully mobilized women who saw their traditional roles threatened. In October 1972, she established a national movement called STOP (Stop Taking Our Privileges) ERA, whose members deluged legislators with letters and lobbied them personally in state capitols. In Illinois, they gave lawmakers apple pies with notes that read, "My heart and my hand went into this dough / For the sake of the family please vote 'no.'" Opponents also brought baby girls to the legislature wearing signs that pleaded, "Please don't draft me."

ERA opponents had an easier task than supporters, because the framers of the Constitution had stacked the odds against revision. All opponents had to do was to convince a minority of legislators in a minority of states to preserve the status quo. In addition, unlike their suffragist predecessors, ERA forces

"The struggle over [ERA] ratification has provided the greatest political training ground for women in the history of the world."

—Feminist SONIA JOHNSON

gerated only somewhat when she called the ratification struggle "the greatest political training ground for women in the history of the world." (See chapter 28 and "Historical Question," above.)

Cast on the defensive, feminists focused more on women's economic and family problems, where they found some common ground with the Reagan administration. The Child Support Enforcement Amendments Act helped single and divorced mothers collect court-ordered child support payments from absent fathers. The Retirement Equity Act of 1984 benefited divorced and older women by strengthening their claims to their husbands' pensions and enabling women to qualify more easily for private retirement pensions.

The Reagan administration had its own concerns about women, specifically about the gender gap in voting — women's tendency to support liberal and Democratic candidates in larger numbers than men did. Reagan eventually appointed three women to cabinet posts

had concentrated on winning Congress and were not prepared for the state campaigns.

The very gains feminists made in the 1960s and 1970s also worked against ratification. Congress had banned sex discrimination in employment, education, and other areas, and the Supreme Court had struck down several discriminatory laws, thus making it harder for ERA advocates to demonstrate the urgency of constitutional revision.

The ERA failed because a handful of men in a handful of state legislatures voted against it. The shift of only a few votes in states such as Illinois and North Carolina would have meant ratification. Schlafly's forces played a key role in the defeat, because men could vote "no" and take cover behind the many women who opposed it. And those women proved willing to commit time, energy, and money to block ratification because conservative leaders convinced them that the ERA threatened their very way of life.

Feminists did not leave the ERA battle empty-handed, however. Thousands of women were mobilized across the political spectrum, participating in the public arena for the first time. Fourteen states passed their own equal rights amendments after 1970. And feminists continued to fight legislative and judicial battles for the expansion of women's rights, struggles that continue to bear fruit in the twenty-first century.

Phyllis Schlafly Derails the ERA in Illinois
Illinois was one of the most hotly contested states in the battle over ratification of the Equal Rights Amendment. Here Schlafly rallies ERA opponents in the state capitol in 1975. Schlafly's STOP ERA movement succeeded in Illinois, her home state and the only northern state that failed to ratify. Despite time-consuming and energetic political activities that involved traveling and speaking across the country, Schlafly insisted on calling herself a housewife.
© Bettmann/Corbis.

Thinking about Beliefs and Attitudes

1. In what ways did the New Right see the Equal Rights Amendment as a threat to traditional values?

2. How did attitudes about the ERA differ from those about woman suffrage in the period leading up to ratification of the Nineteenth Amendment? (See chapter 22.)

and, in 1981, selected the first woman, **Sandra Day O'Connor**, a moderate conservative, for the Supreme Court, despite the Christian Right's objection to her support of abortion. But these actions accompanied a general decline in the number of women and minorities in high-level government positions. And with higher poverty rates than men, women suffered most from Reagan's cuts in social programs.

A powerful antiabortion movement won Supreme Court decisions that placed restrictions on women's ability to obtain abortions, but feminists fought successfully to retain the basic principles of *Roe v. Wade*. Moreover, they won a key decision from the Supreme Court ruling that sexual harassment in the workplace constituted sex discrimination. Feminists also made some gains at the state level in such areas as pay equity, rape, and domestic violence.

The Gay and Lesbian Rights Movement

In contrast to feminism and other social movements, gay and lesbian rights activism grew during the 1980s, galvanized in part by the

The Abortion Debate

After the Supreme Court upheld women's right to abortion in *Roe v. Wade* in 1973, several state legislatures instituted restrictions on that right that fell within the parameters outlined by the Court. In 1989, the Court upheld a Missouri law that prohibited public employees from performing abortions not necessary to save the life of the woman, banned the use of public buildings for providing abortions, and required physicians to perform viability tests on the fetus in pregnancies beyond the twentieth week. Here, activists on both sides of the issue rally before the Supreme Court on the day of its decision. AP Images/Ron Edmonds.

discovery in 1981 of a devastating disease, **acquired immune deficiency syndrome (AIDS)**. Because initially the disease disproportionately affected male homosexuals in the United States, activists mobilized to promote public funding for AIDS education, prevention, and treatment. Such efforts, along with the death from AIDS of a friend, movie star Rock Hudson, spurred President Reagan during his second term to attack the epidemic, which he had previously refused to address.

The gay and lesbian rights movement helped closeted homosexuals experience the relief of "coming out," and their visibility increased awareness, if not always acceptance, of homosexuality among the larger population. Beginning with the election of Elaine Noble to the Massachusetts legislature in 1974, several openly gay politicians won offices ranging from mayor to member of Congress, and the Democrats began to include gay rights in their party platforms. Activists organized gay rights marches throughout the

Gay Pride Parades

Since June 1970, when gays and lesbians marched in New York City on the first anniversary of Stonewall (see chapter 28), annual gay pride parades have taken place throughout the United States. According to history professor Robert Dawidoff, the parades are not about "flaunting private things in public," as some people charged, but a way for gay men and lesbians to express "pride . . . in having survived the thousand petty harassments and reminders of a special status we neither seek nor merit." Friends and families of homosexuals participate in the parades, as this sign from a parade in Los Angeles indicates. © Bettmann/Corbis.

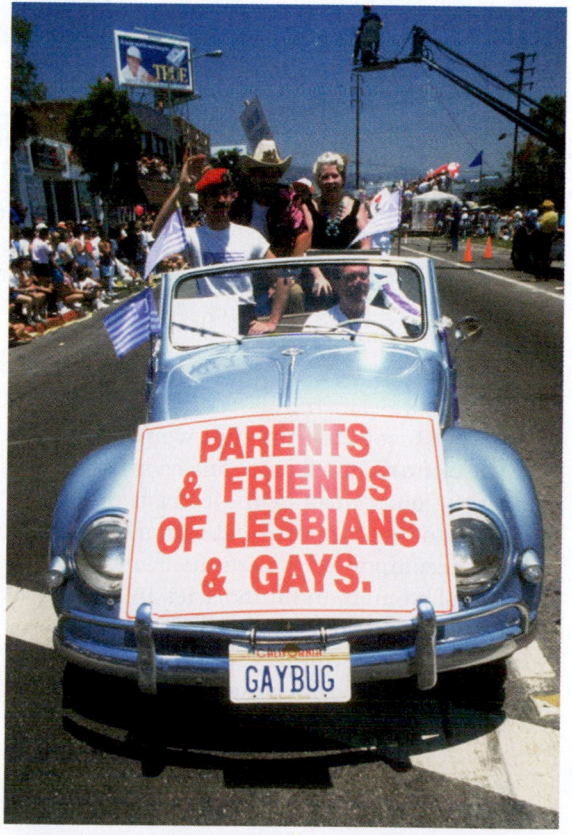

country, turning out half a million people in New York City in 1987.

Popular attitudes about homosexuality moved toward greater tolerance but remained complex, leading to uneven changes in policies. (See "Documenting the American Promise," page 1028.) Dozens of cities banned job discrimination against homosexuals, and beginning with Wisconsin in 1982, eleven states made sexual orientation a protected category under civil rights laws. Local governments and large corporations began to offer health insurance and other benefits to same-sex domestic partners.

Yet a strong countermovement challenged the drive for recognition of gay rights. The Christian Right targeted gays and lesbians as symbols of national immorality and succeeded in overturning some homosexual rights measures, which already lagged far behind antidiscrimination guarantees for minorities and women. Many states removed antisodomy laws from the books, but in 1986 the Supreme Court upheld the constitutionality of such laws. Until the Court reversed that opinion in 2003, more than a dozen states retained statutes that left homosexuals vulnerable to criminal charges for private consensual behavior.

REVIEW What gains and setbacks did minorities, feminists, and gays and lesbians experience during the Reagan years?

▶ Ronald Reagan Confronts an "Evil Empire"

Campaigning for president in the wake of the Soviet invasion of Afghanistan and the Iran hostage crisis, Reagan accused Carter of weakening the military and losing the confidence of the nation's allies and the respect of its enemies. As president, he accelerated Carter's arms buildup and harshly censured the Soviet Union, calling it "an evil empire." Yet despite the new aggressiveness — or, as some argued, because of it — Reagan presided over the most impressive thaw in superpower conflict since the Cold War had begun.

On the periphery of the Cold War, however, Reagan practiced militant anticommunism, assisting antileftist movements in Asia, Africa, and Central America and dispatching troops to the Middle East and the Caribbean. When Congress blocked Reagan's efforts to help overthrow the leftist government in Nicaragua, administration officials resorted to secret and illegal means to achieve their agenda.

Militarization and Interventions Abroad

Reagan expanded the military with new bombers and missiles, an enhanced nuclear force in Europe, a larger navy, and a rapid-deployment force. Despite the growing budget deficit, Congress approved most of these programs, and military expenditures shot up by one-third in the first half of the 1980s. Throughout Reagan's presidency, defense spending averaged $216 billion a year, up from $158 billion in the Carter years and higher even than in the Vietnam era.

Reagan startled many of his own advisers in March 1983 by announcing plans for research on the **Strategic Defense Initiative (SDI)**. Immediately dubbed "Star Wars" by critics who doubted its feasibility, the project would deploy lasers in space to destroy enemy missiles before they could reach their targets. Reagan conceded that SDI could appear to be "an aggressive policy" that would allow the United States to strike first and not fear retaliation. The Soviets reacted angrily because SDI violated the 1972 Antiballistic Missile Treaty and because they would have to make huge investments to develop their own Star Wars technology. Nonetheless, Reagan persisted, and subsequent administrations continued to spend billions on SDI research without producing a working system.

Reagan justified the military buildup and SDI as a means to negotiate with the Soviets from a position of strength, but he provoked an outburst of pleas to halt the arms race. In 1982, a rally demanding a freeze on additional nuclear weapons drew 700,000 people in New York City. That same year the National Conference of Catholic Bishops issued a strong call for nuclear disarmament. Hundreds of thousands demonstrated across Europe, stimulated by fears of new U.S. missiles scheduled for deployment there in 1983.

The U.S. military buildup was impotent before the growing threat of terrorism by nonstate organizations that sought political objectives by attacking civilian populations. Terrorism had a long history throughout the world, but in the 1970s and 1980s Americans saw it escalate in the Middle East, used by Palestinians after the Israeli occupation of the West Bank and by other

Protecting Gay and Lesbian Rights

Since the 1970s, the gay and lesbian rights movement has worked for passage of laws and ordinances to protect homosexuals from discrimination. In 1982, Wisconsin became the first state to ban discrimination on the basis of sexual orientation, following the lead of several cities throughout the United States that passed gay rights ordinances in the 1970s. By 2010, twenty-one states and the District of Columbia outlawed employment discrimination against gays, and dozens of cities did so. These measures ignited controversy, but whether homosexuals should have the right to marry aroused even more contention.

DOCUMENT 1
Ordinance of the City of Minneapolis, 1974

In 1974, the city council of Minneapolis amended its civil rights ordinance to cover discrimination based on sexual preference. The law provided a rationale for banning discrimination and, unlike some laws focusing exclusively on employment, encompassed a broad range of activities.

It is determined that discriminatory practices based on race, color, creed, religion, national origin, sex, or affectional or sexual preference, with respect to employment, labor union membership, housing accommodations, property rights, education, public accommodations, and public services, or any of them, tend to create and intensify conditions of poverty, ill health, unrest, civil disobedience, lawlessness, and vice and adversely affect the public health, safety, order, convenience, and general welfare; such discriminatory practices threaten the rights, privileges, and opportunities of all inhabitants of the city and such rights, privileges, and opportunities are hereby to be declared civil rights, and the adoption of this Chapter is deemed to be an exercise of the policy power of the City to protect such rights.

SOURCE: Excerpt from *The Rights of Gay People: The Basic ACLU Guide to a Gay Person's Rights*, edited by Norman Dorsen and Aryeh Neier, p. 251.

DOCUMENT 2
Letter to the Editor of the *New York Times* from Paul Moore, November 23, 1981

Paul Moore, Episcopal bishop of New York, made a religious argument for gay rights in his letter to the editor of the New York Times.

I quote our diocesan resolution: "Whereas this Convention, without making any judgment on the morality of homosexuality, agrees that homosexuals are entitled to full civil rights. Now therefore be it resolved this Convention supports laws guaranteeing homosexuals all civil rights guaranteed to other citizens." The Bible stands for justice and compassion for all of God's children. To deny civil rights to anyone for something he or she cannot help is against the clear commandment of justice and love, which is the message of the word of God. As a New Yorker I find it incredible that this great city, populated by more gay persons than any other city in the world, still denies them basic human rights. They make an enormous contribution to the commercial, artistic, and religious life of our city.

SOURCE: Paul Moore, reprinted with permission.

DOCUMENT 3
Vatican Congregation for the Doctrine of the Faith, August 6, 1992

The following statement from the Roman Catholic Church reflects the views of many religious groups that take positions against gay rights.

"Sexual orientation" does not constitute a quality comparable to race, ethnic background, etc., in respect to nondiscrimination. Unlike these, homosexual orientation is an objective disorder and evokes moral concern.

There are areas in which it is not unjust discrimination to take sexual orientation into account, for example, in the placement of children for adoption or foster care, in employment of teachers or athletic coaches, and in military recruitment.

SOURCE: Vatican Congregation for the Doctrine of the Faith, *Origins*, August 6, 1992. Reprinted with permission.

groups hostile to Western policies. The terrorist organization Hezbollah, composed of Shiite Muslims and backed by Iran and Syria, arose in Lebanon in 1982 after Israeli forces invaded that country to stop the Palestine Liberation Organization from using sanctuaries in Lebanon to launch attacks on Israel.

Reagan's effort to stabilize Lebanon by sending 2,000 Marines to join an international peacekeeping mission failed. In April 1983, a suicide

DOCUMENT 4
Testimony of Charles Cochrane Jr. before the House Subcommittee on Employment Opportunities of the Committee on Education and Labor, January 27, 1982

Although the U.S. Congress has never enacted legislation banning discrimination on the basis of sexual orientation, it has considered a number of bills for that purpose. Charles Cochrane Jr., an army veteran and police sergeant, testified on behalf of such a bill in 1982.

I am very proud of being a New York City policeman. And I am equally proud of being gay. I have always been gay.

I have been out of the closet for 4 years. November 6 was my anniversary. It took me 34 years to muster enough courage to declare myself openly.

We gays are loathed by some, pitied by others, and misunderstood by most. We are not cruel, wicked, cursed, sick, or possessed by demons. We are artists, business people, police officers, and clergymen. We are scientists, truck drivers, politicians; we work in every field. We are loving human beings who are in some ways different. . . .

During the early years of my association with the New York City Police Department a great deal of energy did go into guarding and concealing my innermost feelings. I believed that I would be subjected to ridicule and harassment were my colleagues to learn of my sexual orientation. Happily, when I actually began to integrate the various aspects of my total self, those who knew me did not reject me.

Then what need is there for such legislation as H.R. 1454? The crying need of others, still trapped in their closets, who must be protected, who must be reassured that honesty about themselves and their lives will not cost them their homes or their jobs. . . .

The bill before you will not act as a proselytizing agent in matters of sexual orientation or preference. It will not include affirmative action provisions. Passage of this bill will protect the inherent human rights of all people of the United States, while in no way diminishing the rights of those who do not see the need for such legislation. Finally, it will signify, quite clearly, recognition and compassion for a group which is often maligned without justification.

SOURCE: U.S. House Subcommittee on Employment Opportunities of the Committee on Education and Labor, Hearing on H.R. 1454, 97th Cong., 2nd sess., 1982, 54–56.

DOCUMENT 5
Carl F. Horowitz, "Homosexuality's Legal Revolution," May 1991

Carl Horowitz, a policy analyst at the Heritage Foundation, a conservative think tank, expresses some of the arguments of those opposed to government protection of homosexual rights.

Homosexual activists have all but completed their campaign to persuade the nation's educational establishment that homosexuality is normal "alternative" behavior, and thus any adverse reaction to it is akin to a phobia, such as fear of heights, or an ethnic prejudice, such as anti-Semitism.

The movement now stands on the verge of fully realizing its use of law to . . . intimidate heterosexuals uncomfortable about coming into contact with it. . . . The movement seeks to win sinecures through the state, and over any objections by "homophobic" opposition. With a cloud of a heavy fine or even a jail sentence hanging over a mortgage lender, a rental agent, or a job interviewer who might be discomforted by them, homosexuals under these laws can win employment, credit, housing, and other economic entitlements. Heterosexuals would have no right to discriminate against homosexuals, but apparently, not vice versa. . . .

These laws will create market bottlenecks. Heterosexuals and even "closeted" homosexuals will be at a competitive disadvantage for jobs and housing. . . .

The new legalism will increase heterosexual anger — and even violence — toward homosexuals.

SOURCE: Carl F. Horowitz, "Homosexuality's Legal Revolution," *Freeman*, May 1991.

Questions for Analysis and Debate

1. Which of these documents discuss how heterosexuals would be affected by laws protecting gay and lesbian rights? What effects did they anticipate?

2. Which of these documents suggest that the civil rights movement influenced the authors' views on homosexual rights?

3. What do you think is the strongest argument for government protection of homosexual rights? What do you think is the strongest argument against government protection?

---

attack on the U.S. Embassy in Beirut killed 63 people, and in October a Hezbollah fighter drove a bomb-filled truck into a U.S. barracks there, killing 241 Marines (see Map 30.3). The attack prompted the withdrawal of U.S. troops, and Lebanon remained in chaos, while incidents of murder, kidnapping, and hijacking by various Middle Eastern extremist groups continued.

Following a Cold War pattern begun under Eisenhower, the Reagan administration sought

Attack on the Marine Barracks in Beirut
On October 23, 1983, members of Islamic Jihad, an anti-Israel, anti-Western terrorist group sponsored by Iran, demonstrated their hostility toward the U.S. troops stationed in Lebanon by exploding a car bomb outside the U.S. Marine compound near the Beirut airport and killing 241 Americans. In the aftermath of the attack, army colonel Colin Powell, assistant to the secretary of defense, approved the decision to withdraw from Lebanon, believing that "America [was] sticking its hand into a thousand-year-old hornet's nest" in the Middle East. Shown here are military personnel searching for and removing bodies of their dead comrades. © Bettmann/Corbis.

to contain leftist movements across the globe. In October 1983, 5,000 U.S. troops invaded Grenada, a small island nation in the Caribbean where Marxists had staged a successful coup. In Asia, the United States moved more quietly, aiding the Afghan rebels' war against Afghanistan's Soviet-backed government. In the African nation of Angola, the United States armed rebel forces against the government supported by both the Soviet Union and Cuba. Reagan also sided with the South African government, which was brutally suppressing black protest against apartheid, forcing Congress to override his veto in order to impose economic sanctions against South Africa.

Administration officials were most fearful of left-wing movements in Central America, which Reagan claimed could "destabilize the entire region from the Panama Canal to Mexico." When a leftist uprising occurred in El Salvador in 1981, the United States sent money and military advisers to prop up the authoritarian government even though it had committed murderous human rights violations. In neighboring Nicaragua, the administration secretly aided the Contras (literally, "opposers"), an armed coalition seeking to unseat the left-wing Sandinistas, who had toppled a long-standing dictatorship.

The Iran-Contra Scandal

The Reagan administration's commitment to the Contras highlighted the issue of presidential versus congressional authority in using force abroad. Fearing another Vietnam, many Americans opposed aligning the United States with reactionary forces not supported by the majority of Nicaraguans. Congress repeatedly instructed the president to stop aiding the Contras, but the administration continued to secretly provide them with weapons and training and helped wreck the Nicaraguan economy. With support for his government undermined, Nicaragua's president, Daniel Ortega, agreed to a political settlement, and when he was defeated by a coalition of all the opposition groups, he stepped aside.

Secret aid to the Contras was part of a larger project that came to be known as the **Iran-Contra**

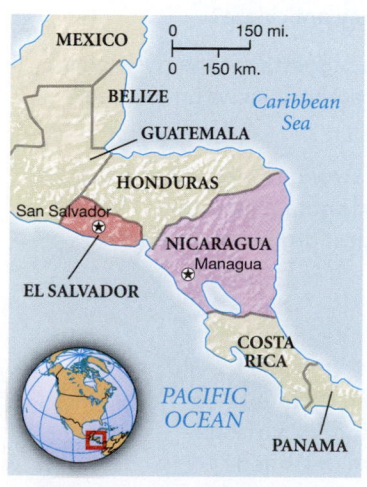

El Salvador and Nicaragua

scandal. It began in 1985 when officials of the National Security Council and CIA secretly arranged to sell arms to Iran, then in the midst of an eight-year war with neighboring Iraq, even while the United States openly supplied Iraq with funds and weapons. The purpose was to get Iran to pressure Hezbollah to release seven American hostages being held in Lebanon (see Map 30.3). Funds from the arms sales were then channeled through Swiss bank accounts to aid the Nicaraguan Contras. Over the objections of his secretary of state and secretary of defense, Reagan approved the arms sales, but the three subsequently denied knowing that the proceeds were diverted to the Contras.

Nuclear Freeze Campaign
Sixteen-year-old Justin Martino made this mask to wear in a 1985 march on the Pentagon in support of disarmament and world peace. Martino wanted to express his belief that "the arms race has no end except the end of life," and he later donated the mask to the Smithsonian Museum of American History. Worldwide demonstrations for nuclear disarmament achieved limited success when the United States and Soviet Union signed arms limitation agreements in 1987. Smithsonian Institution, Washington, D.C.

When news of the affair surfaced in November 1986, the Reagan administration faced serious charges. The president's aides had defied Congress's express ban on military aid for the Contras. Investigations by an independent prosecutor appointed by Reagan led to a trial in which seven individuals pleaded guilty or were convicted of lying to Congress and destroying evidence. One felony conviction was later overturned on a technicality, and President George H. W. Bush pardoned the other six officials in December 1992. The independent prosecutor's final report found no evidence that Reagan had broken the law, but it concluded that he had known about the diversion of funds to the Contras and had "knowingly participated or at least acquiesced" in covering up the scandal — the most serious case of executive branch disregard for the law since Watergate.

A Thaw in Soviet-American Relations

A momentous reduction in Cold War tensions soon overshadowed the Iran-Contra scandal. The new Soviet-American accord depended in part on Reagan's flexibility, his profound desire to end the possibility of nuclear war, and his fortitude in standing up to conservatives and the national security establishment. It also depended on an innovative Soviet head of state who recognized that his country's domestic problems demanded an easing of Cold War antagonism. **Mikhail Gorbachev** assumed power in 1985 determined to revitalize an inefficient Soviet economy incapable of delivering basic consumer goods. As Reagan remarked privately, Gorbachev knew that "his economy is a basket case." Hoping to stimulate production and streamline distribution, Gorbachev introduced some elements of free enterprise and proclaimed a new era of *glasnost* (greater freedom of expression), eventually allowing contested elections and challenges to Communist rule.

Concerns about immense defense budgets moved both Reagan and Gorbachev to the negotiating table. Enormous military expenditures stood between the Soviet premier and his goal of economic revival. With growing popular support for arms reductions, along with a push from his wife, Nancy, Reagan made disarmament a major goal in his last years in office and readily responded when Gorbachev took the initiative. A positive personal chemistry developed between them, and they met four times between 1985 and 1988. Although Reagan's insistence on proceeding with SDI nearly killed the talks, by December 1987 the superpowers had completed an **intermediate-range nuclear forces (INF) agreement**. The treaty marked a major turning point in U.S.-Soviet relations. It eliminated all short- and medium-range missiles from Europe and provided for on-site inspection for the first time. This was also the first time that either nation had agreed to eliminate weapons already in place.

In 1988, Gorbachev further reduced tensions by announcing a gradual withdrawal from Afghanistan, which had become the Soviet equivalent of America's Vietnam. In addition, the Soviet Union, the United States, and Cuba agreed on a political settlement of the civil war in the African nation of Angola. In the Middle East,

The Fireside Summit
This photograph captures the warmth that developed between President Ronald Reagan and Soviet leader Mikhail Gorbachev at their first meeting at Geneva in November 1985. Although the meeting did not produce any key agreements, the two men spent much more time in private meetings than had been scheduled. They began to appreciate each other's concerns and to build trust, launching a relationship that would lead to nuclear arms reductions and the end of the Cold War. Ronald Reagan Presidential Library.

both superpowers supported a cease-fire and peace talks in the eight-year war between Iran and Iraq. Within three years, the Cold War that had defined the world for nearly half a century would be history.

> **REVIEW**   How did anticommunism shape Reagan's foreign policy?

▶ Conclusion: Reversing the Course of Government

"Ours was the first revolution in the history of mankind that truly reversed the course of government," boasted Ronald Reagan in his farewell address in 1989. The word *revolution* exaggerated the change, but his administration did mark the slowdown or reversal of expanding federal budgets for domestic programs and regulations that had taken off in the 1930s. Although he did not deliver on the social or moral issues dear to the heart of the New Right, Reagan represented the "choice not an echo" that Phyllis Schlafly had called for in 1964, as he used his skills as "the Great Communicator" to cultivate antigovernment sentiment and undo the liberal assumptions of the New Deal.

Antigovernment sentiment grew along with the backlash against the reforms of the 1960s and the conduct of the Vietnam War. Watergate and other lawbreaking by Nixon administration

officials further disillusioned Americans. Presidents Ford and Carter restored morality to the White House, but neither could solve the gravest economic problems since the Great Depression — slow economic growth, stagflation, and an increasing trade deficit. Even the Democrat Carter gave higher priority to fiscal austerity than to social reform, and he began the government's retreat from regulation of key industries.

A new conservative movement helped Reagan win the presidency and flourished during his administration. Reagan's tax cuts, combined with hefty increases in defense spending, created a federal deficit crisis that justified cuts in social welfare spending, made new federal initiatives unthinkable, and burdened the country for years to come. These policies also contributed to a widening income gap between the rich and poor, weighing heavily especially on minorities, female-headed families, and children. Many Americans continued to support specific federal programs — especially those, such as Social Security and Medicare, that reached beyond the poor — but public sentiment about the government in general had taken a U-turn from the Roosevelt era. Instead of seeing the government as a helpful and problem-solving institution, many believed that not only was it ineffective at solving national problems, but it also often made things worse. As Reagan appointed new justices, the Supreme Court retreated from liberalism, curbing the government's authority to protect individual rights and regulate the economy.

With the economic recovery that set in after 1982 and his optimistic rhetoric, Reagan lifted the confidence of Americans about their nation and its

promise — confidence that had eroded with the economic and foreign policy blows of the 1970s. He began his presidency voicing harsh rhetoric against the Soviet Union and intensifying the military buildup begun by Carter; he left office having helped move the two superpowers to the highest level of cooperation since the Cold War began. Although that accord was not welcomed by strong anti-Communist conservatives like Phyllis Schlafly, it signaled developments that would transform American-Soviet relations — and the world — in the next decade.

► Selected Bibliography

General Works

Edward D. Berkowitz, *Something Happened: A Political and Cultural Overview of the Seventies* (2006).

Steven F. Hayward, *The Age of Reagan: The Conservative Counterrevolution, 1980–1989* (2009).

Burton I. Kaufman and Scott Kaufman, *The Presidency of James Earl Carter, Jr.* (2006).

Robert Mason, *Richard Nixon and the Quest for a New Majority* (2004).

Keith W. Olson, *Watergate: The Presidential Scandal That Shook America* (2003).

James T. Patterson, *Restless Giant: The United States from Watergate to* Bush v. Gore (2005).

Gil Troy, *Morning in America: How Ronald Reagan Invented the 1980s* (2005).

Sean Wilentz, *The Age of Reagan: A History, 1974–2008* (2008).

Foreign Policy

David Farber, *Taken Hostage: The Iran Hostage Crisis and America's First Encounter with Radical Islam* (2004).

Beth A. Fischer, *The Reagan Reversal: Foreign Policy and the End of the Cold War* (1997).

Frances FitzGerald, *Way Out There in the Blue: Reagan, Star Wars, and the End of the Cold War* (2000).

Scott Kaufman, *Plans Unraveled: The Foreign Policy of the Carter Administration* (2008).

William M. LeoGrande, *Our Own Backyard: The United States in Central America, 1977–1992* (1998).

Douglas Little, *American Orientalism: The United States and the Middle East since 1945* (2002).

James Mann, *The Rebellion of Ronald Reagan: A History of the End of the Cold War* (2009).

The Economy, Energy, and the Environment

W. Carl Biven, *Jimmy Carter's Economy: Policy in an Age of Limits* (2003).

Elizabeth D. Blum, *Love Canal Revisited: Race, Class, and Gender in Environmental Activism* (2008).

Jefferson Cowie, *Stayin' Alive: The 1970s and the Last Days of the Working Class* (2010).

Samuel P. Hays, *A History of Environmental Politics since 1945* (2000).

Christopher Jencks, *The Homeless* (1994).

Hal K. Rothman, *The Greening of a Nation? Environmentalism in the United States since 1945* (1998).

Robert J. Samuelson, *The American Dream in the Age of Entitlement, 1945–1995* (1996).

John W. Sloan, *The Reagan Effect: Economics and Presidential Leadership* (1999).

Judith Stein, *Pivotal Decade: How the United States Traded Factories for Finance in the Seventies* (2010).

Social Movements and Contests over Rights

Terry H. Anderson, *The Pursuit of Fairness: A History of Affirmative Action* (2004).

John A. Andrew, *The Other Side of the Sixties: Young Americans for Freedom and the Rise of Conservative Politics* (1997).

Elizabeth A. Armstrong, *Forging Gay Identities: Organizing Sexuality in San Francisco, 1950–1994* (2003).

Donald T. Critchlow, *The Conservative Ascendancy: How the GOP Right Made Political History* (2007).

Donald T. Critchlow, *Phyllis Schlafly and Grassroots Conservatism: A Woman's Crusade* (2005).

Godfrey Hodgson, *The World Turned Right Side Up: A History of the Conservative Ascendancy in America* (1996).

Laura Kalman, *Right Star Rising: A New Politics, 1974–1980* (2010).

J. Anthony Lukas, *Common Ground: A Turbulent Decade in the Lives of Three American Families* (1986).

William Martin, *With God on Our Side: The Rise of the Religious Right in America* (1996).

Donald G. Mathews and Jane Sherron De Hart, *Sex, Gender, and the Politics of the ERA* (1990).

Lisa McGirr, *Suburban Warriors: The Origins of the New American Right* (2001).

James F. Simon, *The Center Holds: The Power Struggle inside the Rehnquist Court* (1995).

► **FOR MORE BOOKS ABOUT TOPICS IN THIS CHAPTER,** see the Online Bibliography at **bedfordstmartins.com/roark.**

► **FOR ADDITIONAL PRIMARY SOURCES FROM THIS PERIOD,** see Michael Johnson, ed., *Reading the American Past*, Fifth Edition.

► **FOR WEB SITES, IMAGES, AND DOCUMENTS RELATED TO TOPICS AND PLACES IN THIS CHAPTER,** visit Make History at **bedfordstmartins.com/roark.**

Reviewing Chapter 30

REVIEW QUESTIONS

Use key terms and dates to support your answer.

1. How did Nixon's policies reflect the increasing influence of conservatives on the Republican Party? (pp. 1005–1013)

2. How and where did Carter implement his commitment to human rights, and where and why did human rights give way to other priorities? (pp. 1013–1019)

3. Why did economic inequality increase during the Reagan administration? (pp. 1019–1025)

4. What gains and setbacks did minorities, feminists, and gays and lesbians experience during the Reagan years? (pp. 1026–1029)

5. How did anticommunism shape Reagan's foreign policy? (pp. 1029–1034)

MAKING CONNECTIONS

Draw on key terms, the timeline, and review questions.

1. What was Watergate's legacy for American politics in the following decade? In your answer, explain what led to Nixon's resignation. How did Congress try to prevent such abuses of power in the future?

2. Both the Republican and Democratic parties changed significantly in the 1970s and 1980s. Describe these changes, and discuss how they shaped contemporary American politics. In your answer, be sure to cite specific political developments.

3. Recent experiences in Vietnam hung over the foreign policy decisions of Presidents Carter and Reagan. How did each president try to reconcile the lessons of that conflict and the ongoing Cold War? In your answer, be sure to discuss the impact of the Vietnam War on specific policies in the 1970s and 1980s.

4. American regional politics shifted in significant ways during the 1970s and 1980s. Why was grassroots conservatism particularly strong in the Sun Belt? What was its relationship to the civil rights and equal opportunity developments of the 1960s? What was its relationship to economic development?

LINKING TO THE PAST

Link events in this chapter to earlier events.

1. How were the conservatives of the 1980s similar to and different from the conservatives who opposed the New Deal in the 1930s? (See chapter 24.)

2. Presidents Jimmy Carter and Woodrow Wilson both claimed human rights as a central principle of their foreign policy. Which one do you think pursued human rights more consistently? Which one was more successful in spreading human rights? Explain your answers. (See chapter 22.)

▶ FOR PRACTICE QUIZZES AND OTHER STUDY TOOLS, visit the Online Study Guide at bedfordstmartins.com/roark.

TIMELINE 1966–1988

1966
- Republican Ronald Reagan elected governor of California.

1968
- Republican Richard Nixon elected president.

1969
- Warren E. Burger appointed chief justice of U.S. Supreme Court.

1971
- Nixon vetoes comprehensive child care bill.

1972
- Nixon campaign aides arrested at Watergate complex.
- Nixon reelected president.

1974
- Nixon resigns; Gerald Ford becomes president.
- Ford pardons Nixon of any crimes he may have committed while president.

1976
- Democrat Jimmy Carter elected president.

1977
- United States signs Panama Canal treaty.

1978
- *Regents of University of California v. Bakke*.
- Congress deregulates airlines.

1979
- Camp David accords signed.
- Carter establishes formal diplomatic relations with China.
- Soviet Union invades Afghanistan.
- Hostage crisis in Iran begins.
- Moral Majority founded.

1980
- Congress deregulates banking, trucking, and railroad industries.
- Congress passes Superfund legislation.
- Republican Ronald Reagan elected president.

1981
- Researchers discover AIDS virus.
- Economic Recovery Tax Act.

1982
- Large demonstrations against nuclear weapons.

1983
- Terrorist bomb kills 241 U.S. Marines in Beirut, Lebanon.
- Reagan announces plans for Strategic Defense Initiative ("Star Wars").
- Family Research Council founded.
- Reagan reelected president.

1986
- Iran-Contra scandal.

1987
- INF agreement signed.

1988
- Civil Rights Restoration Act.

CONTAINER BOX

Containerized shipping revolutionized the maritime industry and contributed to the intensifying globalization that occurred near the end of the twentieth century. The use of truck-size boxes to move goods without loading and unloading individual items began in the 1950s and became the norm by the 1980s. The container box's efficiency and cost-effectiveness stimulated industrial development around the world and gave Americans access to an unheralded array of cheap consumer goods. After the terrorist attacks against the United States on September 11, 2001, some Americans worried that weapons of mass destruction might be concealed within container boxes. In the background, container ships unload at Port Elizabeth, New Jersey.

Container box: Shutterstock Images LLC;
background: © Bettmann/
Corbis.

31

The Promises and Challenges of Globalization

Since 1989

IN HIS MOSCOW HOTEL ROOM ON APRIL 22, 1988, RONALD REAGAN'S national security adviser, Colin L. Powell, contemplated the plans that Premier Mikhail Gorbachev had just announced, which would dramatically alter the Soviet Union's government and economy. "Lying there in bed," Powell recalled, "I realized that one phase of my life had ended, and another was about to begin. Up until now, as a soldier, my mission had been to confront, contain, and, if necessary, combat communism. Now I had to think about a world without a Cold War." For the next sixteen years, Powell labored to redefine his country's role in a world transformed.

Colin Powell was born in Harlem in 1937 and grew up in the Bronx, the son of Jamaican immigrants. His father headed the shipping department in a garment factory, where his mother worked as a seamstress. After attending public schools, Powell enrolled in City College of New York. There he joined the army's Reserve Officers Training Corps (ROTC) program, the defining experience of his college years. "The discipline, the structure, the camaraderie, the sense of belonging," he said, "were what I craved." When he graduated in 1958, Powell began a lifelong career in military and public service, rising to the highest rank of four-star general. He chose to stay in the army primarily because "I loved what I was doing." But he also recognized that "for a black, no other avenue in American society offered so much opportunity." Powell's two tours of duty in Vietnam taught him that "you do not squander courage and lives without clear purpose, without the country's backing, and without full commitment." In his subsequent positions as national security adviser to Ronald Reagan, chairman of the Joint Chiefs of Staff in the George H. W. Bush and Bill Clinton administrations, and secretary of state under George W. Bush, Powell endeavored to keep his country out of "halfhearted warfare for half-baked reasons that the American people could not understand or support."

Powell's sense that Gorbachev's reforms would ring down the curtain on the Cold War became a reality more quickly than anyone anticipated. Eastern Europe broke free from Communist control in 1989, and the Soviet Union disintegrated in 1991. Throughout the 1990s, as the lone superpower, the United States deployed both military and diplomatic power during episodes of instability in Latin America, the Middle East, eastern Europe, and

Asia, almost always in concert with the major nations of Europe and Asia. In 1991, in its first full-fledged war since Vietnam, the United States led a United Nations–authorized force of twenty-eight nations to repel Iraq's invasion of Kuwait.

During a temporary retirement from public service in the 1990s, Powell remarked that "neither of the two major parties fits me comfortably." Many Americans seemed to agree: They turned Republican George H. W. Bush out of office in 1992 but elected Republican Congresses during Democrat Bill Clinton's administration. When Republican George W. Bush (son of George H. W. Bush) entered the White House in 2001, he faced a nearly evenly divided Congress. Between 1989 and 2000, domestic policies reflected a slight retreat from the conservatism of the Reagan years. The first Bush administration approved tighter environmental protections and new rights for people with disabilities, and President Clinton signed measures strengthening gun control and aiding low-wage earners. But the pendulum swung back to the right in the second Bush presidency.

All three presidents shared a commitment to hastening the globalization processes that were linking nations together in an increasingly connected economy. As capital, products, information, and people crossed national boundaries in greater numbers and at greater speed, a surge of immigration rivaled the stream of a century earlier that had brought Powell's parents to the United States. Powell cheered globalization, predicting that the world would become "defined by trade relations, by the flow of information, capital, technology, and goods, rather than by armies glaring at each other across borders."

He was not so naive as to anticipate a world "without war or conflict," recognizing challenges such as nuclear proliferation, nationalist passions in areas of former Soviet dominance and the Middle East, civil wars in Africa, and Islamic extremism. But he shared other Americans' shock when in September 2001 deadly terrorist attacks in New York City and Washington, D.C., exposed American vulnerability to new and horrifying threats and sent U.S. soldiers into Afghanistan to overthrow the government that harbored the attackers. The administration's response to terrorism overwhelmed Secretary of State Powell's commitments to internationalism, multilateralism, and military restraint. In 2003, George W. Bush began a second war against Iraq, implementing a distinct shift to a foreign policy based on preemptive attacks against presumed threats and going it alone if necessary. The unpopularity of that war and a severe financial crisis helped the Democrats regain power and elect Barack Obama as the first African American president.

Secretary of State Colin Powell

Colin Powell's loyalty and discretion helped him rise through the ranks of the army and serve in four presidential administrations. The U.S. invasion of Iraq in March 2003 ran counter to Powell's commitment to acting through the international community and sacrificing American lives only when a vital interest was at stake and an exit plan had been established. Nonetheless, he stayed in his job until 2005 and defended administration policy. In this photo taken at the White House in February 2003, Powell listens to Secretary of Defense Donald Rumsfeld. National Security Adviser Condoleezza Rice stands behind them. Charles Ommanney/Contact Press Images for *Newsweek*.

▶ Domestic Stalemate and Global Upheaval: The Presidency of George H. W. Bush

Announcing his bid for the presidency in 1988, Vice President **George H. W. Bush** declared, "We don't need radical new directions." Generally satisfied with the agenda set by Ronald Reagan and facing a Democratic-controlled Congress, Bush proposed few domestic initiatives. His dispatch of troops to oust the corrupt dictator of Panama, Manuel Noriega, represented a much longer continuity, following a century of U.S. intervention in Latin America.

Yet as the most dramatic changes since the 1940s swept through the world, Bush confronted situations that did not fit the simpler free world versus communism framework that had guided foreign policy since World War II. Most Americans approved of Bush's handling of two challenges to U.S. foreign policy: the disintegration of the Soviet Union and its hold over Eastern Europe, and Iraq's invasion of neighboring Kuwait. But voters' concern over a sluggish economy limited Bush to one term in the White House.

Gridlock in Government

The son of a wealthy New England senator, George Herbert Walker Bush fought in World War II, earned a Yale degree, and then settled in Texas to make his own way in the oil industry and politics. He served in Congress during the 1960s and headed the CIA during the Nixon and Ford years. When Ronald Reagan achieved a commanding lead in the 1980 presidential primaries, Bush adjusted his more moderate policy positions to fit Reagan's conservative agenda and accepted second place on the Republican ticket. At the end of Reagan's second term, Republicans rewarded him with the presidential nomination.

Several candidates competed for the Democratic nomination in 1988. The Reverend Jesse Jackson — whose Rainbow Coalition campaign centered on the needs of minorities, women, the working class, and the poor — made an impressive bid, winning several primaries and seven million votes. But a more centrist candidate, Massachusetts governor Michael Dukakis, won the nomination. On election day, half the eligible voters stayed home, indicating their disgust with the negative campaigning or their satisfaction with the Republican record on peace and prosperity. Divided government would remain, however, as Bush won 54 percent of the vote but the Democrats gained seats in Congress.

Although President Bush saw himself primarily as guardian and beneficiary of the Reagan legacy, he promised "a kinder, gentler nation" and was more inclined than Reagan to approve government activity in the private sphere. An oil spill from an Exxon tanker that ruined eight hundred miles of Alaska shoreline in 1989 heightened environmental awareness and helped Bush convince Congress to approve the **Clean Air Act of 1990**, the strongest, most comprehensive environmental law in history.

"Let the shameful wall of exclusion finally come tumbling down," proclaimed Bush when he signed another regulatory measure in 1990, the **Americans with Disabilities Act**. Benefiting some forty million Americans, this measure banned discrimination in employment, transportation, public accommodation, communications, and governmental activities, requiring that private businesses and public facilities be accessible to people with disabilities. Cynthia Jones, publisher of a magazine on disability politics, noticed a breeze stirring over the White House lawn at the signing of the bill. She said, "It was kind of like a new breath of air was sweeping across America. . . . People knew they had rights. That was wonderful." (See "Seeking the American Promise," page 1042.)

> "It was kind of like a new breath of air was sweeping across America. . . . People knew they had rights."
> — Disability rights activist **CYNTHIA JONES**

Yet Bush also needed to satisfy conservatives whose strength in the Republican Party continued to rise. His most famous campaign pledge had been "Read my lips: No new taxes," and he opposed most proposals requiring additional federal funds. Bush vetoed thirty-six bills, including those lifting abortion restrictions, extending unemployment benefits, raising taxes, and mandating family and medical leave for workers. Press reports increasingly used the words *stalemate, gridlock,* and *divided government.*

Continuing a trend begun during the Reagan years, states tried to compensate for this paralysis, becoming more innovative than Washington. States passed bills to block corporate takeovers, establish parental leave policies, improve food labeling, and protect the environment. In the 1980s, a few states began to pass

Suing for Access: Disability and the Courts

When the Americans with Disabilities Act (ADA) passed in 1990, Beverly Jones expressed her elation: "For me, the passage of the ADA was like opening a door that had been closed to me for so long." The measure promised to protect people with disabilities from discrimination by private employers, public agencies, and state and local governments. This civil rights act providing equal access and opportunity followed in a long tradition of Americans fighting for their rights, struggles not only to enact laws but also to see them enforced.

Jones, a single mother with two children, joined the ranks of the 2.2 million Americans who use a wheelchair after she was in an automobile accident in 1984 that resulted in paraplegia. Determined not to "allow what I wanted in life to be denied because of . . . physical limitations," she trained as a court reporter and went to work to support her family. But Jones discovered that despite the requirements of the ADA, in Tennessee seven out of ten courthouses were not wheelchair accessible. "I was often forced to ask complete strangers to carry me up the stairs," Jones recalled, and she found the experiences "humiliating and frightening."

Jones pleaded in vain with local, state, and federal officials to obtain compliance with the law. "The door that I thought had been opened was still closed and my freedom to live my dream was turning into a nightmare," she said. Finally, in 1998, after having to ask a judge to carry her to a restroom, she decided to appeal to the courts.

Jones filed a lawsuit against the state of Tennessee, joining five other plaintiffs who alleged that the state was in violation of Title II of the ADA, which prohibits governmental entities from denying public services, programs, and activities to individuals because of a disability. Another plaintiff, George Lane, had injured his hip and pelvis in a car accident. Cited for reckless driving, he went to the courthouse in a wheelchair but had to crawl up the stairs. When the court adjourned for lunch, he crawled back down. That afternoon, he refused to crawl upstairs again and was jailed for failing to appear in court. Lane said that he would never forget the humiliation of having to drag his body up the thirty tile steps of the Polk County Courthouse. Lane, Jones, and the four other plaintiffs sought legal redress and damages of $250,000 each.

Tennessee immediately countersued, challenging the constitutionality of the ADA's requirement that states make public facilities accessible to people with disabilities. Finally, in 2004, the case of *Tennessee v. Lane* reached the Supreme Court, where conservative justices espoused a "new federalism" that challenged the right of Congress to tell the states what to do. Citing sovereign immunity (protection from lawsuits), granted to states by the Eleventh Amendment to the Constitution, courts began to question the right of Congress to make federal laws binding on the states. In 2001, in a dramatic example of the trend to limit Congress's power, the Supreme Court held that Congress lacked a constitutional basis for permitting states

---

measures guaranteeing gay and lesbian rights. In the 1990s, dozens of cities passed ordinances requiring businesses receiving tax abatements or other city benefits to pay wages well above the federal minimum wage. And in 1999, California passed a gun control bill with much tougher restrictions on assault weapons than reformers had been able to get through Congress.

The huge federal budget deficit inherited from the Reagan administration impelled the president in 1990 to abandon his "no new taxes" pledge, outraging conservatives. The new law, which Bush depended on Democrats to pass, authorized modest tax increases for high-income Americans and higher taxes on gasoline, cigarettes, alcohol, and luxury items. Yet it had little effect on the massive tax reductions of the early 1980s, leaving intact a key element of Reagan's legacy. Neither the new revenues nor controls on spending curbed the deficit, which was boosted by rising costs for Social Security, Medicare, and Medicaid and spending on war and natural disasters.

Bush also continued Reagan's efforts to create a more conservative Supreme Court. His first nominee, federal appeals court judge David Souter, was a moderate. But in 1991, when the only African American on the Court, Justice Thurgood Marshall, retired, Bush set off a national controversy. He nominated Clarence Thomas, a conservative black appeals court judge who had to be sued under Title I of the ADA, which applies to state employment.

In *Tennessee v. Lane*, the state cited this decision, claiming sovereign immunity and challenging the constitutionality of the ADA. Carol Westlake, executive director of the Tennessee Disability Coalition, pointed out that Tennessee's claim of states' rights was the same argument used to deny civil rights to African Americans in the 1950s and 1960s. In January 2004, as the Supreme Court heard arguments in the case, activists demonstrated outside the Court, chanting, "Justice for all; we won't crawl."

At stake was not only the right of people with disabilities to sue a state when denied access to public facilities but also the right of Congress to make federal laws binding on the states. In May 2004, in a five-to-four decision, the Supreme Court ruled that states failing to make their courthouses accessible to people with disabilities could be sued for damages under federal disability law. But it confined its ruling to the specific context presented in the case: access to courts. By the narrowest possible margin, with the crucial fifth vote cast by Justice Sandra Day O'Connor, the Court focused on one narrow application of the ADA and upheld it in the face of Tennessee's claim of constitutional immunity.

"My case is over," Jones acknowledged. "We have accomplished what

Beverly Jones

Beverly Jones is shown here in her wheelchair next to one of the Tennessee courthouse stairways that made her job as a court reporter so difficult. "As a single mom supporting myself and two kids," she said, "I could not afford to quit my job or strictly limit my work to accessible courthouses." In 1998, Jones filed suit under the Americans with Disabilities Act. Six years later, in 2004, the Supreme Court upheld her right to enforce the protections the ADA granted to those with disabilities. AP Photo/John Russell.

we wanted to be achieved." Nonetheless, the narrow grounds on which the Court decided her case meant that people with disabilities would continue to seek judicial acknowledgment of their rights to opportunity and access.

Questions for Consideration

1. What arguments did Tennessee use in its effort to defeat Jones's lawsuit?

2. In what ways was the struggle for disability rights similar to and different from minority rights movements?

opposed affirmative action as head of the Equal Employment Opportunity Commission (EEOC) under Reagan. Charging that Thomas would not protect minority rights, civil rights groups and other liberal organizations fought the nomination. Then Anita Hill, a black law professor, accused Thomas of sexually harassing her while she was his employee at the EEOC.

Thomas angrily denied the charges, claiming that he was the victim of a "high-tech lynching for uppity blacks." Hill's testimony failed to sway the Senate, which voted narrowly to confirm Thomas. The hearings angered many women, who noted that only two women sat in the Senate and denounced the male senators for failing to

take sexual harassment seriously. Feminists complained that men "still don't get it" and redirected their anger to electoral politics, making 1992 a banner year for female candidates. Thomas's confirmation solidified the Supreme Court's shift to the right.

Going to War in Central America and the Persian Gulf

President Bush won greater support for his actions abroad than for his domestic policy, and he twice sent U.S. soldiers into battle. In Central America, the United States had tolerated and, in fact, paid Panamanian dictator Manuel Noriega for helping

Bush and Taxes
When George H. W. Bush ran as the Republican candidate for president in 1988, he addressed an issue central to conservative politics. "Read my lips," he said. "No new taxes." Yet the federal budget deficit he inherited from Ronald Reagan grew even larger, compelling Bush to agree to a fiscal package of both budget cuts and tax increases. Many Republicans were outraged, and Bush had to depend on Democrats' votes in Congress to pass the measure. Editorial cartoonists had a field day with the controversy. Here, conservative cartoonist Scott Stantis likened Bush to Pinocchio, whose nose grew when he lied. Scott Stantis/Copley News Service.

the Contras in Nicaragua and providing the CIA with information about Communist activities in the region. But in 1989, after Noriega was indicted for drug trafficking by an American grand jury and after his troops killed an American Marine, President Bush ordered 25,000 military personnel into Panama. In **Operation Just Cause**, U.S. forces quickly overcame Noriega's troops, sustaining 23 deaths, while hundreds of Panamanians, including many civilians, died. Chairman of the Joint Chiefs of Staff Colin Powell noted that "our euphoria over our victory in Just Cause was not universal." Both the United Nations and the Organization of American States censured the unilateral action by the United States.

By contrast, Bush's second military engagement rested solidly on international approval. Considering Iran to be America's major enemy in the Middle East, U.S. officials had quietly assisted the Iraqi dictator **Saddam Hussein** in the Iran-Iraq war, which began in 1980 and ended inconclusively in 1988. In August 1990, Hussein sent troops into the small, oil-rich country of Kuwait to the south (Map 31.1), and within days the invasion neared the Saudi Arabian border, threatening the world's largest oil reserves. President Bush quickly ordered a massive mobilization of American forces and assembled an international coalition to stand up to Iraq. He invoked principles of national self-determination and international law, but long-standing interests in Middle Eastern oil also drove the U.S. response. As the largest importer of oil, the United States

consumed one-fourth of the world's supply, 20 percent of which came from Iraq and Kuwait.

Reflecting the easing of Cold War tensions, the Soviet Union voted for a UN resolution declaring an embargo on Iraqi oil and authorizing the use of force if Iraq did not withdraw from Kuwait by January 15, 1991. By then, the United States had deployed more than 400,000 soldiers to Saudi Arabia, joined by 265,000 troops from some two dozen other nations, including several Arab states. "The community of nations has resolutely gathered to condemn and repel lawless aggression," Bush announced. "With few exceptions, the world now stands as one."

With Iraqi forces still in Kuwait, in January 1991 Bush asked Congress to approve war. Considerable sentiment favored waiting to see if the embargo and other means would force Hussein to back down, a position quietly urged within the administration by Colin Powell. Linking the crisis to the failure of U.S. energy conservation, Democratic senator Edward M. Kennedy insisted, "Not a single American life should be sacrificed in a war for the price of oil." Congress debated for three days and then authorized war by a margin of five votes in the Senate and sixty-seven in the House, with most Democrats in opposition. On January 17, 1991, the U.S.-led coalition launched Operation Desert Storm, a forty-day bombing campaign against Iraqi military targets, power plants, oil refineries, and transportation networks. Having severely crippled Iraq by air, the coalition then stormed into Kuwait

MAP ACTIVITY

Map 31.1   Events in the Middle East, 1989–2011
During the Persian Gulf War of 1991, Egypt, Syria, and other Middle Eastern nations joined the coalition against Iraq, and the twenty-two-member Arab League supported the war as a means to liberate Kuwait. After September 11, 2001, the Arab League approved of U.S. military operations in Afghanistan because the attacks "were an attack on the common values of the world, not just on the United States." Yet, except for the countries where the United States had military bases — Bahrain, Kuwait, Qatar, and Saudi Arabia — no Arab country supported the American invasion and occupation of Iraq in 2003. Arab hostility toward the United States also reflected the deterioration of Israeli-Palestinian relations after 1999, as Arabs charged that the United States allowed Israel to deny Palestinians land and liberty.

READING THE MAP: In what countries are the sources of oil located? In what countries does the United States have military bases?
CONNECTIONS: What conditions prompted the U.S. military interventions in Iraq and Afghanistan in 1991, 2001, and 2003? What were the U.S. goals in each of these interventions? To what extent were those goals realized?

with massive ground forces, forcing Iraqi troops to withdraw (see Map 31.1).

"By God, we've kicked the Vietnam syndrome once and for all," President Bush exulted on March 1. Most Americans found no moral ambiguity in the **Persian Gulf War** and took pride in the display of military prowess. In contrast to the loss of 58,000 American lives in Vietnam, 270 U.S. service members perished in Desert Storm.

The United States stood at the apex of global leadership, steering a coalition in which Arab nations fought beside their former colonial rulers.

Some Americans criticized the Bush administration for ending the war without deposing Hussein. But Bush pointed to the UN mandate that limited the mission to driving Iraqi forces out of Kuwait and to Middle Eastern leaders' concern that an invasion of Iraq would destabilize

The Gulf War
This soldier arriving in Saudi Arabia in September 1990 was part of the massive military buildup in the Persian Gulf area before the U.S.-led coalition drove Iraqi forces out of Kuwait. For the first time, women served in combat-support positions. More than 33,000 women were stationed throughout the area; eleven died, and two were held as prisoners. Among their duties were piloting planes and helicopters, directing artillery, and fighting fires. © Bettmann/Corbis.

the region. His secretary of defense, Richard Cheney, doubted that coalition forces could secure a stable government to replace Hussein and considered the price of a long occupation too high. Administration officials counted on economic sanctions and Hussein's pledges not to rearm or develop weapons of mass destruction, secured by a system of UN inspections, to contain the dictator.

Yet Middle Eastern stability remained elusive. Israel, which had endured Iraqi missile attacks, was more secure, but the Israeli-Palestinian conflict remained intractable. Despite military losses, Saddam Hussein remained in power and turned his war machine on Iraqi Kurds and Shiite Muslims whom the United States had encouraged to rebel. Hussein also found ways to conceal arms from UN weapons inspectors before he threw them out in 1998. Finally, the decision to keep U.S. troops based in Saudi Arabia, the holy land of Islam, fueled the hatred and determination of Muslim extremists like Osama bin Laden and served as a recruiting tool.

The Cold War Ends

Soviet support in the Persian Gulf War marked a momentous change in relations between the United States and the Soviet Union. The progres-

sive forces that Gorbachev had encouraged in the Communist world (see chapter 30) swept through Eastern Europe in 1989, when popular uprisings in Hungary, Poland, East Germany, and elsewhere demanded an end to state repression and inefficient economic bureaucracies. Communist governments toppled like dominoes (Map 31.2), virtually without bloodshed, because Gorbachev refused to prop them up with Soviet armies. East Germany opened its border with West Germany, and in November 1989 ecstatic Germans danced on the Berlin Wall and swung sledgehammers to demolish that dominant symbol of the Cold War, which had separated East and West since 1961. An amazed East Berliner crossed the line exclaiming, "They just let us go. I can't believe it."

Bush assured Gorbachev that he would not "climb the Berlin Wall and make high-sounding pronouncements," taking care not to weaken the Soviet leader at home. The president persuaded Gorbachev that unification of East and West Germany was inevitable, and it sped to completion in 1990. Soon former iron curtain countries such as Hungary and Poland lined up to join NATO. Although U.S. military forces remained in Europe as part of NATO, Europe no longer depended on the United States for its security. Its economic clout also grew as Western Europe formed a common economic market in 1992. The destiny of Europe, to which the United States and the Soviet Union had held the key for forty-five years, now lay in European hands.

Inspired by the liberation of Eastern Europe, republics within the Soviet Union soon sought their own independence. In December 1991, Boris Yeltsin, president of the Russian Republic, announced that Russia and eleven other republics had formed a new entity, the Commonwealth of Independent States, and other former Soviet states declared their independence. With nothing left to govern, Gorbachev resigned. The Soviet Union had dissolved, and with it the Cold War conflict that had defined U.S. foreign policy for decades.

Colin Powell joked that he was "running out of villains. I'm down to Castro and Kim Il Sung," the North Korean dictator who, along with China's leaders, resisted the liberalizing tides sweeping the world. In 1989, Chinese

VISUAL ACTIVITY

Fall of the Berlin Wall
After 1961, the Berlin Wall stood as the prime symbol of the Cold War and the iron grip of communism over Eastern Europe and the Soviet Union. More than four hundred Eastern Europeans were killed trying to flee to the West. After Communist authorities opened the wall on November 9, 1989, permitting free travel between East and West Germany, Berliners from both sides gathered at the wall to celebrate. Eric Bouvet/Gamma Press Images.

READING THE IMAGE: What does the image tell you about the revolutions in Eastern Europe in 1989?
CONNECTIONS: What were the major factors that made possible the dismantling of the Berlin Wall, the major symbol of the Cold War in Europe?

soldiers killed hundreds of pro-democracy demonstrators in Tiananmen Square in Beijing, and the Communist government arrested some ten thousand reformers. North Korea remained a Communist dictatorship, committed to developing nuclear weapons. "The post–Cold War world is decidedly not post-nuclear," declared one U.S. official. In 1990, the United States and the Soviet Union signed the Strategic Arms Reduction Talks (START) treaty, which cut about 30 percent of each superpower's nuclear arsenal. And in 1996, the UN General Assembly overwhelmingly approved a total nuclear test ban treaty. Yet India and Pakistan, hostile neighbors, refused to sign the treaty, and both exploded atomic devices in 1998, increasing the nuclear risk in South Asia. Moreover, the Republican-controlled Senate defeated U.S. ratification of the test ban treaty in October 1999, halting a decade of progress on nuclear weapons control. The potential for rogue nations and terrorist groups to develop nuclear weapons posed an ongoing threat to international peace and security.

The 1992 Election

In March 1991, Bush's chances for reelection in 1992 looked golden. The Gulf War victory catapulted his approval rating to 88 percent, causing the most prominent Democrats to opt out of the presidential race. But that did not deter **William Jefferson "Bill" Clinton**, who at age forty-five had served as governor of Arkansas for twelve years. Like Carter in 1976, Clinton and his running mate, Tennessee senator Albert Gore Jr., presented themselves as "New Democrats" and sought to rid the party of its liberal image.

Clinton promised to work for the "forgotten middle class," who "do the work, pay the taxes, raise the kids, and play by the rules." Disavowing the "tax and spend" label that Republicans pinned on his party, he promised a tax cut for the middle class, pledged to reinvigorate government and the economy, and vowed "to put an end to welfare as we know it." Bush was vulnerable to voters' concerns about the ailing economy, as unemployment reached 7 percent, and to the

MAP ACTIVITY

Map 31.2 Events in Eastern Europe, 1989–2002

The overthrow of Communist governments throughout Eastern Europe and the splintering of the Soviet Union into more than a dozen separate nations were the most momentous changes in world history since World War II.

READING THE MAP: Which country was the first to overthrow its Communist government? Which was the last? In which nations did elections usher in a change in government?

CONNECTIONS: What problems did Mikhail Gorbachev try to solve, and how did he try to solve them? What policy launched by Ronald Reagan contributed to Soviet dilemmas? (See chapter 30.) Did it create any problems in the United States?

Clinton campaign's emphasis on bread-and-butter issues. The popularity of a third candidate, self-made Texas billionaire H. Ross Perot, revealed Americans' frustrations with government and the major parties. Railing against the huge federal budget deficit, Perot mobilized a sizable grassroots movement and established the deficit as a key campaign issue.

Fifty-five percent of those eligible voted, just barely reversing the thirty-year decline in voter turnout. Clinton won 43 percent of the popular vote, Bush 38 percent, and Perot 19 percent — the strongest third-party finish in eighty years. By casting nearly two-thirds of their votes against Bush, voters suggested a mandate for change but not the direction that change should take.

REVIEW How did George H. W. Bush respond to threats to U.S. interests as the Cold War came to an end?

▶ The Clinton Administration's Search for the Middle Ground

Bill Clinton's assertion that "the era of big government is over" reflected the Democratic Party's move to the right that had begun with Jimmy Carter in the 1970s. Clinton did not completely abandon liberal principles. He extended benefits for the working poor; delivered incremental reforms to feminists, environmentalists, and other groups; and spoke out in favor of affirmative action and gay rights. Yet his administration attended more to the concerns of middle-class Americans than to the needs of the disadvantaged.

Clinton's eight-year presidency witnessed the longest economic boom in history and ended

Clinton and Gore on Tour
The gregarious Bill Clinton excelled at political campaigning, and the youth of the first baby boomer candidates appealed to many. During the 1992 presidential campaign, Clinton and his wife, Hillary — accompanied by running mate Al Gore and his wife, Tipper — went out on several bus tours as a way of demonstrating the Democrats' connection to ordinary people. Not far from this campaign stop in Sylvester, Georgia, the bus caravan passed by a handmade sign that read "Bubbas for Clinton/Gore." © Ira Wyman/Sygma/Corbis.

with a budget surplus. Although various factors generated the prosperity, many Americans identified Clinton with the buoyant economy, elected him to a second term, and continued to support him even when his reckless sexual behavior resulted in impeachment. The Senate failed to convict the president, but the scandal crippled Clinton's leadership in his last years in office.

Clinton's Reforms

Clinton wanted to restore confidence in government as a force for good while not alienating antigovernment voters. The huge budget deficit that he inherited — $4.4 trillion in 1993 — further precluded substantial federal initiatives. Moreover, Perot's challenges denied Clinton a majority of the popular vote in both 1992 and 1996, and the Republicans controlled Congress for all but his first two years in office. Throughout most of his presidency, Clinton was burdened by investigations into past financial activities and private indiscretions. While the president had an extraordinary knack for making voters feel that he liked and understood them, he struggled to translate that appeal into gains for his agenda.

Despite these obstacles, Clinton achieved a number of incremental reforms. He used his executive authority to ease restrictions on abortion and signed several bills that Republicans had previously blocked. In 1993, Congress enacted gun control legislation and the Family and Medical Leave Act, which entitled workers in larger companies to unpaid leave for childbirth, adoption, and family medical emergencies. The Violence

against Women Act of 1994 authorized $1.6 billion and new remedies for combating sexual assault and domestic violence. Clinton won stricter air pollution controls and greater protection for national forests and parks. Other liberal measures included a minimum-wage increase, the largest expansion of aid for college students since the GI Bill (see chapter 25), and the creation of AmeriCorps, which enabled students to pay for their education with community service.

Most significantly, Clinton pushed through a substantial increase in the **Earned Income Tax Credit (EITC)** for low-wage earners, a program begun in 1975. The EITC gave tax cuts to people who worked full-time at meager wages or, if they paid no taxes, a subsidy to lift their family income above the poverty line. By 2003, some fifteen million low-income families were benefiting from the EITC, almost half of them minorities. One expert called it "the largest antipoverty program since the Great Society."

> **"The largest antipoverty program since the Great Society."**
> — A policy expert, commenting on the Earned Income Tax Credit

Shortly before Clinton took office, the economy had begun to rebound, and the boom that followed helped boost his popularity through the 1990s. Economic expansion, along with spending cuts, tax increases, and declining unemployment, produced a budget surplus in 1998, the first since 1969. Despite a substantial tax cut in 1997 that reduced levies on estates and capital gains and provided tax credits for families with children and for higher education, the surplus grew. The seemingly inexorable growth of government debt had turned around.

Clinton's Appointments
Not only did President Clinton appoint more women to high government posts than any previous president, but he also broke new ground by appointing them to offices traditionally considered to be male territory. During his presidency, Janet Reno served as attorney general, Laura Tyson as chair of the President's Council of Economic Advisers, Sheila Widnall as secretary of the air force, and Madeleine Albright first as ambassador to the United Nations and then as secretary of state. Here, Albright (left) and Reno (second from right) applaud Clinton's 1999 State of the Union address with other cabinet members. AP Images/Doug Mills.

Clinton failed, however, to provide universal health insurance and to curb skyrocketing medical costs. Under the direction of First Lady Hillary Rodham Clinton and with very little congressional consultation, the administration proposed a complicated plan that drew criticism from both sides. Liberals wanted a single-payer plan similar to Medicare, while conservatives charged that the proposal would increase taxes and government interference in medical decisions. Congress enacted smaller reforms enabling workers who changed jobs to retain health insurance and underwriting health care for five million uninsured children, but affordable health care for all remained elusive.

Pledging to change the face of government to one that "looked like America," Clinton built on the gradual progress women and minorities had made since the 1960s. For example, African Americans and women had become mayors in major cities from New York to San Francisco. Virginia had elected the first black governor since Reconstruction, and Florida the first Latino. In the executive branch, Clinton appointed the most diverse group of department heads ever assembled, including six women,

three African Americans, and two Latinos. Secretary of Commerce Norman Y. Mineta became the first Asian American to hold a cabinet post. Janet Reno became the first female attorney general and Madeleine K. Albright the first female secretary of state. Clinton's judicial appointments had a similar cast, and in 1993 he named the second woman to the Supreme Court, Ruth Bader Ginsburg, whose arguments before she became an appeals court judge had won key women's rights rulings from the Supreme Court.

Accommodating the Right

Although much of Clinton's agenda fell within the liberal tradition, the continuing strength of conservatism and his own determination to move his party to the center led him to make compromises with the right. The 1994 midterm elections swept away the Democratic majorities in Congress. Led by Representative Newt Gingrich of Georgia, Republicans claimed the 1994 election as a mandate for their "contract with America," a conservative platform to end "government that is too big, too intrusive, and too easy with the public's money" and to elect "a Congress that respects the values and shares the faith of the American family." Opposition from Democrats and moderate Republicans blocked passage of most of the contract's pledges, but Gingrich succeeded in moving the debate to the right.

The most extreme antigovernment sentiment developed far from Washington in the form of grassroots armed militias. They celebrated white Christian supremacy and reflected conservatives' hostility to such diverse institutions as taxes and the United Nations. Claiming the need to defend themselves from government tyranny, they stockpiled weapons. The militia movement grew in reaction to the passage of new gun control legislation and after government agents stormed the headquarters of an armed religious cult in Waco, Texas, in April 1993, killing more than 80. On the second anniversary of that event, a bomb leveled a federal building in Oklahoma City, taking 169 lives in the worst terrorist attack in the nation's history up to that point.

Clinton bowed to conservative views on gay and lesbian rights, backing away from a campaign promise to lift the ban on gays in the military. Although many other nations, including France and Israel, welcomed homosexual soldiers, U.S. military leaders and key legislators objected to the proposal, and Clinton reverted to a **"don't ask, don't tell" policy** in 1993. Officials were forbidden to ask military personnel about their sexuality, but soldiers who said they were gay or who engaged in homosexual behavior could be dismissed. Eventually, more than ten thousand homosexuals were discharged, including army Arabic linguist Cathleen Glover, who lamented, "The army preaches integrity, but asks you to lie to everyone around you." In 1996, Clinton signed the Defense of Marriage Act, prohibiting the federal government from recognizing state-licensed marriages between same-sex couples.

Nonetheless, gays and lesbians continued to make strides as attitudes about homosexuality became more tolerant. By 2006, more than half of the country's five hundred largest companies provided health benefits to same-sex domestic partners and included sexual orientation in their nondiscrimination policies. More than twenty-five states banned discrimination in public employment, and many of those laws extended to private employment, housing, and education. By 2010, gay marriage was legal in Massachusetts, Connecticut, Vermont, Iowa, Maine, New Hampshire, and the District of Columbia; moreover, several states recognized civil unions and domestic partnerships, extending to same-sex couples rights available to married

Domestic Terrorism
The most devastating product of anti-government extremism in the 1990s was the explosion of the Alfred P. Murrah Federal Building in Oklahoma City. On the morning of April 23, 1995, Timothy McVeigh, wearing a T-shirt with the words shouted by John Wilkes Booth when he assassinated Abraham Lincoln—*Sic Semper Tyrranis* ("thus ever to tyrants")—drove a bomb-rigged truck to the federal building, where it exploded at 9 A.M. The building housed a day care center, and nineteen infants and toddlers were killed. McVeigh was executed in 2001, and his co-conspirator, Terry Nichols, was sentenced to life imprisonment without parole. Zuma Press.

couples such matters as inheritance, taxation, and medical decisions.

Clinton's efforts to cast himself as a centrist were apparent in his handling of the New Deal program Aid to Families with Dependent Children (AFDC), which most people called welfare. Public sentiment about poverty had shifted since the 1960s. Instead of blaming poverty on the lack of adequate jobs or other external circumstances, more people blamed the poor themselves and believed that welfare programs trapped the poor in cycles of dependency. Many questioned why they should subsidize poor mothers now that so many women had joined the labor force. Nearly everyone considered work to be better than welfare, but supporters of AFDC doubted that the economy could provide sufficient jobs at decent wages.

After vetoing two welfare reform bills, Clinton forced through a less punitive measure, which he signed as the 1996 election approached. The **Personal Responsibility and Work Opportunity Reconciliation Act** abolished AFDC and with it the nation's fifty-year pledge to provide a minimum level of subsistence for all children. The law provided grants to the states to assist the poor, but it limited welfare payments to two years, regardless of whether the recipient could find a job, and it set a lifetime limit of aid at five years. Reflecting growing controversy over immigration, it also barred legal immigrants from obtaining food stamps and other benefits and allowed states to stop Medicaid for legal immigrants. New York senator Daniel Patrick Moynihan called it "the most brutal act of social policy since Reconstruction."

In its first decade, the law produced neither the horrors predicted by its critics nor the successes promised by its advocates. As intended, it did force single mothers to seek employment, cutting welfare rolls from 12.5 million to 4.5 million between 1996 and 2006. Yet not all former welfare recipients became self-supporting. Forty percent of former welfare mothers were not working regularly after being cut from the rolls, and those who did find jobs earned on average only about $12,000 a year. More than one-third of children living in female-headed families still lived in poverty.

Clinton's signature on the new law denied Republicans a partisan issue in the 1996 presidential campaign. The president ran as a moderate who would save the country from extremist Republicans, while the Republican Party also moved to the center, nominating Kansan Robert Dole, a World War II hero and former Senate majority leader. Clinton won 49 percent of the votes; 41 percent went to Dole and 9 percent to third-party candidate Ross Perot. Although Clinton won reelection with room to spare, voters sent a Republican majority back to Congress.

In 1999, Clinton and Congress bowed to calls from the financial industry for deregulation by repealing key aspects of the Glass-Steagall Act, passed during the New Deal to avoid another Great Depression. This Financial Services Modernization Act ended the separation between banking, securities, and insurance services, allowing financial institutions to engage in all three, practices that leading economists would link to the severe financial meltdown of 2008.

The End of Welfare
When Congress ended Aid to Families with Dependent Children, the welfare system established during the New Deal, and replaced it with Temporary Assistance for Needy Families, LuAnne St. Clair wondered how she and her five children would fare when her welfare payments ended. American Indian mothers had to overcome, with other welfare recipients, the problems of acquiring job training and child care so they could find employment. But Indian women also faced the lack of sufficient jobs on reservations, to which they had strong family, cultural, and religious ties. AP/Wide World.

Impeaching the President

Clinton's magnetic and articulate style, his ability to capture the middle ground of the electorate, and the nation's economic resurgence enabled the self-proclaimed "comeback kid" to survive scandals and an impeachment trial in 1999. Early in his presidency, charges related to firings of White House staff, political use of FBI records, and "Whitewater" — the nickname for real estate investments that the Clintons had made in Arkansas — led to an official investigation by an independent prosecutor. The president also faced a sexual harassment lawsuit filed in 1994 by a state employee. A federal court threw out that case in 1998, but another sexual scandal more seriously threatened Clinton's presidency.

In January 1998, Kenneth Starr, independent prosecutor for Whitewater, began to investigate the charge that Clinton had had sexual relations with a twenty-one-year-old White House intern and then lied about it to a federal grand jury. At first, Clinton vehemently denied the charge, but subsequently he bowed to the mounting evidence against him. Starr prepared a case for the House of Representatives, which in December 1998 voted to impeach the president on two counts: perjury and obstruction of justice. Clinton became the second president (after Andrew Johnson, in 1868) to be impeached by the House and tried by the Senate.

The Senate trial took place in early 1999. Most Americans condemned the president's behavior but approved of the job he was doing and opposed his removal from office. Some saw Starr as a fanatic invading individuals' privacy. One man said, "Let him get a divorce from his wife. Don't take him out of office and disrupt the country." Those favoring removal insisted that the president must set a high moral standard for the nation and that lying to a grand jury, even over a private matter, was a serious offense. A number of senators did not believe that Clinton's actions constituted the high crimes and misdemeanors required by the Constitution for conviction. With a two-thirds majority needed for that result, the Senate voted 45 to 55 on the perjury count and 50 to 50 on the obstruction of justice count. A majority, including some Republicans, seemed to agree with a Clinton supporter that the president's behavior, though "indefensible, outrageous, unforgivable, shameless," did not warrant his removal from office.

The investigation that triggered events leading up to impeachment ended in 2000 when the independent prosecutor reported insufficient evidence of illegalities related to the Whitewater land deals. Although more than 60 percent of Americans gave Clinton high marks on his job performance throughout the scandal, it distracted him from domestic and international problems and precluded the possibility of significant policy advances in his last years in office.

The Booming Economy of the 1990s

Clinton's ability to weather the impeachment crisis owed much to the prosperous economy, which in 1991 began its longest period of expansion in U.S. history. During the 1990s, the gross domestic product grew by more than one-third, thirteen million new jobs were created, inflation remained in check, unemployment reached 4 percent — its lowest point in twenty-five years — and the stock market soared.

The president took credit for the thriving economy, and his policies did contribute to the boom. He made deficit reduction a priority, and in exchange the Federal Reserve Board and bond market traders lowered interest rates, encouraging economic expansion by making money easier to borrow. Businesses also prospered because they had lowered their costs through restructuring and laying off workers. Economic problems in Europe and Asia helped American firms become more competitive in the international market. And the computer revolution and the application of information technology boosted productivity.

People at all income levels benefited from the economic boom, but the gaps between the rich and the poor and between the wealthy and the middle class, which had been growing since the 1970s, endured (Figure 31.1). This persistence of inequality was linked in part to the growing use of information technology, which increased demand for highly skilled workers, while the movement of manufacturing jobs abroad diminished opportunities and wages for the less skilled. In addition, deregulation and the continuing decline of unions hurt lower-skilled workers, tax cuts had favored the better-off, and the national minimum wage failed to keep up with inflation.

Although more minorities than ever attained middle-class status, in general people of color remained lowest on the economic ladder, reflecting Colin Powell's observation that "race still casts a shadow over our society." For instance, in 1999 the median income for white households surpassed $45,000, but it stood at only $29,423

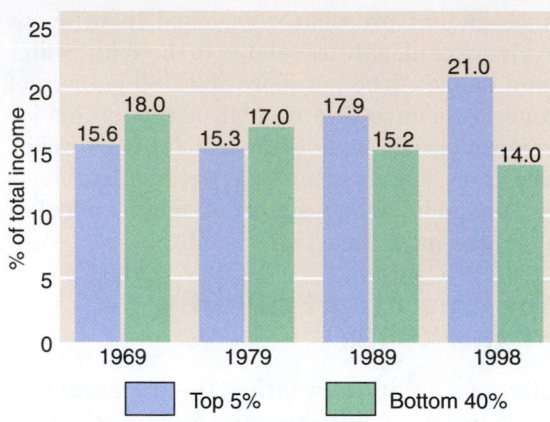

FIGURE 31.1   THE GROWTH OF INEQUALITY: Changes in Family Income, 1969–1998
For most of the post–World War II period, income increased for all groups on the economic ladder. But after 1979, the income of the poorest families actually declined, while the income of the richest 20 percent of the population grew substantially. Adapted from the *New York Times*, 1989.

and $33,676 for African American and Latino households, respectively. In 2000, poverty afflicted about 22 percent of blacks, 21 percent of Latinos, and 10 percent of Asian Americans, in contrast to 7.5 percent of whites.

REVIEW   What policies of the Clinton administration moved the Democratic Party to the right?

▶ The United States in a Globalizing World

America's economic success in the 1990s was linked to its dominance in the world economy. From that position, President Clinton tried to shape the tremendous transformations occurring in a process called **globalization** — the growing integration and interdependence of national citizens and economies. Building on the initiatives of Reagan and Bush, Clinton lowered a number of trade barriers, despite stiff opposition from critics who emphasized the economic deprivation and environmental devastation that often resulted. Debates likewise arose over the large numbers of immigrants entering the United States.

Clinton agreed with Bush that the United States must retain its economic and military dominance over all other nations. The president took military action in Somalia, Haiti, the Middle East, and eastern Europe, and he pushed hard to ease the conflict between Israel and the Palestinians. Yet no new global strategy emerged to replace the containment of communism as the decisive factor in the exercise of American power abroad. And safeguarding American interests from terrorist attacks around the world proved much more difficult than combating communism.

Defining America's Place in a New World Order

In 1991, President George H. W. Bush declared a "new world order" emerging from the ashes of the Cold War. As the sole superpower, the United States was determined to let no nation challenge its military superiority or global leadership (Figure 31.2). Yet policymakers struggled to define guiding principles for deciding when and how to use the nation's military and diplomatic power in a post–Cold War world. Combating Saddam Hussein's naked aggression seemed the obvious course of action in 1991, but dealing with other areas of instability proved more difficult.

Africa, where civil wars and extreme human suffering rarely evoked a strong American response, was a case in point. In 1992, guided largely by humanitarian concern, President Bush had attached U.S. forces to a UN operation in the small northern African country of Somalia, where famine and civil war raged. In 1993, President Clinton allowed that humanitarian mission to turn into "nation building" — an effort to establish a stable government — and eighteen U.S. soldiers were killed. After Americans saw film of Somalis dragging a soldier's corpse through the streets, the outcry at home suggested that most citizens were unwilling to sacrifice lives when no vital interest seemed threatened. Indeed, both the United States and the United Nations stood by in 1994 when more than half a million people were massacred in a brutal civil war in the central African nation of Rwanda.

As always, the United States was more inclined to use force nearer its borders, but in the case of Haiti it gained international support for intervention. In 1994, after a military coup overthrew Jean-Bertrand Aristide, Haiti's democratically elected president, Clinton persuaded the United Nations to impose economic sanctions on Haiti and to authorize military intervention. Hours before U.S. forces were to invade, Haitian military leaders promised to step down. U.S. forces peacefully landed, and Aristide was restored to power. Initially a huge success, U.S. policy continued to be tested as Haiti faced grave economic challenges and political instability.

In eastern Europe, the collapse of communism ignited a severe crisis, triggering U.S.-NATO intervention in Yugoslavia. During the Cold War, the Communist government of Yugoslavia, a federation of six republics, had held ethnic tensions in check, and many Muslims, Croats, and Serbs had grown accustomed to living and working together. After the Communists were swept out in 1989, ruthless leaders exploited ethnic differences to bolster their power, and Yugoslavia splintered into separate states and fell into civil war.

The Serbs' aggression under President Slobodan Milosevic against Bosnian Muslims in particular horrified much of the world, but European and U.S. leaders hesitated to use military force. As reports of rape, torture, and mass killings in Bosnia increased, American leaders worried about the image of the world's strongest nation being unwilling to stop the violence. Finally, in 1995, Clinton ordered U.S. fliers to join NATO forces in intensive bombing of Serbian military concentrations. That effort and successful offensives by the Croatian and Bosnian armies forced Milosevic to the bargaining table. After representatives from Serbia, Croatia, and Bosnia hammered

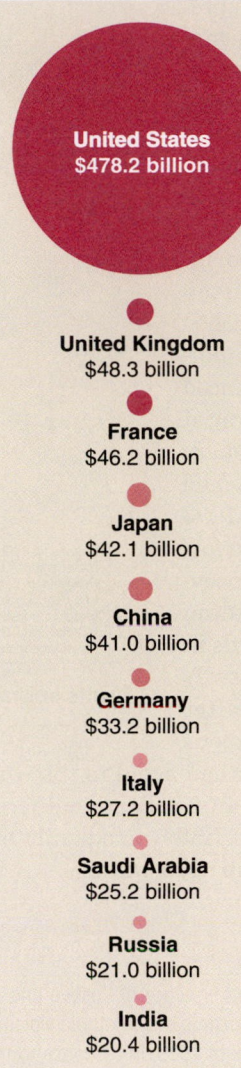

United States
$478.2 billion

United Kingdom
$48.3 billion

France
$46.2 billion

Japan
$42.1 billion

China
$41.0 billion

Germany
$33.2 billion

Italy
$27.2 billion

Saudi Arabia
$25.2 billion

Russia
$21.0 billion

India
$20.4 billion

FIGURE 31.2 GLOBAL COMPARISON: Countries with the Highest Military Expenditures, 2005
During the Cold War, the military budgets of the United States and the Soviet Union were relatively even. For example, in 1983 U.S. military expenditures stood at $217 billion, compared to $213 billion for the Soviet Union. Even before the Iraq War, which began in 2003, the U.S. military budget constituted 47 percent of total world military expenditures. That proportion rose to 48 percent in 2005, with the United States spending nearly ten times as much as its nearest competitor. The U.S. defense budget reflects the determination of Democratic and Republican administrations alike to maintain dominance in the world, even while the capacities of its traditional enemies have been greatly diminished.

Breakup of Yugoslavia

—— Yugoslavia 1945–1991

out a peace treaty, Clinton then agreed to send twenty thousand American troops to Bosnia as part of a NATO peacekeeping mission.

In 1998, new fighting broke out in the southern Serbian province of Kosovo, where ethnic Albanians, who constituted 90 percent of the population, demanded independence. The Serbian army brutally retaliated, driving out one-third of Kosovo's 1.8 million Albanian Muslims. In 1999, NATO launched a U.S.-led bombing attack on Serbian military and government targets that, after three months, forced Milosevic to agree to a peace settlement. Serbians voted Milosevic out of office in October 2000, and he died in 2006 while on trial for genocide by a UN war crimes tribunal.

Elsewhere, Clinton remained willing to deploy U.S. power when he could send missiles rather than soldiers, and he was prepared to act without international support or UN sanction. In August 1998, bombs exploded at the U.S. embassies in Kenya and Tanzania, killing 12 Americans and more than 250 Africans. Clinton retaliated with missile attacks on terrorist training camps in Afghanistan and facilities in Sudan controlled by **Osama bin Laden**, a Saudi-born millionaire who financed the Islamic-extremist terrorist network linked to the embassy attacks. Clinton also launched air strikes against Iraq in 1993 when a plot to assassinate former president Bush was uncovered, in 1996 after Saddam Hussein attacked the Kurds in northern Iraq, and repeatedly between 1998 and 2000 after Hussein expelled UN weapons inspectors. Whereas Bush had acted in the Gulf War with the support of an international force that included Arab states, Clinton acted unilaterally and in the face of Arab opposition.

Israel and PLO sign accords, 1993
Israel and Jordan sign peace treaty, 1994
Progress of Israeli-Palestinian negotiations halts and violence escalates, 2000
Israel withdraws from Gaza, 2005
Israel at war with Hezbollah in Lebanon, 2006
Israel invades Gaza, 2008

Events in Israel since 1989

To defuse the Israeli-Palestinian conflict, a major source of Arab hostility toward the West, Clinton used diplomatic rather than military power. In 1993, largely because of the efforts of the Norwegian government, Yasir Arafat, head of the Palestine Liberation Organization (PLO), and Yitzhak Rabin, Israeli prime minister, recognized the existence of each other's states for the first time and agreed to Israeli withdrawal from the Gaza Strip and Jericho, allowing for Palestinian self-government there. In July 1994, Clinton presided over another turning point as Rabin and King Hussein of Jordan signed a declaration of peace. Yet difficult issues remained to be settled: control of Jerusalem; the fate of Palestinian refugees; and the presence of more than 200,000 Israeli settlers in the West Bank, the land seized by Israel in 1967, where 3 million Palestinians were determined to establish their own state. Clinton's last effort to broker negotiations between the PLO and Israel failed in 2000, and continuing violence between Israelis and Palestinians strengthened anti-American sentiment among Arabs, who saw the United States as Israel's ally.

Debates over Globalization

The Clinton administration moved energetically on the economic side to speed up the growth of a "global marketplace." The process of globalization had begun in the fifteenth century, when Europeans began to penetrate other parts of the world. Between the U.S. Civil War and World War I, products, capital, and labor crossed national boundaries in ever-larger numbers. In that era, globalization was based on imperialism; Western nations took direct control of foreign territories, extracted their natural resources, and restricted manufacturing. By contrast, late-twentieth-century globalization advanced among sovereign nations and involved the industrialization of less developed areas, such as Korea and China. Other distinguishing marks of the more recent globalization were its scope and intensity: New communications technologies such as the Internet and cell phones connected nations, corporations,

Ethnic Strife in Kosovo
These ethnic Albanians seeking to escape the Serbian province of Kosovo into Macedonia were among hundreds of thousands of victims of the ethnic violence that devastated Yugoslavia after the cold war ended. In 1999, in response to the brutality of the Serbian army against the Albanians, the United States first led a NATO bombing campaign against Serbian strongholds and then contributed troops to a NATO peacekeeping unit in Kosovo after the bombing had forced the Serbian army to withdraw. Reuters.

Article 6

No State, without the consent of the United States, in Congress assembled, shall send any embassy to, or receive any embassy from, or enter into any conference, agreement, alliance, or treaty with any king, prince, or state; nor shall any person, holding any office of profit or trust under the United States, or any of them, accept of any present, emolument, office or title, of any kind whatever, from any king, prince, or foreign state; nor shall the United States, in Congress assembled, or any of them, grant any title of nobility.

No two or more states shall enter into any treaty, confederation, or alliance, whatever, between them, without the consent of the United States, in Congress assembled, specifying accurately the purposes for which the same is to be entered into, and how long it shall continue.

No state shall lay any imposts or duties which may interfere with any stipulations in treaties entered into by the United States, in Congress assembled, with any king, prince, or state, in pursuance of any treaties already proposed by Congress to the courts of France and Spain.

No vessels of war shall be kept up in time of peace by any State, except such number only as shall be deemed necessary by the United States, in Congress assembled, for the defence of such State or its trade; nor shall any body of forces be kept up by any State, in time of peace, except such number only as, in the judgment of the United States, in Congress assembled, shall be deemed requisite to garrison the forts necessary for the defence of such State; but every State shall always keep up a well regulated and disciplined militia, sufficiently armed and accoutred, and shall provide, and constantly have ready for use, in public stores, a due number of field pieces and tents, and a proper quantity of arms, ammunition and camp equipage.

No State shall engage in any war without the consent of the United States, in Congress assembled, unless such State be actually invaded by enemies, or shall have received certain advice of a resolution being formed by some nation of Indians to invade such State, and the danger is so imminent as not to admit of a delay till the United States, in Congress assembled, can be consulted; nor shall any State grant commissions to any ships or vessels of war, nor letters of marque or reprisal, except it be after a declaration of war by the United States, in Congress assembled, and then only against the kingdom or state, and the subjects thereof, against which war has been so declared, and under such regulations as shall be established by the United States, in Congress assembled, unless such State be infested by pirates, in which case vessels of war may be fitted out for that occasion, and kept so long as the danger shall continue, or until the United States, in Congress assembled, shall determine otherwise.

Article 7

When land forces are raised by any State for the common defence, all officers of or under the rank of colonel, shall be appointed by the legislature of each State respectively, by whom such forces shall be raised, or in such manner as such State shall direct; and all vacancies shall be filled up by the State which first made the appointment.

Article 8

All charges of war and all other expences, that shall be incurred for the common defence or general welfare, and allowed by the United States, in Congress assembled, shall be defrayed out of a common treasury, which shall be supplied by the several states, in proportion to the value of all land within each State, granted to or surveyed for any person, as such land and the buildings and improvements thereon shall be estimated according to such mode as the United States, in Congress assembled, shall, from time to time, direct and appoint.

The taxes for paying that proportion shall be laid and levied by the authority and direction of the legislatures of the several states, within the time agreed upon by the United States, in Congress assembled.

Article 9

The United States, in Congress assembled, shall have the sole and exclusive right and power of determining on peace and war, except in the cases mentioned in the 6th article; of sending and receiving ambassadors; entering into treaties and alliances, provided that no treaty of commerce shall be made, whereby the legislative power of the respective states shall be restrained from imposing such imposts and duties on foreigners as their own people are subjected to, or from prohibiting the exportation or importation of any species of goods or commodities whatsoever; of establishing rules for deciding, in all cases, what captures on land or water shall be legal, and in what manner prizes, taken by land or naval forces in the service of the United States, shall be divided or appropriated; of granting letters of marque and reprisal in times of peace; appointing courts for the trial of piracies and felonies committed on the high seas, and establishing courts for receiving and determining, finally, appeals in all cases of captures; provided, that no member of Congress shall be appointed a judge of any of the said courts.

The United States, in Congress assembled, shall also be the last resort on appeal in all disputes and differences now subsisting, or that hereafter may arise between two or more states concerning boundary, jurisdiction or any other cause whatever; which authority shall always be exercised in the manner following: whenever the legislative or executive authority, or lawful agent of any State, in controversy with another, shall present a petition to Congress, stating the matter

Resolved, That copies of the Declaration be sent to the several assemblies, conventions, and committees, or councils of safety, and to the several commanding officers of the continental troops; that it be proclaimed in each of the United States, at the head of the army.

THE ARTICLES OF CONFEDERATION AND PERPETUAL UNION

Agreed to in Congress, November 15, 1777.
Ratified March 1781.

BETWEEN THE STATES OF NEW HAMPSHIRE, MASSACHUSETTS BAY, RHODE ISLAND AND PROVIDENCE PLANTATIONS, CONNECTICUT, NEW YORK, NEW JERSEY, PENNSYLVANIA, DELAWARE, MARYLAND, VIRGINIA, NORTH CAROLINA, SOUTH CAROLINA, GEORGIA.*

Article 1

The stile of this confederacy shall be "The United States of America."

Article 2

Each State retains its sovereignty, freedom and independence, and every power, jurisdiction, and right, which is not by this confederation expressly delegated to the United States, in Congress assembled.

Article 3

The said states hereby severally enter into a firm league of friendship with each other for their common defence, the security of their liberties and their mutual and general welfare; binding themselves to assist each other against all force offered to, or attacks made upon them, or any of them, on account of religion, sovereignty, trade, or any other pretence whatever.

Article 4

The better to secure and perpetuate mutual friendship and intercourse among the people of the different states in this union, the free inhabitants of each of these states, paupers, vagabonds, and fugitives from justice excepted, shall be entitled to all privileges and immunities of free citizens in the several states; and the people of each State shall have free ingress and regress to and from any other State, and shall enjoy therein all the privileges of trade and commerce, subject to the same duties, impositions, and restrictions, as the inhabitants thereof respectively; provided, that such restrictions shall not extend so far as to prevent the removal of property, imported into any State, to any other State of which the owner is an inhabitant; provided also, that no imposition, duties, or restriction, shall be laid by any State on the property of the United States, or either of them. If any person guilty of, or charged with treason, felony, or other high misdemeanor in any State, shall flee from justice and be found in any of the United States, he shall, upon demand of the governor or executive power of the State from which he fled, be delivered up and removed to the State having jurisdiction of his offence. Full faith and credit shall be given in each of these states to the records, acts, and judicial proceedings of the courts and magistrates of every other State.

Article 5

For the more convenient management of the general interests of the United States, delegates shall be annually appointed, in such manner as the legislature of each State shall direct, to meet in Congress, on the 1st Monday in November in every year, with a power reserved to each State to recall its delegates, or any of them, at any time within the year, and to send others in their stead for the remainder of the year.

No State shall be represented in Congress by less than two, nor by more than seven members; and no person shall be capable of being a delegate for more than three years in any term of six years; nor shall any person, being a delegate, be capable of holding any office under the United States, for which he, or any other for his benefit, receives any salary, fees, or emolument of any kind.

Each State shall maintain its own delegates in a meeting of the states, and while they act as members of the committee of the states.

In determining questions in the United States, in Congress assembled, each State shall have one vote.

Freedom of speech and debate in Congress shall not be impeached or questioned in any court or place out of Congress: and the members of Congress shall be protected in their persons from arrests and imprisonments, during the time of their going to and from, and attendance on Congress, except for treason, felony, or breach of the peace.

*This copy of the final draft of the Articles of Confederation is taken from the Journals, 9:907–925, November 15, 1777.

For protecting them by a mock trial, from punishment, for any murders which they should commit on the inhabitants of these States:

For cutting off our trade with all parts of the world:

For imposing taxes on us without our consent:

For depriving us, in many cases, of the benefit of trial by jury:

For transporting us beyond seas to be tried for pretended offences:

For abolishing the free system of English laws in a neighboring province, establishing therein an arbitrary government, and enlarging its boundaries, so as to render it at once an example and fit instrument for introducing the same absolute rule into these colonies:

For taking away our charters, abolishing our most valuable laws, and altering, fundamentally, the powers of our governments:

For suspending our own legislatures, and declaring themselves invested with power to legislate for us in all cases whatsoever.

He has abdicated government here, by declaring us out of his protection, and waging war against us.

He has plundered our seas, ravaged our coasts, burnt our towns, and destroyed the lives of our people.

He is, at this time, transporting large armies of foreign mercenaries to complete the works of death, desolation, and tyranny, already begun, with circumstances of cruelty and perfidy scarcely paralleled in the most barbarous ages, and totally unworthy the head of a civilized nation.

He has constrained our fellow citizens, taken captive on the high seas, to bear arms against their country, to become the executioners of their friends, and brethren, or to fall themselves by their hands.

He has excited domestic insurrections amongst us, and has endeavored to bring on the inhabitants of our frontiers, the merciless Indian savages, whose known rule of warfare is an undistinguished destruction of all ages, sexes, and conditions.

In every stage of these oppressions, we have petitioned for redress; in the most humble terms; our repeated petitions have been answered only by repeated injury. A prince, whose character is thus marked by every act which may define a tyrant, is unfit to be the ruler of a free people.

Nor have we been wanting in attention to our British brethren. We have warned them, from time to time, of attempts made by their legislature to extend an unwarrantable jurisdiction over us. We have reminded them of the circumstances of our emigration and settlement here. We have appealed to their native justice and magnanimity, and we have conjured them, by the ties of our common kindred, to disavow these usurpations, which would inevitably interrupt our connections and correspondence. They, too, have been deaf to the voice of justice and consanguinity. We must, therefore, acquiesce in the necessity which denounces our separation, and hold them as we hold the rest of mankind, enemies in war, in peace, friends.

We, therefore, the representatives of the United States of America, in general Congress assembled, appealing to the Supreme Judge of the world for the rectitude of our intentions, do, in the name, and by authority of the good people of these colonies, solemnly publish and declare, that these united colonies are, and of right ought to be, free and independent states: that they are absolved from all allegiance to the British Crown, and that all political connection between them and the state of Great Britain is, and ought to be, totally dissolved; and that, as free and independent states, they have full power to levy war, conclude peace, contract alliances, establish commerce, and to do all other acts and things which independent states may of right do. And, for the support of this declaration, with a firm reliance on the protection of Divine Providence, we mutually pledge to each other our lives, our fortunes, and our sacred honor.

The foregoing Declaration was, by order of Congress, engrossed, and signed by the following members:

JOHN HANCOCK

New Hampshire
Josiah Bartlett
William Whipple
Matthew Thornton

Massachusetts Bay
Samuel Adams
John Adams
Robert Treat Paine
Elbridge Gerry

Rhode Island
Stephen Hopkins
William Ellery

Connecticut
Roger Sherman
Samuel Huntington
William Williams
Oliver Wolcott

New York
William Floyd
Phillip Livingston
Francis Lewis
Lewis Morris

New Jersey
Richard Stockton
John Witherspoon
Francis Hopkinson
John Hart
Abraham Clark

Pennsylvania
Robert Morris
Benjamin Rush
Benjamin Franklin
John Morton
George Clymer

James Smith
George Taylor
James Wilson
George Ross
Caesar Rodney
George Read
Thomas M'Kean

Maryland
Samuel Chase
William Paca
Thomas Stone
Charles Carroll,
  of Carrollton

North Carolina
William Hooper
Joseph Hewes
John Penn

South Carolina
Edward Rutledge
Thomas Heyward, Jr.
Thomas Lynch, Jr.
Arthur Middleton

Virginia
George Wythe
Richard Henry Lee
Thomas Jefferson
Benjamin Harrison
Thomas Nelson, Jr.
Francis Lightfoot Lee
Carter Braxton

Georgia
Button Gwinnett
Lyman Hall
George Walton

THE DECLARATION OF INDEPENDENCE

In Congress, July 4, 1776,

THE UNANIMOUS DECLARATION OF THE THIRTEEN UNITED STATES OF AMERICA

When in the course of human events, it becomes necessary for one people to dissolve the political bands which have connected them with another, and to assume, among the powers of the earth, the separate and equal station to which the laws of nature and of nature's God entitle them, a decent respect to the opinions of mankind requires that they should declare the causes which impel them to the separation.

We hold these truths to be self-evident, that all men are created equal; that they are endowed by their Creator with certain unalienable rights; that among these, are life, liberty, and the pursuit of happiness. That, to secure these rights, governments are instituted among men, deriving their just powers from the consent of the governed; that, whenever any form of government becomes destructive of these ends, it is the right of the people to alter or to abolish it, and to institute a new government, laying its foundation on such principles, and organizing its powers in such form, as to them shall seem most likely to effect their safety and happiness. Prudence, indeed, will dictate that governments long established, should not be changed for light and transient causes; and, accordingly, all experience hath shown, that mankind are more disposed to suffer, while evils are sufferable, than to right themselves by abolishing the forms to which they are accustomed. But, when a long train of abuses and usurpations, pursuing invariably the same object, evinces a design to reduce them under absolute despotism, it is their right, it is their duty, to throw off such government and to provide new guards for their future security. Such has been the patient sufferance of these colonies, and such is now the necessity which constrains them to alter their former systems of government. The history of the present King of Great Britain is a history of repeated injuries and usurpations, all having, in direct object, the establishment of an absolute tyranny over these States. To prove this, let facts be submitted to a candid world: He has refused his assent to laws the most wholesome and necessary for the public good.

He has forbidden his governors to pass laws of immediate and pressing importance, unless suspended in their operation till his assent should be obtained; and, when so suspended, he has utterly neglected to attend to them.

He has refused to pass other laws for the accommodation of large districts of people, unless those people would relinquish the right of representation in the legislature; a right inestimable to them, and formidable to tyrants only.

He has called together legislative bodies at places unusual, uncomfortable, and distant from the depository of their public records, for the sole purpose of fatiguing them into compliance with his measures.

He has dissolved representative houses repeatedly for opposing, with manly firmness, his invasions on the rights of the people.

He has refused, for a long time after such dissolutions, to cause others to be elected; whereby the legislative powers, incapable of annihilation, have returned to the people at large for their exercise; the state remaining in the mean-time exposed to all the danger of invasion from without, and convulsions within.

He has endeavoured to prevent the population of these States; for that purpose, obstructing the laws for naturalization of foreigners, refusing to pass others to encourage their migration hither, and raising the conditions of new appropriations of lands.

He has obstructed the administration of justice, by refusing his assent to laws for establishing judiciary powers.

He has made judges dependent on his will alone, for the tenure of their offices, and the amount and payment of their salaries.

He has erected a multitude of new offices, and sent hither swarms of officers to harass our people, and eat out their substance.

He has kept among us, in times of peace, standing armies, without the consent of our legislature.

He has affected to render the military independent of, and superior to, the civil power.

He has combined, with others, to subject us to a jurisdiction foreign to our Constitution, and unacknowledged by our laws; giving his assent to their acts of pretended legislation:

For quartering large bodies of armed troops among us:

Appendix Directory

LINKING TO THE PAST

Link events in this chapter to earlier events.

1. How did George W. Bush's doctrine of preemption differ from the doctrine of containment? (See chapter 26.)

2. What features did the immigration after 1980 have in common with the immigration between 1880 and 1920? What was different? (See chapter 19.)

▶ For practice quizzes and other study tools, see the Online Study Guide at bedfordstmartins.com/roark.

TIMELINE 1988–2011

1988
- Republican George H. W. Bush elected president.

1989
- Communism collapses in Eastern Europe.
- United States invades Panama.

1990
- Americans with Disabilities Act.

1991
- Persian Gulf War.

1992
- Democrat William Jefferson "Bill" Clinton elected president.

1993
- Israel and PLO sign peace accords.
- North American Free Trade Agreement (NAFTA).

1994
- United States sends troops to Haiti.
- General Agreement on Tariffs and Trade establishes World Trade Organization (WTO).

1995
- Bombing of federal building in Oklahoma City.
- United States, with NATO, bombs Serbia.

1996
- Personal Responsibility and Work Opportunity Reconciliation Act.
- President Clinton reelected.

1998
- United States bombs terrorist sites in Afghanistan and Sudan.

1998–2000
- United States bombs Iraq

1999
- Senate trial fails to approve impeachment of Clinton.

2000
- Republican George W. Bush elected president.

2001
- September 11. Terrorists attack World Trade Center and Pentagon.
- U.S.-led coalition attacks Afghanistan, driving out Taliban government.
- USA Patriot Act.
- $1.35 trillion tax cut.

2002
- No Child Left Behind Act.
- Department of Homeland Security established.

2003
- United States attacks Iraq.
- Prescription drug coverage added to Medicare.

2004
- George W. Bush reelected president.

2005
- Hurricane Katrina.

2007
- Bush begins troop surge in Iraq.

2008
- Worst financial crisis since the Great Depression.
- Troubled Asset Relief Program.
- Democrat Barack Obama elected president.

2009
- American Recovery and Reinvestment Act.

2010
- Patient Protection and Affordable Care Act.
- Wall Street Reform and Consumer Protection Act.
- United States ends combat operations in Iraq, increases troops in Afghanistan.

2011
- U.S. forces kill Osama bin Laden in Pakistan

Reviewing Chapter 31

KEY TERMS

Explain each term's significance.

Domestic Stalemate and Global Upheaval: The Presidency of George H. W. Bush
- George H. W. Bush (p. 1041)
- Clean Air Act of 1990 (p. 1041)
- Americans with Disabilities Act (p. 1041)
- Operation Just Cause (p. 1044)
- Saddam Hussein (p. 1044)
- Persian Gulf War (p. 1045)
- William Jefferson "Bill" Clinton (p. 1047)

The Clinton Administration's Search for the Middle Ground
- Earned Income Tax Credit (EITC) (p. 1049)
- "don't ask, don't tell" policy (p. 1051)
- Personal Responsibility and Work Opportunity Reconciliation Act (p. 1052)

The United States in a Globalizing World
- globalization (p. 1054)
- Osama bin Laden (p. 1056)
- North American Free Trade Agreement (NAFTA) (p. 1057)
- World Trade Organization (WTO) (p. 1057)

President George W. Bush: Conservatism at Home and Radical Initiatives Abroad
- George W. Bush (p. 1061)
- Kyoto Protocol (p. 1063)
- No Child Left Behind Act (p. 1063)
- Hurricane Katrina (p. 1063)
- September 11, 2001 (p. 1064)
- Al Qaeda (p. 1064)
- USA Patriot Act (p. 1065)
- Department of Homeland Security (p. 1066)
- Iraq War (p. 1066)

The Obama Presidency: Reform and Backlash
- Barack Obama (p. 1068)
- Hillary Rodham Clinton (p. 1068)
- American Recovery and Reinvestment Act of 2009 (p. 1069)
- Wall Street Reform and Consumer Protection Act (p. 1069)
- Patient Protection and Affordable Care Act (p. 1069)

REVIEW QUESTIONS

Use key terms and dates to support your answer.

1. How did George H. W. Bush respond to threats to U.S. interests as the Cold War came to an end? (pp. 1041–1048)

2. What policies of the Clinton administration moved the Democratic Party to the right? (pp. 1048–1054)

3. Who criticized free trade agreements and why? (pp. 1054–1061)

4. Why did the United States invade Iraq in March 2003? (pp. 1061–1068)

5. What obstacles stood in the way of Obama's reform agenda? (pp. 1068–1071)

MAKING CONNECTIONS

Draw on key terms, the timeline, and review questions.

1. How did George H. W. Bush continue the policies of his predecessor, Ronald Reagan? How did he depart from them?

2. President Bill Clinton called himself a "New Democrat." How did his policies and goals differ from those of Democrats in the past?

3. In the late twentieth century, economic globalization transformed the United States. Explain what globalization is, and describe how it affected the U.S. economy and population in the 1990s.

4. The terrorist attacks of September 11, 2001, were unprecedented. What gave rise to the attacks? How did the nation respond?

Foreign Policy after the Cold War

Andrew J. Bacevich, *American Empire: The Realities and Consequences of U.S. Diplomacy* (2002).

Ivo H. Daalder and James M. Lindsay, *America Unbound: The Bush Revolution in Foreign Policy* (2003).

Karen DeYoung, *Soldier: The Life of Colin Powell* (2006).

David Halberstam, *War in a Time of Peace: Bush, Clinton, and the Generals* (2001).

Paul Kennedy, *The Parliament of Man: The Past, Present, and Future of the United Nations* (2006).

James Mann, *Rise of the Vulcans: The History of Bush's War Cabinet* (2004).

Terrorism and the Afghan and Iraq Wars

Seth G. Jones, *In the Graveyard of Empires: America's War in Afghanistan* (2009).

Gilles Kepel, *Jihad: The Trail of Political Islam* (2002).

Daniel Levitas, *The Terrorist Next Door: The Militia Movement and the Radical Right* (2002).

National Commission on Terrorist Attacks, *The 9/11 Commission Report: Final Report of the National Commission on Terrorist Attacks upon the United States* (2004).

George Packer, *The Assassins' Gate: America in Iraq* (2005).

Gary Rosen, ed., *The Right War? The Conservative Debate on Iraq* (2005).

Anthony Shadid, *Night Draws Near: Iraq's People in the Shadow of America's War* (2005).

Ron Suskind, *The One Percent Doctrine: Deep Inside America's Pursuit of Its Enemies since 9/11* (2006).

Lawrence Wright, *The Looming Tower: Al-Qaeda and the Road to 9/11* (2006).

▶ **FOR MORE BOOKS ABOUT TOPICS IN THIS CHAPTER,** see the Online Bibliography at **bedfordstmartins.com/roark**.

▶ **FOR ADDITIONAL PRIMARY SOURCES FROM THIS PERIOD,** see Michael Johnson, ed., *Reading the American Past*, Fifth Edition.

▶ **FOR WEB SITES, IMAGES, AND DOCUMENTS RELATED TO TOPICS AND PLACES IN THIS CHAPTER,** visit Make History at **bedfordstmartins.com/roark**.

fusion of cultures, recognized in 2000 on Census Bureau forms, where Americans could check more than one racial category. Only half-joking, the famous golfer Tiger Woods called himself a "Cablinasian" to reflect his mixed heritage of Caucasian, black, American Indian, and Asian.

Like their predecessors, the majority of post-1965 immigrants were unskilled and poor. They took the lowest-paying jobs, constituting, for example, nearly half of all farmworkers and housekeepers and performing other work that employers insisted native-born Americans would not do. Yet a significant number of immigrants were highly skilled workers, sought after by burgeoning high-tech industries. By 2006, nearly one-third of all software developers were foreign-born, as were 28 percent of all physicians.

REVIEW   Who criticized free trade agreements and why?

▶ President George W. Bush: Conservatism at Home and Radical Initiatives Abroad

The election of **George W. Bush** in 2000 marked the second time that a son of a former president gained the White House. But the younger Bush pushed an agenda that was closer to Ronald Reagan's than to that of George H. W. Bush. He signed key legislation to improve public school education and to subsidize prescription drugs for elderly citizens. But he also persuaded Congress to pass enormous tax cuts favoring the wealthy, reduced environmental protections, and tipped the balance on the Supreme Court with two conservative appointments. The tax cuts, along with spending on new international and domestic crises, turned the substantial budget surplus that Bush had inherited into the largest deficit in the nation's history, and a financial crisis near the end of his presidency sent the economy into a recession.

As Islamist terrorism replaced communism as the primary threat to U.S. security, the Bush administration launched a war in Afghanistan in 2001 and expanded the federal government's powers to investigate and detain individuals. In distinct contrast to his father's multilateral and cautious approach to foreign policy, George W.

Bush adopted a policy of unilateralism and pre-emption by going to war against Iraq in 2003. He won reelection in 2004, but stability in Iraq and Afghanistan, despite huge costs, remained elusive, and Bush confronted serious foreign and domestic crises in his second term. Democrats capitalized on widespread dissatisfaction with his administration to gain control of Congress in 2006.

The Disputed Election of 2000

Clinton's presidency ended with a flourishing economy, and public opinion polls indicated that a majority of Americans agreed with the Democrats on most issues. Yet his vice president, Albert Gore, failed to succeed him in 2000. To many voters, Gore seemed stiff and pompous and too willing to change his positions for political advantage. He was further burdened with the taint of Clinton administration scandals.

George W. Bush won the Republican nomination after a series of richly funded, hard-fought primaries. The oldest son of former president George H. W. Bush, he had earned degrees from Yale and Harvard, worked in the oil industry, and served as governor of Texas since 1994. Inexperienced in national and international affairs, Bush chose for his running mate a seasoned official, Richard B. Cheney, who had served in the Nixon, Ford, and first Bush administrations.

Many observers predicted that the amazingly strong economy would give Gore the edge, and he did surpass Bush by more than half a million votes. Once the polls closed, however, it became clear that Florida's 25 electoral college votes would decide the presidency. Bush's tiny margin in Florida prompted an automatic recount of the votes, which eventually gave him an edge of 537 votes in that state.

Meanwhile, the Democrats asked for hand-counting of Florida ballots in several heavily Democratic counties where machine errors and confusing ballots may have left thousands of Gore votes unrecorded. The Republicans, in turn, went to court to try to stop the hand-counts. The outcome of the 2000 election hung in the balance for weeks as cases went all the way to the Supreme Court. Finally, a bitterly divided Court ruled five to four against further recounts, and Gore conceded the presidency to Bush on December 13, 2000. For the first time since 1888, a president who failed to win the popular vote took office (Map 31.3). Despite the lack of a popular mandate, the Bush administration set out to make dramatic policy changes.

The Disputed Election
While attorneys representing George W. Bush and Al Gore pursued lawsuits over the counting of ballots in Florida, partisan supporters took to the streets. Here, backers of both sides rally outside the Supreme Court on December 11, 2000, the day before the Court issued its five-to-four ruling that ended the recounting of ballots and thus secured the presidency for Bush. Critics charged that the five justices in the majority had ruled from partisanship rather than objectivity, pointing out that if those justices had followed their custom of favoring state over federal authority, they would have allowed Florida to continue the recounts. AP Photo.

The Domestic Policies of a "Compassionate Conservative"

Bush's appointments, like Clinton's, brought significant diversity to the executive branch. He chose African Americans Colin Powell as secretary of state and Condoleezza Rice first as national security adviser and subsequently as secretary of state when Powell resigned in January 2005. Five of

Bush's top-level appointees were women, including Secretary of Labor Elaine L. Chao, the first Asian American woman to serve in the cabinet.

Bush had promised to govern as a "compassionate conservative." A devout born-again Christian, he immediately established the White House Office of Faith-Based and Community Initiatives to encourage religious groups to participate in government programs aimed at prison inmates, the unemployed, and others. The religious right praised the initiatives, but others charged that they violated the constitutional separation of church and state, and federal courts ruled in several dozen cases that faith ministries were using government funds to indoctrinate the people they served.

Bush's fiscal policies were more compassionate toward the rich than toward average Americans. In 2001, he signed a bill reducing taxes over the next ten years by $1.35 trillion. A 2003 tax law slashed another $320 billion. The laws heavily favored the rich by reducing income taxes, phasing out estate taxes, and cutting tax rates on capital gains and dividends. They also provided benefits for married couples and families with children and offered tax deductions for college expenses.

The administration insisted that the tax cuts would promote economic growth and jolt the economy out of the recession that had begun in 2000. The economy did recover, but opponents stressed inequities in the tax cuts and pointed to a mushrooming federal deficit — the highest in U.S. history — that surpassed $400 billion in 2004, although Republicans had traditionally railed against budget deficits. In 2009, the deficit surpassed $1

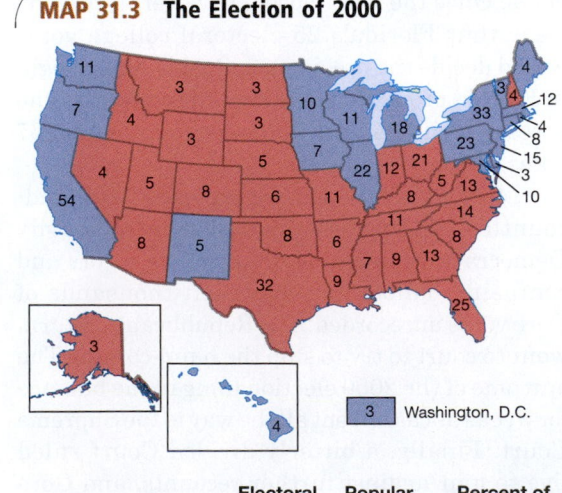

MAP 31.3 The Election of 2000

3 Washington, D.C.

Candidate	Electoral Vote	Popular Vote	Percent of Popular Vote
George W. Bush (Republican)	271	50,456,062	47.8
Al Gore (Democrat)	267	50,996,862	48.4
Ralph Nader (Green Party)	0	2,858,843	2.7
Patrick J. Buchanan (Reform Party)	0	438,760	0.4

trillion as the government struggled to combat a recession. By then, the national debt had risen to $9.6 trillion, making the United States increasingly dependent on China and other foreign investors, who held more than half of the debt.

Bush used regulatory powers that did not require congressional approval to weaken environmental protection as part of his larger goals of reducing government regulation, promoting economic growth, and increasing energy production. The administration opened millions of wilderness acres to mining, oil, and timber industries and relaxed environmental requirements under the Clean Air and Clean Water Acts. To worldwide dismay, the administration withdrew from the **Kyoto Protocol** on global warming, signed in 1997 by 178 nations to reduce greenhouse gas emissions.

While environmentalists pushed for measures to limit American energy consumption, the administration called for more rapid development of energy resources. During his second term, as gasoline prices reached all-time highs in 2005, Bush signed the Energy Policy Act, a compromise bill providing $14 billion in subsidies to producers of oil, coal, nuclear power, and alternative sources of energy. But when gas prices shot up even higher in 2008 and Bush sought to lift restrictions on offshore drilling for oil, Congress blocked the president's efforts, and it continued to thwart his calls to allow drilling for oil in the Arctic National Wildlife Refuge.

Bush had the opportunity to replace two Supreme Court justices, and conservatives hailed his choices. In 2005, John Roberts, who had served in the Reagan and George H. W. Bush administrations, was named chief justice. Bush then replaced the moderate Sandra Day O'Connor with Samuel A. Alito, a staunch conservative who won confirmation by a narrow margin. While the Court stood up to the administration in rulings on the rights of accused terrorists, it tilted right on cases concerning abortion, gun control, sex discrimination in employment, campaign financing, and regulation of business.

In contrast to the partisan conflict over judicial appointments and tax and environmental policy, Bush won bipartisan support for the **No Child Left Behind Act** of 2002, marking the greatest change in federal education policy since the 1960s and substantially extending the role of the federal government in public education. Promising to end, in Bush's words, "the story of children being just shuffled through the system," the law required every school to meet annual testing standards, penalized failing schools, and allowed parents to transfer their children out of such schools. It authorized an increase in federal aid, but not enough for Senator Paul Wellstone of Minnesota, one of the few critics of the measure, who asked, "How can you reach the goal of leaving no child behind on a tin cup budget?" In addition to struggling to finance the new standards, school officials began to criticize the one-size-fits-all approach and pointed to family and community impoverishment as sources of student deficiencies.

The Bush administration's second major effort to co-opt Democratic Party issues constituted what the president hailed as "the greatest advance in health care coverage for America's seniors" since the start of Medicare in 1965. In 2003, Bush signed a bill authorizing prescription drug benefits for the elderly and at the same time expanding the role of private insurers in the Medicare system. Most Democrats opposed the legislation, charging that it left big gaps in coverage, subsidized private insurers with federal funds to compete with Medicare, banned imports of low-priced drugs, and prohibited the government from negotiating with drug companies to reduce prices. Legislators of both parties worried about the cost of the new drug benefit. More than 80 percent of the elderly who signed up for the benefit were at least "somewhat satisfied" with the program, but medical costs overall continued to soar, and the number of uninsured Americans surpassed forty million in 2008.

One domestic undertaking of the Bush administration found little approval anywhere: its handling of **Hurricane Katrina**, which in August 2005 devastated the coasts of Alabama, Louisiana, and Mississippi and ultimately resulted in some fifteen hundred deaths. The catastrophe that ensued when New Orleans's levees broke, flooding 80 percent of the city, shook a deeply rooted assumption held by Americans: that government owed its citizens protection from natural disasters. Federal, state, and local officials failed the citizens of New Orleans in two ways: They had not built the levees to withstand such a deluge, and they failed to rescue citizens when the levees broke and flooded their homes.

New Orleans residents who were too old, too poor, or too sick to flee the flooding spent anguished days waiting on rooftops for help; wading in filthy, toxic water; and enduring the heat, disorder, and lack of basic necessities at the convention center and Superdome, where they had been told to go for safety and protection. "How can we save the world if we can't save our own people?" wondered one Louisianan. Thousands of volunteers rushed to help, and millions more opened their pocketbooks to aid the victims. Yet the immense private generosity and the superb

> **"How can you reach the goal of leaving no child behind on a tin cup budget?"**
> — Minnesota senator PAUL WELLSTONE, on the No Child Left Behind Act

Hurricane Katrina
Residents of the poverty-stricken Lower Ninth Ward of New Orleans plead for help after floods submerged 80 percent of the city in the wake of Hurricane Katrina in August 2005. The boat was useless to these people because it had lost its motor. Some residents waited as long as five days to be rescued. A historian of the disaster wrote, "Americans were not used to seeing their country in ruins, their people in want." AP Photo/David J. Phillip.

response of a few groups, such as the U.S. Coast Guard and the Louisiana Department of Wildlife and Fisheries, could not make up for the feeling that the nation had failed some of its citizens when they needed it most. Since so many of Katrina's hardest-hit victims were poor and black, the disaster also highlighted the severe injustices and deprivations remaining in American society.

The Globalization of Terrorism

The response to Hurricane Katrina contrasted sharply with the Bush administration's decisive

reaction to the horror that had unfolded four years earlier on the morning of **September 11, 2001**. In the most deadly attack ever launched on American soil, nineteen terrorists hijacked four planes and flew two of them into the twin towers of New York City's World Trade Center and one into the Pentagon in Washington, D.C.; the fourth crashed in a field in Pennsylvania. The attacks took nearly 2,800 lives, including U.S. citizens and people from ninety countries. The nation, indeed the world, was stunned.

The hijackers belonged to Osama bin Laden's **Al Qaeda** international terrorist network, and some of them had been living in the United States for several years. Organized from bin Laden's sanctuaries in Afghanistan, where the radical Muslim Taliban government had taken control, the attacks reflected Islamic extremists' rage at the spread of Western goods, culture, and values into the Muslim world, as well as their opposition to the 1991 Persian Gulf War against Iraq and the stationing of American troops in Saudi Arabia. Bin Laden sought to rid the Middle East of Western influence and install puritanical Muslim control.

The 9/11 terrorists and others who came after them ranged from poor to middle-class; some lived in Middle Eastern homelands governed by undemocratic and corrupt governments, others in Western cities where they felt alienated and despised. All saw the West, especially the United States, as the evil source of their humiliation and the supporter of Israel's oppression of Palestinian Muslims. In the wake of the September 11 attacks, President Bush's public approval rating skyrocketed as he sought a global alliance against terrorism and won at least verbal support from most governments.

On October 11, the United States and Britain began bombing Afghanistan, and American special forces aided the Northern Alliance, the Taliban government's main opposition. By December, the Taliban government was destroyed, but bin Laden eluded capture, continuing to direct Al Qaeda forces throughout the world, until U.S. special forces killed him in Pakistan in 2011. Afghans elected a new national government, but the Taliban remained strong in large parts of the county, and economic stability and physical security remained out of reach.

At home, the balance between liberty and security tilted. Throughout the country, anti-immigrant sentiment revived, and anyone appearing to be Middle Eastern or practicing Islam was likely to arouse suspicion. Even though President Bush reminded Americans that "the enemy of America is not our many Muslim friends," authorities arrested more than a thousand Arabs and Muslims, and a

9/11
The magnitude of the destruction and loss of lives in the 9/11 attacks made Americans feel more vulnerable than they had since the Cold War ended. The attacks also affected people around the world who streamed to U.S. embassies or expressed their shock and sympathy in other ways. The surge of patriotism that overtook Americans is demonstrated in this button, which also recognizes the heroism of the first responders. It was made from a photograph taken just hours after the attack, when three firefighters raised an American flag on the ruins. What historic photograph does the image on the button recall? Photograph: Steve Ludlum/The New York Times/Redux; button: Collection of Janice L. and David J. Frent.

Justice Department study later reported that many people with no connection to terrorism spent months in jail, denied their rights. "I think America overreacted . . . by singling out Arab-named men like myself," said Shanaz Mohammed, who was jailed for eight months for an immigration violation.

In October 2001, Congress passed the **USA Patriot Act** by huge majorities. The law gave the government new powers to monitor suspected terrorists and their associates, including the ability to access personal information, while allowing more exchange of information between criminal investigators and those investigating foreign threats. It soon provoked calls for revision from both conservatives and liberals. Kathleen MacKenzie, a councilwoman in Ann Arbor, Michigan, explained why the council opposed the Patriot Act: "As concerned as we were about national safety, we felt that giving up [rights] was too high a price to pay." A security official countered, "If you don't violate someone's human rights some of the time, you probably aren't doing your job."

Insisting that presidential powers were virtually limitless in times of national crisis, Bush

Afghanistan

stretched his authority as commander in chief until he met resistance from the courts and Congress. In 2001, the administration established special military commissions to try prisoners captured in Afghanistan and taken to the U.S. military base at Guantánamo, Cuba. But in 2006, responding to a suit filed by one of the approximately five hundred detainees who had languished there for years, the Supreme Court ruled five to three that Congress had not authorized such tribunals and that they violated international law. That year, congressional leaders became openly critical of the administration for wiretapping phone conversations of U.S. residents without obtaining the warrants required by law.

The government also sought to protect Americans from future terrorist attacks through the greatest reorganization of the executive branch since 1948. In November 2002, Congress authorized the new **Department of Homeland Security**, combining 170,000 federal employees from twenty-two agencies that had responsibilities for various aspects of domestic security. Chief among the department's duties were intelligence analysis; immigration and border security; chemical, biological, and nuclear countermeasures; and emergency preparedness and response.

Unilateralism, Preemption, and the Iraq War

The Bush administration sought collective action against the Taliban, but on most other international issues it adopted a go-it-alone approach. In addition to withdrawing from the Kyoto Protocol on global warming and violating international rules about the treatment of military prisoners, it scrapped the 1972 Antiballistic Missile Treaty in order to develop the space-based Strategic Defense Initiative first proposed by Ronald Reagan. Bush also withdrew the nation from the UN's International Criminal Court, and he rejected an agreement to enforce bans on the development and possession of biological weapons — an agreement signed by all of America's European allies.

Nowhere was the new policy of unilateralism more striking than in a new war against Iraq, a war endorsed by Vice President Dick Cheney and Secretary of Defense Donald H. Rumsfeld, but not by Secretary of State Colin Powell. Addressing West Point graduates in June 2002, President Bush proclaimed a new policy for American security based not on containment but on preemption: "Traditional concepts of deterrence will not work against a terrorist enemy whose avowed tactics are wanton destruction and the targeting of innocents; whose so-called soldiers seek martyrdom in death and whose most potent protection is statelessness." Because nuclear, chemical, and biological weapons enabled "even weak states and small groups [to] attain a catastrophic power to strike great nations," the United States had to "be ready for preemptive action." The president's claim that the United States had the right to start a war was at odds with international law and with many Americans' understanding of their nation's ideals. It distressed most of America's great-power allies.

The Bush administration moved deliberately to apply the doctrine of preemption to Iraq, whose dictator, Saddam Hussein, appeared to be in violation of UN resolutions from the 1991 Gulf War requiring Iraq to destroy and stop further development of nuclear, chemical, and biological weapons. In November 2002, the United States persuaded the UN Security Council to pass a resolution requiring Iraq to disarm or face "serious consequences." When Iraq failed to comply fully with new UN inspections, the Bush administration decided on war. Making claims (subsequently refuted) that Hussein had links to Al Qaeda and harbored terrorists and that Iraq possessed weapons of mass destruction, the president insisted that the threat was immediate and great enough to justify preemptive action. In opposition were the Arab world and most major nations — including France, Germany, China, and Russia — which preferred to give the UN inspectors more time. Nevertheless, the United States and Britain invaded Iraq on March 19, 2003, supported by some thirty nations (see Map 31.1). Coalition forces won an easy and decisive victory, and Bush declared the end of the **Iraq War** on May 1. Saddam Hussein remained at large until December 2003.

Chaos followed the quick victory over Hussein. Damage from U.S. bombing and widespread looting resulting from the failure of U.S. troops to secure order and provide basic necessities left Iraqis wondering how much they had gained. "With Saddam there was tyranny, but at least you had a salary to put food on your family's table," said a young father from Hussein's hometown of Tikrit. A Baghdad hospital worker complained,

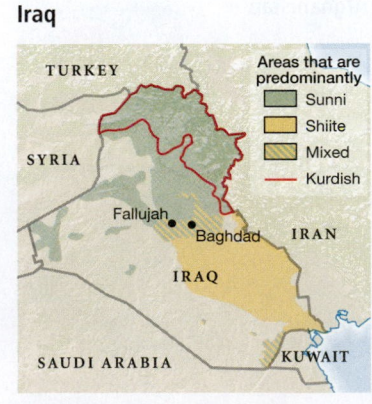

Iraq

Areas that are predominantly

- Sunni
- Shiite
- Mixed
- — Kurdish

TURKEY
SYRIA
Fallujah
Baghdad
IRAN
IRAQ
SAUDI ARABIA
KUWAIT

"They can take our oil, but at least they should let us have electricity and water." Five years after the invasion, Iraqis had less electricity than they had had before the war, and a majority lacked access to clean water. Continuing violence had caused 2 million to flee their country and displaced 1.9 million within Iraq.

The administration had not planned adequately for the occupation and sent far fewer forces to Iraq than it had deployed in 1991 in response to Iraq's invasion of Kuwait. The 140,000 American forces in Iraq came under attack almost daily from remnants of the former Hussein regime, religious extremists, and hundreds of foreign terrorists now entering the chaotic country. Seeking to divide Iraqis and undermine the occupation, terrorists launched deadly assaults on such targets as the UN mission in Baghdad, as well as on major mosques and Iraqi citizens, resulting in the death of tens of thousands.

The war became an issue in the presidential campaign of 2004, which registered the highest voter turnout since 1968. Massachusetts senator John Kerry, the Democratic nominee, criticized Bush's unilateralist foreign policy and the administration's conduct of the war. A slim majority of voters, however, indicated their belief that Bush would better protect American security from terrorist threats than Kerry. The president eked out a 286 to 252 victory in the electoral college, winning 50.7 percent of the popular vote to Kerry's 48.3 percent and carrying Republican majorities into Congress.

In June 2004, the United States transferred sovereignty to an interim Iraqi government, and in January 2005 Iraqis elected a national assembly. The daunting challenge facing the national assembly was to organize a government satisfactory to Iraq's three major groups — Sunnis, Shiites, and Kurds. Violence escalated against government officials, Iraqi civilians, and occupation forces. A nineteen-year-old Iraqi confined to his house by his parents, who feared he could be killed or lured into terrorist activities, said, "If I'm killed, it doesn't even matter because I'm dead right now." By 2006, when U.S. military deaths approached 3,000 and Iraqi civilian casualties reached tens of thousands, public opinion polls in the United States found that a majority of Americans believed that the Iraq War was a mistake.

The president's father, George H. W. Bush, had refused to invade Iraq at the end of the 1991 Gulf War. He explained that Colin Powell, Dick Cheney, and other advisers agreed that "unilaterally exceeding the United Nations' mandate would have destroyed the precedent of international

Transferring Authority to Iraqis
In March 2007, as part of the troop surge in Iraq, U.S. forces set up three joint security stations in Ghazaliya, one of the most dangerous areas around Baghdad. By 2009, the counterinsurgency strategy had produced significant results. Attacks throughout Iraq fell sharply, while U.S. military deaths dropped from 904 in 2007 to 314 in 2008. The improved security fed Iraqis' determination to regain control of their country. In January 2009, U.S. forces transferred control of Joint Security Station III in Ghazaliya to the Iraqi army. Here, U.S. Army Specialist Anthony Perez and an Iraqi soldier raise the Iraqi flag above the station. AP Images/Karim Kadim.

response to aggression that we hoped to establish." The first Bush administration resisted making the nation "an occupying power in a bitterly hostile land," refusing to incur the "incalculable human and political costs" that such an invasion would produce.

By 2006, his son's very different approach was subject to criticism that crossed party lines and included leading military figures. Critics acknowledged that the U.S. military had felled a brutal dictator, but coalition forces were not large enough or adequately prepared for the turmoil that followed the invasion. Nor did they find the weapons of mass destruction or links to Osama bin Laden that administration officials had insisted made the war necessary. Rather, in the chaos induced by the invasion, more than a thousand terrorists entered Iraq — the place, according to one expert, "for fundamentalists to go . . . to stick it to the West."

The war and occupation exacted a steep price not only in dollars but also in American and Iraqi lives, U.S. relations with the other great powers, and the nation's reputation in the world, especially among Arab nations. Revelations of prisoner abuse in the Abu Ghraib prison in Iraq and in the Guantánamo detention camp housing captives from the Afghan war further tarnished the United States' image. Anti-Americanism around the world rose to its highest point in history. The budget deficit swelled, and resources were diverted to Iraq from other national security challenges, including the stabilization of Afghanistan, the elimination of bin Laden and Al Qaeda, and the threats posed by North Korea's and Iran's pursuit of nuclear weapons.

Voters registered their dissatisfaction in 2006, turning control of both houses of Congress over to the Democrats for the first time since 1994. President Bush replaced Secretary of Defense Donald Rumsfeld, and the administration displayed more willingness to work with other nations in dealing with Iraq, Iran, and North Korea. Yet Bush clung to the goal of bringing democracy to the Middle East, even as the situation in Iraq deteriorated. Despite opposition from Democrats in Congress, who wanted a timetable for withdrawal from Iraq, in 2007 the administration began a troop surge that increased U.S. forces there to 160,000. The surge, along with actions by Iraqi leaders, contributed to a significant reduction in terrorist violence, and the administration began planning for the eventual withdrawal of U.S. forces by the end of 2011.

REVIEW Why did the United States invade Iraq in March 2003?

▶ ## The Obama Presidency: Reform and Backlash

Despite the improving situation in Iraq, President Bush's approval ratings sank below 30 percent, posing severe difficulties for the Republican Party in the 2008 elections. The Republicans

nominated John McCain, a Vietnam War hero and longtime senator from Arizona, who chose as his running mate Alaska governor Sarah Palin, the second woman to run for vice president on a major party ticket. Even more historic changes occurred in the Democratic Party when, for the first time, an African American and a woman were the top two contenders. (See "Visualizing History," page 1070.) In hard-fought battles that continued until the last primaries in June, **Barack Obama** edged out New York senator and former First Lady **Hillary Rodham Clinton**, for the presidential nomination.

Born to a white mother and a Kenyan father and raised in Hawai'i and Indonesia, Obama was the first African American to head the *Harvard Law Review*. He settled in Chicago, served in the Illinois Senate, and won election to the U.S. Senate in 2004. At the age of forty-seven, Obama won the Democratic nomination with a combination of a brilliant campaign strategy based on grassroots and Internet organizing and the ability to speak to deep-seated longings for a new kind of politics and racial reconciliation. He won 53 percent of the popular vote and defeated McCain 365 to 173 in the electoral college, while Democrats increased their majorities in the House and Senate (Map 31.4).

Obama hoped to work across party lines, nodding to both conservatives and liberals when he defined "individual responsibility and mutual responsibility" as "the essence of the American promise." The first African American president

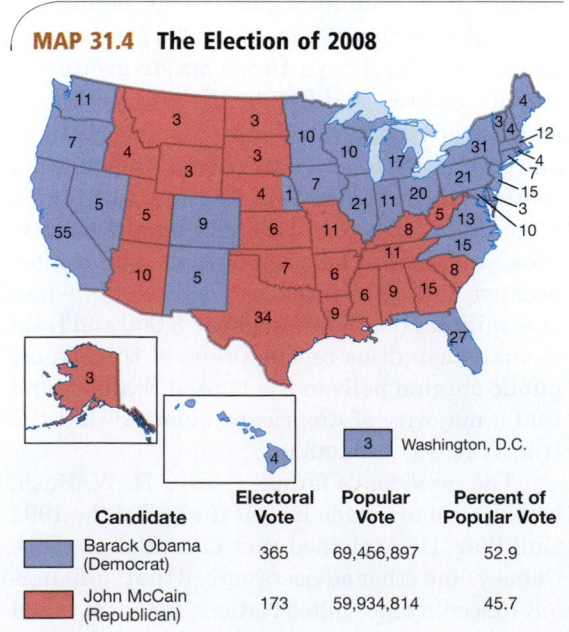

MAP 31.4 The Election of 2008

Candidate	Electoral Vote	Popular Vote	Percent of Popular Vote
Barack Obama (Democrat)	365	69,456,897	52.9
John McCain (Republican)	173	59,934,814	45.7

pledged to pursue a series of reforms in health care, education, the environment, and immigration policy, but he confronted the worst economic crisis since the 1980s. A recession struck in 2008, fueled by a breakdown in financial institutions that had accumulated trillions of dollars of bad debt, largely from the making of loans for over-priced houses to people who lacked the capacity to repay them. As the recession spread to other parts of the world, home mortgage foreclosures skyrocketed, major companies went bankrupt, and unemployment rose to 9.8 percent in late 2010, the highest rate in more than twenty-five years. The financial crisis was so severe that Congress passed the Bush administration's $700 billion Troubled Assets Relief Program in 2008 to inject credit into the economy and shore up banks and other businesses. Obama followed with the **American Recovery and Reinvestment Act of 2009**, $787 billion worth of spending and tax cuts to stimulate the economy and relieve unemployment. Finally, in an effort to prevent the conditions that triggered the financial crisis, he persuaded Congress to expand governmental regulation with the **Wall Street Reform and Consumer Protection Act** in 2010.

Obama's judicial appointments increased the number of women on the Supreme Court to three and included the first ever Latina justice. The president implemented reforms in education, and he signed laws strengthening women's right to equal pay and protecting credit-card holders. His most substantial domestic achievement was passage of a health care reform bill over unanimous Republican opposition. The **Patient Protection and Affordable Care Act** of 2010 extended health insurance to thirty million Americans. It provided subsidies and compelled larger businesses to offer coverage, imposed new regulations on insurance companies to protect their customers, and contained provisions to limit health care costs. Although liberals failed to get a public option to allow government-managed programs to compete with private insurance plans, the law represented the largest expansion of government since the Great Society. One journalist remarked that its passage made Obama "a figure in history for reasons far beyond the color of his skin."

In foreign affairs, Obama reached out to Muslim nations, recommitted the United States to multilateralism, and worked to contain the proliferation of nuclear weapons. He continued the Bush administration's plan to withdraw from Iraq. When the last combat troops departed in 2010, 50,000 U.S. military personnel remained to train and assist Iraqi security forces while leaders struggled to build a stable government that could win the confidence of the three major factions. On Afghanistan, even though corruption permeated its government and a majority of Americans opposed that war, Obama accepted the advice of military leaders that more troops were needed to contain the Taliban insurgents and secure the government. He dispatched an additional 50,000 military personnel to Afghanistan with the promise that the United States could begin to draw down its commitment in mid-2011.

Voters were much more concerned with domestic issues when they issued a sharp rebuke

> **"Individual responsibility and mutual responsibility [are] the essence of the American promise."**
> — President BARACK OBAMA

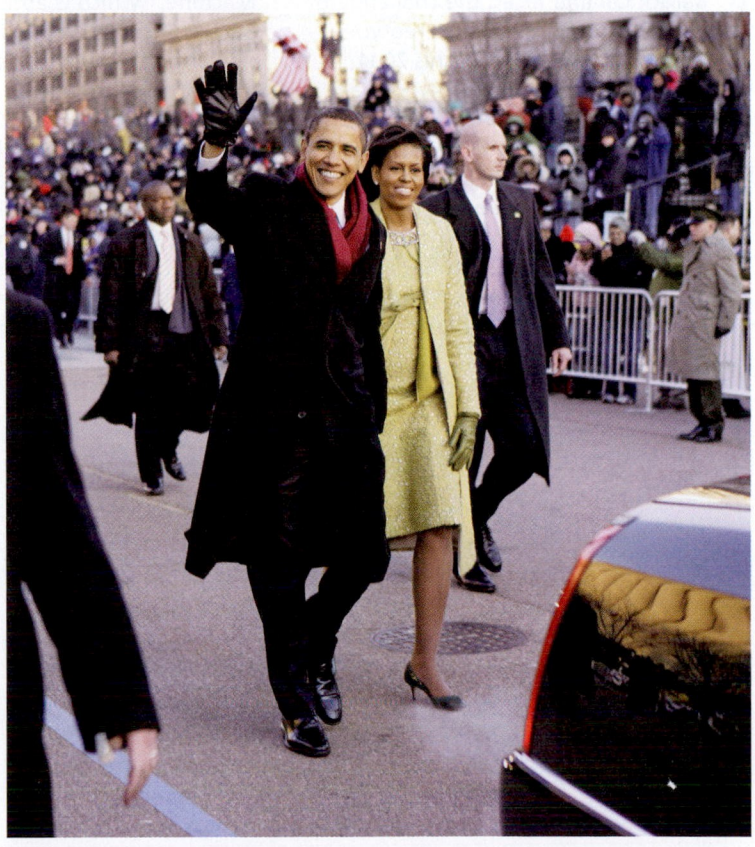

The Inauguration of Barack Obama
President Barack Obama and his wife, Michelle, walk down Pennsylvania Avenue after his inauguration at the Capitol on January 20, 2009. In his inaugural address, Obama spoke of "this winter of our hardship," referring to economic crisis, wars in Iraq and Afghanistan, and other challenges facing the nation. While the most people ever to attend an inauguration absorbed his sober message, they also radiated feelings of sheer joy and hope. AP Images/Doug Mills/Pool.

Caricaturing the Candidates: Clinton and Obama in 2008

In the Democratic presidential primaries of 2008, political cartoonists faced an unusual challenge. For the first time, a woman and an African American squared off as major rivals. Cartoonists had a free hand at portraying the unpopular outgoing president, George W. Bush — often pictured as a simian or monkeylike creature of dim intelligence. But how could they portray a woman and a black man without raising charges of sexism or racism?

Hillary Clinton, of course, had a history in political cartoons as First Lady and then as senator from New York. Her caricatures at the hands of the press had already drawn fire from her supporters for being as personal as they were political. After viewing the cartoons shown here, do you agree that her caricatures are sexist?

Political cartoonists drawing Barack Obama faced the challenge of avoiding obvious racial stereotypes. Fortunately for them, in his 2004 Democratic convention keynote address, Obama had already described himself as "a skinny kid with big ears and a funny name," and cartoonists capitalized on that image. Do you think the cartoons here avoid racism in their portrayal of Obama?

In the first cartoon, from February 2008, Hillary Clinton is in

"The Clinton Machine."

the driver's seat of "The Clinton Machine," which is about to crush Barack Obama. Who is shown as powering the steamroller? How does the portrayal of Obama compare with that of Clinton in this cartoon? What does this cartoon imply about Clinton's chances for capturing the Democratic nomination?

The second cartoon shows Clinton melting, in the style of the Wicked Witch of the West from *The Wizard of Oz*. A smiling Obama,

dressed as Dorothy, holds a pail of water labeled "High Tone Rhetoric," which is apparently responsible for Clinton's demise. The cartoon, inked by the well-known political cartoonist Steve Benson, ran in late February after Obama had won a series of primary contests. What anti-Clinton messages are included in this cartoon? Is Obama depicted as a powerful victor?

In the third cartoon, Clinton appears as "The Incredible Sulk,"

to Obama in the 2010 midterm elections, turning over the House to the Republicans and cutting into the Democratic majority in the Senate. Nearly 10 percent of American workers were unemployed, the federal deficit that Obama had inherited from the Bush administration soared to $1.4 trillion, and a vocal minority of older and mostly white voters expressed their fury at what they considered an overreaching government by joining grassroots movements that took the name the Tea Party revolt. As one Tea Party

supporter put it, "The government is taking over everything — I want my freedom back." The intensely polarized political environment would complicate Obama's efforts to reduce unemployment and cut into the enormous federal debt and would imperil his agenda of reform in environmental and immigration policy.

REVIEW What obstacles stood in the way of Obama's reform agenda?

"I'm Melting."

of Clinton and Obama vary in these three cartoons? For each candidate, would you say there is a progression of change, or do their depictions generally remain static?

Although cartoonists tended to portray Clinton and Obama as bitter enemies throughout the primaries, the two politicians began an effective partnership when president-elect Obama selected Clinton for the position of secretary of state in November 2008.

a monster who threatens a nervous Obama as he contemplates choosing a running mate. The cartoon ran in June 2008, in the lead-up to the Democratic National Convention in Denver. Why do you think the artist styled Clinton as a cartoon character who morphs into a monster when provoked? Why do you think the artist portrayed Obama as cowering before his former rival?

The political cartoons reproduced here are a tiny sample of the larger world of political commentary. Yet they convey many of the beliefs and attitudes held by the American public as the 2008 primary elections played out. How do the portrayals

"The Incredible Sulk."

► Conclusion: Defining the Government's Role at Home and Abroad

More than two hundred years after the birth of the United States, Colin Powell referred to the unfinished nature of the American promise when he declared that the question of America's role in the world "isn't answered yet." In fact, the

end of the Cold War, the rise of international terrorism, and the George W. Bush administration's doctrines of preemption and unilateralism sparked new debates over the long-standing question of how the United States should act beyond its borders.

Nor had Americans set to rest questions about the role of government at home. In a population so greatly derived from people fleeing oppressive governments, Americans had debated for more than two centuries what responsibilities the government should shoulder and what was best left to private enterprise, families, churches, and other voluntary institutions. Far more than most industrialized democracies, the United States had relied on private rather than public obligation, individual rather than collective solutions. In the twentieth century, Americans had significantly enlarged the federal government's powers and responsibilities, but the years since the 1960s had seen a decline of trust in government's ability to improve people's lives, even as a poverty rate of 20 percent among children and a growing gap between rich and poor survived the economic boom of the 1990s.

The shifting of control of the government back and forth between Republicans and Democrats from 1989 to 2010 revealed a dynamic debate over government's role in domestic affairs. The protections enacted for people with disabilities during the first Bush administration and Bill Clinton's incremental reforms both built on a deep-rooted tradition that sought to realize the American promise of justice and human well-being. Those who mobilized against the ravages of globalization worked internationally for what populists, progressives, New Deal reformers, and many activists of the 1960s had sought for the domestic population: protection of individual rights, curbs on capitalism, assistance for victims of rapid economic change, and fiscal policies that placed greater responsibility on those best able to pay for the collective good. Even the second Bush administration, which sought to limit government's reach, supported the No Child Left Behind Act and the Medicare prescription drug program, and it departed from traditional conservative policy in the gigantic program to bail out failing businesses when the financial crisis hit the economy in 2008. The bitter controversy surrounding Obama's health care reform replayed America's long-standing debate about the government's appropriate role.

The United States became ever more deeply embedded in the global economy as products, information, and people crossed borders with amazing speed and frequency. Although the end of the Cold War brought about unanticipated cooperation between the United States and its former enemies, globalization also contributed to international instability and the threat of deadly terrorism to a nation unaccustomed to foreign attacks within its own borders. In response to those dangers, the second Bush administration departed from the multilateral approach to foreign policy that had been built up by Republican

and Democratic administrations alike since World War II. Toward the end of his second term, however, Bush worked to improve international relationships, and Obama promised a new approach in American relations with the world.

▶ Selected Bibliography

Domestic Politics, Policies, and Economic Change

Jonathan Alter, *The Promise: President Obama, Year One* (2010).

David Blumenthal and James A. Morone, *The Heart of Power: Health and Politics in the Oval Office* (2009).

Douglas Brinkley, *The Great Deluge: Hurricane Katrina, New Orleans, and the Mississippi Gulf Coast* (2006).

Alfred D. Chandler Jr., *Inventing the Electronic Century: The Epic Story of the Consumer Electronics and Computer Science Industries* (2001).

Robert Draper, *"Dead Certain": The Presidency of George W. Bush* (2007).

John F. Harris, *The Survivor: Bill Clinton in the White House* (2005).

Bruce D. Meyer and Douglas Holtz-Eakin, *Making Work Pay: The Earned Income Tax Credit and Its Impact on America's Families* (2002).

Richard A. Posner, *A Failure of Capitalism: The Crisis of '08 and the Descent into Depression* (2009).

Jack N. Rakove, ed., *The Unfinished Election of 2000* (2001).

Richard K. Scotch, *From Good Will to Civil Rights: Transforming Federal Disability Policy* (rev. ed., 2001).

David K. Shipler, *The Working Poor: Invisible in America* (2004).

Julian E. Zelizer, ed., *The Presidency of George W. Bush: A First Historical Assessment* (2010).

Kate Zernike, *Boiling Mad: Inside Tea Party America* (2010).

Globalization and Immigration

Frank D. Bean and Gillian Stevens, *America's Newcomers and the Dynamics of Diversity* (2003).

Jeremy Brecher, Tim Costello, and Brendan Smith, *Globalization from Below* (2000).

Thomas L. Friedman, *The World Is Flat* (2005).

Otis L. Graham, *Unguarded Gates: A History of America's Immigration Crisis* (2004).

John R. MacArthur, *The Selling of "Free Trade": NAFTA, Washington, and the Subversion of American Democracy* (2000).

David M. Reimers, *Other Immigrants: The Global Origins of the American People* (2005).

Joseph E. Stiglitz, *Globalization and Its Discontents* (2002).

Globalization was transforming not just the economy but American society as well, as the United States experienced a tremendous surge of immigration, part of a worldwide trend that counted some 214 million immigrants across the globe in 2010. By 2006, the United States' 35.7 million immigrants constituted 12.4 percent of the population. The 20 million who arrived between 1980 and 2005 surpassed the previous peak immigration of the first two decades of the twentieth century and exhibited a striking difference in country of origin. Eighty-five percent of the earlier immigrants had come from Europe; by the 1980s, the vast majority came from Asia and Latin America. Consequently, immigration changed the racial and ethnic composition of the nation. By 2004, Asian Americans numbered 13 million, while 41 million Latinos constituted — at 14 percent — the largest minority group in the nation.

The promise of economic opportunity, as always, lured immigrants to America, and the Immigration and Nationality Act of 1965 enabled them to come. Although the law set an annual limit of 270,000 immigrants, it allowed close relatives of U.S. citizens to enter above the ceiling, thus creating family migration chains. In addition, the Cold War dispersal of U.S. military and other personnel around the world enabled foreigners to learn about the nation and form relationships with citizens. Moreover, during the Cold War, U.S. immigration policy was generous to refugees from communism, welcoming more than 800,000 Cubans after Castro's revolution in 1959 and more than 600,000 Vietnamese, Laotians, and Cambodians after the Vietnam War.

Unlike in the earlier immigration, women comprised more than half of all newcomers to the United States in the 1990s. But it was the racial composition of the new immigration that heightened the century-old wariness of native-born Americans toward newcomers. Pressure for more restrictive policies stemmed from beliefs that immigrants took jobs from the native-born, suppressed wages by accepting low pay, strained the capability of social services, or eroded the dominant culture and language. Americans expressed particular hostility toward immigrants who were in the country illegally — an estimated 12 million in 2008 — even though the economy depended on their cheap labor. The Immigration Reform and Control Act of 1986 did little to stem the tide. It penalized employers who hired undocumented aliens but also granted amnesty to some 2 million illegal immigrants who had been in the country before 1982.

The new immigration was once again making America an international, interracial society. The largest numbers of immigrants flocked to California, New York, Texas, Florida, New Jersey, and Illinois, but new immigrants dispersed throughout the country. Taquerias, sushi bars, and Vietnamese restaurants appeared in southeastern and midwestern towns; cable TV companies added Spanish-language stations; and the international sport of soccer soared in popularity. Mixed marriages displayed the growing

Immigrant Labor
Large commercial farms depended on Latino workers, who constituted more than 45 percent of agricultural labor in 2002. A majority of these workers were citizens, and not all were immigrants, but growers insisted that they could not supply Americans with fresh produce without the labor of immigrants, legal and illegal. The dependence of agriculture and service industries on immigrant labor helped block movements for greater immigration restrictions. The workers here are harvesting strawberries near Carlsbad, California. In 2002, the median weekly pay for migrant farmworkers was $300. Sandy Huffaker/ Getty Images.

of technology to overcome distance and noted, "You can get cracker-jack Java programmers in India right out of college for $5,000 a year versus $60,000."

The flight of jobs has not been entirely one-way. Seeking to move production closer to its market, in 1983 Japan's second-largest automaker, Nissan, opened a plant in Smyrna, Tennessee, which would become the largest auto plant in the United States. The plant was non-union, and wages were lower than those of Michigan autoworkers. Yet Daren Shanks, who came from a Tennessee farming town, felt that his job on the engine line gave him "the opportunity to do stuff for my kids that I'd never have had the opportunity to do." In all, by 2007 nearly 5 percent of all American workers, and more than 10 percent of those in manufacturing, received their paychecks from foreign companies operating in the United States.

The majority of jobs, however, moved in the opposite direction. In 2003, the blue jeans company founded in 1853 by Levi Strauss closed its last plants in the United States, contracting out its work to suppliers in fifty other countries from Latin America to Asia. Marivel Gutierez, a side-seam operator in the San Antonio plant, acknowl-edged that workers in Mexico and elsewhere would benefit, suggest-ing the globalization of the American dream. "But what hap-pens to our American dream?" Workers like Gutierez stood as stark reminders that as the benefits of the free flow of eco-nomic enterprise across national borders reached many, globaliza-tion left multitudes of victims in its wake.

Making Nikes in Vietnam
In 1995 Nike began to contract with Vietnamese factories to produce footwear. The average monthly wage in South Korea, where Nike had been contracting out its production, was nearly $800, but stood at just $45 in Vietnam. In the United States, the Oregon-based company faced protests and boycotts over working conditions in Vietnamese plants, but Nike wages surpassed those available to most Vietnamese. These workers putting the finishing touches on shoes in a plant just outside of Ho Chi Minh City (formerly Saigon) were among some 130,000 Vietnamese producing Nike products in 2005. AP Images.

America in a Global Context

1. Why did manufacturing jobs move from the United States to other countries in the 1980s and beyond?

2. What impact did the outsourcing of jobs have on workers in the United States and elsewhere?

promised in 2000 to provide poor nations more debt relief and a greater voice in decisions about loans and grants. According to World Bank president James D. Wolfensohn, "Our challenge is to make globalization an instrument of oppor-tunity and inclusion — not fear."

The Internationalization of the United States

Globalization was typically associated with the expansion of American enterprise and cul-ture to other countries, yet the United States experienced the dynamic forces of globalization within its own borders. Already in the 1980s, Japanese, European, and Middle Eastern inves-tors had purchased American stocks and bonds, real estate, and corporations such as Firestone and 20th Century Fox. Local communities wel-comed foreign capital, and states competed to recruit foreign automobile plants. American non-union workers began to produce Hondas in Marysville, Ohio, and BMWs in Spartanburg, South Carolina. By 2002, the paychecks of nearly four million American workers came from foreign-owned companies.

Jobs in a Globalizing Era

In November 2001, Paul Sufronko, a supervisor at Rocky Shoes and Boots in Nelsonville, Ohio, handed out final paychecks to the company's last sixty-seven employees in the United States, ending a process of outsourcing jobs that had begun in the 1980s. Before his own job ended, Sufronko traveled to Rocky plants in Puerto Rico and the Dominican Republic to train local workers to replace him. Asked about his job loss, the thirty-six-year-old said, "I had other plans. Things just didn't work out."

Other Americans did not take the loss of their jobs to foreign workers so philosophically. An autoworker believed that "corporations are looking for a disposable workforce. . . . No commitment to community; no commitment to country."

In 1960, American workers made 96 percent of all shoes bought in the United States; by 2000, nearly all shoes came from abroad. The globalizing process was not a new experience for Julio Lopez, a temporary beneficiary of Rocky's outsourcing of labor. After Lopez lost his job of twenty-three years when his employer moved its operations overseas, he found work at Rocky's Puerto Rico plant at a rate of $5.15 an hour, less than half of what Nelsonville workers had earned. Lopez hoped that the factory would stay in Puerto Rico for eight more years. "Then I will be sixty-two, and I can retire." His hopes were not unusual. Lillian Chaparro, the plant manager, spoke about the perpetual motion of jobs: "It's like a chain, you know? The jobs leave the U.S. They come here. Then they go to the Dominican, to China. That's why I push people — we have to be able to compete."

The athletic shoe manufacturer Nike was one of the first companies to exploit the advantages of production abroad, turning to Japan in the 1960s. When labor costs there began to rise, Nike shifted production to South Korea. When Korean workers demanded better wages and working conditions, Nike moved production to China and other Asian countries. Local contractors in Indonesia paid workers as little as fifteen cents an hour as they churned out seventy million pairs of shoes in 1996.

Charles Seitz, who lost his job at Eastman Kodak when the company moved some operations to China and Mexico, was not entirely wrong when he said, "There's nothing made here anymore." The proportion of American workers who held manufacturing jobs fell from one-third in the 1950s to 10 percent by the twenty-first century. Of course, not all the job losses resulted from outsourcing. At Kodak, for example, a machine replaced fourteen workers who previously had mixed film-making ingredients. In the 1980s and 1990s, American corporations sought increased productivity so that they could downsize their workforces and reduce costs. Moreover, some companies built plants abroad to be close to burgeoning markets there. Buick, for example, was China's most popular brand in the early twenty-first century. Because so many companies, like Nike, contracted out production to foreign companies rather than employing foreign workers directly, the number of U.S. jobs lost to foreign workers is difficult to calculate.

The outsourcing of work did not end with manufacturing jobs. By 2003, corporations were relying on workers abroad, especially in India, for a wide range of service and professional work. For example, 1,700 engineers and scientists conducted research for General Electric in Bangalore, India. Technology experts in Bangalore provided telephone help for Dell computer users, and American schoolchildren received online tutoring from teachers in Cochin, India. A research firm executive pointed to the power foreign investment, insisting that wages deemed pitiful by Americans offered their impoverished people a much better living than they could otherwise obtain. At the same time, developing countries often pointed to American hypocrisy in advocating free trade in industry while heavily subsidizing the U.S. agricultural sector. "When countries like America, Britain and France subsidize their farmers," complained a grower in Uganda, "we get hurt."

Whereas globalization's cheerleaders argued that everyone would benefit in the long run, critics focused on the short-term victims. American businessman George Soros conceded that international trade and investments generated wealth, "but they cannot take care of other social needs, such as the preservation of peace, alleviation of poverty, protection of the environment, labor conditions, or human rights." The critics enjoyed a few successes. In 2000, President Clinton signed an executive order requiring an environmental impact review before the signing of any trade agreement. Beyond the United States, officials from the World Bank and the International Monetary Fund, along with representatives from wealthy economies, and individuals at much greater speed and much less cost than ever before.

Building on efforts by Presidents Reagan and Bush, Clinton sought to speed up globalization, seeking new measures to ease restrictions on international commerce. In November 1993, he won congressional approval of the **North American Free Trade Agreement (NAFTA)**, which eliminated all tariffs and trade barriers among the United States, Canada, and Mexico. Organized labor and others fearing loss of jobs and industries to Mexico lobbied vigorously against NAFTA, and a majority of Democrats opposed it, but Republican support ensured approval. In 1994, the Senate ratified the General Agreement on Tariffs and Trade, establishing the **World Trade Organization (WTO)** to enforce substantial tariff reductions and elimination of import quotas among some 135 member nations. And in 2005, Clinton's successor, George W. Bush, lowered more trade barriers with the passage of the Central American–Dominican Republic Free Trade Agreement.

The free trade issue was intensely contested. Much of corporate America welcomed the elimination of trade barriers. "Ideally, you'd have every plant you own on a barge," remarked Jack Welch, CEO of General Electric. Critics linked globalization to the loss of manufacturing jobs, the erosion of the social safety net provided for workers since the 1930s, and the growing gap between rich and poor. (See "Beyond America's Borders," page 1058.) Demanding "fair trade" rather than simply free trade, critics wanted trade treaties to require decent wage and labor standards. Environmentalists insisted that countries seeking increased commerce with the United States agree to eliminate or reduce pollution and prevent the destruction of endangered species.

> **"Ideally, you'd have every plant you own on a barge."**
> — General Electric CEO JACK WELCH, on the outsourcing of jobs

Globalization controversies often centered on relationships between the United States, which dominated the world's industrial core, and the developing nations on the periphery, whose cheap labor and lax environmental standards caught the eye of investors. United Students against Sweatshops, for example, attacked the international conglomerate Nike, which paid Chinese workers $1.50 to produce a pair of shoes selling for more than $100 in the United States. Yet leaders of developing nations actively sought

THE PROMISE OF TECHNOLOGY

The Internet

Like many new technologies, the Internet developed through government funding. In 1958, in response to the Soviet launch of *Sputnik*, President Eisenhower created the Advanced Research Projects Agency (ARPA), one of whose projects led to ARPANET, a system that routed digitized messages between computers to provide security for military secrets and to enable communications during an enemy attack. The technology spread quickly beyond the military; by 2000, even the poorest countries had some access to what came to be called the Internet, and a majority of Americans regularly went online at home or at work. Even more people—some 2 billion throughout the world—had cell phones by 2006, and Internet-enabled "smart phones" were abundant by 2011. Using online social networks such as Facebook and Twitter, people around the world can connect virtually to exchange opinions, coordinate events, and participate in politics. During the revolutions that swept through North Africa and the Middle East in 2011, activists used digital

networks to communicate with one another, organize protests, and broadcast their stories and images. What forms of technology do you see among these Egyptian protesters? What are some pros and cons of using these technologies for political activism? ©Bettmann/Corbis.

in question, and praying for a hearing, notice thereof shall be given, by order of Congress, to the legislative or executive authority of the other State in controversy, and a day assigned for the appearance of the parties by their lawful agents, who shall then be directed to appoint, by joint consent, commissioners or judges to constitute a court for hearing and determining the matter in question; but, if they cannot agree, Congress shall name three persons out of each of the United States, and from the list of such persons each party shall alternately strike out one, the petitioners beginning, until the number shall be reduced to thirteen; and from that number not less than seven, nor more than nine names, as Congress shall direct, shall, in the presence of Congress, be drawn out by lot; and the persons whose names shall be so drawn, or any five of them, shall be commissioners or judges to hear and finally determine the controversy, so always as a major part of the judges who shall hear the cause shall agree in the determination; and if either party shall neglect to attend at the day appointed, without shewing reasons which Congress shall judge sufficient, or, being present, shall refuse to strike, the Congress shall proceed to nominate three persons out of each State, and the secretary of Congress shall strike in behalf of such party absent or refusing; and the judgment and sentence of the court to be appointed, in the manner before prescribed, shall be final and conclusive; and if any of the parties shall refuse to submit to the authority of such court, or to appear or defend their claim or cause, the court shall nevertheless proceed to pronounce sentence or judgment, which shall, in like manner, be final and decisive, the judgment or sentence and other proceedings begin, in either case, transmitted to Congress, and lodged among the acts of Congress for the security of the parties concerned: provided, that every commissioner, before he sits in judgment, shall take an oath, to be administered by one of the judges of the supreme or superior court of the State where the cause shall be tried, "well and truly to hear and determine the matter in question, according to the best of his judgment, without favour, affection, or hope of reward:" provided, also, that no State shall be deprived of territory for the benefit of the United States.

All controversies concerning the private right of soil, claimed under different grants of two or more states, whose jurisdictions, as they may respect such lands and the states which passed such grants, are adjusted, the said grants, or either of them, being at the same time claimed to have originated antecedent to such settlement of jurisdiction, shall, on the petition of either party to the Congress of the United States, be finally determined, as near as may be, in the same manner as is before prescribed for deciding disputes respecting territorial jurisdiction between different states.

The United States, in Congress assembled, shall also have the sole and exclusive right and power of regulating the alloy and value of coin struck by their own authority, or by that of the respective states; fixing the standard of weights and measures throughout the United States; regulating the trade and managing all affairs with the Indians not members of any of the states; provided that the legislative right of any State within its own limits be not infringed or violated; establishing and regulating post offices from one State to another throughout all the United States, and exacting such postage on the papers passing through the same as may be requisite to defray the expences of the said office; appointing all officers of the land forces in the service of the United States, excepting regimental officers; appointing all the officers of the naval forces, and commissioning all officers whatever in the service of the United States; making rules for the government and regulation of the said land and naval forces, and directing their operations.

The United States, in Congress assembled, shall have authority to appoint a committee to sit in the recess of Congress, to be denominated "a Committee of the States," and to consist of one delegate from each State, and to appoint such other committees and civil officers as may be necessary for managing the general affairs of the United States, under their direction; to appoint one of their number to preside; provided that no person be allowed to serve in the office of president more than one year in any term of three years; to ascertain the necessary sums of money to be raised for the service of the United States, and to appropriate and apply the same for defraying the public expences; to borrow money or emit bills on the credit of the United States, transmitting, every half year, to the respective states, an account of the sums of money so borrowed or emitted; to build and equip a navy; to agree upon the number of land forces, and to make requisitions from each State for its quota, in proportion to the number of white inhabitants in such State; which requisitions shall be binding; and thereupon, the legislature of each State shall appoint the regimental officers, raise the men, and cloathe, arm, and equip them in a soldier-like manner, at the expence of the United States; and the officers and men so cloathed, armed, and equipped, shall march to the place appointed and within the time agreed on by the United States, in Congress assembled; but if the United States, in Congress assembled, shall, on consideration of circumstances, judge proper that any State should not raise men, or should raise a smaller number than its quota, and that any other State should raise a greater number of men than the quota thereof, such extra number shall be raised, officered, cloathed, armed, and equipped in the same manner as the quota of such State, unless the legislature of such State shall judge that such extra number cannot be safely spared out of the same, in which case they shall raise, officer, cloathe, arm, and equip as many of such extra number as they judge can be safely spared. And the officers and men so cloathed, armed, and equipped, shall march to the place appointed and within the time agreed on by the United States, in Congress assembled.

The United States, in Congress assembled, shall never engage in a war, nor grant letters of marque and reprisal in time of peace, nor enter into any treaties or alliances, nor coin money, nor regulate the value thereof, nor ascertain the sums and expences necessary for the defence and welfare of the United States, or any of them: nor emit bills, nor borrow money on the credit of the United States, nor appropriate money, nor agree upon the number of vessels of war to be built or purchased, or the number of land or sea forces to be raised, nor appoint a commander in chief of the army or navy, unless nine states assent to the same; nor shall a question on any other point, except for adjourning from day to day, be determined, unless by the votes of a majority of the United States, in Congress assembled.

The Congress of the United States shall have power to adjourn to any time within the year, and to any place within the United States, so that no period of adjournment be for a longer duration than the space of six months, and shall publish the journal of their proceedings monthly, except such parts thereof, relating to treaties, alliances or military operations, as, in their judgment, require secrecy; and the yeas and nays of the delegates of each State on any question shall be entered on the journal, when it is desired by any delegate; and the delegates of a State, or any of them, at his, or their request, shall be furnished with a transcript of the said journal, except such parts as are above excepted, to lay before the legislatures of the several states.

Article 10

The committee of the states, or any nine of them, shall be authorized to execute, in the recess of Congress, such of the powers of Congress as the United States, in Congress assembled, by the consent of nine states, shall, from time to time, think expedient to vest them with; provided, that no power be delegated to the said committee, for the exercise of which, by the articles of confederation, the voice of nine states, in the Congress of the United States assembled, is requisite.

Article 11

Canada acceding to this confederation, and joining in the measures of the United States, shall be admitted into and entitled to all the advantages of this union; but no other colony shall be admitted into the same, unless such admission be agreed to by nine states.

Article 12

All bills of credit emitted, monies borrowed and debts contracted by, or under the authority of Congress before the assembling of the United States, in pursuance of the present confederation, shall be deemed and considered as a charge against the United States, for payment and satisfaction whereof the said United States and the public faith are hereby solemnly pledged.

Article 13

Every State shall abide by the determinations of the United States, in Congress assembled, on all questions which, by this confederation, are submitted to them. And the articles of this confederation shall be inviolably observed by every State, and the union shall be perpetual; nor shall any alteration at any time hereafter be made in any of them, unless such alteration be agreed to in a Congress of the United States, and be afterwards confirmed by the legislatures of every State.

These articles shall be proposed to the legislatures of all the United States, to be considered, and if approved of by them, they are advised to authorize their delegates to ratify the same in the Congress of the United States; which being done, the same shall become conclusive.

THE CONSTITUTION OF THE UNITED STATES*

Agreed to by Philadelphia Convention, September 17, 1787. Implemented March 4, 1789.

Preamble

We the people of the United States, in order to form a more perfect union, establish justice, insure domestic tranquility, provide for the common defense, promote the general welfare, and secure the blessings of liberty to ourselves and our posterity, do ordain and establish this Constitution for the United States of America.

---

*Passages no longer in effect are in italic type.

Article I

Section 1 All legislative powers herein granted shall be vested in a Congress of the United States, which shall consist of a Senate and a House of Representatives.

Section 2 The House of Representatives shall be composed of members chosen every second year by the people of the several States, and the electors in each State shall have the qualifications requisite for electors of the most numerous branch of the State Legislature.

No person shall be a Representative who shall not have attained to the age of twenty-five years, and been seven years a citizen of the United States, and who shall not, when elected, be an inhabitant of that State in which he shall be chosen.

Representatives and direct taxes shall be apportioned among the several States which may be included within this Union, according to their respective numbers, *which shall be determined by adding to the whole number of free persons, including those bound to service for a term of years and excluding Indians not taxed, three-fifths of all other persons.* The actual enumeration shall be made within three years after the first meeting of the Congress of the United States, and within every subsequent term of ten years, in such manner as they shall by law direct. The number of Representatives shall not exceed one for every thirty thousand, but each State shall have at least one Representative; *and until such enumeration shall be made, the State of New Hampshire shall be entitled to choose three, Massachusetts eight, Rhode Island and Providence Plantations one, Connecticut five, New York six, New Jersey four, Pennsylvania eight, Delaware one, Maryland six, Virginia ten, North Carolina five, South Carolina five, and Georgia three.*

When vacancies happen in the representation from any State, the Executive authority thereof shall issue writs of election to fill such vacancies.

The House of Representatives shall choose their Speaker and other officers; and shall have the sole power of impeachment.

Section 3 The Senate of the United States shall be composed of two Senators from each State, *chosen by the legislature thereof,* for six years; and each Senator shall have one vote.

Immediately after they shall be assembled in consequence of the first election, they shall be divided as equally as may be into three classes. The seats of the Senators of the first class shall be vacated at the expiration of the second year, of the second class at the expiration of the fourth year, and of the third class at the expiration of the sixth year, so that one-third may be chosen every second year; *and if vacancies happen by resignation or otherwise, during the recess of the legislature of any State, the Executive thereof may make temporary appointments until the next meeting of the legislature, which shall then fill such vacancies.*

No person shall be a Senator who shall not have attained to the age of thirty years, and been nine years a citizen of the United States, and who shall not, when elected, be an inhabitant of that State for which he shall be chosen.

The Vice-President of the United States shall be President of the Senate, but shall have no vote, unless they be equally divided.

The Senate shall choose their other officers, and also a President pro tempore, in the absence of the Vice-President, or when he shall exercise the office of President of the United States.

The Senate shall have the sole power to try all impeachments. When sitting for that purpose, they shall be on oath or affirmation. When the President of the United States is tried, the Chief Justice shall preside: and no person shall be convicted without the concurrence of two-thirds of the members present.

Judgment in cases of impeachment shall not extend further than to removal from the office, and disqualification to hold and enjoy any office of honor, trust or profit under the United States: but the party convicted shall nevertheless be liable and subject to indictment, trial, judgment and punishment, according to law.

Section 4 The times, places and manner of holding elections for Senators and Representatives shall be prescribed in each State by the legislature thereof; but the Congress may at any time by law make or alter such regulations, except as to the places of choosing Senators.

The Congress shall assemble at least once in every year, and such meeting *shall be on the first Monday in December, unless they shall by law appoint a different day.*

Section 5 Each house shall be the judge of the elections, returns and qualifications of its own members, and a majority of each shall constitute a quorum to do business; but a smaller number may adjourn from day to day, and may be authorized to compel the attendance of absent members, in such manner, and under such penalties, as each house may provide.

Each house may determine the rules of its proceedings, punish its members for disorderly behavior, and with the concurrence of two-thirds, expel a member.

Each house shall keep a journal of its proceedings, and from time to time publish the same, excepting such parts as may in their judgment require secrecy; and the yeas and nays of the members of either house on any question shall, at the desire of one-fifth of those present, be entered on the journal.

Neither house, during the session of Congress, shall, without the consent of the other, adjourn for more than three days, nor to any other place than that in which the two houses shall be sitting.

Section 6 The Senators and Representatives shall receive a compensation for their services, to be ascertained by law and paid out of the treasury of the United States. They shall in all cases except treason, felony and breach of the peace, be privileged from arrest during their attendance at the session of their respective houses, and in going to and returning from the same; and for any speech or debate in either house, they shall not be questioned in any other place.

No Senator or Representative shall, during the time for which he was elected, be appointed to any civil office under the authority of the United States, which shall have been created, or the emoluments whereof shall have been increased, during such time; and no person holding any office under the United States shall be a member of either house during his continuance in office.

Section 7 All bills for raising revenue shall originate in the House of Representatives; but the Senate may propose or concur with amendments as on other bills.

Every bill which shall have passed the House of Representatives and the Senate, shall, before it become a law, be presented to the President of the United States; if he approve he shall sign it, but if not he shall return it with objections to that house in which it shall have originated, who shall enter the objections at large on their journal, and proceed to reconsider it. If after such reconsideration two-thirds of that house shall agree to pass the bill, it shall be sent, together with the objections, to the other house, by which it shall likewise be reconsidered, and, if approved by two-thirds of that house, it shall become a law. But in all such cases the votes of both houses shall be determined by yeas and nays, and the names of the persons voting for and against the bill shall be entered on the journal of each house respectively. If any bill shall not be returned by the President within ten days (Sundays excepted) after it shall have been presented to him, the same shall be a law, in like manner as if he had signed it, unless the Congress by their adjournment prevent its return, in which case it shall not be a law.

Every order, resolution, or vote to which the concurrence of the Senate and House of Representatives may be necessary (except on a question of adjournment) shall be presented to the President of the United States; and before the same shall take effect, shall be approved by him, or being disapproved by him, shall be repassed by two-thirds of the Senate and House of Representatives, according to the rules and limitations prescribed in the case of a bill.

Section 8 The Congress shall have power

To lay and collect taxes, duties, imposts, and excises, to pay the debts and provide for the common defense and general welfare of the United States; but all duties, imposts and excises shall be uniform throughout the United States;

To borrow money on the credit of the United States;

To regulate commerce with foreign nations, and among the several States, and with the Indian tribes;

To establish an uniform rule of naturalization, and uniform laws on the subject of bankruptcies throughout the United States;

To coin money, regulate the value thereof, and of foreign coin, and fix the standard of weights and measures;

To provide for the punishment of counterfeiting the securities and current coin of the United States;

To establish post offices and post roads;

To promote the progress of science and useful arts by securing for limited times to authors and inventors the exclusive right to their respective writings and discoveries;

To constitute tribunals inferior to the Supreme Court;

To define and punish piracies and felonies committed on the high seas and offences against the law of nations;

To declare war, grant letters of marque and reprisal, and make rules concerning captures on land and water;

To raise and support armies, but no appropriation of money to that use shall be for a longer term than two years;

To provide and maintain a navy;

To make rules for the government and regulation of the land and naval forces;

To provide for calling forth the militia to execute the laws of the Union, suppress insurrections and repel invasions;

To provide for organizing, arming, and disciplining the militia, and for governing such part of them as may be employed in the service of the United States, reserving to the States respectively the appointment of the officers, and the authority of training the militia according to the discipline prescribed by Congress;

To exercise exclusive legislation in all cases whatsoever, over such district (not exceeding ten miles square) as may, by cession of particular States, and the acceptance of Congress, become the seat of the government of the United States, and to exercise like authority over all places purchased by the consent of the legislature of the State, in which the same shall be, for erection of forts, magazines, arsenals, dockyards, and other needful buildings;—and

To make all laws which shall be necessary and proper for carrying into execution the foregoing powers, and all other powers vested by this Constitution in the government of the United States, or in any department or officer thereof.

Section 9 *The migration or importation of such persons as any of the States now existing shall think proper to admit shall not be prohibited by the Congress prior to the year one thousand eight hundred and eight; but a tax or duty may be imposed on such importation, not exceeding ten dollars for each person.*

The privilege of the writ of habeas corpus shall not be suspended, unless when in cases of rebellion or invasion the public safety may require it.

No bill of attainder or ex post facto law shall be passed.

No capitation, or other direct, tax shall be laid, unless in proportion to the census or enumeration herein before directed to be taken.

No tax or duty shall be laid on articles exported from any State.

No preference shall be given by any regulation of commerce or revenue to the ports of one State over those of another; nor shall vessels bound to, or from, one State be obliged to enter, clear, or pay duties in another.

No money shall be drawn from the treasury, but in consequence of appropriations made by law; and a regular statement and account of the receipts and expenditures of all public money shall be published from time to time.

No title of nobility shall be granted by the United States: and no person holding any office of profit or trust under them, shall, without the consent of the Congress, accept of any present, emolument, office, or title, of any kind whatever, from any king, prince, or foreign state.

Section 10 No State shall enter into any treaty, alliance, or confederation; grant letters of marque and reprisal; coin money; emit bills of credit; make anything but gold and silver coin a tender in payment of debts; pass any bill of attainder, ex post facto law, or law impairing the obligation of contracts, or grant any title of nobility.

No State shall, without the consent of Congress, lay any imposts or duties on imports or exports, except what may be absolutely necessary for executing its inspection laws: and the net produce of all duties and imposts, laid by any State on imports or exports, shall be for the use of the treasury of the United States; and all such laws shall be subject to the revision and control of the Congress.

No State shall, without the consent of Congress, lay any duty of tonnage, keep troops, or ships of war in time of peace, enter into any agreement or compact with another State, or with a foreign power, or engage in war, unless actually invaded, or in such imminent danger as will not admit of delay.

Article II

Section 1 The executive power shall be vested in a President of the United States of America. He shall hold his office during the term of four years, and, together with the Vice-President, chosen for the same term, be elected as follows:

Each State shall appoint, in such manner as the legislature thereof may direct, a number of electors, equal to the whole number of Senators and Representatives to which the State may be entitled in the Congress; but no Senator or Representative, or person holding an office of trust or profit under the United States, shall be appointed an elector.

The electors shall meet in their respective States, and vote by ballot for two persons, of whom one at least shall not be an inhabitant of the same State with themselves. And they shall make a list of all the persons voted for, and of the number of votes for each; which list they shall sign and certify, and transmit sealed to the seat of government of the United States, directed to the President of the Senate. The President of the Senate shall, in the presence of the Senate and House of Representatives, open all the certificates, and the votes shall then be counted. The person having the greatest number of votes shall be the President, if such number be a majority of the whole number of electors appointed; and if there be more than one who have such majority, and have an equal number of votes, then the House of Representatives shall immediately choose by ballot one of them for President; and if no person have a majority, then from the five highest on the list said house shall in like manner choose the President. But in choosing the President the votes shall be taken by States, the representation from each State having one vote; a quorum for this purpose shall consist of a member or members from two-thirds of the States, and a majority of all the States shall be necessary to a choice. In every case, after the choice of the President, the person having the greatest number of votes of the electors shall be the Vice-President. But if there should remain two or more who have equal votes, the Senate shall choose from them by ballot the Vice-President.

The Congress may determine the time of choosing the electors, and the day on which they shall give their votes; which day shall be the same throughout the United States.

No person except a natural-born citizen, *or a citizen of the United States at the time of the adoption of this Constitution*, shall be eligible to the office of President; neither shall any person be eligible to that office who shall not have attained to the age of thirty-five years, and been fourteen years a resident within the United States.

In cases of the removal of the President from office or of his death, resignation, or inability to discharge the powers and duties of the said office, the same shall devolve on the Vice-President, and the Congress may by law provide for the case of removal, death, resignation, or inability, both of the President and Vice-President, declaring what officer shall then act as President, and such officer shall act accordingly, until the disability be removed, or a President shall be elected.

The President shall, at stated times, receive for his services a compensation, which shall neither be increased nor diminished during the period for which he shall have been elected, and he shall not receive within that period any other emolument from the United States, or any of them.

Before he enter on the execution of his office, he shall take the following oath or affirmation:—"I do solemnly swear (or affirm) that I will faithfully execute the office of the President of the United States, and will to the best of my ability preserve, protect and defend the Constitution of the United States."

Section 2 The President shall be commander in chief of the army and navy of the United States, and of the militia of the several States, when called into the actual service of the United States; he may require the opinion, in writing, of the principal officer in each of the executive departments, upon any subject relating to the duties of their respective offices, and he shall have power to grant reprieves and pardons for offenses against the United States, except in cases of impeachment.

He shall have power, by and with the advice and consent of the Senate, to make treaties, provided two-thirds of the Senators present concur; and he shall nominate, and by and with the advice and consent of the Senate, shall appoint ambassadors, other public ministers and consuls, judges of the Supreme Court, and all other officers of the United States, whose appointments are not herein otherwise provided for, and which shall be established by law: but Congress may by law vest the appointment of such inferior officers, as they think proper, in the President alone, in the courts of law, or in the heads of departments.

The President shall have power to fill up all vacancies that may happen during the recess of the Senate, by granting commissions which shall expire at the end of their next session.

Section 3 He shall from time to time give to the Congress information of the state of the Union, and recommend to their consideration such measures as he shall judge necessary and expedient; he may, on extraordinary occasions, convene both houses, or either of them, and in case of disagreement between them, with respect to the time of adjournment, he may adjourn them to such time as he shall think proper; he shall receive ambassadors and other public ministers; he shall take care that the laws be faithfully executed, and shall commission all the officers of the United States.

Section 4 The President, Vice-President and all civil officers of the United States shall be removed from office on impeachment for, and on conviction of, treason, bribery, or other high crimes and misdemeanors.

Article III

Section 1 The judicial power of the United States shall be vested in one Supreme Court, and in such inferior courts as the Congress may from time to time ordain and establish. The judges, both of the Supreme and inferior courts, shall hold their offices during good behavior, and shall, at stated times, receive for their services a compensation which shall not be diminished during their continuance in office.

Section 2 The judicial power shall extend to all cases, in law and equity, arising under this Constitution, the laws of the United States, and treaties made, or which shall be made, under their authority;—to all cases affecting ambassadors, other public ministers and consuls;—to all cases of admiralty and maritime jurisdiction;—to controversies to which the United States shall be a party;—to controversies between two or more States;—*between a State and citizens of another State*;—between citizens of different States;— between citizens of the same State claiming lands under grants of different States, and between a State, or the citizens thereof, and foreign states, citizens or subjects.

In all cases affecting ambassadors, other public ministers and consuls, and those in which a State shall be party, the Supreme Court shall have original jurisdiction. In all the other cases before mentioned, the Supreme Court shall have appellate jurisdiction, both as to law and fact, with such exceptions, and under such regulations, as the Congress shall make.

The trial of all crimes, except in cases of impeachment, shall be by jury; and such trial shall be held in the State where said crimes shall have been committed; but when not committed within any State, the trial shall be at such place or places as the Congress may by Law have directed.

Section 3 Treason against the United States shall consist only in levying war against them, or in adhering to their enemies, giving them aid and comfort. No person shall be convicted of treason unless on the testimony of two witnesses to the same overt act, or on confession in open court.

The Congress shall have power to declare the punishment of treason, but no attainder of treason shall work corruption of blood, or forfeiture except during the life of the person attainted.

Article IV

Section 1 Full faith and credit shall be given in each State to the public acts, records, and judicial proceedings of every other State. And the Congress may by general laws prescribe the manner in which such acts, records, and proceedings shall be proved, and the effect thereof.

Section 2 The citizens of each State shall be entitled to all privileges and immunities of citizens in the several States.

A person charged in any State with treason, felony, or other crime, who shall flee from justice, and be found in another State, shall on demand of the executive authority of the State from which he fled, be delivered up, to be removed to the State having jurisdiction of the crime.

No Person held to service or labor in one State, under the laws thereof, escaping into another, shall, in consequence of any law or regulation therein, be discharged from such service or labor, but shall be delivered up on claim of the party to whom such service or labor may be due.

Section 3 New States may be admitted by the Congress into this Union; but no new State shall be formed or erected within the jurisdiction of any other State; nor any State be formed by the junction of two or more States, or parts of States, without the consent of the legislatures of the States concerned as well as of the Congress.

The Congress shall have power to dispose of and make all needful rules and regulations respecting the territory or other property belonging to the United States; and nothing in this Constitution shall be so construed as to prejudice any claims of the United States, or of any particular State.

Section 4 The United States shall guarantee to every State in this Union a republican form of government, and shall protect each of them against invasion; and on application of the legislature, or of the executive (when the legislature cannot be convened), against domestic violence.

Article V

The Congress, whenever two-thirds of both houses shall deem it necessary, shall propose amendments to this Constitution, or, on the application of the legislatures of two-thirds of the several States, shall call a convention for proposing amendments, which, in either case, shall be valid to all intents and purposes, as part of this Constitution, when ratified by the legislatures of three-fourths of the several States, or by conventions in three-fourths thereof, as the one or the other mode of ratification may be proposed by the Congress; provided *that no amendments which may be made prior to the year one thousand eight hundred and eight shall in any manner affect the first and fourth clauses in the ninth section of the first article*; and that no State, without its consent, shall be deprived of its equal suffrage in the Senate.

Article VI

All debts contracted and engagements entered into, before the adoption of this Constitution, shall be as valid against the United States under this Constitution, as under the Confederation.

This Constitution, and the laws of the United States which shall be made in pursuance thereof; and all treaties made, or which shall be made, under the authority of the United States, shall be the supreme law of the land; and the judges in every State shall be bound thereby, anything in the Constitution or laws of any State to the contrary notwithstanding.

The Senators and Representatives before mentioned, and the members of the several State legislatures, and all executive and judicial officers, both of the United States and of the several States, shall be bound by oath or affirmation to support this Constitution; but no religious test shall ever be required as a qualification to any office or public trust under the United States.

Article VII

The ratification of the conventions of nine States shall be sufficient for the establishment of this Constitution between the States so ratifying the same.

Done in convention by the unanimous consent of the States present, the seventeenth day of September in the year of our Lord one thousand seven hundred and eighty-seven and of the Independence of the United States of America the twelfth. In witness whereof we have hereunto subscribed our names.

GEORGE WASHINGTON
PRESIDENT AND DEPUTY FROM VIRGINIA

New Hampshire
John Langdon
Nicholas Gilman

Massachusetts
Nathaniel Gorham
Rufus King

Connecticut
William Samuel
    Johnson
Roger Sherman

New York
Alexander Hamilton

New Jersey
William Livingston
David Brearley
William Paterson
Jonathan Dayton

Pennsylvania
Benjamin Franklin
Thomas Mifflin
Robert Morris
George Clymer
Thomas FitzSimons
Jared Ingersoll
James Wilson
Gouverneur Morris

Delaware
George Read
Gunning Bedford, Jr.
John Dickinson
Richard Bassett
Jacob Broom

Maryland
James McHenry
Daniel of St. Thomas
    Jenifer
Daniel Carroll

Virginia
John Blair
James Madison, Jr.

North Carolina
William Blount
Richard Dobbs Spaight
Hugh Williamson

South Carolina
John Rutledge
Charles Cotesworth
    Pinckney
Charles Pinckney
Pierce Butler

Georgia
William Few
Abraham Baldwin

AMENDMENTS TO THE CONSTITUTION WITH ANNOTATIONS (including the six unratified amendments)

▶ *IN THEIR EFFORT TO GAIN Antifederalists' support for the Constitution, Federalists frequently pointed to the inclusion of Article 5, which provides an orderly method of amending the Constitution. In contrast, the Articles of Confederation, which were universally recognized as seriously flawed, offered no means of amendment. For their part, Antifederalists argued that the amendment process was so "intricate" that one might as easily roll "sixes an hundred times in succession" as change the Constitution.*

The system for amendment laid out in the Constitution requires that two-thirds of both houses of Congress agree to a proposed amendment, which must then be ratified by three-quarters of the legislatures of the states. Alternatively, an amendment may be proposed by a convention called by the legislatures of two-thirds of the states. Since 1789, members of Congress have proposed thousands of amendments. Besides the seventeen amendments added since 1789, only the six "unratified" ones included here were approved by two-thirds of both houses and sent to the states for ratification.

Among the many amendments that never made it out of Congress have been proposals to declare dueling, divorce, and interracial marriage unconstitutional as well as proposals to establish a national university, to acknowledge the sovereignty of Jesus Christ, and to prohibit any person from possessing wealth in excess of $10 million.*

Among the issues facing Americans today that might lead to constitutional amendment are efforts to balance the federal budget, to limit the number of terms elected officials may serve, to limit access to or prohibit abortion, to establish English as the official language of the United States, and to prohibit flag burning. None of these proposed amendments has yet garnered enough support in Congress to be sent to the states for ratification.

Although the first ten amendments to the Constitution are commonly known as the Bill of Rights, only Amendments 1–8 actually provide guarantees of individual rights. Amendments 9 and 10 deal with the structure of power within the constitutional system. The Bill of Rights was promised to appease Antifederalists who refused to ratify the Constitution without guarantees of individual liberties and limitations to federal power. After studying more than two hundred amendments recommended by the ratifying conventions of the states, Federalist James Madison presented a list of seventeen to Congress, which used Madison's list as the founda-

tion for the twelve amendments that were sent to the states for ratification. Ten of the twelve were adopted in 1791. The first on the list of twelve, known as the Reapportionment Amendment, was never adopted (see page A-15). The second proposed amendment was adopted in 1992 as Amendment 27 (see page A-24).

Amendment I

Congress shall make no law respecting an establishment of religion, or prohibiting the free exercise thereof; or abridging the freedom of speech, or of the press; or the right of the people peaceably to assemble, and to petition the government for a redress of grievances.

◆ ◆ ◆

▶ *The First Amendment is a potent symbol for many Americans. Most are well aware of their rights to free speech, freedom of the press, and freedom of religion and their rights to assemble and to petition, even if they cannot cite the exact words of this amendment.*

The First Amendment guarantee of freedom of religion has two clauses: the "free exercise clause," which allows individuals to practice or not practice any religion, and the "establishment clause," which prevents the federal government from discriminating against or favoring any particular religion. This clause was designed to create what Thomas Jefferson referred to as "a wall of separation between church and state." In the 1960s, the Supreme Court ruled that the First Amendment prohibits prayer (see Engel v. Vitale, online) and Bible reading in public schools.

Although the rights to free speech and freedom of the press are established in the First Amendment, it was not until the twentieth century that the Supreme Court began to explore the full meaning of these guarantees. In 1919, the Court ruled in Schenck v. United States (online) that the government could suppress free expression only where it could cite a "clear and present danger." In a decision that continues to raise controversies, the Court ruled in 1990, in Texas v. Johnson, that flag burning is a form of symbolic speech protected by the First Amendment.

Amendment II

A well-regulated militia being necessary to the security of a free State, the right of the people to keep and bear arms shall not be infringed.

◆ ◆ ◆

*Richard B. Bernstein, Amending America (New York: Times Books, 1993), 177–81.

▶ *Fear of a standing army under the control of a hostile government made the Second Amendment an important part of the Bill of Rights. Advocates of gun ownership claim that the amendment prevents the government from regulating firearms. Proponents of gun control argue that the amendment is designed only to protect the right of the states to maintain militia units.*

In 1939, the Supreme Court ruled in United States v. Miller *that the Second Amendment did not protect the right of an individual to own a sawed-off shotgun, which it argued was not ordinary militia equipment. Since then, the Supreme Court has refused to hear Second Amendment cases, while lower courts have upheld firearms regulations. Several justices currently on the bench seem to favor a narrow interpretation of the Second Amendment, which would allow gun control legislation. The controversy over the impact of the Second Amendment on gun owners and gun control legislation will certainly continue.*

Amendment III

No soldier shall, in time of peace, be quartered in any house without the consent of the owner, nor in time of war, but in a manner to be prescribed by law.

◆ ◆ ◆

▶ *The Third Amendment was extremely important to the framers of the Constitution, but today it is nearly forgotten. American colonists were especially outraged that they were forced to quarter British troops in the years before and during the American Revolution. The philosophy of the Third Amendment has been viewed by some justices and scholars as the foundation of the modern constitutional right to privacy. One example of this can be found in Justice William O. Douglas's opinion in* Griswold v. Connecticut *(online).*

Amendment IV

The right of the people to be secure in their persons, houses, papers, and effects, against unreasonable searches and seizures, shall not be violated, and no warrants shall issue but upon probable cause, supported by oath or affirmation, and particularly describing the place to be searched, and the persons or things to be seized.

◆ ◆ ◆

▶ *In the years before the Revolution, the houses, barns, stores, and warehouses of American colonists were ransacked by British authorities under "writs of assistance" or general warrants. The British, thus empowered, searched for seditious material or smuggled goods that could then be used as evidence against colonists who were charged with a crime only after the items were found. The first part of the Fourth Amendment protects citizens from "unreasonable" searches and seizures.*

The Supreme Court has interpreted this protection as well as the words search *and* seizure *in different ways at different times. At one time, the Court did not recognize electronic eavesdropping as a form of search and seizure, though it does today. At times, an "unreasonable" search has been almost any search carried out without a warrant, but in the two decades before 1969, the Court sometimes sanctioned warrantless searches that it considered reasonable based on "the total atmosphere of the case."*

The second part of the Fourth Amendment defines the procedure for issuing a search warrant and states the requirement of "probable cause," which is generally viewed as evidence indicating that a suspect has committed an offense.

The Fourth Amendment has been controversial because the Court has sometimes excluded evidence that has been seized in violation of constitutional standards. The justification is that excluding such evidence deters violations of the amendment, but doing so may allow a guilty person to escape punishment.

Amendment V

No person shall be held to answer for a capital, or otherwise infamous crime, unless on a presentment or indictment of a grand jury, except in cases arising in the land or naval forces, or in the militia, when in actual service in time of war or public danger; nor shall any person be subject for the same offence to be twice put in jeopardy of life or limb; nor shall be compelled in any criminal case to be a witness against himself, nor be deprived of life, liberty, or property, without due process of law; nor shall private property be taken for public use without just compensation.

◆ ◆ ◆

▶ *The Fifth Amendment protects people against government authority in the prosecution of criminal offenses. It prohibits the state, first, from charging a person with a serious crime without a grand jury hearing to decide whether there is sufficient evidence to support the charge and, second, from charging a person with the same crime twice. The best-known aspect of the Fifth Amendment is that it prevents a person from being "compelled . . . to be a witness against himself." The last clause, the "takings clause," limits the power of the government to seize property.*

Although invoking the Fifth Amendment is popularly viewed as a confession of guilt, a person may be innocent yet still fear prosecution. For example, during the Red-baiting era of the late 1940s and 1950s, many people who had participated in legal activities that were associated with the Communist Party claimed the Fifth Amendment privilege rather than testify before the House Un-American Activities Committee because the mood of the times cast those activities in a negative light. Since "taking the Fifth" was viewed as an admission of guilt, those people often lost their jobs or became unemployable. (See chapter 26.) Nonetheless, the right to protect oneself against self-incrimination plays an important role in guarding against the collective power of the state.

Amendment VI

In all criminal prosecutions, the accused shall enjoy the right to a speedy and public trial, by an impartial jury of the State and district wherein the crime shall have been committed, which district shall have been previously ascertained by law, and to be informed of the nature and cause of the accusation; to be confronted with the witnesses against him; to have compulsory process for obtaining witnesses in his favor, and to have the assistance of counsel for his defence.

◆ ◆ ◆

▶ *The original Constitution put few limits on the government's power to investigate, prosecute, and punish crime. This process was of great concern to the early Americans, however, and of the twenty-eight rights specified in the first eight amendments, fifteen have to do with it. Seven rights are specified in the Sixth Amendment. These include the right to a speedy trial, a public trial, a jury trial, a notice of accusation, confrontation by opposing witnesses, testimony by favorable witnesses, and the assistance of counsel.*

Although this amendment originally guaranteed these rights only in cases involving the federal government, the adoption of the Fourteenth Amendment began a process of applying the protections of the Bill of Rights to the states through court cases such as Gideon v. Wainwright (online).

Amendment VII

In suits at common law, where the value in controversy shall exceed twenty dollars, the right of trial by jury shall be preserved, and no fact tried by a jury shall be otherwise reexamined in any court of the United States, than according to the rules of the common law.

◆ ◆ ◆

▶ *This amendment guarantees people the same right to a trial by jury as was guaranteed by English common law in 1791. Under common law, in civil trials (those involving money damages) the role of the judge was to settle questions of law and that of the jury was to settle questions of fact. The amendment does not specify the size of the jury or its role in a trial, however. The Supreme Court has generally held that those issues be determined by English common law of 1791, which stated that a jury consists of twelve people, that a trial must be conducted before a judge who instructs the jury on the law and advises it on facts, and that a verdict must be unanimous.*

Amendment VIII

Excessive bail shall not be required, nor excessive fines imposed, nor cruel and unusual punishments inflicted.

◆ ◆ ◆

▶ *The language used to guarantee the three rights in this amendment was inspired by the English Bill of Rights of 1689. The Supreme Court has not had a lot to say about "excessive fines." In recent years it has agreed that, despite the provision against "excessive bail," persons who are believed to be dangerous to others can be held without bail even before they have been convicted.*

Although opponents of the death penalty have not succeeded in using the Eighth Amendment to achieve the end of capital punishment, the clause regarding "cruel and unusual punishments" has been used to prohibit capital punishment in certain cases (see Furman v. Georgia, online) and to require improved conditions in prisons.

Amendment IX

The enumeration in the Constitution, of certain rights, shall not be construed to deny or disparage others retained by the people.

◆ ◆ ◆

▶ *Some Federalists feared that inclusion of the Bill of Rights in the Constitution would allow later generations of interpreters to claim that the people had surrendered any rights not specifically enumerated there. To guard against this, Madison added language that became the Ninth Amendment. Interest in this heretofore largely ignored amendment revived in 1965 when it was used in a concurring opinion in Griswold v. Connecticut (online). While Justice William O. Douglas called on the Third Amendment to support the right to privacy in deciding that case, Justice Arthur Goldberg, in the concurring opinion, argued that the right to privacy regarding contraception was an unenumerated right that was protected by the Ninth Amendment.*

In 1980, the Court ruled that the right of the press to attend a public trial was protected by the Ninth Amendment. While some scholars argue that modern judges cannot identify the unenumerated rights that the framers were trying to protect, others argue that the Ninth Amendment should be read as providing a constitutional "presumption of liberty" that allows people to act in any way that does not violate the rights of others.

Amendment X

The powers not delegated to the United States by the Constitution, nor prohibited by it to the States, are reserved to the States respectively, or to the people.

◆ ◆ ◆

▶ *The Antifederalists were especially eager to see a "reserved powers clause" explicitly guaranteeing the states control over their internal affairs. Not surprisingly, the Tenth Amendment has been a frequent battleground in the struggle over states' rights and federal supremacy. Prior to the Civil War, the Democratic Republican Party and Jacksonian Democrats invoked the Tenth Amendment to prohibit the federal government from making decisions about whether people in individual states could own slaves. The Tenth Amendment was virtually suspended during Reconstruction following the Civil War. In 1883, however, the Supreme Court declared the Civil Rights Act of 1875 unconstitutional on the grounds that it violated the Tenth Amendment. Business interests also called on the amendment to block efforts at federal regulation.*

The Court was inconsistent over the next several decades as it attempted to resolve the tension between the restrictions of the Tenth Amendment and the powers the Constitution granted to Congress to regulate interstate commerce and levy taxes. The Court upheld the Pure Food and Drug Act (1906), the Meat Inspection Acts (1906 and 1907), and the White Slave Traffic Act (1910), all of which affected the states, but struck down an act prohibiting interstate shipment of goods produced through child labor. Between 1934 and 1935, a number of New Deal programs created by Franklin D. Roosevelt were declared unconstitutional on the grounds that they violated the Tenth Amendment. (See chapter 24.) As Roosevelt appointees changed the composition of the Court, the Tenth Amendment was declared to have no substantive meaning. Generally, the amendment is held to protect the rights of states to regulate internal matters such as local government, education, commerce, labor, and business, as well as matters involving families such as marriage, divorce, and inheritance within the state.

Unratified Amendment

Reapportionment Amendment (proposed by Congress September 25, 1789, along with the Bill of Rights)

After the first enumeration required by the first article of the Constitution, there shall be one Representative for every thirty thousand, until the number shall amount to one hundred, after which the proportion shall be so regulated by Congress, that there shall be not less than one hundred Representatives, nor less than one Representative for every forty thousand persons, until the number of Representatives shall amount to two hundred; after which the proportion shall be so regulated by Congress, that there shall not be less than two hundred Representatives, nor more than one Representative for every fifty thousand persons.

◆ ◆ ◆

▶ *If the Reapportionment Amendment had passed and remained in effect, the House of Representatives today would have more than 5,000 members rather than 435.*

Amendment XI
[Adopted 1798]

The judicial power of the United States shall not be construed to extend to any suit in law or equity, commenced or prosecuted against one of the United States by citizens of another State, or by citizens or subjects of any foreign state.

◆ ◆ ◆

▶ *In 1793, the Supreme Court ruled in favor of Alexander Chisholm, executor of the estate of a deceased South Carolina merchant. Chisholm was suing the state of Georgia because the merchant had never been paid for provisions he had supplied during the Revolution. Many regarded this Court decision as an error that violated the intent of the Constitution.*

Antifederalists had long feared a federal court system with the power to overrule a state court.

When the Constitution was being drafted, Federalists had assured worried Antifederalists that section 2 of Article 3, which allows federal courts to hear cases "between a State and citizens of another State," did not mean that the federal courts were authorized to hear suits against a state by citizens of another state or a foreign country. Antifederalists and many other Americans feared a powerful federal court system because they worried that it would become like the British courts of this period, which were accountable only to the monarch. Furthermore, Chisholm v. Georgia prompted a series of suits against state governments by creditors and suppliers who had made loans during the war.

In addition, state legislators and Congress feared that the shaky economies of the new states, as well as the country as a whole, would be destroyed, especially if loyalists who had fled to other countries sought reimbursement for land and property that had been seized. The day after the Supreme Court announced its decision, a resolution proposing the Eleventh Amendment, which overturned the decision in Chisholm v. Georgia, was introduced in the U.S. Senate.

Amendment XII
[Adopted 1804]

The electors shall meet in their respective States, and vote by ballot for President and Vice-President, one of whom, at least, shall not be an inhabitant of the same State with themselves; they shall name in their ballots the person voted for as President, and in distinct ballots the person voted for as Vice-President, and they shall make distinct lists of all persons voted for as President, and of all persons voted for as Vice-President, and of the number of votes for each, which lists they shall sign and certify, and transmit sealed to the seat of government of the United States, directed to the President of the Senate;—the President of the Senate shall, in the presence of the Senate and House of Representatives, open all the certificates and the votes shall then be counted;—the person having the greatest number of votes for President shall be the President, if such number be a majority of the whole number of electors appointed; and if no person have such majority, then from the persons having the highest numbers not exceeding three on the list of those voted for as President, the House of Representatives shall choose immediately, by ballot, the President. But in choosing the President, the votes shall be taken by States, the representation from each State having one vote; a quorum for this purpose shall consist of a member or members from two-thirds of the States, and a majority of all the States shall be necessary to a choice. And if the House of Representatives shall not choose a President whenever the right of choice shall devolve upon them, before the fourth day of March next following, then the Vice-President shall act as President, as in the case of the death or other constitutional disability of the President.

The person having the greatest number of votes as Vice-President shall be the Vice-President, if such number be a majority of the whole number of electors appointed; and if no person have a majority, then from the two highest numbers on the list the Senate shall choose the Vice-President; a quorum for the purpose shall consist of two-thirds of the whole number of Senators, and a majority of the whole number shall be necessary to a choice. But no person constitutionally ineligible to the office of President shall be eligible to that of Vice-President of the United States.

◆ ◆ ◆

▶ *The framers of the Constitution disliked political parties and assumed that none would ever form. Under the original system, electors chosen by the states would each vote for two candidates. The candidate who won the most votes would become president, while the person who won the second-highest number of votes would become vice president. Rivalries between Federalists and Antifederalists led to the formation of political parties, however, even before George Washington had left office. Though Washington was elected unanimously in 1789 and 1792, the elections of 1796 and 1800 were procedural disasters because of party maneuvering (see chapters 9 and 10). In 1796, Federalist John Adams was chosen as president, and his great rival, the Antifederalist Thomas Jefferson (whose party was called the Republican Party), became his vice president. In 1800, all the electors cast their two votes as one of two party blocs. Jefferson and his fellow Republican nominee, Aaron Burr, were tied with 73 votes each. The contest went to the House of*

Representatives, which finally elected Jefferson after 36 ballots. The Twelfth Amendment prevents these problems by requiring electors to vote separately for the president and vice president.

Unratified Amendment

Titles of Nobility Amendment (proposed by Congress May 1, 1810)

If any citizen of the United States shall accept, claim, receive or retain any title of nobility or honor or shall, without the consent of Congress, accept and retain any present, pension, office or emolument of any kind whatever, from any emperor, king, prince or foreign power, such person shall cease to be a citizen of the United States, and shall be incapable of holding any office of trust or profit under them or either of them.

◆ ◆ ◆

▶ *This amendment would have extended Article 1, section 9, clause 8 of the Constitution, which prevents the awarding of titles by the United States and the acceptance of such awards from foreign powers without congressional consent. Historians speculate that general nervousness about the power of the emperor Napoleon, who was at that time extending France's empire throughout Europe, may have prompted the proposal. Though it fell one vote short of ratification, Congress and the American people thought the proposal had been ratified, and it was included in many nineteenth-century editions of the Constitution.*

The Civil War and Reconstruction Amendments (Thirteenth, Fourteenth, and Fifteenth Amendments)

▶ *In the four months between the election of Abraham Lincoln and his inauguration, more than 200 proposed constitutional amendments were presented to Congress as part of a desperate attempt to hold the rapidly dissolving Union together. Most of these were efforts to appease the southern states by protecting the right to own slaves or by disfranchising African Americans through constitutional amendment. None were able to win the votes required from Congress to send them to the states. The relatively innocuous Corwin Amendment seemed to be the only hope for preserving the Union by amending the Constitution.*

The northern victors in the Civil War tried to restructure the Constitution just as the war had restructured the nation. Yet they were often divided in their goals. Some wanted to end slavery; others hoped for social and economic equality regardless of race; others hoped that extending the power of the ballot box to former slaves would help create a new political order. The debates over the Thirteenth, Fourteenth, and Fifteenth Amendments were bitter. Few of those who fought for these changes were satisfied with the amendments themselves; fewer still were satisfied with their interpretation. Although the amendments put an end to the legal status of slavery, it took nearly a hundred years after the amendments' passage before most of the descendants of former slaves could begin to experience the economic, social, and political equality the amendments had been intended to provide.

Unratified Amendment

Corwin Amendment (proposed by Congress March 2, 1861)

No amendment shall be made to the Constitution which will authorize or give to Congress the power to abolish or interfere, within any State, with the domestic institutions thereof, including that of persons held to labor or service by the laws of said State.

♦ ♦ ♦

▶ *Following the election of Abraham Lincoln, Congress scrambled to try to prevent the secession of the slaveholding states. House member Thomas Corwin of Ohio proposed the "unamendable" amendment in the hope that by protecting slavery where it existed, Congress would keep the southern states in the Union. Lincoln indicated his support for the proposed amendment in his first inaugural address. Only Ohio and Maryland ratified the Corwin Amendment before it was forgotten.*

Amendment XIII

[Adopted 1865]

Section 1 Neither slavery nor involuntary servitude, except as a punishment for crime whereof the party shall have been duly convicted, shall exist within the United States, or any place subject to their jurisdiction.

Section 2 Congress shall have power to enforce this article by appropriate legislation.

♦ ♦ ♦

▶ *Although President Lincoln had abolished slavery in the Confederacy with the Emancipation Proclamation of 1863, abolitionists wanted to rid the entire country of slavery. The Thirteenth Amendment did this in a clear and straightforward manner. In February 1865, when the proposal was approved by the House, the gallery of the House was newly opened to black Americans who had a chance at last to see their government at work. Passage of the proposal was greeted by wild cheers from the gallery as well as tears on the House floor, where congressional representatives openly embraced one another.*

The problem of ratification remained, however. The Union position was that the Confederate states were part of the country of thirty-six states. Therefore, twenty-seven states were needed to ratify the amendment. When Kentucky and Delaware rejected it, backers realized that without approval

from at least four former Confederate states, the amendment would fail. Lincoln's successor, President Andrew Johnson, made ratification of the Thirteenth Amendment a condition for southern states to rejoin the Union. Under those terms, all the former Confederate states except Mississippi accepted the Thirteenth Amendment, and by the end of 1865 the amendment had become part of the Constitution and slavery had been prohibited in the United States.

Amendment XIV

[Adopted 1868]

Section 1 All persons born or naturalized in the United States, and subject to the jurisdiction thereof, are citizens of the United States and of the State wherein they reside. No State shall make or enforce any law which shall abridge the privileges or immunities of citizens of the United States; nor shall any State deprive any person of life, liberty, or property, without due process of law; nor deny to any person within its jurisdiction the equal protection of the laws.

Section 2 Representatives shall be appointed among the several States according to their respective numbers, counting the whole number of persons in each State, excluding Indians not taxed. But when the right to vote at any election for the choice of Electors for President and Vice-President of the United States, Representatives in Congress, the executive and judicial officers of a State, or the members of the legislature thereof, is denied to any of the male inhabitants of such State, being twenty-one years of age and citizens of the United States, or in any way abridged, except for participation in rebellion, or other crime, the basis of representation therein shall be reduced in the proportion which the number of such male citizens shall bear to the whole number of male citizens twenty-one years of age in such State.

Section 3 No person shall be a Senator or Representative in Congress, or Elector of President and Vice-President, or hold any office, civil or military, under the United States, or under any State, who, having previously taken an oath, as a member of Congress, or as an officer of the United States, or as a member of any State legislature, or as an executive or judicial officer of any State, to support the Constitution of the United States, shall have engaged in insurrection or rebellion against the same, or given aid or comfort to the enemies thereof. Congress may, by a vote of two-thirds of each house, remove such disability.

Section 4 The validity of the public debt of the United States, authorized by law, including debts incurred for payment of pensions and bounties for services in suppressing insurrection or rebellion, shall not be questioned. But neither the United States nor any State shall assume or pay any debt or obligation incurred in aid of insurrection or rebellion against the United States, or any claim for the loss or emancipation of any slave; but all such debts, obligations, and claims shall be held illegal and void.

Section 5 The Congress shall have power to enforce, by appropriate legislation, the provisions of this article.

◆ ◆ ◆

▶ *Without Lincoln's leadership in the reconstruction of the nation following the Civil War, it soon became clear that the Thirteenth Amendment needed additional constitutional support. Less than a year after Lincoln's assassination, Andrew Johnson was ready to bring the former Confederate states back into the Union with few changes in their governments or politics. Anxious Republicans drafted the Fourteenth Amendment to prevent that from happening. The most important provisions of this complex amendment made all native-born or naturalized persons American citizens and prohibited states from abridging the "privileges or immunities" of citizens; depriving them of "life, liberty, or property, without due process of law"; and denying them "equal protection of the laws." In essence, it made all ex-slaves citizens and protected the rights of all citizens against violation by their own state governments.*

As occurred in the case of the Thirteenth Amendment, former Confederate states were forced to ratify the amendment as a condition of representation in the House and the Senate. The intentions of the Fourteenth Amendment, and how those intentions should be enforced, have been the most debated point of constitutional history. The terms due process and equal protection have been especially troublesome. Was the amendment designed to outlaw racial segregation? Or was the goal simply to prevent the leaders of the rebellious South from gaining political power?

The framers of the Fourteenth Amendment hoped Article 2 would produce black voters who would increase the power of the Republican Party. The federal government, however, never used its power to punish states for denying blacks their right to vote. Although the Fourteenth Amendment had an immediate impact in giving black Americans citizenship, it did nothing to protect blacks from the vengeance of whites once Reconstruction ended. In the late nineteenth and early twentieth centuries, section 1 of the Fourteenth Amendment was often used to protect business interests and strike down laws protecting workers on the grounds that the rights of "persons," that is, corporations, were protected by "due process." More recently, the Fourteenth Amendment has been used to justify school desegregation and affirmative action programs, as well as to dismantle such programs.

Amendment XV
[Adopted 1870]

Section 1 The right of citizens of the United States to vote shall not be denied or abridged by the United States or by any State on account of race, color, or previous condition of servitude.

Section 2 The Congress shall have power to enforce this article by appropriate legislation.

◆ ◆ ◆

▶ *The Fifteenth Amendment was the last major piece of Reconstruction legislation. While earlier Reconstruction acts had already required black suffrage in the South, the Fifteenth Amendment extended black voting rights to the entire nation. Some Republicans felt morally obligated to do away with the double standard between North and South since many northern states had stubbornly refused to enfranchise blacks. Others believed that the freedman's ballot required the extra protection of a constitutional amendment to shield it from white counterattack. But partisan advantage also played an important role in the amendment's passage, since Republicans hoped that by giving the ballot to northern blacks, they could lessen their political vulnerability.*

Many women's rights advocates had fought for the amendment. They had felt betrayed by the inclusion of the word "male" in section 2 of the Fourteenth Amendment and were further angered when the proposed Fifteenth Amendment failed to prohibit denial of the right to vote on the grounds of sex as well as "race, color, or previous condition of servitude." In this amendment, for the first time, the federal government claimed the power to regulate the franchise, or vote. It was also the first time the Constitution placed limits on the power of the states to regulate access to the franchise. Although ratified in 1870, the amendment was not enforced until the twentieth century.

The Progressive Amendments (Sixteenth–Nineteenth Amendments)

▶ *No amendments were added to the Constitution between the Civil War and the Progressive Era. America was changing, however, in fundamental ways. The rapid industrialization of the United States after the Civil War led to many social and economic problems. Hundreds of amendments were proposed, but none received enough support in Congress to be sent to the states. Some scholars believe that regional differences and rivalries were so strong during this period that it was almost impossible to gain a consensus on a constitutional amendment. During the Progressive Era, however, the Constitution was amended four times in seven years.*

Amendment XVI

[Adopted 1913]

The Congress shall have power to lay and collect taxes on incomes, from whatever source derived, without apportionment among the several States, and without regard to any census or enumeration.

♦ ♦ ♦

▶ *Until passage of the Sixteenth Amendment, most of the money used to run the federal government came from customs duties and taxes on specific items, such as liquor. During the Civil War, the federal government taxed incomes as an emergency measure. Pressure to enact an income tax came from those who were concerned about the growing gap between rich and poor in the United States. The Populist Party began campaigning for a graduated income tax in 1892, and support continued to grow. By 1909, thirty-three proposed income tax amendments had been presented in Congress, but lobbying by corporate and other special interests had defeated them all. In June 1909, the growing pressure for an income tax, which had been endorsed by Presidents Roosevelt and Taft, finally pushed an amendment through the Senate. The required thirty-six states had ratified the amendment by February 1913.*

Amendment XVII

[Adopted 1913]

Section 1 The Senate of the United States shall be composed of two Senators from each State, elected by the people thereof, for six years; and each Senator shall have one vote. The electors in each State shall have the qualifications requisite for electors of [voters for] the most numerous branch of the State legislatures.

Section 2 When vacancies happen in the representation of any State in the Senate, the executive authority of such State shall issue writs of election to fill such vacancies: Provided, that the Legislature of any State may empower the executive thereof to make temporary appointments until the people fill the vacancies by election as the Legislature may direct.

Section 3 This amendment shall not be so construed as to affect the election or term of any Senator chosen before it becomes valid as part of the Constitution.

♦ ♦ ♦

▶ *The framers of the Constitution saw the members of the House as the representatives of the people and the members of the Senate as the representatives of the states. Originally senators were to be chosen by the state legislators. According to reform advocates, however, the growth of private industry and transportation conglomerates during the Gilded Age had created a network of corruption*

in which wealth and power were exchanged for influence and votes in the Senate. Senator Nelson Aldrich, who represented Rhode Island in the late nineteenth and early twentieth centuries, for example, was known as "the senator from Standard Oil" because of his open support of special business interests.

Efforts to amend the Constitution to allow direct election of senators had begun in 1826, but since any proposal had to be approved by the Senate, reform seemed impossible. Progressives tried to gain influence in the Senate by instituting party caucuses and primary elections, which gave citizens the chance to express their choice of a senator who could then be officially elected by the state legislature. By 1910, fourteen of the country's thirty senators received popular votes through a state primary before the state legislature made its selection. Despairing of getting a proposal through the Senate, supporters of a direct election amendment had begun in 1893 to seek a convention of representatives from two-thirds of the states to propose an amendment that could then be ratified. By 1905, thirty-one of forty-five states had endorsed such an amendment. Finally, in 1911, despite extraordinary opposition, a proposed amendment passed the Senate; by 1913, it had been ratified.

Amendment XVIII

[Adopted 1919; repealed 1933 by Amendment XXI]

Section 1 After one year from the ratification of this article the manufacture, sale, or transportation of intoxicating liquors within, the importation thereof into, or the exportation thereof from the United States and all territory subject to the jurisdiction thereof, for beverage purposes, is hereby prohibited.

Section 2 The Congress and the several States shall have concurrent power to enforce this article by appropriate legislation.

Section 3 This article shall be inoperative unless it shall have been ratified as an amendment to the Constitution by the legislatures of the several States, as provided by the Constitution, within seven years from the date of the submission thereof to the States by the Congress.

♦ ♦ ♦

▶ *The Prohibition Party, formed in 1869, began calling for a constitutional amendment to outlaw alcoholic beverages in 1872. A prohibition amendment was first proposed in the Senate in 1876 and was revived eighteen times before 1913. Between 1913 and 1919, another thirty-nine attempts were made to prohibit liquor in the United States through a constitutional amendment. Prohibition became a key element of the progressive agenda as reformers linked alcohol and drunkenness to numerous social problems, including the corruption of immigrant voters. While opponents of such an amendment argued that it was undemocratic, supporters claimed that their efforts had widespread public support. The admission of twelve "dry" western states to the Union in the early twentieth century and the spirit of sacrifice during World War I laid the groundwork for passage and ratification of the Eighteenth Amendment in 1919. Opponents added a time limit to the amendment in the hope that they could thus block ratification, but this effort failed. (See also Amendment XXI.)*

Amendment XIX

[Adopted 1920]

Section 1 The right of citizens of the United States to vote shall not be denied or abridged by the United States or by any State on account of sex.

Section 2 Congress shall have the power to enforce this article by appropriate legislation.

♦ ♦ ♦

▶ *Advocates of women's rights tried and failed to link woman suffrage to the Fourteenth and Fifteenth Amendments. Nonetheless, the effort for woman suffrage continued. Between 1878 and 1912, at least one and sometimes as many as four proposed amendments were introduced in Congress each year to grant women the right to vote. While over time women won very limited voting rights in some states, at both the state and federal levels opposition to an amendment for woman suffrage remained very strong. President Woodrow Wilson and other officials felt that the federal government should not interfere with the power of the states in this matter. Others worried that granting suffrage to women would encourage ethnic minorities to exercise their own right to vote. And many were concerned that giving women the vote would result in their abandoning traditional gender roles. In 1919, following a protracted and often bitter campaign of protest in which women went on hunger strikes and chained themselves to fences, an amendment was introduced with the backing of President Wilson. It narrowly passed the Senate (after efforts to limit the suffrage to white women failed) and was adopted in 1920 after Tennessee became the thirty-sixth state to ratify it.*

Unratified Amendment

Child Labor Amendment (proposed by Congress June 2, 1924)

Section 1 The Congress shall have power to limit, regulate, and prohibit the labor of persons under eighteen years of age.

Section 2 The power of the several States is unimpaired by this article except that the operation of State laws shall be suspended to the extent necessary to give effect to legislation enacted by Congress.

♦ ♦ ♦

▶ *Throughout the late nineteenth and early twentieth centuries, alarm over the condition of child workers grew. Opponents of child labor argued that children worked in dangerous and unhealthy conditions, that they took jobs from adult workers, that they depressed wages in certain industries, and that states that allowed child labor had an economic advantage over those that did not. Defenders of child labor claimed that children provided needed income in many families, that working at a young age developed character, and that the effort to prohibit the practice constituted an invasion of family privacy.*

In 1916, Congress passed a law that made it illegal to sell goods made by children through interstate commerce. The Supreme Court, however, ruled that the law violated the limits on the power of Congress to regulate interstate commerce. Congress then tried to penalize industries that used child labor by taxing such goods. This measure was also thrown out by the courts. In response, reformers set out to amend the Constitution. The proposed amendment was ratified by twenty-eight states, but by 1925, thirteen states had rejected it. Passage of the Fair Labor Standards Act in 1938, which was upheld by the Supreme Court in 1941, made the amendment irrelevant.

Amendment XX

[Adopted 1933]

Section 1 The terms of the President and Vice-President shall end at noon on the 20th day of January, and the terms of Senators and Representatives at noon on the 3rd day of January, of the years in which such terms would have ended if this article had not been ratified; and the terms of their successors shall then begin.

Section 2 The Congress shall assemble at least once in every year, and such meeting shall begin at noon on the 3rd day of January, unless they shall by law appoint a different day.

Section 3 If, at the time fixed for the beginning of the term of the President, the President-elect shall have died, the Vice-President-elect shall become President. If a President shall not have been chosen before the time fixed for the beginning of his term, or if the President-elect shall have failed to qualify, then the Vice-President-elect shall act as President until a President shall have qualified; and the Congress may by law provide for the case wherein neither a President-elect nor a Vice-President-elect shall have qualified, declaring who shall then act as President, or the manner in which one who is to act shall be selected, and such person shall act accordingly until a President or Vice-President shall have qualified.

Section 4 The Congress may by law provide for the case of the death of any of the persons from whom the House of Representatives may choose a President whenever the right of choice shall have devolved upon them, and for the case of the death of any of the persons from whom the Senate may choose a Vice-President whenever the right of choice shall have devolved upon them.

Section 5 Sections 1 and 2 shall take effect on the 15th day of October following the ratification of this article.

Section 6 This article shall be inoperative unless it shall have been ratified as an amendment to the Constitution by the Legislatures of three-fourths of the several States within seven years from the date of its submission.

◆◆◆

▶ *Until 1933, presidents took office on March 4. Since elections are held in early November and electoral votes are counted in mid-December, this meant that more than three months passed between the time a new president was elected and when he took office. Moving the inauguration to January shortened the transition period and allowed Congress to begin its term closer to the time of the president's inauguration. Although this seems like a minor change, an amendment was required because the Constitution specifies terms of office. This amendment also deals with questions of succession in the event that a president- or vice president-elect dies before assuming office. Section 3 also clarifies a method for resolving a deadlock in the electoral college.*

Amendment XXI
[Adopted 1933]

Section 1 The eighteenth article of amendment to the Constitution of the United States is hereby repealed.

Section 2 The transportation or importation into any State, Territory, or Possession of the United States for delivery or use therein of intoxicating liquors, in violation of the laws thereof, is hereby prohibited.

Section 3 This article shall be inoperative unless it shall have been ratified as an amendment to the Constitution by conventions in the several States, as provided in the Constitution, within seven years from the date of the submission thereof to the States by the Congress.

◆◆◆

▶ *Widespread violation of the Volstead Act, the law enacted to enforce prohibition, made the United States a nation of lawbreakers. Prohibition*

caused more problems than it solved by encouraging crime, bribery, and corruption. Further, a coalition of liquor and beer manufacturers, personal liberty advocates, and constitutional scholars joined forces to challenge the amendment. By 1929, thirty proposed repeal amendments had been introduced in Congress, and the Democratic Party made repeal part of its platform in the 1932 presidential campaign. The Twenty-first Amendment was proposed in February 1933 and ratified less than a year later. The failure of the effort to enforce prohibition through a constitutional amendment has often been cited by opponents to subsequent efforts to shape public virtue and private morality.

Amendment XXII
[Adopted 1951]

Section 1 No person shall be elected to the office of the President more than twice, and no person who has held the office of President, or acted as President, for more than two years of a term to which some other person was elected President shall be elected to the office of President more than once. But this article shall not apply to any person holding the office of President when this Article was proposed by the Congress, and shall not prevent any person who may be holding the office of President, or acting as President, during the term within which this Article becomes operative from holding the office of President or acting as President during the remainder of such term.

Section 2 This article shall be inoperative unless it shall have been ratified as an amendment to the Constitution by the legislatures of three-fourths of the several States within seven years from the date of its submission to the States by the Congress.

◆◆◆

▶ *George Washington's refusal to seek a third term of office set a precedent that stood until 1912, when former president Theodore Roosevelt sought, without success, another term as an independent candidate. Democrat Franklin Roosevelt was the only president to seek and win a fourth term, though he did so amid great controversy. Roosevelt died in April 1945, a few months after the beginning of his fourth term. In 1946, Republicans won control of the House and the Senate, and early in 1947 a proposal for an amendment to limit future presidents to two four-year terms was offered to the states for ratification. Democratic critics of the Twenty-second Amendment charged that it was a partisan posthumous jab at Roosevelt.*

Since the Twenty-second Amendment was adopted, however, the only presidents who might have been able to seek a third term, had it not existed, were Republicans Dwight Eisenhower, Ronald Reagan, and George W. Bush, and Democrat Bill Clinton. Since 1826, Congress has entertained 160 proposed amendments to limit the president to one six-year term. Such amendments have been backed by fifteen presidents, including Gerald Ford and Jimmy Carter.

Amendment XXIII
[Adopted 1961]

Section 1 The District constituting the seat of Government of the United States shall appoint in such manner as the Congress may direct: A number of electors of President and Vice-President equal to the whole number of Senators and Representatives in Congress to which the District would be entitled if it were a State, but in no event more than the least populous State; they shall be in addition to those appointed by the States, but they shall be considered for the purposes of the election of President and Vice-President, to be electors appointed by a State; and they shall meet in the District and perform such duties as provided by the twelfth article of amendment.

Section 2 The Congress shall have the power to enforce this article by appropriate legislation.

◆ ◆ ◆

▶ *When Washington, D.C., was established as a federal district, no one expected that a significant number of people would make it their permanent and primary residence. A proposal to allow citizens of the district to vote in presidential elections was approved by Congress in June 1960 and was ratified on March 29, 1961.*

Amendment XXIV
[Adopted 1964]

Section 1 The right of citizens of the United States to vote in any primary or other election for President or Vice-President, for electors for President or Vice-President, or for Senator or Representative in Congress, shall not be denied or abridged by the United States or any State by reason of failure to pay any poll tax or other tax.

Section 2 The Congress shall have the power to enforce this article by appropriate legislation.

◆ ◆ ◆

▶ *In the colonial and Revolutionary eras, financial independence was seen as necessary to political independence, and the poll tax was used as a requirement for voting. By the twentieth century, however, the poll tax was used mostly to bar poor people, especially southern blacks, from voting. While conservatives complained that the amendment interfered with states' rights, liberals thought that the amendment did not go far enough because it barred the poll tax only in national elections and not in state or local elections. The amendment was ratified in 1964,*

however, and two years later, the Supreme Court ruled that poll taxes in state and local elections also violated the equal protection clause of the Fourteenth Amendment.

Amendment XXV
[Adopted 1967]

Section 1 In case of the removal of the President from office or of his death or resignation, the Vice-President shall become President.

Section 2 Whenever there is a vacancy in the office of the Vice-President, the President shall nominate a Vice-President who shall take office upon confirmation by a majority vote of both Houses of Congress.

Section 3 Whenever the President transmits to the President pro tempore of the Senate and the Speaker of the House of Representatives his written declaration that he is unable to discharge the powers and duties of his office, and until he transmits to them a written declaration to the contrary, such powers and duties shall be discharged by the Vice-President as Acting President.

Section 4 Whenever the Vice-President and a majority of either the principal officers of the executive departments or of such other body as Congress may by law provide, transmit to the President pro tempore of the Senate and the Speaker of the House of Representatives their written declaration that the President is unable to discharge the powers and duties of his office, the Vice-President shall immediately assume the powers and duties of the office as Acting President.

Thereafter, when the President transmits to the President pro tempore of the Senate and the Speaker of the House of Representatives his written declaration that no inability exists, he shall resume the powers and duties of his office unless the Vice-President and a majority of either the principal officers of the executive department[s] or of such other body as Congress may by law provide, transmit within four days to the President pro tempore of the Senate and the Speaker of the House of Representatives their written declaration that the President is unable to discharge the powers and duties of his office. Thereupon Congress shall decide the issue, assembling within forty-eight hours for that purpose if not in session. If the Congress, within twenty-one days after receipt of the latter written declaration, or, if Congress is not in session, within twenty-one days after Congress is required to assemble, determines by two-thirds vote of both Houses that the President is unable to discharge the powers and duties of his office, the Vice-President shall continue to discharge the same as Acting President; otherwise, the President shall resume the powers and duties of his office.

◆ ◆ ◆

► *The framers of the Constitution established the office of vice president because someone was needed to preside over the Senate. The first president to die in office was William Henry Harrison, in 1841. Vice President John Tyler had himself sworn in as president, setting a precedent that was followed when seven later presidents died in office. The assassination of President James A. Garfield in 1881 posed a new problem, however. After he was shot, the president was incapacitated for two months before he died; he was unable to lead the country, while his vice president, Chester A. Arthur, was unable to assume leadership. Efforts to resolve questions of succession in the event of a presidential disability thus began with the death of Garfield.*

In 1963, the assassination of President John F. Kennedy galvanized Congress to action. Vice President Lyndon Johnson was a chain smoker with a history of heart trouble. According to the 1947 Presidential Succession Act, the two men who stood in line to succeed him were the seventy-two-year-old Speaker of the House and the eighty-six-year-old president of the Senate. There were serious concerns that any of these men might become incapacitated while serving as chief executive. The first time the Twenty-fifth Amendment was used, however, was not in the case of presidential death or illness, but during the Watergate crisis. When Vice President Spiro T. Agnew was forced to resign following allegations of bribery and tax violations, President Richard M. Nixon appointed House Minority Leader Gerald R. Ford vice president. Ford became president following Nixon's resignation eight months later and named Nelson A. Rockefeller as his vice president. Thus, for more than two years, the two highest offices in the country were held by people who had not been elected to them.

Amendment XXVI
[Adopted 1971]

Section 1 The right of citizens of the United States, who are eighteen years of age or older, to vote shall not be denied or abridged by the United States or by any State on account of age.

Section 2 The Congress shall have power to enforce this article by appropriate legislation.

♦ ♦ ♦

► *Efforts to lower the voting age from twenty-one to eighteen began during World War II. Recognizing that those who were old enough to fight a war should have some say in the government policies that involved them in the war, Presidents Eisenhower, Johnson, and Nixon endorsed the idea. In 1970, the combined pressure of the antiwar movement and the demographic pressure*

of the baby boom generation led to a Voting Rights Act lowering the voting age in federal, state, and local elections.

In Oregon v. Mitchell (1970), the state of Oregon challenged the right of Congress to determine the age at which people could vote in state or local elections. The Supreme Court agreed with Oregon. Since the Voting Rights Act was ruled unconstitutional, the Constitution had to be amended to allow passage of a law that would lower the voting age. The amendment was ratified in a little more than three months, making it the most rapidly ratified amendment in U.S. history.

Unratified Amendment
Equal Rights Amendment (proposed by Congress March 22, 1972; seven-year deadline for ratification extended to June 30, 1982)

Section 1 Equality of rights under the law shall not be denied or abridged by the United States or by any State on account of sex.

Section 2 The Congress shall have the power to enforce, by appropriate legislation, the provisions of this article.

Section 3 This amendment shall take effect two years after the date of ratification.

♦ ♦ ♦

► *In 1923, soon after women had won the right to vote, Alice Paul, a leading activist in the woman suffrage movement, proposed an amendment requiring equal treatment of men and women. Opponents of the proposal argued that such an amendment would invalidate laws that protected women and would make women subject to the military draft. After the 1964 Civil Rights Act was adopted, protective workplace legislation was removed anyway.*

The renewal of the women's movement, as a byproduct of the civil rights and antiwar movements, led to a revival of the Equal Rights Amendment (ERA) in Congress. Disagreements over language held up congressional passage of the proposed amendment, but on March 22, 1972, the Senate approved the ERA by a vote of 84 to 8, and it was sent to the states. Six states ratified the amendment within two days, and by the middle of 1973 the amendment seemed well on its way to adoption, with thirty of the needed thirty-eight states having ratified it. In the mid-1970s, however, a powerful "Stop ERA" campaign developed. The campaign portrayed the ERA as a threat to "family values" and traditional relationships between men and women. Although thirty-five states ultimately ratified the ERA, five of those state legislatures voted to rescind ratification, and the amendment was never adopted.

Unratified Amendment

D.C. Statehood Amendment (proposed by Congress August 22, 1978)

Section 1 For purposes of representation in the Congress, election of the President and Vice-President, and article V of this Constitution, the District constituting the seat of government of the United States shall be treated as though it were a State.

Section 2 The exercise of the rights and powers conferred under this article shall be by the people of the District constituting the seat of government, and as shall be provided by Congress.

Section 3 The twenty-third article of amendment to the Constitution of the United States is hereby repealed.

Section 4 This article shall be inoperative, unless it shall have been ratified as an amendment to the Constitution by the legislatures of three-fourths of the several states within seven years from the date of its submission.

◆ ◆ ◆

▶ *The 1961 ratification of the Twenty-third Amendment, giving residents of the District of Columbia the right to vote for a president and vice president, inspired an effort to give residents of the district full voting rights. In 1966, President Lyndon Johnson appointed a mayor and city council; in 1971, D.C. residents were allowed to name a nonvoting delegate to the House; and in 1981, residents were allowed to elect the mayor and city council. Congress retained the right to overrule laws that might affect commuters, the height of federal buildings, and selection of judges and prosecutors. The district's nonvoting delegate to Congress, Walter Fauntroy, lobbied fiercely for a congressional amendment granting statehood to the district. In 1978, a proposed amendment was approved and sent to the states. A number of states quickly ratified the amendment, but, like the ERA, the D.C. Statehood Amendment ran into trouble.*

Opponents argued that section 2 created a separate category of "nominal" statehood. They argued that the federal district should be eliminated and that the territory should be reabsorbed into the state of Maryland. Although these theoretical arguments were strong, some scholars believe that racist attitudes toward the predominantly black population of the city were also a factor leading to the defeat of the amendment.

Amendment XXVII

[Adopted 1992]

No law, varying the compensation for the services of the Senators and Representatives, shall take effect, until an election of Representatives shall have intervened.

◆ ◆ ◆

▶ *While the Twenty-sixth Amendment was the most rapidly ratified amendment in U.S. history, the Twenty-seventh Amendment had the longest journey to ratification. First proposed by James Madison in 1789 as part of the package that included the Bill of Rights, this amendment had been ratified by only six states by 1791. In 1873, however, it was ratified by Ohio to protest a massive retroactive salary increase by the federal government. Unlike later proposed amendments, this one came with no time limit on ratification.*

In the early 1980s, Gregory D. Watson, a University of Texas economics major, discovered the "lost" amendment and began a single-handed campaign to get state legislators to introduce it for ratification. In 1983, it was accepted by Maine. In 1984, it passed the Colorado legislature. Ratifications trickled in slowly until May 1992, when Michigan and New Jersey became the thirty-eighth and thirty-ninth states, respectively, to ratify. This amendment prevents members of Congress from raising their own salaries without giving voters a chance to vote them out of office before they can benefit from the raises.

THE CONSTITUTION OF THE CONFEDERATE STATES OF AMERICA

▶ *In framing the Constitution of the Confederate States, the authors adopted, with numerous small but significant changes and additions, the language of the Constitution of the United States, and followed the same order of arrangement of articles and sections. The revisions that they made to the original Constitution are shown here. The parts stricken out are enclosed in*

brackets, and the new matter added in framing the Confederate Constitution is printed in italics.

Adopted March 11, 1861

WE, the People of the [United States] *Confederated States, each State acting in its sovereign and independent character,* in order to form a [more perfect

Union] *permanent Federal government*, establish Justice, insure domestic Tranquillity [provide for the common defense, promote the general Welfare], and secure the Blessings of Liberty to ourselves and our Posterity, *invoking the favor and guidance of Almighty God*, do ordain and establish this Constitution for the [United] *Confederate* States of America.

Article I

Section I All legislative Powers herein [granted] *delegated*, shall be vested in a Congress of the [United] *Confederate* States, which shall consist of a Senate and House of Representatives.

Section II The House of Representatives shall be composed of Members chosen every second Year by the People of the several States, and the Electors in each State shall *be citizens of the Confederate States, and* have the Qualifications requisite for Electors of the most numerous Branch of the State Legislature; *but no person of foreign birth, and not a citizen of the Confederate States, shall be allowed to vote for any officer, civil or political, State or federal.*

No Person shall be a Representative who shall not have attained to the Age of twenty-five Years, and [been seven Years a Citizen of the United] *be a citizen of the Confederate States*, and who shall not, when elected, be an Inhabitant of that State in which he shall be chosen.

Representatives and direct Taxes shall be apportioned among the several States which may be included within this [Union] *Confederacy*, according to their respective Numbers, which shall be determined by adding to the whole Number of free Persons, including those bound to Service for a Term of Years, and excluding Indians not taxed, three-fifths of all [other Persons] *slaves*. The actual Enumeration shall be made within three Years after the first Meeting of the Congress of the [United] *Confederate States*, and within every subsequent Term of ten Years, in such Manner as they shall by Law direct. The Number of Representatives shall not exceed one for every [thirty] *fifty* Thousand, but each State shall have at Least one Representative; and until such enumeration shall be made, the State of [New Hampshire shall be entitled to choose three, Massachusetts eight, Rhode Island and Providence Plantations one, Connecticut five, New York six, New Jersey four, Pennsylvania eight, Delaware one, Maryland six, Virginia ten, North Carolina five, South Carolina five, and Georgia three] *South Carolina shall be entitled to choose six, the State of Georgia ten, the State of Alabama nine, the State of Florida two, the State of Mississippi seven, the State of Louisiana six, and the State of Texas six.*

When vacancies happen in the Representation from any State, the Executive Authority thereof shall issue Writs of Election to fill such Vacancies.

The House of Representatives shall choose their Speaker and other Officers; and shall have the sole Power of Impeachment; *except that any judicial or other federal officer resident and acting solely within the limits of any State, may be impeached by a vote of two-thirds of both branches of the Legislature thereof.*

Section III The Senate of the [United] *Confederate* States shall be composed of two Senators from each State, chosen by the Legislature thereof, for six Years, *at the regular session next immediately preceding the commencement of the term of service*; and each Senator shall have one Vote.

Immediately after they shall be assembled in Consequence of the first Election, they shall be divided as equally as may be into three Classes. The Seats of the Senators of the first Class shall be vacated at the Expiration of the second Year, of the second Class at the Expiration of the fourth Year, and of the third Class at the Expiration of the sixth Year, so that one-third may be chosen every second Year; and if Vacancies happen by Resignation, or otherwise, during the Recess of the Legislature of any State, the Executive thereof may make temporary Appointments until the next Meeting of the Legislature, which shall then fill such Vacancies.

No Person shall be a Senator who shall not have attained to the Age of thirty Years, and [been nine Years a Citizen of the United] *be a citizen of the Confederate* States, and who shall not, when elected, be an Inhabitant of that State for which he shall be chosen.

The Vice President of the [United] *Confederate* States shall be President of the Senate, but shall have no Vote, unless they be equally divided.

The Senate shall choose their other Officers, and also a President pro tempore, in the Absence of the Vice President, or when he shall exercise the Office of President of the United States.

The Senate shall have the sole Power to try all Impeachments. When sitting for that Purpose, they shall be on Oath or Affirmation. When the President of the [United] *Confederate* States is tried, the Chief Justice shall preside: And no Person shall be convicted without the Concurrence of two-thirds of the Members present.

Judgment in Cases of Impeachment shall not extend further than to removal from Office, and Disqualification to hold and enjoy any Office of honour, Trust or Profit under the [United] *Confederate* States; but the Party convicted shall nevertheless be liable and subject to Indictment, Trial, Judgment and Punishment, according to Law.

Section IV The Times, Places and Manner of holding Elections for Senators and Representatives, shall be prescribed in each State by the Legislature thereof, *subject to the provisions of this Constitution*; but the Congress may at any time by Law make or alter such Regulations, except as to the *times and* places of choosing Senators.

The Congress shall assemble at least once in every Year, and such Meeting shall be on the first Monday in December, unless they shall by Law appoint a different Day.

Section V Each House shall be the Judge of the Elections, Returns and Qualifications of its own Members, and a Majority of each shall constitute a Quorum to do Business; but a smaller Number may adjourn from day to day, and may be authorized to compel the Attendance of absent Members, in such Manner, and under such Penalties as each House may provide.

Each House may determine the Rules of its Proceedings, punish its Members for disorderly Behaviour, and, with the Concurrence of two-thirds *of the whole number* expel a Member.

Each House shall keep a Journal of its Proceedings, and from time to time publish the same, excepting such Parts as may in their Judgment require Secrecy; and the Yeas and Nays of the Members of either House on any question shall, at the Desire of one-fifth of those Present, be entered on the Journal.

Neither House, during the Session of Congress, shall, without the Consent of the other, adjourn for more than three days, nor to any other Place than that in which the two Houses shall be sitting.

Section VI The Senators and Representatives shall receive a Compensation for their Services, to be ascertained by Law, and paid out of the Treasury of the [United] *Confederate* States. They shall in all Cases, except Treason [Felony] and Breach of the Peace, be privileged from Arrest during their Attendance at the Session of their respective Houses, and in going to and returning from the same; and for any Speech or Debate in either House, they shall not be questioned in any other Place.

No Senator or Representative shall, during the Time for which he was elected, be appointed to any civil Office under the Authority of the [United] *Confederate* States, which shall have been created, or the Emoluments whereof shall have been increased during such time; and no Person holding any Office under the [United] *Confederate* States, shall be a Member of either House during his Continuance in Office. *But Congress may, by law, grant to the principal officers in each of the executive departments a seat upon the floor of either House, with the privilege of discussing any measures appertaining to his department.*

Section VII All Bills for raising Revenue shall originate in the House of Representatives; but the Senate may propose or concur with Amendments as on other Bills.

Every Bill which shall have passed [the House of Representatives and the Senate] *both Houses*, shall, before it become a Law, be presented to the President of the [United] *Confederate* States; If he approve he shall sign it, but if not he shall return it, with his Objections to that House in which it shall have originated, who shall enter the Objections at large on their Journal, and proceed to reconsider it. If after such Reconsideration two-thirds of that House shall agree to pass the Bill, it shall be sent, together with the Objections, to the other House, by which it shall likewise be reconsidered, and if approved by two-thirds of that House, it shall become a Law. But in all *such* Cases the Votes of both Houses shall be determined by Yeas and Nays, and the Names of the Persons voting for and against the Bill shall be entered on the Journal of each House respectively. If any Bill shall not be returned by the President within ten Days (Sundays excepted) after it shall have been presented to him, the Same shall be a law, in like Manner as if he had signed it, unless the Congress by their Adjournment prevent its return, in which Case it shall not be a Law. *The President may approve any appropriation and disapprove any other appropriation in the same bill. In such case he shall, in signing the bill, designate the appropriation disapproved, and shall return a copy of such appropriation, with his objections, to the House in which the bill shall have originated; and the same proceedings shall then be had as in case of other bills disapproved by the President.*

Every Order, Resolution, or Vote to which the Concurrence of [the Senate and House of Representatives] *both Houses* may be necessary (except on a question of Adjournment), shall be presented to the President of the [United] *Confederate* States; and before the Same shall take Effect, shall be approved by him, or being disapproved by him, [shall] *may* be repassed by two-thirds of [the Senate and House of Representatives] *both Houses*, according to the Rules and Limitations prescribed in the Case of a Bill.

Section VIII The Congress shall have Power.

To lay and collect Taxes, Duties, Imposts and *Excises, for revenue necessary* to pay the Debts [and], provide for the common Defense [and general Welfare of the United States; but], *and carry on the government of the Confederate States; but no bounties shall be granted from the treasury, nor shall any duties, or taxes, or importation from foreign nations be laid to promote or foster any branch of industry; and* all Duties, Imposts and Excises shall be uniform throughout the [United] Confederate States;

To borrow Money on the credit of the [United] Confederate States;

To regulate Commerce with foreign Nations, and among the several States, and with the Indian Tribes; *but neither this, nor any other clause contained in this Constitution, shall ever be construed to delegate the power to Congress to appropriate money for any internal improvement intended to facilitate commerce; except for the purpose of furnishing lights, beacons, and buoys, and other aids to navigation upon the coasts, and the improvement of harbors, and the removing of obstructions in river navigation; in all such cases such duties shall be laid on the navigation facilitated thereby, as may be necessary to pay the costs and expenses thereof;*

To establish an uniform Rule of Naturalization, and uniform Laws on the subject of Bankruptcies throughout the [United] *Confederate* States; *but no law of Congress shall discharge any debt contracted before the passage of the same;*

To coin Money, regulate the Value thereof, and of foreign Coin, and fix the Standard of Weights and Measures;

To provide for the Punishment of counterfeiting the Securities and current Coin of the [United] *Confederate* States;

To establish Post Offices and post [Roads] *routes; but the expenses of the Postoffice Department, after the first day of March, in the year of our Lord eighteen hundred and sixty-three, shall be paid out of its own revenues;*

To promote the progress of Science and useful Arts, by securing for limited Times to Authors and Inventors the exclusive Right to their respective Writings and Discoveries;

To constitute Tribunals inferior to the supreme Court;

To define and punish Piracies and Felonies committed on the high Seas, and Offences against the Law of Nations;

To declare War, grant Letters of Marque and Reprisal, and make Rules concerning Captures on Land and Water;

To raise and support Armies, but no Appropriation of Money to that Use shall be for a longer Term than two Years;

To provide and maintain a Navy;

To make Rules for the Government and Regulation of the land and naval Forces;

To provide for calling forth the Militia to execute the Laws of the [Union] *Confederate States,* suppress Insurrections and repel Invasions;

To provide for organizing, arming, and disciplining the Militia and for governing such Part of them as may be employed in the Service of the [United] *Confederate* States, reserving to the States respectively, the Appointment of the Officers, and the Authority of training the Militia according to the Discipline prescribed by Congress;

To exercise exclusive Legislation in all Cases whatsoever, over such District (not exceeding ten Miles square) as may, by Cession of particular States, and the Acceptance of Congress, become the Seat of the Government of the [United] *Confederate* States, and to exercise like Authority over all Places purchased by the Consent of the Legislature of the State in which the Same shall be, for the Erection of Forts, Magazines, Arsenals, Dock Yards, and other needful Buildings;—And

To make all Laws which shall be necessary and proper for carrying into Execution the foregoing Powers, and all other Powers vested by this Constitution in the Government of the [United] *Confederate* States or in any Department or Officer thereof.

Section IX [The Migration or Importation of such Persons as any of the States now existing shall think proper to admit, shall not be prohibited by the Congress prior to the Year one thousand eight hundred and eight, but a Tax or Duty may be imposed on such Importation, not exceeding ten dollars for each Person.] *The importation of negroes of the African race from*

any foreign country other than the slaveholding States or territories of the United States of America, is hereby forbidden; and Congress is required to pass such laws as shall effectually prevent the same. Congress shall also have power to prohibit the introduction of slaves from any State not a member of, or territory not belonging to, this Confederacy.

The Privilege of the Writ of Habeas Corpus shall not be suspended, unless when in Cases of Rebellion or Invasion the public Safety may require it. No Bill of Attainder or ex post facto Law, *or law denying or impairing the right of property in negro slaves,* shall be passed.

No Capitation, or other direct, Tax shall be laid, unless in Proportion to the Census or Enumeration herein before directed to be taken.

No Tax or Duty shall be laid on Articles exported from any State, *except by a vote of two-thirds of both Houses.*

No Preference shall be given by any Regulation of Commerce or Revenue to the Ports of one State over those of another; nor shall Vessels bound to, or from, one State, be obliged to enter, clear, or pay Duties in another.

No Money shall be drawn from the Treasury, but in Consequence of Appropriations made by Law; and a regular Statement and Account of the Receipts and Expenditures of all public Money shall be published from time to time.

Congress shall appropriate no money from the Treasury except by a vote of two-thirds of both Houses, taken by yeas and nays, unless it be asked and estimated for by some one of the heads of departments and submitted to Congress by the President; or for the purpose of paying its own expenses and contingencies; or for the payment of claims against the Confederate States, the justice of which shall have been officially declared by a tribunal for the investigation of claims against the Government, which it is hereby made the duty of Congress to establish.

All bills appropriating money shall specify in Federal currency the exact amount of each appropriation and the purposes for which it is made; and Congress shall grant no extra compensation to any public contractor, officer, agent or servant, after such contract shall have been made or such service rendered.

No Title of Nobility shall be granted by the [United] *Confederate States;* and no Person holding any Office of Profit or Trust under them, shall, without the Consent of the Congress, accept of any present, Emolument, Office, or Title, of any kind whatever, from any King, Prince or foreign State.

[*Here the framers of the Confederate Constitution insert the U.S. Bill of Rights.*] Congress shall make no law respecting an establishment of religion, or prohibiting the free exercise thereof; or abridging the freedom of speech, or of the press; or the right of the people peaceably to assemble, and to petition the Government for a redress of grievances.

A well-regulated Militia, being necessary to the security of a free State, the right of the people to keep and bear Arms shall not be infringed.

No Soldier shall, in time of peace, be quartered in any house, without the consent of the Owner, nor in time of war, but in a manner to be prescribed by law.

The right of the people to be secure in their persons, houses, papers, and effects, against unreasonable searches and seizures, shall not be violated, and no Warrants shall issue, but upon probable cause, supported by Oath or affirmation, and particularly describing the place to be searched, and the persons or things to be seized.

No person shall be held to answer for a capital, or otherwise infamous crime, unless on a presentment or indictment of a Grand Jury, except in cases arising in the land or naval forces, or in the Militia, when in actual service in time of War or public danger; nor shall any person be subject for the same offence to be twice put in jeopardy of life or limb; nor shall be compelled in any Criminal Case to be a witness against himself, nor be deprived of life, liberty or property without due process of law; nor shall private property be taken for public use, without just compensation.

In all criminal prosecutions, the accused shall enjoy the right to a speedy and public trial, by an impartial jury of the State and district wherein the crime shall have been committed, which district shall have been previously ascertained by law, and to be informed of the nature and cause of the accusation; to be confronted with the witnesses against him; to have Compulsory process for obtaining Witnesses in his favour, and to have the Assistance of Counsel for his defence.

In Suits at common law, where the value in controversy shall exceed twenty dollars, the right of trial by jury shall be preserved, and no fact tried by a jury shall be otherwise reexamined in any Court of the [United] *Confederate* States, than according to the rules of the common law.

Excessive bail shall not be required, nor excessive fines imposed, nor cruel and unusual punishments inflicted.

Every law or resolution having the force of law, shall relate to but one subject, and that shall be expressed in the title.

Section X No State shall enter into any Treaty, Alliance, or Confederation; grant Letters of Marque and Reprisal; coin Money; [emit Bills of Credit;] make any Thing but gold and silver Coin a Tender in Payment of Debts; pass any Bill of Attainder, or ex post facto Law, or Law impairing the Obligation of Contracts, or grant any Title of Nobility.

No State shall, without the consent of the Congress, lay any Imposts or Duties on Imports or Exports, except what may be absolutely necessary for executing its inspection Laws: and the net Produce of all Duties and Imposts, laid by any State on Imports or Exports, shall be for the Use of the Treasury of the [United] *Confederate* States; and all such Laws shall be subject to the Revision and Control of the Congress.

No State shall, without the Consent of Congress, lay any Duty of Tonnage, *except on seagoing vessels, for the improvement of its rivers and harbors navigated by the said vessels; but such duties shall not conflict with any treaties of the Confederate States with foreign nations; and any surplus of revenue thus derived shall, after making such improvement, be paid into the common treasury;* nor shall any State keep Troops, or Ships of War in time of Peace, enter into any Agreement or Compact with another State, or with a foreign Power, or engage in War, unless actually invaded, or in such imminent Danger as will not admit of Delay. *But when any river divides or flows through two or more States, they may enter into compacts with each other to improve the navigation thereof.*

Article II

Section I [The executive Power shall be vested in a President of the United States of America. He shall hold his Office during the Term of four Years, and, together with the Vice President, chosen for the same Term, be elected, as follows:] *The executive power shall be vested in a President of the Confederate States of America. He and the Vice President shall hold their offices for the term of six years; but the President shall not be reeligible.*

The President and Vice President shall be elected as follows: Each State shall appoint in such Manner as the Legislature thereof may direct, a Number of Electors, equal to the whole Number of Senators and Representatives to which the State may be entitled in the Congress; but no Senator or Representative, or Person holding an Office of Trust or Profit under the [United] *Confederate* States, shall be appointed an Elector.

The Electors shall meet in their respective States, and vote by ballot for President and Vice President, one of whom, at least, shall not be an inhabitant of the same State with themselves; they shall name in their ballots the person voted for as President, and in distinct ballots the person voted for as Vice President, and they shall make distinct lists of all persons voted for as President, and of all persons voted for as Vice President, and of the number of votes for each, which lists they shall sign and certify, and transmit sealed to the seat of the government of the [United] *Confederate* States, directed to the President of the Senate;— The President of the Senate shall, in the presence of the Senate and House of Representatives, open all the certificates and the votes shall then be counted;—The person having the greatest number of votes for President shall be the President, if such number be a majority of the whole number of Electors appointed; and if no person have such majority, then from the persons having the highest numbers not exceeding three on the list of those voted for as President, the House of Representatives shall choose immediately, by ballot, the President. But in choosing the President, the votes shall be taken by States, the representation from each State having one vote; a quorum for this purpose shall consist of a member or members from two-thirds of the States, and a majority of all the States shall be necessary to a choice. And if the House of Representatives shall not choose a President whenever the right of choice shall devolve upon them, before the fourth day of March next following, then the Vice President shall act as President, as in the case of the death or other constitutional disability of the President. The person having the greatest number of votes as Vice President shall be the Vice President, if such number be a majority of the whole number of Electors appointed, and if no person have a majority, then from the two highest numbers on the list the Senate shall choose the Vice President; a quorum for the purpose shall consist of two-thirds of the whole number of Senators, and a majority of the whole number shall be necessary to a choice. But no person constitutionally ineligible to the office of President shall be eligible to that of Vice President of the [United] *Confederate* States.

The Congress may determine the Time of choosing the Electors, and the Day on which they shall give their Votes; which Day shall be the same throughout the [United] *Confederate* States.

No Person except a natural-born Citizen [or a Citizen of the United States] *of the Confederate States, or a citizen thereof,* at the time of the Adoption of this Constitution, *or a citizen thereof born in the United States prior to the 20th of December, 1860*, shall be eligible to the Office of President; neither shall any Person be eligible to that Office who shall not have attained to the Age of thirty-five Years, and been fourteen Years a Resident within the [United States] *limits of the Confederate States, as they may exist at the time of his election.*

In Cases of the Removal of the President from Office, or of his Death, Resignation, or Inability to discharge the Powers and Duties of the said Office, the same shall devolve on the Vice President, and the Congress may by Law provide for the Case of Removal, Death, Resignation, or Inability, both of the President and Vice President, declaring what Officer shall then act as President, and such Officer shall act accordingly, until the Disability be removed, or a President shall be elected.

The President shall, at stated Times, receive for his Services, a Compensation, which shall neither be increased nor diminished during the Period for which he shall have been elected, and he shall not receive within that Period any other Emolument from the [United] *Confederate* States or any of them.

Before he enters on the Execution of his Office, he shall take the following Oath or Affirmation—"I do solemnly swear (or affirm) that I will faithfully execute the Office of President of the [United] *Confederate* States, and will to the best of my Ability, preserve, protect and defend the Constitution [of the United States] *thereof*."

Section II The President shall be Commander in Chief of the Army and Navy of the [United] *Confederate* States, and of the Militia of the several States, when called into the actual Service of the [United] *Confederate* States; he may require the Opinion, in writing, of the principal Officer in each of the executive Departments, upon any Subject relating to the Duties of their respective Offices, and he shall have Power to grant Reprieves and Pardons for Offenses against the [United] *Confederate* States, except in Cases of Impeachment.

He shall have Power, by and with the Advice and Consent of the Senate, to make Treaties, provided two-thirds of the Senators present concur; and he shall nominate, and by and with the Advice and Consent of the Senate, shall appoint Ambassadors, other public Ministers and Consuls, Judges of the supreme Court, and all other Officers of the [United] *Confederate* States, whose Appointments are not herein otherwise provided for, and which shall be established by Law: but the Congress may by Law vest the Appointment of such inferior Officers, as they think proper, in the President alone, in the Courts of Law, or in the Heads of Departments. *The principal officer in each of the executive departments, and all persons connected with the diplomatic service, may be removed from office at the pleasure of the President. All other civil officers of the executive department may be removed at any time by the President, or other appointing power, when their services are unnecessary, or for dishonesty, incapacity, inefficiency, misconduct, or neglect of duty; and when so removed, the removal shall be reported to the Senate, together with the reasons therefor.*

The President shall have Power to fill [up] all Vacancies that may happen during the Recess of the Senate, by granting Commissions which shall expire at the End of their next Session.

Section III [He] *The President* shall from time to time give to the Congress Information of the State of the [Union] *Confederacy*, and recommend to their Consideration such Measures as he shall judge necessary and expedient; he may, on extraordinary Occasions, convene both Houses, or either of them, and in Case of Disagreement between them, with Respect to the Time of Adjournment, he may adjourn them to such Time as he shall think proper; he shall receive Ambassadors and other public Ministers; he shall take Care that the Laws be faithfully executed, and shall Commission all the officers of the [United] *Confederate* States.

Section IV The President, Vice President and all civil Officers of the [United] *Confederate* States, shall be removed from Office or Impeachment for, and Conviction of, Treason, Bribery, or other high Crimes and Misdemeanors.

Article III

Section I The judicial Power of the [United] *Confederate* States shall be vested in one [supreme] *Superior* Court, and in such inferior Courts as the Congress may from time to time ordain and establish. The Judges, both of the supreme and inferior Courts, shall hold their Offices during good Behavior, and shall, at stated Times, receive for their Services a Compensation, which shall not be diminished during their Continuance in Office.

Section II The judicial Power shall extend to all cases [in Law and Equity, arising under this Constitution], *arising under this Constitution, in law and equity,* the Laws of the [United] *Confederate* States, and Treaties made, or which shall be made, under their Authority;—to all Cases affecting Ambassadors, other public Ministers, and Consuls;—to all Cases of admiralty and maritime Jurisdiction;—to Controversies to which the [United] *Confederate* States shall be a Party;—to Controversies between two or more States;—between a State and Citizens of another State *where the State is plaintiff;—between* Citizens *claiming lands under grants* of different States,—[between Citizens of the same State claiming Lands under Grants of different States,] and between a State, or the Citizens thereof, and foreign States, Citizens or Subjects; *but no State shall be sued by a citizen or subject of any foreign State.*

In all Cases affecting Ambassadors, other public Ministers and Consuls, and those in which a State shall be Party, the supreme Court shall have original Jurisdiction. In all the other Cases before mentioned, the supreme Court shall have appellate Jurisdiction, both as to Law and Fact, with such Exceptions, and under such Regulations as the Congress shall make.

The Trial of all Crimes, except in Cases of Impeachment, shall be by Jury; and such Trial shall be held in the State where the said Crime[s] shall have been committed; but when not committed within any State, the Trial shall be at such Place or Places as the Congress may by Law have directed.

Section III Treason against the [United] *Confederate* States shall consist only in levying War against them, or in adhering to their Enemies, giving them Aid and Comfort. No Person shall be convicted of Treason unless on the Testimony of two Witnesses to the same overt Act, or on Confession in open Court.

The Congress shall have Power to declare the Punishment of Treason, but no Attainder of Treason shall work Corruption of Blood, or Forfeiture except during the Life of the Person attainted.

Article IV

Section I Full Faith and Credit shall be given in each State to the public Acts, Records, and judicial Proceedings of every other State. And the Congress may by general Laws prescribe the Manner in which such Acts, Records and Proceedings shall be proved, and the Effect thereof.

Section II The Citizens of each State shall be entitled to all Privileges and Immunities of Citizens in the several States, *and shall have the right of transit and sojourn in any State of this Confederacy, with their slaves and other property; and the right of property in such slaves shall not be impaired.*

A Person charged in any State with Treason, Felony, or other Crime, who shall flee from Justice, and be found in another State, shall on Demand of the executive Authority of the State from which he fled, be delivered up, to be removed to the State having Jurisdiction of the Crime.

No *slave* or Person held to Service or Labor in [one State] *any State or Territory of the Confederate States* under the Laws thereof, escaping *or unlawfully carried* into another, shall, in Consequence of any Law or Regulation therein, be discharged from such Service or Labor, but shall be delivered up on Claim of the Party to whom such *slave belongs, or to whom such* Service or Labor may be due.

Section III [New States may be admitted by the Congress into this Union;] *Other States may be admitted into this Confederacy by a vote of two-thirds of the whole House of Representatives and two-thirds of the Senate, the Senate voting by States*; but no new State shall be formed or erected within the Jurisdiction of any other State; nor any State be formed by the Junction of two or more States, or Parts of States, without the Consent of the Legislatures of the States concerned as well as of the Congress.

The Congress shall have Power to dispose of and make all needful Rules and Regulations [respecting the Territory or other Property belonging to the United States; and nothing in this Constitution shall be so construed as to Prejudice any Claims of the United States, or of any particular State] *concerning the property of the Confederate States, including the lands thereof.*

The Confederate States may acquire new territory, and Congress shall have power to legislate and provide governments for the inhabitants of all territory belonging to the Confederate States lying without the limits of the several States, and may permit them, at such times and in such manner as it may by law provide, to form States to be admitted into the Confederacy. In all such territory the institution of negro slavery as it now exists in the Confederate States shall be recognized and protected by Congress and by the territorial government, and the inhabitants of the several Confederate States and territories shall have the right to take to such territory any slaves lawfully held by them in any of the States or Territories of the Confederate States.

Section IV The [United] *Confederate* States shall guarantee to every State [in this Union] *that now is, or hereafter may become, a member of this Confederacy,* a Republican Form of Government, and shall protect each of them against Invasion; and on Application of the Legislature, or of the Executive (when the Legislature [cannot be convened] *is not in session*) against domestic Violence.

Article V

[The Congress, whenever two-thirds of both Houses shall deem it necessary, shall propose Amendments to this Constitution, or on the Application of the Legislatures of two-thirds of the several States, shall call a Convention for proposing Amendments, which, in either Case, shall be valid to all Intents and Purposes, as Part of this Constitution, when ratified by the Legislatures of three-fourths of the several States, or by Conventions in three-fourths thereof, as the one or the other Mode of Ratification may be proposed by the Congress; Provided that no Amendment which may be made prior to the Year one thousand eight hundred and eight shall in any Manner affect the first and fourth Clauses in the Ninth Section of the first Article; and that no State, without its Consent, shall be deprived of its equal Suffrage in the Senate.] *Upon the demand of any three States, legally assembled in their several Conventions, the Congress shall summon a Convention of all the States, to take into consideration such amendments to the Constitution as the said States shall concur in suggesting at the time when the said demand is made; and should any of the proposed amendments to the Constitution be agreed on by the said Convention—voting by States—and the same be ratified by the Legislatures of two-thirds of the several States, or by Conventions in two-thirds thereof—as the one or the other mode of ratification may be proposed by the general Convention—they shall henceforward form a part of this Constitution. But no State shall, without its consent, be deprived of its equal representation in the Senate.*

Article VI

The Government established by this Constitution is the successor of the Provisional Government of the Confederate States of America, and all laws passed by the latter shall continue in force until the same shall be repealed or modified; and all the officers appointed by the same shall remain in office until their successors are appointed and qualified or the offices abolished.

All Debts contracted and Engagements entered into, before the Adoption of this Constitution, shall be as valid against the [United] *Confederate* States under this Constitution, as under the [Confederation] *Provisional Government.*

This Constitution and the Laws of the [United] *Confederate* States [which shall be] made in Pursuance thereof; and all Treaties made, or which shall be made, under the authority of the [United] *Confederate* States,

shall be the supreme Law of the Land; and the Judges in every State shall be bound thereby, any Thing in the Constitution or Laws of any State to the Contrary notwithstanding.

The Senators and Representatives before mentioned, and the Members of the several State Legislatures, and all executive and judicial Officers, both of the [United] *Confederate* States and of the several States, shall be bound by Oath or Affirmation, to support this Constitution; but no religious Test shall ever be required as a Qualification to any Office or public Trust under the [United] *Confederate* States.

The enumeration in the Constitution, of certain rights, shall not be construed to deny or disparage others retained by the people *of the several States.*

The powers not delegated to the [United] *Confederate* States by the Constitution, nor prohibited by it to the States, are reserved to the States respectively, or to the people.

Article VII

The Ratification of the Conventions of [nine] *five* States shall be sufficient for the Establishment of this Constitution between the States so ratifying the same.

When five States shall have ratified this Constitution, in the manner before specified, the Congress under the Provisional Constitution shall prescribe the time for holding the election of President and Vice President; and for the meeting of the electoral college; and for counting the votes and inaugurating the President. They shall also prescribe the time for holding the first election of members of Congress under this Constitution, and the time for assembling the same. Until the assembling of such Congress, the Congress under the Provisional Constitution shall continue to exercise the legislative powers granted them, not extending beyond the time limited by the Constitution of the Provisional Government.

[Done in Convention by the Unanimous Consent of the States present, the Seventeenth Day of September in the Year of our Lord one thousand seven hundred and eighty-seven and of the Independence of the United States of America the Twelfth.] *Adopted unanimously March 11, 1861.*

U.S. Politics and Government

PRESIDENTIAL ELECTIONS

Year	Candidates	Parties	Popular Vote	Percentage of Popular Vote	Electoral Vote	Percentage of Voter Participation
1789	**GEORGE WASHINGTON (Va.)***				69	
	John Adams				34	
	Others				35	
1792	**GEORGE WASHINGTON (Va.)**				132	
	John Adams				77	
	George Clinton				50	
	Others				5	
1796	**JOHN ADAMS (Mass.)**	Federalist			71	
	Thomas Jefferson	Democratic-Republican			68	
	Thomas Pinckney	Federalist			59	
	Aaron Burr	Dem.-Rep.			30	
	Others				48	
1800	**THOMAS JEFFERSON (Va.)**	Dem.-Rep.			73	
	Aaron Burr	Dem.-Rep.			73	
	John Adams	Federalist			65	
	C. C. Pinckney	Federalist			64	
	John Jay	Federalist			1	
1804	**THOMAS JEFFERSON (Va.)**	Dem.-Rep.			162	
	C. C. Pinckney	Federalist			14	
1808	**JAMES MADISON (Va.)**	Dem.-Rep.			122	
	C. C. Pinckney	Federalist			47	
	George Clinton	Dem.-Rep.			6	
1812	**JAMES MADISON (Va.)**	Dem.-Rep.			128	
	De Witt Clinton	Federalist			89	
1816	**JAMES MONROE (Va.)**	Dem.-Rep.			183	
	Rufus King	Federalist			34	
1820	**JAMES MONROE (Va.)**	Dem.-Rep.			231	
	John Quincy Adams	Dem.-Rep.			1	
1824	**JOHN Q. ADAMS (Mass.)**	Dem.-Rep.	108,740	30.5	84	26.9
	Andrew Jackson	Dem.-Rep.	153,544	43.1	99	
	William H. Crawford	Dem.-Rep.	46,618	13.1	41	
	Henry Clay	Dem.-Rep.	47,136	13.2	37	
1828	**ANDREW JACKSON (Tenn.)**	Democratic	647,286	56.0	178	57.6
	John Quincy Adams	National Republican	508,064	44.0	83	
1832	**ANDREW JACKSON (Tenn.)**	Democratic	687,502	55.0	219	55.4
	Henry Clay	National Republican	530,189	42.4	49	
	John Floyd	Independent			11	
	William Wirt	Anti-Mason	33,108	2.6	7	

*State of residence when elected president.

Year	Candidates	Parties	Popular Vote	Percentage of Popular Vote	Electoral Vote	Percentage of Voter Participation
1836	**MARTIN VAN BUREN (N.Y.)**	Democratic	765,483	50.9	170	57.8
	W. H. Harrison	Whig			73	
	Hugh L. White	Whig	739,795	49.1	26	
	Daniel Webster	Whig			14	
	W. P. Mangum	Independent			11	
1840	**WILLIAM H. HARRISON (Ohio)**	Whig	1,274,624	53.1	234	78.0
	Martin Van Buren	Democratic	1,127,781	46.9	60	
	J. G. Birney	Liberty	7,069		—	
1844	**JAMES K. POLK (Tenn.)**	Democratic	1,338,464	49.6	170	78.9
	Henry Clay	Whig	1,300,097	48.1	105	
	J. G. Birney	Liberty	62,300	2.3	—	
1848	**ZACHARY TAYLOR (La.)**	Whig	1,360,099	47.4	163	72.7
	Lewis Cass	Democratic	1,220,544	42.5	127	
	Martin Van Buren	Free-Soil	291,263	10.1	—	
1852	**FRANKLIN PIERCE (N.H.)**	Democratic	1,601,117	50.9	254	69.6
	Winfield Scott	Whig	1,385,453	44.1	42	
	John P. Hale	Free-Soil	155,825	5.0	—	
1856	**JAMES BUCHANAN (Pa.)**	Democratic	1,832,995	45.3	174	78.9
	John C. Frémont	Republican	1,339,932	33.1	114	
	Millard Fillmore	American	871,731	21.6	8	
1860	**ABRAHAM LINCOLN (Ill.)**	Republican	1,866,452	39.8	180	81.2
	Stephen A. Douglas	Democratic	1,375,157	29.4	12	
	John C. Breckinridge	Democratic	847,953	18.1	72	
	John Bell	Union	590,631	12.6	39	
1864	**ABRAHAM LINCOLN (Ill.)**	Republican	2,213,665	55.1	212	73.8
	George B. McClellan	Democratic	1,805,237	44.9	21	
1868	**ULYSSES S. GRANT (Ill.)**	Republican	3,012,833	52.7	214	78.1
	Horatio Seymour	Democratic	2,703,249	47.3	80	
1872	**ULYSSES S. GRANT (Ill.)**	Republican	3,597,132	55.6	286	71.3
	Horace Greeley	Democratic; Liberal Republican	2,834,125	43.9	66	
1876	**RUTHERFORD B. HAYES (Ohio)**	Republican	4,036,298	48.0	185	81.8
	Samuel J. Tilden	Democratic	4,288,590	51.0	184	
1880	**JAMES A. GARFIELD (Ohio)**	Republican	4,454,416	48.5	214	79.4
	Winfield S. Hancock	Democratic	4,444,952	48.1	155	
1884	**GROVER CLEVELAND (N.Y.)**	Democratic	4,874,986	48.5	219	77.5
	James G. Blaine	Republican	4,851,981	48.3	182	
1888	**BENJAMIN HARRISON (Ind.)**	Republican	5,439,853	47.9	233	79.3
	Grover Cleveland	Democratic	5,540,309	48.6	168	
1892	**GROVER CLEVELAND (N.Y.)**	Democratic	5,555,426	46.1	277	74.7
	Benjamin Harrison	Republican	5,182,690	43.0	145	
	James B. Weaver	People's	1,029,846	8.5	22	
1896	**WILLIAM McKINLEY (Ohio)**	Republican	7,104,779	51.1	271	79.3
	William J. Bryan	Democratic-People's	6,502,925	47.7	176	
1900	**WILLIAM McKINLEY (Ohio)**	Republican	7,207,923	51.7	292	73.2
	William J. Bryan	Dem.-Populist	6,358,133	45.5	155	
1904	**THEODORE ROOSEVELT (N.Y.)**	Republican	7,623,486	57.9	336	65.2
	Alton B. Parker	Democratic	5,077,911	37.6	140	
	Eugene V. Debs	Socialist	402,283	3.0	—	
1908	**WILLIAM H. TAFT (Ohio)**	Republican	7,678,908	51.6	321	65.4
	William J. Bryan	Democratic	6,409,104	43.1	162	
	Eugene V. Debs	Socialist	420,793	2.8	—	

Year	Candidates	Parties	Popular Vote	Percentage of Popular Vote	Electoral Vote	Percentage of Voter Participation
1912	**WOODROW WILSON (N.J.)**	Democratic	6,293,454	41.9	435	58.8
	Theodore Roosevelt	Progressive	4,119,538	27.4	88	
	William H. Taft	Republican	3,484,980	23.2	8	
	Eugene V. Debs	Socialist	900,672	6.1	—	
1916	**WOODROW WILSON (N.J.)**	Democratic	9,129,606	49.4	277	61.6
	Charles E. Hughes	Republican	8,538,221	46.2	254	
	A. L. Benson	Socialist	585,113	3.2	—	
1920	**WARREN G. HARDING (Ohio)**	Republican	16,143,407	60.5	404	49.2
	James M. Cox	Democratic	9,130,328	34.2	127	
	Eugene V. Debs	Socialist	919,799	3.4	—	
1924	**CALVIN COOLIDGE (Mass.)**	Republican	15,725,016	54.0	382	48.9
	John W. Davis	Democratic	8,386,503	28.8	136	
	Robert M. La Follette	Progressive	4,822,856	16.6	13	
1928	**HERBERT HOOVER (Calif.)**	Republican	21,391,381	57.4	444	56.9
	Alfred E. Smith	Democratic	15,016,443	40.3	87	
	Norman Thomas	Socialist	881,951	2.3	—	
	William Z. Foster	Communist	102,991	0.3	—	
1932	**FRANKLIN D. ROOSEVELT (N.Y.)**	Democratic	22,821,857	57.4	472	56.9
	Herbert Hoover	Republican	15,761,841	39.7	59	
	Norman Thomas	Socialist	881,951	2.2	—	
1936	**FRANKLIN D. ROOSEVELT (N.Y.)**	Democratic	27,751,597	60.8	523	61.0
	Alfred M. Landon	Republican	16,679,583	36.5	8	
	William Lemke	Union	882,479	1.9	—	
1940	**FRANKLIN D. ROOSEVELT (N.Y.)**	Democratic	27,244,160	54.8	449	62.5
	Wendell Willkie	Republican	22,305,198	44.8	82	
1944	**FRANKLIN D. ROOSEVELT (N.Y.)**	Democratic	25,602,504	53.5	432	55.9
	Thomas E. Dewey	Republican	22,006,285	46.0	99	
1948	**HARRY S. TRUMAN (Mo.)**	Democratic	24,105,695	49.5	303	53.0
	Thomas E. Dewey	Republican	21,969,170	45.1	189	
	J. Strom Thurmond	States'-Rights Democratic	1,169,021	2.4	38	
	Henry A. Wallace	Progressive	1,156,103	2.4	—	
1952	**DWIGHT D. EISENHOWER (N.Y.)**	Republican	33,936,252	55.1	442	63.3
	Adlai Stevenson	Democratic	27,314,992	44.4	89	
1956	**DWIGHT D. EISENHOWER (N.Y.)**	Republican	35,575,420	57.6	457	60.6
	Adlai Stevenson	Democratic	26,033,066	42.1	73	
	Other	—	—		1	
1960	**JOHN F. KENNEDY (Mass.)**	Democratic	34,227,096	49.9	303	62.8
	Richard M. Nixon	Republican	34,108,546	49.6	219	
	Other	—	—		15	
1964	**LYNDON B. JOHNSON (Texas)**	Democratic	43,126,506	61.1	486	61.7
	Barry M. Goldwater	Republican	27,176,799	38.5	52	
1968	**RICHARD M. NIXON (N.Y.)**	Republican	31,770,237	43.4	301	60.9
	Hubert H. Humphrey	Democratic	31,270,533	42.7	191	
	George Wallace	American Indep.	9,906,141	13.5	46	
1972	**RICHARD M. NIXON (N.Y.)**	Republican	47,169,911	60.7	520	55.2
	George S. McGovern	Democratic	29,170,383	37.5	17	
	Other	—	—		1	
1976	**JIMMY CARTER (Ga.)**	Democratic	40,830,763	50.0	297	53.5
	Gerald R. Ford	Republican	39,147,793	48.0	240	
	Other	—	1,575,459	2.1	—	
1980	**RONALD REAGAN (Calif.)**	Republican	43,901,812	51.0	489	54.0
	Jimmy Carter	Democratic	35,483,820	41.0	49	
	John B. Anderson	Independent	5,719,722	7.0	—	
	Ed Clark	Libertarian	921,188	1.1	—	

Year	Candidates	Parties	Popular Vote	Percentage of Popular Vote	Electoral Vote	Percentage of Voter Participation
1984	RONALD REAGAN (Calif.)	Republican	54,455,075	59.0	525	53.1
	Walter Mondale	Democratic	37,577,185	41.0	13	
1988	GEORGE H. W. BUSH (Texas)	Republican	47,946,422	54.0	426	50.2
	Michael S. Dukakis	Democratic	41,016,429	46.0	112	
1992	WILLIAM J. CLINTON (Ark.)	Democratic	44,908,254	43.0	370	55.9
	George H. W. Bush	Republican	39,102,282	38.0	168	
	H. Ross Perot	Independent	19,721,433	19.0	—	
1996	WILLIAM J. CLINTON (Ark.)	Democratic	47,401,185	49.2	379	49.0
	Robert Dole	Republican	39,197,469	40.7	159	
	H. Ross Perot	Independent	8,085,294	8.4	—	
2000	GEORGE W. BUSH (Texas)	Republican	50,456,062	47.8	271	51.2
	Al Gore	Democratic	50,996,862	48.4	267	
	Ralph Nader	Green Party	2,858,843	2.7	—	
	Patrick J. Buchanan	—	438,760	0.4	—	
2004	GEORGE W. BUSH (Texas)	Republican	61,872,711	50.7	286	60.3
	John F. Kerry	Democratic	58,894,584	48.3	252	
	Other	—	1,582,185	1.3	—	
2008	BARACK OBAMA (Illinois)	Democratic	69,456,897	52.9	365	56.8
	John McCain	Republican	59,934,314	45.7	173	

PRESIDENTS, VICE PRESIDENTS, AND SECRETARIES OF STATE

The Washington Administration (1789–1797)
Vice President	John Adams	1789–1797
Secretary of State	Thomas Jefferson	1789–1793
	Edmund Randolph	1794–1795
	Timothy Pickering	1795–1797

The John Adams Administration (1797–1801)
Vice President	Thomas Jefferson	1797–1801
Secretary of State	Timothy Pickering	1797–1800
	John Marshall	1800–1801

The Jefferson Administration (1801–1809)
Vice President	Aaron Burr	1801–1805
	George Clinton	1805–1809
Secretary of State	James Madison	1801–1809

The Madison Administration (1809–1817)
Vice President	George Clinton	1809–1813
	Elbridge Gerry	1813–1817
Secretary of State	Robert Smith	1809–1811
	James Monroe	1811–1817

The Monroe Administration (1817–1825)
Vice President	Daniel Tompkins	1817–1825
Secretary of State	John Quincy Adams	1817–1825

The John Quincy Adams Administration (1825–1829)
Vice President	John C. Calhoun	1825–1829
Secretary of State	Henry Clay	1825–1829

The Jackson Administration (1829–1837)
Vice President	John C. Calhoun	1829–1833
	Martin Van Buren	1833–1837
Secretary of State	Martin Van Buren	1829–1831
	Edward Livingston	1831–1833
	Louis McLane	1833–1834
	John Forsyth	1834–1837

The Van Buren Administration (1837–1841)
Vice President	Richard M. Johnson	1837–1841
Secretary of State	John Forsyth	1837–1841

The William Harrison Administration (1841)
Vice President	John Tyler	1841
Secretary of State	Daniel Webster	1841

The Tyler Administration (1841–1845)
Vice President	None	
Secretary of State	Daniel Webster	1841–1843
	Hugh S. Legaré	1843
	Abel P. Upshur	1843–1844
	John C. Calhoun	1844–1845

The Polk Administration (1845–1849)
Vice President	George M. Dallas	1845–1849
Secretary of State	James Buchanan	1845–1849

The Taylor Administration (1849–1850)
Vice President	Millard Fillmore	1849–1850
Secretary of State	John M. Clayton	1849–1850

The Fillmore Administration (1850–1853)

Vice President	None	
Secretary of State	Daniel Webster	1850–1852
	Edward Everett	1852–1853

The Pierce Administration (1853–1857)

Vice President	William R. King	1853–1857
Secretary of State	William L. Marcy	1853–1857

The Buchanan Administration (1857–1861)

Vice President	John C. Breckinridge	1857–1861
Secretary of State	Lewis Cass	1857–1860
	Jeremiah S. Black	1860–1861

The Lincoln Administration (1861–1865)

Vice President	Hannibal Hamlin	1861–1865
	Andrew Johnson	1865
Secretary of State	William H. Seward	1861–1865

The Andrew Johnson Administration (1865–1869)

Vice President	None	
Secretary of State	William H. Seward	1865–1869

The Grant Administration (1869–1877)

Vice President	Schuyler Colfax	1869–1873
	Henry Wilson	1873–1877
Secretary of State	Elihu B. Washburne	1869
	Hamilton Fish	1869–1877

The Hayes Administration (1877–1881)

Vice President	William A. Wheeler	1877–1881
Secretary of State	William M. Evarts	1877–1881

The Garfield Administration (1881)

Vice President	Chester A. Arthur	1881
Secretary of State	James G. Blaine	1881

The Arthur Administration (1881–1885)

Vice President	None	
Secretary of State	F. T. Frelinghuysen	1881–1885

The Cleveland Administration (1885–1889)

Vice President	Thomas A. Hendricks	1885–1889
Secretary of State	Thomas F. Bayard	1885–1889

The Benjamin Harrison Administration (1889–1893)

Vice President	Levi P. Morton	1889–1893
Secretary of State	James G. Blaine	1889–1892
	John W. Foster	1892–1893

The Cleveland Administration (1893–1897)

Vice President	Adlai E. Stevenson	1893–1897
Secretary of State	Walter Q. Gresham	1893–1895
	Richard Olney	1895–1897

The McKinley Administration (1897–1901)

Vice President	Garret A. Hobart	1897–1901
	Theodore Roosevelt	1901
Secretary of State	John Sherman	1897–1898
	William R. Day	1898
	John Hay	1898–1901

The Theodore Roosevelt Administration (1901–1909)

Vice President	Charles Fairbanks	1905–1909
Secretary of State	John Hay	1901–1905
	Elihu Root	1905–1909
	Robert Bacon	1909

The Taft Administration (1909–1913)

Vice President	James S. Sherman	1909–1913
Secretary of State	Philander C. Knox	1909–1913

The Wilson Administration (1913–1921)

Vice President	Thomas R. Marshall	1913–1921
Secretary of State	William J. Bryan	1913–1915
	Robert Lansing	1915–1920
	Bainbridge Colby	1920–1921

The Harding Administration (1921–1923)

Vice President	Calvin Coolidge	1921–1923
Secretary of State	Charles E. Hughes	1921–1923

The Coolidge Administration (1923–1929)

Vice President	Charles G. Dawes	1925–1929
Secretary of State	Charles E. Hughes	1923–1925
	Frank B. Kellogg	1925–1929

The Hoover Administration (1929–1933)

Vice President	Charles Curtis	1929–1933
Secretary of State	Henry L. Stimson	1929–1933

The Franklin D. Roosevelt Administration (1933–1945)

Vice President	John Nance Garner	1933–1941
	Henry A. Wallace	1941–1945
	Harry S. Truman	1945
Secretary of State	Cordell Hull	1933–1944
	Edward R. Stettinius Jr.	1944–1945

The Truman Administration (1945–1953)

Vice President	Alben W. Barkley	1949–1953
Secretary of State	Edward R. Stettinius Jr.	1945
	James F. Byrnes	1945–1947
	George C. Marshall	1947–1949
	Dean G. Acheson	1949–1953

The Eisenhower Administration (1953–1961)

Vice President	Richard M. Nixon	1953–1961
Secretary of State	John Foster Dulles	1953–1959
	Christian A. Herter	1959–1961

The Kennedy Administration (1961–1963)

Vice President	Lyndon B. Johnson	1961–1963
Secretary of State	Dean Rusk	1961–1963

The Lyndon Johnson Administration (1963–1969)

Vice President	Hubert H. Humphrey	1965–1969
Secretary of State	Dean Rusk	1963–1969

The Nixon Administration (1969–1974)

Vice President	Spiro T. Agnew	1969–1973
	Gerald R. Ford	1973–1974
Secretary of State	William P. Rogers	1969–1973
	Henry A. Kissinger	1973–1974

The Ford Administration (1974–1977)

Vice President	Nelson A. Rockefeller	1974–1977
Secretary of State	Henry A. Kissinger	1974–1977

The Carter Administration (1977–1981)

Vice President	Walter F. Mondale	1977–1981
Secretary of State	Cyrus R. Vance	1977–1980
	Edmund Muskie	1980–1981

The Reagan Administration (1981–1989)

Vice President	George H. W. Bush	1981–1989
Secretary of State	Alexander M. Haig	1981–1982
	George P. Shultz	1982–1989

The George H. W. Bush Administration (1989–1993)

Vice President	J. Danforth Quayle	1989–1993
Secretary of State	James A. Baker III	1989–1992
	Lawrence S. Eagleburger	1992–1993

The Clinton Administration (1993–2001)

Vice President	Albert Gore	1993–2001
Secretary of State	Warren M. Christopher	1993–1997
	Madeleine K. Albright	1997–2001

The George W. Bush Administration (2001–2009)

Vice President	Richard Cheney	2001–2009
Secretary of State	Colin Powell	2001–2005
	Condoleezza Rice	2005–2009

The Barack Obama Administration (2009–)

Vice President	Joseph Biden	2009–
Secretary of State	Hillary Clinton	2009–

ADMISSION OF STATES TO THE UNION

State	Date of Admission	State	Date of Admission
Delaware	December 7, 1787	Rhode Island	May 29, 1790
Pennsylvania	December 12, 1787	Vermont	March 4, 1791
New Jersey	December 18, 1787	Kentucky	June 1, 1792
Georgia	January 2, 1788	Tennessee	June 1, 1796
Connecticut	January 9, 1788	Ohio	March 1, 1803
Massachusetts	February 6, 1788	Louisiana	April 30, 1812
Maryland	April 28, 1788	Indiana	December 11, 1816
South Carolina	May 23, 1788	Mississippi	December 10, 1817
New Hampshire	June 21, 1788	Illinois	December 3, 1818
Virginia	June 25, 1788	Alabama	December 14, 1819
New York	July 26, 1788	Maine	March 15, 1820
North Carolina	November 21, 1789	Missouri	August 10, 1821

ADMISSION OF STATES TO THE UNION

State	Date of Admission	State	Date of Admission
Arkansas	June 15, 1836	Colorado	August 1, 1876
Michigan	January 16, 1837	North Dakota	November 2, 1889
Florida	March 3, 1845	South Dakota	November 2, 1889
Texas	December 29, 1845	Montana	November 8, 1889
Iowa	December 28, 1846	Washington	November 11, 1889
Wisconsin	May 29, 1848	Idaho	July 3, 1890
California	September 9, 1850	Wyoming	July 10, 1890
Minnesota	May 11, 1858	Utah	January 4, 1896
Oregon	February 14, 1859	Oklahoma	November 16, 1907
Kansas	January 29, 1861	New Mexico	January 6, 1912
West Virginia	June 19, 1863	Arizona	February 14, 1912
Nevada	October 31, 1864	Alaska	January 3, 1959
Nebraska	March 1, 1867	Hawaii	August 21, 1959

SUPREME COURT JUSTICES

Name	Service	Appointed by	Name	Service	Appointed by
John Jay*	1789–1795	Washington	Philip P. Barbour	1836–1841	Jackson
James Wilson	1789–1798	Washington	John Catron	1837–1865	Van Buren
John Blair	1789–1796	Washington	John McKinley	1837–1852	Van Buren
John Rutledge	1790–1791	Washington	Peter V. Daniel	1841–1860	Van Buren
William Cushing	1790–1810	Washington	Samuel Nelson	1845–1872	Tyler
James Iredell	1790–1799	Washington	Levi Woodbury	1845–1851	Polk
Thomas Johnson	1791–1793	Washington	Robert C. Grier	1846–1870	Polk
William Paterson	1793–1806	Washington	Benjamin R. Curtis	1851–1857	Fillmore
John Rutledge†	1795	Washington	John A. Campbell	1853–1861	Pierce
Samuel Chase	1796–1811	Washington	Nathan Clifford	1858–1881	Buchanan
Oliver Ellsworth	1796–1799	Washington	Noah H. Swayne	1862–1881	Lincoln
Bushrod Washington	1798–1829	J. Adams	Samuel F. Miller	1862–1890	Lincoln
Alfred Moore	1799–1804	J. Adams	David Davis	1862–1877	Lincoln
John Marshall	1801–1835	J. Adams	Stephen J. Field	1863–1897	Lincoln
William Johnson	1804–1834	Jefferson	**Salmon P. Chase**	1864–1873	Lincoln
Henry B. Livingston	1806–1823	Jefferson	William Strong	1870–1880	Grant
Thomas Todd	1807–1826	Jefferson	Joseph P. Bradley	1870–1892	Grant
Gabriel Duval	1811–1836	Madison	Ward Hunt	1873–1882	Grant
Joseph Story	1811–1845	Madison	**Morrison R. Waite**	1874–1888	Grant
Smith Thompson	1823–1843	Monroe	John M. Harlan	1877–1911	Hayes
Robert Trimble	1826–1828	J. Q. Adams	William B. Woods	1880–1887	Hayes
John McLean	1829–1861	Jackson	Stanley Matthews	1881–1889	Garfield
Henry Baldwin	1830–1844	Jackson	Horace Gray	1882–1902	Arthur
James M. Wayne	1835–1867	Jackson	Samuel Blatchford	1882–1893	Arthur
Roger B. Taney	1836–1864	Jackson	Lucius Q. C. Lamar	1888–1893	Cleveland
			Melville W. Fuller	1888–1910	Cleveland
			David J. Brewer	1889–1910	B. Harrison
			Henry B. Brown	1890–1906	B. Harrison
			George Shiras	1892–1903	B. Harrison
			Howell E. Jackson	1893–1895	B. Harrison

*Chief Justices appear in bold type.
†Acting Chief Justice; Senate refused to confirm appointment.

Name	Service	Appointed by	Name	Service	Appointed by
Edward D. White	1894–1910	Cleveland	Frederick M. Vinson	1946–1953	Truman
Rufus W. Peckham	1896–1909	Cleveland	Tom C. Clark	1949–1967	Truman
Joseph McKenna	1898–1925	McKinley	Sherman Minton	1949–1956	Truman
Oliver W. Holmes	1902–1932	T. Roosevelt	Earl Warren	1953–1969	Eisenhower
William R. Day	1903–1922	T. Roosevelt	John Marshall Harlan	1955–1971	Eisenhower
William H. Moody	1906–1910	T. Roosevelt	William J. Brennan Jr.	1956–1990	Eisenhower
Horace H. Lurton	1910–1914	Taft	Charles E. Whittaker	1957–1962	Eisenhower
Charles E. Hughes	1910–1916	Taft	Potter Stewart	1958–1981	Eisenhower
Willis Van Devanter	1910–1937	Taft	Byron R. White	1962–1993	Kennedy
Edward D. White	1910–1921	Taft	Arthur J. Goldberg	1962–1965	Kennedy
Joseph R. Lamar	1911–1916	Taft	Abe Fortas	1965–1969	L. Johnson
Mahlon Pitney	1912–1922	Taft	Thurgood Marshall	1967–1991	L. Johnson
James C. McReynolds	1914–1941	Wilson	Warren E. Burger	1969–1986	Nixon
			Harry A. Blackmun	1970–1994	Nixon
Louis D. Brandeis	1916–1939	Wilson	Lewis F. Powell Jr.	1972–1988	Nixon
John H. Clarke	1916–1922	Wilson	William H. Rehnquist	1972–1986	Nixon
William H. Taft	1921–1930	Harding	John Paul Stevens	1975–	Ford
George Sutherland	1922–1938	Harding	Sandra Day O'Connor	1981–2006	Reagan
Pierce Butler	1923–1939	Harding			
Edward T. Sanford	1923–1930	Harding	William H. Rehnquist	1986–2005	Reagan
Harlan F. Stone	1925–1941	Coolidge			
Charles E. Hughes	1930–1941	Hoover	Antonin Scalia	1986–	Reagan
Owen J. Roberts	1930–1945	Hoover	Anthony M. Kennedy	1988–	Reagan
Benjamin N. Cardozo	1932–1938	Hoover	David H. Souter	1990–2009	G. H. W. Bush
Hugo L. Black	1937–1971	F. Roosevelt			
Stanley F. Reed	1938–1957	F. Roosevelt	Clarence Thomas	1991–	G. H. W. Bush
Felix Frankfurter	1939–1962	F. Roosevelt			
William O. Douglas	1939–1975	F. Roosevelt	Ruth Bader Ginsburg	1993–	Clinton
Frank Murphy	1940–1949	F. Roosevelt	Stephen Breyer	1994–	Clinton
Harlan F. Stone	1941–1946	F. Roosevelt	John G. Roberts Jr.	2005–	G. W. Bush
James F. Byrnes	1941–1942	F. Roosevelt	Samuel Anthony Alito Jr.	2006–	G. W. Bush
Robert H. Jackson	1941–1954	F. Roosevelt			
Wiley B. Rutledge	1943–1949	F. Roosevelt	Sonia Sotomayor	2009–	Obama
Harold H. Burton	1945–1958	Truman	Elena Kagan	2010–	Obama

SIGNIFICANT SUPREME COURT CASES

Marbury v. Madison (1803)

This case established the right of the Supreme Court to review the constitutionality of laws. The decision involved judicial appointments made during the last hours of the administration of President John Adams. Some commissions, including that of William Marbury, had not yet been delivered when President Thomas Jefferson took office. Infuriated by the last-minute nature of Adams's Federalist appointments, Jefferson refused to send the undelivered commissions out, and Marbury decided to sue. The Supreme Court, presided over by John Marshall, a Federalist who had assisted Adams in the judicial appointments, ruled that although Marbury's commission was valid and the new president should have delivered it, the Court could not compel him to do so. The Court based its reasoning on a finding that the grounds of Marbury's suit, resting in the Judiciary Act of 1789, were in conflict with the Constitution.

For the first time, the Court had overturned a national law on the grounds that it was unconstitutional. John Marshall had quietly established the concept of judicial review: The Supreme Court had given itself the authority to nullify acts of the other branches of the federal government. Although the Constitution provides for judicial review, the Court had not exercised this power before and did not use it again until 1857. It seems likely that if the Court had waited until 1857 to use this power, it would have been difficult to establish.

McCulloch v. Maryland (1819)

In 1816, Congress authorized the creation of a national bank. To protect its own banks from competition with a branch of the national bank in Baltimore, the state legislature of Maryland placed a tax of 2 percent on all notes issued by any bank operating in Maryland that was not chartered by the state. McCulloch, cashier of the Baltimore branch of the Bank of the United States, was convicted for refusing to pay the tax. Under the leadership of Chief Justice John Marshall, the Court ruled that the federal government had the power to establish a bank, even though that specific authority was not mentioned in the Constitution.

Marshall maintained that the authority could be reasonably implied from Article 1, section 8, which gives Congress the power to make all laws that are necessary and proper to execute the enumerated powers. Marshall also held that Maryland could not tax the national bank because in a conflict between federal and state laws, the federal law must take precedence. Thus he established the principles of implied powers and federal supremacy, both of which set a precedent for subsequent expansion of federal power at the expense of the states.

Scott v. Sandford (1857)

Dred Scott was a slave who sued for his own and his family's freedom on the grounds that, with his master, he had traveled to and lived in free territory that did not allow slavery. When his case reached the Supreme Court, the justices saw an opportunity to settle once and for all the vexing question of slavery in the territories. The Court's decision in this case proved that it enjoyed no special immunity from the sectional and partisan passions of the time. Five of the nine justices were from the South and seven were Democrats.

Chief Justice Roger B. Taney hated Republicans and detested racial equality; his decision reflects those prejudices. He wrote an opinion not only declaring that Scott was still a slave but also claiming that the Constitution denied citizenship or rights to blacks, that Congress had no right to exclude slavery from the territories, and that the Missouri Compromise was unconstitutional. While southern Democrats gloated over this seven-to-two decision, sectional tensions were further inflamed, and the young Republican Party's claim that a hostile "slave power" was conspiring to destroy northern liberties was given further credence. The decision brought the nation closer to civil war and is generally regarded as the worst decision ever rendered by the Supreme Court.

Butchers' Benevolent Association of New Orleans v. Crescent City Livestock Landing and Slaughterhouse Co. (1873)

The *Slaughterhouse* cases, as the cases docketed under the *Butchers'* title were known, were the first legal test of the Fourteenth Amendment. To cut down on cases of cholera believed to be caused by contaminated water, the state of Louisiana prohibited the slaughter of livestock in New Orleans except in one slaughterhouse, effectively giving that slaughterhouse a monopoly. Other New Orleans butchers claimed that the state had deprived them of their occupation without due process of law, thus violating the Fourteenth Amendment.

In a five-to-four decision, the Court upheld the Louisiana law, declaring that the Fourteenth Amendment protected only the rights of federal citizenship, like voting in federal elections and interstate travel. The federal government thus was not obliged to protect basic civil rights from violation by state governments. This decision would have significant implications for African Americans and their struggle for civil rights in the twentieth century.

United States v. E. C. Knight Co. (1895)

Also known as the *Sugar Trust* case, this was among the first cases to reveal the weakness of the Sherman Antitrust Act in the hands of a pro-business Supreme Court. In 1895, American Sugar Refining Company purchased four other sugar producers, including the E. C. Knight Company, and thus took control of more than 98 percent of the sugar refining in the United States. In an effort to limit monopoly, the government brought suit against all five of the companies for violating the Sherman Antitrust Act, which outlawed trusts and other business combinations in restraint of trade. The Court dismissed the suit, however, arguing that the law applied only to commerce and not to manufacturing, defining the latter as a local concern and not part of the interstate commerce that the government could regulate.

Plessy v. Ferguson (1896)

African American Homer Plessy challenged a Louisiana law that required segregation on trains passing through the state. After ensuring that the railroad and the conductor knew that he was of mixed race (Plessy appeared to be white but under the racial code of Louisiana was classified as "colored" because he was one-eighth black), he refused to move to the "colored only" section of the coach. The Court ruled against Plessy by a vote of seven to one, declaring that "separate but equal" facilities were permissible according to section 1 of the Fourteenth Amendment, which calls upon the states to provide "equal protection of the laws" to anyone within their jurisdiction. Although the case was viewed as relatively insignificant at the time, it cast a long shadow over several decades.

Initially, the decision was viewed as a victory for segregationists, but in the 1930s and 1940s civil rights advocates referred to the doctrine of "separate but equal" in their efforts to end segregation. They argued that segregated institutions and accommodations were often not equal to those available to whites, and finally

succeeded in overturning *Plessy* in *Brown v. Board of Education* in 1954 (see below).

Lochner v. New York (1905)

In this case, the Court ruled against a New York state law that prohibited employees from working in bakeries more than ten hours a day or sixty hours a week. The purpose of the law was to protect the health of workers, but the Court ruled that it was unconstitutional because it violated "freedom of contract" implicitly protected by the due process clause of the Fourteenth Amendment. Most of the justices believed strongly in a laissez-faire economic system that favored survival of the fittest. They felt that government protection of workers interfered with this system. In a dissenting opinion, Justice Oliver Wendell Holmes accused the majority of distorting the Constitution and of deciding the case on "an economic theory which a large part of the country does not entertain."

Muller v. Oregon (1908)

In 1905, Curt Muller, owner of a Portland, Oregon, laundry, demanded that one of his employees, Mrs. Elmer Gotcher, work more than the ten hours allowed as a maximum workday for women under Oregon law. Muller argued that the law violated his "freedom of contract" as established in prior Supreme Court decisions.

Progressive lawyer Louis D. Brandeis defended the Oregon law by arguing that a state could be justified in abridging freedom of contract when the health, safety, and welfare of workers was at issue. His innovative strategy drew on ninety-five pages of excerpts from factory and medical reports to substantiate his argument that there was a direct connection between long hours and the health of women and thus the health of the nation. In a unanimous decision, the Court upheld the Oregon law, but later generations of women fighting for equality would question the strategy of arguing that women's reproductive role entitled them to special treatment.

Schenck v. United States (1919)

During World War I, Charles Schenck and other members of the Socialist Party printed and mailed out flyers urging young men who were subject to the draft to oppose the war in Europe. In upholding the conviction of Schenck for publishing a pamphlet urging draft resistance, Justice Oliver Wendell Holmes established the "clear and present danger" test for freedom of speech. Such utterances as Schenck's during a time of national peril, Holmes wrote, could be considered the equivalent of shouting "Fire!" in a crowded theater. Congress had the right to protect the public against such an incitement to panic, the Court ruled in a unanimous decision. But the analogy was a false one. Schenck's pamphlet had little power to provoke a public firmly opposed to its message. Although Holmes later modified his position to state that the danger must relate to an immediate evil and a specific action, the "clear and present danger" test laid the groundwork for those who later sought to limit First Amendment freedoms.

Schechter Poultry Corp. v. United States (1935)

During the Great Depression, the National Industrial Recovery Act (NIRA), which was passed under President Franklin D. Roosevelt, established fair competition codes that were designed to help businesses. The Schechter brothers of New York City, who sold chickens, were convicted of violating the codes. The Supreme Court ruled that the NIRA unconstitutionally conferred legislative power on an administrative agency and overstepped the limits of federal power to regulate interstate commerce. The decision was a significant blow to the New Deal recovery program, demonstrating both historic American resistance to economic planning and the refusal of the business community to yield its autonomy unless it was forced to do so.

Brown v. Board of Education (1954)

In 1950, the families of eight Topeka, Kansas, children sued the Topeka Board of Education. The children were blacks who lived within walking distance of a whites-only school. The segregated school system required them to take a time-consuming, inconvenient, and dangerous route to get to a black school, and their parents argued that there was no reason their children should not be allowed to attend the nearest school. By the time the case reached the Supreme Court, it had been joined with similar cases regarding segregated schools in other states and the District of Columbia. A team of lawyers from the National Association for the Advancement of Colored People (NAACP), led by Thurgood Marshall (who would later be appointed to the Supreme Court), urged the Court to overturn the fifty-eight-year-old precedent established in *Plessy v. Ferguson*, which had enshrined "separate but equal" as the law of the land. A unanimous Court, led by Chief Justice Earl Warren, declared that "separate educational facilities are inherently unequal" and thus violate the Fourteenth Amendment. In 1955, the Court called for desegregation "with all deliberate speed" but established no deadline.

Roth v. United States (1957)

In 1957, New Yorker Samuel Roth was convicted of sending obscene materials through the mail in a case that ultimately reached the Supreme Court. With a six-to-three vote, the Court reaffirmed the historical view that obscenity is not protected by the First Amendment. Yet it broke new ground by declaring that a work could be judged obscene only if, "taken as a whole," it appealed to the "prurient interest" of "the average person."

Prior to this case, work could be judged obscene if portions were thought able to "deprave and corrupt" the most susceptible part of an audience (such as children). Thus, serious works of literature such as Theodore Dreiser's *An American Tragedy*, which was banned in Boston when first published, had received no protection. Although this decision continued to pose problems of definition, it did help to protect most works that attempt to convey ideas, even if those ideas have to do with sex, from the threat of obscenity laws.

Engel v. Vitale (1962)

In 1959, five parents with ten children in the New Hyde Park, New York, school system sued the school board. The parents argued that the so-called Regents' Prayer that public school students in New York recited at the start of every school day violated the doctrine of separation of church and state outlined in the First Amendment. In 1962, the Supreme Court voted six to one in favor of banning the Regents' Prayer.

The decision threw the religious community into an uproar. Many religious leaders expressed dismay and even shock; others welcomed the decision. Several efforts to introduce an amendment allowing school prayer have failed. Subsequent Supreme Court decisions have banned reading of the Bible in public schools. The Court has also declared mandatory flag saluting to be an infringement of religious and personal freedoms.

Gideon v. Wainwright (1963)

When Clarence Earl Gideon was tried for breaking into a poolroom, the state of Florida rejected his demand for a court-appointed lawyer as guaranteed by the Sixth Amendment. In 1963, the Court upheld his demand in a unanimous decision that established the obligation of states to provide attorneys for indigent defendants in felony cases. Prior to this decision, the right to an attorney had applied only to federal cases, not state cases. In its ruling in *Gideon v. Wainwright*, the Supreme Court applied the Sixth through the Fourteenth Amendments to the states. In 1972, the Supreme Court extended the right to legal representation to all cases, not just felony cases, in its decision in *Argersinger v. Hamlin*.

Griswold v. Connecticut (1965)

With a vote of seven to two, the Supreme Court reversed an "uncommonly silly law" (in the words of Justice Potter Stewart) that made it a crime for anyone in the state of Connecticut to use any drug, article, or instrument to prevent conception. *Griswold* became a landmark case because here, for the first time, the Court explicitly invested with full constitutional status "fundamental personal rights," such as the right to privacy, that were not expressly enumerated in the Bill of Rights. The majority opinion in the case held that the law infringed on the constitutionally protected right to privacy of married persons.

Although the Court had previously recognized fundamental rights not expressly enumerated in the Bill of Rights (such as the right to procreate in *Skinner v. Oklahoma* in 1942), *Griswold* was the first time the Court had justified, at length, the practice of investing such unenumerated rights with full constitutional status. Writing for the majority, Justice William O. Douglas explained that the First, Third, Fourth, Fifth, and Ninth Amendments imply "zones of privacy" that are the foundation for the general right to privacy affirmed in this case.

Miranda v. Arizona (1966)

In 1966, the Supreme Court, by a vote of five to four, upheld the case of Ernesto Miranda, who appealed a murder conviction on the grounds that police had gotten him to confess without giving him access to an attorney. The *Miranda* case was the culmination of the Court's efforts to find a meaningful way of determining whether police had used due process in extracting confessions from people accused of crimes. The *Miranda* decision upholds the Fifth Amendment protection against self-incrimination outside the courtroom and requires that suspects be given what came to be known as the "Miranda warning," which advises them of their right to remain silent and warns them that anything they say might be used against them in a court of law. Suspects must also be told that they have a right to counsel.

New York Times Co. v. United States (1971)

With a six-to-three vote, the Court upheld the right of the *New York Times* and the *Washington Post* to print materials from the so-called *Pentagon Papers*, a secret government study of U.S. policy in Vietnam, leaked by dissident Pentagon official Daniel Ellsberg. Since the papers revealed deception and secrecy in the conduct of the Vietnam War, the Nixon administration had quickly obtained a court injunction against their further publication, claiming that suppression was in the interests of national security. The Supreme Court's decision overturning the injunction strengthened the First Amendment protection of freedom of the press.

Furman v. Georgia (1972)

In this case, the Supreme Court ruled five to four that the death penalty for murder or rape violated the cruel and unusual punishment clause of the Eighth Amendment because the manner in which the death penalty was meted out was irregular, "arbitrary," and "cruel." In response, most states enacted new statutes that allow the death penalty to be imposed only after a postconviction hearing at which evidence must be presented to show that "aggravating" or "mitigating"

circumstances were factors in the crime. If the post-conviction hearing hands down a death sentence, the case is automatically reviewed by an appellate court.

In 1976, the Court ruled in *Gregg v. Georgia* that these statutes were not unconstitutional. In 1977, the Court ruled in *Coker v. Georgia* that the death penalty for rape was "disproportionate and excessive," thus allowing the death penalty only in murder cases. Between 1977 and 1991, some 150 people were executed in the United States. Public opinion polls indicate that about 70 percent of Americans favor the death penalty for murder. Capital punishment continues to generate controversy, however, as opponents argue that there is no evidence that the death penalty deters crime and that its use reflects racial and economic bias.

Roe v. Wade (1973)

In 1973, the Court found, by a vote of seven to two, that state laws restricting access to abortion violated a woman's right to privacy guaranteed by the due process clause of the Fourteenth Amendment. The decision was based on the cases of two women living in Texas and Georgia, both states with stringent antiabortion laws. Upholding the individual rights of both women and physicians, the Court ruled that the Constitution protects the right to abortion and that states cannot prohibit abortions in the early stages of pregnancy.

The decision stimulated great debate among legal scholars as well as the public. Critics argued that since abortion was never addressed in the Constitution, the Court could not claim that legislation violated fundamental values of the Constitution. They also argued that since abortion was a medical procedure with an acknowledged impact on a fetus, it was inappropriate to invoke the kind of "privacy" argument that was used in *Griswold v. Connecticut* (see page A-43), which was about contraception. Defenders suggested that the case should be argued as a case of gender discrimination, which did violate the equal protection clause of the Fourteenth Amendment. Others said that the right to privacy in sexual matters was indeed a fundamental right.

Regents of the University of California v. Bakke (1978)

When Allan Bakke, a white man, was not accepted by the University of California Medical School at Davis, he filed a lawsuit alleging that the admissions program, which set up different standards for test scores and grades for members of certain minority groups, violated the Civil Rights Act of 1964, which outlawed racial or ethnic preferences in programs supported by federal funds. Bakke further argued that the university's practice of setting aside spaces for minority applicants denied him equal protection as guaranteed by the Fourteenth Amendment. In a five-to-four decision, the Court ordered that Bakke be admitted to the medical school, yet it sanctioned affirmative action programs to attack the results of past discrimination as long as strict quotas or racial classifications were not involved.

Webster v. Reproductive Health Services (1989)

By a vote of five to four, the Court upheld several restrictions on the availability of abortions as imposed by Missouri state law. It upheld restrictions on the use of state property, including public hospitals, for abortions. It also upheld a provision requiring physicians to perform tests to determine the viability of a fetus that a doctor judged to be twenty weeks of age or older. Although the justices did not go so far as to overturn the decision in *Roe v. Wade* (see at left), the ruling galvanized interest groups on both sides of the abortion issue. Opponents of abortion pressured state legislatures to place greater restrictions on abortions; those who favored availability of abortion tried to mobilize public action by presenting the decision as a major threat to the right to choose abortion.

Cipollone v. Liggett (1992)

In a seven-to-two decision, the Court ruled in favor of the family of Rose Cipollone, a woman who died of lung cancer after smoking for forty-two years. The Court rejected arguments that health warnings on cigarette packages protected tobacco manufacturers from personal injury suits filed by smokers who contract cancer and other serious illnesses.

Miller v. Johnson (1995)

In a five-to-four decision, the Supreme Court ruled that voting districts created to increase the voting power of racial minorities were unconstitutional. The decision threatens dozens of congressional, state, and local voting districts that were drawn to give minorities more representation as had been required by the Justice Department under the Voting Rights Act. If states are required to redraw voting districts, the number of black members of Congress could be sharply reduced.

Romer v. Evans (1996)

In a six-to-three decision, the Court struck down a Colorado amendment that forbade local governments from banning discrimination against homosexuals. Writing for the majority, Justice Anthony Kennedy said that forbidding communities from taking action to protect the rights of homosexuals and not of other groups unlawfully deprived gays and lesbians of opportunities that were available to others. Kennedy based the decision on the guarantee of equal protection under the law as provided by the Fourteenth Amendment.

Bush v. Palm Beach County Canvassing Board (2000)

In a bitterly argued five-to-four decision, the Court reversed the Florida Supreme Court's previous order for a hand recount of contested presidential election ballots in several counties of that battleground state, effectively securing the presidency for Texas Republican governor George W. Bush. The ruling ended a protracted legal dispute between presidential candidates Bush and Vice President Al Gore while inflaming public opinion: For the first time since 1888, a president who failed to win the popular vote took office. Critics charged that the Supreme Court had applied partisanship rather than objectivity to the case, pointing out that the decision went against this Court's customary interpretation of the Constitution to favor state over federal authority.

Lawrence v. Texas (2003)

In the 1986 case *Bowers v. Hardwick*, the Supreme Court upheld the constitutionality of a Georgia law that outlawed sodomy, ruling that sexual privacy was not protected by the Constitution. This decision came into question, however, when *Lawrence v. Texas* arrived at the Supreme Court in 2002, challenging the constitutionality of a Texas anti-sodomy statute. In this case, the Court voted six to three to strike down the statute, asserting that the 1986 decision was based on an interpretation of constitutional liberties that was too narrow. This decision thus overruled *Bowers v. Hardwick*, with the majority holding that the Texas law violated the Fourteenth Amendment's declaration that no state shall "deprive any person of life, liberty, or property, without due process of law." The decision in *Lawrence v. Texas* was hailed as a legal victory for the gay and lesbian community. It was landmark in its implication that laws cannot be made on the basis of morality, without proof of harm.

Hamdan v. Rumsfeld (2005)

In 2001, Salim Ahmed Hamdan, driver for al-Qaeda leader Osama bin Laden, was arrested in Afghanistan as a suspected terrorist. He was charged with conspiracy to commit terrorist offenses after being held in the U.S. military base in Guantanamo Bay, Cuba, for two years. It was decided that Hamdan would be tried by a military commission under an order from President George W. Bush that commissions be established for express non-citizens, including those with connections to al-Qaeda. Hamdan, however, claimed that trial by military commission was unlawful under the Geneva Conventions and Uniform Code of Military Justice (UCMJ).

In the case's first round through the courts, the U.S. District Court of the District of Columbia ruled in Hamdan's favor. Upon appeal, the decision was reversed, the new court ruling that the military commission was indeed lawful, and that the Geneva Conventions could not be enforced by the U.S. judicial systems. The Supreme Court issued a writ of certiorari in 2005 and ultimately upheld Hamdan's case by a vote of five to three, stating that the military commission was unlawful under both the Geneva Conventions and the UCMJ. This decision put a halt to all Guantanamo Bay tribunals, and was praised by human rights activists and lawyers.

Citizens United v. Federal Election Commission (2010)

In 2010, the Supreme Court overruled a ban on political spending by corporations in a vote of five to four. The case went to court after Citizens United, a conservative nonprofit organization, tried to air its critical documentary on Hillary Clinton, *Hillary: The Movie*, during the 2008 presidential campaign. *Citizens United v. Federal Election Commission* quickly became a matter of free speech and raised the sensitive question of whether corporations should be viewed as individuals under the First Amendment.

The Court's decision overturned two precedents and divided the nation in an already heated time in the political sphere. Advocates for the ruling felt that the previous ban would have given the Supreme Court power to prohibit other political outlets, such as newspapers and television programs. Dissenters, including President Barack Obama, believed that the vote created an opening for wealthy corporations to take advantage of the democratic system. In reversing years of policy, the ruling left all to speculate on its possible impact not only on the 2008 election, but also on American politics as a whole.

THE AMERICAN ECONOMY

THESE SIX "SNAPSHOTS" OF THE U.S. ECONOMY show significant changes over the past century and a half. In 1849, the agricultural sector was by far the largest contributor to the economy. By the turn of the century, with advances in technology and an abundance of cheap labor and raw materials, the country had experienced remarkable industrial expansion, and the manufacturing industries dominated. By 1950, the service sector had increased significantly, fueled by the consumerism

of the 1920s and the post–World War II years, and the economy was becoming more diversified. Note that by 1990, the government's share in the economy had grown to more than 10 percent and activity in both the trade and manufacturing sectors had declined, partly as a result of competition from Western Europe and Asia. Manufacturing continued to decline, and by 2008 the service and finance, real estate, and insurance sectors had all grown steadily to eclipse it.

Main Sectors of the U.S. Economy: 1849, 1899, 1950, 1990, 2001, 2008

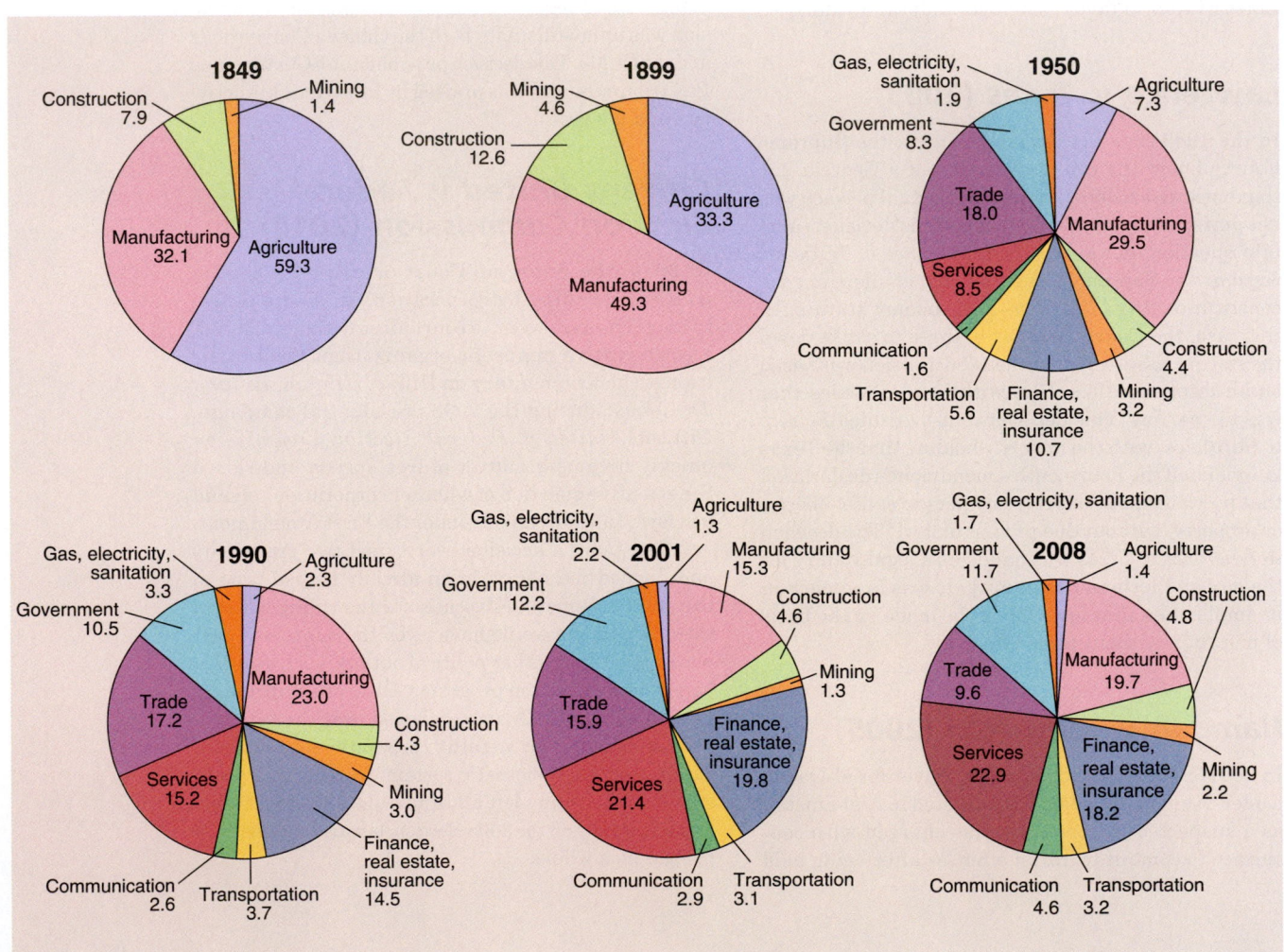

SOURCE: Data from *Historical Statistics of the United States, Colonial Times to 1970* (1975); *Statistical Abstract of the United States, 2010*; U.S. Bureau of Economic Analysis, *Industry Accounts Data*, 2010.

FEDERAL SPENDING AND THE ECONOMY, 1790–2009

Year	Gross Domestic Product (in billions)	Foreign Trade (in billions)		Federal Federal Budget (in billions)	Surplus/Deficit (in billions)	Federal Debt (in billions)
		Exports	Imports			
1790	4.03	0.43	0.50	0.09	0.0032	1.64
1800	7.40	1.10	1.41	0.17	0.0010	1.29
1810	10.6	1.02	1.29	0.12	0.0187	0.81
1820	14.4	1.44	1.52	0.37	−0.0078	1.87
1830	22.2	1.62	1.55	0.33	0.2120	1.07
1840	31.5	2.66	2.16	0.48	−0.0977	0.08
1850	49.6	2.95	3.45	0.78	0.0788	1.24
1860	82.1	7.56	6.84	1.19	−0.1340	1.23
1870	112	6.54	6.70	4.50	1.47	34.8
1880	192	15.8	14.1	4.96	1.22	38.9
1890	319	19.3	17.5	6.73	1.80	23.3
1900	423	30.8	19.1	10.7	0.95	26.7
1910	534	30.6	26.2	11.1	−0.29	17.6
1920	688	67.4	45.0	49.8	2.27	189
1930	893	39.3	34.3	33.7	7.22	159
1940	1,167	46.4	85.6	104	−41.50	495
1950	2,006	94.3	82.1	294	−14.30	257
1960	2,831	145	125	629	2.10	291
1970	4,270	270	246	983	−14.30	381
1980	5,839	470	513	1,369	−171	909
1990	8,034	545	686	1,832	−323	3,206
2000	11,226	1,071	1,449	2,041	270	5,269
2009	12,703	1,571	1,946	3,186	−1,280	11,876

NOTE: All Figures are in 2005 dollars.

SOURCE: *Historical Statistics of the U.S., 1789–1945* (1949), *Statistical Abstract of the U.S., 1965* (1965), *Statistical Abstract of the U.S., 1990* (1990), *Statistical Abstract of the U.S., 2011* (2011), and Louis Johnston and Samuel H. Williamson, "What Was the U.S. GDP Then?" MeasuringWorth, 2011, www.measuringworth.org/usgdp.

A DEMOGRAPHIC PROFILE OF THE UNITED STATES AND ITS PEOPLE

Population

FROM AN ESTIMATED 4,600 white inhabitants in 1630, the country's population grew to a total of more than 308 million in 2010. It is important to note that the U.S. census, first conducted in 1790 and the source of these figures, counted blacks, both free and slave, but did not include American Indians until 1860. The years 1790 to 1900 saw the most rapid population growth, with an average increase of 25 to 35 percent per decade. In addition to "natural" growth—birthrate exceeding death rate—immigration was also a factor in that rise, especially between 1840 and 1860, 1880 and 1890, and 1900 and 1910 (see table on page A-51). The twentieth century witnessed slower growth, partly a result of 1920s immigration restrictions and a decline in the birthrate, especially during the depression era and the 1960s and 1970s. The U.S. population is expected to pass 340 million by the year 2020.

POPULATION GROWTH, 1630–2010

Year	Population	Percent Increase	Year	Population	Percent Increase
1630	4,600	—	1830	12,866,020	33.5
1640	26,600	473.3	1840	17,069,453	32.7
1650	50,400	89.1	1850	23,191,876	35.9
1660	75,100	49.0	1860	31,443,321	35.6
1670	111,900	49.1	1870	39,818,449	26.6
1680	151,500	35.4	1880	50,155,783	26.0
1690	210,400	38.9	1890	62,947,714	25.5
1700	250,900	19.3	1900	75,994,575	20.7
1710	331,700	32.2	1910	91,972,266	21.0
1720	466,200	40.5	1920	105,710,620	14.9
1730	629,400	35.0	1930	122,775,046	16.1
1740	905,600	43.9	1940	131,669,275	7.2
1750	1,170,800	30.0	1950	150,697,361	14.5
1760	1,593,600	36.1	1960	179,323,175	19.0
1770	2,148,100	34.8	1970	203,302,031	13.4
1780	2,780,400	29.4	1980	226,542,199	11.4
1790	3,929,214	41.3	1990	248,718,302	9.8
1800	5,308,483	35.1	2000	281,422,509	13.1
1810	7,239,881	36.4	2010	308,745,538	9.7
1820	9,638,453	33.1			

SOURCE: *Historical Statistics of the U.S.* (1960), *Historical Statistics of the U.S., Colonial Times to 1970* (1975), *Statistical Abstract of the U.S., 1996* (1996), *Statistical Abstract of the U.S., 2003* (2003), and United States Census (2010).

Birthrate, 1820–2007

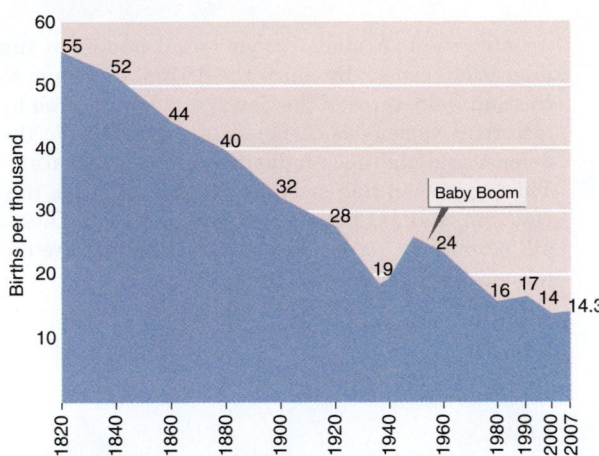

SOURCE: Data from *Historical Statistics of the U.S., Colonial Times to 1970* (1975) and *Statistical Abstract of the U.S., 2007* (2007).

Death Rate, 1900–2007

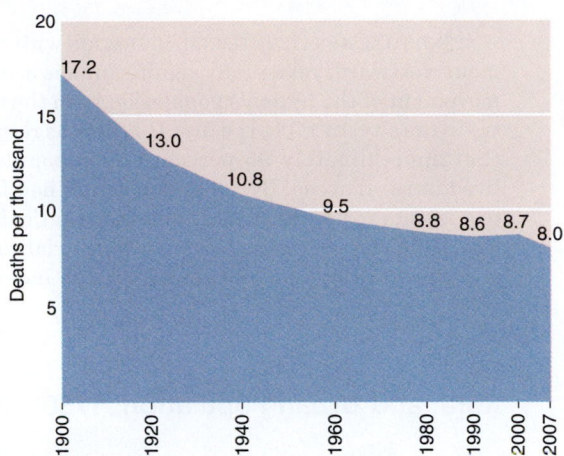

SOURCE: Data from *Historical Statistics of the U.S., Colonial Times to 1970* (1975) and *Statistical Abstract of the U.S., 2007* (2007).

Life Expectancy, 1900–2007

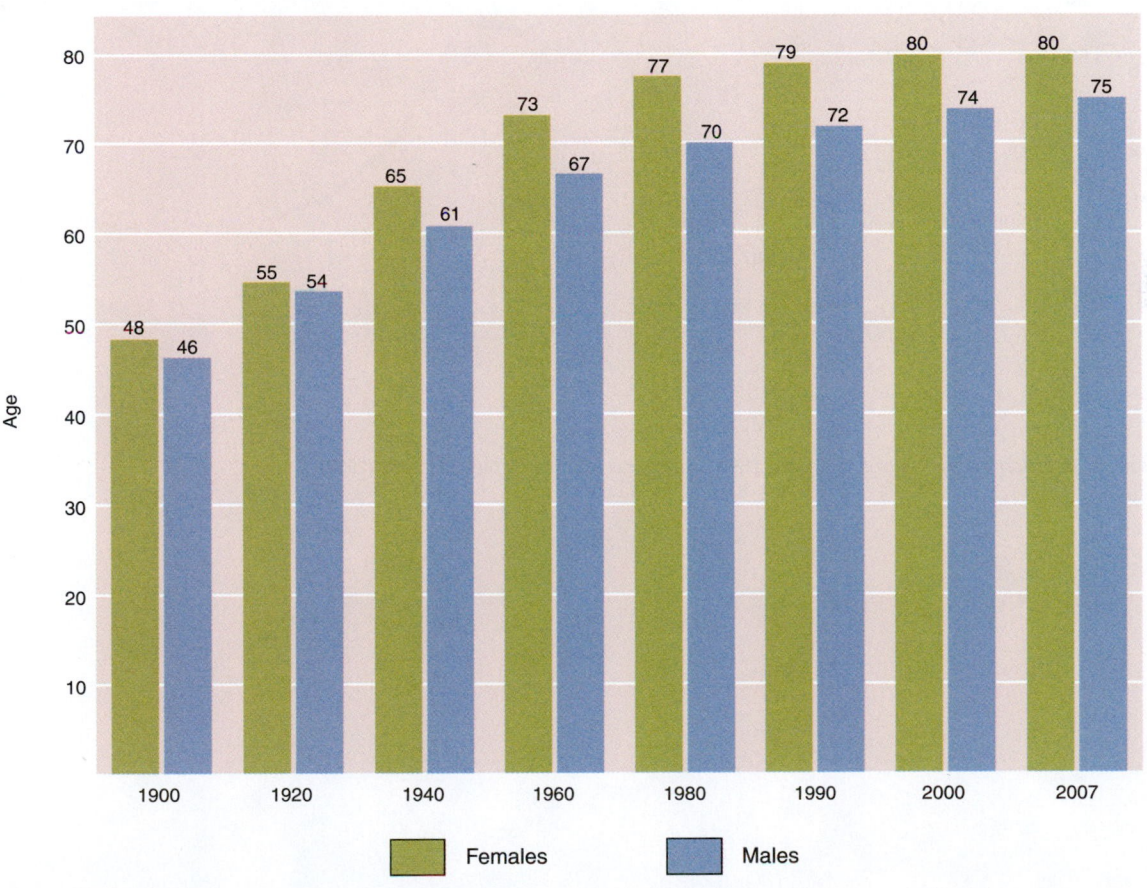

SOURCE: Data from *Historical Statistics of the U.S., Colonial Times to 1970* (1975) and *Statistical Abstract of the U.S., 2007* (2007).

MIGRATION AND IMMIGRATION

WE TEND TO ASSOCIATE INTERNAL MIGRATION with movement westward, yet equally significant has been the movement of the nation's population from the country to the city. In 1790, the first U.S. census recorded that approximately 95 percent of the population lived in rural areas. By 1990, that figure had fallen to less than 25 percent. The decline of the agricultural way of life, late-nineteenth-century industrialization, and immigration have all contributed to increased urbanization. A more recent trend has been the migration, especially since the 1970s, of people to the Sun Belt states of the South and West, lured by factors as various as economic opportunities in the defense and high-tech industries and good weather. This migration has swelled the size of cities like Houston, Dallas, Tucson, Phoenix, and San Diego, all of which in recent years ranked among the top ten most populous U.S. cities.

Rural and Urban Population, 1750–2000

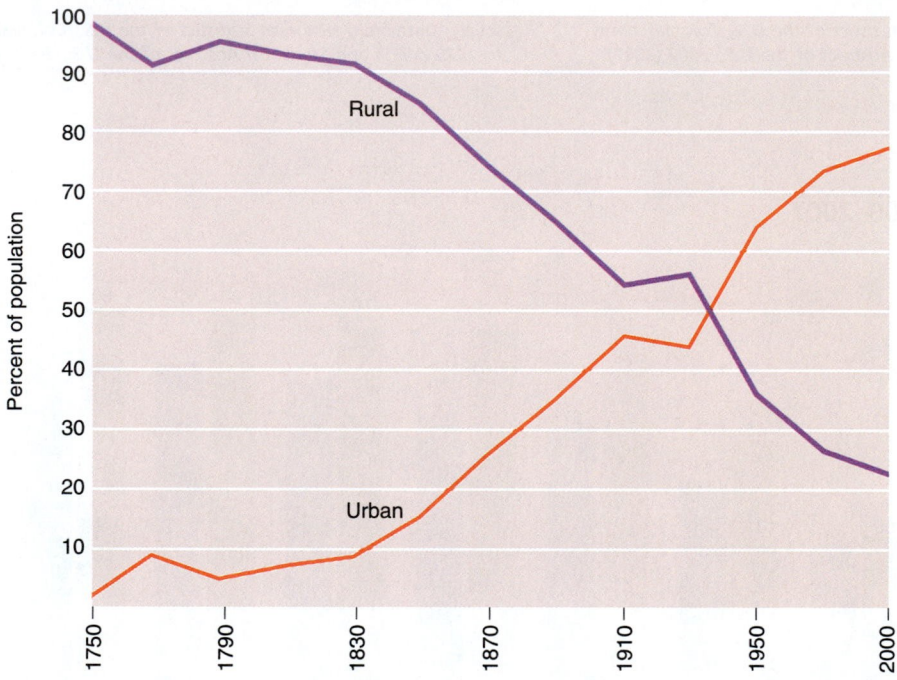

SOURCE: *Statistical Abstract of the U.S., 1991* (1991), *Statistical Abstract of the U.S., 2002* (2002).

THE QUANTITY AND CHARACTER OF IMMIGRATION to the United States has varied greatly over time. During the first major influx, between 1840 and 1860, newcomers hailed primarily from northern and western Europe. From 1880 to 1915, when rates soared even more dramatically, the profile changed, with 80 percent of the "new immigration" coming from central, eastern, and southern Europe. Following World War I, strict quotas reduced the flow considerably. Note also the significant falloff during the years of the Great Depression and World War II. The sources of immigration during the last half century have changed significantly, with the majority of people coming from Latin America, the Caribbean, and Asia. The latest surge during the 1980s and 1990s brought more immigrants to the United States than in any decade except 1901–1910.

RATES OF IMMIGRATION, 1821–2009

Year	Number	Rate per Thousand of Total Resident Population
1821–1830	151,824	1.6
1831–1840	599,125	4.6
1841–1850	1,713,521	10.0
1851–1860	2,598,214	11.2
1861–1870	2,314,824	7.4
1871–1880	2,812,191	7.1
1881–1890	5,246,613	10.5
1891–1900	3,687,546	5.8
1901–1910	8,795,386	11.6
1911–1920	5,735,811	6.2
1921–1930	4,107,209	3.9
1931–1940	528,431	0.4
1941–1950	1,035,039	0.7
1951–1960	2,515,479	1.6
1961–1970	3,321,677	1.8
1971–1980	4,493,300	2.2
1981–1990	7,338,100	3.0
1991	1,827,167	7.2
1992	973,977	3.8
1993	904,292	3.5
1994	804,416	3.1
1995	720,461	2.7
1996	915,900	3.4
1997	798,378	2.9
1998	654,451	2.4
1999	646,568	2.3
2000	849,807	3.0
2001	1,064,318	3.7
2002	1,063,732	3.7
2003	704,000	2.4
2004	958,000	3.3
2005	1,122,000	3.8
2006	1,266,129	4.2
2007	1,052,415	3.5
2008	1,107,126	3.6
2009	1,130,818	3.7

SOURCE: *Historical Statistics of the U.S., Colonial Times to 1970* (1975), *2002 Yearbook of Immigration Statistics* (2002), and *Statistical Abstract of the U.S., 1996, 1999, 2003, 2005,* and *2011* (1996, 1999, 2003, 2005, 2011).

Major Trends In Immigration, 1820–2010

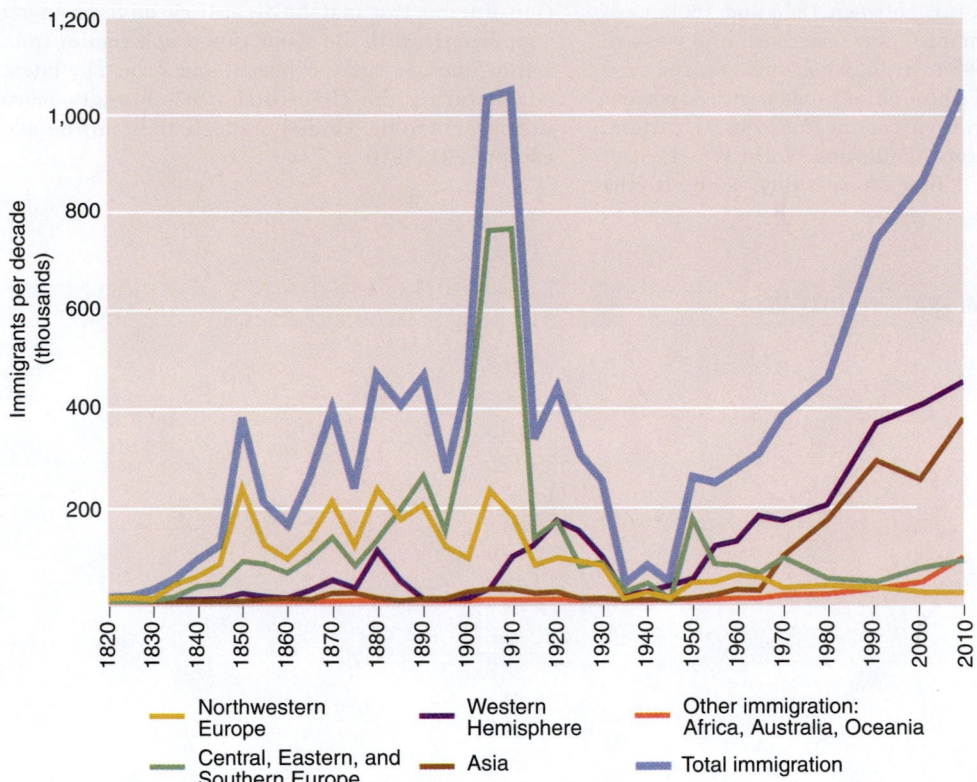

SOURCE: Data from *Historical Statistics of the U.S., Colonial Times to 1970* (1975), *Statistical Abstract of the U.S., 1999* (1999), and *Statistical Abstract of the U.S., 2011* (2011).

Glossary of Historical Vocabulary

A NOTE TO STUDENTS: This list of terms is provided to help you with historical and economic vocabulary. Many of these terms refer to broad, enduring concepts that you may encounter not only in further studies of history but also when following current events. The terms appear in bold at their first use in each chapter. In the glossary, the page numbers of those chapter-by-chapter appearances are provided so you can look up the terms' uses in various periods and contexts. For definitions and discussions of words not included here, consult a dictionary and the book's index, which will point you to topics covered at greater length in the book.

affirmative action Policies established in the 1960s and 1970s by governments, businesses, universities, and other institutions to overcome the effects of past discrimination against specific groups such as racial and ethnic minorities and women. Measures to ensure equal opportunity include setting goals for admission, hiring, and promotion; considering minority status when allocating resources; and actively encouraging victims of past discrimination to apply for jobs and other resources. (pp. 943, 944)

agribusiness Farming on a large scale, using the production, processing, and distribution methods of modern business. Farming became a big business, not just a way to feed a family and make a living, in the late nineteenth century as farms got larger and more mechanized. In the 1940s and 1950s, specialized commercial farms replaced many family-run operations and grew to an enormous scale. (pp. 562, 913)

alliance system The military and diplomatic system formulated in an effort to create a balance of power in pre–World War I Europe. Nations were bound together by rigid and comprehensive treaties that promised mutual aid in the case of attack by specific nations. The system swung into action after the Austrian archduke Franz Ferdinand was assassinated in Sarajevo on June 28, 1914, dragging most of Europe into war. (p. 715)

anarchist A person who rebels against established order and authority. An anarchist is someone who believes that government of any kind is unnecessary and undesirable and should be replaced with voluntary cooperation and free association. Anarchists became increasingly visible in the United States in the late nineteenth and early twentieth centuries. They advocated revolution and grew in numbers through appeals to discontented laborers. Anarchists frequently employed violence in an attempt to achieve their goals. In 1901, anarchist Leon Czolgosz assassinated President William McKinley. (pp. 619, 685, 769)

antebellum A term that means "before a war" and commonly refers to the period prior to the Civil War. (pp. 373, 395, 493, 521)

antinomian A person who does not obey societal or religious laws. In colonial Massachusetts, Puritan authorities accused Anne Hutchinson of antinomianism because she believed that Christians could achieve salvation by faith alone. They further asserted, incorrectly, that Hutchinson also held the belief that it was not necessary to follow God's laws as set forth in the Bible. (p. 103)

archaeology A social science devoted to learning about people who lived in the past through the study of physical artifacts created by humans. Most but not all archaeological study focuses on the history of people who lived before the use of the written word. (p. 5)

Archaic A term applied to various hunting and gathering cultures that descended from Paleo-Indians. The term also refers to the period of time when these cultures dominated ancient America, roughly from 8000 BP to between 2000 and 1000 BP. (p. 11)

artifacts Material remains studied and used by archaeologists and historians to support their interpretations of human history. Examples of artifacts include bones, pots, baskets, jewelry, furniture, tools, clothing, and buildings. (p. 5)

artisan A term commonly used prior to 1900 to describe a skilled craftsman, such as a cabinetmaker. (pp. 50, 124, 614)

Bill of Rights The commonly used term for the first ten amendments to the U.S. Constitution. The Bill of Rights (the last of which was ratified in 1791) guarantees individual liberties and defines limitations to federal power. Many states made the promise of the prompt addition of a bill of rights a precondition for their ratification of the Constitution. (pp. 261, 262, 263, 264)

black nationalism A term linked to several African American movements emphasizing racial pride, separation from whites and white institutions, and black autonomy. Black nationalism gained in popularity with the rise of Marcus Garvey and the Universal Negro Improvement Association (1917–1927) and later with the Black Panther Party, Malcolm X, and other participants of the black power movements of the 1960s. (pp. 762, 946)

bloody shirt A refrain used by Republicans in the late nineteenth century to remind the voting public that the Democratic Party, dominated by the South, was largely responsible for the Civil War and that the Republican Party had led the victory to preserve the Union. Republicans urged their constituents to "vote the way you shot." (pp. 524, 587)

bracero **program** A policy begun during World War II to help with wartime agriculture in which Mexican laborers (*braceros*) were permitted to enter the United States and work for a limited period of time but not to gain citizenship or permanent residence. The program officially ended in 1964. (p. 913)

brinksmanship A cold war practice of appearing willing and able to resort to nuclear war in order to make an enemy back down. Secretary of State John Foster Dulles was the foremost proponent of this policy. (p. 903)

Calvinism The religious doctrine of which the primary tenet is that salvation is predestined by God. Founded by John Calvin of Geneva during the Protestant Reformation, Calvinism required its adherents to live according to a strict religious and moral code. The Puritans who settled in colonial New England were devout Calvinists. (p. 98) *See also* predestination.

capitalism An economic system in which private individuals and corporations own and operate most means of production. Free-market competition—in which supply and demand is minimally regulated by the state or not regulated at all—determines the prices of goods and services. There are three major aspects of capitalism. First, a capitalist system generally includes many workers who do not own what they produce, but instead perform labor for wages. Second, capitalist societies move beyond local trade to the specialized production of goods for large-scale cash markets. Third, people in a capitalist society internalize a social mentality that emphasizes rationality and the pursuit of profit as the primary goal of economic life. In the United States, most regions made the transition to capitalism by the early nineteenth century. Over the following two hundred years, the United States developed an industrial capitalist system, based on new technologies that allowed for self-sustaining economic growth. (pp. 570, 581, 632)

checks and balances A system in which the executive, legislative, and judicial branches of the government curb each other's power. Checks and balances were written into the U.S. Constitution during the Constitutional Convention of 1787. (p. 254)

civil disobedience The public and peaceful violation of certain laws or government orders on the part of individuals or groups who act out of a profound conviction that the law or directive is unjust or immoral and who are prepared to accept the consequences of their actions. Civil disobedience was practiced most famously in U.S. history in the black freedom struggle of the 1960s. (pp. 924, 925)

civil service The administrative service of a government. This term often applies to reforms following the passage of the Pendleton Act in 1883, which set qualifications for U.S. government jobs and sought to remove such jobs from political influence. (pp. 591, 592) *See also* spoils system.

closed shop An establishment in which every employee is required to join a union in order to obtain a job. (p. 752)

cold war The hostile and tense relationship that existed between the Soviet Union on the one hand and the United States and other Western nations on the other from 1947 to 1989. This war was said to be "cold" because the hostility stopped short of armed (hot) conflict, which was warded off by the strategy of nuclear deterrence. (pp. 741, 868, 869) *See also* deterrence.

collective bargaining Negotiation by a group of workers (usually through a union) and their employer concerning rates of pay and working conditions. (pp. 724, 798, 910)

collective security An association of independent nations that agree to accept and implement decisions made by the group, including going to war in defense of one or more members. The United States resolutely avoided such alliances until after World War II, when it created the North Atlantic Treaty Organization (NATO) in response to the threat posed by the Soviet Union. (pp. 753, 873) *See also* North Atlantic Treaty Organization.

colonization The process by which a country or society gains control over another, primarily through settlement. (pp. 343, 344, 388, 475, 476)

Columbian exchange The transatlantic exchange of goods, peoples, and ideas that began when Columbus arrived in the Caribbean in 1492, ending the age-old separation of the hemispheres. (pp. 39, 40, 52, 53, 56)

communism (Communist Party) A system of government and political organization, based on Marxist-Leninist ideals, in which a single authoritarian party controls the economy through state ownership of production, as a means toward reaching the final stage of Marxist theory in which the state dissolves and economic goods are distributed evenly for the common good. Communists around the globe encouraged the spread of communism in other nations in hopes of fomenting worldwide revolution. At its peak in the 1930s, the Communist Party of the United States worked closely with labor unions and insisted that only the overthrow of the capitalist system by its workers could save the victims of the Great Depression. After World War II, the Communist power and aspirations of the Soviet Union were held to be a direct threat to American democracy, prompting the cold war. (pp. 740, 779, 802, 886, 1003, 1004, 1005, 1021) *See also* cold war.

conscription Compulsory military service. Americans were first subject to conscription during the Civil War. The Selective Service Act of 1940 marked the first peacetime use of conscription. (p. 480) *See also* draft.

conservatism A political and moral outlook dating back to Alexander Hamilton's belief in a strong central government resting on a solid banking foundation. Currently associated with the Republican Party, conservatism today places a high premium on military preparedness, free market economics, low taxes, and strong sexual morality. (pp. 511, 517, 528, 586, 1004, 1005, 1006, 1007, 1019, 1021, 1025)

consumer culture (consumerism) A society that places high value on, and devotes substantial resources to, the purchase and display of material goods. Elements of American consumerism were evident in the nineteenth century but really took hold in the twentieth century with installment buying and advertising in the 1920s and again with the postwar prosperity of the 1950s. (pp. 755, 758, 799)

containment The U.S. foreign policy developed after World War II to hold in check the power and influence of the Soviet Union and other groups or nations espousing communism. The strategy was first fully articulated by diplomat George F. Kennan in 1946–1947. (pp. 902, 903, 996, 998)

covenant An agreement or pact; in American history, this refers to a religious agreement. The Pilgrims used this term in the Mayflower Compact to refer to the agreement among themselves to establish a law-abiding community in which all members would work together for the common good. Later, New England Puritans used this term to refer to the agreement they made with God and each other to live according to God's will as revealed through Scripture. (pp. 98, 105) *See also* Halfway Covenant.

cult of domesticity The nineteenth-century belief that women's place was in the home, where they should create a haven for harried men working in the outside world. This ideal was made possible by the separation of the workplace and the home and was used to sentimentalize the home and women's role in it. (pp. 624, 625) *See also* separate spheres.

culture A term used here to connote what is commonly called "way of life." It refers not only to how a group of people supplied themselves with food and shelter but also to their family relationships, social groupings, religious ideas, and other features of their lives. (pp. 3, 13, 14, 16, 139, 298, 482, 572, 574, 586, 587, 915, 1018, 1059, 1064)

de-industrialization A long period of decline in the industrial sector. The term often refers specifically to the decline of manufacturing and the growth of the service sector of the economy in post–World War II America. This shift and the loss of manufacturing resulting from it were caused by more efficient and automated production techniques at home, increased competition from foreign-made goods, and the use of cheap labor abroad by U.S. manufacturers. (p. 1023)

democracy A system of government in which the people have the power to rule, either directly or indirectly, through their elected representatives. Believing that direct democracy was dangerous, the framers of the Constitution created a government that gave direct voice to the people only in the House of Representatives and that placed a check on that voice in the Senate by offering unlimited six-year terms to senators, elected by the state legislatures to protect them from the whims of democratic majorities. The framers further curbed the perceived dangers of democracy by giving each of the three branches of government (legislative, executive, and judicial) the ability to check the power of the other two. (pp. 247, 248, 254, 255, 331, 332, 333, 474, 475, 505, 513, 529, 564, 1068) *See also* checks and balances.

détente French for "loosening." The term refers to the easing of tensions between the United States and the Soviet Union during the Nixon administration. (pp. 990, 1012)

deterrence The linchpin of U.S. military strategy during the cold war. The strategy of deterrence dictated that the United States would maintain a nuclear arsenal so substantial that the Soviet Union would refrain from attacking the United States and its allies out of fear that the United States would retaliate in devastating proportions. The Soviets pursued a similar strategy. (p. 1066)

disfranchisement The denial of suffrage to a group or individual through legal or other means. Beginning in 1890, southern progressives preached the disfranchisement of black voters as a "reform" of the electoral system. The most common means of eliminating black voters were poll taxes and literary tests. (pp. 455, 528, 704, 760, 810, 879)

domino theory The assumption underlying U.S. foreign policy from the early cold war until the end of the Vietnam War. The theory was that if one country fell to communism, neighboring countries also would fall under Communist control. (pp. 870, 904, 996)

doves Peace advocates, particularly during the Vietnam War. (p. 985)

draft (draftee) A system for selecting individuals for compulsory military service. A draftee is an individual selected through this process. (pp. 478, 480, 481, 482, 718, 835) *See also* conscription.

emancipation The act of freeing from slavery or bondage. The emancipation of American slaves, a goal shared by slaves and abolitionists alike, occurred with the passage of the Thirteenth Amendment in 1865. (pp. 343, 344, 388, 475, 476, 477, 485)

English Reformation *See* Reformation.

Enlightenment An eighteenth-century philosophical movement that emphasized the use of reason to reevaluate previously accepted doctrines and traditions. (p. 144)

evangelicalism The trend in Protestant Christianity stressing salvation through conversion, repentance of sin, adherence to Scripture, and the importance of preaching over ritual. During the Second Great Awakening in the 1830s, evangelicals worshiped at camp meetings and religious revivals led by exuberant preachers. (pp. 322, 339, 341, 342) *See also* Second Great Awakening.

fascism An authoritarian system of government characterized by dictatorial rule, disdain for international stability, and a conviction that warfare is the only means by which a nation can attain greatness. Nazi Germany and Mussolini's Italy are the prime examples of fascism. (p. 790)

federal budget deficit The situation resulting when the government spends more money than it takes in. (pp. 1020, 1022)

feminism The belief that men and women have the inherent right to equal social, political, and economic opportunities. The suffrage movement and second-wave feminism of the 1960s and 1970s were the most visible and successful manifestations of feminism, but feminist ideas were expressed in a variety of statements and movements as early as the late eighteenth century and continue to be expressed in the twentyfirst. (pp. 932, 955, 956, 957, 958, 959, 960)

finance capitalism Refers to investment sponsored by banks and bankers and the profits garnered from the sale of financial assets such as stocks and bonds. The decades at the end of the twentieth century are known as a period of finance capitalism because banks and financiers increasingly took on the role of stabilizing markets and reorganizing industries. (p. 581)

franchise The right to vote. The franchise was gradually widened in the United States to include groups such as women and African Americans, who had no vote when the Constitution was ratified. (pp. 310, 516, 652) *See also* suffrage.

free labor Work conducted free from constraint and in accordance with the laborer's personal inclinations and will. Prior to the Civil War, free labor became an ideal championed by Republicans (who were primarily Northerners) to articulate individuals' right to work how and where they wished and to accumulate property in their own name. The ideal of free labor lay at the heart of the North's argument that slavery should not be extended into the western territories. (pp. 364, 365, 388, 397, 398)

free silver The late-nineteenth-century call by silver barons and poor American farmers for the widespread coinage of silver and for silver to be used as a base upon which to expand the paper money supply. The coinage of silver created a more inflationary monetary system that benefited debtors. (pp. 596, 643) *See also* gold standard.

free soil The idea advanced in the 1840s that Congress should prohibit slavery within the western territories. "Free soil, free speech, free labor, and free men" became the rallying cry of the short-lived Free-Soil Party. (pp. 430, 432)

frontier A borderland area. In U.S. history, this refers to the borderland between the areas primarily inhabited by Europeans or their descendants and the areas solely inhabited by Native Americans. (pp. 132, 147, 156, 164, 165)

fundamentalism Strict adherence to core, often religious beliefs. The term has varying meanings for different religious groups. Protestant fundamentalists adhere to a literal interpretation of the Bible and thus deny the possibility of evolution. Muslim fundamentalists believe that traditional Islamic law should govern nations and that Western influences should be banned. (pp. 770, 771, 1006)

gag rule A procedural rule invoked to prohibit discussion or debate on a particular subject in a legislative body. From 1836 to 1844, a series of gag rules prevented the House of Representatives from discussing the large number of antislavery petitions from abolitionist groups that flooded that chamber. (p. 347)

gender gap An electoral phenomenon that became apparent in the 1980s when men and women began to display different preferences in voting. Women tended to favor liberal candidates, and men tended to support conservatives. The key voter groups contributing to the gender gap were single women and women who worked outside the home. (p. 1026)

globalization The spread of political, cultural, and economic influences and connections among countries, businesses, and individuals around the world through trade, immigration, communication, and other means. In the late twentieth century, globalization was intensified by new communications technology that connected individuals, corporations, and nations with greater speed at low prices. This led to an increase in political and economic interdependence and mutual influence among nations. (pp. 1054, 1056)

gold standard A monetary system in which any circulating currency was exchangeable for a specific amount of gold. Advocates for the gold standard believed that gold alone should be used for coinage and that the total value of paper banknotes should never exceed the government's supply of gold. The triumph of gold standard supporter William McKinley in the 1896 presidential election was a big victory for supporters of this policy. (pp. 597, 641) *See also* free silver.

gospel of wealth The idea that wealth garnered from earthly success should be used for good works. Andrew Carnegie promoted this view in an 1889 essay in which he maintained that the wealthy should serve as stewards and act in the best interests of society as a whole. (pp. 585, 678)

government bonds Promissory notes issued by a government in order to borrow money from members of the public. Such bonds are redeemable at a set future date. Bondholders earn interest on their investments. (p. 351)

Great Awakening The widespread movement of religious revitalization in the 1730s and 1740s that emphasized vital religious faith and personal choice. It was characterized by large, open-air meetings at which emotional sermons were given by itinerant preachers. (p. 145)

Great Society President Lyndon Johnson's domestic program, which included civil rights legislation, antipoverty programs, government subsidy of medical care, federal aid to education, consumer protection, and aid to the arts and humanities. (pp. 932, 933, 935)

gross domestic product (GDP) A measure of economic production. GDP is the value of all the goods and services produced within a country during a year, regardless of the nationality of the owners of those goods and services. (p. 816)

gross national product (GNP) A measure of economic production. GNP is the value of all the goods and services produced by a country's citizens, regardless of where production takes place. (p. 915)

guerrilla warfare Fighting carried out by an irregular military force usually organized into small, highly mobile groups. Guerrilla combat was common in the Vietnam War and during the American Revolution. Guerrilla warfare is often effective against opponents who have greater material resources. (pp. 192, 445, 464, 471, 516, 663, 904, 977)

Halfway Covenant A Puritan compromise that allowed the unconverted children of the "visible saints" to become "halfway" members of the church and to baptize their own children even though they were not full members of the church themselves because they had not experienced full conversion. Massachusetts ministers accepted this compromise in 1662, but the compromise remained controversial throughout the seventeenth century. (p. 105)

hard currency (hard money) Money coined directly from, or backed in full by, precious metals (particularly gold). (p. 266)

hawks Advocates of aggressive military action or all-out war, particularly during the Vietnam War. (p. 985) *See also* War Hawks.

holding company A system of business organization whereby competing companies are combined under one central administration in order to curb competition and ensure profit. Pioneered in the late 1880s by John D. Rockefeller, holding companies, such as Standard Oil, exercised monopoly control even as the government threatened to outlaw trusts as a violation of free trade. (p. 577) *See also* monopoly; trust.

horizontal integration A system in which a single person or corporation creates several subsidiary businesses to sell a product in different markets. John D. Rockefeller pioneered the use of horizontal integration in the 1880s to control the refining process, giving him a virtual monopoly on the oil-refining business. (p. 577) *See also* vertical integration; monopoly.

impeachment The process by which formal charges of wrongdoing are brought against a president, a governor, or a federal judge. (pp. 514, 1011, 1053)

imperialism The system by which great powers gain control of overseas territories. The United States became an imperialist power by gaining control of Puerto Rico, Guam, the Philippines, and Cuba as a result of the Spanish-American War. (pp. 525, 537, 543, 544, 545, 667, 668, 669)

indentured servitude A system that committed poor immigrants to four to seven years of labor in exchange for passage to the colonies and food and shelter after they arrived. An indenture is a type of contract. (pp. 71, 73)

iron curtain A metaphor coined by Winston Churchill during his commencement address at Westminster College in Fulton, Missouri, in 1946, to refer to the political, ideological, and military barriers that separated Soviet-controlled Eastern Europe from the rest of Europe and the West following World War II. (pp. 866, 867, 868, 869)

isolationism A foreign policy perspective characterized by a desire to have the United States withdraw from the conflicts of the world and enjoy the protection of two vast oceans. (pp. 658, 753, 825, 826, 873)

Jim Crow The system of racial segregation that developed in the post–Civil War South and extended well into the twentieth century; it replaced slavery as the chief instrument of white supremacy. Jim Crow laws segregated African Americans in public facilities such as trains and streetcars and denied them basic civil rights, including the right to vote. It was also at this time that the doctrine of "separate but equal" became institutionalized. (pp. 519, 588, 704, 705)

Keynesian economics A theory developed by economist John Maynard Keynes that guided U.S. economic policy from the New Deal to the 1970s. According to Keynesians, the federal government has a duty to stimulate and manage the economy by spending money on public works projects and by making general tax cuts in order to put more money into the hands of ordinary people, thus creating demand. (p. 814)

laissez-faire The doctrine, based on economic theory, that government should not interfere in business or the economy. Laissez-faire ideas guided American government policy in the late nineteenth century and conservative politics in the twentieth century. Business interests that supported laissez-faire in the late nineteenth century accepted government interference when it took the form of tariffs or subsidies that worked to their benefit. A broader use of the term refers to the simple philosophy of abstaining from interference. (pp. 585, 586, 640, 654, 674, 788, 789)

land grant A gift of land from a government, usually intended to encourage settlement or development. The British government issued several land grants to encourage development in the American colonies. In the mid-nineteenth century, the U.S. government issued land grants to encourage railroad development and, through the passage of the Land-Grant College Act (also known as the Morrill Act) in 1862, set aside public land to support universities. (pp. 209, 363, 552, 556, 560, 571, 573)

liberalism The political doctrine that government rests on the consent of the governed and is duty-bound to protect the freedom and property of the individual. In the twentieth century, liberalism became associated with the idea that government should regulate the economy and ensure the material well-being and individual rights of all people. (pp. 690, 676, 674, 932, 933, 936, 938, 940, 1013)

liberty The condition of being free or enjoying freedom from control. This term also refers to the possession of certain social, political, or economic rights, such as the right to own and control property. Eighteenth-century American colonists invoked the principle to argue for strict limitations on government's ability to tax its subjects. (pp. 158, 170, 171, 172, 173, 174, 264, 378, 434, 452)

manifest destiny A term coined by journalist John O'Sullivan in 1845 to express the popular nineteenth-century belief that the United States was destined to expand westward to the Pacific Ocean and had an irrefutable right and God-given responsibility to do so. This idea provided an ideological shield for westward expansion and masked the economic and political motivations of many of those who championed it. (pp. 370, 382, 537)

McCarthyism The practice of searching out suspected Communists and others outside mainstream American society, discrediting them, and hounding them from government and other employment. The term derives from Senator Joseph McCarthy, who gained notoriety for leading such repressive activities from 1950 to 1954. (p. 885)

mercantilism A set of policies that regulated colonial commerce and manufacturing for the enrichment of the mother country. Mercantilist policies ensured that the American colonies in the mid-seventeenth century produced agricultural goods and raw materials to be shipped to Britain, where they would increase wealth in the mother country through reexportation or manufacture into finished goods that would then be sold to the colonies and elsewhere. (p. 77)

Middle Passage The crossing of the Atlantic (as a slave destined for auction) in the hold of a slave ship in the eighteenth and nineteenth centuries. Conditions were unimaginably bad, and many slaves died during these voyages. (p. 124)

military-industrial complex A term first used by President Dwight D. Eisenhower to refer to the aggregate power and influence of the armed forces in conjunction with the aerospace, munitions, and other industries that produced supplies for the military in the post–World War II era. (p. 908)

miscegenation The sexual mixing of races. In slave states, despite the social stigma and legal restrictions on interracial sex, masters' almost unlimited power over their female slaves meant that liaisons inevitably occurred. Many states maintained laws against miscegenation into the 1950s. (pp. 397, 400, 588)

monopoly Exclusive control and domination by a single business entity over an entire industry through ownership, command of supply, or other means. Gilded Age businesses monopolized their industries quite profitably, often organizing holding companies and trusts to do so. (pp. 568, 571, 577, 581, 583, 596) *See also* holding company; trust.

Monroe Doctrine President James Monroe's 1823 declaration that the Western Hemisphere was closed to any further colonization or interference by European powers. In exchange, Monroe pledged that the United States would not become involved in European struggles. Although Monroe could not back his policy with action, it was an important formulation of national goals. (pp. 313, 314, 316)

nationalism A strong feeling of devotion and loyalty toward one nation over others. Nationalism encourages the promotion of the nation's common culture, language, and customs. (pp. 947, 972, 973)

nativism Bias against immigrants and in favor of native-born inhabitants. American nativists especially favor persons who come from white, Anglo-Saxon, Protestant lines over those from other racial, ethnic, and religious heritages. Nativists may include former immigrants who view new immigrants as incapable of assimilation. Many nativists, such as members of the Know-Nothing Party in the nineteenth century and the Ku Klux Klan through the contemporary period, voice anti-immigrant, anti-Catholic, and anti-Semitic sentiments. (pp. 439, 680)

Navigation Acts British acts of 1650, 1651, and 1660 that, together with a 1663 law (the Staple Act), set forth three fundamental regulations governing colonial trade. First, all colonial goods imported into England had to be transported on English ships using primarily English crews. Second, specific colonial products could be shipped only to England or to other English colonies. Third, all goods imported into the colonies had to pass through England. The 1660 Navigation Act assessed an explicit import tax of two pence on every pound of colonial tobacco; these tobacco taxes yielded about a quarter of all English customs revenues in the 1660s. The Navigation Acts fueled tension between the colonies and the monarchy in the century leading up to the Revolutionary War (1775–1783). (pp. 77, 112, 168)

New Deal The group of social and economic programs that President Franklin Roosevelt developed to provide relief for the needy, speed economic recovery, and reform economic and government institutions. The New Deal was a massive effort to bring the United States out of the Great Depression and ensure its future prosperity. (pp. 786, 790, 791, 792, 795, 801, 809, 810)

New Right Politically active religious conservatives who became particularly vocal in the 1980s. The New Right criticized feminism, opposed abortion and homosexuality, and promoted "family values" and military preparedness. (p. 1012)

New South A vision of the South, promoted after the Civil War by Henry Grady, editor of the *Atlanta Constitution*, that urged the South to abandon its dependence on agriculture and use its cheap labor and natural resources to compete with northern industry. Many Southerners migrated from farms to cities in the late nineteenth century, and Northerners and foreigners invested a significant amount of capital in railroads, cotton and textiles, mining, lumber, iron, steel, and tobacco in the region. (pp. 587–588)

North Atlantic Treaty Organization (NATO) North Atlantic Treaty Organization (NATO) A post–World War II alliance that joined the United States, Canada, and Western European nations into a military coalition designed to counter the Soviet Union's efforts to expand. Each NATO member pledged to go to war if any member was attacked. Since the end of the cold war, NATO has been expanding to include the formerly Communist countries of Eastern Europe. (pp. 864, 867, 1046)

nullification The idea that states can disregard federal laws when those laws represent an overstepping of congressional powers. The controversial idea was first proposed by opponents of the Alien and Sedition Acts of 1798 and later by South Carolina politicians in 1828 as a response to the Tariff of Abominations. (pp. 337, 432)

oligopoly A competitive system in which several large corporations dominate an industry by dividing the market so each business has a share of it. More prevalent than outright monopolies during the late 1800s, the oligopolies of the Gilded Age successfully muted competition and benefited the corporations that participated in this type of arrangement. (pp. 550, 583)

paternalism The idea that slavery was a set of reciprocal obligations between masters and slaves, with slaves providing labor and obedience and masters providing basic care and direction. The concept of paternalism denied that the slave system was brutal and exploitative. Although paternalism did provide some protection against the worst brutality, it did not guarantee decent living conditions, reasonable work, or freedom from physical punishment. (p. 404–406)

planters Owners of large farms (or, more specifically, plantations) that were worked by twenty or more slaves. By 1860, planters had accrued a great deal of local, statewide, and national political power in the South despite the fact that they represented a minority of the white electorate. Planters' dominance of southern politics demonstrated both the power of tradition and stability among southern voters and the planters' success at convincing white voters that the slave system benefited all whites, even those without slaves. (pp. 400, 404, 407, 408, 409, 416, 421–422, 482)

plutocracy A society ruled by the richest members. The excesses of the Gilded Age and the fact that just 1 percent of the population owned more than half the real and personal property in the country led many to question whether the United States was indeed a plutocracy. (p. 614)

pogrom An organized and often officially encouraged massacre of an ethnic minority; usually used in reference to attacks on Jews. (p. 608)

popular sovereignty The idea that government is subject to the will of the people. Before the Civil War, this was the idea that the residents of a territory should determine, through their legislatures, whether to allow slavery. (pp. 438, 444, 430–431)

Populism A political movement that led to the creation of the People's Party, primarily comprising southern and western farmers who railed against big business and advocated business and economic reforms, including government ownership of the railroads. The movement peaked in the late nineteenth century. The Populist ticket won more than 1 million votes in the presidential election of 1892 and 1.5 million in the congressional elections of 1894. The term *populism* has come to mean any political movement that advocates on behalf of the common person, particularly for government intervention against big business. (pp. 656, 657, 659)

predestination The idea that individual salvation or damnation is determined by God at, or just prior to, a person's birth. The concept of predestination invalidated the idea that salvation could be obtained through either faith or good works. (p. 98) *See also* Calvinism.

progressivism (progressive movement) A wide-ranging twentieth-century reform movement that advocated government activism to mitigate the problems created by urban industrialism. Progressivism reached its peak in 1912 with the creation of the Progressive Party, which ran Theodore Roosevelt for president. The term *progressivism* has come to mean any general effort advocating for social welfare programs. (pp. 614, 640, 643, 1072)

Protestantism A powerful Christian reform movement that began in the sixteenth century with Martin Luther's critiques of the Roman Catholic Church. Over the centuries, Protestantism has taken many different forms, branching into numerous denominations with differing systems of worship. (pp. 54–56, 86, 93, 94, 339, 347, 439, 587)

Protestant Reformation *See* Reformation.

Puritanism The ideas and religious principles held by dissenters from the Church of England, including the belief that the church needed to be purified by eliminating the elements of Catholicism from its practices. (pp. 91–92, 93–97, 101)

Reformation The reform movement that began in 1517 with Martin Luther's critiques of the Roman Catholic Church, which led to the formation of Protestant Christian groups. The English Reformation began with Henry VIII's break with the Roman Catholic Church, which established the Protestant Church of England. Henry VIII's decision was politically motivated; he had no particular quarrel with Catholic theology and remained an orthodox Catholic in most matters of religious practice. (pp. 430–431, 437)

reform Darwinism A social theory, based on Charles Darwin's theory of evolution, that emphasized activism, arguing that humans could speed up evolution by altering the environment. A challenge to social Darwinism, reform Darwinism condemned laissez-faire and demanded that the government take a more active approach to solving social problems. It became the ideological basis for progressive reform in the late nineteenth and early twentieth centuries. (p. 683) *See also* laissez-faire; social Darwinism.

republicanism The belief that the unworkable model of European-style monarchy should be replaced with a form of government in which supreme power resides in the hands of citizens with the right to vote and is exercised by a representative government answerable to this electorate. In Revolutionary-era America, republicanism became a social philosophy that embodied a sense of community and called individuals to act for the public good. (pp. 232, 247–248, 899–900)

scientific management A system of organizing work, developed by Frederick Winslow Taylor in the late nineteenth century, to increase efficiency and productivity by breaking tasks into their component parts and training workers to perform specific parts. Labor resisted this effort because it de-skilled workers and led to the speedup of production lines. Taylor's ideas were most popular at the height of the Progressive Era. (p. 683)

Second Great Awakening A popular religious revival that preached that salvation was available to anybody who chose to take it. The revival peaked in the 1830s, and its focus on social perfection inspired many of the reform movements of the Jacksonian era. (p. 339) *See also* evangelicalism.

separate spheres A concept of gender relations that developed in the Jacksonian era and continued well into the twentieth century, holding that women's proper place was in the world of hearth and home (the private sphere) and men's was in the world of commerce and politics (the public sphere). The doctrine of separate spheres eroded slowly over the nineteenth and twentieth centuries as women became more and more involved in public activities. (pp. 339–340, 588, 761) *See also* cult of domesticity.

social Darwinism A social theory, based on Charles Darwin's theory of evolution, that argued that all progress in human society came as the result of competition and natural selection. Gilded Age proponents such as William Graham Sumner and Herbert Spencer claimed that reform was useless because the rich and poor were precisely where nature intended them to be and intervention would retard the progress of humanity. (pp. 583–586, 686) *See also* reform Darwinism.

social gospel movement A religious movement in the late nineteenth and early twentieth centuries founded on the idea that Christians have a responsibility to reform society as well as individuals. Social gospel adherents encouraged people to put

G-9 GLOSSARY OF HISTORICAL VOCABULARY

Christ's teachings to work in their daily lives by actively promoting social justice. (pp. 677, 678–679)

socialism A governing system in which the state owns and operates the largest and most important parts of the economy. (pp. 351, 611, 622, 643, 779, 802)

social purity movement A movement to end prostitution and eradicate venereal disease, often accompanied by the censorship of materials deemed "obscene." (p. 677)

spoils system An arrangement in which party leaders reward party loyalists with government jobs. This slang term for *patronage* comes from the saying "To the victor go the spoils." Widespread government corruption during the Gilded Age spurred reformers to curb the spoils system through the passage of the Pendleton Act in 1883, which created the Civil Service Commission to award government jobs on the basis of merit. (pp. 333, 525, 586) *See also* civil service.

state sovereignty A state's autonomy or freedom from external control. The federal system adopted at the Constitutional Convention in 1787 struck a balance between state sovereignty and national control by creating a strong central government while leaving the states intact as political entities. The states remained in possession of many important powers on which the federal government cannot intrude. (p. 467)

states' rights A strict interpretation of the Constitution that holds that federal power over the states is limited and that the states hold ultimate sovereignty. First expressed in 1798 through the passage of the Virginia and Kentucky Resolutions, which were based on the assumption that the states have the right to judge the constitutionality of federal laws, the states' rights philosophy became a cornerstone of the South's resistance to federal control of slavery. (pp. 337, 480–481, 507, 508, 699)

strict constructionism An approach to constitutional law that attempts to adhere to the original intent of the writers of the Constitution. Strict construction often produces Supreme Court decisions that defer to the legislative branch and to the states and restrict the power of the federal government. Opponents of strict construction argue that the Constitution is an organic document that must be interpreted to meet conditions unimagined when it was written. (p. 1008)

suffrage The right to vote. The term *suffrage* is most often associated with the efforts of American women to secure voting rights. (pp. 233, 311–312, 443, 500, 554, 683, 703–704, 760) *See also* franchise.

Sun Belt The southern and southwestern regions of the United States, which grew tremendously in industry, population, and influence after World War II. (pp. 909, 912–915)

supply-side economics An economic theory based on the premise that tax cuts for the wealthy and for corporations encourage investment and production (supply), which in turn stimulate consumption. Embraced by the Reagan administration and other conservative Republicans, this theory reversed Keynesian economic policy, which assumes that the way to stimulate the economy is to create demand through federal spending on public works and general tax cuts that put more money into the hands of ordinary people. (p. 1021) *See also* Keynesian economics.

temperance movement The reform movement to end drunkenness by urging people to abstain from the consumption of alcohol. Begun in the 1820s, this movement achieved its greatest political victory with the passage of a constitutional amendment in 1919 that prohibited the manufacture, sale, and transportation of alcohol. That amendment was repealed in 1933. (pp. 589–590, 652–653)

third world Originally a cold war term linked to decolonization, *third world* was first used in the late 1950s to describe newly independent countries in Africa and Asia that were not aligned with either Communist nations (the second world) or non-Communist nations (the first world). Later, the term was applied to all poor, nonindustrialized countries, in Latin America as well as in Africa and Asia. Many international experts see *third world* as a problematic category when applied to such a large and disparate group of nations, and they criticize the discriminatory hierarchy suggested by the term. (pp. 605, 606, 874)

trickle-down economics The theory that financial benefits and incentives given to big businesses in the top tier of the economy will flow down to smaller businesses and individuals and thus benefit the entire nation. President Herbert Hoover unsuccessfully used the trickle-down strategy in his attempt to pull the nation out of the Great Depression, stimulating the economy through government investment in large economic enterprises and public works such as construction of the Hoover Dam. In the late twentieth century, conservatives used this economic theory to justify large tax cuts and other financial benefits for corporations and the wealthy. (pp. 775, 1024)

Truman Doctrine President Harry S. Truman's assertion that American security depended on stopping any Communist government from taking over any non-Communist government—even nondemocratic and repressive dictatorships—anywhere in the world. Beginning in 1947 with American aid to help Greece and Turkey stave off Communist pressures, this approach became a cornerstone of American foreign policy during the cold war. (p. 870)

trust A corporate system in which corporations give shares of their stock to trustees, who coordinate the industry to ensure profits to the participating corporations and curb competition. Pioneered by Standard Oil, such business practices were deemed unfair, were moderated by the Sherman Antitrust Act (1890), and were finally abolished by the combined efforts of Presidents Theodore Roosevelt and William Howard Taft and the sponsors of the 1914 Clayton Antitrust Act. The term *trust* is also loosely applied to all large business combinations. (pp. 568, 577, 595) *See also* holding company.

vertical integration   A system in which a single person or corporation controls all processes of an industry from start to finished product. Andrew Carnegie first used vertical integration in the 1870s, controlling every aspect of steel production from the mining of iron ore to the manufacturing of the final product, thereby maximizing profits by eliminating the use of outside suppliers or services. (p. 576)

virtual representation   The notion, propounded by the British Parliament in the eighteenth century, that the House of Commons represented all British subjects—wherever they lived and regardless of whether they had directly voted for their representatives. Prime Minister George Grenville used this idea to argue that the Stamp Act and other parliamentary taxes on British colonists did not constitute taxation without representation. The American colonists rejected this argument, insisting that political representatives derived authority only from explicit citizens' consent (indicated by elections), and that members of a distant government body were incapable of adequately representing their interests. (p. 169)

War Hawks   Young Republicans elected to the U.S. Congress in the fall of 1810 who were eager for war with Britain in order to legitimize attacks on Indians, end impressment, and avenge foreign insults. (p. 303) *See also* hawks.

welfare capitalism   The idea that a capitalistic, industrial society can operate benevolently to improve the lives of workers. The notion of welfare capitalism became popular in the 1920s as industries extended the benefits of scientific management to improve safety and sanitation in the workplace as well as institute paid vacations and pension plans. (p. 754) *See also* scientific management.

welfare state   A nation or state in which the government assumes responsibility for some or all of the individual and social welfare of its citizens. Welfare states commonly provide education, health care, food programs for the poor, unemployment compensation, and other social benefits. The United States dramatically expanded its role as a welfare state with the provisions of the New Deal in the 1930s. (pp. 804–812)

Yankee imperialism   A cry raised in Latin American countries against the United States when it intervened militarily in the region without invitation or consent from those countries. (p. 1041)

yeoman   A farmer who owned a small plot of land that was sufficient to support a family and was tilled by family members and perhaps a few servants. (pp. 77, 140, 415–416, 421–422, 481–482, 518, 527–528)

Spot Artifact Credits

p. 5 (Anasazi figurine) © Jerry Jacka. 2006; p. 16 (Chaco figurine) Chaco Culture National Historic Park, Photo Archives, Image #CHCU 31104; p. 20 (mica hand) Ohio Historical Society; p. 23 (dolls) Collection of the Oakland Museum of California, Gift of Frank K. Mott and Herbert Avery; p. 34 (astrolabe) © National Maritime Museum, London; p. 41 (knife) © Michael Zabe/AZA; p. 43 (toucan) Werner Forman/Art Resource, NY; p. 49 (crucifix) Florida Museum of Natural History, Fort Mose Exhibition; p. 65 (pot) Archives, Virginia Department of Historic Resources, Richmond. Photograph by Katherine Wetzel; p. 68 (tobacco flower) The Granger Collection, NYC; p. 76 (pipe) Niemeyer Nederlands Tabacologisch Museum; p. 77 (sixpence) Courtesy of Preservation Virginia; p. 100 (bone dice) Courtesy of Preservation Virginia; p. 104 (barrel) Peabody Essex Museum, Salem, MA; p. 105 (cradle) WADSWORTH ATHENAEUM, HARTFORD. Wallace Nutting Collection Gift of J. Pierpont Morgan; p. 114 (dagger) ©Pocumtuck Vallery Memorial Association Memorial Association, Deerfield, MA; p. 127 (pitcher) ©Pocumtuck Vallery Memorial Association Memorial Association, Deerfield, MA; p. 130 (weathercock) Schoharie County Historical Society, Old Stone Fort Museum; p. 135 (*Poor Richard's Almanack*) Courtesy, American Antiquarian Society; p. 139 (doll) The Stagville Center, Division of Archives and History, North Carolina Department of Cultural Resources; p. 142 (mirror) Photograph courtesy of the Concord Museum, Concord, MA; p. 168 (tankard) Bequest from collection of Dr. Joseph H. Kler; 1986; 1986.27.91; Negative number: 71-17851-53; Social History Division; National Museum of American History, Smithsonian Institution; p. 169 (stamps) Courtesy of the Trustees of the British Library; p. 174 (teapot) Peabody Essex Museum, Salem, MA; p. 202 (coat) Nichipor Collection/Picture Research Consultants & Archives; p. 210 (currency) Smithsonian Institution, Washington, D.C., Photo by Douglas Mudd; p. 233 (voting box) Independence National Historic Park; p. 238 (penny note) Library of Congress; p. 248 (inkwell) Independence National Historic Park; p. 261 (button) © Collection of the New-York Historical Society, Gift of William L. Calver; p. 266 (cotton bales) Picture Research Consultants & Archives; p. 268 (coin) The American Numismatic Society; p. 275 (shoes) Joël Garnier/Musée International de la Chaussure, Roman-sur-Isere-France; p. 296 (compass) National Museum of American History, Smithsonian Institution, Behring Center; p. 299 (headdress) National Museum of American Indian, Smithsonian Institution (2/1294) Photos by Photo Services; p. 304 (medal) © Collection of the New-York Historical Society; p. 351 (miniature log cabin) Smithsonian Institution, National Museum of American History, Behring Center; p. 359 (plow) Courtesy Deere & Company; p. 368 (sheet music) Special Collections, Milton S. Eisenhower Library, The Johns Hopkins University; p. 376 (flag) The Center for American History, The University of Texas at Austin; p. 405 (shoe) Archaeological Society of Virginia; p. 412 (whip) Louisiana State Museum; p. 418 (fiddle) National Museum of American History, Smithsonian Institution, Washington, D.C.; p. 431 (ticket) Courtesy, American Antiquarian Society; p. 434 (token) © Collection of the New-York Historical Society; p. 453 (revolver) Ohio Historical Society; p. 466 (Confederate flag) Smithsonian Institution, National Museum of American History, Behring Center; p. 468 (Confederate jacket) National Museum of American History, Smithsonian Institution, Behring Center; p. 472 (Union jacket) Chicago Historical Society; p. 501 (top hat) National Museum of American History, Smithsonian Institution, Behring Center; p. 514 (impeachment ticket) Collection of Janice L. and David J. Frent; p. 521 (plow) National Museum of American History, Smithsonian Institution, Behring Center; p. 524 (election artifact) Collection of Janice L. and David J. Frent; p. 546 (shirt) Image courtesy of National Park Service, Nez Perce National Historical Park. Catalogue #BIHO1256; p. 547 (moccasins) Photo Addison Doty, Santa Fe, NM; p. 549 (silver bar) Collection of the Oakland Museum of California, Museum Purchase; p. 560 (spurs) Courtesy of the High Desert Museum, Bend, Oregon, catalog number 0564AN.04; p. 573 (stock ticker) Collection of John D. Jenkins, www.sparkmanmuseum.com; p. 577 (kerosene lamp) Picture Research Consultants & Archives; p. 587 (cigarette box) Courtesy, Duke Homestead and Tobacco Museum; p. 616 (sewing machine) Smithsonian Institution, National Museum of American History, Behring Center; p. 625 (baseball glove with ball) Smithsonian Institution, National Museum of American History, Behring Center; p. 627 (faucet) Picture Research Consultants & Archives; p. 645 (dagger) Library & Archives Division, Historical Society of Western Pennsylvania; p. 656 (button) Collection of Janice L. and David J. Frent; p. 661 (magazine cover) The Granger Collection, NYC; p. 684 (token) The Western Reserve Historical Society, Cleveland, Ohio; p. 702 (button) Collection of Janice L. and David J. Frent; p. 715 (helmet) Collection of Colonel Stuart S. Corning, Jr. /Picture Research Consultants, Inc.; p. 724 (poster) Herbert Hoover

A NOTE ABOUT THE INDEX:

Names of individuals appear in boldface.

Letters in parentheses following pages refer to:
(i)   illustrations, including photographs and artifacts
(f)   figures, including charts and graphs
(m)   maps
(b)   boxed features (such as "Historical Question")
(t)   tables

ATLAS OF THE TERRITORIAL GROWTH OF THE UNITED STATES

Lake Superior

Lake Michigan

Lake Huron

Lake Ontario

Lake Erie

St. Lawrence R.

N.H.

MASS.

NEW YORK

RHODE ISLAND

CONNECTICUT

Connecticut R.

Hudson R.

PENN.

Delaware R.

Susquehanna R.

NEW JERSEY

DELAWARE

MARYLAND

Potomac R.

Chesapeake Bay

THE ORIGINAL THIRTEEN COLONIES

Proclamation Line of 1763

James R.

VIRGINIA

Ohio R.

NORTH CAROLINA

Cumberland R.

Cape Fear R.

Tennessee R.

ATLANTIC OCEAN

Arkansas R.

SOUTH CAROLINA

Missouri R.

Mississippi R.

Savannah R.

GEORGIA

THE ORIGINAL THIRTEEN COLONIES IN 1776

0   150   300 miles
0   150   300 kilometers

Gulf of Mexico

M-2

Lake Superior

Lake Michigan

Lake Huron

Lake Ontario

Lake Erie

St. Lawrence R.

Missouri R.

Ohio R.

**Gained by treaty
with Britain, 1783**

Cumberland R.

Tennessee R.

Arkansas R.

Mississippi R.

Proclamation Line of 1763

THE ORIGINAL THIRTEEN COLONIES

NEW YORK

N.H.

MASS.

RHODE
ISLAND

CONNECTICUT

Connecticut R.

Hudson R.

PENN.

Delaware R.

Susquehanna R.

NEW JERSEY

DELAWARE

MARYLAND

Potomac R.

*Chesapeake
Bay*

James R.

VIRGINIA

NORTH
CAROLINA

Cape Fear R.

SOUTH
CAROLINA

Savannah R.

GEORGIA

*ATLANTIC
OCEAN*

Gulf of Mexico

**THE UNITED STATES
IN 1783**

| 0 | 150 | 300 miles |
| 0 | 150 | 300 kilometers |

M-3

Area ceded by the United States to Great Britain, 1818

Area ceded by Great Britain, 1818

Columbia R.

Missouri R.

Snake R.

LOUISIANA PURCHASE from France, 1803

N. Platte R.

Platte R.

S. Platte R.

Sacramento R.

San Joaquin R.

Colorado R.

Red R.

PACIFIC OCEAN

Rio Grande

Lake Superior

(MICHIGAN TERRITORY)

Lake Huron

Lake Michigan

Lake Ontario

Lake Erie

Missouri R.

ILLINOIS
(1818)

INDIANA
(1816)

OHIO
(1803)

Ohio R.

KENTUCKY
(1792)

**Gained by treaty
with Britain, 1783**

Cumberland R.

Tennessee R.

TENNESSEE
(1796)

MISSISSIPPI
(1817)

ALABAMA
(1819)

LOUISIANA
(1812)

Mississippi R.

**Areas taken from Spain
in 1810, 1813**

Gulf of Mexico

St. Lawrence R.

Maine
(part of Mass.)

VERMONT
(1791)

N.H.
(1788)

MASS.
(1788)

NEW YORK
(1788)

Connecticut R.

Hudson R.

RHODE
ISLAND
(1790)

CONNECTICUT
(1788)

PENN.
(1787)

Susquehanna R.

NEW JERSEY
(1787)

Delaware R.

DELAWARE
(1787)

MARYLAND
(1788)

*Chesapeake
Bay*

Potomac R.

James R.

VIRGINIA
(1788)

THE ORIGINAL THIRTEEN COLONIES

Proclamation Line of 1763

NORTH
CAROLINA
(1789)

Cape Fear R.

SOUTH
CAROLINA
(1788)

Savannah R.

GEORGIA
(1788)

*ATLANTIC
OCEAN*

THE UNITED STATES
IN 1819

| 0 | 150 | 300 miles |

| 0 | 150 | 300 kilometers |

FLORIDA
**Treaty with Spain,
1819**

(1789) Date of statehood

M-5

Area ceded by
Great Britain,
1818

Area ceded by
the United States
to Great Britain, 1818

Columbia R.

OREGON COUNTRY
Agreement with Britain,
1846

(OREGON TERRITORY)

Snake R.

Missouri R.

LOUISIANA
PURCHASE
from France, 1803

N. Platte R.

Sacramento R.

(UTAH TERRITORY)

MEXICAN CESSION,
1848

Colorado R.

S. Platte R.

Platte R.

San Joaquin R.

CALIFORNIA
(1850)

(NEW MEXICO TERRITORY)

(Claim waived by
Texas, 1850)

Red R.

TEXAS
Annexed, 1845

PACIFIC
OCEAN

GADSDEN PURCHASE
from Mexico, 1853

TEXAS
(1845)

Rio Grande

Areas ceded by Britain, 1842
(Webster-Ashburton Treaty)

St. Lawrence R.

MAINE
(1820)

VERMONT
(1791)

Lake Superior

N.H.
(1788)

Lake Huron

Lake Ontario

NEW YORK
(1788)

Hudson R.

MASS.
(1788)

RHODE
ISLAND
(1790)

CONNECTICUT
(1788)

Connecticut R.

Lake Michigan

Lake Erie

WISCONSIN
(1848)

MICHIGAN
(1837)

PENN.
(1787)

Delaware R.

NEW JERSEY
(1787)

(MINNESOTA
TERRITORY)

OHIO
(1803)

Susquehanna R.

DELAWARE
(1787)

IOWA
(1846)

INDIANA
(1816)

Potomac R.

MARYLAND
(1788)

*Chesapeake
Bay*

ILLINOIS
(1818)

Missouri R.

Ohio R.

KENTUCKY
(1792)

VIRGINIA
(1788)

James R.

THE ORIGINAL THIRTEEN COLONIES

Proclamation Line of 1763

Gained by treaty
with Britain, 1783

MISSOURI
(1821)

NORTH
CAROLINA
(1789)

Cape Fear R.

Cumberland R.

Tennessee R.

ARKANSAS
(1836)

TENNESSEE
(1796)

ATLANTIC
OCEAN

(INDIAN
TERRITORY)

SOUTH
CAROLINA
(1788)

Savannah R.

Mississippi R.

MISSISSIPPI
(1817)

ALABAMA
(1819)

GEORGIA
(1788)

**THE UNITED STATES
IN 1853**

LOUISIANA
(1812)

0   150   300 miles

0   150   300 kilometers

Areas taken from Spain
in 1810, 1813

FLORIDA
(1845)

FLORIDA
Treaty with Spain,
1819

Gulf of Mexico

(1789) Date of statehood

Area ceded by the United States to Great Britain, 1818

Area ceded by Great Britain, 1818

WASHINGTON (1889)
★ Olympia

Missouri R.

★ Helena
MONTANA (1889)

NORTH DAKOTA (1889)
★ Bismarck

Columbia R.

★ Salem

OREGON COUNTRY
Agreement with Britain, 1846

OREGON (1859)

IDAHO (1890)
★ Boise

Snake R.

SOUTH DAKOTA (1889)
★ Pierre

WYOMING (1890)

L O U I S I A N A
P U R C H A S E
from France, 1803

NEBRASKA (1867)

N. Platte R.

★ Salt Lake City

Sacramento R.

★ Carson City
★ Sacramento

NEVADA (1864)

UTAH (1896)

Cheyenne ★

S. Platte R.

Platte R.

★ Denver
COLORADO (1876)

KANSAS (1861)

San Joaquin R.

MEXICAN CESSION
1848

Colorado R.

CALIFORNIA (1850)

ARIZONA (1912)

★ Phoenix

★ Santa Fe

NEW MEXICO (1912)

TEXAS
Annexed, 1845

Red R.

PACIFIC OCEAN

TEXAS (1845)

GADSDEN PURCHASE
from Mexico, 1853

Rio Grande

ARCTIC OCEAN

RUSSIA

ALASKA (1959)
Purchased from Russia, 1867

CANADA

Yukon R.

Bering Sea

Gulf of Alaska

★ Juneau

| 0 | 250 | 500 miles |
| 0 | 250 | 500 kilometers |

HAWAII (1959)
Annexed, 1898

★ Honolulu

PACIFIC OCEAN

| 0 | 50 | 100 miles |
| 0 | 50 | 100 kilometers |

M E X I C O

M-8

Areas ceded by Britain, 1842 (Webster-Ashburton Treaty)

CANADA

St. Lawrence R.

Lake Superior

Lake Huron

Lake Michigan

Lake Ontario

Lake Erie

MAINE (1820)

★ Augusta

VERMONT (1791)

Montpelier ★

Concord ★ N.H. (1788)

NEW YORK (1788)

Albany ★

Hudson R.

Connecticut R.

MASS. (1788)

★ Boston

Hartford ★

★ Providence

RHODE ISLAND (1790)

CONNECTICUT (1788)

PENN. (1787)

Susquehanna R.

Harrisburg ★

Delaware R.

★ Trenton

NEW JERSEY (1787)

★ Dover

DELAWARE (1787)

⊛ Annapolis

MARYLAND (1788)

WASHINGTON, D.C.

Chesapeake Bay

THE ORIGINAL THIRTEEN COLONIES

St. Paul ●

WISCONSIN (1848)

MICHIGAN (1837)

● Lansing

MINNESOTA (1858)

Madison ★

IOWA (1846)

Missouri R.

★ Des Moines

● Lincoln

Topeka ★

ILLINOIS (1818)

INDIANA (1816)

Indianapolis ★

Springfield ★

OHIO (1803)

● Columbus

WEST VIRGINIA (1863)

Charleston ★

Proclamation Line of 1763

Potomac R.

Richmond ★

VIRGINIA (1788)

James R.

Jefferson City ★

MISSOURI (1821)

Frankfort ●

KENTUCKY (1792)

Gained by treaty with Britain, 1783

Ohio R.

Cumberland R.

NORTH CAROLINA (1789)

Raleigh ★

Cape Fear R.

klahoma ity

OKLAHOMA (1907)

ARKANSAS (1836)

Little Rock ●

Arkansas R.

Mississippi R.

Nashville ★

TENNESSEE (1796)

Tennessee R.

SOUTH CAROLINA (1788)

Columbia ●

Topeka ★

ustin

MISSISSIPPI (1817)

ALABAMA (1819)

Montgomery ★

Jackson ★

Atlanta ★

GEORGIA (1788)

Savannah R.

LOUISIANA (1812)

Baton Rouge ★

Tallahassee ★

FLORIDA (1845)

FLORIDA Treaty with Spain, 1819

THE CONTEMPORARY UNITED STATES

0   150   300 miles

0   150   300 kilometers

ATLANTIC OCEAN

Gulf of Mexico

Areas taken from Spain in 1810, 1813

U.S. Territories

ATLANTIC OCEAN

San Juan ★

PUERTO RICO Acquired from Spain, 1898

VIRGIN ISLANDS Acquired from Denmark, 1916–1917

Caribbean Sea

0   50   100 miles

0   50   100 kilometers

(1789)   Date of statehood

BAHAMAS

CUBA

M-9

About the authors

JAMES L. ROARK (Ph.D., Stanford University) is Samuel Candler Dobbs Professor of American History at Emory University. In 1993, he received the Emory Williams Distinguished Teaching Award, and in 2001–2002 he was Pitt Professor of American Institutions at Cambridge University. He has written *Masters without Slaves: Southern Planters in the Civil War and Reconstruction* and coauthored *Black Masters: A Free Family of Color in the Old South* with Michael P. Johnson.

MICHAEL P. JOHNSON (Ph.D., Stanford University) is professor of history at Johns Hopkins University. His publications include *Toward a Patriarchal Republic: The Secession of Georgia*; *Abraham Lincoln, Slavery, and the Civil War: Selected Speeches and Writings*; and *Reading the American Past: Selected Historical Documents*, the documents reader for *The American Promise*. He has also coedited *No Chariot Let Down: Charleston's Free People of Color on the Eve of the Civil War* with James L. Roark.

PATRICIA CLINE COHEN (Ph.D., University of California, Berkeley) is professor of history at the University of California, Santa Barbara, where she received the Distinguished Teaching Award in 2005–2006. She has written *A Calculating People: The Spread of Numeracy in Early America* and *The Murder of Helen Jewett: The Life and Death of a Prostitute in Nineteenth-Century New York*, and she has coauthored *The Flash Press: Sporting Male Weeklies in 1840s New York*.

SARAH STAGE (Ph.D., Yale University) has taught U.S. history at Williams College and the University of California, Riverside, and she was visiting professor at Beijing University and Szechuan University. Currently she is professor of women's studies at Arizona State University. Her books include *Female Complaints: Lydia Pinkham and the Business of Women's Medicine* and *Rethinking Home Economics: Women and the History of a Profession*.

SUSAN M. HARTMANN (Ph.D., University of Missouri) is Arts and Humanities Distinguished Professor of History at Ohio State University. In 1995 she won the university's Exemplary Faculty Award in the College of Humanities. Her publications include *Truman and the 80th Congress*; *The Home Front and Beyond: American Women in the 1940s*; *From Margin to Mainstream: American Women and Politics since 1960*; and *The Other Feminists: Activists in the Liberal Establishment*.

About the cover image

Jeannette Rankin with American Flag, 1918

Congresswoman Jeannette Rankin (1880–1973) is shown receiving the flag that flew over the Capitol when the House of Representatives passed the Nineteenth Amendment, which, when it was ratified in 1920, gave women the right to vote. Rankin, who held office from 1917 to 1919 and from 1941 to 1943, was the first woman elected to Congress and an ardent supporter of woman suffrage. Her election solidified the necessity of a female voice in government and ushered in a new era in women's struggle for equality.

How to analyze primary sources

In their search for an improved understanding of the past, historians look for new evidence, written documents or visual artifacts. When they encounter a written or visual primary source, historians ask certain key questions. You should ask these questions, too. Sometimes historians can't be certain about the answer, but they always ask the question.

Analyzing a written document

- Who wrote the document? Is it a specific person or someone not completely identifiable whom you can merely infer from the context of the document (for example, a parent writing to a child, a traveler writing home)?

- When and where was it written?

- Why was the document written? Is there a clear purpose, or are multiple interpretations possible?

- Who was, or who might have been, its intended audience?

- What point of view does it reflect?

- What can the document tell us about the individual who produced it and the society from which he or she came?

Analyzing a visual source

- Who made the image or artifact, and how was it made?

- When and where was the image or artifact made?

- Who paid for or commissioned it? How can you tell?

- For what audience might it have been intended? Where might it have originally been displayed or used?

- What message or messages is it trying to convey?

- How could it be interpreted differently depending on who viewed or used it?

- What can this image tell us about the individual who produced it and the society from which he or she came?

THE CONTEMPORARY WORLD

80°N

60°N

40°N

20°N

0° Equator

20°S

40°S

60°S

80°S

160°W 140°W 120°W 100°W 80°W 60°W 40°W 20°W

Greenland
(Den.)

ICELAND

UNITED
KINGDOM

IRELAND

FRANCE

SPAIN

PORTUGAL

Azores
(Port.)

MOROCCO

Canary Is.
(Sp.)

Western Sahara
(Mor.)

MAURITANIA

CAPE
VERDE

SENEGAL

GAMBIA

GUINEA-BISSAU

GUINEA

SIERRA LEONE

LIBERIA

CÔTE D'IVOIRE

BURKINA FAS

GHAN

MA

ALASKA

CANADA

UNITED STATES

Hawaii

MEXICO

GUATEMALA
EL SALVADOR

COSTA RICA

PANAMA

BELIZE
HONDURAS
NICARAGUA

CUBA
JAMAICA

BAHAMAS
DOMINICAN
REPUBLIC
HAITI

Puerto Rico (U.S.)

Guadeloupe (Fr.)

Martinique (Fr.)

ST. LUCIA

ST. KITTS AND NEVIS
ANTIGUA AND BARBUDA
DOMINICA
ST. VINCENT AND THE GRENADINES
BARBADOS
GRENADA
TRINIDAD AND TOBAGO
GUYANA
SURINAME
French Guiana (Fr.)

VENEZUELA

COLOMBIA

ECUADOR

Galápagos Is.
(Ec.)

PERU

BRAZIL

BOLIVIA

PARAGUAY

CHILE

URUGUAY

ARGENTINA

SAMOA

TONGA

Easter I.
(Chile)

Falkland Is.
(U.K.)

*ATLANTIC
OCEAN*

PACIFIC OCEAN

*ATLANTIC
OCEAN*

N
W E
S

| 0 | 1,500 | 3,000 miles |
| 0 | 1,500 | 3,000 kilometers |